Merriam-Webster's Crossword Puzzle Dictionary

Merriam-Webster's Crossword Puzzle Dictionary

Fourth Edition

Merriam-Webster, Incorporated
Springfield, Massachusetts

A GENUINE MERRIAM-WEBSTER

The name *Webster* alone is no guarantee of excellence. It is used by a number of publishers and may serve mainly to mislead an unwary buyer.

Merriam-Webster™ is the name you should look for when you consider the purchase of dictionaries or other fine reference books. It carries the reputation of a company that has been publishing since 1831 and is your assurance of quality and authority.

ISBN: 978-0-87779-734-0

Made in the United States of America

6th Printing Data Reproductions Corp. Auburn Hills, MI 8/2020

Preface to the Fourth Edition

In the 35 years since Merriam-Webster first published its *Crossword Puzzle Dictionary,* the style and content of crossword puzzles have changed noticeably. As arcane references have declined, clever and playful clues have proliferated, and the world of popular culture has been increasingly welcomed into the crossword grid. These shifts have been reflected in the changing content of our own dictionary, resulting in a resource quite distinct from the one that first appeared in 1981.

New vocabulary has naturally continued to emerge over the decades, and the eleven years since the appearance of the third edition have resulted in a steady flow of new words and names into our shared experience. Many of these—in such realms as food *(acai, pho, unagi),* sports and entertainment *(Eli* Manning, *Argo, Sela* Ward, *Adele),* and technology and social media *(vlog, iPad, IMHO)*—have made their way into dozens of recent crossword puzzles and from there into the present book.

While incorporating numerous new names and terms, the dictionary has also enhanced its treatment of the reliable staples of "crosswordese"—*ETA, ion, Ono, néné, Obie, Odie, Opie, sloe, tare, yeti, Aleut, arête, tetra,* and scores of others—words that may only occasionally slip the mind of the veteran crossworder but may still be out of reach for the novice.

Most of the challenges of a crossword puzzle will continue to be challenges for the puzzler alone, and no dictionary of this kind can begin to list more than a small fraction of the nearly infinite clue possibilities. But where just a word or two is standing in the way of a completed puzzle, we hope this convenient reference, when used intelligently, will often be able to supply exactly what the frustrated puzzler requires.

The principal editors of this dictionary's first and second editions (1981, 1996) were James G. Lowe and Michael G. Belanger; those for the third edition (2005) were C. Roger Davis and Mark A. Stevens. The present edition was edited by Mark Stevens, with technical assistance from Robert D. Copeland. Like the previous edition, it was typeset by Dianna Logan at Dedicated Book Services, Clarinda, Iowa. Thousands of useful additions were suggested by several users of the third edition—D. Robert Chemberlin, Graham Forbes, Patricia H. Green, Eileen M. Haraty, Will Hutchins, and J. Robert Ramsay—to whom we owe a debt of gratitude.

Explanatory Notes

This dictionary is organized to make it easy to find answer words with a specific number of letters. Every answer word follows a numeral indicating the number of letters it contains. Answers listed here generally run up to 13 letters, but multiword titles of works may run longer, to allow for clues in which a title is missing one or two words. (Two-letter words have been omitted, since crossword puzzles never contain two-letter answers.)

Actual puzzle clues are often intentionally ambiguous as to which meaning is intended, so a list of all possible synonyms together is usually ideal for the puzzle solver. A single list of answer words will very often include words representing various parts of speech, as well as words with very different meanings. Thus, for example, the entry for **fast** includes synonyms for the adjective *(rapid)*, the noun *(diet)*, and the verb *(abstain)*, all in a continuous list.

Since puzzle creators rarely provide a clue whose answer word shares a root with the clue, root-related answers are generally omitted here. Thus, *singular* does not appear at **single**, *basal* does not appear at **basic**, and *papa* does not appear at **pop**. Likewise, where a clue word and an answer word would share a common prefix such as *un-*, the answer word is very often—though not always—omitted.

When one entry word simply adds a suffix to another entry word, as when **shared** follows **share**, the answer list for the suffixed entry word will often omit words that merely add the same suffix to a word in the list for the stem word itself. For example, since **share** includes such answer words as *divide* and *prorate,* the list at **shared** omits *divided* and *prorated.* So the user who encounters a clue with a familiar suffix may want to look at a neighboring entry to be sure of finding all the possible synonyms.

When a personal name is entered as an answer term, the first name generally appears in parentheses and is ignored in the letter count.

In cases where the first name is the one normally encountered, the last name is generally parenthesized: *Napoleon (Bonaparte), Scout (Finch),* etc. In particular, the last name may be parenthesized if the first name is simply the one more likely to appear in a puzzle: *Ella (Fitzgerald), Etta (James),* etc.

When a title begins with an article *(A, An,* or *The),* the article is parenthesized and omitted from the lettter count.

In a list of geographic entities (**river**, **bay**, **peak**, **mountain**, etc.), any generic term that forms part of a proper name (*River, Bay, Peak, Mount,* etc.) is omitted from the answer and the letter count. If no such answer as listed fits the blanks for a given geographic clue, you should naturally consider whether adding a parenthesized or omitted element might produce the desired letter count.

In the many entries that are broken into subentries, the subheadings often consist of a single word, which should usually be read as either preceding or following the main entry word. Thus, at **liquor**, the subheadings include **inferior**, which should be read as "inferior liquor," and **measure**, which should be read as "liquor measure."

Under the subentry **combining form** are listed the kinds of word fragments, usually Greek or Latin in origin, that are commonly called "roots": *omni, derm, geo,* etc.

No crossword dictionary can hope to list more than a fraction of the possible clues for a given answer word, since the possibilities are limited only by the puzzle constructors' imagination. Thus, this dictionary is best used somewhat imaginatively. If a puzzle clue is not listed here in its exact wording, look up a synonym; only rarely will you fail to find one. If a clue takes a form such as "Basque game," "white wine," or "Italian tenor" and the dictionary provides no such entry, be sure to check the entry for the generic term—**game**, **wine**, **tenor**, etc.

A

A1
4 best, tops **5** prime **6** tip-top **7** optimal, perfect **8** splendid, superior, top-notch **9** excellent, first-rate, front-rank, matchless, top-drawer **10** blue-ribbon, first-class

Aaron
brother: **5** Moses
father: **5** Amram
sister: **6** Miriam

aback
7 unaware **8** suddenly, unawares **10** by surprise **12** unexpectedly

abaft
4 back **5** after **6** astern, behind **8** rearward **9** sternward

abalone
7 mollusc, mollusk **9** gastropod
lining: **5** nacre

abandon
4 cede, drop, dump, ease, jilt, junk, play, quit **5** cease, chuck, ditch, leave, let go, scrap, yield **6** desert, disown, give up, laxity, maroon, reject, resign, strand, vacate **7** back out, bail out, cast off, discard, drop out, forsake, freedom, liberty, license, pull out, retreat **8** abdicate, give over, hand over, renounce, wildness, withdraw **9** looseness, repudiate, surrender, throw over **10** enthusiasm, exuberance, relinquish, wantonness **11** discontinue, leave behind, spontaneity, unrestraint **12** carelessness, heedlessness, intemperance, recklessness, unconstraint **13** impulsiveness

abandoned
4 free, lewd, lorn, wild **5** loose **6** gave up, vacant, wanton **7** cast off, corrupt, given up, outcast, uncouth **8** cast away, depraved, derelict, desolate, forsaken **9** cast aside, debauched, destitute, dissolute, lecherous, neglected, reprobate, shameless **10** degenerate, dissipated, friendless, lascivious, left behind, licentious, profligate, unoccupied **11** uninhibited **12** incorrigible, uncontrolled, unrestrained

abase
5 lower, shame **6** defame, demean, demote, grovel, humble, lessen, reduce **7** cheapen, degrade, devalue, put down **8** belittle **9** denigrate, discredit, disparage, downgrade, humiliate **10** depreciate, undervalue

abash
4 faze **5** mix up, shame, upset **6** dismay, puzzle, rattle **7** confuse, mortify, mystify **8** confound **9** discomfit, embarrass **10** discompose, disconcert

abashment
6 unease **7** chagrin **8** disquiet **9** confusion **12** discomfiture, discomposure

abate
3 ebb, end **4** ease, fade, fall, omit, slow, void, stem, wane **5** allay, annul, close, let up, quash, taper **6** deduct, lessen, negate, recede, reduce, relent, weaken **7** abolish, decline, deprive, die down, dwindle, ease off, nullify, slacken, subside **8** decrease, diminish, mitigate, moderate **9** alleviate, eradicate **10** invalidate

abatement
6 ebbing, rebate, waning **8** decrease, discount **9** declining, deduction, dwindling, exemption, lessening, reduction, shrinkage **10** diminution, subsidence **11** subtraction

abattoir
8 shambles

Abba ___
4 Eban

abbey
6 friary **7** convent **8** cloister **9** monastery

abbot
female: **6** abbess

abbreviate
3 cut **4** clip, trim **5** prune **6** cut out, reduce **7** abridge, curtail, cut back, shorten **8** compress, condense, contract, cut short, truncate

abbreviation
5 brief **6** digest, précis, sketch **7** acronym, cutting, outline **8** abstract, clipping, synopsis, trimming **10** abridgment, shortening **11** curtailment **12** condensation

ABC island
5 Aruba **7** Baranof, Bonaire, Curaçao **9** Admiralty, Chichagof

abdicate
4 cede, drop, quit **5** evade, forgo, leave, waive, yield **6** abjure, give up, reject, resign **7** abandon, cast off, discard **8** abnegate, disclaim, hand over, renounce, withdraw **9** repudiate, surrender **10** relinquish

abdomen
3 gut, pot **5** belly, tummy **6** middle, paunch **7** midriff, stomach **8** potbelly **9** bay window **10** midsection **11** breadbasket, solar plexus
depression: **5** navel

abduct
4 grab, take **5** seize **6** kidnap, remove, snatch **8** carry off, draw away, take away **9** carry away, steal away **10** spirit away **11** make off with

Abduction from the Seraglio
character: **5** Osmin, Selim **8** Belmonte, Pedrillo **9** Konstanze
composer: **6** Mozart (Wolfgang Amadeus)

abecedarian
4 tyro **6** novice, rookie **7** amateur, dabbler, learner, trainee **8** beginner, initiate, neophyte **9** beginning **10** apprentice, dilettante, elementary **11** rudimentary **12** alphabetical

Abel
brother: **4** Cain, Seth
father: **4** Adam
mother: **3** Eve
slayer: **4** Cain

Abelard
son: **9** Astrolabe
wife: **7** Heloise

abele
6 poplar

aberrant
3 odd **7** deviant, strange, unusual **8** abnormal, atypical, peculiar, straying **9** anomalous, deviating, different, eccentric, irregular, unnatural, untypical **11** exceptional, nonstandard

aberration
4 slip **5** quirk **6** change, oddity **7** anomaly, mistake **8** mutation, straying **9** curiosity, deviation, exception, wandering **10** deflection, difference, distortion, divergence **11** abnormality, peculiarity **12** eccentricity, irregularity

abet
3 aid, egg **4** ally, back, help, prod, spur, urge **5** boost, egg on **6** assist, second, stir up **7** condone, endorse, forward, promote, support **9** encourage **11** countenance

abettor
4 aide, ally **6** backup, cohort, helper **7** inciter, partner **8** fomenter, henchman, sidekick **9** accessory, supporter **10** accomplice **11** confederate, conspirator **12** collaborator

abeyance
4 lull, rest **5** break, lapse, pause **6** recess **7** respite, time-out, waiting **8** breather, interval **10** inactivity, quiescence, suspension **12** intermission, interruption

abeyant
7 dormant **8** deferred, inactive, recessed **9** postponed, quiescent, suspended **11** interrupted

abhor
4 hate **5** scorn **6** detest, loathe, reject, revile, vilify **7** contemn, despise, disdain, dislike **8** execrate **9** abominate, excoriate, repudiate

abhorrence
4 evil, hate **5** odium **6** hatred, horror **7** disgust **8** aversion, distaste, loathing **9** repulsion, revulsion **10** repugnance **11** abomination, detestation

abhorrent
4 base, foul, vile **5** awful **6** horrid, odious **7** beastly, hateful, heinous **8** damnable, horrible, horrific **9** atrocious, execrable, invidious, loathsome, monstrous, obnoxious, repellent, repugnant, repulsive, revolting **10** abominable, deplorable, despicable, detestable, disgusting **12** contemptible **13** reprehensible

abide
4 bear, last, live, stay, wait **5** await, brook, dwell, exist, stand, tarry **6** accede, accept, comply, endure, keep on, linger, remain, reside, stay on, suffer **7** consent, hang out, inhabit, persist, sojourn, stomach, subsist, swallow, wait for **8** continue, live with, stand for, tolerate **9** put up with, withstand

abiding
4 fast, firm, sure **6** steady **7** durable, eternal, lasting, staying **8** constant, enduring, timeless **9** complying, perpetual, steadfast **10** continuing, persistent, persisting, unchanging **11** everlasting, unfaltering

abigail
4 maid

Abigail
brother: **5** David
husband: **5** David, Nabal
mother: **5** Amasa
son: **7** Chileah

ability
4 bent, gift **5** craft, flair, knack, might, savvy, skill **6** talent **7** aptness, command, faculty, know-how, mastery, prowess **8** aptitude, capacity, facility **9** adeptness, dexterity, expertise, handiness, ingenuity, potential **10** adroitness, capability, cleverness, competence, efficiency **11** proficiency **12** skillfulness **13** qualification

abject
3 low **4** base, mean, poor, vile **5** lowly, sorry **6** dismal, humble, shabby, sordid **7** debased, fawning, forlorn, ignoble, pitiful, servile **8** cast down, degraded, dejected, downcast, hopeless, pathetic, pitiable, rejected, resigned, wretched **9** afflicted, destitute, groveling, miserable, worthless **10** deplorable, obsequious, spiritless, submissive **11** deferential, downtrodden, subservient **12** contemptible, dishonorable, ingratiating

abjure
4 cede, deny **5** avoid, spurn **6** desert, disown, recall, recant, reject, refuse, revoke **7** abandon, disavow, decline, forsake, retract **8** disclaim, forswear, renounce, take back, withdraw

9 repudiate, surrender 10 relinquish 11 abstain from

ablaze
5 afire, aglow, fiery 6 aflame, alight, on fire 7 burning, flaming, excited, flaring, ignited, radiant

able
3 apt, fit 4 keen 5 adept, alert, sharp, smart 6 adroit, clever, expert, facile, suited 7 capable, skilled 8 skillful, talented 9 competent, effective, effectual, efficient, qualified 10 proficient 11 intelligent, resourceful 12 accomplished

able-bodied
3 fit 4 hale 5 hardy, lusty, sound, stout 6 brawny, hearty, robust, strong, sturdy 7 capable, healthy 8 stalwart, vigorous 9 strapping

ablution
4 bath 6 laving 7 bathing, washing 8 lavation 9 cleansing, immersion 12 purification

abnegate
4 cede, deny, drop 5 forgo, waive, yield 6 abjure, give up, recant, revoke, vacate 7 disavow, gainsay 8 disallow, disclaim, forswear, renounce, withdraw 9 repudiate, surrender 10 contradict, contravene, relinquish

abnegation
6 denial 9 surrender 10 abstinence, self-denial 12 renouncement, renunciation

Abner
cousin: 4 Saul
father: 3 Ner
slayer: 4 Joab

abnormal
3 odd 5 freak, outré, undue, weird 6 off-key 7 bizarre, deviant, strange, unusual 8 aberrant, atypical, freakish, peculiar 9 anomalous, divergent, eccentric, irregular, unnatural 11 heteroclite 13 preternatural

abnormality
4 flaw 6 oddity 7 anomaly 8 deviance 9 deviation, exception, weirdness 10 aberration, difference 12 irregularity

abode
3 hut 4 home, nest, tent 5 house 7 address, lodging, sojourn 8 domicile, dwelling 9 residence 10 habitation
conical: 5 tepee 6 teepee

abolish
3 end 4 undo, kill, void 5 abate, annul, erase, quash 6 cancel, negate, recall, repeal, revoke, vacate 7 destroy, nullify, rescind, retract, reverse, wipe out 8 abrogate, disallow, dissolve, overturn, prohibit 9 eliminate, eradicate, terminate 10 do away with, extinguish, invalidate

abolition
6 repeal

abolitionist
4 Mott (Lucretia), Weld (Theodore) 5 Brown (John), Child (Lydia), Lundy (Benjamin), Smith (Gerrit), Stowe (Harriet Beecher), Truth (Sojourner) 6 Birney (James), Lowell (James Russell), Parker (Theodore), Tappan (Arthur), Tubman (Harriet) 7 Lincoln (Abraham) 8 Douglass (Frederick), Garrison (William Lloyd), Phillips (Wendell), Whittier (John Greenleaf)

abominable
5 awful, nasty 6 cursed, horrid, odious 7 hateful, heinous 8 accursed, horrible, shocking, terrible, wretched 9 abhorrent, loathsome, offensive, repellent, repugnant, repulsive, revolting 10 deplorable, despicable, detestable, disgusting 12 contemptible

abominable snowman
4 yeti

abominate
4 damn, hate 5 abhor, curse, scorn 6 detest, loathe, revile 7 despise 8 execrate 9 repudiate

abomination
4 evil, hate 5 scorn 6 hatred, horror, plague 7 disdain, disgust, dislike 8 anathema, aversion, contempt, distaste, loathing 9 repulsion, revulsion 10 abhorrence, repugnance, repugnancy 11 detestation

aboriginal
5 first 6 native 7 ancient, endemic, primary 8 earliest, original, primeval 9 primitive 10 indigenous, primordial 13 autochthonous
Japanese: 4 Ainu

aborigine
6 native 7 ancient 8 indigene 10 autochthon

abort
3 end 4 drop, halt, stop 5 check, expel, scrap, scrub 6 arrest, cancel 7 abandon, call off, scratch, suspend 8 cut short 9 interrupt, terminate

abortive
4 vain 6 futile, otiose, unripe 7 failing, useless 9 fruitless, worthless 10 unavailing, unfruitful 11 ineffective, ineffectual 12 unproductive, unsuccessful

abound
4 flow, teem 5 burst, crawl, crowd, flood, swarm, swell 6 throng 8 overflow

abounding
4 full, rife 5 laden 6 filled, jammed, packed 7 copious, profuse, replete, stuffed, teeming 8 abundant, swarming, thronged 9 alive with, bristling, plenteous, plentiful 11 overflowing

about
4 as to, back, in re, near, nigh, over, some 5 again, anent, circa, round 6 almost, around, nearby, nearly 7 apropos, close to, roughly

8 backward **9** as regards, in general, in reverse, regarding **10** as concerns, concerning, in regard to, more or less, relating to, relative to, respecting **11** dealing with, practically, referring to **12** with regard to **13** approximately, concerned with, in reference to, with respect to

about-face
4 turn **5** U-turn **7** reverse **8** reversal **9** turnabout

above
3 o'er **4** atop, over, past **5** aloft, supra **6** beyond **8** overhead **9** exceeding
prefix: **4** over **5** hyper, super, supra

above all
7 chiefly **9** primarily **10** especially **11** principally **12** particularly

aboveboard
4 free, open **5** frank, overt **6** candid, honest, openly **7** frankly, up front **8** candidly, honestly, straight, truthful **10** truthfully, forthright, scrupulous

abracadabra
5 charm, magic **6** babble, jargon **9** gibberish **10** double talk, hocus-pocus, mumbo jumbo **11** incantation **12** gobbledygook **13** mystification

abrade
3 bug, irk, rub **4** burn, fret, gall, rasp, wear **5** annoy, chafe, erode, grate, graze, upset, weary **6** bother, ruffle, scrape **7** corrode, eat away, perturb, provoke, roughen **8** irritate, wear away, wear down **9** aggravate, grind down

Abraham
brother: **5** Haran, Nahor
concubine: **5** Hagar
father: **5** Terah
grandfather: **5** Nahor
grandson: **4** Esau
nephew: **3** Lot
son: **5** Isaac, Medan, Shuah **6** Midian, Zimran **7** Ishmael
well: **9** Beer-Sheba
wife: **5** Sarah **7** Keturah

abrasion
5 chafe, graze, scuff **6** scrape **7** chafing, erosion, grating, rubbing, scratch **8** friction, grinding, scraping, scuffing **10** irritation, scratching

abrasive
5 emery, rough **6** pumice **7** wearing **8** annoying **10** irritating **11** Carborundum, garnet paper

abreast
6 beside, next to, versed, with-it **7** versant **8** familiar, informed, up-to-date **9** au courant **10** acquainted, conversant, side by side

abridge
3 cut **4** pare, trim **5** limit, prune **6** lessen, narrow, reduce **7** curtail, cut back, shorten **8** boil down, compress, condense, cut short, diminish, restrict, truncate **9** summarize **10** abbreviate

abridgment
5 brief **6** digest **7** capsule, cutting, summary **8** abstract, synopsis **9** lessening, reduction, short form **10** diminution, shortening **11** compression, contraction, curtailment, restriction **12** abbreviation, condensation

abroad
4 afar, away **6** afield, astray, widely **7** touring **8** overseas **9** elsewhere, traveling

abrogate
3 end **4** undo, void **5** abate, annul, quash **6** cancel, negate, repeal, revoke, vacate **7** abolish, blot out, nullify, rescind, reverse **8** dissolve **9** discharge **10** extinguish, invalidate, obliterate

abrupt
4 curt **5** bluff, blunt, brief, brisk, gruff, hasty, sharp, sheer, short, steep **6** cut off, snippy, sudden **7** brusque, hurried **8** headlong **9** impetuous **10** unexpected **11** precipitate, precipitous **13** unceremonious

abruptness
10 brusquerie **12** precipitance

Absalom
commander: **5** Amasa
father: **5** David
mother: **7** Maachah
sister: **5** Tamar
slayer: **4** Joab

abscess
4 boil, sore **5** botch, ulcer **6** trauma **7** blister, pustule **8** furuncle **9** carbuncle

abscond
4 bolt, flee, quit, skip **5** break, leave **6** decamp, escape, run off **7** run away, take off **8** slip away, sneak off **9** disappear, sneak away, steal away

absence
4 AWOL, lack, need, void, want **6** dearth, defect, vacuum **7** default, drought, failure, sick-out, vacancy **9** privation **10** deficiency, inadequacy **11** absenteeism, inattention

absent
4 away, AWOL, gone, lost **6** no-show **7** faraway, lacking, missing, omitted, wanting, without **8** distrait, heedless **9** elsewhere, forgetful **10** abstracted, distracted **11** inattentive, preoccupied

absentminded
4 lost **7** bemused, faraway **8** distrait, dreaming, heedless, unseeing **9** forgetful, oblivious, unheeding, unmindful **10** abstracted, distracted, unnoticing **11** inattentive, inconscient, preoccupied, unconscious, unobserving

absolute
4 full, pure, real, true **5** ideal, sheer, total, utter **6** actual, entire, simple, strict **7** eternal, factual, genuine, perfect, supreme, unmixed **8** autarkic, complete, despotic, flawless, infinite, outright, positive, ultimate, simplest, thorough, unflawed

9 arbitrary, autarchic, boundless, downright, embodying, imperious, masterful, sovereign, unalloyed, undiluted, unlimited **10** autocratic, autonomous, consummate, impeccable, monocratic, tyrannical **11** categorical, dictatorial, domineering, fundamental, independent, unequivocal, unmitigated, unqualified **12** indisputable, totalitarian, unrestrained, unrestricted **13** authoritarian, unconditional

absolutely
4 dead **5** fully **6** wholly **7** utterly **8** entirely **9** doubtless, perfectly **10** completely, definitely, positively, thoroughly **11** doubtlessly **13** unequivocally

absolution
6 pardon **7** amnesty, freeing, release **9** releasing, remission **10** letting off **11** exculpation, exoneration, forgiveness **12** dispensation

absolutism
9 Caesarism, despotism **12** dictatorship

absolve
4 free **5** clear, let go, remit, spare **6** acquit, excuse, exempt, let off, pardon **7** forgive, release, relieve, set free **8** dispense **9** discharge, exculpate, exonerate, vindicate

absorb
4 bear, blot **5** imbue, learn, sop up, use up **6** assume, embody, endure, engage, imbibe, infuse, ingest, soak up, sponge, suck up, take in, take up **7** acquire, consume, drink in, engross, immerse, involve, receive, sustain **8** permeate **9** preoccupy, transform **10** assimilate **11** incorporate

absorbed
4 deep, into, lost, rapt **6** intent **7** engaged, wrapped **8** caught up, immersed, involved **9** engrossed, wrapped up **10** captivated, fascinated **11** preoccupied

absorbing
9 arresting, consuming **10** engrossing, intriguing **11** captivating, fascinating, interesting **12** monopolizing, preoccupying

abstain
4 curb, deny, diet, fast, keep, pass, stop **5** avoid, forgo, spurn **6** abjure, eschew, give up, pass up, refuse, reject **7** decline, forbear, refrain **8** abnegate, forswear, hold back, keep from, renounce, swear off, teetotal, withhold **9** constrain, do without **11** deny oneself

abstemious
5 sober **6** chaste, strict **7** ascetic, austere, sparing, spartan **9** abstinent, continent, temperate **10** restrained **11** self-denying

abstinence
6 denial **7** fasting **8** chastity, sobriety **9** soberness **10** continence, self-denial, temperance **12** renunciation **13** self-restraint

abstract
5 brief, ideal **6** detach, digest, précis **7** epitome, neutral, outline, shorten, summary, utopian **8** academic, breviary, condense, detached, notional, separate, synopsis **9** disengage, summarize **10** abridgment, conceptual, conspectus, disconnect, dissociate, impersonal **11** appropriate, impractical, speculative, theoretical **12** condensation, hypothetical, transcendent **13** disinterested

abstracted
4 lost, rapt **6** absent, intent **7** bemused, faraway **8** absorbed, distrait, heedless **9** engrossed, oblivious, unheeding, unmindful, unminding, withdrawn **11** inattentive, inconscient, preoccupied, unconscious **12** absentminded

abstruse
4 deep **5** heavy **6** arcane, knotty, occult **7** complex **8** esoteric, hermetic, involved, profound **9** difficult, intricate, recondite **11** complicated

absurd
5 balmy, comic, crazy, droll, inane, loony, potty, silly, wacky **6** insane **7** asinine, fatuous, foolish, idiotic, risible **8** derisory, farcical **9** illogical, laughable, ludicrous **10** irrational, ridiculous **11** harebrained, nonsensical **12** preposterous, unreasonable

absurdity
5 farce, folly **7** inanity **8** nonsense **9** craziness, dottiness, silliness **11** foolishness, incongruity, witlessness **13** ludicrousness, senselessness

Abu Dhabi's federation
3 UAE

abundance
5 ocean **6** bounty, excess, plenty, riches, wealth **9** affluence, profusion **10** lavishness, prosperity **11** prodigality
Scottish: 5 routh

abundant
4 full, lush, rich, rife **5** ample **6** filled, galore, lavish, plenty **7** aplenty, copious, crammed, crowded, liberal, profuse, replete **8** fruitful, prolific **9** abounding, bounteous, bountiful, extensive, luxuriant, plenteous, plentiful

abuse
3 mar **4** harm, hurt, rail **5** anger, decry, shame, spoil, wrong **6** damage, debase, deride, impair, injure, misuse, revile, vilify **7** calumny, corrupt, cursing, epithet, exploit, obloquy, oppress, profane **8** belittle, berating, derision, derogate, disgrace, ill-treat, maltreat, mistreat, swearing **9** blaspheme, contumely, desecrate, disparage, harshness, invective, manhandle, mishandle, persecute, profanity **10** defamation, depreciate, malignment, revilement, scurrility **11** disapproval **12** billingsgate, denunciation, vilification, vituperation

abusive
5 dirty, harsh **6** odious **7** corrupt **8** scurrile **9** injurious, insulting, invective, offending, offensive, truculent **10** calumnious, defamatory, scurrilous **11** blasphemous, castigating, opprobrious **12** calumniating, contumelious, sharp-tongued, vituperative, vituperatory

abut
4 join, link **5** flank, touch, verge **6** adjoin, border, butt on **8** border on, neighbor **9** lie beside **11** communicate

abutting
4 next **6** beside, joined, next to **7** joining, verging **8** adjacent, next door, touching **9** adjoining, bordering, impinging **10** connecting, contiguous, juxtaposed **11** bordering on, coextensive, coterminous, neighboring **12** conterminous

abuzz
7 humming

abysmal
4 deep, vast, vile **5** awful **7** endless **8** infinite, profound, terrible, unending, wretched **9** atrocious, boundless, cavernous, execrable, plumbless, soundless, unplumbed **10** bottomless, fathomless, unmeasured **11** illimitable, measureless **12** immeasurable, unfathomable

abyss
3 pit **4** gulf, hell, hole, void **5** chasm, depth, gorge, hades, Sheol **6** Tophet **7** fissure, Gehenna, inferno **8** crevasse, deepness **9** perdition **10** underworld

academia
10 university **12** professoriat

academic
3 don **4** moot **5** pupil, tutor **6** closet, fellow, master **7** bookish, learned, scholar, student **8** abstract, gownsman, lecturer, pedantic **9** professor, scholarly **10** scholastic **11** book-learned, conjectural, impractical, speculative, theoretical **12** conventional, hypothetical

academic period
4 term **7** quarter **8** semester **9** trimester

academy
5 lycée **6** lyceum **7** college, society **9** institute **10** prep school **12** conservatory

Academy Award winner
picture:
1927-28: **5** Wings
1928-29: **14** Broadway Melody
1929-30: **25** All Quiet on the Western Front
1930-31: **8** Cimarron
1931-32: **10** Grand Hotel
1932-33: **9** Cavalcade
1934: **18** It Happened One Night
1935: **17** Mutiny on the Bounty
1936: **16** The Great Ziegfeld
1937: **15** Life of Emile Zola
1938: **20** You Can't Take It with You
1939: **15** Gone with the Wind
1940: **7** Rebecca
1941: **19** How Green Was My Valley
1942: **10** Mrs. Miniver
1943: **10** Casablanca
1944: **10** Going My Way
1945: **11** Lost Weekend (The)
1946: **19** Best Years of Our Lives (The)
1947: **19** Gentleman's Agreement
1948: **6** Hamlet
1949: **14** All the King's Men
1950: **11** All About Eve
1951: **15** American in Paris (An)
1952: **19** Greatest Show on Earth (The)
1953: **18** From Here to Eternity
1954: **15** On the Waterfront
1955: **5** Marty
1956: **26** Around the World in Eighty Days
1957: **20** Bridge on the River Kwai (The)
1958: **4** Gigi
1959: **6** Ben-Hur
1960: **9** Apartment (The)
1961: **13** West Side Story
1962: **16** Lawrence of Arabia
1963: **8** Tom Jones
1964: **10** My Fair Lady
1965: **12** Sound of Music (The)
1966: **16** Man for All Seasons (A)
1967: **19** In the Heat of the Night
1968: **6** Oliver
1969: **14** Midnight Cowboy
1970: **6** Patton
1971: **16** French Connection (The)
1972: **9** Godfather (The)
1973: **5** Sting (The)
1974: **9** Godfather (Part Two, The)
1975: **25** One Flew over the Cuckoo's Nest
1976: **5** Rocky
1977: **9** Annie Hall
1978: **10** Deer Hunter (The)
1979: **14** Kramer vs. Kramer
1980: **14** Ordinary People
1981: **14** Chariots of Fire
1982: **6** Gandhi
1983: **17** Terms of Endearment
1984: **7** Amadeus
1985: **11** Out of Africa
1986: **7** Platoon
1987: **11** Last Emperor (The)
1988: **7** Rain Man
1989: **16** Driving Miss Daisy
1990: **16** Dances with Wolves
1991: **17** Silence of the Lambs (The)
1992: **10** Unforgiven
1993: **14** Schindler's List
1994: **11** Forrest Gump
1995: **10** Braveheart
1996: **14** English Patient (The)

1997: **7** Titanlc
1998: **17** Shakespeare in Love
1999: **14** American Beauty
2000: **9** Gladiator
2001: **13** Beautiful Mind (A)
2002: **7** Chicago
2003: **14** Lord of the Rings (The)
2004: **17** Million Dollar Baby
2005: **5** Crash
2006: **8** Departed (The)
2007: **18** No Country for Old Men
2008: **18** Slumdog Millionaire
2009: **10** Hurt Locker (The)
2010: **11** King's Speech (The)
2011: **6** Artist (The)
2012: **4** Argo
2013: **17** Twelve Years a Slave
2014: **7** Birdman
2015: **9** Spotlight

actor:
1927-28: **8** Jannings (Emil)
1928-29: **6** Baxter (Warner)
1929-30: **6** Arliss (George)
1930-31: **9** Barrymore (Lionel)
1931-32: **5** Beery (Wallace), March (Fredric)
1932-33: **8** Laughton (Charles)
1934: **5** Gable (Clark)
1935: **8** McLaglen (Viotor)
1936: **4** Muni (Paul)
1937: **5** Tracy (Spencer)
1938: **5** Tracy (Spencer)
1939: **5** Donat (Robert)
1940: **7** Stewart (James)
1941: **6** Cooper (Gary)
1942: **6** Cagney (James)
1943: **5** Lukas (Paul)
1944: **6** Crosby (Bing)
1945: **7** Milland (Ray)
1946: **5** March (Fredric)
1947: **6** Colman (Ronald)
1948: **7** Olivier (Laurence)
1949: **8** Crawford (Broderick)
1950: **6** Ferrer (José)
1951: **6** Bogart (Humphrey)
1952: **6** Cooper (Gary)
1953: **6** Holden (William)
1954: **6** Brando (Marlon)
1955: **8** Borgnine (Ernest)
1956: **7** Brynner (Yul)
1957: **8** Guinness (Alec)
1958: **5** Niven (David)
1959: **6** Heston (Charlton)
1960: **9** Lancaster (Burt)
1961: **6** Schell (Maximilian)
1962: **4** Peck (Gregory)
1963: **7** Poitier (Sidney)
1964: **8** Harrison (Rex)
1965: **6** Marvin (Lee)
1966: **8** Scofield (Paul)
1967: **7** Steiger (Rod)
1968: **9** Robertson (Cliff)
1969: **5** Wayne (John)
1970: **5** Scott (George C.)
1971: **7** Hackman (Gene)
1972: **6** Brando (Marlon)
1973: **6** Lemmon (Jack)
1974: **6** Carney (Art)
1975: **9** Nicholson (Jack)
1976: **5** Finch (Peter)
1977: **8** Dreyfuss (Richard)
1978: **6** Voight (Jon)
1979: **7** Hoffman (Dustin)
1980: **6** De Niro (Robert)
1981: **5** Fonda (Henry)
1982: **8** Kingsley (Ben)
1983: **6** Duvall (Robert)
1984: **7** Abraham (F. Murray)
1985: **4** Hurt (William)
1986: **6** Newman (Paul)
1987: **7** Douglas (Michael)
1988: **7** Hoffman (Dustin)
1989: **8** Day-Lewis (Daniel)
1990: **5** Irons (Jeremy)
1991: **7** Hopkins (Anthony)
1992: **6** Paclno (Al)
1993: **5** Hanks (Tom)
1994: **5** Hanks (Tom)
1995: **4** Cage (Nicholas)
1996: **4** Rush (Geoffrey)
1997: **9** Nicholson (Jack)
1998: **7** Benigni (Roberto)
1999: **6** Spacey (Kevin)
2000: **5** Crowe (Russell)
2001: **10** Washington (Denzel)
2002: **5** Brody (Adrien)
2003: **4** Penn (Sean)
2004: **4** Foxx (Jamie)
2005: **7** Hoffman (Philip Seymour)
2006: **8** Whitaker (Forest)
2007: **8** Day-Lewis (Daniel)
2008: **4** Penn (Sean)
2009: **7** Bridges (Jeff)
2010: **5** Firth (Colin)
2011: **8** Dujardin (Jean)
2012: **8** Day-Lewis (Daniel)
2013: **11** McConaughey (Matthew)
2014: **8** Redmayne (Eddie)
2015: **8** DiCaprio (Leonardo)

actress:
1927-28: **6** Gaynor (Janet)
1928-29: **8** Pickford (Mary)
1929-30: **7** Shearer (Norma)
1930-31: **8** Dressler (Marie)
1931-32: **5** Hayes (Helen)
1932-33: **7** Hepburn (Katharine)
1934: **7** Colbert (Claudette)
1935: **5** Davis (Bette)
1936: **6** Rainer (Luise)

1937: **6** Rainer (Luise)
1938: **5** Davis (Bette)
1939: **5** Leigh (Vivien)
1940: **6** Rogers (Ginger)
1941: **8** Fontaine (Joan)
1942: **6** Garson (Greer)
1943: **5** Jones (Jennifer)
1944: **7** Bergman (Ingrid)
1945: **8** Crawford (Joan)
1946: **11** de Havilland (Olivia)
1947: **5** Young (Loretta)
1948: **5** Wyman (Jane)
1949: **11** de Havilland (Olivia)
1950: **8** Holliday (Judy)
1951: **5** Leigh (Vivien)
1952: **5** Booth (Shirley)
1953: **7** Hepburn (Audrey)
1954: **5** Kelly (Grace)
1955: **7** Magnani (Anna)
1956: **7** Bergman (Ingrid)
1957: **8** Woodward (Joanne)
1958: **7** Hayward (Susan)
1959: **8** Signoret (Simone)
1960: **6** Taylor (Elizabeth)
1961: **5** Loren (Sophia)
1962: **8** Bancroft (Anne)
1963: **4** Neal (Patricia)
1964: **7** Andrews (Julie)
1965: **8** Christie (Julie)
1966: **6** Taylor (Elizabeth)
1967: **7** Hepburn (Katharine)
1968: **7** Hepburn (Katharine) **9** Streisand (Barbra)
1969: **5** Smith (Maggie)
1970: **7** Jackson (Glenda)
1971: **5** Fonda (Jane)
1972: **8** Minnelli (Liza)
1973: **7** Jackson (Glenda)
1974: **7** Burstyn (Ellen)
1975: **8** Fletcher (Louise)
1976: **7** Dunaway (Faye)
1977: **6** Keaton (Diane)
1978: **5** Fonda (Jane)
1979: **5** Field (Sally)
1980: **6** Spacek (Sissy)
1981: **7** Hepburn (Katharine)
1982: **6** Streep (Meryl)
1983: **8** MacLaine (Shirley)
1984: **5** Field (Sally)
1985: **4** Page (Geraldine)
1986: **6** Matlin (Marlee)
1987: **4** Cher
1988: **6** Foster (Jodie)
1989: **5** Tandy (Jessica)
1990: **5** Bates (Kathy)
1991: **6** Foster (Jodie)
1992: **8** Thompson (Emma)
1993: **6** Hunter (Holly)
1994: **5** Lange (Jessica)
1995: **8** Sarandon (Susan)
1996: **9** McDormand (Frances)
1997: **4** Hunt (Helen)
1998: **7** Paltrow (Gwyneth)
1999: **5** Swank (Hilary)
2000: **7** Roberts (Julia)
2001: **5** Berry (Halle)
2002: **6** Kidman (Nicole)
2003: **6** Theron (Charlize)
2004: **5** Swank (Hilary)
2005: **11** Witherspoon (Reese)
2006: **6** Mirren (Helen)
2007: **9** Cotillard (Marion)
2008: **7** Winslet (Kate)
2009: **7** Bullock (Sandra)
2010: **7** Portman (Natalie)
2011: **6** Streep (Meryl)
2012: **8** Lawrence (Jennifer)
2013: **9** Blanchett (Cate)
2014: **5** Moore (Julianne)
2015: **6** Larson (Brie)

accede
3 let **5** admit, agree, allow, grant, yield **6** accept, assent, comply, concur, give in, permit **7** agree to, approve, concede, consent **9** acquiesce, cooperate, subscribe

accelerando
6 faster **7** speed up **10** quickening, speeding up

accelerate
3 gun, rev **4** grow, roll **5** hurry, impel, rev up, speed **6** hasten, open up, step up **7** quicken, speed up **8** expedite, increase **9** fast-track **10** peel rubber

acceleration
7 speedup **8** hurrying, spurring **9** hastening, revving up **10** increasing, quickening, speeding up, stepping up

accent
4 beat, lilt, tone **5** acute, grave, meter, pulse, throb **6** rhythm, stress, weight **7** cadence **8** emphasis **9** diacritic, pulsation **10** inflection, intonation
Irish: **6** brogue
Scottish: **4** burr
Southern: **5** drawl
Spanish: **5** tilde
verse: **5** ictus

accept
3 bow, buy, see **4** bear, gain, okay, take **5** admit, adopt, agree, catch, favor, go for, grasp, yield **6** accede, admire, affirm, assent, endure, follow, take in, take on **7** agree to, approve, believe, receive, respect, swallow, welcome **8** assent to, bear with, hold with, live with, stand for, tolerate **9** acquiesce, agree with, undertake **10** capitulate, comprehend, concur with, understand **11** acknowledge, countenance, subscribe to

acceptable
4 good, okay **6** decent, worthy **7** average, welcome **8** adequate, all right, bearable, ordinary, passable, pleasing, standard, suitable **9** endurable, tolerable **10** sufficient **11** commonplace, respectable, supportable **12** satisfactory **13** unexceptional, unimpeachable

acceptably
4 well **5** amply **7** capably **8** properly, suitably **9** fittingly, tolerably **10** becomingly **11** competently **13** appropriately

acceptant
4 open **8** amenable, friendly, swayable **9** favorable, receptive, recipient, welcoming **10** open-minded, responsive **11** persuadable, persuasible, susceptible

acceptation
4 gist **5** point, sense **6** import **7** meaning, message, purport **9** intention **10** intendment **12** significance, significancy **13** signification, understanding

accepted
5 usual **6** common, normal, proper **7** correct, regular, routine **8** approved, everyday, expected, habitual, ordinary, orthodox, received **9** customary **10** accustomed, recognized, sanctioned **11** established, traditional **12** conventional

access
3 fit, way **4** adit, door, gust, pang, path, road, turn **5** burst, entry, get at, onset, route, sally, spell, throe **6** attack, avenue, entrée **7** contact, flare-up, ingress, passage, seizure **8** approach, entrance, eruption, increase, outburst **9** admission, explosion **10** admittance

accessible
4 near, open **5** handy **6** public, usable **8** possible **9** available, operative, reachable **10** attainable, employable, obtainable **11** practicable **12** approachable, unrestricted

accession
4 rise **5** raise **8** addition, approach, increase, outburst, taking on **9** accretion, adherence, increment, induction **10** admittance, assumption, attainment **11** acquisition **12** augmentation, inauguration

accessory
3 aid **4** aide, prop, trim **5** extra, frill **6** helper **7** abettor, adjunct, fitting, insider, partner **8** addition, adjuvant, appendix **9** accretion, adornment, ancillary, appendage, assistant, associate, auxiliary, increment, secondary, tributary **10** accomplice, coincident, collateral, concurrent, decoration, incidental, subsidiary **11** appurtenant, concomitant, confederate, conspirator, subordinate, subservient **12** appurtenance, contributory **13** accompaniment, coconspirator, supplementary

accident
3 hap, lot **4** fate, luck, odds **5** fluke **6** chance, gamble, hazard, kismet, mishap **7** bad luck, destiny **8** calamity, casualty, fortuity, incident **9** mischance **10** misfortune **12** misadventure

accidental
3 odd **4** flat **5** fluky, sharp **6** casual, chance, flukey, random **7** unmeant **8** by chance, careless **9** chromatic, dependent, extempore, impromptu, unplanned, unwitting **10** coincident, contingent, fortuitous, unexpected, unforeseen, unintended **11** conditional, inadvertent **12** coincidental, uncalculated **13** unintentional

acclaim
4 hail, clap, laud **5** cheer, éclat, exalt, extol, glory, honor, kudos, roose **6** homage, praise, salute **7** applaud, approve, commend, glorify, magnify, ovation, plaudit, root for **8** applause, plaudits **10** compliment

acclimate
5 adapt **6** adjust, change, harden, season **7** toughen **9** condition, habituate

accolade
4 bays, fame **5** award, badge, honor, kudos **6** praise **7** laurels, tribute **8** approval **10** decoration **11** distinction

accommodate
3 fit **4** hold, rent, suit **5** adapt, alter, board, defer, favor, house, humor, lodge, put up, yield **6** adjust, attune, bestow, billet, change, encase, harbor, modify, oblige, please, submit, tailor, take in **7** cater to, conform, contain, enclose, furnish, indulge, quarter, receive, shelter **8** accustom, allow for, domicile **9** entertain, harmonize, integrate, reconcile **11** domiciliate, make room for

accommodating
7 amiable, helpful, willing **8** gracious, obliging **9** adaptable **10** hospitable, solicitous, thoughtful **11** considerate, cooperative

accommodations
3 inn **4** digs, keep, room **5** hotel, lodge, motel **6** hostel **7** housing, lodging, shelter **8** hostelry, lodgment, quarters **9** residence **12** room and board

accompaniment
6 backup **7** adjunct **8** addition **9** accessory, associate, attendant, corollary **10** supplement **11** concomitant, enhancement **12** augmentation

accompany
4 join **5** bring, guide, pilot **6** attend, convoy, escort, go with **7** combine, conduct, consort **8** chaperon, come with **9** associate **10** appear with, go together **11** perform with

accompanying
8 incident **9** accessory, ancillary, attendant, attending, secondary **10** associated, coincident, collateral **11** concomitant

accomplice
4 aide, ally **5** aider **6** cohort, flunky, helper, stooge **7** abettor, partner **8** henchman **9** accessory, assistant, associate **11** confederate, conspirator, subordinate **13** coconspirator

accomplish
3 win **4** gain **5** reach, score **6** attain, effect, fulfil, rack up **7** achieve, execute, fulfill, perfect, pull off, realize, succeed **8** bring off, carry out, complete **9** discharge **10** bring about

accomplished
4 able **5** adept **6** expert **7** skilled **8** finished, masterly, skillful, talented, virtuoso **9** practiced **10** proficient

accomplishment
3 act, art **4** deed, feat **5** craft, doing, skill **7** ability **9** adeptness, expertise **10** attainment, capability, completion **11** achievement, acquirement, proficiency

accord
4 deal, fuse, give, jibe, pact **5** agree, award, blend, chime, fit in, grant, match, merge, tally, union **6** affirm, assent, concur, confer, treaty **7** compact, concert, conform, empathy, entente, harmony, rapport **8** affinity, coincide, dovetail, sympathy **9** agreement, harmonize, reconcile **10** attraction, conformity, consonance, correspond, solidarity **11** concordance **13** understanding

accordant
8 agreeing **9** congruous, consonant **10** conforming, harmonious **13** correspondent

accordingly
4 duly, ergo, then, thus **5** hence **9** therefore, thereupon **12** consequently

accost
3 dog **4** call, dare, face, hail **5** annoy, beard, cross, front, hound, worry **6** bother, call to **7** affront, outface, outrage **8** approach, confront **9** challenge **10** buttonhole

accouchement
7 lying-in **8** childbed, delivery **10** childbirth **11** confinement, parturition

account
3 tab, use **4** bill, deem, note, rate, view **5** avail, basis, favor, score, story, track, value, worth **6** assess, client, esteem, reason, reckon, record, regard, report, repute **7** analyze, explain, expound, justify, recital, version **8** appraise, consider, customer, estimate **9** chronicle, narrative, rationale, reckoning, statement **11** explanation **13** consideration
book: **6** ledger

accountable
6 liable **8** amenable **10** answerable **11** explainable, responsible

accounting
11 bookkeeping
method: **4** FIFO, FILO, LIFO

accoutre
3 arm, rig **4** deck, gear **5** adorn, dress, equip, fix up, ready **6** attire, fit out, outfit, supply **7** appoint, furnish, prepare, provide, turn out **9** provision

accoutrement
3 kit **4** gear **6** outfit, tackle **7** regalia **8** tackling **9** accessory, apparatus, equipment, machinery, trappings **10** provisions **11** furnishings, habiliments **12** appointments **13** paraphernalia

accredit
3 lay **4** okay **5** refer **6** assign, attest, charge, credit, enable **7** approve, ascribe, certify, commend, empower, endorse, license, warrant **8** sanction, validate, vouch for **9** attribute, authorize, recognize, recommend **10** commission, credential

accretion
4 rise **5** raise **6** growth **7** buildup **8** addition, increase **9** accession, appendage, increment **10** attachment **11** enlargement **12** accumulation, augmentation

accrue
4 grow **5** amass **6** gather, pile up **7** build up, collect, compile **8** increase **10** accumulate, amalgamate **11** agglomerate

accumulate
4 heap, grow, mass, pile **5** add to, amass, hoard, lay by, lay in, lay up, stock, store **6** accrue, garner, gather, pile up, rack up, roll up **7** acquire, backlog, collect, compile, lay down, stack up, store up **8** assemble, increase **9** stockpile

accumulation
4 bank, heap, mass, pile **5** hoard, stock, store, trove **6** growth **7** backlog, buildup, reserve **8** increase **9** accretion, amassment **10** collection **11** aggregation, enlargement

accumulative
6 heaped **7** growing **8** additive, additory **9** summative **10** collective, increasing **11** aggregative **12** augmentative

accuracy
8 veracity **9** certainty, exactness, precision **10** definition, exactitude **11** correctness, preciseness **12** definiteness

accurate
4 just, nice, true **5** exact, right **6** actual, dead on, proper, spot on **7** certain, correct, factual, precise **8** definite, reliable, rigorous **9** authentic, error-free, errorless **10** dependable

accursed
4 vile **6** odious **7** hateful **8** damnable **9** abhorrent, execrable, loathsome, offensive, repugnant, revolting **10** abominable, despicable, detestable

accusation
3 rap 6 charge 9 aspersion, complaint 10 allegation, indictment 12 denunciation
false: 5 libel, smear 7 calumny, slander

accuse
3 tax 5 blame, brand 6 allege, charge, delate, finger, impute, indict 7 arraign, ascribe, censure, impeach 8 admonish, denounce, reproach 9 criminate, criticize, inculpate, reprobate 10 denunciate 11 incriminate

accustom
3 use 4 wont 5 adapt, enure, inure 6 adjust, harden, season 7 conform 9 habituate 11 acclimatize, familiarize

accustomed
3 set 5 usual 6 normal 7 chronic, regular, routine 8 accepted, everyday, familiar, habitual, ordinary, standard 9 customary 10 habituated 11 commonplace, established, traditional 12 conventional

ace
3 bit, jot, pip, top 4 atom, hair, iota, mite, star 5 crumb, minim, pilot, point, score, speck 6 Bishop (Billy), bullet, defeat, master, winner 7 whisker 8 molecule, particle, Red Baron 9 first rate, hole in one 10 Richthofen (Manfred von) 11 hairbreadth, tennis score 12 Rickenbacker (Eddie)

ace and face card
7 natural 9 blackjack

acedia
5 ennui 6 apathy, torpor 7 boredom, languor 8 lethargy, numbness

acerbate
3 vex 5 anger, annoy, peeve 6 madden 7 incense, inflame 8 embitter, irritate 9 aggravate 10 exasperate

acerbic
4 acid, sour, tart 5 acrid, harsh, rough, sharp 6 barbed, biting 7 caustic, cutting, mordant, satiric 8 sardonic, stinging 9 acidulous, corrosive, sarcastic 10 astringent

acerbity
7 acidity, sarcasm 8 acrimony, asperity, sourness, tartness 9 harshness, roughness, surliness 10 bitterness, causticity

Achates' companion
6 Aeneas

ache
3 yen 4 hurt, long, pain, pang, pine, pity, sigh 5 crave, smart, throb, yearn 6 hanker, hunger, stitch, suffer, thirst, twinge 8 yearning 11 commiserate
Scottish: 6 stound

Achebe novel
15 Things Fall Apart

Acheron
5 Hades, river

achieve
3 get, win 4 gain 5 reach, score 6 attain, effect, finish, obtain, rack up, secure 7 acquire, execute, fulfill, get done, perform, realize, succeed 8 carry out, complete, conclude 9 actualize 10 accomplish

achievement
3 win 4 coup, deed, feat 6 finish 7 exploit, success 10 attainment, completion 11 acquisition, realization, tour de force

Achilles
adviser: 6 Nestor
companion: 9 Patroclus
father: 6 Peleus
horse: 7 Xanthus
lover: 7 Briseis
mother: 6 Thetis
slayer: 5 Paris
victim: 6 Hector
vulnerable part: 4 heel

aching
4 hurt, sore 6 in pain 7 hurtful, hurting, painful 8 yearning 9 disturbed 10 afflictive, distressed 13 compassionate

acicular
5 acute, peaky, piked, sharp 6 peaked, pointy, spiked 7 pointed

acid
3 LSD 4 sour, tart 5 acerb 7 acerbic, acetose, caustic 8 stinging 9 corrosive, sarcastic, vitriolic
bleaching: 6 oxalic
fatty: 6 capric 7 caproic, stearic 8 caprylic
found in apples: 5 malic
found in cranberries: 7 benzoic
found in grapes: 8 tartaric
found in lemons: 6 citric
found in rhubarb: 6 oxalic
found in sour milk: 6 lactic
indicator: 6 litmus
kind: 5 amino, boric, iodic, malic, oleic 6 acetic, bromic, formic, nitric, oxalic, tannic 7 nitrous, silicic 8 carbolic, carbonic, muriatic, sulfuric 9 aqua regia 12 hydrochloric
neutralizer: 4 base 6 alkali
tanning: 6 tannic 8 catechin
vinegar: 6 acetic

acidulous
3 dry 4 sour, tart 5 acerb, harsh, sharp 6 barbed, biting 7 acerbic, acetose, cutting, mordant, piquant, pungent 8 sardonic 9 sarcastic

Acis
lover: 7 Galatea
slayer: 10 Polyphemus

acknowledge
3 own **4** avow, deem, tell, view **5** admit, agree, allow, grant, let on, own up **6** accede, accept, fess up, reveal **7** concede, confess, declare, divulge, profess **8** announce, consider, disclose, proclaim **9** recognize

acknowledgment
6 assent, avowal, credit, notice **9** admission **10** confession **11** affirmation, declaration, recognition

acme
3 cap, top **4** apex, peak **6** apogee, climax, summit, tiptop, vertex, zenith **8** capstone, pinnacle, ultimate **9** high point **10** perfection **11** culmination

acolyte
6 votary **7** apostle, epigone **8** adherent, disciple, follower

aconite
9 monkshood

acorn tree
3 oak

acoustic
5 aural **6** audile **8** auditory **9** unplugged

acquaint
4 clue, tell, warn **6** advise, fill in, inform, notify, orient, reveal **7** apprise, present **8** accustom, disclose **9** enlighten, introduce **11** familiarize

acquaintance
4 mate **5** amigo, crony, grasp **6** friend **7** comrade, contact **9** associate, colleague, companion **10** cognizance **11** familiarity

acquainted
6 versed **7** abreast, in touch **8** familiar, informed, up-to-date **9** au courant **10** conversant

acquiesce
3 bow, yes **5** agree, allow, bow to, yield **6** accede, accept, assent, comply, concur, give in, submit **7** consent, go along **9** reconcile, subscribe

acquiescence
6 assent **7** consent **8** giving in, yielding **9** deference **10** acceptance, compliance, conformity, submission **11** resignation

acquiescent
6 docile **7** passive **8** amenable, biddable, resigned, yielding **9** agreeable **10** submissive **11** unresistant, unresisting **12** nonresistant, nonresisting

acquire
3 add, buy, get, win **4** earn, form, gain, land **5** amass, annex **6** garner, obtain, pick up, secure, take on **7** bring in, collect, develop, procure **10** accumulate

acquirement
8 addition **9** accretion **11** acquisition

acquisition
4 gain **5** prize **7** winning **8** addition, learning, property, purchase **9** accretion

acquisitive
4 avid **5** eager, itchy **6** grabby, greedy **8** covetous, desirous, grasping **10** avaricious

acquit
3 act **4** bear, free **5** carry, clear, let go **6** behave, deport, let off **7** absolve, comport, conduct, perform, release, set free **8** liberate **9** discharge, exculpate, exonerate, vindicate

acreage
4 area, land **5** lands **6** estate **7** demesne, expanse, holding **8** property

acrid
4 acid, sour, tart **5** harsh, nasty, sharp **6** barbed, biting, bitter **7** acerbic, austere, burning, caustic, cutting, piquant, pungent **8** stinging **9** acidulous, trenchant **10** astringent, irritating

acrimonious
3 mad **5** angry, cross, irate, sharp, testy **6** biting, bitter, cranky, ireful **7** acerbic, caustic, cutting, vicious **9** indignant, irascible, rancorous **11** belligerent, contentious, quarrelsome

acrimony
5 anger, spite **6** animus, malice, rancor **7** ill will **8** acerbity, asperity, bad blood, mordancy **9** animosity, antipathy, harshness, virulence **10** bitterness **11** malevolence

Acrisius
daughter: **5** Danaë
slayer: **7** Perseus

acrobat
7 gymnast, tumbler **9** aerialist, trapezist **11** funambulist

across
4 over **6** beyond **7** athwart **12** transversely
prefix: **5** trans

act
3 law, run **4** bear, bill, deed, fake, feat, mime, play, pose, sham, work **5** bluff, feign, front, put-on, serve, stunt **6** affect, appear, behave, shtick **7** exploit, operate, perform, portray, pretend, routine, statute **8** function, pretense, simulate **9** officiate **10** masquerade **11** counterfeit, impersonate
wrongful: **3** sin **4** tort **5** crime, error, fault **7** default, misdeed, offense

acting
6 pro tem **7** interim, playing **9** ad interim, dramatics, imitating, portrayal, temporary, theatrics **10** pro tempore **12** entertaining

action
4 case, deed, feat, move, step, stir, suit, work **5** cause, doing **6** battle, bustle, combat

7 lawsuit, process, service **8** activity, behavior, conflict, fighting, function **9** execution, operation, procedure **10** engagement, proceeding **11** performance

action painter
5 Kline (Franz) **7** Pollock (Jackson) **9** de Kooning (Willem)

action painting
7 tachism

activate
3 arm **4** stir, wake **5** rally, rouse, set up, waken **6** arouse, awaken, call up, turn on **7** trigger **8** energize, mobilize, motivate, vitalize **9** stimulate

active
4 busy, live, spry **5** agile, alert, alive, brisk, going **6** at work, in play, lively, moving **7** driving, dynamic, flowing, on the go, running, working **8** animated, bustling, emitting, erupting, spirited, vigorous **9** effective, energetic, operating, operative, sprightly **11** functioning, industrious **12** enterprising

activity
6 action, bustle, motion **7** process, pursuit, venture **8** exercise, exertion **10** exercising, liveliness **11** undertaking

actor
4 mime, star **5** mimic **6** mummer, player **7** artiste, trouper **8** thespian **9** performer **11** participant **12** impersonator
name: **3** Cox (Wally), Fox (James, Michael J.), Lee (Bruce), Lom (Herbert), Mix (Tom), Ray (Aldo) **4** Alda (Alan, Robert), Bean (Orson), Blue (Ben), Bond (Ward), Caan (James), Cage (Nicholas), Cobb (Lee J.), Coco (James), Culp (Robert), Dean (James), Depp (Johnny), Dern (Bruce), Duff (Howard), Egan (Richard), Falk (Peter), Ford (Glenn, Harrison), Foxx (Redd), Geer (Will), Gere (Richard), Grey (Joel), Hill (Arthur), Hope (Bob), Hurt (John, William), Ives (Burl), Kaye (Danny), Kean (Edmund), Keel (Howard), Ladd (Alan), Lahr (Bert), Lord (Jack), Lowe (Rob), Lunt (Alfred), Marx (Chico, Groucho, Harpo, Zeppo), Muni (Paul), Ngor (Haing S.), Peck (Gregory), Penn (Sean), Pitt (Brad), Raft (George), Reid (Wallace), Roth (Tim), Ryan (Robert), Shaw (Robert), Tati (Jacques), Tone (Franchot), Torn (Rip), Tune (Tommy), Wahl (Ken), Webb (Clifton, Jack), Wynn (Ed, Keenan), York (Michael) **5** Adler (Luther), Allen (Fred, Tim, Woody), Arkin (Adam, Alan), Asner (Ed), Autry (Gene), Ayres (Lew), Bacon (Kevin), Barry (Gene), Bates (Alan), Beery (Wallace), Benny (Jack), Berle (Milton), Boone (Richard), Booth (Edwin), Boyer (Charles), Boyle (Peter), Brand (Neville), Burns (George), Caine (Michael), Candy (John), Chase (Chevy), Clift (Montgomery), Cosby (Bill), Dafoe (Willem), Davis (Clifton, Ossie, Sammy Jr.), Delon (Alain), Donat (Robert), Evans (Maurice), Ewell (Tom), Finch (Peter), Firth (Colin, Peter), Flynn (Errol), Fonda (Henry, Peter), Franz (Dennis), Gabin (Jean), Gable (Clark), Gould (Elliot), Grant (Cary, Hugh), Gwenn (Edmund), Hanks (Tom), Hardy (Oliver), Hauer (Rutger), Hawke (Ethan), Hayes (Gabby), Hogan (Paul), Irons (Jeremy), Jaffe (Sam), Jones (Dean, James Earl, Tommy Lee), Kazan (Elia), Keach (Stacy), Keith (Brian, David), Kelly (Gene), Kiley (Richard), Kline (Kevin), Kotto (Yaphet), Lamas (Fernando, Lorenzo), Lanza (Mario), Lewis (Jerry, Richard), Lloyd (Harold), Lorre (Peter), Lukas (Paul), Lynde (Paul), March (Fredric), Mason (James), McCoy (Tim), Mills (John), Mineo (Sal), Moore (Dudley, Roger, Victor), Neill (Sam), Nimoy (Leonard), Niven (David), Nolte (Nick), Olmos (Edward James), O'Neal (Patrick, Ryan), O'Shea (Milo), Payne (John), Perry (Luke, Matthew), Pesci (Joe), Power (Tyrone), Price (Vincent), Pryce (Jonathan), Quaid (Dennis, Randy), Quinn (Aidan, Anthony), Rains (Claude), Reeve (Christopher), Scott (Campbell, George C., Randolph), Segal (George), Sheen (Charlie, Martin), Smits (Jimmy), Stack (Robert), Stamp (Terence), Sydow (Max von), Tracy (Spencer), Wayne (John), Wilde (Cornel), Wills (Chill), Woods (James), Young (Gig, Robert) **6** Abbott (Bud), Albert (Eddie), Ameche (Don), Arness (James), Backus (Jim), Balsam (Martin), Barker (Lex), Baxter (Warner), Beatty (Ned, Warren), Begley (Ed), Blades (Ruben), Bogart (Humphrey), Bolger (Ray), Brando (Marlon), Brooks (Albert, Mel), Burton (Richard), Caesar (Sid), Cagney (James), Cantor (Eddie), Cariou (Len), Carney (Art), Carrey (Jim), Carvey (Dana), Chaney (Lon), Cleese (John), Coburn (Charles, James), Colman (Ronald), Conrad (Robert, William), Conway (Tim, Tom), Coogan (Jackie), Cooper (Gary), Cotten (Joseph), Coward (Noël), Crabbe (Buster), Crenna (Richard), Cronyn (Hume), Crosby (Bing), Cruise (Tom), Culkin (Macaulay), Curtis (Tony), Dailey (Dan), Dalton (Timothy), Danson (Ted), Danton (Ray), Darren (James), De Niro (Robert), de Sica (Vittorio), De Vito (Danny), Dillon (Matt), Downey (Robert), Dullea (Keir), Duryea (Dan), Duvall (Robert), Ferrer (José, Mel), Fields (W.C.), Finney (Albert), Garcia (Andy), Garner (James), Gibson (Hoot, Mel), Glover (Danny), Graves (Peter), Greene (Lorne), Grodin (Charles), Harris (Ed, Richard), Harvey (Laurence), Hayden (Sterling), Heflin (Van), Heston (Charlton), Hingle (Pat), Holden (Bill), Hopper (Dennis, William), Howard (Leslie, Ron, Trevor), Hudson (Rock), Hunter (Jeffrey, Tab), Huston (John, Walter), Hutton (Jim,

Timothy), Irving (Henry), Jacobi (Derek, Lou), Jagger (Dean), Keaton (Buster, Michael), Keitel (Harvey), Kilmer (Val), Knotts (Don), Landau (Martin), Landon (Michael), Laurel (Stan), Lemmon (Jack), Liotta (Ray), Lugosi (Bela), MacRae (Gordon), Malden (Karl), Martin (Dean, Steve), Marvin (Lee), Massey (Raymond), Mature (Victor), McCrea (Joel), Meeker (Ralph), Menjou (Adolphe), Mifune (Toshiro), Modine (Matthew), Morley (Robert), Mostel (Zero), Murphy (Audie, Eddie), Murray (Bill, Don), Neeson (Liam), Nelson (Ozzie), Newley (Anthony), Newman (Paul), O'Brian (Hugh), O'Brien (Edmund, Pat), Oldman (Gary), O'Toole (Peter), Pacino (Al), Parker (Fess), Poston (Tom), Powell (Dick), Quayle (Anthony), Reeves (Keanu, Steve), Reiner (Carl, Rob), Reiser (Paul), Rennie (Michael), Ritter (John, Tex), Rogers (Roy, Wayne, Will), Romero (Cesar), Rooney (Mickey), Rourke (Mickey), Schell (Maximilian), Seagal (Steven), Sharif (Omar), Slezak (Walter), Snipes (Wesley), Spacey (Kevin), Spader (James), Swayze (Patrick), Taylor (Robert, Rod), Thomas (Danny, Richard), Turpin (Ben), Vallee (Rudy), Vaughn (Robert), Voight (Jon), Wagner (Robert), Walker (Robert), Warden (Jack), Wayans (Damon, Keenen Ivory), Weaver (Dennis, Fritz), Welles (Orson), Werner (Oskar), Wilder (Gene), Willis (Bruce) **7** Abraham (F. Murray), Andrews (Dana), Astaire (Fred), Aykroyd (Dan), Baldwin (Alec, Daniel, Stephen, William), Bellamy (Ralph), Bogarde (Dirk), Branagh (Kenneth), Bridges (Beau, Jeff, Lloyd), Bronson (Charles), Brosnan (Pierce), Brynner (Yul), Burbage (Richard), Bushman (Francis X.), Buttons (Red), Calhern (Louis), Calhoun (Rory), Cameron (Rod), Carroll (Leo G.), Chaplin (Charlie), Clooney (George), Connery (Sean), Connors (Chuck), Conried (Hans), Costner (Kevin), Crystal (Billy), Daniels (Jeff), da Silva (Howard), DeLuise (Dom), Dennehy (Brian), DeWilde (Brandon), Donahue (Troy), Donlevy (Brian), Douglas (Kirk, Melvyn, Michael, Paul), Durante (Jimmy), Edwards (Vince), Estrada (Erik), Feldman (Marty), Fiennes (Ralph), Freeman (Morgan), Garrick (David), Gazzara (Ben), Gielgud (John), Gleason (Jackie), Goodman (John), Gosling (Ryan), Gossett (Lou), Grammer (Kelsey), Granger (Farley, Stewart), Gulager (Clu), Hackman (Gene), Henreid (Paul), Hoffman (Dustin), Homolka (Oscar), Hopkins (Anthony), Hoskins (Bob), Janssen (David), Johnson (Ben, Don, Van), Jourdan (Louis), Jurgens (Curt), Karloff (Boris), Kennedy (Arthur, George), Klugman (Jack), Lawford (Peter), Leonard (Robert Sean, Sheldon), Lithgow (John), MacLane (Barton), Maharis (George), Mathers (Jerry), Matthau (Walter), McCarey (Leo), McGavin (Darren), McQueen (Steve), Milland (Ray), Mitchum (Robert), Montand (Yves), Morales (Esai), Navarro (Ramon), Newhart (Bob), Nielsen (Leslie), Novello (Ivor), O'Connor (Carroll, Donald), Olivier (Laurence), Palance (Jack), Paulsen (Pat), Peppard (George), Perkins (Anthony), Pickens (Slim), Pidgeon (Walter), Poitier (Sidney), Preston (Robert), Randall (Tony), Redford (Robert), Rickman (Alan), Robards (Jason), Robbins (Tim), Robeson (Paul), Roberts (Pernell, Tony), Sanders (George), Savalas (Telly), Scourby (Alexander), Selleck (Tom), Sellers (Peter), Shatner (William), Shepard (Sam), Silvers (Phil), Sinatra (Frank), Skelton (Red), Skinner (Otis), Steiger (Rod), Stewart (James, Patrick), Stooges (Three), Tamblyn (Russ), Ustinov (Peter), Van Dyke (Dick, Jerry), Wallach (Eli), Widmark (Richard), Wilding (Michael), Winters (Jonathan), Woolley (Monty) **8** Banderas (Antonio), Barrault (Jean-Louis), Basehart (Richard), Belmondo (Jean-Paul), Berenger (Tom), Blackmer (Sidney), Borgnine (Ernest), Buchanan (Edgar), Buchholz (Horst), Chandler (Jeff), Costello (Lou), Crawford (Broderick, Michael), Cummings (Robert), Day-Lewis (Daniel), DiCaprio (Leonardo), Dreyfuss (Richard), Eastwood (Clint), Forsythe (John), Garfield (John), Goldblum (Jeff), Griffith (Andy), Guinness (Alec), Harrison (Noel, Rex), Hemmings (David), Holbrook (Hal), Holloway (Stanley), Houseman (John), Jannings (Emil), Kingsley (Ben), Langella (Frank), Laughton (Charles), Marshall (E.G., Herbert), McDowall (Roddy), McDowell (Malcolm), McGregor (Ewan), McKellen (Ian), McLaglen (Victor), Meredith (Burgess), Rathbone (Basil), Redgrave (Michael), Reynolds (Burt), Ritchard (Cyril), Robinson (Edward G.), Sarrazin (Michael), Scofield (Paul), Seinfeld (Jerry), Stallone (Sylvester), Stroheim (Erich von), Sullivan (Barry), Travolta (John), Turturro (John), Van Damme (Jean-Claude), Von Sydow (Max), Whitaker (Forest), Whitmore (James), Williams (Robin) **9** Amsterdam (Morey), Barrymore (John, Lionel), Brandauer (Klaus Maria), Broderick (Matthew), Carnovsky (Morris), Carradine (David, John, Keith, Robert), Courtenay (Tom), Depardieu (Gérard), Fairbanks (Douglas), Fishburne (Larry), Franciosa (Anthony), Hardwicke (Cedric), Harrelson (Woody), Hyde-White (Wilfrid), Lancaster (Burt), MacMurray (Fred), Malkovich (John), Montalban (Ricardo), Nicholson (Jack), Pleasance (Donald), Robertson (Cliff, Dale), Strasberg (Lee), Tarantino (Quentin), Valentino (Rudolph), Zimbalist (Efrem) **10** Fitzgerald (Barry), Hasselhoff (David), Montgomery (Robert), Richardson (Ralph), Sutherland (Donald, Kiefer), Washington (Denzel) **11** Chamberlain (Richard), Greenstreet (Sydney), Mastroianni (Marcello), Trintignant (Jean-Louis) **13** Kristofferson (Kris)

actor Jared
4 Leto

actor Richard
4 Egan, Gere **5** Kiley, Lewis **6** Burton, Crenna, Harris

actor's
quest: 4 part, role
signal: 3 cue
group: 3 SAG **5** AFTRA

actress
3 Bow (Clara), Cox (Courtney), Day (Doris), Dee (Ruby, Sandra), Dru (Joanne), Gam (Rita), Loy (Myrna), May (Elaine), Rae (Charlotte) **4** Alba (Jessica), Ball (Lucille), Bara (Theda), Barr (Roseanne), Cass (Peggy), Cher, Coca (Imogene), Cruz (Penelope), Dahl (Arlene), Daly (Tyne), Dern (Laura), Diaz (Cameron), Dors (Diana), Down (Lesley-Ann), Duke (Patty), Duse (Eleonora), Eden (Barbara), Foch (Nina), Garr (Teri), Gish (Dorothy, Lillian), Grey (Jennifer), Gwyn (Nell), Hawn (Goldie), Holm (Celeste), Hunt (Helen, Linda, Marsha), Hurt (Mary Beth), Hyer (Martha), Ivey (Judith), Kahn (Madeline), Kerr (Deborah), Lake (Veronica), Lisi (Virna), Long (Nia, Shelley), Main (Marjorie), Mayo (Virginia), Neal (Patricia), Olin (Lena), Page (Geraldine), Raye (Martha), Rigg (Diana), Ross (Diana, Katharine), Rush (Barbara), Ryan (Meg, Peggy), Shue (Elisabeth), Skye (Ione), Ward (Sela), Weld (Tuesday), West (Mae), Wood (Natalie, Peggy), Wray (Fay), York (Susannah) **5** Adams (Maude), Aimee (Anouk), Allen (Joan, Gracie, Karen, Nancy), Alley (Kirstie), Arden (Eve), Astor (Mary), Bates (Kathy), Berry (Halle), Black (Karen), Bloom (Claire), Blyth (Ann), Booth (Shirley), Braga (Sonia), Brice (Fanny), Britt (May), Bruce (Virginia), Buzzi (Ruth), Caron (Leslie), Close (Glenn), Crain (Jeanne), Danes (Claire), Davis (Bette, Geena, Judy, Viola), Dench (Judi), Derek (Bo), Dunne (Irene), Eggar (Samantha), Evans (Edith), Falco (Edie), Field (Sally), Fonda (Bridget, Jane), Gabor (Eva, Zsa Zsa), Garbo (Greta), Gless (Sharon), Grant (Lee), Greer (Jane), Grier (Pam), Hagen (Uta), Hasso (Signe), Hayek (Salma), Hayes (Helen), Heche (Anne), Henie (Sonja), Howes (Sally Ann), Jones (Cherry, Jennifer, Shirley), Kazan (Lainie), Kelly (Grace, Patsy), Kurtz (Swoosie), Lahti (Christine), Lange (Hope, Jessica), Leigh (Janet, Jennifer Jason, Vivien), Lenya (Lotte), Lewis (Juliette), Loren (Sophia), Mason (Marsha, Pamela), Meara (Anne), Miles (Sarah, Vera), Moore (Demi, Julianne, Mary Tyler, Terry), Naldi (Nita), North (Sheree), Novak (Kim), O'Hara (Maureen), Olson (Nancy), O'Neal (Tatum), Perez (Rosie), Picon (Molly), Pitts (Zasu), Reese (Della), Ricci (Christina), Roman (Ruth), Ruehl (Mercedes), Russo (Rene), Ryder (Winona), Saint (Eva Marie), Scott (Lizbeth, Martha), Shire (Talia), Smith (Alexis, Maggie), Stone (Emma, Sharon), Storm (Gale), Swank (Hilary), Tandy (Jessica), Terry (Ellen), Tomei (Marisa), Tyler (Liv), Tyson (Cicely), Watts (Naomi), Welch (Raquel), Wiest (Dianne), Worth (Irene), Wyatt (Jane), Wyman (Jane), Young (Sean, Loretta) **6** Adjani (Isabelle), Angeli (Pier), Arthur (Bea, Beatrice, Jean), Ashley (Elizabeth), Bacall (Lauren), Bardot (Brigitte), Barkin (Ellen), Barrie (Wendy), Baxter (Anne), Bening (Annette), Bergen (Candice, Polly), Bisset (Jacqueline), Blaine (Vivian), Brooks (Louise), Bujold (Genevieve), Butler (Brett), Cannon (Dyan), Carter (Dixie, Lynda, Nell), Cooper (Gladys), Crouse (Lindsay), Curtin (Jane), Curtis (Jamie Lee), Danner (Blythe), Davies (Marion), Del Rio (Dolores), Dennis (Sandy), Diller (Phyllis), Draper (Ruth), Driver (Minnie), Dumont (Margaret), Duncan (Sandy), Durbin (Deanna), Duvall (Shelley), Ekberg (Anita), Ekland (Britt), Fabray (Nanette), Farmer (Frances), Farrow (Mia), Feldon (Barbara), Fisher (Carrie), Foster (Jodie), Garner (Peggy Ann), Garson (Greer), Gaynor (Mitzi), Gordon (Ruth), Grable (Betty), Grimes (Tammy), Hannah (Daryl), Harlow (Jean), Harper (Jessica, Tess, Valerie), Harris (Barbara, Julie, Rosemary), Hedren (Tippi), Hiller (Wendy), Hunter (Holly, Kim), Hussey (Ruth), Huston (Anjelica), Hutton (Betty), Irving (Amy), Keaton (Diane), Keeler (Ruby), Kidman (Nicole), Kinski (Nastassja), Knight (Shirley), Lamarr (Hedy), Lamour (Dorothy), Lasser (Louise), Laurie (Piper), Lillie (Bea, Beatrice), Louise (Tina), Lupino (Ida), MacRae (Sheila), Malone (Dorothy), Martin (Mary), Matlin (Marlee), Merkel (Una), Merman (Ethel), Midler (Bette), Miller (Ann), Mirren (Helen), Monroe (Marilyn), Moreau (Jeanne), Moreno (Rita), Oberon (Merle), O'Brien (Margaret), Oliver (Edna May), Palmer (Lili), Paquin (Anna), Parker (Eleanor, Mary-Louise, Sarah Jessica, Suzy), Peters (Bernadette), Powers (Stephanie), Prowse (Juliet), Rainer (Luise), Rashad (Phylicia), Remick (Lee), Ritter (Thelma), Rivera (Chita), Rogers (Ginger), Scales (Prunella), Seberg (Jean), Sidney (Sylvia), Somers (Suzanne), Sommer (Elke), Spacek (Sissy), Streep (Meryl), Taylor (Elizabeth), Temple (Shirley), Theron (Charlize), Thomas (Marlo), Tiffin (Pamela), Tomlin (Lily), Turner (Kathleen, Lana), Walker (Nancy), Warren (Lesley Ann), Watson (Emily), Weaver (Sigourney), Wilson (Marie), Winger (Debra), Wright (Teresa), Wynter (Dana) **7** Allyson (June), Andress (Ursula), Andrews (Julie), Aniston (Jennifer), Bassett (Angela), Bennett (Constance, Joan), Bergman (Ingrid), Binoche (Juliette), Blethyn (Brenda), Buckley (Betty), Bullock (Sandra), Burnett (Carol), Burstyn (Ellen), Colbert (Claudette), Collins (Joan, Pauline),

Cornell (Katherine), Cushman (Charlotte), Darnell (Linda), DeCarlo (Yvonne), Delaney (Dana), Deneuve (Catherine), Dukakis (Olympia), Dunaway (Faye), Dunnock (Mildred), Fawcett (Farrah), Fleming (Rhonda), Fricker (Brenda), Gardner (Ava), Garland (Judy), Gershon (Gina), Gingold (Hermione), Goddard (Paulette), Grahame (Gloria), Grayson (Kathryn), Hatcher (Teri), Hayward (Susan), Heckart (Eileen), Hepburn (Audrey, Katharine), Hershey (Barbara), Jackson (Anne, Glenda, Kate), Langtry (Lillie), Learned (Michael), Lombard (Carole), MacGraw (Ali), Madonna, Magnani (Anna), Mangano (Silvana), McGuire (Dorothy), McKenna (Siobhan), McQueen (Butterfly), Meadows (Audrey, Jayne), Mimieux (Yvette), Miranda (Carmen), Mulgrew (Kate), Natwick (Mildred), Parsons (Estelle), Perlman (Rhea), Perrine (Valerie), Plummer (Amanda), Podesta (Rosanna), Portman (Natalie), Roberts (Julia), Russell (Jane, Rosalind, Theresa), Salonga (Lea), Scacchi (Greta), Sevigny (Chloë), Shearer (Norma), Shields (Brooke), Siddons (Sarah), Simmons (Jean), Sorvino (Mira), Sothern (Ann), Stevens (Connie, Stella), Stritch (Elaine), Swanson (Gloria), Swinton (Tilda), Thaxter (Phyllis), Thurman (Uma), Tierney (Gene), Ullmann (Liv), Verdugo (Elena), Winfrey (Oprah), Winslet (Kate), Winters (Shelley), Withers (Jane), Woodard (Alfre) **8** Anderson (Judith, Loni, Melissa Sue), Arquette (Patricia, Rosanna), Ashcroft (Peggy), Bancroft (Anne), Bankhead (Tallulah), Basinger (Kim), Blondell (Joan), Byington (Spring), Caldwell (Zoe), Campbell (Mrs. Patrick), Channing (Carol, Stockard), Charisse (Cyd), Christie (Julie), Crawford (Joan), DeMornay (Rebecca), Dewhurst (Colleen), Dietrich (Marlene), Dressler (Marie), Fletcher (Louise), Fontaine (Joan), Fontanne (Lynn), Goldberg (Whoopi), Griffith (Melanie), Hayworth (Rita), Holliday (Judy), Lansbury (Angela), Lawrence (Gertrude), Leachman (Cloris), Leighton (Margaret), Lindfors (Viveca), Lockhart (June), Lovelace (Linda), MacLaine (Shirley), McDaniel (Hattie), Mercouri (Melina), Minnelli (Liza), Nelligan (Kate), Neuwirth (Bebe), O'Donnell (Rosie), Pfeiffer (Michelle), Pickford (Mary), Prentiss (Paula), Redgrave (Lynn, Vanessa), Reynolds (Debbie), Roseanne, Rowlands (Gena), Sarandon (Susan), Shepherd (Cybill), Signoret (Simone), Spelling (Tori), Stanwyck (Barbara), Straight (Beatrice), Sullavan (Margaret), Talmadge (Norma), Thompson (Emma, Sada), Van Doren (Mamie), Vardalos (Nia), Williams (Esther), Woodward (Joanne) **9** Alexander (Jane), Barrymore (Drew, Ethel), Bernhardt (Sarah), Blanchett (Cate), Cardinale (Claudia), Christian (Linda), Clayburgh (Jill), Dandridge (Dorothy), DeGeneres (Ellen), Dickinson (Angie), Fairchild (Morgan), Henderson (Florence), Kellerman (Sally), Mansfield (Jayne), McDonnell (Mary), Moorehead (Agnes), O'Sullivan (Maureen), Pleshette (Suzanne), Plowright (Joan), Schneider (Romy), Singleton (Penny), Stapleton (Jean, Maureen), Strasberg (Susan), Streisand (Barbra), Struthers (Sally), Thorndike (Sybil), Vera-Ellen, Zellweger (Renée) **10** Ann-Margret, Lanchester (Elsa), Montgomery (Elizabeth), Richardson (Miranda, Natasha), Rossellini (Isabella), Rutherford (Margaret), Tushingham (Rita) **11** de Havilland (Olivia), McCambridge (Mercedes), Riefenstahl (Leni), Silverstone (Alicia), Steenburgen (Mary) **12** Bonham-Carter (Helena), Lollabrigida (Gina), Mastrantonio (Mary Elizabeth)

actress Christine
5 Lahti

actress Marisa
5 Tomei

actress Rene
4 Russo

actress Ruby
3 Dee

actress Téa
5 Leoni

actual
4 echt, hard, live, real, true **5** exact **6** extant, living **7** certain, current, de facto, factual, genuine **8** absolute, bona fide, concrete, definite, existent, existing, material, physical, positive, tangible **9** authentic, objective, veritable **10** legitimate, phenomenal **12** indisputable

actuality
4 fact **5** being, truth **7** reality **9** existence, substance **10** embodiment **11** incarnation, materiality

actually
5 truly **6** indeed, in fact, really **7** de facto, no doubt **9** genuinely, in reality, veritably **10** absolutely

actuate
4 move, spur, stir **5** drive, impel, rouse **6** arouse, excite, propel, set off, turn on **7** provoke, trigger **8** activate, energize, mobilize, motivate, vitalize

act up
5 cut up **7** show off **9** misbehave **11** misfunction

acumen
3 wit **6** acuity, vision, wisdom **7** insight **8** keenness **9** acuteness, sharpness **10** astuteness, perception, shrewdness **11** discernment, penetration, percipience **12** perspicacity

acute
4 dire, keen **5** sharp **6** shrewd, urgent **7** crucial, exigent, intense, pointed **8** critical, incisive, piercing, shooting, stabbing **9** knifelike, observant, trenchant **10** perceptive **11** penetrating, quick-witted, sharp-witted

ad ___
3 hoc, lib, rem **7** hominem, interim, nauseam **9** infinitum

adage
3 saw **4** rule **5** axiom, maxim, motto **6** byword, saying, truism **7** proverb **8** aphorism, apothegm

adagio
4 slow **5** tempo

Adah
husband: **4** Esau **6** Lamech
son: **5** Jabal, Jubal **7** Eliphaz

Adam
grandson: **4** Enos **5** Enoch
home: **4** Eden
rib: **3** Eve
son: **4** Abel, Cain, Seth
wife: **3** Eve **6** Lilith

Adam ___
4 Bede **5** Smith

adamant
3 set **4** firm, hard **5** rigid, stiff, stone, tough **6** flinty **8** immobile, obdurate, resolute **9** immovable, unbending, unswaying **10** determined, inflexible, unbendable, unyielding **11** unbreakable

adapt
3 fit **4** suit **5** alter, shape, yield **6** adjust, change, modify, revise, square, tailor **7** arrange, conform, get used, remodel **9** acclimate, habituate, reconcile **11** acclimatize, accommodate

adaptable
6 mobile, pliant, supple **7** ductile, plastic, pliable **8** flexible, moldable **9** malleable, versatile

adaptation
6 change **7** version **8** revision **9** reworking **10** adjustment, alteration **12** modification

ad astra per ___
6 aspera

add
3 sum, tot **4** cast, foot, join, tote **5** affix, annex, count, tally, total, unite **6** append, attach, figure, reckon, tack on, take on **7** augment, compute, count up, enlarge, improve, include **8** compound, increase, totalize **9** build onto, calculate **10** supplement

Addams family
3 Itt **5** Gomez **7** Pugsley **8** Morticia **9** Grandmama, Wednesday **11** Uncle Fester
servants: **5** Lurch, Thing

added
3 new **4** else, more **5** extra, fresh, other **7** another, farther, further **9** accessory **10** additional **13** supplementary

addendum
5 extra, rider **8** addition **10** supplement

adder
5 snake, viper **10** calculator **12** hognose snake

addict
3 fan, nut **4** bias, buff, user **5** hound, lover **6** abuser, devote, junkie, zealot **7** booster, devotee, fanatic, groupie, habitué **9** habituate, surrender **10** aficionado, enthusiast

Addis ___
5 Ababa

addition
4 plus, rise **5** annex, extra, raise, rider **7** accrual, adjunct **8** appendix, increase **9** accession, accessory, accretion, extension, increment **10** supplement **11** enlargement **12** appurtenance, augmentation

additional
see **added**

additionally
3 too **4** also, more, then **5** again **6** as well **7** besides, further **8** likewise, moreover **11** furthermore

additive
5 extra **8** extender **9** summative, substance

addle
5 mix up, spoil **6** muddle, puzzle **7** confuse, fluster, nonplus, perplex **8** befuddle, bewilder, confound, distract, throw off **9** dumbfound

addled
5 dizzy, woozy **6** groggy

add-on
3 ell **7** adjunct **9** accessory **11** enhancement

address
3 aim, air, set, URL **4** hail, send, tact, talk **5** apply, court, grace, greet, level, place, point, poise, remit, route, skill, speak, treat **6** call to, devote, direct, pursue, relate, salute, speech **7** bearing, consign, deliver, forward, know-how, lecture, oration, speak to, write to **8** appeal to, approach, converse, deal with, deftness, delivery, demeanor, dispatch, identify, location, petition, position, presence, transmit **9** attention, dexterity, diplomacy, expertise **10** adroitness, competence, directions, efficiency **11** comportment, designation, proficiency, savoir faire
abbreviation: **3** apt., ave.

adduce
3 lay **4** cite **5** claim, offer **6** allege, submit, tender **7** advance, present, proffer, propose, refer to, suggest **8** document **9** exemplify **10** illustrate

add up
3 sum **5** count, tally, total **6** amount, reckon **7** compute **9** make sense

add up to
4 mean **5** spell **6** amount, denote, import, intend **7** compute, connote, express, signify

adept
3 pro **4** able, deft, whiz **5** crack, savvy **6** adroit, expert, master, wizard **7** skilled **8** masterly,

skillful, virtuoso **9** dexterous, masterful **10** proficient **11** crackerjack **12** professional

adequacy
5 might **6** enough **7** ability **8** capacity **10** capability, competence, sufficient **11** sufficiency **13** qualification

adequate
3 due **4** enow **6** common, decent, enough **8** all right, passable, pleasing, standard, suitable **9** competent, sufficing **10** acceptable, sufficient **11** comfortable **12** satisfactory **13** unexceptional, unimpeachable

adequately
4 well **5** amply, right **6** enough **8** all right, passably, properly, suitably **9** fittingly, tolerably **12** sufficiently **13** appropriately

Adeste ___
7 Fideles

adhere
4 bond, glue **5** cling, paste, stick **6** attach, bind to, cement, cleave, cohere, fasten **7** stick to **8** hold fast

adherence
4 bond **5** cling **7** loyalty **8** adhesion, clinging, cohesion, fidelity, sticking **9** constancy **10** attachment **12** faithfulness

adherent
3 fan, ist **6** cohort, minion, votary **7** apostle, devotee, sectary **8** disciple, follower, henchman, partisan, stalwart **9** satellite, supporter **10** aficionado

adhering
6 clingy, sticky **7** binding

adhesive
4 glue **5** epoxy, gluey, gooey, gummy, stamp, tacky **6** cement, clingy, gummed, sticky **7** holding, stickum **8** adhering, fastener, mucilage, sticking **9** attaching

adieu
3 bye **4** by-by, ciao, ta-ta **5** congé **6** bye-bye, so long **7** cheerio, good-bye, parting, toodles **8** farewell, toodle-oo **11** leave-taking

ad interim
6 acting, pro tem **9** temporary **10** pro tempore **11** temporarily

adios
3 bye **4** by-by, ciao, ta-ta **5** adieu, later **6** bye-bye, so long **7** cheerio, goodbye, toodles **8** farewell, toodle-oo **10** hasta luego

adipose
3 fat **4** oily **5** fatty **6** greasy **7** fatlike

adit
3 way **4** door **5** entry **6** access, entrée, tunnel **7** ingress, passage **8** entrance **9** mine entry **10** passageway **12** mine entrance

adjacent
4 near **5** close **6** beside, nearby, next to **8** abutting, next door, touching **9** adjoining, alongside, bordering **10** contiguous, juxtaposed, near-at-hand **11** close-at-hand, neighboring **12** conterminous

adjoin
3 add **4** abut, link, line, meet **5** annex, touch, verge **6** append, attach, border, butt on, couple **7** connect, impinge **8** neighbor **11** communicate

adjourn
4 move, rise, stay **5** defer, delay **6** hold up, put off, recess, shelve **7** hold off, suspend **8** dissolve, hold over, postpone, prorogue **9** prorogate

adjudge
4 deem, rule **5** award, grant **6** decide, settle, umpire **7** mediate, referee **9** arbitrate

adjudicate
6 decide, settle **9** arbitrate

adjunct
5 added, affix **6** joined **8** addendum, addition, appanage, appendix, attached **9** accessory, accretion, appendage, assistant, associate, auxiliary **10** attachment **12** appurtenance

adjure
3 beg, bid **4** urge **6** exhort **7** beseech, entreat, command, implore, require **9** importune **10** supplicate

adjust
3 fit, fix, rig **4** suit, tune **5** adapt, order, right **6** accord, attune, modify, orient, settle, square, tailor, tune up **7** arrange, conform, correct, rectify, resolve **8** modulate, regulate **9** habituate, harmonize, reconcile **11** accommodate

adjutant
4 aide **6** deputy

adjuvant
4 aide **6** aiding, helper **8** enhancer, modifier **9** accessory, ancillary, assisting, auxiliary **10** collateral, subsidiary **11** appurtenant **12** contributory

Adlai's running mate
5 Estes (Kefauver)

ad-lib
9 extempore, improvise, impromptu **10** improvised, off-the-cuff, unprepared **11** extemporize, spontaneous, unrehearsed

Admetus
father: **6** Pheres
wife: **8** Alcestis

administer
3 run **4** boss, deal, give, head, mete **5** issue **6** direct, govern, head up, manage **7** conduct,

control, deal out, deliver, dole out, execute, give out, mete out, oversee, perform, provide **8** carry out, dispense, share out **9** apportion, supervise **10** distribute, portion out

administration
6 regime **7** control **9** direction **10** governance, presidency
system of: 11 bureaucracy

administrator
4 boss, exec, head **5** chief **7** manager, officer **8** director, official, overseer **9** executive **10** supervisor

admirable
6 august, worthy **8** laudable **9** deserving, estimable, excellent, meritable **11** commendable, meritorious, outstanding **12** praiseworthy

admiral
American: 4 Byrd (Richard), Sims (William) **5** Dewey (George), Stark (Harold) **6** Halsey (Bull), Nimitz (Chester) **7** Zumwalt (Elmo) **8** Farragut (David), Rickover (Hyman), Spruance (Raymond)
Chinese: 7 Zheng He
Confederate: 6 Semmes (Raphael)
Dutch: 5 Tromp (Maarten)
English: 5 Drake (Francis) **6** Nelson (Horatio), Rodney (George), Vernon (Edward) **7** Hawkins (John) **8** Beaufort (Francis), Jellicoe (John), Villiers (George) **11** Mountbatten (Louis)
fictional: 10 Hornblower (Horatio)
French: 10 Villeneuve (Pierre-Charles)
German: 4 Spee (Graf Maximilian von) **6** Dönitz (Karl), Raeder (Erich) **7** Doenitz (Karl), Tirpitz (Alfred von)
Japanese: 4 Togo (Hideki) **5** Yonai (Mitsumasa) **8** Yamamoto (Isoroku)
Spanish: 8 Menéndez (Pedro)

admiration
5 favor **6** esteem, praise, regard **7** account, delight, respect **8** applause, approval, pleasure **9** affection **10** estimation **11** approbation **12** appreciation

admire
5 adore, honor, prize, value **6** esteem, praise, regard, relish, revere **7** adulate, applaud, approve, cherish, commend, respect **8** consider, treasure **9** delight in **10** appreciate

admirer
3 fan **4** beau, buff **5** swain **6** suitor **7** booster, devotee, fancier **8** believer, follower, partisan **9** supporter **10** enthusiast

admission
3 way **4** door, gate **5** entry **6** access, assent, avowal, entrée **7** ingress **8** entrance **10** admittance, concession, confession **11** affirmation

admit
3 own **4** avow, take **5** agree, allow, cop to, enter, grant, let in, let on, lodge, own up **6** accept, fess up, harbor, permit, suffer, take in **7** concede, confess, receive, shelter, welcome **9** entertain, introduce, recognize **11** acknowledge

admix
5 blend, merge **6** mingle **7** combine **8** comingle, compound, immingle **9** commingle **11** intermingle

admixture
5 alloy, blend, combo **6** fusion **7** amalgam **8** compound **9** aggregate, composite **12** amalgamation

admonish
4 warn **5** alert, chide **6** lesson, monish, rebuke, talk to **7** caution, counsel, reprove, speak to **8** call down, forewarn, reproach **9** criticize, reprimand

admonition
3 tip **6** caveat, rebuke **7** caution, chiding, reproof, warning **8** reproach **9** criticism, reprimand **11** disapproval, forewarning

ado
4 fuss, stir **5** stink, tizzy, whirl, worry **6** bother, bustle, flurry, hubbub, pother **7** concern, problem, trouble, turmoil **9** commotion, confusion **10** difficulty

adolescence
5 youth **7** puberty **8** minority **9** greenness **10** juvenility, pubescence **12** youthfulness

adolescent
4 teen **5** minor **6** teener **7** teenage **8** immature, preadult, teenager, youthful **9** pubescent
woe: 4 acne

Adolph of the N.Y. Times
4 Ochs

Adonai
3 God **4** YHWH **6** Elohim, Yahweh

Adonijah
brother: 5 Amnon **7** Absalom, Chileab
father: 5 David
mother: 7 Haggith
slayer: 7 Benaiah

Adonis
lover: 5 Venus **9** Aphrodite
mother: 5 Myrrh **6** Myrrha
slayer: 4 boar

adopt
4 pick, take **5** raise **6** accept, affect, assume, choose, select, take on, take up **7** care for, embrace, endorse, espouse

adoption
6 choice **7** raising, support **8** espousal, taking in **9** embracing, selection **11** embracement

adorable
4 cute, dear **7** darling, lovable, winsome **8** charming, pleasing, precious **9** appealing **10** attractive, delightful

adoration
4 love **5** ardor, honor **6** esteem, praise **7** passion, worship **8** devotion, idolatry **9** adulation, affection, reverence **10** admiration **11** idolization

adore
4 love **5** honor, prize **6** admire, dote on, esteem, revere **7** cherish, idolize, respect, worship **8** dote upon, treasure, venerate **9** affection, delight in, reverence

adoring
6 doting **7** devoted

adorn
4 deck, trim **5** fix up, grace **6** bedeck, enrich, pretty **7** dress up, enhance, enliven, furbish, garnish, smarten **8** beautify, decorate, ornament, prettify **9** embellish

adornment
5 decor, frill **6** finery **7** garnish **8** ornament, trimming **9** accessory, caparison **10** decoration **13** embellishment

ad rem
3 apt **7** apropos, fitting, germane **8** apposite, material, relevant **9** pertinent **10** applicable, relevantly, to the point **11** applicative, applicatory

adrift
4 asea, lost **5** at sea, loose **6** afloat **7** aimless, mixed up **8** confused, floating, unmoored **10** anchorless, bewildered **11** disoriented, purposeless

adroit
3 apt **4** able, deft **5** adept, canny, handy, savvy, smart **6** astute, clever, expert, nimble, shrewd **7** cunning, skilled **8** skillful, talented **9** dexterous, ingenious **11** intelligent, quick-witted, resourceful **13** perspicacious

adroitness
3 art **4** gift **5** craft, flair, knack, savvy, skill **7** address, cunning, know-how, prowess **8** deftness **9** adeptness, dexterity, expertise, ingenuity, readiness **10** cleverness, expertness **12** intelligence

adulation
7 acclaim, baloney, blarney, fawning, tribute, worship **8** applause, flattery, soft soap **10** overpraise **11** hero-worship **12** blandishment

adulatory
7 buttery, fawning **8** unctuous **9** kowtowing **10** flattering, obsequious, oleaginous **11** bootlicking, sycophantic

adult
4 aged, ripe **5** grown, of age **6** mature **7** grown-up, matured, ripened **9** full-blown, full-grown **11** full-fledged

adulterate
3 cut **4** thin **5** alloy, dirty, taint, water **6** debase, deflle, dilute, doctor, dope up, impair, weaken **7** cheapen, corrupt, defiled, degrade, devalue, diluted, falsify, pollute, tainted, thinned **8** degraded, denature, impurify, polluted, spurious **9** water down **10** tamper with **11** contaminate

adumbrate
3 dim, fog **4** bode, call, hint, mist, veil **5** augur, cloud **6** darken, shadow, sketch **7** becloud, bespeak, betoken, obscure, outline, portend, predict, presage, suggest **8** block out, disclose, forebode, forecast, foretell, indicate, intimate, prophesy **9** obfuscate, prefigure **10** foreshadow **11** prefigurate **12** characterize

adumbration
4 hint, sign **5** shade, umbra **6** shadow **7** outline **8** penumbra **10** indication, intimation, suggestion

advance
3 aid **4** cite, help, lend, loan, move, rise **5** get on, march, money, raise, serve **6** assist, course, foster, mature, prefer, step up, supply, uplift **7** deposit, develop, elevate, forward, furnish, further, headway, ongoing, present, proceed, promote, propose, upgrade **8** approach, get along, heighten, increase, progress **9** encourage, evolution, provision **10** accelerate, bring about **11** development, furtherance, improvement, progression **12** breakthrough

advanced
3 old **5** first **6** far out **7** forward, in front, leading, liberal, radical **8** far ahead, foremost **9** developed **10** precocious **11** broad-minded, progressive
degree: **3** Ph.D.

advancement
4 gain, rise **5** boost **6** growth **7** headway **8** progress **9** elevation, promotion **10** betterment, preference **11** improvement, progression

advantage
3 use **4** boon, edge, gain, good, help, lead, odds **5** asset, avail, serve **6** better, profit **7** account, benefit, mastery **8** blessing, interest, leverage **9** allowance, head start, upper hand **10** ascendancy, domination, leadership, prosperity **11** superiority **12** running start

advantageous
4 good **6** timely, toward, useful **7** benefic, gainful, helpful **8** favoring, salutary **9** conducive, desirable, expedient, favorable, fortunate, promising **10** beneficial, profitable, propitious, worthwhile

advent
4 dawn **5** onset **6** coming **7** arrival **8** approach **9** beginning

adventitious
5 fluky **6** casual, chance, flukey **8** by chance **9** unplanned **10** accidental, contingent, fortuitous, incidental, unexpected

adventure
3 try **4** feat, risk, trip **5** quest, wager **6** chance, gamble, hazard **7** exploit **8** escapade **9** undertake **10** enterprise, experience

adventurous
4 bold, rash **5** brash, risky **6** daring **8** intrepid, reckless **9** audacious, dangerous, daredevil, foolhardy, hazardous, impetuous, imprudent **10** innovative **12** enterprising

adversary
3 con, foe **4** anti **5** enemy, rival **7** opposer **8** opponent, opposing **10** antagonist, competitor

adverse
3 bad **4** anti **7** counter, harmful, hostile, hurtful, opposed **8** contrary, damaging, negative, opposing, opposite **9** injurious **11** deleterious, detrimental, obstructive, unfavorable **12** antagonistic, antipathetic

adversity
4 dole **5** trial **6** misery, mishap **7** bad luck, bad news, trouble **8** bad break, distress, hard time, hardship **9** mischance, suffering **10** difficulty, ill fortune, misfortune

advert
4 cite, note **5** refer **6** allude, notice, remark **7** bring up, mention, observe **8** indicate, point out

advertent
5 aware **7** heedful, mindful **9** attentive, intentive, observant, regardful

advertise
4 drum, hype, plug, puff, push, tout **5** boost, pitch **6** blazon, herald, inform, notify, report **7** advance, apprise, build up, declare, promote, publish, sponsor **8** announce, ballyhoo, proclaim **9** broadcast, publicize **10** annunciate, promulgate

advertisement
4 bill, plug, sign **5** blurb, flier, flyer, promo **6** notice, poster, want ad **7** affiche **8** circular **9** billboard, broadcast, promotion, publicity **10** commercial **11** declaration, publication **12** announcement, proclamation

advertising award
4 Clio

advice
3 aid, tip **4** help, news, view, word **5** input **6** notice **7** caution, counsel, opinion, tidings, warning **8** guidance, teaching **10** admonition, suggestion **11** information, instruction **12** intelligence

Advil alternative
5 Aleve **6** Anacin, Motrin **7** aspirin, Tylenol

advisable
4 wise **5** sound **6** seemly **7** politic, prudent **8** sensible, suitable, tactical **9** desirable, expedient, practical **10** worthwhile **11** recommended **12** advantageous

advise
3 tip **4** tell, tout, urge, warn **5** guide **6** clue in, confer, enjoin, fill in, inform, notify, tip off, wise up **7** apprise, caution, consult, counsel, suggest **8** acquaint, forewarn, instruct, point out **9** encourage, prescribe, recommend

advised
7 studied, weighed **8** designed, intended **10** calculated, considered, deliberate, thought out **11** intentional **12** premeditated

adviser
5 coach, guide **6** Egeria, mentor **7** counsel, tipster **9** counselor **10** consultant, instructor

advisory
7 guiding, helping **9** educative **10** counseling **12** consultative **13** informational

advocacy
3 aid **6** urging **7** backing, defense, support **9** promotion

advocate
4 back, push, tout, urge **5** favor **6** backer, defend, preach, uphold **7** promote, propose, support **8** argue for, backstop, champion, exponent, plump for, side with **9** encourage, expounder, proponent, recommend, spokesman, supporter **11** countenance

Aeacus
father: **4** Zeus
mother: **6** Aegina
son: **6** Peleus **7** Telamon

Aedon
brother: **7** Amphion
sister-in-law: **5** Niobe
son (victim): **6** Itylus

Aeëtes
daughter: **5** Medea
father: **6** Helios

Aegean island
3 Kos **5** Naxos, Samos **6** Lesbos, Patmos, Rhodes

aegis
4 care, ward **5** armor, guard **6** charge, shield **7** backing, control, defense, support **8** auspices, guidance, security **9** influence, patronage, safeguard **10** protection **11** sponsorship

Aegisthus
father: **8** Thyestes
lover: **12** Clytemnestra
mother: **7** Pelopia
slayer: **7** Orestes
victim: **6** Atreus **9** Agamemnon

Aeneas
companion: **7** Achates
father: **8** Anchises
lover: **4** Dido
mother: **5** Venus **9** Aphrodite
son: **5** Iulus **8** Ascanius
wife: **6** Creusa **7** Lavinia

Aeneid
author: **6** Vergil, Virgil
first words: **16** arma virumque cano
hero: **6** Aeneas

Aeolus
daughter: **7** Alcyone **8** Halcyone
father: **8** Poseidon

aeon
3 age **4** time **6** period **8** blue moon, duration

aerate
7 lighten, freshen, refresh **9** oxygenate, ventilate

aerial
4 high **5** lofty **6** flying, vapory **7** antenna, soaring **8** birdlike, elevated, ethereal, fanciful, towering, vaporous **9** pneumatic **10** impalpable **11** atmospheric, forward pass

aerie
4 nest **7** citadel, lookout **9** penthouse
resident: **4** eyas **5** eagle **6** eaglet

aeroembolism
5 bends

aeronaut
4 Fogg (Phileas) **5** pilot **7** aviator **8** Zeppelin (Ferdinand, Graf von) **10** balloonist

Aerope
husband: **6** Atreus
lover: **8** Thyestes
son: **8** Menelaus **9** Agamemnon

aery
see **aerial**

Aesculapius
daughter: **6** Hygeia **7** Panacea
father: **6** Apollo
slayer: **4** Zeus **7** Jupiter
teacher: **6** Chiron
wife: **6** Epione

Aeson
brother: **6** Pelias
son: **5** Jason

aesthete
4 buff **6** expert **7** devotee **9** authority **10** dilettante **11** appreciator, cognoscente, connoisseur

aesthetic
4 arty **6** artful **8** artistic, creative, pleasing **9** beautiful, sensitive **10** attractive, harmonious

afar
3 yon **4** yond **5** apart **6** remote **7** distant

affable
4 kind, open, warm **6** at ease, genial, gentle, kindly, polite **7** amiable, cordial **8** friendly, gracious, obliging, pleasant, sociable **9** congenial, courteous

affair
4 case, love **5** amour, fling, worry **6** action, matter **7** concern, liaison, palaver, romance **8** business, function, interest, intrigue, occasion **9** dalliance, happening, procedure **10** proceeding **12** relationship

affect
3 act **4** fake, move, sham, stir, sway **5** act on, adopt, alter, bluff, fancy, feign, haunt, put on, touch **6** assume, change, strike **7** act upon, disturb, impress, inspire, pretend **8** frequent, simulate **9** cultivate, influence

affectation
3 air **4** airs, pose, sham, show **6** facade **8** pretense **9** mannerism **10** pretension **13** artificiality

affected
5 apish, false, moved, phony, put-on **6** phoney, too-too **7** altered, assumed, changed, feigned, stilted **8** disposed, inclined, involved, mannered, precious, spurious **9** concerned, conscious, contrived, insincere, pretended, unnatural **10** artificial **11** overrefined, pretentious **13** self-conscious

affecting
3 sad **6** lively, moving **7** pitiful **8** exciting, poignant, touching **9** thrilling **10** disturbing, impressive **11** distressing, influential

affection
4 bias, love **5** trait **6** doting, liking, malady, virtue, warmth **7** ailment, concern, disease, emotion, feature, feeling, illness, leaning, passion, quality **8** devotion, disorder, fondness, interest, penchant, property, sickness, sympathy **9** attention, attribute, character, complaint, condition, sentiment **10** attachment, pretension, propensity, tenderness **12** predilection

affectionate
4 dear, fond, warm **6** caring, doting, loving, tender **7** devoted **8** friendly **11** sympathetic

affective
6 moving **7** emotive **8** stirring, touching **9** emotional

affectivity
7 emotion, feeling, passion **9** sentiment

affectless
4 numb **5** blank, stoic **6** stolid **7** deadpan

affianced
7 engaged, pledged **8** intended, plighted, promised **9** betrothed, committed **10** contracted

affiche
4 bill, list **6** notice, poster **7** placard **8** handbill

affidavit
4 oath **9** testimony **11** affirmation, declaration

affiliate
4 ally, join **5** annex, unite **6** branch **7** combine, connect, partner **9** associate

affiliated
4 akin **5** bound **6** allied, joined, linked **7** kindred, related **9** connected, dependent **10** associated

affiliation
4 club **5** tie-in, union **6** hookup, league **7** cahoots, company, joining **8** alliance **10** connection, fellowship **11** association, combination, conjunction, partnership

affinity
6 simile **7** analogy, kinship, rapport **8** likeness, relation, sympathy **9** alikeness **10** attraction, similarity, similitude **11** resemblance **13** compatibility

affirm
3 say, yes **4** aver, avow, okay **5** posit, state, swear, vouch **6** assent, assert, attest, depose, ratify, uphold **7** certify, confirm, declare, profess, protest, testify, witness **8** dedicate, validate **9** guarantee

affirmative
3 A-OK, aye, yea, yes **4** yeah **5** roger **6** assent, aye-aye, yessir **7** right on **8** approval, positive **9** affirming, approving, asserting, assertion, endorsing, favorable, ratifying **10** confirming, supporting **11** affirmation

affix
3 add, tag **4** bind, glue, join, nail, tack **5** annex, paste, put on, rivet, stick, tag on **6** append, attach, fasten, tack on **7** impress, stick on, subjoin **8** addition **9** appendage **10** attachment

Affleck film
4 Argo

afflict
3 try, vex **4** pain, rack **5** annoy, beset, harry, press, smite, worry, wound, wring **6** bother, burden, harass, harrow, injure, martyr, pester, plague, strike, suffer **7** agonize, anguish, torment, torture, trouble **8** distress

afflicted
6 pained, rueful, woeful **7** doleful, injured, unhappy, worried **8** dolorous, stricken, troubled, wretched **9** disturbed, miserable, sorrowful, tormented **10** distressed

affliction
3 ill, woe **4** care **5** cross, grief, trial **6** malady, ordeal, plague, sorrow **7** anguish, illness, scourge, torment, trouble **8** distress, hardship, sickness **9** adversity, heartache, infirmity **10** misfortune **11** tribulation

afflictive
3 sad **4** dire, sore **6** aching, bitter, woeful **7** galling, hurtful, hurting, painful **8** grievous, mournful **9** sorrowful **10** calamitous, deplorable, lamentable **11** distasteful, distressing, regrettable, troublesome, unfortunate, unpalatable **13** heartbreaking

affluence
5 means, worth **6** bounty, influx, plenty, riches, wealth **8** opulence, property, richness **9** abundance, plenitude, profusion, resources **10** prosperity

affluent
4 full, rich **5** flush **6** loaded **7** copious, flowing, moneyed, opulent, upscale, wealthy, well-off **8** abundant, well-to-do **9** bountiful, plentiful, tributary, well-fixed **10** prosperous, well-heeled

afford
4 able, bear, give **5** allow, grant, incur, offer, spare, stand **6** bestow, confer, donate, impart, manage, supply **7** furnish, present, support, sustain

affordable
5 cheap **6** modest **7** low-cost **8** bearable **10** manageable, reasonable **11** inexpensive

affray
3 row **5** clash, fight, melee, scrap **6** fracas, rumpus **7** dispute, quarrel, ruction, scuffle **8** disorder, skirmish

affront
3 vex **4** face, meet, slap, slur **5** abuse, anger, annoy, wrong **6** injury, insult, offend, slight **7** offense, outrage, put down **8** contempt, rudeness **9** aspersion, criticize, encounter, indignity

Afghanistan
capital: 5 Kabul
city: 5 Herat **8** Kandahar **12** Mazar-i-Sharif
ethnic group: 7 Pashtun
language: 4 Dari **6** Pashto
monetary unit: 3 pul **7** Afghani
neighbor: 4 Iran **5** China **8** Pakistan **10** Tajikistan, Uzbekistan **12** Turkmenistan

aficionado
3 fan **4** buff **5** hound, lover **6** expert **7** admirer, devotee, habitué **10** enthusiast **11** appreciator

afield
4 afar, away, awry **5** amiss, badly, wrong **6** abroad, astray **8** straying **9** elsewhere, off course

afire
3 hot **5** aglow, fiery **6** ablaze, aflame, alight, red-hot **7** blazing, burning, excited, flaming, flaring, ignited, kindled **8** inflamed, in flames **9** energized, excitable **10** passionate **11** conflagrant

aflame
see **afire**

afloat
4 asea **5** at sea **6** adrift, buoyed **9** supported, sustained

afoot
8 under way

afore
3 ere

afraid
4 wary **5** chary, jumpy, loath, scary, sorry, timid **6** averse, scared, trepid **7** anxious, fearful, uneager, worried **8** cautious, hesitant, skittish, timorous **9** concerned, regretful, reluctant, unwilling **10** frightened **11** disinclined **12** apprehensive

afresh
3 new **4** anew, over **5** again, newly **6** de novo, encore **8** once more, repeated **9** once again

Africa
country: **4** Chad, Mali, Togo **5** Benin, Congo, Egypt, Gabon, Ghana, Kenya, Libya, Niger, Sudan, Zaire **6** Angola, Gambia, Guinea, Malawi, Rwanda, Uganda, Zambia **7** Algeria, Burundi, Comoros, Eritrea, Lesotho, Liberia, Morocco, Namibia, Nigeria, Senegal, Somalia, Tunisia **8** Botswana, Cameroon, Djibouti, Ethiopia, Tanzania, Zimbabwe **9** Cape Verde, Mauritius, Swaziland **10** Ivory Coast, Madagascar, Mauritania, Mozambique, Seychelles, South Sudan **11** Burkina Faso, Côte d'Ivoire, Sierra Leone, South Africa **12** Guinea-Bissau
ethnic group: **3** Ibo **4** Akan, Arab, Baya, Boer, Copt, Fula, Issa, Jebu, Moor, Zulu **5** Bantu, Fulah, Galla, Hausa, Kongo, Mande, Pygmy, Swazi, Wolof, Xhosa **6** Berber, Fulani, Hamite, Herero, Kikuyu, Nubian, Somali, Tuareg, Ubangi, Yoruba **7** Ashanti, Bedouin, Bushman, Malinke, Swahili, Touareg **8** Egyptian, Mandingo **9** Hottentot
language: **3** Ibo **4** Taal **5** Bantu, Galla, Hausa, Xhosa **6** Arabic, Berber, Somali, Yoruba **7** Amharic, Bambara, Swahili **8** Malagasy **9** Afrikaans

African antelope
3 gnu **4** kudu, oryx **5** eland

African fever
5 Lassa

African Queen screenwriter
4 Agee (James)

African river
4 Nile, Uele **5** Benue, Congo, Niger, Volta **6** Ubangi **7** Limpopo, Zambezi

Afrikaner
4 Boer

aft
6 astern **8** rearmost, rearward **9** sternward

after
4 back, hind, next, past, rear **5** après, below, later, since **6** astern, back of, behind, beyond, hinder **7** ensuing **8** hindmost **9** following, posterior, sternward **10** subsequent

after all
3 yet **5** still **6** at last, though **7** finally, however **8** in the end **11** nonetheless **12** nevertheless

aftereffect
5 issue **6** result, upshot **7** fallout, outcome **11** consequence, eventuality

afterlife
6 beyond **8** eternity **9** hereafter

aftermath
4 wake **6** effect, result, upshot **12** consequences, repercussion

afterward
4 next, soon, then **5** later **6** behind **7** by and by, thereon **8** latterly **9** hereafter **10** thereafter **12** subsequently

afterword
5 envoi **6** epilog **8** epilogue

Agag
kingdom: **6** Amalek
slayer: **6** Samuel

again
3 bis **4** also, anew, back, over **6** afresh, de novo, encore **8** once more

again and again
3 oft **4** much **5** often **8** ofttimes **10** frequently, oftentimes, repeatedly **11** continually

against
3 con **4** anti **6** contra, facing, versus **7** vis-à-vis **8** fronting, opposite, touching
prefix: **4** anti **6** contra **7** counter

Agamemnon
avenger: **7** Orestes
brother: **8** Menelaus
daughter: **7** Electra **9** Iphigenia
father: **6** Atreus
slayer: **9** Aegisthus
son: **7** Orestes
wife: **12** Clytemnestra

agape
4 love, open **6** amazed **7** yawning **8** wide open **9** astounded, love feast **10** astonished, confounded **11** dumbfounded, overwhelmed **13** thunderstruck

Agassi of tennis
5 Andre

agate
3 taw **4** type **6** marble, quartz **7** shooter **8** type size

agave
4 aloe **5** yucca
drink: **6** mescal, mezcal, pulque **7** tequila
product: **4** hemp **5** sisal

Agave
father: **6** Cadmus
husband: **6** Echion
mother: **8** Harmonia
sister: **3** Ino **6** Semele **7** Autonoë
son: **8** Pentheus

age
3 eon, era **4** aeon, grow, span, time **5** epoch, ripen, stage **6** grow up, mature, mellow, period **7** develop **8** blue moon, division, interval, lifetime, majority, maturate **10** generation

aged
3 old **4** ripe, worn **5** cured, hoary, olden **6** mellow, senior **7** ancient, antique, elderly, matured, ripened **8** grown old, timeworn **9** developed, senescent, venerable **11** patriarchal **12** antediluvian

ageless
7 endless, eternal, lasting **8** dateless, enduring, immortal, timeless **9** immutable **11** everlasting

agency
4 firm **5** cause, force, means, organ, power **6** action, bureau, medium, office **7** company, channel, vehicle **8** activity, auspices, business, division, function, ministry **9** mechanism, operation **10** department, instrument **12** organization **13** establishment

agenda
5 slate **6** docket, lineup **7** program **8** calendar, schedule, to-do list **9** timetable
entry: **4** item

Agenor
brother: **5** Belus
daughter: **6** Europa
father: **7** Antenor, Neptune **8** Poseidon
mother: **5** Libya
son: **6** Cadmus

agent
3 fed, spy **4** G-man, narc, T-man, tool **5** actor, means, organ, proxy, spook **6** broker, deputy, factor, medium **7** channel, proctor, steward, vehicle **8** assignee, attorney, executor, minister, ministry **9** activator, go-between, middleman, operative **10** instrument, procurator

age-old
7 ancient, antique **9** venerable **10** immemorial **11** traditional

ages
3 eon **4** aeon

agglomerate
4 heap, mass, pile, rock **6** gather **7** cluster, collect **9** aggregate **10** collection **11** aggregation

agglomeration
4 heap **5** hoard, trove **7** cluster **9** aggregate, amassment, gathering **10** collection, cumulation **11** aggregation

aggrandize
4 hype **5** boost, exalt **6** beef up, expand, extend, praise **7** augment, build up, enhance, enlarge, ennoble, glorify, inflate, magnify **8** heighten, increase, multiply **11** distinguish

aggravate
3 vex **4** gall **5** anger, annoy, grate, mount, peeve, pique, rouse, upset **6** burn up, deepen, nettle, worsen **7** bedevil, disturb, enhance, inflame, magnify, perturb, provoke **8** heighten, increase, irritate **9** intensify **10** exacerbate

aggravation
4 pain **5** worry **6** bother **9** annoyance, worsening **11** provocation

aggregate
3 all, sum **4** body, bulk, floc **5** add up, gross, total, whole **6** amount, gather **7** collect **8** entirety, quantity, totality **9** composite **10** cumulative **11** agglomerate **12** conglomerate **13** agglomeration

aggregation
4 body, mass **5** crowd, group, hoard, total, trove **7** cluster, company **8** assembly **9** amassment, gathering **10** assemblage, collection, cumulation **11** agglomerate **12** accumulation

aggression
4 push, raid **5** fight, onset **6** attack **7** assault, offense **8** invasion **9** hostility, incursion, offensive, onslaught, pugnacity **10** assailment **12** belligerence **13** combativeness

aggressive
5 pushy **6** fierce, severe **7** hostile, scrappy, vicious, warlike **8** emphatic, forceful, militant **9** assertive, attacking, combative, energetic, intrusive, offensive **11** belligerent, contentious, domineering, hard-hitting **12** enterprising

aggrieve
4 hurt, pain **5** annoy, harry, upset, worry, wrong **6** harass, injure, plague **7** afflict, oppress, torment, trouble **8** distress **9** constrain, persecute

aghast
4 agog, awed **6** afraid, amazed, scared **7** anxious, fearful, shocked, stunned **8** appalled, dismayed, startled **9** awestruck, horrified, terrified **10** astonished, confounded, frightened **11** dumbfounded, overwhelmed **13** thunderstruck

agile
4 deft, spry **5** alert, brisk, catty, lithe, quick, zippy **6** active, adroit, limber, lively, nimble, supple **7** lissome **9** adaptable, dexterous, sprightly

agitate
4 move, rile, roil, rock, stir, toss **5** argue, churn, peeve, shake, slosh, upset **6** arouse, bother,

excite, flurry, joggle, ruffle, stir up **7** discuss, dispute, disturb, fluster, perturb, provoke, tempest, trouble, unhinge **8** disquiet, irritate, unsettle **9** thrash out **10** discompose

agitated
4 edgy **5** het up, jumpy, upset **6** uneasy **7** anxious, jittery

agitation
4 flap, fuss, stir, to-do **5** clash **6** bustle, clamor, debate, flurry, lather, tumult **7** dispute, ferment, tempest, turmoil **9** commotion, confusion **10** turbulence **11** disturbance

agitator
5 rebel **6** shaker **7** inciter, stirrer **8** fomenter, inflamer **9** disrupter **10** instigator **11** provocateur

Aglaia
see **Graces**

Aglauros
father: **7** Cecrops
sister: **5** Herse **9** Pandrosos

aglow
4 warm **5** afire **6** bright, aflame, alight **7** excited, radiant, shining **8** gleaming, luminous

agnate
4 akin, like **5** alike **6** allied, joined, linked **7** cognate, connate, kindred, kinsman, related, similar **8** relation, relative **9** analogous **10** affiliated **11** consanguine **13** corresponding

agnostic
7 doubter, skeptic **8** doubting **10** questioner, undogmatic **11** uncommitted **12** noncommittal

Agnus ____
3 Dei

ago
4 back, gone, past, yore **5** since **6** before

agog
4 avid, keen **5** eager **6** roused **7** excited, fervent **8** desirous **9** expectant, impatient **12** enthusiastic

agon
5 clash **6** battle, strife **7** contest **8** conflict, struggle

agonize
4 fret, gall, hurt, pain, rack **5** chafe **6** harrow, squirm, suffer, writhe **7** afflict, torment, torture, trouble **8** distress, stew over, struggle **10** excruciate

agonizing
6 fierce **7** extreme, intense, painful, racking, tearing **9** harrowing, suffering, torturing, torturous **10** tormenting **12** excruciating

agony
4 pain **5** dolor, pangs **6** misery **7** anguish, passion, torment, torture **8** distress, outburst, struggle **9** suffering **10** affliction

agora
6 market **11** marketplace **12** meeting place

agrarian
5 rural **6** rustic **8** pastoral **10** campestral **12** agricultural

agree
3 buy, set, yes **4** jibe, okay, suit **5** admit, check, equal, fit in, match, tally **6** accede, accept, accord, assent, concur, settle, square **7** comport, concede, concert, concord, conform, consent **8** check out, coincide, dovetail **9** acquiesce, harmonize, recognize, subscribe **10** correspond **11** acknowledge
silently: **3** nod

agreeable
4 nice, open **5** ready **7** affable, welcome, willing **8** amenable, in accord, pleasant, pleasing **9** approving, congenial, congruous, consonant, favorable, receptive **10** acceptable, compatible, concurring, consenting, consistent **11** pleasurable, sympathetic

agreed
3 aye, yea, yep, yes **4** okay **8** all right, of course **9** certainly **10** definitely, positively

agreement
4 bond, deal, pact **6** accord, assent, treaty **7** bargain, compact, concord, consent, entente, harmony **8** contract, covenant **9** concordat **10** acceptance, consonance **11** arrangement, concordance, concurrence

agree with
3 fit **4** suit **5** befit **6** assist, become **7** support **10** go together

agricultural
5 rural **7** bucolic **8** agrarian, pastoral

agriculture
7 farming, tillage **8** agronomy, ranching **9** husbandry **11** cultivation, soil culture

Agrippina
brother: **8** Caligula
husband: **8** Claudius
son: **4** Nero

aground
5 stuck **6** ashore **7** beached **8** disabled, stranded
run: **3** sew

ague
3 flu **5** chill, fever **7** malaria, shivers **9** influenza, shivering **10** blackwater

Ahab
daughter: **8** Athaliah
father: **4** Omri
prey: **8** Moby-Dick
ship: **6** Pequod
wife: **7** Jezebel

Ahasuerus
kingdom: **6** Persia
wife: **6** Esther, Vashti
Ahaz
kingdom: **5** Judah
son: **8** Hezekiah
wife: **3** Abi
Ahaziah
father: **4** Ahab **5** Joram **7** Jehoram
kingdom: **5** Judah **6** Israel
mother: **7** Jezebel **8** Athaliah
sister: **9** Jehosheba **11** Jehosobeath
ahead
4 ante, fore, on top **6** before, dormie, onward **7** earlier, forward, in front, leading, onwards **8** foremost, forwards, previous **9** in advance **10** beforehand
Ahinoam
father: **7** Ahimaaz
husband: **4** Saul **5** David
son: **5** Amnon
Ah, Wilderness! author
6 O'Neill (Eugene)
aid
4 abet, care, hand, help, lift **6** assist, helper, relief, rescue, succor **7** backing, comfort, help out, support, sustain **8** befriend **9** assistant, attendant, subsidize **10** assistance, benefactor, mitigation **11** alleviation
Aida
composer: **5** Verdi (Giuseppe)
father: **8** Amonasro
lover: **7** Radamès
rival: **7** Amneris
aide
4 ass't **6** deputy, helper, second **7** orderly **8** adjutant, sidekick **9** assistant, attendant, coadjutor **10** coadjutant, lieutenant
aikido
10 martial art
ail
4 ache, hurt, pain **5** upset, worry **6** bother **7** afflict, disturb, trouble **8** distress
ailing
3 ill, low **4** down, sick, weak **6** infirm, in pain, poorly, sickly, unwell **8** below par, diseased **9** enfeebled **10** indisposed **11** debilitated
ailment
6 malady, unrest **7** disease, ferment, illness, turmoil **8** disorder, disquiet, sickness, syndrome **9** affection, complaint, condition, infirmity **10** inquietude, uneasiness **11** disquietude, restiveness **12** restlessness
aim
3 end, try **4** cast, goal, head, mark, mean, plan, want, wish **5** angle, essay, focus, level, point, slant, train **6** aspire, design, desire, direct, intend, intent, object, strive, target, zero in **7** address, attempt, propose, purpose **8** ambition, endeavor **9** objective **11** contemplate
aimless
6 random **7** wayward **8** goalless **9** desultory, haphazard, hit-or-miss, irregular, pointless, unplanned **10** designless **11** purposeless
air
3 sky **4** aura, mien, mood, song, tune, vent **5** style **6** manner, melody, reveal, strain **7** bearing, divulge, express, feeling, quality **8** demeanor **9** broadcast, character, ventilate **10** atmosphere, deportment
aircraft
5 blimp, drone, plane **6** glider **7** airship, balloon, chopper **8** aerodyne, aerostat, airplane, jetliner, zeppelin **9** dirigible **10** helicopter
carrier: **7** flattop
designer: **6** Fokker (Anthony), Martin (Glenn) **7** Junkers (Hugo), Tupolev (Andrei) **8** Northrop (Jack), Sikorsky (Igor), Yakovlev (Alexander) **13** Messerschmitt (Willy)
Air France terminal
4 Orly
airhead
4 ditz, yo-yo **6** nitwit **9** birdbrain
airless
5 close **6** stuffy, sultry **8** stagnant, stifling **11** suffocating
airline
3 JAL, KLM, LOT, SAS, TWA **4** BOAC, El Al **5** Delta, Pan Am, USAir, Varig **6** Iberia, Qantas, Sabena, Spirit, United, Virgin **7** Eastern, JetBlue, Olympic **8** Aeroflot, Alitalia, American, Swissair **9** Aer Lingus, Air France, Lufthansa, Northwest, Southwest, U.S. Airways **11** Continental, Pan American
airman
3 ace **5** flier, flyer, pilot **6** flyboy **7** aviator **8** aeronaut
air movement
4 gust, wind **5** draft **6** breath, breeze **7** updraft **9** downdraft
air navigation system
5 loran, navar, radar
airplane
3 jet **5** avion **6** bomber, duster **7** fighter **8** autogiro, autogyro **9** transport **10** crop duster
A-bomb-dropper: **8** Enola Gay
battle: **8** dogfight
body: **8** fuselage
engine: **3** jet **6** fanjet **7** propjet **8** turbofan, turbojet **9** turboprop
engine casing: **7** nacelle

engineless: **6** glider
instrument: **5** radar, radio **7** compass **9** altimeter, gyroscope **10** tachometer **11** transponder
maneuver: **4** buzz, dive, loop, roll **8** nosedive **9** chandelle **10** barrel roll
movement: **3** yaw **4** bank, spin **5** pitch **8** tailspin
part: **3** fin **4** flap, nose, prop, tail, wing **5** cabin, wheel **6** engine, rudder **7** aileron **8** airscrew, elevator **9** empennage, propeller **10** stabilizer
pilotless: **5** drone
pioneer: **6** Cessna (Clyde), Hughes (Howard), Wright (Orville, Wilbur) **7** Blériot (Louis)
safety machine: **6** deicer
shelter: **6** hangar
supersonic: **3** SST
target: **6** drogue
vapor: **8** contrail

air plant
6 orchid **8** epiphyte **9** bromeliad, kalanchoe **11** Spanish moss **12** strangler fig

airport
5 field **7** helipad **8** heliport **9** aerodrome
abbreviation: **3** ETA, ETD
building: **8** terminal
flag: **8** windsock
name:
Atlanta: **10** Hartsfield
Boston: **5** Logan
Chicago: **5** O'Hare **6** Midway
Dublin: **7** Shannon
London: **7** Gatwick **8** Heathrow
Los Angeles: **3** LAX
New York: **3** JFK **7** Kennedy **9** La Guardia
Paris: **4** Orly **8** DeGaulle **9** Le Bourget
Rome: **7** Da Vinci
Tokyo: **6** Narita
Washington: **6** Dulles, Reagan **8** National
part: **5** apron, tower **6** runway **7** taxiway
posting: **3** ETA

Airport author
6 Hailey (Arthur)

airs
4 pose, show **5** front **6** vanity **7** hauteur **8** pretense **9** loftiness, mannerism, vainglory **10** pretension **11** affectation, insincerity, ostentation **13** artificiality

airship
3 jet **5** blimp, plane **8** zeppelin **9** dirigible

airtight
4 shut **6** closed, sealed **7** certain **8** hermetic, ironclad **10** impervious **11** impermeable, irrefutable **12** indisputable, invulnerable **13** incontestable

airwaves regulator
3 FCC

airy
4 open, rare, thin **5** blowy, fresh, gusty, light, lofty, proud, windy **6** aerial, bouncy, breezy, dainty, unreal **7** buoyant, gaseous, soaring, tenuous **8** affected, animated, delicate, ethereal, graceful, illusory, rarefied, spirited, towering, vaporous, volatile **9** expansive, frivolous, pneumatic, resilient, sprightly, vivacious **10** diaphanous, ventilated **11** atmospheric, skyscraping **12** effervescent, high-spirited

Ajax
4 hero **5** Greek **7** warrior
father: **6** Oileus **7** Telamon
opponent: **6** Hector
participant: **9** Trojan War

a.k.a.
5 alias

akin
4 like, same **5** alike **6** allied **7** kindred, related, similar, uniform **8** parallel **9** analogous, consonant **10** affiliated, comparable, compatible **11** consanguine **13** corresponding

Akkadian king
6 Sargon

Alabama
capital: **10** Montgomery
city: **5** Selma **6** Mobile **10** Birmingham, Huntsville, Tuscaloosa **12** Muscle Shoals
college, university: **6** Auburn **8** Tuskegee
mountain: **6** Cheaha
nickname: **6** Cotton (State) **12** Heart of Dixie
river: **6** Mobile **7** Alabama **9** Tombigbee
state bird: **12** yellowhammer
state flower: **8** camellia
state tree: **12** longleaf pine

alacrity
8 dispatch **9** briskness, eagerness, quickness, readiness **10** enthusiasm, expedition, liveliness, promptness **11** promptitude, willingness **12** cheerfulness

____ alai
3 jai

Alamo
city: **10** San Antonio
hero: **5** Bowie (Jim) **6** Travis (William) **8** Crockett (Davy)

alamo
6 poplar **10** cottonwood

à la mode
4 chic, tony **6** trendy **7** dashing, stylish **8** up-to-date **9** exclusive **11** fashionable **12** with ice cream

alarm
3 SOS **4** bell, fear, horn **5** alert, dread, panic, scare, siren, spook, upset **6** dismay, excite,

fright, signal, terror, tocsin **7** anxiety, disturb, red flag, startle, terrify, unnerve, warning **8** distress, frighten **9** terrorize **11** forewarning, trepidation **12** apprehension **13** consternation

alas
3 heu, woe **4** ah me, darn, drat **5** alack, oy vey **7** woe is me

Alaska
capital: **6** Juneau
city: **4** Nome **5** Sitka **6** Barrow **9** Anchorage, Fairbanks **10** Prudhoe Bay
island group: **6** Kodiak **8** Aleutian, Pribilof
mountain, range: **6** Brooks, Denali **8** McKinley, Wrangell
native: **5** Aleut, Inuit
nickname: **12** Last Frontier
park: **6** Denali, Katmai
river: **5** Yukon
state bird: **9** ptarmigan
state flower: **11** forget-me-not
state tree: **11** sitka spruce

alb
4 gown **8** vestment

Albania
capital: **6** Tirana, Tiranë
city: **5** Korçë, Vlorë **6** Durrës **7** Shkodër
ethnic group: **4** Gheg, Tosk
king: **3** Zog
monetary unit: **3** lek
neighbor: **6** Greece **9** Macedonia **10** Montenegro
part of: **7** Balkans
peninsula: **6** Balkan
sea: **8** Adriatic

albatross
5 check, goony, worry **6** burden, gooney **7** anxiety, seabird **9** hindrance, millstone, restraint **11** encumbrance

Albee play
7 Sandbox (The) **8** Seascape, Zoo Story (The) **9** Tiny Alice **13** American Dream (The) **14** Three Tall Women **16** A Delicate Balance **25** Who's Afraid of Virginia Woolf?

albeit
5 still, while **6** even if, much as, though **7** despite, whereas **8** although **10** even though

Alberta
capital: **8** Edmonton
city: **5** Banff **7** Calgary
lake: **6** Claire, Louise **9** Athabasca
mountain, range: **7** Rockies **8** Columbia
provincial flower: **8** wild rose
river: **4** Milk **5** Peace **9** Athabasca

Albion
7 England

album
3 ana **4** book **6** jacket, record **7** garland, omnibus **8** notebook, pictures, register **9** anthology, portfolio, scrapbook **10** collection, miscellany

Alcestis
father: **6** Pelias
husband: **7** Admetus
rescuer: **8** Heracles, Hercules

alchemist
5 Faust **10** Paracelsus

alchemy
5 charm, magic **7** panacea, sorcery **8** wizardry **9** conjuring **10** necromancy

Alcina
sister: **7** Morgana **10** Logistilla
victim: **6** Rogero **8** Astolpho, Ruggiero

Alcinous
daughter: **8** Nausicaa
wife: **5** Arete

Alcmaeon
father: **10** Amphiaraus
mother: **8** Eriphyle
wife: **10** Callirrhoe

Alcmene
husband: **10** Amphitryon
son: **8** Heracles, Hercules

alcohol
4 grog **5** booze, hooch, juice, sauce **6** hootch, liquor, red-eye, rotgut, tipple **7** spirits **8** home brew **9** aqua vitae, firewater, moonshine
name: **4** amyl **5** butyl, cetyl, ethyl **6** glycol, methyl, sterol **7** butanol, ethanol, mannite, menthol **8** glycerin, glycerol, inositol, mannitol, methanol **9** isopropyl **11** cholesterol
used in perfumes: **5** nerol **7** borneol **8** geraniol, linalool

alcoholic
4 hard **5** dipso, drunk **6** brewed **8** drunkard **9** distilled, fermented, inebriant, inebriate, spiritous **10** spirituous **11** dipsomaniac, inebriating **12** intoxicating

alcoholic drink
see under **beverage**

Alcott novel
7 Jo's Boys **9** Little Men **11** Little Women

alcove
4 nook **5** niche **6** gazebo, recess **9** belvedere **11** summerhouse
Japanese: **8** tokonoma

Alcyone
father: **5** Atlas **6** Aeolus
husband: **4** Ceyx
mother: **7** Pleione
sisters: **8** Pleiades

ale
3 nog **4** beer, brew, nogg
aleatory
4 iffy **5** dicey, risky, shaky **6** chancy **9** hazardous, uncertain **10** contingent, precarious, vulnerable **11** problematic, speculative **13** unpredictable
alehouse
3 bar, pub **6** bistro, saloon, tavern **7** taproom **8** beer hall **10** beer garden **11** rathskeller
alembic
5 still **6** filter **9** distiller
alert
3 SOS **4** keen, psst, warn **5** alarm, quick, ready, sharp, smart **6** brainy, bright, clever, lively, notify, tip off, tocsin **7** heedful, mindful, on guard, red flag, wakeful **8** animated, forewarn, open-eyed, vigilant, watchful **9** attentive, mercurial, sprightly, wide-awake **10** perceptive **11** intelligent, quick-witted
Scottish: **4** gleg **8** wakerife
Aleutian island
3 Fox **4** Adak, Atka, Attu, Near **5** Amlia, Kiska **6** Unimak **8** Unalaska **9** Andreanof
town: **11** Dutch Harbor
alewife
4 fish **7** herring **8** menhaden
Alexander
birthplace: **5** Pella
conquest: **4** Tyre **5** Egypt, Issus **6** Greece, Persia **7** Parthia **8** Granicus
father: **6** Philip
general: **9** Antipater
horse: **10** Bucephalus
kingdom: **9** Macedonia
mother: **8** Olympias
teacher: **9** Aristotle
wife: **6** Roxana
alfalfa
3 hay **6** forage, legume **7** lucerne
alfresco
7 open-air, outdoor, outside **8** outdoors **9** out-of-door **10** out-of-doors
alga
6 desmid, diatom **7** seaweed
blue-green: **6** nostoc
brown: **4** kelp **5** fucus **8** rockweed
green: **9** chlorella
red: **4** nori
algebra term
4 root **6** factor **8** binomial, equation, monomial, variable **9** quadratic **10** polynomial
Algeria
capital: **7** Algiers
city: **4** Bône, Oran **6** Annaba **11** Constantine
coast: **7** Barbary
desert: **6** Sahara
ethnic group: **4** Arab **6** Berber
language: **6** Arabic, Berber
monetary unit: **5** dinar
mountain range: **5** Atlas **12** Saharan Atlas
neighbor: **4** Mali **5** Libya, Niger **7** Morocco, Tunisia **10** Mauritania
Algonquian Indian
3 Sac **4** Cree **6** Lenape
Algren novel
17 Walk on the Wild Side (A) **19** Man with the Golden Arm (The)
Ali
son: **5** Hasan **6** Husayn
wife: **6** Fatima
Ali ___
4 Baba
alias
3 AKA **6** anonym, handle **7** moniker, pen name **8** nickname **9** false name, pseudonym, stage name **10** also called, nom de plume **11** nom de guerre
Ali Baba's spell
10 Open Sesame
alibi
3 out **4** plea **5** clear, cover, proof **6** answer, excuse **7** account, cover up, defense, pretext **9** assertion, exonerate **11** explanation
Alice's Restaurant singer
4 Arlo (Guthrie)
alien
6 exotic **7** foreign, opposed, strange **8** estrange, outsider, stranger, transfer **9** estranged, extrinsic, foreigner, outlander **10** extraneous, outlandish **12** incompatible
alienate
4 part **5** repel **6** assign, convey, divide, offend, oppose **7** break up, turn off **8** disunify, disunite, estrange, separate, sign over, transfer **9** disaffect
alienation
5 break **6** anomie, breach **7** discord, divorce, rupture **8** division **10** conveyance, separation **12** disaffection, estrangement
alight
4 land **5** fiery **6** arrive, bright, on fire, settle **7** blazing, burning, deplane, descend, detrain, flaming, flaring, get down, glowing, ignited, shining **8** dismount **9** touch down **11** conflagrant
align
4 ally, join, line, sync, true **5** agree, array, order, range **6** adjust, follow, line up **8** regulate **9** affiliate, associate **10** straighten
alignment
6 camber
alike
4 akin, same **7** similar **8** parallel **9** analogous, consonant **10** comparable **13** corresponding

alikeness
6 simile 7 analogy 8 affinity, alliance, relation 9 closeness, semblance 10 comparison, connection, similarity, similitude 11 resemblance

aliment
4 eats, fare, feed, food, grub 7 nourish, nurture, sustain 9 nutriment 10 sustenance 11 nourishment

alimentary
9 nutritive 10 nourishing, sustaining 11 nutritional
canal: 7 enteron

alimony
4 keep 5 bread 6 living, upkeep 7 support 9 allowance, provision 10 livelihood, sustenance 11 maintenance, subsistence

A-list
5 cream, elite

alive
4 rife, spry 5 alert, awake, aware, brisk, fresh, quick, ready, vital 6 active, extant, living, moving, viable 7 animate, dynamic, knowing, replete, running, teeming, working, zestful 8 animated, existent, existing, sensible, sentient, swarming, thronged 9 abounding, breathing, cognizant, conscious, energetic, operative, sensitive, wide-awake 11 functioning, overflowing

alkali
4 base, salt 9 substance 11 soluble salt
metal: 6 cesium, sodium 7 lithium 8 francium, rubidium 9 potassium 10 monovalent
opposite: 4 acid

alkaline
5 acrid, basic, salty 6 bitter 7 antacid, caustic, soluble 8 chemical
substance: 3 lye 4 lime, soda 5 borax 6 potash 7 ammonia, antacid 8 pearl ash, saltwort 11 caustic soda

alkaloid
4 base
medicinal: 5 ergot 7 codeine, emetine, eserine, quinine 8 atropine, caffeine, lobeline, morphine 9 ephedrine, quinidine, reserpine 11 scopolamine
narcotic: 6 heroin 7 cocaine, codeine 8 morphine
poisonous: 8 atropine, nicotine, solanine 11 scopolamine

all
3 sum 4 each 5 every, gross, total, whole 6 entire, in toto, purely, wholly 7 exactly, totally, utterly 8 complete, entirety, everyone, outright, totality 9 aggregate, everybody 10 altogether, everything
combining form: 3 pan 4 omni, pant

all-around
7 general, overall, skilled 8 complete, sweeping, synoptic 9 adaptable, competent, many-sided, panoramic, universal, versatile 10 consummate, proficient 11 wide-ranging 12 encompassing 13 comprehensive

allay
4 balm, calm, ease, lull 5 abate, quell, quiet, still 6 lessen, reduce, settle, soothe, subdue 7 assuage, compose, lighten, mollify, quieten, relieve 8 decrease, diminish, mitigate, moderate 9 alleviate 11 tranquilize

all but
4 most, much, nigh 5 about 6 almost, nearly 8 as much as, in effect 9 just about, virtually 11 essentially, practically

All Creatures Great and Small author
7 Herriot (James)

allegation
5 claim 6 charge, report 9 assertion, statement 10 contention, profession 11 declaration

allege
3 say 4 aver, avow, cite 5 claim, offer, state 6 adduce, assert, attest, charge, submit 7 advance, contend, declare, present, profess 8 maintain 10 put forward

alleged
7 accused, dubious, reputed, suspect 8 doubtful, so-called, supposed 9 described, pretended, purported, soi-disant 10 ostensible, self-styled 12 questionable

allegiance
4 duty 5 ardor, piety 6 fealty, homage 7 loyalty 8 devotion, fidelity 9 adherence, constancy, obedience 10 dedication, obligation 11 devotedness 12 faithfulness

allegiant
4 firm, true 5 liege, loyal 6 ardent, steady 7 devoted, dutiful, staunch 8 constant, faithful, resolute 9 steadfast 10 dependable

allegorical
5 moral 6 fabled 8 mythical, symbolic 9 legendary, spiritual 10 emblematic, exegetical, fictitious, figurative 12 iconographic, illustrative, metaphorical

allegory
4 myth, tale 5 fable, story 6 emblem, symbol 7 parable 8 apologue 9 symbolism 10 figuration 12 typification

allegro
4 fast 5 brisk 6 bouncy, lively 8 animated, spirited 9 sprightly

allegro con ___
4 brio

Allende novel
17 House of the Spirits (The)

allergy
5 dread 6 hatred 7 disgust, dislike 8 aversion, distaste, hay fever 9 antipathy, disliking, rejection, repulsion

alleviate
4 cure, ease **5** allay **6** lessen, reduce, remedy **7** assuage, lighten, mollify, relieve **8** decrease, diminish, mitigate

alleviation
4 ease **6** relief **7** decline **8** decrease, easement **9** lessening, reduction **10** diminution, mitigation

alley
4 lane, walk **6** marble, street **7** passage **10** backstreet

all-fired
7 totally, utterly **9** extremely **10** absolutely, completely **11** excessively

alliance
3 tie **4** axis, bloc, bond, pact **5** union **6** accord, league, treaty **7** compact, concord, entente **8** affinity, relation **9** coalition **10** connection, federation **11** affiliation, association, combination, confederacy, conjunction, partnership, unification **12** relationship **13** confederation
international: **3** CIS, OAS **4** APEC, EFTA, NATO, OECD, OPEC **5** ASEAN, CENTO, NORAD, SEATO **7** CARICOM **8** Interpol **10** Warsaw Pact

allied
4 akin **5** bound **6** agnate, joined, linked, united **7** cognate, connate, kindred, related, unified **8** in league **9** connected **10** affiliated, associated, connatural **11** consanguine

alligator
11 crocodilian
relative: **4** croc **6** caiman, cayman **9** crocodile

alligator pear
7 avocado

all in
4 dead, used, worn **5** spent, tired **6** bushed, done in, used up **7** drained, far-gone, worn-out **8** depleted **9** dead tired, exhausted, washed-out

all in all
5 in all **6** mainly **7** en masse, largely **9** generally **10** altogether, by and large, on the whole

all, in Mexico
4 todo

All in the Family
character: **5** Edith (Bunker) **6** Archie (Bunker), Gloria **7** Michael
creator: **4** Lear (Norman)
nickname: **7** Dingbat **8** Meathead
setting: **6** Queens **7** Astoria
star: **6** Reiner (Rob) **7** O'Connor (Carroll) **9** Stapleton (Jean), Struthers (Sally)
theme song: **16** Those Were the Days

allocate
4 give **5** allot, slice **6** assign, divide **7** dish out, divvy up, dole out, earmark, mete out, prorate **8** set apart **9** admeasure, apportion, designate **10** distribute

allocution
4 talk **5** spiel **6** sermon, speech **7** address, lecture, oration, oratory, pep talk **11** exhortation

allot
4 give, mete **5** grant, share **6** accord, assign **7** deal out, divvy up, dole out, mete out **8** allocate, dispense, set aside **9** admeasure, apportion **10** distribute

allotment
3 cut, lot **4** bite, part **5** chunk, piece, quota, share, slice **6** ration **7** measure, portion **9** allowance, provision **13** apportionment

all-out
4 full **5** total **6** entire, utmost **7** maximum **8** absolute, complete, thorough **9** full-blown, full-scale, unlimited **12** totalitarian **13** thoroughgoing

all over
8 wherever **9** all around **10** everyplace, everywhere, far and near, far and wide, high and low, thoroughly, throughout

allow
3 let, lot, own **4** avow, give **5** admit, allot, brook, grant, leave, let on, stand **6** assign, endure, permit, suffer **7** concede, confess, consent, entitle, forbear, mete out **8** allocate, tolerate **9** apportion **11** acknowledge

allowed
5 legal, licit

allowance
3 aid, cut, lot, pay, sum **4** bite, edge, help, part, tare, tret **5** grant, leave, piece, quota, share, slice **6** amount, permit, ration **7** consent, measure, partage, portion, quantum, subsidy, vantage **8** handicap, pittance, quantity, sanction **9** advantage, allotment, head start, reduction **10** adjustment, allocation, assistance, concession, permission, sufferance, toleration **13** accommodation, apportionment, authorization

alloy
5 blend **6** fusion **7** amalgam, mixture **8** compound **9** admixture, composite **10** adulterant **11** interfusion **12** amalgamation, intermixture
brass-like: **6** latten
copper-sulfur: **6** niello
copper-tin: **6** bronze
copper-zinc: **5** brass **6** tombac
enamel-like: **6** niello
gold-like: **6** oreide, ormolu, oroide
gold-silver: **8** electrum
iron-carbon: **5** steel
iron-nickel: **5** invar
mercury: **7** amalgam
tin-lead: **5** terne **6** pewter, solder
used in jewelry: **6** tombac

all-powerful
6 mighty 7 supreme 8 absolute, almighty 10 invincible, omnipotent 11 controlling

all right
3 A-OK, aye, yea, yep, yes 4 good, okay, safe, well 5 A-okay 6 agreed, decent, proper, surely 7 average 8 adequate, of course, passable, passably, pleasing, standard, very well 9 agreeable, certainly, tolerable, tolerably 10 acceptably, adequately, definitely, positively, sufficient, well enough 12 satisfactory

all round
see **all-around**

All That Jazz director
5 Fosse (Bob)

All the King's Men author
6 Warren (Robert Penn)

all told
6 in toto 7 overall

allude
4 hint 5 imply, point, refer 7 bring up, suggest 8 indicate, intimate

allure
4 draw, pull 5 charm, tempt 6 appeal, entice, lead on, seduce 7 attract, beguile, enchant, glamour, win over 8 charisma, inveigle, persuade 9 captivate, fascinate, magnetism, magnetize 10 attraction 11 enchantment, fascination

alluring
4 sexy 6 lovely 7 winning, winsome 8 charming, inviting, pleasing 9 appealing, beguiling, glamorous, seductive 10 appetizing, attractive, bewitching, enchanting 11 captivating, fascinating

ally
4 join 5 unite 6 friend, helper 7 comrade, partner 8 federate 9 accessory, affiliate, associate, auxiliary, bedfellow, colleague, supporter 10 accomplice 11 confederate 12 collaborator

almighty
4 very 6 hugely, mighty 7 awfully, godlike, supreme 8 absolute 9 extremely 10 invincible, omnipotent 11 all-powerful, exceedingly

almost
4 nigh 5 about 6 all but, nearly 8 as good as, as much as, not quite, well-nigh 9 just about, virtually 11 essentially, practically 13 approximately
Scottish: 6 feckly

almost sold out
3 SRO

alms
4 gift 6 relief 7 present 8 donation, offering 10 assistance 11 benefaction, beneficence 12 contribution

aloe
9 emollient, succulent

Aloeus
father: 7 Neptune 8 Poseidon
mother: 6 Canace
son: 4 Otus 9 Ephialtes
wife: 9 Iphimedia

aloft
4 high, over 5 above 6 on high, upward 7 skyward 8 in flight, overhead

aloha
4 by-by, ciao, hail 5 hello, howdy 6 bye-bye, good-by, so long 7 good-bye, welcome 8 farewell, greeting 9 greetings
State: 6 Hawaii

alone
4 only, sole, solo, stag 5 apart 6 singly, solely, unique, wholly 7 isolate, removed 8 detached, entirely, isolated, peerless, singular, solitary 9 matchless, unequaled, unmatched, unrivaled 10 nothing but, unequalled, unexampled, unexcelled 11 exclusively, unsurpassed 12 incomparable, unparalleled, unrepeatable 13 unaccompanied

aloneness
8 solitude 9 isolation, seclusion 10 uniqueness

along
3 too, yet 4 also, near, with 5 forth, there 6 as well, at hand, on hand, onward 7 besides, forward 8 likewise, moreover 11 furthermore 12 accompanying, additionally

alongside
6 beside, next to 8 touching 9 adjoining, bordering

aloof
3 shy 4 cold, cool 5 apart, proud 6 casual, chilly, frigid, offish, remote 7 distant, haughty, removed, stuck up 8 arrogant, detached, reserved, reticent, solitary 9 incurious, unbending, uncurious, withdrawn 10 disdainful, restrained, unfriendly, unsociable 11 constrained, indifferent, standoffish, unconcerned 12 uninterested 13 disinterested

alopecia
8 baldness

alp
4 peak 5 mount 8 mountain

alpaca
4 wool 5 cloth 6 mammal
habitat: 4 Peru 5 Andes 7 Bolivia

alpha
4 dawn 5 first, start 6 outset 7 dawning, genesis, opening 9 beginning 12 commencement
follower: 4 beta
opposite: 5 omega

alphabet
4 ABC's 7 letters

Arabic: **3** ayn, dad, dal, gaf, jim, kaf, kha, lam, mim, nun, qaf, sad, sin, tha, waw, zay **4** alif, dhal, shin **5** ghayn
Greek: **3** chi, eta, phi, psi, rho, tau **4** beta, iota, zeta **5** alpha, delta, gamma, kappa, omega, sigma, theta **6** lambda **7** epsilon, omicron, upsilon
Hebrew: **3** mem, nun, sin, taw, tet, vav, waw, yod **4** alef, ayin, beth, heth, kaph, koph, qoph, resh, shin, teth **5** aleph, gimel, lamed, sadhe, tsade, zayin **6** daleth, samekh
Old Irish: **4** ogam **5** ogham
runic: **7** futhark

Alpheus
beloved: **8** Arethusa
father: **7** Oceanus
form: **5** river
mother: **6** Tethys

Alpine
animal: **4** ibex **7** chamois
dress: **6** dirndl
house: **6** chalet
lake: **4** Como, Iseo **5** Garda **6** Geneva **7** Lucerne **8** Bodensee, Maggiore **9** Constance, Neuchâtel
pass: **3** col **5** Cenis **7** Brenner, Simplon **9** St. Bernard
peak: **5** Blanc, Eiger **7** Bernina **8** Jungfrau **10** Matterhorn
plant: **9** edelweiss
primrose: **8** auricula
resort: **5** Davos **7** Bolzano, Zermatt **8** Chamonix, Grenoble, St. Moritz **9** Innsbruck **10** Interlaken **11** Saint Moritz
river: **5** Rhine, Rhône
snowfield: **4** firn, névé
staff: **10** alpenstock
state: **5** Tirol, Tyrol
tunnel: **5** Blanc, Cenis **7** Arlberg, Simplon **10** St. Gotthard
wind: **4** bora, föhn **5** foehn

already
4 even, once **5** by now, prior **6** before, by then **7** earlier, just now **8** formerly **9** before now **10** by this time, heretofore, previously

also
3 and, too **4** more, plus **5** again, along **6** as well **7** besides, further **8** likewise, moreover **9** along with, including, similarly **10** in addition **11** furthermore **12** additionally

also-ran
3 dud **5** loser **7** failure, wannabe, washout **8** defeated, runner-up

altar
6 shrine
boy: **6** server **7** acolyte
cloth: **4** pall **7** frontal
constellation: **3** Ara
hanging: **6** dorsal, dossal
platform: **8** predella
screen: **7** reredos
shelf: **7** retable
site: **4** apse, bema
vessel: **5** cruet, paten **7** chalice **8** ciborium **10** monstrance

alter
3 fix **4** geld, spay, turn, vary **5** adapt **6** adjust, change, doctor, modify, mutate, neuter, revamp **7** remodel **8** castrate, moderate, modulate **9** refashion

alteration
4 turn **5** shift **6** change **8** mutation, revision **9** variation **10** adaptation, adjustment, changeover, conversion, remodeling, transition **12** modification

altercate
4 spat, tiff **5** argue, scrap **6** bicker, hassle **7** dispute, quarrel, wrangle **8** squabble **9** caterwaul

altercation
3 row **4** beef, flap, fray, spat, tiff **5** brawl, clash, fight, melee, run-in **6** affray, blowup, combat, fracas, hassle, kickup **7** contest, dispute, quarrel, rhubarb, wrangle **8** argument, squabble **9** bickering **10** falling-out **11** controversy, embroilment

alternate
3 sub **5** proxy **6** backup, by turn, change, fill-in, rotate, second **7** another, relieve, stand-in **8** periodic, rotating **9** change off, fluctuate, recurrent, recurring, replacing, surrogate **10** equivalent, every other, periodical, substitute **11** every second, pinch hitter, replacement **12** intermittent

alternately
6 in lieu, rather **7** instead **10** preferably

alternative
5 other, proxy **6** backup, choice, option, second **7** another **8** atypical, druthers, election **9** different, selection, surrogate **10** preference, substitute **11** contingency, nonstandard, possibility

Althaea
father: **8** Thestius
husband: **6** Oeneus
son (victim): **8** Meleager

although
4 when **5** still, while **6** albeit, even if, much as **7** despite, howbeit, whereas

altitude
6 height **8** eminence **9** elevation, high level

altitudinous
4 high, tall **7** eminent **8** elevated

alto
3 Day (Doris), Lee (Peggy) **4** Cher, Kitt (Eartha), Piaf (Édith) **5** Baker (Janet), Lenya (Lotte) **6** London (Julie), Merman (Ethel) **7** Clooney (Rosemary), Ferrier (Kathleen), Vaughan (Sarah) **8** Anderson (Marian), Dietrich (Marlene)

9 Forrester (Maureen) 10 Chookasian (Lili) 13 Schumann-Heink (Ernestine)

altogether
4 nude, well 5 fully, in all, quite 6 in toto, wholly 7 all told, en masse, exactly, totally, utterly 8 all in all, entirely 9 generally, perfectly 10 absolutely, by and large, completely, on the whole, thoroughly

altruism
7 charity 8 sympathy 10 compassion, generosity 11 benevolence 12 philanthropy, selflessness 13 unselfishness

altruistic
3 big 6 humane 8 generous 9 unselfish 10 benevolent, bighearted, charitable, open-handed 11 considerate, magnanimous, noble-minded 12 humanitarian 13 philanthropic

alum
4 grad 6 emetic 7 styptic 8 graduate 10 astringent

aluminum source
7 bauxite

always
3 e'er 4 ever 7 forever 8 evermore, for keeps 9 at any rate, endlessly, eternally 10 at all times, constantly, in any event, invariably 11 continually, forevermore, in perpetuum, perpetually, unceasingly 12 consistently, continuously

Amahl and the Night Visitors composer
7 Menotti (Gian Carlo)

amalgamate
3 mix 4 ally, fuse, meld, pool 5 admix, alloy, merge, unify, unite 6 mingle 7 combine 8 coalesce, compound, intermix 9 commingle, integrate 11 consolidate, intermingle

amalgamation
5 alloy, blend, union 6 fusion, merger 7 joining, melding, merging, mixture, uniting 8 alliance, compound 9 admixture, coalition, composite 10 commixture 12 intermixture 13 consolidation

Amalthea
form: 4 goat
horn: 10 cornucopia
nursling: 4 Zeus

amanita
8 death cap, mushroom 9 fly agaric 10 death angel

amanuensis
6 scribe 7 copyist 9 scrivener, secretary 11 transcriber 12 stenographer

___, amas, amat
3 amo

amass
4 bulk, heap, make, pile 5 hoard, lay up, store, uplay 6 accrue, garner, gather, pile up, roll up 7 acquire, collect, compile, round up, store up 8 assemble, cumulate 9 aggregate, stockpile 10 accumulate 12 come together

amassment
4 pile 5 clump, group, hoard, stack, stock, store, trove 7 cluster 8 assembly, quantity 9 gathering, stockpile 10 assemblage, collection, cumulation 11 aggregation 12 accumulation 13 agglomeration

amateur
4 tyro 6 layman, novice, tinker, votary 7 admirer, dabbler, devotee, learner 8 aspirant, beginner, neophyte, putterer 9 greenhorn, smatterer 10 apprentice, dilettante, enthusiast, uninitiate 11 abecedarian

amateurish
3 raw 5 green 6 simple 7 artless 8 dabbling, inexpert 9 deficient, unskilled, untutored 10 dilettante, unfinished, unpolished, unskillful 12 dilettantist, unproficient 13 inexperienced

amative
see **amorous**

amatory
6 ardent, erotic, loving, tender 7 sensual 8 romantic 9 erogenous, seductive 10 passionate 11 aphrodisiac

amaze
3 wow, stun 4 daze 5 floor 6 wonder 7 astound, nonplus, perplex, startle, stupefy 8 astonish, bewilder, blow away, bowl over, confound, surprise 9 dumbfound 10 admiration 11 flabbergast

amazement
3 awe 6 marvel, wonder 8 surprise 9 marveling 10 admiration, perplexity, wonderment 12 astonishment, bewilderment, confoundment

amazing
7 awesome 8 striking, stunning, wondrous 9 marvelous, startling, wonderful 10 astounding, impressive, miraculous, stupendous, surprising 11 astonishing, bewildering, spectacular 12 breathtaking

Amazon
6 parrot 8 giantess 12 woman warrior
founder: 5 Bezos (Jeff)
native: 4 Tupi
snake: 3 boa
tributary: 5 Negro (Rio)

ambassador
5 agent, envoy 6 legate 8 diplomat, emissary 9 messenger
papal: 6 nuncio

amber
5 ocher, ochre, resin, rosin 6 orange, yellow 7 saffron

ambience
4 aura, mood, tone 6 flavor, medium, milieu 7 climate 10 atmosphere 11 environment 12 surroundings

ambient
5 music **6** milieu **7** general, setting **8** everyday **9** prevalent **10** atmosphere, prevailing **11** atmospheric, environment, mise-en-scène **12** encompassing, surroundings **13** environmental

ambiguity
5 doubt **6** enigma, puzzle **7** evasion **9** equivoque, obscurity, vagueness **11** incertitude, uncertainty **12** doubtfulness, equivocality, equivocation **13** double meaning

ambiguous
5 vague **6** opaque, unsure **7** cryptic, dubious, inexact, obscure, unclear **8** doubtful, puzzling, two-edged **9** enigmatic, equivocal, tenebrous, uncertain, unsettled **10** indefinite, inexplicit **11** problematic **12** inconclusive, questionable

ambit
4 area, room **5** field, limit, orbit, range, reach, scope, space, sweep **6** border, bounds, extent, limits, radius, sphere **7** breadth, circuit, compass, expanse, purview **8** boundary, confines **9** extension, perimeter, periphery **13** circumference

ambition
3 aim **4** goal, hope, itch, push, wish, zeal **5** ardor, dream, drive, vigor **6** desire, energy, hunger, spirit, target, thirst **7** avidity, craving, purpose **8** appetite, striving, yearning **9** eagerness, intention, objective **10** aspiration, enterprise, enthusiasm, get-up-and-go, initiative, pretension

ambitious
4 avid, bold, keen **5** eager, pushy **6** driven, hungry, intent **7** driving, zealous **8** aspiring, desirous, striving **9** energetic **10** aggressive **11** hard-working **12** enterprising, enthusiastic

ambivalent
5 mixed **6** unsure **7** warring **8** clashing, wavering **9** equivocal, uncertain, undecided **10** unresolved **11** fluctuating, vacillating **13** contradictory

amble
4 gait, walk **5** dally, drift, mosey **6** dawdle, linger, stroll, wander **7** meander, saunter

ambrosia
6 dainty, regale **7** dessert, perfume **8** delicacy, ointment

ambrosial
5 balmy, spicy, sweet **6** savory **7** scented **8** aromatic, fragrant, heavenly, luscious, perfumed, pleasing, redolent **9** delicious **10** delectable, delightful **11** scrumptious

ambulate
4 hoof, move, pace, step, walk **5** tread, troop **6** foot it, hoof it **7** traipse

ambulatory
6 moving, on foot, roving **7** nomadic, roaming, walking **8** vagabond **9** itinerant **11** peripatetic

ambush
4 jump, lurk, trap **5** snare **6** assail, attack, entrap, lay for, waylay **7** assault, ensnare **8** surprise **9** ambuscade **11** concealment

ameliorate
3 fix **4** help, lift, mend **5** amend, raise **6** better, perk up, remedy, reform **7** elevate, enhance, improve, lighten, relieve, upgrade **8** mitigate **9** alleviate **10** convalesce, recuperate

amen
5 selah

amenable
4 open, tame **6** docile, liable, pliant, suited **7** plastic, pliable, subdued, subject, willing **8** biddable, in accord, obedient, yielding **9** adaptable, agreeable, complying, malleable, receptive, tractable **10** answerable, consenting, responsive, submissive **11** accountable, acquiescent, cooperative, responsible

amend
3 fix **4** help **5** alter, right **6** better, change, modify, reform, remedy, repair, revise, square **7** correct, improve, rectify **8** put right **9** meliorate **10** ameliorate

amendment
5 rider **6** change **7** codicil **8** addendum, revision **10** alteration, attachment, correction **11** enhancement, improvement **12** modification

amends
7 redress **8** reprisal **9** indemnity, quittance **10** recompense, reparation **11** restitution **12** compensation

amenities
5 mores **6** polish **7** decorum, manners **8** civility, courtesy **9** etiquette, propriety **12** social graces

amenity
5 charm, frill **6** luxury **7** comfort, quality **8** civility, courtesy, facility **9** advantage, etiquette, geniality, pleasance **10** affability, amiability, betterment, cordiality, enrichment, pleasantry, politeness **11** convenience, enhancement, improvement, sociability **12** agreeability, graciousness, pleasantness

ament
6 catkin

amerce
3 tax **4** dock, fine, levy **5** exact, mulct **6** punish **7** hit with, make pay **8** penalize

amercement
4 fine **5** mulct **7** damages, forfeit, penalty **10** assessment, punishment, reparation

American Buffalo playwright
5 Mamet (David)

American Express rival
4 Visa

American League
Baltimore: **7** Orioles
Boston: **6** Red Sox
Los Angeles: **6** Angels (of Anaheim)
Chicago: **8** White Sox
Cleveland: **7** Indians
Detroit: **6** Tigers
Houston: **6** Astros
Kansas City: **6** Royals
Los Angeles: **6** Angels
Minnesota: **5** Twins
New York: **7** Yankees
Oakland: **9** Athletics
Seattle: **8** Mariners
Tampa Bay: **9** Rays
Texas: **7** Rangers
Toronto: **8** Blue Jays

American Samoa
capital: **8** Pago Pago
island, island group: **4** Rose **5** Aunuu, Manua **6** Swains **7** Tutuila
language: **6** Samoan

America's Cup winner
6 Ranger **7** Alinghi, Freedom **8** Columbia, Intrepid **9** Weatherly **10** Black Magic, Courageous

America, the Beautiful
music: **4** Ward (Samuel Augustus)
words: **5** Bates (Katherine Lee)

Amfortas
father: **7** Titurel
opera: **8** Parsifal

amiability
7 amenity **9** geniality, pleasance **10** cordiality **11** sociability **12** complaisance, congeniality, friendliness, pleasantness, sociableness **13** agreeableness, enjoyableness

amiable
4 kind, warm **6** genial, gentle, kindly **7** affable, cordial, likable **8** cheerful, friendly, gracious, likeable, obliging, sociable **9** agreeable, congenial, courteous **10** responsive **11** complaisant, good-humored, good-natured, warmhearted

amicable
7 cordial, pacific **8** empathic, friendly, peaceful, sociable **9** congenial, peaceable **10** harmonious, like-minded, neighborly **11** sympathetic **13** understanding

amid
4 over **5** among, midst **6** during **7** amongst, between **10** throughout

amigo
3 pal **4** chum, mate, pard **6** friend **7** comrade, partner **8** sidekick **9** companion, confidant **12** acquaintance

Amin of Uganda
3 Idi

amino acid
4 dopa **6** leucin, lysine, serine, toluid, valine **7** cystein, cystine, glycine, leucine, proline, toluide **8** cysteine, dopamine, histidin, thyroxin, toluidin, tyrosine

Amis, Kingsley
novel: **8** Lucky Jim
son: **6** Martin

Amis, Martin
father: **8** Kingsley
novel: **5** Money **10** Time's Arrow **11** Information (The) **12** London Fields

amiss
3 bad **4** awry, poor **5** badly, wrong **6** afield, astray, faulty, flawed **7** wrongly **8** erringly, faultily **9** defective, imperfect **10** improperly, mistakenly, out of place **11** erroneously, imperfectly, incorrectly, unfavorably **12** inaccurately **13** inappropriate

amity
5 union **6** accord, comity, unison **7** concert, concord, harmony **8** alliance, goodwill **9** agreement **10** cordiality, friendship, kindliness **11** concurrence **12** friendliness

Ammonite
6 Semite
god: **6** Molech, Moloch

ammunition
4 ammo, shot **5** bombs **6** rounds, shells **7** charges **8** armament, grenades, missiles, ordnance **10** cartridges **11** projectiles

Amneris's rival
4 Aïda

amnesty
6 pardon **7** freeing, release **8** immunity, reprieve **9** discharge **10** absolution **11** forgiveness **12** dispensation

Amnon
father: **5** David
half sister: **5** Tamar
mother: **7** Ahinoam

amoeba
4 blob **8** rhizopod **9** protozoan

amok
7 berserk

Amon
father: **8** Manasseh
son: **6** Josiah

Amonasro's daughter
4 Aïda

among
3 mid **4** amid **5** midst **6** amidst, within **7** between
other things: **9** inter alia
prefix: **5** inter

amorist
4 rake, wolf **5** lover, Romeo **7** Don Juan, gallant, playboy **8** Casanova, lothario, paramour **9** womanizer **12** heartbreaker

amorous
6 ardent, erotic, in love **7** amative, amatory, lustful **8** enamored, romantic **10** infatuated, passionate **11** aphrodisiac, impassioned

amorousness
4 love, lust **5** amour, ardor **6** desire **7** passion **9** eroticism

amorphous
7 unclear **8** formless, inchoate, nebulous, unformed, unshaped **9** shapeless, undefined **10** indistinct **11** nondescript **12** disorganized **13** characterless
mass: **4** blob

amortize
5 repay **6** pay off, reduce **7** pay down **8** write off

Amos of song
4 Tori

amount
4 bulk, dose **5** add up, equal, price, total **6** dosage, matter, number, upshot **7** purport, quantum **8** quantity **9** aggregate, substance
owed: **4** debt
small: **3** bit, jot **4** atom, drop, iota, mite, whit **5** minim, spark, speck, trace **7** modicum, smidgen **8** molecule, particle **9** scintilla

amour
4 love **5** fling, lover **6** affair **7** liaison, passion, romance **8** intimacy, intrigue **9** dalliance **10** love affair **12** entanglement, relationship

amour propre
5 pride **6** egoism, vanity **7** conceit, egotism **8** self-love, vainness **9** vainglory **10** narcissism, self-esteem, self-regard **11** self-conceit, self-respect **12** pridefulness **13** conceitedness

amphetamines
5 speed **6** dexies, hearts, uppers **7** bennies, Dexoxyn **8** greenies, pep pills, Preludin **9** Dexedrine **10** Benzedrine, Methedrine

amphibian
burrowing: **9** caecilian
genus: **4** Hyla, Rana
legless: **9** caecilian
tailed: **3** eft **4** newt **10** salamander
tailless: **4** frog, toad **8** bullfrog, tree toad **10** batrachian
wormlike: **9** caecilian
young: **7** tadpole **8** polliwog

Amphion
brother: **6** Zethus
conquest: **6** Thebes
father: **4** Zeus
mother: **7** Antiope
sister: **5** Aedon
wife: **5** Niobe

amphitheater
4 bowl **5** arena **7** stadium **8** coliseum **10** auditorium, hippodrome

Amphitrite
father: **6** Nereus
husband: **7** Neptune **8** Poseidon
mother: **5** Doris
son: **6** Triton

Amphitryon's wife
7 Alcmene

amphora
3 jar, jug, urn **4** ewer, vase **5** crock, flask **6** carafe, flagon, vessel

ample
4 wide **5** buxom, great, large, roomy **6** lavish, plenty, portly **7** copious, liberal, profuse **8** abundant, generous, handsome, spacious **9** bounteous, bountiful, capacious, expansive, extensive, plenteous, plentiful **10** commodious, sufficient **11** substantial

amplify
5 boost, raise, swell **6** dilate, expand, extend, jack up **7** augment, develop, distend, enhance, enlarge, inflate, magnify **8** increase **9** elaborate, intensify **10** supplement

amplitude
4 size **5** range, scale, scope, space **6** amount, extent, spread **7** bigness, breadth, expanse, stretch **8** distance, fullness, wideness **9** abundance, expansion, greatness, largeness, magnitude, roominess **12** spaciousness **13** capaciousness

amulet
4 juju, luck, tiki **5** charm **6** fetish, grigri, mascot, scarab **7** periapt **8** gris-gris, talisman **10** lucky piece, phylactery **11** rabbit's-foot

Amundsen of the South Pole
5 Roald

amuse
4 wile **5** charm, cheer **6** appeal, divert, engage, occupy, please, regale, tickle **7** animate, beguile, delight, enchant, enliven, gladden **8** distract, interest, recreate **9** entertain, fascinate

amusement
3 fun **4** play **7** delight, pastime **8** pleasure **9** diversion, enjoyment **10** recreation **11** distraction

amusing
3 fun **5** droll, funny **7** comical, risible **8** engaging, humorous, pleasing **9** diverting, enjoyable **9** laughable **12** entertaining

Amycus
father: **7** Neptune **8** Poseidon
friend: **8** Heracles, Hercules
mother: **5** Melia

ana
5 album, varia **7** sayings **9** anecdotes, anthology **10** collection, miscellany **11** memorabilia, miscellanea

anabasis
5 march **7** advance, headway, retreat **8** progress **11** advancement, progression

Anacin alternative
5 Advil, Aleve **6** Motrin **7** aspirin, Tylenol

anagogic
6 arcane, hidden, mystic, occult, secret **7** obscure **8** esoteric, mystical, telestic **9** spiritual **10** symbolical **11** allegorical

Anaïs known for memoirs
3 Nin

analects
5 album **6** digest **7** garland, omnibus **8** treasury **9** anthology, selection **10** compendium, miscellany **11** compilation, florilegium

analgesic
6 opiate **7** anodyne **10** anesthetic, painkiller

analogous
4 akin, like **5** alike **7** kindred, similar, related, uniform **8** parallel **9** consonant **10** comparable, equivalent, resembling

analogue
5 match **7** oognate **8** parallel **9** correlate **10** similarity **11** correlation, counterpart, equivalence **13** correspondent

analogy
6 simile **8** affinity, likeness, metaphor, parallel, relation **9** agreement, alikeness, semblance **10** comparison, similarity, similitude **11** correlation, equivalence, resemblance
words: **4** is to

analysis
5 assay, audit, proof, study **6** method, review, report, survey **7** finding, inquiry **8** division **9** breakdown, partition, statement **10** dissection, inspection, resolution, separation **11** examination **13** clarification

analytic
6 cogent, subtle **7** logical, testing **8** studious **9** organized **10** diagnostic, scientific, systematic **11** proposition, questioning **13** investigative, ratiocinative

analyze
4 part, test **5** assay, parse, study **6** divide **7** dissect, examine, inspect, resolve **8** classify, consider, separate **9** anatomize, break down, decompose, interpret **10** decompound, scrutinize **11** deconstruct, distinguish, investigate

Ananias
4 liar **9** falsifier **12** prevaricator
father: **9** Nedebaeus
wife (coconspirator): **8** Sapphira

anarchism
4 riot **6** theory **7** misrule **8** disorder **9** distemper, rebellion **11** lawlessness

anarchist
5 rebel **6** rioter **8** agitator, mutineer, provoker, revolter **9** dissident, insurgent **10** malcontent **11** provocateur **13** revolutionary
famous: **6** Tucker (Benjamin), Zerzan (John) **7** Bakunin (Mikhail), Chomsky (Noam), Goldman (Emma), Stirner (Max) **8** Christie (Stuart), Proudhon (Pierre-Joseph) **9** Kropotkin (Peter)

anarchy
4 riot **5** chaos **7** misrule, mob rule, turmoil **8** disarray, disorder **9** confusion, distemper, mobocracy, rebellion **10** ochlocracy, revolution **11** lawlessness **13** nongovernment

anathema
3 ban **4** bane **5** curse, enemy, odium, taboo **6** pariah **7** bugbear, censure, malison, outcast, reproof **8** loathing **9** damnation, bête noire **10** black beast, execration **11** abomination, commination, detestation, imprecation, malediction **12** condemnation, denunciation

anathematize
3 ban **4** damn, oust **5** curse, expel **6** banish **7** condemn **8** denounce, execrate **9** objurgate, proscribe **13** excommunioate

anatomical depression
5 fossa, fovea

anatomical tube
3 vas **4** duct **5** canal

anatomist
5 Wolff (Kaspar) **6** Harvey (William) **8** Vesalius (Andreas)

anatomize
5 cut up **7** analyze, dissect **8** separate **9** break down, decompose

anatomy
5 frame, mummy **6** makeup **8** analysis, division, skeleton **9** framework, histology, structure **10** dissection, morphology, physiology **11** examination

Anaxo
brother: **10** Amphitryon
daughter: **7** Alcmene
father: **7** Alcaeus
husband: **9** Electryon

ancestor
8 forebear, foregoer **9** ascendant, precursor, prototype **10** antecedent, antecessor, forefather, forerunner, progenitor **11** predecessor **12** primogenitor

ancestral
6 family, inborn, inbred, lineal **7** genetic **8** familial **9** inherited **10** bequeathed, hereditary **11** consanguine, patrimonial
sequence: **8** pedigree **9** bloodline, genealogy

ancestry
4 line, race 5 blood, breed, stock 6 family, origin, source 7 descent, history, kindred, lineage 8 heritage, pedigree 9 parentage 10 derivation, extraction

Anchises' son
6 Aeneas

anchor
4 moor 5 kedge 6 kedger, secure 7 grapnel, mooring 8 mainstay
network news: 4 Daly (John), Hume (Brit), Muir (David) 5 Chung (Connie) 6 Brokaw (Tom), Couric (Katie), Gibson (Charles), Koppel (Ted), Lehrer (Jim), Murrow (Edward R.), Pelley (Scott), Rather (Dan), Sawyer (Diane), Swayze (John Cameron) 7 Blitzer (Wolf), Edwards (Douglas), Huntley (Chet), Walters (Barbara) 8 Brinkley (David), Cronkite (Walter), Jennings (Peter), Reasoner (Harry), Reynolds (Frank), Williams (Brian) 9 Schieffer (Bob) 10 Chancellor (John)
part: 3 arm 4 bill, ring 5 crown, fluke, shank, stock

anchorage
4 port 5 haven, roads 6 harbor, refuge, riding 7 mooring, shelter 9 harborage, roadstead

anchorite
5 loner 6 hermit 7 recluse 8 solitary

anchors ___
6 aweigh

ancient
3 old 4 aged 5 hoary, olden 6 age-old, primal 7 antique, archaic, elderly 8 Noachian, old-timer, primeval, timeworn 9 venerable 10 primordial 12 antediluvian

ancient capital
4 Susa 5 Aksum, Balkh, Calah, Isker, Kalhu, Ninus, Pella, Petra, Sibir 6 Angkor, Bactra, Nimrud, Sardis 7 Babylon, Knossos, Memphis, Nineveh, Samaria, Shushan 10 Persepolis

ancient character
4 rune

ancient city
Asia Minor: 4 Nice, Teos 5 Tyana 6 Edessa, Nicaea 7 Antioch 13 Halicarnassus
Babylonia: 4 Sura 5 Agade, Akkad, Eridu, Larsa 7 Ellasar
Bengal: 4 Gaur 9 Lakhnauti
Canaan: 5 Gezer
Cyprus: 7 Salamis
Egypt: 5 Tanis 6 Thebes 7 Memphis 10 Heliopolis
Etruria: 4 Veii
Euphrates River: 7 Babylon
Greece: 5 Crisa 6 Athens, Sparta 7 Calydon 10 Lacedaemon
Ionia: 4 Myus, Teos 5 Chios, Samos 6 Priene 7 Ephesus, Lebedos, Miletus, Phocaea 8 Colophon, Erythrae 10 Clazomenae
Italy: 5 Locri 7 Pompeii 8 Siracusa, Syracuse 11 Herculaneum
Latium: 5 Gabii 9 Alba Longa
Mayan: 4 Cobá 5 Tikal, Tulum, Uxmal 8 Palenque 11 Chichén Itzá
Nile River: 5 Meroë
North Africa: 5 Utica 8 Carthage
Palestine: 4 Gaza 5 Ekron, Endor, Sodom 6 Beroea, Bethel, Gilead, Hebron 7 Jericho, Samaria 8 Ashkelon 9 Capernaum, Jerusalem
Peloponnesus: 5 Tegea 6 Sparta 7 Corinth
Sumeria: 4 Kish, Uruk 5 Erech, Larsa 6 Lagash
Turkey: 5 Assos, Assus 9 Byzantium

ancient country
Adriatic coast: 7 Illyria
Africa: 10 Mauretania
Arabian Peninsula: 5 Sheba
Asia: 4 Aram 5 Media, Minni, Syria 7 Armenia, Ash Sham, Bactria
Asia Minor: 5 Ionia, Lydia, Mysia 6 Aeolis, Pontus 7 Cilicia, Phrygia 8 Bithynia
Balkan: 7 Macedon 9 Macedonia
Black Sea: 7 Colchis
Dead Sea: 4 Edom
Euphrates River: 9 Babylonia
Europe: 4 Gaul 5 Dacia 6 Gallia
gold-rich: 5 Ophir
Italy: 6 Latium 7 Etruria
Nile valley: 4 Cush
Peloponnesus: 4 Elis 7 Arcadia
Syria: 9 Phoenicia

ancient empire
6 Median 7 Hittite, Persian 8 Assyrian, Athenian, Chaldean, Seleucid 9 Ptolemaic 10 Babylonian

ancient kingdom
Anglo-Saxon: 6 Wessex
Asia: 4 Ghor, Ghur
Celtic: 7 Cumbria
China: 3 Shu
Euphrates valley: 4 Hira 7 Al-Hirah
Greece: 8 Pergamon, Pergamum
North Of Assyria: 3 Van 6 Ararat, Urartu
Palestine: 5 Judah 6 Israel
Persian Gulf: 4 Elam
Portugal: 7 Algarve
Spain: 4 Leon 6 Aragon 7 Castile, Galicia, Granada, Navarre
Syria: 4 Moab
Welsh: 5 Powys
West Sahara: 4 Gana 5 Ghana

Ancient Mariner poem
4 rime

ancient monument
6 sphinx **7** obelisk, pyramid

ancient Roman road
3 via **4** iter

ancient royal forest
4 Dean **8** Sherwood

ancient theater
4 odea (plural) **5** odeum

ancient Tokyo
3 Edo

ancient town
Africa: **4** Zama
Armenia: **4** Dwin, Tvin
Asia Minor: **4** Soli **5** Derbe, Issus, Soloi
Attica: **6** Icaria
Black Sea: **5** Olbia **9** Apollonia
Greece: **4** Abae, Opus **8** Marathon
Italy: **4** Elea, Luna **5** Cumae, Velia
Latium: **5** Ardea, Cures
Macedonia: **5** Pydna, Stobi **9** Apollonia
Peloponnesus: **5** Asine
Persia: **6** Hormuz **8** Harmozia
Sicily: **5** Hybla
Spain: **5** Munda
Tatar: **5** Isker, Sibir
Wendish: **5** Julin

ancilla
3 aid **4** aide, ally, hand, help **6** helper **9** assistant, attendant, supporter

ancillary
5 extra **8** adjuvant, incident **9** accessory, attendant, attending, auxiliary, satellite, secondary **10** additional, coincident, collateral, subsidiary, supporting **11** appurtenant, concomitant, subordinate, subservient **12** accompanying, contributory **13** supplementary

andante
4 slow **5** tempo **7** relaxed, walking **8** moderate

Anderson play
7 High Tor **8** Key Largo **9** Winterset **11** Valley Forge **14** What Price Glory

Anderson book
9 Poor White **12** Dark Laughter **13** Winesburg Ohio

Andes
grazer: **5** llama **6** alpaca, guemal, huemal, vicuña **7** camelid, guanaco
native: **4** Inca
peak: **9** Aconcagua, Huascarán

andiron
7 firedog

Andorra
capital: **7** Andorra
language: **7** Catalan
liberator: **11** Charlemagne
monetary unit: **4** euro
monetary unit, former: **6** peseta **11** French franc
mountain range: **8** Pyrenees
neighbor: **5** Spain **6** France
river: **6** Valira

and others, for short
4 et al.

Andrea ___
5 Doria **8** del Sarto

androgynous
7 epicene **8** bisexual **9** unisexual

android
5 robot **9** automaton

Andromache
husband: **6** Hector
son: **8** Astyanax, Molossus

Andromeda
father: **7** Cepheus
husband: **7** Perseus
mother: **10** Cassiopeia
rescuer: **7** Perseus

Andean country
4 Peru **5** Chile

Andean Indian
4 Inca

and so forth, for short
3 etc.

___ and the Detectives
4 Emil

Andy Griffith Show
actor: **6** Bavier (Francis), Howard (Ron), Knotts (Don), Nabors (Jim)
character: **4** Opie (Taylor) **5** Gomer (Pyle) **6** Barney (Fife) **7** Aunt Bee

anecdote
4 tale, yarn **5** story **7** account, episode, recital **8** relation **9** narration, narrative **12** recollection, reminiscence

anemic
3 wan **4** pale, thin, weak **5** pasty **6** feeble, pallid, sickly, watery **7** insipid **8** ischemic **9** bloodless, colorless **10** spiritless

anemone
9 buttercup **10** windflower

anent
4 as to, in re **5** about, as for **7** apropos **8** touching **9** as regards **10** concerning **13** with respect to

anesthetic
6 opiate **7** anodyne **9** analgesic **10** painkiller, palliative
medical: **5** ether **6** spinal **8** morphine, procaine **9** halothane, novocaine **10** benzocaine, chloroform, tetracaine **11** scopolamine
suffix: **5** caine

anesthetize
4 numb, stun **6** benumb, deaden **8** etherize, knock out **9** narcotize **11** desensitize

anesthetized
4 dead, numb **5** inert **6** asleep, torpid **10** insensible **11** insensitive, unconscious

anew
4 over **5** again **6** afresh, de novo, lately, of late **8** once more, recently

angel
6 backer, cherub, patron, seraph, surety **7** sponsor **8** backer-up, guardian **9** celestial, guarantor, supporter **10** benefactor **11** underwriter
aura: **4** halo
biblical: **5** Uriel **7** Gabriel, Michael, Raphael
fallen: **7** Lucifer
hierarchy: **6** powers **7** thrones, virtues **8** cherubim, seraphim **9** dominions
Mormon: **6** Moroni
of death: **6** Azrael

Angel Clare's bride
4 Tess

angelic
4 holy, pure **5** godly **6** divine **7** saintly **8** cherubic, ethereal, heavenly **9** celestial **11** beneficient

Angelica
father: **9** Galaphron
husband: **6** Medoro
lover: **7** Orlando

Angelina's husband
4 Brad (Pitt)

Angelou work
13 Heart of a Woman (The) **25** I Know Why the Caged Bird Sings

anger
3 ire, vex **4** bile, boil, burn, fume, fury, gall, huff, rage, rant, rave, rile **5** storm, upset, wrath **6** choler, dander, enrage, madden, nettle, offend, seethe **7** affront, bristle, dudgeon, incense, outrage, provoke, steam up, umbrage **8** acrimony **9** animosity, infuriate **10** antagonism, antagonize, exasperate

angle
3 aim, bow **4** axil, bend, bias, fish, hand, skew, turn **5** facet, slant **6** aspect, corner, crotch, dogleg **7** flexure, outlook, turning **9** direction, viewpoint **10** standpoint

angler
6 fisher **8** monkfish **9** fisherman, goosefish

Anglo-Saxon
assembly: **4** moot **5** gemot **6** gemote
council: **9** heptarchy
county: **5** shire
court: **4** moot **5** gemot **6** gemote
crown tax: **4** geld
epic: **7** Beowulf
free servant: **5** thane, thegn
god: **3** Ing
goddess of fate: **4** Wyrd
historian: **4** Bede
king: **3** Ine, Ini **4** Edwy **5** Edgar, Edred **6** Alfred, Edmund, Edward, Egbert **8** Ethelred
kingdom: **4** Kent **5** Essex **6** Mercia, Sussex, Wessex **10** East Anglia **11** Northumbria
king's council: **5** witan
laborer: **4** esne
letter: **3** edh, eth, wen, wyn **4** rune, wynn **5** thorn
nobleman: **4** earl
poet: **4** scop
prince: **8** atheling
sheriff: **5** reeve
slave: **4** esne
warrior: **5** thane, thegn

Angola
capital: **6** Luanda
city: **6** Huambo **7** Lubango **8** Benguela
exclave: **7** Cabinda
language: **10** Portuguese
monetary unit: **6** kwanza
neighbor: **5** Congo **6** Zambia **7** Namibia **11** South Africa
river: **5** Congo

angora
3 cat **4** goat, hair, wool, yarn **6** mohair, rabbit

angry
3 hot, mad **4** sore **5** irate, riled, riley, upset, vexed, wroth **6** fuming, heated, ireful, wrathy **7** enraged, furious, riled up, teed off **8** choleric, incensed, inflamed, maddened, wrathful **9** indignant, irritated **10** aggravated, infuriated **11** acrimonious, exasperated

angst
4 fear **5** agita, worry **6** unease **7** anxiety, concern **8** disquiet, distress **10** insecurity **11** disquietude, fretfulness **12** apprehension

Anguilla
island, island group: **3** Dog **4** Seal **5** Scrub **7** Leeward
location: **10** West Indies
territory of: **7** Britain

anguish
3 rue, woe **4** ache, care, dole, hurt, pain, pang **5** agony, dread, grief, throe, worry **6** misery, regret, sorrow, throes **7** anxiety, torment, torture **8** distress, hardship **9** heartache, suffering **10** affliction, heartbreak **12** wretchedness

angular
4 bony, edgy, lank, lean, thin **5** gaunt, lanky, spare, stiff **6** forked, skinny, zigzag **7** pointed, scraggy, scrawny **8** cornered, rawboned, ungainly **9** roughhewn **10** unfinished, ungraceful, unpolished

ani
6 cuckoo
anima
4 soul **6** psyche, spirit
animadversion
4 slam, slur **7** censure, obloquy **9** aspersion, criticism **10** accusation, imputation, reflection **11** insinuation **12** reprehension
animadvert
6 notice **7** observe **9** criticize
animal
5 beast, brute, feral **6** brutal, carnal, ferine **7** beastly, bestial, brutish, critter, fleshly, sensual, swinish, wilding **8** creature, wildling
antlered: **3** elk **4** axis, deer **5** moose **7** caribou **8** reindeer
aquatic: **3** eel **4** fish, frog, seal **5** otter, whale **6** dugong, sea cow, walrus **7** dolphin, manatee, octopus **8** bryozoan, porpoise **9** alligator, crocodile
arboreal: **4** bird **5** chimp, coati, koala, lemur, sloth **6** gibbon, monkey **7** opossum, tarsier **8** kinkajou, marmoset, squirrel **9** orangutan
burrowing: **4** mole **5** brock, ratel **6** badger, gopher, marmot, rabbit **7** echidna **9** armadillo, groundhog, woodchuck
castrated: **4** oxen (plural) **5** capon, steer **6** barrow, wether **7** gelding
coat: **3** fur **4** hair, hide **6** pelage
draft: **3** yak **4** mule, oxen (plural) **5** burro, horse **6** donkey **8** elephant
exhibit: **3** zoo
extinct: **3** moa **4** dodo, urus **6** quagga **7** mammoth **8** dinosaur, eohippus, mastodon **9** trilobite
female: **3** cow, dam, doe, ewe, hen, pen, roe, sow **4** mare, puss **5** bitch, goose, jenny, nanny, vixen **6** jennet **7** lioness
four-footed: **9** quadruped
four-limbed: **8** tetrapod
free-swimming: **6** nekton
hibernating: **4** bear, frog, toad **5** skunk, snake **7** polecat **8** chipmunk **9** groundhog, woodchuck
horned: **3** ram, yak **4** bull, goat, ibex, kudu, oxen (plural) **5** addax, bison, eland, rhino **6** cattle, koodoo **7** buffalo, gazelle, giraffe, unicorn **8** antelope
humped: **3** elk, yak **4** oxen (plural), zebu **5** bison, camel, moose
imaginary: **5** snark **6** Harvey **10** hippogriff
male: **3** cob, ram, tom **4** boar, buck, bull, cock, stag, stud **5** billy, steer **6** gander **7** gobbler, rooster **8** bachelor, stallion
many-celled: **8** metazoan
many-footed: **9** centipede, millipede
meat-eating: **9** carnivore
mythical: **5** Hydra **6** dragon, kraken, sphinx **7** centaur, griffin, mermaid, Pegasus, unicorn **8** basilisk, Cerberus, Minotaur
one-celled: **9** protozoan
Peruvian: **5** llama **6** alpaca, vicuña
plant-eating: **9** herbivore
skin disease: **5** mange
spotted: **4** axis, paca **6** calico, jaguar, ocelot **7** cheetah, leopard, piebald **8** skewbald **9** dalmatian
striped: **4** kudu **5** tiger, zebra **6** koodoo, quagga
tender: **8** herdsman
trail: **3** pug **4** foil, slot **5** spoor
tusked: **6** walrus **7** warthog **8** elephant
two-footed: **5** biped
web-footed: **4** duck, frog, toad **5** goose, otter **6** beaver **7** muskrat **8** duckbill, platypus
young: **3** cub, kid, kit, pup **4** calf, colt, fawn, foal, joey, lamb **5** bunny, chick, kitty, poult, shoat, stirk, whelp **6** cygnet, farrow, heifer, kitten, piglet **7** bullock, gosling, lambkin **8** suckling, yeanling, yearling **9** fledgling
animal behavior
study of: **8** ethology
animal fat
4 suet **6** tallow
Animal House garment
4 toga
animalism
4 lust **7** abandon **8** vitality **9** carnality **10** sensualism, sensuality **11** lustfulness, physicality, unrestraint
animalize
4 warp **6** debase **7** corrupt, deprave, pervert, vitiate **9** brutalize **10** bestialize, demoralize
animal life
5 fauna
animal skin
4 hide, pelt
animal sound
3 arf, baa, bay, caw, coo, low, mew, moo **4** bark, bray, buzz, crow, hiss, hoot, howl, meow, purr, roar, yelp **5** bleat, chirp, croak, drone, growl, grunt, miaow, neigh, quack **6** bellow, gibber, gobble, warble **7** screech, twitter
animate
4 fire, live, move, spur, stir, urge **5** alert, alive, cheer, drive, exalt, impel, liven, nerve, spark, steel, vital **6** active, arouse, excite, inform, kindle, lively, living, moving, viable, vivify **7** actuate, chirk up, dynamic, enliven, hearten, inspire, quicken, refresh **8** activate, embolden, energize, inspirit, motivate, spirited, vitalize **9** breathing, encourage, energized, enhearten, make alive, stimulate **10** invigorate
animated
3 gay **4** keen **5** alert, alive, peppy, quick, vivid, vital **6** lively, living **7** dynamic, excited, vibrant, zestful **8** spirited, vigorous **9** activated,

energetic, energized, exuberant, sprightly, vitalized, vivacious **12** high-spirited

animation

3 pep, vim, zip **4** brio, dash, élan, life, toon, zing **5** oomph, verve **6** energy, esprit, gaiety, spirit **7** cartoon, dynamic **8** dynamism, vitality, vivacity **10** liveliness

unit: 3 cel **4** cell

animato

5 brisk, tempo **6** lively **8** spirited **9** energetic, sprightly

animator's frame

3 cel

anime film

5 Akira

animosity

4 hate **5** venom **6** animus, enmity, hatred, rancor **7** dislike, ill will **8** acrimony **9** antipathy, hostility **10** antagonism, resentment

animus

4 plan, soul **6** design, enmity, intent, pneuma, psyche, rancor, spirit **7** dislike, ill will, meaning, purpose **8** bad blood **9** antipathy, élan vital, hostility, intention **10** antagonism, intendment, opposition, vital force **11** disposition, malevolence

Anita of jazz

4 O'Day

Anjou

4 pear

capital: 6 Angers

native: 7 Angevin

ankle

5 talus **6** tarsus

Anna Karenina

author: 7 Tolstoy (Leo)

character: 5 Dolly, Kitty, Levin (Konstantin), Stiva **6** Andrei (Karenin) **7** Vronsky (Count Alexei) **8** Ivanovna (Countess Lidia), Seriozha

film star: 4 Bean (Sean) **5** Bloom (Claire), Garbo (Greta), Leigh (Vivien), March (Fredric), Reeve (Christopher) **6** Bisset (Jacqueline) **7** Connery (Sean), Marceau (Sophie) **10** Richardson (Ralph)

radio star: 4 Peck (Gregory) **7** Bergman (Ingrid)

annals

6 record **7** account, history **8** archives, register **9** chronicle

Annapolis freshman

5 plebe

Anna's home

4 Siam

annelid

4 worm **5** leech **9** earthworm

annex

3 add, arm, cop, ell, win **4** gain, hook, join, land, take, wing **5** add on, affix, seize, tag on **6** adjoin, append, attach, fasten, obtain, pick up, secure, tack on, take on **7** acquire, connect, preempt, procure, subjoin **8** accroach, addition, appendix, arrogate, superadd, take over **9** extension **10** attachment, commandeer, subsidiary, supplement **11** appropriate, expropriate, incorporate

Annie Oakley

4 comp, pass **10** free ticket, markswoman

annihilate

4 do in, kill, raze, rout, ruin, undo **5** abate, annul, crush, erase, quash, quell, wrack, wreck **6** murder, negate, quench, rub out, squash, uproot, vanish **7** abolish, blot out, destroy, expunge, nullify, put down, root out, vitiate, wipe out **8** abrogate, demolish, massacre, suppress, vanquish **9** eradicate, extirpate, liquidate, slaughter **10** extinguish, invalidate, obliterate **11** exterminate

annihilation

7 killing **8** massacre **9** abolition **11** destruction, elimination, liquidation, termination **12** obliteration **13** extermination

anniversary

hundredth: 9 centenary **10** centennial

tenth: 9 decennial

thousandth: 10 millennial

Anno ___

6 Domini

annotate

5 gloss **6** remark **7** comment, explain **8** footnote **9** elucidate, interpret **10** commentate

announce

4 call, tell **5** augur, issue, sound, state **6** attest, blazon, herald, impart, report, reveal, signal **7** bespeak, declare, divulge, forerun, give out, portend, predict, presage, present, publish, release, signify, trumpet **8** disclose, forecast, foreshow, foretell, indicate, proclaim **9** advertise, broadcast, harbinger, make known, publicize **10** give notice, make public, promulgate **11** preindicate

announcement

4 news **5** promo **6** notice, report **7** message, release **8** briefing, bulletin **9** broadcast, statement **10** communiqué, disclosure **11** declaration, publication **12** proclamation, promulgation **13** advertisement, communication

announcer

5 emcee **6** deejay, herald, veejay **9** anchorman, voice-over **10** disc jockey, disk jockey, newscaster **11** anchorwoman, broadcaster, commentator **12** anchorperson, sportscaster

annoy

3 bug, irk, vex **4** bait, fret, gall, miff **5** chafe, chivy, harry, peeve, tease, upset, worry **6** badger, bother, harass, heckle, hector, molest,

needle, nettle, pester, plague, ruffle, tee off **7** agitate, bedevil, disturb, hagride, perturb, provoke, tick off **8** distress, irritate **9** beleaguer
Scottish: **4** fash

annoyance
4 drag, to-do **5** trial, upset, worry **6** bother, nettle, plague, strain **7** problem, trouble **8** distress, headache, irritant, nuisance, vexation **10** affliction, harassment, irritation **11** aggravation, botheration, disturbance, indignation, provocation **12** exasperation

annoying
5 pesky **8** tiresome **9** troubling, vexatious **10** disturbing, irritating **11** aggravating, distressing, troublesome **12** exasperating
smell: **4** odor

annual
5 plant **6** flower, yearly **7** almanac **8** each year, yearbook, yearlong **9** every year

annul
4 undo, void **5** abate, erase, quash **6** cancel, delete, efface, negate, revoke, vacate **7** abolish, blot out, expunge, nullify, redress, rescind, retract, reverse, vitiate, wipe out **8** abrogate, dissolve **9** cancel out, discharge, frustrate **10** annihilate, counteract, extinguish, invalidate, neutralize, obliterate **11** countermand

annunciate
see **announce**

anodyne
4 balm **5** bland **6** opiate, relief, remedy **7** soother **8** narcotic, nepenthe, painless, sedative **9** analgesic, calmative, innocuous, soporific **10** anesthetic, depressant, pain-killer, palliative **11** inoffensive, unoffending **12** tranquilizer

anoint
3 rub **4** daub, laud, name **5** anele, apply, bless, honor, smear **6** choose, hallow, ordain **7** confirm, massage **8** dedicate, sanctify, set apart, venerate **9** designate **10** consecrate

anomalous
3 odd **6** off-key **7** deviant, strange, unusual **8** aberrant, abnormal, atypical, peculiar **9** deviating, deviatory, divergent, irregular, unnatural, untypical **10** unexpected **11** heteroclite, incongruous, paradoxical **12** inconsistent **13** nonconforming, preternatural

anomaly
5 freak, quirk **6** oddity **7** paradox **9** departure, deviation, exception **10** aberration, divergence **11** abnormality, incongruity, peculiarity **12** idiosyncrasy, irregularity **13** inconsistency

anomie
4 flux **6** unrest **7** anxiety, inertia **10** alienation, insecurity **11** disquietude, instability, uncertainty **12** disaffection, estrangement, indifference, restlessness

anon
4 soon **5** later **7** by and by, shortly **8** directly, in a while **9** presently **10** before long **11** after a while

anonym
5 alias **6** handle **7** Jane Roe, John Doe, pen name **8** nickname **10** nom de plume **11** assumed name, nom de guerre

anonymous
7 unknown, unnamed **8** nameless, not named, unsigned **9** incognito **11** unspecified **12** unidentified, unrecognized

anorak
5 parka

another
3 new **4** else, more **5** added, fresh **7** farther, further, one more **9** different **10** additional **11** alternative, someone else **13** something else

anschluss
5 union **6** league **8** alliance **9** coalition **10** federation **11** confederacy **13** confederation

answer
4 fill, meet, plea, RSVP **5** atone, plead, rebut, reply, serve, solve **6** come in, refute, rejoin, result, retort, return **7** conform, defense, explain, fulfill, respond, satisfy **8** antiphon, rebuttal, response, solution **9** rejoinder **10** refutation **11** recriminate **13** countercharge

answerable
5 bound **6** liable **7** obliged, subject **8** amenable **9** compelled, duty-bound, obligated **11** accountable, constrained, responsible

ant
5 emmet **9** carpenter
relating to: **6** formic

Antaean
4 huge **5** giant **6** heroic **7** mammoth, titanic **8** colossal, enormous, gigantic **9** cyclopean **10** gargantuan

Antaeus
father: **7** Neptune **8** Poseidon
mother: **4** Gaea
slayer: **8** Heracles, Hercules

antagonism
3 con **6** animus, enmity, hatred, rancor **7** discord **8** conflict, friction **9** animosity, antipathy, hostility **10** antithesis, contention, dissension, opposition, resistance **11** contrariety **12** disagreement

antagonist
3 con, foe **4** anti **5** enemy, match **6** muscle **7** opposer **8** chemical, opponent **9** adversary, contender

antagonistic
4 anti **6** averse **7** adverse, hostile, opposed **8** clashing, contrary, inimical, opposing **9** bellicose, combative, rancorous, truculent **11** belligerent, conflicting, contentious **12** antipathetic

Antarctica sea
4 Ross **7** Weddell **8** Amundsen

ante
3 bet, pay, pot **4** cost, risk **5** level, pay up, price, put up, stake, wager **6** stakes **7** produce

anteater
8 aardvark, pangolin, tamandua

antecede
7 forerun, precede, predate **8** foredate, go before

antecedence
8 priority **10** precedence, precession, preference

antecedent
4 fore, line **5** cause, prior **6** former, reason **7** earlier **8** ancestor, anterior, forebear, foregoer, occasion, previous **9** condition, foregoing, precedent, preceding, precursor, prototype **10** forerunner, progenitor **11** determinant, predecessor

antedate
7 forerun, precede **11** anachronize

antediluvian
3 old **4** aged, fogy **5** hoary, passé **6** age-old, fogram, fossil, square **7** ancient, antique, archaic **8** mossback, Noachian, obsolete, outdated, outmoded, primeval, timeworn **9** out-of-date, primitive **10** antiquated, fuddy-duddy **12** old-fashioned **13** stick-in-the-mud

antelope
3 gnu, kob **4** guib, kudu, oryx, poku, puku, topi, tora **5** addax, bongo, eland, nyala, oribi, serow **6** dik-dik, duiker, impala, koodoo, lechwe, nilgai, rhebok **7** blesbok, chamois, gazelle, gemsbok, gerenuk, sassaby **8** bushbuck, reedbuck, steinbok **9** springbok, waterbuck **10** hartebeest
female: **3** doe
genus: **4** Oryx
male: **4** buck
young: **3** kid
(see also **gazelle**)

antenna
4 wire **6** aerial, device, dipole, sensor **8** monopole, receiver

antennae
4 ears **11** sensitivity **13** receptiveness

anterior
4 past **5** prior **6** former **8** previous **9** foregoing, precedent, preceding **10** antecedent

anteroom
5 entry, foyer, lobby **6** alcove **9** vestibule

Anteros
brother: **4** Eros
father: **4** Ares, Mars
mother: **5** Venus **9** Aphrodite
opposite: **4** Eros

anthem
4 hymn, song **5** chant, paean, psalm **8** canticle

anthology
3 ana **5** album, cento **6** digest, reader **7** garland, omnibus **8** analects, treasury **9** selection **10** assortment, collection, compendium, miscellany **11** compilation, florilegium

anthropoid
3 ape **4** saki, titi **5** biped **6** bonobo, gibbon, monkey, uakari **7** bipedal, gorilla, macaque, manlike, primate, tamarin, tarsier **8** capuchin, hominoid, humanoid, marmoset **9** orangutan **10** chimpanzee

anthropologist
4 Boas (Franz), Dart (Raymond), Mead (Margaret) **5** Sapir (Edward), Tylor (Edward Burnett) **6** Frazer (James George), Geertz (Clifford), Leakey (Louis), Morgan (Lewis Henry) **7** Bateson (Gregory), Kroeber (Alfred Louis) **8** Benedict (Ruth) **10** Malinowski (Bronisław) **11** Lévi-Strauss (Claude)

anti
3 con **6** averse **7** adverse, against, counter, opposed, opposer **8** contrary, opponent, opposing **9** adversary, opposed to **10** antagonist **12** antagonistic, antipathetic, in opposition

antiaircraft fire
4 flak

antibiotic
7 colicin **8** neomycin, viomycin **9** polymyxin **10** bacitracin, novobiocin, penicillin **11** bacteriocin, tyrothricin **12** streptomycin, tetracycline

antic
3 gag **4** dido, joke, lark, romp **5** caper, comic, prank, trick **6** frisky, frolic, lively **7** comical, foolish, playful **8** escapade, farcical, prankish, spirited **9** high jinks, laughable, ludicrous, sprightly **10** frolicsome, rollicking, shenanigan, tomfoollery **11** mischievous, monkeyshine **12** monkeyshines **13** practical joke

anticipate
3 see **4** wait **5** await, check **6** divine, expect **7** counter, count on, foresee, prepare, presage, prevent, wait for **8** forecast, foreknow, foretell **9** apprehend, forestall, prevision, visualize **10** prepare for

anticipation
4 hope **7** inkling, outlook, promise **8** awaiting, forecast, prospect **9** awareness, foresight, foretaste **10** expectancy **11** expectation, realization **12** apprehension **13** visualization

Anticlea
father: **9** Autolycus
husband: **7** Laertes
son: **7** Ulysses **8** Odysseus

antidote
4 cure, drug **6** remedy **7** negator **8** medicine **9** nullifier **10** corrective, counteract, preventive

11 counterstep, neutralizer **12** counteragent **13** counteractant, counteractive

Antigone
brother: **9** Polynices **10** Polyneices
father: **7** Oedipus
mother: **7** Jocasta
sister: **6** Ismene
uncle: **5** Creon

Antigua and Barbuda
capital: **7** St. Johns
island: **7** Antigua, Barbuda, Redonda

Antilochus
father: **6** Nestor
friend: **8** Achilles
slayer: **6** Memnon

Antiope
father: **6** Asopus
husband: **5** Lycus **7** Theseus
queen of: **7** Amazons
son: **6** Zethus **7** Amphion **10** Hippolytus

antipasto
9 appetizer **11** hors d'oeuvre **12** hors d'oeuvres

antipathetic
5 loath **6** averse, loathe **7** adverse, hostile, opposed **8** aversive, clashing, contrary, inimical, opposing, opposite **9** abhorrent, loathsome, repellent, repugnant, repulsive **10** discordant, unfriendly **11** conflicting, distasteful, ill-disposed, uncongenial **12** antagonistic **13** contradictory

antipathy
4 hate **6** animus, enmity, hatred, rancor **7** allergy, dislike, ill will **8** aversion, distaste, loathing **9** animosity, hostility **10** abhorrence, antagonism, opposition, repellency

antiphon
5 psalm, reply, verse **6** answer, anthem, return **7** respond **8** response

antipodal
5 polar **7** adverse, counter, opposed, reverse **8** contrary, converse, opposite **9** diametric **11** conflicting, contrasting, diametrical **12** antithetical **13** contradictory

antipode
6 contra **7** counter, reverse **8** contrary, converse, flip side, opposite **9** other side **11** counterpole

antiquate
7 outdate, outmode **8** obsolete **9** obsolesce **12** superannuate

antiquated
3 old **4** aged **5** dated, fusty, hoary, moldy, passé **6** bygone, old hat **7** ancient, antique, archaic, old-time **8** obsolete, old-timey, outmoded **9** out-of-date **10** oldfangled, out-of-style **11** discredited, obsolescent **12** antediluvian, old-fashioned **13** inappropriate, superannuated

antique
3 old **4** aged **5** dated, hoary, olden, passé, relic **6** age-old, bygone, rarity **7** ancient, archaic, vintage **8** artifact, heirloom, old-timey, outdated, outmoded, timeworn **9** ancestral, objet d'art, out-of-date, venerable **10** antiquated, oldfangled **12** antediluvian, old-fashioned
auto: **3** REO

antiseptic
6 iodine **7** alcohol, sterile **8** hygienic, peroxide, sanitary **9** boric acid, carvacrol, germicide, merbromin **10** gramicidin, sterilized **12** carbolic acid, disinfectant
pioneer: **6** Lister (Joseph)

antisocial
7 ascetic, austere, hostile **8** eremitic, solitary **9** alienated, reclusive, withdrawn **10** unfriendly **11** standoffish **12** antagonistic, misanthropic

antithesis
3 con **6** contra **7** counter, reverse **8** antipode, antipole, contrary, contrast, converse, opposite **10** antagonism, opposition **11** counterpole

antithetical
5 polar **6** contra **7** counter, reverse **8** contrary, converse, opposite **9** antipodal, diametric **10** antipodean **11** diametrical **13** contradictory

antitoxin
4 sera (plural) **5** serum **11** neutralizer

antiwar
6 irenic **8** pacifist **10** nonviolent, pacifistic

antlered animal
3 elk **4** deer **5** moose **6** cervid, wapiti **7** caribou **8** reindeer

Antony, Mark
defeat: **6** Actium
friend: **6** Caesar
lover: **9** Cleopatra
wife: **7** Octavia

antsy
4 edgy **7** jittery, nervous, restive, twitchy

anxiety
4 care, fear **5** agita, doubt, dread, panic, worry **6** nerves, unease **7** concern **8** distress, mistrust, suspense **9** self-doubt, suffering **10** uneasiness **11** disquietude, uncertainty **12** apprehension

anxious
4 avid, keen **5** antsy, eager **6** afraid, ardent, scared, uneasy **7** alarmed, fearful, worried **8** agitated, desirous, troubled, worrying **9** impatient, perturbed, terrified **10** breathless, disquieted, frightened **12** apprehensive

any
3 all **4** a bit, some **5** every **7** a little, several **8** whatever

anyhow
6 random **7** however **8** at random, randomly

9 hit-or-miss 10 carelessly, regardless 11 haphazardly 13 helter-skelter

anymore
3 now 5 today 8 nowadays 9 presently, these days

anyone
3 all 9 everybody

anything
5 aught

anytime
4 ever 8 whenever

anyway
4 ever, once 5 at all 7 however 12 nevertheless

anywise
5 at all

Aoki of golf
4 Isao

apace
4 fast 6 versed 7 abreast, flat-out, hastily, quickly, rapidly, swiftly 8 informed, up-to-date, speedily 9 posthaste 12 lickety-split 13 expeditiously

Apache
chief: 7 Cochise 8 Geronimo
subgroups: 7 Cibecue 9 Jicarilla, Mescalero 10 Chiricahua

apart
5 alone, aside 6 singly 7 asunder, removed 8 detached, isolated, one by one 9 severally 10 separately 12 individually 13 independently, unaccompanied
prefix: 3 dis

apart from
3 bar, but 4 save 6 except, saving 7 barring, besides 9 except for, excepting, excluding, other than, outside of 11 exclusive of

apartheid
8 division 9 partition 10 separation, separatism 11 segregation 12 separateness

apartment
4 flat, room 5 rooms, suite 6 bedsit, rental 7 chamber, housing, lodging 8 building, dwelling 9 residence 10 maisonette 13 accommodation

apathetic
4 dull, flat, limp 5 inert 6 stolid, torpid 7 languid, passive, unmoved 8 sluggish 9 impassive, untouched 10 anesthetic, insensible, phlegmatic, spiritless 11 emotionless, indifferent, insensitive 12 unresponsive 13 disinterested

apathy
6 torpor 8 coldness, dullness, lethargy, obduracy, stoicism 9 aloofness, disregard, inertness, lassitude, passivity, stolidity, torpidity, unconcern 10 detachment, dispassion 11 callousness, disinterest, impassivity 12 heedlessness, indifference, listlessness 13 insensibility, insensitivity

ape
4 copy, mime, mock 5 magot, mimic, orang 6 bonobo, gibbon, parody, pongid, simian 7 copycat, emulate, gorilla, imitate, siamang, take off 8 simulate, travesty 9 burlesque, orangutan 10 anthropoid, caricature, chimpanzee 11 impersonate

aperçu
5 brief 6 digest, précis, sketch, survey 7 insight, outline 8 syllabus 10 compendium, impression

aperitif
3 kir 4 whet 5 drink 6 Pastis, Pernod, sherry 7 Campari, Cinzano 8 cocktail 9 appetizer

aperture
3 gap 4 hole, port, slit, vent 5 chink 6 outlet 7 opening, orifice, pinhole

apery
7 mimicry 9 imitation

apex
3 cap, tip, top 4 acme, cusp, peak, roof 5 crest, crown, limit, point 6 apogee, climax, summit, vertex, zenith 8 capstone, pinnacle, ultimate 9 crescendo, sublimity 11 culmination, ne plus ultra 12 quintessence

aphorism
3 saw 4 rule 5 adage, axiom, maxim, moral 6 dictum, saying, truism 7 precept, proverb 8 apothegm

aphrodisiac
6 erotic 7 amative, amatory, amorous, lustful 8 excitant 10 passionate

Aphrodite
Roman counterpart: 5 Venus
consort: 4 Ares 6 Vulcan 10 Hephaestus
father: 4 Zeus 7 Jupiter
goddess of: 4 love
mother: 4 Leto 5 Dione
sister: 6 Athena 7 Artemis
son: 4 Eros 6 Aeneas 7 Priapus

apiarist
9 beekeeper

apical
3 top 7 highest, topmost 8 loftiest 9 uppermost

apiculture
10 beekeeping

apiece
3 per 4 a pop, each 6 singly, to each 7 for each 8 one by one 9 per capita, severally 10 separately 12 individually, respectively

apish
5 phony, silly 6 phoney 7 slavish 8 affected 9 emulative, imitative 10 artificial

aplenty
4 full 5 ample 6 galore, indeed 7 copious, greatly 8 abundant, very much 9 extremely

aplomb
4 ease **5** poise **6** polish **8** coolness, easiness **9** assurance, certainty, certitude, composure **10** confidence, equanimity **11** nonchalance, savoir faire **12** self-reliance **13** self-assurance

apocalypse
6 augury, oracle, vision **8** disaster, prophecy **10** Armageddon, prediction, revelation

apocalyptic
4 dire **5** awful **7** baleful, baneful, fateful, fearful, ominous **8** Delphian, dreadful, oracular, terrible **9** appalling, climactic, grandiose, prophetic **10** foreboding, predicting **11** foretelling, prophetical, threatening **12** inauspicious
book: 10 Revelation **11** Revelations

apocryphal
5 false, wrong **6** untrue **7** dubious **8** doubtful, spurious **9** incorrect, ungenuine **10** fictitious, inaccurate, unverified **11** unauthentic **12** questionable

apogee
4 acme, apex, peak **6** climax, summit, zenith **8** capstone, meridian, pinnacle **9** high point **11** culmination

Apollo
6 Helios **7** Phoebus
beloved: 6 Cyrene, Daphne **8** Calliope
birthplace: 5 Delos
father: 4 Zeus **7** Jupiter
mother: 4 Leto **6** Latona
oracle: 6 Delphi
sister: 5 Diana **7** Artemis
son: 3 Ion **7** Orpheus
temple: 6 Delphi

apologetic
5 sorry **6** rueful **8** contrite, penitent **9** regretful, repentant **10** remorseful **11** penitential **12** compunctious

apologia
4 plea **6** excuse, reason **7** defense **8** argument **11** elucidation, explanation **13** clarification, justification

apologize
5 atone **6** lament, regret, repent **7** confess **9** beg pardon **10** make amends

apologue
4 myth, tale **5** fable, story **7** parable **8** allegory

apology
4 plea **6** amends, excuse **7** redress, regrets **8** mea culpa **9** admission, makeshift **10** concession, confession

apoplexy
4 esca **6** stroke

apostasy
7 perfidy **9** defection, desertion, disavowal, falseness, rejection **11** abandonment, repudiation **12** disaffection, renunciation

apostate
7 heretic, traitor **8** defector, deserter, recreant, renegade, turncoat **9** turnabout

apostatize
4 turn **6** defect, desert **7** abandon, forsake, sell out **8** renounce **9** repudiate

a posteriori
9 inductive

apostle
4 John, Jude, Paul **5** James, Judas, Peter, Silas, Simon **6** Andrew, Philip, Thomas **7** Matthew **8** Barnabas, disciple, follower, Matthias, preacher **9** missioner **10** colporteur, evangelist, missionary **11** Bartholomew **12** propagandist
of Germany: 8 Boniface
of Ireland: 7 Patrick
of the English: 9 Augustine
of the French: 5 Denis
of the Gauls: 8 Irenaeus
of the Gentiles: 4 Paul
of the Goths: 7 Ulfilas
to the Indians: 9 John Eliot

apothecary
7 chemist **8** druggist, pharmacy **9** drugstore **10** pharmacist

apothegm
see **aphorism**

apotheosis
6 height **7** epitome **8** exemplar, ultimate **9** archetype, elevation **10** embodiment, exaltation **11** deification, ennoblement, idolization, lionization **12** enshrinement, quintessence **13** glorification

appall
3 awe **4** faze **5** alarm, shake, shock **6** dismay **7** horrify, outrage, overawe, perturb **8** confound, distress **10** disconcert **11** consternate

appalled
6 aghast **11** dumbfounded

appalling
5 awful **6** horrid **7** fearful **8** daunting, dreadful, horrible, horrific, shocking, terrible **9** atrocious, dismaying, frightful, loathsome **10** disgusting, formidable, horrifying

appanage
5 grant, right **7** adjunct **8** property **9** endowment, privilege **10** birthright, perquisite **11** prerogative

apparatus
4 gear, tool **5** gismo, gizmo **6** device, gadget, outfit, tackle, widget **7** utensil **8** matériel, tackling **9** equipment, implement, machinery **10** instrument **11** contraption **13** accouterments, accoutrements, paraphernalia

apparel
4 clad, duds, garb, gear, robe, suit, togs **5** adorn, array, dress, getup, habit **6** attire, clothe, livery, outfit **7** clothes, costume, garment, raiment, threads, vesture **8** clothing, enclothe, glad rags, vestment **9** embellish **11** habiliments

apparent
5 clear, overt, plain **6** patent **7** evident, obvious, seeming, visible **8** distinct, manifest, palpable **9** succedent **10** noticeable, observable **11** discernible, perceivable, perceptible

apparition
5 ghost, shade, umbra **6** shadow, spirit, vision, wraith **7** eidolon, fantasm, phantom, specter **8** illusion, phantasm **10** appearance, phenomenon **13** hallucination

appeal
3 ask, beg, bid **4** call, lure, plea, pray, pull, suit, urge **5** apply, brace, charm, crave, plead **6** accuse, allure, charge, excite, invoke, sue for **7** attract, beseech, entreat, glamour, implore, request **8** call upon, charisma, entreaty, interest, intrigue, petition **9** fascinate, importune, magnetism, seduction **10** allurement, attraction, supplicate **11** application, fascination, imploration **12** drawing power, solicitation, supplication

appealing
8 alluring, charming, pleading, pleasant, pleasing **9** agreeable **10** attractive, bewitching, enchanting **11** captivating, fascinating

appear
4 look, loom, rise, seem, show **5** arise, issue, occur **6** arrive, emerge, show up, turn up **7** emanate **8** resemble **9** come forth **11** materialize

appearance
3 air **4** face, form, look, mien, pose, show **5** debut, dress, front, guise, image **6** advent, aspect, facade, manner **7** arrival, bearing, display, seeming **8** attitude, demeanor, illusion **9** semblance **10** impression, occurrence, simulacrum **11** countenance **13** manifestation

appease
4 calm, ease **5** allay, quiet **6** buy off, pacify, soothe **7** assuage, concede, content, gratify, mollify, placate, relieve, satisfy, sweeten **10** conciliate, propitiate

appellation
4 name **5** brand, label, nomen, style, title **7** moniker **8** cognomen **10** identifier **11** designation **12** denomination

append
3 add **5** add on, affix, annex, tag on **6** adjoin, attach, tack on **7** subjoin **10** supplement

appendage
3 arm, fin, leg, tab, tag **4** barb, flap, horn, limb, seta, tail, wing **5** extra **6** cercus, member **7** adjunct, antenna, elytron, stipule **8** pedipalp, pendicle, tentacle **9** accessory, auxiliary, extremity **10** attachment, collateral, incidental, projection, supplement **12** appurtenance, nonessential, protuberance

appendix
5 notes, rider **7** adjunct, codicil **8** addendum, addition **9** accessory, appendage **10** attachment, supplement **12** appurtenance

apperception
5 grasp **9** awareness **10** cognizance **11** realization, recognition **12** apprehension, assimilation **13** comprehension, introspection, understanding

appertain
4 bear **5** apply, refer **6** bear on, belong, relate **8** bear upon **10** be relevant **11** be connected, be pertinent

appetence
3 yen **5** taste **6** desire, hunger, relish, thirst **7** craving, longing, stomach **8** fondness

appetent
4 agog, avid, keen **5** eager **6** ardent **7** anxious, craving, lusting, thirsty **8** desirous, yearning **9** impatient **10** breathless

appetite
3 yen **4** bent, itch, lust, urge **5** taste **6** desire, hunger, liking, relish **7** craving, leaning, longing, passion, stomach **8** cupidity, fondness, gluttony, penchant, soft spot, voracity, weakness, yearning **9** hankering **10** preference, proclivity, propensity **11** inclination

appetizer
4 whet **5** snack **6** canapé, savory, tidbit **7** starter **8** aperitif, cocktail, stimulus **9** antipasto **11** amuse-bouche, hors d'oeuvre

appetizing
5 tasty **6** savory **8** saporous, tempting **9** agreeable, appealing, aperitive, flavorful, palatable, relishing, toothsome **10** delectable, flavorsome **11** scrumptious, tantalizing **13** mouth-watering

applaud
4 clap, hail, laud, root **5** bravo, cheer, extol **6** praise, rise to **7** acclaim, approve, commend **9** recommend **10** compliment

applause
4 hand **5** éclat, round **6** bravos, cheers, praise **7** acclaim, hurrahs, ovation, rooting **8** accolade, approval, cheering, clapping, plaudits **11** acclamation **12** commendation

apple
4 crab, Fuji, Gala, pome **5** Cameo, Mutsu **6** Empire, Macoun, medlar, pippin, russet **7** Baldwin, costard, Duchess, winesap **8** Braeburn, Cortland, greening, Jonagold, Jonathan, McIntosh **9** Delicious **10** Rome Beauty **11** Granny Smith, Gravenstein, Northern Spy, Transparent

acid: **5** malic
dessert: **5** crisp
juice: **5** cider
spray: **4** Alar
sugar: **4** ates **8** sweetsop

Apple product
3 Mac **4** iCar, iMac, iPad, iPod **5** iBook **6** iPhone

applejack
5 cider **6** brandy, liquor **8** calvados **9** hard cider

apple knocker
see **rustic**

apple-polish
4 fawn **5** toady **6** kowtow **7** cater to, flatter, honey up, truckle **8** butter up **10** curry favor, ingratiate

apple-polisher
5 toady **6** yes-man **8** bootlick, groveler, lickspit **9** flatterer, sycophant **11** lickspittle

applesauce
5 hooey **6** bunkum **7** baloney, rubbish, twaddle **8** malarkey, nonsense **9** poppycock

appliance
6 device **7** utensil **9** implement **10** instrument **11** application
kitchen: **4** oven **5** mixer, range, stove **6** fridge **7** blender, toaster **9** can opener, microwave **10** dishwasher **12** refrigerator
maker: **5** Amana **6** Maytag **7** Kenmore **9** Whirlpool

applicability
3 use **7** account, fitness, utility **9** advantage, relevance **10** usefulness

applicable
3 apt, fit **4** just, meet **5** ad rem **6** seemly, suited, useful **7** apropos, fitting, germane **8** apposite, material, relevant, suitable **9** befitting, pertinent **10** felicitous **11** appropriate

applicant
6 seeker **7** hopeful **8** aspirant, inquirer **9** candidate, job-hunter, job-seeker

application
3 use **4** form, heed, plea, suit **5** study **6** appeal, debate, effort, letter **7** request **8** entreaty, exercise, exertion, industry, petition **9** assiduity, attention, diligence, operation, treatment **10** dedication **11** requisition, utilization

appliqué
5 decal

apply
3 dab, use **4** bend, daub, give, turn, urge **5** exert, press, put on, refer **6** accost, affect, appeal, assign, bear on, bestow, devote, direct, employ, engage, handle, relate, resort, take on **7** address, beseech, concern, entreat, execute, implore, involve, pertain, utilize **8** approach, bear upon, exercise, petition, set about **9** appertain, implement, importune, undertake **10** administer, buckle down

appoint
3 arm, fix, rig, set, tap **4** gear, name **5** equip **6** assign, decide, fit out, outfit, supply **7** dress up, furbish, furnish, provide, turn out **8** accouter, accoutre, accredit, delegate, nominate **9** authorize, designate, determine, embellish, provision **10** commission

appointment
3 job **4** date, meet, post, spot **5** berth, place, tryst **6** billet, choice, office **7** meeting **8** election, position **9** equipment, selection, situation **10** assignment, connection, engagement, rendezvous **11** arrangement, assignation, designation

appointments
5 decor **7** fitting **8** equipage **9** equipment, trappings **11** furnishings **13** accouterments, accoutrements

apportion
3 cut, lot **4** give, mete, part **5** allot, allow, cut up, divvy, quota, serve, share, slice, split **6** assign, bestow, divide, parcel, ration **7** deal out, dish out, divvy up, dole out, measure, mete out, prorate, split up **8** allocate, dispense, separate, share out **9** admeasure, partition **10** administer, distribute

apportionment
3 cut, lot **4** part **5** piece, quota, share, slice, split **6** ration **7** measure, quantum **9** allotment, allowance **10** allocation, assignment

apposite
3 apt **4** just **5** ad rem **6** proper, suited, timely **7** apropos, fitting, germane, right on **8** material, on target, relevant, suitable **9** pertinent **10** applicable **11** appropriate

appositeness
7 aptness, fitness **9** relevance **10** pertinence, timeliness **11** suitability

appraisal
5 stock **6** rating, survey **7** pricing **8** estimate, judgment **9** valuation **10** assessment, estimation, evaluation

appraise
3 eye, fix, set, vet **4** rate, size **5** assay, audit, gauge, judge, price, set at, value **6** assess, figure, size up, survey **7** adjudge, examine, inspect, measure, valuate **8** estimate, evaluate, look over **9** calculate, figure out

appreciable
5 clear, plain **6** marked **7** evident, obvious **8** apparent, clear-cut, concrete, manifest, material, palpable, sensible, tangible **10** detectable, measurable, noticeable, observable **11** discernible, perceptible, substantial **12** considerable

appreciate
4 gain, go up, grow, know, like, love, rise **5** enjoy, grasp, judge, prize, savor, value **6** admire, esteem, fathom, regard, relish **7** apprize, cherish, cognize, enhance, improve, inflate, realize, respect **8** evaluate, increase, treasure **9** apprehend, delight in, recognize **10** comprehend, understand

appreciation
4 gain, rise **6** growth, regard, thanks **7** tribute **8** increase, judgment **9** awareness, gratitude, inflation **10** evaluation, perception **11** recognition, sensitivity, testimonial **12** gratefulness

appreciative
8 grateful

apprehend
3 nab **4** bust, fear, grab, know, nail, read, twig **5** catch, grasp, run in, seize, sense **6** absorb, accept, arrest, collar, detain, divine, fathom, pick up, take in **7** capture, catch on, cognize, compass, foresee, make out, preknow, realize **8** conceive **9** recognize, visualize **10** anticipate, appreciate, understand

apprehensible
5 clear, lucid, plain **7** evident, obvious **8** distinct, explicit, knowable, luminous **9** graspable **10** fathomable

apprehension
3 ken **4** care, fear, idea **5** alarm, angst, dread, grasp, pinch, worry **6** arrest, notion, pickup, unease **7** anxiety, capture, concern, seizure, thought **8** disquiet, judgment **9** agitation, awareness, detention, knowledge, misgiving, suspicion **10** conception, foreboding, perception, solicitude, uneasiness **11** disquietude, premonition **13** understanding

apprehensive
5 alive, awake, aware, leary, leery, sharp **6** afraid, astute, scared, uneasy **7** anxious, fearful, knowing, worried **8** sensible, sentient, troubled **9** cognizant, conscious, observant, sensitive **10** discerning, disquieted, insightful, perceptive

apprentice
4 bind, tiro, tyro **5** pupil **6** novice, rookie **7** learner, protégé, starter, student, trainee **8** beginner, freshman, neophyte, newcomer **9** novitiate **10** tenderfoot

apprenticed
5 bound **7** obliged, pledged **8** articled **9** obligated **10** indentured

apprise
4 clue, post, tell, warn **6** advise, clue in, fill in, impart, inform, notify, reveal, wise up **7** let know **8** acquaint, announce, describe, disclose **9** make known **11** communicate

apprize
5 value **6** admire, esteem, regard, relish **7** cherish **8** hold dear, treasure **10** appreciate, rate highly

approach
4 near, nigh **5** reach, rival, verge **6** avenue, border, gain on **7** address, advance, apply to, attempt, descent **8** draw near, overture **11** approximate

approachable
7 affable **8** friendly, sociable **9** agreeable, congenial, reachable, receptive **10** accessible, attainable

approaching
6 coming **7** nearing **8** expected, imminent, oncoming, upcoming **11** forthcoming

approbate
4 back, like **5** favor **6** accept, assent, praise **7** applaud, approve, commend, consent, endorse, support **8** sanction **9** recommend **11** countenance

approbation
3 nod **4** euge, okay **5** bravo, favor **6** esteem, praise **7** acclaim, consent, support **8** applause, approval, sanction **10** admiration, permission **11** endorsement, recognition **12** commendation

appropriate
3 apt, cop, due, fit **4** grab, just, lift, meet, take, true **5** allot, annex, claim, exact, filch, grasp, pinch, right, seize, steal, swipe, usurp **6** assign, assume, budget, devote, pilfer, proper, snatch, snitch, suited, timely, useful, worthy **7** apropos, desired, earmark, fitting, germane, merited, preempt, purloin **8** accroach, apposite, arrogate, deserved, eligible, entitled, relevant, rightful, set apart, set aside, suitable **9** befitting, opportune, pertinent, requisite **10** acceptable, admissible, applicable, commandeer, compatible, confiscate, convenient, felicitous, seasonable

appropriately
4 well **5** amply, aptly, right **8** properly, suitably **9** fittingly **10** acceptably, adequately, becomingly

appropriateness
3 use **5** order **7** account, aptness, fitness, service, utility **8** meetness **9** advantage, propriety, relevance, rightness **10** expediency, usefulness **13** applicability

appropriation
5 grant **7** funding, stipend, subsidy **9** allotment, allowance **10** allocation, assignment, earmarking, subvention

approval
3 nod **4** okay **5** favor, leave, say-so **6** assent **7** consent, go-ahead, license, support **8** applause, blessing, sanction, suffrage **10** acceptance, compliment, green light, permission

11 approbation, benediction, concurrence, endorsement 12 commendation, confirmation, ratification 13 authorization

approve
4 okay 5 clear, favor, go for 6 accept, back up, praise, ratify, uphold 7 applaud, certify, commend, condone, confirm, endorse, initial, mandate, stand by, support, sustain 8 accredit, hold with, sanction 9 approbate, authorize, encourage 10 compliment 11 countenance

approximate
4 near 5 close, rough, touch 6 almost 7 similar, verge on 8 approach, ballpark, come near 10 resembling

approximately
4 most, nigh, or so 5 about, circa 6 all but, almost, nearly 7 close to 8 well-nigh 9 just about 10 more or less 11 practically

approximation
8 likeness, nearness 9 closeness 10 similarity 11 resemblance

appurtenance
7 adjunct 8 addition, appendix, ornament 9 accessory, apparatus, appendage 10 attachment 11 furnishings 13 accompaniment

appurtenant
5 extra 8 adjuvant 9 accessory, ancillary, auxiliary 10 additional, collateral, subsidiary 11 subordinate, subservient 12 accompanying, contributory

apricot
3 ume 4 ansu

a priori
8 provable, reasoned 9 deducible, deductive, derivable, inferable 11 inferential, presumptive

apron
5 stage 6 shield 7 garment 8 pinafore 9 extension

apropos
3 apt 4 as to, in re, meet 5 about, ad rem, anent, aptly, as for 6 proper, timely 7 fitting, germane, related 8 apposite, material, relevant, suitable, suitably, touching 9 as regards, opportune, pertinent, regarding 10 applicable, concerning, respecting 11 applicative, in respect to

apt
3 fit 4 just 5 alert, given, prone, quick, ready, savvy, smart 6 bright, clever, liable, likely, prompt, proper 7 apropos, fitting, germane, tending 8 apposite, disposed, inclined, relevant, suitable 9 befitting, pertinent, qualified 10 felicitous, responsive 11 appropriate, intelligent

aptitude
4 bent, gift 5 flair, knack, savvy 6 genius, liking, talent 7 ability, faculty, fitness 8 capacity, tendency 10 capability, cleverness, proclivity, propensity 11 disposition, inclination, suitability 12 predilection

aptness
4 bent, gift 5 flair, knack, skill 6 genius, talent 7 ability, faculty, fitness 8 tendency 9 propriety, readiness 10 capability, cleverness, expediency, likelihood 11 inclination, suitability 12 intelligence

aquanaut
5 diver 10 scuba diver

aquarium
4 tank 8 fish tank
fish: 4 opah 5 tetra

aquatic mammal
4 seal 5 hippo, otter, whale 6 beaver 7 dolphin, manatee, muskrat, sea lion 8 porpoise

aquatic plant
4 alga 5 algae 7 seaweed

aqua vitae
4 grog 5 booze, drink, hooch 6 brandy, cognac, liquor, tipple 7 alcohol, spirits 8 schnapps

aqueduct
5 canal 6 course 7 channel, conduit, passage 8 waterway 11 watercourse

aqueous
5 fluid 6 liquid, watery 9 liquefied

Aquila
5 eagle 13 constellation
star: 6 Altair

Aquitaine
7 Guienne
queen: 7 Eleanor

aquiver
5 shaky 7 quaking, shaking, trembly 9 shivering, trembling, tremulant, tremulous

Arab
chief: 4 emir 5 sheik 6 sheikh, sultan
country: 4 Iraq, Oman 5 Egypt, Libya, Qatar, Sudan, Syria, Yemen 6 Jordan, Kuwait 7 Algeria, Bahrain, Lebanon, Morocco, Tunisia 11 Saudi Arabia

Arabian Nights bird
3 roc

Arabian Peninsula
country: 3 UAE 4 Oman 5 Yemen
emirate: 5 Dubai, Qatar 7 Bahrain 8 Abu Dhabi
native: 5 Omani, Saudi 6 Yemeni

arable
7 fertile 8 fruitful, tillable 10 cultivable, productive

Arachne
father: 5 Idmon
form: 6 spider
mother: 6 Cyrene
rival: 6 Athena 7 Minerva

arachnid
4 mite, tick **6** acarus, spider **8** scorpion **9** arthropod, phalangid, tarantula **10** harvestman **13** daddy longlegs

Aramis friend
5 Athos **7** Porthos **9** d'Artagnan

arbiter
3 ump **5** judge **6** expert, umpire **7** referee **8** mediator **9** authority, moderator **11** adjudicator

arbitrary
4 rash **6** chance, random **7** erratic, offhand, wayward, willful **8** fanciful, heedless **9** frivolous, impetuous, whimsical **10** capricious, subjective **10** irrational **12** unreasonable **13** discretionary

arbitrate
5 judge **6** settle, umpire **7** adjudge, mediate, referee **9** intervene **10** adjudicate **12** intermediate

arbitrator
5 judge **6** umpire **7** referee, settler **8** mediator **9** moderator **11** adjudicator

arbor
4 axle, beam **5** bower, frame, shaft **7** pergola, shelter, spindle

arc
3 bow, lob **4** arch, bend, path **5** curve, round **7** rainbow **9** curvation, curvature **11** measurement, progression

arcade
6 arches, loggia **7** gallery **10** passageway
game: **8** Skee-Ball
pioneer: **5** Atari

arcadia
4 Eden, Zion **6** heaven, utopia **7** Elysium, nirvana **8** paradise **9** fairyland, Shangri-la **10** wonderland

arcane
6 hidden, mystic, occult, opaque, secret **7** obscure, unknown **8** abstruse, esoteric **9** recondite **10** cabalistic, mysterious, unknowable **11** inscrutable **12** impenetrable **13** unaccountable

Arcas
father: **4** Zeus **7** Jupiter
mother: **8** Callisto

arch
3 bow, coy, sly **4** bend, hump, pert **5** curve, fresh, saucy, vault **6** camber, cheeky, impish **7** playful, roguish, waggish **8** flippant, malapert **9** curvature **10** coquettish **11** mischievous
inner curve: **6** soffit **8** intrados
kind: **4** ogee **5** ogive, round, Tudor **6** lancet **7** rampart, trefoil **9** horseshoe, primitive, segmental **10** shouldered **11** equilateral **12** baskethandle
outer curve: **8** extrados
part: **6** impost **8** keystone, springer, voussoir

archaeological site
Africa: **8** Zimbabwe **13** Great Zimbabwe
Britain: **7** Avebury **9** Skara Brae, Sutton Hoo **10** Stonehenge
Cambodia: **6** Angkor **9** Angkor Wat
Crete: **7** Knossos
Egypt: **4** Giza **5** Luxor **6** Abydos, Karnak, Naqada, Thebes **7** Memphis **9** El-Bahnasa **11** Oxyrhynchus
Greece: **6** Delphi **7** Mycenae, Olympia
Guatemala: **5** Tikal
Honduras: **5** Copán
Indonesia: **9** Borobudur
Iran: **10** Persepolis
Iraq: **4** Isin, Nuzi **6** Nimrud **7** Babylon, Nineveh, Samarra
Israel: **7** Jericho
Italy: **7** Pompeii **11** Herculaneum
Lebanon: **6** Byblos **7** Baalbek
Mexico: **5** Mitla, Tulum, Uxmal **8** Palenque **10** Monte Albán **11** Chichén Itzá
Peru: **11** Machu Picchu
Syria: **7** Palmyra
Tunisia: **8** Carthage, Kairouan
Turkey: **4** Troy **6** Knidos **8** Hisarlik, Pergamon **9** Hissarlik
Uzbekistan: **9** Samarkand

archaeologist
4 Bell (Gertrude), Dart (Raymond) **5** Evans (Arthur) **6** Carter (Howard), Childe (V. Gordon), Kidder (Alfred), Petrie (Flinders) **7** Thomsen (Christian), Woolley (Leonard), Worsaae (Jens) **8** Breasted (James Henry), Goodyear (William) **10** Schliemann (Heinrich) **11** Champollion (Jean-François), Winckelmann (Johann)

archaic
3 old **5** dated, olden, passé **6** bygone **7** ancient, antique **8** obsolete, outdated **9** out-of-date, primitive, unevolved **10** antiquated **11** undeveloped **12** old-fashioned

archangel
5 Uriel **7** Gabriel, Michael, Raphael

arched
4 bent **5** bowed, round **6** curved **7** curving, rounded

archer
4 Tell (William) **5** Cupid **6** bowman **9** Robin Hood **11** Sagittarius

archery
9 toxophily

archetypal
5 ideal, model **7** classic, perfect, typical **9** classical, exemplary **10** consummate **12** paradigmatic, prototypical

archetype
4 idea **5** ideal, model **6** mirror **7** epitome, essence, example, pattern **8** exemplar, original,

paradigm, standard **9** beau ideal, prototype **10** apotheosis, embodiment, protoplast **12** quintessence

archfiend
5 demon, devil, Satan **6** diablo **7** Lucifer

Archie
character: **5** Betty, Lodge (Hiram) **6** Archie, Reggie **7** Andrews (Fred, Mary), Jughead **8** Veronica
creator: **7** Montana (Bob)
Jughead's pet: **6** Hot Dog
school: **9** Riverdale
school staff: **6** Grundy (Geraldine), Kleats (Coach) **7** Beazley (Miss), Clayton (Coach), Svenson (Mr.) **10** Flutesnoot (Prof.), Weatherbee (Mr. Waldo)
shop owner: **7** Pop Tate

Archie's wife
5 Edith

Archimedes
5 Greek **8** inventor
cry: **6** eureka
discovery: **5** screw **8** buoyancy **9** principle **11** water raiser

archipelago
Asian: **5** Malay
Canada: **6** Arctic
Japan: **4** Goto **9** Gotoretto
Norway: **11** Spitsbergen
Papua New Guinea: **8** Bismarck **9** Louisiade
Philippines: **4** Sulu
off Scotland: **7** Orcades, Orkneys
United States: **9** Alexander

architect
5 maker **7** creator **8** designer, inventor **9** generator **10** originator
American: **3** Pei (I. M.) **4** Hood (Raymond), Kahn (Louis) **5** Gehry (Frank), McKim (Charles), Meier (Richard), Roche (Kevin), Stone (Edward Durell), Weese (Harry), White (Stanford) **6** Breuer (Marcel), Fuller (Buckminster), Graves (Michael), Morgan (Julia), Neutra (Richard), Rogers (Isaiah), Soleri (Paolo), Upjohn (Richard), Walter (Thomas), Warren (William), Wright (Frank Lloyd) **7** Burnham (Daniel), Gilbert (Cass), Johnson (Philip), Latrobe (Benjamin), Olmsted (Frederick Law), Renwick (James), Sturgis (John Hubbard), Venturi (Robert) **8** Bulfinch (Charles), Saarinen (Eero, Eliel), Sullivan (Louis), Thornton (William), Yamasaki (Minoru) **9** Libeskind (Daniel) **10** Richardson (Henry Hobson)
Austrian: **4** Loos (Adolf) **6** Wagner (Otto)
Brazilian: **8** Niemeyer (Oscar)
Canadian: **6** Safdie (Moshe)
Dutch: **8** Koolhaas (Rem), Rietveld (Gerrit)
English: **4** Nash (John), Shaw (Richard), Wood (John), Wren (Christopher) **5** Hadid (Zaha), Jones (Inigo), Scott (George Gilbert), Wyatt (James) **6** Foster (Norman), Rogers (Richard), Street (George Edmund), Voysey (Charles) **7** Lutyens (Edwin) **8** Vanbrugh (John)
Finnish: **5** Aalto (Alvar) **8** Saarinen (Eero, Eliel)
French: **6** Nouvel (Jean), Perret (Auguste) **7** Garnier (Tony), L'Enfant (Pierre-Charles) **11** Le Corbusier **12** Viollet-le-Duc (Eugène)
German: **7** Gropius (Walter) **8** Schinkel (Karl) **10** Mendelsohn (Erich)
Iraqi: **5** Hadid (Zaha)
Israeli: **6** Safdie (Moshe)
Italian: **5** Nervi (Pier Luigi), Piano (Renzo) **6** Romano (Giulio), Soleri (Paolo) **7** Alberti (Leon Battista), Bernini (Gian Lorenzo), da Vinci (Leonardo), Orcagna, Peruzzi (Baldassare), Raphael, Vignola (Giacomo da) **8** Bramante (Donato), Leonardo (da Vinci), Palladio (Andrea), Sangallo (Giuliano da), Terragni (Giuseppe) **9** Borromini (Francesco), Sansovino (Jacopo) **12** Michelangelo
Japanese: **4** Ando (Tadao) **5** Tange (Kenzo) **8** Yamasaki (Minoru)
Roman: **9** Vitruvius
Scottish: **10** Mackintosh (Charles Rennie)
Spanish: **5** Gaudí (Antonio) **9** Calatrava (Santiago)
Swedish: **7** Asplund (Erik Gunnar)

architectural order
5 Doric, Ionic **10** Corinthian

architecture
6 design, makeup **9** formation **11** composition **12** constitution, construction
ornament: **4** boss, fret **5** gutta **6** finial, volute **7** cabling, console, crocket, diglyph **8** triglyph, vignette **9** arabesque, modillion
style: **5** Doric, Ionic, Tudor **6** Gothic, Norman, Rococo **7** Baroque **8** Colonial, Georgian **9** Byzantine, Victorian **10** Corinthian, Romanesque

archive
4 file **6** record **7** collect, history, library, records **8** document, register **9** chronicle **10** collection, repository

archon
10 magistrate

arctic
3 icy **4** cold **5** chill, gelid **6** chilly, frigid, frosty, wintry **7** glacial, numbing **8** freezing, hibernal **11** hyperborean
animal: **3** auk, fox **4** bear, hare, seal, vole **5** sable, whale **6** ermine, marten **7** caribou, lemming **8** reindeer **9** polar bear, ptarmigan
base: **4** Etah **5** Thule **6** Barrow **11** Point Barrow
bird: **3** auk **4** skua
cetacean: **7** narwhal
current: **8** Labrador
dog: **5** husky **7** Samoyed **8** malamute
explorer: **4** Byrd (Richard), Cook (Frederick) **5** Bylot (Robert), Davis (John), Peary (Robert)

6 Baffin (William), Bering (Vitus), Henson (Matthew), Hudson (Henry), Nansen (Fridtjof), Nobile (Umberto) **7** Barents (Willem), Bennett (Floyd), Wilkins (George), Wrangel (Ferdinand) **8** Amundsen (Roald) **9** Ellsworth (Lincoln), Mackenzie (Alexander), MacMillan (Donald) **10** Stefansson (Vilhjalmus)
forest: **5** taiga
jacket: **5** parka **6** anorak
ocean hazard: **4** berg, floe **7** iceberg
people: **4** Lapp **5** Aleut, Inuit, Yakut **6** Eskimo, Tungus **7** Chukchi, Samoyed
sea: **4** Kara **6** Laptev **7** Barents, Chukchi **8** Beaufort
transport: **7** dogsled
treeless plains: **6** tundra

ardent
3 hot **4** agog, avid, keen, true **5** eager, fiery, loyal **6** fervid, fierce, heated, intent, red-hot, strong, torrid **7** blazing, burning, devoted, earnest, fervent, flaming, glowing, intense, shining, staunch, zealous **8** constant, desirous, faithful, powerful, resolute, sizzling, vehement, white-hot **9** allegiant, impatient, impetuous, impulsive, perfervid, scorching, steadfast **10** breathless, hot-blooded, passionate **11** impassioned **12** enthusiastic

Arden of Tennyson's poem
5 Enoch

ardor
4 élan, fire, heat, zeal, zest, zing **5** gusto, verve, vigor **6** energy, fealty, fervor, spirit, warmth **7** avidity, loyalty, passion **8** devotion, fidelity **9** eagerness, intensity, vehemence **10** allegiance, enthusiasm, excitement **12** faithfulness

arduous
4 hard **5** harsh, rough, sheer, steep, tight, tough **6** severe, taxing, tiring, trying, uphill **7** labored **8** grueling, rigorous, toilsome **9** difficult, effortful, gruelling, laborious, punishing, strenuous **10** formidable **11** precipitate, precipitous

area
4 belt, turf, zone **5** field, place, range, realm, scene, space, tract **6** domain, locale, region, sector, sphere **7** expanse, stretch **8** district, locality, province, vicinity **9** bailiwick, territory **12** neighborhood
unit: **3** ure **4** acre **7** hectare

arena
5 field, scene, stage **6** sphere **7** stadium, theater **8** activity, building, coliseum, province **10** hippodrome **12** amphitheater
level: **4** tier

Ares
Roman counterpart: **4** Mars
consort: **9** Aphrodite
father: **4** Zeus
mother: **4** Enyo, Hera
sister: **4** Eris
son: **5** Remus **7** Romulus

arête
5 crest, ridge

Arethusa
5 nymph **6** spring **9** wood nymph
pursuer: **7** Alpheus

argent
6 silver **7** silvern, silvery **9** whiteness

Argentina
capital: **11** Buenos Aires
city: **6** Paraná **7** Córdoba, La Plata, Rosario, Santa Fe **11** Mar del Plata
desert: **9** Patagonia
language: **7** Spanish
leader: **5** Perón (Juan)
monetary unit: **4** peso
mountain, range: **5** Andes **9** Aconcagua
neighbor: **5** Chile **6** Brazil **7** Bolivia, Uruguay **8** Paraguay
plain: **5** llano, pampa **6** pampas
river: **5** Plata (Río de la) **6** Paraná **8** Colorado **12** Río de la Plata
volcano: **5** Maipo **9** Tupungato

Arges
7 Cyclops
brother: **7** Brontes **8** Steropes
father: **6** Uranus
mother: **4** Gaea

Argonaut
4 hero **10** adventurer **13** paper nautilus
leader: **5** Jason

argosy
4 ship **5** fleet **6** armada, supply **8** flotilla

argot
4 cant **5** idiom, lingo, slang **6** jargon, patois, patter **7** dialect **10** vernacular

arguable
4 moot **7** dubious **8** doubtful **9** debatable, in dispute, uncertain **10** disputable **11** contestable, problematic **12** questionable

argue
5 claim, clash, prove **6** assert, attest, bicker, debate, differ, induce, object, reason **7** agitate, canvass, contend, discuss, dispute, dissent, justify, protest, quarrel, quibble, stickle, testify, witness, wrangle **8** announce, conflict, consider, disagree, indicate, maintain, persuade, polemize, squabble **9** thrash out **10** polemicize **11** expostulate, remonstrate

argument
3 row **4** case, feud, flap, fuss **5** claim, proof, set-to, theme, topic **6** debate, dustup, hassle, motive, reason, rumpus, thesis **7** defense, dispute,

polemic, sorites, subject, summary, wrangle **8** abstract, evidence, rebuttal **9** amplitude, assertion, discourse **10** contention, discussion, dissension, squabbling **11** controversy, disputation, embroilment **12** disagreement

argumentation
6 debate **7** dispute, oratory **8** forensic, rhetoric **9** dialectic, reasoning **10** discussion **11** controversy, disputation

argumentative
4 moot **9** in dispute, litigious, polemical **11** contentious, quarrelsome **12** disputatious, questionable **13** controversial

Argus
father: **4** Zeus
mother: **5** Niobe
slayer: **6** Hermes

Argus-eyed
5 alert **8** watchful **9** all-seeing

argyle
4 sock **6** design **7** diamond, pattern **8** Campbell

aria
3 air, lay **4** hymn, lied, solo, song, tune **5** ditty **6** melody **7** descant

Ariadne
father: **5** Minos
husband: **7** Theseus
island home: **5** Naxos
mother: **8** Pasiphaë

arid
3 dry **4** drab, dull, sere **5** dusty, vapid **6** barren, boring, desert, dreary, jejune **7** bone-dry, insipid, parched, sterile, tedious, thirsty **8** droughty, lifeless, weariful **9** dryasdust, infertile, unwatered, waterless, wearisome **10** lackluster, spiritless, unfruitful **12** moistureless **13** uninteresting

Ariel
6 spirit
master: **8** Prospero

Aries
3 ram **13** constellation

aright
4 well **5** fitly **6** justly, nicely **8** decently, properly **9** correctly, fittingly, precisely **10** accurately, decorously

Arikara
3 Ree

Ariosto epic
14 Orlando Furioso

arise
4 go up, lift, soar, wake **5** awake, begin, get up, issue, mount, occur, start **6** appear, ascend, aspire, come up, crop up, emerge, spring, uprear, wake up **7** emanate, proceed **8** commence **9** originate

arista
3 awn

Aristaeus
father: **6** Apollo
mother: **6** Cyrene
son: **7** Actaeon
wife: **7** Autonoë

aristocracy
5 elite, state **6** gentry, jet set **7** who's who **8** nobility, noblesse **9** beau monde, blue blood, gentility, haut monde **10** government, patricians, patriciate, upper class, upper crust

aristocrat
9 blue blood, gentleman, patrician
ancient Greek: **8** eupatrid
Russian: **5** boyar **6** boyard

aristocratic
5 aloof, elite, noble **6** lordly **7** courtly, elegant, genteel, haughty, refined, stately **8** highborn, well-born, well-bred **9** dignified, exclusive, patrician **10** privileged, upper-class, upper-crust **11** blue-blooded

Aristophanes play
5 Birds (The), Frogs (The), Wasps (The) **6** Clouds (The), Plutus **10** Lysistrata

arithmetic
4 math **8** addition, counting, figuring **9** ciphering, reckoning **10** estimation **11** calculation, computation, mathematics

Arizona
capital: **7** Phoenix
city: **4** Mesa, Yuma **5** Tempe **6** Bisbee, Sedona, Tucson **8** Glendale, Prescott **9** Flagstaff **10** Scottsdale
mountain: **9** Humphreys (Peak)
nickname: **11** Grand Canyon (State)
park: **15** Petrified Forest
river: **4** Gila, Salt **8** Colorado
state bird: **10** cactus wren
state flower: **7** saguaro (cactus)
state tree: **9** palo verde

Arizona Indian
4 Hopi, Pima, Zuni

ark
3 den **4** ship **5** chest, haven **6** adytum, asylum, refuge **7** convent, retreat, shelter **8** hideaway **9** safe house, sanctuary **10** repository, Torah chest
landfall: **6** Ararat
wood: **6** gopher **7** cypress

Arkansas
capital: **10** Little Rock
city: **4** Hope **9** Fort Smith, Pine Bluff **10** Hot Springs **11** Bentonville **12** Fayetteville
mountain, range: **5** Ozark **8** Magazine
nickname: **17** Land of Opportunity

river: **3** Red
state bird: **11** mockingbird
state flower: **12** apple blossom
state tree: **12** loblolly pine

Arkansas footballers
4 Hogs **10** Razorbacks

arm
3 bay, ell, gun, rig **4** cove, gear, gulf, limb, wing **5** annex, bayou, equip, firth, force, inlet, power **6** fit out, harbor, muscle, outfit, slough, weapon **7** appoint, furnish, turn out **8** accouter, strength **9** extension
bone: **4** ulna **5** ulnae (plural) **6** radius **7** humerus
combining form: **6** brachi **7** brachio
muscle: **6** biceps **7** triceps

armada
4 navy **5** boats, fleet, force, group, ships **7** vessels **8** flotilla, warships

armadillo
4 apar, peba, tatu
relative: **5** sloth **8** anteater, tamandua

armament
4 arms **5** armor **6** weapon **7** defense **8** ordnance, security, weaponry **9** munitions, safeguard **10** ammunition, protection

armamentarium
4 fund **5** stock, store **6** supply **9** inventory

armchair
6 remote **8** fauteuil **9** vicarious **11** theoretical

armed forces
4 army, navy **6** troops **7** marines **8** air force, military **10** servicemen
mail drop: **3** APO

armed robbery
6 hold-up **7** stickup

Armenia
capital: **7** Yerevan
city: **6** Gyumri **8** Vanadzor
lake: **5** Sevan
monetary unit: **4** dram
mountain, range: **7** Aragats **8** Caucasus
neighbor: **4** Iran **6** Turkey **7** Georgia **10** Azerbaijan
river: **5** Araks

armistice
5 truce **9** agreement, cease-fire **10** suspension

armor
4 mail **5** aegis, cover, guard **6** shield **7** buckler **8** security **9** safeguard **10** protection
arm: **8** brassard
body: **6** lorica **7** cuirass
armpit: **8** pallette
buttocks: **5** culet
coat: **7** hauberk **10** brigandine
face: **5** visor **6** beaver
flexible: **4** mail
foot: **8** solleret
hand: **7** gantlet **8** gauntlet
head: **6** helmet
horse: **4** bard **5** barde **8** chamfron
leg: **6** greave **7** jambeau
mail: **4** coif **7** hauberk
suit: **7** panoply
thigh: **4** tace **5** tasse **6** cuisse, tuille
throat: **6** gorget

armory
4 dump **5** depot, plant, range, store **7** arsenal, factory **8** magazine **10** collection, storehouse

armpit
6 axilla **8** underarm
Scottish: **5** oxter

arms
7 ensigns, warfare **8** weaponry

army
4 host **5** flock, horde **6** legion **7** militia **9** multitude
combat arm: **5** armor **8** infantry **9** artillery
commission: **6** brevet **7** reserve
Fort: **3** Dix, Lee, Ord **4** Drum, Hood, Knox, Myer, Polk, Sill **5** Bliss, Bragg, Irwin, Lewis, McCoy, Meade, Riley, Story **6** Carson, Eustis, Gillem, Gordon, Greely, McNair, Monroe, Rucker **7** Belvoir, Benning, Detrick, Jackson, Ritchie, Shafter, Stewart **8** Buchanan, Campbell, Hamilton, Holabird, Huachuca, Monmouth **9** McClellan, McPherson **10** Richardson, Sam Houston, Wainwright **11** Leavenworth
insect: **3** ant
mascot: **4** mule
meal: **3** MRE **4** chow, mess
mine layer: **6** sapper
NCO: **8** corporal, sergeant
officer: **5** major **7** captain, colonel, general, warrant **10** lieutenant
post: **4** base, camp, fort
postal abbreviation: **3** APO
ration: **3** MRE
relating to: **7** martial **8** military
school: **3** OCS, OTS **7** academy **9** West Point
signaler: **6** bugler
store: **10** commissary **12** post exchange
unit: **5** corps, squad, troop **7** brigade, cavalry, company, platoon **8** division, regiment **9** battalion
vehicle: **4** jeep, tank **6** Abrams, Humvee **7** Bradley **9** half-track

Arnaz, Desi
character: **5** Ricky (Ricardo)
company: **6** Desilu
mentor: **6** Cougat (Xavier)
signature song: **6** Babalu
star of: **9** I Love Lucy
wife: **4** Ball (Lucille), Lucy

aroma
4 balm, nose, odor **5** scent, smell, spice **6** flavor **7** bouquet, incense, perfume **9** fragrance, redolence

aromatic
5 balmy, spicy, sweet **6** savory **7** odorous, perfumy, pungent, scented **8** fragrant, perfumed, redolent **9** ambrosial

around
4 near, nigh **5** about, circa **6** nearby **7** through
prefix: **4** ambi, peri **5** amphi **6** circum

around-the-clock
8 constant, unending **9** ceaseless, continual, incessant, perpetual, unceasing **10** continuous **11** unremitting **13** uninterrupted

arouse
4 fire, stir, wake, whet **5** alert, awake, pique, rally, waken **6** awaken, bestir, excite, fire up, foment, incite, kindle, work up **7** agitate, inflame **9** challenge, stimulate

arraign
3 tax, try **5** blame **6** accuse, charge, indict, summon **9** criminate, inculpate **11** incriminate

arrange
4 plan, sort **5** adapt, array, chart, order, score, unify **6** assort, codify, deploy, design, devise, lay out, line up, map out, scheme, set out, settle **7** dispose, marshal, prepare, work out **8** organize, sequence **9** blueprint, harmonize, integrate, methodize **10** bring about, categorize, instrument, symphonize, synthesize **11** choreograph, orchestrate, systematize

arrangement
5 array, order, setup **6** format, layout, lineup, series **8** grouping, ordering, sequence **9** structure **10** adaptation, deployment **11** disposition **12** distribution
floral: **4** posy **7** bouquet, garland, ikebana
Japanese: **7** ikebana

arrant
4 rank **5** gross, total, utter **6** brassy, brazen **7** blatant, extreme, flat-out **8** absolute, complete, impudent, infernal, overbold **9** barefaced, downright, egregious, out-and-out, shameless, unabashed **10** immoderate, unblushing

arras
6 screen **7** drapery **8** curtains, tapestry

array
3 lot **4** clad, garb, pomp, show **5** adorn, batch, bunch, clump, dress, group, order **6** attire, bundle, clothe, draw up, finery, lineup, parade **7** apparel, arrange, cluster, display, dispose, garment, marshal, militia, panoply, raiment, variety **8** clothing, decorate, enclothe, organize, spectrum **9** formation **10** assortment **11** systematize

arrears
3 due **4** debt **5** claim, debit **7** deficit **9** liability **10** balance due, obligation **12** indebtedness

arrest
3 nab, tab, tag **4** bust, grab, halt, hold, jail, slow, snag, stay, stem, stop **5** block, catch, check, pinch, run in, seize, stall **6** collar, detain, haul in, lock up, pick up, pull in, retard, take in **7** capture, contain, seizure **8** imprison, obstruct, restrain **9** apprehend, detention, interrupt **11** incarcerate **12** apprehension

arresting
6 marked, signal **7** salient **8** striking **9** affective, appealing, prominent **10** attractive, compelling, enchanting, impressive, noticeable, remarkable **11** conspicuous, eye-catching, outstanding

arrival
6 advent, coming **7** landing, success **8** entrance, incoming **9** emergence **10** appearance

arrive
4 come, land, show **5** get in, get to, reach **6** appear, show up, thrive, turn up **7** prosper, succeed **8** flourish

arrivederci
4 ciao

arriviste
7 parvenu, upstart **8** roturier **12** nouveau riche

arrogance
3 ego **4** airs, gall **5** brass, cheek, pride **6** hubris **7** conceit, disdain, hauteur **8** self-love **9** loftiness **11** haughtiness

arrogant
5 cocky, proud **6** lordly, snooty **7** haughty, pompous **8** cavalier, fastuous, insolent, superior **9** egotistic **10** disdainful, high-handed, peremptory **11** domineering, magisterial, overbearing **12** supercilious **13** high-and-mighty, self-important

arrogate
4 grab, take **5** annex, claim, seize, usurp **6** assume, demand **7** ascribe, preempt **8** accroach, take over **9** sequester **10** commandeer, confiscate **11** appropriate, expropriate

arrow
4 dart **5** shaft
poison: **4** inée, upas **6** curare

arrowroot
5 plant, tuber **6** starch **7** coontie

Arrowsmith's wife
5 Leora

arroyo
3 gap **4** draw, wadi **5** brook, chasm, cleft, clove, creek, gorge, gulch, gully **6** coulee, ravine **7** channel **11** watercourse

Ars Amatoria poet
4 Ovid

arsenal
4 dump **5** depot, stock, store **6** armory, supply **7** factory, weapons **8** magazine, ordnance **9** stockpile **10** depository, repertoire, repository, storehouse

arson
6 firing **8** torching **9** pyromania **12** incendiarism

arsonist
5 firer, torch **7** firebug, igniter **10** incendiary

art
5 craft, skill **6** métier **7** finesse, know-how **8** artifice, painting, vocation **9** dexterity, expertise, sculpture **10** handicraft
botanical: **6** bonsai
faddish: **6** kitsch
style: **3** pop **4** Dada **6** cubist, rococo **7** fauvist, realist, surreal **8** abstract, futurist **9** classical **10** naturalist, surrealist **12** naturalistic, surrealistic **13** expressionist, impressionist

art deco
5 style **6** design
designer: **4** Erté

Artemis
Roman counterpart: **5** Diana
birthplace: **5** Delos
brother: **6** Apollo
father: **4** Zeus
mother: **4** Leto
priestess: **9** Iphigenia

artery
3 way **4** duct, line, path, road, tube **5** aorta, track **6** avenue, course, street, vessel **7** carotid, channel, conduit, highway, passage, pathway **8** coronary **9** boulevard **12** thoroughfare

artful
3 sly **4** deft, foxy, wily **5** adept, sharp, slick, smart, suave **6** adroit, astute, clever, crafty, shrewd, smooth, tricky **7** cunning **8** guileful, skillful **9** dexterous, ingenious **10** artificial, diplomatic

arthropod
3 bee, fly **4** crab, mite, moth, tick **6** beetle, insect, shrimp, spider **7** lobster **8** arachnid, barnacle, diplopod, myriapod, scorpion **9** butterfly, centipede, cockroach, millipede, trilobite **10** crustacean
body segment: **6** somite, telson **8** metamere

Arthur
see **King Arthur**

Arthur of tennis
4 Ashe

Arthur of TV
3 Bea

article
3 the **4** bind, item, part **5** essay, paper, piece, point, theme, thing **6** matter, object **7** element, feature, passage, section **10** particular **11** composition, stipulation
French: **3** les, une
German: **3** das, dem, den, der, des, die, ein **4** eine
Spanish: **3** las, los, una

articled
5 bound **10** indentured

articulate
3 say **4** join, link, oral, talk **5** clear, hinge, joint, lucid, shape, speak, state, utter, vocal, voice **6** couple, fluent, prolix, relate, spoken, voiced **7** connect, express, jointed **8** coherent, definite, distinct, eloquent, vocalize **9** effective, enunciate, harmonize, integrate, pronounce, verbalize **10** coordinate, expressive **11** concatenate **12** intelligible, smooth-spoken

artifact
5 curio, relic **6** legacy, rarity, trophy **7** remnant, spin-off, vestige **8** creation, heirloom **9** by-product, handcraft, handiwork **10** handicraft **11** contrivance, fabrication

artifice
4 play, ploy, ruse, wile **5** craft, feint, guile, skill, trick **6** deceit, device, gambit **7** cunning, slyness **8** facility, foxiness, trickery, wiliness **9** adeptness, canniness, chicanery, duplicity, ingenuity, stratagem **10** adroitness, artfulness, cleverness, craftiness

artificial
4 fake, faux, mock, sham **5** bogus, dummy, faked, false, phony, put-on **6** ersatz, forced, hollow, unreal **7** assumed, feigned, in vitro, labored, man-made, plastic, pretend **8** affected, mannered, spurious **9** contrived, imitation, insincere, simulated, synthetic, unnatural **10** fabricated, factitious, fictitious, substitute

artillery
4 arms **5** canon, force **6** rocket **7** battery, bazooka, gunnery, weapons **8** cannonry, howitzer, ordnance, weaponry **9** munitions

artisan
6 worker **7** builder, workman **8** producer **9** carpenter, craftsman **12** craftsperson

artist
7 painter **8** sculptor, virtuoso
garb: **5** smock
knife: **7** spatula
medium: **3** oil **5** paint **6** pastel **7** tempera **8** charcoal **10** watercolor
pigment board: **7** palette
stand: **5** easel
workshop: **6** studio **7** atelier
(see also **painter**)

artistic category
5 genre

artist Paul
4 Klee
artist's stand
5 easel
artless
4 free, open, pure, true 5 crude, naive, plain 6 direct, honest, simple 7 genuine, natural, sincere, unaware 8 trusting 9 childlike, guileless, ingenuous, unstudied 10 aboveboard, forthright, unaffected, uncultured, unschooled 12 unartificial, unsuspicious
Art of Love poet
4 Ovid
art supporter
5 easel
arty
5 showy 6 pseudo 8 affected, imposing 9 overblown 11 pretentious 12 high-sounding
Aruba
capital: 10 Oranjestad
language: 5 Dutch 10 Papiamento
monetary unit: 6 florin
part of: 11 Netherlands
as
3 for, who 4 coin, like, that, when 5 being, since, which, while 6 though 7 because 11 considering, for instance
ASAP
4 stat 6 at once 11 immediately
as a rule
6 mainly, mostly 7 usually 8 commonly 9 generally 10 frequently, ordinarily
Ascanius
5 Iulus
father: 6 Aeneas
ASCAP competitor
3 BMI
ascend
4 go up, lift, rise, soar 5 arise, climb, crest, mount, scale 6 aspire, move up, occupy 7 lift off, take off 8 escalade, escalate, surmount
ascendancy
4 rule 5 power, reign 7 command, control, mastery 8 dominion 9 authority, dominance, influence, supremacy 10 domination, prepotency 11 preeminence, sovereignty 13 preponderance
ascendant
6 master, rising 7 regnant 8 ancestor, dominant, forebear, relative, superior 9 paramount, precursor, prevalent, sovereign 10 commanding, forefather, forerunner, prevailing, progenitor 11 controlling, overbearing, predecessor, predominant, predominate 12 preponderant, primogenitor
ascension
4 rise 6 rising 7 going up, scaling 8 climbing, mounting
ascent
4 ramp, rise 5 climb, grade, slope 6 rising 7 advance, incline 8 gradient, progress 9 acclivity, elevation, uplifting
ascertain
5 learn 7 catch on, find out, unearth 8 discover, make sure 9 determine, establish, figure out
ascetic
5 stoic 6 hermit, severe 7 austere, eremite, recluse 9 abstinent, anchoress, anchorite, mortified 10 abstemious, astringent, forbearing, restrained 11 disciplined, self-denying
ancient Hebrew: 6 Essene
Buddhist: 5 bonze
early Christian: 7 stylite
Hindu: 4 yogi 5 fakir, sadhu, Yogin
Muslim: 4 Sufi
Asclepius
see **Aesculapius**
ascribe
3 lay 4 cite 5 infer, refer 6 assign, charge, credit, impute 7 chalk up 8 accredit 9 attribute, reference 10 conjecture
Asenath
husband: 6 Joseph
son: 7 Ephraim 8 Manasseh
aseptic
4 cool, flat 5 clean 7 sterile 8 germ-free, hygienic, sanitary 9 unfeeling 10 restrained, sterilized 11 emotionless, unemotional
asexual
6 agamic
as for
4 in re 5 about, anent 7 apropos 9 regarding 10 concerning, respecting 12 with regard to
as good as
4 nigh 6 all but, almost, nearly 8 in effect, well-nigh 9 basically, in essence, just about, virtually 11 essentially, practically
ash
4 calx, soot, tree, wood 7 cinders, residue 8 clinkers
ashamed
6 abased, abject, guilty 7 abashed, humbled 8 contrite, penitent 9 chagrined, mortified, repentant 10 humiliated 11 discomfited, embarrassed
ashen
3 wan 4 gray, pale 5 faded, pasty, waxen 6 doughy, pallid, sallow, sickly 7 ghostly 8 blanched, bleached 9 bloodless, colorless 10 corpselike

Asher
daughter: 5 Serah
father: 5 Jacob
mother: 6 Zilpah
son: 4 Isui 6 Beriah, Ishuah, Jimnah

ashes
5 ruins 6 pallor 7 remains

ashy
3 wan 4 drab, pale 5 livid, waxen 6 doughy, leaden, pallid 7 ghastly, greyish 8 blanched 9 bloodless, colorless, washed-out 10 cadaverous

Asia
country: 4 Laos 5 Burma, China, India, Japan, Korea, Nepal 6 Bhutan, Russia, Taiwan 7 Armenia, Georgia, Myanmar, Vietnam 8 Cambodia, Malaysia, Mongolia, Pakistan, Sri Lanka, Thailand 9 East Timor, Indonesia, Kampuchea, Kazakstan, New Guinea, Singapore 10 Azerbaijan, Bangladesh, Kazakhstan, Kyrgyzstan, North Korea, South Korea, Tajikistan, Timor-Leste, Uzbekistan 11 Afghanistan, Philippines 12 Turkmenistan
ethnic group: 3 Han, Lao, Tai 4 Arab, Kurd, Moor, Shan 5 Karen, Khmer, Malay, Tajik, Tamil, Uzbek 6 Burman, Lepcha, Manchu, Mongol, Sindhi 7 Baluchi, Bengali, Persian, Punjabi, Tibetan 8 Armenian, Assyrian, Javanese 9 Dravidian, Indo-Aryan, Sinhalese 10 Circassian, Montagnard, Singhalese
language: 3 Lao 4 Ainu, Urdu 5 Hindi, Malay, Tamil, Uzbek 6 Arabic, Bahasa, Korean, Nepali 7 Bengali, Burmese, Khalkha, Kurdish, Persian, Tibetan, Turkish 8 Armenian, Japanese, Javanese, Mandarin 9 Cambodian 10 Vietnamese

Asia Minor
8 Anatolia
country: 6 Turkey
region: 5 Ionia

Asian
buffalo: 4 anoa
cuisine: 4 Thai
desert: 4 Gobi
inland sea: 4 Aral
nanny: 4 amah
ox: 4 anoa
primate: 5 loris
Sasquatch: 4 yeti

aside
4 away 5 apart 7 tangent 8 away from 9 in reserve, privately 10 digression, discursion 11 parenthesis

aside from
3 bar, but 4 save 6 bating, except 7 barring, besides 9 excepting, excluding, other than, outside of

Asimov, Isaac
forte: 5 sci-fi
work: 6 I Robot 9 Nightfall 10 Foundation (Trilogy)

asinine
5 crazy, daffy, inane, silly 6 absurd, simple 7 fatuous, foolish, idiotic, puerile, witless 8 mindless 9 brainless 10 irrational, ridiculous 11 nonsensical

ask
3 beg, bid 4 pray, quiz, seek 5 crave, exact, grill, plead, query 6 appeal, demand, desire, invite 7 beseech, call for, canvass, consult, enquire, entreat, examine, implore, inquire, request, require, solicit 8 petition, question 9 catechize, importune 10 supplicate 11 interrogate
Scottish: 5 speer, speir

askance
8 sidelong, sideways 9 cynically, obliquely 10 critically, doubtfully, doubtingly, scornfully 11 skeptically 12 suspiciously 13 distrustfully, mistrustfully

asker
6 beggar, prayer, suitor 7 speaker 9 suppliant 10 petitioner, questioner, supplicant 11 supplicator

askew
3 off 4 awry 6 turned 8 cockeyed 9 crookedly

aslant
4 awry 5 askew 7 crooked 8 cockeyed, sideways, sidewise 9 obliquely

asleep
4 dead, idle, numb 5 inert 6 dozing, numbed 7 defunct, dormant, napping 8 benumbed, deadened, inactive, in repose, not alert, sluggish 9 senseless, unfeeling 10 insensible, slumbering, unanimated 11 indifferent, unconscious 12 anesthetized

as long as
3 for 5 since 6 seeing 7 because, whereas 8 provided 11 considering 12 provided that

as much as
6 all but, almost 8 well-nigh 11 essentially, practically

aspect
3 air 4 look, mien, side 5 angle, facet, phase, scene, slant 6 regard, status 7 bearing, feature, seeming 8 exposure, position 9 direction 10 appearance 11 perspective

aspen
4 tree 6 poplar

asperity
5 rigor 8 acerbity, acrimony, grimness, hardness, hardship, mordancy, severity, tartness 9 harshness, roughness, sharpness 10 bitterness, difficulty, unevenness 12 irregularity, irritability

asperse
4 slur **5** libel, smear, sully **6** attack, defame, insult, malign, vilify **7** baptize, slander, tarnish, traduce **8** bad mouth, dishonor, sprinkle **9** denigrate, insinuate **10** calumniate

aspersion
4 muck, slam, slur **5** abuse **7** calumny, obloquy, slander **9** invective, stricture **10** defamation, detraction **11** denigration **12** vilification, vituperation **13** animadversion

asphalt
3 tar **4** pave **7** bitumen, macadam, surface **8** blacktop, pavement

asphyxiate
4 kill **5** choke, drown **6** stifle **7** smother **8** strangle, throttle **9** suffocate

aspirant
6 seeker **7** hopeful, seeking **9** applicant, candidate, contender

aspiration
3 aim **4** goal, urge, wish **5** dream **6** desire, intent, object **7** craving, longing, passion, pursuit **8** ambition, striving, yearning **9** breathing, objective **10** pretension **13** ambitiousness

aspire
3 aim, try **4** long, pant, rise, seek, soar, want, wish **5** arise, mount, yearn **6** ascend, desire, hunger, strive, thirst

aspiring
7 longing, seeking, wanting, wishful **8** striving, vaulting, yearning **9** ambitious

as regards
4 in re **7** apropos **8** touching **10** concerning, respecting

ass
4 dolt, fool, jerk, moke, mule **5** burro, dunce, idiot **6** donkey, nitwit **8** bonehead, imbecile **10** nincompoop
female: **5** jenny
male: **4** jack
wild Asian: **5** kiang **6** onager

assai
4 very

assail
4 bash, beat, pelt **5** abuse, beset, blast, pound, storm **6** attack, berate, buffet, charge, fall on, have at, malign, oppugn, pummel, revile, strike, vilify **7** assault, bombard **8** fall upon, lambaste **9** break down

assassin
3 gun **5** bravo **6** gunman, hit man, killer **7** torpedo **8** murderer **9** cutthroat **10** hatchet man, triggerman
of Caesar: **6** Brutus **7** Cassius
of Garfield: **7** Guiteau (Charles Julius)
of J. F. Kennedy: **6** Oswald (Lee Harvey)
of M. L. King: **3** Ray (James Earl)
of Lincoln: **5** Booth (John Wilkes)
of Marat: **6** Corday (Charlotte)
of McKinley: **8** Czolgosz (Leon)
of R. F. Kennedy: **6** Sirhan (Sirhan)

assassinate
4 do in, kill, slay **6** finish, murder, rub out **7** bump off, execute, gun down, put away, take out **8** dispatch, knock off **9** eliminate, liquidate

assault
3 mug, war **4** raid **5** beset, fight, onset, set-to, storm **6** assail, attack, charge, fall on, strike, threat **7** aggress, besiege, mugging, offense **8** fall upon, invasion, storming **9** incursion, offensive, onslaught, violation **10** aggression

assay
3 try **4** rate, seek, test **5** judge, offer, prove, trial, value, weigh **6** assess, result, rating, strive, survey **7** analyze, attempt, examine, inspect, measure, valuate, venture **8** analysis, appraise, endeavor, estimate, evaluate, struggle **9** appraisal, undertake, valuation **10** assessment, evaluation, inspection **11** examination, measurement

assemblage
5 crowd, group **6** muster **7** company, turnout **8** audience **9** gathering **10** collection **11** aggregation, composition, convergence **12** congregation

assemble
4 call, form, make, mass, meet, mold **5** amass, build, clump, group, shape, unite **6** gather, muster, summon **7** cluster, collect, convene, convoke, fashion, marshal, produce, round up **8** congress, contrive **9** aggregate, forgather **10** accumulate, congregate **11** fit together, manufacture, put together **12** call together, come together **13** bring together

assembly
4 bevy **5** bunch, covey, crowd, flock, group, party, plena (plural), rally, set-up **6** muster, plenum, troupe **7** cluster, meeting **8** conclave **9** congeries, gathering **10** collection **11** association, fabrication, get-together, manufacture **12** congregation, construction
American Indian: **6** powwow
ancient Greek: **8** ecclesia
ancient Roman: **7** comitia
Anglo-Saxon: **4** moot **5** gemot **6** gemote **8** folkmoot, folkmote
ecclesiastical: **5** synod **10** consistory
legislative: **4** diet **6** senate **8** congress **10** parliament
place: **4** hall, room **5** agora **10** auditorium
Russian: **4** duma
witches': **6** sabbat **7** sabbath

assent
3 nod, yes, yup **4** okay, yeah **5** agree, uh-huh **6** accede, accord, concur, say yes **7** approve, consent, embrace **8** approval, sanction, thumbs-up **9** accession, acquiesce, admission, agreement, subscribe **10** acceptance, permission **11** affirmation, concurrence **12** acquiescence

assert
3 say **4** aver, avow **5** argue, claim, posit, state, utter, voice **6** adduce, affirm, allege, attest, avouch, defend, depose, insist, submit **7** advance, contend, declare, express, justify, profess, protest, publish, warrant **8** announce, maintain, proclaim **9** broadcast, postulate, predicate **10** promulgate

assertion
6 avowal **8** averment **9** affidavit, statement **10** allegation, avouchment, contention, deposition, disclosure, insistence, profession **11** affirmation, attestation, declaration **12** asseveration **13** pronouncement

assertive
4 firm, sure **5** pushy **6** strong **7** assured, certain, decided, pushing **8** cocksure, emphatic, forceful, positive **9** confident, energetic, insistent **10** aggressive, resounding **11** affirmative, distinctive, self-assured **13** self-confident

assess
3 fix, tax **4** deem, levy, rate **5** assay, exact, judge, put on, set at, value, weigh **6** charge, figure, impose, reckon, survey **7** account, compute, subject, valuate **8** appraise, consider, estimate, evaluate **9** determine

assessment
3 fee, tax **4** duty, levy, toll **6** charge, impost, rating, tariff **8** estimate, judgment **9** appraisal, valuation **10** estimation, evaluation **12** appraisement

asset
4 boon, good, plus **5** merit **6** credit **7** benefit **8** blessing, resource **9** advantage **11** distinction
opposite: **9** liability

assets
5 items, means, money **6** wealth **7** capital **8** bankroll, holdings, property **9** resources, valuables **11** possessions

asseverate
4 aver, avow **5** state **6** affirm, assert, attest, avouch, depose, insist **7** certify, contend, declare, profess **8** maintain, proclaim **9** pronounce

assiduous
4 busy **5** eager **6** active **7** moiling, zealous **8** diligent, sedulous, tireless **9** attentive, laborious **10** persistent, unflagging **11** hard-working, industrious **13** indefatigable

assiduously
4 hard **6** busily **9** earnestly, intensely **10** diligently, thoroughly **11** intensively **12** exhaustively, meticulously, persistently **13** painstakingly, unremittingly

assign
3 fix, lay, set **4** cede, deed, give, name **5** allot, allow, refer **6** charge, convey, credit, define, impute, remise, settle **7** appoint, ascribe, chalk up, earmark, lay down, mete out, specify, station **8** accredit, allocate, delegate, make over, relegate, sign over, transfer **9** admeasure, apportion, attribute, designate, establish, prescribe **10** pigeonhole

assignation
4 date **5** tryst **7** meeting **9** allotment **10** engagement, rendezvous **11** appointment, get-together

assignee
5 agent, proxy **6** deputy, factor **7** officer **8** attorney, delegate

assignment
3 job **4** beat, duty, post, task, work **5** chore, stint **6** office **8** homework, position, transfer **9** allotment **10** allocation, delegation, obligation **11** designation

assimilate
5 adapt, adopt, grasp, learn, liken, match **6** absorb, adjust, digest, equate, imbibe, soak up, take in, take up **7** blend in, compare, conform **8** parallel **10** comprehend, understand **11** incorporate

assimilation
8 taking in **9** awareness **10** absorption, conversion **11** mindfulness, recognition **12** apperception **13** consciousness, incorporation

assist
3 aid **4** abet, back, help, lift **5** boost, do for, serve, stead **6** relief, succor **7** backing, benefit, comfort, help out, secours, service, support, work for **8** benefact, work with **9** accompany, cooperate, open doors

assistance
3 aid **4** hand, help, lift **5** boost **6** relief, succor **7** backing, benefit, comfort, secours, service, subsidy, support **8** abetment **9** upholding **10** subvention, supporting **11** cooperation

assistant
3 aid **4** aide, ally, help **5** aider, gofer **6** backer, backup, deputy, flunky, helper, second **7** acolyte, ancilla, orderly **8** adjutant, factotum, henchman **9** attendant, auxiliary, coadjutor **10** accomplice, aide-de-camp, coadjutant, lieutenant **12** right-hand man

assistive
6 aiding, useful **7** helpful **10** beneficial **11** serviceable

assize
3 law **4** rule, writ **5** canon, edict **6** decree **7** finding, inquest, precept, statute, verdict **8** standard **9** ordinance, prescript **10** regulation

associate
3 pal 4 ally, chum, join, link, mate, pair, yoke 5 blend, buddy, crony, group, match, merge, unite 6 cohort, comate, couple, fellow, friend, hobnob, relate, worker 7 bracket, combine, compeer, comrade, conjoin, connect, consort, partner 8 confrere, coworker, employee, familiar, federate, identify, intimate 9 affiliate, bedfellow, colleague, companion, confidant, copartner, secondary 10 accomplice, amalgamate, compatriot, complement, confidante 11 concomitant, confederate, correlative 12 acquaintance 13 accompaniment

association
3 tie 4 band, bloc, bond, clan, club, crew, hint, team, tong 5 group, guild, order, tie-up, union 6 hookup, league 7 circuit, concert, linkage, linking, society 8 alliance, congress, overtone, relation, sodality, teamwork 9 coalition, undertone 10 conference, connection, federation, fellowship, fraternity, mental link, suggestion 11 affiliation, brotherhood, combination, conjunction, connotation, cooperation, implication, partnership 12 conjointment, organization, relationship, togetherness 13 collaboration

assort
5 class, group, order 6 codify, divide 7 arrange 8 classify, stratify 9 associate, designate, harmonize, methodize 10 categorize, distribute, pigeonhole 11 systematize

assorted
4 like 5 mixed 6 fitted, motley, suited, sundry, varied 7 adapted, diverse, matched, similar, various 9 different 11 diversified, conformable 12 conglomerate, multifarious 13 heterogeneous, miscellaneous

assortment
4 olio 5 array, group 6 choice, jumble, medley 7 mélange, mixture, variety 8 mishmash, mixed bag, pastiche 9 diversity, potpourri, selection 10 collection, hodgepodge, miscellany 11 gallimaufry

assuage
4 calm, cool, ease 5 allay, quiet 6 lessen, pacify, quench, reduce, soften, soothe, temper 7 appease, lighten, mollify, placate, relieve, sweeten 8 decrease, mitigate, moderate 9 alleviate 10 conciliate, propitiate

as such
5 per se 8 by itself 9 in essence, virtually 11 essentially 13 fundamentally, intrinsically

assumably
6 likely, surely 7 no doubt 8 probably 9 doubtless 10 most likely, presumably

assume
3 act, don 4 fake, sham, take 5 adopt, bluff, feign, posit, put on, seize, usurp 6 affect, draw on, expect, reckon, slip on, take in, take on, take up 7 believe, imagine, preempt, premise, presume, pretend, receive, suppose, suspect 8 accroach, arrogate, shoulder, simulate, take over 9 postulate, undertake 10 commandeer, presuppose, understand 11 appropriate, counterfeit

assumed
4 fake, sham 5 bogus, false, given, put on, tacit 6 made-up, phoney 7 feigned 8 affected, delusory, putative, spurious, supposed 9 deceptive, pretended, simulated 10 artificial, fictitious
name: 5 alias 9 pseudonym 10 nom de plume

assumption
5 given, posit 6 belief, thesis 7 conceit, premise, seizure, surmise 8 takeover 9 arrogance, postulate 10 acceptance, arrogation, conjecture, pretension, usurpation 11 expectation, supposition, undertaking 13 appropriation

assurance
3 say 4 oath, word 5 nerve, say-so, troth 6 aplomb, parole, pledge, safety, surety 7 promise, support, warrant 8 audacity, boldness, safeness, security, sureness, temerity, warranty 9 assertion, brashness, certainty, certitude, cockiness, composure, guarantee, hardiness, self-trust 10 brazenness, confidence, conviction, equanimity, profession 11 affirmation, presumption

assure
4 aver 5 bet on, cinch, swear 6 affirm, attest, ensure, insure, pledge, secure, soothe 7 certify, comfort, confirm, promise, satisfy 8 convince, persuade 9 guarantee 11 make certain

assured
3 set 4 cool 5 fixed 6 secure 7 certain, decided, settled 8 clear-cut, composed, definite, positive, sanguine 9 assertive, collected, confident, undoubted, unruffled 10 guaranteed, pronounced 11 beyond doubt, made certain, unflappable 13 imperturbable, self-confident, self-satisfied

assuredly
9 certainly, doubtless 10 positively 11 confidently, undoubtedly, without fail

assuredness
6 surety 9 certainty, certitude 10 confidence, conviction

Assyria
capital: 5 Calah 7 Nineveh
city: 5 Ashur, Assur
god: 3 Sin 4 Asur, Nabu 5 Ashur, Nusku 6 Tammuz 7 Ninurta
goddess: 6 Ishtar
king: 3 Pul 6 Sargon 11 Sennacherib, Shalmaneser 12 Ashurbanipal
language: 7 Aramaic
queen: 9 Semiramis
river: 6 Tigris
writing: 9 cuneiform

asterisk
4 star **6** symbol **9** character

astern
3 aft **4** baft, rear, tail **5** abaft **6** back of, behind **8** backward, rearmost, rearward

asteroid
5 Ceres

Asterope
father: **5** Atlas
mother: **7** Pleione
sisters: **8** Pleiades

asthma
7 allergy **8** disorder

as to
4 in re **5** about, anent **7** apropos **9** regarding **10** concerning, respecting **11** according to

astonish
3 wow **4** daze, stun **5** amaze, floor, shock **7** astound, stagger, startle, stupefy **8** blow away, bowl over, confound, dumfound, surprise **9** dumbfound, take aback **11** flabbergast

astonishing
7 amazing **8** stunning, wondrous **9** marvelous, startling, wonderful **10** astounding, miraculous, prodigious, staggering, stupendous, surprising **11** spectacular **12** breathtaking

astonishment
3 awe **5** shock **6** wonder **8** surprise **9** amazement, confusion **10** perplexity, wonderment **12** bewilderment, stupefaction **13** consternation

astound
3 wow **4** daze, stun **5** amaze, shock **7** confuse **8** astonish, bewilder, confound, dumfound, surprise **9** dumbfound, overwhelm, take aback **11** flabbergast

Astraea
father: **4** Zeus **7** Jupiter
mother: **6** Themis

astral
6 dreamy, starry **7** exalted, highest, stellar **8** elevated, sidereal **9** celestial, top-drawer, unworldly, visionary **10** top-ranking **11** high-ranking **12** otherworldly

astray
4 awry **5** amiss, badly, wrong **6** adrift, afield **7** in error **9** off course
lead: **6** seduce

astride
8 bridging, spanning **10** on each side, straddling

astringent
4 acid, alum, keen **5** acerb, acrid, harsh, sharp, stern **6** biting, bitter, severe, strict **7** acerbic, ascetic, austere, caustic, cutting, puckery, pungent, styptic **8** incisive, stinging **10** irritating **11** contracting **12** constrictive

astrolabe successor
7 sextant

astrologer
5 Dixon (Jeane), Faust, Omarr (Sidney) **9** stargazer, Zoroaster **11** horoscopist, Nostradamus

astrological aspect
5 trine **7** sextile **8** quartile **10** opposition **11** conjunction

astronaut
4 Ride (Sally) **5** Glenn (John), White (Edward), Young (John) **6** Aldrin (Buzz), Borman (Frank), Cooper (Gordon), Lovell (James), Resnik (Judith), Worden (Alfred) **7** Bluford (Guion), Collins (Eileen, Michael), Gagarin (Yuri), Grissom (Gus), Jemison (Mae), Schirra (Walter), Shepard (Alan), Yegorov (Boris) **8** Stafford (Thomas) **9** Armstrong (Neil), Carpenter (Scott), McAuliffe (Christa) **10** Tereshkova (Valentina)

astronomer
American: **3** See (Thomas Jefferson) **5** Sagan (Carl) **6** Hubble (Edwin), Lowell (Percival) **7** Langley (Samuel), Newcomb (Simon), Shapley (Harlow) **8** Bowditch (Nathaniel), Mitchell (Maria), Tombaugh (Clyde) **9** Pickering (Edward) **11** Schlesinger (Frank)
Austrian: **13** Schwarzschild (Karl)
Danish: **5** Brahe (Tycho)
Dutch: **4** Oort (Jan Hendrik) **6** Sitter (Willem de) **7** Huygens (Christiaan)
Egyptian: **7** Ptolemy
English: **4** Ryle (Martin), Wren (Christopher) **6** Halley (Edmond), Lovell (Bernard) **7** Lockyer (Joseph), Parsons (William) **8** Herschel (Caroline, John, William)
French: **6** Picard (Jean) **7** Laplace (Pierre-Simon de), Messier (Charles)
German: **4** Wolf (Maximilian) **5** Vogel (Hermann) **6** Bessel (Friedrich), Kepler (Johannes), Müller (Johann), Struve (Otto)
Greek: **7** Ptolemy **12** Eratosthenes
Italian: **7** Galileo (Galilei) **12** Schiaparelli (Giovanni)
Persian: **11** Omar Khayyám
Polish: **10** Copernicus (Nicolaus)
Swedish: **7** Celsius (Anders)
Swiss: **6** Zwicky (Fritz)

astute
3 sly **4** cagy, deep, foxy, keen, wily **5** cagey, canny, heady, quick, savvy, sharp **6** artful, clever, crafty, shrewd, tricky **7** cunning, knowing **8** guileful **9** insidious, sagacious **11** calculating **13** perspicacious

astuteness
3 wit **6** acumen **8** wiliness **9** canniness **10** craftiness **11** discernment, percipience **12** perspicacity

Astyanax
father: **6** Hector
mother: **10** Andromache

asunder
4 torn **5** apart, split **7** divided **9** into parts, separated

as usual
8 normally, wontedly **9** routinely **10** habitually, ordinarily **11** customarily **12** consistently

as well
3 and, too, yet **4** also, even, just, more, plus **7** besides, further **8** likewise, moreover **9** along with, including, similarly **10** in addition **11** furthermore **12** additionally

as well as
3 and **4** plus **7** besides **9** along with **11** not counting **12** in addition to, together with

as yet
5 so far, to now **7** earlier, thus far **8** hitherto, until now **10** to this time **12** to the present

asylum
4 home, port **5** cover, haven **6** covert, harbor, refuge **7** retreat, shelter **8** hospital, security **9** harborage, safe house, sanctuary **10** protection, sanatorium **11** institution

asymmetric
6 uneven **7** not even, unequal **8** lopsided **9** irregular **10** unbalanced **12** overbalanced

at a distance
4 afar

Atalanta
husband: **8** Melanion
suitor: **10** Hippomenes

at all
4 ever, once **6** anyway **7** anytime **10** whatsoever

at any time
4 ever

atavism
9 reversion, throwback **10** recurrence

ataxia
5 chaos, snarl **6** huddle, muddle **7** clutter **8** disarray, disorder **9** confusion

atelier
6 studio **8** workroom, workshop

Athamas
daughter: **5** Helle
father: **6** Aeolus
son: **7** Phrixos, Phrixus **8** Learchus
wife: **3** Ino **7** Nephele

Athena
Roman counterpart: **7** Minerva
attribute: **3** owl **5** Aegis **7** serpent
city: **6** Athens
father: **4** Zeus
names: **4** Nike **6** Pallas **9** Parthenos
shield: **5** Aegis
statue: **9** Palladium
temple: **9** Parthenon

athenaeum
6 museum **7** library **8** archives **10** repository

Athens
citadel: **9** Acropolis
founder: **7** Cecrops
last king: **6** Codrus
lawgiver: **5** Solon
leader: **7** Pericles
marketplace: **5** agora
rival: **6** Sparta
senate: **5** boule
temple: **9** Parthenon

athirst
4 avid, keen **5** eager **6** ardent **7** anxious **8** desiring, desirous, yearning **9** impatient

athlete
4 jock **5** sport **6** player **7** acrobat, gymnast, tumbler **9** sportsman **10** competitor **11** sportswoman

athlete's foot
8 ringworm **10** tinea pedis

athletic
6 brawny, robust, sinewy **8** sporting, vigorous **9** strapping, strenuous
contest: **4** agon, game **5** match
field: **4** oval, ring, rink **5** arena, court **7** diamond, stadium **8** gridiron
prize: **3** cup **5** medal **6** trophy, wreath

athletics
5 games, races **6** events, sports **7** contest **8** exercise **9** exercises **10** gymnastics, recreation **12** calisthenics

Athos friend
6 Aramis **7** Porthos **9** d'Artagnan

athwart
4 over **5** cross **6** across, beyond **9** crossways, crosswise, opposed to **12** transversely

Atlanta-based TV channel
3 TBS

Atlanta's civic center
4 Omni

Atlas
brother: **10** Prometheus
daughter: **5** Hyads **6** Hyades **8** Pleiades **10** Atlantides
father: **7** Iapetus
mother: **7** Clymene
race: **5** Titan
wife: **7** Pleione

atlas detail
5 inset

Atlas Shrugged author
4 Rand (Ayn)

at last
7 finally

Atli
wife (slayer): **6** Gudrun

atmosphere
3 air **4** aura, mood, tone **6** medium, milieu **7** ambient, climate, feeling, quality **8** ambiance, ambience **11** environment, mise-en-scène **12** surroundings
stratum: **9** exosphere **10** ionosphere, mesosphere **11** chemosphere, ozonosphere, troposphere **12** stratosphere, thermosphere
sun's: **12** chromosphere

atmospheric
4 airy **6** aerial **8** ethereal

atoll
6 island
equatorial area: **5** Baker
Indian Ocean: **4** Male
Kiribati: **4** Beru
Marshall Islands: **6** Bikini **8** Eniwetok
Tuamotu: **4** Anaa **5** Chain
Tuvalu: **8** Funafuti

atom
3 bit, jot **4** iota, mite, whit **5** minim, speck, touch, trace **6** tittle **7** modicum, smidgen **8** particle **9** scintilla
charged: **3** ion **5** anion
group: **7** radical

atomic particle
3 ion **4** beta, muon, pion **5** alpha, boson, meson **6** baryon, hadron, lepton, proton **7** fermion, hyperon, neutron, nucleon **8** electron, mesotron, neutrino, positron, thermion
hypothetical: **5** quark **6** parton

atomic weapon
5 A-bomb, H-bomb **6** Fat Man **9** Little Boy

atomize
4 nuke, ruin **5** smash, spray, wreck **6** divide, rub out **7** break up, destroy, shatter **8** demolish, destruct, disperse, dynamite, fragment, nebulize **9** break down, devastate, pulverize **10** disconnect

at once
3 now, PDQ **4** ASAP, away, both, stat **6** pronto **8** directly, first off, right now, together **9** forthwith, instanter, instantly, right away **11** immediately, straightway **12** concurrently, straightaway

atone
3 pay **6** redeem, repair, repent **7** correct, expiate, rectify, redress, satisfy **10** compensate, make amends, recompense

Atonement author McEwan
3 Ian

atoner
8 penitent

atop
4 upon

Atossa
father: **5** Cyrus
husband: **6** Darius **7** Smerdes **8** Cambyses
son: **6** Xerxes

at random
5 about **6** anyhow **7** anywise **8** by chance **9** aimlessly, haphazard **10** carelessly **11** any which way, haphazardly **12** accidentally **13** helter-skelter

at rest
4 dead **5** still **8** inactive, lifeless, reposing, sleeping, tranquil, unmoving **9** quiescent **10** motionless, stationary, untroubled **11** trouble-free

Atreus
brother: **8** Thyestes
father: **6** Pelops
mother: **10** Hippodamia
slayer: **9** Aegisthus
son: **8** Menelaus **9** Agamemnon **11** Pleisthenes
victim: **11** Pleisthenes
wife: **6** Aerope

atrium
5 court, patio

atrocious
4 foul, vile **5** awful, cruel **6** brutal, horrid, odious, savage, wicked **7** heinous, noisome, obscene **8** barbaric, horrible, shocking, terrible **9** appalling, desperate, execrable, loathsome, monstrous, offensive, repulsive, revolting, sickening **10** abominable, despicable, detestable, disgusting, horrifying, outrageous, scandalous **12** contemptible

atrocity
4 evil **5** crime **6** horror, infamy **7** cruelty, outrage **8** enormity, savagery **9** barbarity, brutality **11** abomination, heinousness **13** monstrousness

atrophy
7 decline, wasting **9** decadence, waste away **10** devolution **11** declination **12** degeneration **13** deterioration

attach
3 fix, tie **4** bind, hook, link **5** affix, annex, latch, rivet, stick, unite **6** adhere, append, assign, fasten, secure **7** ascribe, connect **8** make fast **9** associate, attribute

attached
5 bound, fixed **7** sessile

attachment
3 tag, tie **4** bond, link, love **5** add-on **6** fealty **7** loyalty, seizure **8** addition, adhesion, devotion,

fastener, fidelity, fondness **9** accessory, adherence, affection, connector, constancy **10** allegiance, connection **12** faithfulness

attack
4 bout, jump, pelt, raid, rush **5** beset, blitz, drive, fight, foray, onset, sally, siege, spasm, spell, storm, throe **6** access, ambush, assail, banzai, battle, charge, fall on, harass, have at, invade, irrupt, onrush, pounce, sortie, strike, tackle **7** aggress, assault, barrage, besiege, bombard, lay into, offense, seizure **8** fall upon, invasion, outbreak, paroxysm **9** beleaguer, incursion, offensive, onslaught, pugnacity **10** aggression, blitzkrieg

attain
3 get, win **4** gain **5** reach, score **6** arrive, come to, effect, make it, obtain, rack up **7** achieve, fulfill, pull off, realize, succeed **8** bring off, complete **10** accomplish

attainment
4 feat **6** finish **7** arrival **10** completion **11** achievement, acquirement, acquisition, fulfillment, realization

attempt
3 bid, try **4** dare, seek, shot, stab **5** assay, crack, essay, offer, trial **6** attack, effort, strive, tackle **7** assault, venture **8** endeavor, striving, struggle **9** undertake **11** undertaking **12** make an effort

attend
3 aid, see **4** be at, go to, hear, heed, help, mark, mind, note **5** apply, catch, nurse, see to, serve, visit, watch **6** assist, convoy, doctor, drop in, escort, go with, harken, listen, notice, show up, turn up, wait on **7** be there, care for, conduct, hearken, oversee, pay heed, work for **8** chaperon, stay with, wait upon **9** accompany, chaperone, companion, look after, supervise **11** concentrate

attendant
4 aide, page **5** valet **6** escort, helper, lackey **7** orderly, servant **9** ancillary, assistant **10** bridesmaid, coincident **11** chamberlain, concomitant **12** accompanying
ancient Roman: 6 lictor
in court: 7 bailiff **8** tipstaff

attendants
5 suite, train **7** cortege, retinue **9** entourage

attendee
4 goer

attention
4 care, heed, mark, note **5** study **6** notice, regard, remark **7** amenity, command, concern, respect, service, thought **8** civility, courtesy, industry, scrutiny **9** assiduity, awareness, deference, diligence, gallantry, spotlight, treatment **10** absorption, cognizance, observance, politeness **11** application, mindfulness, observation, sensibility **12** deliberation **13** concentration, consciousness, consideration

attention getter
4 ahem, psst **5** gavel

attentive
4 kind **5** alert, awake, aware, civil **6** intent, polite **7** all ears, devoted, gallant, heedful, mindful **8** gracious, obliging, open-eyed **9** advertent, courteous, observant, regardful **10** interested, respectful, solicitous, thoughtful **11** considerate **13** concentrating

attenuate
3 sap **4** rare, slim, thin **5** abate, blunt, reedy **6** lessen, rarefy, shrink, slight, stalky, subtle, twiggy, weaken **7** cripple, deflate, disable, reduced, slender, squinny, subtile, tenuous, unbrace **8** contract, enfeeble, mitigate, rarefied, tapering, wiredraw **9** constrict, dissipate, undermine **10** become thin, become fine, become less, debilitate

attest
4 aver, show **5** argue, prove, swear, vouch **6** adjure, affirm, assert, verify **7** certify, confirm, declare, display, exhibit, point to, support, sustain, swear to, testify, warrant, witness **8** announce, indicate, manifest **9** establish **10** asseverate **11** bear witness, demonstrate **12** authenticate

attestation
5 proof **7** witness **8** evidence **9** testament, testimony **10** validation **11** declaration, testimonial **12** confirmation

at the summit of
4 atop

attic
4 loft, room **6** garret **7** storage **8** cockloft

Attica
6 Greece
division: 4 deme

at times
9 sometimes **10** now and then, on occasion **11** now and again **12** occasionally

attire
4 clad, duds, garb, gear, togs, wear **5** array, drape, dress, getup, habit, tog up **6** clothe, enrobe, fit out, outfit **7** apparel, clothes, costume, garment, raiment, threads **8** clothing, garments, glad rags **11** habiliments

attitude
4 pose, view **5** angle, stand **6** manner, stance **7** bearing, mind-set, outlook, posture **8** carriage, demeanor, position, pretense **10** standpoint **11** inclination, perspective, point of view

attitudinize
4 mask, pose, sham **6** affect **7** pass for, pass off, posture, pretend, show off **10** masquerade

attorney
5 agent, proxy **6** deputy, factor, lawyer **7** counsel **8** advocate, assignee **9** barrister, counselor, solicitor **10** counsellor, legal eagle, mouthpiece
exam: LSAT

Attorney General Janet
4 Reno

attorneys' org.
3 ABA

attract
4 draw, lure, wile **5** charm, court, tempt **6** allure, appeal, beckon, draw in, entice, invite, seduce **7** beguile, bewitch, enchant, solicit **8** appeal to, interest, intrigue, inveigle **9** captivate, fascinate, influence, magnetize

attraction
4 bait, call, draw, lure, pull **5** charm **6** allure, appeal, liking **8** affinity, cynosure, sympathy **9** affection, chemistry, magnetism, seduction **10** allurement **12** drawing power

attractive
4 cute, fair, sexy **5** bonny, dishy **6** comely, lovely, luring, pretty **7** Circean, likable, winsome **8** alluring, charming, engaging, enticing, fetching, handsome, inviting, magnetic, mesmeric, tempting **9** appealing, beauteous, beautiful, beckoning, glamorous, seductive **10** bewitching, enchanting **11** captivating, fascinating, good-looking, tantalizing **13** prepossessing

attractiveness
5 charm **6** appeal, beauty, glamor **7** glamour

attribute
3 lay **4** mark, sign **5** apply, facet, pin on, point, refer, trait **6** aspect, assign, charge, credit, emblem, impute, symbol, virtue **7** ascribe, connect, earmark, explain, feature, quality **8** accredit, classify, property **9** adjective, character, designate

attrition
3 rue **4** ruth, wear **6** sorrow **7** erosion, penance, remorse, rubbing, wearing **8** abrasion, friction, grinding **9** penitence, penitency, reduction, weakening **10** repentance **12** contriteness

attritional
5 sorry **6** rueful **8** contrite, penitent **9** regretful, repentant **10** apologetic, remorseful **11** penitential

attune
6 accord, adjust **7** balance, conform **9** harmonize, integrate, reconcile **10** coordinate, proportion **11** accommodate

Atwood novel
7 Cat's Eye **12** Oryx and Crake **13** Handmaid's Tale (The)

atypical
3 odd **5** queer **7** deviant, strange, unusual **8** aberrant, abnormal, peculiar **9** anomalous, deviative, different, divergent, irregular, unnatural **11** exceptional, heteroclite, nonstandard **13** preternatural

auberge
3 inn **5** hotel, lodge **6** hostel, tavern **7** hospice **8** hostelry **9** roadhouse **11** caravansary, public house

Auber opera
10 Fra Diavolo

auburn
4 rust **5** henna **6** russet **8** chestnut **11** burnt sienna **12** reddish-brown

Auchincloss novel
9 Embezzler (The) **13** East Side Story **14** Rector of Justin (The)

au courant
3 mod **4** up on **5** awake, aware, hep to, hip to, savvy **6** modern, modish, versed **7** abreast, current, in touch, knowing, stylish, versant, witting **8** familiar, informed, sentient, up-to-date **9** cognizant, conscious, plugged in **10** acquainted, conversant **11** fashionable **12** contemporary **13** up-to-the-minute

auction
4 sale, sell
offer: **3** bid

audacious
4 bold, rash **5** brash, brave, cocky, risky, saucy **6** brazen, cheeky, daring **7** valiant **8** arrogant, fearless, impudent, insolent, intrepid, reckless, unafraid, uncurbed **9** daredevil, dauntless, foolhardy, shameless, undaunted, venturous **10** courageous, ungoverned, unhampered **11** adventurous, impertinent, temerarious, uninhibited, untrammeled, venturesome **12** unrestrained **13** adventuresome

audacity
4 gall **5** brass, cheek, moxie, nerve, spunk **6** mettle, spirit **7** courage **8** boldness, chutzpah, rashness, temerity **9** assurance, arrogance, brashness, cockiness, disregard, hardihood, hardiness, impudence, insolence **10** brazenness, effrontery **12** recklessness

audible
5 aural, clear, heard **8** distinct **9** auricular

audibly
5 aloud **7** aurally, clearly, out loud

audience
5 crowd, group, house **6** public **7** hearing, gallery, hearers, meeting **8** admirers, assembly, audition, devotees **9** clientele, following, gathering, interview, listeners **10** assemblage, spectators

audile
see **auditory**

audio
5 sound
component: 3 amp

audiologist's concern
3 ear

audit
4 scan 5 check, probe 6 go over, report, review, survey, verify 7 analyze, balance, checkup, examine, inspect 8 analysis, scrutiny 9 going-over, reinspect 10 inspection, scrutinize 11 examination 13 investigation

audition
4 test 5 trial 6 tryout 7 hearing, reading
tape: 4 demo

auditor
3 CPA, IRS 8 examiner, listener 9 inspector 10 accountant, bookkeeper, controller 11 comptroller

auditorium
4 hall, odea (plural) 5 arena, odeum 6 lyceum

auditory
5 aural 8 acoustic
suffix: 4 otic

Auel, Jean
novel: 17 Clan of the Cave Bear (The)
series: 14 Earth's Children

au fait
4 able 5 right 6 decent, proper, versed 7 abreast, capable, correct, versant 8 becoming, decorous, familiar, informed, relevant 9 befitting, competent, qualified 10 acquainted, conforming, conversant, to the point

au fond
8 at bottom 9 basically, in essence 11 essentially 13 fundamentally

Augean
9 difficult 10 formidable 11 distasteful
stable: 3 sty 4 sink 5 filth, Sodom 7 cesspit 8 cesspool

auger
3 bit 5 borer, drill, screw 6 gimlet, trepan, wimble 9 corkscrew

Auge's son
8 Telephus

aught
3 all, nil, nix, zip 4 nada, zero 5 zilch 6 cipher 7 nothing 8 anything, goose egg 10 everything

augment
3 wax 4 grow, hike, rise 5 add to, boost, build, exalt, mount, raise 6 beef up, expand, extend 7 amplify, build up, develop, enhance, enlarge, magnify 9 intensify, reinforce 8 compound, heighten, increase, multiply 10 aggrandize, supplement 11 make greater

augmentation
4 rise 5 annex, extra, raise 7 adjunct, buildup 8 addition, increase 9 accession, accretion, increment 10 complement, enrichment 11 enhancement, enlargement

augur
4 bode, seer 6 herald, oracle 7 betoken, diviner, portend, predict, presage, promise, prophet, suggest 8 forebode, forecast, foreshow, foretell, indicate, prophesy, soothsay 9 adumbrate, foretoken, harbinger, predictor, prefigure 10 forecaster, foreshadow, foreteller, prophesier, soothsayer, vaticinate 11 Nostradamus 13 prognosticate

augury
4 omen, sign 5 token 6 herald 7 auspice, portent, presage, warning 8 bodement, forecast, prophecy 9 foretoken, harbinger 10 divination, forerunner, prediction, prognostic 11 forewarning

august
5 grand, noble, regal 6 lordly 7 eminent, stately 8 baronial, imposing, majestic, princely, splendid 9 dignified, grandiose 11 magnificent

auk
5 alcid 7 dovekie, seabird
genus: 4 Alca
relative: 5 murre

au naturel
3 raw 4 nude 5 naked, plain 6 unclad 8 stripped 9 unclothed, undressed 10 stark naked

aunt
French: 5 tante
German: 5 Tante
Italian: 3 zia
Japanese: 6 obasan
Spanish: 3 tía

aura
3 air 4 feel, glow, halo, mood, tone, vibe 5 aroma, nimbi (plural), vibes 6 nimbus 7 aureole, feeling, quality 8 ambience, mystique, radiance, stimulus 9 emanation, semblance, sensation 10 atmosphere

aurae
5 nimbi

aural
8 acoustic
suffix: 4 otic

aureate
6 florid, golden 7 flowery, orotund 8 sonorous 9 bombastic, grandiose, overblown 10 euphuistic, rhetorical 11 declamatory 13 grandiloquent

aureole
4 aura, halo, ring 5 crown, light 6 circle, corona, nimbus 8 radiance

au revoir
4 by-by, ciao, ta-ta **5** adieu, adios **6** bye-bye, so long **7** good-bye **8** farewell **11** arrivederci

auricular
see **aural**

Auriga star
7 Capella

aurora
4 dawn, morn **7** dawning, morning, sunrise **8** cockcrow, daybreak

Aurora
Roman counterpart: 3 Eos
goddess of: 4 dawn
husband: 8 Tithonus
son: 6 Memnon

auslander
5 alien **7** inconnu **8** outsider, stranger **9** foreigner

auspice
4 omen, sign **10** divination

auspices
5 aegis **6** charge **7** backing, support **8** guidance **9** influence, patronage **11** sponsorship, supervision

auspicious
5 lucky **6** bright, timely **7** hopeful **9** favorable, fortunate, opportune, promising, well-timed **10** propitious, prosperous **11** encouraging

Austen, Jane
novel: 4 Emma **10** Persuasion **13** Mansfield Park **15** Northanger Abbey **17** Pride and Prejudice **19** Sense and Sensibility

Auster
see **Notus**

austere
4 bare, cold, dour, firm, grim, hard **5** acrid, bleak, grave, harsh, plain, rigid, sharp, spare, stern **6** bitter, severe, simple, somber, strict **7** ascetic, serious, spartan **8** exacting **9** stringent, unadorned, unfeeling **10** astringent, restrained **11** self-denying

austerity
5 rigor **6** thrift **7** economy **8** acerbity, asperity, coldness, grimness, hardness, rigidity, severity **9** harshness, parsimony, privation, solemnity, spareness, sternness, stiffness **10** self-denial, simplicity, strictness, stringency **11** unadornment **13** self-restraint

Australia
capital: 8 Canberra
city: 5 Perth **6** Darwin, Sydney **8** Adelaide, Brisbane **9** Melbourne, Newcastle
desert: 10 Great Sandy **13** Great Victoria
ethnic group: 9 Aborigine
island: 6 Fraser **8** Kangaroo, Melville, Tasmania
lake: 4 Eyre
monetary unit: 6 dollar
mountain, range: 9 Ayers Rock **9** Kosciusko **13** Great Dividing
reef: 12 Great Barrier
river: 4 Swan **6** Murray **7** Darling **8** Flinders **11** Cooper Creek **12** Coopers Creek
strait: 4 Bass **6** Torres

Australian
"bear": 5 koala
soldier: 5 ANZAC
wild dog: dingo

Austria
capital: 6 Vienna
city: 4 Graz, Linz **8** Salzburg **9** Innsbruck **10** Klagenfurt
lake: 10 Neusiedler
monetary unit: 4 euro
monetary unit, former: 9 schilling
mountain: 3 Alp **13** Grossglockner
mountain range: 4 Alps
neighbor: 5 Italy **7** Croatia, Germany, Hungary **8** Slovakia, Slovenia **11** Switzerland **13** Czech Republic, Liechtenstein
river: 3 Ems **6** Danube

autarchy
see **autocracy**

autarkic
4 free **8** separate **9** sovereign **10** autonomous, self-ruling **11** independent, self-reliant **13** self-governing

autarky
7 freedom **8** autonomy **12** independence, self-reliance

authentic
4 real, true **5** legit, pukka, right, solid, sound, valid **6** actual, trusty **7** certain, factual, for real, genuine **8** accurate, bona fide, credible, faithful, reliable **9** undoubted, veritable **10** convincing, dependable, legitimate, sure-enough **11** indubitable, trustworthy **12** questionless

authenticate
5 prove, vouch **6** adduce, attest, verify **7** bear out, certify, confirm, justify, voucher, warrant **8** accredit, notarize, validate **11** corroborate **12** substantiate

author
5 maker **6** penman, scribe, writer **7** creator **8** inventor, novelist, prosaist **9** generator **10** originator
American: 3 Bly (Robert), Fox (Paula), Nin (Anaïs), Poe (Edgar Allan), Tan (Amy) **4** Agee (James), Baum (L. Frank), Buck (Pearl S.), Cain (James M.), Carr (Caleb), Cook (Robin), Dana (Richard Henry), Díaz (Junot), Fast (Howard), Ford (Richard), Grau (Shirley Ann), Grey (Zane), Jong (Erica), Loos (Anita), Mann (Thomas), Pohl (Frederik), Puzo (Mario), Rand (Ayn),

Rice (Anne), Riis (Jacob), Roth (Philip), Shaw (Irwin), Uris (Leon), West (Nathanael), Wouk (Herman) **5** Aiken (Conrad), Alger (Horatio), Banks (Russell), Barth (John), Benét (Stephen Vincent), Blume (Judy), Boyle (T. Coraghessan), Brown (Rita Mae), Clark (Mary Higgins), Crane (Hart, Stephen), Davis (Lydia), Dunne (Dominick, John Gregory), Elkin (Stanley), Ellis (Bret Easton), Foote (Horton), Haley (Alex), Harte (Bret), Henry (O.), Hurst (Fanny), Jaffe (Rona), Jakes (John), James (Henry), Kesey (Ken), Levin (Ira), Lewis (Sinclair), Lurie (Alison), Mason (Bobbie Ann), Oates (Joyce Carol), O'Hara (John), Ozick (Cynthia), Paine (Thomas), Paley (Grace), Potok (Chaim), Price (Reynolds, Richard), Seton (Anya), Steel (Danielle), Stein (Gertrude), Stone (Irving, Robert), Stout (Rex), Stowe (Harriet Beecher), Tartt (Donna), Turow (Scott), Twain (Mark), Tyler (Anne), Vidal (Gore), Welty (Eudora), White (Edmund, E. B., T. H.), Wolfe (Thomas, Tom), Wylie (Elinor) **6** Alcott (Louisa May), Asimov (Isaac), Auster (Paul), Bellow (Saul), Berger (Thomas), Bierce (Ambrose), Bowles (Paul), Cabell (James Branch), Capote (Truman), Cather (Willa), Chabon (Michael), Chopin (Kate), Clancy (Tom), Conroy (Pat), Cooper (James Fenimore), Dickey (James), Didion (Joan), Ellroy (James), Ephron (Nora), Ferber (Edna), French (Marilyn), Gaddis (William), Gaines (Ernest J.), Gilroy (Frank), Godwin (Gail), Hailey (Arthur), Harris (Frank, Joel Chandler), Hawkes (John), Heller (Joseph), Hersey (John), Hinton (S. E.), Holmes (Oliver Wendell), Hughes (Langston), Hunter (Evan), Irving (John, Washington), Jewett (Sarah Orne), Kidder (Tracy), Koontz (Dean), Krantz (Judith), L'Amour (Louis), L'Engle (Madeleine), Le Guin (Ursula K.), London (Jack), Mailer (Norman), McBain (Ed), Miller (Arthur, Henry, Joaquin, May), Morley (Christopher), Morris (Wright), Mosley (Walter), Norris (Frank), Parker (Dorothy), Piercy (Marge), Porter (Katherine Anne, William Sydney), Proulx (E. Annie), Runyon (Damon), Sarton (May), Sendak (Maurice), Sheehy (Gail), Singer (Isaac Bashevis), Smiley (Jane), Sontag (Susan), Styron (William), Talese (Gay), Taylor (Peter), Terkel (Studs), Updike (John), Walker (Alice), Waller (Robert James), Warren (Robert Penn), Wiesel (Elie), Wilder (Laura Ingalls, Thornton), Wilson (August, Edmund, Harriet, Lanford), Wister (Owen), Wright (James, Richard) **7** Baldwin (Faith, James), Beattie (Ann), Bombeck (Erma), Cheever (John), Clavell (James), Clemens (Samuel Langhorne), Collins (Jackie), Connell (Evan), Cozzens (James Gould), DeLillo (Don), Dreiser (Theodore), Ellison (Ralph), Erdrich (Louise), Farrell (James T.), Francis (Dick), Franzen (Jonathan), Gardner (Erle Stanley), Garland (Hamlin), Glasgow (Ellen), Goldman (William), Grafton (Sue), Grisham (John), Hammett (Dashiell), Heyward (DuBose), Howells (William Dean), Hurston (Zora Neale), Jackson (Shirley), Jarrell (Randall), Johnson (Diane, James), Keillor (Garrison), Kennedy (William), Kerouac (Jack), Kincaid (Jamaica), Lardner (Ring), Leonard (Elmore), Malamud (Bernard), Marquis (Don), Masters (Edgar Lee), McCourt (Frank), Mencken (H. L.), Mumford (Lewis), Nabokov (Vladimir), O'Connor (Flannery), Pynchon (Thomas), Rexroth (Kenneth), Richter (Conrad), Roberts (Elizabeth Madox, Kenneth, Nora), Saroyan (William), Sheehan (Neil), Sheldon (Sidney), Susann (Jacqueline), Theroux (Paul), Thoreau (Henry David), Thurber (James), Vollmann (William T.), Wallace (David Foster, Irving, Lew), Wharton (Edith) **8** Anderson (Maxwell, Poul, Regina, Sherwood), Benchley (Peter), Bradbury (Ray), Bradford (Barbara Taylor), Caldwell (Erskine), Chandler (Raymond), Cornwell (Patricia), Crichton (Michael), Doctorow (E. L.), Faulkner (William), Kingston (Maxine Hong), Marquand (John P.), McCarthy (Cormac, Mary), McMillan (Terry), McMurtry (Larry), Melville (Herman), Michener (James), Mitchell (Donald Grant, Margaret, S. Weir), Morrison (Toni), Paretsky (Sara), Remarque (Erich Maria), Rinehart (Mary Roberts), Salinger (J. D.), Sandburg (Carl), Sinclair (Upton), Spillane (Mickey), Stockton (Frank R.), Vonnegut (Kurt), Wambaugh (Joseph) **9** Burroughs (Edgar Rice, John, William S.), Dos Passos (John), Hawthorne (Nathaniel), Hemingway (Ernest), Hillerman (Tony), Isherwood (Christopher), McCullers (Carson), Steinbeck (John), Wodehouse (P. G.), Woollcott (Alexander) **10** Cunningham (Michael), Fitzgerald (F. Scott), Kingsolver (Barbara), Tarkington (Booth) **11** Auchincloss (Louis), Matthiessen (Peter), Silverstein (Shel)

Argentinian: 6 Borges (Jorge Luis)

Australian: 4 West (Morris L.) **5** Carey (Peter), Stead (Christina), White (Patrick) **7** Clavell (James), Idriess (Ion) **8** Keneally (Thomas) **10** McCullough (Colleen), Richardson (Henry Handel)

Austrian: 5 Kafka (Franz) **6** Handke (Peter) **7** Jelinek (Elfriede), Suttner (Bertha) **8** Bernhard (Thomas) **10** Schnitzler (Arthur)

Brazilian: 6 Coelho (Paulo)

Canadian: 3 Roy (Camille, Gabrielle) **5** Kirby (William), Moore (Brian), Munro (Alice) **6** Atwood (Margaret), Davies (Robertson), Martel (Yann), Mistry (Rohinton) **7** Leacock (Stephen), Raddall (Thomas), Richler (Mordecai), Service (Robert), Shields (Carol) **8** Laurence (Margaret), Woodcock (George) **9** de la Roche (Mazo), MacLennan (Hugh), Ondaatje (Michael)

Chilean: 6 Donoso (José) **7** Allende (Isabel)

Chinese: 3 Lin (Yutang) **5** Han Yu

Colombian: 7 Márquez (Gabriel García)

Czech: **5** Čapek (Karel), Hasek (Jaroslav), Havel (Václav) **7** Kundera (Milan)
Danish: **4** Rode (Helge), Wied (Gustav) **6** Jensen (Johannes Vilhelm) **7** Dinesen (Isak), Holberg (Ludwig)
Dominican: **4** Díaz (Junot)
Dutch: **6** Vondel (Joost van den)
Egyptian: **7** Mahfouz (Naguib)
English: **4** Amis (Kingsley, Martin), Dahl (Roald), Ford (Ford Madox, John), Glyn (Elinor), Lyly (John), Saki, Snow (C. P.), Ward (Mrs. Humphry), West (Rebecca) **5** Byatt (A. S.), Defoe (Daniel), Doyle (Arthur Conan), Eliot (George, Thomas Stearns), Evans (Mary Ann), Frayn (Michael), Hardy (Thomas), James (Henry, P. D.), Lewis (C. S., Monk, Wyndham), Lowry (Malcolm), Milne (A. A.), Munro (H. H.), Powys (John Cowper, Llewelyn, Theodore Francis), Reade (Charles), Spark (Muriel), Waugh (Alec, Evelyn), Wells (Charles Jeremiah, H. G.), White (T. H.), Wilde (Oscar), Woolf (Leonard, Virginia), Young (Arthur, Edward, Francis Brett) **6** Ambler (Eric), Archer (Jeffrey), Austen (Jane), Barnes (Julian), Belloc (Hilaire), Blyton (Enid), Brontë (Anne, Charlotte, Emily), Bunyan (John), Butler (Samuel), Clarke (Arthur C.), Conrad (Joseph), Fowles (John), Graves (Robert), Greene (Graham, Robert), Hilton (James), Hudson (W. H.), Huxley (Aldous), Malory (Thomas), Mantel (Hilary), McEwan (Ian), O'Brian (Patrick), Orwell (George), Potter (Beatrix), Powell (Anthony), Sayers (Dorothy L.), Sterne (Laurence), Stoker (Bram), Storey (David), Walton (Izaak) **7** Bagnold (Enid), Ballard (J. G.), Burgess (Anthony), Burnett (Frances Hodgson), Carroll (Lewis), Clavell (James), Collins (Wilkie), Dickens (Charles), Dodgson (Charles), Durrell (Lawrence), Fleming (Ian), Follett (Ken), Forster (E. M.), Forsyth (Frederick), Golding (Louis, William), Johnson (Samuel), Kipling (Rudyard), Le Carré (John), Lessing (Doris), Lofting (Hugh), Maugham (Robin, W. Somerset), Murdoch (Iris), Naipaul (V. S.), Rendell (Ruth), Rowling (J. K.), Sassoon (Siegfried), Shelley (Mary Wollstonecraft, Percy Bysshe), Sitwell (Edith, Osbert, Sacheverell), Southey (Robert), Stewart (Mary), Surtees (Robert Smith), Tolkien (J. R. R.), Walpole (Horace, Hugh), Wyndham (John) **8** Christie (Agatha), Fielding (Henry), Forester (C. S.), Koestler (Arthur), Lawrence (D. H., T. E.), Macaulay (Rose, Thomas Babington), Meredith (George), Sillitoe (Alan), Smollett (Tobias), Strachey (Lytton), Trollope (Anthony), Zangwill (Israel) **9** De Quincey (Thomas), Du Maurier (Daphne, George), Goldsmith (Oliver), Isherwood (Christopher), Mansfield (Katherine), Masefield (John), Priestley (J. B.), Radcliffe (Ann), Stevenson (Robert Louis), Thackeray (William Makepeace), Wodehouse (P. D.) **10** Chesterton (Gilbert Keith), Galsworthy (John), Richardson (Dorothy, Samuel) **12** Quiller-Couch (Arthur Thomas)
Finnish: **7** Waltari (Mika) **9** Sillanpää (Frans Eemil)
French: **3** Nin (Anaïs) **4** Gide (André), Hugo (Victor), Kock (Charles-Paul de), Sade (Marquis de), Sand (George), Zola (Emile) **5** Beyle (Marie Henri), Camus (Albert), Dumas (Alexandre), Duras (Marguerite), Genet (Jean), Sagan (Françoise), Staël (Germaine de), Verne (Jules), Vigny (Alfred-Victor) **6** Balzac (Honoré de), Daudet (Alphonse), France (Anatole), Lesage (Alain-René, Proust (Marcel), Sartre (Jean-Paul) **7** Cocteau (Jean), Colette, de Staël (Germaine), Gautier (Léon, Théophile), Malraux (André), Mauriac (Claude, François), Maurois (André), Merimée (Prosper), Rolland (Romain), Romains (Jules), Simenon (Georges) **8** Beauvoir (Simone de), Flaubert (Gustave), Marivaux (Pierre), Rabelais (François), Stendhal, Voltaire **9** Giraudoux (Jean), Montaigne (Michel de) **10** Maupassant (Guy de), Saint-Simon (Duke de) **12** Robbe-Grillet (Alain), Saint-Exupéry (Antoine de)
German: **4** Böll (Heinrich), Mann (Thomas) **5** Grass (Gunter), Hesse (Hermann), Kafka (Franz), Storm (Theodor), Tieck (Ludwig), Zweig (Stefan) **6** Goethe (Johann Wolfgang von), Toller (Ernst) **7** Fontane (Theodor), Richter (Jean Paul), Wieland (Christoph Martin) **8** Hoffmann (E. T. A., Heinrich), Remarque (Erich Maria), Schlegel (August Wilhelm von, Friedrich von, Johann Elias) **9** Hauptmann (Gerhart), Sudermann (Hermann) **10** Wassermann (Jakob)
Greek: **5** Homer **6** Hesiod, Lucian, Pindar, Sappho **7** Plautus, Terence **8** Xenophon **9** Aeschylus, Euripedes, Herodotus, Sophocles **10** Thucydides **11** Kazantzakis (Nikos)
Hungarian: **5** Jókai (Mór)
Icelandic: **7** Laxness (Halldór)
Indian: **3** Roy (Arundhati) **7** Narayan (R. K.), Rushdie (Salman)
Irish: **5** Behan (Brendan), Doyle (Roddy), Joyce (James), Moore (Brian), Swift (Jonathan), Synge (J. M.), Wilde (Oscar) **6** O'Brien (Edna), Stoker (Bram), Tóibín (Colm), Trevor (William) **7** Beckett (Samuel), McCourt (Frank), O'Connor (Frank), Russell (George William) **8** Banville (John), Kinsella (Thomas), O'Faolain (Julia, Sean), Stephens (James) **9** Edgeworth (Maria), O'Flaherty (Liam)
Italian: **3** Eco (Umberto) **4** Levi (Primo) **5** Dante (Alighieri), Verga (Giovanni) **6** Silone (Ignazio) **7** Calvino (Italo), Manzoni (Alessandro), Moravia (Alberto) **9** Boccaccio (Giovanni), Vittorini (Elio) **10** Pirandello (Luigi), Straparola (Gianfrancesco)
Japanese: **3** Abe (Kobo) **7** Mishima (Yukio) **8** Kawabata (Yasunari), Murakami (Haruki), Murasaki (Shikibu) **9** Yokomitsu (Riichi), Yoshikawa (Eiji)
Lebanese: **6** Gibran (Khalil)

Mexican: **5** Rulfo (Juan) **7** Fuentes (Carlos)
Nigerian: **6** Achebe (Chinua) **7** Soyinka (Wole), Tutuola (Amos)
Norwegian: **3** Lie (Jonas) **6** Hamsun (Knut), Undset (Sigrid) **7** Rolvaag (Ole) **8** Bjornson (Bjornstjerne), Kielland (Alexander) **10** Knausgaard (Karl Ove)
Peruvian: **11** Vargas Llosa (Mario)
Polish: **3** Lem (Stanislaw) **7** Reymont (Wladyslaw) **8** Zeromski (Stefan) **10** Gombrowicz (Witold) **11** Sienkiewicz (Henryk)
Portuguese: **6** Pessoa (Fernando) **8** Saramago (José)
Roman: **4** Livy **5** Pliny, Varro (Marcus Terentius) **7** Tacitus **8** Apuleius **9** Petronius
Romanian: **6** Wiesel (Elie)
Russian: **5** Babel (Isaac), Bunin (Ivan), Gogol (Nikolai), Gorki (Maxim), Gorky (Maxim) **7** Chekhov (Anton), Nabokov (Vladimir), Pushkin (Alexander), Tolstoy (Leo) **8** Andreyev (Leonid), Turgenev (Ivan), Zamyatin (Yevgeny) **9** Ehrenburg (Ilya), Lermontov (Mikhail), Pasternak (Boris), Sholokhov (Mikhail), Ulitskaya (Lyudmila) **10** Dostoevsky (Fyodor) **11** Dostoyevsky (Fyodor), Yevtushenko (Yevgeny) **12** Solzhenitsyn (Alexander)
Scottish: **3** Tey (Josephine) **4** Lang (Andrew) **5** Banks (Iain), Scott (Alexander, Walter), Walsh (Irvine) **6** Barrie (James M.), Buchan (John) **8** Urquhart (Thomas) **9** Stevenson (Robert Louis)
South African: **5** Paton (Alan) **6** Fugard (Athol) **7** Coetzee (J. M.) **8** Gordimer (Nadine)
Spanish: **6** Baroja (Pio) **7** Alarcón (Pedro Antonio de) **9** Cervantes (Miguel de)
Swedish: **7** Johnson (Eyvind), Rydberg (Viktor) **8** Lagerlöf (Selma) **10** Lagerkvist (Pär), Strindberg (August)
Swiss: **4** Wyss (Johann Rudolf) **5** Spyri (Johanna) **6** Frisch (Max) **9** Spitteler (Carl)
Trinidadian: **7** Naipaul (V. S.)
Welsh: **4** Owen (Alun, Daniel, Goronwy, John) **5** Evans (David, Evan), Wynne (Ellis)
Yiddish: **4** Asch (Sholem) **6** Singer (Isaac Bashevis) **8** Aleichem (Sholem)

authoritarian
5 harsh, rigid **6** despot, severe, strict, tyrant **8** absolute, autocrat, despotic, dictator, dogmatic **9** imperious, stringent **10** absolutist, autocratic, oppressive, totalistic, tyrannical **11** dictatorial, doctrinaire, domineering, magisterial **12** totalitarian

authoritative
4 sure, true **5** legal, legit, sound **6** lawful, proven **7** factual **8** accepted, accurate, approved, attested, dogmatic, official, orthodox, reliable, verified **9** canonical, cathedral, confirmed, imperious, trustable, validated **10** autocratic, commanding, definitive, dependable, documented, dominating, ex cathedra, legitimate, sanctioned **11** dictatorial, doctrinaire, domineering, irrefutable, magisterial, overbearing, trustworthy **12** indisputable

authority
4 rule, sway **5** clout, force, maven, power, right, say-so **6** agency, charge, credit, expert, master, weight **7** command, control, grounds, license, mastery, warrant **8** citation, decision, dominion, prestige **9** influence, testimony **10** domination, governance, government, management **12** jurisdiction

authorization
4 okay, word **5** leave, say-so **6** permit **7** consent, go-ahead, license, mandate **8** approval, sanction **9** agreement, allowance, clearance **10** green light, permission, sufferance **11** approbation

authorize
3 let **4** okay, vest **5** allow **6** affirm, enable, invest, permit **7** approve, confirm, empower, endorse, entitle, license, qualify, warrant **8** accredit, sanction, vouch for **9** give leave, recognize **10** commission **11** countenance

auto
see **automobile**

autobahn
7 highway **8** turnpike **10** expressway **12** superhighway

autobiography
4 life, vita **5** diary **6** memoir **7** account, journal **9** life story **11** confessions **13** reminiscences

autochthonous
6 native **7** endemic **8** original **10** aboriginal, indigenous

autocracy
7 czarism, tyranny **8** monarchy **9** despotism, monocracy **12** absolute rule, dictatorship

autocrat
4 czar, duce, emir, lord, raja, shah, tsar, tzar **5** mogul, rajah, ruler **6** caliph, despot, sultan, tyrant **7** magnate, monarch **8** dictator, oligarch, overlord **9** potentate, sovereign **10** absolutist

autocratic
7 haughty **8** absolute, arrogant, despotic **9** arbitrary, imperious, tyrannous **10** monocratic, tyrannical **11** dictatorial, domineering, overbearing

autodidactic
10 self-taught **12** self-educated

autograph
3 ink, pen **4** sign **5** write **7** endorse **8** original **9** signature, subscribe **11** endorsement, John Hancock

Autolycus
daughter: **8** Anticlea
father: **6** Hermes **7** Mercury

automaker Ferrari
4 Enzo

automated
7 robotic 9 by machine, motorized 10 electrical, electronic, mechanical, mechanized, programmed 12 computerized

automatic
6 reflex 8 habitual 9 impulsive, reflexive 10 mechanical, self-acting, unprompted 11 instinctive, involuntary, perfunctory, spontaneous, unmeditated
prefix: 4 self

automaton
5 droid, golem, robot 7 android, machine 9 mechanism

automne preceder
3 été

automobile
3 ATV, bus, car 5 buggy, coupe, racer, sedan 6 beater, jalopy, tourer, wheels 7 clunker, flivver, hardtop, machine 8 dragster, motorcar, roadster, runabout 9 hatchback, limousine 10 rust bucket 11 convertible
American: 3 Geo, Reo 4 Cord, Dart, Ford, Fury, Jeep, Nash, Neon, Olds, Vega 5 Buick, Dodge, Eagle, Edsel, Essex, Focus, Pinto, T-bird, Tesla 6 Cougar, DeSoto, Duster, Fraser, Hudson, Hummer, Impala, Kaiser, Model A, Model T, Saturn, Tucker, Willys 7 Charger, Cutlass, LaSalle, LeBaron, LeSabre, Lincoln, Maxwell, Mercury, Mustang, Packard, Pontiac, Rambler, Seville 8 Cadillac, Chrysler, Corvette, Eldorado, Franklin, Plymouth 9 Barracuda, Chevrolet, Hupmobile 10 Duesenberg, Oldsmobile, Studebaker 11 Continental, Pierce-Arrow, Thunderbird
British: 3 Jag, MGB 4 Mini 5 Lotus 6 Anglia, Arnage, Austin, Cooper, DeSoto, Jaguar, Morris 7 Bentley, Daimler, Hillman, Phantom, Sunbeam, Triumph 8 Vauxhall 9 Land Rover 10 Range Rover, Rolls-Royce 11 Aston Martin, Silver Ghost 12 Austin-Healey
club: 3 AAA
French: 5 Simca 7 Citroën, Peugeot, Renault
German: 3 BMW 4 Audi, Benz, Golf, Opel 6 Beetle 7 Daimler, Maybach, Porsche, Quattro 8 Mercedes 10 Volkswagen 12 Mercedes-Benz
Italian: 4 Fiat 6 Lancia 7 Bugatti, Ferrari 8 Maserati 9 Alfa-Romeo 11 Lamborghini
Japanese: 5 Acura, Civic, Honda, Isuzu, Lexus, Mazda, Prius 6 Datsun, Altima, Maxima, Nissan, Subaru, Toyota 7 Corolla 8 Daihatsu, Infiniti 10 Mitsubishi
Korean: 3 Kia 6 Daewoo 7 Hyundai
Russian: 4 Lada
Serbian: 4 Yugo
Swedish: 4 Saab 5 Volvo

automobile safety device
3 ABS 6 air bag 8 seat belt

automotive pioneer
4 Benz (Carl Friedrich), Ford (Henry), Olds (Ransom), Otto (Nikolaus), Pope (Albert) 5 Evans (Oliver), Rolls (Charles), Roper (Sylvester) 6 Cugnot (Nicholas Joseph), Duryea (Charles E., J. Frank), Lenoir (Etienne), Winton (Alexander) 7 Bugatti (Ettore), Citroën (André-Gustave), Daimler (Gottlieb), Peugeot (Armand), Stanley (Francis, Freelan) 8 Morrison (William) 10 Lanchester (Frederick William)

Autonoë
father: 6 Cadmus
husband: 9 Aristaeus
mother: 8 Harmonia
sister: 5 Agave
son: 7 Actaeon

autonomous
4 free 8 autarkic, separate 9 sovereign 10 self-ruling 11 independent, self-reliant 12 self-governed, uncontrolled 13 self-contained, self-governing

autonomy
7 autarky, freedom 8 home rule, self-rule 11 sovereignty 12 independence

autopsy
6 assess 7 examine 8 evaluate, necropsy 10 assessment, dissection, evaluation, post-mortem 11 examination

auto racer
4 Foyt (A. J.), Hill (Graham) 5 Clark (Jim), Mears (Rick), Petty (Richard), Rahal (Bobby), Unser (Al, Bobby) 6 Carter (Pancho), Fangio (Juan), Vogler (Rich) 7 Brabham (Jack), Stewart (Jackie) 8 Andretti (Mario, Michael), Johncock (Gordon) 9 Earnhardt (Dale) 10 Rutherford (Johnny)

autumn
4 fall 6 season 8 maturity

auxiliary
4 aide 5 spare 6 backup, helper 7 reserve 8 adjutant, adjuvant 9 accessory, ancillary, assistant, coadjutor, secondary 10 accomplice, additional, collateral, subsidiary 11 appurtenant, subservient 12 contributory 13 complementary, supplementary
verb: 3 are, can, did, had, has, may, was 4 been, does, have, must, were, will 5 could, might, ought, shall, would 6 should

avail
3 aid, use 4 gain, good, help 5 asset, serve 6 profit 7 account, benefit, fitness, satisfy, service 9 advantage, relevance 10 usefulness 13 applicability

available
5 handy, on tap, ready, valid 6 at hand, on hand, usable 7 present, willing 8 prepared 9 qualified 10 accessible, attainable, convenient, obtainable, procurable 11 purchasable

avalanche
4 mass, rush **5** drown, flood, slide **6** deluge **7** overrun, smother **8** inundate, mudslide, overflow, rockfall **9** landslide, overwhelm, rockslide, snowslide **10** inundation **12** accumulation

Avalon
8 paradise

avant-garde
7 radical **8** advanced, contempo **10** innovative, pioneering **11** cutting-edge, leading-edge, progressive **12** experimental **13** up-to-the-minute

avarice
5 greed **7** avidity **8** cupidity, rapacity, voracity **10** greediness **12** covetousness

avaricious
6 grabby, greedy, stingy **7** miserly **8** covetous, esurient, grasping, ravenous **9** mercenary, rapacious **11** acquisitive

avatar
4 type **5** image **7** epitome **8** exemplar **9** archetype **10** apotheosis, embodiment, expression **11** incarnation, reification **13** manifestation
of Vishnu: 4 Rama

avaunt
4 away **5** hence, leave, scram **6** beat it, depart, get out

ave
4 hail **8** farewell, greeting

avenge
5 repay, right **6** punish **7** get even, pay back, redress, requite **9** fight back, retaliate, vindicate

avenue
3 way **4** path, road **5** drive, means, route, track **6** access, artery, course, street **7** channel, parkway, pathway **8** approach **9** boulevard **10** passageway **12** thoroughfare

aver
4 avow **5** prove, state, swear **6** affirm, allege, assert, attest, avouch, depose, insist, verify **7** declare, profess, protest, testify, warrant **8** maintain **9** guarantee, predicate

average
3 par **4** fair, mean, norm, so-so **5** usual **6** common, divide, equate, figure, median, medium, middle, normal **7** balance, even out, typical **8** everyday, midpoint, moderate, ordinary **12** intermediate

averagely
4 so-so **6** enough, fairly, rather **8** passably **9** tolerably **10** moderately

averse
5 balky, loath **6** afraid **7** hostile, opposed, uneager **8** allergic, hesitant **9** reluctant, resistant, unwilling **10** indisposed **11** disinclined **12** antipathetic

aversion
4 fear, hate **5** dread **6** hatred, horror **7** allergy, disgust, dislike **8** disfavor, distaste, loathing **9** antipathy, disliking, repulsion, revulsion **10** abhorrence, antagonism, repugnance **11** abomination, detestation, displeasure **13** indisposition

aversive
8 ungenial **9** repellent, repugnant **11** uncongenial **12** antipathetic **13** unsympathetic

avert
4 foil, halt, turn, veer, ward **5** avoid, check, deter **6** thwart **7** deflect, fend off, forfend, obviate, prevent, rule out, ward off **8** go around, stave off, turn away **9** forestall, turn aside

avian
6 flying, winged **8** birdlike, ornithic

aviary
4 cage **8** birdcage, dovecote **9** birdhouse, enclosure

aviator
3 ace **4** Post (Wiley) **5** flier, pilot **6** airman, Cessna (Clyde), flyboy, Wright (Orville, Wilbur), Yeager (Chuck) **7** birdman, Earhart (Amelia) **8** aeronaut **9** bush pilot, Lindbergh (Charles) **10** Richthofen (Manfred von) **12** Rickenbacker (Eddie)

avid
4 agog, keen **5** eager **6** ardent, greedy, hungry **7** anxious, athirst, craving, fervent, thirsty, zealous **8** appetent, covetous, desirous, grasping **9** impatient **10** breathless, insatiable **12** enthusiastic

avidity
4 zeal **5** greed **6** fervor, thirst **7** avarice, craving **8** cupidity, keenness, rapacity **9** eagerness **10** greediness

Avis competitor
5 Hertz

___ avis
4 rara

avocation
5 hobby **7** pastime, pursuit **8** sideline **9** amusement, diversion **10** recreation

avoid
4 bilk, duck, miss, shun, snub **5** annul, avert, dodge, elude, evade, shirk, skirt **6** bypass, divert, escape, eschew, pass up **7** abstain, prevent, refrain **8** preclude, sidestep, stay away, withdraw **9** keep clear **11** refrain from **12** keep away from

avoidance
5 dodge **6** escape, nonuse **7** dodging, elusion, evasion **8** escaping, escapism, eschewal, shirking, shunning **9** runaround **10** abstinence

avouch
3 own **4** aver, avow **5** admit, claim, state,

swear **6** affirm, assert, depose, insist **7** certify, confess, confirm, declare, profess, testify **9** predicate, pronounce **11** acknowledge, corroborate

avow
3 own **4** aver **5** admit, allow, grant, let on, own up, state, swear **6** affirm, assert, avouch, depose **7** concede, confess, declare, profess, protest **8** disclose, maintain, proclaim **9** predicate **11** acknowledge

avowal
6 assent **9** admission, assertion, statement **10** profession **11** affirmation, attestation, declaration

avowedly
6 openly **7** frankly **8** candidly **9** allegedly **10** apparently, ostensibly, supposedly

await
4 bide, hope, pend, stay **5** abide **6** expect **7** count on, look for **8** watch for **10** anticipate, hang around

awake
4 stir **5** alert, alive, aware, rouse **6** active, arouse, bestir, excite, revive, roused, stir up **7** animate, aroused, excited, on guard **8** activate, sensible, sentient, vigilant, watchful **9** attentive, cognizant, conscious, observant, stimulate, stirred up

award
4 gift, give, kudo **5** allot, badge, endow, grant, honor, kudos, medal, prize **6** accord, bestow, confer, donate, ribbon, trophy **7** concede, laurels, tribute **8** accolade, citation, donation **9** vouchsafe **10** blue ribbon, decoration, distribute **11** distinction
advertising: **4** Addy, Andy, Clio
broadcasting: **7** Peabody
cable: **5** Telly
cartooning: **6** Ignatz, Reuben
comic books: **6** Eisner, Harvey
computing: **6** Turing
horror writing: **10** Bram Stoker
Internet: **5** Webby
motion picture: **5** Annie, Oscar **6** Razzie, Saturn **7** Academy **11** Golden Globe
mystery novel: **5** Edgar **6** Agatha
record: **6** Grammy
remodeling: **9** Chrysalis
romance novel: **4** Rita
science & technology: **11** Enrico Fermi
science-fiction: **4** Hugo **6** Nebula
software: **5** Codie
television: **4** Emmy
theater: **4** Obie, Tony

aware
5 alert, alive, awake **7** heedful, knowing, mindful, tuned in, witting **8** informed, sensible, sentient, vigilant **9** attentive, au courant, cognizant, conscious, observant **10** conversant, perceptive **12** apprehensive **13** knowledgeable
of: **4** in on, onto

awash
4 full **6** afloat, filled, jammed, loaded, packed **7** brimful, covered, crammed, crowded, flooded, run-over, stuffed **8** brimming, chockful **9** chock-full **11** overflowing

away
3 far, fro, now, off, out **4** afar, gone **5** along, apart, aside, forth, hence **6** abroad, absent, afield, far off **7** distant, lacking, missing, not here **9** elsewhere **11** incessantly **12** continuously

away from
6 beyond

awe
5 alarm, amaze, scare **6** wonder **7** inspire, startle **8** astonish **9** amazement, reverence **10** veneration, wonderment **11** flabbergast **12** astonishment

aweless
4 bold **5** brave **7** valiant **8** fearless, intrepid, unafraid **9** dauntless, undaunted **10** courageous

awesome
3 rad **6** august **7** amazing, sublime **8** imposing, terrific, wondrous **10** formidable, impressive **11** astonishing, jaw-dropping **12** breathtaking **13** extraordinary

awestruck
5 agape **6** amazed **9** astounded **10** astonished

awful
3 bad **4** dire, very **5** nasty **6** odious **7** hateful, heinous **8** dreadful, horrible, horrific, shocking, terrible, terrific **9** appalling, atrocious, extremely, frightful, loathsome, offensive **10** deplorable, disgusting, formidable

awfully
4 much, very **6** hugely, vastly **7** greatly **8** terribly, whopping **9** extremely, immensely **10** dreadfully, enormously **11** exceedingly

awhile
7 briefly **8** for a time **11** temporarily

awkward
5 gawky, inept, messy, nerdy, splay **6** clumsy, clunky, gauche, klutzy, wooden **7** artless, gawkish, halting, lumpish, stilted, unhandy, unhappy **8** bumbling, bungling, tactless, ungainly **9** graceless, ham-handed, ill-chosen, inelegant, lumbering, maladroit **10** blundering, ungraceful, unskillful **11** heavy-handed, unfortunate **12** embarrassing, incommodious, inconvenient, infelicitous

awl
4 tool **7** ice pick, piercer

awn
6 arista

awning
6 canopy **7** marquee **8** sunshade
ancient Roman: 8 velarium

awry
5 amiss, askew, atilt, wrong **6** astray **7** askance, crooked **8** cockeyed **9** cock-a-hoop, crookedly
Scottish: 5 agley

ax, axe
3 adz, can, hew **4** adze, boot, chop, fire, sack **6** bounce, lay off **7** boot out, chopper, cleaver, dismiss, hatchet, kick out **8** tomahawk **9** discharge, terminate
blade: 3 bit
handle: 5 helve

axillary
4 alar

axiom
3 law **4** rule **5** adage, maxim, moral, truth **6** dictum, truism **7** precept, theorem **8** aphorism, apothegm **9** postulate, principle **10** principium **11** fundamental

axiomatic
5 given **7** assumed, certain, obvious **8** accepted, absolute, manifest, provable **10** aphoristic, understood **11** fundamental, indubitable, self-evident **12** unquestioned

axis
4 line, pole, stem **5** point, pivot **8** alliance **9** continuum, plant stem **11** partnership **12** straight line, turning point

axle
3 bar, pin, rod **4** beam **5** bogie, shaft **7** spindle, support

axlike tool
3 adz **4** adze

aye
3 yea, yep, yes **4** amen, okay, ever, vote **6** agreed, always **8** all right **11** affirmative, continually

Ayn ___
4 Rand

Azerbaijan
capital: 4 Baku
city: 5 Gäncä **8** Sumqayit
exclave: 8 Naxçivan **11** Nakhichevan
monetary unit: 5 manat
neighbor: 4 Iran **6** Russia **7** Armenia, Georgia
river: 4 Kura **5** Araks
sea: 7 Caspian

Azores
capital: 12 Ponta Delgada
city: 5 Horta
island: 4 Pico **5** Corvo, Faial, Lajes **6** Flores **8** São Jorge, Terceura **9** São Miguel **10** Santa Maria
part of: 8 Portugal

Aztec
capital: 12 Tenochtitlán
conqueror: 6 Cortés, Cortéz
emperor: 9 Moctezuma, Montezuma
god: 4 Xipe **6** Tlaloc **9** Xipetotec **12** Quetzalcoatl
hero: 4 Nata
language: 7 Nahuatl
temple: 8 teocalli

azure
3 sky **4** blue **5** color **7** sky blue

B

baa
5 bleat

Babbitt
10 conformist, middlebrow, philistine
author: 5 Lewis (Sinclair)

babble
3 gab, jaw, yak, yap **4** blab, chat, go on, gush, rant, rave **5** clack, prate, run on **6** burble, drivel, gibber, gossip, jabber, murmur, natter, patter, piffle, rattle, yammer **7** blabber, blather, chatter, maunder, palaver, prattle, twaddle **8** nonsense, idle talk **9** gibberish **11** jabberwocky

babe
3 cub, tot **4** doll, girl **5** bairn, child, chick, cutie, toots, woman **6** infant, hottie **7** bambino, papoose, neonate, newborn **8** bantling, nursling
in the woods: 4 naïf

babel
3 ado, din, row **4** to-do **5** hoo-ha **6** bedlam, clamor, hubbub, jangle, outcry, racket, ruckus, tumult, uproar **7** clangor, discord, ferment, turmoil **8** brouhaha, clangour, foofaraw **9** cacophony, commotion, confusion **10** dissonance, hullabaloo, hurly-burly, turbulence **11** pandemonium **12** vociferation

baboon
3 oaf **4** clod, dolt, goon, lout **6** chacma, galoot, monkey, simian **7** palooka **8** lunkhead, mandrill, meathead **9** hamadryas

babushka
5 scarf **6** granny **7** bandana **8** bandanna, kerchief

baby
3 pet, tot **4** tiny **5** bairn, sissy, spoil **6** cocker, coddle, cosset, dote on, infant, pamper **7** bambino, cater to, indulge, neonate, newborn, papoose, toddler **8** bantling, dote upon, nursling, suckling, weanling **11** mollycoddle
ailment: **5** colic, croup
bed: **4** crib **6** cradle **8** bassinet
bedroom: **7** nursery
breechcloth: **6** diaper
cap: **6** biggin, bonnet
carriage: **4** pram **5** buggy **8** stroller **12** perambulator
doctor: **12** pediatrician
first word: **4** dada, mama
food: **3** pap **4** milk **6** pablum **7** pabulum
garment: **7** rompers
Italian: **7** bambino
napkin: **3** bib
outfit: **7** layette
powder: **4** talc
shoe: **6** bootee
Spanish: **4** bebé, nene

baby grand
5 piano

babyhood
7 infancy **10** diaper days, immaturity

babyish
5 petty **7** foolish, puerile, spoiled **8** childish, immature, juvenile **9** infantile, infantine

Babylonian
6 lavish **9** luxurious
abode of the dead: **5** Aralu
capital: **7** Babylon
chaos: **4** Apsu
city: **5** Akkad **6** Cunaxa
crown prince: **10** Belshazzar
division: **5** Akkad, Sumer
first ruler: **6** Nimrod
god: **3** Bel **4** Adad, Addu, Enki, Enzu, Irra, Nabu, Nebo **6** Marduk, Tammuz **7** Shamash
goddess: **4** Erua, Gula **5** Belit **6** Ishtar
hero: **9** Gilgamesh
king: **6** Sargon **9** Hammurabi **12** Ashurbanipal
river: **6** Tigris **9** Euphrates
tower: **5** Babel **8** ziggurat
waters: **4** Apsu **6** Tiamat
winged dragon: **6** Tiamat

baccalaureate
6 degree **9** bachelor's **10** graduation

bacchanal
6 maenad
see also **bacchanalia**

bacchanalia
4 bash, orgy **5** binge, revel, spree **6** bender, excess **7** blowout, carouse, debauch, revelry, wassail **8** carnival, festival, wingding **11** celebration, dissipation, merrymaking

bacchanalian
4 wild **7** drunken, riotous **8** frenzied **9** debauched, Dionysian, orgiastic **12** intoxicating
cry: **4** evoe **5** evohe

Bacchus
8 Dionysus
attendant: **5** satyr **6** maenad **9** bacchante
father: **4** Zeus **7** Jupiter
lover: **5** Venus **9** Aphrodite
mother: **6** Semele
son: **7** Priapus
staff: **7** thyrsus

Bach, Johann Sebastian
birthplace: **8** Eisenach
genre: **5** fugue, motet, suite **6** sonata **7** cantata, chorale, partita, prelude, toccata **8** concerto, fantasia, oratorio, sinfonia
home: **7** Leipzig
instrument: **5** organ **11** harpsichord
musical style: **7** baroque
religion: **8** Lutheran

back
3 aft, ago, aid **4** abet, fund, help, hind, rear **5** abaft, about, bet on, dorsa (plural), spine, stake, stern **6** assist, astern, dorsum, hinder, recede, uphold **7** endorse, finance, promote, retract, retreat, reverse, sponsor, support **8** advocate, bankroll, champion, rearward, side with **9** in reverse, posterior, retrocede, subsidize **10** retrograde
ailment: **7** lumbago **10** rheumatism
muscle: **3** lat **4** trap **8** rhomboid **9** trapezius
of an arthropod: **6** tergum
of an insect: **5** notum
of the neck: **4** nape **6** scruff
prefix: **4** post **5** retro
relating to: **6** dorsal

back answer
3 lip **6** retort **7** riposte **8** comeback, repartee **9** rejoinder, wisecrack **10** return shot **11** parting shot

backbite
4 slam, slur **5** abuse, decry, knock, libel, smear, sully, taint **6** defame, defile, malign, vilify **7** asperse, put down, run down, slander, traduce **8** bad-mouth, belittle, besmirch, derogate, diminish **9** denigrate, discredit

backbiter
6 gossip **7** defamer, traitor **9** detractor, slanderer **10** talebearer

backbiting
5 abuse, smear, spite **6** gossip **7** abusing, calumny, obloquy, scandal, slander **8** libelous, smearing **9** aspersion, cattiness, gossiping, invective, maligning, traducing, vilifying **10** calumnious, defamation, defamatory, scandalous, slandering, slanderous **11** denigration **12** belittlement, depreciation, spitefulness, vituperation **13** disparagement

backbone
4 base, grit, guts, will **5** basis, moxie, nerve, spine, spunk **6** mettle, pillar, rachis **7** resolve, support **8** mainstay, tenacity **9** character, fortitude, framework, toughness, vertebrae **10** foundation, moral fiber, resolution **12** spinal column **13** determination, steadfastness

backbreaking
6 taxing, tiring **7** arduous, onerous **8** grueling, toilsome **9** fatiguing, gruelling, laborious, punishing, strenuous, torturous, wearisome **10** burdensome, exhausting

backchat
6 banter, gossip **10** persiflage

backcomb
5 tease

backcountry
4 bush **6** sticks **7** boonies, outback **8** frontier, interior **9** boondocks **10** hinterland

backcourtman
5 guard

backdoor
5 shady **6** sneaky **7** furtive **8** stealthy

back down
4 balk **5** admit, blink, demur, welsh, yield **6** beg off, bow out, cry off, give in, give up, recall, recant, renege **7** concede, disavow, retract, retreat **8** take back, withdraw **9** surrender, weasel out **10** chicken out

backdrop
6 milieu **7** climate, context, scenery, setting **8** stage set **10** atmosphere, background **11** environment, mise-en-scène **12** surroundings

backer
4 ally **5** angel **6** patron, surety **7** sponsor **8** advocate, defender, exponent, follower, investor, promoter **9** auxiliary, guarantor, proponent, supporter **10** bankroller, benefactor, meal ticket

backfire
4 fail **5** blast **6** fizzle, go awry **7** go amiss, go wrong, implode **8** miscarry, ricochet **9** boomerang, discharge, explosion **10** disappoint, spring back **11** fall through **13** counteraction

backgammon
board section: **5** table
piece: **5** stone
wedge: **5** point

background
4 base, tone **6** milieu **7** history, scenery, setting **8** heritage, training **9** education **10** experience, supporting **13** circumstances, qualification

backhanded
7 devious, oblique **8** indirect, derisive, sneering **9** insulting, sarcastic **10** roundabout **12** disingenuous **13** condescending
compliment: **6** insult, slight **7** put-down **9** aspersion

backing
3 aid **4** help **5** aegis, funds **7** harmony, support **8** auspices **9** patronage, promotion **10** assistance **11** endorsement, sponsorship **13** accompaniment, encouragement

backland
see **backcountry**

backlash
5 slack **6** recoil **8** kickback, reaction, response, ricochet **11** retaliation **12** repercussion

backless couch
5 divan **8** recamier

backlog
4 pile **5** hoard, stock, store **6** pile up, supply **7** nest egg, reserve **9** inventory, reservoir, stockpile **12** accumulation

back of
5 abaft **6** behind **9** following

back off
see **back down**

back of the neck
4 nape **6** scruff

back out
4 quit **5** leave, welsh, yield **6** beg off, desert, give up, renege **7** forsake **8** withdraw **9** surrender

backpack
4 gear, hike **5** tramp **6** duffel, ramble **8** knapsack, rucksack **9** haversack

backpedal
see **back down**

backset
see **setback**

backside
3 bum **4** butt, duff, rear, rump, seat, tail, tush **5** fanny, hiney, stern **6** behind, bottom, breech, far end, heinie **8** buttocks, derriere, haunches **9** fundament, posterior **12** hindquarters

backslide
4 fall, sink, slip **5** lapse **6** return, revert **7** go wrong, regress, relapse **9** retrovert **10** degenerate, go downhill, recidivate **11** deteriorate

backstabbing
4 slur **5** smear **6** malice **7** calumny, scandal, slander **8** betrayal **9** treachery **10** defamation, detraction, traitorous **11** treacherous **12** belittlement, depreciation, vilification **13** disparagement

backstairs
6 covert, secret, sneaky, sordid **7** furtive **8** hush-hush **9** secretive **10** scandalous **11** clandestine, underhanded **13** surreptitious

backstop
5 fence **6** screen, uphold **7** bolster, support **8** advocate, champion, side with

back talk
3 lip **4** guff, sass **5** cheek, mouth, sauce **9** freshness, impudence, insolence **12** impertinence

backtrack
7 regress, retrace, retreat, reverse **8** turn tail

backward
3 fro **4** dull, slow, rear **5** abaft, dense **6** averse, astern, behind, stupid **7** awkward, delayed, moronic **8** ignorant, inverted, rearward, retarded, reversed, stagnant **9** benighted, dim-witted, in reverse **10** half-witted, retrograde, slow-witted, uncultured **11** thickheaded, undeveloped **12** feebleminded, simpleminded, uncultivated **13** unprogressive

backwoods
see **backcountry**

backwoodsman
4 hick, rube **5** swain, yokel **6** rustic **7** bumpkin, hayseed **9** chawbacon, hillbilly **10** clodhopper, country boy, provincial **11** mountaineer

bacon
side: 6 flitch, gammon
slice: 6 rasher

Bacon, Francis
work: 12 Novum Organum

bacteria
5 cocci **6** coccus **7** bacilli, vibrios **8** bacillus, spirilla **9** spirillum
culture medium: 4 agar
destroyer: 10 antibiotic
pathogenic: 5 E. coli

bacterial disease
6 plague, typhus **7** anthrax, leprosy, tetanus, typhoid **8** botulism, syphilis **9** gonorrhea, infection, pneumonia **10** diphtheria, meningitis **11** shigellosis

bacteriologist
American: 6 Enders (John Franklin) **7** Noguchi (Hideyo), Theiler (Max)
British: 7 Fleming (Alexander)
French: 5 Widal (Fernand) **7** Nicolle (Charles-Jean-Henri), Pasteur (Louis)
German: 4 Cohn (Ferdinand Julius), Koch (Robert) **5** Klebs (Edwin) **7** Behring (Emil von), Ehrlich (Paul), Löffler (Friedrich) **10** Wassermann (August von)
Japanese: 8 Kitasato (Shibasaburo)
Russian: 11 Metchnikoff (Elie)
Swiss: 6 Yersin (Alexandre-Emile-John)

bad
3 ill, low **4** evil, foul, sour **5** amiss, awful, lousy, wrong **6** crummy, putrid, rancid, rotten, sinful, wicked **7** harmful, hateful, hurtful, immoral, naughty, noisome, noxious, spoiled, tainted, vicious **8** damaging, dreadful, inferior, perverse, terrible, wretched **9** abhorrent, defective, execrable, injurious, loathsome, obnoxious, offensive, putrefied, reprobate, repulsive, sickening **10** disgusting, iniquitous **11** deleterious, detrimental, distasteful, intolerable **12** unacceptable **13** objectionable
comparative: 5 worse
prefix: 3 dys, mis
superlative: 5 worst

bad blood
6 enmity, hatred, rancor **7** discord, ill will **9** animosity, antipathy **10** bitterness, ill feeling

Badebec
husband: 9 Gargantua
son: 10 Pantagruel

Baden
3 spa **6** resort **9** hot spring

badge
3 pin **4** arms, logo, mark, seal, sign **5** award, honor, kudos, medal, token **6** button, emblem, ensign **7** laurels **8** accolade, hallmark, insignia **10** coat of arms, decoration **11** distinction, purple heart

badger
3 bug, nag **4** bait, goad, ride **5** annoy, brock, chivy, harry, hound, ratel **6** chivvy, harass, hassle, heckle, hector, needle, pester, plague **7** torment **8** bullyrag **9** importune

Badger State
9 Wisconsin

badinage
4 play **6** banter, joking **7** jesting, joshing, kidding, ribbing, teasing **8** backchat, chitchat, repartee **9** cross talk **10** persiflage

badland
4 wild **5** waste, wilds **6** barren, desert **7** outback **8** wildness **10** wilderneiss **11** hill country

bad mark
3 gig **7** demerit

bad mood
3 pet **4** pout, snit, sulk

bad-mouth
5 decry, trash **6** asperse, defame, malign, vilify **7** slander, traduce **8** belittle **9** denigrate, disparage

bad-tempered
4 dour, sour **5** cross, sulky, surly, testy **6** crabby, cranky, crusty, grumpy, ornery, sullen, tetchy, touchy **7** grouchy, peevish **8** choleric, petulant **9** crotchety, dyspeptic, irascible, irritable,

splenetic **10** ill-humored, ill-natured, unpleasant **11** quarrelsome **12** cantankerous, curmudgeonly, disagreeable, misanthropic

Baedeker
5 guide **6** manual **8** handbook **9** guidebook, vade mecum **10** compendium **11** enchiridion, travel guide

baffle
4 balk, foil **5** addle, block, floor, mix up, stump **6** bemuse, hinder, impede, muddle, puzzle, thwart **7** barrier, confuse, flummox, mystify, nonplus, perplex **8** befuddle, bewilder, confound **9** deflector, dumbfound, frustrate **10** circumvent, disappoint, disconcert

bafflement
9 confusion **10** bemusement, perplexity **12** bewilderment

bag
3 cop, nab, kit, net, sag, win **4** flop, grip, hook, kill, land, nail, poke, sack, tote, trap **5** biddy, bulge, catch, crone, forgo, pouch, purse, seize, shoot, snare, steal, udder **6** beldam, collar, duffel, duffle, give up, secure, valise **7** abandon, acquire, capture, satchel **8** backpack, knapsack, reticule, suitcase **9** apprehend, haversack **12** protuberance

bagatelle
6 trifle, whimsy **9** plaything

baggage
4 gear **5** hussy, stuff, tramp, trull, wench **6** burden, things, wanton **7** carry-on, effects, jezebel, luggage, parcels, trollop **8** obstacle, matériel, slattern, strumpet **9** equipment, hindrance **10** impediment, prostitute **11** impedimenta **13** paraphernalia

baggy
5 loose

Baghdad
country: **4** Iraq **11** Mesopotamia
founder: **6** Mansur
river: **6** Tigris

bagnio
4 crib, stew **7** brothel, lupanar **8** bordello, cathouse **10** bawdy house, whorehouse

bagpipe
part: **5** drone **7** bourdon, chanter
sound: **5** skirl

Bahamas
capital: **6** Nassau
island: **3** Cat **5** Abaco **6** Andros, Inagua **7** Watling **9** Eleuthera, Mayaguana **11** Grand Bahama, San Salvador **13** New Providence
neighbor: **4** Cuba

Bahrain
capital: **6** Manama
island: **6** Sitrah **7** Bahrain **10** Al Muharraq
language: **6** Arabic
monetary unit: **5** dinar
ruler: **4** amir, emir **5** ameer, hakim

bail
3 bar, dip **4** bond, flee, lade **5** ladle, scoop **6** handle, pledge, surety **7** release **8** guaranty, security, warranty **9** guarantee **10** collateral **12** recognizance

bailiff
5 reeve

bailiwick
4 area, turf, zone **5** field, realm **6** domain, sphere **7** demesne, purview, terrain **8** district, dominion, province **9** champaign, specialty, territory **10** discipline **12** jurisdiction

bailout
3 aid **6** relief, rescue **7** subsidy **11** benefaction, deliverance

bairn
3 kid, tot **4** babe, baby, tyke **5** child **6** infant

bait
3 dap, nag, try, vex **4** lure, ride, trap **5** abuse, chase, chivy, decoy, harry, hound, leger, snare, taunt, tease, tempt, worry **6** allure, badger, come-on, entice, entrap, harass, heckle, hector, lead on, molest, pester, seduce **7** beguile, torment, torture **8** bullyrag, inveigle, ridicule **9** persecute, seduction, sweetener **10** attraction, allurement, enticement, temptation
and switch: **4** lure **5** trick **8** inveigle **10** substitute

bake
3 tan **4** bask, burn, char, cook, fire, kiln **5** broil, roast, toast **6** scorch **7** scallop, scollop, swelter

baked clay
7 ceramic

baker's dozen
8 thirteen

bakers' yeast
6 leaven **9** leavening

bakery
lure: **5** aroma
offering: **3** pie **4** cake, loaf, roll **5** bread, scone, torte **6** Danish, muffin, pastry **7** cupcake **9** croissant

baking
3 hot **5** fiery **6** red-hot, torrid **7** burning **8** broiling, scalding, sizzling, white-hot **9** scorching
chamber: **4** kiln, oven

baksheesh
3 tip **4** alms **5** bribe, favor **6** grease, reward **7** payment **8** gratuity **9** emolument **12** compensation

Balaam
beast: **3** ass **6** donkey
father: **4** Beor

balance
4 rest **5** level, poise, scale, weigh **6** adjust, excess, make up, offset, set off, square, stasis **7** harmony, remains, remnant, residue **8** atone for, equalize, outweigh, residual, residuum, symmetry **9** composure, congruity, equipoise, harmonize, remainder, stability **10** compensate, counteract, difference, equanimity, neutralize, proportion, steadiness **11** consistency, countervail, equilibrium, self-control **12** counterpoise

balanced
4 even, fair **5** equal **6** offset, stable, steady **7** equable, weighed **9** equitable, impartial **10** evenhanded, harmonized, stabilized

balcony
6 piazza **7** catwalk, gallery **8** platform **9** mezzanine
section: **4** loge

bald
4 bare, nude **5** blunt, naked, plain, stark **6** barren, severe, shaven, smooth **8** glabrous, hairless, palpable, treeless **9** depilated, unadorned, uncovered **10** deforested, forthright **11** undisguised, unvarnished

baldachin
4 silk **6** canopy, fabric

Balder, Baldur
father: **4** Odin
mother: **5** Frigg **6** Frigga
slayer: **3** Höd **4** Hoth, Loke, Loki **5** Hoder, Hothr
wife: **5** Nanna

balderdash
3 rot **4** bosh, bull, bunk, tosh **5** bilge, crock, hokum, hooey **6** blague, bunkum, drivel **7** baloney, eyewash, garbage, hogwash, palaver, rubbish, twaddle **8** buncombe, claptrap, malarkey, nonsense, tommyrot **9** poppycock **10** tomfoolery **11** foolishness **13** horsefeathers

bald-faced
4 bold **6** arrant, brazen **7** blatant, defiant **8** impudent, insolent **9** audacious, shameless, unabashed **11** impertinent

baldness
8 alopecia **12** hairlessness

baldpate
7 widgeon **8** skinhead

Baldwin, James
essay: **17** Nobody Knows My Name, Notes of a Native Son
novel: **12** Fire Next Time (The) **13** Giovanni's Room **14** Another Country **21** Go Tell It on the Mountain
play: **21** Blues for Mister Charlie

Baldwin of 30 Rock
4 Alec

balefire
6 beacon

baleful
4 dire, evil **6** deadly, malign **7** direful, fateful, harmful, hostile, malefic, ominous **8** menacing, sinister **9** ill-boding, ill-omened, malignant **10** maleficent, malevolent, pernicious **11** apocalyptic, threatening **12** unpropitious

balk
3 bar, gag, jib, shy **4** beam, dash, foil, ruin **5** block, check, demur, plank, stall **6** baffle, boggle, desist, flinch, hinder, rafter, refuse, thwart **7** prevent, scruple, stumble **8** hang back, hesitate, obstruct **9** frustrate, hindrance **10** circumvent, disappoint

Balkan native
4 Serb **5** Croat **7** Bosnian, Kosovar

balky
5 loath **6** averse, ornery, mulish, unruly **7** froward, restive, wayward, willful **8** contrary, hesitant, perverse, stubborn **9** immovable, obstinate, reluctant **10** unreliable **11** intractable, wrongheaded **12** cross-grained, recalcitrant **13** uncooperative, unpredictable

ball
3 orb, wad **4** prom **5** dance, globe, round **6** sphere **8** spheroid
batted high: **3** fly
batted straight: **5** liner
high-arching: **3** lob
of thread or yarn: **4** clew
ornamental: **6** pom-pom, pompon
tiny: **7** globule

ballad
3 lay **4** poem, song
singer: **8** minstrel **10** troubadour

ballast
4 load **5** poise **6** steady **7** balance, freight **8** balancer **9** stabilize, weigh down **10** dead weight, stabilizer **12** counterpoise **13** counterweight

ballerina
6 dancer **8** coryphée, danseuse **9** toe dancer **11** dancing girl
skirt: **4** tutu
see also **dancer**

ballet
4 Agon **6** Apollo, Jewels, Sylvia **7** Giselle, Orpheus **8** Bayadère (La), Coppélia, Firebird (The), Raimonda, Raymonda, Swan Lake, Sylphide (La) **9** Fancy Free, Petrushka, Sylphides (Les) **10** Don Quixote, Nutcracker (The), Petrouchka **12** Rite of Spring (The)
company: **5** Kirov **7** Joffrey **8** Imperial
costume: **4** tutu **6** tights **7** leotard
dancer: **7** danseur **8** coryphée, danseuse **9** ballerina

for two: 9 pas de deux
handrail: 5 barre
jump: 4 jeté 9 entrechat
knee bend: 4 plié
painter: 5 Degas (Edgar)
position: 6 pointe 8 attitude 9 arabesque
step: 3 pas 8 glissade
turn: 6 chaîné 9 pirouette

Ballets ___
6 Russes

ball game
see at **game**

Ballo in Maschera composer
5 Verdi (Giuseppe)

balloon sail
9 spinnaker

ballpark figure
4 stat 5 guess 8 estimate 11 guesstimate

ball-shaped
7 globoid, globose 8 globular, spheroid 9 globulous, spherical

ball up
4 clew, daze 5 addle 6 fuddle, jumble, muddle, puzzle, tangle 7 confuse, fluster 8 befuddle, bewilder, bollix up, confound, distract, throw off 9 disorient

ballyhoo
4 hype, tout 6 blazon, herald, hoopla, hubbub, tumult 7 promote, trumpet 8 brouhaha 9 commotion, publicity 12 extravaganza

balm
4 lull 5 aroma, cream, quiet, salve, scent, spice 6 chrism, relief, remedy, solace 7 anodyne, bouquet, comfort, incense, perfume, soother, unction, unguent 8 easement, ointment 9 emollient, fragrance, redolence 10 palliative 11 consolation, restorative

balmacaan
8 overcoat

balm of Gilead
6 poplar 7 soother 8 restorer 9 balsam fir 11 restorative 12 balsam poplar

balmy
4 calm, daft, mild, nuts, soft 5 crazy, loony, nutty, potty, silly, sweet, wacky 6 gentle, insane, smooth 7 cracked, foolish, lenient, summery 8 aromatic, deranged, fragrant, perfumed, peaceful, pleasant, pleasing, redolent, soothing, tropical 9 agreeable, ambrosial, temperate

baloney
3 rot 4 bosh, bull, bunk, pish, tosh 5 bilge, hokum, hooey 6 bunkum, humbug 7 hogwash, rubbish 8 buncombe, claptrap, nonsense 9 poppycock 10 balderdash 11 foolishness

balsam poplar
9 tacamahac 12 balm of Gilead

Balthazar's gift
5 myrrh

Baltic
city: 4 Riga 7 Tallinn 8 Helsinki 9 Stockholm
native: 4 Lett, Sorb, Wend 7 Latvian 8 Estonian, Prussian 10 Lithuanian
state: 6 Latvia 7 Estonia 9 Lithuania

Baltimore team
5 Blast, Colts 6 Ravens 7 Orioles

balustrade
4 rail 5 fence 7 railing 8 banister, handrail

Balzac character
4 Pons (Cousin) 5 Bette (Cousin) 6 Goriot (Père), Vidocq 7 Chabert (Colonel), Eugénie (Grandet), Grandet, Vautrin 8 Rubempré (Lucien de) 9 Birotteau, Rastignac (Eugène de) 13 Henri de Marsay

Bambi
aunt: 3 Ena
author: 6 Salten (Felix)

bambino
3 kid, tot 4 babe, baby, tyke 5 bairn, child 6 cherub, Christ, infant, moppet, nipper 7 toddler

bamboozle
3 con 4 bilk, dupe, fool, gull, hoax, hose, scam 5 stump, trick 6 baffle, befool, diddle, puzzle 7 chicane, confuse, deceive, defraud, mislead, perplex, swindle 8 befuddle, confound, flimflam, hoodwink, throw off 9 frustrate 11 hornswoggle

ban
3 bar 5 curse, taboo 6 enjoin, forbid, outlaw 7 censure, exclude 8 anathema, prohibit, suppress 9 damnation, interdict, proscribe 10 injunction 11 forbiddance, malediction, prohibition, suppression 12 denunciation, interdiction, proscription

Ban
ally: 6 Arthur
son: 8 Lancelot

banal
4 blah, dull, flat 5 bland, corny, ho-hum, tired, trite, usual, vapid 6 common, jejune, stupid 7 clichéd, humdrum, insipid, prosaic, sapless, trivial 8 ordinary 9 hackneyed, quotidian, wearisome 10 namby-pamby, pedestrian, uninspired, wishy-washy 11 commonplace

banality
5 ennui 6 cliché, old saw, truism 7 bromide, inanity, old song 8 chestnut, monotony, prosaism 9 platitude 10 dreariness, shibboleth, triviality 11 commonplace, old chestnut, tediousness

banana
3 fei
skin: 4 peel

banana-like fruit
8 plantain

banausic
4 blah, drab, dull, poky **6** dreary, earthy, stodgy **7** humdrum, mundane, routine, secular, sensual, tedious, worldly **8** everyday, material, plodding, temporal, workaday **9** practical, pragmatic **10** monotonous, pedestrian **11** acquisitive, utilitarian **13** materialistic, uninteresting

band
4 belt, bevy, club, crew, gang, gird, sash, tape **5** bunch, corps, covey, group, horde, party, strap, strip, troop, unite **6** concur, fillet, girdle, league, outfit, ribbon, team up, troupe **7** cluster, combine, company, coterie **8** cincture, engirdle, ensemble, symphony **9** cooperate, orchestra **10** federation
horizontal: **4** fess
Mexican: **8** mariachi
neck: **6** torque
small: **5** combo

bandage
4 bind **5** cover, dress, gauze, truss **6** swathe **7** plaster, swaddle **8** compress, dressing

bandanna
8 babushka, kerchief **9** headscarf **11** neckerchief

bandeau
3 bra **5** strip **6** fillet, ribbon, stripe **7** tube top **8** swimwear **9** brassiere

banded gemstone
4 onyx

banded rock
5 agate

banderilla
4 dart

banderole
4 flag, jack **6** banner, burgee, colors, ensign, pennon, scroll **7** pennant **8** bannerol, standard, streamer

bandicoot
3 rat

bandit
6 outlaw, raider, robber, sacker **7** brigand, cateran, forager, ravager **8** marauder, pillager **9** cutthroat, desperado, holdup man, plunderer **10** freebooter, highwayman **11** bushwhacker

bandleader
7 maestro **9** conductor
famous: **3** Rey (Alvino) **4** Shaw (Artie), Ward (Hedley), Welk (Lawrence) **5** Arnaz (Desi), Basie (Count), Brown (Les), Cugat (Xavier), Faith (Percy), Heath (Ted), James (Harry), Jones (Spike), Kyser (Kay), Lewis (Ted), Lopez (Vincent), Owens (Buck), Prado (Pérez), Sousa (John Philip) **6** Cotton (Billy), Dorsey (Jimmy, Tommy), Duchin (Eddie, Peter), Herman (Woody), Hylton (Jack), Kenton (Stan), Miller (Glenn), Mingus (Charles), Nelson (Ozzie), Puente (Tito), Waring (Fred) **7** Goodman (Benny), Trotter (John Scott) **8** Calloway (Cab), Giordano (Vince), Lombardo (Guy), Whiteman (Paul) **9** Ellington (Duke), Henderson (Fletcher), Mantovani

bandolier
4 belt, sash

bandwagon
3 fad **4** chic, mode, rage **5** craze, style, trend, vogue **7** fashion

bandy
3 bat **4** flip, swap, toss **5** argue, bowed **6** banter **7** discuss, shuffle **8** exchange **9** bowlegged, pass about **11** interchange

bane
3 woe **4** pest, ruin **5** curse, death, venom, virus **6** blight, burden, plague, poison **7** bugaboo, bugbear, scourge, torment, undoing **8** anathema, calamity, downfall, nuisance **9** bête noire, contagion, destroyer, ruination **10** affliction, pestilence **11** destruction

baneful
4 dire, evil **5** fatal **6** deadly **7** fateful, harmful, hurtful, malefic, noxious, ominous **9** ill-boding, ill-omened, injurious, malignant, pestilent, unhealthy **10** disastrous, pernicious **11** apocalyptic, deleterious, pestiferous, threatening **12** pestilential, unpropitious

bang
3 bat, box, hit, pop, rap **4** bash, beat, belt, blow, boom, bump, clap, peal, push, rape, shot, slam, sock, wham, whop **5** blast, burst, crack, crash, noise, pound, punch, smack, smash, sound, vigor, whack **6** fringe, report, strike, thrill, wallop **7** collide, exactly, resound **8** smack-dab, squarely **9** explosion **10** detonation

banger
7 athlete, sausage

Bangkok native
4 Thai

Bangladesh
capital: **5** Dacca, Dhaka
city: **6** Khulna **10** Chittagong
former name: **6** Bengal
language: **7** Bengali
monetary unit: **4** taka
neighbor: **5** Burma, India **7** Myanmar
river: **5** Padma **6** Ganges, Jamuna **11** Brahmaputra

bangle
4 disk **5** charm **6** anklet, bauble **7** pendant, trinket **8** bracelet, wristlet

bang-up
3 ace **4** fine **5** dandy, primo, super **6** far-out, superb **7** capital **8** champion, fabulous, five-star, splendid, top-notch **9** excellent, first-rate **10** first-class **11** spectacular

banish
3 ban **4** oust **5** debar, eject, evict, exile, expel **6** deport, dispel, put out, run out **7** cast out, dismiss, exclude, shut out, turn out **8** drive out, relegate, send away **9** discharge, ostracize, rusticate, transport **10** expatriate **13** excommunicate

banishment
5 exile **7** banning **8** eviction **9** discharge, expulsion, ostracism **10** dispelling, relegation **11** deportation, dissolution **12** displacement

banister
3 bar **4** rail **7** railing **10** balustrade

banjoist Scruggs
4 Earl

bank
3 row **4** edge, heap, hill, mass, pile, rank, save, tier, tilt **5** amass, array, beach, coast, group, hoard, levee, marge, mound, pitch, shoal, shore, slope, stack, stash **6** coffer, dealer, invest, margin, rivage, strand **7** deposit, incline, lay away, pyramid **8** lakeside, lay aside, salt away, seafront, set aside, sock away, squirrel, treasury **9** riverside **10** repository, storehouse **11** credit union **12** squirrel away
claim: **4** lien
machine: **3** ATM

bank on
5 trust **7** believe

bankroll
4 back, fund **5** endow, funds, stake **6** pay for **7** capital, finance, sponsor, support **9** grubstake, subsidize **10** capitalize, underwrite

bankrupt
4 bare, bust, do in, ruin **5** break, drain, empty, strip, spent, use up, wreck **6** broken, divest, failed, fold up **7** deplete, deprive, exhaust, lacking, sterile **8** depleted, indebted **9** destitute, exhausted, pauperize, penniless **10** impoverish **12** impoverished

bankruptcy
4 lack, ruin **6** penury **7** failure **9** depletion, ruination, sterility, total loss **10** barrenness, exhaustion, insolvency **11** destitution, liquidation

banned
4 tabu **5** taboo **6** barred **7** illegal, illicit, tabooed **8** enjoined, verboten **9** forbidden **10** contraband, disallowed, prohibited, proscribed **11** interdicted
orchard spray: **4** Alar

banner
4 flag, jack **6** burgee, ensign, pennon **7** pendant, pennant **8** banderol, gonfalon, standard, streamer **9** banderole
Roman: **7** labarum **8** vexillum

bannerol
see **banderole**

banquet
4 feed **5** feast, roast **6** dinner, regale, repast, spread

banquette
4 seat, sofa **5** bench, shelf **8** platform, sidewalk

Banquo
5 ghost
murderer: **7** Macbeth

banshee
6 keener, wailer

bantam
3 wee **4** arch, fowl, mini, pert, runt, tiny **5** dwarf, saucy, small **6** cheeky, little, petite **8** insolent, malapert **9** combative, undersize **10** diminutive, undersized

banter
3 fun, kid, rag, rib, wit **4** fool, jest, jive, joke, josh, razz, spar **5** chaff, dally, jolly, tease **7** jesting, joshing, kidding, mockery, ragging, razzing, ribbing, teasing **8** backchat, back talk, badinage, chitchat, drollery, exchange, repartee **9** challenge, small talk **10** persiflage, pleasantry **11** give-and-take

bantling
4 babe, baby **5** bairn **6** infant **7** bambino, newborn, papoose

baptize
3 dip, dub **4** call, name, soak **5** douse, title **6** anoint, drench, purify **7** asperse, cleanse, entitle, immerse **8** christen, dedicate, initiate, sprinkle **9** designate **10** consecrate, denominate, regenerate

bar
3 ban, dam, pub, rod, tap **4** curb, dive, fess, halt, save, stop **5** block, court, estop, ingot, limit, stick, strip **6** bistro, except, impede, lounge, saloon, tavern **7** barrier, cantina, delimit, exclude, gin mill, rule out, taproom **8** alehouse, blockade, count out, obstacle, obstruct, restrict, tribunal **9** barricade, eliminate, honky-tonk, nightclub, roadhouse **11** obstruction, rathskeller **12** circumscribe, watering hole
type: **3** raw **4** cash, fern, open, roll, tiki **6** sports

Bara of silent films
5 Theda

barb
3 dig **4** dart, hook **5** quill, shaft, thorn **6** zinger

Barbados
capital: **10** Bridgetown
location: **10** West Indies

barbarian
3 Hun **4** Goth, lout, rude, wild **5** beast, crude, brute **6** savage, Vandal **7** lowbrow, uncouth **8** Visigoth **9** foreigner, Ostrogoth, primitive **10** uncultured **11** uncivilized **12** uncultivated

barbaric
4 wild 5 crude, rough 6 brutal, coarse, savage 7 beastly, boorish, brutish, loutish, uncouth 8 churlish 9 atrocious, monstrous, primitive, unrefined 11 uncivilized

barbarism
8 malaprop, rudeness, solecism 9 vulgarism, vulgarity 10 coarseness, corruption 11 impropriety, malapropism 12 backwardness, unseemliness

barbarity
7 cruelty 8 atrocity, savagery 9 brutality, depravity 10 inhumanity, savageness 11 viciousness 12 ruthlessness 13 monstrousness

barbarous
4 base, fell, grim, rude, vile, wild 5 cruel, harsh 6 brutal, fierce, Gothic, savage, unholy, vulgar, wicked 7 brutish, Hunnish, inhuman, lowbrow, uncivil, ungodly, vicious, wolfish 8 backward, fiendish, inhumane, ruthless, sadistic 9 benighted, ferocious, graceless, heartless, merciless, monstrous, primitive, tasteless, truculent 10 abominable, outlandish, outrageous, philistine, unmerciful 11 unchristian, uncivilized 12 uncultivated

Barbary ape
5 magot

Barbary state
5 Tunis 7 Algiers, Morocco, Tripoli

barbecue
5 grill, roast 7 cookout, roaster
site: 5 patio

barber
3 bob, cut 4 clip, crop, trim 5 shave, shear 6 shaver, tonsor 7 clipper, cropper 8 coiffeur 9 coiffeuse 10 beautician, haircutter 11 hairdresser, hair stylist

Barber of Seville
author: 12 Beaumarchais (Pierre-Augustin de)
character: 6 Figaro, Rosina, Rosine 7 Bartolo, Basilio 8 Almaviva, Bartholo
composer: 7 Rossini (Gioacchino) 9 Paisiello (Giovanni)

bard
4 muse, poet, scop 5 skald 8 jongleur, minstrel 9 balladist 10 Parnassian, troubadour
fictitious: 6 Ossian

Bard of Avon
11 Shakespeare (William)

bare
4 bald, mere, nude, void 5 empty, naked, shorn, stark, strip 6 barren, denude, devoid, expose, peeled, reveal, unclad, unveil, vacant 7 denuded, disrobe, emptied, exposed, uncover 8 bankrupt, disclose, stripped 9 unclothed, uncovered, undressed

barefaced
4 bald, bold, open 5 blunt, naked 6 arrant, brassy, brazen 7 blatant, glaring, obvious 8 flagrant, impudent, overbold 9 audacious, beardless, shameless, unabashed 10 unblushing 11 temerarious, unconcealed

barefoot
6 unshod 8 shoeless 9 discalced

bareheaded
7 hatless

barely
4 just 6 hardly, scarce 7 faintly 8 meagerly, scarcely

barely get (with "out")
3 eke

barely passing grade
3 dee

bargain
3 buy 4 bond, deal, pact, swap 5 agree, steal, trade, truck, value 6 barter, confer, dicker, haggle, higgle, palter, pledge 7 chaffer, compact, savings, traffic 8 closeout, contract, covenant, exchange, giveaway, good deal, huckster, markdown, transact 9 agreement, good value, negotiate, reduction 10 compromise, convention, loss leader, pennyworth 11 arrangement, transaction 13 understanding

barge
3 hoy 4 scow 5 clump, stump 6 lumber 7 galumph, stumble

baritone
4 Prey (Hermann) 5 Gobbi (Tito) 6 Bailey (Norman), London (George), Milnes (Sherrill), Terfel (Bryn), Warren (Leonard) 7 Hampson (Thomas), MacNeil (Cornell), Merrill (Robert), Tibbett (Lawrence) 8 Raimondi (Ruggero), Warfield (William)

bark
3 arf, bay, yap, yip 4 snap, woof, yelp 5 snarl 6 bellow, scrape
mulberry: 4 tapa

barkeeper
see **bartender**

barker
4 tout 5 shill 6 hawker 8 pitchman

barley-shaped pasta
4 orzo

Barlow epic
9 Columbiad

barman
see **bartender**

Barmecidal
5 empty, false 6 unreal 7 fictive 8 apparent, illusive, illusory 9 imaginary 10 chimerical, ostensible 13 insubstantial

barn
6 stable
area of: **4** loft **7** hayloft

barnacle
5 leech **7** sponger **8** hanger-on, nuisance, parasite **9** dependent, free rider **10** crustacean, freeloader

barnstorm
8 campaign

Barnum
elephant: **5** Jumbo
midget: **8** Tom Thumb
partner: **6** Bailey

barnyard
4 foul, rude **5** crass, crude, dirty, nasty **6** coarse, earthy, filthy, ribald, smutty, vulgar **7** obscene, raunchy, uncouth **8** indecent **9** tasteless **10** indelicate **12** scatological
sound: **3** baa, moo **4** oink **5** neigh

baron
4 lord, peer **5** mogul, noble **6** tycoon **7** kingpin, magnate **8** overlord **13** industrialist

baronial
5 ample, grand, noble **6** august, lordly **7** stately **8** imposing, majestic, princely **9** grandiose **10** commanding, impressive **11** magnificent, resplendent

baroque
6 florid, ornate, rococo **7** complex **8** dramatic **9** excessive, grotesque, irregular **10** flamboyant, ornamented **11** embellished, extravagant **12** ostentatious **13** overdecorated

Baroque
architect: **4** Wren (Christopher) **7** Bernini (Gian Lorenzo), Guarini (Guarino), Maderno (Carlo) **9** Borromini (Francesco)
composer: **4** Bach (Johann Sebastian) **5** Lully (Jean-Baptiste) **6** Handel (George Frideric), Rameau (Jean-Philippe), Schütz (Heinrich) **7** Corelli (Arcangelo), Purcell (Henry), Vivaldi (Antonio) **8** Albinoni (Tommaso), Couperin (François), Telemann (Georg Philipp) **9** Pachelbel (Johann), Scarlatti (Alessandro, Domenico) **10** Monteverdi (Claudio)
painter: **4** Hals (Frans) **5** Steen (Jan) **6** Claude (Lorrain), Rubens (Peter Paul) **7** El Greco, Holbein (Hans), Poussin (Nicolas), Van Dyck (Anthony), Vermeer (Jan) **8** Carracci (Agostino, Annibale, Lodovico), Ter Borch (Gerard) **9** Rembrandt (van Rijn), Velázquez (Diego) **10** Caravaggio
sculptor: **5** Puget (Pierre) **7** Bernini (Gian Lorenzo), Coustou (Guillaume, Nicholas), Pigalle (Jean-Baptiste) **8** Coysevox (Antoine), Girardon (François)

barrack
4 jeer, root **5** cheer, scoff, taunt **6** billet, casern, deride, hector **7** caserne **8** quarters

barrage
3 dam **4** fire, hail, mass **5** blitz, burst, salvo, storm, surge **6** deluge, shower, stream, volley **7** gunfire, torrent **8** drumfire, shelling **9** broadside, cannonade, crossfire, fusillade, onslaught **11** bombardment

barranca
4 bank **5** bluff, gully **6** arroyo

barrel
3 keg, tun, vat **4** butt, cask, drum, peck, race, rush, tear **5** hurry **6** firkin, hasten **8** hogshead
maker: **6** cooper
part: **4** hoop **5** stave
stopper: **4** bung
support: **6** gantry

barrelhouse
4 dive **5** hurry, joint **7** hangout **9** honky-tonk

barren
3 dry **4** arid, bare, poor **5** bleak, empty, stark, stony, waste **6** desert, devoid, effete, futile, fallow **7** badland, lacking, parched, sterile, wanting **8** desolate, heirless, impotent **9** childless, fruitless, infertile, unbearing, unfertile, wasteland **10** unfruitful, untillable **11** unrewarding **12** hardscrabble, unproductive, unprofitable

barricade
5 block, fence **7** barrier **8** blockade, pallsade **9** roadblock
of trees: **6** abatis

Barrie character
4 Hook (Capt.), John, Nana, Smee **5** Peter, Tommy, Wendy **7** Michael **8** Crichton **9** Tiger Lily **10** Tinker Bell **11** Captain Hook

barrier
see **barricade**

barring
3 but **4** save **6** bating, except, saving **7** besides, without **9** aside from, excluding, excepting, outside of **11** exclusive of

barrio
4 slum, turf, ward **6** ghetto **7** quarter, section **8** district, precinct **12** neighborhood

barrister
6 lawyer **7** counsel **8** advocate, attorney **9** counselor

barroom
3 pub **6** lounge, saloon, tavern **7** gin mill, rum room, taproom **8** alehouse, beer hall, dramshop, drinkery, groggery, grogshop **9** beer joint, roadhouse **12** watering hole

bartender
7 tapster **8** boniface **10** mixologist **12** saloonkeeper

barter
4 swap **5** trade, truck **7** bargain, traffic **8** exchange

Bartered Bride composer
7 Smetana (Bedrich)

Barth novel
7 Chimera **12** Giles Goat-Boy **13** Sot-Weed Factor (The)

Bartók of music
4 Béla

Bart Simpson
dad: 5 Homer
mom: 5 Marge
sister: 4 Lisa

Baruch
father: 6 Neriah, Zabbai
occupation: 6 scribe

basal
5 basic, vital **6** bottom, lowest **7** minimal, primary, radical **8** simplest **9** beginning, essential, undermost **10** bottommost, elementary, primordial, underlying **11** fundamental, preliminary, rudimentary **12** foundational
layer: 4 sima

base
3 bad, bed, fix, key, low **4** camp, evil, foot, fort, foul, home, mean, poor, post, prop, rest, root, seat, site, ugly, vile **5** build, cheap, dirty, found, hinge, lousy, lowly, nadir, plant, set up, sorry, stand **6** bottom, coarse, common, depend, derive, filthy, ground, humble, menial, origin, paltry, scurvy, shoddy, sleazy, sordid, source, trashy, wicked **7** bedrock, caitiff, essence, footing, ignoble, lowborn, low-down, pitiful, servile, squalid, support **8** beggarly, buttress, cowardly, garrison, inferior, pedestal, plebeian, recreant, unwashed, unworthy, wretched **9** construct, dastardly, degrading, establish, framework, loathsome, low-minded, predicate, principle **10** abominable, despicable, foundation, groundwork, substratum, unennobled **11** disgraceful, humiliating, ignominious **12** contemptible, meanspirited, substructure, underpinning

baseball
abbreviation: 3 ERA, LOB, MVP, RBI
bat wood: 3 ash
glove: 4 mitt
official: 3 ump **6** umpire
pitch: 4 drop, heat **5** curve, smoke **6** change, heater, sinker, slider, slurve **7** spitter **8** change-up, fadeaway, fastball, fork ball, knuckler, palm ball, spitball **9** brushback, screwball **11** knuckleball **12** change of pace, knuckle curve
player: 6 batter **7** baseman, catcher, fielder, pitcher **9** infielder, shortstop **10** base runner, outfielder **11** left fielder **12** right fielder **13** center fielder
reputed founder: 9 Doubleday (Abner)
term: 3 bag, bat, box, fan, fly, out, run, tag, tap, tip **4** balk, ball, base, bean, bunt, cage, deck, foul, hook, line, mitt, no-no, pill, pole, save, walk **5** alley, apple, bench, bloop, clout, count, drive, error, flare, fungo, glove, homer, liner, mound, pop-up, slide, swing **6** assist, clutch, double, dugout, groove, ground, inning, inside, pop fly, pop-out, powder, putout, relief, rubber, runner, single, strike, triple, windup **7** battery, blooper, bullpen, cleanup, diamond, floater, fly ball, home run, infield, manager, outside, pickoff, rhubarb, sidearm, squeeze, stretch **8** baseline, beanball, delivery, foul ball, grounder, keystone, no-hitter, outfield, pinch-hit, rosin bag, southpaw **9** full count, home plate, hot corner, line drive, sacrifice, strikeout, two-bagger **10** double play, frozen rope, ground ball, scratch hit, strike zone **11** knuckleball, pinch hitter, squeeze play, three-bagger
(see also **American League, National League**)

baseballer
3 Ott (Mel) **4** Alou (Felipe, Jesús, Matty, Moises), Aoki (Nori), A-Rod, Bell (George), Cobb (Ty), Cone (David), Dean (Dizzy), Fisk (Carlton), Ford (Whitey), Foxx (Jimmy), Kaat (Jim), Mays (Willie), Rice (Jim), Rose (Pete), Ruth (Babe), Ryan (Nolan), Sosa (Sammy) **5** Aaron (Henry), Anson (Cap), Banks (Ernie), Belle (Albert), Bench (Johnny), Berra (Yogi), Boggs (Wade), Bonds (Barry), Brett (George), Brock (Lou), Brown (Kevin), Carew (Rod), Clark (Will), Damon (Johnny), Davis (Mark), Green (Shawn), Grove (Lefty), Gwynn (Tony), Henke (Tom), Jeter (Derek), Kiner (Ralph), Maris (Roger), Mauer (Joe), Ortiz (David), Paige (Satchel), Perez (Tony), Perry (Gaylord), Smith (Lee), Spahn (Warren), Staub (Rusty), Tiant (Luis), Torre (Joe), Viola (Frank), Weeks (Rickie), Young (Cy), Yount (Robin) **6** Dawson (Andre), Feller (Bob), Foster (George), Franco (John), Garvey (Steve), Gehrig (Lou), Gibson (Bob, Josh, Kirk), Gooden (Dwight), Herzog (Whitey), Hodges (Gil), Hunter (Catfish), Kaline (Al), Koufax (Sandy), Lajoie (Nap), Maddux (Greg), Mantle (Mickey), Morgan (Joe), Munson (Thurman), Murphy (Dale), Murray (Eddie), Musial (Stan), Palmer (Jim), Piazza (Mike), Pujols (Albert), Raines (Tim), Ripken (Cal), Seaver (Tom), Sisler (George), Snyder (Duke), Sutter (Bruce), Sutton (Don), Thomas (Frank), Vaughn (Mo), Wagner (Honus), Walker (Larry) **7** Bagwell (Jeff), Canseco (José), Carlton (Steve), Clemens (Roger), Coleman (Vince), Collins (Eddie), Delgado (Carlos), Fingers (Rollie), Griffey (Ken), Hornsby (Roger), Hubbell (Carl), Jackson (Joe, Reggie), Johnson (Randy, Walter), Justice (David), Leonard (Buck), McGwire (Mark), Mondesi (Raul), Puckett (Kirby), Ramirez (Manny), Reardon (Jeff), Schmidt (Mike), Simmons (Al), Speaker (Tris) **8** Anderson (Sparky), Blyleven (Bert), Clemente (Roberto), DiMaggio (Joe), Guerrero (Vladimir), Martinez (Pedro), Mitchell (Kevin), Righetti (Dave), Robinson (Brooks, Frank, Jackie), Williams (Bernie, Ted), Winfield (Dave)

9 Alexander (Grover), Eckersley (Dennis), Gehringer (Charlie), Greenberg (Hank), Henderson (Rickey), Hernandez (Willie), Hershiser (Orel), Killebrew (Harmon), Mathewson (Christy), Mattingly (Don), Rodriguez (Alex), Sheffield (Gary), Slaughter (Enos) **10** Campanella (Roy), Conigliaro (Tony), Strawberry (Darryl), Valenzuela (Fernando) **11** Garciaparra (Nomar), Yastrzemski (Carl)

baseball team
see **American League; National League**

Baseball Tonight home
4 ESPN

baseboard
7 molding **8** skirting

baseless
4 idle, thin, vain **5** empty, false, wrong **6** feeble, flimsy **9** frivolous, pointless, senseless, unfounded, untenable **10** fallacious, gratuitous, groundless, inadequate, incredible, ungrounded **11** uncalled-for, unconfirmed, unnecessary, unsupported, unsustained, unwarranted **12** indefensible, contemptible, unpersuasive **13** unjustifiable

basil sauce
5 pesto

basement
6 bottom, cellar, ground **7** bedrock **10** foundation, groundwork, substratum **12** substructure

base on balls
4 walk

bash
3 bat, hit **4** belt, blow, fete, gala, slam, whop **5** beset, blast, crack, crash, knock, party, pound, smack, smash, thump, whack **6** attack, berate, have at, kegger, pummel, soiree, strike, wallop **7** blowout, lay into, shindig **8** lambaste, wingding

Bashemath
father: **7** Ishmael
husband: **4** Esau
sister: **8** Nebaioth

bashful
3 coy, shy **5** chary, mousy, timid **6** demure, modest **7** abashed, nervous **8** blushing, reserved, retiring, timorous **9** diffident, reluctant, shrinking, unassured **11** unassertive

basic
3 key **4** main **5** chief **6** bottom, innate, simple **7** capital, central, element, minimum, primary, radical **8** cardinal, inherent, rudiment **9** beginning, elemental, essential, intrinsic, primitive, principal, unadorned **10** elementary, underlying **11** fundamental **12** foundational

basically
6 au fond, mainly, mostly **7** at heart, chiefly, firstly, overall **8** in effect **9** generally, in essence, primarily

basic point
4 crux, gist, pith **5** heart **6** kernel **7** essence

basics
4 ABCs **9** rudiments **10** essentials

basilica
6 church **7** minster **9** cathedral

basin
3 dip, pan, sag **4** bowl, font, sink **6** cirque, hollow, lavabo **7** sinkage **8** sinkhole, washbowl **9** concavity **10** depression
liturgical: **5** stoup **7** piscina

basis
3 bed **4** crux, root, seat, seed **5** heart, nexus **6** bottom, ground, reason **7** bedrock, essence, footing, grounds, nucleus, premise, support, warrant **9** authority, postulate, principle **10** assumption, foundation, groundwork, substratum **11** fundamental, presumption **12** substructure, underpinning **13** justification

bask
3 sun, tan **4** loll **5** glory, revel, relax **6** lounge, wallow, welter **7** indulge **8** sunbathe **9** luxuriate

basket
6 bushel, gabion **7** pannier
angler's: **5** creel
jai alai: **5** cesta
material: **4** reed **5** osier **6** raffia
pelota: **5** cesta

basketball
inventor: **8** Naismith (James)
official: **6** umpire **7** referee
player: **5** cager, guard **6** center **7** forward **8** hoopster, swingman **10** point guard
team: **4** five **7** quintet
term: **3** gun, jam, key **4** cage, dunk, pass, trey **5** board, hoops, lay-up, press, shoot, tip-in **6** freeze, screen, tap-off, tip-off, travel **7** dribble, keyhole, rebound, throw-in, time-out **8** alley-oop, jump ball, slam dunk **9** backboard, backcourt, field goal, free throw **11** ball control
(see also **National Basketball Association**)

basketballer
3 Bol (Manute) **4** Bing (Dave), Bird (Larry), Daly (Chuck), Kerr (Johnny), Ming (Yao), Nash (Steve), Redd (Michael), Reed (Willis), Ryan (Bob), Shue (Gene), West (Jerry, Mark) **5** Allen (Ray), Barry (Rick), Blake (Marty), Brand (Elton), Brown (Hubie), Cousy (Bob), Davis (Baron), Embry (Wayne), Ewing (Patrick), Hearn (Chuck), Hyatt (Chuck), James (LeBron), Lewin (Leonard), Mikan (George), O'Neal (Shaq, Shaquille), Price (Mark) **6** Albert (Marv), Attles (Al), Baylor (Elgin), Blount (Mark), Boozer (Carlos), Bryant (Kobe), Carter (Vince), Cowens (Dave), Duncan (Tim), DuPree (David), Erving (Julius), Gervin (George), Hannum (Alex), Jasner (Phil), Jordan (Michael), Lanier (Bob), Layden (Frank),

Malone (Jeff, Karl, Moses), McAdoo (Bob), McHale (Kevin), Miller (Brad, Reggie), Parish (Robert), Payton (Gary), Pettit (Bob), Pierce (Paul, Ricky), Pippin (Scottie), Ramsay (Jack), Rodman (Dennis), Skiles (Scott), Thomas (Isiah, Kenny), Thorpe (Otis), Unseld (Wes), Vecsey (Peter), Walton (Bill), Worthy (James) **7** Barkley (Charles), Billups (Chauncey), Bradley (Bill), Dampier (Erick), Dawkins (Darryl), Edwards (James), Frazier (Walt), Garnett (Kevin), Hilario (Nene), Holzman (Red), Houston (Allan), Iverson (Allen), Jackson (Lauren), Jamison (Antawn), Johnson (Magic), Koppett (Leonard), McGrady (Tracy), McGuire (Dick), Pollack (Harvey), Russell (Bill), Rollins (Tree), Schayes (Dolph), Sharman (Bill), Taurasi (Diana), Wallace (Ben), Wilkins (Dominique) **8** Auerbach (Red), Cardinal (Brian), Harrison (Lester), Havlicek (John), Magloire (Jamaal), McCallum (Jack), Nowitzki (Dirk), Olajuwon (Akeem), Randolph (Zach), Robinson (David), Stockton (John), Thompson (Tina), Williams (Buck) **9** Blinebury (Fran), Chortkoff (Mitch), Donaldson (James), Ferdinand (Marie), Gilmartin (Joe), Holdsclaw (Chamique), Robertson (Oscar) **10** Cunningham (Billy), Stojakovic (Predrag), Williamson (Corliss) **11** Abdul-Jabbar (Kareem), Chamberlain (Wilt)

Basmath's father
7 Solomon

Basque
6 bodice
cap: **5** beret
game: **6** pelota **7** jai alai
mountains: **8** Pyrenees
province: **5** Alava **7** Vizcaya **9** Guipúzcoa

bass
3 low **4** deep **6** singer **8** cabrilla
famous: **5** Hines (Jerome), Pinza (Ezio), Ramey (Samuel), Siepi (Cesare), Tozzi (Giorgio) **6** Hotter (Hans), London (George), Morris (James) **7** Plishka (Paul), Robeson (Paul), Talvela (Martti) **8** Flagello (Ezio), Ghiaurov (Nicolai), Raimondi (Ruggero) **9** Chaliapin (Fyodor), Christoff (Boris)

Bassanio's beloved
6 Portia

bassinet
6 cradle, basket

bassist
4 Flea **5** Brown (Ray), Bruce (Jack), Haden (Charlie), Wyman (Bill) **6** Carter (Ron), Clarke (Stanley), Mingus (Charles) **8** Spalding (Esperanza) **9** Entwistle (John)

bassoon, e.g.
4 reed **8** woodwind

bassoon relative
4 oboe

bastard
5 cross **6** by-blow, hybrid **7** mongrel **9** love child **12** natural child
combining form: **4** noth **5** notho

bastardize
4 warp **5** taint **6** debase, defile **7** corrupt, debauch, degrade, deprave, pervert, pollute, vitiate **9** brutalize **10** adulterate, bestialize, demoralize, depreciate **11** contaminate

baste
3 sew **4** beat, drub, lash, mill, pelt, rail, tack, whip **5** paste, scold **6** batter, berate, larrup, pummel, revile, stitch, thrash, wallop **7** bawl out, belabor, chew out, clobber, moisten, tell off, trounce, upbraid **8** bless out, chastise **9** dress down **10** tongue-lash

bastille
4 jail **6** prison **9** bridewell

bastinado
3 bat, rod **4** bash, beat, blow, cane, club **5** birch, crack, pound, smack, smash, stick, whack **6** cudgel, paddle, strike, switch, thwack, wallop **8** bludgeon **9** truncheon

bastion
5 tower **7** bulwark, citadel, parapet, rampart, redoubt **8** fastness, fortress **10** breastwork, stronghold **13** fortification

bat
3 bag, bop, hag **4** belt, biff, blow, bust, club, slam, sock, swat, whop, wink **5** biddy, blink, crone, smack **6** cudgel, thwack **7** meander **8** bludgeon **9** flying fox, truncheon **10** knobkerrie, shillelagh **11** pipistrelle
wood: **3** ash

batch
3 lot, set **5** array, bunch, clump, crowd, group **6** bundle, clutch, parcel **7** cluster **8** quantity, shipment **10** assemblage, assortment, collection **11** aggregation **12** accumulation

bate
3 bar **4** omit **5** check **6** deduct, except, reduce **7** cut back, exclude, suspend **8** diminish, moderate, restrain, subtract

bateau
4 boat, dory **5** craft, skiff **6** dinghy, launch **7** shallop

bath
3 spa, tub **4** soak, wash **5** hydro, wells **6** shower **7** springs **8** ablution **13** watering place
powder: **4** talc

bathe
3 dip, lap, lip, sop, tub, wet **4** bask, lave, soak, soap, swim, wash **5** clean, douse, flood, rinse, flush, souse, steep **6** shower **7** cleanse, immerse, pervade, suffuse **8** irrigate

bathetic
5 mushy, soppy, stale, tired, trite **6** drippy **7** clichéd, cloying, gushing, maudlin, mawkish **9** emotional, hackneyed, schmaltzy **10** lachrymose **11** commonplace, sentimental, stereotyped, tear-jerking **13** anticlimactic, overemotional, stereotypical

bathhouse
5 sauna **6** cabana

bathing suit
6 bikini, trunks **7** bandeau, maillot

bathos
7 letdown **8** banality, comedown **9** triteness **10** anticlimax

bathroom
3 lav, loo **4** john **5** privy **6** toilet **8** lavatory, outhouse

Bathsheba
father: **5** Eliam
husband: **5** David, Uriah
son: **7** Solomon

bathtub gin
5 hooch **6** rotgut **7** bootleg **8** homebrew **9** moonshine **11** mountain dew

Batman
alias: **13** Matches Malone
bat-signal: **11** searchlight
butler: **6** Alfred
creator: **4** Kane (Bob)
film director: **5** Nolan (Christopher) **6** Burton (Tim)
film star: **4** Bale (Christian), West (Adam) **6** Carrey (Jim), DeVito (Danny), Keaton (Michael), Kilmer (Val) **7** Clooney (George), Thurman (Uma) **8** Meredith (Burgess), Pfeiffer (Michelle) **9** Nicholson (Jack)
secret identity: **10** Bruce Wayne
setting: **6** Gotham
sidekick: **5** Robin
TV star: **4** Ward (Burt), West (Adam) **8** McDowall (Roddy)
villain: **5** Chill (Joe), Joker **7** Penguin, Riddler, Two-Face **8** Catwoman, Clayface, Deadshot, Mr. Freeze **9** Mad Hatter, Poison Ivy, Scarecrow

baton
3 rod **4** club, mace, wand **5** billy, staff, stick **6** cudgel **7** war club **8** bludgeon **9** billy club, truncheon **10** nightstick

___ Bator
4 Ulan

batrachian
4 frog, toad **9** amphibian

battalion
4 army, host, unit **5** force, horde **6** legion, throng, troops **8** squadron **10** contingent, detachment

batter
4 bash, beat, drub, hurt, maul, mush **5** baste, break, dough, paste, pound, wreck **6** bruise, buffet, bung up, hitter, mangle, pommel, pummel, thrash, wallop **7** assault, belabor, bombard, clobber, coating, contuse, cripple, lambast **8** demolish, lambaste
stat: **3** RBI

battery
3 lot, set **4** body, guns **5** abuse, array, batch, bunch, clump, group, suite **6** bundle, cannon, series **7** assault, beating, cluster **8** thumping **9** artillery, onslaught **10** energy cell **11** gunnery unit
fluid: **4** acid
size: **3** AAA
terminal: **5** anode **7** cathode

battle
4 feud, fray **5** brush, clash, fight **6** action, assail, attack, combat, sortie **7** assault, contend, contest **8** conflict, skirmish, struggle **9** encounter, onslaught, scrimmage **10** engagement **11** hostilities

battle-ax
5 harpy, scold, shrew **6** virago **8** harridan **9** termagant, Xanthippe

Battle Born State
6 Nevada

battle cry
6 banzai, to arms

battlement
4 wall **7** barrier, bastion, bulwark, parapet, rampart **10** protection

battling
4 at it **5** at war

batty
3 mad **4** daft, nuts, zany **5** barmy, crazy, kooky, loony, nutty, potty, wacky **6** crazed, cuckoo, insane, maniac, screwy, whacko **7** bananas, bonkers, cracked, idiotic, lunatic **8** deranged **9** bedlamite

bauble
3 toy **5** curio **6** gewgaw, trifle **7** bibelot, novelty, trinket, whatnot **8** gimcrack, ornament **9** objet d'art, plaything **10** knickknack

Baucis's husband
8 Philemon

bauxite, e.g.
3 ore

Bavaria
6 Bayern
capital: **6** Munich
city: **8** Augsburg, Bayreuth, Würzburg **9** Nuremberg
king: **6** Ludwig
patron saint: **6** Rupert

bawd
4 drab, moll, tart **5** madam, tramp, whore **6** floozy, harlot, hooker **7** trollop **8** strumpet **10** prostitute **11** nightwalker **12** streetwalker

bawdy
4 blue, lewd **5** crude, dirty **6** coarse, erotic, ribald, risqué, smutty, vulgar **7** obscene **8** indecent, prurient **9** lecherous, offensive, salacious **10** lascivious, libidinous, licentious, suggestive

bawdy house
4 crib, stew **6** bagnio **7** brothel, lupanar **8** bordello

bawl
3 cry, sob **4** howl, roar, rout, wail, weep, yaup, yawp, yell, yowl **5** shout **6** bellow, berate, boohoo, clamor, holler, outcry, scream, shriek, squall **7** blubber, bluster

bawl out
3 wig **4** lash **5** baste, scold **6** berate, rebuke **7** censure, chew out, condemn, tell off, upbraid **8** bless out, denounce, tear into **9** castigate, dress down, reprimand **10** tongue-lash

bay
3 arm **4** cove, gulf, howl, loch, nook, wail **5** award, bight, crown, firth, honor, inlet, niche **6** harbor, laurel, recess **7** garland, laurels **8** accolade **10** decoration
Aegean Sea: **5** Anzac
Africa: **6** Walvis
Alaska: **7** Glacier
Antarctica: **3** Ice **8** Amundsen
Argentina: **6** Blanca
Atlantic Ocean: **6** Baffin
Australia: **5** Anson, Shark **6** Botany, Sharks **7** Repulse **9** Discovery
Baltic: **4** Hano, Kiel **6** Danzig, Kieler **9** Pomerania **10** Pomeranian, Pommersche
Beaufort Sea: **7** Prudhoe **9** Mackenzie
Brazil: **9** Guanabara
Bristol Channel: **10** Carmarthen
California: **5** Morro **8** Monterey, San Diego
Canada: **5** Fundy **6** Hudson **7** Repulse
Capetown: **5** Table
Caribbean Sea: **5** Limón **8** Chetumal
Central America: **7** Fonseca
Cuba: **10** Guantánamo
East River: **8** Flushing
Egypt: **6** Abu Qir
Eire: **4** Clew **7** Brandon
English Channel: **3** Tor **4** Lyme
Europe: **6** Biscay
Florida: **8** Biscayne
Greenland: **6** Baffin **8** Melville
Gulf of Alaska: **12** Resurrection
Gulf of California: **5** Adair
Gulf of Guinea: **5** Benin **6** Biafra
Gulf of Mexico: **5** Tampa **6** Mobile **7** Aransas **8** Campeche, Sarasota **9** Matagorda, Pensacola **10** San Antonio, Terrebonne **11** Atchafalaya, Ponce de Leon **12** Apalachicola **13** Corpus Christi
Gulf of St. Lawrence: **5** Bonne, Gaspé
Hawaii: **5** Koloa, Lawai
Hong Kong: **4** Deep
Honshu: **3** Ise **5** Mutsu, Osaka, Owari, Tokyo **6** Atsuta, Sagami
Indian Ocean: **6** Bengal
Indonesia: **8** Humboldt
Irish Sea: **4** Luce **7** Dundalk
Jamaica: **4** Long
Japan: **4** Tosa
Java Sea: **7** Batavia **8** Djakarta
Lake Erie: **8** Sandusky
Lake Huron: **7** Saginaw, Thunder
Lake Michigan: **5** Green **13** Grand Traverse
Lake Ontario: **11** Irondequoit
Lake Superior: **5** Huron **8** Keweenaw **9** Whitefish
Long Island Sound: **6** Oyster
Maine: **5** Casco **7** Machias **9** Penobscot
Maryland-Virginia: **10** Chesapeake **12** Chincoteague
Massachusetts: **6** Boston **7** Cape Cod **8** Buzzards, Plymouth
New Brunswick: **13** Passamaquoddy
Newfoundland: **4** Hare **5** White **7** Fortune
New Jersey: **5** Great **6** Newark **7** Raritan **8** Barnegat
New York: **7** Jamaica
North Carolina: **6** Onslow
Northwest Territories: **5** Wager **7** Repulse **8** Franklin **9** Frobisher
Oregon: **4** Coos
Puerto Rico: **5** Sucia
Quebec: **6** Ungava
Rhode Island: **12** Narragansett
Sea of Japan: **13** Peter the Great
South Carolina: **4** Bull, Long
South China Sea: **5** Subic, Subig **7** Camranh
Spain: **5** Cadiz
Strait of Gibraltar: **7** Tangier
Sydney: **6** Botany
Tasmania: **5** Storm
Texas: **7** Trinity
Tyrrhenian Sea: **6** Naples **7** Paestum
Wales: **10** Caernarfon, Caernarvon
Washington: **5** Dabob **6** Skagit
West Indies: **5** Coral

bayou
5 creek, marsh **6** slough **9** everglade, tributary
Louisiana: **5** Macon **9** Barataria, Lafourche **10** Terrebonne
Mississippi: **9** Chickasaw

Bay State
13 Massachusetts
bay window
3 gut, pot **5** oriel, tummy **6** paunch **8** potbelly **9** beer belly, spare tire **11** corporation, bread-basket
bazaar
4 fair, mall, mart, souk **6** market **7** benefit **8** emporium, exchange **11** marketplace
bazooka's target
4 tank
be
4 live **5** exist
beach
4 bank **5** Cocoa, coast, Omaha, shore **6** Malibu, Pebble, strand, Venice **7** seaside, shingle, Waikiki **8** cast away, lakeside, littoral, seashore **9** lakeshore **10** Clearwater, Copacabana, oceanfront, run aground
resort: **4** lido
___ Beach
3 Amy **4** Long, Palm, Vero **5** Dover, Miami, Omaha **6** Delray, Myrtle, Ormond **7** Daytona, Riviera, Waikiki **8** Imperial, Virginia
beached
6 ashore **7** aground **8** grounded, marooned, stranded **9** abandoned
beachhead
8 foothold
beachwear
see **bathing suit**
beacon
4 buoy, sign **5** flare, guide **6** pharos, signal **7** bonfire, lantern **8** balefire **9** watchfire **10** lighthouse, signal fire **11** inspiration, transmitter **12** guiding light
bead
3 dab, dot, pea **4** blob, drop **6** bubble **7** driblet, globule **8** spherule
beak
3 neb, nib **4** bill, nose **5** snoot, snout, spout **6** pecker, schnoz **7** schnozz **8** mandible **9** proboscis, schnozzle
beaker
3 cup **6** carafe, goblet, vessel **8** decanter
beaklike part
7 rostrum
be-all and end-all
3 sum **4** pith, root, soul **5** total, whole **6** bottom **7** essence **8** entirety, sum total, totality **9** aggregate, substance **10** prime cause **12** quintessence
beam
3 bar, ray **4** balk, boom, burn, glow, grin, I-bar, spar **5** flare, flash, gleam, joist, plank, shaft, shine, shoot, smile, strut **6** girder, lintel, rafter, signal, streak, stream, timber **7** radiate **8** transmit **9** broadcast
type: **5** laser
beaming
6 bright, joyful, lucent **7** fulgent, lambent, radiant **8** animated, cheerful, luminous **9** brilliant, effulgent, refulgent **12** incandescent
bean
3 soy, wax **4** bush, conk, dome, fava, head, lili, lima, mung, navy, pate, pole, poll, snap, soya **5** baked, brain, broad, horse, jelly, pinto **6** belfry, coffee, frijol, kidney, legume, noddle, noggin, noodle, string **7** jumping **9** headpiece **10** stringless
curd: **4** tofu
of India: **3** urd
beanery
4 café **5** diner, grill **9** hash house **10** coffee shop, restaurant **11** greasy spoon **12** luncheonette
beano
5 bingo
Bean Town
6 Boston
bear
3 lug **4** tote **5** abide, allow, beget, bring, brook, bruin, carry, stand, touch **6** accept, behave, convey, deport, endure, permit, suffer **7** comport, condone, conduct, deliver, stomach, support, sustain, swallow, undergo **8** engender, generate, shoulder, tolerate **9** procreate, propagate, reproduce, transport **10** bring forth **11** countenance
Alaskan: **5** polar **6** Kodiak
Australian: **5** koala
constellation: **4** Ursa **9** Ursa Major, Ursa Minor
genus: **5** Ursus
kind: **3** sun **5** black, brown, honey, koala, polar, sloth **6** Kodiak **7** grizzly **10** spectacled
Kipling: **5** Baloo **7** Adam-zad
lair: **3** den
relating to: **6** ursine
young: **3** cub
bearable
7 livable, tenable **8** adequate, passable **9** allowable, endurable, tolerable **10** acceptable, admissible, good enough, manageable, sufferable **11** supportable, sustainable
bearcat
5 panda **9** binturong
beard
4 dare, defy, face, fuzz **5** brave, front **6** goatee **7** outface, stubble, Vandyke **8** confront, imperial, whiskers **9** challenge, soul patch
on grain: **3** awn **6** arista

bearded
5 bushy, fuzzy, hairy **6** shaggy, tufted **7** bristly, goateed, hirsute, stubbly **8** unshaven **9** whiskered **11** bewhiskered
antelope: 3 gnu
flower: 4 iris

bear down
4 rout **5** crush, quell **6** burden, defeat, reduce, subdue **7** conquer, overrun, trample **8** overcome, vanquish **9** emphasize, overpower, overwhelm, subjugate

bearer
4 mule **5** envoy **6** coolie, porter, runner **7** carrier, courier **8** conveyor, emissary **9** go-between, messenger **11** internuncio

bear hug
6 clinch

bearing
3 air, set **4** look, mien, pose **5** poise **6** aspect, manner, stance **7** address, conduct, display, posture **8** attitude, behavior, carriage, delivery, demeanor, presence, relation **9** demeanour, direction **10** connection, deportment **11** comportment

bearish
4 curt **5** gruff, rough, terse, surly **6** cranky, ornery **7** anxious, dubious, prickly, uncouth **8** cautious, vinegary **9** crotchety, irascible **10** ill-humored **11** pessimistic **12** cantankerous

bearlike
6 ursine

bear out
4 show **5** prove **6** attest, uphold, verify **7** certify, confirm, justify **8** validate, vouch for **9** vindicate **11** corroborate, demonstrate **12** authenticate, substantiate

bear up
4 cope, fare, prop **5** brace, get by **6** endure, uphold **7** bolster, support, sustain **8** buttress, get along, maintain, underpin

beast
5 brute **6** animal **7** critter, monster, varmint **8** behemoth, creature, gargoyle

beastly
4 foul, mean, vile **5** awful, brute, feral, nasty **6** animal, brutal, odious **7** bestial, brutish, inhuman, ogreish, swinish **8** horrible, terrible **9** barbarous, revolting **10** abominable, detestable

beast of burden
3 ass **4** mule, oxen (plural) **5** camel, llama **6** donkey

beat
3 box, get, gyp, hit, lam, rap, tan, top **4** balk, belt, best, cane, dash, drub, drum, dump, flap, flog, foil, lash, lick, maul, pelt, rout, ruin, stir, tick, trim, whip, whop **5** baste, cheat, cozen, excel, forge, lay on, meter, outdo, paste, pound, pulse, punch, rhyme, route, scoop, scour, smear, spent, stick, stomp, stump, swing, throb, tread, tromp, whack, whisk **6** baffle, batter, better, buffet, cudgel, defeat, diddle, exceed, forage, hammer, larrup, muss up, patrol, pummel, rhythm, rounds, strike, thrash, thresh, thwart, wallop **7** belabor, clobber, circuit, conquer, exhaust, fashion, fatigue, lambast, lay down, prevail, pulsate, ransack, rough up, shellac, surpass, swindle, triumph, trounce **8** bewilder, bludgeon, Bohemian, lambaste, outshine, outsmart, outstrip, overcome, precinct **9** exhausted, frustrate, palpitate, pulsation, shattered, transcend, vibration **10** circumvent, pistol-whip **11** oscillation

beating
4 rout **5** lumps **6** defeat, hiding, mayhem **7** assault, setback **9** hammering, pulsation, throbbing **11** palpitation, shellacking

beat it
3 git **4** scat, shoo **5** leave, scoot, scram, split **6** get out **7** buzz off, get lost, skiddoo, vamoose

beatitude
3 joy **5** bliss **7** delight, ecstasy, rapture **8** euphoria, gladness, rhapsody **9** happiness, transport **10** exaltation, joyfulness **11** blessedness **12** blissfulness

Beatles
4 John (Lennon), Paul (McCartney) **5** Ringo (Starr) **6** George (Harrison) **7** Fab Four
album: 8 Revolver **9** Abbey Road, Sgt. Pepper **10** Rubber Soul
early: 4 Best (Pete) **9** Quarrymen (The), Sutcliffe (Stuart)
manager: 5 Klein (Allen) **7** Epstein (Brian)
producer: 6 Martin (George)
wife: 3 Ono (Yoko) **5** Linda

beatnik
5 rebel **6** hippie **7** radical **8** Bohemian **9** dissident **11** flower child **13** nonconformist

beat-up
6 shabby **7** rickety, worn-out **8** decrepit, tattered **9** crumbling **10** broken-down, ramshackle, tumble-down **11** dilapidated

beau
5 dandy, flame, lover, swain, wooer **6** steady, suitor **7** admirer, beloved **8** paramour, truelove, young man **9** boyfriend **10** sweetheart

beau ___
5 geste, ideal, monde

Beau Brummell
3 fop **5** dandy, swell **7** coxcomb, gallant **8** macaroni **11** petit-maître **12** lounge lizard

beau ideal
5 guide, model **6** mirror **7** epitome, example, paragon, pattern **8** exemplar, paradigm, standard **9** archetype **12** quintessence

Beaumarchais hero
6 Figaro

beau monde
5 elite 6 gentry, jet set 7 society 8 smart set 10 glitterati, upper crust

beauteous
see **beautiful**

beautiful
4 fair 5 bonny 6 comely, lovely, pretty 7 radiant 8 glorious, gorgeous, handsome, splendid, stunning 9 exquisite 10 attractive 11 good-looking, resplendent, well-favored

beautiful people
6 jet set 8 smart set 9 haut monde 10 glitterati 11 high society

beautify
4 deck, gild, trim 5 adorn, array, fix up, grace, prank, primp 6 bedeck, doll up 7 dress up, festoon, garland, garnish, gussy up, enhance, improve 8 decorate, ornament, prettify, spruce up 9 embellish, glamorize

beauty
5 asset, belle, dream, merit, peach 6 appeal, eyeful, looker, lovely 7 charmer, dazzler, stunner 8 knockout 9 eye-opener, good looks 10 good-looker, loveliness
mark: 4 mole
parlor: 5 salon

beaver
6 castor, rodent
home: 5 lodge
project: 3 dam
skin: 4 plew
young: 3 kit, pup

Beaver State
6 Oregon

becalm
4 hush, lull, stop 5 allay, quiet, stall, still 6 arrest, pacify, sedate, settle, soothe, steady, subdue 7 assuage, compose, quieten 11 tranquilize

because
3 for, now 4 that 5 since 7 being as, whereas 8 being how, as long as, seeing as 10 inasmuch as

because of
4 over 5 due to 7 owing to, through 8 thanks to 10 by reason of 11 on account of

Beckett work
4 Not I, Play, Watt 6 Molloy, Murphy 7 Endgame 9 Happy Days, Unnamable (The) 10 Eleutheria, Malone Dies 14 Krapp's Last Tape 15 Waiting for Godot

beckon
3 bid, nod 4 lure, wave 6 allure, entice, invite, motion, signal, summon 7 attract

becloud
3 dim, fog 4 blur, hide, veil 5 addle, bedim, befog, cloak, muddy 6 impair, darken, muddle, puzzle, shroud 7 confuse, eclipse, obscure, perplex 8 befuddle 9 obfuscate 10 overshadow

become
3 fit, get, wax 4 grow, suit 5 befit 6 go with 7 enhance, flatter 8 turn into

becoming
3 apt 5 right 6 decent, proper, seemly 7 correct, fitting 8 decorous, suitable, tasteful 9 befitting 10 attractive, flattering, well-chosen 11 appropriate, comme il faut

bed
3 cot 4 base, bunk, crib, doss, sack, twin 5 basis, berth, layer 6 bottom, cradle, double, ground, Murphy, pallet 7 bedrock, stratum, trundle 8 rollaway 10 foundation, substratum
of India: 7 charpoy

bedaub
4 coat 5 cover, smear 6 smudge 7 overlay, plaster

bedazzle
4 daze, stun 5 blind

bedcover
5 duvet, quilt 6 afghan, spread 7 blanket 8 coverlet 9 comforter 11 counterpane

bedeck
4 trim 5 adorn, array, prank 6 attire, bedaub, jazz up 7 appoint, bedizen, dress up, festoon, furbish, garland, garnish, gussy up 8 accouter, accoutre, beautify, decorate, ornament, prettify 9 embellish

bedevil
5 annoy, harry, spoil, tease, worry 6 harass, needle, nettle, pester, plague 7 hagride, provoke, torment, trouble 8 bewilder 10 exasperate

bedevilment
6 bother 7 torment, trouble 8 disorder, vexation 9 annoyance, confusion 10 irritation 11 aggravation 12 bewilderment

bedfellow
4 ally 5 crony 7 comrade 9 associate, colleague 10 compatriot 11 confederate 12 collaborator

bedim
3 fog 4 blur, mask, veil 5 befog, blear, cloud, gloom, shade 6 darken, muddle, shadow, shroud 7 becloud, confuse, eclipse, obscure 9 obfuscate

bedizen
4 deck, garb, gild 5 adorn, array, endue 6 doll up, dude up, invest, outfit, rig out 7 costume, dandify, dress up, garnish, gussy up, turn out 8 beautify, ornament 9 caparison, embellish

bedlam
3 ado 5 chaos, furor 6 asylum, clamor, furore,

hubbub, tumult, uproar, welter **7** turmoil **8** foofaraw, madhouse, upheaval **9** commotion, maelstrom **10** hurly-burly **11** pandemonium

bedlamite
3 mad, nut **4** loon, nuts **5** batty, crazy, loony **6** insane, madman, maniac **7** cracked, lunatic **8** demented, deranged

bedouin
4 Arab **5** nomad

bedraggled
5 faded, seedy **6** shabby, ragtag, untidy **7** muddied, rundown, unkempt **8** decrepit, dripping, slovenly, tattered **10** disheveled, disarrayed, disordered, down-at-heel, ramshackle, threadbare **11** dilapidated

bedridden
6 laid up, shut-in **8** confined **12** hospitalized

bedrock
4 base, core, foot, root **5** axiom, basic, basis, floor, nadir **6** bottom, depths, ground **7** footing, support **10** foundation, groundwork, substratum **11** fundamental **12** substructure, underpinning

bedroom
7 boudoir, chamber

bedspread
8 coverlet **11** counterpane

bed-wetting
8 enuresis

bee
food: **6** nectar
genus: **4** Apis
glue: **8** propolis
group: **5** swarm **6** colony
house: **4** hive **6** apiary
kind: **5** drone, mason, queen **6** mining, sewing, worker **8** quilting, spelling **9** carpenter
nest: **4** hive, skep
product: **3** wax **5** honey
relating to: **5** apian **8** apiarian
wax cells: **9** honeycomb

beechnuts
4 mast

beef
4 crab, fuss, meat, veal **5** bitch, brawn, gripe **6** grouse, muscle **7** grumble **9** bellyache, complaint, grievance
cut: **3** rib **4** loin, rump, side **5** chuck, flank, plate, round, shank **7** brisket, sirloin **10** tenderloin **11** porterhouse
grade: **5** prime **6** choice **7** utility **8** standard **10** commercial
order: **4** rare **6** medium **8** well-done

beefcake
4 hunk, stud **5** himbo

beefeater
5 guard **6** sentry, warder, yeoman

beefy
5 bulky, burly, hefty, husky, meaty **6** brawny, fleshy, robust, stocky, sturdy **7** massive **8** muscular, thickset **9** strapping **11** substantial

beehive
4 skep

Beehive State
4 Utah

beekeeper
4 Ulee **8** apiarist **12** apiculturist

beekeeping
10 apiculture

beeline
3 fly, nip, zip **4** race, whiz **5** hurry, speed **6** bullet, hasten, hustle, rocket **7** hotfoot **8** expedite, highball **10** make tracks **12** shortest path

Beelzebub
5 devil, fiend, Satan **6** diablo **7** Evil One, Lucifer, Old Nick, serpent **8** Apollyon **9** adversary, archfiend

beer
3 ale, IPA **4** bock, brew, suds **5** draft, lager, stout, weiss **6** porter **7** brewski, cerveza, pilsner **8** pilsener
vessel: **3** mug **4** toby **5** stein **6** flagon, seidel **7** tankard **8** schooner **9** blackjack
drinking place: **3** bar, inn, pub **6** saloon, tavern **7** taproom **8** alehouse **11** public house, rathskeller
ingredient: **4** hops, malt **5** yeast **6** barley
Japanese: **5** Asahi, Kirin
maker: **6** brewer
mythical inventor: **9** Gambrinus
plant: **7** brewery
relative: **3** ale
Russian: **5** kvass
Scottish: **10** barley-bree

Beeri
daughter: **6** Judith
son: **5** Hosea

beet
5 chard **6** mangel, wurzel **10** Swiss chard
family: **9** goosefoot

Beethoven, Ludwig van
birthplace: **4** Bonn
concerto: **7** Emperor
dedicatee: **5** Elise
opera: **7** Fidelio
overture: **6** Egmont **7** Leonore **10** Coriolanus
sonata: **7** Tempest **8** Kreutzer **9** Moonlight, Waldstein **10** Pathétique **12** Appassionata
symphony: **6** Choral, Eroica **8** Pastoral

beetle
3 bug, jut **5** bulge **6** insect, scarab, scurry **7** project **8** overhang, protrude, stand out, stick out
click: **6** elater **7** firefly

dung: **6** scarab **9** tumblebug
front wing: **6** elytra (plural) **7** elytron
fruit-eating: **8** curculio
insect-eating: **7** ladybug **8** ladybird
kind: **4** bean, dung, fire, June, stag **5** click, flour, grain, tiger, water **6** carpet, chafer, ground, May bug, museum **7** blister, cadelle, carabid, firefly, goldbug, goliath, June bug, vedalia **8** ambrosia, Japanese **9** longicorn, potato bug **10** cockchafer, rhinoceros
order: **10** Coleoptera
ornament: **6** scarab
snouted: **6** weevil **7** billbug **8** curculio **9** wood borer
young: **4** grub **5** larva **6** larvae (plural) **8** wireworm

Beetle Bailey dog
4 Otto

beet soup
6 borsch **7** borscht

befall
3 hap **5** ensue, occur **6** betide, chance, follow, happen **7** come off, develop, fall out **8** happen to **9** come about, eventuate, transpire

befit
4 meet, suit **6** become, go with **9** agree with, chime with **10** accord with, be right for **11** be proper for

befitting
3 apt **4** just, meet **5** happy, right **6** decent, proper, seemly **7** correct **8** becoming, decorous, suitable **10** conforming, felicitous **11** appropriate, comme il faut

befog
3 dim **4** blur, hide, veil **5** bedim, blear, cloak, cloud, muddy **6** darken, puzzle **7** becloud, confuse, eclipse, envelop, obscure, perplex **8** bewilder, confound **9** obfuscate, overcloud **10** overshadow

befool
4 dupe, gull, hoax, play **5** cozen, trick **6** delude **7** chicane, deceive, mislead **8** hoodwink **9** bamboozle, victimize **11** hornswoggle

before
3 ere **4** ante, once, till, up to **5** ahead, until **6** facing, sooner, up till **7** ahead of, already, earlier, prior to **8** formerly **9** in advance, in front of, preceding **10** previously **11** in advance of
prefix: **3** pre-, pro- **4** ante-, fore-

befoul
3 mar, tar **4** slur, soil **5** dirty, smear, spoil, sully, taint **6** defame, defile, malign, smudge **7** blacken, pollute, profane, spatter, tarnish, traduce **8** besmirch **9** bespatter, denigrate **10** adulterate **11** contaminate

befuddle
4 daze **5** addle, mix up **6** ball up, baffle, bemuse, muddle **7** confuse, fluster, perplex, stupefy **8** bewilder, confound, distract, throw off **9** disorient

befuddlement
3 fog **4** daze, haze, maze **5** mix-up **6** muddle, stupor **9** confusion **10** perplexity, puzzlement **11** distraction

beg
3 ask, bum, dun, nag, sue **4** pray, urge **5** apply, brace, cadge, crave, evade, hit on, mooch, plead, press, worry **6** adjure, appeal, call on, demand, invoke, pester **7** beseech, besiege, conjure, entreat, implore, request, solicit **8** petition, sidestep **9** importune, panhandle **10** supplicate

beget
4 bear, sire **5** breed, bring, cause, forge, hatch, spawn, yield **6** create, effect, father **7** produce **8** engender, generate, multiply, result in **9** procreate, propagate, reproduce **10** bring about

beggar
4 hobo, defy, ruin **5** tramp **6** bummer, cadger, fellow, pauper, prayer, sponge, suitor **7** moocher, sponger **8** bankrupt, deadbeat, vagabond **9** overwhelm, pauperize, schnorrer, suppliant **10** down-and-out, freeloader, impoverish, panhandler, petitioner, supplicant **11** bindle stiff, supplicator **12** street person
request: **4** alms

beggared
4 flat, poor **5** broke, needy **6** ruined **7** drained **8** bankrupt, dirt poor, indigent, strapped, wiped out **9** destitute, insolvent, penniless, penurious, tapped out **10** pauperized **11** impecunious, overwhelmed **12** dispossessed, impoverished

beggarly
3 low **4** base, mean, poor **5** cheap, lowly, nasty, petty, sorry **6** cheesy, meager, measly, paltry, scanty, scurvy, shabby, shoddy, trashy **7** ignoble, miserly, pitiful, squalid **8** pitiable, inferior, wretched **9** miserable, niggardly **10** despicable, despisable **11** ignominious **12** contemptible, parsimonious

Beggar's Opera
music: **7** Pepusch (John)
painting: **7** Hogarth (William)
text: **3** Gay (John)

beggarweed
6 dodder **9** knotgrass **11** tick trefoil

beggary
4 need, want **6** penury **7** bumming, cadging, poverty **8** mooching, pleading **9** indigence, neediness, pauperism, privation **10** meagerness, mendicancy **11** destitution, panhandling

begin
4 dawn, open, rise **5** arise, cause, dig in, enter, found, mount, set to, start **6** appear, attack, be born, broach, create, effect, emerge, get off,

induce, invent, launch, spring, sprout, tackle, take up, tee off **7** break in, emanate, jump off, kick off, lead off, prepare, usher in **8** activate, commence, embark on, engender, initiate **9** establish, instigate, institute, introduce, originate **10** embark upon, inaugurate, issue forth **11** break ground

beginner
4 colt, tiro, tyro **6** newbie, new kid, novice, rookie **7** recruit, starter, student, trainee **8** freshman, neophyte, newcomer **9** fledgling, greenhorn, novitiate **10** apprentice, catechumen, tenderfoot **11** abecedarian

beginning
4 cusp, dawn, font, rise, root **5** alpha, basal, birth, fount, get-go, onset, start **6** day one, origin, outset, primal, source, spring **7** dawning, genesis, infancy, initial, kickoff, nascent, opening **8** creation, exordium, outstart, prologue, rudiment, simplest **9** elemental, emergence, inception, incipient **10** appearance, elementary, incipiency, initiative, initiatory, opening gun, rudimental **11** origination, rudimentary **12** commencement, inauguration, introductory

begird
3 hem **4** belt, bind, ring **5** beset, fence, hem in, round **6** circle, corral, girdle, immure **7** confine, enclose, wreathe **8** encircle, engirdle, surround **9** encompass **12** circumscribe

beg off
5 demur, welsh **6** bow out, cop out, opt out, pass up, refuse, renege **7** back out, bail out, decline, drop out, pull out **8** back down, withdraw

begone
4 scat, shoo **5** leave, scram, split **6** beat it, decamp, depart, get out **7** buzz off, get lost, skiddoo, take off, vamoose **8** clear out, hightail, shove off **9** skedaddle **10** make tracks

begrime
3 tar **4** foul, soil, spot **5** dirty, muddy, smear, spoil, sully, taint **6** defile, mess up, muck up, smirch, smooch, smudge, smutch **7** blacken, corrupt, pollute, tarnish **8** besmirch **11** contaminate

begrudge
4 envy **6** resent

beguile
3 con **4** draw, dupe, fool, hoax, lure, play, snow, wile **5** bluff, charm, fleet, trick **6** allure, beckon, betray, delude, divert, enamor, entice, humbug, lead on, seduce, take in **7** attract, bewitch, deceive, enchant, engross, exploit, finesse, mislead **8** distract, hoodwink, intrigue, maneuver **9** captivate, fascinate, while away **10** manipulate **11** double-cross

beguiling
4 wily **5** false **6** artful, subtle **8** alluring, deluding, delusive, delusory **9** deceitful, deceiving, deceptive, insidious, seductive **10** bewitching, chimerical, enchanting, fallacious, misleading **11** enthralling

Behan's autobiography
10 Borstal Boy

behave
3 act, run **5** carry, react **6** acquit, be good, deport, direct, manage **7** comport, conduct, disport, perform **8** function

behavior
3 act, air, way **4** mien, tone, ways **6** action, aspect, custom, habits, manner **7** bearing, conduct **8** demeanor, presence, response **10** deportment **11** comportment

behead
4 head, kill **7** execute **9** decollate **10** decapitate, guillotine

beheaded noblewoman
8 Jane Grey (Lady) **9** Catherine (Howard) **10** Anne Boleyn

behemoth
5 giant, jumbo, titan, whale **7** goliath, mammoth, monster **8** colossus **9** leviathan **11** monstrosity

behemothic
4 huge **5** jumbo **7** mammoth, massive, titanic **8** colossal, gigantic, towering **9** Herculean, monstrous **10** gargantuan **11** elephantine

behest
3 say **4** will, wish, word, writ **5** edict, order **6** charge, demand, urging **7** bidding, command, dictate, mandate, precept, request **9** direction, enjoinder, ordinance, prescript, prompting **10** injunction **11** commandment, exhortation, instruction **12** solicitation

behind
3 can **4** butt, duff, late, next, rump, tush **5** after, fanny **6** back of, bottom, heinie **7** backing **8** backside, buttocks, derriere, trailing **9** following, posterior **10** supporting **12** subsequent to
prefix: **4** post **5** retro

behindhand
3 lax **4** late, slow **5** slack, tardy **6** in debt, remiss **7** belated, delayed, laggard, overdue **8** backward, careless, derelict **9** in arrears, negligent, unmindful **10** delinquent, neglectful, unpunctual **11** undeveloped

behold
3 see **4** espy, note, view **6** descry, notice **7** discern, observe, witness
French: **5** voilà
Latin: **4** ecce

beholden
5 bound **7** obliged **8** grateful, indebted **9** duty-bound, obligated

beholder
4 seer **6** gawker, viewer **7** watcher, witness

8 observer, onlooker, passerby **9** bystander, spectator **10** eyewitness **12** rubbernecker

beige

3 tan **4** buff, ecru **7** vanilla

being

3 ens, man **4** body, esse, life, self, soul **5** human, stuff, thing **6** entity, matter, mortal, nature, object, person, spirit **7** essence **8** creature, existent, material **9** actuality, character, existence, personage, something, substance **10** individual **11** personality **12** essentiality **13** individuality

celestial: **6** cherub, seraph

bejeweled

7 studded **8** sequined, spangled **9** encrusted **10** bespangled, gem-studded, ornamented

Bel

Sumerian counterpart: **5** Enlil

wife: **5** Belit **6** Beltis

Bel ___

3 Air **5** Paese

bel ___

5 canto **6** esprit

Bela

father: **4** Beor **8** Benjamin

son: **3** Ard

belabor

4 beat, drub, flog **5** baste, pound, scold **6** batter, berate, buffet, pummel, thrash, wallop **7** lambast, scourge, tell off, upbraid **8** chastise, lambaste, tear into **9** criticize, fulminate, overstate **10** flagellate **11** overexplain

Belarus

capital: **5** Minsk

city: **6** Homyel **7** Vitebsk **8** Mahilyow **9** Vitsyebsk

language: **7** Russian **10** Belarusian **11** Belarussian

monetary unit: **5** rubel, ruble **7** kapeyka

neighbor: **6** Latvia, Poland, Russia **7** Ukraine **9** Lithuania

river: **3** Bug **5** Neman **7** Dnieper, Pripyat

belated

4 late, slow **5** tardy **6** remiss **7** delayed, laggard, overdue **10** behindhand, behind time, unpunctual

Belau

see **Palau**

belch

4 burp, emit, gush, spew, vent, void **5** eject, eruct, erupt, expel, issue, spout, spurt, vomit **6** hiccup, irrupt **7** explode, extrude **8** disgorge **10** eructation **11** expectorate

beldam

3 hag **5** crone **8** old woman

beleaguer

3 bug, dog, hem, nag, vex **4** gnaw **5** annoy, beset, harry, hound, siege, storm, tease, worry **6** assail, attack, badger, bother, fall on, harass, invest, pester, plague **7** bedevil, besiege, hagride, put upon, set upon, trouble **8** blockade, fall upon

Belfast group

3 IRA

belfry

7 steeple **8** carillon **9** bell tower, campanile

dweller: **3** bat

Belgium

capital: **8** Brussels

city: **4** Gent **5** Ghent, Liège **7** Antwerp **9** Charleroi

ethnic group: **7** Fleming, Flemish, Walloon

language: **5** Dutch **7** Flemish

monetary unit: **4** euro

monetary unit, former: **5** franc

neighbor: **6** France **7** Germany **10** Luxembourg **11** Netherlands

plain: **8** Flanders

port: **7** Antwerp **8** Oostende

river: **4** Yser **5** Meuse **7** Schlede

sea: **5** North

sleuth: **6** Poirot (Hercule), Suchet (David)

Belgrade resident

4 Serb, Slav

belle

4 deny, hide, warp **5** color, twist **6** expose, doctor, garble, negate **7** conceal, confute, distort, falsify, gainsay, pervert, trump up **8** confront, denounce, disagree, disguise, disprove, miscolor, misstate, negative **9** disaffirm, gloss over, repudiate **10** contradict, contravene, controvert **11** dissimulate **12** misrepresent

belief

3 ism **4** idea, mind, view **5** axiom, credo, creed, dogma, faith, hunch, tenet, trust **6** assent, avowal, credit, surety, theory, thesis **7** concept, feeling, opinion, precept, surmise, theorem **8** credence, doctrine, firmness, religion, sureness **9** assurance, certainty, certitude, intuition, postulate, principle, sentiment **10** acceptance, assumption, confidence, contention, conviction, hypothesis, impression, persuasion **11** supposition

system: **5** credo

believable

5 solid, sound, valid **6** cogent, likely **7** logical, tenable **8** credible, possible, probable, reliable **9** authentic, colorable, plausible **10** convincing, creditable, persuasive, reasonable **11** conceivable, trustworthy

believe

3 buy **4** deem, hold, know **5** lap up, think, trust **6** accept, affirm, assume, credit, expect, reckon **7** fall for, imagine, profess, suppose, suspect, swallow **8** conceive, consider **10** conjecture, presuppose, understand

belittle
3 cut, pan **5** abase, abuse, decry, knock, scorn **6** deride, insult, jeer at, revile **7** cut down, put down, run down, sneer at **8** bad-mouth, derogate, diminish, discount, minimize, write off **9** criticize, discredit, disparage, dispraise, downgrade, underrate **10** depreciate, undervalue **13** underestimate

belittlement
5 abuse, scorn **7** calumny, jeering, scandal, slander **8** derision, ridicule **9** aspersion **10** backbiting, defamation, detraction **11** denigration **12** backstabbing, depreciation

Belize
capital: **8** Belmopan
city: **10** Belize City
ethnic group: **4** Maya **5** Mayan
mountain: **8** Victoria
neighbor: **6** Mexico **9** Guatemala
river: **5** Hondo
sea: **9** Caribbean

bell
4 peal **5** chime, knell **6** tocsin
set: **4** peal, ring **8** carillon

belle
5 siren **6** beauty, eyeful **7** charmer **8** knockout, ornament **11** enchantress, femme fatale

Bellerophon
father: **7** Glaucus **8** Poseidon
grandfather: **8** Sisyphus
horse: **7** Pegasus
victim: **7** Chimera

belles lettres
10 literature

belletrist
8 novelist **4** poet **6** author, writer **9** dramatist **10** playwright

bellflower
9 campanula

____ belli
5 casus

bellicose
6 ornery **7** hawkish, hostile, martial, scrappy, warlike **8** factious, fighting, militant **9** assertive, combative, truculent **10** aggressive, pugnacious, rebellious **11** belligerent, contentious, hot-tempered, quarrelsome **12** disputatious, gladiatorial

belligerence
5 fight **6** attack, enmity, rancor, spleen **7** ill will **9** hostility, militancy, petulance, pugnacity **10** aggression, antagonism, truculence **11** bellicosity **12** churlishness **13** combativeness

belligerent
6 ardent, fierce **7** fighter, hostile, scrappy, soldier, warlike, warring, warrior **8** battling, churlish, fighting, invading, militant, opponent, petulant **9** aggressor, attacking, bellicose, combatant, combative, disputant, splenetic, truculent **10** aggressive, antagonist, pugnacious **11** contentious, hot-tempered, quarrelsome **12** antagonistic, disputatious

Bellini
opera: **5** Norma **6** Pirata (Il) **8** Puritani (I) **10** Sonnambula (La)
heroine: **5** Norma
sleepwalker: **5** Amina

Bell Jar author
5 Plath (Sylvia)

bell metal
6 bronze

bellow
3 bay, cry, moo **4** bark, bawl, bray, howl, roar, rout, yowl **5** shout **6** clamor, holler **7** bluster

Bellow character
4 Rose (Billy) **5** Chick **6** Herzog (Moses E.) **7** Citrine (Charlie), Sammler (Arthur) **8** Humboldt, (Harry) **9** Henderson **10** Ravelstein (Abe), Augie March

bell ringer
6 toller **9** Quasimodo **12** carillonneur **13** campanologist

bell ringing
11 campanology

bell-shaped
11 campanulate

bell sound
4 bong, boom, ding, dong, peal, ring, ting, toll **5** chime, clang, knell **6** tinkle

bell tower
6 belfry **7** clocher **8** carillon **9** campanile

____ bellum
4 ante, post

bellwether
4 dean, lead **5** doyen, guide, pilot **6** leader **7** pioneer **8** lodestar **9** harbinger **10** forerunner **11** trend setter

belly
3 gut, pot, tum **5** tummy **6** paunch, venter **7** abdomen, midriff, stomach **9** bay window **10** front porch, midsection **11** breadbasket
Scottish: **4** wame

bellyache
4 beef, carp, crab, fret, fuss, moan, yawp **5** bitch, bleat, colic, gripe, whine **6** grouse, snivel, squawk, yammer **7** grumble **8** complain **11** let off steam **12** collywobbles

bellyacher
4 crab **5** crank **6** griper, grouch, whiner **7** grouser **8** grumbler, sourpuss **10** complainer, crosspatch, malcontent **11** faultfinder

belly button
5 navel

belong
3 fit, set **4** suit, vest **5** agree, apply, befit, chime, fit in, match, tally **6** accord, attach, become, reside **7** pertain **9** correlate, harmonize **10** correspond

belongings
3 kit **4** gear **5** goods, stuff **6** assets, estate, legacy, things **7** baggage, effects **8** chattels, movables, property **9** patrimony **11** attachments, impedimenta, inheritance, possessions **13** appurtenances

beloved
3 gra, pet **4** baby, beau, dear, idol, love **5** flame, honey, lover, swain, sweet **6** adored, steady **7** darling, dearest, dear one, doted on, sweetie **8** favorite, idolized, ladylove, old flame, precious, truelove **9** boyfriend, cherished, inamorata, treasured **10** girlfriend, heartthrob, sweetheart, sweetie pie

below
5 infra, 'neath, under **7** beneath **10** underneath
prefix: **3** sub **5** infra

belt
3 bat, bop **4** area, band, bash, biff, blow, gird, loop, ring, sash, slam, slug, sock, whap, whop, zone **5** smack, smash, strap, strip **6** begird, cestus, circle, engird, girdle, region, wallop **7** baldric, clobber, stretch **8** begirdle, ceinture, cincture, encircle, engirdle **9** bandoleer, bandolier, territory, waistband **10** cummerbund
celestial: **6** zodiac

beltway
8 ring road

Belus
brother: **6** Agenor
daughter: **4** Dido
father: **7** Neptune **8** Poseidon
mother: **5** Libya
son: **6** Danaus **7** Cepheus, Phineus **8** Aegyptus

belvedere
6 alcove, cupola, gazebo, pagoda **7** balcony, terrace **10** widow's walk **11** garden house, summerhouse, observatory

bemedaled
9 decorated **10** beribboned

bemired
4 miry, oozy **5** boggy, dirty, grimy, gummy, gunky, muddy, stuck **6** filthy, soiled, swampy **7** swamped

bemoan
3 rue **4** wail, weep **6** bewail, grieve, lament, oppose, regret **7** deplore **8** complain, object to **10** sorrow over **12** disapprove of

bemuse
4 daze **5** addle **6** absorb, muddle, puzzle **7** confuse, mystify, nonplus, perplex **8** bewilder, distract **10** disconcert

bemused
3 wry **4** lost **6** absent, remote **7** faraway **8** distrait **9** distraite **10** abstracted, distracted **11** preoccupied **12** absentminded **13** lost in thought

bench
5 court **6** settee, settle, thwart **7** counter **8** platform, prie-dieu **9** worktable
church: **3** pew
outdoor: **6** exedra
upholstered: **9** banquette

benchmark
4 norm **5** basis, gauge, guide, model, scale **7** measure **8** exemplar, paradigm, standard **9** criterion, guideline, milestone, yardstick **10** touchstone

benchwarmer
5 scrub

bend
3 arc, bow, sag **4** arch, bank, cave, curl, flex, hang, hook, lean, mold, sway, tend, tilt, turn, veer, warp **5** angle, crook, curve, round, shape, shift, stoop, twist, yield **6** compel, corner, buckle, direct, double, fasten, kowtow, subdue, submit, zigzag **7** deflect, dispose, distort, flexure, turning **8** lean over **9** curvature, deviation, genuflect **10** compromise, predispose

bendable
5 lithe **6** limber, pliant, supple **7** elastic, plastic, pliable **8** flexible, moldable **9** malleable, tractable **11** manipulable

bender
see **binge**

___ bene
4 nota

beneath
5 below, under
prefix: **3** hyp, sub **4** hypo **5** infra

___ Benedict
4 eggs

benediction
4 boon, okay **5** favor, grace **6** orison, thanks **7** benefit, benison, godsend **8** approval, blessing **9** advantage **11** approbation **12** consecration, thanksgiving

benefaction
4 alms, care, fund, gift, help **5** favor, grant **6** relief **7** charity, comfort, handout, largess, service, subsidy **8** donation, largesse, oblation, offering, windfall **9** endowment, patronage **10** assistance **12** contribution, ministration

benefactor
5 angel, donor **6** backer, patron **7** grantor, sponsor **9** supporter, sustainer **11** contributor, underwriter

beneficence
see **benefaction**

beneficent
4 kind **6** benign, caring, giving **8** generous **10** altruistic, bighearted, charitable, ungrudging **11** kindhearted, magnanimous **13** compassionate, philanthropic

beneficial
4 good **5** brave, tonic **6** benign, toward, useful **7** helpful **8** favoring, salutary, valuable **9** favorable, healthful, nurturing, wholesome **10** profitable, propitious, salubrious **12** advantageous, constructive

beneficiary
4 heir **5** donee, payee **7** grantee, heiress, legatee **8** assignee **9** inheritor, recipient

beneficiate
5 treat **6** reduce **7** prepare, process

benefit
3 aid **4** boon, gain, good, help, perk, sake **5** avail, extra, favor, serve **6** assist, behalf, better, profit, relief, succor **7** account, advance, charity, further, godsend, improve, promote, relieve, welfare **8** blessing, interest **9** advantage, well-being **10** ameliorate, fund-raiser, prosperity **11** good fortune **12** contribute to

benevolence
4 boon, gift, help **5** amity, favor, grant **6** comity, relief **7** caritas, charity **8** altruism, clemency, goodness, goodwill, humanity, kindness **10** compassion, compliment, kindliness **11** magnanimity

benevolent
4 good, kind, warm **6** caring, do-good, humane, kindly **7** helpful, liberal **8** generous, tolerant **10** altruistic, beneficent, bighearted, charitable, openhanded **11** considerate, magnanimous, warmhearted **12** eleemosynary, humanitarian **13** compassionate, philanthropic, tenderhearted

Ben Hur author
7 Wallace (Lew)

benighted
6 obtuse, unread **8** backward, ignorant, untaught **9** untutored, unwitting **10** illiterate, uneducated, uninformed, unlettered, unschooled **11** know-nothing **12** uncultivated **13** unenlightened, unprogressive

benign
4 kind, mild **6** genial, gentle, humane, kindly, mellow **7** amiable, clement **8** gracious, harmless, merciful, pleasant **9** favorable, fortunate, healthful, temperate, wholesome **10** auspicious, benevolent, charitable, forbearing, propitious, remediable **11** good-hearted **12** noncancerous

Benin
capital: **9** Porto-Novo
city: **7** Cotonou
coast: **5** Slave
ethnic group: **3** Fon **6** Fulani, Yoruba
former name: **7** Dahomey
language: **3** Fon **6** French
monetary unit: **5** franc
neighbor: **4** Togo **5** Niger **7** Nigeria **11** Burkina Faso
river: **5** Ouémé

benison
5 grace **8** blessing **11** benediction **12** consecration

Benjamin
brother: **6** Joseph
father: **5** Jacob
mother: **6** Rachel

bent
3 set **4** bias, gift **5** arced, bowed, flair, knack **6** arched, curved, intent, talent **7** decided, faculty, leaning **8** aptitude, capacity, penchant, resolute, resolved, tendency **10** determined, proclivity, propensity **11** disposition, inclination **12** predilection

benumb
4 daze, dull, stun **5** blunt, chill **6** deaden, freeze **7** petrify, stupefy **8** etherize, paralyze **10** immobilize **11** desensitize

benumbed
4 cold **6** frozen **9** unfeeling **10** insensible **11** insensitive **12** anesthetized

Beowulf
drink: **4** mead
monster: **7** Grendel

bequeath
4 gift, will **5** endow, grant, leave **6** bestow, commit, confer, devise, hand on, impart, legate, pass on **7** furnish, present **8** hand down, make over, transmit

bequest
3 lot **4** gift **5** share, trust **6** devise, estate, legacy **7** portion **8** heritage **10** settlement **11** inheritance

berate
3 jaw **4** rail, rate **5** chide, scold **6** rail at, rebuke, revile **7** bawl out, blister, chew out, condemn, reprove, tell off, upbraid **8** admonish, chastise, reproach **9** castigate, criticize, reprimand **10** tongue-lash, vituperate

berceuse
7 lullaby **10** cradlesong

bereave
3 rob **4** lose **5** seize, strip **6** divest, remove **7** deprive **8** take away **10** confiscate, disinherit, dispossess **11** appropriate, requisition

bereaved
8 mourning **9** sorrowful, sorrowing **10** distressed **11** heartbroken **13** grief-stricken

bereavement
3 rue, woe **4** loss **5** dolor, grief **6** misery, pining, regret, sorrow **7** anguish, despair, remorse, sadness **8** grieving, mourning **9** dejection, heartache **10** affliction, depression, desolation **11** deprivation, despondency, lamentation, tribulation

bereft
4 lorn **5** shorn **6** devoid, robbed **7** fleeced, forlorn, wanting **8** beggared, deprived, desolate, divested, stricken, stripped **9** destitute **10** despondent **12** disconsolate, dispossessed, impoverished

Bergen's dummy
7 Charlie (McCarthy) **8** Mortimer (Snerd)

Berger novel
12 Little Big Man

Bergman role
4 Ilsa

berm
4 path **5** ledge, mound, shelf **8** shoulder

Bermuda
capital: **8** Hamilton
territory of: **7** Britain

Bernice
brother: **7** Agrippa
father: **5** Herod
husband: **6** Polemo
lover: **5** Titus **9** Vespasian

berry
3 haw **4** acai, goji **5** cubeb, fruit, grape **7** currant, madrona, madrone **8** allspice **9** saskatoon

berserk
3 ape **4** amok **5** amuck, crazy **6** crazed, insane **7** bonkers, lunatic **8** demented, deranged, frenzied

berth
3 bed, cot **4** dock, moor, pier, port, post, quay, slip, spot **5** cabin, jetty, levee, place, wharf **6** billet, office **8** position **9** anchorage, situation **10** connection **11** appointment, compartment **13** accommodation

Bert
pal: **5** Ernie
twin: **3** Nan

beseech
see **beg**

beset
3 dog, hem, try, vex **4** gird, ring **5** harry, hem in, storm, worry **6** assail, attack, badger, circle, fall on, harass, infest, pester, plague, strike **7** assault, besiege, overrun, trouble, torture **8** blockade, encircle, fall upon, surround **9** beleaguer, encompass, overswarm

besetment
3 nag **4** bane, pain, pest **5** curse, trial **6** blight, bother, gadfly, pester, plague **7** torment **8** irritant, nuisance, vexation **9** annoyance **10** affliction, botherment, holy terror **11** aggravation, botheration

besetting
6 urgent **7** driving **8** dominant **9** obsessive **10** compelling, persistent **11** omnipresent **12** overwhelming

beside
4 near, nigh **6** next to

besides
3 too **4** also, else, plus, save **5** added, extra **6** and all, as well, beyond, except, to boot **7** barring, farther, further, without **8** as well as, likewise, moreover, more than **9** aside from, along with, exceeding, excluding, other than, otherwise, outside of **10** in addition **11** exclusive of, furthermore, not counting **12** additionally, together with

besiege
3 nag **4** ring, trap **5** beset, hem in, hound **6** assail, attack, circle, girdle, harass, pester, plague **7** assault, confine, environ, trouble **8** blockade, encircle, surround **9** beleaguer, encompass

besmear
see **smear**

besmirch
4 blot, foul, slur, soil **5** dirty, libel, stain, sully, taint **6** defile, damage, impugn, malign **7** asperse, slander, tarnish **8** disgrace, dishonor

besom
5 broom

besotted
5 dotty, drunk **7** charmed, muddled, smitten **8** enamored **9** enchanted **10** captivated, fascinated, infatuated, spellbound **11** intoxicated

bespatter
see **spatter**

bespeak
3 ask **4** book, hire, show **5** imply **6** accost, attest, desire, evince, reveal **7** address, apply to, betoken, connote, lecture, portend, request, reserve, signify, solicit, suggest, testify, witness **8** announce, approach, foretell, indicate, intimate, petition **9** preengage **10** prearrange

bespoke
8 tailored **10** custom-made

best
3 gem, top **4** beat, pick, tops **5** cream, elite, excel, model, one-up, outdo, pride, prime, prize **6** choice, defeat, exceed, finest **7** conquer, leading, optimal, optimum, paragon, premium, supreme, surpass **8** exemplar, foremost, greatest, nonesuch, outshine, outstrip, overcome **9** matchless, nonpareil, number-one, paramount,

transcend, unequaled **11** outstanding **12** incomparable
combining form: **6** aristo

bestial
4 vile, wild **5** brute, cruel, feral **6** animal, brutal, carnal, fierce, malign, savage **7** beastly, brutish, inhuman, swinish, vicious **8** depraved, inhumane **9** ferocious **10** degenerate

bestialize
4 ruin, warp **5** abase **6** debase, defile **7** corrupt, debauch, degrade, deprave, pervert, pollute, subvert, vitiate, violate **9** brutalize **10** bastardize, demoralize

bestir
3 fly, rip **4** dash, flit, goad, race, rush, spur, stir, tear, urge, wake, whet **5** rally, rouse, scoot, waken, whirl **6** arouse, awaken, hasten, hustle, kindle **8** get going, scramble **9** challenge

bestow
4 give **5** apply, award, grant **6** confer, devote, donate, impart, lavish **7** hand out, present **8** bequeath, give away
Scottish: **7** propine

bestower
5 donor, giver **6** patron **7** donator **8** altruist **9** conferrer, patroness, presenter **10** benefactor **12** benefactress **13** good Samaritan

bestrew
3 dot, sow **6** pepper, shower **7** diffuse, disject, scatter, speckle, stipple **8** disperse, sprinkle **9** broadcast, interlard **10** distribute **11** disseminate

bestride
5 mount, tower **8** dominate, loom over, straddle **9** stand over

bet
3 pot **4** ante, game, play, risk, shot **5** put on, stake, wager **6** gamble, hazard, parlay, pledge **7** lay odds, venture
racing: **6** exacta **8** perfecta, quinella, quiniela
taker: **6** bookie

___ Beta Kappa
3 Phi

beta preceder
5 alpha

Betelgeuse
4 star
constellation: **5** Orion

betel palm
5 areca

bête noire
4 bane, hate, ruin **5** trial **6** animus, horror **7** bugbear, nemesis, scourge, torment, undoing **8** anathema, aversion, downfall **9** ruination **10** black beast

bethink
4 cite, mind **6** call up, recall, remind, retain, review, revive **7** flash on **8** hark back, look back, remember, summon up **9** conjure up, recollect, reminisce **10** call to mind, retrospect

Bethuel
daughter: **7** Rebekah
father: **5** Nahor
mother: **6** Milcah
son: **5** Laban
uncle: **7** Abraham

betide
4 fall **5** break, ensue, occur **6** befall, chance, happen **7** come off, develop, fall out **8** commence **9** come about, transpire

betimes
4 anon, soon **5** early **6** pronto, seldom, timely **7** too soon **8** directly, far ahead, fitfully, promptly **9** presently **10** before long, now and then, on occasion, seasonably **11** prematurely **12** occasionally, sporadically

betoken
4 bode, omen, show, warn **5** argue, augur **6** attest, denote, hint at **7** bespeak, point to, portend, presage, promise, signify, suggest, testify, witness **8** announce, forebode, evidence, foreshow, foretell, indicate, intimate, prophesy **9** prefigure **10** foreshadow **13** prognosticate

betray
4 dupe, jilt, trap **5** rat on, snare, spill, split **6** desert, entrap, evince, finger, inform, reveal, seduce, take in, tattle, tell on, turn in, unveil **7** abandon, beguile, deceive, divulge, forsake, let down, let slip, sell out, traduce **8** blurt out, denounce, disclose, discover, evidence, give away, manifest **10** apostatize, break faith **11** double-cross

betrayal
4 leak **7** perfidy, sellout, treason **8** exposure **9** duplicity, falseness, Judas kiss, treachery **10** disclosure, infidelity, revelation **13** faithlessness

betrayer
3 rat **4** fink, nark **5** Judas **6** snitch **7** stoolie, tattler, traitor **8** apostate, defector, informer, quisling, renegade, squealer, turncoat **10** talebearer, tattletale **11** backstabber, stool pigeon

betroth
3 wed **5** marry **6** pledge **7** espouse **8** affiance

betrothal
6 pledge **8** espousal **10** engagement

betrothed
6 fiancé **7** engaged, fiancée, pledged **8** intended, plighted, promised, wife-to-be **9** affianced, bride-to-be, spoken for **10** contracted **11** husband-to-be

better
3 fix, top, win **4** beat, help, mend, more, well **5** amend, cured, elder, excel, finer, outdo **6** exceed, fitter, repair **7** advance, correct, enhance, further, greater, improve, largest, mending, rectify, success, surpass, triumph, victory **8** greatest, improved, outshine, outstrip, stronger, superior, whip hand, worthier **9** advantage, desirable, excellent, healthier, improving, meliorate, preferred, transcend, upper hand **10** ameliorate, preferable, preferably, recovering, surpassing

bettor
7 gambler, wagerer

Betty of cartoons
4 Boop

between
4 amid **5** among, twixt **6** within **7** betwixt
prefix: **5** inter, intra

betweentimes
11 at intervals

bevel
4 bias, cant **5** angle, grade, slant, slope **7** chamfer, incline, oblique **8** diagonal

beverage
3 ade, nog, tea **4** chai, cola, kava, milk **5** cider, cocoa, drink, juice, mocha, shake **6** coffee, eggnog, frappe, malted, nectar **7** potable **8** lemonade, libation, potation **9** drinkable, milk shake
alcoholic: **3** ale, gin, rum **4** beer, grog, mead, nipa, wine **5** booze, hooch, negus, sauce, stout, toddy, vodka **6** bishop, bracer, brandy, caudle, cognac, cooler, cordial, grappa, liquor, rotgut, Scotch, shandy, sherry, whisky **7** bourbon, liqueur, tequila, whiskey **8** cocktail, highball, nightcap, vermouth
Arab: **4** arak **6** arrack
Asian: **4** arak **6** arrack, kumiss **7** koumiss
Australasian: **4** kava
Balkan: **9** slivovitz
British: **5** perry, stout **6** porter
carbonated: **4** cola, soda **5** tonic **6** rickey **7** Perrier, seltzer, soda pop **8** club soda, root beer **9** ginger ale
Dutch: **7** schnaps **8** schnapps
from milk: **5** kefir **6** kumiss **7** koumiss
Greek: **4** ouzo **7** retsina
Hawaiian: **3** 'ava **4** kava
herbal: **6** tisane
Irish: **6** poteen **10** usquebaugh
Japanese: **4** sake, saki
medicinal: **6** elixir, tisane
Mexican: **6** mescal, mezcal, pulque **7** tequila
of the gods: **6** nectar
Polynesian: **4** kava
Russian: **5** kefir, kvass, vodka
South American: **4** maté **5** yerba **9** yerba maté
Scandinavian: **5** glogg
Spanish: **7** sangria
Turkish: **4** raki
West Indian: **3** rum
see also **cocktail**

Beverly Hillbillies
patriarch: **3** Jed
star: **5** Ebsen (Buddy)

bevy
3 mob **4** band, club, crew, gang, herd, knot, pack **5** bunch, covey, crowd, drove, flock, group, horde, party, swarm **6** clutch, gaggle, troupe **7** cluster, company, coterie **8** assembly **9** menagerie, multitude **10** assemblage, collection

bewail
3 rue **4** keen, moan, weep **5** mourn **6** bemoan, grieve, lament, regret **7** deplore

beware
4 heed, mark, mind, note, shun **5** avoid, watch **6** attend, notice **7** look out **8** take heed, watch out

bewhiskered
5 bushy **7** bearded, goateed, hirsute, stubbly **8** unshaven

bewilder
3 fog **4** daze, stun **5** addle, amaze, befog, mix up, stump **6** baffle, ball up, bemuse, fuddle, muddle, puzzle, rattle **7** confuse, fluster, mystify, nonplus, perplex, stumble **8** befuddle, confound, distract **9** disorient, dumbfound **10** disconcert

bewildered
5 at sea

bewilderment
3 awe **4** daze **6** wonder **8** surprise **9** amazement, confusion **10** perplexity, puzzlement **11** distraction **12** astonishment, discomfiture, stupefaction **13** consternation

bewitch
3 hex **4** draw, pull, snow, take, wile **5** charm, spell, trick **6** allure, dazzle, seduce, voodoo **7** attract, bedevil, beguile, control, delight, enchant, possess **8** demonize, ensorcel, enthrall, entrance, intrigue, overlook **9** captivate, enrapture, ensorcell, fascinate, hypnotize, magnetize, mesmerize, spellbind

Bewitched
character: **6** Darrin, Endora **7** Maurice, Tabitha **8** Samantha **9** Aunt Clara
creator: **4** Saks (Sol)
film director: **6** Ephron (Nora)
film star: **5** Caine (Michael) **6** Kidman (Nicole) **7** Ferrell (Will) **8** MacLaine (Shirley)
TV star: **4** York (Dick) **7** Sargent (Dick) **9** Moorehead (Agnes) **10** Montgomery (Elizabeth)

bewitching
4 foxy 5 siren 7 magical 8 alluring, charming, engaging, enticing, magnetic, mesmeric 9 seductive 10 attractive 12 irresistible

bewitchment
3 hex 4 jinx 5 charm, magic, spell 6 trance 7 evil eye, sorcery 8 black art, wizardry 9 conjuring 10 necromancy 11 conjuration, enchantment, incantation, thaumaturgy

beyond
4 over, past 5 above, after 6 across, beside, yonder 7 besides, further, outside 8 as well as 9 afterlife, hereafter, otherwise 10 afterworld 12 over and above
prefix: 4 meta, over, para 5 extra, hyper, super, trans, ultra 6 preter

Bhutan
capital: 7 Thimphu
ethnic group: 6 Bhutia 8 Assamese, Nepalese 9 Mongolian, Sharcrops
language: 8 Dzongkha
monetary unit: 8 ngultrum
mountain range: 8 Himalaya 13 Great Himalaya
neighbor: 5 China, India, Tibet
plain: 5 Duars

bias
4 bend, bent, skew, sway, tilt, turn 5 angle, bevel, slant 7 beveled, bigotry, dispose, distort, incline, leaning, oblique, slanted 8 diagonal, penchant, slanting, tendency 9 crosswise, inclining, influence, prejudice, proneness, viewpoint 10 diagonally, favoritism, partiality, propensity, predispose, prepossess, proclivity, standpoint, transverse 11 disposition, inclination 12 one-sidedness, predilection 13 preconception

biased
6 racist, swayed, unfair, warped 7 bigoted, colored, partial, slanted 8 disposed, inclined, one-sided, partisan, slanting 9 jaundiced, sectarian, unneutral 10 influenced, interested, prejudiced 11 opinionated, predisposed, tendentious

bibelot
5 curio 6 bauble, gewgaw, trifle 7 memento, novelty, trinket, whatnot 8 gimcrack, ornament 9 objet d'art 10 knickknack

Bible
abbreviation: 3 Col, Cor, Dan, Eph, Gal, Gen, Hab, Heb, Hos, Jas, Jer, Jon, Lam, Lev, Mal, Mic, Neh, Num, Pet, Rev, Rom, Sam, Tim, Tit 4 Deut, Ezek, Josh, Judg, Obad, Phil, Prov, Zech, Zeph 5 Chron, Thess 6 Eccles, Philem
Apocrypha book: 5 Tobit 6 Baruch, Esdras, Esther, Judith 7 Susanna 8 Manasseh, Manasses 9 Maccabees
New Testament book: 4 Acts, John, Jude, Luke, Mark 5 James, Peter, Titus 6 Romans 7 Hebrews, Matthew, Timothy 8 Philemon 9 Ephesians, Galatians 10 Colossians, Revelation 11 Corinthians, Philippians 13 Thessalonians
Old Testament book: 3 Job 4 Amos, Ezra, Joel, Ruth 5 Hosea, Jonah, Kings, Micah, Nahum 6 Daniel, Esther, Exodus, Haggai, Isaiah, Joshua, Judges, Psalms, Samuel 7 Ezekiel, Genesis, Malachi, Numbers, Obadiah 8 Habakkuk, Jeremiah, Nehemiah, Proverbs 9 Leviticus, Zechariah, Zephaniah 10 Chronicles 11 Deuteronomy 12 Ecclesiastes, Lamentations 13 Song of Solomon
part: 4 book 5 verse 7 chapter 9 testament
translator: 4 Knox (Ronald Arbuthnott) 5 Eliot (John) 6 Jerome, Luther (Martin) 7 Erasmus (Desiderius), Tyndale (William), Zwingli (Huldrych) 8 Andrewes (Lancelot), Wycliffe (John) 9 Coverdale (Miles)
version: 5 Douay 6 Coptic, Gothic, Syriac 7 Vulgate 9 Jerusalem, King James, Masoretic 10 New English, Septuagint

Biblical
animal: 8 behemoth
ascetic order: 6 Essene
battle: 7 Jericho
battle site: 10 Armageddon
brother: 4 Abel, Cain, Esau 5 Aaron
charioteer: 4 Jehu
city, town: 4 Cana, Gaza, Tyre, Zoar 5 Endor, Golan, Haifa, Joppa, Sidon, Sodom 6 Asshur, Bethel, Emmaus, Gilgal, Hebron, Mizpah, Shiloh, Smyrna, Tarsus 7 Antioch, Baalbec, Bethany, Corinth, Ephesus, Ephraim, Jericho, Magdala, Nineveh, Samaria 8 Caesarea, Damascus, Gomorrah, Nazareth, Philippi, Tiberias 9 Beersheba, Bethlehem, Capernaum, Jerusalem
coin: (see at **Hebrew**)
desert: 5 Sinai
garden: 4 Eden 8 Paradise
giant: 7 Goliath
giant slayer: 5 David
hill: 4 Zion 7 Calvary
hunter: 6 Nimrod
judge: 3 Eli 4 Ehud 6 Gideon, Samson, Samuel 7 Deborah, Jephtha 8 Jephthah
king: 3 Asa 4 Ahab, Amon, Elah, Jehu, Saul 5 David, Herod, Hiram 6 Josiah 7 Azariah, Menahem, Solomon 8 Hezekiah, Jeroboam, Manasseh, Rehoboam, Zedekiah 9 Zechariah 11 Jehoshaphat
land: 3 Nod 4 Aram, Elam, Moab, Seba 5 Judah, Judea, Magog 6 Canaan, Goshen, Israel, Judaea 7 Chaldea, Galilee, Samaria 9 Palestine
land of plenty: 6 Goshen
measure: (see at **Hebrew**)
mountain: 4 Nebo 5 Horeb, Sinai, Tabor 6 Ararat, Carmel, Gilboa, Gilead, Hermon, Moriah, Olivet, Pisgah 7 Lebanon

name: **3** Asa, Bel, Dan, Eli, Eve, Gad, Ham, Ira, Job, Lot, Uri **4** Abel, Adam, Ahab, Amon, Boaz, Cain, Elam, Enos, Esau, Jael, Jehu, Joel, John, Lael, Leah, Levi, Mark, Mary, Mica, Moab, Noah, Omar, Onan, Paul, Reba, Ruth, Sara, Saul, Seth, Shem **5** Aaron, Abner, Amram, Asher, Caleb, David, Dinah, Elias, Enoch, Ethan, Hagar, Heman, Herod, Hosea, Isaac, Jacob, James, Jared, Jesse, Jonah, Jubal, Judah, Judas, Laban, Micah, Moses, Naomi, Peter, Rufus, Sarah, Sheba, Simon, Tamar, Tubal, Uriah, Uriel, Zadok **6** Ashhur, Balaam, Baruch, Canaan, Daniel, Elijah, Elisha, Esther, Gideon, Gilead, Hannah, Hebron, Isaiah, Israel, Jeshua, Jethro, Joanna, Joseph, Joshua, Josiah, Judith, Martha, Miriam, Nathan, Nimrod, Pasach, Philip, Pilate, Rachel, Reuben, Salome, Samson, Samuel, Simeon, Thomas, Tobias
patriarch: (see at **Hebrew**)
people: **6** Kenite, Levite **7** Amorite, Edomite, Elamite, Moabite **9** Israelite
plains: **6** Sharon **7** Jericho
plotter: **5** Haman
poem: **5** psalm
pool: **8** Bethesda
priest: **3** Eli **4** Levi **5** Aaron, Annas **8** Caiaphas
Promised Land: **6** Canaan
pronoun: **3** thy **4** thee, thou **5** thine
prophet: (see **prophet**)
Psalmist: **5** David
punishment: **7** stoning
queen: **5** Sheba **6** Esther **7** Jezebel
quotation: **4** text
river: **4** Nile **6** Jordan
sacred object: **4** urim **7** thummin
scribe: **6** Baruch
sea: **3** Red **4** Dead **7** Galilee
sea monster: **9** Leviathan
spice: **5** aloes, myrrh **6** cassia **7** calamus **8** cinnamon **12** frankincense
spy: **5** Caleb
strongman: **6** Samson
temptress: **3** Eve **7** Delilah
text set to music: **8** oratorio
thief: **8** Barabbas
tree: **5** cedar
twin: **4** Esau **5** Jacob
valley: **4** Baca, Elah **6** Hinnon, Kidron, Shaveh, Siddim
wedding site: **4** Cana
weed: **4** tare
witch's home: **5** Endor

bibliography
4 list **7** catalog, history **8** book list **13** reference list

bibliopole
7 bookman **10** book dealer, bookseller

bibulous
6 spongy **7** thirsty **8** drinking **9** absorbent **10** absorptive

bicker
3 row **4** spar, spat, tiff **5** argue, clack, fight, scrap **6** gurgle, hassle **7** brabble, clatter, contend, dispute, fall out, flicker, quarrel, quibble, wrangle **8** squabble

bickering
3 row **4** at it, spat **5** brawl, run-in **6** blowup, fracas, hassle, ruckus, rumpus, strife **7** discord, dispute, quarrel, rhubarb, wrangle **8** squabble **11** altercation, embroilment

bicycle
4 bike
brake: **7** caliper, coaster
for two: **6** tandem
gear shift: **10** derailleur
rider: **6** cycler **7** cyclist
track: **9** velodrome

bid
3 ask, say, try **4** call, tell, warn, wish **5** essay, greet, offer, order **6** amount, charge, direct, effort, enjoin, invite, render, summon, tender **7** attempt, command, proffer, request, require, venture **8** endeavor, instruct, proposal **10** invitation, submission **11** proposition

biddable
4 mild **6** docile, pliant **7** amiable, pliable, willing **8** amenable, obedient, obliging **9** malleable, tractable **10** governable, manageable **11** acquiescent, cooperative, good-natured **13** accommodating

bidding
4 call, word **5** offer, order **6** behest, charge, demand, notice, tender **7** auction, command, dictate, mandate, request, summons **9** ordinance, summoning **10** injunction, invitation **11** commandment, instruction **12** proclamation

biddy
3 bag, bat, hag, hen **4** drab, trot **5** crone, witch **6** beldam **7** chicken

bide
4 live, stay, wait **5** await, dwell, tarry **6** hang in, linger, remain, reside **7** hang out, sojourn **8** continue, sit tight, tolerate **10** hang around **11** stick around

bier
10 catafalque

biff
3 bop, box, hit, jab, zap **4** bash, belt, blow, clip, ding, nail, slam, slug, sock, swat, whop **5** blast, catch, clout, pound, slosh, smack, thump, whack **6** strike, thwack, wallop

bifurcate
3 cut **4** fork **5** halve, split **6** bisect, branch, cleave, divide **8** separate **9** branch out **11** dichotomize, dichotomous

bifurcation
4 fork **6** branch **8** division **9** dichotomy, partition, radiation **10** separation

big
3 fat **4** full, hard, huge, main, mega, tall, vast **5** adult, ample, chief, great, grown, heavy, hefty, husky, large, lofty, major, proud, roomy **6** bumper, hugely **7** capital, copious, crammed, crowded, eminent, grown-up, hulking, leading, liberal, mammoth, massive, monster, notable, popular, replete, sizable, stuffed, swollen, weighty **8** colossal, enormous, generous, gracious, imposing, inflated, material, oversize, princely, spacious, swelling **9** capacious, chock-full, distended, extensive, heavy duty, humongous, important, momentous, overblown, paramount, ponderous, principal, prominent, unselfish **10** commodious, large-scale, preeminent, prodigious, voluminous **11** heavyweight, magnanimous, major-league, overflowing, significant, substantial **12** considerable **13** comprehensive, consequential
prefix: **4** mega

big bang theorist
5 Gamow (George)

Big Bertha
6 cannon **8** howitzer
birthplace: **5** Essen
manufacturer: **5** Krupp

Big ___, Cal.
3 Sur

Big Dipper
constellation: **9** Ursa Major
star: **5** Alcor, Dubhe, Merak, Mizar

bigfoot
9 Sasquatch
relative: **4** yeti

biggety
4 bold, vain, wise **5** fresh, nervy, sassy **6** cheeky, snippy, snooty, uppity **7** forward, stuck-up **8** impudent, insolent, puffed up, snobbish **9** conceited **11** smart-alecky **13** self-important

bighearted
6 giving **7** liberal **8** generous **9** forgiving **10** altruistic, benevolent, charitable, munificent, open-handed **11** magnanimous **13** compassionate

big house
3 can, jug, pen **4** coop, jail **5** clink, joint **6** cooler, lockup, prison **7** slammer **8** bastille, hoosegow, stockade **9** bridewell **11** reformatory **12** penitentiary

bight
3 arm, bay **4** cove, gulf **6** harbor

bigmouthed
4 loud, rude **8** boastful **10** boisterous

bigness
4 size **5** scale, scope **6** extent, volume **9** amplitude, immensity, magnitude **10** dimensions, importance

bigot
6 racist **8** jingoist **9** extremist, racialist **10** chauvinist **11** supremacist

bigoted
6 biased, narrow, unfair **9** hidebound, illiberal, sectarian **10** brassbound, intolerant, prejudiced **11** small-minded **12** narrow-minded

bigotry
4 bias **6** racism **9** apartheid, prejudice **10** xenophobia **11** intolerance

big shot
3 VIP **4** czar **5** celeb, mogul, nabob **6** fat cat, tycoon **7** kingpin, notable, pooh-bah **8** higher-up, luminary, top brass **9** celebrity, dignitary, personage **13** high-muck-a-muck

Big Ten team
4 Iowa (Hawkeyes) **6** Purdue (Boilermakers) **7** Indiana (Hoosiers), Rutgers (Scarlet Knights) **8** Illinois (Fighting Illini), Maryland (Terrapins), Michigan (Wolverines), Nebraska (Cornhuskers) **9** Minnesota (Golden Gophers), Ohio State (Buckeyes), Penn State (Nittany Lions), Wisconsin (Badgers) **12** Northwestern (Wildcats) **13** Michigan State (Spartans)

big-time
5 major **7** eminent, greatly, leading **8** renowned **9** high-level, important, paramount, prominent **10** large-scale **11** influential, major-league

big top
4 tent **6** circus

Big Three conference site
5 Yalta

big top
4 tent

bigwig
3 VIP **5** heavy, mogul, nabob **6** honcho, kahuna **7** kingpin, magnate, notable **8** luminary, somebody **9** dignitary, personage **11** heavy hitter, muckety-muck **13** high-muck-a-muck

bijou
3 gem **5** jewel **8** gemstone

bijouterie
6 jewels **7** jewelry **8** trinkets **10** decoration

bike
5 cycle **7** scooter **10** motorcycle **12** motorscooter

Bikini, e.g.
5 atoll

bile
4 gall **5** anger, spite, venom **6** malice, rancor, spleen **7** vitriol **8** acrimony

bilge
3 rot **4** bull, bunk, guff **5** hooey, trash **6** bunkum **7** baloney, garbage, hogwash, malarky, rubbish,

twaddle **8** claptrap, nonsense **9** poppycock, silliness **10** balderdash **11** foolishness

bilious
5 surly, testy **6** crabby, cranky, tetchy, touchy **7** grouchy, peevish **9** crotchety

bilk
3 con, gyp **4** balk, beat, dash, duck, dupe, foil, fool, hoax, hose, kite, milk, rook, ruin, scam, take **5** avoid, cheat, cozen, dodge, elude, evade, shake, shaft, skirt, stiff, trick **6** baffle, chisel, chouse, diddle, double, escape, eschew, fleece, rip off, sucker, thwart **7** deceive, defraud, prevent, swindle **8** flimflam, hoodwink, sidestep, stave off **9** frustrate **10** circumvent

bill
3 dun, fin, neb, nib, one, tab, ten **4** beak, bone, buck, chit, list, note, skin **5** check, fiver, score, visor **6** charge, damage, dollar, notice, poster, roster, tenner **7** account, charges, invoice, placard, program, sawbuck, smacker, ten-spot **8** Hamilton, mandible **9** greenback, reckoning, smackeroo, statement
part: **4** cere

billet
3 bar, bed, gig, hut, job, rod **4** post, slab, spar, spot **5** berth, board, house, ingot, lodge, place, put up, stick, strip **6** bestow, canton, harbor, office **7** quarter **8** domicile, position, quarters, vocation **9** entertain, situation **10** assignment, connection, employment, encampment, livelihood, profession, occupation **11** appointment

billet-doux
8 mash note **10** love letter

billfold
6 wallet

billiards term
3 cue **4** foot, head, jaws, kiss, long, peas, pool, race, rack, spot **5** break, carom, chalk, count, masse **6** bridge, cannon, corner, crotch, inning, miscue, nurses, pocket, stance, string **7** bricole, cue ball, cushion, ferrule, kitchen, pyramid, scratch, shooter, snooker **8** apex ball, balkline, bank shot, cue stick, dead ball, jump shot, rotation, triangle **9** clean bank, eight ball **10** chuck nurse, head string, object ball **12** balance point

billingsgate
5 abuse **6** tirade **7** obloquy **9** contumely, invective **10** revilement, scurrility **12** vilification, vituperation

billion
British: **8** milliard
combining form: **4** giga-
years: **3** eon **4** aeon

billionth
combining form: **4** nano-

bill of fare
4 menu **7** program **11** carte du jour

billow
4 mass, wave **5** bulge, cloud, surge, swell **6** puff up, roller **7** balloon, upsurge

Billy Budd
author: **8** Melville (Herman)
character: **4** Vere (Captain) **8** Claggert (John)

billy club
4 cane **5** baton **6** cudgel, paddle **8** bludgeon **9** bastinado, truncheon **10** knobkerrie, nightstick

Billy ___ Williams
3 Dee

bin
4 crib **5** frame, stall **6** bunker, hamper, trough **9** container **10** receptacle

binary
4 twin, dual **5** duple **6** double, duplex, paired **7** coupled, matched, twofold **9** dualistic

bind
3 tie **4** frap, gird, tape, wrap **5** chain, cinch, strap, tie up, truss **6** cement, commit, fasten, fetter, ligate, pinion **7** bandage, confine, enchain, shackle, trammel **8** enfetter, restrain **9** constrain, constrict, indenture

binder
4 file **5** cover **6** folder, jacket **7** wrapper **9** harvester

binding
8 required **9** mandatory, requisite **10** obligatory

bindlestiff
4 hobo

binge
3 jag **4** orgy, riot, soak, tear, time, toot **5** blast, booze, fling, party, revel, souse, spree, stint **6** bender **7** blowoff, blowout, carouse, debauch, rampage, revelry, shindig, splurge, surfeit, wassail **8** carousal, gluttony **9** bacchanal, brannigan **10** debauchery, indulgence **11** bacchanalia, celebration **12** intemperance

bingo
3 yes **5** beano **7** correct

biographer
American: **4** Edel (Leon) **5** Weems (Parson) **6** Parton (James) **7** Freeman (Douglas) **8** Bradford (Gamaliel), Sandburg (Carl) **10** McCullough (David)
English: **6** Aubrey (John), Morley (John), Walton (Izaak) **8** Strachey (Lytton)
French: **7** Maurois (André)
German: **6** Ludwig (Emil)
Greek: **8** Plutarch
Italian: **6** Vasari (Giorgio)
Roman: **9** Suetonius
Scottish: **7** Boswell (James)

biography
3 bio 4 life, obit, vita 5 diary, story 6 memoir 7 history, profile 8 obituary 11 confessions

biological category
5 class, genus, order 6 family, phylum 7 kingdom, species, variety 10 subspecies

bionomics
7 ecology

Bip's creator
7 Marceau (Marcel)

bird
3 ani, auk, daw, eme, emu, ern, iwa, jay, kea, mew, moa, owl, poe, tit, tui 4 Alca, Anas, chat, Chen, coot, crow, dove, duck, erne, guan, gull, hawk, ibis, iiwi, kite, kiwi, knot, koko, lark, loon, loro, lory, mina, moho, myna, néné, Olor, Pavo, Pica, rail, rhea, rook, ruff, shag, skua, smew, sora, Sula, swan, teal, tern, Uria, wren, Xema 5 booby, brant, buteo, cahow, crake, crane, eagle, egret, finch, galah, goose, grebe, heron, junco, macaw, merle, murre, mynah, noddy, ousel, ouzel, owlet, pewee, pewit, pipit, quail, raven, robin, stilt, snipe, stork, swift, veery, vireo 6 avocet, barbet, bulbul, canary, chough, chukar, condor, corbie, cuckoo, curlew, drongo, dunlin, falcon, fulmar, gannet, godwit, grouse, hoopoe, jabiru, jacana, jaeger, kakapo, linnet, magpie, martin, merlin, mud hen, oriole, osprey, parrot, peahen, peewit, petrel, phoebe, plover, puffin, raptor, ratite, redleg, scoter, shrike, takahe, thrush, tomtit, toucan, towhee, trogon, turaco, turkey, verdin, wigeon, willet 7 anhinga, apteryx, bittern, blue jay, bunting, bustard, buzzard, catbird, chicken, courser, creeper, dovekie, flicker, goshawk, grackle, harrier, jacamar, jackdaw, kestrel, kinglet, lapwing, limpkin, mallard, marabou, moorhen, oilbird, ostrich, peacock, pelican, penguin, pintail, quetzal, redwing, sawbill, skimmer, skylark, sparrow, swallow, tanager, tattler, titlark, touraco, vulture, wagtail, warbler, waxbill, waxwing, widgeon 8 baldpate, bellbird, blackcap, bobolink, bobwhite, brantail, caracara, cardinal, cockatoo, curassow, dabchick, dotterel, flamingo, guacharo, hornbill, killdeer, lorikeet, lyrebird, marsh hen, moorfowl, murrelet, nightjar, nuthatch, oxpecker, parakeet, pheasant, Philomel, redshank, redstart, screamer, shoebill, shoveler, starling, thrasher, throstle, titmouse, tragopan, troupial, wheatear, whimbrel, wildfowl, woodcock, woodlark 9 accipiter, albatross, broadbill, cassowary, chaffinch, chickadee, cormorant, crossbill, francolin, gallinule, guillemot, gyrfalcon, kittiwake, merganser, nighthawk, owl parrot, partridge, phalarope, ptarmigan, razorbill, sandpiper, snakebird, spoonbill, stonechat, trumpeter, turnstone 10 bufflehead, chiffchaff, flycatcher, goatsucker, kingfisher, shearwater, sheathbill 11 lammergeier, nightingale 12 whippoorwill
beak: 3 neb, nib
class: 4 Aves
colony: 5 roost 7 rookery
combining form: 5 ornis 6 ornith 7 ornitho 8 ornithes (plural)
extinct: 3 moa 4 dodo 9 aepyornis, solitaire
mythical: 3 roc 7 phoenix
relating to: 5 avian 8 ornithic
sound: 3 caw, coo 4 chip, crow, honk, hoot, peep 5 cheep, chirp, cluck, croak, quack, trill, tweet 6 squawk 7 screech, twitter
unfledged: 4 eyas 5 chick 8 nestling

birdbrain
4 clod, ditz, dodo, dolt, dope, fool, goof, loon 5 dummy, dunce, idiot, moron, ninny 6 cretin, dimwit, doofus, nitwit 7 airhead, dullard, halfwit, pinhead 8 dumbbell, imbecile, meathead, numskull 9 dumb bunny, ignoramus, numbskull, simpleton 10 nincompoop 11 featherhead

birdcage
6 aviary

bird dog
6 setter 7 pointer 9 retriever

birdlife
5 ornis 8 avifauna

bird of ——
4 prey

bird of Sindbad fame
3 roc

bird pepper
9 chiltepin

birds' eggs
study of: 6 oology

birth
4 dawn, stem 5 arise, issue, onset, start 6 create, outset, spring 7 emanate, genesis, lineage, opening 8 delivery, generate, geniture, nascence, nascency, nativity, pedigree 9 beginning, originate 10 extraction 11 parturition 12 commencement

birth-control leader
6 Sanger (Margaret)

birth flower
April: 5 daisy
August: 9 gladiolus
December: 10 poinsettia
February: 8 primrose
January: 9 carnation
July: 8 sweet pea
June: 4 rose
March: 6 violet
May: 15 lily of the valley
November: 13 chrysanthemum
October: 6 dahlia
September: 5 aster

birthmark
4 mole **5** nevus, point, trait **7** feature **13** discoloration

birth-name preceder
3 née

Birth of a Nation director
8 Griffith (D. W.)

birthright
3 due, lot **6** legacy **7** bequest, portion **8** appanage, heirloom, heritage **9** patrimony **11** entitlement, inheritance
seller: **4** Esau

birthroot
8 trillium

birthstone
April: **7** diamond **8** sapphire
August: **7** peridot **8** sardonyx
December: **6** zircon **9** turquoise
February: **8** amethyst
January: **6** garnet
July: **4** ruby
June: **5** agate, pearl **11** alexandrite
March: **6** jasper **10** aquamarine, bloodstone
May: **7** emerald
November: **5** topaz
October: **4** opal **10** tourmaline
September: **8** sapphire **10** chrysolite

biscotti flavor
5 anise

biscuit
4 rusk, snap **6** cookie **7** cracker **8** cracknel, hardtack

bishop
district: **7** diocese
headdress: **5** miter, mitre
seat of office: **3** see
skullcap: **9** zucchetto
staff: **7** crosier, crozier
throne: **8** cathedra

Bishop Desmond
4 Tutu

bishopric
3 see **7** diocese

bison
European: **6** wisent **7** aurochs
family: **7** Bovidae
North American: **7** buffalo

bistered
4 dark **5** brown, dusky, swart, tawny **6** brunet, tanned **7** swarthy **8** brunette **11** dark-skinned

bistro
3 bar, pub **4** café **5** joint **6** nitery, tavern **7** barroom, cabaret, hot spot, niterie, taproom **8** snack bar **9** coffee bar, nightclub, night spot **10** coffee shop **11** rathskeller **13** watering place

bit
3 dab, dot, end, jot, tad **4** atom, dash, drop, iota, lump, mite, part, rein, tick, time, whit **5** borer, flake, grain, minim, pinch, scrap, shard, shred, slice, space, speck, spell, trace, while **6** minute, moment, morsel, rather, second, smidge **7** portion, segment, smidgen, stretch, trickle **8** fraction, fragment, molecule, mouthful, particle, smidgeon, somewhat

bit by bit
6 evenly **9** by degrees, gradually, piecemeal **12** continuously **13** slow and steady

bitch goddess
7 success

bite
3 cut, eat, lot, nip **4** chaw, chew, edge, etch, food, gnaw, kick, meal, nosh, pain, part, rust, snap, tang, tapa, zest **5** champ, chomp, erode, munch, piece, quota, share, slice, snack, stink, taste, tooth **6** crunch, morsel, nibble **7** corrode, eat away, eat into, engrave, portion **8** mouthful **9** masticate, occlusion

biting
3 raw **4** cold **5** bleak, crisp, harsh, nippy, sharp **6** bitter, severe **7** acerbic, caustic, cutting, mordant, satiric **8** freezing, incisive, piercing, scathing **9** sarcastic, trenchant **11** penetrating

bit part
5 cameo

bitter
4 acid, tart **5** acerb, acrid, harsh, sharp **6** severe **7** acerbic, caustic, galling, hostile, painful **8** grievous, virulent **9** rancorous, vitriolic **11** acrimonious

bitterness
4 gall **6** rancor **7** ill will **8** acridity, acrimony, asperity, coldness **9** animosity, antipathy **10** resentment

bittersweet
4 vine **8** poignant **10** nightshade

bitumen
3 tar **5** pitch **7** asphalt **8** blacktop

bivalve
4 clam, spat **6** cockle, mussel, oyster **7** geoduck, mollusc, mollusk, piddock, scallop **9** lampshell **10** brachiopod

bivouac
4 camp, tent **5** étape **6** billet, encamp, laager, maroon **7** shelter, sojourn **10** encampment

bizarre
3 odd **5** antic, outré, queer, weird **7** curious, oddball, strange, uncanny, unusual **8** abnormal, atypical, freakish, peculiar, quixotic, singular **9** anomalous, eccentric, fantastic, grotesque, unearthly, unnatural **10** outlandish, outrageous **11** extravagant

bizarrerie
5 freak **6** oddity **7** anomaly, caprice, oddness **9** curiosity, weirdness **10** aberration

Bizet opera
6 Carmen

blab
3 gab, gas, jaw, yak **4** chat, leak, sing, talk, tell **5** run on, spill **6** babble, betray, burble, gabble, gossip, inform, jabber, reveal, snitch, squeal, tattle, tell on, yammer **7** blather, chatter, divulge, let slip, palaver, prattle **8** blurt out, disclose, give away, go public

blabber
3 gab, rat **4** chat, fink **5** clack, drool, prate **6** babble, canary, drivel, gabber, gabble, gossip, jabber, magpie, prater, ramble **7** blather, chatter, palaver, prattle, twaddle **8** idle talk, jabberer, prattler **9** chatterer **10** chatterbox, tattletale

blabbermouth
3 rat **4** fink **5** yenta **6** canary, gabber, gossip, magpie, prater, snitch **7** windbag **8** busybody, jabberer, prattler **10** chatterbox, talebearer, tattletale **11** stool pigeon

black
3 jet **4** ebon, inky, noir, onyx **5** ebony, raven, sable **6** pitchy **8** charcoal, funereal **9** pitch-dark
combining form: **3** mel **4** atro, mela, melo **5** melam, melan **6** melano

black-and-white whale
4 orca

blackball
3 bar **4** veto, shun, snub **5** block, spurn **6** ice out, refuse, reject, strike **7** boycott, exclude, keep out, rule out **9** interdict, ostracize **11** vote against

black bass
7 sunfish

black beast
see **bête noire**

Black Beauty author
6 Sewell (Anna)

black cohosh
7 bugbane

black crappie
7 sunfish **10** calico bass

black cuckoo
3 ani

black death
6 plague **13** bubonic plague

black diamond
4 coal **8** hematite **9** carbonado

blacken
3 dim, fog, ink, tar **4** blot, burn, char, sear, slur, soil, soot **5** cloud, libel, shade, singe, smear, sully, taint **6** bruise, darken, defame, defile, malign, scorch, vilify **7** asperse, cloud up, eclipse, slander, traduce **8** besmirch, dishonor **10** calumniate

black eye
4 blot, onus, slur **5** stain **6** bruise, defeat, shiner, stigma **7** setback

blackfish
5 whale **6** tautog **10** pilot whale

Black Forest
11 Schwarzwald
city: **10** Baden-Baden
peak: **8** Feldberg
product: **11** cuckoo clock
river: **5** Rhein, Rhine **6** Danube, Neckar

black gold
3 oil **9** petroleum

blackguard
4 heel, punk **5** abuse, cheat, knave, rogue **6** rascal **7** hoodlum, lowlife, ruffian, villain **8** hooligan, scalawag **9** charlatan, miscreant, reprobate, scoundrel **10** delinquent, mountebank **11** rapscallion

blackhead
3 zit **4** spot **5** sebum **6** pimple **10** larval clam

blackjack
3 oak, sap **4** bash, club, cosh **6** coerce **7** pontoon, tankard **8** bludgeon **9** twenty-one, vingt-et-un **10** sphalerite

black lead
8 graphite

black letter
6 Gothic **7** Fraktur **10** Old English

blacklist
3 bar **4** oust **5** expel, purge, smear **6** banish, impugn **7** boycott, condemn, exclude, shut out **8** denounce **9** ostracize, proscribe **10** stigmatize

blackmail
5 bleed **6** extort, payoff **7** milking, squeeze **8** chantage, coercion **9** extortion, hush money, shake down

Blackmore novel
10 Lorna Doone

black out
4 edit, wipe **5** annul, erase, faint, swoon **6** cancel, censor, cut off, darken, delete, efface, excise **7** conceal, eclipse, expunge **8** collapse, make dark, sanitize, suppress **9** eradicate, expurgate **10** blue-pencil, obliterate

blackpoll
7 warbler

Black Prince
6 Edward

Black Sea
arm: **4** Azov
city: **5** Yalta **6** Odessa **9** Constanta
peninsula: **6** Crimea **7** Crimean

Blackshirt
7 fascist

blacksmith
6 forger 7 farrier, striker 10 horseshoer

blacktail
8 mule deer

blackthorn
4 plum, sloe

black widow
6 spider

bladder
3 sac 4 cyst 5 pouch 7 blister, vacuole 7 vesicle
gall: 9 cholecyst

blade
4 beau, buck, dude, edge, leaf, shiv 5 knife, sword 6 runner 9 swordsman

blah
4 bosh, dull, flat, tame 5 ho-hum, hooey, tired, vapid 6 boring, bunkum, dreary, humbug, stodgy 7 humdrum 8 banausic, lifeless, mediocre, nonsense, plodding 10 balderdash, lackluster, monotonous, pedestrian 11 indifferent, uninspiring 13 uninteresting

Blake work
5 Tiger (The), Tyger (The) 8 Four Zoas (The) 10 Book of Thel (The) 16 Songs of Innocence 17 Songs of Experience

blamable
see **blameworthy**

blame
3 rap 4 onus 5 fault, guilt, knock 6 accuse, charge, finger, indict 7 censure, condemn 8 denounce, reproach 9 criticize, liability, reprehend, reprobate 10 accusation, imputation 11 culpability 12 condemnation, denunciation, reprehension
Scottish: 4 wite, wyte 6 dirdum

blameless
4 good, pure 5 clean, moral 7 perfect, upright 8 innocent, unguilty, virtuous 9 crimeless, exemplary, faultless, guiltless, honorable, lily-white, righteous, unsullied 10 immaculate, impeccable, inculpable 13 unimpeachable

blameworthy
3 lax 5 amiss 6 guilty, liable, sinful 7 at fault 8 criminal, culpable, derelict 9 negligent 10 answerable, censurable, delinquent, indictable, punishable 11 disgraceful, inexcusable, responsible 12 dishonorable 13 reprehensible, objectionable

Blanc of many voices
3 Mel

blanch
4 fade, pale 5 quail, scald, start 6 bleach, shrink, whiten 7 decolor, lighten, parboil 8 etiolate

blanched
3 wan 4 ashy, pale 5 ashen, faded, livid, peaky, waxen, white 6 anemic, doughy, pallid, peaked 7 ghostly 9 bloodless, colorless, washed out 10 cadaverous

Blancheflor's beloved
6 Flores, Floris

bland
4 dull, flat, blah, mild, soft 5 balmy, banal, vapid 6 boring, gentle, pablum 7 insipid, restful, sapless 8 soothing 9 calmative 10 complacent, flavorless, monotonous, namby-pamby, wishy-washy 12 ingratiating 13 nonirritating

blandish
3 con, woo 4 coax, fawn, urge 5 cozen 6 cajole, stroke 7 blarney, flatter, wheedle 8 butter up, inveigle, soft-soap 9 importune, sweet-talk 10 curry favor

blandishment
3 oil 5 honey 7 blarney, eyewash, incense, promise 8 flattery, soft soap 9 adulation, seduction, sweet talk 10 allurement, compliment, inducement, sycophancy, temptation

blank
3 gap 4 bare, dull, seal, skip, void 5 chasm, dazed, empty, space 6 stupid, vacant, virgin 7 deadpan, obscure, vacuous 8 complete, omission, outright, spotless, unfilled 9 impassive 10 empty space, interstice, obliterate 11 featureless 12 inexpressive, unexpressive

blanket
4 bury, hide 5 cover, quilt, throw 6 afghan, stroud 7 overlay 8 coverlet, mackinaw, sweeping 9 comforter 10 overspread

blankness
6 vacuum 7 nullity, vacancy, vacuity 9 emptiness 10 desolation

blare
4 roar 5 blast, shout 6 clamor, jangle 7 trumpet

blaring
4 loud 5 sharp 6 brassy, shrill 7 clarion, jarring, roaring 8 blinding, piercing, strident 9 deafening, dissonant 10 stentorian 11 ear-piercing, penetrating, stentorious 12 earsplitting

blarney
3 con, oil 4 coax, bunk 5 charm, honey, hooey 6 bunkum, cajole, humbug 7 baloney, incense, wheedle 8 blandish, buncombe, cajolery, flattery, inveigle, nonsense, soft soap 9 adulation, sweet-talk 11 compliments 12 blandishment, inveiglement

blasé
4 cool 5 bored, jaded, sated 6 breezy 7 knowing, offhand, unmoved, worldly 9 apathetic, incurious, surfeited, unexcited 10 world-weary 11 indifferent, unconcerned, worldly-wise

12 disenchanted, uninterested 13 disillusioned, sophisticated

blaspheme
4 cuss 5 abuse, curse, swear 6 revile 7 pollute, profane 8 denounce, execrate 9 castigate, excoriate

blasphemous
6 coarse, sinful 7 godless, impious, obscene, profane, ungodly 10 irreverent 12 sacrilegious 13 disrespectful

blasphemy
3 sin 5 abuse, error 6 heresy 7 cursing, cussing, impiety, mockery 8 swearing 9 profanity, sacrilege, violation 10 execration, heterodoxy, iconoclasm 11 desecration, imprecation, irreverence, malediction, profanation

blast
3 din 4 bang, beat, blow, boom, clap, dash, gale, gust, kill, peal, ruin, slam, toot 5 blare, burst, crack, crash, salvo, shoot, smash, wreck 6 attack, blight, blow up, damage, squall, wallop 7 destroy, lambast, shatter, shrivel, tantara, trumpet 8 dynamite, lambaste, outburst 9 explosion, castigate, discharge, overwhelm, shock wave 10 annihilate, detonation

blasting letters
3 TNT

blat
4 bray 5 blurt 6 cry out 7 exclaim 8 blurt out

blatant
4 bald, loud 5 brash, clear, gaudy, naked, noisy, overt, saucy, stark 6 arrant, brassy, brazen, crying, flashy, garish, patent, tawdry, vulgar 7 glaring, jarring, obvious 8 flagrant, immodest, impudent, insolent, manifest, outright, overbold, strident 9 barefaced, clamorous, obtrusive, shameless, unabashed 10 boisterous, outrageous, scurrilous, unblushing, vociferous 11 conspicuous, loudmouthed, transparent 12 ear-splitting, obstreperous

blather
3 gab, gas, jaw, rot, yak 4 bosh, gush, rave, stir 5 bleat, drool, hokum, prate 6 babble, bunkum, drivel, effuse, gabble, jabber, natter, yammer 7 blabber, chatter, enthuse, palaver, prattle, rubbish, twaddle 8 chitchat, claptrap, idle talk, nonsense 9 commotion 10 balderdash, double-talk, flapdoodle 12 gobbledygook

blaze
4 burn, fire 5 burst, flame, flare, glare, shine 7 flare up 8 eruption, outburst 10 incandesce 13 conflagration
Scottish: 3 low 4 lowe

blazer
6 marker, reefer 9 sport coat 10 sports coat 12 sports jacket

blazes
4 hell 5 abyss, Hades, Sheol 6 Tophet 7 Gehenna, inferno 9 perdition 11 netherworld

blazing
4 keen 5 afire, fiery 6 aflame, alight, ardent, fervid, on fire, red-hot 7 burning, fervent, flaming, flaring, furious, glowing, ignited, intense, lighted 8 dazzling, feverish, powerful, speeding, white-hot 9 brilliant, perfervid 11 conflagrant, impassioned 12 incandescent 13 scintillating

Blazing Saddles creator Brooks
3 Mel

blazon
4 deck 5 adorn, sound 7 declare, display, publish, trumpet 8 announce, proclaim 9 advertise, broadcast 10 coat of arms, promulgate 11 ostentation

bleach
3 dim 4 fade, pale 5 white 6 blanch, blench, purify, whiten 7 decolor, launder, wash out 8 etiolate, peroxide, sanitize 9 whitewash

bleak
3 raw, sad 4 bare, cold, dour, drab, grim, wild 5 chill, drear, empty, harsh, stark 6 barren, chilly, dismal, dreary, gloomy, lonely, severe, somber, wintry 7 austere, exposed, joyless 8 blighted, desolate, funereal, hopeless 9 cheerless, windswept, woebegone 10 depressing, despondent, oppressive, melancholy

blear
3 dim, fog 4 blur, dull, mist, murk, veil 5 bedim, faint, vague 6 hidden, shroud 7 becloud, obscure, shadowy, unclear 10 indistinct

bleary
3 dim 5 all in, faint, filmy, fuzzy, milky, spent, tired, vague 6 pooped, sapped, used-up, wasted 7 blurred, drained, obscure, shadowy, unclear, worn-out 8 depleted 9 enervated, exhausted, washed-out 10 indistinct

bleat
3 baa 4 blat, carp, crab, fuss, yawp 5 gripe, whine 6 bellow, grouse, squawk, yammer 7 blather, grumble, whimper 8 complain 9 bellyache

bleed
3 sap, run 4 milk, ooze, pity, seep 5 drain, exude, leech, mulct 6 extort, fleece 7 diffuse, extract 9 blackmail 10 hemorrhage

bleep
6 censor

blemish
3 mar 4 blot, flaw, harm, mark, maim, mole, scar, spot, vice, wart 5 fault, nevus, spoil, stain 6 blotch, damage, deface, defect, impair, injure, pimple, stigma 7 blacken, distort, freckle, pervert, tarnish, vitiate 8 impurity,

mutilate, pockmark **9** birthmark **12** imperfection **13** dlsfigurement

blench
3 shy **4** balk, duck, fade **5** blink, cower, quail, quake, start, wince **6** flinch, purify, recoil, shrink, whiten **7** launder, shy away, squinch, tremble **8** draw back, etiolate **9** whitewash

blend
3 fit, mix **4** brew, fuse, meld, weld **5** admix, alloy, merge, unify, union, unite **6** commix, fusion, go with, hybrid, mingle **7** amalgam, combine, mélange, mixture **8** beverage, coalesce, compound, conflate, immingle, infusion, intermix, mishmash **9** admixture, commingle, composite, harmonize, integrate **10** amalgamate, commixture, concoction, synthesize **12** adulteration, amalgamation, intermixture

blender setting
3 mix **4** chop, whip **5** grate, mince, puree **7** liquefy

blesbok
8 antelope

bless
4 laud **5** exalt, extol, endow, favor, grace **6** anoint, bestow, hallow, praise, uphold **7** approve, beatify, glorify, magnify **8** enshrine, eulogize, make holy, sanctify **10** consecrate

blessed
4 holy **5** happy, lucky **6** joyous, sacred **7** saintly **8** beatific, hallowed **9** beatified, fortunate, venerated **10** inviolable, sacrosanct, sanctified **11** consecrated

blessedness
5 bliss **8** felicity, sanctity **9** beatitude, godliness, happiness **12** blissfulness

blessing
4 boon, good, okay **5** asset, favor, grace **6** assent, bounty, thanks **7** benefit, benison, consent, fortune, godsend, support **8** approval, good luck, windfall **9** advantage **10** invocation, permission **11** approbation, benediction, endorsement, good fortune, valediction **12** commendation, consecration, thanksgiving **13** encouragement

"___ bleu!"
5 Sacré

blight
3 mar, nip **4** bane, dash, ruin **5** blast, decay, spoil, wreck **6** canker, wither **7** disease, scourge, shrivel **9** withering **10** pestilence **13** deterioration

blimp
7 airship **8** zeppelin **9** dirigible

blind
4 boma, daze, dull **5** decoy, front, shade, shill **6** dazzle **7** eyeless, muddled, shutter **8** bodazzle, jalousie, unseelng **9** enclosure, sightless **10** visionless

blind alley
6 pocket **7** dead end, impasse **8** cul-de-sac, deadlock **9** stone wall **10** standstill **11** obstruction

blind god
4 Eros, Hodr, Hoth **5** Cupid, Hoder, Hodur, Hothr

blindworm
8 slowworm

blink
3 bat **4** wink **5** flash, yield **6** give in, squint **7** flicker, flutter, nictate, twinkle **9** nictitate **11** scintillate

blink at
4 omit **5** clear, let go **6** bypass, excuse, forget, ignore, slight **7** condone, connive, let pass, neglect **8** discount, overlook, pass over **9** disregard, exonerate, whitewash

blip
6 censor, screen **9** deviation, expurgate, radar spot **10** bowdlerize

bliss
3 joy **4** Zion **6** Canaan, heaven **7** ecstasy, elation, elysium, nirvana, rapture **8** empyrean, euphoria, paradise **9** beatitude, cloud nine, happiness **10** exaltation **11** blessedness

blissful
5 happy **6** divine, elated, joyful, joyous **7** elysian **8** beatific, ecstatic, euphoric **9** ambrosial, delighted, entranced, rapturous **10** delightful, entrancing

blissfulness
3 joy **7** ecstasy, elation, nirvana, rapture **8** euphoria **9** beatitude, happiness **10** exaltation **11** contentment

blister
4 bleb, flay, lash **5** blain, bulla, slash **6** assail, canker, scathe, scorch **7** lambast, scarify, scourge, vesicle **8** lambaste **9** castigate, excoriate

blithe
3 gay **4** boon **5** happy, jolly, merry, sunny **6** bouncy, casual, cheery, chirpy, jaunty, jocund, jovial **7** gleeful **8** carefree, careless, cheerful, chirrupy, gladsome, heedless, mirthful **9** lightsome, sprightly, unworried, vivacious **10** untroubled **11** thoughtless **12** lighthearted

blitz
4 raid, rush **6** attack **7** air raid, bombard, bombing **8** shelling **9** offensive, onslaught **10** mass attack **11** bombardment

blitzkrieg
6 attack **7** assault, bombing **9** offensive, onslaught **11** bombardment

blizzard
4 gale **6** squall **8** whiteout **9** snowstorm

bloat
5 bulge, swell **6** billow, expand, fatten, puff up **7** balloon, distend, enlarge, inflate **10** distension

bloated
5 puffy, tumid **6** puffed **7** pompous, swollen **8** arrogant, enlarged, inflated **9** distended, overblown, overlarge **11** pretentious **13** self-important

bloc
4 band, ring **5** cabal, party, union **6** clique, league **7** combine, faction **8** alliance **9** coalition **10** consortium, contingent, federation **11** association, combination **13** confederation

block
3 bar **4** clog, fill, hunk, Lego, plug, slab, stop, wall, wing **5** brick, choke, chunk, close, ingot **6** cut off, hinder, impede **7** barrier, congest, occlude, stopper **8** obstacle, obstruct **9** barricade, hindrance, intercept

blockade
3 bar **4** stop, wall **5** beset, hem in, siege **6** shut in **7** barrier, besiege **8** close off, encircle, obstruct, stoppage **9** barricade, beleaguer, blank wall, hindrance, roadblock **10** impediment **11** obstruction

blockage
3 bar **4** clog, halt **7** barrier **8** obstacle, stoppage **10** impediment **11** obstruction

blockbuster
4 bomb **11** spectacular

blockhead
3 oaf **4** clod, dolt, dope, fool **5** clunk, dummy, dunce, idiot, moron, ninny **6** nitwit **7** halfwit, jackass **8** clodpole, clodpoll, dumbbell, imbecile, numskull **9** ignoramus, lamebrain, numbskull, simpleton **10** nincompoop **12** featherbrain

blockheaded
4 dull, dumb **5** dense, thick **6** obtuse, stupid **7** doltish **9** brainless, dim-witted **10** slow-witted

block out
4 mark **5** chart, close, draft, frame **6** hinder, screen, sketch **7** obscure, outline, prepare, repress, shut off **8** indicate, obstruct **9** adumbrate, formulate

block up
3 dam **4** clog, fill, plug, stop **5** choke **7** congest

bloke
3 guy, man **4** chap, gent **6** fellow **9** gentleman

blond
4 fair, gold, pale **5** light, sandy, straw, tawny **6** flaxen, golden **7** towhead **8** platinum **9** champagne, towheaded **10** fair-haired **11** sandy-haired **12** honey-colored

blood
4 gore **7** descent, kindred, kinship, lineage **8** ancestry **10** extraction
cancer of: **8** leukemia
cell: **3** red **5** white **8** hemocyte, monocyte, platelet **9** corpuscle, leukocyte **10** lymphocyte **11** erythrocyte, granulocyte
clot: **8** thrombus
coloring matter: **10** hemoglobin
combining form: **3** hem **4** hemo
disease: **6** anemia **8** leukemia **10** hemophilia
fluid part: **5** serum **6** plasma
of the gods: **5** ichor
particle in: **7** embolus
plasma: **4** sera (plural) **5** serum
poisoning: **6** pyemia **7** toxemia **10** septicemia
pressure: **8** systolic **9** diastolic
relating to: **5** hemal, hemic
serum: **6** plasma
study of: **10** hematology
sugar: **7** glucose

bloodbath
7 carnage, slaying **8** butchery, massacre **9** slaughter **10** decimation **12** annihilation **13** extermination

bloodless
3 wan **4** ashy, dull, pale, weak **5** ashen, waxen **6** anemic, feeble, pallid, sallow, torpid **8** listless **9** insensate, unfeeling **10** insensible, nonviolent **11** coldhearted, passionless, unemotional

bloodletting
4 gore **7** carnage, killing **8** butchery, shambles, violence **9** slaughter **10** phlebotomy **11** venesection

bloodline
6 family, strain **7** descent, lineage **8** ancestry, pedigree **10** family tree

bloodroot
7 puccoon

bloodshed
4 gore **7** carnage, killing **8** butchery **9** slaughter

bloodstained
4 gory **6** grisly **7** imbrued, wounded **8** sanguine **10** sanguinary **11** ensanguined, sanguineous

bloodstone
10 chalcedony

bloodsucker
3 ked **4** tick **5** lamia, leech **6** lizard, sponge **7** sponger, vampire **8** hanger-on, parasite, sheep ked **10** freeloader **12** lounge lizard

bloodthirsty
5 rabid **8** ravening, sanguine **9** cutthroat, homicidal, murdering, murderous, predatory, voracious **10** sanguinary **11** sanguineous

blood vessel
4 vein **5** aorta **6** artery **7** jugular **9** capillary

combining form: **3** vas **4** angi, vasi, vaso **5** angio

bloody
4 gory, grim, very **5** cruel **6** damage, damned, deadly, grisly **7** blasted, hateful, imbrued, wounded **8** accursed, infernal, sanguine **9** cutthroat, homicidal, murdering, murderous **10** detestable, sanguinary **11** ensanguined, sanguineous **12** death-dealing, slaughtering

bloom
4 blow, glow, open, posy **5** blush **6** floret, flower, thrive, unfold **7** blossom, burgeon, coating, develop, dusting, prosper **8** flourish, rosiness **10** cloudiness, effloresce **13** discoloration

blooper
4 goof, slip, trip **5** boner, break, error, fluff, gaffe, lapse **6** boo-boo, bungle, howler, slipup **7** blunder, faux pas, fly ball, misstep, mistake, offense **8** solecism **9** indecorum, false step **11** impropriety **12** indiscretion

blossom
3 bud, wax **4** blow, glow, grow, open, posy **5** bloom, blush, flush **6** expand, flower, mature, thrive, unfold **7** burgeon, develop, prosper **8** flourish, floweret, progress **10** effloresce, peak period **13** efflorescence

blot
4 blur, mark, onus, slur, smut, soil, spot **5** brand, odium, smear, speck, stain, sully **6** absorb, smudge, stigma **7** bestain, blemish, spatter, tarnish **8** black eye, discolor, disgrace **9** bespatter, moral flaw

blotch
4 mark, spot **5** stain **6** macula, macule, mottle, smudge **7** blemish, splotch **12** imperfection

blot out
4 raze, void **5** annul, crush, erase, quash, quell, scrub **6** cancel, delete, efface, squash **7** abolish, destroy, expunge **9** eliminate, eradicate, extirpate **10** annihilate, extinguish, obliterate **11** exterminate

blotto
see **drunk**

blouse
5 middy, shell, shirt, smock, tunic **6** guimpe

bloviate
4 rail, rant, rave **5** mouth, orate, spout **7** bluster, carry on, declaim, inveigh, soapbox, talk big **8** harangue, perorate, sound off, splutter **9** hold forth **10** vociferate

blow
3 bop, fan, hit, jar **4** bang, bash, belt, biff, bump, cuff, damn, fail, gasp, gust, huff, pipe, puff, slam, slug, swat, toot, whop, wind **5** boast, botch, crack, drive, erupt, leave, pound, punch, shock, slosh, smack, smash, sound, spend, swipe, waste, whack **6** buffet, depart, impact, mishap, thwack, wallop **7** assault, breathe, chagrin, consume, debacle, explode, flutter, fritter, trumpet **8** calamity, disaster, flounder, knockout, squander **9** bombshell, collision, dissipate, throw away **10** concussion, misfortune, trifle away **11** catastrophe

blow-by-blow
4 full **8** detailed, itemized, thorough **10** exhaustive **13** thoroughgoing

blowhard
see **boaster**

blow in
4 land **5** pop by **6** appear, arrive, drop by, show up, turn up **7** hit town **11** materialize

blowout
4 bash, fete, gala, riot, tear **5** binge, blast, break, party, split, spree **6** frolic, shindy **7** shindig, victory **8** carousal, flat tire **9** festivity

blowsy
5 ruddy **6** florid, frowsy, frowzy, sloppy, untidy **7** flushed, healthy, unkempt **8** blushing **10** bedraggled

blow up
4 bomb, burn, fume, rage **5** bloat, burst, erupt, flare, go off, storm, swell **6** expand, lose it, see red, seethe **7** bristle, distend, enlarge, explode, inflate, magnify, rupture, shatter **8** boil over, demolish, detonate, dynamite, heighten, mushroom **9** discredit, fulminate, overstate **10** aggrandize

blowy
4 airy, wild **5** fresh, gusty, windy **6** breezy, stormy **7** squally **8** blustery **9** windswept **11** tempestuous

blubber
3 cry, fat, sob **4** bawl, flab, keen, lard, pipe, wail, weep **5** flesh **6** snivel **7** carry on **8** whale fat

bludgeon
3 bat **4** club **5** baton, billy, bully **6** attack, cudgel, hector **7** bluster, war club **8** browbeat, bulldoze, bullyrag **9** bastinado, billy club, blackjack, strong-arm, truncheon **10** intimidate, nightstick
British: **4** cosh

blue
3 low, sad, sea **4** cyan, down, glum, lewd, navy, racy **5** bawdy, ocean, royal, salty, spicy **6** cobalt, gloomy, risqué **7** naughty, profane, unhappy **8** dejected, downcast, indecent, off-color **9** depressed, woebegone **10** despondent, dispirited, melancholy, suggestive **11** downhearted
combining form: **4** cyan **5** cyano
dark: **4** anil, navy **5** perse **6** indigo **8** Prussian
dye: **4** woad
grayish: **5** merle, slate
greenish: **4** aqua, cyan, teal **5** beryl **6** cobalt **7** azurite **9** turquoise

reddish: **5** smalt **6** marine, purple, violet **7** cyanine, gentian, lobelia
sky: **5** azure **8** cerulean

___ Blue
3 Ben **9** Little Boy

blue blood
4 lady, lord, peer **5** elite, noble **6** aristo **7** royalty **8** nobleman **9** gentility, gentleman, patrician **10** aristocrat, noblewoman **11** gentle birth, gentlewoman

blue-blooded
5 noble **7** wellborn **9** patrician **12** aristocratic

bluebonnet
4 Scot **11** Texas lupine

Blue Boy painter
12 Gainsborough (Thomas)

bluecoat
3 cop, law **4** fuzz **5** bobby **6** copper **9** constable, patrolman, policeman

Bluegrass State
8 Kentucky

Blue Grotto site
5 Capri

bluejacket
4 mate, salt, swab **5** limey **6** sailor, seaman **7** swabbie **9** sailorman

blue jeans
5 Levis **6** denims

blue moon
3 age, eon, era **4** aeon **5** epoch **7** dog's age **8** eternity, lifetime **10** generation

bluenose
4 prig, snob **5** prude **7** puritan **9** Mrs. Grundy, nice Nelly **10** goody-goody

bluenosed
4 prim **5** rigid **6** prissy, proper, square, stuffy **7** prudish **8** overnice, priggish **9** Victorian **10** tight-laced **11** puritanical, straitlaced

blue-pencil
3 cut **4** edit, trim **5** emend **6** cut out, delete, excise, remove, revise **7** clean up **8** boil down, cross out **9** strike out, tighten up

bluepoint
6 oyster

blueprint
3 map **4** cast, plan, plot **5** chart, draft, frame, model, trace **6** design, devise, rubric, scheme, set out, sketch **7** arrange, diagram, outline, picture, project **8** game plan, strategy **9** delineate **10** conception **11** description

blue-ribbon
3 top **4** A-one **5** prime, prize **6** Grade A, tiptop **7** capital, premier, stellar **8** five-star, topnotch, superior **9** excellent, first-rate, top-drawer **10** first-class, top-quality, world-class **11** outstanding **12** prize-winning

blues
4 funk **5** dumps, gloom, grief **6** lament **7** sadness, trouble **8** doldrums, glumness **9** dejection, pessimism **10** depression, desolation, low spirits, melancholy, woefulness **11** despondency, melancholia, unhappiness **12** hopelessness, mournfulness

blues musician
3 Guy (Buddy) **4** Cray (Robert), King (Albert, B. B.), Wolf (Howlin') **5** Bland (Bobby "Blue"), Brown (Clarence "Gatemouth"), Dixon (Willie), Foley (Sue), Handy (W. C.), James (Elmore, Etta), Myers (Sam), Smith (Bessie), Wells (Junior) **6** Hooker (John Lee), Rainey (Gertrude "Ma"), Taylor (Koko), Turner (Joe), Walker (T-Bone), Waters (Ethel, Muddy) **7** Broonzy (Big Bill), Diddley (Bo), Collins (Albert), Hammond (John), Hopkins (Sam "Lightnin'"), Johnson (Robert), Rushing (Jimmy) **8** Burnside (R. L.), Copeland (Johnny) **9** Jefferson (Blind Lemon), Leadbelly, Ledbetter (Huddie) **10** Williamson (John Lee, Sonny Boy)

Blue ___ Shoes
5 Suede

bluff
3 act, con **4** curt, fake, fool, jive, ruse, sham, show **5** blunt, cliff, feign, frank, gruff, rough, trick **6** abrupt, betray, candid, crusty, delude, direct, hearty, humbug **7** beguile, brusque, deceive, fake out, mislead, playact, pretend **8** headland, pretense **9** deception, outspoken, precipice, steep bank **10** escarpment, forthright, no-nonsense, promontory, subterfuge **11** counterfeit, double-cross, plainspoken, short-spoken **13** unceremonious

bluish-green
4 aqua, teal

blunder
3 err **4** bull, gaff, goof, mess, muff, slip, trip **5** boner, botch, error, fluff, gaffe, gum up, lapse, lurch, misdo, snafu **6** bobble, bollix, bumble, bungle, foul up, fumble, goof up, howler, mess up, wander **7** balls-up, blooper, failure, faux pas, louse up, misstep, mistake, screw up, stumble **8** disaster, flounder **12** indiscretion, misadventure

blunderbuss
3 gun **4** dolt **5** klutz **6** galoot, lummox **7** bungler, firearm **8** bonehead, numskull **9** blockhead, numbskull **10** stumblebum **13** butterfingers

blunt
4 bald, calm, curt, dull **5** allay, bluff, brief, frank, gruff, plain, rough, terse **6** abrupt, benumb, candid, crusty, deaden, direct, lessen, obtuse **7** brusque, rounded, uncivil **8** enfeeble, not sharp, snippety **10** forthright **11** desensitize, insensitive, plainspoken, unvarnished **12** discourteous **13** unceremonious

blunted sword
4 épée
blur
3 dim, fog **4** blot, dull, mist **5** befog, blear, cloud, muddy, smear, stain, taint **6** smudge, stigma **7** becloud, besmear, confuse, obscure, tarnish **8** besmirch, discolor
in printing: **6** mackle
blurb
4 hype, plug, puff **5** press, promo **6** notice **7** write-up **8** good word **9** promotion **12** commendation
blurry
4 hazy **5** vague **6** cloudy **7** clouded, unclear **9** undefined, unfocused **10** indistinct
blurt
4 blab, blat, bolt **5** spill **6** cry out, let out **7** divulge, exclaim, let slip, spit out **8** disclose, give away **9** ejaculate
blush
4 burn, glow, rose, view **5** bloom, color, flame, flush, rouge **6** mantle, pinken, redden, ruddle **7** blossom, crimson, redness, turn red **8** mantling, rosiness
bluster
4 bawl, crow, gust, huff, rage, roar, rout **5** blast, bully, prate, storm, strut, vaunt **6** bellow, clamor, hector, lean on **7** bombast, bravado, dragoon, roister, swagger, talk big **8** boasting, browbeat, bulldoze, bullyrag, domineer **9** gasconade **10** grandstand, intimidate **11** braggadocio
blustery
4 wild **5** blowy, gusty, rough **6** drafty, raging, raving, stormy **7** furious, squally, violent **9** truculent, turbulent **10** boisterous, tumultuous **11** tempestuous
BMI rival
5 ASCAP
BMW alternative
4 Audi **7** Porsche **8** Mercedes
boa
5 scarf, snake
Boadicea clan
5 Iceni
boar
3 hog, pig **4** male **5** swine **7** wild pig **9** razorback
board
4 fare, feed, food, lath, slab, slat **5** catch, get on, hop on, house, lodge, meals, panel, plank, put up, table **6** billet, embark **7** emplane, entrain, quarter **9** directors **11** directorate
artist's: **7** palette
mystic: **5** Ouija
boarder
5 guest **6** lodger, renter, roomer, tenant
board game
see at **game**
boarding house
6 hostel **7** hospice, lodging, pension **8** pensione
boardwalk
7 gangway **9** esplanade, promenade
boast
3 own **4** blow, brag, crow, have, puff **5** exalt, exult, glory, mouth, prate, preen, strut, vaunt **6** parade **7** bluster, bombast, bravado, contain, enlarge, exhibit, inflate, possess, show off, swagger, talk big **9** gasconade **10** exaggerate, grandstand **11** rodomontade **12** exaggeration
boaster
6 gascon **7** egotist, peacock, show-off **8** big mouth, blowhard, braggart **11** braggadocio, rodomontade
boastful
4 vain **5** cocky **6** braggy **8** arrogant, braggart, puffed-up, vaunting **9** bigheaded, conceited, egotistic **11** egotistical, pretentious, swellheaded **12** vainglorious **13** swelled-headed
Scottish: **6** vaunty
boat
3 ark, hoy, tug **4** dhow, dory, junk, pram, prau, proa, punt, scow, ship, yawl **5** aviso, balsa, barge, canoe, coble, ferry, kayak, ketch, scull, shell, skiff, sloop, smack, umiak, yacht **6** bateau, bugeye, caïque, cutter, dinghy, hooker, lateen, lugger, packet, sampan, vessel, wherry **7** caravel, coracle, cruiser, currach, curragh, gondola, inboard, lighter, pinnace, pirogue, pontoon, shallop, steamer, trawler, vedette, vidette **8** outboard, runabout, schooner, trimaran **9** catamaran, hydrofoil
bottom projection: **4** keel
captain: **5** pilot **6** master **7** skipper
dock, basin: **6** marina
front end of: **3** bow **4** fore, prow
on a ship: **3** gig **6** launch **7** pinnace
race: **7** regatta
rear end of: **3** aft **5** stern
song: **6** chanty, shanty **7** chantey **9** barcarole **10** barcarolle
boatman
3 tar **4** mate, swab **5** limey **6** Charon, sailor **7** mariner, oarsman, paddler **8** deckhand, water dog **9** gondolier, navigator
boat-shaped
8 scaphoid **9** navicular
Boaz's wife
4 Ruth
bob
3 jig, nod, rap, tap **4** buff, clip, crop, dock, trim **5** bunch, float **6** bounce, curtsy, jiggle, jounce, polish, trifle, wobble **7** cluster, curtsey, nosegay **8** shilling **9** genuflect

bobbery
3 ado, din, row **4** fray, riot **5** babel, noise **6** bedlam, hubbub, racket, ruckus, rumpus **7** ferment, ruction **9** commotion, confusion **10** hullabaloo, hurly-burly **11** disturbance, pandemonium

bobbin
4 pirn **5** quill, spool, wheel **7** spindle **8** cylinder

bobble
3 bob, dud **4** flub, goof, mess, muff **5** botch, error, fluff, gum up **6** ball up, bollix, bumble, bungle, flub up, fumble, goof up, muff up **7** blooper, failure, louse up, mistake

Bobbsey twin
3 Nan **4** Bert

bobby
3 law **6** copper, peeler **7** officer **9** constable, patrolman, policeman

Bobby of hockey
3 Orr

bobwhite
5 quail **9** partridge

Boccaccio
beloved: **9** Fiammetta
tales: **9** Decameron

bode
4 hint **5** augur **6** signal, warn of **7** betoken, portend, presage, promise, signify, suggest **8** foreshow, indicate **9** foretoken, prefigure **10** foreshadow

bodega
3 bar, pub **6** saloon **7** barroom, grocery **8** wineshop **12** general store

bodement
4 omen, sign **5** hunch **6** augury **7** portent, presage **8** prophecy **9** foretoken, harbinger **10** foreboding, intimation, prediction, prognostic **11** premonition **12** presentiment

bodiless
7 ghostly **8** ethereal, spectral **9** unfleshly **10** discarnate, immaterial, unphysical **11** disembodied, incorporeal, nonmaterial **12** apparitional **13** insubstantial

bodily
6 carnal **7** en masse, earthly, fleshly, sensual, somatic, totally **8** corporal, entirely, physical, visceral **9** corporeal **10** altogether, completely **11** unspiritual

bodkin
4 shiv **5** blade, knife, shank **6** dagger, lancet, needle **7** poniard **8** stiletto

____ bodkins
4 odds

body
4 bulk, core, form, hull, mass, soma **5** frame, stiff, stock, torso **6** corpse, corpus **7** anatomy, cadaver, carcass, chassis, corpora (plural), remains **8** physique **9** aggregate, substance
combining form: **4** dema, soma, some, somi (plural) **5** somat, somia, somus **6** somata (plural), somato
human: **4** clay

body art
3 tat **6** tattoo

bodybuilder's pride
3 abs **4** pecs

body cavity
4 ceca (plural) **5** cecum, sinus **6** cloaca, coelom **7** abdomen **8** hemocoel

body check
4 scan **5** block

bodyguard
7 retinue **9** attendant, protector

body of water
3 bay, sea **4** cove, gulf, lake, pond, pool **5** bight, brook, creek, fiord, firth, fjord, inlet, ocean, river **6** harbor, lagoon, puddle, stream **7** channel, estuary **9** reservoir

body passage
4 duct, vein **5** canal **6** artery, meatus, ureter, vagina, venule, vessel **7** trachea, urethra **8** bronchus **9** arteriole, capillary, esophagus, intestine **10** bronchiole **13** bronchial tube, fallopian tube

body politic
5 state **6** nation **11** nation-state

body powder
4 talc

boffo
3 gag, gas, hit **4** wild **5** laugh **6** scream **7** sold-out **8** smash-hit, smashing **10** successful **11** sensational

bog
3 fen **4** mire, quag **5** delay, marsh, swamp **6** impede, morass, muskeg, slough, slow up **8** quagmire **9** swampland

boggy
4 miry **5** mucky **6** marshy, quaggy, swampy **7** sloughy

Bogart, Humphrey
film: **6** Sahara **7** Dead End, Sabrina **8** Big Sleep (The), Key Largo **10** Casablanca, High Sierra **11** Caine Mutiny (The) **12** African Queen (The) **13** Maltese Falcon (The) **15** Petrified Forest (The) **16** To Have and Have Not **24** Treasure of the Sierra Madre (The)
wife: **6** Bacall (Lauren)

bog down
4 flag, mire **5** choke, delay, stall **6** detain, falter, hang up, hinder, impede, retard, slow up **7** embroil, set back, slacken **8** encumber, keep back, obstruct, slow down **9** lose steam **10** decelerate

bogey
5 ghost, haunt, shade, spook **6** scarer, shadow, spirit, wraith **7** phantom, specter, spectre **8** phantasm, revenant **10** apparition

bogeyman
5 spook **7** bugbear, chimera, monster, phantom, specter, spectre **10** apparition

boggle
4 balk, mess, muff, stun **5** amaze, botch, fudge, gum up, shock, wreck **6** bollix, bungle, cobble, goof up, mess up, strain **7** astound, louse up, nonplus, stagger, stumble, stupefy **8** astonish, bewilder, bowl over, confound **9** dumbfound, mishandle, mismanage, overwhelm, take aback **11** flabbergast

boggy
4 miry **5** mucky **6** marshy, quaggy, swampy **7** sloughy

bogus
4 fake, mock, sham **5** false, phony, pseud, snide **6** ersatz, forged, pseudo **7** fictive, pretend **8** invented, specious, spurious **9** brummagem, concocted, imitation, pinchbeck, simulated, trumped up **10** artificial, fabricated, fraudulent, mendacious **11** counterfeit

Bohème, La
character: **4** Mimì **7** Rodolfo
composer: **7** Puccini (Giacomo)
setting: **5** Paris

bohemian
4 arty, boho **5** artsy, gypsy, hippy **6** hippie **7** beatnik, dropout, oddball, offbeat **8** maverick, vagabond, wanderer **9** eccentric **10** avant-garde, free spirit, iconoclast, unorthodox **13** nonconformist

boil
3 jet **4** bolt, brew, burn, cook, dash, foam, fume, gush, moil, race, rage, rush, spew, spot, stew, vent **5** anger, churn, erupt, fling, froth, poach, shoot, storm, swirl **6** blow up, bubble, charge, canker, coddle, decoct, pimple, seethe, simmer **7** abscess, agitate, bristle, ferment, flare up, pustule, smolder **8** furuncle **9** carbuncle, discharge **10** effervesce **11** excrescence

boil down
4 pare, trim **6** amount, decoct, reduce **7** distill **8** compress, condense, simplify, truncate **9** summarize, synopsize **10** streamline **11** concentrate, encapsulate

boiler suit
8 coverall

boiling
3 hot **5** fiery **6** baking, red-hot, sultry, torrid **7** burning, febrile **8** agitated, roasting, scalding, sizzling, tropical **9** scorching **10** blistering

boil over
4 burn, fume, rage **5** erupt **6** blow up, bridle, see red, seethe **7** bristle, flare up

boisterous
4 loud, wild **5** noisy, rowdy **6** lively, stormy, unruly **7** blatant, raucous, riotous **8** strident **9** clamorous, convivial, turbulent **10** disorderly, disruptive, rollicking, tumultuous, uproarious, vociferous **11** loudmouthed, tempestuous **12** high-spirited, obstreperous, rambunctious, ungovernable, unrestrained

Boito opera
11 Mefistofele

bold
4 edgy, free, pert, rude **5** bluff, brave, fresh, gutsy, nervy, sassy, saucy, sheer, showy, steep **6** arrant, brassy, brazen, bright, cheeky, daring, heroic **7** doughty, forward, glaring, obvious, valiant **8** cocksure, fearless, impudent, insolent, intrepid, resolute, unafraid, valorous **9** audacious, dauntless, intrusive, prominent, shameless, undaunted **10** courageous, pronounced **11** adventurous, impertinent, smart-alecky, venturesome **12** enterprising, presumptuous

boldness
4 gall, grit **5** drive, nerve, valor **6** aplomb, mettle, spirit **8** audacity, backbone, chutzpah, temerity **9** arrogance, challenge, hardihood, impudence, insolence **10** brazenness, disrespect, effrontery **11** discourtesy **12** impertinence

Bolero composer
5 Ravel (Maurice)

Bolivia
ancient culture: **4** Inca **10** Tiahuanaco
capital: **5** La Paz, Sucre
city: **6** El Alto **9** Santa Cruz **10** Cochabamba
conqueror: **7** Pizarro (Hernando)
Indian people: **6** Aymara **7** Quechua
lake: **5** Poopó **8** Titicaca
language: **6** Aymara **7** Quechua, Spanish
monetary unit: **9** boliviano
mountain, range: **5** Andes **6** Sajama
neighbor: **4** Peru **5** Chile **6** Brazil **8** Paraguay **9** Argentina
river: **4** Beni **5** Abuna **6** Mamoré **7** Guaporé **9** Pilcomayo

bollix
4 flub, mess, muff, ruin **5** botch, gum up, mix-up, snafu, spoil, upset **6** bobble, bumble, bungle, foul up, fumble, goof up, jumble, mess up, muck up, muddle, muff up **7** balls-up, confuse, louse up, screw up **8** dishevel, disorder, scramble, unsettle **9** mishandle, mismanage

bolo
5 knife **7** machete

Bolshevik
3 Red 6 commie 7 comrade 8 Leninist, tovarich, tovarish 9 communist

bolshevism
7 Marxism 8 Leninism 9 communism

bolster
3 aid 4 buoy, gird, help, husk, prop 5 boost, brace, carry, cheer 6 assist, bear up, buoy up, pillow, upbear, uphold 7 bulwark, cushion, fortify, hearten, shore up, support, sustain 8 backstop, buttress, maintain 9 encourage, reinforce 10 strengthen 12 underpinning 13 reinforcement

bolt
3 bar, fly, rod, run 4 cram, dash, dart, flee, gulp, jump, lock, race, rush, tear, wolf 5 arrow, blurt, bound, chase, dowel, flush, rivet, scarf, scoot, shoot, skirr, slosh, start 6 charge, decamp, devour, gobble, guzzle, secure, spring 7 abscond, exclaim, hotfoot, make off, missile, rigidly, scamper, startle, take off 8 blurt out, hightail 9 skedaddle 10 make tracks, take flight 11 ingurgitate 13 thunderstroke

bomb
3 dud, hit 4 bust, dull, fail, flop, sink, zero 5 blast, blitz, lemon, loser, pound, shell 6 blow up 7 debacle, destroy, failure, home run, success, washout, wipe out 8 detonate, disaster, fall flat, long pass, long shot, spray can

bombard
4 pelt 5 blast, blitz, shell, storm 6 attack, assail, cannon, hammer, pepper, shower, strafe, strike 7 assault, barrage 8 catapult 9 cannonade

bombardment
4 hail 5 burst, salvo 6 attack, shower, volley 7 air raid, barrage, battery 8 drumfire 9 broadside, cannonade, fusillade, onslaught

bombardon
4 bass 8 bass tuba

bombast
4 rant 6 hot air 7 bluster, fustian, oration 8 rhapsody, tumidity 9 fancy talk, pomposity, turgidity 10 pretension 11 rodomontade

bombastic
6 prolix, turgid 7 aureate, orotund, pompous 8 inflated, puffed-up 9 overblown 10 euphuistic, rhetorical 11 declamatory, overwrought 12 magniloquent 13 grandiloquent

____ Bombeck
4 Erma

bombed
4 high 5 drunk, fried, stiff, tight 6 blotto, stinko, soused, stewed, stoned, wasted 8 comatose, tanked up 9 plastered 10 inebriated 11 intoxicated

bombinate
3 hum 4 buzz, purr, whir 5 drone, strum, thrum 6 bumble, rumble 7 grumble

bombshell
4 blow, jolt 5 shock 6 marvel 8 surprise 9 curveball, sensation 10 revelation 11 thunderbolt

bon ____
3 mot

Bon ____ cleaner
3 Ami

Bonaduce role
5 Danny

bona fide
4 real, sure, true 5 valid 6 actual 7 earnest, genuine, sincere 8 sterling 9 authentic, undoubted, veritable 10 legitimate, sure-enough 11 indubitable, in good faith 13 authenticated

bona fides
6 candor 7 probity 8 goodwill 9 good faith, sincerity 10 reputation 11 reliability

bonanza
4 mine 5 catch, hoard 7 pay dirt 8 Golconda, gold mine, treasure, treasury, windfall 10 motherlode 12 extravaganza 13 treasure trove

bonbon
5 candy, sweet 7 fondant 9 sweetmeat, sugarplum 10 confection

bond
3 tie 4 bail, fuse, knot, link, pact, yoke 5 nexus 6 cement, fetter, pledge, surety 7 bargain, compact, linkage, promise, shackle, warrant 8 adhesive, affinity, cohesion, contract, covenant, guaranty, ligament, ligature, security, vinculum, warranty 9 adherence, agreement, coherence, guarantee 10 attachment, connection, connective, obligation

bondage
4 yoke 6 chains, thrall 7 durance, fetters, helotry, peonage, serfage, serfdom, slavery 9 captivity, detention, servitude, thralldom, vassalage, villenage 10 subjection 11 enslavement, subjugation 12 imprisonment

Bond creator Fleming
3 Ian

bondman
4 peon, serf 5 helot, slave 6 vassal

bondsman
4 peon, serf 5 helot, slave 6 surety 7 chattel

bone
4 ossa (plural)
ankle: 4 tali (plural) 5 talus, tarsi (plural) 6 tarsus
arm: 4 ulna 5 radii (plural), ulnae (plural) 6 radius 7 humerus
back: 5 spine 8 vertebra 9 vertebrae (plural)
breast: 7 sternum
calf: 6 fibula
cavity: 5 fossa

change into: 6 ossify
cheek: 5 malar 6 zygoma
chest: 3 rib 6 costal
collar: 8 clavicle
combining form: 4 oste 5 osteo
ear: 5 incus 6 stapes 7 malleus
face: 5 malar, nasal 7 frontal
finger: 7 phalanx 8 phalange
foot: 5 tarsi (plural) 6 tarsus 9 calcaneum, calcaneus 10 astragalus, metatarsus
hand: 10 metacarpus
head: 5 skull, vomer 7 cranium 8 parietal, sphenoid 9 occipital
heel: 9 calcaneum, calcaneus
hip: 5 iliac, ilium, pubis 6 pelvis 7 ischium
jaw: 7 maxilla 8 mandible
kneecap: 7 patella
leg: 5 femur, tibia 6 fibula 7 patella
lower back: 6 coccyx, sacrum
middle ear: 5 anvil, incus 6 hammer, stapes 7 malleus, stirrup
pelvis: 5 ilium
projection: 7 mastoid
relating to: 6 osteal
shin: 5 tibia 6 tibiae (plural)
shoulder blade: 7 scapula 8 scapulae (plural)
small: 7 ossicle
substance: 6 ossein
temporal process: 7 mastoid
thigh: 5 femur
toe: 7 phalanx 8 phalange
U-shaped: 5 hyoid
wrist: 5 carpi (plural) 6 carpus

bone-dry
4 arid, sere

bonehead
4 clod 5 dunce, idiot, moron 6 cretin, dimwit, nitwit 7 half-wit 8 clodpole, clodpoll, numskull 9 ignoramus, lamebrain, numbskull 12 featherbrain

bonelike
7 osseous, osteoid

boner
see **blooper**

bone up
4 cram 5 study 6 review, revise 8 pore over

bong
4 bell, dong, peal, ring, toll 5 chime, knell, sound 6 hookah, strike 7 resound 9 water pipe 11 reverberate

boniface
7 barkeep 8 publican, taverner 9 barkeeper, innkeeper 12 saloonkeeper

Bonjour Tristesse author
5 Sagan (Françoise)

bonkers
3 ape, mad, off 4 daft, loco, nuts, wild 5 batty, crazy, dotty, giddy, loony, potty 6 cuckoo, insane 7 bananas, haywire 8 demented, deranged, unhinged

bon mot
4 jest, quip 5 crack, sally 6 zinger 7 epigram, riposte 8 one-liner, repartee 9 witticism

bonny
4 fair, fine 6 comely, lovely, pretty 7 winsome 8 pleasing 9 beauteous, beautiful, excellent 10 attractive, delightful 11 good-looking

bon ton
4 élan 5 flair, style 6 gentry, jet set 7 fashion, society 8 elegance, smart set 9 beau monde, haut monde, propriety 11 high society

bonus
4 gift, perk, plus 6 reward 7 benefit, payment, premium 8 dividend 13 fringe benefit

bon vivant
7 epicure, flaneur, trifler 8 aesthete, gourmand 10 aficionado, dilettante, gastronome 11 cognoscente, connoisseur 12 boulevardier, gastronomist, man-about-town

bony
4 lank, lean, thin 5 gaunt, lanky, spare 6 barren, osteal, skinny, twiggy 7 angular, osseous, scraggy, scrawny, starved 8 rawboned, skeletal, underfed 9 emaciated 10 cadaverous

boo
4 hiss, hoot, jeer, razz 6 bellow, deride, heckle, revile 7 catcall 9 raspberry, shout down

boob
3 oaf 4 dolt, dope, goof, goon, boor 5 chump, dunce, goose, ninny 6 breast, dumb ox 7 blunder, fathead, mistake, tomfool 8 lunkhead 9 simpleton 10 dunderhead, philistine

boo-boo
see **blooper**

booby hatch
6 asylum, bedlam 8 bughouse, loony bin, madhouse, nuthouse 9 funny farm 11 institution

booby trap
4 mine 5 snare 6 hazard 7 pitfall, springe 8 deadfall, land mine

boodle
3 wad 4 bilk, haul, heap, loot, mint, perk, take 5 prize, spoil 6 packet, payola, spoils 7 fortune, plunder, present 8 kickback 9 incentive 10 bribe money, inducement

book
4 list, text, tome 5 album, bible, codex, enter, folio, novel, tract 6 charge, engage, enroll, folder, line up, manual, octavo, quarto, record, script, volume 7 catalog, edition, reserve 8 hardback, inscribe, register, schedule, softback, treatise 9 hardcover, monograph, paperback, preengage, reference 10 compendium 11 publication

binding: **4** case, sewn, tape, Yapp **5** cloth **7** leather, perfect **9** hardcover
combining form: **6** biblio
liturgical: **5** horae **6** missal **7** gradual, psalter **8** breviary **10** lectionary
part: **4** head, mull, tail **5** board, cover, crash, envoy, hinge, index, joint, spine **6** gutter, jacket, lining **7** chapter, flyleaf, preface **8** appendix, fore edge, foreword **9** text block **10** dedication

bookie
see **bookmaker**

bookish
5 nerdy **7** erudite, learned **8** academic, cerebral, literary, pedantic, studious, well-read **9** scholarly **10** longhaired **12** intellectual, professorial

bookkeeper
3 CPA **10** accountant

bookkeeping term
4 loss **5** asset, audit, check, debit, entry, yield **6** budget, credit, equity, income, ledger, margin, profit, return **7** account, accrual, balance, expense, invoice, revenue, voucher **8** discount, dividend, interest, write off **9** inventory, liability **10** appreciate, depreciate, fiscal year **11** double entry **12** amortization, appreciation, balance sheet, depreciation, variable cost

booklet
8 brochure, opuscule, pamphlet

bookmaker
6 binder, editor **7** printer **9** bet holder, publisher

book of account
6 ledger, record **7** journal **8** register

bookplate
5 label **8** ex libris

bookstall
5 booth, kiosk **9** newsstand

boom
3 wax **4** bang, clap, grow, rise, slam, spar, wham **5** blast, boost, burst, crack, crash, sound, smash, swell **6** do well, expand, growth, rumble, thrive **7** explode, prosper, resound, thunder **8** flourish, kick hard, long beam **9** expansion **10** bull market, detonation, prosperity **11** reverberate
opposite: **4** bust

boomerang
6 recoil **7** rebound **8** backfire, backlash, come back, kick back, ricochet **10** bounce back

booming
4 bass, deep **6** robust **7** roaring **8** affluent, resonant, sonorous, thriving **9** deafening **10** prospering, prosperous, successful **11** flourishing

boon
3 aid, gay **4** gift, good, help **5** asset, grant, favor, jolly, merry, token **6** blithe, bounty, jocund, jovial **7** benefit, festive, gleeful, godsend, largess, present **8** blessing, largesse, mirthful, windfall **9** advantage, convivial, privilege **10** indulgence **11** benediction, benefaction

boondocks
5 wilds **6** sticks **7** outback **8** backland, frontier **9** backwater, backwoods, provinces **10** hinterland **11** backcountry, countryside **12** back of beyond

boondoggle
4 hoax, scam **5** fraud, hokum **6** hustle, rip-off **7** con game, fast one, lanyard, swindle **8** flimflam

boor
3 cad, oaf **4** lout, hick, rube **5** brute, chuff, churl, clown, yahoo, yokel **6** lummox, rustic **7** buffoon, bumpkin, hayseed, peasant **9** ignoramus, vulgarian **10** clodhopper, philistine, provincial

boorish
4 rude **5** crass, crude, rough **6** coarse, common, rugged, vulgar **7** ill-bred, lowbred, uncivil, uncouth **8** impolite, insolent, lubberly **9** graceless, tasteless, unrefined **10** philistine, provincial, robustious, uncultured, ungracious, unmannerly, unpolished, unsociable **11** bad-mannered, clodhopping, ill-mannered, uncivilized **12** discourteous, uncultivated **13** disrespectful

boost
3 aid **4** hike, lift, jump, plug, push, rise **5** raise, steal **6** assist, beef up, expand, extend, foster, jack up **7** advance, amplify, augment, elevate, magnify, promote, support **8** heighten, increase, shoplift **9** advertise, encourage, expansion, promotion **10** assistance **11** helping hand **13** encouragement

booster
3 fan **4** hypo, shot **6** backer, Jaycee, patron, rocket, rooter **7** vaccine **8** champion, defender, promoter, upholder **9** amplifier, expositor, injection, proponent, supporter **10** shoplifter **11** inoculation

boot
3 axe, can **4** bang, fire, kick, oust, sack **5** chuck, eject, evict, expel, start **6** bounce, thrill **7** dismiss, kick out, start up **8** throw out **9** discharge, dismissal, terminate
kind: **5** kamik, wader **6** arctic, brogan, chukka, gaiter, galosh, mukluk **7** jodhpur, shoepac **8** balmoral, cothurni (plural), overshoe, shoepack **9** cothurnus **10** Wellington

Boötes star
8 Arcturus

booth
4 nook **5** berth, bower, kiosk, stall, stand **6** carrel **9** enclosure **11** compartment

bootleg
3 hot, run **5** hooch **6** pirate **7** illicit, smuggle **9** irregular, moonshine **10** bathtub gin, contraband **11** black market, mountain dew **12** unauthorized

bootless
4 vain **5** empty **6** futile, hollow **7** useless **8** abortive, impotent, nugatory **9** fruitless, valueless, worthless **10** profitless, unavailing **11** ineffective, ineffectual **12** unproductive, unprofitable, unsuccessful

bootlick
4 fawn **5** cower, crawl, creep, toady **6** cringe, grovel, kowtow, stroke **7** cater to, flatter, truckle **8** blandish **9** brownnose, importune, seek favor **10** curry favor **11** apple-polish **12** bow and scrape

bootlicker
4 toad **5** toady **6** lackey, lapdog, minion, yesman **7** doormat, spaniel **8** hanger-on **9** sycophant **11** lickspittle

booty
4 butt, duff, haul, lift, loot, pelf, swag, take, tush **5** prize, spoil, yield **6** spoils **7** pillage, plunder, rear end, seizure, takings **8** buttocks

booze
4 brew, grog, swig **5** binge, drink, hooch, juice, quaff, sauce, souse, swill **6** guzzle, imbibe, liquor, rotgut, tank up, tipple **7** alcohol, carouse, put away, spirits, swizzle **8** cocktail, liquor up **9** aqua vitae, firewater, knock back, moonshine

boozehound
3 sot **4** lush, wino **5** drunk, hoser, rummy, souse, toper **7** guzzler **8** drunkard **9** alcoholic, inebriate **11** dipsomaniac

bop
3 bat, box, hit, jab, pop, rap **4** bash, bean, belt, biff, boff, blow, clip, cuff, jive, slug, sock, swat, whop **5** clock, pound, smack, thump, whack **8** plant one

borax
4 junk

Bordeaux wine
district: **5** Médoc **6** Graves
grape: **6** Malbec, Merlot **8** Cabernet
name: **5** Arsac, Ludon, Macau **6** Moulis **7** Labarde, Margaux, Pomerol **8** Cantenac, St. Julien, Pauillac **9** St. Emilion, St. Estèphe, St. Laurent
red: **6** claret

bordello
see **brothel**

border
3 hem, lip, rim **4** abut, brim, edge, join, line, pale, trim **5** bound, brink, flank, frame, limit, march, skirt, touch, verge **6** adjoin, bounds, butt on, define, fringe, limbus, margin, trench **7** contour, outline, selvage **8** approach, boundary, frontier, neighbor, sideline, surround **9** marchland, perimeter, periphery **11** butt against, communicate
heraldry: **4** orle
inlaid: **8** purfling
raised: **7** coaming

bordereau
4 note **6** record **7** account **10** memorandum

bordering
4 nigh **5** close **6** almost, next to **7** meeting, verging **8** abutting, adjacent, touching **9** adjoining, alongside, close upon, impinging **10** approximal, contiguous, juxtaposed **11** coterminous, neighboring, practically

borderland
5 march **6** fringe, margin **8** frontier **9** marchland

borderline
4 pale **6** almost, nearly **7** dubious, unclear **8** boundary, doubtful, marginal, unstable **9** ambiguous, debatable, dubitable, equivocal, perimeter, uncertain, undecided, unsettled **11** demarcation, problematic **12** intermediate **13** indeterminate

border state
8 Delaware, Kentucky, Maryland, Missouri, Virginia

bore
3 irk **4** drag, drip, mine, peer, pill, ream, sink, tire, yawn **5** auger, drill, drone, gouge, prick, punch **6** burrow, pierce, tunnel **7** bromide, caliber, fatigue **8** diameter, puncture **9** penetrate, perforate, soporifio **10** dullsville
tidal: **5** eagre

boreal
3 icy **4** cold, cool **5** chill, gelid, polar **6** arctic, bitter, chilly, frosty, frigid, tundra **7** glacial, wintery **8** freezing, northern **9** northerly

Boreas
beloved: **8** Orithyia
brother: **5** Notus **8** Hesperus, Zephyrus
father: **8** Astraeus
mother: **3** Eos
son: **5** Zetes **6** Calais

boredom
5 blahs, ennui **6** apathy, stupor, tedium, torpor **7** fatigue **8** doldrums, dullness, flatness, monotony **9** lassitude, weariness **11** incuriosity, tediousness **12** indifference

Borges work
5 Aleph (The) **10** Labyrinths

Borgia
4 Juan **6** Alonso, Cesare **7** Alfonso, Rodrigo **8** Lucrezia

boring
3 dry **4** arid, drab, dull, flat, zero **5** ho-hum, vapid **6** dreary, stodgy, tiring **7** humdrum, tedious **8** bromidic, drudging, lifeless, tiresome **9** wearisome **10** lackluster, lacklustre, monotonous, pedestrian, unexciting **13** uninteresting

boring tool
5 drill, auger **6** trepan

Boris Godunov composer
10 Mussorgsky (Modest) **11** Moussorgsky (Modest)

born
3 née **6** innate, native **8** destined, inherent **9** intrinsic **10** congenital, deep-seated
combining form: **3** gen **4** gene **6** genous **7** genetic

borne by the wind
6 aeolic, eolian **7** aeolian

Borneo
ethnic group: **4** Dyak **5** Dayak
mountain: **8** Kinabalu
nation: **6** Brunei
river: **6** Rabang

Borneo ape
5 orang **9** orangutan

Born Free
author: **7** Adamson (Joy)
lion: **4** Elsa

Borodin opera
10 Prince Igor

borough
4 town **5** burgh **7** village **8** township

bosh
see **bunkum**

Bosnia-Herzegovina
capital: **8** Sarajevo
language: **7** Serbian **8** Croatian **13** Serbo-Croatian
monetary unit: **4** mark **5** dinar
neighbor: **6** Serbia **7** Croatia
part of: **7** Balkans
sea: **8** Adriatic

bosom
4 bust, core, soul, teat **5** chest, close, heart **6** breast **7** embrace **8** feelings, intimate **10** affections, conscience

bosomy
5 built, busty, buxom, curvy **6** chesty, zaftig **7** shapely, stacked **9** Junoesque **11** full-figured

boss
4 capo, head, stud **5** chief, neato **6** direct, honcho, leader, manage, master, survey, worthy **7** command, foreman, headman, oversee **8** director, employer, overlook, overseer, superior **9** chieftain, excellent, first-rate, supervise **10** supervisor, taskmaster **11** superintend
African: **5** bwana

bossy
3 cow **4** calf **7** studded **8** despotic, imperial **9** arbitrary, assertive, imperious, masterful **10** autocratic, high-handed, imperative, oppressive, peremptory, tyrannical **11** controlling, dictatorial, domineering, magisterial, overbearing

Boston Bruins star Bobby
3 Orr

Boston fish
3 cod **5** scrod

botanist
American: **4** Gray (Asa) **5** Sears (Paul B.) **6** Bailey (Liberty), Bessey (Charles), Carver (George Washington) **7** Bartram (John, William), Burbank (Luther) **9** Fairchild (David)
Austrian: **6** Mendel (Gregor)
British: **6** Sloane (Sir Hans)
Danish: **7** Warming (Johannes)
Dutch: **7** De Vries (Hugo)
French: **7** Lamarck (Chevalier de)
German: **4** Cohn (Ferdinand), Mohl (Hugo von) **5** Sachs (Julius von)
Irish: **6** Harvey (William)
Scottish: **5** Brown (Robert)
Swedish: **8** Linnaeus (Carolus)
Swiss: **6** Nägeli (Karl) **8** Candolle (Augustin)

botany branch
7 ecology **8** algology, bryology, mycology **9** phycology **10** morphology, palynology, physiology **11** hydroponics, paleobotany, pteridology, systematics **12** bacteriology

botch
4 blow, flop, flub, foul, goof, mess, muck, muff, ruin **5** fluff, gum up, misdo, mix-up, snafu, snarl, spoil **6** bobble, boggle, bollix, bumble, bungle, fiasco, foul up, fumble, goof up, mess up, muddle **7** balls-up, blunder, confuse, louse up, washout **8** bugger up, disaster, disorder, dishevel, mishmash, shambles **9** mishandle, mismanage, patchwork **10** discompose, hodgepodge, misconduct

botchy
5 messy **6** blowsy, blowzy, frowsy, frowzy, sloppy, untidy **7** chaotic **8** careless, confused, slapdash, slipshod, slovenly

both
combining form: **3** bis
prefix: **4** ambi, amph **5** amphi

bother
3 ado, bug, irk, nag, vex **4** drag, fret, fuss, gall, pest, pain **5** annoy, eat at, harry, trial, upset **6** badger, flurry, harass, needle, pester, plague, ruffle **7** afflict, agitate, anxiety, bedevil, concern, disturb, fluster, perturb, provoke, torment, trouble **8** disquiet, headache, irritant, nuisance, vexation **9** aggravate, annoyance **10** discompose, exasperate, irritation **11** aggravation, intrude upon **12** exasperation **13** inconvenience

botheration
4 damn, pain, pest **5** trial **6** plague **7** torment **8** headache, irritant, nuisance, vexation **9** annoyance **10** difficulty, irritation **11** aggravation, provocation **12** exasperation **13** inconvenience

Botswana
capital: **8** Gaborone
city: **11** Francistown
desert: **8** Kalahari
former name: **12** Bechuanaland
language: **6** Tswana
monetary unit: **4** pula
neighbor: **7** Namibia **8** Zimbabwe **11** South Africa
river: **5** Chobe **6** Molopo **7** Limpopo **8** Okavango

bottle
4 vial **5** cruet, cruse, flask, phial **6** ampule, carafe, fiasco, flacon, magnum, vessel **7** ampoule **8** decanter, jeroboam **9** container

bottle gourd
8 calabash

bottleneck
5 choke **6** hinder, impede, narrow **7** impasse **8** obstacle, obstruct, paralyze, slowdown, throttle **9** hindrance **10** choke point, congestion, traffic jam **11** obstruction

bottom
3 bum **4** base, boat, butt, core, duff, foot, root, pith, rump, seat, ship, sole, soul, tail, tush **5** basal, basic, basis, fanny, found, nadir **6** behind, breech, heinie, lowest, source **7** bedrock, essence, footing, primary, rear end **8** backside, buttocks, derriere, pedestal, pediment **9** establish, fundament, lowermost, posterior, predicate, principle, underbody, undermost, underside **10** foundation, nethermost, underbelly, underlying, underneath **11** fundamental, lowest point **12** undersurface

bottomless
4 deep, vast **7** abysmal, endless **8** baseless, enduring, profound, unending **9** boundless, unlimited **10** groundless, unfillable, ungrounded **11** everlasting, inestimable, never-ending **12** immeasurable, incalculable, unfathomable **13** inexhaustible

bottommost
4 last **5** least **6** lowest **7** deepest

bouffe
5 comic

bough
3 arm **4** limb **5** shoot **6** branch **8** offshoot

boulder
4 rock

boulevard
4 road **6** artery, avenue, street **7** terrace **8** main drag **9** esplanade, promenade **10** high street **12** thoroughfare

boulevardier
7 flaneur, trifler **9** bon vivant **10** aficionado, dilettante **11** cognoscente, connoisseur **12** man-about-town

bounce
3 axe, can, hop, pep, vim, zip **4** fire, jump, leap, oust, sack, zest **5** expel, vault, verve, vigor **6** energy, hurdle, spirit, spring **7** bluster, boot out, dismiss, kick out, rebound, saltate, sparkle **8** buoyancy, ricochet, vitality **9** animation, discharge, eliminate, terminate **10** ebullience, elasticity, liveliness

bounce back
5 rally **6** perk up, pick up, recoil, return, revive **7** cheer up, improve, rebound, recover **8** backfire **9** boomerang **10** recuperate, turn around

bounce off
5 carom **7** rebound **8** ricochet

bouncer
4 goon **5** guard **8** houseman, sentinel, watchman **9** muscleman

bouncing ball game
5 jacks

bouncy
3 gay **4** airy **5** peppy, perky **6** blithe, cheery, jaunty, jocund, lively **7** buoyant, elastic **8** animated, volatile **9** ebullient, energetic, expansive, exuberant, resilient, sprightly **10** unsinkable **12** effervescent, high-spirited **13** irrepressible

bound
3 end, hem, hop, rim **4** bolt, edge, jump, leap, term, skip **5** caper, frisk, hem in, limit, skirt, vault, verge **6** border, bounce, define, demark, driven, finite, fringe, gambol, hurdle, margin, spring, sprint **7** confine, delimit, enclose, hotfoot, limited, mark out, obliged, pledged, rebound, saltate **8** articled, beholden, confined, confines, enslaved, resolved, restrain, surround **9** compelled, demarcate, obligated **10** determined, indentured, limitation **11** apprenticed, responsible **12** circumscribe

boundary
3 hem **4** mete, pale **5** ambit, limit **6** limits, margin **7** compass, outline **8** confines, environs, purlieus **9** perimeter, precincts **10** borderline **11** demarcation **13** circumference

bounder
3 cad, cur, dog **4** boor, worm **5** knave, louse, rogue **6** rascal, rotter

boundless
4 vast **5** great **7** endless **8** infinite **9** excessive, limitless, unbounded, unlimited **10** indefinite, unconfined, unmeasured **11** illimitable, measureless **12** immeasurable, unrestricted **13** inexhaustible, unsurpassable

bounteous
5 ample **6** benign, lavish **7** copious, liberal,

profuse **8** abundant, generous, handsome, prodigal **9** bountiful, capacious, expansive, extensive, plenteous, plentiful, unsparing **10** beneficent, big-hearted, freehanded, munificent, openhanded, voluminous **11** magnanimous, overflowing

bountiful
see **bounteous**

bounty
5 grant, prize, yield **6** deluge, plenty, reward, wealth **7** payment, premium **8** plethora, richness **9** abundance, affluence, plenitude, profusion **10** cornucopia, generosity, inducement, liberality, luxuriance, prosperity **11** benevolence, copiousness **12** compensation

Bounty
captain: 5 Bligh (William)
event: 6 mutiny
first mate: 9 Christian (Fletcher)
letters: 3 HMS

bouquet
4 balm, kudo, nose, odor, posy **5** aroma, kudos, scent, spice, spray **6** eulogy, medley **7** acclaim, corsage, essence, garland, incense, nosegay, perfume **8** accolade, encomium **9** fragrance, redolence **10** compliment **11** arrangement, boutonniere **12** commendation

bourgeois
7 burgher **8** ordinary **10** conformist, philistine **11** middle-class **12** conventional

bourgeoisie
11 middle class, third estate

Bourne Identity author
6 Ludlum (Robert)

bout
3 jag, run **4** game, meet, term, tour, turn **5** match, round, shift, siege, spell, spasm, spree, stint, throe, trick **6** attack **7** contest, session **8** outbreak **9** smackdown **10** engagement

boutique
4 shop **8** emporium

boutonniere site
5 lapel

bovine
3 cow, yak **4** anoa, bull, calf, gaur, neat, oxen (plural), zebu **5** bison, steer, stirk **6** heifer, placid, torpid, wisent **7** aurochs, banteng, buffalo, bullock, cowlike **8** longhorn
genus: 3 Bos
sound: 3 low, moo

bow
3 arc, bob, dip, nod **4** arch, bend, knot, lout, prow, turn **5** angle, crook, curve, debut, defer, hunch, round, stoop, yield **6** archer, congee, curtsy, give in, kowtow, relent, salaam, salute, submit **7** concede, curtsey, flexure, incline, rainbow, succumb, turning **9** curvation, curvature, genuflect, obeisance, surrender **10** capitulate **11** buckle under **12** knuckle under
ornament: 10 figurehead

Bow, Clara
6 It girl

bowdlerize
4 blip, edit **6** censor, excise, purify, screen **7** abridge, cleanse, distort, launder **8** sanitize **9** expurgate **10** adulterate, blue-pencil

bowed
4 bent **5** arced, bandy **6** arched, curved **11** bandy-legged, curvilinear

bowel
3 gut **9** intestine

bower
5 arbor **6** anchor **7** enclose, pergola, retreat **9** apartment

bowery
7 skid row

bowfin
4 amia **7** mudfish

bowl
5 arena, basin, jorum, mazer, stade, tazza **6** lavabo, tureen, vessel **7** stadium **8** coliseum **12** amphitheater

bowlegged
5 bandy

bowler
3 hat **5** derby **6** kegler

Bowl game
5 Super
Abilene: 5 Pecan
Anaheim: 7 Freedom
Arlington, Texas: 6 Cotton
Atlanta: 5 Peach
Dallas: 6 Cotton
El Paso: 3 Sun
Fresno: 10 California
Glendale, Ariz.: 6 Fiesta
Honolulu: 5 Aloha
Houston: 10 Bluebonnet
Jacksonville: 5 Gator
Memphis: 7 Liberty
Miami: 6 Orange **8** Carquest
Mobile: 6 Senior
New Orleans: 5 Sugar
Orlando: 6 Citrus
Pasadena: 4 Rose
San Diego: 7 Holiday
Shreveport: 12 Independence
Tampa: 10 Hall of Fame
Tempe: 6 Fiesta
Tucson: 6 Copper

bowling
7 kegling
British: 8 skittles
Italian: 5 bocce, bocci 6 boccie
term: 3 pin 4 hook, lane, spot 5 curve, frame, spare, split 6 gutter, strike, string, turkey 7 duckpin 9 candlepin

bowl over
3 awe, wow 4 daze, fell, slay, stun 5 floor, shock, throw 6 boggle, dismay 7 astound, flatten, impress, stupefy 8 blow away, surprise 9 bring down, dumbfound, knock down, overwhelm 10 disconcert

bow out
4 exit, fold, quit 5 leave, welsh 6 beg off, give up, retire 8 withdraw 9 surrender

box
3 bin 4 case, cell, chop, cuff, duke, inro, loge, slap, sock, spar 5 booth, chest, clout, crate, fight, punch, smack, stall, trunk 6 buffet, carton, casket, coffer, coffin, encase, hopper, packet 7 confine, enclose, package 9 container, enclosure, rectangle 10 pigeonhole, receptacle 11 compartment

boxer
7 fighter, palooka 8 pugilist 9 flyweight 11 heavyweight, lightweight 12 bantamweight, middleweight, welterweight 13 featherweight
call: 3 TKO
champ: 3 Ali (Muhammad) 4 Baer (Max), Bowe (Riddick), Clay (Cassius) 5 Bruno (Frank), Jones (Roy), Lewis (Lennox), Louis (Joe), Moore (Archie), Tyson (Mike) 6 Hagler (Marvin), Hearns (Thomas), Holmes (Larry), McCall (Oliver), Moorer (Michael), Seldon (Bruce), Spinks (Leon, Michael), Tunney (Gene), Walker (Mickey) 7 Charles (Ezzard), Corbett (James), Dempsey (Jack), Douglas (Buster), Foreman (George), Frazier (Joe), Johnson (Jack), LaMotta (Jake), Leonard (Sugar Ray), Sharkey (Jack), Walcott (Joe), Willard (Jess) 8 de la Hoya (Oscar), Marciano (Rocky), Robinson (Sugar Ray), Sullivan (John L.) 9 Armstrong (Henry), Holyfield (Evander), Klitschko (Vitali, Wladimir), Patterson (Floyd), Schmeling (Max)

boxing
8 pugilism 10 fisticuffs 13 prizefighting
term: 3 jab, TKO 4 blow, bout, duck, foul, hook, kayo, ring, rope, spar 5 break, count, feint, glove, match, parry, punch, round, swing 6 bucket, canvas, corner 7 low blow, referee 8 heavy bag, knockout, uppercut 9 knockdown 11 punching bag

boy
3 lad, son, tad 5 gamin, puppy, sonny 6 laddie, nipper, shaver 9 shaveling, stripling, youngster
combining form: 3 ped 4 paed, paid, pedo 5 paedo, paido
errand: 5 gofer 8 lobbygow
French: 6 garçon
from Mayberry: 4 Opie
Italian: 7 ragazzo
Latin: 4 puer
mischievous: 6 urchin
Spanish: 4 niño 8 muchacho

___ boy!
4 Atta

boyfriend
4 beau 5 swain 6 fiancé, old man, suitor 7 main man 9 inamorato
French: 3 ami

Boy Scout
founder: 11 Baden-Powell (Robert)
gathering: 8 jamboree
motto: 10 be prepared
rank: 4 Life (Scout), Star (Scout) 5 Eagle (Scout) 10 Tenderfoot
unit: 5 troop 6 patrol

Boys Town
founder: 8 Flanagan (Edward)
star: 6 Crosby (Bing)
state: 8 Nebraska

bozo
3 oaf 4 boob, clod, dodo, dolt, dope, fool, goof, jerk, mutt, simp, yo-yo 5 chump, dummy, dunce, idiot, moron, ninny, noddy, schmo, stupe 6 dimwit, donkey, dum-dum, nitwit, noodle 7 airhead, dullard, pinhead 8 bonehead, clodpoll, dumbbell, dumbhead, imbecile, lunkhead, meathead, numskull 9 birdbrain, blockhead, ignoramus, lamebrain, numbskull, simpleton, thickhead 10 dunderhead, hammerhead, nincompoop 11 chowderhead, chucklehead, knucklehead

BP acquisition
5 Amoco

B.P.O.E. member
3 Elk

Brabantio's daughter
9 Desdemona

brabble
3 row 4 beef, feud, flap, riot, spat, tiff 5 argue, scrap, set-to 6 bicker, blowup, fracas, grouse 7 dispute, fall out, palaver, quarrel, rhubarb, scuffle, wrangle 8 argument, squabble 9 altercate, bickering, brannigan, caterwaul, wrangling 10 falling-out 11 altercation, disputation, embroilment

brace
3 arm, bar, duo, tie, two 4 dyad, gird, pair, prop, stay 5 clamp, ready, shore, steel, strut, truss 6 accost, bear up, column, couple, demand, splint, steady, uphold 7 bolster, bracket, enliven,

fortify, freshen, prepare, refresh, shore up, support, sustain, tighten, twosome **8** buttress **9** reinforce **10** cantilever, exhilarate, invigorate, strengthen **12** underpinning **13** underpropping

bracelet
6 bangle **7** manacle **8** wristlet

bracing
4 keen **5** brisk, crisp, fresh, nippy, sharp, tonic **6** biting, chilly **7** rousing **8** stirring **9** animating **10** energizing, quickening **11** restorative, stimulating, stimulative **12** exhilarating, invigorating

bracken
4 fern **5** brake, brush, scrub **11** undergrowth

bracket
3 arm **4** join, link, omit **5** brace **6** couple, relate, remove, sconce **7** combine, compare, conjoin, connect, embrace, enclose, include, support **8** buttress, encircle, leave out, put aside, set aside **9** associate, encompass **11** parenthesis **12** strengthener

brackish
4 sour **5** acrid, briny, salty **6** saline, salted **9** repulsive, sickening

bract
4 leaf **5** glume **6** paleat, spathe **8** phyllary

brad
4 nail

Bradamant
brother: **7** Rinaldo
husband: **6** Rogero **8** Ruggiero

Bradbury, Ray
forte: **5** sci-fi **7** fantasy
work: **13** Dandelion Wine **14** Illustrated Man (The) **17** Martian Chronicles (The)

Bradley of World War II
4 Omar

Brady Bunch
actor: **4** Reed (Robert) **5** Davis (Ann B.), Olsen (Susan), Plumb (Eve) **6** Knight (Christopher) **8** Williams (Barry) **9** Henderson (Florence), McCormick (Maureen) **10** Lookinland (Mike)
character: **3** Jan **4** Greg **5** Alice, Bobby, Cindy, Peter, Tiger **6** Marcia **9** Mike Brady
creator: **8** Schwartz (Sherwood)

brae
4 bank, hill **5** slope **8** hillside

brag
3 gas **4** blow, crow, puff **5** boast, mouth, prate, vaunt **7** show off, swagger, talk big **9** cockiness, gasconade **10** grandstand **11** rodomontade

braggadocio
6 hot air **7** boaster, bombast, bravado, conceit, puffery, swagger, windbag **8** blowhard, boasting, braggart, bragging **9** arrogance, cockiness, pomposity **10** cockalorum, pretension, swaggering **11** fanfaronade

braggart
6 blower **7** boaster, egotist, vaunter, windbag **8** big mouth, blowhard **9** big talker, know-it-all, swaggerer, vulgarian **11** braggadocio

Brahmin
8 highbrow **9** blueblood, patrician **10** aristocrat

braid
4 plat **5** plait, queue **6** ricrac **7** galloon, pigtail **8** rickrack, soutache **9** interlace **10** intertwine, interweave

brain
3 wit **4** bean, conk, mind **7** concuss **9** intellect **10** gray matter **12** intelligence
bone: **5** skull **7** cranium
channel: **4** iter
clot: **10** thrombosis
gland: **6** pineal **9** pituitary
layer: **6** cortex
lobe: **6** limbic, vermis **7** frontal **8** parietal, temporal **9** occipital
membrane: **3** pia **4** dura **6** meninx **8** pia mater **9** arachnoid, dura mater
part: **4** lobe **6** fornix **7** medulla **8** cerebrum, thalamus **9** sensorium, ventricle **10** cerebellum, hemisphere **12** diencephalon
relating to: **8** cerebral **10** encephalic
ridge: **4** gyri (plural) **5** gyrus
scan: **3** EEG, MEG, MRI, PET
vertebrate: **10** encephalon
wave record: **3** EEG

brainchild
4 idea, opus, work **6** animus, scheme, theory **7** coinage **9** handiwork, invention **10** hypothesis, innovation **11** achievement, chef-d'oeuvre, contrivance

brainiac
3 wiz **4** whiz **6** genius **7** prodigy

brainless
3 dim **5** dense, silly, thick **6** simple, stupid **7** asinine, foolish, idiotic, moronic, vacuous, witless **9** dim-witted, nitwitted **10** acephalous **12** feebleminded

brainpower
3 wit **5** sense **6** smarts **8** aptitude, capacity, sagacity **9** intellect, mentality, mother wit **12** intelligence

brains
4 mind **6** smarts **9** intellect **12** intelligence

brainsick
3 mad **4** daft **5** batty, crazy, manic, potty **6** crazed, insane, mental **7** cracked, haywire, lunatic **8** aberrant, demented, deranged, maniacal, unhinged **9** bedlamite, delirious, disturbed **10** disordered, incoherent, irrational, unbalanced

brainstorm
3 rap, jaw **4** idea **6** confer, huddle **7** discuss,

dream up, think up **8** cogitate, mull over **10** kick around, toss around **11** inspiration

brainteaser
5 poser, rebus **6** enigma, puzzle, riddle **7** stumper **9** conundrum **10** cryptogram

brainwashing
10 propaganda **11** mind control, reeducation

brainy
4 keen **5** quick, savvy, sharp, smart **6** adroit, astute, bright, clever **8** cerebral **9** eggheaded, brilliant, sagacious **10** discerning, precocious **11** intelligent, quick-witted, ready-witted **13** knowledgeable, perspicacious
organization: 5 Mensa

brake
4 curb, slow, stop **5** block **6** damper, hinder, impede, retard, slough **7** barrier, bracken, slacken **8** blockade, obstacle, obstruct, slow down **9** deterrent, hindrance **10** constraint, decelerate **11** bracken fern

bramble
4 burr **5** briar, brier, furze, gorse, hedge, shrub, thorn **6** nettle **7** thistle

branch
3 arm, leg **4** fork, limb, rami (plural), spur, wing **5** bough, ramus **6** office, ramify **7** chapter, diverge, outpost **8** division **9** tributary **10** subsidiary

branched
6 ramate, ramose

brand
4 blot, blur, logo, make, mark, onus, sear, slur, sort, spot, type **5** badge, class, odium, stain, stamp, sword, taint, torch **6** accuse, charge, impute, stigma, stripe **7** species, variety **8** black eye, disgrace, insignia, logotype **9** trademark **10** stigmatize

brandish
4 wave **5** flash, shake, sport, swing, wield **6** flaunt, parade **7** display, exhibit, show off **8** flourish

brand-new
4 mint **5** fresh **6** latest, unused, virgin **8** up-to-date **9** untouched **11** cutting-edge **13** inexperienced

brandy
4 marc, ouzo, raki **5** Pisco **6** cognac, grappa, kirsch, Metaxa **7** liqueur **8** Armagnac, calvados, digestif, eau-de-vie **9** applejack, framboise, slivovitz
cocktail: 7 sidecar, stinger **9** Alexander

brannigan
3 row **4** bust, flap, spat, tiff **5** binge, fight, set-to, spree **6** bender, blowup, hassle, ruckus **7** brabble, discord, dispute, quarrel, wassail, wrangle **8** squabble **10** falling-out **11** altercation

Braque, e.g.
6 cubist

brash
4 bold, flip, pert **5** cocky, gutsy, hasty, nervy, saucy **6** brassy, brazen, cheeky, madcap, uppish, uppity **7** brittle, forward **8** arrogant, cocksure, flippant, impudent, insolent, reckless, tactless **9** audacious, bumptious, ebullient, energetic, exuberant, hot-headed, impetuous, impolitic, unabashed, untactful **10** ill-advised, incautious **11** overweening, thoughtless **12** high-spirited, presumptuous, undiplomatic, unrestrained **13** disrespectful, inconsiderate, irrepressible, self-assertive

brashness
4 gall, grit, guts **5** brass, cheek, crust, nerve **8** audacity, chutzpah, temerity **10** confidence, effrontery **11** presumption

brass
4 gall **5** cheek, nerve **8** audacity, chutzpah **9** brashness, impudence, insolence **10** confidence, effrontery **11** presumption **12** impertinence
component: 4 zinc **6** copper

brassbound
3 set **5** brash, rigid **6** brazen, narrow **7** adamant, bigoted, forward **8** obdurate **9** illiberal, presuming, obstinate, unbending **10** implacable, inflexible, intolerant, unswayable, unyielding **11** opinionated, small-minded, unrelenting **12** narrow-minded, presumptuous, single-minded **13** dyed-in-the-wool, self-assertive

brasserie
10 restaurant

brass hat
3 VIP **4** boss **5** elder **6** better, senior **7** big shot **8** big wheel, higher-up, superior

brassica
4 kale, rape **5** colza **6** turnip **7** cabbage, mustard **8** broccoli, collards, kohlrabi, rutabaga **11** cauliflower

brass tacks
5 facts **7** details **11** nitty-gritty, particulars

brass worker
7 brazier

brassy
see **brazen**

brat
3 imp **4** punk **6** urchin **10** holy terror

bravado
5 bluff **6** hot air **7** bluster, bombast **8** audacity, boasting, boldness, bragging, defiance, vaunting **9** gasconade **10** blustering, pretension, swaggering **11** braggadocio, grandiosity **12** boastfulness

brave
4 bold, dare, defy, face, game, meet, risk **5** beard, gutsy, hardy, manly, nervy, noble, stout **6** daring, heroic, manful, plucky, spunky, take on **7** defiant, doughty, gallant, valiant, venture **8** confront, face down, fearless, intrepid, reckless, resolute, spirited, splendid, stalwart, unafraid, valorous **9** audacious, challenge, dauntless, excellent, steadfast, undaunted, withstand **10** courageous **11** boldhearted, indomitable, lionhearted, unflinching, venturesome **12** stouthearted

Braveheart star Gibson
3 Mel

Brave New World author
6 Huxley (Aldous)

bravery
4 grit, guts **5** nerve, pluck, valor **6** daring, mettle, spirit **7** courage, heroism **8** audacity, boldness, temerity **9** derring-do, fortitude, gallantry **11** intrepidity **12** fearlessness, intrepidness
false: **7** bravado

bravo
3 olé **4** euge, rave, thug **5** cheer **6** encore, gunman, hit man, killer **7** ovation, plaudit, villain **8** applause, assassin **9** desperado

bravura
4 bold **5** showy **6** daring, florid, ornate **8** dazzling, skillful, virtuoso **9** brilliant

brawl
3 row **4** feud, flap, fray, fuss, maul, riot, spar, spat, tiff **5** clash, broil, fight, melee, scrap, set-to **6** affray, battle, bicker, dustup, fracas, rumble, tussle **7** bobbery, brabble, contend, quarrel, rhubarb, ruction, scuffle, wrangle **8** dogfight, skirmish, slugfest **9** fistfight, imbroglio, scrimmage **10** donnybrook, fisticuffs, free-for-all **11** altercation, disturbance

brawn
4 beef, meat, thew **5** clout, flesh, might, power, sinew **6** muscle **8** strength **9** puissance **10** headcheese

brawny
5 beefy, burly, husky, lusty, tough **6** robust, sinewy, stocky, strong, sturdy **8** athletic, muscular, powerful, thickset, vigorous **9** strapping, well-built **10** able-bodied

bray
4 mill **5** crush, grind, pound **6** bellow, hee-haw, pestle, powder **7** atomize, trumpet **9** pulverize

brazen
4 bold, loud **5** brash, gaudy, noisy, showy **6** arrant, brassy, cheeky **7** blatant, defiant, forward, glaring, jarring **8** flagrant, impudent, insolent **9** audacious, barefaced, obtrusive, shameless, unabashed **10** outrageous, procacious, unblushing **11** conspicuous, impertinent **12** contumelious, presumptuous **13** disrespectful

Brazil
capital: **8** Brasília
city: **3** Rio **5** Belém **6** Recife **8** Salvador, São Paulo **12** Rio de Janeiro **13** Belo Horizonte
discoverer: **6** Cabral (Pedro)
island: **6** Marajó **7** Caviana
language: **10** Portuguese
monetary unit: **4** real **8** cruzeiro
neighbor: **4** Peru **6** Guyana **7** Bolivia, Uruguay **8** Colombia, Paraguay, Suriname **9** Argentina, Venezuela **12** French Guiana
river: **4** Pará **6** Amazon **8** Parnaíba **10** Alto Paraná **12** São Francisco
state: **4** Acre, Pará **5** Amapá, Bahia, Ceará, Goiás, Piauí **6** Paraná

breach
3 gap **4** gash, hole, leap, open, rent, rift, slit **5** break, chasm, cleft, crack, split **6** hiatus, lacuna, schism **7** break in, discord, disrupt, fissure, infract, interim, opening, rupture, violate **8** aperture, disunity, division, fracture, infringe, interval, trespass **9** disregard, severance, violation **10** alienation, contravene, infraction, separation, transgress **11** delinquency, dereliction **12** disaffection, disobedience, estrangement, infringement, interruption **13** contravention, discontinuity, noncompliance, nonobservance, transgression

bread
3 bun **4** food, pita, roll, rusk, wrap **5** bagel, bialy, money, scone, toast **6** living, muffin, sippet **7** biscuit, crouton, edibles, stollen **8** hardtack, victuals, zwieback **9** provender, sourdough **10** livelihood, provisions, sustenance **11** comestibles, maintenance, subsistence
communion: **4** host **5** wafer **9** Eucharist
English: **7** crumpet
French: **7** brioche **8** baguette **9** croissant
from heaven: **5** manna
Indian: **3** nan **4** naan, roti
ingredient: **4** meal **5** flour, yeast **6** leaven
Italian: **8** ciabatta, focaccia **10** bruschetta
Jewish: **5** matzo **6** hallah, matzoh **7** challah
loaf: **8** baguette
maker: **5** baker
Scottish: **7** bannock
spread: **3** jam **4** oleo **5** jelly **6** butter **9** margarine
unleavened: **5** matzo **6** matzoh

bread and butter
4 keep, work **6** basics, living **7** support **8** mainstay, victuals **10** employment, livelihood, occupation, sustenance **9** nutriment **11** maintenance, necessities, subsistence **12** alimentation

breadbasket
3 gut 5 belly, tummy 6 paunch 7 abdomen, stomach 8 potbelly 9 bay window, beer belly

breadth
4 area, size, span 5 range, reach, scope, space, sweep, width 6 extent, spread 7 compass, expanse, stretch 8 distance, fullness, latitude, vastness, wideness 9 amplitude, expansion, magnitude 10 liberality

break
3 gap 4 bust, dash, halt, knap, leak, luck, rest, rift, ruin, snap, tame 5 burst, clear, crack, inure, sever, solve, spell, split 6 breach, chance, decode, divide, escape, exceed, hiatus, impair, lacuna, refute, relief, reveal 7 destroy, divulge, fall out, interim, lighten, opening, respite, rupture, shatter, surpass, suspend, take ten, time-out, violate 8 accustom, bankrupt, breather, decipher, disclose, division, downtime, fracture, good luck, interval, moderate, take five 9 interlude, interrupt 10 annihilate, controvert, impoverish 11 discontinue, disjunction, dislocation, opportunity, suspensions 12 intermission, interruption 13 discontinuity

breakable
4 weak 5 frail 6 flimsy 7 brittle, fragile, friable 8 delicate 9 frangible

breakaway
4 prop 7 escapee 8 offshoot, renegade, seceding

break down
4 fail, fold, sort, wilt 5 class, decay, index 6 cave in, digest, give in 7 analyze, crumble, crumple, give out, give way, go crazy, succumb 8 classify, collapse, dissolve 9 anatomize, decompose, fall apart 12 disintegrate

breakdown
5 crash, decay, smash, study, wreck 6 mishap 7 crack-up, debacle, failure, smashup 8 analysis, collapse, taxonomy 9 cataclysm, partition 10 disruption, dissection, resolution 11 dysfunction, examination, prostration

breaker
4 wave 6 billow, comber, roller

breakfast staple
4 eggs 5 bacon, toast

Breakfast at Tiffany's author
6 Capote (Truman)

breakfront
7 cabinet 8 bookcase

break in
4 tame 5 train 6 breach, burgle, gentle, invade 7 intrude 8 initiate 9 condition, habituate, interfere, interpose, interrupt

breakneck
4 fast 5 fleet, hasty, quick, rapid, swift 6 racing, speedy, unsafe 8 meteoric 10 harefooted 11 precipitous

break off
3 end 4 drop, halt, kill, stop 5 abort, cease, scrub, sever 6 cancel, detach 7 curtail, scratch, suspend 8 cut short 9 terminate 11 discontinue

break out
4 bolt, flee 5 arise, erupt, flare 6 emerge, escape 7 explode 8 mushroom, separate

break through
5 burst 6 breach, emerge, pierce 7 rupture, surface 8 overcome 9 penetrate

breakthrough
4 find, gain, hike, leap, rise 5 boost 7 advance, radical, upgrade 8 advanced, increase, landmark 9 invention, milestone 10 avant-garde, innovation 11 cutting-edge, development, exceptional, progressive, quantum leap

break up
3 end 4 halt, knap, part 6 divide, sunder 7 destroy, disband, disjoin, disrupt, rupture, scatter, shatter 8 disperse, dissever, dissolve, disunite, separate 9 decompose, dismantle, pulverize, terminate 12 disintegrate

breakup
4 rift 5 split 7 divorce, parting 8 analysis 9 dispersal 10 dissection, separation 11 dissolution

breakwater
5 groin, jetty 7 seawall

breast
5 bosom, chest, heart
animal: 7 brisket
combining form: 3 maz 4 mast, mazo 5 masto, stern, steth 6 mastia (plural), sterno, stetho

breastbone
7 sternum

breast-feed
5 nurse 6 suckle 7 nourish

breastwork
7 barrier, bastion, bulwark, defense, parapet, rampart 9 barricade, earthwork 10 embankment 13 fortification, reinforcement

breath
4 gasp, gust, hint, puff 5 let-up, pause, trace, whiff 6 breeze 7 respite 10 exhalation, inhalation, suggestion

breathe
4 emit, sigh 5 exude, utter, voice 6 endure, exhale, expire, inhale, murmur 7 confide, express, give off, inspire, persist, radiate, respire, subsist, survive, whisper

breather
4 lull, rest, stay, vent 5 break, let-up, pause, spell 6 hiatus, recess 7 caesura, respite 8 downtime 9 remission 12 interruption

breathing
normal: **6** eupnea
problem: **5** apnea **7** dyspnea **8** polypnea

breathing apparatus
10 respirator
underwater: **5** scuba

breathing orifice
4 nose **5** mouth **8** blowhole, spiracle

breathless
4 agog, avid, keen **5** eager **6** ardent **7** anxious, gasping, intense **8** gripping **9** expectant, impatient **11** short-winded **13** on tenterhooks

breathtaking
6 moving **7** awesome **8** dramatic, exciting, imposing, stunning, wondrous **9** panoramic, thrilling **10** impressive, staggering **11** astonishing, magnificent, spectacular **12** awe-inspiring, overwhelming **13** heart-stirring

Brecht play
4 Baal **13** Life of Galileo (The), Mother Courage **15** Seven Deadly Sins (The), Threepenny Opera (The) **20** Caucasian Chalk Circle (The)

breech
3 bum **4** duff, rear, rump, seat, tail **5** fanny **6** behind, bottom, heinie **7** keester, keister, rear end **8** backside, buttocks, derriere, haunches **9** fundament, posterior **12** hindquarters

breechclout
5 dhoti **9** loincloth

breed
3 ilk **4** bear, grow, kind, make, mate, race, rear, sire, sort, type **5** beget, brand, cause, class, cross, genus, hatch, likes, raise, stock, yield **6** couple, create, father, induce, nature, strain, stripe **7** bring up, develop, educate, lineage, nurture, produce, species, variety **8** copulate, engender, generate, mate with, multiply **9** cultivate, procreate, propagate, reproduce **10** discipline, extraction, give rise to, impregnate, inseminate

breeding
4 line **5** class, grace, taste **6** polish **7** culture, decorum, lineage, manners **8** ancestry, civility, courtesy, pedigree **9** genealogy, gentility, propriety **10** refinement, upbringing **11** cultivation

breeding ground
6 hotbed, origin **8** hothouse **10** forcing bed, mating spot **12** forcing house

breeze
3 zip **4** flit, sail, snap, waft **5** cinch, draft, waltz **6** zephyr **8** duck soup, kid stuff **10** child's play

breezy
4 airy, cool **5** fresh, gusty, windy **6** blithe, casual, drafty **7** offhand, relaxed **8** carefree, careless, detached, informal **9** easygoing **10** insouciant, nonchalant **11** unconcerned **12** devil-may-care, lighthearted

Breton
4 Celt

____ breve
4 alla

breviary
5 brief **6** digest, précis **7** epitome, essence, outline, rundown, summary **8** abstract, boildown, synopsis **9** reduction **10** abridgment, conspectus, prayer book **11** abridgement **12** condensation, divine office

brevity
7 economy **8** laconism **9** briefness, concision, crispness, pithiness, shortness, terseness **10** transience

brew
3 ale, tea **4** beer, loom, mull, plan, plot, suds **5** drink, lager, stout **6** cook up, foment, gather, impend, infuse, porter, scheme, stir up **7** concoct, ferment **8** contrive

brewery kiln
4 oast

brewpub quaff
3 ale **4** beer

briar
4 burr, pipe **5** furze, gorse, shrub, thorn **6** nettle **7** bramble, thistle

Briareus
7 Aegaeon
father: **6** Uranus
mother: **4** Gaea

bribable
5 venal

bribe
3 buy, fix, sop **6** buy off, payoff, payola, square, suborn **7** corrupt **9** incentive **10** enticement, inducement, tamper with

bric-a-brac
6 curios **8** trinkets **9** ornaments **10** objets d'art **11** gingerbread, knickknacks **13** embellishment
holder: **7** étagère

brick
5 block, gaffe **7** blunder
layer: **5** mason
laying: **7** masonry
material: **4** clay, marl
oven: **4** kiln
row: **6** course
sun-dried: **5** adobe
toy: **4** Lego
trough for carrying: **3** hod

bridal
7 nuptial, spousal **8** conjugal **9** connubial **11** matrimonial
fabric: **5** tulle
path: **5** aisle

bridal wreath
6 spirea

bridewell
3 can, jug, pen **4** coop, jail **5** clink, joint **6** lockup, prison **7** slammer **8** bastille **12** penitentiary

bridge
4 join, link, span **5** unite **7** connect **8** overpass, traverse
fee: **4** toll
great: **8** Brooklyn **10** Golden Gate
kind: **4** arch, draw, rope **5** swing, truss **7** bascule, covered, natural, pontoon, trestle, viaduct **10** cantilever, suspension
term: **3** bid **4** book, east, pass, ruff, slam, suit, void, west **5** bonus, dummy, north, raise, south, trick, trump **6** double, renege, rubber **7** auction, finesse, no-trump, overbid **8** contract, jump call, redouble **9** grand slam, overtrick, singleton **10** little slam, undertrick, vulnerable

bridgelike game
5 whist **6** hearts

Bridges brother
4 Beau, Jeff

bridle
3 bit **4** curb, fume, rein, rule **5** check, flare, quell **6** govern, halter, hold in, manage, master, rein in, ruffle, seethe, subdue **7** bristle, control, flare up, inhibit, repress **8** hold back, moderate, restrain, suppress, withhold **9** constrain, deterrent, hackamore, restraint

brief
4 curt **5** pithy, short, terse **6** abrupt, digest, inform **7** brusque, concise, epitome, laconic, outline, passing, summary **8** abstract, breviary, fleeting, succinct, synopsis **9** momentary, transient **10** abridgment, conspectus **11** abridgement, compendious **12** condensation **13** short and sweet

briefs alternative
6 boxers

brig
3 can, jug, pen **4** coop, jail **5** clink **6** cooler, lockup, prison **7** slammer **8** stockade **9** guardroom **10** guardhouse

brigade
4 army, unit **5** force, group **6** troops **10** contingent, detachment

brigand
6 bandit, bummer, looter, pirate, raider **7** cateran, corsair, forager, rustler **8** marauder, pillager **9** buccaneer, plunderer **10** freebooter, highwayman

brigandage
7 pillage, sacking **10** despoiling, ransacking **11** depredation

bright
4 fair, keen **5** aglow, alert, clear, light, lucid, quick, shiny, smart, sunny, vivid **6** brainy, cheery, clever, lively, lucent, sunlit **7** beaming, blazing, flaming, fulgent, glowing, lambent, lighted, radiant, shining **8** cheerful, dazzling, gleaming, luminous, lustrous, sunshiny **9** brilliant, effulgent, favorable, refulgent, sparkling **10** auspicious, glittering, precocious, propitious, shimmering **11** illuminated, intelligent, quick-witted **12** incandescent **13** scintillating

brighten
4 buoy **5** cheer, clear, shine **6** look up, perk up, polish, revive, solace **7** burnish, cheer up, clear up, enhance, enliven, furbish, gladden, hearten, improve **8** illumine **10** illuminate

brightness
5 éclat, shine **6** luster, lustre **8** radiance, splendor **10** brilliance, effulgence, luminosity
measure of: **3** lux **5** lumen **6** candle **7** candela **10** foot-candle

bright star
4 nova

brilliance
see **brightness**

brilliant
6 ablaze, brainy, genius, lucent, superb **7** beaming, fulgent, lambent, radiant, shining, stellar **8** dazzling, luminous, masterly, striking **9** effulgent, ingenious, refulgent, sparkling **10** glittering **11** exceptional **12** incandescent
success: **5** éclat

brilliantine
6 pomade **9** hair cream

brim
3 hem, lip, rim **4** edge, fill, well **5** brink, skirt, verge, visor **6** border, fill up, fringe, margin **7** run over **8** overflow, well over **9** perimeter, periphery **13** circumference

brimless hat
5 toque

brimming
4 full **5** awash, flush **6** filled, jammed, loaded, packed **7** crammed, crowded, replete, stuffed, teeming, welling **8** bursting, overfull, suffused, swarming, swelling **9** chock-full, jam-packed **11** chockablock, running over

brimstone
6 sulfur

brine
3 sea **4** deep, main **5** ocean **8** seawater **9** salt water

bring
3 lug **4** lead, pack, tote **5** carry, fetch, gross, yield **6** convey **7** attract, produce **9** transport

bring about
3 win **5** beget, cause **6** create, draw on, effect, secure **7** procure, produce, trigger **8** engender, generate, result in **10** accomplish, effectuate, give rise to

bring around
4 hook, sway, turn **7** convert, win over **8** convince, persuade, talk into **9** argue into, prevail on, sweet-talk **11** prevail upon

bring back
5 renew **6** recall, recoup, return, revive **7** recover, reprise, restore, salvage **8** retrieve, revivify **9** reinstate **10** repatriate **11** reestablish

bring down
3 bag, hew **4** drop, fell, raze **5** floor, level, shoot **6** defeat, depose, ground, humble, lay low, reduce **7** depress, flatten **8** demolish, overturn **9** humiliate, overthrow, prostrate, undermine

bring forth
4 bear **5** beget, educe, yield **6** create, elicit, invent **7** deliver, produce **8** generate **9** propagate, reproduce **10** give rise to

bring forward
6 adduce, submit, tender, unveil **7** advance, present, produce, proffer **9** introduce

bring home
4 earn

bring in
3 pay, net, win **4** draw, earn, gain, make, sell **5** fetch, gross, yield **6** garner, return, secure **7** acquire, be worth, realize **9** introduce

bring off
6 effect, finish, rescue **7** achieve, execute, realize, succeed **8** carry out **9** discharge, implement **10** accomplish, consummate, effectuate **12** carry through

bring out
4 cull **5** educe, utter, voice **6** elicit, reveal **7** declare, enhance, explain, extract **8** disclose, showcase **9** elucidate, highlight, introduce

bring together
3 mix, wed **4** herd, join, link, yoke **5** amass, batch, blend, group, marry, merge, rally, unify, unite **6** corral, muster **7** collect, compact, compile, convene, round up **8** assemble **9** aggregate, integrate, reconcile, stockpile **10** synthesize **11** consolidate

bring up
4 moot, rear **5** breed, raise, refer, teach, train, vomit **6** advert, allude, broach, foster, parent, school **7** advance, educate, mention, nurture, propose, suggest, touch on **8** point out, instruct **9** cultivate, introduce **10** put forward **11** regurgitate

brink
3 hem, rim **4** bank, brim, edge **5** point, skirt, verge **6** border, fringe, margin **9** extremity, perimeter, periphery, threshold

Brinker of fiction
4 Hans

briny
5 salty **6** saline

brio
3 pep, vim, zip **4** dash, élan, fire, life, zest, zing **5** ardor, flair, gusto, oomph, style, verve, vigor **6** bounce, esprit, fervor, spirit **7** panache, passion, sparkle **8** dynamism, vivacity **9** animation

brioche
4 roll

Briseis' lover
8 Achilles

brisk
4 busy, fast, keen, spry, yare **5** agile, fresh, nippy, quick, sharp, zippy **6** lively, nimble, snappy, speedy **7** bracing **8** animated, bustling, vigorous **9** energetic, sprightly **10** refreshing **11** stimulating **12** invigorating

bristle
3 awn **4** boil, burn, fume, seta **5** anger, quill, setae (plural), spine **6** arista, chaeta, seethe **7** chaetae (plural)
Scottish: **5** birse

bristle-like appendage
3 awn **4** seta **6** arista

brit
5 krill

British
air force: **3** RAF
cathedral city: **3** Ely **4** York **5** Ripon, Truro, Wells **6** Durham, Exeter **7** Chester, Lincoln **8** Coventry, Hereford, St. David's **9** Lichfield, Salisbury, Wakefield, Worcester **10** Canterbury, Gloucester
Channel Island: **4** Sark **6** Jersey **8** Alderney, Guernsey
coin, current: **5** pence (plural), penny, pound
coin, old: **3** bob **5** crown, groat, noble **6** bawbee, florin, George, guinea, tanner, teston **8** farthing, shilling **9** halfcrown, halfpenny, sovereign **10** threepence
colony, former: **4** Aden, Cape **5** Adana, Kenya, Malta, Natal **6** Ceylon, Cyprus, Gambia **7** Jamaica, Sarawak **9** Gold Coast, Singapore, Transvaal **10** Basutoland, New Zealand **11** Orange River, Sierra Leone **12** Bechuanaland
county: **4** Avon, Kent, York **5** Derby, Devon, Essex, Gwent **6** Dorset, Durham, Oxford, Surrey, Sussex **7** Bedford, Cumbria, Norfolk, Rutland, Suffolk, Warwick **8** Cheshire, Cornwall, Hereford, Hertford, Somerset, Stafford **9** Berkshire, Cleveland, Hampshire, Lancaster, Leicester,

Wiltshire, Worcester **10** Cumberland, Gloucester, Humberside, Lancashire, Merseyside, Shropshire **11** Westmorland **12** Lincolnshire
court, local: **8** hustings
court, medieval: **4** eyre
era: **9** Edwardian, Victorian **11** Elizabethan
forest: **5** Arden, weald **8** Sherwood
honor: **3** DBE, GBE, KBE, MBE, OBE
king, legendary: **3** Lud **4** Beli, Bran **6** Arthur **7** Artegal, Belinus, Elidure **8** Brannius
language, ancient: **6** Celtic, Cymric **9** Brythonic
legislature: **10** Parliament
medical system: **3** NHS
museum: **4** Tate
news agency: **7** Reuters
nobleman: **4** duke, earl, peer **5** baron **6** prince **8** marquess, viscount
order: **6** Garter
people, early: **5** Celts, Iceni, Jutes, Picts **6** Angles, Saxons
political party: **4** Tory, Whig **6** Labour **12** Conservative
pope: **8** Adrian IV
pop star: **5** Adele
prime minister: **4** Eden (Anthony) **5** Blair (Tony), Brown (Gordon), Heath (Edward), Major (John) **6** Attlee (Clement), Wilson (Harold) **7** Cameron (David) **8** Thatcher (Margaret) **9** Callaghan (James), Churchill (Winston), Macmillan (Harold)
prince: **5** Harry **6** Andrew, Edward **7** Charles, William
princess: **4** Anne **5** Diana **8** Margaret
prison: **5** Tower (of London) **7** Newgate **8** Dartmoor
queen, ancient: **8** Boadicea, Boudicca
resort: **4** Bath **7** Margate **8** Brighton **9** Blackpool
restroom: **3** loo
royal house: **4** York **5** Tudor **6** Stuart **7** Hanover, Windsor **9** Lancaster **11** Plantagenet
royal residence: **7** Windsor **8** Balmoral **10** Buckingham
school: **4** Eton **5** Rugby **6** Harrow **10** Winchester
school, military: **9** Sandhurst
spa: **4** Bath **5** Epsom **6** Buxton **7** Malvern, Matlock **8** Brighton **9** Harrogate **10** Cheltenham
weight: **5** tonne

British Columbia
capital: **8** Victoria
city: **6** Surrey **7** Burnaby **8** Richmond **9** Vancouver
mountain: **11** Fairweather
provincial flower: **7** dogwood (Pacific)

British Honduras
6 Belize

Briton of old
4 Celt, Pict

brittle
4 curt **5** crisp, frail, stiff **6** infirm **7** crumbly, fragile, friable **9** breakable, frangible, inelastic, irritable, sensitive **10** perishable, transitory

broach
3 tap **4** moot **6** open up **7** bring up, mention, propose, suggest **8** initiate **9** introduce **10** put forward

broad
4 wide **7** general, liberal **8** extended, generous, spacious, sweeping, tolerant **9** expansive, extensive
combining form: **4** eury, lati, plat **5** platy

broadcast
3 air, sow **4** beam, show **5** radio, strew **6** blazon, report, spread **7** bestrew, declare, publish, scatter **8** announce, proclaim, televise, transmit **9** advertise, publicize **10** bruit about, promulgate **11** communicate, declaration, disseminate, publication **12** announcement, proclamation, promulgation, transmission
regulator: **3** FCC

broadcasting
5 on air

broaden
4 open **5** swell, widen **6** dilate, expand, extend, fatten, spread **7** amplify, augment, distend, enlarge, thicken **8** increase **10** supplement

broadloom
6 carpet

broad-minded
4 open **7** liberal **8** catholic, eclectic, flexible, tolerant, unbiased **9** accepting, indulgent, unbigoted **10** forbearing, undogmatic **11** progressive **12** unjudgmental, unprejudiced

broadsheet
7 tabloid **9** newspaper

broadside
4 hail **5** burst, salvo, sheet, storm **6** shower, volley **7** barrage, torrent **8** at random **9** cannonade, fusillade, laterally, obliquely **11** bombardment

broadtail
4 hawk **5** sheep **7** karakul **8** lambskin

Broadway backer
5 angel

Brobdingnagian
4 huge **5** giant, jumbo **7** hulking, immense, mammoth, massive, titanic **8** colossal, gigantic, towering **9** cyclopean, humongous, monstrous **10** gargantuan, prodigious **11** elephantine

brochette
4 spit **6** skewer

brochure
5 flier, flyer **7** booklet **8** pamphlet
Brockovich of film
4 Erin
brogue
4 lilt, shoe **6** accent, oxford **7** dialect
broil
3 row **4** bake, burn, char, cook, fray, riot, sear **5** brawl, clash, fight, grill, melee, roast, run-in, toast **6** affray, fracas, scorch, tumult **7** bobbery, rhubarb, ruction, swelter, wrangle **8** disorder, squabble **10** donnybrook, free-for-all **11** disturbance
broiling
3 hot **5** fiery **6** baking, red-hot, torrid **7** blazing, burning **8** ovenlike, scalding, sizzling, white-hot **9** scorching **10** blistering, oppressive, sweltering
broke
4 poor **5** needy, spent **6** busted, ruined **7** drained **8** bankrupt, beggared, dirt poor, indigent, strapped, wiped out **9** destitute, insolvent, out of cash, penniless, penurious, played out **10** cleaned out **11** impecunious
Brokeback Mountain director Lee
3 Ang
broke-in
4 tame **5** tamed **6** docile
broken
4 shot **5** tamed **6** beaten, busted, cut off, faulty **7** crushed, haywire, humbled, subdued **8** bankrupt, defeated, violated, weakened **9** depressed, disrupted, fractured, heartsick, shattered, sorrowful **11** discouraged, demoralized, interrupted **12** disconnected, disheartened **13** discontinuous
broken-down
7 rickety **8** battered, decaying, decrepit **9** crumbling, neglected **10** threadbare, ramshackle **11** debilitated, dilapidated **12** deteriorated
brokenhearted
7 crushed, unhappy **8** dejected, dolorous, hopeless, wretched **9** depressed, heartsick, sorrowful **10** despairing, despondent **12** inconsolable **13** grief-stricken
broker
5 agent **6** factor **8** diplomat, mediator **9** financier, go-between, middleman **10** interagent, interceder, matchmaker, negotiator **11** intercessor **12** intermediary **13** intermediator
brolly
8 umbrella **11** bumbershoot
bromide
4 bore, drip, lump, pill, yawn **5** drone, grind **6** cliché, old saw, truism **7** proverb **8** banality, chestnut, prosaism, sedative **9** platitude, soporific **10** shibboleth, triviality **11** commonplace, rubber stamp
bromidic
3 dry **4** arid, dull **5** banal, bland, dusty, stale, trite **6** boring **7** humdrum, insipid, tedious **8** shopworn, tiresome **9** dryasdust, moth-eaten, wearisome **10** monotonous, pedestrian, unoriginal **11** commonplace **13** unimaginative, uninteresting
bronco
5 horse **6** cayuse **7** mustang
Australian: **6** brumby
Brontë
character: **9** Catherine, Rochester **10** Heathcliff
novel: **7** Shirley **8** Jane Eyre, Villette **16** Wuthering Heights
sisters: **4** Anne **5** Emily **9** Charlotte
Bronx Bombers, for short
5 Yanks
Bronx cheer
3 boo **4** hoot, jeer, razz **5** taunt **7** catcall **9** raspberry
brooch
3 pin **4** clip **5** clasp **8** fastener
brood
3 set, sit **4** fret, mope, muse, stew, sulk **5** cover, flock, gloom, hatch, worry **6** litter, ponder, repine **7** despond, progeny **8** children, meditate, ruminate **9** offspring
brook
4 bear, burn, gill, race, rill **5** abide, creek, stand **6** arroyo, endure, rillet, runnel, stream, suffer **7** rivulet, stomach, swallow **8** stand for, tolerate
Scottish: **6** burnie
Brooklyn island
5 Coney
Brookner novel
10 Hotel du Lac
Brooks of comedy
3 Mel
broom
5 besom, brush, shrub, sweep, whisk **7** heather
bro or sis
3 sib
broth
5 stock **8** bouillon, consommé
brothel
4 crib, stew **6** bagnio **7** lupanar **8** bordello, cathouse **9** call house **10** bawdy house, whorehouse
brother
3 kin **4** monk **5** friar **7** comrade, sibling
biblical: **4** Abel, Cain, Esau, Seth
French: **5** frère
Italian: **3** fra **5** frate **8** fratello
Latin: **6** frater
relating to: **9** fraternal
Spanish: **7** hermano
Vincent's: **4** Theo

brotherhood
4 club, gang **5** amity, guild, order, union **6** league **7** kinship, society **8** alliance, sodality **10** fellowship, fraternity, friendship **11** association, camaraderie, comradeship, confederacy **12** togetherness **13** consanguinity, secret society

brotherly
9 fraternal

brother or sister, for short
3 sib

Brothers Karamazov
4 Ivan **5** Mitya **6** Alexei, Alexey, Dmitri, Dmitry **7** Alyosha **10** Smerdyakov

brought up
4 bred **6** raised, reared

brouhaha
3 din **4** coil, flap, fuss, riot, to-do **5** babel, broil, hoo-ha, scene, whirl **6** bedlam, clamor, fracas, furore, hoo-hah, hubbub, hurrah, jangle, pother, racket, ruckus, rumpus, shindy, tumult, uproar **7** ferment **8** ballyhoo, foofaraw **9** agitation, commotion, kerfuffle **10** excitement, hullabaloo, hurly-burly **11** pandemonium

brow
3 top **4** mien **5** front, crest, crown **8** forehead **9** gangplank **10** expression **11** countenance

browbeat
3 cow **5** beset, bully, harry, press **6** badger, carp at, coerce, harass, hector, lean on **7** bluster, dragoon **8** bludgeon, bulldoze, bullyrag, domineer, overbear, pressure **9** tyrannize **10** intimidate

brown
4 sear **5** dusky, toast **6** scorch, tanned **7** swarthy
dark: **5** mocha, sepia, umber **9** chocolate
grayish: **3** dun **6** bister, bistre
light: **3** tan **4** ecru, fawn **5** beige, hazel, khaki, tawny
moderate: **4** teak **6** sienna
reddish: **3** bay **4** roan **5** henna, sepia **6** auburn, russet, sorrel, titian **8** chestnut
yellowish: **6** bronze **12** butterscotch

Brown Bomber
5 Louis (Joe)

brown coal
7 lignite

brownie
3 elf, fay **5** fairy, pixie **6** sprite

Browning poem
8 Prospice, Sordello **11** Aurora Leigh, Pippa Passes **12** Rabbi Ben Ezra **13** Fra Lippo Lippi, My Last Duchess **14** How Do I Love Thee?

brown pear
4 Bosc

brown recluse
6 spider

brownshirt
4 Nazi **12** storm trooper

browse
4 crop, feed, scan, shop, skim, surf **5** graze, munch **6** forage, nibble, peruse **7** dip into, pasture **8** glance at, look over **10** glance over **11** flip through, leaf through, look through, skim through **12** thumb through

browser
5 Opera **6** Chrome, Safari **7** Firefox, Mozilla **8** Explorer

Broz, Josip
4 Tito

bruin
4 bear

Bruins great
3 Orr (Bobby)

bruise
5 pound, wound **6** batter, damage, injure, injury **7** contuse **8** abrasion, discolor **9** contusion **13** discoloration

bruit about
6 blazon, gossip, report, spread **7** declare, publish **8** announce, proclaim **9** advertise, broadcast, circulate **10** annunciate, pass around, promulgate **11** blaze abroad

brume
3 fog **4** film, haze, mist, murk **5** vapor **6** miasma **8** haziness **11** obscuration

brummagem
4 fake, sham **5** bogus, false, gaudy, phony, showy **6** ersatz, pseudo, shoddy, tinsel, tawdry **7** chintzy **8** spurious **9** imitation, pinchbeck, tasteless **10** fabricated, fictitious **11** counterfeit, make-believe

Brummel of Regency England
4 Beau

brunch cocktail
5 shrub **6** mimosa **7** bellini **10** Bloody Mary **11** screwdriver

Brunei
capital: **17** Bandar Seri Begawan
island: **6** Borneo
language: **5** Malay
neighbor: **8** Malaysia
sea: **10** South China

brunet
3 jet **4** dark, onyx **5** dusky, ebony, raven, sable, sooty, swart **6** swarth **7** swarthy **8** bistered, obsidian **10** dark-haired **11** brown-haired

Brunhild
5 queen **7** heroine **8** Valkyrie
husband: **6** Gunnar **7** Gunther
lover: **9** Siegfried

brunt
4 jolt **5** shock **6** burden, impact

brush
4 clip, kiss, skim **5** broom, clash, graze, run-in, scrap, scrub, shave, sweep, whisk **6** glance, scrape, tussle **7** contact, thicket **8** skirmish **9** encounter, shrubbery, sideswipe **11** undergrowth

brusque
4 curt, tart **5** bluff, blunt, brief, gruff, rough, short, surly, terse **6** abrupt, crusty, snippy **7** uncivil **8** impolite, snippety, succinct **10** peremptory, ungracious **11** ill-mannered **12** discourteous

brutal
4 hard **5** cruel, feral, harsh **6** rugged, savage, severe **7** beastly, bestial, callous, inhuman, swinish, vicious **8** barbaric, pitiless, ruthless, sadistic **9** barbarous, ferocious, merciless **10** relentless **11** cold-blooded, remorseless **12** bloodthirsty

brutalize
5 abuse **6** debase, harden **7** corrupt, debauch, deprave, pervert, roughen, subvert, vitiate **8** maltreat, mistreat **9** manhandle **10** bestialize

brute
4 ogre **5** beast, cruel, feral **6** animal, savage **7** beastly, bestial, inhuman, piggish, swinish, varmint **8** creature **10** troglodyte **11** instinctive

brutish
3 low **4** base, vile **5** crude, feral, gross, rough, stony **6** animal, carnal, coarse, scurvy, strong **7** beastly, bestial, boorish, inhuman, obscene, piggish, swinish, uncivil, uncouth **8** barbaric, degraded, depraved, inhumane, physical, sadistic **9** primitive, truculent, unrefined **11** animalistic, uncivilized

Bryn ____
4 Mawr

bryophyte
4 moss **8** hornwort **9** liverwort

Brythonic
see **Cymric**

bubble
3 sac **4** blob, boil, dome, fizz, foam, moil **5** churn, froth, slosh, spume, swash **6** burble, gurgle, seethe, simmer **7** ferment, globule, vesicle **10** effervesce

bubbly
5 alive, fizzy, foamy, jolly, perky, sudsy **6** cheery, frothy, lively **7** buoyant, excited **8** animated, effusive **9** champagne, ebullient, exuberant, sparkling **10** carbonated

buccaneer
5 rover **6** cowboy, pirate, sea dog **7** corsair, sea wolf **8** picaroon, sea rover **9** sea robber **10** freebooter

Buccaneers' base
5 Tampa

buck
3 fop, guy, lad, lug **4** balk, bear, bill, chap, clam, dude, jerk, load, male, move, note, oner, pack, stag, tote, trip **5** cadet, carry, dandy, ferry, fight, money, pitch, repel, stark, throw, token **6** combat, dollar, fellow, oppose, resist, unseat **7** coxcomb, trestle **8** antelope, bank note, sawhorse, traverse **9** greenback, withstand, workhorse **10** completely **11** Beau Brummel

bucket
3 fly, run **4** pail, rush, whiz **5** hurry, speed **6** barrel, basket, hasten, hustle, vessel **9** clamshell **10** receptacle

Buckeye State
4 Ohio

buckle
4 bend, clip, fold, hasp, kink, warp **5** catch, clamp, clasp, heave, yield **6** cave in, fasten **7** contort, crumple, harness **8** collapse **9** fastening **10** coffee cake

buckle under
3 bow **4** cave, fold, give **5** defer, yield **6** cave in, submit **7** concede, succumb **8** collapse **9** surrender **10** capitulate **11** admit defeat

Buck novel
9 Good Earth (The)

buckram
4 taut **5** stiff **6** wooden **8** starched **9** cardboard, unbending **10** inflexible **11** interlining

bucks
4 kale **5** bread, dough, money, moola **6** dinero, do-re-mi, moolah **7** lettuce **10** greenbacks

buck up
4 buoy, lift **5** cheer, rally **6** solace **7** comfort, console, gladden, improve, refresh, smarten **8** brighten **9** encourage **10** strengthen

buckwheat
groats: 5 kasha
pancake: 4 blin **5** blini (plural)

____ buco
4 osso

bucolic
5 rural **6** rustic **7** georgic, halcyon, idyllic **8** agrarian, arcadian, pastoral **10** campestral, provincial **11** countrified, picturesque

bud
3 bro, pal **4** germ, seed **5** gemma, spark **6** sprout **7** burgeon **9** pullulate **10** primordium
combining form: 5 blast **6** blasto

Buddenbrooks author
4 Mann (Thomas)

Buddha
7 Gautama **10** Siddhartha
dialogues: 5 sutra
disciple: 6 Ananda

enemy: **4** Mara
Japanese: **5** Amida, Amita
mother: **4** Maya
son: **6** Rahula
teachings: **6** dharma
wife: **9** Yasodhara

Buddhist
chant: **6** mantra
dialogues: **5** sutra
enlightenment: **6** satori
evil spirit: **4** Mara
fate: **5** karma
language: **4** Pali **8** Sanskrit
monk: **4** lama **5** arhat, bonze
sacred city: **5** Lhasa
saint: **5** arhat
scripture: **5** sutra **6** sutras **9** Pali canon
sect, tradition: **3** Son, Zen **4** Chan **5** Kegon **6** Huayan, Tendai **7** Tiantai **8** Hinayana, Mahayana, Nichiren, Pure Land **9** Theravada, Vajrayana
shrine: **4** tope **5** stupa **7** chorten
spell: **6** mantra
spiritual leader: **4** guru **9** Dalai Lama
state of happiness: **7** nirvana
temple: **6** pagoda
title: **7** mahatma
tree of enlightenment: **5** bodhi, pipal

buddy
3 mac, pal **4** chum, mate **5** crony **6** comate, fellow, friend **7** compeer, comrade, partner **8** coworker, playmate, sidekick **9** associate, companion **10** accomplice **11** confederate

buddy-buddy
5 close, pally, thick, tight **6** chummy **8** intimate **10** palsy-walsy **11** inseparable

budge
4 move **5** shift, yield **7** give way

budgerigar
6 parrot **8** parakeet

budget
5 funds, means **6** amount, ration, supply **8** allocate, estimate **9** allowance, apportion, resources

Budget alternative
4 Avis **5** Hertz

buff
3 fan, fit, nut, rub, tan **4** ecru, fawn, sand, wipe **5** beige, brush, fiend, freak, glaze, gloss, lover, shine, toned **6** addict, expert, polish, votary **7** admirer, burnish, devotee, fanatic, fancier, furbish, groupie, habitué **8** follower **9** yellowish **10** aficionado, altogether, enthusiast **11** connoisseur, yellow-brown

buffalo
4 anoa, arna, bilk, faze **5** bison, bovid, stump **6** baffle, muddlo, rattle **7** carabao, confuse, defraud, flummox, fluster, nonplus, overawe, perplex, swindle **8** befuddle, bewilder, confound, hoodwink **9** bamboozle, dumbfound

Buffalo athlete
5 Sabre

buffalo grass
5 grama

Buffalo's canal
4 Erie

Buffalo's lake
4 Erie

buffer
6 screen, shield **7** buckler, bulwark, cushion **8** absorber, mediator, polisher **9** safeguard **10** protection **12** intermediary

buffet
3 box, hit, rap **4** beat, blip, blow, bump, chop, cuff, drub, jolt, move, poke, slap, sock **5** clout, drive, force, pound, punch, smack, spank **6** batter, hammer, pummel, thrash, wallop **7** belabor, clobber, counter, lambast **8** lambaste, salad bar **9** sideboard

buffoon
4 bozo, dolt, fool, goof, lout, zany **5** antic, clown, comic, droll, dunce, joker, yokel **6** jester **7** bumpkin **8** bonehead **9** blockhead, harlequin **10** clodhopper **11** merry-andrew

bug
3 fad, fan, irk, nag, nut, spy, tap, vex **4** buff, flaw, fret, gall, germ, rage **5** annoy, bulge, craze, fiend, freak, mania, peeve **6** badger, beetle, bother, defect, insect, malady, needle, nettle, pester, plague, zealot **7** disease, fanatic, microbe, provoke, wiretap **8** irritate, listen in, protrude, sickness **9** eavesdrop, infection, obsession **10** enthusiast **12** imperfection **13** microorganism

bugaboo
see **bugbear**

bugbear
4 bane, bogy, fear, ogre **5** bogey, bogie, poser **6** goblin, teaser **7** bugaboo, problem, specter, spectre **8** anathema, bogeyman, phantasm **9** bête noire, boogerman, boogeyman, hobgoblin **10** black beast **11** abomination

buggy
4 cart, tram **6** go-cart, jalopy **8** carriage

bugle
call: **4** mess, taps **5** drill **6** sennet, tattoo **7** fanfare, retreat, tantara **8** assembly, reveille
relative: **6** cornet **7** trumpet **10** flügelhorn
sound: **5** blare

build
3 wax **4** body, form, make, mode, mold, rise

5 boost, erect, forge, frame, habit, mount, put up, raise, set up, shape, swell **6** expand, figure **7** amplify, augment, compose, enlarge, fashion, magnify, produce, upsurge **8** assemble, compound, engineer, escalate, heighten, increase, multiply, physique **9** construct, establish, fabricate, institute, intensify, originate **10** accelerate, inaugurate, strengthen **11** fit together, manufacture **12** conformation, constitution

builder
5 mason **9** carpenter **10** bricklayer, contractor

builder's knot
10 clove hitch

building
3 hut **5** house **7** edifice **8** dwelling **9** structure
addition: **3** ell **4** wing **5** annex
beam: **4** I bar
block: **4** Lego **5** brick
compartment: **3** bay **4** room **6** office
connector: **9** breezeway
farm: **4** barn, crib, shed, silo
for apartments: **8** tenement
for arms: **7** arsenal
for gambling: **6** casino
for grain: **4** silo **7** granary **8** elevator
for horses: **6** stable
for manufacture: **4** shop **5** plant **7** factory
for music: **10** auditorium
for sports: **3** gym **4** bowl **5** arena **7** stadium **8** coliseum **9** gymnasium **10** hippodrome
material: **4** iron, wood **5** adobe, brick, glass, steel, stone **6** cement **8** concrete
projection: **3** bay, ell **4** wing **5** annex **6** dormer **7** cornice
round: **7** rotunda
spot: **4** site

building kit
5 Legos **10** Erector set **11** Lincoln Logs

build up
4 hype, plug, puff **5** boost, brace, erect **6** accrue, expand, extend, praise **7** collect, develop, enhance, fortify, improve, promote **8** buttress, heighten, increase **9** advertise, construct, establish, intensify, publicize **10** accumulate, aggrandize, strengthen

buildup
4 hype, puff, to-do **6** growth, hoopla **8** increase, ballyhoo **9** accretion, expansion, promotion, publicity **10** escalation **11** development, enhancement, enlargement **12** accumulation, augmentation **13** strengthening

built-in
6 inborn, inbred, innate **8** included, inherent **9** essential, ingrained, intrinsic **10** congenital, deep-seated, indwelling **11** established, fundamental **12** constitutive, incorporated

bulb
4 leek, lily, sego **5** onion, tulip **6** allium, dahlia, garlic, squill **8** daffodil, hyacinth **9** amaryllis, narcissus
segment: **5** clove

bulb-like bud
4 corm **5** tuber **7** rhizome

Bulgaria
capital: **5** Sofia
city: **4** Ruse **5** Stara, Varna **6** Burgas, Pleven, Zagora **7** Plovdiv
monetary unit: **3** lev
mountain, range: **6** Balkan, Musala **7** Rhodope
neighbor: **6** Greece, Serbia, Turkey **7** Romania **9** Macedonia
part of: **7** Balkans
river: **6** Danube **7** Maritsa
sea: **5** Black

bulge
3 bag, jut, sac, sag **4** blob, bump, edge, lump, poke **5** bloat, pouch, swell **6** beetle, billow, bubble, bug out, dilate, excess, expand **7** balloon, distend, inflate, project, puff out **8** overhang, protrude, stand out, stick out, swelling **9** allowance, head start **10** distension, projection, promontory, protrusion **11** excrescence, protuberate **12** protuberance

bulk
4 body, core, heft, loom, mass **5** fiber, swell, total **6** amount, corpus, expand, volume **7** bigness, quantum **8** majority, quantity, stand out **9** aggregate, magnitude, substance

bulky
3 fat **5** beefy, hefty, husky, large, obese, stout **7** massive **8** cumbrous, unwieldy **9** corpulent, ponderous **10** cumbersome, overweight **11** substantial

bull
4 bunk, male, slip, toro, trip **5** boner, edict, error, fluff, force, hooey, lapse **6** bovine, bungle, decree, el toro **7** baloney, blooper, blunder, hogwash, mistake **8** nonsense **9** detective
combining form: **4** taur **5** tauri, tauro
sacred: **4** Apis

bulldoze
3 cow **4** move, push, raze **5** abash, bully, clear, cream, elbow, force, level, press, scare, shove **6** coerce, hector, hustle, jostle, lean on, menace, propel, thrust **7** bluster, clobber, dragoon, flatten, oppress, trounce **8** bludgeon, browbeat, bullyrag, demolish, domineer, restrain, shoulder **9** terrorize, tyrannize **10** intimidate, obliterate

bullet
3 ace **4** slug **6** dumdum, tracer **9** cartridge **10** projectile
size: **7** caliber, calibre

bullets, e.g.
4 ammo

bulletin
4 news 5 flash, scoop 6 notice, report 7 account, catalog, gazette, message, missive, release 8 briefing, calendar, dispatch, magazine, register 9 catalogue, statement 10 communiqué, periodical 12 announcement

bull fiddle
10 contrabass, double bass

bullfighter
6 torero 7 matador, picador 8 toreador 11 cuadrillero 12 banderillero
famous: 6 Arruza 7 Ordóñez 8 Belmonte, Joselito, Manolete 9 Dominguin 10 El Cordobés

bullfighting
arena: 5 plaza
cheer: 3 olé
hero: 6 torero 7 matador 8 toreador
lancer: 7 picador
red cloth: 6 muleta
Spanish: 7 corrida
team: 9 cuadrilla

bullheaded
6 mulish 7 adamant, willful 8 contrary, obdurate, perverse, stubborn 9 insistent, obstinate, pigheaded 10 headstrong, refractory, self-willed, unyielding 11 intractable, stiff-necked 12 intransigent, pertinacious, strong-willed

bullish
4 rosy 6 brawny, rising, upbeat 7 booming 9 advancing, expanding, favorable 10 optimistic

bullring cry
3 olé

bully
3 cow 4 goon, pimp, punk, thug 5 abuse, heavy, meany, tease, tough 6 harass, hector, meanie, menace, pander, pick on, rascal 7 bluster, buffalo, dragoon, harrier, oppress, ruffian, torment, torture 8 bludgeon, browbeat, bulldoze, bullyrag, harasser, threaten 9 bulldozer, persecute, victimize, tormenter, tyrannize 10 browbeater, corned beef, intimidate, persecutor 11 intimidator

bullyrag
see **bulldoze**

bulrush
4 reed, tule 5 sedge 7 cattail, papyrus

bulwark
4 wall 6 screen, shield 7 barrier, bastion, parapet, rampart, seawall 8 buttress, fortress, palisade 9 barricade, earthwork, safeguard 10 breakwater, breastwork, embankment, stronghold 13 fortification

bum
3 beg, vag 4 bust, hobo, idle, laze, lazy, loaf, loll, slug, wino 5 binge, cadge, drunk, hit up, idler, mooch, tramp 6 bottom, dawdle, loafer, loiter, lounge, slouch, unfair 7 depress, drifter, feel low, goof off, rear end, vagrant, wheedle 8 buttocks, derelict, fainéant, slugabed, sluggard, vagabond 9 do-nothing, goldbrick, importune, lazybones, panhandle, transient

bumbershoot
6 brolly 8 umbrella

bumble
3 mar 4 blow, flub, muff 5 botch, fluff, gum up, lurch 6 bobble, bollix, bungle, falter, fumble, mess up, muck up, rumble, slip up, teeter, totter 7 blunder, screw up, stagger, stumble 8 flounder

bumbling
5 inept, gawky 6 clumsy, gauche, klutzy 7 awkward, halting, unhandy 8 ungainly 9 all thumbs, graceless, ham-handed, incapable, maladroit, unskilled 11 heavy-handed, incompetent 13 butterfingers, uncoordinated

bummer
3 dud 4 drag, flop, hobo 5 tramp 6 beggar, cadger, downer, sponge, too bad 7 failure, forager, moocher, sponger 8 deadbeat, vagabond 9 tough luck 10 freebooter, panhandler, rotten luck, wet blanket

bump
3 bop, hit, jar, ram, rap, wen 4 bang, bash, bust, jolt, knot, lump, node, oust, slam 5 break, carom, clash, crack, crash, gnarl, knock, prang, shift, shock, shove, wound 6 demote, growth, impact, injury, jostle, jounce, nodule, remove, strike, wallop 7 collide, degrade, demerit, pothole, run into 8 demotion, dislodge, displace, swelling 9 carbuncle, collision, contusion, convexity 10 concussion, projection, protrusion 12 protuberance

bumpkin
3 oaf 4 boor, hick, lout, rube 5 clown, swain, yokel 6 rustic 7 hayseed, peasant 9 chawbacon, hillbilly, simpleton 10 clodhopper, country boy, countryman, provincial

bump off
3 ice 4 do in, kill, slay 5 erase, snuff 6 murder, rub out 7 butcher, execute, take out 9 eliminate, liquidate 11 assassinate

Bumppo, Natty
alias: 7 Hawkeye 10 Deerslayer, Pathfinder
creator: 6 Cooper (James Fenimore)

bumptious
5 cocky, pushy 8 arrogant, impudent 9 audacious, obnoxious, obtrusive, officious 13 self-assertive

bumpy
5 jerky, nubby, ridgy, rough 6 bouncy, jouncy, knobby, knotty, patchy, pimply, uneven 7 jolting, nodular 9 difficult, irregular

bun
4 load, roll **6** pastry **7** brioche

bunch
3 lot, set, wen **4** band, bevy, bump, clot, crew, knot, lump, mass, push, slew **5** batch, clump, covey, crowd, flock, group, party, spray, stack, swell **6** bundle, circle, clutch, gather, huddle, parcel, throng **7** bouquet, collect, cluster **8** assembly, protrude, swelling **9** gathering **10** assemblage, assortment, collection, congregate **11** aggregation **12** accumulation

bunco steerer
3 gyp **6** con man **7** cheater, diddler, grifter, sharper **8** swindler **9** defrauder, trickster **12** double-dealer **13** confidence man

bundle
3 lot, pot, set, wad **4** bale, body, heap, mint, pack, pile, wrap **5** array, batch, bunch, clump, group, sheaf, truss **6** fardel, packet, parcel **7** cluster, fortune **8** fascicle **10** assortment

bung
4 plug **5** cecum, spile **7** stopper

bungalow
5 cabin, lodge **6** chalet **7** cottage

bungle
3 err **4** flub, goof, mess, muff, slip, trip **5** boner, botch, error, fluff, gum up, lapse, misdo, mix up, spoil **6** bollix, bumble, fiasco, foozle, foul up, fumble, goof up, mess up, muck up, muddle **7** blooper, blunder, failure, louse up, misstep, mistake, stumble **9** mishandle, mismanage

bungler
3 oaf **4** clod, dolt, goof **5** klutz **7** screw-up, tomfool **8** bonehead, goofball, shlemiel **9** blunderer, schlemiel **10** stumblebum **11** blunderbuss, incompetent **13** butterfingers

bunglesome
6 clumsy, klutzy **7** awkward **8** bumbling **9** all thumbs **13** uncoordinated

bung up
4 beat, hurt **5** abuse, pound **6** batter, bruise, injure **7** contuse, disable **9** disfigure, manhandle

bunion
4 lump **8** swelling **10** protrusion, tumescence **11** enlargement

bunk
3 bed, cot, kip, rot **4** bosh, bull, guff, jazz **5** bilge, board, crash, hokum, hooey, house, lodge, put up **6** humbug, pallet, piffle **7** eyewash, baloney, hogwash, rubbish, twaddle **8** claptrap, domicile, flimflam, malarkey, nonsense, tommyrot **9** poppycock **10** balderdash

bunker
3 bin **6** dugout **7** bastion, chamber **8** sand trap **10** embankment, stronghold **11** compartment

bunkum
3 rot **4** bosh, bull, guff, jazz **5** bilge, hokum, hooey **6** humbug, piffle **7** baloney, hogwash, rubbish, twaddle **8** claptrap, flimflam, malarkey, nonsense, tommyrot **9** poppycock **10** balderdash

bunny tail
4 scut

bunting
5 finch, flags **8** songbird **9** streamers

Bunyanesque
4 huge **5** giant, jumbo **7** mammoth, massive, titanic **8** behemoth, colossal, gigantic, towering **9** Herculean **10** gargantuan, prodigious

Bunyan's ox
4 Babe

buona ___
4 sera

buoy
4 lift, prop **5** boost, cheer, float, raise **6** assist, beacon, bear up, buck up, signal, solace, uphold, uplift **7** bolster, comfort, gladden, hearten, support, sustain **9** encourage

buoyancy
6 bounce, levity **7** jollity **8** airiness **10** ebullience, exuberance, exuberancy, liveliness, resilience **12** floatability **13** effervescence

buoyant
3 gay **4** airy **5** sunny **6** afloat, bouncy **7** elastic **8** cheerful, floating, volatile **9** expansive, floatable, resilient **10** unsinkable, weightless **12** effervescent, lighthearted

burble
3 gas, yak **4** blab, chat, gush, talk, wash **5** clack, plash, run on, slosh, swash **6** babble, bubble, gabble, gurgle, murmur, rattle, splash, yammer **7** chatter, prattle, sparkle

burden
3 tax, try **4** care, clog, core, duty, gist, haul, lade, load, onus, pile, pith, task, text **5** brunt, cargo, press, theme, weigh **6** amount, charge, chorus, cumber, hamper, lading, lumber, saddle, strain, stress, thrust, upshot, weight **7** afflict, anxiety, freight, oppress, payload, refrain, purport **8** encumber, handicap, obligate, overload, shiralee **9** millstone, substance, weigh down **10** deadweight **11** encumbrance

burdensome
5 tough **6** taxing, trying **7** arduous, exigent, irksome, onerous, weighty **8** crushing, exacting, grievous **9** demanding, difficult, fatiguing, ponderous **10** exhausting, oppressive **11** troublesome **12** backbreaking, unmanageable

bureau
4 unit **5** chest **6** agency **7** dresser, section **8** ministry **10** department, chiffonier **11** writing desk

bureaucrat
8 mandarin, minister, official **11** functionary **12** civil servant, officeholder

burg
4 city, town **7** borough **8** fortress **10** metropolis, walled town **12** municipality

burgee
4 flag **6** banner, ensign, pennon **7** pendant, pennant **8** standard, streamer

burgeon
4 blow, boom, open **5** bloom, build, mount, run up **6** emerge, expand, flower, sprout, thrive, unfold **7** augment, blossom, develop, enlarge, fill out, prosper, run riot **8** flourish, heighten, increase, multiply, mushroom, snowball **9** germinate **10** burst forth, effloresce

Burgess novel
7 Enderby **13** Earthly Powers **15** Clockwork Orange (A)

burghal
5 civic, urban **8** citified **9** municipal **12** metropolitan

burgher
7 citizen, denizen **8** townsman

burglar
4 yegg **5** thief
loot: **4** swag

burglarize
see **burgle**

burglary
5 heist, theft **7** larceny

burgle
3 rob **4** lift, loot **5** heist, steal, strip **6** rip off, thieve **7** despoil, plunder, ransack **9** break into, knock over **10** housebreak

burgomaster
5 mayor **10** magistrate

Burgundy wine
grape: **5** Gamay **9** Pinot Noir **10** Chardonnay
red: **8** Mercurey **10** Beaujolais
white: **5** Rully **6** Chagny **7** Chablis **10** Montrachet **13** Pouilly-Fuissé

burial
4 tomb **5** grave **7** funeral **9** interment, obsequies, sepulcher, sepulchre, sepulture **10** entombment, inhumation
box: **6** casket, coffin
ceremony: **7** funeral, obsequy **9** obsequies
mound: **6** barrow **7** tumulus
tomb: **9** mausoleum, sepulcher, sepulchre

burial ground
8 boot hill, cemetery **8** boneyard, God's acre **9** graveyard **10** churchyard, necropolis **12** memorial park, potter's field
early Christian: **8** catacomb

Burkina Faso
capital: **11** Ouagadougou
ethnic group: **3** Gur **5** Mossi **7** Voltaic
former name: **10** Upper Volta
language: **4** Moré **5** Dyula **6** French
monetary unit: **5** franc
neighbor: **4** Mali, Togo **5** Benin, Ghana, Niger **10** Ivory Coast
river: **5** Volta (Black, Red) **6** Nazion **7** Mouhoun, Nakanbe **8** Red Volta **10** Black Volta

burl
4 knar, knot **5** knaur

burlap
5 gunny **6** fabric **7** bagging, sacking
fiber: **4** hemp, jute

burlesque
3 ape **4** mock, sham **5** farce, spoof **6** parody, satire, send-up **7** lampoon, mockery, mocking, takeoff **8** pastiche, skin show, travesty **10** caricature, distortion, girlie show, lampoonery

burly
4 hale **5** beefy, hefty, husky, tough **6** brawny, robust, strong, stocky **8** athletic, heavyset, muscular, powerful, stalwart, thickset, vigorous **9** strapping

Burma
see **Myanmar**

burn
4 bake, char, cook, fire, fume, rage, sear **5** anger, blaze, broil, creek, flame, flare, gleam, roast, scald, singe, smart, smoke, sting, toast **6** ignite, kindle, scorch, seethe **7** bristle, combust, consume, cremate, flare up, inflame, radiate, smolder, swelter **8** immolate, smoulder **9** carbonize, cauterize **10** incinerate

burnable
8 volatile **9** flammable, ignitable **10** incendiary **11** combustible, inflammable

burned-out
4 beat, shot **5** spent, weary **6** sapped **7** drained, worn-out **8** consumed, fatigued **9** destroyed, exhausted, played-out **10** broken-down **11** debilitated **12** extinguished

burner
3 hob **4** ring **6** Bunsen

Burnett of comedy
5 Carol

burning
3 hot **5** afire, aglow, fiery **6** ablaze, aflame, alight, ardent, fervid, heated, hectic, red-hot, torrid, urgent **7** blazing, fervent, fevered, glowing, ignited, kindled, searing **8** broiling, feverish, pressing, sizzling, white-hot **9** scorching **10** imperative, passionate **11** conflagrant, impassioned **12** incandescent
combining form: **4** igni
malicious: **5** arson

burnish
3 rub, wax **4** buff **5** glaze, gloss, scour, sheen, shine **6** luster, patina, polish, smooth **7** furbish, varnish **8** brighten

burnished
5 shiny **6** glossy, satiny, sheeny **7** lambent, radiant, shining **8** gleaming, lustrous, polished **9** brilliant **10** glistening **11** resplendent

burnsides
8 whiskers **9** sideburns **10** sideboards **11** dundrearies, muttonchops **12** side-whiskers

burp
5 belch, eruct, expel

burrito alternative
4 taco **6** fajita **9** enchilada **10** quesadilla **11** chimichanga

burro
3 ass **6** donkey **7** jackass

Burroughs hero
6 Tarzan

burrow
3 den, dig **4** hole, lair, mine, nook, snug **5** delve, gouge, lodge **6** cavity, cuddle, nestle, nuzzle, tunnel **7** snuggle **10** excavation

burrower
4 mole, vole **5** otter, shrew **6** gopher, marmot **9** woodchuck

burst
3 pop, run **4** bang, boom, clap, gush, gust, rive, rush, slam, wham **5** blast, crack, crash, erupt, flare, go off, lunge, sally, salvo, smash, spasm, split, storm, surge **6** access, blow up, emerge, irrupt, launch, plunge, shiver, spring, shower, volley **7** assault, barrage, dehisce, explode, flare-up, fly open, rupture, shatter, torrent **8** detonate, drumfire, eruption, fragment, outbreak, splinter, splitter **9** broadside, cannonade, explosion, fusillade, onslaught **11** bombardment

Burundi
capital: **9** Bujumbura
ethnic group: **4** Hutu **5** Tutsi
former name: **6** Urundi
lake: **10** Tanganyika
language: **5** Rundi **6** French **7** Kirundi
monetary unit: **5** franc
neighbor: **5** Congo **6** Rwanda **8** Tanzania

bury
4 hide, sink, stow **5** cache, cover, embed, inter, plant, stash **6** absorb, entomb, inhume, mantle, shroud **7** blanket, conceal, cover up, implant, lay away, overlay, put away, secrete **8** ensconce, submerge

bus
5 clear **6** jitney **7** missile, trolley, vehicle **9** hand truck **10** spacecraft

bush
4 rose **5** lilac, shrub, wahoo **6** azalea, cassis, privet **7** currant, thicket, weigela **8** backland, barberry, hazelnut **9** backwater, backwoods, forsythia, manzanita **10** gooseberry, hinterland, wilderness **11** pussy willow **12** rhododendron

bushel
3 ton **4** heap, load, pile **6** basket, hamper **7** pannier

bush-league
5 minor **6** junior, two-bit **8** inferior, mediocre, small-fry **9** small-time **10** inadequate, second-rate **11** lightweight **13** insignificant

Bush or Clinton
3 Eli **5** Yalie

bushranger
6 outlaw **8** woodsman **12** frontiersman

Bush spokesman Fleischer
3 Ari

bushwhack
4 trap **6** ambush, assail, attack, entrap, waylay **7** assault **8** surprise **9** blindside

bushwhacker
6 bandit, outlaw, raider, sniper **8** guerilla, woodsman **9** guerrilla **10** highwayman

bushy
5 bosky, fuzzy, hairy, leafy **6** fluffy, woolly **7** hirsute, unkempt **9** bristling, luxuriant, overgrown **10** disordered **11** flourishing

business
3 job **4** firm, line, work **5** trade **6** affair, custom, matter, métier, office, outfit, racket **7** calling, company, concern, pursuit, traffic **8** commerce, function, industry **9** patronage **10** employment, enterprise, livelihood, occupation **11** corporation **13** establishment
course: **7** finance **8** modeling **9** marketing **10** accounting
degree: **3** MBA
expense: **8** overhead
syndicate: **6** cartel
VIP: **3** CEO

businesslike
6 formal **7** orderly, serious **8** diligent, thorough **9** competent, efficient, practical, pragmatic **10** impersonal, methodical, no-nonsense, purposeful, systematic **11** disciplined, hardworking **12** professional

businessman
6 broker, dealer, trader, tycoon **7** magnate **8** investor, merchant **9** bourgeois, financier, tradesman, executive **10** capitalist, trafficker **12** entrepreneur, merchandiser **13** industrialist

busker
8 minstrel, musician **11** entertainer

buss
4 kiss, peck **5** smack **6** smooch **8** osculate

Bus Stop author
4 Inge (William)

bust
3 bag, cop, dud, hit, jag, nab, net **4** bomb, bump, fail, flop, fold, raid, ruin, slug, sock, tear, tour **5** binge, bosom, break, broke, burst, catch, chest, crash, lemon, loser, punch, smash, spell, spree, stint, torso, trash **6** arrest, bender, breast, collar, demote, pick up **7** break up, carouse, degrade, demerit, destroy, exhaust, failure, rupture, wear out **8** bankrupt, demolish, fracture **9** apprehend, break down, destitute, downgrade, penniless **10** impoverish, police raid
opposite: **4** boom

bustle
3 ado, fly, run **4** flit, fuss, rush, stir, tear, teem, to-do **5** hurry, whirl, whisk **6** action, be busy, bestir, clamor, flurry, furore, hassle, hasten, hubbub, hustle, motion, pother, scurry, tumult, uproar **7** ferment, turmoil **8** activity, to-and-fro **9** commotion, whirlpool, whirlwind **10** hurly-burly, excitement, liveliness

bustling
4 busy, rife **5** brisk, fussy, peppy **6** active, hectic, lively **7** dynamic, festive, hopping, humming, jumping **8** animated, swarming, vigorous **9** energetic **10** tumultuous **11** hard-working, industrious

busty
5 ample, buxom, curvy **6** bosomy, chesty, zaftig **7** shapely, stacked **10** curvaceous, voluptuous **11** full-bosomed, well-rounded

busy
5 brisk, fussy, in use **6** active, at work, lively, on duty, tied up **7** crowded, engaged, hopping, humming, swamped, teeming, working **8** bustling, diligent, employed, hustling, meddling, occupied, overdone, sedulous **9** assiduous, congested, elaborate, energetic, intrusive, obtrusive, officious **10** meddlesome **11** distracting, impertinent, industrious, unavailable

busybody
5 prier, pryer, snoop, yenta **6** butt-in, gossip, old hen **7** meddler **8** informer, kibitzer, quidnunc **9** pragmatic **10** chatterbox, newsmonger, pragmatist, talebearer, tattletale **11** nosey parker, rumormonger **12** gossipmonger, rubbernecker, troublemaker

but
3 bar, yet **4** just, only, save **5** alone **6** except, merely, saving, unless **7** barring, besides, however **8** entirely **9** aside from, excepting, excluding, outside of **13** on the contrary

butcher
4 ruin, slay **5** botch, carve, clean, spoil, wreck **6** bollix, killer, mess up, slayer **7** cut meat, destroy, meat man **8** mutilate **9** slaughter **11** slaughterer

butcher-bird
6 shrike

butcherly
5 cruel **6** bloody, clumsy, savage **7** awkward **8** sadistic **9** ferocious, merciless **10** unskillful

butchery
7 carnage **8** abattoir, genocide, massacre **9** bloodbath, bloodshed, holocaust, slaughter **10** mass murder **12** annihilation **13** extermination

buteo
4 hawk **7** buzzard

butler
5 valet **7** steward **10** manservant

Butler, Samuel
novel: **7** Erewhon **13** Way of All Flesh (The)
poem: **8** Hudibras

butt
3 end, keg, tip, ram, tun, vat **4** base, cask, drum, duff, dupe, join, push, rump, stub, tail **5** chump, fanny, patsy, stump, touch, verge **6** adjoin, barrel, border, bottom, firkin, pigeon, sucker, target, thrust, victim **7** collide, fall guy, rear end, run into **8** derriere, hogshead, neighbor **9** cigarette, fundament, lie beside, pilgarlic, posterior, remainder **11** communicate, sitting duck **12** hindquarters **13** laughingstock

butte relative
4 mesa

butter
artificial: **4** oleo **9** margarine **13** oleomargarine
Indian: **4** ghee
piece: **3** pat
semifluid: **4** ghee
substitute: **4** oleo
tree: **4** shea

butterball
5 blimp, fatso, whale **8** dumpling, elephant **10** bufflehead

butterfish
6 gunnel

butterfly
4 blue **5** diana, satyr, zebra **6** copper, morpho **7** admiral, buckeye, monarch, satyrid, skipper, sulphur, vanessa, viceroy **8** crescent, grayling, milkweed, victoria **9** aphrodite, metalmark, nymphalid, wood nymph **10** fritillary, hairstreak **11** swallowtail
bush: **8** buddleia
case: **6** cocoon

fish: **6** blenny, chiton **7** gurnard
larva: **11** caterpillar
lily: **8** mariposa
order: **11** Lepidoptera
plant: **8** oncidium
pupa: **9** chrysalis
scientist: **13** lepidopterist
Spanish: **8** mariposa

butter up
4 coax **5** charm **6** cajole, kowtow, praise, stroke **7** adulate, beguile, blarney, flatter, massage, wheedle **8** blandish, bootlick, soft-soap **9** brown-nose, sweet-talk **10** overpraise

butt in
6 kibitz, meddle **7** intrude, obtrude **8** busybody, overstep **9** interfere, interlope, interpose, interrupt

buttinsky
5 yenta **7** meddler **8** busybody, kibitzer, quidnunc **9** kibbitzer, loudmouth **10** trespasser **12** troublemaker

buttocks
3 bum **4** duff, rear, rump, seat, tail, tush **5** fanny, nates **6** behind, bottom, breech, heinie **7** hind end, hunkers, keister, rear end, tail end **8** backside, derriere, haunches **9** fundament, posterior

buttonball
8 sycamore **9** plane tree

button-down
6 square, stuffy **8** decorous, orthodox, straight **10** restrained **11** straitlaced, traditional **12** conservative, conventional

buttonhole
5 lobby **6** accost, chat up, detain, waylay **8** confront

buttonwood
8 sycamore **9** plane tree

buttress
4 pier, prop, stay **5** brace, carry, shore, strut, truss **6** back up, bear up, hold up, column, uphold **7** bolster, bulwark, fortify, shore up, support, sustain **9** reinforce, stanchion **10** strengthen **12** underpinning **13** fortification, reinforcement

buxom
5 ample, busty, curvy **6** bosomy, chesty, zaftig **7** shapely, stacked **10** curvaceous, voluptuous **11** full-bosomed, full-figured, well-rounded

buy
5 bribe **6** obtain, ransom, redeem **7** acquire, bargain, believe **8** purchase

buy back
6 ransom, recoup, redeem, regain **8** retrieve **10** repurchase

buyer
6 client, patron, vendee **7** shopper **8** consumer, customer **9** purchaser

buy off
3 fix, sop **5** bribe **6** settle **7** corrupt, silence **9** influence **10** manipulate, tamper with

buzz
3 fad, hum **4** call, fizz, high, hiss, news, purr, ring, talk, whir, whiz **5** craze, drone, hurry, phone, rumor, strum, thrum, whirr, whish **6** bumble, fizzle, gossip, murmur, natter, report, rumble, sizzle, summon, wheeze, whoosh **7** chatter, scandal, whisper **8** sibilate **9** bombinate **11** reverberate, scuttlebutt

buzzard
5 buteo **7** vulture **13** turkey vulture

by
3 per, via **4** away, near, nigh, past **5** along, aside **6** at hand, beside, next to **7** through **9** alongside **10** incidental **11** according to **12** not later than

by and by
4 anon, soon **5** after, later **7** ere long, shortly **8** directly, latterly **9** afterward, presently **10** before long **12** subsequently

by and large
7 all told, broadly, en masse, overall, usually **8** all in all, normally **9** generally, typically **10** altogether, on the whole, ordinarily **11** principally

by dint of
see **by means of**

bye-bye
4 ciao, ta-ta **5** adieu, adios **6** so long **7** cheerio, toodles **8** au revoir, farewell, sayonara, toodle-oo

bygone
3 old **4** dead, late, lost, once, past **5** dated, of old, olden **6** former, fossil, of yore, remote, whilom **7** antique, archaic, belated, defunct, extinct, old-time, onetime, quondam, vintage **8** departed, sometime, obsolete, outdated, outmoded, vanished **9** erstwhile, out-of-date **10** antiquated, oldfangled **12** antediluvian, old-fashioned

by Jove
4 egad **6** zounds

by means of
3 per, via **4** with **5** using **7** through **9** employing, utilizing

byname
6 handle **7** epithet, moniker **8** cognomen **9** sobriquet **10** diminutive, hypocorism **11** appellation

bypass
4 omit, skip **5** avoid, burke, shunt, skirt **6** detour, ignore **7** highway **8** go around, outflank, ring road, sidestep **10** circumvent, pass around **11** deviate from

by-product
5 yield **6** effect, result **7** outcome, residue, spin-off **8** offshoot **9** outgrowth **10** derivative, descendant **11** aftereffect, consequence **12** repercussion

Byron work
4 Cain, Lara **5** Beppo **6** Giaour (The), Werner **7** Corsair (The), Don Juan, Manfred **12** Childe Harold

bystander
6 gawker, viewer **7** watcher, witness **8** beholder, observer, onlooker, passerby **9** spectator **10** eyewitness **12** rubbernecker

by stealth
5 slyly **7** sub rosa **8** covertly, in secret, secretly **9** furtively, privately **10** under cover **11** insidiously **13** clandestinely

by virtue of
see **by means of**

by way of
see **by means of**

byword
3 saw **5** adage, axiom, maxim, motto, nomen **6** dictum, phrase, saying, slogan, truism **7** epigram, epithet, precept, proverb, refrain **8** aphorism, cognomen, nickname **9** platitude, prescript, sobriquet **10** hypocorism, shibboleth **11** catchphrase, commonplace, rallying cry

Byzantine
6 daedal, knotty **7** complex, devious **8** involved **9** elaborate, intricate **10** convoluted **11** complicated **12** labyrinthine **13** sophisticated, surreptitious
emperor: **3** Leo **4** Zeno **5** Basil **6** Bardas, Justin, Phocas **7** Michael, Romanus **9** Heraclius, Justinian **10** Nicephorus, Theodosius
empress: **3** Zoe **5** Irene **8** Theodora

C

cab
4 hack, taxi **6** jitney **7** hackney **8** carriage

cabal
3 mob **4** clan, club, plot, ring **5** coven, group, junta, mafia **6** cartel, circle, clique **7** coterie, faction, in-group **8** intrigue **9** camarilla **10** conspiracy **11** machination

cabaletta
4 aria, song

cabalistic
6 arcane, mystic, occult **8** esoteric **9** recondite **10** mysterious **11** inscrutable **12** impenetrable

caballero
6 knight **7** paladin **8** cavalier, horseman **9** chevalier

cabana
3 hut **5** shack **7** shelter

cabaret
4 café **6** bistro, nitery **7** hot spot **9** nightclub, nightspot **10** supper club **12** watering hole

Cabaret
composer: **6** Kander (John)
director: **5** Fosse (Bob)
lyricist: **3** Ebb (Fred)

cabbage
3 nab, nip **4** cash, gelt, hook, lift, loot, palm **5** bread, dough, filch, kraut, lucre, money, moola, pinch, steal, swipe **6** boodle, dinero, do-re-mi, moolah, pilfer, wampum **7** lettuce, purloin, scratch **10** greenbacks, sauerkraut
disease of: **6** mildew, mosaic **7** root rot, yellows **8** blackleg, club root
family: **4** cole, kale, rape **5** colza, savoy **6** turnip **7** collard, mustard **8** broccoli, colewort, kohlrabi, rutabaga **11** cauliflower
sliced: **4** slaw

cabdriver
4 hack **5** cabby **6** cabbie

cabin
3 hut **4** camp, shed **5** berth, hovel, lodge, shack **6** cabana, chalet, lean-to, shanty **7** bivouac, cottage **9** stateroom

cabin cruiser
5 yacht **9** motorboat, powerboat

cabinet
4 case **6** bureau **7** armoire, chamber, commode, console, council, dresser **8** advisers, advisors, cupboard, ministry **9** presidium **10** chiffonier, collection, counselors

cabinetmaker
American: **5** Eames (Charles, Ray), Phyfe (Duncan) **6** Belter (John Henry) **7** Goddard (John, Stephen, Thomas) **8** McIntire (Samuel), Townsend (Christopher, Edmund, James, Job, John)

English: **4** Adam (James, Robert), Hope (Thomas), Kent (William) **8** Sheraton (Thomas) **11** Chippendale (Thomas), Hepplewhite (George)
French: **6** Boulle (André-Charles) **8** Caffieri (Jacques, Jean-Jacques, Philippe), Cressent (Charles)
German: **10** Weisweiler (Adam)

cable
4 rope, wire **5** braid, chain **6** stitch **8** transmit **9** telegraph

cabriolet
5 coupe **8** carriage

cache
4 bury, hide **5** cover, hoard, plant, stash, store, trove **6** memory, wealth **7** arsenal, conceal, lay away, nest egg, put away, reserve, secrete **8** ensconce, treasure **9** stockpile **10** accumulate **11** hiding place

cachet
4 rank, seal **5** motto, state **6** slogan, status **7** dignity, stature **8** approval, position, prestige, standing **11** consequence

cachinnate
4 crow, howl, roar **5** laugh, whoop **6** guffaw, shriek

cackle
3 gab, jaw **4** blab, chat, crow **5** clack, cluck **6** babble, burble, gabble, gaggle, gobble **7** blabber, blatter, chatter, prattle

cacoëthes
4 zeal **5** mania **6** desire **9** obsession

cacomistle
5 civet **7** raccoon **8** civet cat, ringtail

cacophonic
5 harsh **8** tuneless **9** dissonant, unmusical **10** discordant **11** unmelodious **12** unharmonious

cacophony
3 din **5** babel, noise **6** hubbub, uproar **9** confusion, harshness **10** dissonance

cactus
5 nopal **6** cereus, cholla, mescal, peyote **7** opuntia, saguaro **11** prickly pear

cad
3 cur, dog, rat **4** boor, fink, heel, jerk, lout, rake, roué **5** creep, knave, louse, rogue, skunk, swine **6** rascal, rotter **7** bounder **9** conductor, scoundrel

cadaver
4 body, mort **5** stiff **6** corpse **7** carcass, remains **8** deceased

cadaverous
5 ashen, gaunt, livid **6** pallid, wasted **7** deathly, ghastly, ghostly, shadowy **8** skeletal, spectral **9** deathlike, emaciated, ghostlike **10** corpselike

caddy
3 bin, box **4** aide **5** toter **6** casket **8** canister, tea chest

cadence
4 beat, flow, lilt **5** meter, pulse **6** rhythm **9** pulsation **10** conclusion, inflection, intonation

cadet
4 pimp **5** plebe **7** student, trainee **10** midshipman

cadge
3 beg, bum **5** mooch **6** hustle, sponge **8** freeload, scrounge **9** panhandle

Cadmus
daughter: **3** Ino **5** Agave **6** Semele **7** Autonoë
father: **6** Agenor
sister: **6** Europa
victim: **6** dragon
wife: **8** Harmonia

cadre
4 cell, core **5** frame, staff **6** cohort **7** in-group **9** framework

caducity
3 age **6** dotage, old age **8** senility **10** senescence **11** senectitude

Caesar
assassin: **6** Brutus (Marcus Junius) **7** Cassius (Gaius)
battle: **4** Zela **9** Pharsalus
conquest: **4** Gaul **7** Britain
death date: **4** Ides **11** Ides of March
eulogist: **6** Antony (Marc) **7** Anthony (Mark) **8** Antonius (Marcus)
message: **12** Veni vidi vici
partner: **4** Coca (Imogene)
river: **7** Rubicon
utterance: **4** Et tu **9** Et tu Brute
wife: **7** Pompeia **8** Cornelia **9** Calpurnia

Caesarism
7 tyranny **9** authority, autocracy, despotism **10** absolutism **12** dictatorship

caesura
5 break, pause **12** interruption

café
5 diner **6** bistro, nitery **7** barroom, beanery, cabaret, hot spot **8** cookshop **9** lunchroom, nightclub, nightspot **10** coffee shop, restaurant, supper club **12** luncheonette, watering hole **13** watering place
order: **5** latte

café ___
4 noir **5** latte **6** au lait, filtre **7** society

caftan
4 gown, robe **6** muumuu **12** dressing gown

cage
3 hem, pen **4** cell, coop, jail **5** score **6** aviary, corral, immure, lock up, shut in **7** close

in, enclose, impound **8** imprison **9** enclosure **11** incarcerate

cagey
3 sly **4** foxy, wary, wily **5** canny, sharp **6** astute, clever, crafty, shrewd

cahier
6 record, report, review **7** journal **8** notebook

cahoots
6 hookup, league **8** alliance **9** collusion **10** complicity **11** partnership

caiman
9 crocodile **11** crocodilian

Cain
brother: **4** Abel, Seth
father: **4** Adam
land: **3** Nod
mother: **3** Eve
nephew: **4** Enos
son: **5** Enoch
victim: **4** Abel

Caine Mutiny
author: **4** Wouk (Herman)
character: **5** Keith (Willie), Maryk (Steve), Queeg (Capt. Francis)

Cain novel
8 Serenade **13** Mildred Pierce **23** Postman Always Rings Twice (The)

cajole
3 con **4** coax, dupe **6** entice, seduce **7** beguile, blarney, deceive, wheedle **8** blandish, inveigle, maneuver, persuade, soft-soap **9** sweet-talk

Cajun cookery staple
4 okra

cake
3 dry, set **4** coat, loaf, rime **5** cover, crust, torte **6** gâteau, harden, pastry **7** congeal, encrust, incrust **8** solidify
almond: **8** macaroon
flat: **5** cooky **6** cookie
oatmeal: **4** farl **5** scone **7** bannock
ring-shaped: **5** donut **6** jumble **8** doughnut
rum-soaked: **4** baba
Scottish: **4** farl **5** scone
shell-shaped: **9** madeleine
topping: **5** icing **8** frosting, streusel
twisted: **7** cruller
without shortening: **6** sponge

Cakes and Ale author
7 Maugham (W. Somerset)

cakewalk
4 romp, rout, snap **5** cinch, dance, strut **6** breeze, prance **8** pushover, walkover

calaboose
3 can **4** brig, coop, jail, tank **5** clink, pokey **6** cooler, lockup, prison **7** slammer **8** hoosegow **9** jailhouse

calamitous
4 dire **5** fatal **6** woeful **7** ruinous **8** grievous **10** disastrous, lamentable **11** cataclysmic, devastating, unfortunate **12** catastrophic **13** heartbreaking

calamity
4 ruin **5** wreck **7** tragedy **8** disaster, downfall **9** cataclysm **11** catastrophe, tribulation

calculate
4 rely **5** assay, count, gauge, judge, solve, tally, tot up, value **6** assess, cipher, figure, intend, reckon **7** compute, measure, work out **8** appraise, estimate, evaluate, forecast **9** ascertain, determine, figure out

calculated
6 likely **7** planned **8** intended **9** worked out **10** deliberate **12** aforethought, premeditated

calculating
3 sly **4** wary, wily **5** canny, chary, sharp **6** artful, crafty, shrewd **7** careful, cunning, devious, politic **8** cautious, discreet, guileful, scheming **9** designing **11** circumspect

calculating device
5 abaci (plural) **6** abacus
Peruvian: **5** quipu

calculation
8 analysis, counting, estimate, figuring, prudence **9** ciphering, reckoning **10** arithmetic, estimation, prediction **11** computation

Caledonia
8 Scotland

calendar
3 log **4** card, sked **6** agenda, docket **7** almanac, program **8** schedule **9** timetable
abbreviation: **3** Apr, Aug, Dec, Feb, Fri, Jan, Mar, Mon, Nov, Oct, Sat, Sep, Sun, Tue, Wed **4** Sept **5** Thurs
ecclesiastical: **4** ordo
unit: **3** day **4** week, year **5** month

calenture
4 fire, zeal **5** ardor, fever **6** fervor **7** passion **10** enthusiasm

calf
hide: **3** kip
leather: **3** elk
meat: **4** veal
stray: **5** dogie
unbranded: **8** maverick

calf-length skirt
4 midi

Caliban
5 slave
master: **8** Prospero
witch-mother: **7** Sycorax

caliber
4 bore **5** class, gauge, grade, merit, value, worth **6** virtue **7** ability, quality, stature **8** diameter

calibrate
3 set **6** adjust, polish **7** measure **8** fine-tune, regulate **9** ascertain **11** standardize

California
army fort: 3 Ord
capital: 10 Sacramento
city: 4 Napa **6** Fresno, Sonoma **7** Anaheim, Oakland, San Jose **8** San Diego, Santa Ana **9** Long Beach, Santa Cruz **10** Los Angeles **12** San Francisco
college, university: 3 USC **4** UCLA **5** Mills **6** Pomona **8** Berkeley, Stanford, Whittier **9** Loma Linda **10** Golden Gate, Occidental, Pepperdine, Santa Clara
desert: 6 Mohave
fault zone: 10 San Andreas
lake: 5 Owens, Tahoe **9** Salton Sea
lowest spot: 11 Death Valley
motto: 6 Eureka
mountain, range: 5 Coast **6** Lassen (Peak), Shasta **7** Whitney **12** Sierra Nevada
nickname: 6 Golden (State)
park: 7 Sequoia **8** Yosemite **11** Kings Canyon **14** Channel Islands
river: 10 Sacramento, San Joaquin
state bird: 5 quail
state flower: 11 golden poppy
state tree: 7 redwood, sequoia
wine region: 4 Napa **6** Sonoma

caliginous
3 dim **4** dark, dusk **5** dusky, foggy, misty, murky **6** gloomy **7** obscure, sunless **8** nebulous **9** lightless, tenebrous

Caligula
mother: 9 Agrippina
predecessor: 8 Tiberius
successor: 8 Claudius
uncle: 8 Claudius

caliph's name
3 Ali **7** Abu Bakr

Calista's seducer
8 Lothario

calisthenics
7 workout **9** exercises

call
3 bid, cry **4** buzz, hail, lure, name, page, ring, yell **5** phone, pop in, shout, visit **6** bellow, come by, drop by, drop in, holler, salute, stop by, stop in, summon **7** convene, convoke, summons **8** estimate **9** designate, telephone

calla
4 arum, lily

call down
5 chide, scold **6** rebuke **7** censure, reprove **8** admonish, reproach **9** reprimand

called
5 named **6** chosen, picked, yclept **7** ycleped **8** selected

caller
5 guest **6** suitor **7** visitor

call for
3 ask, beg **4** page, seek **5** crave, plead **6** demand, entail, pick up **7** beseech, entreat, implore, involve, require **11** necessitate

call forth
5 awake, educe, evoke, rouse **6** arouse, elicit **7** conjure, provoke **9** conjure up

calligrapher
6 penman, scribe **7** copyist **9** engrosser, scrivener

calligraphy
4 hand **6** script **7** writing **8** longhand **10** penmanship **11** handwriting

call in
5 phone **6** summon **7** convene, reclaim **8** retrieve, withdraw **9** repossess, telephone

calling
3 job **4** duty, work **5** craft, trade **6** career, métier **7** mission, pursuit, yelling **8** business, lifework, shouting, vocation **10** employment, obligation, occupation, profession

call in sick
7 book off

calliope
5 organ **10** steam organ

Calliope
4 Muse
father: 4 Zeus **7** Jupiter
mother: 9 Mnemosyne
sister: 5 Erato
son: 7 Orpheus

Callisto
lover: 4 Zeus **7** Jupiter
son: 5 Arcas

Call It Sleep author
4 Roth (Henry)

call off
4 halt **5** abort, scrub **6** cancel, divert **8** distract

Call of the Wild
author: 6 London (Jack)
dog: 4 Buck

call on
5 visit **6** oblige **7** require

callosity
8 hardness **9** thickness

callous
5 stony **8** hardened, obdurate, uncaring **9** heartless, indurated, unfeeling **10** hard-bitten, hard-boiled **11** coldhearted, hardhearted, insensitive,

unemotional **12** case-hardened, stonyhearted **13** unsympathetic

callow
3 raw **5** fresh, green, naive, young **7** puerile **8** immature, juvenile, youthful **9** unfledged **10** unseasoned **13** inexperienced, unexperienced

call up
5 draft, evoke **6** summon **8** mobilize, retrieve **9** conscript

calm
4 cool, ease, hush, lull **5** allay, peace, quiet, relax, salve, still **6** hushed, pacify, placid, poised, repose, sedate, serene, settle, smooth, soothe, stable, steady, stilly **7** appease, assuage, compose, halcyon, mollify, pacific, placate, restful, resting **8** composed, inactive, peaceful, reposing, serenity, tranquil **9** collected, composure, easygoing, impassive, possessed, quiescent, unruffled **10** phlegmatic, untroubled **11** tranquility, tranquilize, unflappable **12** even-tempered, self-composed, tranquillity **13** imperturbable, self-possessed

calmative
8 quietive, relaxing, sedative **9** soporific **12** tranquilizer

calmness
4 lull **5** quiet **6** phlegm, repose **8** coolness, serenity **9** composure, placidity, sangfroid **10** equanimity **11** tranquility **12** tranquillity

calumet
4 pipe **9** peace pipe

calumniate
5 libel, smear **6** defame, malign, vilify **7** asperse, slander, tarnish, traduce **8** besmirch **9** denigrate **10** scandalize

calumnious
8 libelous **9** maligning, traducing, vilifying **10** backbiting, defamatory, detracting, scandalous, slanderous

calumny
7 scandal, slander **9** aspersion **10** backbiting, defamation, detraction **11** denigration **12** backstabbing, belittlement, depreciation **13** disparagement

calvados
6 brandy **9** applejack

calvary, Calvary
5 agony, cross, trial **6** misery, ordeal **7** anguish **8** distress **9** suffering **10** affliction, visitation **11** tribulation
inscription: 4 INRI

Calvino of literature
5 Italo

Calypso
beloved: 7 Ulysses **8** Odysseus
island: 6 Ogygia

calyx part
3 cup **5** sepal

camaraderie
5 cheer **7** jollity **10** affability, fellowship **12** conviviality

camarilla
3 mob **4** camp, clan, ring **5** cabal, mafia **6** circle, clique **7** coterie, ingroup

Cambodia
9 Kampuchea
capital: 9 Phnom Penh
city: 10 Battambang **11** Kompong Cham
ethnic group: 8 Mon-Khmer
lake: 8 Tonle Sap
language: 5 Khmer
leader: 6 Lon Nol, Pol Pot
monetary unit: 4 riel
neighbor: 4 Laos **7** Vietnam **8** Thailand
river: 6 Mekong
ruin: 9 Angkor Wat

came down
4 alit

camel
one-humped: 9 dromedary
relative: 5 llama
two-humped: 8 Bactrian

camel-hair fabric
3 aba

camelopard
7 giraffe

Camelot
6 palace
lord: 6 Arthur

Camembert
6 cheese

cameo
6 brooch, relief, walk-on **7** bit part **8** portrait
stone: 4 onyx

camera
feature: 4 lens, zoom **5** flash
type: 3 SLR, spy, TLR **5** video **7** digital, folding, pinhole **9** autofocus, single-use **10** viewfinder **11** rangefinder

cameraman
6 photog **7** lensman **12** photographer

Cameroon
capital: 7 Yaoundé
ethnic group: 4 Fang **5** Duala, Pygmy **6** Fulani **8** Bamileke
largest city: 6 Douala
monetary unit: 5 franc

neighbor: 4 Chad 5 Congo, Gabon 7 Nigeria
river: 5 Nyong 6 Sanaga

Camille's creator
5 Dumas (Alexandre)

Camino ___
4 Real

camouflage
4 mask 5 cloak 7 conceal, deceive 8 disguise 9 dissemble 11 dissimulate

camp
3 hut 4 bloc, shed 5 cabin, lodge, shack 6 clique, shanty 7 bivouac, coterie, cottage, faction 10 settlement

campaign
4 push, race 5 blitz, drive, fight, lobby, stump 6 attack 7 agitate, canvass, crusade 8 movement, politick 9 barnstorm, offensive 10 engagement, expedition 11 electioneer, whistle-stop

campaigner
8 activist 9 candidate

campanile
6 belfry 8 carillon 9 bell tower

Campbell of song
4 Glen

campesino
6 farmer 7 peasant

campestral
5 rural 6 rustic, sylvan 7 bucolic, country, idyllic 8 agrarian, pastoral 10 provincial 11 countrified

camping craft
5 canoe

campsite shelter
4 tent

campus
see **college**

Camus work
4 Fall (The) 5 Rebel (The) 6 Plague (The) 8 Caligula, Stranger (The)

can
3 may, tin 4 boot, fire, sack 5 let go, put up 7 dismiss 8 preserve 9 container, discharge 10 receptacle

Canaan
4 Zion 12 Promised Land
father: 3 Ham
grandfather: 4 Noah

Canaanite god
3 Mot 4 Baal 6 Molech, Moloch

Canada
bay: 5 Fundy, James 6 Baffin, Hudson, Ungava 8 Georgian 9 Frobisher
capital: 6 Ottawa
city: 6 London, Oshawa, Quebec, Regina, Surrey 7 Burnaby, Calgary, Halifax, Moncton, Toronto, Windsor 8 Edmonton, Hamilton, Montreal, Moose Jaw, Victoria, Winnipeg 9 Longueuil, North York, Saskatoon, Vancouver 10 Lethbridge, Thunder Bay 11 Fredericton, Scarborough 13 Charlottetown, Mississisauga
district: 6 riding
explorer: 6 Hudson (Henry) 7 Cartier (Jacques) 9 Champlain (Samuel de)
Indian people: 4 Cree, Inuk 5 Blood, Haida, Huron, Inuit, Métis, Niska, Slave 6 Abnaki, Beaver, Eskimo, Micmac, Mohawk, Nootka, Ojibwa, Ojibwe, Ottawa, Piegan, Seneca, Stoney 7 Kutenai, Naskapi, Ojibway, Siksika, Wyandot 8 Algonkin, Chippewa, Iroquois, Kootenai, Kootenay, Kwakiutl, Salishan, Tsattine 9 Algonkian, Algonquin, Blackfeet, Blackfoot, Chipewyan, Tsimshian 10 Algonquian, Athapascan, Gros Ventre, Montagnais 11 Assiniboine
island, island group: 5 Banks, Devon 6 Baffin 7 Belcher 8 Melville, Victoria 9 Anticosti, Ellesmere, Vancouver 10 Cape Breton 11 Southampton 12 Newfoundland, Prince Edward
lake: 6 Louise 7 Nipigon 8 Reindeer, Winnipeg 9 Athabasca, Champlain, Great Bear 10 Great Slave
language: 6 French 7 English
monetary unit: 6 dollar
mountain, range: 5 Coast, Logan, Rocky 10 Laurentian
national park: 5 Banff, Fundy 6 Jasper 7 Glacier, Nahanni 8 Kootenay 9 Gros Morne 10 Grasslands, Point Pelee 11 Georgian Bay, Wood Buffalo
peninsula: 5 Bruce, Gaspé 6 Ungava 8 Labrador
prime minister: 4 King (W. L. Mackenzie) 5 Clark (Joe) 6 Abbott (John), Borden (Robert Laird), Bowell (Mackenzie), Harper (Stephen), Martin (Paul), Tupper (Charles), Turner (John) 7 Bennett (Richard Bedford), Laurier (Wilfrid), Meighen (Arthur), Pearson (Lester), Trudeau (Pierre Elliott) 8 Campbell (Kim), Chrétien (Jean), Mulroney (Brian), Thompson (John) 9 MacDonald (John), Mackenzie (Alexander), St. Laurent (Louis) 11 Diefenbaker (John)
province: 3 Man., NWT, Ont., PEI, Que. 4 Alta, Sask. 6 Quebec 7 Alberta, Nunavut, Ontario 8 Manitoba 10 Nova Scotia 12 New Brunswick, Newfoundland (and Labrador), Saskatchewan 15 British Columbia 18 Prince Edward Island
provincial park: 3 Gas 7 Rondeau 9 Garibaldi
river: 3 Red 5 Liard, Slave, Yukon 6 Albany, Fraser, Nelson, Ottawa, Severn 8 Columbia, Saguenay 9 Athabasca, Churchill, Mackenzie 10 St. Lawrence
sea: 8 Beaufort, Labrador
symbol: 9 maple leaf
territory: 5 Yukon 9 Northwest

Canadian insurgent
4 Riel (Louis)

Canadian oil brand
4 Esso

Canadian snack
7 poutine

canaille
3 mob 6 masses, rabble 8 riffraff, unwashed 9 hoi polloi 11 proletarian, proletariat

canal
4 duct 6 course 7 channel, conduit 8 aqueduct 11 watercourse
Africa: 4 Suez 8 Ismailia
Belgium: 6 Albert
Canada: 7 Welland
Central America: 6 Panama
China: 7 Da Yunhe
Florida: 10 Saint Lucie
Germany: 4 Kiel 10 Nord-Ostsee
Greece: 7 Corinth
Michigan: 3 Soo
mule: 3 Sal
New York: 4 Erie 6 Oswego 9 Champlain
of song: 4 Erie
Ontario: 6 Rideau
Venice: 5 Grand

canapé
6 morsel 9 appetizer 11 hors d'oeuvre
spread: 4 paté
topper: 3 roe 6 caviar

canard
3 fib, lie 4 tale, yarn 5 fraud, rumor, spoof 6 deceit 7 falsity, untruth 8 chestnut 9 falsehood

canary
3 rat 4 fink, wine 5 finch 6 snitch 7 rat fink, stoolie 8 informer, squealer 11 stool pigeon

Canary Islands
5 Ferro, Lobos, Palma 6 Gomera, Hierro 7 Inferno 8 Graciosa, Tenerife 9 Alegranza, Lanzarote

cancel
3 end 4 drop, lift, undo, x out 5 abort, annul, erase, scrub 6 delete, efface, negate, offset, repeal, revoke 7 blot out, call off, destroy, expunge, nullify, rescind, scratch, wipe out 8 black out, deletion 9 terminate 10 invalidate, neutralize, obliterate

cancer
5 tumor 9 carcinoma 10 malignancy
treatment: 5 chemo, X rays 9 radiation 12 chemotherapy

cancer-causing
12 carcinogenic
substance: 10 carcinogen

candescent
7 glowing 8 dazzling 9 refulgent

Candia
5 Crete

candid
4 fair, just, open 5 blunt, frank, plain 6 honest 7 sincere 8 unbiased 9 equitable, guileless, impartial, objective 10 aboveboard, forthright, scrupulous, unreserved 11 openhearted, unconcealed, undisguised 12 unprejudiced 13 dispassionate

candidate
6 seeker 7 hopeful, nominee, stumper 8 aspirant 9 applicant, contender 10 campaigner, contestant
unlisted: 7 write-in

Candide
author: 8 Voltaire
lover: 9 Cunegonde
tutor: 8 Pangloss (Dr.)
valet: 7 Cacambo

candle
5 taper 6 bougie
holder: 6 sconce 7 menorah, pricket 9 girandole 10 candelabra 11 candelabrum
material: 3 wax 4 wick 6 tallow 7 beeswax, stearin 8 bayberry, paraffin
religious: 6 votive 7 paschal

candlefish
8 eulachon
relative: 5 smelt

candlelit service
5 vigil

candlepins
7 bowling

candor
7 honesty 8 fairness, openness 9 frankness, sincerity, whiteness 11 artlessness 13 guilelessness

candy
7 sweeten 9 sugarcoat 10 confection
kind: 4 rock 5 fudge, lolly, sweet, taffy 6 bonbon, comfit, dragée, jujube, nougat, toffee 7 brittle, caramel, fondant, gumdrop, penuche, praline 8 licorice, lollipop, lollypop, marzipan, sourball 9 chocolate, jelly bean, nonpareil, sweetmeat 10 confection 12 butterscotch
medicated: 7 lozenge 9 cough drop

cane
3 rod 4 beat, drub, flog, lash, reed, stem, swat 5 flail, grass, spank, staff, stave, stick, weave, whale 6 batter, buffet, cudgel, larrup, paddle, rattan, thrash, wallop 7 lambast, sorghum 8 lambaste 12 walking stick

Canea's land
5 Crete

Canetti of literature
5 Elias

canine
3 dog, fox 4 tyke, wolf 5 dhole, dingo, hound, pooch 6 jackal

caning material
5 istle

Canis Major star
6 Sirius

Canis Minor star
7 Procyon

canker
4 rust, sore 5 stain 6 debase, infect 7 corrupt, debauch, deprave, pervert, vitiate 8 necrosis 10 demoralize

cankered
8 infested, infected

canker sore
5 ulcer 6 lesion 10 ulceration

cannabis
3 kef, kif, pot, tea 4 dope, hash, hemp, weed 5 bhang, ganja, grass 7 hashish 8 Mary Jane 9 marijuana

canned
5 drunk, fired 6 potted 11 prerecorded

Cannery Row author
9 Steinbeck (John)

canniness
7 caution, cunning, slyness 8 prudence, wiliness 9 cageyness, foresight 10 artfulness, cleverness, craftiness, discretion, precaution, providence, shrewdness 11 forethought

cannon
6 pom-pom 8 howitzer, ordnance 9 artillery
part: 5 chase 6 breech 8 cascabel, trunnion

cannonade
4 bomb 5 blitz, burst, salvo, shell 6 shower, volley 7 barrage, bombard 8 drumfire, shelling 9 broadside, fusillade 11 bombardment

cannonball
4 dive 5 speed 7 missile

cannoneer
6 gunner

cannon fodder
6 troops 8 infantry, soldiers

canny
3 sly 4 wary, wise 5 acute, cagey, chary, quick, sharp, smart 6 adroit, clever, frugal, saving, shrewd 7 cunning, knowing, prudent, thrifty 9 ingenious, provident 10 economical 11 quick-witted, sharp-witted 12 nimble-witted

canoe
6 dugout 7 pirogue
ancient: 7 coracle
Eskimo: 5 kayak, umiak

canon
3 law 4 list, rule 5 dogma, edict, round, tenet 6 decree 7 precept, statute 8 doctrine, standard 9 clergyman, criterion, ordinance 10 regulation

canonical
5 sound 6 lawful 7 classic 8 accepted, approved, official, orthodox, received 10 authorized, recognized, sanctioned 13 authoritative

canonical hour
4 none, sext 5 lauds, prime, terce 6 matins, tierce 7 vespers 8 compline

canonicals
9 vestments

canoodle
3 hug, pet 5 spoon 6 caress, cuddle, fondle

can opener
9 church key

canopy
5 cover, shade 6 awning, tester 7 marquee, shelter 8 covering, sunshade 9 baldachin 10 baldachino
canvas: 4 tilt

cant
3 tip 4 heel, lean, list, tilt 5 angle, argot, bevel, idiom, lingo, piety, slang, slant, slope 6 humbug, jargon, patois, patter, speech 7 dialect, diction, incline, lexicon, palaver, recline 8 language, singsong 9 hypocrisy 10 dictionary, pharisaism, sanctimony, vernacular 11 inclination, insincerity 12 pecksniffery

cantaloupe
5 melon 9 muskmelon

cantankerous
4 dour, sour 5 cross, huffy, testy, waspy 6 crabby, cranky, crusty, grumpy, morose, ornery 7 bearish, crabbed, grouchy, peevish, prickly, waspish 8 cankered, liverish, petulant, snappish, stubborn, vinegary 9 crotchety, difficult, dyspeptic, irascible, irritable, obstinate 10 ill-natured, irritating, vinegarish 12 cross-grained

canter
3 bum 4 gait, hobo, lope 5 tramp 6 beggar 7 drifter, vagrant 8 derelict, vagabond 11 bindle stiff

Canterbury
Archbishop: 3 Oda 6 Anselm, Becket (Thomas á), Parker (Matthew) 7 Cranmer (Thomas), Dunstan 9 Augustine

Canterbury Tales
author: 7 Chaucer (Geoffrey)
character: 4 host, monk 5 clerk, friar, reeve 6 knight, miller, parson, squire, yeoman 7 plowman, shipman 8 franklin, Griselda, manciple, merchant, pardoner, prioress, summoner 9 physician 10 wife of Bath
inn: 6 Tabard

canticle
3 ode 4 hymn, song 6 Te Deum 10 Benedicite, Benedictus, Magnificat 12 Nunc Dimittis

canticles
11 Song of Songs **13** Song of Solomon

cantilever
4 beam **6** bridge **7** bracket, support

cantillate
4 sing **5** chant **6** intone, recite

cantina
3 bar, pub **6** saloon, tavern **7** barroom

canton
5 state **6** billet **7** quarter, section **8** district, division
Swiss: 3 Uri

cantor
5 hazan **6** singer **9** precentor

canvas
4 duck, sail, tarp, tent **7** tenting **8** painting **9** sailcloth, tarpaulin
coating: 5 gesso
holder: 5 easel

canvasback
4 duck

canvass
3 con, vet **5** argue, study **6** debate, survey **7** discuss, dispute, examine, inspect, solicit **8** campaign **9** check over **10** scrutinize **11** electioneer **12** authenticate

canyon
4 Glen, Zion **5** Bryce, chasm, gorge, Grand, gulch, Hells **6** Copper, coulee, ravine, valley
sound: 4 echo

cap
3 tam, top **4** best, coif **5** beret, cover, crest, crown, limit, trump **6** beanie, exceed, top off **7** calotte **9** culminate
clergyman's: 7 biretta **9** zucchetto
hoodlike: 4 coif
hunter's: 7 montero
jester's: 7 coxcomb **9** cockscomb
Jewish: 8 yarmulke
knitted: 5 toque, tuque **9** balaclava
lace: 5 aglet
military: 4 kepi
mushroom: 6 pileus
part: 4 bill, brim, flap, peak **5** visor **7** earflap
Roman: 6 pileus
Scottish: 3 tam **8** balmoral **9** glengarry **11** tam-o'-shanter
Turkish: 3 fez **6** calpac **7** calpack

capability
5 craft, means, skill **7** ability, potency **8** adequacy, aptitude, capacity, efficacy, facility **9** potential **10** competence, efficiency **12** potentiality **13** effectiveness, qualification

capable
3 apt **4** able **5** adept **6** adroit, au fait **9** competent, efficient, qualified **10** proficient **11** susceptible

capacious
4 wide **5** ample, roomy **7** sizable **8** abundant, spacious **9** extensive **10** commodious **11** substantial

capacitance
jar: 6 Leyden
unit of: 5 farad

capacity
4 bent, gift, rank, role, room **5** knack, range, reach, scope, skill, space **6** output, status, talent **7** ability, caliber, faculty **8** adequacy, aptitude, facility, position, standing **10** capability, competence **11** proficiency **13** qualification
unit of: 4 gill, peck, pint **5** liter, litre, minim, quart **6** bushel, gallon **10** fluid ounce, milliliter

Capaneus
slayer: 4 Zeus
wife: 6 Evadne

caparison
5 adorn **6** finery **7** apparel, panoply, raiment **9** adornment, trappings

cape
4 cope, ness **5** cloak, point, talma **6** capote, mantle, tabard, tippet **7** manteau, pelisse **8** foreland, headland, mantelet, mantilla, pelerine **9** peninsula **10** promontory
clergyman's: 8 mozzetta
papal: 5 fanon, orale

Cape
Africa: 4 Juby, Yubi **5** Blanc **6** Blanco **7** Agulhas
Alaska: 3 Icy **4** Nome **11** Krusenstern
Algeria: 3 Fer
Antarctica: 3 Ann **4** Dart **5** Adare
Arctic: 8 Nordkaap
Asia: 5 Aniva
Australia: 5 Byron, Otway, Sandy, Smoky **6** Arnhem **9** Van Diemen
Baffin Island: 4 Dyer
Black Sea: 5 Yasun
Borneo: 4 Datu **6** Datoek
Brazil: 4 Frio, Raso
California: 9 Mendocino
Colombia: 5 Aguja
Costa Rica: 5 Velas
Crete: 5 Plaka
Croatia: 5 Ploca **6** Planka
Cuba: 4 Cruz **5** Maisi
Denmark: 4 Skaw **6** Skagen
Desolación Island: 5 Pilar **6** Pillar
Djibouti: 3 Bir
Egypt: 5 Banas
England: 8 Bolerium, Lands End
Florida: 5 Sable **7** Kennedy **9** Canaveral

Greece: **4** Busa **5** Gallo, Malea, Papas, Vouxa **6** Araxos, Maleas **7** Akritas
Guinea: **5** Verga
Gulf of California: **5** Lobos
Gulf of Guinea: **5** Lopez
Gulf of Mexico: **4** Rojo
Hawaii: **5** Ka Lae **10** South Point **11** Diamond Head
Hispaniola: **5** Beata
Honshu: **3** Iro, Oma **5** Inubo, Kyoga, Nyudo
Indonesia: **4** Vals **5** False
Japan: **4** Esan, Nomo, Sata, Soya **5** Erimo, Kamui
Libya: **3** Tin **4** Milh
Long Island Sound: **10** Throgs Neck
Malay Peninsula: **5** Bulat
Malaysia: **4** Piai **5** Sirik
Massachusetts: **3** Ann, Cod
Mediterranean: **5** Ajdir
Mexico: **4** Buey
Morocco: **3** Sim **4** Guir, Rhir
Namibia: **4** Fria
Newfoundland: **5** Bauld
New Jersey: **3** May
New Zealand: **5** Brett
North Carolina: **4** Fear **7** Lookout **8** Hatteras
Northwest Territories: **8** Bathurst
Nova Scotia: **5** Canso **6** Breton
Oman: **3** Nus **4** Hadd
Ontario: **4** Hurd, Rich
Pakistan: **5** Monze, Muari
Portugal: **4** Roca
Puerto Rico: **4** Rojo
Quebec: **5** Gaspé
Red Sea: **5** Kasar
Sicily: **4** Boeo, Faro **7** Lilibeo, Passero, Pelorus
Solomon Islands: **5** Zelee
Somalia: **4** Asir **5** Assir, Hafun
South Africa: **8** Good Hope
South America: **4** Horn
Spain: **3** Nao **4** Gata **5** Creus, Penas
Syria: **5** Basit
Taiwan: **5** O-luan **7** Garam Bi
Tierra del Fuego: **5** Penas
Tunisia: **5** Blanc
Turkey: **3** Boz **4** Baba, Ince, Kara, Krio **6** Lectum **8** Bozburun **9** Inceburun, Karaburun
Vancouver Island: **5** Scott
Virginia: **5** Henry
Washington: **5** Alava

Čapek, Karel
coinage: **5** robot
play: **3** R.U.R.

caper
4 dido, lark, leap, romp **5** antic, frisk, heist, prank, revel, shine, theft, trick **6** cavort, frolic, gambol, prance **7** roguery, rollick **8** escapade, mischief **10** shenanigan, tomfoolery **11** monkeyshine

Cape Verde
capital: **5** Praia
city: **7** Mindelo
island: **3** Sal **4** Fogo, Maio **5** Brava **8** Boa Vista, São Tiago **10** São Vicente, São Nicolau, Santa Luzia, Santo Antão
language: **7** Crioulo **10** Portuguese
monetary unit: **6** escudo

capillary
4 tube **6** tubule **8** hairlike **11** blood vessel

capital
4 main **5** basic, chief, funds, major, prime **6** assets, lethal, wealth **8** cardinal **9** essential, excellent, financing, first-rate, principal, resources **10** first-class, investment, preeminent, underlying **11** fundamental, outstanding, predominant, wherewithal
Afghanistan: **5** Kabul
Albania: **6** Tirana, Tiranë
Alberta: **8** Edmonton
Algeria: **7** Algiers
Angola: **6** Luanda
Antigua and Barbuda: **7** St. John's **10** Saint John's
Argentina: **11** Buenos Aires
Armenia: **7** Yerevan
Assam: **6** Dispur
Australia: **8** Canberra
Austria: **4** Wien **6** Vienna
Azerbaijan: **4** Baku
Bahamas: **6** Nassau
Bahrain: **6** Manama
Bangladesh: **5** Dacca, Dhaka
Barbados: **10** Bridgetown
Belarus: **5** Minsk
Belgium: **8** Brussels
Belize: **8** Belmopan
Benin: **9** Porto-Novo
Bhutan: **7** Thimphu
Bolivia: **5** La Paz, Sucre
Bosnia and Herzegovina: **8** Sarajevo
Botswana: **8** Gaborone
Brazil: **8** Brasília
Bulgaria: **5** Sofia
Burkina Faso: **11** Ouagadougou
Burma: **6** Yangon **7** Rangoon
Burundi: **9** Bujumbura
Cambodia: **9** Phnom Penh
Cameroon: **7** Yaoundé
Canada: **6** Ottawa
Cape Verde: **5** Praia
Central African Republic: **6** Bangui
Chad: **8** N'Djamena
Chile: **8** Santiago
China: **6** Peking **7** Beijing

Colombia: **6** Bogotá
Comoros: **6** Moroni
Congo (Zaire): **8** Kinshasa
Costa Rica: **7** San José
Côte d'Ivoire: **7** Abidjan **12** Yamoussoukro
Croatia: **6** Zagreb
Cuba: **6** Havana
Cyprus: **7** Nicosia
Czech Republic: **6** Prague
Denmark: **10** Copenhagen
Dominica: **6** Roseau
Dominican Republic: **12** Santo Domingo
East Timor: **4** Dili
Ecuador: **5** Quito
Egypt: **5** Cairo
El Salvador: **11** San Salvador
Equatorial Guinea: **6** Malabo
Eritrea: **6** Asmara
Estonia: **7** Tallinn
Ethiopia: **10** Addis Ababa
Faeroe Islands: **8** Tórshavn
Falkland Islands: **7** Stanley
Fiji: **4** Suva
Finland: **8** Helsinki
France: **5** Paris
French Guiana: **7** Cayenne
Gabon: **10** Libreville
Galápagos Islands: **12** San Cristóbal
Gambia: **6** Banjul
Georgia, Republic of: **6** Tiflis **7** Tbilisi
Germany: **6** Berlin
Ghana: **5** Accra
Greece: **6** Athens
Greenland: **8** Godthaab
Grenada: **9** St. George's **12** Saint George's
Guam: **5** Agana
Guinea: **7** Conakry
Guyana: **10** Georgetown
Haiti: **12** Port-au-Prince
Honduras: **11** Tegucigalpa
Hungary: **8** Budapest
Iceland: **9** Reykjavík
India: **8** New Delhi
Indonesia: **7** Jakarta **8** Djakarta
Iran: **6** Tehran **7** Teheran
Iraq: **7** Baghdad
Ireland: **4** Tara **6** Dublin
Israel: **7** Tel-Aviv **9** Jerusalem
Italy: **4** Rome
Jamaica: **8** Kingston
Japan: **5** Tokyo
Jordan: **5** Amman
Kazakhstan: **6** Astana **7** Alma-Ata
Kenya: **7** Nairobi
Kiribati: **6** Tarawa **11** South Tarawa
Korea, North: **9** Pyongyang
Korea, South: **5** Seoul
Kosovo: **8** Pristina
Kuwait: **10** Kuwait City
Kyrgyzstan: **7** Bishkek
Laos: **9** Vientiane
Latvia: **4** Riga
Lebanon: **6** Beirut
Lesotho: **6** Maseru
Libya: **7** Tripoli
Liechtenstein: **5** Vaduz
Lithuania: **7** Vilnius
Macedonia: **6** Skopje
Madagascar: **12** Antananarivo
Malawi: **8** Lilongwe
Malaysia: **11** Kuala Lumpur
Maldives: **4** Male
Mali: **6** Bamako
Malta: **8** Valletta
Manitoba: **8** Winnipeg
Marshall Islands: **6** Majuro
Mauritania: **10** Nouakchott
Mauritius: **9** Port Louis
Micronesia: **7** Palikir
Moldova: **8** Chişinău, Kishinev
Mongolia: **9** Ulan Bator **11** Ulaanbaatar
Montenegro: **7** Cetinje **9** Podgorica
Montserrat: **8** Plymouth
Morocco: **5** Rabat
Mozambique: **6** Maputo
Myanmar: **6** Yangon **7** Rangoon
Namibia: **8** Windhoek
Nauru: **5** Yaren
Nepal: **8** Katmandu **9** Kathmandu
Netherlands: **9** Amsterdam
Newfoundland: **10** Saint Johns
New Zealand: **10** Wellington
Nicaragua: **7** Managua
Niger: **6** Niamey
Nigeria: **5** Abuja
Northern Ireland: **7** Belfast
Northern Territory: **6** Darwin
North-West Frontier Province: **8** Peshawar
Northwest Territories: **11** Yellowknife
Norway: **4** Oslo
Nova Scotia: **7** Halifax
Oman: **6** Muscat
Pakistan: **9** Islamabad
Palau: **5** Koror **10** Babelthuap
Papua New Guinea: **11** Port Moresby
Paraguay: **8** Asunción
Peru: **4** Lima
Philippines: **6** Manila
Poland: **6** Warsaw
Portugal: **6** Lisbon
Prince Edward Island: **13** Charlottetown
Puerto Rico: **7** San Juan
Qatar: **4** Doha
Queensland: **8** Brisbane
Réunion: **7** St. Denis **10** Saint Denis
Romania: **9** Bucharest

Russia: **6** Moscow
Rwanda: **6** Kigali
Saint Helena: **9** Jamestown
Saint Kitts and Nevis: **10** Basseterre
Saint Lucia: **8** Castries
Samoa: **4** Apia
Saskatchewan: **6** Regina
Saudi Arabia: **6** Riyadh
Scotland: **9** Edinburgh
Senegal: **5** Dakar
Serbia: **8** Belgrade
Seychelles: **8** Victoria
Shetland: **7** Lerwick
Sicily: **7** Palermo
Sierra Leone: **8** Freetown
Sikkim: **7** Gangtok
Sind: **7** Karachi
Slovakia: **10** Bratislava
Slovenia: **9** Ljubljana
Solomon Islands: **7** Honiara
Somalia: **9** Mogadishu
South Africa: **8** Cape Town, Pretoria **12** Bloemfontein
South Australia: **8** Adelaide
South-West Africa: **8** Windhoek
South Sudan: **4** Juba
Spain: **6** Madrid
Sri Lanka: **7** Colombo
Sudan: **8** Khartoum
Suriname: **10** Paramaribo
Swaziland: **7** Mbabane
Sweden: **9** Stockholm
Switzerland: **4** Bern **5** Berne
Syria: **8** Damascus
Tahiti: **7** Papeete
Taiwan: **6** Taipei
Tajikistan: **8** Dushanbe
Tanzania: **6** Dodoma **11** Dar es Salaam
Tasmania: **6** Hobart
Thailand: **7** Bangkok
Tibet: **5** Lhasa
Tirol: **9** Innsbruck
Togo: **4** Lomé
Tonga: **9** Nuku'alofa
Trinidad and Tobago: **11** Port-of-Spain
Tunisia: **5** Tunis
Turkey: **6** Ankara
Turkmenistan: **8** Ashgabat **9** Ashkhabad
Tuvalu: **8** Funafuti
Uganda: **7** Kampala
Ukraine: **4** Kiev
United Arab Emirates: **8** Abu Dhabi
United Kingdom: **6** London
Uruguay: **10** Montevideo
Uttar Pradesh: **7** Lucknow
Uzbekistan: **8** Tashkent
Vanuatu: **4** Vila
Venezuela: **7** Caracas
Victoria: **9** Melbourne
Vietnam: **5** Hanoi
Wales: **7** Cardiff
Western Australia: **5** Perth
Yemen: **4** Sana **5** Sanaa
Yugoslavia: **8** Belgrade
Yukon: **10** Whitehorse
Zambia: **6** Lusaka
Zimbabwe: **6** Harare

capitalist
6 backer, tycoon **7** magnate **8** investor **9** bourgeois, financier, plutocrat **12** entrepreneur

capitalistic
9 bourgeois

capitalize
4 back, fund **5** stake **6** profit **7** convert, finance, promote, sponsor, support **8** bankroll **9** grubstake, subsidize

capital sin
see **deadly sin**

capitation
3 tax **7** payment, poll tax

Capitol Hill sound
3 aye, nay

capitulate
3 bow **4** cave **5** defer, yield **6** cave in, give in, give up, relent, submit **7** concede, succumb **9** acquiesce, surrender **12** knuckle under

capitulation
9 surrender **10** submission

capo
3 bar **4** boss, head **5** chief **9** godfather

Capone nemesis
4 Ness (Eliot)

capote
4 cope **5** cloak **6** mantle, tabard **7** manteau, pelisse **8** overcoat

Capote work
11 In Cold Blood **19** Breakfast at Tiffany's

capper
4 lure **5** blind, decoy, shill **6** climax, finale **8** clincher

cappuccino alternative
5 latte

Capri, e.g.
4 isle

capriccio
4 whim **5** caper, fancy, prank **6** notion, vagary, whimsy **7** impulse

caprice
3 bee **4** mood, vein, whim **5** fancy, freak, humor **6** foible, maggot, megrim, notion, vagary, whimsy **7** conceit **8** crotchet

capricious
4 iffy **5** flaky, moody **6** chancy, fickle **7** erratic, flighty, wayward **8** fanciful, unstable, variable,

volatile **9** arbitrary, impulsive, mercurial, uncertain, whimsical **10** changeable, inconstant **12** effervescent, incalculable **13** temperamental, unpredictable

caprid
4 goat

capriole
4 leap **5** caper

capsize
4 keel, roll, sink **5** upset **7** founder, tip over **8** collapse, overturn, turn over

capstone
4 acme, apex, peak **6** apogee, climax, coping, summit, zenith **8** pinnacle **9** high point **11** culmination

capsule
6 canned, pocket, potted **7** compact, outline **9** condensed

capsulize
6 reduce **7** enclose **8** compress, condense **9** summarize, synopsize

captain
6 master **7** skipper
fictional: **4** Ahab, Hook, Kirk, Nemo **5** Queeg **10** Hornblower
historical: **4** Cook (James) **5** Bligh (William)
order: **5** avast
pirate: **4** Kidd (William) **6** Morgan (Henry)

Captain Hook's sidekick
4 Smee

Captains Courageous author
7 Kipling (Rudyard)

caption
5 title **6** legend, rubric **7** cutline, heading **8** subtitle **9** underline

captious
5 testy **7** carping, peevish **8** caviling, contrary, critical, exacting, petulant, snappish **9** demanding, irritable **10** censorious, nit-picking **12** faultfinding, overcritical **13** hypercritical

captivate
4 draw, grip, hold, take **5** charm **6** allure, dazzle, enamor, please, ravish, seduce **7** attract, beguile, bewitch, delight, enamour, enchant, gratify **8** enthrall **9** enrapture, fascinate, hypnotize, infatuate, magnetize, mesmerize, spellbind

captivating
8 charming, enticing, fetching, magnetic, riveting **9** appealing, glamorous, seductive **10** bewitching, engrossing, intriguing **11** enthralling, fascinating

captive
5 bound, caged, taken **6** jailed **7** hostage **8** confined, detainee, internee, prisoner **10** enthralled, hypnotized, imprisoned

captivity
7 bondage, custody, slavery **9** detention **10** internment **11** confinement **12** imprisonment

capture
3 bag, get, nab, net, win **4** nail, take, trap **5** catch, lasso, prize, seize, snare **6** arrest, collar, entrap, occupy, secure **7** conquer, ensnare **8** preserve

Capuan
4 lush **5** plush **6** deluxe **7** opulent **8** luscious, palatial **9** luxuriant, luxurious, sumptuous **11** upholstered

car
4 auto, heap **5** buggy, coach, crate, sedan, wreck **6** beater, jalopy, junker, wheels **7** clunker, flivver, hooptie **8** roadster **10** automobile, rattletrap, rust bucket
(see also **automobile**)

carafe
4 ewer **5** cruet **6** bottle, flacon, flagon **8** decanter

caravan
6 convoy, safari
stop: **5** oasis

caravansary
3 inn **4** khan **5** hotel, lodge, serai **6** hostel, tavern **10** campground

carbohydrate
5 sugar **6** starch **7** amylose, glucose, lactose, maltose, sucrose **8** fructose, glycogen **9** cellulose, galactose

carbolic acid
6 phenol

carbon
4 coal, coke, soot **8** charcoal, graphite, plumbago **9** lampblack

carbonate
6 aerate

carbon copy
4 dupe, twin **5** clone, ditto, mimeo, repro, Xerox **7** replica **8** knockoff **9** duplicate, facsimile **10** dead ringer **11** replication **12** reproduction

carbonize
4 burn, char, sear **5** singe, toast **6** scorch

carbuncle
4 boil, sore **5** ulcer **6** garnet, pimple **7** abscess, pustule **8** cabochon

carcass
4 body, hulk, mort **5** frame, shell, stiff **6** corpse **7** cadaver, remains **8** skeleton

carcinoid
5 tumor **8** neoplasm

carcinoma
5 tumor **6** cancer **8** neoplasm

card
3 wag, wit **4** menu, sked **5** joker **6** agenda, docket **7** program **8** calendar, comedian, humorist, schedule **9** timetable
fortune-telling: **5** tarot
game: **3** gin, loo, Uno, war **4** faro, fish, skat, solo, stud **5** monte, ombre, pitch, poker, rummy, whist **6** Boston, bridge, casino, écarté, euchre, fan-tan, hearts, piquet **7** auction, bezique, canasta, cooncan, old maid, primero **8** baccarat, Canfield, conquian, cribbage, gin rummy, pinochle **9** blackjack, solitaire, twenty-one, vingt-et-un **11** chemin de fer
game authority: **5** Hoyle (Edmond)
high: **3** ace
low: **5** deuce
performer's: **3** cue
spot: **3** pip
wild: **5** deuce, joker

cardboard
5 stiff **6** unreal, wooden **7** bristol, buckram, stilted **8** lifeless **10** unlifelike **11** stereotyped, unrealistic

card-carrying
4 true **7** genuine **8** bona fide **9** authentic, certified **11** full-fledged

cardiac stimulant
7 ouabain **9** digitalis

cardinal
3 key **4** main **5** basic, chief, prime, vital **6** ruling **7** central, leading, pivotal, primary **9** essential, important, principal **10** overriding, overruling **11** fundamental **12** constitutive
point: **4** east, west **5** north, south
suffix: **4** teen
title: **8** Eminence
virtue: **7** justice **8** prudence **9** fortitude **10** temperance

care
4 fear, heed, mind, tend, ward **5** alarm, nurse, serve, trust, worry **6** attend, charge, effort, regard, regret, strain, stress, unease, wait on **7** anguish, anxiety, concern, custody, keeping **8** disquiet, handling **9** attention, curiosity, misgiving, oversight **10** management, solicitude **11** maintenance, safekeeping, supervision **12** guardianship **13** consideration

careen
4 race, sway, tilt **5** lurch, pitch, speed, swing, weave **6** repair, wobble **7** stagger

career
3 job **4** race, rush, tear, work **5** chase, speed **6** charge, course **7** calling, passage **8** lifework, vocation **9** encounter **10** livelihood, profession

care for
4 like, love, mind, tend **5** nurse, treat **6** attend, foster **7** cherish, nurture **8** preserve **9** cultivate, look after

carefree
4 wild **6** blithe, breezy, jaunty **8** reckless **10** insouciant, untroubled **12** happy-go-lucky, lighthearted **13** irresponsible

careful
4 safe, wary **5** chary, exact, fussy **7** dutiful, guarded, precise, prudent, studied **8** accurate, cautious, critical, discreet, gingerly, thorough **9** attentive, provident **10** deliberate, meticulous, particular, scrupulous **11** calculating, circumspect, considerate, foresighted, painstaking, punctilious **13** conscientious

carefully
6 warily **8** gingerly **10** cautiously, discreetly **12** meticulously, scrupulously **13** painstakingly, punctiliously

careless
3 lax **5** hasty, messy, slack **6** casual, remiss, sloppy, untidy **7** cursory, offhand, unkempt **8** feckless, heedless, reckless, slapdash, slipshod, slovenly **9** forgetful, negligent, oblivious, unheeding, unmindful, unstudied **10** disheveled, inaccurate, incautious, neglectful, unthinking, untroubled **11** inadvertent, inattentive, indifferent, perfunctory, spontaneous, thoughtless, unconcerned **12** uninterested, unreflective **13** irresponsible

caress
3 pat, pet, toy **4** kiss, love **5** dally, touch **6** coddle, cosset, cuddle, dandle, fondle, nuzzle, pamper, stroke **7** cherish, indulge **8** canoodle **10** endearment

caressive
7 calming **8** soothing

caretaker
6 warden **7** curator, janitor **9** custodian

careworn
3 wan **5** drawn, faded, jaded **7** haggard, pinched, wearied **8** fatigued, troubled **9** exhausted **10** distressed

cargo
4 haul, load **6** burden, lading **7** freight, payload **8** shipload, shipment **11** consignment

Caribbean
island: **5** Aruba, Nevis **6** Tobago **7** Antigua, Barbuda, St. Kitts **8** Anguilla, Barbados, Trinidad **10** Guadeloupe, Hispaniola, Martinique, Montserrat, Saint Kitts
nation: **4** Cuba **5** Haiti **7** Bahamas, Grenada, Jamaica, St. Lucia **8** Dominica **10** Saint Lucia

caribe
7 piranha

caribou
4 deer **8** reindeer
kin: **3** elk **6** wapiti

caricature
4 mock, sham **5** farce, phony **6** parody

7 cartoon, lampoon, mockery, takeoff **8** travesty **9** burlesque **10** distortion, pasquinade **12** exaggeration

Carlsbad feature
4 cave **6** cavern

Carmen
author: 7 Mérimée (Prosper)
composer: 5 Bizet (Georges)
lover: 7 Don José **9** Escamillo

carnage
4 gore **8** butchery, hecatomb, massacre **9** bloodbath, bloodshed, slaughter

carnal
4 lewd **6** animal, bodily, coarse, earthy, sexual, vulgar, wanton **7** earthly, fleshly, lustful, mundane, obscene, sensual, worldly **8** corporal, material, physical, sensuous, temporal **9** corporeal **10** lascivious

carnation
4 pink **5** color **6** flower

Carnegie of self-help
4 Dale

carnival
4 fair, fete **6** fiesta
attraction: 4 ride **6** midway **8** sideshow **10** concession
character: 5 shill **6** barker, hawker **7** grifter, spieler
city: 3 Rio
game: 8 Skee-Ball
New Orleans: 9 Mardi Gras
performer: 4 geek

carnivore
9 meat-eater **10** flesh-eater

carol
4 noel, song **6** ballad
Christmas: 4 noel

carom
6 bounce, glance **7** rebound **8** ricochet

Caron role
4 Gigi, Lili **5** Fanny

carotid's relative
5 aorta

carousal
3 bat, jag **4** bash, tear **5** binge, booze, drunk, fling, revel, spree **6** bender, frolic **7** blowout, debauch, shindig **8** wingding **9** brannigan
Scottish: 6 splore

carouse
5 revel **6** cavort, frolic **7** roister
Scottish: 4 birl

carp
3 nag **4** crab, fuss **5** bream, cavil, scold **6** peck at, pester **7** henpeck **8** complain, cyprinid, sea bream **9** complaint, criticize, find fault

carpe ___
4 diem

carpenter
3 ant, bee **6** joiner, wright **7** builder, workman **10** woodworker

carpentry
7 joinery **10** timberwork
tool: 3 saw **5** auger, drill, plane **6** chisel, hammer, pliers **11** brace and bit, screwdriver

carper
6 critic, nagger **7** caviler, knocker, niggler **9** nitpicker **10** complainer, criticizer **11** faultfinder

carpet
3 mat, rug **4** Agra **5** Herat, Heriz, Koula, Ladik, Sarok, tapis **6** Herati, Kerman, Keshan, Kirman, Sarouk, Tabriz, Wilton **8** moquette **9** Axminster, broadloom

carpet beetle
10 buffalo bug

carping
7 blaming, railing **8** captious, critical **10** censorious **11** reproachful **12** faultfinding, overcritical

carrageen
7 seaweed **9** Irish moss

carrefour
5 plaza **6** square **10** crossroads

car-rental option
4 Avis **5** Hertz **6** Budget

carriage
3 gig, rig **4** mien, pose **5** coach **6** stance **7** posture, transit **8** attitude **9** transport **10** conveyance, deportment
American: 5 buggy **8** rockaway **9** buckboard
attendant: 6 flunky **7** footman
baby: 4 pram **5** buggy **8** stroller **12** perambulator
driver: 4 hack **5** cabby **8** coachman
folding top: 6 calash
four-wheeled: 4 trap **5** buggy, coupe **6** berlin, calash, fiacre, landau, surrey **7** cariole, droshky, hackney, phaeton **8** barouche, brougham, carryall, clarence, rockaway, sociable, stanhope, victoria **9** buckboard
Indian: 6 gharry
man-drawn: 8 rickshaw **10** jinricksha, jinrikisha
Russian: 6 troika **7** droshky
stately: 7 caroche
three-horse: 6 troika
two-wheeled: 3 gig **4** shay, trap **5** buggy, sulky, tonga **6** chaise, dennet, hansom **7** calèche, dogcart, tilbury **8** curricle **9** cabriolet
with attendants: 8 equipage

carriage trade
5 elite **6** gentry **7** quality **9** blue blood, gentility **10** upper class, upper crust **11** aristocracy

carrick bend
4 knot

carried
5 borne
carrier
4 mule 5 envoy 6 bearer, porter, runner, vector 7 airline, courier, shipper, vehicle 8 conveyor, emissary 9 go-between, messenger, stretcher 11 internuncio, transporter
Carroll character
5 Alice, Bruno, snark 6 boojum, Sylvie 8 Dormouse, Red Queen 9 Mad Hatter, March Hare 10 Mock Turtle 11 White Rabbit 12 Humpty Dumpty
carrot
5 prize 6 reward 9 incentive 10 inducement
carry
3 get, lug 4 bear, haul, have, hump, keep, move, pack, send, take, tote, wear 5 bring, ferry, fetch, range, stock 6 affect, bear up, convey, uphold 7 comport, conduct, portage, possess, support, sustain 8 buttress, transfer, transmit 9 influence, transport
carryall
4 tote 7 tote bag
carrying case
7 holdall, satchel
carry off
4 kill 6 abduct, kidnap, remove 7 achieve, destroy, execute, perform, realize 8 complete, conclude, dispatch, shanghai 10 accomplish, spirit away
carry on
3 run 4 go on, keep, rant, rave, wage 6 direct, endure, manage, ordain 7 conduct, operate, persist, prattle, proceed 8 continue, sound off 9 persevere
carry out
6 effect, govern, render 7 achieve, execute, fulfill, oversee, perform, realize 8 bring off, complete, finalize, transact 9 discharge, prosecute 10 accomplish, administer, effectuate 12 administrate
carry over
6 deduct 7 persist 8 postpone, transfer
carry through
4 last 5 abide 6 effect, endure 7 execute, perdure, perform, persist, survive 8 bring off, complete, continue 10 accomplish, effectuate
Carson, Johnny
predecessor: 4 Paar (Jack)
successor: 4 Leno (Jay)
Carson work
11 Sea Around Us (The) 12 Silent Spring
cart
3 gig 4 dray, haul 5 buggy, carry 6 barrow, convey, schlep 7 schlepp, trundle, tumbrel, tumbril 8 carriage 9 transport 11 wheelbarrow
Indian: 5 tonga
racing: 5 sulky

___ carte
3 à la
___ Carte
5 D'Oyly
carte blanche
3 say 5 power, right, say-so 7 freedom, license 8 free hand, free rein 9 authority 10 blank check 11 prerogative
carte du jour
4 menu
cartel
4 bloc, OPEC, pool 5 trust 7 combine 9 syndicate 10 consortium 12 conglomerate
Carthage neighbor
5 Utica
Carthaginian
goddess of the moon: 5 Tanit 6 Tanith
queen: 4 Dido 6 Elissa
cartilage
7 gristle
cartographer
English: 5 Smith (William)
Flemish: 6 Kremer (Gerhard) 8 Mercator (Gerardus), Ortelius
German: 13 Waldseemüller (Martin)
Greek: 7 Ptolemy
Italian: 8 Vespucci (Amerigo)
cartography
9 mapmaking
carton
3 box 4 pack
cartoon
5 anime, manga 10 comic strip
chipmunk: 4 Chip, Dale
dog: 4 Lady 5 Astro, Pluto, Pongo, Tramp 6 Gromit 7 Sherman
frame: 3 cel
(see also **comic strip**)
cartoonist
3 Lee (Stan) 4 Arno (Peter), Auth (Tony), Capp (Al), Kane (Bob), Nast (Thomas), Szep (Paul) 5 Adams (Scott), Block (Herbert), Booth (George), Chast (Roz), Crumb (R.), Davis (Jim), Gould (Chester), Hanna (Bill), Hergé, Jones (Chuck), Keane (Bill), Kelly (Walt), Lantz (Walter), McCay (Winsor), Sempé, Steig (William), Toles (Tom), Young (Chic) 6 Addams (Charles), Caniff (Milton), Conrad (Paul), Disney (Walt), Eisner (Will), Kliban (B.), Larson (Gary), Martin (Don), Peters (Mike), Schulz (Charles), Searle (Ronald), Walker (Mort), Wilson (Gahan) 7 Barbera (Joe), Drucker (Mort), Feiffer (Jules), Ketcham (Hank), Mauldin (Bill), Thurber (James), Trudeau (Garry) 8 Breathed (Burke), Goldberg (Rube), Groening (Matt), Herblock, Herriman (George), Hokinson (Helen), MacNelly (Jeff), Oliphant (Pat), Steadman (Ralph)

9 Fleischer (Max), Steinberg (Saul) **10** Hirschfeld (Al), MacFarlane (Seth)

cartouche
5 frame **6** shield **9** cartridge

cartridge
4 case, tube **5** shell **8** cassette, cylinder **9** cartouche, container

cartwheel
4 coin **6** dollar, tumble **10** handspring

carve
3 cut, hew **4** chip, etch, form, hack **5** shape, slice **6** chisel, cleave, incise, sculpt **7** dissect, engrave, whittle **9** sculpture

carved
6 graven
gem: 5 cameo
pillar: 5 stela, stele **6** stelae (plural)

Casablanca
actor: 5 Lorre (Peter), Rains (Claude) **6** Bogart (Humphrey) **7** Bergman (Ingrid), Henreid (Paul) **11** Greenstreet (Sydney)
character: 4 Ilsa (Lund), Rick (Blaine) **6** Laszlo (Victor)
director: 6 Curtiz (Michael)

Casals's instrument
5 cello

Casanova
4 rake, roué, wolf **5** Romeo **6** lecher, masher, tomcat **7** amorist, Don Juan, gallant, playboy, seducer **8** lothario, paramour **9** adulterer, ladies' man, libertine, womanizer **10** lady-killer, voluptuary **11** philanderer

cascade
4 fall, gush, lace, pour, spew **5** chute, falls, flood, spill **6** deluge, plunge, rapids, shower, tumble **7** Niagara, torrent **8** cataract **9** avalanche, waterfall **10** outpouring

Cascade Mountains peak
6 Lassen, Shasta **7** Rainier

case
3 box, con, vet **4** etui, hull, husk, skin, suit **5** cause, event, shell, trunk **6** action, sample, sheath **7** episode, examine, example, inspect, lawsuit **8** argument, covering, incident, instance, sampling, specimen **9** check over, condition, situation **10** occurrence, proceeding, scrutinize **11** eventuality **12** circumstance
grammatical: 6 dative **8** ablative, genitive, vocative **9** objective **10** accusative, nominative, possessive

casebearer
5 larva **11** caterpillar

case-hardened
5 tough **7** callous **8** obdurate **9** indurated, insensate, toughened, unfeeling **11** insensitive **12** thick-skinned

casement
4 sash **6** window

Casey at the Bat poet
6 Thayer (Ernest Lawrence)

cash
4 coin, jack **5** bread, dough, money, moola, scrip **6** dinero, moolah, redeem, wampum **7** cabbage, lettuce, scratch **8** currency **10** greenbacks, ready money **11** legal tender
drawer: 4 till
machine: 3 ATM

cashier
3 axe, can **4** boot, fire, oust, sack **5** clerk, eject, expel, scrap **6** banker, bounce, bursar, reject, teller **7** boot out, discard, dismiss, kick out **8** jettison, throw out **9** discharge, eliminate, terminate, throw away **10** bookkeeper **11** bean counter, comptroller

cash in
3 die **4** conk, drop **5** croak **6** expire, pop off, redeem, retire **7** kick off, succumb **8** check out, drop dead, pass away, settle up **9** liquidate

casing
4 hull, husk, pipe, rind, skin, tire **5** frame, shell, space **7** wrapper **8** membrane

casino
attendant: 6 dealer **8** croupier
game: 4 faro **5** craps, monte, poker **6** tierce **8** baccarat, roulette **9** blackjack
city: 4 Reno
game: 4 Keno **5** craps, poker **8** baccarat, roulette **9** blackjack

cask
3 keg, tun **4** butt, drum, pipe **6** barrel, firkin **8** hogshead

casket
3 box **5** chest **6** coffer, coffin **8** jewel box

Caspian Sea
city: 4 Baku
feeder: 4 Kura, Ural **5** Volga

Cassandra
4 seer **7** prophet, seeress **8** doomster **9** doomsayer, pessimist, worrywart **10** prophetess
brother: 7 Helenus
father: 5 Priam
lover: 9 Agamemnon
mother: 6 Hecuba
slayer: 12 Clytemnestra

cassava
4 yuca **5** yucca **6** manioc **7** tapioca

casserole
4 dish **5** crock, kugel **6** tureen

cassette
4 tape

Cassini of fashion
4 Oleg

Cassiopeia
13 constellation
daughter: 9 Andromeda
husband: 7 Cepheus

Cassio's mistress
6 Bianca

Cassius Clay, today
3 Ali (Muhammad)

cassock
4 robe 7 soutane 8 vestment

cassowary kin
3 emu, moa

cast
3 add, hue, sum, tot 4 drop, face, fire, form, hurl, kind, look, mold, shed, sort, tint, tone, toss, turn, type 5 color, fling, heave, leave, pitch, range, shade, shape, strew, throw, tinge, total, touch 6 actors, design, devise, direct, figure, nature, reject, slough, troupe, visage 7 arrange, company, quality, replica, scatter 8 abdicate, disperse, jettison, sprinkle 9 character, prognosis, throw away 10 appearance, conjecture, distribute, expression, prediction, strabismus, suggestion 11 countenance
a spell on: 3 hex 5 charm 7 beguile, bewitch 8 enthrall 9 captivate, enrapture, fascinate, hypnotize, infatuate, mesmerize, spellbind
overboard: 7 deep-six 8 jettison

cast about
4 hunt, seek 5 grope 6 search 7 seek out 8 contrive 9 search for, search out

castaway
5 leper, tramp 6 beggar, maroon, pariah 7 Ishmael, outcast, vagrant 8 deadbeat, derelict 10 Ishmaelite

cast down
see **downcast**

caste
5 class 6 degree, estate, status 7 station 8 division, prestige

cast head
4 bust

castigate
4 beat, flay, rail, whip 5 baste, chide, scold, slash 6 berate, pummel, punish, rebuke, scorch, thrash 7 belabor, blister, chasten, chew out, lambast, reprove, scarify, scourge, upbraid 8 chastise, lambaste, penalize 9 criticize, dress down, excoriate, reprimand 10 discipline, tongue-lash

castigation
3 rod 6 rebuke 7 reproof 8 punition, scolding 10 correction, discipline, punishment 12 chastisement

castle
5 manor, villa 7 alcazar, château, citadel, mansion 8 fortress 10 stronghold
adjunct: 4 moat
gate: 10 portcullis
ledge: 7 rampart
structure: 6 turret
tower: 4 keep 6 donjon
wall: 6 bailey 10 battlement

cast off
4 shed 5 fling, flung, let go, loose, untie 6 jilted, untied 7 unhitch 8 cut loose, forsaken, rejected, unfasten, unmoored 9 discarded, unhitched 10 left behind, unfastened

Castor
brother: 6 Pollux 10 Polydeuces
constellation: 6 Gemini
father: 4 Zeus 9 Tyndareus
mother: 4 Leda
sister: 5 Helen
slayer: 4 Idas

castor oil
8 laxative 9 cathartic, lubricant, purgative

cast out
4 oust 5 egest, eject, evict, exile, expel 6 banish, deport 7 discard 9 eliminate, ostracize

castrate
3 fix 4 geld, spay 5 alter, unman, unsex 6 neuter 7 unnerve 8 enervate, mutilate 9 sterilize 10 emasculate 11 desexualize

castrato singer
9 Farinelli

Castro's home
4 Cuba

casual
5 light, minor 6 breezy, chance, random, remote 7 natural, offhand, relaxed, trivial, unfussy 8 detached, informal, laid-back 9 easygoing, impromptu, irregular, uncurious, unplanned, unserious 10 accidental, contingent, fortuitous, improvised, incidental, insouciant, nonchalant, occasional 11 indifferent, low-pressure, spontaneous, unconcerned, unimportant 12 uninterested 13 disinterested, insignificant
shirt: 3 tee

casualty
4 prey 5 death 6 mishap, victim 8 accident, calamity, disaster, fatality 9 mischance 10 misfortune 11 catastrophe 12 misadventure

casuistry
7 sophism 9 deception, sophistry 12 equivocation, speciousness 13 deceptiveness

casus ___
5 belli

cat
4 eyra, lion, lynx, pard, puma, puss 5 felid, kitty, liger, moggy, ounce, pussy, tabby, tiger, tigon 6 cougar, feline, jaguar, margay, mouser, ocelot, serval 7 caracal, cheetah, leopard, panther 10 jaguarundi 12 mountain lion

Alice's: 5 Dinah
Born Free: 4 Elsa
cartoon: 3 Tom 5 Felix, Krazy 6 Stimpy 8 Garfield 9 Sylvester 10 Heathcliff
combining form: 5 ailur 6 ailuro
disease: 9 distemper
domestic: 3 Mau, Rex 4 Manx 5 tabby 6 Angora, Birman, calico, exotic, Ocicat, Somali 7 bobtail, Burmese, Persian, Ragdoll, Siamese 8 longhair, Wirehair 9 Himalayan, Maine coon, shorthair, Tonkinese 10 Abyssinian
extinct: 10 saber-tooth
fastest: 7 cheetah
female: 5 queen 7 lioness, tigress 9 grimalkin
genus: 5 Felis
grinning: 8 Cheshire
hybrid: 5 liger, tigon 6 Bengal, Safari 7 Chausie 8 Savannah
lookalike: 5 civet, genet 7 linsang
male: 3 gib, tom
relating to: 6 feline
sound: 3 mew 4 hiss, meow, purr, roar 5 miaou, miaow 9 caterwaul
tailless: 4 Manx
young: 6 kitten

cataclysm
5 flood 6 deluge 7 Niagara, torrent, tragedy 8 calamity, cataract, disaster, flooding 10 inundation 11 catastrophe, devastation

cataclysmic
5 fatal 7 ruinous 10 calamitous, disastrous 11 devastating 12 catastrophic

catacomb
5 crypt, vault 8 cemetery 10 necropolis, undercroft

catafalque
4 bier

catalepsy
6 trance

catalog
4 list, roll 5 enter, index, tally 6 enroll, roster 7 itemize, program 8 classify, inscribe, register, roll call, schedule, syllabus 9 enumerate, inventory 10 prospectus
of books: 11 bibliotheca
of saints: 9 hagiology

catalyst
4 goad, spur 7 impetus, impulse 8 stimulus 9 incentive, stimulant 10 incitation, incitement, motivation

catamaran
4 boat, raft

catamount
4 lynx, puma 6 bobcat, cougar 7 panther, wildcat 12 mountain lion

cataract
5 falls, flood, rapid 6 deluge, rapids 7 cascade, Niagara, torrent 8 downpour 9 waterfall 10 inundation

catastrophe
3 woe 6 deluge, fiasco 7 debacle, tragedy 8 calamity, disaster, meltdown 9 cataclysm, emergency 11 devastation

catastrophic
5 fatal 6 deadly, tragic 7 ruinous 10 calamitous, disastrous 11 cataclysmic

Catawba
4 wine 5 river 6 Indian

catcall
3 boo 4 hiss, hoot, jeer, razz 9 criticism, raspberry 10 Bronx cheer

catch
3 bag, get, nab, net, see, wed 4 dupe, find, fool, grab, grip, gull, haul, hoax, hook, nail, snag, sock, spot, take, trap 5 block, clasp, clout, grasp, hit on, marry, reach, round, seize, smite, snare, stick, stump, trick, watch, whack 6 accept, anchor, arrest, clutch, collar, cut off, descry, detect, engage, entrap, fasten, flurry, follow, put out, rattle, secure, snatch, strike, take in, tangle, turn up 7 capture, confuse, deceive, disturb, ensnare, grapple, hit upon, perplex, receive 8 confound, contract, entangle, flimflam, fragment, hoodwink, kick over, meet with, overhaul, overtake 9 apprehend, bamboozle, embarrass, encounter, intercept 10 comprehend, understand 12 come down with

Catch-22 author
6 Heller (Joseph)

catchall term
3 etc. 4 et al. 5 and/or 7 and so on 10 and so forth

Catcher in the Rye
author: 8 Salinger (J. D.)
character: 9 Caulfield (Holden)

catcher's glove
4 mitt

catching
10 contagious, infectious 12 communicable

catch on
3 see 4 hear 5 learn 7 find out 8 discover 9 ascertain, determine, figure out

catchphrase
see **catchword**

catch sight of
4 espy 7 glimpse

catch some rays
3 tan

catch up
4 hold 6 gain on 7 close in, ensnare 8 entangle, enthrall 9 fascinate, mesmerize, spellbind

catchword
5 maxim, motto 6 slogan 10 shibboleth

catchy
6 fitful, spotty, tricky **7** erratic **8** sporadic **9** appealing, desultory, irregular, memorable, spasmodic

catechist
7 teacher

catechize
3 ask **4** quiz **5** grill, query, train **7** examine, inquire **8** instruct, question **9** inculcate **11** interrogate

catechumen
6 novice **7** convert, student, trainee **8** initiate, neophyte

categorical
7 certain, decided, express **8** absolute, clear-cut, definite, emphatic, explicit, positive **9** downright **10** definitive, forthright **11** unambiguous, unequivocal, unqualified

categorize
3 peg **4** sort **5** class, group **6** assort **7** put down **8** classify, identify **10** pigeonhole

category
4 rank, tier **5** class, genre, grade, group, taxon **6** league **7** section **8** division, grouping **10** pigeonhole

catenation
4 link **5** chain **6** series, string **7** linkage **10** connection, succession

catercorner
9 obliquely, slantways, slantwise **10** cornerwise, diagonally

caterpillar
5 larva **7** cutworm, webworm **8** armyworm, silkworm **10** casebearer

cater to
5 humor, spoil **6** coddle, oblige, pamper, supply **7** furnish, gratify, indulge

caterwaul
4 howl, meow, yowl **5** miaow **6** squall

catfish
see **fish**

catharsis
5 purge, tonic **7** purging **8** curative **9** cleansing, purgation, purgative **10** lustration **11** expurgation, restorative **12** purification

cathartic
5 purge, tonic **8** curative **9** castor oil, purgative **11** restorative, therapeutic

Cathay
5 China

cathedral
5 duomo **6** church **8** basilica
feature: 4 apse, nave **5** altar **6** chapel **7** chancel **8** buttress, transept **10** clerestory

cathedral city
3 Ely **4** Bath, York **5** Wells **6** Durham, Exeter, London, Oxford **7** Bristol, Chester, Lincoln, Norwich **8** Carlisle, Coventry, Hereford **9** Lichfield, Liverpool, Salisbury, Worcester **10** Canterbury, Chichester, Gloucester, Winchester **11** Westminster **12** Peterborough

Cather novel
8 Lost Lady (A) **9** My Antonia, One of Ours, O Pioneers **13** Song of the Lark **15** Professor's House (The) **16** Shadows on the Rock

catholic, Catholic
5 broad **6** global **7** general, liberal **8** eclectic, tolerant **9** expansive, inclusive, undivided, universal, worldwide **10** ecumenical **12** cosmopolitan **13** comprehensive
district: 7 diocese
tribunal: 4 rota

catholicity
7 breadth **9** tolerance **10** liberality **11** magnanimity **12** universality

catholicon
6 elixir **7** cure-all, nostrum, panacea

catkin
5 ament

catlike
6 feline **7** furtive **8** stealthy

catnap
3 nap **4** doze **6** siesta, snooze **10** forty winks

catnip
3 nep

Cato
title: 6 aedile, censor, consul **7** praetor, tribune **8** quaestor

cat's-paw
4 dupe, knot, pawn, tool **5** patsy **6** puppet, stooge

cattail
4 reed, rush

cattle
4 cows, kine, neat, oxen **7** bovines **9** livestock
breed: 5 Angus, Devon, Kerry **6** Durham, Jersey, Sussex **7** Brahman, Hariana, Red Poll **8** Ayrshire, Galloway, Guernsey, Hereford, Highland, Holstein, Limousin, Longhorn **9** Charolais, Red Polled, Shorthorn, Simmental **10** Brown Swiss **11** Dutch Belted
catching rope: 5 lasso **6** lariat
cry: 3 low, moo
dehorn: 4 poll
disease: 4 loco **5** bloat **6** mad cow, nagana **7** anthrax, locoism, measles, murrain **8** blackleg, lumpy jaw, mastitis, staggers **10** rinderpest, Texas fever **11** brucellosis
dung: 4 tath

extinct breed: **9** Teeswater
family: **7** Bovidae
feed: **6** fodder, silage, stover
genus: **3** Bos
goddess: **6** Bubona
grazing land: **5** range **6** meadow **7** pasture
group: **4** herd **5** drove
herdsman: **6** cowboy, drover, gaucho **7** vaquero **8** neatherd, wrangler **10** cowpuncher
identification: **5** brand
pen: **6** corral
round up: **7** wrangle
stable: **4** barn, byre
steal: **6** rustle
wild flight: **8** stampede

catty
4 mean **5** nasty, snide **6** barbed, feline **7** furtive, vicious **8** spiteful, stealthy **9** malicious **10** backbiting, malevolent

Caucasian
capital: **4** Baku **6** Tiflis **7** Tbilisi, Yerevan
republic: **7** Armenia, Georgia **10** Azerbaijan

Caucasus
peak: **6** Elbrus
people: **5** Osset

caucus
4 bloc, sect **5** cabal, lobby **6** parley, powwow **7** faction

caudal appendage
4 tail

caudillo
6 despot, tyrant **8** dictator **9** strongman

cauldron
3 pot **6** boiler, kettle **8** crucible

cause
4 case, make, root **5** evoke, hatch **6** compel, effect, elicit, induce, motive, origin, reason, source, spring **7** produce, provoke **8** engender, generate, movement **9** necessity, principle **10** antecedent, bring about, inducement, originator **11** determinant, precipitate **13** consideration

cause ___
7 célèbre

causerie
4 chat **5** essay **6** column **7** article, feature **8** colloquy, dialogue **12** conversation

caustic
4 acid, keen, tart **5** acerb, acrid, sharp **6** biting, bitter, ironic **7** acerbic, cutting, mordant, pungent **8** scathing, stinging **9** corrosive, sarcastic, trenchant **10** astringent
solution: **3** lye

cauterize
4 burn, numb, sear **6** deaden **11** anesthetize

caution
4 warn **6** caveat **7** warning **8** forewarn, monition, prudence **9** canniness, chariness, foresight, vigilance **10** admonition, discretion, providence **11** carefulness, forethought, forewarning **12** admonishment, discreetness

cautionary
7 warning **8** monitory **10** admonitory

cautious
4 wary **5** alert, cagey, canny, chary, leery **6** shrewd **7** careful, guarded, politic, prudent **8** discreet, gingerly, vigilant, watchful **9** judicious, provident **11** circumspect, considerate, foresighted

cavalcade
6 parade, series **7** cortege **8** sequence **10** procession, succession

cavalier
5 lofty, proud **6** casual, knight, lordly **7** gallant, haughty, offhand **8** arrogant, debonair, horseman, scornful, superior **9** caballero, gentleman **10** disdainful, dismissive, insouciant, nonchalant **12** aristocratic, supercilious

cavalryman
6 lancer **7** dragoon, trooper
Algerian: **5** spahi
horse: **5** waler
Prussian: **5** uhlan
Russian: **7** cossack
Turkish: **5** spahi
weapon: **5** lance, saber **7** carbine

cave
3 bow, den **4** bend, drop, give, grot, lair **5** antre, break, defer, yield **6** fold up, grotto, hollow, submit **7** crumple, knuckle, succumb **8** collapse **9** break down **10** capitulate, subterrane **11** buckle under **12** knuckle under, subterranean
dweller: **3** bat **4** bear, lion **6** hermit **9** Cro-Magnon **10** troglodite **11** Neanderthal
explorer: **9** spelunker
formation: **10** stalactite, stalagmite
France: **7** Lascaux **10** Rouffignac
Iceland: **7** Singing
Indiana: **9** Wyandotte
Iraq: **8** Shanidar
Kentucky: **7** Mammoth
New Zealand: **7** Waitomo
rock: **8** dolomite **9** limestone
Scotland: **7** Fingal's
South Africa: **5** Cango
Spain: **8** Altamira
study of: **10** speleology

caveat
6 notice **7** caution, warning **8** monition **10** admonition **11** explanation, forewarning

caveat ___
6 emptor
caveman
5 brute **6** savage **9** barbarian, Cro-Magnon **10** troglodyte
cavern
5 antre **6** grotto **12** subterranean
Capri: 10 Blue Grotto
Montana: 13 Lewis and Clark
New Mexico: 8 Carlsbad
Tennessee: 10 Cumberland
Virginia: 5 Luray
cavernous
4 vast **6** gaping, hollow **7** yawning
caviar
3 roe **4** eggs **6** relish
source: 4 shad **6** beluga **8** sturgeon
cavil
4 carp **7** nitpick, quibble **9** criticize, find fault
caviler
6 carper, critic **7** knocker **8** quibbler **10** criticizer **11** faultfinder
caviling
5 fussy **7** carping, finicky, nagging **8** captious, contrary, critical, exacting, niggling **10** censorious, nitpicking **12** faultfinding **13** hairsplitting
cavity
3 pit **4** bore, hole, void **5** decay, fossa **6** caries, hollow **7** vacuity **10** depression, interstice
body: 5 antra (plural), fossa, sinus **6** antrum, fossae (plural) **8** follicle, hemocoel
cavort
4 leap, romp **5** caper, cut up, frisk, sport **6** frolic, gambol, prance **7** carry on, rollick **10** roughhouse **11** horse around
cavy
4 paca **6** rodent **9** guinea pig
caw
4 crow, yawp **6** squall, squawk
cay
3 key **4** isle, reef **5** islet **6** island
cayenne
6 pepper
genus: 8 Capsicum
cayman
see **caiman**
Cayman Islands
capital: 10 George Town
discoverer: 8 Columbus (Christopher)
territory of: 7 Britain
Cayuga chief
5 Logan (James)
cease
3 die, end **4** halt, quit, stop **5** close **6** desist, ending, finish **8** conclude, give over, knock off, leave off **9** terminate **10** conclusion **11** discontinue, termination
cease-fire
5 truce **9** armistice **10** suspension
ceaseless
7 endless, eternal, nonstop **8** constant, immortal, unending **9** continual, incessant, perennial, perpetual, sustained, unabating **10** continuing, continuous **11** everlasting, never-ending, unremitting **12** interminable **13** uninterrupted
Cecrops' daughter
5 Herse **8** Aglauros, Aglaurus **9** Pandrosos, Pandrosus
cede
4 deed **5** grant, leave, yield **6** assign, convey, give up **7** abandon, concede **8** alienate, hand over, make over, part with, renounce, sign over, transfer **9** surrender, vouchsafe **10** relinquish
ceiling
3 cap **5** limit
ceinture
4 belt, sash **6** girdle **9** waistband
Celaeno
father: 5 Atlas
mother: 7 Pleione
sisters: 8 Pleiades
celebrate
4 fete, hold, hymn, keep, laud **5** bless, cry up, exalt, extol, honor, party, revel **6** praise **7** carouse, glorify, maffick, observe, perform, rejoice **8** eulogize **9** solemnize **11** commemorate
celebrated
5 famed, great, noted **6** famous **7** eminent, notable, partied **8** caroused, rejoiced, renowned **9** prominent, well-known **11** illustrious **13** distinguished
celebration
4 bash, fete, gala **5** beano, party **6** fiesta **7** blowout, jubilee, revelry **8** ceremony, festival, jamboree, wingding **10** observance
celebrity
3 VIP **4** fame, hero, idol, lion, name, star **5** éclat, glory **6** renown, repute **7** notable **8** eminence, luminary, prestige, somebody **9** notoriety, personage, superstar **10** notability, prominence, reputation
celerity
4 pace **5** speed **8** alacrity, dispatch, rapidity, velocity **9** briskness, fleetness, quickness, swiftness **10** speediness
celestial
6 divine, uranic **7** blessed, elysian, sublime, uranian **8** beatific, empyreal, empyrean, ethereal, heavenly, Olympian, supernal **9** unearthly **12** otherworldly

celestial body
3 sun **4** moon, star **5** comet **6** meteor, nebula, planet **8** asteroid **9** satellite

Celestial Empire
5 China

celibate
5 unwed **6** chaste, single, virgin **8** virginal, virtuous **9** abstinent, continent

cell
4 room **5** cubby, zooid **6** alcove **7** chamber, cubicle **9** corpuscle, cubbyhole **11** compartment
blood: 8 hemocyte
combining form: 3 cyt **4** cyto
disease: 6 cancer
division: 7 meiosis, mitosis
fertilized egg: 6 zygote
material: 3 DNA, RNA **7** protein **9** chromatin, cytoplasm **10** protoplasm
nerve: 6 neuron
part: 4 gene **7** nucleus, vacuole **8** ribosome **9** centriole **10** chromosome
reproductive: 3 egg **4** germ, ovum **5** sperm **6** gamete **8** gonidium

cellar
5 store **7** shelter **8** basement

cellist
American: 4 Rose (Leonard) **6** Lesser (Laurence), Parnas (Leslie), Yo-Yo Ma **7** Nelsova (Zara), Parisot (Aldo), Starker (Janos) **8** Schuster (Joseph) **10** Greenhouse (Bernard)
English: 5 du Pré (Jacqueline)
French: 8 Fournier (Pierre)
Russian: 11 Piatigorsky (Gregor) **12** Rostropovich (Mstislav)
Spanish: 6 Casals (Pablo)

cellophane
4 wrap **7** wrapper **8** wrapping **9** packaging

cell-phone sound
8 ringtone

celluloid
4 film **7** plastic

Celt
4 Gael, Scot **6** Breton **8** Irishman, Welshman **10** Cornishman, Highlander

Celtic
deity: 4 Bran **5** Epona, Lugus, Macha **6** Brigit **8** Rhiannon **9** Cernunnos
festival: 7 Beltane, Samhain
heroine: 7 Deirdre
priest: 5 druid
queen: 8 Boadicea, Boudicca

cement
4 bind, glue, join **5** grout, unify, unite **6** mastic, mortar, secure **8** concrete
ingredient: 4 lime **6** silica **7** alumina **8** magnesia, pozzolan **9** iron oxide, pozzolana

cemetery
8 boneyard, boot hill **8** God's acre **9** graveyard **10** churchyard, necropolis **12** burial ground, memorial park, potter's field
underground: 8 catacomb

cenacle
7 coterie **9** Upper Room **12** retreat house

cenotaph
4 tomb **6** marker **8** memorial, monument

censer
8 thurible
carrier: 8 thurifer

censor
3 ban, cut **4** blip, edit **5** bleep, purge **6** cut out, delete, excise, purify, screen **7** clean up **8** black out, restrict, suppress, withhold **9** expurgate, red-pencil **10** blue-pencil, bowdlerize

censorious
6 severe **7** carping **8** captious, critical **10** accusatory, condemning **11** reproachful **12** condemnatory, denunciatory, disapproving, faultfinding, overcritical, reprehending **13** hypercritical

censurable
5 wrong **6** guilty, sinful **7** heinous **8** blamable, blameful, culpable, improper, wrongful **9** incorrect **10** deplorable, despicable, detestable **11** blameworthy, disgraceful, impeachable **12** unacceptable **13** discreditable, objectionable, reprehensible

censure
5 blame, chide, scold **6** berate, rebuke, strafe **7** condemn, reprove, upbraid **8** chastise, denounce, disallow, reproach **9** castigate, criticize, reprehend, reprimand, reprobate **10** disapprove

centaur
6 Chiron, Nessus

Centaurus star
4 Beta **5** Alpha

Centennial State
8 Colorado

center
3 hub, mid **4** axis, core, crux, mean, pith, root, seat **5** focus, heart, midst, pivot **6** inside, medial, median, middle, source **7** central, essence **8** interior, midpoint, omphalos **10** focal point **11** equidistant **12** intermediary, intermediate

centerboard
4 keel

centerfold
7 foldout **8** gatefold

centerpiece
7 epergne

central
3 hub, key, mid **4** main, mean **5** basic, chief, focal **6** medial, median, middle **7** leading,

pivotal, primary, salient **8** cardinal, dominant, exchange, foremost, moderate **9** essential, paramount, principal **10** overriding **11** fundamental, outstanding, predominant **12** intermediate

Central African Republic
capital: **6** Bangui
former name: **11** Ubangi-Shari
language: **5** Sango, Zande **6** French
monetary unit: **5** franc
neighbor: **4** Chad **5** Congo, Sudan **8** Cameroon

Central America
country: **6** Belize, Panama **8** Honduras **9** Costa Rica, Guatemala, Nicaragua **10** El Salvador
language: **7** Nahuatl, Spanish

centralize
5 focus, unify **11** concentrate, consolidate

central point
3 hub **4** core, foci (plural) **5** focus, heart, nexus **7** nucleus

centripetal
8 afferent, focusing, unifying **10** converging **11** integrative **12** centralizing **13** concentrating, consolidating

centurion
7 officer **9** commander

century part
6 decade

century plant
5 agave **6** maguey

CEO's degree
3 MBA

cephalopod
5 squid **7** mollusc, mollusk, octopus **10** cuttlefish

Cepheus
daughter: **9** Andromeda
kingdom: **8** Ethiopia
wife: **10** Cassiopeia

ceramic pot
4 olla

cerate
4 balm **5** cream, salve **6** chrism **7** unction, unguent **8** dressing, liniment, ointment **9** demulcent, emollient

Cerberus
5 guard **8** guardian, sentinel, watchdog
father: **6** Typhon
form: **3** dog
mother: **7** Echidna

cereal
4 meal, mush, samp **5** gruel **6** farina **7** oatmeal **8** cornmeal, porridge
disease: **4** bunt, smut **5** ergot
fungus: **5** ergot
grass: **3** rye **4** corn, oats, ragi, rice, teff **5** emmer, maize, spelt, wheat **6** barley, millet **7** sorghum **9** buckwheat
Russian: **5** kasha

cerebral
6 mental **7** bookish **8** highbrow **9** scholarly **10** highbrowed **12** intellectual

cerebrate
5 think **6** reason **7** reflect **8** cogitate **9** speculate **10** deliberate

cerebration
7 thought **9** brainwork **10** cogitation, reflection **11** speculation **12** deliberation

ceremonial
6 august, formal, ritual, solemn **7** courtly, stately, studied **8** mannered, stylized **10** liturgical **11** ritualistic **12** conventional

ceremonious
6 formal, proper, seemly, solemn **7** courtly, stately **8** decorous, imposing, majestic **9** dignified, grandiose **10** impressive **11** punctilious **12** conventional

ceremony
4 form, pomp, rite **6** ritual **7** decorum, liturgy, service **8** protocol **9** formality **10** observance
Jewish: **8** habdalah, havdalah **10** bar mitzvah, bat mitzvah
university: **8** encaenia

Ceres
Greek counterpart: **7** Demeter
daughter: **10** Persephone, Proserpina, Proserpine
father: **6** Cronus, Saturn
mother: **3** Ops **4** Rhea

certain
3 set **4** firm, sure, true **5** fixed **6** stated **7** assured, settled **8** credible, definite, destined, positive, provable, reliable, specific, surefire **9** authentic, confident, convinced **10** conclusive, dependable, guaranteed, inarguable, inevitable, infallible, stipulated, undeniable, verifiable **11** confirmable, indubitable, unavoidable **12** demonstrable, indisputable, well-grounded **13** incontestable, uncontestable

certainty
5 faith **6** surety **8** sureness **9** assurance, sure thing **10** confidence, conviction **12** definiteness

certificate
7 diploma, license, voucher **8** contract, document **9** affidavit **10** credential

certifier
6 notary **7** auditor **9** registrar

certify
4 aver, avow, okay **5** state, swear, vouch **6** assert, assure, attest, verify **7** approve, confirm, endorse, license, testify, warrant,

witness **8** accredit, guaranty, notarize **9** authorize, guarantee, recognize **10** commission **12** authenticate

Cervantes character
10 Don Quixote **11** Sancho Panza

cervid
3 elk **4** deer **5** moose **6** wapiti **7** caribou **8** reindeer

cessation
3 end **4** halt, rest, stop **5** break, cease, close, letup, pause **6** ending, finish, freeze, hiatus, period, recess **7** respite **10** conclusion, suspension **11** termination **12** interruption

cesspool
3 den, pit, sty **4** sink, sump **5** sewer, Sodom **6** cloaca, gutter, pigsty **8** Gomorrah **12** Augean stable

cetacean
4 orca **5** baiji, whale **6** beluga, tucuxi **7** costero, dolphin, narwhal, vaquita **8** narwhale, porpoise

Cetus star
4 Mira

Ceylon
see **Sri Lanka**

cgs unit
3 erg **4** dyne, gram, phot **5** gauss, poise, stilb **6** second, stokes **7** lambert, maxwell, oersted **10** centimeter

Chablis
4 wine **8** Burgundy **9** white wine

Chad
capital: **8** N'Djamena
city: **4** Sarh **6** Abéché **7** Moundou
language: **6** Arabic, French
monetary unit: **5** franc
neighbor: **5** Libya, Niger, Sudan **7** Nigeria **8** Cameroon
river: **5** Chari **6** Logone

chafe
3 irk, rub, vex **4** fret, gall, peel, rage, skin, wear **5** annoy, erode **6** abrade, bother, scrape **7** provoke **8** irritate, vexation

chaff
3 kid, rag, rib **4** jest, joke, josh, razz **5** dregs, husks, tease **6** banter, debris, refuse **7** remains **8** detritus **9** sweepings

chaffer
6 barter, dicker, haggle, higgle, palter **7** bargain, chatter **8** exchange, huckster

chagrin
3 ire, irk, vex **5** abash, annoy, peeve, pique, upset **6** dismay **7** perturb **8** disquiet, distress, unsettle, vexation **9** annoyance, discomfit, displease, embarrass, humiliate, petulance **10** disappoint, discompose, disconcert, irritation **11** frustration, humiliation **12** discomfiture

chagrined
4 hurt **5** upset, vexed **6** shamed **7** ashamed **8** dismayed **9** disturbed, mortified, perturbed, unsettled **10** distressed, humiliated **11** discomposed, embarrassed **12** disappointed, disconcerted

chain
3 row **4** bind, bond, gyve **5** group, train, trust **6** cartel, catena, fetter, hobble, series, string, tether **7** combine, manacle, shackle **8** handcuff, sequence **9** syndicate **10** succession **11** concatenate, progression **12** conglomerate **13** concatenation
adjunct: **8** sprocket
collar: **6** torque
gang: **6** coffle
ornamental: **10** chatelaine
sound: **5** clank

chain ___
3 saw **4** gang, mail **5** store **6** letter **8** reaction

Chained Lady
9 Andromeda

chain store
6 big box

chair
4 seat **5** stool **6** rocker, settee, settle **7** preside
back: **5** splat
bishop's: **8** cathedra
designer: **5** Eames (Charles, Ray) **6** Breuer (Marcel)
maker: **5** caner
portable: **5** sedan
reclining: **6** chaise **12** chaise longue, chaise lounge
royal: **6** throne
type: **4** club, easy **6** morris **7** rocking **8** captain's, electric **9** director's, reclining **10** Adirondack, ladder-back

chaise
4 sofa **5** chair, coach, divan **8** carriage

chalcedony
4 onyx, sard **5** agate, chert **6** jasper, quartz **9** carnelian, cornelian **10** bloodstone **11** chrysoprase

chalet
3 hut **4** camp **5** lodge **7** cottage

chalice
3 cup **5** grail **6** goblet
veil: **3** aer

chalk out
5 draft **6** sketch **7** outline **8** block out, rough out **11** skeletonize **12** characterize

chalk up
3 get, win **4** gain **6** attain, credit, impute, obtain, secure **7** achieve, acquire, ascribe, procure, realize **9** attribute

challenge
3 try **4** dare, defy, face, stir, wake **5** brave, claim, demur, doubt, exact, rouse, waken **6** arouse, awaken, demand, impugn, invite, kindle, oppugn **7** calling, dispute, protest, require, solicit, venture **8** confront, defiance, demurral, demurrer, question, struggle **9** objection, postulate, stimulate **10** difficulty, insistence **12** remonstrance

challenger
5 rival **8** aspirant, opponent **9** adversary, contender **10** antagonist, competitor, contestant

chamber
4 cell, hall, room **5** haven, house **7** cubicle **9** apartment, enclosure **11** compartment
burial: **4** cist
ceremonial: **4** kiva
underground: **8** hypogeum

chambered seashell
8 nautilus

chamberlain
6 priest **7** officer, servant **9** attendant, treasurer

chameleon
5 anole **6** lizard

chameleonic
6 fickle **7** protean **9** mercurial **10** changeable, inconstant

chamfer
5 bevel **6** groove

chamois
5 izard **6** shammy **7** leather **8** antelope, ruminant
habitat: **4** Alps
Old Testament: **6** aoudad

chamois-like animal
4 goat, ibex

champ
3 gum **4** bite, chew, mash **5** gnash, munch **7** trample **8** macerate, ruminate **9** masticate

champagne
4 wine **6** bubbly
brand: **4** Moët
bucket: **4** icer
center: **5** Reims **6** Rheims
type: **3** sec **4** brut, doux

Champagne capital
6 Troyes

champaign
5 field, plain **7** expanse, terrain **11** battlefield

champignon
6 fungus **8** mushroom

champion
4 back, hero **5** first, prime **6** uphold, victor, winner **7** capital, contend, leading, paladin, premier, support, titlist **8** advocate, defender, exponent, fight for, foremost, medalist, unbeaten **9** excellent, nonpareil, number one, principal, proponent, protector, supporter **11** illustrious, outstanding, titleholder, white knight

championship
5 crown, title **6** laurel, trophy **7** contest, defense, laurels, pennant **8** advocacy **10** blue ribbon

chance
3 hap, hit, lot, odd **4** fate, luck, meet, odds, risk, shot **5** break, fluke, light, wager **6** befall, casual, gamble, happen, hazard **7** fortune, offhand, stumble, venture **8** accident, fortuity, occasion, prospect **9** advantage, transpire **10** accidental, fortuitous, incidental, likelihood **11** contingency, opportunity, possibility, probability, serendipity
even: **6** toss-up

chancellor
5 judge **8** minister **9** secretary
German: **4** Kohl (Helmut) **6** Brandt (Willy), Erhard (Ludwig), Hitler (Adolf), Merkel (Angela) **7** Schmidt (Helmut) **8** Adenauer (Konrad), Bismarck (Otto von) **9** Schroeder (Gerhard)

chancy
4 iffy **5** dicey, fluky, hairy, risky **6** touchy, tricky **8** perilous, ticklish **9** dangerous, haphazard, hazardous, uncertain **10** capricious, precarious **11** speculative, treacherous **12** incalculable **13** unpredictable

Chandler, Raymond
character: **7** Marlowe (Philip)
novel: **8** Big Sleep (The) **11** Long Good-Bye (The) **13** Murder My Sweet **16** Farewell My Lovely
screenplay: **10** Blue Dahlia (The) **15** Double Indemnity

Chanel of fashion
4 Coco

Chaney of horror films
3 Lon

change
3 fix **4** flux, swap, turn, vary **5** add-on, alter, amend, coins, emend, money, morph, shift, trade **6** adjust, evolve, modify, mutate, reform, remake, revamp, revert, revise, switch **7** commute, convert, novelty, replace, reverse **8** exchange, mutation, revision, transfer **9** alternate, deviation, diversify, fluctuate, refashion, transform, transmute, transpose, variation **10** alteration, conversion, divergence, innovation, substitute **11** interchange, permutation, transfigure, vicissitude **12** metamorphose, modification, transmogrify **13** metamorphosis, transmutation
sudden: **8** peripety **10** peripeteia

changeable
5 fluid **6** fickle, labile, pliant, shifty **7** flighty, mutable, plastic, protean, unfixed, varying **8** restless, shifting, slippery, ticklish, unstable, unsteady, variable, volatile **9** adaptable,

alterable, impulsive, mercurial, uncertain, unsettled, whimsical **10** capricious, inconstant **11** chameleonic, fluctuating, vacillating **13** kaleidoscopic, temperamental, unpredictable

change course
4 veer **6** swerve **7** deviate

changeless
5 fixed **6** steady **7** abiding, regular, uniform **8** constant, enduring, resolute **9** immutable, perpetual, steadfast, unvarying **10** invariable

change off
6 rotate **9** alternate

change of heart
8 reversal

change of life
9 menopause **11** climacteric

change of pace
5 pitch, shift **9** slow pitch

changeover
5 shift **10** alteration, conversion, transition

Chang's twin
3 Eng

channel
3 way **4** band, duct, kyle, pass, path, pipe **5** agent, canal, carry **6** agency, convey, course, funnel, groove, gutter, medium, siphon, strait, trough, tunnel **7** conduct, conduit, passage, vehicle **8** aqueduct, millrace, pipeline, transmit **10** instrument **11** watercourse
Africa-Madagascar: **10** Mozambique
Atlantic-Nantucket Sound: **8** Muskeget
Atlantic-North Sea: **7** English
Ellesmere-Greenland: **7** Robeson
Ganges: **5** Hugli **7** Hooghly
Hawaii: **5** Kaiwi, Kauai
Japan: **5** Bungo
Northwest Territories: **9** M'Clintock
Pakistan: **4** Nara
Scotland: **5** Minch
Tierra del Fuego: **6** Beagle
Tigris-Euphrates: **11** Shatt al Arab
Virginia: **12** Hampton Roads
West Indies: **9** Old Bahama

channel bass
4 drum **7** red drum, redfish

Channel Islands
capital: **8** St. Helier **11** St. Peter Port
dependency of: **7** Britain
island: **4** Herm, Sark **6** Jersey **8** Alderney, Guernsey

Channing of Broadway
5 Carol

chanson
4 song

Chanson ___
6 Triste

chanson de ___
5 geste

chant
4 sing, tune **5** drone **6** intone **8** vocalize **10** cantillate
Gregorian: **9** plainsong
melody: **12** cantus firmus
Jewish: **6** Hallel **7** Kaddish

chanteuse
6 singer **7** artiste **10** cantatrice
Edith: **4** Piaf

chanticleer
4 cock **7** rooster

chaos
5 havoc, snafu **6** bedlam, muddle **7** anarchy, clutter, entropy, turmoil **8** disarray, disorder **9** confusion **11** lawlessness, pandemonium

Chaos
daughter: **3** Nox, Nyx **4** Gaea
son: **6** Erebus

chaotic
7 jumbled, lawless **8** anarchic, confused, formless **9** amorphous, haphazard, scrambled **10** disordered, disorderly, topsy-turvy, tumultuous **11** harum-scarum, unorganized **12** disorganized **13** helter-skelter, unpredictable

chap
3 guy **4** gent **5** bloke **6** fellow

chaparral
5 scrub **7** thicket

chaparral cock
10 roadrunner

chapeau
3 hat **6** topper

chapel
6 bethel, church, shrine **7** chantry **9** sanctuary

Chapel Hill school, for short
3 UNC

chaperone
5 guide **6** attend, duenna, escort, matron **7** oversee **9** accompany, companion, supervise **11** superintend

chapfallen
see **crestfallen**

chaplain
5 padre **6** pastor **8** minister, sky pilot

chaplet
5 crown **6** anadem, laurel, rosary, wreath **7** coronal, coronet, garland

Chaplin's wife
4 Oona

chapter
4 unit **5** phase, stage **6** branch, period **7** episode, section **8** division **9** affiliate

char
4 burn, sear **5** singe **6** scorch **9** carbonize
character
3 ilk **4** bent, case, cast, kind, mark, mind, name, rank, role, rune, sign, sort, type **5** ethos, state, trait **6** cipher, device, letter, makeup, nature, repute, status, symbol, temper, virtue **7** oddball, persona, quality, variety **8** eminence, identity, standing **9** attribute, eccentric, rectitude **10** reputation **11** disposition, personality, temperament
chief: **4** hero **11** protagonist
defect: **8** hamartia
character assassination
5 libel **7** calumny, scandal, slander **10** backbiting, defamation **12** backstabbing
characteristic
4 mark, sign **5** badge, point, token, trait **6** aspect, innate, normal, proper **7** feature, natural, quality, special, typical **8** especial, peculiar, property, specific, tendency **9** attribute, birthmark, component, mannerism, trademark **10** diagnostic, emblematic, individual, particular **11** distinction, distinctive, peculiarity, singularity **12** idiosyncrasy **13** idiosyncratic
characterize
4 mark **5** draft **6** define, sketch, typify **7** outline, portray **8** describe, identify **10** constitute, pigeonhole **11** distinguish, individuate, personalize **12** discriminate **13** differentiate, individualize
characterless
4 flat **5** mousy **7** humdrum, insipid, vacuous **8** mediocre **9** colorless **10** namby-pamby, wishy-washy **11** nondescript
charade
4 sham **5** farce, put-on **6** parody **8** disguise, pretense, travesty **9** deception, pantomime **11** make-believe
chare
see **chore**
charge
3 ask, bid, fee, lay, tab, tax **4** bill, care, cost, duty, fill, heap, kick, load, onus, race, rate, rush, task, tell, toll, warn **5** choke, debit, order, place, price, refer, trust **6** accuse, assign, attack, burden, credit, direct, enjoin, exhort, impugn, impute, indict, saddle, thrill **7** arraign, ascribe, bidding, command, conduct, entrust, expense, impeach, mandate, request, solicit **8** accredit, handling, instruct, price tag, reproach, stampede **9** attribute, committal, electrify, inculpate **10** accusation, allegation, commitment, injunction, management, obligation **11** incriminate, instruction, requirement, supervision
chargeable
6 liable **7** subject **11** accountable, responsible
charged atom
3 ion
charged particle
5 anion
chargeless
4 free **6** gratis **8** costless **10** gratuitous **13** complimentary
charger
5 horse, mount, steed **6** salver **7** courser, platter **8** trencher, warhorse
chariness
7 caution **8** prudence **9** integrity **10** discretion
chariot
8 carriage
four-horse: **8** quadriga
charioteer
6 Auriga, driver
charisma
5 charm **6** allure, appeal, duende **7** glamour **9** magnetism **10** attraction **11** fascination
charitable
6 benign, giving, humane, kindly **7** clement, lenient, liberal **8** generous, merciful, obliging, tolerant **9** forgiving, indulgent **10** altruistic, beneficent, benevolent, forbearing, thoughtful **11** considerate, kindhearted, sympathetic **12** eleemosynary, humanitarian **13** philanthropic
donation: **4** alms
charity
4 alms, love **5** grace, mercy **6** lenity, relief **7** caritas **8** altruism, clemency, donation, goodwill, leniency, offering **10** generosity, humaneness, kindliness **11** benefaction, beneficence, benevolence **12** contribution
charivari
5 babel, melee **6** jangle, jumble, medley, racket, ruckus, uproar **7** farrago **8** serenade, shivaree **9** cacophony, confusion **10** hodgepodge **11** celebration
charlatan
4 sham **5** bluff, faker, fraud, quack **6** con man **8** imposter, impostor, swindler **10** mountebank **11** quacksalver **13** confidence man
Charlemagne
brother: **8** Carloman
capital: **3** Aix **6** Aachen
father: **5** Pepin
knight: **6** Oliver, Roland **7** Olivier, Orlando, paladin **8** douzeper
nephew: **6** Roland **7** Orlando
sword: **7** Joyeuse
traitor: **4** Gano **7** Ganelon
Charles Lamb pseudonym
4 Elia
Charles's Wain
9 Big Dipper, Ursa Major
charleston
5 dance

Charlie and the Chocolate Factory author
4 Dahl (Roald)

Charlie Brown
see **Peanuts**

Charlie McCarthy
5 dummy **6** stooge
friend: 5 Snerd (Mortimer)
voice: 6 Bergen (Edgar)

charm
3 hex **4** juju, lure, mojo, rune, take, wile **5** grace, quark, spell **6** allure, amulet, appeal, disarm, enamor, fetish, hoodoo, mascot, seduce, voodoo **7** attract, beguile, bewitch, enchant, glamour **8** enthrall, entrance, talisman, witchery **9** captivate, enrapture, ensorcell, fascinate, hypnotize, magnetism, mesmerize **10** allurement, attraction, phylactery, witchcraft **11** fascination, incantation **13** agreeableness

charmed
5 lucky **7** blessed **8** enamored **9** bewitched, enchanted, entranced, fortunate **10** captivated, fascinated, infatuated

charmer
4 roué **5** magus **6** wizard **7** seducer, warlock **8** conjurer, lothario, magician, sorcerer **9** enchanter **11** spellbinder

charming
5 suave **6** quaint **7** winsome **8** adorable, alluring, engaging, inviting, magnetic **9** appealing, glamorous, seductive **10** attractive, delightful, enchanting, entrancing **11** captivating

Charon
7 boatman **8** ferryman
father: 6 Erebus
mother: 3 Nox
river: 4 Styx

Charpentier opera
5 Médée **6** Louise

charpoy
3 bed, cot

chart
3 map **4** plan, plat, plot **5** graph, table **6** design, lay out, map out, sketch **7** arrange, diagram, outline, project **9** blueprint **10** tabulation

charter
3 let **4** deed, hire, rent **5** grant, lease **10** conveyance **12** constitution

Chartreuse
7 liqueur

chary
4 wary **5** cagey, canny **6** frugal, stingy **7** careful, guarded, miserly, prudent, sparing, thrifty **8** cautious, discreet, gingerly, hesitant **9** provident, reluctant **10** economical, restrained, suspicious, unwasteful **11** calculating, circumspect, constrained, disinclined

Charybdis
9 whirlpool
rock associated with: 6 Scylla

chase
3 run **4** bolt, dash, game, hunt, prey, race, rush, tear **5** chivy, drive, eject, evict, hound, shoot, speed, trail **6** career, charge, course, follow, hasten, pursue, quarry **7** boot out, hunting, kick out, pursuit **8** run after, throw out

chase away
4 rout, shoo

chaser
4 wolf **6** masher **7** Don Juan **8** Casanova **9** ladies' man, womanizer **10** lady-killer **11** philanderer

chasm
3 gap **4** gulf, rift **5** abyss, cleft, clove, flume, gorge, gulch, split **6** ravine **8** crevasse

chasmal
6 gaping **7** echoing, yawning **9** cavernous

chassepot
5 rifle

chaste
4 pure **5** clean, moral **6** decent, modest, proper, seemly, vestal, virgin **7** austere, prudish **8** celibate, decorous, innocent, maidenly, platonic, spotless, virginal, virtuous **9** abstinent, continent, stainless, undefiled, unsullied **10** immaculate **11** unblemished

chasten
5 abase, scold **6** humble, punish, rebuke, refine, subdue **7** correct, upbraid **8** chastise **9** castigate, humiliate, reprimand **10** discipline

chastise
4 beat, flog, whip **5** scold **6** punish, rebuke, thrash **7** belabor, censure, chasten, correct, reprove, scourge, upbraid **9** castigate **10** discipline

chastisement
3 rod **7** reproof **8** punition **10** correction, discipline, punishment **11** castigation

chastity
6 purity, virtue **7** modesty **8** celibacy **9** innocence, integrity, virginity **10** abstention, continence, maidenhood

chasuble
8 vestment

chat
3 gab, jaw, rap, yak, yap **4** blab, gush, talk **5** prate, visit **6** babble, confab, gossip, jabber, natter, parley, patter, yak-yak **7** chatter, palaver, prattle, twaddle **8** causerie, colloquy, converse, dialogue, schmooze **9** tête-à-tête, yakety-yak **11** confabulate **12** conversation, tittle-tattle **13** confabulation

château
5 manor, villa 6 castle, estate 7 mansion 8 fortress 12 country house

chateaubriand
5 steak 10 tenderloin

Chateaubriand novel
4 René 5 Atala

chatelain
6 warden 8 governor 9 castellan

chatelaine
4 hook, wife 5 clasp 8 mistress

chattel
4 serf 5 slave 7 bondman 8 bondsman, property

chatter
3 gab, jaw, yak 4 blab, bull 5 prate 6 babble, gabble, gibber, gossip, jabber, natter, patter, yak-yak, yammer 7 blabber, blather, palaver, prattle, vibrate 9 small talk, yakety-yak 12 tittle-tattle

chatterbox
5 yenta 6 gabber, gossip, magpie, prater 7 blabber 8 jabberer, prattler 12 blabbermouth

chatty
5 gabby 7 voluble 9 garrulous, talkative 10 loquacious

Chaucer pilgrim
4 Cook, Monk 5 Clerk, Friar, Reeve 6 Miller, Parson, Squire 8 Franklin, Manciple, Merchant, Summoner 10 Nun's Priest, Wife of Bath

chauffeur
5 drive 6 driver 9 transport

chauvinism
6 sexism 8 jingoism 10 patriotism 11 nationalism

cheap
4 mean, poor 5 junky, tight 6 cheesy, common, cruddy, flashy, measly, paltry, shabby, shoddy, sleazy, stingy, tawdry, trashy 7 chintzy, cut-rate, low-cost, reduced, thrifty 8 inferior, trifling, uncostly 9 brummagem, low-priced 10 economical 11 inexpensive 12 contemptible, meretricious

cheapen
5 decry, lower 6 debase, reduce 7 devalue 8 mark down 9 devaluate, downgrade 10 depreciate, undervalue

cheapjack
5 junky 6 hawker, cheesy, cruddy, shoddy, sleazy, tawdry, trashy 7 haggler, higgler, packman, peddler 8 huckster, inferior, rubbishy 9 worthless

cheapskate
5 miser, piker 7 niggard, scrooge 8 tightwad 9 skinflint 11 cheeseparer

cheat
3 con, gyp 4 bilk, burn, dupe, fool, gull, hoax, hose, milk, ream, rook, scam 5 bunco, cozen, crook, fraud, fudge, gouge, hocus, put-on, screw, shaft, short, slick 6 chisel, chouse, con man, deceit, delude, diddle, extort, fleece, humbug, rip-off, sucker, take in 7 beguile, chicane, deceive, defraud, diddler, mislead, sharper, shyster, swindle, two-time 8 flimflam, hoodwink, swindler, trickery 9 bamboozle, chicanery, deception, defrauder, imposture, overreach, trickster 11 double-cross 12 double-dealer 13 confidence man
on a check: 4 kite

check
3 tab, try, vet 4 bill, curb, halt, jibe, stay, stem, stop, test, tick 5 block, brake, draft, prove, score, stall 6 accord, arrest, baffle, bridle, damage, desist, hold in, square, thwart, verify 7 compare, conform, control, examine, inhibit, repress, setback 8 dovetail, hold back, hold down, preclude, restrain, reversal, suppress 9 constrain, criterion, interrupt, restraint 10 correspond, inspection 11 examination 13 investigation

checkered
5 plaid 6 motley 7 mutable, spotted 9 patchwork, patterned 10 variegated 11 diversified

checklist
7 catalog 9 catalogue, inventory 11 enumeration

checkmate
4 beat 6 corner, defeat 7 outplay 8 vanquish 9 finish off

check out
3 die, eye 4 case 5 leave 6 assess 7 examine, inspect 8 appraise, evaluate, look over

check over
3 con, vet 4 scan 5 audit, study 6 review, survey 7 analyze, canvass, examine, inspect 10 scrutinize

checkup
4 exam 8 physical 10 inspection 11 examination

cheek
4 gall 5 brass, nerve 8 audacity, chutzpah, temerity 9 brashness, impudence, insolence 10 confidence, effrontery 11 presumption 12 impertinence

cheekbone
5 malar

cheeky
4 bold, flip, pert, wise 5 brash, cocky, fresh, lippy, nervy, sassy, saucy, smart 6 brazen, mouthy 7 forward 8 cocksure, flippant, impudent, insolent 11 impertinent, smart-alecky 12 presumptuous

cheep
4 peep 5 chirp, tweet 7 chirrup, chitter, twitter

cheer
3 olé, rah, yay **4** buoy, hail, root **5** bravo, elate, huzza, nerve **6** buck up, gaiety, hoorah, hooray, hurrah, hurray, huzzah, rah-rah, solace, spirit **7** animate, applaud, comfort, console, enliven, gladden, hearten **8** embolden, inspirit **9** animation, encourage **10** strengthen

cheerful
3 gay **4** glad, rosy **5** jolly, merry, perky, riant, sunny **6** blithe, bouncy, bright, chirpy, hearty, jaunty, jocund, lively, upbeat **7** beamish, buoyant, radiant **8** animated, carefree, chirrupy **9** vivacious **12** lighthearted

cheerio
3 bye **4** ciao, ta-ta **5** adieu **6** bye-bye, good-by, so long **7** good-bye, toodles **8** farewell, toodle-oo

cheerless
4 dour, drab, grim **5** bleak **6** dismal, dreary, gloomy, somber, sombre **7** forlorn, joyless **8** desolate, dolorous, funereal, mournful **9** dejecting **10** depressing, melancholy, oppressive, tenebrific **11** dispiriting

cheers
5 salud, skoal **6** cincin, l'chaim, prosit **7** l'chayim, sláinte **8** applause, approval, chinchin **9** bottoms up **10** jubilation **11** acclamation, approbation

Cheers
actor: **4** Long (Shelley) **5** Alley (Kirstie), Wendt (George) **6** Danson (Ted) **7** Grammer (Kelsey), Perlman (Rhea) **8** Neuwirth (Bebe) **9** Harrelson (Woody)
character: **3** Sam **4** Norm **5** Carla, Cliff, Diane, Ernie, Woody **6** Lilith **7** Frasier, Rebecca
creator: **7** Burrows (James), Charles (Glen, Les)

cheery
5 happy, jolly, merry, sunny **6** blithe, bouncy, chirpy, lively, upbeat **7** buoyant, chipper, festive, gleeful **8** animated, carefree, gladsome **9** convivial, sparkling **12** lighthearted

cheese
3 pot **4** bleu, blue, jack **5** brick, cream **6** farmer **7** cottage, process, ricotta **9** smearcase
American: **5** Colby **8** Longhorn **11** Liederkranz **12** Monterey Jack
Belgian: **9** Limburger
curdling agent: **6** rennet, rennin
Danish: **7** Havarti
dish: **6** fondue **7** rarebit, soufflé
Dutch: **4** Edam **5** Gouda **6** Leyden
English: **7** cheddar, Stilton **8** Cheshire **10** Lancashire
French: **4** Brie **7** fromage, Livarot **9** Camembert, Reblochon, Roquefort **10** Neufchâtel **11** Pont l'Évêque, Port du Salut
German: **6** Tilsit **7** Munster **8** Muenster, Tilsiter
Greek: **4** feta
green: **7** sapsago
Italian: **6** Asiago, Romano **7** fontina, ricotta **8** Bel Paese, Parmesan, pecorino **9** provolone **10** Gorgonzola, mozzarella
lover: **9** turophile
main ingredient: **6** casein
Norwegian: **9** Jarlsberg
pickled: **4** feta **5** Ezine **8** Halloumi
protein: **6** casein
red-wax-covered: **4** Edam **5** Gouda
Scottish: **6** Dunlop, Orkney **7** kebbock, kebbuck
Spanish: **8** manchego
Swiss: **6** Saanen **7** Gruyère, sapsago **8** Vacherin **10** Emmentaler **11** Emmenthaler
uncured: **7** cottage
Welsh: **10** Caerphilly

cheesecloth
5 gauze

cheeselike
6 caseic **7** caseous

cheeseparer
5 miser **7** niggard, scrooge **8** tightwad **9** skinflint **10** cheapskate, pinchpenny

cheeseparing
4 mean **5** chary, cheap, mingy, tight **6** frugal, shabby, stingy **7** chintzy, miserly, thrifty **8** grudging, skimping **9** niggardly, penurious **11** closefisted, tightfisted **12** parsimonious **13** penny-pinching

cheesy
4 poor **5** cheap **6** common, shabby, shoddy, sleazy, tawdry, trashy **7** caseous **8** rubbishy

Cheever, John
family: **7** Wapshot
novel: **8** Falconer **14** Wapshot Scandal (The) **16** Wapshot Chronicle (The)
story: **7** Swimmer (The)

chef
4 cook
hat: **5** toque

chef d'oeuvre
7 classic **9** showpiece **10** magnum opus, masterwork **11** masterpiece, tour de force

Chekhov, Anton
play: **6** Ivanov **7** Seagull (The) **10** Uncle Vanya **12** Three Sisters **13** Cherry Orchard (The)
story: **9** Black Monk (The)

chelonian
6 turtle **8** tortoise

chemical
agent: **8** catalyst
combining power: **7** valence
compound: **4** acid, base, diol, enol, imid, oxim, salt, tepa, urea **5** amide, amine, diene, ester,

imide, imine, indol, orcin, oxime, purin, pyran, salol, tolan, triol **6** alkali, benzin, benzol, diamin, emodin, guanin, halide, hydrid, indole, inulin, ionone, isatin, isolog, isomer, ketone, lactam, maltol, metepa, natron, nitril, pterin, purine, pyrone, pyrrol, quinol, retene, silane, skatol, tannin, tetryl, thiram, thymol, tolane, triene, trimer, uracil, ureide, yttria, zeatin **7** barilla, benzene, benzole, cumarin, diamide, diamine, diazine, diazole, diester, flavone, guanine, heptose, hydride, indamin, indican, indoxyl, isatine, levulin, metamer, monomer, naphtol, nitrile, orcinol, oxazine, phytane, picolin, polyene, polymer, pyrrole, quinoid, quinone, salicin, skatole, steroid, taurine, terpene, thiazin, thiazol, thymine, tolidin, triazin, urethan, uridine, vitamer, xylidin **8** cephalin, cyanamid, disulfid, elaterin, fluorene, furfural, guaiacol, hematein, hexamine, indamine, isologue, kephalin, lichenin, limonene, melamine, naloxone, naphthol, palmitin, phenazin, phosphid, phthalin, picoline, piperine, pristane, quinolin, resorcin, salicine, santonin, siloxane, sodamide, sorbitol, spermine, squalene, stilbene, strontia, tautomer, thiazine, thiazole, thiophen, thiotepa, thiourea, tolidine, triazine, triazole, triptane, tyramine, urethane, vanillin, warfarin, xanthene, xanthine, xanthone, xylidine, ytterbia, zaratite, zirconia
(see also **element**)
quantity: **4** mole
radical: **4** acyl, amyl, aryl, cyan **5** allyl, butyl, ethyl, hexyl, tolyl **6** acetyl, formyl, methyl, oxalic, phenyl, propyl, toluyl **7** benzoyl
reaction: **5** redox
salt: **5** niter, nitre, urate, ziram **6** haloid, humate, malate, oleate, phytin **7** ferrate, formate, gallate, maleate, pectate, persalt, picrate, tannate, toluate, zincate **8** fumarate, pyruvate, racemate, selenate, silicate, stearate, tartrate, thionate, titanate, valerate, vanadate, xanthate
suffix: **3** ane, ase, ate, ein, ene, ide, ile, ine, ite, ium, oic, oin, one, ose, ous, yne **4** eine, idin, itol, oate, olic, onic **5** idine, onium, oside, ylene
warfare agent: **7** tear gas **8** vesicant **10** mustard gas

chemin de fer
5 train **7** railway **8** railroad

chemise
4 slip

chemist
7 analyst **8** druggist **10** apothecary, pharmacist
American: **4** Urey (Harold) **6** Remsen (Ira), Sumner (James) **7** Onsager (Lars), Pauling (Linus), Seaborg (Glenn) **8** Hoffmann (Roald), Langmuir (Irving), Mulliken (Robert), Richards (Theodore), Woodward (Robert)
Austrian: **4** Kuhn (Richard) **5** Pregl (Fritz)
British: **4** Abel (Frederick), Davy (Humphry), Todd (Alexander) **5** Boyle (Robert), Soddy (Frederick) **6** Dalton (John), Ramsay (William) **7** Faraday (Michael) **8** Smithson (James) **9** Priestley (Joseph), Wollaston (William) **10** Williamson (Alexander)
Dutch: **8** van't Hoff (Jacobus)
French: **5** Curie (Irene, Marie, Pierre) **7** Moissan (Henri), Pasteur (Louis) **8** Sabatier (Paul) **9** Gay-Lussac (Joseph), Lavoisier (Antoine), Berthelot (Marcellin)
German: **5** Haber (Fritz) **6** Bunsen (Robert), Liebig (Justus von), Nernst (Walther), Wittig (Georg), Wohler (Friedrich) **7** Fischer (Emil, Ernst, Hans), Hofmann (August), Ostwald (Friedrich), Wallach (Otto), Wieland (Heinrich), Windaus (Adolf), Ziegler (Karl) **9** Zsigmondy (Richard) **10** Erlenmeyer (Richard), Staudinger (Hermann) **11** Willstatter (Richard)
Italian: **5** Natta (Giulio) **8** Avogadro (Amedeo)
Russian: **8** Semyonov (Nikolay), Zelinsky (Nikolay) **10** Mendeleyev (Dmitry)
Swedish: **8** Svedberg (The, Theodor) **9** Berzelius (J. J.)
Swiss: **6** Karrer (Paul), Werner (Alfred)
(see also under **Nobel Prize winner**)

chemist's vessel
4 vial **5** flask, phial **6** ampule, beaker, mortar, retort **7** ampoule **8** crucible, test tube

chemoreceptor
8 taste bud

cheongsam
5 dress

Cheops
5 Khufu

cherish
4 keep, save **5** adore, guard, honor, nurse, prize, value **6** admire, cosset, defend, dote on, esteem, foster, harbor, relish, revere, shield **7** apprize, care for, nourish, nurture, shelter, worship **8** conserve, hold dear, preserve, treasure, venerate **9** cultivate, delight in, entertain, reverence, safeguard **10** appreciate

Cherokee
chief: **4** Ross (John)
historian: **7** Sequoia, Sequoya **8** Sequoyah

cherry
dark: **4** bing
family: **4** rose **8** Rosaceae
genus: **6** Prunus
hybrid: **4** Duke
sour: **7** morello
sweet: **4** bing **7** mazzard, oxheart
wild: **7** mazzard **10** maraschino

cherry bomb
11 firecracker

Cherry Orchard author
7 Chekhov (Anton)

cherrystone
4 clam 6 quahog

Chersonese
9 peninsula

cherub
4 amor, babe, baby 5 angel, child, cupid, putto 6 infant 7 bambino 8 amoretto, innocent

cherubic
4 cute, rosy 6 chubby 7 angelic 8 adorable, innocent

chess
champion: 3 Tal (Mikhail) 4 Euwe (Max) 6 Karpov (Anatoly), Lasker (Emanuel), Petrov (Alexander) 7 Fischer (Bobby), Kramnik (Vladimir), Smyslov (Vassily), Spassky (Boris) 8 Alekhine (Alexander), Kasparov (Garry), Steinitz (Wilhelm) 9 Botvinnik (Mikhail), Petrosian (Tigran) 10 Capablanca (José)
draw game: 9 stalemate
goal: 4 mate 9 checkmate
move: 6 castle, gambit
opening: 6 gambit
piece: 4 king, pawn, rook 5 queen 6 bishop, knight
risk: 6 gambit
term: 3 pin 4 draw, FIDE, file, fork, luft, rank 5 check 6 skewer 7 battery, capture, endgame 8 blockade, castling, diagonal 9 promotion

chest
3 box 4 arca, cist, kist 5 bosom, torso, trunk 6 breast, bureau, coffer, thorax 7 cabinet 8 cupboard, treasury 9 exchequer
combining form: 5 stern 6 sterno, thorac
muscles, for short: 4 pecs

chesterfield
4 sofa 5 divan 8 overcoat 9 davenport

chestnut
4 tree 5 color, horse 6 cliché, marron 10 chinquapin
extract: 6 tannin
water: 4 ling

cheval glass
6 mirror

chevalier
5 noble 6 knight 8 horseman 9 caballero, gentleman

chevet
4 apse

chevron
6 stripe

Chevy subcompact
4 Aveo

chew
3 eat, gum 4 bite, gnaw 5 champ, chomp, munch 6 crunch, devour, nibble 7 consume 8 ruminate 9 masticate

chewing gum
6 chicle

chew out
3 jaw 5 scold 6 rebuke, revile 7 bawl out, reprove, tell off, upbraid 8 lambaste, reproach 9 castigate, criticize, reprimand 10 tongue-lash, vituperate

Chiang ___
7 Kai-shek

chic
4 mode, rage, tony 5 nobby, smart, style, swank, swish, vogue 6 modish, trendy, with-it 7 dashing, elegant, fashion, stylish 8 elegance 10 dernier cri 11 fashionable

Chicago
7 Chi-Town 9 Windy City 10 Second City
airport: 5 O'Hare
newspaper: 4 Trib 7 Tribune
team: 4 Cubs 5 Bears, Bulls 8 White Sox 10 Black Hawks

chicane
4 dupe, fool, gull, hoax, ploy, ruse, wile 5 cavil, cheat, feint, fraud, trick 6 gambit 8 artifice, flimflam, hoodwink, trickery 9 bamboozle, deception, duplicity, stratagem, victimize 10 dishonesty, hanky-panky 13 double-dealing

chicanery
4 plot, ruse, wile 5 fraud, guile, trick 6 gambit 8 intrigue, trickery 9 deception, duplicity 10 subterfuge 11 machination, skulduggery 12 skullduggery

chichi
4 arty 5 gaudy, showy, swank 6 dressy, frills, frilly, la-di-da, modish, soigné, trendy 7 soignée, splashy, voguish 8 affected, précieux, precious 10 flamboyant, preciosity 11 affectation, fashionable, overrefined, pretentious 12 ostentatious

chick
3 gal, kid, tot 4 girl 5 child 6 moppet, nipper, pullet 7 toddler 8 juvenile 9 youngster

chickadee
8 titmouse
family: 7 Paridae

chicken
4 fowl, funk 5 sissy, timid 6 coward, craven 7 dastard, gutless 8 cowardly, poltroon 11 lily-livered, yellowbelly 13 pusillanimous
breed: 4 Java 6 Cochin 7 Cornish, Leghorn 9 Dominique, Orpington, Wyandotte 11 Jersey Giant, Rock Cornish
castrated: 5 capon

cooking: **5** fryer **7** broiler, roaster
disease: **8** avian flu, pullorum **11** coccidiosis
female: **3** hen **6** pullet
genus: **6** Gallus
male: **4** cock **7** rooster **8** cockerel
pen: **4** coop **7** hennery **10** chick house
small: **6** bantam
sound: **6** cackle

chicken-dish general
3 Tso

chicken feed
6 bubkes, bupkes, bupkus **7** peanuts **8** pittance **11** chump change **12** pocket change

chicken pox
9 varicella

chickpea
4 gram **8** garbanzo

chickweed
4 pink **7** potherb

chicle
3 gum **10** chewing gum

chicory
6 endive **7** witloof **9** radicchio

chide
3 kid **5** scold **6** berate, rebuke **7** chew out, lecture, reprove, upbraid **8** admonish, call down, reproach **9** castigate, reprimand

chiding
6 rebuke **7** reproof **8** reproach **9** reprimand **10** admonition **12** admonishment

chief
3 key **4** arch, boss, duce, emir, head, jefe, lion, main, star **5** first, major, prime, thane **6** führer, honcho, leader, master, primal, ruling, sachem **7** fuehrer, headman, highest, leading, premier, primary **8** cardinal, champion, dictator, dominant, eminence, foremost **9** number-one, principal, prominent **10** preeminent **11** outstanding, predominant
prefix: **4** arch

Chief Justice
3 Jay (John) **4** Taft (William Howard) **5** Chase (Salmon), Stone (Harlan Fiske), Taney (Roger), Waite (Morrison), White (Edward) **6** Burger (Warren), Fuller (Melville), Hughes (Charles Evans), Vinson (Fred), Warren (Earl) **7** Roberts (John) **8** Marshall (John), Rutledge (John) **9** Ellsworth (Oliver), Rehnquist (William)

chiefly
6 mainly, mostly **7** largely, notably, overall **9** generally, primarily **10** especially **11** principally **12** preeminently **13** predominantly

chief priest
7 primate

chiffchaff
4 bird **7** warbler

chiffon
5 gauze

chiffonier
5 chest **6** bureau **7** armoire, dresser

chigger
4 mite **6** chigoe, red bug

chignon
3 bun **4** knot

chilblain
4 sore **8** swelling **12** inflammation

child
3 kid **4** brat **5** gamin, minor, youth **6** cherub, infant, moppet, nipper, shaver, urchin **7** bambino, toddler **8** juvenile, small fry **9** youngling, youngster
combining form: **3** ped **4** paed, pedo **5** paedo
gifted: **7** prodigy
homeless: **4** waif
Indian: **4** baba
of Japanese immigrants: **5** nisei
parentless: **6** orphan
Scottish: **5** bairn
spoiled: **4** brat
young: **3** tot **4** baby, tike, tyke **6** infant, kiddie, rug rat **8** bantling, weanling

childish
5 naive **7** puerile **8** arrested, immature, juvenile **9** infantile

childless
6 barren **7** sterile

childlike
5 naive **6** docile, filial **7** natural, puerile **8** innocent, trustful, trusting **9** ingenuous

children
4 kids, seed **5** brood, heirs, issue **6** scions **7** progeny **9** offspring, posterity **11** descendants

child's play
4 snap **5** cinch, setup **6** breeze, picnic **8** cakewalk, duck soup, kid stuff, pushover **11** piece of cake

Chile
capital: **8** Santiago
city: **6** Temuco **10** Concepción, Talcahuano, Valparaíso, Viña del Mar **11** Antofagasta
conqueror: **7** Almagro (Diego de) **8** Valdivia (Pedro de)
desert: **7** Atacama
island: **6** Easter **13** Juan Fernández
lake: **10** Llanquihue
language: **7** Spanish
leader: **7** Allende (Salvador) **8** Pinochet (Augusto)

monetary unit: **4** peso
mountain range: **5** Andes
neighbor: **4** Peru **7** Bolivia **9** Argentina
passage: **5** Drake
poet: **6** Neruda (Pablo) **7** Mistral (Gabriela)
river: **6** Bío-Bío
strait: **8** Magellan

Chileab
father: **5** David
mother: **7** Abigail

chili con ___
5 carne

Chilion
father: **9** Elimelech
mother: **5** Naomi

chill
3 ice, icy, raw **4** ague, cold, cool, hang **5** algid, gelid, nippy, relax **6** arctic, cool it, formal, freeze, frigid, frosty, wintry **7** distant, glacial, hostile **8** dispirit, freezing **10** demoralize, discourage, dishearten **11** emotionless, refrigerate

chiller
7 shocker **8** thriller

chilling
5 frore, gelid, scary **6** frigid, frosty **8** alarming **9** unnerving **10** disturbing, terrifying **11** distressing, frightening

chill out
5 relax **6** cool it

chills and fever
4 ague

chilly
3 raw **4** cold **5** algid, brisk, crisp, nippy **6** frigid **7** bracing, coldish, hostile **10** unfriendly

chilopod
9 centipede

chime
4 bell, bong, dong, peal, ring, toll, tune **5** agree, clang, knell, sound **6** accord, strike **7** concord, harmony **8** carillon **9** agreement, harmonize **10** consonance, correspond

chime in
3 say **4** tell **5** offer, opine, state, utter **6** inject, pipe up **7** declare **9** interrupt

chimera
5 dream, fancy **7** fantasy, figment, monster, specter, spectre **8** illusion, phantasy **9** nightmare, pipe dream

Chimera
father: **6** Typhon
mother: **7** Echidna
slayer: **11** Bellerophon

chimerical
6 absurd, unreal **7** fictive, utopian **8** delusive, delusory, fabulous, fanciful, illusory, mythical, spurious **9** ambitious, beguiling, deceptive, fantastic, fictional, imaginary, visionary **10** far-fetched, fictitious, improbable, outlandish **11** extravagant, unrealistic **12** preposterous, suppositious

chiming
8 harmonic **9** consonant **10** harmonious

chimney
3 lum **4** flue, tube, vent **5** stack **10** smokestack
corner: **8** fireside **9** inglenook
output: **4** soot **5** fumes, smoke

chimpanzee
3 ape **7** primate **10** anthropoid
kin: **5** orang **6** bonobo, gibbon **7** gorilla **9** orangutan

chin
3 gab, jaw, rap, yak **4** blab, chat, talk **8** converse
hair: **5** beard **6** goatee **7** Vandyke **9** soul patch

china
6 dishes **7** ceramic **8** crockery **9** porcelain, tableware **11** earthenware
maker: **3** Bow **5** Hizen, Imari, Spode **6** Doccia, Sèvres **7** Bristol, Chelsea, Dresden, Limoges, Meissen **8** Caughley, Haviland, Wedgwood

China
bay: **8** Hangzhou
capital: **7** Beijing
city: **4** Sian, Xi'an **5** Wuhan **6** Canton, Harbin, Mukden **7** Nanjing, Nanking, Tianjin **8** Shanghai, Shenyang, Tientsin **9** Chongqing, Guangzhou
desert: **4** Gobi **10** Taklimakan
dynasty: **3** Ch'i, Han, Qin, Sui, Wei, Yin **4** Ch'en, Ch'in, Chou, Hsia, Ming, Qing, Song, Sung, T'ang, Tsin, Yüan **5** Ch'ing, Liang, Shang **6** Manchu, Mongol, Shu Han
emperor, legendary: **7** Huangdi, Huang-ti
ethnic group: **3** Han
feudal state: **3** Wei
gulf: **5** Bo Hai
heritage site: **9** Great Wall
island: **6** Hainan **8** Hong Kong
lake: **5** Tai Hu **8** Hongze Hu, Poyang Hu **10** Dongting Hu
language: **3** Han **8** Mandarin
leader: **3** Mao (Tse-tung, Zedong) **8** Hu Jintao **9** Kubla Khan, Mao Zedong, Sun Yat-sen, Zhou Enlai **10** Kublai Khan, Mao Tse-tung **12** Deng Xiaoping **13** Chiang Kai-shek, Teng Hsiao-p'ing
monetary unit: **4** jiao, yuan **8** renminbi
monetary unit, former: **4** tael
mountain, range: **6** Kunlun **8** Himalaya **9** Altai Shan, Altay Shan, Himalayan **10** Gongga Shan

old name: 6 Cathay
peninsula: 7 Leizhou 8 Liaodong, Shandong
province: 5 Anhui, Gansu, Hevei, Henan, Hubei, Hunan, Jilin 6 Fujian, Shanxi, Yunnan 7 Guizhou, Jiangsu, Jiangxi, Qinghai, Shaanxi, Sichuan 8 Liaoning, Shandong, Szechuan, Szechwan, Zhejiang 9 Guangdong 12 Heilongjiang
region: 5 Macao, Tibet 6 Xizang 8 Hong Kong 10 Nei Monggol 12 Ningxia Huizu 13 Inner Mongolia, Xinjiang Uygur
river: 4 Amur 5 Chang, Huang, Tarim 6 Mekong, Yellow, Zangbo 7 Salween, Yangtze

china clay
6 kaolin

chinchilla
3 fur 6 rodent

chine
5 crest, ridge, spine 7 hogback 8 backbone

Chinese
aromatic root: 7 ginseng
bamboo: 7 whangee
boat: 4 junk 6 sampan
bow: 6 kowtow
broadsword: 3 dao
cabbage: 7 bok choy, pak choi
calculator: 6 abacus
card game: 6 fan-tan
cauterizing agent: 4 moxa
conveyance: 7 pedicab 8 rickshaw 10 jinricksha, jinrikisha
cuisine: 5 Hunan 7 Sichuan
date: 6 jujube
dialect: 4 Amoy 8 Mandarin 9 Cantonese, Pekingese
dog: 4 chow, Peke 8 chow chow 9 Pekingese
fabric: 6 pongee, tussah 8 shantung
feminine principle: 3 yin
food: 6 dim sum, lo mein, mantou, subgum, wonton 8 chop suey, chow mein 9 fried rice 10 egg foo yong, egg foo yung, Peking duck 11 egg foo young
fruit: 6 lichee, litchi, lychee, loquat 7 kumquat 8 mandarin
gambling game: 6 fan-tan
general: 3 Tso
gong: 6 tam-tam
gruel: 6 congee
healing art: 6 qigong
herb: 5 ramie 7 ginseng
idol: 4 joss
laborer: 6 coolie
mandarin's residence: 5 yamen
masculine principle: 4 yang
money, silver: 5 sycee
musical instrument: 3 kin 4 pipa
nurse: 4 amah
official: 8 mandarin
official seal: 4 chop
oil: 4 tung
ox: 4 zebu
penal system: 6 laogai
poet: 4 Du Fu, Li Po, Tu Fu 5 Li Bai 7 Wang Wei
porcelain: 4 Ming 7 celadon, Nankeen 8 mandarin 9 cloisonné
pottery: 4 Kuan, Ming 5 Chien
preceder: 4 Indo
prefix: 4 Sino
puzzle: 7 tangram
race: 9 Mongoloid
religion: 6 Taoism 8 Buddhism 12 Confucianism
sauce: 3 soy
secret society: 4 tong
sheep: 5 urial
silkworm: 6 tussah
tea: 5 bohea, hyson 6 congou, oolong 8 souchong
temple: 6 pagoda 9 joss house
tree: 4 tung 6 ginkgo, loquat 7 kumquat
unicorn: 3 lin
vine: 5 kudzu
vital energy: 3 chi

Chinese-American architect
5 I. M. Pei

chink
4 rift, slit 5 caulk, cleft, crack, split 6 cranny 7 crevice, fissure, opening 8 aperture

chinquapin
3 nut 8 chestnut

chintzy
5 cheap, gaudy, showy, tacky 6 flashy, garish, stingy, tawdry, vulgar 9 tasteless 12 meretricious

chip
4 flaw, nick 5 flake, notch, shard, slice, split, wafer, wedge 6 chisel, defect, paring, sliver 7 counter

chip in
6 ante up, kick in 7 pitch in 10 contribute 11 come through

Chipmunk of cartoons
4 Dale

chipper
4 spry 5 alert, brisk, perky, zesty 6 bright, lively, nimble 8 animated, spirited 9 sprightly, vivacious

Chip's partner
4 Dale

chirk
4 buoy 5 cheer 7 animate, enliven, hearten 8 energize, inspirit 9 encourage 10 strengthen

chirography
6 script **8** longhand **10** penmanship **11** calligraphy, handwriting

chiromancy
9 palmistry

Chiron
7 centaur
father: **6** Cronus
mother: **7** Philyra
pupil: **5** Jason **8** Achilles, Heracles, Hercules **9** Asclepius **11** Aesculapius

chiropody
8 podiatry

chiropractic founder
6 Palmer (Daniel)

chirp
4 chip, peep, sing **5** cheep, trill, tweet **6** warble **7** chirrup, twitter

chirpy
3 gay **5** sunny **6** blithe, cheery, sparky **7** buoyant, sparkly **8** cheerful, sunbeamy **9** lightsome

chirrup
4 chip, peep, sing **5** cheep, tweet **6** warble **7** chipper, twitter

chisel
3 gad, gyp, hew **4** beat, bilk, scam **5** carve, cheat, cozen, cut in, gouge, trick **6** butt in, diddle, fleece, horn in, sculpt **7** defraud, engrave, intrude, swindle

chit
3 IOU, kid **4** memo, note, slip **5** child **6** moppet **7** invoice, voucher **8** notation **9** youngster **10** memorandum

chitchat
3 gab **5** chaff **6** babble, banter, gossip **7** chatter, palaver, prattle **8** badinage **9** small talk **12** tittle-tattle

Chi-Town
7 Chicago

chitter
4 chip, peep, sing **5** cheep, chirp, tweet **6** warble **7** chatter, chirrup, twitter

chivalric
see **chivalrous**

chivalrous
5 lofty, manly, noble **7** courtly, gallant, valiant **8** generous, gracious, knightly **9** honorable **10** benevolent, courageous **11** considerate, gentlemanly, magnanimous

chivy, chivvy
4 bait, ride **5** annoy, tease **6** badger, heckle, hector **7** torment **8** bullyrag

Chloe
11 shepherdess
beloved: **7** Daphnis

chlordane
11 insecticide

Chloris
father: **7** Amphion
husband: **6** Neleus **8** Zephyrus
mother: **5** Niobe
son: **6** Nestor

chloroform
7 anodyne, solvent **10** anesthetic **11** anaesthetic

chockablock
4 full **6** jammed, loaded, packed **7** brimful, crammed, crowded, stuffed **9** jam-packed

chocolate
5 brown, cacao, cocoa
tree: **5** cacao

Chocolate Soldier composer
6 Straus (Oscar)

choice
3 top **4** best, pick, rare, vote **5** cream, elite, prime, prize **6** chosen, dainty, option, rating, select **7** elegant, verdict **8** decision, delicate, druthers, election, free will, judgment, selected, superior, volition **9** exquisite, selection **10** preference **11** alternative **13** determination
even: **6** toss-up

choir
6 chorus **7** chorale
area: **4** loft **7** chancel, gallery
leader: **6** cantor **8** choragus **9** precentor
member: **9** chorister
section: **4** alto, bass **5** tenor **7** soprano
vestment: **4** gown, robe **5** cotta **8** surplice

choke
3 gag **4** clog, plug, stop **5** block, close **6** stifle **7** congest, occlude, silence, smother **8** obstruct, strangle, throttle **9** constrict, suffocate **10** asphyxiate

choking
8 quashing, stifling **10** repression, smothering, squelching, strangling **11** suppression

choleric
5 angry, fiery, irate **6** fierce, heated **7** enraged **8** incensed, wrathful **9** irascible, splenetic **10** infuriated **11** hot-tempered **13** quick-tempered

cholla
6 cactus **7** opuntia

Chomolungma
7 Everest (Mt.)

chomp
4 bite, chaw, chew **5** munch **6** crunch **9** masticate

choose
3 opt, tap **4** cull, mark, pick, take, want **5** adopt, elect, favor **6** decide, desire, opt for, prefer,

select **7** embrace, pick out **8** decide on, hand-pick **9** single out

choosy
5 fussy, picky **7** finical, finicky **9** finicking, selective **10** fastidious, particular, pernickety **11** persnickety

chop
3 cut, hew **4** dice, fell, hack, hash, seal, veer **5** cut up, grade, mince **7** quality

chop-chop
4 fast **5** quick **6** presto, pronto **7** quickly, rapidly **8** promptly, speedily **9** posthaste **12** lickety-split

chophouse
10 restaurant

Chopin, Frédéric
birthplace: 6 Poland
instrument: 5 piano
lover: 4 Sand (George)
work: 5 étude **7** mazurka, prelude **8** nocturne **9** polonaise **11** Minute Waltz

chopped down
4 hewn

chopper
3 hog **5** cycle, teeth (plural), tooth **6** copter **9** eggbeater **10** whirlybird **10** motorcycle

chopping tool
3 axe

choppy
4 wavy **5** jerky, rough **6** ripply, stormy, uneven **7** erratic **8** variable **9** turbulent, unsettled

choral section
4 alto, bass **5** tenor **7** soprano

choral work
5 motet **6** anthem **7** cantata, passion **8** oratorio

chord
5 triad **6** tetrad **7** harmony
sequence: 7 cadence **11** progression

chore
3 job **4** duty, task **5** stint, trial **6** devoir, effort **7** routine **10** assignment, obligation **11** tribulation

choreograph
6 devise, direct, map out **7** arrange, compose **11** orchestrate

choreographer
American: 4 Feld (Elliot), Holm (Hanya), Lang (Pearl) **5** Ailey (Alvin), Fosse (Bob), Limón (José), Shawn (Ted), Tharp (Twyla) **6** Duncan (Isadora), Dunham (Katherine), Fokine (Michel), Graham (Martha), Morris (Mark), Taylor (Paul), Tetley (Glen) **7** de Mille (Agnes), Jamison (Judith), Joffrey (Robert), Martins (Peter), Massine (Leonide), Robbins (Jerome), St. Denis (Ruth), Tamiris (Helen), Weidman (Charles) **8** Champion (Gower, Marge), Humphrey (Doris), Nikolais (Alwin), Villella (Edward) **10** Balanchine (George), Cunningham (Merce)
Australian: 8 Helpmann (Robert)
Cuban: 6 Alonso (Alicia)
Danish: 5 Bruhn (Erik) **7** Martins (Peter) **12** Bournonville (August)
English: 5 Dolin (Anton), Tudor (Antony) **6** Ashton (Frederick), Weaver (John) **7** Markova (Alicia), Rambert (Marie) **8** de Valois (Ninette), Helpmann (Robert) **9** MacMillan (Kenneth)
French: 5 Lifar (Serge) **6** Béjart (Maurice), Perrot (Jules), Petipa (Marius) **7** Camargo (Marie), Massine (Léonide), Noverre (Jean-Georges)
German: 5 Jooss (Kurt)
Hungarian: 5 Laban (Rudolf)
Mexican: 5 Limón (José)
Russian: 5 Lifar (Serge) **6** Fokine (Michel), Petipa (Marius) **8** Nijinska (Bronislava), Nijinsky (Vaslav)

chorography
3 map **7** mapping **8** features **9** mapmaking

chortle
5 laugh **6** giggle, guffaw, hee-haw, titter **7** chuckle, snicker

chorus
5 choir **7** refrain
section: 4 alto, bass **5** tenor **7** soprano
syllable: 3 tra

chorus girl
7 chorine

chosen
4 pick **5** elect, elite, named **6** called, marked, pegged, picked, select **7** blessed **8** selected **9** appointed, delegated, exclusive

Chou ___
5 Enlai

chouse
3 gyp **4** bilk, clip, dupe, herd **5** cheat, cozen, drive, trick **6** diddle, fleece **7** defraud, swindle **8** flimflam

chow
4 eats, feed, food, grub, meal, mess

chowchow
6 medley, relish **7** mélange

chowderhead
4 boob, clod, dodo, dolt, dope, fool **5** chump, dunce, idiot, noddy **6** dimwit, nitwit, noodle **7** halfwit, schnook **8** dumbbell, numskull **9** lamebrain, numbskull

chowhound
7 glutton **8** gourmand

chrism
3 oil **4** balm **5** cream, salve **6** cerate **7** unction, unguent **8** ointment

christen
3 dub **4** call, name, term **5** title **7** asperse, baptize, immerse **8** dedicate, sprinkle **9** designate

christening
7 baptism

Christian
denomination: 6 Mormon, Quaker 7 Baptist, Friends 8 Anglican, Catholic, Lutheran, Moravian, Nazarene, Reformed 9 Calvinist, Episcopal, Mennonite, Methodist, Unitarian 10 Anabaptist 11 Pentecostal 12 Episcopalian, Presbyterian, Universalist
Eastern rite: 5 Uniat 6 Uniate
Egyptian: 4 Copt
love feast: 5 agape
martyr, first: 7 Stephen
symbol: 3 IHS 4 fish, rood 5 cross 6 Chi-Rho 7 ichthus

Christiania, today
4 Oslo

Christian Science founder
4 Eddy (Mary Baker)

Christie, Agatha
character: 6 Marple (Jane), Poirot (Hercule)
novel: 14 Death on the Nile 16 Ten Little Indians 24 Murder on the Orient Express
play: 9 Mousetrap (The) 24 Witness for the Prosecution

Christina's World painter
5 Wyeth (Andrew)

Christmas
4 Noel, yule 8 Nativity, yuletide
crumpet: 7 pikelet
drink: 3 nog 5 glogg 6 eggnog
French: 4 Noël
Italian: 6 Natale
song: 4 noel 5 carol
Spanish: 7 Navidad
symbol: 7 yule log

Christmas Carol, A
author: 7 Dickens (Charles)
character: 7 Scrooge (Ebenezer), Tiny Tim 8 Cratchit (Bob)

Christogram
6 Chi-Rho

Christopher Robin creator
5 Milne (A. A.)

chromatic
8 colorful 10 accidental

chromatin thread
7 spireme

chromosome component
3 DNA 4 gene 8 telomere 10 centromere, chromomere

chronic
5 usual 6 wonted 7 routine 8 constant, enduring, habitual 9 ceaseless, confirmed, continual, customary, incessant, perennial, perpetual, recurrent, recurring 10 accustomed, continuing, habituated, inveterate, persisting 11 unrelenting

chronicle
4 list, saga, tale 6 annals, record, relate, report 7 account, history, narrate, recital, recount 8 describe 9 narration, narrative

chronicler
8 annalist, narrator, recorder, reporter 9 historian

chronograph
5 clock, watch 9 timepiece

chronology
5 annal 6 annals, record 7 history 8 calendar, register, schedule 9 timetable

chronometer
5 clock, watch 9 timepiece

chrysalis
4 pupa 8 covering

Chryseis
captor: 9 Agamemnon
father: 7 Chryses

Chrysippus
father: 6 Pelops
slayer: 6 Atreus 8 Thyestes

chthonic
6 Hadean, nether 7 hellish, satanic 8 accursed, infernal, plutonic 9 plutonian, Tartarean 10 sulphurous

chubby
5 hefty, husky, plump, podgy, pudgy, round, tubby 6 chunky, fleshy, portly, rotund, stocky, zaftig 8 plumpish, roly-poly

chuck
3 pat, tap 4 beef, cast, hurl, junk, oust, shed, toss 5 ditch, fling, heave, nudge, pitch, scrap, throw 6 give up, reject 7 abandon, boot out, discard, dismiss, kick out 8 jettison, throw out 9 throw away

chucker
7 bouncer

chuckle
5 laugh 6 giggle, guffaw, hee-haw, titter 7 chortle, snicker

chucklehead
see **chowderhead**

chuff
3 oaf 4 boor, lout, rube 5 churl, clown, yahoo, yokel 7 bumpkin, hayseed 10 clodhopper

chum
3 pal 4 mate, pard 5 buddy, crony 6 friend, salmon 7 comrade 8 sidekick 9 companion

chummy
4 cozy 5 close, matey, pally, palsy, thick 8 familiar, intimate 10 buddy-buddy, palsy-walsy

chump
3 oaf, sap 4 boob, dolt, dope, dupe, fool, goof, goon, gull, mark, shmo 5 booby, dummy, dunce, loser, patsy, schmo 6 pigeon, sucker, turkey 7 failure, fall guy, fathead 8 dolthead, lunkhead

chunk
3 sum, wad **4** clod, hunk, lump, slab **5** clump **6** nugget

chunky
5 beefy, dumpy, hefty, husky, plump, pudgy, squat, stout **6** chubby, fleshy, portly, rotund, stocky, stubby, stumpy **8** heavyset, thickset

church
4 cult, fane, kirk, sect **5** creed, faith **6** temple **7** minster **8** basilica, religion **9** cathedral, communion **10** tabernacle **12** denomination
adjunct: **6** belfry **7** steeple **9** bell tower
basin: **4** font **5** stoup
bench: **3** pew
bishop's: **9** cathedral
calendar: **4** ordo
caretaker: **6** sexton
chapel: **7** oratory
code: **8** canon law
council: **5** synod
court: **4** rota **10** consistory
creed: **6** Nicene **8** Apostles'
district: **6** parish **7** diocese
father: **5** Basil **6** Jerome, Justin, Origen **7** Ambrose, Clement **8** Ignatius **9** Augustine **10** Chrysostom, Tertullian, theologian
fund-raiser: **5** bingo **6** bazaar, raffle
governing body: **5** curia **7** classis **10** consistory, presbytery
head: **4** pope **7** pontiff
law: **5** canon
member: **11** communicant
of a monastery: **7** minster
music: **5** motet
officer: **5** elder, vicar **6** beadle, deacon, sexton, verger, warden **9** presbyter, sacristan
part: **4** apse, bema, loft, nave **5** aisle, altar, choir **6** vestry **7** chancel, gallery, narthex, steeple **8** sacristy, transept **9** baptistry, sanctuary **10** baptistery, clerestory
porch: **6** parvis **7** galilee
reader: **6** lector
recess: **4** apse
response: **4** amen
revenue: **5** tithe
room: **6** vestry **8** sacristy
Scottish: **4** kirk
seats for clergy: **7** sedilia
service: **4** mass **6** matins **7** vespers **8** evensong **9** communion
small: **6** chapel
song: **4** hymn
tribunal: **4** rota
vault: **5** crypt

Churchill, Winston
daughter: **4** Mary **5** Diana, Sarah
estate: **8** Checkers
father: **8** Randolph
gesture: **5** V-sign
mother: **6** Jennie (Jerome)
phrase: **11** Iron Curtain
son: **8** Randolph
successor: **4** Eden (Anthony)
trademark: **5** cigar
wife: **10** Clementine

Churchill Downs event
5 Derby

church key
9 can opener

churchman
6 bishop, cleric, divine, parson, pastor, priest **7** pontiff, prelate **8** cardinal, minister, preacher, reverend **12** ecclesiastic

churl
3 cad, oaf **4** boor, clod, lout, rube **5** chuff, clown, yahoo, yokel **6** mucker **7** bumpkin, hayseed **10** clodhopper

churlish
4 base, curt, dour, rude **5** blunt, crude, gruff, surly **6** coarse, crusty, oafish, vulgar **7** boorish, brusque, loutish, lowbred, uncivil **8** cloddish, clownish **10** unmannerly **11** clodhopping, uncivilized **12** discourteous

churn
4 boil, foam, roil, stir **5** froth, swirl **6** bubble, seethe, simmer, stir up **7** agitate, ferment, smolder

chute
4 fall, ramp **5** falls, rapid, slide, spout **6** rapids **7** cascade, channel, descent **8** cataract **9** spinnaker, waterfall

chutzpah
4 gall **5** brass, cheek, moxie, nerve, spunk **8** audacity, temerity **10** effrontery

CIA predecessor
3 OSS

ciao
4 by-by, ta-ta **5** adieu, adios, aloha, hello, howdy **6** bye-bye, good-by, so long **7** cheerio, good-bye, toodles **8** farewell, toodle-oo

CIA mole Aldrich
4 Ames

cicatrix
4 scar **13** scarification

Cicero
forte: **7** oratory
speech: **9** philippic
target: **8** Catiline **10** Mark Antony

cicerone
4 guru **5** coach, guide, tutor **6** docent, escort, mentor **7** adviser **9** counselor, tour guide

Cid, El (Le)
4 epic, hero, play, poem **5** opera
composer: **8** Massenet (Jules)

meaning: 4 lord
name: 4 Díaz (Rodrigo, Ruy) 5 Bivar
playwright: 9 Corneille (Pierre)
sword: 6 Colada, Tizona
wife: 6 Jimena, Ximena

cigar
5 claro, stogy 6 corona, Havana, stogie 7 cheroot 8 panatela, perfecto
case: 7 humidor
color: 5 claro 6 maduro 8 colorado
residue: 3 ash

cigarette
3 fag 4 butt 5 smoke 6 gasper 10 coffin nail

cilium
4 hair, lash 7 eyelash

Cimmerian
4 dark 5 dusky, murky 6 gloomy 7 hellish, shadowy, stygian 8 infernal, plutonic 9 plutonian

cinch
4 snap 5 girth, setup 6 assure, breeze, ensure, fasten, insure, latigo, picnic, secure, shoo-in 8 duck soup, kid stuff, pushover 9 certainty 10 child's play

cinchona bark extract
7 quinine

cincture
4 band, belt, sash 6 girdle 9 waistband

cinders
3 ash 4 coal, lava, slag 5 ashes, dross 6 embers 8 clinkers
of old comics: 4 Ella

cinema
4 film, nabe, show 5 flick, movie 6 movies 7 picture, theater, theatre 12 silver screen 13 motion picture

cinereous
4 ashy, gray, grey 5 ashen 7 ashlike

cinnabar
3 ore 7 mineral, pigment 9 vermilion
color: 3 red

cinnamon bark
6 cassia

cinnamon stone
6 garnet 8 essonite

cipher
4 code, zero 5 aught, count, digit 6 figure, naught, nobody, number, reckon, symbol 7 compute, integer, numeral 8 estimate, monogram 9 calculate, nonentity 11 whole number

ciphering
8 figuring 9 computing, reckoning 10 arithmetic 11 calculation, computation

circa
4 near, nigh 5 about 6 approx., around 7 roughly 13 approximately

circadian
5 daily 6 cyclic 7 diurnal, regular 9 quotidian

Circe
5 siren, witch 9 sorceress 11 enchantress
brother: 6 Aeëtes
father: 3 Sol 6 Helios
home: 5 Aeaea
lover: 7 Ulysses 8 Odysseus
niece: 5 Medea
son: 5 Comus 9 Telegonus

Circean
6 luring 8 alluring, enticing, fetching, tempting 10 bewitching

circinate
6 coiled 7 rounded

circle
4 belt, gyre, hoop, loop, ring 5 crowd, cycle, group, orbit, wheel, whorl 6 clique, corona, girdle, gyrate, rotary, rotate 7 compass, coterie, cronies, friends, revolve, rondure 8 surround 9 encompass 10 associates, companions, revolution
bisector: 8 diameter
colored: 6 areola
combining form: 3 gyr 4 cycl, gyro 5 cyclo
dance: 4 hora
graph: 8 pie chart
luminous: 4 aura, halo 6 corona, nimbus 7 aureole
part: 3 arc 6 sector 8 quadrant
small: 4 disk 7 annulet

circlet
4 band, ring 6 bangle, diadem 8 bracelet, headband
for head or helmet: 7 coronal

circling current
4 eddy

circuit
3 lap, way 4 beat, loop, tour, trip, turn 5 ambit, cycle, orbit, round, route, track 6 course, hookup, league 7 compass, journey, pathway, travels 8 district, rotation 9 perimeter, periphery, round trip 10 revolution, roundabout 11 association, circulation 13 circumference

circuitous
7 devious, oblique, winding 8 circular, indirect, tortuous 10 collateral, convoluted, meandering, roundabout

circuit rider
5 judge 8 minister, preacher 9 clergyman

circular
4 bill 5 flier, flyer, round 7 annular, cycloid, discoid, handout, leaflet 8 handbill 9 throwaway
file: 11 wastebasket
fort: 8 martello
motion: 4 eddy, gyre, spin 5 whirl 8 gyration, rotation 10 revolution
plate: 4 disc, dish, disk

circularize
4 poll **6** survey **7** canvass **9** advertise, publicize

circulate
4 flow **6** rotate, spread **7** diffuse, radiate, revolve **8** disperse **9** propagate **10** distribute **11** disseminate

circulation
4 flow **6** spread **8** currency **9** diffusion **11** propagation **12** transmission **13** dissemination

circumciser
5 mohel

circumcision, Jewish
4 bris **9** Brit Milah

circumference
3 rim **5** ambit, girth **6** border, bounds, limits, margin **7** circuit, compass **8** boundary, confines **9** perimeter, periphery

circumflex
9 diacritic

circumjacent
11 surrounding

circumlocution
8 pleonasm, verbiage **9** euphemism, loquacity, prolixity, verbosity, wordiness **10** redundancy **11** periphrasis, verboseness

circumnavigate
5 skirt **6** bypass, detour **8** sidestep

circumnavigator
4 Cook (James) **5** Drake (Francis) **8** Magellan (Ferdinand), van Noort (Olivier) **9** Cavendish (Thomas)

circumscribe
5 cramp, limit **6** fetter, hamper **7** confine, delimit, enclose, mark off, outline, trammel **8** restrict, surround **9** constrict

circumscribed
5 bound, fixed **6** finite, narrow, strait **7** bounded, cramped, limited, precise **8** confined, definite, hampered **10** restrained, restricted **11** determinate

circumscription
5 cramp, limit, stint **6** border, margin **8** boundary **9** perimeter, restraint, stricture **10** constraint, definition, limitation **11** confinement, restriction **12** ball and chain, delimitation

circumspect
4 safe, wary **5** chary **7** careful, guarded, prudent **8** cautious, discreet, gingerly **11** calculating

circumstance
4 fact, item **5** event, thing **6** detail, factor **7** adjunct, element, episode, feature **8** accident, incident, occasion **9** component, condition, happening **10** occurrence, particular **11** concomitant, constituent, eventuality
unforeseen: **8** exigency **9** emergency

circumstantial
4 full **5** close, exact **6** strict **7** precise, replete **8** accurate, complete, detailed, thorough **9** elaborate, pertinent **10** blow-by-blow, ceremonial, exhaustive, incidental, particular

circumvent
5 avoid, dodge, elude, evade, hem in, skirt **6** bypass, detour **8** outflank, sidestep

circumvolution
4 gyre, turn **5** wheel, whirl **8** gyration, rotation **10** revolution

circus
4 ring **5** arena **6** big top **9** spectacle **12** amphitheater
animal: **4** bear, flea, lion, seal **5** horse, tiger **8** elephant
attraction: **5** freak **8** sideshow
owner: **6** Bailey (James), Barnum (P. T.) **8** Ringling (Bros.)
performer: **5** clown, tamer **7** acrobat, athlete, juggler, tumbler **9** aerialist, fire eater, strong man
worker: **10** roustabout

Cisco Kid
9 caballero
actor: **4** Beck (Jackson) **6** Baxter (Warner), Roland (Gilbert), Romero (Cesar) **7** Renaldo (Duncan)
horse: **6** Diablo
sidekick: **6** Pancho **7** Gordito

citadel
4 fort **7** redoubt **8** fastness, fortress **10** stronghold
of Carthage: **5** Bursa, Byrsa
Russian: **7** kremlin

citation
5 quote **6** eulogy **7** endnote, excerpt, mention, summons, tribute **8** accolade, encomium, footnote **9** panegyric, quotation, reference **12** commendation

cite
4 name, tell **5** offer, quote **6** adduce, recall, summon **7** arraign, mention, present, refer to, specify **8** point out, remember **9** recollect

Citi Field predecessor
4 Shea

citizen
7 burgess, burgher, subject **8** civilian, national, resident, townsman **10** inhabitant

Citizen Kane director
6 Welles (Orson)

citron
4 tree **5** melon

citrus
family: **3** rue **8** Rutaceae
fruit: **4** lime, ugli **5** lemon **6** citron, orange, pomelo **7** kumquat, tangelo **8** bergamot, mandarin, shaddock **9** tangerine **10** grapefruit

city
4 burg **5** urban **7** burghal **9** municipal **10** metropolis
combining form: **5** polis
Eternal: **4** Rome
fortress: **7** citadel
French: **5** ville
heavenly: **4** Sion, Zion
Latin: **4** urbs
Motor: **7** Detroit
of Bells: **10** Strasbourg
of Bridges: **6** Bruges
of Brotherly Love: **12** Philadelphia
of David: **9** Jerusalem
official: **5** mayor **7** manager **8** alderman **10** councilman
of God: **6** heaven **8** paradise
of Gold: **8** Eldorado
of Kings: **4** Lima
of Lights: **5** Paris
of Lilies: **8** Florence
of Masts: **6** London
of Rams: **6** Canton
of Refuge: **6** Medina
of Saints: **8** Montreal
of Seven Hills: **4** Rome
of the dead: **10** necropolis
of Victory: **5** Cairo
planner: **8** urbanist
section: **4** slum, ward **5** block, plaza **6** barrio, ghetto, square, uptown **8** business, downtown, red-light **11** residential
slicker: **4** dude
windy: **7** Chicago

city-state, Greek
5 Argos, polis **6** Athens, Delphi, poleis (plural), Sparta, Thebes **7** Corinth

city, town, village
(see also **capital**)
Afghanistan: **5** Balkh, Farah, Herat, Kushk **6** Konduz **8** Kandahar, Qandahar **9** Jalalabad
Alabama: **3** Opp **4** Arab, Boaz, Elba **5** Selma **6** Athens, Dothan, Mobile **7** Decatur, Florala **8** Prichard **10** Birmingham, Huntsville, Scottsboro, Tuscaloosa **12** Muscle Shoals
Alaska: **4** Nome **5** Kenai, Sitka **6** Barrow, Bethel, Kodiak, Valdez **9** Anchorage, Fairbanks, Ketchikan **11** Point Barrow
Albania: **4** Fier **5** Berat, Korçë, Kukës, Vlorë
Alberta: **4** Olds **5** Hanna, Leduc, Taber **7** Calgary **10** Lethbridge **11** Medicine Hat
Algeria: **4** Bône, Oran **5** Batna, Blida, Médéa, Saïda, Sétif **6** Annaba, Bechar **11** Constantine
Angola: **6** Huambo **7** Lubango **8** Benguela
Argentina: **4** Azul, Goya **5** Junin, Lanus, Lujan, Merlo, Salta, Tigre **6** Parana **7** Córdoba, La Plata, La Rioja, Mendoza, Rosario, San Juan, Santa Fe **9** Catamarca **11** Bahía Blanca, Mar del Plata
Arizona: **3** Ajo **4** Eloy, Mesa, Yuma **5** Globe, Tempe **6** Tucson **7** Sun City, Winslow **8** Glendale, Prescott **9** Flagstaff, Tombstone **10** Casa Grande, Scottsdale
Arkansas: **4** Mena **5** Beebe, Cabot, Earle, Ozark, Wynne **9** Fort Smith, Pine Bluff, Texarkana **10** Hot Springs
Armenia: **6** Gyumri **8** Vanadzor
Australia: **3** Ayr **5** Dalby, Dubbo, Perth, Unley **6** Darwin, Sydney **8** Adelaide, Brisbane, Randwick **9** Bankstown, Blacktown, Gold Coast, Melbourne, Newcastle **10** Kalgoorlie, Parramatta, Sutherland, Wollongong **12** Alice Springs
Austria: **4** Enns, Graz, Linz, Wels **5** Steyr, Traun **8** Salzburg **9** Innsbruck **10** Klagenfurt
Azerbaijan: **5** Gäncä **8** Sumqayit **9** Kirovabad
Bahamas: **8** Freeport
Bangladesh: **5** Bogra, Pabna **6** Khulna, Sylhet **7** Barisal, Comilla, Jessore, Rangpur, Saidpur **10** Chittagong
Belarus: **5** Brest, Gomel, Mozyr, Pinsk **6** Grodno, Homyel', Hrodna **7** Mogilev, Vitebsk **8** Babruysk, Mahilyow **9** Vitsyebsk
Belgium: **3** Ath, Hal, Huy, Mol **4** Amay, Dour, Geel, Genk, Gent, Hoei, Luik, Mons, Vise **5** Aalst, Arlon, Diest, Evere, Ghent, Halle, Ieper, Jumet, Leuze, Liège, Namur, Ronse, Theux, Wavre, Ypres **6** Bruges, Brugge **7** Antwerp, Hasselt, Louvain **8** Oostende **9** Charleroi
Benin: **5** Kandi **6** Abomey **7** Parakou
Bolivia: **5** Oruro, Uyuni **6** Potosí **9** Santa Cruz **10** Cochabamba
Bosnia and Herzegovina: **5** Bihac, Brcko, Jajce, Tuzla **6** Mostar, Zenica **9** Banja Luka
Botswana: **4** Maun **5** Kanye **11** Francistown
Brazil: **4** Codo, Pará **5** Bahia, Bauru, Belém, Ceara, Natal **6** Campos, Canoas, Caxias, Ilheus, Maceio, Manaus, Olinda, Recife, Santos **7** Aracaju, Caruaru, Goiania, Jundiai, Marilia, Niteroi, Pelotas, São Luis, Uberaba, Vitória **8** Campinas, Colatina, Curitiba, Londrina, Salvador, Santarém, São Paulo, Sorocaba, Teresina **9** Caratinga, Fortaleza, Guarulhos, Rio Grande **10** Guarapuava, Joao Pessoa, Juiz de Fora, Nova Iguaçu, Pernambuco, Petropolis, Piracicaba, Pôrto Velho, Santa Maria, Santo André, São Gonçalo, Uberlândia **11** Campo Grande, Caxias do Sul, Ponta Grossa, Pôrto Alegre **12** Montes Claros, Rio de Janeiro, Teófilo Otoni, Volta Redonda **13** Belo Horizonte
British Columbia: **5** Comox **6** Surrey **7** Burnaby **8** Richmond **9** Vancouver
Bulgaria: **3** Lom **4** Ruse **5** Varna, Vidin **6** Burgas **7** Plovdiv **11** Stara Zagora
Burma: see **Myanmar**
California: **4** Brea, Galt, Lodi, Ojai **5** Arvin, Azusa, Ceres, Chico, Chino, Dixon, Hemet, Indio, Norco, Ripon, Ukiah, Wasco, Yreka **6** Downey, Encino, Fresno, Oxnard, Pomona,

Sonoma **7** Anaheim, Burbank, Compton, Fremont, Hayward, Modesto, Oakland, San Jose, Seaside, Soledad, Van Nuys **8** Berkeley, Glendale, Palo Alto, Pasadena, San Diego, Santa Ana, Stockton, Torrance, Yuba City **9** El Segundo, Hollywood, Long Beach, Menlo Park, Riverside, Sausalito **10** Chula Vista, Culver City, Los Angeles, San Leandro, Santa Clara **11** Bakersfield, Laguna Beach, Pebble Beach, Redwood City, San Clemente, Santa Monica **12** Beverly Hills, Mission Viejo, Redondo Beach, San Francisco, Santa Barbara **13** San Bernardino, San Luis Obispo

Cambodia: 8 Siem Reap **10** Battambang **11** Kompong Cham

Cameroon: 4 Buea, Edea **5** Kribi, Lomie **6** Douala **7** Bamenda, Foumban **9** Bafoussam

Canada: 4 York **5** Banff **6** London, Oshawa, Regina, St. John **7** Brandon, Burnaby, Calgary, Halifax, Iqaluit, Red Deer, St. John's, Sudbury, Toronto, Windsor **8** Hamilton, Montreal, Moose Jaw, North Bay, Victoria, Winnipeg **9** Dartmouth, Kitchener, Longueuil, North York, Saint John, Saskatoon, Vancouver **10** Lethbridge, Saint John's, Sherbrooke, Thunder Bay, Whitehorse **11** Fredericton, Medicine Hat, Mississauga, Scarborough, Yellowknife **12** Peterborough, Prince Albert, Prince George **13** Charlottetown, Trois-Rivières

Central African Republic: 5 Bouar **7** Bambari

Chad: 4 Sarh **6** Abéché

Chile: 4 Lebu, Lota, Tomé **5** Ancud, Angol, Arica, Maipu, Penco, Rengo, Talca **6** Temuco **7** Copiapó, Iquique **8** Rancagua **10** Concepción, Talcahuano, Valparaíso **11** Antofagasta

China: 4 Amoy, Jian, Luan, Xi'an, Yaan **5** Hefei, Jilin, Jinan, Lhasa, Qinan, Ssuan, Wuhan, Yibin, Yumen **6** Andong, Anqing, Anshan, Anshun, Anyang, Beihai, Canton, Dalian, Datong, Foshan, Fushun, Fuzhou, Guilin, Haikou, Handan, Harbin, Hohhot, Hoihao, Jilong, Luzhou, Mukden, Ningbo, Pengbu, Suzhou, Ürümqi, Xiamen, Xining, Xuzhou, Yanggu, Yichun, Yining, Zhangi, Zhaoan **7** Baoding, Changan, Chengdu, Dandong, Guiyang, Huainan, Jiamusi, Jiaxing, Kaifeng, Kunming, Lanzhou, Luoshan, Luoyang, Nanking, Nanjing, Nanning, Shantou, Tianjin, Taiyuan **8** Changchi, Changsha, Hangzhou, Hanzhong, Huangshi, Jiangmen, Shanghai, Shaoyang, Shenyang, Shenzhen, Zhenjing **9** Changchun, Chenjiang, Chongqing, Chungking, Guangzhou, Zhengzhou, Zhenjiang

Colombia: 4 Buga, Cali **5** Bello, Mocoa, Neiva, Ocaña, Pasto, Tuluá, Tunja **6** Cúcuta, Ibagué **7** Ciénaga, Palmira, Pereira, Popayán **8** Medellín, Montería **9** Cartagena, Manizales **10** Santa Marta **11** Bucaramanga **12** Barranquilla

Colorado: 6 Arvada, Aurora, Golden, Salida **7** Alamosa, Boulder, Durango, Greeley, La Junta **8** Brighton, Gunnison, Lakewood, Longmont, Loveland, Montrose, Thornton **9** Englewood, Estes Park, Leadville, Littleton, Rocky Ford, Telluride **10** Broomfield, Castle Rock **11** Fort Collins **13** Grand Junction

Congo (Zaire): 4 Boma **6** Bukavu **7** Kolwezi **8** Bandundu **9** Kisangani **10** Lubumbashi **12** Stanleyville

Congo-Brazzaville: 11 Pointe-Noire

Connecticut: 6 Darien, Granby, Groton, Haddam **7** Danbury, Enfield, Meriden, Milford, Newtown, Norwalk, Norwich, Old Lyme, Pomfret, Windham **8** Guilford, New Haven, Simsbury, Stamford, Suffield, Westport **9** Greenwich, New Canaan, New London, Waterbury, Waterford **10** Bridgeport, Farmington, Kensington, Litchfield, New Britain, Ridgefield, Stonington, Torrington

Costa Rica: 8 Alajuela **10** Puntarenas **11** Puerto Limón

Croatia: 4 Pula **5** Sisak, Split, Zadar **6** Osijek, Rijeka **9** Dubrovnik

Cuba: 5 Banes, Bauta **6** Bayamo **7** Holguín **8** Camagüey, Marianao, Matanzas, Santiago **10** Cienfuegos, Guantánamo **11** Pinar del Río

Cyprus: 7 Kyrenia, Larnaca **8** Limassol **9** Famagusta

Czech Republic: 4 Brno, Zlín **5** Plzen **7** Liberec, Olomouc, Ostrava **10** Bratislava

Delaware: 5 Lewes **7** Seaford **10** Harrington, Wilmington, Winterthur

Denmark: 5 Arhus, Skive, Vejle **6** Alborg, Odense, Viborg **13** Frederiksberg

Dominican Republic: 4 Azua, Bani, Moca **5** Bonao, Nagua **8** Barahona, Santiago

Ecuador: 4 Loja **5** Canar, Daule, Manta, Pinas **7** Machala **8** Riobamba **9** Guayaquil

Egypt: 4 Giza, Idfu, Isna, Qena **5** Aswan, Asyut, Benha, Disuq, Girga, Luxor, Minuf, Tahta, Tanta **6** Helwan **7** El Arish, Zagazig **8** Damanhur, Damietta, El Faiyum, Ismailia, Port Said **10** Alexandria

Eire: see **Ireland,** below

El Salvador: 7 La Unión **8** Santa Ana **9** Sonsonate

England: 4 Bath, Eton, Hove, Ryde, York **5** Brent, Brigg, Colne, Corby, Cowes, Derby, Dover, Egham, Eling, Esher, Eston, Goole, Leeds, Lelgh, Lewes, Luton, Poole, Ryton, Wigan **6** Bexley, Bolton, Dudley, Durham, Exeter, Merton, Oldham, Oxford, Torbay, Warley, Welwyn **7** Bristol, Bromley, Croydon, Hackney, Ipswich, Malvern, Norwich, Salford, Seaford, Walsall **8** Abingdon, Basildon, Bradford, Brighton, Coventry, Hastings, Hatfield, Havering, Hertford, Kingston, Lewisham, Plymouth, Wallsend **9** Aylesbury, Blackpool, Cambridge, Islington, Leicester, Liverpool, Newcastle, Sheffield, Stratford **10** Birkenhead, Birmingham,

Canterbury, Colchester, Manchester, Nottingham, Portsmouth, Sunderland **11** Bournemouth, Northampton, Southampton **12** Peterborough, Stoke-on-Trent, West Bromwich **13** Southend-on-Sea, Wolverhampton
Estonia: 5 Narva, Pärnu, Tartu
Ethiopia: 5 Aksum, Harer **6** Nazret **8** Dire Dawa
Finland: 4 Kemi, Oulu, Pori **5** Espoo, Hango, Kotka, Lahti, Rauma, Turku, Vaasa **6** Vantaa **7** Tampere
Florida: 5 Largo, Miami, Ocala, Ocoee, Oneco, Tampa **6** DeLand, Naples **7** Hialeah, Key West, Orlando, Sebring **8** Gulfport, Key Largo, Lakeland, Opa-Locka, Sarasota **9** Boca Raton, Bradenton, Fort Myers, Kissimmee, Palm Beach, Pensacola, Vero Beach **10** Clearwater, Cocoa Beach, Miami Beach, Punta Gorda, Titusville **11** Coral Gables, Gainesville, Key Biscayne, St. Augustine, Winter Haven **12** Apalachicola, Daytona Beach, Ft. Lauderdale, Jacksonville, Pompano Beach, St. Petersburg **13** Chattahoochee
France: 3 Dax, Pau **4** Agde, Agen, Albi, Ales, Auch, Caen, Gien, Laon, Lyon, Metz, Nice, Orly, Rezé, Sens, Sète, Vire **5** Arles, Arras, Auray, Auton, Avion, Berck, Blois, Bondy, Brest, Creil, Digne, Dijon, Douai, Dreux, Flers, Gagny, Laval, Le Puy, Lille, Lunel, Lyons, Mâcon, Meaux, Melun, Muret, Nîmes, Niort, Noyon, Reims, Revin, Rodez, Rouen, Royan, Tours, Tulle, Vichy, Vitre **6** Amiens, Angers, Calais, Cannes, Dieppe, Evreux, Le Mans, Nantes, Nevers, Rennes, Rheims, Thiers, Toulon, Troyes **7** Ajaccio, Antibes, Avignon, Béthune, Bourges, Le Havre, Limoges, Lorlent, Lourdes, Orléans, Roubaix **8** Beauvais, Besançon, Biarritz, Bordeaux, Chartres, Gentilly, Grenoble, Nanterre, Poitiers, Toulouse **9** Cherbourg, Dunkerque, Marseille, Perpignan **10** Marseilles, Strasbourg, Versailles **11** Carcassonne, Montpellier **13** Aix-en-Provence
Gabon: 4 Oyem **5** Bitam **10** Port-Gentil **11** Franceville
Gambia: 9 Serekunda
Georgia: 4 Adel, Alma, Arco **5** Jesup, Macon, McRae **6** Albany, Athens **7** Augusta, Calhoun **8** Americus, Columbus, Marietta, Savannah, Valdosta **9** Brunswick
Georgia, Republic of: 6 Batumi **7** Kutaisi, Rustavi, Sukhumi
Germany: 3 Aue, Hof, Ulm **4** Bonn, Gera, Goch, Hamm, Jena, Kehl, Kiel, Köln, Marl, Suhl **5** Aalen, Ahlen, Borna, Bruhl, Calbe, Celle, Düren, Emden, Essen, Forst, Fulda, Furth, Gotha, Greiz, Hagen, Halle, Hanau, Herne, Hurth, Kleve, Lemgo, Lobau, Mainz, Trier **6** Aachen, Bremen, Coburg, Dachau, Dessau, Erfurt, Kassel, Lübeck, Munich **7** Cologne, Cottbus, Dresden, Hamburg, Hanover, Koblenz, Krefeld, Leipzig, München, Munster, Potsdam, Rostock, Zwickau **8** Augsburg, Bayreuth, Chemnitz, Cuxhaven, Dortmund, Duisburg, Freiburg, Hannover, Mannheim, Nürnberg, Würzburg **9** Bielefeld, Brunswick, Darmstadt, Frankfurt, Göttingen, Karlsruhe, Magdeburg, Nuremberg, Stuttgart, Wiesbaden, Wuppertal **10** Baden-Baden, Düsseldorf, Heidelberg, Regensburg **11** Brandenburg, Bremerhaven, Saarbrücken **12** Braunschweig **13** Gelsenkirchen
Ghana: 4 Axim, Keta, Tema **5** Lawra, Yendi **6** Kumasi
Greece: 3 Kos **4** Arta **5** Argos, Lamia, Nemea, Volos **6** Sparta, Thebes **7** Corinth, Khalkis, Larissa, Piraeus, Tríkala **8** Salonika **12** Thessaloniki
Guatemala: 5 Cobán **13** Quezaltenango
Guinea: 4 Labé **6** Kankan, Kindia
Haiti: 8 Gonaïves **10** Cap Haitien
Hawaii: 4 Aiea, Hilo, Laie **5** Kapaa, Lihue, Maili **6** Kailua **7** Kaneohe, Waikiki, Wailuku
Honduras: 5 Danlí **7** La Ceiba **12** San Pedro Sula
Hong Kong: 7 Kowloon
Hungary: 3 Ozd **4** Eger, Györ, Pécs **5** Abony, Bekes **6** Szeged **7** Miskolc **8** Debrecen
Idaho: 4 Buhl **5** Nampa **6** Dubois, Moscow **7** Gooding, Payette, Rexburg **8** Caldwell **9** Blackfoot, Pocatello, Sandpoint, Sun Valley, Twin Falls **11** Coeur d' Alene, Grangeville
Illinois: 6 DeKalb, Galena, Hardin, Joliet, Macomb, Moline, Paxton, Peoria, Skokie, Urbana **7** Chicago, Decatur, Glencoe, Oak Lawn, Oak Park, Tuscola, Watseka, Wheaton **8** Carthage, Evanston, Kankakee, La Grange, Monmouth, Rockford, Vandalia, Waukegan **9** Belvidere, Effingham, Galesburg, Park Ridge, Yorkville **10** Belleville, Carbondale, Carrollton, Des Plaines, Northbrook, Rock Island
India: 3 Mau **4** Agra, Ahwa, Bhuj, Durg, Gaya, Kota, Mhow, Pune, Puri, Rewa, Tonk, Ziro **5** Adoni, Aimer, Akola, Alwar, Arcot, Arrah, Banda, Barsi, Bidar, Bihar, Churu, Damoh, Delhi, Dewas, Eluru, Gonda, Jalna, Jammu, Karur, Miraj, Morvi, Nasik, Patan, Patna, Poona, Sagar, Satna, Sikar, Simla, Surat, Thana **6** Baroda, Bhopal, Bombay, Cochin, Guntur, Howrah, Indore, Jaipur, Jhansi, Kanpur, Madras, Meerut, Mysore, Nagpur, Raipur, Rajkot, Ranchi, Ujjain **7** Aligarh, Asansol, Belgaum, Bikaner, Burdwan, Cuttack, Gauhati, Gwalior, Jodhpur, Kurnool, Lucknow, Madurai, Mathura, Nellore, Patiala, Vellore **8** Amritsar, Bhatpara, Calcutta, Dehra Dun, Kolhapur, Ludhiana, Sholapur, Srinagar, Varanasi **9** Ahmadabad, Allahabad, Bangalore, Hyderabad **10** Ahmadnagar, Chandigarh, Trivandrum **11** Pondicherry
Indiana: 4 Gary **5** Berne, Paoli, Vevay **6** Delphi, Kokomo, Marlon, Muncie, Tipton **7** Bedford, Corydon, Elkhart, La Porte, Winamac **8** Bluffton, Kentland **9** Boonville, Fort Wayne, New Albany, Rushville, South Bend, Vincennes **10** Crown

Point, Evansville, Logansport, Scottsburg, Terre Haute, Valparaiso **11** Bloomington
Indonesia: 4 Pati **5** Ambon, Bogor, Garut, Kudus, Medan, Tegal, Turen **6** Batang, Kediri, Madiun, Malang, Manado, Padang **7** Bandung, Kendari **8** Semarang, Surabaja, Surabaya, Tjirebon **9** Palembang, Pontianak, Surakarta **10** Pekalongan **11** Tasikmalaja **12** Bandjarmasin
Iowa: 5 Onawa, Pella **6** Eldora, Harlan, Keokuk, Le Mars, Red Oak **7** Allison, Anamosa, Carroll, Clinton, Corydon, Denison, Dubuque, Marengo, Osceola, Waverly **8** Clarinda, Ida Grove, Waterloo **9** Davenport, Fort Dodge, Indianola, Mason City, Muscatine, Oskaloosa, Sioux City, Storm Lake, West Union, Winterset **10** Emmetsburg, Rock Rapids, Spirit Lake **11** Cedar Rapids, Fort Madison **13** Council Bluffs
Iran: 3 Qom, Qum **4** Amul, Arak, Khoi, Sari, Yazd, Yezd **5** Ahvaz, Ahwaz, Babol, Rasht **6** Abadan, Meshed, Shiraz, Tabriz **7** Esfahan, Hamadan, Isfahan, Mashhad **9** Bakhtaran
Iraq: 3 Ana, Kut **4** Kufa **5** Al Kut, Amara, Basra, Erbil, Hilla, Mosul, Najaf, Rutba **6** Amarah, Hillah, Kirkuk, Ramadi, Rutbah **7** Falluja, Samarra **8** Fallujah, Nasiriya **9** Nasiriyah
Ireland: 4 Athy, Birr, Cobh, Cork, Naas, Tuam **5** Ennis, Sligo **6** Carlow, Galway, Tralee **7** Dundalk, Kildare, Wexford, Wicklow **8** Drogheda, Kilkenny, Limerick, Monaghan **9** Castlebar, Killarney, Tipperary, Waterford **10** Balbriggan
Israel: 5 Afula, Haifa, Holon, Jaffa **7** Rehovot **8** Ashqelon, Nazareth, Ramat Gan **9** Beersheba
Italy: 4 Acri, Alba, Asti, Bari, Enna, Este, Fano, Gela, Iesi, Lodi, Lugo, Pisa **5** Adria, Agira, Anzio, Aosta, Arola, Cantù, Capua, Carpi, Crema, Cuneo, Eboli, Fermo, Fondi, Forli, Gaeta, Genoa, Imola, Ivrea, Lecce, Lecco, Lucca, Massa, Melfi, Menfi, Milan, Monza, Padua, Parma, Prato, Siena, Turin **6** Ancona, Assisi, Foggia, Mantua, Milano, Modena, Naples, Napoli, Rimini, Torino, Venice, Verona **7** Bergamo, Bologna, Bolzano, Brescia, Catania, Firenze, Leghorn, Messina, Palermo, Perugia, Pescara, Potenza, Ravenna, Salerno, San Remo, Taranto, Trieste, Venezia **8** Brindisi, Cagliari, Florence, La Spezia, Piacenza, Siracusa, Syracuse
Ivory Coast: 6 Bouaké
Jamaica: 6 May Pen **10** Montego Bay
Japan: 3 Ina, Ise, Ito, Ota, Tsu, Ube, Uji, Yao **4** Ageo, Anan, Gifu, Hagi, Himi, Hofu, Iida, Joyo, Kaga, Kobe, Kofu, Kure, Miki, Mito, Naha, Nara, Noda, Oita, Otsu, Saga, Saku, Soka, Tosu, Ueda, Yono **5** Akita, Atami, Beppu, Chiba, Imari, Itami, Iwaki, Iwata, Izumi, Izumo, Kiryu, Kochi, Kyoto, Minoo, Odate, Ogaki, Okawa, Okaya, Omiya, Omuta, Osaka, Otaru, Oyama, Sabae, Saiki, Sakai, Sanjo, Suita, Tenri, Urawa **6** Akashi, Aomori, Himeji, Kadoma, Kurume, Matsue, Mitaka, Nagano, Nagoya, Numazu, Sasebo, Sendai, Suzuka, Toyama, Yonago **7** Fukuoka, Hitachi, Ibaraki, Imabari, Muroran, Niigata, Niihama, Nobeoka, Obihiro, Odawara, Okayama, Okazaki, Sapporo **8** Ashikaga, Fujisawa, Fukuyama, Hirakata, Hirosaki, Ichihara, Ichikawa, Kakogawa, Kamakura, Kanazawa, Kawasaki, Miyazaki, Nagasaki, Onomichi, Shizuoka, Takasaki, Toyonaka, Wakayama, Yamagata, Yokohama, Yokosuka **9** Hiroshima
Jordan: 5 Aqaba, Irbid
Kansas: 4 Gove, Iola **5** Colby, Hoxie, Lakin, Leoti, Paola, Pratt **6** Atwood, Beloit, Girard, Holton, Salina **7** Abilene, Emporia, Garnett, Kinsley, Wichita **8** Cimarron, Goodland, La Crosse, Sublette **9** Coldwater, Fort Scott, Great Bend, Oskaloosa **10** Hutchinson **11** Leavenworth **12** Council Grove, Overland Park **13** Medicine Lodge
Kazakhstan: 5 Semey **6** Almaty, Aqtöbe, Guryev, Uralsk **7** Alma-Ata, Zhambyl **8** Balkhash, Chimkent, Dzhambul, Kyzl Orda, Pavlodar, Shymkent **9** Karaganda **10** Aktyubinsk
Kentucky: 4 Inez **5** Cadiz, Hyden, McKee **6** Elkton, Harlan **7** Ashland, Campton, Greenup, Hindman, Paducah, Stanton **8** Fort Knox, Mayfield **9** Bardstown, Covington, Cynthiana, Lexington, Maysville, Owensboro, Pikeville, Pineville, Southgate, Vanceburg **10** Booneville, Hawesville, Louisville, Whitesburg **12** Bowling Green
Kenya: 4 Embu **5** Nyeri **6** Kisumu, Nakuru **7** Mombasa
Kyrgyzstan: 3 Osh **5** Naryn
Laos: 5 Pakse **11** Savannakhet
Latvia: 7 Jelgava, Liepaja **9** Ventspils **10** Daugavpils
Lebanon: 4 Tyre **5** Sidon, Zahlé **7** Juniyah, Tripoli
Libya: 4 Homs **5** Derna, Zawia **6** Tobruk **8** Benghazi, Misratah
Lithuania: 6 Kaunas **8** Klaipeda
Louisiana: 4 Jena **5** Amite, Arabi, Houma, Mamou, Norco, Rayne **6** Colfax, Edgard, Gretna, Minden, Ruston **7** Arcadia, Bastrop, Marrero, Oberlin **8** Bogalusa, De Ridder, Metairie, New Roads, Oak Grove, Westwego **9** Abbeville, Chalmette, Hahnville, Leesville, New Iberia, Opelousas, Port Allen, Thibodaux, Winnfield, Winnsboro **10** New Orleans, Plaquemine, Shreveport **11** Lake Charles **12** Natchitoches
Macedonia: 6 Bitola, Prilep, Tetovo
Maine: 4 Saco **5** Orono **6** Auburn, Bangor, Gorham **7** Berwick, Kittery, Machias, Rumford **8** Lewiston, Portland, Rockland **9** Bar Harbor, Biddeford, Brunswick, Ellsworth, Kennebunk, Skowhegan, Wiscasset **11** Millinocket, Presque Isle **13** Kennebunkport
Malawi: 5 Mzuzu, Zomba **8** Blantyre

Malaysia: **4** Ipoh **5** Gemas, Klang **6** Kelang, Penang, Pinang **11** Johore Bahru
Mali: **5** Kayes, Mopti, Ségou **7** Sikasso
Malta: **10** Birkirkara
Maryland: **5** Bowie **6** Denton, Elkton, Towson **8** Bethesda, Landover, Snow Hill **9** Baltimore, Rockville **10** Beltsville, Hagerstown **11** Chestertown, College Park, Leonardtown **12** Havre de Grace, Silver Spring
Massachusetts: **5** Lenox, Salem **6** Boston, Dedham, Lowell, Malden, Monson, Natick, Saugus, Woburn **7** Amherst, Duxbury, Holyoke, Hyannis, Methuen, Needham, Swansea, Taunton, Walpole, Waltham, Wareham **8** Brockton, Chicopee, Falmouth, Plymouth, Rockport, Yarmouth **9** Brookline, Cambridge, Edgartown, Fall River, Fitchburg, Haverhill, Lexington, Nantucket, Worcester **10** Framingham, Gloucester, Greenfield, Leominster, New Bedford, North Adams, Pittsfield, Somerville **11** Northampton **11** Springfield **12** Provincetown, Williamstown
Mauritania: **4** Atar **5** Kaedi **6** Dakhla
Mexico: **4** León **5** Ameca, Choix, Tepic **6** Cancún, Celaya, Colima, Jalapa, Juárez, Mérida, Oaxaca, Puebla, Toluca, Tuxtla **7** Durango, Guasave, Morelia, Obregón, Reynosa, Tampico, Tijuana, Tlalpán, Torreón, Uruapan, Zapopan **8** Chetumal, Coyoacán, Culiacán, Ensenada, Mazatlan, Mexicali, Saltlllo, Tuxtepec **9** Chihuahua, Fresnillo, Ixtacalco, Monterrey, Querétaro, Salamanca, Tapachula, Zacatecas **10** Cuernavaca, Hermosillo, Ixtapalapa, Xochimilco **11** Guadalajara, Nuevo Laredo **13** San Luis Potosí
Michigan: **4** Alma, Holt **5** Flint, Ionia, L'Anse, Niles **6** Otsego, Paw Paw, Warren **7** Allegan, Corunna, Detroit, Gladwin, Livonia, Midland, Saginaw **8** Ann Arbor, Bessemer, Dearborn, Escanaba, Grayling, Hastings, Houghton, Muskegon, Sandusky **9** Cheboygan, Coldwater, Kalamazoo, Menominee, Port Huron, Ypsilanti **10** Charlevoix, Grand Haven **11** Battle Creek, Grand Rapids
Minnesota: **3** Ely **4** Mora **5** Anoka, Edina, Osseo **6** Aitkin, Benson, Duluth, Waseca, Windom, Winona **7** Glencoe, Hibbing, Mankato, Red Wing, St. Cloud, Wabasha **8** Brainerd, Elk River, Moorhead, Shakopee **9** Caledonia, Crookston, Faribault, Pipestone, Rochester, Saint Paul, Silver Bay **10** Park Rapids, Saint Cloud, Saint James, Saint Peter, Stillwater, Two Harbors **11** Bloomington, Fergus Falls, Long Prairie, Minneapolis, Worthington **12** Breckenridge, Granite Falls, Redwood Falls
Mississippi: **4** Iuka **5** Amory **6** Biloxi, Leland, McComb, Purvis, Sardis, Sumner, Tupelo, Winona **7** Belzoni, Brandon, Okolona, Quitman, Wiggins **8** Gulfport, Hernando, Meridian, Paulding, Rosedale, Walthall **9** Greenwood, Indianola, New Albany, Pittsboro, Vicksburg **10** Batesville, Booneville, Brookhaven, Clarksdale, Ellisville, Greenville, Hazlehurst, Pascagoula, Port Gibson, Starkville, Waynesboro **11** Hattiesburg **12** Holly Springs
Missouri: **3** Ava **4** Linn **5** Eldon, Hayti, Ladue, Rolla **6** Galena, Neosho, Potosi **7** Hermann, Ironton, Kennett, Linneus, Osceola, Palmyra, Sedalia, St. Louis **8** Gallatin, Hannibal **9** Boonville, Hartville, Hillsboro, Maryville, Pineville, Tuscumbia, Warrenton **10** Kansas City, Kirksville, Marble Hill, Marshfield, Perryville, Saint Louis, Springfield **11** Saint Joseph **12** Independence, Saint Charles
Moldova: **5** Balti **7** Tighina **8** Tiraspol
Mongolia: **5** Kobdo **6** Darhan **10** Choybalsan
Montana: **5** Butte, Havre, Libby **6** Hardin, Polson **7** Bozeman **8** Billings, Missoula, Red Lodge **10** Great Falls
Montenegro: **8** Titograd
Morocco: **3** Fès **4** Safi, Salé, Taza **5** Nador, Oujda **6** Agadir, Meknès **7** Kenitra, Tangier **9** Marrakech, Marrakesh **10** Casablanca
Mozambique: **5** Beira **7** Chimoio, Nampula **9** Quelimane, Quilimane
Myanmar: **3** Pyu **4** Paan **5** Akyab, Bhamo, Chauk, Katha, Magwe, Minbu, Mogok, Tavoy **7** Bassein **8** Mandalay, Moulmein
Namibia: **5** Outjo **6** Tsumeb **8** Oshakati **12** Keetmanshoop
Nebraska: **3** Ord **5** Cozad, Omaha, Ponca, Tryon, Wahoo **6** Elwood, Gering, McCook, Minden, Wilber **7** Burwell, Fremont, Kearney, Kimball, Osceola, Tekamah **8** Beatrice, Fairbury, Hastings, Ogallala, Red Cloud, Schuyler, Tecumseh, Thedford **9** Fullerton, Papillion **10** Springview, Stockville **11** Grand Island, Hayes Center, North Platte, Plattsmouth
Netherlands: **3** Ede, Epe, Oss **4** Echt, Tiel, Uden **5** Aalst, Assen, Breda, Delft, Emmen, Hague, Soest, Vaals, Venlo, Vught, Weert, Weesp, Zeist **6** Arnhem **7** Haarlem, Tilburg, Utrecht **8** Enschede, Nijmegen, The Hague **9** Apeldoorn, Eindhoven, Groningen, Rotterdam, Zandvoort **10** Maastricht
Nevada: **3** Ely **4** Elko, Reno **6** Fallon, Minden, Pioche **7** Tonopah **8** Las Vegas, Lovelock **9** Goldfield, Yerington **10** Winnemucca
New Brunswick: **5** Minto **6** St. John **7** Moncton **9** Dalhousie, Saint John **10** Edmundston, Richibucto **12** Hopewell Cape, Perth Andover, Saint Andrews
Newfoundland: **5** Burin **6** Wabana **10** Mount Pearl **11** Corner Brook
New Hampshire: **5** Derry, Dover, Keene **6** Berlin, Exeter, Gorham, Nashua **7** Hanover, Laconia, Lebanon, Ossipee **8** Hinsdale, Seabrook **9** Littleton, Merrimack **10** Manchester, Portsmouth, Woodsville

New Jersey: **4** Atco, Lodi **6** Camden, Newark, Nutley, Rahway, Rumson **7** Bayonne, Cape May, Clifton, Hoboken, Paramus, Passaic, Raritan, Teaneck **8** Freehold, Metuchen, Paterson, Vauxhall, Woodbury **9** Elizabeth, Glassboro, Lakehurst, Menlo Park, Montclair, Princeton, Riverside, Toms River **10** Asbury Park, Bloomfield, Cherry Hill, Hackensack, Jersey City, Morristown, Mount Holly, Perth Amboy, Piscataway, Plainfield, Somerville **11** Mays Landing **12** Atlantic City, New Brunswick **13** Palisades Park
New Mexico: **4** Taos **5** Belen, Hobbs, Raton **6** Clovis, Deming, Grants **7** Roswell, Socorro **8** Estancia, Los Lunas, Portales **9** Carrizozo, Las Cruces, Los Alamos, Lovington, Tucumcari **10** Alamogordo, Bernalillo, Fort Sumner **11** Albuquerque
New York: **4** Elma, Ovid, Troy **5** Depew, Ilion, Islip, Le Roy, Nyack, Olean, Owego, Utica **6** Attica, Cohoes, Delmar, Elmira, Hudson, Ithaca, Oneida **7** Batavia, Buffalo, Corning, Geneseo, Katonah, Mineola, Yonkers **8** Bay Shore, Cortland, Hyde Park, Kingston, Lockport, Ossining, Syracuse **9** Greenport, Hempstead, Patchogue, Rochester, Scarsdale, Schoharie **10** Binghamton, Glens Falls, Huntington, Lackawanna, Lake George, Lake Placid, Mamaroneck, Massapequa, Mount Kisco **11** Cooperstown, Plattsburgh, Port Chester, Saint George, Schenectady, Southampton, Watkins Glen, White Plains **12** Poughkeepsie
New Zealand: **4** Hutt, Tawa **5** Levin, Taupo, Waihi **7** Dunedin, Manukau **8** Auckland **12** Christchurch
Nicaragua: **4** León **5** Boaco, Rivas **6** Masaya **7** Granada
Nigeria: **3** Aba, Ado, Ede, Ife, Ila, Iwo, Jos, Owo, Oyo **4** Kano, Ondo **5** Akure, Enugu, Gusau, Lagos, Okene, Zaria **6** Ibadan, Ilesha, Ilorin, Kaduna, Mushin, Sokoto **7** Onitsha, Oshogbo **8** Abeokuta **9** Maiduguri, Ogbomosho **12** Port Harcourt
North Carolina: **4** Dunn **5** Ayden, Elkin, Erwin, Oteen, Sylva **6** Dobson, Durham, Lenoir, Manteo, Marlon, Shelby, Winton **7** Bayboro, Brevard, Edenton, Roxboro, Sanford, Tarboro **8** Asheboro, Beaufort, Gastonia, Hatteras, Snow Hill **9** Albemarle, Asheville, Charlotte, Kitty Hawk, Morganton **10** Chapel Hill, Greensboro, Smithfield, Wilkesboro **12** Murfreesboro, Winston-Salem
North Dakota: **4** Mott **5** Cando, Fargo, Minot, Rolla **6** Amidon, Ashley, Bowman, Formon, Lakota, Linton, Medora, Mohall **8** Wahpeton, Washburn **9** Dickinson, Williston **10** Devils Lake, Grand Forks
Northern Ireland: **5** Derry, Larne, Newry, Omagh **6** Antrim, Armagh **9** Bally-mena, Coleraine, Craigavon, Dungannon **10** Ballymoney **11** Ballycastle, Downpatrick, Enniskillen, Londonderry **13** Carrickfergus
North Korea: **5** Haeju, Nampo **6** Wonsan **7** Hamhung, Kaesong, Sinuiju **8** Ch'ongjin, Kimchaek
Northwest Territories: **6** Dawson **10** Whitehorse
Norway: **4** Bodo **5** Hamar, Skien, Vardo **6** Bergen, Tromso **8** Kirkenes **9** Stavanger, Trondheim **10** Hammerfest **12** Kristiansand
Nova Scotia: **5** Digby **6** Pictou **7** Arichat, Baddeck **8** Port Hood **9** Dartmouth, Kentville, Lunenburg, Shelburne, Westville **10** Antigonish **11** Guysborough
Ohio: **4** Kent **5** Akron, Berea, Bryan, Carey, Eaton, Heath, Logan, Niles, Parma, Piqua, Solon, Xenia **6** Canton, Celina, Dayton, Elyria, Euclid, Kenton, Lorain, Marion, Medina, Sidney, Tiffin, Toledo **7** Ashland, Batavia, Bucyrus, Chardon, Findlay, Ironton, Oakwood, Pomeroy, Ravenna, Wauseon, Wooster **8** Conneaut, Marietta, Sandusky **9** Ashtabula, Cleveland, Coshocton, Mansfield **10** Cincinnati, Gallipolis, Zanesville **11** Chillicothe, Mount Gilead, Port Clinton **12** Steubenville
Oklahoma: **3** Ada **4** Alva, Enid **5** Altus, Atoka, Sayre, Tulsa **6** Durant, El Reno, Guymon, Idabel, Lawton, Okemah, Poteau, Wewoka **7** Antlers, Ardmore, Cordell, Eufaula, Newkirk, Purcell, Sapulpa, Watonga **8** Anadarko, Okmulgee, Pawhuska, Sallisaw, Stilwell **9** Chickasha, Claremore, Frederick, McAlester, Wilburton **10** Stillwater, Tishomingo
Oman: **3** Sur **6** Matrah **7** Salalah
Ontario: **4** Ajax, Wawa, York **6** Barrie, Guelph, Kenora, London, Oshawa, Sarnia, Simcoe **7** Cobourg, Markham, Napanee, Sudbury, Windsor **8** Brampton, Cochrane, Goderich, Hamilton, North Bay, Pembroke, Prescott **9** Brantford, Etobicoke, Kitchener, L'Original, Newmarket, North York, Owen Sound, Walkerton **10** Belleville, Brockville, Burlington, Haileybury, Parry Sound, Thunder Bay **11** Bracebridge, Fort Frances, Mississauga, Scarborough **12** Peterborough, St. Catharines
Oregon: **5** Canby, Nyssa **6** Eugene **8** Coquille, La Grande, Portland, Roseburg **9** Clackamas, Corvallis, Gold Beach, Pendleton, The Dalles, Tillamook **10** Grants Pass **12** Klamath Falls
Pakistan: **5** Bannu, Bhera, Kasur, Kohat **6** Gujrat, Lahore, Mardan, Multan, Quetta, Sukkur **7** Karachi, Sialkot **8** Lyallpur, Peshawar, Sargodha **9** Hyderabad **10** Bahawalpur, Faisalabad, Gujranwala, Rawalpindi
Papua New Guinea: **3** Lae **10** Mount Hagen, Popondetta
Paraguay: **3** Itá **4** Yuty **5** Luque, Pilar **7** Caacupé, Caazapa **9** Paraguarí **10** San Lorenzo

Pennsylvania: **4** Erie, York **5** Avoca, Darby, Muncy, Paoli **6** Easton **7** Altoona, Bedford, Clarion, Hanover, Hershey, Latrobe, Reading, Ridgway, Sunbury **8** Carlisle, Edinboro, Hazleton, Montrose, Scranton, Somerset **9** Allentown, Ebensburg, Honesdale, Jim Thorpe, Lancaster, Lewisburg, Lock Haven, Meadville, New Castle, Wellsboro **10** Bloomsburg, Brookville, Carbondale, Clearfield, Gettysburg, McKeesport, Middleburg, Pittsburgh, Pottsville, Waynesburg **11** Valley Forge, Wilkes-Barre **12** Philadelphia, State College
Peru: **3** Ica, Ilo **5** Ancon, Cuzco, Jauja, Junin, Lamas, Pisco, Piura, Tacna **6** Callao **8** Arequipa, Chiclayo, Chimbote, Trujillo
Philippines: **3** Iba **4** Bago, Bais, Boac, Bogo, Cebu, Daet, Jolo, Lipa, Mati **5** Basco, Bulan, Cadiz, Danao, Davao, Digos, Gapan, Gubat, Iriga, Laoag, Ormoc, Pasay, Silay, Tagum, Vigan **6** Butuan, Iloilo, Quezon **7** Angeles, Bacolod, Basilan **8** Batangas, Calbayog, Caloocan **9** Zamboanga **10** Quezon City
Poland: **4** Lodz, Nysa, Pila, Zary **5** Bytom, Bytow, Chelm, Kutno, Lomza, Luban, Lubin, Plock, Radom, Torun, Tychy **6** Elblag, Gdansk, Gdynia, Kalisz, Kielce, Krakow, Lublin, Poznan, Rybnik, Zabrze **7** Chorzow, Dabrowa, Gliwice, Rzeszow, Wroclaw **8** Gornicza, Katowice, Szczecin **9** Bialystok, Bydgoszcz, Sosnowiec, Walbrzych **11** Czestochowa
Portugal: **4** Faro **5** Braga, Evora, Porto **6** Almada, Oporto, Queluz **7** Amadora **8** Barreiro, Santarém
Prince Edward Island: **10** Summerside
Puerto Rico: **5** Ponce **6** Caguas **7** Arecibo, Bayamón **8** Carolina, Guaynabo, Mayagüez
Quebec: **4** Alma **5** Amqui, Anjou, Gaspé, Laval, Lévis, Magog, Percé, Rouyn **6** Granby, Ham Sud, Matane, Ste.-Foy, Val d'Or **7** Bedford, Lachute **8** Beauport, Cap Santé, Joliette, Lac Brome, Maniwaki, Montreal, Rimouski, Roberval, Sept-Iles, Waterloo **9** Bécancour, Cookshire, Iberville, Inverness, La Malbaie, La Prairie, Longueuil, Montmagny, Sainte-Foy, Saint Jean, Tadoussac, Vaudreuil **10** Baie-Comeau, Chicoutimi **11** Beauharnois, Louiseville, Mont-Laurier **12** Charlesbourg **13** Trois-Rivières
Rhode Island: **7** Newport, Rumford, Warwick **8** Apponaug, Coventry, Cranston, Tiverton, Westerly **9** Hopkinton, Pawtucket **10** Woonsocket **12** Narragansett
Romania: **3** Dej **4** Aiud, Arad, Cluj, Deva, Husi, Iasi **5** Anina, Bacau, Buzau, Carei, Lugoj, Sibiu, Turda **6** Braila, Brasov, Galati, Oradea **7** Craiova **8** Ploiesti **9** Constanta, Timisoara **10** Cluj-Napoca
Russia: **3** Kem, Ufa **4** Inta, Luga, Okha, Omsk, Orel, Orsk, Perm, Tula, Tura, Zima **5** Aldan, Artem, Chita, Ishim, Kansk, Kazan, Lysva, Onega, Penza, Pskov, Rzhev, Salsk, Serov, Sochi, Sokol, Tomsk, Tulun, Volsk, Yurga **6** Bratsk, Grozny, Kaluga, Kovrov, Kurgan, Rostov, Ryazan, Samara, Syzran, Tambov, Tyumen, Vyborg, Yelets **7** Irkutsk, Ivanovo, Izhevsk, Kalinin, Kolomna, Lipetsk, Magadan, Norilsk, Rybinsk, Saransk, Saratov, Shakhty, Vologda, Yakutsk, Zhdanov **8** Belgorod, Kemerovo, Kostroma, Murmansk, Nakhodka, Novgorod, Orenburg, Smolensk, Taganrog, Vladimir, Volzhski, Voronezh **9** Archangel, Astrakhan, Krasnodar, Stavropol, Ulyanovsk, Volgograd **10** Dzerzhinsk **11** Arkhangel'sk, Chelyabinsk, Kaliningrad, Krasnoyarsk, Novosibirsk, Vladivostok **12** St. Petersburg **13** Yekaterinburg
Saskatchewan: **8** Moose Jaw **9** Saskatoon **10** Assiniboia **12** Prince Albert
Saudi Arabia: **4** Jauf, Taif **5** Jedda, Jidda, Mecca, Tabuk **6** Jeddah, Jiddah, Medina **8** Buraydah
Scotland: **3** Ayr **4** Alva, Caol, Dyce, Oban **5** Alloa, Annan, Beith, Cowie, Cupar, Dalry, Ellon, Kelso, Kelty, Largs, Leven, Nairn, Patna, Troon **6** Dundee **7** Glasgow, Paisley **8** Aberdeen, Greenock, Hamilton **9** Inverness, Lockerbie **10** Kilmarnock **11** Dunfermline, John o' Groats
Senegal: **5** Thiès **6** Kaolak **7** Kaolack **10** Saint-Louis
Serbia: **3** Bor, Nis, Pec **4** Ruma **5** Becej, Cacak, Pirot, Sabac, Senta, Vrbas, Vrsac **7** Novi Sad **8** Subotica **10** Kragujevac
Slovakia: **5** Nitra **6** Kosice, Presov, Zilina
Slovenia: **4** Bled **5** Celje, Koper, Kranj **7** Maribor
Somalia: **3** Eil **5** Afgoi, Alula, Brava, Burao, Marka, Obbia **7** Berbera, Kismayu **8** Hargeysa, Kismaayo
South Africa: **5** Brits, Ceres, De Aar, Nigel, Paarl **6** Benoni, Durban, Soweto **7** Springs **8** Boksburg, Mafeking **9** Germiston, Kimberley, Ladysmith, Uitenhage **10** East London **11** Krugersdorp, Vereeniging **12** Johannesburg **13** Port Elizabeth
South Carolina: **5** Aiken, Cayce, Saxon **6** Sumter **7** Gaffney, Laurens, Manning, Pickens **8** Beaufort, Newberry, Rock Hill, Walhalla **9** Abbeville, Allendale, Greenwood, Kingstree, McCormick, Winnsboro **10** Charleston, Darlington, Greenville, Hilton Head, Orangeburg, Walterboro **11** Myrtle Beach, Spartanburg
South Dakota: **7** Sturgis, Yankton **8** Deadwood, Elk Point **9** Brookings, Rapid City **10** Sioux Falls
South Korea: **3** Iri **4** Yosu **5** Cheju, Masan, Mokpo, Pusan, Suwon, Taegu, Ulson, Wonju **6** Chinju, Chonju, Inchon, Kunsan, Taejon **7** Kwangju

Spain: **4** Adra, Baza, Elda, Jaca, Jaén, León, Loja, Lugo, Olot, Reus, Vich, Vigo **5** Albox, Alcoy, Alora, Avila, Baena, Cádiz, Ceuta, Cieza, Ecija, Eibar, Elche, Gijón, Ibiza, Jodar, Lorca, Mahon, Oliva, Osuna, Palma, Ronda, Soria, Ubeda **6** Bilbao, Burgos, Cuenca, Huelva, Lérida, Málaga, Mérida, Murcia, Oviedo, Toledo **7** Almadén, Almería, Cáceres, Córdoba, Durango, Granada, Segovia, Sevilla, Seville, Tarrasa, Vitoria **8** Albacete, Alicante, La Coruña, Pamplona, Sabadell, Valencia, Zaragoza **9** Algeciras, Barcelona, Salamanca, Santander, Saragossa, Tarragona **10** Hospitalet, Valladolid **12** San Sebastián
Sri Lanka: **5** Galle, Kandy **6** Jaffna **8** Dehiwala, Moratuwa **10** Batticaloa
Sudan: **4** Juba **5** Kodok, Kosti **7** El Obeid, Kassala **8** Omdurman
Sweden: **4** Lund, Täby, Umea **5** Falun, Gävle, Lulea, Malmö, Växjö, Visby **6** Orebro **7** Uppsala **8** Göteborg, Halmstad **9** Jönköping, Linköping **12** Kristianstad
Switzerland: **3** Zug **4** Biel, Chur, Sion, Thun **5** Aarau, Arbon, Baden, Basel, Koniz **6** Geneva, Lugano, St. Gall, Zürich **7** Lucerne, Zermatt **8** Lausanne, Montreux, St. Moritz **9** Neuchâtel, Saint Gall **11** Saint Moritz
Syria: **4** Hama, Homs **5** Idlib **6** Aleppo, Tartus **7** Latakia
Taiwan: **5** Chia-i **6** T'ai-nan **7** Chi-lung, Hsin-chu **8** Feng-shan, Pan-ch'iao, San-ch'ung, T'ai-chung **9** Kao-hsiung
Tanzania: **5** Lindi, Mbeya, Tanga **6** Arusha, Kigoma, Mwanza **8** Morogoro, Zanzibar **11** Dar es Salaam
Tennessee: **5** Alcoa, Erwin, Rives **6** Loudon, Ripley, Selmer **7** Memphis, Waverly **8** Gallatin, Oak Ridge, Rutledge, Tazewell, Wartburg **9** Dandridge, Dyersburg, Jacksboro, Jonesboro, Knoxville, Lewisburg, Maryville **10** Cookeville, Crossville, Somerville, Waynesboro **11** Blountville, Chattanooga, Clarksville, Greeneville, McMinnville, Rogersville, Sevierville, Shelbyville **12** Elizabethton, Lawrenceburg, Madisonville, Murfreesboro
Texas: **4** Azle, Waco **5** Alvin, Anson, Baird, Bowie, Bryan, Clute, Cuero, Emory, Ennis, Freer, Hondo, Marfa, Mexia, Olney, Pampa, Pecos, Pharr, Plano, Sealy, Vidor, Wylie **6** Belton, Boerne, Bonham, Burnet, Dallas, Denton, El Paso, Lamesa, Laredo, Linden, Lufkin, Odessa, Seguin **7** Abilene, Bandera, Denison, Houston, Kaufman, Lubbock, Midland, Wharton **8** Amarillo, Angleton, Beaumont, Eastland, Giddings, Gonzales, Granbury, Groveton, Hemphill, La Grange **9** Fort Worth, Galveston **10** Brownfield, Port Arthur, San Antonio, Sweetwater, Waxahachie **11** Brownsville, Littlefield, Nacogdoches, Weatherford **12** New Braunfels **13** Corpus Christi
Thailand: **3** Nan, Tak **5** Phrae, Roi Et, Surin **8** Songkhla **9** Chiang Mai **10** Nonthaburi
Tunisia: **4** Béja, Sfax **5** Gabès, Gafsa, Susah **6** Ariana **7** Bizerte, Safaqis
Turkey: **5** Adana, Bursa, Izmir, Konya, Sivas **6** Edirne, Erzurm, Samsun **7** Antakya, Antalya, Antioch, Kayseri, Malatya **8** Istanbul **9** Eskisehir, Gallipoli, Gaziantep **10** Diyarbakir
Turkmenistan: **8** Nebit Dag **9** Chardzhou, Dashhowuz
Uganda: **5** Jinja, Mbale **7** Entebbe
Ukraine: **4** Lviv, Lvov, Sumy **5** Lutsk, Rovno, Yalta **6** Odessa **7** Donetsk, Kharkiv, Kharkov, Kherson, Luhansk, Poltava **8** Mariupol, Vinnitsa, Zhitomir **9** Chernigov, Chernobyl, Krivoy Rog, Krivyy Rih, Nikolayev **10** Kirovograd, Sebastopol, Sevastopol, Simferopol, Zaporozhye
United Arab Emirates: **5** Ajman, Dubai **6** Dubayy **8** Fujairah, Fujayrah
Uruguay: **4** Melo **5** Minas, Pando, Rocha, Salto **6** Rivera **8** Paysandú **10** Las Piedras
Utah: **3** Loa **4** Lehi, Orem **5** Manti, Ogden, Provo, Sandy **6** Dugway, Tooele **7** Parowan **8** Duchesne **9** Coalville **11** Saint George
Uzbekistan: **5** Nukus **6** Kokand **7** Bukhara, Fergana **8** Andizhan, Chirchik, Namangan **9** Samarkand, Samarqand
Venezuela: **4** Coro **5** Anaco, Cagua **6** Cumaná, Mérida, Petare **7** Cabimas, Guayana, Maracay **8** Valencia **9** Maracaibo **12** Barquisimeto, San Cristóbal
Vermont: **5** Barre **7** Rutland **8** St. Albans **10** Bennington, Burlington, Middlebury **11** Brattleboro, Saint Albans, St. Johnsbury
Vietnam: **3** Hue **4** Vinh **5** Da Lat, Hoi An, My Tho **6** Can Tho, Da Nang, Saigon **7** Bien Hoa, Nam Dinh, Qui Nhon **8** Haiphong, Nha Trang, Thanh Hoa **9** Long Xuyen
Virginia: **4** Tabb **5** Luray **6** Grundy **7** Accomac, Boydton, Fairfax, Hampton, New Kent, Norfolk **8** Abingdon, Culpeper, Leesburg, Manassas, Montross, Nottoway, Powhatan, Tazewell **9** Arlington, Clintwood, Courtland, Eastville, Farmville, Lunenburg, Lynchburg **10** Alexandria, Appomattox, Front Royal, Hillsville, King George, Portsmouth, Rocky Mount **11** King William, Newport News **12** Prince George, Spotsylvania, Williamsburg
Wales: **4** Rhyl **5** Neath, Risca, Tenby, Tywyn **7** Cwmbran, Denbigh, Harlech, Newport, Swansea **8** Aberdare, Bridgend **10** Caernarfon, Caernarvon, Llangollen **11** Aberystwyth
Washington: **4** Omak **5** Brier, Camas, Kelso, Lacey, Pasco, Selah **6** Asotin, Colfax, Tacoma, Yakima **7** Ephrata, Everett, Prosser, Redmond, Seattle, Spokane **8** Bellevue, Chehalis, Colville,

Okanogan **9** Montesano, Ritzville, Snohomish, Wenatchee **10** Bellingham, Coupeville, Ellensburg, Goldendale, Walla Walla, Waterville **11** Port Angeles
West Virginia: **5** Nitro, Welch **6** Elkins, Hamlin, Hinton, Keyser, Ripley **7** Beckley, Weirton **8** Kingwood, Philippi, Wheeling **9** Pineville, Wellsburg **10** Buckhannon, Clarksburg, Huntington, Moorefield, Morgantown, Petersburg, Williamson **11** Harrisville, Martinsburg, Moundsville, Parkersburg **12** Harpers Ferry
Wisconsin: **4** Kiel **5** Ripon, Tomah **6** Antigo, Barron, Oconto, Racine, Wausau **7** Baraboo, Chilton, Elkhorn, Hayward, Kenosha, Mauston, Merrill, Oshkosh, Shawano, Viraqua, Waupaca, Wautoma **8** Appleton, Green Bay, Kewaunee, La Crosse, Washburn, Waukesha, West Bend **9** Eau Claire, Ellsworth, Fond du Lac, Green Lake, Manitowoc, Marinette, Menomonie, Milwaukee, Sheboygan, Whitehall **10** Balsam Lake, Darlington, Dodgeville **12** Stevens Point
Wyoming: **6** Casper, Lander **7** Laramie, Rawlins **8** Gillette, Kemmerer, Sheridan **10** Green River **11** Rock Springs
Yemen: **4** Aden **5** Taizz **7** Hodeida, Mukalla **8** Hudaydah
Zambia: **5** Kabwe, Kitwe, Mansa, Mbala, Mongu, Ndola **6** Kasama **7** Chipata
Zimbabwe: **5** Gweru **6** Hwange, Kadoma, Kwekwe, Mutare, Umtali **7** Mashava **8** Bulawayo, Masvingo

civet
3 cat **5** rasse
Madagascar: **5** fossa
relative: **5** genet

civic
5 urban **6** public, social **8** communal, national, societal **9** municipal

civil
6 polite, public, seemly, urbane **7** affable, cordial, courtly, genteel, refined **8** decorous, gracious, mannerly, national, obliging, well-bred **9** courteous, political **10** diplomatic **12** well-mannered **13** accommodating

civilian clothes
5 mufti

civility
6 comity **7** amenity, decency, decorum, manners **8** courtesy **9** etiquette, gentility, propriety **10** politeness **11** correctness

civilization
7 culture

civilized
6 decent, proper, urbane **7** genteel, refined **8** decorous, mannerly, tasteful **9** courteous **10** cultivated **13** sophisticated

civil rights
organization: **4** CORE, SCLC **5** NAACP
pioneer: **4** King (Martin Luther) **5** Evers (Medgar), Lewis (John), Parks (Rosa) **6** Du Bois (W. E. B.), Garvey (Marcus) **7** Jackson (Jesse) **8** Malcolm X, Marshall (Thurgood) **10** Washington (Booker T.)

Civil War
admiral: **8** Buchanan (Franklin), Farragut (David)
alliance (abbrev.): **3** CSA
battle: **6** Shiloh **7** Bull Run **8** Antietam, Manassas **9** Mobile Bay, Nashville, Vicksburg **10** Cold Harbor, Gettysburg **11** Chattanooga, Chickamauga
general: **3** Lee (Robert E.) **4** Hood (John Bell), Pope (John) **5** Bragg (Braxton), Buell (Don Carlos), Ewell (Richard Stoddart), Grant (Ulysses S.), Meade (George), Sykes (George) **6** Hooker (Joseph) **7** Forrest (Nathan Bedford), Jackson (Thomas "Stonewall"), Sherman (Thomas West, William Tecumseh) **8** Burnside (Ambrose), Johnston (Albert Sidney, Joseph Eggleston), Sheridan (Philip) **9** McClellan (George Brinton), Rosecrans (William), Schofield (John) **10** Beauregard (Pierre)
ship: **7** Monitor **9** Merrimack
soldier: **3** reb **4** yank **9** Billy Yank, Johnny Reb

civil wrong
4 tort

clabber
5 curds

clack
3 gab, jaw, yak **4** blab, chat **5** prate **6** babble, cackle, gabble, gossip, jabber, rattle **7** blabber, chatter, clatter, palaver, prattle **9** yakety-yak

clad
4 face, side, skin **5** dress, faced **6** clothe, decked, garbed, outfit **7** attired, clothed, covered, dressed, overlay, sheathe **8** costumed, overlaid, sheathed **9** outfitted

claim
4 call, dibs, hold, lien, plea, take **5** argue, exact, right, share, stake, title **6** adduce, allege, assert, defend, demand, insist **7** advance, call for, contend, declare, justify, profess, purport, require, solicit, warrant **8** interest, maintain **9** assertion, challenge, postulate, privilege **10** allegation, birthright **11** affirmation, declaration, prerogative, requisition **12** protestation

clairvoyance
3 ESP **7** insight **9** intuition, telepathy **10** sixth sense **11** penetration, second sight **12** precognition

clairvoyant
4 seer **5** sibyl **7** diviner **8** telepath **10** soothsayer

clam
4 buck **5** razor **6** dollar, quahog **7** bivalve, coquina, geoduck, mollusc, mollusk, smacker, steamer **11** cherrystone
genus: **3** Mya

clamant
4 dire **6** crying, urgent **7** blatant, burning, exigent **8** pressing **9** insistent **10** compelling, imperative

clamber
5 climb, crawl, scale, swarm **8** scrabble, scramble, struggle

clammy
4 cool, dank, damp **5** close, moist, slimy **6** sticky

clamor
3 cry, din, row **4** bawl, roar, to-do **5** babel, hoo-ha, noise **6** bellow, demand, hoo-hah, hubbub, jangle, outcry, racket, ruckus, tumult, uproar **7** agitate, dispute, ferment, protest, turmoil **8** brouhaha, foofaraw, shouting **9** agitation, commotion **10** hullabaloo, hurly-burly **11** pandemonium

clamorous
5 noisy, vocal **6** crying, shrill, urgent **7** blatant, exigent, raucous, voluble **8** strident, vehement **9** insistent **10** boisterous, imperative, tumultuous, vociferous **11** importunate **12** obstreperous

clamp
4 grip, hold, vise **5** clasp, grasp **6** clench, clinch, clutch, fasten, secure **7** grapple

clamshell
6 bucket **7** grapple

clan
3 mob **4** camp, folk, ring, sept **5** cabal, house, stock, tribe **6** circle, clique, family **7** coterie, kindred, lineage **9** camarilla
emblem: **5** totem

Clancy novel
12 Patriot Games **13** Sum of All Fears (The) **17** Hunt for Red October (The) **21** Clear and Present Danger

clandestine
6 covert, secret, sneaky **7** furtive, illicit, sub rosa **8** hush-hush, stealthy **10** undercover, under wraps **11** underhanded **12** hugger-mugger, illegitimate **13** surreptitious, under-the-table

clang
3 cry, din **4** ding, peal, slam **6** jangle **8** ding-dong

clangor
3 din **5** noise **6** clamor, jangle, racket, rattle, tumult, uproar **7** clatter, ringing **9** stridency **13** reverberation

clangorous
5 noisy **7** booming, rackety, ringing **8** clattery, sonorous **9** deafening **12** earsplitting

Clan of the Cave Bear author
4 Auel (Jean M.)

clap
3 pat **4** bang, blow, boom, slam, slap **5** blast, burst, crack, crash, whack **6** strike **7** applaud **8** applause

Clapton of rock
4 Eric

claptrap
4 bull, bunk **5** cheap, hokum, showy, trash, tripe **6** bunkum, drivel, humbug, vulgar **7** baloney, eyewash, hogwash, twaddle **8** malarkey, nonsense **9** poppycock **10** balderdash, flapdoodle

Clara Bow
6 It girl

claret
3 red **4** wine **8** Bordeaux

clarified butter
4 ghee

clarify
5 clean, clear **6** define, filter, purify **7** analyze, cleanse, clear up, explain, resolve **8** simplify **9** elucidate **10** illuminate **13** straighten out

clarinet, e.g.
4 reed

clarion
5 clear **7** ringing, rousing, trumpet **8** gleaming, stirring **9** brilliant

clarity
6 purity **8** accuracy, lucidity **9** clearness, limpidity, precision **10** exactitude, simplicity **12** transparency

Clarke novel
10 Earthlight **13** Childhood's End

clash
4 bump, jolt **5** brawl, crash, melee, set-to, smash **6** battle, fracas, impact, jangle **7** collide **8** conflict, mismatch, skirmish **9** collision, encounter **10** engagement **11** embroilment

clasp
3 hug, pin **4** clip, grip, hold **5** clamp, grasp, press **6** brooch, buckle, clench, clinch, clutch, enfold **7** embrace, grapple, squeeze **10** chatelaine

class
3 ilk **4** hold, kind, mark, part, rank, rate, sort, tier, type **5** allot, brand, caste, gauge, genre, genus, grade, grain, group, judge, order, score, stamp, style **6** assess, assign, assort, branch, course, league, nature, reckon, regard, stripe **7** bracket, caliber, quality, section, species, variety **8** appraise, category, consider, division, evaluate, grouping, separate **10** categorize, pigeonhole **11** description **12** denomination
middle: **11** bourgeoisie

school: **6** junior, senior **8** freshman **9** sophomore
working: **11** proletariat

classic
5 ideal, model, prime **7** capital, typical, vintage **8** champion, enduring, standard, superior, topnotch **9** authentic, canonical, classical, excellent, exemplary, memorable, tradition **10** magnum opus, masterwork **11** chef d'oeuvre, masterpiece, tour de force, traditional **12** paradigmatic, prototypical **13** authoritative

classical
4 pure **5** Attic, Greek, ideal, Latin, Roman **7** ancient, fitting, Grecian, perfect, typical, vintage **8** Hellenic, standard, sterling **9** canonical, exemplary **10** consummate **11** traditional **13** authoritative

classical architectural order
5 Doric, Ionic **10** Corinthian

classical musician
4 Böhm (Karl), Hess (Myra), Lind (Jenny), Muti (Riccardo), Pons (Lily), Shaw (Robert) **5** Arrau (Claudio), Biggs (E. Power), Borge (Victor), Boult (Adrian), Chang (Sarah), Davis (Colin), du Pré (Jacqueline), Gould (Glenn), Masur (Kurt), Mehta (Zubin), Melba (Nellie), Ozawa (Seiji), Patti (Adelina), Pinza (Ezio), Price (Leontyne), Ramey (Samuel), Sills (Beverly), Stern (Isaac), Szell (George) **6** Abbado (Claudio), Battle (Kathleen), Boulez (Pierre), Callas (Maria), Caruso (Enrico), Casals (Pablo), Galway (James), Levine (James), Maazel (Lorin), Midori, Norman (Jessye), Peters (Roberta), Previn (André), Rampal (Jean-Pierre), Rattle (Simon), Reiner (Fritz), Serkin (Peter, Rudolf), Terfel (Bryn), Tucker (Richard), Upshaw (Dawn), Walter (Bruno) **7** Bartoli (Cecilia), Beecham (Thomas), Bocelli (Andrea), Brendel (Alfred), Cliburn (Van), Corelli (Franco), Domingo (Plácido), Farrell (Eileen), Fiedler (Arthur), Fleming (Renée), Glennie (Evelyn), Haitink (Bernard), Heifetz (Jascha), Karajan (Herbert von), Menuhin (Yehudi), Nelsons (Andris), Nilsson (Birgit), Ormandy (Eugene), Perlman (Itzhak), Pollini (Maurizio), Sargent (Malcolm), Segovia (Andrés), Tebaldi (Renata) **8** Anderson (Marian), Argerich (Martha), Bergonzi (Carlo), Carreras (José), Flagstad (Kirsten), Horowitz (Vladimir), Kreisler (Fritz), Marriner (Neville), Netrebko (Anna), Oistrakh (David), Schnabel (Artur), Te Kanawa (Kiri), Zukerman (Pinchas) **9** Barenboim (Daniel), Bernstein (Leonard), Chaliapin (Feodor), Klemperer (Otto), Landowska (Wanda), Pavarotti (Luciano), Stokowski (Leopold), Toscanini (Arturo) **10** Rubinstein (Arthur), Sutherland (Joan), Tetrazzini (Luisa) **11** Furtwängler (Wilhelm), Kostelanetz (André), Schwarzkopf (Elisabeth) **12** Rostropovich (Mstislav)

classification
4 sort, type **5** genre, genus, grade, order **6** family, phylum, rating **7** sorting, species **8** category, division, grouping, ordering, taxonomy, typology **11** arrangement, cataloguing

classified
6 secret, sorted **7** divided, ordered **9** top secret **11** categorized **12** confidential

classified-ad abbreviation
3 ABS, AKC, APR, apt, brm, CDL, CPA, EDP, EOE, est, exc, exp, flr, FSH, FWD, gar, gdn, GWO, ISO, kit, LPN, lux, lwd, max, mgr, min, MLS, neg, OBO, opp, pkg, PWO, rec, ref, rep, sal, sep, sig, spd, TLC, wgn **4** appl, bldg, bdrm, bsmt, demo, flex, frpl, furn, HVAC, pass, pref, priv, prof, prop, temp, util, vacc, warr **5** specs (see also **real estate term**)

classify
4 rank, rate, sort **5** grade, group **6** assort **7** arrange **9** break down **10** categorize, pigeonhole

classy
4 chic, tony **5** swank **6** modish **7** dashing, elegant, refined, stylish **8** gracious, tasteful, wellbred **9** courteous **11** fashionable

clatter
4 to-do **6** clamor, hubbub, pother, racket, rattle, tumult, uproar **10** hurly-burly
Scottish: **7** brattle

clattery
5 noisy **7** rackety **10** clangorous

Claudia's husband
6 Pilate

Claudio's beloved
4 Hero

Claudius
nephew: **6** Hamlet
predecessor: **8** Caligula
slayer: **6** Hamlet **9** Agrippina
successor: **4** Nero
wife: **8** Gertrude **9** Agrippina

Clavell novel
6 Gai-Jin, Shogun, Tai-Pan **7** King Rat

claw
3 dig **4** nail, rake, tear **5** chela, talon, uncus **6** pincer, scrape, ungula **7** scratch

clay
3 cob **4** loam, lute, marl **5** argil, brick, earth, gault, loess, ocher, ochre **6** kaolin **10** terra-cotta
baked: **4** tile **5** adobe, brick
box: **6** saggar, sagger
brick: **5** adobe
building: **5** adobe
ceramic: **10** terra-cotta
constituent: **6** silica **8** feldspar, silicate **9** kaolinite

in glass: **4** tear
made of: **7** fictile
porcelain: **6** kaolin
red: **8** laterite
rock: **5** shale
tobacco pipe: **6** dudeen
watery mixture: **4** slip
white: **6** kaolin

clay pigeon
6 target

clean
4 dust, fair, pure, swab, tidy, wash, wipe **5** bathe, fresh, groom, purge, scour, scrub, sweep **6** bright, chaste, decent, neaten, purify, spruce, vacuum, washed **7** clarify, launder, sinless **8** hygienic, innocent, sanitary, sanitize, spotless, unsoiled **9** blameless, faultless, sparkling, stainless, undefiled, unsullied, untainted, wholesome **10** antiseptic, immaculate **11** unblemished **12** spick-and-span

clean-cut
4 trim **7** defined, precise **8** definite, explicit, specific **9** wholesome **10** definitive **11** categorical, unambiguous, well-groomed

cleaner
see **cleanser**

cleanhanded
8 innocent **9** blameless

clean-limbed
4 trim **7** shapely **8** handsome **10** statuesque

cleanse
4 lave, wash **5** purge, rinse **6** purify, refine **7** clarify, deterge, launder **8** lustrate, sanitize **9** disinfect, expurgate, sterilize

cleanser
3 lye **4** soap **9** detergent **10** antiseptic **12** disinfectant

cleansing
7 purging **8** ablution **9** catharsis, purgation **10** lustration **11** expurgation **12** purification

clear
3 bus **4** earn, fair, fine, pure **5** deice, erase, lucid, overt, plain, repay, solve, stark, sunny **6** acquit, limpid, secure, settle, simple, starry **7** absolve, audible, clarify, clarion, defined, evident, legible, obvious, precise **8** apparent, definite, distinct **9** authorize, cloudless, elucidate, exculpate, exonerate, liquidate, meliorate, unblurred, unclouded, vindicate **10** ameliorate, illuminate, see-through **11** disentangle, open-and-shut, perceptible, transparent, unambiguous, unequivocal **12** unmistakable

clearance
3 gap **4** sale **7** go-ahead, removal **8** approval **10** green light, permission **13** authorization

clear away
6 remove **7** take out

clear-cut
5 crisp, exact, plain **7** decided, precise **8** definite, distinct, explicit, manifest **10** definitive, pronounced, undisputed **11** categorical, indubitable, unambiguous, unequivocal **12** unquestioned

clear-eyed
6 astute **9** judicious, observant **10** discerning, perceptive

clearheaded
4 calm, cool **10** perceptive

clearing
3 gap **5** field, glade **7** opening **10** settlement

clear out
5 scoot, scram, split **6** beat it, begone, bug off, decamp, depart **7** buzz off, skiddoo, take off, vamoose **8** shove off **9** drive away, skedaddle **10** hightail it

clear-sightedness
6 acuity, acumen **8** sagacity **11** discernment, penetration, percipience **12** perspicacity

clear up
5 solve **6** cipher, unfold **7** clarify, dope out, explain, resolve, unravel **8** decipher **9** elucidate, figure out **10** illuminate

clearwing
4 moth

cleat
4 bitt **5** chock **6** batten **7** bollard, dolphin

cleavage
4 rift **5** chasm, cleft, split **6** schism **7** fissure **8** crevasse **9** splitting

cleave
3 cut, hew **4** chop, join, link, rend, rive **5** carve, cling, sever, slice, split, stick, unite **6** adhere, divide, sunder **7** combine **8** dissever, separate

cleft
3 gap **4** rift **5** chasm, chink, clove, crack, gorge, gulch, split **6** clough, ravine, schism **7** crevice, divided, fissure **8** cleavage

clemency
5 grace, mercy **6** lenity **7** caritas, charity **8** kindness, lenience, leniency, mildness **9** tolerance **10** compassion, gentleness, indulgence, sufferance, toleration **11** forbearance

clement
4 fair, kind, mild **5** balmy **6** benign, humane, kindly **7** lenient **8** merciful, tolerant **9** indulgent **10** benevolent, charitable, forbearing **13** compassionate

clench
4 grip, grit, hold **5** clamp, clasp, grasp **6** clutch **7** grapple

Cleopatra
attendant: **4** Iras **8** Charmian
brother: **7** Ptolemy
husband: **7** Ptolemy

killer: 3 asp
lover: 6 Antony (Marc), Caesar (Julius) 7 Anthony (Mark)
river: 4 Nile

Cleopatra's Needle
7 obelisk

clepsydra
9 timepiece 10 water clock

clerestory
7 gallery

clergy
7 canonry 8 ministry 9 churchmen, diaconate, pastorate, rabbinate 10 priesthood 11 cardinalate 13 ecclesiastics

clergyman
4 abbé 5 clerk, padre, vicar 6 bishop, cleric, curate, divine, father, parson, pastor, priest, rector 7 dominie, prelate 8 chaplain, clerical, minister, preacher, reverend, shepherd, sky pilot 9 churchman, pulpiteer 10 evangelist, missionary, sermonizer 12 ecclesiastic
American: 4 Hale (Edward Everett), King (Martin Luther, Thomas Starr) 5 Eliot (John), Moody (Dwight), Stone (Barton Warren), Swift (Jonathan), Weems (Parson) 6 Dwight (Timothy), Finney (Charles), Graham (Billy), Holmes (John Haynes), Hooker (Thomas), Mather (Cotton, Increase, Richard), Merton (Thomas), Parker (Samuel, Theodore), Sunday (Billy), Taylor (Edward, Graham, Nathaniel William) 7 Beecher (Henry Ward, Lyman), Edwards (Jonathan), Harvard (John), Russell (Charles Taze) 10 Muhlenberg (Frederick Augustus, Henry Melchior, John Peter Gabriel)
English: 4 Ward (Nathaniel, Seth, William George) 5 Donne (John), Paley (William), Smith (Henry "Silver-Tongued," John "The Sebaptist," Sidney) 6 Cotton (John), Fuller (Andrew, Thomas), Taylor (Jeremy, Rowland), Wesley (Charles, John) 7 Cranmer (Thomas), Parsons (Robert) 8 Kingsley (Charles) 10 Whitefield (George)
home: 5 manse 6 priory 7 rectory 8 vicarage 9 monastery, parsonage
traveling: 12 circuit rider

cleric
see **clergyman**

clerical vestment
3 alb 4 cope 8 chasuble, dalmatic

clerisy
8 literati 10 illuminati 13 intellectuals

clerk
7 cashier 8 salesman 9 secretary 10 accountant, bookkeeper 11 salesperson 12 stenographer

Cleveland
baseball team nickname: 5 Tribe
basketballers, for short: 4 Cavs

clever
3 apt, sly 4 able, deft, foxy, good, keen, wily 5 adept, alert, canny, funny, handy, quick, savvy, sharp, smart, witty 6 adroit, astute, brainy, bright, crafty, expert, shrewd, tricky 7 amusing, capable, cunning, knowing, skilled 8 fanciful, humorous, pleasing, skillful, talented 9 competent, dexterous, ingenious 10 proficient 11 intelligent, quick-witted, resourceful

cliché
3 saw 5 trope 6 truism 7 bromide 8 banality, buzzword, chestnut 9 platitude 10 shibboleth, stereotype 11 commonplace

clichéd
5 banal, bland, musty, stale, tired, trite, vapid 6 canned, old-hat 7 humdrum, insipid, worn-out 8 bromidic, shopworn, timeworn 9 hackneyed, moth-eaten 10 pedestrian, unoriginal 11 stereotyped 13 platitudinous, unimaginative

click
3 fit, tsk 4 snap, tick, work 5 agree, match 6 go over, pan out 7 come off, succeed

client
6 patron 7 patient, protégé 8 customer 9 dependent

clientele
4 fans 5 trade, train 6 custom, market, public 7 patrons, traffic 8 audience, patients, regulars, shoppers 9 customers 10 purchasers, supporters 12 constituency

cliff
4 crag, pali 5 bluff, scarp 8 headland, palisade 9 precipice 10 escarpment

Clifford of drama
5 Odets

climacteric
4 apex, crux, cusp 5 acute 6 crisis 7 crucial 8 critical 9 menopause 11 culmination 12 change of life, turning point

climactic
4 peak 7 crucial, pivotal 8 critical, decisive, dramatic 9 momentous 10 definitive 11 culminating, determining

climate
6 medium, milieu 7 ambient 8 ambience 10 atmosphere 11 environment 12 surroundings

climax
3 cap 4 acme, apex, peak 5 crown 6 apogee, summit, top off 8 capstone, meridian, pinnacle 9 culminate 11 culmination

climb
4 go up, rise, soar 5 mount, scale, slope 6 ascend, ascent, shinny 7 clamber 8 escalate, increase

climbing
8 scandent

climbing device
3 cam, nut **5** biner, cinch, piton **7** crampon **9** carabiner

clinch
3 hug, ice **4** grip, hold, nail, seal **5** clamp, clasp, grasp, sew up **6** decide, ensure, lock up, settle **7** confirm, embrace, grapple, squeeze **8** nail down

clincher
4 tire **5** proof **6** capper, kicker **7** crusher, quietus **9** deathblow **10** smoking gun **11** affirmation, coup de grâce **12** confirmation **13** corroboration

cling
4 bond **5** stick **6** adhere, cleave, clutch, hold on, linger **8** adhesion **9** adherence

clingstone
5 peach

clink
3 can, jug, pen **4** brig, cell, coop, jail, stir **5** pokey, pound **6** cooler, jingle, lockup, prison, tingle, tinkle **7** slammer **8** hoosegow **9** calaboose

clinker
3 dud **4** bomb, bust, flop, goof, slag **5** botch, brick, error, lemon, loser **6** bummer, bungle, fiasco, fizzle, howler, turkey **7** bloomer, blunder, failure, faux pas, mistake

clinkers
3 ash **4** slag **5** ashes **7** cinders

clinquant
5 gaudy, showy **6** flashy, garish, glitzy, tawdry, tinsel **8** specious **10** glittering

Clio
see **Muse**

clip
3 bob, cut, mow, pin **4** crop, hasp, pare, snip, sock, trim **5** block, clasp, prune, punch, shave, shear, slash **6** broach, brooch, fleece, reduce **7** curtail, cut back, cut down, shorten **8** magazine, truncate **10** abbreviate, overcharge

clipped
3 cut, hit **4** curt, taut **5** brief, crisp, shorn, short, terse **6** abrupt, cut off, docked, pruned **7** blocked, clasped, cropped, trimmed **8** cut short, fastened **9** curtailed, shortened, truncated

clique
3 set **4** camp, clan, club, gang, ring **5** cabal, crowd, mafia **6** circle **7** coterie, enclave, faction, in-group **9** camarilla

cloak
4 cape, hide, mask, robe, veil, wrap **5** cover, guise, talma **6** domino, facade, joseph, mantle, poncho, screen, shroud, veneer **7** blanket, conceal, curtain, dress up, manteau, obscure **8** disguise **9** dissemble, semblance **10** camouflage **11** dissimulate
ancient Greek: **7** chlamys
ancient Roman: **7** pallium
Arab: **3** aba
fur: **7** pelisse
hooded: **6** capote **7** burnous **8** burnoose
liturgical: **4** cope
Moroccan: **8** djellaba
over armor: **6** tabard **7** surcoat
Spanish: **5** manta

clobber
4 belt, drub, flay, lick, slam, slug, sock, whip, whup **5** blast, brain, clout, cream, pound, smash **6** hammer, thrash, wallop **7** lambast, shellac, trounce **8** demolish, lambaste

clochard
3 bum, vag **4** hobo **5** tramp **6** beggar, canter **7** drifter, floater, moocher, vagrant **8** deadbeat, derelict, vagabond **9** transient **10** freeloader, panhandler **11** bindle stiff

cloche
3 hat **5** cover, toque, tuque

clock
4 time **9** timepiece **11** chronometer
water: **9** clepsydra

clocklike
5 exact **6** minute, prompt, strict, timely **7** precise, regular **8** accurate, punctual, reliable, thorough **10** dependable, meticulous, scrupulous

clockmaker
10 horologist

clockwise
6 deasil **7** dextral **11** right-handed

Clockwork Orange author
7 Burgess (Anthony)

clod
3 gob, oaf, wad **4** boob, dolt, dope, hunk, lout, lump, soil **5** chump, chunk, clump, dummy, dunce, earth **6** dimwit **8** dumbbell **9** blockhead, lamebrain

cloddish
7 boorish, ill-bred, loutish, uncouth **8** churlish, clownish **9** unrefined **10** uncultured, unpolished **11** uncivilized

clodhopper
3 oaf **4** boor, boot, hick, lout **5** chuff, churl, clown, yokel **6** rustic **7** bumpkin, hayseed, redneck **9** chawbacon

clog
3 gum, jam, tax **4** fill, glut, load, plug, stop **5** block, choke, close, sabot, stuff **6** hamper, hinder **7** congest **8** encumber, obstruct, overload **10** impediment **11** encumbrance

cloisonné
6 enamel

cloister
5 abbey, court **6** arcade, garden **7** convent, retreat, seclude, shelter **9** courtyard, monastery, sequester

Cloister and the Hearth author
5 Reade (Charles)

cloistered
7 recluse **8** confined, hermetic, secluded **9** seclusive, withdrawn **11** sequestered

cloistered one
3 nun **4** monk

clone
4 copy **5** ditto **6** double, carbon **7** replica **9** duplicate, facsimile, replicate, reproduce **10** carbon copy, simulacrum **12** reproduction

Clorinda
beloved: **7** Tancred
father: **6** Senapo
guardian: **6** Arsete
slayer: **7** Tancred

close
3 end **4** near, nigh, shut, slam **5** block, cease, choke, humid, muggy, tight **6** ending, finale, finish, narrow, nearby, stuffy, sultry, windup, wrap up **7** airless, compact, crowded, stopper **8** adjacent, complete, conclude, finalize, intimate, obstruct, stifling **9** adjoining, cessation, condensed, terminate **10** conclusion, consummate, convenient, near-at-hand **11** constricted, neighboring, termination **12** confidential

closed-minded
4 deaf **6** narrow **8** obdurate **9** hidebound, obstinate, pigheaded, unbending **10** bullheaded, hardheaded **11** intractable

closefisted
5 cheap, mingy **6** frugal, stingy **7** miserly, thrifty **9** niggardly, penurious **13** penny-pinching

close in
3 hem **4** cage **5** fence, hedge **6** corral, immure **7** advance, confine, enclose, envelop, impound **8** approach, converge, encircle, enshroud, imprison, surround

close-knit
8 intimate

close match
6 toss-up

closemouthed
3 mum **4** mute **6** silent **7** laconic **8** reserved, reticent, taciturn

closeness
8 intimacy

close off
4 clog, plug **5** block **6** stop up **7** isolate, occlude **8** insulate **9** segregate, sequester

closet
6 covert, inside, office, secret **7** cabinet, chamber, furtive, private **8** wardrobe

closing
3 end **4** coda, last, stop **5** final **6** finish, latest, period, windup, wrap-up **7** curtain **8** eventual, terminal, ultimate **9** cessation **11** termination

closure
3 cap, end, lid **6** ending, finish **8** fastener **9** cessation

clot
3 gel, set **4** curd, glob, jell, lump **5** clump **6** curdle, gelate **7** congeal **8** coagulum, thrombus **9** coagulate **10** gelatinize
combining form: **6** thromb **7** thrombo

cloth
see **fabric**

clothe
3 tog **4** deck, do up, garb, robe **5** array, cloak, couch, drape, dress, endow, endue, equip **6** attire, bedeck, outfit, swathe **7** apparel, costume, dress up **8** accouter

clothes
3 rig **4** duds, garb, rags, togs **5** array, dress, getup, habit **6** attire, outfit, things **7** apparel, costume, raiment, rigging, threads, toggery, vesture **8** garments, glad rags **9** vestments **11** habiliments
basket: **6** hamper
civilian: **5** mufti

clothes-moth genus
5 Tinea

clothespress
7 armoire **8** wardrobe

cloud
3 dim, fog, tar **4** blur, haze, mist, murk **5** addle, befog, brume, gloom, muddy, plume, smear, sully, taint **6** muddle, nebula, puzzle, shadow, smudge **7** besmear, confuse, obscure, perplex, tarnish **8** befuddle, besmirch, discolor, distract, overcast **9** obfuscate
type: **4** nine **5** cirri (plural), nimbi (plural) **6** cirrus, cumuli (plural), nimbus, strati (plural) **7** cumulus, stratus **11** altocumulus, altostratus **12** cirrocumulus, cirrostratus, cumulonimbus, interstellar, nimbostratus **13** stratocumulus

cloudburst
6 deluge, shower **7** monsoon, torrent **8** downpour, drencher, rainfall **10** outpouring

clouded
5 dusky, murky, shady **6** dreary, gloomy, somber, sombre **7** dubious, ominous, sunless, unclear **8** doubtful, overcast **9** ambiguous, equivocal, uncertain, unsettled **11** problematic

cloudless
4 fair, fine 5 clear, sunny 7 clarion 8 pleasant, sunshiny
cloud-like mass
6 nebula
cloud nine
5 bliss 6 heaven 7 ecstasy, elation, nirvana, rapture 8 euphoria
cloudy
4 dull, hazy 5 dusky, foggy, heavy, misty, murky, roily, vague 6 gloomy, opaque, somber, sombre 7 louring, obscure, tainted, unclear 8 confused, darkened, lowering, nebulous, overcast, vaporous 10 indistinct
clout
3 box, hit, rag 4 blow, cuff, poke, pull, slam, slap, slug, sock, swat, sway 5 paste, power, punch, smack, smite, whack 6 strike 9 influence
clove
4 bulb 5 spice 7 chopped, severed
clove hitch
4 knot
clover
5 lotus 6 alsike, ladino, lucern 7 alfalfa, berseem, lucerne, melilot, trefoil 8 four-leaf, shamrock 9 lespedeza
family: 3 pea
genus: 9 Trifolium
clown
3 wag 4 bozo, mime, zany 5 cutup, joker, Punch 6 jester 7 buffoon 8 comedian, jokester 9 harlequin, prankster 11 merry-andrew
French: 7 Pierrot
operatic: 5 buffo
Spanish: 8 gracioso
clownish
4 rude 6 clumsy, gauche 7 awkward, ill-bred, uncouth 9 unrefined
cloy
4 fill, glut, jade, pall, sate 5 gorge 6 sicken 7 satiate, surfeit 8 overfill
cloying
4 icky 5 gushy, mushy, sappy, soppy 6 sticky, sugary 7 fulsome, gushing, maudlin, mawkish, treacly 9 excessive, schmaltzy, sickening 10 disgusting, lovey-dovey, nauseating, saccharine 11 sentimental
club
3 bat, sap 4 beat, cosh, frat, iron, mace 5 baton, billy, guild, lodge, order, union 6 cudgel, league 7 society 8 bludgeon, sodality, sorority 9 blackjack, truncheon 10 fellowship, fraternity, knobkerrie, nightstick 11 association, brotherhood
Australian: 5 waddy
Irish: 10 shillelagh
Maori: 4 patu
singing: 4 glee
clubfoot
7 talipes
cluck
4 dodo, dolt, dope, fool 5 dunce 6 dimwit, nitwit 7 pinhead
clue
3 cue 4 hint, idea, lead, sign, tell, warn 6 advise, inform, notify, notion, tip-off 7 inkling 8 evidence, telltale 10 indication, intimation, suggestion
Clue character
4 Plum (Prof.) 5 Green (Mr., Rev.), White (Mrs.) 7 Mustard (Col.), Peacock (Mrs.), Scarlet (Miss)
clueless
4 a-sea, lost 5 at sea 10 out to lunch
clump
3 gob, wad 4 clod, hunk, lump, mass, mess, plod 5 batch, bunch, chunk, group, stomp, tramp 6 bumble, bundle, lumber, parcel 7 cluster, galumph, stumble
of grass: 4 tuft 6 tuffet 7 tussock
clumsy
5 bulky, gawky, inept, splay 6 clunky, gauche, klutzy, oafish, wooden 7 awkward, hulking, lumpish, uncouth, unhandy 8 bumbling, bungling, tactless, ungainly, unsubtle, unwieldy 9 all thumbs, graceless, ham-handed, inelegant, lumbering, maladroit 11 heavy-handed, inefficient
person: 3 oaf 4 clod, goon, lout, slob 5 klutz 6 baboon, galoot, lummox 7 bumpkin, bungler, palooka 13 butterfingers
clunk
4 thud 5 clout, thump, whack 6 thwack, wallop
clunker
3 car 4 bomb, heap 5 crate, lemon, wreck 6 beater, jalopy, junker 7 hooptie, stinker 10 rattletrap, rust bucket
clunky
7 awkward 8 ungainly 9 graceless
cluster
3 lot, set 4 band, bevy, crew, knot, pack 5 array, batch, bunch, clump, covey, group 6 bundle, clutch, gather 7 collect, package 8 assemble, assembly 9 aggregate 10 accumulate
cluster bean
4 guar
clutch
4 grab, grip, hold, keep 5 catch, clamp, clasp, grasp, pinch, seize 6 bundle, clench, clinch, snatch 7 cluster, grapple
clutter
4 hash, mash, mess, muss, ruck 5 chaos, snarl, strew 6 jumble, litter, muddle 7 mélange, rummage 8 disarray, disorder, mishmash, shambles 9 confusion 10 hodgepodge, hotchpotch
Clydesdale
5 horse 10 draft horse

Clymene
father: **7** Oceanus
husband: **7** Iapetus
mother: **6** Tethys
son: **5** Atlas **10** Epimetheus, Prometheus

Clytemnestra
brother: **6** Castor, Pollux **10** Polydeuces
daughter: **7** Electra **9** Iphigenia
father: **9** Tyndareus
husband: **9** Agamemnon
lover: **9** Aegisthus
mother: **4** Leda
slayer: **7** Orestes
son: **7** Orestes
victim: **9** Agamemnon, Cassandra

Clytie
beloved: **6** Apollo
form: **9** sunflower **10** heliotrope

coach
3 bus, car, pro **5** drill, stage, train, tutor **6** chaise, mentor **7** prepare, trainer **8** carriage, instruct **10** instructor

coach Parseghian
3 Ara

coadjutor
3 aid **4** aide **6** bishop, deputy **9** assistant **10** aide-de-camp, lieutenant

coagulate
3 gel, set **4** clot, jell **6** curdle **7** congeal, jellify, thicken **8** coalesce, condense, solidify **10** gelatinize, inspissate

coal
carrier: **3** hod **7** scuttle
distillate: **3** tar
dust: **4** culm, smut, soot **5** slack
element: **6** carbon
fused leavings: **4** slag **7** clinker
glowing: **5** ember, gleed
hard: **10** anthracite
lump: **3** cob
miner: **7** collier
region: **4** Saar
residue: **4** coke
soft: **6** cannel **10** bituminous

coalesce
3 mix **4** fuse, join, link **5** blend, merge, unite **6** mingle **7** combine, conjoin **10** amalgamate

coalition
4 bloc, ring **5** party, union **6** fusion, league, merger **7** combine, melding, merging **8** alliance **9** anschluss **10** federation **11** affiliation, association, combination, confederacy, integration, unification **13** confederation, consolidation

coarse
3 raw **4** rude **5** bawdy, crass, crude, dirty, gross, harsh, rough, tacky **6** common, filthy, grainy, ribald, smutty, vulgar **7** boorish, obscene, raffish, raunchy, uncouth **8** granular, indecent **9** inelegant, roughneck, unrefined **10** uncultured **11** particulate **12** uncultivated

coast
4 bank **5** beach, drift, shore, slide **6** strand **7** seaside **8** littoral, seashore **9** freewheel
of Antarctica: **4** Knox

coastal
7 seaside **8** littoral
inlet: **3** ria **5** firth, fjord **7** estuary

coaster
4 sled, tray **6** trader **8** toboggan

coat
5 crust, glaze, gloss, layer, parka, plate, tunic **6** blazer, duster, finish, jacket, patina, raglan, reefer, ulster, veneer **7** cutaway **8** covering, mackinaw, tegument **9** newmarket, redingote **10** integument, mackintosh **11** windbreaker **12** Prince Albert
animal: **3** fur **4** hide, pelt, wool **6** pelage
fur-lined: **7** pelisse
kind: **3** pea, top **5** frock **6** trench
Levantine: **6** caftan
of arms: **5** crest **6** blazon, emblem, shield, tabard **8** blazonry **10** escutcheon
of egg white: **5** glair **6** glaire
of mail: **7** hauberk
soldier's: **5** frock, tunic **6** capote
waterproof: **3** mac **4** mack **7** slicker **10** mackintosh

coating
4 film, leaf, scum, skin **5** glaze, gloss, layer **6** finish, patina, veneer **7** dusting, lacquer, overlay, surface, varnish **8** covering
winter: **3** ice **4** snow **5** sleet

coat rack part
3 leg, peg **4** base, hook **5** stand **6** hanger

coax
4 lure, urge **5** cable, press, tempt **6** cajole, entice, induce **7** blarney, wheedle **8** blandish, butter up, inveigle, persuade, soft-soap **9** importune, sweet-talk

cob
3 ear **4** swan **5** adobe, horse

cobble
4 mend **5** patch, stone **6** repair **11** paving stone

cobbler
3 pie **5** drink **8** cocktail **9** shoemaker
form: **4** last
tool: **3** awl

cobelligerent
4 ally

cobweb
3 net **4** mesh, trap **8** gossamer **9** confusion, spiderweb **12** entanglement

coccyx
8 tailbone

cochineal
3 dye **6** insect

cock
3 tap **4** boss, head, heap, hill, lord, mass, pile, rick, tilt **5** chief, mound, stack, strut, valve **6** faucet, honcho, leader, master, spigot **7** headman, hydrant, rooster, swagger **11** chanticleer

cock-a-hoop
4 awry **5** askew **7** askance, crooked **8** boastful, exultant, exulting, jubilant **9** triumphal

Cockaigne
6 utopia **7** arcadia **9** Shangri-la **10** wonderland

cockalorum
7 bluster, bombast, bravado **8** blowhard, boasting, braggart, leapfrog **11** braggadocio

cockamamy
5 batty, crazy, daffy, flaky, kooky, loony, nutty, wacky **6** absurd **9** ludicrous **10** incredible, ridiculous **11** harebrained

cock-and-bull story
5 crock **6** canard **7** whopper **9** fairy tale

cockcrow
4 dawn, morn **5** sunup **7** morning, sunrise **8** daybreak, daylight

cocker
4 baby **5** humor, spoil **6** coddle, cosset, pamper **7** indulge, spaniel **11** mollycoddle

cockeyed
4 awry **5** askew **6** aslant **8** lopsided **11** harebrained

cockle
5 shell **6** dimple, furrow, groove, pucker, ripple **7** bivalve, mollusc, mollusk, wrinkle

cockleshell
4 boat

cockscomb
see **coxcomb**

cocksure
5 brash **6** cheeky **9** bumptious **13** overconfident

cocktail
3 kir **5** Bronx, cosmo, drink, G and T, julep **6** Gibson, gimlet, mai tai, mimosa, mojito, Rob Roy, zombie **7** gin fizz, martini, sidecar, stinger **8** aperitif, daiquiri, highball, pink lady, salty dog, sombrero **9** Cuba libre, manhattan, margarita, mint julep, pisco sour, rusty nail **10** Bloody Mary, caipirinha, piña colada, Tom Collins, wallbanger **11** grasshopper, screwdriver, whiskey sour **12** Black Russian, cosmopolitan, old-fashioned
fruit: 9 macedoine
gasoline: 7 Molotov

Cocktail Party author
5 Eliot (T. S.)

cocky
4 bold, sure **5** brash, nervy, pushy, sassy, saucy **6** brassy, cheeky, jaunty **8** arrogant, impudent, insolent **9** bumptious, conceited **10** swaggering **11** self-assured **12** enterprising **13** overconfident, self-confident

coconspirator
7 abettor **9** accessory **10** accomplice **11** confederate

coconut
husk fiber: 4 coir
meat: 5 copra

coda
5 envoi, envoy **6** ending, finale **7** summary **8** epilogue, follow-up **9** afterword **10** conclusion

coddle
4 baby **5** humor, spoil **6** cosset, pamper **7** cater to, indulge

code
6 cipher, symbol **7** encrypt **8** encipher
kind: 3 PIN, zip **4** area **5** Morse, legal, penal
message in: 10 cryptogram **11** cryptograph

code word
see **communications code word**

codger
4 coot, fogy **5** crank, fogey **6** duffer, fellow, fossil, geezer **7** old coot, old fogy **8** old fogey

codicil
5 rider **8** addendum, addition, appendix **10** attachment, postscript, supplement

codswallop
see **nonsense**

coefficient
6 factor **7** measure **8** constant

coelenterate
5 coral **7** anemone, hydroid **9** cnidarian, jellyfish **10** sea anemone

coerce
3 cow **5** bully, force, impel, press **6** compel, menace, oblige **8** browbeat, bulldoze, dominate, pressure, threaten **9** blackjack, constrain, strong-arm, terrorize **10** intimidate

coercion
5 force **6** duress, menace, threat **8** pressure **10** compulsion, constraint

Coetzee novel
8 Disgrace

Coeur d'___
5 Alene

coeval
see **contemporary**

coexistent
see **contemporary**

coffee
3 joe, mud **4** java **6** jamoke

alkaloid: **8** caffeine
bean: **3** nib
cake: **6** kuchen
cup: **9** demitasse
dispenser: **3** urn
drink: **5** latte, mocha **9** macchiato **10** café au lait, cappuccino
French: **4** café
grinder: **4** mill
kind: **4** drip **5** decaf **7** arabica, instant **8** espresso **9** Americano **10** café au lait, cappuccino
maker: **10** percolator

coffee shop
4 café **5** diner **8** snack bar **9** cafeteria, hash house, lunchroom **11** greasy spoon **12** luncheonette

coffer
5 chest **6** casket **8** treasury **9** exchequer, strongbox

coffin
3 box **4** kist **6** casket
carrier: **6** hearse **10** pallbearer
cover: **4** pall
nail: **9** cigarette
stand: **4** bier **10** catafalque

cog
4 gear **5** tooth

cogency
5 force, point, power, punch **7** potency **8** strength, validity **9** relevance **10** conviction, pertinence **13** effectiveness

cogent
5 solid, sound, valid **6** potent **7** telling, weighty **8** forceful, powerful, relevant **9** pertinent **10** compelling, convincing, meaningful, persuasive **11** influential, well-founded **12** well-grounded

cogitate
4 muse **5** think **6** ponder, reason **7** reflect **8** conceive, consider, meditate, mull over, ruminate **9** cerebrate, speculate **10** deliberate

cogitation
7 thought **10** meditation, reflection, rumination **11** cerebration, speculation **12** deliberation **13** consideration

cogitative
7 pensive **10** meditative, reflective, ruminative, thoughtful **11** speculative **13** contemplative

Cogito ___ sum
4 ergo

cognac
6 brandy
relative: **5** pisco **6** grappa **8** armagnac

cognate
4 akin, like **5** alike **6** allied, common **7** kindred, related, similar **8** parallel **10** affiliated, associated

cognition
9 awareness, knowledge, sentience **10** perception

cognizance
4 heed, note **6** notice **9** attention, awareness, knowledge **12** jurisdiction

cognizant
5 aware **7** knowing, mindful **8** informed, sensible **9** conscious **13** knowledgeable

cognize
4 know **5** grasp **6** fathom **7** realize **8** perceive **9** apprehend **10** appreciate, comprehend, understand

cognomen
4 name **5** alias, title **7** epithet, moniker, surname **8** nickname **11** appellation, appellative

cognoscente
5 judge **6** expert **7** epicure **8** aesthete **9** authority **10** specialist **11** connoisseur

cognoscible
8 knowable **10** fathomable **13** apprehensible

cogwheel
4 gear

cohere
4 fuse, join **5** agree, blend, cling, merge, stick, unite **6** accord **7** combine, comport, conform, connect **8** coalesce, dovetail

coherence
4 bond **5** union, unity **8** adhesion, cohesion **9** agreement, congruity, integrity **10** conformity, conneotion, consonance, solidarlty **11** Integration

coherent
5 sound **7** logical, ordered, unified **8** rational **10** consistent, integrated, meaningful **11** coordinated

cohesion
see **coherence**

coho
6 salmon **12** silver salmon

cohort
3 pal **4** ally, band, chum, crew, gang, mate **5** buddy, crony, group **6** clique, fellow, friend **7** comrade, partner **8** adherent, confrere, disciple, follower, henchman, sidekick **9** assistant, associate, colleague, companion, supporter **10** accomplice **11** demographic **12** collaborator

coif
3 cap, cut **4** hood, perm **6** hairdo **7** haircut **8** skullcap

coiffeur
6 barber **10** haircutter **11** hairdresser, hairstylist

coiffure
6 hairdo
aid: **3** net, rat **5** snood

coil
4 curl, loop, ring, turn, wind **5** helix, twine, twist **6** rotate, spiral **7** entwine, revolve, wreathe **8** curlicue **9** corkscrew

coiled
6 spiral, volute **7** helical, voluted, whorled **9** circinate

coin
4 mint **6** invent, make up, strike
Afghanistan: **3** pul **7** afghani
Albania: **3** lek **9** quindarka
Algeria: **5** dinar **7** centime
ancient Greek: **4** obol
ancient Muslim: **5** dinar
ancient Roman: **8** denarius
Argentina: **4** peso **7** centavo
Austria: **4** euro **8** groschen **9** schilling
Bahrain: **4** fils **5** dinar
Belgium: **4** euro **5** franc **7** centime
Benin: **5** franc **7** centime
Bhutan: **7** chetrum **8** ngultrum
Bolivia: **7** centavo **9** boliviano
Botswana: **4** pula **5** thebe
Brazil: **4** real **7** centavo **8** cruzeiro
Bulgaria: **3** lev **8** stotinka
Burma: **4** kyat
Burundi: **5** franc **7** centime
Cameroon: **5** franc **7** centime
Canada: **6** loonie, toonie, twonie
Cape Verde Islands: **6** escudo **7** centavo
Chile: **4** peso **7** centavo
China: **3** fen **4** jiao, yuan
Colombia: **4** peso **7** centavo
Costa Rica: **5** colón **7** centimo
Cuba: **4** peso **7** centavo
Czech Republic: **5** haler **6** koruna
defective: **4** fido
Denmark: **3** ore **5** krone
Dominican Republic: **4** peso **7** centavo
Ecuador: **5** sucre **7** centavo
edge: **7** milling
Egypt: **7** piastre
European gold: **5** ducat
Finland: **4** euro **5** penni **6** markka
former: **3** ecu, mil, pie, sol, sou **4** anna, besa, doit, duit, fels, kran, para, pice, reis (plural) **5** fanam, litas, mohur, paisa, rupia, shahi, soldo, taler, toman **6** besant, centas, denier, heller, macuta, pagoda, tangka **7** santims, sapeque **8** maravedi, skilling **9** rigsdaler **10** Indian head, reichsmark **13** reichspfennig
France: **3** ecu, sou **4** euro **5** franc **7** centime
Gambia: **5** butut **6** dalasi
Germany: **4** euro, mark **7** pfennig
Ghana: **4** cedi **6** pesewa
Great Britain: **3** bob **4** quid **5** crown, penny, pound **6** guinea **7** ha'penny **8** farthing, shilling, sixpence **9** halfpenny, sovereign **10** threepence
Greece: **4** euro **6** lepton **7** drachma
Guatemala: **7** centavo, quetzal
Guinea-Bissau: **4** peso
Guyana: **3** bit
Haiti: **6** gourde **7** centime
Honduras: **7** centavo, lempira
Hungary: **5** pengo **6** filler, forint
Iceland: **5** aurar (plural), eyrir, krona
India: **3** pie **4** anna **5** paisa, rupee
Indonesia: **3** sen **6** rupiah
Iran: **4** rial **5** dinar
Iraq: **4** fils **5** dinar
Ireland: **4** euro **5** penny **8** farthing
Israel: **5** agora **6** shekel
Italy: **4** euro, lira **5** scudo
Japan: **3** rin, sen, yen
Jordan: **4** fils **5** dinar
Kenya: **8** shilling
Korea, North and South: **3** won **4** chon
Kuwait: **4** fils **5** dinar
large: **9** cartwheel
Lebanon: **5** livre **7** piastre
Lesotho: **4** loti **7** licente, lisente
Libya: **5** dinar **6** dirham
Luxembourg: **4** euro **5** franc
Macao: **3** avo
Madagascar: **5** franc
Malawi: **6** kwacha **7** tambala
Mauritania: **5** khoum **7** ouguiya
Mauritius: **5** rupee
Mexico: **4** peso **7** centavo
Moldova: **3** leu
Monaco: **4** euro **5** franc
Morocco: **6** dirham
Mozambique: **7** metical
Nepal: **5** paisa, rupee
Netherlands: **4** euro **6** florin, gulden **7** guilder
Nicaragua: **7** centavo, córdoba
Nigeria: **4** kobo **5** naira
Norway: **3** ore **5** krone
Oman: **4** rial **5** baiza
Pakistan: **4** anna **5** paisa, rupee
Palestine: **3** mil
Panama: **6** balboa **9** centesimo
Papua New Guinea: **4** kina, toea
Paraguay: **7** centimo, guarani
Peru: **3** sol **7** centimo
Philippines: **4** peso, piso **7** sentimo
Poland: **5** grosz, zloty
Portugal: **4** euro **6** escudo **7** centavo
Qatar: **5** riyal **6** dirham
Roman: **6** aureus, bezant **7** solidus
Romania: **3** ban, leu
Russia: **5** kopek, ruble **6** kopeck
Samoa: **4** sene, tala
San Marino: **4** lira
Saudi Arabia: **4** rial **6** halala
Scandinavia: **3** ore
Seychelles: **5** rupee

Siam: 3 att
side of a: 7 obverse
Slovakia: 5 haler 6 koruna
South Africa: 4 rand 10 Krugerrand
Spain: 4 euro 6 peseta 7 centimo
Sri Lanka: 5 rupee
stamping metal: 8 planchet
Suriname: 6 florin, gulden 7 guilder
Swaziland: 9 lilangeni
Sweden: 3 ore 5 krona 8 skilling
Switzerland: 5 franc 6 rappen
Syria: 7 piastre
Tanzania: 8 shilling
Thailand: 4 baht 5 tical 6 satang
Timor: 3 avo
Tonga: 6 pa'anga, seniti
Tunisia: 5 dinar
Turkey: 4 lira, para 5 kurus
Uganda: 8 shilling
United Arab Emirates: 6 dirham
United Kingdom: see **Great Britain**
United States: 4 dime 5 penny 6 dollar, nickel 7 quarter 10 half-dollar
Uruguay: 4 peso 9 centesimo
Vatican City: 4 lira
Venezuela: 7 bolivar
Virgin Islands: 3 bit
Zambia: 5 ngwee 6 kwacha

coinage
7 new word 8 creation, currency 9 invention, neologism 10 brainchild 11 contrivance

coincide
4 jibe 5 agree, equal, match, tally 6 accord, concur, square 7 comport, conform 8 dovetail 9 harmonize 10 correspond

coincident
7 similar 9 consonant 10 concurrent 11 concomitant, synchronous 12 accompanying, contemporary, simultaneous

coincidentally
8 by chance, together 12 accidentally, concurrently, fortuitously

coin-shaped
8 nummular

col
3 gap 4 pass 5 ridge 6 saddle

___ colada
4 piña

colander's cousin
5 sieve 6 sifter 8 strainer

cold
3 icy, raw 4 cool, dead, iced 5 aloof, chill, crisp, frore, gelid, nippy, polar 6 arctic, biting, chilly, frigid, frosty, frozen, wintry 7 bracing, glacial, shivery 8 chilling, comatose, freezing, lifeless 11 emotionless, passionless, unconscious, unemotional 12 unresponsive
combining form: 4 cryo, kryo
common: 6 coryza
symptom: 5 cough, fever 6 sneeze 7 catarrh

cold ___
3 war 4 call, cash, cuts, feet, fish, sore, wave 5 cream, frame, front, patch, steel, sweat, water 6 turkey 7 comfort, storage 8 shoulder

cold-blooded
5 cruel 6 brutal 7 callous 8 hardened, obdurate, pitiless, ruthless 9 heartless, impassive, unfeeling 10 hard-boiled, impersonal 11 ectothermic, emotionless, hard-hearted 12 stonyhearted 13 dispassionate

coldcock
4 deck, kayo 5 floor 8 knock out

cold feet
4 fear 5 alarm, doubt, dread, panic, worry 6 dismay, fright, terror 7 anxiety, jitters 8 timidity 9 cowardice 11 trepidation

coldhearted
see **cold-blooded**

cold-shoulder
3 cut 4 snub 6 ignore, slight 9 ostracize

cold storage
8 abeyance, dormancy 10 quiescence, suspension 12 intermission

Cold War weapon
4 ICBM

cole
4 kale, rape 7 cabbage 8 brassica, broccoli, kohlrabi 11 cauliflower

Coleridge poem
9 Dejection, Kubla Khan 10 Christabel

Colette character
4 Gigi 5 Chéri 8 Claudine

colewort
4 kale 7 cabbage

colic
5 gripe 9 bellyache 11 stomachache 12 collywobbles

coliseum
4 bowl 5 arena, stade 6 circus 7 stadium

collaborate
6 team up 7 collude 8 conspire 9 cooperate

collaborator
4 ally 6 helper 7 abettor, partner, traitor 8 coworker, henchman, quisling 9 accessory, assistant, associate, auxiliary, colleague 10 accomplice 11 confederate, conspirator

collapse
4 cave, drop, fail, ruin 5 break, crash, plotz, smash, wreck 6 buckle, cave in, fold up 7 breakup, crack-up, crumple, debacle, deflate, failure, founder, give out, give way, pass out, shatter, smashup, succumb 8 condense,

downfall **9** breakdown, cataclysm, fall apart, ruination **10** disruption **11** catastrophe, destruction, prostration **12** disintegrate

collar
3 bag, nab **4** grab, hook, nail, take **5** catch, seize **6** arrest, secure **7** capture **9** apprehend
armor: 6 gorget
boy's: 4 Eton
chain: 4 torc **6** torque
jeweled: 8 carcanet
lace-edged: 6 rebato
metal: 4 torc **6** torque
pleated: 4 ruff

collarbone
8 clavicle

collate
5 group, order **7** arrange, collect, compare, compile **8** assemble, organize **9** integrate

collateral
4 bond **6** allied, lineal, pledge, surety **7** cognate, kindred, oblique, related, subject **8** indirect, parallel, security **9** accessory, ancillary, attendant, auxiliary, dependent, secondary, tributary **10** coincident, coordinate, reciprocal, subsidiary **11** concomitant **12** accompanying, confirmatory, contributory **13** complementary, corresponding, corroborative

colleague
4 aide **6** cohort, fellow, helper **7** partner **8** confrere, coworker, teammate **9** assistant, associate, companion **10** compatriot **11** confederate **12** collaborator

collect
4 draw **5** amass, glean, group, infer, raise **6** deduce, derive, gather, muster, prayer **7** build up, compile, compose, convene, dispose, marshal, round up **8** assemble, converge **10** accumulate, congregate

collected
4 calm, cool **5** quiet, still **6** poised, serene **7** assured **8** complete, composed, sanguine, tranquil **9** assembled, confident, unruffled **11** unflappable **13** imperturbable, self-possessed

collection
3 ana, kit, lot **4** band, bevy, crew, olio, ruck **5** bunch, cento, crowd, hoard, trove **6** medley, muster **7** cluster, variety **8** assembly, caboodle **9** aggregate, anthology, congeries, gathering, stockpile **10** assemblage, assortment, cumulation, miscellany **11** aggregation **12** accumulation, congregation **13** agglomeration
miscellaneous: 4 hash, olio **6** jumble, medley **7** mélange, mixture **8** mishmash, pastiche **9** potpourri **10** hodgepodge, hotchpotch, salmagundi **11** olla podrida
of anecdotes: 3 ana
of animals: 3 zoo **9** menagerie
of artistic works: 6 museum **7** gallery
of clothes: 8 wardrobe
of dried plants: 9 herbarium
of literary pieces: 8 analects **9** anthology
of reports: 4 file **7** dossier
of trinkets: 10 bijouterie

collective
5 joint **7** commune, kibbutz, kolkhoz **11** cooperative

collector
of bird's eggs: 8 oologist
of books: 11 bibliophile
of coins: 11 numismatist
of fares: 9 conductor
of phonograph records: 10 discophile
of stamps: 11 philatelist

colleen
4 girl, lass **6** lassie, maiden
country: 4 Eire, Erin **7** Ireland

college
9 alma mater
application part: 5 essay
building: 3 gym, lab **4** dorm, hall
campus area: 4 quad **10** quadrangle
class meeting: 3 lab **7** lecture, seminar **8** tutorial, workshop
climber: 3 ivy
degree: 3 BLS, DST, MBA, MEd, MFA, MLS, PhD **5** LittD
graduate: 4 alum **6** alumna, alumni (plural) **7** alumnae (plural), alumnus
military org.: 4 ROTC
official: 4 dean **5** prexy **6** bursar, regent **7** proctor, provost **9** registrar
oldest in U.S.: 7 Harvard
oldest women's in U.S.: 12 Mount Holyoke
relating to: 8 academic **10** collegiate
social group: 4 frat **8** sorority **10** fraternity
song: 9 alma mater
student class: 4 soph **5** frosh **6** junior, senior **8** freshman **9** sophomore
teacher: 3 don **4** prof **8** academic **9** professor
term: 7 quarter, session **8** semester **9** trimester
VIP: 4 BMOC
woman: 4 coed

college team
Air Force: 7 Falcons
Alabama: 11 Crimson Tide
Arizona: 8 Wildcats
Arizona State: 9 Sun Devils
Arkansas: 10 Razorbacks
Arkansas State: 7 Indians
Army: 6 Cadets
Auburn: 6 Tigers
Baylor: 5 Bears

Boston College: 6 Eagles
Boston University: 8 Terriers
Brigham Young: 7 Cougars
Brown: 5 Bears
California: 11 Golden Bears
Central Michigan: 9 Chippewas
Cincinnati: 8 Bearcats
Citadel: 8 Bulldogs
Clemson: 6 Tigers
Colgate: 10 Red Raiders
Colorado: 9 Buffaloes
Colorado State: 4 Rams
Columbia: 5 Lions
Connecticut: 7 Huskies
Cornell: 6 Big Red
Dartmouth: 8 Big Green
Davidson: 8 Wildcats
Delaware State: 7 Hornets
Drake: 8 Bulldogs
Duke: 10 Blue Devils
Eastern Kentucky: 8 Colonels
Eastern Michigan: 6 Eagles
Florida: 6 Gators
Florida State: 9 Seminoles
Fresno State: 8 Bulldogs
Furman: 8 Palidans
Georgia: 8 Bulldogs
Georgia Tech: 13 Yellow Jackets
Harvard: 7 Crimson
Hawaii: 15 Rainbow Warriors
Holy Cross: 9 Crusaders
Houston: 7 Cougars
Howard: 6 Bisons
Idaho: 7 Vandals
Idaho State: 7 Bengals
Illinois: 14 Fighting Illini
Illinois State: 8 Redbirds
Indiana: 8 Hoosiers
Indiana State: 9 Sycamores
Iowa: 8 Hawkeyes
Iowa State: 8 Cyclones
Kansas: 8 Jayhawks
Kansas State: 8 Wildcats
Kent State: 13 Golden Flashes
Kentucky: 8 Wildcats
Lehigh: 9 Engineers
Louisiana State: 6 Tigers
Louisiana Tech: 8 Bulldogs
Maine: 10 Black Bears
Maryland: 5 Terps 9 Terrapins
Massachusetts: 9 Minutemen
Miami (Florida): 10 Hurricanes
Miami (Ohio): 8 Redskins
Michigan: 10 Wolverines
Michigan State: 8 Spartans
Minnesota: 7 Gophers
Mississippi: 6 Rebels
Mississippi State: 8 Bulldogs
Missouri: 6 Tigers
Montana: 9 Grizzlies
Montana State: 7 Bobcats
Navy: 10 Midshipmen
Nebraska: 11 Cornhuskers
Nevada: 6 Rebels 8 Wolfpack
New Hampshire: 8 Wildcats
New Mexico: 5 Lobos
New Mexico State: 6 Aggies
North Carolina: 8 Tar Heels
North Carolina State: 8 Wolfpack
Northeastern: 7 Huskies
Northwestern: 8 Wildcats
Notre Dame: 13 Fighting Irish
Ohio State: 8 Buckeyes
Ohio University: 7 Bobcats
Oklahoma: 7 Sooners
Oklahoma State: 7 Cowboys
Oregon: 5 Ducks
Oregon State: 7 Beavers
Pennsylvania: 7 Quakers
Pennsylvania State: 12 Nittany Lions
Pittsburgh: 8 Panthers
Princeton: 6 Tigers
Purdue: 12 Boilermakers
Rhode Island: 4 Rams
Rice: 4 Owls
Rutgers: 14 Scarlet Knights
San Diego State: 6 Aztecs
San Jose State: 8 Spartans
South Carolina: 9 Gamecocks
South Carolina State: 8 Bulldogs
Southern California: 7 Trojans
Southern Illinois: 7 Salukis
Southern Methodist: 8 Mustangs
Stanford: 9 Cardinals
Syracuse: 9 Orangemen
Temple: 4 Owls
Tennessee: 10 Volunteers
Tennessee State: 6 Tigers
Tennessee Tech: 12 Golden Eagles
Texas: 9 Longhorns
Texas A&M: 6 Aggies
Texas Christian: 11 Horned Frogs
Texas Southern: 6 Tigers
Texas Tech: 10 Red Raiders
Toledo: 7 Rockets
Tulane: 9 Green Wave
UCLA: 6 Bruins
UNLV: 12 Runnin' Rebels
Utah: 4 Utes
Utah State: 6 Aggies
Vanderbilt: 10 Commodores
Villanova: 8 Wildcats
Virginia: 9 Cavaliers
Virginia Tech: 6 Hokies
VMI: 7 Keydets
VPI: 6 Hokies

Wake Forest: **12** Demon Deacons
Washington: **7** Huskies
Washington State: **7** Cougars
West Virginia: **12** Mountaineers
William & Mary: **5** Tribe
Wisconsin: **7** Badgers
Wyoming: **7** Cowboys
Yale: **4** Elis **8** Bulldogs

collide
3 hit, ram **4** bump **5** clash, crash, smash **6** impact, strike **7** impinge **8** conflict

collier
4 ship **5** miner **6** choker

Collins novel
9 Moonstone (The) **12** Woman in White (The)

collision
4 bump, jolt **5** clash, crash, shock, smash, wreck **6** impact **7** crack-up, smashup **10** concussion

collocate
7 arrange **8** position **9** juxtapose

collogue
6 confer, huddle, parley, powwow **7** consult

colloid
3 gel, sol **4** agar **7** mixture **8** hydrogel, hydrosol

colloquial
6 casual, slangy, vulgar **7** demotic **8** familiar, informal **9** idiomatic **10** vernacular

colloquium
5 forum **7** palaver, seminar **9** symposium **10** conference, roundtable

colloquy
4 chat, talk **5** forum **6** debate, parley **7** palaver, seminar **8** dialogue **9** symposium **10** conference, discussion, roundtable **12** conversation **13** confabulation

collude
4 plot **6** devise, scheme **7** connive **8** conspire, contrive, intrigue **9** machinate

collusion
4 plot **8** intrigue, skin game **10** conspiracy

collywobbles
5 colic, gripe **9** bellyache **11** stomachache

Colombia
capital: **6** Bogotá
city: **4** Cali **6** Ibagué **8** Medellín **9** Cartagena **12** Barranquilla
language: **7** Spanish
liberator: **7** Bolivar (Simón)
monetary unit: **4** peso
mountain, range: **5** Andes, Chita **6** Puracé, Tolima **9** Cristóbal
neighbor: **4** Peru **6** Brazil, Panama **7** Ecuador **9** Venezuela
river: **6** Chauca **7** Orinoco **9** Magdalena
sea: **9** Caribbean

Colonel Blimp
4 fogy, Tory **5** fogey **6** fossil **7** old fogy **8** mossback, old fogey **10** fuddy-duddy **11** reactionary

colonial regime in India
3 Raj

colonist
6 émigré, nester **7** evacuee, pilgrim, pioneer, settler **8** emigrant, squatter **9** immigrant **10** expatriate **11** homesteader

colonize
6 settle **8** populate

colonnade
4 stoa **9** peristyle

colony
7 outpost **9** satellite **10** settlement
Greek: **4** Elea **5** Ionia

color
3 dun, dye, hue, red, tan **4** aqua, blue, buff, cast, cyan, ecru, glow, gold, gray, grey, jade, lime, navy, pink, puce, rose, teal, tint, tone **5** amber, azure, beige, belie, black, blush, brown, coral, cream, ebony, flush, green, hazel, henna, ivory, khaki, lemon, lilac, mauve, ocher, ochre, olive, paint, peach, rouge, sepia, shade, stain, taupe, tinge, umber **6** auburn, bronze, canary, cherry, copper, indigo, maroon, orange, purple, redden, russet, salmon, sienna, silver, violet, yellow **7** crimson, emerald, fuchsia, magenta, mustard, pigment, saffron, scarlet **8** amethyst, burgundy, chestnut, dyestuff, lavender, tincture **9** embellish, embroider, turquoise, vermilion **10** aquamarine, exaggerate, vermillion **12** pigmentation
band: **5** facia, vitta **6** fascia
combining form: **5** chrom **6** chromo **7** chromat **8** chromato
primary: **3** red **4** blue **6** yellow
relating to: **9** chromatic
secondary: **5** green **6** orange, purple
soft: **6** pastel

Colorado
capital: **6** Denver
city: **4** Vail **5** Aspen **6** Aurora, Pueblo **7** Boulder **8** Lakewood **11** Fort Collins
college, university: **5** Regis **9** Fort Lewis
mountain, range: **5** Longs (Peak), Pikes (Peak), Rocky **6** Elbert **7** Rockies
nickname: **10** Centennial (State)
park: **9** Mesa Verde
river: **8** Arkansas **9** Rio Grande
state bird: **11** lark bunting
state flower: **9** columbine
state tree: **10** blue spruce

Colorado resort
4 Vail **5** Aspen **8** Snowmass **9** Telluride

colorant
3 dye **5** stain **7** pigment **8** dyestuff, tincture

colored
6 biased, warped **8** one-sided, partisan **9** jaundiced **10** prejudiced **11** tendentious

colorful
3 gay **5** gaudy, showy, vivid **6** bright, flashy, florid, garish, motley **7** splashy

coloring
4 cast, tint **5** front, tinge **6** facade, nuance **7** pigment **8** overtone **10** camouflage, complexion **12** embroidering **13** embellishment

colorless
3 wan **4** ashy, drab, dull, flat, pale **5** ashen, pasty, prosy, waxen, white **6** albino, doughy, pallid **7** insipid, neutral, prosaic **8** abstract, blanched, bleached **10** achromatic, lackluster

Color Purple author
6 Walker (Alice)

colossal
4 huge, vast **5** giant **7** immense, mammoth, massive, titanic **8** enormous, gigantic, towering **9** cyclopean, humongous, monstrous, towering **10** gargantuan, prodigious, stupendous, tremendous **11** astonishing, elephantine

colossus
5 giant, titan **6** statue **7** goliath, mammoth, monster **8** behemoth **9** leviathan

Colossus of ___
6 Rhodes

colporteur
10 evangelist, missionary

colt
4 foal, tyro **6** novice, rookie **8** beginner, freshman, neophyte, newcomer **9** fledgling **10** tenderfoot

coltish
6 frisky, impish **7** playful **10** frolicsome

Columbine
beloved: **9** Harlequin
father: **9** Pantaloon

Columbus, Christopher
birthplace: **5** Genoa
patron: **8** Isabella **9** Ferdinand
ship: **4** Niña **5** Pinta **10** Santa Maria
son: **5** Diego
starting point: **5** Palos

column
3 row **4** pier **5** shaft, stela **6** pillar **7** obelisk **8** pilaster
angle: **5** arris
base: **4** dado, ordo **5** socle **6** plinth **9** stylobate
bulge: **7** entasis
female figure: **8** caryatid
male figure: **5** atlas **7** telamon **8** atlantes (plural)
style: **5** Doric, Ionic **10** Corinthian
top: **7** capital **8** chapiter

columnists' page
4 op-ed

coma
6 stupor, torpor **8** blackout, hebetude, lethargy, oblivion **9** lassitude

comate
3 pal **4** chum **5** buddy, crony **7** comrade, partner **9** associate, colleague, companion

comatose
3 out **6** torpid **7** out cold **8** sluggish **9** lethargic **10** insensible **11** unconscious

comb
4 rake, sift, sort **5** crest, curry, probe, scour, sweep, tease **6** search, winnow **7** ransack **8** untangle **10** straighten

combat
3 war **4** buck, duel, fray **5** fight, repel **6** action, battle, oppose, resist, strife **7** contend, contest, dispute **8** skirmish, struggle **9** withstand

combatant
7 battler, fighter, soldier, warrior **8** militant, opponent **9** adversary, aggressor, assailant, contender, disputant, mercenary **10** antagonist, challenger, competitor, contestant **11** belligerent

combative
6 feisty **7** scrappy, warlike **8** militant **9** agonistic, bellicose, truculent **10** aggressive, pugnacious **11** belligerent, contentious, quarrelsome **12** disputatious, militaristic

combativeness
9 pugnacity **10** aggression, truculence **11** bellicosity **12** belligerence

combe
4 dale, dell, glen, vale **6** dingle, valley

combination
3 mix **4** bloc, pool, ring **5** blend, union **6** fusion, hookup, merger **7** melding, merging **8** alliance **9** aggregate, coalition, composite, synthesis **10** connection **11** affiliation, association, conjunction, partnership, unification **13** consolidation

combine
3 add, mix, wed **4** band, bloc, fuse, join, link, pool, ring **5** blend, chain, group, marry, merge, trust, unify, union, unite **6** cartel, league, mingle **7** bracket, conjoin, connect, faction **8** coadjute, coalesce **9** associate, coalition, commingle, cooperate, integrate, syndicate **10** amalgamate **11** consolidate, incorporate **12** conglomerate
Japanese: **8** keiretsu, zaibatsu
Korean: **7** chaebol, jaebeol

combined action
7 synergy **9** synergism

combo
4 band, trio **5** group, nonet, octet **6** septet, sextet **7** quartet, quintet **8** ensemble

combust
4 burn **6** ignite, kindle **10** incinerate

combustible
4 edgy, fuel **8** burnable, volatile **9** excitable, flammable, ignitable **11** inflammable
material: 3 gas, oil **4** coal, peat, wood **6** tinder

combustion
4 riot **7** burning **8** eruption, ignition, kindling **9** explosion, oxidation **13** thermogenesis

come
4 flow, hail, stem **5** arise, issue, occur **6** arrive, derive, show up, spring, turn up **7** advance, emanate, proceed **8** approach **9** originate
a cropper: 4 fail, fall
across: 4 find, meet **8** discover **9** encounter
apart: 12 disintegrate
at: 6 attack
away: 5 leave **6** depart
before: 7 precede
clean: 7 confess
forth: 5 arise, issue **6** appear, emerge **7** emanate
forward: 7 advance **9** volunteer
into: 5 enter **7** acquire
near: 5 verge **8** approach
round: 5 rally **7** get well, recover
to pass: 5 occur **6** happen
up: 5 arise

comeback
5 rally **6** answer, retort, return **7** rebound, revival, riposte **8** rebuttal, recovery, repartee, response **11** improvement **12** counterclaim, recuperation

come by
4 call **5** pop in, visit **6** drop in, look in **7** acquire, collect, inherit

comedian
3 wag, wit **4** card **5** clown, comic, droll, joker **6** jester **7** farceur **8** funnyman, humorist, jokester, quipster **11** entertainer
famous: 3 Cho (Margaret), Fey (Tina), Fry (Stephen), Nye (Louis) **4** Ball (Lucille), Barr (Roseanne), Chan (Jackie), Coca (Imogene), Cook (Peter), Dana (Bill), Foxx (Redd), Hill (Benny), Hope (Bob), Idle (Eric), Kaye (Danny), King (Alan), Leno (Jay), Levy (Eugene), Marx (Chico, Groucho, Gummo, Harpo, Zeppo), Mull (Martin), Raye (Martha), Rock (Chris), Sahl (Mort), Wise (Ernie), Wood (Victoria) **5** Abbot (Bud), Allen (Gracie, Steve, Woody), Benny (Jack), Berle (Milton), Black (Lewis), Borge (Victor), Bruce (Lenny), Burns (George), Candy (John), Chase (Chevy), Chong (Tommy), Cosby (Bill), David (Larry), Guest (Christopher), Hardy (Oliver), Lewis (Jerry), Lloyd (Harold), Lopez (George), Maher (Bill), Marin (Cheech), Meara (Anne), Moore (Dudley), Myers (Mike), Palin (Michael), Pearl (Minnie), Perry (Tyler), Pryor (Richard), Rogen (Seth), Rowan (Dan), Sales (Soupy) **6** Berman (Shelley), Caesar (Sid), Carell (Steve), Carlin (George), Carrey (Jim), Carson (Johnny), Carvey (Dana), Cheech (Marin), Cleese (John), DeVito (Danny), Diller (Phyllis), Fallon (Jimmy), Farley (Chris), Fields (Totie, W. C.), Gosden (Freeman), Izzard (Eddie), Keaton (Buster), Kimmel (Jimmy), Knotts (Don), Kovacs (Ernie), Laurel (Stan), Lehrer (Tom), Lemmon (Jack), Little (Rich), Mabley (Moms), Martin (Dean, Dick, Steve), Meyers (Seth), Midler (Bette), Murphy (Eddie), Murray (Bill), O'Brien (Conan), Oliver (John), Radner (Gilda), Reiner (Carl), Rivers (Joan), Rogers (Will), Thomas (Danny), Tomlin (Lily), Turpin (Ben), Ullman (Tracey), Wayans (Damon, Keenan Ivory, Marlon, Shawn), Wilson (Flip) **7** Aykroyd (Dan), Belushi (Jim, John), Buttons (Red), Burnett (Carol), Chaplin (Charlie), Colbert (Stephen), Crystal (Billy), Durante (Jimmy), Farrell (Will), Feldman (Marty), Freberg (Stan), Gervais (Ricky), Gleason (Jackie), Grammer (Kelsey), Hackett (Buddy), Keillor (Garrison), Louis CK, Matthau (Walter), Moranis (Rick), Newhart (Bob), Nielsen (Leslie), Paulsen (Pat), Rickles (Don), Poehler (Amy), Russell (Mark), Sandler (Adam), Sedaris (Amy, David), Sellers (Peter), Sherman (Allan), Silvers (Phil), Skelton (Red), Stewart (Jon), Stiller (Ben, Jerry), Winters (Jonathan) **8** Atkinson (Rowan), Bernhard (Sandra), Costello (Lou), Goldberg (Whoopi), Grenfell (Joyce), Jankovic (Weird Al), Mulligan (Spike), O'Donnell (Rosie), Seinfeld (Jerry), Smothers (Dick, Tom), Williams (Robin), Youngman (Henny) **9** Carrot Top, Chappelle (Dave), DeGeneres (Ellen), Leguizamo (John), Letterman (David), Morecambe (Eric) **10** Poundstone (Paula) **11** Dangerfield (Rodney)

comedian Mort
4 Sahl

comedienne Martha
4 Raye

comedo
9 blackhead

comedown
4 dive, fall, ruin **5** crash **7** decline, descent, failure, setback **8** collapse **9** ruination

come down with
3 get **5** catch **7** develop **8** contract

comedy
5 farce, humor **6** levity **8** drollery, hilarity **9** drollness, slapstick, wittiness
Muse: 6 Thalia
show: 3 SNL **6** Hee-Haw **7** Laugh-In **9** Daily Show (The)

come in
5 enter, reply 6 answer 7 respond

comely
4 fair 5 bonny, sonsy 6 lovely, pretty, proper, sonsie 7 winsome 8 becoming, decorous, handsome, pleasing 9 beauteous, beautiful, befitting 10 attractive 11 good-looking

come off
4 fare, seem 5 click, occur 6 appear, go over, happen, pan out 7 develop, succeed 8 prove out 9 transpire

come-on
4 bait, lure, trap 5 decoy, snare 9 seduction 10 allurement, enticement, inducement, invitation, temptation 12 blandishment, inveiglement, solicitation

come out
4 leak 5 break, debut, end up 6 emerge 9 transpire

come out with
3 say 4 tell 5 state, utter 6 report 7 declare, deliver, publish, release 8 announce, proclaim

comestible
6 edible 7 eatable 8 esculent

comestibles
4 feed, food 6 viands 7 edibles 8 victuals 9 provender 10 provisions

comet
4 West 7 Halley's 8 Hale-Bopp, Kohoutek, McNaught 9 Hyakutake

Comet competitor
4 Ajax 6 Bon Ami

come through
6 chip in, endure 7 pitch in, prevail, survive 8 transmit 10 contribute

come together
4 mass, meet 5 merge, swarm 6 gather, huddle 7 cluster, collect, combine, convene 8 assemble, converge 10 congregate

come to terms
5 agree

come upon
4 find, meet 7 run into, uncover, unearth 8 bump into, discover, trip over 9 encounter, run across

comeuppance
3 due 5 lumps 7 deserts

comfort
3 aid 4 ease, help 5 cheer 6 assist, buck up, luxury, relief, solace, soothe, succor 7 amenity, cheer up, console, relieve, support 8 reassure, sympathy 10 assistance, sympathize 11 commiserate, consolation, contentment

comfortable
4 cozy, easy, homy, snug, soft 5 ample, cushy, homey, roomy 7 content, easeful, restful, well-off 8 adequate, homelike, pleasant, pleasing, spacious, well-to-do 9 agreeable, satisfied, well-fixed 10 commodious, prosperous, sufficient, well-heeled 11 substantial 12 satisfactory

comforter
4 down, pouf, puff 5 duvet, quilt 9 eiderdown

comic
3 wag, wit 5 antic, droll, funny, joker 6 jester 7 risible 8 comedian, farcical, funnyman, humorist, jokester, quipster 9 laughable, ludicrous 10 ridiculous

comical
4 zany 5 droll, funny, goofy, silly 6 absurd 7 amusing, foolish, risible, waggish 8 farcical 9 laughable, ludicrous 10 ridiculous

comic opera
6 bouffe

comic strip
4 Pogo, Shoe 5 Hazel, Henry, Nancy 6 Archie, Popeye 7 Blondie, Dilbert, Far Side (The), Peanuts 8 Alley Oop, Andy Capp, Etta Kett, Garfield, Krazy Kat, Li'l Abner, Superman 9 Betty Boop, Dick Tracy, Marmaduke, Mary Worth, Spider-Man, Yellow Kid (The) 10 Doonesbury, Joe Palooka, Little Nemo 11 Bloom County, Brenda Starr, Flash Gordon, Hogan's Alley, Mutt and Jeff, Rex Morgan M.D., Steve Canyon 12 Beetle Bailey 13 Captain Marvel, Gasoline Alley, Prince Valiant
character: 3 Arn, Jon, Kim, Liz, Owl, Roz 4 Asok, Elmo, Flip, Herb, Honi, Irma, Lizz, Loon, Lucy, Nemo, Odie, Opus, Otto, Phil, Rube, Tess, Thun, Zero 5 Abner, Aleta, Alice, Bella, Betty, Carol, Cosmo, Foozy, Hägar, Helga, Honey, Itchy, Krazy, Lacey, Linus, Mammy, Oola, Pappy, Patty, Percy, Phred, Plato, Porky, Rerun, Rocky, Rollo, Sally, Shmoo, Spike, Wally 6 Albert, Arlene, Belfry, Cookie, Doc Boy, Dottie, Frieda, Joanie, Junior, Lt. Flap, Lt. Fuzz, Marcie, Nermal, Pig-Pen, Reggie, Skyler, Sluggo, Snoopy, Vultan, Zipper, Zonker 7 Aunt May, Boopsie, Chalkie, Churchy, Dagwood, Dithers, Flattop, Florrie, Ignatz, Jughead, Mr. Butts, Mumbles, Phyllis, Portnoy, Skeezix, Tootsie, Wolf Gal 8 Black Cat, B. O. Plenty, Bull Pupp, Daisy Mae, Dr. Sivana, June Gale, Lana Lang, Lois Lane, Olive Oyl, Pete Ross, Shroeder, Veronica 9 Alexander, Brilliant, Chip Gizmo, Clark Kent, Dale Arden, Diet Smith, Gwen Stacy, Pat Patton, Pruneface, Uncle Duke 10 Aunt Fritzi, Betty Brant, Bill the Cat, Cutter John, Dragon Lady, Hans Zarkov, Hodge-Podge, Jimmy Olsen, Joe Btfsplk, Louise Lugg, Marryin' Sam, Miss Buxley, Perry White, Sam Catchem, Scott Sloan, Sgt. Snorkel, Walt Wallet 11 Happy Easter, Harry Osborn, Ignatz Mouse, Lola Granola, Mickey Dugan, Peter Parker, Steve Dallas, Summer Olson 12 Charlie Brown, Felicia Hardy, Gen. Halftrack, Gravel Gertie

coming
3 due **4** next **5** ahead, fated, onset **6** advent, future **7** arrival, ensuing, nearing **8** approach, expected, foreseen, imminent **9** following, impending **11** approaching
forth: **7** issuant

comity
5 amity **7** concord, harmony **8** goodwill **10** friendship **11** benevolence, camaraderie **12** friendliness

comma
4 lull **5** pause **8** interval

command
3 bid **4** rule, sway **5** order **6** adjure, behest, charge, compel, direct, enjoin **7** bidding, conduct, control, dictate, mandate, mastery, precept **9** authority, direction, directive, expertise, ordinance **10** domination, imperative, injunction **11** instruction **12** jurisdiction
to Fido: **3** beg, sit **4** stay
to go: **4** mush **6** avaunt, begone **7** giddyap, giddyup
to stop: **4** whoa **5** avast

commandeer
4 take **5** annex, seize, usurp **6** assume, hijack **7** preempt **8** accroach, arrogate **9** conscript, sequester **10** confiscate **11** appropriate, expropriate, requisition

commander
4 boss, head **6** honcho, leader, master **7** captain, general, headman, officer

commandment
3 law **4** fiat, rule **5** edict, order **6** decree **7** mitzvah, precept, statute

commedia dell' ___
4 arte

comme il faut
6 decent, polite, proper, seemly **7** correct **8** becoming, decorous, suitable

commemorate
4 keep **7** observe **8** eulogize, monument **9** celebrate, solemnize **11** memorialize **13** monumentalize

commemorative
8 memorial **10** dedicatory **11** celebratory

commence
5 begin, start **6** launch, set out **7** kick off **8** embark on, initiate **10** embark upon, inaugurate

commencement
4 dawn **5** birth, onset, start **6** outset **7** dawning, genesis, opening **9** beginning, inception **10** graduation **12** inauguration

commend
4 cite, hail, laud **5** extol **6** commit, kudize, praise, salute, tender **7** acclaim, applaud, approve, consign, entrust **8** hand over, relegate, turn over **10** compliment

commendable
6 worthy **8** laudable **9** admirable, deserving, estimable, meritable, venerable **10** creditable **11** meritorious **12** praiseworthy

commensurable
see **commensurate**

commensurate
4 even **5** equal **10** comparable **11** coextensive **12** proportional **13** corresponding, proportionate

comment
4 note **5** opine **6** remark **7** mention, observe **8** critique, point out **9** criticism, interject **10** animadvert **11** observation **12** obiter dictum

commentary
5 gloss **6** review **8** analysis, critique, exegesis **9** editorial, narration, voice-over **10** annotation, exposition **11** explanation, observation **12** appreciation, obiter dictum

commerce
5 trade **7** contact, traffic **8** business, congress, dealings, exchange, industry **9** communion **11** interchange **13** communication

commercial
4 spot **6** advert **8** economic **10** mercantile **13** advertisement
award: **4** Clio
tune: **6** jingle

commie
3 Red **5** pinko **6** bolshy **7** bolshie **9** Bolshevik

commination
5 curse **8** anathema **10** accusation, execration **11** imprecation, malediction **12** denunciation

commingle
3 mix **4** meld **5** blend, merge, unify **8** compound, intermix **9** integrate **10** amalgamate

comminute
4 bray **5** crush, grind **9** granulate, pulverize

commiserate
4 pity **7** condole, feel for **9** empathize **10** sympathize

commiseration
4 pity, ruth **7** empathy **8** sympathy **10** compassion, condolence

commission
3 bid, fee **4** name **5** board, order, panel **6** agency, assign, charge, enable, engage, enjoin, enlist **7** appoint, command, council, empower, license, warrant **8** accredit, delegate, deputize **9** authorize, designate **10** delegation, deputation, percentage **11** certificate

commit
4 bind **5** allot, grant, refer **6** assign, convey, invest, ordain, pledge, record, reveal **7** achieve,

consign, deposit, entrust, execute, perform, promise, pull off, trustee **8** allocate, carry out, hand over, obligate, relegate, turn over **10** accomplish, perpetrate

commitment
3 vow **4** bond, deal, duty **6** charge, devoir, pledge **7** promise **8** contract **9** agreement, assurance, guarantee **10** obligation **11** undertaking

committal
see **commitment**

committee type
5 ad hoc

commixture
5 blend **6** fusion **7** amalgam, melange **8** compound, mingling **9** composite

commodious
4 wide **5** ample, roomy **8** spacious **9** capacious, expansive, luxurious **11** comfortable

commodities
5 goods, items, wares **8** articles, products **9** vendibles **11** merchandise

common
4 park **5** banal, daily, joint, plaza, trite, usual **6** mutual, normal, shared **7** general, generic, prosaic, regular, routine, typical **8** adequate, communal, conjoint, conjunct, déclassé, everyday, familiar, frequent, habitual, ordinary, standard, workaday **9** customary, prevalent, tolerable, universal **10** collective, pedestrian, prevailing, unexciting, widespread **12** conventional, run-of-the-mill, satisfactory **13** unexceptional, uninteresting

commonalty
3 mob **5** plebs **6** masses, people, plebes, public, rabble **7** commune **8** populace **9** hoi polloi, multitude, plebeians **11** proletariat, rank and file, third estate

commoners
see **commonalty**

commonplace
5 banal, stale, tired, trite, usual **6** cliché, normal, truism **7** bromide, clichéd, humdrum, mundane, obvious, prosaic, regular, routine, typical **8** banality, bromidic, chestnut, everyday, habitual, mediocre, ordinary, well-worn, workaday **9** hackneyed, platitude, prevalent **10** pedestrian, shibboleth, stereotype, uneventful **11** stereotyped **12** conventional, run-of-the-mill, unremarkable **13** stereotypical, unexceptional, uninteresting

common sense
6 wisdom **8** judgment, prudence **10** shrewdness

Common Sense author
5 Paine (Thomas)

commotion
3 ado, din, row **4** flap, fuss, moil, riot, stew, stir, to-do **5** furor, hoo-ha, scene, storm, whirl **6** clamor, dither, flurry, fracas, furore, hoo-hah, hoopla, hubbub, hurrah, lather, outcry, pother, racket, ruckus, rumpus, shindy, tumult, uproar, upturn **7** ferment, tempest, turmoil **8** brouhaha, foofaraw **9** agitation, confusion **10** hullabaloo, hurly-burly, turbulence **11** pandemonium

commove
5 rouse **6** excite **7** agitate, inspire, provoke **9** electrify, galvanize, stimulate

communal
5 civil, joint **6** common, mutual, public, shared **10** collective **11** socialistic

commune
10 collective
Dutch: **3** Ede
Israeli: **7** kibbutz
Russian: **3** mir **7** kolkhoz

communicable
8 catching **10** contagious, infectious **13** transmissible, transmittable

communicate
4 tell **6** convey, impart, inform, pass on, relate, reveal, signal **7** connect, contact, divulge **8** disclose, transmit **9** make known

communication
4 talk **7** contact, message, missive, talking **8** converse, exchange **9** directive **10** discussing, discussion **11** interchange, intercourse **12** conversation
means: **3** Web **4** drum, mail, note, text **5** e-mail, media, phone, radio, tweet **6** letter, medium, pigeon, speech **7** Twitter **8** Internet **9** telegraph, telephone **10** television

communications code word
4 Alfa, Echo, Golf, Kilo, Lima, Mike, Papa, Xray, Zulu **5** Alpha, Bravo, Delta, Hotel, India, Oscar, Romeo, Tango **6** Quebec, Sierra, Victor, Yankee **7** Charlie, Foxtrot, Juliett, Uniform, Whiskey **8** November

communicative
5 vocal **6** fluent, prolix **7** verbose, voluble **8** eloquent **9** expansive, garrulous, talkative **10** articulate, expressive, loquacious

communion
7 rapport, sharing **9** Eucharist, sacrament **10** connection, fellowship
cloth: **8** corporal
cup: **7** chalice
plate: **5** paten

communism
7 Marxism **8** Leninism **10** bolshevism **12** collectivism

Communist
3 red **5** lefty, pinko **6** bolshy, Maoist **7** bolshie, comrade, Marxist **8** Leninist **9** Bolshevik, Stalinist **10** Bolshevist, Trotskyist

Communist leader
Chinese: 3 Hua (Guofeng), Kim (Jong-il, Jong-un), Mao (Tse-tung, Zedong) **4** Deng (Xiaoping), Zhou (Enlai) **5** Jiang (Zemin) **8** Hu Jintao **9** Kim Jong-il, Kim Jong-un, Mao Zedong, Xi Jinping **10** Jiang Zemin, Mao Tse-tung **12** Deng Xiaoping **13** Teng Hsiao-p'ing
Cuban: 6 Castro (Fidel, Raúl)
Russian: 5 Lenin (Vladimir Ilyich) **6** Stalin (Joseph) **7** Kosygin (Aleksey), Trotsky (Leon) **8** Andropov (Yuri), Brezhnev (Leonid) **9** Chernenko (Konstantin), Gorbachev (Mikhail) **10** Khrushchev (Nikita)

community
4 town **7** enclave, society **12** neighborhood
closed: 5 abbey **6** priory **7** convent, nunnery **8** cloister **9** monastery
ecological: 10 biocenosis **11** biocoenosis

commute
5 alter **6** change, make up, modify, soften, travel **7** convert, curtail, shorten, shuttle **8** decrease, exchange, mitigate, transfer **9** transform, translate, transmute, transpose **10** compensate, substitute **11** interchange

Comoros
capital: 6 Moroni
island: 6 Mohéli **7** Anjouan **12** Grande Comore
language: 6 Arabic, French **8** Comorian
monetary unit: 5 franc
volcano: 8 Karthala

cómo ___ usted?
4 está

compact
4 bond **5** close, dense, unify **7** bargain, bunched, crowded, entente, pressed **8** compress, condense, contract, covenant **9** agreement, concordat **10** convention **11** concentrate, consolidate, transaction

compadre
3 pal **4** chum, mate **5** amigo, buddy, crony **6** cohort, friend **7** partner **8** confrere, sidekick, intimate **9** associate, colleague, companion

companion
3 pal **4** chum, mate **5** buddy, crony **6** cohort, escort, fellow **7** comrade, consort, partner **8** sidekick **9** associate, attendant, colleague

companionable
6 genial, social **7** affable, amiable **8** outgoing, sociable **9** agreeable, congenial, convivial **10** gregarious **11** good-natured

companionship
7 company, society **8** intimacy **10** fellowship **11** camaraderie

company
4 band, club, crew, firm, gang, team **5** corps, group, party, troop **6** circle, clique, guests, outfit, troupe **7** concern, coterie, retinue, society, visitor **8** assembly, business, ensemble, visitors **9** gathering **10** assemblage, enterprise, fellowship **11** association, camaraderie, corporation **12** congregation **13** establishment

comparable
4 akin, like **5** alike **6** agnate **7** similar, uniform **8** parallel **9** analogous **10** equivalent, homologous **12** commensurate **13** corresponding

comparative
4 near **8** relative **11** approximate
phrase: 4 is to

compare
5 liken, match **6** equate, relate **7** collate **8** contrast, parallel **9** correlate **10** assimilate

comparison
6 simile **7** analogy **8** affinity, contrast, likeness **9** collation, semblance **10** similarity, similitude **11** correlation, resemblance

compartment
3 bay **4** cell, nook, part, slot **5** berth, booth, niche, stall **6** alcove, carrel, locker **7** chamber, cubicle, section **8** division **9** cubbyhole **10** pigeonhole **11** subdivision

compass
3 hem **4** ring **5** ambit, field, grasp, orbit, range, reach, scope, sweep **6** bounds, circle, domain, extent, girdle, limits, radius, sphere **7** circuit, environ, purview **8** boundary, confines, environs **9** enclosure, extension, perimeter, periphery **13** circumference
kind: 4 gyro **5** solar **8** magnetic
stand: 8 binnacle

compassion
4 pity, ruth **5** mercy **7** charity, empathy **8** clemency, humanity, kindness, sympathy **10** condolence, humaneness **11** benevolence **13** commiseration, fellow feeling

compassionate
4 pity, warm **6** humane, tender **7** clement **8** merciful **10** benevolent, charitable, solicitous **11** commiserate, kindhearted, softhearted, sympathetic, warmhearted

compassionless
5 stony **7** callous **8** obdurate **9** heartless, unfeeling **11** coldblooded, hard-hearted, ironhearted **12** stonyhearted

compass point
3 ENE, ESE, NNE, NNW, SSE, SSW, WNW, WSW **4** east, west **5** north, rhumb, south **7** bearing
Scottish: 4 airt

compatible
8 suitable **9** agreeable, congenial, congruous, consonant **10** consistent, harmonious, likeminded **11** appropriate, sympathetic

compatriot
7 paisano **8** confrere **9** associate, colleague, companion **10** countryman

compel
4 hale, urge **5** drive, force **6** coerce, impose, oblige **7** enforce **9** constrain

compelling
4 dire **5** acute **6** cogent, crying, urgent **7** clamant, exigent, telling, weighty **8** forceful, pressing **10** convincing, persuasive **11** importunate **12** well-grounded

compendious
5 brief, pithy, short **7** compact, concise, summary **8** succinct **9** condensed **11** abbreviated

compendium
4 list **5** brief, guide **6** aperçu, digest, manual, précis, sketch, survey **7** epitome, summary **8** abstract, Baedeker, handbook, overview, syllabus, synopsis **9** anthology, guidebook, vade mecum **10** abridgment, collection, conspectus **11** abridgement, compilation, enchiridion

compensate
3 pay **5** atone, repay **6** make up, offset, pay off, redeem, set off **7** balance, guerdon, requite, satisfy **8** outweigh **9** indemnify, reimburse **10** counteract, neutralize, recompense, remunerate **11** countervail

compensation
6 amends, reward, salary **7** damages, payment, redress **8** earnings, reprisal, requital, solatium **9** atonement, indemnity, quittance, repayment **10** recompense, reparation **11** restitution **12** remuneration
unexpected: **4** gift **5** bonus **8** windfall

compete
3 vie **4** spar **5** fight **6** battle, strive **7** contend, contest **8** struggle

competence
5 skill **7** ability, know-how **8** adequacy, aptitude, capacity, facility **9** expertise **10** capability **11** proficiency, sufficiency **13** qualification

competent
3 fit **4** able **5** adept **6** au fait, decent, proper **7** capable, skilled **8** adequate **9** efficient, qualified **10** proficient, sufficient **12** satisfactory

competition
4 bout, game, meet, race **5** clash, fight, match, rival **6** strife **7** contest, matchup, rivalry **8** concours, conflict, striving, struggle, tug-of-war **10** antagonism, contention, tournament

competitive advantage
4 edge

competitor
5 enemy, rival **7** entrant **8** opponent **9** adversary, contender **10** antagonist, contestant, opposition

compilation
3 ana **5** album, cento **9** anthology **10** collection, compendium **11** florilegium

compile
4 edit **5** amass **6** gather, select **7** build up, collate, collect **8** assemble **9** construct **10** accumulate **11** anthologize

complacency
5 pride **7** conceit **8** smugness **10** narcissism

complacent
4 smug **9** conceited **11** unconcerned **13** self-contented, self-satisfied

complain
3 nag **4** beef, carp, crab, fret, fuss, moan, wail **5** gripe, grump, whine **6** grouch, grouse, lament, repine, yammer **7** grizzle, grumble, protest **9** bellyache

complainer
4 crab **5** crank **6** griper, grouch **7** grouser **8** grumbler, sourpuss **10** malcontent **11** fault-finder

complaint
4 beef **5** gripe **6** grouse, lament, malady **7** ailment, disease, protest **8** disorder, sickness, syndrome **9** condition, criticism, grievance, infirmity, objection **10** affliction, allegation **12** protestation

complaisant
4 easy, mild **7** amiable, lenient **8** generous, obliging **9** agreeable, easygoing, indulgent **11** deferential, good-humored, good-natured **12** good-tempered **13** accommodating

complement
4 crew, rest **9** correlate, remainder **11** counterpart

complete
3 end **4** done, full, halt **5** close, ended, sew up, total, utter, whole **6** entire, finish, intact, wind up, wrap up **7** achieve, fulfill, perfect, perform, plenary **8** absolute, conclude, finalize, finished, integral, round out, thorough **9** concluded, out-and-out, terminate **10** accomplish, consummate, exhaustive, unabridged **11** categorical, unmitigated **13** thoroughgoing

completed
4 done, over **5** ended **7** through **8** done with, executed, finished **9** concluded, fulfilled **10** terminated **11** consummated **12** accomplished

completely
4 A to Z **5** fully **6** wholly **7** totally, utterly **8** entirely **9** inside out, up and down **10** thoroughly

completion
3 end **6** finish, windup, wrap-up **8** fruition **10** conclusion

complex
6 daedal, knotty, system, varied **7** chelate, gordian, network **8** abstruse, compound, involved,

syndrome, tortuous **9** aggregate, Byzantine, composite, elaborate, intricate **10** convoluted **11** complicated **12** conglomerate, labyrinthine **13** heterogeneous, sophisticated

complexion
3 hue **4** cast, tint, tone **5** color, humor, tinge **6** aspect, makeup, nature, temper **8** tincture **9** character **10** appearance, coloration **11** disposition, temperament **12** pigmentation **13** individuality

compliance
7 consent **8** docility **9** agreement, deference, obedience **10** acceptance, conformity, submission **11** amenability, flexibility, resignation **12** acquiescence, tractability

complicate
5 mix up, ravel, snarl **6** jumble, muddle, tangle **7** confuse, involve **8** confound, disorder, entangle **9** aggravate, convolute **10** disarrange, exacerbate

complicated
6 daedal, knotty **7** complex, gordian, tangled **8** abstruse, involved, tortuous **9** Byzantine, elaborate, intricate, recondite **10** convoluted **12** labyrinthine **13** heterogeneous, sophisticated

complication
4 snag **5** catch **6** glitch **7** setback

complicity
8 abetment **9** collusion **10** connivance **11** involvement

compliment
4 hail, kudo, laud **5** extol, honor, kudos, paean **6** praise, salute **7** acclaim, applaud, bouquet, commend, flatter, regards, tribute **8** accolade, encomium **9** laudation, recommend **11** recognition **12** appreciation, commendation, congratulate

complimentary
4 free **6** gratis **8** costless **9** favorable, laudatory **10** chargeless, flattering, gratuitous **12** appreciative

comply
4 obey **5** yield **6** accede, submit **7** conform **9** acquiesce

component
4 part **5** piece **6** factor **7** element, segment **10** ingredient **11** constituent

comport
4 bear, jibe **5** agree, carry, fit in, match, tally **6** accord, acquit, behave, demean, square **7** conduct **8** coincide, dovetail **9** harmonize **10** correspond

comportment
3 air **4** mien **7** address, bearing, conduct **8** attitude, behavior, carriage, demeanor, presence

compose
3 pen **4** calm, cool, form, lull, make **5** forge, quiet, relax, still, write **6** becalm, create, devise, draw up, indite, invent, make up, settle, solace, soothe **7** collect, console, contain, control **8** comprise **9** construct, fabricate, formulate, originate **10** constitute
type: **3** set

composed
4 calm, cool **5** staid **6** poised, sedate, serene **9** collected, unruffled **11** unflappable **13** imperturbable, self-possessed

composer
6 scorer **8** melodist **9** balladist, songsmith, tunesmith **10** songwriter
American: **3** Kay (Hershy, Ulysses) **4** Ager (Milton), Bock (Jerry), Cage (John), Hill (Edward Burlingame), Ives (Charles), Kern (Jerome), Lane (Burton), Monk (Thelonious), Work (Henry Clay) **5** Adams (John, John Luther), Arlen (Harold), Beach (Amy), Blake (Eubie), Bland (James A.), Bloch (Ernest), Cohan (George M.), Friml (Rudolf), Glass (Philip), Gould (Morton), Grofé (Ferde), Handy (W. C.), Loewe (Frederick), Mason (Daniel Gregory, Lowell), Moore (Douglas), Reich (Steve), Rorem (Ned), Sousa (John Philip), Still (William Grant), Styne (Jule), Zappa (Frank) **6** Barber (Samuel), Carter (Elliott), Cowell (Henry), Emmett (Daniel), Foster (Stephen), Hanson (Howard), Harris (Roy), Herman (Jerry), Joplin (Scott), Kander (John), Menken (Alan), Morton ("Jelly Roll"), Oliver ("King"), Parker (Horatio), Piston (Walter), Porter (Cole), Previn (André), Seeger (Pete), Taylor (Deems), Varèse (Edgard), Warren (Harry) **7** Babbitt (Milton), Brubeck (Dave), Copland (Aaron), Gilbert (Henry F.), Gilmore (Patrick), Goldman (Edwin Franko), Herbert (Victor), Loesser (Frank), Mancini (Henry), Menotti (Gian Carlo), Rodgers (Richard), Romberg (Sigmund), Schuman (William), Thomson (Virgil), Tiomkin (Dimitri), Willson (Meredith) **8** Anderson (Leroy), Billings (William), Burleigh (Henry Thacker), Damrosch (Leopold, Walter), Gershwin (George), Hamlisch (Marvin), Herrmann (Bernard), Korngold (Erich Wolfgang), Kreisler (Fritz), Marsalis (Wynton), Schifrin (Lalo), Schuller (Gunther), Sessions (Roger), Sondheim (Stephen), Williams (John) **9** Bacharach (Burt), Bernstein (Elmer, Leonard), Ellington (Duke), Hovhaness (Alan), Lauridsen (Morton), MacDowell (Edward) **10** Blitzstein (Marc), Gottschalk (Louis Moreau)
Argentinian: **9** Ginastera (Alberto)
Australian: **8** Grainger (Percy)
Austrian: **4** Berg (Alban), Wolf (Hugo) **5** Haydn (Franz Joseph), Lehár (Franz) **6** Czerny (Karl), Mahler (Gustav), Mozart (Leopold, Wolfgang Amadeus), Straus (Oscar), Webern (Anton)

7 Strauss (Eduard, Johann, Josef) **8** Bruckner (Anton), Schubert (Franz) **10** Schoenberg (Arnold)
Belgian: 5 Ysaÿe (Eugène) **6** Franck (César)
Brazilian: 5 Jobim (Antonio Carlos) **10** Villa-Lobos (Heitor)
Czech: 3 Suk (Josef) **4** Hába (Alois) **5** Friml (Rudolf) **6** Dvŏrák (Antonín) **7** Janáček (Leoš), Martinu (Bohuslav), Smetana (Bedřich)
Danish: 7 Nielsen (Carl)
Dutch: 9 Sweelinck (Jan Pieterszoon)
English: 3 Eno (Brian) **4** Adès (Thomas), Arne (Thomas Augustine), Byrd (William) **5** Elgar (Edward), Holst (Gustav) **6** Davies (Peter Maxwell), Delius (Frederick), Morley (Thomas), Tallis (Thomas), Walton (William), Wesley (Charles, Samuel) **7** Britten (Benjamin), Dowland (John), Gibbons (Orlando), Purcell (Henry), Tippett (Michael), Weelkes (Thomas) **8** Sullivan (Arthur) **9** Dunstable (John) **11** Lloyd Webber (Andrew)
Estonian: 4 Pärt (Arvo)
Finnish: 8 Palmgren (Selim), Sibelius (Jean)
Flemish: 5 Dufay (Guillaume), Lasso (Orlando di) **6** Lassus (Orlande de) **8** Willaert (Adriaan)
French: 4 Indy (Vincent d'), Lalo (Edouard) **5** Auber (Esprit), Bizet (Georges), Dukas (Paul), Fauré (Gabriel), Ibert (Jacques), Jarre (Maurice), Lully (Jean-Baptiste), Ravel (Maurice), Satie (Erik), Widor (Charles-Marie) **6** Boulez (Pierre), Campra (André), Franck (César), Gounod (Charles), Rameau (Jean-Philippe), Thomas (Ambroise) **7** Berlioz (Hector), Debussy (Claude), Delibes (Léo), Machaut (Guillaume de), Milhaud (Darius), Poulenc (Francis), Roussel (Albert) **8** Chabrier (Emmanuel), Couperin (François, Louis), Honegger (Arthur), Massenet (Jules), Messiaen (Olivier) **9** Meyerbeer (Giacomo), Offenbach (Jacques) **10** Saint-Saëns (Camille)
German: 4 Bach (C. P. E., Johann Christian, Johann Sebastian, Wilhelm Friedemann), Orff (Carl) **5** Bruch (Max), Gluck (Christoph Willibald von), Reger (Max), Spohr (Louis, Ludwig), Weber (Carl Maria von), Weill (Kurt) **6** Brahms (Johannes), Handel (George Frideric), Schütz (Heinrich), Vogler (Abt), Wagner (Richard) **7** Hassler (Hans Leo), Strauss (Richard) **8** Korngold (Erich Wolfgang), Schumann (Robert), Telemann (Georg Philipp) **9** Beethoven (Ludwig van), Buxtehude (Dietrich), Hindemith (Paul), Meyerbeer (Giacomo), Pachelbel (Johann) **10** Praetorius (Michael) **11** Humperdinck (Engelbert), Mendelssohn (Felix), Stockhausen (Karlheinz)
Hungarian: 5 Léhar (Franz), Liszt (Franz) **6** Bartók (Béla), Kodály (Zoltán), Ligeti (György) **8** Dohnányi (Erno)
Italian: 4 Peri (Jacopo), Rota (Nino) **5** Berio (Luciano), Boito (Arrigo), Verdi (Giuseppe) **6** Busoni (Ferruccio) **7** Bellini (Vincenzo), Caccini (Giulio), Corelli (Arcangelo), Martini (Padre), Puccini (Giacomo), Rossini (Gioacchino), Salieri (Antonio), Tartini (Giuseppe), Vivaldi (Antonio) **8** Albinoni (Tomaso), Clementi (Muzio), Gabrieli (Andrea, Giovanni), Mascagni (Pietro), Paganini (Niccolò), Respighi (Ottorino) **9** Cherubini (Luigi), Donizetti (Gaetano), Pergolesi (Giovanni Battista), Scarlatti (Alessandro, Domenico), Tommasini (Vincenzo) **10** Boccherini (Luigi), Monteverdi (Claudio), Palestrina (G. P. da), Ponchielli (Amilcare), Zingarelli (Niccolò) **11** Frescobaldi (Girolamo), Leoncavallo (Ruggero) **12** Dallapiccola (Luigi)
Japanese: 4 Taki (Rentaro) **5** Satoh (Somei) **6** Tomita (Isao) **7** Ifukube (Akira) **9** Katsuhisa (Hattori), Takemitsu (Toru)
Mexican: 6 Chávez (Carlos)
Norwegian: 5 Grieg (Edvard)
Polish: 6 Chopin (Frédéric) **7** Gorecki (Henryk) **10** Paderewski (Ignacy Jan), Penderecki (Krzysztof), Wieniawski (Henryk) **11** Lutoslawski (Witold), Szymanowski (Karol)
Romanian: 6 Enescu (Gheorghe, George) **7** Xenakis (Iannis)
Russian: 6 Glinka (Mikhail) **7** Borodin (Aleksandr) **8** Glazunov (Aleksandr), Scriabin (Aleksandr) **9** Balakirev (Mily), Prokofiev (Sergey), Schnittke (Alfred) **10** Kabalevsky (Dmitri), Mussorgsky (Modest), Rubinstein (Anton), Stravinsky (Igor), Tcherepnin (Nikolay) **11** Tchaikovsky (Pyotr Ilich) **12** Khachaturian (Aram), Rachmaninoff (Sergey), Shostakovich (Dmitry)
Spanish: 5 Falla (Manuel de) **7** Albéniz (Isaac), Rodrigo (Joaquin) **8** Granados (Enrique), Victoria (Tomas Luis de)
Swiss: 5 Bloch (Ernest) **6** Martin (Frank) **8** Honegger (Arthur)
(see also **songwriter**)

composer Brian
3 Eno

composer of Bolero
5 Ravel (Maurice)

composer Schifrin
4 Lalo

composer's creation
4 opus

composer's org.
3 BMI **5** ASCAP

composite
3 mix **5** blend **6** fusion, hybrid **7** amalgam, complex, mixture **8** compound **11** combination **12** amalgamation

composition
4 opus **5** essay, paper, theme **6** design, layout, makeup **7** article **9** formation **11** arrangement **12** architecture, constitution, construction

choral: **4** mass **5** motet **7** cantata, passion **8** oratorio
for eight: **5** octet
for five: **7** quintet
for four: **7** quartet
for nine: **5** nonet
for one: **4** aria, solo **6** arioso
for seven: **6** septet
for six: **6** sextet
for three: **4** trio
for two: **3** duo **4** duet
instrumental: **3** jig **4** reel **5** étude, fugue, gigue, march, rondo, suite **6** sonata **7** caprice, partita, prelude, scherzo **8** concerto, fantasia, overture, rhapsody, saraband, sinfonia, symphony, tone poem **9** allemande, capriccio, sarabande **10** intermezzo
vocal: **4** aria, lied, mass, song **5** carol, chant, motet, opera, round **6** arioso, ballad, chanty **7** cantata, chanson, chantey, chorale, lullaby, requiem **8** berceuse, madrigal, oratorio **9** plainsong, spiritual **10** plainchant

compos mentis
4 sane **5** lucid, sound **6** normal

composure
4 calm **5** poise **7** balance, dignity **8** calmness, coolness, evenness, serenity, sobriety **9** sangfroid **10** equanimity **11** equilibrium

compound
3 mix **4** join, link **5** admix, alloy, blend, union, unite **6** expand, extend, fusion, make up, mingle **7** amalgam, augment, complex, compost, enlarge, magnify, mixture **8** coalesce, comingle, heighten, increase, intermix, multiply **9** admixture, aggravate, associate, commingle, composite, intensify, synthesis **10** commixture, exacerbate **11** intermingle **12** amalgamation
aroma: **5** neral **6** citral **7** menthol **8** vanillin
chemical: (see at **chemical**)
protein: **7** peptone

comprehend
4 know **5** catch, grasp **6** absorb, accept, embody, fathom, take in **7** cognize, compass, contain, discern, embrace, include, involve, subsume **8** comprise, perceive **9** encompass **10** appreciate, understand

comprehensible
8 knowable **9** graspable **10** fathomable **12** intelligible

comprehension
3 ken **5** grasp **6** uptake **9** awareness, knowledge **10** cognizance, conception, perception **11** discernment **12** apperception **13** understanding

comprehensive
4 full, wide **5** broad **6** global **7** general, overall **8** catholic, complete, sweeping **9** all-around, extensive, inclusive, universal **10** exhaustive **11** compendious **12** all-inclusive, encyclopedic

comprehensiveness
5 range, reach, scope **7** breadth **8** entirety, fullness, totality **9** amplitude

compress
3 jam **4** cram, push **5** crush, press **6** reduce, shrink, squash, squish, shrink **7** bandage, compact, squeeze **8** condense, contract **11** concentrate

comprise
4 form **6** make up **7** contain, embrace, include, subsume **10** comprehend, constitute

compromise
4 mean, pact, risk **6** settle **7** bargain, compact **8** contract, endanger, trade off **9** agreement, middle way **10** concession, golden mean, jeopardize, settlement **12** middle ground

compulsion
4 itch, need, urge **5** drive, force **6** duress **8** coercion **9** necessity **10** constraint

compulsive
6 driven **7** driving **9** besetting, obsessive **12** irresistible, overwhelming

compulsory
7 binding **8** coercive, enforced, required **9** mandatory, requisite **10** imperative, obligatory

compunction
4 pang **5** demur, qualm **6** regret, unease **7** remorse, scruple **8** distress **9** hesitancy, misgiving **10** conscience, hesitation

compunctious
5 sorry **8** contrite, penitent **9** regretful, repentant **10** apologetic, remorseful **11** penitential

computation
8 figuring **9** ciphering, reckoning **10** arithmetic, estimation **11** calculation

compute
5 tally, total **6** cipher, figure, reckon **8** estimate **9** calculate, determine

computer
6 abacus, laptop **7** desktop **9** mainframe **10** calculator
brand: **4** Acer, Dell **5** Apple
code: **5** ASCII
command: **4** undo
component: **3** CPU **4** chip **5** mouse, tower **7** monitor **8** keyboard **9** hard drive
connection: **3** LAN
disc: **5** CD-ROM
early: **5** ENIAC **6** UNIVAC
expert: **4** geek, nerd **6** techie
fodder: **4** data
graphics application: **3** CGI, FMV

information: 4 data
instruction: 5 macro
inventor: 7 Babbage (Charles)
key: 3 Alt, Esc, Tab 4 Ctrl 5 Enter, Shift
language: 3 Ada, APL, SQL 4 Java, Lisp, Perl 5 ALGOL, BASIC, COBOL 6 Pascal 7 FORTRAN
see also **programming language**
type: 6 analog 7 digital
operating system: 4 Unix 5 Linux, MS-DOS 7 Android

computer-game genre
3 FPS, RPG, RTS 6 action, puzzle, racing, sports 8 fighting, platform 9 adventure 10 simulation

comrade
3 pal 4 ally, chum, mate 5 buddy, crony 6 cohort, comate, fellow 7 consort 8 sidekick, tovarich, tovarish 9 associate, colleague, companion

con
3 gyp, vet 4 anti, bilk, coax, dupe, fool, hoax, rook, scam 5 cheat, fraud, grift, learn, study, trick 6 cajole, fleece, gammon, inmate, survey 7 against, blarney, canvass, chicane, convict, deceive, defraud, examine, inspect, swindle, wheedle 8 blandish, flimflam, hoodwink, inveigle, jailbird, memorize, negative, opponent, persuade, prisoner, soft-soap 9 bamboozle, check over, sweet-talk 10 antithesis, manipulate, scrutinize 11 hornswoggle 12 tuberculosis

concatenate
4 join, link 5 unite 7 connect

concavity
3 dip, sag 4 bowl, dent, sink 5 basin 6 crater, hollow, trough 7 sinkage 8 sinkhole 10 depression

conceal
4 bury, hide, mask, veil 5 cache, cloak, cover, stash 6 screen 7 obscure, secrete 8 ensconce, enshroud, palliate 10 camouflage

concealed
3 hid 5 privy 6 buried, covert, hidden, secret 8 obscured, shrouded, ulterior 11 clandestine

concede
3 own 4 avow, fold 5 admit, allow, award, grant, yield 6 accept, accord 7 confess 9 surrender, vouchsafe 10 capitulate, relinquish 11 acknowledge

conceit
4 idea, whim 5 fancy, pride 6 egoism, megrim, notion, vagary, vanity 7 caprice, egotism, thought 8 crotchet, metaphor, self-love, smugness, snobbery 9 self-pride, vainglory 10 narcissism, self-esteem 11 complacence, complacency, self-opinion, swelled head

conceited
4 vain 6 snobby, snooty, uppish, uppity 7 pompous, stuck-up 8 egoistic, immodest, puffed up, snobbish 9 egotistic 12 narcissistic, vainglorious

conceitedness
6 vanity 8 self-love 9 vainglory 10 narcissism

conceivable
8 possible 9 plausible, thinkable 10 imaginable, supposable

conceive
4 form 5 beget, fancy, grasp, think 6 devise, expect, ideate, ponder 7 dream up, feature, imagine, realize, suppose, suspect, think up 8 envisage, envision 9 formulate, originate, speculate, visualize 10 excogitate, mastermind

concentrate
4 mass 5 focus 6 gather, shrink 7 collect, compact 8 assemble, compress, condense, contract, converge 10 accumulate 11 consolidate

concentrated
5 thick 6 intent, strong 7 focused, intense 9 intensive, undiluted

concentration
5 field, major, study 9 attention 10 absorption 11 application

concept
4 idea 5 image 6 notion, theory 7 conceit, thought 10 impression, perception

conception
4 idea 5 birth, image, start 6 notion, origin, outset, theory 7 conceit, genesis, thought 9 beginning 10 impression, perception

conceptual
5 ideal 8 abstract, notional 9 imaginary, visionary 10 ideational 11 theoretical 12 hypothetical, intellectual

concern
4 care, firm, heed 5 doubt, worry 6 affair, bear on, bother, engage, gadget, matter, occupy, outfit, regard, unease 7 anxiety, company, disturb, involve, perturb, trouble 8 business, deal with, disquiet, interest, mistrust 9 attention, curiosity, misgiving, suspicion 10 enterprise, skepticism, solicitude, uneasiness 11 carefulness, contrivance, uncertainty 12 apprehension 13 consciousness, consideration, establishment

concerned
7 anxious, worried 8 affected, involved 10 implicated, interested

concerning
4 as to, in re 5 about, anent, as for 7 apropos 9 as regards, regarding 10 relating to, relative to, respecting

concert
5 agree, union 6 accord, concur, settle, soiree

7 arrange, concord, harmony, recital 8 coincide, musicale 9 agreement, cooperate, harmonize, negotiate 11 performance
venue: 4 hall, odea (plural) 5 arena, odeum 10 auditorium

concerted
5 joint 6 mutual, united 7 unified 8 combined 11 coordinated 13 collaborative

concession
3 sop 5 favor, grant 8 giveback 9 admission, allowance, privilege 10 compromise 12 acquiescence

conch
5 shell 7 mollusc, mollusk

concierge
5 super 6 porter, warden 7 doorman, janitor 9 custodian 10 doorkeeper

conciliate
4 calm, ease 6 disarm, pacify, soothe 7 appease, assuage, mollify, placate, sweeten, win over 9 reconcile 10 propitiate

concise
5 brief, pithy, short, terse 7 compact, laconic, summary 8 abridged, succinct 9 condensed 10 compressed, contracted 11 compendious 13 short and sweet

conclave
5 forum, synod 6 caucus, powwow 7 meeting, session 8 assembly 9 gathering 10 conference, consistory, convention 11 convocation, get-together

conclude
3 end 4 halt, stop 5 close, infer, judge 6 decide, deduce, derive, effect, figure, finish, gather, reason, settle, wind up, wrap up 7 collect, resolve 8 complete 9 determine, terminate

concluding
4 last 5 final 6 latest, latter 7 closing 8 eventual, terminal, ultimate

conclusion
3 end 4 coda, stop 5 cease, close 6 ending, epilog, finale, finish, period, result, windup 7 closing, closure, outcome, verdict 8 decision, epilogue, judgment, sequitur 9 cessation, deduction, inference, summation 10 completion, denouement, resolution, settlement 11 culmination, termination 13 determination
musical: 4 coda
poetic: 5 envoi

conclusive
4 last 5 final 6 cogent 8 deciding, decisive, ultimate 9 clinching 10 compelling, convincing, definitive, undeniable 11 determinant, determinate, irrefutable 12 irrefragable, unanswerable 13 determinative

concoct
3 mix 4 brew, cook 5 frame, hatch 6 cook up, create, devise, invent 7 dream up 8 conceive, contrive 9 fabricate, formulate, originate

concoction
4 brew, plan 5 blend 7 mixture, project 8 compound, creation 9 invention 11 combination, contrivance, fabrication, preparation

concomitant
7 adjunct 8 adjuvant 9 accessory, ancillary, associate, attendant, attending, companion, satellite 10 coincident, collateral 12 accompanying 13 accompaniment, supplementary

concord
4 pact 5 amity, peace, unity 6 comity, treaty, unison 7 entente, harmony, rapport 8 goodwill 9 agreement 10 consonance

concordant
8 agreeing 9 congruous, consonant 10 compatible, consistent, harmonious 11 appropriate

Concorde
3 SST

concourse
5 foyer 6 throng 7 joining, meeting 8 junction 9 gathering 10 confluence, crossroads

concrete
5 solid 6 actual 8 specific, tangible 10 particular 11 substantial
component: 4 sand 5 water 6 gravel

concubine
7 hetaera, hetaira, odalisc, odalisk 8 mistress 9 courtesan, odalisque

concupiscence
4 lust 5 ardor 6 desire, libido, venery 7 lechery, passion 9 prurience, pruriency 11 lustfulness 13 lickerishness

concupiscent
3 hot 5 randy 6 wanton 7 aroused, goatish, lustful 8 prurient 9 lecherous, lickerish, salacious 10 lascivious, libidinous, lubricious, passionate

concur
4 jibe 5 agree, unite 6 accord, assent 7 approve, combine, concord, consent, go along 8 coincide 9 cooperate, harmonize

concurrent
6 coeval 8 parallel 10 coexistent, coexisting, convergent, synchronic 11 synchronous 12 contemporary, simultaneous

concurrently
6 at once 8 together 12 coincidently

concuss
3 jar 4 rock, stun 5 shake, shock 7 agitate

concussion
3 jar 4 bump, jolt 5 clout, crash, shock 6 impact

7 jarring, jolting, shaking 8 pounding 9 agitation, collision

condemn
3 rap 4 damn, doom 5 blame, decry, knock, seize 7 censure, convict, deplore 8 denounce, sentence 9 criticize, deprecate, proscribe, reprehend, reprobate 10 denunciate

condensation
3 dew 5 brief 6 digest, précis 7 epitome, outline, summary 8 abstract, synopsis 9 reduction 10 abridgment, conspectus 11 abridgement

condense
5 sum up 6 digest, reduce, shrink 7 abridge, compact, shorten 8 boil down, compress, contract 9 constrict, epitomize, summarize, synopsize 10 abbreviate 11 concentrate, consolidate, precipitate

condensed
7 concise, summary 10 boiled down 11 compendious

condenser
9 capacitor

condescend
5 deign, stoop 6 unbend

condescending
5 lofty 6 lordly, snobby, snooty, uppish, uppity 7 haughty, pompous 8 affected, arrogant, cavalier, snobbish, superior 10 disdainful 11 patronizing, pretentious 12 supercilious

condign
3 apt, due, fit 4 fair, just 5 right 6 proper 7 fitting, merited 8 deserved, rightful, suitable 9 equitable, justified 11 appropriate

condiment
5 curry, sauce, spice 6 catsup, relish, tamari 7 chutney, ketchup, mustard 8 dressing, soy sauce 9 seasoning 10 mayonnaise

____ con Dios!
4 Vaya

condition
5 enure, inure, shape, state, terms 6 fettle, malady, status 7 ailment, disease, fitness, proviso 8 syndrome 9 complaint, essential, exception, necessity, provision, requisite, situation 10 limitation, sine qua non 11 requirement, reservation, stipulation 12 prerequisite 13 qualification

conditional
7 reliant 8 relative 9 dependent, provisory, qualified, tentative, uncertain 10 contingent, restricted 11 provisional

condolence
3 rue 4 pity, ruth 6 solace 7 comfort 8 sympathy 10 compassion 13 commiseration

condonable
7 tenable 9 excusable, tolerable 10 acceptable, defensible, pardonable 11 justifiable

condone
5 remit 6 excuse, pardon 7 forgive 8 overlook

conduce
4 lead, tend 7 redound 10 contribute

conducive
7 helpful, leading, tending 9 favorable 10 beneficial, salubrious 11 efficacious, serviceable, stimulating 12 advantageous, contributory, instrumental 13 accommodating

conduct
3 act, run 4 bear, head, lead, show 5 guide, pilot, steer, usher 6 attend, behave, charge, convey, demean, deport, direct, escort, handle, manage 7 arrange, bearing, comport, control, manners, operate, oversee 8 behavior, demeanor, handling, shepherd, transmit 9 accompany, oversight, supervise 10 administer, deportment, management 11 comportment, supervision

conductor
5 guide 6 escort, leader 7 maestro 8 motorman 10 bandleader
American: 4 Shaw (Robert) 5 Stock (Frederick), Szell (George) 6 Levine (James), Maazel (Lorin), Previn (André), Reiner (Fritz), Thomas (Theodore, Michael Tilson), Walter (Bruno) 7 Fennell (Frederick), Fiedler (Arthur), Monteux (Pierre), Ormandy (Eugene), Schwarz (Gerard), Slatkin (Leonard) 8 Damrosch (Leopold, Walter), Williams (John) 9 Bernstein (Leonard), Leinsdorf (Erich), Rodzinski (Artur), Steinberg (William), Stokowski (Leopold) 11 Kostelanetz (André), Mitropoulos (Dimitri)
Argentinian: 7 Kleiber (Carlos) 9 Barenboim (Daniel)
Australian: 7 Bonynge (Richard)
Austrian: 4 Böhm (Karl) 6 Mahler (Gustav) 7 Karajan (Herbert von) 11 Weingartner (Felix)
Belgian: 5 Ysaÿe (Eugene)
Canadian: 6 Dutoit (Charles) 9 MacMillan (Ernest)
Czech: 7 Kubelik (Jan, Rafael)
Dutch: 7 Haitink (Bernard) 10 Mengelberg (Willem)
English: 4 Wood (Henry) 5 Boult (Adrian), Davis (Colin) 6 Rattle (Simon) 7 Beecham (Thomas), Leppard (Raymond), Malcolm (George), Pinnock (Trevor), Sargent (Malcolm) 8 Goossens (Eugene), Marriner (Neville) 9 Mackerras (Charles) 10 Barbirolli (John)
Finnish: 7 Salonen (Esa-Pekka)
French: 5 Munch (Charles) 6 Boulez (Pierre), Prêtre (Georges) 7 Monteux (Pierre)

German: **4** Böhm (Karl), Muck (Carl, Karl) **5** Masur (Kurt) **6** Jochum (Eugen) **7** Kleiber (Erich) **9** Klemperer (Otto), Scherchen (Hermann) **10** Sawallisch (Wolfgang) **11** Furtwängler (Wilhelm), Mendelssohn (Felix)
Greek: **11** Mitropoulos (Dimitri)
Hungarian: **5** Seidl (Anton), Solti (Georg), Szell (George) **6** Doráti (Antal), Reiner (Fritz) **7** Nikisch (Arthur), Ormandy (Eugene), Richter (Hans)
Indian: **5** Mehta (Zubin)
Italian: **4** Muti (Riccardo) **6** Abbado (Claudio) **7** Chailly (Riccardo), Giulini (Carlo Maria) **8** Cantelli (Guido), Sinopoli (Giuseppe) **9** Toscanini (Arturo)
Japanese: **5** Ozawa (Seiji)
Latvian: **7** Nelsons (Andris)
Polish: **9** Rodzinski (Artur)
Russian: **7** Gergiev (Valery) **10** Temirkanov (Yuri) **12** Koussevitzky (Serge)
Spanish: **6** Iturbi (José)
Swiss: **8** Ansermet (Ernest)
Venezuelan: **7** Dudamel (Gustavo)
stick: **5** baton

conduit
4 duct, main, pipe **5** canal **6** course **7** channel **8** aqueduct, penstock, pipeline **11** watercourse

coney
4 pika **5** hyrax, lapin **6** rabbit **10** butterfish

confab
4 chat, talk **6** confer, huddle, parley, powwow **7** consult **8** collogue, colloquy, dialogue **10** conference, discussion **12** conversation, deliberation

confabulate
see **confab**

confabulation
see **confab**

confection
see **candy**

confederacy
5 cabal, union **6** league **7** compact **8** alliance **9** coalition, syndicate **10** conspiracy, federation

confederate
3 reb **4** ally **5** rebel, unite **6** fellow **7** abettor, partner **9** accessory, associate, colleague, Johnny Reb **10** accomplice **11** conspirator **12** collaborator **13** coconspirator
admiral: **6** Semmes
capital: **8** Richmond
color: **4** gray
general: **3** Lee (Robert E.) **4** Hill (Ambrose), Hood (John Bell) **5** Bragg (Braxton), Ewell (Richard Stoddart), Price (Sterling), Smith (Edmund Kirby) **6** Morgan (John Hunt), Stuart (J. E. B.) **7** Forrest (Nathan Bedford), Hampton (Wade), Jackson (Thomas Jonathan "Stonewall"), Pickett (George) **8** Johnston (Albert Sidney, Joseph Eggleston) **9** Pemberton (John Clifford) **10** Beauregard (Pierre G. T.), Longstreet (James)
president: **5** Davis (Jefferson)
soldier: **3** reb **9** butternut
spy: **4** Boyd (Belle)
vice-president: **8** Stephens (Alexander)

confederation
see **confederacy**

confer
4 give, meet, talk **5** allot, award, grant, speak **6** accord, advise, bestow, confab, donate, huddle, parley, powwow **7** consult, discuss, present **8** collogue, converse **10** deliberate **11** confabulate

conference
4 talk **5** forum, synod **6** caucus, league, parley, powwow **7** meeting, palaver, seminar **8** assembly, colloquy, congress **9** symposium **10** colloquium, discussion, round-robin, roundtable **11** association, convocation **12** consultation, deliberation **13** confabulation
site: **5** Yalta

confess
3 own **4** avow, sing **5** admit, allow, grant, let on, own up **6** reveal **7** concede, divulge, profess **8** disclose **9** come clean **11** acknowledge

confession
5 creed **6** avowal **7** peccavi **9** admission, statement **10** disclosure

confidant
8 familiar, intimate

confide
4 tell **5** trust **6** bestow, commit, reveal **7** commend, consign, entrust, whisper **8** hand over, relegate, turn over

confidence
5 faith, poise, stock, trust **6** aplomb, surety **8** credence, reliance, sureness **9** assurance, certainty, certitude **10** conviction, equanimity
game: **4** scam **5** bunco, bunko, fraud, grift, sting **6** hustle **7** swindle **8** flimflam

confidence man
3 gyp **5** shark **7** diddler, grifter, scammer, sharper, sharpie **8** swindler **9** charlatan, defrauder, trickster **11** bunco artist

confident
4 bold, sure **5** brash, brave, cocky **6** secure **7** assured, certain **8** cocksure, fearless, intrepid, positive, sanguine, unafraid **9** dauntless, undaunted **10** courageous, undoubtful **11** self-assured, self-reliant **13** self-assertive, self-possessed

confidential
5 close, privy **6** hushed, inside, secret **7** private **8** familiar, hush-hush, intimate **9** auricular **10** classified

configuration
4 cast, form **5** shape **6** figure, layout, makeup **7** contour, gestalt, outline, pattern **9** structure **12** conformation

confine
3 box, mew, pen **4** cage, coop, crib, jail, term **5** bound, cramp, hem in, limit **6** immure, intern, lock up, shut in, shut up **7** delimit, enclose, impound, put away **8** encircle, imprison, localize, restrict **9** constrain **11** incarcerate **12** circumscribe

confinement
7 custody, lying-in **8** childbed **9** captivity, detention, restraint **10** constraint **12** accouchement, imprisonment **13** incarceration

confines
6 bounds, limits **7** borders, compass **8** boundary, environs, purlieus **9** precincts **10** boundaries

confirm
3 fix, set **5** check, prove, vouch **6** attest, ratify, uphold, verify **7** approve, bear out, certify, concede, endorse, justify, support **8** buttress, check out, validate **9** ascertain, reinforce **10** strengthen **11** corroborate **12** authenticate, substantiate

confirmation
5 proof **7** support, witness **8** approval, evidence **9** testimony **10** validation **11** attestation, endorsement, testimonial **12** ratification, verification **13** certification, corroboration

confirmed
3 set **5** fixed, sworn **6** proven **7** chronic, settled **8** deep-dyed, definite, habitual, hardened, ratified **10** accustomed, deep-rooted, deep-seated, entrenched, habituated, inveterate, persistent **13** bred-in-the-bone, dyed-in-the-wool

confiscate
4 grab, take **5** annex, seize, usurp **7** escheat, impound, preempt **8** arrogate **9** sequester **10** commandeer **11** appropriate, expropriate

confiture
3 jam **8** conserve, preserve **9** marmalade, preserves

conflagrant
5 afire, fiery **6** ablaze, aflame, alight **7** blazing, burning, flaming

conflagration
3 war **4** fire **5** blaze **7** inferno **8** conflict **9** holocaust

conflate
3 mix **4** fuse, join, meld, weld **5** blend, merge, mix up **6** mingle, muddle **7** combine, confuse, mistake **8** coalesce, confound **9** commingle

conflict
3 row, war **4** bout, duel, rift, vary **5** brawl, clash, fight, melee, set-to **6** battle, combat, differ, fracas, strife **7** contend, contest, discord, dispute, rivalry, warfare **8** argument, disagree, mismatch, struggle, tug-of-war, variance **9** encounter, rencontre **10** contention, engagement **11** competition

conflicting
6 at odds **7** opposed, warring **8** clashing, contrary, opposing **9** dissonant **10** contending, discordant, discrepant **11** incongruent, incongruous, inconsonant **12** antagonistic, antipathetic, incompatible, inconsistent, inharmonious **13** contradictory

confluence
6 merger **7** joining, meeting, merging **8** junction **9** concourse, gathering **11** convergence

conform
3 fit **4** jibe, obey, suit **5** adapt, agree, fit in, match, yield **6** accord, adjust, attune, comply, follow, square, submit, tailor **8** dovetail **9** acquiesce, harmonize, reconcile **10** coordinate, correspond, proportion **11** accommodate

conformable
6 fitted, suited **7** adapted, matched **8** amenable, obedient, suitable **9** agreeable, compliant, congenial, consonant **10** submissive

conformation
4 cast, form **5** shape **6** figure **7** anatomy **9** structure **10** adaptation **11** arrangement **13** configuration

conforming
3 apt **6** decent, proper, seemly **7** correct, uniform **8** becoming, decorous, suitable **9** befitting, civilized **10** compatible, consistent **11** comme il faut

conformity
6 accord **7** decorum, harmony **9** agreement, coherence, congruity, obedience, orthodoxy **10** accordance, allegiance, compliance, consonance, observance, submission **11** consistency **12** acquiescence

confound
4 damn, faze **5** abash, befog, mix up, stump **6** baffle, puzzle, rattle, refute **7** confuse, mistake, mystify, nonplus, perplex, stupefy **8** befuddle, bewilder, disprove **9** discomfit, dumbfound, embarrass, frustrate **10** controvert, disconcert **11** misidentify

confounded
5 at sea, utter **6** blamed, cursed, cussed, damned **7** blasted, blessed, doggone, shocked **8** absolute, accursed, dismayed, infernal, outright **9** consarned, dad-blamed, execrable, out-and-out **11** dumbfounded, overwhelmed, unmitigated **13** thunderstruck

confrere
see **colleague**

confront
4 defy, face, meet **5** beard, brave, cross **6** accost, breast, oppose, take on **9** challenge, encounter

confuse
3 fog **4** blur, daze, faze **5** abash, addle, befog, cloud, dizzy, mix up, muddy, stump, upset **6** baffle, ball up, bemuse, flurry, foul up, fuddle, garble, jumble, mess up, muddle, puzzle, rattle **7** agitate, becloud, derange, disrupt, distort, flummox, fluster, mislead, mistake, mystify, nonplus, perplex, perturb, snarl up **8** bedazzle, befuddle, bewilder, confound, disorder, disquiet, distract, throw off, unsettle **9** discomfit, disorient, embarrass **10** complicate, disarrange, discompose, disconcert **11** disorganize, misidentify **12** misrepresent

confused
4 a-sea, lost **5** at sea, dazed, messy, muddy, muzzy, vague **6** addled **7** at a loss, chaotic, mixed up, muddled, puzzled **9** flustered, perplexed, unsettled **10** bewildered, nonplussed, topsy-turvy **11** disoriented **12** disconcerted

confusion
3 ado, din **4** flap, mess, stew **5** babel, chaos, havoc, mix-up, snafu, snarl **6** bedlam, dither, foul-up, hubbub, huddle, jumble, lather, muddle, tumult, unease **7** anarchy, clutter, turmoil **8** disarray, disorder, shambles **9** abashment, agitation, commotion, imbroglio **10** hullabaloo, perplexity, puzzlement, turbulence, uneasiness **11** derangement, disturbance, pandemonium **12** bewilderment

confute
4 deny **5** evert, rebut **6** defeat, negate **8** confound, disprove, puncture **10** controvert, disconfirm

congé
3 bow **5** adieu **6** good-by **7** good-bye, molding, parting, sendoff **8** farewell **9** dismissal **11** leave-taking

congeal
3 dry, gel, set **4** clot, jell **5** jelly **6** curdle, harden **7** stiffen, thicken **8** solidify **9** coagulate **10** gelatinize

congener
6 agnate **7** cognate, sibling **8** relation, relative

congenial
4 nice **6** social **7** affable, amiable, cordial, kindred, welcome **8** amicable, friendly, gracious, pleasant, pleasing, sociable, suitable **9** agreeable, congruous, consonant, favorable **10** compatible, consistent, gratifying, harmonious **11** cooperative, pleasurable, sympathetic **13** companionable

congenital
6 inborn, inbred, innate, native **7** natural **8** inherent **9** essential, ingrained, intrinsic **10** deep-seated, indigenous, indwelling

conger
3 eel
catcher: **5** eeler

congeries
5 group **7** company **8** assembly **9** gathering **10** assemblage, collection **11** aggregation **12** congregation

congest
3 jam **4** clog, fill, plug, stop **5** block, choke, close, crowd **6** plug up **7** occlude **8** obstruct

conglobate
4 ball **6** sphere **8** ensphere **9** spherical

conglomerate
4 mass, pool **5** chain, group, mixed, trust **6** cartel, motley **7** chaebol, combine **8** keiretsu, zaibatsu **9** aggregate, syndicate **11** aggregation

conglomeration
5 hoard, trove **8** mishmash **9** aggregate **10** collection, cumulation, hodgepodge, hotchpotch, miscellany **11** agglomerate, aggregation **12** accumulation

Congo, Democratic Republic of the
capital: **8** Kinshasa
city: **7** Kolwezi **9** Kisangani, Mbuji-Mayi **10** Lubumbashi
explorer: **7** Stanley (Henry Morton)
former name: **5** Zaire **12** Belgian Congo
lake: **4** Kivu **5** Mweru **6** Albert, Edward **10** Tanganyika
language: **6** French **7** English
monetary unit: **5** franc
neighbor: **5** Sudan **6** Angola, Rwanda, Uganda, Zambia **7** Burundi **8** Tanzania
river: **4** Uele

Congo, Republic of
capital: **11** Brazzaville
city: **11** Pointe-Noire
former name: **11** Middle Congo
language: **6** French
monetary unit: **5** franc
neighbor: **5** Gabon **6** Angola **7** Cabinda **8** Cameroon

congratulate
4 laud **6** salute **10** compliment, felicitate

congregate
4 meet **5** swarm **6** gather, muster **7** collect, convene **8** assemble, converge **9** forgather **10** foregather, rendezvous

congregation
4 mass **5** crowd, flock, group **7** meeting **8** assembly, audience **9** gathering **10** assemblage, collection **11** churchgoers **12** parishioners

congress
4 diet **5** synod **6** league **7** meeting, society

8 assembly, conclave 10 convention, parliament 11 association, Capitol Hill, legislature

congressman
5 solon 7 senator 8 delegate, lawmaker 10 legislator

congruity
9 agreement, coherence 10 conformity 11 consistency

congruous
3 apt, fit 7 fitting 9 agreeable, befitting, congenial, consonant 10 compatible, concordant, consistent, harmonious 11 appropriate, sympathetic

conical dwelling
5 tepee

conifer
3 fir, yew 4 pine 5 cedar, larch 6 spruce 7 cypress, hemlock, juniper, redwood, sequoia 8 softwood 9 evergreen 10 arborvitae

conjectural
7 reputed 8 putative, supposed 11 speculative, theoretical 12 hypothetical, suppositious 13 suppositional

conjecture
5 guess, infer 6 assume, theory 7 presume, suppose, surmise, suspect 8 theorize 9 inference, speculate 11 hypothesize, proposition, speculation, supposition

conjoin
3 wed 4 band, link, yoke 5 unite 6 couple 7 combine, connect 8 federate 9 affiliate, associate, cooperate 11 consolidate

conjoint
6 common, mutual, public, shared, united 7 unified 8 combined, communal 9 concerted 10 collective 11 coefficient, cooperative, intermutual

conjointly
8 mutually, together

conjugal
6 wedded 7 marital, married, nuptial, spousal 8 hymeneal 9 connubial 11 matrimonial

conjugality
7 wedlock 8 marriage 9 matrimony

conjugate
4 fuse, join, link, pair, yoke 5 yoked 6 couple, joined, linked 7 bracket, combine, conjoin, connect, coupled 9 associate, connected

conjunct
5 joint 6 common, joined, mutual, shared, united

conjunction
3 and, but, for, nor, yet 4 lest, once, than, then, when 5 after, since, union, until, where, which, while 6 before, either, though, unless 7 because, however, neither, whereas, whether 8 alliance, although, moreover, whenever 9 therefore 10 connection 11 affiliation, association, combination, concurrence

conjuration
4 oath 5 charm, spell, trick 7 sorcery 10 adjuration, hocus-pocus, invocation 11 abracadabra, incantation

conjure
3 beg 4 urge 6 appeal, invoke, summon 7 beseech, entreat, imagine, implore 8 contrive 9 importune 10 supplicate

conjurer
4 mage 5 magus 6 Magian, wizard 7 warlock 8 magician, sorcerer 9 enchanter, trickster 11 illusionist, necromancer

conjuring
5 magic 7 sorcery 8 wizardry 10 hocus-pocus, necromancy 11 abracadabra, legerdemain, thaumaturgy

conk
3 die, hit, rap 4 belt, swat 5 croak, faint, knock, thump, whack 8 knock out

con man
see **confidence man**

connate
4 akin 6 allied, inborn, native 7 kindred, related 8 inherent 9 congenial, elemental, essential, ingrained, inherited, intrinsic 10 affiliated, congenital, indigenous, indwelling 11 consanguine

connect
3 tie, wed 4 ally, bind, join, link, yoke 5 hitch, marry, unite 6 attach, bridge, couple, fasten, relate 7 combine, conjoin 8 transfer 9 affiliate, associate, interlock

Connecticut
capital: 8 Hartford
city: 4 Avon 6 Darien 8 New Haven, Stamford 9 Greenwich, New London, Waterbury 10 Bridgeport
college, university: 4 Yale 7 Trinity 8 Wesleyan 9 Fairfield 10 Quinnipiac
nickname: 6 Nutmeg (State) 12 Constitution (State)
river: 6 Thames 10 Housatonic 11 Connecticut
state bird: 5 robin (American)
state flower: 14 mountain laurel
state tree: 8 white oak

connection
3 tie 4 bond, link 5 joint, nexus, tie-in, union 6 hookup, splice 7 joining, kinship, network 8 affinity, alliance, coupling, junction, juncture 9 coherence, communion, fastening 10 attachment, catenation, continuity 11 affiliation, association, combination, conjunction, partnership 12 relationship

connective
3 and, nor, not 4 then 6 either 7 neither 8 syndetic 11 conjunction, conjunctive

Connery of 007 fame
4 Sean

conniption
3 fit **4** bout, snit **5** furor, spasm, spate, spell, throe **6** attack, frenzy **7** seizure, tantrum **8** outburst, paroxysm **10** convulsion

connivance
8 intrigue **9** collusion **10** complicity, conspiracy

connive
4 plot, wink **5** blink **6** devise, scheme, wink at **7** blink at, collude **8** conspire, contrive, intrigue **9** machinate

connoisseur
4 buff **6** expert **7** epicure, esthete, gourmet **8** aesthete, gourmand, highbrow **9** authority, bon vivant **10** dilettante, gastronome **11** cognoscente

connotation
4 hint **7** meaning **8** overtone **9** undertone **10** intimation, suggestion **11** association, implication **13** signification

connote
4 hint, mean **5** imply, spell **6** hint at, intend **7** betoken, express, signify, suggest **8** indicate, intimate **9** insinuate

connubial
6 wedded **7** marital, married, nuptial, spousal **8** conjugal, hymeneal **11** matrimonial

connubiality
7 wedlock **8** marriage **9** matrimony **11** conjugality

conquer
4 beat, best, lick, tame, whip **5** crush **6** defeat, master, subdue **8** overcome, surmount, vanquish **9** checkmate, overpower, overthrow, overwhelm, subjugate

conquest
3 win **4** rout **7** triumph, victory **9** overthrow, seduction **11** subjugation

Conrad, Joseph
character: 3 Jim **4** Axel, Lena **5** Flora, Kurtz **6** Marlow, Verloc **7** Almayer **8** MacWhirr, Nostromo
work: 5 Youth **6** Chance **7** Lord Jim, Typhoon, Victory **8** Nostromo **11** Secret Agent (The) **13** Almayer's Folly **15** Heart of Darkness

Conroy novel
10 Beach Music **11** Water Is Wide (The) **12** Great Santini (The) **13** Prince of Tides (The) **17** Lords of Discipline (The)

consanguineous
4 akin **6** agnate **7** cognate, connate, kindred, related

conscience
5 demur, honor, qualm **6** ethics, virtue **7** decency, remorse, scruple **8** morality, scruples, superego **9** integrity **10** contrition **11** compunction

conscienceless
6 amoral **7** immoral **9** unethical **12** unprincipled, unscrupulous

conscientious
4 fair, just **6** honest **7** careful, dutiful, upright **8** diligent, reliable, studious **9** honorable **10** high-minded, meticulous, principled, scrupulous **11** hard-working, painstaking, punctilious

conscious
5 alive, awake, aware **7** knowing, mindful, witting **8** sensible, sentient **9** attentive, cognizant **10** deliberate, perceptive

consciousness
4 heed, mind **6** regard **7** concern **9** alertness, awareness, knowledge **10** cognizance, perception **11** realization, recognition

conscribe
5 draft, limit **6** call up, enlist, enroll, muster **7** recruit

conscript
5 draft, elect **6** called, choose, chosen, enlist, enroll, induct, select **7** drafted, dragoon, impress, recruit, soldier **8** selected

consecrate
5 bless **6** anoint, devote, hallow, ordain, pledge **8** dedicate, sanctify

consecrated
4 holy **6** sacred **7** blessed **8** hallowed **10** sanctified
oil: 6 chrism

consecution
see **sequence**

consecutive
4 next **5** later **6** serial **7** ensuing, ordered, sequent **9** following, succedent **10** sequential, subsequent, succeeding, successive **11** progressive **12** successional

consent
3 yes **4** okay **5** agree, allow, leave, yield **6** accede, accord, assent, comply, concur, permit **7** approve, go-ahead **8** approval, sanction **9** acquiesce, agreement, allowance, subscribe **10** compliance, permission **12** acquiescence **13** authorization, understanding

consequence
4 fame, note, rank **5** issue, state **6** cachet, effect, import, moment, renown, repute, result, sequel, status, upshot, weight **7** account, conceit, fallout, outcome, stature **8** eminence, position, prestige, reaction **9** aftermath, magnitude **10** importance, reputation **11** aftereffect, weightiness **12** repercussion, significance

consequent
5 later, sound **7** ensuant, ensuing, logical **8** rational **9** deduction, following, resulting

consequential
3 big **5** major **7** serious, weighty **8** indirect, material **9** important, momentous **10** collateral, incidental, meaningful, subsidiary **11** significant, substantial **12** considerable

consequently
4 ergo, thus **5** hence **9** as a result, therefore, thereupon **10** inevitably **11** accordingly

conservation
4 care **7** control **9** attention, husbandry **10** management, protection **11** safekeeping **12** guardianship, preservation

conservative
4 tory **6** proper **7** diehard, old-line **8** cautious, discreet, old-guard, orthodox, rightist, standpat **9** right-wing, temperate **10** restrained **11** circumspect, reactionary, right-winger, standpatter, traditional
preceder: 3 neo

conservatory
6 school **7** academy, nursery **8** hothouse **10** greenhouse **11** music school

conserve
3 can, jam **4** keep, save **5** hoard, lay up, put up, skimp, store **6** keep up **7** husband, protect, support, sustain **8** maintain, set aside, withhold **9** confiture, economize, safeguard, sweetmeat

consider
3 see **4** deem, feel, mind, muse, note, rate, view **5** fancy, judge, sense, study, think, weigh **6** credit, look at, notice, ponder, reason, reckon, regard **7** account, believe, examine, imagine, inspect, reflect, respect, suppose **8** appraise, cogitate, conclude, envisage, meditate, mull over, ruminate **9** speculate, think over **10** deliberate, excogitate, scrutinize, think about **11** contemplate

considerable
3 big **5** ample, hefty, large, major **7** notable, sizable, weighty **8** material, sensible, sizeable **9** extensive, important, momentous, plentiful **10** large-scale, meaningful **11** respectable, significant, substantial **13** consequential

considerably
3 far **4** well **5** quite **6** rather **7** notably **8** somewhat **10** noticeably **11** appreciably **13** significantly, substantially

considerate
4 kind, nice **6** kindly, polite, tender **7** amiable, careful, patient, tactful **8** discreet, generous, obliging **9** attentive **10** chivalrous, forbearing, solicitous, thoughtful **11** circumspect, complaisant, sympathetic, warmhearted **13** compassionate

consideration
3 fee **4** heed, tact **5** cause, favor, issue, study **6** esteem, factor, motive, reason, regard **7** account, concern, payment, respect, thought **8** kindness **9** attention, awareness **10** admiration, cogitation, discussion, reflection, solicitude **11** application, forbearance, mindfulness **12** deliberation

considered
7 advised, studied, weighed **8** studious **10** deliberate, thought-out **11** intentional **12** aforethought, premeditated

consign
4 give, send, ship **5** agree, allot, award, remit, yield **6** commit, convey, devote, submit **7** address, commend, confide, deliver, entrust, forward **8** dispatch, hand over, relegate, transmit, turn over **9** surrender

consist
3 lie **4** rest **5** abide, agree, dwell, exist, fit in **6** accord, inhere, reside **7** comport, conform, consort, subsist **8** dovetail **10** correspond

consistency
7 aptness, concord, density, fitness, harmony, texture **8** evenness, firmness, likeness **9** agreement, coherence, congruity, thickness, viscosity **10** conformity, consonance, similarity **11** suitability

consistent
4 even, true **6** steady **7** regular, uniform **8** constant **9** accordant, agreeable, congenial, congruous, consonant, unfailing, unvarying **10** compatible, conforming, dependable, invariable, unchanging **11** homogeneous, sympathetic, undeviating

consistently
8 wontedly **9** regularly, routinely **10** habitually, invariably **11** customarily

console
4 calm, case **5** cheer **6** buck up, solace **7** cabinet, comfort, hearten **9** sideboard

consolidate
3 mix, set **4** fuse, join, meld, pool **5** blend, merge, unify, unite **6** firm up, secure **7** compact, fortify **8** compress, condense, federate, solidify **9** integrate **10** amalgamate, strengthen **11** concentrate

consolidation
5 union **6** merger **7** melding, merging **9** coalition **11** combination, integration, unification **12** amalgamation

consonance
6 accord **7** concord, harmony **9** agreement, congruity, resonance **10** congruence

consonant
4 akin, like **6** agnate **7** musical, similar **8** blending, harmonic, resonant **9** congruous **10** compatible, harmonious **11** conformable **13** corresponding

kind: **4** stop, surd **5** nasal, velar **6** atonic, voiced **7** lateral, palatal, spirant **8** alveolar, bilabial, unvoiced **9** fricative, voiceless

consort
3 set **4** mate, wife **5** agree, group, tally, unite **6** accord, attend, fellow, spouse, square, troupe **7** company, comport, conform, husband, partner **8** assembly, chaperon, dovetail **9** accompany, associate, companion, harmonize **10** correspond

consortium
4 bloc, club, ring **5** guild, trust, union **6** cartel, league **7** combine, society **8** alliance, congress **9** coalition, syndicate **10** federation **11** association **12** conglomerate

conspectus
5 brief **6** digest, précis, sketch, survey **7** epitome, outline, summary **8** abstract, overview, synopsis **9** reduction **10** abridgment **11** abridgement **12** condensation

conspicuous
5 clear, overt, showy **6** marked, patent, signal **7** blatant, evident, glaring, notable, obvious, pointed, salient **8** apparent, distinct, flagrant, manifest, striking **9** arresting, egregious, notorious, obtrusive, prominent **10** noticeable, pronounced, remarkable **11** eye-catching, outstanding **12** ostentatious

conspiracy
4 plan, plot **5** cabal **6** scheme **8** intrigue **11** machination

conspirator
7 abettor, plotter, schemer **9** accessory, intriguer **10** accomplice **11** confederate

conspire
4 plot **5** cabal **6** scheme **7** collude, connive **8** intrigue **9** machinate

constable
6 deputy, lawman, warden **7** marshal, sheriff

constancy
5 faith **6** fealty **7** loyalty, resolve **8** adhesion, devotion, fidelity, firmness **9** adherence, diligence, endurance, fortitude **10** allegiance, attachment, dedication, resolution, steadiness **11** staunchness **12** faithfulness, perseverance **13** dependability, steadfastness

constant
4 even, fast, firm, true **5** fixed, loyal **6** dogged, stable, steady, trusty **7** abiding, chronic, endless, equable, lasting, nonstop, staunch, uniform **8** enduring, faithful, habitual, resolute, unending **9** ceaseless, confirmed, continual, immovable, immutable, incessant, obstinate, perpetual, steadfast, sustained, unceasing, unfailing, unmovable, unvarying **10** changeless, consistent, continuous, dependable, inflexible, invariable, inveterate, persistent, persisting, unchanging, unwavering **11** everlasting, inalterable, unalterable, unrelenting, unremitting **12** interminable, unchangeable

Constantine
birthplace: **3** Nis **4** Nish
mother: **6** Helena
son: **7** Crispus
victim: **6** Fausta **7** Crispus
wife: **6** Fausta

constantly
4 ever **5** often **6** always **7** forever **9** eternally **10** frequently, invariably, repeatedly **11** incessantly, perpetually **12** continuously

constellation
5 group **7** pattern **10** assemblage, collection **11** arrangement
Altar: **3** Ara
Archer: **11** Sagittarius
Arrow: **7** Sagitta
Balance: **5** Libra
Bear: **4** Ursa (Major, Minor)
Big Dipper: **9** Ursa Major
Bird of Paradise: **4** Apus
Bull: **6** Taurus
Centaur: **9** Centaurus
Chained Lady: **9** Andromeda
Chameleon: **10** Chamaeleon
Champion: **7** Perseus
Charioteer: **6** Auriga
Clock: **10** Horologium
Colt: **8** Equuleus
Crab: **6** Cancer
Crane: **4** Grus
Cross: **4** Crux
Crow: **6** Corvus
Crown: **6** Corona
Cup: **6** Crater
Dolphin: **9** Delphinus
Dove: **7** Columba
Dragon: **5** Draco
Eagle: **6** Aquila
Fishes: **6** Pisces
Fly: **5** Musca
Flying Fish: **6** Volans
Furnace: **6** Fornax
Graving Tool: **6** Caelum
Great Bear: **9** Ursa Major
Greater Dog: **10** Canis Major
Hare: **5** Lepus
Herdsman: **6** Boötes
Horned Goat: **11** Capricornus
Hunter: **5** Orion
Indian: **5** Indus
Keel: **6** Carina
Lady in the Chair: **10** Cassiopeia
Larger Bear: **9** Ursa Major
Larger Dog: **10** Canis Major
Lesser Dog: **10** Canis Minor
Lion: **3** Leo

Little Bear: 9 Ursa Minor
Little Dipper: 9 Ursa Minor
Little Fox: 9 Vulpecula
Lizard: 7 Lacerta
Lyre: 4 Lyra
Mariner's Compass: 5 Pyxis
Monarch: 7 Cepheus
Net: 9 Reticulum
Painter's Easel: 6 Pictor
Pair of Compasses: 8 Circinus
Peacock: 4 Pavo
Pump: 6 Antlia
Ram: 5 Aries
Rescuer: 7 Perseus
River Po: 8 Eridanus
Sails: 4 Vela
Scorpion: 8 Scorpius
Serpent: 7 Serpens
Serpent Holder: 9 Ophiuchus
Sextant: 7 Sextans
Shield: 6 Scutum
Smaller Bear: 9 Ursa Minor
Square: 5 Norma
Stern: 6 Puppis
Swan: 6 Cygnus
Table: 5 Mensa
Toucan: 6 Tucana
Triangle: 10 Triangulum
Twins: 6 Gemini
Unicorn: 9 Monoceros
Virgin: 5 Virgo
Water Carrier: 8 Aquarius
Water Monster: 5 Hydra
Water Snake: 6 Hydrus
Whale: 5 Cetus
Winged Horse: 7 Pegasus
Wolf: 5 Lupus

consternate
5 alarm, daunt, shake, shock **6** appall, dismay **7** horrify, unnerve **8** distress

consternation
4 fear **5** alarm, dread, panic, shock **6** dismay, fright, horror, terror **11** trepidation **12** bewilderment

constituent
4 part **5** piece, voter **6** factor, member **7** element, portion **8** division, fraction **9** component, elemental, principal **10** ingredient

constitute
4 form, make **5** enact, found, set up, start **6** create, embody, make up **7** appoint, compose **8** complete, comprise, organize **9** establish, institute, represent

constitution
3 law **4** code **5** build, canon **6** design, makeup, nature **7** charter **8** physique **9** formation, structure **11** composition **12** architecture, construction

constitutional
4 walk **6** inborn, inbred, innate, lawful **7** built-in, organic **8** inherent **9** essential, ingrained, intrinsic **10** congenital, deep-seated

Constitution State
11 Connecticut

Constitution, U.S.S.
12 Old Ironsides

constitutive
5 vital **8** cardinal **9** essential **11** fundamental **12** constructive

constrain
3 bar **4** curb, deny, jail **5** chain, check, crush, force, impel, limit, press **6** bridle, coerce, compel, enjoin, oblige, secure, squash, squish **7** confine, deprive, inhibit, refrain, squeeze **8** compress, hold back, hold down, imprison, restrain, restrict **11** incarcerate

constraint
4 bond **5** check, force **6** duress **8** coercion, pressure **9** captivity, detention, restraint **10** compulsion, diffidence, inhibition, limitation, repression **11** confinement, restriction, suppression **13** embarrassment

constrict
4 curb **5** cramp, limit, pinch, strap **6** hamper, narrow, shrink **7** confine, inhibit, squeeze, tighten **8** compress, condense, contract, restrain, strangle, stultify **9** constrain **12** circumscribe

constrictor
3 boa **5** snake **6** muscle **8** anaconda **9** sphincter, strangler

construct
4 form, make **5** build, erect, forge, frame, put up, raise, set up, shape **6** create, devise **7** build up, compile, fashion, produce **8** assemble, engineer **9** establish, fabricate **11** manufacture, put together

construction
6 design, makeup **7** edifice, shaping **8** assembly, building **9** formation **10** fashioning **11** arrangement, engineering, fabrication, manufacture **12** architecture, constitution
girder: 4 I bar
locale: 4 site

constructive
6 useful **7** helpful, implied, virtual **8** implicit, positive, valuable **9** practical **10** beneficial

construe
5 educe, gloss, parse **6** induct **7** analyze, explain, expound **9** explicate, interpret **10** paraphrase, understand

consuetude
5 habit, usage **6** custom, manner **8** practice **10** convention

consult
3 ask **6** advise, confer, huddle, parley **7** examine, refer to **8** collogue, consider **11** confabulate

consume
3 eat, use **4** down, gulp, ruin **5** drain, drink, eat up, gorge, spend, use up, waste **6** absorb, devour, expend, finish, ingest, obsess, take up **7** deplete, destroy, engross, exhaust, put away, put down, swallow **8** squander **9** dissipate, finish off, polish off **10** annihilate, extinguish, monopolize, run through

consumer
4 user **5** buyer **6** client **7** shopper, end user **8** customer **9** purchaser

consumer advocate
5 Nader (Ralph)

consuming
6 ardent **7** fervent, intense **8** gripping, riveting **9** absorbing **10** engrossing **11** enthralling **12** monopolizing

consummate
3 end **4** ripe **5** close, crown, ideal, utter **6** finish, superb, wind up, wrap up **7** achieve, perfect, supreme **8** absolute, complete, conclude, finished, flawless, peerless, ultimate **9** faultless, matchless, perfected, virtuosic **10** accomplish, impeccable, inimitable **11** superlative **12** accomplished **13** thoroughgoing

consumption
3 use **5** decay, waste **6** intake **7** wasting **8** phthisis **9** depletion, ingestion **10** absorption **11** dissipation **12** tuberculosis

contact
4 meet **5** reach, touch **8** tangency, touching **9** closeness, communion, proximity **10** connection, contiguity **11** association, contingence **13** communication

contagion
3 pox **4** bane, meme **5** taint, venom, virus **6** miasma, plague, poison **7** disease, scourge **8** epidemic **9** infection, pollution **10** corruption, pestilence **13** contamination

contagious
6 catchy **8** catching, epidemic **9** spreading **10** infectious **12** communicable, pestilential **13** transmissible, transmittable

contain
4 hold, keep **5** check, house **6** embody, take in **7** collect, control, embrace, enclose, include, receive, repress, subsume **8** comprise, restrain **9** encompass **10** comprehend **11** accommodate

container
3 bag, bin, box, can, cup, jar, jug, keg, mug, pod, pot, tin, tub, urn, vat **4** cage, case, cask, drum, etui, ewer, pail, sack, silo, tank, vase, vial, well **5** chest, crate, cruet, flask, glass, gourd, phial, pouch **6** basket, bottle, carafe, carton, casket, coffin, cooler, goblet, hamper, hatbox, holder, inkpot, shaker **7** bandbox, capsule, chalice, inkwell, package, pitcher, thermos **8** canister, catchall, decanter, envelope, hogshead, jerrican, puncheon **10** receptacle
liturgical: **3** pyx **7** chalice **8** ciborium
weight: **4** tare

contaminate
4 foul, soil **5** dirty, spoil, stain, sully, taint **6** befoul, debase, defile, infect, injure, poison **7** corrupt, deprave, pervert, pollute, profane, tarnish, vitiate **9** desecrate **10** adulterate

conte
4 tale **5** story **9** narrative

contemn
4 snub **5** abhor, scorn, spurn **6** deride **7** deplore, despise, disdain **8** ridicule **10** look down on

contemplate
3 eye **4** mull, muse, view **5** study, think, weigh **6** behold, debate, gaze at, intend, look at, ponder, regard **7** examine, inspect, propose, reflect **8** consider, gaze upon, look upon, meditate, mull over, ruminate, think out **9** think over **10** deliberate, excogitate, scrutinize

contemplation
5 study **6** musing **7** thought **8** thinking **9** intention, pondering **10** cogitation, meditation, reflection, rumination **11** cerebration, expectation, speculation **12** deliberation **13** consideration

contemplative
6 musing **7** pensive **10** cogitative, meditative, reflecting, reflective, ruminative, thoughtful **11** speculative **13** introspective

contemporary
3 new **6** coeval, extant, modern, recent **7** current, present, topical **8** existent, existing, up-to-date **9** au courant **10** coexistent, coexisting, coincident, concurrent, present-day, synchronic **11** synchronous **12** simultaneous

contempt
5 scorn, shame **7** despite, disdain, mockery **8** aversion, defiance, disfavor, disgrace, dishonor, distaste, ignominy **9** antipathy, discredit, disesteem, disrepute **10** disrespect, opprobrium, repugnance **12** disobedience, stubbornness

contemptible
3 low **4** base, mean, poor, vile **5** cheap, sorry **6** abject, odious, paltry, scummy, scurvy, shabby, sordid **7** hateful, ignoble, pitiful, squalid **8** inferior, pitiable, shameful, unworthy, wretched **9** abhorrent, loathsome **10** despicable, detestable, disgusting **11** ignominious **12** dishonorable

contemptuous
7 haughty **8** arrogant, derisive, scornful **10** disdainful **12** supercilious **13** condescending, disrespectful

contend
3 vie, war **4** aver, avow, cope, face, urge **5** argue, brawl, claim, fight **6** affirm, allege, assert, battle, charge, combat, debate, defend, insist, oppose, report, strive **7** compete, contest **8** confront, maintain, struggle **9** encounter, withstand

contender
5 match, rival **6** player **8** opponent **9** adversary, candidate, combatant **10** antagonist, challenger, competitor, contestant

___ contendere
4 nolo

content
4 cozy, gist **5** happy **6** at ease, serene **7** appease, gratify, meaning, placate, satisfy **9** gratified, satisfied, substance **11** comfortable **12** significance

contention
3 war **4** beef, feud **6** combat, rumpus, strife, thesis **7** discord, dispute, dissent, quarrel, rivalry, wrangle **8** argument, conflict, disunity, squabble **10** difference, dissension, dissidence **11** altercation, competition, controversy
Scottish: 5 sturt

contentious
5 fiery **7** carping, froward, peppery, scrappy, warlike **8** captious, caviling, contrary, militant, perverse **9** bellicose, combative, hotheaded, litigious, polemical, truculent **10** pugnacious **11** belligerent, quarrelsome **12** disputatious, faultfinding **13** argumentative, controversial

conterminous
10 coincident **11** coextensive

contest
3 vie **4** bout, duel, feud, fray, game, meet, race, tilt **5** clash, fight, match, repel, rival, trial **6** battle, combat, debate, oppose, resist, strife, strive **7** compete, dispute, rivalry, warfare **8** argument, conflict, endeavor, skirmish, struggle, tug-of-war **9** challenge, encounter, rencontre **10** engagement, tournament **11** competition

contestant
5 rival **7** also-ran, entrant, opposer, wannabe **8** opponent **9** adversary, contender **10** challenger, competitor

contiguity
9 adjacency, immediacy, proximity **11** propinquity

contiguous
4 next **8** abutting, adjacent, touching **9** adjoining, bordering **10** juxtaposed

continence
6 purity, virtue **8** chastity, sobriety **9** austerity **10** abnegation, abstinence, asceticism, chasteness, moderation, temperance **11** forbearance **12** renunciation **13** self-restraint

continent
4 Asia, mass **5** sober **6** Africa, chaste, Europe **8** celibate, landmass, mainland **9** abstinent, Australia, temperate **10** abstemious, Antarctica, restrained **11** abstentious **12** North America, South America
lost: 8 Atlantis

continental currency
4 euro

contingence
5 touch **7** contact **8** tangency, touching

contingency
4 pass **5** event, pinch **6** chance, crisis **8** exigency, juncture, occasion **9** emergency **10** likelihood **11** opportunity, possibility, probability, uncertainty

contingent
3 odd **4** band **5** group, party, troop **6** casual, chance, likely **7** reliant **8** possible, probable, relative **9** dependent, empirical, entourage, uncertain **10** accidental, delegation, deputation, detachment, fortuitous, incidental, unforeseen **11** conditional **13** unanticipated, unforeseeable, unpredictable

continual
5 solid **6** steady **7** abiding, endless, nonstop, regular, running **8** constant, enduring, timeless, unbroken, unending **9** ceaseless, incessant, perpetual, perennial, recurrent, recurring, unceasing, unfailing, unvarying **10** persistent, persisting, relentless, unchanging, unflagging **11** everlasting, unremitting **12** interminable **13** uninterrupted

continually
4 ever **5** on end **6** always **7** forever **8** steadily, together **9** endlessly **10** constantly **11** incessantly, night and day **12** interminably, persistently, relentlessly, successively **13** consecutively

continuance
3 run **4** stay **5** delay **6** sequel **8** duration, survival **9** longevity **10** permanence **11** adjournment, persistence **12** postponement, prolongation

continuation
3 run **4** coda **6** sequel **8** appendix, duration, epilogue **9** endurance, extension **10** resumption **11** persistence, protraction **12** prolongation

continue
4 go on, last, stay **5** abide, renew, run on, segue **6** endure, hang in, keep at, keep on, keep up, pick up, push on, remain, reopen, resume, retain, take up **7** carry on, persist, press on, proceed, prolong, restart, survive **8** maintain, postpone **9** carry over, persevere **10** recommence

continuing
5 fixed **6** steady **7** abiding, chronic, durable, eternal, lasting, ongoing **8** constant, enduring,

lifelong, stubborn **9** long-lived, obstinate, perennial, prolonged, steadfast, tenacious, unabating **10** inveterate, persistent, persisting **11** long-lasting

continuity
4 flow **6** script **8** duration, scenario, sequence **9** endurance **11** persistence, progression

continuous
see **continual**

continuously
see **continually**

contort
4 knot, warp **5** twist, wring **6** deform, wrench, writhe **7** distort, grimace, torture **9** convolute, corkscrew, disfigure

contortionist
7 acrobat

contour
4 form, line **5** curve, lines, shape **6** figure **7** outline, pattern, profile **9** lineament, lineation **10** silhouette **11** delineation

contra
6 facing, toward **7** against, counter, reverse, vis-à-vis **8** converse, fronting, opposite **10** conversely

contraband
3 hot **5** taboo **6** banned **7** bootleg, illegal, illicit, smuggle **8** unlawful **9** forbidden **10** prohibited, proscribed **11** black market, bootlegging, trafficking

contract
4 bond, hire, pact, sink **5** catch, incur, lease **6** engage, induce, lessen, reduce, shrink, treaty, weaken **7** abridge, acquire, afflict, bargain, decline, dwindle, shorten, shrivel **8** compress, condense, covenant, decrease, diminish **9** agreement, constrict, succumb to **11** concentrate, transaction **12** come down with
part: **6** clause **7** article, proviso

contraction
3 he'd, he's, I'll, it's, I've, tic **4** ain't, can't, don't, flex, he'll, isn't, let's, she'd, she's, won't, you'd **5** aren't, cramp, didn't, hadn't, hasn't, she'll, spasm, they'd, wasn't, you'll, you're, you've **6** haven't, mustn't, needn't, they'll, they've, weren't **7** couldn't, elision, mightn't, wouldn't **8** shouldn't **9** reduction, shrinkage **10** abridgment **11** abridgement **12** abbreviation
heart's: **7** systole
poetic: **3** e'en, e'er, o'er, 'tis **4** ne'er, 'twas **5** 'twere, 'twill

contradict
4 deny **5** belie, cross, rebut **6** impugn, negate, refute, take on **7** confute, dispute, gainsay **8** negative, traverse **9** challenge, disaffirm

contradiction
6 denial **7** paradox **8** antinomy, negation, rebuttal, variance **9** disparity **10** gainsaying, opposition, refutation **11** discrepancy, incongruity **12** disagreement, protestation **13** inconsistency

contradictory
7 counter, reverse **8** contrary, converse, negating, opposite **9** antipodal **10** antipodean, antithesis, nullifying **12** antithetical

contraption
3 rig **5** gizmo **6** device, doodad, gadget **7** machine **9** apparatus, doohickey **11** contrivance

contrariety
10 antagonism, antithesis, opposition, perversity, unlikeness

contrariwise
9 vice versa **10** conversely, oppositely

contrary
5 balky **6** averse, ornery, unruly **7** adverse, counter, froward, reverse, wayward **8** converse, opposite, perverse, stubborn **9** antipodal, diametric, dissident, obstinate, vice versa **10** conversely, discordant, headstrong, oppositely, rebellious, refractory **11** conflicting, intractable, wrongheaded **12** antagonistic, antipathetic, antithetical, contumacious, cross-grained, recalcitrant
prefix: **7** counter

contrast
6 differ **7** collate, compare, diverge **8** conflict, disagree **9** disparity **10** comparison, difference, divergence **11** distinction, distinguish

contravene
4 defy, deny **5** break, cross, fight **6** abjure, breach, disown, impugn, negate, offend, oppose, reject **7** disobey, gainsay, violate **8** disclaim, infringe, renege on **9** disaffirm, go against, repudiate **10** contradict, transgress

contravention
6 breach **7** offense **8** trespass **9** violation **10** infraction **12** infringement **13** nonobservance, transgression

contretemps
3 row **4** slip, tiff **5** clash, run-in **6** dustup, mishap, slip-up **7** dispute, quarrel **8** argument **9** mischance **10** falling-out, misfortune

contribute
3 add **4** give, help, tend **5** grant **6** chip in, donate, kick in, submit, supply **7** conduce, pitch in, redound **9** subscribe **11** come through

contribution
4 alms, gift **5** input, share, tithe **7** charity, payment, present **8** donation, offering **11** benefaction, beneficence

contributory
8 adjuvant **9** accessory, ancillary, auxiliary **10** collateral, subsidiary, supporting **11** appurtenant, subservient

contrite
5 sorry **8** penitent **9** regretful, repentant **10** apologetic, remorseful **11** penitential

contrition
3 rue **4** ruth **6** regret **7** penance, remorse **9** penitence **10** repentance **11** compunction **12** self-reproach

contrivance
4 ruse **6** device, gadget **7** gimmick **8** artifice **9** apparatus, expedient, invention, stratagem **10** brainchild **11** contraption

contrive
3 rig **4** fake, make, move, plan, plot **5** frame, hatch **6** cook up, devise, invent, make up, manage, scheme, vamp up, wangle **7** arrange, concoct, connive, develop, dream up, fashion, project, work out **8** cogitate, conspire, engineer, intrigue **9** construct, elaborate, fabricate, formulate, machinate

contrived
5 hokey **6** forced **7** labored **8** strained **9** concocted, insincere **10** artificial, engineered, fabricated, factitious

control
3 run **4** curb, rein, rule, sway **5** guide, power, steer **6** bridle, direct, govern, handle, manage, master, rein in, subdue **7** command, conduct, mastery, oversee, repress, reserve **8** dominate, dominion, regulate, restrain **9** authority, direction, restraint, supervise, supremacy **10** discipline, domination, management **11** supervision **12** jurisdiction

controlled
8 discreet, reserved **9** temperate **10** restrained

controversial
5 risky **6** touchy **7** awkward, charged, eristic **8** delicate, disputed, ticklish **9** debatable, explosive, litigious, polemical **11** contentious, problematic **12** disputatious **13** argumentative

controversy
3 row **5** clash **6** debate, rumpus, strife **7** dispute, quarrel, wrangle **8** argument, squabble **10** contention, falling-out **11** altercation, disputation, embroilment

controvert
4 deny **5** rebut **6** debate, oppose, oppugn, refute **7** confute, counter, dispute, gainsay **8** disprove, question **9** challenge, repudiate

contumacious
7 froward **8** contrary, insolent, mutinous, obdurate, perverse **9** obstinate **10** rebellious, refractory **11** disobedient, intractable **12** recalcitrant **13** insubordinate

contumacy
8 contempt, defiance **9** insolence **10** perversity **12** stubbornness **13** recalcitrance

contumelious
7 abusive **8** derisive, insolent, scornful **9** insulting, truculent **10** disdainful, scurrilous **11** opprobrious **12** vituperative

contumely
5 abuse **6** insult **7** affront, mockery, obloquy **8** contempt, ridicule, sneering **9** aspersion, invective **10** scurrility **12** vituperation

contuse
6 batter, bruise, injure **7** blacken

conundrum
5 poser **6** enigma, puzzle, riddle **7** baffler, mystery, problem, puzzler, stumper **10** puzzlement **13** Chinese puzzle

convalesce
4 heal, mend **7** improve, recover **10** recuperate

convene
4 call, meet **6** call in, gather, muster, summon **7** convoke, summons **8** assemble **9** forgather **10** congregate **12** come together

convenience
4 ease **7** amenity, benefit, comfort, leisure **8** facility **9** handiness **10** assistance **13** accessibility

convenient
3 fit **4** near **5** close, handy, ready **6** at hand, nearby, proper, useful **7** close by, helpful **8** suitable **9** available, immediate, opportune **10** accessible **11** appropriate, comfortable **12** advantageous

convent
5 abbey **6** priory **7** nunnery **8** cloister **9** monastery, sanctuary
dweller: 3 nun

convention
3 law **4** bond, code, pact, rule **5** canon, usage **6** accord, custom, treaty **7** compact, meeting, precept **8** assembly, congress, contract, covenant, practice, protocol **9** agreement, concordat, formality, gathering, propriety, tradition **11** convocation

conventional
5 trite, usual **6** formal, normal, proper, seemly, solemn, square **7** correct, regular, routine, typical, uptight **8** everyday, habitual, moderate, ordinary, orthodox, standard, straight **9** bourgeois, customary **10** button-down, conforming, prevailing, restrained, unoriginal **11** commonplace, traditional **12** conservative

conventionalize
5 adapt **7** conform **9** normalize

converge
4 join, meet **5** focus, merge, unite **11** concentrate **12** come together

conversant
8 familiar **9** au courant **10** acquainted **11** experienced

conversation
4 chat, talk **6** confab, debate, parley **7** palaver, talking **8** causerie, colloquy, dialogue, duologue, exchange, repartee **9** discourse, tête-à-tête **10** discussion **13** confabulation

conversation piece
5 curio **6** oddity **9** curiosity, objet d'art

converse
3 gab **4** chat, chin, talk **5** speak, visit **6** confer, contra, parley **7** chatter, counter, reverse **8** antipode, contrary, opposite **9** antipodal, diametric **10** antithesis **12** antithetical **13** contradictory

conversely
9 vice versa **10** oppositely **12** contrariwise

conversion
5 shift **6** change, switch **7** novelty, rebirth, turning **8** metanoia, mutation, reversal **9** about-face **10** alteration, changeover **11** permutation **12** modification, regeneration **13** metamorphosis, transmutation

convert
4 sway **5** alter **6** change, modify, redeem, reform, switch **7** commute, remodel **8** persuade, renovate **9** proselyte, transform, translate, transmute, transpose **11** transfigure **12** metamorphose, transmogrify
Christian: **10** catechumen

convex
5 bowed, toric **6** arched, curved **7** bulging, curving, gibbous, rounded

convexity
4 arch **6** camber

convey
3 lug **4** bear, cart, cede, deed, pack, send, tell, tote **5** bring, carry, ferry **6** assign, impart, pass on **7** channel, conduct, consign, deliver, express, project **8** make over, sign over, transfer, transmit **9** transport **11** communicate

conveyance
3 car **4** auto, cart, deed, sled **5** coach, sedan, stage, title, wagon **7** charter, trailer, transit, vehicle **8** carriage, carrying **9** transport **10** automobile **12** transporting
public: **3** bus, cab **4** taxi, tram **5** plane, train **6** subway **7** trolley **8** airplane, monorail, railroad, rickshaw **9** streetcar **10** jinricksha, jinrikisha

convict
4 perp **5** felon, lifer **6** inmate, send up **7** condemn, put away **8** criminal, jailbird, prisoner, sentence, yardbird **10** find guilty

conviction
4 view **5** creed, faith **6** belief, surety **7** opinion **8** doctrine, sentence, sureness **9** assurance, certainty, certitude, sentiment **10** confidence, persuasion **12** condemnation

convince
6 assure, induce, prompt **7** satisfy, win over **8** persuade, talk into **9** influence, prevail on **11** bring around, prevail upon

convincing
5 solid, sound, valid **6** cogent **8** credible, faithful **9** plausible **10** believable, conclusive, persuasive, satisfying **11** trustworthy

convivial
3 gay **5** jolly, merry **6** hearty, jocund, jovial, lively, social **7** festive **8** mirthful, sociable **9** fun-loving, vivacious **10** gregarious **13** companionable

convocation
5 synod **7** council, meeting **8** assembly, conclave **9** gathering **10** assemblage **12** congregation

convoke
4 call **6** gather, invite, muster, summon **7** collect, convene **8** assemble **12** call together

convoluted
6 coiled **7** complex, tangled, winding **8** involved, tortuous **9** intricate **10** circuitous **11** anfractuous, complicated **12** labyrinthine

convoy
6 attend, escort **7** conduct **9** accompany

convulse
4 rock **5** shake **7** agitate, concuss **8** tetanize

convulsion
3 fit **5** spasm **6** attack, tumult, uproar **7** quaking, rocking, seizure, shaking **8** disaster, paroxysm, upheaval **9** commotion, trembling

cook
3 fix, fry **4** bake, boil, chef, heat, melt, stew **5** broil, grill, poach, roast, sauté, steam **6** braise, doctor, simmer **7** falsify, parboil, prepare, swelter

cookbook
abbreviation: **3** tsp **4** tbsp
term: **3** cup, fry, mix **4** bake, beat, boil, chop, pare, peel, roux, sift, stew, stir, toss, whip, zest **5** baste, blend, broil, cream, glaze, grate, grind, knead, mince, pinch, poach, roast, sauté, scald, steam, stock **6** blanch, braise, fillet, season, simmer **7** al dente, deglaze, parboil **8** dissolve, emulsify, julienne, marinate, meringue **10** caramelize

cooked
4 done, sham **5** bogus, faked, phony **6** made-up **7** altered **8** doctored, spurious **10** fictitious

cookery
7 cuisine

expert: **3** Ray (Rachael), Yan (Martin) **4** Chen (Joyce), Deen (Paula), Kerr (Graham), Puck (Wolfgang), Root (Waverley) **5** Beard (James), Child (Julia), David (Elizabeth), Hines (Duncan), Pépin (Jacques), Smith (Jeff), Tower (Jeremiah) **6** Batali (Mario), Bocuse (Paul), Carême (Marie-Antoine), Farmer (Fannie), Fisher (M. F. K.), Franey (Pierre), Keller (Thomas), Reichl (Ruth), Waters (Alice) **7** Bittman (Mark), Crocker (Betty), Ducasse (Alain), Lagasse (Emeril), Stewart (Martha) **8** Bourdain (Anthony), Rombauer (Irma) **9** Claiborne (Craig), Escoffier (Auguste), Prudhomme (Paul)

cookie
4 Oreo, snap **5** wafer **7** biscuit, brownie **10** gingersnap

cooking
appliance: **4** oven **5** mixer, range, stove **7** blender, toaster **9** microwave **10** rotisserie
implement: **3** cup, pan, pot, wok **4** olla **5** ladle, sieve, spoon, whisk **6** grater, masher, sifter, tureen **7** griddle, skillet, spatula, steamer **8** colander, teaspoon **9** eggbeater, frying pan **10** rolling pin, tablespoon **12** measuring cup
measure: **3** cup, tsp. **4** tbsp. **8** teaspoon **10** tablespoon
room: **6** galley **7** kitchen

Cook Islands
capital: **6** Avarua
dependency of: **10** New Zealand
island: **9** Rarotonga

cookout area
5 patio

cool
3 hep, hip, icy, rad **4** calm, cold, phat **5** abate, aloof, chill, funky, gelid, neato, nippy **6** arctic, chilly, frigid, frosty, with-it **7** assured, awesome, compose, control, decline, distant, dwindle, repress, subside **8** composed, decrease, detached, diminish, reserved, suppress **9** collected, confident, impassive, unruffled **10** nonchalant, phlegmatic, unsociable **11** indifferent, standoffish, unflappable **13** dispassionate, imperturbable, self-possessed

cooler
3 fan, jug, pen **4** brig, coop, jail **5** clink, pokey **6** fridge, icebox, lockup, prison **7** freezer, slammer **9** calaboose **11** refrigerant **12** refrigerator

cooling device
3 fan **6** fridge, icebox **7** freezer **12** refrigerator

coolness
5 chill, poise **6** aplomb, phlegm **7** reserve **9** composure, frigidity, sangfroid **10** dispassion, equanimity **11** nonchalance, self-control

coop
3 hem, jug, mew, pen **4** brig, cage, cote, jail **5** cramp, fence, pokey **6** cooler, corral, lockup, prison, shut in **7** close in, confine, enclose, slammer **9** calaboose, enclosure

cooperate
5 agree, unite **6** concur, league **7** combine, conjoin, pitch in **8** coincide, conspire **11** collaborate, participate **12** work together

cooperation
8 alliance, teamwork **13** confederation

cooperative
5 joint **6** common, mutual, shared **8** coactive, conjoint, obliging **9** collegial, concerted **10** collective, synergetic **11** coordinated **13** accommodating, collaborative, uncompetitive
craft society: **5** artel

Cooper hero
5 Natty (Bumppo) **7** Hawkeye **10** Deerslayer, Pathfinder

coordinate
4 mate, mesh **5** align, equal, match, order **6** adjust, relate **7** coequal, conform **8** organize, parallel **9** companion, correlate, harmonize, integrate, reconcile **10** proportion, reciprocal **11** accommodate, correlative, counterpart
system: **9** Cartesian

coot
4 bird, fogy **5** crank, fogey **6** codger, dotard, duffer, fellow, geezer, oddity, scoter, weirdo **7** oddball **9** character, eccentric

cootie
5 louse **9** body louse

cop
3 nab **4** lift, take **5** adopt, catch, filch, pinch, steal, swipe **6** pilfer **7** capture, officer **8** bluecoat **9** patrolman, policeman

copacetic
3 A-OK **4** fine, jake, okay **5** dandy, great, nifty **8** all right **9** excellent **12** satisfactory

cope
4 cape, hack **5** cloak, cover, get by, match, vault **6** canopy, endure, make do, manage, mantle **7** carry on, survive **8** vestment

copestone
5 crown

copier need
5 toner

copious
4 lush, rich **5** ample **6** lavish, plenty **7** liberal, profuse, replete **8** abundant, generous **9** abounding, bounteous, bountiful, exuberant, luxuriant, plenteous, plentiful

Copland, Aaron
work: **5** Rodeo **11** Billy the Kid **17** Appalachian Spring

cop-out
5 dodge **6** excuse **7** evasion, pretext, retreat

copper
4 cent, coin **5** bobby, metal, penny, token **8** flatfoot **9** butterfly, policeman
coating: **6** patina
item: **4** cent **5** penny **6** kettle
sulfate: **7** vitriol **9** bluestone **11** blue vitriol

copperhead
5 snake, viper **8** pit viper

coppice
4 bosk, wood **5** copse, grove, woods **6** bosque, forest, growth **7** thicket **9** brushwood, underwood

copse
see **coppice**

Copt
8 Egyptian

copter
7 chopper **9** eggbeater **10** whirlybird

copula
4 bond, link **5** joint, union **7** coupler

copy
3 ape **4** echo, fake, mock, sham **5** clone, ditto, forge, mimic, model, repro **6** carbon, parrot, repeat **7** emulate, forgery, imitate, replica, takeoff **8** knockoff, likeness, simulate **9** duplicate, facsimile, imitation, replicate, reproduce **10** impression, simulacrum, simulation, transcribe, transcript **11** counterfeit, counterpart, reduplicate, replication **12** reproduction

copycat
3 ape **4** aper **5** mimic **6** parrot **8** imitator

copyist
5 clerk **6** scribe **8** imitator **9** engrosser **10** plagiarist **11** transcriber

copyread
4 edit

coquet
3 toy **4** fool, vamp **5** dally, flirt, tease **6** trifle

coquette
4 minx, vamp **5** flirt, tease

coquettish
3 coy **6** fickle **9** frivolous, kittenish **11** flirtatious

coral
3 red **4** pink, rosy **5** polyp **9** limestone

coral reef
3 cay, key **5** atoll
off Australia: **5** Wreck
world's largest: **12** Great Barrier

cord
3 tie **4** band, lace, pile, rick, rope, whip, yarn **5** cable, nerve, stack, twine **6** strand, string, tendon **7** lanyard
twisted: **7** torsade

cordage
4 rope **5** ropes **7** rigging
fiber: **4** bast, hemp, jute, pita **5** istle, sisal

Corday's victim
5 Marat (Jean-Paul)

Cordelia
father: **4** Lear
sister: **5** Regan **7** Goneril

cordial
4 warm **6** genial, hearty, jovial, tender **7** affable, liqueur, sincere **8** cheerful, friendly, gracious, sociable **9** congenial, convivial, heartfelt **10** hospitable **11** sympathetic, warmhearted **12** wholehearted

cordiality
6 warmth **7** amenity **9** geniality **10** amiability **12** agreeability, friendliness

cordon
4 lace, line, ring **5** braid **6** circle, ribbon **7** barrier **8** espalier
bleu: **4** chef, cook **6** ribbon **10** blue ribbon, decoration, master chef

core
3 hub, nub **4** base, crux, gist, meat, pith, root **5** basis, focus, heart, midst **6** center, depths, kernel, middle, upshot **7** essence, nucleus **8** interior, midpoint **9** substance **10** foundation

corium
5 cutis **6** dermis

cork
4 bark, plug, seal, stop **5** float **6** bobber **7** stopper, stopple

corker
3 pip **4** lulu **5** beaut, daisy, dandy, dilly, doozy **6** doozie, killer **8** jim-dandy, knockout **9** humdinger **11** crackerjack **12** lollapalooza

corkscrew
4 coil, wind **5** helix, twist **6** spiral

cormorant
4 bird, shag **7** glutton

corn
5 grain, maize **6** hominy **9** granulate
bread: **4** pone **7** bannock, hoecake
Indian: **5** maize **6** mealie
kind: **3** pop **5** flint, flour, sweet **6** Indian
pest: **5** borer
piece: **3** cob, ear **5** spike **6** kernel, nubbin

Corn Belt state
4 Iowa

Corncracker State
8 Kentucky

Cornell founder
4 Ezra

corner
3 box, fix, jam, nab **4** hole, nook, trap, tree **5** angle, catch, coign, niche, seize **6** collar, cranny, dogleg, pickle, plight, recess, scrape **7** capture, dilemma, impasse, trouble **8** bottle up, monopoly **10** bring to bay **11** predicament **12** intersection
of eye: **7** canthus

cornerstone
4 base **5** basis **7** support **8** rudiment **10** foundation, groundwork

cornet
4 cone, horn **7** officer **10** instrument
relative: **7** trumpet **10** flügelhorn

Cornhusker State
8 Nebraska

cornice
3 cap **4** band, eave **5** crown **7** molding

cornmeal
4 masa, mush, samp **5** grits **6** hominy **7** hoecake
bread: **10** johnnycake
mush: **7** polenta

cornucopia
4 cone, horn **6** bounty, plenty, wealth **9** abundance, profusion **12** horn of plenty

Cornwallis, Charles
adversary: **6** Greene (Nathanael)
surrender site: **8** Yorktown

corny
5 banal, sappy, stale, trite **6** old hat **7** clichéd, mawkish **8** shopworn **9** hackneyed, schmaltzy **11** sentimental, stereotyped

corollary
6 effect, result, sequel, upshot **8** parallel, sequence **9** resulting **10** associated, end product, equivalent **11** aftereffect, consequence
logical: **9** inference

corona
4 aura, glow, halo **5** cigar, crown, glory **6** circle, nimbus **7** aureola, aureole

coronate
5 crown **8** enthrone

coroner
8 examiner

coronet
5 crown, tiara **6** anadem, circle, diadem, wreath **7** chaplet, circlet, garland **8** headband

Coronis
form: **4** crow
son: **9** Asclepius **11** Aesculapius

corporal
3 NCO **6** bodily, carnal **7** fleshly, somatic **8** physical

corporate
7 unified **8** combined **9** aggregate
symbol: **4** logo
VIP: **3** CEO

corporeal
6 bodily, carnal, mortal **7** fleshly, somatic **8** material, physical, tangible **9** objective **10** phenomenal **11** substantial

corposant
11 St. Elmo's fire

corps
4 band, body, crew **5** group, party, squad, troop **6** cohort, outfit, troupe **7** company

corpse
4 body **5** bones, stiff **7** cadaver, carcass, carrion, remains
combining form: **4** necr **5** necro

corpselike
4 ashy, dead **5** ashen, gaunt **6** wasted **7** deathly, ghastly, macabre **8** lifeless, skeletal **10** cadaverous

corpulence
7 fatness, obesity **9** adiposity, rotundity **10** fleshiness, overweight, portliness

corpulent
3 fat **5** bulky, gross, heavy, obese, plump, stout **6** fleshy, portly, rotund **7** porcine, weighty **9** overblown **10** overweight

corpus
4 body, bulk, core, mass **6** oeuvre **9** principal, substance **10** collection **11** compilation

corpuscle
4 cell **8** hemocyte, monocyte **9** blood cell, leukocyte **10** lymphocyte **11** erythrocyte, granulocyte

corral
3 mew, pen **5** fence **6** gather, shut in **7** close in, collect, confine, enclose, round up **8** surround **9** enclosure

correct
3 fit, fix **4** edit, just, mend, true **5** amend, emend, exact, right **6** adjust, dead on, decent, proper, punish, reform, remedy, repair, revise, seemly, spot on **7** chasten, fitting, improve, perfect, precise, rectify, redress **8** accurate, becoming, chastise, decorous, flawless, set right **9** castigate, faultless **10** conforming, discipline, impeccable, legitimate, meticulous, scrupulous **11** appropriate, comme il faut, punctilious **12** conventional
combining form: **4** orth **5** ortho

correction
3 rod **6** rebuke **7** reproof **8** revision **9** amendment **10** adjustment, discipline, emendation, punishment **11** castigation

corrective
4 cure **6** remedy **8** antidote, punitive, remedial **10** beneficial **11** counterstep, restorative **12** counteragent **13** counteractive

correctness
7 decorum **8** accuracy, fidelity **9** precision, propriety **10** exactitude

correlate
5 match **6** analog **7** pendant **8** analogue, coincide, dovetail, parallel **9** harmonize **10** complement, correspond **11** counterpart

correlative
3 and, nor **4** both, then **6** either **7** neither, related **10** complement, reciprocal **11** counterpart **13** complementary, corresponding

correspond
4 jibe **5** agree, equal, match, write **6** accord, concur **7** comport, conform **8** dovetail **9** harmonize **11** communicate

correspondence
4 mail **7** analogy, letters **8** symmetry **9** agreement, congruity **10** conformity, similarity **11** consistency, correlation
mathematical: **7** mapping **8** function

correspondent
5 match **6** analog, pen pal, writer **7** fitting **8** analogue, parallel, reporter, suitable **9** correlate **10** conforming, journalist **11** commentator, contributor, counterpart

corresponding
4 akin, like **5** alike **6** agnate **7** related, similar **8** matching, parallel **9** analogous, consonant **10** comparable **11** correlative

correspondingly
4 also **7** equally **8** likewise **9** similarly **11** analogously

corrida
9 bullfight
combatant: **4** bull, toro **7** matador **8** toreador
shout: **3** olé

corridor
4 hall, lane, path **5** aisle, route, strip **6** artery, avenue **7** hallway, passage **10** passageway

corroborate
5 prove **6** uphold, verify **7** approve, bear out, certify, confirm, endorse, justify, support **8** document, validate **9** vindicate **12** authenticate, substantiate

corroborative
9 ancillary, auxiliary **10** collateral, supporting, supportive **12** confirmatory

corrode
4 rust **7** eat away, eat into, oxidize **8** wear away **9** undermine

corrosion
4 rust

corrosive
4 acid **5** acerb **6** biting **7** acerbic, caustic, cutting **9** sarcastic

corrosiveness
7 sarcasm **8** acerbity

corrugation
4 fold, ruck **5** plica, ridge **6** crease, furrow, groove **7** crinkle, wrinkle

corrupt
3 rot **5** bribe, decay, spoil, stain, taint, venal **6** befoul, debase, defile, molder, rotten, smirch **7** crooked, debauch, degrade, deprave, pervert, putrefy, tarnish, vitiate **8** bribable, degraded, depraved, infected, perverse **9** decompose, dishonest, miscreant, reprobate, unethical **10** bastardize, degenerate **12** unprincipled, unscrupulous **13** untrustworthy

corruptible
5 venal **7** buyable **8** bribable

corruption
4 vice **5** decay, fraud, graft **7** bribery, jobbery **9** barbarism, depravity, turpitude **10** immorality, wickedness **11** impropriety

corsair
5 rover **6** pirate **8** picaroon, sea rover **9** buccaneer, pickaroon, privateer **10** freebooter

corset
5 stays **6** bodice, girdle **7** support

Corsica
city: **6** Bastia **7** Ajaccio
hero: **8** Napoleon (Bonaparte)
patriot: **5** Paoli (Pasquale)

cortege
5 train **6** parade **7** retinue **8** equipage **9** entourage **10** attendants, procession

cortex
4 bark, husk, peel, rind **6** casing **8** peridium

Cortland, e.g.
5 apple

corundum
4 ruby **5** emery, topaz **7** emerald **8** abrasive, amethyst, sapphire

coruscate
5 flash, gleam, glint, shine **7** glisten, glitter, sparkle, twinkle **11** scintillate

corvid
3 jay **4** crow **5** raven **6** magpie **9** passerine

Corvino's wife
5 Celia

corybantic
3 mad **4** wild **5** rabid **6** crazed **7** frantic, furious **8** ecstatic, frenetic, frenzied **9** delirious

coryphée
6 dancer 8 danseuse 9 ballerina

Cosby Show son
4 Theo

Cosí Fan Tutte composer
6 Mozart (Wolfgang Amadeus)

cosine reciprocal
6 secant

cosmetic
4 kohl 5 blush, rouge 6 ceruse, lotion, makeup, powder 7 blusher, bronzer, mascara 8 lip gloss, lipstick 9 eye shadow 10 decorative, nail polish, ornamental 11 beautifying, superficial
ingredient: 4 aloe

cosmetics queen Lauder
5 Estée

cosmetologist
10 beautician

cosmic
4 huge, vast 7 immense 8 infinite 9 planetary, spiritual, unbounded, universal 12 astronomical, metaphysical

cosmopolitan
6 global, urbane 7 worldly 8 catholic, cultured, polished 9 civilized, universal, worldwide 10 cultivated, ecumenical 11 worldly-wise 13 sophisticated

cosmos
6 flower 8 creation, universe

Cossack
army: 3 Don 4 Ural 5 Kuban
land: 7 Ukraine
leader: 5 Razin (Stenka) 6 ataman, hetman, Mazepa (Ivan) 7 Bulavin (Kondraty) 8 Pugachov (Yemelyan)
novel: 10 Taras Bulba

cosset
3 pet 4 baby, lamb, love 5 humor, spoil 6 caress, cocker, coddle, cuddle, dandle, dote on, fondle, pamper 7 cater to, indulge 11 mollycoddle

cost
3 tab 4 rate, toll 5 price 6 charge, damage, outlay, tariff 7 expense, payment 8 price tag 9 sacrifice 11 expenditure 12 disbursement
business: 8 overhead

Costa del ___
3 Sol

Costa Rica
bay: 8 Coronado
capital: 7 San José
city: 8 Alajuela 10 Puntarenas 11 Puerto Limón
discoverer: 8 Columbus (Christopher)
language: 7 Spanish
leader: 5 Arias (Oscar)
monetary unit: 5 colón
neighbor: 6 Panama 9 Nicaragua
peninsula: 3 Osa 6 Nicoya
river: 7 San Juan
volcano: 5 Barba, Irazú 9 Turrialba

costermonger
6 hawker, pedlar, vendor 7 peddler 9 barrow boy

costive
4 mean, slow 5 bound, close, tight 6 frugal, stingy 7 miserly 9 penurious 10 hardfisted, pinchpenny 11 closefisted 12 cheeseparing, parsimonious

costless
4 free 6 gratis 10 gratuitous 13 complimentary

costly
4 dear, rich 5 fancy 6 lavish, pricey 7 opulent, premium 8 precious, splendid, valuable 9 expensive, luxurious, priceless 10 exorbitant, high-priced, invaluable 11 extravagant

costume
3 rig 4 duds, garb, mode 5 dress, getup, guise, habit, style 6 attire, outfit 7 apparel, clothes, fashion, threads, turnout, uniform 8 disguise, ensemble, garments 9 trappings

cot
3 bed, hut 4 camp 5 cabin, lodge, shack 6 shanty
wheeled: 6 gurney

cote
4 coop, shed

coterie
4 band, camp, clan, club, ring 5 cabal 6 circle, clique 7 in-group 9 camarilla

cotillion
4 ball, prom 5 dance
girl: 3 deb 9 debutante

cottage
3 hut 4 camp 5 cabin, lodge, shack 6 shanty 8 bungalow
Russian: 5 dacha
Swiss: 6 chalet

cotton
cleaner: 3 gin 6 linter
cloth: 4 duck, jean, mull 5 baize, chino, denim, drill, khaki, scrim, terry, toile, wigan 6 calico, canvas, chintz, dimity, muslin, oxford, sateen, velour 7 batiste, etamine, fustian, gingham, jaconet, nankeen, organdy, percale 8 corduroy, dungaree, moleskin, nainsook, tarlatan 9 grenadine, percaline, stockinet, swansdown 10 balbriggan 11 stockinette
cloth, Indian: 5 surah 6 madras 7 dhurrie, khaddar
comb: 4 card

fuzz remover: **6** linter
high-grade: **4** pima
measure: **4** hank, pick, yard **5** count, skein
pad: **7** pledget
pest: **6** weevil
pod: **4** boll
refuse: **5** flock
seed separator: **3** gin
sheet: **4** batt
thread: **5** lisle
variety: **4** pima

cotton-gin inventor Whitney
3 Eli

Cotton State
7 Alabama

cottontail's tail
4 scut

cottonwood
5 alamo **6** poplar

cottony
4 soft **6** fluffy

___ Coty
4 René

couch
3 den, put **4** lair, sofa, word **5** divan, lodge **6** burrow, chaise, daybed, lounge, phrase **7** express, lie down, recline **8** recamier **9** davenport, formulate **12** chesterfield

couch potato
5 idler **6** loafer **7** slacker **8** sluggard

cougar
3 cat **4** puma **7** panther **9** catamount **12** mountain lion

cough
4 hack, hawk

cough drop
6 troche **7** lozenge

cough up
3 pay **5** spend **6** lay out, pay out **7** deliver, dole out, fork out **8** fork over, hand over, shell out

couloir
5 chasm, gorge, gulch, gully **6** ravine

council
4 diet **5** board, junta **6** powwow, senate **7** cabinet, meeting **8** assembly, conclave, congress, ministry **10** conference, federation **12** consultation
ancient Greek: **5** boule
church: **5** synod **10** consistory
medieval English: **4** moot **5** gemot **6** gemote **8** hustings
Muslim: **5** divan
Russian: **4** duma **6** soviet
secret: **5** cabal, junto **9** camarilla
Spanish: **7** cabildo

counsel
4 rede, urge, warn **6** advice, advise, charge, direct, enjoin, lawyer **7** consult, suggest **8** advocate, attorney **9** prescribe, recommend **10** advisement **12** deliberation
British: **9** barrister, solicitor

count
3 add, sum, tot **4** bank, earl, mean, rely, tote **5** issue, score, tally, total, tot up, weigh **6** census, charge, depend, expect, figure, matter, number, reckon, result, tote up **7** compute, signify **8** estimate, militate, numerate, quantify **9** calculate, enumerate **10** allegation

countenance
3 let, mug **4** back, cast, face, look, mien, phiz **5** allow, favor, go for **6** accept, aspect, permit, visage **7** approve, commend, condone, endorse, support **8** advocate, features, hold with, sanction, tolerate **9** approbate, composure, encourage **10** expression **11** physiognomy

counter
3 bar, pit, vie **4** anti, desk **5** asset, check, match, polar, shelf, table **6** contra, offset, oppose **7** adverse, against, hostile, obverse, opposed, reverse **8** antipode, contrary, converse, opposing, opposite **9** antipodal, diametric **10** antipodean, antithesis, contravene **12** antagonistic, antipathetic, antithetical **13** contradictory

counteract
3 fix **4** foil **5** annul **6** cancel, negate, oppose, resist, thwart **7** balance, correct, nullify, prevent, rectify, redress **8** negative **9** cancel out, frustrate **10** balance out, neutralize

counteragent
4 cure **6** remedy **8** antidote **9** antitoxin, antivenin **10** corrective

counterbalance
6 cancel, make up, offset, redeem, set off **7** ballast, correct, even out, rectify, redress **8** equalize, outweigh **10** compensate

counterblow
7 revenge **8** reprisal, requital, revanche **9** vengeance **11** retaliation, retribution

counterclockwise
4 levo **12** levorotatory

counterfeit
4 copy, fake, hoax, sham **5** bluff, bogus, dummy, false, feign, forge, fraud, mimic, phony **6** affect, assume, deceit, ersatz, forged, pseudo **7** feigned, imitate, pretend **8** delusive, delusory, knock off, simulate, spurious **9** brummagem, deception, deceptive, fabricate, imitation, imposture, insincere, pinchbeck, pretended, simulated **10** fraudulent, misleading, simulacrum
prefix: **5** pseud **6** pseudo

counterpane
4 pouf, puff **5** duvet **6** spread **8** bedcover, coverlet **9** bedspread, comforter, eiderdown

counterpart
4 like, twin **5** equal, match **6** analog, double **7** vis-à-vis **8** alter ego, analogue, parallel **9** correlate, duplicate **10** complement, coordinate, equivalent **11** correlative **13** correspondent

counterpoise
6 make up, offset, redeem, set off **7** balance, ballast **8** outweigh **9** stabilize **10** compensate

countersign
8 password **9** watchword

countervail
4 foil **6** cancel, offset, oppose, redeem, set off, thwart **7** balance, correct, nullify, rectify **8** outweigh **9** frustrate **10** compensate, neutralize

countess's husband
4 earl

countless
6 legion, myriad, untold **7** umpteen **11** innumerable

Count of Monte Cristo
6 Dantès (Edmond)
author: **5** Dumas (Alexandre)

count out
5 expel **6** except **7** exclude **9** disregard, eliminate

countrified
5 rural **6** rustic **7** bucolic **8** homespun, pastoral **10** campestral

country
4 home, land, soil **5** rural **6** nation, region, rustic, sticks **7** boonies, bucolic, outland **8** homeland, pastoral **9** backwoods, boondocks **10** campestral, fatherland, motherland, provincial
dance: **3** jig **4** reel **10** strathspey
estate: **5** manor
home: **5** dacha, manor, ranch, villa **8** hacienda
music: **9** bluegrass
lodging: **3** inn
road: **4** lane, path **5** byway
(see also **nation**)

country-music star
4 Cash (Johnny), Ford (Tennessee Ernie), Gill (Vince), Lynn (Loretta), Rich (Charlie), Tubb (Ernest) **5** Acuff (Roy), Autry (Gene), Black (Clint), Clark (Roy), Cline (Patsy), Davis (Skeeter), Jones (George), Owens (Buck), Pearl (Minnie), Pride (Charley), Swift (Taylor), Twain (Shania), Urban (Keith), Wells (Kitty), Wills (Bob) **6** Arnold (Eddy), Atkins (Chet), Brooks (Garth), Carter (A. P., June, Maybelle, Sara), Harris (Emmylou), McGraw (Tim), Miller (Roger), Milsap (Ronnie), Monroe (Bill), Nelson (Willie), Parton (Dolly), Ritter (Tex), Rogers (Kenny, Roy), Skaggs (Ricky), Strait (George), Tillis (Mel), Travis (Randy), Tucker (Tanya), Twitty (Conway) **7** Chesney (Kenny), Haggard (Merle), Millsap (Ronnie), Paisley (Brad), Robbins (Marty), Rodgers (Jimmie), Shelton (Blake), Wynette (Tammy) **8** Campbell (Glen), Jennings (Waylon), Mandrell (Barbara), McEntire (Reba), Williams (Hank) **9** Underwood (Carrie)

country of G.B.
3 Eng.

coup
4 blow, feat **5** upset **6** putsch, stroke **8** takeover **9** overthrow

coup d'___
4 état

coup de ___
5 grâce

couple
3 duo, twa, two **4** bond, dyad, fuse, item, join, link, mate, pair, span, team, yoke **5** brace, hitch, marry, merge, unite **6** hook up, link up **7** bracket, combine, conjoin, connect, doublet, harness, twosome

coupler
4 link, ring **5** hitch, joint **6** hookup **7** shackle **8** ligature
railroad: **7** drawbar

couplet
3 duo **4** dyad, pair **5** twins **7** distich, doublet, twosome

coupling
4 link, seam **5** joint, union **6** yoking **7** joining, pairing **8** junction, juncture **9** connector **10** connection

courage
4 dash, grit, guts **5** heart, moxie, nerve, pluck, spunk, valor **6** daring, mettle, spirit **7** bravery, heroism **8** audacity, backbone, boldness, firmness, temerity, tenacity, valiance, valiancy **9** assurance, fortitude, gallantry **10** resolution **11** doughtiness, intrepidity **12** fearlessness **13** dauntlessness

courageous
4 bold **5** brave, gutsy, nervy, stout **6** daring, heroic, manful, plucky, spunky, strong **7** doughty, gallant, valiant **8** fearless, intrepid, resolute, stalwart, unafraid, valorous **9** audacious, dauntless, tenacious, undaunted **11** venturesome **12** stouthearted

courier
5 envoy, gofer **6** legate, runner **8** emissary **9** go-between, messenger **11** internuncio

course
3 row, run, way **4** dart, dash, duct, flow, line, path, plan, race, road, rush, tack, tear **5** canal,

chain, chase, class, hurry, orbit, order, range, route, scoot, scope, speed, surge, track, trend **6** career, design, hasten, hustle, manner, policy, polity, scheme, sequel, series, string, system **7** advance, channel, circuit, conduit, passage, pattern, program, regimen, routine, seminar **8** aqueduct, duration, progress, sequence, syllabus **9** procedure, racetrack **10** curriculum, succession **11** progression
curving: **4** coil, curl, turn, wind **5** swing, twist **6** spiral **9** corkscrew
dinner: **4** soup **5** salad **6** entrée **7** dessert **9** appetizer, blue plate

courser
4 bird **5** horse, mount, steed **7** charger **8** huntsman, warhorse

court
3 bar, woo **4** date, quad, yard **5** atria (plural), charm, motel, spark, suite, tempt **6** allure, atrium, homage, invite, palace, pursue **7** address, flatter, justice, retinue, romance, solicit **8** assembly, cloister, tribunal **9** captivate, curtilage, enclosure, entourage **10** magistrate, parliament, quadrangle **11** legislature
action: **4** suit **5** trial **6** appeal, assize **7** hearing, inquest, lawsuit **10** proceeding
calendar: **6** docket
call to: **7** summons **8** subpoena **11** arraignment
circuit: **4** eyre
crier's call: **4** oyez
decision: **6** assize **7** finding, verdict **8** judgment
ecclesiastical: **4** rota **5** Curia **10** consistory
Indian: **6** durbar
kind: **4** moot **5** civil **6** county, family **7** circuit, customs, federal, supreme **8** chancery, criminal, district, juvenile, kangaroo, superior **9** appellate, municipal **11** territorial
medieval English: **4** eyre, moot **5** gemot **6** gemote **8** hustings
of equity: **8** chancery
official: **3** ref
officer: **5** clerk, crier, judge **7** bailiff, justice, marshal, sheriff **10** prosecutor
order: **4** writ **5** edict **6** decree **7** summons **8** mandamus, subpoena
panel: **4** jury
relating to: **8** judicial **9** juridical
roofed: **5** atria (plural) **6** atrium
session: **6** assize **7** sitting **8** sederunt

courteous
5 civil **6** polite **7** courtly, gallant, genteel **8** mannerly, well-bred **9** attentive **10** chivalrous, thoughtful **11** considerate **12** well-mannered

courtesan
7 cocotte, demirep, odalisc, odalisk **9** odalisque **12** demimondaine

courtesy
7 amenity, decorum, manners, service **8** chivalry, civility **9** attention, etiquette, gallantry **10** cordiality, indulgence **11** courtliness **12** graciousness **13** attentiveness, consideration

court game
see under **game**

courtly
5 noble **6** august, formal, urbane **7** elegant, gallant, refined, stately **8** gracious **9** dignified **10** chivalrous, flattering **11** ceremonious

courtship
4 suit **6** dating, wooing **7** romance **10** flirtation
former custom of: **8** bundling

courtyard
4 quad **5** atria (plural), garth, patio **6** atrium **9** curtilage **10** quadrangle

cousin
3 kin **7** kinsman **8** relative

Cousteau, Jacques
ship: **7** Calypso
vehicle: **11** bathysphere

couturier
8 clothier, costumer, designer **10** dressmaker (see also **fashion designer**)

cove
3 arm, bay **4** nook **5** bight, firth, inlet, niche **6** harbor, recess **9** concavity

covenant
3 vow **4** bond, pact **5** agree, swear **6** pledge, treaty **7** compact, promise **8** contract **9** agreement **10** convention

Covent Garden offering
5 opera **6** ballet

cover
3 cap, lid **4** bury, hide, hood, mask, veil, wrap **5** alibi, cloak, front, guise, stash, track **6** clothe, enfold, enwrap, facade, hiding, insure, mantle, refuge, screen, secure, shield, shroud, sleeve, travel **7** blanket, conceal, embrace, enclose, envelop, obscure, overlay, protect, secrete, shelter, write up **8** disguise, ensconce, enshroud, traverse **9** encompass, safeguard, sanctuary, superpose **10** overspread **11** concealment, superimpose
rooflike: **6** awning, canopy
story: **5** alibi
the eyes: **4** loup **9** blindfold
the face: **4** mask, veil
the head: **4** hood
the mouth: **6** muzzle
with asphalt: **4** pave
with cloth: **5** drape
with dirt: **7** begrime, blacken **8** besmirch
with straw: **6** thatch

coverall
8 jumpsuit **10** boilersuit

covered wagon
9 Conestoga

covering
anatomical: **5** theca, velum **6** tegmen **7** velamen **8** tegument **10** integument
apex of roof: **3** épi
close-fitting: **6** sheath **9** sheathing
cloth: **5** sheet
flap: **9** operculum
for a book: **4** case **6** jacket
for a cigar: **7** wrapper
for a coffin: **4** pall
for a corpse: **6** shroud **8** cerement
for a package: **7** wrapper
for concealment: **10** camouflage
for food: **4** cosy, cozy
for soil: **5** mulch
metal: **4** mail **5** armor
of a diatom: **6** lorica
of a plant ovary: **8** pericarp
of a seed: **4** aril, case **5** testa
of fruits: **4** peel, rind
of gloom: **4** pall
of grain: **4** hull, husk **5** chaff
shell-like: **7** testudo **8** carapace
thin: **4** film **6** patina, veneer
waterproof: **4** tarp **9** tarpaulin

coverlet
4 pouf, puff **5** duvet **6** spread **8** bedcover **9** bedspread, comforter **11** counterpane

covert
4 lair **5** haven, privy **6** hidden, masked, refuge, secret, veiled **7** feather, furtive, retreat, shelter, sub-rosa, thicket **8** hush-hush, shrouded, stealthy **9** concealed, disguised, sanctuary, sheltered **10** undercover **11** camouflaged, clandestine, hiding place, underhanded **12** hugger-mugger **13** surreptitious, under-the-table

covertly
7 sub-rosa **9** by stealth **12** hugger-mugger

covet
4 want **5** crave **6** desire

covetous
4 avid, keen **5** itchy **6** grabby, greedy **7** envious **8** desirous, esurient, grasping, ravenous **9** rapacious, voracious **10** avaricious, gluttonous **11** acquisitive

covey
4 band, bevy, crew, nest **5** brood, bunch, flock, group, party, troop **6** gaggle, troupe **7** cluster, company

cow
(see also **cattle**)
4 faze, kine (plural), neat **5** abash, bossy, bully, daunt **6** appall, bovine, dismay, hector, rattle **7** bluster, dragoon **8** bludgeon, browbeat, bulldoze, bullyrag **9** discomfit, embarrass, strong-arm **10** disconcert, intimidate
breed: **6** Jersey **8** Ayrshire, Guernsey, Hereford, Holstein **10** Brown Swiss
cud: **5** rumen
French: **5** vache
hornless: **5** muley **7** pollard
mammary gland: **5** udder
pen: **6** corral
shed: **4** barn, byre
Spanish: **4** vaca
young: **4** calf **5** stirk **6** heifer

coward
6 craven **7** caitiff, chicken, dastard, milksop, nebbish **8** poltroon, recreant **9** jellyfish **10** scaredy-cat **11** yellowbelly

Coward of the stage
4 Noël

cowardly
5 timid, wimpy **6** afraid, craven, yellow **7** caitiff, chicken, fearful, gutless **8** poltroon, recreant, timorous **9** dastardly, spineless **11** lily-livered, milk-livered, poltroonish **12** apprehensive, fainthearted, poor-spirited, white-livered **13** pusillanimous

Cowardly Lion portrayer
4 Lahr (Bert)

cowboy
5 rogue, waddy **6** drover, herder, waddie **7** puncher, rancher **8** buckaroo, herdsman, maverick, wrangler **9** cattleman, ranch hand **10** cowpuncher **12** broncobuster
contest: **5** rodeo
gear: **5** cuffs, quirt, spurs **6** duster **7** bedroll, slicker, Stetson
legendary: **9** Pecos Bill
leggings: **5** chaps
movie: **3** Mix (Tom) **4** Hart (William S.) **5** Autry (Gene), oater, Wayne (John) **6** Gibson (Hoot), McCrea (Joel), Murphy (Audie), Ritter (Tex), Rogers (Roy, Will) **8** Cisco Kid, Eastwood (Clint)
rope: **5** lasso, reata, riata **6** lariat
Spanish-American: **6** charro, gaucho **7** vaquero

cowcatcher
5 pilot

cower
5 quail, wince **6** blench, cringe, flinch, recoil, shrink

cowfish
6 dugong, sea cow **7** grampus, manatee **8** sirenian

cowl
4 cape, hood **5** cloak **6** capote, domino, mantle **7** capuche

coworker
8 confrere **9** associate, colleague

cowpox
8 vaccinia

cowpuncher
see **cowboy**

coxcomb
3 fop **4** beau, buck, dude, fool **5** blood, dandy, swell **7** peacock **8** macaroni **9** exquisite **11** Beau Brummel **12** clotheshorse, fashion plate, lounge lizard

coy
3 shy **4** arch, cute, pert **5** saucy, timid **6** demure, modest **7** bashful, evasive, playful **8** blushing, decorous, skittish **9** diffident, kittenish **10** capricious, coquettish **11** flirtatious, mischievous **12** noncommittal

Coyote State
11 South Dakota

coypu
6 nutria, rodent **8** river rat

cozen
3 gyp **4** bilk, scam **5** cheat, trick **6** diddle, fleece, take in **7** beguile, deceive, defraud, swindle, wheedle **8** flimflam **9** bamboozle **11** double-cross

cozy
4 safe, snug, soft **5** comfy, cushy, pally, tight **6** chummy, secure **8** familiar, intimate **11** comfortable

cpl. or sgt.
3 NCO

CPR expert
3 EMT

crab
3 nag **4** beef, fuss, yawp **5** gripe, sidle **6** grinch, griper, grouch, kvetch, squawk, yammer **7** decapod, grouser, growler **8** arthopod, complain, grumbler, sourpuss **9** bellyache, shellfish **10** bellyacher, complainer, crosspatch, crustacean, curmudgeon **11** faultfinder
claw: **5** chela **6** nipper
constellation: **6** Cancer
genus: **3** Uca **6** Birgus **7** Limulus, Pagurus
kind: **3** pea **4** blue, king, pine, rock **5** ghost, purse **6** hermit, spider **7** fiddler **9** Dungeness, horseshoe
king, horseshoe: **7** limulus

crabbed
4 dour, glum, grim, sour **5** gruff, surly **6** crusty, gloomy, morose, sullen **9** illegible, irascible, saturnine, splenetic

crablike
8 cancroid

crabwise
8 sidelong, sideward, sideways **9** laterally

crab-walk
5 sidle

crack
3 gag, gap, rap, try **4** bang, barb, bash, belt, blow, boom, clap, flaw, jest, joke, open, peal, quip, rift, roll, shot, slam, slap, snap, stab, wham, whop **5** adept, break, burst, chink, cleft, crash, craze, knock, smack, smash, solve, split, whack, whirl, wreck **6** breach, cranny, decode, expert, master, moment, thwack, zinger **7** break up, crevice, decrypt, destroy, fissure, instant, shatter, skilled **8** crevasse, decipher, disorder, interval, masterly, skillful, superior **9** break into, excellent, interrupt, masterful, witticism **10** percussion, proficient

crackbrain
3 nut **4** kook **5** crank, wacko **6** cuckoo, nitwit **7** dingbat, half-wit, lunatic **9** ding-a-ling, fruitcake, screwball

crackdown
5 purge **8** quashing **10** repression **11** suppression

cracked
3 mad **4** ajar, daft, nuts **5** balmy, batty, crazy, daffy, loony, nutty **6** broken, crazed, cuckoo, insane, screwy **7** bonkers, lunatic, smashed **8** demented, deranged

cracker
4 hick, HiHo, Ritz, rube **5** wafer, yokel **6** rustic **7** biscuit, hillbilly, saltine **8** Georgian **9** Floridian

crackerjack
3 ace **4** lulu **5** daisy, dandy, dilly, doozy, nifty, sharp **6** corker, killer **8** jim-dandy, knockout **9** humdinger **12** lollapalooza

crackle
4 snap **7** glitter, sparkle, twinkle **9** crepitate **10** effervesce **13** effervescence

crackpot
3 nut **4** case, kook, loon **5** crank, loony, wacko **6** cuckoo, madman **7** dingbat, lunatic, oddball **9** ding-a-ling, eccentric, fruitcake, harebrain, screwball

crack-up, crack up
5 crash, smash, wreck **6** fiasco **7** debacle **8** accident, collapse, disaster **9** breakdown **11** catastrophe

cradlesong
7 lullaby **8** berceuse

craft
3 art, job **4** boat, ship **5** guile, knack, skill, trade, wiles **6** career, deceit, métier **7** ability, calling, cunning, know-how, slyness **8** artifice, caginess, foxiness, vocation, wiliness **9** adeptness, canniness, dexterity, duplicity, expertise, ingenuity, technique **10** adroitness, artfulness, competence, occupation, profession, shrewdness **11** proficiency
(see also **boat**)

craftiness
5 guile **7** cunning **8** artifice, subtlety

craftsman
5 smith **6** carter, carver, potter, weaver, wright **7** artisan, builder, cobbler, jeweler **9** carpenter **10** blacksmith

crafty
3 sly **4** foxy, keen, wily **5** acute, cagey, canny, sharp, slick **6** adroit, artful, astute, clever, shrewd, tricky **7** cunning, devious, vulpine **8** guileful, scheming, skillful, slippery **9** deceitful, designing, ingenious, insidious **11** calculating, duplicitous
Scottish: **7** sleekit

crag
3 tor **5** cliff

craggy
5 erose, harsh, rocky, rough **6** jagged, rugged, uneven

crake
4 rail

cram
3 jam, ram **4** bolt, fill, gulp, heap, load, pack, wolf **5** crowd, crush, drive, force, press, shove, study, stuff, wedge **6** gobble, review, squash, thrust **7** jam-pack, overeat, squeeze

crammed
4 full **5** awash, flush **7** brimful **8** brimming **9** chock-full

cramp
4 kink, pain, pang **5** crick, limit, spasm **6** hamper, stitch **7** confine, inhibit, shackle **8** confined, restrain, restrict **9** restraint, stricture **10** constraint, limitation **11** confinement, restriction

cramped
5 close, tight **6** narrow **9** confining, two-by-four

crane
4 bird, boom, rail **5** heron **7** derrick, stretch
arm: **3** jib
genus: **4** Grus
ship's: **5** davit

Crane hero
12 Henry Fleming

cranium
5 skull **9** braincase

crank
3 nut **4** crab, kook **5** fancy **6** griper, grouch, notion, rotate, turn up, vagary **7** caprice, conceit, fanatic, grouser, oddball **8** crackpot, crotchet, grumbler, sourpuss **9** eccentric, screwball **10** bellyacher, crosspatch

cranky
5 cross, testy **6** crabby, crusty, cussed, grumpy, morose, ornery, tetchy, touchy **7** bearish, crabbed, peevish, prickly **8** contrary, petulant, tortuous, vinegary **9** crotchety, irascible, irritable, obstinate **10** bad-humored, ill-humored **12** cantankerous, disagreeable **13** unpredictable

cranny
3 gap **4** nook, slit **5** chink, crack, niche **6** corner **7** crevice

crash
3 din, jar, ram **4** bang, boom, bump, bust, clap, fail, fold, jolt, peal, slam, wham **5** blast, break, burst, crack, shock, smash, wreck **6** impact, pileup **7** collide, crack-up, debacle, decline, failure, smashup **8** accident, collapse **9** breakdown, collision **10** concussion

crass
4 rude **5** crude, gross **6** coarse, vulgar **7** boorish, loutish, uncouth **8** churlish **9** unrefined **13** materialistic

crate
3 box **4** heap **5** wreck **6** jalopy, junker **7** clunker

crater
3 pit **4** dent, hole, pock **5** crash **6** cavity, dimple, hollow, trough **7** caldera **8** collapse **10** depression
Hawaiian: **7** Kilauea

cravat
3 tie **4** band **5** ascot, scarf **7** necktie

crave
3 ask, beg **4** need, want, wish **5** covet **6** demand, desire **7** call for, entreat, implore, long for, require **8** yearn for

craven
4 funk **6** abject, coward **7** caitiff, chicken, dastard, fearful, gutless, ignoble **8** cowardly, cringing, poltroon, recreant **9** dastardly **11** lily-livered, poltroonish, yellowbelly **13** pusillanimous, yellowbellied

craving
3 yen **4** itch, lust, need, urge **5** jones **6** desire, hunger, thirst **7** longing, passion **8** appetite, yearning **9** hankering

crawl
4 flow, inch, teem **5** creep, swarm **6** abound, grovel **7** slither, wriggle **9** pullulate

crawling
6 repent

craze
3 fad **4** chic, rage **5** crack, fever, furor, mania, trend, vogue **6** dement, enrage, frenzy, furore, madden **7** derange, fashion, unhinge **9** unbalance **10** dernier cri, enthusiasm

craziness
5 folly, mania **6** lunacy **8** hysteria, insanity **9** absurdity

crazy
3 fey, mad **4** amok, bats, daft, gaga, loco, nuts, wild, zany **5** balmy, barmy, batty, daffy, dotty, goofy, kooky, loony, loopy, nutty, rabid, silly,

wacko, wacky **6** absurd, cuckoo, fruity, insane, mental, psycho, screwy, teched, whacky **7** berserk, bonkers, cracked, foolish, frantic, lunatic, meshuga, smitten, tetched, touched, unsound **8** cockeyed, crackpot, demented, deranged, frenetic, frenzied, maniacal, meshugge, unhinged **9** bedlamite, delirious, eccentric, fanatical, foolhardy, ludicrous, possessed, screwball, senseless **10** crackbrain, moonstruck, ridiculous, unbalanced **11** harebrained, nonsensical **12** preposterous
British: **5** potty **6** scatty
Scottish: **3** wud

creak
4 rasp **5** grate, grind **6** scrape, squeak, squeal **7** grating, screech **9** squeaking

creaky
4 aged **5** rusty **7** rickety, run-down, squeaky, unsound, worn-out **8** decrepit **9** tottering **10** broken-down, ramshackle

cream
3 top **4** balm, beat, best, drub, pick, whip, whup **5** A-list, blast, elite, prime, salve **6** cerate, choice, defeat, finest, thrash **7** clobber, destroy, trounce, unguent **8** lambaste, liniment, ointment

creamy cheese
4 Brie

crease
4 fold, ruck **5** graze, plica, ridge **6** furrow, groove, rumple **7** crinkle, wrinkle

create
3 dub **4** form, make, sire **5** beget, build, cause, forge, found, hatch, set up, spawn, start **6** author, design, devise, father, invent **7** compose, concoct, develop, fashion, produce **8** conceive, engender, generate, occasion **9** construct, establish, fabricate, formulate, institute, originate **10** constitute

creation
5 birth, world **6** cosmos, nature **7** genesis **8** universe **9** inception, macrocosm **10** conception **11** macrocosmos

creative
4 arty **5** artsy **7** fertile **8** artistic, inspired, original **9** deceptive, demiurgic, ingenious, inventive **10** innovative, innovatory **11** imaginative **12** innovational

creator
3 god **6** author **8** inventor **9** architect, generator, patriarch **10** originator, progenitor

creature
3 man **5** beast, being, brute, human **6** animal, mortal, person **7** critter, varmint
fabled: **3** elf, imp, orc, roc **4** ogre, puck, yeti **5** dwarf, fairy, ghost, giant, gnome, harpy, nymph, pixie, troll **6** dragon, goblin, gorgon, kraken, merman, Nessie, sphinx, sprite, wyvern **7** bigfoot, brownie, bugbear, centaur, chimera, gremlin, griffin, mermaid, monster, unicorn, vampire, wendigo, windigo **8** chimaera, minotaur, werewolf **9** hobgoblin, manticore, sasquatch **10** cockatrice, hippogriff, leprechaun
(see also **monster**)

credence
5 faith, trust **6** belief, credit **8** reliance **9** sideboard **10** acceptance, confidence

credentials
6 papers **9** documents **10** references **12** certificates, testimonials **13** documentation

credenza
6 buffet **7** console **8** bookcase **9** sideboard

credible
5 solid, sound, valid **6** trusty **8** reliable **9** authentic, colorable, plausible **10** believable, convincing, persuasive, reasonable **11** trustworthy **12** satisfactory

credit
4 deem, feel **5** asset, faith, honor, refer, sense, think, trust **6** accept, assign, belief, charge, impute, notice, weight **7** ascribe, believe **8** consider, credence, prestige, reliance **9** attribute, authority, influence **10** confidence, reputation **11** recognition

creditable
6 worthy **8** laudable, reliable **9** colorable, deserving, estimable, plausible, reputable **10** believable **11** commendable, meritorious, respectable **12** praiseworthy

credo
5 canon, creed, dogma, tenet **6** belief, tenets **7** beliefs, precept **8** doctrine, ideology **9** catechism, principle

credulous
5 naive **6** unwary **8** gullible, trustful, trusting **9** believing **12** unsuspecting, unsuspicious **13** unquestioning

creed
4 sect **5** canon, dogma, faith, tenet **6** belief, church, tenets **7** beliefs, precept **8** doctrine, ideology, religion **9** catechism, communion, principle **12** denomination
Christian: **6** Nicene

creek
3 ria **4** burn, rill **5** brook **6** arroyo, rillet, runlet, runnel, stream **7** freshet, rivulet **8** brooklet **9** streamlet

creep
4 drag, edge, inch, jerk, lurk, slip **5** crawl, freak, glide, schmo, shirk, sicko, skulk, slide, slink, snake, sneak, steal **6** shmuck, sickie, spread, tiptoe, weirdo **7** gumshoe, oddball, pervert, schmuck, slither, wriggle **9** pussyfoot

creeping
6 repent **7** gradual **9** prostrate
creepy
5 eerie, weird **6** spooky **7** anxious, macabre, ominous, strange, uncanny **8** ghoulish, menacing, sinister **9** unnerving **10** disturbing, unpleasant, unsettling **11** hair-raising
crème de ___
5 cacao, noyau **6** menthe
crème de la crème
4 best **5** A-list, elect, elite **6** finest
Cremona family
5 Amati **8** Guarneri **10** Stradivari **12** Stradivarius
Creole
dish: 5 gumbo **9** andouille, dirty rice, jambalaya
music: 6 zydeco
vegetable: 4 okra
Creon
daughter: 6 Creusa, Glauce, Glauke
sister: 7 Jocasta
son: 6 Haemon
victim: 8 Antigone
crepe
4 blin **5** blini (plural) **6** blintz **7** blintze, pancake
crescendo
4 acme, apex, peak, rise **5** crest, surge, swell **6** apogee, climax, growth, height, zenith **8** increase, pinnacle **9** high point **11** culmination
crescent
6 bicorn
crescent-shaped
5 bowed **6** lunate, sickle **7** falcate
body or surface: 4 lune **8** meniscus
crest
3 cap, top **4** acme, apex, brow, comb, noon, peak, roof, tuft **5** arête, chine, crown, plume, ridge **6** apogee, climax, summit, vertex **7** hogback **8** pinnacle, surmount **9** high point **10** coat of arms, prominence **11** culmination
of a wave: 8 whitecap
crestfallen
3 low, sad **4** blue, down **6** droopy **8** dejected, downcast, drooping **9** depressed **10** dispirited **11** discouraged, downhearted **12** disappointed, disconsolate, disheartened
Crete
ancient city: 7 Cnossus, Knossos **8** Phaistos
ancient name: 6 Candia
capital: 5 Canea
goddess: 8 Dictynna **11** Britomartis
guard: 5 Talos
king: 5 Minos **9** Idomeneus
maze: 9 labyrinth
monster: 8 Minotaur
mountain: 3 Ida
princess: 7 Ariadne
cretin
3 oaf **4** boob, clod, dolt, dope, fool, lout **5** dumbo, dummy, dunce, idiot, moron **6** dimwit, nitwit **7** half-wit **8** imbecile, lunkhead, numskull **9** lamebrain, numbskull, simpleton
Creusa
brother: 6 Haemon
father: 5 Priam
husband: 6 Aeneas
mother: 6 Hecuba
sister: 6 Glauce, Glauke
son: 3 Ion **8** Ascanius
crevice
3 gap **4** rift, seam, slit **5** chink, cleft, crack **6** cranny **7** fissure **8** cleavage **10** interstice
crew
4 band, bevy, gang, team **5** bunch, covey, group, party **6** rowers, rowing **7** company, sailors
leader: 3 cox **8** coxswain
crib
3 bed, bin, box, hut, key **4** pony, trot **5** cheat, crate, hovel, shack, stall, steal, theft **6** cradle, crèche, manger, pilfer **7** barrier, brothel **8** bassinet, bedstead, bordello **9** enclosure **10** plagiarism, plagiarize
Crichton novel
11 Terminal Man (The) **12** Jurassic Park **15** Andromeda Strain (The)
cricket
period of play: 7 innings
team: 6 eleven
term: 3 leg, off, rot **4** bowl **5** pitch **6** bowler, wicket, yorker **7** batsman, striker **9** fieldsman
turn at bat: 4 over
crime
3 sin **4** evil, tort, vice **5** caper **6** breach, delict, felony **7** misdeed, offense **8** atrocity, iniquity **9** diablerie, violation **10** corruption, illegality, infraction, wrongdoing **11** misdemeanor **13** transgression
instructor: 5 Fagin
lab evidence: 3 DNA
syndicate head: 4 capo
Crimea
city: 5 Kerch, Yalta **10** Sebastopol, Sevastopol, Simferopol
river: 4 Alma
sea: 4 Azov **5** Black
strait: 5 Kerch
criminal
4 hood, thug **5** crook, felon, shady **6** outlaw **7** convict, corrupt, crooked, hoodlum, illegal, illicit, lawless, mobster **8** culpable, fugitive,

gangster, jailbird, offender, scofflaw, unlawful, wrongful **9** desperado, felonious, miscreant, nefarious, racketeer, wrongdoer **10** delinquent, lawbreaker, malefactor, trespasser **12** illegitimate, transgressor
habitual: **8** repeater **10** recidivist
intent: **7** mens rea
slang: **5** argot

criminate
see **incriminate**

crimp
4 bend, curb, wave **5** frizz **6** crease, hamper, hold in **7** crinkle, inhibit, wrinkle **8** hold back, obstacle, restrain **9** constrain, restraint **10** impediment **11** obstruction

crimson
3 red **4** rose **5** blush, color, flush **6** redden
team of Atlanta: **4** Tide

cringe
4 duck **5** cower, hunch, quail, wince **6** blench, flinch, grovel, recoil, shrink

crinkle
4 ruck **5** crimp, plica, ridge **6** crease, furrow, pucker, ruck up, rumple, rustle **7** crackle, crumple, scrunch, wrinkle **11** corrugation

crinkly
5 crepy **6** crepey, frizzy **7** frizzed **8** wrinkled

cripple
4 lame, maim **6** mangle **7** disable **8** mutilate, paralyze **9** hamstring, undermine **10** debilitate **12** incapacitate

crippled
4 halt, lame **6** maimed **7** gnarled, mangled **8** battered, deformed, disabled, weakened **9** enfeebled, misshapen, mutilated, paralyzed **11** debilitated, handicapped

crisis
4 crux, pass **5** pinch **6** climax, crunch, height, strait **7** impasse, straits **8** disaster, exigency, juncture, zero hour **9** emergency, extremity **10** crossroads **11** catastrophe, contingency **12** turning point

crisp
4 cold, cool, curl, deft, keen, neat, wavy **5** brisk, clean, crimp, curly, fresh, nippy, pithy, sharp, short **6** biting, chilly, lively, ripple, spruce **7** bracing, brittle, crunchy, cutting, wrinkle **8** clean-cut, clear-cut, incisive **9** trenchant **11** stimulating **12** invigorating

crisscross
3 net **4** grid, mesh **5** weave **7** network, overlap **8** reticule **9** confusion, decussate, intersect, reticular **10** reticulate

criterion
4 norm **5** canon, gauge, ideal, model, tenet **7** measure, precept **8** exemplar, paradigm, standard **9** benchmark, yardstick **10** touchstone

critic
5 judge **6** carper, pundit **7** arbiter, caviler **8** caviller, censurer, quibbler, reviewer **9** belittler, nitpicker **10** disparager, mudslinger **11** commentator, connoisseur, faultfinder

critical
4 dire **5** acute, fussy **7** carping, crucial, finicky, pivotal, weighty **8** captious, caviling, decisive **9** desperate, important, momentous **10** belittling, censorious, conclusive, precarious **11** disparaging, significant **12** faultfinding **13** consequential, determinative, hairsplitting
study: **6** examen **8** exegesis

criticism
4 flak, slap **5** blame, cavil, swipe **6** rebuke, review **7** censure, comment, opinion, potshot, reproof **8** analysis, brickbat, judgment, reproach **9** appraisal, objection **10** assessment, commentary, evaluation, nitpicking **11** examination, observation **12** faultfinding

criticize
3 pan, rap **4** bash, carp, flay **5** blame, blast, cavil, chide, fault, judge, knock, roast, scold **6** assess, rebuke, review, scathe **7** blister, censure, condemn, nitpick, reprove **8** appraise, badmouth, chastise, denounce, evaluate, lambaste **9** castigate, disparage, dress down, excoriate, find fault, reprehend, reprimand, reprobate

critique
see **criticism**

critter
5 beast **6** animal **7** varmint

Crius
father: **6** Uranus
mother: **4** Gaea
son: **8** Astraeus

croak
3 die **6** cackle, cash in, expire, go west, squawk **7** go south, grumble, snuff it **8** check out

croaker
4 drum, fish, frog **6** doctor

croaky
5 gruff, husky, raspy **6** hoarse **8** gravelly

Croatia
capital: **6** Zagreb
city: **5** Split, Zadar **6** Osijek, Rijeka **9** Dubrovnik
monetary unit: **4** kuna
neighbor: **6** Bosnia, Serbia **7** Hungary **8** Slovenia
part of: **7** Balkans
region: **8** Dalmatia, Slavonia

crock
3 jar, lie, pot **4** tale **6** tureen **7** cripple, disable, fiction **9** break down **11** fabrication

crocked
3 lit **4** high **5** drunk, lit up, oiled, tipsy **6** bashed, blotto, bombed, juiced, potted, soaked, soused,

stewed, stoned, tanked, wasted, zonked
7 drunken, pickled, pie-eyed, sloshed, smashed
9 plastered **10** inebriated, liquored up **11** intoxicated

Crockett's last stand
5 Alamo

crocodile
7 reptile
bird: **6** plover
Indian: **6** gavial **7** gharial
relative: **9** alligator
South American: **6** caiman, cayman
Southeast Asian: **6** mugger

Croesus' kingdom
5 Lydia

croft
4 farm **5** field

Croft of Tomb Raider
4 Lara

crofter
4 hind **6** farmer

Cromwell, Oliver
13 lord protector
battle: **6** Naseby **11** Marston Moor
party: **10** Roundheads
regiment: **9** Ironsides
son: **7** Richard
victim: **7** Charles (I)

crone
3 hag **4** trot **5** biddy, witch **6** beldam **7** beldame

Cronus
5 Titan **6** Saturn
daughter: **4** Hera **6** Hestia **7** Demeter
father: **6** Uranus
mother: **4** Gaea
sister: **4** Rhea **6** Cybele, Tethys
son: **4** Zeus **5** Hades **7** Jupiter, Neptune **8** Poseidon
wife: **4** Rhea **6** Cybele

crony
3 pal **4** chum **5** buddy **6** cohort **7** comrade
8 sidekick **9** associate, companion **10** accomplice **11** confederate

crook
3 bow **4** bend, flex, hook, wind **5** angle, curve, staff, thief **6** bandit, robber **7** burglar, crosier, hoodlum, pothook **8** criminal

crooked
4 awry **5** askew, lying, shady, venal **6** curved, errant, jagged, shifty, skewed, zigzag **7** bending, corrupt, devious, illegal, illicit, slanted
8 cockeyed, criminal, ruthless, tortuous, twisting **9** deceitful, dishonest, nefarious, underhand, unethical **10** fraudulent, mendacious, untruthful
11 duplicitous, underhanded **12** unscrupulous
13 double-dealing

croon
4 sing **6** murmur, warble

crooner
4 Cole (Nat "King"), Como (Perry), Eddy (Nelson) **5** Laine (Frankie), Tormé (Mel) **6** Crosby (Bing), Martin (Dean), singer, Vallee (Rudy)
7 Bennett (Tony), Sinatra (Frank) **8** Eckstine (Billy), vocalist, Williams (Andy)

crop
3 bob, cut, hew, lop, mow **4** chop, clip, pare, snip, trim **5** prune, shave, shear, stock, yield
6 gullet, handle, output **7** harvest, produce
8 fruitage, truncate **10** collection

croquet
5 roque

crosier
5 crook, staff

cross
3 mad **4** mule, rood, span **5** angry, surly, testy, trial **6** betray, bridge, crabby, cranky, grumpy, hybrid, negate, oppose, tetchy, touchy **7** athwart, calvary, grouchy, mongrel, peevish **8** captious, choleric, traverse **9** half blood, half-breed, hybridize, intersect, irascible, irritable, querulous, splenetic **10** affliction, contradict, interbreed, transverse **12** cantankerous
a river: **4** ford
bearer: **8** crucifer
decoration: **4** Iron **8** Victoria
kind: **3** tau **4** ankh **5** Greek, Latin, papal
6 Celtic, fleury, formée, moline, pommée, potent
7 avellan, botonée, Calvary, Maltese, saltire
8 crucifix, fourchée, Lorraine, quadrate **11** patriarchal **12** Saint Andrew's **13** Saint Anthony's
letters: **4** INRI
section: **5** slice

crossbow
8 arbalest, arbalist

crossbreed
4 mule **6** hybrid **7** bastard, mongrel **9** half blood, hybridize

cross-eye
6 squint **10** strabismus

crossing
8 junction, overpass, traverse **9** traversal, underpass **10** transverse **11** decussation, interchange, transversal **12** intersection

cross out
5 erase **6** cancel, delete, efface, excise **7** expunge

crosspatch
4 crab **5** crank, grump **6** griper, grouch
7 grouser **8** grumbler, sorehead, sourpuss
10 complainer, curmudgeon

crossroads
4 crux, pass **5** pinch **6** crisis, strait **8** exigency,

juncture, zero hour **9** carrefour, emergency **11** contingency **12** intersection, turning point
goddess: **6** Hecate, Hekate, Trivia

cross-shaped
8 cruciate **9** cruciform

crossways
6 aslant **7** athwart, oblique **8** diagonal **9** obliquely **10** diagonally, transverse **11** cater-corner, cattycorner, kitty-corner **12** transversely

crotchet
3 bee **4** whim **5** fancy, freak, quirk, trick **6** foible, megrim, notion, vagary **7** caprice, conceit **11** quarter note **12** eccentricity

crotchety
5 testy **6** crabby, cranky, crusty, ornery, tetchy, touchy **7** bearish, peevish, prickly **8** contrary, snappish, vinegary **9** difficult, eccentric, irascible **10** vinegarish **11** ill-tempered **12** cantankerous, cross-grained

crouch
4 bend, duck **5** cower, hunch, squat, stoop **6** cringe, huddle, shrink **10** hunker down

croup
3 bum **4** butt, hack, rear, rump, seat, tail **5** cough, edema, whoop **6** behind **7** keister, rear end, tail end **8** backside, buttocks, derriere, haunches **9** posterior

croupier tool
4 rake

crow
4 blow, brag, puff **5** boast, exult, gloat, prate, vaunt **6** cackle **7** bluster **9** gasconade, humble pie
colony: **7** rookery
cry: **3** caw
family: **6** corvid **8** Corvidae
genus: **6** Corvus
relating to: **7** corvine, corvoid
relative: **3** daw, jay **4** rook **5** raven **6** chough, magpie **7** jackdaw, jaybird

crowbar
3 pry **5** jimmy, lever

crowd
3 jam, mob **4** army, bear, cram, fill, herd, host, mass, pack, pile, push, rout, ruck **5** bunch, crush, drove, flock, flood, group, horde, hurry, press, serry, shove, surge, swarm, troop **6** circle, clique, gaggle, huddle, jostle, legion, rabble, squash, squish, stream, throng **7** cluster, collect, company, coterie, squeeze **8** assembly **9** gathering, multitude **10** assemblage, collection **11** aggregation **12** congregation

crowded
4 full **5** awash, close, dense, thick, tight **6** loaded **7** brimful, compact, teeming **8** brimming, populous, swarming **9** chock-full, congested, jam-packed

crown
3 cap, top **4** acme, apex, pate, peak, roof **5** cover, crest, tiara **6** climax, diadem, laurel, summit, top off, vertex, wreath, zenith **7** chaplet, coronal, coronet, garland, overlay, perfect **8** pinnacle, round off, surmount **9** culminate, finish off **10** consummate **11** culmination

crucial
4 dire **5** acute, vital **6** urgent **7** central, pivotal **8** critical, deciding, decisive **9** desperate, essential, important, momentous, necessary **10** imperative **11** climacteric, significant

crucible
4 test **5** trial **6** ordeal **8** acid test **10** melting pot

crucifix
4 rood **5** cross
letters: **4** INRI

crucifixion
aftermath: **5** pietà
site: **7** Calvary **8** Golgotha

crucify
4 rack **6** impale, martyr **7** mortify, pillory, torment, torture **10** excruciate

crud
3 goo **4** glop, gook, gunk, junk, muck **5** dreck, filth, slime, trash **6** debris, sludge **7** deposit, garbage, rubbish **12** incrustation

crude
3 raw **4** poor **5** crass, dirty, gross, rough **6** coarse, earthy, gauche, impure, ribald, risqué, vulgar **7** boorish, ill-bred, loutish, lowbred, obscene, obvious, raunchy, uncivil, uncouth **8** backward, cloddish, homespun, ignorant, indecent, inferior **9** elemental, graceless, inelegant, makeshift, primitive, rough-hewn, unrefined **10** amateurish, unfinished, unpolished

cruel
4 fell, grim, mean **5** harsh **6** brutal, fierce, savage **7** bestial, brutish, callous, heinous, vicious **8** inhumane, ruthless, sadistic **9** atrocious, barbarous, ferocious, heartless, merciless, monstrous, truculent **12** bloodthirsty

cruise
4 roam, rove, sail, surf, tour **5** drift, jaunt **6** junket, voyage **9** excursion

cruiser
4 boat **5** yacht **7** warship **8** squad car **9** patrol car, powerboat

cruising
4 a-sea

crumb
3 bit, ort **4** iota **5** ounce, scrap, shred **6** morsel, sliver, smidge **7** smidgen, smidgin **8** fragment, particle, smidgeon

crumble
5 decay **8** collapse **9** break down, decompose **11** deteriorate **12** disintegrate

crumbly
7 friable

crummy
4 poor **5** dingy, lousy, seedy, tacky **6** cruddy, flimsy, shoddy, sleazy **8** inferior

crumple
3 wad **4** cave **5** crimp **6** buckle, cave in, ruck up **7** crinkle, scrunch, wrinkle **8** collapse

crunch
4 chew **5** champ, chomp, grind, munch, sit-up **6** crisis **7** compute, process, squeeze **8** shortage, showdown
target: **3** abs

crusade
5 cause, drive **6** appeal **7** holy war **8** campaign, movement **9** offensive **10** expedition **11** undertaking

Crusader
English: **7** Richard (Lionheart)
foe: **7** Saladin, Saracen
French: **5** Louis (IX) **6** Philip, Robert **7** Baldwin, Charles, Godfrey, Raymond, Raymund **8** Boniface, Montfort, Philippe, Theobald
German: **6** Conrad **9** Frederick, Friedrich **10** Barbarossa
Norman: **7** Tancred **8** Bohemund
preacher: **5** Peter (the Hermit), Urban (II) **7** Adhémar, Bernard **8** Innocent (III), Pelaglus

crusading
11 evangelical **12** evangelistic

crush
3 jam, mob **4** cram, mash, pulp, push, ruin **5** crowd, drove, grind, horde, pound, press, quash, quell, smash, wreck **6** bruise, burden, defeat, mangle, reduce, squash, squish, subdue, throng **7** conquer, destroy, mortify, oppress, passion, put down, repress, scrunch, squeeze, squelch, squoosh, trample **8** bear down, beat down, demolish, overcome, suppress, vanquish **9** humiliate, multitude, overpower, overwhelm, pulverize, puppy love, subjugate **10** annihilate, extinguish, obliterate **11** infatuation

crust
4 cake, coat, rime, scab **7** coating, deposit **8** covering

crustacean
4 crab, flea **5** louse, prawn **6** isopod, shrimp, slater, sow bug **7** copepod, daphnia, decapod, lobster, pill bug **8** amphipod, barnacle, crawfish, crayfish, ostracod, sand flea **9** arthropod, beach flea, shellfish, water flea, wood louse **10** hermit crab, stomatopod, whale louse **11** branchiopod, fiddler crab
aggregate of: **5** krill
appendage: **7** pleopod
body segment: **6** somite, telson **8** metamere
claw: **5** chela **6** pincer
covering substance: **6** chitin
larva: **8** nauplius

crusty
4 curt **5** bluff, blunt, gross, gruff, short, surly **6** cranky **7** brusque, crabbed, prickly **8** choleric **9** irascible, irritable, saturnine, splenetic

crux
3 nub **4** core, gist, meat, pith **5** focus, heart **6** kernel, thrust **7** essence, purport **9** substance

cry
(see also **exclamation**)
3 sob **4** bawl, blub, call, howl, keen, mewl, moan, pule, wail, weep, yawp, yell, yelp, yowl **5** bleat, motto, mourn, shout, whine, whoop **6** boohoo, furore, holler, lament, scream, snivel, squall, squawk, squeak, squeal **7** blubber, screech, ululate, whimper **10** vociferate
bacchanals': **4** evoe
calf: **5** bleat
cat: **3** mew **4** meow **5** miaow
cattle: **3** low, moo
chick: **4** peep **5** cheep
court: **4** oyez
crane: **5** clang
crow: **3** caw
dog: **3** arf **4** bark, woof
donkey: **4** bray **6** hee-haw
duck: **5** quack
frog: **5** croak
goat: **5** bleat
goose: **4** honk **5** clang
hen: **6** cackle
horse: **5** neigh **6** nicker, whinny **7** whicker
lion: **4** roar
owl: **4** hoot
pig: **4** oink **5** grunt
raven: **3** caw **5** croak
rook: **3** caw
sheep: **5** bleat
songbird: **5** chirp, tweet
turkey: **6** gobble

cry down
5 decry **6** defame, deride, malign, revile, vilify **7** condemn **8** belittle, denounce, derogate, diminish **9** denigrate, deprecate, discredit, disparage **10** calumniate, depreciate **11** detract from, opprobriate

crying
4 dire **5** acute, vital **6** urgent **7** blatant, burning, clamant, exigent, heinous **8** flagrant, pressing, shocking **9** atrocious, clamorous, desperate, monstrous, notorious **10** compelling, imperative, outrageous, scandalous **11** importunate

Crying Game actor
3 Rea (Stephen)

crypt
5 vault **7** chamber **8** catacomb **9** mausoleum **10** undercroft

cryptic
5 vague **6** arcane, occult, opaque, secret **7** Delphic, obscure, unclear **8** abstruse, Delphian, esoteric, puzzling **9** ambiguous, enigmatic, recondite, tenebrous **10** mysterious, mystifying **12** unfathomable

crystal
4 lens **5** clear, lucid, macle **6** limpid, lucent, quartz **8** clear-cut, luminous, pellucid **9** glassware, unblurred **11** translucent, transparent **12** transpicuous
gazer: **4** seer **7** psychic **11** clairvoyant
set: **5** radio

cry up
4 laud, puff **5** boost, extol **6** praise **7** acclaim

cub
3 pup **4** baby, tyro **6** novice, rookie **8** neophyte **9** offspring, youngster **10** apprentice

Cuba
capital: **6** Havana
city: **7** Holguín **8** Camagüey, Santiago **10** Guantánamo, Santa Clara
discoverer: **8** Columbus (Christopher)
language: **7** Spanish
leader: **6** Castro (Fidel, Raúl) **7** Batista (Fulgencio), Guevara (Che)
monetary unit: **4** peso
sea: **9** Caribbean

Cuban hero
5 Martí (José)

cubbyhole
5 niche **6** alcove, recess **7** cubicle

cube
4 dice **5** mince
game creator: **5** Rubik (Ernö)
type: **6** Rubik's

Cub Scout
rank: **4** Bear, Lion, Wolf **6** Bobcat **7** Webelos
unit: **3** den **4** pack

Cuchulain
father: **3** Lug **4** Lugh **5** Lugus
foe: **4** Medb **5** Maeve
kingdom: **6** Ulster
lord: **9** Conchobar
mother: **8** Dechtire
son: **8** Conlaoch
victim: **8** Conlaoch
wife: **4** Emer

cuckoo
3 mad, nut **4** daft, kook, nuts **5** batty, crank, crazy, daffy, loony, loopy, nutty, potty, silly, wacko, wacky **6** crazed, fruity, insane, screwy, whacky **7** bonkers, cracked, idiotic, lunatic, nutcase **8** crackpot, demented **9** ding-a-ling, harebrain, screwball **12** crackbrained
bird: **3** ani **8** keelbill

cucumber
4 pepo **7** gherkin

cuddle
3 hug, pet **4** neck, snug **5** spoon **6** burrow, caress, clinch, cosset, dandle, fondle, nestle, nuzzle **7** embrace, snuggle, squeeze **8** canoodle

cuddly
7 lovable, snuggly **8** huggable **11** embraceable

cudgel
3 bat, sap **4** club, cosh, mace **5** baton, billy **7** war club **8** bludgeon **9** bastinado, billy club, blackjack, truncheon **10** knobkerrie, nightstick, shillelagh

cue
3 key, nod, rod, tip **4** clue, hint, lead, prod, sign **5** alert **6** insert, notion, prompt, signal, tip-off **7** heads-up, inkling, warning **8** high sign, reminder, telltale **10** indication, intimation, suggestion

cuff
3 box, hit **4** belt, blip, clip, poke, slap, sock **5** clout, fight, punch, smack, whack **6** bangle, buffet, wallop **7** clobber, scuffle **8** bracelet, wristlet

cul-de-sac
5 pouch **6** pocket **7** dead end, impasse **10** blind alley **12** diverticulum

cull
4 pick, sift, thin **5** elect, glean **6** choose, garner, gather, select, winnow **7** extract, thin out

culminate
4 peak **5** crest **6** climax

culmination
3 top **4** acme, apex, peak **6** apogee, capper, climax, height, payoff, summit, zenith **8** capstone, pinnacle **11** ne plus ultra **12** consummation

culpability
4 onus **5** blame, fault, guilt

culpable
6 guilty, liable, sinful **7** at fault **8** blamable, blameful **10** censurable, delinquent **11** blameworthy, impeachable, responsible **13** reprehensible

culprit
4 perp

cult
3 fad **4** sect **5** creed, faith **6** church **8** religion **10** persuasion **12** denomination

cultivable
6 arable 8 tillable

cultivate
4 farm, grow, tend, till 5 breed, nurse, raise 6 enrich, foster, refine 7 cherish, develop, further, improve, nourish, nurture, produce, promote 9 encourage, propagate

cultivated
6 urbane 7 genteel, refined 8 cultured, polished, well-bred

cultivation
6 polish 7 culture, tillage 8 breeding 10 refinement 11 development

cultural values
5 ethic, ethos 6 ethics

culture
4 grow 5 taste 6 foster 7 nurture 9 cultivate, erudition, gentility 10 refinement 11 cultivation 12 civilization 13 enlightenment

cultured
6 urbane 7 erudite, genteel, learned, refined 8 educated, highbrow, literate, polished, well-bred 9 civilized 10 cultivated 11 enlightened

culture medium
4 agar

cum ___ salis
5 grano

cumber
4 clog, lade, load 6 burden, hinder, hobble, impede, saddle 7 clutter 8 handicap 9 hindrance

cumbersome
5 bulky, heavy, hefty 6 clumsy 7 awkward 8 unwieldy 9 lumbering, ponderous 10 slow-moving

cumshaw
3 fee, tip 5 bribe 6 payoff 7 present 8 gratuity, largesse 9 baksheesh, lagniappe, pourboire 10 perquisite

cumulate
4 heap 5 amass, hoard, lay up, store 6 garner, gather, pile up 7 collect, combine, store up 9 stockpile

cumulation
4 heap, mass, pile 5 cache, hoard, trove 9 stockpile 10 collection 11 aggregation 13 agglomeration

cumulative
8 additive, compound 9 summative 10 compounded, increasing

cunning
3 sly 4 cute, foxy, keen, wary, wily 5 acute, cagey, canny, craft, guile, savvy, sharp, skill, slick, smart 6 adroit, artful, astute, clever, crafty, deceit, shifty, shrewd, tricky 7 finesse, know-how, slyness 8 artifice, caginess, deftness, facility, foxiness, guileful, slippery, subtlety, wiliness 9 adeptness, cageyness, canniness, dexterity, dexterous, duplicity, ingenious, ingenuity, insidious, sharpness, slickness 10 adroitness, artfulness, cleverness, craftiness, shiftiness, shrewdness, trickiness

cup
3 mug 4 toby 5 grail, jorum, stein 6 beaker, goblet, rummer, seidel 7 chalice, tankard 8 schooner
handle: 3 ear, lug
holder: 6 saucer
liturgical: 3 ama 5 calix 7 chalice
Scottish: 4 tass
small: 6 noggin 8 cannikin, pannikin 9 demitasse
sports: 5 Davis, Ryder, World 6 Curtis, Nextel 7 Stanley 8 America's, Wightman

cupbearer of the gods
4 Hebe 8 Ganymede

cupboard
5 ambry, cuddy 6 buffet, closet, larder, pantry 7 armoire, cabinet 8 credence, credenza 9 sideboard

Cupid
4 Amor, Eros 5 putto 6 cherub 8 amoretto
beloved: 6 Psyche
brother: 7 Anteros
father: 6 Hermes 7 Mercury
mother: 5 Venus 9 Aphrodite
title: 3 Dan

cupidity
4 lust 5 greed 6 desire 7 avarice, avidity, craving, lechery, passion 8 rapacity, voracity 9 eagerness, esurience 10 greediness 11 infatuation 12 covetousness 13 rapaciousness

cupola
4 dome 5 vault 6 turret 7 furnace, lookout

cupped
7 concave

cur
3 dog 4 mutt 7 mongrel

curate
6 cleric, priest 9 churchman, clergyman

curative
4 pill 5 tonic 6 elixir, relief, remedy 7 healing, nostrum, panacea, therapy 8 antidote, remedial, salutary, sanative, solution 9 healthful, medicinal, remedying, treatment, wholesome 10 beneficial, corrective 11 restorative, therapeutic 12 health-giving

curator
6 keeper, warden 9 caretaker, custodian 11 conservator

curb
3 bit **4** deny, rein, stem **5** check, frame, leash, tie up **6** border, bridle, edging, fetter, hamper, hobble, hold in, rein in, subdue **7** abstain, contain, control, inhibit, refrain, repress **8** hold back, hold down, restrain, suppress, withhold **9** constrain, entrammel, restraint
British: **4** kerb

curdle
4 clot, sour, turn **5** spoil **7** clabber, congeal, thicken **9** coagulate

curdling substance
6 rennet

cure
3 age, spa **4** heal, mend **5** treat **6** elixir, kipper, physic, pickle, relief, remedy **7** rectify, relieve, restore, therapy **8** antidote, medicant, medicine, preserve, recovery, solution **10** ameliorate, corrective **12** counteragent **13** counteractive

cure-all
6 elixir **7** nostrum, panacea **10** catholicon

curio
6 oddity, whimsy **7** novelty, whatsit **9** objet d'art

curiosity
5 freak **6** marvel, oddity, rarity, whimsy, wonder **7** anomaly, concern, novelty **8** interest, nonesuch

curious
3 odd **4** nosy **5** nosey, novel, queer, weird **6** exotic, prying, quaint, snoopy **7** bizarre, oddball, strange, unusual **8** meddling, peculiar, puzzling, singular **9** inquiring, intrusive **11** inquisitive, questioning

curl
4 coil, kink, wind **5** frizz, twine, twist **6** spiral **7** contort, crinkle, entwine, frizzle, ringlet, wreathe **9** corkscrew

curling
match: **8** bonspiel
period of play: **3** end
team: **4** four
term: **3** tee **4** hack, rink **5** house, stone

curly
4 wavy **5** kinky **6** frizzy

curmudgeon
4 crab **5** grump **6** grinch, grouch

currency
4 cash, coin **5** dough, lucre, money, scrip **7** coinage **8** banknote **10** acceptance, prevalence **11** legal tender
since 1999: **4** euro
unit: see **individual country**

current
4 eddy, flow, flux, race, rush, tide **5** drift, flood, spate, tenor, trend **6** extant, modern, strain, stream **7** instant, ongoing, popular, present, regnant, topical **8** accepted, existent, existing, tendency, up-to-date **9** prevalent **10** present-day, prevailing, widespread **11** fashionable **12** contemporary
air: **4** gale, gust, wind **5** blast, draft **6** breeze, squall, zephyr **7** cyclone, indraft, updraft **9** downdraft **10** slipstream
ocean: **7** riptide **8** undertow **9** maelstrom, whirlpool
unit: **3** amp **6** ampere

Currier's partner
4 Ives (James)

curry
4 beat, comb, seek, whip **5** groom **6** thrash

curse
3 hex, pox **4** bane, cuss, damn, evil, jinx, oath **5** swear **6** blight, plague, whammy **7** afflict, damning, malison, scourge, torment **8** anathema, cussword, execrate **9** bête noire, blaspheme, blasphemy, expletive, imprecate, profanity, swearword **10** affliction, execration, misfortune, pestilence **11** commination, imprecation, malediction, profanation **12** anathematize, denunciation

cursed
6 damned **7** blasted, dratted **8** damnable, infernal **9** execrable **10** confounded **13** blankety-blank

cursive
6 fluent, smooth **7** flowing, running

cursory
5 hasty, quick, rapid **6** casual **7** hurried, shallow, sketchy **8** careless **10** uncritical **11** perfunctory, superficial

curt
4 rude **5** bluff, blunt, brief, gruff, short, terse **6** abrupt, crusty **7** brusque, concise **8** succinct **10** peremptory

curtail
3 cut **4** clip, dock, trim **5** prune, slash **6** lessen, reduce **7** abridge, cut back, shorten **8** diminish, pare down, retrench, truncate **10** abbreviate

curtain
4 drop, veil **5** drape **6** screen **7** barrier
doorway: **8** portiere
holder: **3** rod
Indian: **6** purdah
material: **4** lace, silk **5** gauze **6** damask, velvet **8** chenille, jacquard
rod concealer: **7** valance
sash: **7** tieback
stage: **4** drop **5** scrim **8** backdrop

curtains
3 end **4** ruin **5** death **6** demise, finish **7** decease **8** disaster

curtilage
4 quad, yard **5** court **8** cloister **9** courtyard, enclosure **10** quadrangle

curvaceous
5 buxom **7** rounded, shapely **9** Junoesque **10** statuesque, voluptuous **13** well-developed

curvature
of the spine: **8** kyphosis, lordosis **9** scoliosis

curve
3 arc, bow **4** arch, bend, coil, curl, turn, veer, wind **5** crook, round, swing, swirl, twist **6** convex, spiral, swerve **7** concave, flexure, rondure **9** corkscrew
drawing device: **6** spline
of an arch: **8** extrados, intrados
pitcher's: **4** hook
plane: **7** cycloid, limaçon **8** parabola, sinusoid, trochoid **9** hyperbola
S-shaped: **3** ess **4** ogee **7** sigmoid

curved
4 bent **5** arced, bowed, round **6** arched, convex **7** arcuate, bending, embowed, falcate, rounded, sigmoid, sinuous, twisted
implement: **6** sickle
molding: **4** ogee
path: **3** arc
sword: **5** kukri, saber, sabre **7** cutlass **8** scimitar

curvilinear
see **curved**

curvy
see **curvaceous; curved**

Cush
father: **3** Ham
son: **6** Nimrod

cushion
3 mat, pad **5** squab **6** absorb, buffer, pillow, soften **7** bolster, hassock, pillion **8** palliate, woolsack

cushy
4 cozy, easy, soft **11** comfortable, undemanding

cusp
3 eve, tip **4** apex, edge, peak **5** point, verge **12** turning point

cuspid
6 canine **8** eyetooth

cuspidate
5 sharp **6** peaked, pointy **7** pointed

cuss
3 guy, man **4** chap, damn, dude, oath **5** curse, swear **6** fellow **9** expletive

cussed
4 dour **5** crude, gruff **6** crusty, cursed, grumpy, ornery **7** boorish, brusque, grouchy **8** churlish **9** obstinate **10** unyielding **11** contentious **12** antagonistic, cantankerous

cussword
4 oath **5** curse **9** expletive, swearword

custard
4 flan **7** pudding

custodian
5 super **6** keeper, porter, warden **7** curator, steward **8** guardian, overseer, watchdog, watchman **9** caretaker, concierge, protector **10** supervisor **11** conservator

custody
4 care, ward **5** guard, trust **6** charge **7** keeping **9** captivity, detention **10** caretaking, management, protection **11** confinement, safekeeping, supervision **12** guardianship

custom
3 use **4** norm **5** habit, mores (plural), trade, usage **6** groove, manner, praxis, ritual **7** folkway, precept, routine, traffic **8** business, habitude, practice **9** patronage **10** consuetude, convention

customary
5 usual **6** common, normal, wonted **7** general, regular, routine **8** accepted, everyday, familiar, frequent, habitual, ordinary, orthodox, standard **10** accustomed **11** established, traditional **12** conventional

custom-built
7 bespoke **10** tailor-made **11** made-to-order

customer
5 buyer **6** client, patron **7** shopper **8** consumer **9** purchaser
frequent: **7** habitué

customized
see **custom-built**

custom-made
see **custom-built**

cut
3 bob, hew, lop, mow, saw **4** bite, chop, clip, crop, dice, dock, fell, gash, hack, nick, pare, reap, sawn, skip, slit, snip, snub, trim **5** carve, filet, lathe, lower, mince, notch, piece, prune, quota, sawed, sever, share, shave, shear, slash, slice, split, wound **6** cleave, delete, dilute, divide, excise, fillet, incise, reduce, scythe, sickle, sunder **7** abridge, curtail, dissect, portion, section, segment, shorten **8** division, separate, truncate **9** allotment, allowance, reduction **10** abbreviate
of beef: **3** rib **4** loin, rump **5** chine, chuck, flank, roast, shank, steak, T-bone **6** saddle **7** brisket, sirloin **9** aitchbone **11** porterhouse

cut across
6 bisect **8** transect **9** transcend

cut-and-dried
5 stock **7** routine **9** formulaic **10** unoriginal **11** predictable **13** unimaginative

cutaneous
6 dermal

cutaway
4 coat, dive **5** tails

cut back
3 zag 4 clip, curb, dock, pare, trim 5 lower, prune, shave, slash 6 lessen, reduce 7 abridge, curtail, shorten 8 decrease, retrench, truncate 10 abbreviate

cut down
3 axe, hew, mow 4 chop, clip, fell, pare 5 lower, shave, slash 6 digest, reduce 7 abridge, shorten 10 abbreviate

cute
4 twee 6 dainty, pretty 7 cunning 8 affected 10 attractive 11 impertinent, smart-alecky

cut in
7 include, intrude, obtrude 9 introduce

cutlass
5 saber, sabre, sword 7 machete 8 scimitar

cut off
3 axe, bar, end, lop 4 halt, kill, stop 5 abort, block, sever 6 disown 7 curtail, destroy, isolate, suspend 8 amputate, obstruct, renounce, separate, truncate 9 intercept, interrupt, terminate 10 disinherit 11 discontinue

cut out
3 end 4 halt 5 cease, leave, scram, usurp 6 beat it, delete, depart, escape, excise, remove, resect 7 defraud, deprive, take off 8 displace, supplant 9 eliminate, extirpate 10 disconnect

cutpurse
5 thief 10 pickpocket

cut short
3 bob 4 clip, crop, dock, halt, poll 5 abort, check, scrub, shear 7 abridge, curtail 8 break off 9 interrupt, terminate 10 abbreviate

cuttable
7 sectile 8 scissile

cutthroat
5 bravo 6 gunman, hit man, killer 7 torpedo 8 assassin, murderer 10 hatchet man, triggerman

cutting
5 acerb 7 acerbic 8 incisive, piercing 9 sarcastic, trenchant 11 penetrating
edge: 5 blade
remark: 3 dig 4 barb 5 taunt
tool: 3 adz, axe, hob, saw 4 adze 5 knife, lathe, mower, plane, razor 6 reaper, scythe, shears, sickle 7 hatchet 8 scissors, tomahawk

cuttlefish
7 mollusc, mollusk 10 cephalopod
ink: 5 sepia
relative: 5 squid 7 octopus

cut up
4 dice, hash, romp 5 caper, clown, mince, slash 6 cavort 7 carry on, show off 9 misbehave 10 roughhouse

cutup
3 wag 4 zany 5 clown, joker 6 madcap 7 buffoon, farceur 8 jokester

cyan
4 blue

Cybele
4 Rhea
beloved: 5 Attis
brother: 6 Cronus
father: 6 Uranus
husband: 6 Cronus
mother: 4 Gaea
son: 4 Zeus 7 Jupiter, Neptune 8 Poseidon

cyber
5 wired 10 electronic

cyberjunk
4 spam

cybernetics founder
6 Wiener (Norbert)

cycle
3 age, lap, set 4 bike, loop, ring 5 chain, orbit, recur, round, wheel 6 course, period, series 7 circuit 8 rotation, sequence 9 vibration 10 revolution, succession, two-wheeler, velocipede 11 oscillation

cycle track
9 velodrome

cyclic
7 regular 8 periodic, repeated, rhythmic 9 iterative, recurring, repeating 10 isochronal 12 intermittent

cyclone
7 tornado, twister

cyclopean
4 huge 7 immense, mammoth, massive, titanic 8 colossal, enormous, gigantic 9 monstrous 10 gargantuan, tremendous 11 elephantine

Cyclops
5 Arges 7 Brontes 8 Steropes 10 Polyphemus

Cycnus
father: 4 Ares, Mars
slayer: 8 Heracles, Hercules

cygnet
4 swan
dam (mother): 3 pen
sire (father): 3 cob

Cygnus
form: 4 swan
friend: 7 Phaeton
star: 5 Deneb

cylinder
4 drum, pipe, tube 5 spool 6 barrel, bobbin, platen, roller

cylindrical
6 terete 7 tubular 8 tubelike

Cymbeline
daughter: **6** Imogen
son: **9** Arviragus, Guiderius
son-in-law: **9** Posthumus

Cymric
5 Welsh **6** Celtic **9** Brythonic
bard: **8** Taliesin
Elysium: **6** Annwfn
god: **5** Lludd
of Elysium: **5** Arawn
of the dead: **5** Pwyll
of the seas: **3** Ler **4** Llyr **5** Dylan
of the sky: **7** Gwydion
of the sun: **4** Lleu, Llew
of the underworld: **4** Gwyn
goddess: **3** Don **9** Arianrhod
magician: **6** Merlin

Cymru
5 Wales

cynical
8 derisive, sardonic, scornful **12** misanthropic

Cynthia
4 Luna, moon **5** Diana **7** Artemis

cyprian
4 bawd, jade, slut, tart **5** hussy, tramp **6** floozy, harlot, hooker, wanton **7** jezebel, trollop **8** slattern, strumpet **10** prostitute

Cyprus
capital: **7** Nicosia **8** Lefkosia
city: **7** Larnaca **8** Limassol
language: **5** Greek **7** Turkish
monetary unit: **4** lira **5** pound
mountain: **7** Olympus
port: **9** Famagusta
sea: **13** Mediterranean

Cyrano de Bergerac
4 poet **7** duelist **8** duellist
author: **7** Rostand (Edmond)
beloved: **6** Roxane **7** Roxanne
feature: **4** nose
rival: **9** Christian

Cyrus
conquest: **5** Lydia, Media **7** Babylon
daughter: **6** Atossa
empire: **7** Persian
father: **8** Cambyses
son: **8** Cambyses

cyst
3 sac, wen **4** sore **5** pouch, spore **6** growth **7** abscess, blister, capsule, vesicle **8** swelling

Cytherea
4 isle **5** Venus **6** island **9** Aphrodite

czar
5 chief, mogul **6** despot, honcho, tycoon, tyrant **7** emperor, kingpin, magnate **8** autocrat
Russian: **4** Ivan **5** Basil, Boris, Peter **6** Alexis, Dmitry, Feodor, Fyodor, Vasily **7** Dimitri, Michael, Romanov **8** Nicholas, Romanoff, Theodore **9** Alexander **12** Boris Godunov
son: **10** czarevitch
wife: **7** czarina

czar's wife
7 czarina

Czech Republic
capital: **6** Prague
city: **4** Brno **7** Ostrava
monetary unit: **6** koruna
neighbor: **6** Poland **7** Austria, Germany **8** Slovakia
region: **7** Bohemia, Moravia
river: **4** Labe, Oder **5** March **6** Morava

D

dab
3 bit, pat **4** blob, blow, daub, peck, poke, spot **5** smear, touch **6** bedaub **7** besmear, plaster, splotch **8** flatfish

dabble
3 dip, dot, toy **4** fool, stud **5** fleck **6** dampen, fiddle, monkey, pepper, putter, splash, tinker **7** freckle, spatter, stipple **8** sprinkle **9** bespeckle, muck about **10** muck around

dabbler
4 duck, tyro **7** amateur **8** putterer, tinkerer **9** smatterer **10** dilettante

dabchick
5 grebe

dacha
5 villa **7** cottage **12** country house

dad
3 pop **4** papa **5** padre, pater **6** father, old man, parent

Dadaist
3 Arp (Jean), Ray (Man) **4** Ball (Hugo) **5** Ernst (Max), Grosz (George), Tzara (Tristan) **7** Duchamp (Marcel), Picabia (Francis) **10** Schwitters (Kurt)

daedal
6 knotty **7** complex **8** artistic, involved, skillful **9** elaborate, intricate **11** complicated **12** labyrinthine **13** sophisticated

Daedalus
7 builder **9** architect, artificer
construction: **9** Labyrinth
father: **6** Metion
son: **6** Icarus
victim: **5** Talos **6** Perdix

daffy
see **daft**

daft
3 mad **4** loco, nuts **5** balmy, crazy, dopey, flaky, loony, nutty, potty, silly, wacko, wacky **6** absurd, crazed, cuckoo, insane, screwy **7** cracked, foolish, idiotic, lunatic, witless **8** demented **10** unbalanced **11** harebrained

Dag
father: **7** Delling
horse: **9** Skinfaksi
mother: **4** Nott

Dagda
daughter: **6** Brigit
instrument: **4** harp
son: **6** Aengus
wife: **5** Boann

dagger
4 dirk, snee **5** skean, skene **6** bodkin, stylet **7** dudgeon, poniard **8** stiletto
double: **6** diesis
handle: **4** hilt
Malay: **4** kris

___ Dahl
5 Roald **6** Arlene

daikon
6 radish

daily
7 diurnal **8** everyday **9** circadian, quotidian
grind: **7** rat race

Daily Planet reporter
5 Olsen (Jimmy)

dainty
5 goody, tasty, treat **6** choice, morsel, select, tidbit **7** elegant, fragile **8** delicacy, delicate, ethereal, graceful, kickshaw **9** exquisite, recherché **10** delightful

daiquiri liquor
3 rum

dairy
8 creamery

dais
4 bema, bima **5** bimah, stage **6** podium **7** almemar, rostrum **8** platform

daisy
5 oxeye **6** Shasta
British: **10** moonflower
Scottish: **5** gowan

Daisy Miller author
5 James (Henry)

Daisy ___ of Dogpatch
3 Mae

Dakota dialect
5 Teton

Daksha's father
6 Brahma

dale
4 dell, glen, vale **6** dingle, valley

Dallas basketballers
4 Mavs **9** Mavericks

Dallas series
character: **3** Liz, Ray **4** Jack, Jock, Lucy **5** April, Bobby, Cally, Cliff, Donna, James, Jenna **6** Carter **7** Clayton, J. R. Ewing, Kristin **8** Michelle, Sue Ellen **9** Miss Ellie
family: **5** Ewing
ranch home: **9** Southfork
star: **4** Gray (Linda), Keel (Howard), Reed (Donna) **5** Davis (Jim), Duffy (Patrick), Rambo (Dack) **6** Crosby (Mary), Hagman (Larry), Howard (Susan), Kanaly (Steve), Tilton (Charlene), Wilson (Sheree) **7** Presley (Priscilla) **9** Bel Geddes (Barbara), Kercheval (Ken), Principal (Victoria)

dally
3 lag, pet, toy **4** drag, idle, play **5** flirt, tarry **6** coquet, dawdle, diddle, linger, loiter, trifle **8** lollygag **9** hang about, waste time **10** fool around

dam
4 weir **5** block, check **7** barrier **8** hold back, restrain
major: **4** Oahe **6** Aswan, Hoover **7** San Luis **8** Fort Peck, Garrison, Oroville **10** Bonneville, Glen Canyon **11** Grand Coulee

damage
3 mar **4** blot, harm, hurt, loss, maim, ruin **5** abuse, burst, cloud, spoil, stain, wound **6** blight, deface, impair, injure, injury, mangle, ravage, scathe **7** blemish, destroy, marring, tarnish, vitiate **8** maltreat, mischief, mistreat, mutilate, sabotage **9** devastate, vandalism **10** impairment **11** devastation

damaged
4 hurt, rent **6** broken, busted, dinged, flawed, marred **7** injured, spoiled, totaled **8** battered, impaired, ruptured **9** blemished, fractured, imperfect, shattered **10** fragmented
merchandise tag: 3 irr.

damaging
6 nocent **7** harmful, hurtful, nocuous **9** injurious **11** deleterious, detrimental, prejudicial

dame
4 lady **5** woman **6** gammer, matron **7** dowager **9** matriarch
of comedy: 4 Edna (Everage)

Damien's island
7 Molokai

Damkina's son
6 Marduk

damn
4 cuss, darn, doom, drat **5** curse, swear **7** condemn, doggone **8** execrate, sentence **9** imprecate **10** vituperate **12** anathematize

damnable
6 blamed, cursed, cussed **7** blasted, dratted **8** accursed, infernal **9** abhorrent, execrable **10** abominable, detestable

damned
5 utter **6** blamed, cursed, cussed, darned, dashed, doomed **7** awfully, blasted, doggone, dratted, goldarn **8** accursed, infernal **9** condemned **10** confounded **13** anathematized

Damn Yankees temptress
4 Lola

Damocles' ____
5 sword

Damon's friend
7 Pythias

damp
3 wet **4** dank, dewy **5** check, choke, humid, moist, musty **6** clammy **7** bedewed **8** humidify, humidity

dampen
4 cool, curb **5** chill **6** deaden **7** depress, moisten **8** diminish

damsel
3 gal **4** girl, lass, maid, miss **5** filly, wench **6** lassie, maiden

Dan
father: 5 Jacob
mother: 6 Bilhah
son: 6 Hushim

Danaë
father: 8 Acrisius
lover: 4 Zeus
son: 7 Perseus

Danaus
brother: 8 Aegyptus
daughters: 7 Danaïds **8** Danaïdes
father: 5 Belus
founder of: 5 Argos
grandfather: 7 Neptune **8** Poseidon

dance
3 dip, hop, jig, tap **4** ball, flit, foot, heel, hoof, hula, juba, leap, lope, reel, step, trip **5** bamba, brawl, galop, gigue, hover, lindy, mambo, mixer, polka, rumba, stomp, swing, tread, waltz **6** ballet, bolero, boogie, Boston, cancan, chassé, foot it, formal, frolic, German, hoof it, rhumba, shimmy **7** beguine, coranto, courant, flicker, flitter, flutter, hoedown, one-step, shuffle **8** cakewalk, flamenco, galliard, glissade, rigadoon, rigaudon **9** allemande, cotillion, jitterbug, pas de deux
Argentinian: 5 tango
art of: 12 choreography
Austrian: 7 ländler
ballroom: 5 rumba, tango **6** cha-cha, rhumba **7** fox-trot, mazurka, two-step **8** merengue **9** cotillion **10** Charleston
Bohemian: 5 polka
Brazilian: 5 samba **6** maxixe **7** carioca, lambada **8** capoeira **9** bossa nova
combining form: 5 chore **6** choreo, chorio
country: 3 hay **4** reel **8** hornpipe
couple: 5 polka **9** cotillion, malaguena **11** square dance
court: 6 canary, pavane **8** saraband **9** allemande, sarabande
Cuban: 5 conga, mambo, rumba **6** rhumba **8** habanera
designer: 13 choreographer
English: 6 morris
formal: 4 ball, prom **9** cotillion
French: 6 cancan **7** bourrée, gavotte **9** allemande **10** carmagnole
garment: 4 tutu **7** leotard
Haitian: 4 juba **8** merengue
Hawaiian: 4 hula
Hungarian: 7 czardas
Indian: 6 nautch **7** bhangra
instrument: 8 castanet
Israeli: 4 hora
Italian: 10 saltarello, tarantella, villanella **11** passacaglia
line: 5 conga
lively: 3 jig **4** reel, trot **5** galop, gigue, polka, rumba **6** rhumba **7** bourrée **8** fandango, hornpipe, rigadoon, rigaudon **9** farandole, shakedown **10** Charleston, saltarello, tarantella
Maori: 4 haka
movement: 4 plié, step **8** capriole, glissade **9** pirouette
Muse of: 11 Terpsichore

1920's: **10** Charleston
Polish: **5** polka **7** mazurka **9** polonaise
Polynesian: **4** hula
ragtime: **10** turkey trot
Scottish: **3** bob **4** reel **5** fling **10** strathspey **11** schottische **13** Highland fling
shoes: **5** pumps **8** slippers
slipper: **7** toeshoe
slow: **6** adagio, minuet, pavane **8** habanera
Spanish: **4** jota **6** bolero **7** zapateo **8** cachucha, chaconne, fandango, flamenco, saraband **9** malaguena, sarabande **10** seguidilla
spectator: **10** wallflower
springy: **3** jig
square: **7** hoedown, lancers **9** cotillion, quadrille
stately: **5** pavan **6** pavane **8** saraband **9** polonaise, sarabande
step: **3** pas
woman's: **6** cancan

dancer
6 hoofer **7** chorine, clogger, danseur, stepper **8** coryphée, danseuse **9** ballerina, chorus boy **10** cakewalker, chorus girl
American: **4** Feld (Elliot), Holm (Hanya), Lang (Pearl), Tune (Tommy) **5** Ailey (Alvin), Fosse (Bob), Kelly (Gene), Shawn (Ted), Tharp (Twyla), Watts (Heather) **6** Castle (Irene, Vernon), Duncan (Isadora), Dunham (Katherine), Graham (Martha), Morris (Mark), Taylor (Paul), Verdon (Gwen), Zorina (Vera) **7** Astaire (Adele, Fred), Bujones (Fernando), de Mille (Agnes), Farrell (Suzanne), Gregory (Cynthia), Jamison (Judith), Joffrey (Robert), Kistler (Darci), Martins (Peter), Massine (Leonide), McBride (Patricia), Robbins (Jerome), St. Denis (Ruth), Tamiris (Helen) **8** Champion (Gower, Marge), d'Amboise (Jacques), Humphrey (Doris), Kirkland (Gelsey), LeClercq (Tanaquil), Mitchell (Arthur), Nikolais (Alwin), Villella (Edward) **9** Tallchief (Maria) **10** Cunningham (Merce)
Cuban: **6** Alonso (Alicia)
Danish: **5** Bruhn (Erik) **7** Martins (Peter) **8** Tomasson (Helgi)
English: **5** Dolin (Anton), Somes (Michael), Tudor (Antony) **7** Fonteyn (Margot), Markova (Alicia), Rambert (Marie) **8** de Valois (Ninette), Helpmann (Robert)
French: **5** Lifar (Serge) **6** Béjart (Maurice), Perrot (Jules), Petipa (Marius) **7** Camargo (Marie), Massine (Leonide)
German: **5** Jooss (Kurt)
Italian: **5** Grisi (Carlotta)
Mexican: **5** Limón (José)
Russian: **5** Lifar (Serge) **6** Fokine (Michel), Petipa (Marius) **7** Massine (Leonide), Nureyev (Rudolf), Pavlova (Anna), Ulanova (Galina) **8** Danilova (Aleksandra), Makarova (Natalia), Nijinska (Bronislava), Nijinsky (Vaslav), Vaganova (Agrippina) **9** Karsavina (Tamara), Semyonova (Marina) **11** Baryshnikov (Mikhail), Plisetskaya (Maya)
Scottish: **7** Shearer (Moira)

dancing
6 ballet **12** choreography
mania: **9** tarantism

Dancing Queen group
4 ABBA

dandle
3 pet **4** play **6** caress, cosset, cradle, cuddle, pamper

dandruff
5 scall, scurf

dandy
3 fop, pip **4** beau, buck, dude, fine, lulu, toff **5** dilly, doozy, nifty, swell **6** doozie, peachy **7** coxcomb, foppish **8** terrific **9** excellent, first-rate, humdinger, hunky-dory **11** Beau Brummel, crackerjack **12** lounge lizard

dang
4 damn, darn **6** cursed, cussed, damned, darned **7** blasted, dratted, goldarn **8** infernal **10** confounded

danger
4 risk **5** peril **6** crisis, hazard, menace, plight, threat **7** pitfall, trouble **8** distress, jeopardy **9** emergency
signal: **4** bell **5** alarm, siren **6** tocsin

dangerous
5 risky **6** unsafe **7** parlous **8** insecure, menacing, perilous, unstable **9** hazardous **10** precarious **11** threatening

dangle
4 hang **5** droop, swing **6** depend **7** suspend

Daniel ____
pioneer: **5** Boone
statesman: **7** Webster

Danish
hero: **5** Ogier
king: **9** Christian, Frederick
physicist: **4** Bohr (Niels)
prince: **6** Hamlet
queen: **9** Margrethe
writer: **7** Dinesen (Isak)

dank
4 damp **5** humid, moist **6** clammy

Dante
beloved: **8** Beatrice
birthplace: **8** Florence
daughter: **7** Antonia
deathplace: **7** Ravenna
party: **6** Guelph **7** Bianchi
patron: **5** Scala
teacher: **6** Latini
wife: **5** Gemma

work: 5 canto 7 Inferno 8 Commedia, Paradiso 9 Vita Nuova 10 Purgatorio 12 Divine Comedy (The)

Danton's colleague
5 Marat (Jean-Paul) 11 Robespierre (Maximilien)

Danzig
6 Gdańsk

Daphne
father: 5 Ladon 6 Peneus
form: 6 laurel 10 laurel tree
pursuer: 6 Apollo 9 Leucippus

Daphnis' lover
5 Chloe

dapper
4 neat, trim 5 doggy, natty, sassy, smart, swank 6 classy, jaunty, rakish, snazzy, spiffy, spruce, sprucy 7 bandbox, dashing, doggish, foppish, stylish 11 well-groomed

dapple
4 spot 5 fleck, patch 6 mottle 7 speckle, stipple

dappled
4 pied 6 motley 7 flecked, mottled, patched, piebald, spotted 8 brindled 10 variegated 11 varicolored

Dardanelles
10 Hellespont

Dardanus
descendants: 7 Trojans
father: 4 Zeus 7 Jupiter
mother: 7 Electra

dare
3 try 4 defy, risk 5 beard, brave 6 hazard 7 attempt, venture 8 confront, defiance 9 challenge

daredevil
see **daring**

daredevil Knievel
4 Evel

daring
4 bold, guts, rash 5 brash, brave, gutsy, moxie, nerve, nervy, pluck, valor 6 heroic, plucky 7 bravery, courage, heroism 8 audacity, boldness, fearless, reckless 9 audacious, derring-do, fortitude, venturous 10 courageous 11 adventurous, venturesome 13 adventuresome

Darius
battle: 8 Marathon
father: 9 Hystaspes
country: 6 Persia 7 Parthia
son: 6 Xerxes
wife: 6 Atossa

Darjeeling
3 tea

dark
3 dim 4 dusk, inky, murk 5 black, blind, cloud, dingy, dusky, ebony, murky, night, sable, shady, sooty, swart, umber, unlit, vague 6 brunet, cloudy, dismal, gloomy, opaque, somber, sombre, wicked 7 obscure, ominous, rayless, satanic, shadowy, stygian, subfusc, sunless, swarthy, unclear 8 bistered, brunette, infernal, sinister 9 enigmatic, lightless, plutonian, secretive, tenebrous, unlighted 10 caliginous, indistinct, mysterious, mystifying, pitch-black 11 crepuscular 13 unilluminated
poetic: 4 ebon

darken
3 dim 5 bedim, cloud, gloom, lower, shade, sully, umber 6 shadow 7 becloud, blacken, eclipse, obscure, tarnish 8 melanize, overcast 9 obfuscate, overcloud 10 overshadow
Scottish: 5 gloam

dark-haired
6 brunet 8 brunette

darkness
4 dusk, evil, murk 5 black, gloom, night, shade 6 shadow 8 blackout 9 nightfall, obscurity

darkroom liquid
3 fix 8 emulsion, hardener

darling
3 gra, hon, pet 4 dear, duck, love 5 angel, deary, ducky, flame, honey, loved, sugar, sweet 7 beloved, dearest, sweetie 8 adorable, charming, favorite, precious 10 sweetheart, sweetie pie

darn
4 drat, knit, mend 5 patch 6 blamed, cursed, cussed, damned, shucks 7 blasted, doggone, dratted 8 infernal 9 embroider 10 confounded
French: 3 zut

Darrow client
4 Debs (Eugene), Loeb (Richard) 6 Scopes (John) 7 Haywood (William), Leopold (Nathan)

dart
3 fly, run, zip 4 barb, bolt, buzz, dash, flit, leap, rush, sail, scud, skim, tear 5 arrow, bound, hurry, lance, pitch, scamp, scoot, shaft, shoot, skirr, spear, speed, spurt 6 glance, hasten, scurry, spring, sprint 7 javelin, missile, scamper
barbed: 10 banderilla

D'Artagnan's friends
5 Athos 6 Aramis 7 Porthos 10 musketeers

Dartmouth location
5 Devon 7 Hanover 12 New Hampshire

darts term
3 leg 4 bust 5 split 6 double, flight, hockey, treble 8 bull's-eye

Darwin, Charles
colleague: 7 Wallace (Alfred Russel)
ship: 6 Beagle
theory: 9 evolution, selection

dash
3 fly, nip, run **4** bolt, brio, cast, damn, dart, élan, foil, hurl, race, ruin, rush, slam, tear, zing **5** break, chase, flair, fling, pinch, smash, style, trace **6** esprit, hyphen, pizazz, scurry, smidge, splash, sprint, thrust, thwart **7** bravura, depress, destroy, pizzazz, shatter, smidgen, spatter **8** confound, smidgeon **9** animation, frustrate

dashboard reading
3 GPS, mpg, rpm **4** fuel **5** speed **7** mileage **8** pressure **11** temperature

dashing
4 bold **6** dapper, jaunty, modish **7** gallant, stylish **8** animated, spirited **11** adventurous, fashionable

Das Kapital author
4 Marx (Karl)

dassie
4 pika **5** coney, hyrax

dastard
6 coward, craven **7** caitiff, chicken, quitter **8** poltroon, recreant **9** scoundrel

dastardly
3 low **4** base, mean **6** craven, yellow **7** caitiff **8** cowardly, shameful, skulking **11** treacherous, underhanded **13** pusillanimous

data
4 info **5** facts, input **7** figures **9** documents **11** information
numerical: **5** stats **10** statistics

data-sharing connection
3 LAN

date
3 age, era, woo **5** court, epoch, tryst **6** cutoff, escort **7** take out **8** deadline **9** accompany **10** engagement, rendezvous **11** anniversary, appointment, assignation

dated
3 old **5** passé, stale **6** démodé, old hat **7** archaic, outworn **8** obsolete, outmoded **10** antiquated **12** old-fashioned **13** unfashionable
fashionably: **5** retro

datum
4 fact

daub
4 blob, blot, spot **5** fleck, paint, smear **6** dapple, smudge, splash **7** besmear, dribble, plaster, speckle, splotch

daughter
Blythe Danner's: **7** Paltrow (Gwyneth)
Bruce Dern's: **5** Laura
Bush's: **5** Jenna **7** Barbara
Carter's: **3** Amy
Cash's: **7** Rosanne
Cher's: **8** Chastity (Bono)
Clinton's: **7** Chelsea
Cole's: **7** Natalie
Coppola's: **5** Sofia
Danny Thomas's: **5** Marlo
Debbie Reynolds's: **6** Carrie (Fisher)
Eddie Fisher's: **6** Carrie
Elizabeth II's: **4** Anne
Elvis's: **9** Lisa Marie
Fonda's: **4** Jane
Ford's: **5** Susan
Freud's: **4** Anna
Garland's: **4** Liza (Minnelli)
Goldie Hawn's: **10** Kate Hudson
Ingrid Bergman's: **8** Isabella (Rossellini)
Janet Leigh's: **8** Jamie Lee (Curtis)
Joel Grey's: **8** Jennifer
Johnson's: **4** Lucy **5** Linda
Jon Voight's: **8** Angelina (Jolie)
Kennedy's: **8** Caroline
Klaus Kinski's: **9** Nastassja
Maureen O'Sullivan's: **3** Mia (Farrow)
Naomi Judd's: **7** Wynonna
Nixon's: **5** Julie **6** Tricia
Obama's: **5** Malia, Sasha
Pat Boone's: **5** Debby
Priam's: **4** Ilia
Ravi Shankar's: **10** Norah Jones
Reagan's: **5** Patti **7** Maureen
Richard Burton's: **4** Kate
Ryan O'Neal's: **5** Tatum
Sinatra's: **5** Nancy
Tony Curtis's: **8** Jamie Lee

Daughter of the Moon
7 Nokomis

daunt
3 cow **5** alarm, deter **6** dismay, subdue **7** terrify, unnerve **8** frighten **10** disconcert, discourage, dishearten, intimidate

daunting
7 awesome **8** imposing **9** dismaying, unnerving **10** forbidding, formidable **11** dispiriting **12** discouraging, intimidating, overwhelming

dauntless
4 bold, game **5** brave **6** daring **7** gallant, valiant **8** fearless, unafraid, valorous **9** unfearful, unfearing **10** courageous **11** lionhearted **12** stouthearted

dauntlessness
4 guts **5** heart, nerve, pluck, spunk, valor **6** daring, mettle, spirit **7** bravery, cojones, courage **8** boldness **10** resolution

davenport
4 desk, sofa **5** couch, divan **6** daybed **12** chesterfield

David
commander: **4** Joab **5** Amasa
companion: **8** Jonathan
daughter: **5** Tamar
father: **5** Jesse

rebuker: **6** Nathan
son: **5** Amnon **7** Absalom, Solomon **8** Adonijah
song of: **5** psalm
wife: **6** Michal **7** Abigail, Ahinoam **9** Bathsheba

___ David
4 Camp **5** Magen, Mogen **6** Star of

David Copperfield
author: **7** Dickens (Charles)
character: **4** Dora, Heep (Uriah) **6** Barkis **8** Micawber, Peggotty **9** Murdstone **10** Steerforth

Da Vinci Code author
5 Brown (Dan)

davit
5 crane

dawdle
3 lag **4** idle, laze, loaf, loll **5** dally, delay, tarry **6** diddle, linger, loiter, lounge **8** lollygag **10** dillydally

dawn
4 morn **5** onset, sunup **6** aurora **7** morning, sunrise **8** cockcrow, daybreak, daylight **9** beginning **10** first light
goddess: **3** Eos **6** Aurora
pertaining to: **4** eoan

___ Dawn Chong
3 Rae

day
abbreviation: **3** Fri, Mon, Sat, Sun, Thu, Tue, Wed **4** Thur, Tues **5** Thurs
before: **3** eve
church calendar: **5** feria
French: **4** jour
German: **3** Tag
holy: **5** feast
hour: **4** noon
Latin: **4** dies
Spanish: **3** día

daybreak
4 dawn, morn **5** sunup **6** aurora **7** dawning, morning, sunrise **8** cockcrow, daylight

daydream
4 muse **5** fancy **6** vision **7** fantasy, reverie **8** phantasy **9** fantasize **10** woolgather **13** woolgathering

daystar
3 Sol, sun **5** Venus **7** phoebus

daze
3 fog **4** haze, stun **5** amaze, blind **6** dazzle, stupor, trance **7** astound, confuse, stupefy **8** astonish, bedazzle, befuddle, confound **9** dumbfound

dazed
5 woozy **6** groggy, punchy **7** dazzled, stunned **8** confused **9** stupefied **10** punch-drunk

___ d'Azur
4 Côte

dazzle
3 wow **4** stun **5** amaze, blind, éclat, glitz, shine **7** impress **8** astonish, bewilder, confound, outshine **9** overpower

dazzling
6 flashy, garish **7** radiant **8** splendid, stunning **9** brilliant **11** confounding, resplendent **12** overpowering

DC baseballers, for short
4 Nats

DC footballers' nickname
4 Hogs

DC hockey team, for short
4 Caps

DC VIP
3 Rep., Sen.

D-Day town
4 St. Lo

DDE
predecessor: **3** HST
successor: **3** JFK
World War II command: **3** ETO

DEA agent
4 narc

deacon
6 clergy, cleric, layman **8** reverend **9** churchman

dead
4 cold, gone, late **5** kaput, passé, slain, stiff **6** buried, fallen **7** defunct, done for, expired, extinct **8** deceased, departed, lifeless **9** senseless **10** corpselike **11** unconscious **12** extinguished

deadbeat
3 bum **5** idler **6** debtor, loafer, slouch **7** lounger, shirker, slacker **10** delinquent, malingerer

dead duck
5 goner **8** casualty, fatality

deaden
4 dull, kill, mute, numb, stun **5** blunt, quiet **6** benumb, dampen, lessen, muffle, obtund, reduce, stifle **7** smother, stupefy **8** suppress **11** anesthetize, desensitize

dead end
4 halt, stop **6** pocket, unruly **7** impasse **8** cul-de-sac, standoff **9** stalemate, terminate **10** blind alley, bottleneck, standstill

deadened
4 numb **6** asleep, dulled, killed, numbed **7** blunted, muffled **8** benumbed, impaired **12** anesthetized

deadeye
5 block **8** marksman **12** sharpshooter

deadfall
4 trap **7** springe **9** booby trap, mousetrap

deadliness
8 fatality **9** lethality, mortality

deadlock
3 tie **4** draw **7** impasse **8** standoff, stoppage **9** checkmate, stalemate **10** standstill

deadly
5 fatal, toxic **6** lethal, mortal **7** capital, killing **8** lethally, unerring **10** implacable **11** destructive, internecine **12** pestilential
sin: **4** envy, lust **5** greed, pride, sloth, wrath **6** acedia, hubris **7** avarice **8** gluttony **9** vainglory

deadpan
5 blank, empty **6** vacant **9** impassive **10** poker-faced **11** inscrutable **12** inexpressive, unexpressive

Dead Souls author
5 Gogol (Nikolay)

dead to rights
9 red-handed

deadweight
4 load **6** weight

deal
4 dole, sale, sell **5** allot, serve, shake, share, trade, treat **6** barter, dicker, parcel **7** bargain, deliver, dish out, dole out, mete out, package, portion, traffic, wrestle **8** contract, disburse, dispense, share out **9** agreement, apportion, negotiate **10** administer, compromise, distribute, measure out **11** arrangement, transaction **13** understanding
great: **4** gobs, heap, lots, tons **5** heaps, horde, loads, scads **6** oodles, plenty, stacks
out: **8** disburse, dispense **9** apportion **10** administer, distribute
with: **5** serve, treat **6** handle, regard **7** concern, involve

dealer
5 agent **6** broker, seller, trader, vendor **8** chandler, merchant, operator **9** tradesman **10** negotiator, trafficker **11** businessman, distributer, distributor **12** merchandiser
British: **5** coper **6** draper, jobber, mercer **7** chapman

dealings
5 trade, truck **7** affairs, matters, traffic **8** business, commerce, concerns **11** intercourse **12** interactions, transactions, undertakings

dean
4 head **5** chief, doyen, elder **6** leader

dear
3 gra, pet **4** fond, lamb, love **5** honey, loved, sugar, sweet **6** costly, doting, loving, prized, scarce **7** beloved, darling, devoted, lovable, machree, querida, tootsie **8** favorite, precious, valuable **9** cherished, expensive, heartfelt, treasured **10** fair-haired, honeybunch, sweetheart **12** affectionate
French: **4** cher **5** chère **6** chérie

dearth
4 lack, want **6** famine **7** absence, default, paucity **8** scarcity, shortage, sparsity **9** privation, scantness **10** deficiency, meagerness, scantiness

death
3 end **4** exit **6** demise, ending, expiry **7** decease, passing, quietus **8** casualty, curtains, fatality, necrosis, thanatos **9** bloodshed, departure **10** expiration, extinction, grim reaper **11** dissolution, termination **12** annihilation
after: **10** posthumous
combining form: **6** thanat **7** thanato
music: **5** dirge, elegy **8** threnody
notice: **4** obit **8** obituary **9** necrology
of tissue: **8** gangrene
personification: **10** grim reaper
put to: **3** gas, hit, ice, zap **4** do in, hang, kill, slay **5** drown, lynch, snuff, waste **6** murder, poison, rub out **7** bump off, butcher, execute, smother, wipe out **8** blow away, dispatch, immolate, knock off, strangle, throttle **9** slaughter, suffocate **10** asphyxiate **11** assassinate, electrocute
rate: **9** mortality
rites: **7** funeral **8** exequies **9** interment, obsequies

Death in the Family author
4 Agee (James)

Death in Venice author
4 Mann (Thomas)

deathless
7 abiding, eternal, lasting, undying **8** enduring, immortal **11** everlasting **12** imperishable

deathlike
see **deathly**

deathly
5 fatal **6** lethal, mortal **7** macabre, stygian **12** pestilential
pale: **4** ashy **5** ashen

death notice
4 obit

debacle
4 rout **6** defeat, fiasco **7** breakup, failure **8** collapse, disaster **9** breakdown, cataclysm **10** disruption

debar
3 ban **4** stop **6** forbid, outlaw **7** exclude, prevent, rule out **8** preclude, prohibit **9** interdict

debark
4 land **6** alight, get off

debase
3 mar **4** harm **5** lower, stain **6** damage, dilute, impair, reduce, weaken **7** cheapen, corrupt, pervert, pollute, vitiate **8** dishonor **9** undermine **10** adulterate, depreciate **11** contaminate

debatable
4 iffy, moot **7** dubious **8** arguable, doubtful **9** contested, uncertain, undecided **10** disputable, unresolved **11** problematic **12** questionable

debate
4 moot **5** argue, bandy, plead **7** contend, contest, discuss, dispute, quarrel, wrangle **8** argument, consider, forensic, question **9** dialectic, thrash out **10** controvert, toss around **11** application, controversy, disputation **12** deliberation **13** argumentation
again: **6** rehash
art of: **9** forensics
expert: **7** eristic
place for: **5** forum
side: **3** con, pro

debauch
4 orgy, warp **6** seduce **7** corrupt, deprave, pervert, vitiate **9** bacchanal, brutalize **10** lead astray, saturnalia **11** bacchanalia

debauched
6 wanton **8** vitiated **9** corrupted, dissolute, libertine, perverted **10** degenerate, licentious

debauchee
4 roué **8** hedonist, sybarite **9** libertine **10** sensualist, voluptuary

debilitate
3 sap **6** impair, weaken **7** cripple, disable, exhaust, wear out **8** enervate, enfeeble, wear down **9** attenuate, undermine **10** devitalize

debilitated
4 weak **6** feeble, infirm, sapped **7** run-down, worn-out **8** decrepit, weakened **9** enfeebled

debility
7 disease, frailty, malaise **8** weakness **9** infirmity **10** feebleness, infirmness, sickliness **11** decrepitude

Debir
kingdom: **5** Eglon
slayer: **6** Joshua

debit
4 bill, levy **6** charge **7** deficit **8** drawback **9** liability **11** encumbrance, shortcoming
opposite: **5** asset

debonair
5 suave **6** smooth, svelte, urbane **7** dashing, elegant **8** polished **10** nonchalant **12** lighthearted

Deborah's husband
9 Lappidoth

debouch
5 empty, issue **6** emerge **8** march out **9** discharge

debris
4 junk, slag **5** trash, waste **6** litter, refuse, rubble, spilth **7** garbage, rubbish **8** detritus, riffraff, wreckage
rock: **5** scree, talus **8** colluvia **9** colluvium

debt
3 due, sin **6** arrear, red ink **7** arrears, default, deficit **8** mortgage, trespass **9** arrearage, liability **10** obligation **11** delinquency
acknowledgment: **3** IOU **4** bill **5** check

debtless
7 solvent **10** in the black

debtor's letters
3 IOU

debunk
6 expose, reveal, show up, unmask **7** lay bare, lay open, uncloak, uncover, undress **8** unshroud **9** demystify, discredit

Debussy's La ___
3 Mer

debut
3 bow **4** open **5** entry **6** entree **7** come out, opening, present **8** entrance, premiere **9** beginning, coming out, introduce **12** introduction, presentation

decadence
5 decay **7** decline **8** hedonism **10** degeneracy, regression, sybaritism **11** degradation, dissipation **12** degeneration **13** deterioration

decadent
6 effete, wanton **7** debased **8** decaying, degraded, depraved **9** debauched, declining, dissolute, sybaritic **10** degenerate, dissipated, hedonistic **11** incontinent **13** self-indulgent

Decalogue
12 Commandments
verb: **5** shalt

Decameron, The
author: **9** Boccaccio (Giovanni)
heroine: **8** Griselda

decamp
4 blow, bolt, exit, flee **5** leave, scram, split **6** beat it, begone, cut out, escape, get out, retire **7** abscond, make off, pull out, run away, skiddoo, take off, vamoose **8** clear out, withdraw **9** skedaddle

decant
4 pour **7** draw off, pour out **8** transfer

decanter
5 cruet, flask **6** bottle, carafe, flagon, vessel

decapitate
4 head **6** behead **9** decollate **10** guillotine

decapod
7 mollusc, mollusk **10** crustacean

decathlon champ
5 Eaton (Ashton) **6** Jenner (Bruce), Morris (Glenn), O'Brien (Dan), Schenk (Christian), Sebrle (Roman), Toomey (Bill), Zmelik (Robert) **7** Doherty (Ken), Johnson (Rafer), Mathias (Bob) **8** Campbell (Milton), Thompson (Daley)

decay
3 rot **4** ruin, wane **5** spoil, waste **6** molder, wither **7** atrophy, crumble, decline, putrefy, rotting **8** putresce, spoilage **9** decompose **11** deteriorate **12** dilapidation, putrefaction **13** deterioration

decayed
6 putrid, rotted, rotten, ruined **7** carious, spoiled **8** decadent, moldered, overripe **9** putrefied **10** decomposed, degenerate

decease
3 die, end **4** fail, pass **5** death, dying, sleep **6** demise, depart, expire, finish, pass on, perish **7** passing, quietus, release, succumb **8** pass away **9** departure **10** expiration

deceased
4 body, dead, late **6** corpse **7** cadaver, carcass, expired, remains **8** departed, lifeless **9** inanimate

deceit
3 gyp **4** hoax, ruse, sham **5** fraud, guile, trick **6** humbug **7** swindle **8** artifice, flimflam, trickery **9** chicanery, deception, duplicity, imposture **10** dishonesty **13** double-dealing

deceitful
3 sly **4** wily **5** false, lying **6** crafty, sneaky, tricky **7** crooked, cunning, knavish, roguish **8** two-faced **9** deceptive, dishonest, underhand **10** mendacious, untruthful **11** underhanded **13** double-dealing

deceive
3 con **4** bilk, dupe, fool, gull, hoax **5** bluff, cozen, lie to, trick **6** delude, humbug, palter, take in **7** beguile, mislead, sandbag, two-time **8** flimflam, hoodwink **9** bamboozle, four-flush **11** double-cross

deceiving
5 false **6** tricky **8** deluding, delusive, delusory, guileful, two-faced **9** beguiling, deceptive **10** fallacious, misleading **11** duplicitous, underhanded

decelerate
4 slow **5** delay **6** retard, slow up **7** slacken **8** slow down

decency
7 decorum, dignity, fitness, modesty **8** civility **9** etiquette, propriety **10** conformity, seemliness

decennium
6 decade

decent
4 fair, good **5** right **6** honest, modest, proper, seemly **7** correct, fitting, upright **8** adequate, all right **9** competent, honorable, tolerable **10** acceptable, conforming, sufficient **11** comme il faut, presentable, respectable **12** satisfactory

deception
3 gyp, lie **4** gaff, hoax, hype, ruse, scam, sham, wile **5** cheat, feint, fraud, grift, guile, put-on, trick **6** deceit, dupery, humbug, mirage **7** chicane, cunning, fallacy, fantasm, knavery, sophism **8** flimflam, illusion, intrigue, phantasm, trickery, trumpery, wiliness **9** casuistry, chicanery, duplicity, imposture, mare's nest, sophistry, treachery **10** dishonesty, hanky-panky, subterfuge

deceptive
4 fake **5** false, phony **6** tricky **8** deluding, delusory, illusory, specious **9** beguiling, deceitful, deceiving **10** fallacious, misleading

decide
3 opt **4** rule, will **5** judge **6** settle **7** adjudge, resolve **8** conclude **9** determine **10** adjudicate

decided
3 set **4** firm **5** fixed **6** intent **7** assured, certain, obvious, settled **8** definite, resolute, resolved **10** determined, pronounced **11** established, unequivocal

decimate
4 raze, ruin **5** wreck **7** abolish, destroy, wipe out **8** demolish, massacre **9** slaughter **10** annihilate, obliterate **11** exterminate

decipher
4 read **5** break, crack, solve **6** decode, reveal **7** decrypt, resolve, unravel **8** unriddle **9** figure out, interpret, puzzle out, translate **12** cryptanalyze

decision
4 fiat **6** choice, ruling **7** finding, resolve, verdict **8** firmness, judgment, sentence **9** judgement, selection **10** conclusion, resolution, settlement **13** determination
rabbinical: **9** responsum

decisive
3 set **7** crucial, settled **8** critical, resolute **10** conclusive, convincing, determined, imperative, peremptory **11** determining **12** unmistakable

deck
4 trim **5** adorn, array, dress, equip, floor, level, porch, prank **6** attire, blazon, clothe **7** apparel, appoint, festoon, furnish, garland, garnish, terrace **8** accouter, accoutre, beautify, decorate, emblazon, ornament, platform **9** embellish
chief: **4** bos'n **9** boatswain
contents: **5** cards
high: **4** poop

lowest: **5** orlop
out: **5** array, fix up, slick, spiff, tog up **6** clothe, doll up **7** dress up, gussy up **8** spruce up
part: **7** scupper

deckhand
3 gob, tar **4** jack, swab **6** sailor, seaman **7** jack-tar, rouster, swabbie **10** bluejacket

declaim
4 rant **5** mouth, orate, speak **6** preach, recite **7** deliver, lecture **8** bloviate, harangue, perorate **9** hold forth, sermonize, speechify

declamatory
5 tumid, windy, wordy **6** florid, turgid **7** aureate, flowery, fustian, orotund, pompous, ranting, verbose **8** sonorous **9** bombastic, high-flown, overblown **10** euphuistic, oratorical, rhetorical **12** magniloquent **13** grandiloquent

declaration
4 fiat **5** edict **6** avowal, report **7** promise **8** pleading **9** affidavit, manifesto, statement, testimony, utterance **10** confession, deposition, disclosure, expression, profession **11** affirmation, attestation **12** announcement, notification, proclamation **13** pronouncement

declare
3 say, vow **4** aver, avow, tell, vent **5** claim, sound, state, swear, utter, voice **6** affirm, allege, assert, avouch, blazon, depone, depose, insist, ordain, report, reveal **7** certify, confirm, deliver, divulge, express, profess, signify, testify **8** announce, disclose, indicate, maintain, manifest, proclaim, propound **9** broadcast, enunciate, predicate, pronounce **10** annunciate, asseverate, promulgate **11** come out with
a saint: **8** canonize
in cards: **3** bid **4** meld
invalid: **5** annul

declass
4 bump, bust **5** abase, lower **6** reduce **7** set back **9** downgrade

déclassé
4 mean, poor **6** common, vulgar **7** ignoble, lowered **8** inferior, lowgrade, mediocre, middling **10** second-rate **11** second-class

declension
5 class, slope **7** descent **8** downfall **9** downgrade **10** inflection **12** dégringolade **13** deterioration

declination
3 ebb **5** slant, slide **6** ebbing **7** refusal, incline **8** downturn **9** downgrade **10** deflection **12** dégringolade, turning aside **13** deterioration

decline
3 dip, ebb, jib, rot, sag, set **4** balk, dive, drop, fade, fail, fall, flag, loss, sink, slip, wane **5** abate, avoid, demur, droop, lapse, lower, say no, slide, slope, slump, spurn **6** ebbing, go down, recede, refuse, reject, renege, waning, weaken, worsen **7** abstain, atrophy, descend, descent, devolve, dismiss, drop-off, dwindle, failure, falloff, forbear, refrain, relapse, sell-off, sinkage, subside **8** comedown, decrease, downfall, downturn, languish, lowering, turn down **9** backslide, decadence, downgrade, downslide, downswing, downtrend, reprobate, repudiate, weakening **10** degeneracy, degenerate, depression, devolution, disapprove, falling off **11** backsliding, deteriorate **12** degeneration, dégringolade **13** deterioration

declivitous
5 steep **6** sloped **7** pitched, sloping **8** inclined **9** inclining **10** descending

declivity
3 dip **4** drop, fall **5** slope **7** descent **8** downturn, gradient **9** downgrade **11** inclination

decode
see **decipher**

decollate
4 head, kill **6** behead **10** decapitate, guillotine

___ de cologne
3 eau

decolor
6 blanch, bleach, blench, whiten **7** wash out **11** achromatize

decompose
3 rot **5** decay, spoil, taint **6** fester, molder **7** analyze, break up, crumble, putrefy, resolve **8** dissolve, separate **9** anatomize, break down **12** disintegrate

decor
7 setting **8** backdrop, stage set **11** furnishings, mise-en-scène **13** ornamentation

decorate
4 do up, pink, trim **5** adorn, dress, frill **6** bedeck **7** bedizen, dress up, enhance, festoon, furnish, garnish **8** appliqué, beautify, emblazon, ornament **9** embellish
a border: **6** purfle
anew: **4** redo

decorated
6 ornate **7** adorned, honored, opulent, wrought **9** bemedaled, decked out, garnished **10** beribboned, ornamented **11** embellished

decoration
4 bays **5** award, badge, honor, kudos, medal **6** doodad, plaque **7** garnish, laurels, regalia **8** accolade, filigree, fretting, fretwork, frippery, froufrou, furbelow, ornament, trimming, vignette **9** caparison, garniture **11** distinction
cutout: **8** appliqué
furniture: **4** buhl **6** boulle

decorative case
4 etui
decorous
3 fit **4** prim **6** au fait, decent, proper, seemly **7** correct, elegant, fitting, refined **8** becoming, mannerly, suitable, tasteful **9** befitting, civilized, de rigueur, dignified **11** appropriate, respectable, well-behaved
decorousness
7 decency **8** civility **9** propriety, rightness **10** seemliness **11** correctness **12** correctitude
decorticate
4 bare, bark, flay, hull, husk, pare, peel, skin **5** scale, scalp, shell, shuck, strip **6** denude **7** lay bare, pull off
decorum
5 order **7** civility, decency, dignity, fitness, modesty **8** protocol **9** etiquette, propriety **10** properness, seemliness **11** correctness, orderliness **12** correctitude
decoy
4 bait, fake, lure **5** plant, shill, tempt **6** allure, capper, delude, entice, lead on, pigeon, seduce **7** deceive, mislead **8** inveigle **10** red herring
decrease
3 cut, ebb **4** bate, drop, ease, fall, loss, wane **5** allay, lower **6** lessen, reduce, shrink **7** abridge, curtail, cut back, cutback, cut down, decline, die down, drop off, dwindle, fall off, lighten, shorten, slacken, subside **8** diminish, downturn, moderate, rollback, taper off **9** abatement, alleviate, reduction **10** abbreviate, depreciate, diminution, falling off
decree
4 fiat, rule **5** canon, edict, enact, judge, order, ukase **6** assize, behest, charge, dictum, impose, ordain, ruling **7** adjudge, appoint, bidding, command, declare, dictate, lay down, mandate, precept, statute **8** judgment, proclaim, sentence **9** directive, judgement, ordinance, prescribe, prescript, pronounce **10** adjudicate, injunction, regulation **11** declaration **12** adjudication, announcement, proclamation, promulgation **13** pronouncement
Muslim: 5 fatwa
decrepit
4 aged, weak, worn **5** anile, frail, seedy, tacky **6** creaky, feeble, infirm, senile, shabby, wasted, weakly **7** fragile, run-down, worn-out **8** battered, impaired, weakened **10** bedraggled, broken-down, down-at-heel, ramshackle **11** dilapidated
decrepitude
4 ruin **5** decay **7** frailty, wasting **8** collapse, debility, weakness **9** disrepair, infirmity **10** exhaustion, feebleness, infirmness **12** dilapidation, enfeeblement **13** deterioration
decretal
4 fiat, writ **5** edict, order, ukase **6** assize, dictum, letter, ruling **7** dictate **8** decision, judgment **11** declaration **13** pronouncement
decry
3 boo **4** bash, slam, slur **5** abuse **6** berate, malign, vilify **7** asperse, censure, condemn, degrade, devalue, put down **8** bad-mouth, belittle, denounce, derogate, reproach **9** criticize, deprecate, discredit, disparage, dispraise, reprehend, reprobate **10** depreciate, disapprove **11** rail against
decrypt
see **decipher**
decumbent
4 flat **5** prone **6** supine **9** lying down, prostrate, reclining **10** horizontal
decussate
5 cross **8** crosscut **9** intersect **10** crisscross, intercross
dedicate
3 vow **5** bless **6** commit, devote, hallow, pledge **7** address **8** inscribe, restrict, set apart **10** consecrate
deduce
5 infer, judge, trace **6** derive, evolve, gather, reason, reckon **7** discern, make out, surmise **8** conclude **9** figure out
deduct
4 bate **5** abate, infer, judge **6** gather, remove **7** make out, take off, take out **8** conclude, knock off, perceive, subtract, take away
deduction
3 cut **4** tare **8** discount, illation, judgment, sequitur, write-off **9** abatement, inference, reasoning **10** conclusion **11** subtraction
deductive
7 a priori **8** dogmatic, illative, provable, reasoned **9** derivable, inferable **10** consequent **11** inferential **13** ratiocinative
deed
3 act **4** cede, fact, feat, pact **5** doing, title **6** action, assign, convey, escrow, remise **7** charter, exploit **8** alienate, contract, covenant, make over, sign over, transfer **9** adventure **10** conveyance, enterprise **11** achievement, performance, tour de force
brutal: 8 atrocity
evil: 3 sin **11** malefaction
good: 7 mitzvah
deem
4 feel, hold **5** judge, think **7** account, adjudge, believe **8** consider
de-emphasize
8 downplay, minimize, play down **9** gloss over, soft-pedal, underplay **13** underestimate

deep
3 low **4** bass, rapt, sunk **5** abyss, grave, ocean **6** occult, orphic, secret **7** abyssal, obscure **8** abstruse, esoteric, hermetic, profound **9** engrossed, recondite **10** bottomless, fathomless, mysterious
combining form: **5** bathy

deepen
6 darken, worsen **7** enhance, enlarge, magnify, thicken **8** heighten **9** aggravate, intensify **10** strengthen

deepness
5 abyss **9** intensity **10** profundity

deep-seated
6 inborn, inbred, innate **7** settled **8** inherent, lifelong, profound, stubborn **9** confirmed, ingrained, intrinsic **10** congenital, entrenched, indwelling, inveterate **11** established **12** long-standing **13** bred-in-the-bone, dyed-in-the-wool, thoroughgoing

deep-six
4 dump, toss **5** chuck, scrap **6** unload **7** discard **8** jettison **9** eliminate

deep water
7 trouble **8** distress **10** difficulty

deer
3 elk, roe **4** buck, musk, stag **5** moose **6** wapiti **7** caribou, venison
Asian: **4** axis, maha **6** sambar **7** muntjac
British: **4** hart
female: **3** doe **4** hind
Japanese: **4** sika
male: **4** buck, hart, stag **7** roebuck
meat: **5** jerky **7** venison
path: **3** run **5** trail
red: **7** brocket
relating to: **7** cervine
relative: **3** elk **4** pudú **6** wapiti **7** brocket, muntjac
track: **4** slot **5** spoor
young: **3** kid **4** fawn

Deere rival
4 Case, Ford, Toro **6** Kubota **7** Farmall

Deerslayer, The
author: **6** Cooper (James Fenimore)
character: **5** Harry (Hurry), Natty (Bumppo) **6** Hutter (Thomas), Judith (Hutter) **11** Natty Bumppo **12** Chingachgook

deface
3 mar **4** harm, ruin **6** damage, impair, injure **9** disfigure, vandalize

de facto
4 real **6** actual, really **8** actually, existing

defalcation
7 default, failing, failure **10** embezzling, inadequacy, negligence **12** embezzlement

defamation
5 libel, smear **7** calumny, obloquy, slander **10** backbiting **11** traducement **12** backstabbing **13** disparagement

defamatory
8 libelous **9** maligning, traducing, vilifying **10** backbiting, calumnious, slanderous **11** denigrating

defame
5 abase, libel, smear **6** malign, vilify **7** asperse, blacken, blemish, slander, traduce **8** dishonor **9** denigrate, discredit **10** calumniate

default
4 fail **5** welsh **7** absence, exclude, failure, forfeit, neglect **9** selection

defeasance
4 deed **6** defeat **9** overthrow **11** termination

defeat
3 tan **4** beat, best, down, drub, edge, foil, lick, loss, rout, sink, undo, whip, whup **5** crush, excel, outdo, skunk, smoke, swamp, upset, waste, whomp **6** outgun, reduce, subdue, wallop **7** beating, conquer, destroy, eclipse, failure, licking, mow down, nose out, nullify, outplay, overrun, setback, shellac, trounce, wipe out **8** confound, dispatch, knock out, outfight, outflank, outstrip, overcome, surmount, vanquish, waterloo **9** frustrate, overpower, overthrow, overtrump, subjugate, thrashing, trouncing **10** obliterate **11** shellacking

defeatist
8 doomster, naysayer **9** doomsayer, Gloomy Gus, pessimist, worrywart

defect
3 bug **4** flaw, kink, lack, vice, want **5** botch, error, fault, taint **6** damage, dearth, desert, foible, glitch, injury **7** blemish, default, failing **8** drawback, weakness **9** birthmark, deformity **10** apostatize, deficiency **11** shortcoming **12** imperfection, tergiversate
timber: **4** knot
visual: **6** myopia, squint **9** amblyopia, hyperopia **10** presbyopia, strabismus

defection
8 apostasy **9** desertion, forsaking, recreancy **10** disloyalty **11** abandonment

defective
6 broken, faulty, flawed **7** damaged, lacking, unsound, wanting **8** impaired **9** corrupted, deficient, imperfect

defector
5 Judas **7** traitor **8** apostate, quisling, recreant, renegade, turncoat **9** turnabout **13** double-crosser

defend
4 back, hold, save **5** argue, cover, guard **6** screen, secure, shield, uphold **7** contend,

justify, protect, support **8** advocate, champion, maintain, plead for, preserve **9** safeguard

defendable
see **defensible**

defendant
7 accused, libelee **8** libellee
declaration: 4 plea

defender
7 paladin, tribune **8** advocate, champion, guardian **9** protector **11** white knight

defense
4 fort, ward **5** aegis, alibi, armor, guard **6** excuse, sconce, shield **7** bulwark, rampart, shelter **8** apologia, armament, fastness, fortress, muniment, security **9** safeguard **10** protection, stronghold **11** exculpation, explanation **13** justification
organization: 4 NATO **5** ANZUS, NORAD, SEATO **10** Warsaw Pact

defenseless
7 exposed, unarmed **8** helpless, wide open **9** unguarded **10** vulnerable **11** unprotected

defensible
5 valid **7** tenable **8** passable **9** excusable, plausible **10** condonable, reasonable **11** justifiable

defer
3 bow **4** stay, wait **5** delay, remit, stall, table, yield **6** accede, hold up, put off, shelve, submit **7** hold off, lay over, put over, suspend **8** hold over, postpone, prorogue **9** acquiesce **13** procrastinate

deference
5 honor **6** esteem, homage, regard **7** respect **8** courtesy **9** obeisance **11** recognition

deferential
8 obliging **9** disarming, regardful **10** respectful **11** complaisant

defiance
4 dare **5** moxie **7** bravado **8** audacity, obduracy **9** challenge, contumacy, impudence, insolence **10** brazenness, effrontery **12** contrariness, stubbornness

defiant
5 brash, gutsy, sassy, saucy **6** brazen, cheeky, daring **8** arrogant, impudent, insolent **9** audacious, obstinate, resistant **10** refractory **12** recalcitrant

deficiency
4 flaw, lack, want **5** fault, minus **6** dearth **7** absence, blemish, demerit, failing, failure, paucity **8** scarcity, shortage, weakness **9** privation **10** inadequacy, scantiness **11** defalcation, shortcoming **12** imperfection
mental: 6 idiocy **7** amentia
pigmentation: 8 albinism

deficient
3 shy **5** minus, scant, short **6** faulty, flawed, meager, meagre, measly, scanty, scarce **7** failing, lacking, unsound, wanting **8** exiguous, impaired **9** defective, imperfect **10** inadequate, incomplete

deficit
4 lack, loss **6** red ink **8** shortage **9** shortfall **10** impairment, inadequacy **12** disadvantage **13** insufficiency

defile
3 tar **4** foul, pass, rape, soil **5** dirty, gorge, march, shame, smear, spoil, stain, sully, taint **6** befoul, debase, ravish **7** besmear, corrupt, pollute, profane, tarnish, violate **8** deflower, dishonor **9** desecrate **11** contaminate

defiled
6 impure **7** stained, unclean **8** profaned, polluted, ravished, violated **9** corrupted **10** deflowered, desecrated **12** contaminated

define
3 fix, hem, rim, set **4** edge **5** limit **6** assign, border, detail **7** clarify, delimit, lay down, mark off, mark out, outline, specify **9** delineate, demarcate, determine, establish **11** distinguish **12** characterize

definite
3 set **4** sure **5** clear, final, fixed, sharp, solid **7** certain, decided, express, precise, settled **8** clear-cut, distinct, explicit, specific **10** conclusive, pronounced **11** unambiguous, unequivocal **12** unmistakable

definiteness
8 accuracy, sureness **9** certainty, certitude, exactness, precision **10** exactitude

definitive
5 final **7** express **8** clear-cut, complete, explicit, settling, specific, ultimate **10** concluding, conclusive, exhaustive **11** categorical, determining, unambiguous **13** authoritative

deflate
4 dash **6** humble, reduce, shrink **7** devalue, put down **8** contract, ridicule **9** humiliate, shoot down

deflect
5 avert, parry **6** divert **7** deviate, diverge, hold off **9** turn aside

deflection
3 yaw **4** bend, tack, turn, veer **5** carom, curve, shift **6** double, swerve **7** bending, rebound, turning, veering **8** swerving **9** departure, deviation, diversion **10** divergence

deflower
4 rape **5** spoil **6** defile, ravish **7** despoil, violate **9** desecrate

Defoe, Daniel
character: 4 Moll (Flanders) 6 Crusoe (Robinson), Friday, Roxana

deform
4 warp 5 spoil 6 deface 7 contort, distort 8 misshape 9 disfigure

deformed
4 awry, bent 5 askew, bowed 6 warped 7 buckled, crooked 8 crippled 9 contorted, misshapen, unshapely

deformity
4 flaw 6 defect 7 blemish 11 abnormality 12 imperfection, irregularity, malformation 13 disfigurement

____ de France
3 Île

defraud
3 con, gyp 4 bilk, dupe, rook, scam 5 cheat, cozen, mulct, trick 6 fleece, rip off 7 swindle 8 flimflam 9 bamboozle

deft
3 apt 4 able 5 adept, agile, handy 6 adroit, clever 7 skilled 8 dextrous, skillful 9 dexterous

deftness
5 knack, skill 7 address, prowess 8 facility 9 adeptness, dexterity 10 capability

defunct
4 cold, dead, late 5 kaput 7 extinct 8 deceased, departed, lifeless, vanished

defy
4 dare, face, gibe, jeer, mock 5 beard, brave, flout, stump 6 resist 7 affront, outdare, outface 8 confront 9 challenge, disregard, withstand

dégagé
6 breezy, casual 7 relaxed, unfussy 8 informal 9 easygoing 10 nonchalant, unreserved 13 unconstrained

De Gaulle alternative
4 Orly

degeneracy
see **degeneration**

degenerate
4 sink 6 rotten, sunken, worsen 7 corrupt, debased, decayed, decline, descend, immoral, pervert, vicious, vitiate 8 decadent, degraded, depraved 9 backslide, dissolute 11 deteriorate

degeneration
7 atrophy, decline 8 downfall, lowering 9 decadence, depravity, downgrade 10 debasement, perversion, regression 12 dégringolade

degradation
4 fall 7 decline, descent 8 demotion 9 abasement, decadence, depravity, downgrade, reduction 10 corruption, debasement, degeneracy, perversion 11 downgrading 12 degeneration

degrade
4 bump, bust 5 abase, break, decry, lower 6 debase, demean, demote, impair, lessen, reduce 7 corrupt, declass, pervert, put down 8 belittle, cast down, derogate, diminish 9 decompose, discredit, disparage, downgrade, humiliate

degree
3 nth, peg 4 heat, rank, rate, rung, step, term, tier 5 grade, honor, notch, order, pitch, point, ratio, scale, shade, stage, stair 6 amount, extent, status 7 measure, station 8 standing 9 dimension, gradation, intensity, magnitude 10 proportion
academic: 3 BFA, BSc, DDS, LLB, LLD, LLM, MBA, MFA, MSc, PhD 5 MPhil 7 master's 9 bachelor's, doctorate
highest: 5 magna, summa 8 cum laude 13 magna cum laude, summa cum laude
seeker: 9 candidate

dégringolade
see **degeneration**

____ de guerre
3 nom

dehydrate
3 dry 4 sear 5 parch 9 desiccate, exsiccate

Deianira
brother: 8 Meleager
father: 6 Oeneus
husband: 8 Heracles, Hercules
mother: 7 Althaea
victim: 8 Heracles, Hercules

deific
5 godly 6 divine 7 godlike

deification
8 idolatry 10 apotheosis, glorifying 13 glorification

deify
5 exalt 7 glorify, idolize, worship 8 sanctify, venerate 11 apotheosize

Deighton of spy novels
3 Len

deign
5 stoop 7 descend 9 vouchsafe 10 condescend

Deiphobus
brother: 5 Paris 6 Hector
father: 5 Priam
mother: 6 Hecuba
wife: 5 Helen

Deirdre
beloved: 5 Noisi
father: 5 Felim

deity
3 god 4 Baal, Lord 7 goddess, godhead, godhood 8 Almighty, divinity 12 supreme being (see also *god* and *goddess* at **Egyptian; Greek; Hindu; Norse; Roman**)

deject
5 chill, cloud, daunt **6** dampen, dismay **7** depress **8** dispirit **9** disparage **10** demoralize, discourage, dishearten

dejected
3 low, sad **4** blue, down, glum, sunk **6** bummed, gloomy, morose, somber, sombre **7** doleful, hangdog, humbled, unhappy **8** downcast, wretched **9** cheerless, depressed, woebegone **10** despondent, spiritless **11** crestfallen, downhearted **12** disconsolate, disheartened

dejection
5 dumps, gloom **7** despair, sadness **10** melancholy **11** despondency, unhappiness **12** mournfulness

Delaware
capital: 5 Dover
city: 10 Wilmington
nickname: 5 First (State) **7** Diamond (State)
state bird: 14 blue hen chicken
state flower: 12 peach blossom
state tree: 13 American holly

delay
3 lag **4** drag, hold, slow, stay, wait **5** dally, defer, stall, tarry, trail **6** dawdle, detain, hang up, hinder, holdup, impede, linger, loiter, put off, retard, slow up **7** bog down, hold off, respite, set back, slacken, suspend **8** hesitate, hold over, postpone, prorogue, reprieve, slow down **10** dillydally, moratorium, suspension **13** procrastinate

delaying
8 dawdling, dilatory **10** postponing, putting off

dele
see **delete**

delectable
5 tasty, yummy **6** choice, savory **8** charming, heavenly, luscious, pleasing **9** ambrosial, delicious, enjoyable, exquisite, toothsome **10** delightful, enchanting **11** scrumptious **13** mouthwatering

delectation
3 fun, joy **4** zest **5** gusto **6** relish **7** delight **8** gladness, pleasure **9** enjoyment

delegate
4 name, send **5** agent, envoy, proxy **6** assign, depute, deputy, legate **7** appoint, consign, entrust **8** deputize, emissary, transfer **9** authorize, catchpole, designate, spokesman **10** commission, mouthpiece, procurator

delete
4 drop, omit, x out **5** erase, purge **6** cancel, censor, cut out, efface, excise, remove **7** blot out, destroy, expunge, take out, wipe out **8** black out, cross out **9** eliminate, eradicate, strike out **10** blue-pencil, obliterate

deleterious
3 bad **6** nocent **7** baneful, harmful, hurtful, nocuous, noxious, ruinous **8** damaging **9** injurious **10** pernicious **11** destructive, detrimental, mischievous, prejudicial

deletion
7 erasure, voiding **9** canceling **10** deficiency **11** elimination **12** cancellation

deliberate
4 chaw, cool, muse, pore, slow **5** chary, meant, study, think, weigh **6** chew on, ponder, reason **7** careful, heedful, planned, reflect, studied, willful, willing, witting **8** cautious, cogitate, consider, intended, measured, meditate, mull over, ruminate, talk over **9** cerebrate, conscious, unhurried **10** calculated, considered, purposeful, thought-out **11** circumspect, intentional **12** premeditated

deliberately
9 knowingly, on purpose, purposely, willfully, wittingly **11** consciously **12** purposefully **13** intentionally

deliberation
5 study **6** debate **7** thought **10** conference, discussion, reflection **13** consideration

Delibes, Léo
ballet: 6 Sylvia **8** Coppélia, La Source
opera: 5 Lakmé
waltz: 5 Naila

delicacy
4 tact **5** goody, treat **6** dainty, luxury, morsel, nicety, tidbit **7** frailty **8** kickshaw, fineness **9** fragility, precision **10** daintiness, difficulty, indulgence, stickiness **11** awkwardness **12** ticklishness

delicate
4 fine, lacy, twee, weak **5** frail **6** choice, dainty, flimsy, petite, queasy, sickly, slight, subtle, tender, touchy, tricky **7** elegant, fragile, refined, tactful, tenuous **8** ethereal, feathery, finespun, gossamer, graceful, pleasing, ticklish **9** exquisite, sensitive, squeamish **10** precarious

Delicate Balance playwright
5 Albee (Edward)

delicatessen
11 charcuterie
loaf: 3 rye

delicious
5 tasty, yummy **6** choice, divine, savory **8** heavenly, luscious **9** ambrosial, exquisite, toothsome **10** delectable, delightful **11** scrumptious **13** mouthwatering

delight
3 joy **4** glee **5** amuse, bliss, charm, enjoy, exult, glory, mirth, revel **6** divert, please, regale, relish **7** ecstasy, enchant, gladden, gratify, jollity,

rapture, rejoice **8** enravish, entrance, fruition, hilarity, pleasure **9** captivate, delectate, enjoyment, enrapture, entertain, fascinate **11** delectation

in: **4** love **5** adore, enjoy, savor **6** admire, relish **7** cherish **10** appreciate

delighted
4 glad **5** happy **6** joyful **8** ecstatic, euphoric

delightful
5 yummy **6** dreamy, lovely **8** charming, heavenly, luscious, pleasant, pleasing **9** congenial, enjoyable **10** delectable, enchanting, satisfying **11** captivating, fascinating, pleasurable, scrumptious **12** entertaining

Delilah's victim
6 Samson

DeLillo novel
5 Libra, Mao II **10** Underworld, White Noise

delimit
3 bar **5** bound, hem in **6** demark, define **7** confine, enclose **8** restrict **9** demarcate, determine **12** circumscribe

delineate
3 map **4** etch, limn **5** chart, image, trace **6** define, depict, detail, render **7** mark out, outline, picture, portray **8** describe, spell out **9** elucidate, interpret, represent **10** illustrate

delineation
5 draft, story **6** report **7** account, contour, drawing, outline, picture, profile **9** depiction, rendering **11** presentment

delinquency
4 debt **5** crime, fault, lapse **7** default, failure, misdeed, neglect, offense **8** omission **9** oversight **10** misconduct, nonpayment, wrongdoing **11** dereliction, misbehavior

delinquent
3 lax **5** slack **6** debtor **7** overdue **8** careless, offender **9** defaulter, in arrears, negligent **10** behindhand, neglectful

deliquesce
3 rot, run **4** flux, fuse, melt, thaw **5** decay **6** render, soften **7** liquefy, putrefy **8** dissolve, fluidize **9** decompose, disappear, waste away **12** disintegrate

delirious
3 mad **4** wild **5** crazy **6** crazed, insane, raving **7** frantic, lunatic **8** confused, demented, deranged, ecstatic, frenetic, frenzied, rambling **9** rapturous **10** bewildered, corybantic, distracted, irrational **11** lightheaded, overexcited

delirium
5 furor, mania **6** fervor, frenzy **7** ecstasy, jimjams, rapture, seizure **8** dementia, hysteria **13** hallucination

delirium ____
7 tremens

deliver
4 bear, deal, feed, find, give, hand, save, send, ship, sing, take **5** bring, serve, speak, state, throw, utter **6** convey, redeem, rescue, strike, supply **7** consign, present, produce, provide, set free, release **8** hand over, liberate, turn over **9** pronounce, surrender **10** bring forth, emancipate **11** come out with, come through

deliverance
6 rescue **7** freeing, opinion, release, verdict **8** decision **9** acquittal, discharge, salvation **10** absolution, liberation

Deliverance author
6 Dickey (James)

delivery
4 drop **5** birth, labor **6** rescue **7** address, bearing **8** birthing, shipment **9** elocution, rendition, salvation **10** childbirth, conveyance, liberation **11** consignment, parturition, transferral **12** childbearing, transmission

dell
4 dale, glen, vale **6** dingle, hollow, valley

Delphic
4 dark **5** vatic **6** arcane, hidden, mantic, mystic, occult, veiled **7** cryptic, obscure **8** auguring, divining, esoteric, mystical, oracular **9** ambiguous, enigmatic, equivocal, prophetic, recondite, sibylline, vaticinal **10** mystifying, portentous **11** prophesying, prophetical

delta
6 letter, symbol **7** deposit **8** triangle **9** increment

delude
3 con **4** dupe, fool, gull, hoax **5** bluff, cozen, trick **6** betray, humbug, juggle, take in **7** beguile, deceive, mislead **8** flimflam, hoodwink **11** double-cross

deluge
5 drown, flood, spate, swamp **6** drench, engulf **7** Niagara, torrent **8** cataract, downpour, drencher, flooding, inundate, overflow **9** cataclysm, overwhelm **10** cloudburst, outpouring, inundation

delusion
5 dream, fancy, snare **6** mirage **7** chimera, fallacy, fantasy, figment, phantom, specter, spectre **8** daydream, paranoia, phantasm **9** deception **10** apparition **11** ignis fatuus **13** hallucination

delusive
5 false **8** fanciful, illusory, specious **9** beguiling, deceiving, deceptive, imaginary **10** chimerical, fallacious, misleading

delusory
see **delusive**

deluxe
4 lush, posh **5** grand, plush, ritzy, swank **6** choice, costly, swanky **7** elegant, opulent **8** luscious, splendid **9** expensive, exquisite, luxuriant, luxurious, sumptuous **10** first class

delve
3 dig, dip **4** mine **5** probe **6** dredge, fathom, hollow, quarry, search, shovel **7** inquire **8** excavate
into: **4** sift **5** probe **7** explore **8** prospect **11** investigate

delving
6 asking **7** inquest, inquiry, probing **8** research **9** inquiring, searching

demagnetize
7 degauss

demagogue
6 leader **7** inciter **8** agitator, fomenter **9** firebrand **10** instigator **11** provocateur **12** rabble-rouser

demand
3 ask, use **4** call, need, urge, want **5** claim, crave, exact, force, order **6** compel, direct, expect, insist **7** call for, request, require **11** requirement, requisition

demanding
4 hard **5** pushy, tough **6** taxing, trying **7** exigent, onerous, weighty **8** exacting, forceful, rigorous **9** assertive, difficult, insistent, strenuous, stringent **10** aggressive, burdensome, oppressive **11** challenging

demarcate
5 bound, limit **6** define, set off **7** delimit, mark off, outline **8** separate, set apart **9** delineate, determine **11** distinguish **12** circumscribe **13** differentiate

demarcation
9 outlining **10** border line, separation **11** distinction **12** delimitation

démarche
4 plan, ploy, ruse **5** feint **6** action, device, gambit, scheme, tactic **7** protest **8** artifice, maneuver, petition **9** stratagem **10** initiative **11** contrivance, machination

demean
4 bear **5** abase, carry, decry, lower **6** acquit, behave, debase, deport, humble **7** comport, conduct, degrade, detract **8** bad-mouth, belittle **9** disparage, humiliate

demeanor
3 air **4** look, mien **6** aspect, manner **7** address, bearing, conduct **8** behavior, carriage, presence **10** deportment **11** comportment

demented
3 mad **5** crazy, loony, nutty, wacko **6** crazed, insane, psycho **7** lunatic, unsound **8** deranged, frenzied, maniacal **9** delirious **10** hysterical, unbalanced **12** psychopathic

___ de mer
3 mal

demerit
4 mark **5** fault, stain **6** defect **7** blemish, penalty **9** downgrade **10** deficiency, punishment **11** shortcoming **12** imperfection

demesne
4 fief **5** field, realm **6** estate, region, sphere **7** fiefdom, terrain **8** dominion, province **9** bailiwick, champaign, territory
house: **5** manor

Demeter
see **Ceres**

demigod
4 idol **6** Aeneas **7** Orpheus, Perseus, Theseus **8** Achilles, Heracles, Hercules, superman **9** Gilgamesh, superstar

demise
3 die, end **4** drop, pass **5** death, dying, sleep **6** cash in, depart, ending, expire **7** decease, passing, quietus, release, silence, succumb **8** pass away **9** cessation, departure **10** expiration, extinction

demit
4 quit **6** bow out, give up, resign **8** abdicate, renounce, step down, withdraw

demiurgic
8 creative, original **9** formative, inventive **10** innovative **11** originative

demobilize
7 break up, disband, dismiss, scatter **8** disperse, separate **9** discharge, disengage, muster out

democratic
7 popular **8** populist **10** self-ruling **11** egalitarian **13** self-governing

Democrats' symbol
6 donkey

démodé
5 dated, passé **7** antique, archaic, outworn **8** obsolete, old-timey, outdated **9** out-of-date **12** old-fashioned

demoiselle
4 maid **6** lassie, maiden **7** ingenue **10** damselfish

demolish
4 raze, ruin **5** crush, level, smash, total, wrack, wreck **7** destroy, flatten, scuttle, wipe out **8** decimate, tear down **9** finish off **10** annihilate, obliterate

demolition
6 razing **8** leveling, wrecking **10** bulldozing **11** destruction **12** annihilation

demolition bomb
11 blockbuster

demon
3 imp **4** jinn **5** devil, fiend, genie, ghoul, jinni, Satan **7** hellion, incubus **9** archfiend
Arabic: 5 afrit **6** afreet
female: 5 lamia **6** Lilith **7** succuba, succubi (plural) **8** succubae (plural), succubus

demonic
4 evil **6** wicked **7** satanic **8** devilish, diabolic, fiendish, infernal **9** possessed **10** diabolical

demonize
6 malign, revile, vilify **7** bedevil, censure, slander **8** denounce

demonstrate
3 try **4** mark, show, test **5** prove, rally **6** act out, evince **7** confirm, display, exhibit, explain, make out, protest **8** evidence, manifest, proclaim, validate **9** determine, establish **10** illustrate **12** authenticate

demonstration
4 expo, show, test **5** march, proof, rally, trial **6** picket **7** display, protest **9** spectacle **10** exhibition, exposition, validation **12** presentation **13** corroboration, manifestation

demonstrative
4 open **8** effusive, outgoing, specific **9** emotional, expansive, exuberant, outspoken **10** outpouring, unreserved, validating **12** affectionate, unrestrained **13** unconstrained

demoralize
5 chill, daunt, shake, unman, upset **6** dampen, debase, deject, rattle, weaken **7** corrupt, debauch, deprave, unnerve, vitiate **8** dispirit, psych out **9** undermine **10** discourage, dishearten

Demosthenes
6 orator
oration: 9 Philippic

demote
4 bump, bust **5** lower **6** reduce **9** downgrade

demulcent
4 balm **5** salve **7** unguent **8** liniment, ointment, soothing **9** softening

demur
5 qualm **6** object, oppose, resist **7** dispute, protest **8** hesitate, question **9** challenge, hesitancy, objection **10** hesitation, indecision, reluctance **11** compunction, remonstrate

demure
3 coy, mim, shy **5** timid **6** modest **7** bashful **8** reserved, reticent, retiring **9** diffident **11** unassertive **12** self-effacing

demurral
7 protest **9** challenge, objection **12** remonstrance **13** remonstration

demurrer
see **demurral**

den
4 base, cave, home, lair, nest, room **5** study **6** burrow, cavern, hollow **7** dayroom, hideout, man cave, sanctum **8** hideaway, playroom
rabbit: 6 warren

denial
3 nay, nix **6** heresy **7** refusal **8** disproof, negation, rebuttal **9** disavowal, rejection **10** abnegation, gainsaying, refutation **11** repudiation **12** renunciation

denigrate
5 decry, libel, smear, stain, sully **6** darken, defame, defile, impugn, malign, vilify **7** asperse, devalue, put down, slander, tarnish, traduce **8** belittle, dishonor, tear down **9** discredit, disparage **10** calumniate, scandalize

denims
5 jeans **8** overalls **9** blue jeans, dungarees

denizen
5 liver **6** native **7** dweller, habitué, haunter, resider **8** habitant, occupant, resident **9** indweller, inhabiter **10** frequenter, inhabitant

Denmark
capital: 10 Copenhagen
city: 5 Århus **6** Ålborg, Odense **11** Helsingborg **13** Frederiksberg
island: 3 Fyn **7** Falster, Zealand **8** Bornholm **9** Sjaelland
monetary unit: 5 krone
neighbor: 6 Sweden **7** Germany
part of: 11 Scandinavia
peninsula: 7 Jutland
possession: 9 Greenland **12** Faroe Islands **13** Faeroe Islands
sea: 5 North **6** Baltic
strait: 5 Lille, Store **9** Langeland

denominate
3 dub **4** call, name, term **5** label, style, title **7** baptize, entitle **8** christen **9** designate

denomination
4 cult, name, sect **5** creed, faith, style, title **6** church **8** category, cognomen, religion **9** communion **10** persuasion
religious: 5 Amish **6** Mormon **7** Baptist **8** Catholic, Lutheran, Moravian, Mormonism, Reformed **9** Adventist, Episcopal, Mennonite, Methodism, Methodist, Unitarian **11** Pentecostal **12** Episcopalian, Presbyterian, Unitarianism, Universalist **13** Roman Catholic

denotation
4 name, sign **5** sense **6** import **7** meaning **10** indication, signifying **11** designation **13** signification, specification

denote
4 mark, mean, name, show **5** spell **6** import **7** add up to, betoken, express, signify **8** announce, indicate **9** designate, represent

denouement
3 end **6** effect, result, upshot **7** outcome **10** conclusion **11** consequence, culmination

denounce
3 rap **4** skin **5** blame, blast, decry, knock **6** rebuke, scathe **7** censure, condemn, upbraid **8** derogate, reproach **9** castigate, criticize, dress down, excoriate, reprehend, reprobate **10** denunciate, vituperate **11** incriminate **12** anathematize

de novo
4 anew, over **5** again, newly **6** afresh **8** once more **9** over again **11** from scratch

dense
4 dull, dumb **5** close, heavy, solid, thick, tight **6** obtuse, opaque, stupid **7** compact, crammed, crowded, doltish, serried **9** fatheaded, jam-packed **10** numskulled **11** blockheaded, numbskulled, thickheaded **12** impenetrable

dent
4 bash, ding, flaw, nick **5** tooth **6** dimple, hollow **10** depression, impression
producer: 4 hail

dental addition
5 inlay, plate **6** braces, bridge **7** denture, filling, implant **8** dentures

denticulate
6 ridged **7** dentate, notched, serrate, serried, toothed **8** saw-edged, sawtooth, serrated **10** saw-toothed

dentin
6 enamel

dentine
5 ivory

denude
4 bare **5** strip **6** divest **7** disrobe, uncover, undress **8** unclothe

denunciate
see **denounce**

deny
5 cross, rebut **6** disown, forbid, negate, refuse, refute, reject, renege **7** disavow, gainsay **8** abnegate, disallow, disclaim, forswear, renounce, traverse, withhold **9** disaffirm, repudiate **10** contradict, contravene

depart
3 die **4** exit, flee, pass, quit **5** leave, scram, split **6** begone, decamp, demise, desert, escape, expire, go away, move on, pass on, perish, skidoo **7** decease, deviate, go forth, move out, pull out, skiddoo, take off, vamoose **8** pass away, shove off, slip away, withdraw **9** skedaddle, take leave

departing
6 egress, exodus **7** good-bye **8** farewell **9** desertion **11** leave-taking, valedictory

department
5 arena **6** branch, domain, sphere **7** section **8** category, division, province **9** bailiwick, territory **11** subdivision

departure
4 exit **5** adieu, break, congé, going **6** egress, exodus, flight **7** leaving **8** farewell **9** deviation, diversion **10** aberration, decampment, deflection, divergence, embarkment, setting-out, withdrawal **11** embarkation, leave-taking
of a ship: 6 sortie
point: 7 outport

dependable
4 sure, true **5** loyal, solid, tried **6** secure, steady, trusty **7** certain, staunch **8** accurate, constant, faithful, reliable, surefire **9** authentic, steadfast, unfailing **11** responsible, trustworthy **12** tried and true **13** authoritative
Scottish: 6 sicker

dependence
4 need **5** faith, habit, stock, trust **8** reliance **9** addiction **11** contingency, habituation

dependent
5 child **6** minion, vassal **7** reliant, relying **9** secondary **10** contingent, equivalent **11** conditional, subordinate

depend on
5 bet on, trust **6** bank on, hang on, look to, rely on, turn on **7** build on, count on, hinge on, stand on, swear by

depict
4 draw, etch, limn, show **5** image, paint **6** relate, render, sketch **7** express, picture, portray **8** describe **9** delineate, represent **10** illustrate

depiction
5 image **6** sketch **7** drawing, picture **9** portrayal, rendering **11** delineation, portraiture, presentment **12** illustration, presentation

deplete
3 sap **4** milk **5** bleed, drain, eat up, empty, leech, use up **6** expend, lessen, reduce **7** consume, draw off, exhaust **8** decrease, diminish, draw down **9** undermine **10** run through

depleted
4 beat **5** all in, spent **6** bushed, pooped, sapped, used up **7** drained, reduced, run-down, worn-out **8** consumed, expended, fatigued **9** enervated, exhausted, knackered, washed-out

deplorable
5 awful **6** rotten, woeful **8** dreadful, god-awful,

grievous, terrible, wretched **9** execrable, miserable, sickening **10** calamitous, disastrous, lamentable **11** distressing, intolerable **12** contemptible, disreputable, heartrending **13** heartbreaking, reprehensible

deplore
3 rue **5** abhor, mourn **6** bemoan, bewail, grieve, lament, regret **7** condemn **8** denounce, object to **9** deprecate **10** disapprove

deploy
3 use **5** array **6** muster, unfold **7** arrange, display, dispose, marshal, utilize **8** position

____ de plume
3 nom

depone
5 state, swear **6** affirm, assert, attest **7** certify, confirm, declare, testify, warrant **11** corroborate **12** authenticate

deport
3 act **4** bear **5** carry, exile, expel **6** acquit, banish, behave, demean **7** conduct **8** displace, relegate **10** expatriate

deportee
5 exile **8** expellee

deportment
3 air, set **4** mien, port **6** aspect, manner **7** address, bearing, conduct, manners **8** behavior, carriage, demeanor, presence

depose
4 aver, avow, oust **5** state, swear **6** affirm, assert, avouch, remove, topple, unmake **7** declare, profess, testify, uncrown **8** dethrone, displace, throw out, unthrone **9** overthrow

deposit
3 lay **4** bank, drop, dump, fund, lees, pawn, save, stow **5** cache, chest, dregs, place, put by, stash, store **6** settle **7** consign, grounds, lay away **8** put aside, security, sediment, sock away **9** settlings **11** precipitate **13** precipitation
alluvial: **5** delta
black: **4** soot
calcium carbonate: **10** stalactite, stalagmite
containing gold: **6** placer
eggs: **5** spawn
geologic: **7** horizon
glacial: **4** till **5** drift, esker **7** moraine
loam: **5** loess
mineral: **4** lode **10** concretion
muddy: **6** sludge
sand: **4** bank **5** beach
sedimentary: **4** silt
skeletal: **5** coral
stream: **4** tufa **8** alluvium, sediment
tooth: **6** tartar

deposition
6 avowal **7** ousting, placing **9** affidavit, dismissal, testimony **10** testifying **11** attestation, declaration

depository
4 bank, dump, safe **5** attic, cache, depot, store, vault **7** archive, arsenal **8** magazine **9** warehouse **10** storehouse
for bones: **7** ossuary

depot
4 dump **5** cache, store **6** armory, garage **7** arsenal, station **8** magazine, terminal, terminus **9** warehouse **10** depository, repository, storehouse **12** station house

deprave
4 warp **6** debase **7** corrupt, debauch, pervert, vitiate **9** brutalize **10** bastardize, bestialize, demoralize

depraved
3 bad, low **4** base, evil **6** rotten, wanton, warped, wicked **7** bestial, corrupt, debased, immoral, twisted, vicious **8** degraded, perverse, vitiated **9** corrupted, debauched, miscreant, nefarious, perverted **10** degenerate

depravity
3 sin **4** vice **8** baseness, iniquity **9** abasement, decadence, turpitude **10** corruption, debasement, debauchery, degeneracy, immorality, perversion

deprecate
7 frown on, put down **8** belittle, derogate, disfavor, object to, play down, pooh-pooh **9** disparage **10** disapprove **12** disapprove of

depreciate
4 drop, fall **5** abate, decry, erode, lower **6** lessen, reduce, slight **7** cheapen, devalue, put down **8** belittle, decrease, derogate, diminish, discount, mark down, write off **9** devaluate, disparage, downgrade, underrate **10** devalorize, undervalue **11** detract from

depreciation
8 discount **11** denigration **12** belittlement **13** disparagement

depreciative
9 slighting **10** derogatory, detracting, pejorative **11** disparaging

depredate
4 sack **5** waste **6** ravage **7** despoil, pillage, plunder **8** desolate, lay waste, prey upon, spoliate **9** desecrate, devastate, vandalize

depredation
4 sack **5** havoc **7** pillage, plunder, sacking **8** ravaging **9** marauding, ruination **10** spoliation **11** desecration, destruction, devastation **12** despoliation

depredator
6 looter, raider, vandal **7** forager, spoiler **8** marauder **9** plunderer **10** freebooter

depress
4 damp, dent **5** daunt, lower **6** dampen, deject, sadden **7** trouble **8** dispirit **9** disparage, weigh down **10** discourage, dishearten

depressed
3 low, sad **4** blue, dour, down, glum, sunk **6** broody, gloomy, glumpy, lonely, morose, somber, woeful **7** forlorn, joyless **8** cast down, dejected, desolate, downcast **9** bummed out, flattened, heartsick, miserable, woebegone **10** dispirited, lugubrious, melancholy, spiritless **11** crestfallen, downhearted, melancholic **12** disconsolate

depressing
3 sad **5** bleak **6** dismal, dreary, gloomy, somber, sombre **7** joyless **8** desolate, funereal, mournful **9** cheerless, saddening **10** melancholy, oppressive **11** melancholic **13** disheartening

depression
3 dip, low, pit, sag **4** bust, drop, funk, glen, hole, sink, vale **5** basin, blues, dolor, dumps, ennui, gloom, scoop, slump **6** cavity, crater, hollow, pocket, valley **7** cyclone, decline, sadness, sinkage **8** downturn, sinkhole **9** concavity, dejection **10** desolation, melancholy **11** melancholia, unhappiness
anatomical: **5** fossa, fovea **6** foveae (plural)
geographic: **7** Qattara
in ridge: **3** col
in snow: **8** sitzmark
small: **4** dent **6** dimple

depressive
4 blue, dour, glum **6** morose, woeful **7** doleful **8** downbeat, downcast, mournful **9** miserable, woebegone **10** despondent, melancholy **11** low-spirited

deprivation
4 lack, loss **6** denial **7** forfeit, removal **10** forfeiture **11** bereavement, divestiture **13** dispossession

deprive
3 rob **5** strip **6** divest **8** disseise, disseize **10** disinherit, dispossess
of brilliancy: **4** dull **6** deaden
of courage: **7** unnerve
of sensation: **6** benumb

depth
4 base, drop, gulf **5** abyss, chasm, gorge **7** lowness **10** profundity
charge: **6** ash can
measure: **6** fathom
of water: **5** draft **7** draught

depthless
7 cursory, shallow, sketchy **10** uncritical **11** superficial

Dept. of ___
5 Labor, State **6** Energy **7** Defense, Justice **8** Commerce, Interior, Treasury **9** Education **11** Agriculture

deputize
4 name **6** assign **7** appoint, empower, warrant **8** delegate **9** authorize, designate **10** commission

deputy
4 aide **5** agent, proxy **6** backup, factor **8** delegate, sidekick **9** assistant, catchpole, surrogate

derange
5 craze, upset **6** madden, mess up **7** confuse, perturb, unhinge **8** confound, disarray, disorder, distract, unsettle **9** interrupt, unbalance **10** discompose **11** disorganize

deranged
3 mad **4** loco **5** crazy, wacko **6** crazed, insane, maniac **7** berserk, bonkers, cracked, haywire, lunatic, unsound **8** demented, maniacal, unhinged **9** disturbed **10** disordered, flipped out, unbalanced

derangement
5 chaos, mania **6** lunacy, muddle **7** madness **8** delirium, dementia, disorder, hysteria, insanity **9** confusion, psychosis, unbalance **11** distraction, disturbance, psychopathy

derby
3 hat **4** race **6** bowler **7** contest **9** horse race

derelict
3 bum **4** hobo, lorn **5** tramp **6** remiss, shabby **7** drifter, outcast, run-down, uncouth, vagrant **8** careless, deserted, vagabond **9** abandoned, neglected, negligent **10** neglectful **11** dilapidated **12** disregardful, undependable **13** irresponsible

dereliction
5 fault **7** default, failure, neglect **9** deviation, disregard, oversight **10** negligence **11** abandonment, delinquency, shortcoming

deride
3 rag, rap **4** bait, gibe, jeer, jibe, lout, mock, quiz, razz, twit **5** fleer, rally, scoff, scout, sneer, taunt **6** dump on, insult **7** catcall **8** belittle, ridicule **9** disparage

de rigueur
5 right **6** au fait, decent, proper **7** correct, genteel **8** becoming, decorous, required **9** essential, mandatory, requisite **10** compulsory, obligatory, prescribed **11** comme il faut

derision
5 abuse, scorn **7** disdain, mockery, ribbing **8** contempt, raillery, ridicule, scoffing **9** contumely, invective

derisive
5 snide **7** abusive, jeering, mocking **8** sardonic, scoffing, scornful, taunting **9** insulting, sarcastic **10** disdainful **12** contemptuous

derivable
7 a priori **9** deducible, deductive, traceable **10** obtainable **11** extractable **12** attributable, determinable

derivation
4 root **6** origin, source **7** descent **8** ancestry **9** etymology **10** provenance, wellspring **11** origination, provenience

derivative
5 banal **7** spin-off **8** acquired, borrowed, offshoot **9** by-product, imitative, outgrowth, secondary **10** descendant, unoriginal

derive
3 get **4** draw, flow, rise, stem, take **5** adapt, arise, educe, infer, issue, trace **6** deduce, deduct, evolve, gather, obtain **7** descend, emanate, extract, proceed, work out **8** arrive at, conclude **9** formulate, originate

dernier cri
3 fad **4** chic, rage **5** craze, vogue **8** last word

derogate
5 decry **6** berate, dump on, insult **7** put down **8** bad-mouth, belittle, diminish, minimize, write off **9** disparage, dispraise **10** depreciate **11** detract from

derogatory
5 snide **8** decrying, scornful, spiteful **9** degrading, demeaning, maligning, slighting **10** belittling, detracting, disdainful, pejorative **11** disparaging **12** contumelious, depreciative

derrick
5 crane, davit, hoist

derriere
3 bum **4** beam, butt, rear, rump, seat, tail, tush **5** fanny **6** behind, bottom **7** rear end **8** backside, buttocks **9** posterior

derring-do
4 guts **5** nerve, pluck, spunk, valor **6** daring, mettle **7** bravado, bravery, bravura, courage **8** boldness **12** fearlessness **13** dauntlessness

dervish
4 monk, Sufi **9** mendicant
in Arabian Nights: **4** Agib
practice: **8** whirling
wandering: **5** fakir **8** calender

descant
4 sing **6** melody, treble **7** discuss, melisma, melodia, oration, soprano **9** discourse, expatiate **12** counterpoint

Descartes, René
axiom: **13** cogito ergo sum

descend
4 dive, drop, fall, pass, sink **5** slide, stoop, swoop **6** alight, go down, plunge, worsen **7** decline **8** come down, dismount **9** originate **10** degenerate, retrograde
by rope: **6** rappel

descendant
4 heir **5** issue, scion **7** progeny, spin-off **8** offshoot, relative **9** by-product, offspring, outgrowth **10** derivative

descendants
4 seed **5** brood, heirs, issue, spawn **6** litter **7** progeny **8** children **9** offspring, posterity **11** progeniture

descent
3 dip **4** drop, fall **5** birth, blood, slide, slope **6** origin, plunge, tumble **7** decline, drop-off, incline, lineage, sinkage **8** ancestry, comedown, gradient, pedigree **9** declivity, downgrade **10** derivation, devolution, extraction
airplane: **8** approach
parachute: **4** jump **7** bailout

describe
4 etch, limn **6** depict, recite, relate, render, report **7** explain, express, mark out, narrate, outline, picture, portray, recount **9** delineate, represent **10** illustrate **12** characterize

description
3 ilk **4** kind, sort, type **6** nature, report **7** account, picture, species **9** character, depiction, narrative, portrayal **10** recounting

descry
3 see **4** espy, spot **6** behold, detect, glimpse, spy out, turn up **7** discern, find out, hit upon **8** discover, meet with, perceive **9** encounter, recognize **12** catch sight of

Desdemona
father: **9** Brabantio
husband: **7** Othello
slanderer: **4** Iago
slayer: **7** Othello

desecrate
4 sack **5** stain, sully, waste **6** befoul, debase, defile, ravage **7** corrupt, degrade, despoil, pillage, pollute, profane, violate **8** spoliate **9** depredate, devastate, vandalize

desecration
5 abuse **7** impiety **9** blasphemy, sacrilege **10** debasement, defilement, spoliation **11** profanation **12** despoliation

desensitize
4 dull, numb **5** blunt **6** benumb, dampen, deaden, freeze, sedate **11** anesthetize

desert
4 flee, quit **5** leave, waste **6** barren, betray, decamp, defect, escape, go AWOL, maroon,

strand **7** abandon, abscond, badland, forsake **8** renounce **9** repudiate, wasteland **10** apostatize, wilderness **12** tergiversate
African: **5** Namib **6** Libyan, Nubian, Sahara **7** Arabian **8** Kalahari
Arizona: **7** Painted
Asian: **4** Gobi, Thar **6** Syrian **7** Kara-Kum **8** Kyzyl Kum, Qizilkum **10** Great Sandy
Australian: **6** Gibson, Tanami **7** Simpson
basin bottom: **5** playa
beast: **5** camel **9** dromedary
California: **6** Mohave, Mojave
Chilean: **7** Atacama
clay: **5** adobe
dweller: **4** bedu **5** nomad **6** Beduin, Berber, Nubian **7** bedouin **8** Maghrebi, Maghribi
Egyptian: **7** Arabian
fertile area: **5** oases (plural), oasis
garb: **3** aba **7** burnous **8** burnoose
hallucination: **6** mirage
Israeli: **5** Negev
Mexican: **7** Sonoran
plant: **5** agave, cacti (plural), yucca **6** cactus, maguey
region: **3** erg
Saudi Arabia: **7** Al-Nafud, An Nafud **10** Rub Al-Khali
travel group: **7** caravan
wind: **7** sirocco **8** scirocco

deserted
4 bare, lorn **6** barren, vacant **8** derelict, desolate, forsaken, solitary **9** abandoned, neglected **11** uninhabited

deserter
3 rat **4** AWOL **6** bolter **7** runaway **8** apostate, defector, fugitive, renegade, runagate, turncoat

desertion
7 perfidy **8** apostasy **9** defection, forsaking **11** abandonment, dereliction

desertlike
3 dry **4** arid, sere **6** rainless **7** parched

deserts
3 due **6** reward **8** requital **9** reckoning **10** recompense **11** comeuppance

deserve
3 win **4** earn, gain, rate **5** merit **6** demand **7** justify, warrant

deserved
3 apt, due **4** just **5** right **7** fitting, merited **8** rightful, suitable **9** befitting **11** appropriate

deserving
3 due **6** worthy **8** laudable **9** admirable, estimable **10** creditable **11** commendable, meritorious, thankworthy **12** praiseworthy

desex
4 geld, spay **5** unman **6** neuter

desiccate
3 dry **4** bake **5** dry up, parch, wizen **6** wither **7** shrivel **9** dehydrate **10** devitalize

desiccated
3 dry **4** arid, sere **7** parched, wizened

desiderate
4 want, wish **5** covet, crave **6** desire **7** long for, wish for **8** yearn for

design
3 aim **4** cast, draw, form, mean, mind, plan, plot, will **5** chart, draft, frame, model, motif **6** create, device, devise, figure, intend, intent, invent, lay out, makeup, map out, motive, scheme, set out, sketch, tailor **7** arrange, diagram, drawing, execute, fashion, meaning, outline, pattern, prepare, project, propose, tracing **8** contrive, creation, game plan, intrigue, strategy, thinking **9** blueprint, construct, delineate, direction, formation, intention, invention **10** decoration, figuration **11** arrangement, composition **12** architecture, construction
book: **8** vignette
carpet: **3** gul **9** medallion
incised: **8** intaglio
Indonesian: **5** batik
inlaid: **6** mosaic
intricate: **9** arabesque
of squares: **5** check
openwork: **8** filigree
perforated: **7** stencil
raised: **8** repoussé
skin: **6** tattoo
textile: **8** polka dot
velvety: **8** flocking

designate
3 dub, tap **4** call, name, pick, term **5** allot, elect, label, style, title **6** assign, choose, denote, depute, select **7** appoint, declare, earmark, reserve, signify, specify **8** allocate, christen, delegate, identify, set aside, stand for **9** apportion, stipulate **10** decide upon **11** appropriate **12** characterize

designation
4 name, sign **5** class, nomen, style, title **6** naming **8** cognomen, monicker **11** appellation

designed
7 devised, planned **8** intended, resolved **9** contrived, patterned **10** considered, deliberate, determined, thought-out **12** premeditated

designedly
9 expressly, knowingly, on purpose, purposely, willfully, wittingly **11** consciously, purposively **12** deliberately **13** intentionally

designer
see **fashion designer, furniture designer**

desirable
8 enviable, fetching 9 advisable, agreeable, preferred 10 attractive, beneficial 12 advantageous

desire
3 aim, yen 4 envy, eros, itch, lust, need, urge, want, wish 5 covet, crave, fancy, go for, greed, jones 6 hunger, libido, pining, thirst 7 avarice, craving, long for, longing, passion 8 appetite, cupidity, petition, yearn for, yearning 9 eroticism, hankering, prurience, pruriency 10 aphrodisia, attraction, preference 11 inclination, lustfulness 13 concupiscence, lickerishness

desired
6 wanted 8 hoped-for 9 preferred, requested

desirous
4 avid 6 greedy 7 athirst, craving, envious, longing, wishful, wishing 8 covetous, grasping 10 solicitous

desist
4 halt, quit, stop 5 cease, yield 7 forbear, hold off, refrain 8 knock off, leave off, surcease 11 discontinue

desistance
3 end 4 halt, stop 5 cease, close 6 ending, finish, period 8 stoppage, stopping 9 cessation 10 conclusion 11 termination

desk
5 booth, stand, table 7 counter, lectern, rolltop 8 lapboard 9 secretary 10 escritoire
adjunct: 8 inkstand, standish
item: 3 pad 7 blotter, inkwell
library: 6 carrel

Desmond of South Africa
4 Tutu

desolate
4 bare, lorn, sack 5 alone, bleak, drear, stark, waste 6 barren, devoid, dismal, dreary, gloomy, ravage 7 despoil, forlorn, joyless, pillage, plunder 8 dejected, derelict, deserted, desolate, downcast, forsaken, lay waste, lifeless, lonesome, solitary, spoliate 9 abandoned, cheerless, depredate, desecrate, destitute, devastate, sorrowful 10 despondent 11 dilapidated 12 inconsolable 13 disheartening

desolation
3 woe 4 ruin 5 gloom, grief, waste 6 misery, sorrow 7 anguish, despair, sadness 8 bareness 9 bleakness, dejection, wasteland 10 loneliness 11 abandonment, devastation 12 wretchedness

despair
6 give up 8 lose hope

despairing
7 anxious, doleful, forlorn 8 dejected, desolate, hopeless, wretched 9 depressed 10 despondent 11 downhearted 12 disconsolate 13 brokenhearted

desperado
6 bandit, gunman, outlaw 7 bandito, brigand, convict, ruffian 8 criminal 9 cutthroat 10 gunslinger, highwayman, lawbreaker

desperate
4 bold, dire, rash 5 acute, risky 6 daring, futile 7 crucial, forlorn, frantic, useless, violent 8 critical, headlong, hopeless, reckless 9 foolhardy, impetuous 10 despondent, frustrated, outrageous

Desperate Housewives
actress: 5 Cross (Marcia) 7 Hatcher (Teri), Huffman (Felicity) 8 Longoria (Eva), Sheridan (Nicollette)
creator: 6 Cherry (Marc)
character: 4 Bree (Van De Kamp), Edie (Britt), Mike (Delfino) 5 Betty (Applewhite), Orson (Hodge), Susan (Mayer) 7 Lynette (Scavo) 9 Gabrielle (Solis)
narrator: 6 Strong (Brenda)
setting: 8 Fairview 12 Wisteria Lane

desperation
5 agony 7 anguish, despair 8 distress 11 distraction 12 hopelessness, wretchedness

despicable
3 low 4 base, foul, mean, vile 5 awful, gross 6 scurvy, sordid 7 beastly, hateful, ignoble, pitiful 8 pitiable, shameful, wretched 9 degrading, loathsome 10 deplorable, detestable, disgusting 11 disgraceful, ignominious 12 contemptible, disreputable 13 reprehensible

despise
4 hate, shun, snub 5 abhor, avoid, scorn, spurn 6 detest, loathe, reject 7 contemn 8 execrate 9 abominate

despised one
5 leper 6 pariah 7 outcast

despisement
4 hate 5 scorn 6 hatred, malice 7 disdain, ill will 8 aversion, contempt, loathing 9 antipathy, contumely 10 abhorrence 11 detestation

despite
12 regardless of

despiteful
4 evil, mean 5 catty 6 bitchy, horrid, malign, odious, wicked 7 baleful, baneful, hostile, vicious 8 vengeful 9 malicious, rancorous, repellent 10 despicable, malevolent

despoil
4 sack 5 waste, wreck 6 ravage 7 pillage, plunder 8 spoliate 9 depredate, desecrate, devastate, strip away, vandalize

despoiler
6 looter, sacker, vandal 7 ravager, wrecker 8 marauder, pillager 9 plunderer, spoliator 10 depredator, freebooter

despond
4 fret, mope, wilt **5** brood, droop, worry **6** give up, sorrow **8** languish **9** dejection **12** hopelessness

despondency
5 blues, dumps, gloom **6** misery, sorrow **7** anguish, despair, sadness **8** glumness **9** dejection **10** depression, melancholy **11** desperation, unhappiness **12** hopelessness

despondent
3 low, sad **4** blue, down, glum **7** doleful, forlorn **8** cast down, dejected, downcast, grieving, hopeless, mourning **9** depressed, desperate, heartsick, heartsore, sorrowful, woebegone **10** dispairing, dispirited, melancholy **11** discouraged, downhearted **12** disconsolate, disheartened

despot
4 czar, duce, tsar, tzar **5** ruler **6** tyrant **7** autarch, emperor **8** autocrat, dictator, overlord **9** oppressor, strong man

despotic
8 absolute **9** arbitrary, autarchic, imperious, tyrannous **10** autocratic, monocratic, tyrannical **11** dictatorial **12** totalitarian

despotism
7 czarism, tsarism, tyranny, tzarism **8** autarchy **9** autocracy **10** absolutism, domination **12** dictatorship

desquamate
4 pare, peel **5** scale **7** peel off **8** flake off, scale off **9** exfoliate

dessert
3 ice, pie **4** cake, flan, fool, tart **5** Betty, bombe, crepe, crisp, fruit, grunt, halva, Jell-O, melba, s'more, sweet, torte **6** afters, blintz, cookie, Danish, éclair, fondue, frappe, gâteau, gelato, halvah, hermit, junket, kuchen, mousse, pastry, sorbet, sundae, trifle **7** baklava, brownie, cannoli, cobbler, compote, cupcake, custard, gelatin, parfait, pudding, sabayon, sherbet, soufflé, spumoni, strudel, tapioca **8** ambrosia, Bismarck, clafouti, crostata, flummery, ice cream, macaroon, meringue, napoleon, pandowdy, streusel, tiramisu, turnover **9** charlotte, cream puff, fruitcake, petit four, shortcake **10** blancmange, brown Betty, cheesecake, frangipane, icebox cake, peach Melba, zabaglione **11** baked Alaska, banana split, crème brûlée, gingerbread **12** hasty pudding, zuppa inglese
French: **5** bombe **6** éclair, frappe, gâteau, mousse **7** parfait, sabayon **9** petit four **10** blancmange, frangipane
frozen: **5** bombe **7** parfait, sherbet
German: **6** kuchen **7** strudel
Italian: **7** cannoli, spumoni **8** tiramisu **10** zabaglione **12** zuppa inglese
Turkish: **5** halva **6** halvah

destination
3 aim, end, use **6** object, target **7** purpose **8** terminus **9** objective **10** appointing

destine
4 fate **6** assign, direct, intend **8** dedicate, set aside **9** designate, determine, preordain **10** foreordain **12** predetermine

destiny
3 lot **4** doom, fate **5** karma **6** design, future, kismet, Moirai **7** fortune, portion **8** prospect **9** hereafter **12** circumstance

destitute
4 bare, poor, void **5** broke, empty, needy **6** bereft, devoid, ruined **7** drained, lacking **8** bankrupt, depleted, dirt poor, divested, indigent, strapped, stripped **9** deficient, exhausted, penurious **10** bankrupted, stone-broke **11** impecunious **12** impoverished

destitution
6 penury **7** poverty **9** indigence, privation

destroy
3 axe, zap **4** doom, down, kill, nuke, raze, ruin, sack, slay, undo **5** crush, erase, quash, quell, smash, total, trash, waste, wrack, wreck **6** finish, lay low, mangle, ravage, rubble, rub out, unmake **7** abolish, atomize, despoil, expunge, nullify, pillage, shatter, wipe out **8** decimate, demolish, dispatch, dynamite, lay waste, pull down, snuff out, stamp out, tear down **9** devastate, dismantle, eradicate, extirpate, liquidate, pulverize **10** annihilate, extinguish, obliterate **11** exterminate

destroyer
4 bane, ruin **6** tin can, vandal **7** undoing, warship **8** downfall

destruction
4 loss, ruin **5** havoc **7** killing, sacking, undoing **8** downfall **9** ruination **10** extinction **11** devastation, liquidation **12** annihilation

destructive
7 baneful, harmful, ruinous **8** damaging **9** corrosive, injurious **10** shattering **11** deleterious, detrimental

desuetude
6 disuse **7** closure, neglect **11** abandonment

desultory
6 casual, chance, fitful, random, spotty **7** aimless, erratic, offhand, vagrant **8** shifting, slipshod, sporadic, wavering **9** haphazard, hit-or-miss, unplanned **10** capricious, digressive, disjointed **12** unmethodical, unsystematic

detach
4 free, part, undo, wean **5** sever **6** cut off, remove, sunder **7** disjoin, divorce, release **8** separate, uncouple, withdraw **9** disengage **10** disconnect **12** disaffiliate

detached
5 alone, aloof, apart **6** remote **7** distant, neutral, removed, severed **8** abstract, isolated, separate, unbiased **9** incurious, withdrawn **10** impersonal **11** indifferent, unconcerned, unconnected **12** uninterested **13** disinterested, dispassionate, unaccompanied

detachment
5 squad **7** divorce, rupture **8** disunion, division **9** partition **10** neutrality, separation **11** dissolution

detail
4 item, list, part **5** point **6** assign, nicety, relate, report **7** appoint, article, element, itemize, listing, minutia, specify **8** allocate, spell out **9** enumerate, stipulate **10** assignment, particular **12** circumstance **13** particularize

detailed
4 full **6** minute **8** itemized, complete, thorough **10** blow-by-blow, exhaustive, meticulous, particular **13** thoroughgoing

detain
3 nab **4** bust, curb, hold, keep, mire, snag **5** check, delay, run in **6** arrest, collar, hang up, hinder, hold up, impede, pick up, retard, slow up **7** bog down, reserve, set back **8** hold back, keep back, restrain, slow down, withhold **9** apprehend **10** buttonhole
in conversation: **10** buttonhole

detect
4 espy, find, note, spot **5** catch, dig up, hit on, scent, smell **6** descry, notice, turn up **7** discern, hit upon, uncover, unearth **8** discover, meet with **9** ascertain, encounter, ferret out, track down

detectable
6 patent **7** evident, visible **8** sensible, tangible **10** noticeable, observable **11** discernible, perceptible

detection
9 discovery **10** unearthing
system: **5** radar, sofar

detective
3 tec **4** dick, G-man **6** shamus, sleuth **7** gumshoe **8** hawkshaw, informer, sherlock **9** inspector **10** private eye **12** investigator
fictional: **3** Pym (Lucy) **4** Chan (Charlie), Drew (Nancy), Gray (Cordelia), Monk (Adrian), Moto (Mr.) **5** Banks (Alan), Bosch (Harry), Brown (Father), Dupin (Auguste), Hardy (Frank, Joe), Lecoq, Lewis (Inspector), Lupin (Arsène), McGee (Travis), Morse (Inspector), Queen (Ellery), Rebus (John), Saint, Spade (Sam), Trent (Philip), Vance (Philo), Wolfe (Nero) **6** Alleyn (Roderick), Archer (Lew), Carter (Nick), Hammer (Mike), Holmes (Sherlock), Marple (Miss Jane), McCone (Sharon), Poirot (Hercule), Wimsey (Peter) **7** Cadfael (Brother), Campion (Albert), Charles (Nick, Nora), Columbo, Maigret (Jules), Marlowe (Philip), Rawlins (Easy), Reacher (Jack) **8** Drummond (Bulldog), Lestrade (G.), Millhone (Kinsey) **9** Dalgliesh (Adam), Scarpetta (Kay), Wallander (Kurt) **10** Robicheaux (Dave), Warshawski (V. I.) **11** Father Brown
lead: **4** clue

detective-story writer
3 Poe (Edgar Allan), Tey (Josephine) **4** Carr (John Dickson), Knox (Ronald) **5** Blake (Nicholas), Block (Lawrence), Child (Lee), Cross (Amanda), Dixon (Franklin W.), Doyle (Arthur Conan), Green (Anna Katherine), Innes (Michael), James (P. D.), Keene (Carolyn), Marsh (Ngaio), Queen (Ellery), Stout (Rex) **6** Bramah (Ernest), Buchan (John), Dexter (Colin), Hansen (Joseph), McBain (Ed), Mosley (Walter), Parker (Robert), Peters (Ellis), Sayers (Dorothy L.) **7** Bentley (E. C.), Biggers (Earl Derr), Collins (Wilkie), Francis (Dick), Freeman (Austin), Gardner (Erle Stanley), Grafton (Sue), Hammett (Dashiell), Hiaasen (Carl), Hornung (E. W.), Leonard (Elmore), Rendell (Ruth), Simenon (Georges), Van Dine (S. S.), Wallace (Edgar) **8** Chandler (Raymond), Christie (Agatha), Cornwell (Patricia), Gaboriau (Emile), Marquand (John), Mortimer (John), Paretsky (Sara), Rinehart (Mary Roberts), Spillane (Mickey) **9** Allingham (Margery), Highsmith (Patricia), Hillerman (Tony), Lockridge (Frances, Richard), Macdonald (John, Ross) **10** Chesterton (Gilbert Keith)

detent
4 pawl

detention
6 arrest **7** holding **10** internment **11** confinement **12** imprisonment

deter
5 avert, block **6** divert, hamper, hinder, impede, thwart **7** forfend, inhibit, obviate, prevent, rule out, shut out, ward off **8** dissuade, preclude, restrain, stave off **9** forestall, turn aside **10** discourage

deterge
4 wash **7** cleanse, wash off

detergent
4 soap **8** cleanser

deteriorate
3 rot **4** fade, fail, flag, sink, wear **5** decay, lapse, slide, spoil **6** weaken, worsen **7** decline, regress **8** languish **9** decompose, fall apart **10** debilitate, degenerate, depreciate, go downhill, retrograde, retrogress **12** disintegrate

deterioration
4 ruin **5** decay **6** ebbing, waning **7** atrophy, decline, erosion, failing, rotting **8** decaying, spoiling **9** crumbling, decadence, downgrade **10** debasement, degeneracy **12** degeneration, dégringolade

determinant
4 gene **5** agent, basis, cause, trait **6** factor, ground, reason **7** epitope, radical **9** attribute, influence

determinate
5 fixed **6** cymose **7** limited, precise, settled **8** constant, definite **10** definitive, restricted **11** established **13** circumscribed

determination
5 drive, spunk **6** mettle **7** finding, opinion, purpose, resolve, verdict **8** decision, firmness, judgment, tenacity **9** hardihood, impulsion, intention, willpower **10** conclusion, dedication, definition, doggedness, resolution **11** decidedness, intrepidity **12** perseverance, resoluteness, stubbornness

determine
3 fix, set **4** rule **5** bound, limit, prove **6** decide, figure, ordain, settle **7** control, delimit, find out, mark out, measure, preform, unearth **8** conclude, discover, regulate **9** ascertain, demarcate, establish, preordain, resolve on **10** delimitate, foreordain, predestine, predispose

determined
3 set **4** bent **5** fixed **6** driven, intent **7** decided, settled **8** decisive, hellbent, resolute, resolved, stubborn **9** tenacious **10** persistent, purposeful, unwavering **11** established, persevering, unfaltering **12** foreordained, unhesitating

deterrent
4 snag **6** hurdle **8** handicap, holdback, obstacle **9** hindrance **10** impediment

detest
4 hate **5** abhor, spurn **6** loathe **7** despise, dislike **8** execrate **9** abominate

detestable
4 foul, vile **6** damned, horrid, odious **7** hateful, heinous **9** abhorrent, atrocious, execrable, loathsome **10** abominable, despicable **12** contemptible

detestation
4 hate **6** hatred **8** anathema, aversion, loathing **9** repulsion, revulsion **10** abhorrence, execration, repugnance

dethrone
4 oust **6** depose, topple, unseat **7** uncrown **8** displace **9** overthrow

detonate
5 blast, burst, go off, spark **6** blow up, ignite, set off **7** explode **8** touch off

detonator
3 cap **4** fuse **9** explosive **11** blasting cap

detour
5 avoid, skirt **6** bypass **8** side trip **9** diversion

detract
6 divert, lessen, reduce **8** decrease, diminish, minimize **10** depreciate

detraction
9 aspersion, maligning, traducing **10** backbiting, belittling, derogation, slandering **11** denigration, deprecation, traducement **12** backstabbing, belittlement **13** disparagement

detractive
9 maligning, slighting, traducing, vilifying **10** defamatory, derogatory, pejorative **11** denigrating, disparaging **12** depreciative, depreciatory

detriment
4 harm, loss **5** debit, minus **6** damage, injury **7** marring **8** downside, drawback **9** liability **10** impairment **12** disadvantage

detrimental
3 bad, ill **7** adverse, harmful, hurtful, nocuous **8** damaging, negative **9** injurious **10** pernicious **11** deleterious, unfavorable

___ de Triomphe
3 Arc

detritus
4 tufa, tuff **5** scree, talus **6** debris, rubble **7** remains **11** odds and ends

Detroit
county: **5** Wayne
founder: **8** Cadillac (Sieur de)
lake: **4** Erie **10** Saint Clair
sobriquet: **6** Motown **9** Motor City

de trop
5 extra, spare **7** too much, surplus **9** excessive, redundant **10** gratuitous **11** superfluous **13** supernumerary

Deucalion
father: **10** Prometheus
kingdom: **6** Phthia
mother: **7** Clymene
son: **6** Hellen
wife: **6** Pyrrha

deuce
3 tie, two **4** card, draw **5** devil **7** dickens **10** even-steven
beater: **4** trey
follower: **4** ad in **5** ad out

Deutschland über ___
5 alles

Devaki's son
7 Krishna

De Valera of Ireland
5 Eamon

devaluate
5 abase, decry, lower **6** debase, reduce, weaken **7** cheapen, degrade **8** mark down, write off **9** undermine, underrate, write down **10** depreciate

devaluation
7 decline **10** debasement, declension **11** declination

devalue
see **depreciate**

devastate
4 ruin, sack **5** waste **6** ravage **7** despoil, pillage, plunder **8** demolish, desolate, lay waste, overcome, spoliate **9** depredate, desecrate, overpower, overwhelm

devastation
4 loss, ruin **5** havoc, waste **6** ravage **7** pillage, plunder **9** ruination **10** demolition, desolation, spoliation **11** depredation

develop
3 age **4** form, grow **5** ripen **6** attain, emerge, evolve, expand, grow up, happen, mature, mellow, open up, thrive, unfold **7** advance, burgeon, enlarge, promote **8** flourish **9** actualize, establish, transpire **11** come to light, materialize

development
5 phase **6** growth, result, spread **7** advance, buildup, outcome **8** ontogeny, progress, ripening **9** evolution, expansion, flowering, phylogeny, unfolding **10** maturation **11** elaboration, progression
of life: **10** biogenesis

Devi
7 goddess
consort: **5** Shiva
father: **7** Himavat
name: **3** Uma **4** Kali **5** Durga, Gauri **6** Chandi **7** Parvati

deviant
4 bent **5** kinky, outré, queer **6** off-key **7** twisted, wayward **8** aberrant, abnormal, atypical, perverse **9** anomalous, different, divergent, eccentric, irregular, unnatural **11** heteroclite

deviate
3 err, yaw **4** turn, vary, veer **5** sheer, stray **6** depart, detour, swerve, wander **7** digress, diverge **8** aberrant **9** eccentric, turn aside

deviation
3 yaw **4** bend, tack, turn **5** error, shift **6** change **7** anomaly, turning, veering **8** variance **9** departure, diversion **10** aberration, alteration, deflection, divergence

device
4 ploy, tool **5** feint, gizmo, means, motif, motto, shift, thing, trick **6** dingus, doodad, emblem, figure, gadget, gambit, hickey, jigger, medium, motive, symbol, widget **7** gimmick, machine, utensil, whatnot, whatsit **8** artifice, creation, insignia **9** apparatus, appliance, doohickey, expedient, implement, invention, makeshift, mechanism, thingummy **10** instrument **11** contraption, contrivance, inclination, thingamabob, thingamajig, thingumajig
automatic: **5** servo
binding: **5** clamp
fastening: **6** zipper
grasping: **4** tong
heating: **8** radiator
hoisting: **5** crane, lewis **8** windlass
holding: **4** vise **5** clamp
paging: **6** beeper
suction: **4** pump

____ de vie
3 eau

devil
3 imp **5** beast, cloot, demon, fiend, rogue, Satan, scamp **6** Belial, diablo, dybbuk, rascal, spirit **7** Clootie, dickens, Lucifer, Old Nick, serpent, tempter, villain **8** Apollyon, Mephisto, scalawag, succubus **9** archfiend, Beelzebub, cacodemon, scoundrel, skeezicks **10** blackguard, Old Scratch **11** rapscallion

devilfish
3 ray **5** manta **7** octopus **8** manta ray **10** cephalopod

devilish
3 bad **4** evil **6** cursed, wicked **7** demonic, hellish, roguish, satanic **8** accursed, damnable, diabolic, fiendish, infernal, sinister **9** nefarious **10** diabolical, iniquitous, villainous **11** mischievous

devil-may-care
4 bold, rash, wild **6** blithe, daring, rakish, sporty **7** raffish **8** rakehell, reckless **9** easygoing, foolhardy

devilry
7 knavery, roguery, sorcery, waggery **8** mischief **9** diablerie **10** wickedness, witchcraft **11** roguishness, waggishness **12** sportiveness

devious
3 sly **4** foxy, wily **6** artful, crafty, errant, erring, roving, shifty, sneaky, tricky **7** bending, crooked, cunning, curving, erratic, winding **8** aberrant, guileful, indirect, scheming, sneaking, twisting **9** deceptive, underhand, wandering **10** roundabout **11** out-of-the-way, underhanded

devise
4 form, plan, plot, will **5** chart, forge, frame, shape **6** cook up, create, design, invent, legacy, legate, scheme **7** arrange, bequest, concoct, connive, dope out, dream up, hatch up, project **8** bequeath, property **9** determine, formulate **11** inheritance

devitalize
3 sap **5** drain **6** deaden, weaken **7** exhaust **8** enfeeble, etiolate **9** desiccate **10** eviscerate

devoid of
7 lacking, wanting **8** free from

devoir
3 job **4** duty, task **5** chore, stint **6** charge **9** committal **10** assignment, commitment, obligation

devolution
5 decay **7** decline, passing **8** receding, transfer **9** conferral, decadence, recession, surrender **10** conveyance, declension, degeneracy, regression, relegation, transferal **11** degradation, transferral **12** degeneration, dégringolade, retrograding, transference **13** retrogression

devolve
4 give, pass **6** pass on **8** hand down, hand over, relegate, transfer **10** degenerate

devote
5 apply **6** commit, direct, donate, hallow **7** reserve **8** dedicate, give over, sanctify **9** confirm in, habituate **10** consecrate

devoted
4 dear, fond, true **5** loyal **6** ardent, caring, doting, fervid, loving **7** dutiful, fervent, zealous **8** constant, faithful **9** dedicated **10** thoughtful **12** affectionate
religiously: 6 oblate

devotee
3 fan, nut **4** buff **5** hound, lover **6** addict, votary, zealot **7** admirer, amateur, fanatic, fancier, habitué **8** follower **9** supporter **10** aficionado, enthusiast

devotion
4 love, zeal **5** ardor, piety **6** fealty, fervor, prayer, Rosary **7** loyalty, passion **8** fidelity, fondness **9** adherence, adoration, reverence **10** allegiance, attachment, dedication, enthusiasm **12** faithfulness

devour
3 eat **5** eat up, enjoy, scarf, scoff **6** absorb, feed on, gobble, inhale **7** consume, destroy, feast on, pillage **8** prey upon, wolf down **9** delight in, feast upon, polish off, scarf down, scoff down, swallow up

devouring
4 avid **6** greedy **8** esurient, ravenous **9** voracious **10** gluttonous

devout
4 holy **5** godly, loyal, pious **6** ardent **7** earnest, fervent, serious, sincere, zealous **8** faithful, reverent **9** pietistic, prayerful, religious

devoutness
4 zeal **5** ardor, piety **9** reverence **10** commitment

dew
5 sweat, tears **8** moisture **11** precipitate **12** perspiration **13** precipitation

dewy
3 wet **4** damp, pure **5** fresh, moist, naive **7** artless, natural **8** innocent, wide-eyed **9** credulous, guileless, ingenuous, unworldly

dexter
5 right

dexterity
4 ease **5** craft, grace, skill **7** ability, aptness, know-how, prowess, sleight **8** deftness, facility **9** adeptness, expertise, readiness **10** adroitness, nimbleness, smoothness **12** skillfulness

dexterous
3 apt **4** able, deft **5** adept, agile, handy **6** adroit, artful, facile, nimble **7** skilled **8** masterly, skillful **10** proficient

____ Dhabi
3 Abu

diablerie
4 evil **6** hoodoo **7** devilry, hexerei, roguery, sorcery, waggery **8** deviltry, iniquity, mischief, satanism **9** devilment **10** black magic, wickedness, witchcraft, wrongdoing

diabolical
4 evil **5** awful **6** impish, wicked **7** beastly, demonic, heinous, hellish, puckish, roguish, satanic **8** demoniac, devilish, dreadful, fiendish, god-awful, hellborn, infernal, rascally, sinister **9** execrable, malicious, monstrous, nefarious **10** degenerate, demoniacal, horrendous, iniquitous, scandalous, villainous **11** mischievous

diabolism
see **diablerie**

diacritic
5 acute, breve, grave, haček, tilde **6** accent, macron, umlaut **7** cedilla **8** dieresis **9** diaeresis **10** circumflex
Arabic: 5 hamza **6** hamzah

diadem
5 crown, tiara **6** wreath **7** chaplet, coronal, coronet **8** headband

diagnose
8 identify, pinpoint **9** determine, interpret, recognize **11** distinguish

diagnostic
8 analytic **10** analytical, expository, indicating, indicative **11** explanatory, exploratory **12** interpretive

diagonal
4 bias **5** bevel **6** biased **7** beveled, oblique, slanted **8** inclined, slanting **9** inclining, slantways, slantwise

diagonally
5 askew **7** athwart **9** slantways, slantwise **10** cornerwise **11** catercorner, kitty-corner

diagram
3 map **5** chart, graph **6** design, layout, sketch **7** drawing, isotype **9** represent
type: 4 Venn

dial
4 call, knob, tune, turn **5** phone **6** rotate

dialect
5 argot, idiom, koine, lingo **6** creole, jargon, patois, patter, pidgin, speech, tongue **8** language, localism **10** vernacular **11** regionalism, terminology **13** provincialism
Georgia: 6 Gullah
London: 7 cockney

dialectic
5 logic **6** debate **8** dialogue, forensic **9** reasoning **10** discussion **11** disputation **13** argumentation

dialogue
4 chat, talk **6** confab, confer, debate, parley, script **8** colloquy, converse, exchange **10** discussion **12** conversation **13** confabulation

diameter
4 bore **5** chord, width **7** breadth, caliber **8** bisector, wideness **9** broadness

diametric
7 counter, opposed **8** contrary, converse, opposite **12** antithetical **13** contradictory

diamond
3 gem **5** field, stone **7** lozenge, rhombus
cover: 4 tarp
element: 6 carbon
famous: 4 Hope, Pitt **5** Sancy **6** Orloff, Regent **8** Braganza, Cullinan, Kohinoor **9** Excelsior **10** Great Mogul
holder: 3 dop
inferior: 4 bort
measure: 5 carat
mistake: 5 error
official: 3 ump **6** umpire
oval: 9 briolette
pattern: 6 argyle
state: 8 Delaware
surface: 5 facet

Diana
see **Artemis**

diapason
4 peal, stop **5** range, scale, scope **7** compass, measure **8** spectrum **10** tuning fork

diaper
5 nappy **7** pattern **8** ornament

diaphanous
5 filmy, gauzy, sheer, vague **6** flimsy **8** ethereal, gossamer **11** transparent **13** insubstantial

diaphragm
6 septum **8** membrane **9** partition

diarist
3 Nin (Anaïs) **4** Gide (André), Mann (Thomas) **5** Frank (Anne), Inman (Arthur Crew), Jones (Bridget), Kahlo (Frida), Pepys (Samuel), Plath (Sylvia), Rorem (Ned), Scott (Walter), Swift (Jonathan), Woolf (Virginia) **6** Burney (Fanny), Evelyn (John) **7** Boswell (James), Thoreau (Henry David) **8** Robinson (Henry Crabb) **9** Lindbergh (Anne Morrow) **10** chronicler, journalist

diary
3 log **6** record **7** daybook, diurnal, journal, logbook **8** notebook, register **9** chronicle

diastase
6 enzyme **8** catalyst, reactant

diatribe
4 rant, rave **6** screed, tirade **7** polemic **8** harangue, jeremiad **9** criticism, philippic **11** castigation **12** denunciation

dibs
4 gelt **5** claim, dough, money, title **6** rights **11** reservation

dice
4 cast, cube **5** bones, cubes, ivory, mince **11** devil's-bones
game: 5 craps
losing throw: 7 missout
singular: 3 die
throw: 7 boxcars **9** snake eyes

dicer
5 loser **6** risker **7** gambler

dicey
4 iffy **5** risky **6** chancy, tricky **8** ticklish **9** uncertain, whimsical **10** precarious **11** problematic, speculative **13** unpredictable

dichotomize
5 halve **7** dissect **8** hemisect **9** bifurcate

dichotomous
5 split **6** forked **7** pronged **9** bifurcate **10** bifurcated

dichotomy
7 forking **8** division **9** bisection, branching, splitting **11** bifurcation **13** contradiction

Dickens, Charles
birthplace: 10 Portsmouth
captain: 6 Cuttle
character: 3 Ada (Clare), Pip, Tim **4** Dick (Mr.), Dora, Gamp (Sairey), Heep (Uriah), Nell **5** Drood (Edwin), Emily, Fagin, Lucie (Manette), Sikes (Bill), Uriah (Heep) **6** Barkis, Bumble (Mr.), Carton (Sydney), Cuttle (Capt.), Darnay (Charles), Dombey (Fanny, Florence, Paul), Dorrit (Amy), Oliver (Twist) **7** Barnaby (Rudge), Dedlock (Lady), Defarge, Gargery (Joe), Manette (Dr.), Scrooge (Ebenezer), Tiny Tim **8** Cratchit (Bob), Havisham (Miss), Jarndyce (John), Magwitch (Abel), Micawber (Mr.), Nickleby (Nicholas), Peggotty (Clara, Daniel, Ham), Pickwick (Mr.) **9** Bill Sikes, Gradgrind (Mr.), Murdstone (Mr.), Pecksniff (Mr.), Uriah Heep **10** Chuzzlewit (Anthony, Jonas, Martin), Steerforth **11** Copperfield (David)

hero: **6** Carton (Sydney)
nationality: **7** English
pen name: **3** Boz
villain: **5** Fagin
work: **9** Hard Times **10** Bleak House **11** Oliver Twist **12** Barnaby Rudge, Dombey and Son, Little Dorrit **14** Christmas Carol (A), Pickwick Papers (The) **15** Our Mutual Friend, Tale of Two Cities (A) **16** David Copperfield, Martin Chuzzlewit, Nicholas Nickleby **17** Great Expectations

dicker
4 deal, swap **5** argue, trade **6** barter, haggle, higgle, palter **7** bargain, chaffer **8** contract, huckster **9** negotiate

dickey
10 shirtfront

Dickey novel
11 Deliverance

dictate
3 set **4** lead, rule, word **5** edict, order, tenet **6** behest, decree, direct, enjoin, govern, impose, ordain, recite **7** bidding, command, control, lay down, mandate, read off, summons **9** determine, direction, directive, prescribe, principle, pronounce, verbalize **10** injunction **12** prescription

dictative
5 bossy **8** despotic, dogmatic **9** imperious **10** peremptory **11** doctrinaire, magisterial **13** authoritarian

dictator
4 czar, duce, tsar, tzar **6** caesar, despot, tyrant **8** autocrat, martinet **9** oppressor, strongman
Chinese: **3** Mao **9** Mao Zedong **10** Mao Tsetung
German: **6** Hitler (Adolf)
Italian: **9** Mussolini (Benito)
military: **8** caudillo
Russian: **5** Lenin (Vladimir) **6** Stalin (Joseph)
Spanish: **6** Franco (Francisco)
Ugandan: **4** Amin (Idi)

dictatorial
5 bossy **8** despotic, dogmatic **9** arbitrary, imperious, masterful **10** autocratic, iron-handed, peremptory, tyrannical **11** doctrinaire, domineering, overbearing **12** totalitarian **13** authoritarian

dictatorship
7 tyranny **9** autocracy, Caesarism, despotism, supremacy **10** absolutism

diction
6 phrase, speech **7** wordage, wording **8** delivery, language, parlance, phrasing, rhetoric, verbiage **9** elocution, verbalism **11** enunciation, phraseology

dictionary
7 lexicon **8** glossary, wordbook **10** repository **13** reference book
compiler: **7** Johnson (Samuel), Webster (Noah) **13** lexicographer
geographical: **9** gazetteer
of synonyms: **8** thesauri (plural) **9** thesaurus

dictum
4 fiat **5** adage, axiom, edict, maxim, moral **6** ruling **7** mandate, opinion, precept, proverb **11** declaration **13** pronouncement

didactic
5 moral **6** teachy **7** donnish, preachy **8** advisory, edifying, pedantic, sermonic, teaching **9** hortative, pedagogic, teacherly **10** moralizing **11** informative, instructive

diddle
3 con, gyp, toy **4** beat, bilk, dupe, hoax, fool, idle, laze, loaf, loll, rook, scam **5** cheat, cozen, delay, drone, trick **6** chisel, chouse, dabble, dawdle, delude, fiddle, fleece, loiter, lounge, rope in, take in **7** deceive, defraud, goof off, mislead, swindle **8** flimflam, fool with, hoodwink, lollygag **9** bamboozle, overreach, victimize, waste time **10** dilly-dally, fool around, hang around

diddler
3 gyp **4** sham **5** cheat, faker, fraud, rogue **6** con man **7** grifter, shammer, sharper **8** swindler **9** con artist, defrauder, trickster **11** flimflammer **12** double-dealer **13** confidence man

dido
4 jest, lark **5** antic, caper, curio, frill, prank **6** bauble, frolic, gewgaw, trifle, whimsy **7** bibelot, novelty, trinket **8** furbelow, gimcrack, kickshaw, mischief **9** bagatelle, plaything **10** knickknack, tomfoolery

Dido
6 Elissa
brother: **9** Pygmalion
city founded by: **8** Carthage
father: **5** Belus **6** Mutton
husband: **7** Acerbas **8** Sichaeus
lover: **6** Aeneas

Dido and Aeneas composer
7 Purcell (Henry)

die
4 drop, fall, mold, pass, stop, wane **5** buy it, cease, croak **6** cash in, demise, expire, go west, matrix, pass on, peg out, perish, pop off **7** decease, go south, kick off, snuff it, succumb **8** cash it in, check out, drop dead, flat-line, pass away **9** disappear **10** buy the farm **11** bite the dust **12** join the choir **13** kick the bucket
from hunger: **6** starve
loaded: **6** fulham

___ die
4 sine

diehard
7 devoted, fanatic **8** true-blue **9** dogmatlst

10 determined **11** bitter-ender, doctrinaire, reactionary, standpatter **12** conservative, intransigent **13** stick-in-the-mud

___ diem
3 per **5** carpe

Dies ___
4 Irae

diet
4 bant, eats, fare, fast, feed, menu, slim **6** ration, reduce, regime **7** regimen **8** assembly, victuals **10** parliament **11** legislature, nourishment
type: 5 vegan **7** freegan **8** locavore **10** fruitarian, omnivorous, vegetarian **11** carnivorous, flexitarian, herbivorous, pescatarian

Diet of ___
5 Worms **6** Speyer, Spires **8** Augsburg

Dieu ___ (British motto)
10 et mon droit

___-dieu
4 prie

differ
4 vary **5** demur **7** deviate, diverge **8** disagree

difference
3 gap **7** discord, dispute, dissent **8** conflict, contrast, variance **9** departure, deviation, disparity, otherness, variation **10** dissension, divergence, unlikeness **11** controversy, discrepancy, distinction **12** disagreement **13** dissimilarity

different
5 other **6** divers, single, sundry, unlike, varied **7** another, deviant, distant, diverse, several, special, unalike, unequal, unusual, various **8** discrete, distinct, peculiar, separate **9** disparate, divergent **10** dissimilar, individual, particular **11** contrasting, distinctive

differentiate
4 vary **5** adapt **6** change, modify **8** contrast, separate **9** diversify, transform **11** distinguish, individuate **12** characterize, discriminate

difficult
4 hard **5** tight, tough **6** thorny, uphill **7** arduous, awkward, labored, obscure, operose **8** exacting, perverse, puzzling, stubborn **9** demanding, effortful, herculean, laborious, strenuous **10** refractory **11** problematic

difficulty
3 ado, fix, jam **4** beef, pass, snag **5** hitch, nodus, pinch, rigor, worry **6** hang-up, hassle, pickle, plight, scrape, strait **7** dilemma, pitfall, problem, trouble **8** distress, hardship, hot water, obstacle, quandary, quagmire, question **9** adversity, challenge **10** impediment **11** aggravation, arduousness, predicament, vicissitude

diffidence
7 modesty, reserve, shyness **8** distrust, meekness, timidity **9** quietness, restraint, timidness **10** hesitation **11** bashfulness

diffident
3 coy, shy **4** meek **5** timid **7** bashful **8** hesitant, reserved, retiring, timorous **9** reluctant, unassured **11** unassertive **12** self-effacing

diffuse
5 strew, vague, wordy **6** osmose, prolix, spread **7** scatter, verbose **8** disperse, rambling **9** broadcast, dispersed, propagate, scattered, spreading, spread out **10** distribute, long-winded, widespread **11** disseminate, distributed

diffusion
6 spread **7** osmosis **9** broadcast, dispersal, prolixity, spreading **10** dispersion, scattering **11** circulation, propagation **12** broadcasting, promulgation

DiFranco of song
3 Ani

dig
3 jab **4** barb, grub, hole, like, mine, poke, prod, root, site, slur, stab **5** delve, ditch, enjoy, gouge, nudge, probe, scoop, spade, taunt **6** burrow, plunge, quarry, relish, rootle, shovel, thrust, trench, tunnel **7** explore, root out, unearth **8** excavate, prospect **10** excavation **11** investigate
up: 6 exhume **7** unearth

digest
5 sum up **6** absorb, codify, précis **7** consume, stomach, summate, swallow **8** abstract, boil down, classify, compress, condense, syllabus, synopsis **9** summarize, summation, synopsize **10** abridgment **12** condensation

digger
4 plow **5** miner **6** shovel **7** soldier

digit
3 toe **5** thumb **6** cipher, figure, finger, number, pinkie **7** integer, numeral **9** character **11** whole number

digital image
3 PDF **4** JPEG

dignified
4 prim **6** august, formal, proper, seemly **7** courtly, elegant, stately **8** cultured, decorous, ennobled, polished **9** distingué, patrician

dignify
5 adorn, exalt, grace, honor **7** ennoble, elevate, glorify, sublime **11** distinguish

dignitary
3 VIP **4** lion **5** nabob **6** leader, worthy **7** notable **8** eminence, luminary **9** personage **10** notability **11** muckety-muck **13** high-muck-a-muck

dignity
4 rank **5** honor, merit, poise, pride, worth **6** cachet, status, virtue **7** address, decorum,

gravity, hauteur, majesty, stature **8** grandeur, nobility, position, prestige, standing **9** propriety **10** augustness, seemliness **11** consequence, self-respect

digress
5 stray **6** depart, ramble, swerve, wander **7** deviate, diverge **8** divagate

digression
5 aside **7** episode, tangent **8** drifting, excursus, rambling, straying **9** deviation, wandering **10** deflection, divagation, divergence **11** parenthesis

dig up
4 find **6** expose, reveal **7** nose out, root out, uncover, unearth **8** discover **9** ferret out, run across, search out, track down

dik-dik
8 antelope

dike
3 dam **4** bank **5** ditch, drain, levee **7** barrier **8** causeway **10** embankment **11** watercourse

dilapidate
4 ruin **5** decay, wreck **7** break up, crumble, decline, neglect **9** break down, decompose, disregard **10** deliquesce **12** disintegrate

dilapidated
5 dingy, seedy **6** beat-up, ragtag, ruined, shabby **7** decayed, rickety, run-down **8** battered, crumbled, decrepit **9** crumbling, neglected **10** broken-down, down-at-heel, ramshackle, tumbledown **12** deteriorated

dilapidation
4 ruin **5** decay **7** atrophy **8** collapse, decaying **9** crumbling, decadence, disrepair **11** decrepitude **13** decomposition, deterioration

dilate
5 swell, widen **6** expand, extend **7** distend, enlarge, expound **9** discourse, expatiate

dilatory
4 idle, late, slow **5** slack, tardy **7** laggard **8** dallying, delaying, sluggish **9** leisurely, lingering, unhurried **11** time-wasting

dilemma
3 box, fix, jam **4** bind, spot **6** choice, corner, pickle **7** problem **8** argument, quandary **11** predicament

dilettante
7 amateur, dabbler **8** aesthete **9** smatterer

dilettantish
7 amateur **8** dabbling

diligence
4 care, zeal **8** industry, sedulity, tenacity **9** assiduity **10** commitment **11** application, persistence **12** perseverance, sedulousness **13** assiduousness

diligent
8 sedulous **9** assiduous **10** persistent, persisting, unflagging **11** hardworking, industrious, painstaking, persevering

dilly
3 pip **4** lulu **5** beaut, daisy, dandy, doozy, peach **6** corker, doozie, hummer, pippin, ripper, rouser **8** jim-dandy, knockout **9** humdinger **10** ripsnorter **11** crackerjack

dillydally
6 dawdle, diddle, loiter **8** lollygag

dilute
3 cut **4** thin, weak **5** water **6** watery, weaken **8** diminish, weakened **9** attenuate, water down **11** watered-down

dim
4 dull, dumb, hazy, pale, slow **5** befog, blear, blind, cloud, dense, dusky, faint, muddy, murky, muted, thick, vague **6** bleary, gloomy, stupid **7** becloud, low beam, obscure, shadowy, subdued, unclear **9** tenebrous **10** ill-defined, indistinct, lackluster, lusterless **11** unpromising

dime novel
4 pulp **7** chiller, shocker **8** dreadful, thriller **12** bloodcurdler **13** penny dreadful

dimension
4 size **5** reach, scale, scope, width **6** aspect, extent, spread **7** compass, expanse, measure, quality **9** amplitude, magnitude

diminish
3 ebb **4** bate, wane **5** abate, peter, quell, taper **6** lessen, recede, reduce, shrink, subdue, temper, weaken **7** curtail, decline, dwindle, subside **8** belittle, decrease, minimize, moderate, restrain, taper off **9** attenuate, disparage, dispraise **10** depreciate **11** detract from

diminutive
3 wee **4** tiny **5** bitsy, dwarf, pygmy, small, teeny, weeny **6** bantam, little, midget, minute, peewee, petite, teensy **9** miniature, pint-sized, undersize **10** teeny-weeny **11** lilliputian **12** teensy-weensy

___ dimittis
4 Nunc

dimple
3 pit **4** dent, dint, fret, nick **5** notch **8** pockmark **9** concavity **10** depression **11** indentation

dimwit
3 oaf **4** clod, dodo, dolt, dope, fool, simp, yo-yo **5** booby, chump, cluck, dummy, dunce, idiot, moron, stupe **6** dum-dum **7** airhead, dullard, fathead, pinhead **8** bonehead, dumbbell, imbecile, lunkhead, meathead, numskull **9** birdbrain, blockhead, dumb bunny, dumb cluck, ignoramus, lamebrain, numbskull, simpleton **10** dunderhead, nincompoop **11** featherhead, knucklehead **12** featherbrain

dim-witted
4 dull, dumb, slow **6** stupid **7** doltish, foolish, idiotic, moronic **8** backward, imbecile, retarded **9** brainless, half-baked, imbecilic **11** birdbrained, lamebrained **12** feebleminded, simpleminded

din
3 row **4** roar **5** babel, clash, noise **6** bedlam, clamor, deafen, hubbub, racket, rattle, tumult, uproar **7** clangor, clatter, resound **8** brouhaha **9** cacophony, commotion, stridency **10** hullabaloo, hurly-burly **11** pandemonium

Dinah
brother: **4** Levi **6** Simeon
father: **5** Jacob
mother: **4** Leah

dine
3 eat, sup **4** feed **5** feast **6** eat out **7** banquet, nourish

diner
4 café **5** eater **6** eatery **7** canteen **8** snack bar **9** hash house **10** coffee shop, restaurant **11** greasy spoon **12** lunch counter, luncheonette, sandwich shop
sign: **4** eats

Dinesen, Isak
6 Blixen (Karen)
work: **11** Out of Africa **12** Winter's Tales **16** Seven Gothic Tales

ding
3 mar **4** dent, nick **5** clang **7** blemish

ding-a-ling
3 nut **4** kook, yo-yo **5** flake, loony, wacko **6** cuckoo, nitwit **7** airhead, lunatic **8** crackpot **9** fruitcake, harebrain, lamebrain, screwball **10** crackbrain **12** scatterbrain

dinghy
5 skiff **7** rowboat, shallop **8** lifeboat, life raft, sailboat

dingle
4 dale, dell, glen, vale **6** ravine, valley

dingus
5 gizmo **6** doodad, gadget, jigger, widget **7** whatsit **9** doohickey, thingummy **11** thingamabob, thingamajig, thingumajig

dingy
5 dirty, grimy, seedy, tacky **6** cruddy, filthy, grotty, grubby, grungy, scuzzy, shabby, soiled, sordid **7** squalid, sullied, unclean **8** begrimed

dinky
3 toy **4** puny, tiny **5** small, teeny **6** little **7** shrimty **9** undersize **10** locomotive

dinner
4 meal **5** feast **6** regale, repast, spread, supper **7** banquet **8** luncheon **9** collation **10** table d'hôte
course: **4** meat, soup **5** salad **6** entrée **7** dessert **9** appetizer
jacket: **3** tux **6** tuxedo

dinosaur
4 fogy **5** fogey **6** fossil **7** has-been **8** mossback, theropod **11** anachronism
fictional: **8** Godzilla

dinosauric
4 huge **5** passé **6** bygone **7** extinct, mammoth **8** colossal, enormous, obsolete, outmoded **9** out-of-date **10** antiquated, behemothic, fossilized, gargantuan, mastodonic, oldfangled **11** elephantine **12** antediluvian, old-fashioned **13** anachronistic

dint
4 nick **5** force, might, power **6** dimple, virtue **7** drive in, impress **10** impression **11** indentation

diocese
3 see **9** bishopric
Eastern Orthodox: **7** eparchy
subdivision: **6** parish

diode
9 rectifier **10** vacuum tube **12** electron tube
component: **5** anode **7** cathode **9** electrode

Diomedes
city founded by: **4** Arpi
father: **4** Ares, Mars **6** Tydeus
foe: **6** Aeneas, Hector
slayer: **8** Heracles, Hercules
victim: **6** Rhesus

Dione
5 Titan
cult partner: **4** Zeus
daughter: **5** Venus **9** Aphrodite
father: **7** Oceanus
lover: **4** Zeus
mother: **6** Tethys

Dionysus
7 Bacchus
attendant: **6** maenad **9** bacchante
father: **4** Zeus
lover: **9** Aphrodite
mother: **6** Semele
son: **7** Priapus
staff: **7** thyrsus

Dionyza's husband
5 Cleon

Dioscuri
5 twins **6** Castor, Gemini, Pollux
father: **4** Zeus **9** Tyndareus
mother: **4** Leda
sister: **5** Helen

dip
3 sag **4** bail, draw, drop, duck, dunk, fall, lade, paté, sink, skid, slip, slue, swim **5** basin, ladle, lower, pitch, sauce, scoop, slope, slump, spoon,

stoop **6** go down, hollow, plunge **7** decline, descend, descent, falloff, immerse, sinkage **8** decrease, downturn, sinkhole, submerge, submerse **9** concavity, declivity, downswing, downtrend, immersion **10** depression

diphthong
7 digraph **8** ligature

diploma
6 degree **7** charter **8** document **9** sheepskin **10** credential

diplomacy
4 tact **7** address, finesse **8** delicacy **10** artfulness, discretion, statecraft **11** negotiation, savoir faire, tactfulness

diplomatic
4 deft **5** bland, suave **6** artful, astute, polite, smooth, urbane **7** courtly, politic, tactful **8** delicate, discreet **9** courteous **12** conciliating, conciliatory

diplomat's office
7 embassy, mission

diplopod
9 millipede

dipper
3 cup **4** bird **5** ladle, ouzel, scoop, stars **6** bucket **10** pickpocket, water ouzel

dippy
4 daft, zany **5** crazy, daffy, flaky, goofy, kooky, loony, nutty, silly, wacky **7** doltish, foolish, witless **9** half-baked **11** harebrained

dipsomania
10 alcoholism

dire
4 grim **5** acute, awful **6** dismal, horrid, tragic, urgent, woeful **7** baleful, baneful, crucial, extreme, fateful, ominous, ruinous **8** alarming, critical, dreadful, grievous, horrible, horrific, menacing, shocking, sinister, terrible **9** appalling, desperate, frightful, ill-boding **10** calamitous, deplorable, foreboding, malevolent, pernicious **11** apocalyptic, distressing, threatening

direct
4 head, lead, show **5** apply, frank, guide, label, level, order, pilot, plain, point, route, steer, train **6** assign, charge, define, devote, divert, enjoin, escort, extend, govern, lineal, linear, manage, ordain, settle **7** address, carry on, command, conduct, control, genuine, nonstop, operate, oversee, preside, project, request **8** dispatch, instruct, regulate, shepherd, straight, unbroken, verbatim **9** determine, firsthand, immediate, prescribe **10** administer, contiguous, continuous, inevitable **11** categorical, undeviating, unequivocal, word for word
a helmsman: **4** conn
proceedings: **7** preside

direction
3 way **4** east, line, path, side, west **5** angle, north, point, south, trend **6** course, design **7** bearing, channel, command, purpose **8** guidance, tendency **9** clockwise, oversight, viewpoint **10** management, standpoint, trajectory **11** instruction, supervision
blowing: **7** leeward **8** windward
horizontal: **7** azimuth
main line of: **4** axis
(see also **compass point**)

directive
4 fiat, memo, word, writ **5** edict, order, ukase **6** charge, decree, dictum, notice, ruling **7** bidding, command, dictate, mandate **8** deciding, managing **9** presiding **10** assignment, injunction, memorandum **11** instruction, supervising, supervisory **12** policy-making **13** communication, pronouncement

directly
3 due **4** anon, soon **5** right, spang **6** at once, head-on, pronto **7** bluntly, by and by, shortly **8** first off, in person, promptly, squarely, straight, verbatim **9** forthwith, instanter, instantly, presently, right away **10** face-to-face **11** immediately, straight off, straightway, word for word **12** contiguously, straightaway

director
4 boss, head **5** chief **6** leader, top dog **7** manager **8** overseer **9** conductor, organizer **10** head honcho, supervisor
(see also **movie director**)

director Ang
3 Lee

director Spike
3 Lee **5** Jonze

directory
4 list **5** guide, index **6** folder **7** catalog **8** register **9** catalogue **11** compilation

dirge
6 lament **7** requiem **8** threnody **11** lamentation
Gaelic: **8** coronach

dirigible
5 blimp **7** airship **8** zeppelin **9** steerable

dirk
4 shiv, stab **5** skean, skene, sword **6** bodkin, dagger, stylet **7** poniard

dirt
3 mud **4** clay, dust, land, loam, mire, muck, porn, smut, soil, spot **5** earth, filth, fraud, grime, stain **6** gossip, ground **7** chicane, squalor **9** chicanery, indecency **10** corruption, hanky-panky

dirt-poor
4 bust **5** broke **8** beggared, indigent **9** destitute, flat broke, penniless, penurious **10** stone-broke **12** impoverished

dirty
3 tar **4** base, foul, lewd, racy, smut, soil **5** bawdy, grimy, mucky, muddy, murky, nasty, smear, sooty, stain, sully, taint **6** befoul, coarse, debase, defile, filthy, grubby, impure, smudge, smutty, soiled, sordid, vulgar **7** begrime, corrupt, defiled, immoral, naughty, obscene, raunchy, smutchy, spotted, squalid, squally, sullied, tainted, tarnish, unclean, unkempt **8** begrimed, besmirch, indecent, off-color, polluted, unchaste, unwashed **9** ill-gotten, uncleanly **10** abominable, scandalous, scurrilous **11** unlaundered **12** contaminated

Dis
see **Pluto**

disability
7 ailment **8** drawback, handicap **9** detriment, hindrance, infirmity, unfitness **10** affliction, impairment, impediment, incapacity **11** restriction, shortcoming

disable
4 maim **5** spoil **6** hobble, weaken **7** cripple **8** enfeeble, handicap, paralyze, sabotage **9** hamstring, undermine **10** debilitate, immobilize **12** incapacitate
a racehorse: **6** nobble

disabled
4 halt, lame **6** maimed **7** hobbled **8** crippled **9** arthritic, paralyzed, rheumatic **11** handicapped **13** incapacitated

disabuse
4 free **5** emend, purge **7** correct, deliver, rectify, redress, release, relieve **8** liberate, unburden **9** enlighten, undeceive **10** illuminate **11** disencumber, disillusion

disaccharide
7 lactose, maltose, sucrose

disaccord
3 jar, war **4** vary **5** brawl, clash **6** combat, debate, differ **7** contest, contend, dispute, dissent, quarrel **8** conflict

disadvantage
3 bar **4** harm, loss **6** burden, damage, hamper **7** barrier, setback **8** drawback, handicap, obstacle **9** detriment, hindrance, liability, prejudice **10** impairment, impediment, imposition, limitation **11** deprivation, obstruction

disadvantaged
7 lacking **8** deprived **11** handicapped

disaffect
4 wean **5** alien, repel **8** alienate, disquiet, disunite, estrange **10** antagonize

disaffirm
4 deny **5** annul, belie, cross **6** abjure, impugn, negate, refute, reject **7** confute, gainsay **8** disclaim, disprove, negative **9** repudiate **10** contradict, contravene

disagree
4 vary **5** argue, clash **6** bicker, differ, divide, haggle **7** contend, contest, dispute, dissent **8** conflict

disagreeable
5 surly, testy **6** crabby, cranky, grumpy, ornery **7** bearish, bilious, grouchy, peevish **8** annoying, petulant **9** irascible, offensive, querulous **10** unpleasant **11** disobliging, distressing, ill-tempered

disagreement
5 clash **6** debate **7** discord, dispute, quarrel, wrangle **8** argument, conflict, squabble, variance **9** disparity **10** contention, difference, dissension, divergence **11** altercation, controversy, discrepancy, incongruity

disallow
4 deny, veto **5** debar **6** enjoin, forbid, refuse, reject **7** exclude, rule out, shut out **8** prohibit **9** interdict, proscribe, repudiate

disallowance
4 veto **5** taboo **6** denial **7** refusal **9** disavowal, dismissal, exclusion, rejection **11** prohibition, repudiation **12** interdiction, proscription

____-disant
3 soi

disappear
3 die **4** fade, melt **5** clear, leave **6** depart, die out, vanish **8** dissolve, evanesce, fade away, melt away, pass away, slip away **9** evaporate, sneak away, steal away **13** dematerialize

disappearing Asian sea
4 Aral

disappoint
4 dash, foil, ruin **6** baffle, defeat, thwart **7** let down **9** frustrate **10** discourage, dishearten

disappointment
4 blow **6** bummer, defeat, downer **7** failure, letdown **8** comedown **9** bringdown **11** frustration

disapproval
4 veto **6** rebuke **7** censure, dislike, obloquy, reproof **8** reproach **9** criticism, objection, rejection
expression of: **3** boo **4** hiss, hoot, jeer **7** catcall **9** raspberry **10** Bronx cheer, thumbs-down

disapprove
4 veto **6** oppose, reject, tut-tut **7** decline, dislike, dismiss, frown on **8** disfavor, turn down **9** dispraise

disarm
5 charm **6** allure **7** win over **8** sideline **9** captivate **10** neutralize

disarming
7 amiable, likable, winning, winsome **8** likeable **9** endearing **10** convincing, persuasive **11** insinuating **12** ingratiating

disarrange
4 mess **5** mix up, upset **6** jumble, mess up, mislay, muddle, muss up **7** confuse, disturb **8** disorder, displace, misplace, unsettle **10** discompose **11** disorganize

disarray
5 chaos **6** bedlam, jumble, mess up, muddle **7** clutter, undress **8** disorder, shambles, unsettle **9** confusion **10** discompose, dishabille

disassemble
6 detach **7** scatter **8** separate, take down, tear down **9** break down, come apart, take apart

disassociate
5 sever, unfix **6** detach, sunder **7** back off **8** abstract, alienate, back down, liberate, separate, uncouple, withdraw **9** disengage

disaster
3 woe **6** fiasco **7** debacle, failure, tragedy **8** calamity **9** cataclysm, ruination **11** catastrophe, devastation

disastrous
4 dire **5** fatal **6** tragic **7** fateful, ruinous **8** terrible **10** calamitous, horrendous **11** cataclysmic, destructive, devastating **12** catastrophic

disavow
4 deny **6** abjure, disown, impugn, negate, recant, reject **7** forsake, gainsay, retract **8** abnegate, disclaim, forswear, negative, renounce **9** repudiate

disband
3 end **4** part **5** sever **6** divide, sunder **7** break up, dissect, divorce, scatter **8** disperse, dissolve, separate

disbelieve
5 doubt, scorn, scout **6** eschew, reject **7** scoff at, suspect **8** discount, distrust, mistrust, question **9** discredit, repudiate

disbeliever
5 cynic **7** doubter, sceptic, scoffer, skeptic **9** dissenter **10** questioner **11** freethinker

disbelieving
4 wary **5** leery **6** show-me **7** cynical, dubious **8** doubting **9** quizzical, skeptical **11** incredulous, mistrustful, questioning, unconvinced

disburden
4 shed **6** unlade, unload, unship, unstow **7** offload, relieve **8** disgorge **9** discharge

disburse
3 pay **5** allot, issue **6** lay out, pay out, supply **7** deliver, dole out, furnish, mete out, provide **8** dispense, disperse **9** apportion, partition **10** distribute, measure out

disbursement
4 cost **5** funds **6** outlay **7** expense, payment **9** allotment **11** expenditure **12** distribution

discard
4 cast, drop, dump, junk, shed, toss, waif **5** chuck, ditch, eject, let go, scrap **6** reject **7** cast off, cast-off, deep-six, wash out **8** get rid of, jettison, shuck off, throw out **9** throw away, toss aside

discarnate
8 bodiless, ethereal, spectral **9** asomatous, unfleshly **10** immaterial, unembodied, unphysical, wraithlike **11** disembodied, incorporeal, nonphysical **12** otherworldly **13** insubstantial

discern
3 see **4** espy, know, note **5** grasp, sense **6** behold, detect, divine, notice **7** glimpse, observe **8** identify, perceive **9** apprehend, ascertain, recognize **10** comprehend **11** distinguish **12** discriminate **13** differentiate

discernible
7 visible **8** apparent, palpable **10** detectable, noticeable, observable **11** appreciable, perceivable **12** recognizable

discerning
4 keen **5** acute, aware **6** astute **7** knowing **9** clear-eyed, insighted, observant, sagacious **10** insightful, perceptive **12** clear-sighted **13** knowledgeable, perspicacious

discernment
5 taste **6** acuity, acumen **7** insight **8** keenness, sagacity **9** intuition **10** astuteness, perception, shrewdness **11** penetration, percipience **12** perspicacity **13** comprehension, sagaciousness

discharge
3 axe, can, pay **4** drop, emit, fire, free, gush, oust, quit, sack, spew, vent, void **5** annul, clear, demob, egest, eject, empty, expel, exude, let go, loose, pay up, quash, salvo, shoot, utter **6** bounce, excuse, exempt, let fly, let off, loosen, outlet, remove, settle, unbind, unload, vacate **7** absolve, boot out, barrage, cashier, deliver, dismiss, exclude, excrete, execute, fulfill, give off, kick out, manumit, off-load, release, relieve, removal, satisfy, unchain **8** abrogate, aquittal, dispense, displace, dissolve, ejection, emission, get rid of, liberate, separate, throw off **9** acquittal, dismissal, eliminate, explosion, expulsion, muster out, pour forth, send forth, terminate, unshackle **10** deactivate, demobilize **11** exoneration, fulfillment
electrical: **5** spark **6** leader **8** streamer **9** lightning

disciple
3 fan **6** minion **7** apostle, devotee, learner **8** adherent, follower, henchman, partisan, retainer **9** supporter **10** enthusiast

disciplinarian
8 enforcer, martinet **10** taskmaster **11** slave driver

disciplinary
8 punitive 9 punishing 10 corrective

discipline
4 curb, rule, will 5 check, drill, field, guide, order, teach, train 6 bridle, direct, ferule, method, punish, school, subdue 7 chasten, conduct, control, correct, educate 8 approach, chastise, instruct, penalize, restrain, training 9 castigate, obedience, subjugate, will-power 10 correction, punishment 11 castigation, self-control, self-mastery 12 chastisement 13 self-restraint

disclaim
4 deny 6 abjure, reject 7 disavow, gainsay, retract 8 disallow, forswear, renounce, traverse 9 repudiate 10 contradict

disclaimer in a text message
4 IMHO

disclose
3 own 4 avow, tell 5 admit, spill 6 expose, impart, relate, report, reveal, unmask, unveil 7 display, divulge, uncover 8 discover, give away, unclothe 9 make known

disclosure
6 exposé 8 exposure 9 admission 10 revelation 11 declaration

discolor
3 tar 4 blot, dull, fade, smut, soil 5 smear, stain, sully, taint, tinge 6 defile, smudge 7 besmear, bestain, tarnish 8 besmirch

discoloration
4 spot 5 stain, taint 6 blotch, bruise, smudge 7 blemish 9 birthmark

discomfit
3 irk, vex 4 faze 5 abash, annoy, upset 6 baffle, bother, defeat, rattle, thwart 7 fluster, nonplus, perturb, unnerve 8 confound 9 embarrass 10 discompose, disconcert

discomfiture
5 upset 6 unease 8 disquiet 9 abashment, agitation, confusion 10 uneasiness 11 frustration 12 discomposure, perturbation 13 embarrassment, inconvenience

discomfort
3 irk, vex 4 ache, pain 5 annoy 6 bother, unease 7 malaise 8 vexation 9 annoyance 10 uneasiness 13 embarrassment

discommend
5 decry 7 censure, frown on, put down 8 admonish, disfavor, object to 9 criticize, deprecate, disesteem, disparage, reprehend 10 disapprove

discommode
3 irk, vex 5 annoy, upset 6 bother, burden, flurry, put out 7 disturb, fluster, perturb, trouble 8 encumber 9 aggravate, disoblige 13 inconvenience

discompose
3 irk, vex 5 abash, annoy, harry, upset, worry 6 bother, dismay, flurry, harass, pester, plague, ruffle, untune 7 agitate, disturb, fluster, perturb, unhinge 8 disarray, disorder, unsettle 9 embarrass 10 disarrange 11 disorganize

discomposure
5 upset, worry 6 bother, unease 8 vexation 9 abashment, agitation, annoyance, confusion 10 discomfort, irritation, perplexity, uneasiness 11 disquietude 12 discomfiture, perturbation 13 consternation, embarrassment

disconcert
3 jar 4 faze 5 abash, upset, worry 6 bemuse, bother, puzzle, rattle, ruffle 7 confuse, disturb, nonplus, perplex, perturb, trouble, unnerve 8 bewilder, confound, disquiet 9 discomfit, embarrass, frustrate

disconfirm
4 deny 5 rebut 6 refute, negate 7 gainsay 8 abnegate, confound, disclaim, disprove 10 contradict, controvert

disconnect
3 cut, gap 5 break, sever, unfix 6 cut off, detach 7 disjoin 8 separate, uncouple 9 disengage 10 dissociate

disconnected
7 muddled 8 detached, separate 10 disjointed, incoherent, unattached 11 fragmentary, unorganized 13 discontinuous

disconsolate
3 low, sad 4 blue, down 5 bleak, drear 6 abject, dreary, gloomy, woeful 7 doleful, forlorn, joyless, unhappy 8 dejected, downcast, wretched 9 cheerless, depressed, miserable, sorrowful, woebegone 10 dispirited, melancholy 11 comfortless, crestfallen, downhearted

discontent
4 envy 7 malaise, unhappy 9 dysphoria 10 depression, inquietude, uneasiness 12 restlessness

discontented
5 upset 6 uneasy 7 annoyed, fretful, unhappy 8 restless 9 disturbed, irritated, perturbed 10 displeased 11 complaining, disgruntled, ungratified, unsatisfied 12 dissatisfied

discontinuation
3 end 4 stop 5 cease, close, pause 6 ending, finish 7 closing 8 abeyance 9 cessation 10 conclusion, desistance, moratorium, suspension 12 postponement

discontinue
3 end 4 halt, quit, stay, stop 5 cease, close, sever 6 desist, give up, wind up, wrap up 8 break off, close out, conclude, knock off, leave off, shut down, surcease 9 terminate

discontinuity
3 gap **4** hole, rent, rift **5** break, cleft, crack, split **6** breach, lacuna **7** fissure, opening, rupture

discontinuous
6 fitful **7** muddled **8** discrete, separate **9** spasmodic **10** incoherent, incohesive **11** unconnected **12** disconnected, intermittent **13** nonsequential

discord
5 clash **6** enmity, rancor, strife **7** rupture **8** conflict, contrast, disunity, division, friction, mismatch, variance **9** animosity, antipathy, hostility **10** antagonism, contention, difference, dissension, dissidence, dissonance, opposition **12** inconsonance, polarization **13** inconsistency
goddess: **3** Ate **4** Eris

discordant
5 harsh **6** at odds **7** grating, jarring **8** clashing, contrary, jangling, strident **9** dissonant, out of tune **10** cacophonic, unpleasant **11** cacophonous, conflicting, disagreeing, inconsonant, quarrelsome, unmelodious **12** unharmonious

discotheque
6 bistro, nitery **7** hot spot **9** dance club, nightclub, night spot

discount
4 agio **5** doubt, lower **6** deduct, ignore, rebate, reduce, slight **7** neglect, take off **8** belittle, derogate, decrease, diminish, knock off, mark down, markdown, minimize, overlook, roll back, rollback, subtract, take away **9** abatement, deduction, disregard, reduction, substract, underrate **13** underestimate
label abbrev.: **3** irr.

discountenance
4 faze **5** abash **6** rattle **7** frown on **8** confound, disfavor **9** deprecate, discomfit, embarrass **10** disapprove, disconcert, discourage

discourage
4 damp **5** daunt, check, chill, deter **6** dampen, deject, divert, hinder, impede **7** depress, inhibit, trouble **8** disfavor, dissuade, suppress **10** demoralize, dishearten

discouraging
5 bleak **7** unhappy **8** daunting **9** deterring, troubling **10** depressing **11** unfavorable, unpromising **12** unpropitious **13** disappointing, disheartening

discourse
4 talk **5** argue, essay, orate, speak, spiel, voice **6** sermon, speech, thesis **7** amplify, descant, enlarge, explain, expound, lecture **8** converse, harangue, perorate, rhetoric, speaking, treatise **9** expatiate, hold forth, monograph, sermonize, utterance **10** expression **11** interchange **12** conversation **13** verbalization
art of: **8** rhetoric
religious: **6** homily, sermon

discourteous
4 rude **6** unkind **7** boorish, brusque, ill-bred, uncivil, uncouth **8** impolite **10** ungracious, unmannerly **11** ill-mannered, impertinent **13** disrespectful

discover
4 espy, find, spot **5** learn **6** betray, detect, expose, reveal, unmask **7** divulge, find out, observe, unearth **8** come upon, perceive, proclaim, unshroud **9** ascertain, determine, encounter, make known **10** come across

discovery
4 find **5** trove **6** espial, strike **7** finding **8** locating, sighting **9** detection **10** revelation, unearthing

discredit
4 slur, ruin **5** doubt, shame **6** defame, malign, show up **7** asperse, degrade, put down, run down, slander, traduce **8** disgrace, ignominy **9** disparage, disrepute **10** disbelieve, opprobrium

discreditable
5 shady **6** shabby, shoddy **8** shameful, unworthy **9** degrading **10** inglorious **11** blameworthy, disgraceful, ignominious **12** contemptible, dishonorable, disreputable

discreet
4 wary **5** chary, muted, plain **6** modest, simple **7** careful, guarded, prudent, tactful **8** cautious, moderate **9** unadorned **10** controlled, reasonable, restrained **11** circumspect, considerate, unelaborate, unobtrusive **12** unnoticeable **13** unpretentious

discrepancy
3 gap **8** alterity, conflict, variance **9** disparity, otherness, variation **10** difference, divergence, divergency, unlikeness **12** disagreement **13** inconsistency

discrepant
6 unlike **7** diverse, varying **8** contrary **9** different, differing, disparate, divergent **11** conflicting, disagreeing **12** incompatible, inconsistent **13** contradictory

discrete
8 detached, distinct, separate **9** countable, different **10** individual **12** disconnected **13** discontinuous, noncontinuous

discretion
4 care, tact **7** caution, reserve **8** delicacy, judgment, prudence, wariness **9** canniness, chariness, restraint **13** judiciousness

discriminate
5 judge **6** assess, secern **7** compare, discern, make out **8** contrast, disfavor, evaluate, perceive, separate **9** segregate, tell apart **11** distinguish **13** differentiate

discriminating
6 choosy, select **7** finical, finicky **8** eclectic **9** judicious, selective **10** discerning **11** prejudicial

discrimination
5 taste **6** acumen **7** bigotry, insight **8** inequity, judgment **9** prejudice **10** astuteness, favoritism, partiality, perception **11** discernment, intolerance, penetration

discriminatory
6 biased **7** partial, unequal **8** partisan **9** jaundiced **10** prejudiced **11** inequitable, predisposed

discursive
5 windy, wordy **6** chatty, prolix **7** diffuse, logical, verbose **8** rambling, tortuous **9** desultory **10** analytical, circuitous, digressive, long-winded, meandering **11** wide-ranging

discuss
4 moot **5** argue, weigh **6** debate, parley **7** canvass, expound **8** consider, converse, hash over, talk over **9** elucidate, expatiate, interpret, talk about, thrash out, ventilate **10** deliberate, toss around
business: **8** talk shop
lightly: **5** bandy
thoroughly: **7** exhaust

discussion
3 rap **4** chat, talk **6** confab, debate, parley, powwow **7** canvass, palaver **8** argument, colloquy **10** conference, rap session **11** bull session, ventilation **12** conversation, deliberation **13** confabulation

discus thrower
6 Alekna (Virgilijus), Marten (Maritza), Oerter (Al) **10** discobolus **11** Rashchupkin (Viktor)

disdain
5 abhor, scorn, scout, spurn **6** deride, refuse, reject, slight **7** contemn, despise, despite, hauteur, put down **8** aversion, belittle, contempt, disprize, misprize **9** antipathy **10** repugnance, undervalue

disdainful
5 aloof, proud **6** averse, lordly, sniffy, snooty, uppity **7** haughty **8** arrogant, cavalier, derisive, insolent, scorning, snobbish, spurning, superior, toplofty **11** overbearing **12** antipathetic, contemptuous, supercilious **13** high and mighty

disease
3 bug, ill **5** upset, virus **6** blight, malady **7** ailment, anthrax, illness, malaise, mycosis, purpura **8** debility, epidemic, myxedema, pandemic, sickness, syndrome, zoonoses (plural), zoonosis **9** affection, black lung, contagion, ill health, infection, infirmity, sclerosis **10** affliction, blackwater, bronchitis, infirmness, sickliness
animal: **5** mange, surra **6** rabies **7** bighead **8** enzootic, zoonosis **9** distemper, tularemia **10** rinderpest
blood: **8** leukemia, leukoses (plural), leukosis
cabbage: **8** clubroot
cattle: **6** cowpox **7** foot rot, locoism, murrain **8** blackleg, vaccinia **9** vibriosis **10** rinderpest **11** brucellosis
cereal grass: **4** bunt, smut **5** ergot
children's: **5** mumps **7** measles, rubella **10** chicken pox **13** whooping cough
citrus tree: **8** tristeza
classification: **8** nosology
combining form: **4** path **5** patho
communicable: **3** flu **4** mono **5** mumps, polio **6** dengue, herpes, plague, rabies **7** bird flu, cholera, leprosy, malaria, measles, rubella, tetanus, typhoid **8** avian flu, impetigo **9** hepatitis, influenza **10** giardiasis **12** tuberculosis
deficiency: **6** scurvy **7** rickets **8** beriberi, pellagra
disseminator: **6** vector **7** carrier
eye: **6** iritis **8** glaucoma, trachoma **9** retinitis
hair follicle: **7** sycoses (plural), sycosis
heart: **11** cardiopathy
horse: **6** nagana, spavin **7** locosim, sarcoid **8** glanders **9** strangles
identification of: **9** diagnosis
industrial: **10** byssinosis
infectious: **4** mono, yaws **6** dengue, typhus **7** leprosy, malaria, tetanus, typhoid **9** tularemia, vibriosis **10** rinderpest **13** whooping cough
liver: **9** cirrhosis, hepatitis
livestock: **7** locoism **9** vibriosis **10** rinderpest
lung: **8** phthisic, phthisis **9** pneumonia **10** byssinosis **12** tuberculosis
lymph glands: **8** scrofula
metabolic: **4** gout
nervous system: **4** kuru **6** rabies **10** diphtheria
of beets: **8** heartrot
of mammals: **6** rabies **7** malaria **9** distemper **10** babesiosis, rinderpest
parasitic: **3** rot **4** smut **5** mange **7** malaria **8** hookworm, kala-azar **9** heartworm
plant: **4** rust, scab, smut, wilt **5** blast, edema, scald, scurf, stunt **6** blight, blotch, canker, mosaic, streak **7** blister, crinkle, foot rot, frogeye, red leaf, root rot **8** clubroot, curly top, fusarium, gummosis, leaf curl, leaf roll, leaf rust, leaf spot, ring spot, root knot, stem rust **9** chlorosis, crown gall, white rust **10** blackheart, leaf scorch
poultry: **8** leukosis
respiratory: **6** asthma, coryza **10** byssinosis
sheep: **3** gid **7** scrapie **9** vibriosis **10** bluetongue
silkworm: **3** uji
skin: **4** acne, yaws **5** favus, hives, lupus, mange, pinta, tinea **6** eczema, tetter **7** leprosy, prurigo, sarcoid, scabies, serpigo **8** impetigo, miliaria, pyoderma, ringworm, vitiligo **9** pemphigus, psoriasis **10** erysipelas **11** scleroderma

syphilitic: 5 tabes
throat: 5 croup, strep
thyroid: 6 struma
tropical: 4 yaws 5 pinta, sprue, surra 6 dengue 7 malaria 8 kala-azar
venereal: 6 herpes 8 syphilis 9 chancroid, gonorrhea
viral: 3 flu 4 AIDS, noma 5 Ebola, mumps, polio 6 dengue, grippe, herpes, rabies, zoster 7 bird flu, measles, rubella, rubeola, variola 8 avian flu, morbilli, shingles, smallpox 9 hepatitis, influenza, monkey pox, varicella 13 poliomyelitis

diseased
3 ill 6 ailing, infirm, sickly, unwell 7 fevered, unsound 8 feverish, infected

disembark
4 land 6 alight 7 deplane, detrain 8 go ashore

disembarrass
3 rid 4 free 7 release, relieve 8 liberate, unburden, untangle 9 extricate 11 disencumber, disentangle

disembodied
7 ghostly 8 ethereal, spectral 9 asomatous, unfleshly 10 immaterial, unphysical, wraithlike 11 incorporeal, nonmaterial, nonphysical 13 insubstantial

disembogue
4 flow, gush, pour, spew 5 empty 7 pour out 9 discharge

disembowel
3 gut 10 eviscerate, exenterate

disemploy
3 axe, can 4 boot, fire, sack 7 cashier 9 discharge, terminate

disenchanted
5 blasé, jaded 6 soured 7 cynical 9 jaundiced 10 undeceived 11 worldly-wise 12 disappointed, dissatisfied 13 disenthralled, disillusioned

disencumber
3 rid 4 free 7 lighten, release, relieve, sort out 8 free from, liberate, unburden 9 alleviate, disburden, extricate

disengage
4 free, part 5 loose, unfix 6 detach, opt out, unbind 7 back out, drop out, release, unloose 8 cut loose, liberate, separate, uncouple, unfasten, unloosen, withdraw 10 disconnect

disentangle
5 untie 6 detach 7 resolve, sort out, unravel, unsnarl, untwine 8 separate 9 extricate 10 unscramble 11 disencumber 13 straighten out

disenthrall
4 free 7 manumit, release 8 liberate 10 emancipate

disfavor
7 dislike 8 aversion, distrust, mistrust 9 deprecate, disesteem, disregard, disrepute 10 disrespect 11 disapproval 12 disadvantage, unpopularity

disfigure
3 mar 4 maim, scar 6 deface, defile, deform, impair, injure, mangle 7 blemish, distort 8 mutilate

disfranchise
3 bar 7 exclude 8 take away 9 deprive of 10 disentitle

disgorge
4 barf, spew 5 belch, eject, eruct, erupt, expel, vomit 6 give up, irrupt, spit up 7 release, throw up, upchuck 9 discharge

disgrace
5 odium, shame 6 infamy, stigma 7 attaint, mortify, obloquy 8 black eye, contempt, dishonor, ignominy, reproach 9 discredit, disrepute, humiliate 10 opprobrium, stigmatize 11 degradation, humiliation

disgraceful
7 ignoble 8 shameful 9 degrading 10 deplorable, inglorious, unbecoming 11 humiliating, ignominious, reproachful 12 dishonorable, disreputable

disgruntled
5 vexed 6 cranky, put out 7 annoyed, beefing, griping 8 grousing 9 irritated 10 discontent, displeased, ill-humored, malcontent 11 ungratified 12 discontented, malcontented

disguise
4 hide, mask, sham, veil 5 belie, cloak, feign, put on 6 facade 7 conceal, falsify, obscure 8 artifice, pretense 9 deception 10 camouflage, false front, pretension 12 misrepresent

disguised
6 masked, veiled 7 cloaked, feigned 9 incognito 10 undercover 11 camouflaged

disguisement
4 mask, veil 5 cloak, front 6 facade 8 pretense 9 deception 10 false front, pretention

disgust
6 appall, nausea, offend, revolt, sicken 8 aversion, gross out, loathing, nauseate 9 antipathy, repulsion, revulsion 10 abhorrence, repugnance 11 abomination 13 squeamishness

disgusted
5 fed up 8 offended, repelled, repulsed, revolted, sickened 9 nauseated, squeamish 10 grossed out

disgusting
3 ugh 4 foul, icky, vile 5 gross, nasty, yucky 7 noisome 9 loathsome, offensive, repellent, repugnant, repulsive, revolting, sickening 10 nauseating

dish
4 bowl, buzz, food, talk, tray **5** plate **6** course, gossip, tureen **7** chatter, hearsay, platter, scandal, slander **9** casserole, container **11** scuttlebutt
baked: **7** soufflé
baking: **7** cocotte, scallop **9** casserole **12** scallop shell
cheese: **6** fondue **7** ramekin, rarebit **8** raclette, ramequin
Chinese: **6** dim sum, lo mein, subgum, wonton **8** chop suey, chow mein **10** egg foo yong, egg foo yung **11** egg foo young
deep: **9** casserole
Hungarian: **7** goulash
Italian: **5** pasta, penne, pesto, pizza **6** scampi **7** cannoli, lasagna, polenta, ravioli **8** calamari, focaccia, linguine, linguini, osso buco, rigatoni **9** manicotti **10** cannelloni, scaloppine, tortellini **11** saltimbocca
Japanese: **5** sushi **7** sashimi, tempura **8** sukiyaki
Mexican: **4** taco **5** chili **6** fajita, flauta, nachos, tamale **7** burrito, chalupa **8** frijoles **9** enchilada, guacamole **10** carne asada **11** chimichanga **12** refried beans **13** chili con carne
Middle Eastern: **5** kebab, kibbe, kibbi **6** hummus, kibbeh **7** falafel **8** couscous, moussaka **10** shish kebab **11** baba ghanouj **12** baba ghanoush
principal: **6** entrée
rice: **5** pilaf **7** risotto
Scottish: **5** brose **6** haggis
serving: **7** charger
shallow: **6** saucer
Thai: **7** pad thai

disharmonize
3 jar, war **5** clash **6** jangle **7** discord **8** conflict, mismatch **9** disaccord

disharmony
6 strife **7** discord **8** conflict, disunion, disunity, friction, variance **9** cacophony **10** contention, difference, dissension, dissonance

dishearten
3 cow **5** chill, crush, daunt, shake **6** dampen, deject, dismay, sadden **7** depress, unnerve **8** dispirit, distress **10** demoralize, discourage, intimidate

dishes
4 ware
clay: **7** pottery
porcelain: **5** china

dishevel
5 touse **6** muss up, rumple, tousle **8** disarray, disorder **10** disarrange, discompose

disheveled
5 messy **6** mussed **7** unkempt **8** ill-kempt, uncombed

dishonest
5 false, lying, rogue, snide **6** tricky, unfair **7** corrupt, crooked, knavish **8** cheating, cozening, two-faced **9** deceitful, deceiving, deceptive, swindling **10** defrauding, fraudulent, mendacious, untruthful **13** double-dealing, untrustworthy

dishonesty
5 fraud, guile **6** deceit **7** falsity, knavery, roguery **8** flimflam, pretense, trickery **9** chicanery, deception, duplicity, falsehood, hypocrisy **10** corruption **11** crookedness **13** double-dealing

dishonor
see **disgrace**

dishonorable
see **disgraceful**

dish out
5 ladle, serve **6** pile on, supply **7** deliver, present, serve up **8** allocate, disburse, dispense **10** distribute

disillusioned
see **disenchanted**

disinclination
7 dislike **8** aversion, distaste **9** antipathy, objection **10** reluctance **13** indisposition, unwillingness

disinclined
5 loath **6** averse **7** opposed **8** hesitant **9** reluctant, resistant, unwilling **10** indisposed

disinfect
6 purify **8** sanitize **9** autoclave, sterilize **13** decontaminate

disingenuous
3 sly **4** foxy, wily **5** false **6** artful, crafty, tricky **7** cunning, devious, feigned **8** delusive, guileful, indirect, specious **9** deceitful, deceiving, deceptive, dishonest, insidious, insincere, sophistic **10** misleading **11** calculating, casuistical, sophistical

disinherit
6 cut off **7** bereave, exclude **9** deprive of, repudiate **10** dispossess

disintegrate
3 rot **4** turn **5** break, burst, decay, spoil, taint **6** molder **7** crumble, scatter, shatter **8** splinter **9** break down, decompose, fall apart **10** deliquesce

disinter
5 dig up **6** exhume, unbury **7** unearth **8** exhumate **9** resurrect

disinterest
6 apathy **7** neglect **8** coolness, lethargy **9** aloofness, disregard, unconcern **10** detachment, dispassion, neutrality **11** impassivity, inattention, insouciance, nonchalance, objectivity **12** indifference

disinterested
4 fair, just **5** aloof **6** candid **7** neutral **8** detached, unbiased **9** impartial, impassive, incurious, objective **10** even-handed, impersonal, neglectful, nonchalant **11** inattentive, indifferent, unconcerned

disjoin
4 part **5** sever, unfix **6** detach, divide, sunder, unlink **7** break up, divorce **8** disunite, separate, uncouple, unfasten **9** disengage, take apart **10** dissociate **12** disaffiliate, disassociate

disjointed
7 jumbled, muddled **8** confused, inchoate, rambling **9** displaced **10** disordered, incoherent, incohesive **11** unconnected, unorganized **13** discontinuous

disk
4 puck **5** paten, wafer **6** record
metal: 4 slug
ornamental: 6 bangle, sequin

dislike
4 shun **5** scorn, spurn **6** animus, oppose, reject, resent **7** deplore, frown on **8** aversion, disfavor, distaste **9** animosity, antipathy **10** alienation, disapprove, repugnance **11** disapproval

dislimn
3 dim **5** bedim **6** darken **7** becloud, obscure **9** obfuscate

dislocate
5 break **7** disrupt, unhinge **9** disengage **10** disconnect **13** disarticulate

dislodge
4 oust **5** eject, evict, expel **6** remove, uproot **8** displace, drive out, force out

disloyal
5 false **6** untrue **8** apostate, recreant **9** alienated, faithless **10** perfidious, traitorous, unfaithful **11** disaffected, treacherous

disloyalty
7 falsity, perfidy, treason **8** apostasy **9** falseness, recreancy, treachery **10** alienation, infidelity **12** disaffection **13** faithlessness

dismal
4 grim **5** bleak, drear **6** dreary, gloomy, horrid, somber, sombre **7** joyless **8** desolate, dreadful, funereal, lowering **9** atrocious, cheerless, depressed, tenebrous **10** depressing, depressive **11** dispiriting **12** discouraging **13** disheartening

dismantle
4 raze, undo **5** strip, unrig, wreck **6** denude, divest **7** break up, destroy **8** demolish, pull down, take down **9** break down, knock down, take apart **11** disassemble

dismay
4 faze, fear **5** abash, alarm, daunt, dread, panic, scare, shake, upset **6** appall, fright, horror, rattle **7** agitate, fluster, horrify, perturb, unnerve **8** affright, bewilder, confound, dispirit, distress, frighten **9** discomfit, dumbfound, embarrass **10** discompose, disconcert, discourage, dishearten **11** trepidation **12** perturbation **13** consternation
expression: 4 alas

dismayed
5 upset **6** afraid, aghast, scared, shaken **7** fearful, shocked **9** disturbed

dismember
4 maim **5** cut up **7** disjoin, dissect **8** mutilate **9** dismantle, take apart

dismiss
3 axe, can **4** drop, fire, oust, sack, shed **5** chuck, eject, evict, let go, scorn, spurn **6** bounce, depose, deride, lay off, reject, remove, retire, shelve, unseat **7** boot out, cashier, contemn, decline, disband, kick out, kiss off, turn off **8** displace, furlough, pooh-pooh, ridicule, throw out, turn away, turn down **9** discharge, repudiate, terminate **11** send packing

dismissal
5 congé, scram **6** beat it, firing, layoff, ouster **7** removal **8** brush-off, bum's rush **9** discharge, expulsion **10** cashiering

dismount
6 alight, debark, get off **7** deplane, detrain **9** disembark **10** alight from **11** descend from

Disney, Walt
10 cartoonist
character: 4 Gyro, Huey, Lady, Nemo **5** Ariel, Baloo, Bambi, Belle, Daisy, Dewey, Dumbo, Goofy, Louie, Mulan, Pluto, Simba, Tramp **6** Beauty, Donald, Grumpy, Mickey, Minnie, Mowgli, Sleepy **7** Aladdin, Cruella (De Vil), Scrooge, Thumper **9** Gladstone, Pinocchio, Snow White **10** Beagle Boys, Clarabelle, Pocahontas
classic: 5 Bambi, Dumbo **8** Fantasia **9** Pinocchio **10** Jungle Book (The) **15** Lady and the Tramp
frame: 3 cel
mermaid: 5 Ariel
middle name: 5 Elias

disobedient
6 unruly **7** naughty, wayward, willful **8** contrary **10** headstrong, ill-behaved, rebellious, refractory **11** misbehaving, uncompliant **12** contumacious, noncompliant, obstreperous, recalcitrant **13** insubordinate

disoblige
5 annoy **6** bother, offend, put out **7** affront, disturb, trouble **9** displease, incommode **10** discommode **13** inconvenience

disorder
3 ill **4** mess, riot **5** chaos, havoc, mix up, snarl, upset **6** ataxia, hubbub, jumble, malady, mess up, muddle, muss up, ruckus, rumple, tumble, tumult, unrest, uproar **7** ailment, anarchy, clutter, confuse, disease, embroil, illness, misdeed, shuffle, turmoil **8** disarray, sickness, syndrome, unsettle, upheaval **9** affection, agitation, commotion, complaint, confusion, infirmity **10** affliction, turbulence, untidiness
mental: 5 mania **8** delirium, insanity, neurosis, paranoia **9** psychosis **11** psychopathy **13** schizophrenia

disordered
6 roiled **7** chaotic, jumbled, muddled **8** confused, inchoate, shuffled **9** displaced **10** disjointed, dislocated, incoherent, incohesive **11** disarranged, unconnected, unorganized **13** discontinuous

disorderly
5 rowdy **6** unruly, untidy **7** jumbled, raucous, unkempt **8** confused **9** cluttered, offensive, turbulent **10** boisterous, topsy-turvy, tumultuous **12** disorganized, rambunctious, unsystematic

disorganize
5 upset **6** jumble, mess up **7** break up, confuse, derange, disband, disrupt **8** disorder, disperse, unsettle **10** disarrange

disoriented
4 lost **7** mixed up **8** confused **9** displaced, perplexed, unsettled **10** bewildered

disown
4 deny, dump **6** desert, reject **7** cast off, disavow **8** disclaim, renounce **9** repudiate

disparage
5 abase, decry **6** defame, slight **7** condemn, degrade, devalue, dismiss, put down, run down, slander **8** bad-mouth, belittle, derogate, discount, downplay, minimize, pooh-pooh **9** denigrate, deprecate, discredit, dispraise, downgrade, underrate **10** demoralize, depreciate, undervalue **11** detract from

disparagement
5 scorn **7** calumny, censure, despite, scandal, slander **8** contempt, despisal, reproach **9** aspersion, discredit, stricture **10** backbiting, defamation, derogation, detraction, diminution **11** degradation **12** backstabbing, depreciation **13** animadversion

disparate
6 at odds, divers, unlike, varied **7** diverse, unalike, unequal, various, varying **8** discrete, distinct, separate **9** different, divergent, unsimilar **10** dissimilar **11** distinctive, incongruous, inconsonant **12** incompatible, inconsistent

disparity
3 gap **8** contrast **9** imbalance **10** difference, divergence, divergency, inequality **11** discrepancy **13** disproportion, dissimilarity

dispassionate
4 calm, fair, just **7** neutral **8** composed, detached, unbiased **9** equitable, impartial, objective, unruffled **10** impersonal **11** unemotional **12** unprejudiced **13** disinterested

dispatch
4 kill, send, ship, slay **5** haste, hurry, scrag, speed **6** defeat, murder **7** bump off, execute, forward, killing, message, put away **8** alacrity, get rid of, shipment, transmit **9** dispose of, eliminate, swiftness **10** expedition, put to death, speediness **11** assassinate, promptitude
boat: 5 aviso

dispel
6 banish **7** cast out, scatter **8** disperse **9** clear away, dissipate, drive away

dispensable
5 minor **7** trivial **8** needless, unneeded **10** disposable, expendable, unrequired **11** superfluous, unessential, unimportant, unnecessary **12** nonessential

dispensary
6 clinic

dispensation
4 plan **5** favor, share **7** license, portion, service **8** bestowal, courtesy, kindness, ordering **9** allotment, exception, exemption, privilege, remission **10** indulgence, management **12** disbursement, distribution **13** apportionment, authorization

dispense
5 allot, apply, wield **6** assign, divide, excuse, exempt, ration, supply **7** absolve, deal out, deliver, dish out, dole out, furnish, give out, mete out, portion, provide, release **8** allocate, carry out, disburse, share out, transfer **9** apportion, discharge, partition **10** administer, distribute, measure out, portion out

disperse
3 sow **5** spray, strew **6** dispel, divide, spread, vanish **7** break up, diffuse, disband, radiate, scatter **9** broadcast, dissipate, partition, propagate **10** distribute

dispersion
6 spread **7** breakup, colloid **9** diffusion, spreading **10** scattering **11** dissipation **12** distribution **13** dissemination

dispirit
3 cow **5** chill, daunt **6** deject, dismay, sadden **7** depress, oppress **8** distress **10** demoralize, discourage, dishearten

dispirited
3 low, sad **4** blue, down, glum **5** cowed **6** morose **7** daunted **8** cast down, dejected, dismayed, downcast, saddened **9** bummed out, depressed, oppressed, woebegone **10** distressed, melancholy **11** crestfallen, demoralized, discouraged, downhearted **12** disconsolate, disheartened

dispiriting
4 blue **6** dismal, dreary, gloomy **8** daunting, dolorous, funereal **9** cheerless, dismaying, saddening **10** depressing, oppressive **12** demoralizing, disconsolate, discouraging **13** disheartening

displace
4 bump, oust, sack **5** exile, expel, usurp **6** banish, deport, depose, remove **7** succeed **8** dethrone, supplant **9** supersede, transport **10** expatriate, substitute

display
4 pomp, show **5** array, éclat, model **6** evince, expose, flaunt, lay out, parade, reveal, spread, unfold, unfurl, unveil **7** exhibit, panoply, present, showing, show off, trot out, uncover **8** brandish, evidence, manifest, showcase **9** showiness, spectacle **10** exhibiting, exhibition **11** demonstrate, ostentation **13** demonstration, manifestation

displeasing
6 vexing **7** irksome **8** annoying **10** bothersome, unpleasant **12** disagreeable **13** objectionable

displeasure
5 anger **8** aversion, disfavor, vexation **9** annoyance **10** discomfort, discontent, irritation, uneasiness **11** indignation, unhappiness **13** indisposition

disport
4 show **5** amuse **6** acquit, behave, divert, expose, flaunt, frolic, parade **7** conduct, display, exhibit, show off, trot out **9** entertain

disposal
5 order **7** removal **8** bestowal, chucking, jettison, ordering, transfer **9** clearance **10** allocation, assignment, demolition, discarding, regulation, relegation **11** arrangement, consignment, destruction, disposition **12** distribution, transference

dispose
4 bend, bias, rank **5** array, order, range **6** settle **7** arrange, incline, marshal, prepare **8** organize, regulate **9** make ready **11** systematize
of: **4** dump, junk, sell **5** chuck, scrap **6** finish, handle, unload **7** deep-six, destroy, discard **8** deal with, throw out, transfer **9** eighty-six, eliminate **10** distribute

disposed
3 apt **4** fain, game **5** prone, ready **6** biased, minded **7** partial, willing **8** arranged, inclined **9** persuaded

disposition
4 bent, cast, mood, tone, type, vein **5** being, order, stamp **6** makeup, nature, temper **7** control, leaning, mind-set **8** ordering, penchant, riddance, sequence, tendency, transfer **9** character, direction **10** management, proclivity, propensity, settlement **11** arrangement, inclination, personality, temperament **12** constitution, predilection **13** individuality
favorable: **8** optimism
unfavorable: **9** pessimism

dispossess
3 rob **4** oust **5** eject, evict, strip **6** divest **7** bereave, deprive

dispossession
4 loss **6** ouster **7** seizure **9** privation **10** divestment **11** deprivation, divestiture **13** expropriation

dispraise
3 pan **5** decry **6** censor, deride, dump on **7** put down, run down **8** bad-mouth, belittle, derogate **9** criticize, deprecate, discredit, disparage **10** depreciate, disapprove **11** detract from **12** depreciation

disproportion
8 imparity, mismatch **9** disparity **10** inequality, unevenness **12** lopsidedness

disproportionate
6 uneven **7** unequal **8** lopsided **10** unbalanced

disprove
5 belie, rebut **6** refute, negate **7** confute, explode **8** confound, overturn, puncture, traverse **9** discredit, overthrow **10** invalidate

disputable
4 iffy, moot **7** dubious **8** arguable, doubtful **9** debatable, uncertain, unsettled **10** unresolved **11** problematic **12** questionable **13** controversial

disputation
6 debate **8** argument, forensic, polemics **9** dialectic **11** controversy **13** argumentation

dispute
4 buck, duel, moot, tiff **5** argue, fight, rebut, repel **6** bicker, combat, debate, hassle, impugn, negate, oppose, refute, resist, rumpus, strife **7** confute, contend, contest, discuss, gainsay, quarrel, quibble, wrangle **8** argument, conflict, question, squabble **9** bickering, challenge, thrash out, withstand **10** contention, controvert, falling-out **11** altercation, controversy, embroilment

disputed
7 debated **8** arguable **9** contested, uncertain **12** questionable **13** controversial

disqualified
5 unfit **8** unfitted **10** ineligible, unequipped

disqualify
3 bar **5** debar **6** except **7** exclude, rule out, suspend **9** eliminate
as judge: **6** recuse

disquiet
5 alarm, angst, upset, worry **6** bother, flurry, unease, unrest **7** agitate, anxiety, concern, disturb, ferment, fluster, perturb, trouble, turmoil **10** discompose, uneasiness **11** disturbance, restiveness **12** restlessness **13** Sturm und Drang

disquietude
4 care **5** worry **6** unease, unrest **7** anxiety, concern, ferment, turmoil **9** agitation, misgiving **10** foreboding, uneasiness **11** nervousness, restiveness **12** apprehension, restlessness **13** Sturm und Drang

Disraeli, Benjamin
novel: **5** Sybil **7** Lothair, Tancred **8** Endymion **9** Coningsby
opponent: **4** Peel (Robert) **9** Gladstone (William)
queen: **8** Victoria

disregard
4 skip **6** forget, ignore, slight **7** neglect, tune out **8** overlook **9** unconcern **12** heedlessness, indifference

disregardful
3 lax **5** slack **6** remiss **8** careless, derelict, heedless **9** forgetful, unheeding, negligent, unmindful **10** neglectful, regardless, unthinking **11** indifferent, unconcerned **12** absent-minded

disremember
6 forget

disreputable
4 base **5** dingy, ratty, seamy, seedy, shady **6** scurvy, shabby, shoddy, sordid **7** run-down **8** decrepit, infamous, shameful **10** inglorious **11** dilapidated, disgraceful, ignominious **12** contemptible, unprincipled **13** discreditable, unrespectable

disrepute
5 odium, shame **7** obloquy **8** disfavor, disgrace, dishonor, ignominy **9** disesteem **10** opprobrium

disrespect
6 insult **7** disdain **8** boldness, contempt, rudeness **9** disregard, flippancy, impudence, insolence **10** incivility **11** discourtesy, presumption **12** impertinence, impoliteness

disrespectful
4 flip, rude **5** sassy, saucy **7** ill-bred, uncivil **8** flippant, impolite, impudent, insolent **10** ungracious **11** ill-mannered, impertinent **12** contemptuous, discourteous

disrobe
4 bare, peel **5** strip **6** denude, divest **7** undress **8** unclothe

disrupt
5 upset **6** mess up **7** break up, rupture **8** disorder, unsettle

dissatisfaction
6 dismay **9** annoyance, complaint **10** discontent, irritation, uneasiness **11** displeasure, frustration

dissatisfied
5 irked, vexed **7** annoyed, unhappy **8** bothered **10** begrudging, discontent, displeased, malcontent **11** complaining, disaffected, unfulfilled **12** disappointed, discontented, malcontented

dissect
5 probe, study **7** analyze, examine, inspect **9** anatomize, break down, take apart **10** scrutinize

dissection
7 autopsy **8** analysis, necropsy
of animals: **7** zootomy

dissemble
4 hide, mask **5** cloak, feign **7** conceal, cover up, dress up, falsify **8** disguise, simulate **9** whitewash **10** camouflage **11** counterfeit

dissembler
4 fake **5** faker, fraud, phony **8** deceiver, imposter, impostor, pharisee **9** hypocrite, pretender

disseminate
3 sow **5** strew **6** blazon, spread **7** bestrew, diffuse, pass out, publish, scatter, send out **8** announce, disperse, proclaim **9** advertise, broadcast, circulate, propagate, publicize **10** promulgate

dissension
5 fight **6** strife **7** discord, dispute, faction, quarrel, wrangle **8** argument, clashing, conflict, disunity, friction, variance **9** bickering **10** contention, difference, quarreling **11** altercation, controversy **12** disagreement

dissent
5 demur **6** differ, heresy, object **7** protest **8** conflict, variance **9** misbelief **10** contention, difference, heterodoxy, opposition, resistance **11** unorthodoxy **12** nonagreement **13** nonconformism, nonconformity

dissenter
7 heretic **8** apostate, defector, deserter, partisan, recreant **10** schismatic, separatist **11** misbeliever, schismatist **13** nonconformist

dissertation
6 thesis **8** tractate, treatise **9** discourse, monograph **10** commentary, exposition **11** disputation **12** disquisition **13** argumentation

dissever
3 cut, hew **4** hack, part **5** carve, slice, split **6** cleave, detach, divide, sunder **7** disjoin, divorce **8** disjoint, disunite, separate, uncouple **10** disconnect

dissidence
6 heresy, schism, strife **7** discord, dispute, dissent, faction **8** conflict, friction, variance

10 contention, disharmony, dissension, heterodoxy, opposition 11 discordance, unorthodoxy 12 disagreement 13 nonconformism, nonconformity

dissident
7 heretic 8 partisan, recusant 9 differing, dissenter, heretical, heterodox, protestor 10 schismatic, separatist, unorthodox 11 contentious, disagreeing, misbeliever, nonbeliever, quarrelsome, schismatist 12 disputatious, unharmonious 13 nonconformist

dissimilar
6 unlike 7 diverse, unalike, unequal, various 8 distinct 9 different, disparate, divergent 13 heterogeneous

dissimilarity
8 contrast, variance 9 disparity, diversity, variation 10 difference, divergence, divergency, unlikeness 11 incongruity 13 heterogeneity, inconsistency

dissimulate
see **dissemble**

dissimulation
5 fraud, guile, lying 6 deceit 7 cunning 8 artifice, flimflam, pretense 9 deception, duplicity, hypocrisy, mendacity, sophistry 10 craftiness, pharisaism 11 beguilement, smoke screen

dissipate
4 blow 5 use up, waste 6 burn up, spread, vanish 7 break up, scatter 8 disperse, evanesce, melt away, misspend, squander 9 evaporate, throw away 11 fritter away

dissipated
6 rakish, wanton, wasted 8 depraved 9 debauched, reprobate 10 degenerate, licentious, profligate 11 intemperate

dissociate
4 part 5 unfix 6 cut off, detach 7 disband, disjoin 8 alienate, disunite, estrange, separate, uncouple 9 disengage 10 disconnect

dissolute
3 lax 4 fast, wild 5 loose, slack 6 rakish, wanton 7 raffish, wayward 8 decadent, depraved 9 abandoned, debauched, indulgent, reprobate 10 degenerate, dissipated, licentious, profligate 12 unprincipled, unrestrained

dissolution
5 death, decay, split 6 demise 7 breakup, divorce, rupture, split-up 8 division 9 dispersal, partition 10 detachment, disbanding, profligacy 11 evaporation 12 liquefaction

dissolvable
7 soluble 8 meltable

dissolve
3 end 4 flux, melt, thaw, undo, void 5 annul, quash 6 recess, vacate, vanish 7 adjourn, break up, diffuse, liquefy 8 abrogate, disperse, evanesce, fade away, get rid of, melt away, prorogue, separate 9 decompose, dissipate, evaporate, prorogate, terminate, waste away 10 deliquesce, do away with 12 disintegrate

dissonance
5 noise 6 strife 7 discord 8 clashing, conflict 9 cacophony, harshness 10 contention, difference, disharmony 11 incongruity 12 disagreement 13 inconsistency

dissonant
5 harsh 7 grating, jarring, raucous 8 strident 9 unmusical 10 cacophonic, discordant, inharmonic 11 cacophonous, conflicting, incongruous 12 incompatible, inharmonious

dissuade
5 deter 7 turn off 10 discourage, disincline

distaff
6 female 8 maternal

distance
4 area 5 ambit, lapse, orbit, range, reach, scope, space, sweep 6 course, degree, extent, length, radius, remove, spread 7 breadth, compass, expanse, horizon, mileage, reserve, spacing, stretch 8 interval 9 amplitude, disparity, expansion, extension 10 divergence, divergency, remoteness, separation 11 distinction
between levels: 4 drop
between rails: 4 gage
between supports: 4 span
from bottom to top: 6 height
geometric: 8 altitude
greatest perpendicular: 6 camber
measuring instrument: 8 odometer 9 pedometer, telemeter 11 range finder
perpendicular: 5 depth
shortest: 7 beeline 12 straight line

distant
3 far, shy 4 afar, cold, cool 5 aloof, apart 6 absent, far-off, remote 7 faraway, haughty, obscure, removed, spacial, spatial 8 far-flung, isolated, outlying, reserved, secluded, solitary 9 separated, unsimilar, withdrawn 10 unsociable 11 out-of-the-way, sequestered, standoffish
combining form: 3 tel 4 tele, telo

distaste
7 disgust, dislike 8 aversion, loathing 9 antipathy, hostility, revulsion 10 abhorrence, repugnance 13 indisposition

distasteful
8 unsavory 9 loathsome, obnoxious, offensive, repellent, repugnant, repulsive 10 abominable, unpleasant 11 displeasing, unpalatable 12 disagreeable, unappetizing 13 objectionable

distemper
6 malady **7** ailment, disease **8** disorder **9** contagion, strangles **10** affliction **11** derangement **13** panleucopenia

distend
5 bloat, bulge, swell, widen **6** dilate, expand, extend, puff up **7** amplify, augment, enlarge, inflate, stretch **8** increase, lengthen **10** stretch out

distill
6 refine **7** extract **8** boil down **11** concentrate, precipitate

distinct
4 sole **5** clear, lucid, plain **6** marked, patent, single, unique **7** audible, defined, diverse, evident, express, notable, obvious, special, unusual **8** apparent, clear-cut, definite, discrete, especial, explicit, manifest, palpable, peculiar, separate, specific **9** different, divergent **10** individual, noticeable, particular **11** categorical, unambiguous, unequivocal **12** unmistakable

distinction
4 bays, rank **5** award, badge, grade, honor, kudos **6** nicety, renown **7** laurels **8** accolade, eminence, prestige **10** difference, divergence, divergency, prominence, unlikeness **11** differentia, peculiarity, preeminence, recognition **12** significance **13** dissimilarity

distinotive
6 proper, single, unique **7** special, unusual **8** peculiar, separate, singular **10** individual **13** idiosyncratic
flair: 4 élan
period: 3 era

distingué
6 classy, urbane **7** courtly, elegant, eminent, genteel, refined **8** cultured, decorous, highbrow, mannerly, polished, well-bred **9** dignified, high-class **10** cultivated **13** sophisticated

distinguish
4 mark, note, spot, view **5** honor, place **6** descry, notice, set off **7** dignify, make out, mark off, observe, pick out **8** classify, identify, perceive, separate **9** recognize, single out **10** categorize **12** characterize, discriminate **13** differentiate, individualize

distinguished
5 famed, noted **6** famous **7** eminent, notable, stately **8** esteemed, imposing, renowned **9** dignified, prominent **10** celebrated **11** illustrious

distort
4 bend, skew, warp, wind **5** alter, color, twist **6** deform, garble **7** contort, falsify, pervert, torture **8** misstate **11** misconstrue **12** misinterpret, misrepresent

distortion
8 twisting **9** deformity

distract
5 addle, mix up **6** ball up, bemuse, divert, puzzle **7** confuse, fluster, mislead, perplex **8** befuddle, bewilder, confound, throw off **9** sidetrack, unbalance

distracted
8 confused, deranged, maddened, troubled **9** oblivious **10** nonplussed **11** disoriented, inattentive, preoccupied **12** absent-minded

distraction
5 upset **9** agitation, amusement, confusion, diversion **10** perplexity **12** interruption **13** entertainment

distrait
5 upset **7** anxious, bemused, faraway, worried **8** confused, deranged, harassed, maddened, troubled **9** tormented, withdrawn **10** abstracted, distracted, distraught **11** inattentive, preoccupied **12** absentminded, apprehensive

distraught
5 upset **6** addled, crazed, torn up **7** anxious, frantic, muddled, rattled, shook up, unglued, worried **8** agitated, confused, demented, deranged, frenzied, harassed, troubled, worked up **9** flustered, perturbed, tormented, wigged-out **10** distressed, bewildered, freaked out, nonplussed **11** overwrought

distress
3 ail, irk, mar, try, vex, woe **4** ache, care, hurt, pain, pang, rack **5** agony, annoy, cross, dolor, grief, rigor, throe, trial, upset, worry **6** bother, grieve, harass, misery, pester, plague, sorrow, strain, strait, twinge **7** afflict, anguish, anxiety, exhaust, torment, torture, trouble **8** aggrieve, calamity, exigency, hardship **9** adversity, constrain, hard times, suffering **10** affliction, difficulty, heartbreak, misfortune, visitation **11** tribulation, vicissitude
call: 6 Mayday
signal: 3 SOS **5** alarm

distressing
4 dire **6** woeful **8** alarming, grievous, shocking **9** offensive **10** deplorable, lamentable **11** dispiriting, regrettable, unfortunate **13** heartbreaking

distribute
4 deal, mete **5** allot, place, strew **6** assign, assort, divide, donate, parcel, ration, spread **7** deal out, deliver, diffuse, dish out, divvy up, dole out, dribble, give out, hand out, mete out, prorate, radiate, scatter, slice up **8** allocate, classify, disburse, dispense, position, separate **9** apportion, circulate, partition, propagate, spread out **10** administer, measure out **11** disseminate

distribution
7 density **8** delivery, dividend, grouping, ordering, sequence **9** allotment, allotting, diffusion,

dispersal, marketing, placement, spreading **10** dispersion, scattering **11** arrangement, probability, propagation **12** apportioning, dispensation **13** apportionment, dissemination

distributor
5 agent **6** broker, jobber **7** carrier **9** middleman **10** wholesaler **12** intermediate

district
4 area, ward **5** tract **6** barrio, locale, parcel, region, sector **7** borough, quarter, section **8** division, locality, precinct, vicinage, vicinity **11** subdivision **12** neighborhood
Danish: 3 amt
ecclesiastical: 5 synod **6** parish **7** diocese
Greek: 4 deme
Indian: 6 tahsil
judicial: 7 circuit
London: 4 Soho **7** Chelsea, Mayfair **9** Docklands, Greenwich, Southwark **10** Kensington, Piccadilly **11** Canary Wharf, Notting Hill **13** Knightsbridge
New York: 4 Soho **7** Chelsea, Tribeca
theater: 6 rialto

District of Columbia
college, university: 6 Howard **8** American, Catholic **9** Gallaudet **10** Georgetown
motto: 13 E Pluribus Unum
official bird: 10 wood thrush
official flower: 18 American Beauty rose

distrust
5 doubt **7** suspect **8** question, wariness **9** disbelief, discredit, misgiving, suspicion **10** disbelieve

distrustful
4 wary **5** chary, leery **7** cynical, dubious, jealous **8** doubtful, doubting **10** suspicious **12** questionable

disturb
4 faze, rile, roil **5** alarm, daunt, rouse, upset, worry **6** bother, harass, meddle, mess up, pester, stir up **7** agitate, break up, disrupt, fluster, perplex, trouble, unnerve **8** bewilder, distress, unsettle **9** incommode, interrupt **10** discompose, disconcert, tamper with **13** inconvenience, interfere with

disturbance
4 flap, fuss, stir, to-do **5** hoo-ha, stink **6** clamor, hoo-hah, hubbub, rumpus, tumult, unrest, uproar **7** bobbery, turmoil **8** disorder **9** agitation, commotion, confusion, kerfuffle **10** alteration, disruption, turbulence **11** derangement, distraction **12** interruption
atmospheric: 5 storm **7** cyclone, tornado **9** hurricane
mental: 6 frenzy **8** delirium, neurosis **9** psychosis

disturbed
5 upset **6** insane, shaken **7** anxious, puzzled, rattled, worried **8** bothered, demented, deranged, troubled **9** concerned, psychotic, unsettled **10** distracted, distressed **12** disconcerted

disunion
7 divorce, rupture, split-up **8** division, severing, variance **9** partition **10** detachment, difference, separation **13** disconnection

disunite
4 part **6** divide, sunder **7** break up, disjoin, divorce, split up **8** dissever, separate, uncouple **9** disengage, fall apart **10** disconnect **12** disaffiliate

disunity
6 strife, schism **7** discord **8** conflict, division, variance **10** alienation, contention, disharmony, dissension **12** disaffection, disagreement, estrangement

disused
5 passé **8** obsolete, outdated, outmoded **9** abandoned, discarded **10** antiquated, superseded

ditch
3 dig, pit **4** drop, dump, foss, ha-ha, junk, lose, moat **5** chuck, fosse, leave, scrap, swale **6** haw-haw, reject, trench, trough **7** abandon, cashier, discard, dismiss, forsake, foxhole **8** jettison, throw out **9** crash-land, dispose of, throw away **10** excavation

dither
4 fuss, stew **5** quake, shake, tizzy, waver **6** falter, flurry, quaver, shiver **7** flutter, tremble, twitter, whiffle **8** hesitate **9** agitation, commotion, confusion, vacillate **10** excitement, turbulence **12** shilly-shally

dithyramb
4 hymn, poem **5** chant

dithyrambic
6 ardent, fervid **9** perfervid, rhapsodic **10** boisterous, passionate **11** impassioned

ditto
4 copy, ibid., idem, same **5** clone, me too, mimeo, repro, Xerox **6** carbon, repeat **7** replica, reprint, similar **9** duplicate, facsimile, photocopy **10** carbon copy, mimeograph **11** replication **12** reproduction **13** reduplication

ditty
3 air, lay **4** song, tune **5** carol, chant **6** ballad

ditz
7 airhead, dingbat **9** birdbrain

diurnal
5 daily **7** daytime **8** daylight **9** circadian, ephemeral, quotidian

diva
7 goddess 10 prima donna 11 leading lady
solo: 4 aria

divagate
4 turn, veer 5 drift, stray 6 depart, ramble, wander 7 digress, diverge

divan
4 sofa 5 couch 6 settee 7 chamber, council 9 davenport 12 chesterfield

dive
3 bar, pub 4 dash, dump, hole, jump, leap 5 joint, lunge, pitch, sound, swoop 6 header, lounge, plunge, saloon, tavern 7 barroom, decline, descend, descent, hangout, plummet, taproom 8 submerge 9 honky-tonk, roadhouse 10 cannonball
type: 4 pike, swan, tuck 6 gainer 7 cutaway 9 belly flop, jackknife

diver
4 loon

diverge
4 part, vary 5 stray 6 depart, differ, swerve 7 deflect, deviate, digress 8 disagree, separate 9 bifurcate, branch off, draw apart

divergence
7 parting 9 departure, deviation, differing 10 aberration, deflection, difference, digression, separation 11 disagreeing, discrepancy, distinction 12 disagreement

divergent
6 unlike 8 aberrant, abnormal, atypical 9 anomalous, different, differing, disparate, irregular 10 dissimilar

divers
6 sundry 7 several, various 8 assorted 9 different, disparate 13 miscellaneous

diverse
5 mixed 6 motley, sundry, unlike, varied 7 several, unalike, unequal, various, varying 8 assorted, discrete, distinct, manifold, separate 9 different, differing, disparate, multiform, multiplex, unsimilar 10 contrasted, dissimilar 11 contrasting, contrastive 12 multifarious 13 contradictory, miscellaneous
combining form: 4 vari 5 vario
meanings: 8 polysemy

diversion
5 sport 7 pastime, turning 8 pleasure, sideshow 9 amusement, deviation, enjoyment 10 aberration, deflection, recreation, red herring 11 distraction 13 entertainment

diversity
7 variety 10 assortment, difference, unlikeness 11 variegation 12 multiformity 13 dissimilarity, heterogeneity

divert
4 turn, veer 5 amuse 6 regale, swerve 7 beguile, deflect, delight, deviate, digress 8 distract, redirect 9 entertain, turn aside

divest
3 rid, rob 4 free 5 spoil, strip 6 denude 7 bereave, deprive, despoil, disrobe, undress 8 take away 9 dismantle 10 disinherit, dispossess

divide
3 cut 4 fork, part 5 allot, cut up, sever, share 6 assign, cleave, parcel, ration, schism, sunder 7 break up, dissect, divorce, dole out, isolate, prorate, quarter, share in, split up 8 allocate, classify, dispense, disunite, separate 9 apportion, branch out, partition, watershed 10 distribute, measure out 11 dichotomize, distinguish
into four parts: 7 quarter
into three parts: 7 trisect
into two parts: 5 halve 6 bisect 9 bifurcate

divided
4 rent 5 cleft, riven, split 6 cloven 7 asunder, partite 8 ruptured

dividend
5 bonus, share 6 return, reward 7 benefit, guerdon, portion, premium 9 allotment 12 dispensation

divider
6 border, screen 9 partition

divination
6 augury 7 insight 8 prophecy 11 foretelling, soothsaying
by communication with the dead: 10 necromancy
by figures: 8 geomancy
by lots: 9 sortilege
by numbers: 10 numerology
by rods: 7 dowsing 11 rhabdomancy
by stars: 9 astrology

divine
4 holy 5 clerk, godly, infer 6 cleric, deduce, deific, intuit, parson, priest, sacred, superb 7 foresee, godlike 8 clerical, foreknow, foretell, heavenly, luscious, minister, preacher, prophesy, reverend 9 apprehend, churchman, clergyman, marvelous, religious, visualize 10 anticipate, conjecture, sanctified, superhuman, theologian 11 scrumptious 12 ecclesiastic

Divine Comedy
guide: 6 Vergil, Virgil
poet: 5 Dante (Alighieri)
section: 5 canto 7 Inferno 8 Paradiso 10 Purgatorio

diviner
4 seer 5 augur, sibyl 6 oracle 7 palmist, prophet 8 haruspex 10 forecaster, prophetess, soothsayer

diving bird
3 auk **4** coot, loon, smew **5** grebe, murre **7** pelican

divinity
3 god **5** deity, fudge **7** goddess, godhead, godhood **8** theology

division
3 cut **4** part, unit **5** class, piece, slice, split **6** branch, moiety, parcel, schism, sector **7** breakup, discord, dissent, divorce, parting, portion, rupture, section, segment, split-up **8** category, conflict, district, disunion, disunity, variance **9** partition **10** detachment, difference, disharmony, dissidence, separation **11** dissolution **12** disagreement **13** apportionment
Bible: **5** verse
book: **7** chapter
British territorial: **5** shire
building: **4** wing
cell: **7** meiosis, mitosis
city: **4** ward **7** borough **8** precinct
contest: **4** heat **6** inning, period
corolla: **5** petal
country: **5** state **6** canton **8** province **10** department, prefecture
family: **4** side **6** branch
geologic time: **3** eon, era **5** epoch **6** period
hospital: **4** ward, wing
into two: **9** bisection **11** bifurcation, bipartition
meal: **6** course
music: **3** bar **4** beat **7** measure **8** movement
opera, play: **3** act **5** scena, scene
poem: **5** canto, verse **6** stanza
population: **7** segment, stratum
race: **3** lap **4** heat
social: **5** caste, class, tribe
state: **6** county, parish
term: **8** quotient
time: **3** day, eon **4** week, year **5** month **6** decade, minute, moment, second **7** century, weekend **9** fortnight **10** millennium
tribal: **4** clan
word: **8** syllable
zodiac: **4** sign

divisive
8 factious **11** disunifying

divorce
4 part **5** sever, split **6** divide, sunder **7** break up, breakup, disjoin, rupture **8** disjoint, dissever, disunion, disunite, separate **9** partition, severance **10** detachment, separation **11** dissolution

divot
3 sod **4** turf **5** clump

divulge
4 blab, leak, tell **5** spill **6** betray, expose, gossip, reveal, tattle **7** let slip, uncover **8** disclose, give away

Dixie composer
6 Emmett (Daniel D.)

dizziness
7 vertigo **9** giddiness

dizzy
5 addle, dazed, giddy, mix up, silly, tipsy **6** addled **7** confuse, dazzled, flighty, foolish, fuddled, muddled, puzzled, reeling **8** confused, swimming, whirling **9** befuddled, confusing **10** bewildered, confounded, distracted, exorbitant, immoderate, inordinate **11** extravagant, lightheaded, vertiginous

Djibouti
language: **6** Arabic, French
monetary unit: **5** franc
neighbor: **7** Eritrea, Somalia **8** Ethiopia
sea: **3** Red

DNA
component: **7** adenine, guanine, thymine **8** cytosine **10** nucleotide **11** deoxyribose
segment: **4** exon, gene **7** cistron
spiral: **5** helix

doable
8 feasible, possible, workable **9** realistic **10** achievable, attainable **11** performable

do away with
3 end, nix, zap **4** kill, slay **5** annul, erase, whack **6** cancel, finish, murder, remove, repeal, revoke, rub out **7** abolish, bump off, deep-six, destroy, discard, expunge, rescind, squelch, wipe out **8** abrogate, blow away, demolish, dispatch, dissolve, massacre, stamp out **9** dispose of, eliminate, eradicate, extirpate, finish off, liquidate, slaughter **10** extinguish, obliterate **11** discontinue, exterminate

docent
5 guide **6** leader **7** teacher **8** lecturer **10** instructor

docile
4 tame **6** pliant **7** ductile, pliable **8** amenable, biddable, obedient, yielding **9** adaptable, compliant, teachable, tractable **10** submissive **11** acquiescent

dock
3 bob, cut **4** crop, fine, pier, quay, rump, slip **5** berth, jetty, levee, tie up, wharf **6** anchor, hangar, lessen, marina, reduce **7** abridge, landing, shorten **8** cut short, platform, truncate
union: **3** ILA
worker: **6** lumper **9** stevedore **12** longshoreman

docket
4 card **6** agenda, lineup, record **7** program **8** abstract, calendar, caseload, register, schedule **9** timetable

doctor
3 fix, vet **4** mend **5** adapt, alter, medic, treat **6** medico, repair **7** croaker, dentist, falsify, scholar, surgeon **8** sawbones **9** clinician, internist, physician **10** adulterate, specialist **11** medicine man, recondition, reconstruct
animal: **3** vet **12** veterinarian
children's: **12** pediatrician
famous: **4** Koop (C. Everett), Weil (Andrew) **5** Apgar (Virginia), Galen, Spock (Benjamin) **6** Atkins (Robert), Chopra (Deepak), Mehmet (Oz), Ornish (Dean) **9** Blackwell (Elizabeth), Kevorkian (Jack) **10** Schweitzer (Albert) **11** Hippocrates, Livingstone (David)
foot: **10** podiatrist **11** chiropodist
heart: **12** cardiologist
organization: **3** AMA
teeth: **7** dentist **10** exodontist
women's: **12** gynecologist

Doctor of the Church
5 Basil **6** Jerome **7** Ambrose, Gregory **9** Augustine **10** Athanasius

Doctorow novel
7 Ragtime **9** City of God (The) **10** Waterworks, World's Fair **12** Book of Daniel (The) **13** Billy Bathgate **18** Welcome to Hard Times

Doctor Zhivago
author: **9** Pasternak (Boris)
character: **4** Lara **7** Larissa
film director: **4** Lean (David)
film star: **6** Sharif (Omar) **8** Christie (Julie)

doctrinaire
5 rigid **8** dogmatic **9** obstinate **10** unyielding **11** domineering, magisterial **13** authoritarian

doctrine
3 ism **5** axiom, basic, canon, credo, creed, dogma, faith, tenet **7** precept **8** teaching **9** principle **11** fundamental

document
4 deed, writ **5** paper **6** record **8** evidence, monument **9** testimony **10** instrument **11** certificate
travel: **8** passport

dodder
4 limp **5** shake **6** falter, hobble, totter **7** shamble, shuffle, stagger, tremble **12** morning glory

doddering
5 anile, shaky **6** doting, feeble, senile **7** fragile **8** unsteady, weakened **9** faltering

dodge
4 duck, jink, ploy, ruse, slip **5** avert, avoid, elude, evade, fence, parry, shirk, skirt, slide, trick **6** escape, scheme, weasel **7** evasion **8** sidestep **9** avoidance, deception, expedient

Dodge City lawman
4 Earp (Wyatt)

Dodger
5 Davis (Tommy) **6** Garvey (Steve), Karros (Eric), Koufax (Sandy), Piazza (Michael), Snider (Duke), Sutton (Don) **8** Newcombe (Don), Robinson (Jackie) **9** Hershiser (Orel) **10** Campanella (Roy)
field: **7** Ebbetts
home: **8** Brooklyn **10** Los Angeles
manager: **6** Alston (Walter) **7** Lasorda (Tommy)

dodger
6 outlaw, screen **7** escapee **8** circular, deceiver, deserter, fugitive, handbill, runagate **9** throwaway

dodgy
4 iffy **5** fishy, vague **6** tricky **7** cryptic, obscure **8** doubtful, unproven **9** ambiguous, enigmatic, uncertain **10** indefinite, suspicious, unreliable **11** problematic **12** questionable **13** controversial

dodo
3 oaf **4** bird, boob, clod, ditz, dolt, dope, goof, yo-yo **5** chump, dummy, dunce, idiot, moron, ninny, noddy, stupe **6** dimwit, dum-dum, nitwit **7** airhead, dullard, pinhead **8** bonehead, dumbbell, imbecile, lunkhead, meathead, numskull **9** birdbrain, blockhead, ignoramus, lamebrain, numbskull, simpleton **10** dunderhead, nincompoop **11** chowderhead, chucklehead

doe
4 deer **6** female, rabbit **8** kangaroo

doff
4 shed **6** remove **7** take off

dog
3 cur, pom, pug, pup, tag **4** alan, bird, chow, fice, mutt, peke, puli, tail, tyke **5** Akita, boxer, canid, corgi, dhole, dingo, feist, frank, hound, husky, lemon, pooch, puppy, spitz, trail **6** Afghan, beagle, borzoi, bowwow, briard, canine, collie, detent, poodle, pursue, rascal, saluki, setter, shadow, Talbot, vizsla, wiener, wretch **7** andiron, basenji, harrier, Maltese, mastiff, mongrel, pointer, redbone, Samoyed, Scottie, shar-pei, spaniel, terrier, whippet **8** Airedale, Brittany, elkhound, foxhound, inferior, keeshond, komondor, malamute, malemute, papillon, Pekinese, pinscher, sheepdog, Shiba Inu, spurious, wirehair **9** Chihuahua, dachshund, dalmation, deerhound, Great Dane, greyhound, Lhasa apso, Pekingese, retriever, schnauzer, wolfhound **10** bloodhound, Pomeranian, rottweiler, Weimaraner **11** basset hound, bullmastiff, frankfurter, wienerwurst **12** border collie, Newfoundland, Saint Bernard **13** cocker spaniel
breeders' org.: **3** AKC
Bush's: **6** Millie
Buster Brown's: **4** Tige
Charlie Brown's: **6** Snoopy

Chinese: **7** shar-pei, shih tzu **9** Pekingese
command: **3** sit **4** heel, stay
crime-fighting: **7** McGruff
Dagwood's: **5** Daisy
Dorothy's: **4** Toto
family: **5** canid **7** Canidae
FDR's: **4** Fala
fictional: **3** Max **4** Buck, Cujo, Lady, Tige **5** Astro, Pluto, Scamp, Tramp **6** Big Red, Marley **8** McBarker **9** Marmaduke, Old Yeller, Scooby-Doo, White Fang
"Garfield": **4** Odie
genus: **5** Canis
Grinch's: **3** Max
heroic: **5** Balto
Japanese: **5** Akita **8** Shiba Inu
L.B.J.'s: **3** Her
monster: **8** Barghest
movie: **4** Asta, Lady, Toto **5** Benji, Pongo, Tramp **6** Gromit, Lassie **9** Beethoven, Old Yeller, Rin Tin Tin
name: **3** Max **4** Fido, Spot **5** Bella, Buddy, Rover **6** Bowser
Nixon's: **8** Checkers
Obama's: **5** Sunny
Odysseus's: **5** Argos
of Hades: **8** Cerberus
Orphan Annie's: **5** Sandy
Peanuts: **6** Snoopy
RCA: **6** Nipper
Roy Rogers's: **6** Bullet
Sgt. Snorkel's: **4** Otto
sled command: **4** mush
small: **3** toy
space traveler: **5** Laika
Steinbeck's: **7** Charley
television: **4** King **5** Eddie, Tramp **6** Lassie, Murray **8** Wishbone **9** Rin Tin Tin
three-headed: **8** Cerberus
tooth: **4** fang
treat: **4** bone
two-headed: **6** Orthos
Wallace's: **6** Gromit
Welsh: **5** corgi
Wendy's: **4** Nana
wild: **5** dingo
young: **3** pup **5** puppy, whelp

dog days
6 August **9** canicular

dogfight
3 row **4** fray **5** brawl, broil, melee, set-to **6** fracas, ruckus **7** ruction **10** donnybrook, free-for-all

dogfish
6 bowfin, burbot **8** mud puppy

dogged
7 adamant **8** obdurate, resolute, stubborn **9** insistent, steadfast, obstinate, tenacious, unbending **10** bullheaded, determined, hard-headed, persistent, persisting, unshakable, unyielding **11** persevering, unremitting **12** pertinacious

doggone
4 damn, dang, darn, rank **5** utter **6** cursed, damned, darned **7** blasted, blessed, dratted **8** absolute, accursed, infernal, outright **9** out-and-out **10** confounded **11** unmitigated **13** blankety-blank

dogma
4 code, rule **5** canon, credo, creed, tenet **6** belief, gospel **7** precept **8** doctrine, ideology **9** orthodoxy, postulate, teachings **10** conviction, persuasion

dogmatic
8 oracular, orthodox **9** assertive, canonical, doctrinal **11** dictatorial, doctrinaire, magisterial, opinionated

Dog of Flanders author
5 Ouida

dog-paddle
4 swim

Dogpatch creator
4 Capp (Al)

dog's age
3 eon **4** aeon **8** blue moon, eternity

Dog Star
6 Sirius

dogwood
6 cornel, Cornus **8** red osier

do in
4 kill, ruin, slay **5** cheat, wreck **6** defeat, finish, murder, rub out **7** blot out, bump off, destroy, execute, exhaust, frazzle, take out, wear out, wipe out **8** dispatch, knock off, knock out **9** eliminate, liquidate, prostrate, run ragged, shipwreck **11** assassinate

doing
3 act **6** action **8** activity
good: **10** beneficent
evil: **10** maleficent

doit
3 bit, jot **4** coin, damn, dram, drop, hoot, iota, mite, whit **6** trifle **8** particle

doldrums
5 blahs, blues, dumps, ennui, gloom, slump **6** apathy, tedium, torpor **7** boredom **9** dejection **10** depression, inactivity, quiescence, stagnation **12** listlessness

doleful
3 sad **4** down **7** forlorn, ruthful **8** cast down, dejected, dolorous, downcast, grieving, mournful, mourning **9** afflicted, cheerless, depressed, miserable, plaintive, sorrowful, sorrowing,

woebegone **10** dispirited, lamentable, lugubrious, melancholy **11** crestfallen, downhearted **12** disconsolate

dole out
4 dealmete **5** allot **6** divide, parcel, ration **7** divvy up **8** disburse, dispense, disperse **9** apportion, partition **10** administer, distribute

doll
3 Ken **6** Barbie, figure, Kewpie, puppet **7** kachina **10** Betsy Wetsy, Raggedy Ann **11** Raggedy Andy
grotesque: 8 golliwog

dollar
3 one **4** bill, buck, clam, oner, peso **5** taler **6** single **7** ringgit, smacker **8** simoleon **9** cartwheel, greenback

dollop
4 blob, glob, lump **7** portion

Doll's House, A
author: 5 Ibsen (Henrik)
heroine: 4 Nora

dolly
4 cart **7** stirrer **8** platform **10** locomotive

dolomite
6 marble **9** limestone

dolor
5 agony, grief **6** misery, sorrow **7** anguish, passion **8** distress **9** suffering **10** affliction

dolorous
6 rueful, woeful **7** ruthful **8** grievous, mournful, wretched **9** afflicted, anguished, miserable, plaintive, sorrowful **10** lamentable, lugubrious, melancholy **13** heartbreaking

dolphin
5 whale **7** bollard **8** porpoise

dolt
3 ass, oaf **4** boob, clod, dodo, dork, fool, goof, goon, lout, yo-yo **5** booby, chump, dunce, idiot **6** nitwit **7** dullard, fathead, halfwit, jughead, pinhead, saphead, schnook **8** bonehead, dumbbell, dummkopf, imbecile, lunkhead, meathead, numskull **9** blockhead, lamebrain, numbskull, simpleton **11** chowderhead

doltish
4 dull, dumb **5** dense, thick **6** oafish, obtuse, stupid **7** idiotic, moronic **8** ignorant, mindless **9** dim-witted, fatheaded, imbecilic

domain
4 fief, land, rule, turf **5** field, realm **6** estate, sphere **7** barony, fiefdom, kingdom, terrain **8** dominion, province **9** bailiwick, territory

dome
4 head, hill, roof **5** mound, vault **6** bubble, cupola **7** ceiling, stadium **8** mountain
shape: 4 cone **5** onion **8** geodesic

domestic
4 help, home, maid, tame **6** butler, family, native **7** servant **8** houseboy, internal, national **9** charwoman, household **10** indigenous **11** chambermaid

domesticate
4 tame **5** adapt, adopt, train **10** housebreak

domicile
3 pad **4** home **5** abode, house, lodge, put up **6** bestow, billet, harbor **7** quarter **8** dwelling, quarters **9** residence, residency **10** habitation

domiciliate
4 bunk, tame **5** house, lodge, put up **6** billet, harbor, reside **7** quarter

dominance
4 rule, sway **5** power **7** command, control **7** mastery **9** supremacy **10** ascendancy, prepotency **11** preeminence, sovereignty

dominant
4 main **5** chief, first, major **6** ruling **7** leading, supreme **8** foremost, powerful, reigning **9** ascendant, governing, number-one, paramount, prevalent, principal **10** commanding, preeminent, prevailing, surpassing **11** controlling, overbearing **12** preponderant

dominate
4 rule **5** reign **6** direct, govern, obsess **7** control, prevail, repress **8** bestride, hold sway, look down, loom over, overlook **9** subjugate, tower over, tyrannize **10** tower above

domination
4 rule, sway **5** might, power **7** command, control, mastery **9** authority, supremacy **10** ascendancy, prepotency, suzerainty **11** preeminence, sovereignty **13** preponderancy

dominator
4 boss, head **5** chief, ruler **6** honcho, leader, master, top dog **7** headman **8** director, hierarch, kingfish **9** chieftain, commander

domineer
5 bully **6** hector **7** swagger **8** browbeat, bulldoze **9** tyrannize **10** intimidate

domineering
5 bossy **6** lordly **8** arrogant, despotic **9** imperious, masterful **10** autocratic, high-handed, oppressive, tyrannical **11** dictatorial, magisterial, overbearing

Domingo, e.g.
5 tenor

Dominica
capital: 6 Roseau
discoverer: 8 Columbus (Christopher)
location: 10 West Indies
sea: 9 Caribbean

Dominican Republic
capital: **12** Santo Domingo
island: **10** Hispaniola
language: **7** Spanish
location: **10** West Indies
monetary unit: **4** peso
mountain: **6** Duarte
neighbor: **5** Haiti
sea: **9** Caribbean

dominion
3 raj **4** rule, sway, turf **5** realm, power **6** domain, empery, empire, regnum, sphere **7** demesne, kingdom, terrain **8** province **9** ascendant, ownership, supremacy, territory **10** ascendancy, possession **11** preeminence, sovereignty

domino
4 bone, cape, mask **5** amice, cloak, visor **6** vizard **8** disguise
spot: **3** pip

don
3 sir **4** lord **5** get on, put on, tutor **6** assume, fellow, take on **9** professor, undertake

Donalbain
brother: **7** Malcolm
father: **6** Duncan

Donald's ex
5 Ivana, Marla

donate
4 give **5** grant **6** bestow, chip in, supply **7** dish out, hand out, present, provide **8** give away, shell out, transfer **10** contribute

donation
3 aid **4** alms, gift **5** grant **7** bequest, handout **8** offering **9** endowment **11** benefaction, beneficence **12** contribution, philanthropy

Don Carlos
author: **8** Schiller (Friedrich von)
composer: **5** Verdi (Giuseppe)
father: **6** Philip

done
4 over **5** all in, ended, ready, spent **6** bushed, gone by, used up **7** drained, dressed, far-gone, settled, through, worn-out **8** complete, depleted, finished, washed-up **9** completed, concluded, exhausted **10** terminated **12** accomplished
poetic: **3** o'er

donee
7 grantee **8** receiver **9** recipient **11** beneficiary

done for
4 gone, sunk **5** kaput **6** beaten, doomed, ruined **7** wrecked **8** finished, stricken

done in
5 spent **6** bushed, effete, used up **7** drained, far gone, worn-out **8** depleted **9** exhausted, shattered, washed out

Don Giovanni
composer: **6** Mozart (Wolfgang Amadeus)
conquest: **4** Anna (Donna) **6** Elvira (Donna) **7** Zerlina
servant: **9** Leporello

Donizetti, Gaetano
hero: **7** Roberto (Devereux)
opera: **5** Lucia (di Lammermoor) **10** Anna Bolena, La Favorita **11** Don Pasquale **12** Maria Stuarda

Don Juan
4 rake, roué, wolf **5** Romeo **6** chaser, masher **7** amorist, gallant, playboy, seducer **8** Casanova, lothario, paramour **9** ladies' man, libertine, womanizer **10** lady-killer, profligate **11** philanderer
drama: **10** Stone Guest (The)
home: **7** Seville
mother: **4** Inez
poet: **5** Byron (Lord) **7** Pushkin (Alexander)

donkey
3 ass **4** mule **5** burro **7** jackass
female: **5** jenny **6** jennet
male: **4** jack
wild: **5** kiang **6** onager

donkeywork
4 moil, toil **5** grind, labor **7** travail **8** drudgery

donnybrook
3 row **4** fray, riot **5** brawl, broil, fight, melee, set-to **6** fracas, ruckus, rumpus, tumult, uproar **7** dispute, quarrel, rhubarb, ruction **10** free-for-all **11** altercation

donor
5 giver, Type O **6** patron **7** granter, grantor **8** bestower **9** conferrer, presenter **10** benefactor **11** contributor

do-nothing
3 bum **4** slug **5** idler **6** loafer, slouch **7** goof-off, slacker **8** deadbeat, fainéant, layabout, slugabed, sluggard **9** lazybones, vegetable **11** couch potato

Don Pasquale composer
9 Donizetti (Gaetano)

Don Quixote
author: **9** Cervantes (Miguel de)
beloved: **8** Dulcinea
companion (squire): **11** Sancho Panza
giant: **8** windmill
home: **8** La Mancha
horse: **9** Rocinante, Rosinante, Rozinante

doodad
5 gizmo, thing **6** bauble, dingus, entity, gadget, gewgaw, jigger, widget **7** trinket, whatsit **8** gimcrack **9** doohickey, thingummy **10** attachment, decoration, knickknack **11** thingamabob, thingamajig, thingumajig

doodle
6 dabble, dawdle, fiddle, potter, putter, sketch, tinker, trifle 7 cartoon, drawing 8 scribble 10 mess around

doodlebug
7 ant lion, missile 8 buzz bomb

doohickey
see **doodad**

doom
4 damn, fate, ruin 5 death 6 decree, demise, kismet 7 condemn, destiny, tragedy 8 calamity, disaster, judgment, sentence 11 catastrophe 12 annihilation, last judgment

doomful
4 dire 7 baleful, baneful, direful, fateful, malefic, ominous, unlucky 8 dreadful, ill-fated, sinister 10 foreboding, portentous 11 apocalyptic

doomsayer
7 killjoy 9 Cassandra, defeatist, Gloomy Gus, pessimist

___ Doone
5 Lorna

door
3 way 4 adit, exit, gate 5 entry 6 access, egress, entrée, portal 7 gateway, ingress, opening 8 entrance, entryway 9 admission 10 admittance 11 entranceway
fasterne: 4 hasp
rear: 7 postern

doorkeeper
5 usher 6 porter 7 ostiary

doorway
5 entry 6 portal 8 entrance, entryway 11 entranceway

doozy
3 ace, pip 4 lulu 5 beaut, daisy, dandy, dilly, peach 6 corker 7 paragon 8 jim-dandy, standout 9 humdinger 10 ripsnorter 10 phenomenon 11 crackerjack

dope
3 oaf 4 bozo, clod, ditz, dodo, dolt, drug, goof, info, news, yo-yo 5 chump, drugs, dummy, dunce, facts, idiot, moron, ninny, noddy, stupe 6 dimwit, doofus, dum-dum, heroin, nitwit, opiate, sedate, skinny 7 airhead, cocaine, details, dullard, lowdown, pinhead 8 bonehead, dumbbell, imbecile, lunkhead, meathead, narcotic, numskull 9 birdbrain, blockhead, ignoramus, lamebrain, marijuana, narcotize, numbskull, simpleton 10 dunderhead, nincompoop 11 anesthetize, chowderhead, chucklehead, information, preparation

doped
4 high 5 dazed 6 stoned, zonked 7 drugged, tuned-in 8 hopped-up, tripping, turned on, wiped out 9 spaced-out, strung out, stupefied 10 narcotized

do penance
5 atone

dopey
4 dumb 5 silly 6 dulled, stupid, torpid 7 fatuous, fuddled, muddled 8 comatose, sluggish 9 lethargic, senseless, stupefied

Doris
brother: 6 Nereus
daughters: 7 Nereids
father: 7 Oceanus
husband: 6 Nereus

dork
4 geek, nerd, wonk

dormancy
5 sleep 6 repose 7 latency, slumber 8 abeyance, diapause, doldrums, downtime 9 torpidity 10 inactivity, quiescence, suspension 11 cold storage 12 intermission, interruption

dormant
5 inert 6 asleep, drowsy, fallow, latent, torpid 7 abeyant 8 comatose, inactive, sluggish 9 lethargic, potential, quiescent, suspended 10 slow-moving, slumbering

dormer
3 bay 4 nook 5 niche 6 window

Dorothy's dog
4 Toto

dorsal
6 aboral 7 abaxial

___ d'Orsay
4 Quai

dorsum
4 back

Dorus
brother: 6 Aeolus
father: 6 Hellen

dory
4 bark, boat 5 craft, skiff 6 barque, bateau 7 shallop 8 lifeboat

dose
3 fix, hit 4 dram, shot, slug 7 measure, portion 8 medicate, quantity

Dos Passos trilogy
3 U.S.A.

dossier
4 file 6 folder 9 portfolio

dot
3 pip 4 mark, mote, stud 5 dower, dowry, pixel, point, speck 6 bestud, pepper, period 7 freckle, speckle, stipple 8 flyspeck, sprinkle 9 bespeckle 12 decimal point
in the ocean: 4 isle 5 islet

dotage
8 senility 11 decrepitude, senectitude

dote on
5 adore, enjoy, fancy, prize **7** cherish, idolize **8** treasure **9** delight in

doting
4 dear, fond, gaga **6** loving **7** adoring, devoted **12** affectionate

dotted
4 semé, sown **6** spotty, strewn **8** punctate, stippled

dotty
4 gaga **5** crazy, loony, wacky **6** absurd, insane **7** foolish, smitten **8** enamored **9** eccentric **10** captivated, enraptured, infatuated **12** preposterous

double
4 copy, dual, fold, mate, tack, twin **5** clone, duple, image, match, twice **6** bifold, binary, duplex, paired, ringer **7** dualize, enlarge, magnify, replica, twofold **8** alter ego, geminate, increase **9** companion, dualistic, duplicate, look-alike, replicate **10** dead ringer, reciprocal, simulacrum, understudy **13** spitting image

double-barreled
4 dual **5** duple **6** bifold, binary, duplex, paired **7** twofold **9** dualistic

double bass
10 bull fiddle

double-cross
3 con **4** dupe **5** cheat, rat on, trick **6** betray, delude, humbug, juggle, take in **7** beguile, deceive, sell out, two-time **8** flimflam, hoodwink **9** four-flush

double curve
3 ess **4** ogee

double dagger
6 diesis

double-dealer
3 gyp **5** cheat, knave **6** con man **7** cozener, diddler, sharper **8** deceiver, swindler **9** defrauder **11** flimflammer **13** confidence man

double-dealing
5 fraud **6** deceit **7** chicane **8** flimflam, trickery **9** chicanery, deceitful, deception, duplicity, two-timing **10** hanky-panky **11** duplicitous

double-dome
7 egghead **8** Einstein, highbrow **10** pointy-head **12** intellectual

double-faced
9 deceitful, deceptive, equivocal, insincere **10** reversible **12** hypocritical **13** untrustworthy

doublet
3 duo **4** dyad, pair, span **5** brace **6** couple, jacket **7** twosome

double-talk
4 bosh, bunk **5** hokum, hooey **6** babble, bunkum, drivel, jabber **7** blather, hogwash, twaddle **8** flimflam, nonsense **9** gibberish, poppycock **10** balderdash **12** gobbledygook

double vision
8 diplopia

doubt
5 qualm **7** concern, dispute, dubiety, suspect **8** distrust, mistrust, question **9** challenge, disbelief, misgiving, suspicion **10** skepticism **11** dubiousness, incertitude, incredulity, uncertainty

doubtable
4 hazy, iffy, moot **7** dubious, suspect **8** arguable **9** ambiguous, debatable, equivocal, uncertain, undecided **10** disputable, borderline, indefinite **11** problematic **12** questionable

doubter
5 cynic **6** Thomas **7** sceptic, skeptic **8** agnostic **10** Pyrrhonist, questioner, unbeliever **11** freethinker

doubtful
4 hazy, iffy, moot **5** fishy, shady, shaky **6** chancy, unsure **7** clouded, dubious, obscure, suspect, unclear **8** arguable, unlikely **9** ambiguous, debatable, dubitable, equivocal, uncertain, undecided, unsettled **10** borderline, disputable, improbable **11** problematic, speculative **12** questionable

doubtfulness
7 concern, dubiety **8** mistrust **9** ambiguity, misgiving, suspicion **10** indecision, skepticism, uneasiness **11** dubiousness, incertitude, uncertainty **13** indeterminacy

doubting Thomas
see **doubter**

doubtless
6 likely, surely **7** certain, clearly **8** of course, probably **10** absolutely, definitely, positively, presumably **11** indubitably **12** indisputably **13** presumptively, unequivocally

douceur
3 tip **4** gift **5** bribe **7** present **8** gratuity **9** baksheesh

dough
4 cash, masa **5** bread, money **6** dinero, moolah **7** cabbage, lettuce, scratch **8** currency **11** legal tender
inflator: 5 yeast

doughboy
7 dogface **11** infantryman

doughty
4 bold **5** brave, gutsy, manly, stout **6** daring, heroic, plucky, spunky, strong **7** gallant, valiant **8** fearless, intrepid, resolved, stalwart, unafraid, valorous **9** dauntless, undaunted **10** courageous **12** stouthearted

doughy
3 wan **4** pale **5** pasty, waxen **6** pallid **8** blanched **9** colorless

do up
3 can, fix **4** mend, wash, wrap **5** clean, patch **6** clothe, doctor, fasten, repair, revamp **7** exhaust, festoon, launder, package, prepare, rebuild, wear out **8** decorate, gift wrap, ornament, overhaul **9** embellish **11** recondition, reconstruct

dour
4 glum, grim **5** bleak, harsh, rigid, stern, surly **6** gloomy, morose, severe, strict, sullen **7** austere, crabbed, peevish **9** obstinate, saturnine, stringent **10** forbidding, unyielding

douse
3 sop **4** duck, dunk, soak **5** bathe, drown, plash, slosh, souse **6** drench, put out, quench, splash, strike **7** immerse, slacken **8** inundate, saturate, snuff out, submerge, submerse **10** extinguish

dove
6 culver, pigeon **8** pacifist
call: **3** coo
genus: **7** Columba
pen: **4** cote

dovecote
6 aviary **9** birdhouse

dovetail
3 fit **4** jibe, mesh **5** agree, match, tally **6** accord, splice, square **7** comport, conform **8** check out **9** harmonize, interlock, intermesh **10** correspond

dovish
4 mild **6** gentle **7** antiwar, pacific **8** pacifist **9** peaceable **10** nonviolent, pacifistic **11** peace-loving **12** conciliatory

dowager
4 dame **5** widow **6** matron **9** matriarch **10** grande dame **11** grandmother

dowdy
4 drab **5** dated, frump, passé, seedy, tacky **6** blowsy, bygone, démodé, frowsy, frowzy, frumpy, old hat, shabby **7** rundown, unkempt **8** frumpish, outdated, outmoded, slattern, slovenly **9** out-of-date, unstylish **10** antiquated, bedraggled, slatternly **11** draggle-tail **12** old-fashioned **13** draggletailed

dowel
3 bar, peg, pin, rod **5** stick

dower
4 gift **5** endow, endue **6** legacy, talent **8** bequeath

dowitcher
5 snipe **9** sandpiper

do without
5 forgo, waive **6** abjure, eschew, give up, pass up **8** renounce

down
3 eat, fur, ill, low, off, sad **4** blue, fell, fuzz, lint, pile, sick **5** below, ended, floor, floss, fluff, level, lower, under **6** defeat, fallen, finish, lay low, nether **7** conquer, consume, destroy, flatten, swallow, unhappy **8** bowl over, complete, defeated, dejected, dispatch, feathers, finished, inferior, overcome, sluggish, surmount **9** completed, concluded, depressed, earthward, miserable **10** dispirited, groundward

down-and-out
5 broke, needy **6** hard-up, ruined **8** beggared, derelict, homeless **9** destitute, penniless, penurious **12** impoverished

down-and-outer
3 bum **6** beggar, pauper, wretch **7** have-not **9** mendicant **10** supplicant

down-at-heels
4 mean **5** dingy, ratty, seedy, tacky **6** ragged, ragtag, shabby, shoddy **7** ignoble, run-down, worn-out **8** decrepit, tattered **10** bedraggled, threadbare **11** dilapidated **12** deteriorated, disreputable

downbeat
3 low, sad **4** blue, glum **6** droopy, gloomy, morose **7** decline, doleful **8** dejected **9** depressed **10** dispirited, melancholy **11** discouraged, pessimistic **12** disconsolate, disheartened, heavy-hearted

downcast
3 low, sad **4** blue, glum, sunk **5** moody, mopey **6** droopy, gloomy, morose **7** doleful, forlorn, unhappy **8** dejected, dismayed, listless, soulsick, troubled **9** depressed, heartsick, heartsore, miserable, oppressed, woebegone **10** chapfallen, despondent, dispirited, distressed, melancholy, spiritless **11** crestfallen, discouraged, low-spirited **12** disconsolate, disheartened

downer
4 drag **6** bummer **8** sedative

downfall
4 bane, ruin **6** demise **7** decline, undoing **8** collapse, Waterloo **9** ruination **10** devolution **11** declination, destruction **12** degeneration, dégringolade **13** deterioration

downgrade
4 bump, bust **5** abase, lower **6** demote **7** decline, demerit, descent, devalue **8** belittle, diminish, discount, minimize, relegate **9** denigrate, deprecate, devaluate, discredit, disparage, humiliate **10** depreciate, undervalue **12** degeneration, dégringolade **13** deterioration

downhearted
see **downcast**

down-in-the-mouth
see **downcast**

down payment
5 token **6** pledge **7** advance, deposit, earnest

downplay
8 belittle, discount, minimize, pooh-pooh **11** de-emphasize

downpour
6 deluge **7** monsoon **8** drencher **9** drenching, rainstorm **10** cloudburst, inundation **11** gully washer

downright
5 blunt, gross, total, truly, utter **7** blatant, flat-out **8** absolute, complete, explicit, positive, thorough **9** out-and-out **10** absolutely, sure-enough **11** indubitable, unequivocal, unmitigated, unqualified **13** thoroughgoing

downslide
3 dip, sag **4** drop, slip **5** slump **7** decline, drop-off, falloff **8** decrease **9** declivity, reduction

downstairs
6 cellar **8** basement

down-to-earth
8 rational **9** practical, pragmatic, realistic **10** hard-boiled, hardheaded, no-nonsense, reasonable **11** common-sense, plain-spoken **12** matter-of-fact **13** unpretentious, unsentimental

downtown district
4 Soho

downtrend
see **downslide**

downtrodden
6 abject, abused **9** oppressed **10** maltreated, mistreated, persecuted, tyrannized

downturn
see **downslide**

Down Under soldier
5 ANZAC

downward
8 dropping **9** declining **10** descending

downy
4 soft **5** fuzzy **6** fleecy, fluffy **7** velvety **8** feathery
duck: **5** eider
filler: **5** eider

dowry
4 gift **6** talent
French: **3** dot

doxy
4 bawd, drab, minx, moll, slut, tart **5** hussy, wench **6** floozy, harlot **7** trollop **8** mistress, slattern **10** prostitute

doyen
4 dean, head **5** chief, maven **6** expert, leader, master, wizard **7** maestro **8** virtuoso **9** authority, patriarch **10** past master

Doyle's detective
6 Holmes (Sherlock)

D'Oyly Carte offering
8 operetta

doze
3 nap, nod **5** sleep **6** catnap, drowse, nod off, snooze **7** drop off, slumber **8** drift off **10** forty winks

dozy
see **drowsy**

DP
5 exile **6** émigré **7** evacuee, outcast, refugee **8** deportee, emigrant, fugitive **10** expatriate

drab
4 dull, flat **5** bleak, brown, dingy, faded, mousy, muddy, olive, vapid **6** dismal, dreary, mousey **7** subfusc **8** lifeless **9** cheerless, colorless **10** lackluster **11** dispiriting

draconian
5 cruel, harsh, rigid **6** severe, strict **7** callous **8** ironclad, rigorous, ruthless **9** merciless, stringent **10** inflexible, ironfisted, ironhanded

Dracula author
6 Stoker (Bram)

draft
3 tap **4** dose, haul, plan, plot, pull, pump, swig **5** check, claim, drink, frame, press, swill **6** breeze, call up, demand, design, devise, enlist, enroll, induct, potion, scheme, select, siphon, sketch **7** compose, concoct, current, outline, portion, prepare, project, recruit **8** block out, contrive, rough out, skeleton, traction **9** adumbrate, allowance, blueprint, conscribe, conscript, fabricate, formulate, muster out **11** delineation, skeletonize
animals: **4** oxen
avoider: **6** dodger
of a law: **4** bill

drag
3 lug, tow, tug **4** bore, haul, puff, pull, swig **5** dally, delay, draft, shlep, tarry, trail **6** burden, dawdle, harrow, loiter, schlep, search, sledge **7** schlepp **8** friction, straggle **9** lag behind **13** procrastinate

dragging
4 beat, long **5** all in, spent, weary **6** pooped **7** drained, lengthy, tedious **8** drawn-out, extended, fatigued, overlong, sluggish, wiped out **9** exhausted, lethargic, long-drawn, pooped out, prolonged, washed-out, wearisome **10** protracted, slow-moving **12** interminable, long-drawn-out

draggle
3 lag **4** rove **5** stray, trail **8** straggle, trail off **10** fall behind

draggle-tail
4 bawd, drab, slut **5** wench, whore **6** harlot **8** slattern **10** prostitute **11** nightwalker **12** streetwalker

draggletailed
6 blowsy, frowsy, frowzy, sordid, untidy **8** slattern, sluttish **10** slatternly

dragnet
4 trap **5** snare, trawl **7** network

drag off
4 cart, haul

dragon
5 beast **8** basilisk **10** cockatrice
biblical: 5 Rahab
Canaanite: 3 Yam **4** Yamm **5** Lotan
Chinese: 4 lung
French: 8 Tarasque
genus: 5 Draco
Greek: 5 Ladon **9** Eurythion
slayer: 4 Baal, Enki, Zeus **5** Indra **6** Cadmus, George (St.), Marduk, Sigurd **7** Beowulf, Jupiter, Michael (St.), Ninurta, Perseus **8** Margaret (St.)
Sumerian: 3 Kur
Wagnerian: 6 Fafnir

dragoon
3 cow **5** bully **6** badger, coerce, harass, hector **8** bludgeon, browbeat, bulldoze, bullyrag, threaten **9** persecute, strong-arm, terrorize **10** cavalryman, intimidate

drain
3 dry, sap, tap **4** pump, sink, sump, swig, tire, vent, wear **5** bleed, draft, drink, empty, leech, sewer, swill, use up, weary **6** burden, gutter, siphon, trench **7** conduit, culvert, deplete, dwindle, draw off, exhaust, fatigue, outflow **8** bankrupt, draw down, enervate, wear down **9** discharge **10** impoverish **11** watercourse

drain away
3 ebb **4** drop, sink, wane **5** abate **6** lessen, reduce, remove **7** draw off, dwindle, retreat, subside **8** decrease, diminish, draw back, taper off, withdraw

drained
4 beat **5** all-in, spent, weary **6** bleary, pooped, used up **7** far-gone, worn-out **8** depleted, dragging, weakened, wiped out **9** exhausted, pooped out, washed-out

drainpipe
4 duct **5** sewer, spout **7** conduit **9** downspout

dram
3 bit, dab, nip, tot **4** atom, dash, drop, iota, jolt, mite, shot, slug, spot, swig, whit **5** crumb, grain, ounce, pinch, scrap, shred, snort, speck **6** morsel, sliver **7** modicum, smidgen, snifter, snippet, soupçon **8** particle

drama
4 play **7** pageant, theater, theatre, tragedy
award: 4 Tony
former English: 6 masque
Japanese: 3 Noh
main part: 8 epitasis
musical: 5 opera **8** operetta, zarzuela
suspenseful: 11 cliff-hanger

dramatic
5 vivid **8** striking, thespian **10** histrionic, theatrical
conflict: 4 agon

dramatis personae
4 cast **5** parts, roles **6** actors, troupe **7** company **10** characters

dramatist
10 playwright
American: 4 Hart (Moss), Inge (William), Rabe (David), Rice (Elmer), Uhry (Alfred) **5** Akins (Zoë), Albee (Edward), Barry (Philip), Foote (Horton), Guare (John), Hecht (Ben), Kanin (Garson), Mamet (David), Odets (Clifford), Parks (Suzan-Lori), Payne (John Howard), Shawn (Wallace), Simon (Neil) **6** Ferber (Edna), Gurney (A. R.), Henley (Beth), Miller (Arthur), Norman (Marsha), O'Neill (Eugene), Thomas (Augustus), Wilder (Thornton), Wilson (August, Lanford, Robert) **7** Belasco (David), Hellman (Lillian), Kaufman (George S.), Kushner (Tony), McNally (Terrence), Shanley (John Patrick), Shepard (Sam) **8** Anderson (Maxwell, Robert), Caldwell (Erskine), Connolly (Marc), Sherwood (Robert), Williams (Tennessee) **9** Chayefsky (Paddy), Fierstein (Harvey), Hansberry (Lorraine) **11** Hammerstein (Oscar), Wasserstein (Wendy)
Austrian: 10 Schnitzler (Arthur)
Belgian: 11 Maeterlinck (Maurice)
Czech: 5 Havel (Vaclav)
English: 3 Fry (Christopher), Gay (John) **4** Behn (Aphra), Bolt (Robert), Bond (Edward), Gray (Simon), Hare (David), Rowe (Nicholas), Tate (Nahum) **5** Frayn (Michael), Milne (A. A.), Orton (Joe), Peele (George) **6** Barrie (James), Coward (Nöel), Dryden (John), Jonson (Ben), Pinero (Arthur Wing), Pinter (Harold), Steele (Richard), Storey (David) **7** Bennett (Alan), Delaney (Shelagh), Marlowe (Christopher), Marston (John), Osborne (John), Shaffer (Anthony, Peter), Webster (John) **8** Congreve (William), Rattigan (Terrence), Shadwell (Thomas), Stoppard (Tom), Tourneur (Cyril), Vanbrugh (John), Zangwill (Israel) **9** Ayckbourn (Alan), Churchill (Caryl), Goldsmith (Oliver), Middleton (Thomas), Wycherley (William) **11** Shakespeare (William)
French: 5 Camus (Albert), Genet (Jean) **6** Musset (Alfred de), Racine (Jean), Sardou

(Victorien), Sartre (Jean-Paul), Scribe (Eugène) **7** Anouilh (Jean), Ionesco (Eugène), Labiche (Eugène), Molière, Rostand (Edmond) **8** Marivaux (Pierre) **9** Corneille (Pierre), Crébillon, Giraudoux (Jean) **12** Beaumarchais (P. A. Caron de)
German: **5** Weiss (Peter) **6** Brecht (Bertolt), Goethe (Johann Wolfgang von), Kleist (Heinrich von) **8** Schiller (Friedrich von) **9** Hauptmann (Gerhart), Zuckmayer (Carl)
Greek: **8** Menander **9** Aeschylus, Euripides, Sophocles **12** Aristophanes
Hindu: **8** Kalidasa
Irish: **4** Shaw (George Bernard) **5** Behan (Brendan), Friel (Brian), Synge (John Millington), Wilde (Oscar), Yeats (William Butler) **6** O'Casey (Sean) **7** Beckett (Samuel), Gregory (Lady Augusta) **8** Sheridan (Richard Brinsley)
Italian: **5** Gozzi (Carlo), Verga (Giovanni) **7** Alfieri (Vittorio), Ariosto (Ludovico), Giacosa (Giuseppe), Goldoni (Carlo) **8** Trissino (Gian Giorgio) **9** D'Annunzio (Gabriele) **10** Metastasio (Pietro), Pirandello (Luigi)
Japanese: **5** Zeami
Nigerian: **7** Soyinka (Wole)
Norwegian: **5** Ibsen (Henrik) **8** Bjornson (Bjornstjerne)
Roman: **6** Seneca **7** Plautus, Terence
Romanian: **7** Ionesco (Eugene)
Russian: **7** Chekhov (Anton) **8** Zamyatin (Yevgeny)
South African: **6** Fugard (Athol)
Spanish: **4** Vega (Lope de) **5** Lorca (Federico García) **7** Alberti (Rafael), Arrabal (Fernando) **8** Quintero (Serafín, Joaquín) **9** Benavente (Jacinto) **11** García Lorca (Federico), Valle-Inclán (R. M. del)
Swedish: **5** Sachs (Nelly) **10** Strindberg (August)
Swiss: **6** Frisch (Max)

drape
4 fold, hang, roll **5** adorn, array, cloak, cover **6** clothe, enfold, enwrap, swathe, wrap up **7** curtain, swaddle **8** enswathe, envelope, swathe in

drapery
7 curtain, hanging **8** curtains, hangings

drastic
4 dire **5** harsh **6** severe **7** extreme, radical **9** desperate **10** exorbitant

drat
4 damn, dang, darn **6** phooey, shucks **7** doggone

draw
3 gut, tie, tow, tug **4** etch, haul, limn, lure, puff, pull, pump **5** draft, drain, infer, judge, trace **6** allure, appeal, deduce, depict, derive, elicit, entice, extend, gather, indite, inhale, pencil, siphon, sketch **7** attract, deplete, exhaust, extract, outline, portray, prolong, spin out, win over **8** conclude, contract, convince, dead heat, deadlock, lengthen, protract, standoff **9** delineate, formulate, represent, stalemate **10** allurement, attraction, disembowel, eviscerate, exenterate
forth: **5** educe **6** elicit **7** extract
from: **4** milk, pump **5** bleed
together: **3** tie **4** join, lace

draw a bead on
3 aim

draw back
4 duck **5** cower, quail, wince **6** blench, cringe, flinch, recoil, shrink **7** back off, retreat, take off **9** turn aside

drawback
4 flaw, snag **5** fault, hitch **6** defect, refund **7** failing, trouble **8** weakness **9** detriment, hindrance **10** deficiency, difficulty, impediment **11** shortcoming **12** disadvantage

draw down
4 milk **5** drain, spend, use up **6** expend, reduce **7** deplete, exhaust **8** decrease, diminish **9** reduction, siphon off

drawer
9 draftsman
for money: **4** till

drawers
5 pants **6** undies **8** knickers, trousers **10** underpants

draw in
6 enmesh, entice, induce, prompt **7** involve, retract, win over **8** convince, persuade, pull back **9** prevail on **11** bring around, prevail upon

drawing
6 doodle, sketch **7** cartoon, outline

drawing power
4 lure, pull **6** allure, appeal **9** magnetism **10** attraction

drawing room
5 salon

drawn
4 taut, worn **6** peaked **7** fraught, haggard, pinched **8** careworn, fatigued, pictured, strained, stressed **9** attracted **10** delineated

drawn-out
4 long **7** lengthy, tedious **8** extended, overlong **9** prolonged **10** protracted

draw off
3 tap **4** pump **5** bleed, draft, drain **6** siphon

draw out
5 educe **6** extend **7** prolong, stretch **8** elongate, lengthen, protract

draw up
4 balk, halt, lift, make, stop **5** array, draft, frame,

order, raise, write **6** deploy, map out **7** compose, concoct, dispose, marshal, prepare, set down **8** organize, write out **9** formulate

dray
4 cart, drag **5** wagon **6** barrow, sledge **7** travois **9** stoneboat

dread
4 fear **5** alarm, panic **6** dismay, fright, horror, phobia, terror **7** anxiety **10** foreboding **11** trepidation **12** apprehension **13** consternation

dreadful
4 dire **5** awful **6** horrid, tragic **7** awesome, extreme, fearful, ghastly, heinous, hideous, ominous **8** alarming, horrible, horrific, shocking, terrible **9** appalling, frightful, revolting **11** distressing, frightening

dreadnought
10 battleship

dream
4 ache, long, wish **5** crave, fancy, ideal **6** aspire, bubble, desire, hanker, vision **7** chimera, fantasy, imagine, rainbow, reverie, specter, spectre **8** ambition, delusion, illusion, phantasm, phantasy **9** fantasize, nightmare **10** aspiration
divination by: 11 oneiromancy
god: 8 Morpheus
sleep: 3 REM

dreamer
7 utopian **8** idealist **9** visionary **10** Don Quixote, lotus-eater **13** castle-builder

dreamlike
5 ideal, vague **6** unreal **7** shadowy, surreal **8** fanciful, illusory, nebulous **9** imaginary, visionary **12** otherworldly

Dream of Gerontius composer
5 Elgar (Edward)

dream on
4 as if **7** you wish

dream up
5 frame, hatch **6** cook up, create, devise, invent **7** concoct, imagine **8** conceive, contrive, envisage, envision **9** formulate, visualize

dreamy
7 pensive **9** unworldly, visionary **10** idealistic **11** impractical **12** otherworldly

dreary
4 blah, drab, dull **5** bleak **6** boring, dismal, gloomy, somber, sombre **7** forlorn, humdrum, joyless, tedious **8** banausic, tiresome, wretched **9** cheerless **10** depressing, depressive, monotonous, oppressive, pedestrian **11** dispiriting

dreck
3 mud **4** junk, muck, slop **5** offal, swill, trash, waste **6** litter, refuse, sewage **7** garbage, rubbish **9** sweepings

dredge
3 dig **5** barge, scoop **6** deepen, dig out, gather **8** excavate, scoop out **9** hollow out, scrape out

dregs
4 lees, scum **5** trash **6** grouts **7** deposit, grounds, remains, residue **8** sediment **9** settlings **11** precipitate

drei
5 three

dreidel
3 top

Dreiser, Theodore
character: 5 Clyde (Griffiths) **6** Carrie (Meeber), Eugene (Witla), Sondra (Finchley) **7** Roberta (Alden) **9** Hurstwood (George) **10** Cowperwood (Frank)
novel: 5 Stoic (The), Titan (The) **6** Genius (The) **9** Financier (The) **12** Sister Carrie **14** Jennie Gerhardt **15** American Tragedy (An)

drench
3 sop **4** dunk, soak **5** douse, souse, steep, swill **6** deluge, seethe **7** immerse **8** inundate, saturate, submerge, waterlog

drenched
6 sodden **7** soaking, sopping

dress
3 gut **4** bind, clad, deck, doll, duds, garb, gown, sack, togs **5** adorn, align, A-line, array, frock, getup, guise, habit, smock, weeds **6** attire, bedeck, caftan, clothe, dirndl, enrobe, outfit, sacque **7** apparel, bandage, bedizen, chemise, clothes, costume, garment, garnish, raiment, threads, turnout, uniform **8** beautify, clothing, covering, decorate, ensemble, ornament, wardrobe **9** embellish, make ready **11** habiliments
a wound: 7 bandage
line: 3 hem
mode of: 5 habit
ordinary: 5 mufti
oriental: 9 cheongsam
part: 5 skirt **6** bodice
South Seas: 6 sarong

dress designer
see **fashion designer**

dress down
5 chide, scold **6** berate, rail at, rebuke, revile **7** bawl out, reprove, tell off, upbraid **8** admonish, chastise, reproach **9** castigate, reprimand **10** tongue-lash

dresser
5 chest, valet **6** bureau **7** commode, highboy **10** chiffonier
gaudy: 9 butterfly

dressing
5 sauce **6** catsup **7** bandage, catchup, ketchup **8** stuffing

salad: **5** ranch **6** French **7** Italian, Russian **10** blue cheese **11** vinaigrette **12** green goddess

dressing room
6 vestry **8** vestiary

dressmaker
7 modiste **9** couturier **10** couturiere, seamstress

dress up
6 attire, clothe, rig out, tog out **7** apparel, deck out **8** beautify, disguise, prettify, trick out **9** embellish **10** camouflage

dressy
4 chic **5** showy, smart **6** classy, formal, frilly, ornate **7** duded up, elegant, stylish **9** rigged out

Dreyfus's defender
4 Zola (Emile) **6** Proust (Marcel)

dribble
4 drip, leak, weep **5** drool **6** bounce, drivel, slaver **7** distill, drizzle, slobber, trickle **8** salivate, sprinkle

driblet
4 drop **6** gobbet **7** globule, smidgen **8** particle, pittance

dried grape
6 raisin

dried meat
5 jerky

dried plum
5 prune

drift
3 bat, gad **4** flow, flux, gist, roam, sail, skim, tide, waft, wash **5** amble, coast, creep, float, mosey, range, slide, stray, trend **6** bummel, linger, ramble, stream, stroll, wander **7** current, maunder, meander, meaning, saunter **8** movement, penchant, sideslip, tendency **9** deviation **10** propensity **11** disposition, inclination, progression **12** predilection

drifter
3 bum, vag **4** hobo **5** gypsy, nomad, tramp **7** floater, migrant, vagrant **8** derelict, vagabond **9** transient **11** beachcomber **12** rolling stone

drill
3 bit, dig **4** bore **5** auger, borer, punch, train **6** pierce, trepan, wimble **7** routine, wildcat, workout **8** exercise, practice, practise, rehearse **9** penetrate, rehearsal **10** discipline
command: **6** at ease **8** left face **9** about face, attention, right face

drink
3 ade, lap, nip, sea, sip, tea **4** belt, brew, chug, deep, down, grog, gulp, soak, swig, tope, toss **5** booze, draft, drain, ocean, quaff, slurp, snort, swill, toast **6** absorb, brandy, cassis, cognac, embibe, guzzle, imbibe, jigger, liquid, liquor, pledge, potion, tank up, tipple, tisane **7** consume, potable, schnaps, spirits, swallow, swizzle, toss off **8** aperitif, beverage, libation, liquor up, schnapps **9** aqua vitae
after-dinner: **6** frappé **7** cordial, liqueur
drugged: **6** Mickey **10** Mickey Finn
honey: **4** mead
hot: **5** negus, toddy
liquor: **5** booze, hooch **6** red-eye **9** firewater, moonshine
mixed: **3** kir, nog **5** julep **6** Gibson, gimlet, mai tai, mimosa, mojito, rickey, Rob Roy, zombie **7** gin fizz, martini, sidecar, stinger **8** daiquiri, pink lady **9** alexander, Cuba libre, manhattan, margarita, mint julep, rusty nail **10** Bloody Mary, piña colada, Tom Collins **11** gin and tonic, grasshopper, screwdriver, whiskey sour **12** black Russian, old-fashioned
mixer: **7** swirler
noisily: **5** slurp
of liquor: **4** dram, shot, slug **5** snort **6** bracer **8** highball
of the gods: **6** nectar
soft: **3** pop **4** cola, soda **5** tonic **7** soda pop **8** root beer **9** ginger ale **12** sarsaparilla
stimulating: **6** bracer
Vedic ritual: **4** soma
(see also **beverage**)

drinkable
6 liquor **7** potable **8** beverage, libation, potation

drinker
(see **drunkard**)

drinking
8 potation
fountain: **7** bubbler
glass: **6** rummer **7** tumbler
horn: **6** rhyton
spree: **3** jag **4** tear, toot **5** binge, spree **6** bender **7** carouse **8** carousal

drip
4 leak, plop, weep **7** dribble, droplet, trickle **8** sprinkle

dripping
3 wet **5** runny, soppy **6** soaked, soused **7** drizzly, soaking, sopping **8** drenched **9** saturated **11** wringing-wet

drippy
5 mushy, rainy, sappy, sobby, soppy, soupy, teary, weepy **6** slushy, syrupy **7** drizzly, maudlin, mawkish, soaking, sopping, tearful **9** schmaltzy **11** sentimental

drive
3 pep, ram **4** goad, herd, push, spur, taxi, tool, trip, urge **5** chase, force, guide, impel, jaunt, lunge, motor, moxie, oomph, pilot, pound, spunk,

steer, surge, vigor **6** compel, convey, exhort, hammer, outing, plunge, propel, strike, thrust **7** actuate, impetus, operate, produce **8** ambition, mobilize, momentum, navigate, shepherd, vitality **9** chauffeur, excursion, urge along **10** enterprise, get-up-and-go, initiative, motivation
away: 4 shoo **5** exile

drive away
see **expel**

drivel
3 rot **4** bosh, bunk **5** drool, hokum, hooey, prate **6** babble, bunkum, gabble, jabber, slaver **7** baloney, blabber, blather, dribble, hogwash, prattle, rubbish, slobber, twaddle **8** claptrap, flimflam, nonsense, salivate **9** gibberish, poppycock **10** balderdash, double-talk, flapdoodle **12** blatherskite, gobbledygook

driver
4 hack, jehu **5** cabby **6** cabbie, cabman, hackie, mallet **7** hackman **8** coachman, motorist, muleteer, operator **9** chauffeur, dowitcher **10** taskmaster **11** tamping iron
of an elephant: 6 mahout
org.: 3 AAA
Roman: 10 charioteer
truck: 8 teamster

driving
7 dynamic, powered **8** forceful, vigorous **9** energetic, inspiring **10** compelling

drizzle
4 mist, rain **7** dribble, spatter **8** droplets, sprinkle **10** sprinkling **13** precipitation

Dr. Jekyll and Mr. ___
4 Hyde

droll
3 odd **5** comic, funny, nutty, witty **7** comical, risible **8** farcical, humorous **9** eccentric, laughable, ludicrous, whimsical

drollery
5 humor **6** comedy, joking, whimsy **7** jesting

dromedary
5 camel

drone
3 bee, hum **4** buzz, idle, laze, loaf, loll **5** idler **6** drudge, intone, loiter, lounge, murmur, worker **7** bagpipe **8** aircraft, parasite **9** bombinate **10** pedal point

drool
4 gush, rave **5** froth **6** dote on, drivel, saliva, slaver **7** blather, dribble, enthuse, slobber **8** salivate **10** rhapsodize

droop
3 sag **4** fall, flag, hang, loll, sink, swag, wilt **5** slump **6** dangle, slouch, weaken **7** decline, let down, subside **8** languish

droopy
4 blue, down, limp, weak **5** baggy **6** gloomy **7** doleful, languid, sagging, slouchy, wilting **8** cast down, dejected, downcast **9** depressed **10** dispirited **11** downhearted

drop
3 dip, nip, sag, tad, tot **4** down, drib, dump, fall, fell, jilt, jolt, lose, omit, plop, slip, slug, tear **5** cease, depth, lapse, lower, pitch, plump, scrub, slide, snort, speck, spend **6** cancel, cave in, demise, depart, expire, fumble, give up, go down, ground, plunge, reduce, smitch, topple, unload, vanish **7** abandon, decease, decline, deposit, descend, descent, distill, dribble, driblet, fall off, forfeit, give out, globule, pendant, plummet, trickle **8** bowl over, break off, collapse, comedown, downturn, keel over, nose-dive **9** declivity, discharge, downslide, downswing, downtrend, prostrate, reduction, terminate **10** depository

drop by
4 call **5** pop in, visit **6** stop in **8** come over

dropdown list
4 menu

droplet
4 bead, drib, tear **7** globule

drop off
3 nap, sag **4** doze, fall, slip **5** slide, slump **6** catnap, drowse, lessen, snooze **7** decline, deliver, deposit, slacken **8** diminish, fall away, hand over **10** fall asleep

dropsical
5 puffy, tumid **6** turgid **7** swollen **8** inflated **9** edematous, tumescent

dropsy
5 edema **8** anasarca

dross
4 junk, scum, slag **5** dregs, offal, waste **6** debris, scoria **7** remains, residue, schlock **8** detritus, impurity, leavings

drossy
4 base **6** impure, scummy **7** trivial **8** inferior, unworthy **9** worthless

drought
4 lack, need, want **6** dearth **7** aridity, dryness **8** scarcity, shortage **10** deficiency

droughty
3 dry **4** arid, sere **7** bone-dry, dried up, parched, thirsty **10** desiccated

drove
3 mob **4** army, herd, host, mass, pack **5** crowd, flock, horde, troop **6** myriad, pushed, school, throng **7** phalanx **9** multitude

drover
6 cowboy **8** shepherd

drown
4 sink, soak **5** douse, flood, souse, swamp **6** deluge, drench, engulf **7** immerse, repress, smother **8** inundate, submerge **9** overpower, overwhelm, suffocate **10** asphyxiate, extinguish

drowse
3 nod **4** doze **5** sleep **6** catnap, snooze **7** doze off, drop off, shut-eye, slumber **10** forty winks

drowsy
4 dozy **5** dopey **6** droopy, sleepy, torpid **7** languid **8** indolent, sluggish **9** lethargic, somnolent, soporific **10** slumberous **13** lackadaisical

Dr. Seuss
6 Geisel (Theodor Seuss)
book: 11 Cat in the Hat (The) **15** Green Eggs and Ham, Yertle the Turtle **19** Horton Hatches the Egg **26** How the Grinch Stole Christmas

drub
3 tan, wax, zap **4** bash, beat, club, deck, drum, flay, flog, lash, lick, mash, maul, pelt, trim, whip **5** baste, cream, crush, paste, pound, score, slash, smash, smear, spank, stamp, thump, wreck **6** batter, berate, bruise, buffet, deface, hammer, master, pummel, punish, revile, scorch, thrash, thresh, wallop **7** belabor, blister, censure, clobber, cripple, lambast, scourge, shatter, shellac, trounce **8** bulldoze, lambaste, lash into, outclass, outshine **9** castigate, excoriate, overwhelm

drubbing
4 loss, rout **6** defeat **7** setback **10** defeasance **11** shellacking

drudge
4 grub, hack, moil, peon, plod, serf, slog **5** grind, slave **6** menial, slavey **7** grubber, plodder **8** dogsbody

drudgery
4 moil, toil **5** chore, grind **7** travail **9** grunt work **10** donkeywork **11** backbreaker

drudging
6 boring, tiring **7** irksome, tedious **8** dragging, tiresome **9** fatiguing, laborious, wearisome **10** monotonous

drug
4 dope, lull **5** sulfa **6** downer, ipecac, opiate, physic, poison, potion, remedy, statin **7** fen-phen, generic, stupefy **8** biologic, medicine, narcotic, nepenthe, relaxant, sedative **9** ibuprofen, medicinal, methadone **10** antibiotic, medicament, medication **11** thalidomide
addict: 6 junkie
agent: 4 narc
calming: 8 sedative
experience: 4 trip
illicit: 3 ice, kif, LSD, pot **4** acid, coke, dope, hash, meth, scag, snow, weed **5** crack, grass, opium, smack, speed **6** heroin, peyote **7** cocaine, crystal, hashish **8** cannabis, goofball **9** mescaline **10** methadrine, psilocybin
seller: 10 pharmacist
sleep-inducing: 8 hypnotic **9** soporific **11** barbiturate

drugged
4 high **5** dazed, doped, dopey **6** flying, loaded, stoned, zonked **8** benumbed, hopped-up, turned on **9** spaced-out, stupefied **10** narcotized

druggist
7 chemist **10** apothecary, pharmacist

drugstore
8 pharmacy **10** apothecary

druid
4 Celt **6** priest **7** prophet
sacred object: 3 oak **9** mistletoe

drum
3 keg, vat **4** beat, cask **5** conga, naker, tabor, thrum **6** atabal, barrel, timbal, tom-tom, tympan **7** tambour, timpani (plural), tympani (plural) **8** cylinder, timbales (plural)
Indian: 5 tabla **8** mridanga
Irish: 7 bodhran
large: 4 bass
small: 5 bongo, tabor **7** timbrel
string: 5 snare

drumbeat
4 flam, roll, tuck **6** ruffle, tattoo **7** booming, pit-a-pat, rat-a-tat **8** rataplan

drumfire
5 salvo **6** volley **7** barrage, booming **9** broadside, cannonade, fusillade **11** bombardment

drumhead
4 skin **7** summary

drummer
4 Hart (Mickey), Helm (Levon), Moon (Keith), Rich (Buddy) **5** Krupa (Gene), Roach (Max), Starr (Ringo), Watts (Charlie) **6** Blakey (Art), hawker, Puente (Tito), vendor **7** peddler **8** pitchman, salesman

drum up
6 arouse, invent **7** canvass, solicit **9** originate
interest: 4 plug, tout **8** ballyhoo

drunk
3 lit, sot **4** lush, soak, wino **5** dipso, lit up, oiled, souse, tight, tipsy **6** blotto, boozer, gassed, juiced, looped, soused, stewed, stinko, tiddly, wasted, zonked **7** crocked, guzzler, pie-eyed, sloshed, smashed, squiffy, tippler, tosspot **8** squiffed **9** inebriate, plastered **10** boozehound, inebriated **11** intoxicated

drunkard
3 sot **4** lush, soak, wino **5** dipso, rummy, souse, stiff, toper **6** bibber, boozer, soaker **7** guzzler, swiller, tippler, tosspot **9** alcoholic, inebriate, juicehead **10** boozehound **11** dipsomaniac

Drusilla
brother: **8** Caligula
father: **5** Herod **10** Germanicus
husband: **5** Felix
mother: **9** Agrippina
sister: **8** Berenice **9** Agrippina

dry
3 set **4** arid, brut, dull, sere, sour, tart **5** baked, dusty, parch, stale, wizen **6** barren, desert, harden, stolid, thirst, wither **7** congeal, deadpan, parched, Saharan, shrivel, sterile, thirsty **8** rainless, solidify, tearless, teetotal, withered **9** anhydrous, dehydrate, desiccate, evaporate, unwatered **10** dehydrated, desiccated **11** unemotional **12** matter-of-fact **13** uninteresting
combining form: **3** xer **4** xero
goods: **6** linens, napery **8** clothing, textiles
out: **5** sober **8** soberize
period: **7** drought
river bed: **4** wadi **5** gully **6** arroyo
wine: **3** sec **4** brut

dryasdust
4 arid, dull **5** banal, inane, vapid **6** boring, stodgy **7** insipid, prosaic, tedious **9** wearisome **10** uninspired **13** uninteresting

dryer
4 kiln, oast

dry measure
4 peck, pint **5** quart **6** bushel

Dryope
form: **5** lotus
husband: **9** Andraemon
sister: **4** Iole

dry up
4 wilt **5** wizen **6** wither **7** deplete, exhaust, mummify, shrivel **9** desiccate, disappear, evaporate

dual
3 two **4** twin **5** duple **6** bifold, binary, double, duplex, paired **7** coupled, matched, twofold **8** matching **9** duplicate

dualistic
5 duple **6** bifold, binary, double, duplex, paired **7** twofold **9** Manichean **10** Manichaean

dualize
4 copy, dupe **5** clone **6** double **9** duplicate, replicate, reproduce

dub
4 call, name, term, trim **5** style, title **6** duffer **7** baptize, bungler, entitle, fumbler **8** christen, nickname, rerecord **9** blunderer, designate **10** denominate

Dubai's federation
3 UAE

dubiety
5 doubt **7** concern **8** mistrust **9** confusion, suspicion **10** skepticism **11** incertitude, incredulity, uncertainty **12** doubtfulness

dubious
4 iffy **5** fishy **6** unsure **7** suspect, unclear **8** doubtful, hesitant, unlikely **9** equivocal, sceptical, skeptical, uncertain, undecided **10** improbable, unreliable **11** mistrustful, problematic, questioning, unconvinced, unpromising **12** questionable, undependable, undetermined

dubitable
5 fishy **7** suspect **8** doubtful, marginal **9** ambiguous, uncertain, unsettled **10** borderline **11** problematic **13** indeterminate

duce
5 ruler **6** despot, leader, tyrant **8** dictator **9** Mussolini (Benito), strongman

duck
3 bob, bow, dip, shy **4** bend, dive, dunk, shun **5** avoid, dodge, douse, elude, evade, fence, parry, shirk, stoop **6** escape, plunge **7** back out, immerse **8** sidestep, submerge, submerse **10** canvasback
Asian: **5** Pekin **8** mandarin
dabbling: **7** gadwall, mallard
diving: **4** smew **7** pochard **9** merganser **10** bufflehead
down: **5** eider
Eurasian: **4** smew
European: **8** shelduck
genus: **3** Aix **4** Anas
group: **4** team **5** brace, flock, skein **6** flight
hunter's screen: **5** blind
male: **5** drake
red-wattled: **7** Muscovy
river: **4** teal **6** wigeon **7** pintail, widgeon
scaup: **8** bluebill
sea: **5** eider, scaup **6** scoter

duckbill
8 platypus **9** hadrosaur, monotreme

duck soup
4 easy, snap **5** cinch **6** breeze, picnic, simple **8** kid stuff, painless, pushover **10** child's play **11** piece of cake

ducky
4 cute **5** swell **6** lovely, peachy **7** darling **9** hunky-dory **10** peachy-keen

duct
4 flue, pipe, tube **5** canal **6** course, runway **7** channel, conduit **11** watercourse
anatomical: **3** vas **4** vasa (plural)

ductile
6 pliant, supple **7** plastic, pliable **8** flexible, moldable **9** adaptable, compliant, malleable, tractable
metal: **4** wire

ductless gland
see **endocrine gland**

dud
3 dog **4** bomb, bust, flop **5** lemon, loser **6** bummer, misfit, turkey **7** debacle, failure, washout **8** abortion

dude
3 bro, fop, guy **4** beau, buck, rake **5** blood, dandy **6** fellow **7** coxcomb **8** macaroni, popinjay 9 exquisite **12** Beau Brummell, lounge lizard

dudgeon
3 ire **4** fury, huff, miff, rage **5** anger, pique, wrath **7** chagrin, offense, outrage, umbrage **8** vexation **10** resentment **11** indignation **12** exasperation

duds
3 rig **4** garb, gear, rags, togs **5** dress, getup, weeds **6** attire, things **7** apparel, clothes, raiment, threads, toggery **8** clothing, garments **9** trappings, vestments **11** habiliments

due
4 debt, just, owed **5** lumps, owing **6** direct, earned, lawful, proper, unpaid **7** arrears, condign, deserts, merited, payable, payment, regular **8** adequate, deserved, expected, rightful, suitable **9** deserving, equitable, requisite, scheduled **10** obligatory, receivable, sufficient **11** appropriate, outstanding

duel
4 tilt **5** fight, joust **6** combat **7** contest, dispute **8** conflict **9** smackdown

dueling sword
4 épée

duenna
8 chaperon **9** chaperone, companion, governess

duet
dancer's: **9** pas de deux

due to
4 over **7** owing to, through **9** because of **11** considering

duff
3 can **4** buns, butt, rear, rump, tail, tush **5** fanny, slack **6** bottom **7** keester, keister, pudding, rear end **8** backside, buttocks, coal dust, derriere **10** leaf litter

duffer
4 boob, clod, dolt, dope, yo-yo **5** chump, dunce, klutz **6** dimwit, dum-dum, lubber, nitwit **7** dullard, fumbler, peddler, pinhead **8** bonehead, dumbbell, lunkhead, numskull **9** blockhead, ignoramus, numbskull, simpleton **10** nincompoop, stumblebum **11** incompetent

dugout
5 canoe **6** trench **7** piragua, pirogue, shelter

duiker
8 antelope

dukedom
5 duchy **6** domain

dulcet
5 sweet **7** melodic, tuneful **8** charming, cheerful, engaging, euphonic, pleasant, pleasing, soothing **9** agreeable, melodious **10** euphonious **11** mellifluous

dulcimer
6 zither **8** psaltery
Hungarian: **8** cimbalom
Persian: **6** santir **7** santour

dull
3 dim, dun, mat **4** arid, blah, blur, drab, flat, numb **5** blunt, dense, dusty, faded, ho-hum, inert, matte, muddy, muted **6** benumb, blurry, boring, deaden, dreary, gloomy, leaden, obtuse, stodgy, stupid **7** blunted, humdrum, insipid, muffled, prosaic, stupefy, subdued, tarnish, tedious **8** banausic, bromidic, deadened, discolor, lifeless, listless, monotone, plodding, sluggish **9** colorless, dim-witted, dryasdust, ponderous, wearisome **10** indistinct, lackluster, lusterless, monotonous, pedestrian **11** commonplace, desensitize, insensitive, thickheaded, thick-witted, unsharpened **12** simpleminded **13** uninteresting

dullard
3 oaf **4** bird, boob, bore, clod, dolt, dope, yo-yo **5** chump, dummy, dunce, idiot, moron, ninny, noddy, stupe **6** dimwit, dum-dum, nitwit **7** airhead, pinhead **8** bonehead, dumbbell, imbecile, lunkhead, meathead, numskull **9** birdbrain, blockhead, ignoramus, lamebrain, numbskull, simpleton **10** dunderhead **11** chowderhead, chucklehead

dullness
5 ennui **6** apathy, stupor, tedium, torpor **7** boredom, languor **8** hebetude, lethargy, monotony **9** bluntness, denseness, lassitude, stupidity, torpidity **12** indifference, listlessness, sluggishness

duly
8 properly, suitably **9** correctly, regularly **12** sufficiently **13** appropriately

duma
7 council **8** assembly, congress **11** legislature

Dumas character
5 Athos **6** Aramis, Dantès (Edmond) **7** Camille, Porthos **9** d'Artagnan

dumb
3 mum **4** dull, mute **5** dense, quiet, thick **6** deaden, obtuse, silent, stupid **7** doltish, foolish, idiotic, moronic **8** ignorant, taciturn, wordless **9** dim-witted, fatheaded, voiceless **10** speechless, tongue-tied **11** blockheaded, thick-witted **12** closemouthed, inarticulate, simple-minded

dumbbell
see **dullard**

dumbfound
4 stun **5** amaze, floor **6** boggle, puzzle

7 astound, nonplus, perplex, stagger 8 astonish, bewilder, bowl over, confound, distract, surprise 9 take aback 11 flabbergast

dumbfounded
5 agape 6 amazed 7 puzzled, shocked 8 startled 9 astounded, perplexed, staggered, surprised 10 astonished, bewildered, bowled over, confounded, distracted, nonplussed, taken aback 13 thunderstruck

dumbstruck
6 aghast, amazed 7 stunned 9 astounded, stupefied 10 astonished, blindsided

dummkopf
3 oaf 4 boob, clod, dodo, dolt, dope, fool, goof, jerk, mutt, simp, yo-yo 5 chump, dunce, idiot, moron, ninny, noddy, stupe 6 dimwit, donkey, nitwit, noodle 7 airhead, dullard, pinhead, schnook 8 bonehead, clodpoll, dumbbell, dumbhead, imbecile, lunkhead, meathead, numskull 9 birdbrain, blockhead, ignoramus, lamebrain, numbskull, simpleton, thickhead 10 dunderhead, hammerhead, nincompoop 11 chowderhead, chucklehead, knucklehead

dummy
4 boob, clod, dodo, dolt, mock, sham, yo-yo 5 chump, dunce, false, idiot, model, moron, ninny, noddy, stupe 6 dimwit, dum-dum, effigy, ersatz, layout, mock-up, nitwit, puppet, stooge 7 airhead, dullard, manikin, pinhead, stand-in 8 bonehead, dumbbell, imbecile, lunkhead, mannekin, meathead, numskull 9 birdbrain, blockhead, ignoramus, imitation, lamebrain, numbskull, simpleton, simulated 10 artificial, dunderhead, fictitious, nincompoop, substitute 11 chowderhead, chucklehead

dump
3 sty 4 drop, junk 5 chuck, depot, ditch, scrap 6 armory, midden, pigpen, pigsty, plunge 7 abandon, arsenal, deep-six, discard 8 jettison, landfill, magazine, throw out 9 stockpile, throw away 10 depository

dumpling
5 dough 8 quenelle 10 butterball

dumps
4 funk 5 blues, dolor, gloom, mopes, slump 7 sadness 8 doldrums 9 dejection 10 depression, gloominess, melancholy 11 despondency, unhappiness

dumpy
5 dingy, seedy, squat, stout 6 chubby, chunky, shabby, slummy, stocky, stubby, stumpy 7 rundown 8 heavyset, thickset 9 shapeless

dun
3 dim, fly 4 dull, drab, gray 5 annoy, brown, dusky, horse, murky, press 6 demand, gloomy, mayfly, needle, pester, plague, somber, sombre 9 ephemerid, importune

Duncan's slayer
7 Macbeth

dunce
3 oaf 4 boob, clod, dodo, dolt, dope, goof, mutt, simp, yo-yo 5 booby, chump, dummy, idiot, moron, ninny, noddy, stupe 6 dimwit, donkey, duffer, dum-dum, nitwit, noodle, stupid 7 airhead, dullard, fathead, pinhead 8 bonehead, clodpoll, dumbbell, imbecile, lunkhead, meathead, numskull 9 birdbrain, blockhead, ignoramus, lamebrain, numbskull, simpleton 10 dunderhead, hammerhead, nincompoop 11 chowderhead, chucklehead, knucklehead

Dunciad author
4 Pope (Alexander)

dundrearies
9 burnsides, sideburns 11 muttonchops 12 sidewhiskers

dune
8 sandbank
area: 3 erg 5 beach, shore 6 desert

dung
4 muck 6 manure, ordure 9 excrement
beetle: 6 scarab 9 tumblebug

dungeon
4 jail 5 vault 6 prison 9 black hole, oubliette

dunghill
6 midden

Dunham of TV
4 Lena

dunk
3 dip, sop 4 soak 5 douse, drown, souse 6 drench 7 immerse 8 saturate, submerge, submerse

dunlin
9 sandpiper

duo
4 dyad, pair 5 brace 6 couple 7 doublet, twosome

dupe
3 con, kid, sap 4 butt, fool, gull, hoax, mark, pawn 5 cheat, chump, cozen, patsy, spoof, trick 6 befool, delude, double, outwit, pigeon, sucker 7 chicane, deceive, defraud, mislead 8 flimflam, hoodwink 9 bamboozle, victimize 11 double-cross, hornswoggle

dupery
3 con 4 scam, sham 5 cheat, fraud 6 deceit, humbug, hustle 7 chicane 8 cheating, flimflam, trickery 9 chicanery, deception, duplicity, imposture, swindling 10 dishonesty, hanky-panky 11 hoodwinking 13 double-dealing, sharp practice

duple
4 dual, twin **6** bifold, binary, double, paired **7** coupled, doubled, twofold **9** dualistic

duplex
see **duple**

duplicate
4 copy, fake, mate, redo, same, twin **5** clone, ditto, equal, match, mimeo, repro, Xerox **6** carbon, double **7** dualize, imitate, replica **8** knock-off **9** companion, facsimile, identical, imitation, look-alike, photocopy, replicate, reproduce **10** carbon copy, dead ringer, equivalent, reciprocal **11** counterfeit, counterpart, replication **12** reproduction

duplicitous
5 phony **6** shifty, sneaky **7** devious **8** delusive, guileful, scheming, sneaking, two-faced **9** deceitful, deceiving, deceptive, dishonest, underhand **10** fraudulent **11** underhanded **12** disingenuous **13** double-dealing

duplicity
5 fraud, guile **6** deceit **7** cunning, perfidy **8** scheming, trickery **9** chicanery, deception, treachery **10** dishonesty, doubleness **11** skulduggery **12** dissemblance, skullduggery **13** dissimulation, double-dealing

durability
4 wear **8** firmness **9** endurance, longevity, stability **10** permanence

durable
5 stout **6** stable, strong, sturdy **7** lasting **8** enduring **9** permanent, tenacious **10** dependable **11** long-lasting

durance
7 bondage **9** captivity, detention, restraint **11** confinement **12** enthrallment, imprisonment **13** incarceration

duration
3 run **4** term, time **6** extent, period **7** interim **8** interval **11** persistence

D'Urberville daughter
4 Tess

duress
5 force **6** menace, threat **8** bullying, coercion, menacing, pressure **9** restraint **10** compulsion, constraint **11** restriction **12** intimidation

during
4 amid **10** throughout

durra
7 sorghum **12** grain sorghum

Durrell work
4 Cleo **7** Justine **9** Balthazar **10** Mountolive **17** Alexandria Quartet

durum
5 wheat

dusk
3 e'en **4** dark **7** evening **8** darkness, evenfall, eventide, gloaming, twilight **9** nightfall **12** semi-darkness

dusky
3 dim **4** dark **5** murky, swart **6** brunet, gloomy, opaque, twilit **7** obscure, shadowy, swarthy **8** funereal, nubilous, overcast, twilight **9** tenebrous **10** caliginous **11** dark-skinned

dust
4 grit, sand, sift, soot **5** ashes, grime **6** powder **8** sprinkle **10** besprinkle, sprinkling

dust-bowl victim
4 Okie

dustup
3 row **4** spat **5** brawl, fight, melee, run-in, set-to **6** battle, fracas, hassle, tussle **7** dispute, quarrel, rhubarb, scuffle **8** argument, skirmish **9** bickering, brannigan **10** falling-out **11** altercation

dusty
3 dry **4** arid, dull **5** stale **7** parched, powdery, tedious, unswept

Dutch
7 trouble **8** hot water
African: 9 Afrikaans
ceramics: 5 delft
cheese: 4 Edam **5** Gouda
commune: 3 Ede
dog breed: 7 griffon **8** keeshond
painter: 3 Dou (Gerrit, Gerard) **4** Cuyp (Aelbert Jacobsz), Gogh (Vincent van), Hals (Frans) **5** Bosch (Hieronymus), Hooch (Pieter de), Steen (Jan) **6** Rubens (Peter Paul) **7** de Hooch (Pieter), Hobbema (Meindert), van Gogh (Vincent), Vermeer (Jan) **8** Mondrian (Piet), Ruysdael (Jacob van, Salomon van), Terborch (Gerard) **9** de Kooning (Willem), Honthorst (Gerrit van), Rembrandt (van Rijn)
philosopher: 7 Spinoza (Benedict de)
scholar: 7 Erasmus (Desiderius)

Dutch South African
4 Boer

dutiful
7 devoted **8** faithful **9** compliant **10** respectful **13** conscientious

duty
3 job, tax, use **4** levy, onus, role, task, work **5** chare, chore, stint **6** burden, charge, devoir, impost, office, tariff **7** respect, service **8** function **10** allegiance, assessment, assignment, commitment, dedication, obligation

DVR option
4 TiVo

dwarf
4 runt **5** gnome, pygmy, stunt, troll **6** midget, peewee **7** manikin **8** Tom Thumb **9** miniature **10** diminutive, homunculus
in Snow White: 3 Doc **5** Dopey, Happy **6** Grumpy, Sleepy, Sneezy **7** Bashful
Scottish: 7 blastie

dwarfish
5 pygmy, small **6** midget **7** minikin, stunted **8** inferior, pint-size **9** miniature, pint-sized **10** diminutive, undersized

dweeb
4 dork, drip, geek, nerd, wimp, wuss **5** loser **7** nebbish

dwell
3 lie **4** bide, live, stay **5** abide, exist **6** locate, remain, repose, reside, settle **7** hang out

dweller
7 citizen, denizen, settler **8** habitant, occupant, resident **10** inhabitant

dwelling
3 pad **4** casa, digs, home, nest **5** abode, haunt, house **7** address, habitat, lodging **8** domicile, quarters **9** residence **10** brownstone, habitation
American Indian: 4 tipi **5** hogan, tepee **6** pueblo, teepee, wigwam
clergyman's: 5 manse **7** rectory **8** vicarage **9** parsonage
crude: 3 hut **4** camp **5** cabin, hovel, shack **6** cabana, shanty **7** barrack **8** barracks
Eskimo: 5 igloo
grand: 5 manor, manse, villa **6** palace **7** château, mansion
Hindu: 6 ashram
Navajo: 5 hogan
Russian: 5 dacha
small: 3 cot, hut **5** cabin, hovel, shack **6** shanty **7** cottage **8** bungalow

Dwight's opponent
5 Adlai (Stevenson)

dwindle
3 ebb **4** fade, fall, wane **5** abate, taper **6** lessen, recede, reduce, shrink, weaken, wither **7** decline, die away, die down, shrivel, slacken, subside **8** decrease, diminish, taper off **9** attenuate, drain away

dyad
3 duo, two **4** pair, yoke **5** brace, twins **6** couple **7** doublet, twosome

dye
4 tint **5** color, stain, tinge **7** pigment **8** colorant, pyronine, tincture
blue: 4 woad **6** indigo **7** cyanine
plant: 4 woad **5** sumac **6** madder
red: 5 eosin, henna **6** kermes, ruddle **7** cudbear, fuchsin, magenta **8** alizarin, fuchsine, amaranth, safranin **9** cochineal, rhodamine, safranine **10** erythrosin
violet: 6 archil
yellow: 7 flavine **8** orpiment
yellowish red: 7 annatto

dyed-in-the-wool
5 loyal, sworn **7** devoted, die-hard, old-line, settled, staunch **8** faithful, hard-core, orthodox, standpat, true-blue **9** confirmed, hard-shell, steadfast **10** deep-rooted, deep-seated, entrenched, inveterate, unwavering **11** established **13** bred-in-the-bone, thoroughgoing

dyewood
6 fustic **10** brazilwood

dying
6 demise **7** done for, quietus **8** moribund **9** departure **10** extinction, in extremis **12** annihilation

dynamic
7 driving, intense **8** forceful, forcible, powerful, vigorous **9** energetic, strenuous **10** compelling, energizing

dynamite
4 raze **5** blast **6** blow up **7** destroy, explode, shatter **8** demolish **9** explosive **10** annihilate
inventor: 5 Nobel (Alfred)

dynamo
8 go-getter, live wire **9** generator **10** ball of fire **11** self-starter

dynasty
Chinese: 3 Han, Qin, Sui **4** Hsia, Ming, Qing, Sung, Tang
Mongol: 4 Yuan

Dynasty series
character: 3 Ben, Dex **4** Adam, Dana **5** Blake, Sable **6** Alexis, Amanda, Fallon, Leslie, Monica, Steven **7** Claudia, Jeffery, Krystie **8** Samantha **9** Dominique
family: 5 Colby **10** Carrington
setting: 6 Denver
spin-off: 6 Colbys (The)
star: 5 Evans (Linda), James (John), Nader (Michael), Samms (Emma) **6** Corley (Al), Garber (Terri), Hunley (Leann), Martin (Pamela Sue) **7** Beacham (Stephanie), Carroll (Diahann), Cellini (Karen), Coleman (Jack), Collins (Joan), Thomson (Gordon) **8** Bellwood (Pamela), Cazenove (Christopher), Forsythe (John), Locklear (Heather), Oxenberg (Catherine), Scoggins (Tracy)

dysentery
4 flux 6 scours 8 diarrhea

dyslogistic
7 adverse 10 derogatory, pejorative 11 deleterious, disparaging, prejudicial, unfavorable

dyspepsia
5 gloom 6 dismay 7 chagrin, pyrosis 8 glumness 9 dejection, heartburn 10 gloominess 11 frustration, indigestion

dyspeptic
5 cross, surly 6 crabby, morose, ornery 9 irritable 10 ill-humored, ill-natured 11 disgruntled, ill-tempered

dysphoria
4 funk 5 blues, dumps, gloom, mopes 6 sorrow 7 sadness 9 dejection 10 depression, gloominess, melancholy 11 unhappiness 12 mournfulness, wretchedness 13 cheerlessness

E

each
3 all, per 4 a pop 5 every 6 apiece 8 everyone 9 per capita, everybody

eager
4 avid, keen 5 antsy, hyper, itchy, ready 6 ardent, fervid, gung ho, intent, raring 7 anxious, athirst, earnest, fervent, restive 8 appetent, aspiring, desirous, restless, yearning 9 ambitious, hankering, impatient 10 breathless 12 enthusiastic

eagerness
4 urge, zeal, zest, zing 5 ardor, gusto 6 desire, fervor, spirit, thirst 7 avidity, craving, itching, longing 8 alacrity, ambition, appetite, fervency 9 intensity 10 enthusiasm, impatience

eagle
4 hawk 9 accipiter
claw: 5 talon
nest: 4 aery 5 aerie, eyrie
North American: 4 bald 6 golden
sea: 3 ern 4 erne 6 osprey

eagle-eyed
8 vigilant, watchful 9 attentive, observant 10 perceptive 12 sharp-sighted

ear
6 notice 7 auricle 9 attention
bone: 5 anvil, incus 6 hammer, stapes 7 malleus, stirrup
canal: 5 scala
combining form: 3 aur, oto 4 auri, otic
doctor: 9 otologist
inner: 9 labyrinth
middle: 8 tympanum
outer: 5 pinna
part: 4 drum, lobe 5 canal 6 tragus 7 cochlea
relating to: 5 aural 9 auricular
science: 7 otology

eardrum
8 tympanum

___ Earhart
6 Amelia

earl
4 lord, peer 5 count, noble 8 nobleman, seigneur 9 patrician 10 aristocrat
executed by Elizabeth: 5 Essex

Earl Grey, e.g.
3 tea

earlier
3 ere, yet 4 once 5 as yet, so far 6 before, sooner 7 already, thus far 8 formerly, hitherto, previous 9 erstwhile, preceding 10 beforehand, heretofore, previously

earlier than
3 pre 6 before
Latin: 4 ante

earliest
5 first, prime 6 maiden, primal 7 initial, pioneer, primary 8 original, primeval, pristine 10 aboriginal, primordial

earlike projection
3 lug

early
3 old 5 first, prior 6 primal, timely 7 ancient, betimes 8 original, previous, primeval, pristine, untimely 9 preceding, premature, primitive 10 antecedent, antiquated, precocious, primordial 11 prematurely
prefix: 5 paleo

early computer
5 ENIAC 6 UNIVAC

earn
3 bag, get, net, win 4 gain, make, rate, reap 5 amass, clear, gross, merit, score 6 attain, come by, obtain, pick up, rack up, secure,

wangle 7 acquire, bring in, collect, deserve, harvest, procure, produce, realize, receive 8 pull down 9 bring home, knock down

earnest

3 vow 4 bond, busy, firm, keen, pawn, true, warm 5 grave, sober, token 6 active, ardent, intent, pledge, solemn, somber, surety 7 deposit, genuine, intense, serious, sincere, up front, warrant, zealous 8 contract, covenant, diligent, interest, security, sedulous, studious 9 assiduous, heartfelt 10 determined, no-nonsense, passionate, sobersided, thoughtful, unaffected 11 industrious 12 enthusiastic, wholehearted

earnestly

5 madly 7 for real, like mad

earnings

3 net, pay 4 gain 5 lucre, wages 6 EBITDA, income, profit, return, salary 7 profits 8 proceeds, take-home 9 emolument 10 bottom line

earring

site: 4 lobe
type: 4 cuff, hook, hoop, stud 5 huggy, slave 6 clip-on, dangle 7 barbell, stick-on

ear shell

7 abalone

earshot

5 range, sound 7 hearing

earsplitting

4 loud 6 shrill 7 blaring, grating, raucous, roaring 8 piercing, strident 9 deafening, dissonant 10 screeching, stentorian 11 fullmouthed

earth

3 orb, sod 4 dirt, land, soil, turf 5 globe, world 6 ground, planet, sphere 7 dry land, terrain 8 creation 10 terra firma
brick: 4 pisé 5 tapia
combining form: 3 geo 4 geog 6 tellur 7 telluro
core: 12 centrosphere
crust: 4 sial, sima 11 lithosphere
god: 3 Geb, Keb, Seb 5 Dagan
goddess: 4 Erda, Gaea 5 Ceres, Nintu 6 Kishar 7 Demeter, Nerthus
pigment: 5 ocher, ochre, umber 6 sienna
relating to: 8 telluric 11 terrestrial
satellite: 4 moon
science: 7 geology 9 geography

earthenware

4 clay 5 china, delft 7 biscuit, faience, pottery 8 clayware, crockery, majolica 9 porcelain, stoneware 10 terra-cotta
pot: 4 olla

earthlike

11 terrestrial

earthling

6 Terran

earthly

6 mortal 7 mundane, terrene, worldly 8 material, physical, temporal 9 corporeal 11 terrestrial

earthquake

5 seism, shake, shock 6 tremor 7 temblor
measuring device: 11 seismograph, seismometer
relating to: 7 seismic
science: 10 seismology 11 seismometry

earthwork

4 bank, berm, wall 7 bulwark, rampart 10 embankment 13 fortification

earthworm

7 annelid 12 night crawler

earthy

3 low 4 base, real 5 crude, dirty, dusty, gross, muddy, ocher, ochre, sandy 6 clayey, coarse, common, simple 7 mundane, worldly 8 temporal 9 corporeal, inelegant, practical, pragmatic, realistic, unrefined 10 hard-boiled, hardheaded, indelicate, uncultured, unpolished 11 terrestrial 12 matter-of-fact

earwax

7 cerumen

ease

3 aid 4 bate, calm, dull, free, help, rest 5 allay, loose, peace, poise, relax, slack 6 assist, deaden, loosen, relief, repose, soften 7 assuage, comfort, fluency, improve, leisure, lighten, mollify, relieve, slacken 8 calmness, deftness, diminish, dispatch, facility, idleness, mitigate, moderate, pleasure, serenity 9 abundance, affluence, alleviate, expertise, reduction, untighten, well-being 10 ameliorate, efficiency, facilitate, inactivity, moderation, prosperity, relaxation, smoothness 11 alleviation, contentment, nonchalance, spontaneity
off: 3 ebb 4 bate, fade, fall, flag, wane 5 abate, let up, loose, relax, slack 6 lessen, loosen, relent, unbend, unwind 7 die away, die down, slacken, subside 8 diminish, loosen up, moderate 9 untighten

easel

4 desk 5 frame, stand 7 support 9 workbench, worktable

easement

6 relief 7 comfort 10 mitigation, palliative 11 alleviation, consolation, restorative 13 mollification

easily

6 simply 7 handily, lightly, readily 8 facilely, smoothly 11 dexterously, efficiently 12 effortlessly

East

4 Asia 6 Levant, Orient

Easter
5 Pasch
relating to: 7 paschal
symbol: 3 egg 4 lamb, lily 5 bunny 6 rabbit

Easter Island
7 Rapa Nui

eastern
8 oriental 9 Levantine
countries: 6 Orient
European: 4 Slav

East Indies
country: 8 Malaysia 9 Indonesia, Singapore

East of Eden twin
4 Aron

East Timor
capital: 4 Dili
neighbor: 9 Indonesia

easy
3 lax 4 calm, cozy, mild, soft, snug 5 basic, clear, comfy, cushy, light, loose, naive, plain 6 facile, fluent, placid, polite, secure, serene, simple, smooth 7 amiable, evident, lenient, obvious, patient, relaxed 8 apparent, composed, familiar, graceful, gullible, informal, obliging, peaceful, pleasant, sociable, tolerant, trusting 9 collected, forgiving, indulgent 10 charitable, effortless, elementary 13 uncomplicated

easygoing
3 lax 4 calm, cool, lazy 5 quiet 6 breezy, casual, dégagé, folksy 7 affable, offhand, patient, relaxed, unfussy 8 amenable, carefree, down home, flexible, indolent, informal, laid-back, together, tranquil 9 apathetic, indulgent, unhurried 10 nonchalant, permissive, unaffected 11 comfortable, complaisant, low-pressure, pococurante, unconcerned, unflappable 12 devil-may-care, even-tempered, happy-go-lucky

easy mark
3 sap 4 butt, dupe, fool, gull 5 chump, patsy, sport 6 pigeon, softie, sucker, turkey, victim 7 fall guy 8 pushover 9 soft touch 11 sitting duck

eat
3 sup, vex 4 bite, chow, dine, gnaw, meal, nosh, pick, take, wolf 5 erode, feast, gorge, graze, lunch, mouth, munch, scarf, scoff, scour, snack, use up 6 devour, feed on, gobble, ingest, inhale, nibble, pester, pick at, pig out, take in 7 banquet, consume, corrode, gorge on, swallow, torment 8 chow down, dissolve, take food, wear away 9 breakfast, decompose, masticate, partake of, polish off 10 break bread, gormandize, nibble away

eatable
6 edible 8 esculent, harmless 9 palatable 10 comestible, digestible

eatery
4 café 5 diner, grill 10 coffee shop, restaurant 11 greasy spoon 12 luncheonette

eating place
3 pub 4 café, mess 5 diner, grill, joint 6 bistro, tavern 7 automat, beanery, canteen, commons, dinette, tearoom 8 cookshop, messroom, pizzeria, snack bar 9 brasserie, cafeteria, chophouse, hash house, lunchroom, trattoria 10 coffee shop, restaurant, steak house 11 greasy spoon 12 luncheonette

eavesdrop
3 bug, tap 4 lurk 5 snoop 7 monitor 8 listen in, overhear

Eban of Israel
4 Abba

ebb
4 drop, fade, fall, flag, tide, wane 5 abate, droop, let up 6 lessen, recede, reduce, relent, shrink, wither 7 decline, descent, die away, die down, ease off, retreat, slacken, subside 8 decrease, diminish, languish, moderate, withdraw 10 retrograde

Eblis
5 Satan
son: 3 Tir 4 Awar 5 Dasim 8 Zalambur

ebon, ebony
3 jet 4 inky 5 black, jetty, raven, sable 6 brunet 8 brunette, jet-black 9 pitch-dark 10 pitch-black

ebullience
3 vim, zip 4 brio, élan, zing 5 gusto 6 gaiety 7 abandon, elation 8 buoyancy, vitality, vivacity 9 animation 10 enthusiasm, exuberance, liveliness 11 high spirits 13 effervescence

ebullient
5 brash, zingy, zippy 6 bouncy, bubbly, elated, frothy, geeked, pumped, raring 7 boiling, excited, gleeful, gushing, vibrant 8 hopped-up 9 sprightly, vivacious 11 exhilarated 12 enthusiastic, high-spirited 13 irrepressible

Ecce ___
4 homo

eccentric
3 odd, nut 4 coot, kook 5 batty, crank, crazy, droll, flaky, freak, funky, funny, goofy, kooky, nutty, outré, queer, wacky, weird 6 far out, oddity, quaint, quirky, screwy, weirdo, whacko, whacky 7 bizarre, deviant, erratic, heretic, oddball, offbeat, strange, unusual 8 aberrant, abnormal, bohemian, cockeyed, crackpot, goofball, maverick, peculiar, singular, uncommon 9 anomalous, character, deviating, fantastic, fruitcake, grotesque, irregular, off-center, screwball, whimsical 10 elliptical, off-balance, unbalanced, uncentered 11 exceptional 13 idiosyncratic, nonconformist

eccentricity
4 kink **5** quirk, twist **8** crotchet, quiddity **9** deviation, weirdness **10** aberration **11** strangeness **12** idiosyncrasy

ecclesiastic
see **clergyman**

ecclesiastical
4 holy **5** papal **6** church, sacred **8** churchly, clerical, pastoral, priestly **9** apostolic, canonical, episcopal, spiritual, synagogal **10** churchlike, pontifical, rabbinical, sacerdotal **11** ministerial, theological **12** episcopalian, evangelistic, tabernacular

ecdysiast
6 peeler, teaser **8** stripper **10** stripteuse **11** stripteaser

echelon
3 row **4** file, line, rank, tier **5** grade, group, level, order, queue **6** string **7** chevron **9** formation

echidna
8 anteater **9** monotreme **13** spiny anteater

Echidna
father: **7** Phorcys **8** Chrysaor
mother: **4** Ceto **10** Callirrhoë
offspring: **5** Hydra **6** dragon, Orthus, Sphinx **7** Chimera **8** Cerberus, Chimaera

echinoderm
6 urchin **7** crinoid, sea star **8** starfish **9** coelomate, sea urchin **11** sea cucumber

echo
3 ape **4** mime, ring **5** evoke, mimic, trace **6** mirror, parrot, repeat, result, reverb, second **7** imitate, iterate, reflect, resound, revoice, vestige **8** resonate, response **9** duplicate, imitation, reiterate **10** reflection, repetition **11** reverberate **12** repercussion **13** reverberation

Echo
5 nymph, oread
beloved: **9** Narcissus

echoic
7 mimetic **9** imitative **10** derivative **12** onomatopoeic **13** onomatopoetic

éclat
4 bang, dash, fame, pomp **5** glory, honor, kudos **6** luster, lustre, praise, renown, repute **7** acclaim, display, laurels, stardom, success **8** applause, eminence, prestige, standing **9** celebrity, notoriety, publicity **10** brilliance, brilliancy, exaltation, prominence, reputation **11** distinction, ostentation

eclectic
5 broad, fussy, mixed, picky **6** choosy, select, varied **7** diverse, finicky, mingled **8** assorted, catholic, elective **9** inclusive, selective **10** discerning, fastidious, particular **11** diversified **12** dilettantish, multifarious **13** heterogeneous

eclipse
3 dim **5** bedim, cloud, cover, excel, outdo, shade **6** darken, exceed, shadow **7** becloud, decline, obscure, surpass **8** downfall, outshine **9** adumbrate, obfuscate, overcloud **10** extinguish, overshadow
phenomenon: **5** umbra **6** corona, shadow **7** annulus **8** penumbra **11** Diamond Ring **12** Bailey's Beads

eclogue
3 ode **4** idyl, poem **5** idyll, lyric **8** pastoral

école student
5 élève

ecological
5 green **8** bionomic
community: **5** biome

ecology
9 bionomics **11** environment

economic
6 fiscal **8** material, monetary **9** budgetary, financial, pecuniary **10** mercantile, profitable
doctrine: **12** laissez-faire
system: **9** communism, socialism **10** capitalism **11** syndicalism **12** mercantilism

economical
4 mean **5** canny, close, spare, tight **6** frugal, saving, stingy **7** careful, miserly, prudent, sparing, thrifty **8** skimping **9** efficient, niggardly, penny-wise, penurious, provident, scrimping **10** unwasteful **12** cheeseparing, parsimonious **13** penny-pinching

economist
American: **5** Arrow (Kenneth), Simon (Herbert, Julian), Solow (Robert), Tobin (James) **6** Becker (Gary), George (Henry), Thurow (Lester), Veblen (Thorstein), Walker (Amasa), Weaver (Robert) **7** Krugman (Paul), Kuznets (Simon), Stigler (George), Volcker (Paul) **8** Friedman (Milton), Stiglitz (Joseph) **9** Galbraith (John Kenneth), Greenspan (Alan), Samuelson (Paul) **10** Schumpeter (Joseph)
Austrian: **5** Hayek (Friedrich von), Mises (Ludwig von)
Canadian: **7** Leacock (Stephen)
Dutch: **9** Tinbergen (Jan)
English: **3** Sen (Amartya) **4** Mill (John Stuart) **5** Coase (Ronald), Hayek (Friedrich von), Pigou (Arthur) **6** Engels (Friedrich), Keynes (John Maynard) **7** Bagehot (Walter), Malthus (Thomas), Ricardo (David)
French: **3** Say (Jean-Baptiste) **6** Monnet (Jean), Turgot (Anne-Robert-Jacques), Walras (Léon) **7** Quesnay (François)
German: **4** Marx (Karl) **5** Weber (Max) **6** Engels (Friedrich) **7** Schacht (Hjalmar)
Indian: **3** Sen (Amartya)

Scottish: **4** Mill (James) **5** Smith (Adam)
Swedish: **6** Myrdal (Gunnar)
Swiss: **8** Sismondi (Simonde de)

economist Amartya
3 Sen

economize
4 save **5** skimp, stint **6** manage, scrimp **7** husband **8** conserve **10** cut corners **12** pinch pennies

economy
6 saving, thrift **8** prudence, skimping **9** concision, frugality, husbandry, parsimony, restraint, scrimping **10** discretion, efficiency, providence, stinginess **11** carefulness, conciseness, miserliness, thriftiness **13** niggardliness

Eco novel
9 Baudolino **13** Name of the Rose (The) **17** Foucault's Pendulum

ecru
3 tan **4** buff **5** beige, khaki **7** vanilla

ecstasy
3 joy **5** bliss **6** frenzy, heaven, trance **7** delight, elation, madness, rapture **8** euphoria, paradise, rhapsody **9** beatitude, transport **10** exaltation, joyfulness **11** blessedness, derangement, enchantment, high spirits, inspiration **12** blissfulness, exhilaration, intoxication **13** seventh heaven

ecstatic
6 elated, joyful **7** gleeful **8** euphoric, exultant, jubilant, thrilled **9** delirious, delighted, entranced, overjoyed, rapturous, rhapsodic **11** exhilarated, transported

ectothermic
11 cold-blooded

Ecuador
capital: **5** Quito
city: **6** Ambato, Cuenca **7** Machala **9** Guayaquil
Indian people: **7** Quechua
island group: **9** Galápagos
language: **7** Spanish
monetary unit: **5** sucre
mountain range: **5** Andes
neighbor: **4** Peru **8** Colombia
volcano: **6** Sangay **7** Cayambe **8** Cotopaxi **10** Chimborazo

ecumenical
6 cosmic, global **7** general, generic **8** catholic **9** inclusive, planetary, universal, worldwide **12** all-inclusive, cosmopolitan **13** comprehensive

ecumenical council
4 Lyon **5** Basel, Lyons, Trent **6** Nicene **7** Ephesus, Ferrara, Lateran, Vatican **8** Florence **9** Chalcedon, Constance

eczema
6 tetter

edacious
7 piggish **8** ravenous **9** voracious **10** gluttonous

eddy
4 purl **5** swirl, twirl, whirl, whorl **6** vortex **8** backwash **9** backwater, maelstrom, whirlpool **11** counterflow

edema
5 croup, tumor **6** dropsy **8** anasarca, swelling
treatment: **8** diuretic

Eden
6 heaven, utopia **7** arcadia, elysium **8** paradise
dweller: **3** Eve **4** Adam
river: **5** Gihon **6** Pishon **8** Hiddekel **9** Euphrates

edentate
5 sloth **8** aardvark, anteater, pangolin **9** armadillo, toothless

Edessa's king
5 Abgar

edge
3 cut, end, hem, lip, rim **4** bank, bite, brim, cusp, draw, ease, hone, inch, lead, limb, line, pink, side, whet, worm **5** arris, bound, brink, bulge, force, ledge, picot, point, ridge, sidle, skirt, sting, strop, verge **6** border, fringe, margin, nosing **7** acidity, contour, chamfer, outline, serrate, sharpen, vantage **8** acerbity, acridity, boundary, emborder, handicap, keenness, surround, thinness **9** acuteness, advantage, extremity, harshness, head start, perimeter, periphery, sharpness, threshold, upper hand **10** causticity, shrillness, stringency **11** astringency **12** incisiveness **13** effectiveness

edge city
5 exurb **6** suburb

edged
4 acid, tart **5** acerb, acute, sharp **6** barbed, strong **7** acerbic, cutting **8** incisive, piercing

edge in
6 inject **9** interject, interpose, insinuate **10** infiltrate **11** interpolate

edging
3 hem **4** lace **5** braid, frill, limit **6** border, fringe, lacing, margin, piping **7** flounce, selvage **8** rickrack, selvedge, trimming

edgy
3 hip **5** funky, nervy, sharp, tense, testy, wired **6** daring, touchy, uneasy **7** excited, keyed up, offbeat, restive, uptight **8** Bohemian, out-there, renegade, restless, skittery, skittish, volatile **9** excitable, impatient, irascible, irritable **10** high-strung, outlandish **11** provocative

edible
8 esculent **9** palatable **10** comestible
root: **3** oca, yam **4** beet, taro, yuca **6** carrot, daikon, ginger, jicama, potato, radish, turnip,

wasabi **7** burdock, cassava, ginseng, malanga, parsnip, salsify **8** celeriac, galangal, kohlrabi, rutabaga **11** horseradish, sweet potato
seed: **3** nut, pea **4** bean **6** peanut

edibles
4 chow, eats, feed, food, grub **6** viands **7** aliment, goodies, nurture **8** victuals **9** provender **10** provisions, sustenance **11** comestibles

edict
3 law **4** bull, fiat, rule **5** canon, order, ukase **6** decree, dictum, ruling **7** command, dictate, mandate, precept, statute **9** directive, manifesto, ordinance, prescript **10** injunction, regulation **12** proclamation **13** pronouncement
Islamic: **5** fatwa
papal: **4** bull **8** decretal

Edict of ___
5 Milan, Worms **6** Nantes

edifice
4 pile **8** building, erection **9** structure

edify
5 teach **6** better, fill in, illume, inform, update, uplift **7** educate, elevate, enhance, improve **8** illumine, instruct **9** elucidate, enlighten **10** illuminate

Edison
middle name: **4** Alva
rival: **5** Tesla (Nikola)

edit
3 cut **4** cull, omit **5** adapt, alter, amend, emend, fix up **6** delete, doctor, excise, polish, redact, refine, review, revise, reword, select **7** abridge, compile, correct, rewrite **8** annotate, assemble, condense, copyread, fine-tune **9** proofread, rearrange **10** blue-pencil, bowdlerize
out: **4** dele

Edith of French song
4 Piaf

editing term
4 dele, stet **5** caret **7** jump cut

edition
4 copy, form **5** issue, print **7** reissue, reprint, version **8** printing, variorum **10** impression, reprinting **12** reproduction

editor
8 redactor **9** scrivener, wordsmith **10** copyreader **11** proofreader

editor's request
4 SASE

Edmonton player
5 Oiler

Edomite's ancestor
4 Esau

educate
4 rear **5** brief, coach, drill, edify, nurse, teach, train, tutor **6** inform, school **7** explain, nurture **8** instruct **9** brainwash, enlighten **10** discipline **12** indoctrinate

education
7 culture, tuition **8** breeding, coaching, guidance, learning, literacy, pedagogy, teaching, training, tutelage, tutorage, tutoring **9** erudition, knowledge, schooling, tutorship **11** instruction, learnedness, scholarship **13** enlightenment

educational
11 informative, instructive **13** informational, instructional
institution: **6** school **7** academy, college **10** university **12** conservatory

educator
5 tutor **7** teacher **9** professor **10** instructor
American: **4** Mann (Horace) **5** Dewey (John) **6** Butler (Nicholas Murray), Conant (James Bryant), Harris (William Torrey) **7** Barnard (Henry), Beecher (Catharine), Peabody (Elizabeth) **8** Hutchins (Robert Maynard), McGuffey (William) **10** Washington (Booker T.)
Austrian: **7** Steiner (Rudolf)
Czech: **8** Comenius (John Amos)
English: **6** Arnold (Thomas) **7** Spencer (Herbert)
German: **7** Froebel (Friedrich), Herbart (Johann)
Italian: **10** Montessori (Maria)
Scottish: **5** Neill (A. S.)
Swiss: **10** Pestalozzi (Johann Heinrich)
org.: **3** NEA

educe
4 drag, draw, milk, pull **5** evoke, wrest, wring **6** derive, elicit, evince, evolve, extort, obtain, secure **7** distill, draw out, extract, procure **8** bring out **10** excogitate

eel
5 moray, siren, unagi **6** conger **7** hagfish, lamprey, sniggle
young: **5** elver

eelpout
6 blenny, burbot **10** muttonfish

eely
5 slimy **6** slippy, wiggly **7** elusive, wriggly **8** slippery, slithery **9** wriggling

eerie
5 scary, weird **6** creepy, spooky **7** bizarre, strange, uncanny **8** chilling, spectral **9** fantastic, grotesque, unearthly **10** mysterious **11** frightening, hair-raising **12** otherworldly

Eeyore creator
5 Milne (A. A.)

efface
4 dele, x out **5** annul, erase **6** cancel, delete, rub out **7** blot out, destroy, expunge, scratch, wipe out **8** black out, wear away **9** eliminate, eradicate, extirpate **10** obliterate

effect
3 end **4** make **5** cause, enact, event, fruit **6** create, draw on, induce, intent, invoke, render, result, upshot **7** achieve, execute, fulfill, outcome, perform, produce, realize, turn out **8** bring off, carry out, conceive, generate **9** actualize, aftermath, discharge, implement, outgrowth **10** accomplish, bring about, conclusion, denouement **11** consequence **12** carry through, ramification, repercussion

effective
4 able **5** sound, valid **6** causal, cogent, direct, potent, useful **7** capable, operant **8** adequate **9** competent, operative **10** compelling, convincing, productive

effectiveness
5 clout, force, point, power, vigor **6** weight **7** cogency, potency **8** strength, validity **10** capability

effects
4 gear **5** goods, stuff **6** things **8** chattels, movables, property **9** equipment, moveables, trappings **10** belongings **11** impedimenta, possessions **13** accoutrements

effectual
5 sound, valid **6** potent, strong, useful **7** capable **8** decisive, powerful, workable **10** conclusive, fulfilling, productive **11** influential, practicable **13** authoritative, determinative

effectuate
see **effect**

effervescence
5 giddy **7** fizzing, foaming, sparkle **8** bubbling, buoyancy, vivacity **9** animation **10** ebullience, ebullition, exuberance, exuberancy, liveliness **12** exhilaration

effervescent
3 gay **4** airy **5** jolly **6** bouncy, bubbly, lively **7** boiling, buoyant, excited **8** animated, mirthful, volatile **9** sparkling, sprightly, vivacious **10** carbonated **12** high-spirited **13** irrepressible

effete
4 soft, weak **5** frail, spent **6** barren **7** decayed, drained, worn-out **8** decadent, decaying, delicate, depleted, fatigued **9** declining, dissolute, enfeebled, exhausted, infertile, washed-out **10** degenerate

efficacious
6 active, potent, strong **8** forceful, powerful, puissant **9** operative **10** productive **11** influential

efficacy
see **effectiveness**

efficiency
see **effectiveness**

efficient
4 able, lean **5** adept **6** expert **7** capable, elegant, skilled **8** economic, masterly, skillful **9** competent **10** economical, productive

effigy
3 guy **4** icon, idol **5** dummy, image **6** figure **7** waxwork **8** likeness

effloresce
4 blow **5** bloom, burst **6** flower, sprout **7** blossom, burgeon **9** bear fruit

effluvium
3 air **4** odor, reek **5** smell, vapor, waste **6** miasma **7** exhaust **8** effusion, emission **9** by-product, discharge, emanation **10** exhalation

efflux
see **effluvium**

effort
3 job, try **4** dint, feat, push, task, toil, work **5** chore, essay, force, labor, might, nisus, pains, sweat, while **6** energy, strain **7** attempt, travail, trouble, venture **8** endeavor, exertion, industry, struggle **11** application, elbow grease

effortful
4 hard **6** tiring, uphill **7** arduous, labored, operose **8** exacting, toilsome **9** ambitious, difficult, laborious, strenuous **11** challenging

effortless
4 easy **5** adept, light, ready **6** expert, facile, fluent, simple, smooth **8** masterly, skillful **10** proficient **11** undemanding

effrontery
4 face, gall **5** brass, cheek, nerve **8** audacity, boldness, chutzpah, temerity **9** arrogance, assurance, brashness, hardihood, impudence, insolence **10** brazenness **11** presumption **12** impertinence

effulgence
4 glow **5** blaze, glory **6** luster, lustre **8** radiance, splendor **9** splendour **10** brightness, brilliance, brilliancy, luminosity

effulgent
5 vivid **6** bright, lucent **7** beaming, glowing, lambent, radiant, shining **8** dazzling, glorious, luminous, lustrous, splendid **9** brilliant **11** resplendent **12** incandescent

effuse
4 flow, gush, pour, shed **5** exude, issue **6** stream **7** emanate, enthuse, flow out, radiate

effusive
5 gushy **6** lavish, sloppy, smarmy **7** cloying, fulsome, gushing, profuse, verbose **9** expansive, exuberant **10** loquacious, outpouring, unreserved **11** extravagant **12** enthusiastic, unrestrained **13** demonstrative, unconstrained

eft
4 newt **6** triton **10** salamander

e.g.
3 say **10** for example **11** for instance **13** exempli gratia

egad
6 zounds **7** criminy **8** gadzooks **11** odds bodkins

egg
3 ova (plural) **4** ovum, seed **5** ovule
case: **5** shell **7** ootheca
cell: **3** ova (plural) **4** ovum
combining form: **3** ovi, ovo
dish: **6** omelet **8** omelette
fertilized: **6** zygote **7** oospore
fish: **3** roe **6** caviar
French: **4** oeuf
holder: **4** nest
immature: **6** oocyte
louse: **3** nit
part: **4** yolk **5** glair, shell, white
receptacle: **6** ovisac
shaped: **5** ovate, ovoid **7** ovoidal
white: **5** glair **7** albumen

egghead
4 whiz **6** genius, pundit **8** brainiac, highbrow, longhair **10** double-dome **12** intellectual

egg on
4 goad, prod, spur, urge **5** prick, rally **6** arouse, exhort, excite, incite, prompt, stir up **7** agitate **9** instigate, stimulate

eggplant
6 purple **9** aubergine **10** nightshade

egg-shaped
4 oval **5** ovate, ovoid **7** oviform

Eglah
husband: **5** David
son: **7** Ithream

eglantine
7 dog rose **10** sweetbriar, sweetbrier

Eglantine
father: **5** Pepin
husband: **9** Valentine

Eglon
king: **5** Debir
slayer: **4** Ehud

ego
4 self **5** pride **6** vanity **7** conceit **10** self-esteem

egocentric
7 selfish **9** conceited **10** self-loving **11** self-seeking **12** narcissistic, self-absorbed, self-affected, self-centered, self-involved, vainglorious **13** individualist, self-conceited, self-concerned, self-indulgent

egoism
5 pride **6** vanity **7** conceit **8** self-love **9** self-glory, self-pride, vainglory **10** narcissism, self-regard **11** selfishness, self-opinion

egoistic
4 smug, vain **7** selfish **9** conceited **12** self-absorbed, self-centered **13** self-concerned, self-contented, self-satisfied

egomaniacal
12 self-exalting, vainglorious

egotism
5 pride **6** vanity **7** conceit **8** boasting, bragging, self-love, vainness, vaunting **9** arrogance, pomposity, self-glory, self-pride, vainglory **10** narcissism, self-esteem **11** megalomania, self-opinion **12** boastfulness **13** conceitedness

egotistic
4 vain **5** cocky, proud **7** selfish, stuck-up **8** arrogant, boastful, inflated, puffed-up **9** conceited **11** pretentious, self-serving **12** self-absorbed, self-centered, self-involved **13** self-concerned, self-satisfied

egregious
4 rank **5** gross, stark **6** arrant, brazen **7** blatant, glaring, heinous **8** flagrant, infamous, outright, shocking **9** atrocious, notorious, shameless **10** deplorable, outrageous **11** conspicuous

egress, egression
4 door, exit **5** issue, leave **6** depart, escape, exodus, outlet **7** doorway, exiting, opening, passage **9** departure, emergence

egret
5 heron, wader

Egypt
ancient city: **6** Thebes **7** Memphis
capital: **5** Cairo
city: **4** Giza **6** Karnak **8** Port Said **10** Alexandria
dam: **5** Aswan
desert: **6** Libyan **7** Arabian, Western
gulf: **4** Suez **5** Aqaba
lake: **6** Nasser
language: **6** Arabic
leader: **5** Sadat (Anwar el-) **6** Nasser (Gamal Abdul) **7** Mubarak (Hosni)
monetary unit: **5** pound
neighbor: **5** Libya, Sudan **6** Israel
oasis: **4** Siwa **6** Dakhla, Kharga **7** Farafra
peninsula: **5** Sinai
river: **4** Nile
sea: **3** Red **13** Mediterranean

Egyptian
burial jar: **7** canopic
Christian: **4** Copt
cross: **4** ankh
dynasty: **5** Saite, Xoite **6** Hyksos, Tanite, Theban **7** Persian, Thinite **8** Memphite **9** Bubastite, Ethiopian **10** Diospolite
flower: **5** lotus
god:
bull: **4** Apis
chief: **4** Amen, Amun **6** Amen-Ra, Amun-Ra
crocodile-headed: **5** Sebek
falcon-headed: **4** Ment **5** Horus, Mentu **6** Sokari **7** Sokaris

ibis-headed: **5** Thoth **6** Dhouti
jackal-headed: **6** Anubis
of creation: **4** Ptah **5** Phtha
of day: **5** Horus
of death: **6** Anubis
of earth: **3** Geb, Keb, Seb
of evil: **3** Set **4** Seth **5** Sebek
of life: **4** Amen, Amon **5** Ammon
of magic: **5** Thoth **6** Dhouti
of Memphis: **4** Ptah **5** Phtha **6** Sokari **7** Sokaris
of the heavens: **5** Horus
of the morning sun: **5** Horus **7** Khepera
of the sun: **4** Amen, Amun, Aten, Aton **6** Amen-Ra, Amun-Ra
of Thebes: **4** Amen **6** Khensu, Khonsu
of the underworld: **6** Osiris
of war: **4** Ment **5** Mentu
of wisdom: **5** Thoth **6** Dhouti
ram-headed: **4** Amen, Amon **5** Ammon, Khnum **6** Khnemu
snake: **4** Apep **5** Apepi

goddess:
cat-headed: **4** Bast **5** Pakht
cow-headed: **5** Athor **6** Hathor
lioness-headed: **4** Bast **5** Pakht **6** Sekhet
of fertility: **4** Isis
of love and mirth: **5** Athor **6** Hathor
of motherhood: **4** Apet, Isis
of Thebes: **3** Mut
of the heavens: **3** Nut
queen of the gods: **4** Sati
vulture-headed: **3** Mut **7** Nekhebt **8** Nekhebet

hat: **3** fez
king: (see **king** entry)
language: **6** Arabic, Coptic
native: **4** Arab, Copt **5** Nilot
queen: **9** Cleopatra, Nefertiti
sacred bird: **4** ibis **5** bennu
sacred bull: **4** Apis
snake: **3** asp
solar disk: **4** Aten, Aton
sultan: **7** Saladin
symbol of life: **4** ankh
talisman: **6** scarab
underworld: **4** Aaru, Duat **6** Amenti
wind: **7** khamsin, sirocco

eider
4 down, duck **7** sea duck

eidetic
5 exact, vivid **7** perfect, precise **8** absolute, lifelike

eidolon
4 icon **5** ghost, ideal, image, model, shade **6** mirage, vision, wraith **7** epitome, fantasm, figment, paragon, phantom, specter, spectre **8** exemplar, illusion, paradigm, phantasm **9** archetype, prototype **10** apparition

eight
combining form: **4** octa, octo
group of: **5** octad, octet **6** octave

eight bells
4 noon

eighteen-wheeler
3 rig **4** semi **11** semitrailer

eighth note
6 quaver

eighty-six
4 boot, junk, toss **5** chuck, eject, evict, scrap **6** bounce **7** discard, kick out **8** get rid of, jettison, throw out

Einstein, Albert
birthplace: **3** Ulm
theory: **10** relativity

Eire
see **Ireland**

Eisenhower, Dwight
3 Ike
home: **7** Abilene
initials: **3** DDE
wife: **5** Mamie
World War II command: **3** ETO

eject
4 boot, bump, dump, fire, oust, sack, spew **5** chuck, evict, expel **6** banish, bounce **7** boot out, cast out, dismiss, kick out **8** disgorge, throw out **9** discharge

eke out
6 extend **7** augment, enhance, fill out, squeeze, stretch **8** increase **10** supplement

elaborate
4 busy **5** fancy, showy **6** daedal, dressy, evolve, expand, knotty, minute, ornate, refine, unfold **7** amplify, build up, careful, clarify, comment, complex, develop, discuss, elegant, enlarge, explain, expound, profuse, work out **8** detailed, involved, overdone, thorough **9** Byzantine, decorated, embellish, extensive, interpret, intricate **10** overworked **11** complicated, embellished, extravagant, painstaking **12** labyrinthine

Elaine
father: **6** Pelles
lover: **8** Lancelot **9** Launcelot
son: **7** Galahad

Elam
capital: **4** Susa **7** Shushan
father: **4** Shem
king: **12** Chedorlaomer

élan
3 pep, vim, zip **4** brio, dash, fire, life, zeal, zest, zing **5** ardor, flair, gusto, oomph, verve, vigor **6** energy, esprit, fervor, spirit **7** impetus **8** vivacity **9** animation, eagerness, intensity **10** enthusiasm

élan vital
4 soul **5** anima **6** animus, pneuma, psyche, spirit

elapse
4 go by, pass **6** expire, run out, slip by **8** pass away

elastic
6 bouncy, limber, pliant, rubber, supple **7** ductile, pliable, rubbery, springy **8** animated, flexible, moldable, stretchy, volatile **9** adaptable, expansive, malleable, resilient **10** extendable, extensible, rubber band, rubberlike **11** stretchable

elate
4 buoy **5** cheer, exalt, flush, set up **6** excite, perk up, uplift **7** cheer up, delight, enliven, gladden, gratify, hearten, inspire, overjoy **8** brighten, embolden, inspirit, spirit up **9** encourage **10** exhilarate, invigorate

elated
4 glad, high **5** happy **7** exalted, excited **8** ecstatic, euphoric, exultant, gladsome, jubilant **9** overjoyed **10** enraptured **11** exhilarated, intoxicated, on cloud nine **12** high-spirited

elation
3 joy **4** glee **7** delight, ecstasy, rapture **8** buoyancy, euphoria **9** happiness, transport **10** exaltation, excitement, jubilation **12** exhilaration, intoxioation

Elbe tributary
4 Eger, Iser, Ohre **5** Saale **6** Moldau, Vltava

elbow
4 poke, push **5** joint, nudge, shove **6** hustle, jostle

eld
4 yore **6** old age **8** old times

elder
6 senior **8** old-timer **9** patriarch, presbyter **10** golden-ager

elderliness
3 age **6** dotage, old age **8** caducity **10** senescence **11** senectitude

elderly
3 old **4** aged, gray **5** aging, hoary **7** ancient **9** declining, venerable

eldritch
5 eerie, weird **6** creepy, spooky **7** uncanny

Eleanor
husband: **7** Henry II **8** Franklin
terrier: **4** Fala

elect
3 opt, tap **4** name, pick **5** co-opt, saved **6** choice, choose, chosen, decide, opt for, ordain, picked, vote in **7** resolve, vote for **8** destined, nominate, ordained, redeemed **9** delivered, designate, determine, exclusive, single out **10** designated, singled out

election
6 ballot, choice, voting **7** primary **8** choosing, decision **9** balloting **10** preference, referendum **11** alternative

electioneer
5 stump **7** canvass **8** campaign, politick **9** barnstorm

elective
6 chosen **8** optional **9** voluntary **11** sympathetic **13** discretionary, noncompulsory, nonobligatory

Electra
brother: **7** Orestes
father: **9** Agamemnon
husband: **7** Pylades
mother: **12** Clytemnestra
sister: **9** Iphigenia
victim: **9** Aegisthus **12** Clytemnestra

electric
appliance: **3** fan **4** iron, oven **5** clock, drier, dryer, mixer, range, stove **6** stereo, washer **7** blender, freezer, toaster **10** dishwasher, television **12** refrigerator
coil: **5** tesla **8** solenoid
device: **4** coil, fuse, plug **6** dynamo, magnet, switch **7** battery **8** resistor, rheostat, varistor **9** amplifier, capacitor, condenser, generator **11** transformer
generator: **6** dynamo
outlet: **6** socket
particle: **3** ion
unit: **3** amp, ohm **4** volt, watt **5** farad, henry, joule **6** ampere **7** coulomb, faraday **8** kilowatt

electric-car brand
5 Tesla

electric current
5 juice
kind: **4** AC/DC **6** direct **11** alternating
power: **7** wattage
strength: **8** amperage
unit: **3** amp **6** ampere

electricity
5 juice, spark **7** current **9** galvanism, lightning
kind: **6** static **7** current
pioneer: **5** Tesla (Nikola) **6** Edison (Thomas) **7** Faraday (Michael)

electrify
3 jar **4** jolt, stun **5** amaze, power, shock **6** charge, excite, thrill **7** astound, enthuse, inflame, provoke, stagger, startle **8** astonish, energize

electrode
6 dynode
negative: **7** cathode
positive: **5** anode

electron
3 ion **7** polaron
stream: **10** cathode ray
tube: **6** triode **7** tetrode **8** dynatron, klystron

Electryon
brother: 6 Mestor
daughter: 7 Alcmene
father: 7 Perseus
mother: 9 Andromeda
wife: 5 Anaxo

eleemosynary
6 humane 8 generous 10 altruistic, beneficent, benevolent, charitable, munificent, openhanded 12 humanitarian 13 philanthropic

elegance
4 chic, pomp, tone 5 charm, grace, style, taste 6 luxury, polish 7 culture, dignity 8 chicness, poshness, richness, splendor, urbanity 9 gentility, precision 10 ornateness, refinement 11 cultivation 12 tastefulness

elegant
4 chic, fine, posh 5 fancy, grand, noble, swank 6 choice, classy, dainty, lovely, modish, ornate, swanky, urbane 7 courtly, genteel, opulent, refined, stately, stylish 8 cultured, polished, splendid, tasteful 9 exquisite, luxurious, recherché, sumptuous 10 cultivated 11 fashionable

elegiac
7 pensive 8 dactylic 9 lamenting, sorrowful 10 melancholy

elegy
4 poem, song 5 dirge 6 lament, monody 8 threnody

___ eleison
5 Kyrie

Elektra composer
7 Strauss (Richard)

element
4 item, part 5 basic, facet, piece, point 6 aspect, detail, factor, member, sector 7 article, feature, portion, section 8 division, particle, rudiment 9 component, essential, principle 10 ingredient, particular 11 constituent, fundamental
chemical: 3 tin 4 gold, iron, lead, neon, zinc 5 argon, boron, radon, xenon 6 barium, carbon, cerium, cesium, cobalt, copper, curium, erbium, helium, indium, iodine, nickel, osmium, oxygen, radium, silver, sodium 7 arsenic, bismuth, bohrium, bromine, cadmium, calcium, dubnium, fermium, gallium, hafnium, hassium, holmium, iridium, krypton, lithium, mercury, niobium, rhenium, rhodium, silicon, sulphur, terbium, thorium, thulium, uranium, yttrium 8 actinium, aluminum, antimony, astatine, chlorine, chromium, europium, fluorine, hydrogen, illinium, lutecium, masurium, nitrogen, nobelium, platinum, polonium, rubidium, samarium, scandium, selenium, tantalum, thallium, titanium, tungsten, vanadium 9 americium, berkelium, beryllium, columbium, germanium, lanthanum, magnesium, manganese, neodymium, neptunium, palladium, plutonium, potassium, ruthenium, strontium, tellurium, virginium, ytterbium, zirconium 10 dysprosium, gadolinium, lawrencium, meitnerium, molybdenum, seaborgium 11 californium, copernicium, einsteinium, mendelevium, phosphorous 12 darmstadtium, praseodymium 13 rutherfordium, protoactinium

elemental
3 key 4 pure 5 basal, basic, crude, prime 6 inborn, innate, primal, simple 7 central, connate, primary, radical 8 cardinal, inherent, integral, intimate, simplest 9 beginning, essential, ingrained, intrinsic, primitive 10 deep-seated, primordial, underlying 11 fundamental 13 uncomplicated

elementary
4 easy 5 basal, basic 6 simple 7 initial 9 beginning, essential, primitive 10 rudimental, underlying 11 fundamental, preliminary, rudimentary 12 introductory

elemi
5 resin 9 oleoresin

elephant
5 Babar 6 Horton, tusker 9 pachyderm
boy: 4 Sabu
driver: 6 mahout
enclosure: 5 kraal
extinct: 7 mammoth 8 mastodon
female: 3 cow
group: 4 herd
keeper: 6 mahout
male: 4 bull
maverick: 5 rogue
nose: 5 trunk 9 proboscis
seat: 6 howdah
sound: 6 bellow 7 trumpet
tooth: 4 tusk
tusk: 5 ivory
young: 4 calf

elephant-headed god
6 Ganesa, Ganesh 7 Ganesha

elephantine
4 huge 6 clumsy 7 awkward, hulking, mammoth, massive 8 colossal, enormous, gigantic 9 graceless, humongous, monstrous, ponderous 10 gargantuan, mastodonic, prodigious, ungraceful 11 heavy-footed

Elephant Man
7 Merrick (Joseph)

elevate
4 lift, rear, rise 5 boost, elate, erect, exalt, hoist, raise 6 buoy up, jack up, lift up, pick up, uplift 7 advance, dignify, ennoble, glorify, hearten, improve, inspire, promote, upgrade 8 heighten 10 exhilarate

elevated
4 high **5** grand, lofty, moral, noble **6** aerial, formal, superb **7** ethical, refined, soaring, stately, sublime **8** eloquent, majestic, virtuous **9** dignified, grandiose, high-flown, honorable, righteous

elevation
4 hill, rise **5** boost **6** ascent, height, uplift **7** advance, raising **8** altitude, mountain **9** acclivity, promotion, upgrading **10** apotheosis, preference, preferment **11** advancement, ennoblement
indication: **9** benchmark

elevator
4 cage, lift, silo **5** hoist
maker: **4** Otis (Elisha)

elf
3 fay, imp **4** peri, puck **5** fairy, gnome, pixie, troll **6** goblin, sprite **7** brownie, gremlin **10** leprechaun

elfin
5 antic **6** frisky, impish **7** implike, playful, puckish **8** pixieish **11** mischievous

Elgin ___
7 Marbles

Eli
4 Yale **5** Yalie

Eli ___
4 Yale **5** Lilly **7** Whitney

Elia
4 Lamb (Charles)

Eliab
brother: **5** David
daughter: **7** Abihail
father: **5** Helon, Pallu
son: **6** Abiram, Dathan

Eliada
father: **5** David
son: **5** Rezon

Eliam's daughter
9 Bathsheba

elicit
5 educe, evoke **6** derive, evince, extort **7** extract, provoke **8** bring out **9** call forth, draw forth

elide
4 fail, omit, skip, slur **6** cut off, excise, forget, ignore, remove, slight **7** abridge, curtail, neglect **8** condense, cross out, discount, overlook, pass over, suppress **9** disregard, strike out

eligible
3 fit **6** fitted, likely, nubile, seemly, suited, worthy **7** capable **8** entitled, suitable **9** desirable, qualified **10** acceptable **11** appropriate **12** marriageable

Elihu ___
4 Root, Yale

Elijah
5 Elias **7** prophet **8** Tishbite
father: **5** Harim **7** Jeroham

Elimelech's wife
5 Naomi

eliminate
3 bar **4** bate, drop, oust, void **5** debar, egest, eject, erase, evict, expel, purge **6** delete, except, remove **7** abolish, discard, dismiss, exclude, expunge, obviate, rule out, take out **8** count out **9** clear away, eradicate, liquidate **11** exterminate

Eliot, George
lover: **5** Lewes (George Henry)
novel: **6** Romola **8** Adam Bede **11** Middlemarch, Silas Marner **13** Daniel Deronda **14** Mill on the Floss (The)
pseudonym of: **5** Evans (Mary Ann)

Eliot, T. S.
character: **8** Prufrock (J. Alfred)
play: **13** Cocktail Party (The) **20** Murder in the Cathedral
poem: **9** Gerontion, Hollow Men (The), Waste Land (The) **12** Ash Wednesday, Four Quartets

Eliphaz
father: **4** Esau
mother: **4** Adah
son: **5** Teman

Elisabeth
husband: **9** Zacharias
son: **4** John (the Baptist)

Elisha
father: **7** Shaphat
servant: **6** Gehazi

Elisheba
brother: **7** Nahshon
father: **9** Amminadab
husband: **5** Aaron
son: **5** Abihu, Nadab **7** Eleazar, Ithamar

elite
3 top **4** best, pick **5** A-list, cream, elect, pride, prime, prize **6** choice, flower, gentry, select **7** quality, society **9** exclusive, gentility, patrician **10** upper class, upper crust **11** aristocracy **12** aristocratic
unit: **5** A team

elixir
4 balm, cure **6** potion **7** arcanum, cure-all, nostrum, panacea, philter, philtre **10** catholicon

Elizabeth I
6 Oriana **8** Gloriana

elk
4 deer **6** wapiti
relative: **5** moose **6** sambar **7** brocket, muntjac, red deer

ell
3 arm **4** wing **5** annex, elbow, joint **8** addition **9** extension

ellipse
4 oval **5** curve, orbit

elliptical
5 brief, ovate, short **6** gnomic **7** concise, cryptic, laconic, obscure, summary **9** condensed, enigmatic **11** abbreviated

Ellison work
10 Juneteenth **12** Invisible Man

elm
5 wahoo

elocution
7 diction, oratory **8** delivery, rhetoric **11** declamation, speechcraft

elongate
4 draw **6** extend **7** draw out, lengthy, spin out, stretch **8** extended, lengthen **10** lengthened

elope
4 flee **6** escape, run off **7** abscond, run away **9** steal away

eloquence
5 force, power **6** fervor, spirit **7** fluency, oratory, passion **8** rhetoric **10** expression **12** expressivity, forcefulness

eloquent
5 lofty **6** ardent, fervid, fluent, moving **7** fervent, voluble **8** elevated, forceful, powerful, stirring **9** affecting **10** articulate, expressive, impressive, meaningful, passionate, persuasive, rhetorical **11** impassioned, sententious **12** smooth-spoken **13** silver-tongued

El Salvador
capital: 11 San Salvador
city: 8 Santa Ana **9** San Miguel
ethnic group: 5 Pipil
lake: 8 Ilopango
language: 7 Spanish
monetary unit: 5 colón **6** dollar
neighbor: 8 Honduras **9** Guatemala
river: 5 Lempa

else
5 if not **7** besides, further **9** otherwise **10** additional **11** differently **12** additionally

elucidate
7 clarify, clear up, explain, expound **8** annotate, spell out **9** exemplify, explicate, interpret **10** illuminate, illustrate

elude
4 defy, duck, flee, foil **5** avert, avoid, dodge, evade **6** baffle, escape, outwit, thwart **8** confound **9** frustrate **10** circumvent

elusive
6 subtle, tricky **7** evasive, phantom **8** baffling, fleeting, fugitive, slippery **10** evanescent, intangible, mysterious **13** insubstantial

elute
7 extract

elver
3 eel

Elvis
daughter: 4 Lisa
middle name: 4 Aron **5** Aaron
mother: 6 Gladys
wife: 9 Priscilla

elvish
see **elfin**

Elysium
5 bliss **6** heaven **7** nirvana **8** empyrean, paradise

elytron
4 wing

emaciated
4 bony, lean, thin **5** gaunt **6** skinny, wasted **7** scrawny, starved, wizened **8** skeletal, underfed **10** cadaverous

emaciation
5 tabes **7** atrophy **8** marasmus **10** starvation **11** attenuation

e-mail abbreviation
3 AKA, BAK, BBL, BRB, BTW, FYI, HTH, IMO, IOW, KIT, LOL, NRN, OBO, POV, PDQ, TIA, UKW **4** ASAP, BCNU, BION, FWIW, GMTA, GTGB, IMHO, TTYL, YMMV

e-mail nuisance
4 spam

emanate
4 emit, flow, rise, stem **5** arise, exude, issue **6** derive, emerge, spring **7** come out, give off, give out, proceed, radiate **9** come forth, originate **10** derive from

emanation
4 aura, flow **6** efflux **8** effusion, emission **9** effluence

emancipate
4 free **5** let go, loose **6** loosen, redeem, unbind **7** manumit, release, set free, unchain **8** liberate, unfetter **9** discharge, unshackle **11** enfranchise

emancipation
7 release **10** liberation **11** deliverance

emancipator
5 Moses **7** Bolívar (Simón), Lincoln (Abraham) **9** deliverer, liberator

emasculate
3 fix **4** geld **5** alter, unman **6** neuter, soften, weaken **7** unnerve **8** castrate, enervate, unstring **10** debilitate, devitalize

embalm
7 mummify, perfume **8** preserve

embankment
4 berm, bund, dike, quay 5 levee, mound 6 escarp

embargo
3 ban, bar 5 edict, order 8 blockade, stoppage 10 impediment 11 prohibition

embark
5 board, enter, start 6 set out 7 set sail 8 commence

embarrass
4 faze 5 abash, upset 6 flurry, hamper, hinder, impede, rattle 7 confuse, flummox, fluster, mortify, nonplus, perturb 8 confound, distress 9 discomfit, humiliate 10 complicate, discomfort, discompose, disconcert

embarrassing
7 awkward

embarrassment
5 shame, upset 7 chagrin 8 distress 9 confusion 10 discomfort 11 humiliation 12 discomfiture, perturbation 13 mortification

embassy
5 envoy 7 mission 8 legation 10 ambassador, delegation, deputation
relative: 9 consulate

embay
4 trap 5 catch, seize 7 capture 8 encircle, surround

embed
3 fix, set 4 bury, root 5 infix, inlay, lodge 7 implant, ingrain 8 entrench

embellish
3 pad 4 deck, gild, trim 5 adorn, color 6 bedeck, blazon, emboss, enrich 7 amplify, dress up, enhance, festoon, garnish 8 beautify, decorate, ornament 9 elaborate, embroider 10 exaggerate 11 romanticize

embellishment
4 trim 5 filip, frill 6 fillip, frills 7 garnish, gilding, melisma, mordent 8 coloring, frippery, ornament, trimming 9 fioritura, floridity, hyperbole 10 decoration 11 elaboration 12 embroidering, exaggeration 13 ornamentation

ember
3 ash 4 coal 6 cinder

embezzle
4 loot, skim 5 filch, steal 6 pilfer 7 purloin 8 peculate 9 defalcate

embitter
4 sour 6 poison 7 envenom 9 acidulate

emblazon
4 laud 5 extol 7 glorify 8 inscribe 9 celebrate

emblem
4 arms, flag, logo, mace, seal, sign 5 badge, brand, crest, image, token, totem 6 banner, device, symbol 7 pennant 8 colophon, hallmark, insignia, monogram, standard 9 attribute, trademark 10 coat of arms

emblematic
8 symbolic 10 figurative, indicative 11 allegorical 12 illustrative, metaphorical

embodiment
6 avatar 7 epitome 8 exemplar 9 archetype 11 incarnation 13 manifestation

embody
5 reify 6 evince, mirror, typify 7 compose, contain, exhibit, realize, subsume 8 manifest 9 actualize, encompass, epitomize, exemplify, incarnate, integrate, objectify, personify, represent, symbolize 10 constitute, illustrate 11 emblematize, externalize, hypostatize, incorporate, materialize 12 substantiate

embolden
5 steel 7 fortify, hearten, inspire 8 inspirit 9 encourage 10 strengthen

embolus
4 clog, clot

embosom
3 hug 7 embrace, enclose, envelop, shelter

embouchure
10 mouthpiece

embowel
3 gut 4 draw 10 eviscerate, exenterate

embrace
3 hug 4 hold, lock, love, wrap 5 admit, adopt, clasp, cling, press 6 accept, cradle, cuddle, embody, enfold, fondle, nuzzle, take in, take on, take up 7 bear hug, cherish, contain, embosom, enclose, entwine, envelop, espouse, include, receive, snuggle, squeeze, subsume, welcome 8 comprise, encircle 9 encompass 10 comprehend 11 accommodate, incorporate 12 encirclement

embrangle
see **embroil**

embrocation
5 salve 7 unguent 8 liniment

embroider
3 pad, sew, tat 4 gild 5 color 6 expand, overdo, play up, stitch 7 amplify, build up, enhance, garnish, magnify, stretch 8 decorate, ornament 9 dramatize, elaborate, embellish 10 exaggerate 11 hyperbolize, romanticize

embroidery
6 crewel 7 cutwork, orphrey 8 bargello, couching, smocking, tapestry 10 crewelwork, needlework 11 needlepoint

embroil
4 mire 6 tangle 7 confuse, ensnare, involve 8 disorder, entangle 9 implicate

embroilment
4 tiff **6** fracas **7** dispute, quarrel, wrangle **8** squabble **9** bickering **10** falling-out **11** altercation, controversy

embryo
3 bud **4** germ, seed **5** fetus, spark **7** nucleus **8** blastula, gastrula

emcee
4 host

emend
4 edit **5** alter, right **6** polish, revise **7** correct, improve, rectify, retouch

emerald
3 gem **5** beryl, green, stone **8** gemstone

Emerald Isle
4 Eire, Erin **7** Ireland

emerge
4 flow, loom, rise, stem **5** arise, issue **6** appear, derive, evolve, spring **7** come out, debouch, develop, emanate, proceed, surface **9** originate, transpire **11** come to light, materialize

emergency
3 fix **4** hole, pass **5** pinch **6** climax, clutch, crisis, crunch, strait **7** squeeze **8** accident, exigency

emeritus
7 retired

Emerson, Ralph Waldo
essay: **12** Self-Reliance
forte: **5** essay
friend: **7** Thoreau (Henry David)
home: **7** Concord

emery
6 powder **8** abrasive, corundum

emetic
8 vomitive **9** cathartic, purgative

émeute
4 riot **6** mutiny, revolt, rising, tumult **8** outbreak, upheaval, uprising **9** rebellion **12** insurrection

emigrant
7 pioneer, settler **8** colonist **10** expatriate

émigré
5 alien, exile, expat **7** evacuee, migrant, refugee **8** colonist **10** expatriate

Emilia
husband: **4** Iago **7** Palamon
slayer: **4** Iago

eminence
3 VIP **4** fame, peak, rise **5** honor, power **6** bigwig, esteem, height, leader, renown, repute **7** dignity, notable, stature **8** altitude, big-timer, luminary, prestige, standing **9** authority, dignitary, elevation, greatness, loftiness **10** importance, projection, prominence, promontory, reputation **11** distinction, superiority

eminent
4 high **5** famed, grand, great, large, lofty, noble, noted **6** august, famous **7** exalted, notable **8** esteemed, renowned, towering **9** important, well-known **10** celebrated, noteworthy, projecting **11** conspicuous, illustrious, outstanding, prestigious **13** distinguished

eminently
4 very **6** highly **7** notably **9** extremely **10** remarkably, strikingly **11** exceedingly **12** surpassingly **13** exceptionally

emir
5 chief, ruler, sheik, title **6** sheikh **9** chieftain, commander

emissary
5 agent, envoy **6** legate, nuncio **8** delegate **10** ambassador

emission
4 flow **7** venting **9** discharge, effluvium, emanation, radiation

emit
4 beam, glow, ooze, pour, shed, spew, vent, void **5** eject, expel, exude, issue, loose, utter **6** exhale, let out **7** emanate, excrete, extrude, give off, give out, radiate, release, secrete, send out **8** evacuate, throw off **9** circulate, discharge

emmer
5 grain, spelt, wheat

emmet
3 ant **7** pismire

emollient
4 aloe, balm **5** salve **7** lenient, unguent **8** aloe vera, lenitive, liniment, ointment, sedative, soothing **9** analgesic, softening **10** mollifying

emolument
3 fee, pay **4** wage **5** wages **6** income, reward, salary **7** guerdon, stipend **8** earnings **10** recompense **11** pay envelope **12** compensation

emotion
3 ire, joy **4** fear, glee, hate, love **5** agony, ardor, grief, shame **6** affect, hatred, relief, sorrow, warmth **7** ardency, despair, disgust, ecstasy, feeling, passion, sadness **8** jealousy, surprise **9** affection, agitation, happiness, sentiment

emotional
4 warm **6** ardent, fervid, heated, moving **7** feeling, fervent, intense, soulful, zealous **8** effusive, stirring, touching, vehement **9** affecting, affective, excitable, heartfelt, impetuous, rhapsodic, sensitive **10** hysterical, passionate **11** impassioned, overwrought, rhapsodical, softhearted, susceptible, sympathetic

emotionless
3 icy **4** cold, cool **5** chill, staid, stoic, stony **6** frigid, remote, torpid **7** callous, deadpan,

distant, glacial **8** detached, reserved **9** apathetic, immovable, impassive, unfeeling **10** impersonal **11** cold-blooded, indifferent **12** matter-of-fact **13** dispassionate, unimpassioned

empathy
4 pity **6** lenity, warmth **7** rapport **8** affinity, sympathy **9** communion **10** compassion **12** congeniality **13** compatibility, comprehension, fellow feeling, understanding

emperor
4 czar, shah, tsar, tzar **5** ruler **6** caesar, kaiser **7** monarch **8** autocrat, dictator **9** potentate, sovereign
French: 8 Napoleon (Bonaparte) **9** Bonaparte (Napoleon) **11** Charlemagne
Indian: 5 Babur
Japanese: 6 mikado **7** Akihito **8** Hirohito
Mexican: 8 Iturbide (Agustín de) **10** Maximilian
Roman: 4 Nero, Otho **5** Galba, Nerva, Titus **6** Decius, Julian, Trajan **7** Gratian, Hadrian, Severus **8** Augustus, Aurelian, Caligula, Claudius, Commodus, Domitian, Honorius, Tiberius, Valerian **9** Antoninus, Caracalla, Justinian, Vespasian, Vitellius **10** Diocletian, Elagabalus **11** Constantine

emphasis
5 focus, foroe **6** accent, stress, weight **9** attention, intensity **10** insistence, prominence **12** accentuation

emphasize
6 accent, play up, stress **7** feature **8** pinpoint **9** highlight, italicize, spotlight, underline **10** accentuate, underscore

emphatic
4 firm **6** marked **7** decided, earnest, pointed **8** accented, decisive, forceful, positive, stressed, vigorous **9** assertive, energetic, insistent **10** resounding, underlined **11** accentuated

empire
5 realm **6** domain **7** demesne, kingdom **8** dominion
ancient: (see **ancient empire**)

Empire Falls author Richard
5 Russo

Empire State
7 New York

empirical
7 factual **9** fact-based, pragmatic **12** experiential, experimental **13** observational

emplacement
7 battery **8** position

employ
3 job, use **4** busy, hire, work **5** apply, avail **6** devote, engage, occupy, retain, secure, take on **7** exploit, utilize **8** exercise, practice **9** make use of **10** occupation

employee
4 hand, help **5** agent **6** worker **7** servant **8** factotum **9** underling
bank: 5 clerk, guard **6** teller
hotel: 7 bellboy, bellhop, doorman **9** concierge, desk clerk **11** chambermaid

employer
4 boss **6** master **10** supervisor

employment
3 job, use **4** line, post, task, toil, work **5** trade, usage **6** hiring, métier, office **7** calling, mission, purpose, pursuit **8** business, exercise, function, position, vocation **9** appliance, operation, situation **10** engagement, occupation **11** application, recruitment, utilization **12** exploitation

emporium
4 mall, mart, shop **5** store **6** bazaar, market **8** exchange **11** marketplace

empower
5 endow **6** charge, enable, invest **7** entitle, entrust, license **8** accredit, delegate, deputize, sanction **9** authorize, privilege **10** commission

empress
5 queen
Byzantine: 3 Zoe
French: 7 Eugénie **9** Josephine
Japanese: 5 Suiko
of India: 8 Victoria
Mexican: 7 Carlota
Roman: 6 Fausta
Russian: 4 Anna **7** czarina, tsarina, tzarina **9** Alexandra, Catherine, Elizabeth

empressement
6 fervor, warmth **10** cordiality

emprise
4 feat, gest **5** geste **7** exploit, venture **9** adventure **11** undertaking

emptiness
4 void **5** blank **6** hunger, vacuum **7** inanity, vacancy, vacuity

emptor
5 buyer **6** vendee **8** consumer, customer **9** purchaser

____ emptor
6 caveat

empty
3 rid **4** bare, dump, pour, vain, void **5** blank, clear, drain **6** barren, devoid, hollow, unload, vacant, vacate **7** deplete, drained, exhaust, vacated, vacuous **8** depleted, deserted, evacuate, forsaken **9** abandoned, destitute **10** unoccupied, untenanted
Scottish: 4 toom

empty-headed
5 ditzy **6** simple, vacant **7** vacuous, witless **8** ignorant, untaught **9** benighted, brainless, frivolous **10** illiterate, uneducated, unlettered, unschooled **11** know-nothing **12** uninstructed **13** rattlebrained

empyreal
4 airy, holy **6** aerial, divine **7** sublime **8** beatific, ethereal, heavenly **9** celestial, spiritual, unearthly **12** transcendent

empyrean
3 sky **4** Zion **5** bliss, ether **6** heaven, welkin **7** Elysium, heavens, nirvana **8** paradise **9** firmament

EMT's skill
3 CPR

emu
4 bird **6** ratite
relative: **3** moa **4** kiwi, rhea **7** ostrich **9** cassowary

emulate
3 ape **4** copy **5** equal, mimic, rival **6** follow, mirror **7** compete, imitate **9** challenge

emulation
7 rivalry **8** striving, tug-of-war **9** imitation **10** contention **11** competition

emulous
5 vying **8** aspiring, striving, vaulting **9** ambitious **11** competitive

emulsifier
4 soap **5** algin

enable
3 fit, let **5** allow, ready **6** permit **7** empower, entitle, license, prepare, qualify **8** accredit, sanction **9** authorize, condition **10** commission, facilitate **12** make possible

enact
4 pass, play **6** decree, depict, effect, ordain, ratify **7** execute, perform, portray **8** proclaim **9** authorize, discourse, establish, institute, legislate, represent **10** accomplish, bring about, constitute, effectuate **11** impersonate

enactment
3 law **6** action, decree **7** statute **9** depiction, ordinance, portrayal **11** legislation, performance **12** ratification

enamel
5 glaze, gloss, japan, paint **7** lacquer

enamored
4 fond **6** loving **7** devoted, smitten **8** besotted **9** bewitched, enchanted, entranced, infatuate **10** captivated, infatuated

encamp
4 tent **6** settle **7** bivouac

encampment
6 billet, laager **7** bivouac, hutment

encase
3 box **4** pack **7** confine, enclose, envelop, sheathe

enceinte
6 gravid **8** pregnant **9** expectant, expecting **10** parturient

enchain
4 bind **6** fetter **7** manacle, shackle

enchant
3 hex **4** lure, wile **5** charm, spell, witch **6** allure, enamor, seduce, thrill, voodoo **7** attract, beguile, bewitch, delight **8** ensorcel, enthrall **9** captivate, enrapture, ensorcell, fascinate, hypnotize, magnetize, mesmerize, spellbind

enchanter
4 mage **5** magus **6** Merlin, wizard **7** charmer, warlock **8** conjurer, conjuror, magician, sorcerer **11** necromancer, spellbinder

enchanting
5 siren **7** magical **9** glamorous, seductive **10** attractive, delectable, delightful, intriguing

enchantment
3 hex **5** charm, magic, spell **6** allure **7** glamour, sorcery **8** witchery, wizardry **9** conjuring, seduction **10** necromancy, witchcraft **11** incantation

enchantress
3 hex **5** bruja, Circe, lamia, Medea, siren, witch **9** sorceress

enchiridion
4 text **5** guide **6** manual **8** Baedeker, handbook **9** guidebook, vade mecum

encipher
4 code

encircle
3 hem **4** band, gird, girt, halo, hoop, ring **5** girth **6** begird, begirt, engird, enlace, girdle **7** compass, embrace, enclose, environ, wreathe **8** surround **9** encompass **12** circumscribe

enclave
6 colony, ghetto, sector **7** quarter **8** district, homeland

enclose
3 box, hem, mew, pen, rim **4** cage, coop, mure, wall, wrap **5** bound, fence, hedge, limit **6** circle, closet, corral, hold in, immure, shroud, shut in, wall in **7** compass, confine, contain, embosom, include **8** fence off, imprison, surround **9** capsulize **12** circumscribe

enclosed
6 obtect
court: **5** atria (plural) **6** atrium

enclosure
3 box, mew, pen, sty **4** boma, cage, camp, cell, coop, cote, fold, jail, pale, quad, SASE, tank, trap, wall, weir, yard **5** court, fence, kraal, pound, stall **6** aviary, corral, cowpen, kennel,

paling, prison **7** chamber, enclave, paddock **8** cloister, stockade **9** courtyard **10** quadrangle

encomiast
7 praiser **8** eulogist **10** panegyrist

encomiastic
9 adulatory, laudative, laudatory **10** eulogistic **11** panegyrical

encomium
4 laud **5** kudos, paean **6** eulogy, homage, praise **7** acclaim, plaudit, tribute **8** accolade, citation, plaudits **9** laudation, panegyric **10** compliment, salutation **11** acclamation **12** commendation

encompass
3 hem **4** belt, gird, ring **5** bound **6** begird, circle, girdle, take in **7** contain, embrace, enclose, include, subsume **8** encircle, surround **10** accomplish, bring about, comprehend

encore
6 recall, repeat, return **10** repetition

encounter
4 face, find, fray, meet **5** brush, clash, fight, run-in, scrap, set-to **6** battle, engage, take on **7** collide, contest, meeting, quarrel, run into **8** argument, bump into, come upon, conflict, confront, meet with, skirmish, struggle **10** contention, experience

encourage
3 egg **4** abet, back, buoy, push, spur, stir, urge **5** boost, cheer, egg on, rally, rouse, serve, steel **6** assist, assure, buck up, excite, foster, incite, induce, praise, spur on **7** advance, animate, approve, bolster, cheer up, endorse, fortify, further, hearten, improve, inspire, promote, provoke, quicken, support, sustain **8** advocate, embolden, energize, inspirit, reassure, sanction **9** enhearten, galvanize, instigate, patronize, reinforce, stimulate, subsidize **10** invigorate, strengthen

encouragement
4 lift, push **5** boost **7** backing, support **8** approval **9** promotion **11** inspiration

encouraging
4 rosy **6** bright, likely **7** hopeful **9** favorable, promising **10** auspicious, propitious

encroach
5 poach **6** invade, meddle, trench **7** impinge, intrude **8** entrench, infringe, overstep, trespass

encrypt
4 code **6** cipher, encode **7** convert **8** disguise, encipher

encumber
4 lade, load **6** burden, charge, fetter, hamper, hinder, impede, saddle, weight **7** freight, oppress **8** handicap, obstruct, overload **9** weigh down **10** overburden

encumbrance
4 lien, load, onus **5** claim **6** burden **7** baggage **8** easement, handicap, mortgage **9** albatross, millstone **10** impediment

encyclical
6 letter **7** general **8** circular

encyclopedic
5 broad **7** general **8** complete, thorough **9** extensive, inclusive, universal **11** compendious, wide-ranging **12** all-embracing, all-inclusive **13** comprehensive

encyclopedist
7 Diderot (Denis)

end
3 aim, tip **4** coda, doom, goal, halt, quit, stop, tail, term **5** cease, close, death, finis, lapse, limit **6** demise, expire, finale, finish, object, period, result, scotch, windup, wrap up **7** abolish, closing, closure, extreme, lineman, outcome, purpose **8** complete, conclude, curtains, surcease, terminal, terminus **9** cessation, extremity, objective, terminate **10** completion, conclusion, denouement, expiration **11** culmination, discontinue, termination **12** consummation

endanger
4 risk **5** peril **6** expose **7** imperil **8** threaten **10** compromise, jeopardize

endearment term
3 hon, pet **4** baby, dear, duck, lamb **5** bubby, bunny, honey, romeo, sugar **6** kitten, poopsy, poppet, sparky **7** darling, dearest, gumdrop, ladybug, lambkin, pumpkin, sweetie **8** cutie pie, doll-face, gorgeous, honey-bun, lady-love, lover-boy, precious, princess, pussycat, snookums, snuggles, sunshine, sweet pea, sweetums **9** angel-face, babycakes, buttercup, sugar-lips **10** heartthrob, honey bunch, honeychild, love-muffin, sweetheart, sweetie pie, tootsie pie

endeavor
3 aim, try **4** push, seek, toil, work **5** assay, essay, labor, trial **6** effort, intend, strain, strive **7** attempt, purpose, travail, venture **8** exertion, striving, struggle **9** determine, undertake **10** enterprise **11** undertaking

ended
4 done, over, past **7** through **8** complete

endemic
5 local **6** innate, native **8** homebred, inherent, primeval **9** homegrown, prevalent **10** aboriginal, indigenous, native-born

ending
4 coda, stop **5** close **6** finale, finish, period, windup **7** closing, closure **8** terminus **9** cessation **10** completion, conclusion, denouement **11** termination

endive
7 lettuce, witloof **8** escarole

endless
7 eternal, undying **8** constant, enduring, immortal, infinite, unending **9** ceaseless, continual, incessant, limitless, perpetual, unbounded, unceasing, unlimited **10** continuous, indefinite, unmeasured **11** everlasting, illimitable, measureless **12** immeasurable, interminable

endmost
4 last **5** final **8** farthest, furthest, ultimate **10** concluding

endnote abbrev.
4 ibid., idem **5** op. cit. **6** loc. cit.

endocrine gland
5 gonad, ovary **6** pineal, testis, thymus **7** adrenal, thyroid **8** pancreas **9** pituitary **11** parathyroid **12** hypothalamus

end-of-week cry
4 TGIF

endomorphic
5 beefy, heavy, husky, plump, pudgy, stout **6** chubby, portly, pyknic, rotund

endorse
4 back, okay, sign **5** bless, vouch **6** attest, ratify, second, uphold **7** approve, certify, command, confirm, stand by, support, witness **8** accredit, advocate, champion, inscribe, make over, notarize, sanction **9** autograph, recommend **10** underwrite **12** authenticate

endorsement
4 okay **7** backing, support **8** approval, sanction, thumbs-up **9** signature **10** green light **12** confirmation, ratification **13** authorization

endow
4 back, fund **5** found **6** bestow, confer, enrich, supply **7** empower, enhance, finance, furnish, promote, provide, sponsor, support **8** bequeath **9** subsidize

endowment
4 fund, gift **5** award, dower, dowry, grant, power, skill **6** legacy, talent **7** ability, bequest **8** appanage, aptitude, bestowal, capacity, donation **11** benefaction

end product
5 fruit, issue **6** effect, payoff, result, upshot **7** outcome **11** consequence

endue
3 don **4** vest **5** dower, equip, imbue, put on **6** clothe, invest, outfit **7** furnish, provide **8** accouter **9** crown with, transfuse

endurance
4 grit, guts, wind **5** moxie, pluck **6** mettle **7** stamina **8** patience, strength, tenacity **9** fortitude **10** permanence, resolution **11** persistence **12** perseverance

endure
4 bear, bide, go on, last **5** abide, brook, stand **6** accept, hold on, linger, pocket, remain, suffer **7** carry on, persist, ride out, stomach, survive, sustain, swallow, undergo, weather **8** continue, submit to, tolerate, tough out **9** withstand

enduring
3 old **4** fast, firm, sure **6** steady **7** abiding, durable, eternal, lasting, staunch **8** constant, lifelong **9** long-lived, perennial, permanent, steadfast **10** continuing, inveterate, persistent **11** long-lasting, unfaltering **12** never-failing

Endymion
father: 8 Aethlius
lover: 5 Diana **6** Selene
author: 5 Keats (John)

enemy
3 foe **5** rival **8** attacker, opponent **9** adversary, assailant, bête noire **10** antagonist, competitor

energetic
4 hale, spry **5** brisk, fresh, hardy, lusty, peppy, zippy **6** active, lively **7** driving, dynamic, vibrant **8** spirited, tireless, vigorous **9** sprightly, strenuous, vivacious **13** indefatigable

energize
3 pep **4** fuel, stir **5** liven, pep up, rouse, spark **6** enable, excite, stir up, turn on **7** empower, enliven, fortify, inspire, juice up **8** activate, inspirit, vitalize **9** electrify, galvanize, stimulate **10** invigorate, strengthen

energy
3 chi, pep, vim, zip **4** dash, life, tuck **5** drive, force, juice, moxie, pluck, power, steam, verve, vigor **6** effort, muscle, spirit **7** current, potency, stamina, voltage **8** activity, dynamism, exertion, strength, vitality **9** animation, puissance **10** enterprise, get-up-and-go, initiative
source: 4 fuel
unit: 3 erg **4** dyne, volt **5** joule **7** quantum **10** horsepower

enervate
3 sap **4** jade, tire **5** weary **6** soften, weaken **7** disable, exhaust, fatigue, unnerve **8** enfeeble, unstring **10** debilitate, devitalize

enfant terrible
3 imp **5** scamp **6** bad boy, urchin **7** skeezix **9** skeezicks

enfeeble
3 sap **6** soften, weaken **7** deplete, disable, exhaust, fatigue **8** enervate **9** attenuate, undermine **10** debilitate, devitalize

enfold
3 hug **4** wrap **5** clasp, cover, press **6** shroud, swathe **7** contain, embrace, squeeze **8** surround

enforce
5 exact, impel 6 compel, effect, impose, invoke, oblige 7 execute, fulfill 8 carry out 9 constrain, discharge, implement, prosecute 10 accomplish, administer, strengthen

enfranchise
4 free 6 rescue 7 deliver, manumit, release, set free 8 liberate 10 emancipate

engage
4 bind, grip, hire, mesh 5 fight, tie up, troth 6 absorb, attack, battle, commit, employ, enlist, pledge, take on 7 assault, betroth, engross, immerse, involve, promise 8 affiance, interact 9 captivate, encounter, interlace, interlock, intermesh, interplay, preoccupy, undertake

engaged
4 busy, rapt 6 intent 7 working 8 absorbed, employed, immersed, intended, occupied, plighted 9 affianced, betrothed, committed, engrossed, wrapped up 10 contracted 11 preoccupied
person: 6 fiancé 7 fiancée

engage in
4 wage 5 enter 6 pursue, tackle, take up 7 conduct 8 embark on, practice 9 prosecute, undertake

engagement
3 gig 4 date, fray, word 5 fight, troth, tryst 6 action, battle, combat, hiring, pledge, plight 7 booking, meeting, promise 8 espousal, skirmish 9 betrothal, encounter 10 commitment, employment, rendezvous 11 appointment, assignation

engaging
7 likable, winning, winsome 8 charming, pleasant, pleasing 9 appealing 10 attractive 13 prepossessing

engender
4 sire, stir 5 beget, breed, cause, hatch, rouse, spawn 6 arouse, create, excite, father, induce, lead to, work up 7 develop, produce, provoke 8 generate 9 originate, procreate, stimulate

engine
5 motor, turbo 7 turbine 10 locomotive
fluid: 7 coolant 10 antifreeze
kind: 3 gas, jet 5 steam 6 diesel 7 turbine 8 gasoline 9 hydraulic
jet: 8 turbofan, turbojet
part: 3 cam, rod 4 gear, plug, pump 5 choke 6 filter, piston, tappet 8 cylinder, manifold, throttle 9 condenser, crankcase 10 carburetor 12 transmission
siege: 3 ram 6 onager 8 ballista, catapult 9 trebuchet 12 battering ram
sound: 4 chug, roar 6 rattle

engineer
4 plan, plot 5 set up, swing 6 devise, driver, manage, scheme, wangle 7 arrange, finagle 8 contrive, intrigue, maneuver, motorman 9 machinate, negotiate 10 manipulate, mastermind 11 orchestrate
kind: 5 civil 6 mining 8 chemical, sanitary 10 electrical, mechanical 12 aeronautical
military: 6 sapper

engineers' group
4 ASME, IEEE

England
6 Albion 7 Britain 9 Britannia 12 Great Britain
see also **United Kingdom**

English
7 British
cathedral city: 3 Ely 4 York 5 Wells 6 Durham, Exeter 7 Lincoln, Norwich 8 Coventry, Hereford 9 Salisbury, Worcester 10 Canterbury, Winchester
china: 5 Spode
coin: 5 crown, groat, pence 6 florin, guinea 8 farthing, shilling, sixpence, twopence 9 fourpence, half crown, halfpenny, sovereign 10 threepence
combining form: 5 Anglo
farm: 5 croft
forest: 5 Arden 8 Sherwood
honor: 3 CBE, DBE, GBE, KBE, MBE, OBE
letter: 3 zed
measure: 3 rod, tun 4 gill, hand, peck, span 5 chain 6 barrel, bushel, fathom, firkin 7 furlong 8 hogshead 10 barleycorn
military college: 9 Sandhurst
noble: 4 duke, earl 5 baron 8 marquess, viscount
patron saint: 6 George
person: 4 chap, mate 5 bloke 6 Briton
pirate: 4 Kidd (Capt. William) 5 Avery (Henry), Teach (Edward) 6 Morgan (Henry) 7 Dampier (William) 10 Blackbeard
prince: 5 Harry 6 Andrew, Edward, Philip 7 Charles, William
princess: 4 Anne 5 Diana 8 Margaret
professor: 3 don
restroom: 3 loo
royal family: 5 Tudor 6 Stuart 7 Hanover, Windsor 11 Plantagenet
saint: 7 Dunstan 8 Cuthbert
school: 4 Eton 6 Harrow
spa: 4 Bath
sport: 5 darts, rugby 7 cricket
tavern: 3 pub
time: 3 GMT
university: 5 Leeds 6 Oxford 9 Cambridge
weight: 5 stone 6 firkin 7 quintal 8 quartern

English Channel
French: 6 Manche (La)
swimmer: 6 Ederle (Gertrude)

Englishman in colonial India
5 sahib
engrave
3 cut, fix 4 etch 5 carve, chase 6 incise, scrive 7 instill 8 inscribe
engraver
6 chaser, etcher
German: 5 Dürer (Albrecht) 10 Schongauer (Martin)
Italian: 8 Raimondi (Marcantonio)
tool: 5 styli (plural) 6 stylus
engraving
7 etching, linecut, woodcut 8 drypoint, intaglio 9 xylograph
engross
4 bury, busy, copy, grip 5 apply, write 6 absorb, engage, indite, occupy, scribe 7 consume, immerse, involve 8 enthrall, inscribe 9 captivate, preoccupy 10 transcribe
engrossed
4 rapt 6 intent 7 engaged, riveted 8 absorbed, immersed 9 attentive 10 enraptured 11 preoccupied 12 concentrated
engrosser
6 scribe 7 copyist 9 scrivener 12 calligrapher 13 calligraphist
engulf
4 bury 5 drown, flood, swamp, whelm 6 deluge, devour 7 immerse, overrun, swallow 8 flow over, inundate, overflow, submerge 9 overwhelm, swallow up
enhance
4 lift 5 add to, adorn, exalt, raise 6 deepen 7 amplify, augment, build up, elevate, enlarge, flatter, improve, magnify 8 beautify, heighten, increase 9 aggravate, embellish, embroider, intensify, reinforce 10 exaggerate, strengthen
enigma
4 crux, knot 5 poser, rebus 6 puzzle, riddle, sphinx, teaser 7 mystery, problem, puzzler 9 conundrum 10 closed book, perplexity, puzzlement 12 question mark 13 Chinese puzzle, mystification
enigmatic
6 mystic 7 cryptic, Delphic, obscure 8 Delphian, oracular, puzzling 9 ambiguous 10 mysterious, mystifying, perplexing 11 inscrutable
Enigma Variations composer
5 Elgar (Edward)
enisle
6 cut off 7 isolate 8 insulate, separate 9 segregate, sequester
enjoin
3 ban, bid 4 deny, rule, tell, urge, warn 5 order, taboo 6 adjure, charge, decree, direct, forbid, impose, outlaw 7 caution, command, counsel, dictate, inhibit 8 admonish, disallow, forewarn, instruct, prohibit 9 interdict, prescribe, proscribe
enjoy
4 like, love 5 eat up, fancy, savor 6 relish 9 delight in 10 appreciate
enjoyable
3 fun 8 pleasant, pleasing 9 agreeable 10 delightful, satisfying 11 pleasurable 12 entertaining
enjoyment
4 zest 5 gusto, savor 6 relish 7 benefit, delight 8 felicity, fruition, pleasure 9 diversion 10 indulgence, recreation, relaxation 11 delectation 12 satisfaction 13 gratification
Enki
consort: 5 Nintu
son: 6 Ninsar
enkindle
4 fire 5 flame, light 6 ignite 7 inflame 8 touch off 9 set fire to
enlarge
3 wax 4 grow, rise 5 add to, boost, build, mount, widen 6 beef up, dilate, expand, extend 7 amplify, augment, broaden, develop, greaten, inflate, magnify, stretch 8 heighten, increase, multiply 9 elaborate, embroider 10 exaggerate
enlargement
4 node 5 tumor 6 blowup, growth, nodule 7 buildup 8 addition, increase, swelling 9 accretion, expansion, extension 12 augmentation 13 amplification
enlighten
5 edify, guide, teach 6 advise, illume, inform, uplift 7 educate, improve 8 illumine, instruct 10 illuminate
enlightened Buddhist
5 arhat
enlist
4 join 5 draft, enter 6 employ, enroll, join up, muster, sign on, sign up 7 attract, recruit 8 register 9 volunteer 11 participate
again: 4 reup
enliven
3 pep 4 buoy, fire, warm 5 amuse, cheer, pep up, renew, rouse 6 excite, jazz up, perk up, vivify, wake up 7 animate, cheer up, inspire, quicken, refresh, restore, spice up 8 energize, recreate 9 entertain, galvanize, stimulate 10 exhilarate, invigorate, rejuvenate
en masse
5 as one 6 bodily 8 together 12 collectively
enmesh
4 hook, mire, trap 5 catch, snare 6 draw in, tangle 7 embroil, ensnarl, involve, trammel 8 drag into, entangle 9 embrangle, implicate

enmity
4 hate **6** animus, hatred, rancor, spleen **7** ill will **8** aversion, bad blood, loathing **9** animosity, antipathy, hostility **10** abhorrence, antagonism **11** detestation

ennoble
5 exalt, honor, raise **6** uplift, uprear **7** dignify, elevate, glorify, magnify, sublime **10** aggrandize **11** distinguish

ennui
6 apathy, tedium **7** boredom, fatigue, languor **8** doldrums, dullness, lethargy **9** jadedness, lassitude, tiredness, weariness **11** languidness **12** listlessness

Enoch
father: 4 Cain
son: 10 Methuselah

Enoch Arden author
8 Tennyson (Alfred)

enormity
6 infamy **7** outrage **8** atrocity, hugeness, rankness, savagery, vastness **9** barbarity, depravity, flagrancy, graveness, greatness, grossness, immensity, magnitude **11** abomination, heinousness, massiveness, monstrosity, seriousness, weightiness

enormous
4 huge, vast **5** great **7** immense, mammoth, massive, titanic **8** colossal, gigantic **9** humongous, monstrous **10** astronomic, gargantuan, prodigious, stupendous, tremendous **12** astronomical

Enos
father: 4 Seth
grandfather: 4 Adam
grandmother: 3 Eve
uncle: 4 Abel, Cain

enough
5 ample **6** fairly, plenty **8** adequate, decently, passably **9** competent, tolerably **10** acceptably, adequately, sufficient **11** comfortable, sufficiency **12** satisfactory, sufficiently
poetic: 4 enow

enounce
3 say **5** state, utter **6** intone **8** proclaim, set forth **10** articulate

enrage
3 ire **4** rile **5** anger **6** madden **7** incense, inflame, steam up **9** infuriate

enraged
3 mad **5** angry, irate. livid **6** fuming, raving **7** furious, hopping **8** wrathful

enrapture
5 charm, elate **6** ravish, trance **7** delight, enchant, rejoice **8** enthrall, entrance **9** captivate, transport

enraptured
6 elated **7** charmed **8** ecstatic, thrilled **9** bewitched, delighted, enchanted, entranced **10** captivated, enthralled, mesmerized, spellbound **11** transported

enrich
5 adorn, endow **6** fatten **7** enhance, improve **8** beautify, ornament **9** embellish, fertilize **10** supplement

enroll
4 book, file, join, list **5** draft, enter **6** enlist, induct, join up, muster, record, sign on, sign up, wrap up **7** catalog, engross, recruit **8** inscribe, register **9** conscript, subscribe **10** transcribe **11** matriculate

ensconce
4 bury, hide **5** cache, cover, place, plant, stash **6** hole up, locate, settle **7** conceal, install, secrete, shelter **9** establish

ensemble
3 duo **4** band, crew, suit, trio **5** choir, combo, decor, group, octet, suite, troop, whole **6** chorus, outfit, septet, sextet, troupe **7** chorale, company, costume, en masse, quartet, quintet **8** together **9** aggregate, orchestra

enshrine
6 hallow, revere **7** cherish **8** dedicate, preserve, sanctify, treasure **10** consecrate **11** memorialize

enshroud
4 hide, veil, wrap **5** cloak **6** clothe, enfold, enwrap, invest **7** blanket, conceal, envelop, obscure

ensign
4 flag, jack, sign **5** badge, crest **6** banner, colors, emblem, pennon **7** officer, pennant **8** gonfalon, insignia, standard, streamer **9** oriflamme

enslave
4 yoke **5** chain **6** fetter, thrall **7** enchain, oppress, shackle, subject **8** dominate, enthrall **9** indenture, subjugate **12** disfranchise

enslavement
4 yoke **6** thrall **7** bondage, helotry, peonage, serfdom, slavery **9** servitude, thralldom

ensnare
3 bag, net **4** hook, lure, mesh, snag, trap **5** benet, catch, decoy **6** enmesh, entrap, tangle **7** capture **8** entangle, inveigle

ensnarl
4 mire **6** enmesh, tangle **7** embroil, perplex, trammel **8** entangle **9** embrangle

ensorcell
3 hex **5** charm, spell, witch **6** allure, voodoo **7** beguile, bewitch, enchant **8** enthrall **9** captivate, enrapture, hypnotize, magnetize, mesmerize, spellbind

ensorcellment
5 magic **7** sorcery **8** witchery, wizardry **9** conjuring **10** necromancy, witchcraft **11** bewitchment, enchantment

ensphere
4 ball **8** conglobe **10** conglobate

ensue
4 stem **5** issue **6** attend, derive, follow, result **7** emanate, proceed, succeed **9** supervene

ensuing
4 next **5** later **9** resultant **10** consequent, subsequent, succeeding

ensure
5 cinch **6** clinch, secure **7** certify, confirm, warrant **9** establish, guarantee

enswathe
4 roll, wrap **5** cloak, drape **6** bundle, enwrap, shroud, wrap up **7** envelop, swaddle

entail
5 imply **6** assign, confer, demand, impose, lead to **7** call for, involve, require **8** occasion, restrict, result in, transmit **11** necessitate

entangle
4 mesh, mire, trap **5** catch, ravel, snare, snarl, tie up, twist **6** enmesh, entrap **7** capture, catch up, embroil, ensnare, ensnarl, involve, perplex, trammel **10** complicate, intertwine, interweave

entanglement
3 web **4** knot, mesh, mess, toil **5** skein, snare **6** affair, cobweb, muddle **8** intrigue **9** confusion, imbroglio **11** embroilment, involvement **12** complication

entente
4 pact **6** league, treaty **7** compact **8** alliance, covenant **9** agreement, coalition, concordat **13** understanding

enter
3 key **4** go in, join, list, open **5** admit, begin, input, key in, start **6** come in, enlist, enroll, go into, insert, join up, muster, record, sign on, sign up **7** intrude **8** come into, embark on, inscribe, register **9** introduce, penetrate **10** embark upon

enterprise
4 deed, feat, firm, push, task **5** cause, drive, pluck, vigor **6** action, daring, effort, energy, hustle, outfit, scheme **7** attempt, company, concern, courage, exploit, project, pursuit, venture **8** activity, ambition, audacity, boldness, business, campaign, endeavor, gumption, industry **9** adventure, eagerness **10** enthusiasm, get-up-and-go, initiative **11** corporation, undertaking **12** organization, self-reliance **13** establishment

Enterprise crew member
4 Kirk (Jim), Sulu (Hikaru) **5** Spock, Uhura **6** Scotty

enterprising
4 bold **5** eager **6** daring, hungry **7** driving, go-ahead **8** aspiring, hustling **9** ambitious, audacious, energetic **10** aggressive **11** adventurous, hardworking, industrious, up-and-coming, venturesome

entertain
4 host **5** amuse **6** divert, regale **7** delight, receive **8** consider

entertainer
4 mime **5** actor, clown, comic **6** busker, dancer, jester, singer **7** actress, artiste, diseuse, trouper **8** comedian, minstrel **10** comedienne

entertaining
6 lively **7** amusing **8** engaging **9** diverting, enjoyable

entertainment
4 fete, play, show, skit **5** revue, sport **6** circus **7** banquet, concert, pastime, ridotto **8** pleasure **9** amusement, diversion, enjoyment **10** recreation **11** distraction, performance

enthrall
4 grip **5** charm **6** absorb, subdue **7** beguile, bewitch, enchant, engross, enslave **9** fascinate, hypnotize, mesmerize, spellbind, subjugate

enthralled
4 rapt

enthralling
8 exciting, gripping, riveting **9** absorbing, arresting **10** enchanting, engrossing, entrancing **11** captivating, charismatic, provocative **12** spellbinding

enthuse
4 gush, rave **6** excite, thrill **7** animate, delight, inspire **8** energize **10** rhapsodize

enthusiasm
4 élan, fire, zeal, zest **5** ardor, craze, fever, mania, verve **6** fervor, spirit **7** ardency, passion, rapture **9** eagerness, intensity **10** ebullience, excitement, fanaticism

enthusiast
3 bug, fan, nut **4** buff **5** fiend, freak, lover, maven **6** addict, junkie, maniac, votary, zealot **7** booster, devotee, fanatic, groupie, habitué **8** believer, partisan **9** extremist **10** aficionado

enthusiastic
4 avid, gaga, keen **5** eager, rabid **6** ardent, fervid, geeked, gung ho, hearty, hipped, juiced, pumped, rah-rah, raring, stoked **7** devoted, excited, fervent, intense, zealous **8** hopped-up, obsessed, spirited, vascular **9** fanatical **10** passionate

entice
4 bait, coax, draw, lure, toll, wile **5** charm, decoy, tempt **6** allure, cajole, entrap, invite, lead on, seduce **7** attract, wheedle **8** inveigle, persuade

enticement
4 bait, lure, trap **5** decoy, snare **6** allure, come-on **9** seduction **10** allurement, attraction, seducement, temptation **12** blandishment, inveiglement

enticer
4 bait, vamp **5** Circe, decoy, siren **7** Lorelei **9** attractor, temptress **10** attraction, seductress **11** enchantress, femme fatale

enticing
5 siren **8** fetching, witching **9** seductive **10** attractive, bewitching, intriguing **11** captivating, fascinating

entire
3 all **4** full **5** gross, total, whole **6** intact **7** perfect, plenary, unified **8** complete, integral, outright **10** integrated **12** consolidated
combining form: 3 hol, pan **4** holo

entirely
5 fully, quite **6** wholly **7** utterly **9** perfectly **10** altogether, completely, thoroughly **11** exclusively

entirety
3 sum **5** total, whole **8** sum total, totality **9** aggregate, wholeness **10** everything **12** completeness, universality

entitle
3 dub, let **4** call, name, term **5** allow **6** enable, permit **7** baptize, empower, license, qualify **8** christen **9** authorize, designate **10** denominate

entity
3 sum **4** body, item, unit **5** being, thing, whole **6** object **7** article, integer **8** quiddity, totality **9** existence, something, substance **10** individual

entomb
4 bury **5** inter, inurn **6** immure, inhume, shrine **7** mummify **8** enshrine **9** sepulcher, sepulchre

entombment
6 burial **7** funeral, obsequy **9** obsequies, sepulture **10** inhumation

entourage
5 staff, suite, train **6** escort, milieu **7** cortege, coterie, retinue **8** henchmen **9** courtiers, followers, following, hangers-on, retainers **10** associates, attendants **12** surroundings

entr'acte
8 interval **9** interlude **12** intermission

entrails
4 guts **5** pluck, tripe **6** bowels, tripes, umbles, vitals **7** giblets, innards, insides, viscera **8** stuffing **10** intestines

entrance
4 door, gate, port **5** charm, foyer, inlet, lobby, mouth **6** access, portal, ravish **7** arrival, attract, bewitch, delight, doorway, enchant, gateway, ingress, opening **8** aperture, enthrall, open door **9** admission, captivate, enrapture, fascinate, hypnotize, mesmerize, spellbind, threshold, transport, vestibule **10** admittance, ingression **11** penetration
mine: 4 adit

entranced
4 rapt

entrant
7 starter **10** competitor, contestant **11** participant

entrap
3 bag, nab, net **4** bait, lure, toll **5** catch, decoy, snare, tempt **6** allure, ambush, entice, entoil, lead on, seduce, tangle **7** beguile, catch up, ensnare **8** entangle, inveigle

entre ___
4 nous

entreat
3 ask, beg, bid **4** pray, urge **5** crave, plead, press **6** adjure, appeal **7** beseech, implore, wheedle **8** blandish **9** importune **10** supplicate

entreaty
4 plea, suit **6** appeal, orison, prayer **7** request **8** petition **11** application, importunity **12** supplication

entrechat
4 leap

entrée
6 access **7** ingress **8** main dish **9** admission **10** admittance, main course

entrench
3 fix **4** root **5** embed, lodge **6** define, furrow, ground, hole up, invade, settle **7** confirm, impinge, implant, intrude **8** encroach, ensconce, infringe, trespass **9** establish **10** strengthen

entrenched
3 set **4** firm **5** rigid, sworn **8** accepted, deep-dyed **9** hard-shell **10** deep-rooted, deep-seated, inveterate **13** bred-in-the-bone, dyed-in-the-wool

entrepôt
3 hub **4** mart **5** depot **6** bazaar, market **8** emporium, exchange **9** concourse, warehouse **10** depository, storehouse **11** marketplace

entrepreneur
10 capitalist, contractor, impresario

entresol
9 mezzanine

entropy
5 chaos, decay **7** decline **8** disorder **10** randomness **11** degradation

entrust
4 give **5** allot, leave **6** assign, charge, commit, confer, impose **7** commend, confide, consign, deliver, deposit **8** allocate, delegate, hand over, relegate, turn over

entry
3 way **4** adit, door, gate, item, port **5** debit, foyer, inlet, lobby **6** access, credit, portal, record **7** doorway, ingress, opening **8** headword **9** admission, threshold, vestibule **10** admittance, enlistment, enrollment, ingression
permit: **4** visa

entryway
4 door, gate **5** foyer, lobby **6** portal **7** ingress, narthex, portico **9** vestibule

entwine
4 coil, wind **5** braid, plait, twist **6** enmesh **7** wreathe **8** entangle **9** interlace **10** interweave

enumerate
3 sum, tot **4** cite, list, tell, tote **5** add up, count, tally, total, tot up **6** detail, number, recite, reckon, tote up **7** compute, itemize, recount, specify, tick off **8** identify **9** calculate, inventory **13** particularize

enunciate
3 say **5** speak, state, utter, voice **6** affirm, intone **7** declare, express, lay down **8** announce, proclaim, propound, vocalize **9** formulate, postulate, pronounce, verbalize **10** articulate

envelop
3 hem **4** hide, roll, veil, wrap **5** cloak, cover, drape **6** cocoon, enfold, engulf, enwrap, invest, sheath, shield, shroud, swathe, wrap up **7** blanket, embrace, enclose, swaddle **8** encircle, enshroud, enswathe, surround **10** circumfuse

envelope abbreviation
4 ADSR, ATTN

envenom
6 poison **8** embitter **10** exacerbate

envious
7 jealous **8** coveting, covetous, grudging **9** green-eyed, invidious, resentful **10** begrudging

environment
6 medium, milieu **7** ambient, climate, context, habitat, setting, terrain **8** ambiance, ambience, backdrop **9** situation **10** atmosphere, background **11** mise-en-scène **12** surroundings
combining form: **3** eco
science: **7** ecology

environmentalist
4 Gore (Al), Muir (John) **6** Brower (David), Carson (Rachel), Hansen (James), Nelson (Gaylord), Wilson (Edward O.) **7** Ehrlich (Paul), Leopold (Aldo), Thoreau (Henry David) **8** Commoner (Barry), Cousteau (Jacques-Yves), McKibben (Bill) **9** Burroughs (John), ecologist, Roosevelt (Theodore)

environs
4 nabe **6** bounds, limits **7** compass, fringes, suburbs **8** boundary, confines, locality, purlieus, vicinity **9** districts, outskirts, precincts **12** neighborhood, surroundings

envisage
4 view **5** dream, fancy, grasp, image, think **6** ideate, regard, vision **7** dream up, feature, foresee, imagine, picture, realize **8** conceive, look upon, summon up **9** conjure up, objectify, visualize

envoy
5 agent **6** bearer, consul, deputy, legate, nuncio **7** attaché, carrier, courier **8** diplomat, emissary, minister **9** messenger **10** ambassador **11** internuncio **12** intermediary

envy
5 covet **6** grudge **8** begrudge, grudging, jealousy **10** resentment **12** covetousness **13** invidiousness

enwrap
4 roll, veil **5** clasp, drape **6** enfold, invest, shroud, swathe **7** enclose, engross, envelop, sheathe, swaddle **8** enshroud, enswathe

enzyme
3 ase **5** ficin, lyase, renin, urase **6** kinase, ligase, lipase, mutase, papain, pepsin, rennin, urease, zymase **7** amidase, amylase, cyclase, enolase, guanase, hydrase, inulase, isozyme, lactase, maltase, oxidase, pectase, pepsine, plasmin, ptyalin, rennase, sucrase, trypsin, zymogen **8** aldolase, diastase, elastase, esterase, fumarase, lyzozyme, nuclease, protease, steapsin, thrombin, zymogene **9** cellulase, invertase

eon
3 age, era **5** epoch **8** blue moon, coon's age, eternity

Eos
6 Aurora
goddess of: **4** dawn

épée
5 blade, sword **6** rapier

epergne
5 stand **11** centerpiece

ephemeral
5 brief, short **7** passing **8** episodic, fleeting, fugitive, volatile **9** fugacious, momentary, temporary, transient **10** evanescent, short-lived, transitory **11** impermanent

Ephialtes
5 giant
brother: **4** Otus
father: **6** Aloeus **8** Poseidon
mother: **9** Iphimedia
slayer: **6** Apollo

Ephraim
brother: **8** Manasseh
father: **6** Joseph
grandfather: **5** Jacob
mother: **7** Asenath

epic
4 Edda, poem, saga **5** grand, Iliad **6** Aeneid, heroic **7** Beowulf, Odyssey **8** imposing, sweeping **9** Gilgamesh, narrative **12** Heimskringla

epicene
10 effeminate **11** intersexual, transsexual **13** hermaphrodite

epicure
7 gourmet **8** aesthete, hedonist, sybarite **9** bon vivant **10** gastronome **11** connoisseur **12** gastronomist

epicurean
7 gourmet, sensual **8** aesthete, hedonist, sensuous, sybarite **9** bon vivant, luxurious **10** gastronome, voluptuous **11** connoisseur **12** gastronomist, sensualistic

epidemic
3 flu **4** rash, wave **5** Ebola **6** plague **7** rampant, scourge **8** catching, outbreak **9** contagion, prevalent **10** contagious, pestilence

epidermis
4 skin **7** cuticle **10** integument

epigram
3 saw **4** poem **5** adage, axiom, maxim **6** bon mot, dictum, saying, truism **7** proverb **8** aphorism, apothegm

epigrammatic
5 meaty, pithy, terse, witty **6** cogent **7** compact, concise, marrowy, piquant, pointed

epigraph
5 motto **9** quotation **11** inscription

epilogue
4 coda **5** close **6** ending, finale, windup **7** closing **8** postlude **9** afterword **10** conclusion, postscript

Epimetheus
brother: **10** Prometheus
father: **7** Iapetus
wife: **7** Pandora

epiphany
6 aperçu, vision **7** insight **9** discovery, intuition **10** appearance, disclosure, revelation **11** inspiration, realization **13** manifestation

episode
5 event, phase **7** passage **8** incident, occasion **9** happening, interlude **10** occurrence **12** circumstance

episodic
5 brief **7** passing **8** fleeting, sporadic **9** ephemeral, irregular, temporary, transient **10** evanescent, occasional, short-lived **12** intermittent

epistaxis
9 nosebleed

epistle
4 note **6** letter **7** lection, missive **13** communication

epitaph
3 R.I.P. **5** elegy **6** eulogy **8** hic jacet **11** inscription

epithet
4 name **5** label, title **7** agnomen, moniker **8** cognomen, nickname **9** sobriquet **11** appellation

epitome
3 sum **4** acme, type **5** brief, short **6** digest, précis, résumé **7** essence, example, outline, summary **8** abstract, breviary, exemplar, synopsis, ultimate **9** archetype, summation, summing-up **10** abridgment, apotheosis, conspectus, embodiment **11** abridgement **12** condensation, quintessence

epitomize
5 sum up **6** digest, embody, mirror, typify **7** abridge, outline, summate **8** abstract, boil down, condense, manifest, tabulate **9** capsulize, exemplify, incarnate, inventory, objectify, personify, represent, summarize, symbolize, synopsize **10** abbreviate, illustrate **11** concentrate, emblematize, incorporate, personalize

epoch
3 age, eon, era **4** aeon, term, time **6** period **8** interval, time span

equable
4 calm, even, just **6** serene, stable, steady **7** orderly, regular, stabile, uniform **8** composed, constant **9** immutable, temperate, unvarying **10** consistent, invariable, unchanging **12** unchangeable

equal
3 tie **4** even, fair, like, mate, peer, same, twin **5** agree, alike, match **7** uniform **8** alter ego, amount to, parallel **9** duplicate, identical, impartial, objective **10** fifty-fifty **11** counterpart, symmetrical **12** commensurate, correspond to, proportional **13** commensurable, proportionate
combining form: **3** iso **4** equi, pari
French: **4** égal

equality
3 par **6** equity, parity **7** balance, égalité **8** evenness, fairness, sameness **10** uniformity

Equality State
7 Wyoming

equalize
4 even **5** level **6** square **7** balance, even out **9** harmonize

equalizer
3 gun **6** pistol **8** handicap **10** tying score

equally
10 fifty-fifty **11** impartially

equanimity
4 calm, cool **5** poise **6** aplomb, phlegm **7** balance **8** calmness, coolness, evenness, serenity

9 **assurance**, composure, equipoise, placidity, sangfroid **10** detachment, steadiness **11** tranquility **12** tranquillity

equate
4 even **5** liken, match, treat **6** adjust, regard, relate, square **7** compare **8** consider, equalize, parallel **10** assimilate

Equatorial Guinea
capital: **6** Malabo
island, island group: **5** Bioko **6** Elobey, Pagulu **7** Corisco
language: **5** Bantu **6** French **7** Spanish
mainland: **5** Mbini **7** Río Muni
monetary unit: **5** franc
neighbor: **5** Gabon **8** Cameroon

equestrian
5 rider **6** horsey **8** horseman, knightly **10** horsewoman
sport: **4** polo

equidistant
3 mid **6** medial, median, middle, midway **7** central, halfway, midmost

equilibrium
5 poise **6** aplomb, stasis **7** balance **8** evenness, symmetry **9** composure, stability **10** steadiness **12** counterpoise **13** stabilization

equine
4 colt, mare **5** filly, horse, steed **6** horsey **8** stallion **9** horselike

equip
3 arm, fit, rig **5** array, dress, endow, rig up **6** attire, fit out, outfit, rig out, supply **7** appoint, furnish, prepare, provide **8** accouter, accoutre **9** provision

equipment
3 rig **4** gear **5** traps **6** attire, outfit, tackle, things **7** baggage, panoply **8** fittings, material, matériel, ordnance, supplies, tackling **9** apparatus, endowment, machinery, trappings **10** provisions **11** accessories, attachments, habiliments, impedimenta **12** accouterment, accoutrement, provisioning **13** accouterments, accoutrements, appurtenances, paraphernalia

equitable
4 even, fair, just **5** level **6** proper, square **7** condign **8** balanced, deserved, unbiased **9** identical, impartial, objective, uncolored **10** evenhanded, impersonal **12** unprejudiced **13** dispassionate

equity
3 law, par **7** justice **8** equality, interest, justness

equivalence
3 par **6** parity, simile **7** analogy **8** equality, identity, likeness, sameness **10** conformity **11** correlation

equivalent
4 akin, copy, like, peer, same, twin **5** alike, match **6** agnate **7** identic, similar **8** parallel **9** analogous, duplicate, identical **10** comparable, homologous, substitute, tantamount **11** convertible, correlative, counterpart **12** commensurate **13** corresponding, proportionate

equivocal
4 hazy **5** fishy, vague **6** unsure **7** clouded, dubious, obscure, suspect, unclear **8** doubtful **9** ambiguous, debatable, enigmatic, uncertain, undecided **10** ambivalent, indecisive, indistinct, irresolute, unresolved **11** problematic **12** disreputable, inconclusive, questionable **13** indeterminate

equivocate
3 fib, lie **5** cavil, dodge, evade, fudge, hedge **6** palter, waffle, weasel **7** shuffle **8** sidestep **9** pussyfoot **11** prevaricate **12** tergiversate

equivocation
3 fib **7** evasion, fibbing, hedging, sophism **8** waffling **9** ambiguity, casuistry, duplicity, sophistry **12** speciousness

equivoque
3 pun **8** wordplay

era
3 age, day, eon **4** aeon, date, term, time **5** epoch, stage **6** period

eradicate
4 dele, raze **5** abate, erase, purge **6** delete, efface, remove, uproot **7** abolish, blot out, destroy, expunge, root out, weed out, wipe out **8** demolish, stamp out **9** eliminate, extirpate, liquidate **10** annihilate, do away with, extinguish, obliterate **11** exterminate

erase
4 dele, void, x out **6** cancel, delete, efface, excise, remove, rub out **7** abolish, blot out, expunge, nullify, scratch, take out, wipe out **8** black out, blank out, cross off, cross out **9** eliminate, extirpate, sponge out, strike out **10** extinguish, obliterate

Erato
4 Muse

Erbin
father: **9** Custennin
nephew: **6** Arthur
son: **7** Geraint

ere
5 afore **6** before

Erebus
daughter: **3** Day **6** Hemera
father: **5** Chaos
home: **5** Hades
sister, wife: **3** Nox, Nyx
son: **6** Aether, Charon

Erec et ___
5 Enide
Erechteus
daughter: 8 Chthonia
father: 6 Vulcan 10 Hephaestus
mother: 4 Gaea
slayer: 4 Zeus 7 Jupiter
erect
4 form 5 build, put up, raise, set up 6 create, raised 7 build up, stand-up, upright 8 assemble, elevated, standing, straight, vertical 9 construct, establish 10 upstanding 13 perpendicular
erelong
4 anon, soon
eremite
6 hermit 7 ascetic, recluse, stylite 9 anchoress, anchorite
Erewhon
6 utopia 7 nowhere
author: 6 Butler (Samuel)
ergo
4 then, thus 5 and so, hence 9 therefore 11 accordingly 12 consequently
Erichthonius
father: 8 Dardanus
son: 4 Tros
Eridanus star
8 Achernar
Erin
see **Ireland**
Erinyes
6 Alecto, Furies 7 Megaera 9 Eumenides, Tisiphone
Eris
brother: 4 Ares, Mars
daughter: 3 Ate
fruit: 5 apple
goddess of: 6 strife 7 discord
mother: 3 Nox, Nyx
Eritrea
archipelago: 6 Dahlak
capital: 6 Asmara
island: 5 Zuqar
language: 8 Tigrinya
monetary unit: 5 nakfa
neighbor: 5 Sudan 8 Djibouti, Ethiopia
river: 6 Baraka
sea: 3 Red
ermine
3 fur 5 stoat 6 weasel
Ernie of golf
3 Els
erode
3 eat, mar, rot, rub 4 rust, wear 5 decay, scour 6 abrade, rub off 7 consume, corrade, crumble, eat away, oxidize, rub away 8 wear away 9 scrape off 10 scrape away 11 deteriorate 12 disintegrate
Eroica composer
9 Beethoven (Ludwig van)
Eros
4 Amor 5 Cupid, putto 6 cherub 8 amoretto
lover: 6 Psyche
erose
6 craggy, jagged, uneven 9 irregular
erotic
4 lewd, racy, sexy 5 bawdy, spicy 6 carnal, earthy, ribald, risqué 7 fleshly, obscene, profane, sensual 8 off-color, prurient, sensuous 9 salacious 10 voluptuous 11 aphrodisiac, titillating
err
3 sin 4 goof, slip, trip 5 lapse, stray 6 bollix, bungle, foul up, fumble, mess up, slip up 7 balls-up, blunder, deviate, screw up, stumble 8 trespass 10 transgress
errand
3 job 4 task 5 chore 7 mission 10 assignment
errand boy
4 page 5 gofer 7 bellboy, bellhop, courier 9 go-between
errant
5 stray 6 fickle, roving 7 aimless, deviant, erratic, naughty, ranging, roaming, wayward, willful 8 drifting, fallible, rambling, shifting, straying 9 deviating, itinerant, traveling, wandering 10 meandering, unreliable 11 mischievous
erratic
5 flaky 6 fitful, spotty 7 wayward 8 freakish, shifting, unstable, variable, volatile 9 arbitrary, desultory, eccentric, fluctuant, irregular, mercurial, spasmodic, uncertain, wandering, whimsical 10 capricious, changeable, inconstant, meandering 12 inconsistent 13 idiosyncratic, unpredictable
erring
see **errant**
erroneous
3 off 4 awry 5 amiss, askew, false, wrong 6 untrue 7 unsound 8 mistaken, specious, spurious 9 defective, incorrect, misguided 10 fallacious, inaccurate, misleading
error
4 flub, goof, muff, slip, trip 5 boner, botch, fault, fluff, gaffe, lapse, snafu 6 boo-boo, bungle, fumble, howler, miscue, slipup 7 blooper, blunder, fallacy, falsity, faux pas, misdeed, misstep, mistake, screwup, stumble, untruth 8 delusion, illusion, screamer 9 falsehood, indecorum, oversight 10 inaccuracy, misreading 11 impropriety, misjudgment
printing: 4 typo 6 errata (plural) 7 erratum

ersatz
4 copy, fake, sham **5** bogus, dummy, faked, false, phony, pseud **6** phoney, pseudo **8** spurious **9** imitation, simulated, synthetic **10** artificial, factitious, simulacrum, substitute **11** counterfeit

Erse
5 Irish **6** Celtic, Gaelic

erstwhile
3 old **4** late, once, past **5** prior **6** before, bygone, former, whilom **7** already, earlier, onetime, quondam **8** formerly, previous **10** heretofore, previously

eruct
4 burp, emit, gush, spew **5** belch, eject, expel **7** explode **8** detonate, disgorge

erudite
7 bookish, learned **8** lettered, literate, studious, well-read **9** scholarly **10** scholastic

erudition
7 culture **8** learning, literacy **9** knowledge **11** bookishness, cultivation, learnedness, scholarship **12** studiousness **13** scholarliness

erupt
3 jet **4** spew **5** belch, burst, eject, expel, go off, spout, spurt **7** explode **8** break out, burst out, detonate **9** discharge **10** break forth, burst forth

eruption
4 gust, rush **5** blast, burst, flare, sally **6** access **7** flare-up **8** outbreak, outburst **9** commotion, explosion
skin: **3** zit **4** rash **6** pimple

Esau
brother: **5** Jacob
country: **4** Edom
descendant: **7** Edomite
father: **5** Isaac
father-in-law: **4** Elon
grandson: **6** Amalek
mother: **7** Rebecca, Rebekah
new name: **4** Edom
son: **5** Korha, Reuel **7** Eliphaz
wife: **4** Adah **10** Aholibamah

escalade
5 climb, mount, scale **6** ascend **7** scaling

escalate
4 grow, rise, soar **5** boost, climb, mount, widen **6** expand, extend, spread, step up **7** amplify, augment, broaden, enlarge, inflate **8** heighten, increase, multiply **9** intensify **11** proliferate

escapade
4 lark, romp **5** antic, caper, fling, folly, prank, spree, stunt **6** frolic, vagary **7** roguery, rollick **8** mischief **9** adventure

escape
3 fly, lam **4** bolt, duck, flee, shun, skip, slip **5** avoid, break, dodge, elude, evade, shake **6** bypass, depart, eschew, flight, hegira, outlet **7** abscond, duck out, evasion, get away, make off, release, run away, skip out **8** breakout **9** avoidance, desertion, disappear, steal away **10** circumvent, liberation **11** deliverance, evasiveness
artist: **7** Houdini (Harry)
narrow: **9** close call **10** close shave

escargot
5 snail

escarole
6 endive

escarpment
5 bluff, cliff, slope

eschar
4 scab **5** crust **6** lesion

eschew
4 shun **5** avoid, elude, evade, forgo, spurn **6** abjure, forego, pass up, refuse, reject **7** decline **8** turn down

eschewal
7 elusion, evasion, refusal **8** shunning, spurning **9** avoidance, rejection

escort
4 beau, date, lead, show **5** guard, guide, pilot, steer, usher **6** attend, convoy, direct, gigolo, squire **7** company, conduct, consort, retinue **8** cavalier, chaperon, henchman, shepherd **9** accompany, bodyguard, chaperone, companion, entourage, safeguard **13** accompaniment

escritoire
4 desk **9** secretary **11** writing desk

escrow
4 bond, deed, fund **7** deposit

esculent
6 edible **7** eatable **10** comestible, digestible

escutcheon
6 flange, shield

Eshcol
ally: **7** Abraham
brother: **4** Aner **5** Mamre

esker
4 kame **5** mound, ridge

Eskimo
4 Inuk **5** Aleut, Inuit
boat: **5** kayak, umiak
boot: **5** kamik **6** mukluk
dog: **5** husky **8** malamute, malemute
dwelling: **5** igloo
knife: **3** ulu
outer garment: **5** parka **6** anorak
sledge: **7** komatik

esophagus
6 gullet

esoteric
5 inner **6** arcane, mystic, occult, orphic, secret **7** cryptic, private **8** abstruse, hermetic, profound **9** recondite **10** cabalistic, mysterious **12** confidential

ESP
9 telepathy **10** sixth sense **12** clairvoyance, precognition

espadrille
4 shoe **6** sandal

espalier
7 lattice, railing, trellis

esparto
5 grass

especial
4 main **5** close **7** express, notable, unusual **8** dominant, intimate, peculiar, singular, specific, uncommon **9** paramount **10** individual, particular **11** exceptional

especially
7 notably **8** markedly **9** expressly, primarily, unusually **10** peculiarly, remarkably, singularly **11** principally **12** particularly, specifically **13** distinctively, exceptionally

espial
6 notice **9** detection, discovery **11** observation

espionage
6 spying **9** sleuthing **12** surveillance
org.: **3** CIA, NSA, OSS **6** Mossad

espousal
5 troth, union **6** mating **7** embrace, support, wedding **8** adoption, advocacy, approval, ceremony, marriage **9** betrothal, embracing, matrimony, promotion **10** acceptance

espouse
3 wed **4** back **5** adopt, marry **6** accept, take on, take up **7** approve, embrace, support **8** advocate

esprit
3 vim, wit **4** brio, dash, élan, zest, zing **5** oomph, verve, vigor **6** fervor, gaiety, mettle, morale, spirit **7** courage, loyalty, panache, passion, sparkle **8** devotion, vibrancy, vitality **9** animation **10** brightness, enthusiasm, fellowship **11** camaraderie

esprit de corps
6 morale

espy
3 see **4** mark, spot **5** sight **6** descry, detect, notice **7** discern, glimpse, make out **9** recognize

___ es Salaam
3 Dar

essay
3 try **4** seek, test **5** labor, paper, piece, study, theme, tract, trial **6** effort, strive, thesis **7** article, attempt, venture **8** endeavor, treatise **9** undertake **10** discussion, exposition **11** composition, undertaking **12** dissertation

essayist
American: **4** Agee (James), Will (George) **5** Baker (Russell), Cooke (Alistair), Gould (Stephen Jay), White (E. B.) **6** Brooks (Cleanth), Fisher (M. F. K.), Holmes (Oliver Wendell), Lowell (James Russell), Sontag (Susan), Thomas (Lewis) **7** Buckley (William F.), Cousins (Norman), Emerson (Ralph Waldo), Mencken (Henry Louis), Thoreau (Henry David) **8** Benchley (Robert), Lippmann (Walter), Repplier (Agnes) **10** Crèvecoeur (Jean de)
English: **4** Elia, Lamb (Charles) **5** Bacon (Francis), Cecil (Lord David), Pater (Walter), Smith (Sydney) **6** Arnold (Matthew), Cowley (Abraham), Morris (Jan), Ruskin (John), Steele (Richard) **7** Addison (Joseph), Hazlitt (William) **8** Beerbohm (Max) **9** De Quincey (Thomas) **12** Chesterfield (Lord)
French: **9** Montaigne (Michel de)
Scottish: **7** Carlyle (Thomas)

essence
3 nub **4** base, core, crux, gist, odor, pith, root, soul **5** attar, basis, being, fiber, fibre, point, stuff **6** center, entity, kernel, marrow, nature, spirit **7** extract, perfume, quality **9** substance **10** distillate **12** distillation, significance

essential
3 key **4** main, must, need **5** basal, basic, chief, prime, vital **6** inborn, inbred, innate, primal **7** connate, crucial, element, primary **8** cardinal, foremost, inherent, required, rudiment **9** condition, elemental, intrinsic, necessary, necessity, principal, requisite, substance **10** congenital, deep-seated, elementary, idiopathic, imperative, sine qua non, underlying **11** fundamental, requirement **12** precondition, prerequisite **13** indispensable, part and parcel
oil: **5** attar

essentially
6 almost, au fond, really **7** largely **8** actually, as good as, as much as, well-nigh **9** basically, virtually **11** practically **13** fundamentally, substantially

essonite
6 garnet **13** cinnamon stone

establish
3 fix, lay, put, set **4** base, form, root, show **5** build, enact, endow, erect, found, place, prove, set up, start **6** attest, create, decree, effect, ground, impose, secure, settle, verify **7** build up, certify, clarify, confirm, find out, implant, install, instill, provide, set down **8** document, ensconce, organize **9** authorize, construct, determine,

formulate, institute, legislate, originate, prescribe **10** bring about, constitute, inaugurate **11** corroborate, demonstrate **12** authenticate, substantiate

establishment
4 firm **6** outfit **7** company, concern **8** business, old guard **9** institute, workplace **10** enterprise, foundation **11** institution, ruling class

estate
4 farm, land **5** manor, ranch, villa **6** domain, legacy, quinta **7** demesne **8** dominion, hacienda, property **10** plantation
agent: **7** Realtor
feudal: **4** fief **7** fiefdom
first: **6** clergy
fourth: **5** press
manager: **7** steward **8** executor, guardian
second: **6** nobles **8** nobility
third: **7** commons

esteem
4 deem **5** favor, honor, prize, think, value **6** admire, liking, regard, revere **7** account, believe, cherish, idolize, respect, worship **8** approval, consider, treasure, venerate **9** valuation **10** admiration, appreciate **12** appreciation **13** consideration

ester
6 oleate **7** acetate **8** compound **9** phosphate

Esther
cousin: **8** Mordecai
enemy: **5** Haman
father: **7** Abihail
festival: **5** Purim
Hebrew name: **8** Hadassah
husband: **6** Xerxes **9** Ahasuerus

estimable
5 noble **6** august, valued, worthy **7** admired **8** laudable, sterling **9** admirable, deserving, honorable, reputable, respected, venerable **10** creditable **11** commendable, meritorious, respectable **12** praiseworthy

estimate
3 put **4** call, rank, rate **5** assay, gauge, guess, infer, judge, price, set at, value **6** assess, deduce, figure, rating, reckon, survey **7** imagine, opinion, project, suppose, surmise **8** appraise, conclude, discover, evaluate, forecast, judgment, round off **9** appraisal, calculate, determine, reckoning, valuation **10** assessment, conjecture, evaluation, impression, projection **11** approximate, calculation, measurement

estimation
4 fame **5** favor, honor, stock **6** esteem, regard **7** account, opinion, respect **8** figuring, judgment **9** appraisal, reckoning, valuation **10** admiration, assessment, evaluation, impression **11** calculation **13** consideration

Estonia
capital: **7** Tallinn
city: **5** Tartu
gulf: **4** Riga **7** Finland
inhabitant: **4** Balt
island: **4** Muhu **6** Vormsi **7** Hiiumaa **8** Saaremaa
lake: **5** Pskov **6** Peipus **9** Vorts-Jarv
monetary unit: **5** kroon
neighbor: **6** Latvia, Russia
river: **5** Narva, Pärnu **6** Kasari
sea: **6** Baltic

estop
3 bar **6** enjoin, forbid **7** prevent **8** disallow, preclude, prohibit, restrain

Estrada of TV
4 Erik

estrange
4 part **5** split **7** break up, divorce **8** alienate, disunite, separate **9** disaffect

estrangement
4 rift **5** split **6** breach, schism **7** breakup, cooling, divorce, rupture **8** disunity, division **10** alienation, falling-out, withdrawal **12** disaffection

estuary
5 firth, frith, mouth **10** tidal river

esurient
4 avid **6** greedy, hungry **8** covetous, grasping, ravening, ravenous **9** rapacious, voracious **10** avaricious, gluttonous **11** acquisitive

et ___ ("and others")
4 alia, alii **5** aliae

étagère
7 cabinet, whatnot

Etats-___
4 Unis

etch
3 cut **5** carve, stamp **6** depict, incise **7** engrave, impress, imprint, portray **8** inscribe **9** delineate, represent

etcher
American: **7** Pennell (Joseph) **8** Whistler (James McNeill)
Dutch: **9** Rembrandt (van Rijn)
French: **5** Redon (Odilon) **6** Villon (Jacques)
Italian: **8** Piranesi (Giambattista)
Spanish: **6** Ribera (José)
Swiss: **4** Zorn (Anders)

Eteocles
brother: **9** Polynices **10** Polyneices
father: **7** Oedipus
mother: **7** Jocasta
slayer: **9** Polynices **10** Polyneices

eternal
7 abiding, ageless, endless, lasting, undying **8** constant, enduring, immortal, infinite, timeless, unending **9** ceaseless, continual, deathless, immutable, incessant, permanent, perpetual, unceasing **10** immemorial, unchanging **11** amaranthine, everlasting, illimitable, inalterable, never-ending, unalterable, unremitting **12** imperishable, interminable

Eternal City
4 Rome

eternally
3 e'er **4** ever **6** always **7** forever **8** evermore, for keeps **11** forevermore, in perpetuum **12** in perpetuity

eternity
3 age, eon **4** aeon **7** dog's age **8** blue moon, coon's age, infinity **9** afterlife **10** infinitude, perpetuity **11** endlessness, immortality **12** infiniteness, timelessness

Etesian
4 wind **6** annual

Ethan ___
5 Allen, Brand, Frome

Ethbaal's daughter
7 Jezebel

ether
3 air, gas, sky **6** heaven **7** heavens **8** airwaves, empyrean **10** anesthetic, atmosphere

ethereal
4 aery, airy **5** filmy, light **6** aerial **7** fragile **8** delicate, empyreal, empyrean, gossamer, heavenly, rarefied, vaporous **9** celestial, spiritual, unearthly, unworldly **10** immaterial, intangible **13** unsubstantial

ethical
4 good **5** moral, noble **6** decent **7** upright, virtual **8** elevated, virtuous **9** righteous **10** principled, upstanding **11** right-minded **13** conscientious

ethics
5 mores **6** morals, values **8** morality **9** moral code, standards **10** principles

Ethiopia
battle site: 5 Adowa
biblical name: 4 Cush
capital: 10 Addis Ababa
city: 6 Gonder **8** Dire Dawa
desert: 4 Haud **7** Danakil
emperor: 7 Menelik, Menilek **8** Selassie **9** Ras Tafari **13** Haile Selassie
former name: 9 Abyssinia
language: 5 Oromo **7** Amharic
monetary unit: 4 birr
mountain: 9 Ras Dashen
neighbor: 5 Kenya, Sudan **7** Eritrea, Somalia **8** Djibouti
region: 5 Tigre **6** Ogaden, Tigray **7** Danakil
river: 4 Abay **5** Awash **6** Tekeze **8** Blue Nile

Ethiopian princess of opera
4 Aida

ethnic
6 racial, tribal **8** minority

etiolate
4 fade, pale **6** bleach, weaken **7** lighten, wash out **8** enfeeble

etiquette
4 code, form **5** mores **7** conduct, customs, decency, decorum, manners **8** behavior, protocol **9** amenities, propriety **10** civilities, convention, deportment, seemliness **11** conventions, formalities, proprieties

Etna output
4 lava

Etruscan
city, town: 4 Roma, Veii **5** Caere, Vulci **6** Arezzo **7** Clusium, Felsina, Perugia **8** Volsinii **9** Florentia, Tarquinia, Vetulonia
deity: 3 Tin, Tiv, Uni **4** Turm, Usil **5** Tinia, Turan, Turms **6** Menfra, Menrva, Nethun, Trithn **7** Velchan **8** Sethlans, Voltumna
king: 7 Porsena, Tarquin **10** Tarquinius **11** Lars Porsena
kingdom: 7 Etruria

étude
5 study **8** exercise **11** composition

etui
4 case

etymology
11 word history

etymon
4 root **5** radix **6** source **8** morpheme

eucalyptus eater
5 koala

Eucharist
container: 3 pyx
plate: 5 paten
service: 4 Mass **9** Communion
vessel: 8 ciborium
wafer: 4 host **8** viaticum

Euclid
subject: 8 geometry
work: 8 Elements

___ Eulenspiegel
4 Till, Tyll

eulogistic
9 adulatory, laudative, laudatory **11** encomiastic, panegyrical **12** commendatory **13** complimentary

eulogize
4 hymn, laud 5 cry up, exalt, extol 6 praise 7 acclaim, applaud, commend, glorify, magnify 9 celebrate 10 panegyrize

eulogy
5 paean 6 praise 7 oration, tribute 8 accolade, citation, encomium 9 laudation, panegyric 10 salutation 12 commendation 13 glorification

Eumenides
see **Erinyes**

eunuch
7 gelding 8 castrate, castrato

euphony
7 harmony 8 lyricism 9 sweetness 10 consonance

euphoria
3 joy 4 glee 5 bliss 7 ecstasy, elation, rapture 9 transport 10 exaltation, jubilation 11 high spirits 12 exhilaration, intoxication

Euphrosyne, e.g.
5 Grace

euphuistic
5 fancy, tumid 6 florid, ornate, prolix, purple, turgid 7 elegant, flowery, fustian, orotund, verbose 8 colorful, elevated, inflated, sonorous 9 bombastic, elaborate, high-flown, overblown 10 figurative, flamboyant, rhetorical 11 highfalutin, overwrought 12 magniloquent 13 grandiloquent

eureka
3 aha

Euridice's husband
7 Orpheus

Euripides play
3 Ion 5 Helen, Medea 6 Hecuba 7 Bacchae (The), Cyclops, Electra, Orestes 8 Alcestis 10 Andromache, Hippolytus, Suppliants (The) 11 Trojan Women (The)

Europa
brother: 6 Cadmus
father: 6 Agenor 7 Phoenix
husband: 8 Asterius
son: 5 Minos 8 Sarpedon

Europe
9 continent
country: 4 Eire 5 Italy, Malta, Spain 6 Cyprus, France, Greece, Latvia, Monaco, Norway, Poland, Russia, Serbia, Sweden, Turkey 7 Albania, Andorra, Armenia, Austria, Belarus, Belgium, Croatia, Denmark, Estonia, Finland, Georgia, Germany, Hungary, Iceland, Ireland, Moldova, Romania, Rumania, Ukraine 8 Bulgaria, Portugal, Slovakia, Slovenia 9 Lithuania, Macedonia, San Marino 10 Azerbaijan, Luxembourg, Montenegro 11 Netherlands, Switzerland, Vatican City 13 Czech Republic, Liechtenstein, United Kingdom
ethnic group: 4 Celt, Finn, Lapp, Lett, Pole, Serb, Sorb, Turk, Wend 5 Croat, Czech, Dutch, Greek, Gypsy, Irish, Latin, Swede, Swiss, Welsh 6 Basque, Celtic, French, German, Magyar, Polish, Scotch, Slovak 7 Bosnian, Catalan, English, Finnish, Fleming, Italian, Lettish, Maltese, Russian, Slovene, Spanish, Swedish, Walloon 8 Albanian, Andorran, Armenian, Croatian, Romanian 9 Belarusan, Bulgarian, Hungarian, Ukrainian 10 Belarusian, Macedonian, Monegasque, Phoenician 11 Belarussian 12 Byelorussian, Scandinavian
language: 4 Lapp 5 Czech, Dutch, Greek, Irish, Latin, Welsh 6 Basque, Breton, Danish, French, Gaelic, German, Magyar, Polish, Slovak 7 Catalan, English, Finnish, Flemish, Italian, Maltese, Romansh, Russian, Serbian, Slovene, Spanish, Swedish, Turkish, Wendish 8 Albanian, Croatian, Lusatian, Romanian, Rumanian 9 Bulgarian, Hungarian, Icelandic, Norwegian 10 Macedonian, Portuguese 13 Serbo-Croatian
mountain range: 4 Alps 8 Pyrenees 11 Carpathians

European farewell
4 ciao

European Union member
5 Italy, Malta, Spain 6 Cyprus, France, Greece, Latvia, Poland, Sweden 7 Austria, Belgium, Denmark, Estonia, Finland, Germany, Hungary, Ireland, Romania, Rumania 8 Bulgaria, Portugal, Slovakia, Slovenia 9 Lithuania 10 Luxembourg 11 Netherlands 13 Czech Republic, United Kingdom

Euryale, e.g.
6 Gorgon

Eurytus
daughter: 4 Iole
slayer: 8 Hercules

Euterpe, e.g.
4 Muse

evacuate
4 exit, void 5 clear, empty, expel, leave 6 decamp, depart, remove, vacate 7 abandon, excrete, exhaust, pull out, retreat 8 clear out, pull back, withdraw 9 eliminate

evacuee
6 émigré 7 refugee 8 fugitive

evade
4 duck, flee, foil 5 avoid, dodge, elude, hedge, parry, shirk, skirt 6 baffle, bypass, escape, eschew, outwit, thwart, weasel 7 shuffle 8 sidestep, slip away 9 pussyfoot, turn aside 10 circumvent, equivocate 11 prevaricate 12 tergiversate

evaluate
4 rank, rate, test **5** assay, class, gauge, grade, set at, weigh **6** assess, figure, reckon, size up, survey **7** eyeball **8** appraise, classify, estimate **9** calculate, criticize

evaluation
6 rating **7** judging, measure, opinion **8** estimate, judgment **9** appraisal **10** assessment **12** appreciation

Evander
father: **6** Hermes **7** Mercury
mother: **8** Carmenta **9** Carmentis
son: **6** Pallas

evanesce
4 fade **5** clear **6** vanish **7** scatter **8** disperse, dissolve, melt away **9** disappear, dissipate, evaporate **13** dematerialize

evanescent
6 fading **7** elusive, melting, passing **8** fleeting, fugitive, volatile **9** ephemeral, fugacious, momentary, transient, vanishing **10** dissolving, short-lived, transitory **12** disappearing

evangelical
6 ardent, fervid **7** fanatic, fervent, zealous **8** militant **9** crusading **10** missionary **13** proselytizing

Evangeline
author: **10** Longfellow (Henry Wadsworth)
beloved: **7** Gabriel
home: **6** Acadia

evangelist
4 John, Luke, Mark **5** Moody (Dwight) **6** Bakker (Jim, Tammy Faye), Dobson (James), Graham (Billy, Franklin), Sunday (Billy), Warren (Rick), Wesley (John) **7** apostle, Edwards (Jonathan), Falwell (Jerry), Matthew, Roberts (Oral) **8** Schuller (Robert), Swaggart (Jimmy) **9** McPherson (Aimee Semple), missioner, Robertson (Pat) **10** colporteur, missionary, revivalist, Whitefield (George)

evangelistic
9 crusading, reforming **10** missionary, revivalist **13** proselytizing

evangelize
6 preach **7** convert **9** sermonize

evaporate
4 fade, melt **5** clear **6** vanish **8** diminish, disperse, dissolve, evanesce, melt away, vaporize **9** disappear, dissipate

evasion
5 dodge, fudge **6** escape, excuse **7** dodging, elusion, fudging **8** escaping **9** avoidance **13** circumvention

evasive
3 sly **5** cagey, dodgy, vague **6** shifty **7** elusive, elusory **8** slippery **9** ambiguous, equivocal

Eve
home: **4** Eden
husband: **4** Adam
son: **4** Abel, Cain, Seth
temptation: **5** apple, fruit

even
3 tie **4** fair, flat, just, same, tied **5** align, equal, exact, flush, grade, level, plane, still, truly **6** as well, equate, smooth, square, stable, steady **7** balance, equable, flatten, uniform **8** balanced, constant, equalize, smoothen, straight **9** equitable, expressly, identical, precisely, unvarying **10** absolutely, comparable, consistent, continuous, fifty-fifty, unchanging **13** fair and square, proportionate

evening
4 dusk **6** soiree, sunset, vesper **7** sundown **8** gloaming, twilight **9** nightfall
French: **4** soir
Italian: **4** sera
service: **7** vespers
star: **5** Venus **6** Vesper **8** Hesperus

evenness
6 equity, parity **7** balance **8** equality **9** stability **10** equanimity, uniformity **11** consistency, equilibrium

even so
3 yet **5** still **6** withal **7** however **10** regardless **11** nonetheless **12** nevertheless

event
3 act **4** case, deed, fact, feat, meet **5** issue, match **6** action, affair, chance, effect, result, upshot **7** contest, episode, outcome, product **8** accident, function, incident, occasion **9** aftermath, happening **10** occurrence, phenomenon **11** achievement, competition, consequence, eventuality **12** circumstance, happenstance

eventful
4 busy **6** lively **9** important, momentous

eventual
4 last **5** final **6** ending **7** closing, endmost, ensuing **8** terminal, ultimate **9** resulting **10** concluding, consequent, inevitable, succeeding

eventuality
4 case **6** effect, result **7** outcome **11** consequence, contingency, possibility

eventually
6 at last, in time, one day **7** finally, someday **8** sometime **9** hereafter **10** ultimately **13** sooner or later

eventuate
5 ensue, occur **6** befall, follow, happen, result **9** come about, take place

ever
4 once **5** at all **6** always **7** forever **9** at any

time, eternally, regularly **10** constantly, invariably **11** perpetually **12** consistently, continuously
poetic: 3 e'er

evergreen
3 fir, ivy, yew **4** ilex, pine, tawa, tree **5** cedar, holly, savin **6** laurel, myrtle, spruce **7** conifer, cypress, hemlock, juniper, lasting, redwood, sequoia, undying **8** magnolia, mangrove, timeless, unfading **9** mistletoe, perennial **10** arborvitae **12** rhododendron

Evergreen State
10 Washington

everlasting
7 abiding, ageless, endless, eternal, forever, lasting, undying **8** constant, immortal, infinite, termless, timeless, unending **9** boundless, ceaseless, continual, deathless, limitless, permanent, perpetual, unceasing **10** continuous, perdurable **11** amaranthine, never-ending, unremitting **12** imperishable

evermore
6 always **7** for good **8** for keeps **9** eternally **12** in perpetuity

every
3 all **4** each
prefix: 3 pan

everybody
3 all **4** each

everyday
5 banal, plain, usual **6** common, normal **7** mundane, prosaic, routine **8** familiar, habitual, ordinary **9** customary, quotidian **11** commonplace **12** conventional, run-of-the-mill, unremarkable

everything
3 all
French: 4 tout
German: 5 alles
Spanish: 4 todo

everywhere
7 all over, overall **8** all round, wherever **9** all around **10** far and near, far and wide, high and low, throughout

Évian, e.g.
3 spa **5** water

evict
3 out **4** boot, oust **5** eject, expel **6** bounce, put out **7** boot out, dismiss, extrude, kick out **8** dislodge, force out, throw out **10** dispossess

evidence
4 clue, mark, show, sign **5** goods, proof, prove **6** attest, evince, expose, reveal **7** confirm, display, exhibit, symptom, testify, witness **8** indicate **9** testament, testimony **10** indication, smoking gun **11** attestation, demonstrate, testimonial **12** confirmation **13** documentation

evident
5 clear, overt, plain **6** marked, patent **7** obvious, visible **8** apparent, distinct, manifest, palpable, tangible **9** prominent **10** noticeable, pronounced **11** conspicuous, perceptible, unambiguous

evidently
9 outwardly, seemingly **10** officially, ostensibly

evil
3 bad, sin **4** foul, vice, vile **5** black **6** infamy, malice, sinful, wicked **7** badness, baleful, baneful, devilry, hateful, heinous, malefic, satanic, vicious **8** damnable, iniquity, satanism, villainy **9** atrocious, diablerie, diabolism, execrable, loathsome, malicious, malignant, nefarious **10** flagitious, iniquitous, maleficent, malevolent, pernicious, sinfulness, wickedness **11** maleficence
combining form: 3 mal

evildoer
6 sinner **7** villain **8** criminal **9** miscreant **10** malefactor

evil spirit
3 imp **5** demon, devil, fiend, Satan **6** daemon

evince
4 mark, show **5** educe, evoke, prove **6** attest, betray, elicit, expose, reveal **7** bespeak, betoken, confirm, display, exhibit, signify **8** evidence, indicate, manifest, proclaim **10** illustrate **11** demonstrate

eviscerate
3 gut **4** draw **5** bowel **7** embowel **8** protrude **10** disembowel, exenterate

evocative
6 moving **8** redolent, stirring **9** affecting, emotional, nostalgic **10** expressive, meaningful, suggestive **11** stimulating

evoke
4 cite, stir **5** educe, raise, waken **6** arouse, awaken, call up, elicit, evince, excite, induce, recall **7** conjure **8** recreate, summon up **9** call forth, conjure up, stimulate **11** summon forth

evolution
6 change, growth **8** progress, upgrowth **9** flowering, phylogeny, unfolding **10** biogenesis, maturation **11** development, progression

evolve
4 grow **5** educe, ripen **6** change, derive, emerge, mature, open up, unfold **7** advance, develop, work out **8** progress **9** elaborate

ewe
5 sheep
mate: 3 ram

ewer
3 jug **4** olpe, vase **7** pitcher

ex
4 from, past **5** out of, prior **6** former **7** earlier, without **9** erstwhile

exacerbate
6 worsen **7** envenom, inflame, provoke **8** embitter, heighten **9** aggravate, intensify

exact
4 levy, true **5** claim, force, gouge, pinch, screw, wrest, wring **6** coerce, compel, dead-on, demand, extort, spot-on, strict **7** correct, extract, literal, precise, require, solicit, squeeze **8** accurate, rigorous, selfsame **9** identical, postulate, shake down **10** meticulous, scrupulous **11** painstaking, punctilious, requisition

exacting
5 fussy, rigid, stern, tough **6** severe, strict, taxing, trying **7** exigent, finicky, onerous **8** critical, rigorous **9** demanding, stringent **10** fastidious, nitpicking, particular, scrupulous **11** persnickety **13** hypercritical

exactitude
5 rigor **8** accuracy **9** precision **10** definitude **11** correctness, preciseness **12** definiteness

exactly
4 bang, just **5** quite, right, sharp, spang **6** bang on, square, to a tee, wholly **7** totally, utterly **8** entirely, on the dot, smack-dab, squarely **9** on the nose, precisely **10** absolutely, accurately, altogether, completely, positively **12** specifically

exaggerate
6 overdo **7** amplify, enlarge, inflate, magnify, overact, romance **8** overdraw, overrate **9** embellish, embroider, overstate **11** hyperbolize **13** overemphasize

exaggeration
8 travesty **9** hyperbole **10** caricature, stretching **11** enlargement, overdrawing **12** embroidering **13** embellishment, overstatement

exalt
4 fete, laud, lift **5** boost, elate, ensky, extol, honor, raise **6** praise, uplift **7** acclaim, adulate, build up, dignify, elevate, enhance, ennoble, glorify, inspire, magnify, promote **8** eulogize, heighten, inspirit **9** intensify **10** aggrandize **11** apotheosize

exaltation
3 joy **5** bliss, glory **6** homage, praise **7** delight, ecstasy, elation, rapture, tribute **8** euphoria, rhapsody **9** panegyric, transport, uplifting **10** apotheosis, jubilation **11** deification **12** exhilaration, intoxication **13** glorification

exalted
4 high **5** grand, lofty, noble **6** august **7** eminent, highest, sublime **9** venerable **11** high-ranking, illustrious, outstanding, prestigious

examination
3 ACT, SAT **4** LAST, oral, PSAT, quiz, scan, test **5** assay, final, probe, trial **6** review, survey **7** canvass, checkup, hearing, inquest, inquiry, perusal, sifting, testing **8** analysis, scrutiny **9** breakdown, check-over, diagnosis **10** dissection, inspection **11** inquisition **13** catechization, investigation, perlustration
kind: **3** bar **4** oral **5** final **7** medical, midterm **8** physical
of accounts: **5** audit
of a corpse: **7** autopsy **10** postmortem
type: **4** oral

examine
3 con, vet **4** pump, quiz, scan, sift, test **5** assay, audit, check, grill, probe, query, study **6** go over, look at, peruse, survey **7** canvass, check up, inquire, inspect, observe **8** check out, look into, look over, question **9** catechize, check over **10** scrutinize **11** interrogate, investigate

examiner
6 censor **7** auditor, coroner **9** inspector **10** inquisitor, prosecutor **12** investigator

example
4 case **5** ideal, model **7** paragon, pattern **8** instance, paradigm, specimen, standard **9** archetype, precedent, prototype **11** case history **12** illustration

exanimate
4 dead **5** inert **8** lifeless, listless, sluggish, stagnant **9** lethargic **10** spiritless

exasperate
3 irk, vex **4** gall, rile, roil **5** anger, annoy, peeve, pique, upset **6** enrage, madden, nettle, rankle **7** agitate, incense, inflame, provoke **8** irritate **9** aggravate, infuriate

exasperation
8 vexation **9** annoyance **10** irritation **11** aggravation

ex cathedra
8 official **9** ex officio **13** authoritative

excavate
3 dig **4** grub **5** scoop, spade **6** dig out, dredge, expose, hollow, quarry, shovel **7** unearth **8** gouge out, scoop out **9** hollow out, scrape out

excavation
3 dig, pit **4** hole, mine **5** ditch, stope **6** dugout, hollow, quarry, trench, trough

exceed
3 cap, top **4** beat, best, pass **5** break, excel, outdo **6** better, outrun, overdo **7** eclipse, outpace, overrun, surpass **8** go beyond, outreach, outshine, outstrip, outweigh, overstep, overtake **9** overreach, transcend

exceedingly
4 very **6** hugely, vastly **7** awfully, notably, vitally **9** extremely **10** remarkably, strikingly **12** surpassingly **13** exceptionally
prefix: 5 ultra

excel
3 cap, top **4** beat, best, pass **5** outdo, shine **6** better, exceed, outrun, overdo **7** eclipse, outpace, overrun, surpass **8** go beyond, outclass, outreach, outshine, outstrip, outweigh, overstep, overtake **9** overreach, transcend

excellence
5 class, merit, value, worth **6** virtue **7** quality **8** fineness **9** greatness **10** perfection **11** distinction, superiority

excellent
3 top **4** A-one, boss, fine **5** bully, model, neato, prime **6** bang-up, banner, famous, Grade A, superb, tip-top, worthy **7** capital, premium, supreme **8** champion, five-star, splendid, stunning, superior, terrific, top-notch **9** classical, exemplary, first-rate, high-class, high-grade, marvelous, number one, top-drawer, wonderful **10** blue-ribbon, first-class **11** exceptional, magnificent, meritorious, sensational, superlative, unsurpassed **12** incomparable

except
3 bar, but, yet **4** omit, only, save **6** beside, exempt, object, reject, unless **7** barring, besides, exclude, however, outside, rule out, suspend **8** pass over **9** apart from, aside from, eliminate, excluding, outside of **11** exclusive of

exception
5 demur **7** anomaly, dissent **8** question **9** allowance, deviation, exclusion, objection **10** aberration

exceptionable
8 unwanted **9** unwelcome **10** unsuitable **11** regrettable, undesirable **12** unacceptable **13** objectionable

exceptional
4 rare **6** scarce, unique **7** notable, special, unusual **8** abnormal, atypical, distinct, singular, superior, uncommon, unwonted **9** anomalous, excellent, marvelous, wonderful **10** infrequent, noteworthy, phenomenal, remarkable **11** outstanding, uncustomary **13** extraordinary

exceptionally
4 very **6** hugely **7** notably **9** extremely **10** especially, remarkably, strikingly **11** exceedingly **12** particularly, stupendously

excerpt
4 cite, clip, cull, pick **5** glean, quote **6** choose, sample, select **7** extract, passage, pick out, portion, snippet **8** fragment **9** quotation

excess
3 fat **4** glut, rest **5** extra, flood, spare, waste **7** nimiety, overage, surfeit, surplus **8** leavings, leftover, overflow, overkill, overmuch **9** indulgent, overstock, redundant, remainder **10** oversupply, surplusage **11** dissipation, prodigality, superfluity, superfluous, unessential **12** extravagance, immoderation, intemperance **13** overabundance, supernumerary

excessive
4 over **5** dizzy, steep, super, undue **6** de trop, too-too **7** extreme, sky-high **8** overmuch, prodigal **10** exorbitant, immoderate, inordinate, profligate **11** extravagant, intemperate, overweening, superfluous **12** supernatural, unrestrained

excessively
3 too **6** overly, unduly **8** overmuch
prefix: 5 hyper

exchange
4 swap, swop **5** bandy, trade, truck **6** barter, market, switch **7** bargain, commute, convert, pay back, replace, traffic **8** displace **9** transpose **10** conversion, substitute **11** reciprocate
fee: 4 agio

exchange-rate premium
4 agio

exchequer
5 funds **8** treasury

excise
3 fee, tax **4** toll **5** elide, slash **6** cut out, delete, remove, resect **9** expurgate, extirpate, strike out, surcharge

excision
3 cut **7** removal, surgery **8** deletion **9** resection **11** extirpation

excitable
4 rash **8** volatile **9** impetuous **10** high-strung

excite
4 fire, goad, move, spur, stir **5** elate, evoke, key up, pique, prime, rouse, waken **6** appeal, arouse, elicit, fire up, induce, kindle, stir up, thrill, turn on **7** agitate, animate, commove, inflame, inspire, provoke, quicken **8** activate, charge up, energize, motivate **9** galvanize, impassion, innervate, stimulate **10** exhilarate

excited
3 hot **4** avid **5** eager, het up **6** aflame **7** fevered **8** aflutter, worked up **10** passionate **12** enthusiastic

excitement
3 ado **4** buzz, stir, to-do **5** fever, furor **6** flurry, frenzy, furore, hubbub, thrill **7** turmoil **8** delirium, hysteria **9** agitation, commotion **10** enthusiasm, hullabaloo **11** disturbance, pandemonium **12** exhilaration

exclaim
4 blat, bolt **5** blurt **6** cry out **8** blurt out, burst out **9** ejaculate

exclamation
3 aah, aha, bah, boo, cry, eek, feh, fie, gee, hah, hey, huh, oho, ooh, pah, tsk, tut, ugh, wow **4** ahem, alas, amen, damn, dang, darn, drat, egad, gosh, heck, hell, oops, ouch, phew, pish, posh, rats, whew, yell **5** alack, bravo, faugh, golly, humph, pshaw, shout **6** clamor, hurrah, indeed, outcry, phooey, shucks **7** doggone, gee whiz, hosanna, jeepers, whoopee **9** expletive **10** hallelujah **12** interjection
of disappointment: **4** damn, darn, rats
of disapproval: **3** tsk **6** tsk-tsk
of discovery: **3** aha **6** eureka
of disgust: **3** bah, boo, feh, fie, ugh **4** yech, yuck **5** faugh, yecch **6** phooey
of dismay: **4** oh no, uh-oh **5** yikes
of enthusiasm: **4** whee **5** wahoo **7** whoopie
of fear: **3** eek
of pain: **4** ouch
of relief: **4** phew
of sorrow: **3** woe **4** alas **5** alack
of surprise: **3** wow **4** gosh **5** golly
of triumph: **3** aha, hah **5** yahoo **6** eureka
(see also **interjection**)

exclude
3 ban, bar **4** oust **5** block, debar **6** banish, disbar, reject **7** keep out, lock out, obviate, prevent, rule out, shut out, suspend **8** count out, preclude, prohibit **9** blackball, blacklist, eliminate, ostracize

excluding
3 bar, but **4** less, save **6** except **7** barring, besides **9** apart from, aside from, other than, outside of

exclusion
3 bar **6** ouster **7** barring, lockout, removal **8** ejection, eviction, omission **9** blackball, expulsion, ostracism **10** banishment **12** blackballing, nonadmission

exclusive
4 lone, only, sole **5** elect, elite, prime, scoop, smart, swank, swish **6** choice, chosen, picked, select, single **7** cliquey, high-hat, stylish **8** clannish, cliquish, selected, snobbish **9** preferred, undivided **10** privileged **11** fashionable, prohibitive, restrictive **12** aristocratic, concentrated, preferential

exclusively
4 only **5** alone **6** wholly **8** entirely **10** completely **12** particularly

excogitate
6 derive, devise, invent **7** develop, think up **8** contrive, think out

excommunicate
7 cast out **8** unchurch

excoriate
4 flay, lash, skin **5** roast, slash **6** abrade, scathe, scorch **7** blister, censure, scarify, scourge **8** chastise, lambaste, lash into **9** castigate

excrement
6 ordure
of animals: **4** dung, muck **6** manure
of sea birds: **5** guano

excrescence
4 blot, lump, mole, wart **5** tumor **6** growth, nodule, pimple **7** blemish, process **9** by-product, outgrowth

excrete
4 emit, spew **5** egest, eject, expel, exude **9** discharge

excruciate
4 rack **6** martyr **7** afflict, crucify, torment, torture **9** martyrize

excruciating
5 acute, sharp **6** severe **7** extreme, intense **8** piercing, shooting, stabbing **9** agonizing, harrowing, torturous **10** unbearable **11** unendurable

exculpate
4 free **5** clear, remit **6** acquit, excuse, let off, pardon **7** absolve, amnesty, condone, forgive, justify **9** exonerate, vindicate **11** rationalize

excursion
4 ride, tour, trek, trip, walk **5** aside, drive, jaunt, paseo, sally, tramp **6** cruise, junket, outing, ramble, safari **7** day trip, journey **9** round trip **10** digression, divagation, expedition **11** parenthesis **12** pleasure trip

excusable
6 venial

excuse
3 out **4** plea **5** alibi, clear, remit **6** acquit, copout, defend, exempt, let off, pardon, reason, wink at **7** absolve, apology, condone, defense, forgive, justify, pretext, regrets, relieve **8** mitigate, overlook, palliate, pass over, shrug off, tolerate **9** discharge, exculpate, exonerate, extenuate, gloss over, makeshift, vindicate, whitewash **10** substitute **11** explanation, rationalize **13** justification

excuse me
4 ahem **6** pardon **9** beg pardon

execrable
4 base, foul, vile **6** cursed **7** heinous **8** accursed, damnable, horrific, infernal, wretched **9** abhorrent, atrocious, loathsome, monstrous, repulsive, revolting **10** abominable, deplorable, despicable, detestable, horrifying

execrate
4 damn, hate **5** abhor, curse **6** detest, loathe, revile, vilify **7** censure, condemn, despise **8** denounce **9** abominate, imprecate **12** anathematize

execute
3 act **4** do in, kill, play, slay **5** cause, lynch **6** effect, finish, murder, render **7** achieve, bump off, conduct, enforce, fulfill, perform, realize **8** carry out, complete, dispatch, knock off, transact **9** discharge, eliminate, implement, liquidate **10** accomplish, administer, bring about, put through, put to death **11** assassinate **12** administrate

execution
6 murder **7** killing **11** performance

executioner
7 hangman, headman **8** headsman

executive
4 dean, suit **6** leader **7** manager **8** director, governor **9** president **10** supervisor **13** administrator
degree: 3 MBA
ineffective: 9 empty suit

exegesis
5 gloss **8** analysis **9** construal **10** commentary, exposition **11** elucidation, explanation, explication **12** construction

exemplar
4 copy **5** ideal, model **7** epitome, paragon, pattern **8** instance, paradigm, specimen, standard **9** archetype, criterion, prototype **12** illustration

exemplary
4 pure **5** ideal, model **7** classic, typical **8** laudable, monitory, virtuous **9** admirable, blameless, classical, estimable, faultless, honorable, righteous **10** impeccable, inculpable, prototypal **11** commendable, meritorious **12** illustrative, paradigmatic, praiseworthy, prototypical

exemplify
4 copy **6** embody, mirror, typify **7** clarify **9** enlighten, epitomize, personify, represent, symbolize **10** concretize, illuminate, illustrate

exempt
4 free **5** spare **6** except, excuse, let off, spared **7** absolve, excused, relieve **8** dispense **9** discharge

exemption
7 freedom, release **8** immunity, impunity **9** discharge, exception

exenterate
3 gut **4** draw **7** embowel **10** disembowel, eviscerate

exercise
3 use, vex **4** fret, gall, hone **5** alarm, annoy, apply, drill, étude, exert, sit-up, train, upset, wield **6** chin-up, crunch, employ, pull-up, push-up **7** agitate, develop, exploit, improve, prepare, problem, provoke, utilize, work out **8** activity, maneuver, practice, rehearse **9** athletics, condition, cultivate, discharge, operation **10** employment **11** application **12** calisthenics

exert
3 use **5** apply, wield **6** employ, expend, put out, strain **8** exercise, put forth

exertion
4 toil, work **5** labor, pains **6** effort, strain **7** trouble **8** activity, exercise, striving **11** application, elbow grease

exfoliate
4 peel, shed **5** scale **7** cast off, leaf out **8** flake off **10** desquamate

exhalation
6 breath **8** emission **9** breathing, effluvium, emanation

exhale
4 blow, emit, sigh **6** expire, let out **7** breathe, respire **10** breathe out
audibly: 4 sigh

exhaust
3 fag, sap **4** do in, tire **5** drain, eat up, empty, spend, use up, waste, weary **6** expend, finish, tucker, wash up, weaken **7** burn out, consume, deplete, fatigue, frazzle, tire out, wear out **8** draw down, enervate, squander, wear down **9** discharge, dissipate, prostrate, tucker out **10** debilitate, overextend, run through

exhausted
4 beat, limp, weak **5** all in, spent, tired **6** bushed, gassed **7** run-down, worn out **8** dog-tired

exhaustion
7 burnout, fatigue **8** collapse **9** lassitude, tiredness, weariness **11** prostration

exhaustive
8 complete, sweeping, thorough **9** full-blown, full-scale, intensive **10** scrupulous **11** painstaking **13** comprehensive, thoroughgoing

exhibit
4 fair, show **6** evince, expose, flaunt, parade, reveal **7** display, feature, show off **8** evidence, manifest, proclaim, showcase **10** exposition **11** demonstrate

exhibition
4 expo, fair, show **5** rodeo **7** display, pageant, showing **9** trade show **12** presentation **13** demonstration, manifestation

exhibitionist
3 fop **4** toff **6** hot dog **7** peacock, show-off **8** showboat **12** grandstander

exhilarate
4 buoy, lift **5** boost, cheer, elate, exalt, pep up **6** buck up, excite, thrill, uplift **7** animate, cheer up, commove, delight, enliven, gladden, inspire, refresh **8** inspirit, vitalize **9** stimulate **10** invigorate

exhilaration
3 joy **4** glee **7** ecstasy, elation **8** euphoria,

gladness **10** exaltation, excitement **11** inspiration **12** vitalization, vivification **13** galvanization

exile's island
4 Elba

exhort
4 goad, prod, spur, urge, warn **5** egg on, plead, press, prick **6** adjure, call on, incite, prompt, propel **7** beseech, entreat **8** admonish, call upon **9** stimulate

exhortation
4 plea **6** advice, urging **7** caution, warning **8** entreaty, jeremiad **10** admonition, incitement, injunction **11** inspiration **13** encouragement

exhume
5 dig up **6** redeem **7** reclaim, recover, unearth **8** disinter **9** resurrect

exigency
3 fix, jam **4** need, pass **5** pinch, rigor **6** crisis, demand, pickle, plight, strait **7** urgency **8** juncture, pressure, zero hour **9** extremity, necessity **10** compulsion, constraint, crossroads, difficulty, insistence **11** predicament, requirement

exigent
5 acute, vital **6** crying, taxing **7** burning, clamant, instant, onerous **8** exacting, grievous, pressing **9** clamorous, demanding, insistent, necessary **10** burdensome, imperative **11** importunate

exiguous
4 poor, puny, thin, tiny **5** scant, spare, token **6** meager, meagre, measly, paltry, scanty, shabby, skimpy, slight, sparse **7** minimal, scrimpy **9** miserable **10** inadequate, straitened

exile
4 oust **5** eject, expel **6** banish, deport, émigré **7** cast out, outcast, refugee **8** diaspora, displace, drive out, evacuate, expellee **9** exclusion, expulsion, extradite, migration, ostracism, ostracize **10** banishment, dispossess, expatriate, scattering **11** deportation, extradition **12** displacement, expatriation
place of: **4** Elba **7** Siberia **8** St. Helena

exist
3 are, lie **4** live **5** occur

existence
4 esse, life **5** being **7** reality **8** duration **9** actuality

existent
4 live, real **5** being, thing **6** actual, entity, extant, living **7** current, instant, present **10** present-day **12** contemporary

existentialist writer
5 Buber (Martin), Camus (Albert) **6** Marcel (Gabriel), Sartre (Jean-Paul) **7** Jaspers (Karl) **8** Beauvoir (Simone de) **9** Heidegger (Martin), Nietzsche (Friedrich) **11** Kierkegaard (Søren)

existing
5 alive, being, ontic **6** extant, living
from birth: **6** innate **10** congenital
Latin: **6** in esse

exit
3 die **4** door, gate, quit **5** death, going, leave, scram, split **6** depart, egress, escape, outlet, portal, retire **7** doorway, get away, off-ramp **8** withdraw **9** departure, egression **10** withdrawal

____ ex machina
4 deus

exodus
6 flight **9** migration **10** emigration

Exodus
author: **4** Uris (Leon)
hero: **3** Ari (Ben Canaan) **5** Moses

exonerate
4 free **5** clear, remit **6** acquit, excuse, exempt, let off, pardon **7** absolve **8** reprieve **9** exculpate, vindicate

exorbitant
5 undue **7** extreme **9** excessive **10** immoderate, inordinate, outrageous **11** extravagant, unwarranted **12** preposterous

exordium
5 intro, proem **6** lead-in **7** opening, preface, prelude **8** foreword, overture, preamble, prologue **12** introduction, prolegomenon

exotic
4 rare **5** alien **7** bizarre, foreign, strange, unusual **8** alluring, enticing, imported, romantic **9** different, glamorous, nonnative **10** introduced, mysterious **11** fascinating

expand
3 wax **4** grow, open, rise **5** boost, mount, swell, widen **6** beef up, bulk up, dilate, pad out, spread, unfold **7** amplify, augment, bolster, develop, distend, enlarge, inflate, magnify, prolong, stretch **8** escalate, increase, lengthen, multiply, mushroom, protract **9** discourse, elaborate, expatiate, spread out

expanse
4 area, room **5** field, ocean, range, reach, scope, space, sweep, tract **6** domain, extent, sphere, spread **7** breadth, stretch **8** distance **9** territory

expansion
6 growth, spread **8** increase **9** unfolding **11** enlargement **12** augmentation

expansive
3 big **4** wide **5** ample, broad, large, roomy **6** lavish **7** buoyant, elastic, liberal, sizable **8** effusive, extended, generous, outgoing, spacious **9** capacious, garrulous, talkative **10** gregarious, openhanded, unreserved **11** extroverted **13** demonstrative

expatiate
6 ramble, wander **7** dissert, enlarge **8** dilate on, perorate **9** discourse, elaborate, sermonize **10** dilate upon, dissertate

expatriate
5 exile, expel **6** banish, deport, émigré **8** displace, expellee, relegate

expect
4 feel, hope, take **5** await, sense, think, trust **6** assume, divine, gather, look to **7** believe, count on, foresee, imagine, look for, predict, presume, suppose, surmise **8** forecast, foreknow **9** apprehend, count upon **10** anticipate, presuppose

expectant
5 alert **6** gravid **7** anxious, hopeful **8** enceinte, pregnant, vigilant, watchful **10** breathless, parturient **12** anticipatory, apprehensive

expectation
4 hope **5** hunch **8** prospect **9** assurance, intuition **10** assumption, likelihood **11** presumption, probability **12** anticipation, presentiment

expectorate
4 spit

expediency
5 means **6** resort, tactic **7** aptness, fitness, measure, stopgap **8** meetness, recourse, resource, strategy **9** makeshift, propriety, rightness **11** opportunism, suitability **12** appositeness, practicality, suitableness

expedient
3 fit **5** ad hoc, means, shift **6** resort, timely, useful **7** fitting, politic, prudent, stopgap **8** feasible, recourse, resource, suitable, tactical **9** advisable, judicious, makeshift, opportune, practical, pragmatic, well-timed **10** convenient **11** appropriate, practicable, utilitarian **12** advantageous

expedite
4 send **5** hurry, issue, speed **6** hasten **7** quicken, speed up **8** dispatch **10** accelerate, facilitate

expedition
4 trek, trip **5** hurry, speed **6** voyage **7** journey **8** campaign, dispatch **9** excursion, swiftness **10** efficiency, speediness **11** punctuality

expeditious
4 fast **5** brisk, quick, rapid, swift **6** prompt, speedy **9** efficient **11** efficacious

expeditiousness
5 hurry, speed **6** hustle **8** dispatch

expel
4 boot, oust, spew **5** egest, eject, evict, exile **6** banish, bounce, deport, disbar **7** cast out, dismiss, drum out, kick out, turn out **8** disgorge, displace, throw out **9** discharge, eliminate **10** expatriate

expellee
5 exile **6** émigré **7** outcast **8** deportee, emigrant

expend
3 pay, sap **4** blow **5** drain, spend, use up, waste **6** lay out, outlay, pay out **7** consume, deplete, dig into, dole out, exhaust, fork out, utilize **8** disburse, dispense, shell out, squander **9** dissipate **10** run through

expendable
10 disposable **11** dispensable, inessential, replaceable **12** nonessential

expenditure
4 cost **5** outgo **6** outlay, payoff, payout **12** disbursement

expense
4 cost, loss, toll **5** debit, price **6** burden, charge, outlay **7** forfeit, payment **8** overhead **9** decrement, sacrifice **10** forfeiture **12** disbursement

expensive
4 dear, high, posh **5** fancy, pricy, ritzy, steep, stiff **6** costly, deluxe, lavish, pricey **7** upscale **8** precious, valuable, wasteful **9** big-ticket, luxurious **10** exorbitant, high-priced, overpriced **11** extravagant **12** uneconomical

experience
4 know, live **5** event, savor, skill, trial **6** ordeal, suffer, wisdom **7** episode, know-how, sustain, undergo **8** incident, practice **9** encounter, go through **10** background **11** familiarity, savoir faire
anew: 6 relive

experienced
4 wise **6** mature, versed **7** old-line, veteran, worldly **8** broken in, seasoned **9** practiced, qualified **12** accomplished

experiential
9 empirical, objective

experiment
3 try **4** test **5** assay, probe, trial **6** try out **7** test out **8** research, trial run **13** trial and error

experimental
9 empirical, tentative **10** innovative **11** exploratory, preliminary, preparatory, provisional **13** developmental, trial-and-error

experimentation
4 test **5** trial **7** testing **8** research, trial run **13** trial and error

expert
3 ace, dab, pro, wiz **4** deft, whiz **5** adept, crack, doyen, maven, mavin **6** adroit, master, mayvin, wizard **7** hotshot, skilled **8** masterly, skillful, virtuoso **9** authority, dexterous, masterful, virtuosic **10** past master, proficient, specialist **11** crackerjack **12** passed master, professional

expertise
5 craft, skill 7 ability, command, know-how, mastery 8 facility 10 adroitness, competence 11 proficiency 12 skillfulness

expiate
6 offset, pay for, redeem 7 redress 8 atone for

expiation
9 atonement, indemnity 10 recompense, reparation 11 restitution 12 satisfaction

expiatory
7 atoning, lustral 9 purgative 11 penitential, purgatorial 12 propitiatory

expiration
3 end 5 death 10 exhalation 11 termination

expire
3 die, end 4 pass 5 lapse 6 elapse, exhale, pass on, perish, run out 7 decease 8 pass away 9 terminate 10 breathe out

explain
5 gloss, solve 7 analyze, clarify, clear up, condone, expound, justify, resolve, unravel 8 construe, decipher, spell out, unriddle, untangle 9 break down, elucidate, interpret 10 account for, illuminate, illustrate, unscramble 11 disentangle, rationalize

explain away
6 excuse 7 justify 8 minimize 9 extenuate 10 account for 11 rationalize

explanation
3 key 5 gloss 6 excuse, motive, reason 7 account, example, grounds, meaning 8 exegesis 9 construal, rationale 11 elucidation 12 significance 13 clarification

explanatory
10 discursive, exegetical 12 enlightening, illuminating, illustrative, interpretive

expletive
4 cuss, oath 5 curse, swear 8 cussword 9 swearword 12 interjection (see also **exclamation**)

explicate
7 amplify, develop, explain, expound 8 construe, spell out 9 elucidate, interpret

explication
5 gloss 8 exegesis 9 construal 10 commentary 11 development

explicative
10 discursive, exegetical, scholastic 12 interpretive 13 hermeneutical

explicit
4 open, sure 5 clear, exact, frank, lucid, overt, plain 7 certain, correct, express, obvious, precise 8 clear-cut, definite, distinct, specific 10 definitive 11 categorical, perspicuous, unambiguous, unequivocal

explode
3 pop 4 blow, fire 5 blast, burst, erupt, go off 6 blow up, debunk, negate, refute 7 burgeon, deflate 8 break out, burst out, detonate, disprove, dynamite, mushroom, puncture 9 discharge, discredit 10 burst forth 11 proliferate

exploit
3 act, use 4 coup, deed, feat, gest, play 5 abuse, geste, stunt 6 bestow, effort, employ, parlay, play on 7 emprise, utilize, venture 8 escapade, exercise 9 adventure, cultivate 10 enterprise, manipulate 11 achievement, performance, tour de force

explore
5 probe, scout 6 burrow, go into, search 7 dig into, examine 8 look into, prospect, traverse 9 delve into 11 inquire into, investigate

explorer
African: 3 Cam, Cão (Diogo) 4 Park (Mungo) 5 Grant (James), Laird (Macgregor), Speke (John Hanning) 6 Akeley (Carl, Mary), Burton (Richard), Lander (John, Richard) 7 Covilhã (Pero da), Stanley (Henry) 8 Covilhâo (Pero da) 10 Clapperton (Hugh) 11 Livingstone (David)
American: 4 Byrd (Richard), Hall (Charles Francis), Kane (Elisha Kent), Pike (Zebulon) 5 Beebe (Charles William), Clark (William), Lewis (Meriwether), Peary (Robert) 6 Henson (Matthew), Powell (John Wesley), Wilkes (Charles) 7 Ballard (Robert), Frémont (John Charles)
Antarctic: 4 Byrd (Richard), Cook (Frederick), Ross (James Clark) 5 Fuchs (Vivian), Ronne (Finn), Scott (Robert Falcon) 6 Palmer (Nathaniel), Rymill (John Riddoch), Wilkes (Charles) 7 Weddell (James), Wilkins (George) 8 Amundsen (Roald), d'Urville (Dumont) 9 Ellsworth (Lincoln) 10 Shackleton (Ernest)
Arctic: 3 Rae (John) 4 Byrd (Richard), Cook (Frederick) 5 Davis (John), Peary (Robert) 6 Baffin (William), Bering (Vitus), Henson (Matthew), Hudson (Henry), Nansen (Fridtjof), Nobile (Umberto) 7 Barents (Willem), Bennett (Floyd), Wilkins (George), Wrangel (Ferdinand von) 8 Amundsen (Roald) 9 Mackenzie (Alexander), MacMillan (Donald) 10 Stefansson (Vilhjalmur)
Australian: 7 Wilkins (George)
Austrian: 9 Weyprecht (Carl)
Canadian: 9 Mackenzie (Alexander) 10 Stefansson (Vilhjalmur)
Danish: 9 Rasmussen (Knud)
Dutch: 6 Tasman (Abel Janszoon)
English: 4 Cook (James) 5 Cabot (John, Sebastian), Drake (Francis), Scott (Robert Falcon), Smith (John) 6 Baffin (William), Burton (Richard), Hudson (Henry) 7 Raleigh (Walter), Stanley (Henry) 9 Vancouver (George)

10 **Shackleton** (Ernest) **12** Younghusband (Francis)
fictional: **4** Dora, Nemo (Capt.) **8** Gulliver
French: **7** Cartier (Jacques), La Salle (Sieur de), Nicolet (Jean) **8** Cousteau (Jacques-Yves) **9** Champlain (Samuel de), La Perouse (Comte de), Marquette (Jacques)
French Canadian: **6** Joliet (Louis) **7** Jolliet (Louis) **9** Iberville (Sieur d')
German: **6** Peters (Carl) **8** Humboldt (Alexander von)
Italian: **5** Cabot (John) **6** Nobile (Umberto) **8** Vespucci (Amerigo)
New Zealand: **7** Hillary (Edmund)
Norwegian: **6** Nansen (Fridtjof) **8** Amundsen (Roald), Sverdrup (Otto) **9** Heyerdahl (Thor)
Portuguese: **4** Gama (Vasco da) **5** Cunha (Tristão da) **6** Cabral (Pedro) **8** Cabrilho (João Rodrigues), Magellan (Ferdinand)
Scottish: **3** Rae (John) **4** Park (Mungo), Ross (James Clark) **7** Thomson (Joseph) **11** Livingstone (David)
Spanish: **6** Balboa (Vasco Núñez de), Cortés (Hernán, Hernando), de Soto (Hernando), Pinzón (Martín Alonso, Vicente Yáñez) **7** Mendoza (Pedro de), Pizarro (Francisco) **8** Bastidas (Rodrigo de), Coronado (Francisco de) **11** Ponce de León (Juan)

explosion
3 pop, pow **4** bang, boom, clap **5** blast, burst, crack, crash, sally, salvo, storm **6** report, volley **7** barrage, blowout, torrent **8** eruption, outburst, paroxysm **9** discharge **10** detonation
cosmic: **7** big bang

explosive
3 TNT **5** nitro, tense **6** charge, napalm, petard, powder **7** cordite, violent **8** dynamite **9** gunpowder **13** nitroglycerin
device: **3** cap **4** bomb, mine **5** shell **6** petard **7** grenade **8** firework
inventor: **5** Maxim (Hudson), Nobel (Alfred)
letters: **3** TNT
sound: **3** pop, pow **4** bang, blam, boom **5** crack

exponent
6 backer **7** booster **8** advocate, champion, defender, partisan, promoter, upholder **9** supporter **12** practitioner

expose
3 air **4** bare, open, show **5** dig up, flash **6** debunk, flaunt, parade, reveal, show up, unmask, unveil **7** abandon, display, exhibit, lay open, publish, show off, subject, uncover, undress **8** brandish, disclose, discover, endanger, unclothe

exposé
10 disclosure, revelation, uncovering

exposed
4 bare, open **5** naked **6** liable **7** evident, subject, visible **8** manifest, stripped, unhidden **9** uncovered **11** susceptible, unconcealed, unprotected

exposition
4 fair, show **6** bazaar **7** display, exhibit **9** trade show

expostulate
5 argue **6** debate, reason **7** discuss, dispute

exposure
4 risk **5** peril **6** airing, baring, danger **8** betrayal, jeopardy, openness **9** liability, publicity **10** revelation **12** helplessness **13** vulnerability

expound
5 state **6** defend **7** clarify, comment, explain, present **8** construe, set forth, spell out **9** discourse, explicate, interpret

expounder
7 teacher **8** advocate, champion, defender, promoter **9** proponent, supporter

express
3 air, say **4** mean, tell, vent **5** couch, crush, frame, state, utter, voice **6** broach, convey, denote, impart, intend, voiced **7** connote, declare, signify, special, uttered **8** announce, clear-cut, definite, disclose, explicit, intended, proclaim, specific **9** enunciate, formulate, high-speed, pronounce, symbolize, ventilate **10** definitive, particular **11** categorical, communicate, intentional, unambiguous
gratitude: **5** thank
regret: **9** apologize

expression
4 cast, face, form, look, mien, sign, vent, word **5** idiom, issue, motto, token, voice **6** symbol, visage **7** diction, gesture **8** locution **9** eloquence, statement, utterance, verbalism, vividness **10** embodiment, indication **11** countenance, enunciation, observation **13** demonstration, manifestation
facial: **4** grin, moue, phiz, pout **5** frown, glare, scowl, smile, smirk, sneer, wince **7** grimace
of assent: **3** aye, nod, yea, yes **4** okay
of sorrow: **4** alas, tear
trite: **6** cliché **7** bromide **8** banality
witty: **4** quip **5** sally **6** bon mot

expressionless
5 blank **6** stolid, vacant, wooden **7** deadpan **9** impassive **10** poker-faced **11** inscrutable

expressive
5 vivid **7** graphic **8** eloquent **9** revealing **10** meaningful, passionate

expressly
9 precisely, purposely **10** explicitly **12** particularly, specifically **13** intentionally

expressway
4 road **7** freeway, highway, parkway **8** turnpike **12** thoroughfare

expropriate
4 take **5** annex, seize **7** impound, preempt **8** arrogate **9** sequester **10** commandeer, confiscate, dispossess

expulsion
5 exile, purge **6** ouster **7** ousting, removal **8** ejection, eviction **9** ostracism **10** banishment, relegation **11** deportation **12** displacement

expunge
4 dele, x out **5** annul, erase **6** cancel, delete, efface **7** blot out, destroy, exclude, wipe out **8** black out **9** eliminate, eradicate, strike out **10** annihilate, obliterate

expurgate
4 blip **5** bleep, purge **6** censor, purify, screen **7** cleanse **8** sanitize **10** bowdlerize

expurgation
8 ablution **9** catharsis, cleansing **10** lustration **12** purification

exquisite
3 fop **4** fine, keen, rare **5** acute, dandy **6** choice, dainty, select, superb **7** coxcomb, elegant, extreme, intense, refined **8** delicate, finished, flawless, macaroni **9** recherché **10** fastidious, immaculate, impeccable

exsiccate
3 dry **4** bake, sear **5** parch, wizen **6** wither **7** shrivel **9** dehydrate

extant
4 live **5** alive **6** actual, living **7** current, present **9** surviving **10** present-day **12** contemporary

extemporaneous
5 ad-lib **6** casual **7** offhand **8** ad-libbed, informal **9** impromptu, impulsive, makeshift, unplanned **10** improvised, unprepared, unscripted **11** spontaneous, unrehearsed **12** unthought-out

extempore
see **extemporaneous**

extemporize
5 ad-lib **6** wing it **7** dash off, toss off **8** knock off **9** improvise

extend
4 draw, span, vary **5** award, offer, range, reach **6** bestow, spread, unbend, unfold **7** advance, augment, broaden, drag out, draw out, enlarge, further, hold out, proceed, proffer, project, prolong, spin out, stretch **8** continue, elongate, increase, lengthen, protract **10** outstretch, stretch out

extension
3 arm, ell **4** wing **5** add-on, annex, delay, range, reach, scope, sweep **6** radius, spread **7** adjunct, compass, purview **8** addition, increase **9** appendage, magnitude **10** broadening, elongation **11** enlargement, lengthening, protraction **12** augmentation, continuation, postponement, prolongation

extensity
5 ambit, orbit, range, reach, scope, sweep **6** radius **7** compass, purview

extensive
3 big **4** long, vast, wide **5** broad, large, major **7** general, immense, lengthy, sizable **8** far-flung, sizeable, spacious, sweeping, thorough **9** wholesale **10** large-scale, widespread **11** far-reaching, wide-ranging **12** considerable

extent
4 size **5** ambit, limit, orbit, range, reach, scope, sweep, width **6** amount, degree, domain, radius **7** breadth, compass, measure, purview **8** vicinity **9** magnitude **10** dimensions, proportion

extenuate
6 dilute, excuse, lessen, soften, temper, weaken **7** explain, justify, qualify, varnish **8** diminish, enervate, mitigate, moderate, palliate **9** gloss over **11** rationalize

exterior
4 skin **5** outer, shell **6** facade **7** outmost, outside, outward, surface **8** apparent **9** outermost **11** superficial

exterminate
4 kill **6** rub out **7** destroy, wipe out **8** massacre **9** eliminate, eradicate, finish off, liquidate, slaughter **10** annihilate, extinguish, obliterate

external
3 out **4** over **5** outer **7** foreign, outside, outward, surface **9** outermost **10** peripheral **11** superficial

externalize
4 show **6** embody, evince, excuse, expose, reveal **7** display, exhibit, justify **8** manifest **9** extenuate, incarnate, objectify, personify **11** rationalize **12** substantiate

extinct
4 cold, dead, gone, late **5** passé **6** bygone **7** archaic, defunct **8** deceased, departed, obsolete, perished, vanished **10** superseded
bird: 3 moa **4** dodo
mammal: 6 quagga **7** aurochs, mammoth **8** dire wolf **10** sabertooth

extinction
3 end **4** doom **5** death **6** demise **11** destruction, eradication, liquidation **12** annihilation, obliteration **13** disappearance, extermination

extinguish
3 end **5** crush, douse, erase, quash, quell, snuff **6** put out, quench, squash, stifle **7** abolish, blot out, blow out, destroy, eclipse, expunge, nullify, put down, wipe out **8** snuff out, stamp out, suppress **9** eliminate, eradicate, extirpate **10** annihilate, obliterate

extirpate
5 erase **6** cut out, efface, excise, resect, uproot **7** abolish, blot out, destroy, expunge, kill off, root out, wipe out **8** demolish **9** eliminate, eradicate **10** annihilate, deracinate, extinguish

extol
4 hymn, laud **5** cry up, exalt **6** praise **7** acclaim, applaud, commend, glorify, magnify **8** eulogize **9** celebrate **10** panegyrize

extort
5 gouge, wrest, wring **6** coerce **7** extract

extortion
8 exaction **9** blackmail

extra
3 odd **4** more, over, perk, plus **5** added, add-on, bonus, spare **6** de trop, excess, rarely **7** overage, reserve, surplus **8** leftover **9** lagniappe, redundant, unusually **10** additional, especially, perquisite **11** superfluous **12** particularly, supplemental **13** supernumerary, supplementary

extract
4 pull, yank **5** evoke, glean, quote, wring **6** derive, eke out, elicit, remove **7** abridge, distill, essence, excerpt, passage, pull out, squeeze, take out **8** citation, condense, infusion **9** quotation, selection **11** concentrate

extraction
5 birth, blood, stock **6** origin **7** descent, essence, lineage **8** ancestry, pedigree **9** parentage **10** derivation **12** distillation

extraneous
5 alien, outer **6** exotic **7** foreign, outside **8** external **9** unrelated **10** immaterial, inapposite, incidental, irrelevant, peripheral **11** impertinent, inessential, superfluous, unessential **12** adventitious, inapplicable, nonessential

extraordinary
3 odd **4** rare **6** unique **7** amazing, notable, special, unusual **8** abnormal, atypical, singular, terrific, uncommon, unwonted **9** wonderful **10** noteworthy, phenomenal, remarkable, stupendous, tremendous **11** exceptional, outstanding

extraterrestrial
5 alien

extravagance
5 frill, waste **6** excess, luxury **9** hyperbole, profusion **10** indulgence, lavishness **11** ostentation, prodigality, superfluity **12** immoderation, wastefulness

extravagant
4 wild **5** outré, undue **6** lavish **7** bizarre, extreme, profuse **8** overdone, prodigal, reckless, wasteful **9** elaborate, excessive, fantastic, grandiose, overblown **10** exorbitant, hyperbolic, immoderate, inordinate, profligate **11** exaggerated, implausible, intemperate, nonsensical **12** ostentatious, preposterous, unrestrained

extreme
3 max, nth, top **4** apex, dire, last, peak, wild **5** crown, final, limit, ultra, undue **6** climax, excess, height, summit, utmost, zenith **7** drastic, fanatic, intense, maximal, maximum, outmost, radical, violent **8** farthest, furthest, pinnacle, remotest, ultimate **9** desperate, excessive, outermost, uttermost **10** immoderate, inordinate, outlandish, outrageous **11** furthermost, unwarranted **12** unmeasurable, unreasonable **13** revolutionary
degree: 3 nth

extremely
4 mega, most, unco, very **5** ultra **6** highly, hugely, mighty, overly, plenty, wildly **7** acutely, awfully, greatly, utterly **8** severely, terribly **9** immensely, seriously, unusually **10** remarkably, strikingly **11** exceedingly **12** terrifically

extremist
5 rabid, ultra **6** zealot **7** die-hard, fanatic, radical **8** militant, ultraist **9** fanatical **10** monomaniac, ultraistic **11** reactionary **13** revolutionary

extremity
3 arm, end, leg, tip **4** acme, apex, foot, hand, tail **5** limit, verge **6** apogee, vertex, zenith **8** terminal, terminus

extricate
4 free **5** loose **6** detach, redeem, rescue **7** bail out, deliver, resolve, set free, untwine **8** liberate, untangle **9** disengage **11** disencumber, disentangle, distinguish, individuate **12** discriminate, disembarrass **13** differentiate

extrinsic
5 alien, outer **6** exotic **7** foreign, outside, outward **8** exterior, external, imported **10** incidental, extraneous

extrude
4 spew **5** eject **7** push out **8** press out **10** squeeze out

exuberance
4 glee, life, zest **5** ardor **6** gaiety, spirit **7** abandon **8** buoyancy, hilarity, vivacity **9** profusion **10** ebullience, enthusiasm, friskiness, liveliness **11** flamboyance, high spirits, zestfulness **12** exhilaration **13** effervescence, sprightliness

exuberant
3 gay **4** lush, rank **5** happy **6** bouncy, elated, fecund, hearty, lavish, lively **7** buoyant, profuse, rampant, riotous, zestful **8** fruitful, prodigal, prolific, spirited **9** ebullient, luxuriant, sprightly, vivacious **10** flamboyant **11** exhilarated **12** effervescent, enthusiastic, high-spirited

exude
4 emit, leak, ooze, seep, shed **5** issue **7** diffuse, display, emanate, excrete, exhibit, give off, ooze out, radiate, secrete **9** discharge

exult
4 crow **5** cheer, gloat, glory, revel **7** delight, rejoice **8** jubilate **9** celebrate

exultant
6 elated, joyful, joyous **7** gleeful **8** ecstatic, euphoric, jubilant **9** cock-a-hoop, overjoyed, rejoicing, triumphal **10** triumphant **11** over the moon

exultation
3 joy **4** glee **7** delight, ecstasy, elation, rapture, triumph **8** euphoria, gloating **9** jubilance, rejoicing **10** jubilation

Exxon predecessor
4 Esso **11** Standard Oil

eye
3 orb **4** lamp, ogle, scan, view **5** sight, watch **6** behold, goggle, look at, ocular, oculus, peeper, regard, size up, vision **7** inspect, observe **8** check out, consider, gaze upon, scrutiny **9** headlight **10** scrutinize
combining form: **4** ocul, opia **5** oculo **8** ophthalm **9** ophthalmo
defect: **6** myopia **9** hyperopia **10** emmetropia, presbyopia **11** astigmatism
disease: **8** cataract, glaucoma, trachoma
doctor: **7** oculist **11** optometrist
lasciviously: **4** leer, ogle
layer: **4** uvea
opening: **5** pupil
part: **4** iris, lens, uvea **5** pupil **6** cornea, retina, sclera
relating to: **5** optic **7** optical
socket: **5** orbit
Spanish: **3** ojo
test: **10** Amsler Grid **12** Snellen Chart

eyeball
4 scan **5** check, study **6** go over, look at, peruse, survey **7** examine, inspect, observe **8** appraise, check out, evaluate, pore over **10** scrutinize

eye-catching
4 bold **5** gaudy, showy **6** flashy **7** salient **8** striking **9** arresting, prominent **10** noticeable, remarkable **11** conspicuous

eyeful
6 looker **7** stunner **8** knockout

eyeglass
7 monocle **9** lorgnette

eyeglasses
5 specs **6** lenses **7** lorgnon **8** bifocals, pince-nez **9** lorgnette **10** spectacles

eyelash
6 cilium **11** hairbreadth

eyelet
4 hole **7** grommet **8** loophole, peephole

eyelid growth
3 sty **4** cyst, stye **5** nevus **9** chalazion, hordeolum

eyepiece
4 lens **5** loupe **6** ocular

eye-popping
7 amazing **8** exciting, stirring **9** thrilling **10** astounding **11** astonishing, mind-blowing, spectacular **12** breathtaking

eyesore
4 blot, dump, mess **6** blight **7** blemish **8** atrocity **11** monstrosity

eyespot
6 blight, fungus **7** ocellus

eyetooth
6 canine

eyewash
3 rot **4** bunk **5** bilge, hooey, tripe **6** bunkum **7** baloney, garbage, hogwash, rubbish, twaddle **8** malarkey, nonsense **9** poppycock **10** balderdash **13** horsefeathers

eyewitness
8 observer, onlooker **9** bystander, spectator

eyrie
4 nest
resident: **4** eyas **5** eagle **6** eaglet

F

Fabergé product
3 egg **9** Easter egg

Fabian
4 Shaw (George Bernard), Webb (Beatrice, Sidney) **7** politic **8** cautious, dilatory **9** socialist **11** circumspect, calculating

fable
4 myth, tale, yarn **5** story **6** legend **7** fantasy, fiction, figment, parable **8** allegory, tall tale
animal: **8** bestiary
conclusion: **5** moral

fabled
5 famed **6** famous, unreal **7** storied **8** fanciful, mythical, renowned **9** fictional, imaginary, legendary, pretended **10** fictitious **11** make-believe **12** mythological
bird: **3** roc

fabric
3 aba, rep, web **4** lamé, repp **5** cloth, fiber, grain **7** texture **8** building, material, shirting **9** structure
coarse: **4** tapa **5** crash, gunny **6** burlap, linsey, ratiné **7** cheviot, hopsack, sacking **8** homespun

colorer: **4** dyer
corded: **3** rep **4** repp **5** piqué **6** calico, dimity, moreen, poplin **7** pinwale **8** corduroy, paduasoy **9** bengaline
cotton: **4** jean, leno **5** baize, chino, denim, domet, drill, lisle, scrim, wigan **6** chintz, dimity, faille, madras, muslin, sateen **7** etamine, gingham, nankeen, percale, ticking **8** chambray, dungaree, nainsook, tarlatan **9** crinoline **10** seersucker
cotton and linen: **4** huck **7** fustian **9** huckaback
crepe: **8** marocain
dealer: **6** draper, mercer
durable: **4** huck, jean **5** chino, denim, drill, scrim **6** frieze, moreen **7** lasting, ticking **8** cretonne, dungaree
embroidered: **9** baldachin **10** baldachino
finishing process: **8** lustring **9** mercerize
flag material: **7** bunting
glazed: **4** ciré **6** chintz **7** cambric, holland
knitted: **6** tricot **10** balbriggan
linen: **7** cambric, lockram
looped: **6** bouclé
lustrous: **4** silk **5** moiré, satin, surah **6** sateen **7** taffeta **12** brilliantine
metallic: **4** lamé
net: **5** tulle **8** bobbinet, illusion
openwork: **4** lace **8** filigree
ornamental: **4** lace **5** braid **6** ribbon **7** bunting
pebbly-surface: **8** barathea
pile-surface: **5** panne, plush, terry **6** velour, velvet **7** duvetyn, velours **8** chenille, moleskin **9** velveteen
plaid: **6** tartan
pleated: **5** ruche
printed: **5** batik, toile **6** calico, chintz, damask **7** allover, challis **8** cretonne, jacquard **11** toile de Jouy
puckered: **6** plissé **10** seersucker
raised pattern: **4** lamé **7** brocade **10** brocatelle
satin weave: **5** panne
sheer: **4** lawn, mull **5** gauze, ninon, voile **6** dimity **7** batiste, chiffon, organdy, organza, tiffany **8** tarlatan
silk: **6** faille, pongee, samite **7** foulard, grogram **8** paduasoy, sarcenet, sarsenet, shantung **9** bombazine
stretch: **5** Lycra **7** spandex **8** elastane
striped: **3** aba **7** ticking **8** bayadere
synthetic: **5** Arnel, ninon, nylon, Orlon, rayon **6** Dacron
trim: **5** ruche
twill: **4** jean **5** chino, drill, serge **7** foulard, nankeen, ticking **8** dungaree, shalloon **9** bombazine **10** broadcloth
unfinished: **6** greige
waterproof: **7** oilskin
wool: **5** baize, loden, tweed **6** alpaca, caddis, camlet, duffel, duffle, melton, merino, wadmal, wadmel, wadmol, woolen **7** woollen **8** mackinaw, prunella **9** cassimere
wool, poor quality: **5** mungo **6** shoddy
wool mixture: **6** saxony **7** drugget, ratteen **8** moquette, shalloon, zibeline **9** zibelline
woven: **4** weft **7** textile

fabricate
4 coin, fake, form, make **5** build, erect, frame, set up, shape **6** cook up, create, devise, invent, make up **7** concoct, dream up, fashion, produce, think up **8** assemble, contrive **9** construct, structure **11** manufacture, put together

fabrication
3 fib, lie **4** bull, jive **6** canard, deceit **7** fiction, figment, hogwash, product, untruth **8** assembly, building, creation **9** deception, fairy tale, falsehood, invention **10** concoction, production **11** manufacture **12** construction

fabulist
4 liar
French: **10** La Fontaine (Jean de)
Greek: **5** Aesop
Roman: **8** Phaedrus
Russian: **6** Krylov (Ivan)

fabulous
5 super **7** amazing **8** mythical, terrific, wondrous **9** fantastic, legendary, marvelous, wonderful **10** astounding, fictitious, incredible, outrageous, phenomenal, prodigious, remarkable, stupendous **11** astonishing, extravagant, spectacular **12** mythological
animal: **6** dragon **7** centaur, unicorn
bird: **3** roc
serpent: **8** basilisk **10** cockatrice

facade
4 face, mask **5** color, front, guise, put-on **6** veneer **8** disguise, exterior, frontage, pretense **10** appearance, camouflage, false front

face
3 mug, pan **4** dare, defy, dial, meet, phiz, puss, show, side **5** abide, brave, front, guise, honor, image, nerve **6** endure, facade, kisser, makeup, mazard, oppose, resist, suffer, take on, visage **7** compete, contend, dignity, surface **8** confront, cope with, deal with, disguise, features, prestige, war paint **9** assurance, encounter, lineament, semblance, withstand **10** appearance, confidence, experience, expression, maquillage, reputation **11** countenance, self-respect

face-off
5 clash, set-to **13** confrontation

facet
4 edge, item, part, side **5** angle, bezel, front,

phase, plane, point, trait **6** aspect, detail **7** element, feature, surface **9** attribute, component **10** appearance, particular

facetious
4 flip **5** comic, droll, jokey, smart, witty **6** blithe, breezy, joking **7** amusing, comical, jesting, jocular, joshing, kidding, risible, waggish **8** flippant, humorous **9** ludicrous, unserious, whimsical **10** irreverent, ridiculous **12** wisecracking **13** tongue-in-cheek

face-to-face
6 direct **7** contact, present, vis-à-vis **8** directly, in person, personal **10** personally

facile
4 deft, easy, glib, snap **5** light, quick, ready **6** adroit, expert, fluent, poised, simple, smooth **7** assured, cursory, offhand, shallow, voluble **8** skillful, untaxing **9** dexterous **10** effortless, simplistic **13** uncomplicated

facilitate
3 aid **4** abet, ease, help **6** assist, enable, smooth **7** advance, forward, further, promote **8** expedite, make easy, simplify

facility
3 aid, wit **4** bent, ease **5** knack, privy, skill **6** talent, toilet **7** ability, amenity, comfort, fluency, leaning **8** aptitude, bathroom, building, capacity, lavatory, washroom **9** advantage, dexterity **10** adroitness, competence, smoothness **11** convenience, institution, proficiency **12** installation **13** accommodation, establishment

facing
5 front, panel **6** contra, lining, toward, veneer **7** surface, vis-à-vis **8** covering, opposite, paneling **11** over against
down: 5 prone
up: 6 supine

facsimile
4 copy, dupe, fake, twin **5** clone, ditto, match, mimeo, repro, Xerox **6** carbon, double **7** replica **8** knockoff, likeness **9** duplicate, imitation, photocopy **10** carbon copy, dead ringer, similitude **11** counterpart, duplication, replication **12** reproduction

fact
4 dope **5** datum, event, truth **6** detail, gospel, truism, verity **7** episode, reality **8** evidence, incident **9** actuality **10** occurrence, particular, phenomenon **11** information **12** circumstance, intelligence

faction
4 band, bloc, camp, part, ring, sect, side, wing **5** cabal, group, party **6** caucus, circle, clique, sector, strife **7** combine, coterie, discord, section **8** alliance, disunity, splinter **10** contingent

factious
7 warring **8** contrary, divisive, partisan **9** dissident, insurgent, sectarian, seditious, turbulent **10** contending, malcontent **11** contentious, disaffected, dissentious, quarrelsome **12** disputatious **13** troublemaking

factitious
4 sham **5** bogus, false, phony **6** ersatz, forced, made-up, unreal **7** assumed, created, feigned, man-made, shammed **8** affected, invented, spurious **9** concocted, contrived, fashioned, pretended, simulated, synthetic, unnatural **10** artificial, fabricated **11** constructed, counterfeit **12** manufactured **13** counterfeited

____ facto
4 ipso **6** ex post

factor
4 gene, item **5** agent, cause, proxy **6** broker, lender, number, symbol **7** divisor, element, exclude, include, resolve **8** attorney, emissary, quantity **9** component, majordomo, substance **10** antecedent, ingredient, multiplier **11** determinant **12** intermediary

factory
4 mill, shop **5** plant, works **8** workshop **9** sweatshop **11** machine shop

factotum
4 grub **5** gofer **6** drudge **7** servant **9** assistant, gal Friday, man Friday, operative **11** functionary

factual
4 real, true **5** exact, valid **6** actual **7** certain, genuine, literal **8** absolute, positive **9** authentic, undoubted **10** undisputed **12** indisputable

faculty
4 bent, body, gift **5** flair, knack, power **6** talent **7** ability, college **8** aptitude, capacity, facility, function, instinct **9** educators, lecturers **10** department, professors **11** instructors

fad
4 chic, kick, mode, rage, whim **5** craze, furor, mania, style, trend **6** furore, latest, whimsy **7** caprice, fashion **9** bandwagon **10** dernier cri

faddish
3 hot **4** chic **5** today **6** modish, red-hot, trendy, with-it **7** stylish, voguish **8** contempo **9** au courant **11** cutting-edge, fashionable

fade
3 die, dim, ebb **4** fail, pale, wane, wilt **6** lessen, vanish, weaken, wither **7** decline, lighten, wash out **8** decrease, discolor, diminish **9** disappear, evaporate

faded
3 dim, wan **4** drab, dull, pale **6** pallid **8** bleached, vanished, withered **9** etiolated, washed-out

Faerie Queene, The
author: **7** Spenser (Edmund)
character: **3** Ate, Una **4** Alma **5** Guyon, Irena, Talus **6** Abessa, Amavia, Amoret, Arthur, Cambel, Duessa, Palmer **7** Artegal, Corceca, Fidessa, Maleger, Sansloy **8** Calidore, Florimel, Fradubio, Gloriana, Lucifera, Orgoglio, Satyrane **9** Archimago, Britomart **11** Britomartis

Fafnir
6 dragon
brother: **5** Regin **6** Fasolt, Reginn
father: **8** Hreidmar
slayer: **6** Sigurd **9** Siegfried
victim: **6** Fasolt **8** Hreidmar

fa follower
3 sol

fag
4 do in, moil, tire, toil **5** serve, smoke, stick, weary **6** drudge, overdo, tucker **7** exhaust, fatigue, servant, wear out **8** drudgery, knock out **9** cigarette

fag end
4 butt, edge, fray **7** remnant

faience
7 pottery **11** earthenware

fail
3 die, end **4** bomb, fade, lack, lose, miss, sink, slip, stop, wane **5** break, flunk **6** fizzle, forget, ignore, lessen, weaken **7** decline, default, founder, give out, go under, neglect **8** fall flat, languish, miscarry **9** break down, fall short **10** disappoint, go bankrupt **11** deteriorate
to include: **4** omit

failing
4 flaw, vice **5** fault **6** defect **8** weakness **9** weak point **10** deficiency **11** shortcoming **12** imperfection

failure
3 bum, dud **4** bomb, bust, flop, miss **5** decay, loser **6** fiasco, fizzle, no-good, outage **7** default, washout **8** collapse, fracture, omission **9** breakdown, cessation, oversight, unconcern **10** bankruptcy, deficiency, insolvency, negligence **11** defalcation, dysfunction, miscarriage **12** interruption **13** deterioration

fain
3 apt **5** eager, prone, ready **6** gladly, minded **7** willing **8** amenable, inclined **9** agreeable

fainéant
3 bum **4** idle, lazy **5** idler, sloth **6** loafer, torpid **7** goof-off, slacker **8** deadbeat, inactive, indolent, layabout, slothful, sluggard, sluggish **9** do-nothing, lazybones, shiftless **11** couch potato, ineffectual **13** lackadaisical

faint
3 dim, low, wan **4** hazy, pale, soft, weak, wilt **5** dizzy, light, plotz, swoon, vague, woozy **6** feeble, subtle **7** conk out, obscure, pass out, shadowy, syncope, unclear **8** black out, collapse, keel over **9** undefined **10** ill-defined, indistinct

fainthearted
5 timid **6** craven **7** fearful **8** cowardly, timorous

fair
3 due **4** even, expo, fine, join, just, mild, okay, open, so-so **5** blond, bonny, clear, equal, fresh, light, sunny **6** bazaar, blonde, comely, decent, honest, kermis, lovely, market, pretty, square **7** cricket **8** adequate, all right, balanced, carnival, festival, mediocre, middling, pleasant, pleasing, rational, sunshiny, unbiased **9** beautiful, cloudless, equitable, favorable, fortunate, impartial, objective, tolerable, trade show, unclouded **10** acceptable, attractive, evenhanded, exhibition, exposition, open-minded, reasonable **11** indifferent, nonpartisan, respectable **12** satisfactory, unprejudiced **13** disinterested, dispassionate, sportsmanlike

fair food
10 candy apple, candy floss, fried dough, funnel cake **11** cotton candy, elephant ear

fair-haired
3 pet **5** blond **6** blonde **7** beloved, darling, favored **8** favorite **9** fortunate

fairly
5 quite **6** nearly, rather **7** plainly **8** passably, properly, somewhat **9** tolerably **10** acceptably, deservedly, distinctly, moderately, reasonably **11** practically

fairness
6 candor, equity **7** honesty **8** justness **9** good faith **12** impartiality

fairy
3 elf, imp, nix **4** peri, puck **5** elfin, nixie, nymph, pixie, sylph **6** goblin, kobold, sprite **7** brownie, gremlin **10** leprechaun
king: **6** Oberon
queen: **3** Mab **4** Oona **7** Titania **8** Gloriana
shoemaker: **10** leprechaun

fairy tale
author: **4** Lang (Andrew) **5** Grimm (Jacob, Wilhelm), Wilde (Oscar) **7** Kipling (Rudyard) **8** Andersen (Hans Christian), Perrault (Charles)
character: **4** Jack, Puck **6** Gretel, Hansel **8** Rapunzel, Tom Thumb **9** Snow White **10** Cinderella, Goldilocks, Thumbelina
monster: **4** ogre

faith
4 cult, sect **5** credo, creed, stock, troth, trust **6** belief, church, credit **8** credence, reliance, religion **9** certainty, certitude, communion, credulity **10** confidence, persuasion **12** denomination
article of: **5** tenet

faithful
4 fast, just, true **5** liege, loyal, pious, tried **6** steady, trusty **7** devoted, dutiful, staunch **8** constant, follower, reliable, resolute, true-blue **9** religious, steadfast **10** dependable, scrupulous, unwavering **11** truehearted, trustworthy

faithfulness
5 piety, troth **6** fealty **7** loyalty **8** devotion, fidelity **9** adherence, constancy **10** allegiance, attachment

faithless
5 false, Punic **6** fickle, untrue **8** disloyal, recreant **10** perfidious, traitorous **11** treacherous **13** untrustworthy

faithlessness
7 perfidy, treason **8** betrayal **9** falseness, treachery **10** disloyalty, infidelity

fake
3 act, gyp **4** hoax, mock, sham **5** bluff, bogus, false, feign, fraud, phony, pseud, put on, spoof **6** affect, doctor, ersatz, forged, framed, humbug, pseudo **7** falsify, pretend **8** impostor, invented, simulate, spurious **9** brummagem, charlatan, concocted, fabricate, imitation, imposture, pinchbeck, pretended, simulated **10** artificial, fabricated, fictitious, fraudulent, simulation **11** counterfeit
combining form: **5** pseud **6** pseudo

faker
4 sham **5** fraud, phony, quack **6** con man, hoaxer **8** deceiver, impostor **9** charlatan, con artist, pretender **10** mountebank **11** four-flusher **12** double-dealer **13** confidence man

fakir
7 ascetic, dervish **9** mendicant

falafel holder
4 pita, wrap **5** pitta

Falco of Sopranos fame
4 Edie

falcon
4 hawk **5** hobby, saker **6** lanner, merlin **7** kestrel **9** peregrine
eye cover: **4** seel
male: **4** jack **6** tercel **7** tiercel **8** lanneret
mature: **7** haggard
young: **4** eyas

falcon-headed god
4 Ment **5** Horus, Mentu **6** Sokari **7** Sokaris

falconry
7 hawking
equipment: **4** bell, hood, jess, lure
procedure: **3** imp **4** cope, seel

Falkland Islands
capital: **7** Stanley
claimant: **9** Argentina
colony of: **7** Britain

fall
3 dip, ebb, sag **4** dive, drip, drop, dump, hang, plop, sink, slip, trip, wane **5** abate, crash, lapse, slide, slump, spill **6** autumn, drowse, give up, go down, header, plunge, sprawl, tumble **7** cascade, decline, descend, descent, devolve, go under, plummet, scatter, stumble, subside **8** collapse, decrease, diminish, keel over, nose-dive **9** hairpiece **10** depreciate **11** precipitate

fallacious
6 untrue **7** invalid **8** delusive, delusory **9** deceitful, deceptive, erroneous, sophistic **10** fraudulent

fallacy
5 error **6** canard **7** falsity, sophism, untruth **8** delusion **9** falsehood **11** non sequitur **13** misconception

fall apart
6 lose it **7** crumble **9** break down, decompose **10** go to pieces **11** come unglued, deteriorate **12** disintegrate

fall back
3 ebb, lag **6** recede, recoil, retire **7** retract, retreat **8** withdraw **9** disengage, retrocede **10** retrograde

fall behind
3 lag, owe **4** drag **5** delay, tarry, trail **6** dawdle, linger, loiter

fall flat
4 bomb, fail, flop, miss **6** fizzle

fall flower
5 aster

fall guy
4 dupe, fool, goat, gull **5** chump, front, patsy **6** stooge, sucker **8** front man **9** scapegoat **11** whipping boy

fallible
4 iffy, weak **5** dicey, frail, human **6** errant, erring, faulty **9** imperfect **10** unreliable

falling-out
3 row **4** beef, feud, fuss, spat, tiff **5** break, run-in, words **6** bicker, fracas, hassle **7** dispute, quarrel, rhubarb, wrangle **8** argument, conflict, squabble **9** brannigan **11** altercation, controversy **12** disagreement, estrangement

falloff
3 sag **4** drop, slip **5** slump **7** decline **8** downturn **9** downslide, downswing, downtrend **13** deterioration

Fall of the House of Usher author
3 Poe (Edgar Allan)

fall out
5 argue, break, leave, occur **6** bicker **7** brabble, quarrel, wrangle **8** disagree, squabble

fallow
4 idle **5** inert **6** unsown **7** dormant, resting **8** inactive, unseeded, untilled **9** neglected, quiescent, unplanted **12** uncultivated

false
4 fake, faux, mock, sham **5** bogus, dummy, hokey, lying, phony, wrong **6** ersatz, forged, hollow, pseudo, untrue **7** crooked, devious, feigned, seeming, unloyal **8** apostate, apparent, deluding, delusive, delusory, disloyal, recreant, specious, spurious **9** brummagem, deceitful, deceiving, deceptive, dishonest, distorted, erroneous, faithless, illogical, imitation, incorrect, pinchbeck, simulated **10** artificial, fictitious, fraudulent, inaccurate, misleading, perfidious, traitorous, unfaithful, untruthful **11** counterfeit, treacherous
combining form: **5** pseud **6** pseudo

falsehood
3 fib, lie **5** fable **6** canard **7** fallacy, fiction, untruth, whopper **8** roorback **9** mendacity **11** fabrication **12** misstatement **13** prevarication

falseness
6 deceit **7** fallacy, perfidy **8** apostasy **9** treachery **10** disloyalty, infidelity **11** insincerity

false teeth
8 dentures

falsify
3 fib, lie **4** cook, deny **5** belie, fudge, slant **6** doctor, refute **7** deceive, distort, mislead **8** disprove, misstate **10** contradict **11** prevaricate **12** misrepresent

falsity
3 fib, lie **4** tale, yarn **5** fable **6** canard **7** untruth, whopper **9** falsehood, mendacity **11** fabrication **13** prevarication

Falstaff
companion: **3** Nym **4** Peto **6** Pistol **8** Bardolph
composer: **5** Verdi (Giuseppe)
creator: **11** Shakespeare (William)
drink: **4** sack
play: **7** Henry IV
prince: **3** Hal
tavern: **9** Boar's Head

Falstaffian
3 fat **5** obese **6** jovial **7** roguish **8** boastful **9** convivial, dissolute

falter
4 halt, limp, reel, sway, trip **5** quail, waver **6** flinch, teeter, totter, wobble **7** give way, stagger, stammer, stumble **8** hesitate **9** vacillate **12** shilly-shally

fame
4 note **5** éclat, glory, honor, kudos **6** esteem, regard, renown, repute **7** acclaim, stardom **8** standing **9** celebrity, notoriety **10** popularity, prominence, reputation **11** acclamation, immortality, recognition

famed
5 noted **6** marked **7** eminent, notable **8** renowned **9** notorious, prominent, well-known **10** celebrated **11** illustrious **13** distinguished

familiar
4 cozy **6** common, folksy **8** domestic, everyday, frequent, informal, intimate, standard **10** accustomed **11** comfortable, commonplace **12** conventional, recognizable **13** garden-variety
with: **4** onto

familiarity
4 ease **8** intimacy **9** closeness, knowledge **11** informality **12** acquaintance

family
3 kin **4** clan, folk, home, line, race **5** brood, folks, house, issue, stirp, stock, tribe **6** ménage, strain **7** dynasty, kindred, lineage, progeny **8** pedigree **9** bloodline, household, offspring
branch: **5** stirp
car: **5** sedan
lineage: **4** tree **6** stemma **7** kinship **8** pedigree **9** genealogy

Family Guy creator MacFarlane
4 Seth

famine
4 want **6** dearth, hunger **10** starvation

famished
6 hungry **7** starved **8** ravenous, starving

famous
5 famed, noble, noted **6** fabled **7** eminent, notable, popular **8** historic, renowned **9** legendary, notorious, prominent, well-known **10** celebrated **11** illustrious, prestigious, redoubtable

fan
3 bug, nut **4** blow, buff, open, wind **5** freak, lover, maven, rouse **6** addict, arouse, expand, extend, kindle, rooter, ruffle, spread, stir up, unfold, votary, whip up, winnow **7** admirer, devotee, habitué **8** adherent, enkindle, follower, railbird **9** stimulate **10** aficionado, enthusiast
dance: **11** balletomane
horseracing: **7** turfman
India: **6** punkah
movie: **7** cineast **8** cineaste **9** cinephile

fanatic
3 bug, nut **4** buff **5** fiend, freak, rabid **6** addict, maniac, votary, zealot **7** devotee, die-hard, habitué **10** aficionado, enthusiast

fanatical
5 fiery, rabid **6** ardent, fervid **7** extreme, fervent, zealous **8** frenetic, frenzied, maniacal, obsessed **9** perfervid **10** passionate **11** impassioned

fanaticism
4 zeal **5** mania **6** frenzy **8** zealotry **9** extremism, monomania, obsession

fancier
6 grower **7** amateur, admirer, breeder, devotee

fanciful
6 absurd, unreal **7** bizarre, fictive **8** fabulous, illusory, imagined, mythical, notional, romantic

9 fantastic, fictional, grotesque, imaginary **10** chimerical, fictitious **11** fantastical **12** preposterous

fancy
3 bee, fad **4** idea, like, posh, whim **5** dream, ritzy, shine, smart, taste **6** dressy, liking, megrim, notion, relish, snazzy, swanky, vision, whimsy **7** caprice, chimera, conceit, concept, dream up, elegant, fantasy, feature, imagine, picture **8** conceive, daydream, envision, fondness, judgment, velleity **9** capriccio, elaborate, intricate, inventive, visualize, whimsical **10** decorative, ornamental, partiality, propensity **11** extravagant, highfalutin, imagination, inclination

fandango
5 dance **9** malaguena

fanfare
4 pomp, show, ta-da **5** array, ta-dah **6** hoopla **7** display, hooplah, panoply **8** ballyhoo, flourish
trumpet: **6** tucket **7** tantara

fanlike
7 plicate

Fannie ___
3 Mae

fanny
3 bum, can **4** buns, butt, duff, moon, rear, rump, seat, tail, tush **5** booty, nates **6** behind, bottom, breech, heinie **7** caboose, hind end, keister, rear end, tail end **8** backside, buttocks, derriere **9** fundament, posterior

fan-tan
6 sevens

fantasia
6 vision **8** daydream, illusion, rhapsody **9** fairyland **10** apparition

fantasize
4 moon **5** dream, fancy **7** imagine **8** daydream **10** woolgather

fantastic
3 odd **4** wild **6** absurd, unreal **7** bizarre, surreal **8** fanciful, singular **9** eccentric, grotesque, imaginary, marvelous, monstrous, unearthly, whimsical **10** chimerical, far-fetched, improbable, incredible, outlandish, outrageous, prodigious, stupendous, tremendous **11** implausible, nonsensical, sensational, superlative **12** preposterous, unbelievable

Fantastic Mr. Fox author
5 Roald (Dahl)

fantasy
4 moon, whim **5** dream, fancy, freak **6** vagary, vision, whimsy **7** caprice, chimera, fiction, reverie **8** daydream, delusion, phantasm **9** imagining, invention, pipe dream **10** bizarrerie **11** imagination **12** grotesquerie

far
4 long **6** remote **7** distant **8** outlying
combining form: **3** tel **4** tele, telo

far and wide
7 all over **10** everyplace, everywhere, throughout

faraway
4 lost **5** moony **6** absent, dreamy, remote **7** distant, removed **8** outlying **9** oblivious, unheeding **10** abstracted, distracted **11** preoccupied, inattentive **12** absentminded

farce
4 sham **5** stuff **6** comedy, satire **7** mockery **8** travesty **9** burlesque, slapstick **10** caricature

farceur
5 clown, cutup, joker **7** buffoon

farcical
5 comic **6** absurd **7** comical, foolish, risible **9** laughable, ludicrous **10** ridiculous **12** preposterous

fare
4 diet, dine, food, pass, rate, toll **5** get on, price, track **6** manage, travel **7** come off, journey, make out, proceed, succeed **8** get along, progress, victuals **9** passenger, surcharge **10** provisions **11** comestibles

farewell
3 ave, bye **4** ciao, ta-ta, vale **5** adieu, adios, aloha, congé **6** bye-bye, pip-pip, shalom, so long **7** aloha oe, cheerio, good-bye, send-off, toodles **8** au revoir, swan song, toodle-oo **9** bon voyage, departure **11** arrivederci, leave-taking, valediction, valedictory

far-fetched
5 fishy **6** absurd **7** dubious **8** doubtful, strained, unlikely **10** improbable, incredible **11** implausible, unrealistic **12** preposterous, unbelievable

far-flung
6 remote **7** distant, removed **8** outlying **10** widespread

farinaceous
5 mealy **6** floury **7** starchy
food: **4** meal **5** flour, grits **6** cereal, hominy **7** polenta, pudding, tapioca

farm
4 till **5** croft, ranch **6** grange, rancho **7** hennery **8** estancia, hacienda, hatchery **9** cultivate, farmstead **10** plantation
building: **4** barn, shed, silo
Dutch: **6** bowery
female: **3** cow, ewe, hen, sow **4** mare **5** nanny **6** heifer
Israeli collective: **7** kibbutz
Russian: **7** kolkhoz, sovkhoz
storage building: **4** silo
team: **4** oxen

farmer
6 grower, tiller, yeoman **7** granger, planter, rancher **8** ranchero, ranchman **13** agriculturist
Russian: **5** kulak
South African: **4** Boer
tenant: **6** cottar, cotter **7** crofter **12** sharecropper

farming
7 tillage **8** agronomy **9** husbandry **11** agriculture, cultivation

faro
5 monte
bet: **7** sleeper
card: **4** case, hock, soda

far-off
6 remote **7** distant, removed **8** outlying

far-out
3 rad **4** cool **5** outré, weird **6** groovy **7** bizarre, offbeat, radical **9** eccentric **10** avant-garde, off-the-wall, outlandish

farrago
4 hash, mess, olio **5** gumbo **6** jumble, medley, muddle **7** goulash, mélange, mixture **8** mishmash, shambles **9** potpourri **10** hodgepodge, miscellany

far-reaching
5 broad **8** sweeping **9** extensive, momentous, pervasive **10** portentous, widespread **11** significant, wide-ranging **13** comprehensive, consequential

farrier
5 smith **10** blacksmith, horseshoer

farsighted
4 sage, wise **9** hyperopic, prescient, sagacious **10** discerning

farthest
3 nth, ult. **6** utmost **7** apogean, extreme, outmost **8** remotest, ultimate **9** outermost, uttermost

Fasching
8 carnival

fascinate
4 draw, wile **5** charm **6** allure, enamor, entice, please **7** attract, beguile, bewitch, enchant **8** enthrall, intrigue, transfix **9** captivate, enrapture, magnetize, mesmerize, spellbind

fascination
5 charm **6** allure, appeal **7** glamour **8** charisma **9** magnetism **10** attraction, witchcraft **11** enchantment **12** enthrallment

Fascist
4 Nazi **6** despot, Hitler (Adolf), tyrant **8** autocrat **9** Falangist, Mussolini (Benito) **10** Blackshirt

fashion
3 fad, fit, ton, way **4** chic, form, mode, mold, suit, tone, vein, wear **5** craze, shape, style, trend, usage, vogue **6** create, custom, design, devise, manner, method, sculpt, tailor **7** compose, costume, pattern **8** contrive **9** bandwagon, construct, fabricate **10** dernier cri **12** haute couture
magazine: **3** WWD **4** Elle **5** Vogue **6** Hilary **7** Glamour, InStyle

fashionable
3 hip **4** chic, cool, posh, tony **5** fresh, ritzy, sharp, smart, swank, swish **6** chichi, du jour, modish, trendy, with-it **7** à la mode, current, dashing, faddish, popular, stylish, voguish **8** up-to-date **9** au courant, exclusive, happening **12** silk-stocking

fashionably nostalgic
5 retro

fashion designer
7 modiste **9** couturier **10** couturiere
American: **3** Sui (Anna) **4** Cole (Kenneth), Ford (Tom), Head (Edith), Kors (Michael), Wang (Vera) **5** Beene (Geoffrey), Blass (Bill), Daché (Lilly), Ellis (Perry), Karan (Donna), Klein (Anne, Calvin) **6** Jacobs (Marc), Lauren (Ralph), Mackie (Bob) **7** Galanos (James), Halston, Mizrahi (Isaac) **8** Galliano (John), Hilfiger (Tommy) **9** Claiborne (Liz), de la Renta (Oscar), Gernreich (Rudi)
Anglo-French: **5** Worth (Charles Frederick)
Dominican: **9** de la Renta (Oscar)
English: **5** Quant (Mary) **6** Bailey (Christopher) **7** McQueen (Alexander) **8** Westwood (Vivienne) **9** McCartney (Stella)
French: **3** YSL **4** Dior (Christian) **5** Bohan (Marc) **6** Cardin (Pierre), Chanel (Coco), Poiret (Paul), Ungaro (Emanuel) **7** Balmain (Pierre), Lacroix (Christian), Montana (Claude) **8** Gaultier (Jean-Paul), Givenchy (Hubert de) **9** Courrèges (André), Lagerfeld (Karl) **12** Saint-Laurent (Yves), Schiaparelli (Elsa)
German: **9** Lagerfeld (Karl)
Israeli: **7** Mizrahi (Isaac)
Italian: **5** Ferrè (Gianfranco), Prada (Miuccia), Pucci (Emilio), Ricci (Nina), Zegna (Ermenegildo) **6** Armani (Giorgio) **7** Cassini (Oleg), Versace (Gianni) **9** Valentino **12** Schiaparelli (Elsa)
Japanese: **6** Miyake (Issey)
Spanish: **10** Balenciaga (Cristóbal)

fast
3 set **4** ASAP, diet, easy, firm, Lent, soon, sure, true, wild **5** apace, fixed, fleet, hasty, hitch, loose, loyal, quick, rapid, swift **6** firmly, presto, prompt, snappy, speedy, stable **7** abstain, hastily, hurried, lasting, quickly, rapidly, staunch, swiftly **8** chop-chop, constant, faithful, full tilt, immobile, promptly, resolute, speedily

9 breakneck, dissolute, immovable, libertine 10 abstinence, profligate, recklessly, stationary 11 expeditious, promiscuous 12 lickety-split 13 expeditiously

fasten
3 fix, peg, pin, set, sew, tie, zip 4 bind, bolt, clip, hook, join, lace, lash, link, lock, moor, nail, seal, shut, weld 5 affix, belay, cable, catch, chain, cinch, clamp, clasp, close, cramp, dowel, girth, hitch, latch, rivet, screw, stake, stick, strap, tie up, truss 6 anchor, attach, batten, buckle, button, couple, secure, skewer, solder, staple, tether 7 connect, mortise 8 buckle up

fastener
3 nut, peg, pin, tie 4 bolt, brad, clip, cord, frog, hasp, link, lock, nail, rope, snap, stud, tack, tape 5 catch, clamp, clasp, dowel, girth, hinge, hitch, latch, rivet, screw, spike, stake, strap 6 buckle, button, cotter, skewer, staple, tether, toggle, Velcro, zipper 7 grommet, padlock, netsuke, shackle 8 coupling, cuff link, handcuff, seat belt, shoelace 9 connector, cotter pin, safety pin, thumbtack 10 clothespin

fastidious
5 fussy, picky 6 choosy, dainty, queasy 7 choosey, finical, finicky, refined 8 exacting 9 demanding, squeamish 10 meticulous, particular, pernickety 11 persnickety

fastness
4 fort, hold, keep 6 bunker, castle, refuge 7 alcazar, bastion, citadel, crannog, redoubt, sanctum 8 casemate, fortress, presidio 10 stronghold, tower house 11 strongpoint

fast-talking
4 glib 5 slick 6 facile 8 slippery 13 silver-tongued

fat
3 big, oil 4 flab, lard, suet, wide 5 beefy, broad, bulky, burly, cream, dumpy, gross, heavy, husky, large, lipid, obese, plump, pudgy, round, stout, thick, tubby 6 chunky, excess, fleshy, grease, portly, rotund, stocky, stubby, tallow 7 adipose, blubber, paunchy, pinguid, porcine, surfeit, surplus, weighty 8 heavyset, oversize, thickset 9 corpulent 10 full-bodied, overweight, potbellied 11 superfluity

fatal
6 deadly, lethal, mortal 7 deathly, ruinous 8 terminal 9 incurable, pestilent 10 pernicious 12 pestilential

fatality
4 doom 5 death 8 casualty 10 deadliness

fata morgana
6 mirage 8 illusion

fat cat
5 mogul, nabob 6 big gun, bigwig, tycoon 7 big shot, magnate, pooh-bah 8 big wheel 9 moneybags, plutocrat 11 muckety-muck 13 high-muck-a-muck

fat chance
4 as if

fate
3 end, lot 4 doom, luck, ruin 5 death, karma 6 chance, kismet, upshot 7 destiny, fortune, outcome, portion 13 inevitability

fateful
6 deadly 7 ominous, ruinous 8 decisive 9 momentous, prophetic 10 portentous

Fates
see at **Greek; Norse; Roman**

fathead
3 ass, oaf 4 boob, clod, dodo, dope, dolt, gawk, goof, goon, jerk, lump, mutt, yo-yo 5 cluck, clunk, dummy, dunce, idiot, moron, stock, stupe, yahoo 6 cretin, dimwit, donkey, doofus, dumdum, nitwit, noodle, schlub, turkey 7 buffoon, dullard, jackass, schnook 8 dumbbell, imbecile, numskull 9 birdbrain, ignoramus, lamebrain, numbskull, simpleton

fatheaded
4 dull, dumb 5 dense, dopey, thick 6 obtuse, simple, stupid 7 doltish, idiotic 8 gormless 9 brainless, dim-witted, imbecilic 10 numskulled 11 numbskulled, thick-witted

father
3 dad, pop 4 dada, papa, père, sire 5 beget, breed, daddy, hatch, padre, pappy, pater, poppa, spawn 6 author, create, old man, parent, priest 7 builder, creator, founder, produce 8 ancestor, engender, generate, inventor, producer 9 architect, initiator, originate, patriarch, procreate 10 originator, prime mover
combining form: 4 patr 5 patri, patro
French: 4 père
German: 5 Vater
Italian: 5 padre
Portuguese: 3 pai
Spanish: 5 padre

Father Brown creator
10 Chesterton (Gilbert Keith)

fatherland
4 home, soil 7 country

Father Time's implement
6 scythe

fathom
4 know 5 probe, sound 7 discern, explore, measure 9 apprehend, figure out, penetrate 10 comprehend, understand 11 investigate

fathomless
7 abysmal, abyssal 8 profound 12 immeasurable

fatidic
5 vatic **6** mantic **7** Delphic, sibylic **8** Delphian, oracular, sibyllic **9** prophetic, prescient, sibylline, vaticinal **10** divinatory, predictive

fatigue
3 fag **4** poop, tire, wear **5** drain, weary **6** tucker **7** deplete, burn out, exhaust, frazzle, wear out **8** drudgery, wear down **9** tiredness, weariness **10** enervation, exhaustion
combat: **7** frazzle **10** shell shock

Fatima
father: **8** Mohammed, Muhammad
husband: **9** Bluebeard
son: **5** Hasan **6** Husayn
stepbrother: **3** Ali

fatness
7 obesity **9** adiposity **10** corpulence, overweight

fatty
4 oily, rich **6** greasy **7** adipose **8** unctuous **10** oleaginous
combining form: **4** lipo **5** adipo

fatuous
4 dumb, fond **5** inane, sappy, silly **6** jejune, simple **7** asinine, foolish, puerile, witless

faucet
3 tap **4** bung, cock, gate **5** valve **6** spigot **7** hydrant, petcock **8** stopcock

Faulkner, William
character: **3** Ike (Snopes), Joe (Christmas) **4** Eula (Varner Snopes), Flem (Snopes), Mink (Snopes) **5** Benjy (Compson), Caddy (Compson), Gavin (Stevens), Henry (Sutpen), Jason (Compson), Lucas (Beauchamp) **6** Dilsey, Temple (Drake) **7** Candace (Compson), Quentin (Compson) **8** Benjamin (Compson)
county: **13** Yoknapatawpha
family: **6** Benbow, Snopes, Sutpen **7** Compson **8** McCaslin, Sartoris **9** Beauchamp
novel: **4** Town (The) **6** Hamlet (The) **7** Mansion (The), Reivers (The) **8** Sartoris **9** Sanctuary, Wild Palms (The) **11** As I Lay Dying **13** Light in August **14** Absalom Absalom **15** Sound and the Fury (The) **17** Intruder in the Dust

fault
3 err, nag, sin **4** flaw, rift, slip, spot, vice, want **5** blame, break, knock, error, scold **6** accuse, defect, foible, miscue **7** censure, demerit, failing, fissure, frailty, mistake, upbraid **8** fracture, weakness **9** criticize, infirmity **10** San Andreas **11** culpability, dereliction, shortcoming **12** imperfection
line: **4** rift **5** split **6** breach **7** fissure **8** crevasse

faultfinder
4 crab **5** grump **6** critic, griper, grouch, nagger, whiner **7** grouser **8** grumbler **10** bellyacher, complainer, criticizer, crosspatch

faultfinding
7 carping **8** captious, critical, nitpicky **9** criticism **10** censorious, nit-picking, pernickety **11** persnickety **12** overcritical **13** hypercritical

faultless
4 pure **7** perfect **8** innocent, unerring **9** guiltless **10** immaculate, impeccable, inculpable

faulty
4 awry **5** amiss, wrong **6** flawed, marred **7** botched, damaged, defaced, inexact, unsound **8** fallible, specious **9** blemished, defective, deficient, erroneous, imperfect, incorrect **10** fallacious, inaccurate
prefix: **3** dys

faun
5 satyr

fauna
7 animals

Faunus
grandfather: **6** Saturn
son: **4** Acis **7** Latinus

Faust
author: **6** Goethe (Johann Wolfgang von)
beloved: **8** Gretchen
composer: **6** Gounod (Charles)

faux
4 fake, mock, sham **5** bogus, false, phony **6** ersatz **9** imitation, pretended, simulated, synthetic **10** substitute

faux pas
4 flub, goof, slip **5** boner, error, gaffe **6** booboo, howler, miscue, slipup **7** blooper, blunder, misstep, mistake, stumble **8** pratfall, solecism **9** gaucherie **11** impropriety

favor
4 baby, back, bias, boon, gift, okay **5** bless, bribe, grace, mercy, token, value **6** accept, behalf, choose, oblige, pamper, prefer, regard **7** indulge, present, support, sustain **8** courtesy, goodwill, interest, keepsake, kindness, resemble, sanction, sympathy **9** attention, patronage, privilege, take after **10** admiration, facilitate, indulgence, partiality **11** approbation, benevolence, countenance

favorable
4 fair **5** lucky **6** benign, biased, golden, timely, toward, useful **7** helpful, partial **8** pleasant, pleasing, positive **9** agreeable, benignant, fortunate, promising **10** auspicious, benevolent, propitious, prosperous **11** affirmative **12** advantageous **13** complimentary

favoring
4 rosy **6** timely, toward, useful **7** helpful **9** opportune **10** auspicious, beneficial, propitious **12** advantageous
prefix: **3** pro

favorite
3 pet 4 idol 7 dearest, popular, special 8 precious 9 preferred, well-liked 10 fair-haired, preference 11 front-runner, teacher's pet, white-haired

favoritism
4 bias 8 cronyism, nepotism 10 partiality 12 one-sidedness

fawn
3 kid, tan 4 deer, ecru 5 beige, toady 6 bister, grovel, kowtow 7 flatter, truckle, wheedle 8 blandish, bootlick 9 sweet-talk 11 apple-polish

fawning
6 smarmy 8 unctuous 9 parasitic 10 obsequious 11 sycophantic

fay
3 elf, nix 4 puck 5 elfin, fairy, nixie, pixie 6 elfish, goblin, sprite 7 brownie 10 leprechaun

faze
3 cow 5 abash, daunt, throw 6 dismay, rattle 7 confuse, disturb, nonplus, perturb 8 befuddle, bewilder, confound, unsettle 9 discomfit, dumbfound, embarrass 10 disconcert 11 flabbergast

FBI
agent: 4 G-man
director: 5 Comey (James), Freeh (Louis) 6 Hoover (J. Edgar) 7 Mueller (Robert), Webster (William)

FDR
affliction: 5 polio
successor: 3 HST
terrier: 4 Fala
wife: 7 Eleanor

fealty
5 faith, troth 7 loyalty 8 devotion, fidelity 9 adherence, constancy, vassalage 10 allegiance, attachment 11 devotedness 12 faithfulness

fear
3 awe 5 alarm, angst, dread, panic, qualm, scare, worry 6 dismay, fright, horror, phobia, terror 7 anxiety, jitters 8 cold feet, disquiet, timidity 9 agitation, cowardice, misgiving 10 foreboding 11 disquietude, trepidation 12 apprehension, cowardliness, perturbation, presentiment, timorousness
of animals: 9 zoophobia
of being buried alive: 11 taphephobia
of cats: 12 ailurophobia
of crowds: 11 ochlophobia
of darkness: 11 nyctophobia
of dirt: 10 mysophobia
of fire: 10 pyrophobia
of heights: 10 acrophobia
of men: 11 androphobia
of new things: 9 neophobia
of open areas: 11 agoraphobia
of pain: 10 algophobia
of strangers: 10 xenophobia
of thunder: 12 brontophobia
of water: 11 hydrophobia
of women: 10 gynophobia

fearful
5 timid 6 afraid, aghast, scared, trepid 7 alarmed, anxious, jittery, panicky 8 alarmist, paranoid, timorous 9 terrified, tremulous 12 apprehensive

fearless
4 bold 5 brave 6 daring 7 gallant, valiant 8 intrepid, unafraid 9 dauntless 10 courageous 11 lionhearted 12 greathearted, stouthearted

fearmonger
8 alarmist

Fear of Flying author
4 Jong (Erica)

fearsome
3 shy 5 scary, timid 6 afraid 7 extreme, intense 8 daunting, timorous 9 frightful 10 terrifying 11 frightening 12 intimidating

feasible
6 doable, likely, viable 8 possible, suitable, workable 10 reasonable 11 practicable 12 tried-and-true

feast
3 eat 4 dine, meal 5 gorge 6 dinner, regale, repast, spread 7 banquet, indulge 8 potlatch
Hawaiian: 4 luau
Scottish: 3 foy

Feast of Lights
8 Chanukah, Hanukkah

Feast of Lots
5 Purim

Feast of Tabernacles
6 Sukkot 7 Sukkoth

feat
3 act 4 coup, deed, gest 5 stunt, trick 6 action 7 exploit 11 achievement, performance, tour de force

feather
3 ilk 4 down, kind, sort, type 5 breed, order, pinna, plume, quill 6 fledge, fletch, pinion 7 species, variety
kind: 4 down 6 covert 7 contour, plumule, rectrix 8 scapular
part: 3 web 4 barb, vane 5 shaft 7 barbule, calamus 8 barbicel

featherbrained
5 dizzy, giddy, silly 7 flighty, foolish 8 heedless 9 frivolous 11 light-headed, thoughtless

feathered
7 plumose

feathers
4 down **7** plumage

feathery neckwear
3 boa

feature
4 item, mark, part **5** add-on, trait **6** aspect, detail, factor **7** article, element, fixture, gimmick, quality **8** hallmark, property **9** attribute, component, lineament **10** attraction, ingredient **11** drawing card, peculiarity

febrile
3 hot **5** fiery **7** fevered, pyretic **8** feverish

feckless
4 weak **5** inept **7** useless **8** carefree, impotent **11** incompetent, ineffective, ineffectual **12** undependable **13** irresponsible

fecund
4 rich **7** fertile **8** fruitful, prolific **9** inventive **10** productive

fecundity
9 abundance, fertility **11** prodigality **12** fruitfulness, productivity

federal agent
4 G-man, T-man

Federalist writer
3 Jay (John) **7** Madison (James) **8** Hamilton (Alexander)

federation
5 union **6** league, nation **7** council **8** alliance **10** government **11** confederacy

fed up
4 sick **9** disgusted **11** exasperated

fee
3 cut, pay, tax **4** bill, cost, dues, hire, rate, toll, wage **5** price **6** charge **7** expense, payment, rake-off, stipend, tuition **8** retainer **9** emolument **10** commission, recompense
minting: **10** seignorage **11** seigniorage
wharf: **7** quayage

feeble
3 wan **4** lame, puny, weak **5** anile, frail **6** infirm, senile, sickly, weakly **7** doddery **8** decrepit **9** doddering, unhealthy **10** inadequate

feebleminded
4 daft, dull, slow **5** dense, thick **6** senile, stupid **7** doltish, foolish, idiotic, moronic, witless **8** imbecile, retarded **9** brainless, dim-witted, imbecilic **10** half-witted, slow-witted **11** harebrained, thick-headed

feebleness
7 frailty **8** debility **9** fragility, infirmity **10** enervation, inadequacy **11** decrepitude

feed
3 eat **4** grub, hand, meal **5** feast, gorge, graze, stuff **6** browse, devour, fatten, fodder, ingest, regale, repast, supply, viands **7** banquet, consume, deliver, dish out, edibles, furnish, nourish, nurture, provide, sustain **8** bonemeal, dispense, hand over, victuals **9** partake of, provender, provision, refection **10** provisions

feedback
5 input **8** critique, reaction, response **9** criticism **10** evaluation

feedbag grain
3 oat **4** oats

feed the kitty
4 ante

feel
5 grope, sense, touch **6** caress, fondle, handle, stroke **7** palpate

feeler
4 palp **5** probe **6** palpus **7** antenna **8** proposal, tentacle **12** trial balloon

feeling
3 air **4** aura, mood, vibe **5** hunch, sense, touch **6** notion, temper **7** emotion, inkling, opinion, outlook, passion, sensate **8** attitude, instinct, sentient **9** affection, emotional, intuition, sensation, sentiment, suspicion **10** atmosphere, impression, persuasion **11** sensibility, sensitivity

feel poorly
3 ail

feel regret
3 rue

feign
3 act **4** fake, play, sham **5** bluff, put on **6** affect, assume **7** pretend **8** simulate **9** dissemble **11** counterfeit, make believe

feigned
4 fake, sham **5** false, phony, put-on **7** assumed **8** imagined **9** imitation, insincere, pretended, simulated **10** fabricated, fictitious **11** counterfeit

feint
4 fake, hoax, play, ploy, ruse, sham, wile **5** trick **6** gambit **8** maneuver **9** stratagem
hockey: **4** deke

feisty
6 frisky, plucky, spunky, touchy **7** bristly, fidgety, scrappy **8** petulant, snappish, spirited **9** fractious, irascible **10** aggressive **11** quarrelsome

feldspar
6 albite **8** andesine **9** anorthite, moonstone **10** microcline, orthoclase **11** plagioclase
clay: **6** kaolin

felicitate
6 salute **7** commend **10** compliment **12** congratulate

felicitous
3 apt, fit **4** meet **5** happy **6** proper, timely **7** apropos, fitting **8** apposite, pleasant, suitable **9** agreeable **10** delightful **11** appropriate

feline
3 cat, sly, tom **4** lion, lynx, pard, puma, puss **5** catty, felid, pussy, sleek, tiger **6** bobcat, cougar, jaguar, margay, ocelot, serval, slinky, sneaky, tomcat **7** caracal, catlike, cheetah, furtive, leonine, leopard, lioness, panther, tigress, wildcat **8** graceful, pussycat, stealthy
hybrid: **5** liger, tigon **6** tiglon

Felipe of baseball
4 Alou

fell
3 cut, hew, mow **4** down, drop, kill, raze **5** floor **6** poleax **7** cut down, flatten **8** knock off **9** bring down, knock down

Fellini film
8 Amarcord, Casanova, La Strada **9** Satyricon **10** I Vitelloni **11** La Dolce Vita **15** Nights of Cabiria **18** Juliet of the Spirits

fellow
3 bub, guy, joe, lad, man **4** buck, chap, dude, gent, mate, peer, twin **5** bloke, match **6** codger, cohort, hombre, person **7** comrade, consort, partner **8** confrere **9** associate, companion, copartner, gentleman **10** coordinate, reciprocal

fellow feeling
5 agape **7** concern, empathy, rapport **8** affinity, kindness, sympathy **9** affection **10** compassion, kindliness **11** consolation **13** understanding

fellowship
4 club **5** guild **6** league **7** coterie, society, stipend **8** sodality **9** communion, community **10** fraternity **11** association, brotherhood

felon
3 con **7** convict, whitlow **8** criminal **10** malefactor

felt
6 groped, sensed

felt hat
3 fez **5** derby, terai **6** fedora, trilby **7** homburg, stetson **8** snap-brim **9** wideawake

female
3 dam **4** girl **5** woman **7** girlish, womanly **8** feminine
deer: **3** doe
goat: **5** nanny
horse: **4** mare
pig: **3** sow
sheep: **3** ewe
singer: **4** alto **5** mezzo **7** soprano
suffix: **3** ess **4** esse, ette, trix

Feminine Mystique author
7 Friedan (Betty)

feminist
10 suffragist **11** suffragette

femme fatale
4 Bara (Theda), vamp **5** Circe, siren **6** Carmen, Judith, Salome **7** Delilah, Jezebel, Lorelei **8** Mata Hari **9** temptress **10** seductress **11** enchantress

femur
9 thighbone

fen
3 bog **4** mire, moor, quag, wash **5** marsh, swale, swamp **6** morass, muskeg, slough **9** marshland

fence
3 bar, pen **4** cage, ha-ha, rail, pale, weir **5** hedge, parry **6** corral, haw-haw, paling, picket **7** barrier, enclose, railing **8** backstop, boundary, hoarding, palisade, receiver, sidestep, stockade **9** barricade, stone wall
sunk: **4** ha-ha

fencer
7 duelist, épéeist **8** foilsman **9** swordsman

fencing
9 swordplay
attack: **5** lunge **6** thrust **7** reprise, riposte
cry: **6** touché **7** en garde
defense: **5** parry
movement: **4** volt
term: **4** jury **5** forte, lunge **6** flèche, foible, touché
touch: **3** cut, hit
weapon: **4** épée, foil **5** blade, guard, saber, sabre **6** pommel

fender
4 skid **5** guard **6** buffer, bumper, shield **7** cushion, railing **8** mudguard

fennec
3 fox

Fenrir
chain: **8** Gleipnir
father: **4** Loki
form: **4** wolf
mother: **9** Angerboda **10** Angerbotha
slayer: **5** Vidar **6** Vithar
victim: **4** Odin **5** Woden

Fenway Park
fence: **12** Green Monster
site: **6** Boston
team: **6** Red Sox

feral
4 wild **5** brute **6** brutal, savage **7** beastly, bestial, brutish, inhuman, untamed

Ferber, Edna
novel: **5** Giant, So Big **8** Cimarron, Show Boat **9** Ice Palace **13** Saratoga Trunk

Ferdinand
beloved: **7** Miranda
father: **6** Alonso

Ferdinand, King
conquest: **7** Granada
daughter: **6** Joanna
wife: **7** Isabela **8** Germaine, Isabella

fermata
4 hold 5 pause
ferment
4 boil, brew, stir 5 rouse, sweat 6 clamor, enzyme, excite, incite, leaven, seethe, simmer, unrest, work up 7 smolder, turmoil 9 agitation, commotion 12 restlessness
fermentation
7 zymosis 13 bioconversion
fermented drink
4 mead 5 kvass 6 kumiss, pulque 7 koumiss 8 kombucha
fermented soy soup
4 miso
fern
4 tree 5 brake, holly, royal 6 Boston 7 bracken 8 polypody 10 maidenhair, spleenwort
leaf: 5 frond
ferocious
4 fell, grim, wild 5 brute, cruel 6 brutal, fierce, savage 7 bestial, extreme, inhuman, intense, vicious, violent 8 barbaric, inhumane, ruthless 9 barbarous, rapacious, truculent
Ferrari founder
4 Enzo
ferret out
4 find 5 dig up, flush 6 elicit 7 unearth 8 discover 9 ascertain
ferrule
3 cap, tip 4 band, ring, virl 6 collet
ferry
5 carry 6 convey 7 shuttle 9 transport
ferryman
6 Charon 9 gondolier
fertile
4 lush, rich 6 fecund 8 abundant, creative, fruitful, pregnant, prolific 9 bountiful, ingenious, inventive, luxuriant, plenteous 10 productive 12 reproductive
fertilize
5 beget, breed 6 enrich 8 generate 9 fecundate, pollinate 10 impregnate, inseminate
fertilizer
4 dung 5 guano, mulch, niter, nitre 6 manure 7 compost 8 bonemeal 9 plant food
ferule
3 rod 5 stick
fervent
3 hot 4 avid, keen 5 eager, fiery 6 ardent, devout, gung-ho 7 blazing, burning, earnest, glowing, intense, zealous 8 vehement 9 heartfelt 10 hot-blooded, passionate 11 impassioned, warm-blooded 12 enthusiastic, wholehearted
fervor
4 fire, heat, zeal 5 ardor 6 warmth 7 passion 8 devotion, violence 9 vehemence 10 devoutness, enthusiasm
fescennine
7 obscene 10 scurrilous
fess up
3 own 5 admit 9 come clean
fester
3 rot 6 rankle 7 inflame, putrefy 8 ulcerate 9 suppurate
festina ____
5 lente
festival
4 fair, fete, gala 5 feast 6 fiesta 7 jubilee 8 carnival, jamboree 11 celebration, merrymaking
festive
3 gay 4 gala 5 jolly, merry 6 joyful, joyous 7 gleeful 8 mirthful 11 celebratory
occasion: 4 fete, gala 5 revel 7 jubilee
festivity
4 bash, fair, fete, gala 5 feast, party, revel 6 affair, frolic, gaiety 7 blowout, jubilee, revelry, whoopee 8 carnival, jamboree 9 rejoicing, merriment 11 celebration, merrymaking
festoon
4 deck, hang 5 adorn 6 bedeck 7 garland 8 decorate, ornament 9 embellish
fetch
3 get 4 draw, earn 5 bring, yield 6 take in 7 attract, bring in, realize 8 retrieve
fetching
4 fair 6 comely, lovely, pretty 7 winsome 8 alluring, charming, enticing, engaging, handsome, pleasing 9 appealing 10 attractive
fete
4 ball, bash, fair, gala 5 feast, honor, party 6 affair, fiesta, soiree 7 banquet, jubilee, shindig 8 carnival, festival, jamboree, wingding 9 celebrate, entertain 11 celebration, commemorate 13 entertainment
fetid
4 foul, high, rank 5 funky 6 putrid, rancid, smelly, strong 8 mephitic, stinking 10 malodorous
fetish
4 idol, juju, luck 5 charm 6 amulet 7 periapt 8 fixation, gris-gris, talisman 10 phylactery
fetor
4 funk, odor, reek 5 stink 6 stench
fetter
3 tie 4 bind, bond, gyve 5 chain, check, irons 6 hobble, hog-tie, impede 7 enchain, manacle, shackle, trammel 8 handcuff, restrain 9 restraint

fettle
5 shape **6** health **7** fitness **9** condition **12** constitution

feud
6 enmity, strife **7** dispute, quarrel **8** argument, vendetta **9** hostility **11** controversy

feudal
estate: **3** fee **4** feud, fief **5** manor **6** domain
house: **5** manor
jurisdiction: **4** soke
laborer: **4** esne, serf
lord: **5** laird, liege, mesne, thane **8** suzerain
status: **9** vassalage
tax: **7** tallage
tenant: **6** vassal **7** homager, socager, vavasor **8** vavasour
tenure of land: **6** socage
tribute: **6** heriot
warrior: **5** bushi, ronin **7** samurai

feuilleton
5 essay

fever
4 ague, fire, heat **5** craze, flush, Lassa, mania **6** dengue, frenzy **7** ferment, passion, pyrexia **8** delirium **9** calenture
recurrent: **7** malaria, quartan, tertian
type: **3** hay **6** dengue, hectic **7** scarlet

fevered
6 crazed, heated **7** burning, febrile, flushed **8** agitated, frenetic, restless **9** delirious **10** distracted, overheated **11** overwrought

feverish
3 hot **5** fiery **6** hectic **7** burning, febrile, flushed, pyretic **8** frenetic, frenzied **10** passionate **11** overwrought

fever tree
6 acacia **7** blue gum

few
4 rare **5** scant **6** meager, meagre, scanty, scarce, sparse **7** handful, limited **8** sporadic **9** scattered **10** infrequent, occasional, scattering, smattering, spattering, sprinkling
combining form: **4** olig **5** oligo

fey
4 daft **5** campy, crazy, vatic **7** touched **8** oracular, precious **9** pixilated, prophetic, sibylline, visionary **11** clairvoyant **12** otherworldly

Fey of 30 Rock
4 Tina

fiasco
3 dud **4** bomb, flop **5** farce, flask **6** bottle, defeat **7** blunder, debacle, failure, washout **8** abortion, disaster **11** miscarriage **13** embarrassment

fiat
5 edict, order **6** decree **7** command, dictate, mandate, warrant **8** sanction **11** endorsement **12** proclamation **13** authorization

fib
3 lie **4** tale **5** story **7** falsify, falsity, untruth **8** white lie **9** falsehood, mendacity **10** taradiddle **11** fabrication, prevaricate

fiber
3 web **4** bast, noil, pita **5** grain, istle **6** fabric, strand, thread **7** texture
basketry: **5** istle
brain: **4** pons
coarse: **4** jute **8** piassava
coconut husk: **4** coir
rope: **4** bast, hemp **5** sisal **8** henequen
silky: **5** kapok
small: **6** fibril
substructure: **7** micelle, spongin
synthetic: **5** nylon, Orlon, rayon, saran, vinal **6** Dacron, olefin **7** spandex
woody: **4** bast
woollike: **7** lanital

fibrous
4 ropy, wiry **5** tough, woody **6** sinewy **7** stringy

fibula
4 bone **5** clasp

fichu
5 scarf **8** kerchief

fickle
7 flighty **8** unstable, variable, volatile **9** mercurial **10** capricious, changeable, inconstant, unfaithful, unreliable **12** undependable **13** temperamental, unpredictable

fiction
4 tale, yarn **5** fable, story **7** fantasy, figment **8** pretense **9** falsehood, fish story, invention, narrative **10** concoction **11** fabrication

fictional
6 made-up, unreal **8** notional **9** imaginary **11** make-believe **12** suppositious

fictitious
4 fake, mock, sham **5** bogus, faked, false, phony **6** ersatz, made-up, unreal, untrue **7** assumed, created **8** cooked-up, fanciful, illusory, imagined, invented, mythical, spurious **9** concocted, fantastic, imaginary, simulated, trumped-up **10** apocryphal, artificial, chimerical, fabricated **11** make-believe **12** suppositious

fiddle
3 toy **4** fool, play, rack **5** alter, cheat **6** dawdle, diddle, doodle, finger, meddle, monkey, potter, putter, tamper, tinker, trifle, violin **7** swindle **9** interfere **10** fool around, manipulate, mess around

fiddle-faddle
3 rot **4** bosh, bull, bunk, nuts **5** fudge, drool, hokum, hooey, pshaw **6** bunkum, drivel, hoodoo, humbug, piffle **7** baloney, blarney, hogwash, rubbish, twaddle **8** nonsense, pishposh, tommyrot **9** poppycock **10** applesauce, balderdash, flapdoodle **13** horsefeathers

fiddler in Rome
4 Nero

Fiddler on the Roof role
5 Golde, Tevye, Yenta

___ Fideles
6 Adeste

Fidelio
composer: **9** Beethoven (Ludwig van)
hero: **9** Florestan
heroine: **7** Leonora

fidelity
5 ardor, piety, troth **6** fealty **7** loyalty **8** devotion **9** adherence, constancy **10** allegiance, attachment **11** staunchness **12** faithfulness **13** dependability, steadfastness

Fidel's comrade
3 Che

fidget
6 fantod, fiddle, jitter, squirm, twitch **7** wriggle

fidgety
5 antsy, jumpy **6** uneasy **7** jittery, nervous, restive, squirmy, twitchy **8** restless

fiduciary
7 trustee

field
3 lea **4** area, mead, turf **5** green, major, milpa, orbit, range **6** domain, meadow, métier, region, sphere **7** demesne, pasture, purview, terrain **8** dominion, gridiron, precinct, vocation **9** bailiwick, champaign, specialty, territory **10** department, discipline, occupation

field crop
3 hay **4** corn, oats **5** grain, wheat **6** cotton **7** alfalfa **8** soybeans

field deity
3 Pan **4** Faun **5** Fauna **6** Faunus

field glasses
6 binocs **10** binoculars

field hand
4 hoer **5** sower **6** picker **7** laborer, planter

Fielding novel
6 Amelia **8** Tom Jones **13** Joseph Andrews

field marshal
Austrian: **8** Radetzky (Joseph)
British: **6** Napier (Robert), Raglan (Baron), Wavell (Archibald), Wilson (Henry) **7** Roberts (Frederick) **8** Wolseley (Garnet) **9** Kitchener (Horatio) **10** Montgomery (Bernard)
French: **3** Ney (Michel) **4** Foch (Ferdinand) **6** Joffre (Joseph-Jacques-Césaire), Pétain (Philippe)
German: **6** Keitel (Wilhelm), Paulus (Friedrich), Rommel (Erwin), Rupert (Prince) **9** Mackensen (August von), Rundstedt (Karl von), Waldersee (Alfred von) **10** Kesselring (Albert)
Japanese: **8** Sugiyama (Hajime)
Prussian: **6** Moltke (Helmuth von)
Russian: **7** Kutuzov (Mikhail), Suvorov (Aleksandr) **8** Potemkin (Grigory)

field mouse
4 vole

field officer
5 major **7** colonel

field of study
4 area **10** discipline

fieldwork
5 redan

fiend
3 bug, imp, nut **5** demon, devil, freak, Satan **6** addict, Belial, diablo, maniac, zealot **7** devotee, fanatic, habitué, Lucifer, monster, Old Nick, serpent **8** Apollyon, succubus **9** Beelzebub **10** enthusiast, Old Scratch **13** Old Gooseberry

fiendish
3 bad **4** evil **5** cruel **6** malign, savage, wicked **7** baleful, demonic, hellish, inhuman, malefic, satanic, vicious **8** demoniac, devilish, diabolic, infernal, sinister **9** barbarous, difficult, ferocious, malicious, malignant **10** diabolical

fierce
4 fell, grim, wild **5** cruel **6** brutal, savage, wicked **7** brutish, hostile, inhuman, intense, vicious, violent, wolfish **8** inhumane, pitiless, ruthless, terrible, vehement **9** barbarous, bellicose, ferocious, merciless, truculent **10** aggressive, determined

fiery
3 hot, red **5** afire **6** ablaze, aflame, ardent, fervid, fierce, heated, red-hot, torrid **7** burning, febrile, fervent, flaming, flaring, igneous, intense, peppery **8** broiling, feverish, spirited, vehement, white-hot **9** flammable, hotheaded, irritable, perfervid **10** mettlesome, passionate **11** combustible, inflammable, impassioned

fiesta
4 fete **5** party **6** frolic **8** carnival, festival, jamboree **9** merriment

fife
4 pipe **5** flute

fifth
combining form: **5** quint
scale note: **3** sol

fifth columnist
3 spy **5** Judas **7** traitor **8** apostate, quisling, turncoat

fig
genus: **5** Ficus
sacred: **5** pipal
variety: **5** elemi **6** Smyrna

fight
3 row, war **4** bout, buck, duel, feud, fray, spat, tiff **5** brawl, broil, clash, joust, match, melee, repel, scrap, set-to **6** affray, attack, battle, combat, fracas, oppose, oppugn, rassle, resist, rumble, scrape, tussle **7** contend, contest, dispute, grapple, quarrel, scuffle, wrangle, wrestle **8** conflict, skirmish, slugfest, squabble, struggle, traverse **10** aggression, donnybrook, free-for-all **11** altercation

fighter
3 pug **4** swad **5** boxer **7** brawler, soldier, warrior **8** champion, pugilist, scrapper **9** combatant, gladiator, man-at-arms, mercenary **11** interceptor
pilot: **3** ace

fighter plane
3 MiG, Roc **4** Zero **5** Sabre **6** bomber, Fokker, Hawker, Mirage, Voodoo **7** Corsair, Harrier **8** Spitfire **11** interceptor

fighting fish
5 betta

figment
5 dream, fable, fancy **7** chimera, fiction **8** daydream, illusion, phantasm **9** invention, unreality **11** contrivance, fabrication

figure
3 add, sum, tot **4** cast, form, mold, rule, tote **5** count, digit, frame, image, model, motif, shape, total **6** cipher, decide, design, device, effigy, motive, number, reckon, settle, symbol **7** compute, integer, numeral, outline, pattern, resolve **8** conclude, estimate, physique **9** calculate, character, determine, enumerate
geometric: **4** cone, cube **5** rhomb **6** circle, isogon, square **7** decagon, ellipse, hexagon, nonagon, octagon, polygon, rhombus **8** pentacle, pentagon, rhomboid, tetragon, triangle **9** rectangle **10** hexahedron, octahedron **11** icosahedron **12** dodecahedron, rhombohedron
human: **4** nude **5** atlas **7** telamon **8** caryatid
ornamental: **6** statue **8** gargoyle

figurehead
4 pawn, tool **5** front **6** minion, puppet **7** cat's-paw **8** creature **10** instrument, mouthpiece

figure of speech
5 trope **6** aporia, simile **7** litotes **8** metaphor, metonymy **10** synecdoche

figure out
5 crack, learn, solve **6** decide, decode, fathom **7** resolve, unravel **8** decipher, discover, unriddle **9** ascertain, determine

figure skater
see **ice skater**

figure skating
jump: **4** axel, loop, lutz **5** split **6** rocker **7** bracket, counter, salchow **11** spreadeagle
spin: **5** camel

figurine
9 statuette

Fiji
capital: **4** Suva
explorer: **4** Cook (Capt. James) **6** Tasman (Abel)
island: **3** Gau **4** Koro **6** Ovalau **8** Viti Levu **9** Vanua Levu
island group: **3** Lau **6** Yasawa
language: **6** Fijian
neighbor: **5** Samoa **7** Vanuatu

filch
3 cop, nip **4** crib, lift, take **5** boost, pinch, steal, swipe **6** pilfer, snitch **7** purloin

file
3 row, rub **4** line, rank, rasp, tier **5** lodge, march, place, queue **6** smooth **7** archive, arrange, corrupt, dossier **10** emery board

filial
5 sonly **7** duteous, dutiful

filibuster
5 delay, stall **10** adventurer

filigree
4 lace **6** design **7** pattern **8** fretwork, openwork, ornament **10** decoration **13** embellishment, ornamentation

fill
3 jam **4** clog, cloy, cram, glut, heap, lade, load, pack, pile, plug, sate, stop **5** block, choke, close, gorge, stock, stuff **6** charge, stodge **7** congest, engorge, inflate, occlude, pervade, satiate, satisfy, stopper, surfeit **8** permeate
interstices: **4** calk **5** caulk, chink, putty

filled
5 awash, flush, sated **6** packed **7** replete **9** saturated

filler
5 squib **7** packing, padding, tobacco, wadding **8** stuffing

fillet
4 band **5** slice, snood, strip **6** debone, ribbon, stripe **7** bandeau, banding **8** headband
anatomical: **9** lemniscus
architectural: **6** listel, reglet, taenia
meat: **10** tenderloin

fill in
3 sub **4** clew, clue, post **6** advise, detail, insert, notify **7** apprise **8** acquaint, complete **10** substitute

fill-in
3 sub 4 temp 6 backup 7 stopgap 9 alternate, expedient, makeshift, surrogate, temporary 10 substitute 11 locum tenens, pinch hitter, replacement, succedaneum

filling
5 kapok

fillip
3 tap 4 goad, kick, spur 5 boost, tonic 6 buffet, strike 7 impetus, wrinkle 8 catalyst, stimulus 9 incentive, stimulant, stimulate 10 inducement, motivation 13 embellishment

film
4 coat, scum, skim, skin 5 glaze, layer, Mylar 6 lamina, patina 7 tarnish 8 membrane, pellicle
holder: 4 reel
(see also **movie**)

film ___
4 noir

film director
see **movie director**

film producer
see **movie producer**

filmy
4 hazy 5 gauzy, misty, sheer, wispy 6 dainty 8 delicate, gossamer 10 diaphanous 11 transparent

fils
3 son

filter
4 sift 5 clean, leach, sieve 6 purify, refine, screen, strain 7 clarify, cleanse 9 percolate

filth
4 crud, dirt, dung, muck, slop, smut 5 dreck, grime, slime, trash 6 ordure, refuse, sludge 7 squalor 9 obscenity

filthy
4 base, foul, vile 5 black, dirty, grimy, gross, gunky, mucky, muddy, nasty 6 coarse, cruddy, grubby, grungy, ribald, scuzzy, skanky, smutty, sordid 7 obscene, raunchy, squalid, unclean 8 indecent 9 loathsome, offensive, repulsive, revolting 12 scatological
money: 5 lucre

filthy lucre
4 cash, loot, pelf 5 bread, bucks, dough, money, moola 6 boodle, riches, moolah, wampum 7 cabbage, scratch 8 currency

fin
3 arm 4 bill 5 fiver, pinna 7 airfoil, flipper
type: 6 caudal, dorsal 7 ventral 8 pectoral

finagle
5 cheat, trick 6 wangle 7 snaffle, swindle, wheedle 8 fast-talk, maneuver, scrounge 9 bamboozle, machinate

final
3 end, ult. 4 last 6 ending, latest 7 closing 8 hindmost, terminal, ultimate 10 concluding, conclusive, definitive 11 examination

finale
3 end 4 coda 5 close, finis 6 capper, climax, ending, payoff, windup, wrap-up 7 closing 10 conclusion, denouement 11 culmination, termination

finalize
3 end 5 close, sew up, tie up 6 decide, finish, wind up, wrap up 7 approve 8 complete, conclude, solidify 9 terminate 10 consummate

finally
6 at last, lastly 7 someday 8 at length 9 belatedly 10 at long last, eventually, ultimately 12 subsequently

finance
4 back, bank, fund 5 endow, funds, money, stake 6 credit 7 banking, promote, revenue, sponsor, support 8 bankroll 9 grubstake, patronize, subsidize 10 capitalize, investment, underwrite

financial
6 fiscal, pocket 8 business, economic, monetary 9 pecuniary 10 commercial
plan: 6 budget
statement: 12 balance sheet

financier
American: 4 Hill (James Jerome), Ryan (Thomas Fortune), Sage (Russell) 5 Astor (John Jacob), Baker (George Fisher), Eaton (Cyrus), Field (Cyrus West), Gould (Jay), Grace (William Russell), Green (Hetty), Soros (George) 6 Biddle (Nicholas), Boesky (Ivan), Girard (Stephen), Mellon (Andrew), Morgan (John Pierpont, Junius Spencer), Morris (Robert), Rogers (Henry Huttleston), Yerkes (Charles Tyson) 7 Buffett (Warren), Peabody (George) 10 Vanderbilt (Cornelius, William)
British: 6 Baring (Alexander), Rhodes (Cecil) 7 Gresham (Thomas)
French: 6 Necker (Jacques) 7 Colbert (Jean-Baptiste)
German: 7 Schacht (Hjalmar) 10 Rothschild (Amschel, Jakob, Karl, Mayer, Nathan, Salomon)

finch
4 pape 5 junco, serin, zebra 6 canary, linnet, siskin, towhee 7 bunting, chewink, redpoll, sparrow 8 cardinal, grosbeak, longspur 9 crossbill, seedeater

find
3 gem 4 gain, meet, spot 5 catch, dig up, hit on, reach, sight 6 attain, detect, locate, supply, turn up 7 discern, furnish, scare up, uncover, unearth 8 bump into, come upon, discover, meet with, perceive, treasure 9 determine, discovery, encounter 10 experience 13 treasure trove

Finding Nemo heroine
4 Dory

find out
4 hear **5** catch, learn **6** detect **7** catch on **8** discover, perceive **9** ascertain, determine

fine
3 A-OK, end, top **4** fair, keen, levy, pure, thin **5** bonny, close, clear, dandy, mulct, sheer **6** amerce, choice, minute, ornate, punish, purify, subtle **7** clarion, damages, elegant, forfeit, penalty **8** all right, delicate, penalize, pleasant, splendid, superior **9** beautiful, enjoyable, excellent, first-rate **10** punishment, reparation

fine china
5 Spode

finery
5 array **6** attire **7** apparel, regalia **8** clothing, frippery, glad rags, ornament **9** caparison, full dress, trappings, trimmings **10** decoration, Sunday best

finesse
5 dodge, evade, skill, skirt **6** jockey **7** beguile, cunning, exploit **8** maneuver, subtlety **9** dexterity **10** adroitness, artfulness, manipulate

fine-tune
4 true **5** tweak **6** adjust

Fingal's Cave
composer: **11** Mendelssohn (Felix)
island: **6** Staffa

finger
5 blame, digit, index, pinky, strum, touch **6** accuse, pinkie **7** palpate **8** identify, pinpoint
bone: **7** phalanx
combining form: **6** dactyl

finial
3 épi

finicky
5 fussy, picky **6** choosy, dainty, prissy **7** choosey **8** exacting **9** squeamish **10** fastidious, meticulous, particular, pernickety **11** persnickety

finis
3 end **5** close **6** finale **10** completion, conclusion

finish
3 end **4** do in, kill, slay, stop **5** cease, close, glaze, use up **6** cut off, ending, finale, murder, patina, polish, windup, wrap up **7** closing, consume, destroy, execute, exhaust, surface **8** complete, conclude, dispatch, finalize, terminus **9** cessation, liquidate, terminate **10** completion, conclusion, denouement, run through **11** termination
dull: **3** mat **4** matt **5** matte
second: **5** place
third: **4** show

finished
4 done, over, ripe **5** ideal **7** done for, perfect, refined, through **8** achieved, complete, over with, polished, washed-up **9** perfected **10** consummate

finishing nail
4 brad

finite
5 bound, fixed **7** bounded, limited, precise **9** definable **10** restricted **12** determinable

fink
3 rat **5** Judas **6** betray, snitch, squeal **7** traitor **8** betrayer, informer, quisling, snitcher **11** backstabber, stool pigeon **13** strikebreaker

Finland
5 Suomi
Arctic region: **7** Lapland
capital: **8** Helsinki
city: **5** Espoo, Lahti, Turku **6** Vantaa **7** Tampere
ethnic group: **4** Lapp, Sami
gulf: **7** Bothnia
invader: **9** Alexander
island: **5** Karlö **6** Kimito **9** Vallgrund
island group: **5** Åland
lake: **5** Inari **6** Saimaa **7** Keitele **8** Pielinen
language: **7** Finnish, Swedish
monetary unit: **4** euro
monetary unit, former: **6** markka
neighbor: **6** Norway, Russia, Sweden

Finlandia composer
8 Sibelius (Jean)

Finnigans Wake
author: **5** Joyce (James)
first word: **8** riverrun
last word: **3** the

Finnish
architect: **4** Eero (Saarinen) **5** Aalto (Alvar), Eliel (Saarinen)
bath: **5** sauna
epic: **8** Kalevala
god: **6** Jumala

fir
4 pine **6** balsam, Fraser **7** conifer, Douglas **9** evergreen
genus: **5** Abies

fire
3 axe, can, pep, vim, zip **4** bake, boot, brio, burn, cast, dash, hurl, sack, stir, toss, zeal, zest, zing **5** ardor, blaze, drive, flame, flare, fling, glare, ingle, light, pitch, rouse, salvo, shoot, spark, throw, torch, verve, vigor **6** arouse, energy, excite, fervor, flames, ignite, kindle, lay off, spirit **7** animate, boot out, dismiss, enthuse, inferno, inflame, inspire, kick out, passion, provoke **8** enkindle **9** calenture, discharge, holocaust, terminate **10** combustion, enthusiasm, liveliness **13** conflagration
combining form: **3** pyr **4** igni, pyro
god: **4** Agni, Loki **6** Vulcan **10** Hephaestus
residue: **3** ash

firearm
see **gun**

firebrand
8 agitator **10** incendiary, instigator

firebug
5 torch **8** arsonist **10** incendiary, pyromaniac

firecracker
5 squib **6** banger **9** explosive **10** cherry bomb, noisemaker

firedog
7 andiron

firedrake
6 dragon

firefly
12 lightning bug

fire opal
7 girasol

fireplace
5 grate, ingle
equipment: 6 fender, screen **7** andiron
part: 3 hob **4** flue **6** hearth, mantel

fireplug
7 hydrant

Fireside Chat president
3 FDR

fire up
5 anger, annoy, rouse, spark **6** arouse, excite, ignite, incite, kindle **7** enliven, inflame, inspire, provoke **8** enkindle, irritate

firework
6 petard, rocket **8** pinwheel, sparkler **11** pyrotechnic, Roman candle
cluster: 9 girandole

firkin
3 keg, tun, vat **4** butt, cask, pipe **6** barrel, vessel **8** hogshead

firm
3 set **4** fast, hard, sure **5** fixed, rigid, solid, sound, stiff, tight, tough **6** harden, outfit, secure, settle, stable, steady, strong, sturdy **7** abiding, adamant, certain, company, concern, improve, settled, staunch, unmoved **8** business, constant, definite, enduring, faithful, resolute, specific, vigorous **9** steadfast, tenacious **10** determined, enterprise, inflexible, stipulated, strengthen, unwavering, unyielding **11** established, partnership, substantial, unfaltering, well-founded **13** establishment

____ firma
5 terra

firmament
3 sky **5** vault **6** sphere, welkin **7** expanse, heavens **8** empyrean

firmness
7 resolve **8** decision, security, solidity, strength, tenacity **9** constancy, stability **10** durability, resolution **13** determination

firn
4 névé

first
4 arch, head **5** alpha, chief, prime **6** maiden, primal **7** highest, initial, leading, lead-off, opening, pioneer, premier, primary, supreme **8** champion, dominant, earliest, foremost, headmost, original **9** inaugural, initially, paramount, principal, sovereign **10** aboriginal, preeminent, primordial
prefix: 4 prot **5** proto

firstborn
4 heir **6** eldest, oldest

first-class
3 top **4** A-one, best, fine **5** prime, primo **6** tip-top **7** capital, supreme **8** five-star, superior, top-notch **9** excellent, top-drawer

First Family daughter
5 Jenna, Malia, Sasha **7** Barbara, Chelsea

first Greek letter
5 alpha

firsthand
6 direct **7** primary **9** immediate

first Hebrew letter
4 alef **5** aleph

first lady
3 Eve
of jazz: 4 Ella (Fitzgerald)

First Lady
5 Laura, Nancy **7** Barbara, Hillary **8** Michelle

first man
4 Adam

first man in space
7 Gagarin (Yury)

first name in fashion
4 Coco (Chanel)

first name in mysteries
4 Erle

first-rate
4 A-one **5** great, prime **6** superb, tip-top **7** capital, stellar, topping **8** splendid, terrific, top-notch **9** excellent, top-drawer

first showing
5 debut **7** opening **8** premiere

First State
8 Delaware

first string
5 A team

first-to-twelfth-grade
4 elhi

firth
3 arm, bay **4** cove, gulf **5** inlet **6** harbor, slough **7** estuary

fiscal
8 monetary **9** budgetary, financial

fish
3 aku, bob, cod, dab, eel, gar, ide, koi, net, ray **4** barb, bass, carp, cast, cero, char, chub, chum, coho, cusk, dace, dory, drum, gata, gill, goby, hake, hint, jack, ling, mero, opah, parr, pike, rudd, scup, shad, sild, sisi, sole, spet, tuna, ulua **5** angle, betta, bream, brill, charr, cisco, cobia, danio, fluke, grunt, guppy, jurel, loach, moray, perch, platy, porgy, roach, scrod, seine, shark, skate, smelt, smolt, snook, sprat, tench, tetra, trawl, troll, trout, tunny, wahoo **6** blenny, bonito, burbot, caribe, conger, dorado, grilse, kipper, marlin, minnow, mullet, permit, plaice, pompon, puffer, remora, salmon, sauger, sebago, shiner, sucker, tarpon, tautog, tomcod, turbot, warsaw, wrasse **7** alewife, anchovy, buffalo, capelin, catfish, cavalla, chimera, chinook, cichlid, corbina, cowfish, crappie, dolphin, escolar, gillnet, gourami, grouper, grunion, haddock, hagfish, halibut, herring, hogfish, jewfish, lamprey, mudfish, oarfish, pigfish, pinfish, piranha, pollack, pollock, pompano, pupfish, rainbow, rasbora, sardine, sawfish, sculpin, sea carp, snapper, sniggle, sockeye, sunfish, tilapia, torpedo, whiting **8** albacore, blowfish, bluefish, bluegill, bocaccio, bonefish, brisling, bullhead, chimaera, crevalle, filefish, flounder, gambusia, goldfish, grayling, halfbeak, hornpout, kingfish, ladyfish, lionfish, lookdown, lumpfish, lungfish, mackerel, menhaden, moonfish, pickerel, pilchard, pipefish, porkfish, rock bass, rockfish, rosefish, sailfish, seahorse, sea trout, skipjack, stingray, sturgeon, tilefish, warmouth, weakfish, wolffish **9** amberjack, angelfish, barracuda, brandling, cutthroat, goosefish, greenling, pilotfish, spadefish, stargazer, swordfish, topminnow, trunkfish, whitebait, whitefish **10** butterfish, flying fish, needlefish, parrotfish, sheepshead, silverside, squeteague, tripletail, victorfish, yellowtail **11** Dolly Varden, hatchetfish, jacksmelt, killifish, lanternfish, mummichog, muskellunge, pumpkinseed, stickleback, triggerfish
basket: **5** creel
character: **4** Nemo **5** Wanda
combining form: **6** ichthy
dish: **7** ceviche, seviche **8** cioppino, matelote **13** bouillabaisse
eggs: **3** roe **5** spawn
genus: **4** Amia, Lota
relating to: **7** piscine
spear: **3** gig **7** harpoon, trident
trap: **4** weir
young: **3** fry **4** parr **5** larva, smolt **6** alevin, grilse

fisherman
6 angler

fish hawk
6 osprey

fishhook
adjunct: **5** snell
part: **4** barb **5** shank

fishing line
4 trot **7** setline **8** longline, trotline
float: **3** bob **5** quill
leader: **5** snell

fishing lure
3 fly **4** bait **5** spoon **7** spinner

fishing need
3 rod **4** bait, lure, reel

fishing net
5 seine, trawl

fishlike mammal
4 orca **5** whale **6** dugong, sea cow **7** dolphin, grampus, manatee, narwhal **8** cetacean, porpoise

fish story
3 fib, lie **4** bunk, yarn **11** fabrication **12** exaggeration **13** overstatement

fishwife
5 harpy, scold, shrew, vixen **6** virago **9** termagant, Xanthippe

fishy
7 dubious, suspect **8** doubtful, unlikely **9** ambiguous, dubitable, equivocal, uncertain **10** suspicious **11** problematic **12** questionable

fission element
7 uranlum **9** plutonium

fissure
3 gap **4** gash, hole, part, rent, rift **5** break, chasm, chink, cleft, crack, split **6** breach, cleave, divide, schism **7** crevice, discord, opening, rupture **8** crevasse, fracture **10** disharmony, separation

fist
4 duke, grip, hand **5** clamp, grasp **6** clench, clinch, clutch

fit
3 apt, set **4** able, buff, hale, jibe, just, sane, suit, turn **5** adapt, agree, frame, ready, sound, spasm, spell, tally, throe, toned **6** access, accord, adjust, attack, become, belong, decent, go with, proper, seemly, square, tailor, useful **7** capable, conform, healthy, prepare, qualify, seizure, tantrum **8** assemble, decorous, dovetail, eligible, paroxysm, suitable **9** agree with, congruous, consonant, harmonize, reconcile **10** applicable, convenient, correspond, felicitous, go together **11** accommodate, appropriate
for a king: **5** regal

fitful
6 random, spotty **7** erratic **8** periodic, sporadic, variable **9** haphazard, hit-or-miss, irregular,

spasmodic, uncertain **10** changeable, convulsive, herky-jerky, inconstant **12** intermittent

fitness
4 trim **5** order, shape **6** fettle, health, kilter, repair **7** account, decorum, service, utility **8** capacity **9** condition, propriety, relevance **11** eligibility, suitability **13** applicability

fit out
3 arm, rig **5** equip **6** outfit **7** appoint, furnish **8** accouter, accoutre

fitting
3 apt, due **4** able, just, meet, part, true **5** happy, right **6** proper, seemly **7** apropos, germane **8** apposite, relevant, suitable **9** accessory, befitting, pertinent, qualified **10** applicable, attachment, felicitous, harmonious **11** appropriate

fit together
4 hook, join, mesh **6** hook up **7** connect **8** dovetail **9** integrate

Fitzgerald novel
10 Last Tycoon (The) **11** Great Gatsby (The) **16** Tender Is the Night **17** Tales of the Jazz Age **18** This Side of Paradise **17** All the Sad Young Men **21** Beautiful and the Damned (The)

Fitzgerald of jazz
4 Ella

five
combining form: **4** pent **5** penta **6** quinqu **7** quinque
group of: **6** pentad **7** quintet

five-dollar bill
3 fin

fivefold
9 quintuple

Five Nations
8 Iroquois
member: **7** Cayugas, Mohawks, Oneidas, Senecas **9** Onondagas

five-sided figure
8 pentagon

five-star
6 deluxe, superb **8** superior, top-notch **9** excellent, first-rate **10** first-class **11** outstanding

five-year period
6 luster, lustre **7** lustrum

fix
3 jam, rig, set **4** cook, cure, geld, mend, mess, moor, root, spay, spot, work **5** affix, alter, catch, patch, ready, renew, rivet, solve, state, stick **6** adjust, anchor, assign, attach, change, decide, doctor, fasten, neuter, pickle, plight, repair, revamp, scrape, secure, settle, square, steady **7** appoint, arrange, correct, dilemma, impress, ingrain, resolve, restore, specify, work out **8** castrate, discover, overhaul, position, renovate, solution **9** condition, establish, stabilize, sterilize **11** predicament

fixation
5 craze, mania **6** fetish **9** obsession **11** fascination, infatuation

___ fixe
4 idée, prix

fixed
3 pat, set **4** fast, firm, sure **6** frozen, secure, stable, stated, steady **7** abiding, certain, limited, precise, settled **8** anchored, constant, definite, enduring, immobile, resolute **9** exclusive, immovable, immutable, permanent, steadfast, tenacious **10** inflexible, invariable, restricted, stationary, stipulated, unswerving, unwavering **11** determinate, unalterable **12** concentrated, unchangeable **13** circumscribed

fixture
9 appliance **10** attachment

fizz
4 buzz, foam, hiss **5** froth **6** bubble, spirit **7** bubbles, sparkle, sputter **10** effervesce, liveliness **13** effervescence

fizzle
4 bomb, fail, flop **6** fiasco **7** failure, misfire **8** miscarry, peter out **10** effervesce **11** fall through

fjord
Baffin Island: **9** Admiralty
Denmark: **3** Ise, Lim **5** Lamme
Iceland: **4** Axar, Eyja **5** Horna, Skaga, Vopna
Norway: **3** Tys **4** Bokn, Nord, Salt, Stor, Tana, Vest **5** Lakse, Ranen, Sogne **9** Stavanger, Trondheim
Spitsbergen: **3** Ice
Svalbard: **4** Stor

flab
3 fat **4** bulk, lard **5** flesh **7** blubber, fatness **9** cellulite **10** corpulence **11** love handles

flabbergast
3 awe **4** stun **5** amaze, shock, throw **7** astound, nonplus **8** astonish, bowl over, dumfound, surprise **9** dumbfound, overwhelm

flabby
4 soft **5** slack **6** doughy, fleshy **7** flaccid

flaccid
4 limp, soft, weak **6** droopy, feeble, flabby, floppy

flag
3 ebb, lag, sag, tag **4** fade, fail, hail, iris, jack, sign, swag, tail, tire, waft, wane, wave, wilt **5** abate, color, droop, stone **6** banner, burgee, colors, ensign, falter, guidon, pennon, signal, weaken **7** bunting, decline, pendant, pennant **8** bannerol, gonfalon, languish, Old Glory, penalize, registry, standard, streamer, tricolor,

vexillum **9** banderole, blue peter, oriflamme, Union Jack **10** Jolly Roger **11** deteriorate **12** Stars and Bars

flagellate
4 beat, flog, hide, lash, whip **5** whale **6** larrup, lather, stripe, switch, thrash **7** scourge **9** horsewhip

flagitious
4 evil **6** sinful, wicked **7** corrupt, vicious **8** criminal, depraved, infamous, perverse, shameful **9** miscreant, nefarious, perverted **10** degenerate, outrageous, scandalous, villainous **11** disgraceful

flagon
3 jug **4** ewer **5** stein, stoup **6** vessel **7** tankard

flagpole
4 mast **5** staff
rope: **7** halyard

flag-raising site
7 Iwo Jima

flagrant
4 bold, rank **5** gross **6** wanton **7** blatant, glaring, heinous, obvious **8** striking **9** atrocious, egregious, monstrous **10** outrageous **11** conspicuous

flagstone
5 shale, slate

flag-waver
7 patriot **8** jingoist, loyalist **10** chauvinist **11** nationalist **12** superpatriot

flail
4 club, beat, flog, whip **6** strike, thrash, thresh **7** scourge **8** flounder, thresher

flair
4 bent, chic, élan, gift **5** éclat, knack, style **6** genius, talent **7** ability, aptness, faculty, panache **8** aptitude, tendency **10** proclivity **11** inclination

flak
4 fire **5** abuse **6** shells **7** censure, vitriol **9** brickbats, criticism, hostility **10** opposition **11** disapproval **12** condemnation, fault-finding

flake
3 bit **4** chip, kook, peel **5** scale **6** lamina **7** oddball **8** crackpot, fragment **9** eccentric

flake off
4 chip, peel **5** scale **9** exfoliate **10** desquamate

flaky
3 odd **5** ditsy, ditzy, goofy, nutty, wacky, weird **6** fickle, screwy **7** bizarre, erratic, offbeat **9** eccentric

flambé
6 ablaze, aflame, alight **7** blazing, flaming

flambeau
5 torch

flamboyant
4 loud **5** gaudy, showy **6** flashy, florid, ornate, rococo **7** baroque, splashy **8** colorful, luscious **10** over-the-top **12** ostentatious

flame
4 beau, dear, fire, glow, love **5** ardor, blaze, flare, flash, honey, light, lover **7** beloved, darling, passion, sweetie **8** ladylove, truelove **9** boyfriend, inamorata, inamorato **10** brilliance, brightness, girlfriend, heartthrob, sweetheart

flamen
6 priest

flaming
5 afire, fiery **6** ablaze, alight, ardent, red-hot **7** blazing, burning, fervent, flaring, ignited, intense **10** hot-blooded, passionate **11** conflagrant, impassioned

flammable
8 burnable **9** ignitable **10** incendiary **11** combustible
liquid: **3** gas, oil **7** acetone, alcohol, ethanol **8** gasoline, kerosene **9** petroleum **10** turpentine

Flanders
capital: **5** Lille
language: **7** Flemish
river: **4** Yser

flaneur
5 idler **12** boulevardier, man-about-town

flank
4 abut, side **6** adjoin, border

flap
3 tab, tap **4** beat, flog, fold, slap, stew, to-do, wave, wing **5** fling, hoo-ha, panel, tizzy **6** crisis, dither, furore, hoo-hah, hubbub, lather, pother, ruckus, tumult, uproar **7** aileron, flutter, turmoil **8** foofaraw **9** agitation, commotion, confusion, kerfuffle

flapdoodle
3 rot **4** bosh, bull, nuts **5** drool, fudge, hokum, hooey **6** bunkum, drivel **7** baloney, blarney, hogwash, rubbish **8** malarkey, nonsense, tommyrot **9** poppycock **10** applesauce, balderdash **12** blatherskite, fiddle-faddle, fiddlesticks

flapjack
7 hotcake, pancake **11** griddle cake

flare
4 burn **5** blaze, burst, flame, flash **6** signal **7** flicker **8** outburst
type: **5** Hyder **9** air-assist **11** steam-assist

flare-up
5 blaze, burst, flame, flash, surge **8** eruption, outburst **9** explosion

flaring
5 afire, fiery **6** ablaze, aflame, alight **7** blazing, burning **11** conflagrant

flash
3 ray **4** beam, rush, snap, show **5** blaze, bling, blink, crack, flame, flare, glare, gleam, glint, jiffy, shake, shine, showy, spark, speed **6** dazzle, expose, flaunt, glance, minute, moment, second **7** display, disport, exhibit, flicker, glamour, glimmer, glisten, glitter, instant, pizzazz, shimmer, show off, spangle, sparkle, twinkle **8** brandish **9** coruscate **11** coruscation, scintillate, split second **13** scintillation

flashy
4 loud **5** gaudy, jazzy, showy **6** brazen, florid, garish, glitzy, ornate, snazzy, sporty, tawdry, tinsel **7** blatant, chintzy, glaring, insipid **9** sparkling **10** flamboyant, glittering **12** meretricious, ostentatious

flask
4 olpe, vial **5** phial **6** bottle, fiasco, flacon **7** ampulla, canteen, costrel, thermos

flat
3 dim, mat **4** dead, drab, dull, even **5** banal, bland, exact, fixed, flush, level, muted, plane, prone, rooms, stale, vapid **7** insipid, prosaic **8** lodgings, tenement, unsavory **9** apartment, colorless, innocuous **10** flavorless, lackluster, monotonous

flat boat
4 scow **5** barge

flatfish
4 sole **6** plaice, turbot **7** halibut **8** flounder

flatland
4 mesa **5** plain **6** steppe, tundra **7** plateau **9** tableland

flat-out
8 absolute **9** downright **10** absolutely

flatten
4 deck, down, dull, even, fell, raze **5** crush, floor, level **6** smooth, squash **9** knock down, prostrate

flattened at the poles
6 oblate

flatter
4 coax, suit **5** toady **6** become, cajole, praise, stroke **7** adulate, blarney, gratify, wheedle **8** blandish, bootlick, butter up, soft-soap **9** sweet-talk

flattery
5 smarm **6** butter, praise **7** blarney **8** cajolery, soft soap, toadyism **9** adulation, sweet talk **10** sycophancy **11** compliments **12** blandishment, ingratiation, unctuousness

flat-topped hill
4 mesa **5** butte

Flaubert, Gustave
birthplace: **5** Rouen
heroine: **4** Emma (Bovary)
novel: **8** Salammbô **12** Madame Bovary

flaunt
4 show, wave **5** flash, flout, vaunt **6** expose, parade **7** display, disport, exhibit, show off **8** brandish, flourish

flavor
4 race, tang, zest, zing **5** sapor, savor, smack, spice, taste, tinge **6** relish, season **7** variety, version
enhancer: **3** MSG

flavorless
4 flat **5** bland, stale **7** insipid **8** unsavory **11** unpalatable

flavorsome
5 sapid, tasty, yummy **6** savory **9** delicious, palatable **10** appetizing, delectable **11** good-tasting

flaw
3 gap, rip, sin **4** blot, chip, tear, vice **5** crack, fault **6** defect **7** blemish **8** weakness **9** deformity **12** imperfection

flawed
5 amiss **6** faulty, marred **7** damaged, spoiled **8** impaired **9** defective, imperfect

flawless
4 pure **5** ideal, model **6** intact **7** perfect **8** seamless, unmarred **9** exquisite **10** immaculate, impeccable **11** unblemished

flax
5 linen
fiber: **3** tow
prepare: **3** ret **4** card **5** dress **6** hackle, scutch

flaxen
4 fair **5** blond, straw **6** blonde, golden, yellow **7** towhead

flay
4 beat, lash, peel, skin **7** blister, censure, lambast, upbraid **8** lambaste **9** castigate, criticize, excoriate

flea
6 chigoe, jigger **7** chigger
water: **7** daphnid

Fleance's father
6 Banquo

flèche
5 spire

fleck
3 dot **4** mark, mote, spot **5** flake, speck **6** dapple, mottle, streak, stripe **7** spatter, speckle, stipple **8** particle **9** bespeckle

Fledermaus, Die
3 bat
character: **5** Adele, Falke, Frank **6** Alfred **9** Rosalinde **10** Eisenstein
composer: **7** Strauss (Johann)

fledge
4 rear **7** feather

fledgling
4 colt, tyro **6** novice, rookie **8** beginner, freshman, neophyte, newcomer **10** apprentice

flee
3 fly, lam, run **4** bolt, scat, skip **5** elude, scoot, scram, skirr, steal **6** decamp, escape **7** abscond, make off, run away, scamper, vamoose **8** stampede, turn tail **9** skedaddle **10** make tracks

fleece
3 rob **4** bilk, clip, gaff, milk, rook, skin, soak, wool **5** bleed, cheat, cozen, mulct, shear, stick, sweat **6** extort, hustle, rip off **7** defraud, swindle **8** flimflam **10** overcharge

fleecy
5 downy **6** fluffy, pilose, woolly **7** hirsute **9** whiskered **10** flocculent

fleer
4 gibe, gird, jeer, jest, mock, quip **5** flout, laugh, scoff, scout, sneer, taunt

fleet
4 fast, navy, spry **5** agile, brisk, group, hasty, quick, rapid, swift **6** argosy, armada, nimble, speedy **8** flotilla **9** breakneck **10** harefooted

fleeting
5 brief **7** passing **8** fugitive, volatile **9** ephemeral, fugacious, momentary, temporary, transient **10** evanescent, short-lived, transitory

Fleming, Ian
see **James Bond**

flesh
4 beef, meat, skin **5** stock **7** kindred **9** offspring, relatives, substance

fleshly
5 obese **6** animal, bodily, carnal **7** lustful, profane, secular, sensual **8** corporal, physical, sensuous, temporal **9** corporeal, epicurean, luxurious, sybaritic **10** voluptuous

fleshy
3 fat **5** ample, beefy, burly, gross, heavy, hefty, husky, meaty, obese, plump, pudgy, stout, tubby **6** chubby, chunky, portly, rotund **7** porcine, weighty **9** corpulent **10** overweight, well-padded
fruit: **4** plum, pome **5** berry, drupe, grape, mango, peach **6** cherry **8** cucumber

Fletcher's partner
8 Beaumont (Francis)

fleur-de-lis
4 iris

flex
4 bend **5** tense

flexible
5 lithe, loose **6** docile, floppy, limber, pliant, supple **7** elastic, pliable, springy, willowy **8** amenable, bendable, stretchy, yielding **9** adaptable, compliant, malleable, tractable

flexion
3 bow **4** bend, fold, turn **5** angle

flexuous
5 fluid, lithe, snaky **7** sinuous, winding **8** tortuous **10** circuitous, convoluted, meandering, serpentine **11** anfractuous

flick
4 film, show **5** movie **13** motion picture, moving picture

flicker
4 bird, film, flit, hint **5** flash, gleam, glint, movie, waver **6** quiver **7** twinkle **10** woodpecker **13** motion picture, moving picture

flickering
7 lambent **8** unsteady

flier
3 ace **5** pilot **6** airman, insert **7** aviator, birdman, handout **8** aviatrix, brochure, circular **9** throwaway

flight
3 hop, lam **4** rout, soar, slip, wing **5** flock, floor, flush, flyby, story **6** escape, flying, series **7** getaway **8** breakout
formation: **7** echelon
info: **3** ETA
overnight: **6** redeye

flightless bird
3 emu, moa **4** kiwi, rhea **7** ostrich

flighty
5 dizzy, giddy, silly, swift **7** foolish **8** freakish, skittish, unstable, volatile **9** frivolous, mercurial, transient **10** capricious, changeable, inconstant **11** empty-headed, harebrained **13** irresponsible

flimflam
3 con, gyp **4** bilk, dupe, fake, fool, gull, hoax, jazz, sham **5** cheat, cozen, fraud, hokum, trick **6** chouse, deceit, diddle, humbug **7** chicane, deceive, defraud, swindle **8** hoodwink, trickery **9** bamboozle, deception, moonshine **10** balderdash, double-talk **11** hornswoggle

flimflammer
3 gyp **5** cheat **6** con man **7** diddler, sharper **8** swindler **9** defrauder **11** four-flusher **12** double-dealer

flimsy
4 limp, weak **5** cheap, filmy, frail, gauzy, sheer **6** feeble, flabby, sleazy, slight **7** flaccid, fragile, rickety, spindly, tenuous, unsound **8** decrepit, delicate, gossamer **10** diaphanous, improbable **11** implausible, transparent **12** unconvincing **13** insubstantial

flinch
5 quail, start, wince **6** blench, cringe, recoil, shrink

fling
3 peg **4** cast, emit, fire, flap, hurl, plop, rush,

shot, slap, stab, tear, toss **5** binge, chuck, heave, pitch, shoot, spree, throw **6** affair, charge, hurtle, launch **7** splurge **8** catapult

Flintstones, The
character: **4** Dino, Fred **5** Betty (Rubble), Wilma **6** Barney (Rubble) **8** Bamm-Bamm
creator: **5** Hanna (Bill) **7** Barbera (Joe)
setting: **7** Bedrock
voice: **5** Blanc (Mel)

flip
4 glib, leaf, pert, riff, toss, wise **6** breezy, invert, riffle, ruffle, switch **8** turn over **10** somersault **11** impertinent, smart-alecky

flip-flop
5 U-turn, waver **6** sandal, switch, waffle **7** reverse **8** reversal **9** about-face, turnabout, vacillate, volte-face **10** turnaround **11** vacillation

flippancy
5 cheek **6** levity **8** archness, pertness **9** cockiness, freshness, frivolity **10** cheekiness, impishness **11** roguishness

flippant
4 glib, pert **5** sassy, saucy **6** breezy, cheeky **11** impertinent, smart-alecky **13** disrespectful

flirt
3 toy **4** flit, fool, minx, ogle, vamp, wink **5** dally, tease **6** coquet, trifle, wanton **8** coquette **10** experiment, mess around

flit
3 fly, zip **4** dart, pass, rush, sail, scud, whiz, wing **5** flash, hurry, scoot, speed **7** flicker, flutter, twinkle

flitter
4 dart, flap, wing **5** hover, waver **6** quiver **7** skitter **9** fluctuate

flivver
6 jalopy **9** tin lizzie

float
3 bob, fly **4** buoy, cork, hang, raft, ride, sail, scud, swim, waft **5** drift, hover **6** wander **7** pontoon, propose **8** levitate **9** negotiate

floater
3 bum, vag **4** hobo, raft **5** tramp **7** drifter, vagrant **8** derelict, vagabond **10** roustabout

floating
5 fluid, loose **6** adrift, natant **7** buoyant, movable **8** moveable, shifting, variable **10** adjustable **11** fluctuating

flocculent
5 flaky **6** fleecy, fluffy, woolly

flock
3 mob **4** army, bevy, herd, host, mass, pack, rout, wisp **5** brood, bunch, cloud, covey, crowd, drove, group, laity, skein **6** flight, gaggle, gather, legion, scores, throng **8** assemble, assembly, converge **9** multitude **11** aggregation **12** congregation

floe
3 ice **4** berg **7** glacier, iceberg **8** ice field

flog
3 tan **4** beat, cane, flap, hide, lash, slog, whip **5** birch, drive, flail, whale **6** larrup, lather, stripe, switch, thrash **7** cowhide, leather, scourge **10** flagellate

flood
4 fill, flow, flux, glut, pour, rush, tide **5** burst, drown, float, spate, swamp **6** deluge, engulf, stream **7** current, freshet, immerse, Niagara, torrent **8** alluvion, cataract, inundate, overflow, submerge **9** avalanche, cataclysm, overwhelm **10** inundation, outpouring

floor
3 awe **4** base, down, drop, fell, stun, tier **5** amaze, étage, level, shock, story **6** ground **7** astound, flatten **8** astonish, audience, bowl down, bowl over, surprise **9** dumbfound, knock down **11** flabbergast

floor covering, for short
4 lino

floor model
4 demo

flop
3 dud **4** bomb, bust, fail, fall **5** lemon, loser **6** bummer, fizzle, turkey **7** clinker, failure

flophouse
4 doss **7** fleabag

floppy
4 disk, limp **6** flimsy **7** flaccid **8** diskette, flexible

flora
6 plants **10** vegetation

flora and fauna
5 biota

floral necklace
3 lei

floral perfume
4 atar **5** attar

Florence
bridge: **12** Ponte Vecchio
cathedral: **5** Duomo
family: **6** Medici
museum: **6** Uffizi **8** Bargello
palace: **5** Pitti
river: **4** Arno

florid
3 red **5** flush, gaudy, ruddy, showy **6** ornate, rococo **7** baroque, flowery, flushed, glowing **8** rubicund, sanguine, sonorous **9** bombastic, elaborate, overblown **10** euphuistic, flamboyant, rhetorical **11** declamatory **12** magniloquent **13** grandiloquent

Florida
capital: **11** Tallahassee

city: **5** Miami, Ocala, Tampa **6** Naples, Venice **7** Hialeah, Key West, Orlando **8** Sarasota **9** Palm Beach **11** St. Augustine **12** Jacksonville, St. Petersburg
college, university: **7** Rollins, Stetson
county: **3** Lee **4** Dade **6** Orange **7** Broward, Volusia **8** Pinellas, Sarasota
key: **4** Long, Vaca, West **5** Largo **7** Big Pine **9** Matecumbe, Sugarloaf
lake: **9** Kissimmee **10** Okeechobee
nickname: **8** Sunshine (State)
park: **10** Everglades
race site: **7** Daytona
river: **6** Indian **7** St. Johns **8** Suwannee **12** Apalachicola
state bird: **11** mockingbird
state flower: **13** orange blossom
state tree: **9** sabal palm

florilegium
5 album **6** reader **7** garland, omnibus **8** analects **9** anthology **10** collection, miscellany

Florimel's husband
7 Marinel

floss
4 down, fuzz, lint **5** fluff **6** thread

flotilla
5 fleet **6** argosy, armada

Flotow opera
5 Indra **6** L'Ombre, Martha

flotsam
6 debris, jetsam **7** remains **8** wreckage **9** driftwood

flounce
5 frill, mince, strut, waltz **6** bounce, prance, ruffle, sashay

flounder
3 dab **5** slosh **6** fumble, muddle, plaice, splash, thrash, wallow **7** blunder, flounce **8** flatfish, struggle

flour
4 meal **6** pinole, powder
beetle: **6** weevil
merchant: **6** miller

flourish
3 wax **4** grow, wave **5** adorn, bloom **6** flower, stroke, thrive **7** blossom, burgeon, develop, fanfare, prosper, succeed **8** brandish, curlicue, ornament **13** embellishment, ornamentation

flout
4 defy, mock **5** scorn, spurn **6** deride, insult **7** scoff at

flow
3 run **4** emit, flux, gush, ooze, pour, rill, rise, rush, stem, tide, well **5** arise, drift, flood, issue, spate, spill, surge, swarm **6** course, deluge, onrush, sluice, spring, stream **7** cascade, current, emanate, give off, outflow, proceed **8** inundate, sequence **9** discharge, originate **10** continuity, inundation, succession **11** progression **12** continuation

flower
4 best, blow, pick, posy **5** bloom, cream, elite, pride, prime, prize **6** choice, thrive **7** blossom, burgeon, develop **10** effloresce **13** inflorescence
autumn: **5** aster
buttonhole: **11** boutonniere
cluster: **4** cyme **5** spike, umbel **6** corymb, floret, raceme, spadix **7** panicle **8** spikelet **9** capitulum, dichasium, glomerule **11** monochasium **13** inflorescence
cup: **5** calyx
garden: **4** iris, lily, pink, rose **5** aster, canna, daisy, oxlip, pansy, peony, phlox, poppy, tulip **6** azalia, cosmos, crocus, dahlia, orchid, violet **7** jonquil, petunia **8** camellia, daffodil, gardenia, geranium, gloxinia, hyacinth, larkspur, marigold, primrose **9** carnation, gladiolus, narcissus **10** delphinium, heliotrope **13** chrysanthemum
necklace: **3** lei
opening: **8** anthesis
part: **5** bract, calyx, ovary, ovule, petal, sepal, style **6** anther, pistil, spathe, stamen, stigma **7** corolla, nectary, pedicel, petiole **8** calyptra, filament, peduncle, perianth
spike: **5** ament **6** catkin, spadix
stalk: **7** pedicel **8** peduncle
type: **3** ray **4** disk **6** annual, simple **9** composite, perennial
wild: **4** flag **5** bluet, daisy, vetch **6** lupine **7** anemone, arbutus, cowslip, gentian, vervain **8** bluebell, hepatica, trillium **9** buttercup, columbine, dandelion, saxifrage **10** cinquefoil **12** lady's slipper

flower arranging
7 ikebana

flowering
6 abloom, growth **8** progress **9** evolution **11** development, florescence, progression

flowerless plant
4 fern, moss **6** lichen **9** liverwort

flowery
5 wordy **6** florid, ornate, prolix **7** aureate, diffuse, verbose **8** sonorous **9** overblown **10** euphuistic, rhetorical **11** declamatory **12** magniloquent **13** grandiloquent

Flowery Kingdom
5 China

flowing
4 easy **5** fluid **6** fluent, liquid, smooth **7** cursive, running **10** effortless
back: **6** reflux **8** refluent
in: **6** influx **8** influent
together: **7** conflux **9** confluent

flow regulator
4 cock, gate **5** valve **8** throttle

flu
6 grippe
symptom: **4** ache, ague
type: **5** avian

flub
3 err **4** goof, mess, muff, slip **5** boner, botch, error, fluff, gaffe, lapse, snarl **6** bobble, bollix, bungle, foul up, goof up, mess up **7** blunder, faux pas, louse up

fluctuate
4 sway, yo-yo **5** swing, waver **6** seesaw **8** undulate **9** alternate, oscillate, vacillate

flue
4 duct, pipe, tube, vent **6** funnel, uptake **7** channel, chimney, outtake

fluent
4 easy, glib **5** fluid **6** facile, liquid, smooth, supple **7** cursive, flowing, voluble **8** eloquent, polished **10** articulate, effortless

fluff
4 down, flub, fuzz, goof, lint, mess, muff, slip, trip **5** boner, botch, error, floss, gaffe, lapse, whisk **6** bobble, bollix, bungle, goof up, mess up **7** blooper, blunder, faux pas, louse up, mistake

fluffy
5 downy **6** flossy **7** cursory, shallow **8** puffed up **10** flocculent **11** superficial **13** unsubstantial

fluid
4 free, sera (plural) **5** lymph, serum, water **6** liquid, mobile, molten, serous, watery **7** mutable, protean **8** flexible, shifting, unstable, unsteady, variable **9** adaptable, changeful, unsettled **10** changeable
excessive: **5** edema

fluke
3 hap **4** lobe, worm **5** quirk **6** chance **8** flatfish, fortuity **9** trematode

fluky
3 odd **6** casual, chance, chancy, random **9** arbitrary **10** accidental, fortuitous

flume
5 chute **6** sluice, stream **7** channel **8** aqueduct **11** watercourse

flummox
5 abash, addle **6** baffle, rattle, stymie **7** confuse, fluster, perplex **8** befuddle, bewilder, confound **9** discomfit, embarrass **10** disconcert

flunk
4 fail

flunky
4 peon **5** gofer, toady **6** drudge, lackey, stooge, yes-man **7** footman, servant, steward **8** factotum, follower

flurry
3 ado, fit **4** fuss, gust, spit, stir, to-do **5** haste, whirl **6** bother, bustle, furore, pother, tumult **7** barrage, flutter, turmoil **8** snowfall **9** agitation, commotion, confusion, whirlpool, whirlwind **10** excitement, turbulence

flush
4 even, flat, glow, pink, rich, rose, wash **5** bloom, color, level, plane, raise, rinse, rouge **6** florid, filled, mantle, redden, sluice **7** cleanse, crimson, glowing, inflame, opulent, suffuse, wealthy **8** abundant, abutting, irrigate, rubicund, sanguine, squarely **9** turn color

fluster
5 abash, addle, dizzy, shake, upset **6** ball up, bother, fuddle, muddle, rattle, ruffle **7** agitate, confuse, disturb, nonplus, perturb, unhinge **8** befuddle, bewilder, confound, disquiet, distract **10** discompose

flustered
5 upset **7** abashed, anxious, rattled **8** agitated, confused, troubled **9** chagrined, disturbed, flummoxed, perplexed, perturbed **10** bewildered, disquieted, distracted, distraught, distressed, nonplussed **11** discomposed, embarrassed **12** disconcerted

flute
4 fife, roll **5** pleat **6** goffer, groove **7** chamfer, channel, piccolo **8** recorder **9** wineglass
Japanese: **10** shakuhachi
oval: **7** ocarina
player: **5** piper **7** flutist **8** flautist

flutist
American: **5** Baker (Julius), Baron (Samuel) **7** Robison (Paula) **8** Zukerman (Eugenia)
French: **6** Rampal (Jean-Pierre)
Irish: **6** Galway (James)

flutter
4 beat, flap, flit **5** hover, quake, shake **6** flurry, quaver, quiver, wobble **7** flicker, flitter, pulsate, tremble, vibrate **9** agitation, commotion, confusion, palpitate, vibration **11** fluctuation

flu type
4 bird **5** Asian, avian, swine

flux
3 run **4** flow, fuse, melt, rush, thaw, tide **5** drift, flood, spate **6** change, stream **7** current, flowing, outflow, torrent **8** dissolve
unit: **5** tesla

fly
3 zip **4** bolt, dart, dash, flee, flit, lure, scud, skip, soar, whiz, wing **5** fleet, float, glide, hover, hurry, pilot, scoot, shoot, skirr, sweep, whish, whisk **6** aviate, escape, hasten, hustle **7** abscond, flutter
insect: **3** ked **4** gnat **5** midge **6** botfly, gadfly, mayfly, tsetse **7** deerfly, sandfly **8** blackfly,

dipteron, horsefly, housefly, tachinid **10** bluebottle
larva: **6** maggot

fly-by-night
5 shady **7** passing **9** transient **10** transitory, unreliable **12** disreputable, undependable **13** untrustworthy

flycatcher
5 pewee **6** phoebe, tyrant **8** bellbird, kingbird **9** passerine

flyer
(see **flier**)

flying
5 aloft **6** volant **8** airborne

Flying Dutchman, The
composer: **6** Wagner (Richard)
heroine: **5** Senta

flying fish
7 gurnard

flying fox
3 bat **8** fruit bat

flying horse
7 Pegasus **10** hippogriff

flying island
6 Laputa

flying lemur
6 oolugo

flying mammal
3 bat

flying saucer
3 UFO

fly in the ointment
5 catch **8** drawback

foam
4 head, scud, scum, suds, surf **5** churn, froth, spume **6** bubble, lather, seethe **7** bubbles **10** effervesce

fob
4 seal **5** chain **6** pocket, ribbon **8** ornament

fob off
5 foist **6** put off **7** palm off, pass off

focus
3 fix, hub **4** node, zoom **5** heart, rivet **6** adjust, center, fixate, home in **8** converge, emphasis, meditate, polestar **9** concenter, epicenter **10** hypocenter **11** concentrate, nerve center

fodder
4 feed, food **6** forage, silage, stover **9** provender
crop: **3** hay, oat, rye **4** corn **5** maize, vetch, wheat **6** barley, clover, millet **7** alfalfa, sorghum
storage structure: **4** silo
store: **6** ensile

foe
5 enemy, rival **8** opponent **9** adversary **10** antagonist

fog
4 blur, daze, foam, haze, mist, murk, soup **5** brume, cloud, vapor **6** miasma, muddle **7** pea soup, pogonip

foggy
4 hazy **5** dirty, grimy, misty, murky, soupy, vague **7** brumous, muddled, obscure, tenuous **8** confused, pea soupy, vaporous

fogy
4 coot **5** crank **6** codger, dotard, fossil, square **7** diehard **8** mossback **10** fuddy-duddy **12** antediluvian, conservative **11** standpatter **13** stick-in-the-mud

fogyish
7 old-line **8** outmoded, standpat **9** hidebound, out-of-date **10** antiquated, fuddy-duddy, mossbacked **11** reactionary **12** conservative, old-fashioned

foible
4 vice **5** fault **6** defect **7** failing, frailty **8** weakness **11** shortcoming **12** imperfection, idiosyncrasy

foil
4 balk, beat, curb, dash, faze **5** check, sword **6** baffle, defeat, rattle, thwart **7** buffalo **8** contrast, restrain **9** discomfit, embarrass, frustrate **10** circumvent, disappoint, disconcert **11** straight man

foist
6 fob off **7** palm off, pass off

fold
3 pen, ply **4** bend, fail, tuck **5** drape, flock, knead, pleat, plica, ridge **6** crease, double, furrow, pucker **7** flexure, plicate **9** plication **11** corrugation
skin: **4** ruga **5** plica, rugae (plural) **6** dewlap, plicae (plural)

folder
4 file **6** binder **9** portfolio

foliage
6 growth, leaves **7** verdure **8** greenery, lushness **10** vegetation

folk
4 race, trad **6** people **9** community

folklore
4 myth, tale **5** fable **6** belief, custom, legend, mythos, wisdom **9** mythology, tradition **12** superstition

folks
6 family **7** parents **9** relatives

folksinger
4 Baez (Joan), Ives (Burl), Ochs (Phil) **5** Dylan (Bob), Niles (John Jacob), White (Josh) **6** Odetta, Seeger (Pete) **7** Collins (Judy), Guthrie (Arlo, Woody), Leadbelly, Robeson (Paul), Van Ronk (Dave), Weavers (The) **9** Belafonte (Harry), Ledbetter (Huddie)

folksy
5 homey **6** casual, earthy, mellow, rustic, simple **7** natural **8** down-home, familiar, informal, laid-back, sociable **9** easygoing, ingenuous **10** unaffected, unpolished **13** unpretentious

folktale
4 lore, myth **5** fable **6** legend **7** märchen

follies
5 revue

follow
3 dog, spy, tag **4** hunt, keep, obey, seek, tail, walk **5** catch, chase, ensue, grasp, hound, trace, track, trail **6** accept, comply, convoy, pursue, search, shadow, travel **7** conform, imitate, proceed, replace, succeed **8** practice, supplant **9** supersede
closely: **5** draft **10** slipstream

follower
3 fan **5** toady **6** addict, cohort, minion, sequel, votary **7** acolyte, apostle, devotee, groupie, habitué, sectary, trailer, wannabe **8** adherent, advocate, disciple, faithful, hanger-on, henchman, myrmidon, parasite, partisan, tagalong **9** dependent, satellite, supporter, sycophant **10** aficionado

following
4 next **5** after, below, later, since **6** behind, public **7** ensuing, retinue **8** audience **9** adherents, afterward, believers, disciples, entourage, partisans **10** afterwards, sequential, supporters, subsequent, succeeding, successive **12** subsequently, subsequent to

follow-up
6 sequel

folly
4 whim **6** lunacy, vanity **7** fatuity, foolery, inanity, madness **8** insanity, nonsense **9** absurdity, craziness, dottiness, silliness, stupidity **10** indulgence **11** foolishness **12** extravagance
goddess: **3** Atë

foment
3 sow **4** brew, goad, spur **5** rouse, set on **6** arouse, excite, foster, incite, stir up, whip up **7** agitate, nurture, provoke **9** cultivate, encourage, instigate

fond
4 dear, warm **5** silly **6** doting, loving, tender **7** devoted, fatuous, foolish, partial **8** desirous, enamored, romantic **9** indulgent **10** infatuated **11** sentimental **12** affectionate

Fond du ___
3 Lac

fondle
3 paw, pet **5** grope, touch **6** caress, cosset, dandle, stroke **7** embrace **8** canoodle

fondness
4 love **5** fancy, taste **6** liking, relish **8** appetite, devotion, penchant, soft spot, weakness **9** affection, tendresse **10** attachment, partiality, preference, propensity **11** inclination **12** predilection

font
4 root, type **5** basin **6** origin, source **8** fountain **10** receptacle
feature: **5** serif

food
3 pap **4** chow, diet, eats, fare, grub, meal, meat **5** bread, manna **6** fodder, viands **7** aliment, cuisine, edibles, nurture, pabulum, vittles **8** delicacy, victuals **9** nutriment, provender **10** provisions, sustenance **11** comestibles, nourishment
additive: **3** MSG
disorder: **7** bulimia **8** anorexia
divine: **8** ambrosia
element: **5** fiber, fibre, sugar **6** starch **7** mineral, protein, vitamin **12** carbohydrate
from heaven: **5** manna
lover: **7** epicure, gourmet **8** gourmand
provision: **4** mess **6** ration **7** serving
scarcity: **6** famine
scrap: **3** ort
thickener: **4** agar
waste: **7** garbage

food-poisoning cause
5 E. coli

foofaraw
3 ado **4** fuss, stir, to-do **5** hoo-ha, stink **6** bother, finery, frills, furore, hoo-hah, hurrah, pother, ruckus, rumpus **8** brouhaha **9** commotion **11** disturbance

fool
3 ass, kid, oaf, rag, rib, sap, toy **4** boob, butt, clod, dolt, dope, dupe, fish, gull, hoax, jerk, jest, joke, josh, mook, zany **5** chump, clown, comic, dally, dummy, dunce, goose, idiot, loser, moron, ninny, patsy, schmo, trick **6** banter, cretin, dawdle, delude, diddle, dimwit, doodle, galoot, gammon, jester, lead on, meddle, monkey, motley, nitwit, pigeon, schmoe, stooge, sucker, tamper, trifle, victim **7** beguile, buffoon, chicane, deceive, fake out, fall guy, fritter, half-wit, jackass, mislead, pinhead, saphead, schmuck **8** bonehead, comedian, dumbbell, flimflam, hoodwink, imbecile, lunkhead, numskull, pushover **9** bamboozle, birdbrain, blockhead, interfere, simpleton **10** nincompoop **11** hornswoggle, merry-andrew, string along **13** laughingstock
around: **4** futz, idle, laze, loaf, loll **5** flirt **6** dawdle, diddle, lounge **8** lollygag, womanize **9** philander

foolhardy
4 bold, rash **6** daring, madcap **8** headlong, reckless **9** audacious, daredevil, impetuous **11** precipitate, temerarious

foolish
3 mad **4** daft, gaga, rash, zany **5** balmy, batty,

crazy, dippy, dizzy, dorky, dotty, goofy, inane, inept, kooky, loony, loopy, nutty, sappy, silly, wacky **6** absurd, insane, simple, stupid, unwise **7** asinine, doltish, fatuous, idiotic, lunatic, meshuga, moronic, witless **8** clueless, meshugge, reckless, trifling **9** cockamamy, half-baked, brainless, fantastic, frivolous, half-baked, imbecilic, insensate, laughable, ludicrous, senseless **10** cockamamie, half-cocked, half-witted, irrational, ridiculous **11** harebrained, nonsensical

foolishness
4 bull, bunk **5** folly, fudge **6** bêtise, bunkum, lunacy **7** fatuity, inanity, rubbish **8** claptrap, drollery, insanity, nonsense, tommyrot **9** absurdity, craziness, silliness, stupidity **10** imbecility, imprudence **12** fiddle-faddle **13** horsefeathers

fool's gold
6 pyrite

foot
3 paw, pay **4** hoof
ailment: 4 corn **6** bunion, callus
animal: 3 pad, paw **4** hoof
bones of: 5 talus, tarsi (plural) **6** cuboid, tarsal, tarsus **7** phalanx **9** calcaneus, cuneiform, navicular, phalanges (plural) **10** metatarsal
combining form: 3 ped, pod **4** pedi, pedo, podo
doctor: 10 podiatrist **11** chiropodist
metric: 4 iamb **5** arsis, paeon **6** dactyl, thesis **7** anapest, pyrrhic, spondee, trochee
part: 3 toe **4** arch, ball, claw, nail **5** ankle, digit, talon **6** hallux, instep

football
4 nerf **5** rugby **6** rugger, soccer **7** pigskin
field: 8 gridiron
foul: 7 holding, offside **8** clipping **12** interference
official: 6 umpire **7** referee **8** linesman **9** back judge, line judge **10** field judge
play: 4 dive, trap **5** sneak, sweep **6** option, screen **7** audible, counter, handoff, rollout, runback **8** dropback **9** crossbuck, off-tackle **10** buttonhook
player position: 3 end **4** back, half, wing **5** guard **6** center, kicker, safety, tackle **7** flanker, lineman, wideout **8** defender, fullback, halfback, linesman, receiver, scatback, slotback, split end, tailback, tight end, wingback **9** noseguard **10** cornerback, linebacker, nose tackle **11** placekicker, quarterback, running back, snapper-back **12** defensive end, strong safety, wide receiver
scoring: 6 safety **9** field goal, touchdown **10** conversion
starting play: 7 kickoff
team: 6 eleven
term: 4 down, kick, pass, punt, rush, snap **5** blitz, block, squad **6** fumble, huddle, kicker, onside, option, player, safety, spiral **7** end zone, handoff, kickoff, offside, pigskin, quarter, spinner, tweener, yardage **8** clipping, crossbar, goal line, goalpost, gridiron, halftime **9** backfield, defensive, field goal, intercept, offensive, placekick, scrimmage, touchback, touchdown **11** ballcarrier, broken field **12** interception, triple threat
(see also **National Football League**)

footballer
4 Kemp (Jack), Long (Howie), Lott (Ronnie), Levy (Marv), Monk (Art), Moon (Warren), Reed (Andre), Rice (Jerry) **5** Allen (Marcus), Baugh (Sammy), Berry (Raymond), Brady (Tom), Brown (Bob, Jim), Clark (Gary), Ditka (Mike), Elway (John), Eller (Carl), Favre (Brett), Gibbs (Joe), Grier (Rosie), Groza (Lou), Jones (Bert, Deacon), Kelly (Jim), Kosar (Bernie), Leahy (Pat), Lomax (Neil), Muñoz (Anthony), Shula (Don), Simms (Phil), Smith (Emmitt), Stagg (Amos Alonzo), Starr (Bart), Stram (Hank), Swann (Lynn), Young (Steve) **6** Aikman (Troy), Blanda (George), Butkus (Dick), Carter (Chris, Ki-Jana), Csonka (Larry), Dawson (Len), Ellard (Henry), Graham (Otto), Grange (Red), Greene (Joe), Harris (Franco), Jaeger (Jeff), Joiner (Charlie), Lofton (James), Lowery (Nick), Marino (Dan), Murray (Eddie), Namath (Joe), Payton (Walter), Rypien (Mark), Sayers (Gale), Slater (Jackie), Taylor (Lawrence), Thorpe (Jim), Tittle (Y. A.), Turner (Jim), Unitas (Johnny), Walker (Herschel) **7** Bledsoe (Drew), Dorsett (Tony), Esiason (Boomer), Gifford (Frank), Hornung (Paul), Johnson (Norm), Largent (Steve), Luckman (Sid), Manning (Eli, Peyton), Montana (Joe), Newsome (Ozzie), Riggins (John), Rozelle (Pete), Sanders (Barry, Deion), Simpson (O. J.), Stabler (Ken), Thurman (Thomas) **8** Andersen (Morten), Anderson (Gary, Ottis), Bradshaw (Terry), Lombardi (Vince), Nagurski (Bronko), Plunkett (Jim), Staubach (Roger) **9** Dickerson (Eric), Jurgensen (Sonny), Hostetler (Jeff), Tarkenton (Fran) **10** Parseghian (Ara), Stallworth (John), Singletary (Mike), Stephenson (Dwight), Youngblood (Jack)
(see also **soccer**)

Foote play
15 Trip to Bountiful (The) **19** Young Man from Atlanta (The)

footfall
4 step **5** tread

footing
4 base, rank, seat, term **5** basis, place, state **6** bottom, ground, status **7** bedrock, seating, station, warrant **8** basement, capacity, pedestal, position, standing **9** character, situation **10** foundation, groundwork, substratum **12** underpinning

footless
4 dull, dumb **5** crass, dense, inept, unfit **6** apodal, stupid **7** foolish

foot lever
5 pedal 7 treadle
footman
7 servant 10 pedestrian 11 infantryman
footnote abbrev.
4 ibid., idem 5 op. cit. 6 loc. cit.
footpad
5 thief 6 mugger, robber 8 criminal 10 highwayman, pickpocket
footprint
3 pug 4 sign, step 5 spoor, trace, track, tract 7 pugmark, vestige
footslog
4 plod, slop, toil 5 tramp, tromp 6 trudge
footstone
6 ledger, marker 8 monument 11 grave marker
footstool
7 cricket, hassock, ottoman
fop
3 jay 4 beau 5 blade, blood, dandy, spark, swell 7 coxcomb, gallant 8 cavalier, macaroni, popinjay 9 exquisite, ladies' man, pretty boy 11 Beau Brummel, petit-maître 12 fashion plate, lounge lizard
foppish
6 chichi 8 dandyish, peacocky 10 peacockish
for
3 pro 7 in favor
forage
4 beat, comb, grub, prog, raid, rake, sack 5 scour 6 browse, fodder, ravage, rustle, search 7 plunder, ransack, rummage 8 finecomb, scrounge 9 pasturage
crop: 5 grass 6 clover, kochia 7 alfalfa, sorghum
(see also **fodder**)
foray
4 raid 6 inroad, sortie 8 invasion 9 incursion, irruption
forbear
4 shun 5 avoid, forgo, spare 6 endure, eschew, resist, suffer 7 abstain, decline, refrain 8 hold back, restrain, tolerate
forbearance
5 grace, mercy 6 lenity 7 charity 8 clemency, lenience, leniency, mildness, patience 9 restraint, tolerance 10 abstinence, toleration 13 consideration
forbearing
4 easy, kind, mild 6 gentle 7 clement, lenient, patient 8 merciful, tolerant 9 indulgent 10 charitable, thoughtful 11 considerate, magnanimous
Forbes hero
8 Tremaine (Johnny)
forbid
3 ban, bar, nix 4 curb, deny, halt, stop, veto 5 block, check, debar 6 enjoin, hinder, impede, outlaw, refuse 7 inhibit, prevent, rule out, shut out 8 disallow, obstruct, preclude, prohibit, restrain 9 interdict, proscribe
forbidden
5 taboo 6 banned, barred 7 illegal, illicit 8 verboten 10 prohibited
perfume: 4 Tabu
thing: 5 taboo
Forbidden City
5 Lhasa 6 Gu Gong 7 Beijing
forbidding
4 grim 5 drear, harsh 6 dreary, severe 8 daunting, menacing, sinister 9 repellent 10 formidable 11 threatening
force
3 jam 4 cram, dint, mana, push 5 drive, foist, impel, might, power, press, vigor, wreak, wreck, wrest 6 coerce, compel, demand, duress, effort, energy, extort, impose, legion, muscle, oblige 7 command, impetus, inflict, potency, require, sandbag 8 coercion, manpower, momentum, obligate, pressure, shoehorn, strength, violence 9 constrain, intensity, puissance, strong-arm 10 compulsion, constraint
apart: 5 wedge
unit: 4 dyne
forced
8 strained 9 contrived, unnatural 10 artificial, compulsory 11 involuntary
forceful
5 stiff, stout 6 mighty, potent, punchy, strong, virile 7 dynamic 8 emphatic, powerful, puissant, vigorous 9 assertive 10 compelling
forceless
4 lame, weak 5 wimpy 6 feeble 8 impotent, nugatory 9 powerless 10 inadequate 11 ineffective, ineffectual
force out
4 oust 5 eject, evict, expel 6 banish 7 extrude
forcible
8 coercive 9 compelled 10 compulsory, obligatory, peremptory
ford
5 cross
Ford's folly
5 Edsel
for each
3 per 6 apiece
forearm bone
4 ulna 5 radii (plural), ulnae (plural) 6 radius
forebear
8 ancestor 9 precursor 10 antecedent, progenitor 11 predecessor 12 primogenitor
forebode
5 augur 7 betoken, portend, predict, presage 8 foretell, prophesy, soothsay 13 prognosticate

foreboding
4 omen, sign **5** dread **6** augury **7** anxiety, portent, presage, warning **10** prediction, prognostic **11** premonition **12** apprehension, presentiment

forecast
5 augur **6** divine **7** foresee, portend, predict, presage **8** estimate, foretell, indicate, prophecy, prophesy **9** adumbrate, calculate, prevision, prognosis **10** prediction **13** prognosticate

forecaster
4 seer **5** augur **6** oracle **7** diviner, prophet **8** haruspex **9** predictor **10** prophesier, soothsayer, weatherman **11** Nostradamus **13** meteorologist, weatherperson

foreclose
3 bar **5** debar **6** cut off, hinder **7** prevent, shut out **8** preclude

forefather
see **forebear**

forefeel
6 divine **9** apprehend, prevision

forefinger
5 index

forefront
3 van **4** lead **8** vanguard **10** avant-garde, firing line **11** cutting edge

foregoer
6 herald **8** ancestor, forebear **9** harbinger, precursor, prototype **10** antecedent, antecessor, forerunner, progenitor **11** predecessor **12** primogenitor

foregoing
5 prior **6** former **7** earlier **8** anterior, previous **9** precedent, preceding **10** antecedent

forehanded
6 frugal **7** prudent, thrifty **8** sensible, well-to-do **9** provident **10** prosperous

forehead
4 brow **5** frons, front **8** sinciput **9** sincipita (plural)

foreign
5 alien **6** exotic **7** strange **8** external, offshore, overseas **9** extrinsic, nonnative **10** accidental, extraneous, immaterial, irrelevant **11** incongruous **12** adventitious, inapplicable, incompatible, inconsistent **13** inappropriate
prefix: **4** xeno

foreigner
5 alien **8** outsider, stranger **9** outlander **10** tramontane

Foreign Legion hat
4 kepi

foreknow
6 divine **9** apprehend, prevision **10** anticipate

foreland
4 beak, cape, head, ness **5** point **10** promontory

forelock
5 bangs, quiff **7** cowlick

foreman
4 bos'n, boss **5** bosun, chief **6** gaffer, ganger, honcho, leader **7** captain, manager, steward **8** overseer **9** boatswain **10** supervisor

foremost
4 arch, head, high, main **5** chief, first, front, grand **7** leading, premier, supreme **9** number one, paramount, principal **10** preeminent **11** cutting-edge, outstanding

forenoon
4 morn **7** morning **12** ante meridiem

forensic
8 judicial **9** debatable **10** rhetorical **13** argumentative

foreordain
4 doom, fate **9** determine **10** predestine **12** predetermine

forerunner
4 omen, sign **5** envoy **6** augury, herald **7** pioneer, portent, presage, symptom, warning **8** ancestor, exemplar, outrider **9** announcer, harbinger, initiator, messenger **10** antecedent, originator, prognostic **11** anticipator, predecessor

foresee
6 divine **7** predict, presage **8** perceive, prophesy **9** apprehend, prefigure, prevision **10** anticipate **13** prognosticate

foreseer
5 augur **6** auspex, oracle **7** diviner, prophet **8** haruspex **9** predictor **10** soothsayer **11** Nostradamus

foreshadow
4 bode, hint **5** augur **6** herald **7** betoken, portend, predict, presage, promise, suggest **8** forecast, intimate **9** adumbrate, prefigure **13** prognosticate

foresight
6 vision **7** caution **8** prudence, sagacity **10** discretion, perception, precaution, prescience, providence

forest
4 bosk, wood **5** copse, grove, weald, woods **6** bosque **7** coppice, thicket, woodlot **8** wildwood, woodland **10** timberland, wilderness
deity: **5** dryad **6** sylvan **8** Sylvanus
English: **4** Dean **5** Arden **8** Sherwood
German: **5** Black **11** Schwarzwald
opening: **5** glade
relating to: **6** sylvan
subarctic: **5** taiga
tropical: **5** selva **6** jungle

forestall
5 avert, block, deter **6** hinder **7** obviate,

preempt, prevent, rule out, ward off **8** preclude, stave off **10** anticipate

Forester, C. S.
hero: **10** Hornblower (Horatio)
novel: **12** African Queen (The)

foretell
4 bode, warn **5** augur **6** divine **7** portend, predict, presage, promise **8** proclaim, prophesy, soothsay **9** adumbrate, apprehend, prefigure **10** anticipate, vaticinate **13** prognosticate

forethought
8 judgment, planning, prudence **10** discretion, precaution **12** deliberation **13** premeditation

foretoken
4 bode, hint, omen, sign, warn **5** augur **6** augury, herald **7** portend, portent, presage, promise, symptom, warning **8** forecast **9** harbinger, precursor **10** intimation

forever
3 aye **6** always **7** endless **8** eternity, evermore **9** endlessly, eternally **10** in aeternum **11** ad infinitum, ceaselessly, continually, everlasting, incessantly, permanently, perpetually, unceasingly **12** in perpetuity **13** everlastingly

forewarning
5 alarm **6** caveat, threat, tip-off **7** caution **8** monition **11** premonition

foreword
5 intro, proem **7** preface, prelude **8** exordium, overture, preamble, prologue **12** introduction, prolegomenon

for example
3 say **6** such as

for fear that
4 lest

forfeit
4 cede, fine, lose **5** mulct **6** give up **7** penalty **9** sacrifice **10** amercement, relinquish

forfend
4 ward **5** avert, deter **6** secure **7** obviate, prevent, protect, rule out, ward off **8** preclude, preserve, stave off

forge
4 copy, fake, form, make **5** pound, shape **6** smithy **7** advance, fashion, imitate, produce, turn out **8** continue **9** construct, fabricate **11** counterfeit, manufacture
Vulcan's: **4** Etna

forget
4 fail, omit **6** ignore, slight **7** neglect **8** discount, overlook, pass over **9** disregard

forgetful
3 lax **5** slack **6** absent, remiss **7** amnesic **8** amnesiac, careless, heedless **9** negligent, oblivious, unwitting **10** abstracted, neglectful **11** inattentive, thoughtless **12** absentminded

forgetfulness
5 lethe **7** amnesia **8** oblivion **10** negligence **11** inattention

forgivable
6 venial **10** remissible

forgive
5 remit **6** excuse, pardon **7** absolve, condone **8** overlook

forgiveness
6 pardon **7** amnesty **9** remission **10** absolution

forgo
3 bag **5** leave, waive, yield **6** eschew, give up, resign **7** abandon **8** abnegate, jettison, renounce **9** sacrifice, surrender **10** relinquish

fork
6 bisect, branch, crotch **7** diverge, utensil **9** branch off
prong: **4** tine

fork out
3 pay **5** spend **10** contribute

forlorn
5 alone **6** bereft, futile, lonely **8** desolate, forsaken, hopeless, lonesome, solitary, wretched **9** abandoned, depressed, destitute, miserable **10** despairing, despondent **12** disconsolate

form
3 way **4** body, cast, make, mode, mold **5** build, forge, found, frame, image, model, shape, style **6** create, design, devise, figure, make up, manner **7** compose, contour, develop, fashion, outline, process, produce, profile **8** comprise, organize, practice **9** construct, establish, fabricate, framework, procedure, structure, take shape **10** constitute, convention, regulation **11** materialize **13** configuration
combining form: **5** morph
set: **10** stereotype

formal
3 set **4** prim **5** exact, legal, rigid, stiff **6** dressy, lawful, proper, seemly, solemn **7** distant, orderly, regular, stately, starchy, stilted **8** abstract, black-tie, decorous, elevated, official, reserved **10** ceremonial, methodical, systematic **11** ceremonious, syntactical **12** conventional
agreement: **4** pact **6** treaty

form a lap
3 sit

formality
4 form, rite **6** ritual **7** liturgy, service **8** ceremony, insignia **10** ceremonial, convention, observance

formalize
6 codify **9** establish, normalize **10** regularize **11** standardize

format
4 plan, size **5** shape, style **6** makeup, method **11** arrangement **12** organization

formation
4 rank **6** design, makeup **9** structure **11** arrangement, composition, development **12** architecture, construction

former
3 old **4** late, once, past **5** prior **6** bygone, whilom **7** earlier, onetime, quondam **8** anterior, previous, sometime **9** erstwhile, precedent, preceding **10** antecedent
anesthetic: **5** ether
Chevrolet subcompact: **4** Aveo
oil giant: **5** Amoco
software: **3** DOS **5** MS-DOS

formerly
3 née **4** erst, once **6** before, whilom **7** already, earlier **9** erstwhile **10** heretofore, previously

formidable
8 daunting **9** difficult **10** impressive **11** redoubtable

formless
5 vague **7** chaotic, obscure, unclear **8** inchoate, nebulous, unshaped **9** amorphous, undefined, unordered **10** immaterial, indefinite, indistinct **11** unorganized

Formosa
6 Taiwan
capital: **6** Taipei

formula
4 rite, rule **5** canon, maxim, tenet **6** method, recipe, ritual **7** precept, theorem **8** equation **9** algorithm, blueprint, principle, yardstick **10** touchstone **12** prescription

formulate
5 couch, draft, frame, hatch **6** codify, devise, invent, make up, phrase **7** concoct, dream up, express, prepare, work out **8** contrive

forsake
4 quit **5** avoid, leave, spurn **6** defect, depart, desert, give up, reject, resign **7** abandon **8** abdicate, renounce **9** throw over **10** relinquish

forsaken
4 lorn **6** bereft **7** forlorn **8** derelict, deserted, desolate, solitary **9** abandoned

Forseti
father: **6** Balder, Baldur
palace: **7** Glitnir

Forster work
7 Maurice **10** Howards End **13** Room with a View (A) **14** Passage to India (A)

forswear
4 deny **5** unsay **6** abjure, recall, recant, reject **7** perjure, retract **8** renounce, take back, withdraw

fort
4 base **6** castle **7** bastion, bulwark, citadel, outpost, redoubt **8** fastness, fortress, garrison, martello, stockade **10** stronghold
Baltimore: **7** McHenry
California: **3** Ord
Kentucky: **4** Knox
New Jersey: **3** Dix
New York: **7** Niagara, Stanwix **8** Schuyler **11** Ticonderoga
Ontario: **9** Frontenac
San Antonio: **5** Alamo
South Carolina: **6** Sumter
Spanish: **7** alcazar **8** presidio

forte
3 bag **4** loud **5** thing **6** métier **8** long suit, strength **9** specialty **10** strong suit **11** strong point

forth
6 onward **7** forward

forthcoming
7 pending **8** imminent **9** impending, proximate **10** responsive **11** approaching

for the most part
9 generally, typically **10** on the whole

for the time being
3 now **6** pro tem **9** at present, currently, presently **10** pro tempore

forthright
4 open **5** blunt, frank, plain **6** candid, direct **7** up-front **8** straight **10** aboveboard, foursquare **11** openhearted, straight-out, undisguised, unvarnished

forthwith
3 now **6** at once **8** directly **9** instantly, right away, thereupon **11** immediately, straightway **12** straightaway

fortification
4 moat, wall **5** redan **6** abatis, buffer, glacis **7** barrier, bastion, bulwark, citadel, parapet, rampart, redoubt **8** barbican, enceinte, fastness, garrison, palisade, presidio, stockade **9** barricade, earthwork **10** breastwork, stronghold
part: **7** salient

fortify
3 arm **4** gird, stir **5** brace, rally, ready, renew, rouse, steel **6** enrich, secure **7** hearten, prepare, protect, refresh, restore **8** embolden, energize **9** encourage, reinforce **10** invigorate, strengthen

fortitude
4 grit, guts, pith **5** fiber, heart, nerve, pluck, spunk, valor **6** mettle, phlegm, spirit **7** bravery, courage, stamina **8** backbone, boldness, strength, tenacity **9** constancy, endurance, tolerance **10** resolution **11** intrepidity **12** fearlessness, perseverance, resoluteness, staying power **13** dauntlessness, determination

fortress
see **fort**

fortuitous
5 fluky, happy, lucky **6** casual, chance **10** accidental, auspicious **12** providential

fortuity
3 hap **4** luck **5** fluke **6** chance **8** accident **9** happening **10** occurrence

Fortuna
5 Tyche
symbol: **5** wheel **6** rudder

fortunate
5 happy, lucky **9** favorable **10** auspicious, propitious **12** providential

Fortunate Islands
8 Canaries

fortune
3 lot, pot, wad **4** doom, fate, luck, mint, pile, ship **5** worth **6** boodle, bundle, chance, happen, hazard, packet, riches, wealth **7** destiny, success, weather **8** property **9** resources

Fortune founder
4 Luce (Henry)

fortune-teller
4 seer **5** augur, sibyl **6** auspex, oracle **7** diviner, palmist **9** wisewoman **10** soothsayer

fortune-telling
6 augury **8** geomancy **10** necromancy

forty winks
3 nap **6** catnap, siesta, snooze **7** shut-eye

forum
5 court, panel **6** medium **8** congress, tribunal **9** symposium **10** colloquium, conference, discussion, roundtable **11** convocation, marketplace

forward
3 aid **4** abet, bold, pert, send, ship **5** ahead, brash, eager, pushy, ready, relay, remit, sassy, saucy **6** cheeky, foster, onward, uphold **7** address, advance, consign, further, promote, support **8** advanced, champion, dispatch, impudent, transmit **9** encourage, in advance **11** smart-alecky **12** presumptuous **13** self-assertive
prefix: **4** ante

For Whom the Bell Tolls
author: **9** Hemingway (Ernest)
character: **5** Maria, Pablo, Pilar **6** Jordan

Forza del Destino composer
5 Verdi (Giuseppe)

fossa
3 pit **5** fovea **6** cavity, groove **10** depression

fosse
4 dike, moat **5** canal, ditch **6** trench **7** acequia, channel

fossil
4 fogy **5** amber, fogey, relic **6** dotard **7** antique **8** calamite, conodont, mossback **10** antiquated, fuddy-duddy **12** antediluvian **13** stick-in-the-mud
fuel: **3** gas, oil **4** coal, peat **9** petroleum **10** natural gas

foster
4 back, help, rear, tend **5** nurse **6** assist, harbor, parent **7** advance, bring up, nourish, nurture, promote, support, sustain **8** champion **9** cultivate, encourage

fou
3 mad **5** crazy, drunk

foul
4 base, rank, soil, vile **5** botch, dirty, fetid, funky, muddy, nasty, yucky **6** coarse, defile, filthy, grubby, horrid, impure, odious, putrid, rotten, scuzzy, smutty, stormy, turbid, vulgar, wicked **7** abusive, noisome, obscene, pollute, profane, raunchy, squalid, tarnish, unclean **8** indecent, obstruct, polluted, stinking, wretched **9** collision, loathsome, obnoxious, offensive, repellent, repugnant, repulsive, revolting **10** abominable, detestable, disgusting, malodorous **11** contaminate, treacherous **12** dishonorable, scatological

foul play
3 hit **5** blood **6** murder **7** killing, outrage **8** homicide, violence **12** manslaughter

found
4 base, cast, rear **5** begin, erect, raise, set up, start **6** bottom, create, invent **7** fashion, support **8** commence, initiate, organize **9** establish, institute, originate, predicate

foundation
3 bed **4** base, rock **5** basis **6** bottom, corset, makeup **7** bedding, footing, support **8** pedestal **9** endowment **10** groundwork, substratum **11** institution **12** organization, substructure, underpinning

foundational
5 basic **6** bottom **7** primary **10** supportive, underlying **11** fundamental

founder
4 fail, sink **5** wreck **6** author, father, go down **7** creator **8** collapse, inventor, submerge, submerse **9** architect, generator, patriarch, shipwreck **10** originator
of Carthage: **4** Dido

foundling
6 infant, orphan

fountain
3 jet **4** head, root **5** spout **6** geyser, origin, source, spring **7** bubbler **8** wellhead **9** inception, reservoir **10** wellspring
nymph: **6** Egeria
Roman: **5** Trevi

Fountainhead author
4 Rand (Ayn)

four
6 tetrad **7** quartet **10** quaternion
bagger: **5** homer **7** home run
combining form: **4** tetr **5** quadr, tetra **6** quadri, quadru, quater, tessar **7** tessara, tessera
gills: **4** pint
hundred: **5** elite **10** upper crust
inches: **4** hand
pecks: **6** bushel
quarts: **6** gallon

four-flush
4 dupe **5** bluff **6** delude, take in **7** deceive

four-footed animal
8 tetrapod **9** quadruped

Four Horsemen
3 War **5** Death **6** Famine **8** Conquest **10** Pestilence

four-in-hand
3 tie **5** coach **7** necktie

fourpence
5 groat

four-poster
3 bed

fourscore
6 eighty

four-sided figure
5 rhomb **6** square **7** rhombus **9** rectangle **13** quadrilateral, parallelogram

foursquare
8 straight **10** forthright **13** quadrilateral

fourteen pounds
5 stone

fourth
7 quarter **8** quadrant, quartern
combining form: **5** quadr, quart **6** quadri, quadru

fowl
3 hen **4** bird, cock, duck **5** chick, goose, poult **6** bantam, pullet, turkey **7** chicken, rooster (see also **chicken; poultry**)

Fowles novel
5 Magus (The) **9** Collector (The) **22** French Lieutenant's Woman (The)

fox
4 fool **5** trick **6** baffle, outwit **7** confuse, reynard **8** bewilder, slyboots
African: **4** asse
female: **5** vixen
kind: **3** kit, red **5** swift **6** arctic, fennec, silver **8** bat-eared
Scottish: **3** tod
young: **3** cub

foxglove
9 digitalis

fox grape
9 muscadine **11** scuppernong

foxiness
4 wile **5** craft, guile **7** cunning, slyness **8** wiliness **10** artfulness, craftiness, cleverness

foxlike
7 vulpine

foxy
3 sly **4** wily **5** canny, slick **6** artful, astute, clever, crafty, shrewd, tricky **7** cunning, vulpine **8** guileful **9** insidious

foyer
5 lobby **8** anteroom, entrance **9** vestibule

fracas
3 row **4** feud, spat, to-do **5** brawl, broil, fight, melee, run-in, set-to **6** affray, hassle, kickup, shindy, uproar **7** dispute, quarrel, ruction, wrangle **8** squabble **9** bickering **10** donnybrook, free-for-all **11** altercation

fraction
3 bit, cut **4** part **5** piece, scrap **6** divide, little **7** portion, section **8** fragment

fractious
6 unruly **7** peevish, pettish, willful **8** contrary **9** bellicose, irritable **10** headstrong, pugnacious, refractory **11** belligerent, contentious, intractable, quarrelsome **12** recalcitrant, ungovernable, unmanageable

fracture
4 rent, rift, tear **5** break, cleft, crack, split **6** breach, schism **7** rupture

Fra Diavolo composer
5 Auber (Esprit)

fragile
4 weak **5** frail **6** feeble, flimsy, infirm **7** brittle, tenuous, unsound **8** decrepit, delicate **9** breakable, frangible

fragment
3 bit **4** chip, iota, part, rive **5** burst, crumb, flake, grain, piece, scrap, shard, sherd, shred, smash **6** morsel, shiver, sliver **7** break up, flinder, shatter **8** fraction, particle, splinter **9** fall apart **12** disintegrate

fragmentary
6 broken **7** partial **10** fractional, incomplete, unfinished

fragrance
4 musk, nose, odor **5** aroma, attar, scent, smell, spice **7** bouquet, cologne, incense, perfume **9** redolence **11** eau de parfum, toilet water **13** eau de toilette

fragrant
7 odorous, scented **8** aromatic, perfumed, redolent **11** odoriferous
compound: **5** ester
oil: **4** atar **5** attar

frail
4 puny, slim, thin, weak **5** anile, petty, reedy, wispy **6** feeble, flimsy, infirm, sickly, slight **7** brittle, fragile, slender, spindly, tenuous, unsound **8** decrepit, delicate **9** breakable, frangible

frailty
4 vice **5** fault **6** foible **7** failing **8** delicacy, weakness **9** infirmity **10** feebleness

frame
3 cel **4** body, form, mold, plan, sash **5** build, draft, erect, forge, mount, shape, shell **6** border, casing, cook up, devise, draw up, figure, invent, make up, sketch, system **7** arrange, chassis, fashion, prepare **8** assemble, casement, conceive, contrive, skeleton **9** cartouche, construct, fabricate, formulate, structure
part: **4** sill, stud **5** joist, plate

framework
4 rack **5** shell, truss **7** trestle **8** cribbing, cribwork, scaffold, skeleton, studding, studwork, trussing **9** bare bones, structure
of crossed strips: **7** lattice, trellis

France
bay: **6** Biscay
capital: **5** Paris
channel: **6** Manche (La) **7** English
city: **3** Pau **4** Caen, Lyon, Metz, Nice **5** Brest, Lyons, Reims **6** Amiens, Calais, Nancy, Nantes, Rennes, Rheims **8** Bordeaux, Grenoble, Toulouse **9** Marseille, Orléans **10** Marseilles, Strasbourg, Versailles **11** Montpellier
conqueror: **6** Caesar (Julius)
department: **3** Var **4** Aude, Gard, Jura, Orne **5** Marne, Rhône, Somme **6** Savoie, Vosges **7** Bas-Rhin **8** Ardennes, Calvados
emperor: **5** Pepin (III, the Short) **8** Napoleon (Bonaparte) **11** Charlemagne
enclave: **6** Monaco
former name: **4** Gaul **6** Gallia
hero: **6** Clovis
heroine: **9** Joan of Arc
historic province: **4** Foix **5** Anjou, Aunis, Bearn, Berry, Maine **6** Alsace, Artois, Marche, Poitou, Vendée **7** Gascony, Guyenne, Picardy **8** Auvergne, Bretagne, Brittany, Burgundy, Dauphine, Flanders, Gascogne, Limousin, Lorraine, Lyonnais, Normandy, Picardie, Provence, Touraine **9** Angoumois, Bourgogne, Champagne, Languedoc, Nivernois, Orléanais, Saintonge, Venaissin **10** Roussillon **11** Bourbonnais, Île-de-France **12** Franche-Comté
island: **3** Yeu **6** Hyères, Oléron, Ushant **7** Corsica **8** Belle-Île **11** Noirmoutier
monarch: **5** Henri, Henry, Louis **6** Philip **7** Charles **8** Philippe
monetary unit: **4** euro
monetary unit, former: **3** ecu, sou **5** franc
mountain, range: **4** Alps, Jura **6** Vosges **8** Auvergne, Pyrenees **9** Mont Blanc
neighbor: **5** Italy, Spain **7** Andorra, Belgium, Germany **10** Luxembourg **11** Switzerland
president: **6** Chirac (Jacques) **8** de Gaulle (Charles) **10** Mitterrand (François)
region: **4** Midi **5** Corse **6** Alsace, Centre **7** Corsica, Picardy **8** Auvergne, Bretagne, Brittany, Burgundy, Limousin, Normandy, Picardie **9** Aquitaine, Bourgogne, Champagne, Languedoc, Normandie **10** Rhône-Alpes **11** Île-de-France **12** Franche-Comté, Midi-Pyrénées
river: **4** Aire, Aube, Aude, Aure, Odon, Oise, Orne, Yser **5** Adour, Isère, Loire, Marne, Rhone, Saône, Seine, Somme, Yonne **7** Garonne
sea: **13** Mediterranean
southern: **4** Midi
spa city: **5** Evian
strait: **5** Dover
symbol: **8** Marianne

Francesca's lover
5 Paolo

franchise
4 vote **6** ballot **7** freedom, license **8** suffrage **9** privilege

frangible
7 brittle, fragile, friable **8** delicate **9** breakable

frank
3 dog **4** fair, free, open **5** blunt, plain **6** candid, direct, honest, hot dog, weenie, wiener, wienie **7** upright **8** man-to-man, out-front, straight **9** barefaced, outspoken **10** forthright, scrupulous, unreserved **11** openhearted, plainspoken, transparent, unconcealed, undisguised, uninhibited, unvarnished, wienerwurst **12** heart-to-heart, unmistakable

Frankenstein
author: **7** Shelley (Mary)
helper: **4** Igor

frankfurter
3 dog **6** hot dog, weenie, wiener, wienie **11** wienerwurst

Frankie's lover
6 Johnny

Frankish hero
6 Roland

Franklin, Benjamin
birthplace: **6** Boston
invention: **5** stove **8** bifocals
pen name: **11** Poor Richard

frankness
6 candor **7** honesty

Frank's wife
3 Ava (Gardner)

frantic
3 mad 4 wild 5 upset, wired 7 fraught, shook up, unglued 8 feverish, frenetic, frenzied, maniacal, worked up 10 distraught 11 overwrought

Franzen novel
7 Freedom 11 Corrections (The)

frappe, frappé
5 shake 6 frozen 7 chilled, liqueur 9 milk shake

fraternal
6 clubby 8 sociable 9 brotherly, comradely, dizygotic 10 like-minded
counterpart: 7 sororal

fraternal society
3 FOE, KOC, SAR 4 BPOE, Elks 5 Lions, Moose 6 Eagles, Masons, Rotary 7 Kiwanis, Woodmen 8 Shriners 10 Freemasons, Hibernians, Odd Fellows

fraternity
4 club 5 guild, order, union 6 league 7 company 8 sodality 10 fellowship 11 association, brotherhood 13 brotherliness
letter: (see **Greek letter**)
party garment: 4 toga

Frau's husband
4 Herr, Mann

fraud
3 con, gyp 4 fake, gaff, hoax, scam, sham 5 cheat, faker, phony, quack, trick 6 deceit, dupery, humbug, hustle, phoney 7 chicane, con game, swindle 8 cozenage, flimflam, impostor, operator, trickery 9 charlatan, chicanery, deception, imposture, mare's nest, pretender, shell game, trickster 10 dishonesty, mountebank, subterfuge 11 counterfeit 12 double-dealer 13 double-dealing, sharp practice

fraudulence
6 deceit 8 quackery, trickery 9 chicanery, deception, phoniness 10 dishonesty

fraudulent
4 fake 5 false, phony 7 crooked 8 cheating, guileful 9 deceitful, deceptive, dishonest 10 fallacious 11 duplicitous

fraught
4 full 5 laden, tense 6 filled, uneasy 7 charged, replete, stuffed 8 pregnant 9 stressful

fräulein
4 maid, Miss 6 maiden 9 governess 12 mademoiselle

fray
3 row 4 fret, wear 5 brawl, broil, brush, clash, fight, melee, ravel, scrap, set-to, shred 6 combat, fracas, strain, strife, tussle 7 dispute, frazzle, quarrel, ruction, scuffle 8 irritate, skirmish, struggle 9 commotion, scrimmage 10 donnybrook 11 disturbance

frayed
4 worn 6 tatty 6 ragged, shabby 8 tattered 9 moth-eaten 10 threadbare

frazzle
4 do in, fray, poop, tire, wear 5 upset 6 tucker 7 exhaust, fatigue, wear out

frazzled
4 beat 5 upset 6 bushed, sapped, shaken 7 drained, rattled 8 agitated, confused, fatigued, tired out 9 exhausted, fagged out, perturbed, unsettled 10 distressed 11 overwrought 12 disconcerted

freak
3 bug, nut 4 buff, geek, whim 5 go ape, fancy, fiend, maven 6 addict, hippie, maniac, megrim, oddity, vagary, weirdo, whimsy, zealot 7 anomaly, caprice, chimera, conceit, deviate, fanatic, monster 8 crotchet, flimflam 9 androgyne, curiosity 10 aberration, enthusiast 11 abnormality, monstrosity 12 lusus naturae, malformation

freakish
3 odd 5 kooky, outré, weird 6 far-out, quirky 7 bizarre, erratic, oddball, strange 8 aberrant, abnormal 9 arbitrary, eccentric, grotesque 10 outlandish

freckle
3 dot 4 mole, spot 5 fleck 7 speckle, stipple

Fred's dancing sister
5 Adele (Astaire)

free
3 rid 4 comp, open 5 frank, loose, untie 6 acquit, exempt, gratis, loosen, unbind, untied 7 absolve, at large, donated, liberal, manumit, movable, pro bono, release, unbound, unchain, unleash, unloose 8 detached, generous, liberate, separate, unfasten, unloosen 9 at liberty, discharge, exculpate, exonerate, extricate, sovereign, unchained, unchecked, unimpeded, unshackle, unsparing, voluntary 10 autonomous, democratic, emancipate, gratuitous, unconfined, unfettered, unshackled 11 disentangle, emancipated, independent, spontaneous, untrammeled 12 unrestrained, unrestricted 13 complimentary, self-governing, unconstrained

freebie
3 tip 4 comp, gift, pass, perk 5 bonus 7 present 8 giveaway, gratuity 9 lagniappe

freebooter
5 rover 6 bandit, pirate, raider 7 brigand, corsair 8 marauder, picaroon, pillager, rapparee, sea rover 9 buccaneer, pickaroon, plunderer, ransacker

freedom
5 right 7 liberty, license, release 8 autonomy, immunity, latitude, mobility 9 exemption,

franchise, privilege **11** prerogative **12** emancipation, independence **13** outspokenness
Swahili: 5 uhuru

free-for-all
4 fray **5** brawl, broil, melee, mix-up **6** affray, fracas, rumble **7** ruction **8** slugfest **10** donnybrook

freehanded
7 liberal **8** generous **9** bounteous, bountiful **10** munificent

freeloader
3 bum **5** leech **6** cadger, sponge **7** moocher **8** barnacle, hanger-on, parasite **11** bloodsucker

Free State
8 Maryland

free ticket
4 pass **11** Annie Oakley

freewheeling
9 footloose

freeze
4 halt, stop **5** chill, stall **6** benumb **7** congeal **8** glaciate, solidify, stoppage **10** immobilize

freezing
3 icy **4** cold **5** chill, gelid, nippy, polar **6** arctic, bitter, chilly, frigid, frosty, wintry **7** glacial, shivery
combining form: 4 cryo, kryo

freight
4 haul, lade, load **5** cargo **6** burden, charge, lading **7** payload **9** transport

freighter
4 scow, ship **7** carrier, shipper **9** cargo ship **11** bulk carrier

Freischütz composer
5 Weber (Carl Maria von)

French
Art Deco designer: 4 Erté
article: 3 les, une
attendant: 9 concierge
aunt: 5 tante
back: 3 dos
battle site: 4 St. Lo
bed: 3 lit **6** couche
black: 4 noir
born: 3 née
boy: 6 garçon
bread: 8 baguette
brother: 5 frère
cake: 6 gâteau
cap: 5 beret
cardinal: 7 Mazarin (Jules) **9** Richelieu (Duc de)
castle: 7 château
cathedral city: 4 Albi **5** Paris, Reims, Rouen **6** Amiens, Nantes, Rheims **8** Chartres
chanteuse: 4 Piaf (Edith)
cheese: 4 Brie
clergyman: 4 abbé, curé, père
coin: 3 ecu
cold: 5 froid
combining form: 5 Gallo **6** Franco
conjunction: 4 mais
daughter: 5 fille
day: 5 jeudi, lundi, mardi **6** samedi **8** dimanche, mercredi, vendredi
dear: 4 cher
department head: 7 prefect
direction: 3 est, sud **4** nord **5** ouest
down with: 4 à bas
dream: 4 rêve
drink: 5 boire
dynasty: 5 Capet **6** Valois **7** Bourbon
egg: 4 oeuf
emblem: 10 fleur-de-lis
empress: 7 Eugénie **9** Joséphine
evening: 4 soir
exclamation: 3 zut **4** eheu, hein **9** sacrebleu
eye: 4 oeil
farewell: 5 adieu **8** au revoir
farmhouse: 5 ferme
father: 4 père
forest: 7 Argonne, Belleau
friend: 3 ami **4** amie
game: 3 jeu **4** jeux (plural)
girl: 5 fille
God: 4 dieu
good: 3 bon **5** bonne
gray: 4 gris
hat: 7 chapeau
head: 4 tête
here: 3 ici
house: 6 maison
income: 5 rente
island: 3 île
king: 3 roi
language: 9 Provençal
leather: 4 cuir
length: 4 aune
mask: 4 loup
military hat: 4 kepi
milk: 4 lait
month: 3 mai **4** août, juin, mars, mois **5** avril **7** février, janvier, juillet
mother: 4 mère
nail: 4 clou
national anthem: 12 Marseillaise (La)
nose: 3 nez
nothing: 4 rien
number: 3 dix, six **4** cinq, deux, huit, neuf, onze, sept **5** douze, trois **6** quatre
opera: 5 Faust, Lakmé, Manon, Thaïs **6** Carmen, Mignon **7** Werther
pancake: 5 crêpe
pastry: 6 éclair **8** napoleon
poem: 3 dit

policeman: **4** flic **8** gendarme
porcelain: **6** Sèvres **7** Limoges
preposition: **3** par, sur **4** avec, dans, pour, sans, sous
pretty: **4** joli **5** jolie
prison: **8** Bastille
pronoun: **3** eux, ils, mes, moi, toi, une **4** elle, nous, vous
Protestant: **6** Calvin (John) **8** Huguenot
pupil: **5** élève
queen: **5** reine
quick: **4** vite
rabbit: **5** lapin
railroad station: **4** gare
resort: **3** Pau **4** Nice **5** Vichy **6** Cannes, Menton **7** Antibes **8** Biarritz
resort area: **7** Riviera
restaurant: **6** bistro
revolutionist: **5** Marat (Jean-Paul) **6** Danton (Georges) **11** Robespierre (Maximilien)
Revolution party: **7** Gironde, Jacobin **8** Mountain
Revolution song: **5** Ça Ira
roasted: **4** rôti
room: **5** salle
saint: **4** Joan (of Arc) **5** Denis **6** Martin (of Tours) **7** Thérèse (of Lisieux)
school: **5** école, lycée
sea: **3** mer
season: **3** été **5** hiver **7** automne **9** printemps
servant: **5** valet
sherry: **5** xérès
shooting match: **3** tir
shop: **8** boutique
shrine: **7** Lourdes
singer: **4** Piaf (Edith) **8** chanteur **9** chanteuse
sister: **5** soeur
small: **5** petit **6** petite
soldier: **5** poilu **6** soldat, Zouave **8** chasseur
son: **4** fils
song: **3** dit **7** chanson
soup: **6** potage
star: **6** étoile
state: **4** état
stock exchange: **6** bourse
street: **3** rue
student: **5** élève
subway: **5** metro
summer: **3** été
there!: **5** voilà
too much: **4** trop
verb: **4** être
very: **4** très
wartime capital: **5** Vichy
water: **3** eau
well: **4** bien
wine: **3** vin
wineshop: **6** bistro
wood: **4** bois
yes: **3** oui
yesterday: **4** hier

French Guiana
capital: **7** Cayenne
ethnic group: **6** Creole
island: **6** Devil's
mountain range: **10** Tumac-Humac
neighbor: **6** Brazil **8** Suriname
river: **4** Mana **6** Maroni **7** Oyapock

French Polynesia
archipelag: **7** Tuamotu
capital: **7** Papeete
island, island group: **6** Tahiti **7** Austral, Gambier, Society **9** Marquesas

frenetic
3 mad **4** amok, loco, wild **5** crazy, wired **6** crazed, hectic **7** berserk, frantic **8** agitated, feverish, frenzied, maniacal **9** delirious, orgiastic **10** corybantic

frenzied
see **frenetic**

frenzy
4 amok, fury, rage **5** amuck, craze, furor, mania **6** madden **7** derange, madness, unhinge **8** delirium, distract, hysteria, insanity, paroxysm **9** unbalance **11** derangement

frequency unit
5 hertz **7** fresnel **9** gigahertz

frequent
5 haunt, often, usual, visit **6** common, hourly **7** regular **8** everyday, familiar, habitual **9** customary

frequenter
7 denizen, habitué, haunter

frequently
4 a lot **5** often **8** commonly **9** routinely **10** oftentimes, repeatedly **11** customarily, recurrently

fresh
3 new, raw **4** rude **5** green, lippy, naive, novel, sassy, saucy, smart **6** callow, cheeky, recent, unused, vernal, virgin **8** brand-new, impudent, insolent, original **9** unspoiled **11** impertinent, smart-alecky **12** invigorating **13** inexperienced

freshet
5 flood, spate **6** influx

freshly
4 anew

freshman
4 pleb, tyro **5** frosh, plebe **6** novice, rookie **8** beginner, neophyte, newcomer **10** apprentice, tenderfoot

fret
4 fume, fuss, stew **5** brood, chafe, worry **6** dither, pother

fretful
5 angry, cross **6** crabby, cranky **7** carping, chafing, peevish, pettish, whining **8** captious, caviling, critical, perverse, petulant, restless, snappish **9** fractious, impatient, irascible, irritable, querulous

Freudian term
3 ego **5** drive **6** denial, libido **7** complex, Oedipal **8** analysis, cathexis, fixation, neurosis, superego **9** analysand, disavowal, dreamwork, fetishism, psychosis **10** parapraxis, projection, regression, repression **11** association, sublimation, unconscious **12** condensation, displacement, preconscious, transference

Frey
father: **5** Njörd **6** Njörth
god of: **3** sun **4** rain **5** peace **9** fertility
sister: **5** Freya
wife: **4** Gerd **5** Gerda, Gerth

Freya
brother: **4** Frey
domain: **9** Folkvangr
father: **5** Njörd **6** Njörth

friable
5 mealy **7** brittle, crumbly, fragile **9** frangible

friar
7 brother **8** cenobite **9** mendicant

fribble
3 toy **5** dally, flirt **6** coquet, trifle **7** trifler **8** trifling **9** dalliance, frivolity **10** dillydally, fool around

friction
4 drag **7** discord, rubbing **8** abrasion **9** animosity, attrition **10** disharmony, dissension, resistance **12** disagreement

friction match
5 vesta **7** lucifer **8** vesuvian

Friday's rescuer
6 Crusoe (Robinson)

friend
3 pal **4** ally, chum, mate, pard **5** buddy, crony, matey, serve **6** cohort **7** comrade, partner **8** alter ego, compadre, confrere, familiar, intimate, playmate, sidekick **9** colleague, companion, confidant **10** confidante
French: **3** ami **4** amie
Maori: **4** ehoa
Spanish: **5** amiga, amigo

Friend
6 Quaker
founder: **3** Fox (George)

friendly
4 warm **6** amical, chummy, folksy, genial **7** affable, amiable, cordial **8** amicable, cheerful, familiar, sociable **9** congenial, favorable **10** buddy-buddy, compatible, hospitable, neighborly **12** affectionate, well-disposed **13** accommodating

Friendly Islands
5 Tonga

Friends series
character: **4** Joey, Ross **6** Monica, Phoebe, Rachel **8** Chandler
setting: **9** Manhattan
star: **3** Cox (Courteney) **5** Perry (Matthew) **6** Kudrow (Lisa) **7** Aniston (Jennifer), LeBlanc (Matt) **9** Schwimmer (David)

friends and neighbors
4 kith

friendship
5 amity **6** accord, comity **7** concord, empathy, harmony **8** affinity, alliance, goodwill

frigate bird
3 ioa, iwa **8** alcatras **11** man-o'-war bird
genus: **7** Fregata

Frigga, Frigg
husband: **4** Odin **5** Woden
son: **6** Balder, Baldur

fright
4 fear **5** alarm, dread, panic, scare, shock **6** dismay, horror, terror **11** trepidation

frighten
3 cow **5** alarm, bully, daunt, scare, shock, spook **6** appall, dismay **7** horrify, perturb, scarify, startle, terrify, unnerve **9** terrorize **10** intimidate

frightful
4 ugly **5** awful, scary **6** horrid **7** fearful, ghastly, hideous **8** alarming, dreadful, fearsome, horrible, horrific, shocking, terrible, terrific **9** appalling, startling **10** formidable, horrendous, terrifying

frigid
3 icy **4** cold **5** chill **6** arctic, chilly, frosty **7** glacial **8** freezing **11** emotionless, indifferent, passionless, unemotional **12** unresponsive

frijoles
5 beans

frill
4 ruff **5** jabot, ruche **6** doodad, luxury, ruffle **7** flounce, ruching **8** furbelow **11** affectation, superfluity **12** extravagance

fringe
3 hem, rim **4** brim, ruff **5** bound, brink, skirt, thrum, verge **6** border, edging, margin **7** fimbria **8** penumbra, trimming **9** perimeter, periphery **10** borderland

frippery
6 finery, frills, tawdry **7** regalia **8** foofaraw, trumpery **9** trappings **11** ostentation

frisée
6 endive **7** lettuce

frisk
4 leap, play, romp, skip **5** caper, dance **6** cavort, frolic, gambol, search **7** disport, pat down, rollick

frisky
3 gay 5 antic 6 feisty, lively 7 coltlsh, playful 8 animated, gamesome, sportive 9 sprightly, vivacious 10 frolicsome

fritter away
4 blow 5 spend, waste 7 consume 8 squander 9 dissipate

frivolity
3 fun 4 play 6 gaiety, levity, whimsy 8 nonsense 12 childishness

frivolous
3 gay 4 idle 5 ditsy, ditzy, dizzy, giddy, inane, light, silly 6 breezy, frothy, yeasty 7 flighty, playful, shallow, trivial 8 carefree, careless, heedless, trifling 11 light-headed, superficial

frizzy
5 kinky, nappy 6 coiled, curled 7 twisted
hair style: 4 Afro

frock
4 gown 5 dress, habit 6 jersey, mantle

Frodo's pal
3 Sam

frog
5 ranid 6 anuran 7 croaker 9 amphibian 10 batrachian
family: 7 Ranidae
genus: 4 Rana
kind: 4 hyla 5 coqui 6 peeper 7 leopard 8 bullfrog, tree toad
larva: 7 tadpole
relative: 4 toad

frolic
3 fun 4 lark, play, romp 5 antic, caper, dance, frisk, party, prank, revel, sport, spree 6 cavort, didoes, gaiety, gambol, prance 7 disport, skylark 8 escapade, hilarity 9 festivity, merriment 10 shenanigan, tomfoolery

frolicsome
3 gay 5 antic 6 frisky, impish 7 coltish, jocular, playful, roguish 8 sportful, sportive 9 sprightly 10 rollicking 11 mischievous

from
German: 3 von
Scottish: 4 frae

From Here to Eternity author
5 Jones (James)

from scratch
4 anew

frondeur
5 rebel 8 mutineer, renegade 9 anarchist, dissident, insurgent 10 malcontent

front
3 bow, van 4 face, fore, lend, look, mask, prow 5 beard 6 facade, facing 7 forward 8 anterior, disguise 9 challenge, encounter 10 appearance, figurehead 11 countenance

frontier
5 bound, field, march 6 border 8 backland, backwash, boundary 9 up-country 10 borderland, hinterland 11 backcountry

frontiersman
5 Boone (Daniel), Clark (George Rogers, William) 6 Carson (Kit) 7 Frémont (J. C.), pioneer, settler 8 Crockett (Davy) 10 bushranger

fronton game
7 jai alai

frontward
4 fore 8 anterior

frost
4 hoar, rime 6 freeze

frostfish
5 smelt 6 tomcod

frost heave
5 pingo

frosting
5 icing 7 topping 8 trimming

Frost poem
7 Birches 10 Fire and Ice 11 Mending Wall 12 Road Not Taken (The) 18 Death of the Hired Man (The) 30 Stopping By Woods on a Snowy Evening

frosty
3 icy 4 cold, rimy 5 chill, frore, hoary, nippy 6 chilly, frigid 7 glacial 8 freezing 10 unfriendly

Frosty's eyes
4 coal

froth
4 foam, head, suds 5 cream, spume, yeast 6 lather 8 airiness 9 frivolity, lightness

froufrou
6 frills 8 rustling

froward
5 balky 6 mulish, ornery 7 peevish, restive 8 contrary, perverse, petulant, stubborn 9 obstinate 10 headstrong, refractory 11 disobedient

frown
4 pout, sulk 5 glare, lower, scowl 6 glower

frowsy
5 dowdy, funky, fusty, messy, musty, stale 6 shabby, smelly, sordid, untidy 7 squalid, unkempt 8 slattern, slovenly 10 disheveled, disordered, slatternly 13 draggletailed

frozen
4 cold, hard 5 fixed, frore, rigid, stiff 6 frigid, iced up, numbed 7 chilled 8 benumbed, immobile 9 congealed, petrified

frugal
4 mean 5 canny, scant, spare 6 Scotch, stingy 7 careful, prudent, scrimpy, sparing, thrifty 8 discreet, stinting 9 niggardly, penurious, provident 10 economical, unwasteful 12 cheeseparing, parsimonious 13 penny-pinching

frugality
6 thrift **7** economy **8** prudence **9** husbandry **10** providence **11** thriftiness

fruit
3 fig, nut **4** ansu, date, kiwi, lime, pear, pepo, plum, pome, seed, sloe, Ugli **5** apple, berry, drupe, gourd, grape, guava, issue, lemon, mango, melon, olive, papaw, peach, prune, young **6** achene, banana, casaba, cherry, citron, durian, legume, loment, loquat, medlar, orange, papaya, pawpaw, pomelo, quince, result, samara **7** acerola, apricot, avocado, capsule, coconut, currant, kumquat, outcome, progeny, silique, syconia (plural), tangelo, utricle **8** bergamot, dewberry, mandarin, plantain, rambutan, shaddock, syconium, tamarind **9** blueberry, cherimoya, cranberry, muskmelon, nectarine, offspring, persimmon, pineapple, raspberry, tangerine **10** blackberry, calamondin, gooseberry, grapefruit, loganberry, mangosteen, strawberry **11** boysenberry, hesperidium, huckleberry, pomegranate
dried: **5** prune **6** raisin
drink: **3** ade **5** juice, punch
residue: **4** marc **6** pomace
seed: **3** pip
skin: **4** peel
study of: **8** pomology **9** carpology
sugar: **7** glucose **8** fructose, levulose
undeveloped: **6** nubbin

fruit-bearing palm
4 acai, coco

fruitful
6 fecund **7** copious, fertile **8** abundant, prolific **9** bountiful, fructuous, plenteous, plentiful **10** productive **11** proliferant

fruition
7 delight **8** pleasure **9** enjoyment **10** attainment, conclusion **11** achievement, delectation, fulfillment, realization

fruitless
4 vain **6** barren, futile, otiose **7** sterile, useless **8** abortive **10** unavailing **11** ineffective, ineffectual **12** unproductive, unsuccessful

frumpy
4 drab, dull **5** dated, dowdy, tacky **6** stodgy **8** outmoded **9** out-of-date, unstylish **12** old-fashioned

frustrate
4 balk, bilk, dash, foil, halt **5** block, check, stump **6** arrest, baffle, defeat, hinder, impede, stymie, thwart **7** inhibit, prevent **8** confound, obstruct, preclude, prohibit **9** discomfit, forestall, interrupt **10** disappoint

frustration
6 defeat, dismay **7** chagrin, letdown **8** vexation **9** annoyance, hindrance **10** impediment, irritation **11** displeasure, obstruction

fry
4 burn, sear **5** frizz, grill, sauté **6** fishes, picnic **7** frizzle **11** electrocute

frying pan
6 spider **7** griddle, skillet

fuddle
5 befog, booze **6** ball up, jumble, tipple **7** confuse, fluster, stupefy **8** bewilder **10** intoxicate

fuddy-duddy
4 fogy **5** fogey **6** fossil, square, stodgy **8** mossback, outdated, outmoded **12** antediluvian, Colonel Blimp, old-fashioned, stuffed shirt **13** stick-in-the-mud

fudge
3 pad **4** blur, bosh, fake **5** candy, cheat, color, dodge, hedge, hooey, welsh **6** bunkum **7** distort, falsify, hogwash, penuche **8** contrive, divinity, nonsense **9** embellish, embroider, overstate, poppycock **10** equivocate, flapdoodle **11** foolishness

fuel
3 gas, oil **4** coal, coke, fire, peat, wood **5** stoke **6** biogas, diesel, petrol, Sterno **7** ethanol, gasohol, inflame, propane **8** charcoal, gasoline, kerosene **9** biodiesel, petroleum, stimulate **10** natural gas **13** reinforcement
additive: **3** STP
jelled: **6** napalm

Fuentes novel
4 Aura **9** Old Gringo (The)

fugacious
7 brittle, passing **8** fleeting, fugitive, volatile **9** ephemeral, momentary, transient **10** evanescent, short-lived, transitory

fugitive
5 exile **6** outlaw **7** escapee, lamster, nomadic, passing, refugee, runaway **8** deserter, fleeting, runagate, vagabond **9** ephemeral, fugacious, momentary, transient, wandering **10** evanescent, short-lived, transitory

fugue master
4 Bach (Johann Sebastian)

Führer, der
6 Hitler (Adolf)

fulcrum
3 hub **4** axis, prop **5** hinge, nexus, pivot **7** support

fulfill
4 meet **5** honor **6** effect, finish, redeem **7** achieve, execute, perform, satisfy **8** complete **9** discharge, implement **10** accomplish

fulgent
6 bright **7** beaming, glowing, radiant, shining **8** luminous, lustrous **9** brilliant

fuliginous
4 dark **5** dingy, dusky, grimy, murky, sooty **7** obscure

full
5 sated, total, whole **6** entire, gorged, jammed, loaded, packed, utmost **7** crammed, crowded, glutted, maximum, plenary, replete, stuffed **8** brimming, complete, satiated **9** jam-packed, plentiful, surfeited **11** chockablock

full-blooded
4 rich **5** flush, ruddy **6** ardent, florid **7** flushed, genuine, glowing **8** forceful, purebred, rubicund, sanguine **9** pedigreed **10** compelling **12** thoroughbred

full-blown
4 lush, ripe **5** adult, total **6** all-out, mature **7** grown-up

full-bodied
4 rich **5** husky, lusty, stout **6** potent, robust, strong **9** corpulent **10** meaningful **11** significant, substantial

full dress
6 finery **7** regalia **8** frippery, glad rags **10** Sunday best

full-figured
5 ample, buxom, plump **6** chubby, fleshy, zaftig **10** curvaceous, overweight, Rubenesque, statuesque, voluptuous

full-fledged
4 ripe **5** adult, grown, total **6** mature **7** genuine, grown-up **8** complete **9** full-blown

full-grown
4 ripe **5** adult **6** mature

fullness
6 plenty **7** satiety **9** abundance, amplitude, repletion **10** perfection **12** completeness

full-scale
5 total **6** all-out **8** complete, life-size **9** unlimited

full tilt
7 flat-out, rapidly, swiftly **8** pell-mell, speedily **9** posthaste **12** lickety-split

fulminate
4 boil, burn, foam, fume, rage, rail, rant, rave **5** curse, flare, storm **7** bluster, explode, inveigh

fulsome
4 oily **5** plump, slick, soapy, suave **6** lavish, smarmy, smooth **7** buttery, cloying, copious, profuse **8** abundant, effusive, generous, overdone, unctuous **9** excessive **10** flattering, oleaginous **11** extravagant, pharisaical **12** ingratiating, Pecksniffian

Fulton's steamboat
8 Clermont

fumarole
4 vent

fumble
3 bob, err, paw **4** feel, flub, mess, muff **5** botch, grope **6** bobble, bollix, bungle, muddle **7** blunder, misplay **8** flounder

fume
3 gas **4** boil, burn, odor, rage, rant, rave, reek, snit, stew **5** smoke, vapor **6** seethe, swivet **7** sputter

fun
4 play **5** sport **6** frolic, gaiety **7** amusing, jollity, pastime, whoopee **8** hilarity, pleasant, ridicule **9** amusement, diversion, diverting, enjoyment, frivolity, horseplay, jocundity, joviality, merriment **10** pleasantry **12** entertaining **13** entertainment

function
3 act, job, run, use **4** duty, goal, mark, role, task, work **5** party, power, react, serve **6** affair, behave, object, office, target **7** concern, faculty, operate, perform, purpose, service **8** activity, behavior, business, capacity, ceremony, occasion, province **9** objective, officiate, operation, reception
trigonometric: **4** sine **6** cosine, secant **7** tangent **8** cosecant **9** cotangent

functional
5 handy, utile **6** usable, useful **7** working **9** practical **11** practicable, serviceable, utilitarian **12** occupational

functioning
6 active, usable **7** dynamic **9** operative

fund
4 back, bank, pool **5** endow, stake, stock, store **6** coffer, supply **7** capital, finance, reserve, support, tontine **8** bankroll, treasury **9** inventory, subsidize **10** accumulate, capitalize

fundament
3 bum **4** butt, rear, rump, seat **5** basis, fanny **6** behind, bottom **8** backside, buttocks, derriere **9** posterior, principle **10** foundation, groundwork

fundamental
3 key **4** ABCs (plural) **5** axiom, basal, basic, prime, vital **6** bottom, factor, primal, simple **7** bedrock, organic, primary, radical, theorem **8** absolute, cardinal, dominant, rudiment, ultimate **9** component, essential, important, necessary, paramount, primitive, principal, principle, requisite **10** deep-rooted, elementary, grassroots, primordial, rock-bottom, underlying **11** constituent, irreducible, nitty-gritty **12** constitutive, foundational

fund-raiser
8 telethon

funeral
6 burial **7** obsequy **9** obsequies
car: **6** hearse
director: **9** mortician **10** undertaker
oration: **6** eulogy **8** encomium **9** panegyric
procession: **7** cortege
service: **7** requiem **9** obsequies
song: **5** dirge, elegy **8** threnody

funereal
3 sad **4** dark **5** black, bleak, grave **6** dismal, dreary, gloomy, solemn, somber, sombre **7** elegiac **8** mournful **9** deathlike, sorrowful **10** depressing, depressive, lugubrious, oppressive, sepulchral

fungus
4 conk, mold, rust, smut **5** ergot, yeast **6** agaric, dry rot, mildew **7** candida, truffle **8** mushroom, puffball **9** earthstar, stinkhorn, toadstool
combining form: 4 myco **5** myces, mycet **6** mycete, myceto
part: 3 cap **4** gill **5** ascus, hypha, stipe, volva **7** annulus **8** basidium, conidium, mycelium
rust: 5 Uredo

fungus disease
3 rot **4** mold, rust, scab, smut **5** ergot, tinea **6** blight, mildew, thrush **7** mycosis **8** lumpy jaw, ringworm **12** athlete's foot

funk
4 odor, reek **5** blues, dolor, dumps, ennui, gloom, smell, stink, slump **6** recoil, stench **7** sadness **9** dejection **10** depression, melancholy

funky
3 hip, odd **4** foul, rank **5** fetid, reeky **6** earthy, frowsy, grungy, quaint, quirky, smelly, stinky **7** natural, noisome, oddball, offbeat **8** down-home **10** malodorous

funnel
4 flue, pipe **5** stack **6** hopper **7** channel, conduct, tornado, tundish, twister **8** transmit **10** smokestack

funny
3 odd **4** joke, zany **5** antic, comic, droll, fishy, queer **7** amusing, bizarre, comical, jocular, risible, strange **8** farcical, humorous, peculiar **9** facetious, fantastic, hilarious, laughable, ludicrous **10** ridiculous

Funny Girl
5 Brice (Fanny)
composer: 5 Styne (Jule)
star: 9 Streisand (Barbra)

funnyman
3 wag, wit **4** card, zany **5** clown, comic, cutup, droll, joker **6** jester **7** buffoon, farceur, gagster **8** comedian, humorist, jokester, quipster

fur
4 down, hide, pelt, pile **5** floss, fluff, stole **6** pelage, peltry
kind: 3 fox **4** mink, seal **5** coypu, fitch, otter, sable **6** ermine, fisher, marten, nutria, rabbit, tanuki **7** raccoon **10** chinchilla
lamb: 7 caracul, karakul **9** broadtail
medieval: 4 vair **7** miniver

furbelow
5 frill **6** ruffle **7** flounce

furbish
4 buff **5** fix up, renew, shine **6** polish, revive **7** burnish, refresh, restore **8** renovate

Furies
6 Alecto **7** Erinyes, Megaera **9** Eumenides, Tisiphone

furious
3 mad **4** wild **5** angry, livid, irate, rabid, upset **6** crazed, fierce, insane, raging, stormy **7** enraged, excited, extreme, frantic, intense, violent **8** feverish, frenetic, frenzied, incensed, maddened, outraged, vehement, wrathful **9** impetuous, turbulent

furl
4 curl, fold, roll, wrap **6** take in

furlough
4 pass **5** leave **6** lay off **7** liberty **10** shore leave **13** authorization

furnace
4 kiln, oven **5** forge, stove **6** heater **7** smelter **8** tryworks **11** incinerator
part: 4 port, vent **6** tuyere
tender: 6 stoker

furnish
3 arm, rig **4** give, hand, lend **5** endow, endue, equip **6** fit out, outfit, supply **7** apparel, appoint, deliver, provide, turn out **8** accouter, accoutre, dispense, hand over, transfer **9** provision **10** contribute

furnishings
4 gear **5** decor **8** equipage **9** equipment, trappings **10** housewares **11** appointment **13** accouterments, accoutrements, paraphernalia

furniture chain
4 IKEA

furniture designer
American: 5 Eames (Charles, Ray), Phyfe (Duncan) **7** Goddard (John, Stephen, Thomas), Haldane (William) **8** Stickley (Gustav)
British: 6 Morris (William) **7** Gibbons (Grinling), Shearer (Thomas) **8** Sheraton (Thomas), Stickley (Gustav) **11** Chippendale (Thomas), Hepplewhite (George)
French: 5 Marot (Daniel) **6** Boulle (André-Charles)
German: 6 Breuer (Marcel)
Scottish: 4 Adam (James, Robert)

furniture style
4 Adam **6** Empire, Shaker **7** Bauhaus, Federal, Mission **8** Colonial, Georgian, Jacobean, Sheraton, Stickley **9** Queen Anne **11** chinoiserie, Chippendale, Duncan Phyfe, Hepplewhite **13** Arts and Crafts

furor
3 ado, cry, fad, wax **4** chic, mode, rage, stir, todo **5** anger, craze, mania, style, vogue **6** flurry,

frenzy, pother, ruckus, rumpus, uproar **7** fashion, madness **8** foofaraw **9** commotion **10** dernier cri, excitement **11** controversy

furrow
3 rut **4** knit, ruck **5** plica, ridge, stria, sulci (plural) **6** course, crease, groove, striaea (plural), sulcus, trench **7** channel, crinkle, wrinkle **8** entrench **9** corrugate **11** corrugation

furrowed
5 lined **6** rugose **7** grooved, sulcate **8** wrinkled **10** corrugated

further
4 abet, also, help **5** again, fresh **6** beyond **7** advance, besides, forward, promote **8** engender, moreover **9** encourage, propagate **10** additional, in addition **12** additionally

furthermore
3 and, too **4** also **6** as well, withal **7** besides **8** likewise, moreover **9** what's more **12** additionally

furthermost
4 last **7** extreme **8** farthest, remotest, ultimate

furtive
3 sly **4** foxy, wary, wily **6** artful, covert, crafty, feline, masked, secret, shifty, sneaky, stolen, tricky **7** catlike, cunning, evasive, sub-rosa **8** guileful, hush-hush, scheming, stealthy **9** disguised, insidious **11** circumspect, clandestine **12** hugger-mugger **13** surreptitious, under-the-table
look: **4** peek, peep

fur trader
8 voyageur

furuncle
4 boil **7** abscess

fury
3 ire **4** burn, rage **5** anger, wrath **6** choler, frenzy **7** madness, passion **8** violence **9** vehemence **10** fierceness

furze
4 Ulex, whin **5** gorse
genus: **4** Ulex **7** Genista

fuse
3 mix **4** flux, meld, melt, weld **5** blend, merge, smelt, unify, unite **6** anneal, solder **7** liquefy **8** coalesce, conflate, dissolve, intermix **9** commingle, integrate **10** amalgamate **11** consolidate, incorporate

fusillade
4 hail **5** burst, salvo **6** shower, volley **7** barrage **8** drumfire, outburst **9** broadside, cannonade **11** bombardment

fusion
5 alloy, blend, union **6** merger **7** amalgam, mixture **8** compound **9** coalition, immixture, synthesis

fuss
3 ado, nag, row **4** beef, crab, flap, fret, miff, stew, stir, to-do **5** gripe, hoo-ha, stink, upset, whine, worry **6** bother, bustle, hassle, hoo-hah, hurrah, pother, ruckus, rumpus, squawk **7** protest **8** complain, foofaraw, squabble **9** commotion, complaint, kerfuffle, objection **11** controversy

fussbudget
3 hen **6** granny **8** stickler **10** fuddy-duddy **13** perfectionist

fusspot
8 stickler **9** nitpicker, worrywart

fussy
5 picky **6** dainty, ornate **7** careful, finicky, fretful **9** crotchety, irritable, querulous **10** fastidious, meticulous, nitpicking, particular, pernickety, scrupulous **11** painstaking, persnickety, punctilious **13** conscientious

fustian
4 rant **6** hot air **7** bombast, pompous **8** affected, inflated, rhetoric **9** high-flown **11** exaggerated, highfalutin, pretentious **13** grandiloquent

fusty
4 rank **5** close, dated, fetid, moldy, passé, stale **6** bygone, old-hat, smelly **7** archaic **8** outdated **10** antiquated, malodorous **11** reactionary **12** old-fashioned

futhark letter
4 rune

futile
4 idle, vain **5** empty **6** hollow, otiose **7** useless **8** abortive, bootless, hopeless, nugatory **9** fruitless, worthless **10** unavailing **11** ineffective, ineffectual **12** unproductive, unsuccessful

future
5 later **6** mañana, offing, to come **7** by-and-by **8** oncoming, tomorrow **9** hereafter

future attorney's exam
4 LSAT

Futurism
founder: **9** Marinetti (Filippo Tommaso)
painter: **5** Balla (Giacomo), Carra (Carlo) **7** Russolo (Luigi) **8** Boccioni (Umberto), Severini (Gino)
sculptor: **8** Boccioni (Umberto)

fuzz
3 cop **4** down, lint **6** police

fuzzy
3 dim **5** faint, gauzy, linty, vague, woozy **6** bleary, blurry **7** blurred, muddled, obscure, shadowy, unclear **8** confused **9** distorted, undefined **10** ill-defined, incoherent, indefinite, indistinct

fylfot
8 swastika **10** Hakenkreuz

G

gab
3 jaw, rap, yak **4** blab, chat, talk **5** clack, drool, prate, speak **6** babble, drivel, gibber, gossip, jabber, natter, yammer **7** blabber, blather, chatter, palaver, prattle, twaddle **8** chitchat, converse, idle talk **9** gibberish, small talk

gabber
5 yenta **6** gossip, magpie **7** blabber **9** chatterer **10** chatterbox **12** blabbermouth, gossipmonger

gabby
4 glib **5** talky, windy **6** chatty **7** voluble **8** effusive **9** garrulous, talkative **10** long-winded, loquacious **11** loose-lipped **12** loose-tongued

gaberdine
4 coat, suit **5** cloak, cloth **6** capote, fabric **7** garment, manteau **8** material

gabfest
6 confab, klatch **7** chin-wag, klatsch, palaver

gable
4 wall **8** pediment
ornament: **6** finial

Gabon
capital: **10** Libreville
city: **10** Port-Gentil
ethnic group: **4** Fang **5** Bantu
language: **6** French
monetary unit: **5** franc
neighbor: **5** Congo **8** Cameroon
river: **6** Ogooué

gad
3 bat **4** flit, roam, rove **5** amble, drift, mooch, range, stray, tramp **6** chisel, ramble, wander **7** maunder, meander, traipse **9** gallivant

Gad
brother: **5** Asher
father: **5** Jacob
mother: **6** Zilpah
son: **3** Eri **5** Ezbon, Haggi

Gaddis novel
12 Recognitions (The) **14** Frolic of His Own (A) **16** Carpenter's Gothic

gadfly
3 nag **4** pest, pill **6** bother, critic, insect, nudnik **8** nuisance

gadget
4 tool **5** gizmo, thing **6** device, dingus, doodad, hickey, jigger, widget **7** concern, gimmick, utensil **9** apparatus, appliance, doohickey, implement, mechanism, thingummy **10** instrument **11** contraption, thingamabob, thingamajig, thingumajig

gadwall
4 bird, duck, fowl **9** waterfowl

gadzooks
4 drat, egad **6** crikey, zounds

Gaea
husband: **6** Uranus
offspring: **6** Furies, Giants, Titans, Typhon, Uranus **7** Erinyes **8** Cyclopes **9** Eumenides
parent: **5** Chaos

Gael
4 Celt

Gaelic
4 Erse **5** Irish **6** Celtic **8** Scottish
god: **3** Ler **5** Dagda
hero: **5** Oisin **6** Cormac, Ossian **8** Diarmaid **11** Finn MacCool
king: **9** Conchobar, Conchobor
language: **4** Manx
poet: **4** bard **6** Ossian
queen: **4** Medb
soldier: **4** kern **6** Fenian
spirit: **7** banshee

gaff
3 fix, rig **4** hoax, hook, spar, spur **5** abuse, fraud, spear, trick **6** fleece, ordeal **7** deceive, gimmick **8** raillery **12** climbing iron

gaffe
4 flub, goof, muff **5** boner, error, fault, fluff, lapse **6** bollix, boo-boo, bungle, foul-up, howler, slipup **7** blooper, blunder, clinker, faux pas, misstep, mistake **8** solecism **9** gaucherie **11** impropriety, misjudgment **12** indiscretion

gag
4 balk, gasp, hoax, jape, jest, joke, quip **5** choke, crack, heave, prank, retch, trick **6** muffle, muzzle, shtick, stifle, strain **7** repress, silence, squelch **8** throttle **9** restraint, wisecrack, witticism

gaga
4 agog, wild **5** crazy, giddy, nutty, wacky **6** doting, fervid, gung ho **7** foolish, gushing, excited, smitten **8** animated, enamored, obsessed, thrilled **9** ebullient, exuberant **10** captivated, infatuated **12** enthusiastic

gage
3 vow **4** bond **5** token **6** pledge, surety **8** gauntlet, security
(see also **gauge**)

gaggle
4 crew, gang, pack **5** array, bunch, flock, group

6 clutch, number 7 cluster 10 assemblage, collection 11 aggregation

Gaheris
brother: 6 Gareth, Gawain
father: 3 Lot
mother: 8 Margawse, Morgause
uncle: 6 Arthur
victim: 8 Margawse, Morgause

gaiety
3 fun, joy 4 glee 5 mirth, revel 6 finery, frolic, hoopla 7 elation, jollity, revelry, whoopee 8 elegance, hilarity, reveling, vivacity 9 animation, festivity, happiness, joviality, merriment 10 ebullience, exuberance, hullabaloo, joyousness, jubilation, liveliness 11 high spirits, merrymaking 12 conviviality

gain
3 get, net, win 4 earn, land, make, reap 5 clear, cover, reach, score 6 attain, expand, obtain, pick up, profit, rack up, secure 7 achieve, acquire, advance, attract, augment, benefit, bring in, enlarge, procure 8 earnings, increase, persuade, proceeds, windfall 10 accomplish

gainful
6 paying 8 fruitful, generous 9 lucrative, rewarding 10 beneficial, productive, profitable, well-paying, worthwhile 12 advantageous, remunerative

gainsay
4 buck, defy, deny 6 impugn, negate, oppose, refute, resist 7 dispute 8 disclaim, disprove, negative, traverse 9 disaffirm, repudiate, withstand 10 contradict, contravene, controvert

Gainsborough painting
7 Blue Boy

gait
3 air, run 4 clip, dash, lope, pace, rate, step, trot, walk 5 amble, speed, strut, train, tread 6 canter, gallop, stride 7 bearing 8 demeanor

gaiter
4 boot, shoe, spat 7 legging 8 overshoe

gal
4 babe, doll 5 chick

gala
4 ball, bash, fete, prom 5 merry, party 6 lively 7 festive, jubilee, pageant, shindig 8 festival, jamboree, wingding 9 festivity, spectacle 11 celebration 13 entertainment

Galactica commander
5 Adama (Adm. William)

galago
5 lemur 8 bush baby

Galahad
father: 8 Lancelot 9 Launcelot
mother: 6 Elaine
quest: 5 Grail 9 Holy Grail

Galatea
father: 6 Nereus
husband: 9 Pygmalion
lover: 4 Acis
mother: 5 Doris

galaxy
6 nebula 8 Milky Way, universe

Galba
predecessor: 4 Nero
successor: 4 Otho

gale
4 blow, gust, wind 5 blast, storm 6 squall 7 cyclone, tempest, typhoon 8 outburst 9 hurricane

galena
3 ore 4 lead

Galen's forte
7 healing 8 medicine

galilee
5 porch 6 chapel

Galilee town
4 Cana 7 Gergesa 8 Nazareth, Tiberias 9 Bethsaida, Capernaum

Galileo's birthplace
4 Pisa 5 Italy 7 Tuscany

gall
3 irk, nag, rub, vex 4 bile, fray, fret, rile, roil, sore, wear 5 annoy, brass, chafe, cheek, erode, grate, graze, nerve 6 abrade, bother, burn up, harass, pester, plague, rancor, ruffle, scrape 7 conceit, disturb, frazzle, inflame, provoke, scratch, torment 8 audacity, boldness, chutzpah, irritate, temerity 9 aggravate, arrogance, brashness, impudence, insolence 10 bitterness, effrontery
bladder: 9 cholecyst

gallant
3 fop 4 beau, bold, buck, dude, hero 5 blade, blood, brave, civil, dandy, lover, manly, Romeo, showy, suave, swain, wooer 6 daring, heroic, suitor, urbane 7 courtly, coxcomb, dashing, Don Juan, stately, valiant 8 Casanova, gracious, lothario, paramour, spirited, valorous 9 attentive, courteous, dauntless, ladies' man 10 chivalrous, courageous

gallantry
5 honor, poise, valor 6 daring, mettle, spirit 7 amenity, bravery, courage, heroism, prowess, suavity 8 boldness, chivalry, courtesy, urbanity, valiance, valiancy 9 attention, manliness 10 resolution 11 courtliness 12 fearlessness

galleon
7 warship 12 square-rigger

gallery
5 patio, porch, salon 6 arcade, loggia, museum, piazza 7 balcony, passage, portico, veranda

8 audience, corridor, showroom 9 colonnade, onlookers, promenade
ancient Greek: 4 stoa

galley
3 gig 4 boat, mess, ship, tray 5 cuddy, proof 6 bireme 7 canteen, kitchen, trireme, warship 8 scullery 9 cookhouse

Gallic
6 French

gallimaufry
3 mix 4 hash, mess, olio, stew 5 chaos 6 jumble, medley 7 clutter, goulash, mélange, mixture, variety 8 mishmash, pastiche 9 patchwork, potpourri 10 assortment, hodgepodge, hotchpotch, miscellany, salmagundi

gallinaceous bird
3 hen 5 quail 6 grouse, turkey 7 chicken, hoatzin, peacock 8 curassow, pheasant 9 partridge 10 guinea fowl

galling
6 bitter, vexing 8 rankling 9 upsetting, vexatious 10 afflictive, irritating, nettlesome 11 aggravating, distressing, troublesome 12 exasperating

gallivant
3 bat, bum, gad 4 flit, roam, rove 5 amble, drift, jaunt, mooch, range, stray 6 cruise, ramble, travel, wander 7 meander, traipse 8 vagabond 10 knock about

gallop
4 dash, race 6 sprint

gallows
6 gibbet
bird: 7 villain 8 criminal

galoot
3 ape, guy, oaf 4 dupe, goon, lout, slob 5 chump 6 fellow, lummox 7 palooka

galore
4 full, lush, rich 5 ample, great 6 lavish 7 aplenty, copious, endless, profuse 8 abundant, generous 9 bountiful, expansive, plentiful 11 overflowing

galosh
4 boot, shoe 6 rubber 8 overshoe

Galsworthy work
7 Justice 11 Forsyte Saga (The)

galumph
4 plod 5 barge, clomp, clump, stomp, stump, tramp 6 lumber, trudge

galvanize
3 jar, zap 4 coat, fire, jolt, stir, spur, stun 5 pep up, pique, prime, react, rouse, shock 6 arouse, excite, perk up, thrill 7 animate, enliven, immerse, inspire, provoke, quicken 8 activate, astonish, energize, motivate, vitalize 9 electrify, innervate, magnetize, stimulate 10 invigorate

gam
3 leg, pin, pod, rap 4 chat, flap, limb, talk 5 visit 6 confab 9 drumstick 12 conversation

Gambia
capital: 6 Banjul
city: 9 Serekunda
monetary unit: 6 dalasi
neighbor: 7 Senegal

gambit
3 con, jig 4 move, play, ploy, ruse, wile 5 dodge, topic, trick 6 design, device, remark, tactic 7 gimmick 8 artifice, maneuver, trickery 9 expedient, stratagem 10 subterfuge

gamble
3 bet, lay, set 4 dare, game, play, punt, risk 5 put on, stake, wager 6 chance, hazard, plunge, raffle 7 imperil, lottery, venture 8 cast lots, long shot 9 crapshoot, speculate 10 jeopardize

gambler
5 dicer, piker, shark, sharp 6 bettor, punter 7 sharper 8 gamester 9 cardsharp 10 cardplayer 11 cardsharper

gambling
game: 4 keno 5 bingo, poker 6 Hold'em 8 baccarat 9 blackjack 10 Texas Hold'em
place: 3 den 4 club, dive, Reno 5 joint, Vegas 6 casino 8 Las Vegas, pool hall 9 roadhouse 10 Monte Carlo 12 Atlantic City, betting house

gambol
3 hop 4 jump, lark, leap, romp, skip 5 bound, caper, frisk, revel, sport 6 cavort, frolic, prance, spring 7 carry on, roister, rollick

Gambrinus' invention
3 ale 4 beer 5 lager

game
3 bet, fun, lay, RPG 4 bold, jest, joke, lark, play, prey, romp 5 brave, chase, eager, hardy, sport, stake, trick, wager 6 gamble, quarry, spunky 7 contest, pastime, valiant, willing 8 fearless, intrepid, resolute, unafraid, valorous 9 amusement, dauntless, diversion, undaunted 10 courageous, recreation
arcade: 7 Gremlin 8 Carnival, Skee-Ball
ball: 4 golf, polo, pool 5 bocce, bocci, fives, rogue, rugby 6 boccie, hockey, pelota, soccer, squash, tennis 7 cricket, croquet, jai alai 8 baseball, football, handball, hardball, lacrosse, racquets, rounders, softball 9 bagatelle, billiards 10 basketball, volleyball 11 racquetball
Basque: 6 pelota 7 jai alai
bird: 4 duck 5 quail 6 chukar, turkey 7 bustard 8 bobwhite, pheasant 9 partridge
board: 4 Clue, Risk, wari 5 chess, chuba, oware, shogi 7 mancala, pachisi 8 checkers, Monopoly, Scrabble 9 crokinole, Parcheesi 10 backgammon

child's: **3** tag **5** jacks **7** marbles, ringtaw **8** leapfrog, peekaboo **9** hopscotch, tic-tac-toe
confidence: **4** scam **5** bunco, bunko, sting
court: **5** roque **6** pelota, squash, tennis **7** jai alai **8** handball, racquets **9** badminton **10** basketball, volleyball **11** racquetball
electric: **7** pinball
English: **5** rugby **7** cricket **8** draughts
Irish: **7** hurling
of chance: **4** faro, keno **5** beano, bingo, boule, craps, lotto, rondo **6** fan-tan, hazard, policy, raffle **7** lottery, rondeau **8** roulette
official: **3** ref, ump **6** umpire **7** referee
parlor: **8** Carnelli, charades
piece: **3** die **4** tile **5** token **6** domino, marble, top hat **7** checker
racket: **6** squash, tennis **8** lacrosse, ping-pong, racquets **9** badminton **11** racquetball, table tennis
roulette-like: **5** boule
rule maker: **5** Hoyle (Edmond)
string: **10** cat's cradle
table: **4** pool **5** craps **7** mah-jong, snooker, Yahtzee **8** dominoes, mah-jongg, ping-pong, roulette **9** bagatelle, billiards **11** table tennis
word: **5** rebus **6** crambo **7** anagram, hangman **8** acrostic, charades, Scrabble **9** crossword, logogriph
(see also **card game**)

game plan
6 scheme, tactic **8** scenario, strategy **9** blueprint **10** big picture

gamete
3 egg **4** ovum **5** sperm **8** germ cell

gamin
3 elf, imp, tad **4** brat, tyke, waif **5** scamp **6** monkey, rascal, urchin **11** guttersnipe **12** street urchin

gamine
3 elf, imp **4** brat, waif **5** scamp **6** hoyden, rascal, tomboy, urchin **11** guttersnipe **12** street urchin

gaming cubes
4 dice **5** bones

gammon
3 ham **4** dupe, fool, rook **5** bacon, feign **6** delude, fleece, humbug **7** deceive, pretend, swindle **8** flimflam, hoodwink **9** bamboozle **11** hornswoggle

gamut
4 A to Z **5** range, scale, scope, sweep **6** extent, series, spread **7** compass **8** diapason, spectrum

gamy
3 off **4** foul, racy, rank, vile **5** brave, fetid, funky **6** plucky, putrid, rancid, rotten, smelly, sordid, stinky, strong **7** corrupt, decayed, noisome, noxious, reeking **10** decomposed, malodorous, scandalous **12** disagreeable, disreputable

gander
4 look, peek **5** goose **6** glance **7** glimpse **9** simpleton, waterfowl

___ Gandhi
5 Rajiv **6** Indira **7** Mahatma **8** Mohandas

Gandalf portrayer McKellen
3 Ian

gandy dancer
10 railroader, tracklayer

ganef
5 thief **6** rascal **9** scoundrel

Ganesa, Ganesh
father: **4** Siva **5** Shiva
head: **8** elephant
mother: **7** Parvati

gang
3 lot, mob, set **4** band, clan, club, crew, pack, ring, team **5** bunch, crowd, group, horde **6** circle, clique, outfit **7** arrange, cluster, collect, combine, company, coterie **8** assemble **10** accumulate, assemblage **11** combination

gangling
4 bony, lean, slim **5** gaunt, lanky, rangy **6** meager, meagre, skinny **7** angular, scrawny, slender, spindly, stringy **8** rawboned **9** spindling

ganglion
5 tumor **7** nucleus

gangrene
3 rot **5** decay **7** mortify, putrefy **8** necrosis **9** decompose

gangster
4 goon, hood, thug **5** cholo, rough, thief, tough **6** bandit, gunman **7** hoodlum, mafioso, mobster, ruffian **8** criminal **9** cutthroat, racketeer
girlfriend: **4** moll
gun: **3** gat, rod **6** heater

gangway
4 hall, path **5** aisle **7** passage, walkway **8** corridor **10** passageway

ganja
3 kef, kif, pot, tea **4** hemp, herb, weed **5** grass, smoke **7** hashish **8** cannabis, Mary Jane **9** marijuana

gannet
4 bird **5** booby **7** seabird

ganoid fish
3 gar **6** beluga, bowfin **7** dogfish, garfish, teleost **8** billfish, sturgeon **10** paddlefish

Ganymede
abductor: **4** Zeus **7** Jupiter
brother: **4** Ilus
father: **4** Tros
function: **9** cupbearer

gaol
3 jug, pen 4 jail 5 clink, joint, pokey 6 cooler, lockup, prison 7 slammer 8 bastille 9 calaboose, jailhouse 12 penitentiary

gap
3 cut, pit 4 gash, gulf, hole, lull, pass, rent, rift, skip, slit, slot, tear, vent, void, yawn 5 abyss, blank, break, chasm, chink, cleft, clove, crack, gorge, gulch, gully, pause, space, split 6 arroyo, breach, canyon, cavity, cranny, divide, hiatus, hollow, lacuna, ravine, recess, schism, vacuum 7 caesura, crevice, fissure, interim, lacunae (plural), opening, orifice, rupture, vacancy, vacuity 8 aperture, cleavage, division, fracture, interval 9 disparity, interlude 10 deficiency, difference, interstice, separation 12 intermission, interruption 13 discontinuity

gape
3 eye, yaw 4 bore, gawk, gawp, gaze, glom, leer, look, ogle, open, part, peer, yawn 5 crack, glare, gloat, space, split, stare 6 glance, goggle 7 eyeball 10 rubberneck

gaping
4 huge, open, vast, wide 5 broad, great 7 chasmal 9 cavernous

gar
4 fish, pike 8 billfish 10 needlefish

garage
4 shop 7 cabinet, car park, carport, shelter

Garand
5 rifle

garb
4 clad, duds, wear 5 array, cover, dress, getup, style 6 attire, clothe, livery, outfit 7 apparel, clothes, garment, raiment, threads 9 trappings 10 appearance

garbage
4 junk, muck, slop 5 dreck, dregs, filth, offal, trash, waste 6 debris, litter, refuse, sewage 7 rubbish 8 detritus, riffraff
hauler: 4 scow
heap: 6 midden

garble
4 sift, warp 5 alter, belie, color, twist 6 jumble, mangle, muddle 7 becloud, confuse, contort, distort, falsify, obscure, pervert 8 miscolor, misstate, mutilate 9 obfuscate 10 impurities 12 misrepresent

garçon
3 boy 6 waiter 7 servant

garden
4 Eden, park 7 nursery 8 parterre
shelter: 5 arbor 6 arbour

gardener
6 grower 7 yardman 9 topiarist

garden house
6 alcove, gazebo 9 belvedere

Garden State
9 New Jersey

garden tool
3 hoe 4 claw, fork, rake 5 edger, mower, spade 6 dibble, pruner, scythe, shears, shovel, sickle, trowel, weeder 8 clippers

Gardner of film
3 Ava

Gardner, Erle Stanley
character: 5 Della (Street) 10 Perry Mason

Gareth
brother: 6 Gawain 7 Gaheris
father: 3 Lot
mother: 8 Margawse, Morgause
slayer: 8 Lancelot 9 Launcelot
uncle: 6 Arthur
wife: 6 Liones

Garfield
creator: 5 Davis (Jim)
dog: 4 Odie

Gargamelle's son
9 Gargantua

Gargantua
abbey: 7 Thélème
author: 8 Rabelais (François)
father: 12 Grandgousier
first word: 5 drink
mother: 10 Gargamelle
son: 10 Pantagruel

gargantuan
see **gigantic**

Garibaldi follower
8 redshirt

garish
4 loud 5 gaudy, showy, vivid 6 brassy, brazen, flashy, glitzy, tawdry, tinsel, vulgar 7 blatant, chintzy, glaring, raffish, splashy 8 tinselly 12 meretricious

garland
3 ana, lei 5 album, crown 6 anadem, digest, laurel, wreath 7 chaplet, coronal, coronet, laurels, omnibus 8 analects 9 anthology, selection 10 collection, compendium, miscellany 11 florilegium

garlic
4 moly, ramp 5 aglio, clove 6 allium
mayonnaise: 5 aioli

garment
4 garb, gear 5 array, habit 6 attire 7 apparel, raiment 8 clothing, vestment 10 habiliment
African: 6 kaross 7 dashiki
Arab: 3 aba 4 haik
British: 10 mackintosh

clergy's: **3** alb **4** cope **7** cassock, soutane **8** vestment
close-fitting: **6** girdle, tights **7** leotard
for sleeping: **6** pajama **7** nightie **9** nightgown
Greek: **5** tunic **6** chiton, peplos **7** chlamys **8** himation
Hawaiian: **6** muumuu
Hindu: **4** sari **6** patola
hooded: **8** djellaba
Japanese: **6** kimono
lace: **10** chemisette
Malay: **6** sarong
Mexican: **6** sarape, serape
Middle Eastern: **6** caftan, kaftan
outer: **4** cape, coat, robe, wrap **5** apron, cloak, parka, shawl, smock, stole **6** anorak, capote, jacket, kimono, poncho, sarong, ulster, wammus **7** overall, pelisse, surtout, sweater, topcoat **8** overcoat, pinafore, pullover, scapular **9** coveralls, gaberdine, polonaise
Polynesian: **5** pareo, pareu **6** sarong
rain: **6** poncho **7** oilskin, slicker
Roman: **4** toga **5** tunic
Scottish: **4** jupe, kilt **7** sporran
sleeveless: **3** aba **4** cape **6** mantle, tabard
Turkish: **6** dolman
women's: **4** cami, gown **5** dress, skirt, teddy **6** blouse, halter, vestee **7** blouson, chemise, nightie, partlet, tank top **8** camisole, negligee, peignoir, pelerine

garner
4 cull, earn, hive, reap **5** amass, glean, hoard, lay up, store **6** gather, pick up, roll up **7** collect, extract, harvest, store up **8** cumulate, ingather **9** stockpile **10** accumulate

garnet
5 jewel, stone **6** pyrope **8** essonite **9** hessonite
black: **8** melanite
red: **9** almandine, almandite

garnish
4 deck, trim **5** adorn **6** bedeck **7** dress up, enhance **8** beautify, decorate, ornament **9** embellish

garret
4 loft, room **5** attic **8** cockloft

garrison
4 camp, fort, post **6** assign, billet, occupy, troops **7** station **8** fortress **10** stronghold

Garr of film
4 Teri

garrote
5 choke **8** strangle, throttle **11** strangulate

garrulous
5 gabby **6** blabby, mouthy **7** verbose, voluble **9** talkative **10** loquacious

garter
4 band, belt **5** strap **7** support **9** supporter

garth
4 yard **5** close **9** enclosure

gas
4 fuel, fume **5** fumes, steam, vapor **6** petrol **8** gasoline **9** petroleum
atmospheric: **4** neon **5** argon, oxide, ozone, xenon **6** helium, oxygen **7** krypton, methane **8** hydrogen, nitrogen
flammable: **6** butane, ethane, ethyne **7** methane, propane, propene **8** ethylene
inert: **4** neon **5** argon, radon, xenon **6** helium **7** krypton
mine: **8** firedamp **9** black damp
oxygen: **5** ozone
toxic: **5** sarin, soman, tabun **6** arsine, ketene **7** mustard **8** phosgene **9** phosphine

gasconade
4 brag **7** bravado **8** boasting, bragging **11** braggadocio

gash
3 cut, rip **4** rend, slit, tear **5** carve, cleft, gouge, slash, slice, split **6** incise **8** lacerate **10** depression, laceration

gasket
4 ring, seal **5** O-ring **6** sealer

gasoline
4 fuel **6** petrol
additive: **3** STP
brand of Canada: **4** Esso
rating: **6** octane

gasp
4 blow, huff, pant, puff **5** heave **6** wheeze **11** exclamation

Gaspar
companion: **8** Melchior **9** Balthazar
gift: **12** frankincense

gassy
5 windy **7** verbose **8** inflated, vaporous **9** flatulent

gastronome
7 epicure, gourmet **8** gourmand **9** bon vivant **11** connoisseur

gastropod
4 slug **5** conch, murex, snail, whelk **6** cowrie, limpet, volute **7** abalone, mollusc, mollusk, sea slug **8** pteropod, univalve **10** periwinkle

gat
3 gun, rod **6** heater, pistol, roscoe **7** channel, firearm, handgun, passage **8** revolver

gate
3 tap **4** cock, door, exit, port **5** entry, hatch, toril, valve **6** faucet, portal, spigot, switch, wicket **7** hydrant, opening, petcock **8** entrance, entryway, stopcock **9** turnstile **10** attendance

gâteau
4 cake

gatefold
6 insert 7 foldout

Gates of Hercules
9 Gibraltar 12 promontories

gateway
4 arch, door, exit 5 pylon, toril 6 portal 7 archway, doorway, opening 8 entrance

gather
4 brew, cull, gain, grow, heap, herd, loom, mass, meet, pick, pile, pool, reap 5 amass, bunch, flock, glean, group, horde, infer, judge, pluck, shirr, swarm 6 assume, deduce, derive, expect, garner, muster, pick up, pucker, rake in, summon, take in 7 cluster, collect, compile, convene, extract, harvest, marshal, round up, suppose, surmise, suspect 8 assemble, conclude, converge, increase 9 aggregate, intensify 10 accumulate, congregate, understand 11 concentrate

gathering
4 bevy, crew, gang, herd, mass, ruck 5 bunch, crowd, crush, drove, flock, group, horde, party, press, rally, swarm 6 caucus, klatch, muster, throng 7 company, harvest, klatsch, meeting, reunion, turnout 8 assembly, congress, junction 9 concourse, congeries 10 assemblage, collection, conference, confluence 11 aggregation, get-together 12 congregation

Gath's giant
7 Goliath 10 Philistine

gator's relative
4 croc

gauche
5 crude, gawky, inept 6 clumsy 7 awkward, halting, loutish, uncouth 8 bumbling, tactless 9 graceless, ham-handed, inelegant, maladroit 10 blundering

gaucho
6 cowboy 8 herdsman
lariat: 4 bola
turf: 5 llano, pampa 6 pampas
weapon: 4 bola 5 bolas 7 machete

gaudeamus ____
6 igitur

gaudy
4 loud 5 showy 6 brassy, brazen, coarse, flashy, garish, tawdry, tinsel, vulgar 7 blatant, chintzy, glaring 9 brummagem, tasteless 10 outlandish 12 meretricious, ostentatious

Gaugamela
loser: 6 Darius, Persia
victor: 9 Alexander (the Great)

gauge
4 bore, rule, size 5 check, judge, meter, scale, weigh, width 6 assess, degree 7 compute, measure 8 diameter, estimate, evaluate, quantify, standard 9 benchmark, criterion, dimension, thickness, yardstick 10 instrument, touchstone 11 measurement

Gauguin's island
6 Tahiti

Gaul
4 Celt 6 France 9 Frenchman
ancient inhabitants: 4 Remi 6 Belgae

Gaulish
6 French
god: 4 Esus 7 Taranis
goddess: 8 Belisama
priest: 5 druid

gaunt
4 bare, bony, grim, lank, lean, thin 5 harsh, lanky, spare 6 barren, gangly, skinny, wasted 7 angular, scraggy, scrawny 8 gangling, rawboned, skeletal 9 emaciated 10 cadaverous

gauntlet
4 dare, test 5 glove, trial 6 attack, ordeal 9 challenge, onslaught

Gautama
6 Buddha 10 Siddhartha
mother: 4 Maya 8 Mahamaya
son: 6 Rahula
wife: 9 Yasodhara

gauze
4 film, haze, leno, mesh, mist 5 cloth, crepe, tulle 6 fabric, tissue 7 bandage, chiffon, tiffany 8 compress, dressing 11 cheesecloth

gauzy
4 thin 5 filmy, fuzzy, sheer, vague 6 flimsy 8 delicate, pellucid 9 gossamery 10 diaphanous 11 transparent

gavel
6 hammer, mallet

gavial
7 gharial, reptile 9 crocodile

gavotte
4 tune 5 dance

Gawain
brother: 6 Gareth 7 Gaheris
father: 3 Lot
mother: 8 Margawse, Morgause
slayer: 8 Lancelot 9 Launcelot
uncle: 6 Arthur
victim: 6 Uwayne 7 Lamerok 9 Pellinore

gawk
3 oaf 4 bore, gape, gaze, hick, look, lout, lump, peer, rube 5 churl, glare, gloat, klutz, looby, stare, yokel 6 goggle, lubber

gawky
5 inept, splay 6 clumsy, coarse, gauche, oafish

7 awkward, loutish, lumpish, uncouth 8 bumbling, bungling, lubberly, ungainly 9 graceless, ham-handed, lumbering, maladroit

gay
4 glad 5 happy, jolly, merry, queer, showy, sunny, vivid 6 blithe, bouncy, bright, cheery, festal, frisky, jocund, jovial, joyful, lively 7 excited, festive, gleeful, lesbian, playful, raffish 8 animated, cheerful, colorful, mirthful, spirited, sportive 9 exuberant, sparkling, vivacious 10 frolicsome, homosexual, insouciant, nonchalant 12 light-hearted

___ Gay
4 John 5 Enola

Gaza victor
7 Allenby (Edmund)

gaze
3 eye 4 bore, gape, gawk, leer, look, ogle, peer, pore, scan, view 5 glare, gloat, stare, watch 6 goggle 7 eyeball, observe 8 consider 10 rubberneck 11 contemplate

gazebo
6 alcove 8 pavilion 9 belvedere 11 garden house, summerhouse

gazelle
3 goa 4 cora, kudu, mohr, oryx 5 eland, nyala 6 koodoo 7 gemsbok 8 antelope

gazette
5 paper 6 record 7 journal, publish 9 newspaper 10 periodical 11 publication 12 announcement

gazetteer
5 atlas, guide, index

gear
3 cam, cog, rig 5 dress, goods, shift, stuff, wheel 6 adjust, tackle, things 7 apparel, harness, rigging 8 clothing, cogwheel, garments, materiel, property, sprocket, tackling, trapping 9 apparatus, equipment, machinery 10 belongings 11 accessories, habiliments, possessions 13 accouterments, accoutrements, paraphernalia

Geats
king: 7 Hygelac
prince: 7 Beowulf

Geb
daughter: 4 Isis 8 Nephthys
father: 3 Shu
mother: 6 Tefnut
sister: 3 Nut
son: 3 Set 6 Osiris
wife: 3 Nut

gecko
6 lizard 7 reptile

Gedaliah
father: 6 Ahikam 7 Pashhur 8 Jeduthun
slayer: 7 Ishmael

gee
3 wow 4 gosh, turn 5 golly, right 8 goodness, gracious 9 turn right

geek
4 buff, guru, nerd, whiz 5 carny, fiend, freak 6 carney, carnie, expert, pundit, techie, weirdo 7 devotee, egghead, fanatic, oddball 9 authority, eccentric 10 enthusiast 12 intellectual

geezer
4 coot, fogy 5 bloke, crank, fogey 6 codger, dotard, fossil

Gehenna
3 pit 4 hell 5 abyss, hades, Sheol 6 Tophet 7 inferno 8 Tartarus 9 perdition 10 underworld 11 netherworld

Geisel pseudonym
7 Dr. Seuss

geisha wear
3 obi 6 kimono

gel
3 dry, set 4 agar, clot 6 harden, mousse 7 colloid, congeal, thicken 8 solidify 9 coagulate

gelatin
3 jam 4 agar 5 aspic, jelly 7 sericin

geld
3 cut, fix, tax 5 alter, desex, unsex 6 change, neuter 7 deprive 8 castrate, mutilate 9 sterilize 10 emasculate 11 desexualize

gelid
3 icy 4 cold 5 chill, nippy, polar 6 arctic, chilly, frigid, frosty, frozen, steely 7 glacial 8 freezing

Geller of paranormal fame
3 Uri

gelt
5 money

gem
3 jet 4 jade, onyx, opal, rock, ruby, sard 5 agate, amber, beryl, bijou, coral, jewel, lapis, pearl, stone, topaz 6 amulet, garnet, jasper, scarab, sphene, spinel, zircon 7 bejewel, cat's-eye, citrine, diamond, emerald, enjewel, olivine, peridot 8 amethyst, corundum, diopside, fluorite, intaglio, lazurite, obsidian, sapphire, sardonyx, sparkler, tigereye 9 brilliant, carnelian, jadestone, moonstone, phenakite, scapolite, spodumene, tiger's-eye, turquoise 10 aquamarine, cordierite, tourmaline 11 alexandrite, chrysoberyl, chrysoprase, lapis lazuli, masterpiece
blue: 6 zircon 8 sapphire 9 turquoise 10 aquamarine 11 lapis lazuli
carved: 5 cameo 8 intaglio
changeable: 9 chatoyant
cut: 7 marquis 8 baguette, cabochon, marquise 9 brilliant
face: 5 culet, facet

green: **4** jade **7** emerald, peridot, smaragd **10** chrysolite **11** chrysoprase
red: **4** ruby, sard **6** garnet, pyrope, spinel **9** carnelian
support: **7** setting
weight: **5** carat
yellow: **5** amber, topaz **6** sphene **7** citrine

Gemini star
6 Castor, Pollux

gemmule
3 bud

gemsbok
4 oryx **8** antelope

Gem State
5 Idaho

gemütlich
see **genial**

gendarme
3 cop **5** bobby **7** officer, soldier **8** flatfoot **9** constable, patrolman, policeman

gender
3 sex **4** kind, male, sort, type **5** class **6** female, neuter **8** feminine **9** masculine

genealogy
5 roots, stirp, stock **6** origin, stemma **7** descent, history, lineage **8** ancestry, heredity, pedigree **9** bloodline **10** family tree

general
4 wide **5** broad, usual, vague **6** common, global, normal, public **7** blanket, generic, overall, regular, routine, typical **8** catholic, everyday, sweeping **9** all-around, prevalent, universal **10** collective, prevailing, unspecific, widespread **11** commonplace **13** comprehensive
American: **3** Lee (Robert E.) **4** Haig (Alexander), Pike (Zebulon), Wood (Leonard) **5** Clark (Mark, Wesley, William), Grant (Ulysses S.), Meade (George), Scott (Charles, Hugh, Winfield), Smith (Andrew Jackson, Giles, Holland, Morgan, Samuel, Walter, Bedell), Stark (John), Worth (William) **6** Abrams (Creighton), Custer (George Armstrong), Franks (Tommy), Hooker (Joseph), Kearny (Philip, Stephen), Patton (George S.), Porter (Fitz-John), Powell (Colin), Slocum (Henry), Spaatz (Carl), Taylor (Maxwell, Richard, Zachary) **7** Bradley (Omar), Frémont (John Charles), Houston (Samuel), Jackson (Andrew, Thomas “Stonewall”), Lejeune (John), Ridgway (Matthew B.), Sherman (William Tecumseh), Twining (Nathaniel), Wallace (Lewis), Wheeler (Joseph) **8** Burnside (Ambrose), Goethals (George Washington), Marshall (George), Mitchell (Billy), Pershing (John J.), Petraeus (David), Sheridan (Philip), Stilwell (Joseph) **9** MacArthur (Arthur, Douglas), McClellan (George), Rosecrans (William), Schofield (John), Wilkinson (James) **10** Beauregard (P. G. T.), Eisenhower (Dwight D.), Vandegrift (Alexander), Wainwright (Jonathan) **11** Schwarzkopf (Norman) **12** Westmoreland (William)
American Revolutionary: **4** Knox (Henry), Ward (Artemas) **5** Gates (Horatio), Wayne (“Mad Anthony”) **6** de Kalb (Baron), Greene (Nathanael), Morgan (Daniel), Putnam (Israel, Rufus) **8** Moultrie (William), Sullivan (John) **10** Washington (George)
Austrian: **11** Wallenstein (Albrecht von)
British: **4** Gage (Thomas), Howe (William) **5** Clive (Robert), Monck (George), Wolfe (James) **6** Rupert (Prince) **7** Amherst (Jeffery), Wingate (Orde Charles, Reginald) **8** Burgoyne (John), Cromwell (Oliver) **10** Abercromby (Ralph, Robert), Cornwallis (Charles), Wellington (Duke of)
Carthaginian: **8** Hamilcar, Hannibal **9** Hasdrubal
Chinese: **3** Tso, Yan (Xishan), Yen (Hsi-shan) **4** Feng (Guozhang, Kuo-chang, Yü-hsiang, Yuxiang) **5** Chang (Tso-lin), Zhang (Zuolin)
Confederate: **3** Lee (Robert E.) **4** Hill (Ambrose), Hood (John Bell) **5** Bragg (Braxton), Ewell (Richard Stoddart), Price (Sterling), Smith (Edmund Kirby) **6** Morgan (John Hunt), Stuart (Jeb) **7** Forrest (Nathan Bedford), Hampton (Wade), Jackson (Thomas “Stonewall”), Pickett (George) **8** Johnston (Albert Sidney, Joseph Eggleston) **9** Pemberton (John) **10** Beauregard (Pierre G. T.), Longstreet (James)
French: **3** Ney (Michel) **4** Foch (Ferdinand) **6** Moreau (Victor), Pétain (Philippe) **7** Weygand (Maxime) **8** de Gaulle (Charles), Lefebvre (Pierre), Montcalm (Marquis de), Saint-Cyr (Laurent de Gouvion-) **9** Frontenac (Comte de) **10** Rochambeau (Comte de)
German: **4** Jodl (Alfred) **6** Kleist (Paul Ludwig von), Rommel (Erwin) **9** Rundstedt (Gerd von) **10** Kesselring (Albert), Ludendorff (Erich)
Greek: **6** Nicias **9** Miltiades **10** Alcibiades **12** Themistocles
Japanese: **4** Tojo (Hideki) **5** Koiso (Kuniaki) **6** Yasuda (Yoshisada) **8** Yamagata (Aritomo) **9** Yamashita (Tomoyuki)
Mexican: **9** Santa Anna (Antonio López de)
Prussian: **11** Scharnhorst (Gerhard von)
Roman: **5** Sulla (Lucius Cornelius) **6** Caesar (Julius), Fabius (Quintus), Marius (Gaius), Pompey (the Great), Scipio (Gnaeus Cornelius, Publius Cornelius) **7** Regulus (Marcus Atilius), Ricimer (Flavius) **8** Agricola (Gnaeus Julius), Lucullus (Lucius Licinius), Stilicho (Flavius) **9** Marcellus (Marcus Claudius), Sertorius (Quintus) **10** Theodosius (the Great) **11** Cincinnatus (Lucius Quinctius)

Russian: **6** Zhukov (Georgy) **7** Kutuzov (Mikhail), Trotcky (Loon), Wrangel (Pyotr), Zhdanov (Andrey) **9** Yeremenko (Andrey)
Spanish: **4** Alba (Duke of), Alva (Duke of) **6** Franco (Francisco)
Swedish: **7** Wrangel (Karl Gustav)

general assembly
4 diet **6** plenum **8** congress **10** parliament **11** legislature

generalize
5 infer, widen **6** derive, extend, induce, spread **7** broaden **8** conclude **12** universalize

generally
6 mainly, mostly, widely **7** all told, as a rule, broadly, chiefly, en masse, largely, overall, usually **8** all in all, commonly, normally **9** on average, primarily, typically **10** altogether, by and large, frequently, on the whole, ordinarily **11** customarily, principally

generate
4 bear, make, sire **5** beget, breed, cause, hatch, spawn, yield **6** create, effect, father, induce, work up **7** achieve, develop, produce, provoke **8** engender, initiate, multiply **9** originate, procreate, propagate, reproduce **10** bring about, bring forth

generator
6 dynamo, selsyn

generic
5 broad **6** common, global **7** blanket **9** inclusive, unbranded, universal **10** indistinct **12** nonexclusive

___ generis
3 sui

generosity
7 charity **8** altruism, kindness, largesse **9** abundance **10** liberality **11** beneficence, benevolence, magnanimity, munificence **12** philanthropy **13** unselfishness

generous
4 free, kind **5** ample **6** lavish **7** copious, helpful, liberal, profuse, willing **8** abundant **9** bounteous, bountiful, plenteous, plentiful, unselfish, unsparing **10** altruistic, benevolent, bighearted, charitable, munificent, openhanded, ungrudging, unstinting **11** considerate, kindhearted, magnanimous, overflowing **12** greathearted

genesis
4 dawn, root **5** alpha, birth, start **6** origin, outset, source **7** dawning, opening **8** creation **9** beginning, formation, inception **10** provenance **12** commencement

Genesis
brother: **4** Abel, Cain, Esau
garden: **4** Eden

genetic
10 congenital, hereditary
material: **3** DNA, RNA **7** cistron **9** chromatid **10** chromosome
term: **8** synapsis **9** backcross

Genet play
5 Maids (The) **6** Blacks (The) **7** Balcony (The)

genial
4 kind, warm **5** jolly, merry **6** benign, blithe, hearty, jocund, jovial, kindly, mellow, social **7** affable, amiable, cordial **8** amicable, friendly, gracious, pleasant, sociable **9** agreeable, congenial, convivial, easygoing **10** neighborly **11** good-humored, good-natured, warmhearted

genie
3 imp **4** jann, jinn, puck **5** afrit **6** afreet, spirit, sprite

geniture
4 dawn **5** birth, start **6** origin **8** nativity **9** beginning, inception

genius
3 wiz **4** bent, gift, head, turn, whiz **5** flair, jinni, knack **6** acumen, brains, master, spirit, talent, wizard **7** aptness, faculty, prodigy **8** aptitude, brainiac, capacity, penchant **9** ingenuity, intellect **10** brilliance, creativity, mastermind, propensity **12** intelligence **13** inventiveness

Genoa's liberator
5 Doria (Andrea)

genre
3 ilk **4** kind, sort, type **5** class, style **6** family, stripe **7** species, variety **8** category, division

gens
3 kin **4** clan **5** group **6** family, people **7** kinfolk **9** relations, relatives

Genseric's subjects
7 Vandals

gent
(see **gentleman**)

genteel
4 nice, prim **5** civil **6** formal, polite, prissy, strict, stuffy, urbane **7** courtly, elegant, prudish, refined, stilted, stylish **8** affected, cultured, graceful, gracious, ladylike, mannerly, polished, priggish, well-bred **9** courteous **10** cultivated **11** gentlemanly, pretentious, straitlaced, well-behaved

gentile
3 goy **5** pagan **7** heathen **9** Christian, non-Jewish

gentility
5 elite **6** gentry **7** decorum, manners, quality, society **8** breeding, courtesy, nobility **9** blue blood **10** aristocrat, refinement, upper class, upper crust **11** aristocracy

gentle
4 calm, easy, kind, meek, mild, soft, tame **5** balmy, quiet, tamed **6** benign, docile, genial, kindly, mellow, placid, serene, smooth, tender **7** amiable, lenient **8** delicate, peaceful, pleasant, soothing, tranquil **9** agreeable **11** softhearted, sympathetic, warmhearted **13** compassionate
creature: **4** lamb

gentleman
3 sir **6** aristo, fellow, mister **8** cavalier **9** blue blood, chevalier, patrician **10** aristocrat
English: **6** milord
French: **8** monsieur
Hindu: **4** babu
Spanish: **3** don **5** señor

gentleman friend
4 beau **5** lover, swain **6** fiancé, squire, suitor **7** gallant

gentlemanly
5 civil, noble, suave **6** polite, urbane **7** elegant, gallant, genteel, refined **8** mannerly, well-bred **9** courteous, honorable **10** chivalrous, cultivated **11** considerate

Gentlemen Prefer Blondes author
4 Loos (Anita)

gentry
5 elite, folks **7** quality, society **8** nobility **9** gentility, patrician **10** gentlefolk, patriciate, upper class, upper crust **11** aristocracy, high society, ruling class

genuflect
3 bow **4** fawn **5** kneel **6** kowtow

genuine
4 echt, pure, real, true **5** plain, pucka, pukka, valid **6** actual, dinkum, honest, tested **7** factual, natural, sincere **8** absolute, bona fide, positive, trueborn **9** authentic, certified, unalloyed, undoubted, unfeigned, veritable **10** sure-enough, unaffected

genus
3 ilk **4** kind, mode, sort, type **5** class, group, order **6** family **7** species, variety **8** category
amphibian: **4** Hyla, Rana
antelope: **4** Oryx
bee: **4** Apis
bird: **4** Alca, Anas, Chen, Olor, Pavo, Pica, Rhea, Sula, Uria, Xema **5** Sitta
fish: **4** Amia, Lota
herb: **4** Arum, Geum
insect: **4** Nepa
lily: **4** Aloe
orchid: **4** Disa
owl: **4** Bubo, Otus
palm: **4** Nipa
sheep: **4** Ovis
shrub: **4** Ilex, Itea, Ulex
snake: **4** Eryx
tree: **4** Acer, Cola, Maba, Olea
turtle: **4** Emys

geode
4 rock **5** stone **6** cavity, nodule

geoduck
4 clam

geographer
American: **10** Huntington (Ellsworth)
Flemish: **8** Mercator (Gerardus)
German: **6** Ratzel (Friedrich)
Greek: **6** Strabo **7** Ptolemy
Italian: **8** Vespucci (Amerigo)

geologic period
3 eon **4** aeon **5** azoic **6** Eocene, Hadean **7** Archean, Miocene, Permian **8** Cambrian, Cenozoic, Devonian, Holocene, Jurassic, Mesozoic, Pliocene, Silurian, Triassic **9** Oligocene, Paleocene, Paleozoic **10** Cretaceous, Ordovician **11** Phanerozoic, Pleistocene, Precambrian, Proterozoic **13** Mississippian, Pennsylvanian

geometer
6 Euclid **13** mathematician

geometric
coordinate: **8** abscissa, ordinate
curve: **3** arc **6** spiral **7** ellipse, evolute **8** parabola
figure: **5** rhomb **6** circle, oblong, square **7** ellipse, hexagon, octagon, polygon, rhombus **8** heptagon, pentagon, rhomboid, triangle **9** rectangle
solid: **4** cone, cube **5** prism **6** sphere **7** pyramid **8** cylinder, spheroid, spherule
surface: **5** nappe, torus **6** toroid

geometry subject
4 area

geophagy
4 pica

Georgia
capital: **7** Atlanta
city: **5** Macon **6** Albany, Athens **7** Augusta **8** Columbus, Marietta, Savannah
college, university: **5** Clark, Emory **6** Mercer **7** Spelman **8** Valdosta **9** Morehouse
founder: **10** Oglethorpe (James)
nickname: **5** Peach (State)
river: **8** Ocmulgee **13** Chattahoochee
state bird: **13** brown thrasher
state flower: **12** Cherokee rose
state tree: **7** live oak
swamp: **10** Okefenokee

Georgia, Republic of
ancient kingdom: **6** Iberia **7** Colchis
capital: **6** Tiflis **7** Tbilisi
city: **7** Kutaisi, Rustavi
includes: **6** Ajaria **8** Abkhazia, Adzharia **12** South Ossetia

monarch: 6 Tamara (Queen)
monetary unit: 4 lari
mountain range: 8 Caucasus
neighbor: 6 Russia, Turkey 7 Armenia 10 Azerbaijan
river: 4 Kura 5 Rioni
sea: 5 Black

Georgics author
6 Vergil, Virgil

Geraint's wife
4 Enid

Gerda's husband
4 Frey

geriatric
3 old 4 aged 5 aging 6 senior 7 elderly 8 outmoded 12 old-fashioned 13 superannuated

germ
3 bud, bug 4 seed 5 spark, spore, virus 6 embryo, origin, source 7 microbe, nucleus 8 pathogen 9 bacterium
cell: 3 egg 4 ovum 5 sperm

German
3 Hun 4 Goth 6 Teuton
after: 4 nach
airport: 9 Flughafen
always: 5 immer
article: 3 das, der, die, ein 4 eine
attention: 7 Achtung
automaker: 3 BMW 4 Audi, Benz, Opel 7 Porsche 8 Mercedes 10 Volkswagen
bad: 8 schlecht
battle: 4 Kampf 8 Schlacht
bomber: 5 Gotha, Stuka
beneath: 5 unter
border: 6 Grenze
breakfast: 9 Frühstück
cabbage: 5 Kraut
child: 4 Kind
city: 5 Stadt
coin: 4 Mark 5 Taler 6 Thaler 7 Pfennig
count: 4 Graf
day: 3 Tag
doctor: 4 Arzt
dog: 4 Hund
empire: 5 Reich
entire, whole: 4 ganz
fairy tale: 7 Märchen
fast: 7 schnell
forbidden: 8 verboten
fruit: 4 Obst
good: 3 gut 4 gute
hardly, scarcely: 4 kaum
head: 4 Kopf
hero: 4 Held
highway: 8 Autobahn
history, story: 10 Geschichte
honor: 4 Ehre
hope: 8 Hoffnung
horse: 5 Pferd
husband: 4 Herr, Mann
I: 3 ich
industrial region: 4 Ruhr
interjection: 3 ach
labor: 6 Arbeit
leader: 6 Führer, Kaiser
lightning: 5 Blitz
liquor: 8 Schnapps
little: 5 klein 6 kleine
love: 5 Liebe
measles: 7 rubella
Miss: 8 Fräulein
money: 4 Geld
moon: 4 Mond
mountain: 4 Berg
musical: 9 Singspiel
no: 4 nein
Mr.: 4 Herr
Mrs.: 4 Frau 4 nein
nobleman: 6 Junker
nothing: 6 nichts
numbers: 3 elf 4 acht, drei, eins, fünf, neun, vier, zehn, zwei 5 sechs, zwölf 6 sieben
or: 4 oder
over: 4 über
picture: 4 Bild
please: 5 bitte
portion: 4 Teil
prince: 5 Fürst
pronoun: 3 ich, sie, wir 4 dich, mich, sich
proud: 5 stolz
railroad: 9 Eisenbahn
rifle: 6 Gewehr, Mauser
rule: 5 Regel
silence: 4 Ruhe 6 Stille
song: 4 Lied 6 Lieder (plural)
space: 4 Raum
spirit: 5 Geist
strength, power: 5 Kraft, Macht
submarine: 5 U-boat, U-boot
success: 6 Erfolg
tank: 6 Panzer
television: 9 Fernseher
thank you: 5 danke
three: 4 drei
today: 5 heute
tomorrow: 6 morgen
train: 3 Zug
train station: 7 Bahnhof
tree: 4 Baum
truth: 8 Wahrheit
two: 4 zwei
valley: 3 Tal
value: 4 Wert
victory: 4 Sieg
war: 5 Krieg
weight: 3 Lot 5 Pfund, Stein 8 Vierling
with: 3 mit

work: **6** Arbeit
world: **4** Welt
woman: **4** Frau **8** Fräulein
youth: **6** Jugend

germane
3 apt **5** ad rem **7** apropos, fitting, related **8** material, relevant **9** pertinent **10** applicable **11** appropriate

Germany
11 Deutschland
capital: **6** Berlin
city: **3** Ulm **4** Bonn, Jena, Kiel **5** Essen, Mainz **6** Bremen, Erfurt, Lübeck, Munich **7** Cologne, Dresden, Hamburg, Hanover, Leipzig, München, Potsdam **8** Augsburg, Dortmund, Duisburg, Freiburg, Hannover, Schwerin **9** Frankfurt, Nuremberg, Stuttgart, Wiesbaden **10** Baden Baden, Düsseldorf
leader: **4** Kohl (Helmut) **6** Brandt (Willy), Hitler (Adolf), Merkel (Angela) **7** Schmidt (Helmut), Wilhelm (Kaiser) **8** Bismarck (Otto)
monetary unit: **4** euro
monetary unit, former: **4** mark **5** taler **6** thaler **12** deutsche mark
mountain, range: **4** Harz **7** Brocken
neighbor: **6** France, Poland **7** Austria, Belgium, Denmark **10** Luxembourg **11** Netherlands, Switzerland **13** Czech Republic
region: **4** Ruhr **6** Saxony **7** Bavaria **11** Black Forest
river: **4** Eder, Elbe, Isar, Main, Oder, Ruhr, Saar **5** Fulda, Mosel, Rhein, Rhine, Weser **6** Danube **7** Moselle
sea: **5** North **6** Baltic
state: **5** Hesse **6** Saxony **7** Bavaria **8** Saarland **9** Thuringia **11** Brandenburg

Germinal author
4 Zola (Émile)

germinate
3 bud **6** evolve, spring, sprout **7** blossom, develop **9** originate, pullulate

Gershom, Gershon
father: **4** Levi
son: **5** Libni **6** Shimei

Gershwin
3 Ira **6** George
opera: **12** Porgy and Bess
piece: **14** Rhapsody in Blue **15** American in Paris (An)
show: **5** Oh Kay **9** Funny Face, Girl Crazy **10** Lady Be Good **11** Of Thee I Sing **15** Strike Up the Band
song: **10** I Got Rhythm, Summertime

Gertrude
husband: **8** Claudius
son: **6** Hamlet
of literature: **5** Stein

Gervaise's daughter
4 Nana

Geryon
dog: **6** Orthus
father: **8** Chrysaor
mother: **10** Callirrhoë
slayer: **8** Hercules

gestalt
4 form **5** shape **6** figure **7** pattern **9** structure **13** configuration

Gestapo chief
7 Himmler (Heinrich)

geste
4 deed, feat **7** emprise, exploit, romance, venture **9** adventure **10** enterprise **11** undertaking

gesticulate
3 nod **4** move, wave **6** beckon, motion, signal

gesticulation
4 wave **6** motion **7** gesture **8** high sign **9** pantomime **12** body language, sign language

gesture
3 nod **4** sign, wave **5** shrug, token **6** motion, salute, signal **8** reminder **9** signalize **10** expression, indication
graceful: **9** beau geste

get
3 bag **4** draw, earn, gain, land **5** catch, cause, seize **6** access, attain, become, elicit, extort, obtain, pick up, secure **7** achieve, acquire, bring in, capture, chalk up, deliver, extract, procure, receive **8** contract **10** understand **12** come down with

get around
4 roam, rove, tour, trek, walk **5** avoid, dodge, elude, evade, skirt **6** cruise, detour, escape, ramble, travel, wander **8** ambulate, outflank, sidestep **10** circumvent

getaway
3 lam **4** exit, slip **6** escape, flight **7** retreat **8** breakout, vacation

get back
6 go home, recoup, regain, return, revert **7** recover, reclaim, revenge, revisit **8** retrieve **9** repossess, retaliate

get by
4 cope, fare, pass **5** slide **6** eke out, endure, manage **7** carry on, survive **8** maintain

get-go
5 start **6** outset **9** beginning

get off
4 walk **5** leave **6** alight, depart, go free, launch **7** pull out **8** dismount **9** disembark **10** beat the rap

get off the fence
3 opt **6** decide

get out
4 exit, kite, leak 5 break, issue, leave, scram, split 6 alight, beat it, begone, decamp, depart, egress, escape 7 buzz off, publish, skiddoo, take off, vamoose 8 dispatch, hightail 9 circulate, skedaddle 10 make tracks

get rid of
4 lose, shed 7 discard 8 throw out 9 throw away

Gettysburg general
3 Lee (Robert E.) 5 Meade (George)

get up
4 gain 5 arise, breed, cause, dress, hatch, mount, raise, stand 6 create, induce, summon 7 acquire, prepare, produce 8 engender, generate 12 rise and shine

getup
3 rig 4 duds, garb, togs 5 array, dress, guise 6 outfit 7 costume, threads

get-up-and-go
3 pep, vim, zip 4 bang, push, snap, zeal, zest 5 drive, moxie, oomph, punch, spunk, steam, verve, vigor 6 energy, spirit, starch 8 ambition 10 enterprise, initiative

gewgaw
3 toy 4 dido 5 bijou, curio 6 bangle, bauble, doodad, trifle 7 bibelot, novelty, trinket, whatnot 8 gimcrack, kickshaw 9 bagatelle, objet d'art 10 knickknack

geyser
3 jet 5 fount, spout, spurt 6 gusher, spring 8 fountain 10 wellspring 11 Old Faithful

Ghana
capital: 5 Accra
city: 4 Tema 6 Kumasi, Tamale
ethnic group: 4 Akan 5 Mossi
former name: 9 Gold Coast
gulf: 6 Guinea
lake: 5 Volta
monetary unit: 4 cedi
neighbor: 4 Togo 10 Ivory Coast 11 Burkina Faso
river: 5 Volta

___ ghanoush
4 baba

ghastly
4 grim, pale 5 awful, lurid 6 grisly, horrid, pallid 7 ghostly, hideous, macabre 8 dreadful, ghoulish, gruesome, horrible, shocking, spectral, terrible 9 appalling, deathlike, frightful, ghostlike, repulsive, sickening 10 cadaverous, corpselike, disgustful, disgusting, horrifying, nauseating, terrifying 11 frightening
pale: 4 ashy 5 ashen

ghee
3 fat 6 butter

gherkin
4 vine 6 pickle 8 cucumber

ghetto
4 slum

ghost
4 soul 5 demon, haunt, shade, spook, trace 6 kelpie, shadow, spirit, wraith, zombie 7 eidolon, phantom, specter 8 phantasm 10 apparition 11 poltergeist
cartoon: 6 Casper

Ghostbusters goo
5 slime

ghostly
5 eerie, scary 6 spooky 7 shadowy 8 ethereal, spectral 9 deathlike, spiritual, unearthly, unworldly 10 cadaverous, corpselike, phantasmal 12 supernatural

Ghosts author
5 Ibsen (Henrik)

ghoul
4 ogre 5 fiend 7 monster 11 grave robber

GI
5 grunt 7 dogface, fighter, soldier, warrior 8 doughboy 9 man-at-arms 10 serviceman
entertainers: 3 USO

Gianni Schicchi composer
7 Puccini (Giacomo)

giant
4 huge, hulk, ogre, Otus, vast 5 gross, Gyges, Hymir, jumbo, titan, whale 6 Cottus, Typhon 7 Aloadae (plural), Antaeus, Cyclops, Goliath, immense, mammoth, monster, titanic, whopper 8 behemoth, Briareus, colossal, colossus, enormous, gigantic, Orgoglio 9 cyclopean, Enceladus, Ephialtes, Gargantua, humongous, leviathan, monstrous 10 gargantuan, prodigious 11 elephantine
biblical: 4 Anak 7 Goliath
cactus: 7 saguaro
hundred-armed: 9 Enceladus
hundred-eyed: 5 Argus
killer: 4 Jack 5 David
movie monster: 6 Mothra 8 Godzilla, King Kong
one-eyed: 5 Arges 7 Cyclops 10 Polyphemus
rime-cold: 4 Ymer, Ymir
sea god: 5 Aegir

Giant author Ferber
6 Edna

Giant Mel
3 Ott

giaour
7 infidel 10 unbeliever 11 nonbeliever

gib
3 tom 6 tomcat

gibber
3 gab, yak **4** blab **5** prate **6** babble, drivel, gabble, jabber, yammer **7** blabber, blather, chatter, palaver, prattle, twaddle

gibberish
3 gab **5** Greek, hokum **6** babble, bunkum, burble, drivel, gabble, jabber, yammer **7** blabber, blather, chatter, palaver, prattle, twaddle **8** claptrap, flimflam, nonsense **10** balderdash, double-talk, hocus-pocus, mumbo jumbo **11** abracadabra, jabberwocky **12** gobbledygook

gibbet
4 hang **5** lynch, noose, scrag **7** execute, gallows **8** string up

gibbon
3 ape, lar **7** primate, siamang **10** anthropoid

gibbous
6 arched, convex, humped **7** bulging, rounded, swollen **10** humpbacked **11** protuberant

gibe
4 gird, jape, jeer, jest, mock, quip, rail **5** fleer, flout, scoff, scorn, scout, sneer, taunt, tease **6** deride, insult **8** ridicule

Gibraltar
colony of: **7** Britain, England
conqueror: **5** Tarik, Tariq
neighbor: **5** Spain
opposite: **5** Ceuta

Gibran work
7 Prophet (The)

Gibson of film
3 Mel

giddy
4 gaga **5** dizzy, inane, light, silly, woozy **6** elated, yeasty **7** flighty, foolish, vacuous **8** euphoric **9** frivolous, slaphappy **10** hoity-toity **11** empty-headed, harebrained, light-headed, vertiginous

___ Gide
5 André

Gideon
father: **5** Joash
servant: **5** Purah
son: **9** Abimelech

Gidget portrayer Sandra
3 Dee

gift
3 set, tip **4** alms, bent, boon, head, turn **5** award, bonus, endow, favor, flair, forte, grant, knack **6** genius, legacy, reward, talent **7** ability, aptness, bequest, cumshaw, faculty, freebie, handout, present, subsidy **8** aptitude, bestowal, capacity, donation, gratuity, largesse, oblation, offering **9** endowment, lagniappe **11** benefaction, benevolence **12** contribution, presentation

gifted
4 able **5** smart **6** expert **7** hotshot, skilled **8** masterly, skillful, talented **9** ingenious, masterful

gig
3 jab, job, top **4** boat, fool, goad, prod, spur **5** annoy, freak, rotor, spear **6** chaise, harass **7** booking, demerit, provoke, rowboat **8** carriage **10** engagement

gigantic
4 huge, vast **5** giant, jumbo **7** hulking, immense, mammoth, massive, titanic **8** behemoth, colossal, enormous, king-size, whopping **9** cyclopean, humongous, king-sized, monstrous, walloping **10** gargantuan, prodigious, stupendous **11** elephantine

giggle
5 laugh **6** guffaw, hee-haw, titter **7** chortle, chuckle, snicker, snigger, twitter

Gigi author
7 Colette

Gilbert and Sullivan opera
6 Mikado (The) **8** Iolanthe, Patience, Sorcerer (The) **9** Grand Duke (The), Ruddigore **10** Gondoliers (The) **11** H.M.S. Pinafore, Princess Ida, Trial by Jury

Gil Blas author
6 Lesage (Alain-René)

gild
4 coat, deck **5** adorn, cover, tinge **6** bedeck, tinsel **7** enhance, overlay **8** brighten, ornament **9** embellish, embroider

Gilda's father
9 Rigoletto

Gilead
father: **6** Machir
grandfather: **8** Manasseh
son: **7** Jephtha **8** Jephthah

Gilgamesh
4 epic
companion: **6** Eabani, Enkidu
goddess: **5** Aruru **6** Ishtar, Siduri
home: **4** Uruk **5** Erech
mother: **6** Ninsun
victim: **6** Huwawa **7** Humbaba

gill
4 race **5** brook, creek **6** runnel, stream, wattle **7** rivulet
relating to: **9** branchial

Gillette razor
4 Atra

gillyflower
4 pink **9** carnation, clove pink

Gilroy play
15 Subject Was Roses (The)

gilt
3 hog, pig, sow **4** bond, gold **5** swine **6** gilded, golden **7** aureate **10** brilliance

gimcrack
5 cheap **6** bauble, gewgaw, shoddy, trifle **7** bibelot, chintzy, trinket **8** kickshaw **10** knickknack

gimlet
4 tool **5** drill, drink **8** cocktail
ingredient: **3** gin **5** vodka **9** lime juice

gimmick
3 con **4** ploy, ruse, wile **5** angle, catch, dodge, feint, gizmo, trick **6** device, gadget, gambit, jigger, scheme, widget **8** artifice, maneuver **9** stratagem **10** subterfuge

gimp
3 vim **4** cord, halt **5** braid, hitch **6** dodder, falter, hobble, spirit **7** cripple **8** lameness

gimpy
4 game, halt, lame **7** hobbled, limping **8** crippled

gin
3 net **4** trap **5** catch, rummy, snare **6** device, liquor **7** springe **8** generate, separate
flavoring: **4** sloe

ginger
3 fig, pep, vim, zip **4** herb, stir, zing **5** liven, spice, verve, vigor **6** energy, mettle, revive, spirit **7** sparkle
cookie: **4** snap

gingerly
4 safe, wary **5** canny, chary **7** careful, guarded **8** cautious, delicate, discreet

gingery
4 tart **5** fiery, peppy, sharp, spicy, tangy, zesty **6** snappy, spunky **7** peppery, piquant, pungent **8** spirited **10** mettlesome **12** high-spirited

gingham
5 cloth **6** fabric **7** textile **8** material

gingiva
3 gum

Gingrich of Congress
4 Newt

gin mill
3 bar, pub **4** dive **5** joint **6** saloon, tavern **7** barroom, taproom **8** alehouse **9** roadhouse **11** public house **12** watering hole

Ginsberg poem
4 Howl **7** Kaddish

ginseng
4 herb, root

Gioconda, La
8 Mona Lisa
composer: **10** Ponchielli (Amilcare)
painter: **7** da Vinci (Leonardo) **8** Leonardo (da Vinci)

giraffe
8 ruminant **9** quadruped **10** camelopard
relative: **5** okapi

girandole
7 earring **10** candelabra **11** candelabrum, candlestick, composition

girasol
3 gem **4** opal **5** jewel, stone **7** mineral **8** fire opal **9** artichoke

gird
3 hem **4** band, belt, bind, ring, wrap **5** brace, equip, hem in, ready, round, steel **6** circle **7** bolster, enclose, fortify, prepare, provide, shore up, wreathe **8** buttress, cincture, encircle, surround **9** encompass, reinforce **10** strengthen

girder
4 beam **5** brace, I-beam **7** support **8** crossbar **9** crossbeam **10** crosspiece, transverse

girdle
4 band, belt, ring, sash **6** cestus, circle **8** ceinture, cincture, encircle, surround **9** encompass, waistband
of Aphrodite: **6** cestus

girl
4 babe, bird, coed, doll, lass, maid, miss **5** chick, filly, missy, wench **6** damsel, lassie, maiden **8** daughter **10** sweetheart

____ girl!
4 atta

girlfriend
8 ladylove **9** inamorata
French: **4** amie

Girls creator Dunham
4 Lena

girth
4 band, belt, bind, size **5** brace, cinch, strap **6** circle, fasten, girdle **7** measure **8** cincture, encircle, surround **9** thickness **10** dimensions **13** circumference

Giselle composer
4 Adam (Adolphe)

gist
3 nub, sum **4** core, crux, meat, pith **5** sense **6** burden, ground, kernel, marrow, matter, thrust, upshot **7** essence **9** main point, substance

Giuseppe of opera
5 Verdi

give
3 pay **4** deal, hand **5** allot, allow, award, grant, issue, offer, remit **6** accord, afford, assign, bestow, commit, confer, convey, devote, direct, donate, extend, market, pony up, render, supply, tender **7** deliver, dish out, display, dole out, fall out, fork out, furnish, hand out, mete out, present, produce, proffer, provide **8** allocate, bequeath, disburse, dispense, give away, hand

over, shell out, turn over **9** apportion, sacrifice **10** administer, contribute, distribute

give-and-take
6 banter **8** exchange, repartee, trade-off **10** compromise **11** cooperation, reciprocity

give away
4 blab, leak **5** award, grant, spill **6** bestow, betray, confer, devote, donate, expose, reveal, tattle **7** deliver, divulge, hand out, let slip, present **8** bequeath, disclose

giveaway
4 deal, gift, leak **5** steal, value **6** tip-off **7** bargain, freebee, freebie, premium, present, sellout **8** betrayal, exposure **10** disclosure, revelation

give back
6 refund, retire, return **7** replace, restore, retreat **8** withdraw **9** reinstate

give in
4 cave, fold, quit, stop **5** yield **6** assent, comply, desist, relent, submit **7** concede, deliver, indulge, succumb **8** back down, cry uncle **9** surrender **10** relinquish

given
5 prone **6** donnée **7** assumed, granted **8** inclined **9** presented, specified **10** particular **11** considering, susceptible

give off
4 beam, emit, flow, vent **5** exude, issue **6** effuse **7** emanate, radiate, release **9** discharge

give out
4 deal, dole, emit, fail, mete, vent **5** issue **6** cave in **7** declare, release, succumb **8** collapse, throw off **9** break down **10** distribute

giver
5 donor **7** donator, grantor

give up
4 cede, quit **5** allow, cease, forgo, waive, yield **6** abjure, devote, resign, vacate **7** abandon, despair **8** abdicate, hand over, renounce, withdraw **9** sacrifice, surrender **10** relinquish

give way
5 yield **6** buckle, cave in **7** retreat, succumb **8** collapse **9** surrender

gizmo
6 dingus, doodad, hickey, jigger, widget **9** doohickey, thingummy

glabrous
4 bald, bare **6** shaven, smooth **8** hairless **9** beardless **10** bald-headed **12** smooth-shaven

glacial
3 icy, raw **5** chill, gelid, nippy, polar **6** arctic, biting, chilly, frigid, frosty, frozen, wintry **8** freezing **11** Pleistocene

glacier
3 ice **6** ice cap **8** ice field, ice sheet
Alaska: **4** Muir, Taku **6** Bering **10** Mendenhall
Antarctica: **9** Beardmore
deposit: **4** kame **5** esker **6** placer **7** moraine
fissure: **8** crevasse
fragment: **4** berg **7** iceberg
Greenland: **8** Humboldt
hill: **7** drumlin
Karakoram: **5** Biafo **7** Baltoro
lake: **4** tarn
New Zealand: **6** Tasman
pinnacle: **5** serac
surface: **4** névé

glacis
5 grade, slope **7** incline **10** buffer zone **11** buffer state

glad
3 gay **4** fain **5** happy, jolly, merry **6** blithe, bright, cheery, genial, jocund, jovial, joyful, joyous **7** beaming, gleeful, pleased, radiant, tickled, willing **8** cheerful, mirthful, pleasant, rejoiced **9** delighted, gratified

gladden
4 buoy **5** cheer, elate **6** buck up, perk up, please, uplift **7** cheer up, delight, gratify, hearten

glade
6 meadow **8** clearing **9** open space

gladiator
7 fighter **9** combatant, Spartacus

gladly
4 fain, lief **6** freely **7** happily, readily **8** heartily **9** willingly **10** cheerfully, with relish **12** with pleasure

gladness
3 joy **4** glee **5** bliss, cheer, mirth **6** gaiety **7** delight, jollity **9** happiness, merriment

gladstone
3 bag **8** suitcase

glamorous
7 elegant **8** alluring, charming, dazzling, enticing, magnetic **9** seductive **10** attractive, bewitching, enchanting **11** captivating, fascinating **13** sophisticated

glamour
5 charm, magic, spell **6** allure, appeal **7** romance **8** charisma, witchery **9** magnetism, sex appeal **10** attraction, witchcraft **11** fascination **12** razzle-dazzle

glance
4 peek, peep, skim, skip **5** brush, carom, flash, glaze, graze, shine **6** bounce, careen **7** glimpse **8** ricochet
lascivious: **4** leer

gland
5 gonad, liver, organ **6** pineal, thymus **7** adrenal, mammary, parotid, thyroid **8** exocrine, pancreas, prostate, salivary **9** endocrine, pituitary **11** parathyroid
secretion: **7** hormone

combining form: **4** aden **5** adeno
swelling: **4** bubo

glare
4 gaze, glow, peer **5** blaze, flame, flash, frown, gleam, light, lower, scowl, shine, stare **6** dazzle, glower **7** obtrude **8** stand out **10** garishness

glaring
4 loud, rank **5** gaudy, plain, vivid **6** brazen, flashy, garish, tawdry, tinsel **7** blatant, obvious **8** blinding, flagrant **9** audacious, egregious, obtrusive **10** noticeable **11** conspicuous, outstanding **12** ostentatious

glass
4 lens, pane **5** image, lense, prism **6** mirror **7** reflect **9** barometer, telescope
combining form: **5** vitro
container: **3** jar **6** beaker, bottle
decorative: **7** schmelz **8** schmelze
drinking: **4** pony **5** flute **6** goblet, jigger, rummer, seidel **7** snifter, tumbler **8** schooner, stemware
gem: **5** paste **6** strass
magnifying: **5** loupe
milky: **7** opaline
volcanic: **7** perlite **8** obsidian

glasses
5 specs **6** shades **7** goggles **8** bifocals, pince-nez, tumblers **9** lorgnette, trifocals **10** spectacles

glass-like
5 clear **6** glazed, limpid, smooth **8** pellucid, vitreous **9** vitrified **11** translucent, transparent

glassmaker
4 Neri (Antonio) **6** Blenko (William) **7** Lalique (René), Tiffany (Louis Comfort) **9** Waterford

glassmaking tool
5 punty **6** pontil **8** blowpipe

Glass Menagerie author
8 Williams (Tennessee)

Glass of public radio
3 Ira

glassy
5 blank, dazed, shiny **6** glazed, smooth, vacant **7** hyaloid **8** polished, vitreous **9** burnished

glaucous
4 waxy **7** frosted, powdery

Glaucus
beloved: **6** Scylla
father: **5** Minos **8** Sisyphus
mother: **6** Merope **8** Pasiphaë
son: **11** Bellerophon

glaze
3 rub **4** buff, coat, film **5** cover, glint, gloss, sheen, shine **6** enamel, finish, luster, patina, polish **7** burnish, coating, furbish, lacquer, overlay, varnish

glazed
5 blank **6** glassy

gleam
3 ray **4** beam, burn, glow **5** flare, flash, glint, sheen, shine **6** glance **7** glimmer, glisten, glitter, radiate, shimmer, sparkle, twinkle **8** radiance **11** coruscation, scintillate **13** scintillation

gleaming
5 aglow, shiny **6** glossy, sheeny **7** beaming, burning, glowing, lambent, radiant, shining **8** flashing, luminous, lustrous, polished **9** brilliant, burnished, refulgent, sparkling, twinkling **10** glimmering, glistening, glittering, shimmering **13** scintillating

glean
4 cull, reap, sift **5** amass, learn **6** garner, gather, pick up **7** extract, find out, harvest

glebe
4 land **5** field, tract **7** acreage **8** cropland, farmland

glee
3 joy **5** mirth **6** gaiety, levity **7** delight, elation, jollity **8** gladness, hilarity, part-song **9** enjoyment, festivity, good cheer, happiness, jocundity, joviality, merriment **10** exuberance, joyfulness, jubilation **12** exhilaration

gleeful
3 gay **5** jolly, merry **6** blithe, elated, jocund, jovial, joyous **8** cheerful, exultant, jubilant, mirthful **9** exuberant **12** lighthearted

glen
4 dale, vale **5** swale **6** dingle, valley
deep: **5** gorge **6** ravine

glengarry
3 cap **6** bonnet

Glengarry Glen Ross playwright
5 Mamet (David)

glib
4 easy **5** slick **6** facile, fluent, smooth **7** offhand, shallow, voluble **8** eloquent, flippant **9** insincere **10** articulate, nonchalant **11** superficial

glide
3 fly **4** flow, sail, skim, slip, soar, waft **5** coast, creep, drift, float, skate, skirr, skulk, slide, slink, sneak, steal **7** descend, slither **8** glissade, volplane **10** portamento

glimmer
4 glow, hint **5** blink, flash, gleam, glint, shine, spark, trace **6** glance **7** flicker, glisten, glitter, inkling, shimmer, sparkle, twinkle **9** coruscate **10** suggestion **11** coruscation, scintillate **13** scintillation

glimpse
4 espy, peek, peep **5** flash, glint, stime **6** aperçu glance

glint
3 ray **5** flash, glaze, gleam, sheen, shine, trace **6** glance, luster **7** glimmer, glisten, glitter, shimmer, sparkle, twinkle **9** coruscate **11** coruscation, scintillate **13** scintillation

glissade
4 skim, slip **5** glide, slide

glissando
3 run **5** slide **7** gliding, sliding

glisten
4 glow **5** flash, gleam, glint, shine **6** glance **7** flicker, glimmer, glitter, shimmer, spangle, sparkle, twinkle **9** coruscate **11** coruscation, scintillate **13** scintillation

glitch
3 bug **4** flaw, snag **5** fault, snafu **6** defect **7** failing, failure, gremlin, problem **8** obstacle **10** difficulty **11** malfunction

glitter
5 flash, gleam, glint, shine **7** glimmer, glisten, shimmer, spangle, sparkle, twinkle **9** coruscate **11** coruscation, scintillate **13** scintillation

glittering
5 gaudy, shiny, showy **6** flashy **7** fulgent **9** brilliant, clinquant, coruscant, effulgent **11** spectacular

glitz
5 bling, flash **6** dazzle

glitzy
5 gaudy **6** flashy **10** flamboyant

gloaming
3 eve **4** dusk **5** gloom **7** evening **8** eventide, twilight **9** nightfall

gloat
4 crow **5** exult, revel, vaunt **6** relish **7** triumph **9** celebrate

glob
4 clot, lump **6** dollop

global
5 grand **6** cosmic **7** blanket, general, overall **8** all-round, catholic **9** inclusive, planetary, spherical, universal, worldwide **12** encyclopedic **13** comprehensive

globe
3 orb **4** ball **5** earth, round, world **6** planet, sphere **7** rondure
half: 10 hemisphere

globetrotter's need
4 visa

globule
4 ball, bead, drip, drop **6** gobbet, pellet **7** driblet, droplet **8** spherule

glom
4 grab, take **5** catch, latch, seize, steal

gloom
3 dim **4** dusk, funk, loom, murk **5** bedim, blues, cloud, dumps, frown, lower, mopes, scowl **6** darken, glower, shadow **7** becloud, despair, dimness, obscure, sadness **8** darkness, overcast, twilight **9** adumbrate, bleakness, dejection **10** blue devils, depression, melancholy, overshadow **11** despondency, unhappiness **12** mournfulness

gloomy
3 dim, dun, sad **4** cold, dark, dour, down, drab, dull, glum **5** black, bleak, drear, dusky, mopey, murky, muzzy, sulky, surly **6** dismal, dreary, morose, solemn, somber, sullen **7** forlorn, joyless, obscure, stygian, unhappy **8** dejected, desolate, downcast, funereal, mournful **9** cheerless, depressed, mirthless, oppressed, saturnine, tenebrous, woebegone **10** caliginous, chapfallen, depressing, depressive, dispirited, despondent, forbidding, lugubrious, melancholy, oppressive, tenebrific **11** dispiriting, pessimistic **12** disconsolate, discouraging

glorify
4 hymn, laud **5** bless, cry up, erect, exalt, extol, honor **6** admire, praise, revere **7** acclaim, dignify, elevate, ennoble, light up, lionize, magnify, sublime, worship **8** eulogize, venerate **9** celebrate **10** aggrandize

glorious
5 grand, great, noble, proud **6** august, divine, superb **7** eminent, exalted, radiant, sublime **8** esteemed, gorgeous, lustrous, majestic, renowned, splendid, stunning **9** beautiful, brilliant, effulgent, excellent, marvelous, ravishing, wonderful **11** illustrious, magnificent, resplendent, splendorous

glory
4 crow, fame, halo, pomp **5** exalt, exult, gloat, honor, revel **6** heaven, praise, relish, renown **7** acclaim, aureole, delight, majesty, rejoice, triumph **8** eminence, eternity, grandeur, jubilate, radiance, splendor **9** greatness, hereafter **10** effulgence, exaltation, exultation **11** distinction **12** magnificence, resplendence

gloss
4 buff **5** glaze, glint, sheen, shine **6** define, enamel, facade, finish, luster, patina, polish, veneer **7** burnish, comment, explain, furbish, varnish **8** annotate **9** interpret, sleekness, slickness, translate **10** annotation, appearance, brilliance, commentary, definition **11** elucidation, explanation, translation

glossary
7 lexicon **8** wordbook **9** word-hoard **10** dictionary, vocabulary

gloss over
4 mask **5** slant **6** veneer **7** conceal, cover

up, distort, falsify, varnish **8** disguise, palliate **9** dissemble, extenuate, sugarcoat, whitewash **10** camouflage

glossy
5 glacé, shiny, sleek, slick **7** shining **8** gleaming, lustrous, polished **9** burnished **10** glistening
fabric: **4** silk **5** satin
paint: **6** enamel

glove
4 gage, mitt **5** catch, cover **6** mitten, sheath **8** covering, gauntlet
material: **5** suede

glow
4 burn, pink, rose **5** bloom, blush, flush, gleam, rouge, shine **6** mantle, redden **7** blossom, crimson, fox fire, glisten, glitter, radiate **8** brighten, radiance **10** brilliance, luminosity **13** incandescence

glower
5 frown, scowl, stare **11** look daggers

glowing
3 hot, red **4** avid **5** flush, ruddy, shiny **6** ardent, fervid, florid, heated, red-hot **7** beaming, burning, fervent, flushed, lambent, radiant, vibrant **8** blushing, dazzling, gleaming, luminous, lustrous, rubicund, sanguine, suffused, white-hot **9** brilliant **10** candescent, hot-blooded, passionate **11** impassioned **12** enthusiastic, incandescent

Gluck opera
5 Orfeo **6** Armide **7** Alceste

glucose
5 sugar, syrup

glue
3 fix, gum **4** bind, join **5** epoxy, paste, stick **6** adhere, attach, cement, fasten **7** plaster, stickum **8** adhesive, mucilage

gluey
5 gummy, tacky **6** sticky, viscid **7** viscous **8** adhesive **12** mucilaginous

glum
3 sad **4** blue, dour, down **5** moody, sulky, surly **6** dismal, dreary, gloomy, morose, sullen, woeful **7** crabbed **8** brooding, dejected, downcast, taciturn **9** depressed, oppressed, saturnine, sorrowful, woebegone **10** despondent, dispirited, melancholy **11** downhearted, melancholic

glut
4 clog, cloy, cram, fill, pack, pall, sate **5** feast, flood, gorge, stuff **6** deluge, excess, stodge **7** satiate, surfeit, surplus, swallow **8** saturate **10** oversupply **13** overabundance

glutinous
4 ropy **5** gluey, gooey, gummy, pasty, tacky, thick **6** sticky, viscid **7** viscous **10** gelatinous **12** mucilaginous

glutton
3 hog, pig **8** gourmand **9** chowhound, wolverine **11** gormandizer

gluttonous
7 hoggish, piggish **8** edacious, ravening, ravenous **9** dissolute, indulgent, rapacious, voracious **10** insatiable **11** intemperate

gluttony
6 excess **7** edacity **8** gulosity, rapacity, voracity **11** piggishness

glyph
6 figure, groove, symbol **7** graphic **9** character

G-man
3 fed **4** narc, Ness (Eliot) **5** agent **6** Hoover (J. Edgar) **10** gangbuster

GM-Toyota brand
3 Geo

gnarl
4 bend, knot, warp **5** growl, snarl, twist **6** deform **7** contort, distort

gnash
4 bite **5** grind

gnat
3 bug, fly **4** pest **5** midge **6** insect, punkie **7** no-see-um

gnaw
3 eat, nag, vex **4** bite, chaw, chew **5** annoy, chomp, erode, munch, scour, tease, worry **6** bother, crunch, nibble, pester, plague, rankle **7** bedevil, corrode, eat away **8** irritate, wear away **9** masticate

gnome
3 elf, saw **4** rule **5** adage, axiom, dwarf, maxim, moral, troll, truth **6** dictum, goblin, saying, truism **7** proverb **8** aphorism, apothegm **10** shibboleth

gnostic
6 occult, secret **8** abstruse **10** mysterious

gnu
10 wildebeest

go
against: **4** defy **5** fight **6** oppose, resist **7** counter, protest **10** contradict
ahead: **4** lead **7** precede, proceed **8** continue, progress
along: **5** agree, yield **6** accede, comply, concur **7** consent **9** acquiesce
around: **5** avoid, skirt **6** bypass, detour **7** compass **8** outflank, sidestep **10** circumvent
ashore: **6** debark **9** disembark
astray: **3** sin
at: **6** assail, attack, tackle **7** assault
away: **3** git **4** exit, scat, shoo **5** leave, scram, split **6** beat it, begone, cut out, depart, move on, retire **7** buzz off, get lost, pull out, take off

8 clear out, run along, shove off, withdraw 9 skedaddle
back: 6 recede, return, revert 7 regress, retreat
back on: 6 betray, renege 7 abandon 8 abrogate
back over: 6 rehash, review, rework 7 recheck, retrace
bad: 3 rot 4 sour, turn 5 spoil 6 curdle 7 putrefy
before: 4 lead 7 precede, predate 8 antedate
beyond: 4 pass 5 excel, outdo 6 exceed, outrun 7 eclipse, surpass 8 outshine, outstrip, overtake 9 transcend
forward: 6 move on, push on 7 advance, press on, proceed 8 continue, progress
in: 5 enter 9 penetrate
out: 4 exit 5 leave 6 expire
Scottish: 3 gae
through: 4 bear 5 audit, brave, check, spend 6 endure, suffer 7 consume, deplete, examine, exhaust, ride out, survive, sustain, undergo 8 squander 9 penetrate, withstand 10 experience
together: 3 fit 4 date, jibe, suit 5 agree, match, tally 6 accord, square 7 conform 8 dovetail 9 accompany, harmonize 10 correspond
with: 4 suit 5 befit, match 9 accompany

goad
3 egg, rod, sic 4 prod, push, spur, urge 5 drive, egg on, impel, prick, thorn 6 coerce, exhort, incite, motive, needle, prompt, propel 7 impetus, impulse 8 catalyst, motivate, stimulus 9 encourage, impulsion, incentive, stimulant, stimulate 10 inducement

go-ahead
4 okay 7 consent 8 spirited 9 ambitious, authority, clearance, energetic 10 green light, permission 11 progressive, up-and-coming 12 enterprising 13 authorization

goal
3 aim, end, use 4 duty, hope, mark 5 score 6 design, intent, object, target 7 mission, purpose 8 ambition, function 9 intention, objective

goat
3 kid, ram 4 lech 5 billy, letch, nanny 6 alpaca, angora, lecher, Saanen 8 cashmere 10 Toggenburg
female: 3 doe 5 nanny
genus: 5 Capra
Himalayan: 4 tahr, thar
male: 4 buck 5 billy
neutered: 6 wether
relating to: 7 caprine
wild: 4 ibex, tahr, thar
wool: 6 mohair 8 cashmere, pashmina

goat antelope
5 serow 7 chamois

goatee
5 beard 7 Vandyke 8 imperial, whiskers

goatfish
6 mullet

goatish
3 hot 4 lewd 6 carnal 7 caprine, lustful, satyric 8 prurient 9 indulgent, lecherous, lickerish 10 lascivious, libidinous, passionate 12 concupiscent

goat-man deity
3 Pan 4 faun 5 satyr 7 silenus

goat nut
6 jojoba, pignut

gob
3 wad 4 blob, clod, glob, hunk, lump, mass 5 chunk, mouth 6 nugget, sailor 7 extract

gobbet
4 drib, drip, drop, hunk, lump, mass 5 chunk, piece 7 driblet, droplet, globule, portion 8 fragment

gobble
3 eat 4 bolt, cram, grab, glut, gulp, slop, wolf 5 gorge, scarf, scoff, snarf 6 devour, guzzle 7 swallow 11 ingurgitate

gobbledygook
6 babble, gabble, jabber 8 nonsense

go-between
5 agent, envoy, proxy 6 broker, deputy, factor 7 courier, liaison 8 emissary, mediator, procurer 9 middleman 10 arbitrator, interagent, interceder, matchmaker, negotiator, procurator 11 intercessor 12 intermediary, intermediate

goblet
3 cup 5 glass, grail 6 vessel 7 chalice

goblin
3 elf, fay, hob, imp 4 puck 5 bogey, bogle, fairy, ghost, gnome 6 sprite 7 brownie, bugbear 8 bogeyman

____ go bragh
4 Erin

gobs
4 lots, tons, wads 5 heaps, loads, lumps, piles, rafts, reams, scads 6 oodles 8 slathers 10 quantities

god
4 idol 5 deity 7 creator 8 Almighty, divinity, immortal
combining form: 4 theo
false: 4 baal
French: 4 dieu
Hebrew: 6 Adonai, Elohim, Yahweh
Latin: 4 deus
Spanish: 4 dios
(see also **Egyptian, Greek, Hindu, Roman**)

god-awful
4 foul **6** horrid, rotten **7** beastly **8** dreadful, horrible, shameful, shocking, terrible, wretched **9** appalling, atrocious, miserable **10** abominable, deplorable, despicable, detestable, disgusting, outrageous

God Bless America composer
6 Berlin (Irving)

goddess
4 idol **5** deity **8** divinity, immortal
Italian: **4** diva
Latin: **3** dea
(see also **Egyptian, Greek, Hindu, Roman**)

godfather
3 don **4** boss, capo **6** leader, patron **7** sponsor

Godfather, The
8 Corleone (Don)
actor: **6** Brando (Marlon), De Niro (Robert), Pacino (Al)
author: **4** Puzo (Mario)
director: **7** Coppola (Francis Ford)

God-fearing
5 pious **6** devout **8** faithful, reverent **9** pietistic, religious, righteous

godforsaken
4 bare **5** bleak **6** barren, dismal, gloomy, remote **7** pitiful **8** deserted, desolate, pitiable, wretched **9** miserable, neglected **11** unfortunate

Godiva's husband
7 Leofric

godless
5 pagan **6** unholy, wicked **7** atheist, heathen, impious, infidel, profane **8** agnostic **9** athelstic **11** irreligious, unreligious

godlike
4 holy **6** divine **7** blessed, supreme **8** almighty, immortal **10** omniscient **11** all-powerful

godliness
5 piety **6** purity **8** devotion, divinity, holiness, sanctity **9** beatitude, reverence **10** devoutness, sacredness **11** religiosity, saintliness **12** spirituality, virtuousness

godly
4 holy **5** pious **6** devout, divine **7** angelic, blessed, saintly, supreme **8** almighty, hallowed, immortal, virtuous **9** pietistic, prayerful, religious **10** omniscient **11** all-powerful

go down
3 dip, set **4** drop, fall, fold, lose, sink **5** ensue, lower, occur, pitch, slide, slump **6** cave in, happen, plunge, settle, topple, tumble **7** crumple, decline, descend, founder, succumb **8** collapse, keel over, submerge, submerse **9** surrender, take place

God's acre
8 boneyard, catacomb, cemetery **9** graveyard **10** churchyard, necropolis **12** burial ground, memorial park, potter's field

godsend
4 boon, gift, good **5** manna **7** benefit **8** blessing, windfall **9** advantage **11** benevolence, serendipity

Goethe work
5 Faust **6** Egmont, Stella **7** Clavigo **10** Prometheus

gofer
4 aide, peon **5** toady **6** drudge, flunky, helper, lackey, menial **7** courier, servant **8** factotum **9** assistant, attendant

goffer
5 crimp, flute, pinch, plait, pleat

go-getter
6 dynamo **7** hustler, rustler **8** live wire **10** ball of fire, powerhouse **11** self-starter

goggle
3 eye **4** bore, gape, gawk, gaze, look, ogle, peer **5** glare, gloat, stare **10** rubberneck

goggles
5 specs **7** glasses **10** eyeglasses, spectacles

go-go
5 hyper **6** hectic **7** frantic **8** frenetic, frenzied

Gogol novel
novel: **9** Dead Souls
story: **8** Overcoat (The) **10** Taras Bulba **14** Diary of a Madman

goiter
6 struma **8** swelling

Golconda
see **gold mine**

gold
4 gilt **5** aurum, money **6** riches, wealth, yellow **7** bullion **8** treasure
bar: **5** ingot
combining form: **4** auri, auro **5** chrys **6** chryso
fool's: **6** pyrite
imitation: **6** ormolu
measure: **5** carat, karat
Spanish: **3** oro

Golda of Israel
4 Meir

goldbrick
3 bum **4** idle, laze, lazy, loaf, loll **5** cheat, dally, dog it, idler, shirk, slack **6** dawdle, loafer, loiter, lounge **7** lounger, shirker, slacker, swindle **8** lollygag, malinger, sluggard **9** lazybones **10** dilly-dally, malingerer

Gold Bug author
3 Poe (Edgar Allan)

gold cloth
4 lamé

gold-covered
4 gilt **6** gilded

golden
4 gilt, rich **5** auric, blond, shiny, straw **6** blonde, flaxen, gilded, mellow, superb, yellow **7** aureate, honeyed, shining **8** glorious, lustrous, resonant **9** favorable **10** auspicious, prosperous **11** flourishing

golden-ager
5 elder **6** senior **7** ancient, oldster, retiree **8** old-timer **13** senior citizen

golden-apples guardian
5 Ithun **6** Ithunn

golden bough
9 mistletoe

Golden Bough author
6 Frazer (James George)

Golden Boy playwright
5 Odets (Clifford)

Golden Calf, e.g.
4 idol

golden-crowned accentor
7 warbler **8** ovenbird

goldeneye
3 bug **4** duck, fowl **6** insect **8** lacewing

Golden Fleece seeker
5 Jason **8** Argonaut

Golden Girl
3 Bea (Arthur)

Golden Hind captain
5 Drake (Francis)

Golden Horde
6 Tatars **7** Mongols
leader: 4 Batu

golden horse
7 Trigger **8** palomino

Golden Rule preposition
4 unto

golden shiner
4 dace, fish

golden song
5 oldie

Golden State
10 California

goldfinch
4 bird **8** songbird **12** yellowhammer

Golding novel
14 Lord of the Flies

gold mine
7 bonanza, pay dirt **8** El Dorado, Golconda, treasure, treasury **13** treasure trove

golem
3 oaf **4** clod, dolt, dope **5** dunce, idiot, robot **6** nitwit **7** halfwit, machine **8** imbecile **9** automaton, blockhead **10** nincompoop **11** blunderhead

golf
assistant: 5 caddy **6** caddie
ball material: 6 balata **11** gutta-percha
club: 4 iron, wood **5** billy, spoon, wedge **6** driver, mashie, putter **7** niblick, pitcher **9** metal wood, sand wedge
club part: 3 toe **4** face, grip, head, heel, neck, sole **5** hosel, shaft
course: 5 links
cup: 5 Ryder **6** Curtis, Walker
hazard: 4 trap **6** bunker **8** sand trap
org.: 3 PGA **4** LPGA, USGA
score: 3 ace, par **5** bogey, eagle **6** birdie
stroke: 4 baff, chip, draw, fade, hook, putt **5** drive, pitch, shank, slice **6** sclaff
target: 3 cup, par, pin **4** flag **5** green **7** fairway
term: 3 lie, tee **4** club, fore, hole, loft **5** divot, rough, swing **6** dormie, hazard, marker, stance, stroke **8** foursome, handicap, mulligan **9** backswing, downswing, flagstick

golfer
8 linksman
man: 3 Els (Ernie) **4** Aoki (Isao), Daly (John), Ford (Doug), Haas (Jay), Kite (Tom), Lyle (Sandy), Mize (Larry), Seve (Ballesteros), Tway (Bob) **5** Atwal (Arjun), Boros (Julius), Faldo (Nick), Floyd (Ray), Grady (Wayne), Green (Hubert), Hagen (Walter), Hogan (Ben), Jones (Bobby), Irwin (Hale), North (Andy), Pavin (Corey), Peete (Calvin), Price (Nick), Shute (Denny), Singh (Vijay), Snead (Sam), Woods (Tiger) **6** Casper (Billy), Graham (David), Janzen (Lee), Langer (Bernhard), Miller (Johnny), Nelson (Byron, Larry), Norman (Greg), Ouimet (Francis), Palmer (Arnold), Player (Gary), Sluman (Jeff), Sutton (Hal), Vardon (Harry), Watson (Tom) **7** Azinger (Paul), Couples (Fred), Guldahl (Ralph), Mayfair (Billy), McIlroy (Rory), Sarazen (Gene), Simpson (Scott), Stewart (Payne), Strange (Curtis), Trevino (Lee), Woosnam (Ian), Zoeller (Fuzzy) **8** Crenshaw (Ben), Nicklaus (Jack), Olazabal (José), Weiskopf (Tom) **9** Mickelson (Phil), Rodriguez (Chi Chi), Elkington (Steve) **10** Middlecoff (Cary) **11** Ballesteros (Seve)
woman: 3 Pak (Se Ri) **4** Berg (Patty), King (Betsy) **5** Baker (Kathy), Lopez (Nancy), Rawls (Betsy), Stacy (Hollis), Suggs (Louise) **6** Alcott (Amy), Carner (Joanne), Daniel (Beth), Davies (Laura), Geddes (Jane), Mallon (Meg), Merten (Lauri), Wright (Mickey) **7** Bradley (Pat), Inkster (Juli), Mochrie (Dottie), Sheehan (Patty) **8** Zaharias (Babe) **9** Didrikson (Babe), Sorenstam (Annika), Whitworth (Kathy) **10** Stephenson (Jan)

Golgotha
7 Calvary

Goliath
5 giant 10 Philistine
deathplace: 4 Elah
home: 4 Gath
slayer: 5 David

Gollum creator
7 Tolkien (J. R. R.)

golly
3 gee, wow 4 geez, gosh, jeez 6 crikey

Gomorrah's sister city
5 Sodom

gonad
5 gland, ovary 6 testis 8 testicle

gondola
3 car 4 boat 7 ski lift 11 railroad car

gone
4 away, dead, left, lost, past 5 flown 6 absent 7 defunct, extinct, lacking, missing 8 departed, vanished

gonef
5 thief 6 rascal 9 scoundrel

goner
8 dead duck 9 lost cause

Goneril
father: 4 Lear (King)
husband: 6 Albany
sister: 5 Regan 8 Cordelia
victim: 5 Regan

Gone with the Wind
author: 8 Mitchell (Margaret)
character: 5 Rhett (Butler) 6 Ashley (Wilkes) 7 Melanie (Wilkes) 8 Scarlett (O'Hara)
plantation: 4 Tara

gonfalon
4 flag, jack 6 banner, ensign 7 pendant, pennant 8 banderol, standard 9 banderole

gong
6 cymbal, tam-tam

gonzo
6 far-out 7 bizarre, offbeat 9 wigged-out 10 outrageous

goo
4 crud, glop, guck, gunk, muck 5 slime

goober
6 peanut

good
4 pure 5 right, sound, whole 6 decent, humane, kindly, worthy 7 benefit, upright, welfare 8 innocent, virtuous 9 admirable, blameless, exemplary, favorable, honorable, righteous, well-being, wholesome 10 altruistic, beneficent, beneficial, benevolent, charitable, worthwhile 11 respectable, well-behaved
French: 3 bon 5 bonne
German: 3 gut 4 gute
Spanish: 5 buena, bueno

good-bye
4 ciao, ta-ta 5 adieu, congé, later 6 so long 7 cheerio, parting, send-off, toodles 8 farewell, toodle-oo 9 departing, departure 11 leave-taking, valediction, valedictory
French: 5 adieu 8 au revoir 9 bon voyage
German: 8 lebe wohl
Italian: 11 arrivederci
Japanese: 8 sayonara
Spanish: 5 adios 10 hasta luego 12 hasta la vista

Good Earth
author: 4 Buck (Pearl S.)
heroine: 4 O-Lan

good-for-nothing
3 bum 6 rascal, waster 7 inutile, rounder, useless, wastrel 8 fainéant, feckless, rascally, unworthy 9 dissolute, scoundrel, valueless, worthless 10 ne'er-do-well, profligate, scapegrace 11 purposeless

good-looking
4 cute, fair, foxy 5 bonny, dishy, hunky 6 comely, lovely, pretty 8 alluring, drop-dead, fetching, handsome, stunning 9 beauteous, beautiful, bodacious, ravishing 10 attractive

goodly
4 fair, tidy 5 ample, hefty, large 7 sizable 8 generous 9 bountiful, plentiful 11 significant, substantial 12 considerable

good-natured
4 easy, kind, mild, warm 6 genial, jovial, mellow 7 affable, amiable, cordial, lenient 8 cheerful, friendly, laid-back, obliging, pleasant, pleasing, sanguine 9 agreeable, congenial, easygoing, gemütlich 10 altruistic, benevolent, charitable 11 complaisant

goodness
5 honor, merit, worth 6 purity, virtue 7 decency, honesty, probity, quality 8 morality 9 integrity, rectitude 11 benevolence

Goodnight girl
5 Irene

goods
4 gear 5 cargo, stock, stuff, wares 7 effects 8 chattels, movables, property 9 vendibles 10 belongings 11 commodities, merchandise, possessions 13 paraphernalia
smuggled: 10 contraband
stolen: 4 loot, swag 5 booty 6 boodle, spoils 7 plunder
thrown overboard: 5 lagan 6 jetsam

good sport
7 trouper

good-tasting
5 sapid, yummy **6** delish, savory, toothy **8** luscious **9** delicious, palatable, relishing, toothsome **10** appetizing, delectable, flavorsome **11** scrumptious **13** mouthwatering

goodwill
5 amity, favor **6** comity **7** charity, rapport **8** altruism, kindness, sympathy **9** tolerance **10** compassion, friendship, generosity, kindliness **11** benevolence, helpfulness **12** friendliness

goody
5 candy, treat **6** bonbon, dainty, morsel, tidbit **8** delicacy, kickshaw

goody-goody
4 prig **5** prude **6** Grundy **7** prudish, puritan, uptight **8** bluenose, Comstock, priggish **9** Mrs. Grundy, nice-nelly **11** puritanical

gooey
5 gluey, gummy, mushy, sappy, soupy **6** cloggy, drippy, slushy, sticky, viscid **7** maudlin, viscous **8** adhesive **9** glutinous **11** sentimental **12** mucilaginous

goof
3 err, kid **4** boob, dolt, flub, fool, mess, muff, slip **5** boner, booby, botch, chump, dunce, error, fluff, gaffe, gum up, idiot, put on **6** bobble, boggle, bollix, boo-boo, bumble, bungle, fumble, mess up, slip-up **7** blooper, blunder, fathead, louse up, mistake **8** dolthead, lunkhead **9** blockhead

go off
4 blow **5** blast, burst, erupt, leave, sound **6** blow up, depart **7** explode **8** detonate

goofy
5 balmy, batty, crazy, daffy, dippy, loony, nutty, potty, silly **6** simple, stupid **7** foolish, idiotic **9** ludicrous **10** ridiculous **11** harebrained

gook
4 crud, glop, gunk, muck **5** gumbo, slime **6** debris, sludge

go on
4 last, stay **5** occur **6** endure, happen, keep up **7** persist, proceed **8** continue **9** persevere

goon
3 oaf, sap **4** boob, dodo, dolt, dope, fool, hood, thug **5** dummy, idiot **6** dimwit, hit man, nitwit **7** hoodlum **8** dumbbell, enforcer **10** triggerman

gooney
7 seabird **9** albatross

goop
4 crud, gunk, muck **5** gumbo, tripe

Goops author
7 Burgess (Gelett)

goose
4 poke, spur **9** stimulate
cry: **4** honk **5** clang
formation: **3** vee **5** skein, wedge **6** gaggle
genus: **5** Anser
Hawaiian: **4** nene
male: **6** gander
wild: **5** brant **7** greylag **8** barnacle
young: **7** gosling

gooseberry
4 poha **7** currant

Goosebumps author
5 Stine (R. L.)

goose egg
3 nil, nix, zip **4** nada, zero **5** aught, zilch **6** bubkes, bupkes, bupkus, cipher, naught, nought **7** no score, nothing

gooseflesh
5 bumps **7** pimples

go over
4 scan, skim **5** study **6** peruse, review **7** examine, inspect

gopher
6 rodent **8** tortoise

Gopher State
9 Minnesota

Gordian knot cutter
9 Alexander

Gordius' son
5 Midas

gore
3 jab **4** stab **5** blood, slime, wound **6** gusset, pierce **7** carnage **12** gruesomeness

gorge
3 gap **4** cloy, fill, glut, jade, pall, sate **5** abyss, chasm, cleft, clove, flume, gulch, stuff **6** arroyo, canyon, clough, defile, pig out, ravine **7** couloir, overeat, satiate, surfeit **11** overindulge
Arizona: **11** Grand Canyon
Colorado: **5** Royal

gorgeous
5 grand, plush **6** comely, lavish, lovely, pretty, superb **7** opulent, sublime **8** alluring, dazzling, glorious, splendid **9** beautiful, brilliant, exquisite, luxurious, sumptuous **10** attractive, glittering **11** magnificent, resplendent, splendorous

gorgon
3 hag **5** crone, harpy, witch **6** Medusa, ogress, virago **8** battle-ax, fishwife, harridan, slattern **9** battle-axe, termagant
father: **7** Phorcus, Phorcys
mother: **4** Ceto

gorilla
3 ape **4** goon, hood, Koko, thug **5** tough **6** simian **7** primate **8** gangster **10** anthropoid

Gorky drama
11 Lower Depths (The)

gormless
4 dumb, slow **6** stupid

gorse
4 whin **5** furze, shrub **6** legume

gory
5 lurid **6** bloody, grisly **8** gruesome, sanguine **10** sanguinary **11** ensanguined, sanguineous, sensational **12** bloodstained **13** bloodcurdling

gosh
3 gee, wow **4** dang, darn, drat, egad, geez, heck **5** golly **6** crikey, cripes, shucks **7** doggone **8** goodness, gracious

gospel
5 truth **6** truism **7** message **8** doctrine **9** scripture **11** evangelical

gossamer
4 airy, film, fine, webs **5** filmy, gauzy, sheer **6** flimsy **7** cobwebs, tenuous **8** delicate **10** diaphanous **11** transparent

gossip
4 blab, buzz, chat, dirt, dish, talk **5** clack, prate, rumor, yenta **6** babble, rumble, tattle **7** babbler, chatter, hearsay, prattle, tattler **8** bigmouth, busybody, informer, prattler, quidnunc, telltale **10** talebearer **11** rumormonger, scandalizer, scuttlebutt **12** blatherskite
bit: **4** item

gossipy
5 gabby, talky **6** chatty **8** babbling, blabbing **9** garrulous, talkative

Gotham
7 New York (City)

Gothic
4 dark, wild **5** crude **6** brutal, coarse, savage **7** uncouth **8** barbaric, Germanic, medieval, Teutonic **9** barbarian, barbarous, sans serif **11** black letter, uncivilized

Götterdämmerung composer
6 Wagner (Richard)

got up
5 arose, stood

Gouda
6 cheese
relative: **4** Edam

gouge
3 dig **4** milk, ream, tool **5** cheat, exact, pinch, screw, wrest, wring **6** chisel, coerce, extort, groove, wrench **7** squeeze **8** scoop out **9** blackmail, extortion, shake down **10** overcharge

goulash
4 olio, stew **6** jumble, medley **7** mélange **8** mishmash **9** potpourri **10** bridge hand, hodgepodge, hotchpotch, salmagundi **11** gallimaufry

go under
4 fall, flop, fold, lose, sink **5** drown **6** plunge, submit **7** founder, immerse, succumb **8** collapse, submerge, submerse **9** surrender **10** capitulate

Gounod work
5 Faust **8** Ave Maria

gourd
4 pepo **5** fruit, melon **6** bottle, squash, vessel **7** chayote, gherkin, pumpkin **8** calabash, cucumber, cucurbit
instrument: **6** maraca

gourmand
3 hog, pig **6** gorger **7** stuffer, swiller

gourmet
6 foodie **7** epicure **9** bon vivant, epicurean **10** gastronome **11** connoisseur **12** gastronomist

gout
4 blob, clot, gush **5** spurt **6** splash **7** disease, podagra **8** eruption, swelling

govern
4 head, lead, rule **5** guide, order, reign, steer **6** direct, manage, master **7** command, conduct, control, execute, oversee **8** dominate, hold sway, regulate **9** supervise **10** administer **11** superintend

governess
5 nanny, nurse **6** duenna **8** mistress **9** nursemaid **10** babysitter **11** Mary Poppins

government
4 rule **5** power **6** polity, regime **7** regency, regimen **8** monarchy, republic, Uncle Sam **9** authority, autocracy, democracy, hierarchy, oligarchy **10** Big Brother **11** aristocracy, sovereignty
autocratic: **7** czarism, fascism, tyranny **9** despotism **10** absolutism **12** dictatorship
by a few: **9** oligarchy
by one: **8** monarchy
by three: **8** triarchy **11** triumvirate
by women: **8** gynarchy
official: **10** bureaucrat **11** functionary
without: **7** anarchy

government agency
3 ATF, BIA, BLM, CDC, CIA, DEA, EPA, FAA, FBI, FCC, FDA, FEC, FHA, GAO, GPO, HUD, ICC, INS, IRS, NBS, NEA, NIH, NRC, TVA **4** FDIC, FEMA, FEPC, NASA, NOAA, NTSB, OSHA

governor
3 bey, dey **4** head **5** chief, nabob, ruler **6** leader, regent **7** manager, viceroy **8** director **9** executive, regulator **10** commandant, magistrate
Chinese: **6** tuchun
of a fort: **7** alcaide, alcayde **9** castellan, chatelain
Persian: **6** satrap

gown
4 robe, toga **5** dress, frock, habit, tunic **6** camise, kimono, kirtle, mantua **7** cassock, chemise **8** peignoir
fabric: **5** tulle
dressing: **8** bathrobe
hospital: **6** johnny

goy
6 non-Jew **7** gentile
grab
3 nab **4** glom, grip, snag, take **5** catch, clasp, grasp, pluck, seize **6** clutch, collar, snatch, tackle **7** capture, grapple, seizure
grab bag
4 olio **6** jumble **7** mélange **10** assortment, hodgepodge, hotchpotch, miscellany
grabby
6 greedy **8** covetous, desirous, grasping **9** rapacious **10** avaricious, prehensile **11** acquisitive
grace
4 ease **5** adorn, charm, favor, mercy, poise **6** allure, lenity, pardon, polish, prayer, thanks, virtue **7** charity, dignify, dignity, enhance **8** approval, blessing, clemency, easiness, elegance, goodness, kindness, leniency, petition, reprieve **9** embellish, privilege **10** indulgence, invocation, refinement **11** benediction, forbearance **12** thanksgiving
graceful
4 airy, deft, easy **5** lithe **6** nimble, poised, smooth **7** elegant, flowing **8** debonair, polished
graceless
4 rude **5** crude, gawky, inept **6** clumsy, coarse, gauche, klutzy, vulgar **7** awkward, boorish, uncouth **8** barbaric, ungainly **9** barbarian, barbarous **10** outlandish, unmannered **12** infelicitous
Graces
6 Charis **8** Charites (plural)
brilliance: **6** Aglaia
bloom: **6** Thalia
joy: **10** Euphrosyne
mother: **5** Aegle
gracious
4 kind **5** suave **6** benign, genial, kindly, urbane **7** affable, amiable, cordial, courtly, gallant, stately, tactful **8** charming, generous, mannered, merciful, obliging, sociable **9** congenial, courteous **11** complaisant, good-natured **13** compassionate
grackle
4 myna **5** mynah **7** jackdaw **8** starling **9** blackbird
grad
4 alum
gradation
4 rank, step **5** order, range, scale, shade, stage **6** ablaut, change, degree, nuance, series **8** ordering, position, spectrum **9** continuum, variation **10** difference, succession
grade
3 peg **4** cant, form, kind, lean, mark, rank, rate, rung, sort, step, tier, tilt **5** blend, class, group, level, notch, order, pitch, place, slant, slope, stage **6** assess, assort, degree, league, rating **7** arrange, caliber, echelon, incline, leaning, quality **8** appraise, category, classify, division, evaluate, grouping, position, standard **9** hierarchy **10** categorize **11** inclination
Grade A
3 ace, top **4** best, boss, fine, tops **5** grand, great, prime, primo, super **6** choice, tip-top **7** capital, supreme **8** five-star, superior, topnotch **9** excellent, first-rate, nonpareil, number one, top-drawer **10** first-class **11** outstanding **13** par excellence
gradient
4 lean, ramp, rise, tilt **5** angle, pitch, slant, slope **7** incline, leaning **9** acclivity, declivity **11** inclination
gradual
4 even, slow **6** Psalms, steady **7** ongoing **8** bit-by-bit, creeping **9** piecemeal, prolonged **10** continuous, developing, protracted, step-by-step **11** progressive
gradually
6 slowly **7** by steps **8** bit by bit **9** by degrees, piecemeal **10** step by step **12** deliberately **13** imperceptibly, incrementally
decrease: **5** taper
graduate
4 alum
acquisition: **6** degree **7** diploma
female: **6** alumna **7** alumnae (plural)
male: **6** alumni (plural) **7** alumnus
Graeae, Graiae
4 Enyo **5** Deino **8** Pephredo
father: **7** Phorcus, Phorcys
mother: **4** Ceto
sisters: **7** Gorgons
Graf ___
4 Spee
graffiti artist
6 tagger
signature: **3** tag
graft
3 imp **4** join, mend, scam, skim **5** affix, crime, fraud, scion, unite **6** attach, boodle, fasten, payola, splice **7** implant, swindle, topwork **8** kickback **10** corruption
Grafton character
8 Millhone (Kinsey)
Grahame, Kenneth
character: **3** Rat **4** Toad, Mole **6** Badger
novel: **16** Wind in the Willows (The)
grail
3 cup, end **4** goal **6** goblet, object, target **7** chalice **9** objective
seeker: **7** Galahad

grain
3 bit, jot, rye **4** corn, flax, iota, meal, mite, oats, rice **5** crumb, fiber, kamut, maize, speck, spelt, trace, wheat **6** barley, cereal, millet, quinoa, tittle **7** granule, smidgen, sorghum, texture **8** amaranth, molecule, particle **9** buckwheat, triticale
beard: **3** awn
bristle: **3** awn
bundle: **4** bale **5** sheaf
chute: **6** hopper
ear: **5** spike
elevator: **4** silo
for horses: **3** oat **4** oats
mixture: **6** fodder
row: **5** swath **7** windrow

grainy
5 rough **6** coarse **8** granular **10** unfinished, unpolished

grammarian
7 Donatus (Aelius)

grammatical case
6 dative **7** oblique **8** ablative, genitive, locative, vocative **9** objective **10** accusative, nominative, possessive, subjective

grampus
3 orc **5** whale **7** dolphin **8** cetacean, porpoise, scorpion **9** blackfish **12** whip scorpion

Granada
building: **8** Alhambra
citadel: **8** Alcazaba
last Moorish king: **7** Boabdil

granary
3 bin **4** silo **10** repository, storehouse

grand
3 fab **4** epic, fine, huge, vast **5** gaudy, lofty, noble, regal, royal, showy, super **6** august, garish, lavish, lordly, mighty, ornate, superb **7** exalted, opulent, pompous, stately, sublime **8** baronial, elevated, gorgeous, imposing, majestic, princely, splendid **9** first-rate, inclusive, luxurious, sumptuous, wonderful **10** first-class, impressive, monumental, prodigious, stupendous, tremendous **11** magnificent **12** ostentatious

Grand Canyon
explorer: **6** Powell (John Wesley)
state: **7** Arizona

grande dame
5 queen **6** matron **7** dowager, doyenne **9** matriarch

grandee
4 duke, earl, king, lord, peer **5** baron, noble, pasha **6** bashaw, prince **8** mandarin, marquess, nobleman, viscount **10** panjandrum **11** mucketymuck

grandeur
4 pomp **5** glory **7** dignity, majesty **8** nobility, opulence, splendor, vastness **9** greatness, immensity, largeness, loftiness, nobleness, sublimity **10** augustness **11** stateliness **12** magnificence

grandiloquent
5 lofty **7** aureate, bloated, fustian, orotund, pompous **8** inflated **9** bombastic, flatulent, high-flown, overblown **10** histrionic, portentous **11** declamatory, highfalutin, pretentious **12** magniloquent

grand inquisitor
10 Torquemada (Tomás de)

grandiose
4 epic, vast **5** lofty, noble, regal, royal, showy **6** august, cosmic, lavish, lordly **7** pompous, stately, sublime, utopian **8** affected, imposing, majestic, princely, splendid **9** ambitious, high-flown **11** extravagant, highfalutin, magnificent, pretentious **12** ostentatious

grand mal
7 seizure **8** epilepsy

grandmother
4 nana
Russian: **8** babushka

Grand Ole Opry star
4 Tubb (Ernest) **5** Acuff (Roy), Cline (Patsy), Macon (Uncle Dave), Pearl (Minnie), Wells (Kitty) **6** Monroe (Bill) **8** Williams (Hank)

Grandson of Adam and Eve
4 Enos

grange
4 farm **9** farmhouse, farmstead

granite
3 ore **4** rock **5** stone **6** aplite **7** mineral **11** igneous rock

Granite State
12 New Hampshire

granola bit
3 oat

grant
3 aid **4** alms, avow, cede, dole, gift, give **5** admit, allow, award, endow, yield **6** accord, assert, assign, assume, bestow, confer, convey, donate, permit **7** charity, concede, consent, entitle, handout, present, subsidy, suppose **8** bequeath, donation, property, transfer **9** endowment, vouchsafe **10** assistance, concession, relinquish, subvention **11** acknowledge, benefaction **12** contribution **13** appropriation

Grant's counterpart
3 Lee (Robert E.)

granular
5 rough, sandy **6** coarse, grainy **7** powdery **8** powdered **10** unfinished, unpolished
snow: **4** névé

granule
3 bit, jot **4** iota, pill, spot **5** grain **6** pellet **8** fragment, particle

grape
3 fox, uva **4** Bual **5** Gamay, Pinot, Syrah **6** Arinto, Burger, Gentil, merlot, muscat, Shiraz **7** Albillo, Aligote, Barbera, Catawba, Concord, Furmint, Niagara, sultana **8** Aleatico, Cabernet, Charbono, Delaware, Friularo, Grenache, Isabella, malvasia, muscadel, Muscadet, Nebbiolo, Riesling, Semillon, Sylvaner, Thompson, Traminer, vinifera, Viognier **9** Carmenère, Chasselas, Lambrusco, Malvoisie, muscadine, Pinot Gris, pinot noir, Sauvignon, Trebbiano, zinfandel **10** chardonnay, Grignolino, muscadelle, pinot blanc, Sangiovese, Verdicchio **11** Chenin Blanc, Petite Sirah, pinot grigio, scuppernong
disease: **4** esca
dried: **6** raisin
drink: **4** wine
pulp: **4** rape **6** pomace
residue: **4** marc

grapefruit
6 pomelo

Grapes of Wrath, The
author: **9** Steinbeck (John)
family: **4** Joad
people: **5** Okies

grapevine
4 buzz **5** rumor **6** gossip **7** hearsay **9** rumor mill **11** scuttlebutt

graph
3 map **4** plot **5** chart **6** sketch **7** diagram, outline **8** nomogram, pie chart

graphic
3 map **5** clear, lucid, photo, vivid **6** cogent, visual **7** picture, precise, telling, written **8** clear-cut, definite, detailed, explicit, incisive, striking **9** pictorial, realistic **10** compelling, photograph **11** descriptive, picturesque

graphite
4 lead **6** carbon **8** plumbago

grapnel
4 hook **6** anchor

grappa
6 brandy

grapple
3 nab **4** bind, cope, grab, grip, hold **5** catch, clamp, clasp, fight, grasp, seize **6** battle, bucket, clench, clinch, clutch, fasten, tackle, tussle **7** contest, scuffle, wrestle **8** struggle

grasp
3 dig, ken, see **4** glom, grip, hold, know, take **5** catch, clamp, clasp, cling, seize **6** accept, clench, clinch, clutch, fathom, follow, handle, take in, tenure **7** cognize, compass, control, embrace, grapple, realize **8** envisage, perceive **9** apprehend, awareness **10** appreciate, comprehend, take hold of, understand **12** apprehension **13** comprehension, understanding

graspable
5 clear, lucid **6** lucent **8** coherent, knowable, palpable **10** fathomable **11** perspicuous **12** intelligible **13** apprehensible

grasping
4 avid **6** grabby, greedy **8** covetous, desirous **9** rapacious **10** avaricious, prehensile **11** acquisitive

grass
3 Poa, pot, sod, tea, Zea **4** lawn, reed, turf, weed **6** redtop **7** herbage, panicum, pasture **8** cannabis, Mary Jane **9** cocksfoot, marijuana
African: **6** imphee
annual: **6** darnel **8** teosinte
Asian: **7** vetiver, whangee
Australian: **8** spinifex
beach: **6** marram
cereal: **3** oat, rye, Zea **4** milo, teff **5** kafir, maize, proso, sorgo, wheat **6** millet **7** sorghum **8** triticum
clump: **4** tuft **7** tussock
cover: **3** dew
dried: **3** hay **5** straw
European: **7** Bermuda, timothy
fiber: **4** flax
fragrant: **10** citronella
Hawaiian: **4** hilo
meadow: **3** Poa
pasture: **5** Bahia, grama
perennial: **6** fescue, quitch, zoysia **7** esparto, galleta
prairie: **8** bluestem
second growth: **5** rowen
tropical: **5** cogon **6** bamboo

grasshopper
6 locust **7** katydid **8** cocktail

grassland
3 lea **5** field **6** meadow **7** pasture, prairie
African: **4** veld **5** veldt
flat: **7** savanna **8** savannah
South American: **5** pampa **6** pampas

grasslike marsh plant
5 sedge

Grass novel
7 Tin Drum (The) **8** Dog Years, Flounder (The) **11** Cat and Mouse

grassy field
3 lea

grate
3 irk, jar, rub, vex **4** file, fray, fret, gall, rasp, rile **5** annoy, chafe, gnash, grill, grind, peeve, pique **6** abrade, grille, nettle, rankle, scrape **7** provoke, scratch **8** irritate **9** aggravate, fireplace

grateful
7 obliged, pleased, restful, welcome **8** beholden, indebted, pleasant, pleasing, thankful **9** agreeable, congenial, favorable **10** refreshing **11** restorative **12** appreciative

Gratiano
brother: **9** Brabantio
friend: **7** Antonio **8** Bassanio
niece: **9** Desdemona
wife: **7** Nerissa

gratify
4 baby, sate **5** favor, humor, spoil **6** coddle, oblige, pamper, pander, please **7** appease, cater to, content, delight, gladden, indulge, satisfy

gratin
5 crust

grating
3 dry **4** grid, rasp **5** grill, harsh, rough **6** grille, hoarse **7** irksome, jarring, lattice, rasping, raucous **8** gridiron, strident **9** vexatious **10** stridulous

gratis
4 comp, free **6** comped **8** costless **10** chargeless **13** complimentary

gratitude
6 thanks **12** appreciation, gratefulness, thankfulness

gratuitous
6 wanton **8** baseless **9** unfounded, voluntary **10** groundless, reasonless, ungrounded **11** uncalled-for, unnecessary, unwarranted **12** indefensible

gratuity
3 tip **4** gift, perk **5** bonus **6** reward **7** cumshaw, douceur **8** donation, largesse, offering **9** baksheesh, lagniappe, pourboire **10** perquisite **11** benefaction **12** contribution

grave
3 pit, sad **4** dire, dour, fell, grim, tomb **5** acute, awful, crypt, fatal, heavy, major, sober, staid, vault **6** burial, deadly, gloomy, sedate, severe, solemn, somber, sombre, urgent **7** austere, ghastly, ominous, ossuary, serious, subdued, weighty **8** catacomb, critical, dreadful, perilous, pressing, terrible **9** dangerous, mausoleum, momentous, ponderous, saturnine, sepulcher, sepulchre, sepulture, unsmiling
marker: **5** stela, stele **8** memorial, monument **9** footstone, headstone, tombstone **11** sarcophagus
mound: **6** barrow **7** tumulus
robber: **5** ghoul

gravel
4 dirt, grit, sand
ridge: **5** esker

gravelly
5 raspy, rough **6** gritty, hoarse **7** rasping, grating **8** abrasive, granular, guttural, scratchy

graven image
4 icon, idol

graver
4 tool **5** burin **8** sculptor

graveyard
8 boot hill, catacomb, cemetery, God's acre **10** necropolis **12** burial ground, memorial park, potter's field

gravid
5 heavy **8** enceinte, pregnant **9** expectant, expecting, with child **10** parturient **12** childbearing

gravity
5 force **6** weight **7** dignity, urgency **8** sobriety **9** heaviness, solemnity **10** importance, somberness **11** consequence, seriousness **12** significance

gravlax
3 lox **6** salmon

gravy
4 perk **5** bonus, bribe, graft, juice, sauce **6** payola **8** dressing, windfall
French: **3** jus

gray
3 ash, old **4** aged, ashy, blah, drab, dull **5** ashen, bleak, color, hoary, slate, slaty **6** dismal, gloomy, leaden **7** elderly, grizzly, neutral **8** grizzled, gunmetal, overcast **9** cinereous, colorless
brownish: **3** dun **5** taupe **7** fuscous

gray duck
7 gadwall, pintail

grayfish
5 shark **7** dogfish

gray matter
3 wit **4** head, mind **5** brain **6** brains, noddle, noggin, noodle **8** cerebrum **9** intellect **10** encephalon **12** intelligence, neural tissue

graze
3 eat, rub **4** feed, gall, kiss, skim, skip, wear **5** brush, chafe, erode, shave, touch **6** abrade, browse, bruise, forage, glance, scrape **7** contuse, corrade, pasture **8** abrasion, ricochet

grazier
7 rancher

grease
3 fat, oil **4** lard **5** smear **6** smooth **7** lanolin **9** lubricant, lubricate
combining form: **4** sebi, sebo

greasy
4 oily **5** fatty, slick **8** slippery, unctuous **10** lubricious, oleaginous

greasy spoon
4 café **5** diner, grill **6** eatery **7** beanery, hashery **9** chophouse, hash house, lunchroom **10** coffee shop **12** luncheonette

great
3 big, fat **4** huge, vast **5** boffo, grand, jumbo, large, noble, socko **6** famous, heroic **7** awesome, eminent, exalted, immense, mammoth, notable, sublime, supreme, titanic **8** colossal, enormous, gigantic, glorious, renowned, terrific, towering **9** excellent, fantastic, humongous, paramount, prominent, wonderful **10** celebrated, impressive, noteworthy, prodigious, remarkable, stupendous, tremendous **11** illustrious, magnificent, outstanding, superlative **13** distinguished
combining form: **4** mega **6** megalo

Great Bear
9 Big Dipper, Ursa Major **13** constellation

Great Britain
see **England, United Kingdom**

Great Commoner, the
4 Pitt (William) **5** Bryan (William Jennings) **7** Lincoln (Abraham)

Great Emancipator, the
7 Lincoln (Abraham)

greater
4 more **5** metro **6** better, bigger, higher, larger **8** superior **9** exceeding **10** surpassing **12** metropolitan

greatest
4 best, most **6** utmost **7** maximum, supreme **8** foremost

Great Expectations
author: **7** Dickens (Charles)
character: **3** Joe (Gargery), Pip **5** Biddy **7** Estella, Jaggers **8** Havisham (Miss), Magwitch (Abel)

greathearted
4 bold, kind **5** brave, lofty, noble **6** heroic **7** gallant **8** fearless, generous, princely **10** benevolent, chivalrous, courageous, high-minded **11** considerate, magnanimous

Great Lake
4 Erie **5** Huron **7** Ontario **8** Michigan, Superior
acronym: **5** HOMES
city: **4** Erie, Gary **6** Duluth **7** Buffalo, Chicago, Toronto **9** Milwaukee

Great Lake State
8 Michigan

great Scott
4 egad

greave
7 legging

grebe
4 bird, fowl **8** dabchick **10** diving bird

Greece
6 Hellas
ancient city-state: **5** Argos **6** Athens, Sparta, Thebes **7** Corinth
ancient town: **6** Delphi
capital: **6** Athens
city: **6** Patras **7** Larissa, Piraeus **8** Salonika **12** Thessaloníki
conqueror: **6** Philip (of Macedonia) **9** Alexander (the Great)
island, island group: **5** Crete **6** Aegean, Euboea, Ionian **8** Cyclades, Sporades
monetary unit: **4** euro
monetary unit, former: **6** lepton **7** drachma
mountain, range: **3** Ida **4** Ossa **5** Athos **6** Pelion, Pindus **7** Olympus **9** Parnassus
neighbor: **6** Turkey **7** Albania **8** Bulgaria **9** Macedonia
part of: **7** Balkans
peninsula: **6** Balkan **10** Chalcidice **11** Peloponnese
region: **6** Attica, Epirus, Thrace **8** Thessaly
sea: **6** Aegean, Ionian **13** Mediterranean
vale: **5** Tempe

greed
4 lust **6** excess, hunger **7** avarice, avidity, craving, edacity, longing **8** cupidity, gluttony, rapacity, voracity **12** covetousness, ravenousness

greedy
4 avid **5** itchy **6** grabby **7** hoggish, miserly, selfish **8** covetous, desirous, edacious, esurient, grasping **10** avaricious, gluttonous **11** acquisitive

Greek
6 Argive, babble, drivel, jabber **7** Achaean, Hellene **8** Hellenic, nonsense **9** gibberish
architectural order: **5** Doric, Ionic **10** Corinthian
assembly: **5** agora, boule
café: **7** taverna
cheese: **4** feta
coin: **4** obol **6** lepton, stater **7** drachma
colony: **5** Ionia
column: **5** Doric, Ionic **10** Corinthian
contest: **4** agon
counselor: **6** Nestor
cross: **3** tau
dictator: **7** Metaxas (Ioannis)
dragon: **9** Eurythion
drink: **4** ouzo
epic: **5** Iliad **7** Odyssey
Fates: **6** Clotho, Moirae **7** Atropos **8** Lachesis
flask: **4** olpe
gift: **11** Trojan Horse
god:
chief: **4** Zeus
messenger: **6** Hermes
of agriculture: **6** Cronus
of death: **8** Thanatos
of dreams: **8** Morpheus
of fire: **10** Hephaestus

of healing: **9** Asclepius **11** Aesculapius
of love: **4** Eros
of marriage: **5** Hymen
of physicians: **6** Hermes
of sleep: **6** Hypnos
of the sea: **6** Nereus, Triton **7** Oceanus **8** Poseidon
of the sun: **6** Apollo, Helios
of the underworld: **5** Pluto
of the winds: **5** Eurus, Notus **6** Aeolus, Boreas **8** Zephyrus
of war: **4** Ares
of wine: **8** Dionysus
of woods: **3** Pan
goddess:
of agriculture: **7** Demeter
of beauty: **9** Aphrodite
of dawn: **3** Eos
of discord: **4** Eris
of fertility: **6** Cybele
of flowers: **7** Chloris
of fortune: **5** Tyche
of harvests: **4** Rhea
of hunting: **7** Artemis
of justice: **7** Astraea
of love: **9** Aphrodite
of marriage: **4** Hera
of night: **3** Nyx
of peace: **5** Irene
of retribution: **7** Nemesis
of ruin: **3** Ate
of the earth: **4** Gaea, Gaia
of the hearth: **6** Hestia
of magic: **6** Hecate, Hekate
of the moon: **6** Hecate, Hekate, Selena, Selene **7** Artemis, Astarte
of the rainbow: **4** Iris
of the seasons: **5** Horae
of the underworld: **6** Hecate, Hekate **10** Persephone
of vengeance: **7** Nemesis
of victory: **4** Nike
of war: **4** Enyo
of wisdom: **6** Athena
of witchcraft: **6** Hecate, Hekate
of womanhood: **4** Hera
of youth: **4** Hebe
hero: **4** Aias, Ajax **5** Jason **7** Theseus **8** Achilles, Argonaut, Heracles, Hercules, Odysseus **9** Achilleus
historian: **8** Xenophon **9** Herodotus **10** Thucydides
lawgiver: **5** Draco, Solon
leader: **9** Agamemnon
letter: **3** chi, eta, phi, psi, rho, tau **4** beta, iota, zeta **5** alpha, delta, gamma, kappa, omega, sigma, theta **6** lambda **7** epsilon, omicron, upsilon
magistrate: **6** archon
marketplace: **5** agora
Muse: **4** Clio **5** Erato **6** Thalia, Urania
physician: **5** Galen
porch: **4** stoa
portico: **4** stoa
sandwich: **4** gyro
singer: **4** Nana (Mouskouri)
slave: **5** helot
soldier: **7** hoplite
theater: **4** odea (plural) **5** odeon, odeum
underworld: **5** Hades
war cry: **5** alala
warrior: **4** Ajax **7** Ulysses **8** Achilles, Diomedes, Odysseus **9** Agamemnon, Palamedes
weeper: **5** Niobe
wine: **7** retsina

green
3 raw **4** jade, lime, moss **5** alive, fresh, kelly, leafy, naive, virid, young **6** callow, forest, unripe **7** avocado, celadon, emerald, envious, untried, verdant **8** immature, juvenile, unversed, youthful **9** unfledged **10** unseasoned **11** unpracticed **13** inexperienced
bluish: **8** glaucous
combining form: **4** verd **6** chloro
grayish: **5** olive
heraldry: **4** vert
prefix: **3** eco
yellowish: **7** luteous **10** chartreuse

greenbacks
4 cash, jack, loot **5** bread, bucks, dough, lucre, money, moola **6** moolah, wampum **7** dollars, scratch **8** currency, smackers **11** legal tender

green beryl
7 emerald

greenery
7 foliage, leafage **8** verdancy

green-eyed
7 envious, jealous **9** invidious
monster: **8** jealousy

greenfly
5 aphid

greengage
4 plum

greenhead
3 fly **8** horsefly

greenheart
6 laurel **9** evergreen

greenhorn
4 babe, hick, jake, naïf, rube, tiro, tyro **6** newbie, novice, rookie **7** ingenue **8** beginner, neophyte, newcomer **10** provincial

greenhouse
7 nursery **12** conservatory

greenish blue
4 aqua, teal
Greenland
capital: 4 Nuuk **7** Godthåb
city: 5 Thule
ethnic group: 5 Inuit **6** Eskimo
explorer: 4 Eric (the Red), Erik (the Red), Leif (Eriksson) **9** Rasmussen (Knud)
language: 6 Danish
monetary unit: 5 krone
possession of: 7 Denmark
green light
3 nod **4** okay **5** leave **6** assent **7** consent, go-ahead, mandate **8** approval, blessing, sanction, thumbs-up **9** authority, clearance **10** permission **11** endorsement **13** authorization
Green Mansions
author: 6 Hudson (W. H.)
character: 4 Rima
green monkey
6 guenon, simian, vervet
green moth
4 luna
Green Mountain State
7 Vermont
greenness
5 youth **6** spring **7** puberty **8** verdancy, viridity **9** youthhood **10** immaturity, juvenility, pubescence, springtide, springtime **11** adolescence **12** inexperience
green osier
6 willow **7** dogwood
green plover
7 lapwing **9** shorebird
greenroom
6 lounge
green sauce
5 pesto
greenstone
4 jade **7** diabase **8** nephrite **9** tremolite **10** actinolite
greet
3 bow **4** hail, meet **6** accost, call to, salaam, salute **7** address, react to, receive, welcome
greeting
3 ave, bow, nod **4** ahoy, ciao, g'day, hail **5** aloha, hello, howdy **6** salaam, salute **7** address, welcome **9** handshake, reception **10** salutation
gregarious
6 clubby, genial, social **7** affable **8** outgoing, sociable **9** clubbable, congenial, convivial **11** extroverted **13** companionable
gremlin
3 bug, elf, imp **5** dwarf, gnome **6** defect, glitch **7** brownie
Grenada
capital: 9 St. George's
discoverer: 8 Columbus (Christopher)
former name: 10 Concepción
location: 10 West Indies
nickname: 11 Isle of Spice
grenade
4 bomb **5** shell **7** missile **9** explosive, pineapple
grenadier
7 rattail, soldier
grenadine
4 pink, yarn **5** syrup **6** fabric **9** carnation
Grendel's slayer
7 Beowulf
Gretchen's lover
5 Faust
greylag
5 goose
Grey's forte
7 anatomy
grid
3 net **5** grate, grill **6** grille **7** grating, lattice, network, trellis
griddle
3 pan **5** grill
griddle cake
7 hotcake, pancake **8** flapjack
gridiron
3 net **5** field, grate, grill **7** grating, network
official: 3 ref
grief
3 rue, woe **4** care **5** agony, dolor, gloom, tears **6** mishap, regret, sorrow **7** anguish, chagrin, sadness, trouble **8** disaster, distress, hardship **9** adversity, heartache, suffering **10** affliction, heartbreak, misfortune **11** despondency
Grieg work
8 Peer Gynt
grievance
4 beef **5** cross, gripe, trial, wrong **6** burden, grouse, injury, squawk **8** hardship, jeremiad **9** complaint, injustice **10** affliction, allegation, unfairness **11** tribulation
grieve
3 cry **4** ache, keen, moan, wail, weep **5** mourn **6** burden, lament, sadden, sorrow, suffer **7** afflict, agonize **8** distress
grievous
3 sad **4** dire, fell, sore **5** cruel, grave, great, major **6** bitter, severe, taxing, tragic, woeful **7** galling, heinous, onerous, painful, serious, weighty **9** egregious **10** abominable, burdensome, calamitous, deplorable, lamentable, oppressive **11** distressing, regrettable, troublesome, unfortunate **12** heartrending

grift
3 con, gyp **4** bilk, rook **7** defraud, swindle **8** flimflam

grifter
3 gyp **5** cheat, crook, thief **6** con man, gouger **7** cheater, scammer, sharper, slicker **8** swindler **9** defrauder, trickster **13** confidence man

grill
3 fry, vex **4** cook, grid, pump, quiz **5** broil, grate, sauté, toast **6** eatery **7** afflict, debrief, grating, griddle, torment **8** gridiron, question **10** restaurant **11** interrogate **12** cross-examine

grilse
6 salmon

grim
3 set **4** cold, dour, fell, firm, hard **5** bleak, cruel, fixed, grave, harsh, rigid, stern **6** dismal, dogged, dreary, fierce, grisly, intent, savage, severe, somber **7** adamant, austere, inhuman, joyless, ominous **8** gruesome, inhumane, obdurate, resolute, ruthless, stubborn **9** merciless, offensive, truculent **10** determined, forbidding, implacable, inevitable, inexorable, inflexible, melancholy, relentless, unyielding, vindictive **11** unforgiving, unrelenting

grimace
3 mow, mug **4** face, moue, pout **5** frown, lower, mouth, scowl, sneer

grimalkin
3 cat **5** tabby **6** feline **9** female cat

grime
4 crud, dirt, gunk, muck, smut, soot **5** filth

grim reaper
5 death

grimy
5 dingy, dirty **6** filthy, grubby, grungy, soiled, scuzzy, smutty **10** besmirched

grin
4 beam **5** smile, smirk **6** rictus

grind
3 rut, vex **4** chew, grub, mill, moil, pace, plod, plug, rote, slog, toil, whet **5** crank, crush, gnash, grate, labor, slave, sweat **6** abrade, crunch, drudge, groove, harass, kibble, powder, rotate **7** oppress, routine, travail **8** drudgery, monotony, wear down **9** pulverize, treadmill **10** donkeywork

grinder
3 sub **4** gyro, hero **5** molar, tooth **6** hoagie **8** sandwich **9** submarine

grinding
5 harsh **6** severe **7** arduous, grating, wearing **9** fatiguing, strenuous
stone: 4 mano **6** mortar, muller, pestle

griot
11 storyteller

grip
4 glom, hold, take **5** clamp, clasp, grasp, seize **6** clench, clinch, clutch, handle, tenure, valise **7** grapple **8** enthrall, suitcase **9** fascinate, mesmerize, restraint, spellbind, stagehand **10** constraint

gripe
3 bug, vex **4** beef, carp, crab, fuss, yawp **5** annoy, bitch, bleat, cavil, croak, groan, whine **6** bother, grouch, grouse, kvetch, murmur, mutter, object, squawk, yammer **7** afflict, grumble **8** complain, distress, irritate **9** bellyache, complaint, grievance, objection

griper
4 bear, crab **5** crank, grump **10** crosspatch, curmudgeon, malcontent

grippe
3 flu **9** influenza

gripper
4 clip, hand, vise **5** clamp, clasp, tongs **6** pliers

gris-gris
4 juju **5** charm, spell **6** amulet, fetish **8** talisman **11** incantation

Grisham novel
4 Firm (The) **6** Broker (The), Client (The) **7** Chamber (The), Partner (The) **8** Brethren (The) **12** Pelican Brief (The)

grisly
4 gory, grim **5** awful, lurid **6** horrid **7** ghastly, hideous, macabre **8** fearsome, god-awful, gruesome, horrible, terrible **9** frightful, repellent, repulsive, sickening **10** disgusting, horrifying, terrifying

grist
3 lot **5** grain, input, stint **6** amount, output **7** product **8** quantity

gristle
9 cartilage

grit
4 guts, sand **5** grate, grind, heart, moxie, nerve, pluck, spunk **6** gravel, mettle, powder, smooth, spirit **7** bravery, courage, granule **8** backbone, tenacity **9** fortitude **10** doggedness **13** determination

gritty
4 game **5** dirty, gutsy, rough, sandy **6** dogged, plucky, spunky **8** abrasive, gravelly, resolute, spirited **9** steadfast, tenacious **10** courageous, determined

groan
4 beef, carp, moan **5** cavil, creak, gripe **6** bemoan, grouse, lament, object, repine **7** grumble **8** complain **9** bellyache

grocery
5 store **11** supermarket
Spanish: 6 bodega

grog
3 rum **5** booze, drink, hooch, juice, sauce **6** liquor, tipple **7** alcohol, spirits **9** firewater

groggy
4 dull, hazy, logy, weak **5** dazed, dopey, foggy, muzzy, tired, woozy **6** dulled, sleepy **7** muddled **8** befogged, confused, sluggish **9** befuddled, slaphappy, stupefied **10** punch-drunk

groin
4 fold **6** crotch

grok
6 intuit

grommet
6 eyelet **7** cringle

groom
4 comb, tend, tidy **5** brush, clean, curry, primp, ready, shave **6** neaten, ostler, polish **7** hostler, prepare, servant **8** benedict **9** attendant
Indian: **4** syce

groove
3 rut **4** dado, pace, rote, slot **5** canal, flute, glyph, gouge, grind, niche, score, stria **6** furrow, gutter, hollow, rabbet, rhythm **7** chamfer, channel, routine, top form **8** monotony **10** depression

groovy
3 hip **4** cool, neat **5** ducky, great, nifty, sharp, slick, super, swell **6** choice, gnarly, peachy **7** right-on **8** smashing **9** copacetic, excellent, hunky-dory, marvelous, wonderful **10** delightful, marvellous, peachy keen

grope
4 feel, grub, poke, root **6** fondle, fumble, search **7** grabble **8** scrabble

grosbeak
5 finch **8** hawfinch, songbird

gross
3 fat, raw, sum, ugh **4** earn, foul, mass, rude **5** brute, bulky, crude, obese, rough, utter, whole **6** carnal, coarse, entire, vulgar **7** blatant, boorish, capital, extreme, glaring, hulking, obscene, overall, porcine, uncouth **8** absolute, complete, flagrant, ignorant, improper, indecent, outright, sum total, tangible, totality **9** aggregate, before tax, corporeal, corpulent, downright, egregious, excessive, loathsome, offensive, out-and-out, repulsive, revolting, unrefined **10** disgusting, exorbitant, immoderate **11** twelve dozen

grotesque
6 absurd, rococo, unreal **7** baroque, bizarre, extreme **8** aberrant, abnormal, deformed, fanciful, freakish **9** distorted, fantastic, ludicrous, misshapen, monstrous **11** incongruous

grotto
4 cave, hole **5** crypt, vault **6** cavern
Capri: **4** Blue

grouch
4 beef, carp, crab, kick, sulk, yawp **5** crank, croak, growl, grump, pique **6** carper, griper, grouse, grudge, kicker, kvetch, murmur, mutter, repine, squawk, whiner, yawper **7** crabber, grouser, growler, grumble **8** complain, grumbler, kvetcher, sorehead, sourpuss, squawker **9** bellyache, complaint **10** bellyacher, complainer, crosspatch, malcontent

ground
3 bed, sod **4** base, dirt, land, root, seat, soil, turf **5** basis, cause, earth, floor, proof **6** bottom, reason **7** bedrock, dry land, footing, support, sustain, terrain **8** argument, buttress, evidence **9** establish, testimony **10** foundation, terra firma

groundbreaking
10 innovative, innovatory, pioneering **11** cutting-edge, leading-edge

grounded
6 stable **7** beached **8** marooned, sensible, stranded **9** realistic **13** unpretentious

groundhog
6 marmot **9** woodchuck

grounding
8 practice, training, tutelage **11** instruction, preparation

groundless
4 idle **5** empty, false **6** hollow **8** baseless **9** causeless, unfounded **10** gratuitous **11** uncalled-for, unjustified, unwarranted

grounds
4 lees **5** basis, dregs **6** campus, estate, reason **7** residue **8** premises, property

groundwork
3 bed **4** base, foot, root **5** basis **6** bottom **7** bedrock, footing, support **8** basement **10** foundation, substratum **11** cornerstone, preparation **12** substruction, substructure, underpinning

ground zero
5 focus, get-go **6** center, outset, target **8** bull's-eye **9** epicenter, square one

group
3 lot, set **4** band, bevy, body, club, crew, gang, pack, ruck, sect, team, tier **5** array, batch, bunch, cadre, class, clump, combo, covey, crowd, horde, panel, squad, taxon, troop **6** assort, bundle, cartel, circle, clique, clutch, huddle, klatch, league, passel **7** battery, brigade, cluster, combine, company, coterie, council, echelon, klatsch, platoon **8** assemble, assembly, category, classify, ensemble, organize **9** congeries, gathering, syndicate **10** assemblage, categorize, collection
of angels: **4** host
of ants: **6** colony
of bees: **4** hive **5** swarm
of birds: **6** flight

of cats: **7** clowder, clutter
of cattle: **5** drove
of chicks: **5** brood **6** clutch
of clams: **3** bed
of crows: **6** murder
of ducks: **5** brace
of eight: **5** octad, octet
of elephants: **4** herd
of elks: **4** gang
of fish: **5** shoal **6** school
of five: **5** quint **6** pentad **7** quintet
of four: **6** tetrad **7** quartet
of foxes: **5** leash, skulk
of geese: **5** flock, skein **6** gaggle
of gnats: **5** cloud, horde
of goats: **5** tribe
of gorillas: **4** band
of greyhounds: **5** leash
of grouse: **5** covey
of hares: **4** down, husk
of hawks: **4** cast
of hounds: **3** cry **4** mute, pack
of kangaroos: **3** mob **5** troop
of kittens: **6** litter
of larks: **10** exaltation
of lions: **5** pride
of locusts: **6** plague
of monkeys: **5** troop
of mules: **4** span
of nine: **5** nonet **6** ennead
of oysters: **3** bed
of partridges: **5** covey
of peacocks: **6** muster
of pheasants: **4** nest
of plovers: **4** wing **12** congregation
of quail: **4** bevy **5** covey
of seals: **3** pod **5** patch
of seven: **6** pleiad, septet
of sheep: **5** drove, flock
of six: **6** sextet
of swans: **4** bevy
of teals: **6** spring
of ten: **6** decade
of three: **4** trio **5** triad **7** ternary, trinity, triplet
of vipers: **4** nest
of whales: **3** gam, pod
of wolves: **4** pack

grouper
8 rockfish

grouse
4 beef, carp, crab **5** croak, gripe, quail, scold **6** mutter, yammer **7** grumble **8** complain, pheasant **9** bellyache, blackcock, ptarmigan **12** capercaillie
extinct: **8** heath hen
red: **8** moorfowl
strut: **3** lek

grout
4 lees, lute **5** dregs **6** cement, filler, mortar **7** grounds, plaster **8** concrete

grove
4 holt, wood **5** copse **7** boscage, coppice, orchard, thicket

grovel
3 beg **4** fawn **5** abase, cower, crawl, creep, toady **6** cajole, cringe, kowtow, snivel, wallow **7** eat dirt, truckle **8** blandish, bootlick **9** brownnose **10** curry favor, ingratiate **11** apple-polish

grow
3 age, wax **4** flow, gain, rise, tend **5** amass, breed, nurse, raise, ripen, swell **6** abound, become, expand, foster, mature, sprout, thrive **7** burgeon, care for, develop, enlarge, gestate, nurture, produce **8** escalate, flourish, increase, multiply, mushroom, spring up **9** cultivate, propagate

growl
4 beef, carp, crab, fuss, gnar, roar **5** bitch, gripe, gnarr, groan, snarl **6** grouse, kvetch, mutter, repine, rumble, yammer **7** grumble **8** complain **9** bellyache

growler
3 can **4** crab, floe **5** crank, grump **6** grouch, vessel **7** ice floe, iceberg, pitcher **8** sorehead, sourpuss **9** container **10** crosspatch, malcontent **11** faultfinder

grown-up
5 adult **6** mature **8** seasoned **9** developed **11** full-fledged

grow old
3 age **4** wane **5** ripen, wizen **6** mature, mellow

growth
4 gain, rise **5** spurt, surge, swell, tumor **7** buildup **8** increase, progress, swelling **9** accretion, evolution, expansion, flowering, unfolding **11** development, enlargement, progression
malignant: **6** cancer
skin: **3** tag, wen **4** corn, cyst, mole, wart **5** nevus **6** bunion, callus, keloid **7** verruca

grow up
3 age **5** ripen **6** evolve, mature, mellow **7** advance, develop **8** maturate **9** come of age

grub
3 dig **4** chow, comb, eats, feed, food, hack, moil, plod, poke, rake, root, slog, toil **5** cadge, grind, larva, scour, slave, spade, stump **6** burrow, drudge, forage, menial, shovel, slavey, uproot, viands **7** edibles, ransack, rummage, unearth, vittles **8** excavate, hireling, victuals **9** provender **11** comestibles

grubby
4 foul **5** dirty, grimy, messy, seedy **6** filthy, frowsy, frowzy, grungy, scuzzy, shabby, sloppy,

soiled **7** scruffy, squalid, unclean, unkempt **8** slovenly, unwashed

grubstake
3 aid **4** back, fund, help, loan **5** funds **6** assist **7** backing, capital, finance, support **8** bankroll **9** financing **10** assistance, capitalize, underwrite

grudge
4 deny, envy **5** spite **6** refuse, spleen **7** ill will **9** grievance **10** resentment **12** hard feelings, spitefulness

gruel
4 mush **5** atole, kasha **6** burgoo, congee, sowens **8** flummery, loblolly, porridge **9** stirabout

grueling
6 taxing **7** arduous **9** difficult, strenuous

gruesome
7 macabre **8** dreadful, horrible, horrific **9** appalling **10** horrifying

gruff
4 curt, dour **5** bluff, blunt, cross, harsh, husky, stern, surly **6** abrupt, crabby, crusty, hoarse, morose, sullen **7** bearish, brusque, crabbed, grating, grouchy **8** churlish, croaking, snappish, snippety **9** saturnine **10** ill-natured **11** bad-tempered

grumble
4 beef, carp, crab, fuss, moan, yawp **5** bitch, croak, gripe, groan, growl, snarl, whine **6** bemoan, grouch, grouse, murmur, mutter, repine, squawk **8** complain **9** bellyache

grumbler
4 crab **5** crank, grump **6** grouch **8** sorehead **10** crosspatch, malcontent

grump
3 pet **4** beef, carp, crab, pout, sulk **5** crank, gripe, growl **6** griper, grouch **7** growler, grumble **8** complain, sorehead, sourpuss **9** bellyache **10** bellyacher, malcontent

grumpy
4 dour, sour **5** cross, moody, sulky, surly, testy **6** crabby, cranky, sullen **7** crabbed, peevish **8** petulant, vinegary **9** crotchety, irascible **11** bad-tempered, ill-tempered **12** cantankerous

grungy
5 dirty **6** cruddy, filthy **7** scruffy, unkempt **8** unwashed

grunion
10 silverside

grunt
3 ugh **5** groan, growl, snort **7** dogface, draftee, soldier

G sharp
5 A flat

guacharo
7 oilbird

Guadeloupe
capital: 10 Basse-Terre
department of: 6 France
dependency: 8 Désirade, St. Martin **12** Marie-Galante, St. Barthélemy
discoverer: 8 Columbus (Christopher)
island: 10 Basse-Terre **11** Grande-Terre
location: 10 West Indies
volcano: 9 Soufrière

Guam
capital: 5 Agana
ethnic group: 8 Chamorro
island group: 7 Mariana

guanaco
5 llama **6** alpaca
kin: 5 camel

guano
6 manure **9** excrement

Guantánamo's home
4 Cuba

guarantee
3 vow **4** bail, bond, oath, seal, word **5** token, vouch **6** assert, assure, ensure, insure, pledge, surety **7** certify, earnest, promise, warrant **8** security, warranty **9** agreement, assurance, insurance, undertake **11** stand behind, undertaking

guarantor
5 angel **6** backer, patron, surety **7** ensurer, insurer, sponsor **8** bondsman **11** underwriter

guard
4 fend, mind, tend, ward **5** aegis, alert, armor, cover, watch **6** convoy, defend, escort, jailer, keeper, minder, patrol, picket, police, screen, secure, sentry, shield, warden, warder **7** bulwark, defense, lookout, oversee, protect, turnkey **8** chaperon, overseer, preserve, security, sentinel, shepherd, watchdog, watchman **9** chaperone, custodian, look after, patrolman, protector, watch over **10** protection

guarded
4 kept, safe, wary **5** cagey, chary, leery **7** careful, politic, prudent **8** cautious, discreet, gingerly, reserved **11** circumspect, considerate

guardhouse
4 brig, jail, keep **5** clink **6** lockup, prison **8** stockade

guardian
6 escort, keeper, patron, warden, warder **7** curator, trustee **8** Cerberus, defender, overseer, watchdog **9** custodian, protector **10** genius loci **11** conservator

guardianship
4 care, keep, ward **5** aegis, trust **6** charge **7** custody, keeping **8** auspices **10** protection **11** safekeeping

Guare play
17 House of Blue Leaves (The) **22** Six Degrees of Separation

Guatemala
capital: **9** Guatemala (City)
ethnic group: **4** Maya **5** Mayan
lake: **6** Izabal **7** Atitlán **9** Petén Itzá
language: **7** Spanish
monetary unit: **7** quetzal
mountain, range: **6** Tacaná **9** Tajumulco **10** Acatenango, Santa María **11** Sierra Madre
neighbor: **6** Belize, Mexico **8** Honduras **10** El Salvador
peninsula: **7** Yucatán
river: **7** Motagua **8** Polochic, Sarstoon **10** Usumacinta

guck
3 bog, goo, mud **4** clay, crud, dirt, glop, goop, mire, ooze, smut **5** filth, slime **7** stickum

gudgeon
3 pin **4** fish **5** pivot **6** socket **7** journal

Gudrun
brother: **6** Gunnar **7** Gunther
father: **5** Hetel
husband: **4** Atli **5** Etzel **6** Sigurd **9** Siegfried

guerrilla
8 partisan **9** irregular
Greek: **6** klepht

guess
4 call, shot, stab **5** fancy, hunch, infer **7** believe, predict, presume, suppose, surmise **8** estimate **9** speculate **10** conjecture, prediction **11** presumption, supposition, speculation

guest
6 caller, lodger, roomer **7** boarder, company, visitor **9** sojourner

guff
3 jaw, lip **4** bosh, sass **5** bilge, cheek, hokum, hooey, mouth, sauce, trash **6** bunkum, drivel, hot air, humbug **7** baloney, hogwash, palaver, twaddle **8** back talk, claptrap, malarkey, nonsense, tommyrot **9** poppycock **10** balderdash **13** horsefeathers

guffaw
6 cackle, hee-haw **7** chortle

guidance
6 advice **7** control, counsel **8** handling **9** direction, oversight **10** leadership, management **11** instruction, supervision

guide
4 dean, guru, help, lead, show **5** doyen, pilot, route, steer, usher **6** beacon, convoy, direct, docent, escort, handle, leader, manage, manual, mentor **7** adviser, conduct, control, marshal, oversee **8** Baedeker, chaperon, director, handbook, instruct, maneuver, navigate, shepherd, signpost **9** accompany, chaperone, conductor, vade mecum, Sacagawea **10** bellwether, compendium, instructor, pathfinder **11** enchiridion

guidebook
6 Fodor's, manual **8** Baedeker, Frommer's, handbook, Michelin **9** itinerary, vade mecum **10** compendium **11** enchiridion

guided missile
3 ABM **4** Hawk, ICBM, IRBM, Nike, Scud, Thor, Zuni **5** Atlas, drone, Snark, Titan **6** Bomarc, cruise, Exocet, Falcon, Navaho, rocket **7** Bullpup, Matador, Polaris, Regulus, Terrier **8** Redstone, Tomahawk **9** Minuteman **10** projectile, Sidewinder

Guiderius
brother: **9** Arviragus
father: **9** Cymbeline

guidon
4 flag **6** banner, burgee, ensign, pennon

guild
4 club **5** lodge, order, union **6** cartel, league **7** society **8** sodality **10** fellowship, fraternity **11** association, brotherhood
medieval: **5** Hansa, Hanse

guile
4 wile **5** craft, fraud **6** deceit **7** cunning **8** artifice, trickery, wiliness **9** deception, duplicity, stratagem **10** cleverness **13** dissimulation

guileful
3 sly **4** foxy, wily **5** cagey, canny, slick **6** artful, astute, crafty, shifty, shrewd, sneaky, tricky **7** cunning, devious **8** indirect, slippery, sneaking **9** designing, insidious, underhand **11** calculating, duplicitous, underhanded

guileless
4 open **5** frank, naive **6** candid, direct, honest **7** genuine, natural, sincere, up-front **8** innocent, truthful **9** ingenuous **10** aboveboard, forthright

guillemot
3 auk **5** murre **7** seabird

guillotine
6 behead **9** decollate **10** decapitate

guilt
4 onus **5** blame, fault, shame **6** regret, stigma **7** offense, remorse **10** contrition **11** culpability **12** self-reproach

guiltless
4 pure **5** clean **6** chaste **8** innocent, virtuous **9** blameless, exemplary, faultless, righteous, stainless **10** immaculate, inculpable

guilty
6 liable, rueful, sinful **7** ashamed, at fault **8** blamable, contrite, culpable, indicted, penitent **9** impeached, regretful **10** answerable, remorseful **11** accountable, blameworthy, responsible

guimpe
6 blouse

Guinea
capital: 7 Conakry
city: 4 Labé 6 Kankan, Kindia
ethnic group: 6 Fulani 7 Malinke
island, island group: 3 Los 5 Tombo
language: 6 French
monetary unit: 5 franc
mountain: 5 Nimba
neighbor: 4 Mali 7 Liberia, Senegal 10 Ivory Coast 11 Sierra Leone 12 Guinea-Bissau
river: 5 Niger 6 Gambia 7 Senegal

Guinea-Bissau
archipelago: 7 Bijagós
capital: 6 Bissau
ethnic group: 6 Fulani 7 Malinke 8 Mandyako
language: 10 Portuguese
monetary unit: 5 franc
neighbor: 6 Guinea 7 Senegal
river: 4 Gêba

guinea fowl
genus: 6 Numida
young: 4 keet

guinea pig
4 cavy 6 rodent
genus: 5 Cavia

Guinevere
court: 7 Camelot
husband: 6 Arthur
lover: 8 Lancelot 9 Launcelot

guise
4 mask 5 cloak, cover, dress, getup 6 aspect, facade, outfit, veneer 7 costume, pretext 8 coloring, pretense 9 posturing, semblance 10 appearance, false front

guitar
accessory: 4 capo
alternative: 3 uke 5 banjo 7 ukelele, ukulele
attachment: 4 capo
horizontal: 10 pedal steel
make: 6 Fender, Gibson, Martin
Mexican: 5 tiple 6 cuatro 8 charango
part: 3 nut, peg 4 fret, neck 5 brace 6 bridge, string 7 peghead
small: 3 uke 7 ukelele, ukulele
tool: 4 pick 8 plectrum

guitarist
American: 3 Guy (Buddy) 4 Byrd (Charlie), Dale (Dick), King (Albert, B. B., Freddie), Page (Jimmy), Pass (Joe), Paul (Les) 5 Berry (Chuck), Ellis (Herb), Isbin (Sharon), Zappa (Frank) 6 Allman (Duane), Atkins (Chet), Cobain (Kurt), Cooder (Ry), Garcia (Jerry), Kessel (Barney), Kottke (Leo), Watson (Doc) 7 Burrell (Kenny), Hendrix (Jimi), Johnson (Robert), Metheny (Pat), Santana (Carlos), Vaughan (Stevie Ray) 8 Van Halen (Eddie) 9 Christian (Charlie), Parkening (Christopher) 10 Montgomery (Wes), Pizzarelli (Bucky, John)
Australian: 8 Williams (John)
British: 4 Beck (Jeff) 5 Bream (Julian) 7 Clapton (Eric) 8 Richards (Keith) 9 Townshend (Pete)
French: 9 Reinhardt (Django)
Italian: 7 Ghiglia (Oscar)
Spanish: 5 Yepes (Narciso) 6 Romero (Celedonio) 7 Segovia (Andrés)

guitarlike instrument
3 uke 4 lute, vina 5 banjo, sitar 7 bandore, pandora, samisen, ukelele, ukulele 8 mandolin, shamisen

gulch
3 gap 4 glen 5 gorge, gully 6 arroyo, canyon, coulee, hollow, ravine, valley 7 couloir

gules
3 red

gulf
3 bay, pit 4 cove 5 abysm, abyss, bayou, bight, chasm, firth, gorge, gulch, inlet 6 cavity, harbor, hollow, ravine, slough 8 crevasse
Adriatic Sea: 6 Venice
Aegean Sea: 7 Saronic 8 Salonika
Africa: 6 Guinea
Arabian Sea: 4 Oman 7 Persian
Australia: 9 Van Diemen 11 Carpentaria
Baltic Sea: 4 Riga 6 Danzig, Gdansk 7 Bothnia, Finland
Bering Sea: 6 Anadyr
Canada: 13 Saint Lawrence
Central America: 7 Fonseca
Djibouti: 6 Tajura 8 Tadjoura
Europe: 7 Bothnia, Gascony 8 Gascogne
Greece: 7 Corinth, Lepanto
Indian Ocean: 4 Aden
Ionian Sea: 4 Arta 7 Taranto
Iran: 7 Arabian
Italy: 5 Genoa
Mediterranean Sea: 5 Sidra, Tunis 8 Valencia 10 Khalij Surt 11 Syrtis Major
Middle East: 7 Persian
New Guinea: 5 Papua 7 McCluer
New Zealand: 7 Hauraki
North America: 6 Mexico
Northwest Territories: 7 Boothia 8 Amundsen 9 Queen Maud
Philippines: 4 Asid 5 Davao, Leyte, Panay, Ragay
Red Sea: 4 Suez 5 Aqaba 11 Aelaniticus
Russia: 8 Sakhalin
Solomon Sea: 4 Huon, Kula 5 Vella
South China Sea: 4 Siam 6 Tonkin 8 Lingayen
Tyrrhenian Sea: 7 Paestum
Yellow Sea: 6 Chihli

Gulf State
5 Texas **7** Alabama, Florida **9** Louisiana **11** Mississippi

gull
3 con, mew, sap **4** bird, dupe, fool, hoax, scam, Xema **5** chump, cozen **6** fleece, pigeon, sea mew, stooge, sucker, take in **7** chicane, fall guy **8** flimflam, hoodwink **9** bamboozle **11** hornswoggle
relative: **4** skua, tern

gullet
3 maw **4** crop, tube **6** dewlap, throat **7** channel **9** esophagus

gullible
4 easy **5** green, naive **8** innocent, trusting **9** believing, credulous **11** susceptible **12** unsuspecting
person: **3** sap **4** dupe **5** chump **6** sucker

Gulliver's Travels
author: **5** Swift (Jonathan)
horses: **10** Houyhnhnms
land: **6** Laputa **8** Lilliput **11** Brobdingnag
people: **6** Yahoos

gully
3 gap **4** glen, wadi, wash **5** gorge, gulch **6** arroyo, coulee, hollow, nullah, ravine, valley **7** couloir

gulp
4 bolt, chug, cram, down, glut, slop, swig, wolf **5** gorge, quaff, scarf, scoff, stuff, swill **6** devour, gobble, guzzle **7** swallow **8** mouthful **11** ingurgitate

gum
4 chew **5** botch **6** bobble, bollix, bungle, chicle, gluten, goof up, tupelo **7** exudate, gingiva, louse up **8** adhesive, mucilage **9** sapodilla **10** eucalyptus
kind: **6** acacia, Arabic, balata, bubble **7** chewing, dextrin
resin: **5** myrrh **7** gamboge **8** ammoniac, galbanum, scammony **9** asafetida **10** asafoetida **12** frankincense

gumbo
3 mud **4** okra, olio, soil, soup, stew **6** creole **7** mélange, mixture
ingredient: **4** crab, duck, filé, okra **5** quail, tasso **6** shrimp **8** crawfish

gummy
5 gooey, pasty **6** cloggy, sticky, viscid **7** viscous **8** adhesive **9** glutinous **10** gelatinous **12** mucilaginous

gumption
5 drive, moxie, nerve, savvy **6** energy **8** industry **10** enterprise, get-up-and-go, initiative

gumshoe
3 cop, tec **4** bull, dick, fuzz, G-man, heat, narc **6** copper, peeler, shamus, sleuth **7** officer **8** flatfoot, hawkshaw, Sherlock **9** detective, policeman **10** bloodhound, private eye **12** investigator

gun
3 gat, rev, rod **4** Colt **5** piece, rev up, rifle, Ruger **6** cannon, Garand, heater, mortar, musket, pistol, roscoe, weapon **7** bazooka, carbine, firearm **8** Browning, howitzer, revolver **9** derringer, Remington **10** Winchester **11** Springfield
antiaircraft: **6** ack-ack, Bofors
Austrian: **5** Glock
British: **4** Bren, Sten
French: **8** arquebus **9** harquebus
German: **5** Luger
Israeli: **3** Uzi
Italian: **7** Beretta
mount: **6** turret
owners' org.: **3** NRA
part: **3** pin **4** bolt, bore, butt, lock **5** sight, stock **6** barrel, breech, hammer, muzzle, safety **7** chamber, trigger **8** cylinder, magazine **9** buttstock
stun: **5** Taser
Swiss: **8** SIG Sauer

gunfire
4 shot **5** blast, salvo **6** volley **7** barrage **9** broadside, discharge, fusillade

gung ho
4 avid, keen **6** ardent, fervid, raring **7** fervent, zealous **9** exuberant **11** impassioned **12** enthusiastic

Guni's father
8 Naphtali

gunk
3 goo **4** crud, glop, gook, goop, muck **5** slime

gunman
5 bravo **6** hit man, killer **7** shooter, torpedo **8** assassin, enforcer

Gunnar
brother-in-law: **6** Sigurd
father: **5** Hetel
sister: **6** Gudrun
wife: **8** Brunhild, Brynhild

gunner
6 sniper **7** shooter **8** marksman, rifleman **9** musketeer **11** infantryman **12** artilleryman

Gunther
sister: **7** Gutrune **9** Kriemhild
slayer: **5** Hagen
uncle: **5** Hagen
wife: **8** Brunhild **9** Brynhilde

gurgle
3 lap **4** flow, purl, wash **5** plash, slosh, swash **6** babble, bubble, burble, ripple

Gurkha knife
5 kukri

gurney
3 cot 9 stretcher

guru
4 sage 5 guide, swami, tutor 6 expert, leader, master, mentor 7 teacher 9 maharishi

gush
3 jet 4 emit, flow, pour, rave, roll, rush, spew, teem, well 5 burst, flood, flush, issue, spout, spurt, surge 6 babble, effuse, sluice, spring, stream 7 cascade, emanate 10 effervesce, outpouring

gushy
5 gooey, mushy, sappy, soppy 6 sloppy, slushy, sticky 7 cloying, maudlin, mawkish, tearful 8 bathetic, effusive 9 schmaltzy, sickening 10 nauseating, saccharine 11 sentimental

gusset
4 fold, gore, tuck 5 armor, plate, pleat 6 insert 7 bracket

gussy up
5 adorn 6 bedeck 7 furbish 8 decorate, renovate

gust
3 fit 4 blow, gale, rush, scud, wind 5 blast, burst, draft, sally, surge, whiff 6 breeze, flurry, squall 7 bluster, delight, flare-up 8 eruption, outburst, paroxysm

gusto
3 vim 4 brio, élan, zeal, zest 5 ardor, heart, oomph, taste, verve 6 fervor, palate, relish, spirit 7 delight, passion 9 enjoyment 10 enthusiasm

gusty
5 blowy, windy 6 breezy 8 blustery

gut
4 draw, loot, silk 5 belly, bowel, dress, empty, tummy 6 bowels, paunch 7 abdomen, ransack, stomach 8 clean out, entrails, visceral 9 intestine 10 disembowel, eviscerate, exenterate, intestines 11 instinctive

Gutenberg, Johannes
city: 5 Mainz
invention: 11 movable type
partner: 4 Fust (Johann)

Guthrie son
4 Arlo

gutless
5 sissy, wimpy, wussy 6 coward, craven, yellow 7 chicken, unmanly 8 cowardly, timorous 9 spineless, spunkless, weak-kneed 11 lily-livered, poltroonish 12 fainthearted 13 pusillanimous

guts
4 grit, sand 5 bowel, heart, moxie, nerve, pluck, spunk, tripe 6 bowels, mettle, spirit 7 bravery, courage, innards, insides, stamina, viscera 8 backbone, entrails, stuffing 9 fortitude, intestine 10 intestines, resolution

gutsy
4 bold 5 brave 6 plucky, spunky 7 valiant 8 intrepid, resolute 10 courageous, determined, mettlesome

gutter
5 chase, ditch, flume, gully 6 furrow, groove, trench, trough 7 channel, conduit
site: 4 eave 5 eaves

guttersnipe
3 bum 4 hobo, scum, waif 5 gamin 6 beggar, gamine, urchin 7 outcast, vagrant, wastrel 8 derelict, riffraff, vagabond 10 ragamuffin

guttural
4 deep 5 gruff, harsh, husky, rough, velar 6 croaky, hoarse 7 grating, palatal, rasping, throaty 8 gravelly
warning: 5 growl

guy
3 cat, joe, lad, man 4 buck, chap, dude, male, rope, stud, wire 5 bloke, brace, chain, guide 6 effigy, fellow, steady 7 support

Guyana
capital: 10 Georgetown
mountain range: 9 Pacaraima
neighbor: 6 Brazil 8 Suriname 9 Venezuela
river: 9 Essequibo

Guy of radio
4 Noir

Guys and Dolls
author: 6 Runyon (Damon)
character: 3 Sky (Masterson) 6 Nathan (Detroit) 8 Adelaide (Miss)
composer: 7 Loesser (Frank)

guzzle
4 belt, chug, gulp, slop, soak, swig, toss, tope 5 booze, drink, quaff, slosh, swill 6 imbibe, tank up, tipple 7 consume, swizzle

Gwendolen's husband
7 Locrine

gym goal
3 abs, bod

gymnast
7 acrobat, athlete, tumbler
American: 4 Hamm (Paul) 5 Rigby (Cathy) 6 Conner (Bart), Miller (Shannon), Retton (Mary Lou), Thomas (Kurt)
Romanian: 8 Comaneci (Nadia)
Russian: 3 Kim (Nelly) 6 Korbut (Olga)
Ukrainian: 5 Baiul (Oksana)

gymnastics
5 sport 8 exercise, tumbling 9 athletics 10 acrobatics 12 calisthenics
apparatus: 3 bar 4 bars, beam, buck, ring, rope 5 horse 11 balance beam
feat: 3 kip 4 flip 5 vault 6 tumble 9 handstand, headstand 10 handspring, headspring, somersault

gyp
3 con **4** bilk, dupe, fake, hoax, rook, scam, sham **5** bunco, cheat, cozen, cross, fraud, spoof, trick **6** chisel, chouse, con man, diddle, fleece, humbug, rip-off, rip off **7** cheater, deceive, defraud, diddler, finagle, sharper, swindle **8** chiseler, hoodwink, swindler **9** bamboozle, defrauder, imposture, trickster **10** mountebank **11** double-cross, flimflammer **12** double-dealer

gypsum
7 drywall, mineral **8** selenite **9** alabaster, wallboard

gypsy
3 Rom **5** caird, nomad, rover **6** roamer, Romany, tinker **7** drifter, tzigane **8** Bohemian, vagabond, wanderer
Spanish: 6 gitano

gyrate
4 coil, purl, roll, spin, turn, wind **5** orbit, twirl, whirl **6** circle, rotate **7** revolve **9** oscillate, pirouette

gyration
4 coil, turn **5** cycle, orbit, twirl, wheel, whirl **6** circle **7** circuit, turning **8** rotation **10** revolution

gyre
4 coil, gird, ring, spin, wind **5** cycle, orbit, twirl, whirl **6** circle, girdle, rotate, spiral, vortex **7** circuit, revolve **8** rotation **10** revolution

gyro
8 sandwich
bread: 4 pita

gyve
4 bond, iron **5** chain **6** fetter **7** shackle **8** restrain **9** restraint

H

Habakkuk
7 prophet

habeas corpus
4 writ **5** right **7** mandate

habiliments
4 gear **5** dress **6** attire, outfit **7** apparel, clothes **8** clothing **9** apparatus, equipment, trappings

habilitate
5 dress **6** clothe **7** qualify

habit
3 rut **4** bent, form, garb, mode, rote, wont **5** dress, quirk, style, usage **6** attire, clothe, custom, groove, manner, outfit **7** costume, fashion, pattern, routine **8** behavior, clothing, practice, tendency **9** addiction, mannerism **10** consuetude, convention, proclivity **11** disposition, inclination
riding: 8 jodhpurs
wearer: 3 nun **5** rider

habitable
7 livable

habitant
5 liver **7** denizen, dweller, resider **8** occupant, resident

habitat
4 home, site, turf **5** abode, haunt, range **6** locale, milieu **7** terrain **8** domicile **9** territory **11** environment **12** surroundings

habitation
3 pad **4** digs, flat, home, nest, seat **5** abode, haunt, haven, house, place, roost **7** housing, lodging, tenancy **8** domicile, dwelling, lodgment, quarters **9** homestead, residence, residency **10** settlement

habitual
3 set **5** fixed, usual **6** addict, inborn, native, normal, steady, wonted **7** chronic, regular, routine, settled **8** accepted, addicted, constant, familiar, frequent, inherent **9** automatic, confirmed, continual, customary, ingrained **10** accustomed, inveterate, persistent **11** established, instinctive, involuntary

habitually
8 commonly, normally, wontedly **9** generally, regularly, routinely **10** ordinarily **11** customarily **12** consistently

habituate (to)
4 bear **5** enure, inure, train **6** addict, adjust, endure, harden, school, season, take to **7** break in, prepare, support **8** accustom, tolerate **9** acclimate, condition **11** familiarize

habitué
3 fan **4** buff, user **5** hound, lover **6** addict, patron **7** denizen, devotee, haunter **8** adherent, customer **10** enthusiast, frequenter

hacienda
4 farm **5** ranch, villa **6** estate, quinta **8** estancia **10** plantation

hack
3 cab, cut, hew, try, vex **4** blow, chip, chop, dull, gash, grub, jade, loaf, mean, ride, taxi **5** annoy, cabby, cough, grind, horse, petty, sever, usual

6 cabbie, cliché, drudge, lackey, mangle, stroke, writer **7** clichéd, machine, plodder, taxicab, trivial **8** inferior, low-grade, mediocre, tolerate **9** cab-driver, mercenary, potboiler **10** second-rate, uninspired

hacker
4 geek, nerd **6** duffer

hackney
3 cab **4** taxi **5** horse **6** jitney **7** taxicab **8** carriage

hackneyed
4 dull, worn **5** banal, corny, stale, stock, tired, trite **6** cliché, common, old hat, old saw **7** archaic, clichéd, worn-out **8** everyday, obsolete, outdated, overused, outmoded, timeworn **9** out-of-date **10** antiquated, overworked, pedestrian

Hadad
father: **5** Bedad **7** Ishmael
victim: **6** Midian

haddock, e.g.
5 scrod

Hades
4 Hell **5** Pluto, Sheol **6** blazes, Tophet **7** Gehenna, inferno **8** Tartarus **9** perdition **10** underworld **11** netherworld
Babylonian: **5** Aralu
entrance: **7** Avernus
god: **3** Dis **5** Orcus, Pluto
goddess: **10** Persephone
guard: **8** Cerberus
lake: **7** Avernus
passage: **6** Erebus **8** Tartarus
river: **4** Styx **5** Lethe **7** Acheron, Cocytus **10** Phlegethon

haft
4 grip, hilt, knob **5** helve **6** handle

hag
3 hex **5** biddy, crone, harpy, shrew, vixen, witch **6** beldam, gorgon, virago **7** beldame **8** battle-ax, fishwife, harridan, slattern **9** hobgoblin

Hagar
9 concubine
lover: **7** Abraham
rival: **5** Sarah, Sarai
son: **7** Ishmael

Hägar the Horrible
daughter: **4** Honi
wife: **5** Helga

Hagen
father: **8** Alberich
nephew: **7** Gunther
slayer: **9** Kriemhild
victim: **9** Siegfried

Hagen of Broadway
3 Uta

haggard
3 wan **4** hawk, lank, pale, thin, weak, wild, worn **5** ashen, drawn, faded, gaunt, tired **6** fagged, pallid, skinny, wasted **7** angular, pinched, scraggy, scrawny, starved, wearied, wizened **8** careworn, fatigued, shrunken, worn-down **9** emaciated, exhausted

Haggard, H. Rider
novel: **3** She **17** King Solomon's Mines

Haggith
husband: **5** David
son: **8** Adonijah

haggle
4 deal **5** argue, cavil, trade **6** barter, bicker, dicker **7** bargain, chaffer, dispute, quibble, stickle, wrangle **8** squabble **10** horse-trade

hagiography subject
5 saint

hail
3 ave **4** ahoy, call **5** greet, salvo, shout, storm **6** accost, call to, holler, praise, salute, shower, volley **7** acclaim, address, applaud, barrage, call out, commend **8** greeting **9** broadside, cannonade, fusillade, originate, recommend **10** salutation **11** acclamation, bombardment

Haile Selassie
9 Ras Tafari
follower: **5** Rasta **11** Rastafarian
nation: **8** Ethiopia

hair
3 bit, jot **4** hint, mite, wool **5** cilia (plural), pilus, trace **6** cilium, trifle **7** eyelash, whisker **8** fraction, particle
animal: **3** fur **4** mane, pelt, wool **8** vibrissa **9** vibrissae (plural)
braid: **5** plait, queue **7** pigtail
clip: **8** barrette
coarse: **7** bristle
coloring: **3** dye **5** henna
combining form: **3** pil **4** pili, pilo **5** trich **6** tricho
covering of: **3** wig
dressing: **3** gel **6** mousse **6** pomade **7** pomatum **8** macassar **12** brilliantine
facial: **5** beard, patch **6** goatee **7** Vandyke **8** mustache, whiskers **9** burnsides, handlebar, moustache, sideburns, soul patch **11** mutton-chops
fine: **6** lanugo
fringe: **5** bangs
head of: **9** chevelure
holder: **5** snood
knot: **3** bun
lock of: **4** curl **5** tress **7** cowlick
loose roll: **4** pouf
matted: **6** dreads **10** dreadlocks

net: **5** snood
ornament: **7** topknot
preparation: **3** gel **6** mousse, pomade **12** brilliantine
relating to: **5** pilar
root: **6** fibril
set: **4** perm
stiff: **4** seta **5** setae (plural)
tangled: **7** elflock
tuft of: **5** quiff **7** cowlick, fetlock
unruly: **3** mop
without: **4** bald

haircutter
6 barber **7** stylist **8** coiffeur **9** coiffeuse

hairdo
3 bob, bun, 'fro **4** Afro, coif, flip, part, perm, pomp, shag, trim, updo **5** bangs, braid, butch, taper, wedge **6** Caesar, dreads, Mohawk, mullet **7** beehive, bowl cut, buzz cut, chignon, crew cut, flattop, pageboy, pigtail, tonsure **8** bouffant, brush cut, coiffure, cornrows, ducktail, pigtails, ponytail, razor cut **9** permanent, pompadour **10** dreadlocks

hairdresser
see **haircutter**

hair-raising
5 eerie, scary **6** spooky **7** amazing, awesome **8** exciting **9** thrilling **10** terrifying **11** astonishing, frightening

hairsplitting
7 finicky **8** exacting **9** quibbling **10** nit-picking **12** overcritical **13** hypercritical

hairstyle
see **hairdo**

hairy
5 bushy, downy, furry, fuzzy, nappy, risky, rough **6** chancy, fleecy, fluffy, shaggy, tufted, woolly **7** bristly, hirsute, scraggy, unshorn, villous **8** perilous, strigose **9** dangerous, difficult, hazardous, tomentose, whiskered **11** treacherous
son: **4** Esau

Haiti
capital: **12** Port-au-Prince
island: **7** Tortuga **10** Hispaniola
language: **6** Creole, French
leader: **8** Aristide (Jean-Bertrand), Duvalier (François, Jean-Claude)
location: **10** West Indies
monetary unit: **6** gourde
passage: **8** Windward
peninsula: **7** Tiburon
river: **10** Artibonite

hajj
5 Umrah **10** pilgrimage
site: **4** Mina **5** Mecca **6** Arafat **10** Muzdalifah

hake
4 fish, ling **7** codling, whiting
relative: **3** cod

halcyon
4 calm **5** happy, lucky, quiet, still **6** golden, hushed, placid, serene **8** affluent, peaceful, tranquil **9** favorable **10** auspicious, felicitous, kingfisher, prosperous, untroubled

Halcyone
father: **6** Aeolus
husband: **4** Ceyx

hale
3 fit **4** sane, well **5** sound, stout **6** hearty, robust **7** healthy **8** vigorous **9** strapping, wholesome

Hale character
5 Nolan (Philip)

Haley epic
5 Roots

half
6 moiety
prefix: **4** demi, hemi, semi

half of an African fly
3 tse

half-baked
8 slapdash, slipshod **9** imbecilic, senseless, underdone **11** harebrained, impractical, nonsensical, unrealistic **12** ill-conceived, shortsighted **13** irresponsible

half-cocked
4 rash **5** brash **8** reckless **9** foolhardy, imprudent, impulsive, misguided, premature **10** incautious, unprepared **11** precipitate

halfhearted
4 weak **5** tepid **6** feeble **8** lukewarm **12** uninterested

half-moon
4 arch **5** curve **6** lunule **8** crescent

halfway
3 mid **6** center, medial, median, middle **7** midmost **10** centermost **11** equidistant **12** intermediate

half-wit
4 boob, dolt, dope, fool **5** dunce, idiot, moron **6** cretin **8** imbecile **9** blockhead, simpleton

half-witted
4 dull, slow **7** moronic **8** backward, imbecile **9** imbecilic **12** feebleminded, simpleminded

hall
4 dorm **5** foyer, lobby **6** lyceum **7** passage **8** corridor **9** dormitory **10** auditorium, passageway
exhibition: **5** salon
Salvation Army: **7** citadel

Halley's ___
5 comet

hallmark
4 logo, seal, sign **5** badge, stamp, trait **6** device, emblem, symbol, virtue **7** feature, imprint, quality **8** logotype **9** attribute **11** distinction

hallow
5 bless, honor **6** anoint, devote, revere **8** dedicate, make holy, sanctify, venerate **10** consecrate

hallowed
4 holy **6** sacred

hallucination
4 trip **5** ghost **6** mirage, vision, wraith **7** fantasy, phantom, specter, spectre **8** delusion, illusion, phantasm **10** apparition **11** fata morgana, ignis fatuus

hallucinogen
3 LSD, STP **6** peyote **9** mescaline **10** psilocybin **11** scopolamine

halo
4 aura, nimb **5** nimbi (plural) **6** corona, nimbus **7** aureole

halogen
6 iodine **7** bromine, element **8** astatine, chlorine, fluorine

halt
3 bar, end **4** lame, limp, quit, stay, stop **5** avast, cease, check, close, hitch, lapse, stall, waver **6** arrest, desist, dither, falter, finish, pull up **7** adjourn, bring up, stagger, suspend **8** conclude, cut short, hesitate, knock off, leave off **9** determine, interrupt, terminate, vacillate **10** standstill **11** discontinue

halter
3 bit **4** hang, rope **5** noose **6** blouse, bridle, hamper **8** restrain, trammels **9** hackamore, headstall, restraint

halvah base
6 sesame

ham
4 hock **5** bacon, emote, thigh **7** buttock, overact **8** overplay, strutter **10** scene-eater **13** exhibitionist

Ham
brother: **4** Shem **7** Japheth
father: **4** Noah
son: **4** Cush, Phut **6** Canaan **7** Mizraim

Haman's adversary
6 Esther

Hamburg's river
4 Elbe

ham-handed
5 inept **6** clumsy, gauche **8** bumbling **9** all thumbs, graceless, inelegant, maladroit **10** blundering, unskillful

Hamilcar
conquest: **5** Spain
home: **8** Carthage
son: **8** Hannibal
surname: **5** Barca

hamlet
4 dorp **7** village
Irish, Scottish: **7** clachan

Hamlet
author: **11** Shakespeare (William)
beloved: **7** Ophelia
castle: **8** Elsinore
country: **7** Denmark
friend: **7** Horatio
mother: **8** Gertrude
slayer: **7** Laertes
uncle: **8** Claudius
victim: **7** Laertes **8** Claudius, Polonius

Hamlet, The
author: **8** Faulkner (William)
family: **6** Snopes

hammer
4 drub, maul, peen **5** forge, gavel, pound **6** batter, mallet, pummel, sledge **7** malleus **8** lambaste
end: **4** peen
type: **3** air **4** claw, maul **6** sledge **8** ball-peen **9** pneumatic

hammerhead
4 dolt, dope, fool **5** dunce, idiot, shark **8** clodpoll, numskull **9** numbskull **10** thickskull

Hammerin' Hank
5 Aaron

hammer's other head, sometimes
4 peen

hammer-wielding deity
4 Thor

Hamm of soccer
3 Mia

hamper
3 bin, tie **4** balk, curb, snag **5** block, check, cramp, crimp, leash, limit **6** baffle, basket, fetter, hinder, hobble, hold up, impede, retard, stymie, thwart **7** inhibit, manacle, pannier, prevent, trammel **8** encumber, handicap, obstacle, obstruct, restrain, restrict, slow down **9** frustrate

hamstring
4 lame **6** muscle, tendon **7** cripple, disable **10** immobilize **12** incapacitate

Hamutal
father: **8** Jeremiah
husband: **6** Josiah
son: **8** Jehoahaz, Zedekiah

hand
3 aid, paw **4** fist, mitt, pass **5** manus **6** script, worker **7** deliver, dish out, laborer, workman **8** employee, transfer **10** assistance, penmanship **11** calligraphy, chirography

clenched: **4** fist
combining form: **4** chir **5** chiro
counting zero: **8** baccarat
covering: **5** glove **6** mitten
down: **8** bequeath
gesture: **5** mudra
on hip: **6** akimbo
part: **4** palm **5** thumb **6** finger
poker: **5** flush **8** straight **9** full house
protector: **5** glove **7** gantlet **8** gauntlet

handbag
4 grip **5** purse **6** clutch **8** reticule, suitcase **10** pocketbook

handbill
5 flier, flyer **6** poster **7** affiche, leaflet, placard **8** circular

handbook
5 guide **6** manual **8** Baedeker **9** vade mecum **10** compendium **11** enchiridion
religious: **9** catechism

handcuff
6 fetter **7** manacle, shackle
British: **7** darbies (plural)

hand down
4 will **6** bestow, pass on **7** deliver **8** bequeath, transmit

Handel, George Frideric
aria: **5** Largo
birthplace: **5** Halle **7** Germany
opera: **4** Nero **5** Serse **6** Admeto, Alcina, Almira, Ottone, Xerxes **7** Arminio, Orlando, Rinaldo, Rodrigo **8** Berenice **9** Agrippina, Ariodante **12** Giulio Cesare, Julius Caesar
oratorio: **4** Saul **6** Esther, Joshua, Samson, Semele **7** Athalia, Deborah, Jephtha, Messiah, Solomon **8** Theodora

handgun
3 gat, rod **6** heater, pistol, roscoe **8** revolver **9** derringer

handicap
4 edge, load, odds **6** burden, hamper, hinder, impede **8** drawback, encumber, restrict **9** advantage, allowance, detriment, head start, hindrance **10** disability, limitation **11** encumbrance **12** disadvantage

handicraft
5 skill **8** artefact, artifact

hand in
6 submit, tender **7** deliver, present

handkerchief
5 hanky **6** hankie **7** bandana **8** bandanna, mouchoir **9** accessory

handle
3 paw, use **4** ansa, feel, grip, haft, hilt, knob, name, test **5** crank, see to, touch, trade, treat, wield **6** manage **7** control, moniker, operate **8** deal with, doorknob, exercise, maneuver, nickname **10** manipulate
scythe: **5** snath **6** snathe

handling
4 care **6** charge **9** packaging, treatment
partner: **8** shipping

handout
4 alms, dole **6** relief **7** charity **8** donation

hand out
4 give, mete **6** bestow, donate **7** deliver, present, provide **8** disburse, dispense, give away **10** administer, distribute

hand over
4 cede, feed, give **5** leave, yield **6** commit, donate, fork up, give up, supply **7** commend, confide, consign, deliver, entrust, present **8** dispense, give back, relegate, transfer **9** deliver up, surrender **10** relinquish

handrail
8 banister

handsome
4 buff, cute, fair **5** hunky, noble **6** comely **7** dashing **10** attractive **11** good-looking
man: **4** hunk, stud **6** Adonis **7** demigod

handspring
6 tumble
lateral: **9** cartwheel

handwriting
6 script **8** longhand **10** autography, manuscript, penmanship **11** calligraphy, chirography, copperplate
bad: **10** cacography
study of: **10** graphology

handy
4 able, deft, near, yare **5** adept, close, utile **6** adroit, clever, nearby, nimble, useful **7** close-by, skilled **8** adjacent, skillful **9** adaptable, available, dexterous **10** accessible, convenient, proficient **11** practicable, within reach

handyman
6 helper **7** go-to guy **8** factotum

hang
3 jut, sag **4** hook, idle, loll **5** cling, drape, droop, float, hoist, knack, lynch, sling, swing **6** dangle, depend **7** suspend
back: **3** lag **4** drag, poke **5** trail **6** dawdle, schlep **7** schlepp **8** straggle
loosely: **3** sag **6** dangle

hang around
4 stay, wait **5** abide, dally, tarry **6** dawdle, linger, loiter **7** goof off **8** frequent

hangdog
3 sad **4** blue, glum **5** cowed **6** guilty **7** abashed, ashamed, pitiful, unhappy **8** dejected, sheepish **9** chagrined, depressed **11** embarrassed

hanger-on
5 leech 6 sponge, sucker 7 sponger 8 barnacle, follower, parasite 9 sycophant 10 freeloader 11 bloodsucker

hang fire
4 pend, wait 5 pause

hanging
5 arras, slope 7 curtain, drapery, pendant, pendent 8 covering, tapestry 9 declivity, execution, pendulous, suspended

Hanging Gardens site
7 Babylon

hang on
4 grip 5 cling, grasp 6 clutch, endure, remain 7 persist, survive 8 continue, hold fast 9 persevere

hang out
4 idle, loaf 5 chill, dally, relax 6 loiter, lounge 7 goof off

hangout
5 haunt, joint 6 resort 7 purlieu, retreat 10 rendezvous 12 watering hole

hang up
4 mire, snag 5 delay 6 detain, impede, retard 7 bog down, set back, suspend 8 slow down

hang-up
5 block 7 dilemma, problem 9 obsession 10 difficulty, inhibition

hank
4 clip, coil, loop, ring 6 bundle

hanker
3 yen 4 ache, itch, long, lust, want, wish 5 covet, crave, yearn 6 desire, hunger, thirst

hankering
3 yen 4 ache, itch, lust, urge 5 ardor 6 desire, hunger, pining, thirst 7 craving, longing, passion 8 appetite, yearning

Hank of baseball
5 Aaron

hanky-panky
5 fraud, trick 7 chicane 8 mischief, trickery 9 chicanery, dalliance, deception 13 double-dealing, sharp practice

Hannibal
defeat: 4 Zama
father: 8 Hamilcar
home: 8 Carthage
surname: 5 Barca
vanquisher: 6 Scipio
victory: 6 Cannae

Han of Star Wars
4 Solo

Hansa
5 guild 6 league

Hans Brinker author
5 Dodge (Mary Mapes)

Hanseatic League city
6 Bremen, Lübeck, Wismar 7 Cologne, Hamburg, Rostock

Hänsel und Gretel composer
11 Humperdinck (Engelbert)

Hansen's disease
7 leprosy

Han's love
4 Leia

hansom
3 cab 5 coach 8 carriage

haole
5 white 9 Caucasian

haphazard
6 casual, chance, random 7 aimless 8 at random, careless, slipshod 9 desultory, hit-or-miss, irregular, unplanned 10 accidental, willy-nilly 11 unorganized 12 adventitious, unsystematic 13 helter-skelter

hapless
4 poor 6 woeful 7 unhappy, unlucky 8 ill-fated, wretched 9 miserable 10 ill-starred 11 star-crossed, unfortunate

happen
4 pass 5 occur 6 befall, betide 7 develop, fall out, turn out 8 bechance 9 transpire
again: 5 recur
next: 5 ensue 6 follow
together: 6 concur 8 coincide

happening
3 new 5 event, scene, thing 7 episode 8 incident, occasion 9 adventure 10 experience, occurrence, phenomenon 11 fashionable 12 circumstance

happen on
4 find 8 bump into, discover

happenstance
5 event 6 chance 8 incident, occasion 9 condition, situation 11 coincidence

happiness
3 joy 4 glee 5 bliss, cheer, mirth 6 gaiety 7 aptness, content, delight, elation, jollity 8 felicity, gladness, pleasure 9 enjoyment, well-being 11 contentment 12 satisfaction

happy
4 glad 5 jolly, lucky, merry 6 joyful, joyous, upbeat 7 blessed, content, pleased 8 friendly, jubilant 9 contented, favorable, satisfied 12 enthusiastic, lighthearted

Happy Days
character: 5 Chuck 6 Chachi, Fonzie, Howard, Joanie, Marion, Potsie, Richie

family: **10** Cunningham
site: **9** Milwaukee
star: **4** Baio (Scott), Ross (Marion) **5** Moran (Erin) **6** Bosley (Tom), Howard (Ron) **7** Winkler (Henry) **8** O'Herlihy (Gavan), Williams (Anson)

happy-go-lucky
4 easy **6** blithe, breezy, casual **8** carefree, careless, cheerful, heedless, laid-back, reckless **9** easygoing, unworried **10** insouciant, nonchalant **11** unconcerned **12** devil-may-care, lighthearted

hara-kiri
7 seppuku, suicide **8** felo-de-se

Haran
brother: **7** Abraham
daughter: **5** Iscah **6** Milcah
father: **5** Terah **6** Shimei
son: **3** Lot

harangue
4 rant, rave **5** orate, spiel **6** exhort, hassle, tirade **7** declaim, lecture, oration **8** bloviate, diatribe, jeremiad **9** discourse, philippic **11** declamation, exhortation

harass
3 irk, vex **4** bait, raid, ride **5** annoy, beset, bully, chivy, harry, hound, tease, worry **6** badger, chivvy, hassle, heckle, hector, molest, pester, plague, stress **7** bedevil, besiege, exhaust, fatigue, torment, trouble **8** bullyrag, distress **9** beleaguer, persecute

harbinger
4 omen, sign **5** augur **6** augury, herald **7** apostle, portent **9** messenger, precursor **10** forerunner, indication

harbor
3 bay **4** cove, port **5** haven, inlet, lodge, put up **6** billet, refuge, shield, take in **7** nurture, protect, seaport, shelter **9** anchorage, safeguard, sanctuary
Hawaii: **5** Pearl

hard
4 firm, iron **5** cruel, harsh, solid, stern, tough **6** brutal, knotty, packed, rugged, tiring, trying **7** arduous, callous, onerous **8** absolute, concrete, exacting, granitic, grinding, indurate, pitiless, rigorous **9** demanding, difficult, fatiguing, intensely, intensive, laborious, unfeeling **10** adamantine, exhausting, spirituous, thoroughly, vigorously **11** complicated, intensively, intractable, troublesome, unrelenting, unremitting **12** backbreaking
cover: **5** crust
to please: **7** finicky

hard-boiled
4 grim **5** rough, stoic, tough **6** coarse **7** callous **8** seasoned **9** impassive, pragmatic, unfeeling **11** insensitive, unemotional **12** stonyhearted, thick-skinned **13** unsympathetic
crime genre: **4** noir

harden
3 dry, set **5** enure, inure, steel **6** anneal, freeze, ossify, season, temper **7** calcify, compact, congeal, densify, lithify, petrify, stiffen, toughen **8** solidify **9** acclimate, fossilize, habituate **10** strengthen

hardfisted
4 mean **5** close, tight **6** stingy, strict **13** penny-pinching

hardheaded
5 sober, tough **6** mulish, shrewd **7** willful **8** obdurate, perverse, stubborn **9** obstinate, practical, pragmatic, realistic **10** determined **11** down-to-earth, intractable

hardhearted
4 cold **5** stony **8** pitiless, uncaring **9** merciless, unfeeling

hard-hitting
6 strong **8** emphatic, forceful, powerful **9** effective

hardihood
3 pep **4** gall, grit, guts **5** cheek, moxie, nerve, pluck, vigor **6** daring **7** courage **8** audacity, boldness, temerity **9** assurance, brashness, cockiness, fortitude, impudence, insolence **10** brazenness, robustness

hard-line
4 firm **5** fixed, rigid, tough **8** obdurate **9** obstinate, unbending **10** inflexible, unyielding **11** stiff-necked **12** intransigent

hardness
5 rigor **7** density **8** rigidity, severity **10** difficulty, resistance
scale: **4** Mohs'

hardscrabble
6 barren **8** marginal **9** infertile, unbearing, unfertile **12** impoverished, unproductive

hardship
3 woe **4** need, toil **5** rigor, trial **6** burden **7** travail **8** asperity, distress, drudgery **9** adversity, privation, suffering **10** affliction, difficulty, discomfort, misfortune **11** tribulation

Hard Times author
7 Dickens (Charles)

hard to find
4 rare **6** scarce

hard up
4 poor **5** broke, needy **6** bad off **8** beggared, bankrupt, deprived, indigent, strapped **9** desperate, destitute, penniless **10** down-and-out **11** necessitous **12** impoverished

hardwood
3 ash, oak **4** teak **5** beech, birch, maple **6** cherry, poplar

hardy
4 bold, hale **5** brave, tough **6** daring, robust, rugged, strong **7** healthy **8** intrepid, resolute **9** audacious

Hardy, Thomas
character: **3** Sue (Bridehead) **4** Alec (D'Urberville), Clym (Yeobright), Jude (Fawley), Tess (Durbeyfield) **5** Angel (Clare) **7** Gabriel (Oak) **8** Arabella (Donn), Eustacia (Vye), Henchard (Michael) **9** Bathsheba (Everdene)
novel: **11** Woodlanders (The) **14** Jude the Obscure **17** Return of the Native (The) **19** Mayor of Casterbridge (The) **21** Tess of the D'Urbervilles **22** Far from the Madding Crowd
setting: **6** Wessex

Hardy Boys
author: **5** Dixon (Franklin W.) **9** McFarlane (Leslie)
character: **3** Joe **4** Biff (Hooper), Chet (Morton), Iole **5** Frank, Laura **6** Callie, Fenton **12** Aunt Gertrude
city: **7** Bayport
jalopy: **5** Queen
motorboat: **6** Napoli, Sleuth

hare
5 lapin **6** rabbit
female: **3** doe
genus: **5** Lepus
male: **4** buck
tail: **4** scut
young: **7** leveret

harebrained
5 crazy, loony, silly, wacky **6** absurd, insane, stupid **7** asinine, foolish **9** frivolous **10** ridiculous **12** preposterous

harem
5 serai **6** zenana **8** seraglio
attendant: **6** eunuch
concubine: **8** odalisc, odalisk **9** odalisque
room: **3** oda

haricot
3 pod **4** bean **10** kidney bean

hark
4 hear, heed, mind, note **6** attend, listen, notice

harlequin
5 clown, joker **6** jester, mottle **7** buffoon **9** prankster

Harlequin
beloved: **9** Columbine
rival: **7** Pierrot

harm
3 mar **4** hurt, maim, ruin **5** abuse, spoil, wound, wrong **6** damage, ill-use, impair, injure, injury, misuse, molest **7** tarnish **8** ill-treat, maltreat, mischief, mistreat **9** undermine **10** disservice, misfortune

harmful
3 bad **4** evil **5** risky, toxic **6** malign, unsafe **7** noisome, noxious **8** damaging **9** dangerous, hazardous, injurious, malignant, unhealthy **10** pernicious **11** deleterious, detrimental, unhealthful

harmless
4 safe **6** benign **8** innocent, nontoxic **9** innocuous **11** inoffensive

Harmonia
daughter: **3** Ino **5** Agave **6** Semele **7** Autonoë
father: **4** Ares, Mars
husband: **6** Cadmus
mother: **5** Venus **9** Aphrodite
son: **9** Polydorus

harmonious
5 sweet **7** chiming, chordal, musical, pacific **8** blending, friendly, in accord, peaceful, pleasing **9** agreeable, congenial, congruous, consonant, en rapport, symphonic **10** compatible, concordant **11** cooperative, symmetrical, sympathetic

harmonize
3 fit **4** jibe, sing **5** agree, blend, match **6** accord, attune **7** arrange, concert, conform **8** coincide, dovetail **9** integrate **10** coordinate, correspond, synthesize **11** orchestrate

harmony
4 sync **5** grace, order, peace, unity **6** accord **7** balance, concert, concord, oneness, rapport **8** affinity, sonority, symmetry **9** agreement, congruity, polyphony **10** accordance, concinnity, conformity, consonance, proportion **11** concordance, consistency, cooperation
lack of: **7** discord **10** dissonance
of movement: **8** eurythmy

harness
4 curb, gear, yoke **5** hitch, leash **6** bridle, tackle **7** utilize **11** domesticate
part: **3** bit **4** rein **5** girth, trace **6** collar **7** blinder, crupper **9** bellyband, breeching, checkrein **12** breast collar
ring: **6** terret

harp
4 lyre **9** harmonica
ancient: **6** trigon
Celtic: **5** telyn **8** clarsach **10** clairseach
Greek: **7** cithara, kithara
Japanese: **4** koto

Harper Valley ____
3 PTA

harpsichord
7 cembalo **8** clavecin
relative: **5** piano **10** clavichord, pianoforte

harpsichordist
American: **6** Fuller (Albert, David), Kipnis (Igor), Newman (Anthony) **7** Marlowe (Sylvia), Pinkham (Daniel), Valenti (Fernando) **11** Kirkpatrick (Ralph)
Dutch: **9** Leonhardt (Gustav)
English: **7** Malcolm (George), Pinnock (Trevor)
German: **7** Richter (Karl)
Italian: **7** Sgrizzi (Luciano)
Polish: **9** Landowska (Wanda)

harpy
3 nag **5** leech, scold, shrew, vixen **6** virago **8** fishwife, harridan **9** termagant

Harpy
5 Aello **7** Celaeno, Ocypete
father: **7** Thaumas
mother: **7** Electra
sister: **4** Iris

harridan
3 hag **4** fury **5** biddy, harpy, shrew, vixen, witch **6** dragon, gorgon, ogress, virago **7** hellcat **8** battle-ax, fishwife **9** battle-axe, termagant

harrier
3 dog **4** hawk **6** hector, runner **10** persecutor

Harris, Joel Chandler
character: **7** Brer Fox **8** Brer Bear **10** Brer Rabbit
narrator: **10** Uncle Remus

Harrison Ford role
4 Solo (Han)

harrow
3 try, vex **4** bait, rack **5** devil, tease **6** badger, heckle, hector, needle, pester, suffer **7** afflict, bedevil, torment, torture, trouble **8** distress, irritate **9** cultivate **10** excruciate

Harrow rival
4 Eton

harry
3 dog, irk, vex **4** gnaw, raid, ride, sack **5** annoy, tease, upset, worry **6** attack, badger, harass, hassle, maraud, pester, plague, ravage **7** assault, bedevil, despoil, perturb, pillage, plunder, torment **8** desolate, maltreat **9** beleaguer, depredate

Harry Potter character
5 Draco (Malfoy), Snape (Severus) **6** Sirius (Black) **7** Minerva (McGonagall), Neville (Longbottom), Weasley (Audrey, Molly, Percy, Ron) **8** Hermione (Granger) **9** Voldemort **10** Dumbledore (Albus)

harsh
5 cruel, gruff, rough, stern **6** biting, brutal, coarse, severe, uneven, unkind **7** austere, caustic, grating, jarring, painful, pungent, raucous, stubbly **8** exacting, grinding, jangling, scraping, scratchy, strident, unsmooth **9** dissonant, inclement **10** discordant, irritating, unpleasant

harshness
8 asperity **9** roughness

hart
4 deer, stag **7** red deer
mate: **4** hind

hartebeest
4 tora **8** antelope
family: **7** Bovidae

Harte story
17 Luck of Roaring Camp (The) **19** Outcasts of Poker Flat (The)

Hartford
college: **7** Trinity
specialty: **9** insurance

Hart, Moss
autobiography: **6** Act One
collaborator: **7** Kaufman (George S.)
musical: **13** Lady in the Dark
play: **15** Once in a Lifetime **18** Man Who Came to Dinner (The) **20** You Can't Take It with You

haruspex
4 seer **5** augur **7** diviner, prophet **8** foreseer **9** predictor **10** forecaster, foreteller, soothsayer

harvest
4 crop, pick, reap **5** amass, cache, glean, hoard, stash, yield **6** garner, gather **7** collect, reaping, store up, vintage **8** ingather, squirrel, stow away **9** garnering, gathering
bug: **4** mite **7** chigger
fly: **6** cicada
festival: **6** Lammas **7** Cerelia **10** Michaelmas **12** Thanksgiving
god, goddess: **3** Ops **5** Ceres **6** Consus **7** Demeter

harvester
7 gleaner
grain: **6** binder, header
of grapes: **8** vintager

Harvey
5 pooka **6** rabbit
author: **5** Chase (Mary)
character: **6** Elwood (P. Dowd)

hash
4 chop, mess, stew **5** botch, mince, mix-up **6** jumble, medley, muddle, review **7** clutter, confuse, mélange, mixture **8** consider, shambles **9** patchwork **10** assortment, hodgepodge, miscellany

hash house
4 café **5** diner **6** bistro, eatery **7** beanery, pit stop **10** coffee shop **11** greasy spoon **12** luncheonette

hashish
5 bhang, ganja 6 charas 8 cannabis, narcotic
plant: 4 hemp

hash out
6 review 7 discuss 8 talk over 9 talk about

hasp
5 catch 6 fasten 8 fastener 9 fastening

hassle
3 row 4 beef, to-do 5 annoy, argue, brawl, fight, run-in 6 bicker, clamor, harass, hubbub, tumult, uproar 7 dispute, problem, quarrel, rhubarb, trouble, turmoil, wrangle 8 argument, squabble, struggle 9 commotion 11 altercation, controversy

hassock
4 pouf 7 cushion, kneeler, ottoman 9 footstool

haste
3 hie, run 4 dash, rush 5 hurry, speed 6 barrel, bustle, flurry, hustle 7 beeline, hotfoot 8 celerity, dispatch, rapidity, velocity 9 fleetness, quickness, swiftness 10 speediness 11 hurriedness, impetuosity

hasten
3 fly, hie, run 4 rush, urge 5 hurry, press, speed 6 barrel, hustle, step up, urge on 7 hurry up, quicken, speed up 8 expedite 10 accelerate

hasty
4 fast, rash 5 brisk, eager, fleet, quick, rapid, swift 6 abrupt, rushed, speedy, sudden 7 cursory, hurried, rushing 8 careless, fleeting, headlong, heedless, reckless, slapdash 9 hotheaded, impatient, impetuous, irritable, quickened 10 ill-advised, incautious 11 expeditious, perfunctory, precipitate, precipitous, superficial, thoughtless

hat
5 beret, derby, toque, tuque 6 boater, cloche, fedora, panama, topper 7 bicorne, chapeau, homburg, porkpie, Stetson, tricorn 8 sombrero, tricorne 9 headpiece 11 deerstalker
ancient Greek: 7 petasos, petasus
brimless: 7 pillbox
close-fitting: 4 kufi 5 toque, tuque 6 cloche, turban
felt: 5 busby, derby 6 bowler, trilby
fur: 5 busby 6 castor
helmetlike: 4 topi 5 topee
maker: 7 modiste 8 milliner
Middle Eastern: 3 fez
military: 4 kepi 5 busby, shako 8 bearskin
Muslim: 3 fez 6 turban 8 tarboosh
Scottish: 3 tam 9 glengarry 11 tam-o'-shanter
sheepskin: 6 calpac 7 calpack
soft: 5 toque, tuque
straw: 6 boater, panama, sailor 7 bangkok, leghorn, skimmer 8 sombrero
sun: 5 terai
tall: 9 stovepipe
waterproof: 9 sou'wester
woman's: 4 coif 5 toque, tuque 6 bonnet 7 pillbox

hatch
4 door, plan, plot 5 breed, brood, cover, inlay, spawn 6 cook up, create, design, devise, emerge, invent, make up, work up 7 concoct, dream up, opening, produce, think up 8 contrive, engender, generate, incubate, occasion 9 floodgate, formulate, give birth, give forth, originate, procreate 11 compartment

Hatcher of TV
4 Teri

hatchet
3 axe 8 tomahawk

hatchet man
5 bravo 6 killer 7 torpedo 8 assassin, enforcer, murderer 9 attack dog, cutthroat 10 eliminator, triggerman

hate
5 abhor, scorn 6 animus, detest, enmity, loathe, malice, rancor 7 despise 8 aversion, execrate, loathing 9 abominate, animosity, antipathy 10 abhorrence, repugnance

hateful
4 evil, foul, mean, vile 5 nasty 6 horrid, malign, odious, scurvy 7 vicious 8 accursed, damnable, infamous 9 abhorrent, execrable, malicious, obnoxious, repellent, repulsive 10 abominable, despicable, detestable, malevolent 11 blasphemous, opprobrious, unspeakable 13 reprehensible

Hatfields vs. ——
6 McCoys

hatred
5 odium, spite 6 animus, enmity, rancor 7 dislike 8 aversion, loathing 9 animosity, antipathy, hostility, repulsion, revulsion 10 abhorrence, repugnance 11 abomination, detestation, malevolence
of change: 9 misoneism
of humankind: 11 misanthropy
of marriage: 8 misogamy
of men: 8 misandry
of women: 8 misogyny

hats
9 millinery

hauberk
5 armor 9 chain mail, habergeon

haughtiness
4 airs 5 pride, scorn 7 conceit, disdain, hauteur 8 snobbery 9 arrogance, insolence, pomposity 12 snobbishness

haughty
5 aloof, proud 6 lordly, sniffy 7 distant

8 arrogant, cavalier, scornful, snobbish, superior **9** egotistic **10** disdainful **11** overbearing **12** contemptuous, supercilious

haul
3 lug, tow, tug **4** cart, drag, draw, hump, lift, load, loot, pull, swag, take, tote **5** boost, booty, cargo, hoist, raise, truck **6** burden, lading, schlep, spoils **7** freight, payload, schlepp
with a tackle: 5 bowse

haul up
5 hoise, hoist
with a rope: 5 trice

haunch
3 hip **11** hindquarter

haunches
4 butt, rump **7** hind end, rear end **8** backside, buttocks **9** posterior **12** hindquarters

haunt
4 site **5** spook **6** obsess, prey on **7** habitat, hang out, inhabit, torment, trouble **8** frequent **9** preoccupy **10** hang around, rendezvous, stay around, visit often

haunter
5 ghost **7** denizen, habitué

hautbois
4 oboe

hauteur
see **haughtiness**

haut monde
5 elite **6** jet set **7** society, who's who **10** glitterati, upper crust **11** aristocracy, high society **13** carriage trade

Havana's land
4 Cuba

have
3 own **4** hold **7** contain, include, possess

haven
4 port, roof **5** house, oases (plural), oasis **6** asylum, harbor, refuge **7** retreat, shelter **9** anchorage, sanctuary

haversack
3 bag **4** pack **8** backpack

havoc
4 loss, ruin, sack **5** chaos, waste **6** mayhem **8** calamity, disorder, ravaging **9** confusion, ruination **11** catastrophe, destruction, devastation, pandemonium

haw
4 left, tree **5** berry, fruit, shrub **8** turn left **10** equivocate
partner: 3 hem

Hawaii
author: 8 Michener (James A.)
beach: 7 Waikiki
capital: 8 Honolulu
city: 4 Hilo
coast: 4 Kona
discoverer: 4 Cook (Capt. James)
island: 4 Maui, Oahu **5** Kauai, Lanai **6** Niihau **7** Molokai
mountain: 7 Kilauea **8** Mauna Kea, Mauna Loa
nickname: 5 Aloha (State)
park: 9 Haleakala
state bird: 4 nene
state flower: 8 hibiscus
state tree: 5 kukui **9** candlenut

Hawaiian
crop: 4 taro
dance: 4 hula
dress: 6 muumuu
farewell: 5 aloha
feast: 4 luau
food: 3 poi
god: 4 Kane, Lono **5** Wakea **7** Kanaloa
goddess: 4 Pele
goose: 4 nene
gooseberry: 4 poha
grass: 4 hilo
greeting: 5 aloha
instrument: 3 uke **7** ukelele, ukulele
neckwear: 3 lei
nonnative: 5 haole **8** malihini
porch: 5 lanai
president: 5 Obama (Barack)
resident: 8 kamaaina
shaman: 6 kahuna
soup: 6 saimin
thrush: 4 omao
tree: 3 koa

hawk
4 kite, sell, vend **5** buteo **6** falcon, monger, osprey, peddle **7** Cooper's, goshawk, haggard, harrier, redtail **8** caracara, huckster, roughleg **9** accipiter, red-tailed, warmonger **10** militarist **11** ferruginous, rough-legged
claw: 5 talon
male: 6 tercel **7** tiercel
young: 4 eyas

hawker
6 coster, monger, seller, vendor **7** packman, peddler **8** pitchman **12** costermonger

hawkeyed
11 keen-sighted **12** sharp-sighted

Hawkeye portrayer
4 Alda (Alan)

Hawkeye State
4 Iowa

hawkish
7 martial, warlike **9** combative **10** aggressive **11** belligerent **12** militaristic

___ Hawley Tariff
5 Smoot

Hawthorne, Nathaniel
birthplace: 5 Salem
character: 6 Hester (Prynne) 8 Clifford (Pyncheon), Hepzibah (Pyncheon), Pyncheon (Judge) 10 Dimmesdale (Rev. Arthur) 13 Chillingworth (Roger)
novel: 10 Marble Faun (The) 13 Scarlet Letter (The) 21 House of the Seven Gables (The)

hay
3 bed 4 feed 5 grass 6 fodder, reward 7 herbage
crops: 6 clover 7 alfalfa, timothy

Haydn oratorio
7 Seasons (The) 8 Creation (The)

hay fever
7 allergy 10 pollenosis, pollinosis
cause: 6 pollen 7 ragweed

haying machine
5 baler

haymaker
3 box 4 blow, sock 5 clout, punch 6 wallop

hayseed
see **hick**

haywire
4 amok, awry 5 amuck, crazy, upset 6 faulty 8 confused 10 out of order 12 out of control

Hayworth of film
4 Rita

hazard
3 bet, try 4 dare, game, luck, risk 5 peril, shoal, wager 6 chance, danger, gamble, menace 7 fortune, imperil, venture 8 accident, endanger, jeopardy, obstacle

hazardous
5 hairy, risky 6 chancy, unsafe 7 unsound 8 perilous 9 dangerous, unhealthy 10 precarious

haze
3 fog 4 film, mist, murk, smog 5 brume, cloud, drive, smoke, vapor 6 harass 7 dimness, obscure 8 dullness, initiate, overcast 9 mistiness, murkiness, vagueness 10 cloudiness

hazel
4 wood 5 birch, shrub 7 filbert

hazy
3 dim 5 faint, filmy, foggy, fuzzy, misty, murky, smoky, vague 6 cloudy, unsure 7 blurred, clouded, obscure, unclear 8 nebulous, vaporous 9 uncertain 10 indefinite, indistinct

head
3 nob, nut, top 4 bean, boss, capo, dome, foam, john, main, mind, pate, poll 5 brain, caput, chief, first, gourd, poise, prime, privy, scalp, skull 6 honcho, leader, master, noggin, noodle, talent, toilet 7 cranium, faculty, latrine, premier, supreme 8 director, foremost, lavatory 9 chieftain, principal 10 promontory
area: 5 crown 6 temple
back part: 7 occiput
bone: 5 skull 7 cranium 8 parietal
combining form: 6 cranio 7 cephalo
covering: 3 cap, hat 6 bonnet 8 kerchief
monastery: 4 dean 5 abbot 8 superior
nunnery: 6 abbess 8 superior
of hair: 4 mane 6 fleece 9 chevelure
relating to: 8 cephalic
shaving of: 7 tonsure
skin: 5 scalp
top: 4 pate 5 crown

headache
4 pain 5 worry 6 bother, megrim 7 problem 8 migraine, nuisance, vexation 9 annoyance 10 irritation

headband
7 bandeau, circlet, coronal
ancient Greek: 6 taenia 7 taeniae (plural)

headdress
7 topknot
American Indian: 9 warbonnet
Arab: 8 kaffiyeh, keffiyeh
bishop's: 5 miter, mitre
medieval: 4 barb
Eastern: 6 turban
nobleman's: 7 coronet
royal: 5 crown, tiara 6 diadem
Spanish women's: 8 mantilla
women's: 6 bonnet
(see also **hat**)

headland
4 cape, ness 5 point 10 promontory

headline
6 banner 7 feature, promote 8 screamer 9 emphasize, publicize, spotlight 10 noteworthy

headlong
4 rash 5 brash, hasty 6 abrupt, daring, rashly, sudden 7 hurried, rushing 8 heedless, reckless 9 foolhardy, impetuous, impulsive 10 heedlessly, recklessly 11 precipitate, precipitous

headmaster
6 leader 9 principal

head off
4 stop 5 avert, block 6 thwart 7 deflect, obviate, prevent, ward off 8 stave off, turn back 9 forestall, intercept

headquarters
3 hub 4 base, seat 6 center

head start
4 edge, jump, lead, odds 5 boost 7 advance, vantage 8 handicap 9 advantage, allowance

headstone
6 marker **8** memorial, monument **11** grave marker

headstrong
6 dogged, mulish, unruly **7** willful **8** contrary, perverse, stubborn **9** obstinate **10** bullheaded, refractory, self-willed **11** intractable, stiff-necked

heads-up
5 alarm, alert **6** signal, tip-off **7** warning **8** high sign **11** resourceful

headway
4 gain **6** growth **7** advance **8** anabasis, progress **11** advancement, improvement

heady
4 rash, rich **5** giddy **6** elated, potent **7** willful **8** exciting **9** impetuous **11** exhilarated, intoxicated **12** intoxicating

heal
3 fix **4** cure, knit, mend **5** sew up, treat **6** cement, remedy, repair **7** patch up, restore **8** make well

healer
6 doctor, shaman

healing
8 curative, remedial, salutary, sanative **9** vulnerary, wholesome **10** salubrious **11** restorative, therapeutic **12** convalescent
combining form: 5 iatro
goddess of: 3 Eir

health
7 fitness, welfare **8** haleness, vitality, wellness **9** soundness, well-being, wholeness
club: 3 gym, spa

healthful
8 curative, hygienic, remedial, salutary **9** favorable, wholesome **10** beneficial, corrective, profitable, salubrious **11** restorative

healthy
3 fit **4** hale, spry, well **5** sound, tonic **6** benign, robust, strong, sturdy **7** chipper **8** blooming, hygienic, positive, salutary, thriving, vigorous **9** wholesome **10** able-bodied, beneficial, prosperous, salubrious **11** flourishing

Heaney work
5 North **9** Field Work **12** Wintering Out
translation: 7 Beowulf

heap
3 lot **4** cock, fill, gobs, hill, load, lump, mass, much, pack, pile, rick, scad **5** amass, bunch, clump, crate, loads, mound, shock, stack, wreck **6** barrel, charge, gather, jalopy, junker, lumber, oodles **7** clunker, collect, deposit, jillion **8** assemble, mountain, slathers **9** abundance, profusion, stockpile

hear
4 heed, oyez **5** catch, learn **8** listen to, perceive **9** apprehend

hearing
4 oyer, test **5** trial **6** tryout **7** earshot, inquiry **8** audience, audition **9** interview **10** conference, discussion
distance: 7 earshot

hearken
4 heed, mind, note **6** attend, listen, notice **7** observe

hearsay
4 buzz, news, talk **5** rumor **6** gossip, report **7** account, chatter **9** grapevine **11** scuttlebutt

heart
3 cor, hub **4** core, crux, gist, guts, love, pith, root, seat, soul, zest **5** ardor, bosom, focus, gusto, moxie, pluck, spunk **6** breast, center, kernel, mettle, relish, spirit, ticker **7** courage, resolve **8** feelings, sympathy **9** character, fortitude **10** compassion
chart: 3 ECG, EKG
combining form: 6 cardio
contraction: 7 systole
dilation: 8 diastole
part: 5 valve **6** atrium, septum **9** ventricle

heartache
3 rue, woe **4** care, pain, pang **5** grief **6** regret, sorrow **7** anguish, sadness **8** distress **10** affliction

heartbeat
5 flash, jiffy, pulse, throb, trice **6** moment, second **9** pulsation
irregular: 10 arrhythmia

heartbreak
3 rue, woe **5** agony, grief **6** misery, regret, sorrow **7** anguish, despair, torment, torture **9** suffering **10** desolation **12** wretchedness

heartbreaking
6 bitter, tragic **8** grievous **9** agonizing **10** calamitous, deplorable, lamentable **11** devastating, distressing

heartbroken
7 crushed, grieved **8** mournful, overcome, wretched **9** sorrowful **10** despairing, despondent **12** disconsolate

heartburn
7 pyrosis

hearten
4 buoy, stir **5** cheer, rally, rouse **6** arouse, buck up, buoy up, perk up **7** animate, cheer up, enliven, inspire **8** embolden, energize, inspirit **9** encourage

heartfelt
4 deep, true **6** honest **7** earnest, fervent, genuine, sincere **8** profound **9** unfeigned

hearth
4 home **5** abode **8** domicile, dwelling, fireside **9** fireplace, residence
goddess: **5** Vesta

heartily
6 wholly **9** sincerely, with gusto, zestfully **10** completely, thoroughly

heartless
4 cold, hard **5** cruel **6** unkind **7** callous **8** uncaring **9** unfeeling **10** hard-boiled **11** insensitive, unemotional **13** unsympathetic

Heart of Dixie
7 Alabama

heartsease
5 pansy, viola **6** violet **11** peace of mind, tranquility **12** johnny-jump-up, tranquillity

heart-shaped
7 cordate

heartsick
4 blue, down **8** dejected, desolate, dismayed, downcast **9** depressed **10** despondent, dispirited **11** demoralized **12** disconsolate

heartthrob
4 idol, love **5** flame, honey, sweet **7** beloved, darling, passion **9** dreamboat **10** sweetheart

heart-to-heart
4 open, talk **5** frank **6** candid, honest **7** sincere **8** truthful **12** conversation

hearty
4 hale, warm **5** ample **6** jovial, robust, sailor, strong **7** cordial, healthy, profuse, sincere **8** abundant, vehement, vigorous **9** approving, energetic, exuberant, flavorful, unfeigned **12** enthusiastic, unrestrained

heat
4 cook, rage, warm, zeal **5** ardor, fever **6** fervor, simmer, warmth **7** caloric, inflame, passion, swelter **8** pyrolyze
combining form: **4** pyro **6** calori, thermo **7** thermia
measuring device: **11** calorimeter, thermometer
quantity: **3** BTU

heated
3 hot, mad **5** angry, fiery, irate **6** ardent, fervid, fierce, ireful, raging, steamy **7** boiling, burning, fevered, furious **8** broiling, feverish, scalding, sizzling, vehement, wrathful **9** indignant, scorching **10** passionate **11** acrimonious

heater
3 gat, gun, rod **4** etna **5** stove **6** boiler, pistol, roscoe **7** furnace, handgun **8** fastball, radiator

heath
4 ling, moor **5** broom, Erica, shrub **7** Calluna **9** crowberry, wasteland

heathen
5 pagan **7** infidel **8** barbaric **11** irreligious, uncivilized
figurine: **4** idol

heat-producing
9 calorific

heave
3 lob **4** cast, draw, fire, gasp, haul, heft, huff, hurl, lift, pant, puff, pull, push, toss **5** fling, hoist, labor, pitch, raise, retch, sling, surge, throw, vomit **6** launch

heave-ho
4 boot **6** ouster **8** bum's rush **9** dismissal

heaven
4 Eden, Zion **5** bliss, glory **6** Asgard, utopia **7** arcadia, ecstasy, elysium, nirvana, rapture **8** empyrean, eternity, paradise **9** firmament, Shangri-la **10** wonderland **11** immortality, kingdom come **12** promised land

heavenly
4 lush **6** divine, sacred **7** blessed, elysian **8** beatific, empyreal, empyrean, ethereal **9** ambrosial, celestial, delicious **10** delectable, delightful, enchanting

heavy
3 big, fat **5** beefy, bulky, gross, hefty, obese, stout, thick **6** bad guy, chunky, fleshy, leaden, portly **7** labored, porcine, villain, weighty **8** cumbrous, sluggish, unwieldy **9** corpulent, laborious, lumbering, ponderous, strenuous **10** burdensome, cumbersome, oppressive, overweight
volume: **4** tome

heavy-handed
5 crude, harsh, inept **6** clumsy, gauche, klutzy **7** awkward **8** bumbling, despotic **9** maladroit **10** oppressive **11** domineering, overbearing

heavyhearted
3 sad **4** glum **5** sorry **7** unhappy **8** dejected, downcast, mournful, saddened **9** depressed, miserable, sorrowful **10** despondent, dispirited, melancholy

heavyset
5 beefy, husky, stout, thick **6** chunky, portly, stocky **11** thick-bodied

heavyweight
3 VIP **4** lion **5** boxer, chief **6** big gun, bigwig, honcho, leader **7** big shot, notable **8** big-timer
great: **3** Ali (Muhammad)

Hebe
father: **4** Zeus **7** Jupiter
husband: **8** Hercules
mother: **4** Hera, Juno
successor: **8** Ganymede

hebetude
6 stupor, torpor **7** languor **8** dullness, lethargy **9** lassitude, torpidity **10** drowsiness

hebetudinous
4 dull, logy **5** dopey **6** drowsy, stupid, torpid **8** listless, sluggish **9** lethargic

Hebrew
3 Jew **6** Jewish
coin: **6** lepton, shekel
feast: **5** seder
festival: **5** Purim **6** Pesach, Sukkot **7** Hanukah, Sukkoth **8** Chanukah, Lag b'Omer, Passover, Shabuoth **9** Tishah-b'Ab, Yom Kippur **12** Rosh Hashanah, Simchas Torah
God: **6** Adonai, Elohim, Yahweh **7** Jehovah
judge: **6** Gideon
lawgiver: **5** Moses
leader: **4** Saul **5** Moses **6** Joshua **7** Solomon
letter: (see at **alphabet**)
lyre: **4** asor **6** kinnor
measure: **4** beka, omer **5** bekah, cubit, ephah
month: **4** Abib, Adar, Elul, Iyar **5** Nisan, Sivan, Tebet **6** Kislev, Shebat, Tammuz, Tishri, Veadar (in leap year) **7** Heshvan
patriarch: **3** Dan, Gad **4** Cain, Levi, Seth **5** Asher, David, Isaac, Jacob, Judah **6** Joseph, Lamech, Reuben, Simeon **7** Abraham, Zebulun **8** Benjamin, Issachar, Naphtali
sacred city: **5** Safad, Safed **6** Hebron **8** Tiberias **9** Jerusalem
tribe: **3** Dan, Gad **4** Levi **5** Asher, Judah **6** Reuben, Simeon **7** Ephraim, Zebulon **8** Benjamin, Issachar, Manasseh, Naphtali
(see also **Jewish**)

Hebrides Island
4 Eigg, Iona, Rhum, Skye, Uist **5** Lewis **6** Harris

Hecate
father: **6** Perses
goddess of: **5** night **10** underworld, witchcraft
mother: **7** Asteria

hecatomb
7 killing, slaying **8** butchery **9** bloodbath, sacrifice, slaughter

heck
3 d'oh **4** darn, drat, geez, gosh, hell, jeez **5** golly **6** shucks

heckle
3 nag **4** bait, faze, gibe, ride **5** annoy, chivy, hound, tease, worry **6** badger, bother, harass, hassle, hector, molest, needle, pester, plague, rattle **7** disrupt, disturb, torment **9** interrupt **10** disconcert

hectic
3 red **6** fervid **7** burning, excited, fevered, flushed **8** confused, exciting, feverish, frenetic, restless **9** turbulent **10** persistent

hector
3 cow, nag **4** bait, ride **5** bully, chivy, hound **6** badger, harass, lean on **7** bedevil, swagger **8** browbeat, bullyrag, domineer **10** intimidate

Hector
brother: **5** Paris **7** Helenus, Troilus **9** Deiphobus, Polydorus
father: **5** Priam
mother: **6** Hecuba
sister: **6** Creusa **8** Polyxena **9** Cassandra
slayer: **8** Achilles
victim: **9** Patroclus
wife: **10** Andromache

Hecuba
daughter: **6** Creusa **8** Polyxena **9** Cassandra
father: **5** Dymas
husband: **5** Priam
son: **5** Paris **6** Hector **7** Helenus, Troilus **9** Deiphobus, Polydorus
victim: **11** Polymnestor

Hedda Gabler author
5 Ibsen (Henrik)

hedge
4 trim **5** avoid, evade, fence, guard, hem in, limit **6** hinder **7** barrier, defense, enclose, evasion, protect **8** boundary, encircle, restrict **9** shrubbery **10** protection

hedgehog
9 porcupine **10** stronghold

hedonist
4 rake **7** epicure, gourmet **8** gourmand, sybarite **9** bon vivant, epicurean, libertine **10** sensualist, voluptuary

heebie-jeebies
5 jumps **6** creeps, nerves, shakes **7** jitters, shivers, willies **11** nervousness

heed
4 care, hark, mark, mind, note, obey **5** watch **6** attend, harken, listen, notice, regard, remark **7** be aware, concern, hearing, hearken, observe, respect **8** consider, interest, listen to **9** attention **10** observance

heedful
5 alert, aware **7** on guard **8** vigilant **9** attentive, observant, observing **10** interested, meticulous, scrupulous **13** conscientious

heedless
9 negligent, oblivious, unmindful **10** unthinking **11** inadvertent, inattentive, unobservant **12** unreflective **13** inconsiderate

heedlessness
7 neglect **9** disregard, unconcern **11** disinterest, inattention, insouciance **12** indifference

hee-haw
4 bray **5** laugh **6** guffaw **10** horse laugh

heel
3 bum, cad, tip **4** cant, hock, lean, list, rake,

tilt 5 creep, knave, louse, rogue, skunk, slope 6 rascal, rotter 7 bounder, incline, lowlife, villain 9 scoundrel
bone: 8 calcanea (plural), calcanei (plural) 9 calcaneum, calcaneus

heft
4 bulk, lift, load 5 hoist, raise, weigh 6 weight 7 heave up 9 heaviness, influence 10 importance

hefty
3 big 5 beefy, burly, bulky, heavy, husky, large, major, stout 6 brawny, mighty, rugged, strong 7 massive, sizable 8 imposing, powerful 9 extensive, good-sized, plentiful, ponderous, strapping 11 substantial

hegira
6 escape, exodus, flight 7 journey 10 emigration, evacuation 11 deliverance

Heidi
author: 5 Spyri (Johanna)
goatherd: 5 Peter
setting: 4 Alps

heifer
4 calf

___ Heifetz
6 Jascha

height
3 top 4 acme, apex, cusp, peak, rise 6 apogee, climax, heyday, summit, vertex, zenith 7 stature 8 altitude, pinnacle 9 elevation, loftiness 10 prominence
combining form: 4 acro

heighten
3 wax 5 boost, mount, raise 6 beef up, expand, extend 7 amplify, augment, build up, elevate, enhance, enlarge, improve, magnify 8 increase 9 highlight, intensify 10 aggrandize

heinie
3 bum 4 butt, rear, rump, tush 5 fanny 6 bottom 7 hind end, keister, rear end 8 backside

heinous
4 evil 6 odious 7 hateful 8 infamous, shocking 9 abhorrent, atrocious, execrable, monstrous 10 abominable, detestable, outrageous

heinousness
4 evil 6 horror, infamy 8 atrocity, enormity 13 monstrousness

heir
5 scion 7 grantee, heritor, legatee 9 inheritor, successor 11 beneficiary
joint: 8 parcener 10 coparcener

heist
3 cop, rob 4 lift, loot 5 boost, caper, filch, pinch, steal, swipe, theft 6 holdup, rip off 7 larceny, purloin, robbery 8 burglary 9 strong-arm

Helen of Troy
abductor: 5 Paris
husband: 8 Menelaus

Helenus
brother: 5 Paris 6 Hector 7 Troilus 9 Deiphobus, Polydorus
father: 5 Priam
mother: 6 Hecuba
sister: 6 Creusa 8 Polyxena 9 Cassandra
wife: 10 Andromache

Hel, Hela
father: 4 Loki
hall: 7 Niflhel 8 Niflheim
mother: 9 Angerboda

helical
6 spiral

helicopter
7 chopper 9 eggbeater 10 whirlybird
armed: 5 Cobra 6 Apache 7 gunship 9 Black Hawk
blade: 5 rotor
manufacturer: 8 Sikorsky (Igor)

Helios
6 Apollo
daughter: 5 Circe 8 Pasiphaë
father: 8 Hyperion
mother: 5 Theia
sister: 3 Eos 6 Aurora, Selene
son: 8 Phaethon

heliotrope
4 herb 5 shrub 6 borage 10 bloodstone

hell
5 hades, Sheol 6 blazes, Tophet 7 Gehenna, inferno 9 perdition, tarnation 10 blue blazes

hell-bent
6 driven, intent 8 obsessed, resolved 10 determined

Hellen
father: 9 Deucalion
mother: 6 Pyrrha
son: 5 Dorus 6 Aeolus, Xuthus

hellhole
3 pit 8 dystopia, snake pit 9 mare's nest

hellion
3 elf, imp 4 puck, punk 5 demon, rogue, scamp 6 rascal 7 gremlin

hellish
6 horrid 7 ghastly, hideous, satanic, stygian 8 damnable, diabolic, dreadful, gruesome, horrible, infernal, terrible 9 appalling, frightful, monstrous, plutonian 10 diabolical

Hellman play
11 Little Foxes (The) 13 Children's Hour (The) 15 Watch on the Rhine

hello
3 hey **4** ciao, hail **5** aloha, howdy **7** hi there, welcome **8** greeting **9** greetings

helm
4 head **5** wheel **7** cockpit **8** controls

helmet
6 casque, sallet, tin hat **7** morrion **8** burgonet, headgear
medieval: 6 sallet **7** basinet
part: 5 nasal **7** ventail **8** aventail
sun: 4 topi **5** topee

helmsman
5 pilot **7** skipper

Heloïse
husband: 7 Abelard (Peter)
son: 9 Astrolabe

helot
4 peon, serf **5** slave **6** vassal **7** laborer, peasant, servant

helotry
4 yoke **6** thrall **7** bondage, peonage, serfdom, slavery **9** servitude, thralldom **11** enslavement

help
3 aid, SOS **4** abet, back, mend **5** avail, boost, guide, serve **6** assist, relief, remedy, succor **7** advance, benefit, bolster, further, promote, relieve, secours, service, support **8** mitigate, palliate **9** alleviate, meliorate **10** ameliorate, assistance, facilitate **11** cooperation
forward: 7 further
hired: 5 labor

helper
4 aide, ass't **6** deputy, server **7** ancilla, servant **8** employee **9** assistant, associate, attendant, auxiliary **10** apprentice **11** subordinate

helpful
5 of use **6** usable, useful **8** salutary, valuable **9** effective, favorable, practical **10** beneficial, profitable, propitious **11** encouraging **12** advantageous, constructive

helping
4 dose **5** share **7** portion, serving **9** auxiliary

helpless
4 weak **6** feeble, futile, unable **7** forlorn **8** desolate **9** abandoned, dependent **11** unprotected

helter-skelter
6 anyhow **7** anywise, flighty, hastily, turmoil **8** at random, disorder, pell-mell, randomly **9** confusion, haphazard, hit-or-miss **11** any which way, haphazardly, in confusion, precipitate

helve
4 haft **6** handle

Helvetian
5 Swiss

hem
3 pen, rim **4** brim, edge, gird, ring, seam, shut **5** alter, bound, brink, fence, hedge, skirt, verge **6** border, circle, corral, edging, fringe, immure, margin, stitch **7** close in, enclose, selvage, shorten **8** encircle, surround **9** encompass, perimeter, periphery
turned-back: 4 cuff

he-man
4 hunk, stud **5** macho

Heman
father: 4 Joel
grandfather: 6 Samuel

hematite
3 ore **7** mineral **12** black diamond

Hemingway, Ernest
work: 9 In Our Time **12** Sun Also Rises (The) **13** Moveable Feast (A) **14** Farewell to Arms (A) **15** Old Man and the Sea (The) **16** To Have and Have Not **18** Islands in the Stream, Snows of Kilimanjaro (The) **19** For Whom the Bell Tolls
sobriquet: 4 Papa

hemipterous insect
3 bug

hemlock
4 drug, herb, tree, wood **6** poison

hemophiliac
7 bleeder

hemp
3 kef, kif **7** hashish **8** cannabis **9** marijuana
fiber: 5 oakum
kind: 4 aloe

hen
5 biddy, layer
broody: 6 sitter
spayed: 8 poularde
young: 6 pullet

hence
4 away, ergo, thus **5** since **6** hereat **9** as a result, from now on, therefore, thereupon **11** accordingly **12** consequently

henceforth
9 from now on, hereafter

henchman
6 cohort, lackey, minion, stooge **7** abettor **8** adherent, disciple, follower, partisan, retainer **9** attendant, supporter **10** accomplice

Hendrix hairdo
3 'fro **4** Afro

Henley poem
8 Invictus

henpeck
3 nag **4** carp, fuss **5** annoy **6** badger, carp at, harass, hector **8** domineer **9** find fault

Henrik of drama
5 Ibsen

Henry II
adversary: 6 Becket (Thomas à)
son: 4 John (Lackland) 7 Richard (Lionheart)
surname: 5 Anjou 11 Plantagenet
wife: 7 Eleanor

Henry IV
11 Bolingbroke
surname: 9 Lancaster
victim: 10 Richard III

Henry VIII
archbishop: 6 Wolsey (Thomas) 7 Cranmer (Thomas) 10 Thomas More
daughter: 4 Mary 9 Elizabeth
son: 6 Edward
surname: 5 Tudor
victim: 4 Anne (Boleyn) 8 Cromwell (Thomas) 9 Catherine (Howard) 10 Thomas More
wife: 4 Anne (Boleyn, of Cleves), Jane (Seymour) 9 Catherine (Howard, of Aragon, Parr), Katherine

hepatic
9 liverwort

Hephaestus
6 Vulcan
father: 4 Zeus 7 Jupiter
milieu: 5 forge
mother: 4 Hera, Juno
wife: 5 Venus 6 Charis 9 Aphrodite

Hephzibah
husband: 8 Hezekiah
son: 8 Manasseh

hepped up
5 eager, wired 7 charged, excited, fervent 8 enthused 12 enthusiastic

Hera
4 Juno
father: 6 Cronus, Saturn
husband: 4 Zeus 7 Jupiter
messenger: 4 Iris
mother: 4 Rhea
son: 4 Ares

Heracles
beloved: 4 Iole
brother: 8 Iphicles
charioteer: 6 Iolaus
father: 4 Zeus 7 Jupiter
mother: 7 Alcmene
son: 6 Hyllus
victim: 5 Hydra, Ladon 6 Geryon, Megara, Orthus 10 Nemean lion
wife: 4 Hebe 6 Megara 8 Deianira

herald
4 hail, tout 5 crier, greet 6 signal 7 courier, declare, portend, precede, presage, trumpet 8 announce, ballyhoo, exponent, outrider, proclaim 9 advertise, harbinger, messenger, precursor, publicize, spokesman 10 forerunner, foreshadow

heraldic
border: 7 bordure
cross: 6 fleury, formée, moline, pommée 8 fourchée
term: 4 aile, bend, fess, orle, pale, semé, vair, vert 5 crest, flank, gules 6 argent, blazon, canton, charge, device, dexter, emblem, impale, manche, sejant, voided, volant 7 chevron, nombril, passant, purpure, rampant, saltire, statant, urinant 8 guardant, sinister, tincture 9 regardant 10 escutcheon

heraldry
6 armory 9 pageantry

herb
3 Iva, oca, pia, udo 4 arum, dill, flax, forb, geum, hemp, leek, mint, nard, sage, wort 5 basil, canna, chive, cumin, senna, tansy, thyme 6 allium, arnica, borage, catnip, endive, eryngo, fat hen, fennel, garlic, hyssop, lovage, orpine, squill, yarrow 7 boneset, caraway, catmint, chervil, chicory, comfrey, episcia, ginseng, milfoil, mullein, oregano, parsley, pinesap, pussley, salsify, sanicle 8 angelica, camomile, capsicum, cardamom, centaury, cilantro, costmary, feverfew, freewort, hepatica, lungwort, mandrake, marjoram, origanum, pokeweed, purslane, rapeseed, rosemary, selfheal, tarragon, turmeric, euphrasy, valerian, woodruff, wormwood 9 birthwort, bush basil, chamomile, goosefoot, patchouli, spikenard 10 basil thyme, cuckoo pint 12 balm of Gilead
beverage: 6 tisane
genus: 4 Arum, Geum
mythical: 4 moly
poisonous: 4 atis 7 aconite, dogbane, hemlock, henbane 8 veratrum 9 hellebore, monkshood

herbicide
6 dioxin, diquat, diuron 7 monuron, Roundup 8 atrazine, Paraquat, picloram, simazine 10 glyphosate 11 Agent Orange

Herculean
4 huge, vast 5 giant 7 arduous, immense, mammoth, titanic 8 colossal, enormous, gigantic, powerful 10 formidable, superhuman

Hercules
see **Heracles**

herd
3 mob, pod 4 bevy, lead 5 covey, crowd, drive, drove, flock, swarm 6 gather, throng 9 associate, multitude

herdsman
6 Boötes, cowboy 7 breeder 8 shepherd
Latin American: 6 gaucho 7 vaquero 8 ranchero

here and there
6 passim 7 at times 9 sometimes 11 irregularly

hereditary
6 inborn, inbred, innate, lineal 7 genetic 9 ancestral, inherited 10 congenital 11 traditional, transmitted

heredity
7 lineage 8 ancestry 9 tradition 11 inheritance
unit: 4 gene

heresy
6 schism 7 dissent, fallacy, impiety 9 defection, deviation, misbelief 10 dissidence, heterodoxy, infidelity, radicalism 11 revisionism, unorthodoxy 13 nonconformism, nonconformity

heretic
7 infidel 8 apostate, defector, recusant, renegade 9 dissenter, dissident 10 iconoclast, schismatic, separatist, unbeliever 11 misbeliever, nonbeliever, revisionist 13 nonconformist

heretical
7 infidel 8 apostate 9 dissident, heterodox, miscreant, sectarian 10 dissenting, schismatic, unorthodox 11 revisionist 12 misbelieving 13 nonconformist

heretofore
6 ere now 7 till now, up to now 8 formerly, until now 10 previously

heritage
6 legacy 7 bequest 9 patrimony, tradition 10 birthright

Hermes
7 Mercury
attribute: 7 petasos, petasus 8 caduceus
father: 4 Zeus 7 Jupiter
mother: 4 Maia
sandals: 7 talaria

hermetic
6 arcane, closed, occult, sealed, secret 7 recluse 8 abstruse, airtight, profound, secluded, solitary 9 recondite 10 cloistered, impervious 11 sequestered

Hermia
beloved: 8 Lysander
father: 5 Egeus

Hermione
father: 8 Menelaus
husband: 7 Orestes, Pyrrhus 11 Neoptolemus
mother: 5 Helen

hermit
5 loner 6 cookie 7 eremite, recluse, stylite 8 solitary 9 anchorite

hermitage
5 abbey 7 retreat 8 cloister, hideaway 9 monastery

hernia
6 breach 7 rupture 10 protrusion
support: 5 truss
type: 6 cystic, hiatal 7 femoral 9 umbilical 10 incisional

hero
4 idol, lion 6 knight 7 demigod, paladin 8 champion 11 protagonist
American: 6 Bunyan (Paul) 8 Superman
Armenian: 10 Skanderbeg
Babylonian: 9 Gilgamesh
Celtic-French: 7 Tristan 8 Tristram
Crusades: 7 Tancred 8 Tancredi
English: 6 Arthur 7 Beowulf 9 Robin Hood
French: 6 Roland 11 Charlemagne
German: 5 Etzel 8 Arminius 9 Siegfried
Greek: 4 Ajax 5 Jason 7 Perseus, Ulysses 8 Achilles, Heracles, Hercules, Leonidas, Odysseus 11 Bellerophon
Hebrew: 5 David 6 Daniel, Samson
Hungarian: 5 Arpad 7 Hunyadi (János)
Irish: 9 Cuchulain, Cuchulinn, Cuchullin
Italian: 7 Orlando
Roman: 7 Romulus 8 Horatius
Scandinavian: 6 Sigurd 9 Siegfried
Scottish: 5 Bruce (Robert) 6 Rob Roy
Spanish: 3 Cid 5 El Cid
Spartan: 8 Leonidas
Trojan: 6 Aeneas, Hector

Herod
daughter: 6 Salome
father: 7 Antipas 9 Antipater
kingdom: 5 Judea 6 Judaea
mother: 6 Cyprus
son: 5 Herod (Antipas) 6 Joseph 7 Pheroas 9 Phasaelus

Herodias
daughter: 6 Salome
father: 11 Aristobulus
husband: 5 Herod (Antipas)

heroic
4 bold, epic 5 brave, noble 6 daring 7 drastic, extreme, radical, valiant 8 fearless, intrepid, unafraid, valorous 9 dauntless, Herculean, undaunted 10 courageous
deed: 4 gest
poem: 4 epos
story: 4 epic, saga

heroin
4 gear, skag, snow 5 horse, smack 8 narcotic 11 diamorphine

heroism
5 valor 6 daring, spirit 7 bravery, courage, prowess 8 boldness, chivalry, nobility, valiance 9 gallantry 11 intrepidity

heron relative
5 egret 7 bittern

Hero's lover
7 Leander

herring
7 sardine 8 brisling, pilchard
measure: 4 cran
relative: 4 shad
smoked: 7 bloater

Herr's partner
4 Frau

Herse
father: 7 Cecrops
sister: 8 Aglauros
son: 8 Cephalus

Hersey
novel: 4 Wall (The) 12 Bell for Adano (A)
town: 5 Adano

Hershiser of baseball
4 Orel

Hertz rival
4 Avis

Hesione
brother: 5 Priam
father: 8 Laomedon
husband: 7 Telamon
rescuer: 8 Heracles, Hercules
son: 6 Teucer

hesitant
4 slow 5 chary, loath, timid 6 afraid, averse, unsure 7 halting, uneager 9 faltering, reluctant, tentative, uncertain, unwilling 10 irresolute 11 disinclined, vacillating

hesitate
4 balk 5 delay, demur, hedge, pause, stall, stick, waver 6 dawdle, dither, falter, waffle 7 stammer, stutter 8 hang back, hold back 9 temporize, vacillate 12 shilly-shally

Hesperides
6 nymphs

Hesperus
5 Venus 11 evening star
father: 8 Astraeus
mother: 3 Eos

Hesse novel
6 Demian 10 Siddhartha 11 Steppenwolf 12 Magister Ludi

Hestia
5 Vesta
father: 6 Cronus, Saturn
mother: 4 Rhea

Heston, Charlton
org.: 3 NRA
role: 5 El Cid, Moses 6 Ben-Hur (Judah)

heterodox
9 dissident, heretical, sectarian 10 schismatic, unorthodox 13 nonconformist

heterodoxy
6 heresy, schism 7 dissent 9 misbelief 10 dissidence 13 nonconformism, nonconformity

heterogeneous
5 mixed 6 motley, sundry, varied 7 diverse, various 8 assorted 9 disparate 12 conglomerate

het up
5 irate, upset 7 excited 8 agitated

hew
3 axe, cut 4 chop, fell, form 5 shape, stick 6 adhere 7 conform, cut down

hex
4 jinx 5 charm, curse, spell, witch 6 voodoo, whammy 7 bad luck, bewitch, enchant 9 sorceress 11 enchantment, enchantress

hey
4 psst

heyday
4 acme, peak 5 prime 6 height, zenith 9 high point

Hezekiah
father: 4 Ahaz 7 Neariah
mother: 3 Abi
son: 8 Manasseh
wife: 9 Hephzibah

H. G. Wells race
4 Eloi

H. H. Munro pseudonym
4 Saki

hiatus
3 gap 5 break, space 6 breach, lacuna 7 interim 8 aperture, downtime, interval 10 suspension 12 interruption 13 discontinuity

Hiawatha
author: 10 Longfellow (Henry Wadsworth)
craft: 5 canoe
grandmother: 7 Nokomis
mother: 7 Wenonah
tribe: 6 Ojibwa, Ojibwe 7 Ojibway 8 Onondaga
wife: 9 Minnehaha

hibernal
6 wintry 8 winterly

Hibernia
4 Eire, Erin 7 Ireland

hick
4 rube 5 yokel 6 rustic 7 bumpkin, hayseed 8 cornball 10 clodhopper, provincial

hidden
5 privy 6 buried, covert, occult, secret, veiled 7 obscure 8 obscured, shrouded, ulterior 9 concealed 11 undisclosed
combining form: 6 crypto, krypto
supply: 5 cache, stash

hide
3 fur 4 bury, lurk, mask, pelt, skin, veil 5 cache, cloak, cover, inter, shade, stash 6 harbor, lie low, screen, shroud 7 conceal, cover up, leather, obscure, seclude, secrete, shelter 8 ensconce

hideaway
see **hideout**

hidebound
8 obdurate **9** parochial **10** inflexible, provincial **11** reactionary, straitlaced **12** conservative, narrow-minded **13** straightlaced

hideous
4 ugly **5** awful, gross, lurid, nasty **6** grisly, horrid **7** ghastly, hateful **8** gruesome, horrible, shocking, terrible **9** appalling, dismaying, frightful, loathsome, monstrous, offensive, repellent, repugnant, repulsive, revolting, sickening **10** disgusting, horrifying

hideout
3 den **4** lair **5** cache, haven **6** covert, refuge **7** retreat, shelter **9** hermitage, safe house, sanctuary

hiding
5 doggo

hie
3 run **4** dash, push, trot **5** hurry, scoot **6** hasten, hustle

hierarch
4 boss, head **5** chief **6** honcho, leader, master **7** headman **9** chieftain **10** high priest

hierarchy
5 group, order, ranks **6** ladder, system **7** pyramid **9** food chain, structure **11** bureaucracy **12** pecking order

hieratic
6 formal **8** priestly, stylized **10** priestlike, sacerdotal

high
4 tall **5** drunk, giddy, grand, lofty, noble, tipsy **6** elated, raised, stoned, treble, zonked **7** drugged, keyed up, soaring, supreme **8** abstruse, elevated, eloquent, euphoric, hopped-up, piercing, towering **9** climactic, delirious, prominent, spaced-out **11** extravagant, intoxicated
ball: 3 lob
combining form: 4 alti
nest: 4 aery **5** aerie, eyrie

high ___
3 hat, tea **4** card, five, noon, road, sign, tech, tide, time **5** chair, heels, hopes, jinks **6** priest, roller, school

high-and-mighty
5 bossy, proud **6** lordly **7** haughty **8** arrogant, cavalier, insolent, superior **9** imperious **10** disdainful **11** domineering, overbearing **12** supercilious

highball
3 fly, run **4** dash, rush, whiz **5** hurry, speed **6** barrel, hustle, signal **7** hotfoot **8** cocktail

highboy
5 chest **6** bureau **7** dresser **9** furniture

highbrow
4 snob **7** egghead **8** cerebral, cultured, educated **9** intellect **12** intellectual

high-class
7 elegant **8** five-star, superior **9** exclusive, exquisite, first-rate, patrician **11** fashionable **12** aristocratic **13** sophisticated

highest
3 top **5** chief **6** apical, upmost **7** exalted, maximal, maximum, supreme, topmost **9** top-drawer, uppermost **10** top-ranking
degree: 3 nth
point: 4 acme, apex **5** crest **6** summit, zenith **8** pinnacle

highfalutin
5 fancy, windy **6** florid **7** aureate, flowery, fustian, orotund, pompous **8** affected **9** bombastic, grandiose, overblown, rhapsodic **10** oratorical, rhetorical **11** declamatory, pretentious

high-flown
5 showy, tumid, windy **6** turgid **7** aureate, flowery, fustian, orotund, pompous, swollen **8** elevated, inflated, sonorous **9** bombastic, grandiose, overblown **10** flamboyant **11** declamatory, pretentious **12** magniloquent, ostentatious **13** grandiloquent

high-handed
5 bossy **8** arrogant, dogmatic, imperial **9** arbitrary, imperious **10** autocratic, disdainful, imperative, peremptory **11** dictatorial, domineering, magisterial, overbearing, overweening

high-hat
4 snub **6** slight, snobby, snooty **7** disdain, haughty **8** arrogant, snobbish **9** conceited, disregard **11** pretentious **12** supercilious

high-IQ group
5 Mensa

high jinks
3 fun **6** antics **7** fooling, revelry **9** horseplay, rowdiness, whoop-de-do **12** monkeyshines

Highland cap
3 tam

Highlander
4 Celt, Gael, Scot

Highland language
4 Erse

highlight
4 mark **5** focus **6** accent, stress **7** feature **8** point out **9** emphasize, underline **10** accentuate, focal point

high-minded
5 lofty, moral, noble **7** ethical, upright **8** elevated **10** principled

high-muck-a-muck
3 VIP **5** nabob **6** bigwig **7** big shot, notable

high-pitched
6 shrill **7** excited **8** agitated, feverish, frenetic, piercing

high point
3 top **4** acme, peak **6** apogee, summit, zenith **8** best part, pinnacle

high-powered
6 driven, strong **7** dynamic **8** animated, forceful, vigorous **9** energetic, strenuous **10** aggressive, compelling **12** enterprising

high-pressure
7 intense **8** forceful **9** insistent, stressful **10** aggressive

high roller
7 gambler, spender, wastrel **8** prodigal **10** big spender, profligate, squanderer **11** spendthrift

high-school dance
4 prom

high-school exam
3 ACT, SAT **4** PSAT

high sign
3 nod, tip **4** wink **5** alarm **6** signal, tipoff **7** gesture, warning **8** thumbs-up

Highsmith novel
11 Ripley's Game **16** Talented Mr. Ripley (The)

high-sounding
7 fustian, pompous **8** affected, imposing, inflated, puffed-up **9** grandiose, overblown **11** pretentious, sententious **13** grandiloquent

high-speed jet
3 SST

high-spirited
4 bold **5** brash, fiery, jolly, merry **6** bubbly, daring, joyful, lively, plucky, spunky **7** excited, gleeful **9** ebullient, energetic, exuberant, vivacious **12** effervescent, lighthearted

high-strung
4 edgy, taut **5** hyper, jumpy, nervy, tense, tight, wired **6** touchy **7** fidgety, jittery, keyed up, nervous, uptight **8** restless **9** excitable, sensitive

hightail it
3 git, run **4** bolt, dash, flee **5** scoot, scram **6** get out, run off **7** take off **8** clear out **9** skedaddle

highway
4 pike, road **5** track **6** artery **8** corridor, turnpike **10** interstate **12** thoroughfare
fee: **4** toll
German: **8** autobahn
Italian: **10** autostrada

highwayman
5 thief **6** bandit, robber **7** brigand

hijack
5 seize, steal **6** abduct, kidnap **8** take over **10** commandeer **11** appropriate

hike
4 jump, rove, snap, trek, walk **5** boost, raise, tramp, tromp **6** jack up, rise up, travel **7** journey, traipse, upgrade **8** backpack, increase

hilarious
5 funny, merry **7** comical **8** humorous, mirthful **9** laughable, priceless **10** rollicking

hilarity
4 glee **5** cheer, mirth **6** gaiety **7** delight **8** jocosity, laughter **9** merriment **12** cheerfulness

hill
4 bank, brae, bump, cock, dune, heap, knob, pile, rick, rise **5** bluff, butte, knoll, mound, ridge, shock, slope, stack **6** cuesta, height **7** hummock, incline **8** mountain **9** elevation, monadnock
African veld: **5** kopje **6** koppie
Boston: **6** Bunker
craggy: **3** tor
Cuba: **7** San Juan
D.C.: **7** Capitol
elongate: **7** drumlin
level-topped: **4** mesa **5** butte
of stratified drift: **4** kame
rounded: **5** swell
sand: **4** dune
small: **5** knoll, kopje, mound **6** koppie
surrounded by ice: **7** nunatak

hillbilly
4 rube **5** yokel **6** rustic **7** bumpkin, hayseed **10** clodhopper **12** backwoodsman

hillock
4 rise **5** knoll, mound

hillside
5 slope
Scottish: **4** brae

hilt
4 grip, haft **6** handle **8** handgrip

Himalayan
capital: **5** Lhasa
country: **5** Nepal **6** Bhutan
creature: **4** yeti
peak: **6** Makalu **7** Everest **9** Annapurna **10** Dhaulagiri **11** Nanga Parbat **13** Kangchenjunga

hind
3 doe **4** back, deer, rear **5** after **7** grouper **9** posterior
mate: **4** hart

hinder
4 balk, curb, mire **5** block, check, delay, deter **6** baffle, burden, fetter, hamper, hold up, impede, retard, stymie, thwart **7** inhibit, prevent, shackle, trammel **8** handicap, hold back, obstruct, restrain **9** frustrate, hamstring, interfere, interrupt

hindmost
3 end 4 back, last, rear 5 after, final 6 latter 7 closing 8 farthest, terminal, ultimate 9 posterior 10 concluding

hindquarters
4 butt, rump, tush 8 buttocks, haunches

hindrance
3 bar 4 snag 6 hurdle 7 barrier 8 obstacle 9 impedance 10 impediment 11 obstruction

Hindu
age: 4 yuga
ascetic: 4 yogi 5 fakir, swami
camel: 4 oont
caste (varna): 5 Sudra 6 Vaisya 7 Brahman 9 Kshatriya
class: 5 caste, varna
community: 6 ashram
demon: 4 Rahu 6 Ravana
essence: 5 atman
force: 5 karma
garment: 4 sari 5 saree
gentleman: 3 sri 4 babu 5 baboo
god: 4 deva, Rama, Siva 5 Shiva 6 Brahma, Vishnu
goddess: 4 devi
goddess of beauty: 7 Lakshmi
goddess of destruction: 4 Kali
goddess of speech: 4 Vach
god of destruction: 4 Siva 5 Shiva
god of fire: 4 Agni
god of love: 4 Kama
god of the heavens: 7 Krishna
god of the wind: 4 Vayu
god of war: 6 Skanda 10 Karttikeya
god of wisdom: 6 Ganesa, Ganesh
hell: 6 Naraka
holy man: 5 sadhu
honorific: 3 Sri 5 Swami 6 Pandit
hundred thousand: 4 lakh
instrument: 5 sitar, tabla
leader: 6 Gandhi (Mahatma)
loincloth: 5 dhoti
lowest caste: 5 Sudra
music: 4 raga
nobleman: 4 raja 5 rajah
philosophy: 7 Vedanta
precept: 5 sutra
prince: 4 raja 5 rajah 8 maharaja 9 maharajah
queen: 4 rani 5 ranee 8 maharani 9 maharanee
salvation: 7 nirvana
scripture: 4 Veda 6 Purana 12 Bhagavad Gita
social group: 5 caste, varna
suicide: 4 sati 6 suttee
teacher: 4 guru 5 swami 9 maharishi
term of respect: 5 sahib
treatise: 9 Upanishad
twice-born: 6 Vaisya 7 Brahman 9 Kshatriya
weaver: 5 tanti

hinge
4 pawl 5 joint, mount 12 turning point
kind: 4 butt 5 piano 10 hook-and-eye

hinged fastener
4 hasp

hint
3 cue, tip 4 clue, dash, sign, wisp 5 imply, taste, tinge, touch, trace 6 allude, notion, shadow, tipoff 7 inkling, soupçon, suggest 8 allusion, indicate, innuendo, intimate 9 insinuate, scintilla, suspicion 10 indication, intimation, suggestion 11 implication, insinuation

hinterland
4 bush 6 sticks 8 frontier, interior 9 backwater, backwoods, boondocks, up-country 10 wilderness 11 backcountry

hip
3 hot 4 chic, coxa 5 aware, savvy 6 haunch, trendy, with-it 7 tuned in 11 fashionable
bone: 4 ilia (plural) 5 ilium, pubis 6 pelvis 7 ischium
cattle: 5 thurl
disorder: 8 sciatica

hip-hop
3 rap
Spanish: 9 reggaeton
star: 3 DMC, DMX, Nas 4 Dash (Damon), Jay-Z, West (Kanye), Zola 5 Combs (Sean "Diddy"), Diddy (Combs), Drake, Dr. Dre, Kelis, Minaj (Nicki) 6 Eminem, Franti (Michael), Ja Rule, Lil' Kim 7 Birdman, Ice Cube, LL Cool J, OutKast, Pitbull, Simmons (Russell) 8 Jadakiss, Lil Wayne, Ludacris 9 Biz Markie, Fifty Cent, Foxy Brown, Snoop Dogg 11 Busta Rhymes, Tupac Shakur
term: 3 dap, def, dip, dis 4 bima, simp, wack 5 busta, chill, crunk, floss, freak, homey, peeps, props, sherm, stilo, whodi 6 gaffle, hottie, nucker, step to 7 all that, be geese, down low, homeboy, hooptie, puff lye, shizzle, wangsta 9 dukey rope, freestyle, throw bows 10 bling bling, ghetto bird, scrap a lick 12 South Central

hippie
8 bohemian, longhair 11 flower child 13 nonconformist

Hippocratic ___
4 oath

Hippodamia
father: 8 Oenomaus
husband: 6 Pelops 9 Pirithous 10 Peirithous
son: 6 Atreus 8 Thyestes

Hippolytus
father: 7 Theseus
mother: 7 Antiope 9 Hippolyte
stepmother: 7 Phaedra

hire
3 fee, let, pay 4 rent, wage 5 lease, wages 6 employ, engage, retain, sign on, take on 7 charter, payment, recruit 8 contract 10 employment 11 contract for

hireling
4 hack 6 worker 7 servant 8 employee 9 mercenary

Hirschfeld's daughter
4 Nina

hirsute
5 hairy 6 shaggy, woolly 9 whiskered

Hispania
6 Iberia 9 peninsula
part: 5 Spain 8 Portugal

Hispaniola country
5 Haiti

hiss
3 boo 4 hoot, jeer 5 decry 6 deride, revile, sizzle, wheeze 7 catcall, whisper, whistle 8 sibilate

historian
8 annalist 10 chronicler
American: 4 Webb (Charles Richard) 5 Adams (Brooks, Charles Kendall, Hannah, Henry, Herbert Baxter), Beard (Charles, Mary), Foote (Shelby) 6 Brooks (Van Wyck), Catton (Bruce), DeVoto (Bernard), Durant (Ariel, Will), Malone (Dumas), Miller (Perry), Muzzey (David), Nevins (Allen), Sarton (George Alfred), Shirer (William), Sparks (Jared), Turner (Frederick Jackson) 7 Ambrose (Stephen), Morison (Samuel Eliot), Parkman (Francis), Ridpath (John Clark), Tuchman (Barbara), Woodson (Carter G.) 8 Bancroft (George), Boorstin (Daniel), Channing (Edward), Commager (Henry Steele), Prescott (William H.), Robinson (James Harvey), Woodward (C. Vann) 10 McCullough (David) 11 Schlesinger (Arthur)
Arab: 10 Ibn Khaldun
Danish: 4 Saxo (Grammaticus)
Dutch: 8 Huizinga (Johan)
English: 4 Bede (Venerable), Stow (John), Ward (Adolphus) 5 Acton (Lord), Grote (George), Wells (Herbert George) 6 Camden (William), Gibbon (Edward), Keegan (John), Namier (Lewis Bernstein), Stubbs (William), Taylor (A. J. P.) 7 Hakluyt (Richard), Raleigh (Walter), Toynbee (Arnold), Whewell (William) 8 Geoffrey (of Monmouth), Macaulay (Thomas Babington) 9 Holinshed (Raphael), Trevelyan (George)
French: 5 Bloch (Marc), Renan (Ernest), Taine (Hippolyte) 6 Guizot (François), Thiers (Louis-Adolphe), Volney (Comte de) 7 Braudel (Ferdinand) 8 Hanotaux (Gabriel), Michelet (Jules)
German: 5 Ranke (Leopold von) 7 Mommsen (Theodor), Niebuhr (Barthold Georg) 8 Spengler (Oswald)
Greek: 8 Plutarch, Polybius, Xenophon 9 Dionysius, Herodotus 10 Thucydides
Italian: 4 Vico (Giovanni) 5 Croce (Benedetto) 9 Salvemini (Gaetano)
Jewish: 8 Josephus (Flavius)
Roman: 4 Livy 7 Sallust, Tacitus (Cornelius) 9 Suetonius
Scottish: 7 Carlyle (Thomas) 9 Robertson (William)
Swiss: 6 Müller (Johannes von)
Welsh: 7 Nennius

historical period
3 age, era 5 epoch

history
4 past, saga 5 diary 6 annals, memoir, record 7 account, done for, journal 9 chronicle, narrative, treatment 10 chronology
Muse: 4 Clio

histrionic
5 showy, stagy 6 staged 8 affected, dramatic 10 artificial, theatrical

hit
3 bop, jab, rap 4 bang, bash, bean, biff, blow, bump, bunt, butt, conk, cosh, cuff, ding, lick, slap, slug, sock, swat 5 clout, knock, paste, pound, punch, smack, smash, smite, swipe, whack 6 batter, buffet, chance, larrup, strike, stroke, thwack, wallop 7 clobber, sellout, success 8 bludgeon, lambaste 9 collision, sensation
baseball: 5 homer, liner 6 double, single, triple 7 home run 9 line drive
topposite: 4 bomb, flop, miss
golf ball: 5 shank

hitch
4 jerk, join, halt, hook, knot, lift, limp, snag, yoke 5 delay, thumb, unite 6 attach, couple, fasten, hobble, tether 7 connect, harness 8 make fast, stoppage 10 connection, difficulty, impediment 11 obstruction 12 entanglement

Hitchcock, Alfred
film: 4 Rope 5 Birds (The), Topaz 6 Frenzy, Marnie, Psycho 7 Rebecca, Vertigo 8 Lifeboat, Sabotage 9 Notorious, Suspicion 10 Rear Window, Spellbound 12 Lady Vanishes (The) 13 To Catch a Thief 14 Shadow of a Doubt 16 North by Northwest
forte: 8 suspense

hitchhike
5 thumb

hither
4 here 6 nearer 11 to this place

hitherto
5 as yet, so far 7 earlier, thus far, till now 8 formerly, until now 10 previously

Hitler, Adolf
follower: **4** Nazi
title: **6** Führer **7** Fuehrer
wife: **5** Braun (Eva)

hit man
4 goon, thug **5** bravo **6** killer **7** torpedo **8** assassin, enforcer, hired gun, murderer **9** cutthroat

hit-or-miss
6 casual, chance, random **7** aimless, erratic **8** careless, slapdash **9** arbitrary, desultory, haphazard, irregular, unplanned **11** scattershot

hit the bottle
4 swig, tope **5** drink, swill **6** guzzle, imbibe, tipple

hive
6 apiary, colony **7** cluster **9** stockpile

HMS Pinafore
composer: **8** Sullivan (Arthur)
librettist: **7** Gilbert (W. S.)

hoagie
3 sub **4** hero **5** po'boy **7** grinder, torpedo **8** sandwich **9** submarine

hoar
4 rime **5** frost

hoard
4 save **5** amass, cache, lay by, lay up, stash, stock, store, trove **6** supply **7** collect, lay away, nest egg, reserve **8** squirrel, treasure **9** stockpile **10** accumulate, collection, cumulation **11** aggregation **12** accumulation

hoarder
5 miser **7** pack rat, scrooge **8** tightwad **9** skinflint

hoarse
5 gruff, husky, raspy, rough, thick **6** croaky **7** grating, rasping, raucous, throaty **8** croaking, gravelly, guttural

hoary
3 old **4** aged **5** stale **6** age-old **7** ancient, antique, graying **8** grizzled, timeworn **9** venerable

hoax
3 con **4** dupe, fake, fool, gull, scam, sham **5** fraud, phony, trick **6** befool, canard, delude, humbug, take in **7** deceive, mislead **8** flimflam, hoodwink, trickery **9** bamboozle, deception, imposture

Hobbit creator
7 Tolkien (J. R. R.)

hobble
4 lame, limp **6** fetter, hamper, hinder, hog-tie, impede **7** cripple, trammel **8** handicap

hobby
6 falcon **7** pastime, pursuit **8** activity, sideline **9** avocation, diversion

hobgoblin
4 Puck **5** bogey **6** sprite **7** bugaboo

hobnob
3 mix **6** mingle **7** consort **9** associate, rub elbows, socialize **10** fraternize **11** get together

hobo
3 bum **5** gypsy, tramp **7** drifter, floater, swagman, vagrant **8** derelict, vagabond

hock
4 debt, pawn **5** ankle **6** prison

hockey
6 shinny
arena: **4** rink
cup: **7** Stanley
implement: **4** puck **5** stick
official: **7** referee **8** linesman
player: **3** Orr (Bobby), Roy (Patrick) **4** Bure (Pavel), Fuhr (Grant), Hall (Glenn), Howe (Gordie), Hull (Bobby, Brett), Jagr (Jaromir), wing **5** Bossy (Mike), Bucyk (John), Hasek (Dominik), Kurri (Jari), Maruk (Dennis), Sakic (Joe), Shore (Eddie), Shutt (Steve) **6** center, Clarke (Bobby), Coffey (Paul), Dionne (Marcel), Dryden (Ken), goalie, Harvey (Doug), Juneau (Joe), Kariya (Paul), Leetch (Brian), Mikita (Stan), Morenz (Howie), Parent (Bernie), Plante (Jacques), Potvin (Denis), Recchi (Mark), Savard (Denis), Sundin (Mats) **7** Belfour (Ed), Bourque (Ray), Brodeur (Martin), Chelios (Chris), Fedorov (Sergei), forward, Francis (Ron), Gretzky (Wayne), Lafleur (Guy), Lemieux (Claude, Mario), Lindros (Eric), Messier (Mark), Mogilny (Alexander), Richard (Maurice), Richter (Mike), Sawchuk (Terry), Selanne (Teemu), Stastny (Peter), Yzerman (Steve) **8** Beliveau (Jean), Esposito (Phil, Tony), Forsberg (Peter), Nicholls (Bernie), pointman, Shanahan (Brendan), Trottier (Bryan), Ysebaert (Paul) **9** Hawerchuk (Dale) **10** Carbonneau (Guy), defenseman, goalkeeper
term: **3** box **4** cage, deke, goal, puck, rink **5** bandy, bench, check, icing, stick **6** charge, crease, shinny **7** face-off, offside **8** blue line **9** back-check, body-check **10** center line, penalty box
variation of: **9** broomball
(see also **National Hockey League**)

hockey great Bobby
3 Orr

hocus-pocus
4 sham **8** artifice, nonsense, trickery **9** conjuring, deception, imposture **10** mumbo jumbo **11** abracadabra, incantation, legerdemain **13** sleight of hand

hod
4 tray **6** trough **7** scuttle **11** coal scuttle

Hoder, Hoth
brother: **6** Balder, Baldur
slayer: **4** Vali
victim: **6** Balder, Baldur

hodgepodge
4 hash, olio, stew **6** jumble, medley **7** mélange, mixture **8** mishmash, mixed bag **9** patchwork, potpourri **10** assortment, miscellany, salmagundi **11** gallimaufry

hoe
4 till, weed **6** tiller, weeder **9** cultivate

hoedown
9 barn dance **11** contra dance, square dance

hog
3 pig, sow **4** boar, suid **5** swine
family: **6** Suidae
female: **3** sow **4** gilt
genus: **3** Sus
home: **3** sty **6** pigsty
red: **5** duroc
young: **5** shoat

hogback
5 crest, ridge

hogshead
3 keg, tun **4** butt, cask **6** barrel **9** container

hog-tie
4 bind **6** fetter **7** shackle, trammel

Hogwarts lesson
6 charms, spells **7** Muggles, potions

hogwash
3 rot **4** bosh, bunk, slop **5** bilge, hokum, hooey, swill **6** piffle **7** baloney, garbage, rubbish **8** nonsense, tommyrot **9** moonshine, poppycock **10** applesauce, balderdash, flapdoodle, taradiddle **12** gobbledygook

hog wild
5 crazy **6** crazed, madcap **7** berserk

ho-hum
4 dull, so-so **5** bored **6** boring **7** tedious **8** tiresome **10** unexciting **11** indifferent

hoi polloi
3 mob **5** horde **6** masses **8** populace **9** multitude **10** lower class **11** proletariat

hoist
4 lift **5** drink, raise, winch **6** lift up, pick up, take up **7** capstan, derrick, elevate **8** windlass

hoity-toity
4 smug **5** dizzy, giddy, silly **6** la-de-da, la-di-da **7** flighty, pompous **8** lah-de-dah, lah-di-dah **9** conceited, frivolous, lah-dee-dah **11** highfalutin

hokey
4 fake, mock, sham **5** banal, bogus, corny, hammy, phony, stale, stagy, trite **6** ersatz, pseudo **7** clichéd **8** cornball, outdated **9** contrived, hackneyed **12** melodramatic

Hokkaido native
4 Ainu

hokum
4 bosh **5** hooey **7** baloney, hogwash **8** malarkey, nonsense **9** moonshine, poppycock **10** applesauce, balderdash, flapdoodle, taradiddle **11** foolishness **12** gobbledygook

Holbrook of Mark Twain fame
3 Hal

hold
3 own **4** bear, deem, grab, grip, keep **5** carry, clamp, clasp, cling, grasp, gripe, judge, sense, think, value **6** arrest, clench, clinch, clutch, detain, harbor, regard, retain **7** contain, convene, convoke, fermata, grapple, keep out, possess, reserve, support, sustain **8** keep back, maintain, preserve, restrict
close: **6** cuddle
dear: **7** cherish
in check: **7** repress
in common: **5** share
out: **4** last **6** endure
together: **4** bond **5** clamp **6** fasten
wrestling: **6** nelson **8** headlock, scissors **10** full nelson, half nelson

hold back
4 curb, keep, stop **5** check, delay **6** bridle, detain, impede, retain **7** inhibit, keep out, prevent, refrain, reserve **8** restrain, suppress, withhold **9** constrain

holder
3 cup, pot **4** bowl, cone, vase **5** owner **6** tenant **7** pitcher

hold forth
4 rant **5** orate, speak, spout **7** declaim, expound, lecture **8** harangue, proclaim **9** expatiate **10** dilate upon

hold off
4 stay, wait **5** defer, delay, pause, repel **6** rebuff, resist **7** abstain, adjourn, repulse, suspend **8** hesitate, postpone, prorogue **9** withstand **11** discontinue

holdup
5 heist, theft **7** mugging, robbery

hold up
3 rob **4** halt, last, lift, stay **5** check, defer, delay, hoist, raise **6** endure, hinder, impede, put off, retard **7** support, suspend **8** postpone, prorogue, slow down

hole
3 den, gap, jam, pit **4** cave, flaw, lair, rent, spot, void **5** fault, niche **6** breach, burrow, cavity, cranny, defect, eyelet, lacuna, outlet **7** dilemma, opening, orifice **8** aperture, weakness **9** perforate **10** excavation, interstice **11** perforation, predicament

hole in one
3 ace

hole-making tool
3 awl

holiday
4 Xmas **5** leave **6** May Day **7** Flag Day **8** Labor Day, New Year's, vacation **9** Christmas, Hallowmas, Halloween **10** Father's Day, Mother's Day **11** Memorial Day, Veterans Day **12** All Saints' Day, Groundhog Day, Thanksgiving **13** Presidents' Day, St. Patrick's Day, Valentine's Day
British: **9** Boxing Day
Canadian: **11** Dominion Day, Victoria Day
drink: **3** nog **5** glogg **6** eggnog
Jewish: **8** Passover **9** Yom Kippur **12** Rosh Hashanah
song: **5** carol
Vietnamese: **3** Tet

holiness
5 piety **6** purity **8** devotion, divinity, sanctity **9** beatitude **11** religiosity **12** consecration, spirituality

Holland
see **Netherlands**

holler
3 cry **4** call, yell **5** shout **6** bellow, clamor, cry out, outcry **7** call out **8** complain **9** complaint

hollow
3 dip, sag **4** void **5** basin, empty, false **6** cavity, ravine, sunken, vacant **7** concave, echoing, sinkage **8** sinkhole, thorough **9** cavernous, concavity **10** depression, sepulchral
out: **3** dig, gut **4** mine **5** gouge **8** excavate

holly
4 tree **5** shrub
genus: **4** Ilex

Hollywood
10 Tinseltown
street: **4** Vine

holm oak
4 ilex

holocaust
4 fire **7** inferno **8** genocide **9** sacrifice **10** mass murder **11** destruction **13** conflagration

Holofernes' slayer
6 Judith

holy
6 adored, divine, sacred **7** angelic, blessed, revered, sainted, saintly, sublime **8** hallowed **9** glorified, religious, spiritual, venerated, worshiped **10** reverenced, sacrosanct, sanctified **11** consecrated
combining form: **5** hagio, hiero
communion: **9** Eucharist
oil: **6** chrism
person: **5** saint **6** zaddik **7** tzaddik
Spirit: **9** Paraclete
vessel: **5** grail **7** chalice **8** ciborium

holy place
6 church, shrine, temple **7** sanctum **9** sanctuary

Holy Roman Emperor
4 Karl, Otto **5** Adolf, Franz, Henry, Louis **6** Albert, Arnulf, Conrad, Joseph, Lothar, Ludwig, Philip, Rudolf, Rupert, Wenzel **7** Charles, Francis, Leopold, Lothair **8** Heinrich **9** Ferdinand, Frederick, Friedrich, Sigismund **10** Maximilian **11** Charlemagne

Holy Thursday
6 Maundy (Thursday) **9** Ascension (Day)

holy war
5 jihad **7** crusade

holy writ
5 Bible **9** Scripture

homage
5 honor **6** praise **7** respect, tribute **9** deference, obeisance, reverence

hombre
3 cat, guy, lad, man **4** buck, chap, dude, gent, stud **6** fellow, honcho **7** comrade

home
3 den **4** digs, lair, land, site **5** abode, haunt, house, range **6** family, hearth **7** country, habitat, housing **8** domicile, dwelling, locality **9** household, residence **10** fatherland, habitation, motherland **12** headquarters
country: **5** cabin **7** cottage **8** bungalow

homeless
5 stray **6** exiled **7** outcast, vagrant **8** derelict **9** abandoned, displaced, wandering **12** dispossessed

homely
4 cozy **5** plain **6** direct, modest, simple **7** natural **8** familiar, ordinary **11** comfortable, commonplace **12** unattractive **13** unpretentious
fruit: **4** Ugli

homemade knife
4 shiv

Homeric epic
5 Iliad **7** Odyssey

Homer Simpson
daughter: **4** Lisa
exclamation: **3** d'oh
son: **4** Bart
wife: **5** Marge

HOMES lake
4 Erie **5** Huron

homesickness
7 longing **9** nostalgia

homespun
5 plain **6** fabric, folksy, russet, simple **8** ordinary **9** practical **13** unpretentious

Home, Sweet Home
music: **6** Bishop (Henry)
words: **5** Payne (John Howard)

homicidal
6 bloody **8** sanguine **9** murdering, murderous **10** sanguinary **11** sanguineous **12** bloodthirsty

homicide
5 blood **6** killer, murder, slayer **7** killing **8** foul play, murderer **9** manslayer **12** manslaughter

homily
6 sermon **7** lecture **9** discourse

hominy
4 mush, samp

homogeneous
7 uniform **10** consistent

Homo sapiens
3 man **7** mankind **8** humanity **9** humankind, human race

homunculus
5 dwarf, pygmy **6** midget, peewee **7** manikin **8** Tom Thumb

honcho
4 boss, head **5** chief, Mr. Big **6** bigwig, leader, master, top gun **7** big shot, foreman, headman **8** hierarch, overseer **9** chieftain, Mister Big

Honduras
capital: **11** Tegucigalpa
city: **7** La Ceiba **9** Choluteca **10** El Progreso **12** San Pedro Sula
coast: **8** Mosquito
discoverer: **8** Columbus (Christopher)
Indian people: **4** Maya **5** Mayan
language: **7** Spanish
monetary unit: **7** lempira
neighbor: **9** Guatemala, Nicaragua **10** El Salvador
river: **4** Coco, Ulúa **5** Aguán **6** Patuca
sea: **9** Caribbean

hone
4 edge, whet **6** finish, polish, refine, smooth **7** perfect, sharpen **9** whetstone

honest
4 fair, just, open, real, true **5** frank, plain **6** candid **7** genuine, sincere, upright **8** innocent, reliable, truthful **9** objective, reputable, unfeigned, veracious **10** creditable, forthright, legitimate, scrupulous **13** conscientious, unimpeachable
president: **3** Abe (Lincoln)

honesty
4 herb **5** honor **6** candor, virtue **7** probity **8** fairness, goodness, justness, veracity **9** integrity, rectitude, sincerity **11** uprightness **12** truthfulness

honey
3 mel **4** dear **7** darling, sweetie **8** beloved **10** sweetheart
combining form: **3** mel **4** meli, mell **5** melli
drink: **4** mead

honey badger
5 ratel

honeybee genus
4 Apis

honeycomb
3 pit **4** fill, fret **5** cells **6** impair, infest, riddle, weaken **7** subvert **9** perforate

honeydew
5 melon

honeyed
5 sweet **6** golden, liquid, mellow **9** sweetened **10** flattering **11** mellifluous

Honeymooners, The
bus company: **6** Gotham
character: **5** Alice (Kramden) **6** Trixie (Norton) **8** Ed Norton **12** Ralph Kramden
lodge: **7** Raccoon
setting: **8** Brooklyn **11** Bensonhurst
star: **6** Carney (Art) **7** Gleason (Jackie), Meadows (Audrey) **8** Randolph (Joyce)

honeysuckle
6 azalea **9** columbine **13** pinxter flower

honey wine
4 mead

honk
4 blow, toot **5** blare, blast **7** trumpet

honker
4 beak, nose **5** snoot, snout **6** schnoz **7** schnozz

honky-tonk
4 dive **5** joint **7** hangout **9** juke joint, roadhouse **11** barrelhouse

Honolulu's island
4 Oahu

honor
4 fete, laud **5** adorn, asset, award, badge, exalt, glory, kudos, medal **6** credit, esteem, homage, praise, purity, regard, trophy **7** commend, dignify, ennoble, fulfill, glorify, laurels, respect **8** accolade, approval, carry out, chastity, decorate, devotion, good name **9** adulation, deference, integrity, privilege, recognize, reverence **10** admiration, decoration, reputation, veneration **11** distinction, distinguish, recognition **12** commendation

honorable
4 just, true **5** moral, right **6** honest, worthy **7** ethical, upright **8** laudable **9** dignified **10** creditable, scrupulous **11** illustrious **13** conscientious

honorarium
7 payment **8** gratuity **10** recompense **12** compensation **13** consideration

honorific in India
3 sri

Honshu city
5 Osaka

hooch
5 booze, sauce 6 liquor, rotgut 7 bootleg 8 dwelling, home brew 9 firewater, moonshine 10 bathtub gin

hood
4 cowl, thug 5 tough 6 bonnet, helmet 7 capuche 8 covering, gangster, hooligan 10 delinquent

hoodlum
4 punk, thug 5 bully 7 mobster, ruffian 8 criminal, gangster, hooligan 10 delinquent

hoodoo
3 hex 4 jinx, juju, rock 5 curse, haunt, hokum, magic, spell, spook 6 harass, whammy 7 bewitch, evil eye, sorcery, terrify, torment 8 nonsense 9 conjuring 10 black magic, hocus-pocus, mumbo jumbo, witchcraft

hoodwink
3 con 4 bilk, dupe, fool, gull, hoax, rook, scam 5 trick 6 befool, take in 7 deceive, mislead 8 flimflam 9 bamboozle

hooey
3 rot 4 bunk 5 bilge 6 bunkum 7 baloney, eyewash, hogwash 8 claptrap, malarkey, nonsense, tommyrot 10 balderdash

hoof
4 foot, walk 5 troop 6 ungula 7 traipse 8 ambulate
cloven: 5 cloot
sound: 4 clop 8 clip-clop

hoofer
6 dancer 7 danseur 8 coryphée, danseuse, showgirl 9 ballerina, tap dancer

hooflike
6 ungual

hook
3 nab, nip 4 gaff, gore, hasp 5 catch, curve, hitch, pinch, steal 6 anchor, fasten, pilfer 7 hamulus 8 crotchet
a fish: 4 gaff, snag
for keys: 10 chatelaine

hooklike
7 falcate 8 unciform, uncinate
part: 5 uncus 7 hamulus

Hook's sidekick
4 Smee

hookup
7 circuit, linkage 8 alliance 10 assemblage, connection 11 affiliation, association, combination, conjunction, partnership

hooky
6 truant 7 truancy 8 truantry

hooligan
see **hoodlum**

hoop
4 band, ring 6 circle 7 circlet
for kids: 4 hula

hoopla
4 bash, fuss, stir, to-do 6 bustle, frolic 7 revelry, shindig, whoopee 8 ballyhoo, wingding 9 commotion, festivity, merriment, promotion

hoops
5 b-ball 10 basketball

hooray
3 rah, yay 5 cheer, huzza 6 huzzah, yippee 7 acclaim, whoopee 10 hallelujah

hoosegow
3 jug, pen 4 brig, cage, coop, jail, keep, stir 5 clink, pokey 6 cooler, lockup, prison 7 slammer 8 bastille, big house 9 calaboose, jailhouse 12 penitentiary

Hoosier State
7 Indiana

hoot
3 bit, boo, jot 4 hiss, iota, jeer, whit 5 laugh, scrap, shout, whoop 6 assail, deride, heckle 7 catcall, modicum 8 particle

hooter
3 owl 5 owlet

Hoover Dam lake
4 Mead

hop
4 jump, leap, trip, vine 5 bound, dance 6 bounce, spring, wait on 7 rebound 8 jump over

hope
4 goal, wish 5 await, dream, faith, trust 6 aspire, desire, expect 7 count on, longing, promise 8 ambition, optimism, prospect 9 count upon 10 anticipate, aspiration, confidence
loss of: 7 despair

hopeful
4 rosy 5 eager, sunny 6 bright, cheery, golden, seeker, upbeat 7 assured 8 aspirant, aspiring 9 candidate, confident, expectant, promising 10 auspicious, contestant, optimistic, propitious 11 encouraging 12 advantageous

hopeless
4 glum, lost, vain 6 futile, gloomy, morose 7 forlorn 8 downcast 9 desperate, incurable, insoluble 10 despairing, despondent, impossible 11 ineffectual, irreparable, pessimistic 12 incorrigible, irredeemable, irremediable

hoper
7 truster 8 optimist 9 expectant, Pollyanna

hopped-up
4 high 5 giddy 6 stoned, zonked 7 drugged, excited 9 delirious 12 enthusiastic

hopper
3 box, mix 4 frog, hare, tank, toad 5 bunny,

chute **6** rabbit **7** cricket **10** freight car, receptacle

___ Hopper
5 Grace (Murray), Hedda **6** Edward

hopping
4 busy **5** irate, livid **6** lively **7** furious **9** extremely, violently **10** infuriated

hops-drying kiln
4 oast

Horae
4 Dike **6** Eirene **7** Eunomia, seasons

Horam
kingdom: **5** Gezer
slayer: **6** Joshua

horde
3 mob **4** army **5** crowd, crush, drove, press, swarm **6** throng **9** multitude

horizon
4 goal **5** limit, range, reach, scope, vista **6** extent **7** purview, skyline **8** prospect **11** perspective

horizontal
4 flat **5** level **8** parallel

hormone
4 ACTH **5** kinin **6** estrin **7** estriol, estrone, gastrin, insulin, relaxin **8** autacoid, estrogen, glucagon, kallidin, secretin
female: **8** estrogen
insect: **8** ecdysone
pituitary: **8** oxytocin

horn
4 toot **5** cornu **6** antler, klaxon, shofar **7** trumpet **10** cornucopia, projection
ancient Greek: **5** rhyta (plural) **6** rhyton
animal: **6** antler

Hornblower, Horatio
creator: **8** Forester (C. S.)
ship: **6** Le Reve **7** Atropos, Hotspur **10** Sutherland

Horne of stage and screen
4 Lena

horn in
6 meddle **7** intrude, obtrude **9** insinuate, interfere, interlope, interrupt

hornlike
8 corneous **10** keratinous

hornswoggle
3 con **4** dupe, fool, gull, hoax, hose, rook, scam **5** trick **6** take in **7** deceive **8** flimflam, hoodwink **9** bamboozle

horrendous
5 awful **7** fearful, ghastly, heinous, hideous **8** alarming, dreadful, gruesome, horrible, horrific, shocking, terrible **9** abhorrent, appalling, execrable, frightful, repugnant, revolting **11** distressing, unspeakable

horrible
4 grim **5** awful, lurid **6** grisly **7** fearful, ghastly, hateful, hellish, hideous **8** dreadful, gruesome, shocking **9** abhorrent, appalling, frightful, loathsome, repellent, repugnant, repulsive, revolting **10** abominable, disgusting, terrifying

horrid
5 nasty **7** noisome **8** shocking **9** loathsome, offensive, repulsive, sickening **10** detestable, disgusting

horrific
5 awful **7** fearful **8** dreadful, shocking, terrible **9** appalling, dismaying, frightful, harrowing

horrified
6 aghast **8** appalled

horrify
5 daunt, shock **6** appall, dismay

horrifying
4 grim **5** awful, lurid **6** grisly **7** ghastly, hideous **8** gruesome, terrible **9** appalling, atrocious

horror
4 fear, hate, pain **5** alarm, dread, panic, shock **6** dismay, fright, hatred, terror **7** disgust **8** aversion, loathing **9** repulsion, revulsion **10** abhorrence, repugnance **11** abomination, detestation, trepidation

hors d'oeuvre
4 whet **5** snack **6** canape, tidbit **7** crudité **9** antipasto, appetizer
Spanish: **4** tapa
spread: **4** paté

horse
3 nag **4** buck **5** bronc, mount, pacer, steed **6** bronco, brumby, equine **7** cavalry, courser, palfrey, sawbuck, trestle, trotter **8** footrope, jackstay, stallion, traveler
Australian-bred: **5** waler
battle: **7** charger
breed: **4** Arab **5** pinto **6** Morgan **7** Arabian, Belgian, Iceland **8** Palomino, Shetland **9** Appaloosa, Percheron **10** Lippizaner **12** standardbred, Thoroughbred
champion: **7** Barbaro, Man o' War **8** Affirmed, Citation **10** Seabiscuit **11** Seattle Slew, Secretariat, Smarty Jones
collar part: **4** hame
color: **3** bay, dun **4** roan **6** grullo, sorrel **8** buckskin, chestnut, palomino
combining form: **4** hipp **5** hippo
command: **3** gee, haw
covering: **8** trapping
draft: **5** shire **10** Clydesdale
extinct: **8** eohippus
farm: **6** dobbin
feature: **4** mane
female: **4** mare **5** filly
foot part: **7** pastern
gait: **4** trot **6** canter, gallop

gear: 3 bit 4 rein 6 saddle 7 harness 9 check-rein
leg joint: 7 fetlock
leg part: 6 gaskin 7 gambrel
male: 4 colt 8 stallion
mark: 5 blaze
of the movies: 4 Fury 6 Flicka, Silver 7 Trigger 8 Champion 11 Black Beauty
pace: 4 gait
race: 5 Ascot, derby 7 Belmont 9 Preakness
rump: 7 crupper
small: 4 pony 6 garron, jennet
spotted: 5 pinto 7 piebald
talking: 4 Mr. Ed
tan: 8 palomino
thoroughbred: 8 hotblood
tooth: 4 tush
war: 8 destrier
wild: 7 mustang

horsefeathers
3 rot 4 bull, bunk, nuts 5 bilge, hokum, hooey, trash 6 bunkum, drivel, piffle 7 baloney, garbage, hogwash, rubbish, twaddle 8 claptrap, flimflam, nonsense, tommyrot 9 poppycock 10 applesauce, balderdash

horseman
5 rider 6 cowboy 7 vaquero 8 cavalier 9 caballero, chevalier 10 equestrian

horsemanship
6 manège 10 equitation

horse opera
5 oater 7 western

horseplay
6 antics 7 fooling 8 clowning, rowdyism 9 high jinks, rowdiness 10 buffoonery, roughhouse 11 shenanigans 12 roughhousing

horse-racing term
3 bug, cup 4 bolt, calk, gait, oaks, pill, prop, show, tack 5 float, place, purse, silks, washy 6 bobble, closer, exacta, impost, mudder, router, stayer 7 also-ran, blowout, clocker, paddock, spit box 8 breakage, claiming, climbing, dead heat, handicap, hand ride, off track, perfecta, post time, quiniela 9 hot walker 10 allowances, in the money, parimutuel, shadow roll 11 backstretch, daily double, morning line, triple crown 12 morning glory

horseshoer
5 smith 6 smithy 7 farrier 10 blacksmith

hortative
8 advisory 9 exhorting, homiletic

horticulturist
6 Carver (George Washington) 7 Burbank (Luther)

Horus
brother: 6 Anubis
father: 6 Osiris
mother: 4 Isis
victim: 3 Set 4 Seth

hose
4 sock, tube, wash 5 cheat, spray, trick, water 6 tights 8 stocking

hoser
6 barfly, boozer 7 redneck

hosiery shade
4 ecru 5 taupe

hospice
see **hostel**

hospitable
4 kind, open 6 social 7 cordial 8 friendly, generous, gracious 9 convivial, receptive, welcoming 10 gregarious

hospital
6 clinic 7 lazaret 9 infirmary, lazaretto
attendant: 7 orderly
ship's: 7 sickbay

Hospitallers' island
5 Malta 6 Rhodes

host
4 army 5 array, cloud, crowd, emcee, flock, horde 6 angels, legion, myriad, scores, server 7 compere, present, receive 8 assemble 9 innkeeper, introduce, moderator, multitude, presenter

hostage
4 pawn 5 token 6 pledge, surety 7 captive, earnest 8 guaranty, prisoner, security 9 guarantee

hostel
3 inn 4 stay 5 lodge 6 tavern, travel 7 auberge, lodging 11 caravansary, public house

hostile
4 anti, mean 5 enemy 6 bitter, fierce 7 adverse, opposed, warlike 8 contrary, inimical, opposite 9 bellicose, combative, resistant, resisting 10 malevolent, pugnacious, unfriendly 11 belligerent, contentious 12 antagonistic 13 argumentative

hostility
3 war 6 animus, enmity, hatred, rancor 7 ill will 8 conflict 9 antipathy 10 aggression, antagonism, opposition, resistance 12 belligerence

hot
3 new 4 fast, heat, sexy 5 angry, close, eager, fiery, lucky, spicy 6 ardent, baking, banned, heated, hectic, on fire, raging, stolen, sultry, torrid, urgent 7 boiling, burning, excited, fevered, illicit, lustful, on a roll, peppery, popular, pungent, zealous 8 broiling, feverish, in demand, scalding, sizzling, tropical, vehement 9 energized, lecherous, scorching 10 blistering, contraband, passionate, sweltering 11 radioactive

hot air
4 bosh 6 bunkum 7 blather, prattle, twaddle 8 malarkey, nonsense 9 empty talk, poppycock 10 double-talk

hotbed
3 hub **4** core, seat **5** heart **6** center **7** nucleus **10** focal point **11** nerve center

hot-blooded
5 fiery, lusty **6** ardent **7** burning, fervent, flaming **9** excitable, impetuous, impulsive **10** passionate **11** impassioned **12** high-spirited

hotchpotch
see **hodgepodge**

hot dog
5 frank **6** weenie, wiener, wienie **7** sausage, show-off **8** showboat **11** frankfurter, wienerwurst

hotel
3 inn **4** doss **5** lodge **6** tavern **7** auberge, hospice, pension **8** motor inn **11** public house **12** lodging house, rooming house **13** boardinghouse
chain: **5** Hyatt **6** Hilton, Ramada, Westin **7** Days Inn **8** Marriott, Radisson, Sheraton, Stouffer **10** Holiday Inn **11** Best Western, Four Seasons
inferior: **7** fleabag **9** flophouse

hothead
5 rebel **7** fanatic, inciter, radical **8** agitator **9** demagogue, firebrand **10** incendiary **12** rabble-rouser, troublemaker **13** revolutionary

hotheaded
4 rash **5** brash, fiery, hasty **6** madcap **8** reckless **9** excitable, impetuous, imprudent, impulsive, irritable

Hotpoint alternative
5 Amana

hotshot
3 ace, VIP **4** star, whiz **5** comer **6** expert, master, wizard **8** virtuoso **10** powerhouse **11** heavyweight

Hot Springs, e.g.
3 spa

hot-tempered
see **quick-tempered**

hot tub
3 spa

hot water
3 box, fix, jam **4** bind, hole **6** corner, pickle **7** dilemma, trouble **9** tight spot **11** predicament
in: **10** up the creek

____ Houdini
5 Harry

hound
3 cur, dog, fan **4** bait, buff, ride **5** chivy **6** badger, basset, beagle, bowwow, canine, harass, hassle, heckle, hector, pester, pursue, Talbot **7** devotee **8** bullyrag **9** dachshund, persecute **10** aficionado
Russian: **6** borzoi

hour, canonical
4 none, sext **5** lauds, nones, prime, terce **6** matins **7** vespers **8** compline

hourglass
5 timer

house
3 cot, hut, ken **4** home, shed **5** abode, board, cabin, dwell, hovel, lodge, put up, shack, villa **6** billet, chalet, harbor, shanty **7** contain, cottage, enclose, mansion, quarter, saltbox, shelter, theater **8** audience, bungalow, domicile, dwelling, quarters **9** residence
clergyman's: **5** manse **7** rectory **9** parsonage
country: **5** manor **7** cottage **8** bungalow
dog: **6** kennel
earth: **5** adobe
Eskimo: **5** igloo
lot: **4** plat, site
mean: **5** hovel, shack
of prostitution: **4** crib **6** bagnio **7** brothel **8** bordello
religious: **5** abbey **6** priory **7** convent, nunnery **9** monastery
rooming: **5** lodge
Russian: **5** dacha
small: **4** camp **5** cabin, shack **6** shanty **7** cottage **8** bungalow
Spanish: **4** casa

housebreaker
4 yegg **5** thief **7** burglar, prowler **8** picklock

household
4 home **5** folks **6** family, ménage **8** domestic, familiar
gods (Roman): **5** lares **7** penates

house of worship
6 bethel, chapel, church, mosque, pagoda, shrine, temple **7** chantry, minster, oratory **8** basilica **9** cathedral, sanctuary, synagogue **10** tabernacle **11** conventicle

housing
4 case, room **7** shelter **8** barracks, quarters **9** enclosure

Houston player
5 Astro

hovel
3 hut, sty **4** dump, shed **5** hutch, shack **6** burrow, pigpen, pigsty, shanty **7** shelter

hover
4 flit, hang, loom **5** dance, drift, float, poise, waver **7** flitter, flutter, suspend **9** fluctuate, hang about

howbeit
3 yet **4** when **5** still, while **6** even if, much as, though **7** whereas **8** after all, although **11** nonetheless **12** nevertheless

Howe of sewing-machine fame
5 Elias

however
3 but, yet **4** only **5** still **6** except, though **8** after all **11** nonetheless **12** nevertheless

howl
3 bay, cry **4** bark, keen, wail, yell, yelp **6** cry out **9** caterwaul

howler
4 flub, gaff, goof **5** boner, fluff, gaffe **6** boo-boo **7** blooper, blunder

HST
predecessor: 3 FDR
successor: 3 DDE

huarache
6 sandal

hub
4 axis, core **5** focus, heart, pivot **6** center **8** polestar **10** focal point **11** nerve center
opposite: 3 rim

hubbub
3 ado, din **4** fuss, stir, to-do **5** babel, furor, hoo-ha, noise **6** clamor, furore, hassle, hoo-hah, jangle, pother, racket, rumpus, tumult, uproar **7** turmoil **8** brouhaha, foofaraw **9** commotion, confusion **10** hullabaloo, hurly-burly **11** disturbance, pandemonium

hubris
3 ego **4** gall **5** brass, cheek, nerve, pride **7** conceit, hauteur, swagger **8** audacity, chutzpah **9** arrogance, cockiness, vainglory **11** braggadocio

hubristic
4 vain **5** cocky, proud **7** haughty **8** arrogant, insolent, superior **11** overbearing, overweening **13** overconfident

Huckleberry Finn
author: 5 Twain (Mark) **7** Clemens (Samuel)
character: 3 Jim, Tom (Sawyer) **4** Duke, King
river: 11 Mississippi

huckster
4 hawk, plug, tout, vend **5** pitch **6** dicker, haggle, hawker, peddle, vendor **7** bargain, chaffer, haggler, packman, peddler, promote **8** pitchman

huddle
4 lump, mass **5** bunch, crowd, group, hunch **6** confab, confer, crouch, curl up, gather, parley, powwow **7** cluster, consult, meeting **8** assemble **10** conference, discussion

Hudson's ship
8 Half Moon

hue
4 cast, tint, tone **5** color, shade, shape, tinge, value **6** aspect, manner **8** coloring, tincture **10** coloration, complexion

huff
3 pet **4** blow, gasp, pant, rile, roil, snap, snit, tiff **5** annoy, grate, heave, peeve, pique, storm **6** nettle, put out **7** bluster, inflate **8** irritate

huffy
5 angry, proud, testy **6** piqued, snippy, tetchy, touchy **7** annoyed, fretful, haughty, peevish, pettish, prickly, waspish **8** arrogant, petulant, snappish **9** irascible, irritable, irritated, querulous

hug
4 hold **5** clasp, press, prize, value **6** clench, clinch, clutch, cuddle, enfold **7** cherish, embrace, envelop, squeeze **8** hold fast, hold onto **12** congratulate

huge
4 epic, vast, wide **5** bulky, giant, grand, great, jumbo, mondo **6** heroic, mighty, untold **7** immense, mammoth, massive, titanic **8** colossal, enormous, gigantic, whopping **9** extensive, monstrous **10** monumental, prodigious, stupendous, tremendous **11** magnificent, mountainous

hugeness
8 enormity **9** immensity, magnitude

hugger-mugger
4 hash **6** jumble, muddle, secret, tangle **7** clutter, furtive, jumbled, secrecy **8** confused, covertly, disorder, secretly **9** by stealth, confusion, furtively, mare's nest **10** disordered, disorderly, stealthily, undercover **11** clandestine **13** clandestinely

Hugo, Victor
character: 6 Javert (Inspector) **7** Cosette, Fantine, Valjean (Jean) **9** Esmeralda, Quasimodo
novel: 13 Les Misérables **20** Hunchback of Notre Dame (The)

Huguenot
10 Protestant
leader: 5 Condé (Prince de), Rohan (Henri) **6** Mornay (Philippe) **7** Coligny (Gaspard II de)

Huguenots composer
9 Meyerbeer (Giacomo)

hulk
4 body, loom, ship **5** shell, wreck **8** skeleton **9** shipwreck

hulking
4 huge **5** beefy, bulky, burly, husky **7** immense, mammoth, massive **8** colossal, enormous, gigantic, oversize **9** humongous, lumbering, monstrous, ponderous, strapping **11** heavyweight

hull
3 pod **4** bark, body, case, husk, peel, rind, skin **5** chaff, frame, shell, shuck **6** casing **8** covering **11** decorticate

hullabaloo
3 ado, din **4** roar, to-do **5** furor, hoo-ha, noise

6 **clamor**, hoo-hah, hubbub, jangle, pother, racket, ruckus, tumult, uproar **8** ballyhoo, foofaraw **9** commotion, hue and cry **11** pandemonium

hum
4 buzz, purr, sing, zing **5** drone **6** murmur **7** vibrate

human
5 being, party **6** mortal, person **7** hominid **8** hominoid **10** individual
race: **7** mankind

Human Comedy author
6 Balzac (Honoré de) **7** Saroyan (William)

humane
4 kind **6** gentle, kindly, tender **8** merciful **10** altruistic, benevolent, charitable **11** considerate, kindhearted, soft-hearted, sympathetic, warmhearted **13** compassionate, philanthropic

humanitarian
5 giver **8** generous **10** altruistic, benefactor, beneficent, benevolent, charitable **13** compassionate, philanthropic

humanity
6 people **7** mankind **8** kindness, sympathy **10** compassion, generosity **11** benevolence, Homo sapiens

humble
3 low **4** meek **5** abase, abash, crush, lowly, quiet **6** demean, modest, simple **7** chagrin, deflate, degrade, subdued **8** cast down, disgrace, ordinary **9** compliant, diffident, discomfit, embarrass, humiliate **10** submissive, unassuming **11** acquiescent, deferential **13** insignificant, unpretentious

humbug
3 con, rot **4** fake, fool, hoax, sham **5** faker, fraud, hokum, phony, spoof, trick **6** bunkum, delude, drivel, take in **7** beguile, deceive, mislead **8** flimflam, impostor, malarkey, nonsense, pretense, quackery **9** deception, hypocrite, imposture, pretender, trickster **10** balderdash

humdinger
3 ace, gem, pip **4** lulu **5** beaut, daisy, dandy, dilly, doozy, jewel, peach, prize **6** doozer, doozie **8** jim-dandy, knockout **11** crackerjack

humdrum
4 blah, dull, flat **6** boring, dreary, stodgy **7** prosaic, tedious **8** monotone, monotony, plodding, unvaried, workaday **10** monotonous, uneventful **13** uninteresting

humid
3 wet **4** damp, dank **5** close, moist, muggy, soggy **6** clammy, sodden, steamy, sticky, stuffy **10** oppressive

humidify
6 dampen **7** moisten

humiliate
5 abase, crush, lower, shame **6** bemean, debase, demean, humble **7** chagrin, degrade, mortify **8** belittle, cast down, disgrace **9** embarrass

humiliation
5 shame **7** chagrin, put-down **8** disgrace, ignominy, reproach **9** abasement, disrepute, indignity **11** degradation **13** embarrassment, mortification

humility
7 modesty, shyness **8** meekness **9** abasement, lowliness **10** diffidence, submission **12** subservience **13** self-abasement

humming
4 busy **5** abuzz, brisk **6** active, lively **8** bustling, hustling **9** energetic

hummock
4 hump **5** couch, knoll, mound **7** hillock

hummus holder
4 pita

humongous
4 huge, vast **5** giant, jumbo **7** immense, mammoth, massive, titanic **8** colossal, enormous, gigantic **9** ginormous, monstrous **10** gargantuan, prodigious, tremendous

humor
3 wit **4** baby, bent, mind, mood, tone, vein, whim **5** fancy, fluid, spoil, yield **6** banter, coddle, comedy, cosset, esprit, joking, levity, nature, pamper, temper **7** caprice, cater to, conceit, gratify, indulge, jesting, kidding **8** crotchet, drollery, jocosity, repartee **9** character, drollness, flippancy, funniness, witticism, wittiness **10** complexion, jocularity, pleasantry **11** disposition, temperament

humorist
3 Ade (George), wag, wit **4** card, Nash (Ogden), Saki, Shaw (Henry Wheeler), Ward (Artemus, Edward) **5** Adams (Franklin Pierce), Allen (Fred), Barry (Dave), clown, comic, cutup, droll, Dunne (Finley Peter), joker, Munro (H. H.), Twain (Mark), White (E. B.) **6** Blount (Roy), Browne (Charles Farrar), Buchwald (Art), Diller (Phyllis), gagman, jester, kidder, Martin (Steve), Parker (Dorothy), Rogers (Will), Rourke (P. J.), Runyon (Damon), Sedaris (David), Thorpe (Thomas Bangs) **7** buffoon, Bombeck (Erma), Burgess (Gelett), Clemens (Samuel Langhorne), gagster, Hubbard (Kin), Keillor (Garrison), Marquis (Don), punster, Sedaris (David), Thurber (James), Trillin (Calvin) **8** Aleichem (Shalom), Benchley (Robert), comedian, funnyman, jokester, Perelman (S. J.), quipster **9** jokesmith, prankster, Wodehouse (P. G.)
Canadian: **7** Leacock (Stephen)
pen name: **4** Saki

humorous
5 comic, droll, funny, jokey, merry, witty **6** jocose

7 amusing, comical, jocular, risible, waggish 8 mirthful 9 facetious, laughable, whimsical

hump
3 lug 4 bump, race, tote 5 bulge, carry, hunch, mound, range 6 hustle, schlep 7 hummock, schlepp 8 mountain, obstacle, swelling 9 transport 10 protrusion

humpback
5 whale 8 kyphosis 10 pink salmon

humpbacked
6 convex, curved 7 gibbous

Humperdinck opera
15 Hansel and Gretel

humus
3 mor 4 mull, soil 7 compost 8 material

hunch
4 arch, clod, idea, lump, hump, push 5 chunk, clump, crook, squat, stoop 6 crouch, curl up, huddle, jostle, notion, nugget 7 feeling, inkling 9 intuition

Hunchback of Notre Dame
author: 4 Hugo (Victor)
character: 9 Esmeralda, Quasimodo

hundred
combining form: 5 centi, hecto
dollar bill: 5 C-note

Hungary
capital: 8 Budapest
city: 4 Pécs 6 Szeged 7 Miskolc 8 Debrecen
ethnic group: 6 Magyar
lake: 7 Balaton
monetary unit: 6 forint
mountain range: 10 Carpathian
national hero: 5 Árpád
neighbor: 6 Serbia 7 Austria, Croatia, Romania, Ukraine 8 Slovakia, Slovenia
plain: 11 Great Alföld
river: 4 Eger 5 Tisza 6 Danube

hunger
3 yen 4 ache, itch, long, lust, need, pine, want 5 crave, greed, yearn 6 desire, hanker, thirst 7 craving, longing

hungry
4 avid, keen, poor 5 eager 6 barren 7 craving, peckish, starved, thirsty 8 desirous, famished, ravenous, starving, underfed, yearning 9 hankering, motivated

hunk
3 gob, wad 4 clod, lump, stud 5 chunk, clump, himbo, piece, wedge 6 Adonis, nugget 7 portion

hunker down
5 dig in, squat 6 crouch 8 settle in

hunky
4 buff 5 burly 6 buffed 7 muscled 8 athletic, muscular 9 strapping, well-built

hunky-dory
4 fine, okay 5 dandy, ducky, nifty, primo, swell 6 peachy 9 copacetic 10 peachy keen 12 satisfactory

Hun leader
4 Atli 5 Etzel 6 Attila

Hunnish
4 rude, wild 6 savage 7 fearful, uncivil 9 barbarian, barbarous, ferocious 11 uncivilized

hunt
3 dog, run 4 hawk, seek 5 chase, hound, prowl, quest, shoot, snare, stalk, track, trail 6 battue, course, dig out, prey on, pursue, safari, search 7 explore, pursuit, rummage 9 ferret out, search for, search out
birds: 4 fowl
illegally: 5 poach

hunted one
4 mark, prey 6 quarry, target

hunter
6 jaeger, nimrod 8 predator
biblical: 6 Nimrod
cap: 7 montero
constellation: 5 Orion
mythological: 5 Orion 7 Actaeon

hunting
5 chase 6 venery 7 gunning, hawking 8 coursing, falconry 9 predatory 10 predacious
bird: 6 falcon
call: 7 recheat
cry: 6 yoicks 7 tallyho 10 view halloo
dog: 5 hound 6 basset, beagle, borzoi, saluki, setter, vizsla 7 harrier, pointer, spaniel 9 ridgeback, wolfhound 10 bloodhound
expedition: 6 safari
garb: 4 camo 10 camouflage
horn: 5 bugle

huntress
5 Diana 7 Artemis 8 Atalanta

hurdle
3 bar 4 leap, snag 5 bound, clear, vault 6 hamper, spring 7 barrier 8 leap over, obstacle, overcome, overleap, surmount, traverse 9 negotiate 10 difficulty, impediment 11 obstruction

hurl
4 cast, fire 5 chuck, fling, heave, pitch, sling, throw, vomit 6 launch, thrust 8 catapult

hurly-burly
3 ado, din 4 riot, to-do 5 melee 6 clamor, furore, hassle, hubbub, racket, rumpus, tumult, uproar 7 turmoil 8 confused 9 commotion, confusion

hurrah
3 olé, yay 4 fuss, to-do, zeal 5 cheer 6 fervor, rumpus 7 fanfare, ovation 8 approval 9 commotion 10 enthusiasm 11 acclamation

hurricane
7 typhoon
of 2011: **5** Irene

hurried
4 fast, sped **5** hasty, quick, swift **6** abrupt, rushed, sudden **7** cursory, rushing **8** headlong **9** impetuous **11** precipitant, precipitate

hurry
3 fly, hie, jog, run, zip **4** dash, post, prod, push, rush **5** fleet, haste, scoot, speed, whirl, whish, whisk **6** barrel, breeze, bullet, bustle, hasten, hustle, rocket, rustle, step up, tumult **7** beeline, hotfoot, quicken, shake up, skelter, speed up, swiften **8** celerity, dispatch, expedite, highball, make time **9** commotion, make haste, swiftness **10** accelerate, speediness

hurt
3 ail, mar **4** ache, blow, harm, pain **5** smart, wound, wrong **6** damage, grieve, hamper, harmed, impair, injure, injury, in pain, misuse, offend, pained, suffer **7** afflict, anguish, blemish, damaged, wounded **8** aggrieve, distress, mischief, mistreat **9** constrain, detriment, prejudice, resentful, suffering **10** resentment

hurtful
4 mean, sore **6** aching, unkind **7** harmful, painful **8** damaging, wounding **9** injurious **11** deleterious, destructive, detrimental, distressing, prejudicial

hurtle
3 fly **4** race, rush, tear **5** fling, shoot, speed, throw **6** charge, plunge, rocket

husband
3 man **4** mate, save **6** manage, mister, spouse **7** consort, partner **8** conserve, helpmate, helpmeet **9** economize, other half **10** bridegroom
German: **4** Herr, Mann

husbandry
6 thrift **7** control, economy, farming **8** prudence **9** frugality **10** management **11** agriculture, thriftiness **12** conservation, preservation

hush
4 calm **5** quell, quiet **6** shut up, stifle **7** cover up, mollify, secrecy, silence **8** choke off, suppress **9** cessation, quietness, stillness

hush-hush
6 covert, secret **7** private, sub-rosa **9** top secret **11** clandestine **12** confidential **13** surreptitious, under-the-table

husk
3 bur, pod **4** case, hull, peel, rind, skin **5** shell, shuck, strip **6** casing

husky
3 big, dog **5** beefy, burly, great, hefty, large, rough, stout **6** brawny, croaky, hoarse, mighty, robust, strong, sturdy **7** throaty **8** muscular, oversize, stalwart, thickset **9** strapping

hussy
4 doxy, minx **5** bimbo, tramp, wench **6** floozy **7** floozie, trollop

hustings
5 stump

hustle
3 fly, rob, run **4** earn, move, push, rush, sell, urge, work **5** cheat, elbow, fraud, haste, hurry, press, shove, speed **6** hasten **7** hotfoot, promote, solicit, swindle **8** bulldoze, dispatch **9** deception, swiftness

hustler
4 doer **6** dynamo, vendor **8** go-getter, live wire **10** powerhouse

hustling
4 busy **5** eager **6** active, lively, speedy **7** hopping, humming **9** energetic **10** aggressive

hut
3 cot **4** camp, crib, shed **5** cabin, dacha, hooch, hovel, hutch, jacal, lodge, roost, shack **6** cabana, chalet, lean-to, Nissen, shanty **7** cottage, Quonset **8** bungalow
American Indian: **6** wigwam **7** wickiup
Scottish: **5** bothy, shiel **8** shieling

hutch
3 bin, pen **4** cage, coop **5** chest, shack **6** locker, shanty **8** cupboard **9** enclosure

Huxley novel
8 Antic Hay **11** Crome Yellow **13** Brave New World, Eyeless in Gaza

Hyacinthus
father: **7** Amyclas
slayer: **6** Apollo

hybrid
5 blend, cross, mixed, Prius, spork **7** amalgam, mixture **8** combined, compound **9** composite, crossbred **10** crossbreed **11** combination
animal: **4** mule **5** hinny, liger, tigon
fruit: **4** Ugli, yuzu **5** pluot **7** tangelo

hybridize
4 join **5** blend, cross **7** combine **10** crossbreed, interbreed, intercross

Hydra
5 polyp **6** plague **7** monster, serpent **13** constellation
father: **6** Typhon
mother: **7** Echidna
slayer: **8** Heracles, Hercules

hydrant
3 tap **4** pipe **5** valve **6** faucet, spigot **7** petcock **8** fireplug

hydraulic device
3 ram **4** jack, lift, pump **5** brake, press **8** elevator

hydrocarbon
5 xylol **6** alkane, dioxin, ethane, olefin, xylene

7 benzene, methane, styrene, toluene **8** biphenyl, butylene, ethylene, paraffin
liquid: 6 octane **7** retinol, styrene **8** menthene

hydroid
5 polyp **6** medusa, obelia **9** jellyfish

hydrometer scale
4 Brix **5** Baumé

hydrophobia
5 lyssa **6** rabies

hyena
5 dingo **6** jackal **9** scavenger

Hygeia
5 Salus
father: 9 Asclepius **11** Aesculapius
goddess of: 6 health

hygiene
6 health **10** sanitation **11** cleanliness

hygienic
5 clean **7** aseptic, healthy, sterile **8** sanitary **9** healthful **10** antiseptic, unpolluted

Hyllus' father
8 Heracles, Hercules

hymeneal
6 bridal, wedded **7** marital, married, nuptial, spousal **8** conjugal **9** connubial **11** matrimonial

hymn
4 laud, song **5** bless, carol, chant, extol, paean, psalm **6** anthem, choral, praise, Te Deum **7** chorale, glorify **8** canticle, doxology, eulogize

hype
4 plug, tout **5** boost, thump **7** acclaim, enliven, fanfare, glorify, promote, puffery, trumpet **8** ballyhoo, increase **9** advertise, excellent, publicity, publicize, stimulate **11** advertising

hyper
4 edgy **5** antsy, jumpy, wired **6** on edge **7** anxious, frantic **8** agitated, frenetic, hopped-up **9** excitable **10** high-strung, overactive **11** overwrought

hyperbole
6 excess **12** embroidering, exaggeration **13** embellishment, overstatement

hypercritical
6 severe **7** carping **8** captious, exacting **10** censorious, nit-picking **12** faultfinding

Hyperion
daughter: 3 Eos **6** Aurora, Selene
father: 6 Uranus
mother: 4 Gaea
son: 6 Helios
wife: 5 Theia

hypnotic
6 opiate, sleepy **8** mesmeric, narcotic, sedative **9** somnolent, soporific **11** mesmerizing, somniferous **12** somnifacient, spellbinding

hypnotize
4 drug **5** charm **6** dazzle, trance **8** enthrall, entrance, overcome **9** captivate, fascinate, mesmerize, overpower, spellbind

hypocorism
7 epithet, pet name **8** nickname **9** sobriquet

hypocrisy
4 cant, sham **6** deceit, humbug **7** falsity, pietism **8** quackery **9** deception, duplicity, phoniness **10** sanctimony **11** insincerity, religiosity

hypocrite
4 fake, sham **5** actor, faker, fraud, phony, poser **6** humbug, poseur **7** bluffer, pietist **8** deceiver, impostor, pharisee **9** charlatan, pretender **10** dissembler **11** masquerader **12** dissimulator

hypocritical
5 false **7** canting **8** affected, specious, two-faced **9** deceitful, insincere, pietistic **10** Janus-faced **11** dissembling, double-faced, duplicitous **12** mealymouthed, pecksniffian **13** sanctimonious

hypothesis
6 belief, theory **7** premise **8** position, supposal **9** condition, inference **10** antecedent, assumption, conjecture **11** explanation, speculation, supposition

hypothetical
7 assumed **8** abstract, academic, supposed **10** assumptive **11** conditional, conjectural, suppositous, theoretical **12** suppositious **13** suppositional

hyrax
4 cony **5** coney **6** dassie, mammal **8** ungulate

hysteria
4 fear **5** craze, furor, mania, panic **6** excess, frenzy **7** madness **8** delirium

hysterical
5 rabid **6** crazed, raving **7** berserk, frantic **8** agitated, frenzied, neurotic **9** delirious, hilarious **10** convulsive, distraught, uproarious **11** overexcited, overwrought **13** side-splitting

I

I in Latin
3 ego

Iago
general: **7** Othello
victim: **6** Cassio, Emilia **7** Othello **9** Desdemona
wife: **6** Emilia

Iapetus
father: **6** Uranus
mother: **4** Gaea
son: **5** Atlas **9** Menoetius **10** Epimetheus, Prometheus
wife: **7** Clymene

Iasion
brother: **8** Dardanus
father: **4** Zeus **7** Jupiter
lover: **5** Ceres **7** Demeter
mother: **7** Electra
son: **6** Plutus

ibex
4 tahr **8** wild goat
family: **7** Bovidae
genus: **5** Capra

Ibhar's father
5 David

ibis-headed god
5 Thoth

ibis relative
5 heron,. stork

Ibiza, por ejemplo
4 isla

Ibsen, Henrik
character: **3** Ase **4** Nora (Helmer) **5** Brack (Judge), Brand, Hedda (Gabler), Helen (Alving), Werle (Gergers) **6** Ejlert (Lovberg), Hedvig (Ekdal), Jorgen (Tesman), Oswald (Alving) **7** Solness (Halvard), Solveig, Torvald (Helmer) **8** Peer Gynt **9** Stockmann (Thomas)
country: **6** Norway
play: **6** Ghosts **8** Peer Gynt, Wild Duck (The) **10** Doll's House (A) **11** Hedda Gabler, Little Eyolf, Rosmersholm **13** Master Builder (The) **16** Enemy of the People (An)

Icarus' father
8 Daedalus

ICBM part
4 MIRV **7** booster, warhead

ice
area: **4** rink
dessert: **6** sorbet **7** sherbet
floating: **4** berg, floe
hanging: **6** icicle
pinnacle: **5** serac
sheet: **7** glacier

icebox
6 cooler, fridge **12** refrigerator

ice cream
6 gelato **7** spumoni, tortoni
brand: **4** Edy's **7** Breyers **8** Klondike **9** Good Humor
dish: **6** sundae **11** baked Alaska
drink: **4** soda **6** frappe
headache: **11** brain freeze
holder: **4** cone

iced
5 glacé **6** glazed **7** chilled

ice field
4 floe **7** glacier

ice game
6 hockey **7** curling

ice house
5 igloo

Iceland
capital: **9** Reykjavik
monetary unit: **5** eyrir, krona
possession: **9** Greenalnd
sea: **9** Norwegian
snowfield: **11** Vatnajökull
strait: **7** Denmark
volcano: **5** Hekla

Icelandic
epic: **4** Edda, saga
hero: **5** Njáll **6** Gunnar **7** Grettir

ice skater
figure skater: **4** Witt (Katarina) **5** Baiul (Oksana), Henie (Sonja), Kulik (Ilia) **6** Hughes (Sarah), Umanov (Alexei) **7** Arakawa (Shizuka), Boitano (Brian), Cousins (Robin), Fleming (Peggy), Yagudin (Alexei) **8** Hamilton (Scott), Lipinski (Tara) **9** Plushenko (Evgeny)
speed skater: **4** Koss (Johann Olav), Ohno (Apolo Anton), Yang (Yang) **5** Blair (Bonnie), Davis (Shani) **6** Heiden (Eric), Timmer (Marianne) **7** Hedrick (Chad), Klassen (Cindy), Zhurova (Svetlana) **9** Pechstein (Claudia)

ice smoother
7 Zamboni
Ichabod Crane's beloved
7 Katrina
icicle's spot
4 eave 5 eaves
icing
7 topping 8 frosting
icky
4 vile 5 awful, gross, nasty 9 loathsome, offensive, repellent, repulsive, revolting, sickening 10 disgusting 11 distasteful
icon
4 idol, sign 5 image 6 emblem, symbol
iconoclastic
9 dissident, heretical 10 rebellious, unorthodox 13 nonconformist
icy
4 cold 5 gelid, polar 6 arctic, chilly, frigid, frosty, frozen, steely 7 glacial 8 freezing 11 emotionless, unemotional
precipitation: 4 hail 5 sleet
Idaho
capital: 5 Boise
city: 6 Moscow 9 Pocatello, Twin Falls 10 Idaho Falls 11 Coeur d'Alene
mountain: 5 Borah (Peak)
nickname: 3 Gem (State)
river: 5 Snake 6 Salmon
state bird: 8 bluebird
state flower: 7 syringa
state tree: 9 white pine
Idas
brother: 7 Lynceus
father: 8 Aphareus
slayer: 4 Zeus
victim: 6 Castor
wife: 8 Marpessa
id counterpart
3 ego
idea
4 whim 5 fancy, guess, motif 6 belief, notion, theory, thesis, vagary 7 caprice, conceit, concept, inkling, meaning, opinion, subject, surmise, thought 8 estimate 9 sentiment, suspicion 10 assumption, brainchild, brainstorm, conception, conclusion, conjecture, conviction, estimation, hypothesis, impression, perception, reflection 11 abstraction, formulation, supposition
ideal
4 best, goal 5 model 7 chimera, classic, epitome, paragon, perfect, utopian 8 absolute, ensample, exemplar, flawless, nonesuch, paradigm, standard, ultimate 9 archetype, classical, exemplary, nonpareil 10 archetypal, conceptual, consummate 11 theoretical
idealist
7 dreamer, quixote, utopian 9 ideologue, visionary
idealistic
6 dreamy 7 utopian 8 poetical, quixotic, romantic 9 visionary 10 starry-eyed 11 impractical, unrealistic
idealize
5 deify, exalt, extol 7 elevate, ennoble, glorify, worship 8 venerate
ideate
5 think 7 imagine 8 conceive, envisage, envision
idée fixe
5 mania 6 fetish, phobia 7 complex 8 fixation 9 obsession 13 preoccupation
identical
3 one 4 like, same, very 5 alike, equal, exact 8 selfsame 9 duplicate 10 equivalent, synonymous
identification mark
4 logo 5 badge, brand, label 6 emblem
identify
3 peg, tag 4 mark, name, spot 5 brand, place 6 finger, select 7 make out, pick out 8 pinpoint 9 determine, recognize 11 distinguish
identity
4 name, self 7 oneness 8 sameness, selfhood 9 character 10 congruence, uniformity, uniqueness 11 personality, singularity 13 individuality, particularity
ideological
8 notional 10 conceptual, ideational 11 speculative 13 philosophical
ideologue
6 zealot 8 believer, idealist, militant, partisan, theorist
ideology
3 ism 5 credo, creed 7 beliefs 8 doctrine 10 philosophy, principles
Idi ___
4 Amin
idiocy
5 folly 6 bêtise 7 fatuity 9 cretinism, stupidity 10 imbecility 11 foolishness
idiom
6 phrase 8 language 10 expression
idiomatic
7 demotic 8 peculiar 9 dialectal 10 colloquial, vernacular
idiosyncrasy
3 tic 5 quirk 6 oddity 7 anomaly 11 peculiarity, singularity 12 eccentricity

idiosyncratic
3 odd **5** kooky, queer, weird **6** quirky **7** erratic, oddball, offbeat, unusual **8** peculiar, singular **9** eccentric **11** distinctive

idiot
3 ass **4** dolt, fool, jerk, simp **5** dummy, dunce, moron, ninny **6** cretin, doofus, nitwit, stupid **7** airhead, dullard, half-wit, jackass, natural, tomfool **8** dumbbell, imbecile, numskull **9** ignoramus, numbskull, simpleton **10** nincompoop

idiotic
5 dopey **6** stupid **7** foolish, moronic **8** ignorant **9** brainless, imbecilic, senseless

idle
3 bum **4** laze, lazy, loaf, loll, rest, vain **5** dally, drone, empty, inert, slack, tarry **6** asleep, dawdle, diddle, fallow, futile, linger, loiter, lounge, otiose, unused, vacant **7** aimless, dormant, passive **8** inactive, indolent, slothful **9** shiftless **10** unemployed, unoccupied

idleness
4 ease **5** sloth **6** vanity **7** leisure, loafing **8** lethargy **9** indolence **10** inactivity

Idle of Monty Python
4 Eric

idler
3 bum **4** slug **5** drone **6** loafer, slouch **7** dawdler **8** deadbeat, fainéant, loiterer, slugabed, sluggard **9** do-nothing, lazybones **11** couch potato

Idmon
daughter: 7 Arachne
father: 6 Apollo
mother: 6 Cyrene

idol
3 god **4** Baal, hero, icon, star **5** deity, image, totem **6** fetish, minion, symbol **8** likeness
Chinese: 4 joss

idolatry
7 worship **8** devotion, paganism **9** adoration **10** exaltation, heathenism, veneration **11** deification **13** glorification

idolize
5 adore, deify, exalt **6** revere **7** adulate, cherish, glorify, worship **8** venerate

Idomeneo composer
6 Mozart (Wolfgang Amadeus)

idyllic
5 ideal **6** rustic **7** bucolic, halcyon, perfect, utopian **8** arcadian, heavenly, pastoral, peaceful, romantic **9** idealized, unspoiled **11** picturesque, sentimental
spot: 4 Eden

Idylls of the King
author: 8 Tennyson (Alfred)
character: 4 Enid **6** Arthur, Elaine, Gareth, Merlin, Vivien **7** Geraint, Lynette **8** Lancelot

iffy
5 dicey, risky **6** chancy, unsure **7** dubious, erratic **8** doubtful **9** uncertain **10** unreliable **12** inconsistent **13** unpredictable

igneous rock
4 lava **5** magma **6** basalt, gabbro **7** diabase, granite **8** porphyry

ignis fatuus
6 mirage **7** chimera **8** delusion, illusion, phantasm **9** pipe dream **12** will-o'-the-wisp **13** hallucination

ignitable
8 burnable **9** excitable, flammable **10** incendiary **11** combustible, inflammable

ignite
4 fire **5** light, spark **6** excite, kindle **7** inflame **8** enkindle, touch off

ignited
3 lit **5** afire, fiery **6** ablaze, aflame, alight **7** blazing, burning, flaming, flaring **11** conflagrant

ignoble
3 low **4** base, mean, poor, vile **5** lowly **6** abject, coarse, common, scurvy, sordid, vulgar **7** lowborn, servile **8** baseborn, indecent, inferior, plebeian, shameful, unwashed, wretched **10** despicable, inglorious **11** disgraceful **12** contemptible, dishonorable

ignominious
6 odious **8** infamous, shameful **9** degrading **10** despicable, inglorious **11** disgraceful, humiliating, opprobrious **12** contemptible, dishonorable, disreputable **13** discreditable, unrespectable

ignominy
5 odium, shame **6** infamy **7** obloquy, scandal **8** disgrace, dishonor **9** discredit, disesteem, disrepute **10** opprobrium **11** humiliation **13** mortification

ignoramus
4 dolt **5** dummy, dunce, idiot, moron **6** dimwit, nitwit, stupid **7** airhead, dullard, half-wit **8** dumbbell, imbecile, numskull **9** numbskull, simpleton

ignorance
7 naïveté **9** innocence, nescience, stupidity **10** illiteracy, simpleness, simplicity **11** unawareness **12** incognizance

ignorant
5 naive **6** simple **7** unaware **8** clueless, nescient, untaught **9** benighted, ingenuous, oblivious, unknowing, unlearned, untutored, unwitting **10** illiterate, uncultured, uneducated, uninformed, unlettered, unschooled **11** incognizant, know-nothing **12** uninstructed **13** unenlightened

ignore
4 omit, snub **5** avoid **6** forget, reject, slight **7** let ride, neglect **8** overlook **9** disregard

Igraine
husband: **5** Uther **7** Gorlois
son: **6** Arthur

iguana
5 anole **6** lizard **8** basilisk **10** chuckwalla

Ike
command: **3** ETO
monogram: **3** DDE
opponent: **5** Adlai (Stevenson)

ilex
4 maté **5** holly **6** yaupon **7** holm oak **8** inkberry

Iliad
4 epic
author: **5** Homer
character: **4** Ajax **5** Helen, Paris, Priam **6** Aeneas, Hector **8** Achilles, Diomedes, Odysseus **9** Agamemnon, Patroclus
city: **4** Troy

Ilium
4 Troy

ilk
4 kind, sort, type **5** breed, class, genre **6** family, kidney, nature, stripe **7** variety

ill
4 sick **6** ailing, infirm, laid up, malady, peaked, queasy, unwell **7** ailment, disease, trouble, unlucky **8** diseased, disorder, distress, feverish, nauseous, scarcely, sickness, syndrome **9** afflicted, infirmity, nauseated, unhealthy **10** misfortune

ill-adapted
8 unfitted, unsuited **10** unsuitable

ill-advised
4 rash **5** brash, hasty **6** madcap, unwise **7** foolish **8** careless, heedless, reckless **9** foolhardy, impolitic, imprudent **10** incautious, indiscreet, unthinking **11** inexpedient, injudicious, thoughtless

ill at ease
3 shy **4** edgy **5** tense **6** on edge **7** anxious, awkward, fidgety, nervous **8** insecure, restless **9** unsettled **11** discomfited **12** apprehensive **13** self-conscious, uncomfortable

ill-boding
4 dire **7** baleful, doomful, fateful, ominous, unlucky **8** sinister **10** portentous **11** apocalyptic **12** inauspicious, unpropitious

ill-bred
4 rude **5** crude **7** boorish, loutish, uncivil, uncouth **8** impolite **9** unrefined **10** uncultured, ungracious, unmannered, unmannerly, unpolished **11** uncivilized **12** discourteous

ill-defined
5 faint, fuzzy, vague **7** shadowy **10** indistinct

illegal
3 hot **6** banned **7** bootleg, illicit, lawless **8** criminal, outlawed, unlawful, wrongful **9** felonious, forbidden **10** actionable, prohibited, proscribed, unlicensed **12** illegitimate
act: **5** crime **6** felony
payment: **5** bribe **6** payola
scheme: **4** scam

illegible
8 scrawled **10** unreadable **11** inscrutable

illegitimacy
8 bastardy **11** bar sinister **12** unlawfulness

illegitimate
7 bastard, bootleg, erratic, invalid, lawless, natural **8** criminal, improper, spurious, unlawful **11** misbegotten **12** unauthorized

ill-fated
6 cursed, doomed **7** unhappy, unlucky **8** accursed, luckless, untoward **10** disastrous **11** star-crossed, unfortunate

ill-favored
4 ugly **5** plain **6** homely **12** unattractive

ill-humored
4 dour, sour **5** cross, surly, testy **6** crabby, cranky, crusty, grumpy, morose, ornery, sullen, tetchy, touchy **7** crabbed, grouchy, peevish, prickly **8** choleric, churlish, snappish **9** dyspeptic, irascible, irritable, saturnine, splenetic **12** cantankerous, disagreeable, misanthropic

illiberal
6 biased, narrow **7** bigoted, insular **9** hidebound, parochial, penurious **10** intolerant, prejudiced, provincial **11** reactionary, small-minded **12** conservative, narrow-minded, uncharitable

illicit
7 bootleg, crooked, lawless **8** criminal, unlawful **9** forbidden **10** contraband, prohibited **11** black-market, clandestine **12** unauthorized

illimitable
7 endless **8** infinite, unending **9** boundless **11** measureless

Illinois
capital: **11** Springfield
city: **6** Aurora, Cicero, Joliet, Peoria **7** Chicago **8** Rockford
college, university: **4** Knox **6** DePaul **7** Wheaton **12** Northwestern
nickname: **7** Prairie (State)
river: **6** Wabash
state bird: **8** cardinal
state flower: **6** violet
state tree: **8** white oak

illiterate
6 unread 8 untaught 9 untutored 10 uneducated, unlettered, unschooled

ill-mannered
4 rude 6 coarse 7 boorish, loutish, uncivil, uncouth 8 churlish, impolite 10 ungracious 12 discourteous

ill-natured
4 sour 5 cross, huffy, surly, testy 6 bitchy, crabby, grumpy, ornery, tetchy 7 grouchy, peevish, waspish 8 choleric, churlish, snappish, spiteful 9 dyspeptic, fractious, irascible, irritable 10 malevolent 11 belligerent, contentious, quarrelsome 12 cantankerous, disagreeable

illness
6 malady 7 ailment, disease, malaise 8 cachexia, disorder, sickness 9 infirmity 10 affliction 13 indisposition

illogical
6 absurd 7 invalid, unsound 8 specious 9 plausible, senseless, sophistic 10 fallacious, irrational, unreasoned 11 nonrational 12 preposterous, unreasonable

ill-starred
6 cursed, doomed, malign 7 fateful, ominous, unhappy, unlucky 8 luckless, untoward 10 disastrous, foreboding, portentous 11 unfavorable, unfortunate, unpromising 12 inauspicious, unpropitious

ill-tempered
4 sour 5 cross, huffy, surly 6 crabby, bitchy, grumpy, ornery, snippy 7 grouchy, peevish, waspish 8 choleric, churlish, petulant, shrewish, snappish, spiteful 9 dyspeptic, fractious, irascible, irritable 11 belligerent, contentious, quarrelsome 12 cantankerous, disagreeable

ill-timed
11 inopportune 12 unseasonable

ill-treat
4 harm, hurt 5 abuse 6 injure, misuse, molest 7 torment 8 aggrieve 10 traumatize

illuminate
5 clear, edify, exalt, gloss, light 6 uplift 7 clarify, clear up, emblaze, explain, lighten 8 brighten, decorate 9 elucidate, embellish, enlighten, highlight, irradiate, spotlight

illuminati
5 elite 7 clerisy, scholar 8 academic 11 academician 13 intellectuals

illumination
5 light 8 lighting
unit of: 3 lux 4 phot 5 lumen 6 candle 7 candela 10 footcandle

illusion
4 myth 5 dream, fancy, ghost 6 facade, mirage 7 chimera, fantasy 8 phantasm, phantasy 9 invention, pipe dream, semblance 11 ignis fatuus 12 will-o'-the-wisp 13 hallucination

illusionist
8 conjurer, magician 9 trickster

illusive
see **illusory**

illusory
4 sham 6 unreal 7 seeming 8 apparent, fanciful 9 deceptive, fictional, imaginary, visionary 10 chimerical, fallacious, fictitious, misleading, ostensible

illustrate
4 mark, show 6 depict, evince, expose, reveal 7 clarify, display, exhibit, explain, picture, portray 8 decorate, describe, evidence, instance, manifest 9 elucidate, epitomize, exemplify 11 demonstrate

illustration
4 case 6 sample 7 diagram, drawing, example, picture, problem 8 instance

illustrative
7 graphic 9 pictorial 10 clarifying 11 descriptive 12 iconographic

illustrator
American: 4 Kent (Rockwell), Pyle (Howard) 5 Abbey (Edwin Austin), Flagg (James Montgomery), Moser (Barry), Smith (Jessie Willcox), Wyeth (Newell Convers) 6 Gibson (Charles Dana), Sendak (Maurice) 7 Burgess (Gelett), Dr. Seuss, Parrish (Maxfield) 8 Rockwell (Norman) 9 Remington (Frederic)
English: 5 Crane (Walter) 6 Morris (William), Potter (Beatrix) 7 Nielsen (Kay), Rackham (Arthur), Tenniel (John) 9 Beardsley (Aubrey), Caldecott (Randolph), du Maurier (George), Greenaway (Kate)
French: 4 Doré (Gustave) 5 Dulac (Edmund)
German: 5 Dürer (Albrecht)

illustrious
5 famed, great, lofty, noted 6 famous 7 eminent, exalted, notable, sublime 8 glorious, renowned, splendid 9 acclaimed, prominent 10 celebrated, preeminent 11 outstanding, prestigious 13 distinguished

illustriousness
4 fame 5 glory 6 renown 8 eminence, prestige 9 celebrity 10 prominence 11 distinction, preeminence

ill will
5 spite, venom 6 animus, enmity, malice, rancor, spleen 7 despite, dislike 8 acrimony, aversion, bad blood 9 animosity, antipathy, hostility, malignity 10 resentment 11 malevolence 12 spitefulness 13 maliciousness

Ilus
father: **4** Tros
grandson: **5** Priam
mother: **10** Callirrhoë
son: **8** Laomedon

image
4 copy, form, icon, idea, idol, ikon **5** equal, match **6** double, effigy, figure, mirror, notion, ringer, vision **7** concept, fantasm, feature, picture **8** likeness, phantasm, portrait **9** facsimile, semblance **10** conception, equivalent, impression, reflection, simulacrum **12** illustration
digital: **3** PDF **4** JPEG
Polynesian: **4** tiki
Semitic: **6** teraph **8** teraphim (plural)

imaginary
5 ideal **6** made-up, unreal **7** fancied, fictive **8** abstract, fabulous, fanciful, illusive, illusory, notional, quixotic **9** dreamlike, fantastic, fictional, legendary, visionary **10** apocryphal, chimerical, fictitious, phantasmal **11** make-believe **12** hypothetical, suppositious

imagination
5 fancy **7** fantasy **8** phantasy **9** invention **10** creativity **11** inspiration **13** inventiveness

imaginative
5 false **7** blue-sky, fictive **8** artistic, creative, fanciful, original, poetical **9** ingenious, inventive, visionary, whimsical **11** resourceful **12** enterprising

imagine
5 dream, fancy **6** assume, invent, make up **7** dream up, feature, picture, suspect **8** conceive, envisage, envision **9** fabricate, visualize **10** conjecture

imbecile
4 dodo, dolt, dull, fool, jerk **5** dunce, idiot, moron, ninny **6** cretin, dimwit, nitwit **7** half-wit, jackass, moronic, pinhead, tomfool **8** numskull **9** birdbrain, blockhead, numbskull **10** dunderhead, nincompoop

imbibe
3 sip, sup **4** chug, soak, swig, tope, toss **5** booze, drink, quaff, swill **6** absorb, guzzle, tipple **7** consume, swallow, swizzle **10** assimilate

imbricate
3 lap **7** overlap, shingle **11** overlapping

imbroglio
3 row **4** maze, mess, spat, to-do **5** brawl, broil, mix-up **6** fracas, muddle, ruckus, tangle **7** dispute, quarrel, rhubarb, scandal, wrangle **8** argument, disorder, squabble **9** confusion, intricacy **10** falling-out **11** altercation, predicament **12** complication, entanglement

imbrue
4 soil **5** stain **8** discolor

imbue
3 dye **4** soak **5** bathe, endow, steep, tinge **6** infuse, invest, leaven **7** ingrain, instill, pervade, suffuse **8** permeate, saturate **9** influence, inoculate

imitate
3 ape **4** copy, echo, mime, mock **5** forge, mimic, spoof **6** parody **7** emulate, take off **8** resemble, simulate, travesty **9** burlesque, duplicate, replicate, reproduce **11** counterfeit, impersonate

imitation
4 copy, fake, mock, sham **5** clone, ditto, dummy, false, match, phony **6** ersatz, parody, ringer **7** forgery, mimicry, replica **8** likeness, parallel, spurious, travesty **9** duplicate, semblance, simulated **10** artificial, simulacrum, simulation, substitute **11** counterfeit, counterpart **12** reproduction, substitution

imitative
4 mock **5** apish **6** echoic **7** copycat, mimetic, parodic, slavish **11** counterfeit **12** onomatopoeic **13** onomatopoetic

imitator
4 aper, mime **5** mimic **6** parrot **7** copycat

immaculate
4 pure **5** clean **6** chaste, virgin **7** cleanly, perfect, sinless **8** flawless, pristine, spotless, unsoiled, virtuous **9** stainless, undefiled, unsullied **11** spic-and-span, unblemished **12** spick-and-span

immaterial
7 trivial **8** bodiless, ethereal **10** extraneous, inapposite, intangible, irrelevant **11** disembodied, incorporeal, nonphysical, unimportant **12** inapplicable **13** insignificant, insubstantial, unsubstantial

immature
3 raw **5** crude, green, young **6** callow, infant, unripe **7** puerile **8** childish, juvenile, youthful **9** infantile, primitive, unfledged **10** unfinished **11** undeveloped

immaturity
6 nonage **7** infancy **8** minority **9** childhood, salad days **11** adolescence **12** juvenescence

immeasurable
4 vast **6** untold **7** endless **8** infinite **9** boundless, extensive, limitless, unbounded, unlimited **11** illimitable, inestimable, uncountable **12** incalculable, unfathomable

immediate
4 next, nigh **5** close **6** at hand, direct, nearby, urgent **7** current, instant, ongoing, primary **9** firsthand, proximate **10** unmediated **12** straightaway **13** instantaneous

immediately
3 now, PDQ **4** anon, ASAP, stat **6** at once, presto, pronto **8** directly, promptly **9** forthwith, instanter, instantly, right away **11** straightway **12** straightaway

immense
4 huge, mega, vast **5** great, large, mondo **6** mighty **7** mammoth, massive, titanic **8** colossal, enormous, gigantic **9** humongous, monstrous **10** gargantuan, monumental, prodigious, tremendous **11** elephantine

immensely
4 a lot **8** terribly **9** extremely **11** exceedingly **12** inordinately

immensity
8 enormity, hugeness, vastness **9** greatness **12** enormousness

immerse
3 dip **4** duck, dunk, sink, soak **5** bathe, douse **6** drench, engage, plunge **7** baptize, engross, involve **8** saturate, submerge

immigrant
5 alien **7** settler **8** newcomer **10** transplant
Japanese: 5 issei

immigrant's study
3 ESL

imminent
4 near **6** at hand, coming **7** brewing, nearing, ominous, pending **8** upcoming **9** gathering, proximate **11** approaching, overhanging

immobile
3 set **5** fixed, inert, still **6** frozen, stable, static **9** unmovable **10** motionless, stationary

immobilize
5 still **7** cripple, disable **8** paralyze **9** hamstring **12** incapacitate

immoderate
5 undue **7** extreme **9** excessive **10** exorbitant, inordinate, untempered **11** extravagant, intemperate **12** unreasonable, unrestrained **13** extraordinary, overindulgent

immoderation
6 excess **11** exorbitance, prodigality **12** extravagance, intemperance

immodest
4 lewd, vain **7** stuck-up **8** arrogant, boastful, indecent, puffed-up, unchaste **9** conceited, egotistic **11** pretentious

immolate
4 burn, kill **7** destroy **9** sacrifice

immoral
4 evil, vile **5** dirty, wrong **6** sinful, unholy, wanton, wicked **7** corrupt, unclean, vicious **8** depraved, indecent, unchaste **9** dissolute, reprobate, uncleanly **10** degenerate, iniquitous, licentious

immorality
3 sin **4** vice **8** iniquity **9** depravity **10** corruption, unchastity, wickedness

immortal
7 endless, eternal, godlike, undying **8** timeless, unending **9** ceaseless, deathless, perpetual **11** amaranthine, everlasting, sempiternal

immotile
5 fixed, inert **6** rooted, static **9** paralyzed **10** stationary

immovable
3 pat, set **4** fast, firm **5** fixed, rigid **6** rooted, stable **7** adamant **8** constant, obdurate, stubborn **9** steadfast **10** inflexible, invariable, stationary, unyielding

immune
4 free, safe **6** exempt, secure **9** protected **10** impervious **12** invulnerable, unassailable

immunity
7 defense, freedom **9** exemption, privilege **10** protection

immure
3 pen **4** cage, coop, jail, wall **6** entomb, intern, shut in **7** confine, enclose **8** imprison **11** incarcerate

immutable
4 firm **5** fixed **8** constant **9** permanent, steadfast **10** changeless, inflexible, invariable, unchanging **11** inalterable, unalterable **12** unchangeable

Imogen
father: 9 Cymbeline
husband: 9 Posthumus

imp
3 elf **4** brat, puck **5** demon, devil, fiend, gamin, gnome, pixie, scamp **6** goblin, kobold, rascal, sprite, urchin **7** gremlin **9** hobgoblin

impact
3 hit, jar, rap **4** blow, bump, jolt, rock, slam, slap **5** brunt, embed, pound, punch, shock, smash, smite **6** affect, buffet, effect, strike, wallop **9** collision, influence **10** concussion, percussion

impair
3 mar, sap **4** harm, hurt **5** spoil **6** damage, injure, lessen, weaken, worsen **7** cripple, tarnish, vitiate **8** enfeeble **9** prejudice, undermine **10** debilitate

impala
8 antelope

impale
4 gore, spit, stab **5** lance, prick, spear, spike, stick **6** pierce, skewer **8** puncture, transfix **11** transpierce

impalpable
4 fine **7** powdery **8** ethereal **10** intangible

11 disembodied, incorporeal **12** imponderable **13** imperceptible, indiscernible

impart

4 cede, give, lend, tell **5** grant, share, yield **6** afford, bestow, confer, convey, pass on, relate, render **8** disclose, transmit **11** communicate **knowledge: 5** teach **6** inform **7** educate **8** instruct

impartial

4 even, fair, just **5** equal **7** neutral **8** detached, unbiased **9** equitable, objective, uncolored **10** evenhanded **12** unprejudiced **13** disinterested, dispassionate

impassable

6 closed **7** blocked **10** obstructed **12** impenetrable

impasse

3 box, fix, jam **6** aporia, corner, logjam, pickle, pocket **7** dead end, dilemma **8** cul-de-sac, deadlock, standoff **9** stalemate **10** blind alley, bottleneck

impassioned

3 hot **5** fiery **6** ardent, fervid, fierce, heated, red-hot, torrid **7** burning, fervent, intense, zealous **8** feverish, romantic, vehement, white-hot **9** emotional, perfervid **10** hot-blooded, overheated **11** dithyrambic **12** melodramatic

impassive

4 calm, cold, cool **5** stoic **6** serene, stolid, vacant **7** deadpan **8** composed, hardened, reserved, reticent, taciturn **9** heartless **10** insensible, insentient, phlegmatic, poker-faced **11** cold-blooded, emotionless, insensitive, unconcerned, unemotional, unexcitable, unflappable **12** inexpressive, unexpressive, unresponsive **13** dispassionate, self-possessed

impassivity

6 apathy, phlegm **8** stoicism **9** sangfroid, stolidity **12** indifference **13** insensibility

impatient

4 edgy **5** antsy, eager, hasty **7** anxious, fretful, restive **8** restless

impeach

5 blame, doubt **6** accuse, charge, indict **7** censure **9** inculpate, reprehend **11** incriminate

impeccable

4 pure **5** exact **7** perfect, precise **8** absolute, accurate, flawless, unerring **9** blameless, errorless, faultless, guiltless **10** infallible **11** unblemished

impecunious

4 poor **5** broke, needy **7** pinched **8** bankrupt, beggarly, indigent **9** destitute, insolvent, penniless, penurious **10** down-and-out **11** necessitous

impecuniousness

4 need, want **6** penury **7** poverty **9** indigence, neediness, pauperism, privation **11** destitution

impedance

3 bar **4** clog **5** block **8** blockage, obstacle **9** hindrance **10** opposition **11** obstruction

impede

3 bar, dam **4** clog, slow **5** block, check, debar, delay, deter, stall **6** hinder, hang up, hold up, stymie, thwart **7** bog down **8** encumber, obstruct **9** embarrass, interfere, stonewall

impediment

3 bar **4** clog, snag **5** block, hitch **6** hurdle **7** barrier **8** obstacle **9** barricade, hindrance, roadblock **10** difficulty **11** encumbrance, obstruction

impel

4 goad, prod, push, spur, urge **5** drive, force, rouse **6** excite, incite, prompt **7** actuate, inspire **8** mobilize, motivate **9** instigate, stimulate

impend

4 loom, near **6** menace **8** approach, overhang, threaten

impenetrable

5 dense **6** arcane **7** obscure **9** enigmatic, recondite **10** impervious, invincible, mysterious, unknowable **11** impermeable, bulletproof, inscrutable, ungraspable **12** unfathomable

imperative

4 duty, need, rule, writ **5** acute, vital **6** crying, urgent **7** burning, clamant, command, crucial, exigent **8** critical, pressing, required **9** clamorous, essential, insistent, mandatory, necessary, necessity, requisite **10** compulsory, obligation, obligatory **11** fundamental, necessitous **12** prerequisite

imperceptible

3 dim **5** faint, vague **6** slight, subtle **7** gradual **9** invisible **10** impalpable, indistinct, insensible, intangible, unapparent **12** undetectable, unnoticeable, unobservable **13** inappreciable, inconspicuous, indiscernible

imperceptive

4 dull **7** shallow, unaware **11** inattentive, insensitive

imperfect

6 faulty, flawed **9** defective, deficient, irregular **10** defeasible, inadequate

imperfection

3 sin **4** flaw, wart **5** fault **6** defect, foible **7** blemish, demerit, failing, frailty **8** weakness **10** deficiency **11** shortcoming

imperial

5 regal, royal **6** kingly, lordly **7** haughty **8** absolute, majestic **9** masterful, sovereign **10** high-handed, peremptory **11** domineering, magisterial, monarchical

imperil

4 risk **6** hazard, menace **7** venture **8** endanger, threaten **10** jeopardize

imperious
5 bossy **6** urgent **7** haughty **8** absolute, arrogant, despotic, dominant **9** arbitrary, masterful **10** autocratic, commanding, high-handed, oppressive, peremptory, tyrannical **11** dictatorial, domineering, heavy-handed, magisterial, overbearing

impermanent
7 passing **8** fleeting, fugitive **9** ephemeral, fugacious, momentary, temporary, transient **10** evanescent, short-lived, transitory

impersonal
4 cold **5** aloof **8** abstract, detached **11** cold-blooded, emotionless **13** dispassionate, unimpassioned

impersonate
3 ape **4** play **5** mimic **6** act out **7** imitate, play-act, portray **9** represent **11** counterfeit

impersonator
3 ape **4** aper, mime **5** actor, mimic **6** mummer, player, ringer **7** actress, copycat **8** thespian
female: 9 drag queen

impertinence
3 lip **4** gall, guff, sass **5** brass, cheek **8** audacity, boldness, chutzpah, rudeness, temerity **9** brashness, impudence, insolence **10** brazenness, effrontery, incivility **11** discourtesy, irrelevance

impertinent
4 bold, busy, rude **5** brash, fresh, sassy, saucy **6** brazen, cheeky **7** uncivil **8** insolent, meddling **9** audacious, intrusive, obtrusive, officious **10** inapposite, irrelative, irrelevant, meddlesome **11** ill-mannered **12** discourteous, inapplicable, presumptuous

imperturbability
5 poise **6** aplomb, phlegm **8** calmness, coolness, serenity, stoicism **9** composure, placidity, sangfroid **10** dispassion, equanimity **11** equilibrium, nonchalance, tranquility **12** tranquillity

imperturbable
4 calm, cool **5** stoic **6** placid, poised, serene, smooth, steady, stolid **7** unmoved **8** composed, tranquil **9** collected, unruffled **10** nonchalant, phlegmatic, unaffected **11** unflappable

impervious
4 safe **6** immune **8** hardened **10** inviolable **12** inaccessible, invulnerable

impetuous
3 hot **4** rash, wild **5** fiery, hasty **6** ardent, fervid, madcap, sudden **8** headlong, vehement, volatile **9** hotheaded, mercurial **10** irrational, passionate **11** precipitant, precipitate, precipitous, spontaneous **13** temperamental

impetus
4 goad, push, spur **5** force **6** motive **8** catalyst, momentum, stimulus **9** incentive, stimulant **10** incitement, motivation **13** encouragement

impinge
5 press **6** border **7** intrude, obtrude **8** encroach

impious
6 sinful, unholy, wicked **7** godless, infidel, profane, secular, ungodly **8** agnostic, apostate **9** atheistic **10** irreverent, unfaithful, unhallowed **11** blasphemous, irreligious, unrighteous **12** iconoclastic, sacrilegious **13** unconsecrated

impish
4 arch **5** elfin **6** elvish **7** playful, puckish, roguish, waggish **11** mischievous

impishness
7 devilry, roguery, waggery **8** deviltry, mischief **9** devilment **11** roguishness, waggishness

implacable
4 grim **8** ruthless **9** merciless **10** inexorable, unyielding **11** intractable **12** unappeasable

implant
3 fix **4** root **5** embed, graft, infix **6** enroot, infuse, insert **7** ingrain, inspire, instill **9** establish, inculcate, inoculate, introduce **10** inseminate **12** augmentation

implausible
5 fishy **6** flimsy **7** dubious, suspect **8** doubtful, fanciful, unlikely **10** far-fetched, incredible **12** questionable, unbelievable, unconvincing

implement
4 tool **6** device, effect, enable, gadget **7** enforce, execute, fulfill, perform, realize, utensil **8** carry out, complete, make good **9** actualize, apparatus, appliance **10** accomplish, instrument, supplement **11** contraption, contrivance
carpentry: 3 adz, die, saw **4** adze, file **5** brace, clamp, drill, punch, tongs **6** chisel, hammer, pliers, reamer, sander, wrench **7** hacksaw, scraper **9** blowtorch **11** screwdriver
cleaning: 3 mop **5** broom, brush, whisk **6** duster, vacuum **7** sweeper **10** whiskbroom
cutting: 5 knife, mower, razor **6** scythe, shears, sickle **8** scissors
digging: 5 spade **6** dibber, dibble, shovel
drawing: 3 pen **6** eraser, pencil **7** compass **8** template
eating: 4 fork **5** knife, spoon, spork **9** chopstick
engraving: 5 burin **6** graver
farm: 4 plow **6** binder, harrow, plough, scythe, seeder, sickle **8** gangplow, reaphook, spreader, thresher **9** pitchfork **10** cultivator
fireplace: 5 poker, tongs **7** andiron
fishing: 3 rod **4** hook, lure, reel **6** sinker **7** harpoon, trident
garden: 3 hoe **4** rake **5** edger, spade **6** dibber, dibble, digger, tiller, trowel **7** mattock
grooming: 4 comb, file **5** brush, razor **7** clipper **8** clippers, nail file, tweezers **10** toothbrush
kitchen: 3 pan, pot **4** mold **5** mixer, whisk **6** grater, kettle, mortar, pestle **7** blender, skillet, spatula **8** colander, saucepan, stockpot

logging: **5** peavy **6** peavey **8** cant hook
measuring: **3** cup **4** gage, rule **5** gauge, ruler, scale **7** caliper, divider, trammel, T-square **10** micrometer, protractor
stone: **5** burin **7** neolith **9** paleolith

implicate
4 link, mire **5** blame **6** tangle **7** concern, embroil, entwine, include, involve **8** entangle, intimate **11** incriminate

implication
4 hint **8** allusion, overtone **9** inference, undertone **10** connection, intimation, suggestion **11** association, connotation **12** significance

implicit
5 tacit **6** unsaid **8** inherent, unspoken **9** doubtless, potential, unuttered **10** undeclared, understood **11** unexpressed

implied
5 tacit **6** unsaid **8** inherent, unspoken **9** suggested **10** undeclared, understood **11** unexpressed

implore
3 ask, beg **4** coax, pray **5** crave, plead **6** adjure, appeal **7** beseech, entreat, solicit **10** supplicate

imply
4 hint, mean **5** get at **7** connote, include, involve, signify, suggest **8** indicate, intimate **9** insinuate

impolite
4 rude **5** crude **7** ill-bred, uncivil, uncouth **10** ungracious, unladylike, unmannered, unmannerly **11** ill-mannered **12** discourteous **13** ungentlemanly

impolitic
5 brash **6** unwise **8** tactless **9** imprudent, maladroit, untactful **10** ill-advised, indiscreet **11** inadvisable, inexpedient, injudicious **12** shortsighted, undiplomatic

import
4 bear, gist, mean, pith **5** sense, value, worth **6** convey, denote, intend, intent, matter, moment, stress, thrust, weight **7** concern, connote, express, meaning, message, purpose, signify **8** emphasis, indicate, transfer **9** magnitude, substance **10** intendment **11** acceptation, consequence **12** significance **13** signification

importance
4 mark, note, pith **5** value, worth **6** moment, weight **7** account, gravity **8** eminence, priority, salience, standing **9** greatness, magnitude, substance **10** prominence, worthiness **11** consequence, distinction, seriousness, weightiness **12** significance

important
3 big **5** chief, grave, great, heavy, major, noted, vital **6** famous, marked, potent, urgent, worthy **7** big-time, capital, crucial, eminent, fateful, notable, salient, serious, telling, weighty **8** critical, eventful, foremost, material, powerful, pressing, valuable **9** essential, estimable, imperious, memorable, momentous, prominent **10** meaningful, noteworthy, preeminent, worthwhile **11** outstanding, significant, substantial **12** considerable **13** consequential, distinguished, indispensable

importune
3 beg **4** pray, urge **5** annoy, plead, worry **6** appeal, invoke, plague **7** beseech, besiege, entreat, solicit, trouble **8** petition

impose
3 fob **4** lade, levy **5** abuse, enact, exact, foist, force, order, place, put on, visit, wreak **6** assess, burden, charge, compel, decree, demand, enjoin, fob off, ordain, saddle **7** command, dictate, exploit, inflict, intrude, lay down, obtrude, palm off, pass off, require **8** encroach, encumber, infringe, trespass **9** authorize, constrain, establish

imposing
4 huge **5** grand, noble, regal, royal **6** august **7** awesome, massive, pompous, stately **8** baronial, majestic, towering **9** dignified **10** commanding, monumental **11** magnificent, outstanding **12** high-sounding **13** distinguished

imposition
3 tax **4** duty, fine, levy **6** burden, demand **7** penalty **9** deception **13** inconvenience

impossible
6 absurd **8** hopeless **10** infeasible, unfeasible, unworkable **11** unthinkable **12** preposterous, unacceptable, unattainable, unbelievable, unimaginable, unrealizable, unreasonable **13** inconceivable

impost
3 fee, tax **4** duty, levy, toll **6** charge, tariff **7** tribute **9** surcharge **10** assessment

impostor
4 fake, sham **5** actor, cheat, faker, fraud, mimic, phony, poser, quack **6** humbug, poseur **8** deceiver **9** charlatan, con artist, hypocrite, pretender **10** dissembler, mountebank **11** masquerader **12** impersonator

imposture
4 fake, hoax, sell, sham, wile **5** cheat, fraud **6** deceit, humbug **8** flimflam **9** deception, mare's nest, stratagem **11** counterfeit

impotence
8 weakness **9** sterility **10** inadequacy **12** helplessness **13** powerlessness

impotent
4 lame, weak **6** effete, feeble **7** sterile **8** helpless **9** forceless, incapable, powerless **11** ineffective, ineffectual **12** invertebrate

impound
5 seize **6** immure, lock up **7** confine, enclose, put away **8** imprison **10** confiscate

impoverish
4 bust, ruin **5** break **6** beggar **8** bankrupt **9** pauperize

impoverished
4 poor **5** broke, needy **8** bankrupt, indigent **9** destitute, penniless, penurious

impoverishment
4 need, want **6** penury **9** indigence, neediness, privation **11** destitution

impracticable
8 unusable **10** infeasible, unfeasible, unworkable **11** insuperable, unrealistic **12** inaccessible, unattainable

impractical
7 blue-sky, utopian **8** quixotic, romantic, unusable **9** visionary **10** idealistic, infeasible, ivory-tower, starry-eyed, unfeasible, unworkable **11** theoretical, unrealistic

imprecation
3 hex **4** cuss **5** curse **7** malison **8** anathema **11** malediction

imprecise
5 rough, vague **7** inexact **9** estimated **10** indefinite **11** approximate, unspecified

impregnable
4 safe **6** immune, secure **9** protected **10** invincible, inviolable, unbeatable **11** indomitable, insuperable **12** unassailable **13** unconquerable

impregnate
3 sop **4** fill, soak **5** imbue, souse, steep **6** drench, infuse **7** pervade **8** conceive, permeate, saturate **9** fecundate, fertilize, penetrate, transfuse **10** inseminate

impresario
4 Bing (Rudolf) **5** Carte (Richard D'Oyly), Hurok (Sol) **6** Pastor (Tony) **7** manager **8** director, Kirstein (Lincoln), producer, promoter **9** Diaghilev (Sergei) **10** D'Oyly Carte (Richard)

impress
3 fix, set **4** dent, etch, mark, move, seal, sway **5** brand, carry, drive, exert, force, grave, infix, print, stamp, touch **6** affect, effect, excite, strike **7** engrave, ingrain, inspire **8** inscribe, transfer, transmit **9** establish, influence, stimulate

impressible
8 gullible, immature, moldable **9** malleable, receptive, sensitive **10** affectable, susceptive, vulnerable **11** persuadable, suggestible, susceptible

impression
4 dent, idea, mark, sign, take **5** image, print, stamp, trace, track **6** effect, hollow, notion **7** concept, edition, feeling, reissue, thought, vestige **8** printing, reaction **9** influence

impressionable
8 sensible, sentient **9** malleable, receptive, sensitive **10** responsive **11** suggestible, susceptible

impressionist
composer: **5** Ravel (Maurice) **7** Debussy (Claude)
mimic: **6** Carrey (Jim), Carvey (Dana), Little (Rich)
painter: **5** Degas (Edgar), Manet (Edouard), Monet (Claude) **6** Renoir (Auguste), Sisley (Alfred) **7** Cassatt (Mary), Morisot (Berthe) **8** Pissarro (Camille)
(see also **postimpressionist**)

impressive
5 grand, noble **6** moving, superb **7** amazing, awesome, notable, stately, sublime **8** dazzling, dramatic, gorgeous, majestic, powerful, splendid, stirring, striking, touching **9** admirable, affecting, arresting, inspiring **11** magnificent

imprimatur
6 permit **7** license **8** approval, sanction **10** permission **13** authorization

imprint
3 fix **4** dent, etch, mark **5** grave, press, stamp **6** dimple, effect **7** engrave **8** inscribe **9** engraving, influence **10** depression **11** indentation, inscription

imprison
3 jug **4** cage, jail **6** coop up, detain, immure, intern, send up **7** confine, enclose **8** restrain, restrict, stockade **9** constrain **11** incarcerate

improbable
5 fishy **7** dubious **8** doubtful, fanciful, unlikely **10** far-fetched **11** implausible

impromptu
5 ad-lib **7** offhand **9** extempore, makeshift, unplanned, unstudied **10** off-the-cuff, unprepared, unscripted **11** extemporary, spontaneous, unrehearsed

improper
5 inapt, inept, outré, undue, wrong **6** gauche, risqué **7** illicit, naughty **8** ill-timed, indecent, tactless, unseemly, untimely, untoward **9** incorrect, unethical, unfitting **10** inaccurate, inapposite, indecorous, indelicate, malapropos, unbecoming, undecorous, unsuitable **11** impertinent, unbefitting **12** illegitimate, inadmissible, inapplicable, infelicitous, unseasonable **13** inappropriate

impropriety
5 gaffe **7** blooper, blunder, faux pas **8** solecism **9** barbarism, gaucherie, indecorum, vulgarism **12** unseemliness **13** incorrectness

improve
4 edit, help, mend **5** amend, boost, edify, emend, raise **6** better, enrich, look up, perk up, refine, reform, remedy, revise, revive, update,

uplift **7** advance, amplify, augment, build up, correct, develop, enhance, enlarge, further, perfect, recover, rectify, upgrade **8** increase, progress **9** cultivate, intensify, meliorate **10** ameliorate, recuperate, strengthen

improvident
4 rash **6** lavish **8** careless, feckless, heedless, prodigal, reckless, wasteful **9** impetuous, negligent, unthrifty **10** profligate **11** extravagant, spendthrift **12** shortsighted

improvise
4 scat, vamp **5** ad-lib **6** cook up, invent, make up, wing it **7** concoct **8** contrive **9** fabricate **11** extemporize

improvised
5 ad hoc **7** offhand **9** extempore, unstudied **10** off-the-cuff, unprepared, unscripted **11** extemporary, unrehearsed

imprudent
4 rash **6** unwise **7** foolish **8** reckless **9** foolhardy **10** ill-advised, incautious, indiscreet **11** inadvisable, inexpedient, injudicious **12** shortsighted

impudence
4 gall **5** brass, cheek, nerve **8** audacity, boldness, chutzpah, temerity **9** brashness, cockiness, hardihood, insolence, nerviness **10** disrespect, effrontery **11** presumption

impudent
4 bold, flip, pert, rude, wise **5** brash, cocky, fresh, lippy, nervy, sassy, saucy, smart **6** brassy, brazen, cheeky **7** blatant, forward **8** flippant, insolent, overbold **9** audacious, barefaced, boldfaced **11** brazen-faced, smart-alecky **12** contumelious **13** disrespectful

impugn
5 cross **6** assail, attack, defame, malign, oppose, vilify **7** asperse, gainsay, impeach **8** chastise, reproach, traverse **9** castigate, criticize, denigrate, deprecate, disparage, reprehend

impugnable
5 fishy, shady **6** guilty **7** suspect **8** doubtful **9** equivocal, uncertain **10** assailable, suspicious **11** problematic **12** disreputable

impulse
4 goad, push, spur, urge, whim **5** drive, force **6** motive, thrust, whimsy **7** caprice, passion **8** catalyst, excitant, stimulus **9** actuation, incentive, stimulant **10** incitation, incitement, motivation **11** inspiration, instigation
conductor: **4** axon

impulsive
4 rash **5** brash, hasty **6** abrupt, fickle, sudden **7** erratic, flighty, offhand **8** headlong, volatile **9** extempore, mercurial, unplanned, whimsical **10** capricious **11** instinctive, precipitate, spontaneous

impunity
7 freedom, liberty, license **8** immunity **9** exception, exemption, indemnity, privilege **10** absolution, protection

impure
3 raw **5** mixed **6** soiled, sordid, unholy **7** alloyed, defiled, profane, sullied, unclean **8** indecent, polluted, unchaste **9** uncleanly, unrefined **10** desecrated, unhallowed **11** adulterated

impute
3 lay **4** cite **5** blame, refer **6** accuse, adduce, assign, charge, credit, indict **7** ascribe **8** accredit **9** attribute, implicate

inaccessible
5 aloof **6** arcane, closed, far-off, remote **7** cryptic, distant, faraway, obscure **8** abstruse, esoteric, hermetic **9** recondite **11** unavailable, unreachable **12** unattainable, unobtainable

inaccurate
5 false, wrong **6** all wet, faulty, untrue **7** unsound **8** specious **9** distorted, erroneous **10** fictitious

inaction
6 repose **7** latency **8** dormancy, idleness, lethargy **9** desuetude, indolence, passivity, slackness, torpidity **10** quiescence

inactive
4 idle, lazy **5** inert, quiet, slack, still **6** asleep, latent, sleepy, static, torpid **7** abeyant, dormant, passive, resting **8** slothful, sluggish **9** do-nothing, lethargic, quiescent, sedentary

in addition
4 also **6** as well, to boot, withal **7** besides, further **8** moreover **11** furthermore

inadequacy
4 lack, want **6** dearth **7** deficit, failure, paucity **8** shortage, weakness **9** impotence **10** deficiency, scantiness **11** shortcoming

inadequate
3 shy **5** scant, short **6** meager, scanty, scarce, skimpy **7** lacking, scrimpy, wanting **8** impotent **9** defective, deficient

inadmissible
5 unapt, unfit **8** unusable, unworthy **9** unwelcome **10** unsuitable **11** unqualified **12** unacceptable

inadvertent
8 careless, heedless **9** negligent, unmindful, unplanned, unwitting **10** accidental, unintended, unthinking **13** unintentional

inadvisable
4 rash **6** unwise **7** foolish **8** careless, reckless **9** foolhardy, impolitic, imprudent, pointless **10** ill-advised **11** harebrained

inalterable
5 fixed **6** stable **8** constant **9** immovable, immutable, steadfast, unmovable, unvarying **12** unchangeable

inamorata, inamorato
4 beau, dear **5** flame, honey, lover **6** steady **7** beloved, darling, squeeze, sweetie **8** ladylove, mistress, paramour, truelove **9** boyfriend **10** girlfriend, heartthrob, sweetheart

inane
4 idle, vain **5** blank, dotty, empty, silly, vapid **6** absurd, jejune, vacant **7** asinine, fatuous, foolish, idiotic, insipid, trivial, vacuous, witless **8** mindless **9** frivolous, laughable, pointless, senseless

inanimate
4 dead, dull **5** inert, still **6** asleep, torpid **7** dormant **8** immotile, lifeless **9** quiescent **10** motionless **11** unconscious

inanity
5 folly **6** idiocy, lunacy **7** fatuity, vacuity **8** vapidity **9** absurdity, dottiness, emptiness, silliness **10** hollowness **11** foolishness, vacuousness, witlessness **13** senselessness

inappreciable
6 meager, scanty, skimpy, slight **10** impalpable, unapparent **13** imperceptible

inappropriate
5 amiss, undue, unfit **6** unmeet **8** improper, unseemly, untimely, untoward **9** ill-suited **10** malapropos, unsuitable **11** impertinent

inapt
5 unfit **6** clumsy, gauche, jejune, unmeet **7** awkward, unhandy **8** improper, unfitted, unsuited, untimely **9** maladroit, unfitting, unskilled **10** amateurish, irrelevant, malapropos, unskillful, unsuitable

inarticulate
4 dumb, mute **5** tacit **6** silent **7** halting, unvocal **8** mumbling, unspoken, wordless **9** voiceless **10** maundering, speechless, tongue-tied, undeclared **11** unexpressed

inasmuch as
5 since **7** because, whereas **11** considering

inattentive
6 absent, remiss **8** distrait, heedless **9** forgetful, negligent, unheeding, unmindful **10** abstracted, distracted, unthinking **12** absentminded

inaugural
5 first **6** maiden, speech **7** address, initial, leading, opening, premier **8** foremost **9** beginning

inaugurate
5 begin, set up, start **6** launch **7** kick off **8** commence, dedicate, initiate **9** establish, institute, originate **10** consecrate

inauspicious
4 dire **7** adverse, baleful, direful, fateful, ominous, unlucky **8** sinister **9** ill-boding **11** threatening, unfavorable, unpromising **12** unpropitious

inborn
6 innate, native **7** connate, natural **8** inherent **9** intrinsic **10** congenital, connatural, hereditary, unacquired

in-box junk
4 spam

inbred
7 connate, genetic, natural **8** inherent **9** intrinsic **10** congenital, connatural, deep-seated, hereditary

Inca
capital: **5** Cuzco
conqueror: **7** Pizarro (Francisco)
god: **4** Inti **9** Viracocha **10** Pachacamac
home: **4** Peru
language: **7** Quechua
record: **5** quipu
ruin: **11** Machu Picchu
ruler: **9** Atahualpa, Pachacuti **10** Atahuallpa

incalculable
4 huge, iffy, vast **6** untold **8** enormous **9** boundless, countless, limitless, uncertain **10** tremendous, unnumbered **11** illimitable, measureless, uncountable **12** immeasurable, unmeasurable **13** unpredictable

in camera
7 privily, sub rosa **8** covertly, secretly **9** furtively, privately **10** stealthily **13** clandestinely

incandescent
3 hot **5** lucid **6** ardent, bright, lucent **7** beaming, fulgent, glowing, intense, lambent, radiant **8** dazzling, luminous **9** brilliant, effulgent, refulgent **11** resplendent

incantation
3 hex **4** rune **5** chant, charm, magic, spell **10** hocus-pocus, mumbo-jumbo, necromancy **11** abracadabra, conjuration, enchantment
Buddhist, Hindu: **6** mantra

incapable
5 unfit **6** unable **8** impotent, unexpert, unfitted **9** powerless, unskilled **10** unequipped, unskillful **11** unqualified **12** disqualified

incapacitate
6 disarm **7** cripple, disable **8** paralyze **10** debilitate, devitalize, disqualify, immobilize

incapacity
9 impotence, unfitness **10** impairment **11** disablement **12** fecklessness

incarcerate
3 jug **4** jail **6** coop up, immure, intern, send up **7** confine, enclose, impound **8** imprison

incarnadine
3 red **4** rosy **5** ruddy **6** redden **7** pinkish **8** bloodred

incarnate
5 human, reify **6** embody **7** realize **8** embodied, manifest **9** actualize, corporeal, personify **11** materialize, personalize **12** substantiate

incarnation
6 avatar **10** embodiment **11** reification
of Christ: 7 kenosis
of Vishnu: 4 Rama

incautious
4 rash **5** brash, hasty **6** daring, madcap, unwary **8** careless, heedless, reckless **9** daredevil, foolhardy, impetuous, imprudent, negligent, unmindful **10** ill-advised, neglectful, regardless **11** precipitate, thoughtless

incendiary
5 fiery, torch **7** firebug **8** agitator, arsonist, arsonous **9** explosive, firebrand, ignitable **10** pyromaniac **12** pyromaniacal

incense
3 ire, mad, oil **4** balm, burn, rile **5** anger, aroma, scent, spice **6** arouse, enrage, homage, incite, madden **7** inflame, provoke **8** irritate **9** infuriate
vessel: 6 censer **8** thurible

incensed
3 mad **4** sore **5** angry, irate **7** furious

incentive
4 goad, spur **5** spark **6** motive **7** impetus, impulse **8** catalyst, stimulus **9** stimulant **10** inducement, motivation **11** provocation **13** encouragement

inception
4 root **5** birth, get-go, onset, start **6** origin, outset, source **7** genesis, kickoff, opening **9** beginning **10** derivation, provenance **11** provenience **12** commencement

inceptive
7 initial, leadoff, nascent **9** beginning **10** initiatory

incertitude
5 doubt **7** dubiety **8** mistrust **9** suspicion **10** skepticism **11** dubiousness, uncertainty, vacillation **12** irresolution

incessant
6 steady **7** endless, eternal, nonstop **8** constant **9** ceaseless, continual, perpetual, unceasing **10** continuous **11** everlasting, unremitting **12** interminable **13** uninterrupted

inch
3 bit **5** crawl, creep **7** modicum

inchoate
8 formless, immature, unformed, unshaped **9** amorphous, embryonic, incipient, potential, shapeless **10** disjointed, incoherent **11** rudimentary, unorganized **12** disconnected

incident
5 event **7** episode **8** occasion **9** happening **10** affiliated, collateral, occurrence **11** concomitant

incidental
5 fluky, minor **6** casual, chance **9** accessory **10** contingent, fortuitous **11** subordinate **12** nonessential

incidentally
7 by the by **8** by the bye, by the way, casually **12** fortuitously

incinerate
4 burn **7** cremate

incipient
7 nascent **9** beginning, embryonic **10** commencing

incipit
5 start **7** opening **9** beginning

incise
3 cut **4** etch, gash, kerf, slit **5** carve **6** chisel **7** engrave

incision
3 cut **4** gash, slit **5** blaze, notch **10** laceration

incisive
4 keen **5** acute, crisp, sharp, terse **6** direct **7** cutting, mordant **8** clear-cut, piercing, slashing, succinct **9** trenchant **11** penetrating **13** perspicacious

incite
3 egg **4** abet, goad, prod, spur, urge **5** egg on, raise, rouse, set on, spark **6** arouse, exhort, foment, kindle, set off, spur on, stir up, whip up **7** actuate, agitate, provoke, trigger **8** motivate **9** instigate, stimulate

incitement
see **incentive**

inclement
3 raw **5** harsh, rough **6** bitter, brutal, severe, stormy **8** rigorous

inclination
3 bow, nod **4** bent, bias, lean, tilt, will **5** fancy, grade, pitch, slant, slope, taste, trend **6** ascent, liking **7** descent, incline, leaning **8** affinity, appetite, fondness, gradient, penchant, soft spot, tendency, velleity, weakness **9** affection **10** attachment, partiality, proclivity, propensity **11** disposition **12** predilection

incline
3 tip **4** bend, bias, cant, cast, heel, lean, list, sway, tend, tilt, turn **5** grade, impel, slant, slide, slope **6** affect, induce **7** dispose, leaning **8** gradient, persuade **9** influence, prejudice

inclined
3 apt **5** atilt, given, leant, prone, raked, ready **6** liable, likely, minded **7** dipping, leaning, oblique, sloping, tilting, willing **8** diagonal, pitching **11** predisposed
way: 4 ramp

include
5 admit, bound, cover **6** enfold, number, take in **7** confine, contain, embrace, enclose, receive, subsume **8** comprise, encircle **9** encompass **10** comprehend **11** accommodate

inclusive
4 A to Z **5** all up, broad **6** global **7** general, overall **8** complete, sweeping **9** all-around, embracive **11** compendious **12** encompassing, encyclopedic **13** comprehensive

___ incognita
5 terra

incognito
6 veiled **7** cloaked **9** anonymous, disguised **11** camouflaged

incognizant
7 unaware **8** ignorant **9** oblivious, unknowing, unmindful, unwitting **10** unfamiliar, uninformed **11** unconscious **12** unacquainted

incoherent
5 loose **6** broken, raving **7** muddled, unclear **8** confused **9** illogical **10** disjointed, disordered, irrational, maundering, tongue-tied **11** unconnected, unorganized **12** disconnected, disorganized **13** discontinuous

incombustible
9 fireproof **10** unburnable **12** nonflammable

income
4 gain, take **5** wages **6** profit **7** revenue **8** entrance, proceeds, receipts **9** emolument

incommode
3 irk, vex **5** annoy, upset **6** bother, burden, hinder, plague, put out **7** disturb, perturb, trouble **8** disquiet, distress, irritate **9** disoblige **10** disconcert

incommodious
7 awkward, cramped, crowded **8** confined **9** congested

incommunicable
8 reserved, taciturn **9** ineffable, withdrawn **11** unspeakable, unutterable **13** undescribable, unexpressible

incomparable
6 unique **7** supreme **8** peerless, singular, ultimate **9** matchless, nonpareil, paramount, unequaled, unmatched, unrivaled **10** preeminent, surpassing, unequalled, unrivalled **11** outstanding, superlative, unequalable, unmatchable **12** transcendent, unparalleled **13** unsurpassable

incompatible
7 adverse, counter **8** contrary, opposite **9** dissonant, unmixable **10** discordant, discrepant **11** conflicting, disagreeing, uncongenial, unfavorable **12** antagonistic, antithetical **13** contradictory, unsympathetic

incompetence
9 unfitness **10** disability, ineptitude **12** fecklessness

incompetent
5 inept, unfit **6** clumsy **8** helpless, inexpert, unfitted **9** incapable, maladroit, unskilled **10** unequipped **11** inefficient, unqualified

incomplete
4 part **5** short **6** broken, undone **7** partial, sketchy **8** abridged, immature **9** truncated **10** unfinished **11** fragmentary

incompliant
5 rigid, stiff **6** mulish **7** defiant **8** perverse, stubborn **9** obstinate, pigheaded, resistant, unbending **10** bullheaded, headstrong, inflexible, self-willed, unyielding **11** intractable **12** pertinacious, recalcitrant

incomprehensible
7 cryptic, obscure, unclear **8** abstruse, baffling, esoteric **9** fantastic **10** fathomless, mysterious, mystifying, unknowable **11** ungraspable **12** impenetrable, unfathomable, unimaginable

inconceivable
10 improbable, unknowable **11** implausible, unthinkable **12** unbelievable, unconvincing, unimaginable

in conclusion
6 lastly **7** finally

inconclusive
4 open **9** equivocal, uncertain, undecided, unsettled **10** unfinished

incongruous
5 alien **6** absurd **7** foreign, variant **9** anomalous, dissonant **10** discordant, discrepant, unsuitable **11** conflicting, disagreeing **12** disconsonant

inconsequential
5 petty, small **6** measly, paltry **7** trivial **8** nugatory, picayune, trifling **9** illogical, small-time **10** immaterial, irrelevant, negligible **11** impertinent, superficial, unimportant

inconsiderable
4 puny **5** minor, petty **6** meager, meagre, paltry, scanty, skimpy, slight **7** scrimpy, trivial **8** picayune, trifling **9** frivolous, small-beer **10** negligible **11** unimportant

inconsiderate
4 rash **5** brash, hasty **6** unkind **8** careless, heedless, impolite, reckless **9** hotheaded, impulsive **10** ill-advised, ungracious **11** precipitate, thoughtless **12** discourteous, uncharitable

inconsistent
6 fickle **7** erratic **8** contrary **9** dissonant, illogical, mercurial **10** capricious, changeable, discordant, discrepant **11** conflicting **13** contradictory

inconsolable
7 forlorn **8** desolate **9** heartsick **11** comfortless, heartbroken

inconspicuous
6 hidden, subtle **7** obscure **9** concealed **11** unobtrusive **12** unnoticeable

inconstant
6 fickle, untrue **7** erratic, mutable, protean, vagrant **8** unstable, unsteady, variable, volatile, wavering **9** changeful, faithless, fluctuant, irregular, mercurial, uncertain, unsettled **10** capricious, changeable, irresolute, perfidious, unfaithful **11** chameleonic, vacillating **13** temperamental

incontestable
4 sure **7** certain **8** absolute, clear-cut, ironclad, positive **9** apodictic, undoubted **10** conclusive, inarguable, undeniable **11** irrefutable, unequivocal **12** unassailable, undisputable **13** unimpeachable

incontinent
5 loose **6** wanton **9** dissolute **10** licentious, profligate **12** unrestrained

incontrovertible
4 sure **7** certain **8** absolute, clear-cut, definite, positive **10** conclusive, undeniable **11** irrefutable, unequivocal **12** undisputable

inconvenience
3 irk, vex **5** annoy **6** bother, meddle, put out **7** disrupt, disturb, trouble **8** handicap, vexation **9** annoyance **10** discomfort, discommode, disruption, exasperate **11** aggravation

inconvenient
7 awkward, unhandy **8** annoying **10** bothersome, unsuitable **11** pestiferous, troublesome

incorporate
3 mix **4** form, fuse, join **5** blend, merge, unite **6** absorb, embody, imbibe, mingle **7** combine **8** organize **9** establish **10** amalgamate, assimilate

incorporeal
8 bodiless, formless **9** spiritual **10** discarnate, immaterial, unphysical **11** disembodied, nonmaterial, nonphysical **12** metaphysical **13** unsubstantial

incorrect
5 false, wrong **6** faulty, untrue **7** unsound **8** improper, specious **9** erroneous, imprecise **10** fallacious, inaccurate, unbecoming

incorrigible
6 unruly **8** depraved **9** incurable **10** delinquent, inveterate **11** unalterable **12** irredeemable

increase
3 add, wax **4** gain, grow, hike, jump, plus, rise, soar, teem **5** add to, boost, build, mount, raise, run up, spike, surge, swarm, swell **6** accrue, amount, beef up, dilate, expand, extend, growth, jack up, markup, step up **7** accrual, advance, amplify, augment, burgeon, enhance, enlarge, inflate, magnify, prolong, upsurge **8** addition, compound, escalate, flourish, heighten, lengthen, manifold, multiply, protract, snowball **9** accession, accretion, expansion, extension, increment, inflation, intensify, reinforce **10** accelerate, accumulate, aggrandize, appreciate **11** enlargement **12** augmentation **13** amplification

incredible
7 amazing, awesome **8** unlikely **9** cockamamy, fantastic **10** astounding, cockamamie, far-fetched, impossible, improbable, outlandish, phenomenal, remarkable **11** astonishing, implausible **12** preposterous, unbelievable, unconvincing, unimaginable **13** extraordinary

incredulity
7 unfaith **8** distrust, mistrust, unbelief **9** disbelief, nonbelief, suspicion **10** skepticism

incredulous
6 show-me **7** dubious **8** doubting **9** quizzical, sceptical, skeptical **10** suspicious **11** distrustful, mistrustful, questioning, unbelieving, unconvinced **12** disbelieving

increment
4 gain, hike, rise, step **5** raise **6** degree, growth **7** quantum **8** addition **9** accession, accretion **11** enlargement **12** augmentation

incriminate
6 accuse, charge **7** arraign, impeach **9** implicate

incrustation
4 film, rime, scab **5** scale **6** tartar **7** coating

incubate
5 hatch

incubus
5 demon, fiend **9** nightmare

inculcate
5 teach, train **6** impart **7** educate, implant, impress, instill

inculpable
4 pure **5** clean **8** innocent, spotless, virtuous **9** blameless, guiltless, righteous **10** impeccable

incumbent
7 leaning, resting **8** occupant, required **9** overlying **10** obligatory **12** officeholder

incur
7 acquire, bring on, sustain **8** contract

incurable
5 fatal **6** deadly, lethal **8** hopeless, terminal

9 immutable **11** immedicable, irreparable **12** irremediable, unchangeable **13** uncorrectable

incursion
4 raid **5** blitz, foray, sally **6** attack, sortie **7** assault **9** irruption

incus
4 bone **5** anvil

indebted
5 bound **7** obliged **8** beholden **9** obligated

indebtedness
3 due, IOU **7** arrears **9** arrearage, gratitude, liability **10** obligation **11** delinquency **12** thankfulness

indecent
4 blue, lewd, racy **5** bawdy, dirty, gross **6** coarse, filthy, impure, risqué, smutty, vulgar **7** obscene, profane, raunchy **8** immodest, improper, off-color, unseemly, untoward **9** offensive **10** scurrilous **13** objectionable

indecision
5 doubt **6** abulia **8** wavering **9** hesitancy **11** ambivalence, uncertainty, vacillation **12** equivocation, irresolution, shilly-shally

indecisive
5 vague **6** abulic, unsure **7** dubious, unclear **8** wavering **9** equivocal, tentative, uncertain, undecided, unsettled **10** irresolute **11** problematic, vacillating

indecorous
4 rude **5** gross, rough **6** coarse, vulgar **7** uncivil **8** impolite, improper, unseemly, untoward **9** graceless, irregular, offensive, tasteless, unrefined **10** unbecoming **11** ill-mannered, undignified **12** discourteous

indecorum
5 gaffe **6** breach **7** blooper, blunder, faux pas, offense **8** solecism **11** impropriety

indeed
4 amen **5** truly **6** really, surely, verily **8** forsooth, honestly **9** assuredly, certainly **10** positively, undeniably **11** doubtlessly, undoubtedly **13** unequivocally

indefatigable
6 dogged **8** tireless, untiring, vigorous **9** energetic, tenacious **10** persistent, relentless, unflagging, unwearying **11** unrelenting

indefensible
9 unguarded, untenable **10** assailable, vulnerable **11** unprotected **12** unforgivable, unpardonable **13** unjustifiable

indefinable
5 vague **7** elusive **9** uncertain **11** unspeakable, unutterable **13** undescribable

indefinite
4 wide **5** broad, loose, vague **7** endless, general, inexact, obscure, unclear, unfixed **8** infinite **9** ambiguous, boundless, imprecise, limitless, unbounded, uncertain, undefined, unlimited **10** indistinct, inexplicit, unmeasured, unspecific **12** inconclusive **13** indeterminate
pronoun: **3** all, any, few **4** each, many, most, none, some **6** anyone, nobody **7** anybody, several, someone **8** everyone, somebody **9** everybody

indehiscent fruit
3 key, nut **4** pepo **5** berry, grain, grape, melon **6** achene, loment, samara, squash **7** pumpkin **8** cucumber **9** caryopsis **10** schizocarp

indelible
4 fast **5** fixed **7** lasting **8** enduring **9** memorable, permanent **13** unforgettable

indelicate
3 raw **4** lewd, rude **5** crude, gross, rough **6** coarse, vulgar **7** uncouth **8** impolite, immodest, improper, tactless, unseemly, untoward **9** unrefined **10** unbecoming

indemnify
5 repay **6** secure **7** redress, requite **9** reimburse **10** compensate, recompense, remunerate

indemnity
6 amends **7** redress **8** requital, security **9** exemption, quittance, reprisals **10** protection, recompense, reparation **11** restitution **12** compensation, remuneration **13** fee-for-service

indentation
4 dent, nick, pock **5** notch **6** dimple, recess **10** depression

indenture
4 nick **5** notch **8** contract **9** agreement **11** certificate

indentured
5 bound **10** controlled **11** apprenticed

independence
7 freedom, liberty **8** autonomy

independent
4 free **8** absolute, autarkic, separate **9** autarchic, sovereign **10** autonomous **11** self-reliant **13** self-contained

indescribable
11 unspeakable, unutterable **13** unexplainable

indestructible
7 lasting **8** enduring, immortal **9** permanent **12** imperishable, irrefragable, unperishable

indeterminate
5 vague **9** imprecise, uncertain, unlimited

index
4 list, mark, sign **5** ratio, table **7** catalog, symptom **8** classify, evidence, regulate **9** catalogue **11** systematize

India
bay: **6** Bengal
capital: **8** New Delhi

city: **5** Delhi **6** Bombay, Kanpur, Madras, Mumbai, Nagpur **7** Benares, Chennai, Kolkata, Lucknow **8** Calcutta **9** Ahmadabad, Bangalore, Hyderabad
coast: **7** Malabar **10** Coromandel
colonial regime: **3** Raj
European discoverer: **4** Gama (Vasco da)
language: **5** Hindi
leader: **3** Rao (P. V. N.) **4** Modi (Narendra) **5** Nehru (Jawaharlal) **6** Gandhi (Indira, Mohandas, Rajiv)
monetary unit: **5** rupee
mountain range: **7** Vindhya **9** Himalayas
neighbor: **5** Burma, China, Nepal **6** Bhutan **7** Myanmar **8** Pakistan **10** Bangladesh
pass: **5** Bolan, Gumal **6** Khyber
plateau: **6** Deccan
river: **5** Indus **6** Ganges, Yamuna **7** Krishna **11** Brahmaputra
sea: **7** Arabian
state: **5** Assam **6** Kerala, Punjab

Indian
4 Desi
bread: **3** nan **4** naan **7** chapati
butter: **3** ghi **4** ghee
caste: **4** Bahr **5** Sudra **6** Vaisya **7** Brahman **9** Kshatriya
cattle: **4** dhan
cavalry commander: **8** risaldar
crop-related: **4** rabi **6** kharif
dress: **4** sari **5** saree
female dancer: **8** bayadere
groom: **4** syce
harem: **6** zenana
honorific: **3** sri
instrument: **4** vina **5** sarod, sitar, tabla, veena **7** tambura
lady: **4** bibi **5** begum **8** memsahib
lentil dish: **3** dal
musical term: **4** raga, tala
musician: **7** Shankar (Ravi)
noble: **4** raja **5** rajah
nurse: **4** amah, ayah
outcast: **6** pariah
peasant: **4** ryot
primate: **5** loris
prince: **4** raja, rana **5** rajah **8** maharaja **9** maharajah
princess: **4** rani **5** begum, ranee
queen: **4** rani **5** ranee
scholar: **6** pandit, pundit
screen: **6** purdah
seal, stamp: **4** chop
soldier: **4** peon **5** sepoy
steps: **4** ghat
teacher: **4** guru
title: **5** sahib
viceroy: **5** nabob, nawab
weight unit: **3** ser **4** cash, dhan, pank, pice, powe, rati, tank, tola **5** adpao, fanam, hubba, masha, maund, pally, pouah, ratti **6** dhurra, pagoda, pollam **7** chinnam, chittak

Indian, American
baby: **7** papoose
ball game: **8** lacrosse
carrier: **7** travois
Central and South American: **3** Mam, Ona **4** Cana, Cora, Cuna, Inca, Maya, Moro **5** Arara, Aztec, Carib, Huave, Mayan, Olmec, Taino, Yagua **6** Arawak, Aymara, Jivaro, Omagua, Toltec, Yahgan **7** Chibcha, Quechua, Zapotec **8** Tarascan, Yanomamo **10** Araucanian **11** Tupi-Guaraní
food: **4** samp **5** maize **8** pemmican
home: **5** hogan, lodge, tepee **6** pueblo, teepee, wigwam **7** wickiup
leader: **4** Gall, Popé **6** Wovoka **7** Cochise, Metacom, Osceola, Pontiac, Sequoia, Sequoya **8** Geronimo, Hiawatha, Powhatan, Red Cloud, Sequoyah, Tecumseh **9** Black Hawk, Massasoit, Red Jacket **10** Crazy Horse, Poundmaker **11** Cornplanter, Sitting Bull
money: **6** wampum
North American: **3** Aht, Fox, Hoh, Kaw, Oto, Sac, Sia, Ute, Wea **4** Coos, Cora, Cree, Crow, Erie, Hopi, Hupa, Iowa, Otoe, Otos, Pima, Pomo, Sauk, Taos, Yuma, Zuni **5** Aleut, Caddo, Creek, Haida, Huron, Kansa, Kiowa, Maidu, Miami, Modoc, Omaha, Osage, Otoes, Sioux, Uinta **6** Apache, Cayuga, Dakota, Lenape, Mandan, Micmac, Mohawk, Munsee, Navaho, Navajo, Nootka, Oglala, Ojibwa, Oneida, Paiute, Pawnee, Pequot, Pueblo, Quapaw, Salish, Santee, Seneca, Siwash **7** Anasazi, Arapaho, Arikara, Bannock, Chilkat, Chinook, Choctaw, Dakotah, Esselen, Klamath, Kutenai, Mohican, Naskapi, Natchez, Ojibway, Pontiac, Shawnee, Tlingit **8** Cherokee, Cheyenne, Chippewa, Comanche, Delaware, Illinois, Iroquois, Kickapoo, Kwakiutl, Nez Percé, Onondaga, Powhatan, Seminole, Shoshoni **9** Blackfoot, Chickasaw, Menominee, Tsimshian, Tuscarora, Wampanoag, Winnebago **10** Assiniboin, Chiricahua, Gros Ventre, Potawatomi **11** Massachuset, Narraganset
pipe: **7** calumet
spirit: **5** totem **6** manitu **7** kachina, manitou

Indiana
capital: **12** Indianapolis
city: **4** Gary **6** Muncie **9** Fort Wayne, South Bend **10** Evansville, Terre Haute **11** Bloomington
college, university: **6** DePauw, Purdue **9** Ball State, Notre Dame
nickname: **7** Hoosier (State)
river: **5** White **6** Wabash

state bird: **8** cardinal
state flower: **5** peony
state tree: **5** tulip

Indian paintbrush
8 hawkweed **10** painted cup

indicate
4 bode, hint, mark, mean, show **5** augur, imply, point, prove **6** attest, convey, denote, evince, import, reveal **7** bespeak, betoken, connote, display, exhibit, express, presage, signify, suggest **8** disclose, evidence, foretell, manifest, register **9** designate **10** foreshadow, illustrate **11** demonstrate

indication
3 cue **4** clue, hint, mark, sign **5** proof, token, trace **6** augury, signal **7** gesture, inkling, portent, symptom **8** evidence, reminder, telltale **9** testimony **10** expression, suggestion **13** foreshadowing, manifestation

indicative
10 expressive, suggestive **11** evidentiary, symptomatic **12** illustrative **13** demonstrative

indicia
5 marks, signs **8** imprints, markings

indict
5 blame **6** accuse, charge **7** arraign, censure, impeach **9** criticize

indifference
6 apathy **9** aloofness, unconcern **10** detachment, dispassion **11** disinterest **12** carelessness, impartiality

indifferent
4 cold, cool, numb, so-so **5** aloof, blasé, stoic **6** casual, remote **7** average, neutral **8** careless, detached, mediocre, middling, moderate, ordinary, passable, unbiased, uncaring **9** apathetic, impartial, impassive, objective **10** nonchalant, unaffected **11** unconcerned, unemotional **12** uninterested, unprejudiced **13** disinterested, dispassionate

indigence
4 need, want **6** penury **7** poverty **9** neediness, pauperism, privation **11** deprivation, destitution

indigene
6 native **9** aborigine **10** aboriginal

indigenous
6 native **7** endemic, natural **10** aboriginal, congenital, connatural, unacquired **13** autochthonous

indigent
4 poor **5** broke, needy **9** destitute, penniless **11** impecunious, necessitous **12** impoverished

indigestion
9 dyspepsia, heartburn

indignant
3 mad **5** irate, riled, upset, vexed **6** galled, heated **7** annoyed **8** offended, outraged, provoked **9** affronted, irritated, resentful

indignation
5 pique **7** dudgeon **10** irritation, resentment

indignity
3 cut **4** slap **6** injury, insult, slight **7** affront, outrage **9** contumely, grievance **10** disrespect **11** humiliation **13** disparagement, embarrassment

indigo
4 anil, blue **8** deep blue

indigo bird
5 finch **7** bunting

Indira's father
5 Nehru (Jawaharlal)

indirect
7 devious, oblique, vagrant, winding **8** circular, sidelong, tortuous **9** deceitful, underhand, wandering **10** backhanded, circuitous, collateral, meandering, roundabout **11** duplicitous, underhanded

indiscreet
5 gabby **6** unwise **7** foolish, gossipy **8** tactless **9** impolitic, imprudent, untactful **10** ill-advised **11** loose-lipped

indiscretion
4 slip **5** folly, gaffe, lapse **7** blunder, faux pas, mistake, misstep **8** solecism **10** imprudence **11** impropriety

indiscriminate
5 mixed **6** hybrid, motley, random, varied **7** aimless, jumbled, vagrant **8** assorted, careless **9** arbitrary, desultory, haphazard, hit-or-miss, unplanned, wholesale **10** uncritical **11** promiscuous **12** conglomerate, multifarious, unrestrained **13** heterogeneous, miscellaneous

indispensable
5 basic, vital **6** needed **7** crucial, needful, pivotal **8** cardinal, critical **9** essential, necessary, requisite **10** imperative, obligatory **11** fundamental

indisposed
3 ill **4** down, sick **5** loath **6** ailing, averse, poorly, sickly, unwell **7** uneager **8** hesitant **9** reluctant, resistant, unwilling **11** disinclined

indisposition
6 malady **7** ailment, dislike, illness, malaise **8** aversion, disfavor, distaste, sickness, unhealth **10** affliction, reluctance

indisputable
4 sure, true **7** certain, evident, obvious **8** absolute, ironclad, positive **9** apodictic **10** undeniable **11** irrefutable, unequivocal **12** irrefragable, unassailable

indistinct
3 dim **4** hazy **5** faint, foggy, misty, murky, vague **6** bleary, blurry, cloudy **7** blurred, obscure, shadowy, unclear **8** confused **9** uncertain, undefined **12** undetermined

indistinguishable
4 same **5** alike, equal, vague **7** unclear **9** duplicate, identical **10** equivalent

indite
3 pen **5** write **6** record, scribe **7** compose, engross **10** transcribe

individual
3 one **4** body, lone, self, sole, soul, unit **5** being, human, party, thing **6** entity, mortal, person, proper, single **7** special **8** creature, discrete, distinct, peculiar, personal, separate, singular, solitary, specific **10** particular, respective **11** distinctive **13** idiosyncratic
combining form: **4** idio

individualist
5 loner **6** hermit **8** lone wolf, maverick **13** nonconformist

individuality
4 self **7** essence, oneness **8** identity, selfhood **9** character **10** uniqueness **11** personality, singularity **12** idiosyncrasy, separateness

individualize
4 mark **7** specify **9** customize **10** specialize **11** distinguish, personalize, singularize **12** characterize **13** differentiate, particularize

Indochinese country
4 Laos **5** Burma **7** Myanmar, Vietnam **8** Cambodia, Thailand **9** Kampuchea

indoctrinate
5 teach, tutor **7** educate, program **8** convince, persuade **9** brainwash, inculcate

indolence
4 laze **5** sloth **7** inertia, languor **8** idleness, laziness, lethargy **9** torpidity **12** slothfulness, sluggishness **13** shiftlessness
fruit of: **5** lotus

indolent
4 idle, lazy **6** torpid **8** fainéant, slothful, sluggish **9** lethargic, shiftless

indomitable
7 staunch **9** steadfast **10** invincible, unbeatable **11** impregnable **13** unconquerable

Indonesia
archipelago: **5** Malay
capital: **7** Jakarta **8** Djakarta
city: **5** Medan **7** Bandung, Cilacap **8** Semarang, Surabaja, Surabaya **9** Palembang
island: **4** Bali, Java **7** Sumatra **8** Sulawesi
island group: **5** Sunda **8** Moluccas
language: **6** Bahasa
leader: **7** Suharto, Sukarno
monetary unit: **6** rupiah
regions: **4** Bali, Java **5** Coram, Timor **6** Bangka, Borneo, Flores, Lombok, Madura **7** Celebes, Sumatra **8** Sulawesi **9** Irian Jaya
volcano: **8** Krakatau, Krakatoa

Indonesian boat
4 prau, proa

indubitable
4 sure **6** patent **7** certain, evident, obvious **8** definite, ironclad, positive **9** apodictic, veritable **10** undeniable **11** irrefutable, self-evident, unequivocal **12** irrefragable

induce
5 cause **6** effect, elicit, prompt **7** actuate, procure **8** convince, engender, generate, motivate, occasion, persuade **9** encourage

inducement
4 bait, lure **6** come-on, motive **10** attraction, motivation **13** consideration

induct
4 lead **5** admit **6** enlist, enroll **7** appoint, install

inductance unit
5 henry

induction
8 entrance **9** accession, reasoning **10** enlistment **11** appointment **13** ratiocination

inductive
7 logical **9** prefatory, prelusive **11** a posteriori

indulge
3 pet **4** baby, bask **5** allow, favor, humor, spoil **6** cocker, coddle, cosset, oblige, pamper, permit, please, wallow **7** cater to, delight, gratify, satisfy **9** luxuriate **11** mollycoddle

indulgence
5 favor, mercy, treat **6** luxury **7** charity **8** clemency, courtesy, kindness, lenience, leniency **9** allowance, remission, tolerance **10** compassion, kindliness, permission, toleration **11** forbearance, forgiveness **12** dispensation, mercifulness **13** gratification

indulgence seller
5 Tezel (Johann) **6** Tetzel (Johann)

indulgent
4 easy, kind **7** clement, lenient **8** generous, merciful, tolerant **9** forgiving **10** charitable, permissive

indurate
6 harden **7** callous, confirm, congeal **8** hardened, solidify, stubborn **9** unfeeling **11** hardhearted

industrialist
6 tycoon **7** magnate **12** manufacturer

industrious
4 busy **8** diligent, sedulous **9** assiduous, laborious
insect: **3** ant, bee

industry
4 work **5** labor **8** business, commerce **9** assiduity, diligence **10** enterprise

Indy 500 winner
4 Foyt (A. J.) **5** Mears (Rick), Unser (Al, Bobby) **8** Andretti (Mario)

inebriant
see **intoxicant**

inebriate
3 sot **4** lush, soak **5** drunk, souse, tight, tipsy, toper **6** bibber, boozer **7** stupefy, tippler, tosspot **8** drunkard **10** intoxicate

inebriated
3 lit **5** drunk, lit up, oiled, stiff, tight, tipsy **6** blotto, juiced, loaded, plowed, potted, soused, stewed, tanked, wasted **7** crocked, pickled, pie-eyed, sloshed, smashed **8** polluted **9** plastered

inedible
9 poisonous **12** unappetizing

ineffable
5 taboo **9** forbidden **11** unspeakable, unutterable **13** undescribable

ineffaceable
7 lasting **8** enduring **9** indelible, permanent

ineffective
4 vain, weak **6** effete, futile **7** useless **8** abortive, bootless, feckless, impotent **9** fruitless, powerless **10** emasculate, unavailing **12** unproductive, unsuccessful

ineffectiveness
8 futility **9** impotence

ineffectual
see **ineffective**

inefficient
5 slack **6** clumsy **8** careless, slipshod, wasteful **9** negligent

inelastic
5 rigid, stiff **7** brittle **9** unbending **10** unyielding

inelegant
5 crass, crude, gross, rough **6** coarse, gauche, vulgar **7** awkward, uncouth **9** graceless, unrefined **10** uncultured, ungraceful **12** uncultivated

ineligible
5 unfit **8** unfitted, unworthy **10** unequipped, unsuitable **11** unqualified **12** disqualified

ineluctable
4 sure **5** bound, fated **6** doomed **7** certain **8** destined **9** necessary **10** inevitable, unevadable **11** unavoidable, unescapable **13** unpreventable

inept
5 unfit **6** clumsy, gauche, klutzy **7** artless, awkward, foolish, halting, unhandy **8** bumbling, bungling, feckless **9** all thumbs, ham-handed, maladroit, unskilled **10** malapropos, unskillful, unsuitable **11** heavy-handed, undexterous, unfortunate

inequality
8 imparity **9** disparity **10** unevenness **12** irregularity, variableness **13** disproportion, heterogeneity

inequitable
6 biased, unfair, unjust **7** partial **10** prejudiced **11** unjustified, unrighteous

inequity
4 bias **5** wrong **9** prejudice **10** unfairness, unjustness

ineradicable
6 innate **7** chronic **8** constant, inherent, stubborn **9** ingrained **10** deep-rooted, deep-seated, entrenched, inveterate **11** established, ever-present, never-ending

inert
4 calm, dead, idle **5** quiet, still **6** asleep, sleepy **7** dormant, passive **8** immobile, lifeless, sluggish **9** apathetic, lethargic **10** motionless

inert gas
4 neon **5** argon, radon, xenon **6** helium **7** krypton

inertia
5 sloth **6** apathy, stupor, torpor **7** languor **8** idleness, laziness, lethargy **9** indolence, inertness, lassitude, passivity, torpidity **10** immobility, inactivity **11** disinterest **12** listlessness, sluggishness

inescapable
see **inevitable**

inessential
see **unessential**

inestimable
9 priceless **11** measureless **12** immeasurable, unmeasurable, unfathomable

inevitable
4 sure **5** bound, fated **6** doomed **7** certain **8** destined **9** necessary **11** unavoidable, unescapable **12** foreordained **13** unpreventable

inevitably
8 perforce **10** willy-nilly **11** like it or not, unavoidably

inexact
5 rough **8** ballpark

inexcusable
6 guilty **8** blamable, culpable **9** untenable **10** censurable **11** blameworthy, condemnable **12** criticizable, unforgivable, unpardonable **13** reprehensible, unjustifiable

inexhaustible
8 tireless, untiring **9** unfailing, weariless **10** bottomless, unflagging **13** indefatigable

inexorable
5 rigid 6 strict 7 adamant 8 immobile, obdurate, stubborn 9 immovable, unbending 10 implacable, relentless, unyielding 11 unrelenting

inexpensive
3 low 5 cheap 7 cut-rate 8 moderate 10 reasonable

inexperience
7 naïveté, rawness 8 verdancy 9 freshness, greenness 10 callowness

inexperienced
3 raw 5 fresh, green, naive, young 6 callow 7 untried 8 unversed 9 unskilled, untrained, unworldly 10 amateurish, unseasoned

inexpert
9 maladroit, unskilled, untrained 10 amateurish

inexplicable
6 arcane, obtuse, opaque 7 cryptic 9 enigmatic 10 mysterious, mystifying, unsolvable 12 impenetrable, unfathomable 13 unaccountable, unexplainable

inexpressible
8 nameless 11 unspeakable, unutterable 13 undescribable, unexplainable

inexpressive
5 blank, stoic 6 stolid, vacant, wooden 7 deadpan 9 impassive 10 poker-faced 13 straight-faced

inextricable
9 insoluble 10 unsolvable

infallible
4 sure 5 exact 6 trusty 7 certain, correct, perfect 8 absolute, accurate, flawless, surefire, unerring 9 errorless, unfailing 10 dependable, impeccable 11 trustworthy 12 tried-and-true 13 unimpeachable

infamous
4 evil, vile 6 odious 7 hateful, heinous 8 flagrant, shameful 9 abhorrent, miscreant, nefarious, notorious 10 abominable, despicable, detestable, flagitious, scandalous, villainous 11 disgraceful, ignominious, opprobrious 12 contemptible, disreputable

infamy
5 odium, shame 7 obloquy 8 disgrace, dishonor, ignominy 9 disrepute, notoriety 10 opprobrium

infancy
6 nonage 8 babyhood 9 childhood

infant
4 babe, baby 5 bairn, child, green 7 bambino, neonate, newborn, papoose, toddler 8 bantling, immature, nursling 9 unfledged
bed: 4 crib 6 cradle 8 bassinet
condition: 5 colic
food: 3 pap 4 milk 7 pabulum
room: 7 nursery

infanta
8 princess

infantile
7 babyish, puerile 8 childish, immature

infantryman
7 dogface 8 doughboy 11 foot soldier
Algerian: 6 Zouave

infatuated
4 gaga 5 dotty, silly 7 foolish 8 besotted, enamored, obsessed 9 bewitched, rapturous 10 captivated, passionate

infatuation
4 rage 5 ardor, craze, crush, folly 7 passion, rapture 8 devotion 9 obsession, puppy love 11 fascination

infect
5 taint 6 defile, poison 7 corrupt, pollute 11 contaminate

infection
3 bug 6 sepses (plural), sepsis
carrier: 6 vector
fungous: 8 mycetoma

infectious
8 catching, epidemic, virulent 9 pestilent 10 contagious, corrupting 12 communicable 13 contaminating, transmittable

infelicitous
5 unapt, unfit 6 unmeet 7 awkward, unhappy 8 improper 9 imperfect 10 malapropos, unsuitable 11 regrettable, unfortunate

infer
5 judge 6 deduce, deduct, derive, gather, reason 7 collect, make out, suppose, surmise 8 conclude, construe 10 conjecture 11 extrapolate, hypothesize

inference
7 surmise 8 illation, sequitur 9 deduction 10 assumption, conclusion, conjecture, derivation 11 presumption, supposition

inferior
3 low 4 base, fair, hack, mean, poor, puny 5 cheap, lousy, lower, minor, petty, scrub, sorry, under, worse 6 common, deputy, feeble, impure, junior, lesser, nether, no-good, paltry, satrap, shoddy, sleazy, tawdry, tinpot, vassal 7 average, subject, unequal 8 declassé, low-grade, mediocre, middling, ordinary, unworthy, wretched 9 attendant, auxiliary, no-account, satellite, secondary, subaltern, subjacent, underling, worthless 10 inadequate, second-rate 11 substandard
prefix: 3 sub 4 demi 5 infra

infernal
6 Hadean, nether 7 demonic, hellish, satanic 8 chthonic, damnable, demoniac, devilish, diabolic, plutonic 9 chthonian, plutonian, Tartarean 10 diabolical, sulphurous

inferno
3 pit **4** fire, hell **5** Hades, Sheol **6** blazes, Tophet **7** Gehenna **9** holocaust, perdition **10** underworld **11** netherworld **13** conflagration

Inferno
division: **5** canto
poet: **5** Dante (Alighieri)
verse form: **9** terza rima

infertile
6 barren, effete **7** sterile **8** impotent **10** unfruitful **12** hardscrabble, unproductive

infest
4 teem **5** beset, swarm **6** plague **7** overrun **10** parasitize

infidel
5 pagan **7** atheist, heathen, heretic, skeptic **8** agnostic **10** unbeliever

infidelity
7 perfidy, treason **8** adultery, betrayal, cheating **9** disbelief, treachery **10** disloyalty **13** faithlessness

infinite
4 vast **7** endless, eternal, immense **8** unending **9** boundless, countless, limitless, perpetual, unlimited **11** everlasting, illimitable, measureless, sempiternal **12** immeasurable

infinity
8 eternity **10** perpetuity **11** endlessness **12** sempiternity **13** boundlessness, limitlessness

infirm
4 lame, sick, weak **5** frail **6** ailing, feeble, sickly **7** failing, fragile, unsound **8** decrepit, unstable **9** doddering **11** debilitated

infirmity
3 ill **4** flaw **5** decay **6** malady **7** ailment, disease, frailty, illness, malaise **8** debility, disorder, sickness, syndrome, weakness **9** complaint, condition **10** affliction, feebleness, sickliness **11** decrepitude **12** debilitation, enfeeblement

infix
4 root **5** embed, lodge **6** fasten, pierce **7** engrave, implant, impress

inflame
4 fire, gall, goad, rile, roil **5** anger, light, rouse **6** arouse, enrage, excite, foment, ignite, kindle, madden, redden, stir up **7** provoke **8** enkindle, irritate **9** aggravate **10** exacerbate, exasperate

inflammable
5 fiery **6** ardent **8** burnable, volatile **9** excitable, ignitable, irascible **11** combustible

inflammation
4 gout, sore **6** otitis, quinsy **7** catarrh, colitis **8** adenitis, bursitis, cystitis, neuritis, pleurisy, rachitis, swelling **9** arthritis, chilblain, gastritis, nephritis, phlebitis **10** bronchitis, cellulitis, combustion, dermatitis, gingivitis, laryngitis, tendinitis **12** encephalitis **13** poliomyelitis
eye: **6** iritis **7** pinkeye **9** keratitis
horse: **7** fistula, quittor
intestines: **7** ileitis **9** enteritis
suffix: **4** itis

inflammatory
8 exciting **9** explosive, seditious **11** provocative **13** rabble-rousing, revolutionary

inflate
4 fill **5** bloat, elate, swell **6** expand **7** amplify, distend **9** supersize **10** aggrandize

inflated
5 tumid, windy **6** turgid **7** bloated, swollen, verbose **9** bombastic, distended, dropsical, flatulent, overblown **10** heightened **11** exaggerated, pretentious

inflection
4 bend, tone **5** curve, pitch **6** accent, change, stress, timbre **8** emphasis, tonality **9** accidence **10** modulation

inflexible
3 set **4** grim, hard, iron **5** fixed, rigid, stiff **6** strict **7** adamant, die-hard **8** dogmatic, granitic, hard-line, ironclad, obdurate, stubborn **9** immovable, immutable, obstinate, steadfast, unbending **10** adamantine, brassbound, implacable, rock-ribbed, unbendable, unyielding **11** unalterable, unrelenting **12** unchangeable

inflict
5 visit, wreak **7** mete out, subject **8** dispense **10** administer

in-flight info
3 ETA

inflow
4 rush **7** arrival

influence
4 move, pull, sway **5** alter, bribe, clout, force, impel, lobby, touch **6** affect, compel, impact, modify, moment, strike, weight **7** command, control, impress, mastery **8** dominate, militate, persuade, prestige **9** authority, dominance

influenceable
8 gullible **9** malleable, receptive, tractable **11** persuadable, persuasible, suggestible

influential
6 potent **8** forceful, powerful **9** effective **10** persuasive **13** authoritative

influx
7 arrival **8** entrance, invasion **9** accession

info
4 dope, poop **6** skinny **7** lowdown

inform
3 rat, tip **4** blab, clue, leak, post, tell, warn **5** brief, edify, endow, endue, imbue, teach **6** advise,

betray, fill in, impart, leaven, notify, reveal, snitch, squeal, tattle, turn in, update **7** animate, apprise, caution, educate **8** acquaint, disclose, forewarn **9** advertise, enlighten **11** familiarize

informal
6 casual, dégagé, folksy **7** natural, offhand, relaxed **8** down-home, familiar, laid-back **9** easygoing **10** colloquial, unofficial **13** unceremonious

information
3 tip **4** data, fact, lore, news, poop, word **5** scoop **6** advice, notice, skinny, wisdom **7** lowdown, tidings **9** knowledge **12** intelligence
manager: 9 cybrarian
secondhand: 7 hearsay

information bureau
abbreviation: 4 USIA, USIS

informative
8 edifying, exegetic **10** exegetical **11** educational, elucidative, explanatory **12** enlightening, illuminating

informed (about)
4 onto, up on, wise **5** aware **6** au fait, versed, wise to **7** abreast, knowing **8** apprised, educated **9** au courant, cognizant, in the know **10** acquainted, conversant **11** enlightened **13** knowledgeable

informer
3 rat, spy **4** fink, mole, narc **5** stool **6** canary, gossip, snitch **7** rat fink, stoolie, tattler, tipster **8** squealer, telltale **10** deep throat, talebearer, tattletale **11** stool pigeon **13** whistle-blower

infra
5 after, below, later, under **7** beneath

infract
3 sin **6** breach, offend **7** violate **8** trespass **10** contravene, transgress

infraction
3 sin **4** foul **5** crime, error **6** breach **7** faux pas, misdeed, offense **8** trespass **9** violation **12** encroachment **13** contravention, transgression

infrastructure
4 base **5** basis **9** framework **10** foundation, groundwork, substratum **12** underpinning

infrequent
3 odd **4** rare **6** scarce, seldom **7** unusual **8** isolated, sporadic, uncommon, unwonted **10** occasional **11** exceptional

infringe
6 breach, impose, meddle, offend **7** disturb, obtrude, violate **8** encroach, entrench, trespass **10** transgress

infuriate
3 ire, mad **4** rile **5** anger, pique **6** enrage, madden, rankle **7** incense, inflame, outrage, provoke, steam up

infuse
4 fill, soak **5** imbue, steep **6** leaven **7** animate, implant, pervade, suffuse **8** permeate, saturate **9** introduce **10** impregnate

ingenious
5 acute, canny, sharp, smart, witty **6** adroit, clever, crafty **7** cunning, fertile **8** creative, original **11** imaginative, resourceful

ingenue
4 naïf

ingenuity
5 knack, savvy, skill **6** acumen, smarts, talent **7** know-how, mastery **8** deftness, keenness **9** adeptness, handiness **10** adroitness, capability, cleverness, perception, shrewdness **11** proficiency **12** intelligence, skillfulness **13** inventiveness

ingenuous
4 open **5** naive **6** simple **7** artless, natural **8** innocent **9** childlike, guileless, unstudied **10** unaffected

ingest
3 eat **4** feed **6** devour **7** consume, partake, swallow

Inge work
6 Picnic **7** Bus Stop **18** Splendor in the Grass **19** Come Back Little Sheba

inglorious
8 shameful **11** disgraceful, ignominious, opprobrious **12** dishonorable, disreputable **13** discreditable, unrespectable

ingot
3 bar, pig, rod **4** mold **6** billet

ingrain
4 etch **5** imbue

ingrained
6 innate **8** inherent **9** essential **10** congenital, deep-rooted, deep-seated

ingratiating
5 silky **6** silken, smarmy **7** fawning **8** pleasing, unctuous **9** adulatory **10** flattering **11** sycophantic

ingredient
4 part **5** piece **6** factor **7** element **9** component **11** constituent

ingress
4 door **5** entry **6** access, entrée, portal **7** doorway, passage **8** entrance, entryway **9** admission, vestibule **10** admittance **11** entranceway

Ingrid Bergman role
4 Ilsa (Lund)

ingurgitate
4 bolt, cram, gulp, slop, wolf **5** gorge, scarf, stuff, swill **6** devour, gobble, guzzle **7** swallow

inhabit
4 live **5** dwell, haunt **6** occupy, people, settle, tenant **8** populate

inhabitant
5 liver **6** inmate, native **7** citizen, denizen, dweller, resider **8** indigene, resident **9** aborigine **10** autochthon
foreign: 5 alien
indigenous: 6 native **9** aborigine

inhale
7 breathe, consume, respire, swallow

inharmonious
6 atonal **7** jarring **9** dissonant, unmusical **10** discordant **11** cacophonous, conflicting, conflictive, disagreeing, quarrelsome, uncongenial **12** antagonistic

inhere
3 lie **5** dwell **6** belong, reside

inherent
4 born **5** basic, per se **6** inborn, native **7** built-in, connate, natural **8** immanent **9** elemental, essential, intrinsic **10** congenital, deep-seated **11** fundamental

inherit
7 acquire, receive, succeed

inheritance
3 DNA **4** gene, gift **5** dower **6** devise, estate, legacy **7** bequest **8** heirloom, heritage **9** patrimony, tradition **10** birthright **13** primogeniture

inherited
6 native **7** connate, genetic, natural **10** bequeathed, congenital, connatural, handed-down, hand-me-down

inheritor
4 heir **7** heiress, legatee **11** beneficiary

inhibit
4 curb, slow **5** check, cramp **6** arrest, bridle, enjoin, fetter, hamper, hinder, hobble, impede **7** prevent, repress, trammel **8** hold back, obstruct, restrain, suppress, withhold **9** constrain **10** discourage

inhibition
4 curb **5** taboo **6** hang-up **7** barrier **9** hindrance, restraint, stricture **10** impediment, repression **11** suppression

inhuman
5 cruel, feral **6** brutal, savage **7** beastly, bestial, brutish **8** fiendish **9** barbarous, monstrous **10** diabolical

inhumane
4 fell, grim **5** cruel **6** brutal, fierce, malign, savage **8** ruthless, sadistic **9** barbarous, ferocious, heartless, merciless, truculent

inhumation
6 burial **9** interment, sepulture **10** entombment

inhume
4 bury **5** plant **6** entomb **7** put away **9** lay to rest

inimical
7 adverse, harmful, hostile **10** malevolent, unfriendly **11** belligerent, contentious **12** antagonistic, antipathetic

iniquitous
3 bad **4** base, evil, vile **5** wrong **6** sinful, unjust, wicked **7** immoral, vicious **9** nefarious

iniquity
3 sin **4** evil **5** crime, wrong **7** offense **8** trespass **9** turpitude **10** immorality, wickedness, wrongdoing **13** transgression

initial
5 first, prime **6** anlage, letter, maiden **7** approve, engrave, leading, opening, primary **8** earliest, foremost, monogram, original **9** beginning

initials of fashion
3 YSL

initiate
4 open **5** begin, enter, set up, start **6** enroll, get off, induct, invest, launch, take up **7** install, kick off, start up, usher in **8** commence, strike up **9** originate **10** inaugurate

initiation
5 debut **7** baptism **9** admission, beginning, induction **10** admittance **11** investiture, origination **12** commencement, introduction

initiative
4 push **5** drive, spunk **6** energy **8** ambition, aptitude, gumption **9** beginning **10** enterprise, get-up-and-go

inject
3 add **6** insert **7** implant, instill **9** inoculate, introduce, vaccinate

injection
3 fix **4** hypo, shot **5** serum **7** booster, vaccine **10** hypodermic **11** inoculation, vaccination

injudicious
4 rash **5** hasty **6** unwise **8** heedless, reckless **9** ill-judged, impolitic, imprudent **10** ill-advised, indiscreet **11** inexpedient **12** shortsighted

injunction
3 ban, bar **4** writ **5** order **6** behest, charge **7** bidding, command, dictate, mandate **9** direction **11** prohibition

injure
3 mar **4** foul, harm, hurt, maim **5** spoil, wound, wrong **6** blight, bruise, damage, deface, deform, impair, mangle **7** contort, cripple, disable, torture **8** maltreat, mutilate **9** disfigure **12** incapacitate

injurious
6 nocent **7** abusive, adverse, harmful, hurtful **8** damaging **9** offensive **10** defamatory **11** detrimental

injury
3 ill **4** harm, hurt **5** wound, wrong **6** bruise, damage, trauma **8** distress **9** detriment

injustice
4 tort **5** crime, wrong **6** breach, damage **7** outrage **8** inequity, trespass **9** grievance, violation **10** favoritism, wrongdoing

ink
3 dye, pen **4** sign **8** inscribe **9** autograph, signature, subscribe
roller: **6** brayer

inkling
3 cue, tip **4** clue, hint, idea, lead, wind **5** hunch **6** notion, tip-off **8** telltale **9** suspicion **10** indication, intimation, suggestion

inky
3 jet **4** ebon **5** black, ebony, jetty, raven, sable **9** Cimmerian, pitch-dark **10** pitch-black

inlaid
5 piqué **6** boolle **7** hatched **8** enchased, nielloed **9** damascene, incrusted

Inland Empire
8 Illinois

inlet
3 arm, bay, ria **4** cove, gulf, loch **5** bayou, bight, creek, fiord, firth, fjord, sound **6** harbor, slough, strait **7** estuary
Admiralties: **4** Kali
Adriatic Sea: **5** Vlorë
Aegean Sea: **7** Saronic
Alaska: **4** Cook **5** Cross, Taiya **8** Chilkoot
Aleutians: **5** Holtz, Nazan
Angola: **5** Bengo, Tiger **6** Tigres
Antarctica: **7** McMurdo **8** Amundsen **10** Shackleton
Arabian Sea: **4** Qamr **5** Kamar
Australia: **4** King **7** Repulse **10** Broad Sound
Baffin Island: **9** Admiralty
Baltic Sea: **6** Gdansk
Barents Sea: **4** Kola **7** Pechora
Bismarck Sea: **5** Kimbe
Canada: **9** Howe Sound
Cape Breton Island: **4** Mira
Chile: **5** Otway
Crete: **4** Suda **5** Canea
Denmark: **3** Ise
Djibouti: **6** Tajura **8** Tadjoura
Ecuador: **5** Manta
Florida: **10** Saint Lucie
Georgia: **8** Altamaha
Gulf of Alaska: **3** Icy **5** Woman
Gulf of Mexico: **8** Suwannee **9** Matagorda **10** Terrebonne
Hawaii: **11** Pearl Harbor
Honshu: **3** Ise **5** Owari **6** Atsuta
Iceland: **4** Axar, Eyja, Huna **5** Horna, Skaga, Vopna **8** Hunafloi
Indonesia: **4** Bima **5** Saleh
Ionian Sea: **7** Taranto
Java: **4** Lada **5** Peper
Kara Sea: **6** Enisei **7** Yenisei
Labrador: **8** Hamilton
Lake Erie: **8** Put-in-Bay, Sandusky
Long Island: **8** Rockaway
Madagascar: **8** Antongil
Massachusetts: **9** Annisquam
Massachusetts Bay: **10** Lynn Harbor
Mediterranean Sea: **8** Valencia **9** Famagusta **10** Khalij Surt **11** Syrtis Major
Mozambique: **5** Memba, Pemba
Nantucket Sound: **5** Lewis
New Guinea: **3** Oro **5** Berau, Hansa **11** McCluer Gulf
New Jersey: **9** Little Egg
New Zealand: **5** Hawke **6** Tasman
North Carolina: **9** Albemarle
Northern Ireland: **12** Belfast Lough
North Sea: **4** Lyse **9** Hardanger
Northwest Territories: **5** Wager **8** Bathurst, Franklin **9** Frobisher **12** Prince Albert
Norway: **3** Tys **4** Bokn, Tana **5** Lakse, Sogne
Norwegian Sea: **4** Nord, Salt, Stor, Vest **5** Ranen **8** Scoresby **9** Trondheim
Ontario: **4** Owen
Potomac: **10** Tidal Basin
Philippines: **5** Baler, Pilar, Sogod **6** Butuan **9** Davao Gulf, Leyte Gulf, Panay Gulf
Puget Sound: **4** Carr, Case
Quebec: **6** Ungava
Red Sea: **4** Foul
Russia: **5** Chaun **8** Sakhalin
Santa Cruz Islands: **8** Basilisk
Solomon Islands: **4** Deep **8** Huon Gulf
South Africa: **5** Table
South Carolina: **4** Bull
South China Sea: **4** Bias, Datu, Siam, Taya **5** Dasol **6** Brunei, Paluan **8** Lingayen
Spitsbergen: **3** Ice **4** Bell **5** Kings
Sumatra: **5** Bajur **10** Koninginne
Wales: **5** Burry
Washington: **11** Grays Harbor
(see also **bay**)

inmate
7 convict **8** occupant, prisoner, resident **10** inhabitant

inmost part
4 core, pith **5** heart **6** center, depths, kernel, marrow **7** nucleus

inn
5 hotel, lodge, motel, serai **6** hostel, tavern **7** auberge, hospice, pension **8** hostelry **9** roadhouse **11** caravansary, public house **12** caravansarai **13** boardinghouse
French: **7** auberge

German: **7** Gasthof **8** Gasthaus
Spanish: **5** fonda **6** posada **7** parador
Turkish: **6** imaret

innards
4 guts **5** belly **6** bowels, tripes **7** viscera **8** entrails, stuffing **10** intestines

innate
see **inherent**

inner
3 gut **5** focal **6** hidden, middle, secret **7** central, nuclear, private **8** familiar, interior, internal, personal, visceral **9** concealed, essential
prefix: **3** ent **4** ento

innervate
4 jolt, move **5** pique, rouse **6** excite **7** animate, provoke, quicken **8** motivate, vitalize **9** electrify, galvanize, stimulate

Innisfail
4 Eire, Erin **7** Ireland

innkeeper
4 host **8** boniface, hosteler, hotelier, landlord, publican

innocence
6 purity **7** naiveté **8** chastity **10** simplicity **11** artlessness, sinlessness

innocent
4 good, lamb, naïf, pure, void **5** clean, legal, licit, naive **6** chaste, devoid, lawful **7** artless, natural, unaware **8** harmless, ignorant, virtuous **9** blameless, childlike, exemplary, faultless, guileless, guiltless, ingenuous, innocuous, righteous, stainless, unstained, unsullied, untainted **10** inculpable, legitimate **12** unsuspecting

innocuous
5 banal, bland **6** pallid **7** insipid **8** harmless **11** inoffensive, unoffending **13** insignificant

innovation
6 change **7** novelty

innovative
3 new **5** novel **8** creative, original **9** inventive **10** newfangled **11** cutting-edge, leading-edge **12** trailblazing

innovator
9 architect, developer **10** originator **11** trailblazer **13** revolutionary

innuendo
4 clue, hint, slur **7** calumny **8** allusion **9** aspersion **10** backbiting, intimation **11** implication, insinuation

innumerable
4 many **6** legion, myriad, untold **7** umpteen **9** countless, uncounted **10** numberless **13** multitudinous

Ino
brother: **9** Polydorus
father: **6** Cadmus
grandfather: **6** Agenor
husband: **7** Athamas
mother: **8** Harmonia
sister: **5** Agave **6** Semele **7** Autonoë
son: **8** Learchus, Palaemon **10** Melicertes

inobtrusive
4 meek **5** muted, quiet **6** modest **7** subdued **8** discreet, tasteful **10** restrained

inoculate
5 imbue, shoot, steep **6** infuse **7** implant, suffuse **9** vaccinate

inoffensive
5 bland **7** neutral **8** harmless **9** innocuous, peaceable

inopportune
8 ill-timed, mistimed, untimely **12** unseasonable

inordinate
5 undue **6** wanton **7** extreme **8** overmuch **9** excessive **10** exorbitant, gratuitous, immoderate, irrational **11** extravagant, intemperate, superfluous, uncalled-for **12** unreasonable **13** extraordinary

inorganic
7 mineral **10** artificial

in passing
5 aside **6** obiter **7** by the by **8** by the bye, by the way **12** incidentally

in perpetuum
4 ever **6** always **7** forever, for good **8** evermore, for keeps **9** eternally **10** enduringly **11** forevermore

input
4 data **6** advice, energy **7** comment, counsel, opinion **8** feedback, guidance, material, stimulus **11** information

inquest
5 probe **7** hearing, inquiry **11** examination **13** investigation

inquietude
5 angst **6** unease, unrest **7** anxiety, ferment, turmoil **8** distress **10** uneasiness **11** restiveness **12** restlessness **13** Sturm und Drang

inquire
3 ask, pry **4** seek **5** probe, query **7** examine **8** question **9** catechize **11** interrogate, investigate

inquiry
5 audit, probe, query **7** hearing **8** grilling, question, research, scrutiny **11** examination, questioning **13** investigation

inquisition
4 hunt **5** probe, quest, trial **6** search **7** inquiry **8** grilling, research **11** examination **13** interrogation, investigation

inquisitive
4 nosy **5** nosey **6** prying, snoopy **7** curious **8** meddling, snooping **9** intrusive **10** meddlesome **11** questioning

inquisitor
10 Torquemada (Tomás de)

in re
4 as to **5** about, as for **7** apropos **9** as regards, regarding **10** as respects, concerning, respecting **12** with regard to **13** with respect to

in respect to
see **in re**

inroad
4 raid **5** foray **7** advance **8** invasion **9** incursion **12** encroachment

ins and outs
5 ropes **6** quirks **7** details **8** minutiae, oddities **11** incidentals, particulars **12** lay of the land

insane
3 mad, off **4** daft, loco, nuts **5** batty, crazy, daffy, dotty, loony, manic, nutsy, nutty, rabid, silly, wacky **6** absurd, crazed, cuckoo, maniac, raving, schizo, screwy, teched **7** berserk, bonkers, cracked, haywire, lunatic, tetched, touched, unsound **8** demented, deranged, unhinged **9** eccentric, psychotic **10** disordered, irrational, moonstruck, unbalanced **11** harebrained **12** crackbrained, preposterous, unreasonable

insane asylum
6 bedlam **8** loony bin, madhouse, nuthouse, snake pit **10** sanatorium, sanitarium

insanity
5 folly, mania **6** frenzy, lunacy **7** madness **8** delirium, delusion, dementia, hysteria, illusion **9** craziness, dottiness, psychosis **11** derangement, psychopathy

insatiable
6 crying, greedy, urgent **7** exigent **8** pressing, ravenous **9** clamorous, demanding, voracious **10** quenchless **11** importunate **12** unappeasable, unquenchable

inscribe
4 etch, list **5** carve, enter, print, write **6** enroll, record **7** engrave, engross, impress, imprint **8** dedicate, enscroll, register

inscription
5 title **6** legend **7** epigram, epitaph, heading **8** epigraph **10** dedication
Calvary: 4 INRI

inscrutable
6 arcane **7** deadpan **10** mysterious, poker-faced, sphinxlike, unknowable, unreadable **12** impenetrable, unfathomable

insect
3 bee, bug, fly **6** beetle
adult: 5 imago
antenna: 4 palp **6** feeler, palpus
combining form: 5 entom **6** entomo
covering: 6 chitin
genus: 4 Nepa
immature: 4 grub, pupa **5** larva, nymph **6** larvae (plural), maggot **8** wriggler **9** chrysalis **11** caterpillar
kind: 3 ant, bee **4** flea, moth, wasp **5** aphid, scale **6** bedbug, beefly, beetle, cicada, earwig, hornet, mantid, mantis, mayfly **7** ant lion, cricket, firefly, June bug, katydid, ladybug, termite **8** honeybee, horsefly, housefly, lacewing, mosquito, stinkbug **9** bumblebee, butterfly, damselfly, dragonfly **10** silverfish, springtail **11** grasshopper **12** walkingstick
luminous: 7 firefly **8** glowworm
molt: 7 ecdysis
moth: 4 luna **5** gypsy **6** miller, sphinx **7** noctuid, pyralid, tortrix, tussock **8** cecropia, cinnabar, forester, sphingid **9** clearwing, geometrid, saturniid, tortricid **10** Polyphemus
multi-legged: 8 diplopod **9** centipede, millipede
noisy: 6 cicada
part: 4 palp **5** cerci (plural) **6** arista, cercus, labium, labrum, ocelli (plural), palpus, thorax **7** antenna, maxilla, ocellus **8** antennae (plural), mandible, maxillae (plural) **9** proboscis, spiracles **10** ovipositor **11** exoskeleton
pest: 4 flea, lice (plural), mite **5** louse, midge, scale **7** blowfly, termite **8** horsefly, housefly, mealybug **9** cockroach, gypsy moth **10** boll weevil, Hessian fly, silverfish
resin: 3 lac
science: 10 entomology
stage: 6 instar
sucking: 5 aphid
winged: 5 alate
wingless: 4 flea, lice (plural) **5** louse **8** firebrat **10** silverfish, springtail **11** bristletail

insecticide
3 DDT **5** mirex, naled **6** aldrin, endrin **7** lindane, phorate **8** carbaryl, dieldrin, rotenone **9** chlordane, malathion, parathion **10** permethrin

insecure
5 shaky **6** unsafe, unsure, wobbly **7** anxious **8** unstable **9** uncertain **10** precarious **11** unconfident **12** apprehensive

inseminate
7 implant, instill **9** fertilize, pollinate **10** impregnate

insensate
4 dull, hard, numb **5** stony **6** brutal, numbed **7** callous **8** comatose **9** bloodless, heartless, impassive, unfeeling

insensibility
4 coma **6** apathy, torpor **8** lethargy, stoicism **12** indifference

insensible
4 cold, dead, dull, hard, numb, rapt **5** stoic **6** asleep, intent, numbed, obtuse, stolid **7** callous **8** absorbed, comatose, deadened, hardened, obdurate **9** apathetic, bloodless, engrossed, impassive, unfeeling **11** unconscious **12** anesthetized

insensitive
4 dull, hard, numb, rude **5** crass **6** numbed, obtuse, unkind **7** callous **8** benumbed, deadened, hardened, tactless, uncaring **9** bloodless, heartless, unfeeling **10** anesthetic, impossible **11** indifferent, unconcerned **12** anesthetized, unresponsive

insert
3 add **5** enter **7** implant, obtrude **9** interpose **10** interleave **11** intercalate, interpolate

insertion
8 addendum, addition **13** interpolation
symbol: 5 caret

in short
7 briefly, tersely **9** concisely **10** succinctly

inside
6 closet, secret, within **7** private **8** hush-hush, interior **12** confidential
combining form: 4 endo

insidious
3 sly **4** foxy, wily **6** artful, crafty, subtle, tricky **7** cunning, gradual **8** creeping, guileful **9** deceitful **13** surreptitious

insight
6 acumen, aperçu, wisdom **8** sagacity, sapience **9** intuition **11** discernment, penetration **13** understanding

insightful
4 keen, sage, wise **7** gnostic, knowing **9** intuitive, sagacious **10** discerning, perceptive **11** penetrating

insignia
4 mark, sign **5** badge **6** emblem **8** brassard **10** decoration

insignificant
4 mere, puny **5** dinky, minor, petty, small **6** casual, little, minute, paltry **7** minimal, trivial **8** nugatory, trifling **9** secondary, small-time **10** fractional, negligible **11** Mickey Mouse, minor-league, unimportant

insincere
4 glib **5** false, lying, phony **6** double, forced, hollow, phoney, shifty, tricky **7** feigned **8** mala fide, slippery, spurious **9** deceitful, deceptive, dishonest, pretended, simulated **10** left-handed, mendacious, untruthful **11** dissembling, double-faced **12** hypocritical

insinuate
4 hint **5** imply **6** inject, insert, work in, worm in **7** implant, instill, suggest **9** introduce

insipid
4 drab, dull, mild, pale, thin, weak **5** banal, bland, vapid **6** jejune, watery **7** mundane, prosaic, tedious **8** bromidic, lifeless, ordinary **9** innocuous, tasteless **10** flavorless, monotonous, namby-pamby, wishy-washy **11** commonplace

insist
4 hold **5** argue, claim, swear **6** affirm, assert, demand, stress **7** certify, contend, declare, require, testify **8** maintain

insistent
6 crying, dogged, urgent **7** adamant, burning, clamant, exigent **8** emphatic, forceful, pressing, resolute **9** assertive, clamorous, obtrusive **10** determined, imperative, relentless **11** persevering

insolence
4 gall, guff, sass **5** brass, cheek, nerve **8** audacity, boldness, chutzpah, contempt, rudeness **9** arrogance, impudence **10** brazenness, disrespect, effrontery **11** haughtiness, presumption **12** impertinence

insolent
4 bold, flip, pert, rude **5** cocky, lofty, sassy, saucy **6** brazen, cheeky **7** haughty, uncivil **8** arrogant, cavalier, flippant, impolite, impudent, superior **9** audacious, barefaced, bold-faced **10** disdainful, peremptory **11** impertinent **12** contumelious, discourteous

insouciance
6 aplomb **9** disregard, unconcern **10** breeziness **11** disinterest, nonchalance **12** carelessness, heedlessness, indifference

insouciant
4 airy, flip **6** blithe, breezy, casual, jaunty **8** carefree, flippant, heedless **9** easygoing **10** nonchalant, untroubled **11** indifferent, thoughtless, unconcerned **12** devil-may-care, happy-go-lucky, lighthearted

inspect
3 con, vet **4** scan, view **5** audit, check, probe, study **6** review, size up, survey **7** canvass, examine, observe **8** appraise, check out, look over, question **9** check over **10** scrutinize **11** investigate

inspection
4 exam, scan **5** audit, check **7** checkup

inspiration
4 idea, muse **6** animus, genius, vision **7** insight **8** afflatus **9** brainwave, influence **10** brainchild, brainstorm, creativity **13** enlightenment

inspire
4 fire, stir **5** elate, exalt, imbue, rouse **6** arouse, excite, foment, incite, prompt, strike **7** animate, enliven, impress, instill, quicken **8** motivate **9** encourage, galvanize, influence, stimulate **10** exhilarate

inspiring
6 moving **7** awesome, rousing **8** exalting, stirring **9** animating, uplifting **10** vitalizing

inspirit
4 fire, lift, spur, stir **5** cheer, elate, exalt, liven, rally, rouse, spark, steel **6** arouse, excite, incite, kindle, revive, uplift, vivify **7** animate, comfort, console, delight, enliven, gladden, hearten, nourish, quicken, refresh, restore **8** activate, embolden, energize, revivify, vitalize **9** encourage, stimulate **10** invigorate, strengthen

instability
6 anomie **8** fluidity **9** shakiness **10** insecurity, volatility **11** inconstancy **12** unsteadiness

install
4 seat, vest **5** put in, set up **6** induct, invest **8** ensconce, enthrone, entrench **9** establish

instance
4 case, cite, item **6** detail, ground, reason, sample **7** example **8** specimen **10** particular **12** illustration

instant
3 sec **4** wink **5** flash, jiffy, point, shake, trice **6** moment, second, urgent **7** current, exigent, present **8** existent, occasion, pressing **9** heartbeat, immediate, insistent, twinkling **10** imperative, present-day

instantaneous
4 fast **5** quick, rapid **6** prompt **9** immediate, ligntning, momentary **11** hair-trigger, split-second

instantly
3 now, PDQ **4** ASAP, stat **6** at once, pronto **8** directly **9** forthwith, posthaste, right away **11** immediately

instead
4 else **6** in lieu, rather **11** alternately **13** alternatively

instigate
4 abet, fire, goad, plan, plot, prod, spur, urge **5** egg on, impel, raise **6** excite, foment, incite, stir up, whip up **7** provoke, suggest **8** motivate **9** stimulate **10** bring about

instill
5 imbue **6** impart, infuse, inject **7** implant, suffuse **8** engender **9** inculcate, introduce

instinct
4 nose **5** hunch, sense **7** feeling, impulse **8** aptitude, behavior **9** intuition **10** proclivity, sixth sense **11** gut reaction

instinctive
3 gut **6** inborn, innate, normal **7** natural **8** habitual, inherent, visceral **9** automatic, ingrained, intrinsic, intuitive, reflexive, unlearned **10** congenital, unprompted **11** involuntary, spontaneous, unmeditated

instinctual
6 reflex **7** natural, routine **8** habitual, knee-jerk, untaught **9** automatic, impulsive, intuitive, reflexive **10** mechanical, unthinking **11** involuntary, spontaneous, unconscious

institute
5 begin, found, set up, start **6** decree, launch, ordain **7** academy, pioneer, usher in **8** initiate, organize **9** establish, introduce, originate **10** inaugurate **12** organization

institution
4 firm, rite **5** habit **6** custom **9** enactment **10** foundation **13** establishment
kind: **6** asylum, school **7** academy, college **8** hospital, seminary **10** sanatorium, sanitarium, sanitorium, university

instruct
4 show **5** coach, drill, guide, order, steer, teach, train, tutor **6** direct, enjoin, inform, school **7** apprise, command, counsel, educate, lecture **9** enlighten, prescribe

instruction
5 drill **6** advice, lesson **7** precept **8** coaching, guidance, teaching, training, tutelage **9** catechism, education, schooling **10** directions
place of: **6** school **7** academe, academy, college **10** university

instructive
8 didactic, edifying, pedantic **9** pedagogic **11** educational, explanatory, explicative, informative **12** enlightening

instructor
3 don **4** guru **5** coach, guide, swami, tutor **6** mentor **7** teacher, trainer **8** educator, lecturer **9** pedagogue, preceptor

instrument
4 deed, gear, mean, tool **5** agent, means, organ **6** agency, device, gadget, medium **7** utensil, vehicle **9** apparatus, appliance, machinery, mechanism **11** contraption, contrivance **13** paraphernalia
aircraft: **5** radar, radio **7** compass **9** altimeter, gyroscope **10** altazimuth, tachometer **11** transponder
calculating: **6** abacus **8** computer **9** slide rule
graphic: **6** camera **8** otoscope **9** telescope **10** binoculars, microscope **11** fluoroscope, stethoscope, stroboscope **12** bronchoscope, oscilloscope, spectrograph, spectroscope
measuring: **4** gage **5** clock, gauge, radar, scale, sonar **7** alidade, ammeter, balance, caliper, sextant, transit **8** quadrant **9** altimeter, astrolabe, barometer, bolometer, manometer, pedometer, sonometer, voltmeter **10** anemometer, Fathometer, hydrometer, hygrometer, micrometer, radiometer, radiosonde, spirometer, tachometer, theodolite **11** chronometer, lie

detector, range finder, seismograph, speedometer, thermometer **12** electroscope, galvanometer, oscillograph, oscilloscope **13** Geiger counter, potentiometer
medical: **6** lancet, trocar **7** curette, forceps, specula (plural) **8** tenacula (plural) **9** tenaculum
radiation-producing: **5** laser, maser
(see also **implement; musical instrument; tool**)

instrumental
5 vital **6** useful **7** crucial, helpful **9** conducive, essential, necessary, requisite **10** imperative **13** indispensable

instrumentality
5 agent, force, means, organ **6** agency, energy, medium **7** channel, vehicle **8** ministry **9** mechanism

insubordinate
6 unruly **8** factious, mutinous **9** fractious, seditious **10** headstrong, rebellious, refractory **11** disobedient, intractable, uncompliant **12** contumacious, recalcitrant, ungovernable

insubstantial
4 airy, weak **5** frail **6** feeble, flimsy, jejune **7** fragile, tenuous **8** bodiless, ethereal **9** unfleshly **10** intangible **11** disembodied **12** apparitional

insufferable
10 unbearable **11** intolerable, unendurable **13** insupportable

insufficiency
4 lack **6** dearth **7** paucity, poverty **8** scarcity, shortage **10** deficiency, inadequacy, scantiness, scarceness **11** defalcation

insufficient
5 scant **6** scanty, scarce, skimpy **7** lacking, wanting **10** inadequate, incomplete

insular
5 local **6** narrow **7** bigoted, limited **8** confined, isolated, secluded **9** illiberal, parochial, sectarian, small-town **10** prejudiced, provincial, restricted

insulate
6 cut off, enisle **7** isolate **8** close off **9** segregate, sequester

insult
3 dis **4** gibe, jeer, mock, slap, slur **5** abuse, fleer, scoff, scorn, shame, sneer, taunt **6** debase, deride, offend, revile **7** affront, disdain, obloquy, offense, outrage **8** brickbat, derision, disgrace, ignominy, ridicule **9** contumely, humiliate **10** opprobrium **12** vituperation

insurance
8 guaranty, warranty **10** protection
agency: **7** actuary **8** adjuster **11** underwriter
giant: **5** Aetna
term: **6** policy **7** annuity **8** coverage **9** bordereau **11** beneficiary
type: **4** crop, fire **5** crime, flood, title **6** dental **7** no-fault **8** accident, casualty **9** liability **10** disability, homeowner's **11** workers' comp

insure
5 cinch, guard **6** shield **7** confirm, protect **9** guarantee, safeguard **10** underwrite

insurgent
5 rebel **6** anarch **8** factious, frondeur, mutineer, mutinous, revolter **9** anarchist, seditious **10** incendiary, rebellious **12** contumacious **13** insubordinate, revolutionary

insurrection
4 coup **6** mutiny, putsch, revolt, rising **8** uprising **9** rebellion

insurrectionist
5 rebel **6** anarch **8** frondeur, mutineer, revolter **10** malcontent

insusceptible
6 exempt, immune **9** resistant **10** impervious **11** unreceptive

intact
5 sound, whole **6** entire, unhurt, virgin **7** perfect **8** complete, unbroken, unmarred, virginal **9** undamaged, uninjured, untouched **10** unimpaired

intangible
4 airy **5** vague **7** elusive, ghostly **8** ethereal **10** evanescent, immaterial, impalpable **11** incorporeal

integer
4 unit **5** digit **6** entity, figure, number **7** numeral **11** whole number

integral
4 full **5** whole **6** entire **7** perfect **8** complete, inherent **9** composite, elemental, essential, necessary, requisite **11** constituent **13** indispensable

integrate
3 mix **4** fuse, join, link **5** blend, merge, unify, unite **6** embody, mingle **7** combine, conjoin **8** coalesce **9** harmonize, reconcile **10** amalgamate, assimilate, coordinate, synthesize **11** consolidate, desegregate

integrity
5 honor **6** virtue **7** honesty, probity **8** cohesion **9** coherence, constancy, rectitude, soundness, wholeness **12** completeness

integument
4 coat **5** testa **7** coating, cuticle **8** covering, envelope

intellect
3 wit **4** mind **5** brain **6** acumen, brains, genius, reason, smarts **9** intuition, mentality **12** intelligence **13** comprehension, understanding

intellectual
5 brain **6** brainy, mental, pundit **7** bookish, egghead, erudite, psychic, thinker **8** academic, cerebral, highbrow, longhair **9** scholarly

intelligence
3 wit **4** dope, info, mind, news, word **5** brain, savvy, sense **6** acuity, acumen, brains, notice, reason, smarts, wisdom **7** hearsay, tidings **8** aptitude, judgment, learning, sagacity **9** knowledge, mentality, mother wit **10** brainpower, shrewdness
organization: **3** CIA, NSA

intelligent
4 keen, wise **5** acute, alert, aware, quick, sharp, smart, sound **6** adroit, astute, brainy, bright, clever, shrewd **7** cunning, knowing, logical **8** rational, sensible **9** brilliant, ingenious, sagacious **10** reasonable **11** quick-witted, ready-witted **13** perspicacious

intelligentsia
7 clerisy **8** literati, vanguard **10** avant-garde, illuminati

intelligible
5 clear, lucid, plain

intemperance
6 excess **7** license **9** depravity **10** debauchery, profligacy **11** dissipation, drunkenness **12** immoderation, incontinence

intemperate
5 harsh **6** bitter, brutal, severe **7** drunken, extreme, violent **8** bibulous **9** crapulous, dissolute, excessive **10** dissipated, exorbitant, gluttonous, immoderate, inordinate, profligate **12** unrestrained **13** overindulgent

intend
3 aim, try **4** mean, plan **5** essay, spell **6** assign, denote, design, scheme, strive **7** attempt, connote, propose, purpose, signify **8** endeavor **9** designate

intended
6 fiancé **7** engaged, fiancée **8** destined, plighted, promised, proposed **9** affianced, betrothed **10** calculated, deliberate

intense
4 keen **5** acute, vivid **6** ardent, fervid, fierce, severe, strong **7** extreme, fervent, furious, violent, zealous **8** powerful, vehement **9** assiduous, excessive, exquisite **10** heightened **12** concentrated

intensify
4 rise **5** mount, rouse **6** accent, heat up, stress **7** enhance, sharpen **8** escalate, heighten, increase, redouble **9** aggravate, emphasize **10** accentuate, aggrandize, exacerbate **11** concentrate

intensity
4 zeal **5** ardor **6** energy, fervor **7** passion **8** emphasis, ferocity, fervency, loudness **9** vehemence

intensive
6 all-out **7** zealous **8** sweeping, thorough **10** exhaustive **12** concentrated
pronoun: **6** itself, myself **7** herself, himself **8** yourself **9** ourselves **10** themselves, yourselves

intent
3 aim, set **4** bent, goal, plan, rapt, will **5** eager, fixed **6** design, import, object **7** decided, earnest, engaged, meaning, purport, purpose, riveted, wrapped **8** absorbed, conation, decisive, diligent, immersed, resolute, resolved, sedulous, volition **9** engrossed, objective, wrapped up **10** determined

intention
3 aim, end **4** goal, hope, plan, wish **6** design, desire, object **7** meaning, purpose **8** ambition **9** objective **10** aspiration

intentional
5 meant **7** advised, studied, willful, willing, witting **8** designed, proposed **9** voluntary **10** considered, deliberate **12** premeditated

intentionally
9 on purpose, purposely

inter
4 bury **5** plant **6** entomb, inhume **9** lay to rest

inter ___
4 alia

interact
9 cooperate **11** collaborate

interbreed
5 cross **9** hybridize **10** mongrelize

intercede
6 step in **7** mediate **9** arbitrate

intercept
4 grab **5** catch, seize, steal **6** cut off, hijack

intercessor
5 agent **6** broker **8** advocate, mediator **9** go-between, middleman

interconnect
4 join, link, mesh **5** unite **6** couple, hook up, link up

intercourse
3 sex **5** trade, truck **7** contact, dealing, traffic **8** business, commerce, dealings **9** communion **10** connection, networking **11** give-and-take **12** conversation **13** communication

intercross
9 hybridize **10** mongrelize

interdict
3 ban, bar **4** veto **5** block, taboo **6** cut off, enjoin, forbid, outlaw **7** censure, condemn, embargo **8** disallow, prohibit, sanction **9** proscribe **11** prohibition

interest
4 gain, grab, hook, lure, pull **5** pique, stake, tempt **6** appeal, arouse, behalf, engage, profit, regard **7** attract, concern, engross, involve, welfare **8** appeal to, intrigue **9** attention, curiosity, fascinate, tantalize, well-being **10** prosperity

interested
4 rapt **5** drawn **7** curious, partial **8** invested, partisan **9** attentive

interface
3 GUI **6** border **8** boundary **9** cooperate **11** communicate

interfere
6 butt in, horn in, meddle, step in **7** barge in, intrude

interim
3 gap **5** break, pause **6** acting, breach, hiatus, lacuna, pro tem **7** stopgap, time-out **8** downtime, meantime **9** makeshift, temporary **10** pro tempore **11** provisional

interior
3 gut **4** pith **5** belly, bosom, heart, inner **6** center, inland, inside, inward, marrow **8** visceral **9** heartland **10** hinterland

interject
3 add **6** fill in, insert **7** throw in

interjection
agreement: **4** amen **5** roger **6** righto **7** right on
attention-getter: **3** hey **4** ahem, ahoy, psst **6** yoo-hoo
cheer: **3** rah, yay **5** wahoo **6** hooray, hurrah, hurray
contempt: **4** pooh **5** pshaw
disappointment: **4** rats **5** shoot **6** shucks
disapproval: **3** boo, fie
disbelief: **3** huh
disgust: **3** bah, boo, pah, ugh **4** rats, yuck **5** faugh, yecch **6** phooey
dismay: **4** alas, oh no, uh-oh
dismissal: **3** git **4** shoo
German: **3** ach
in golf: **4** fore
in hunting: **6** yoicks
in marching: **3** hup, hut
joy: **4** whee **6** hooray, hurrah, hurray, yippee **7** hosanna, whoopee **8** alleluia **10** hallelujah
mild apology: **4** oops **6** whoops
mild oath: **3** gad **4** darn, drat, egad, geez, gosh, heck, jeez **5** egads, golly, zooks **6** jiminy, zounds **7** begorra, gee whiz, jeepers **8** gadzooks **13** gee whillikers
O.K.: **5** roger, wilco
pain: **4** ouch
regret: **3** woe **4** alas **5** alack **8** lackaday
relief: **4** phew
silence: **3** shh
sneeze: **5** achoo **6** atchoo **7** kerchoo
sorrow: **4** alas **5** alack **8** lackaday
stop: **4** whoa **5** avast
surprise: **3** aha, huh, oho, wow **4** gosh, oops **5** blimy, yikes, yipes, zowie **6** blimey
triumph: **3** aha, hah **6** eureka
(see also **exclamation**)

interlace
3 mix **5** braid, plait, twine, weave **6** splice **7** entwine **9** alternate

interlard
3 mix **6** mingle

interlock
4 mesh **5** unite **6** enmesh

interlocuter
4 host **5** emcee

interlope
6 butt in, horn in, meddle **7** intrude **8** encroach, infringe **9** interfere

interlude
4 halt, lull, rest **5** break, idyll, letup, pause, spell **6** hiatus, recess **7** episode, respite **8** breather, entr'acte, meantime, stoppage **9** meanwhile **10** suspension

intermediary
3 mid **4** mean **5** agent, envoy, organ **6** agency, broker, center, medium, middle, midway **7** central, channel, vehicle **8** delegate, emissary, mediator, ministry **9** go-between, middleman

intermediate
3 mid **4** fair, mean, so-so **5** mesne **6** broker, center, middle, midway, step in **7** arbiter, average, between, central, halfway **8** middling **9** arbitrate, go-between, middleman

intermediator
6 broker **7** arbiter, liaison, referee **9** go-between, middleman

interment
6 burial **9** sepulture **10** inhumation

intermesh
4 lock **6** engage **8** dovetail

interminable
7 endless, eternal, lasting **8** constant, infinite, unending **9** boundless, ceaseless, continual, limitless, permanent, perpetual, unceasing **10** protracted **11** everlasting, never-ending

intermission
4 lull, rest, stop **5** break, pause, spell **6** hiatus, recess **7** latency, respite, time-out **8** abeyance,

dormancy, interval **10** quiescence, suspension **11** parenthesis

intermit
4 halt, stay **5** break, defer, delay **6** arrest, hold up, put off **7** suspend **8** postpone, prorogue **9** interrupt **11** discontinue

intermittent
6 broken, cyclic, fitful, serial **8** cyclical, metrical, periodic, seasonal, sporadic **9** irregular, recurrent, recurring, spasmodic, stop-and-go **10** occasional

intermix
4 meld **5** blend **6** mingle **8** comingle, compound **9** commingle, integrate **10** amalgamate

intermixture
4 brew **5** blend **7** amalgam **8** compound **9** composite, synthesis **12** amalgamation **13** miscegenation

intern
4 jail **6** immure **7** confine, impound, put away, trainee **8** imprison **11** incarcerate

internal
6 native **7** private **8** visceral **10** subjective
concretion: **9** gallstone
prefix: **5** intra

internal organs
4 guts **6** bowels, vitals **7** innards, viscera **8** entrails **10** intestines, penetralia

international organization
3 FAO, IAM, ICJ, IFC, ILO, IMF, ITO, ITU, OAS, WHO, WMO, WTO **4** IAAF, IABA, IAEA, IARU, IATA, ICAO, IFIP, IMCO, NATO **5** ICFTU, SEATO **6** UNESCO, UNICEF

Internet forum
9 newsgroup

internuncio
5 envoy **6** bearer, legate **7** carrier, courier **8** delegate, emissary **9** go-between, messenger, middleman

interpolate
3 add **5** admit, annex, enter **6** append, fill in, inject, insert **7** throw in **9** introduce

interpose
6 butt in, fill in, insert, meddle, step in **7** intrude, mediate, obtrude, throw in **8** moderate **9** arbitrate, insinuate, introduce, negotiate **11** come between

interpret
5 gloss **6** decode **7** explain, expound **8** annotate, construe **9** elucidate, explicate **10** paraphrase

interpretation
5 gloss **7** meaning, reading, version **8** exegesis **9** construal, rendering **11** explanation, translation

interpretive
8 exegetic **10** diagnostic, exegetical, expository **11** explanatory, explicatory

interregnum
5 break, lapse, pause **6** hiatus **7** time-out

interrogate
3 ask **4** pump, quiz **5** grill, query **7** examine **8** question **9** catechize **12** cross-examine

interrupt
4 halt, stay, stop **5** abort, break, cut in **7** break in, chime in, suspend **8** cut short

interruption
3 gap **4** halt **5** break, pause, split **6** breach, cutoff, hiatus, lacuna, recess **7** caesura **8** stoppage

intersect
4 meet **5** cross **9** decussate **10** crisscross

intersection
3 hub **4** node **8** crossing, junction, juncture **10** crossroads

intersperse
7 diffuse, scatter **8** sprinkle

interstice
3 gap **4** slit, slot, vent **5** chink, cleft, crack, space **6** breach, cavity, cranny **7** crevice, fissure, opening, orifice **8** aperture

intertwine
4 mesh **5** braid, plait, twist, weave **6** enlace **7** network **9** convolute **10** crisscross

interval
3 gap **4** lull, wait **5** break, comma, delay, letup, pause, space **6** breach, hiatus, lacuna **7** caesura, interim, respite, time-out **8** downtime **9** pausation **11** parenthesis
music: **4** rest

intervene
6 butt in, meddle, step in **7** intrude, mediate, obtrude

interweave
3 mix **4** fuse, join, knit, link, mesh **5** blend, plait, twine **6** enmesh, mingle **7** entwine, wreathe

intestinal
5 ileal **7** colonic, enteric, jejunal **8** duodenal

intestinal fortitude
4 grit, guts **5** nerve, pluck, spunk **6** mettle, spirit **7** courage **8** backbone **10** resolution

intestine
3 gut **4** tube **5** bowel, canal **7** viscera (plural)
combining form: **4** coli, colo **6** entero
part: **4** ilea (plural) **5** cecum, colon, ileum **7** jejunum **8** duodenum

in the same place
6 ibidem

intimacy
9 closeness **11** familiarity **12** acquaintance

intimate
3 gut **4** cozy, dear, fond, hint **5** amigo, close, crony, imply, inner, privy **6** attest, friend, impart, loving, secret **7** comrade, connote, devoted, nearest, suggest **8** familiar, inherent **9** close-knit, companion, confidant, ingrained, insinuate, intrinsic **12** confidential

intimation
3 cue **4** clue, hint **5** shade, tinge, trace **6** breath **7** inkling **8** telltale **10** suggestion

intimidate
3 awe, cow **4** bait **5** bully, chivy, daunt, scare **6** badger, coerce, hector **7** buffalo, overawe **8** browbeat, bulldoze, bullyrag **9** strong-arm, terrorize

intolerable
10 unbearable **11** unendurable **12** insufferable **13** insupportable

intolerant
6 biased, narrow **7** bigoted **8** dogmatic **9** hidebound, illiberal **10** inflexible, prejudiced **11** small-minded **12** narrow-minded

intonation
5 chant, pitch **6** accent, timbre **7** cadence **8** chanting **10** inflection, modulation, recitation

intone
5 chant, croon, drone **10** cantillate

in toto
3 all **6** wholly **7** all told, en masse **10** altogether

intoxicant
5 booze, drink, hooch, sauce **6** hootch, liquor, rotgut **7** alcohol, spirits **9** aqua vitae, firewater, moonshine

intoxicated
3 lit, wet **4** high **5** blind, drunk, fried, giddy, lit up, oiled, stiff, tight, tipsy **6** blotto, bombed, canned, elated, juiced, loaded, looped, potted, sodden, soused, stewed, stoned, tanked, tiddly, zonked **7** blitzed, crocked, drunken, excited, maudlin, muddled, pickled, pie-eyed, sloshed, smashed, sozzled **8** cockeyed, polluted, squiffed **9** crapulous, plastered **11** exhilarated

intoxication
3 joy **5** bliss **6** frenzy **7** ecstasy, elation, rapture **8** delirium, euphoria **9** transport **10** exaltation **11** drunkenness, inebriation

intractable
4 wild **5** balky **6** mulish, ornery, unruly **7** froward, willful **8** mutinous, obdurate, perverse, stubborn **9** fractious, obstinate, pigheaded, unbending **10** bullheaded, headstrong, inflexible, rebellious, refractory, unyielding **12** pertinacious, recalcitrant, ungovernable **13** undisciplined

intransigent
5 rigid, tough **7** willful **8** obdurate, perverse, resolute, stubborn **9** obstinate, unbending, unpliable **10** refractory, self-willed, unyielding **12** contumacious, pertinacious

intraoffice note
4 memo

intrepid
4 bold, game **5** brave, gutsy, hardy **6** daring, heroic **7** doughty, gallant, valiant **8** fearless, resolute, stalwart, unafraid, valorous **9** audacious, dauntless, undaunted **10** courageous **11** adventurous, temerarious

intricate
4 mazy **6** daedal, knotty **7** complex, gordian, tangled **8** abstruse, involved, tortuous **9** Byzantine, elaborate **10** circuitous, convoluted **11** complicated **12** labyrinthine **13** sophisticated

intrigue
4 plot, wile **5** amour, cabal, cheat, pique, trick **6** affair, appeal, excite, scheme **7** attract, beguile, collude, connive, liaison, romance **8** cogitate, conspire, contrive, interest **9** machinate **10** conspiracy **11** machination

intriguing
8 enticing **9** absorbing, beguiling **10** engrossing, entrancing **11** captivating, fascinating, stimulating

intrinsic
see **inherent**

intrinsically
5 per se **6** as such **7** at heart **10** inherently

introduce
5 begin, enter, found, set up **6** broach, fill in, infuse, insert, launch, unveil, work in **7** bring up, implant, install, instill, precede, preface, present, propose, throw in, usher in **8** initiate, innovate **9** insinuate, institute, interject, interpose, originate **10** inseminate

introduction
5 debut, proem **6** lead-in **7** introit, opening, preface, prelude **8** entrance, exordium, foreword, overture, preamble, prologue, protases (plural), protasis **12** prolegomenon

introductory
5 basic **7** initial, nascent, opening **8** proemial **9** beginning, prefatory **10** elementary **11** preliminary, preparatory

intrude
5 cut in **6** butt in, horn in, impose, invade, meddle **7** barge in, burst in, presume **8** encroach, infringe, trespass **9** interfere, interlope, interrupt

intrusive
4 busy, nosy **5** nosey **6** prying, snoopy **7** curious **8** meddling, snooping **9** officious **10** meddlesome **11** impertinent

in truth
6 indeed, really, verily **8** actually, candidly **9** veritably

intuit
4 grok **5** infer, sense **6** deduce, divine **7** surmise

intuition
5 hunch **7** feeling, inkling, insight **8** instinct **10** sixth sense **11** premonition, second sight **12** presentiment

intuitive
6 innate **7** natural **8** unwilled, visceral **10** unthinking **11** instinctive, instinctual, involuntary, spontaneous, unconscious

Inuit
6 Eskimo
boat: **5** kayak, umiak **6** oomiak **7** oomiack

inundate
4 glut **5** drown, flood, swamp, whelm **6** deluge, engulf **7** overrun **8** overflow, submerge **9** overwhelm

inundation
5 flood, spate **6** deluge **7** Niagara, torrent **8** cataract, flooding, overflow **9** avalanche, cataclysm, landslide **10** cloudburst

inure
5 steel, train **6** harden, season **7** prepare, toughen **8** accustom **9** acclimate, habituate **10** discipline **11** familiarize

inutile
6 no-good **7** useless **8** unusable **9** valueless, worthless

invade
4 loot, raid **6** breach, occupy, ravage **7** overrun, pillage, plunder **8** encroach, infringe, trespass **9** penetrate

invader
8 intruder **10** encroacher, interloper, trespasser **11** infiltrator

invalid
3 bad **4** null, sick, void **5** false **6** ailing, infirm, shut-in, sickly **7** expired, unsound **8** baseless, disabled **9** bedridden, illogical, sophistic **10** fallacious, irrational **11** null and void **12** convalescent

invalidate
4 undo, void **5** annul, quash **6** cancel, offset, vacate **7** abolish, nullify **9** discredit, repudiate **10** counteract, disqualify, neutralize

invaluable
7 crucial **8** precious **9** essential, priceless **11** beyond price, inestimable **13** irreplaceable

invariable
4 same **5** fixed **6** static, steady **7** uniform **8** constant **9** continual, immovable, immutable, unfailing, unvarying **10** changeless, consistent, unchanging **11** inalterable, unalterable **12** unchangeable

invariably
4 ever **6** always **7** forever

invasion
4 raid **5** foray **6** attack, inroad **7** assault, offense **8** trespass **9** incursion, intrusion, offensive, onslaught **12** encroachment
date: **4** D-day

invective
5 abuse **6** tirade **7** abusive, obloquy **8** diatribe, jeremiad **9** contumely, philippic, truculent **10** opprobrium, scurrility, scurrilous **11** opprobrious **12** billingsgate, contumelious, vituperation, vituperative

inveigh
4 kick, rail, rant **6** object **7** protest **8** complain **9** fulminate **11** expostulate, remonstrate

inveigle
4 coax, lure **5** decoy, snare, tempt **6** allure, cajole, entice, entrap, lead on, rope in, seduce, wangle **7** blarney, win over **8** blandish, butter up, maneuver, persuade

invent
4 coin, mint **6** cook up, create, design, devise, make up, patent, vamp up **7** concoct, dream up, fashion, hatch up, pioneer, think up **8** conceive, contrive, discover, engineer, envision **9** fabricate, formulate, originate

invention
7 coinage, fiction **8** creation **10** brainchild, innovation **11** contrivance

inventive
7 fertile, teeming **8** creative, fruitful, original **9** demiurgic, ingenious **10** innovative, innovatory **11** imaginative

inventor
5 maker **6** author, coiner, father, mother **7** creator, founder **8** engineer **9** architect, generator, innovator **10** discoverer, introducer, originator
air brake: **12** Westinghouse (George)
air conditioning: **7** Carrier (Willis)
automobile: **7** Daimler (Gottlieb)
ballpoint pen: **4** Loud (John)
barbed wire: **7** Glidden (Joseph Farwell)
barometer: **10** Torricelli (Evangelista)
bifocal lens: **8** Franklin (Benjamin)
camera: **7** Eastman (George)
cash register: **5** Ritty (James)
cotton gin: **7** Whitney (Eli)
cylinder lock: **4** Yale (Linus)
dirigible: **8** Zeppelin (Ferdinand von)
dynamite: **5** Nobel (Alfred)
electric battery: **5** Volta (Alessandro)
electric fan: **7** Wheeler (George)
electric organ: **7** Hammond (Laurens)
electric razor: **6** Schick (Jacob)
electric stove: **7** Hadaway (W. S.)

elevator: 4 Otis (Elisha)
fountain pen: 8 Waterman (Lewis)
friction match: 6 Walker (John)
gyrocompass: 6 Sperry (Elmer)
helicopter: 8 Sikorsky (Igor)
hot-air balloon: 11 Montgolfier (Jacques, Joseph)
incandescent lamp: 6 Edison (Thomas Alva)
induction motor: 5 Tesla (Nikola)
lawn mower: 5 Hills (Amariah)
Linotype: 12 Mergenthaler (Ottmar)
logarithm: 6 Napier (John)
machine gun: 7 Gatling (Richard)
microphone: 8 Berliner (Emile)
microwave oven: 7 Spencer (Percy)
movable type: 9 Gutenberg (Johannes)
parachute: 9 Blanchard (Jean-Pierre)
pendulum clock: 7 Huygens (Christiaan)
phonograph: 6 Edison (Thomas Alva)
photography: 6 Niepce (Nicéphore), Talbot (W. H. Fox) **8** Daguerre (Louis)
piano: 10 Cristofori (Bartolomeo)
radio: 7 Marconi (Guglielmo)
reaper: 9 McCormick (Cyrus)
revolver: 4 Colt (Samuel)
rocket engine: 7 Goddard (Robert)
safety pin: 4 Hunt (Walter)
safety razor: 8 Gillette (King)
sewing machine: 4 Howe (Elias)
sleeping car: 7 Pullman (George)
spinning jenny: 10 Hargreaves (James)
steamboat: 5 Fitch (John) **6** Fulton (Robert), Miller (Patrick), Rumsey (James) **8** Jouffroy (Claude de)
steam engine: 4 Watt (James)
steam locomotive: 10 Stephenson (George)
stethoscope: 7 Laënnec (René)
submarine: 7 Holland (John Philip)
synthesizer: 4 Moog (Robert)
tank: 7 Swinton (Ernest)
telegraph: 5 Morse (Samuel F. B.)
telephone: 4 Bell (Alexander Graham)
telescope: 10 Lippershey (Hans)
television: 5 Baird (John) **6** Nipkow (Paul) **8** Zworykin (Vladimir) **10** Farnsworth (Philo)
thermometer: 7 Galileo (Galilei)
torpedo: 9 Whitehead (Robert)
tractor: 5 Deere (John)
transistor: 7 Bardeen (John) **8** Brattain (Walter), Shockley (William)
vulcanized rubber: 8 Goodyear (Charles)
writing for the blind: 7 Braille (Louis)
zipper: 6 Judson (Whitcomb)

inventor Nikola
5 Tesla

inventory
3 sum **4** fund, list **5** hoard, stock, store, tally **6** assets, digest, record, supply, survey **7** account, backlog, catalog, itemize, reserve, specify, summary **8** register, tabulate **9** catalogue, checklist, enumerate, reservoir, stockpile, summarize, synopsize

inverse
8 contrary, opposite

inversion
7 reverse **8** flipping, reversal, upending **9** about-face, turnabout, volte-face

invert
4 flip **5** upend **7** reverse **8** overturn, turn over **9** transpose

invertebrate
4 weak **5** timid **7** chicken, doormat, milksop **8** boneless, impotent, weakling **9** jellyfish, spineless **10** namby-pamby **11** ineffectual, milquetoast
kind: 4 worm **6** insect, sponge **7** mollusc, mollusk **8** arachnid **9** arthropod **12** coelenterate

invest
4 gird, veil, wrap **5** adorn, array, dress, endow, imbue **6** clothe, confer, enfold, induct, infuse, ordain **7** empower, enclose, envelop, ingrain, install, suffuse

investigate
3 pry **4** sift **5** audit, check, probe, study **6** go into, search **7** dig into, examine, explore, inquire, inspect **8** check out, look into, muckrake, prospect, research **9** delve into **10** scrutinize **11** inquire into

investigation
5 audit, probe **6** survey **7** inquest, inquiry **8** research, scrutiny **11** fact-finding, inquisition

investigator
3 spy, tec **4** dick **5** hound **6** shamus, sleuth **7** gumshoe **8** hawkshaw, sherlock **9** detective **10** private eye

investiture
9 inaugural, induction **10** initiation, ordination **12** inauguration, installation, ratification

investment option
3 IRA **7** Roth IRA

inveterate
3 old, set **5** fixed, sworn **6** rooted **7** abiding, chronic, settled **8** deep-dyed, enduring, habitual, hard-core, hardened, lifelong **9** confirmed, ingrained, perennial **10** continuing, deep-rooted, deep-seated, entrenched, habituated, persistent, persisting **11** established **12** incorrigible **13** dyed-in-the-wool

Invictus author
6 Henley (William Ernest)

invidious
4 mean **5** snide **7** envious, envying, jealous **9** green-eyed, obnoxious, resentful

invigorate
4 stir **5** brace, liven, pep up, rally, renew, rouse **6** perk up, vivify **7** animate, brace up, enliven, fortify, juice up, liven up, refresh, restore **8** energize, vitalize **9** reinforce, stimulate **10** rejuvenate, revitalize, strengthen

invincible
10 inviolable, unbeatable **11** impregnable, indomitable, insuperable **12** invulnerable, unassailable, undefeatable **13** unconquerable

in vino ___
7 veritas

inviolable
4 safe **6** secure **10** impervious, sacrosanct **11** consecrated, hard-and-fast, impregnable **12** unassailable **13** incorruptible

invisible
6 hidden, unseen **9** concealed **10** intangible **12** unnoticeable **13** imperceptible

Invisible Man
author: 5 Wells (H. G.) **7** Ellison (Ralph)
character: 7 Griffin (Herbert)

invitation
4 call, lure **6** come-on **7** bidding, proffer **8** entreaty, proposal **10** enticement **11** proposition **12** solicitation

invite
3 ask, bid **4** call, lure **5** tempt **6** allure, call in, entice, summon **7** propose, request, solicit

inviting
8 engaging, enticing, tempting **9** appealing, beguiling, seductive **10** attractive, intriguing

invocation
6 appeal, prayer **8** entreaty, petition **11** conjuration, incantation **12** supplication

invoice
3 tab **4** bill, list **5** score **7** account **8** manifest **9** reckoning, statement **11** consignment

invoke
3 beg **4** pray **5** crave, plead **6** appeal, call on, effect **7** beseech, conjure, enforce, entreat, implore, solicit **8** call upon, petition **9** call forth, conjure up, implement, importune **10** supplicate

involuntary
6 forced, reflex **8** knee-jerk **9** automatic, impulsive, reflexive, unwitting **10** compulsory, unintended, unprompted **11** instinctive, spontaneous, unconscious, unmeditated **13** unintentional

involve
4 mire **6** affect, embody, engage, entail, take in **7** call for, concern, contain, embrace, embroil, include, require, subsume **8** comprise, entangle **9** encompass, implicate **10** complicate, comprehend **11** necessitate

involved
6 daedal, knotty **7** complex, gordian **8** confused **9** Byzantine, elaborate, intricate **10** convoluted **11** complicated **12** labyrinthine

invulnerable
6 immune, secure **10** impervious, invincible, unbeatable **11** impregnable, indomitable **12** unassailable

Io
father: 7 Inachus
guard: 5 Argus
son: 7 Epaphus

iodine source
4 kelp

Iolanthe
composer: 8 Sullivan (Arthur)
librettist: 7 Gilbert (W. S.)

Iolcus king
5 Aeson **6** Pelias

Iole
captor: 8 Heracles, Hercules
father: 7 Eurytus
husband: 6 Hyllus

ion
6 ligand
kind: 5 anion **6** cation **8** thermion

Ion
father: 6 Apollo
mother: 6 Creusa
stepfather: 6 Xuthus

Ionesco, Eugène
play: 6 Chairs (The), Lesson (The) **10** Rhinoceros **11** Bald Soprano (The)

iota
3 bit, jot, ray **4** atom, hint, mite, whit **5** crumb, grain, ounce, scrap, shred, speck, trace **6** smidge, tittle **7** smidgen, smidgin **8** molecule, particle, smidgeon **9** scintilla

IOU
4 chit, debt
part: 3 owe, you

Iowa
capital: 9 Des Moines
city: 4 Ames **7** Dubuque **8** Waterloo **9** Davenport, Sioux City **11** Cedar Rapids **13** Council Bluffs
college, university: 3 Coe **5** Drake **8** Grinnell
nickname: 7 Hawkeye (State)
river: 9 Des Moines
state bird: 9 goldfinch
state flower: 15 wild prairie rose
state tree: 3 oak

Ipcress File author Deighton
3 Len

Iphicles
brother: 8 Heracles, Hercules
mother: 7 Alcmene
son: 6 Iolaus

Iphigenia
avenger: **12** Clytemnestra
brother: **7** Orestes
father: **9** Agamemnon
mother: **12** Clytemnestra
sister: **7** Electra

Iran
ancient civilization: **4** Elam **5** Medes, Media **6** Persia
capital: **6** Tehran **7** Teheran
city: **3** Qom, Qum **6** Shiraz, Tabriz **7** Esfahan, Isfahan, Mashhad
conqueror: **9** Alexander (the Great)
gulf: **4** Oman **7** Persian
island: **5** Qeshm
language: **3** Tat **5** Farsi **7** Persian
leader: **4** Shah **7** Pahlavi (Mohammad Reza, Reza Shah) **8** Khomeini (Ayatollah Ruholla)
monetary unit: **4** rial
mountain, range: **6** Elburz, Zagros **8** Damavand **9** Hindu Kush
neighbor: **4** Iraq **6** Turkey **7** Armenia **8** Pakistan **10** Azerbaijan **11** Afghanistan **12** Turkmenistan
river: **5** Atrek, Karun, Safīd **7** Karkheh
sea: **7** Caspian
strait: **6** Hormuz

Iranian
7 Persian
parliament: **6** Majlis
religious movement: **5** Baha'i
sect: **4** Shia
sect member: **6** Shiite

Iraq
ancient civilization: **5** Akkad, Sumer **8** Akkadian, Sumerian **9** Babylonia **10** Babylonian
ancient name: **11** Mesopotamia
capital: **7** Baghdad
city: **5** Basra, Mosul, Najaf **6** Kirkuk **7** Falluja, Karbala **8** Fallujah
conqueror: **9** Alexander (the Great)
desert: **6** Syrian
gulf: **7** Persian
leader: **6** Faisal **7** Hussein (Saddam)
monetary unit: **5** dinar
neighbor: **4** Iran **5** Syria **6** Jordan, Kuwait, Turkey **11** Saudi Arabia
port: **5** Basra **7** Umm Qasr
river: **6** Tigris **9** Euphrates

irascible
4 tart **5** huffy, surly, testy **6** crabby, cranky, feisty, tetchy, touchy **7** bristly, grouchy, peevish, peppery, prickly **8** choleric, petulant, snappish **9** crotchety, fractious, irritable, querulous, splenetic **11** hot-tempered **12** cantankerous **13** quick-tempered

irate
3 mad **5** angry, livid, riled, vexed, wroth **6** fuming **7** enraged, furious, steamed **8** choleric, incensed, provoked, wrathful **9** indignant **10** infuriated

ire
4 fury, rage, rile **5** anger, wrath **6** choler, enrage, madden, temper **7** incense, steam up, umbrage **9** infuriate **10** exasperate **11** indignation **12** exasperation

Ireland
4 Eire, Erin **8** Hibernia
capital: **6** Dublin
city: **4** Cork **5** Kerry, Louth, Meath, Sligo **6** Galway **7** Donegal, Kildare, Wexford, Wicklow **8** Kilkenny, Limerick **9** Waterford **12** Dun Laoghaire
county: **4** Cork, Mayo **5** Clare, Kerry, Louth, Meath, Sligo **6** Galway **7** Donegal, Kildare, Wexford **8** Limerick
flag color: **5** green, white **6** orange
flower: **8** shamrock
island group: **4** Aran **8** Hibernia
king: **4** Boru (Brian)
lake: **3** Ree (Lough) **4** Derg (Lough) **5** Neagh (Lough) **6** Corrib (Lough)
language: **4** Erse **5** Irish **6** Gaelic **7** English
legislature: **4** Dail
monetary unit: **4** euro
nickname: **11** Emerald Isle
province: **7** Munster **8** Connacht, Leinster
river: **4** Erne, Nore **5** Boyne **6** Barrow, Liffey **7** Shannon
symbol: **4** harp

Irene
3 Pax
father: **4** Zeus **7** Jupiter
mother: **6** Themis

irenic
4 calm **7** pacific **8** pacifist **9** peaceable, placative, placatory **10** nonviolent **12** conciliatory, propitiatory

iridescent
8 gleaming, lustrous **10** opalescent
gem: **4** opal **5** pearl **7** apatite **8** ammolite **9** fire agate, moonstone
shell: **7** abalone

Iris
father: **7** Thaumas
mother: **7** Electra

iris location
4 uvea

Irish
4 Erse **6** Celtic, Gaelic
accent: **6** brogue
actor: **3** Rea (Stephen) **5** O'Shea (Milo)
airline: **9** Aer Lingus
alphabet: **4** ogam **5** ogham
cattle: **5** Kerry

chief heir-elect: **6** tanist
olan: **4** sept
combining form: **7** Hiberno
coronation stone: **7** Lia Fail
cudgel: **9** shillalah **10** shillelagh
death spirit: **7** banshee
design: **8** claddagh
dog: **6** setter **7** terrier
dramatist: **4** Shaw (George Bernard) **5** Synge (John Millington), Wilde (Oscar)
elf: **10** leprechaun
fortification: **4** liss
girl: **4** lass **6** lassie **7** colleen
god: **3** Ler **5** Dagda **6** Aengus
goddess: **4** Badb, Bodb **6** Brigit **8** Morrigan
hero: **9** Cuchulain **10** Cú Chulainn
heroine: **7** Deirdre
king: **9** Brian Boru
kings' home: **4** Tara
lake: **5** lough
language: **4** Erse
militant force: **3** IRA
nationalist: **4** Tone (Wolfe) **6** Pearse (Padraig) **7** Collins (Michael), Parnell (Charles) **8** De Valera (Eamon), O'Connell (Daniel) **9** Sarsfield (Patrick)
nationalist society: **8** Sinn Fein
patron saint: **7** Patrick
police officer: **5** garda
singer: **4** Enya **5** Makem (Tommy), Margo **6** Clancy (Bobby, Liam, Paddy, Patrick, Tom) **8** O'Donnell (Daniel)
symbol: **4** harp
theater: **5** Abbey
writing system: **4** ogam **5** ogham
(see also **Gaelic; Celtic**)

Irishman, e.g.
4 Celt

Irish moss
7 seaweed **9** carrageen

irk
3 try, vex **4** fret, gall, miff, pain, rile **5** annoy, peeve, pique, upset **6** abrade, bother, harass, nettle, ruffle, strain, stress **7** provoke, trouble **8** exercise, irritate **10** exasperate

irksome
6 vexing **7** tedious **8** annoying, rankling **9** provoking, upsetting, vexatious **10** bothersome, irritating, nettlesome, unpleasant **11** aggravating, troublesome, unpalatable

iron
4 firm, gyve, hard **5** press, rigid **6** fetter, strong **7** adamant, manacle, shackle **8** handcuff, obdurate **9** unbending **10** inexorable, inflexible
combining form: **5** ferro **6** sidero
German: **5** Eisen
relating to: **6** ferric **7** ferrous **11** ferruginous

ironbound
5 harsh, rocky, rough, stern **6** craggy, jagged, rugged, severe, strict, uneven **7** scraggy **8** asperous, exacting, rigorous, scabrous **9** stringent **10** inflexible

Iron City
10 Pittsburgh

ironclad
5 fixed **7** binding **8** constant **9** immovable, immutable **10** inflexible, invariable **11** inalterable, irrefutable, unalterable **12** indisputable, irrefragable, unchangeable **13** unimpeachable

ironfisted
4 grim, hard, mean **5** harsh **6** brutal, severe, stingy **7** callous, miserly **8** pitiless, ruthless **9** penurious **10** implacable, unmerciful **11** hardhearted, intractable, remorseless **12** unappeasable

ironhanded
5 harsh, rigid **6** severe, strict **8** despotic, rigorous **9** draconian, stringent **10** tyrannical **12** unpermissive

ironhearted
5 stony **7** callous **8** hardened, obdurate, ruthless **9** merciless, unfeeling **10** hard-boiled **11** cold-blooded **13** unsympathetic

iron horse
10 locomotive

ironic
3 wry **6** biting **7** caustic, cutting, cynical, mordant, satiric **8** sardonic **9** sarcastic, trenchant

iron ore
8 goethite, hematite, limonite, siderite, taconite **9** magnetite

Iron Pants
6 Patton (George)

irons
5 bonds, gyves **6** chains **7** bilboes, darbies, fetters **8** manacles, shackles

Iroquois tribe
4 Erie **6** Cayuga, Mohawk, Oneida, Seneca **8** Onondaga **9** Tuscarora

irradiate
4 beam, glow **5** edify, light, shine **6** uplift **7** light up **8** illumine **9** enlighten **10** illuminate

irrational
3 mad **5** crazy **6** absurd, insane **7** invalid **8** demented **9** cockamamy, illogical, senseless, sophistic **10** cockamamie, fallacious, ridiculous **12** preposterous, unreasonable
number: **4** surd

irrefutable
4 sure **6** proven **7** certain **8** airtight, ironclad, positive **9** apodictic, veracious **10** conclusive, inarguable **11** indubitable **12** indisputable **13** incontestable

irregular
3 odd **5** erose, queer **6** fitful, patchy, random, spotty, uneven **7** aimless, erratic, unequal **8** aberrant, abnormal, atypical, informal, lopsided, peculiar, singular, sporadic, unstable, unsteady, variable **9** anomalous, desultory, divergent, eccentric, guerrilla, haphazard, hit-or-miss, spasmodic, unregular, unsettled **10** asymmetric, capricious, changeable, inconstant, off-balance, unbalanced, unofficial **11** exceptional, fluctuating **12** intermittent, unsystematic

irregularity
5 freak, quirk **6** oddity, vagary **7** anomaly **8** deviance **9** deviation, roughness **10** aberration, inequality, unevenness **11** abnormality

irrelevant
5 inapt **9** unrelated **10** extraneous, immaterial, inapposite, peripheral **11** inessential, unessential, unimportant **12** inapplicable **13** insignificant

irreligious
6 unholy **7** godless, impious, profane, ungodly **11** blasphemous

irreparable
8 cureless, hopeless **9** incurable **11** immedicable **12** irredeemable, irremediable **13** irretrievable, unrecoverable

irreproachable
4 pure **8** flawless, innocent, spotless, virtuous **9** blameless, errorless, exemplary, faultless, guiltless, righteous **10** immaculate, impeccable, inculpable, unblamable

irresolute
5 shaky **6** fickle, unsure, wobbly **7** halting **8** doubtful, hesitant, unstable, waffling, wavering **9** equivocal, faltering, tentative, uncertain, undecided **10** ambivalent, changeable, inconstant, wishy-washy **11** fluctuating, half-hearted, vacillating

irresponsible
4 rash, wild **8** carefree, careless, feckless, reckless **10** incautious, unreliable **12** undependable **13** unaccountable, untrustworthy

irreverent
4 flip **7** impious, profane, ungodly **8** flippant **9** satirical **11** blasphemous **12** sacrilegious

irrevocable
4 firm **5** final **9** immutable **11** unalterable **12** irreversible, unchangeable **13** nonreversible

irrigate
3 wet **4** soak **5** flush, water

irrigation ditch
5 flume **6** sluice **7** acequia

irritability
5 pique **6** choler **8** edginess **9** petulance **10** crabbiness, impatience **11** fretfulness, peevishness
abnormal: **8** erethism

irritable
4 edgy, sour **5** cross, huffy, ratty, testy, waspy, whiny **6** crabby, cranky, crusty, grumpy, ornery, snappy, tetchy, touchy **7** fretful, grouchy, peevish, pettish, prickly, waspish **8** captious, choleric, petulant, snappish **9** crotchety, fractious, impatient, irascible, querulous, splenetic **12** cantankerous, disagreeable

irritant
4 itch, pest **5** nudge, peeve, thorn **6** bother, gadfly, noodge, nudnik, pester, plague **7** nudnick **8** headache, nuisance, vexation **9** annoyance **11** botheration

irritate
3 bug, irk, rub, vex **4** fret, gall, goad, rile, roil **5** anger, annoy, chafe, grate, peeve, pique, spite **6** abrade, badger, bother, burn up, harass, hector, madden, needle, nettle, offend, ruffle **7** inflame, provoke **9** aggravate, stimulate **10** exacerbate, exasperate

irritated
5 irate, testy **7** fretful, peevish **8** choleric **9** impatient, irascible

irritation
4 itch, pest, rash, sore **5** thorn **6** bother, plague **7** chagrin **8** nuisance, vexation **9** annoyance

irrupt
5 belch, eruct, surge **6** invade **7** intrude

irruption
4 raid **5** foray **6** inroad **7** upsurge **8** invasion **9** incursion, intrusion

I.R.S. employee
7 auditor **10** accountant

Irving novel
15 Cider House Rules (The) **17** Hotel New Hampshire (The) **20** World According to Garp (The)

Isaac
father: **7** Abraham
mother: **5** Sarah
son: **4** Esau **5** Jacob
wife: **7** Rebekah

Isabella I
country: **5** Spain
home: **7** Castile
husband: **9** Ferdinand

Isaiah
7 prophet
father: **4** Amoz

Iscah
brother: **3** Lot
father: **5** Haran
sister: **6** Milcah

Iseult, Isolde
beloved: **7** Tristan **8** Tristram
husband: **4** Mark

Ishbak
father: 7 Abraham
mother: 7 Keturah

Ishbosheth's father
4 Saul

Ishmael
6 pariah 7 outcast 8 castaway, outsider 11 untouchable
captain: 4 Ahab
father: 7 Abraham
mother: 5 Hagar
ship: 6 Pequod

Ishtar
brother: 7 Shamash
father: 3 Anu, Sin
lover: 6 Tammuz

Ishui's father
4 Saul 5 Asher

isinglass
4 mica

Isis
brother: 6 Osiris
father: 3 Geb
husband: 6 Osiris
mother: 3 Nut
son: 4 Sept 5 Horus

Islam
adherent: 6 Moslem, Muslim
founder: 8 Mohammed, Muhammad
god: 5 Allah
holy city: 5 Mecca
holy month: 7 Ramadan
law: 6 Sharia
place of worship: 6 mosque
priest: 4 imam
scriptures: 5 Koran, Quran
sect: 4 Shia, Sufi 5 Sunni 6 Salafi, Shiite, Sufism 7 Ismaili, Wahhabi 8 Salafism
(see also **Muslim**)

island
3 ait, cay, key 4 holm 5 atoll, oasis 6 skerry 7 crannog
Adriatic Sea: 3 Vis 4 Brac, Cres, Hvar 5 Brach, Ciovo, Mljet, Solta 6 Lesina, Pharus
Aegean Sea: 4 Scio 5 Chios, Khios, Samos, Thira 6 Ikaria, Lemnos, Lesbos, Limnos 7 Nikaria 8 Mitilini, Mytilene, Santorin 10 Sakis-Adasi, Susam-Adasi
Alaska: 4 Adak, Atka, Attu, Kuiu 8 Wrangell
American Samoa: 3 Ofu, Tau 4 Rose 6 Swains
Andaman Sea: 4 Mali 5 Tavoy
Antarctica: 5 Scott, Young
Arafura Sea: 5 Dolak
Arctic Archipelago: 6 Baffin 8 Victoria
Arctic Ocean: 5 Senja
Australian: 5 Cocos 8 Tasmania
Azores: 4 Pico 5 Corvo, Faial
Bahamas: 3 Cat, Rum 4 Long 5 Abaco, Exuma 6 Andros, Inagua 7 Acklins, Crooked 8 Watlings 9 Eleuthera, Mayaguana 11 San Salvador
Bahrain: 5 Sitra 8 Muharraq
Baltic Sea: 4 Moon, Muhu 5 Faron, Mukhu, Rugen, Worms 6 Vormsi 7 Gotland 8 Bornholm, Gothland, Gottland
Barents Sea: 4 Bear
Bay of Naples: 5 Capri
Bay of Panama: 4 Naos
Bering Sea: 5 Medny 7 Nunivak 10 Big Diomede 13 Little Diomede
Bismarck Archipelago: 5 Lihir 10 New Britain
Bristol Channel: 5 Lundy
Buzzards Bay: 9 Cuttyhunk
Canadian: 5 Banks, Devon 6 Baffin 8 Bathurst, Melville, Somerset, Victoria 9 Anticosti, Ellesmere 10 Cape Breton 11 Axel Heiberg, Southampton 12 Newfoundland, Prince Edward
Canaries: 6 Gomera 7 La Palma 8 Tenerife 9 Lanzarote
Cape Verde: 4 Fogo, Maio, Mayo 5 Brava, Rombo
Caribbean Sea: 4 Cuba 5 Aruba, Utila, Vache 6 Tobago 7 Antigua, Curaçao, Jamaica 8 Barbados, Dominica, Trinidad 10 Guadeloupe, Martinique, Puerto Rico
(see also **Virgin group**)
Carolines: 3 Uap, Yap 4 Truk 5 Chuuk, Nomoi, Sorol 6 Ponape 7 Hogoleu, Pohnpei 9 Ascension
Chagos Archipelago: 11 Diego Garcia
Chesapeake Bay: 4 Deal, Kent 5 Smith, Watts
Chukchi Sea: 6 Herald
Comoro group: 7 Mayotte
Congo River: 4 Bamu
Croatia: 3 Krk, Pag, Rab 5 Susak, Unije
Cyclades: 3 Ios, Kea, Nio 4 Ceos, Keos, Milo 5 Delos, Melos, Milos, Naxos, Paros, Siros, Syros 6 Andros, Dhilos 7 Amorgos, Cythnos, Kithnos, Kythnos, Mykonos
Denmark: 3 Als, Fyn, Mon 4 Aero, Fano, Moen, Mors 5 Alsen, Funen, Moers, Samso 8 Bornholm 9 Greenland 13 Fanum Fortunae
East River: 5 Ward's 7 Welfare 9 Roosevelt
England's: 7 Britain 9 Britannia 12 Great Britain
English Channel: 5 Wight
Fiji: 4 Koro 5 Mango, Vatoa
French: 7 Corsica 12 New Caledonia
French Polynesia: 4 Rapa, Reao, Ua Pu 5 Ua Pau
Futunas: 5 Alofi
Galápagos: 5 Pinta 7 Chatham, Isabela 8 Abingdon 10 Albermarle
Georgia: 5 Tybee
Germany: 4 Fohr 7 Fehmarn 9 Helgoland 10 Heligoland

Greater Antilles: **4** Cuba **7** Jamaica **10** Hispaniola, Puerto Rico
Greece: **4** Milo, Rodi **5** Creta, Crete, Hydra, Idhra, Kriti, Rodos, Tenos, Tinos **6** Euboea, Evvoia, Hydrea, Lesbos, Rhodes, Rhodus **9** Negropont **10** Negroponte
Grenadines: **5** Union
Gulf of Alaska: **6** Kodiak
Gulf of Bothnia: **5** Karlö
Gulf of Carpentaria: **5** Maria **6** Groote **7** Eylandt
Gulf of Guinea: **7** Sao Tomé **8** Príncipe, Sao Thomé **11** Saint Thomas
Gulf of Mexico: **3** Cat **5** Lobos
Gulf of Panama: **3** Rey
Gulf of St. Lawrence: **5** Brion
Gulf of Thailand: **3** Kut **5** Samui
Haiti: **6** Gonâve
Hawaii: **4** Maui, Oahu **5** Kauai, Lanai **6** Niihau **7** Molokai **9** Kahoolawe
Hudson Bay: **5** Coats
Indian Ocean: **4** Mahé, Nias **5** Heard, Pemba **7** La Dique, Praslin, Réunion **8** Sri Lanka, Zanzibar **9** Mauritius **10** Madagascar
Indonesia: **4** Bali, Biak, Java, Maja, Muna, Nias, Rhio, Riau, Roma, Roti, Savu, Sawu **5** Batam, Boano, Buton, Djawa, Japen, Lakor, Moena, Riouw, Rotti, Rupat, Sawoe, Solor, Sumba, Wetar, Wokam **6** Butung, Flores, Jappen, Lombok, Madura, Padang, Roepat, Romang, Soemba **7** Celebes, Madoera, Sumatra, Sumbawa **8** Boetoeng, Soembawa, Sulawesi **10** Bandanaira, Banda Neira, Sandalwood
Iran: **5** Shahi
Ireland: **4** Aran
Irish Sea: **3** Man
Italy: **4** Elba **6** Sicily **8** Sardinia
Japan: **3** Iki, Uku **4** Naru, Yezo **5** Awaji, Fukae, Fukue, Hondo, Shodo **6** Honshu, Kyushu **7** Shikoku **8** Hokkaido **10** Shodoshima
Java Sea: **4** Laut
Kiribati: **6** Tarawa
Lake Champlain: **5** Grand
Lake Erie: **9** North Bass, South Bass **10** Middle Bass
Lake Huron: **8** Drummond **10** Manitoulin
Lake Michigan: **3** Hog **4** High **6** Beaver
Lake Ontario: **5** Wolfe
Lake Superior: **4** Sand **6** Royale **7** Manitou
Lake Winnipeg: **5** Hecla
largest: **9** Greenland
Leeward group: **5** Nevis **7** Antigua, Barbuda, Redonda **8** Anguilla, Sombrero **10** Montserrat, Saint Kitts **13** St. Christopher
legendary: **7** Cipango
Lesser Sundas: **4** Alor **5** Ombai
Long Island Sound: **4** City, Hart **5** Goose, Harts
Malay Archipelago: **5** Kisar, Larat, Timor **6** Borneo **9** New Guinea
Malaysia: **6** Penang, Pinang **13** Prince of Wales
Malta: **4** Gozo
Massachusetts: **9** Nantucket
Mediterranean Sea: **4** Elba **5** Corfu, Crete, Malta **6** Cyprus, Euboea, Rhodes, Sicily **7** Corsica **8** Sardinia
Moluccas: **4** Buru **5** Ambon, Ceram, Seram **6** Boeroe
Mozambique channel: **10** Juan de Nova
Myanmar: **5** Daung, Kadan, Lanbi
Narragansett Bay: **5** Rhode **8** Prudence **9** Aquidneck, Conanicut
Netherlands: **5** Texel **7** Ameland **8** Vlieland
Netherlands Antilles: **7** Curaçao
New York: **4** Fire, Long **5** Coney, Ellis **6** Staten **7** Liberty **9** Gardiners, Governors, Manhattan, Roosevelt
New York Bay: **5** Ellis **6** Staten **7** Liberty **9** Governors, Manhattan
New Zealand: **5** South, White **7** Chatham, Stewart **8** D'Urville
Niagara River: **4** Goat
Nile River: **4** Argo, Roda, Ruda **5** Rhoda **6** Rawdah **11** Elephantine
North Channel: **3** Mew **8** Manihiki **9** Tongareva
North Pacific: **4** Wake
Northwest Territories: **5** Banks, Bylot, Devon **8** Bathurst, Melville **9** Ellesmere **10** Cornwallis, Resolution **13** Prince of Wales
Norwegian: **8** Jan Mayen
Norwegian Sea: **5** Donna, Smola, Vikna
Nova Scotia: **5** Sable **10** Cape Breton
off Alaska: **4** Dall **5** Kayak
off Albania: **5** Sazan **6** Saseno
off Australia: **4** Dunk
off Belize: **9** Ambergris
off Brazil: **4** Apeu **5** Rocas
off British Columbia: **4** King, Pitt **9** Vancouver
off Cape Cod: **8** Muskeget **9** Nantucket
off Chile: **5** Guafo, Mocha
off China: **4** Amoy **5** Ma-tsu **6** Hainan, Quemoy, Taiwan
off Crete: **3** Dia
off Ecuador: **4** Puna
off England: **3** Man **4** Sark **5** Wight **6** Jersey, Walney **8** Alderney, Guernsey
off Florida: **3** Dog **4** Pine **6** Amelia **7** Pelican, Sanibel **9** Anastasia
off French Guiana: **6** Devil's
off Georgia: **10** Cumberland **11** Saint Simons
off Germany: **4** Sylt
off Greenland: **5** Disko
off Guinea: **5** Tombo
off Hispaniola: **5** Beata
off Honduras: **5** Tigre
off Iceland: **7** Surtsey

off India: **5** Sagar
off Ireland: **4** Tory **5** Clare, Clear
off Kenya: **4** Lamu
off Long Island: **7** Fishers
off Louisiana: **5** Marsh
off Maine: **4** Deer, Orrs **5** Swans **8** Monhegan **11** Mount Desert
off Malay Peninsula: **6** Phuket **9** Singapore
off Maryland: **10** Assateague
off Massachusetts: **4** Plum **7** Naushon
off Mexico: **7** Cozumel
off Mississippi: **4** Horn, Ship
off Mozambique: **3** Ibo
off New Brunswick: **10** Campobello
off Newfoundland: **4** Bell
off Nigeria: **5** Lagos
off North Carolina: **5** Bodie
off Norway: **5** Bomlo, Froya, Hitra, Sotra, Stord, Vardo **8** Hitteren
off Panama: **4** Naos **5** Coiba **6** Parida
off Poland: **5** Wolin **6** Wollin
off Puerto Rico: **4** Crab **7** Culebra, Vieques
off Rhode Island: **5** Block
off Scotland: **4** Bute, Iona, Jura **5** Arran, Islay
off South Carolina: **5** North **6** Parris **10** Hilton Head
off Sri Lanka: **5** Delft
off Staten Island: **7** Hoffman
off Sumatra: **3** Weh
off Sweden: **5** Graso, Oland, Vaddo
off Syria: **5** Arvad, Arwad, Rouad **6** Aradus
off Tanzania: **5** Mafia, Pemba
off Tasmania: **5** Bruni, Bruny
off Tunisia: **5** Jerba **6** Djerba, Meninx
off Venezuela: **5** Aruba **7** Bonaire **8** Buen Aire
off Virginia: **5** Wreck
off Wales: **5** Caldy **6** Caldey
Orkneys: **3** Hoy
Outer Hebrides: **5** Barra, Scarp
Palmer Archipelago: **6** Anvers **7** Antwerp, Brabant
Pearl Harbor: **4** Ford
Persian Gulf: **4** Qeys **5** Kharg, Khark
Philippines: **4** Buad, Cebu, Fuga, Ilin, Poro, Sulu **5** Balut, Batan, Bohol, Coron, Daram, Leyte, Luzon, Panay, Samal, Samar, Sugbu, Talim, Ticao, Verde **6** Negros **7** Masbate, Mindoro, Palawan, Paragua **8** Limasawa, Mindanao **10** Corregidor
Puerto Rico: **4** Mona
Quebec: **4** Alma
Red Sea: **5** Tiran, Zugur, Zuqar
Russia: **7** Wrangel
St. Lawrence River: **4** Hare **5** Jesus **8** Montreal
San Francisco Bay: **5** Angel
Santa Cruz: **5** Anuda, Ndeni **6** Cherry
Scotland: **5** Arran
Sea of Japan: **4** Sado **5** Rebun
Sea of Marmara: **4** Avsa
second largest: **9** New Guinea
Senegal: **5** Gorée
Seychelles: **4** Mahé **7** La Digue, Praslin
Shetland archipelago: **4** Unst, Yell **5** Foula
Sierra Leone: **5** Tasso
South Atlantic: **5** Gough **6** Gough's **11** Saint Helena
South Korea: **5** Cheju
South of Tokyo: **3** Iwo **7** Iwo Jima, Naka Iwo
South Orkneys: **10** Coronation
South Pacific: **3** Hiu **4** Niue **5** Raoul **6** Savage, Sunday **7** Norfolk **8** Pitcairn
Spitsbergen archipelago: **4** Edge
Strait of Hormuz: **5** Qeshm, Qishm
Sulu Archipelago: **4** Jolo **5** Lapac
Svalbard: **4** Hope
Sverdrup: **11** Axel Heiberg **12** Amund Ringnes
Swedish: **3** Ven **4** Hven **5** Hveen, Orust
Tanzania: **8** Zanzibar
Texas: **5** Padre
Thames River: **7** Sheppey
third largest: **6** Borneo
Tierra del Fuego: **5** Hoste
Tonga: **3** Eua, Foa **4** Uiha **5** Haano
Tuamotu Archipelago: **4** Anaa **5** Chain
Turkish: **5** Imroz **6** Imbros
Tuvalu: **7** Nanumea **9** Nukufetau
Tyrrhenian Sea: **6** Ischia **11** Montecristo
Vanuatu: **3** Api, Epi, Oba **4** Aoba, Gaua, Tana, Vate **5** Efate, Maewo, Tanna
Venezuelan: **5** Patos **9** La Tortuga
volcanic: **5** Tofua **7** Iwo Jima
Wales: **8** Anglesea, Anglesey, Holyhead
Weddell Sea: **4** Ross **6** Hearst
Western Samoa: **5** Upolu **6** Savaii
West Indies: **4** Mona, Saba, Salt **5** Nevis, Peter, Saona **6** Tobago, Tortue **7** Grenada, Tortuga **8** Trinidad **9** Santa Cruz **10** Concepción, Hispaniola, Montserrat, Saint Croix (see also **Bahamas; Greater Antilles; Leeward group; Virgin group; Windward group**)
West of England: **7** Ireland
West Pacific: **5** Dyaul, Fauro, Ocean **6** Banaba, Marcus **7** Iwo Jima, Kita Iwo **9** Minami Iwo
with former penitentiary: **8** Alcatraz

island dance
4 hula

island farewell, island greeting
5 aloha

island feast
4 luau

island group
Admiralty: **5** Manus
Alaska: **3** Rat **8** Aleutian, Pribilof **9** Andreanof, Catherine

Aleutians: **4** Near
Aleutian: **3** Rat **4** Adak, Akun, Attu **5** Amlia, Kiska, Umnak **6** Kanaga, Tanaga, Unimak **8** Amchitka, Unalaska
American Samoa: **5** Manua
Apostle: **3** Oak **4** Long, Sand **5** Outer **8** Madeline, Michigan, Stockton
Arabian Sea: **9** Laccadive
Arctic Archipelago: **8** Sverdrup
Arctic Ocean: **8** Svalbard **12** Novaya Zemlya
Bahamas: **5** Berry, Exuma **6** Bimini
Balearic: **5** Ibiza **7** Majorca, Menorca, Minorca **8** Mallorca
Banda Sea: **5** Damar
Bangladesh: **5** Hatia, Hatya
Bay of Bengal: **7** Andaman, Nicobar
between England and France: **7** Channel
Bismarck Archipelago: **4** Feni **5** Tabar, Tanga
Bismarck Sea: **4** Vitu
British: **7** Bermuda
Caribbean Sea: **4** Swan **5** Pearl **6** Cayman, Perlas, Pigeon **8** Pichones **10** Grenadines, West Indies
Central Pacific Ocean: **4** Line **5** Samoa, Union **6** Danger, Midway **7** Phoenix, Tokelau **8** Manihiki **9** Polynesia **12** Northern Cook
Channel: **4** Herm, Sark **5** Lihou, Sercq **6** Jersey **8** Guernsey
Cook: **4** Atiu **5** Mauke
Coral Sea: **4** Huon
Cuba: **8** Camagüey
Denmark: **6** Faroes **7** Faeroes
D'Entrecasteaux: **8** Kaluwawa **9** Fergusson
Dodecanese: **3** Coo, Cos, Kos **4** Caso, Lero, Simi, Syme **5** Kasos, Leros, Lipso, Lisso, Patmo, Telos **6** Calino, Lipsos, Nisiro, Patmos **7** Calimno, Nisiros, Nisyros **8** Kalymnos
east of Philippines: **10** Micronesia
East Siberian Sea: **4** Bear **8** Medvezhi
Ecuador: **5** Colón **9** Galápagos
England: **5** Farne
Faeroes, Faroes: **4** Vago **5** Bordo, Sando
Fiji: **3** Lau **7** Eastern
Florida Keys: **4** Long, Vaca, West **5** Largo **7** Big Pine **9** Matecumbe, Sugarloaf
Formosa Strait: **4** Hoko **6** Peng hu **10** Pescadores
Fox: **5** Umnak **6** Akutan, Unimak **8** Unalaska
France: **5** Salut **6** Safety **9** Kerguelen
French Polynesia: **3** Low **6** Tubuai **7** Austral, Paumotu, Société, Society, Tuamotu **9** Marquesas, Touamotou
Frisian: **3** Rom **4** Föhr, Sylt **5** Amrum, Juist, Mando, Texel **6** Borkum **7** Ameland **8** Langeoog, Pellworm, Vlieland **9** Helgoland, Norderney
Germany: **8** Halligen
Greece: **6** Aegean, Ionian **8** Cyclades **10** Dodecanese **11** Dodecanesus
Hudson Bay: **7** Belcher
Indian Ocean: **7** Aldabra
Indonesia: **4** Asia, Batu, Pagi, Sula **5** Babar, Batoe, Pagai, Pageh, Penju, Spice, Wakde **6** Maluku
Inner Hebrides: **4** Coll, Eigg, Iona, Jura, Muck, Mull, Skye **5** Canna, Gigha, Islay, Tiree, Tyree
Ionian: **5** Corfu, Paxos, Zante **6** Cerigo, Ithaca, Leukas, Levkas **10** Santa Maura
Ireland: **4** Aran
Italy: **6** Lipari
Japan: **5** Osumi
Kuril: **4** Urup **5** Ketoi, Matua **6** Iturup **7** Etorofu, Matsuwa **8** Kunashir **9** Kunashiri
largest: **5** Malay **8** Malaysia
Lesser Antilles: **8** Windward
Leti: **3** Moa **5** Lakor
Line: **5** Flint **6** Malden, Vostok **7** Fanning, Palmyra **8** Starbuck **9** Christmas
Loyalty: **3** Uea **4** Lifu, Maré, Uvea **5** Lifou
Malay Archipelago: **5** Sunda **6** Soenda
Marianas: **4** Maug, Rota **5** Pagan **6** Saipan
Marquesas: **4** Eiào, Ua Pu **6** Hatutu, Hiva Oa, Ua Huka **7** Tahuata **8** Fatu Hiva, Nuku Hiva
Marshall: **5** Wotho, Wotje **8** Eniwetok **9** Kwajalein
Mediterranean Sea: **8** Baleares, Balearic
Midway: **4** Sand **7** Eastern
Moluccas: **3** Kai, Kei, Obi **4** Buru, Leti **5** Ambon, Banda, Letti, Seram **6** Boeroe **8** Tanimbar **9** Timorlaut
New Caledonia: **7** Loyalty **9** Loyalties
Northern Cook: **7** Penrhyn
north of Australia: **9** Melanesia
north of British Isles: **5** Faroe **7** Faeroes
north off Fiji: **5** Hoorn **6** Futuna
north of Madagascar: **7** Aldabra **8** Farquhar
north of New Caledonia: **5** Belep
north of New Guinea: **8** Bismarck **9** Admiralty **11** Admiralties
Northwest Territories: **5** Parry
off Alaska: **3** Fox
off Alaska Peninsula: **8** Shumagin
off Cape Cod: **9** Elizabeth
off eastern Asia: **5** Kuril **6** Kurile
off England: **6** Scilly
off Florida: **11** Dry Tortugas
off Guinea: **3** Los **4** Loos
off Honduras: **5** Bahia
off Morocco: **7** Madeira
off New Guinea: **3** Aru **4** Aroe
off Nicaragua: **4** Corn
off northern Africa: **6** Canary **8** Canaries
off northern Australia: **6** Wessel **7** Dampier
off Sicily: **5** Egadi **8** Aegadian
Okinawa: **4** Kume
Outer Hebrides: **4** Uist

Papua New Guinea: **5** Green
Persian Gulf: **4** Tunb
Philippines: **4** Cuyo **5** Tapul **6** Lubang **7** Basilan, Bisayas, Visayan
Phoenix: **4** Hull, Mary **6** Birnie, Canton **9** Enderbury
Portuguese: **6** Azores
Quebec: **8** Magdalen **9** Madeleine
Queen Charlotte: **7** Moresby
Ryukyus: **5** Amami **7** Okinawa
St. Lawrence River: **8** Thousand
Sea of Japan: **3** Oki
Sea of Marmara: **5** Kizil **7** Princes **11** Kizil Adalar
Shumagin: **4** Unga
Society: **5** Eimeo, Tahaa, Tahao, Taiti **6** Moorea, Tahiti **8** Otaheite
Solomon: **4** Buka, Gizo, Savo **7** Malaita **11** Guadalcanal **12** Bougainville
South Atlantic Ocean: **8** Falkland, Malvinas
South China Sea: **6** Hirata **7** Paracel, Spratly
south of New Zealand: **8** Auckland
South Pacific: **11** Austronesia
Sulu Sea: **7** Cagayan **9** Cagayanes
Tonga: **5** Vavau
Treasury: **4** Mono
Truk: **3** Tol **4** Haru, Moen, Udot, Uman **5** Fefan
Tyrrhenian Sea: **5** Ponza
Venezuelan: **4** Aves, Bird **9** Los Roques
Virgin, American: **9** Saint John **10** Saint Croix **11** Saint Thomas
Virgin, British: **5** Peter **6** Norman **7** Anegada, Tortola **11** Jost Van Dyke
West Europe: **12** British Isles
West Indies: **6** Virgin **10** Guadeloupe
west of French Polynesia: **4** Cook
west of Scotland: **7** Western **8** Hebrides
west Pacific Ocean: **4** Duff **5** Belau, Bonin, Mapia, Palau, Pelew **7** Ladrone, Mariana, Solomon, Vanuatu **8** Marshall, Treasury **9** Ogasawara **10** Saint David
Windward: **10** Martinique

island in a river
3 ait

island nation
Atlantic Ocean: **9** Cape Verde
Indian Ocean: **8** Malagasy, Malgache, Sri Lanka **9** Mauritius **10** Madagascar, Seychelles
Mediterranean Sea: **6** Cyprus
Mozambique Channel: **6** Comoro **7** Comores
off southern China: **6** Taiwan
south of Greenland: **7** Iceland
West Indies: **4** Cuba **7** Jamaica **8** Barbados **10** Saint Lucia
West Pacific Ocean: **4** Fiji **5** Belau, Nauru, Palau, Samoa **6** Tuvalu **7** Vanuatu
Windward group: **8** Dominica

island province
12 Prince Edward

island state
6 Hawaii

isle
see **island**

isle of exile
4 Elba

islet
3 cay, key

Ismene
brother: **9** Polynices **10** Polyneices
father: **7** Oedipus
mother: **7** Jocasta
sister: **8** Antigone
uncle: **5** Creon

isochronous
7 regular **8** cyclical, periodic, rhythmic **9** recurrent, recurring **10** periodical **12** intermittent

isolate
6 cut off, detach, enisle **7** seclude **8** close off, insulate, pinpoint, separate, set apart **9** segregate, sequester **10** quarantine

isolated
5 alone, apart **6** random, remote, unique **7** unusual **8** solitary, sporadic **9** separated, withdrawn **11** exceptional, quarantined

Isolde
see **Iseult**

Israel
airline: **4** El Al
ancient name: **4** Zion **5** Judea **6** Canaan, Judaea **9** Palestine
capital: **9** Jerusalem
city: **4** Acre **5** Haifa, Jaffa **7** Tel Aviv **9** Beersheba
desert: **5** Negeb, Negev
gulf: **5** Aqaba
intelligence service: **6** Mossad
lake: **8** Tiberias **12** Sea of Galilee
language: **6** Arabic, Hebrew
leader: **4** Meir (Golda) **5** Barak (Ehud), Begin (Menachem), Peres (Shimon), Rabin (Yitzhak) **6** Olmert (Ehud), Shamir (Yitzhak), Sharon (Ariel) **9** Ben-Gurion (David), Netanyahu (Benjamin)
monetary unit: **6** shekel
parliament: **7** Knesset
neighbor: **5** Egypt, Syria **6** Jordan **7** Lebanon
plain: **9** Esdraelon
river: **6** Jordan
sea: **4** Dead **13** Mediterranean

Israeli
5 sabra
dance: **4** hora **5** horah
diplomat: **4** Eban (Abba)
gun: **3** Uzi

Israelite
see **Hebrew; Jewish**

Issachar
father: **5** Jacob
mother: **4** Leah

issue
4 emit, flow, gush, pour, rise, seed, stem, vent **5** arise, birth, brood, child, empty, fruit, scion, topic **6** affair, appear, effect, emerge, get out, matter, put out, result, scions, sequel, source, spring, upshot **7** concern, debouch, descent, edition, emanate, give off, give out, outcome, problem, proceed, progeny, publish, release, subject **8** bulletin, children, question, throw off **9** come forth, offspring, originate, posterity **10** derive from, distribute, end product, promulgate **11** consequence, descendants, progeniture, publication

Istanbul
ancient name: **9** Byzantium
business section: **6** Galata
country: **6** Turkey
foreign quarter: **4** Pera **7** Beyoglu
park: **8** Seraglio
residential section: **7** Uskudar

isthmus
Africa-Asia: **4** Suez
America: **6** Panama
Greece: **7** Corinth
Malay Peninsula: **3** Kra

Italian
after: **4** dopo
against: **6** contro
ahead: **6** avanti
apple: **4** mela
aunt: **3** zia
automobile: **4** Alfa (Romeo), Fiat **6** Lancia **7** Ferrari **8** Maserati **9** Alfa Romeo **11** Lamborghini
be: **6** essere
book: **5** libro
brandy: **6** grappa
brother: **8** fratello
cake: **5** torta
cat: **5** gatto
cathedral: **5** duomo
cheers: **6** cin cin
chicken: **5** pollo
child: **7** bambino
coffee: **5** caffè
come: **6** venire
day: **6** giorno
deer: **5** cervo
dialect: **6** Tuscan **8** Sicilian
dictator: **9** Mussolini (Benito)
die: **6** morire
dinner: **6** pranzo
dish: **5** pasta
do, make: **4** fare
dog: **4** cane
enough: **5** basta
evening: **4** sera
everyone: **5** tutti
family: **4** Este **5** Cenci, Savoy **6** Borgia, Medici, Orsini, Pepoli, Savoia, Sforza **7** Colonna, Gonzaga, Spinola **8** Visconti
fascist: **10** Blackshirt
game: **5** bocce, bocci **6** boccie
gentleman: **6** signor **7** signore
give: **4** dare
go: **6** andare
goat: **5** capra
good-bye: **4** ciao
grape: **3** uva
hear: **7** sentire
hello: **4** ciao
highway: **10** autostrada
honey: **5** miele
how much: **6** quanto
ice cream: **6** gelato
lady: **5** donna **7** signora **9** signorina
leave: **7** partire
magistrate: **7** podestà
maybe: **5** forse
meat: **5** carne **6** salami **8** pancetta **9** pepperoni, salsiccia **10** mortadella, prosciutto
man: **4** uomo
milk: **5** latte
mountain soldier: **6** Alpino
much: **5** molto
mushroom: **5** fungo
night: **5** notte
nothing: **6** niente
numbers: **3** due, sei, tre, uno **4** nove, otto **5** dieci, sette **6** cinque **7** quattro
often: **6** spesso
oil: **4** olio
open: **6** aprire
opera house: **7** La Scala
over: **5** sopra
patriot: **6** Cavour (Conte di), Rienzo (Cola di) **7** Mazzini (Giuseppe) **9** Garibaldi (Giuseppe)
peach: **5** pesca
pencil: **6** matita
please: **9** per favore
red: **5** rosso
religious reformer: **10** Savonarola (Girolamo)
resort: **4** Lido **5** Abano, Capri **8** Sorrento, Taormina
road: **6** strada
sandwich: **6** panino
sell: **7** vendere
shrimp: **6** scampi
sing: **7** cantare

sister: 7 sorella
skier: 5 Tomba (Alberto)
soldier: 7 soldato
soup: 5 zuppa 10 minestrone
speak: 7 parlare
square: 6 piazza
squid: 8 calamari
star: 6 stella
street: 3 via 5 corso
summer: 6 estate
sun: 4 sole
tell, say: 4 dire
thanks: 6 grazie
think: 7 pensare
toward: 5 verso
uncle: 3 zio
under: 5 sotto
voice: 4 voce
weight: 5 libra, oncia
white: 6 bianco
wine: 4 vino
wine region: 4 Asti
with: 3 con
without: 5 senza
write: 8 scrivere

Italy
bay: 6 Naples
capital: 4 Roma, Rome
city: 4 Asti, Bari, Pisa 5 Aosta, Genoa, Milan, Ostia, Padua, Parma, Siena, Turin 6 Genova, Mantua, Milano, Modena, Naples, Napoli, Padova, Torino, Venice, Verona 7 Bergamo, Bologna, Bolzano, Catania, Cremona, Firenze, Leghorn, Livorno, Mantova, Palermo, Perugia, Ravenna, Salerno, Taranto, Trieste, Venezia 8 Florence, Siracusa, Syracuse
enclave: 9 San Marino 11 Vatican City
gulf: 5 Gaeta 7 Salerno, Taranto 11 Sant' Eufemia
island, island group: 4 Elba, Lido 5 Capri 6 Ischia, Lipari, Sicily 7 Aeolian, Capraia 8 Sardinia
lake: 4 Como 5 Garda 7 Bolsena 8 Maggiore 9 Bracciano
leader: 9 Mussolini (Benito)
monetary unit: 4 euro
monetary unit, former: 4 lira, lire (plural) 5 scudi (plural), scudo, soldi (plural), soldo
mountain, range: 4 Alps, Etna 9 Apennines, Mont Blanc, Monte Rosa 10 Monte Corno
neighbor: 6 France 7 Austria 8 Slovenia 11 Switzerland
peninsula: 9 Salentina
river: 4 Arno, Liri 5 Adige, Piave, Tiber 6 Isonzo, Tevere 8 Volturno
sea: 6 Ionian 8 Adriatic, Ligurian 10 Tyrrhenian 13 Mediterranean
strait: 7 Messina, Otranto
volcano: 4 Etna 8 Vesuvius
wine region: 4 Asti

itch
3 yen 4 ache, long, lust, pine, urge 5 crave, yearn 6 desire, hanker, hunger, thirst 7 craving, longing 8 appetite, pruritus, yearning 9 hankering

itchy
4 avid, edgy, keen 5 antsy, eager, jumpy 7 fidgety, restive 8 prurient, pruritic, restless 9 impatient

item
3 bit 5 entry, point, scrap, story, thing, topic 6 detail, matter 7 account, article, element, feature, product 8 clipping 9 commodity 10 particular

itemize
4 list 5 count, tally 6 number 7 catalog, run down, specify, tick off 8 document, spell out 9 catalogue, enumerate, inventory

iterate
5 drill, recap, renew 6 rehash, repeat, replay, retell 7 reprise, restate 12 recapitulate

Ithaca king
8 Odysseus

Ithamar's father
5 Aaron

itinerant
5 gypsy, nomad 6 roving 7 migrant, nomadic, roaming, vagrant 8 drifting, rambling, traveler, vagabond, wanderer 9 migratory, transient, unsettled, wandering, wayfaring 11 peripatetic

itty-bitty
3 wee 4 tiny 5 teeny, weeny 6 teensy 10 teeny-weeny 12 teensy-weensy

Ivanhoe
author: 5 Scott (Walter)
character: 5 Isaac 6 Cedric, Rowena, Ulrica 7 Rebecca, Wilfred 9 Robin Hood

Ivory Coast
11 Côte d'Ivoire
capital: 7 Abidjan 12 Yamoussoukro
city: 6 Bouaké
language: 6 French
monetary unit: 5 franc
mountain: 5 Nimba
neighbor: 4 Mali 5 Ghana 6 Guinea 7 Liberia 11 Burkina Faso
river: 7 Bandama 9 Sassandra

ivory-tower
8 academic 11 conjectural, impractical, theoretical, unrealistic

Ivy League
4 Penn, Yale 5 Brown 7 Cornell, Harvard 8 Columbia 9 Dartmouth, Princeton 12 Pennsylvania

J

ja opposite
4 nein

jab
3 hit **4** barb, blow, poke, prod, sock, stab **5** nudge, prick, punch **6** pierce, strike, thrust **8** puncture

jabber
3 gab, jaw, yak, yap **5** prate **6** babble, drivel, gabble, yammer **7** blather, chatter, prattle **8** nonsense **9** gibberish

jabberer
6 gabber, magpie **7** babbler, blabber, gabbler **8** prattler **9** chatterer **10** chatterbox

Jabberwocky author
7 Carroll (Lewis), Dodgson (Charles)

jabot
4 fall **5** frill **6** ruffle

J'accuse author
4 Zola (Émile)

___ jacet
3 hic

jack
3 tar **4** bird, card, fish, flag, hike, lift, move, salt **5** boost, brace, bread, dough, knave, knife, money, put up, raise **6** brandy, cheese, device, donkey, rabbit, sailor, seaman **7** laborer, mariner, servant **8** increase, standard **9** criticize, mechanism **10** take to task

jackal
4 dupe, pawn **5** agent, canid, patsy **6** canine, flunky, lackey, minion, stooge **7** cat's-paw **9** accessory, auxiliary **10** accomplice **11** stool pigeon
god: **4** Anpu **6** Anubis

jackanapes
3 ape, imp **4** brat, fool **6** monkey

jackass
4 dolt, dope, fool, jerk **5** burro, dunce, idiot, schmo **6** donkey, nitwit **7** nebbish **8** bonehead, imbecile, numskull **9** blockhead, numbskull **10** nincompoop
deer: **3** kob **8** antelope

jackdaw
7 grackle **9** blackbird

jacket
3 tux **4** Eton **5** Nehru, parka, tunic **6** anorak, blazer, bolero, jerkin, reefer, sacque, tuxedo **7** doublet, Norfolk, peacoat, spencer **8** camisole **10** roundabout
armored: **7** hauberk **9** habergeon
part: **5** lapel
sleeveless: **4** vest **6** bolero, jerkin **9** waistcoat

jackhammer
5 drill **9** rock drill

Jackie's second
3 Ari (Onassis)

jack-in-the-pulpit
4 arum

jackknife
4 dive **6** barlow
game: **11** mumblety-peg

jackleg
6 make-do, novice **7** amateur, shyster, stopgap **9** dishonest, greenhorn, makeshift, temporary, unskilled **10** substitute **11** pettifogger **12** unscrupulous

jack-of-all-trades
6 tinker **7** go-to guy **8** factotum, handyman

Jack of late-night TV
4 Paar

jack-o'-lantern
6 fungus **7** pumpkin

jackpot
3 sum **4** pool **5** award, kitty, prize **6** reward, stakes **7** bonanza, success **8** windfall

jackrabbit
4 hare

Jackson 5 brother
4 Tito **6** Jackie, Marlon **7** Michael **8** Jermaine

jackstay
3 bar, rod **4** rope **7** rigging, support

Jacob
brother: **4** Esau
daughter: **5** Dinah
father: **5** Isaac
father-in-law: **5** Laban
mother: **7** Rebekah
new name: **6** Israel
son: **3** Dan, Gad **4** Levi **5** Asher, Judah **6** Joseph, Reuben, Simeon **7** Zebulun **8** Benjamin, Issachar, Naphtali
variant: **5** James
wife: **4** Leah **6** Rachel

Jacobin
7 radical **9** Dominican, extremist

Jacob's ladder
4 herb 5 phlox 9 perennial

jade
3 gem, nag 4 bore, cloy, dull, minx, pall, tire, wear 5 color, drain, flirt, green, hussy, jewel, stone, tramp, weary, wench 6 wanton 7 fatigue, jezebel, mineral, trollop, wear out 8 gemstone, nephrite, strumpet, wear down

jaded
4 worn 5 blasé, bored, sated, tired, weary 6 dulled 7 cynical, wearied, worn-out 8 fatigued, satiated, worn down 9 apathetic, exhausted, surfeited 10 overworked

jaeger
4 skua 6 hunter 8 huntsman

Jael
husband: 5 Heber
victim: 6 Sisera

jag
3 cut 4 barb, jerk, load, pink, tear 5 binge, notch, prick, spell, spree 6 bender, indent, thrill, thrust 7 serrate

jagged
5 erose, harsh, rough, sharp 6 broken, craggy, rugged, spiked, uneven 7 scraggy 8 serrated, unsmooth 9 irregular

Jaguar model
3 XKE

jai alai
6 pelota
basket: 5 cesta
court: 6 cancha 7 fronton

jail
3 can, jug, pen 4 coop, gaol, poky 5 clink, pokey 6 cooler, lockup, prison 7 confine, freezer, slammer 8 hoosegow, imprison, stockade 9 constrain 11 confinement, incarcerate

jailbird
3 con 5 felon, loser 7 convict 8 criminal, prisoner, repeater 10 recidivist

jailer
5 guard, screw 6 keeper, warden 7 turnkey 8 overseer

jakes
3 loo 5 privy 7 latrine 8 outhouse 9 backhouse

jalopy
3 car 4 auto, heap 5 crate, wreck 6 beater, junker 7 clunker, vehicle 10 automobile, rattletrap

jalousie
5 blind 6 window 7 shutter

jam
3 box, fix 4 bind, clog, cram, dunk, pack, push 5 block, crowd, crush, force, jelly, press, stuff, wedge 6 bruise, impede, plight, scrape, squash, squish 7 dilemma, squeeze 8 compress, conserve, obstacle, preserve 9 confiture, preserves 10 difficulty 11 predicament

Jamaica
capital: 8 Kingston
cay: 5 Pedro 6 Morant
city: 10 Montego Bay 11 Spanish Town
discoverer: 8 Columbus (Christopher)
location: 10 West Indies
mountain range: 4 Blue 10 Dry Harbour
sea: 9 Caribbean

Jamaican
export: 3 rum 5 sugar
hair style: 6 dreads 10 dreadlocks
music: 3 dub, ska 5 ragga 6 reggae
musician: 5 Cliff (Jimmy) 6 Marley (Bob, Ziggy) 7 Wailers
nationalist: 6 Garvey (Marcus)

jambalaya
4 olio 5 gumbo 6 medley 7 mélange, mixture 8 mishmash 10 hodgepodge, hotchpotch, salmagundi

jamboree
4 gala 5 revel 6 fiesta, frolic 7 carouse, shindig 8 carnival, festival, wingding 9 merriment 11 celebration 13 entertainment

James
brother: 4 John 5 Jesus, Joses
cousin: 5 Jesus
father: 7 Zebedee 8 Alphaeus
mother: 4 Mary 6 Salome

James, Henry
biographer: 4 Edel (Leon)
novel: 8 American (The) 9 Europeans (The) 10 Bostonians (The), Confidence, Golden Bowl (The), Tragic Muse (The) 11 Ambassadors (The), Daisy Miller 14 Turn of the Screw (The), Wings of the Dove (The) 15 Portrait of a Lady (The) 16 Washington Square

James, P. D.
detective: 9 Dalgliesh (Adam)

James and the Giant Peach author
5 Roald (Dahl)

James Bond
actor: 5 Craig (Daniel), Moore (Roger) 6 Dalton (Timothy) 7 Brosnan (Pierce), Connery (Sean), Lazenby (George)
author: 7 Fleming (Ian)
cocktail: 12 vodka martini
film: 4 Dr. No 7 Skyfall 9 GoldenEye, Moonraker, Octopussy 10 Goldfinger 11 Thunderball, View to a Kill (A) 12 Casino Royale 13 Die Another Day, License to Kill, Live and Let Die, Spy Who Loved Me (The) 15 For Your Eyes Only, Living Daylights (The), Quantum of Solace 16 World Is Not Enough (The), You Only Live

Twice **17** Tomorrow Never Dies **18** Diamonds Are Forever, From Russia with Love **19** Man with the Golden Gun (The) **26** On Her Majesty's Secret Service
gun: **7** Beretta, Walther **8** Lilliput
novel: **4** Dr. No **9** Moonraker **10** Goldfinger **11** Thunderball **12** Casino Royale **13** Live and Let Die, Spy Who Loved Me (The) **15** For Your Eyes Only **16** You Only Live Twice **18** Diamonds Are Forever, From Russia with Love **19** Man with the Golden Gun (The) **26** On Her Majesty's Secret Service
secretary: **10** Moneypenny (Miss)
villain: **4** Drax (Sir Hugo), Dr. No, Khan (Kamal), King (Elektra) **5** Klebb (Rosa), Largo (Emilio), Mr. Big, Zorin **6** Carver (Elliot), Graves (Gustav), Renard **7** Blofeld (Ernst Stavro), Mr. White, Sanchez (Franz) **8** Gen. Orlov, Whitaker (Brad) **9** Dr. Kananga, Gen. Koskov, Kristados (Aristotle), Le Chiffre, Stromberg (Karl), Trevelyan (Alec) **10** Goldfinger (Auric), Scaramanga (Francisco)

Jammu and ___
7 Kashmir

Jane Eyre
author: **6** Brontë (Charlotte)
lover: **9** Rochester

jangle
3 jar **4** ring **5** babel, clash **6** clamor, excite, hubbub **7** discord, quarrel **8** conflict **11** discordance, discordancy **12** disharmonize

jangling
5 harsh, noisy, tense **7** grating **9** dissonant **10** discordant, quarreling

Janis of popular music
3 Ian

janitor
5 super **6** porter **7** cleaner **9** caretaker, concierge, custodian **10** doorkeeper

Jannings of the movies
4 Emil

January in Mexico
5 enero

japan
4 coat **7** coating, varnish **11** lacquerware

Japan
5 Nihon **6** Nippon
capital: **3** Edo **4** Nara **5** Tokyo
city: **4** Kobe **5** Kyoto, Osaka, Otaru **6** Nagano, Nagoya **7** Fukuoka, Okinawa, Sapporo **8** Kawasaki, Nagasaki, Yokohama **9** Hiroshima
island: **6** Honshu, Kyushu **7** Shikoku **8** Hokkaido
lake: **4** Biwa **8** Chuzenji
monetary unit: **3** yen
mountain: **4** Fuji **8** Fujiyama

Japanese
aborigine: **4** Ainu
art: **6** bonsai, ukiyo-e **7** origami
baron: **6** daimyo
battle cry: **6** banzai
beer: **5** Asahi, Kirin **7** Sapporo
Buddha: **5** Amida, Amita
business alliance: **8** keiretsu
cartoons: **5** anime
comics: **5** manga
dancing girl: **6** geisha
deer: **4** sika
dish: **4** miso, soba **5** gyoza, katsu, kombu, ramen, sushi **7** sashimi, tempura **8** sukiyaki, teriyaki
dog: **5** Akita **8** Shiba Inu
drama: **3** Noh **6** Bugaku, Kabuki **7** Bunraku
drink: **4** sake, saki
emperor: **6** Mikado **7** Akihito **8** Hirohito
fencing: **5** kendo
festival: **3** Bon
fish: **4** fugu
flower arrangement: **7** ikebana
garment: **6** kimono
gateway: **5** torii
general: **4** Tojo (Hideki)
god: **5** Ebisu, Hotei **7** Daikoku, Jurojin **8** Bishamon
goddess: **6** Benten **9** Amaterasu
governor: **6** shogun
grill: **7** hibachi
honorific: **3** san
horseradish: **6** wasabi
houseplant: **6** bonsai
immigrant: **5** issei
instrument: **4** biwa, koto **7** samisen **8** shamisen **10** shakuhachi
language: **4** Ainu
martial art: **4** judo **5** kendo **6** aikido, karate **7** jujitsu
martial artist: **5** ninja
mat: **6** tatami
native: **4** Ainu
plum: **6** loquat
poem: **5** haiku, tanka
porcelain: **5** imari
pottery: **4** raku **7** satsuma
race: **4** Ainu
radish: **6** daikon
religion: **6** Shinto **8** Buddhism **9** Shintoism
rice wine: **4** sake, saki
robe: **6** kimono
samurai clan: **5** Taira **8** Minamoto
sash: **3** obi
sci-fi film: **5** Akira
song: **3** uta
soup: **4** miso

suicide: **7** seppuku **8** hara-kiri, hari-kari, kamikaze
theater: **3** Noh **6** Bugaku, Kabuki **7** Bunraku
tidal wave: **7** tsunami
vegetable: **3** udo **7** edamame
vehicle: **8** rickshaw
warrior: **7** samurai
warrior code: **7** bushido
wine: **4** sake, saki
wrestling: **4** sumo
writing: **4** kana **5** kanji **8** hiragana, katakana
zither: **4** koto

Japanese-American
5 Issei, Nisei
second-generation: **6** Sansei

jape
3 gag, kid, rib **4** gibe, jest, jibe, joke, mock, quip **5** crack, laugh, prank, tease **7** waggery **8** drollery **9** wisecrack, witticism

Japheth
brother: **3** Ham **4** Shem
father: **4** Noah
son: **5** Gomer, Javan, Madai, Magog, Tiras, Tubal **7** Meshech

jar
4 bump, jolt, olla **5** cruse, quake, shake, shock, upset **6** jangle, jounce **7** tremble, vibrate **8** mismatch **9** container
ancient: **6** krater **7** amphora, canopic

jardiniere
5 stand **6** holder **7** garnish

Jared of film
4 Leto

jargon
4 cant **5** argot, idiom, lingo, slang **6** patois, pidgin **7** dialect, lexicon, palaver **8** language **9** gibberish **10** mumbo-jumbo, vernacular, vocabulary **11** terminology
lawyer's: **8** legalese
tinkers': **6** shelta

jarl
4 earl **5** noble **8** nobleman **12** Scandinavian

jarring
5 harsh, rough **6** hoarse, jangly **7** grating, rasping, raucous **8** strident **9** dissonant **10** discordant, unsettling

jasmine
3 tea **4** vine **5** shrub **6** flower, yellow **7** perfume

Jason
father: **5** Aeson
helper: **5** Medea
lover: **5** Medea **6** Creusa, Glauce, Glauke
quest: **6** Fleece **12** Golden Fleece
ship: **4** Argo
shipmate: **8** Argonaut
teacher: **6** Chiron **7** Cheiron
uncle: **6** Pelias
wife: **5** Medea

jasper
6 morlop, quartz **9** stoneware **10** chalcedony

jaundice
4 bias **7** disease, icterus **9** prejudice

jaundiced
6 biased, warped, yellow **7** colored, cynical, envious, hostile, jealous **9** distorted **10** suspicious

jaunt
4 ride, trip **5** drive, sally **6** junket, outing, ramble **7** journey **9** excursion

jaunty
4 airy, pert, spry **5** fresh, light, peppy, perky **6** breezy, lively **7** buoyant **8** debonair **9** sprightly **10** nonchalant

java
3 joe, mud **6** jamoke **6** coffee

Java
almond: **7** talisay
cotton: **5** kapok
jute: **5** kenaf
lake: **4** Ijen **5** Dieng, Kelut
neighbor: **4** Bali **7** Sumatra
plum: **5** jaman **6** jambul **7** jambool
strait: **4** Bali **5** Sunda
volcano: **4** Gede, Kawi, Lawu **5** Bromo, Kelut, Raung **7** Ciremai

Javanese
civet: **5** rasse
orchestra: **7** gamelan
tree: **4** upas

Javan squirrel
8 jelerang

javelin
5 lance, shaft, spear **7** assagai, assegai, harpoon

Javert's prey
7 Valjean (Jean)

jaw
3 gab, yak **4** chat, rail, talk **5** chops, clack, prate **6** babble, gabble **7** chatter, prattle **9** yakety-yak

jawbone
7 maxilla **8** arm-twist, mandible, persuade, talk into

jawbreaker
9 hard candy

jay
4 bird, blue, hick, rube **5** dandy **6** rustic **7** bumpkin, hayseed **9** chatterer, greenhorn

Jayhawker
9 guerrilla
State: **6** Kansas **8** Missouri

jazz
3 bop **4** guff, jive **5** bebop, swing **6** boogie **7** ragtime **8** malarkey, nonsense
group: **5** combo
term: **3** axe **4** blow, riff, scat, tune, vamp **5** chart, chops **6** bridge, groove, improv **7** changes **8** stop time **9** front line **10** broken time
up: **5** rouse **6** vivify **7** animate, enliven **9** stimulate

jazz musician
3 Ory (Kid) **4** Cole (Nat "King"), Getz (Stan), Hirt (Al), Mann (Herbie), Monk (Thelonious), Rich (Buddy), Shaw (Artie), Sims (Zoot) **5** Baker (Chet), Basie (Count), Brown (Clifford), Corea (Chick), Davis (Miles), Evans (Bill, Gil), Hines (Earl "Fatha"), James (Harry), Jones (Hank), Krall (Diana), Krupa (Gene), Moran (Jason), Roach (Max), Shepp (Archie), Smith (Jimmy), Sun Ra, Tatum (Art), Terry (Clark), Young (Lester) **6** Bechet (Sidney), Blakey (Art), Burton (Gary), Carter (Benny), Dorsey (Jimmy, Tommy), Farmer (Art), Garner (Erroll), Gordon (Dexter), Herman (Woody), Hodges (Johnny), Jordan (Louis), Kenton (Stan), Miller (Glenn), Mingus (Charles), Morton (Jelly Roll), Oliver (King), Parker (Charlie "Bird"), Pepper (Art), Powell (Bud), Puente (Tito), Silver (Horace), Taylor (Cecil), Waller (Fats), Wilson (Teddy) **7** Brubeck (Dave), Coleman (Ornette), Connick (Harry), Goodman (Benny), Hampton (Lionel), Hancock (Herbie), Hawkins (Coleman), Jarrett (Keith), Mehldau (Brad), Metheny (Pat), Rollins (Sonny), Russell (Pee Wee), Shorter (Wayne), Webster (Ben) **8** Adderley (Cannonball), Calloway (Cab), Coltrane (John), Eldridge (Roy), Marsalis (Branford, Wynton), Mulligan (Gerry), Peterson (Oscar), Tristano (Lennie), Williams (Mary Lou) **9** Armstrong (Louis), Blanchard (Terence), Christian (Charlie), Ellington (Duke), Gillespie (Dizzy), Grappelli (Stéphane), Henderson (Fletcher), Lunceford (Jimmie), Reinhardt (Django), Teagarden (Jack) **10** Montgomery (Wes) **11** Beiderbecke (Bix)

jazz singer
3 Lee (Peggy) **4** Cole (Nat "King"), Ella (Fitzgerald), Etta (James), O'Day (Anita) **5** James (Etta), Krall (Diana), McRae (Carmen), Tormé (Mel) **6** Carter (Betty), Elling (Kurt), Simone (Nina) **7** Bennett (Tony), Clooney (Rosemary), Connick (Harry), Holiday (Billie), Jarreau (Al), Rushing (Jimmy), Vaughan (Sarah) **8** Eckstine (Billy), Williams (Joe) **10** Fitzgerald (Ella), Washington (Dinah)

jazzy
5 gaudy **6** brassy, flashy, glitzy, lively, rakish, sporty **7** raffish, splashy **8** animated, colorful, exciting, spirited **9** vivacious **10** flamboyant

jealous
5 green **7** envious **9** green-eyed, invidious, resentful **10** possessive

____ Jean Baker
5 Norma

Jeannie portrayer Barbara
4 Eden

jeans brand
3 Lee **4** Levi **5** Levi's **8** Wrangler

Jed Clampitt portrayer
5 Ebsen (Buddy)

jeer
4 gibe, jibe, mock **5** fleer, flout, scoff, scorn, sneer, taunt **6** deride, heckle, hector, insult **7** catcall, contemn, laugh at, mockery **8** derision, ridicule

Jeeves
creator: **9** Wodehouse (P. G.)
employer: **7** Wooster (Bertie)
position: **5** valet **6** butler

jeez
4 gosh, heck **5** golly, shoot **6** shucks **7** jeepers

jefe
4 boss, head, lord **5** chief, ruler **6** honcho, leader **9** chieftain, commander

Jefferson, Thomas
home: **10** Monticello
lover: **5** Sally (Hemings)
state: **8** Virginia

Jehoram
brother: **7** Ahaziah
father: **4** Ahab **11** Jehoshaphat
kingdom: **5** Judah
slayer: **4** Jehu
wife: **8** Athaliah

Jehoshaphat
father: **3** Asa **6** Ahilud, Nimshi, Paruah
father-in-law: **4** Ahab
son: **4** Jehu **7** Jehoram
wife: **8** Athaliah

Jehovah
3 God **6** Adonai, Elohim, Yahweh

Jehu
6 driver
father: **6** Hanani **11** Jehoshaphat
grandfather: **6** Nimshi
son: **8** Jehoahaz
victim: **5** Joram **7** Jehoram

jejune
4 dull, flat **5** banal, bland, empty, inane, silly, trite, vapid **7** insipid, puerile **8** lifeless **9** colorless **13** uninteresting

Jekyll's alter ego
4 Hyde (Mr.)

jell
3 set 4 form 6 cohere, gelate 7 congeal, thicken 8 coalesce 9 coagulate, take shape

jelly
3 set 4 mass 5 aspic 6 spread 7 congeal, thicken 9 coagulate

jellyfish
6 coward, medusa 7 doormat, medusan 8 medusoid, pushover, weakling 10 ctenophore 12 coelenterate, invertebrate, siphonophore

jennet
3 ass 5 hinny, horse 6 donkey

jenny
4 bird 6 donkey, female

jeopardize
4 risk 5 peril 6 chance, expose, hazard 7 imperil 8 endanger

jeopardy
4 risk 5 peril 6 danger, hazard, menace 8 exposure 9 liability 12 endangerment

jeremiad
6 lament, screed, tirade 7 lecture 8 diatribe, harangue 9 complaint, philippic 11 declamation, lamentation

Jeremiah's scribe
6 Baruch

Jericho's conqueror
6 Joshua

jerk
3 ass, cad, lug, tic, tug 4 dolt, dope, fool, jolt, pull, push, snap, twit, yank 5 brute, creep, idiot, lurch, ninny, spasm, twist, wrest 6 bounce, nitwit, thrust, twitch, wrench 7 jackass 8 preserve 10 nincompoop

jerkin
6 jacket

jerky
4 meat 5 inane 6 abrupt, stupid, sudden 7 foolish, idiotic, jolting, spastic 8 saccadic 9 senseless

Jerome's Bible
7 Vulgate

jersey
6 fabric 7 sweater 8 pullover

Jerusalem
4 Sion, Zion 5 Salem 8 Holy City
hill: 4 Sion, Zion 6 Moriah
mosque: 4 Omar 6 Al-Aqsa 13 Dome of the Rock
pool: 6 Siloam 8 Bethesda

Jerusalem artichoke
5 tuber 8 girasole 9 sunflower

Jerusalem thorn
9 horsebean

jess
5 strap

Jesse
daughter: 7 Abigail, Zeruiah
father: 4 Obed
grandfather: 4 Boaz
son: 4 Ozem 5 David, Eliab, Elihu 6 Raddai 7 Shammah 8 Abinadab, Nethanel
youngest son: 5 David

Jessica
father: 7 Shylock
husband: 7 Lorenzo

jest
3 fun, gag, kid, rag, rib 4 butt, game, gibe, jape, jeer, joke, josh, mock, quip, razz 5 crack, fleer, flout, humor, prank, scoff, sneer, spoof, sport, tease 6 banter, gaiety 7 mockery, waggery 8 derision, drollery, ridicule 9 merriment, wisecrack, witticism

jester
3 wag, wit 4 fool 5 actor, clown, comic, joker 7 buffoon 8 comedian, funnyman, humorist, jokester, quipster 9 prankster 11 entertainer

Jesuit
founder: 6 Loyola (Ignatius)
leader: 6 Xavier (St. Francis)

Jesus-and-Mary scene
5 pietà

jet
4 coal, ebon, emit, gush, inky, rush, spew 5 black, ebony, plane, spout, spurt 6 engine, nozzle, squirt, stream, travel 7 current, jewelry 8 airplane 9 pitch-dark 10 pitch-black
maker: 4 Lear

Jethro
daughter: 8 Zipporah
son-in-law: 5 Moses

jetsam
7 flotsam 8 wreckage 9 driftwood

jet set
5 A-list, elite 9 beau monde, haut monde 10 glitterati

jettison
4 drop, dump, junk, omit 5 eject, forgo, scrap 6 reject, remove 7 deep-six, discard 8 disposal, get rid of, throw out 9 sacrifice, throw away

jetty
4 dock, ebon, inky, pier, quay 5 black, ebony, groin, wharf 7 project, seawall 9 pitch-dark 10 breakwater, pitch-black

Jew
6 Essene, Hebrew, Semite 7 Israeli, Judaist 9 Israelite

jewel
3 gem 4 rock 5 adorn, bijou, ideal, prize, stone

7 **bearing** 8 gemstone, ornament, treasure 9 embellish

jeweled headband
5 tiara

jeweler
8 lapidary
famous: 7 Cartier (Jacques, Louis, Pierre), Fabergé (Carl), Lalique (René), Tiffany (Charles Lewis)
eyepiece: 5 loupe
measure: 5 carat

jewelry
5 bling **10** bijouterie, bling-bling
artificial: 5 glass, paste **6** strass **7** costume
piece: 3 pin **4** ring **6** brooch **7** earring **8** bracelet, cufflink, necklace, tieclasp **9** lavaliere
set: 6 parure

Jewish
ascetic: 6 Essene
bread: 5 matzo **6** matzoh
ceremony: 4 bris **5** seder **8** havdalah **10** bar mitzvah, bas mitzvah, bat mitzvah
combining form: 5 Judeo **6** Judaeo
credo: 5 shema
doctrine: 6 Mishna **7** Mishnah
feast: 5 seder
New Year: 12 Rosh Hashanah
holy day: 5 Purim **9** Yom Kippur **12** Rosh Hashanah
month: 4 Adar, Elul, Iyar **5** Nisan, Sivan, Tebet **6** Kislev, Shebat, Tammuz, Tishri **7** Heshvan
organization: 8 Hadassah **9** B'nai B'rith
prayer: 7 kaddish, kiddush
prayer book: 6 siddur
sabbath: 8 Saturday
scripture: 5 Torah **6** Talmud
synagogue: 4 shul
teacher: 5 rabbi, rebbe **6** Hillel
village: 6 shtetl
(see also **Hebrew**)

Jezebel
4 slut **5** hussy, tramp, trull, wench **6** wanton **7** trollop **8** slattern, strumpet
deity: 4 Baal
father: 7 Ethbaal
home: 5 Sidon
husband: 4 Ahab
slayer: 4 Jehu
victim: 6 Naboth

JFK
predecessor: 3 DDE
successor: 3 LBJ

jib
3 arm, shy **4** balk, boom, sail, stop **5** demur **6** refuse **9** stop short

jibe
5 agree, fit in, match, shift, tally **6** accord, concur, square **7** conform **8** dovetail **9** harmonize **10** correspond, go together **12** change course

jiffy
3 sec **4** snap, tick, wink **5** flash, hurry, shake, trice **6** minute, moment, second **7** instant **11** split second

jig
4 fish, game, hoax, hook, jerk, play, ploy, ruse, sham, wile **5** catch, dance, feint, trick **6** device, gambit **7** gimmick **9** deception

jigger
4 jerk, mold, sail **5** alter, gismo, gizmo **6** device, dingus, doodad, gadget, widget **7** gimmick, machine, measure **9** doohickey, rearrange, shot glass, thingummy **10** manipulate

jiggle
4 jerk **5** shake **7** agitate **9** oscillate

jigsaw
3 cut **4** tool **6** puzzle **7** arrange, machine

jihad
3 war **6** strife **7** crusade, holy war **8** campaign, struggle

jilt
4 drop **5** ditch, leave **6** desert, reject **7** abandon, cast off, discard

jim-dandy
3 ace, gem, pip **4** A-one, lulu **5** beaut, daisy, dilly, doozy, great, ideal, nifty, peach, super, swell **6** corker, doozie **7** perfect **8** knockout **9** excellent, first-rate, humdinger **11** outstanding

jimmy
3 bar, pry **4** open **5** crack, force, lever **7** crowbar **9** break open, force open

jimsonweed
6 datura **10** thorn apple

jingle
4 call, ring, song **5** clink, rhyme, sound, verse **6** tinkle

Jingle Bells contraction
3 o'er

jingoistic
7 hawkish **11** belligerent **12** chauvinistic, militaristic **13** nationalistic

jinn
5 afrit, genie **6** afreet, spirit

jinx
3 hex **5** charm, curse, spell **6** plague, whammy **7** bad luck, evil eye **8** foredoom **10** affliction, misfortune

jinxed
7 unlucky

jitters
5 jumps, panic **6** nerves, shakes **7** anxiety, shivers, willies **9** whim-whams **11** nervousness, stage fright **13** heebie-jeebies

jittery
4 edgy 5 antsy, hinky, jumpy, nervy 6 goosey, spooky 7 anxious, fearful, fidgety, nervous, panicky 10 high-strung

jive
3 kid 4 fool, jazz, talk 5 dance, music, swing, tease 6 banter, cajole, hot air, jargon

Joab
brother: 6 Asahel 7 Abishai
father: 7 Seraiah, Zeruiah
slayer: 7 Benaiah
uncle: 5 David
victim: 5 Abner, Amasa

Joan of Arc
birthplace: 7 Domremy
epithet: 7 Pucelle (La) 13 Maid of Orléans
king: 7 Charles (VII)
victory: 7 Orléans

Joan's husband
5 Darby

Joash
father: 4 Ahab 7 Ahaziah 8 Jehoahaz
son: 6 Gideon 7 Amaziah 8 Jeroboam
victim: 9 Zechariah

job
3 gig 4 duty, hire, item, post, role, spot, task, work 5 chore, stint, trade 6 effort, office 7 calling, posting, pursuit, robbery 8 business, function, position, vocation 9 situation 10 assignment, employment, engagement, livelihood, occupation, profession 11 undertaking

Job
daughter: 6 Keziah 7 Jemimah
father: 8 Issachar
friend: 6 Bildad, Zophar 7 Eliphaz

jobber
6 broker, dealer, seller, trader 8 merchant 10 contractor, wholesaler

job-safety agency
4 OSHA

job-training program
4 JTPA

Jocasta
daughter: 6 Ismene 8 Antigone
husband: 5 Laius 7 Oedipus
son: 7 Oedipus 8 Eteocles 9 Polynices 10 Polyneices

jock
5 pilot 7 athlete

jockey
4 play 5 rider, trick 7 beguile, exploit, finesse 8 maneuver 10 manipulate
famous: 3 Day (Pat) 5 Baeza (Braulio), Krone (Julie), Woolf (George) 6 Arcaro (Eddie), Bailey (Jerry), Murphy (Isaac), Pincay (Laffit) 7 Cauthen (Steve), Cordero (Angel), Hartack (Bill), Longden (Johnny), Piggott (Lester), Stevens (Gary) 8 McCarron (Chris), McHargue (Darrel), Turcotte (Ron) 9 Shoemaker (Willie)
garb: 5 silks
whip: 4 crop

jocular
5 comic, funny, jolly, merry, witty 6 jocose, jocund, jovial, lively 7 amusing, comical, jesting, playful 8 cheerful, humorous 9 facetious

jocularity
3 fun, wit 4 glee 5 humor, mirth 6 gaiety 7 jollity 8 hilarity 9 joviality, merriment 11 high spirits, playfulness

jocund
3 gay 5 happy, jolly, merry 6 elated, jovial, lively 7 festive, gleeful, playful 8 mirthful 12 lighthearted

joe
3 guy, mud 4 dude, java 6 coffee, fellow, jamoke

jog
3 dig, jab, run 4 lope, move, pace, poke, prod, push, ride, stir, trot 5 nudge, punch, rouse, shake 6 bounce, change, jounce, prompt, remind

joggle
4 join, trot 5 dowel, joint, notch, shake, tooth 6 jostle

john
3 lav, loo 4 head 5 jacks, privy 6 toilet 7 latrine 8 bathroom, lavatory 11 water closet

John
French: 4 Jean
Gaelic: 3 Ian
Russian: 4 Ivan
Spanish: 4 Juan

John Hancock
9 autograph, signature

John in legal cases
3 Doe

Johnny ___
3 Reb 6 Carson, Mathis, Mercer, Unitas

john of England
3 lav, loo

Johnson, Samuel
biographer: 7 Boswell (James)
work: 8 Rasselas 10 dictionary

John the Baptist
father: 9 Zacharias
mother: 9 Elisabeth

John the Evangelist
brother: 5 James
father: 7 Zebedee
mother: 6 Salome

joie de vivre
4 élan, zest 5 gusto 6 esprit 10 love of life

join
3 tie, wed **4** abut, ally, bind, bond, fuse, line, link, mate, yoke **5** affix, align, blend, marry, merge, piece, touch, unify, union, unite **6** attach, border, couple, engage, enlist, enroll, sign on, sign up, splice **7** combine, connect **8** compound, federate, side with **9** affiliate, associate, integrate **12** come together

joint
3 bar, ell, hip, tie **4** butt, crux, dado, dive, knee, link, node, seam **5** ankle, elbow, hinge, miter, mitre, nexus, union, wrist **6** common, mutual, public, shared, suture, united **7** hangout, knuckle, shiplap **8** abutment, combined, communal, conjunct, coupling, junction, juncture, shoulder **9** concerted, honky-tonk **10** collective, connection **11** cooperative **12** articulation
combining form: **5** arthr **6** arthro, condyl **7** condylo
disease: **9** arthritis **10** rheumatism

joist
4 beam **6** rafter, timber **7** support

joke
3 gag, kid, pun, rag, rib, yak **4** fool, jape, jest, josh, quip, razz **5** crack, humor, prank, sally **6** banter, corker, parody **7** mockery, sarcasm, waggery **8** drollery, one-liner **9** burlesque, wisecrack, witticism **11** monkeyshine
hilarious: **12** sidesplitter
stale: **8** chestnut

joker
3 guy, wag, wit **4** card, fool **5** catch, clown, comic, cutup **6** fellow, jester, kicker **7** proviso **8** comedian, humorist **9** condition **10** limitation **11** stipulation

jollity
3 fun **4** glee **5** cheer, mirth **6** gaiety, revels **7** revelry, whoopee **8** hilarity **9** festivity, jocundity, joviality, merriment **10** ebullience, jocularity **11** high spirits, merrymaking **12** cheerfulness, conviviality

jolly
3 fun, gay, kid **4** glad, jest, josh, very **5** humor, merry **6** banter, jocund, jovial, joyful, joyous **7** festive, gleeful, jocular, playful, roguish, waggish **8** cheerful, mirthful **9** convivial **10** frolicsome **12** lighthearted

Jolly Roger
4 flag **6** ensign
user: **6** pirate

jolt
3 hit, jar **4** blow, bump, jerk, shot, slug, stun **5** check, clash, crash, knock, lurch, shake, shock, upset **6** impact, jounce, rattle **7** disturb, shake up, startle **8** astonish, surprise **9** collision

Jonah
7 prophet
swallower: **4** fish **5** whale

Jonathan
brother: **7** Johanan
father: **4** Saul
friend: **5** David

Jones, John Paul
ship: **15** Bonhomme Richard
victim: **7** Serapis

Jones novel
11 Thin Red Line (The) **15** Some Came Running **18** From Here to Eternity

jongleur
4 bard **6** singer **7** juggler **8** minstrel **10** troubadour **11** entertainer

jonquil
8 daffodil **9** narcissus, perennial

Jonson play
7 Volpone **9** Alchemist (The) **15** Bartholomew Fair

Joplin creation
3 rag **7** ragtime **11** Entertainer (The) **12** Maple Leaf Rag

Joram
brother: **7** Ahaziah
father: **3** Toi **4** Ahab **11** Jehoshaphat
slayer: **4** Jehu
son: **7** Ahaziah

Jordan
capital: **5** Amman
city: **5** Irbid, Zarqa
gulf: **5** Aqaba
language: **6** Arabic
monarch: **7** Hussein **8** Abdullah
monetary unit: **5** dinar
mountain: **4** Ramm
neighbor: **4** Iraq **5** Syria **6** Israel **11** Saudi Arabia
sea: **4** Dead

jorum
3 cup, jug **6** vessel

Joseph
brother: (see **Jacob** son)
buyer: **8** Potiphar
father: **5** Asaph, Jacob **9** Zacharias **10** Mattathias
mother: **6** Rachel
son: **5** Jesus **7** Ephraim **8** Manasseh
wife: **4** Mary **7** Asenath

josh
3 kid, rag, rib **4** jest, joke, razz **5** chaff, jolly, tease **6** banter

Joshua's victory
7 Jericho

Joshua tree
5 yucca

joss
4 idol **5** image **8** figurine

Jo's sister
3 Amy, Meg 4 Beth

jostle
3 jar, jog 4 bump, push 5 crowd, elbow, nudge, press, shove 7 agitate, collide, compete, contend, vie with 8 shoulder

jot
3 bit 4 atom, iota, note, whit 5 grain, minim, speck, write 6 tittle 7 smidgen 8 particle

joule component
3 erg

jounce
3 bob, jar, jog 4 bump, jolt 5 shake, shock, thump 6 impact

journal
3 log 4 blog 5 diary, organ 6 ledger, record 7 account, gazette, minutes 8 magazine, register 9 chronicle, newspaper 10 periodical

journalist
3 Bly (Nellie) 4 Dowd (Maureen), Drew (Elizabeth), Kalb (Bernard, Marvin), King (Larry), Polk (George), Pyle (Ernie), Reed (John), Riis (Jacob), Rose (Charlie), Will (George F.), Zahn (Paula) 5 Baker (Russell), Brown (George), Chung (Connie), Cooke (Alistair), Dunne (Finley Peter), Evans (Rowland), Hersh (Seymour), Ifill (Gwen), Kroft (Steve), Novak (Robert), Rowan (Carl), Royko (Mike), Safer (Morley), Simon (Bob, Scott), Smith (Hedrick), Stahl (Lesley), Stone (I. F.), Szulc (Tad), Wells (Ida B.), White (Theodore, William Allen), Wolfe (Tom) 6 Arnett (Peter), Bierce (Ambrose), Broder (David), Brokaw (Tom), Cooper (Anderson), Couric (Katie), Ephron (Nora), Hamill (Pete), Koppel (Ted), Gibson (Charles), Kuralt (Charles), Lehrer (Jim), Moyers (Bill), Murrow (Edward R.), Osgood (Charles), Pelley (Scott), Rather (Dan), Reston (James), Reuter (Paul Julius), Rivera (Geraldo), Runyon (Damon), Safire (William), Sawyer (Diane), Shirer (William L.), Thomas (Helen, Lowell), Zenger (John Peter) 7 Blitzer (Wolf), Bradlee (Benjamin), Bradley (Ed), Breslin (Jimmy), Cousins (Norman), Greeley (Horace), Gunther (John), Fallaci (Oriana), Hentoff (Nat), Huntley (Chet), Kempton (Murray), MacNeil (Robert), McGrory (Mary), Mencken (H. L.), Pearson (Drew), Remnick (David), Royster (Vermont), Russert (Tim), Sheehan (Neil), Tarbell (Ida), Trillin (Calvin), Wallace (Chris, Mike), Walters (Barbara) 8 Amanpour (Christiane), Anderson (Jack, Terry), Atkinson (Brooks), Brinkley (David), Cronkite (Walter), Garrison (William Lloyd), Gellhorn (Martha), Jennings (Peter), Lippmann (Walter), Pulitzer (Joseph), Reasoner (Harry), Salinger (Pierre), Sevareid (Eric), Steffens (Lincoln), Thompson (Dorothy, Hunter), Williams (Brian), Winchell (Walter), Woodward (Bob) 9 Bernstein (Carl), Donaldson (Sam), Frederick (Pauline), Salisbury (Harrison), Schieffer (Bob) 10 Halberstam (David)

journey
3 hie 4 hadj, hajj, hike, roam, tour, trek, trip 5 jaunt, quest 6 cruise, junket, safari, travel, voyage 7 caravan, odyssey, proceed, travels 8 progress 9 excursion 10 expedition, pilgrimage
route: 9 itinerary
stage: 3 leg

joust
4 duel, feud, spar, tilt 5 clash, fight 6 combat 7 contest 8 conflict 10 tournament
arena: 5 lists 8 tiltyard

Jove
see **Jupiter**

jovial
5 happy, jolly, merry 6 cheery 7 amiable 8 cheerful 9 convivial 11 good-humored, good-natured

jowl
3 jaw 5 cheek 6 dewlap, wattle 8 mandible

joy
4 glee 5 bliss, mirth 6 gaiety 7 delight, elation 8 felicity, fruition, gladness, pleasure 9 enjoyment, happiness, merriment 11 delectation

Joyce, James
birthplace: 6 Dublin
character: 5 Bloom (Leopold), Bloom (Molly) 7 Dedalus (Stephen)
work: 6 Exiles 7 Ulysses 9 Dubliners 13 Finnegans Wake

joyful
3 gay 4 glad 5 happy, jolly, merry 6 elated, jocund 7 buoyant, gleeful, pleased 8 ecstatic, jubilant, mirthful 9 delighted, rapturous 12 lighthearted

joyless
3 sad 4 glum, grim 5 bleak, drear 6 dismal, dreary, gloomy, morose, somber, sombre 7 unhappy 8 desolate 9 miserable 10 depressing

Joy of Cooking's Rombauer
4 Irma

jubilant
5 happy 6 elated, joyful, joyous 8 euphoric, exultant, exulting 9 cock-a-hoop, delighted, overjoyed, triumphal 10 triumphant 11 over the moon

jubilate
5 exult, glory 7 delight, rejoice 9 celebrate

jubilation
3 joy 4 glee 7 ecstasy, rapture 8 euphoria, rhapsody 9 rejoicing, transport 10 exaltation, exultation, joyfulness, joyousness 11 celebration 12 exhilaration

jubilee
6 flambé **8** festival **9** festivity **10** indulgence **11** anniversary, celebration **13** commemoration

Judah
brother: (see **Jacob** son)
father: **5** Jacob
king: **3** Asa **4** Ahaz, Amon **5** Joash **6** Abijam, Josiah, Jotham, Uzziah **7** Ahaziah, Amaziah, Jehoram **8** Hezekiah, Jehoahaz, Manasseh, Rehoboam, Zedekiah **9** Jehoiakim **10** Jehoiachin **11** Jehoshaphat
mother: **4** Leah
son: **4** Onan **6** Shelah

Judas
7 traitor **8** betrayer, informer, turncoat
father: **5** Simon **7** Chalphi **10** Mattathias
replacement: **8** Matthias
suicide place: **8** Aceldama, Akeldama

judge
3 ref, try, ump **4** call, deem, rate, rule, test **5** infer **6** critic, decide, deduce, jurist, reckon, settle, umpire **7** arbiter, justice, mediate, referee **8** assessor, critique, estimate, mediator **9** arbitrate, criticize, determine, moderator **10** adjudicate, arbitrator, chancellor, magistrate, negotiator **11** conciliator **12** intermediary
bench: **4** banc
biblical: **7** Solomon
chamber: **6** camera
in Hades: **5** Minos **6** Aeacus **12** Rhadamanthus
Islamic: **4** cadi
mallet: **5** gavel
Muslim: **4** cadi, qadi **5** mufti

Judge Lance
3 Ito

judgment
5 award, dicta (plural), sense **6** acumen, decree, dictum, ruling, result, wisdom **7** finding, insight, opinion, verdict **8** decision, sagacity, sentence **9** appraisal, deduction, good sense, inference **10** assessment, conclusion, discretion, estimation, evaluation, horse sense, punishment **11** common sense, discernment **13** determination

judgmental
7 carping **8** captious, critical **10** belittling, censorious, derogatory **11** disparaging, reproachful **12** disapproving, faultfinding **13** hypercritical

Judgment Day
8 doomsday

___ judicata
3 res

judicial
assembly: **5** court
document: **4** writ
order: **10** injunction

judicious
3 apt **4** fair, just, sage, sane, wise **5** right, sound **6** astute **7** careful, politic, prudent, sapient **8** accurate, discreet, rational, sensible **9** equitable, objective, sagacious **10** discerning, reasonable

Judith
father: **5** Beeri
home: **8** Bethulia
husband: **4** Esau
victim: **10** Holofernes

judo
10 martial art
school: **4** dojo
teacher: **6** sensei

Judy's husband
5 Punch

jug
3 jar, pen **4** coop, ewer, gaol, jail, olla, olpe, stew, stir, toby **5** clink, pokey **6** cooler, flagon, immure, intern, lockup, prison, vessel **7** confine, pitcher, slammer **8** demijohn, imprison **9** constrain, container **11** incarcerate

jug-band instrument
5 kazoo **6** bottle **7** washtub **9** stovepipe, washboard

juggernaut
11 steamroller

juggle
3 fix **4** fool, toss **5** bluff, trick **6** change, delude, doctor, handle, humbug, take in **7** balance, beguile, deceive, mislead, shuffle **9** rearrange **10** manipulate

juice
3 sap **4** fuel, must **5** fluid **7** current, essence **8** vitality **10** succulence **11** electricity
fermented: **4** wine **5** cider, perry

juicy
4 racy **5** lusty **7** piquant **8** dripping **9** succulent **10** profitable **11** sensational

juju
4 luck, mojo, zemi **5** charm, magic **6** amulet, fetish, grigri, mascot **7** periapt **8** gris-gris, talisman **10** lucky charm

jujube
4 tree **5** fruit **7** gumdrop, lozenge

julep
5 drink

Jules Verne captain
4 Nemo

Juliet
betrothed: **5** Paris
father: **7** Capulet
lover: **5** Romeo

July 14
11 Bastille Day

jumble
3 mix 4 cake, hash, mess, olio 5 chaos, mix up, shake 6 cookie, medley, mess up, muddle, muss up 7 clutter, confuse, disturb, mélange, rummage, shuffle 8 disarray, disorder, entangle, mishmash, pastiche, scramble 9 confusion, patchwork, potpourri 10 assortment, hodgepodge, hotchpotch, miscellany

jumbo
4 huge, vast 5 giant 6 mighty 7 immense, mammoth, massive 8 colossal, enormous, gigantic, oversize 9 ginormous, humongous, oversized 10 prodigious 11 elephantine

jump
3 hop 4 bolt, hike, leap, move, trip 5 avoid, begin, boost, bound, clear, flush, hurry, leave, put up, raise, shift, start, vault 6 attack, bounce, bustle, change, hurdle, hustle, jack up, pounce, spring 7 bail out, elevate, startle 8 increase, leap over

jumper
4 sled 5 dress, horse, smock 6 blouse, jacket

jumping-frog county
9 Calaveras

jumpy
4 edgy 5 hinky 6 on edge 7 anxious, jittery, nervous 9 excitable 10 high-strung

junction
4 node, seam 5 joint, union 7 joining, meeting 8 coupling 9 interface 10 confluence, connection, crossroads 12 intersection

juncture
4 seam 5 joint, point, union 6 crisis, moment 7 instant, joining 8 coupling 10 connection, crossroads 11 concurrence, convergence 12 turning point

jungle
3 web, zoo 4 hash, mash, maze 5 selva, snarl 6 jumble, morass, muddle, tangle 7 clutter, thicket 8 mishmash 9 labyrinth
vine: 5 liana

Jungle Books, The
author: 7 Kipling (Rudyard)
bear: 5 Baloo
boy: 6 Mowgli
panther: 8 Bagheera
python: 3 Kaa
tiger: 9 Shere Khan
wolf: 5 Akela

Jungle, The
author: 8 Sinclair (Upton)
locale: 7 Chicago 10 stockyards

junior
3 son 5 lower, minor, sonny, youth 6 lesser 7 student, younger 8 inferior, young man, youthful 9 secondary, youngster 11 subordinate

juniper
4 cade, cone 5 cedar, fruit, savin, shrub 7 conifer 9 evergreen

junk
4 boat, dope, drug, ship 5 dreck, scrap, trash, waste 6 debris, heroin, litter, refuse, reject 7 cashier, clutter, discard, garbage, rubbish, rummage 8 get rid of, jettison, throw out 9 narcotics, throw away
e-mail: 4 spam

junker
4 heap 5 crate, wreck 6 beater, jalopy 10 rattletrap, rust bucket

junket
4 tour, trip 5 feast, jaunt, spree 6 outing, picnic 7 banquet, dessert, journey 9 excursion

junkie
4 user 5 doper 6 addict 7 hophead

junk mail
4 spam

junkyard dog
3 cur

Juno
bird: 7 peacock
epithet: 6 Moneta
Greek equivalent: 4 Hera
husband: 7 Jupiter
(see also **Hera**)

Junoesque
7 stately 10 curvaceous, statuesque

junta
5 cabal, group 7 council, faction 9 camarilla, committee

Jupiter
4 Jove, Zeus
angel: 7 Zadkiel
cupbearer: 8 Ganymede
daughter: 5 Venus 7 Minerva
epithet: 6 Fidius, Fulgur, Stator, Tonans 7 Pluvius
father: 6 Saturn
lover: 6 Europa 8 Callisto
mother: 3 Ops
satellite: 6 Europa 8 Callisto, Ganymede
son: 5 Arcas 6 Castor, Pollux
temple: 7 Capitol
wife: 4 Juno

juridical
5 legal 6 lawful 8 juristic 10 legalistic

jurisdiction
3 law, see 4 sway, zone 5 might, orbit, power, range, reach, scope, venue 6 county, domain, parish, sphere 7 circuit, command, compass, control, diocese, mastery, purview 8 dominion, hegemony, province 9 authority, bailiwick, territory 10 domination 11 supervision

jurisprudence
3 law **7** case law

jurist
5 judge

jury
5 panel
decision: **7** verdict

jury-rigged
5 crude, rough **6** make-do **7** stopgap **9** makeshift, temporary **10** improvised

just
3 apt, due, fit **4** even, fair, good, meet, only, true **5** equal, legal, right **6** barely, hardly, honest, lawful, proper, simply, square **7** correct, ethical, exactly, fitting, merited, precise, upright **8** accurate, deserved, rightful, suitable, unbiased **9** equitable, honorable, impartial, objective, requisite, righteous **10** legitimate, reasonable, scrupulous **11** appropriate, well-founded **12** unprejudiced

___ juste
3 mot

justice
3 law **5** court, judge, right **6** equity **7** honesty **8** evenness, fairness, fair play **10** lawfulness, magistrate **11** correctness **12** impartiality

Justice Fortas
3 Abe

Justice Kagan
5 Elena

justification
6 excuse, reason **7** account, apology, defense, grounds **8** apologia **9** rationale **10** validation **11** explanation, vindication

justify
5 argue, claim, prove **6** assert, defend, uphold, verify **7** account, bear out, confirm, contend, explain, support, warrant **8** maintain, make even, validate **9** vindicate **10** legitimate, legitimize **11** corroborate, rationalize **12** authenticate, legitimatize, substantiate

jut
4 hang, poke **5** bulge, pouch **6** beetle, thrust **7** project **8** extend up, overhang, protrude, stand out, stick out **9** extend out, extension **10** projection, protrusion **12** protuberance

jute
5 gunny **6** burlap **7** hessian, sacking

Juvenal
4 poet **5** Roman
forte: **6** satire

juvenile
3 kid **5** actor, child, green, young, youth **6** callow, jejune, junior, moppet **7** preteen, puerile **8** childish, immature, youthful **9** childlike, fledgling, unfledged, youngling, youngster **11** undeveloped

juvenility
5 youth **9** childhood, greenness **10** immaturity, springtide, springtime **12** youthfulness

juxtaposed
4 next **8** abutting, adjacent, neighbor, proximal, touching **9** adjoining, bordering **10** appositive, contiguous, side-by-side **11** coterminous, neighboring **12** conterminous

K

kabob
8 shashlik

kachina
4 doll **6** spirit
maker: **4** Hopi

kaddish, e.g.
6 prayer

Kafka, Franz
character: **4** Olga **6** Gregor (Samsa), Joseph (K.)
novel: **5** Trial (The) **6** Castle (The) **7** Amerika
story: **8** Judgment (The) **12** Hunger Artist (A) **13** Metamorphosis (The)

Kagan of the Supreme Court
5 Elena

kaiser
5 ruler **7** emperor, monarch **8** autocrat **9** sovereign

kaka, e.g.
6 parrot

kale
4 cash, cole **5** bucks, lucre, money, moola **6** moolah **8** Brassica, colewort
relative: **5** savoy **7** cabbage **8** broccoli, collards, kohlrabi **11** cauliflower

kaleidoscopic
8 changing, colorful **10** variegated

Kali
aspect: **5** Durga **7** Parvati
husband: **4** Siva **5** Shiva

Kama
god of: **4** love
mount: **6** parrot **7** sparrow
wife: **4** Rati

Kama ___
5 Sutra

kamikaze
5 pilot **7** suicide **8** suicidal

kampong
6 hamlet **7** village

Kampuchea
see **Cambodia**

kangaroo
6 boomer, hopper, leaper **7** wallaby **8** wallaroo **9** marsupial
herd: **3** mob
young: **4** joey

Kansas
capital: **6** Topeka
city: **4** Iola **6** Olathe, Salina **7** Abilene, Emporia, Shawnee, Wichita **8** Lawrence
nickname: **9** Jayhawker (State), Sunflower (State)
prison: **11** Leavenworth
river: **8** Arkansas
state bird: **10** meadowlark
state flower: **9** sunflower
state tree: **10** cottonwood

kaolin, e.g.
4 clay

kaput
4 shot **5** spent **6** broken, busted, ruined **7** done for, useless **8** defeated, finished, outmoded **9** destroyed

karakul
5 sheep **9** broadtail **11** Persian lamb

karate
belt: **3** obi
blow: **4** chop
level: **4** belt
relative: **4** judo **5** kendo **6** aikido **7** jujitsu, jujutsu **8** jiujitsu
school: **4** dojo
teacher: **6** sensei

karma
4 fate **7** destiny **9** emanation

kaross, e.g.
3 rug

kasha
5 grain **8** porridge **9** buckwheat

Katharina
father: **8** Baptista
suitor: **9** Petruchio

Katrina's suitor
9 Brom Bones **12** Ichabod Crane

katydid
6 insect **11** grasshopper

katzenjammer
3 din **5** hoo-ha, noise **6** clamor, hoo-hah, hubbub, racket, rumpus **7** clamour **8** brouhaha, distress, foofaraw, hangover, headache **9** cacophony, commotion

kava
5 shrub **6** pepper **8** beverage

kayo
4 deck **5** floor **6** defeat, finish **8** knockout **9** finish off **11** coup de grace

Kazakhstan
capital: **6** Akmola, Astana
city: **5** Semey **8** Pavlodar, Shymkent
lake: **6** Tengiz **8** Balkhash
language: **6** Kazakh **7** Russian
monetary unit: **5** tenge
mountain: **10** Khan-Tengri
neighbor: **5** China **6** Russia **10** Kyrgyzstan, Uzbekistan **12** Turkmenistan
river: **4** Ural **6** Irtysh **8** Syr Dar'ya
sea: **4** Aral **7** Caspian

Kazan of film
4 Elia

Kazantzakis hero
5 Zorba (Alexis)

kea
6 parrot

___ Kea
5 Mauna

Keanu role
3 Neo

Keats poem
5 Lamia **8** Endymion, Hyperion, Isabella, To Autumn **11** Ode to Psyche **12** Eve of St. Agnes (The) **16** Ode on a Grecian Urn **17** Ode to a Nightingale

kebab
8 shashlik

kedge, e.g.
6 anchor

keel
4 boat, lean, ship **5** barge, pitch, ridge, slump **6** carina **7** capsize **8** overturn **11** centerboard

keen
4 avid, fine, wail, yowl **5** acute, alert, eager, honed, mourn, neato, nifty, sharp, smart, super **6** ardent, astute, bewail, bright, clever, gung ho, intent, lament, peachy, shrewd **7** anxious,

fervent, intense, whetted, zealous **8** animated, spirited **9** fine-edged, impatient, sensitive, wonderful **10** perceptive, razor-sharp **11** lamentation, penetrating, quick-witted, sharp-witted **12** enthusiastic, sharp-sighted

keenness
3 wit **4** edge, zeal **6** acuity, acumen **10** enthusiasm **11** discernment, penetration **12** incisiveness, perspicacity

keep
3 own **4** hold, jail, mind, obey, save, stay, stet, tend **5** lodge, stock **6** castle, comply, detain, living, lockup, manage, prison, retain **7** abstain, conduct, confine, forbear, fulfill, possess, refrain, reserve **8** conserve, fortress, maintain, preserve, withhold **9** constrain **10** livelihood, sustenance **11** maintenance, subsistence

keep back
3 bar, dam **4** curb, hold, save, stay **6** detain, retain, retard, stifle **7** contain, inhibit, repress, reserve **8** restrain, restrict, suppress, withhold

keeper
5 guard **6** warden **7** big fish, curator **8** Cerberus, guardian, watchdog **9** custodian, protector

keeping
4 care, ward **5** aegis, trust **6** charge **7** custody, support **8** wardship **9** provision **10** caretaking, conformity, observance **11** maintenance **12** conservation, guardianship

keep on
4 last **5** abide **6** endure, retain **7** persist **8** continue **9** hang tough, persevere

keep out
3 ban, bar **4** hold, stop **5** block, check, debar **6** forbid **7** embargo, exclude **8** prohibit, turn back **9** blackball

keepsake
5 relic, token **6** trophy **7** memento **8** memorial, reminder, souvenir **11** remembrance

keep up
7 persist, prolong, sustain **8** continue, maintain, preserve **9** persevere

kef
3 pot **4** dope, hash, hemp, weed **5** grass **7** hashish **8** Mary Jane **9** marijuana **10** dreaminess **11** tranquility **12** tranquillity

Kefauver of Tennessee
5 Estes

keg
3 tun **4** butt, cask, pipe **6** barrel, firkin, vessel **8** hogshead **9** container

kegler
6 bowler

keister
3 bum, end **4** buns, butt, duff, rear, rump, seat, tail, tush **5** fanny **6** behind, bottom, heinie **8** backside, buttocks, derriere **9** posterior

keloid
4 scar

kelp
5 kombu **7** seaweed
relative: **4** nori **5** arame, dulse **6** hijiki, wakame

kelpie
3 dog, nix **5** naiad, nixie **6** sprite **8** sheepdog

Kemo Sabe
10 Lone Ranger

ken
4 view **5** grasp, range, reach, scope, sight **7** horizon, purview **9** knowledge **10** perception **13** comprehension, understanding

kenaf
5 fiber **8** hibiscus

Kenilworth author
5 Scott (Walter)

Kennedy Library architect
3 Pei (I. M.)

Kennedy novel
8 Ironweed

kennel
4 pack **5** board **6** gutter **7** shelter **9** enclosure

keno
4 game
relative: **5** beano, bingo, lotto

Kentucky
capital: **9** Frankfort
city: **9** Lexington **10** Louisville **12** Bowling Green
nickname: **9** Bluegrass (State)
park: **11** Mammoth Cave
racecourse: **14** Churchill Downs
river: **4** Ohio
state bird: **8** cardinal
state flower: **9** goldenrod
state tree: **11** tulip poplar

Kentucky bluegrass
3 Poa

Kenya
capital: **7** Nairobi
city: **6** Kisumu, Nakuru **7** Mombasa
lake: **7** Turkana **8** Victoria
monetary unit: **8** shilling
mountain: **5** Elgon, Kenya
neighbor: **5** Sudan **6** Uganda **7** Somalia **8** Ethiopia, Tanzania
river: **4** Tana

Kenyan rebel
6 Mau Mau

kepi
3 cap, hat

kerchief
6 hankie **7** bandana **8** babushka, bandanna, kaffiyeh, keffiyeh
Scottish: 5 curch

kerf
3 cut **4** nick, slit **5** cleft, notch **6** groove

kerfuffle
3 ado, row **4** flap, fuss, moil, stir, to-do **5** hoo-ha **6** dust-up, hoo-hah, pother, ruckus, rumpus **7** bobbery, turmoil **8** ballyhoo, foofaraw **9** commotion **11** disturbance

kermis
4 fair **8** carnival, festival

kernel
3 nub, nut **4** core, crux, gist, meat, pith, seed **5** grain **6** nubbin, upshot **7** essence, nucleus **9** substance

Kerouac novel
6 Big Sur **9** On the Road **10** Dharma Bums (The) **13** Subterraneans (The)

Kesey novel
21 Sometimes a Great Notion **25** One Flew over the Cuckoo's Nest

kestrel
4 bird, hawk **6** falcon **9** windhover

ketch
4 boat **6** vessel **8** sailboat **10** watercraft

ketone
7 acetone, camphor

kettle
3 pot **6** hollow, vessel **7** caldron, marmite, pothole **8** cauldron
handle: 4 bail

kettledrum
5 naker **7** timpani (plural), timpano
Moorish: 6 atabal

key
4 clue, isle, reef **5** basic, islet, ivory, vital **6** cotter, island, legend, master, opener, samara, spline, ticket, tip-off **7** central, crucial, digital, pivotal **8** critical, password, solution, tonality **9** essential, important, requisite **10** open sesame **11** fundamental
combining form: 5 clavi, clavo
notch: 4 ward
type: 8 skeleton

keyboard
6 manual **7** clavier
instrument: 5 organ, piano **6** spinet **7** celesta, celeste **8** carillon **9** accordion **10** clavichord **11** harpsichord
key: 3 Alt, Esc **4** Ctrl

key fruit
6 samara

Key Largo
director: 6 Huston (John)
star: 6 Bacall (Lauren), Bogart (Humphrey)

key man
5 chief **7** kingpin **9** locksmith

keynote
4 core, crux, gist, pith, tone **5** theme, tonic

keynoter
6 orator **7** speaker

Keystone Kops director
7 Sennett (Max)

Keystone State
12 Pennsylvania

khaki
3 tan **4** buff, ecru **5** brown, cloth, color **7** garment, uniform

khamsin
4 wind
relative: 7 mistral, sirocco **8** scirocco

khan
5 chief, ruler **9** chieftain, sovereign **11** caravansary

___ Khan
3 Aga **5** Chaka, Kubla, Shere **6** Kublai **7** Genghis

Khayyám of poetry
4 Omar

khedive
5 ruler **7** viceroy

Khomeini, e.g.
4 imam **9** ayatollah

Ki
mother: 5 Nammu
son: 5 Enlil

kiang
3 ass **7** wild ass

kibble
4 meal **5** grain, grind **9** pulverize

kibbutz
4 co-op, farm **7** commune **10** collective, settlement **11** cooperative

kibe
4 heel, sore **8** swelling **9** chilblain

kibitz
4 chat **6** banter, butt in, meddle **7** comment, intrude, obtrude **9** interfere

kibitzer
7 meddler **8** busybody, observer **9** buttinsky, spectator **10** rubberneck

kibosh
3 hex **4** jinx, stop **5** check, curse

kick
4 bang, boot, punt **6** recoil, thrill, wallop

kicker
5 catch **6** clause, punter **9** condition, fine print

kick in
3 die, pay **4** give **5** begin, put up, start **6** donate, pony up **7** cough up, fork out **8** fork over, hand over **10** contribute

kick off
3 die **4** open **5** begin, croak, start **6** launch **8** commence, drop dead, embark on, initiate **10** inaugurate

kick out
3 axe, can **4** dump, fire, oust, sack **5** eject, evict, expel **6** bounce **7** cashier, dismiss **9** discharge

kickshaw
5 curio, goody, treat **6** bauble, dainty, gewgaw, morsel, tidbit, trifle **7** bibelot, trinket **8** delicacy **9** bagatelle **10** knickknack

kid
3 guy, rag, rib, tot **4** dupe, fool, gull, hoax, jest, joke, josh, razz, tyke **5** bairn, child, jolly, trick, youth **6** banter, befool, moppet, nipper **7** deceive, toddler, younger **8** flimflam, hoodwink, juvenile **9** bamboozle, youngling, youngster

kidnap
6 abduct, snatch **8** shanghai

kidney
3 ilk **4** kind, sort, type **5** gland, organ
combining form: **4** reni, reno **5** nephr **6** nephro
related to: **5** renal

kidney-shaped
8 reniform
nut: **6** cashew

kielbasa
7 sausage

kif
3 pot **4** hash, hemp, weed **5** grass **7** hashish **8** Mary Jane **9** marijuana **10** dreaminess **11** tranquility **12** tranquillity

kilderkin
3 keg, tun **4** butt, cask **6** barrel, firkin **8** hogshead

kilim
3 mat, rug **6** carpet

kill
3 axe, end, ice, nix, off, zap **4** do in, prey, slay, stop, veto **5** creek, croak, erase, quash, scrag, snuff, waste, whack **6** defeat, delete, finish, murder, quarry, rub out, stifle **7** bump off, butcher, channel, destroy, execute **8** blow away, carry off, dispatch, knock off, massacre **9** sacrifice, slaughter **10** annihilate **11** assassinate, exterminate

killer
5 bravo **6** gunman, hit man **7** butcher, torpedo **8** assassin, homicide **9** cutthroat
combining form: **4** cide

Killer Angels author
6 Shaara (Michael)

killer whale
4 orca

killing
5 blood, fatal **6** deadly, lethal, mortal, murder **7** carnage **8** butchery, foul play, homicide **9** bloodbath, bloodshed, slaughter **12** manslaughter
of a race: **8** genocide
of bacteria: **11** bactericide
of a brother: **10** fratricide
of a father: **9** patricide
of a king: **8** regicide
of a mother: **9** matricide
of a relative: **9** parricide
of a sister: **10** sororicide
of oneself: **7** suicide
of plants: **9** herbicide

killjoy
6 downer, grinch, grouch **7** spoiler **8** doomster, sourpuss **9** Cassandra, defeatist, doomsayer, gloomy Gus, pessimist, worrywart **10** spoilsport, wet blanket

Kilmer poem
5 Trees

kiln
4 oast, oven **7** furnace

kilt
5 skirt
accessory: **7** sporran
fabric: **5** plaid **6** tartan

kilter
4 trim **5** order, shape **6** fettle, repair **7** fitness **9** condition

kimono
4 gown, robe
sash: **3** obi

kin
3 sib **4** clan, folk, sept **5** blood, flesh, house, stock, tribe **6** family **7** lineage, related **8** relation, relative

kind
3 ilk **4** good, like, sort, type, warm **5** breed, class, genre **6** benign, gentle, humane, loving, nature, stripe, tender **7** affable, amiable, clement, essence, feather, lenient, quality, species, variety **8** category, merciful, tolerant **9** character **10** altruistic, benevolent, charitable, forbearing, responsive **11** considerate, good-hearted, good-humored, good-natured, openhearted, soft-hearted, sympathetic, warmhearted

kindergarten lesson
4 ABCs

kindle
4 bear, fire, stir, wake, whet **5** light, rally, rouse, spark, start, waken **6** arouse, awaken, bestir,

excite, foment, ignite, incite **7** inflame, provoke **8** activate **9** galvanize, instigate, stimulate **10** illuminate

kindliness
8 goodwill, sympathy **9** affection **10** solicitude **11** benevolence

kindly
6 benign, gentle **7** benefic **8** friendly, generous, gracious, pleasant **9** agreeable, benignant **10** beneficent, beneficial **11** considerate, goodhearted, sympathetic

kindness
5 favor, mercy **7** service **8** clemency, courtesy, goodwill, sympathy **10** compassion, generosity, indulgence **11** benevolence **13** consideration

kind of
5 quite **6** fairly, pretty, rather **8** passably, somewhat **9** tolerably **10** more or less, reasonably, relatively

kindred
3 sib **4** clan, folk, like, sept **5** alike, blood, flesh, house, stock, tribe **6** agnate, allied, family **7** cognate, connate, lineage, related, similar **9** relatives **10** affiliated, connatural **11** consanguine

king
3 rex **4** czar, tsar, tzar **5** mogul, ruler **6** tycoon **7** magnate, monarch **9** sovereign
Albanian: **3** Zog **7** William
Assyrian: **6** Sargon **11** Sennacherib, Shalmaneser
Babylonian: **6** Sargon **9** Hammurabi **10** Belshazzar
Belgian: **6** Albert **7** Leopold **8** Baudouin
Bohemian: **9** Wenceslas **10** Wenceslaus
Bulgarian: **5** Boris **6** Simeon
Damascus: **8** Benhadad
Danish: **4** Abel, Eric, Gorm, Hans, John, Olaf **5** Sweyn **6** Canute, Harold, Magnus **8** Nicholas, Waldemar **9** Christian, Frederick **11** Christopher
Dutch: **7** William
Egyptian: **3** Tut **4** Pepi, Seti **5** Khufu, Menes, Necho **6** Cheops, Ramses **7** Harmhab, Osorkon, Psamtik, Ptolemy **8** Ikhnaton, Thothmes, Thutmose **9** Amenhotep, Sesostris **11** Tutankhamen
English: **4** John **5** Henry, James **6** Alfred, Canute, Edmund, Edward, Egbert, George, Harold **7** Charles, Richard, Stephen, William **8** Ethelred **9** Athelstan, Ethelbald, Ethelbert
French: **3** Odo, roi **4** Jean, John **5** Henri, Henry, Louis, Pepin, Raoul **6** Philip, Robert, Rudolf **7** Charles, Francis, Lothair **8** François **9** Hugh Capet **11** Charlemagne
German: **4** Carl, Karl **5** König, Louis **6** Lothar, Ludwig **7** Charles, Lothair
Greek (modern): **4** Paul **6** George **9** Alexander **11** Constantine
Hawaiian: **10** Kamehameha
Hungarian: **4** Atli **6** Attila
Hunnish: **4** Atli **6** Attila
Indian: **4** raja **5** rajah
Irish: **9** Brian Boru
Italian: **7** Humbert, Umberto
Jordanian: **5** Talal **7** Hussein **8** Abdullah
Judah: (see at **Judah**)
Judean: **5** Herod
legendary: **3** Lud **4** Cole, Ludd, Nudd **6** Arthur
Lydian: **5** Gyges **7** Croesus **8** Alyattes
Norwegian: **4** Eric, Erik, Inge, Olaf **5** Sweyn **6** Haakon, Harald, Harold, Magnus, Sigurd, Sverre
Ostrogothic: **9** Theodoric
Persian: **5** Cyrus **6** Darius, Xerxes
Portuguese: **4** John **5** Henry, Louis, Peter **6** Carlos, Edward, Manuel, Sancho **7** Alfonso **9** Ferdinand, Sebastian
Prussian: **7** Wilhelm, William **9** Frederick, Friedrich
relating to: **5** regal, royal
Saudi Arabian: **4** Saud **6** Faisal **9** Abdul-Aziz
Scottish: **4** John **5** David, Edgar, James **6** Duncan **7** Macbeth, Malcolm, William **9** Alexander, Donalbane **10** David Bruce **11** Robert Bruce
Shakespearean: **4** John, Lear **5** Henry **7** Richard
Spanish: **3** rey **5** Louis **6** Philip **7** Alfonso, Amadeus, Charles **9** Ferdinand **10** Juan Carlos
Spartan: **8** Leonidas
Swedish: **4** Eric, John **5** Oscar **6** Birger, Gustav, Haakon, Magnus **7** Charles **8** Gustavus, Waldemar **9** Frederick, Sigismund, Sten Sture
Visigothic: **6** Alaric

King and I land
4 Siam

King Arthur
birthplace: **8** Tintagel
chronicler: **8** Geoffrey (of Monmouth)
court site: **7** Camelot **8** Caerleon
deathplace: **6** Camlan
father: **5** Uther
father-in-law: **9** Laodogant, Leodegran **11** Leodegrance
foster father: **5** Ector
jester: **7** Dagonet
knight: **3** Kay **4** Bors **5** Balan, Balin **6** Gareth, Gawain, Modred **7** Galahad, Geraint, Lamerok, Mordred, Tristan **8** Bedivere, Lancelot, Parsifal, Percival, Tristram **9** Launcelot
lance: **3** Ron
last abode: **6** Avalon
last name: **9** Pendragon
magician: **6** Merlin
mother: **6** Ygerne **7** Igraine
nephew: **6** Gareth, Modred **7** Mordred

queen: 9 Guinevere
shield: 7 Pridwin
sister: 7 Morgain 11 Morgan le Fay
slayer: 6 Modred 7 Mordred
son: 6 Modred 7 Mordred
steward: 3 Kay
sword: 9 Excalibur
victim: 6 Modred 7 Mordred
wife: 9 Guinevere

king crab
7 limulus

kingdom
5 realm 6 domain, empire 7 demesne 8 monarchy

kingdom come
4 Zion 6 heaven 8 paradise 9 hereafter 10 afterworld

kingfish
4 boss 6 bigwig, honcho, master 7 big shot, croaker 8 mackerel

kingfisher
7 halcyon 10 kookaburra

King Kong
3 ape
director: 6 Cooper (Merian C.) 7 Jackson (Peter) 10 Guillermin (John)
film studio: 3 RKO
home: 11 Skull Island
star: 4 Wray (Fay) 5 Lange (Jessica), Watts (Naomi)

King Lear
author: 11 Shakespeare (William)
daughter: 5 Regan 7 Goneril 8 Cordelia
servant: 6 Oswald
son: 5 Edgar 6 Edmund

kingly
5 regal, royal 6 august, lordly, regnal 7 exalted 8 imperial, majestic 9 imperious, masterful, monarchal, sovereign 10 monarchial 11 monarchical

King novel
6 Carrie, Misery 7 Shining (The) 8 Dead Zone (The) 9 Dark Tower (The), Green Mile (The), Salem's Lot 11 Firestarter, Pet Sematary

King Philip
7 Metacom 9 Metacomet

kingpin
4 boss, capo, guru, head 5 chief, mogul 6 bigwig, honcho, top dog 7 big shot, magnate 9 top banana 10 head honcho, mastermind

Kingsley or Martin
4 Amis

Kings Peak range
5 Uinta

Kingu
consort: 6 Tiamat
slayer: 6 Marduk

kink
4 bend, curl, knot, whim 5 cramp, crick, quirk, snarl, spasm, twist 6 tangle 8 crotchet 11 peculiarity 12 eccentricity, idiosyncrasy, imperfection

Kinks' lady
4 Lola

kinky
3 odd 4 bent 5 curly, outré, ultra, weird 6 curled, far-out, frizzy, quirky 7 bizarre, deviant, knotted, strange, twisted 9 eccentric 10 outlandish

kiosk
5 booth, stand 8 pavilion 9 newsstand 11 summerhouse

kip
3 bed, nap 4 hide, pelt, skin 5 sleep

Kipling work
3 Kim 6 L'Envoi 8 Gunga Din, Mandalay 10 Fuzzy Wuzzy 11 Jungle Books (The), Recessional 13 Just So Stories, Soldiers Three 15 Light That Failed (The), Puck of Pook's Hill 18 Captains Courageous

Kiribati
capital: 6 Tarawa
island, island group: 4 Line 6 Banaba 7 Gilbert, Phoenix
location: 7 Oceania

kirk
6 church

kirsch, e.g.
6 brandy 7 liqueur

kirtle
4 coat, gown 5 dress, tunic

Kish
father: 3 Ner 4 Abdi 5 Abiel, Jeiel 6 Jehiel
son: 4 Saul

kismet
3 lot 4 doom, fate, luck 6 Moirai 7 destiny, fortune
relative: 5 karma

kiss
4 buss, neck, peck 5 graze, smack, spoon 6 cookie, glance, smooch 7 lip-lock 8 osculate, pucker up 10 osculation

kisser
3 gob, mug, pan 4 face, lips, puss 5 mouth 7 piehole

kissing disease
4 mono

Kiss sculptor
5 Rodin (Auguste)

kit
3 set 4 gear, pelt 5 group 6 outfit, tackle, violin 7 package 8 caboodle 9 container 10 collection

kitchen
4 mess **6** galley **7** cuisine **8** scullery
abbreviation: 3 tsp. **4** tbsp.
appliance: (see at **appliance**)
boss: 4 chef
(see also **cooking**)

kite
4 hawk, sail, soar **5** check, glede, hurry, mosey **7** saunter, take off **8** clear out, hightail, predator **9** spinnaker

kith
3 kin, sib **4** clan, folk **6** family **7** friends, kindred, kinfolk **9** neighbors, relatives

kitsch
4 camp, junk **9** vulgarity

kittenish
3 coy **6** frisky **7** playful **10** frolicsome **11** mischievous

kitty
3 cat, pot **4** ante, fund, pool, puss **5** pussy **6** feline, stakes **7** jackpot

kiwi
4 bird **5** fruit **6** ratite **7** Apteryx **12** New Zealander
relative: 3 emu **4** rhea **7** ostrich

klatch
5 bunch, group **7** meeting **9** gathering **11** get-together

Klemperer on the podium
4 Otto

kleptomaniac
5 thief **7** booster **10** shoplifter

Klondike's territory
5 Yukon

klutz
3 oaf **4** boob, clod, gawk, lout, lump **5** looby **6** lubber, lummox **7** bungler, palooka **8** shlemiel **9** schlemiel **10** stumblebum

klutzy
5 inept **6** clumsy **7** awkward **8** bumbling **9** all thumbs, maladroit **10** blundering

knack
4 bent, gift, head **5** flair, forte, skill, trick **6** genius, talent **7** ability, aptness, command, faculty, know-how, mastery **8** aptitude, capacity, facility **9** dexterity, expertise, stratagem

knapsack
4 pack **8** backpack

knar
4 burl

knave
3 cad **4** heel, jack **5** fraud, rogue, scamp **6** rascal, varlet **7** bounder, lowlife, villain **8** scalawag, swindler **9** miscreant, scoundrel **10** blackguard **11** rapscallion

knavery
5 fraud **6** deceit **8** mischief, trickery, villainy **9** chicanery, deception, rascality **10** dishonesty

knavish
5 lying **6** shifty, tricky **7** devious, roguish **8** rascally **9** deceitful, deceptive, dishonest **10** mendacious **12** unscrupulous

knead
4 form, mold, work **5** press, shape **7** massage **10** manipulate

knee
5 joint
bend: 9 genuflect **12** genuflection
bone: 7 patella

kneeler
5 stool **7** cushion **8** prie-dieu **9** footstool

knell
4 bong, peal, ring, toll **5** chime **6** summon **7** warning **8** announce, proclaim

knickknack
3 toy **4** dido **5** curio **6** bauble, gadget, gewgaw, trifle **7** bibelot, novelty, trinket, whatnot, whatsit **8** gimcrack, ornament, souvenir **9** bagatelle, bric-a-brac, objet d'art
shelf: 7 étagère, whatnot

Knievel of motorcyle fame
4 Evel

knife
3 ulu **4** bolo, kris, shiv, snee **5** blade, bowie, panga, shank, sword **6** barong, cutter, dagger, lancet, parang, sickle **7** cleaver, machete, scalpel **8** stiletto, yataghan **11** switchblade
case: 6 sheath
handle: 4 haft, hilt
maker: 6 cutler **7** grinder

knifelike
4 keen **5** acute, sharp **7** cutting **8** piercing, stabbing **11** penetrating

knight
3 dub, sir **5** eques **8** cavalier, chessman, horseman **9** caballero, chevalier
code: 8 chivalry
competition: 7 listing, tilting **8** jousting **10** tournament
German: 6 Ritter
servant: 4 page **5** valet **6** squire
title: 3 sir
wife: 4 lady

knighthood
8 chivalry

knightly
4 bold **5** brave, noble **6** heroic **7** gallant, valiant **10** chivalrous

Knight of the Round Table
see **King Arthur**

Knight of the Rueful Countenance
7 Quixote (Don)

knit
4 bind, heal, join, link, mend, purl **5** plait, unite, weave **6** fabric, stitch **7** conjoin, crochet **8** contract **9** interlace **10** intertwine, interweave

knitting
material: 4 yarn
stitch: 3 rib **4** purl **6** garter
tool: 6 needle

knob
3 bun, bur, nub **4** bump, burl, burr, dial, hill, hump, lump, node, umbo **5** bulge, gnarl, knoll, mound, tuner **6** button, finial, handle, nubble, pommel **7** hillock **12** protuberance

knobkerrie
3 bat **4** club, mace **5** billy **6** cudgel, weapon **7** war club **8** bludgeon **9** billy club, shillalah, truncheon **10** shillelagh

knock
3 bob, hit, rap, tap **4** bash, blow, bump, cuff, lick, swat **5** blame, clout, fault, pound, swipe, thump **6** strike **7** censure, condemn, setback **8** denounce, reversal **9** criticize **10** denunciate

knockabout
5 rough, rowdy, sloop, tough **7** roaming, vagrant **10** boisterous

knock down
4 drop, earn, fell, gain, raze **5** floor, level, lower **6** lay low, reduce **7** acquire, bring in, flatten **9** dismantle **11** disassemble

knocker
6 carper, critic **7** caviler **8** caviller, quibbler **10** complainer, criticizer **11** fault-finder

knock off
3 rob **4** copy, do in, halt, kill, quit, slay, stop **5** cease, whack **6** deduct, defeat, desist, finish, murder, rub out **7** execute, imitate, take out, take ten **8** discount, overcome, subtract, take five **9** liquidate **11** assassinate, call it quits, counterfeit

knockout
4 kayo, lulu **5** beaut, daisy, dandy, dilly, doozy, final **6** beauty, corker, doozie, eyeful, looker, lovely **7** stunner **8** decisive, jim-dandy, striking, stunning **9** deathblow, finishing, humdinger **10** attractive **11** coup de grace, crackerjack, sockdolager

knock over
3 rob **4** down, drop, fell **5** amaze, floor, steal, upset **6** boggle, hijack, hold up, lay low, topple **7** flatten, stick up **9** bring down, eliminate, overpower, overthrow, overwhelm, prostrate

knoll
4 hill, knob, rise **5** mound **7** hillock

knot
3 bow, tie **4** bond, burl, burr, link, loop, lump, node **5** bunch, gnarl, hitch, nexus **6** jungle, tangle **8** ligament, ligature, vinculum
hair: 7 chignon
in fiber: 3 nep
kind: 4 bend, loop, slip **5** hitch **6** granny, splice, square **7** bowline **9** sheet bend **10** clove hitch, sheepshank

knotty
4 hard **6** sticky **7** complex, gnarled, Gordian **8** involved **9** byzantine, difficult, elaborate, intricate **10** formidable **11** complicated, problematic

knout
4 flog, lash, whip **7** scourge

know
3 wot **5** grasp **6** fathom, intuit **7** discern, realize **9** apprehend, recognize **10** comprehend, understand
Scottish: 3 ken

knowable
9 graspable **10** cognizable, fathomable **12** intelligible **13** apprehensible

know-how
5 craft, knack, skill **6** talent **7** ability, cunning, faculty, mastery **8** aptitude **9** dexterity, expertise **10** adroitness, expertness **11** proficiency

knowing
3 hep, hip **4** sage, wise **5** aware, blasé, canny, savvy, smart **6** bright, clever, with-it **7** witting, worldly **8** sentient **9** cognizant, conscious, sagacious **10** conversant, discerning, insightful, perceptive **11** worldly-wise **13** sophisticated

know-it-all
6 smarty **7** wise guy **8** wiseacre **10** smart aleck **11** smarty-pants, wisenheimer

knowledge
3 ken **4** data, info, lore, news **5** facts **6** wisdom **7** science **8** learning **9** cognition, education, erudition **10** cognizance **11** information, scholarship **12** intelligence
lack of: 9 ignorance, nescience
mystical: 6 gnosis

knowledgeable
5 savvy **7** erudite, learned **8** educated, informed

know-nothing
4 dolt, dope, fool **5** dummy, dunce, idiot, yahoo **6** dimwit **7** pinhead **8** agnostic, ignorant, numskull **9** benighted, blockhead, brainless, ignoramus, lamebrain, numbskull **10** illiterate, uneducated **11** empty-headed

knuckle
5 joint
combining form: 6 condyl **7** condylo

knucklehead
4 bozo, dolt, dope, fool **5** dummy, dunce, idiot, yahoo **6** dimwit **8** clodpole, numskull **9** ignoramus, lamebrain, numbskull

knuckle under
3 bow **4** cave **5** yield **6** cave in, give in, submit **7** succumb **8** say uncle **9** surrender **10** capitulate

knurl
3 nub **4** bead, knob **5** ridge **12** protuberance

KO
8 knockout

koan
7 paradox

kobold
3 nis **5** dwarf, gnome **6** goblin, spirit, sprite

Kohinoor
3 gem **7** diamond

kohlrabi
7 cabbage **8** Brassica
relative: **4** kale **5** savoy **7** cabbage **8** broccoli **11** cauliflower

kola, e.g.
3 nut **4** tree

komatik
4 sled **6** sledge

kook
3 nut **5** crank, flake, loony, wacko **6** cuckoo, weirdo **7** dingbat, lunatic, oddball **8** crackpot **9** ding-a-ling, fruitcake, screwball **10** crackbrain

kooky
4 bats, daft, nuts **5** batty, crazy, daffy, ditsy, ditzy, dotty, flaky, loony, nutty, silly, wacky, weird **6** freaky, fruity, insane, screwy **7** bizarre, idiotic, lunatic, offbeat, touched **8** demented **9** eccentric, fantastic **10** flipped out, freaked-out, off-the-wall, outlandish

kopeck
4 coin
one hundred: **5** ruble

Koran
chapter: **4** sura
revealer of: **7** Gabriel
scholar: **5** ulama, ulema

Korea, North
capital: **9** Pyongyang
city: **7** Hamhung **8** Ch'ongjin
leader: **9** Kim Il Sung, Kim Jong Il, Kim Jong Un **10** Kim Chong-Il
monetary unit: **3** won
mountain: **6** Paektu
neighbor: **5** China **6** Russia **10** South Korea
sea: **6** Yellow

Korea, South
capital: **5** Seoul
city: **5** Pusan, Taegu **6** Inch'on, Taejon **7** Kwangju
island: **5** Cheju
monetary unit: **3** won
neighbor: **10** North Korea
river: **3** Han **7** Naktong
sea: **5** Japan **6** Yellow

Korean
dynasty: **5** Silla **7** Koguryo
national dish: **6** kimchi

kosher
3 fit **4** pure **5** clean, legit **6** proper **10** acceptable, legitimate, sanctioned **12** satisfactory
not: **4** tref **5** trayf, treif, treyf **7** terefah

Kosinski novel
5 Steps **10** Being There **11** Painted Bird (The)

Kosovo
capital: **8** Priština
city: **7** Prizren
lake: **6** Badovc **8** Gazivoda
monetary unit: **4** euro **5** dinar
neighbor: **6** Serbia **7** Albania **9** Macedonia **10** Montenegro
river: **3** Lab **4** Ibar **6** Erenik **7** Sitnica **9** White Drin

Koussevitzky of music
5 Serge

kowtow
3 bow **4** fawn **5** cower, defer, kneel, toady **6** cringe, grovel **7** honey up, truckle **8** bootlick **11** apple-polish

kraal
3 pen **6** corral **7** village **9** enclosure

kraken
5 squid **9** leviathan **10** giant squid, sea monster

krater
3 jar **4** vase **6** vessel

Kriemhild
brother: **7** Gunther
husband: **5** Etzel **6** Attila **9** Siegfried
slayer: **10** Hildebrand
victim: **5** Hagen

krill
4 brit

kris
6 dagger

Krishna
avatar of: **6** Vishnu
brother: **8** Balarama
father: **8** Vasudeva
mother: **6** Devaki
uncle: **5** Kansa
victim: **5** Kansa

krone fraction
3 ore

Krupa of jazz
4 Gene

Krupp works site
5 Essen

Kubla Khan
author: 9 Coleridge (Samuel Taylor)
intruder's home: 7 Porlock
palace: 6 Xanadu
river: 4 Alph

kudos
4 bays, fame **5** award, glory, honor **6** honors, praise, renown **7** acclaim, bouquet, laurels **8** accolade, bouquets **10** compliment **11** distinction, recognition

kudu
8 antelope
relative: 3 gnu **6** duiker **10** wildebeest

kukri
5 sword

kumquat
5 fruit
kin: 6 orange

Kushner play
15 Angels in America

Kuwait
gulf: 7 Persian
island: 7 Bubiyan **8** Faylakah
language: 6 Arabic **7** Persian
monetary unit: 5 dinar
neighbor: 4 Iraq **11** Saudi Arabia
oasis: 8 Al-Jahrah
ruler: 4 amir, emir **5** ameer, emeer

kvass
4 beer

kvetch
4 beef, crab, fret, fuss **5** gripe, whine **6** grouch, grouse **7** grumble **8** complain **9** bellyache

kyphosis
8 humpback **9** curvature, hunchback

Kyrgyzstan
capital: 7 Bishkek
city: 3 Osh
conqueror: 9 Jöchi Khan
lake: 8 Issyk-Kul
language: 6 Kyrgyz **7** Russian
monetary unit: 3 som
mountain, range: 4 Alai **6** Pobedy **7** Victory **8** Tian Shan **10** Khan-Tengri **11** Kok Shaal-Tau
neighbor: 5 China **10** Kazakhstan, Tajikistan, Uzbekistan
river: 5 Naryn

L

Laadah
father: 6 Shelah
grandfather: 5 Judah

laager
4 camp **6** encamp **7** bivouac

lab
see **laboratory**

Laban
daughter: 4 Leah **6** Rachel
father: 7 Bethuel
grandfather: 5 Nahor
sister: 7 Rebekah

lab culture medium
4 agar

label
3 tag **4** band, mark **6** marker, ticket **7** epithet, sticker **8** classify, hallmark, identify, insignia

labium
3 lip

La Bohème
composer: 7 Puccini (Giacomo)
librettist: 6 Illica (Luigi) **7** Giacosa (Giuseppe)
role: 4 Mimi **6** Benoit **7** Colline, Musetta, Rodolfo **8** Marcello **9** Alcindoro, Schaunard
setting: 5 Paris
source author: 6 Murger (Henri)

labor
4 moil, task, toil, work **5** chore, grind, sweat **6** drudge, effort, strain, strive **7** slavery, travail **8** drudgery, endeavor, exertion, struggle **10** birth pangs, childbirth, donkeywork **12** childbearing
camp: 5 gulag
group: 3 AFL, CIO **5** ILGWU, union **6** AFL-CIO
leader: 5 Hoffa (James, Jimmy), Lewis (John L.), Meany (George) **6** Chavez (Cesar) **7** Gompers (Samuel), Reuther (Walter), Sweeney (John J.) **8** Kirkland (Lane), Randolph (A. Philip)

laboratory
13 proving ground

device: **5** flask **6** beaker, mortar, pestle, retort **7** burette, pipette **8** crucible, test tube **9** petri dish **12** Bunsen burner

Labor Dept. watchdog
4 OSHA

labored
4 hard **6** forced, taxing, tiring **7** arduous **8** strained **9** difficult, effortful, fatiguing, strenuous

laborer
4 esne, hack, hand, peon **5** grind, navvy, prole, slave **6** coolie, drudge, menial **7** workman **10** roustabout, workingman
Mexican: **7** bracero

laborious
4 hard **6** tiring, uphill **7** arduous, onerous, operose **8** diligent, grueling, sedulous, toilsome **9** assiduous, difficult, effortful, strenuous **10** burdensome, unflagging **11** hardworking, industrious, persevering **12** backbreaking

La Brea
4 pits **7** tar pits
fossil: **7** mammoth **8** mastodon **10** saber-tooth

labyrinth
3 web **4** coil, knot, maze, mesh **5** skein, snarl **6** jungle, morass, tangle
builder: **8** Daedalus
hero: **7** Theseus
monster: **8** Minotaur

labyrinthine
4 mazy **6** daedal, knotty **7** complex, Gordian **8** involved, mazelike, tortuous **9** Byzantine, elaborate, intricate **10** convoluted, perplexing **11** bewildering, complicated

lac
5 resin

lace
3 net, tat, tie **4** cord, trim **5** adorn, braid, frill, plait, twine **6** fasten, string **7** entwine, netting, tatting **8** filigree, openwork **9** embroider **10** embroidery, intertwine **11** needlepoint
edge: **5** picot
fall: **5** jabot
ground: **6** reseau
into: **5** abuse **6** attack **7** condemn
kind: **6** bobbin **7** Alençon, guipure, macramé, Maltese, Mechlin, torchon **8** Brussels, Venetian **9** Chantilly **11** needlepoint **12** Valenciennes
make: **3** tat
pattern: **5** toilé

Lacedaemon
6 Sparta

lacerate
3 cut, rip **4** gash, rend, tear **5** slash, wound **6** mangle, pierce **7** afflict, mangled, torment **8** distress

lacework
7 tatting

lachrymose
3 sad **5** teary, weepy **7** doleful, tearful, weeping **8** dolorous, mournful **11** tear-jerking

lack
4 need, want **6** dearth, defect **7** absence, default, deficit, failure, paucity, poverty, require **8** scarcity, shortage **9** privation **10** deficiency, inadequacy, scantiness **13** insufficiency

lackadaisical
4 idle, lazy, limp, slow **5** moony **6** dreamy **7** languid, passive **8** fainéant, indolent, listless, slothful **9** apathetic, enervated **10** languorous, spiritless **11** halfhearted

lackey
5 toady **6** fawner, flunky, minion, vassal **7** footman, servant **8** truckler **9** attendant, sycophant

lacking
3 shy **4** sans **5** minus, needy, short **6** absent, flawed, needed **7** missing, needing, omitted, wanting, without **8** devoid of, impaired **9** defective, deficient **10** deprived of, inadequate, incomplete **11** halfhearted **12** insufficient

lackluster
3 dim **4** arid, blah, drab, dull, flat **5** blind, ho-hum, matte, muted, prosy, rusty, vapid **6** boring, leaden **7** prosaic **8** lifeless, mediocre **9** colorless, tarnished **10** uninspired **13** unimaginative

Laconian
7 Spartan
king: **5** Lelex, Myles **8** Menelaus

laconic
4 curt **5** bluff, blunt, brief, pithy, short, terse **7** brusque, concise **8** succinct

lacquer
5 glaze, gloss **6** enamel, finish **7** shellac, varnish

lacrosse
relative: **7** jai alai
term: **5** clamp **6** crease, crosse, pocket **7** face-off
team: **3** ten

lactate
4 salt **5** ester, nurse **6** suckle **7** secrete **8** wet-nurse **10** breast-feed

lacteal
5 milky **6** cloudy, pearly

lacuna
3 gap, pit **4** void **5** blank, break, space **6** breach, cavity, hiatus **7** caesura **10** deficiency **12** interruption

lacy
4 fine **5** meshy **6** dainty **7** netlike **8** delicate, gossamer **9** filigreed **10** diaphanous

lad
3 boy, son, tad **4** tike, tyke **5** youth **6** shaver **9** shaveling, stripling
Irish: 4 boyo **5** bucko
Scottish: 5 chiel **7** callant

ladder
3 run **5** ranks, scale **6** series **7** ranking **9** hierarchy
piece: 4 rung **6** rundle

ladderlike
6 scalar, scaled **7** stepped **11** scalariform

lade
3 dip, tax **4** bail, load, pack, ship, stow **5** ladle, scoop **6** burden, saddle, weight **8** encumber

la-di-dah
6 chichi, snobby, snooty, too-too **7** elegant, genteel, haughty, stuck-up **8** affected, snobbish **9** conceited, grandiose, high-flown **10** hoity-toity **11** pretentious

ladies' man
4 beau, roué, stud, wolf **5** Romeo **7** amorist, Don Juan, gallant **8** Casanova, lothario **9** womanizer **11** philanderer

lading
4 haul, load **5** cargo, goods **6** burden **7** bailing, dipping, freight, loading, payload **8** shipment **11** consignment

ladle
3 dip **4** bail **5** scoop, spoon **6** dipper

Ladon
6 dragon
father: 7 Phorcus, Phorcys
mother: 4 Ceto
slayer: 8 Heracles, Hercules

___ la Douce
4 Irma

lady
4 dame **5** madam, woman **6** female, madame, matron
French: 4 dame
German: 4 Frau
Italian: 5 donna **7** signora
Muslim: 5 begum
Spanish: 4 doña **6** señora

lady ___
4 luck **5** apple **6** beetle, chapel

ladybug
6 beetle
Australian: 7 vedalia

Lady Chatterley's Lover
author: 8 Lawrence (D. H.)
character: 6 Connie **7** Mellors (Oliver) **9** Constance

Lady Hamilton
4 Emma

lady-killer
4 dude, hunk, roué, stud **5** Romeo **7** amorist, Don Juan, gallant, playboy, seducer **8** Casanova, lothario **11** philanderer **12** heartbreaker

Lady of song
3 Day **4** Gaga

Lady of the Lake, The
5 Ellen (Douglas), Nimue **6** Vivien
author: 5 Scott (Walter)

Lady Windermere's Fan author
5 Wilde (Oscar)

Laertes
father: 8 Acrisius, Polonius
sister: 7 Ophelia
son: 7 Ulysses **8** Odysseus
victim: 6 Hamlet
wife: 8 Anticlea

La Fontaine's forte
5 fable

lag
4 drag, last, poke, slow, tire **5** dally, delay, tarry, trail **6** dawdle, linger, loiter **7** slacken **8** hang back, hindmost, interval **10** dillydally **13** procrastinate

lager
4 beer, brew, malt, suds **7** brewski
alternative: 3 ale

laggard
3 lax **4** slow **5** tardy **6** loafer **7** dawdler **8** dallying, dawdling, delaying, dilatory, flagging, lingerer, loiterer, slowpoke, sluggish, tarrying **9** apathetic, lazybones, lethargic, loitering, straggler **10** behindhand

La Gioconda
8 Mona Lisa
composer: 10 Ponchielli (Amilcare)
painter: 7 da Vinci (Leonardo) **8** Leonardo (da Vinci)

lagniappe
3 tip **4** gift, perk **5** bonus, extra **7** cumshaw, largess **8** dividend, gratuity, largesse **9** baksheesh, pourboire **10** perquisite

lagomorph
4 hare, pika **6** rabbit

lagoon
4 pond, pool **5** bayou, sound **6** strait **7** channel, narrows
rim: 5 atoll

La Guardia of New York
7 airport **8** Fiorello

Lahmi
brother: 7 Goliath
slayer: 7 Elhanan

laid-back
4 cool **6** breezy, casual, mellow **7** relaxed

8 carefree, informal **9** easygoing, hang-loose **10** nonchalant

lair
3 den **4** cave **5** haunt, lodge **6** burrow, refuge **7** hideout, man cave, retreat **8** hideaway **9** sanctuary

Laius
father: 8 Labdacus
slayer, son: 7 Oedipus
wife: 7 Jocasta

lake
4 loch, mere, pond, pool, tarn **5** lough **6** lagoon
Adriatic: 6 Varano
Alberta: 6 Louise
Algeria: 5 Hodna
Alps: 6 Annecy
Arizona-Nevada: 4 Mead
Armenia: 5 Sevan **6** Gokcha, Sevang **9** Lychnitis
Aswan's: 6 Nasser
Australia: 4 Eyre **5** Carey, Cowan, Frome, Wells **6** Barlee **7** Amadeus, Everard, Torrens **8** Gairdner
Austria: 5 Atter, Traun **6** Kammer **8** Attersee **9** Kammersee
Bolivia: 5 Poopó
Botswana: 5 Ngami
British Columbia: 4 Pitt **5** Atlin
California: 4 Mono, Tule **5** Clear, Eagle, Honey
Cambodia: 8 Tonle Sap
Canada: 4 Dyke **8** Manitoba
central Africa: 4 Kivu **5** Mweru **6** Albert
Central America: 5 Guija
central Europe: 5 Leman **6** Geneva, Lugano **7** Ceresio **8** Bodensee **9** Constance
central North America: 5 Rainy
Chile: 4 Laja **5** Ranco
China: 6 Poyang **8** Dongting
Colorado: 5 Grand
Denmark: 5 Esrum
east Africa: 6 Rudolf **7** Turkana
east Asia: 6 Khanka **7** Xingkai **8** Hsingkai
east central Africa: 8 Victoria **10** Tanganyika
east China: 3 Tai **5** Dalai, Hulun
Ethiopia: 4 Tana, Zwai **5** Abaya, Shala, Shamo, Tsana **8** Stefanie **9** Chew Bahir
Finland: 5 Inari
Florida: 5 Worth **10** Okeechobee
Germany: 5 Ammer, Chiem **8** Ammersee, Chiemsee
Ghana: 5 Volta
Great: 4 Erie **5** Huron **7** Ontario **8** Michigan, Superior
Greece: 5 Bolbe, Volvi
Guatemala: 7 Atitlán
Honduras: 5 Yojoa
Honshu: 3 Omi **4** Biwa, Suwa, Yodo
Hungary: 7 Balaton **10** Plattensee
Idaho: 4 Waha **5** Grays **6** Priest **11** Coeur d'Alene, Pend Oreille
India: 3 Dal **5** Wular **6** Chilka
Indonesia: 4 Poso, Toba **5** Ranau
Iowa: 5 Storm
Iran: 5 Niriz, Shahi, Urmia **8** Matianus, Urumiyeh **9** Bakhtigan
Ireland: 3 Gur, Ree **4** Conn, Derg, Mask **5** Allen, Arrow, Leane
Israel: 12 Bahr Tabariya, Sea of Galilee
Israel-Jordan: 7 Dead Sea
Italy: 4 Como, Iseo, Nemi **5** Garda **6** Albano **7** Bolsena, Perugia **8** Maggiore **9** Trasimene
Japan: 4 Imba **8** Imbanuma
Kazakhstan: 7 Balqash **8** Balkhash
Louisiana: 4 Soda **9** Catahoula **13** Pontchartrain
Maine: 6 Sebago **9** Moosehead
Mali: 4 Debo
Manitoba: 4 Gods **5** Cedar, Moose **8** Winnipeg
Mexico: 7 Chapala
Michigan: 4 Burt
Minnesota: 3 Red **4** Cass, Gull, Swan **5** Leech **6** Itasca **9** Mille Lacs **10** Minnetonka, of the Woods **11** Lac qui Parle
Minnesota-Wisconsin: 5 Pepin
Mongolian: 3 Har **5** Har Us, Khara **8** Khara Usu
Montana: 8 Medicine
mountain: 4 tarn
Myanmar: 4 Inle
Nevada: 4 Ruby **7** Pyramid
Nevada-California: 5 Tahoe
New Hampshire: 5 Squam **13** Winnipesaukee
New Jersey: 5 Union
New York: 4 Long **5** Chazy, Keuka **6** Cayuga, George, Oneida, Otsego, Owasco, Placid, Seneca **7** Crooked, Saranac **8** Onondaga, Saratoga **9** Champlain **10** Chautauqua **11** Canandaigua, Skaneateles
New Zealand: 4 Ohau **5** Hawea, Taupo **6** Pukaki, Wanaka **8** Wakatipu
Nicaragua: 7 Managua
North Africa: 4 Chad
Northern Ireland: 5 Neagh
Northwest Territories: 4 Gras **5** Baker, Garry, Pelly **9** Great Bear **10** Great Slave
Norway: 5 Mjosa
Nova Scotia: 7 Bras d'Or
Ontario: 4 Rice, Seul **5** Trout
Oregon: 5 Abert **6** Crater **7** Malheur, Wallowa
Paraguay: 4 Ypoá
Peru: 5 Junín **13** Chinchaycocha
Philippines: 4 Bato, Taal **5** Lanao **6** Bombon
Poland: 5 Mamry, Mauer
Quebec: 5 Minto, Payne

Russia: **3** Seg **5** Chany, Ilmen, Lacha, Onega **6** Baikal, Ladoga **7** Rybinsk **10** Eltonskoye **11** Ladozhskoye
Saskatchewan: **4** Cree **5** Ronge
Scotland: **3** Ard, Awe **4** Doon, Earn, Ness, Oich, Shin, Sloy **5** Leven, Lochy, Maree, Morar, Shiel **6** Lomond
Siberia: **6** Baikal, Baykal
South Africa: **4** Kosi
South America: **5** Merin, Mirim **8** Titicaca
South Carolina: **7** Wateree
South Dakota: **5** Andes
southeast Africa: **5** Nyasa **6** Nyassa
southwest Europe: **5** Ohrid **7** Okhrida
Sweden: **5** Asnen, Roxen **6** Siljan, Vänern, Vetter **7** Malaren, Vattern
Switzerland: **3** Zug **4** Biel, Joux **5** Zuger **6** Bieler, Bienne, Brienz, Sarnen, Sarner, Zurich **7** Lucerne, Lungern **8** Brienzer, Züricher **9** Neuchâtel, Zürichsee
Tajikistan: **7** Karakul
Tanzania: **5** Rukwa
Texas-Louisiana: **5** Caddo
Tibet: **4** Na-mu **6** Nam Tso, Tengri
Turkey: **3** Tuz, Van **4** Bafa, Nice **5** Iznik, Sugla **6** Nicaea
Uganda: **5** Kyoga
Utah: **6** Powell, Sevier **9** Great Salt
Vermont: **9** Champlain
Wales: **4** Bala
Washington: **4** Omak **5** Moses **6** Chelan **9** Wenatchee
western China: **4** Ai-pi **6** Ebinur
western United States: **4** Bear **5** Tahoe
Wisconsin: **5** Green **9** Winnebago
Yellowstone National Park: **5** Heart, Lewis **8** Shoshone
Zaire: **5** Tumba
Zambia: **9** Bangweolo, Bangweulu

lake group
central North America: **5** Great, HOMES
Egypt: **5** Balah
Maine: **8** Rangeley
New York: **6** Finger
Saskatchewan: **5** Quill
Twin: **8** Washinee **9** Washining

lake herring
5 cisco

Lake poet
7 Southey (Robert) **9** Coleridge (Samuel Taylor) **10** Wordsworth (William)

Lake Wobegon Days author
7 Keillor (Garrison)

Lakmé
aria: **8** Bell Song
composer: **7** Delibes (Léo)

Lakshmi
husband: **6** Vishnu
son: **4** Kama

la-la leader
3 tra

L. A. Law
actor: **3** Dey (Susan) **5** Drake (Larry), Smits (Jimmy) **6** Dysart (Richard), Greene (Michele), Hamlin (Harry), Ruttan (Susan), Tucker (Michael) **7** Bernsen (Corbin), Rachins (Alan) **10** Eikenberry (Jill)
character: **5** Kuzak (Michael) **6** Becker (Arnie), Kelsey (Ann), Melman (Roxanne) **7** Van Owen (Grace), Perkins (Abby) **8** Brackman (Douglas), McKenzie (Leland) **9** Markowitz (Stuart), Sifuentes (Victor)
creator: **6** Bochco (Steven)

lam
3 hit **4** beat, blow, bolt, drub, flay, flee, flog, pelt, skip, whip **5** baste, paste, pound, scram, smack, split, whale **6** batter, beat it, buffet, cut out, decamp, escape, flight, hammer, pummel, strike, thrash, wallop **7** getaway, take off, vamoose **8** breakout, escaping **9** skedaddle

La Mancha's knight
7 Quixote (Don)

lamb
4 cade **5** sheep **6** cosset **8** yeanling
coat: **6** fleece
leg of: **5** gigot
parent: **3** ewe, ram

lambaste
3 pan **4** beat, drub, flay, flog, lash, lick, pelt, slam, slap, trim, whip **5** paste, pound, roast, scold, score, slash, smear **6** assail, attack, berate, cudgel, hammer, pummel, scathe, scorch, thrash, wallop **7** assault, blister, censure, clobber, reprove, scourge, shellac, upbraid **8** bludgeon, denounce, harangue, lash into **9** castigate, excoriate **10** tongue-lash

lambent
5 aglow **6** ardent, bright, lucent **7** beaming, glowing, radiant, shining **8** gleaming, luminous, lustrous **9** brilliant, effulgent, refulgent, twinkling **10** flickering, glittering, shimmering **12** incandescent

lamblike
4 meek **6** docile

lamb of God
5 Jesus **6** Christ **8** Agnus Dei

Lamb's pseudonym
4 Elia

lame
4 gimp, halt, limp **5** gimpy, stiff **6** feeble, flimsy **7** cripple, disable, halting, limping **8** crippled,

disabled, hobbling, inferior **10** inadequate **11** ineffectual **12** contemptible, unconvincing

lamebrain
3 oaf **4** dolt, dope, goof, mutt, simp, yo-yo **5** chump, dummy, dunce, idiot, moron, ninny, noddy, stupe **6** dimwit, donkey, dum-dum, nitwit, noodle **7** airhead, dullard, pinhead, schnook **8** bonehead, clodpoll, dumbbell, dumbhead, imbecile, lunkhead, meathead, numskull **9** blockhead, ignoramus, numbskull, simpleton, thickhead **10** dunderhead, hammerhead, nincompoop **11** chowderhead, chucklehead, knucklehead

Lamech
daughter: **6** Naamah
father: **10** Methuselah
son: **4** Noah **5** Jabal, Jubal **9** Tubalcain
wife: **4** Adah **6** Zillah

lament
3 cry, rue **4** alas, keen, moan, pine, wail, weep **5** alack, dirge, elegy, mourn, oy vey **6** bemoan, bewail, grieve, plaint, regret, repent, sorrow **7** deplore, elegize, wailing, woe is me **8** jeremiad, threnody **9** complaint, ululation

lamentable
6 rueful, woeful **7** doleful, pitiful **8** dolorous, grievous, mournful **9** plaintive, sorrowful **10** afflictive, deplorable, lugubrious, melancholy **11** distressing, regrettable, unfortunate **13** heartbreaking

lamentation
5 elegy, grief **6** plaint **7** anguish, keening, remorse, wailing **8** grieving, mourning, threnody **9** sorrowing, ululation

Lamerok
father: **9** Pellinore
lover: **8** Margawse
slayer: **6** Gawain

lamia
3 hex **5** witch **7** hellcat, vampire **8** succubus **9** sorceress **11** enchantress

Lamia
country: **5** Libya
form: **7** serpent
lover: **4** Zeus

lamina
5 blade, flake, layer, plate, scale

lamp
3 arc **4** bulb, davy **5** klieg, light, torch **7** lantern **10** candelabra **11** candelabrum
floor: **8** torchère **9** torchiere
hanging: **10** chandelier

lampblack
4 soot **6** carbon

Lampetia
father: **6** Apollo, Helios
husband: **9** Asclepius
mother: **6** Neaera
sister: **9** Phaethusa

lampoon
4 mock **5** roast, spoof, squib **6** parody, satire, send-up **7** take off **8** ridicule, satirize **9** burlesque **10** caricature, pasquinade

lamprey
3 eel **8** nine-eyes
hunter: **5** eeler

lanai
5 patio, porch **6** piazza **7** terrace, veranda

lance
4 gash, hurl, open **5** slash, spear **6** impale, pierce, skewer **7** javelin **8** transfix

Lancelot, Launcelot
cousin: **6** Lionel
father: **3** Ban
lover: **6** Elaine **9** Guinevere
son: **7** Galahad
victim: **6** Gawain

lancer
10 cavalryman
Prussian: **5** uhlan

lancet
4 arch **5** blade, knife **6** cutter, window **7** scalpel

land
4 dirt, dock, gain, soil **5** acres, berth, earth, light, manor, shore, terra, tract **6** alight, estate, ground, obtain, pick up, secure **7** acquire, acreage, country, expanse, grounds, procure, set down, terrain, terrene **9** touch down **10** terra firma
alluvial: **5** delta
barren: **5** waste **6** desert
cultivated: **4** farm **5** glebe, tilth **7** tillage
for grazing: **3** lea, ley **5** range **6** meadow **7** pasture
high: **4** hill, mesa **7** plateau **8** mountain
level: **4** mesa **5** plain **7** plateau
low: **4** vale **6** valley **9** intervale
measure: **3** rod **4** acre
open: **3** lea **5** field, green, plain **6** meadow **7** pasture
piece: **3** lot **4** plat, plot **5** tract **6** estate, parcel
reclaimed: **6** polder
sloping: **6** cuesta
strip: **7** isthmus
unit: **4** acre **7** hectare
wet: **3** bog, fen **5** marsh, swamp **6** marish

land east of Eden
3 Nod

landed
4 alit

landing
4 dock, ghat, pier, quay 5 berth, jetty, wharf 7 pierage 8 wharfage

landlord
6 lessor, squire 9 innkeeper 10 freeholder

landmark
5 cairn, guide 9 benchmark, milestone, watershed 11 achievement 12 breakthrough, turning point

Land of Enchantment
9 New Mexico

Land of Lakes
8 Michigan

Land of Opportunity
3 USA 8 Arkansas 12 United States

Land of the Midnight Sun
6 Norway

landowner
6 squire, yeoman
Anglo-Saxon: 5 thane, thegn
Dutch: 7 patroon
Scottish: 5 laird

landscape
5 scene, vista 7 scenery, setting, terrain 8 backdrop, prospect

lane
3 way 4 path, road 5 aisle, alley, byway, track 6 street 7 pathway, roadway 8 footpath 10 passageway

Lane's Daily Planet suitor
5 Olsen (Jimmy)

Langland work
12 Piers Plowman

lang syne
4 past, yore 10 yesteryear

___ Lang Syne
4 Auld

language
4 cant 5 argot, idiom, lingo, prose, slang 6 jargon, patois, speech, tongue 7 dialect, lexicon, palaver 10 vernacular, vocabulary 11 terminology
ambiguous: 8 newspeak 10 double-talk
ancient: 5 Greek, Latin 6 Hebrew 8 Etruscan, Sanskrit
artificial: 3 Ido 7 Volapük 9 Esperanto
Bantu: 3 Ila
classical: 5 Greek, Latin
combining form: 4 glot 5 gloss, glott 6 glosso, glotto
criminal: 5 argot
expert: 8 linguist, polyglot
informal: 4 jive 5 lingo, slang
meaningless: 6 babble, jabber 7 blather 9 gibberish 10 mumbo-jumbo
mixed: 6 creole, pidgin
Pakistani: 4 Urdu
pretentious: 7 bombast, fustian 8 claptrap
regional: 7 dialect
relating to: 10 linguistic
Romance: 6 French 7 Catalan, Italian, Spanish 8 Romanian, Rumanian 10 Portuguese
Scotch-Irish: 4 Erse 6 Gaelic
secret: 4 cant, code 5 argot
Siamese: 3 Lao, Tai
structure: 6 syntax 7 grammar
suffix: 3 ese
written: 5 prose

languid
4 lazy, limp 5 inert 6 draggy, supine, torpid 8 drooping, flagging, inactive, listless, slothful, sluggish 9 apathetic, enervated, impassive, lethargic 10 languorous, phlegmatic, spiritless 13 lackadaisical

languish
4 fade, fail, pine, tire, wilt 5 brood, droop 6 weaken 7 decline 9 waste away

languishing
4 limp, weak 6 feeble, pining 7 languid 8 fainéant, indolent, listless, weakened 9 depressed, enervated, enfeebled 10 dispirited, spiritless 11 debilitated, devitalized 13 lackadaisical

languor
3 kef, kif 5 ennui 6 stupor, tedium, torpor 7 fatigue 8 doldrums, dullness, hebetude, lethargy 9 heaviness, inertness, lassitude, torpidity, weariness 10 exhaustion

languorous
4 lazy, limp 5 inert 6 draggy, supine, torpid 7 laggard, languid, passive, relaxed 8 dilatory, drooping, fainéant, flagging, inactive, indolent, indulged, listless, pampered, slothful, sluggard 9 apathetic, enervated, impassive, lethargic 10 phlegmatic, spiritless 13 lackadaisical

lank
4 bony, lean, limp, thin 5 rangy, spare 6 gangly 7 angular, scraggy, slender 8 gangling

lanky
4 bony, lean, thin 5 gaunt, spare 6 gangly 7 scraggy, scrawny 8 gangling, rawboned

lanyard
4 cord, line, rope 7 cordage

Laocoön
city: 4 Troy
killer: 8 serpents

Laodamia
father: 7 Acastus
husband: 11 Protesilaus

Laomedon
daughter: 7 Hesione

father: 4 Ilus
kingdom: 4 Troy
mother: 8 Eurydice
slayer: 8 Heracles, Hercules
son: 5 Priam 8 Tithonus

Laos
capital: 9 Vientiane
city: 11 Savannakhet
ethnic group: 5 Hmong
monetary unit: 3 kip
neighbor: 5 Burma, China 7 Myanmar, Vietnam 8 Cambodia, Thailand 9 Kampuchea
river: 6 Mekong

lap
3 sip 4 fold, join, wind 5 drink 6 cuddle, splash, swathe 7 circuit, control, custody, shingle 9 imbricate

lapidary
6 cutter 7 elegant, jeweler 8 engraver, polisher

lapillus
4 lava 6 cinder

lapin
6 rabbit

Lapiths
foes: 8 centaurs
king: 5 Ixion

lappet
4 flap, fold 5 lapel

lapse
3 err, gap, sin 4 fall, flub, goof, sink, slip, vice 5 boner, cease, error, fluff, gaffe, slide 6 breach, bungle, expire, foible, miscue 7 blooper, blunder, decline, failing, failure, faux pas, forfeit, frailty, mistake, screwup, subside 8 abeyance, apostasy, interval, trespass 9 backslide, deviation, oversight, violation 10 apostatize 11 backsliding, impropriety 12 indiscretion, interruption

lapsed
4 sunk 5 ended 6 ceased 7 expired 8 obsolete 9 forfeited

Laputan
6 absurd 9 visionary

lapwing
5 pewit 6 peewit, plover

Lar
3 god 6 spirit 12 household god

larboard
4 left, port 8 leftward

larcenist
5 thief 6 bandit, robber 7 burglar, filcher, stealer 8 pilferer 9 embezzler, plunderer, purloiner 10 pickpocket, shoplifter

larcenous
7 robbing 8 thieving 9 pilfering 10 plunderous 13 light-fingered

larceny
5 theft 7 looting, robbery 8 burglary, stealing, thievery, thieving
kind: 5 grand, petit, petty

lard
3 fat 6 fatten, grease 10 shortening

larder
6 pantry

large
3 big, fat 4 bull, huge, vast 5 ample, bulky, giant, grand, great, gross, hefty, jumbo, major 6 goodly 7 copious, immense, mammoth, massive, outsize, sizable 8 colossal, enormous, gigantic, king-size, oversize, spacious, whopping 9 capacious, excessive, extensive, humongous, monstrous 10 exorbitant, large-scale, monumental, prodigious, stupendous, tremendous, voluminous 11 extravagant, substantial
combining form: 4 macr, mega 5 macro 6 megalo

largesse
4 alms, gift 6 bounty 7 bequest, charity, cumshaw, gifting, present 8 donation, gratuity 9 endowment, pourboire 10 almsgiving, generosity, liberality 11 benefaction, beneficence, benevolence, magnanimity, munificence 12 philanthropy

largest continent
4 Asia

largo
4 slow 5 broad, tempo

lariat
4 bola, bolo, rope 5 lasso, noose, reata, riata
user: 6 cowboy, drover 7 vaquero 10 cowpuncher

lark
4 bird, dido, romp 5 antic, caper, prank, shine, stunt, trick 6 frolic 7 rollick 8 escapade, songbird 9 diversion 10 tomfoolery 11 distraction, shenanigans 12 monkeyshines

larrup
3 tan 4 beat, cane, drub, dust, flay, flog, hide, lash, lick, whip, whup 5 pound, spank, whale 6 cudgel, lather, paddle, thrash, wallop 7 clobber, scourge, shellac, trounce 8 lambaste 10 flagellate

larva
3 bot 4 grub, worm 6 dobson, maggot 8 cercaria, hornworm, mealworm 10 casebearer 11 caterpillar 12 hellgrammite
amphibian: 7 tadpole
crustacean: 4 zoea
flatworm: 5 redia
free-swimming: 7 planula
mollusk: 7 veliger
moth: 8 leafworm
tapeworm: 6 measle

larynx
7 trachea **8** voice box

lasagna
5 pasta **7** noodles

La Scala
home: 5 Milan
production: 5 opera
star: 4 diva

lascivious
4 lewd **5** bawdy, loose, randy **6** carnal, coarse, rakish, wanton **7** fleshly, goatish, immoral, lustful, satyric **8** depraved, prurient **9** lecherous, libertine, lickerish, salacious **10** libidinous, licentious, lubricious, profligate **12** concupiscent

lash
4 beat, bind, dash, flay, flog, hide, whip **5** baste, birch, fling, pound, scold, slash, whale **6** assail, berate, buffet, pummel, scathe, strike, stripe, switch, thrash **7** blister, scarify, scourge, upbraid **8** lambaste **9** castigate, excoriate, horsewhip **10** flagellate

lass
3 gal **4** girl, maid **5** wench **6** damsel, maiden **7** colleen

lassitude
5 ennui, sloth **6** apathy, stupor, tedium, torpor **7** fatigue, languor **8** debility, doldrums, dullness, hebetude, laziness, lethargy **9** indolence, tiredness, torpidity, weariness **10** exhaustion **11** insouciance **12** heedlessness, indifference, listlessness, sluggishness

lasso
see **lariat**

last
3 end, lag, nth, ult. **4** bide, stay **5** abide, final **6** endure, hold up, latest, latter, linger, remain, utmost **7** closing, extreme, perdure, persist, survive **8** continue, crowning, eventual, farthest, furthest, hindmost, rearmost, remotest, terminal, ultimate **9** umpteenth, uttermost **10** concluding, conclusive **11** terminating
French: 7 dernier
next to: 6 penult **11** penultimate

last-ditch
5 final **7** defiant **8** ultimate **9** desperate **10** concluding

last Greek letter
5 omega

lasting
6 stable **7** abiding, durable, undying **8** enduring, lifelong, long-term, longtime **9** continual, indelible, perennial, permanent, unceasing **10** continuing, continuous, perdurable, persisting **12** indissoluble, long-standing

Last of the Mohicans, The
5 Uncas
author: 6 Cooper (James Fenimore)
character: 4 Cora **5** Alice, Magua, Uncas **11** Natty Bumppo **12** Chingachgook

Last Supper, The
painter: 7 da Vinci (Leonardo) **8** Leonardo (da Vinci)
location: 5 Milan

last word
4 amen

latch
4 bolt, glom, hasp, hook **5** catch **6** fasten, secure **8** fastener
British: 5 sneck

latchet
4 band, cord, lace **5** strap, thong **8** shoelace

late
4 dead, past, slow **5** tardy **6** former, recent, whilom **7** defunct, delayed, onetime, overdue, quondam **8** deceased, departed, sometime **9** preceding

latent
4 idle **5** inert **6** covert, fallow, hidden, innate, unripe **7** abeyant, dormant, lurking **8** immature, inactive, inherent **9** concealed, intrinsic, potential, quiescent

later
4 anon, soon **5** after, infra **6** behind **7** by and by, ensuing **9** afterward, following, posterior **10** subsequent, succeeding **12** subsequently

lateral
4 pass, side **6** branch **8** crabwise, flanking, sidelong, sideward, sideways, sidewise

laterally
8 crabwise, sideward, sideways, sidewise

latest
6 newest, red-hot **7** current **8** contempo **9** au courant **10** dernier cri **13** up-to-the-minute

latex
6 balata **8** emulsion
product: 5 paint **6** chicle, rubber **11** gutta-percha

lath
4 slat **5** board, frame, stave, stick, strip

lather
4 flap, flog, foam, hide, lash, soap, stew, suds, whip **5** froth, spume, tizzy, yeast **6** dither, hoopla, pother, thrash, welter **7** scourge, turmoil **8** soapsuds

Latin
5 Roman **7** Italian **8** Hispanic
after: 4 post

always: **6** semper
as directed: **6** ut dict
be, being: **4** esse
before: **4** ante, prae
beginner's word: **3** amo
behold: **4** ecce
believe: **5** credo
book: **5** liber
boy: **4** puer
brother: **6** frater
but: **3** sed
day: **4** dies
dog: **5** canis
earth: **5** terra
egg: **3** ova
father: **5** pater
foot: **3** pes
friend: **6** amicus
girl: **6** puella
god: **4** deus
goddess: **3** dea
good-bye: **4** vale **5** salve
grammarian: **7** Donatus (Aelius)
greeting: **3** ave
hail and farewell: **12** ave atque vale
hand: **5** manus
handle: **4** ansa
hello: **3** ave
horse: **5** equus
house: **5** domus
I: **3** ego
is: **3** est
law: **3** ius, jus, lex
let it stand: **4** stet
life: **4** vita
light: **3** lux
love: **3** amo **4** amas, amat, amor
man: **4** homo
mother: **5** mater
moon: **4** luna
night: **3** nox
nothing: **5** nihil
now: **4** nunc
peace: **3** pax
pronoun: **3** ego, nos, vos
road: **3** via **4** iter
same: **4** idem
sea: **4** mare
see: **4** vide
sister: **5** soror
step: **6** gradus
sun: **3** sol
that is: **5** id est
thing: **3** res
this: **3** hic, hoc **4** haec
thus: **3** sic
truth: **7** veritas
verb: **3** amo
war: **6** bollum
welcome: **5** salve
wife: **4** uxor
woman: **6** femina
year: **4** anno **5** annus

Latin American
country: **4** Cuba, Peru **5** Chile **6** Belize, Brazil, Guyana, Mexico, Panama **7** Bolivia, Ecuador, Uruguay **8** Colombia, Honduras, Paraguay, Suriname **9** Argentina, Costa Rica, Guatemala, Nicaragua, Venezuela **10** El Salvador
revolutionary: **6** Castro (Fidel) **7** Bolívar (Simón), Guevara (Che), Hidalgo (Father Miguel) **8** O'Higgins (Bernardo) **9** San Martín (José de)

Latin dance
4 juba **5** bamba, bomba, conga, mambo, plena, rumba, salsa, samba, tango, tumba **6** cha-cha, cumbia, maxixe, rhumba **7** bachata, carioca, lambada **8** capoeira, habanera, merengue **9** bossa nova, cha-cha-cha, paso doble

Latinus
daughter: **7** Lavinia
father: **6** Faunus **8** Odysseus
son-in-law: **6** Aeneas
wife: **5** Amata

latitude
4 play, room **5** range, scope, space, width **6** leeway, margin **7** breadth, compass, freedom, liberty, license **9** elbowroom **10** discretion **12** independence

latke
7 pancake **13** potato pancake

Latona
4 Leto
daughter: **5** Diana **7** Artemis
father: **5** Coeus
mother: **6** Phoebe
son: **6** Apollo

Latter-day Saint
6 Mormon

lattice
4 grid, mesh **5** grate, grill **7** grating, network, trellis **12** reticulation

Latvia
capital: **4** Riga
city: **7** Liepaja **10** Daugavpils
gulf: **4** Riga
language: **7** Lettish
monetary unit: **3** lat
native: **4** Balt, Lett
neighbor: **6** Russia **7** Belarus, Estonia **9** Lithuania
river: **7** Daugava **12** Western Dvina
sea: **6** Baltic

laud
5 adore, bless, cry up, extol, glory, honor **6** admire, praise, revere **7** acclaim, flatter, glorify, magnify, worship **8** eulogize, venerate **9** celebrate, reverence

laudable
6 worthy **9** admirable, deserving, estimable **11** commendable, meritorious, thankworthy **12** praiseworthy

laudatory
7 glowing **9** adulatory, approving **10** eulogistic, flattering **11** approbative, encomiastic, panegyrical **12** commendatory **13** complimentary

Lauder of cosmetics
5 Estée

laugh
3 yuk **4** ha-ha, roar, yuck **5** tehee, whoop **6** cackle, giggle, guffaw, hee-haw, tee-hee, titter **7** chortle, chuckle, snicker, snigger **10** cachinnate

laughable
4 rich **5** comic, droll, funny, goofy, witty **6** absurd, jocose **7** amusing, comical, jocular, mocking, risible **8** derisive, derisory, farcical, humorous **9** ludicrous **10** ridiculous

Laugh-In
cast: **4** Sues (Alan), Hawn (Goldie) **5** Buzzi (Ruth), Carne (Judy), Owens (Gary) **6** Dawson (Richard), Gibson (Henry), Tomlin (Lily) **7** Johnson (Arte)
catch phrase: **10** sock it to me **12** go to your room
guest: **6** Wilson (Flip) **7** Tiny Tim **8** Youngman (Henny)
host: **5** Rowan (Dan) **6** Martin (Dick)

laughing
5 merry, riant **6** blithe **8** mirthful **9** sparkling

laughingstock
4 butt, dupe, fool, jest, joke, mark, mock **5** sport **6** target **7** mockery **8** derision

launch
4 boat, cast, fire, hurl **5** begin, debut, fling, heave, pitch, sling, start, throw **6** get off **7** jump off, kick off, lift off, release, take off, usher in **8** blast off, catapult, commence, embark on, initiate **9** inception, institute, introduce, motorboat, set afloat **10** inaugurate, initiation **12** inauguration

launder
4 wash **5** clean **6** trough **7** cleanse **8** sanitize, transfer

Laura's lover
8 Petrarch

laurels
4 bays, fame **5** award, honor, kudos, prize **6** awards, badges, honors, prizes, renown **7** acclaim **8** accolade, citation **9** accolades, citations **10** decoration, reputation **11** decorations, distinction **12** achievements, distinctions

laurel-tree nymph
6 Daphne

lav
3 bog, can, loo **4** head, john **5** jakes, privy

lava
4 slag **5** magma **6** pumice, scoria **8** andesite, trachyte
fragment: **8** lapillus
stream: **4** flow **6** coulee

lavalava
4 wrap **5** cloth, pareu, skirt **6** sarong

lavaliere
7 pendant **8** necklace

lavatory
3 can, loo **4** head, john **5** basin, jakes, potty, privy **6** johnny, toilet **7** latrine **8** bathroom, restroom, washroom **11** water closet

lave
4 pour, wash **5** bathe

Lavinia
father: **7** Latinus
husband: **6** Aeneas
mother: **5** Amata

Lavinium's founder
6 Aeneas

lavish
4 lush, posh, pour **5** plush, spend, waste **6** swanky **7** liberal, opulent, profuse **8** effusive, prodigal, splendid, squander **9** bountiful, excessive, exuberant, luxuriant, luxurious, sumptuous **10** immoderate, inordinate, munificent **11** extravagant

law
3 act, lex **4** bill, code, rule **5** axiom, canon, edict, Torah **6** assize, decree, equity **7** dictate, justice, mandate, precept, statute, theorem **8** exigency **9** enactment, ordinance, principle **10** principium, regulation **11** commandment, fundamental **12** prescription
body of: **4** code **7** pandect **12** constitution
degree: **3** LLB, LLD
expert: **5** judge **6** jurist **7** justice
practitioner: **6** lawyer **7** counsel **8** attorney **9** barrister, solicitor
relating to: **5** jural, legal **7** canonic **8** forensic, juristic **9** judiciary
violation of: **4** tort **5** crime **6** felony **11** misdemeanor

law-abiding
6 decent **7** duteous, dutiful, orderly, upright **8** obedient, obliging, straight **9** compliant, peaceable **10** forthright, respectful **11** respectable, well-behaved

Law & Order
actor: **4** Röhm (Elisabeth) **6** Govich (Milena), Martin (Jesse), Orbach (Jerry) **7** Hendrix (Leslie) **8** Thompson (Fred) **9** Merkerson (S. Epatha), Waterston (Sam)
character: **5** Green (Ed), McCoy (Jack) **6** Branch (Arthur) **7** Briscoe (Lennie), Cassady (Nina), Rodgers (Elizabeth) **8** Van Buren (Anita) **10** Southerlyn (Serena)
creator: **4** Wolf (Dick)

lawbreaker
3 con **4** hood, perp, thug **5** crook, felon **6** outlaw, sinner **7** convict, culprit, hoodlum, mobster **8** criminal, gangster, hooligan, jailbird, offender, scofflaw, violator **9** desperado, wrongdoer **10** malefactor, trespasser **12** transgressor

lawful
3 due **4** just **5** legal, legit, licit, valid **6** kosher **7** condign **8** bona fide, innocent, mandated, ordained **9** allowable, canonical, juridical, legalized **10** authorized, legitimate **11** permissible

lawgiver
5 Draco, Moses, solon **7** senator **8** alderman **10** councilman, legislator **11** congressman, thesmothete

lawlessness
5 chaos **6** strife **7** anarchy, discord, misrule, turmoil **8** conflict, disorder **9** mobocracy **10** illegality, misconduct, ochlocracy, unruliness, wrongdoing **11** criminality, pandemonium

lawman
3 cop **4** fuzz **6** copper **7** marshal, officer, sheriff **9** constable, policeman

Lawrence novel
7 Rainbow (The) **8** Kangaroo, Lost Girl (The) **9** Aaron's Rod **11** Women in Love **13** Plumed Serpent (The), Sons and Lovers

lawsuit
4 case **5** cause, claim **6** action **8** replevin **9** assumpsit **10** litigation, proceeding **11** presentment, prosecution
subject: **4** tort

lawyer
6 jurist, legist **7** counsel, pleader **8** advocate, attorney **9** barrister, counselor, solicitor **10** counsellor
dishonest: **7** shyster **11** pettifogger
exam: **4** LSAT
fictional: **5** Finch (Atticus) **7** Matlock (Ben), Rumpole (Horace) **10** Perry Mason
French: **6** avocat
title: **3** Esq. **7** Esquire

lawyers' group
3 ABA

lax
5 loose, slack **6** casual, remiss, sloppy **7** lenient **8** careless, derelict, lacrosse **9** deficient, forgetful, negligent **10** neglectful, permissive **11** inattentive

laxative
5 purge **6** emetic, physic **8** aperient, evacuant **9** cathartic, purgative

lay
3 bet, put, set **5** apply, hatch, place, wager **6** assert, assign, ballad, charge, credit, devise, impute, settle, spread **7** amateur, arrange, ascribe, concoct, deposit, prepare, present **11** nonclerical

lay by
4 keep, save, stow **5** amass, hoard, store **7** deposit, discard, store up **8** preserve, salt away, set aside **10** accumulate

lay down
3 set **4** rule **5** order, store, yield **6** assert, decree, define, give up, impose, ordain, record, resign **7** abandon, command, dictate, specify **8** hand over, preserve, proclaim **9** establish, prescribe, surrender **10** relinquish

layer
3 hen, ply **4** coat, film, seam, tier **5** paver, sheet **6** folium, lamina, strata (plural), veneer **7** coating, stratum **8** covering, laminate, membrane, sandwich, stratify
inner: **6** lining
of iris: **4** uvea
of skin: **6** dermis **9** epidermis
outer: **4** skin **6** veneer

lay for
6 ambush **8** surprise

lay in
see **lay by**

layman
6 novice, oblate **7** amateur, secular **11** parishioner

lay off
4 fire, halt, quit, stop **5** avoid, cease, let go, lie by **6** desist **7** abstain, dismiss, measure, release **9** discharge, terminate **10** inactivity **11** discontinue

lay out
3 pay **4** give, plan **5** chart, dummy, place, spend **6** design, expend **7** arrange, display, exhibit, prepare **8** disburse

lay waste
4 ruin **5** wreck **6** ravage **7** destroy **8** desolate, demolish **9** devastate

lazar
5 leper

Lazarus' sister
4 Mary **6** Martha

laze
3 bum, lag **4** bask, hang, idle, loaf, loll **5** chill **6** dawdle, loiter, lounge, slouch **7** goof off, hang out **8** chill out **9** goldbrick **10** hang around

laziness
5 sloth **6** torpor **7** inertia, languor, laxness, loafing **8** idleness, lethargy, otiosity **9** indolence, lassitude, loitering, slackness **10** inactivity **11** languidness **12** listlessness

lazy
3 lax **4** idle **5** inert, slack **6** droopy, remiss, supine, torpid **7** languid, loafing, passive **8** fainéant, inactive, indolent, listless, slothful, sluggish **9** lethargic, negligent, shiftless, slowgoing **10** languorous

lazybones
4 slug **5** drone, idler **6** loafer, slouch **7** slacker **8** sluggard

lazy Susan
9 turntable

leach
4 drip, leak, ooze, perk, seep, suck, weep **5** bleed, drain, exude, issue **7** draw out, dribble, trickle **8** filtrate, perspire **9** discharge, lixiviate, percolate

lead
3 tip **4** clue, head, hint, show, star **5** guide, metal, plumb, route, steer, trace, usher **6** bullet, ceruse, direct, escort, leader **7** captain, conduct, precede, preface **8** graphite, persuade, shepherd **9** spearhead **10** bellwether
combining form: **5** plumb **6** plumbo
ore: **6** galena **9** anglesite
oxide: **6** sinter
sounding: **5** plumb **7** plummet

lead astray
6 seduce **7** corrupt

lead balloon
3 dud **4** bomb, bust, flop

leaden
4 drab, dull, flat, gray **5** bleak, heavy, inert **6** dismal, gloomy, somber **7** languid, weighty **8** dragging, lifeless, sluggish **9** ponderous

leader
4 boss, dean, duce, guru, head, jefe, lord **5** chief, guide, pilot **6** despot, honcho, rector **7** captain, foreman, general, headman, manager, warlord **8** chairman, director, hierarch, superior **9** chieftain, commander, conductor, demagogue, harbinger, precursor, president, principal, straw boss **10** bellwether, forerunner, pacesetter
authoritarian: **10** Big Brother
Cossack: **6** ataman, hetman
German: **6** führer **7** fuehrer
Japanese: **6** shogun
military: **7** admiral, general, warlord **9** commander **12** field marshal
Muslim: **3** aga **4** agha, amir, emir, imam **5** ameer, emeer **6** caliph, mullah **9** ayatollah
national: **7** premier **9** president **12** chief of state

leading
4 arch, head, main **5** ahead, chief, first, major **6** famous, master **7** premier, primary **8** champion, foremost, headmost, peerless **9** paramount, principal, prominent, well-known **10** preeminent
lady: **4** diva

lead on
3 con **4** bait, dupe, fool, gull, hoax, lure, scam, tole, toll, wile **5** cozen, flirt, tempt **6** allure, betray, cajole, coquet, delude, entice, entrap, humbug, seduce, suck in, take in, trifle **7** beguile, deceive, toy with **8** coquette, hoodwink, inveigle **9** bamboozle **11** string along

leaf
4 flip, foil, page, riff, scan, skim **5** blade, bract, folio, frond, petal, scale, sepal, thumb **6** browse, glance, riffle, spathe
angle: **4** axil
aperture: **5** stoma
axis: **6** rachis
combining form: **5** phyll **6** phyllo **7** phyllum
edge: **9** crenation
lily: **3** pad
palm: **3** ola
part: **4** lobe, vein **5** blade, costa, stoma **7** petiole, stipule, tendril
pine: **6** needle
pore: **5** stoma **7** stomata (plural)
vein: **5** costa

leafage
7 foliage, umbrage, verdure

leaflet
5 flier, flyer, pinna, sheet, tract **6** folder **7** handout **8** brochure, circular, handbill, pamphlet

leafy
4 lush **5** green, shady **6** shaded, wooded **7** foliate, verdant **8** foliated, laminate **9** verdurous

league
4 band, bond, club, crew **5** class, grade, group, guild, order, union, unite **6** circle **7** circuit, combine, society **8** alliance, category, division, grouping, sodality **9** coalition **10** conference, consortium, federation, fellowship, fraternity **11** association, brotherhood, confederacy **13** confederation

Leah
daughter: **5** Dinah
father: **5** Laban
husband: **5** Jacob
sister: **6** Rachel
son: **4** Levi **5** Judah **6** Reuben, Simeon **7** Zebulun **8** Issachar

leak
4 drip, ooze, seep **5** break, crack, spill **6** escape, get out, reveal, source **7** come out, divulge, seepage **8** disclose **9** discharge **10** make public

leaky
6 broken, faulty, porous **7** cracked, damaged

lea, ley
4 veld **5** field, veldt **6** fallow, meadow **7** pasture **9** grassland, pasturage

lean
3 sag, tip **4** bend, bony, cant, heel, lank, list, slim, tend, thin, tilt **5** gaunt, lanky, shift, slant, slope, spare **6** meager, meagre, skinny, slight, wasted **7** angular, deviate, haggard, incline, pinched, scraggy, scrawny, slender, stringy, wizened **8** gradient, rawboned **9** deficient **11** inclination

Leander's beloved
4 Hero

leaning
4 bent, bias, list **5** atilt, drift **6** canted, sloped, tilted **8** diagonal, penchant, tendency **10** proclivity, propensity

Leaning Tower site
4 Pisa

lean-to
3 hut **4** shed **5** shack **6** shanty **7** bivouac, shelter

leap
3 hop **4** axel, buck, jump, loup, lutz, rise, soar **5** bound, caper, clear, mount, vault **6** ascend, gambol, hurdle, spring **7** saltate, upsurge **8** capriole, surmount **9** saltation
ballet: 4 jeté **9** entrechat
by a horse: 7 gambade, gambado

Lear, King
daughter: 5 Regan **7** Goneril **8** Cordelia
son: 5 Edgar **6** Edmund

learn
3 con **4** hear **5** grasp, study **6** attain, detect, master, pick up **7** acquire, catch on, discern, find out, realize, uncover, unearth **8** discover, memorize **9** apprehend, ascertain, determine **10** comprehend, understand **11** stumble onto

learned
4 sage, wise **6** expert, versed **7** bookish, erudite, sapient, studied **8** abstruse, academic, cultured, educated, esoteric, highbrow, lettered, pedantic, well-read **9** recondite, scholarly **10** cultivated, scholastic **12** intellectual

learner
4 tiro, tyro **5** pupil **6** novice, rookie **7** student, trainee **8** beginner, disciple, initiate, neophyte **9** greenhorn, postulant **10** apprentice, catechumen **11** abecedarian

learning
4 lore **6** wisdom **7** science, tuition **8** booklore, pedantry **9** education, erudition, knowledge **11** scholarship
person of: 7 egghead, scholar **9** professor **12** intellectual

lease
3 let **4** hire, rent **6** sublet, tenure **7** charter, compact **8** contract, covenant, document **11** continuance

leash
3 tie **4** bind, cord, curb, rein, rope **5** strap **6** bridle, fetter, hamper, tether **7** shackle, trammel **8** restrain **9** entrammel

least
6 fewest **7** minimal, minimum **8** smallest

leather
3 tan **4** hide, skin, whip **6** thrash
kind: 3 kid, kip, oak **4** bock, buff, calf, roan **5** crown, grain, mocha, strap, suede, whang **6** castor, latigo, oxhide, patent, roller, saddle, skiver **7** buffalo, chamois, morocco, ostrich, peccary **8** capeskin, cordovan, cordwain, shagreen
maker: 5 tawer **6** tanner **7** tannery
piece: 4 welt **5** strap, thong
prepare: 3 tan, taw **5** curry
soft: 5 mocha, suede **8** cabretta

leatherneck
6 marine

Leatherstocking Tales, The
author: 6 Cooper (James Fenimore)
hero: 5 Natty (Bumppo)
title: 7 Prairie (The) **8** Pioneers (The) **10** Deerslayer (The), Pathfinder (The) **17** Last of the Mohicans (The)

leave
3 fly, let **4** blow, cede, exit, flee, move, part, quit, will **5** allow, scram, split **6** assent, assign, beat it, begone, commit, cut out, decamp, depart, desert, devise, escape, get off, legate, permit, resign, retire, set out, vacate **7** abandon, abscond, absence, consent, consign, entrust, forsake, get away, head out, liberty, pull out, take off, vamoose **8** bequeath, clear out, farewell, furlough, hand down, transmit, vacation, withdraw **9** departure, disappear, surrender, terminate **10** permission, relinquish, sabbatical **13** authorization

leaved
5 green **7** foliate, verdant **8** foliated

leave in
4 keep, stet **6** retain

leaven
5 imbue, steep, yeast **6** infuse, invest, modify, temper, vivify **7** enliven, ingrain, lighten, suffuse **8** moderate **9** alleviate, inoculate, sourdough **12** baking powder

leavening
5 yeast 9 sourdough 10 baking soda 12 baking powder

leave of absence
8 furlough

leave off
3 end 4 halt, quit, stop 5 cease 6 desist, give up 7 abstain 8 give over, surcease 9 terminate 11 discontinue

leave out
4 omit, skip 5 elide 6 ignore 7 exclude 8 overlook, pass over

Leaves of Grass author
7 Whitman (Walt)

leavings
4 lees, orts, rest 5 chaff, dregs, dross, offal, scrap, trash 6 debris, grouts, spilth 7 balance, remains, remnant, residue, rubbish 8 detritus, discards, oddments, remnants, residual, residuum 9 fragments, leftovers, remainder

Lebanon
capital: 6 Beirut
city: 4 Tyre 5 Sidon 6 Zahlah 7 Tripoli
language: 6 Arabic, French
monetary unit: 5 pound
mountain: 6 Hermon
neighbor: 5 Syria 6 Israel
river: 6 Litani 7 Orontes
sea: 13 Mediterranean
valley: 5 Bekaa

Le Carré, John
character: 6 Smiley (George)
novel: 11 Russia House (The) 17 Little Drummer Girl (The) 22 Tinker Tailor Soldier Spy 23 Spy Who Came in from the Cold (The)

lecher
4 rake, roué, wolf 5 satyr 7 Don Juan, seducer 8 Casanova, lothario 9 debauchee, reprobate, libertine, womanizer 10 degenerate, profligate, voluptuary 11 philanderer

lecherous
4 lewd 5 bawdy, loose, randy 6 carnal, coarse, rakish, wanton 7 fleshly, goatish, immoral, lustful, satyric 8 depraved, prurient, scabrous 9 debauched, libertine, lickerish, salacious 10 lascivious, libidinous, licentious, lubricious, profligate 11 promiscuous 12 concupiscent
look: 4 leer, ogle

lectern
4 ambo, desk 5 podia (plural), stand 6 podium, pulpit

lecture
4 talk 5 chide, scold, speak 6 berate, preach, rebuke, sermon, speech 7 address, declaim, expound, oration, reproof, reprove, upbraid 8 admonish, briefing, harangue, scolding 9 chalk talk, criticism, criticize, discourse, hold forth, reprimand, talking-to 10 allocution 12 disquisition, dressing-down

lecturer
3 don 6 docent, fellow, master, orator, reader 7 scholar, speaker, teacher, trainer 9 pedagogue, preceptor, professor 10 instructor 11 academician

Leda
daughter: 5 Helen 12 Clytemnestra
father: 8 Thestius
husband: 9 Tyndareus
lover: 4 swan, Zeus
son: 6 Castor, Pollux

ledge
3 bar, rim 4 berm, lode, reef, sill, vein 5 bench, ridge, shelf 6 mantle 7 bedrock, molding 10 projection

ledger
4 book 5 tally 6 record 7 account, balance 8 notebook, register 9 reckoning 11 spreadsheet
entry: 5 asset, debit

LED part
5 diode

lee
5 haven 7 shelter 9 protected, sheltered

leech
4 milk, worm 5 bleed, drain 6 sponge, sucker 7 exhaust, sponger 8 barnacle, hanger-on, parasite 10 freeloader 11 bloodsucker 12 lounge lizard

Lee of film
3 Ang 5 Spike

leer (at)
3 eye 4 ogle 5 gloat, smirk, sneer, stare 6 glance, goggle, squint 7 grimace

leery
4 wary 5 chary 6 unsure 7 dubious, guarded 8 cautious, doubtful, doubting 10 suspicious 11 circumspect, distrustful, mistrustful

lees
5 dregs 6 grouts, refuse 7 deposit, grounds, residue 8 leavings, residual, residuum, sediment 9 settlings 11 precipitate

leeward
8 downwind
opposite: 8 windward

leeway
4 play, room 5 scope, space 6 margin 7 breadth, compass, freedom, liberty 8 latitude 9 elbowroom, tolerance

left
4 port 5 aport 7 liberal, radical 8 departed, deserted, larboard, residual, sinister 9 abandoned, discarded, remaining, sinistral

left-handed
5 inept **6** clumsy, gauche **7** awkward, dubious **8** fumbling, southpaw **9** ambiguous, equivocal, insincere, maladroit **10** morganatic

left-hand page
5 verso

leftover
5 extra, spare **6** excess, unused **7** remnant, reserve, residue, surplus, uneaten, vestige **8** residual, unneeded **9** redundant, remainder, remaining **10** unconsumed **11** superfluous

leftovers
see **leavings**

leftward
4 levo, port **5** aport
go: **3** haw

leg
3 bow, gam, lap **4** limb **5** shank, stage **6** branch **7** support, upright **8** cabriole **9** appendage, drumstick
bone: **5** femur, tibia **6** fibula **7** patella
part: **4** calf, crus, foot, knee, shin **5** ankle, thigh

legacy
4 gift **5** trust **6** devise, estate **7** bequest **8** heirloom, heritage **9** endowment, patrimony, tradition **10** birthright **11** benefaction, inheritance

legal
5 legit, licit **6** lawful **7** allowed **8** innocent **9** juridical, statutory **10** legitimate, sanctioned
hold: **4** lien
matter: **3** res **4** case, suit
order: **4** writ **7** summons **8** subpoena
organization: **3** ABA
party: **6** suitor **8** litigant **9** defendant, plaintiff
restraint: **8** estoppel

legal tender
3 wad **4** cash **5** bread, dough, money, moola, notes **6** moolah, specie **7** coinage **8** banknote, currency **9** long green

legate
4 will **5** endow, envoy, grant, leave **6** bestow, commit, consul, devise, deputy, devise, nuncio, pass on **7** entrust, leave to **8** bequeath, delegate, emissary, hand down, transmit **10** ambassador

legatee
4 heir **7** devisee **9** inheritor

legato
5 fluid **6** smooth **7** flowing

legend
3 key **4** lore, myth, saga, tale, yarn **5** fable, motto, story **6** mythos **7** caption, fiction **8** epigraph, folklore, folktale, tall tale **9** mythology, tradition **11** inscription

legendary
5 famed **6** fabled, famous, mythic **7** fabular, fancied, fictive, storied **8** fabulous, mythical, renowned, supposed **9** well-known **10** apocryphal, celebrated **11** illustrious, traditional **12** mythological

legendary bird
3 roc

legerdemain
5 magic **8** prestige, trickery **9** chicanery, conjuring, deception **13** sleight of hand

leggings
5 chaps **7** puttees **9** gambadoes

leghorn
3 hat **4** fowl **5** straw **7** chicken

legible
5 clear **8** distinct, readable **12** decipherable, intelligible

legion
4 army, host, many, mass, rout **5** cloud, crowd, drove, flock, horde **6** myriad, scores, sundry, throng **7** phalanx, various **8** numerous, populous **9** countless, multitude **10** numberless

legionnaire's hat
4 kepi

legislate
5 enact, order **6** codify, decree, ordain, permit, ratify **7** empower, mandate **8** legalize, regulate, sanction **9** establish

legislation
3 act, law **4** acts, bill, code, laws **5** bills, codes, rules **6** edicts **7** statute **8** charters, dictates, statutes **9** enactment, lawmaking **10** enactments, ordinances, regulation **11** regulations **12** codification

legislator
5 solon **7** senator **8** alderman, lawgiver, lawmaker **10** councilman **11** assemblyman, congressman, thesmothete

legislature
4 diet **5** house, junta **6** senate **7** council **8** assembly, congress **10** parliament
Communist: **6** soviet **9** politburo, presidium
Danish: **9** Folketing
Finnish: **9** Eduskunta
German: **9** Bundesrat, Bundestag
Iceland: **7** Althing
Ireland: **4** Dáil
Israel: **7** Knesset
Norway: **8** Storting
one-house: **10** unicameral
Poland: **4** Sejm
Russian: **4** duma
Spain: **6** Cortes
Sweden: **7** Riksdag
two-house: **9** bicameral
Ukraine: **4** Rada

legitimate
4 fair, just, true **5** legal, licit, sound, usual, valid **6** kosher, lawful, normal, proper **7** genuine,

regular, typical **8** accepted, innocent, orthodox, rightful **9** allowable, authentic, canonical, customary **10** admissable, authorized, reasonable, recognized **11** justifiable, well-founded

Le Guin, Ursula K.
novel: 7 Telling (The) **8** Solitude (The) **12** Dispossessed (The) **18** Left Hand of Darkness (The)
series: 8 Earthsea

legume
3 dal, pea, pod, soy **4** bean, dhal, guar, peas, seed, soya **5** beans, lupin, pulse, vetch **6** clover, lentil, lupine, peanut **7** alfalfa, soybean

leg up
3 aid **4** edge, lift **5** boost **6** assist **9** advantage, head start

lei
6 wreath **7** garland **8** necklace

Leibniz's invention
8 calculus

Leif Eriksson
discovery: 7 Vinland
father: 4 Eric, Erik (the Red)

leisure
4 ease, rest, time **6** casual, chance, repose **7** freedom, liberty **8** downtime **10** relaxation **11** opportunity

leisurely
4 easy, slow **6** lazily, slowly **7** relaxed, restful **8** laid-back **9** unhurried

leitmotiv
4 idea **5** theme, topic **6** burden, motive, thesis **7** subject **8** idée fixe

lemma
5 bract, theme **7** heading, premise, theorem **8** argument **11** proposition

lemon
3 dud **4** bomb, bust, flop **5** fruit, loser, scent **6** flavor, yellow **7** failure
drink: 3 ade

lemur
5 indri **6** colugo
relative: 4 lori **5** loris, potto **6** aye-aye, galago **7** tarsier **8** bush baby

lend
4 give, loan **5** allow, grant **6** afford, oblige, supply **7** advance, furnish, provide **11** accommodate

Lendl of tennis
4 Ivan

L'Engle novel
10 Many Waters **13** Wind in the Door (A), Wrinkle in Time (A)

length
4 span **5** ambit, range, reach, realm, scope **6** extent, radius **7** compass, expanse, measure, purview, section, stretch, yardage **8** distance, duration

lengthen
6 expand, extend, let out **7** draw out, prolong, spin out, stretch **8** elongate, increase, protract **9** string out
Scottish: 3 eke

lengthy
4 long **8** dragging, drawn-out, extended, overlong **9** elongated, prolonged **10** long-winded, protracted, voluminous **12** interminable

leniency
5 mercy **7** quarter **8** clemency **9** tolerance **10** indulgence, toleration **11** forbearance

lenient
4 easy, kind, mild, soft **6** benign, gentle, kindly **7** amiable, clement **8** merciful, obliging, tolerant **9** benignant, forgiving, indulgent **10** forbearing, permissive

lenity
5 mercy **7** quarter **8** clemency **9** tolerance **10** humaneness, indulgence **11** forbearance

Lennon, John
son: 4 Sean **6** Julian
wife: 3 Ono (Yoko) **7** Cynthia

lens
5 glass **6** lentil **8** meniscus
kind: 5 toric **6** convex **7** bifocal, concave **8** trifocal

lentil dish
3 dal **4** dahl

lento
4 slow **5** tempo

Leofric's wife
6 Godiva

Leoncavallo opera
9 Pagliacci (I) **10** Chatterton

Leonhard of mathematics
5 Euler

leonine
8 lionlike

Leonora
7 heroine
alias: 7 Fidelio
husband: 9 Florestan

leopard
3 cat **4** pard **5** ounce **7** panther

leper
6 pariah **7** Ishmael, outcast **8** castaway, derelict **9** incurable **10** Ishmaelite **11** untouchable
hospital: 9 lazaretto
island: 7 Molokai
priest: 6 Damien (Father)

Leper Priest
6 Damien (Father)
lepers' hospital
9 lazaretto
lepers' island
7 Molokai
lepidoptera
5 moths 8 skippers 11 butterflies 12 caterpillars
Leporello's master
11 Don Giovanni
leprechaun
3 elf 5 dwarf, fairy 6 sprite 7 brownie
trade: 8 cobbling
leprechauns' land
4 Eire, Erin 7 Ireland
lepton
4 coin, muon 8 electron, neutrino
Lesage hero
7 Gil Blas
Lesbos poet
6 Sappho 7 Alcaeus
___ LeShan
3 Eda
lesion
3 cut 4 boil, flaw, harm, sore 5 ulcer, wound 6 injury 7 blister
Leslie Caron role
4 Gigi, Lili
Lesotho
capital: 6 Maseru
ethnic group: 5 Sotho
former name: 10 Basutoland
language: 5 Sotho
monetary unit: 4 loti
mountain: 9 Ntlenyana
neighbor: 11 South Africa
river: 6 Orange 7 Caledon
less
5 lower, minus 7 reduced, without
lessen
3 cut 4 clip, crop, ease, thin, wane 5 abate, erode, lower, taper 6 dilute, impair, minify, recede, reduce, shrink, weaken 7 abridge, assuage, curtail, degrade, dwindle, lighten, relieve, subside 8 decrease, diminish, minimize, mitigate, taper off 9 attenuate
lessening
4 drop, fall 5 letup 8 decrease, slowdown 9 abatement, reduction, remission 10 curtailing, diminution 11 degradation
lesser
5 lower, minor 7 smaller 8 inferior 9 secondary, small-time, subjacent 11 minor-league, subordinate 13 insignificant
lesson
4 text 5 chide, moral, study 6 rebuke 7 example, lecture, reading, reprove, warning 8 admonish, exercise, homework, reproach 9 reprimand 10 admonition, assignment 11 instruction
lessor
8 landlady, landlord 9 landowner 10 freeholder
let
4 make, rent 5 allow, grant, lease, leave 6 assign, permit, suffer 9 authorize 11 obstruction
letdown
5 slump 6 defeat 7 decline, descent, failure, reverse, setback 10 anticlimax, depression, misfortune 11 frustration
let go
3 axe, can 4 boot, fire, free, sack 5 remit 6 unhand 7 dismiss, neglect, release, set free 8 liberate 9 discharge, terminate
lethal
4 fell 5 fatal 6 deadly, mortal, poison 7 baleful, deathly 8 poisoned, virulent 9 murderous, poisonous 11 destructive, devastating
lethargic
4 dull, idle, slow 5 dopey, heavy, inert 6 draggy, supine, torpid 7 dormant, laggard, languid, passive 8 comatose, dilatory, inactive, listless, slothful, sluggish 9 apathetic, impassive 10 languorous, phlegmatic, spiritless 11 indifferent 12 hebetudinous 13 lackadaisical
lethargy
5 ennui, sloth 6 apathy, phlegm, stupor, torpor 7 inertia, languor, slumber 8 dullness, hebetude, idleness, laziness 9 disregard, inanition, indolence, inertness, lassitude, torpidity 10 inactivity, supineness 11 impassivity, passiveness 12 listlessness
lethe
7 amnesia 8 oblivion 13 forgetfulness
let it stand
4 stet
Leto
see **Latona**
let off
5 spare 6 excuse, exempt 7 absolve, relieve 8 dispense 9 discharge
let on
3 own 5 admit, allow, grant, own up, spill 6 betray, fess up, reveal 7 concede, confess, confirm, divulge, pretend 8 disclose, give away
let out
5 blurt, loose 6 exhale 7 release, set free, unloose 8 lengthen, liberate, set loose 9 discharge, turn loose
letter
3 bee, cee, cue, dee, eff, ell, ess, gee, jay, kay,

pee, tee, vee, wye, zed, zee **4** line, mail, memo, note, rune **5** aitch, print, vowel **6** report, screed, symbol **7** epistle, message, missive **8** dispatch, inscribe **9** consonant
airmail: **8** aerogram
Anglo-Saxon: (see **Anglo-Saxon**)
Arabic: (see **alphabet**)
Greek: (see **alphabet**)
flourish: **5** serif
Hebrew: (see **alphabet**)
kind: **4** open **5** chain, roman **6** italic, uncial **8** Dear John
large: **7** capital **9** majuscule, uppercase
papal: **4** bull **10** encyclical
small: **9** lowercase, minuscule
start: **4** Dear

lettuce
3 cos **4** Bibb, head **6** Boston **7** iceberg, romaine, Simpson **10** butterweed

let up
3 ebb **4** fall, stop, wane **5** abate, cease **6** lessen, relent **7** die away, die down, dwindle, ease off, slacken, subside **8** decrease, diminish, moderate, taper off

letup
4 lull **5** break, pause **6** hiatus **7** respite **8** breather **9** abatement, cessation, lessening, reduction **10** slackening

levee
4 dike, dock, pier, quay **5** jetty, ridge, wharf **7** seawall **8** assembly, function **9** reception **10** breakwater, embankment, riverfront

level
3 aim, lay, par **4** calm, even, flat, raze, same, tier, true **5** equal, floor, flush, grade, plane **6** direct, ground, smooth, status, steady **7** aligned, flatten, mow down **8** balanced, bulldoze, demolish, equalize, parallel, smoothen, standing **9** bring down, intensity, knock down, magnitude **10** equivalent, horizontal, reasonable **11** equilibrium

lever
3 bar, pry **4** jack, tool **5** jimmy, peavy, prize **6** peavey, tappet **7** crowbar

leverage
4 sway **5** clout, power **7** exploit **9** advantage, dominance, influence **11** superiority **13** effectiveness

leveret
4 hare

Levi
father: **5** Jacob
mother: **4** Leah
son: **6** Kohath, Merari **7** Gershon

leviathan
4 huge **5** giant, jumbo, large, titan, whale **7** Goliath, immense, mammoth, massive, monster, titanic **8** behemoth, colossal, colossus, enormous, gigantic **9** cyclopean, monstrous **10** formidable, gargantuan **11** elephantine, monstrosity

Leviathan author
6 Hobbes (Thomas)

levitate
4 lift, rise **5** float, raise **7** elevate, suspend

levity
5 folly, humor **8** buoyancy **9** absurdity, flippancy, frivolity, giddiness, lightness, silliness **10** jocularity, volatility

levy
3 tax **4** duty, toll, wage **5** exact, lay on **6** assess, charge, custom, enlist, impose, impost, tariff **7** carry on, collect **9** conscript **10** assessment, enlistment **12** conscription

lewd
4 blue, racy **5** bawdy, gross **6** coarse, ribald, risqué, smutty, vulgar **7** fleshly, goatish, lustful, obscene, satyric **8** depraved, improper, indecent, off-color, prurient, unchaste **9** debauched, lecherous, libertine, lickerish, salacious **10** indelicate, lascivious, libidinous, licentious, lubricious, suggestive

Lewis and Clark interpreter
9 Sacagawea, Sacajawea

Lewis work
7 Babbitt **9** Dodsworth **10** Arrowsmith, Main Street **11** Elmer Gantry **16** Screwtape Letters (The) **18** Chronicles of Narnia (The)

lexicographer
8 compiler
American: **6** Porter (Noah) **7** Webster (Noah) **9** Worcester (Joseph)
English: **4** Wyld (Henry) **6** Fowler (Francis, Henry), Murray (James), Onions (Charles) **7** Craigie (William), Johnson (Samuel) **9** Partridge (Eric)
French: **6** Littré (Paul-Emile) **8** Larousse (Pierre)
German: **5** Grimm (Jakob, Wilhelm)

lexicon
4 cant **6** jargon **8** glossary, language, wordbook **9** inventory, word-hoard **10** dictionary, repertoire, vocabulary **11** terminology

Lhasa ____
4 apso

liable
3 apt **4** open **5** given, prone **6** likely **7** exposed, subject **8** inclined **9** sensitive **10** answerable, assailable, vulnerable **11** accountable, responsible, susceptible

liaison
4 bond, link **5** amour, fixer **6** affair, broker,

hookup 7 contact, romance 8 intrigue 9 go-between 10 connection 12 entanglement, intermediary, relationship 13 communication

liana
4 vine

liar
6 fibber 7 Ananias 8 deceiver, fabulist, perjurer 9 falsifier 12 prevaricator
female: 8 Sapphira

libation
5 drink 6 liquid, liquor 7 potable 8 beverage, oblation, offering, potation

libel
4 slur 5 smear 6 defame, malign, vilify 7 asperse, calumny, obloquy, slander, traduce 8 bad-mouth, tear down 9 aspersion, denigrate 10 calumniate, defamation, scandalize 11 denigration

libelous
6 untrue 9 injurious, invidious, maligning, traducing, vilifying 10 backbiting, calumnious, defamatory, derogative, derogatory, detracting, detractive, malevolent, pejorative, scandalous, slanderous

liberal
4 full, open 5 ample, broad, loose 6 lavish 7 copious, leftish, leftist, profuse, radical 8 abundant, generous, prodigal, tolerant 9 bounteous, bountiful, indulgent, plentiful, unsparing 10 benevolent, bighearted, charitable, freehanded, munificent, openhanded, permissive, unorthodox 11 broad-minded

liberal arts
quadrivium: 5 music 8 geometry 9 astronomy 10 arithmetic
trivium: 5 logic 7 grammar 8 rhetoric

liberate
4 free 5 loose 7 manumit, release, unchain 9 discharge, unshackle 10 commandeer, emancipate 11 appropriate, expropriate

liberator
6 savior 7 messiah 9 deliverer
of Argentina: 9 San Martín (José de)
of Chile: 8 O'Higgins (Bernardo)
of Ecuador: 5 Sucre (Antonio José de)
of Scotland: 5 Bruce (Robert the)
of South America: 7 Bolívar (Simón)

Liberia
capital: 8 Monrovia
coast: 3 Kru 5 Grain
neighbor: 6 Guinea 10 Ivory Coast 11 Côte d'Ivoire, Sierra Leone

Liberian
language: 3 Kwa
native: 3 Kru, Vai 4 Gola, Toma 5 Bassa, Grebo 6 Kruman

libertine
4 lewd, rake, roué 5 bawdy, loose, randy 6 carnal, rakish, wanton 7 Don Juan, lustful, raffish, satyric 8 Casanova 9 debauched, debauchee, dissolute, lecherous, salacious 10 degenerate, dissipated, lascivious, libidinous, licentious, profligate, voluptuary 11 promiscuous

liberty
4 risk 5 leave 6 chance 7 freedom, license 8 autonomy 9 franchise, privilege 10 permission 11 familiarity 12 emancipation, independence

libidinous
4 lewd 5 bawdy, loose, randy 6 carnal, rakish, wanton 7 fleshly, goatish, lustful, satyric 8 depraved, prurient, unchaste 9 debauched, lecherous, libertine, lickerish, salacious 10 lascivious, licentious, lubricious, profligate 11 promiscuous 12 concupiscent

librarian
5 Dewey (Melvil)

library
7 archive 8 atheneum 9 athenaeum 11 bibliotheca
desk: 6 carrel

___ libre
4 Cuba

Libya
capital: 7 Tripoli
city: 8 Benghazi
desert: 6 Sahara
gulf: 5 Sidra
language: 6 Arabic 7 Hamitic
leader: 7 Gadhafi, Qaddafi (Mu'ammar)
monetary unit: 5 dinar
neighbor: 4 Chad 5 Egypt, Niger, Sudan 7 Algeria, Tunisia
sea: 13 Mediterranean

lice
4 nits 5 crabs 7 cooties

license
3 let, tag 5 allow, grant, leave 6 enable, laxity, permit, suffer, ticket 7 certify, empower, freedom, go-ahead, liberty 8 accredit, document, sanction, variance 9 authority, authorize, slackness 10 permission, profligacy 11 certificate, impropriety 12 carte blanche 13 authorization

licentious
4 lewd 5 bawdy, loose, randy 6 amoral, carnal, rakish, wanton 7 fleshly, goatish, immoral, lustful, satyric 8 depraved, prurient, scabrous 9 abandoned, debauched, dissolute, lecherous, libertine, salacious 10 lascivious, libidinous, lubricious, profligate 11 promiscuous 12 concupiscent

lichen
4 moss 6 archil, litmus 7 oakmoss
genus: 5 Usnea

licit
4 okay **5** legal **6** lawful **7** allowed **8** approved, innocent, licensed **9** allowable, permitted **10** admissible, authorized, legitimate, sanctioned **11** permissible

lick
3 bit, dab, dig, hit, lap, rap, tan **4** beat, dash, deck, down, drub, hint, swat, whip, wipe **5** cream, pinch, pound, smack, smear, spank, taste, touch, trace, whiff **6** defeat, master, punish, thrash, tongue, wallop **7** clobber, conquer, shellac, trounce **8** lambaste, outstrip, overcome, surmount **9** overwhelm

lickerish
see **libidinous**

lickety-split
4 fast **5** apace **6** presto, pronto **7** flat out, hastily, quickly, rapidly, swiftly **8** chop-chop, full tilt, headlong, pell-mell, speedily **9** posthaste **13** expeditiously, precipitately

lick up
3 lap

licorice
4 root **5** anise, candy
pill: **6** cachou

lid
3 cap, top **5** cover **8** covering
moss: **9** operculum

lie
3 fib **4** rest, tale **5** exist, fable, libel, story **6** belong, canard, covert, delude, extend, inhere, remain, repose, reside **7** consist, falsify, falsity, perjure, recline, untruth, whopper **8** misspeak, misstate, tall tale **9** dissemble, falsehood, fish story, mendacity **10** inaccuracy, taradiddle **11** prevaricate **12** misstatement

Liechtenstein
capital: **5** Vaduz
language: **6** German
monetary unit: **4** euro
mountain range: **4** Alps
neighbor: **7** Austria **11** Switzerland
river: **5** Rhein, Rhine

lied
4 song **7** art song

lieder
5 songs **8** art songs

lief
4 fain, soon **6** freely, gladly **7** happily, readily **9** willingly **11** contentedly

liege
4 lord, true **5** loyal **6** ardent, master, vassal **7** abiding, staunch **8** constant, enduring, faithful, reliable, resolute, stalwart **9** dedicated, steadfast **10** dependable

lien
5 claim **6** charge, demand **8** interest, mortgage **10** imposition

lieu
5 place, stead

lieutenant
4 aide **5** looey, looie **6** backup, deputy **7** officer **9** assistant, coadjutor **10** aide-de-camp, coadjutant **11** subordinate

life
3 vim **4** brio, dash, élan, soul **5** verve **6** energy, esprit, spirit **8** vitality **9** animation, existence
animal: **5** fauna
animal and plant: **5** biota
combining form: **3** bio
plant: **5** flora
relating to: **5** vital **8** biologic **10** biological
science: **7** biology

life jacket
7 Mae West

lifeless
4 dead, drab, dull **5** inert **6** asleep, barren, torpid, wasted **7** defunct, extinct **8** comatose, deceased, departed **9** inanimate, inorganic, insensate **10** lackluster

lifelike
5 exact **7** natural, precise **8** accurate, faithful, veristic **9** realistic

life of ___
5 Riley **8** the party

Life of Pi director Lee
3 Ang

lift
4 heft, hike, jack, load, rear, rise **5** boost, exalt, filch, heave, hoist, pinch, raise, steal, swipe, theft **6** assist, pick up, pilfer, repeal, revoke, snitch, take up **7** elevate, purloin, rescind, reverse, support, upraise **8** levitate, stealing, thievery **10** plagiarize

lift-off
6 ascent, launch **7** takeoff **9** launching

ligament
3 tie **4** band, bond, link, yoke **5** nexus, sinew **8** ligature, vinculum **10** connection

ligature
see **ligament**

Ligeia author
3 Poe (Edgar Allan)

light
4 airy, dawn, deft, easy, fair, fire, lamp, land, luck, neon **5** blond, flash, minor, perch, roost, sunny, torch **6** beacon, blithe, bright, candle, casual, facile, flimsy, fluffy, ignite, kindle, settle, simple, slight, strobe **7** lantern, sunrise, trivial

8 cheerful, daybreak, enkindle, illumine, luminous, trifling **9** frivolous, touch down **10** chandelier, effortless, illuminate
and shade interplay: 11 chiaroscuro
combining form: 4 luci, phot **5** lumin, photo **6** lumini, lumino
measure: 3 lux **4** phot **5** lumen **6** candle **7** candela
refractor: 5 prism
relating to: 6 photic
ring: 4 halo **6** corona **7** aureola, aureole
science: 6 optics
source: 3 sun **4** lamp

light brown
3 tan **4** ecru **5** beige, khaki

light-emitting
6 lasing, lucent **7** beaming, fulgent, glowing, lambent, shining **8** luminous **9** effulgent, refulgent

light-emitting ___
5 diode

lighten
4 dawn, ease, fade **5** allay, cheer **6** bleach, lessen, reduce **7** assuage, gladden, hearten, mollify, relieve **8** decrease, mitigate, unburden **9** alleviate, attenuate, extenuate **11** disencumber

light-footed
5 agile, lithe **6** nimble **7** lissome

light-headed
5 dizzy, faint, giddy, silly **6** swimmy **7** flighty **9** frivolous, slaphappy **10** unbalanced **11** disoriented, vertiginous

lighthearted
3 gay **4** glad **5** happy, jolly, merry, sunny **6** blithe, cheery, jocund, jovial, joyful, joyous, lively, upbeat **7** buoyant, festive, gleeful, playful **8** carefree, cheerful, mirthful, volatile **9** easygoing, expansive, sprightly, vivacious **10** blithesome, insouciant **12** effervescent, happy-go-lucky, high-spirited

lighthouse
6 beacon, pharos **7** warning

lighting crew member
6 gaffer

lightless
4 dark **5** unlit **7** aphotic, stygian **9** tenebrous, pitch-dark **10** caliginous, pitch-black **11** unillumined

lightness
6 bounce, gaiety, levity **8** buoyancy, vivacity **9** animation, frivolity **10** cheeriness, liveliness, resiliency, volatility **12** cheerfulness **13** effervescence

lightning bug
7 firefly

lignite
4 coal **9** brown coal
relative: 4 peat

likable
4 nice **6** genial **7** affable, amiable, popular, winning, winsome **8** charming, engaging, friendly, pleasant, pleasing **9** agreeable, appealing, congenial **10** attractive, personable **11** good-natured

like
3 à la, dig **4** akin, same, such **5** close, enjoy, equal, match **6** admire, agnate, akin to, allied, prefer, relish **7** approve, cognate, kindred, related, similar, uniform **8** parallel, selfsame **9** analogous, consonant, identical **10** appreciate, comparable, comprehend, equivalent, resembling

likelihood
6 chance **8** prospect **11** eventuality, possibility, presumption, probability

likely
3 apt **5** given, prone **6** liable, odds-on **7** assumed **8** credible, inclined, possible, presumed, probable, probably, reliable, suitable **9** doubtless, plausible, promising **10** achievable, attractive, believable, presumably

liken
5 match **6** equate **7** compare **8** parallel **10** assimilate

likeness
4 copy, twin **5** clone, image **6** double, effigy **7** analogy, picture, replica **8** affinity, portrait, sameness **9** depiction, facsimile, look-alike, semblance **10** appearance, photograph, similarity, similitude, uniformity **11** resemblance

likewise
3 and, too **4** also **5** ditto **6** as well, withal **7** besides **8** moreover **9** similarly **10** in addition **11** furthermore

liking
4 bent **5** fancy, taste **6** desire **8** affinity, appetite, fondness, penchant, pleasure, soft spot, weakness **9** affection **10** attraction, partiality **11** inclination **12** appreciation, predilection

Lilith
husband: 4 Adam
successor: 3 Eve

lilliputian
3 wee **4** runt, tiny **5** dwarf, petty, pygmy, small **6** bantam, little, midget, peanut, peewee, shrimp **7** manikin **8** mannikin, pint-size, Tom Thumb **9** miniature, pint-sized, undersize **10** diminutive, homunculus

lilt
3 air **4** flow, purl, sing, song, tune **5** carol, pulse, swing, tempo **6** melody, rhythm **7** cadence **8** buoyancy

lily
3 pad 4 aloe, sego 5 calla, tiger, yucca 6 flower 7 leopard 8 mariposa
genus: 4 Aloe

lily-like flower
4 arum

lily-livered
5 sissy, wimpy 6 craven, yellow 7 caitiff, chicken, fearful, gutless 8 cowardly, cowering, poltroon, recreant, timorous 9 spineless, spunkless, weak-kneed 12 fainthearted, poor-spirited 13 pusillanimous

lily-white
4 pure 6 chaste 7 upright 8 innocent, virtuous 9 blameless, estimable, exclusive, exemplary, guiltless, righteous, untainted 10 inculpable 11 uncorrupted

Lima's country
4 Peru

limb
3 arm, fin, gam, leg 4 lobe, twig, wing 5 bough, shoot, spray, sprig 6 branch, member, pinion 7 flipper 8 offshoot 9 appendage, dismember, extremity

limber
4 spry 5 agile, lithe, loose 6 nimble, pliant, supple 7 elastic, lissome, pliable, springy 8 flexible 9 lithesome, resilient

limbo
5 dance 7 neglect 8 oblivion 9 detention, purgatory 11 confinement, uncertainty

lime
4 tree 5 color, fruit, green 6 citrus, linden 7 calcium
drink: 3 ade

limen
8 doorsill, doorstep 9 threshold

limerick
4 poem 5 verse
writer: 4 Lear (Edward)

limestone
4 tufa, tuff 5 chalk 6 marble, oolite 7 coquina 10 travertine

lime tree
6 linden

limit
3 bar, cap, end, fix, max, set 4 curb 5 check, quota 6 border, bounds, curfew, define, extent, hinder, lessen 7 confine, curtail, enclose, extreme, mark out, measure 8 boundary, deadline, restrain, restrict 9 constrict, demarcate, determine, extremity, prescribe 12 circumscribe

limitless
4 vast 7 endless 8 infinite, wide-open 9 boundless, unbounded 10 indefinite 11 illimitable, innumerable, measureless 12 immeasurable, incalculable 13 inexhaustible

limn
4 draw 5 image, paint 6 depict, render, sketch 7 outline, picture, portray 8 describe 9 delineate, interpret, represent

Limoges product
5 china 9 porcelain

limp
3 lax 4 bent, halt, lame, wilt 5 hitch, loose, slack, spent, tired, weary 6 dodder, droopy, falter, hobble 7 flaccid, languid, shamble, shuffle, slumped 8 drooping 9 enervated, exhausted 10 spiritless

limpid
4 pure 5 clear, lucid 6 glassy, serene 8 pellucid 10 see-through, untroubled 11 crystalline, translucent, transparent 12 crystal clear

limping
4 halt, lame 5 gimpy 7 halting 8 hobbling, lameness 9 faltering 12 claudication

linchpin
8 backbone, mainstay

Lincoln
assassin: 5 Booth (John Wilkes)
biographer: 8 Sandburg (Carl)
debater: 7 Douglas (Stephen)
law partner: 7 Herndon (William)
mother: 5 Nancy (Hanks)
nickname: 9 Honest Abe 12 Railsplitter
photographer: 5 Brady (Mathew)
secretary of state: 6 Seward (William)
secretary of war: 7 Stanton (Edwin)
wife: 8 Mary Todd

Lindsay poem
5 Congo (The)

line
3 row 4 file, rank, rope 5 array, goods, queue, route 6 border, column, cordon, series, strain, string 7 contour, descent 8 business, pedigree, sequence 10 employment, occupation, succession
curved: 3 arc
mathematical: 6 vector
metrical: 5 verse 6 verset 8 versicle
of rulers: 7 dynasty
weather map: 6 isobar

lineage
3 kin 4 clan, folk, race 5 birth, blood, breed, house, stirp, stock, tribe 6 family, origin, strain 7 descent, kindred 8 ancestry, breeding, pedigree 9 forebears, genealogy 10 derivation, extraction, succession 11 forefathers, progenitors

lineal
6 direct 8 familial 9 ancestral, inherited 10 bequeathed, hereditary

lineament
4 form 6 figure, relief 7 contour, feature, outline, profile 10 figuration, silhouette

lined
5 drawn, ruled 7 aligned, striate, striped 8 streaked, wrinkled

linen
4 lawn 5 cloth, toile 6 byssus, damask, fabric, napery, sheets 7 batiste, bedding, cambric, taffeta 8 cretonne, lingerie
fiber: 3 tow
source: 4 flax

lineup
5 array, order 6 roster 8 sequence

linger
3 lag 4 bide, drag, loll, mope, poke, stay, wait 5 abide, dally, delay, mosey, tarry 6 dawdle, loiter, put off, remain 7 saunter 8 hesitate 10 dillydally 11 stick around 13 procrastinate

lingerie
8 negligee
item: 4 cami, slip 5 teddy 7 chemise 8 babydoll, camisole

lingo
4 cant, jive 5 argot, idiom, slang 6 jargon, patois, patter, speech, tongue 7 dialect 10 vernacular, vocabulary

linguist
8 polyglot 11 philologist

linguistics
9 philology

linguist Chomsky
4 Noam

___ Lingus
3 Aer

liniment
3 oil 4 aloe, balm 5 salve 6 lotion 7 anodyne, unction, unguent 8 aloe vera, lenitive, ointment 9 demulcent 11 embrocation

lining
6 facing, insert 8 wainscot

link
3 tie 4 bind, bond, join, knot, ring, yoke 5 hitch, nexus, unite 6 attach, copula, couple, hookup, relate, splice 7 bracket, combine, conjoin, connect, contact, joining 8 catenate, division, vinculum 9 associate, conjugate 10 attachment, connection 11 association 12 relationship

linksman
6 golfer

linnet
5 finch

lint
3 fur, nap 4 down, fuzz, pile 5 floss, fluff 9 ravelings

lion
3 cat, Leo 4 Elsa, Nala, puma 5 Aslan, Simba 6 cougar 7 notable 8 eminence, luminary 9 carnivore, personage
feature: 4 mane
group: 5 pride
young: 3 cub

lionhearted
4 bold 5 brave 6 heroic 7 doughty, valiant 8 fearless, intrepid, stalwart, unafraid, valorous 9 dauntless 10 courageous

lionize
4 fete 5 exalt, extol, honor 7 glorify 8 venerate 9 celebrate

Lion King, The
character: 4 Nala, Scar, Zazu 5 Simba, Timon 6 Banzai, Mufasa, Pumbaa, Rafiki, Sarabi, Shenzi 8 Sarafina
composer: 4 John (Elton)
film score: 6 Zimmer (Hans)
lyricist: 4 Rice (Tim)
setting: 10 Pride Lands
voice: 5 Irons (Jeremy), Jones (James Earl), Marin (Cheech) 8 Atkinson (Rowan), Goldberg (Whoopi) 9 Broderick (Matthew)

lion monkey
7 tamarin 8 marmoset

Lion of Judah
8 Selassie (Haile)

lip
3 rim 4 brim, edge, guff, kiss, sass 5 sauce 6 labium, labrum, margin 8 back talk
relating to: 6 labial

lipid
3 fat, wax

lipped
7 labiate 9 bilabiate

liquefy
3 run 4 flux, melt, thaw 5 smelt 6 render 8 dissolve 10 deliquesce

liqueur
4 arak, ouzo, raki 5 crème 6 arrack, brandy, cassis, Kahlua, kirsch, kummel, pastis, Pernod 7 absinth, Campari, Cinzano, cordial, curaçao, ratafia, sambuca, sloe gin 8 absinthe, amaretto, anisette, Chambord, Drambuie, Galliano, schnapps, Tía Maria 9 Cointreau 10 Chartreuse, pousse-café

liquid
5 drink, fluid, sauce, water 6 watery 7 flowing 8 beverage, emulsion 11 mellifluous
container: 3 cup, jug, keg, mug 4 vial 5 glass 6 bottle, goblet 7 pitcher, tumbler
flammable: 3 gas, oil 5 ether, furan 6 butane, toluol 7 alcohol, toluene 8 gasoline, pyridine

measure: 3 cup, gal. 4 pint 5 liter, litre, ounce, quart 6 gallon
thick: 5 syrup 8 molasses

liquidate
3 pay 4 do in, kill 5 pay up, purge 6 murder, remove, rub out, settle, square 7 bump off, cash out, convert, satisfy, sell off 8 amortize, dispatch, dissolve, knock off 9 eliminate, terminate 10 annihilate 11 assassinate

liquor
5 booze, drink, hooch 7 alcohol, potable, spirits 8 potation 9 firewater, inebriant 10 intoxicant
add: 4 lace 5 spike
Asian: 4 arak 6 arrack
homemade: 5 hooch 9 moonshine 10 bathtub gin
inferior: 5 hooch 6 red-eye, rotgut
Japanese: 4 sake, saki
kind: 3 gin, rum, rye 5 vodka 6 brandy, geneva, scotch, whisky 7 aquavit, bourbon, schnaps, whiskey 8 schnapps, vermouth 9 aqua vitae 10 barley-bree
malt: 3 ale 4 beer 5 nappy, stout 6 porter
measure: 4 dram, shot 6 jigger 7 shooter
Mexican: 5 sotol 6 mescal 7 tequila

Lisa Simpson
brother: 4 Bart
dad: 5 Homer
mom: 5 Marge

lissome
5 agile, lithe 6 limber, nimble, supple, svelte 7 slender 8 flexible, graceful

list
3 tip 4 book, cant, file, heel, lean, menu, note, post, roll, tilt 5 arena, count, index, slant, slate, slope, tally 6 agenda, census, docket, lineup, litany, record, roster 7 catalog, incline, itemize, specify 8 calendar, glossary, manifest, register, roll call, schedule, tabulate 9 chronicle, enumerate, inventory 13 particularize
extender: 3 etc. 4 et al. 7 and so on
type: 3 hit 4 life, to-do, wish 5 punch, short 6 linked 7 laundry, mailing, waiting 8 shopping 10 best-seller

listen
4 hark, hear, heed, hist, note 5 audit 6 attend, harken 7 hearken, monitor 8 overhear 9 eavesdrop

listeners
8 audience

listless
4 dull, limp, weak 5 inert, slack 6 torpid, vacant 7 languid 8 indolent, sluggish 9 apathetic, enervated, lethargic, lymphatic 10 languorous, phlegmatic, spiritless 11 indifferent, languishing 13 lackadaisical

listlessness
5 ennui 6 apathy, stupor, torpor 7 fatigue, inertia, languor 8 doldrums, lethargy 9 indolence, lassitude, torpidity 10 enervation

litany
4 list 5 chant 6 prayer 7 account, listing, recital, refrain 8 petition, rogation 9 catalogue 10 invocation, recitation 11 enumeration 12 supplication

literal
4 bald, bare 5 blunt, exact, stark 6 actual, simple, strict 7 precise 8 accurate, bona fide, faithful, verbatim 9 authentic 11 unvarnished, word-for-word 13 unembellished

literally
5 truly 6 direct, indeed, openly, simply 7 plainly, totally, utterly 8 candidly, directly, verbatim 9 genuinely, virtually 11 word for word

literary
7 bookish, erudite, learned 8 lettered, well-read 9 authorial, scholarly 12 belletristic

literary work
4 book, opus, play, poem 5 drama, essay, novel 10 short story

literature
5 prose 6 poetry 7 fiction 13 belles-lettres

lithe
4 lean, slim 5 agile, spare 6 limber, supple, svelte 7 lissome, pliable, slender 8 flexible, graceful

lithographer
4 Ives (James Merritt) 7 Currier (Nathaniel)

Lithuania
capital: 7 Vilnius
city: 6 Kaunas 8 Klaipeda
monetary unit: 5 litas
neighbor: 6 Latvia, Poland, Russia 7 Belarus
river: 5 Neman, Venta 7 Lielupe
sea: 6 Baltic

litigant
4 suer 6 suitor 9 defendant, disputant, plaintiff

litigate
3 sue 6 indict 7 arraign, contest, dispute 9 prosecute

litigation
4 case, suit 7 lawsuit 11 prosecution, proceedings

litter
3 bed 4 cubs, junk 5 brood, couch, issue, strew, trash, waste, young 6 clutch, debris, refuse 7 bedding, clutter, garbage, kittens, piglets, progeny, puppies, rubbish, scatter 8 detritus 9 offspring, stretcher 10 scattering

little
3 bit, dab, toy, wee 4 dash, hint, mean, puny,

tiny **5** brief, dinky, minor, petty, pinch, runty, short, small, taste, trace, young **6** bantam, meager, meagre, minute, narrow, paltry, petite, skimpy **7** limited, trivial **8** dwarfish, slightly, smallish, trifling **9** miniature, small-beer **10** diminutive, short-lived, undersized **11** microscopic, unimportant

Little Bighorn
state: **7** Montana
victim: **6** Custer (George Armstrong)
victor: **5** Sioux **6** Lakota **7** Arapaho **10** Crazy Horse **11** Sitting Bull

little by little
6 slowly **8** inchmeal, steadily **9** gradually, piecemeal

Little Caesar role
4 Rico

Little Dipper
constellation: **9** Ursa Minor
star: **5** North **7** Polaris

little mermaid
5 Ariel

Little Women
author: **6** Alcott (Louisa May)
character: **3** Amy, Meg **4** Beth **6** Laurie, Marmee
surname: **5** March

littoral
5 beach, coast, shore **6** strand **7** coastal, seaside **8** seaboard, sea front, seashore **9** shoreline **10** oceanfront

liturgy
4 rite **6** ritual **7** service **8** ceremony **9** sacrament **10** ceremonial, observance, repertoire

livable
6 viable **8** adequate, bearable, passable **9** endurable, habitable, tolerable **11** inhabitable, supportable

live
4 fare, stay **5** abide, dwell, exist, on air, vital, vivid **6** actual, reside, thrive **7** breathe, current, subsist, survive

livelihood
3 job **4** game, keep, work **5** craft, trade **7** support **8** business, vocation **10** employment, handicraft, occupation, profession, sustenance **11** subsistence

liveliness
3 pep, zip **4** brio, élan, zing **5** verve, vigor **6** energy, hustle, spirit **8** dispatch, vibrance, vibrancy, vitality, vivacity **9** animation

lively
3 gay **4** busy, keen, pert, spry, yare **5** agile, alert, brisk, fresh, jazzy, jolly, merry, peppy, zippy **6** active, bouncy, bright, chirpy, frisky, jocund, nimble **7** animate, buoyant, chipper, intense, rousing **8** animated, bustling, hustling, spirited, vigorous, volatile **9** energetic, resilient, sparkling, sprightly, vivacious **11** stimulating

liven up
6 vivify **7** animate, freshen, quicken **8** energize, inspirit, vitalize **10** invigorate

liver
7 denizen **8** habitant, occupant, resident **10** inhabitant
combining form: **5** hepat **6** hepato
disease: **9** cirrhosis, hepatitis
French: **4** foie
lobster's: **8** tomalley

liverwort
8 hepatica **9** bryophyte

livestock
4 cows, hogs, pigs **5** bulls, goats, sheep, swine **6** beasts, calves, cattle, horses **7** animals
feed: **6** silage **8** ensilage

live wire
6 dynamo **7** hustler, rustler **8** fireball, go-getter, promoter **9** energizer, generator **11** self-starter

livid
3 hot, mad, wan **4** ashy, pale **5** ashen, lurid, waxen **6** fuming, leaden, pallid, sultry **7** boiling, bruised, enraged, furious, reddish **8** blanched, contused, incensed **9** colorless **10** discolored, infuriated **12** black-and-blue **13** beside oneself

living
5 means, vital **6** extant, income **8** animated, existent **10** livelihood, sustenance
combining form: **3** bio

living room
6 parlor **10** lebensraum
Spanish: **4** sala

lizard
3 eft, Uta **4** Gila, newt, seps, uran **5** agama, anole, gecko, skink, teiid **6** dragon, goanna, iguana **7** monitor, reptile, saurian **8** basilisk, mosasaur, slowworm, squamate, whiptail **9** alligator, blindworm, chameleon, crocodile **10** chuckwalla, salamander **11** Gila monster
combining form: **4** saur **5** saura, sauro

llama
7 camelid
country: **4** Peru **7** Bolivia, Ecuador
habitat: **5** Andes
relative: **6** alpaca, vicuña **7** guanaco

Lloyd's business
9 insurance

Lloyd Webber musical
4 Cats **5** Evita

lo
4 ecce, hark, heed, look, mark, mind **6** attend, behold **7** observe

___ Loa
5 Mauna

load
3 tax **4** bias, copy, fill, haul, heap, lade, onus, pack, pile, stow, task **5** cargo, laden, swamp, weigh **6** burden, debase, doctor, dope up, eyeful, lading, saddle, weight **7** freight **8** encumber, shipment, transfer **9** liability, millstone, transport **11** consignment, encumbrance

loaded
4 full, high, rich **5** awash, doped **6** aboard, biased, filled, packed, stoned **7** boarded, brimful, crowded, wealthy **8** affluent, brimming, chockful, tripping, turned on **9** chock-full

loaf
3 bum, bun **4** idle, laze, lazy, loll **5** bread, dough **6** dawdle, loiter, lounge **7** goof off, hang out **8** lollygag **9** bum around, goldbrick **10** fool around

loafer
3 bum **4** shoe, slug **5** idler **6** slouch **7** goof-off, lounger **8** deadbeat, dolittle, fainéant, slugabed, sluggard **9** do-nothing, goldbrick, lazybones **11** beachcomber, lollygagger

loam
4 clay, dirt, sand, silt, soil **7** topsoil
deposit: **5** loess

loan
3 pay **4** lend **6** credit **7** advance, imprest **9** grubstake
figure: **3** APR
reminder: **3** IOU

loan shark
6 lender, usurer **7** Shylock **10** pawnbroker **11** moneylender

loath
6 afraid, averse **8** hesitant **9** reluctant, unwilling **10** indisposed **11** disinclined **12** antipathetic

loathe
4 hate **5** abhor, scorn, spurn **6** detest, refuse, reject, revile **7** contemn, despise **8** execrate **9** abominate

loathsome
4 foul, ugly, vile **5** gross, nasty **6** odious **7** beastly, hateful, hideous **8** horrible **9** abhorrent, execrable, obnoxious, offensive, repellent, repugnant, repulsive, revolting **10** abominable, deplorable, detestable, disgusting, nauseating

loathing
4 hate **5** odium **6** hatred **8** aversion **9** repulsion, revulsion

lob
4 loft, toss **5** chuck, fling, heave, pitch, sling, throw **6** propel

lobby
4 hall **5** foyer **7** promote **8** anteroom, corridor **9** influence, vestibule **10** passageway **11** waiting room
gun owners': **3** NRA

lobe
4 flap **7** pendant

lobo
4 wolf **8** gray wolf **10** timber wolf

lobster
8 crawfish **10** crustacean
claw: **5** chela **6** pincer
female: **3** hen
male: **4** cock
trap: **3** pot **5** creel

local
6 native **7** endemic, insular, topical **9** parochial **10** provincial

locale
4 area, belt, site, turf, ward **5** place, scene, venue **6** milieu, parish, region, sector **7** commune, quarter, setting **8** district, precinct, vicinage, vicinity **9** community, territory **11** mise-en-scène **12** neighborhood

locality
4 area, belt, city, site, turf, zone **5** block, field, haunt, place, tract **6** county, domain, hamlet, region, sector, sphere, square **7** habitat, section **8** district, environs, precinct, province, purlieus, township, vicinage, vicinity **9** bailiwick, situation, territory **12** neighborhood

localize
4 mass **5** amass, focus **7** cluster, collect **8** coalesce, pinpoint **10** accumulate **11** concentrate, consolidate **12** conglomerate

locate
3 fix, spy **4** espy, find, site, spot **5** dwell, place, trace **6** detect, reside, settle **7** nose out, situate, station, uncover **8** come upon, discover, pinpoint, position **9** establish, ferret out, search out **10** come across

location
4 area, site, post, site, spot **5** locus, place, point, scene, venue, where **7** bearing, habitat, setting **8** position **9** situation **11** mise-en-scène, whereabouts

loch
3 bay **4** lake
Scottish: **4** Ness **5** Leven **6** Lomond

lock
4 bolt, curl, hank, hold, tuft **5** latch, tress **6** fasten, secure **7** ringlet **8** fastener **9** enclosure, fastening

lockjaw
7 tetanus, trismus

lock up
3 ice **4** seal **5** sew up **6** assure, clinch, ensure, ratify, secure, settle **7** confirm **8** complete, conclude, finalize, validate **9** guarantee

lockup
3 can, jug, pen **4** brig, cell, coop, gaol, jail, stir, tank **5** clink, pokey, pound **6** cooler, prison **7** slammer **8** bastille, hoosegow **9** calaboose

loco
3 ape, mad **4** bats, nuts **5** balmy, batty, crazy, kooky, loony, nutty **6** crazed, insane, screwy **7** bananas, berserk, bonkers, cracked, flipped, lunatic **8** demented, deranged, frenzied, unhinged **10** flipped out

locomotive
5 cheer, dolly, train **6** engine
small: **5** dinky **6** dinkey
type: **5** steam **6** diesel **8** electric

locum tenens
3 sub **5** proxy **6** backup, fill-in, supply **7** stand-in **9** alternate, auxiliary, surrogate **10** substitute **11** pinch hitter, replacement, succedaneum

locus
3 hub **4** seat, site **5** focus, heart, stage **6** center **7** setting **8** cynosure, location, polestar **10** focal point **11** nerve center **12** headquarters

locust
4 tree, wood **5** carob **6** cicada, insect **11** grasshopper

locution
4 word **5** argot, idiom, lingo **6** jargon, patois, phrase **7** dialect **8** parlance, phrasing **9** utterance **10** expression **11** phraseology

lode
4 seam, vein **5** store **6** source, supply **7** deposit
mother: **7** bonanza

lodestar
4 guru **5** gauge, guide, ideal, model **6** beacon, leader, mentor **7** epitome **8** exemplar, paradigm **9** archetype, guidepost **11** inspiration

lodestone
6 magnet **9** magnetite

lodge
3 den, fix, inn **4** bunk, camp, club, file, lair, nest, root, stay **5** abide, abode, board, cabin, couch, dwell, embed, guild, hotel, house, motel, order, put up **6** billet, burrow, hostel, league, remain, shanty, tavern, wigwam **7** auberge, contain, cottage, deposit, hospice, quarter, receive, shelter **8** domicile, hostelry, sodality **9** gatehouse **10** fellowship **11** accommodate, brotherhood, caravansary, public house
letters: **4** BPOE
member: **3** Elk **5** Mason, Moose **7** Shriner **9** Freemason, Odd Fellow

lodger
5 guest **6** renter, roomer, tenant **7** boarder, resider

lodging
3 inn, pad **4** dorm, room **5** abode, hotel, motel, place **7** shelter **8** chambers, diggings, domicile, dwelling, quarters **9** apartment, residence **10** pied-à-terre **13** accommodation

loess
4 clay, loam, marl **7** deposit **8** sediment

loft
4 rise **5** attic, raise **6** dormer, garret, propel **7** gallery

loftiness
5 pride **6** height **7** disdain, hauteur, stature **8** altitude, eminence **9** aloofness, arrogance, elevation, pomposity, sublimity **11** haughtiness, superiority **13** condescension

lofty
4 airy, epic, high, tall **5** grand, noble, proud **6** aerial, august, raised, remote, superb **7** exalted, haughty, soaring, stately, sublime, utopian **8** arrogant, cavalier, elevated, eloquent, imposing, insolent, majestic, superior, towering **9** ambitious, grandiose, visionary **10** disdainful **11** overbearing, pretentious, skyscraping **12** supercilious

log
5 diary, tally **6** record, timber **7** journal **8** register
cutter: **8** chain saw
mover: **5** peavy **6** peavey **7** cant dog
type: **4** yule

loge
3 box **5** booth, stall **7** balcony **9** mezzanine

logger
9 lumberman **10** lumberjack, woodcutter
legendary: **10** Paul Bunyan

loggerhead
6 shrike, turtle

loggia
6 arcade **7** balcony, gallery, veranda

logic
6 reason **9** reasoning **10** syntactics
specious: **7** sophism **9** sophistry

logical
5 sound, valid **6** cogent **8** analytic, sensible **9** deducible, deductive, plausible **10** analytical, compelling, convincing, diagnostic, reasonable, scientific, systematic
prefix: **4** theo

logjam
5 crowd **7** impasse **8** blockage, deadlock, stoppage **11** obstruction

logo
5 badge, brand, motto **6** cipher, device, emblem, symbol **8** colophon, hallmark, monogram **9** trademark

logogriph
6 puzzle **7** anagram

logroll
4 birl

logy
4 dull, slow **5** dopey, heavy **6** drowsy, groggy, torpid **8** listless, sluggish

Lohengrin
composer: **6** Wagner (Richard)
father: **8** Parsifal, Parzival
wife: **4** Elsa

loincloth
5 dhoti **11** breechcloth, breechclout

Loire
city: **5** Blois, Tours **6** Nantes **7** Orléans
region: **5** Anjou

Lois of the Daily Planet
4 Lane

loiter
3 bum, lag **4** drag, idle, laze, lazy, loaf, loll, poke **5** dally, delay, tarry, trail **6** dawdle, diddle, linger, lounge, put off, putter **8** lollygag **10** dilly-dally, fool around, hang around **11** screw around **13** procrastinate

Loki
father: **8** Farbauti
mother: **3** Nal **6** Laufey
offspring: **3** Hel **4** Hela **6** Fenris **7** Midgard
slayer: **8** Heimdall
victim: **6** Balder, Baldur
wife: **5** Sigyn **9** Angurboda

Lolita
author: **7** Nabokov (Vladimir)
suitor: **7** Humbert (Humbert)

loll
3 bum, lag **4** drag, idle, laze, lazy, loaf, poke **5** chill, dally, delay, droop, slump, tarry, trail **6** dangle, dawdle, diddle, linger, lounge, putter, slouch **8** chill out **10** dillydally, fool around, hang around **13** procrastinate

lollapalooza
4 lulu **5** beaut, daisy, dilly, doozy **6** corker, doozie **8** jim-dandy, knockout **9** humdinger **11** crackerjack, sockdolager

Lollards' leader
8 Wycliffe (John)

lollygag
4 idle, loaf, loll, poke, drag **5** chill **6** dawdle, diddle, loiter, piddle, putter **10** dilly-dally, fool around

Lombard
6 banker **11** moneylender
king: **5** Cleph **6** Alboin, Audoin **7** Aistulf, Aripert, Authari **9** Liudprand

London
attraction: **3** Eye **5** Tower
borough: **5** Brent **6** Barnet, Bexley, Ealing, Harrow, Sutton **7** Barking, Bromley, Chelsea, Croydon, Enfield, Hackney, Lambeth **8** Haringey, Havering, Hounslow, Lewisham **9** Greenwich, Islington, Redbridge **10** Kensington **11** Westminster
cathedral: **7** St. Paul's
clock: **6** Big Ben
district: **4** Soho **5** Acton **7** Chelsea, Mayfair **9** Belgravia, Southwark
gallery: **4** Tate
gardens: **3** Kew
policeman: **5** bobby
prison: **7** Newgate
river: **6** Thames
square: **9** Leicester, Trafalgar
street: **4** Bond **5** Fleet **6** Strand **7** Downing **9** Whitehall **10** Piccadilly
subway: **4** tube

London novel
7 Sea Wolf (The) **8** Iron Heel (The) **9** White Fang **10** Martin Eden **13** Call of the Wild (The)

lone
4 only, sole, solo **5** alone **6** single, unique **8** deserted, forsaken, isolated, secluded, separate, singular, solitary **13** unaccompanied

lonely
4 left, lorn **5** alone **7** forlorn **8** deserted, forsaken, homesick, lonesome, rejected, solitary **9** abandoned

Lonely Boy singer
4 Anka (Paul)

loneness
8 solitude **9** isolation, seclusion **10** detachment **12** separateness, solitariness

loner
6 hermit **7** isolate, outcast, recluse **8** outsider, solitary **13** individualist

Lone Ranger, The
creator: **7** Striker (Fran)
companion: **5** Tonto
epithet: **8** Kemo Sabe
horse: **6** Silver
trademark: **4** mask **12** silver bullet

Lone Star State
5 Texas

long
3 far, yen **4** ache, itch, pine, tall **5** wordy,

yearn **6** hanker, hunger, prolix, thirst **7** endless, lengthy **8** dragging, drawn-out, extended, unending **9** extensive **10** full-length, protracted

long ago
4 yore

long-billed wader
4 ibis, rail **5** heron

long-drawn-out
7 endless, lengthy **8** dragging, unending **10** protracted **12** interminable

longest river
4 Nile

Longfellow poem
8 Christus, Hiawatha, Hyperion, Kavanagh **10** Evangeline **11** My Lost Youth, Psalm of Life (A)

long for
4 want **5** covet, crave, mourn **6** desire, repine **8** aspire to

longing
3 yen **4** itch, lust, urge, wish **5** greed **6** desire, hunger, thirst **7** avidity, craving, passion **8** appetite

long-jawed fish
3 gar

long-range weapon
4 ICBM

long-running satire show
3 SNL

longshoreman
9 stevedore **10** roustabout
union: 3 ILA

long-suffering
7 patient, stoical **8** enduring, resigned **9** compliant **10** forbearing, submissive **13** accommodating, uncomplaining

long suit
3 bag **4** gift **5** forte **6** métier, talent **8** strength **9** specialty

long time
3 age, eon **4** aeon

long-winded
5 wordy **6** prolix **7** diffuse, lengthy, verbose **8** rambling **9** garrulous, redundant **10** loquacious

loo
3 can, lav **4** head, john **5** jakes, privy **6** toilet **7** latrine **8** bathroom, outhouse

look
3 air, eye **4** gape, gawk, gaze, leer, mien, ogle, peek, peep, peer, seem, view **5** glare, stare, watch **6** admire, appear, aspect, behold, expect, eyeful, glance, glower, goggle, regard, squint, survey, visage **7** bearing, examine, eyeball, glimpse, observe **8** demeanor, once-over **10** appearance, rubberneck

look after
4 mind, tend **5** nurse, serve, watch **6** attend, wait on **7** care for, husband **8** wait upon **9** watch over **10** provide for

look-alike
4 twin **5** clone **6** double **7** similar **8** matching **9** duplicate

look at
3 eye, see **4** face, ogle, scan, view **5** check **6** behold, ponder, regard **7** examine, inspect **8** confront, consider **11** investigate

look back
6 recall, review **7** reflect **8** remember **9** reminisce

look down on
5 abhor, scorn, scout, spurn **7** contemn, despise, disdain **8** dominate **9** tower over **10** tower above

looker
6 beauty, eyeful, lovely, vision **7** stunner, witness **8** knockout, ornament **9** bystander, sightseer, spectator **10** eyewitness

looker-on
5 gaper **6** viewer **7** watcher, witness **8** beholder, observer **9** bystander, spectator **10** eyewitness **12** rubbernecker

look for
4 seek **5** await **6** expect, plan on **9** search out **10** anticipate

looking glass
6 mirror **9** reflector

look into
5 check, probe, study **6** pursue, survey **7** examine, explore, inspect **8** check out, question, research **10** scrutinize **11** investigate

look lasciviously
4 leer, ogle

look out
4 mind **6** beware

lookout
4 aery, view **5** aerie, eyrie, guard, perch, scout, tower, vista, watch **6** cupola, picket, sentry **7** spotter **8** panorama, prospect, sentinel, watchman **9** belvedere, crow's nest, firetower **10** watchtower, widow's walk **11** observatory, perspective

look over
3 con, vet **4** read, scan **5** audit, check **6** peruse, review, size up, survey **7** examine, inspect **8** appraise, evaluate

loom
4 brew, bulk, near, rear **5** hover, mount, tower **6** appear, come on, emerge, gather, impend **7** portend **8** approach, overhang, stand out, threaten **9** take shape
part: 6 heddle **7** harness, shuttle, treadle, trundle

loon
3 nut, oaf **4** bird, clod, dodo, dolt, goof, lout, yo-yo **5** chump, dummy, dunce, ninny, noddy, stupe, yokel **6** dimwit, dum-dum, nitwit **7** airhead, buffoon, dullard, pinhead **8** bonehead, dumbbell, crackpot, imbecile, lunkhead, meathead, numskull **9** birdbrain, blockhead, ignoramus, lamebrain, numbskull, simpleton **10** dunderhead, nincompoop **11** chowderhead, chucklehead

loony
3 nut **4** bats, loco, nuts **5** balmy, batty, crazy, daffy, dippy, goofy, nutty, silly, wacky **6** absurd, insane, madman, screwy **7** fatuous, foolish, idiotic **8** demented **9** bedlamite, half-baked, ludicrous, senseless **10** ridiculous **11** harebrained **12** preposterous

loony bin
6 asylum, bedlam **8** bughouse, madhouse, nuthouse **9** funny farm **10** booby hatch, crazy house

loop
3 arc, eye **4** ansa, ring **5** curve, noose, picot **6** circle, eyelet, league, staple **7** circlet, circuit **8** doubling

looped
3 lit **4** high **5** bowed, drunk, stiff **6** blotto, bombed, curved, juiced, loaded, potted, soused, stewed, tanked, zonked **7** crocked, drunken, pickled, pie-eyed, sloshed, smashed **9** plastered **10** inebriated **11** curvilinear, intoxicated

loophole
3 out **6** escape, outlet **7** opening

loopy
4 bats, daft, loco, nuts, wavy **5** arced, batty, bowed, crazy, daffy, ditzy, dotty, flaky, nutty, silly, snaky, wacky **6** arched, curved, freaky, fruity, screwy, swirly **7** bizarre, idiotic, lunatic, offbeat, sinuous, touched **8** demented **9** eccentric **10** flipped out, off-the-wall, outlandish

loose
3 lax **4** easy, fast, free, lewd, limp **5** baggy, slack, untie, vague **6** flabby, wanton **7** flaccid, relaxed, unleash **8** flexible **9** debauched, desultory, dissolute, imprecise **10** disjointed, dissipated, ill-defined, licentious, unattached, unconfined **12** disconnected, unrestrained

loose end
6 detail **8** fragment

loose-lipped
see **loquacious**

loosen
4 ease, free, undo **5** relax, slack, untie **6** unbind **7** ease off, manumit, release, slacken, unchain **8** liberate, unbuckle, unfasten **10** emancipate

loosen up
5 chill, relax **6** unbend, unwind **7** chillax, ease off, stretch **8** chill out, kick back

loot
3 rob **4** haul, lift, pelf, raid, sack, swag **5** boost, booty, dough, lucre, money, moola, reave, rifle, spoil **6** boodle, moolah, ravish, spoils **7** despoil, pillage, plunder, ransack, stick up **9** knock over

looter
5 thief **6** bandit **7** brigand, burglar **8** marauder

lop
3 cut **4** chop, clip, crop, snip, trim **5** prune, sever, shear **6** cut off, excise **8** amputate, truncate **9** dismember **10** guillotine

lope
3 jog, run **4** gait, romp, trot **5** amble **6** canter

Lopez of pop music
5 Trini

lopsided
4 awry **5** askew, atilt **6** aslant, tilted, uneven **7** crooked, leaning, tilting **8** cockeyed, top-heavy **9** off-kilter **10** asymmetric, off-balance, unbalanced **12** asymmetrical **13** unsymmetrical

loquacious
4 glib **5** gabby, talky, wordy **6** chatty, mouthy, prolix **7** verbose, voluble, yakking **8** babbling, effusive **9** garrulous, jabbering, talkative **10** blathering, chattering, long-winded **11** loose-lipped **12** motormouthed

Lorca play
5 Yerma **12** Blood Wedding

lord
3 sir **4** boss, duke, earl, peer **5** count, noble, ruler **6** master, prince **7** marquis **8** governor, marquess, nobleman, viscount **9** sovereign, tyrannize
feudal: 5 liege, thane **8** seigneur, suzerain
Muslim: 6 sayyid

Lord High Executioner
4 Koko

Lord Jim author
6 Conrad (Joseph)

lordly
5 grand, lofty, noble, proud **6** august, uppity **7** exalted, haughty, pompous, stately, swollen **8** affected, arrogant, cavalier, gracious, imposing, insolent, majestic, princely, snobbish, superior **9** dignified, egotistic, grandiose **10** disdainful, high-handed **11** dictatorial, magisterial,

magnificent, overbearing, patronizing **12** aristocratic, supercilious **13** authoritarian, high-and-mighty

Lord of the Flies
author: **7** Golding (William)
character: **4** Jack **5** Piggy, Ralph

Lord of the Rings
author: **7** Tolkien (J. R. R.)
book: **9** Two Towers (The) **15** Return of the King (The) **19** Fellowship of the Ring (The)
character: **3** Sam **5** Arwen, Frodo, Gimli **6** Elrond, Gollum, Sauron **7** Aragorn, Baggins (Bilbo, Frodo), Boromir, Gandalf, Legolas, Saruman, Théoden **9** Galadriel, Treebeard
film director: **7** Jackson (Peter)
illustrator: **3** Lee (Alan) **4** Howe (John)
race: **4** ents, orcs **5** wargs **6** huorns **7** hobbits **11** ringwraiths
realm: **5** Arnor, Moria, Rohan **6** Gondor, Mordor **10** Lothlórien **11** Middle-earth **12** Undying Lands
site: **5** Shire (The) **8** Isengard **9** Mount Doom, Rivendell
star: **3** Lee (Christopher) **4** Hill (Bernard), Holm (Ian), Wood (Elijah) **5** Astin (Sean), Baker (Sala), Bloom (Orlando), Tyler (Liv) **6** Serkis (Andy) **7** Weaving (Hugo) **8** McKellen (Ian), Monaghan (Dominic) **9** Blanchett (Cate), Mortensen (Viggo)
sword: **5** Sting **6** Narsil **7** Andúril **9** Glamdring

lord's estate
5 manor **7** demesne

Lord's Prayer
9 Our Father **11** Paternoster

lore
6 mythos, wisdom **7** history **8** folkways, learning **9** knowledge, mythology, tradition **11** information **12** superstition

Lorelei
5 siren **9** temptress **10** seductress **11** femme fatale
poet: **5** Heine (Heinrich)
river: **5** Rhein, Rhine
victim: **6** sailor **7** mariner

lorgnette
10 eyeglasses, spectacles **12** opera glasses

Lorna Doone
author: **9** Blackmore (Richard)
hero: **4** Ridd (John)

____ Lorraine
6 Alsace

lorry
3 rig, van **4** semi **5** truck

lose
4 miss, shed **5** evade, shake, waste, yield **6** escape, give up, mislay **7** destroy, forfeit, succumb **8** misplace, shake off, throw off **9** sacrifice, surrender

lose it
4 snap **5** go ape **7** crack up, flip out, go crazy, run amok **8** freak out, run amuck

loser
3 dud **4** bomb, bust, flop **5** lemon **6** bummer, fiasco, misfit, turkey **7** also-ran, debacle, failure, washout **8** deadbeat **11** incompetent

loss
4 bath, harm, ruin **5** waste **6** damage, defeat, injury **7** deficit, failure, forfeit **8** casualty, decrease, fatality **9** depletion, privation, sacrifice, shrinkage **10** divestment, forfeiture, misfortune, misplacing **11** bereavement, deprivation, destruction
allowance: **4** tret

lost
4 asea, dead, gone, rapt **6** absent, astray, bygone, damned, doomed, futile, hidden, wasted **7** defunct, faraway, lacking, mislaid, missing **8** absorbed, departed, distrait, helpless, hopeless, vanished **9** condemned, desperate, destroyed **10** abstracted, insensible, overlooked **11** irrevocable, preoccupied **12** irredeemable, unregenerate

Lost Horizon
author: **6** Hilton (James)
character: **6** Conway (Hugh)
land: **9** Shangri-La

lot
3 cut, ilk **4** doom, fate, heap, kind, mass, plat, yard **5** batch, block, bunch, field, moira, patch, quota, share, slice, tract, weird **6** assign, barrel, bundle, parcel, stripe **7** acreage, cluster, destiny, fortune, mete out, portion, species **8** allocate, clearing, frontage **9** aggregate, allowance, apportion

Lot
father: **5** Haran
sister: **5** Iscah **6** Milcah
son: **4** Moab **5** Ammon
uncle: **7** Abraham

lothario
4 lech, stud, wolf **5** letch, Romeo **6** lecher, tomcat **7** amorist, Don Juan, gallant, seducer **8** Casanova, paramour **9** debaucher, ladies' man, womanizer **10** lady-killer **11** philanderer

lotion
3 oil **4** balm **5** cream, salve **6** cerate **7** unguent **8** ablution, cosmetic, lenitive, liniment, ointment **9** demulcent **11** embrocation
rating: **3** SPF

lottery
6 raffle **7** drawing **11** sweepstakes

lotus-eater
7 dreamer **8** escapist, romantic **10** daydreamer **13** castle-builder

louche
5 seamy, seedy **6** rakish, sordid, wanton **7** raffish, wayward **8** depraved **9** debauched, dissolute, libertine **10** dissipated, licentious, profligate

loud
5 forte, gaudy, noisy, showy **6** brassy, brazen, flashy, garish, glitzy, shrill, tawdry, vulgar **7** blaring, blatant, booming, chintzy, glaring, pealing, raucous, roaring **8** piercing, resonant, sonorous, strident **9** clamorous, deafening, obnoxious, obtrusive, offensive, tasteless **10** bigmouthed, boisterous, flamboyant, fortissimo, resounding, stentorian, thunderous, vociferous **12** earsplitting

loudmouth
6 ranter **7** stentor **8** blowhard, braggart **9** blusterer

loudspeaker
3 amp **6** Tannoy, woofer **7** tweeter **9** amplifier

Louisiana
capital: 10 Baton Rouge
city: 10 New Orleans, Shreveport
college, university: 6 Tulane
county: 6 parish
lake: 13 Pontchartrain
nickname: 7 Pelican (State)
river: 11 Mississippi
state bird: 12 brown pelican
state flower: 8 magnolia
state tree: 11 bald cypress

lounge
3 bar, bum, lie, pub, tap **4** idle, laze, loaf, loll, sofa **5** chill, couch, dally, drift, lobby, relax **6** dawdle, loiter, parlor, repose, saloon **7** barroom, goof off, lie down, recline, taproom **8** chill out, restroom, kill time **10** living room

lounge lizard
3 fop **4** rake, toff **5** blade, dandy, leech **6** gigolo, sponge **9** ladies' man

Lourdes saint
10 Bernadette

louse
3 cad, cur, dog, rat **4** fink, heel, jerk, toad **5** aphid, creep, skunk, snake **6** cootie, psylla, rotter, slater, wretch **7** bounder, schmuck, stinker
egg: 3 nit

louse up
4 blow, flub, muff, ruin **5** botch, spoil, wreck **6** bobble, bollix, bumble, bungle, fumble

lousy
3 ill **4** poor, rife **5** awful **6** crummy, shoddy, rotten **7** replete, teeming **8** crawling, horrible, inferior, infested, terrible **9** miserable, repulsive **10** despicable **12** contemptible

lout
3 cad, oaf **4** boob, boor, dolt, gawk, hick, rube **5** brute, chuff, churl, klutz, looby, scorn, yahoo, yokel **6** galoot, lubber, lummox, rustic **7** bumpkin, hayseed, palooka, schmuck **9** simpleton **10** clodhopper

Louvre masterpiece
8 Mona Lisa **11** Venus de Milo

Louvre Pyramid architect
3 Pei (I. M.)

lovable
4 dear **5** sweet **6** cuddly **7** winning, winsome **8** adorable **9** appealing, endearing **11** embraceable

love
4 zeal **5** adore, ardor, crush, Cupid, prize, value **6** desire, dote on, fervor, revere **7** adulate, cherish, idolize, passion, romance, worship **8** devotion, fondness, idolatry, treasure, venerate, yearning **9** adoration, adulation, delight in **10** attachment **11** amorousness, infatuation
combining form: 4 phil **5** philo, phily **6** philia
French: 5 amour
Italian: 5 amore
tennis: 3 nil **4** zero **7** nothing

love apple
6 tomato

lovebird
6 budgie, parrot **10** budgerigar

love-bite
3 nip **6** hickey

love feast
5 agape

love god
4 Amor, Eros, Kama **5** Bhaga, Cupid

love goddess
5 Athor, Freya, Venus **6** Hathor, Inanna, Ishtar **7** Astarte **9** Aphrodite, Ashtoreth

Lovelace of computer fame
3 Ada

love letter
8 mash note **9** valentine **10** billet-doux

lovely
4 fair **5** sweet, swell **6** comely, dainty, pretty **7** elegant **8** adorable, alluring, charming, delicate, engaging, graceful, knockout **9** beauteous, beautiful, exquisite **10** attractive, delightful, enchanting, entrancing **11** captivating, good-looking

love potion
7 philter, philtre **11** aphrodisiac

lover
3 fan **4** beau, buff **5** flame, leman, Romeo, swain **6** addict, steady, suitor, votary **7** amorist, darling, devotee, Don Juan, gallant, habitué, squeeze **8** fancy man, lothario, mistress,

paramour **9** boyfriend, inamorata, inamorato **10** aficionado, girlfriend, sweetheart

lovey-dovey
5 mushy, sappy **6** doting **7** amorous **12** affectionate

loving
4 dear, fond **6** ardent, erotic, tender **7** amatory, amorous, cordial, devoted, fervent **8** attached, enamored, faithful **10** benevolent, infatuated, passionate, solicitous **11** impassioned **12** affectionate

low
3 moo **4** base, blue, dead, deep, flat, mean, neap **5** cheap, seamy, seedy **6** abject, ailing, humble, hushed, lesser, nether, poorly, sickly, sordid, unwell **7** cut-rate, debased, reduced, scrubby **8** cast down, dejected, depleted, downcast, inferior, mediocre, wretched **9** declining, depressed, miserable, subnormal, woebegone **10** inadequate, indisposed **11** crestfallen, downhearted, unfavorable

lowbred
4 base, rude **6** coarse, oafish, vulgar **7** boorish, brutish, loutish, uncouth **8** churlish, cloddish, lubberly **11** uncivilized

low-cost
5 cheap **6** budget, cheapo **7** bargain, cut-rate **8** discount **10** affordable, reasonable **11** inexpensive

low-down
4 base, mean, ugly, vile **6** grubby, odious, scurvy, sleazy, sordid **7** ignoble, squalid **8** shameful, wretched **9** abhorrent, worthless **10** despicable, disgusting **11** ignominious **12** contemptible

lowdown
4 dope, info **5** facts, goods, scoop, specs **6** skinny **8** briefing **11** information

lower
3 cut **4** clip, drop, fall, sink **5** abase, frown, gloom, scowl, shave, slash, under **6** debase, demean, demote, humble, lesser, menace, nether, reduce **7** cut down, deflate, degrade, demerit, depress, descend, devalue, let down **8** discount, inferior, mark down, overcast, submerge, threaten **9** devaluate, downgrade
prefix: **5** infra

Lower Depths author
5 Gorki, Gorky (Maksim, Maxim)

lower the lights
3 dim

lowest point
5 nadir **6** bottom
in the U.S.: **11** Death Valley
on earth's crust: **13** Mariana Trench
on earth's surface: **7** Dead Sea

low-grade
4 hack **5** junky, lousy **6** cheesy, cruddy, shabby, shoddy, sleazy, tawdry **8** below par, déclassé, inferior, mediocre **9** deficient **10** second-rate **11** second-class, substandard **12** second-drawer

low-key
4 soft **5** muted, quiet **7** relaxed, subdued **8** laid-back, softened, tasteful **9** easygoing, minimized, temperate, toned down **10** played down, restrained **11** understated

lowland
4 dale, flat, sump, vale **5** basin, swale **6** bottom, slough, valley **7** bottoms
Scottish: **6** lallan **7** lalland

lowlife
4 fink, heel **5** knave, rogue **6** no-good, outlaw, rascal, wretch **7** hoodlum, ruffian, villain **9** miscreant, reprobate, scoundrel **10** blackguard, black sheep, ne'er-do-well, sleazeball **11** rapscallion, slimebucket **12** bottom-feeder

lowly
4 base, mean, meek **6** abject, humble, menial, modest **7** ignoble, mundane, obscure, prosaic, servile **8** baseborn, plebeian, unwashed

low point
5 nadir

low-pressure
4 calm **6** casual, dégagé, folksy, mellow **7** relaxed **8** flexible, informal, laid-back **9** easygoing **10** nonchalant

low-spirited
3 sad **4** blue, down, glum **6** abject, droopy, gloomy, morose **7** doleful **8** cast down, dejected, downcast, saddened **9** bummed out, cheerless, depressed, woebegone **10** dispirited, melancholy **11** discouraged, downhearted **12** disheartened, heavyhearted

low tide
3 ebb **4** neap

loyal
4 firm, true **5** liege **6** ardent, trusty **7** devoted, dutiful, staunch **8** constant, faithful, resolute, true-blue **9** allegiant, steadfast, unfailing **10** dependable **11** trustworthy

loyalist
4 Tory **7** patriot **8** partisan **10** countryman **11** nationalist

loyalty
6 fealty **8** adhesion, devotion, fidelity **9** adherence, constancy **10** allegiance, attachment, dedication **11** staunchness **12** faithfulness **13** dependability, steadfastness

lozenge
4 pill **6** troche **7** diamond, rhombus **8** pastille

LSD
4 acid
user: **8** acidhead

luau
dish: **3** poi
instrument: **3** uke **7** ukelele, ukulele

lubricant
3 oil **6** grease

lubricate
3 oil **6** grease, smooth **7** moisten

lubricious
4 lewd, oily **5** slick **6** carnal, greasy, slippy, wanton **7** lustful, sensual **8** prurient, slippery, slithery, ticklish **9** lecherous, salacious **10** lascivious, libidinous **12** concupiscent

lucent
5 clear **6** bright, limpid **7** beaming, crystal, glowing, lambent, radiant, shining **8** clear-cut, luminous, pellucid **9** brilliant, effulgent, refulgent **11** unambiguous

Lucia di Lammermoor
character: **7** Edgardo
composer: **9** Donizetti (Gaetano)
novelist: **5** Scott (Walter)

lucid
4 sane **5** clear **6** bright, limpid **7** crystal, lambent, radiant **8** clear-cut, knowable, luminous **9** brilliant, effulgent, graspable, refulgent, unblurred **10** articulate, fathomable **11** translucent, transparent, unambiguous **12** compos mentis, incandescent, intelligible, transpicuous

lucidity
6 acumen, sanity **7** clarity **8** sagacity, saneness **9** clearness, plainness, soundness **10** cognizance, perception **12** clairvoyance

Lucifer
5 devil, fiend, Satan, Venus **7** Old Nick **8** Apollyon **9** archfiend, Beelzebub **10** Old Scratch **13** Old Gooseberry

Lucinde
beloved: **7** Leandre **9** Clitandre
father: **7** Geronte **10** Sganarelle

luck
3 hap, hit **4** juju, meet **5** fluke, light **6** chance, happen, hazard, kismet **7** fortune, godsend, stumble **8** fortuity, occasion, windfall **9** advantage **11** opportunity
token: **5** charm **6** amulet, clover, fetish, mascot **8** talisman **9** horseshoe **11** rabbit's foot

luckless
6 jinxed **7** adverse, hapless, unhappy **8** ill-fated, snakebit, untoward, wretched **9** miserable **10** ill-starred **11** star-crossed, unfavorable, unfortunate **12** misfortunate, unpropitious

lucky
6 golden, timely **7** favored **9** favorable, fortunate **10** auspicious, beneficial, felicitous, fortuitous, propitious **12** advantageous, providential **13** serendipitous
Scottish: **5** canny

Lucky Jim author
4 Amis (Kingsley)

lucrative
6 paying **7** gainful **8** fruitful **10** high-income, productive, profitable, well-paying, worthwhile **11** moneymaking **12** advantageous, remunerative

lucre
3 pay **4** cash, gain, jack, loot, pelf, swag **5** booty, dough, green, money, moola **6** boodle, dinero, do-re-mi, moolah, profit, wampum **7** cabbage, revenue **9** long green **10** greenbacks

Lucrezia ____
6 Borgia

Lucy's husband
4 Desi (Arnaz)

ludicrous
4 zany **5** antic, comic, droll, funny, goofy, nutty, silly **6** absurd **7** amusing, bizarre, comical, foolish, risible **8** farcical **9** fantastic, grotesque, laughable **10** off-the-wall, outlandish, ridiculous **11** incongruous **12** preposterous

Ludlum, Robert
hero: **6** Bourne (Matthew)
novel: **14** Bourne Identity (The) **15** Bourne Supremacy (The), Bourne Ultimatum (The)

lug
3 nut, oaf, tow, tug **4** bear, buck, drag, draw, haul, hump, jerk, pull, tote **5** carry, ferry, shlep **6** convey, schlep **7** bruiser, schlepp **9** transport

luge
4 sled
relative: **7** bobsled **8** skeleton

luggage
4 bags, gear **7** baggage

Lugosi of horror films
4 Bela

lugubrious
3 sad **4** blue, dour, down, glum **5** bleak **6** dismal, dreary, gloomy, morose, rueful, somber, sullen, woeful **7** doleful, joyless **8** cast down, dejected, dolesome, downcast, mournful **9** cheerless, depressed, plaintive, saturnine, sorrowful, woebegone **10** depressing, despondent, lamentable, melancholy, oppressive **11** discouraged, dispiriting, downhearted **12** disconsolate

Luke's sister
4 Leia

lukewarm
5 blasé, tepid **7** dubious, offhand **8** hesitant **9** uncertain, undecided **10** wishy-washy **11** half-hearted, indifferent

lull
3 ebb **4** balm, calm, hush, wane **5** letup, pause, quiet, still **6** becalm, pacify, soothe, temper **7** compose, decline, ease off, slacken **8** abeyance, interval **9** stillness **10** quiescence **11** tranquilize

lullaby
8 berceuse **10** cradlesong

lulu
3 ace, gem, pip **5** beaut, daisy, dandy, dilly, doozy, dream, honey **6** corker, doozie, hummer, wonder **7** delight **8** jim-dandy, knockout **9** humdinger, sensation **11** crackerjack, sockdolager

lumber
3 tax **4** clog, lade, load, logs, plod, slog, wood **5** barge, clump, stump, weigh **6** burden, charge, rumble, saddle, timber, trudge **8** encumber

lumberjack
6 logger **10** woodcutter
legendary: **10** Paul Bunyan

luminance
10 brightness

luminary
3 sun, VIP **4** lion, name, star **5** celeb, light, nabob **6** leader, worthy **7** big name, notable **8** big-timer, eminence, somebody **9** celebrity, dignitary, superstar **10** notability **12** leading light

luminous
5 clear, lucid **6** bright, lucent **7** beaming, crystal, fulgent, lambent, radiant, shining **8** clear-cut, lustrous, pellucid **9** brilliant, effulgent, refulgent **11** illustrious, translucent, transparent **12** enlightening, incandescent

lummox
3 oaf **4** boor, clod, gawk, goon, hulk, lout **5** klutz, looby **6** lubber **7** palooka

lump
3 gob, lot, oaf, wad **4** blob, bulk, chip, clod, gawk, glob, heap, hunk, lout, mass, pile, welt **5** abide, batch, block, brook, bulge, bunch, chunk, hunch, klutz, knurl, looby, piece, scrap, stand, tumor **6** digest, endure, entire, lubber, morsel, nugget **7** handful, palooka, portion, stomach, swallow **8** swelling, totality **9** aggregate **10** protrusion, tumescence **12** protuberance

lumpy
5 crude, gawky, rough **6** choppy, clumsy, coarse, oafish **8** clumpish, unformed **9** roughhewn

lunacy
5 folly, mania **6** idiocy **7** fatuity, foolery, inanity, madness **8** delirium, dementia, insanity **9** absurdity, craziness, silliness, stupidity **10** imbecility **11** derangement, foolishness **13** senselessness

lunar
dark area: **4** mare **5** maria (plural)
valley: **4** rill **5** rille

lunar New Year
3 Tet

lunatic
3 mad, nut **4** bats, daft, kook, loco, yo-yo, zany **5** balmy, batty, crank, crazy, nutty, raver, wacko, wacky **6** absurd, crazed, cuckoo, insane, madman, maniac, nitwit, psycho, screwy **7** bonkers, cracked, foolish **8** crackpot, demented, demoniac, deranged, frenzied, maniacal, paranoid, schizoid, unhinged **9** bedlamite, ding-a-ling, fruitcake, harebrain, screwball **10** crackbrain **11** nonsensical

lunch
3 eat **4** meal, nosh **5** snack

luncheonette
4 café **5** diner **6** bistro, eatery **7** beanery, canteen, tearoom **8** snack bar **9** cafeteria **10** coffee shop, restaurant **11** greasy spoon

lune
3 bow **5** curve **6** sickle **8** crescent, meniscus

lung
combining form: **5** pneum, pulmo **6** pneumo, pulmon
disease: **9** emphysema, pneumonia **10** byssinosis **12** tuberculosis

lunge
3 jab **4** dash, dive, go at, stab **5** bound, drive, pitch, surge **6** charge, plunge, pounce, thrust

lunkhead
3 oaf **4** boob, clod, dodo, dolt, goof, yo-yo **5** booby, chump, dummy, dunce, idiot, moron, ninny, noddy, stupe **6** dimwit, dum-dum, nitwit **7** dullard **8** dumbbell, imbecile, numskull **9** birdbrain, ignoramus, lamebrain, numbskull, simpleton **10** nincompoop

lupine
5 feral **6** brutal, fierce **7** wolfish **8** ravening **9** predatory, rapacious **10** bluebonnet, sanguinary

Lupino of the stage
3 Ida

lurch
3 bob, yaw **4** jerk, lean, list, reel, rock, roll, sway, tilt, toss **5** heave, pitch, slide, swing **6** bumble, careen, falter, plunge, seesaw, swerve, teeter, totter **7** blunder, stagger, stumble **8** flounder

lure
3 bag **4** bait, call, draw, fake, hook, pull, rope, toll, trap, wile **5** blind, catch, charm, decoy, snare, tempt, trick **6** appeal, cajole, come-on, draw in, draw on, entice, entrap, invite, lead on, seduce **7** attract, beguile, bewitch, capture, con game, enchant, ensnare, gimmick, wheedle **8** blandish, delusion, illusion, inveigle **9** captivate, fascinate, incentive, seduction, siren song

10 attraction, camouflage, enticement, inducement, seducement, temptation
fishing: 3 fly 4 worm 5 spoon 6 minnow 8 bucktail

lurid
4 ashy, gory, gray, grim, pale 5 ashen, fiery, gross, livid, waxen 6 grisly, malign, sultry 7 baleful, ghastly, graphic, hideous, macabre, malefic, tabloid 8 blanched, gruesome, horrible, shocking, sinister, terrible 9 colorless 10 horrifying, maleficent, terrifying 11 sensational 12 melodramatic

Lurie novel
14 Foreign Affairs 18 War Between the Tates (The)

lurk
4 hide, slip 5 creep, prowl, skulk, slide, slink, sneak, snoop, steal 9 pussyfoot

luscious
4 rich, sexy 5 sapid, sweet, tasty, yummy 6 delish, divine, ornate, savory 7 opulent, piquant, sensual 8 sensuous 9 ambrosial, epicurean, exquisite, flavorful, luxurious, seductive, sumptuous, toothsome 10 delectable, delightful, flamboyant, flavorsome, voluptuous 11 scrumptious 13 mouth-watering

lush
3 sot 4 rank, rich, wino 5 dense, drink, drunk, yummy 6 bibber, boozer, deluxe, lavish, savory 7 fertile, opulent, profuse, sensual, teeming, tippler 8 abundant, drunkard, palatial, prodigal, sensuous, thriving 9 ambrosial, epicurean, exuberant, inebriate, luxuriant, luxurious, plentiful, sumptuous, toothsome 10 boozehound, delectable, delightful, profitable, prosperous, voluptuous 11 extravagant, flourishing

Lusitania
8 Portugal

lust
3 rut, yen 4 ache, itch, pine, urge, wish, zeal, zest 5 ardor, crave, drive, greed, letch, yearn 6 desire, fervor, hanker, hunger, libido 7 avidity, craving, lechery, longing, passion 8 appetite, coveting, cupidity, lewdness, priapism, salacity, satyrism, yearning 9 carnality, eagerness, eroticism, lubricity, prurience, pruriency 10 enthusiasm, excitement, satyriasis, wantonness 11 nymphomania 13 concupiscence, lecherousness, salaciousness

luster
4 glow 5 glaze, gleam, glint, gloss, sheen, shine 6 polish 7 burnish, shimmer 8 lambency, radiance 9 afterglow 10 brightness, brilliance, brilliancy, effulgence, luminosity, refulgence 11 candescence, iridescence

lusterless
3 dim, wan 4 blah, drab, dull, flat, gray, matt 5 brown, dingy, dusky, faded, matte, muddy, muted, vapid 6 boring 10 uninspired

lustful
3 hot 4 lewd 5 bawdy, horny 6 carnal, erotic, wanton 7 burning, goatish, itching, ruttish, satyric 8 prurient 9 debauched, lecherous, libertine, lickerish, salacious 10 hot-blooded, lascivious, libidinous, licentious, lubricious, passionate 12 concupiscent
look: 4 leer, ogle

lustrate
5 purge 6 purify 7 cleanse

lustration
6 ritual 8 ablution 9 catharsis, cleansing, purgation 10 sprinkling 12 purification

lustrous
4 naïf 5 nitid, shiny 6 bright, gleamy, glossy, pearly, sheeny 7 fulgent, glowing, lambent, radiant, shining 8 gleaming, luminous, polished, splendid 9 brilliant, burnished, effulgent, refulgent 10 glimmering, glistening 11 resplendent 12 incandescent

lusty
4 hale 5 hardy, vital 6 brawny, hearty, mighty, potent, robust, strong, virile 7 dynamic, healthy, rousing 8 vigorous 9 energetic, strapping, strenuous 10 prodigious, red-blooded 12 enthusiastic

lute
4 clay, seal 5 grout 6 cement 7 bandora, theorbo 8 mandolin 10 chitarrone, instrument
Indian: 5 sarod, sitar
Japanese: 4 biwa 7 samisen 8 shamisen
Middle Eastern: 3 oud, tar

lutenist
5 Bream (Julian) 7 Dowland (John) 8 Gaultier (Denis)

Lutetia
5 Paris

luxe
8 opulence, richness

Luxembourg
capital: 10 Luxembourg
monetary unit: 4 euro
monetary unit, former: 5 franc
mountain range: 8 Ardennes
neighbor: 6 France 7 Belgium, Germany
river: 4 Sûre 7 Alzette

luxuriant
4 lush, rank, rich 5 dense 6 fecund, lavish 7 copious, fertile, opulent, profuse, rampant, riotous, teeming 8 abundant, fruitful, luscious, prodigal, prolific 9 excessive, exuberant, sumptuous

luxuriate
4 bask 5 bloom, enjoy, feast, revel 6 abound, relish, thrive, wallow 7 delight, indulge 8 flourish

luxurious
4 lush, posh, rich 5 fancy, grand, plush, ritzy, showy 6 costly, deluxe, lavish, plushy 7 opulent, sensual, stately 8 imposing, majestic, palatial,

splendid **9** elaborate, epicurean, expensive, grandiose, sumptuous **10** impressive **11** extravagant, magnificent
situation: **7** fat city **10** bed of roses, easy street

luxury
5 frill, treat **6** dainty **7** amenity, comfort **8** delicacy, opulence **9** abundance, affluence **10** indulgence **11** superfluity **12** extravagance

lycée
6 school **10** high school

lyceum
4 hall **6** school **7** academy, chamber **9** institute

Lycidas author
6 Milton (John)

Lycomedes
daughter: **8** Deidamia
victim: **7** Theseus

Lycus
brother: **7** Nycteus
father: **7** Pandion
slayer: **6** Zethus **7** Amphion
wife: **5** Dirce

Lydian
capital: **6** Sardis
king: **5** Gyges **7** Croesus **8** Alyattes
queen: **7** Omphale

lye
7 caustic **9** hydroxide

lynch
4 hang **5** scrag **6** gibbet, murder **7** execute **8** string up

lynx
4 puma **6** bobcat, cougar **7** caracal, wildcat **9** catamount

Lyra star
4 Vega

lyre
4 asor, harp

lyric
3 ode **4** odic, poem **5** melic, verse **6** poetic **7** melodic, musical **8** operatic **9** exuberant, rhapsodic

lyrical
7 lilting, melodic, musical, songful, tuneful **8** operatic **9** melodious

lyricist
4 poet **10** librettist
see **songwriter**

Lysander's beloved
6 Hermia

M

macabre
4 grim **5** lurid **6** grisly, horrid, morbid **7** deathly, ghastly, hideous **8** ghoulish, gruesome, horrible **9** deathlike **10** horrifying

macadam
3 tar **7** asphalt, roadway **8** pavement

macaque
6 monkey, rhesus

macaroni
3 fop **4** beau, buck, dude, toff **5** dandy, pasta, swell **7** coxcomb, gallant

macaw
3 Ara **6** parrot

Macbeth
character: **4** Ross **5** Angus **6** Hecate, Lennox **7** Fleance
slayer: **7** Macduff
successor: **7** Malcolm
title: **5** thane
victim: **6** Banquo, Duncan

mace
4 club **5** baton, staff **6** cudgel, nutmeg **8** bludgeon

Macedonia
capital: **6** Skopje
city: **6** Tetovo
monetary unit: **5** denar
neighbor: **6** Greece, Serbia **7** Albania **8** Bulgaria
part of: **7** Balkans
peninsula: **6** Balkan

macerate
3 ret **4** soak **5** steep **6** drench, soften **7** immerse, suffuse **8** saturate

MacFarlane of Family Guy fame
4 Seth

MacGraw of film
3 Ali

machete
4 bolo **5** knife **6** scythe

Machiavellian
4 wily **6** shrewd **7** cunning, devious **8** guileful, scheming **9** conniving, deceitful, insidious **10** conspiring **11** duplicitous, treacherous **12** unscrupulous

Machiavelli work
6 Prince (The) **8** Mandrake (The) **10** Mandragola (La)

machinate
4 plot **6** scheme **7** connive, finagle **8** conspire, intrigue, maneuver

machination
4 plot, ploy, ruse **5** cabal, dodge **6** gambit, scheme **8** artifice, intrigue, maneuver, scheming, trickery **9** chicanery, collusion, deception, dirty work, expedient, stratagem **10** hanky-panky, subterfuge **11** contrivance, skulduggery **12** gamesmanship, skullduggery

machine
6 device, engine, gadget **9** apparatus, appliance, automaton **11** contraption
part: **3** cam **4** gear **5** lever, shaft, valve **6** caster, flange, router, switch **7** bearing

machine-gun
4 rake **6** strafe **8** enfilade **9** rapid-fire

machine-gun inventor
7 Gatling (Richard)

machinery
5 works **9** apparatus, equipment, mechanism

machismo
7 swagger **8** virility **9** manliness **11** masculinity

macho
4 stud **5** he-man, manly **6** virile **9** masculine

Machu Picchu resident
4 Inca

mackinaw
4 coat **5** cover, trout **7** blanket

mackintosh
7 slicker **8** raincoat

macrocosm
5 world **6** cosmos **8** creation, universe

mad
4 bats, daft, gaga, loco, nuts, rash, sore, wild **5** angry, crazy, irate, irked, kooky, livid, loony, loopy, nutty, rabid, upset, wacky **6** absurd, crazed, cuckoo, heated, insane, ireful, screwy **7** berserk, bonkers, cracked, enraged, foolish, frantic, furious, lunatic **8** choleric, demented, deranged, frenetic, frenzied, incensed, offended, outraged, seething, unhinged, worked up, wrathful **9** delirious, fanatical, fantastic, hilarious, illogical, senseless **10** distracted, infuriated, irrational, unbalanced

Madagascar
capital: **10** Tananarive **12** Antananarivo
channel: **10** Mozambique
city: **9** Mahajanga, Toamasina
language: **6** French **8** Malagasy
monetary unit: **6** ariary
mountain range: **9** Ankaratra

Madagascar primate
5 lemur

madame
3 Mrs. **4** wife **6** milady, missus
German: **4** Frau
Spanish: **3** Sra. **6** Señora

Madame Bovary
author: **8** Flaubert (Gustave)
character: **4** Emma (Bovary) **7** Charles (Bovary) **8** Rodolphe

Madame Butterfly
character: **9** Cho-Cho-San, Cio-Cio-San, Pinkerton, Sharpless
composer: **7** Puccini (Giacomo)

madcap
4 rash, wild, zany **5** antic **7** foolish **8** reckless **9** frivolous, hotheaded **10** capricious, incautious

Mad Cavalier
6 Rupert (Prince)

madden
3 ire, vex **4** goad **5** anger, craze **6** enrage **7** derange, incense, inflame, outrage, possess, steam up, unhinge **9** infuriate, unbalance

Madeira Islands
capital: **7** Funchal
export: **4** wine
part of: **8** Portugal

mademoiselle
4 girl, lass, Miss **6** maiden **9** governess **10** yellowtail **11** silver perch

made-to-order
6 custom **7** bespoke **10** customized **11** custom-built

made-up
5 bogus, faked, false, phony **6** phoney **7** painted **8** invented, mythical, specious **9** fictional, imaginary, pretended, trumped-up **10** apocryphal, fabricated, fictitious **11** make-believe **12** cosmeticized

madhouse
6 asylum, bedlam **8** loony bin **9** funny farm **10** booby hatch

madman
3 nut **4** kook, loon **5** loony, raver **6** cuckoo, maniac, psycho **7** lunatic, nutcase **9** bedlamite, psychotic, fruitcake

Mad Men
actor, actress: **4** Hamm (Jon), Moss (Elisabeth) **5** Jones (January) **9** Hendricks (Christina)
character: **4** Joan (Holloway) **5** Betty (Draper), Peggy (Olson), Sally (Draper) **6** Cooper (Bertram), Draper (Don) **8** Campbell (Pete) **8** Sterling (Roger)

madness
4 rage **5** folly, mania **6** lunacy **8** insanity **9** psychosis **11** derangement

Madonna initials
3 BVM

Madonna musical
5 Evita

Madras
9 Tamil Nadu
founder: **3** Day (Francis)

Madrid museum
5 Prado

madrigal
4 glee, poem, song **8** part-song

madrigalist
English: **4** Byrd (William) **6** Morley (Thomas), Wilbye (John) **7** Tomkins (Thomas), Weelkes (Thomas)
Flemish: **8** Willaert (Adrian)
Italian: **5** Lasso (Orlando di) **6** Lassus (Orlandus) **8** Marenzio (Luca) **10** Monteverdi (Claudio)

maelstrom
4 eddy **5** whirl, whorl **6** vortex **7** turmoil **9** whirlpool **10** tourbillon **11** tourbillion

maenad
9 bacchante, priestess
cry: **4** evoe

maestro
8 batonist **9** conductor **10** bandleader
(see also **conductor)**

Mafia
3 mob **4** ring **6** clique **7** rackets **8** gangland **9** Black Hand, syndicate **10** Cosa Nostra, underworld
code: **6** omertà
don: **4** capo

mafioso
4 capo, goon **6** hit man **7** goombah, made man, mobster **8** gangster **9** racketeer

magazine
4 dump **5** cache, depot, organ, store **6** armory, digest, review, weekly **7** arsenal, gazette, journal, monthly **8** biweekly **9** bimonthly, quarterly, warehouse **10** depository, periodical, repository, storehouse **11** publication
type: **3** box, pan **4** drum, tube **6** rotary

mage
6 priest, wizard **7** warlock **8** sorcerer

maggot
3 bee **4** grub, whim **5** fancy, larva **6** megrim, vagary **7** caprice, conceit

Magi
6 Caspar, Gaspar **8** Melchior **9** Balthasar, Balthazar
gift: **4** gold **5** myrrh **7** incense **12** frankincense

magic
4 juju, mojo **5** obeah, wicca **6** hoodoo, voodoo **7** alchemy, devilry, hexerei, sorcery **8** satanism, witchery, witching, wizardry **9** conjuring, diablerie, diabolism, occultism, sortilege **10** hocus-pocus, mumbo jumbo, necromancy, witchcraft **11** abracadabra, bewitchment, enchantment, legerdemain, thaumaturgy

magical
5 runic **6** occult **8** wizardly **10** bewitching, entrancing **11** necromantic **12** thaumaturgic
expression: **6** presto, shazam **8** alakazam **11** abracadabra

Magic Flute composer
6 Mozart (Wolfgang Amadeus)

magician
5 brujo, witch **6** shaman, wizard **7** Houdini, warlock **8** conjurer, satanist, sorcerer **9** diabolist, enchanter, trickster, voodooist **11** medicine man, necromancer, thaumaturge
Arthurian: **6** Merlin
Shakespearean: **8** Prospero
stage: **3** Uri (Geller) **4** Penn **5** Randi (James) **6** Teller **11** Copperfield (David), illusionist
Tolkien's: **7** Gandalf

Magic Mountain, The
author: **4** Mann (Thomas)
character: **7** Castorp (Hans)

magisterial
6 lordly **7** pompous **8** dogmatic, masterly **9** imperious, masterful **10** high-handed **11** doctrinaire, domineering, overbearing **13** authoritative, self-important

Magister Ludi author
5 Hesse (Hermann)

magistrate
5 court, judge **7** bencher, justice **8** official
ancient Greek: **5** ephor **6** archon
ancient Roman: **6** aedile **7** duumvir, praetor, questor **8** quaestor
Italian: **4** doge **7** podesta
Scottish: **6** bailie
Venetian: **4** doge

Magna Carta
king: **4** John
locale: **9** Runnymede

magnanimous
5 noble **7** liberal **8** generous, princely **9** forgiving, unselfish **10** beneficent, benevolent, bighearted, charitable, chivalrous, high-minded, munificent

magnate
5 baron, mogul, nabob **6** fat cat, prince, tycoon **9** personage, plutocrat

magnet
4 draw, lure **9** lodestone **10** attraction

magnetic
8 alluring **9** appealing, seductive **10** attractive **11** captivating, charismatic, fascinating **12** irresistible
substance: **4** iron **7** ferrite

magnetism
4 draw, lure, pull **5** charm **6** allure, appeal **7** glamour **8** charisma **10** attraction **11** fascination

magnetize
4 draw, lure, wile **5** charm **6** seduce **7** attract, bewitch, enchant **9** captivate, fascinate

magnificence
4 pomp **7** majesty **8** grandeur, splendor **9** pageantry, splendour **13** sumptuousness

magnificent
5 grand, noble, regal, royal **6** august, lavish, lordly, superb **7** exalted, opulent, stately, sublime **8** glorious, imposing, majestic, palatial, princely, splendid **9** brilliant, grandiose, luxurious, sumptuous **11** extravagant, resplendent, splendorous **13** splendiferous

magnifier
4 lens **9** telescope
jeweler's: **5** loupe

magnify
4 hymn, laud **5** add to, boost, cry up, exalt, extol, swell **6** expand, extend, praise **7** amplify, augment, enhance, enlarge, ennoble, glorify, inflate **8** heighten, increase, maximize, multiply, overplay **9** aggravate, celebrate, embellish, embroider, intensify, overstate **10** aggrandize, exaggerate **13** overemphasize

magniloquent
5 tumid, windy **6** florid, turgid **7** aureate, flowery, fustian, orotund, pompous, swollen **8** sonorous **9** bombastic, grandiose, high-flown, overblown, rhapsodic **10** euphuistic, histrionic, rhetorical **11** declamatory

magnitude
4 size **5** order, range **6** extent, import, number, volume **7** bigness, caliber, measure, quality **8** enormity, hugeness, quantity, vastness **9** greatness, immensity, largeness **10** dimensions, importance, proportion **11** consequence

Magnolia State
11 Mississippi

magnum opus
7 classic **10** masterwork **11** chef d'oeuvre, masterpiece, tour de force

Magog's king
3 Gog

magpie
3 jay **4** bird **6** gabber, prater **7** blabber, hoarder **8** jabberer, prattler **9** chatterer, collector **10** chatterbox **12** blabbermouth

Magritte of art
4 René

maguey
5 agave, fiber **7** cantala **12** century plant
relative: **4** aloe
product: **6** pulque **7** tequila

magus
6 wizard **7** diviner, warlock **8** conjurer, magician, sorcerer **9** enchanter **10** astrologer **11** necromancer

Magyar
9 Hungarian
leader: **4** Atli **6** Attila

Mahalath
father: **7** Ishmael **8** Jerimoth
husband: **4** Esau **8** Rehoboam

Mahfouz work
12 Cairo Trilogy

mah-jongg piece
4 tile

Mahler's wife
4 Alma

Mahlon
father: **9** Elimelech
mother: **5** Naomi
wife: **4** Ruth

mai ____
3 tai

Maia
father: **5** Atlas
mother: **7** Pleione
sisters: **8** Pleiades
son: **6** Hermes **7** Mercury

maid
4 girl, lass, miss **5** biddy, bonne, houri, nymph, wench **6** au pair, damsel, lassie, live-in, virgin **7** servant **8** domestic **9** charwoman, hired girl **10** au pair girl
Asian: **4** amah, ayah
lady's: **7** abigail
stage: **9** soubrette

maiden
3 gal **4** girl, lass, miss **5** first, fresh, missy, prime, wench **6** damsel, lassie, unused, virgin **7** colleen, initial, pioneer, primary **8** earliest, original, spinster, virginal **10** spinsterly

maidenhair tree
6 ginkgo

maidenhead
5 hymen **6** purity **9** virginity

maidenhood
9 virginity

maiden-name preceder
3 née

Maid of Astolat
6 Elaine
Maid of Orleans, The
7 Pucelle (La) **9** Joan of Arc
author: 8 Schiller (Friedrich von)
mail
4 post **5** armor **7** hauberk, letters **8** messages
___ mail
3 air **5** chain, snail
mail drop for GIs
3 APO
maim
4 maul **6** mangle **7** cripple, disable **8** mutilate, paralyze **9** disfigure
main
3 sea **5** chief, great, major, ocean, prime, trunk **7** central, high sea, leading, premier, primary **8** cardinal, foremost, high seas **9** paramount, principal **10** preeminent, prevailing **11** fundamental, outstanding, predominant
Maine
capital: 7 Augusta
city: 6 Bangor **8** Lewiston, Portland
college, university: 5 Bates, Colby **7** Bowdoin
college town: 5 Orono
lake: 6 Sebago
motto: 6 Dirigo
mountain: 8 Cadillac, Katahdin
nickname: 8 Pine Tree (State)
park: 6 Acadia
river: 8 Kennebec **9** Penobscot
state bird: 9 chickadee
state flower: 22 white pine cone and tassel
state tree: 9 white pine
mainly
6 mostly **7** chiefly, largely **8** above all **9** primarily **10** especially **11** principally **13** predominantly
main point
3 nub **4** crux, gist, pith
mainstay
4 prop **5** brace **6** pillar **7** bulwark, standby, support **8** backbone, buttress **9** supporter, sustainer
Main Street author
5 Lewis (Sinclair)
maintain
4 aver, avow **5** argue, claim **6** affirm, allege, assert, back up, defend, insist, keep up, manage, stress, uphold **7** care for, carry on, contend, declare, justify, persist, profess, support, sustain, warrant **8** continue, preserve **9** cultivate, emphasize, look after **10** provide for
maintenance
4 care, keep **6** living, upkeep **7** alimony, support **10** livelihood **11** subsistence **12** alimentation, preservation
worker: 7 janitor **9** custodian
maize
4 corn, milo **10** Indian corn
majestic
5 grand, noble, regal, royal **6** august, kingly, lordly, superb **7** exalted, stately **8** elevated, imperial, imposing, princely, splendid **9** dignified, grandiose **11** ceremonious, magnificent
majesty
4 pomp **5** glory **8** eminence, grandeur, splendor **9** greatness, loftiness **11** stateliness **12** magnificence
major
3 big **4** main, star **5** chief, grave, large **6** higher, larger **7** capital, greater, notable, primary, serious, sizable **8** sizeable, superior **9** principal, prominent **10** large-scale, preeminent **11** outstanding, predominant, significant **12** considerable
___ Major
4 Ursa
Major Barbara author
4 Shaw (George Bernard)
Majorca, por ejemplo
4 isla
majority
4 bulk, edge **6** margin **13** preponderance
make
3 net **4** earn, form, mold **5** build, cause, craft, erect, forge, frame, hatch, shape, spawn **6** create, effect, output **7** achieve, bring in, compose, fashion, prepare, produce **8** comprise, conclude, generate **9** construct, establish, fabricate, originate **10** constitute **11** manufacture, put together
amends: 5 atone
believe: 7 pretend
certain: 6 assure **8** convince
fast: 3 fix **4** gird **6** secure
good: 7 succeed **9** indemnify
known: 3 air **6** expose, reveal, spread **7** declare, divulge, uncover **8** announce, disclose, proclaim
lace: 3 tat
make-believe
4 mock, sham **7** charade, fantasy, feigned, fiction **8** disguise, pretense **9** fictional, imaginary, insincere, pretended, simulated **10** fictitious
make do
4 cope **5** get by, get on, shift **6** endure, fake it, manage, wing it **7** survive **8** get along **9** improvise **11** extemporize **13** muddle through
make off
3 fly, run **4** flee, skip **5** leave, scoot, scram **6** decamp, depart, escape **7** abscond, run away **9** skedaddle
make out
3 pet, see **4** fare, neck **5** grasp, infer, spoon

6 accept, cuddle, deduce, derive, follow, gather, manage, take in, thrive 7 discern, prosper, succeed 8 conclude, flourish, get along, perceive 9 apprehend, determine, establish, interpret 10 comprehend, understand

make over
4 cede, deed, redo 6 assign, convey, reform 7 remodel, reshape 8 renovate, transfer

maker
7 builder, creator 8 borrower, designer, inventor, producer 10 originator 11 constructor 12 manufacturer

makeshift
6 resort 7 stopgap 8 recourse, resource 9 expedient, temporary 10 expediency, jerry-built, jury-rigged, substitute 11 provisional 13 quick-and-dirty, rough-and-ready

make up
4 form 5 atone 6 devise, invent 7 arrange, compile, compose, concoct, fashion, prepare 8 comprise, contrive 9 apologize, construct, fabricate, formulate, improvise, reconcile 10 compensate

makeup
4 camo, cast, form, kohl, mold 5 blush, fiber, gloss, grain, paint, rouge, shape, stamp, style 6 design, nature, powder, stripe, temper 7 blusher, content, mascara 8 eyeliner, lip gloss, lipstick, war paint 9 character, cosmetics, eye shadow, formation, substance 10 camouflage, complexion, maquillage 11 arrangement, composition, disposition, greasepaint, personality, temperament 12 architecture, constitution, construction, organization

make use of
6 employ 7 exploit, utilize

maladroit
5 inept 6 clumsy, gauche, klutzy 7 awkward, unhandy 8 bumbling, bungling, tactless 9 ham-handed, impolitic 10 blundering, ungraceful 11 heavy-handed 12 undiplomatic

malady
3 ill 7 ailment, disease, illness 8 disorder, sickness, syndrome 9 complaint, condition, infirmity 10 affliction

malaise
4 funk 5 dumps, ennui 8 debility, doldrums 10 enervation

Malamud, Bernard
novel: 5 Fixer (The) 7 Natural (The) 9 Assistant (The)
story: 11 Magic Barrel (The)

malapert
4 rude 5 brash, fresh, nervy, sassy, saucy, smart 6 brassy, brazen, cheeky 7 forward 8 impudent, insolent 12 presumptuous

Malaprop creator
8 Sheridan (Richard Brinsley)

malapropos
5 inapt, undue 8 improper, unseemly, untimely 10 unsuitable 11 inopportune 13 inappropriate, inopportunely

malaria
4 ague 6 miasma
medicine: 7 quinine 8 Atabrine, cinchona 10 quinacrine
mosquito: 9 anopheles

malarkey
4 bosh, bull, bunk, guff 5 bilge, hokum, hooey, tripe 6 bunkum, drivel, humbug 7 baloney, eyewash, hogwash, rubbish, twaddle 8 nonsense, tommyrot 9 poppycock 10 balderdash 12 blatherskite

Malawi
capital: 8 Lilongwe
city: 8 Blantyre
explorer: 11 Livingstone (David)
former name: 9 Nyasaland
lake: 5 Nyasa 6 Malawi
language: 8 Chichewa
monetary unit: 6 kwacha
neighbor: 6 Zambia 8 Tanzania 10 Mozambique
river: 5 Shire

Malay boat
4 prau, proa

Malaysia
capital: 11 Kuala Lumpur
city: 4 Ipoh 6 Penang 11 Johor Baharu
island: 6 Borneo
monetary unit: 7 ringgit
neighbor: 8 Thailand 9 Indonesia
peninsula: 5 Malay
sea: 10 South China
strait: 7 Malacca

malcontent
5 rebel 6 griper, grouch, unruly 8 agitator, factious, frondeur, grumbler, mutinous, restless 9 alienated 10 bellyacher, complainer, rebellious 11 disaffected, disgruntled 12 contumacious, dissatisfied

mal de mer
6 nausea 8 vomiting 10 queasiness 11 seasickness

Maldives
capital: 4 Male
language: 6 Divehi
monetary unit: 7 rufiyaa

male
3 guy, ram, tom 4 boar, buck, bull, gent, jack, stag 5 drake, macho, manly 6 manful, virile 7 manlike 8 stallion 9 masculine, staminate

malediction
4 jinx, oath **5** curse **7** malison **8** anathema **10** execration **11** imprecation

malefactor
5 felon, knave, rogue **6** sinner **8** criminal, evildoer, offender **9** miscreant, reprobate, scoundrel, wrongdoer **10** blackguard, lawbreaker

maleficent
4 evil, vile **5** toxic **6** malign, sinful, wicked **7** baleful, baneful, beastly, harmful, noxious, vicious **8** damnable, sinister, virulent **9** execrable, injurious, nefarious, repugnant **10** pernicious, villainous **11** destructive

malevolence
4 evil **5** spite **6** grudge, malice, spleen **7** ill will **9** hostility, malignity **12** spitefulness **13** maliciousness

malevolent
4 evil **6** malign, wicked **7** baleful, hateful, hurtful, vicious **8** sinister, spiteful, venomous **9** injurious, malicious, malignant, poisonous

malfunction
6 glitch **7** misfire

Mali
capital: **6** Bamako
city: **5** Mopti, Ségou **7** Sikasso **8** Timbuktu **10** Tombouctou
desert: **6** Sahara
former name: **11** French Sudan
language: **6** French
monetary unit: **5** franc
neighbor: **5** Niger **6** Guinea **7** Algeria, Senegal **10** Ivory Coast, Mauritania **11** Burkina Faso, Côte d'Ivoire
river: **5** Niger

malice
4 bile, hate **5** spite, venom **6** animus, enmity, grudge, hatred, poison, spleen **7** ill will **8** meanness **9** animosity, antipathy **10** bitterness, resentment **11** hatefulness, malevolence **12** spitefulness **13** invidiousness

malicious
4 evil, mean **5** nasty, petty **6** wicked **7** baneful, hateful, heinous, jealous **8** spiteful, vengeful, venomous, virulent **9** poisonous, poison-pen, rancorous **10** malevolent

maliciousness
see **malevolence**

malign
4 evil, soil **5** abuse, decry, libel, smear, stain, sully, taint **6** befoul, defame, defile, revile, smirch, vilify, wicked **7** asperse, baleful, baneful, blacken, detract, hateful, hostile, noxious, slander, tarnish, traduce, vicious **8** besmirch, derogate, inimical, sinister, spiteful, tear down, virulent **9** denigrate, disparage, injurious, rancorous **10** calumniate, depreciate, maleficent, malevolent, pernicious, scandalize, vituperate **11** deleterious, opprobriate **12** antagonistic, antipathetic

malignant
4 evil **5** fatal **6** deadly, lethal, wicked **7** baleful, hateful, vicious **8** devilish, fiendish, spiteful **9** injurious, rancorous **10** diabolical, malevolent

malison
4 jinx **5** curse **8** anathema **11** commination, imprecation, malediction

mall
4 lane **5** alley, plaza, strip **7** passage **9** concourse, esplanade, promenade **10** passageway **11** median strip

malleable
6 pliant, supple **7** ductile, plastic, pliable **8** flexible **9** adaptable

mallet
6 hammer

Mallorca, por ejemplo
4 isla

malodorous
4 foul, gamy, rank **5** fetid, fuggy, funky, fusty, musty, stale **6** frowsy, putrid, rancid, rotten, smelly, stinky **7** noisome, noxious, reeking, spoiled **8** mephitic, stinking **9** offensive **10** nauseating **11** ill-smelling **12** pestilential

Malraux novel
8 Man's Fate

Malta
capital: **8** Valletta
city: **5** Qormi **10** Birkirkara
island: **4** Gozo **6** Comino
language: **6** French **7** Maltese
monetary unit: **4** lira
sea: **13** Mediterranean

Maltese Falcon, The
actor: **5** Astor (Mary), Lorre (Peter) **6** Bogart (Humphrey) **11** Greenstreet (Sydney)
author: **7** Hammett (Dashiell)
detective: **5** Spade (Sam)
director: **6** Huston (John)

maltreat
5 abuse **6** ill-use, misuse, molest

Mamet, David
film: **5** Heist **7** Verdict (The) **9** Wag the Dog **12** House of Games, Untouchables (The)
play: **7** Oleanna, Romance **14** Boston Marriage **15** American Buffalo **17** Glengarry Glen Ross

mammal
3 ass, bat, cat, cow, dog, elk, fox, pig, rat **4** bear, cavy, deer, degu, goat, Homo, lion, mink, mole, mule, oxen (plural), pika, saki, seal, tahr, titi, unau, urva, wolf **5** bilby, camel, civet, coati,

dingo, fossa, genet, hippo, horse, hyena, hyrax, koala, lemur, llama, moose, okapi, otter, panda, quoll, ratel, sable, sheep, shrew, sloth, takin, tapir, tiger, tigon, zebra **6** agouti, alpaca, badger, beaver, brucie, colugo, coyote, dassie, donkey, grison, hyaena, jackal, jaguar, margay, marten, numbat, ocelot, possum, quokka, rabbit, racoon, rodent, sifaka, tenrec, tiglon, uakari, vicuña, wombat **7** bettong, caracal, giraffe, guanaco, hyraces (plural), leopard, lioness, opossum, linsang, peccary, polecat, primate, raccoon, tamarin, tigress, wallaby **8** aardvark, aardwolf, edentate, elephant, hedgehog, hocicudo, javelina, kangaroo, kinkajou, marmoset, mongoose, pangolin, pinniped, ruminant, squirrel, starnose, tamandua, tuco-tuco, ungulate, viscacha **9** armadillo, bandicoot **10** cacomistle, chinchilla **12** hippopotamus
aquatic: **4** orca, seal **5** coypu, otter, whale **6** beaver, dugong, sea cow, walrus **7** cowfish, dolphin, grampus, manatee, muskrat, narwhal, platypi (plural), sea lion **8** capybara, cetacean, platypus, porpoise, sirenian
extinct: **6** quagga **7** mammoth **8** mastodon, stegodon **10** sabertooth

Mamma Mia! group
4 ABBA

mammon
4 pelf **5** lucre **6** riches, wealth **8** treasure **9** abundance, affluence **10** prosperity **11** possessions

mammoth
4 huge, vast **5** giant, jumbo **6** mighty **7** immense, massive, monster, titanic **8** colossal, enormous, gigantic **9** ginormous, humongous, leviathan, monstrous **10** gargantuan, mastodonic, monumental **11** elephantine

man
3 guy, joe **4** buck, chap, cuss, dude, gent, jack, male **5** being, bloke **6** fellow, hombre, mister, mortal, person **7** husband **8** creature, paramour **9** boyfriend, mortality, personage **10** individual **11** Homo sapiens
castrated: **6** eunuch
combining form: **4** andr **5** andro, homin **6** homini
common: **7** Joe Blow, John Doe **11** John Q. Public
French: **5** homme
Italian: **4** uomo
Latin: **3** vir **4** homo
old: **6** codger, geezer
Spanish: **6** hombre
Yiddish: **6** mensch

Man, e.g.
4 isle

manage
3 run **4** cope, fare, head, keep, mind, tend **5** get by, get on, shift **6** afford, direct, effect, govern, handle **7** achieve, carry on, conduct, control, execute, finagle, operate, oversee, succeed **8** carry out, contrive, cope with, deal with, dominate, engineer, get along, maintain **9** cultivate, supervise **10** accomplish, administer, bring about **11** orchestrate, superintend

manageable
6 docile, pliant **8** amenable, bearable, biddable, passable **9** agreeable, compliant, endurable, tractable **10** responsive **11** cooperative, supportable, sustainable **13** accommodating

management
4 care **5** brass **6** charge **7** conduct, control, running **8** guidance, handling **9** direction, oversight **10** conducting **11** front office, supervising, supervision

manager
4 boss, exec **6** gerent **7** handler, officer **8** director, official, overseer, producer **9** conductor, executive **10** impresario, supervisor **13** administrator
museum: **7** curator

mañana
7 someday **8** sometime, tomorrow

Man and Superman author
4 Shaw (George Bernard)

Manassas battle
7 Bull Run

Manasseh, Manasses
brother: **7** Ephraim
father: **6** Hashum, Joseph **8** Hezekiah **10** Pahathmoab
grandfather: **5** Jacob
grandson: **6** Gilead
mother: **7** Asenath
son: **6** Machir

man-at-arms
7 fighter, soldier, warrior **10** serviceman

Mandalay author
7 Kipling (Rudyard)

mandarin
5 elder **6** orange **8** official **9** tangerine **10** bureaucrat, panjandrum

mandate
4 fiat, word **5** edict, order, ukase **6** behest, charge, decree **7** bidding, command, dictate **9** authority, directive **10** imperative, injunction **13** authorization

mandatory
6 forced **7** binding **8** required **9** de rigueur, necessary, requisite **10** compulsory, imperative, obligatory **11** involuntary

mandible
3 jaw **8** lower jaw

mane
4 ruff

man-eater
4 lion, ogre, vamp **5** shark, siren, tiger **8** cannibal **9** temptress **11** femme fatale **13** mackerel shark

Manette's daughter
5 Lucie

maneuver
3 ply **4** move, plan, plot, ploy, step **5** feint, trick, wield **6** design, device, gambit, handle, jockey, scheme, tactic, wangle **7** exploit, finagle, finesse **8** artifice, démarche, engineer, exercise, intrigue, movement, navigate **9** machinate, procedure, stratagem **10** manipulate, proceeding, subterfuge **11** contrivance, machination **12** manipulation

maneuverable, as a ship
4 yare

maneuvering room
8 latitude

Man for All Seasons, A
author: **4** Bolt (Robert)
subject: **4** More (Thomas)

manga relative
5 anime

manger
4 rack **6** cratch, feeder, trough

mangle
3 mar **4** iron, maim, maul **5** press **6** damage, deface, deform, impair, injure **7** butcher, contort, distort **8** lacerate, mutilate **9** disfigure

mangy
5 seedy **6** ragtag, shabby **7** scruffy, squalid **8** decrepit, tattered **9** moth-eaten **10** down-at-heel, threadbare

manhandle
5 abuse **6** batter **7** rough up **8** maltreat, mistreat **10** push around, slap around

Manhattan
building: **8** Chrysler **11** Empire State
district: **4** Soho **6** Harlem **7** Chelsea, Tribeca
entertainment district: **11** Times Square
financial district: **10** Wall Street
museum: **3** Met **4** MOMA **7** Whitney **10** Guggenheim **12** Metropolitan
opera house: **3** Met **12** Metropolitan
purchaser: **6** Minuit (Peter)
river: **4** East **6** Hudson
school: **3** NYU **6** Hunter **8** Columbia **9** Juilliard

mania
4 rage, zeal **5** craze, fancy **6** frenzy, lunacy **7** madness, passion **8** fixation, idée fixe, insanity **9** cacoëthes, obsession **10** compulsion, enthusiasm **11** infatuation

maniac
3 bug, nut **4** loon **5** fiend, freak **6** madman, psycho, zealot **7** fanatic, lunatic, nutcase **8** crackpot **9** bedlamite **10** enthusiast

manifest
4 show **5** clear, overt, plain, shown, utter, voice **6** appear, embody, evince, expose, patent, reveal **7** display, evident, evinced, exhibit, express, invoice, obvious, visible **8** apparent, distinct, evidence, palpable, proclaim, revealed **9** evidenced, incarnate, objectify, prominent **10** illustrate, noticeable, observable **11** demonstrate, exteriorize, externalize, perceptible, unambiguous

manifestation
4 show, sign **5** proof **7** display, symptom **8** epiphany **10** appearance, revelation

manifesto
4 fiat, rule, writ **5** credo, creed, edict, ukase **6** decree, dictum, gospel, notice, policy, ruling **7** mandate **8** doctrine, document, platform **9** directive, statement, testament, testimony, ultimatum **10** deposition, injunction, resolution **11** declaration **12** announcement, notification, proclamation **13** pronouncement

manifold
7 diverse, various **8** compound, multiple, multiply, numerous **9** multiform, multiplex **10** multiphase **12** multifarious

manikin
4 runt **5** dummy, dwarf, gnome, model, pygmy **6** midget, peewee **8** Tom Thumb **10** homunculus

Manila
founder: **7** Legazpi (Miguel López de)
site: **5** Luzon **11** Philippines
victor: **5** Dewey (George)

manioc
4 yuca **5** yucca **6** casava **7** cassava, tapioca

manipulate
3 ply, rig **4** play **5** steer, swing, tweak, wield **6** adjust, direct, doctor, handle, jockey, juggle, manage **7** beguile, conduct, control, exploit, finagle, finesse, massage **8** engineer, maneuver **9** machinate **10** tamper with

Man, Isle of
capital: **7** Douglas
cat: **4** Manx
possession of: **7** Britain
sea: **5** Irish

Manitoba
capital: **8** Winnipeg
lake: **8** Winnipeg **12** Winnipegosis
mountain: **5** Baldy
provincial flower: **13** prairie crocus
river: **6** Nelson **9** Churchill

mankind
6 humans, people **8** humanity **11** Homo sapiens

manlike
4 male **6** virile **8** hominoid, humanoid **9** masculine **10** anthropoid

manly
4 male **5** macho **6** virile **9** masculine

man-made
9 synthetic **10** artificial, factitious
object: **8** artefact, artifact

Mann character
6 Joseph **9** Leverkühn (Adrian) **10** Aschenbach (Gustav von), Felix Krull **11** Hans Castorp, Tonio Kröger

manner
3 air, way **4** form, kind, mien, mode, sort, vein, wont **5** habit, modus, style, usage **6** aspect, custom, method **7** bearing, conduct, fashion **8** behavior, demeanor, habitude, practice, presence **9** demeanour, etiquette, technique **10** consuetude, deportment **11** affectation, comportment **12** idiosyncrasy

mannered
7 stilted **8** affected, precious **10** artificial **13** self-conscious

mannerism
3 tic **4** pose **5** quirk **10** preciosity **11** affectation, peculiarity, singularity **12** eccentricity, idiosyncrasy **13** artificiality

mannerless
4 rude **6** coarse **7** boorish, ill-bred, uncivil, uncouth **8** impolite **12** discourteous

mannerly
5 civil **6** polite **7** genteel, refined **8** decorous, gracious, well-bred **9** civilized, courteous **10** respectful

Manning of the Giants
3 Eli

Manon composer
8 Massenet (Jules)

Manon Lescaut
author: **7** Prévost (Abbé)
composer: **7** Puccini (Giacomo) **8** Massenet (Jules)
lover: **9** des Grieux

manor
5 villa **6** estate, quinta **7** château, demesne **12** landed estate

manservant
5 valet **6** butler

mansion
4 hall **5** villa **6** palace **7** château

manslayer
6 killer **8** homicide, murderer

manta
3 ray **5** cloak, cloth, shawl **7** blanket

manteau
4 coat, robe, wrap **5** cloak **6** capote, domino, mantle, tabard

mantic
5 vatic **6** orphic **7** Delphic, fatidic **8** Delphian, oracular **9** prophetic, sibylline, vaticinal **10** divinatory

mantilla
4 cape, wrap **5** cloak, fichu, scarf, shawl **8** kerchief

mantle
4 cope, glow, pink, robe, rose **5** blush, cloak, color, cover, flush, rouge **6** capote, casing, pinken, redden **7** crimson

man-to-man
4 open **5** frank, plain **6** candid, direct, honest **10** forthright, unreserved **11** openhearted

mantra
5 chant, motto **6** prayer, slogan **9** watchword **10** invocation **11** incantation

manual
4 text **5** guide **6** primer **8** Baedeker, handbook, hornbook, textbook **9** guidebook, vade mecum **10** compendium **11** abecedarium, enchiridion
religious: **9** catechism
worker: **6** menial **7** laborer

manufacture
4 form, make **6** create **7** fashion, produce **8** assemble **9** construct, fabricate **11** put together

manumit
4 free **6** unbind **7** release, set free, unchain **8** liberate **9** unshackle **10** emancipate

manure
4 dung **6** ordure **7** excreta **9** excrement **10** fertilizer

manuscript
4 hand **6** scrawl **8** longhand **9** autograph **10** penmanship **11** calligraphy, handwriting
ancient: **5** codex **6** scroll **7** codices (plural)
enclosure: **4** SASE
red part: **6** rubric
style: **6** uncial
symbol: **6** obelus

many
5 scads **6** divers, legion, myriad, sundry **7** copious, diverse, umpteen, various **8** abundant, manifold, multiple, numerous **9** abounding, bounteous, bountiful, countless, multitude, plentiful **12** multifarious **13** multitudinous
combining form: **4** poly **5** multi, pluri

many-sided
7 diverse **8** all-round, talented **9** all-around, versatile **10** variegated **11** diversified **12** multifaceted, multifarious **13** comprehensive

Mao's successor
3 Hua (Guofeng, Kuo-feng) **4** Deng (Xiaoping), Teng (Hsiao-p'ing)

map
4 plan, plat **5** chart, draft, globe, graph **6** design, lay out, set out, sketch, survey **7** arrange, diagram, drawing, outline, tracing **9** delineate
closeup: **5** inset
collection: **5** atlas
line: **6** isobar **7** contour, isogram, isohyet **8** isogloss, isogonic, isopleth, isotherm
maker: **12** cartographer
making: **11** cartography

maple
genus: **4** Acer
product: **5** syrup
seed: **6** samara
type: **3** red **5** sugar **8** box elder

maple sugar source
3 sap

map projection
5 conic **8** Mercator **9** polyconic **10** sinusoidal **12** orthographic **13** stereographic

maquillage
6 makeup

mar
4 ding, harm, hurt, scar, warp **5** spoil, stain **6** bruise, damage, deface, deform, impair, injure **7** blemish, scratch, tarnish, vitiate **9** disfigure

marabou
5 stork

Marat/Sade author
5 Weiss (Peter)

Marat, Jean-Paul
colleague: **6** Danton (Georges) **11** Robespierre (Maximilien)
slayer: **6** Corday (Charlotte)

maraud
4 loot, raid, sack **5** foray, harry **6** harass, ravage, ravish **7** despoil, pillage, plunder, ransack

marauder
6 bandit, pirate **7** brigand, spoiler, wrecker **9** buccaneer, desperado **10** freebooter

marble
3 mib, mig, taw **4** immy, migg **5** agate, aggie, alley, rance **6** blotch, miggle, mottle, streak **7** cat's-eye, cipolin, glassie, steelie **9** limestone

marbled
6 veined **7** dappled, flecked, mottled **8** speckled, streaked

Marble Faun, The
author: **9** Hawthorne (Nathaniel)
character: **5** Hilda **6** Kenyon, Miriam **9** Donatello
setting: **4** Rome

Marc Anthony ex
3 J. Lo

marcel
4 wave

Marcel Marceau, e.g.
4 mime

march
3 hem, rim **4** abut, file, line **5** étape, skirt **6** adjoin, border, parade **7** advance, headway, proceed **8** anabasis, boundary, frontier, outlands, progress, traverse **9** periphery **10** borderland

March
date: **4** ides
mother: **6** Marmee
sisters: **3** Amy, Meg **4** Beth

March King
5 Sousa (John Philip)

Mardi Gras
8 carnival **10** Fat Tuesday
city: **10** New Orleans
group: **5** crewe

Marduk
city: **7** Babylon
consort: **8** Zarbanit, Zarpanit
victim: **5** Kingu **6** Tiamat

mare
3 sea **5** horse **6** equine

mare's nest
3 con, din **4** hoax, scam **5** babel, cheat, fraud, put-on, spoof **6** bedlam, clamor, hubbub, humbug, racket, ruckus, tumult, uproar **7** swindle, turmoil **8** brouhaha, flimflam, illusion **9** confusion, imposture **10** hullabaloo **11** pandemonium

Margaret of anthropology
4 Mead

margarine
4 oleo

Marge's son
4 Bart

margin
3 hem, rim **4** brim, edge, join, line, play, room, side **5** bound, brink, frame, scope, shore, skirt, verge **6** border, fringe, leeway **7** minimum, outline, selvage **8** boundary, latitude, selvedge, surround, trimming **9** elbowroom, perimeter, periphery **13** circumference
tiny: **4** hair

marginal
5 minor **7** limited, minimal **9** bordering **10** borderline, negligible, peripheral, subsidiary **13** insignificant

Marguerite's lover
5 Faust

Maria ___
5 Elena **7** Stuarda
___ Maria
3 Ave
Marianas
discoverer: **8** Magellan (Ferdinand)
island: **4** Guam, Rota **5** Pagan **6** Guguan, Saipan, Tinian **7** Agrihan, Aguijan
marijuana
3 kef, kif, pot **4** dope, hash, hemp, weed **5** bhang, grass **6** reefer **7** hashish **8** cannabis
Marilyn, originally
5 Norma **9** Norma Jean
marina
4 dock, pier, quay **5** basin, berth, wharf **8** boatyard
marinate
4 soak **5** steep **6** drench, pickle **7** immerse **8** macerate
marine
5 naval **7** abyssal, aquatic, deep-sea, oceanic, pelagic **8** nautical, seagoing, seascape **9** seafaring, thalassic **10** oceangoing **12** hydrographic **13** oceanographic
crustacean: **6** shrimp **7** lobster **8** barnacle
deposit: **5** coral
plant: **4** kelp, nori **5** dulse **6** wakame **7** seaweed
mariner
3 gob, tar **4** jack, salt, swab **5** limey **6** hearty, rating, sailor, sea dog, seaman **7** jack-tar, old salt, swabbie **8** seafarer **9** sailorman, shellback, tarpaulin **10** bluejacket
Marisa of film
5 Tomei
marital
6 wedded **7** married, nuptial, spousal **8** conjugal, hymeneal **9** connubial
maritime
7 oceanic, pelagic **8** nautical **9** thalassic **12** navigational
mark
3 aim, jot, sap, tee **4** butt, dupe, fool, goal, gull, heed, look, nick, note, pick, show, sign, view **5** blaze, bound, brand, chart, chump, elect, grade, label, notch, stamp, token, trait **6** behold, choose, denote, evince, lay off, notice, object, opt for, rating, record, select, sucker, target, victim, virtue **7** betoken, delimit, discern, exhibit, fall guy, feature, gudgeon, indicia, initial, measure, observe, qualify, scratch, signify, symptom **8** function, indicate, perceive, register **9** attribute, character, designate, objective, single out **10** indication **11** differentia, distinction, distinguish **12** characterize
distinctive: **7** indicia **8** indicium
identifying: **4** logo, seal **6** emblem, signet, symbol **8** colophon, logotype
of insertion: **5** caret
of omission: **4** dele **8** ellipsis **10** apostrophe
of retention: **4** stet
over a vowel: **5** breve, haček **6** accent, macron, umlaut **8** dieresis **9** diaeresis **10** circumflex
over n: **5** tilde
punctuation: **4** dash **5** brace, colon, comma, slant, slash **6** hyphen, period **7** bracket, solidus **9** backslash, guillemet, semicolon **10** apostrophe
under a letter: **7** cedilla
Mark
6 Gospel
cousin: **8** Barnabas
mother: **4** Mary
mark down
3 cut **4** pare **5** shave, slash **6** reduce **7** devalue **8** discount **9** devaluate **10** depreciate, undervalue
markdown abbrev.
3 irr.
marked
5 noted **6** patent, signal **7** evident, notable, obvious, pointed, salient **8** distinct, manifest, striking **9** arresting, prominent **10** noticeable, remarkable **11** conspicuous, outstanding **12** considerable **13** distinguished
man: **4** Cain
marker
3 IOU, run **5** cairn, score **7** felt-tip
market
3 suq **4** fair, mall, sell, shop, souk, vend **5** agora, store **6** bazaar, outlet, retail, rialto **8** emporium, exchange, showroom **9** advertise, traffic in, wholesale **11** merchandise
kind: **4** flea **5** money, stock
marketable
5 sound **7** salable **8** vendible **10** commercial
marketplace
3 suq **4** mall, souk **5** agora **6** bazaar, rialto **8** emporium
marksman
4 shot **6** sniper **7** deadeye, shooter **12** sharpshooter
Mark Twain portrayer Holbrook
3 Hal
marl
4 clay, silt
marlin
8 billfish **9** spearfish
Marlowe play
8 Edward II **9** Dr. Faustus **10** Jew of Malta (The) **11** Tamburlaine **13** Doctor Faustus

marmoset
4 mico
marmot
6 rodent 9 woodchuck 10 prairie dog
maroon
3 red 6 claret, desert, enisle, strand 7 abandon, crimson, forsake, isolate, outcast 8 burgundy, castaway
Marquand character
4 Gray (Charles), Moto (Mr.) 5 Apley (George), Wayde (Willis) 6 Pulham (H.M.) 7 Goodwin (Melville)
Marquis, Don
cat: 9 Mehitabel
cockroach: 5 Archy
marriage
5 match, union 6 bridal 7 nuptial, spousal, wedding, wedlock 8 coupling, espousal, monogamy, nuptials, polygamy 9 matrimony 11 conjugality 12 connubiality
combining form: 4 gamy 6 gamous
notice: 5 banns
outside a group: 7 exogamy
within a group: 8 endogamy
marriageable
6 nubile 8 eligible
marriage broker
5 yenta 9 go-between 10 matchmaker
Marriage of Figaro composer
6 Mozart (Wolfgang Amadeus)
marrow
4 core, meat, pith, soul 5 heart, stuff 6 kernel 7 essence 12 quintessence
marry
3 tie, wed 4 join, link, mate, wive, yoke 5 hitch, merge, unite 6 couple, splice, spouse 7 combine, conjoin, espouse 9 conjugate
on the run: 5 elope
Mars
4 Ares 6 planet
combining term: 4 areo
feature: 4 face 5 basin 6 canyon, crater 7 volcano 8 polar cap
lover: 5 Venus
mission: 6 Viking 7 Mariner 10 Pathfinder
moon: 6 Deimos, Phobos
relating to: 7 martian
(see also **Ares**)
Marseillaise composer
13 Rouget de Lisle (Claude-Joseph)
marsh
3 bog, fen 4 mire, ooze, quag 5 bayou, glade, swale, swamp 6 morass, muskeg, salina, slough 7 wetland 8 quagmire 9 swampland
plant: 4 forb, reed, rush 5 sedge 7 bulrush, cattail
marshal
5 align, array, guide, order, rally, usher 6 deploy, direct, escort, muster 7 arrange, officer, round up 8 assemble, mobilize, organize, shepherd 9 methodize, systemize
(see also **field marshal**)
Marshall Islands
atoll: 6 Bikini 8 Enewetak 9 Kwajalein
capital: 6 Majuro
ethnic group: 11 Micronesian
island chain: 5 Ralik, Ratak 6 Sunset 7 Sunrise 11 Marshallese
marshy
4 miry 5 boggy, mucky 6 quaggy, swampy 7 sloughy
marsupial
3 roo 4 euro 5 bilby, koala, quoll 6 numbat, possum, quokka, wombat 7 bettong, opossum, wallaby 8 kangaroo, wallaroo 9 bandicoot
marten
5 sable 6 fisher, weasel
Martha
brother: 7 Lazarus
sister: 4 Mary
Martha of comedy
4 Raye
martial
7 warlike 8 militant, military, spirited 9 bellicose, combative, soldierly 11 belligerent 12 militaristic
martial art
4 judo 5 kendo 6 aikido, karate, kung fu, neijia, tai chi 7 shaolin 8 capoeira, jiujitsu 9 tae kwon do 11 tai chi chuan
expert: 5 ninja
school: 4 dojo
teacher: 6 sensei
Martial's forte
7 epigram
Martin Chuzzlewit author
7 Dickens (Charles)
martini garnish
5 olive
Martinique
capital: 12 Fort-de-France
department of: 6 France
discoverer: 8 Columbus (Christopher)
island group: 8 Windward
location: 10 West Indies
neighbor: 8 Dominica 10 Saint Lucia
volcano: 5 Pelée
Martinique, par exemple
3 île
martyr
4 Paul, rack 5 Agnes, Alban, James, Peter, saint, wring 6 George, harrow, Justin 7 afflict,

agonize, Clement, crucify, Cyprian, Stephen, torment, torture **8** Ignatius, Lawrence, Polycarp, sufferer **9** Joan of Arc, Sebastian **10** excruciate, Thomas More
Protestant: **6** Ridley (Nicholas) **7** Cranmer (Thomas), Latimer (Hugh)

marvel
4 gape **6** wonder **7** miracle, portent, prodigy, stunner **9** curiosity, sensation **10** phenomenon **12** astonishment

marvelous
5 super, swell **6** divine **7** amazing, awesome, ripping **8** glorious, striking, stunning, superior, terrific, wondrous **9** excellent, wonderful **10** astounding, incredible, miraculous, phenomenal, prodigious, remarkable, staggering, stupendous, surprising **11** astonishing, exceptional, sensational, spectacular **12** awe-inspiring, supernatural **13** extraordinary

Marx brother
5 Chico, Gummo, Harpo, Zeppo **7** Groucho

Marxist
9 socialist **9** communist

Marx, Karl
book: **7** Kapital (Das)
collaborator: **6** Engels (Friedrich)

Mary
husband: **6** Clopas, Joseph **8** Alphaeus
kinswoman: **9** Elisabeth
son: **4** Mark **5** James, Jesus

Mary Kay rival
4 Avon

Maryland
bay: **10** Chesapeake
capital: **9** Annapolis
city: **9** Baltimore, Frederick
college, university: **6** Towson **7** Goucher **9** Annapolis **12** Johns Hopkins, Naval Academy (U.S.)
fort: **7** McHenry
nickname: **7** Old Line (State)
river: **7** Potomac **8** Patuxent
state bird: **15** Baltimore oriole
state flower: **14** black-eyed Susan
state tree: **8** white oak

marzipan nut
6 almond

mascot
4 juju **5** charm **6** amulet, fetish, symbol **8** grisgris, talisman

masculine
4 male **5** macho, manly **6** manful, virile **7** manlike

masculinity
8 machismo, virility **9** manliness

Masefield work
7 Cargoes **8** Sea Fever

mash
4 pulp **5** crush, smash **6** squash, squish **7** squoosh **8** macerate **9** pulverize

masher
4 wolf **5** flirt **6** chaser **7** Don Juan, seducer **8** Casanova, lothario **9** ladies' man, womanizer **10** lady-killer **11** philanderer, skirt chaser

mash note
10 billet-doux, love letter

MASH's Alan
4 Alda

mask
4 hide, pose, sham, veil **5** cover, front, guard, guise, visor **6** facade, screen, vizard **7** dress up, frisket, pretext **8** coloring, disguise, pretense **9** dissemble, semblance **10** appearance, camouflage, false front, simulation **11** dissimulate

masonry
9 brickwork, stonework
in a frame: **7** nogging

masquerade
4 pose **6** facade **7** costume, posture **8** carnival, disguise **10** camouflage, masked ball **11** costume ball

mass
3 lot, sum, wad **4** bank, body, bulk, clot, core, glob, heap, hill, lump, pack, peck, pile **5** bolus, clump, mound **6** corpus, volume **7** expanse, globule, wadding **8** assemble, quantity **9** aggregate, stockpile, substance **11** aggregation **12** conglomerate
compacted: **4** cake
for the dead: **7** requiem
of individuals: **3** mob **4** host **5** crowd, crush, flock, horde, swarm **6** throng **12** congregation **13** agglomeration
part: **5** Kyrie **6** proper **8** Agnus Dei, ordinary

Massachusetts
cape: **3** Ann, Cod
capital: **6** Boston
city: **6** Lowell, Quincy **9** Cambridge, Worcester **10** New Bedford **11** Springfield
college, university: **3** MIT **5** Clark, Smith, Tufts **7** Amherst, Berklee, Harvard, Wheaton **8** Brandeis, Williams **9** Hampshire, Holy Cross, Radcliffe, Wellesley **12** Mount Holyoke, Northeastern
island: **9** Nantucket **15** Martha's Vineyard
mountain, range: **8** Greylock **9** Berkshire
nickname: **3** Bay (State) **9** Old Colony (State)
river: **11** Connecticut
state bird: **9** chickadee
state flower: **9** mayflower
state tree: **3** elm (American)
symbol: **3** cod

massacre
4 kill **6** mangle, murder, pogrom **7** butcher, carnage **8** butchery, decimate, genocide, mangling, mutilate **9** bloodbath, bloodshed, slaughter **10** annihilate, blood purge, decimation, mutilation **11** exterminate **12** annihilation

massage
3 rub **5** knead **7** flatter, rubdown, shiatsu **8** blandish **10** manipulate
target: **4** ache

Massenet opera
5 Le Cid, Manon, Sapho, Thaïs **7** Werther

massive
4 huge, mega, vast **5** bulky, giant, great, jumbo, mondo, solid **6** mighty **7** hulking, immense, mammoth, weighty **8** colossal, cumbrous, enormous, gigantic, towering **9** humongous, monstrous **10** gargantuan, monumental, prodigious, stupendous, tremendous **11** elephantine, mountainous

master
4 best, boss, guru, head, lick, rule, tame **5** adept, bwana, chief, crack, learn, ruler, sahib, tutor **6** artist, expert, genius, honcho, leader, subdue, victor **7** captain, conquer, headman, maestro, padrone, prevail, skilled, triumph **8** dominant, dominate, employer, governor, overcome, overlord, overseer, regulate, skeleton, skillful, superior, surmount, virtuoso **9** authority, chieftain, conqueror, dominator, paramount, principal, sovereign **10** proficient **11** predominant
of ceremonies: **4** host **5** emcee **7** compere

MasterCard rival
4 Visa

masterful
4 deft **5** adept **6** adroit, expert **7** skilled **8** skillful **10** high-handed, proficient **11** magisterial **13** authoritative

masterly
5 adept, crack **6** adroit, expert **7** skilled **8** skillful **9** dexterous **10** proficient **11** crackerjack **12** accomplished

Master of Ballantrae, The
6 Durrie
author: **9** Stevenson (Robert Louis)

masterpiece
7 classic **10** magnum opus **11** chef d'oeuvre, tour de force

mastery
5 knack, skill **7** ability, command, control, knowhow, prowess **8** dominion **9** authority, expertise **10** ascendancy, domination, expertness, virtuosity **11** proficiency, superiority

masticate
4 chaw, chew, pulp **5** champ, chomp, crush, munch **6** crunch **7** scrunch **8** macerate, ruminate **9** break down

mat
3 rug **4** felt **6** border, carpet, tangle, tatami

matador
6 torero **8** Manolete, toreador **11** bullfighter
adjunct: **6** muleta
assistant: **7** picador **12** banderillero
bout: **7** corrida
march: **5** paseo
move: **4** pase **5** faena **8** veronica
opponent: **4** bull, toro

Mata Hari
3 spy **10** seductress **11** femme fatale

match
3 pit **4** bout, game, mate, meet, peer, suit, twin **5** array, equal, rival, touch, union **6** double, equate, oppose **7** compare, contest, counter, paragon, play off **8** alliance, analogue, marriage, opponent, parallel **9** adversary, correlate, duplicate, encounter, measure up, smackdown **10** antagonist, complement, coordinate, engagement, equivalent, reciprocal, supplement, tournament **11** counterpart **12** correspond to
a bet: **3** see
friction: **7** lucifer

matchless
6 unique **7** supreme **8** peerless, singular **9** nonpareil, unequaled, unrivaled **10** inimitable **12** incomparable, unparalleled

matchmaker
5 yenta **9** go-between

mate
3 bud, pal, tie, wed **4** chum, pair, twin **5** amigo, breed, buddy, crony, equal, hitch, marry **6** cohort, couple, double, fellow, friend, helper, splice, spouse **7** compeer, comrade, consort, partner **8** confrere, sidekick **9** associate, companion, copartner, duplicate, procreate **10** complement, equivalent, reciprocal **11** concomitant

maté
3 tea **5** holly **8** beverage

mater
3 mom, mum **6** mother **9** matriarch

____ mater
4 alma

material
4 real, true **5** cloth, stuff **6** actual, fabric, matter, object **7** element, germane, worldly **8** palpable, physical, relevant, sensible, tangible **9** component, corporeal, essential, important, objective, pertinent, substance **10** applicable, ingredient, meaningful, phenomenal **11** appreciable, constituent, fundamental, perceptible, significant, substantial
building: **5** adobe, brick **6** stucco **7** lagging, plaster, plywood, shingle **8** concrete

materialistic
7 secular, worldly **11** acquisitive

materialize
4 loom, rise **5** arise, issue **6** appear, embody, emerge, evolve, show up **7** develop, surface **8** manifest **9** come about, incarnate, take shape **12** substantiate

matériel
4 gear **5** stock **8** supplies **9** apparatus, equipment, machinery **10** provisions **13** accouterments, accoutrements, paraphernalia

maternal
8 motherly

maternally related
5 enate

matey
5 pally, tight **6** clubby **7** affable **8** amicable, familiar, friendly, intimate, sociable **9** congenial

math comparison
5 ratio

mathematician
American: **5** Wiles (Andrew) **6** Peirce (Charles S.), Veblen (Oswald), Wiener (Norbert)
Austrian: **5** Gödel (Kurt)
British: **6** Stokes (George)
Dutch: **7** Huygens (Christiaan)
English: **6** Newton (Isaac), Taylor (Brook), Turing (Alan), Wallis (John) **7** Pearson (Karl), Russell (Bertrand) **8** Hamilton (James Rowan) **9** Sylvester (James Joseph), Whitehead (Alfred North, Henry)
French: **4** Weil (André) **5** Borel (Emile), Comte (Auguste), Viète (François) **6** Galois (Evariste), Pascal (Blaise), Picard (Charles-Emile) **7** Fourier (Jean-Baptiste), Laplace (Marquis de), Vernier (Pierre) **8** Painlevé (Paul), Poincaré (Jules-Henri) **9** Descartes (René)
German: **5** Gauss (Carl Friedrich), Wolff (Freiherr von) **6** Staudt (Karl von) **7** Leibniz (Gottfried Wilhelm), Riemann (Georg) **11** Weierstrass (Karl)
Greek: **6** Euclid **10** Archimedes, Pythagoras
Hungarian: **5** Erdos (Paul)
Italian: **8** Volterra (Vito) **10** Torricelli (Evangelista)
Norwegian: **7** Stormer (Fredrik)
Russian: **11** Lobachevsky (Nikolay)
Scottish: **4** Tait (Peter) **6** Napier (John) **8** Stirling (James)
Swiss: **5** Euler (Leonhard), Sturm (Jacques) **7** Steiner (Jakob)

mathematics
branch: **4** trig **7** algebra **8** calculus, geometry, topology **10** arithmetic, statistics **12** trigonometry
proven statement in: **7** theorem

____ Mather
6 Cotton **8** Increase

matinee star
4 idol

mating arena
3 lek

matriarch
4 dame **6** mother **7** dowager **10** grande dame

matriculate
4 join **5** enrol, enter **6** enroll, sign on **8** register

matrimonial
6 bridal, wedded **7** marital, married, nuptial, spousal **8** conjugal, hymeneal **9** connubial **11** epithalamic

matrimony
7 wedlock **8** marriage **11** conjugality **12** connubiality

matrix
3 die, net, web **4** grid, mesh **5** array **6** cradle, gangue **7** complex, network **10** groundmass, truth table

Matrix, The
hero: **3** Neo
star: **5** Keanu (Reeves)

matron
4 dame **7** dowager **8** chaperon **9** chaperone **10** grande dame

matter
4 body, core, gist, meat, pith, text **5** being, cause, order, point, sense, stuff, theme, thing, topic, value, weigh **6** affair, amount, burden, entity, import, object **7** concern, signify, subject **8** argument, material **9** grievance, magnitude, substance **11** constituent **12** circumstance

Matterhorn, e.g.
3 Alp

matter-of-fact
3 dry **5** plain, prose, sober, stoic **6** stolid **7** prosaic **9** impassive, objective, practical, pragmatic, realistic **10** hard-boiled, hardheaded, impersonal, phlegmatic **11** down-to-earth **13** unimpassioned, unsentimental

mattress
3 pad **4** sack
case: **4** tick
fabric: **7** ticking
straw: **6** pallet

Matty of baseball
4 Alou

mature
3 age, due **4** aged, grow, ripe **5** adult, grown, owing, ready, ripen **6** flower, grow up, mellow, season, unpaid **7** advance, blossom, decline, develop, grown-up, overdue, payable, ripened **8** progress **9** developed, full-blown, full-grown **11** full-fledged

maudlin
5 gushy, mushy, silly, sappy, soppy **6** slushy, sticky **7** cloying, gushing, mawkish **8** bathetic **11** sentimental, tear-jerking

Maugham character
4 Kear, Liza **5** Carey, Rosie, Sadie **7** Mildred **8** Ashenden, Craddock **10** Strickland

maul
4 bang, bash, beat, club, drub, flog, whip **5** abuse, flail, pound **6** batter, bruise, buffet, cudgel, hammer, injure, mangle, molest, pummel, sledge, thrash **7** clobber, rough up **8** bludgeon, lambaste **9** manhandle

Mauna ___
3 Kea, Loa

maunder
3 bat, gad **4** rove **5** drift, mooch, range **6** mumble, mutter, ramble, wander **7** blather, digress, traipse **8** divagate

Mauritania
capital: **10** Nouakchott
desert: **6** Sahara
language: **5** Wolof **6** Arabic, Fulani **7** Soninke
monetary unit: **7** ouguiya
neighbor: **4** Mali **6** Guinea **7** Algeria, Senegal **13** Western Sahara
river: **7** Senegal

Mauritius
capital: **9** Port Louis
island group: **9** Mascarene
language: **6** Creole
monetary unit: **5** rupee

mauve
5 lilac **6** purple, violet

maven
3 ace **4** buff, whiz **5** adept, freak, shark **6** addict, expert, master, savant **7** devotee, fanatic, hotshot **8** virtuoso **9** authority **10** enthusiast **11** connoisseur

maverick
5 rogue, stray **7** heretic **8** unmarked **9** dissident, unbranded **10** iconoclast **11** independent, loose cannon **13** nonconformist

maxim
3 saw **5** adage, axiom, motto **6** saying, truism **7** epigram, precept, proverb **8** aphorism, apothegm

maw
4 crop **5** chasm, mouth **6** cavity, gullet **7** stomach

mawkish
5 gushy, mushy, sappy, soppy **6** sloppy, slushy, sticky, syrupy **7** cloying, gushing, insipid, maudlin **8** bathetic, romantic **9** schmaltzy, sickening **10** lovey-dovey, nauseating **11** sentimental, tear-jerking

___ Mawr
4 Bryn

maxilla
3 jaw **4** bone

maxim
3 law, saw **4** rule **5** adage, axiom, gnome, moral, motto, tenet, truth **6** byword, dictum, saying, truism **7** precept, proverb, theorem **8** aphorism, apothegm **9** platitude, prescript, principle **11** commonplace

maximal
3 nth, top, ult. **6** utmost **7** highest, largest, supreme, topmost **8** complete, greatest, ultimate **9** paramount

maximum
3 nth, top, ult. **6** utmost **7** highest, largest, supreme, topmost **8** extremum, greatest, ultimate **9** paramount

may
5 might, shrub **6** spirea **8** hawthorn

maybe
7 perhaps **8** possibly **9** perchance **11** conceivably, uncertainty

Mayberry
actor: **6** Bavier (Frances), Howard (Ron), Knotts (Don) **8** Griffith (Andy)
resident: **4** Andy (Taylor), Opie (Taylor), Otis **5** Floyd, Gomer (Pyle) **6** Barney (Fife) **7** Aunt Bee

Mayday
3 SOS

Mayflower
document: **7** Compact
passengers: **8** Pilgrims

mayhem
4 maim, riot **5** chaos, havoc **7** cripple, dislimb **8** mutilate **9** dismember **10** mutilation

mayonnaise with garlic
5 aioli

mayor
11 burgomaster
Boston: **6** Curley (James Michael)
Chicago: **5** Daley (Richard)
New York: **4** Koch (Edward) **6** Walker (Jimmy) **7** Lindsay (John) **8** de Blasio (Bill), Giuliani (Rudolph) **9** Bloomberg (Michael), La Guardia (Fiorello)
Spanish: **7** alcalde

Mayor of Casterbridge, The
author: **5** Hardy (Thomas)
character: **8** Henchard (Michael)

maze
3 web **4** knot, mesh **5** skein, snarl **6** jungle, morass, tangle **7** confuse, network, perplex **8** bewilder, mishmash **9** labyrinth

Mazel ___!
3 tov

McCarthy novel
4 Road (The) **8** Crossing (The) **13** Blood Meridian **16** Cities of the Plain **18** All the Pretty Horses, No Country for Old Men

McCourt memoir
3 'Tis **10** Teacher Man **12** Angela's Ashes

McCullers, Carson
novel: 18 Ballad of the Sad Café (The), Member of the Wedding (The) **20** Heart Is a Lonely Hunter (The) **23** Reflections in a Golden Eye

McCullough novel
10 Thorn Birds (The)

McEntire of country
4 Reba

McEwan, Ian
novel: 8 Saturday **9** Amsterdam, Atonement, Black Dogs **12** Enduring Love

McGregor of film
4 Ewan

McKellen of film
3 Ian

McMurtry novel
12 Buffalo Girls, Lonesome Dove **14** Horseman Pass By **15** Last Picture Show (The), Streets of Laredo **17** Terms of Endearment

McTeague author
6 Norris (Frank)

MD
3 doc **6** doctor, medico **8** sawbones **9** physician

mea culpa
5 error, fault **7** apology **9** admission **10** concession, confession

meadow
3 lea, ley **4** vega **5** field, green **7** pasture **9** grassland
historic: 9 Runnymede
low-lying: 4 inch **5** haugh

meadow mushroom
6 agaric

meager
4 bare, bony, lean, mere, thin **5** gaunt, lanky, scant, short, spare **6** paltry, scanty, shabby, skimpy, skinny, slight, sparse **7** angular, minimum, scraggy, scrawny, scrimpy **8** exiguous, rawboned **9** deficient, miserable **10** inadequate **12** insufficient

meal
4 chow, fare, feed, grub **5** board, feast, lunch, snack **6** brunch, dinner, farina, picnic, repast, spread, supper **7** high tea, nooning **8** luncheon, victuals **9** breakfast, collation, elevenses, refection
army: 3 MRE **4** mess

mealy
6 spotty, uneven **11** farinaceous

mean
3 low, mid, par **4** base, fair, hint, norm, poor, want, wish **5** catty, cheap, cruel, imply, lousy, lowly, mingy, nasty, petty, rough, small, snide, spell, tight, weigh **6** attest, center, common, denote, design, humble, intend, malign, matter, medial, medium, middle, paltry, scummy, scurvy, shabby, shoddy, sleazy, sordid, stingy, unwell **7** average, betoken, connote, express, lowborn, miserly, pitiful, portend, propose, purport, signify, suggest, vicious **8** déclassé, indicate, inferior, mediocre, middling, midpoint, moderate, ordinary, pitiable, plebeian, spiteful, stand for **9** designate, malignant, penurious, represent, symbolize **10** despicable, second-rate, vindictive **11** closefisted, tightfisted **12** contemptible, intermediary, intermediate

meander
4 roam, rove, turn, wind **5** amble, drift, range, snake, stray, twist **6** ramble, wander **7** traipse, winding **8** vagabond **9** gallivant, labyrinth

meandering
5 snaky **7** sinuous **8** flexuous, tortuous **10** convoluted, serpentine **11** anfractuous

meaning
3 aim **4** gist, pith **5** drift, force, point, sense **6** effect, import, intent **7** essence, message, purport **9** intention, substance **10** definition, denotation, intimation **11** connotation, implication **12** significance **13** signification

meaningful
5 valid **7** pointed, serious, weighty **8** eloquent, material **9** important, momentous **10** expressive **11** sententious, significant, substantial **13** consequential

meaningless
5 empty, inane **6** absurd, futile, hollow, jejune **7** trivial **8** nugatory **11** nonsensical **13** insignificant

meanings
diverse: 8 polysemy
study of: 9 semantics

means
5 funds, money **6** assets, avenue, income, wealth **7** backing, capital **8** finances, holdings, property, reserves **9** equipment, resources, substance **11** wherewithal

meantime
5 nonce **7** interim **8** interval

measly
4 poor, puny **5** petty, scant **6** meager, meagre, paltry, scanty, skimpy **7** pitiful, trivial **8** niggling, pathetic, picayune, piddling, trifling **9** miserable **10** picayunish **13** insignificant

measure
3 bar, ken **4** bill, size, step, test **5** bound, gauge, index, quota, scale, share, weigh **6** amount, bounds, effort, extent, figure, ration, reckon, resort, size up, survey **7** caliper, compute, delimit, mark out, portion **8** calliper, estimate, regulate, resource, standard **9** allotment, benchmark, calculate, calibrate, criterion, demarcate, determine, expedient, magnitude, yardstick **10** dimensions, indication, proportion, touchstone
area: **3** are, cho, mou, tan **4** acre **7** hectare
capacity: **3** cab, cor, pin, zak **4** fass, gill, peck, pint **5** liter, minim, quart, stere **6** bushel, gallon **8** fluidram **9** fluid dram **10** fluid ounce, milliliter
cloth: **3** ell
combining form: **6** metric **8** metrical
depth: **5** plumb, sound
dry: **4** peck **6** bushel
electrical: **3** amp, mho, ohm **4** volt, watt **6** ampere **7** coulomb
energy: **3** erg
force: **4** dyne
horse height: **4** hand
interstellar space: **6** parsec
length: **3** mil, pik, rod **4** alen, aune, foot, hiro, inch, link, mile, tsun, vara, yard **5** chain, cubit, meter **6** league **7** braccio, furlong **9** kilometer **10** centimeter, hectometer
liquid: **3** hin, tun **4** gill, pint **5** minim, quart **6** gallon
mixed drinks: **6** jigger
of comparison: **8** standard
paper: **4** ream
printer's: **4** pica **5** point
radioactive decay: **8** halflife
rotation: **5** angle
strength of solution: **7** titrate
surface: **3** are
thermodynamic: **7** entropy **8** enthalpy
yarn: **3** lea
(see also **weight**)

measured
7 regular, stately **8** metrical **9** regulated, temperate, unhurried **10** calculated, controlled, deliberate, restrained **13** proportionate

Measure for Measure
character: **6** Angelo, Juliet **7** Claudio, Mariana **8** Isabella **9** Vincentio
setting: **6** Vienna

measurement
4 area **6** degree **8** capacity, quantity **9** dimension, magnitude **11** calibration, mensuration

measure up to
3 tie **4** meet **5** equal, match, rival, touch **7** emulate **10** qualify for

measuring device
4 gage, tape **5** buret, gauge, ruler, scale, timer **7** burette, caliper, sextant, venturi **8** calipers, dipstick **9** altimeter, barometer, dosimeter, pedometer, yardstick **11** tensiometer, velocimeter

meat
4 core, food, gist, pith, pork, veal **5** flesh, jerky, steak **6** thrust, upshot **7** edibles **8** victuals **9** foodstuff, provender, substance **10** provisions **11** comestibles
broth: **8** bouillon
cake: **6** burger **9** hamburger
cured: **7** biltong
cut: **3** rib **4** loin, rump **5** chuck, flank, plate, round, shank **7** brisket, sirloin **8** rib roast **9** club steak, rump roast, short loin, short ribs **10** blade roast, flank steak, round steak, T-bone steak **12** sirloin steak
dealer: **7** butcher
deer: **7** venison
dried: **5** jerky
fastening pin: **6** skewer
holding rod: **4** spit **10** rotisserie
juices: **5** gravy
packer: **5** Swift **6** Armour
raw: **6** gobbet
roasted: **8** barbecue
roasting shop: **10** rotisserie
seasoned: **7** sausage **8** pastrami, scrapple
sheep: **6** mutton
side: **8** sowbelly
skewered: **5** kebab, kebob
slice: **6** cutlet, rasher
small portion: **6** collop
tough part: **7** gristle

meat-eating
11 carnivorous

meathead
3 lug, oaf **4** clod, dodo, dolt, gawk, goon, lout **5** chump, klutz, looby **6** dimwit, lubber **7** bungler, palooka **8** dumbbell, numskull **9** birdbrain, ignoramus, lamebrain, numbskull **10** nincompoop

Mebd
husband: **6** Ailill
victim: **10** Cuchulainn

Mecca
4 goal
country: **11** Saudi Arabia
pilgrim: **4** haji **5** hadji, hajji
pilgrimage: **4** hadj, hajj
port: **5** Jedda, Jidda **6** Jeddah, Jiddah
shrine: **5** Kaaba

mechanic
7 artisan **9** machinist, repairman **10** technician **12** grease monkey

mechanical
4 cold, rote **7** cursory, pasteup, robotic **8** lifeless **9** automated, automatic, unfeeling **10** impersonal, repetitive **11** emotionless, instinctive, involuntary, perfunctory, unemotional

mechanism
4 gear **5** gizmo, means, motor, works **6** agency, doodad, engine, jigger, medium, widget **7** whatsit **8** dohickey **9** apparatus, appliance, procedure, technique, thingummy **10** instrument **11** contraption, contrivance, thingamabob, thingamajig, thingumajig

medal
5 badge, honor, prize **6** reward **7** laurels **8** accolade **10** decoration **13** commemoration

meddle
3 pry **4** fool, nose **5** snoop **6** butt in, dabble, horn in, kibitz, monkey, putter, tamper, tinker **7** intrude, obtrude **8** trespass **9** interfere, interlope, intervene **10** mess around

meddler
5 snoop, yenta **7** snooper **8** busybody, intruder, kibitzer **9** buttinsky **12** troublemaker

meddlesome
4 busy, nosy **5** nosey **6** prying **9** intrusive, obtrusive, officious **11** impertinent, interfering

Medea
5 witch **9** sorceress **11** enchantress
aunt: **5** Circe
brother: **8** Absyrtus
father: **6** Aeëtes
husband: **5** Jason **6** Aegeus
sister: **5** Circe
son: **6** Medeus
victim: **6** Creusa, Glauce, Glauke

medial
3 mid **4** mean **6** center, middle **7** average, central, halfway, midmost **8** middling, moderate **10** centermost, middlemost **11** equidistant **12** intermediary, intermediate

median
see **medial**

mediate
5 judge **6** broker, convey, liaise, settle, step in, umpire **7** adjudge, referee, resolve **8** moderate, transmit **9** arbitrate, intercede, interfere, interpose, intervene, negotiate **10** conciliate

mediator
3 ref, ump **5** judge **6** broker, umpire **7** arbiter, liaison, referee **9** go-between, middleman **10** interceder, negotiator, peacemaker **11** intercessor

medical group
3 HMO

medical instrument
6 needle **7** forceps, scalpel, scanner, syringe **8** otoscope, speculum **9** endoscope **11** cardiograph, stethoscope

medical practitioner
3 doc, LPN **5** nurse **6** doctor, intern **7** interne, surgeon **9** physician

medicament
4 cure, pill **6** elixir, physic, remedy **7** nostrum **8** antidote, curative **10** palliative
inert: **7** placebo

medicate
4 cure, dose, drug, heal **5** treat

medicinal
8 curative, remedial, salutary, sanative **9** healthful **12** health-giving, pharmaceutic

medicine
4 cure, pill **5** bromo **6** physic, remedy **7** anodyne, nostrum **8** busulfan, poultice **11** antipyretic
African: **4** muti
bottle: **4** vial
branch: **7** surgery **8** oncology **9** neurology, pathology **10** bariatrics, cardiology, geriatrics, gynecology, nephrology, obstetrics, pediatrics, psychiatry
cathartic: **8** evacuant **9** purgative
combining form: **5** iatro **8** pharmaco
quantity of: **4** dose **6** dosage
shell: **7** capsule
soothing: **7** anodyne **8** lenitive, narcotic, sedative **9** calmative, soporific

medicine man
6 doctor, kahuna, shaman **9** curandero

medieval hero
English: **6** Gawain **7** Beowulf, Galahad **8** Lancelot
French: **6** Roland **7** Orlando
Norse: **6** Sigurd **9** Siegfried
Spanish: **3** Cid (El) **5** El Cid

medieval study
5 logic **7** grammar, trivium **8** rhetoric **10** quadrivium

mediocre
4 dull, fair, hack, so-so **6** common **7** average, fairish **8** inferior, middling, moderate, ordinary, passable **9** tolerable **10** pedestrian, uninspired **11** commonplace, indifferent **12** run-of-the-mill **13** unexceptional

meditate
4 mull, muse **5** weigh **6** chew on, intend, ponder **7** purpose, reflect, revolve **8** cogitate, consider, mull over, ruminate, turn over **9** reflect on **10** deliberate **11** contemplate

meditative
6 broody **7** pensive **8** brooding **10** reflective, ruminative, thoughtful
sect: **3** Zen

meditator
4 yogi

Mediterranean
11 Mare Nostrum **12** Mare Internum
coastal region: **7** Riviera

eastern shores: **6** Levant
island: (see at **island**)
port: **4** Oran
wind: **7** mistral, sirocco **8** scirocco

medium
3 par **4** fair, mean, so-so **5** agent, organ **6** agency, métier, milieu, normal **7** ambient, average, channel, climate, culture, neutral, vehicle **8** ambience, middling, moderate, passable, standard **9** tolerable **10** atmosphere **11** clairvoyant, environment **12** run-of-the-mill
of exchange: **5** money **8** currency **11** legal tender

medley
4 brew, olio, stew **5** combo, gumbo **6** jumble, ragout **7** farrago, mélange, mixture **8** mishmash, pastiche **9** pasticcio, patchwork, potpourri **10** assortment, hodgepodge, hotchpotch, miscellany, salmagundi **11** gallimaufry

Medusa
6 Gorgon
father: **7** Phorcus, Phorcys
hair: **6** snakes
mother: **4** Ceto
offspring: **7** Pegasus **8** Chrysaor
sister: **6** Stheno **7** Euryale
slayer: **7** Perseus

medusa
9 jellyfish

meed
3 due **4** part **5** quota, share **6** amount, desert, ration, return, reward **7** guerdon, measure, portion **8** dividend **9** allotment, allowance **10** recompense

meek
3 shy **4** mild, tame **5** lowly, timid **6** docile, gentle, humble, modest **7** patient **8** tolerant **10** submissive, unassuming **11** deferential **13** long-suffering

meerschaum
4 pipe **9** sepiolite

meet
3 apt, fit **4** face, fair, fill, find, join, just, open, spot **5** cross, event, hit on, match, right, touch, unite **6** answer, chance, engage, oppose, proper, settle, take on **7** contest, convene, fitting, fulfill, hit upon, satisfy, stumble **8** approach, assemble, come upon, concours, conflict, confront, converge, suitable **9** encounter, measure up **10** congregate **11** competition, reencounter
a bet: **3** see
a need: **7** suffice
athletic: **8** gymkhana **10** tournament
by appointment: **10** rendezvous

meeting
4 moot, talk **5** tryst **6** huddle, parley, powwow **7** session **8** assembly, conclave, concours, congress, junction **9** concourse, encounter, gathering, interview, rencontre **10** conference, confluence, convention, rendezvous **11** competition, convocation, get-together **12** intersection
Anglo-Saxon: **5** gemot **6** gemote
place: **5** forum
spiritual: **6** séance

Mefistofele composer
5 Boito (Arrigo)

megaphone
8 bullhorn **10** mouthpiece

Megara
father: **5** Creon
husband: **8** Heracles, Hercules
king: **5** Nisus

megillah
5 story **7** account

megrim
3 bee **4** urge, whim **5** fancy, freak, humor **6** notion, vagary, whimsy **7** caprice, conceit, impulse, vertigo **8** crotchet, migraine **9** dizziness

Mehitabel
3 cat
creator: **7** Marquis (Don)
friend: **5** Archy

Mein Kampf author
6 Hitler (Adolf)

meiosis
7 litotes **12** cell division

Meissen
5 china **8** ceramics **9** porcelain

Meistersinger
5 Sachs (Hans) **9** Frauenlob

Meistersinger, Die
beloved: **3** Eva
composer: **6** Wagner (Richard)
critic: **10** Beckmesser (Sixtus)
hero: **6** Walter **7** Walther
mentor: **5** Sachs (Hans)

melancholia
4 funk **5** dolor, dumps, gloom **6** misery, sorrow **7** despair, sadness **9** dejection, morbidity **10** depression, desolation, gloominess **11** despondency, dolefulness

melancholic
3 low, sad **4** blue, glum **6** gloomy, morose, triste **7** joyless **8** dejected, downcast, mournful **9** depressed, saddening **10** depressing, despondent, dispirited, lugubrious

melancholy
3 low, sad **4** blue, funk, glum **5** blues, dumps, ennui, gloom **6** dismal, dreary, gloomy, misery, morose, rueful, somber, tedium, triste, woeful **7** boredom, despair, doleful, joyless, sadness,

unhappy **8** dejected, dolorous, downcast, funereal, mournful, saddened **9** black bile, dejection, depressed, plaintive, saddening, sorrowful **10** depressing, depression, despondent, dispirited, lachrymose, lugubrious **11** despondency, unhappiness **12** heavyhearted, wretchedness

mélange
4 brew, hash, olio, stew **5** combo, gumbo **6** jumble, motley, ragbag, ragout, welter **7** farrago, grab bag, mixture **8** mishmash, mixed bag, pastiche **9** macédoine, pasticcio, patchwork, potpourri **10** assortment, hodgepodge, hotchpotch, miscellany, salmagundi **11** gallimaufry, smorgasbord

Melanippus
father: 7 Theseus
slayer: 10 Amphiaraus
victim: 6 Tydeus

Melchior
companion: 6 Caspar, Gaspar **9** Balthasar, Balthazar
gift: 4 gold

Melchizedek's kingdom
5 Salem

meld
3 mix **4** fuse **5** blend, merge **6** mingle **7** combine, mixture **8** compound **9** commingle, interfuse **10** amalgamate **11** intermingle

Meleager
beloved: 8 Atalanta
father: 6 Oeneus
mother: 7 Althaea
victim: 4 boar

melee
3 row **4** fray, riot **5** brawl, broil, clash, fight, set-to **6** affray, fracas, kickup, ruckus, rumpus **7** ruction, scuffle **8** skirmish **9** scrimmage **10** donnybrook, free-for-all

meliorate
4 help **5** amend **6** better, soften **7** improve **8** mitigate, palliate

Mélisande's lover
7 Pelléas

melisma
7 cadenza, descant

mellifluous
5 sweet **6** dulcet, fluent, golden, liquid, smooth **7** flowing, honeyed, silvery **8** euphonic, soothing **10** euphonious **13** silver-tongued

mellow
3 age **4** aged, ripe **5** ripen **6** genial, golden, grow up, mature, season, serene, smooth **7** honeyed, matured, relaxed, ripened **8** laid-back, pleasant, seasoned **9** agreeable

melodic
5 sweet **6** ariose, dulcet **7** musical, songful, tuneful **8** canorous, euphonic **10** euphonious

melodious
5 lyric, sweet **6** dulcet **7** musical, songful, tuneful **8** euphonic **9** cantabile **10** euphonious

melody
3 air, lay **4** aria, lilt, song, tune **5** canto, music, theme **6** chorus, strain, warble **7** descant, refrain **11** tunefulness

Mel of baseball
3 Ott

melon
4 pepo **5** gourd **6** casaba, profit **8** crenshaw, honeydew, windfall **10** cantaloupe

Melpomene
see **Muse**

melt
3 run **4** flux, fuse, thaw **5** deice **6** relent, soften **7** liquefy **8** dissolve, liquesce, unfreeze **9** disappear **10** deliquesce
down: 6 render
together: 4 fuse

Melville, Herman
character: 3 Pip **4** Ahab, Toby **5** Bembo, Chase **6** Cereno (Benito), Jermin, Pierre **7** Fayaway, Ishmael **8** Bartleby, Queequeg, Starbuck
work: 4 Omoo **5** Mardi, Typee **6** Pierre **7** Redburn **8** Moby Dick **11** White-Jacket **12** Benito Cereno **13** Confidence-Man (The)

member
3 cut **4** part **5** piece **6** clause, parcel **7** portion, section, segment **8** division **9** appendage, component **10** ingredient
political party: 4 Tory, Whig **7** Liberal **8** Democrat, Laborite **9** Labourite **10** Republican **12** Conservative
service club: 3 Elk **4** Lion **8** Kiwanian, Rotarian

membrane
4 film, tela **5** velum **6** pleura **7** pleurae (plural)
bodily: 6 serosa
brain: 3 pia
diffusion through: 7 osmosis
dividing: 5 septa (plural) **6** septum
ear: 8 tympanum
enclosing: 5 tunic **8** indusium
thin: 6 lamina **7** lamella, laminae (plural) **8** lamellae (plural)
wing: 8 patagium

memento
5 relic, token, trace **6** trophy **7** vestige **8** keepsake, reminder, souvenir **11** remembrance

memento ____
4 mori

Memnon
father: 8 Tithonus
mother: 3 Eos 6 Aurora
slayer: 8 Achilles

memoir
3 bio 4 life 5 diary 6 record, report, thesis 7 account, journal 8 anecdote 9 biography 11 confessions 12 recollection, reminiscence 13 autobiography

memoirist
5 Anaïs (Nin), Jones (Bridget), Pepys (Samuel) 7 Boswell (James), diarist

memorable
7 lasting, notable 8 historic 9 deathless, indelible, momentous, red-letter 10 noteworthy 11 significant 13 distinguished
period: 3 era

memorandum
4 chit, note 6 minute, notice, record 7 tickler 8 notation, reminder 12 announcement

memorial
4 note 5 relic, token, trace 6 record, trophy 7 relique 8 keepsake, monument, reminder, souvenir 10 dedicatory 11 celebrative, remembrance 12 consecrative, remembrancer 13 commemoration, commemorative
mound: 5 cairn

memorial park
8 cemetery, God's acre 9 graveyard

memorize
3 con, get 6 retain 8 remember

memory
6 recall 8 mind's eye, souvenir 9 anamnesis, awareness, flashback, retention 10 reflection 11 remembrance 12 recollection, reminiscence 13 retentiveness, retrospection
assisting: 8 mnemonic
loss: 7 amnesia
trace: 6 engram
unit: 3 meg

menace
4 risk 5 alarm, peril, scare 6 danger, hazard, threat 7 imperil, jeopard, torment 8 endanger, frighten, jeopardy, threaten 9 terrorize 10 intimidate, jeopardize

ménage
4 clan 5 house 6 family 8 quarters 9 household 12 housekeeping

menagerie
3 zoo 7 mixture

mend
3 fix, sew 4 cure, darn, heal, knit 5 patch, renew 6 cobble, doctor, look up, perk up, reform, remedy, repair, revamp 7 correct, improve, patch up, rebuild, rectify, redress, restore 8 overhaul, renovate 9 condition, refurbish 10 ameliorate, convalesce, recuperate 11 recondition, reconstruct

mendacious
5 false, lying 6 shifty 7 fibbing 9 deceitful, deceptive, dishonest, paltering 10 untruthful 11 dissembling 13 prevaricating

mendacity
3 lie 6 deceit 9 deception, duplicity, falsehood 10 dishonesty 12 equivocation 13 truthlessness

mendicancy
7 beggary, begging, bumming, cadging 8 mooching, sponging 11 panhandling

mendicant
5 friar 6 beggar 7 begging

Mending Wall author
5 Frost (Robert)

Menelaus
brother: 9 Agamemnon
father: 6 Atreus
kingdom: 6 Sparta
mother: 6 Aerope
wife: 5 Helen

menial
4 dull 5 lowly 6 humble 7 servant, servile, slavish 8 obeisant, retainer 9 unskilled 10 obsequious 11 subservient, undignified
worker: 4 peon, serf 5 prole 6 lackey

meniscus
4 lens 9 cartilage

Menlo Park inventor
6 Edison (Thomas Alva)

Mennonite sect
5 Amish

menopause
11 climacteric 12 change of life

menorah
10 candelabra

Menotti, Gian Carlo
character: 5 Amahl
opera: 6 Consul (The), Medium (The) 9 Telephone (The)

men's store
12 haberdashery

mental
5 inner 7 psychic 8 cerebral, rational, thinking 9 reasoning, spiritual 10 immaterial, telepathic 11 intelligent 12 intellective, intellectual 13 psychological
faculty: 6 memory

mentalist
3 Uri (Geller) 7 Kreskin 8 Banachek

mentality
3 wit **5** sense **6** brains **7** mindset, outlook **9** intellect, mother wit **10** brainpower **12** intelligence

mention
4 cite, name, note **7** refer to, specify **8** advert to, allude to, citation, instance **9** reference

mentor
4 guru **5** coach, guide, tutor **7** teacher **9** counselor **10** counsellor

Mentor's pupil
10 Telemachus

menu
4 card, diet **5** carte **10** bill of fare **11** carte du jour
item: **4** soup **5** salad **6** entrée **7** dessert **9** appetizer

Mephistophelian
7 satanic **8** devilish, diabolic **10** diabolical

mephitic
4 rank **5** fetid, funky, musty **6** putrid, smelly **7** noisome, noxious, reeking **8** stinking **9** poisonous **10** malodorous

Merab
father: **4** Saul
husband: **6** Adriel

Mercedes competitor
3 BMW **4** Audi **7** Porsche

mercenary
4 hack **5** ninja, ronin, venal **6** greedy **7** corrupt, Hessian, soldier **8** hireling **10** gun for hire

merchandise
4 line, sell **5** cargo, goods, stock, trade, wares **6** deal in, job lot, market, retail **7** effects, promote, staples, traffic **8** products **9** publicize, vendibles **11** commodities

merchandiser
6 dealer, trader, vendor **8** retailer **9** tradesman **10** wholesaler **11** businessman **13** businesswoman

merchant
5 buyer **6** dealer, jobber, seller, trader, vendor **7** peddler **8** purveyor, retailer **9** tradesman **10** trafficker, wholesaler **11** businessman, storekeeper
guild: **5** Hansa, Hanse
League: **9** Hanseatic
ship: **5** oiler **6** argosy, coaler, galiot, packet, tanker, trader **7** collier, galliot, steamer **8** Indiaman **9** freighter
wine: **7** vintner

Merchant of Venice, The
7 Antonio
character: **6** Portia **7** Jessica, Lorenzo, Nerissa, Shylock **8** Bassanio

merciful
4 kind **6** benign, humane, kindly **7** clement, lenient **8** tolerant **9** forgiving, indulgent **10** charitable, forbearing **11** softhearted **13** compassionate

merciless
4 grim **5** cruel, harsh **6** brutal, savage, wanton **9** cutthroat, ferocious, unfeeling **10** gratuitous, implacable, ironfisted, unyielding **11** hardhearted, unrelenting **12** unappeasable

mercurial
5 flaky **6** fickle, mobile **7** erratic **8** unstable, variable, volatile **9** impulsive **10** capricious, changeable, inconstant **13** temperamental, unpredictable

mercury
5 azoth **11** quicksilver
ore: **8** cinnabar

Mercury
6 planet
(see also **Hermes**)

Mercutio
friend: **5** Romeo
slayer: **6** Tybalt

mercy
4 pity, ruth **5** grace **6** lenity **7** caritas, charity **8** clemency, goodwill, kindness, leniency **9** benignity, tolerance **10** compassion, generosity, kindliness **11** benevolence, forbearance **13** commiseration
petition for: **5** kyrie **8** miserere

mere
4 bare, lake, pool, pure **6** meager, meagre, paltry **7** trivial **8** boundary, landmark, piddling **9** undiluted

merely
4 just, only **6** simply, solely, wholly

meretricious
4 loud, sham **5** gaudy, phony, showy **6** flashy, garish, glitzy, sleazy, tawdry, tinsel, trashy **7** chintzy **8** delusive, delusory, illusory **9** contrived, deceptive **10** misleading **11** counterfeit, pretentious

merganser
4 duck, smew

merge
3 mix **4** fuse, join **5** blend, unify, unite **6** mingle **7** combine **8** coalesce, compound **9** commingle, interfuse **10** amalgamate, assimilate **11** consolidate, intermingle

merger
5 union **6** fusion **7** melding **8** alliance, takeover **9** coalition **10** absorption **11** combination, unification **12** amalgamation **13** consolidation

meridian
4 acme, apex, peak **6** apogee, climax, summit, zenith **8** pinnacle

merit
3 due **4** earn, rate **5** arete, value, worth **6** virtue

7 caliber, deserts, deserve, entitle, justify, quality, stature, warrant **10** excellence, perfection, recompense **11** achievement

merited
3 due **4** fair, just **5** right **7** condign, fitting **8** deserved, rightful, suitable **9** justified, requisite **11** appropriate

meritorious
6 worthy **8** laudable **9** admirable, deserving, estimable, honorable **10** creditable **11** commendable, thankworthy **12** praiseworthy

Merlin
4 seer **5** augur, magus **6** shaman, wizard **7** prophet **8** magician **10** soothsayer **11** necromancer, thaumaturge

merlin
6 falcon **10** pigeon hawk

mermaid
3 nix **5** Ariel, nixie **7** manatee **8** sirenian **10** water nymph **11** water sprite

Merope
father: **5** Atlas **8** Oenopion
husband: **7** Polybus **8** Sisyphus **11** Cresphontes
lover: **5** Orion
mother: **7** Pleione
sisters: **8** Pleiades
son: **7** Aepytus, Glaucus

merriment
4 glee **5** mirth, revel **6** gaiety **7** jollity, revelry, whoopee **8** hilarity, reveling **9** festivity, jocundity, joviality **10** jocularity, jubilation **13** entertainment

merry
3 gay **4** glad **5** happy, jolly **6** blithe, jocund, jovial, joyful, joyous, lively **7** festive, gleeful **8** animated, cheerful, mirthful **9** hilarious, sprightly, vivacious **12** high-spirited, lighthearted

merry-andrew
4 fool, zany **5** clown, joker **6** jester, madcap **7** buffoon **9** harlequin **10** mountebank

merrymaker
7 partyer, reveler **8** carouser

merrymaking
5 party, revel **6** frolic, gaiety **7** jollity, revelry, whoopee **8** hilarity **9** festivity **12** conviviality

Merry Widow composer
5 Lehár (Franz)

Merry Wives of Windsor character
3 Nym **4** Ford, Page **5** Caius **6** Fenton, Pistol **7** Slender **8** Falstaff

mesa
5 bench, butte **7** plateau **9** tableland

mescal
5 agave **6** cactus, liquor, maguey, peyote

mesh
3 net, web **4** jibe, maze **5** skein, snare, snarl **6** engage, morass, screen, tangle **7** entwine, netting, network **8** dovetail, entangle **9** harmonize, interlock, labyrinth **10** coordinate **12** reticulation

meshuga
3 mad **4** nuts **5** crazy, goofy, kooky, loony, nutty, wacky **6** insane, screwy **7** foolish

mesmeric
8 alluring, hypnotic **9** glamorous, seductive **10** bewitching, enchanting **11** captivating, fascinating

mesmerize
4 vamp **6** dazzle, seduce **7** bewitch **8** ensorcel, enthrall, entrance **9** captivate, ensorcell, fascinate, hypnotize, spellbind

mesmerized
4 rapt

Mesopotamia
4 Iraq
civilization: **4** Elam **5** Akkad, Sumer **7** Assyria, Elamite **8** Akkadian, Assyrian, Sumerian **9** Babylonia **10** Babylonian
river: **6** Tigris **9** Euphrates

mess
4 hash **5** botch, snafu **6** fright, jumble, muddle **7** clutter, eyesore **8** botchery, disarray, disorder, shambles, wreckage **9** confusion **10** hodgepodge, hotchpotch, miscellany
around: **4** hang, idle **5** chill, dally **6** dawdle, doodle, fiddle, potter, putter **7** goof off, hang out **8** chill out, lollygag **10** dilly-dally
up: **3** err **4** blow, flub, muff, ruin **5** botch, fluff, fudge, spoil, touse **6** bungle, fumble, tousle **7** butcher

message
4 note, post **5** sense, theme **6** letter, report **7** epistle, meaning, mission, missive, purport **8** bulletin, dispatch, telegram **9** directive, telegraph **10** communiqué **12** significance **13** communication, signification

Messalina's husband
8 Claudius

mess around
4 fool, idle **5** flirt **6** dabble, dawdle, fiddle, meddle, monkey, potter, putter, tamper, tinker **8** womanize **9** associate, interfere, interlope, philander

messenger
4 page, post **5** envoy **6** herald, runner **7** apostle, courier **8** emissary **9** go-between, harbinger **10** ambassador **11** internuncio **12** intermediary
God's: **5** angel
of the gods: **4** Iris **6** Hermes **7** Mercury
Turkish: **6** chiaus

messiah
6 savior 7 saviour 8 defender 9 deliverer, liberator

Messiah composer
6 Handel (George Frideric)

messy
6 frowsy, frowzy, sloppy, unneat, untidy 7 chaotic, rumpled, unkempt 8 careless, confused, ill-kempt, slapdash, slipshod, slovenly 10 disheveled, disorderly 11 dishevelled
abode: 3 sty 6 pigpen, pigsty

mestizo
5 métis 6 ladino 10 mixed-blood

Mestor
father: 7 Perseus
mother: 9 Andromeda

Met
offering: 3 art 5 opera
solo: 4 aria
star: 4 diva 10 prima donna

metal
3 tin 4 gold, iron, lead, zinc 5 brass, steel 6 bronze, copper, nickel, pewter, silver 7 uranium 8 aluminum, chromium, platinum, titanium
alloy: (see **alloy**)
casting mold: 5 ingot
corrosion: 4 rust
fuse: 6 solder
in mass: 7 bullion
layer: 7 plating
lump: 6 nugget
magnetic: 4 iron
refuse: 4 calx, slag 5 dross 6 scoria
sheath: 5 armor
source: 3 ore
thin: 4 foil, leaf 5 plate
worker: 5 smith 10 blacksmith

metallic element
3 tin 4 gold, iron, lead, zinc 6 barium, cobalt, copper, nickel, radium, silver, sodium 7 arsenic, bismuth, cadmium, calcium, lithium, mercury, uranium 8 aluminum, chromium, platinum, titanium, tungsten, vanadium 9 magnesium, manganese, potassium, strontium 10 molybdenum

metamere
6 somite 7 segment

metamorphic rock
5 slate 6 gneiss, marble, schist 9 quartzite, soapstone

metamorphose
6 change, mutate 7 convert, develop 9 transform, translate, transmute 11 transfigure 12 transmogrify

Metamorphoses author
4 Ovid

metamorphosis
6 change 8 changing, mutation 9 evolution, sea change 10 changeover 13 transmutation

Metamorphosis, The
author: 5 Kafka (Franz)
character: 6 Gregor (Samsa)

___ me tangere
4 noli

metaphor
5 trope 6 simile, symbol 7 analogy 8 allegory 10 comparison, similitude

metaphorical compound
7 kenning

metaphysical
8 bodiless, numinous 9 unearthly, unfleshly 10 immaterial, suprahuman 12 supermundane, supramundane, supranatural, transcendent 13 preternatural
poet: 5 Donne (John) 6 Cowley (Abraham) 7 Crashaw (Richard), Herbert (George), Marvell (Andrew), Vaughan (Henry) 9 Cleveland (John)

mete (out)
4 deal, dole, give 5 allot, bound 6 border, parcel, ration 7 portion 8 allocate, boundary, disburse, dispense 9 apportion 10 distribute

meteor
8 fireball 12 shooting star
exploding: 6 bolide
shower: 5 Lyrid 6 Leonid, Taurid 7 Aquarid, Geminid, Orionid, Perseid 10 Quadrantid

meteorite
8 aerolite 10 siderolite

meter
4 beat, scan 6 rhythm 7 cadence, measure, pattern
poetic: 6 iambic 8 dactylic, spondaic, trochaic 9 anapestic

meter maid of song
4 Rita

metheglin
4 mead 8 beverage
ingredient: 5 honey

method
3 way 4 mode, modi (plural), plan 5 means, modus, order, style 6 course, design, manner, schema, scheme, system 7 fashion, formula, pattern, process, routine, wrinkle 8 practice 9 procedure, technique 11 orderliness 13 modus operandi
careful: 8 strategy
of employing troops: 6 tactic 7 tactics
of procedure: 4 game

methodical
5 exact 7 careful, logical, orderly, precise,

regular **9** efficient, organized **10** deliberate, scrupulous, systematic, systemized **12** systematized

Methuselah
father: **5** Enoch
grandson: **4** Noah
son: **6** Lamech

meticulous
5 exact, fussy, picky **6** strict **7** careful, finicky, precise **8** detailed, thorough **10** fastidious, nit-picking, pernickety, scrupulous **11** microscopic, painstaking, persnickety, punctilious **13** conscientious

métier
4 work **5** craft, field, forte, trade **7** calling, pursuit **8** business, strength, vocation **9** specialty **10** employment, occupation, profession

MetLife rival
5 Aetna

metrical foot
4 iamb **5** ionic, paeon **6** cretic, dactyl, iambic, iambus **7** anapest, pyrrhic, pyrrhus, spondee, triseme, trochee **8** bacchius, choriamb, dactylic, spondaic, tribrach, trochaic **9** anapestic **10** tribrachic

metric unit
area: **3** are **7** hectare
capacity: **5** liter, litre **9** decaliter, deciliter, kiloliter **10** centiliter, hectoliter, milliliter
length: **5** meter **9** decameter, decimeter, dekameter, kilometer **10** centimeter, hectometer, millimeter
mass and weight: **4** gram **5** tonne **7** quintal **8** decagram, decigram, dekagram, kilogram **9** centigram, hectogram, metric ton, milligram
volume: **5** liter, litre

metro
4 tube **6** subway **11** underground

metronome setting
5 tempo

metropolis
4 city **7** capital

metropolitan
5 urban **6** urbane **7** primate **9** municipal **10** archbishop

Mets home, formerly
4 Shea

mettle
4 fire, grit, guts **5** heart, moxie, nerve, pluck, spunk, steel, valor, vigor **6** daring, spirit, starch, temper **7** cojones, courage, resolve, stamina **8** backbone, boldness, tenacity, vitality **9** fortitude **10** resolution

mettlesome
4 bold, game **5** brave, fiery, gutsy **6** plucky, spunky **7** doughty, staunch, valiant **8** intrepid, resolute, spirited, vigorous **9** tenacious **10** courageous, determined

mew
3 hem, pen **4** cage, coop, gull **5** alley, fence **6** corral, immure, shut in, stable **7** enclose, seagull **8** hideaway

mewl
4 moan, pule **5** whine **6** snivel **7** whimper

Mexican
crop: **5** sisal **8** henequen
estate: **8** hacienda
food: **4** masa, taco **5** chili, salsa, tamal **6** fajita, tamale **7** burrito, panocha, penuche, tamales, tostada **8** frijoles, tortilla **9** enchilada, guacamole **10** quesadilla **11** chimichanga
hut: **5** jacal
liquor: **6** mescal, mezcal, pulque **7** tequila

Mexico
ancient city: **12** Tenochtitlán
ancient culture: **4** Maya **5** Aztec, Mayan, Olmec **6** Toltec
bay: **8** Campeche
capital: **10** Mexico City
city: **4** León **6** Juárez, Mérida, Oaxaca, Puebla **7** Nogales, Tijuana **8** Acapulco, Mexicali, Saltillo **9** Chihuahua, Matamoros, Monterrey **10** Cuernavaca **11** Guadalajara **12** Ciudad Juárez
conqueror: **6** Cortés (Hernán, Hernando)
discoverer: **7** Córdoba (Fernández de)
emperor: **10** Maximilian
gulf: **10** California
island: **7** Cozumel
island group: **13** Revillagigedo
lake: **7** Chapala, Cuitzeo, Texcoco **9** Pátzcuaro
language: **7** Spanish
leader: **4** Díaz (Porfirio) **6** Juárez (Benito) **8** Carranza (Venustiano)
monetary unit: **4** peso
mountain, range: **8** Malinche **11** Sierra Madre
neighbor: **6** Belize **9** Guatemala
peninsula: **4** Baja **7** Yucatán
port: **7** Tampico **8** Ensenada, Mazatlán, Veracruz
resort: **6** Cancún **8** Acapulco
revolutionist: **5** Villa (Pancho) **6** Zapata (Emiliano) **7** Hidalgo (Padre Miguel)
river: **4** Mayo **5** Bravo, Yaquí **6** Balsas, Grande, Pánuco **7** Conchos **8** Grijalva, Río Bravo, Santiago **9** Rio Grande **10** Usumacinta
ruined city: **5** Tulum, Uxmal **7** Mayapán **8** Palenque **11** Chichén Itzá
state: **6** Oaxaca, Puebla, Sonora **7** Chiapas, Durango, Hidalgo, Tabasco, Yucatán **8** Veracruz
sea: **9** Caribbean
volcano: **6** Colima **9** Paricutín **11** Ixtacihuatl **12** Citlaltépetl, Ixtaccihuatl, Popocatépetl

Meyers of late-night talk
4 Seth
mezzanine
4 loge **5** story **7** balcony **8** entresol
mezzo
4 half **6** singer **7** soprano
mezzo-soprano
American: 5 Elias (Rosalind), Horne (Marilyn), Jones (Sissieretta) **6** Bumbry (Grace), Graham (Susan), Graves (Denyce) **7** Stevens (Risë), Verrett (Shirley) **8** DiDonato (Joyce), Troyanos (Tatiana), von Stade (Frederica)
Austrian: 6 Ludwig (Christa)
English: 5 Baker (Janet)
Italian: 7 Bartoli (Cecilia) **8** Cossotto (Fiorenza)
Miami
bowl: 6 Orange
chief: 12 Little Turtle
county: 4 Dade
stadium: 9 Joe Robbie
team: 4 Heat **7** Marlins **8** Dolphins, Panthers
miasma
3 fog **4** haze, mist, murk, smog **5** brume, vapor **9** effluvium
mica
7 biotite **8** silicate **9** isinglass, muscovite
Michelangelo Buonarotti
painting: 10 Holy Family (The) **12** Last Judgment (The)
statue: 5 David, Moses, Pietà **7** Bacchus
Michener novel
5 Space, Texas **6** Hawaii, Iberia, Poland, Source (The) **8** Caravans, Covenant (The), Drifters (The), Sayonara **10** Centennial, Chesapeake **13** Fires of Spring (The) **15** Bridges at Toko-Ri (The)
Michigan
capital: 7 Lansing
city: 5 Flint **7** Detroit, Pontiac **8** Ann Arbor, Dearborn **9** Kalamazoo **11** Grand Rapids **13** Sault Ste. Marie
college, university: 6 Calvin **9** Kalamazoo **10** Wayne State
lake: 4 Erie **5** Huron **8** Michigan, Superior
nickname: 9 Wolverine (State) **10** Great Lakes (State)
state bird: 5 robin
state flower: 12 apple blossom
state tree: 9 white pine
Michigan northerner
6 Yooper
mickey
5 flask, split
Mickey Mouse
5 dinky, petty **7** trivial **8** trifling **9** pointless, small-time, worthless **10** irrelevant
microbe
3 bug **4** germ **5** virus **8** bacillus, pathogen **9** bacterium **13** microorganism
see **microorganism**
microfilm sheet
5 fiche
Micronesia
capital: 7 Palikir
island, island group: 3 Yap **5** Chuuk **6** Kosrae **7** Pohnpei **8** Caroline
microorganism
3 bug **4** germ **5** ameba, virus **6** aerobe, amoeba **7** bacilli (plural), microbe, protist **8** bacillus, bacteria (plural), pathogen, protozoa (plural) **9** bacterium, protozoan, protozoon
microphone
3 bug **4** mike
shield: 4 gobo
microscope
9 magnifier
inventor: 11 Leeuwenhoek (Antoni van)
part: 5 stage **6** mirror **8** eyepiece **9** objective
microscopic
4 tiny **5** small **6** minute **13** infinitesimal
Microsoft
founder: 5 Gates (Bill)
software, formerly: 3 DOS **5** MS-DOS
microwave
3 zap **4** nuke
Mid-Atlantic state
7 New York **8** Delaware, Maryland, Virginia **9** New Jersey **12** Pennsylvania, West Virginia
midday
4 noon, sext **8** high noon, noontide, noontime
middle
4 core, mean **5** mesne, waist **6** center, medial, median **7** average, central, halfway **8** interior **10** centermost **11** equidistant, intervening **12** intermediary, intermediate
combining form: 3 mes **4** meso
Middle American country
4 Cuba **5** Haiti **6** Belize, Mexico, Panama **7** Bahamas, Grenada, Jamaica **8** Barbados, Dominica, Honduras **9** Costa Rica, Guatemala, Nicaragua **10** El Salvador
middlebrow
7 Babbitt
middle class
11 bourgeoisie
middle-class
9 bourgeois
middle ear
bone: 5 incus **6** stapes **7** malleus
membrane: 7 eardrum **8** tympanum

Middle Earth inhabitant
3 elf, ent, orc **5** troll **6** hobbit

Middle Eastern
airline: **4** El Al
country: **3** UAE **4** Iran, Iraq, Oman **5** Egypt, Libya, Qatar, Sudan, Syria, Yemen **6** Cyprus, Israel, Jordan, Kuwait, Turkey **7** Bahrain, Lebanon **11** Saudi Arabia
food: **4** pita **6** hummus **7** baklava, falafel, felafel, tabouli **8** shawarma, tabouleh **9** tabbouleh
hat: **3** fez
native: **4** Arab, Kurd **5** Druze **6** Beduin, Berber **7** Bedouin
streambed: **4** wadi

Middle Kingdom
5 China

middleman
5 agent **6** broker **8** mediator **9** go-between **11** distributor, intercessor **12** intermediary, intermediate

Middlemarch author
5 Eliot (George), Evans (Mary Ann)

middle name
Edison: **4** Alva
Elvis: **4** Aron **5** Aaron

middle-of-the-road
7 neutral **8** moderate **9** impartial **11** nonpartisan

middling
4 fair, okay, so-so **6** decent, fairly, medium, rather **7** average, fairish, typical **8** adequate, mediocre, moderate, ordinary, passable **9** tolerable **10** moderately, second-rate **11** indifferent **12** intermediate, run-of-the-mill

midge
3 fly **4** gnat **6** punkie **7** no-see-um **8** dipteran **10** chironomid
larva: **9** bloodworm

midget
4 runt **5** dwarf, pygmy **6** bantam, peewee **7** manikin **8** Tom Thumb **10** homunculus **11** hop-o'-my-thumb, Lilliputian

Midian
father: **7** Abraham
mother: **7** Keturah
son: **5** Abida, Ephah, Epher **6** Eldaah, Hanoch

mid-month dates
4 ides

midpoint
3 par **4** mean, norm **6** center, median, middle **7** average, centrum, halfway **8** bull's-eye, standard

Midwest hub
5 O'Hare

midwife
4 dhai **5** doula **6** granny, Lucina **10** accoucheur

mien
3 air, set **4** look **6** aspect, manner **7** address, bearing **8** carriage, demeanor, presence **9** mannerism **10** appearance, deportment, expression **11** comportment

miff
3 fit, irk, vex **4** beef, flap, spat **5** annoy, pique, run-in, upset **6** bother, fracas, nettle, offend, put out **7** dispute, provoke, quarrel, rhubarb **8** irritate, squabble **10** conniption, falling-out **11** altercation

might
3 may **4** sway **5** brawn, clout, force, means, power **6** energy, muscle **7** ability, command, control, mastery, potency **8** capacity, strength **9** authority, resources **12** forcefulness

mighty
4 huge, very **5** grand, great **6** heroic, potent, strong **7** eminent, immense, massive, titanic **8** enormous, forceful, gigantic, imposing, powerful, puissant **10** impressive, monumental, prodigious, stupendous, tremendous

Mignon composer
6 Thomas (Ambroise)

mignonette
4 herb **5** sauce **6** annual, reseda

migrant
4 hobo, Okie **5** exile, mover, nomad, tramp **7** bracero, drifter, nomadic, refugee **8** traveler, vagabond, wanderer **9** itinerant, transient **10** expatriate **12** rolling stone

migrate
4 move, trek **5** drift, range, shift **6** wander **8** transfer

migration
6 exodus **8** diaspora
of professionals: **10** brain drain

migratory
5 nomad **6** errant, mobile, moving, roving **7** nomadic, ranging **9** wandering

Mikado, The
character: **4** Ko-Ko **6** Yum-Yum **7** Pooh-Bah **8** Nanki-Poo, Pish-Tush **9** Pitti-Sing
composer: **8** Sullivan (Arthur)
librettist: **7** Gilbert (W. S.)

milady
6 madame **10** noblewoman **11** gentlewoman

Milan
family: **6** Sforza **8** Visconti
opera house: **7** La Scala

Milcah
brother: **3** Lot
father: **5** Haran **10** Zelophehad
husband: **5** Nahor
son: **7** Bethuel

mild
4 calm, easy, meek, soft, tame **5** balmy, bland, faint, tepid **6** benign, docile, gentle, placid, serene, smooth, tender **7** amiable, clement, equable, insipid, lenient, patient, subdued **8** moderate, obliging **9** benignant, temperate **10** forbearing, submissive

mildew
4 mold, rust **6** fungus, growth

___ mile
7 country, statute **8** nautical

mileage recorder
8 odometer

milestone
5 event **6** marker **8** landmark, occasion

milieu
5 scene **6** medium, sphere **7** ambient, climate, setting **8** ambiance, ambience **10** atmosphere, background **11** environment, mise-en-scène **12** surroundings

militant
7 fighter, martial, warlike, warrior **8** activist, fighting **9** assertive, bellicose, combatant, combative, truculent **10** aggressive, pugnacious **11** belligerent, contentious, quarrelsome **12** gladiatorial

military
5 troop **6** forces, troops **7** martial, warlike **8** soldiery **9** soldierly **10** servicemen **11** armed forces, soldierlike
alert protocol: 6 DEFCON
alliance: 4 NATO
base: 4 camp, fort, post **5** depot, field **6** billet **8** barracks, garrison, quarters **10** encampment
hat: 4 kepi **5** shako
officer: 5 major **7** captain, colonel, general **9** brigadier **10** lieutenant
prisoner: 3 POW
school: 3 OCS, OTS **4** ROTC, USMA **9** Annapolis, West Point
sector: 10 combat zone, front lines **11** battlefront
store: 10 commissary
storehouse: 5 depot **6** armory **7** arsenal
supplies: 8 matériel, ordnance
unit: 5 corps, squad, troop **7** company, platoon **8** division, regiment **9** battalion **11** battle group
vehicle: 4 jeep, tank **6** Abrams, Humvee **7** Bradley **9** Black Hawk, half-track

militate
4 tell **5** count, weigh **6** matter **11** carry weight

militia
7 reserve

milk
4 pump, rook, suck **5** drain, educe, empty, evoke, exact, mulct, nurse, wring **6** elicit, extort, fleece **7** exhaust, exploit, extract
coagulated: 4 curd
combining form: 4 lact **5** lacti, lacto
curdled: 7 clabber
fermented: 5 kefir **6** kumiss, yogurt **7** koumiss, yoghurt
liquid part: 4 whey
store: 5 dairy
sugar: 7 lactose

milkfish
3 awa

milk shake
6 frappe **7** frosted

milky
4 fair, meek, mild, pale, tame **5** white **6** chalky, cloudy, gentle **7** lacteal, whitish **8** timorous
gem: 4 opal
lymph: 5 chyle

mill
5 grind, plant, shape, works **7** factory, machine **9** circulate, pulverize **11** manufactory

millenary
8 thousand

Miller, Arthur
film: 7 Misfits (The)
play: 5 Price (The) **9** All My Sons **8** Crucible (The) **12** After the Fall **16** Death of a Salesman **17** View from the Bridge (A)
salesman: 5 Loman (Willy)

milliner
6 hatter

million
combining form: 3 meg **4** mega

millionth
combining form: 4 micr **5** micro

Mill on the Floss author
5 Eliot (George), Evans (Mary Ann)

millstone
4 duty, load, onus **6** burden, charge, weight **9** albatross **10** affliction, deadweight

Milne character
3 Roo **4** Pooh (Winnie the) **5** Kanga **6** Eeyore, Piglet, Tigger, Winnie (the Pooh)

Milo of film
5 O'Shea

milord
8 nobleman **9** gentleman, patrician **10** aristocrat **12** silk stocking

milquetoast
see **milksop**

Miltiades' victory
8 Marathon

Milton work
5 Comus **7** Lycidas **8** L'Allegro **12** Areopagitica, Paradise Lost

mime
3 act **5** actor **6** act out **7** Marceau (Marcel) **9** performer, represent **11** impersonate **12** impersonator

mimic
3 act, ape, tui **4** aper, copy, echo, mock, play **5** actor, enact **6** mummer, parody, parrot, player **7** copycat, imitate **8** resemble, simulate, travesty **9** burlesque, pantomime **11** impersonate **12** impersonator

mimicry
4 echo **6** parody **8** travesty **9** imitation, parroting **10** caricature **13** impersonation

minatory
4 dire, grim **7** baleful, baneful, direful, hostile, malefic, ominous **8** menacing, sinister **9** ill-boding **10** forbidding, foreboding, maleficent **11** frightening, threatening **12** intimidating

mince
4 chop, dice, hash **5** cut up, strut **6** prance, sashay, soften **8** moderate, restrain, tone down **9** euphemize

mincing
5 fussy **6** dainty, la-di-da, too-too **7** finical, finicky, stilted **8** affected, delicate **10** fastidious, pernickety **11** persnickety

mind
3 wit **4** mood, obey, soul, tend, will, wits **5** brain, fancy, watch, weigh **6** attend, belief, beware, brains, follow, memory, notice, psyche, reason, senses, spirit **7** care for, discern, dislike, feeling, observe, oversee, purpose **8** consider **9** intellect, intention, mentality, supervise **10** brainpower, gray matter **11** disposition, temperament **12** intelligence **13** consciousness
combining form: **5** psych **6** psycho

Minderbinder of Catch-22
4 Milo

mindful
5 alert, awake, aware **7** knowing **8** sensible, vigilant **9** attentive, cognizant, conscious, observant **10** conversant **13** conscientious

mindless
4 rash **5** ditsy, ditzy, inane, silly **6** jejune, simple, stupid **7** asinine, foolish, unaware, vacuous **9** nitwitted, oblivious **10** irrational, unthinking **13** unintelligent

mine
3 dig, pit, sap **4** fund, lode, vein, well **5** delve, drill, hoard, stock, store, trove **6** burrow, quarry, spring **7** bonanza, deposit, extract **8** eldorado, excavate, Golconda **10** excavation, wellspring **13** treasure trove
coal: **8** colliery
entrance: **4** adit

Mineo of the movies
3 Sal

miner
6 pitman **7** collier

mineral
5 beryl, topaz, trona **6** augite, barite, garnet, iolite, pinite, rutile, sphene, spinel, sulfur, zircon **7** apatite, axinite, azurite, bornite, calcite, citrine, coesite, cyanite, jadeite, kernite, kunzite, olivine, zeolite **8** boracite, cinnabar, dolomite, epsomite, fayalite, feldspar, fluorite, hematite, lazulite, lazurite, siderite, sodalite, stibnite, triplite, wellsite **9** aragonite, celestite, cerussite, danburite, fosterite, kaolinite, lawsonite, magnetite, malachite, muscovite, phenakite, scapolite, tridymite, turquoise, wulfenite **10** chalcedony, orthoclase, pyrrhotite, tourmaline **11** alexandrite, chrysoberyl, melanterite **12** brazilianite, chalcopyrite, tincalconite **13** rhodochrosite
deposit: **4** lode
flaky: **4** mica
greasy: **4** talc **10** serpentine
hard: **6** spinel **7** diamond **8** corundum
iridescent: **4** opal
nonmetallic: **5** boron **6** gypsum, halite **8** asbestos, graphite
scale: **4** Mohs'
shiny: **4** gold **6** galena, pyrite, silver
soft: **4** talc **6** gypsum **8** graphite
source: **3** ore
transparent: **6** quartz

mineral water
7 seltzer **8** club soda

miner's quest
3 ore **4** lode

Minerva
see **Athena**

mingle
3 mix **4** meld **5** blend, merge **6** commix **7** combine **8** intermix **9** associate, socialize

mingy
4 mean **5** cheap, tight **7** chintzy, miserly, scrimpy **8** grudging, ungiving **9** niggardly, penurious **10** pinchpenny **11** closefisted, tightfisted

miniature
3 wee **4** tiny **5** small, teeny, weeny **6** little, minute, petite, teensy **9** itsy-bitsy, itty-bitty **10** diminutive, small-scale, teeny-weeny **11** Lilliputian **12** illumination

minify
4 trim **6** lessen, shrink **7** abridge, curtail **8** decrease, diminish **10** abbreviate

minim
3 bit, jot **4** atom, iota **5** grain, speck **7** modicum, smidgen **8** particle
music: **8** half note

minimal
5 basic, least, token **6** lowest **7** nominal **8** littlest, smallest **9** slightest

minimize
5 decry **6** reduce **7** run down **8** belittle, derogate, discount, downplay, play down **9** disparage, soft-pedal, underrate **10** depreciate **13** underestimate

minimum
3 dab, jot **4** iota, whit **5** least, speck **6** lowest, margin **7** smidgen **8** particle, pittance, smallest

minion
4 idol **5** toady **6** flunky, lackey, vassal, yes-man **7** devotee, flunkey, flunkie, spaniel **8** favorite, follower, parasite, truckler **9** sycophant, toadeater, underling **10** bootlicker **11** lickspittle, subordinate

minister
3 Rev. **4** tend **5** agent, clerk, serve **6** cleric, curate, divine, parson, pastor **8** clerical, preacher, reverend **9** churchman, clergyman **10** ambassador **12** ecclesiastic
of state: **10** chancellor
plenipotentiary: **5** envoy **6** consul **8** diplomat, emissary

ministry
5 agent, organ **6** agency, clergy, medium **7** cabinet **10** department, instrument **11** bureaucracy

mink kin
5 otter, skunk, stoat **6** ermine, ferret, fisher, weasel

Minnehaha's husband
8 Hiawatha

Minnesota
capital: **6** St. Paul
city: **5** Edina **6** Duluth **9** Rochester **11** Minneapolis
college, university: **8** Carleton **9** Saint Olaf **10** Macalester
nickname: **6** Gopher (State) **9** North Star (State)
park: **9** Voyageurs
river: **7** St. Croix **9** Minnesota **11** Mississippi
state bird: **4** loon (common)
state flower: **12** lady's slipper
state tree: **7** red pine

minor
5 lower, petty, small, youth **6** casual, lesser, little, paltry, slight **7** trivial **8** inferior, mediocre, piddling, small-fry, trifling, underage **9** dependent, secondary, small-beer, small-time **10** bush-league, second-rate, shoestring **11** indifferent, unimportant **13** insignificant

____ Minor
4 Ursa

minority
5 youth **6** nonage **7** infancy **9** childhood **10** immaturity

minor-league
5 small **6** lesser **9** secondary, small-time **11** unimportant

Minos
daughter: **7** Ariadne, Phaedra
father: **4** Zeus **7** Jupiter
kingdom: **5** Crete
monster: **8** Minotaur
mother: **6** Europa
son: **9** Androgeos
wife: **8** Pasiphaë

Minotaur
father: **4** bull
home: **9** labyrinth
mother: **8** Pasiphaë
slayer: **7** Theseus

minstrel
4 bard, wait **6** harper, singer **7** gleeman **8** jongleur **9** balladist **10** troubadour
end man: **5** Bones (Mr.), Tambo (Mr.)
instrument: **4** lute, lyre **5** naker, rebec, shawm, tabor **8** crumhorn, psaltery **9** krummhorn **10** tambourine

mint
3 pot **4** cast, coin, heap, pile, sage **5** basil, bugle, forge, issue, stamp, trove **6** boodle, bundle, create, intact, packet, savory, strike, unused **7** fortune, like-new, menthol, perfect, produce **8** brand-new, lavender, marjoram, original **9** blue curls, bugleweed, undamaged **10** pennyroyal

Minuit's purchase
9 Manhattan

minus
4 flaw, lack, less, sans **6** absent, defect **7** lacking, missing, wanting, without **8** drawback, negative, subtract **10** deficiency

minuscule
4 tiny **5** small **6** letter, little, minute **7** trivial **9** lowercase, miniature **10** negligible, small-scale **11** meaningless, microscopic **13** imperceptible, inappreciable, insignificant

minute
3 wee **4** jiff, memo, note, tiny **5** draft, flash, jiffy, small, teeny, weeny **6** little, moment, record, teensy **7** careful, instant, precise, trivial **8** detailed, itemized, thorough, trifling **9** itsy-bitsy, itty-bitty, miniature, minuscule **10** diminutive, memorandum, meticulous, scrupulous, teeny-weeny **11** Lilliputian, punctilious **13** infinitesimal

minutes
3 log **6** annals, record **7** summary **10** transcript **11** proceedings

minutiae
6 trivia **7** details **10** fine points, triviality **11** particulars
minx
4 bawd, moll, slut, tart **5** bimbo, tramp, wench, whore **6** floozy, harlot, hooker **7** hustler, trollop **8** strumpet **10** prostitute
miracle
4 boon, feat **6** marvel, wonder **7** godsend, portent, prodigy, stunner **8** windfall **9** sensation **10** phenomenon
miraculous
7 amazing **8** wondrous **9** marvelous, unearthly, wonderful **10** astounding, prodigious, superhuman **11** astonishing, spectacular **12** inexplicable, supernatural **13** preternatural
mirage
6 vision, wraith **8** delusion, illusion, phantasm **11** fata morgana, ignis fatuus **13** hallucination
mirage, maybe
5 oasis
Miranda
father: 8 Prospero
lover: 9 Ferdinand
mire
3 bog, fen, mud **4** muck, ooze, sink, trap **5** delay, marsh, slush, swamp **6** detain, enmesh, entrap, hang up, morass, slough, tangle **7** bog down, embroil, ensnare, involve, set back **8** entangle **9** imbroglio, implicate, quicksand
Miriam's brother
5 Aaron, Moses
mirror
5 glass **6** embody, typify **7** reflect **8** speculum **9** exemplify, personify, reflector **10** illustrate **11** cheval glass **12** looking glass
signaling: 10 heliograph
mirth
3 fun, joy **4** glee **5** cheer **6** gaiety, levity **7** jollity, revelry **8** gladness, hilarity **9** festivity, frivolity, happiness, jocundity, joviality, merriment **10** jocularity **11** merrymaking **12** cheerfulness
mirthful
3 gay **5** jolly, merry, riant **6** jocund, jovial **7** festive **9** exuberant, hilarious **12** lighthearted
miry
4 oozy **5** boggy, mucky, muddy **6** marshy, slushy, swampy
misadventure
4 slip **5** boner, error, lapse **6** howler, mishap **7** blunder, faux pas **8** accident, calamity, casualty, disaster **9** cataclysm **10** misfortune **11** catastrophe
misanthrope
5 cynic, grump, loner **6** grinch **7** killjoy, recluse, scoffer **10** curmudgeon
misanthropic
7 cynical **10** antisocial
misappropriate
5 filch, steal **6** pilfer **7** purloin **8** embezzle, peculate **9** defalcate
misbegotten
7 bastard, illicit, natural **8** baseborn, deformed, spurious **10** fatherless, unfathered **12** contemptible, disreputable, ill-conceived, illegitimate
misbehave
5 act up, cut up, lapse, rebel, stray **6** act out, offend **7** carry on, disobey **8** trespass **10** roughhouse, transgress
misbehavior
7 misdeed **8** rudeness **9** high jinks **10** misconduct, wrongdoing **11** delinquency, dereliction, naughtiness **13** transgression
miscalculate
3 err **8** miscount, misgauge
miscarry
4 fail, flop **5** abort **6** fizzle **7** go wrong
miscellaneous
3 odd **5** mixed **6** motley, sundry, varied **7** diverse **8** assorted **9** different, disparate, scrambled **13** heterogeneous
miscellany
3 ana **4** hash, olio, stew **5** salad **6** jumble, medley, motley, muddle **7** farrago, mélange, mixture, omnibus **8** mixed bag, pastiche, sundries **9** anthology, congeries, pasticcio, patchwork, potpourri **10** assortment, hodgepodge, hotchpotch, salmagundi **11** aggregation, gallimaufry, odds and ends, olla podrida, smorgasbord
mischance
6 mishap **7** bad luck, tragedy **8** accident, casualty **9** adversity **10** misfortune **11** contretemps
mischief
3 ill **4** evil, harm **5** prank **6** damage, strife **7** devilry, roguery, trouble, waggery **8** deviltry, sabotage **9** devilment, diablerie, vandalism **10** wrongdoing **11** naughtiness, shenanigans **12** monkeyshines
mischief-maker
3 imp **4** puck **5** devil, knave, rogue, scamp **6** rascal **7** villain **8** agitator, scalawag **9** prankster, trickster **11** rapscallion **12** rabble-rouser
mischievous
3 sly **4** arch, foxy **5** antic, saucy **6** artful, bratty, impish, tricky, vexing **7** harmful, irksome, larkish, naughty, playful, puckish, roguish, tricksy, waggish **8** annoying, damaging, perverse, prankish, rascally, sportive **9** injurious, malicious **10** bothersome, frolicsome, ill-behaved
misconception
5 error **7** fallacy, mistake **8** delusion, illusion

misconduct
8 adultery **10** wrongdoing **11** dereliction, impropriety, malfeasance, malpractice, misbehavior **12** malversation **13** transgression

miscreant
4 heel **5** felon, knave, rogue **6** outlaw, rascal, sinner, wretch **7** corrupt, culprit, heretic, hoodlum, infidel, lowlife, vicious, villain **8** apostate, criminal, depraved, infamous, perverse **9** heretical, nefarious, scoundrel, unhealthy, wrongdoer **10** blackguard, degenerate, delinquent, unbeliever, villainous

miscue
4 goof, miss, slip, trip **5** error, fluff, lapse **6** slipup **7** blooper, blunder, mistake

misdeed
3 sin **5** crime, wrong **6** breach **7** offense **9** violation **10** infraction **13** transgression

misdoubt
4 fear **5** dread **7** suspect

mise-en-scène
3 set **4** site **6** locale, medium, milieu **7** ambient, climate, context, scenery, setting **8** ambiance, ambience, stage set **10** atmosphere, background **11** environment **12** stage setting, surroundings

miser
5 piker **7** hoarder, niggard, scrooge **8** tightwad **9** skinflint **10** cheapskate, pinchpenny

miserable
6 gloomy, meager, meagre, paltry, rueful, sordid, woeful **7** doleful, forlorn, piteous, pitiful, squalid **8** desolate, dolorous, downcast, hopeless, shameful, tortured, wretched **9** afflicted, destitute, sorrowful, worthless **10** despairing, despondent, melancholy

Miserables, Les
author: 4 Hugo (Victor)
character: 6 Javert (Inspector) **7** Cosette, Fantine, Valjean (Jean)

miserly
4 mean **5** close, tight **6** greedy, stingy **7** scrimpy **8** covetous, grasping **9** niggardly, penurious, scrimping **10** avaricious **11** closefisted, tightfisted **12** cheeseparing, parsimonious **13** penny-pinching

misery
3 woe **5** agony, dolor, grief **6** sorrow **7** anguish, squalor **8** calamity, distress **9** adversity, dejection, suffering **10** affliction, depression, desolation **11** despondency **12** wretchedness

misfit
6 oddity, weirdo **7** oddball **8** maverick **9** eccentric, screwball

misfortune
3 ill, woe **4** blow, harm, loss **5** cross, trial **7** reverse, setback, tragedy, trouble **8** accident, calamity, casualty, disaster, hardship **9** adversity, cataclysm **10** affliction, visitation **11** catastrophe, contretemps, tribulation

misgiving
4 fear **5** doubt, dread, qualm **6** unease **7** anxiety, scruple **8** distrust **9** suspicion **10** foreboding **11** premonition, reservation, trepidation **12** apprehension, presentiment

misguided
5 wrong **9** erroneous **10** ill-advised **11** injudicious **12** short-sighted

mishandle
4 flub **5** abuse, botch **6** bungle, fumble, mess up **7** rough up **8** maltreat **10** knock about, slap around

mishap
7 bad luck, tragedy **8** accident, casualty **9** adversity **11** contretemps

mishmash
4 olio, stew **6** jumble, litter, medley, motley, muddle **7** clutter, farrago, mélange, mixture, rummage **8** pastiche, scramble **9** pasticcio, patchwork, potpourri **10** hodgepodge, hotchpotch, salmagundi **11** gallimaufry

misidentify
5 mix up **7** confuse **8** confound

misinterpret
7 confuse, misread

mislay
4 lose

mislead
4 dupe, fool, gull, lure **5** bluff, cheat **6** betray, delude, entice, seduce, take in **7** beguile, deceive **8** hoodwink, inveigle **11** double-cross

misleading
5 false, wrong **8** delusive, delusory, specious **9** deceitful, deceptive **10** fallacious, inaccurate **11** casuistical, sophistical

mismatch
3 jar **5** clash **6** jangle **7** discord **8** conflict

misplace
4 lose

misprint
4 typo

misprision
5 scorn **7** despite, disdain, neglect **8** contempt, sedition **9** contumely, disregard **10** misconduct, negligence **11** concealment, dereliction, impropriety, malpractice

misrepresent
4 skew, warp **5** belie, twist **6** garble **7** distort, falsify, varnish **8** disguise **9** embellish, embroider **10** camouflage **11** counterfeit

misrepresentation
3 fib, lie **4** tale **5** story **6** canard **7** falsity, untruth **9** falsehood **10** distortion

miss
3 err, gal **4** fail, girl, lass, maid, omit, skip **5** avoid **6** damsel, escape, forget, ignore, lassie, maiden **7** failure, misfire, neglect **8** discount, leave out, overlook **9** disregard
French: **4** Mlle. **12** Mademoiselle
German: **8** Fräulein
Spanish: **4** Srta. **8** Señorita

___ Miss
3 Ole

Missa Solemnis composer
9 Beethoven (Ludwig van)

misshape
4 warp **6** deform **7** contort, distort, torture **9** disfigure

missile
4 bolt, dart **5** arrow, shell, spear **6** bullet, rocket **10** cannonball, projectile
shelter: **4** silo
underwater: **7** torpedo
(see also **guided missile**)

missing
4 AWOL, lost **6** absent

mission
3 aim, job **4** duty, goal, task **5** quest, recon **6** charge, errand, object, sortie **7** calling, embassy, purpose **8** legation, lifework, ministry, vocation **9** objective **10** assignment

Mission: Impossible theme composer
4 Lalo (Schifrin)

missionary
7 apostle **8** emissary **10** evangelist, revivalist **12** propagandist, proselytizer

Mississippi
capital: **7** Jackson
city: **6** Biloxi **8** Gulfport **10** Greenville
college, university: **8** Millsaps **12** Jackson State
nickname: **8** Magnolia (State)
river: **5** Pearl **11** Mississippi
state bird: **11** mockingbird
state flower: **8** magnolia
state tree: **8** magnolia

missive
4 memo, note **6** letter, report **7** epistle, message **8** dispatch

Miss Julie author
10 Strindberg (August)

Miss Lonelyhearts author
4 West (Nathanael)

Miss. neighbor
3 Ala., Ark. **4** Tenn.

Missouri
capital: **13** Jefferson City
city: **7** St. Louis **10** Kansas City **11** Springfield **12** Independence
college, university: **10** Washington
lake: **15** Lake of the Ozarks
nickname: **6** Show Me (State)
river: **8** Missouri **11** Mississippi
state bird: **8** bluebird
state flower: **8** hawthorn
state tree: **7** dogwood

Miss Piggy herself
3 moi

misstate
4 warp **5** color, twist **6** garble **7** distort, falsify

misstatement
3 fib, lie **4** tale **7** falsity, untruth **9** falsehood **13** prevarication

misstep
4 flub, goof, slip **5** boner, error, fluff, gaffe, lapse **6** slipup **7** blooper, blunder, faux pas

mist
3 dim, fog **4** blur, film, haze, murk **5** befog, brume, cloud **7** becloud, obscure

mistake
4 flub, slip **5** boner, error, fluff, folly, gaffe, lapse, snafu **6** boo-boo, bungle, howler, slipup **7** blooper, blunder, confuse, faux pas, take for **8** confound **10** inaccuracy

mistaken
5 false, wrong **6** all wet, faulty, flawed, untrue **7** invalid **8** specious **9** defective, erroneous, incorrect, misguided, unfounded **10** fallacious, fraudulent, inaccurate **11** misinformed

mister
3 sir **7** husband
French: **8** Monsieur
German: **4** Herr
Italian: **6** Signor
Spanish: **5** Señor

mistreat
5 abuse **6** ill-use, molest **7** rough up **9** brutalize, manhandle

mistress
4 doxy, moll **5** lover, woman **7** hetaira **8** dulcinea, ladylove, paramour **9** concubine, courtesan, inamorata, kept woman **10** chatelaine, girlfriend
of Charles II: **8** Nell Gwyn **8** Barbara (Villiers)
of Edward III: **5** Alice (Perrers)
of Henry II (England): **8** Rosamund (Clifford)
of Henry II (France): **5** Diane (de Poitiers)
of Louis XV: **9** Pompadour (Madame de)
of Ludwig I: **10** Lola Montez

mistrust
5 doubt **7** concern, dispute, dubiety, surmise, suspect **8** wariness **9** apprehend, misgiving, suspicion **10** foreboding, skepticism **11** incertitude, uncertainty **12** apprehension

mistrustful
4 wary **5** leery **6** uneasy **7** dubious, jealous **8** doubting **9** skeptical **10** suspicious

misty
3 dim **4** hazy **5** foggy, vague **6** cloudy, vapory **7** blurred, obscure, tearful, unclear **8** confused, nebulous, vaporous **10** indistinct

misunderstanding
4 rift, spat, tiff **5** mix-up **6** breach **7** dispute, quarrel, rupture **8** squabble **10** falling-out **12** disagreement

misuse
5 waste
of a word: 8 malaprop **11** malapropism

Mitchell novel
15 Gone with the Wind

mite
3 bit, jot **4** atom, iota **5** grain, minim, ounce, speck **6** acarid, tittle **7** chigger, modicum, smidgen **8** molecule, particle
family: 8 oribatid

miter
5 crown, joint **9** headdress

mitigate
4 ease **5** abate, allay, relax, slake **6** lessen, soften, subdue, temper **7** assuage, lighten, mollify, relieve **8** palliate, moderate, tone down **9** alleviate, extenuate, meliorate

mitigation
4 ease **6** relief **8** easement

mitosis
12 cell division, karyokinesis
stage: 8 anaphase, prophase **9** metaphase, telophase

mix
4 beat, fuse, link, lump, meld, stir **5** blend, merge, unite **6** fusion, jumble, mingle, tangle, work in **7** amalgam, combine, concoct, confuse, conjoin **8** coalesce, compound, confound **9** associate, commingle, interfuse **10** amalgamate, crossbreed **11** intermingle **12** amalgamation

mixed
6 hybrid, impure, motley, sundry, varied **7** diluted, diverse, mongrel **8** assorted, compound **9** composite, crossbred, interbred, irregular **12** multifarious **13** heterogeneous, miscellaneous

mixed bag
4 hash, olio **5** gumbo, salad **6** jumble, medley **7** mélange **8** mishmash, pastiche **9** potpourri **10** assortment, hodgepodge, hotchpotch, miscellany, salmagundi **11** gallimaufry

mixed-up
5 fazed **6** addled **7** jumbled **8** confused **9** flustered, nonplused, perplexed **10** bewildered, disjointed, distracted, incoherent, nonplussed **12** disconcerted

mixologist
6 barman **7** tapster **9** barkeeper, bartender

mixture
4 brew, hash, olio, stew **5** alloy, blend, gumbo **6** fusion, hybrid, jumble, medley **7** amalgam, farrago, mélange **8** compound, mishmash, solution **9** composite, potpourri **10** concoction, confection, miscellany, salmagundi **11** combination **12** amalgamation

mix up
5 addle **6** fuddle, jumble, muddle **7** confuse, fluster, mistake **8** befuddle, bewilder, confound **10** disarrange, discompose **11** disorganize, misidentify

mix-up
4 hash, mess, muss **5** botch, chaos, error, melee **6** muddle, tangle **7** mistake **8** shambles **9** commotion, confusion

___ Miz
3 Les

MKS unit
3 lux, ohm **4** mole, volt, watt **5** farad, henry, hertz, joule, lumen, meter, metre, tesla, weber **6** ampere, kelvin, newton, pascal, second **7** candela, coulomb, siemens **8** kilogram

Mnemosyne
6 Memory
daughters: 5 Muses
father: 6 Uranus
lover: 4 Zeus
mother: 4 Gaea

Moabite
city: 3 Kir
god: 7 Chemosh
king: 5 Eglon, Mesha

Moab's father
3 Lot

moan
4 beef, carp, wail, weep **5** gripe, groan, whine **6** bewail, grieve, grouse, kvetch, lament, repine, whinge **7** deplore, grumble **8** complain **9** bellyache

mob
3 jam **4** clan, gang, herd, pack, push, ring, riot **5** crowd, crush, horde, mafia, press, swarm **6** jostle, masses, rabble, throng **8** canaille, riffraff **9** hoi polloi, multitude **11** proletariat

mobile
5 fluid **6** moving, orrery **7** migrant, movable **8** cellular, moveable, variable **9** itinerant, migratory, unsettled, versatile **10** ambulatory **11** peripatetic

mobile home
4 tent **6** camper **7** trailer **9** Airstream

mobile-phone area
4 cell

mobilize
5 drive, impel, rally, ready, rouse **6** arouse, call up, muster, prompt, propel **7** actuate, animate, marshal **8** activate, assemble, organize **9** circulate

mobster
4 capo, goon, thug **6** hit man **7** goombah, made man, mafioso **8** criminal, gangster **9** godfather, racketeer

Moby Dick
5 whale **10** white whale
author: 8 Melville (Herman)
character: 3 Pip **6** Daggoo, Parsee **7** Ishmael **8** Queequeg, Starbuck, Tashtego
pursuer: 4 Ahab
ship: 6 Pequod

moccasin
3 pac **4** pack **6** loafer **7** slipper **8** larrigan

mock
3 ape **4** defy, fake, gibe, jape, jeer, razz, twit **5** bogus, chaff, dummy, false, feign, mimic, phony, quasi, sneer, taunt, tease **6** deride, ersatz, jeer at, parody, pseudo, send up **7** deceive, feigned, imitate, lampoon, mislead **8** ridicule, satirize, so-called, spurious **9** imitation, simulated **10** artificial **11** counterfeit

mockery
4 sham **5** farce, scorn, sport **6** japery, parody, satire **7** take-off **8** contempt, derision, raillery, ridicule, travesty **9** burlesque, imitation **10** caricature **13** laughingstock

mocking
8 derisive, sardonic, scornful **9** sarcastic

mode
3 fad, way **4** chic, rage **5** state, style, vogue **6** custom, manner, method, status, system **7** fashion **9** condition, procedure, situation, technique **10** convention, dernier cri

model
4 copy, type **5** dummy, ideal, shape **6** design, effigy, mirror, mockup, symbol **7** classic, epitome, example, imitate, manikin, paragon, pattern, perfect, replica, typical **8** ensample, exemplar, flawless, mannikin, maquette, nonesuch, paradigm, standard **9** archetype, beau ideal, blueprint, classical, criterion, exemplary, miniature, nonpareil **10** apotheosis, embodiment, prototypal, touchstone **12** paradigmatic, prototypical, reproduction
famous: 4 Elle (MacPherson), Iman, Klum (Heidi), Moss (Kate) **5** Banks (Tyra), Tiegs (Cheryl) **6** Hutton (Lauren), Parker (Suzy), Twiggy **8** Brinkley (Christie), Bündchen (Gisele), Campbell (Naomi), Crawford (Cindy), Schiffer (Claudia) **9** Shrimpton (Jean) **10** MacPherson (Elle), Turlington (Christy)

modem speed unit
4 baud

moderate
3 ebb **4** bate, curb, ease, even, fair, mild, so-so, wane **5** abate, sober **6** lessen, medium, reduce, relent, soften, steady, subdue, temper **7** average, control, ease off, equable, lighten, limited, neutral, relieve, subside, trivial **8** centrist, constant, discreet, middling, mitigate, restrain **9** alleviate, constrain, temperate **10** abstemious, controlled, reasonable, restrained **11** indifferent **12** conservative

moderation
7 control, measure **9** restraint **10** abstinence, constraint, limitation, temperance **13** temperateness

moderator
5 judge **7** arbiter **8** chairman, examiner, governor, mediator **10** peacemaker **11** chairperson

modern
3 new **5** fresh, novel **6** recent **7** current **8** neoteric, up-to-date **10** newfangled, present-day **12** contemporary

modernize
4 redo **5** renew **6** update **7** remodel **8** renovate **9** refurbish **10** rejuvenate

modest
3 coy, shy **4** meek, prim **5** plain, timid **6** decent, demure, humble, proper, seemly, simple **7** bashful, prudish **8** decorous, discreet, maidenly, moderate, reserved, reticent, retiring **9** diffident **10** unassuming **11** straitlaced, unassertive **12** self-effacing **13** unpretentious

Modest Proposal author
5 Swift (Jonathan)

modesty
7 decency, reserve **8** chastity, humility, timidity **9** propriety, reticence **10** diffidence

modicum
3 bit, jot, tad **4** atom, iota, mite, whit **5** grain, minim, ounce, pinch, scrap, speck, trace **6** dollop **7** smidgen, soupçon **8** particle

modify
4 vary **5** adapt, alter, amend, limit, tweak **6** adjust, change, mutate, revise, rework, temper **7** qualify **8** mitigate, moderate, restrain **9** refashion

modish
4 chic **5** smart, swank **6** chichi, trendy, with-it **7** dashing, stylish **11** fashionable

modiste
8 designer, milliner **9** couturier **10** couturiere

Modred
father: 6 Arthur
mother: 8 Margawse
slayer, victim: 6 Arthur

module
4 item, unit 7 element 9 component 11 constituent

modulate
4 vary 5 tweak 6 adjust, attune, temper 8 fine-tune, regulate, restrain

modus operandi
5 style 6 custom, manner, method, system 7 process, program, routine 8 approach, practice, strategy 9 procedure, technique

modus vivendi
9 way of life

mogul
4 czar, king, lord 5 baron, nabob, ruler 6 bigwig, honcho, prince, sachem, top gun, tycoon 7 kingpin, magnate 9 plutocrat, potentate

Mohammed
see **Muhammad**

Mohawk chief
5 Brant (Joseph) 8 Hiawatha

Mohican chief
5 Uncas

moiety
3 cut 4 half, part 5 piece 7 element, portion, section, segment 8 division 9 component

moil
3 tug, wet 4 grub, to-do, work 5 churn, dirty, drive, grind, labor, swirl 6 bustle, clamor, drudge, hubbub, lather, seethe, strain, strive, uproar 7 ferment, travail, trouble, wrangle 8 drudgery 9 agitation, commotion, confusion 10 hurly-burly, turbulence

Moisés of baseball
4 Alou

moist
3 wet 4 damp, dank, dewy 5 humid 6 clammy, steamy, sticky 7 dampish, maudlin, tearful, wettish

moisten
3 wet 5 bedew 6 dampen 8 humidify, saturate

moisture
4 damp 5 vapor 7 wetness 8 humidity 13 precipitation

moisturizing ingredient
4 aloe

mojo
3 hex 4 jinx 5 charm, magic, power, spell 6 hoodoo, whammy

molar
5 tooth 7 grinder
neighbor: 6 canine

molasses
7 treacle 10 blackstrap

mold
3 die 4 cast, form, sort, type 5 forge, ingot, knead, shape, stamp 6 design, fungus 7 fashion, pattern 8 template 9 construct

moldable
6 pliant, supple 7 ductile, plastic, pliable 9 adaptable, malleable

molded dish
5 aspic

molder
3 rot 5 decay, waste 7 crumble 9 break down, decompose 11 deteriorate 12 disintegrate

molding
4 bead, gula, ogee 5 congé, ogive, talon, torus 6 reglet 7 annulet, beading, cavetto, cornice, reeding 8 cincture 9 baseboard
compound: 4 beak, cyma, ogie 10 serpentine
edge: 5 arris
flat: 5 splay 6 fascia, fillet, listel, regula 7 chamfer
simple curve: 4 roll 5 flute, ovolo, torus 6 scotia 8 astragal

Moldova
capital: 8 Chisinau, Kishinev
former name: 8 Moldavia
language: 8 Romanian
monetary unit: 3 leu
neighbor: 7 Romania, Ukraine
river: 8 Dniester

moldy
5 dated, fusty, musty, passé 6 bygone, old hat 7 ancient, antique, archaic, outworn 8 mildewed, outdated 9 crumbling, moth-eaten 10 antiquated 12 old-fashioned

mole
3 spy 4 pier, quay 5 jetty, nevus 6 burrow, tunnel 9 birthmark 10 breakwater

molecule
3 bit, jot 4 iota 5 minim, speck 7 modicum 8 particle
part: 4 atom

molest
3 vex 4 bait 5 abuse, annoy, harry, tease 6 badger, bother, harass, heckle, hector, pester, plague 7 disturb, torment, trouble 9 persecute

Moll Flanders author
5 Defoe (Daniel)

mollify
4 calm, ease 5 allay 6 pacify, soften, soothe, temper 7 appease, assuage, lighten, placate, relieve, sweeten 8 mitigate 9 alleviate 10 ameliorate, conciliate, propitiate

mollusk
6 chiton

bivalve: 4 clam 6 cockle, mussel, oyster, teredo 7 geoduck, scallop 8 shipworm
cephalopod: 5 squid 7 octopus 8 argonaut, nautilus 10 cuttlefish
part: 6 mantle, radula, siphon
tooth shell: 9 dentalium
univalve: 4 slug 5 conch, cowry, murex, snail, whelk 6 cowrie, limpet, triton 7 abalone 10 nudibranch, periwinkle

Molly ___
7 Maguire, Pitcher

mollycoddle
3 pet 4 baby 5 humor, spoil 6 cocker, cosset, dandle, pamper 7 cater to, indulge, milksop 8 mama's boy 11 milquetoast

Moloch's pit
6 Tophet

molt
4 cast, shed, slip 6 change, slough 7 cast off, discard, ecdysis 9 slough off

molted skins
7 exuviae

molten
6 melted 7 glowing 9 liquefied

molten rock
4 lava 5 magma

moment
3 sec 4 jiff 5 flash, jiffy, point, shake, trice 6 import, minute, second 7 instant 8 juncture, occasion 9 magnitude 10 importance 11 consequence, split second 12 significance

momentary
5 brief, quick 8 fleeting, fugitive 9 ephemeral, fugacious, transient 10 evanescent, short-lived, transitory

momentous
5 grave 7 epochal, fateful, serious, weighty 9 important 10 meaningful 11 significant, substantial 12 considerable 13 consequential

momentousness
6 import, weight 9 magnitude 10 importance 11 consequence, weightiness 12 significance

momentum
5 drive 6 energy, thrust 7 impetus, impulse 10 propulsion

Momo author
4 Ende (Michael)

momus
6 carper, critic, mocker 7 caviler 8 caviller 9 detractor 11 faultfinder

Monaco
commune: 10 Monte Carlo
language: 6 French
monetary unit: 4 euro
monetary unit, former: 5 franc
neighbor: 6 France
prince: 6 Albert 7 Rainier
princess: 5 Grace 8 Caroline

monad
3 one 4 atom, unit 8 zoospore 9 protozoan

Mona Lisa
10 La Gioconda
painter: 7 da Vinci (Leonardo) 8 Leonardo (da Vinci)

monarch
4 czar, king, raja, tsar, tzar 5 queen, rajah, ruler 6 kaiser, prince 7 emperor, empress, majesty 9 butterfly, potentate, sovereign
daughter: 7 infanta 8 princess
heir: 7 dauphin 11 crown prince
son: 6 prince 7 infante

monarchical
5 regal, royal 6 kingly 8 imperial, kinglike, majestic 9 sovereign

monarchy
4 rule 5 realm, reign 7 kingdom 8 kingship 9 autocracy, monocracy 11 sovereignty

monastery
5 abbey 6 friary, priory 7 convent, nunnery 8 cloister
Buddhist: 8 lamasery
Eastern Orthodox: 5 laura
head: 5 abbot, prior

monastic
4 abbé, monk 7 ascetic, brother 8 isolated, secluded 9 reclusive 10 cloistered 11 sequestered

Monday Night Football home
4 ESPN

___ Mondrian
4 Piet

monetary
6 fiscal 9 financial, pecuniary 10 numismatic
gain: 3 net 5 lucre 6 profit

monetary rate
7 millage

monetary unit
see at individual countries

money
4 cash, coin, gelt, jack, kale, loot, pelf, swag 5 bread, chips, dough, funds, lolly, lucre, means, moola, rhino, scrip 6 boodle, change, dinero, do-re-mi, mammon, moolah, riches, specie, wampum, wealth 7 cabbage, capital, coinage, lettuce, needful, scratch, stipend 8 bankroll, currency, finances, treasure 9 resources 10 greenbacks 11 filthy lucre, legal tender
dispenser: 3 ATM
drawer: 4 till

moneyed
4 rich **5** flush **6** loaded **7** opulent, wealthy, well-off **8** affluent, well-to-do **10** prosperous, well-heeled

money-grubber
5 miser **7** hoarder, niggard, scrooge **8** tightwad **9** skinflint **10** cheapskate **12** penny-pincher

moneymaking
6 paying **7** gainful **9** lucrative **10** profitable, well-paying, worthwhile **12** advantageous, remunerative

monger
4 hawk, sell, vend **6** broker, dealer, hawker, peddle, trader, vendor **7** higgler, packman, peddler **8** huckster

Mongol
conqueror: **9** Tamerlane **10** Kublai Khan **11** Genghis Khan, Tamburlaine
peoples: **4** Daur, Olöt, Urat **5** Ordos **6** Bargut, Buryat, Buzawa, Chahar, Dorbet, Torgut **7** Karchin, Khalkha, Monguor

Mongolia
capital: **9** Ulan Bator **11** Ulaanbaatar
conqueror: **6** Ögödei **11** Genghis Khan
desert: **4** Gobi
lake: **6** Baikal
monetary unit: **6** tugrik
mountain range: **5** Altai, Altay **6** Kentai **7** Hentiyn **9** Altai Shan, Altay Shan
neighbor: **5** China **6** Russia
river: **4** Yalu **5** Orhun **7** Selenga

mongoose
4 urva

mongrel
3 cur **4** mule, mutt **5** cross **6** hybrid **7** bastard, mixture **8** half-bred **9** crossbred, half blood, half-breed **10** crossbreed

moniker
3 tag **4** name **6** handle **8** cognomen, nickname **9** sobriquet **11** appellation, designation

monish
4 warn

monition
6 caveat **7** caution, portent, warning **11** fore-warning

monitor
4 test **5** check, watch **6** screen **7** adviser, observe, oversee **8** watchdog **11** keep track of

Monitor
designer: **8** Ericsson (John)
opponent: **8** Virginia **9** Merrimack

monitory
7 warning **8** advisory **10** cautionary

monk
4 abbé **5** friar **7** brother **8** cenobite, monastic **9** anchorite
Buddhist: **4** lama **5** bonze
counterpart: **3** nun
Hindu: **8** sannyasi
home: **5** abbey **9** monastery
Roman Catholic: **8** Capuchin, Salesian, Trappist **9** Carmelite, Dominican **10** Carthusian, Cistercian, Franciscan **11** Augustinian
room: **4** cell
shaven crown: **7** tonsure
title: **3** Dom, Fra **5** Padre

monkey
3 imp **4** mess **5** gamin **6** meddle, simian, tamper, urchin **8** busybody **9** interfere, interlope
Ceylon: **4** maha
Cochin China: **4** douc
New World: **4** mico, saki, titi **6** howler, spider, uakari, woolly **7** sapajou, tamarin **8** capuchin, marmoset, squirrel **11** douroucouli
Old World: **4** mona **5** Diana, drill **6** guenon, langur, rhesus, vervet **7** colobus, hanuman, macaque **8** mandrill, mangabey **9** proboscis **10** Barbary ape
relative: **3** ape

monkeyshine
3 gag **4** dido, jape, lark **5** antic, caper, prank, stunt, trick **6** frolic **10** shenanigan, tomfoolery

monkshood
4 atis **7** aconite

monocratic
8 absolute, despotic **9** arbitrary, autarchic, tyrannous **10** autocratic, tyrannical

monogram
8 initials

monograph
5 study **6** thesis **8** tractate, treatise **9** discourse **12** disquisition, dissertation

monopolize
3 hog **5** sew up **6** absorb, corner **7** control, engross **8** dominate, take over

monopoly
5 trust **6** cartel, corner **7** control **9** ownership, syndicate **10** consortium, domination **11** exclusivity

monotone
5 drone, thrum **8** sameness

monotonous
4 blah, dull **6** boring, dreary **7** droning, humdrum, one-note, uniform **8** singsong, unvaried **9** unvarying **10** pedestrian, repetitive **11** repetitious

monotony
6 tedium **7** humdrum **8** flatness, sameness **10** uniformity

monsoon
6 deluge **8** downpour **9** rainstorm **10** cloudburst

monster
3 orc **4** ogre **5** Argus, beast, freak, giant, golem, Harpy, Hydra, whale **6** dragon, Geryon, gorgon, kraken, Medusa, Mothra, mutant, ogress, Orthos, Scylla, Sphinx, Typhon **7** Chimera, Cyclops, Echidna, Godzilla, griffin **8** behemoth, bogeyman, Briareos, Cerberus, Chimaera, colossus, giantess, Tarasque **9** Enceladus, hellhound, leviathan, manticore **10** cockatrice **11** hippocampus
study of: 10 teratology
(see also **dragon, giant**)

monster's loch
4 Ness

monstrosity
5 freak **6** horror **7** eyesore, outrage, prodigy **8** atrocity, enormity **11** abomination **12** malformation

monstrous
4 huge, vast **5** awful, giant, large **7** glaring, heinous, hellish, hideous, immense, inhuman, mammoth, massive, titanic **8** aberrant, abnormal, colossal, deformed, dreadful, enormous, fiendish, freakish, gigantic, god-awful, gruesome, horrible, infamous, shocking, towering **9** atrocious, egregious, fantastic, frightful, grotesque, humongous, loathsome, malformed, unnatural **10** diabolical, flagitious, gargantuan, horrendous, impressive, monumental, outrageous, prodigious, scandalous, stupendous, tremendous

montage
4 olio **6** jumble, medley **7** mélange, mixture **9** composite, patchwork, potpourri **10** assortment, miscellany **12** conglomerate

Montagues' enemies
8 Capulets

Montaigne's forte
5 essay

Montana
capital: 6 Helena
city: 5 Butte **7** Bozeman **8** Billings, Missoula **10** Great Falls
lake: 8 Flathead
motto: 9 Oro y plata
mountain: 7 Granite (Peak)
nickname: 8 Treasure (State)
park: 7 Glacier
river: 8 Missouri **11** Yellowstone
state bird: 10 meadowlark
state flower: 10 bitterroot
state tree: 13 ponderosa pine

Mont Blanc, e.g.
3 Alp

Montenegro
capital: 7 Cetinje **9** Podgorica
language: 7 Serbian
monetary unit: 4 euro
park: 8 Durmitor
river: 3 Lim **4** Piva, Tara, Zita **6** Morača
sea: 8 Adriatic

Monteverdi opera
5 Orfeo **7** Arianna

___ Montez
4 Lola

Montezuma
capital: 12 Tenochtitlán
conqueror: 6 Cortés, Cortéz (Hernán, Hernando)
people: 6 Aztecs
revenge: 8 diarrhea

month
Hindu: 3 Pus **4** Asin, Jeth, Magh **5** Aghan, Chait, Sawan **6** Asargh, Bhadon, Kartik, Phagun **7** Baisakh
Jewish: 4 Adar, Elul, Iyar **5** Nisan, Sivan, Tebet **6** Kislev, Shebat, Tammuz, Tishri **7** Heshvan
Muslim: 4 Rabi **5** Rajab, Safar **6** Jumada, Sha'ban **7** Ramadan, Shawwal **8** Muharram **9** Dhu'l-Hijja, Dhu'l-Qa'dah

Montmartre church
10 Sacré Coeur

Mont. neighbor
3 Ida., Wyo. **4** N. Dak., S. Dak.

Montreal hockey team
4 Habs **9** Canadiens

Montserrat
capital: 8 Plymouth
discoverer: 8 Columbus (Christopher)
location: 10 West Indies
territory of: 7 Britain
volcano: 9 Soufrière

monument
5 cairn, stela, stupa **7** memento, tribute **8** archives, cenotaph, document, memorial **9** footstone, headstone, tombstone **10** gravestone **11** grave marker, testimonial
prehistoric: 6 dolmen, menhir **8** cromlech, megalith

monumental
4 epic, huge, vast **6** mighty, mortal **7** awesome, immense, mammoth, massive **8** enormous, gigantic, historic, majestic, towering **9** monstrous **10** prodigious, stupendous, tremendous **11** mountainous, outstanding **12** overwhelming

mooch
3 bat, beg, bum **4** grub, roam, rove **5** amble, cadge, drift, range, slink, sneak, steal, stray **6** ramble, sponge, wander **7** maunder, meander, saunter **8** freeload, scrounge **9** panhandle

mooching
7 beggary **9** mendicity **10** mendicancy

mood
3 air **4** aura, feel, tone, whim **5** fancy, humor

6 spirit, temper, vagary 7 caprice, emotion, feeling, mind-set 8 ambiance, ambience 9 character, semblance 10 atmosphere 11 disposition, personality, temperament

moody
4 glum 5 mopey 6 fickle, gloomy 7 pensive 8 unstable 9 mercurial, whimsical 10 capricious, changeable, depressive, inconstant, melancholy 13 temperamental

moola
4 cash, coin, pelf, swag 5 bread, dough, money 6 dinero, specie, wampum 7 cabbage, scratch 9 long green

moon
4 gape, mope 5 dream 6 dawdle 8 languish 9 satellite
dark area: 4 mare 5 maria (plural) 7 farside
god: 3 Sin 5 Nanna 6 Meztli
goddess: 4 Luna 5 Diana, Tanit 6 Hecate, Hekate, Selena, Selene, Tanith 7 Artemis, Astarte
of Saturn: 5 Titan
period: 5 phase
valley: 4 rill
vehicle: 3 LEM
(see also **satellite**)

Moon and Sixpence author
7 Maugham (W. Somerset)

mooncalf
4 dolt, fool 5 dunce, ninny 7 jackass, tomfool 9 simpleton

moonfish
4 opah 5 platy

Moon River composer
7 Mancini (Henry)

moonshine
4 bosh, jake 5 hokum 6 bunkum, humbug 7 bootleg, eyewash, hogwash 8 homebrew, malarkey, nonsense, tommyrot 9 poppycock 10 balderdash, bathtub gin, contraband, flapdoodle 11 mountain dew 12 blatherskite

moonstone
4 opal

Moonstone, The
author: 7 Collins (Wilkie)
detective: 4 Cuff

moonstruck
4 daft, nuts 5 batty, corny, flaky, kooky, mushy, nutty, sappy, wacko, wacky 6 crazed, cuckoo, fruity, insane, screwy 7 berserk, bonkers, lunatic, maudlin, touched 8 romantic 9 nostalgic, schmaltzy 10 lovey-dovey, saccharine, unbalanced 11 sentimental

moor
3 bog, fen 4 dock, fell 5 berth, catch, heath, tie up 6 anchor, Berber, fasten, Muslim, secure, tether 7 peat bog 8 make fast, Moroccan 9 wasteland
fictional: 7 Othello

moose
6 cervid
female: 3 cow
male: 4 bull
relative: 3 elk 4 deer 6 wapiti 7 caribou 8 reindeer

moot
5 argue, plead 6 broach, debate 7 agitate, bring up, canvass, discuss, dispute, dubious, suggest, suspect 8 abstract, academic, arguable, disputed, doubtful 9 debatable, introduce, thrash out, uncertain, unsettled, ventilate 10 disputable, unresolved 11 problematic 12 questionable 13 controversial

mop
4 swab, wipe

mope
4 fret, idle, moon, pine, pout, sigh, stew, sulk 5 brood, drift, mosey 6 dawdle, linger 7 maunder, meander, saunter 8 languish

moped
7 scooter

mopes
4 funk 5 blues, dumps, ennui, slump 7 dismals, malaise, sadness 8 dolefuls 10 depression, melancholy 11 unhappiness

mopey
3 low 4 blue, down, glum 6 broody, droopy, morose 7 doleful 8 cast down, dejected, downcast 9 depressed 10 dispirited, melancholy, spiritless

moppet
3 kid, tot 4 tike, tyke 5 chick, child 7 toddler 8 juvenile 9 youngster

mop up
4 beat, drub, dust, lick, whip 6 absorb, garner, gather 7 shellac, trounce 8 complete, lambaste 9 overwhelm

moral
3 saw 4 good, just, pure, rule 5 adage, axiom, gnome, maxim, noble, right 6 chaste, decent, dictum, honest, lesson, proper, saying, truism 7 epigram, ethical, message, preachy, precept, proverb, upright, virtual 8 aphorism, apothegm, didactic, elevated, sermonic, virtuous 9 honorable, righteous 10 high-minded, principled, scrupulous, upstanding 11 right-minded 13 conscientious
code: 5 ethic, ethos

morale
4 mood 5 heart 6 esprit, mettle, spirit, temper 7 resolve 10 confidence 13 esprit de corps

Morales of TV
4 Esai

moralistic
5 noble, pious **7** canting, ethical **8** didactic, virtuous **9** righteous **10** principled **11** pharisaical, right-minded **13** sanctimonious

morality
5 ethic, honor, mores **6** purity, virtue **7** decency, probity **8** goodness **9** integrity, rectitude, rightness **11** saintliness, uprightness **13** righteousness

moralize
6 preach **7** lecture **9** preachify, sermonize **11** pontificate

morals
5 mores **6** ethics, ideals **8** scruples **9** integrity, standards **10** principles

morass
3 bog, fen, web **4** knot, maze, mesh, mire, quag, trap **5** marsh, skein, snarl, swamp **6** jungle, muddle, tangle **8** quagmire **9** imbroglio

moratorium
3 ban **5** delay **8** interval **10** suspension

moray
3 eel
catcher: **5** eeler

morbid
4 dark, sick **5** moody **6** gloomy, grisly, morose, sickly, sullen **7** unsound **8** diseased, gruesome **9** saturnine, unhealthy **11** melancholic, unwholesome **12** pathological

mordancy
7 acidity **8** acerbity, acridity, acrimony, asperity, pungency **9** harshness, sharpness **10** causticity, trenchancy **11** astringency

mordant
4 acid, keen **5** acerb, acrid, salty, sharp **6** biting **7** acerbic, burning, caustic, cutting, pungent **8** incisive, sardonic, scathing **9** sarcastic, trenchant

Mordecai
cousin: **6** Esther
father: **4** Jair
mother: **6** Esther

more
3 new, too **4** also, else, plus **5** added, again, along, extra, fresh, older, other, spare **6** as well, better, nearer, withal **7** another, besides, farther, further, greater **8** likewise, moreover **9** increased **10** additional

More book
6 Utopia

Moreno of Broadway
4 Rita

more or less
4 or so **5** about, circa **6** around **7** roughly **13** approximately

moreover
3 and, too **4** also **6** as well, withal **7** besides, further **8** likewise **10** in addition **11** furthermore **12** additionally

mores
6 ethics, habits, values **7** beliefs, customs, manners **8** folkways **9** amenities, etiquette **10** civilities **11** proprieties

Morgan le Fay
9 sorceress
brother: **6** Arthur (King)

moribund
5 dying **6** ebbing, fading **7** dormant, outworn **8** decaying, expiring, inactive **9** declining **11** obsolescent **13** deteriorating

Mork and Mindy planet
3 Ork

Morlocks' prey
4 Eloi

Mormon Church
3 LDS
administrative unit: **4** ward **5** stake
founder: **5** Smith (Joseph)
leader: **5** Young (Brigham)
priest: **5** elder

Mormon State
4 Utah

morning
4 dawn **5** sunup **6** aurora **7** dawning, sunrise **8** cockcrow, daybreak, daylight, forenoon
moisture: **3** dew **8** dewdrops
song: **6** aubade

Morocco
capital: **5** Rabat
city: **3** Fès, Fez **6** Agadir, Meknès **7** Tangier **9** Marrakech, Marrakesh **10** Casablanca
coast: **7** Barbary
language: **6** Arabic, Berber
monetary unit: **6** dirham
mountain, range: **3** Rif **5** Atlas **7** Toubkal
neighbor: **5** Spain **7** Algeria **13** Western Sahara
sea: **13** Mediterranean

moron
4 dodo, dolt, dope, fool **5** dummy, dunce, idiot **6** cretin, dimwit, stupid **7** dullard, half-wit **8** dumbbell, imbecile, numskull **9** ignoramus, lamebrain, numbskull, simpleton

moronic
4 dull, dumb **6** simple, stupid **8** backward, retarded **9** brainless, dim-witted, imbecilic **10** half-witted, slow-witted **12** feebleminded, simpleminded

morose
4 dour, glum, sour **5** moody, sulky **6** cranky, crusty, gloomy, morbid, sullen **7** crabbed,

unhappy **9** depressed, saturnine **10** depressive, ill-humored, melancholy

morph
6 change, mutate **7** convert **9** transform, transmute **12** metamorphose, transmogrify

Morpheus
father: **6** Hypnos
god of: **5** sleep

Morrison novel
4 Jazz, Love, Sula **7** Beloved **9** Bluest Eye (The) **13** Song of Solomon

Morse code
dash: **3** dah
dot: **3** dit

morsel
3 bit, ort **4** bite **5** crumb, goody, piece, scrap, snack, taste, treat **6** dainty, nibble, tidbit **7** soupçon **8** delicacy, fragment, kickshaw, mouthful

mortal
3 man **5** awful, being, fatal, frail, human, party **6** deadly, lethal, person **7** deathly, earthly, extreme, fleshly, tedious, worldly **8** creature, ruthless, temporal **9** merciless, personage **10** implacable, individual, perishable **11** conceivable

mortality
5 flesh **7** mankind **8** fatality, humanity **9** death rate, humankind, lethality **10** deadliness

mortar
5 grout **6** binder, cannon, cement, vessel **7** plaster, sealant **8** howitzer, ordnance

Morte d'Arthur author
6 Malory (Thomas)

mortgage
4 hock, lien, pawn **6** pledge **10** obligation

mortician
8 embalmer **10** undertaker

mortified
6 shamed **7** ascetic, ashamed, austere **8** redfaced **9** chagrined **10** humiliated, shamefaced **11** embarrassed

mortify
5 abash, shame **6** deaden, dismay **7** chagrin, perturb **8** disgrace **9** discomfit, embarrass, humiliate

Mort of early TV
4 Sahl

mortise and ___
5 tenon

mortuary
8 funereal **10** sepulchral **11** funeral home

mosaic
5 inlay **7** chimera **8** terrazzo **9** composite, patchwork **12** tessellation
piece: **6** smalto **7** tessera **8** tesserae (plural)

Moscow
cathedral: **8** St. Basil's **11** Saint Basil's
citadel: **7** Kremlin
resident: **9** Muscovite

Moses
brother: **5** Aaron
brother-in-law: **5** Hobab
deathplace: **4** Nebo
father-in-law: **6** Jethro
sister: **6** Miriam
son: **7** Eliezer, Gershom
spy: **5** Caleb
successor: **6** Joshua
wife: **8** Zipporah

mosey
4 mope **5** amble, drift **6** dawdle, linger, ramble, stroll, wander **7** maunder, meander, saunter

mosh
4 slam **9** slam-dance

Moslem
see **Muslim**

mosque
leader: **4** imam **6** masjid
niche: **6** mihrab
prayer caller: **7** muezzin
turret: **7** minaret

mosquito
5 culex **7** skeeter
eater: **3** bat **4** bird, frog **9** dragonfly
genus: **5** Aëdes, Culex **9** Anopheles

moss
9 bryophyte
kind: **4** peat **8** sphagnum
part: **4** seta **7** capsule, rhizoid
study of: **8** bryology

mossback
4 fogy **6** fossil **10** fuddy-duddy **11** reactionary **12** antediluvian, conservative **13** stick-in-the-mud

mostly
6 mainly **7** chiefly, largely, overall, usually **9** generally, primarily **11** principally **13** predominantly

mote
3 bit, dot, jot **4** iota, whit **5** grain, point, speck, trace **8** flyspeck, particle

moth
immature: **5** larva **6** larvae (plural) **11** caterpillar
kind: **4** luna **5** egger **7** codling, tussock **8** Cecropia, silkworm **9** browntail
order: **11** Lepidoptera

moth-eaten
4 worn **5** dated, dingy, faded, mangy, moldy, musty, passé, ratty, seedy **6** bygone, old hat,

patchy, shabby **7** antique, archaic, raggedy, rundown, unkempt **8** decrepit, outdated, outmoded, tattered, timeworn **10** antiquated, down-at-heel, threadbare **11** dilapidated

mother
3 dam, mom **4** mama, root **5** fount, mammy, mater, momma, mommy, mummy, nurse **6** matrix, origin, source **7** care for, nurture **9** prototype, rootstock **10** provenance, wellspring
Apollo's: **4** Leto
combining form: **4** matr **5** matri, matro
French: **4** mère
German: **6** Mutter
Italian: **5** madre
Peer Gynt's: **3** Ase
Portuguese: **3** mãe
Spanish: **5** madre

mother country
8 homeland **10** fatherland

Mother Courage author
6 Brecht (Bertolt)

motherly
8 maternal **9** nurturing **10** protective

mother-of-pearl
5 nacre
source: **6** oyster **7** abalone

Mother of Presidents
8 Virginia

Mother of the Gods
3 Ops **4** Rhea **6** Cybele

motif
4 idea, text **5** point, theme, topic **6** design, device, figure, matter **7** pattern, subject **8** idée fixe **13** subject matter

motion
4 stir, sway **6** signal **7** gesture **8** movement, proposal, stirring **9** agitation

motionless
5 fixed, inert, still **6** frozen, static **7** stalled **8** becalmed, immobile, stagnant, unmoving **9** immovable, steadfast **10** stationary, stock-still

motion picture
see **movie**

motivate
4 fire, goad, move, spur **5** impel, pique, rouse **6** arouse, excite, incite, induce, prompt **7** actuate, inspire, provoke, quicken, trigger **8** inspirit, persuade **9** galvanize, influence, stimulate

motivation
4 spur **5** drive **7** impetus, impulse **8** ambition, catalyst, stimulus **9** impulsion, incentive, stimulant **10** incitation, incitement **11** inspiration, instigation, provocation

motive
3 aim, end **4** spur **5** angle, cause, point, theme, topic **6** design, device, figure, intent, matter, object, reason, spring **7** impulse, pattern, purpose, subject **8** stimulus **9** incentive, intention, rationale **10** incitement, inducement **11** inspiration

motley
4 olio, pied, stew **5** mixed, salad **6** jumble, medley, ragtag, varied **7** dappled, diverse, piebald **8** assorted, pastiche **9** disparate, multihued **10** assortment, hodgepodge, hotchpotch, miscellany, multicolor, salmagundi, variegated **11** gallimaufry, varicolored **12** conglomerate, multicolored, multifarious, parti-colored **13** heterogeneous, miscellaneous, polychromatic

motor
3 car **4** auto, ride **5** buggy, drive **6** cruise, engine **7** machine **10** automobile

motorboat
6 launch **7** cruiser, inboard **8** outboard, runabout **12** cabin cruiser

motorcycle
7 chopper **8** minibike **9** trail bike
adjunct: **7** sidecar

motorcyclist Knievel
4 Evel

motorists' org.
3 AAA

Motown
7 Detroit
founder: **5** Gordy (Berry)
group: **8** Four Tops, Miracles, Supremes **9** Vandellas **11** Temptations

mottle
4 spot **5** fleck **6** blotch, dapple, marble **7** spatter, speckle, stipple, splotch

mottled
4 pied **5** tabby **7** blotchy, dappled, flecked, spotted **8** blotched, brindled, speckled **9** checkered **10** variegated

motto
3 cry **5** adage, axiom, maxim **6** byword, saying, slogan, war cry **7** precept, proverb **8** aphorism **9** battle cry, catchword, watchword **10** shibboleth **11** catchphrase

moue
3 mow, mug **4** face, pout **7** grimace

mound
4 bank, berm, cock, heap, hill, hump, mass, pile, terp **5** cairn, drift, knoll, shock, stack **6** barrow, tumuli (plural) **7** bulwark, hillock, rampart, tumulus **9** elevation **10** embankment
Buddhist: **5** stupa
burial, Eastern Europe: **6** kurgan
of detritus: **4** kame
of sand: **4** dune
of stones: **5** cairn

mount
3 alp, wax 4 lift, peak, rise, show, soar 5 arise, build, climb, frame, horse, put on, raise, rouse, scale, set up, stage, steed, swell 6 ascend, aspire, deepen, expand, launch, uprear 7 advance, augment, display, enhance, enlarge, install, magnify, produce, support, upsurge 8 bestride, escalade, escalate, heighten, increase, multiply, redouble 9 aggravate, intensify 10 promontory

mountain
3 alp, lot 4 bank, crag, dome, heap, hill, hulk, lump, mass, mesa, much, peak, pile, slew 5 bluff, butte, drift, mound, shock, stack 6 height, massif
Adirondack: 9 Whiteface
Africa's highest: 4 Kibo
Alaska: 4 Bona 6 Denali 7 Foraker, Sanford 8 McKinley, Wrangell
Alaska-Canada: 10 Saint Elias
Alberta: 6 Castle 10 Eisenhower
Alps: 4 Rosa (Monte) 5 Blanc, Eiger 8 Jungfrau 10 Matterhorn
Andes: 4 Ruiz 5 Torrá
Angola: 4 Moco
Antarctica: 4 Mohl 6 Vinson (Massif) 7 Gardner 9 Elizabeth
Apennines: 5 Amaro
Appalachians: 8 Mitchell 10 Kittatinny, Washington 13 Clingmans Dome
Argentina: 4 Azul 5 Negra, Payún 9 Aconcagua
Asia Minor: 3 Ida
Australia: 4 Ziel 5 Bruce 6 Cradle 9 Kosciusko
Bavaria: 5 Arber
Berkshires: 8 Greylock
biblical: 4 Nebo 5 Horeb, Sinai, Tabor 6 Ararat, Carmel, Gilboa, Gilead, Hermon, Moriah, Olivet, Pisgah 7 Lebanon 8 Har Tavor
Black Hills: 6 Harney (Peak) 8 Rushmore
Bolivia: 5 Cuzco, Tahua, Ubina 6 Sajama, Sorata 8 Illimani
Borneo: 4 Raja 8 Kinabalu, Kinabulu
California: 5 Guyot 6 Shasta, Sonora 7 Palomar, Whitney 8 Half Dome, Tuolumne 9 Excelsior 10 Buena Vista, Stanislaus
Canada: 5 Keele, Logan
Canaries: 5 Telde 8 Tenerife
Carpathian: 4 Rysy
Cascades: 7 Rainier
Catskill: 6 Pisgah
Caucasus: 5 Ushba 6 Elbrus
Chile: 4 Mayo, Pili 5 Paine, Pular
China: 4 Emei, Song
Colombia: 4 Tama 5 Neiva
Colorado: 3 Ute 5 Eolus, Pikes (Peak) 9 Purgatory (Peak)
Costa Rica: 6 Blanco 14 Chirripó Grande
Crete: 3 Ida
Cuba: 8 Turquino
Cyprus: 7 Olympus, Troodos
depression: 3 col
Dominican Republic: 6 Duarte 8 Trujillo
Ecuador: 10 Chimborazo
Egypt: 4 Musa 5 Sinai
England: 11 Scafell Pike
Ethiopia: 4 Guna 5 Holla
Europe: 3 Alp
Fiji: 8 Victoria 9 Tomaniivi
foot: 8 piedmont
France: 5 Blanc (Mont), Pilat
French Guiana: 5 Amana
Gabon: 8 Iboundji
Georgia: 8 Springer 10 Oglethorpe
Germany: 7 Zollern 9 Zugspitze 11 Fichtelberg
Glacier National Park: 8 Kootenal
Greece: 3 Ida 4 Ossa 5 Athos, Levka 6 Pelion 7 Helicon, Olympus 9 Parnassus, Psiloriti 10 Pendelikon, Pentelicus
Greenland: 9 Gunnbjorn
Himalayas: 3 Api 6 Khamet, Lhotse 7 Everest 9 Annapurna 10 Gasherbrum
Honshū: 4 Yari 10 Yarigatake
Idaho: 11 Pend Oreille
India: 5 Japvo
Indonesia: 4 Lawu 5 Kwoka, Lawoe, Raung 6 Raoeng, Semeru 7 Kerinci
Iran: 8 Damavand
Israel: 5 Meron 6 Carmel
Italy: 4 Etna 8 Vesuvius
Ivory Coast: 5 Nimba
Japan: 4 Fuji, Sobo 5 Iwate, Oyama 7 Fujisan, Sobozan 8 Fujiyama
Java: 5 Liman 6 Slamet
Jordan: 3 Hor 4 Nebo 5 Hārūn 6 Gilead
Karakoram Range: 7 Dapsang 10 Masherbrum 12 Godwin Austen
Maine: 8 Katahdin 10 Saddleback
Malaysia: 5 Ophir, Tahan 6 Ledang
Mediterranean entrance: 5 Calpe 9 Gibraltar
Mexico: 7 Orizaba (Pico de)
Montana: 8 Gallatin
Nevada: 3 Ely
Newfoundland: 9 Gros Morne
New Hampshire: 9 Monadnock
New York: 4 Bear 5 Marcy
New Zealand: 3 Una 4 Cook 7 Aorangi 8 Aspiring
North America's highest: 6 Denali 8 McKinley
North Carolina: 8 Mitchell
Oahu: 5 Kaala
Oman: 4 Sham
Oregon: 4 Hood
Pakistan: 9 Tirich Mir
Papua New Guinea: 7 Wilhelm 8 Victoria
peak: 3 top 4 acme, apex, roof 5 crest, crown 6 summit, vertex, zenith 8 pinnacle

Pennine Alps: **4** Rosa (Monte) **10** Matterhorn, Mont Cervin
Philippines: **3** Apo, Iba **4** High, Labo **5** Silay
Pyrenees: **11** de Vignemale
ridge: **4** spur **5** arête, crest **7** sawbuck
Romania: **11** Moldoveanul
Russia's highest: **6** Elbrus
Scotland: **8** Ben Nevis
Sicily: **4** Etna
South America: **7** Roraima **9** Aconcagua
South Dakota: **6** Custer (Peak)
Spain: **5** Yelmo **8** Mulhacén **11** Pico de Aneto
Switzerland: **3** Dom **4** Dôle, Rosa (Monte), Tödi **5** Eiger, Mönch **6** La Dôle, Rusein **7** Pilatus **8** Jungfrau **10** Matterhorn
Syria: **4** Druz **5** Duruz
Tanzania: **11** Kilimanjaro
Tasmania: **4** Ossa
Tennessee: **13** Clingmans Dome
Togo: **4** Agou
Turkey: **3** Ida
Utah: **5** Kings
Vermont: **8** Ascutney, Haystack, Stratton **9** Mansfield
Vietnam: **8** Ngoo Linh
Virginia: **6** Rogers
Washington: **7** Olympus, Rainier **11** Saint Helens
Western Hemisphere's highest: **9** Aconcagua
White Mts.: **10** Washington
world's highest: **7** Everest
Wyoming: **3** Elk **5** Cloud **7** Gannett (Peak) **10** Grand Teton
Yukon: **4** King **5** Logan

mountain climbing
equipment: **3** axe, nut **5** piton **7** crampon **9** carabiner
maneuver: **6** rappel **10** rappelling

mountain dew
5 hooch **6** rotgut **7** bootleg **8** home brew **10** bathtub gin

mountain formation
7 orogeny **10** orogenesis

mountain goat
4 ibex

mountain lion
4 puma **6** cougar

mountain nymph
5 oread

mountainous
4 huge, vast **6** alpine, mighty **7** immense, mammoth, massive **8** enormous, gigantic, towering **10** monumental, prodigious

mountain pass
3 col, gap
Afghanistan-Pakistan: **6** Khyber
Alps: **5** Gries
California: **4** Muir **6** Sonora
China-Myanmar: **5** Namni
Colorado: **3** Ute **5** Mosca, Muddy, Music, Raton
Europe: **8** Moravian
Greece: **5** Rupel
Hindu Kush Mts.: **5** Dorah, Durah
Pakistan: **5** Bolan, Gomal, Gumal
Sierra Nevada: **4** Mono
Switzerland: **5** Furka, Gemmi **7** Grimsel **8** Lötschen
Tunisia: **4** Faïd
Ukrainian: **5** Uzhok
Wyoming: **5** Union

mountain range
6 sierra
Asia: **5** Altai, Altay **8** Himalaya, Tien Shan **9** Altai Shan, Altay Shan, Himalayan, Himalayas, Hindu Kush
Australia: **8** Flinders
Europe: **4** Alps **10** Carpathian
Germany: **4** Harz **5** Hartz
Greece: **4** Oeta
India: **5** Ghats
Iran: **6** Zagros
Italy: **9** Apennines, Dolomites
Mexico: **11** Sierra Madre
North Africa: **5** Atlas
North America: **5** Rocky **7** Rockies **11** Appalachian
Russia: **4** Ural
Scotland: **9** Grampians
Sinai: **9** Gebel Musa
Slovakia: **5** Tatra, Tatry **9** High Tatra
South America: **5** Andes
Spain: **8** Pyrenees
Turkey: **3** Ida **6** Taurus **7** Kazdagi
United States: **5** Rocky, White **6** Brooks **7** Cascade, Olympic, Rockies, Sawatch, Wasatch **8** Absaroka, Aleutian, Catskill, Wrangell **9** Blue Ridge, Wind River **10** Adirondack, Bitterroot, Black Hills, Clearwater, Grand Teton
Zimbabwe: **6** Matopo (Hills) **7** Matoppo (Hills)

mountain ridge
5 arête

Mountain State
7 Montana **12** West Virginia

mountebank
5 quack **6** con man **8** swindler **9** charlatan **11** flimflammer, quacksalver **13** confidence man

Mount St. Helens, e.g.
7 volcano

mourn
3 rue **6** bemoan, bewail, grieve, lament, sorrow **7** deplore, protest

mournful
3 sad **6** dismal, gloomy, rueful, triste, woeful **7** doleful, elegiac, forlorn, unhappy **8** dejected, desolate, dolorous, funereal, grievous, wretched **9** dirgelike, plaintive **10** depressing, despondent, dispirited, lugubrious, melancholy **11** melancholic **12** heavyhearted

mournfulness
5 blues, dumps, gloom **7** dismals, sadness **9** dejection **10** blue devils, depression, melancholy

mourning
5 grief **7** keening, remorse, wailing, weeping **8** grieving **9** lamenting, morbidity, sorrowing, ululation **10** heartbreak **11** bereavement, lamentation

Mourning Becomes Electra author
6 O'Neill (Eugene)

mourning period, Jewish
5 shiva **6** shivah

mourning symbol
7 armband

mouse
6 rodent, shiner **8** black eye
meadow: **4** vole

mousy
3 shy **4** drab, dull **5** plain, quiet, timid **7** bashful **8** retiring, timorous **9** colorless, diffident, shrinking **11** unassertive **12** self-effacing

mouth
3 gob, maw **4** trap **5** chops **6** kisser **8** entrance **10** embouchure

mouthlike opening
5 stoma **7** stomata (plural)

mouthpiece
5 organ **6** puppet **7** speaker **8** front man **9** spokesman **10** figurehead **11** spokeswoman **12** spokesperson

mouthwatering
5 sapid, tasty, yummy **6** savory, toothy **9** delicious, palatable, succulent, toothsome **10** appetizing, delectable **11** good-tasting

mouthy
4 glib **5** gabby, talky, windy **7** verbose, voluble **8** effusive **9** bombastic, garrulous, talkative

movable
5 loose **6** mobile, motile, roving **8** portable **10** changeable

movables
5 goods **7** effects **8** chattels **10** belongings **11** furnishings

move
4 relo **5** budge, leave, march, shift, start, touch **6** affect, depart, incite, induce **7** advance, conduct, inspire, migrate, proceed, propose, request **8** dislodge, displace, motivate, persuade, progress, relocate, resettle, transfer, withdraw **9** influence, instigate, stimulate, transport **10** relocation
gingerly: **4** edge **5** creep
sideways: **4** edge **5** sidle

movement
4 flow, stir **5** tempo, trend **6** action, motion **7** crusade **8** activity, campaign, dynamism, maneuver, progress, stirring, tendency, velocity **9** migration
music: **4** moto
reflex: **5** taxis
stimulated: **7** kinesis

movie
4 cine, film, show **5** flick **6** cinema, talkie **7** picture **9** photoplay **11** picture show **13** motion picture **7** western
genre: **3** war **4** cult, epic **5** adult, anime, crime, oater **6** action, comedy, cowboy, family, horror, silent **7** cartoon, fantasy, Western **9** adventure, animation **11** documentary, martial arts **12** mockumentary
short: **4** clip **8** newsreel

movie director
American: **3** Lee (Spike), Ray (Nicholas) **4** Coen (Ethan, Joel), Ford (John), Hill (George Roy), Mann (Anthony), Penn (Arthur), Ritt (Martin), Ross (Herbert), Sirk (Douglas), Wise (Robert) **5** Allen (Woody), Ashby (Hal), Brown (Clarence), Capra (Frank), Cukor (George), Demme (Jonathan), Donen (Stanley), Fosse (Bob), Hawks (Howard), Ivory (James), Jonze (Spike), Kazan (Elia), LeRoy (Mervyn), Logan (Joshua), Lucas (George), Lumet (Sidney), Lynch (David), Moore (Michael), Payne (Alexander), Roach (Hal), Stone (Oliver), Vidor (King), Walsh (Raoul), Whale (James), Wyler (William), Zwick (Ed) **6** Altman (Robert), Beatty (Warren), Benton (Robert), Brooks (Richard), Burton (Tim), Cimino (Michael), Corman (Roger), Curtiz (Michael), Fuller (Samuel), Gibson (Mel), Hanson (Curtis), Howard (Ron), Huston (John), Kramer (Stanley), Malick (Terrence), Pakula (Alan), Parker (Alan), Seaton (George), Waters (John), Welles (Orson), Wilder (Billy) **7** Borzage (Frank), Cameron (James), Chaplin (Charlie), Coppola (Francis Ford, Sofia), Costner (Kevin), De Mille (Cecil B.), De Palma (Brian), Fleming (Victor), Gilliam (Terry), Jewison (Norman), Kubrick (Stanley), McCarey (Leo), Nichols (Mike), Pollack (Sydney), Redford (Robert), Russell (David O.), Siodmak (Robert), Stevens (George), Sturges (Preston), Van Sant (Gus), Wellman (William) **8** Anderson (Wes), Avildsen (John), Eastwood (Clint), Flaherty (Robert), Friedkin

(William), Griffith (David Wark), Grosbard (Ulu), Jarmusch (Jim), Levinson (Barry), Lubitsch (Ernst), Marshall (Penny), Minnelli (Vincente), Mulligan (Robert), Scorsese (Martin), Zemeckis (Robert) **9** Carpenter (John), Hitchcock (Alfred), Milestone (Lewis), Peckinpah (Sam), Preminger (Otto), Spielberg (Steven), Sternberg (Josef von), Streisand (Barbra), Tarantino (Quentin), Zinnemann (Fred) **10** Cassavetes (John), Heckerling (Amy), Mankiewicz (Joseph), Soderbergh (Steven) **11** Bogdanovich (Peter) **13** Frankenheimer (John)
Australian: **4** Weir (Peter) **6** Noonan (Chris) **9** Armstrong (Gillian), Beresford (Bruce)
Austrian: **4** Lang (Fritz) **6** Haneke (Michael) **8** Stroheim (Erich von) **9** Sternberg (Josef von)
British: **4** Lean (David), Reed (Carol) **5** Boyle (Danny), Leigh (Mike), Loach (Ken), Losey (Joseph), Reisz (Karel), Scott (Ridley) **6** Figgis (Mike), Frears (Stephen), Jordan (Neil), Madden (John), Newell (Mike), Parker (Alan), Powell (Michael) **7** Boorman (John), Branagh (Kenneth), Forsyth (Bill) **8** Anderson (Lindsay) **9** Hitchcock (Alfred) **10** Richardson (Tony) **11** Schlesinger (John)
Chinese: **3** Lee (Ang) **4** Chen (Kaige) **5** Zhang (Yimou)
Czech: **6** Forman (Milos)
French: **4** Demy (Jacques), Tati (Jacques), Vigo (Jean) **5** Malle (Louis) **6** Godard (Jean-Luc), Ophüls (Marcel), Renoir (Jean), Rohmer (Eric) **7** Bresson (Robert), Chabrol (Claude), Cocteau (Jean), Resnais (Alain), Rivette (Jacques) **8** Truffaut (François)
German: **4** Sirk (Douglas) **6** Herzog (Werner), Ophüls (Max) **7** Wenders (Wim) **8** Petersen (Wolfgang) **10** Fassbinder (Rainer Werner) **11** Riefenstahl (Leni), Schlöndorff (Volker)
Italian: **5** Leone (Sergio) **6** De Sica (Vittorio) **7** Fellini (Federico) **8** Pasolini (Pier Paolo), Visconti (Luchino) **9** Antonioni (Michelangelo) **10** Bertolucci (Bernardo), Rossellini (Roberto), Wertmüller (Lina), Zeffirelli (Franco)
Japanese: **3** Ozu (Yasujiru) **5** Itami (Juzo) **8** Kurosawa (Akira), Miyazaki (Hayao) **9** Mizoguchi (Kenji)
Mexican: **6** Cuarón (Alfonso), del Toro (Guillermo)
New Zealand: **7** Campion (Jane), Jackson (Peter)
Polish: **5** Wajda (Ardrzej) **7** Holland (Agnieszka) **8** Polanski (Roman)
Russian: **9** Tarkovsky (Andrei) **10** Eisenstein (Sergei)
Spanish: **6** Buñuel (Luis) **9** Almodóvar (Pedro)
Swedish: **7** Bergman (Ingmar) **10** Zetterling (Mai)
Taiwanese: **3** Ang (Lee)

movie dog
3 Lad **4** Asta, Toto **5** Benji **6** Lassie, Marley **9** Rin-Tin-Tin

movie producer
American: **3** Fox (William) **4** Cohn (Jack) **5** Lasky (Jesse), Mayer (Louis B.), Zukor (Adolph) **6** Warner (Jack L.), Zanuck (Darryl, Richard) **7** Goldwyn (Samuel), Laemmle (Carl) **8** Selznick (David O.) **9** Weinstein (Bob, Harvey)
Austrian: **9** Reinhardt (Max)

moving
5 astir **6** mobile **7** emotive, rousing **8** arousing, exciting, gripping, pathetic, poignant, stirring, touching **9** affecting, emotional, inspiring, transient **11** stimulating

moving stairs
9 escalator

mow
3 cut **4** clip, crop, fell, heap, moue, pile, raze, rick **5** level, shave, shear, stack **7** grimace **9** knock down

moxie
3 pep, vim, zip **4** grit, guts **5** brass, heart, nerve, oomph, pluck, savvy, spunk, vigor **6** energy, mettle, spirit, starch **7** cojones, courage, know-how **8** backbone **9** fortitude **10** get-up-and-go, resolution **13** determination

Mozambique
capital: **6** Maputo
language: **5** Bantu **7** Swahili **10** Portuguese
monetary unit: **7** metical
neighbor: **6** Malawi, Zambia **8** Tanzania, Zimbabwe **9** Swaziland **11** South Africa
river: **6** Ruvuma **7** Limpopo, Zambezi

Mozart, Wolfgang Amadeus
birthplace: **8** Salzburg
cataloger: **6** Köchel (Ludwig)
deathplace: **6** Vienna
opera: **8** Idomeneo **10** Magic Flute (The) **11** Don Giovanni, Il Rè Pastore **12** Così Fan Tutte **16** Marriage of Figaro (The)

MP's prey
4 AWOL **8** deserter

Mr.
French: **8** Monsieur
German: **4** Herr
India: **3** Sri
Italian: **6** Signor
Spanish: 5 Señor

Mr. Moto star
5 Lorre (Peter)

Mrs.
French: **3** Mme. **6** Madame
German: **4** Frau
Italian: **3** Sra. **7** Signora
Spanish: **3** Sra. **6** Señora

Mrs. Bunker
5 Edith
Mrs. Grundy
4 prig **5** prude **7** puritan **8** bluenose
much
3 oft **4** long, many, most **5** often **6** highly, hugely, plenty **7** greatly, notably **8** abundant **9** eminently, extremely
combining form: **4** poly **5** multi
Much Ado About Nothing character
4 Hero **7** Claudio, Don John **8** Beatrice, Benedick, Dogberry
muck
3 goo, mud **4** crap, crud, dirt, dung, glop, gook, goop, grub, gunk, junk, mess, mire, murk, plod, slog, slop, soil, toil **5** dirty, dreck, filth, grime, gumbo, slave, slime, swill, trash, waste **6** drudge, litter, manure, meddle, putter, sleaze, sludge, smirch, tinker **7** garbage, rubbish **8** nonsense **9** interfere
muckety-muck
3 VIP **5** nabob **6** bigwig, fat cat, honcho, poobah **7** big shot, kingpin, notable, pooh-bah **8** kingfish, somebody **9** dignitary
muckraker
4 Riis (Jacob) **7** Tarbell (Ida) **8** Sinclair (Upton), Steffens (Lincoln)
mucky
4 foul **5** dirty, grimy, muddy, muggy, murky, nasty, soggy **6** cruddy, filthy, grubby, grungy **7** squalid, unclean
mucous
5 slimy **6** viscid
mud
4 dirt, mire, muck, ooze **5** dregs, slime **6** depths, sludge
muddle
3 mix **4** hash, mess, muck, rile, roil **5** addle, botch, mix up, snarl **6** ataxia, bungle, drivel, foul up, fumble, jumble, jungle, litter, mess up, tangle, tumble **7** clutter, confuse, fluster, perplex, rummage, shuffle, snarl up, stumble, stupefy **8** befuddle, bewilder, confound, disarray, disorder, distract, entangle, mishmash, scramble, shambles, throw off, unsettle **9** confusion, throw away **10** complicate, disarrange, discompose **11** disorganize
muddled
5 drunk, tight, tipsy, vague **7** mixed-up **8** inchoate **10** disjointed, disordered, incoherent, inebriated **11** intoxicated, unorganized
muddle through
4 cope, fare **5** get by, get on **6** manage **7** carry on, make out **8** get along
muddy
3 dim, fog **4** base, blur, drab, dull, fade, foul, hazy, oozy, roil, soil **5** befog, cloud, dingy, dirty, grime, grimy, murky **6** cloudy, gloomy, grubby, sordid, turbid **7** becloud, begrime, confuse, obscure, squalid, tarnish, unclean, unclear **8** confused
muff
4 blow, flub **5** botch, fluff **6** bobble, bollix, bungle, fumble, goof up, mess up **7** louse up, misplay, screw up **9** mishandle
muffle
3 gag **4** dull, mute, veil **5** shush **6** dampen, deaden, lessen, shroud, soften, stifle, subdue, wrap up **7** envelop, repress, silence, smother, squelch **8** bundle up, suppress, tone down
muffled
5 muted **6** dulled **7** stifled, subdued **8** deadened, obscured, silenced **9** distorted, enveloped **10** indistinct, suppressed
muffler
4 mask, veil **5** cloak, scarf
mug
3 cup, ham, mop, mow, pan, rob **4** boob, dolt, dope, face, fool, moue, phiz, punk, puss, thug **5** dunce, idiot, mouth, rowdy, stein, tough **6** ambush, dimwit, kisser **7** assault, grimace, tankard **8** bullyboy, dumbbell, features, numskull **9** blockhead, bushwhack, ignoramus, roughneck
mugger
4 thug **6** robber **9** assailant, crocodile
muggy
4 damp **5** humid, moist **6** sticky, sultry **7** dampish
Muhammad
adopted son: **3** Ali
birthplace: **5** Mecca
camel: **5** Kaswa
daughter: **6** Fatima
deathplace: **6** Medina
deity: **5** Allah
father: **8** Abdallah, Abdullah
father-in-law: **7** Abu Bakr
flight: **6** hegira, hejira
follower: **6** Moslem, Muslim
horse: **5** Buraq **7** Alborak
religion: **5** Islam
scripture: **5** Koran
son: **7** Ibrahim
son-in-law: **3** Ali
successor: **6** caliph **7** Abu Bakr
tribe: **7** Koreish, Quraysh
uncle: **8** Abu Talib
wife: **5** Aisha **6** Ayesha **7** Khadija
mulatto
5 métis, mixed **7** mestizo **9** half-breed, halfcaste **10** crossbreed
mulberry
3 fig **10** breadfruit
bark: **4** tapa **5** tappa
type: **6** banyan **11** India rubber, osage orange

mulct
4 fine, milk, rook 5 bleed, cheat, gouge 6 extort, fleece 7 deceive, defraud, forfeit, penalty, swindle 8 penalize 9 blackmail

mule
5 cross, scuff 6 bagman, hybrid 7 bastard, courier, mongrel 8 smuggler 9 crossbred, half blood, half-breed 10 crossbreed
on the canal: 3 Sal

mulish
8 contrary, perverse, stubborn 9 obstinate, pigheaded 10 bullheaded, headstrong, inflexible, refractory, unyielding 11 stiff-necked

mull
4 hash, muse 5 brood, think, weigh 6 ponder 7 reflect 8 cogitate, consider, meditate, ruminate, turn over 9 pulverize 10 deliberate 11 contemplate

multicolored
4 pied 6 motley 7 dappled 9 prismatic 10 variegated 13 polychromatic

multifarious
5 mixed 6 motley, sundry, varied 7 diverse, various 8 assorted, manifold 13 heterogeneous, miscellaneous

multiform
6 sundry, varied 7 diverse, various 8 assorted, manifold 9 disparate 12 multifarious

multigenerational story
4 saga

multilateral
9 many-sided

multiple
4 many 6 shared, sundry 7 diverse, several, various 8 assorted, manifold, numerous 9 composite

multiplicity
3 lot 4 heap, load, mass, peck 5 flood, hoard, horde 6 barrel 7 variety 8 mountain, plethora 9 diversity, great deal, profusion

multiply
3 wax 4 rise 5 boost, breed, build, mount 6 expand, extend, spread 7 amplify, augment, enlarge, magnify 8 generate, heighten, increase 9 procreate, propagate, reproduce 10 aggrandize 11 proliferate

multitude
3 mob 4 army, herd, host, mass, slew 5 crowd, crush, drove, flock, horde, swarm 6 legion, myriad, public, throng 8 populace

multitudinous
4 many 6 legion, myriad, sundry 7 copious, various 8 abundant, manifold, numerous, populous 9 countless 10 numberless, voluminous 11 innumerable

mum
4 dumb, mute 5 quiet 6 silent 8 wordless 10 speechless, tongue-tied

mumble
6 murmur, mutter 7 maunder

mumbo jumbo
4 juju 6 fetish 9 gibberish 10 hocus-pocus 11 abracadabra 12 gobbledygook, superstition

mummer
4 mime 5 actor, mimic 12 impersonator

mummify
5 dry up, wizen 6 embalm, wither 7 shrivel 9 desiccate

munch
3 eat 4 chaw, chew 5 champ, chomp, snack 6 crunch 9 masticate

mundane
5 lowly 6 earthy, normal 7 earthly, humdrum, prosaic, routine, terrene, worldly 8 banausic, day-to-day, everyday, familiar, ordinary, telluric, workaday 9 practical, sublunary, tellurian 11 commonplace, terrestrial, uncelestial 13 materialistic

municipal
5 civic, local, urban 12 metropolitan

munificent
6 lavish 7 liberal 8 generous, handsome 9 bounteous, bountiful 10 benevolent, freehanded, openhanded 11 magnanimous 13 philanthropic

munitions maker
5 Krupp

Munro pen name
4 Saki

muon, e.g.
6 lepton

Muppets character
4 Elmo 6 Kermit

muralist
4 Sert (José María) 6 Benton (Thomas Hart), Giotto, Orozco (José Clemente), Rivera (Diego) 7 La Farge (John) 9 Siqueiros (David Alfaro) 12 Michelangelo (Buonarotti)

murder
3 hit, off 4 do in, kill, slay 5 blood, lynch, scrag, snuff, waste 6 rub out 7 bump off, execute, garrote, killing, smother, take out 8 foul play, homicide, knock off, strangle 9 eradicate, liquidate, slaughter 10 annihilate, asphyxiate, decapitate, extinguish 11 assassinate, electrocute, exterminate 12 manslaughter
brother: 10 fratricide
father: 9 patricide
king: 8 regicide
mother: 9 matricide
parent: 9 parricide
sister: 10 sororicide

murderer
6 hit man, killer, slayer **7** butcher **8** assassin, homicide **9** cutthroat, manslayer **11** slaughterer

Murder in the Cathedral
author: **5** Eliot (Thomas Stearns)
character: **5** Henry (II) **6** Becket (Thomas à)

murderous
6 deadly, lethal **10** sanguinary **12** bloodthirsty

murk
3 fog **4** haze, mist **5** brume, gloom **6** miasma **8** darkness **9** obscurity

murky
3 dim **4** dark, dull, foul, gray **5** dirty, dusky, foggy, misty, muddy, roily, vague **6** cloudy, gloomy, opaque, somber, turbid **7** obscure **8** nebulous **9** ambiguous, equivocal, tenebrous **10** caliginous

murmur
3 hum **4** buzz, purr **5** drone, rumor, sough **6** grouch, grouse, mumble, mutter, rumble **7** grumble, whisper **8** complain **9** grumbling, undertone **11** scuttlebutt, susurration

murre
3 auk **9** razorbill

Muscat
dweller: **5** Omani
home: **4** Oman

muscle
4 beef, thew **5** brawn, force, might, power, sinew **6** energy **7** potency **8** strength **9** strong arm
abdomen: **3** abs **7** abdomen
arm: **3** bis **4** tris **6** biceps **7** triceps
back: **4** lats **5** traps **9** trapezius
buttock: **6** glutes
calf: **6** soleus
chest: **4** pecs **10** pectoralis
jaw: **8** masseter
kind: **6** flexor, tensor **7** dilator, evertor, levator, rotator **8** abductor, adductor, extensor
leg: **4** hams
loin: **5** psoas
neck: **5** traps **8** platysma **9** trapezius
shoulder: **5** delts **7** deltoid **10** deltoideus
side: **4** lats
stomach: **3** abs
straight: **6** rectus
study of: **7** myology
thigh: **5** quads **8** gracilis **9** sartorius

muscle-bound
5 rigid, stiff **6** wooden

muscle car
3 GTO **4** Fury **7** Charger

muscular
4 ropy **5** beefy, built, burly, husky **6** brawny, mighty, robust, sinewy, strong, sturdy **8** athletic, forceful, powerful, resolute, stalwart, vigorous **9** Herculean, strapping, well-built
strength: **5** sinew

muse
5 angel, brood, guide, think **6** genius, ponder, trance **7** reflect, reverie **8** cogitate, meditate, mull over, ruminate, turn over **10** deliberate **11** contemplate

Muse
father: **4** Zeus **7** Jupiter
home: **7** Helicon
leader: **6** Apollo
mother: **9** Mnemosyne
of astronomy: **6** Urania
of choral song: **11** Terpsichore
of comedy: **6** Thalia
of dancing: **11** Terpsichore
of epic poetry: **8** Calliope
of history: **4** Clio
of love poetry: **5** Erato
of lyric poetry: **5** Erato
of music: **7** Euterpe
of pastoral poetry: **6** Thalia
of sacred poetry: **8** Polymnia **10** Polyhymnia
of tragedy: **9** Melpomene

museum
5 salon **7** archive, exhibit, gallery **8** atheneum **10** collection, repository
famous: **3** Met **4** Fogg, MoMA, Tate **5** Brera, Field, Frick, Getty, Orsay, Prado **6** Louvre, Uffizi **7** Peabody, Walters, Whitney **9** Henry Ford, Hermitage, Hirshhorn **10** Guggenheim **11** Norton Simon, Smithsonian

mush
4 slop **5** grits, gruel, hokum **6** bathos, drivel, hominy **8** porridge, schmaltz

mushroom
4 grow **6** expand, spread **7** burgeon, explode, inflate **8** snowball **11** proliferate
combining form: **3** myc **4** myco **5** mycet **6** myceto
edible: **5** enoki, morel **6** bolete **7** cremini, crimini, porcini **8** shiitake **9** mousseron **10** champignon, portabella, portabello, portobello **11** chanterelle
kind: **6** agaric, bolete **7** inky cap, russula
part: **3** cap **4** gill, ring **5** stipe, volva **6** pileus **7** annulus **8** mycelium
poisonous: **7** amanita **8** death cap **9** fly agaric, toadstool

mushy
4 soft **5** pulpy, soppy, vague **6** quaggy, spongy **7** amorous, maudlin, mawkish, squashy, squishy **8** bathetic, effusive, romantic, squooshy **9** schmaltzy **10** lovey-dovey, saccharine **11** sentimental

music
abbreviation: **3** fff, ppp, sfz **5** cresc
bass staff lines: **5** GBDFA
bass staff spaces: **4** ACEG
characteristic phrase: **9** leitmotif, leitmotiv
chord: **5** major, minor, tonic **7** harmony **8** dominant **9** augmented **10** diminished
closing: **4** coda
embellishment: **3** run **4** turn **5** trill **7** cadenza, mordent, roulade **8** arpeggio, flourish **9** grace note
for eight: **5** octet
for five: **7** quintet
for four: **7** quartet
for nine: **5** nonet
for one: **4** solo
for seven: **6** septet
for six: **6** sextet
for three: **4** trio
for two: **3** duo **4** a due, duet
god: **6** Apollo
hall: **5** odeum **7** cabaret, theater
instrumental form: **3** jig, rag **4** jazz, reel **5** étude, fugue, gigue, march, polka, rondo, suite, waltz **6** minuet, pavane, sonata **7** bourrée, gavotte, mazurka, prelude, toccata **8** chaconne, concerto, courante, fantasia, galliard, nocturne, overture, rhapsody, ricercar, saraband, serenade, symphony, tone poem **9** allemande, polonaise
morning: **6** aubade
Muse: **7** Euterpe
night: **8** nocturne, serenade
note: **4** half **5** breve, minim, neume, whole **6** eighth, quaver **7** quarter **8** crotchet **9** sixteenth **10** semiquaver
patron saint: **7** Cecilia
period: **6** Modern, Rococo **7** Baroque **8** Medieval, Romantic **9** Classical
speed: **5** tempi (plural), tempo
symbol: **3** bar, key **4** clef, flat, note, rest, slur, turn **5** G clef, neume, sharp, staff **7** fermata, mordent **8** bass clef **9** alla breve **10** accidental, treble clef
treble staff lines: **5** EGBDF
treble staff spaces: **4** FACE
voice: **4** alto, bass **5** basso, mezzo, tenor **7** soprano **8** baritone **9** contralto
vocal form: **3** air **4** aria, hymn, lied, mass, song **5** chant, motet, opera, round **6** anthem, arioso, ballad **7** cantata, chanson, chorale **8** cavatina, madrigal, operetta, oratorio, serenade **9** cabaletta

musical
4 show **5** revue **6** choral **7** lyrical, melodic, songful, tuneful **8** harmonic, operetta, zarzuela **9** melodious, symphonic **10** euphonious, harmonious
famous: **4** Cats, Hair, Mame, Rent **5** Annie, Evita, Gypsy **6** Grease, Kismet, Les Miz, Oliver, Wicked **7** Cabaret, Camelot, Candide, Chicago, Company, Follies **8** Carousel, Fiorello, Godspell, King and I (The), Lion King (The), Mamma Mia, Music Man (The), Oklahoma, Show Boat **9** Brigadoon, Footloose, Funny Girl, Girl Crazy, Hairspray, On the Town, Over There, State Fair **10** Chorus Line (A), Dreamgirls, Hello Dolly, Kiss Me Kate, Miss Saigon, My Fair Lady, Pajama Game (The), She Loves Me **11** Damn Yankees, Of Thee I Sing, Sweeney Todd **12** Anything Goes, Bye Bye Birdie, Guys and Dolls, Into the Woods, Sound of Music (The), South Pacific, Sweet Charity **13** Les Misérables, Man of La Mancha, Silk Stockings, West Side Story, Wonderful Town **14** Finian's Rainbow, Flower Drum Song, Paint Your Wagon **15** Annie Get Your Gun **16** Fiddler on the Roof **17** Phantom of the Opera (The) **20** Jesus Christ Superstar

musical composition
4 aria, coda, hymn, lied, opus, song, trio **5** chant, canon, carol, dirge, étude, fugue, march, motet, octet, opera, rondo, suite **6** anthem, arioso, ballad, lieder (plural), septet, sextet, sonata **7** cantata, chanson, chorale, prelude, quartet, quintet, requiem, scherzo, toccata **8** concerto, fantasia, madrigal, nocturne, operetta, oratorio, overture, postlude, serenade, sonatina, symphony **9** bagatelle, barcarole, cabaletta, interlude **10** intermezzo, recitative

musical direction
accented: **7** marcato **8** sforzato **9** sforzando
all: **5** tutti
bowed: **4** arco
brisk: **4** brio, vivo **6** vivace **7** allegro, animato
connected: **6** legato
detached: **8** spiccato, staccato
dignified: **8** maestoso
disconnected: **8** staccato
emotional: **12** appassionato
emphatic: **7** marcato
excited: **7** agitato
fast: **4** vite, vivo **6** presto, veloce, vivace **7** allegro
faster: **7** stretto **11** accelerando
fluctuating tempo: **6** rubato
forcefully: **7** furioso
freely: **9** ad libitum
from the beginning: **6** da capo
gay: **7** giocoso
gentle: **5** dolce **7** amabile, amoroso **10** affettuoso
graceful: **8** grazioso
half: **5** mezzo
heavy: **7** pesante
held firmly: **6** tenuto

less: 4 meno
little: 4 poco
little by little: 9 poco a poco
lively: 4 vite, vivo 6 vivace 7 allegro, animato, giocoso
loud: 3 fff 5 forte
louder: 9 crescendo
majestic: 8 maestoso
moderate: 7 andante 8 moderato
moderately loud: 10 mezzo forte
moderately soft: 10 mezzo piano
playful: 10 scherzando
plucked: 9 pizzicato
quick: 4 vite, vivo 6 presto, veloce, vivace 7 allegro
quickening: 11 affrettando
repeat: 3 bis 6 da capo
run: 8 arpeggio 9 glissando
sad: 7 dolente 8 doloroso
separate: 6 divisi
silent: 5 tacet
singing: 9 cantabile
sliding: 9 glissando
slow: 5 grave, largo, lento 6 adagio 7 andante 9 larghetto
slowing: 3 rit 6 ritard 10 ritardando 11 rallentando
smooth: 6 legato
soft: 3 ppp 5 dolce, piano
softening: 10 diminuendo 11 decrescendo
solemn: 5 grave
spirited: 4 vivo 6 vivace 7 animato 9 spiritoso
stately: 7 pomposo 8 maestoso
sustained: 6 tenuto 9 sostenuto
sweet: 5 dolce
tender: 7 amabile, amoroso 10 affettuoso
together: 4 a due 5 tutti
very: 5 assai
very fast: 11 prestissimo
very loud: 10 fortissimo
very soft: 10 pianissimo

musical drama
5 opera 8 operetta, zarzuela 9 singspiel

musical exercise
5 étude

musical group
4 band, trio 5 choir, combo 6 chorus, sextet 7 quartet, quintet 8 ensemble, glee club 9 orchestra

musical instrument
African: 5 mbira, rebab 7 kalimba
ancient: 4 asor, lyre, rote 5 crwth 6 syrinx 7 cithara, kithara, sistrum, timbrel 8 psaltery
Arabic: 3 oud 5 rebab
bagpipe: 7 musette, pibroch
brass: 4 horn, tuba 5 bugle 6 cornet 7 althorn, clarion, helicon, saxhorn, trumpet 8 trombone 10 flügelhorn, French horn, sousaphone
electronic: 8 Theremin 11 synthesizer
Indian: 4 vina 5 sarod, sitar, tabla, veena
Japanese: 4 biwa, koto 7 samisen 8 shamisen 10 shakuhachi
keyboard: 5 organ, piano 6 spinet 7 celesta, cembalo, clavier 8 calliope, melodeon, virginal 9 accordion 10 clavichord, concertina, pianoforte 11 harpsichord
medieval: 4 lute 5 naker, rebab, rebec, shawm, tabor 7 gittern, mandola 8 cornetto, gemshorn, hornpipe, oliphant, psaltery 9 monochord 10 hurdy-gurdy
percussion: 4 bell, drum 5 anvil, güiro, piano 6 cymbal, maraca 7 maracas, marimba, timpani, tympani 8 bass drum, castanet, triangle 9 castanets, snare drum, xylophone 10 kettledrum, tambourine, vibraphone
Persian: 6 santir
reed: 4 oboe 7 bassoon 8 clarinet 9 harmonica, saxophone 11 English horn
Renaissance: 4 viol 5 rebec, regal, shawm 6 curtal, spinet 7 bagpipe, bandora, cittern, rackett, sackbut, serpent, theorbo, vihuela, violone 8 crumhorn, recorder, virginal 9 krummhorn, virginals 10 chitarrone, colascione 11 harpsichord
Russian: 9 balalaika
stringed: 3 uke 4 harp, lute, lyre, viol 5 banjo, cello, piano, rebab, rebec, viola 6 fiddle, guitar, violin, zither 7 bandora, cittern, gittern, kantele, pandura, ukelele, ukulele 8 autoharp, dulcimer, mandolin 10 contrabass, double bass 11 harpsichord, violoncello
toy: 5 kazoo 7 ocarina
woodwind: 4 oboe 5 flute 7 bassoon, piccolo 8 clarinet 9 saxophone 11 English horn

musical interval
5 fifth, major, minor, ninth, sixth, third 6 fourth, octave, second 7 perfect, seventh, tritone

musical rights group
3 BMI 5 ASCAP

musical syllable
3 sol

music hall
4 odea (plural) 5 odeum

musician
4 bard 5 piper 6 player 7 jazzman, maestro 8 minstrel, virtuoso 9 performer 10 troubadour

musician Brian
3 Eno

musicians' org.
3 BMI 5 ASCAP

Music Man setting
4 Iowa

muskeg
3 bog, fen 4 mire, quag 5 marsh, swamp 6 morass, slough 8 quagmire

musket
5 fusil **9** flintlock, matchlock **12** muzzleloader

Musketeer
5 Athos **6** Aramis **7** Porthos
author: 5 Dumas (Alexandre)
friend: 9 d'Artagnan

muskmelon
10 cantaloupe

Muslim
ascetic: 4 Sufi **5** fakir **7** dervish **8** marabout
body of scholars: 5 ulama, ulema
branch: 4 Shia **5** Sunni **6** Shiite
caller to prayer: 7 muezzin
decree: 5 fatwa, irade
devil: 5 Iblis
garment: 4 izar **5** burka, burqa **6** chador
god: 5 Allah
heavenly virgin: 5 houri
holiday: 3 Eid
holy city: 5 Mecca **6** Medina
holy war: 5 jihad
honorific: 3 Aga **4** Agha
judge: 4 qadi **5** mufti
lady: 5 begum
law: 6 Sharia
leader: 3 aga **4** agha, amir, emir, imam **5** ameer, emeer **6** caliph, sayyid, sultan **9** ayatollah
lord: 5 omrah
mendicant: 5 fakir
messiah: 5 Mahdi
month: (see at **month**)
month of fasting: 7 Ramadan
mosque: 6 masjid
mystic: 4 Sufi
official: 3 dey **6** mullah, vizier
pilgrim: 5 hadji, hajji
pilgrimage: 4 hadj, hajj **5** omrah
prayer: 5 salat
priest: 4 imam
prohibition: 5 haram
prophet: 8 Mohammed, Muhammad
religion: 5 Islam
ruler: 4 amir, emir **5** ameer, emeer **6** caliph
scripture: 5 Koran, Quran
school: 7 madrasa **8** madrasah, madrassa **9** madrassah
shrine: 5 Kaaba
spirit: 4 jinn **5** djinn, jinni **6** djinni
temple: 6 masjid, mosque
theological student: 5 softa
title: 3 aga **4** agha, amir, emir **6** ameer, caliph, emeer
tradition: 5 sunna
veil: 7 yashmak
(see also **mosque; Muhammad**)

muss
3 row **4** mess **5** botch, chaos, mix-up, upset **6** jumble, mess-up, muddle, rumple, tousle **7** disrupt, rummage **8** disarray, dishevel, disorder, shambles **9** confusion **10** disarrange **11** disorganize

mussel
5 naiad
genus: 4 Unio **7** Mytilus **8** Anodonta
larva: 9 blackhead

Mussolini, Benito
4 Duce (Il)
son-in-law: 5 Ciano (Galeazzo)

mussy
6 sloppy, untidy **7** tousled, unkempt **8** slovenly **9** cluttered **10** disheveled

must
4 duty, mold, need, want **5** gotta, has to, juice, ought **6** devoir, have to, should **9** condition, essential, necessity, requisite **10** obligation, sine qua non **11** requirement **12** precondition, prerequisite

mustached painter
4 Dalí (Salvador)

muster
4 call, roll **5** crowd, group, raise, rally, rouse **6** enlist, enroll, gather, induce, invoke, join up, roster, sample, sign on, sign up, summon, work up **7** collect, convene, develop, include, marshal, produce **8** assemble, assembly, comprise, congress, generate, mobilize, organize, roll call, specimen **9** gathering, inventory, nose count **10** accumulate, assemblage, collection, congregate, rendezvous **12** accumulation, congregation

muster out
5 demob, let go **9** discharge **10** demobilize

musty
4 dank **5** funky, moldy, stale, tired, trite **6** frowsy, frowzy, old hat, smelly **7** airless, antique, mildewy, squalid **8** shopworn, timeworn **10** antiquated, malodorous, threadbare

Mut
husband: 4 Amen, Amon
son: 5 Chons **6** Chonsu, Khonsu

mutable
5 fluid **6** fickle, mobile, shifty **7** erratic, protean **8** slippery, unstable, unsteady, variable, volatile, wavering **9** changeful, mercurial, unsettled **10** capricious, changeable, inconstant **11** fluctuating, vacillating **12** inconsistent

mutate
4 vary **5** alter, morph **6** change, modify **9** refashion, transform, transmute **11** transfigure **12** metamorphose, transmogrify

mutation
5 sport **6** change **7** novelty **9** deviation, variation **10** alteration **11** vicissitude **12** modification **13** metamorphosis

mute
3 mum **4** dumb **5** quiet **6** dampen, deaden, muffle, muzzle, reduce, silent, soften, stifle, subdue **7** silence **8** silencer, wordless **9** voiceless **10** speechless, tongue-tied

muted
3 dim, mat **4** dull **6** low-key, silent **10** speechless

mutilate
3 mar **4** maim **6** damage, deface, injure, mangle **7** cripple **9** disfigure, dismember

mutineer
5 rebel

mutinous
6 unruly **8** factious **9** insurgent, seditious, turbulent **10** rebellious **12** contumacious **13** insubordinate

mutiny
5 rebel **6** revolt, rise up **8** uprising **9** rebellion **12** insurrection

mutt
3 cur, dog **4** mule **5** cross **6** hybrid **7** mixture, mongrel **9** half blood, half-breed **10** crossbreed

Mutt and ___
4 Jeff

mutter
5 growl **6** grouch, grouse, mumble, murmur **7** grumble **9** undertone

muttonchops
9 burnsides, sideburns **10** sideboards **11** dundrearies **12** side-whiskers

mutual
5 joint **6** common, public, shared, united **7** related **8** communal, conjoint, conjunct **9** bilateral, connected **10** associated, reciprocal, respective
prefix: **5** inter

muumuu
6 caftan

muzzle
3 gag **4** hush, mute, nose, phiz **5** snout **7** silence, squelch

muzzy
3 dim **4** dull, hazy **5** faint, vague **6** blurry, gloomy **7** blurred, muddled, unclear **8** confused, nebulous **9** imprecise

myalgia
4 ache, pain **5** cramp **6** strain **8** soreness

Myanmar
5 Burma
bay: **6** Bengal
capital: **6** Yangon **7** Rangoon
monetary unit: **4** kyat
neighbor: **4** Laos **5** China, India **8** Thailand **10** Bangladesh
peninsula: **9** Indochina
river: **7** Salween **9** Irrawaddy
sea: **7** Andaman

My Antonia author
6 Cather (Willa)

My Cherie ___
5 Amour

My Cousin Vinnie star
5 Tomei (Marisa)

My Dinner with ___
5 Andre

My Fair Lady racecourse
5 Ascot

My Last Duchess author
8 Browning (Robert)

My Lost Youth author
10 Longfellow (Henry Wadsworth)

My Name Is Asher ___
3 Lev

My Way songwriter
4 Anka (Paul)

Myra Breckenridge author
5 Vidal (Gore)

myriad
3 lot **4** heap, host, raft, slew **5** flood, horde, swarm **6** throng **9** countless, multitude **10** infinitude, numberless **11** innumerable **12** incalculable **13** multitudinous

myrmecology subject
3 ant **4** ants

myrmidon
6 minion **8** follower, retainer **9** attendant, underling **11** subordinate

Myron's statue
10 Discobolos, Discobolus **13** Discus Thrower (The)

Myrrha's son
6 Adonis

mysterious
6 arcane, mystic, occult, secret **7** cryptic, obscure, strange **8** abstruse, esoteric, numinous **9** ambiguous, enigmatic, equivocal, recondite **10** cabalistic, unknowable **11** inscrutable **12** impenetrable, inexplicable, unfathomable **13** unaccountable

mystery
5 poser **6** enigma, puzzle, riddle, secret **7** arcanum, problem, stumper **8** whodunit **9** conundrum **10** closed book, perplexity, puzzlement **13** Chinese puzzle
writer: **3** Poe (Edgar Allan), Tey (Josephine) **5** Blake (Nicholas), Cross (Amanda), Doyle (Arthur Conan), Innes (Michael), James (P. D.), Lynds (Dennis), Marsh (Ngaio), Oates (Joyce Carol), Queen (Ellery), Stout (Rex), Waugh (Hillary) **6** Dexter (Colin), Parker (Robert B.), Peters (Ellis), Sayers (Dorothy) **7** Barnard (Robert), Collins (Michael, Wilkie), Gardner (Erle Stanley), Grafton (Sue), Hammett (Dashiell), MacLeod

(Charlotte), Rendell (Ruth), Upfield (Arthur) **8** Chandler (Raymond), Christie (Agatha), Paretsky (Sara), Spillane (Mickey) **9** MacDonald (John D.), Macdonald (Ross) **10** Chesterton (G. K.)

mystic
4 seer **6** arcane, medium, occult, oracle, secret **7** obscure **8** anagogic, esoteric, hermetic, numinous **9** enigmatic, visionary **10** cabalistic, unknowable **11** inscrutable, necromantic **12** impenetrable, thaumaturgic **13** unaccountable

mystical
4 holy **6** arcane, covert, divine, occult, orphic, sacred, secret **7** cryptic, sub-rosa **8** anagogic, esoteric, hermetic, oracular, profound **9** recondite, spiritual **10** miraculous, symbolical **11** clandestine **12** supernatural, supranatural
glow: **4** aura

mysticism
7 Orphism **8** cabalism, quietism **11** hermeticism

mystify
6 baffle, puzzle **7** confuse, obscure, perplex **8** befuddle, bewilder, confound **9** obfuscate

mystifying
7 cryptic, delphic **8** Delphian **9** enigmatic

mystique
4 aura **5** charm, magic **6** glamor **7** glamour **8** charisma **9** magnetism

myth
4 lore, saga, tale **5** fable, story **6** legend **7** fiction, figment, parable **8** allegory, folklore **9** tradition **11** fabrication

mythical
6 fabled, made-up, unreal **7** created, fictive **8** fabulous, fanciful, invented **9** fantastic, fictional, imaginary, legendary **10** apocryphal, fictitious
bird: **3** roc
monster: **3** orc **4** ogre

mythologist
4 Jung (Carl Gustav), Ovid **5** Tylor (Edward Burnett) **6** Eliade (Mircea), Frazer (James George), Müller (Friedrich Max) **8** Campbell (Joseph) **9** Euhemerus **10** Malinowski (Bronislaw)

mythology
see **myth**

N

Naamah
brother: **9** Tubalcain
father: **6** Lamech
husband: **7** Solomon
mother: **6** Zillah
son: **8** Rehoboam

nab
4 grab, nail, nick, trap **5** catch, pinch, run in, seize, snare **6** arrest, clutch, collar, detain, pick up, pull in, snatch **7** capture **9** apprehend

Nabisco treat
4 Oreo

nabob
3 VIP **5** mogul, noble **6** bigwig, fat cat, poo-bah, tycoon **7** bigfoot, big shot, kingpin, magnate, notable, pooh-bah **8** big chief, eminence, governor, kingfish **9** big cheese, dignitary, personage **10** notability

Nabokov novel
3 Ada **4** Gift (The), Pnin **6** Lolita **7** Defense (The), Despair **8** Pale Fire **14** King Queen Knave

nacre
13 mother-of-pearl

nada
3 nil, nix, zip **4** zero **5** zilch **6** naught **7** nothing, nullity **11** nothingness

nadir
4 base, foot **5** depth **6** bottom **8** low point **10** rock bottom
opposite: **6** zenith

nag
3 irk, vex **4** bait, carp, goad, ride **5** annoy, chivy, harry, horse, hound, shrew, worry **6** badger, bother, carp at, harass, heckle, hector, needle, peck at, pester, plague **7** henpeck, torment **8** complain, harangue, irritate

naiad
3 nix **5** nixie, nymph **6** sprite, undine

naïf
7 ingenue

nail
3 ace, bag, get, nab **4** brad, grab, spad, stud, tack, trap **5** catch, clone, spike, sprig **6** arrest, collar, secure **7** capture **9** apprehend

naive
6 simple **7** artless, natural **8** gullible, innocent, wide-eyed **9** childlike, credulous, guileless,

ingenuous, unstudied **10** self-taught, unaffected, unschooled **11** susceptible

naïveté
9 innocence

naked
3 raw **4** bald, bare, mere, nude, pure **5** clear, sheer **6** peeled, scanty, simple, unclad **7** denuded, evident, exposed, obvious **8** revealed, starkers, stripped **9** au naturel, disclosed, unclothed, uncovered, undressed
combining form: **4** gymn **5** gymno

Naked and the Dead author
6 Mailer (Norman)

namby-pamby
4 weak **5** banal, bland, inane, sissy, vapid **6** effete, jejune **7** insipid, milksop, nebbish **8** nebbishy, weakling **9** spineless **10** effeminate, indecisive, pantywaist, wishy-washy **11** milquetoast **12** milk-and-water **13** characterless

name
3 dub, nom, tab, tag, tap **4** cite, term **5** alias, label, nomen, title **6** finger, repute, rubric **7** appoint, baptize, epithet, moniker, specify **8** christen, identify, nominate **9** designate, incognito, sobriquet **10** denominate, reputation **11** appellation, appellative, designation
ancient Rome: **7** agnomen **8** prenomen
assumed: **5** alias **9** sobriquet
family: **8** cognomen
fictitious: **6** anonym **9** pseudonym
source: **6** eponym

nameless
6 unsung **7** obscure, unknown **9** anonymous **11** indefinable, unutterable **12** uncelebrated, unidentified

namely
3 viz. **5** id est, to wit **6** that is **8** scilicet **9** expressly, specially, videlicet **10** especially **12** particularly, specifically

Name of the Rose author
3 Eco (Umberto)

Namibia
capital: **8** Windhoek
city: **8** Oshakati, Rehoboth
desert: **5** Namib **8** Kalahari
language: **5** Bantu **6** German **9** Afrikaans
neighbor: **6** Angola **8** Botswana **11** South Africa
river: **6** Cunene, Orange **8** Okavango

nana
7 grandma **11** grandmother

Nana
author: **4** Zola (Emile)
mother: **8** Gervaise

Nancy Drew
aunt: **6** Eloise
author: **5** Keene (Carolyn)
boyfriend: **3** Ned
creator: **11** Stratemeyer (Edward)
dog: **4** Togo
father: **6** Carson
friend: **4** Bess **5** Helen **6** George
housekeeper: **6** Hannah

Nanna
brother: **6** Nergal, Ninazu
father: **5** Enlil
husband: **6** Balder, Baldur
mother: **6** Ninlil
son: **3** Utu
wife: **6** Ningal

nanny
4 amah, ayah **5** nurse **9** caregiver, governess, nursemaid **11** Mary Poppins

Naomi
4 Mara
daughter-in-law: **4** Ruth **5** Orpah
husband: **9** Elimelech
son: **6** Mahlon **7** Chilion

nap
4 doze, pile, rest, shag, wale, warp, weft, woof **5** sleep, weave **6** drowse, nod off, siesta, snooze **7** drop off, surface **10** forty winks

nape
6 scruff

Naphtali
brother: **3** Dan
father: **5** Jacob
mother: **6** Bilhah
son: **4** Guni **5** Jezer **7** Jahzeel, Jahziel, Shallum

naphtha
3 oil **7** solvent **9** petroleum

napkin
5 cloth, doily, towel **9** serviette

napoleon
4 boot **6** pastry **8** card game **9** solitaire
bid: **7** blucher **10** wellington

Napoleon Bonaparte
adversary: **6** Nelson (Horatio) **7** Kutuzov (Mikhail) **10** Wellington (Duke of)
birthplace: **7** Ajaccio, Corsica
brother: **5** Louis **6** Jérome, Joseph, Lucien
brother-in-law: **5** Murat (Joachim)
deathplace: **8** St. Helena
defeat: **7** Leipzig **8** Waterloo **9** Trafalgar
doctor: **11** Antommarchi (Francesco)
father: **5** Carlo
island of exile: **4** Elba **8** St. Helena
marshal: **3** Ney (Michel) **5** Murat (Joachim), Soult (Nicolas-Jean) **6** Suchet (Louis-Gabriel)
sister: **5** Maria **8** Carlotta, Carolina
victory: **3** Ulm **4** Jena, Lodi **5** Ligny **6** Abukir, Abu Qir, Arcole, Wagram **7** Bautzen, Dresden, Marengo **8** Borodino **10** Austerlitz
wife: **9** Josephine **11** Marie Louise

naproxen brand
5 Aleve

narcissism
3 ego 6 egoism, vanity 7 conceit, egotism 8 self-love, vainness 9 vainglory 11 egocentrism, self-conceit 13 conceitedness

narcissistic
4 vain 7 stuck-up 9 conceited, egotistic 10 self-loving 11 egotistical 12 self-absorbed, self-admiring, self-centered, vainglorious

Narcissus
admirer: 4 Echo
father: 9 Cephissus
mother: 7 Liriope

narcotic
3 hop 4 coca, dope, drug, junk 5 opium 6 heroin, opiate 7 anodyne, cocaine, codeine, Demerol, hashish 8 cannabis, hypnotic, morphine, nepenthe 9 marijuana, methadone, somnolent, soporific 10 somnorific 11 somniferous
peddler: 6 dealer, pusher

narrate
4 spin, tell 5 state 6 detail, recite, relate, report, retail 7 express, outline, recount 8 describe 9 chronicle

narrative
4 epic, idyl, myth, saga, tale, yarn 5 fable, idyll, story 6 legend, report 7 account, history, recital, version 8 anecdote 9 chronicle
medieval French: 5 roman 7 romance
prose: 5 novel 7 novella

narrator
6 teller 7 reciter 8 reporter 9 describer, performer 10 chronicler

narrow
5 close, small, taper 6 lessen, strait 7 bigoted, limited, precise, slender 8 contract, decrease, straiten 9 confining, constrict, hidebound, illiberal, parochial 10 brassbound, inflexible, intolerant, prejudiced, provincial, restricted

narrowly
6 barely 7 closely 8 scarcely, strictly

narrow-minded
5 petty 7 bigoted, insular 9 hidebound, illiberal, parochial 10 brassbound, intolerant, prejudiced, provincial

nasal
6 rhinal, twangy 9 nosepiece
combining form: 4 rhin 5 rhino
sprayer: 9 nebulizer

NASCAR champion
5 Busch (Kurt), Petty (Lee, Richard) 6 Gordon (Jeff), Martin (Mark), Newman (Ryan) 7 Jarrett (Dale), Johnson (Jimmie), Kenseth (Matt), Labonte (Bobby, Terry), Pearson (David), Stewart (Tony), Waltrip (Darrell) 9 Earnhardt (Dale)

nascency
5 birth 6 origin 7 genesis 8 birthing, creation, nativity 9 inception 11 parturition

nascent
7 budding, growing, newborn 8 emergent 9 beginning, embryonic, fledgling, incipient, sprouting 10 blossoming, burgeoning, initiative, initiatory

Naseby victor
7 Fairfax (Thomas) 8 Cromwell (Oliver)

___ Nastase
4 Ilie

nasty
4 evil, foul, icky, mean, vile 5 awful, dirty, gross, snide 6 filthy, grubby, horrid, malign, odious, wicked 7 beastly, harmful, hateful, ill-bred, painful, raunchy, squalid, vicious 8 god-awful, indecent, spiteful 9 loathsome, malicious, malignant, obnoxious, offensive, repugnant, repulsive 10 disgusting, malevolent 11 distasteful 12 disagreeable

natant
8 floating, swimming

Nathan
father: 4 Bani 5 Attai, David
son: 5 Zabad

nation
4 race 5 realm, state, tribe 6 domain, people, polity 7 country, kingdom, society 8 dominion, populace, republic 11 sovereignty 12 commonwealth, principality
Africa: 4 Chad, Mali, Togo 5 Benin, Congo, Egypt, Gabon, Ghana, Kenya, Libya, Niger, Sudan 6 Angola, Gambia, Guinea, Malawi, Rwanda, Uganda, Zambia 7 Algeria, Burundi, Comoros, Eritrea, Lesotho, Liberia, Morocco, Namibia, Nigeria, Senegal, Somalia, Tunisia 8 Botswana, Cameroon, Djibouti, Ethiopia, Tanzania, Zimbabwe 9 Cape Verde, Mauritius, Swaziland 10 Ivory Coast, Madagascar, Mauritania, Mozambique, Seychelles, South Sudan 11 Burkina Faso, Côte d'Ivoire, Sierra Leone, South Africa 12 Guinea-Bissau 16 Equatorial Guinea 18 São Tomé and Principe 22 Central African Republic
Americas: 4 Peru 5 Chile 6 Belize, Brazil, Canada, Guyana, Mexico, Panama 7 Bolivia, Ecuador, Uruguay 8 Colombia, Honduras, Paraguay, Suriname 9 Argentina, Costa Rica, Guatemala, Nicaragua, Venezuela 10 El Salvador 12 United States
Asia: 4 Laos 5 Burma, China, India, Japan, Korea, Nepal 6 Bhutan, Brunei, Ceylon, Taiwan 7 Armenia, Georgia, Myanmar, Vietnam 8 Cambodia, Malaysia, Maldives, Mongolia, Pakistan, Sri Lanka, Thailand 9 East Timor, Indonesia, Singapore 10 Azerbaijan, Bangladesh, Kazakhstan, Kyrgyzstan, North Korea, South

Korea, Tajikistan, Timor-Leste **11** Afghanistan, Philippines **12** Turkmenistan
Caribbean: 4 Cuba **5** Haiti **7** Bahamas, Grenada, Jamaica **8** Barbados, Dominica **10** Saint Lucia **15** St. Kitts and Nevis **17** Antigua and Barbuda, Dominican Republic, Trinidad and Tobago **18** Saint Kitts and Nevis **25** St. Vincent and the Grenadines **28** Saint Vincent and the Grenadines
Europe: 5 Italy, Malta, Spain **6** Bosnia, Cyprus, France, Greece, Kosovo, Latvia, Monaco, Norway, Poland, Russia, Serbia, Sweden, Turkey **7** Albania, Andorra, Austria, Belarus, Belgium, Croatia, Denmark, Estonia, Finland, Germany, Hungary, Iceland, Ireland, Moldova, Romania, Ukraine **8** Bulgaria, Portugal, Slovakia, Slovenia **9** Lithuania, Macedonia, San Marino **10** Luxembourg, Montenegro, Yugoslavia **11** Netherlands, Switzerland **13** Czech Republic, Liechtenstein, United Kingdom
Middle East: 3 UAE **4** Iraq, Iran, Oman **5** Egypt, Libya, Qatar, Syria, Yemen **6** Israel, Jordan, Kuwait **7** Bahrain, Lebanon **11** Saudi Arabia **18** United Arab Emirates
Oceania: 4 Fiji **5** Belau, Nauru, Palau, Samoa, Tonga **6** Tuvalu **7** Vanuatu **8** Kiribati **9** Australia, New Guinea **10** Micronesia, New Zealand **14** Papua New Guinea, Solomon Islands **15** Marshall Islands

national
6 native **7** citizen, federal, subject **8** resident **10** countryman **11** countrywide

National Basketball Association
Atlanta: 5 Hawks
Boston: 7 Celtics
Brooklyn: 4 Nets
Charlotte: 7 Hornets
Chicago: 5 Bulls
Cleveland: 9 Cavaliers
Dallas: 9 Mavericks
Denver: 7 Nuggets
Detroit: 7 Pistons
Golden State: 8 Warriors
Houston: 7 Rockets
Indiana: 6 Pacers
Los Angeles: 6 Lakers **8** Clippers
Memphis: 9 Grizzlies
Miami: 4 Heat
Milwaukee: 5 Bucks
Minnesota: 12 Timberwolves
New Orleans: 8 Pelicans
New York: 6 Knicks
Oklahoma City: 7 Thunder
Orlando: 5 Magic
Philadelphia: 13 Seventy-sixers
Phoenix: 4 Suns
Portland: 12 Trail Blazers
Sacramento: 5 Kings
San Antonio: 5 Spurs
Toronto: 7 Raptors
Utah: 4 Jazz
Washington: 7 Wizards

National Football League
Arizona: 9 Cardinals
Atlanta: 7 Falcons
Baltimore: 6 Ravens
Buffalo: 5 Bills
Carolina: 8 Panthers
Chicago: 5 Bears
Cincinnati: 7 Bengals
Cleveland: 6 Browns
Dallas: 7 Cowboys
Denver: 7 Broncos
Detroit: 5 Lions
Green Bay: 7 Packers
Houston: 6 Texans
Indianapolis: 5 Colts
Jacksonville: 7 Jaguars
Kansas City: 6 Chiefs
Miami: 8 Dolphins
Minnesota: 7 Vikings
New England: 8 Patriots
New Orleans: 6 Saints
New York: 4 Jets **6** Giants
Oakland: 7 Raiders
Philadelphia: 6 Eagles
Pittsburgh: 8 Steelers
St. Louis: 4 Rams
San Diego: 8 Chargers
San Francisco: 11 Forty-niners
Seattle: 8 Seahawks
Tampa Bay: 4 Bucs **10** Buccaneers
Tennessee: 6 Titans
Washington: 8 Redskins

National Hockey League
Anaheim: 5 Ducks
Arizona: 7 Coyotes
Atlanta: 9 Thrashers
Boston: 6 Bruins
Buffalo: 6 Sabres
Calgary: 6 Flames
Carolina: 10 Hurricanes
Chicago: 10 Blackhawks
Colorado: 9 Avalanche
Columbus: 11 Blue Jackets
Dallas: 5 Stars
Detroit: 8 Red Wings
Edmonton: 6 Oilers
Florida: 8 Panthers
Los Angeles: 5 Kings
Minnesota: 4 Wild
Montreal: 9 Canadiens
Nashville: 9 Predators
New Jersey: 6 Devils
New York: 7 Rangers **9** Islanders
Ottawa: 8 Senators
Philadelphia: 6 Flyers
Phoenix: 7 Coyotes

Pittsburgh: **8** Penguins
St. Louis: **5** Blues
San Jose: **6** Sharks
Tampa Bay: **9** Lightning
Toronto: **10** Maple Leafs
Vancouver: **7** Canucks
Washington: **8** Capitals
Winnipeg: **4** Jets

nationalism
8 jingoism **10** chauvinism, patriotism

National League
Arizona: **12** Diamondbacks
Atlanta: **6** Braves
Chicago: **4** Cubs
Cincinnati: **4** Reds
Colorado: **7** Rockies
Florida: **7** Marlins
Houston: **6** Astros
Los Angeles: **7** Dodgers
Miami: **7** Marlins
Milwaukee: **7** Brewers
New York: **4** Mets
Philadelphia: **8** Phillies
Pittsburgh: **7** Pirates
St. Louis: **9** Cardinals
San Diego: **6** Padres
San Francisco: **6** Giants
Washington: **9** Nationals

national military park
Alabama: **13** Horseshoe Bend
Arkansas: **8** Pea Ridge
Mississippi: **9** Vicksburg
Pennsylvania: **10** Gettysburg
South Carolina: **13** Kings Mountain
Tennessee: **6** Shiloh

national monument
Alabama: **11** Russell Cave
Alaska: **9** Aniakchak
Arizona: **5** Tonto **6** Navajo **7** Saguaro, Wupatki **8** Tuzigoot **10** Chiricahua, Pipe Spring, Tumacacori **11** Hohokam Pima **12** Sunset Crater, Walnut Canyon
California: **8** Cabrillo, Lava Beds **9** Muir Woods, Pinnacles **10** Joshua Tree **11** Death Valley
Colorado: **10** Yucca House
Colorado-Utah: **8** Dinosaur **9** Hovenweep
Florida: **12** Fort Matanzas **13** Fort Jefferson
Georgia: **8** Ocmulgee **11** Fort Pulaski **13** Fort Frederica
Iowa: **12** Effigy Mounds
Louisiana: **12** Poverty Point
Maryland: **11** Fort McHenry
Minnesota: **9** Pipestone **12** Grand Portage
Nebraska: **9** Homestead **11** Scotts Bluff
New Mexico: **5** Pecos **7** El Morro **9** Bandelier, El Malpais, Fort Union **10** Aztec Ruins, White Sands
New York: **11** Fort Stanwix **13** Castle Clinton
South Carolina: **10** Fort Sumter **13** Congaree Swamp
South Dakota: **9** Jewel Cave
Utah: **11** Cedar Breaks **13** Rainbow Bridge
Wyoming: **11** Devils Tower, Fossil Butte

national park
Alaska: **6** Denali, Katmai **9** Lake Clark **10** Glacier Bay **11** Kenai Fjords, Kobuk Valley
Angola: **4** Iona, Mupa
Arizona: **11** Grand Canyon
Arkansas: **10** Hot Springs
Botswana: **5** Chobe
California: **7** Redwood, Sequoia **8** Yosemite **11** King's Canyon
Chad: **5** Manda
Colombia: **5** Uraba
Colorado: **9** Mesa Verde **13** Rocky Mountain
eastern Africa: **10** Mount Kenya
Florida: **8** Biscayne **10** Everglades
Hawaii: **9** Haleakala
India: **5** Kanha
Japan: **5** Nikko
Kentucky: **11** Mammoth Cave
Kenya: **4** Meru **5** Tsavo **10** Royal Tsavo
Lake Superior: **10** Isle Royale
Maine: **6** Acadia
Malaysia: **8** Kinabalu
Minnesota: **9** Voyageurs
Montana: **7** Glacier
Nevada: **10** Great Basin
Oregon: **10** Crater Lake
Poland: **5** Ojcow, Tatra
South Africa: **6** Kruger
South Dakota: **8** Badlands, Wind Cave
Sri Lanka: **4** Yala
Sweden: **5** Sarek
Tanzania: **5** Ruaha **9** Serengeti
Texas: **7** Big Bend
Utah: **4** Zion **6** Arches **11** Bryce Canyon, Canyonlands, Capitol Reef
Virginia: **10** Shenandoah
Washington: **7** Olympic **12** Mount Rainier **13** North Cascades
Wyoming: **10** Grand Teton
Wyoming-Idaho-Montana: **11** Yellowstone
Zambia: **5** Kafue
Zimbabwe: **13** Rhodes Inyanga, Victoria Falls

National Velvet author Bagnold
4 Enid

native
3 raw **4** wild **5** local **6** inborn, innate **7** connate, endemic, natural **8** domestic, indigene, inherent, internal, national **9** inherited **10** aboriginal, congenital, connatural, indigenous, unacquired
Acadian Louisiana: **5** Cajun
Arizona: **4** Hopi, Pima
China: **3** Han **9** Celestial
group: **5** tribe

India: **5** sepoy
Japan: **4** Ainu **9** Nipponese
London: **7** Cockney
Mexico: **4** Maya **5** Mayan
Mindanao: **3** Ata
New England: **4** Yank **6** Yankee
New Mexico: **4** Zuni
New York: **13** Knickerbocker
New Zealand: **5** Maori
Peruvian: **4** Inca

Native American
see **Indian, American**

Native Son author
6 Wright (Richard)

Nativity
4 Noel, Xmas, yule **8** yuletide **9** Christmas
scene: **6** crèche

nativity
5 birth, start **6** origin, outset **7** genesis **8** delivery **9** beginning, horoscope, inception **11** parturition

natter
3 gab, jaw, yak, yap **4** blab, buzz, chat, go on **5** prate, run on **6** babble, gabble, gossip, jabber, tattle **7** blather, chatter, prattle, twaddle **8** chitchat, converse

natty
4 neat, tidy, trim **5** doggy, nobby, sassy, smart, swank **6** classy, dapper, jaunty, snazzy, spiffy, spruce, sprucy, swanky **7** bandbox, doggish, stylish **9** turned out **11** well-groomed

natural
4 pure, wild **5** naive, usual **6** candid, inborn, innate, native, normal, simple **7** artless, connate, organic **8** homespun, inherent, innocent **9** childlike, ingenuous, ingrained, primitive **10** congenital, indigenous, legitimate, unaffected **11** commonplace, instinctive, spontaneous

naturalist
American: **4** Muir (John) **5** Gould (Stephen Jay), Hyatt (Alpheus) **6** Carson (Rachel), Wilson (Edward O.) **7** Agassiz (Louis), Audubon (John James), Thoreau (H. D.), Verrill (Addison, Alpheus) **9** Burroughs (John)
English: **3** Ray (John) **5** White (Gilbert) **6** Darwin (Charles) **7** Wallace (Alfred Russel) **10** Williamson (William)
French: **5** Fabre (Jean-Henri) **7** Lamarck (Chevalier de), Réaumur (René-Antoine)
German: **8** Humboldt (Alexander von)
Scottish: **6** Wilson (Alexander) **10** Richardson (John)

nature
3 ilk, way **4** kind, sort, type **6** makeup, manner, stripe, temper **7** essence, scenery **8** creation, tendency, universe **9** character, landscape **10** complexion **11** description, disposition, personality, temperament **12** constitution

naught
3 nil, nix, zip **4** love, nada, zero **5** zilch **6** cipher **7** nothing, nullity **8** goose egg **11** nothingness

naughty
3 bad **4** lewd, racy **5** bawdy **6** unruly, ribald, risqué, smutty, vulgar **7** froward, obscene, raunchy, wayward, willful **8** contrary, improper, perverse, rascally **10** ill-behaved **11** disobedient, mischievous **12** obstreperous, recalcitrant

Nauru
capital: **5** Yaren
former name: **8** Pleasant (Island)

nauseate
5 repel **6** offend, sicken **7** disgust, repulse

nauseated
6 queasy **7** carsick **8** qualmish **9** disgusted, squeamish **10** grossed out

nauseating
5 gross **6** putrid **7** noisome **9** loathsome, offensive, repellant, repugnant, repulsive, revolting, sickening **10** disgusting

Nausicaa
father: **8** Alcinous
mother: **5** Arete

nautical
5 naval **6** marine **7** oceanic **8** maritime, seagoing **12** navigational
direction: **3** aft **4** alee **5** abaft, aport **6** astern
instrument: **3** aba **7** compass, pelorus, sextant **9** astrolabe

nautical "Halt!"
5 Avast

Nautilus skipper
4 Nemo

Navajo dwelling
5 hogan

naval hero
5 Dewey (George), Drake (Francis), Jones (John Paul), Perry (Matthew, Oliver Hazard) **6** Nelson (Horatio) **8** Farragut (David, George), Lawrence (James)

naval officer
3 adm., ens. **4** capt. **6** ensign **7** admiral, captain

navel
6 middle **7** nombril **8** omphalos **9** umbilicus **11** belly button
combining form: **6** omphal **7** omphalo
type: **5** innie, outie

navigate
4 helm, plot, sail **5** guide, pilot, steer **6** cruise **8** maneuver, traverse

navigation
8 piloting **10** seamanship **12** helmsmanship

navigational system
5 loran **6** shoran
navigator
5 flyer, pilot **6** airman **7** copilot
Danish: 6 Bering (Vitus)
Dutch: 6 Tasman (Abel) **7** Barents (Willem)
English: 4 Cook (Captain James) **5** Cabot (John, Sebastian), Drake (Francis) **6** Hudson (Henry) **7** Gilbert (Humphrey), Raleigh (Walter) **9** Vancouver (George)
French: 7 Cartier (Jacques) **9** La Perouse (Comte de)
Italian: 6 Caboto (Giovanni) **8** Columbus (Christopher), Vespucci (Amerigo) **9** Verrazano (Giovanni) **10** Verrazzano (Giovanni)
Norwegian: 4 Eric (the Red), Erik (the Red) **8** Ericsson (Leif), Eriksson (Leif) **12** Leif Ericsson, Leif Eriksson
Portuguese: 4 Dias (Bartolomeu, Dinis) **6** Cabral (Pedro Alvares), da Gama (Vasco) **8** Magellan (Ferdinand)
Spanish: 9 Fernández (Juan)
navy
4 blue **5** fleet **6** argosy, armada **8** flotilla
officer: 3 adm., ens. **4** capt. **6** ensign **7** admiral, captain **9** commander **10** lieutenant
Nazi
9 Hitlerite **10** brownshirt
admiral: 6 Dönitz (Karl), Raeder (Erich) **7** Doenitz (Karl)
air force: 9 Luftwaffe
armed forces: 9 Wehrmacht
cheer: 8 Siegheil
collaborator: 5 Laval (Pierre) **8** Quisling (Vidkun)
concentration camp: 6 Belsen, Dachau **9** Auschwitz, Treblinka **10** Buchenwald, Nordhausen
field marshal: 5 Model (Walter) **6** Keitel (Wilhelm), Paulus (Friedrich), Rommel (Erwin) **9** Rundstedt (Karl von) **10** Kesselring (Albert)
greeting: 4 heil **10** heil Hitler
leader: 3 Ley (Robert) **4** Hess (Rudolf), Röhm (Ernst) **5** Roehm (Ernst) **6** Führer, Göring (Hermann), Hitler (Adolf) **7** Fuehrer, Goering (Hermann), Himmler (Heinrich) **8** Goebbels (Joseph), Heydrich (Reinhard) **9** Rosenberg (Alfred)
police: 7 Gestapo
propagandist: 8 Goebbels (Joseph)
submarine: 5 U-boat
surrender signer: 4 Jodl (Alfred) **6** Keitel (Wilhelm)
symbol: 6 fylfot **8** swastika
tactic: 10 blitzkrieg
tank: 6 Panzer
NBC satire show
3 SNL
NCO
3 cpl, SFC, sgt **8** corporal, sergeant
neap
3 low **4** tide
near
4 nigh **5** about, circa, close, local, round **6** almost, around, at hand **7** close by, close on **8** adjacent, approach **9** immediate, proximate **11** approximate
nearby
4 nigh **5** about, aside, close, handy **6** around, beside **8** adjacent **9** adjoining, proximate **10** contiguous, convenient **11** neighboring
nearest
4 next **7** closest **8** adjacent, next-door, proximal **9** proximate **10** contiguous
nearly
4 nigh **6** all but, almost, next to **9** virtually
nearsighted
6 myopic
neat
4 deft, nice, prim, snug, tidy, trig, trim **5** clean, clear, kempt **6** bovine, cattle, clever, smooth, spruce **7** orderly, precise, unmixed **8** straight, well-kept **9** shipshape, undiluted **10** methodical, systematic **11** spic-and-span, uncluttered, well-groomed **12** spick-and-span **13** unadulterated
neato
3 fab **4** cool, keen **5** nifty **6** groovy, peachy **7** awesome
neb
3 tip **4** beak, bill, nose, prow **5** snoot, snout **9** proboscis
Nebraska
capital: 7 Lincoln
city: 5 Omaha
college, university: 9 Creighton
nickname: 10 Cornhusker (State)
river: 6 Platte **8** Missouri
state bird: 10 meadowlark
state flower: 9 goldenrod
state tree: 10 cottonwood
Nebraskan tribe
3 Oto **4** Otoe
nebula
6 galaxy
nebulous
4 hazy **5** vague **6** cloudy, turbid **7** clouded, obscure, unclear **9** ambiguous, amorphous, uncertain **10** indefinite, indistinct **13** indeterminate
necessary
5 basic, vital **6** needed **7** crucial, needful **8** cardinal, integral, required **9** de rigueur, essential, mandatory, requisite **10** compulsory, imperative, inevitable, obligatory, undeniable **11** fundamental, ineluctable, inescapable,

unavoidable **12** all-important, prerequisite **13** indispensable

necessitate
5 cause, exact, force **6** compel, demand, entail **7** call for, involve, require **8** occasion

necessity
4 must, need **6** crisis, duress **7** poverty **8** exigency **9** essential, privation, requisite **10** compulsion, desiderata (plural), imperative, obligation, sine qua non **11** desideratum, dire straits, needfulness, requirement **12** precondition, prerequisite

neck
3 pet **4** kiss **5** scrag, spoon **6** fondle, smooch
back of: 4 nape **5** nucha, nuque **6** scruff
ornament: 6 gorget, torque

necklace
5 chain **6** choker **7** rivière **8** carcanet
floral: 3 lei

necktie
4 bolo **10** four-in-hand

neckwear
3 boa, tie **5** ascot, scarf **6** cravat

necrology
4 obit **8** obituary

necromancy
4 juju, mojo **5** magic, obeah, vodun **6** hoodoo, voodoo **7** devilry, sorcery **8** witchery, wizardry **9** conjuring, diabolism, magicking **10** black magic, witchcraft **11** bewitchment, conjuration, enchantment, incantation, thaumaturgy

necropolis
8 boneyard, boot hill, cemetery, God's acre **9** graveyard **10** churchyard **12** memorial park, potter's field

necropsy
7 anatomy, autopsy **10** dissection, postmortem

née
4 born **8** formerly **10** originally

need
3 use **4** call, duty, lack, must, want **5** crave **6** demand, devoir, hunger, penury, thirst **7** poverty, require **8** distress, exigency, occasion, shortage **9** indigence, necessity, privation, requisite **10** compulsion, deficiency, obligation **11** deprivation, destitution, requirement

neediness
4 want **6** penury **7** poverty **9** essential, indigence, privation **11** deprivation, destitution **13** insufficiency

needle
3 rib **5** annoy, tease **6** harass, pester, plague **7** bedevil, hagride, obelisk, pricker, syringe **10** hypodermic
case: 4 etui
hole: 3 eye

needlefish
3 gar **8** pipefish

needlelike
7 styloid **8** belonoid
part: 7 acicula

needlepoint
4 lace **7** alençon, crochet, tatting **8** bargello **10** embroidery **11** cross-stitch

needlework
4 lace **6** sewing **7** alençon, crochet, sampler, tatting **8** bargello, knitting **9** stitching **10** crocheting, embroidery **11** cross-stitch

needy
4 poor **5** broke **6** hard up **8** beggared, dirt-poor, indigent, strapped **9** destitute, penniless, penurious **10** down-and-out **11** impecunious, necessitous **12** impoverished

ne'er-do-well
3 bum, dud **5** loser **6** loafer, no-good **7** failure, wastrel **8** derelict, fainéant **9** shiftless **10** profligate, scapegrace

Neeson of film
4 Liam

nefarious
4 evil, vile **6** savage, wicked **7** heinous, impious, noxious **8** depraved, dreadful, flagrant, infamous, perverse **9** execrable, miscreant, monstrous, offensive **10** abominable, degenerate, detestable, iniquitous, outrageous, villainous **11** opprobrious **13** reprehensible

negate
4 deny, undo, void **5** annul, belie, quash, rebut **6** cancel, impugn, refute, vacate **7** abolish, gainsay, nullify, redress, vitiate **8** abrogate, disallow, disprove, overturn, traverse **9** cancel out, disaffirm, repudiate **10** contradict, contravene, counteract, invalidate, neutralize

negative
3 nay, nix **4** deny, kill, veto **5** annul, cross, minus **6** impugn **7** adverse, gainsay, nullify, redress, refusal **8** abrogate, disprove, traverse **9** cancel out, frustrate **10** contradict, contravene, counteract, invalidate, neutralize **11** detrimental, unfavorable
battery terminal: 5 anode
French: 3 non
German: 4 nein
ion: 5 anion
Russian: 4 nyet
Scottish: 3 nae
sign: 5 minus
vote: 3 nay

neglect
4 fail, omit **5** let go, shirk **6** forget, ignore, laxity, slight **7** failure, laxness **8** omission, overlook, overpass, pass over **9** avoidance, disregard,

oversight, pretermit **10** negligence **11** dereliction, inattention **12** carelessness

neglectful
see **negligent**

negligee
4 gown **5** teddy **7** chemise, nightie **8** camisole, peignoir **9** nightgown

negligent
3 lax **5** slack **6** remiss **8** careless, derelict, heedless **9** forgetful, imprudent **10** delinquent, neglectful, nonchalant, regardless, unthinking **11** inattentive, pococurante, unconcerned **13** irresponsible, lackadaisical

negligible
4 puny, slim **5** minor, petty, small **6** meager, meagre, minute, remote, paltry, skimpy, slight **7** minimal, slender, trivial **8** nugatory, picayune, trifling **9** minuscule **11** meaningless, unimportant **13** imperceptible, insignificant

negotiable
8 passable **11** convertible **12** transferable

negotiate
4 cash **6** confer, dicker, hurdle, manage, parley, settle **7** arrange, bargain, develop, mediate, work out, wrangle **8** contract, covenant, moderate, surmount, transact, transfer **9** arbitrate **10** horse-trade

Negri of early film
4 Pola

neigh
6 nicker, whinny

neighbor
4 abut **5** flank, frame, skirt, touch **6** adjoin, border **7** abutter **8** border on

neighborhood
4 area, nabe, turf, ward **5** block, range **6** barrio, parish **8** district, environs, locality, precinct, purlieus, vicinage, vicinity **9** community, proximity

neighborly
6 genial **7** amiable, cordial, helpful **8** amicable, friendly, obliging, sociable **9** congenial **10** gregarious, hospitable **11** considerate, cooperative, good-natured **13** accommodating

nematode
4 worm **7** eelworm **9** roundworm

Nemean predator
4 lion

nemesis
4 bane, doom **5** curse, enemy, rival **7** avenger, scourge **8** opponent **9** bête noire **11** retribution

Neo portrayer
5 Keanu (Reeves)

neologism
7 coinage, new word

neonate
4 baby **6** infant **7** newborn **8** nursling

neophyte
4 tyro **6** newbie, novice, rookie **7** convert **8** beginner

Neoptolemus
7 Pyrrhus
father: **8** Achilles
slayer: **7** Orestes
victim: **5** Priam
wife: **8** Hermione

neoteric
6 modern, recent

Nepal
capital: **8** Katmandu **9** Kathmandu
city: **7** Pokhara **8** Lalitpur
monetary unit: **5** rupee
mountain, range: **7** Everest **8** Himalaya **9** Himalayan, Himalayas **10** Dhaulagiri **11** Gauri Sankar **12** Kanchenjunga
neighbor: **5** China, India
river: **6** Ganges

nepenthe
6 opiate, potion **7** anodyne **8** lenitive, narcotic, oblivion **9** analgesic **10** anesthetic, painkiller **11** anaesthetic

Nephthys
brother, husband: **3** Set **4** Seth

nepotism
10 favoritism, partiality

Neptune
6 planet
satellite: **6** Nereid, Triton
(see also **Poseidon**)

nerd
4 dork, drip, geek, wonk **5** dweeb **6** misfit, weenie **7** egghead, nebbish, oddball **10** pointy-head

Nereid
5 nymph **6** Thetis **7** Galatea **8** sea nymph **10** Amphitrite
father: **6** Nereus
mother: **5** Doris

Nereus
daughters: **8** Nereides
emblem: **7** trident
father: **6** Pontus
mother: **4** Gaea
wife: **5** Doris

Nergal
brother: **5** Nanna **6** Ninazu
father: **5** Enlil
mother: **6** Ninlil

Nero
birthplace: **4** Rome
mother: **9** Agrippina

predecessor: **8** Claudius
successor: **5** Galba
tutor: **6** Seneca
victim: **5** Lucan **6** Seneca **7** Octavia, Poppaea **9** Agrippina
wife: **7** Octavia, Poppaea

Nero Wolfe creator
5 Stout (Rex)

nerve
4 face, gall, grit, guts **5** brass, cheek, crust, heart, moxie, pluck, spunk **6** daring, mettle **7** sciatic **8** audacity, backbone, boldness, chutzpah, temerity **9** assurance, brashness, fortitude, hardihood, hardiness **10** confidence, effrontery **11** presumption
cell: **6** neuron
cell group: **7** ganglia (plural) **8** ganglion
cell part: **4** axon **8** dendrite, receptor
combining form: **4** neur **5** neura, neuro
cranial: **4** vagi (plural) **5** optic, vagus **8** abducens
lesion: **8** neuritis
network: **4** rete

nerve center
3 hub **4** core, seat **5** focus, heart, locus, nexus **7** capital **8** cynosure, polestar **10** crossroads, focal point **12** headquarters

nerve gas
5 sarin, soman, tabun

nervous
4 edgy **5** antsy, jerky, jumpy, tense, timid **6** fitful, goosey, on edge, spooky, uneasy **7** erratic, fidgety, fretful, jittery, restive, twitchy, uptight **8** aflutter, agitated, skittery, skittish, spirited, twittery, unsteady, vigorous, volatile **9** excitable, irritable **10** high-strung **12** apprehensive
twitch: **3** tic

nervy
4 bold, edgy, flip, pert **5** brash, cocky, fresh, jerky, jumpy, sassy, tense **6** brassy, cheeky, goosey, plucky, uneasy **7** fidgety, forward, jittery, restive, twitchy, uptight **8** flippant, impudent, intrepid, twittery **9** excitable **10** high-strung **11** smart-alecky

nescience
9 ignorance

ness
4 cape **8** foreland, headland **9** peninsula **10** promontory

Ness, e.g.
4 T-man

Nessus' victim
8 Heracles, Hercules

nest
3 den **4** aery, home, lair, nidi (plural) **5** aerie, eyrie, nidus **7** hangout, shelter **11** aggregation
eagle's: **4** aery **5** aerie, eyrie
pheasant's: **4** nide
resident: **4** eyas
wasp's: **8** vespiary

nest egg
5 cache, funds, hoard, kitty, stash **6** assets **7** reserve, savings

nest-egg savings option
3 IRA **7** Roth IRA

nestle
4 snug **6** bundle, burrow, cuddle, huddle, nuzzle **7** snuggle

nestling
4 eyas

Nestor
father: **6** Neleus
kingdom: **5** Pylos

net
3 web **4** gain, gist, mesh **5** basic, catch, clear, seine, tulle, yield **6** maline **7** clean up, essence, malines, trammel
conical: **5** trawl
fishing: **5** seine
hair: **5** snood

nether
3 low **4** down **5** below, lower, under **6** lesser **8** chthonic, inferior **9** subjacent **10** underworld **11** underground **12** subterranean

Netherlands
7 Holland
capital: **9** Amsterdam
city: **5** Hague (The) **7** Utrecht **8** The Hague **9** Rotterdam
former inlet: **9** Zuider Zee
island group: **11** West Frisian
lake: **10** IJsselmeer
language: **5** Dutch
monetary unit: **4** euro
monetary unit, former: **6** gulden, stiver **7** guilder
neighbor: **7** Belgium, Germany
river: **4** Maas **5** Meuse, Rhein, Rhine **7** Scheldt
sea: **5** North

Netherlands Antilles
capital: **10** Willemstad
discoverer: **8** Columbus (Christopher)
former name: **7** Curaçao
island: **4** Saba **7** Bonaire **7** Curaçao
location: **10** West Indies

netherworld
3 pit **4** hell **5** abyss, hades, Sheol **6** blazes, Tophet **7** Gehenna, inferno **8** hellfire **9** perdition **10** no-man's-land, underworld **11** underground

netlike
9 reticular **10** reticulate

nettle
3 Irk, nag, vex **4** gall, huff, rlle, roll **5** annoy, chafe, peeve, pique, upset **6** abrade, badger, harass, incite, put out, pester, ruffle, stir up **7** agitate, disturb, perturb, provoke **8** irritate **10** exasperate

nettle rash
5 hives **9** urticaria

nettlesome
5 pesky **6** vexing **7** galling, irksome, prickly **8** annoying, rankling **9** irritable, upsetting, vexatious **10** irritating

network
3 ABC, CBS, CNN, CTV, Fox, HBO, NBC, PBS, QVC, TBS, TNT, web **4** ESPN, grid, INHD, mesh, NESN, rete **7** complex **8** gridiron, Internet **9** reticulum, Telemundo, Univision
anatomical: **4** rete **5** retia (plural)

neurotic
6 phobic, touchy **7** anxious, nervous **8** abnormal, unstable **9** disturbed, obsessive **10** compulsive, disordered

neuter
3 fix **4** geld, spay **5** alter, desex, unsex **7** sexless **8** castrate, mutilate **9** sterilize **10** genderless **11** desexualize **12** intransitive

neutral
7 hueless **8** detached, middling, unbiased **9** colorless, impartial, unaligned **10** achromatic, disengaged, evenhanded, impersonal, nonaligned, pokerfaced **11** indifferent, nonpartisan **13** disinterested, dispassionate
shade: **4** buff, ecru **5** beige

neutralize
4 undo **5** annul **6** defang, disarm, negate, offset **7** balance, nullify, redress, reverse **9** cancel out **10** counteract, invalidate **11** countervail **12** countercheck, counterpoise

neutrino
6 lepton

Nevada
capital: **10** Carson City
city: **4** Elko, Reno **8** Las Vegas
dam: **6** Hoover **7** Boulder
lake: **4** Mead **5** Tahoe
mountain: **8** Boundary (Peak)
nickname: **6** Silver (State)
river: **8** Humboldt
state bird: **8** bluebird (mountain)
state flower: **9** sagebrush
state tree: **5** piñon **6** pinyon **15** bristlecone pine

névé
4 firn, snow

Nev. neighbor
3 Cal., Ida., Ore. **4** Ariz. **5** Calif.

never-ending
7 eternal **8** constant, enduring, immortal **9** ceaseless, permanent, perpetual **11** everlasting

Never-Ending Story author
4 Ende (Michael)

nevertheless
3 but, yet **5** still **6** anyhow, anyway, even so, though, withal **7** howbeit, however **8** after all **10** regardless **11** still and all

nevus
4 mole **9** birthmark

new
5 fresh, novel **6** modern, recent **7** another, nascent, revived **8** neoteric, original, pristine **9** fledgling **10** additional, unfamiliar **11** modernistic **12** contemporary
combining form: **3** neo, nov **4** novo
word: **7** coinage **9** neologism

New Age
belief: **5** karma **6** cabala, holism, kabala **7** kabbala **8** kabbalah **9** occultism, pantheism, shamanism, theosophy, wholeness **10** numerology, soul travel **12** spiritualism **13** reincarnation, synchronicity
community: **6** Esalen, Sedona, Totnes **7** Dornach **8** Byron Bay, Damanhur, Findhorn **9** Arcosanti, Auroville
healing technique: **5** auras **8** Ayurveda, crystals **9** iridology **10** homeopathy **11** acupressure, acupuncture, biofeedback **12** aromatherapy
musician: **3** Eno (Brian) **5** Yanni
practice: **4** yoga **5** reiki **7** fasting **10** channeling, meditation, syncretism
singer: **4** Enya
teacher: **3** Orr (Leonard) **4** Long (Barry), Myss (Caroline) **5** Cohen (Andrew) **6** Chopra (Deepak), Walsch (Neale Donald), Wilber (Ken) **7** Kabbani (Hisham), Quanjer (Johan), Ram Dass **8** Cottrell (Douglas James), Rajneesh (Bhagwan Shree), Spangler (David) **9** Castaneda (Carlos), Helminski (Kabir) **10** Williamson (Marianne)

newborn
6 infant **7** neonate

New Brunswick
capital: **11** Fredericton
city: **6** St. John **7** Moncton
mountain: **8** Carleton
provincial flower: **12** purple violet
river: **9** Miramichi, Saint John **10** Nepisiguit **11** Restigouche

New Caledonia
capital: **6** Nouméa
department of: **6** France
discoverer: **4** Cook (Capt. James)
island: **7** Loyalty, Walpole **11** Isle of Pines

newcomer
4 colt, tiro, tyro **6** novice, rookie **7** trainee **8** beginner, freshman, initiate, neophyte **9** greenhorn, immigrant, novitiate **10** apprentice, tenderfoot

New Deal
agency: 3 CCC, NRA, REA, RFC, SEC, TVA, WPA **4** FDIC, NLRB
initials: 3 FDR

New England catch
3 cod **5** scrod

New England footballers
4 Pats **8** Patriots

Newfoundland and Labrador
capital: 7 St. John's
mountain: 8 Caubvick
provincial flower: 12 pitcher plant
river: 6 Gander **8** Exploits **9** Churchill

New Hampshire
capital: 7 Concord
city: 6 Nashua **10** Manchester, Portsmouth
college, university: 9 Dartmouth
motto: 13 Live Free or Die
mountain, range: 5 White **10** Washington
nickname: 7 Granite (State)
river: 9 Merrimack **11** Connecticut
state bird: 11 purple finch
state flower: 11 purple lilac
state tree: 10 white birch

New Haven student
3 Eli **5** Yalie

New Jersey
capital: 7 Trenton
city: 6 Camden, Newark **7** Cape May **8** Paterson **9** Elizabeth **10** Jersey City
college, university: 4 Drew **7** Rutgers **9** Princeton, Seton Hall
nickname: 6 Garden (State)
river: 6 Hudson **7** Raritan **8** Delaware
state bird: 9 goldfinch
state flower: 6 violet
state tree: 6 red oak

New Mexico
capital: 7 Santa Fe
caverns: 8 Carlsbad
city: 4 Taos **7** Roswell **9** Las Cruces, Los Alamos **10** Farmington **11** Albuquerque
mountain, range: 7 Wheeler (Peak) **14** Sangre de Cristo
nickname: 17 Land of Enchantment
river: 5 Pecos **9** Rio Grande
state bird: 10 roadrunner
state flower: 5 yucca
state tree: 5 piñon **6** pinyon

new prefix
3 neo

news
4 dope, info, poop, word **5** rumor **6** advice, gossip, report, skinny, tattle **7** lowdown, tidings **9** knowledge, speerings **11** information, scuttlebutt **12** announcement, intelligence
agency: 3 AFP, UPI **4** TASS **7** Reuters **8** ITAR-TASS

newspaper
3 rag **5** daily, organ **6** review **7** gazette, journal, tabloid **10** periodical
goof: 4 typo
publisher: 4 Ochs (Adolph) **6** Hearst (William Randolph) **7** Murdoch (Rupert), Scripps (E. W.) **11** Beaverbrook (Lord)
section: 4 arts, op-ed, roto **6** comics, sports **8** business **10** classified

newt
3 eft **6** triton
green: 5 ebbet

New Testament
see at **Bible**

New Year's word
4 Auld

New York
capital: 6 Albany
city: 4 Rome, Troy **5** Utica **6** Elmira, Ithaca **7** Buffalo, Yonkers **8** Saratoga, Syracuse **9** Rochester
college, university: 3 RPI **4** Pace, CUNY, SUNY **5** Pratt, Siena **6** CW Post, Hunter, Vassar **7** Adelphi, Barnard, Colgate, Cornell, Fordham, Hofstra, St. Johns, Yeshiva **8** Columbia, Skidmore, Syracuse **9** Juilliard, West Point **13** Sarah Lawrence
county: 5 Tioga **6** Albany, Oneida, Queens **7** Clinton, Niagara **8** Dutchess, Onandaga
island: 4 Fire, Long **5** Coney **6** Staten **9** Manhattan
lake, lake group: 4 Erie **6** Cayuga, Finger, Oneida **7** Saranac **9** Champlain
motto: 9 Excelsior
mountain, range: 5 Marcy **8** Catskill **10** Adirondack
nickname: 6 Empire (State)
prison: 6 Attica
river: 6 Hudson **7** Niagara **10** St. Lawrence
state bird: 8 bluebird
state flower: 4 rose
state tree: 10 sugar maple

New York baseballers, for short
5 Yanks

New York City
6 Gotham **8** Big Apple
borough: 5 Bronx **6** Queens **8** Brooklyn, Richmond **9** Manhattan **12** Staten Island

mayor: **4** Koch (Ed) **5** Beame (Abe) **9** Bloomberg (Michael), La Guardia (Fiorello)
neighborhood: **4** Soho **6** Harlem **7** Tribeca

New York Times dynasty
4 Ochs **10** Sulzberger

New Zealand
capital: **10** Wellington
city: **8** Auckland **12** Christchurch
ethnic group: **5** Maori
evergreen: **4** tawa
explorer: **4** Cook (Capt. James) **6** Tasman (Abel)
island: **7** Chatham, Stewart
island group: **4** Cook **8** Manihiki **12** Northern Cook
lake: **5** Taupo
language: **5** Maori
mountain, range: **4** Cook **6** Egmont **12** Southern Alps
native: **4** Kiwi **5** Maori
parrot: **3** kea **4** kaka
shrub: **4** tutu
strait: **4** Cook
volcano: **7** Ruapehu **9** Ngauruhoe

next
4 then **5** after, later **6** behind, beside, second **7** closest, ensuing, nearest **8** abutting, adjacent, touching **9** adjoining, afterward, alongside, following, proximate **10** contiguous, subsequent, succeeding **11** neighboring

next to
4 near **6** almost, beside **7** abreast, close by **8** abutting, adjacent, opposite, touching **9** adjoining, alongside, bordering **11** neighboring

nexus
3 tie **4** bond, knot, link, yoke **5** focus, joint **6** center, linkup **7** linkage **8** ligament, ligature, vinculum **10** connection

Nez Percé chief
6 Joseph

Niagara
5 flood, spate **6** deluge **7** torrent **8** alluvion, cataract, flooding, overflow **9** cataclysm, waterfall **10** inundation

nib
3 tip **4** beak, bill, nose, prow **5** prong, snoot, snout, tooth **8** pen point **9** proboscis

nibble
3 eat, nip **4** bite, chew, crop, gnaw, nosh, peck, pick **5** graze, munch, snack, taste **6** morsel, tidbit

Nicaragua
capital: **7** Managua
city: **4** León **6** Masaya **7** Grenada
coast: **8** Mosquito
ethnic group: **4** Maya **5** Mayan
discoverer: **8** Columbus (Christopher)
language: **7** Spanish
monetary unit: **7** córdoba
neighbor: **8** Honduras **9** Costa Rica
sea: **9** Caribbean

nice
4 fine, good, kind, mild, neat **5** right **6** benign, decent, polite, proper, seemly **7** affable, cordial, correct, fitting, refined **8** becoming, charming, decorous, obliging, pleasant, pleasing, suitable, virtuous, well-bred **9** admirable, agreeable, courteous, congenial, enjoyable, favorable **10** attractive, personable **11** appropriate, respectable

niche
4 nook **6** alcove, corner, cranny, recess **7** calling **8** vocation **9** cubbyhole **11** compartment

Nicholas Nickleby author
7 Dickens (Charles)

nick
3 cut **4** chip, gash **5** cheat, graze, notch, score **6** groove, record **10** overcharge **11** indentation

Nick and Nora's dog
4 Asta

nickname
3 tag **5** label **6** byword, handle **7** agnomen, epithet, moniker **8** cognomen **9** sobriquet **10** diminutive, hypocorism

Nicomede
conquest: **10** Cappodocia
dramatist: **9** Corneille (Pierre)
half-brother: **6** Attale
stepmother: **7** Arsinoë

nictitate
3 bat **4** wink **5** blink **7** flutter, twinkle

nifty
3 fab **4** cool, keen, neat **5** dandy, ducky, neato, super, swell **6** clever, groovy, peachy **7** stylish **8** jim-dandy, splendid, terrific **9** ingenious

Niger
capital: **6** Niamey
city: **6** Maradi, Zinder
desert: **5** Sahel **6** Sahara
ethnic group: **5** Hausa
language: **5** Hausa **6** Arabic, French
monetary unit: **5** franc
neighbor: **4** Chad, Mali **5** Benin, Libya **7** Algeria, Nigeria **11** Burkina Faso
river: **5** Niger

Nigeria
capital: **5** Abuja, Lagos
city: **4** Kano **6** Ibadan, Ilorin **7** Oshogbo **9** Ogbomosho
ethnic group: **3** Ibo **4** Igbo **5** Hausa **6** Fulani, Yoruba

gulf: **6** Guinea
lake: **4** Chad
language: **5** Hausa
monetary unit: **5** naira
neighbor: **4** Chad **5** Benin, Niger **8** Cameroon
river: **5** Benue, Niger **6** Kaduna

niggard
5 churl, miser, piker, screw **7** hoarder, scrooge **8** tightwad **9** skinflint **10** cheapskate, curmudgeon **12** money-grubber, penny-pincher

niggardly
5 tight **6** scanty, stingy **7** chintzy, miserly **9** penurious **10** begrudging **11** closefisted, tightfisted **12** cheeseparing, parsimonious **13** penny-pinching

niggling
5 minor, petty **6** measly, paltry, two-bit **7** trivial **8** picayune, piddling, tiresome, trifling **9** small-time **10** bothersome, picayunish **11** Mickey Mouse, small-minded

nigh
4 near **5** about, close, round **6** all but, almost, around, beside, nearby, nearly **7** close to **8** approach **9** immediate, just about, proximate, virtually **10** near at hand **11** practically

night before
3 eve

night blindness
10 nyctalopia

nightclub
5 boîte, disco **6** bistro, casino **7** cabaret **9** honky-tonk, speakeasy **11** discotheque

nightfall
3 e'en, eve **4** dusk, even **6** sunset **7** evening, sundown **8** eventide, gloaming, twilight

nighthawk
6 petrel **7** bullbat **10** goatsucker

nightjar
9 nighthawk **10** goatsucker **12** whip-poor-will

nightly
9 nocturnal

nightmare
5 dream, fancy, worry **6** fright, horror, ordeal, vision **7** bugbear, fantasy, incubus, torment **8** phantasm, phantasy, succubus **12** apprehension **13** hallucination

nightmare street of film
3 Elm

night-school subject
3 ESL

nightshade
6 tomato **7** henbane **8** eggplant **10** belladonna **11** bittersweet

nightstick
3 bat **4** club, mace **5** baton, billy, staff **6** cudgel **8** bludgeon **9** billy club, blackjack, shillalah, truncheon **10** shillelagh

Nike
father: **6** Pallas
goddess of: **7** victory
mother: **4** Styx

nil
3 nix, zip **4** love, nada, wind, zero **5** zilch **6** naught **7** nothing

Nile
6 Al-Bahr
dam: **5** Aswan **6** Makwar **10** Gebel Aulia
enclave: **4** Lado
explorer: **5** Baker (Sir Samuel), Bruce (James), Grant (James Augustus), Speke (John Hanning)
queen: **4** Cleo **9** Cleopatra
section: **4** Abay **5** Abbai
source lake: **4** Tana **8** Victoria

nilgai
8 antelope

nimbi
5 aurae, auras

nimble
4 deft, spry, yare **5** agile, alert, fleet, handy, light, quick, zippy **6** adroit, limber, lively **7** lissome **9** dexterous, sprightly **10** responsive **11** quick-witted

nimbus
4 aura, halo **5** glory **6** corona **7** aureole

Nimrod
6 hunter
father: **4** Cush

Nin, Anaïs
7 diarist
father: **7** Joaquin
friend: **6** Miller (Henry)

Ninazu
brother: **5** Nanna **6** Nergal
father: **5** Enlil
mother: **6** Ninlil

nincompoop
3 oaf **4** boob, clod, dodo, fool, goof, mutt, simp, twit, yo-yo **5** chump, dummy, dunce, idiot, moron, ninny, noddy, stupe **6** dimwit, donkey, dumdum, nitwit **7** airhead, dullard, pinhead, schnook, tomfool **8** bonehead, clodpoll, dumbbell, dumbhead, imbecile, lunkhead, meathead, numskull **9** birdbrain, blockhead, ignoramus, lamebrain, numbskull, simpleton, thickhead **10** dunderhead, hammerhead **11** chowderhead, chucklehead, knucklehead, ninnyhammer

nine
12 baseball team
combining form: **3** non **4** nona **5** ennea
goddesses: **5** Muses

group: **6** ennead
inches: **4** span
instruments: **5** nonet

nine-eyes
7 lamprey

Nine Worlds
3 Hel **6** Asgard **7** Alfheim, Midgard **8** Niflheim, Vanaheim **10** Jotunnheim **12** Muspellsheim **13** Svartalfaheim

ninny
see **nincompoop**

Ninsum's son
9 Gilgamesh

Nintendo
predecessor: **5** Atari
rival: **4** Sega

Nintu
consort: **4** Enki
son: **6** Ninsar

Ninurta
father: **5** Enlil
victim: **3** Kur

Ninus
father: **5** Belus
wife: **9** Semiramis

Niobe
6 weeper
brother: **6** Pelops
father: **8** Tantalus
husband: **7** Amphion
sister-in-law: **5** Aedon

nip
3 bit, nab, sip **4** bite, dart, dash, dram, drop, jolt, peck, shot, slug, swig **5** chill, clamp, hurry, pinch, sever, snort, steal **6** imbibe, snatch, thwart, tipple **7** cabbage, snifter, swallow **9** frustrate

nipper
3 kid **4** tike, tyke **5** child **6** moppet, shaver **7** pincers **9** youngling, youngster

nipple
3 pap **4** teat **7** mammila

Nippon
5 Japan

nippy
3 icy, raw **4** cold, cool **5** algid, chill, crisp, sharp **6** arctic, biting, bitter, chilly, frosty, wintry **7** caustic, glacial, numbing, shivery **8** chilling, freezing

nirvana
5 bliss, dream **6** heaven **7** Elysium, rapture **8** empyrean, euphoria, oblivion, paradise **9** Shangri-la

Nisus
betrayer, daughter: **6** Scylla
father: **7** Pandion

nitid
6 bright, glossy, lucent **7** fulgent, glowing, shining **8** gleaming, glinting, luminous, lustrous, polished **9** burnished

nitpick
4 carp **5** cavil **7** quibble **10** split hairs

nitpicker
6 carper, critic **7** niggler **8** quibbler

nitrogen
5 azote
combining form: **3** azo

nits
4 lice

nitty-gritty
4 core, gist, meat, pith **5** heart, stuff **6** burden, kernel **7** essence **9** substance **10** bottom line, brass tacks

nitwit
3 oaf **4** boob, clod, dodo, dolt, dope, goof, mutt, simp **5** chump, cluck, dummy, dunce, idiot, moron, ninny, noddy, stupe **6** donkey, dum-dum **7** airhead, dullard, pinhead, schnook **8** bonehead, clodpoll, dumbbell, imbecile, lunkhead, meathead, numskull **9** birdbrain, blockhead, ignoramus, lamebrain, numbskull, simpleton, thickhead **10** dunderhead, hammerhead, nincompoop **11** chowderhead, chucklehead, knucklehead

nix
3 nay, nil, zap **4** kill, nada, nope, veto, zero **5** quash **6** cancel, naught, reject, scotch, sprite **7** call off, nothing, nullify

Njord, Njorth
daughter: **5** Freya
son: **4** Frey
wife: **6** Skadhi, Skathi

no
3 nay, nix **4** uh-uh **6** denial **7** refusal **8** negative **10** thumbs-down
German: **4** nein
Russian: **4** nyet
Scottish: **3** nae

no-account
see **no-good**

Noachian
3 old **4** aged **5** fusty, hoary **6** age-old **7** ancient, antique, archaic **8** timeworn **9** venerable **10** antiquated, oldfangled **12** antediluvian, old-fashioned **13** superannuated

Noah
father: **6** Lamech **10** Zelophehad
grandson: **4** Aram **6** Canaan
great-grandson: **3** Hul
landing place: **6** Ararat
son: **3** Ham **4** Shem **6** Canaan **7** Japheth

Nobel Prize winner
chemistry:
1901: 8 van't Hoff (Jacobus)
1902: 7 Fischer (Emil)
1903: 9 Arrhenius (Svante)
1904: 6 Ramsay (William)
1905: 9 von Baeyer (Adolf)
1906: 7 Moissan (Henri)
1907: 7 Buchner (Eduard)
1908: 10 Rutherford (Ernest)
1909: 7 Ostwald (Wilhelm)
1910: 7 Wallach (Otto)
1911: 5 Curie (Marie)
1912: 8 Grignard (François), Sabatier (Paul)
1913: 6 Werner (Alfred)
1914: 8 Richards (Theodore)
1915: 11 Willstatter (Richard)
1918: 5 Haber (Fritz)
1920: 6 Nernst (Walther)
1921: 5 Soddy (Frederick)
1922: 5 Aston (Francis)
1923: 5 Pregl (Fritz)
1925: 9 Zsigmondy (Richard)
1926: 8 Svedberg (Theodor)
1927: 7 Wieland (Heinrich)
1928: 7 Windaus (Adolf)
1929: 6 Harden (Athur) **12** Euler-Chelpin (Hans von)
1930: 7 Fischer (Hans)
1931: 5 Bosch (Karl) **7** Bergius (Friedrich)
1932: 8 Langmuir (Irving)
1934: 4 Urey (Harold)
1935: 11 Joliot-Curie (Frédéric, Irene)
1936: 5 Debye (Peter)
1937: 6 Karrer (Paul) **7** Haworth (Walter)
1938: 4 Kuhn (Richard)
1939: 7 Ruzicka (Leopold) **9** Butenandt (Adolf)
1943: 6 Hevesy (Georg de)
1944: 4 Hahn (Otto)
1945: 8 Virtanen (Artturi)
1946: 6 Sumner (James) **7** Stanley (Wendell) **8** Northrop (John Howard)
1947: 8 Robinson (Robert)
1948: 8 Tiselius (Arne)
1949: 7 Giauque (William)
1950: 5 Alder (Kurt), Diels (Otto)
1951: 7 Seaborg (Glenn) **8** McMillan (Edwin)
1952: 5 Synge (Richard) **6** Martin (Archer)
1953: 10 Staudinger (Hermann)
1954: 7 Pauling (Linus)
1955: 10 du Vigneaud (Vincent)
1956: 7 Semenov (Nikolay) **11** Hinshelwood (Cyril)
1957: 4 Todd (Alexander)
1958: 6 Sanger (Frederick)
1959: 9 Heyrovsky (Jaroslav)
1960: 5 Libby (Willard)
1961: 6 Calvin (Melvin)
1962: 6 Perutz (Max) **7** Kendrew (John)
1963: 5 Natta (Giulio) **7** Ziegler (Karl)
1964: 7 Hodgkin (Dorothy) **8** Woodward (Robert)
1966: 8 Mulliken (Robert)
1967: 5 Eigen (Manfred) **6** Porter (George) **7** Norrish (Ronald)
1968: 7 Onsager (Lars)
1969: 6 Barton (Derek), Hassel (Odd)
1970: 6 Leloir (Luis)
1971: 8 Herzberg (Gerhard)
1972: 5 Moore (Stanford), Stein (William) **8** Anfinsen (Christian)
1973: 7 Fischer (Ernst) **9** Wilkinson (Geoffrey)
1974: 5 Flory (Paul)
1975: 6 Prelog (Vladimir) **9** Cornforth (John)
1976: 8 Lipscomb (William)
1977: 9 Prigogine (Ilya)
1978: 8 Mitchell (Peter)
1979: 5 Brown (Herbert) **6** Wittig (Georg)
1980: 4 Berg (Paul) **6** Sanger (Frederick) **7** Gilbert (Walter)
1981: 5 Fukui (Kenichi) **8** Hoffmann (Roald)
1982: 4 Klug (Aaron)
1983: 5 Taube (Henry)
1984: 10 Merrifield (R. Bruce)
1985: 5 Karle (Jerome) **8** Hauptman (Herbert)
1986: 3 Lee (Yuan) **7** Polanyi (John) **10** Herschbach (Dudley)
1987: 4 Cram (Donald), Lehn (Jean-Marie) **8** Pedersen (Charles)
1988: 5 Huber (Robert) **6** Michel (Hartmut) **11** Deisenhofer (Johann)
1989: 4 Cech (Thomas) **6** Altman (Sidney)
1990: 5 Corey (Elias)
1991: 5 Ernst (Richard)
1992: 6 Marcus (Rudolph)
1993: 5 Smith (Michael) **6** Mullis (Kary)
1994: 4 Olah (George)
1995: 6 Molina (Mario) **7** Crutzen (Paul), Rowland (F. Sherwood)
1996: 4 Curl (Robert) **5** Kroto (Harold) **7** Smalley (Richard)
1997: 4 Skou (Jens) **5** Boyer (Paul) **6** Walker (John)
1998: 4 Kohn (Walter) **5** Pople (John)
1999: 6 Zewail (Ahmed)
2000: 6 Heeger (Alan) **9** Shirakawa (Hideki) **10** MacDiarmid (Alan)
2001: 6 Noyori (Ryoji) **7** Knowles (William) **9** Sharpless (K. Barry)
2002: 4 Fenn (John) **6** Tanaka (Koichi) **8** Wüthrich (Kurt)
2003: 4 Agre (Peter) **9** MacKinnon (Roderick)
2004: 4 Rose (Irwin) **7** Hershko (Avram) **11** Ciechanover (Aaron)
2005: 6 Grubbs (Robert) **7** Chauvin (Yves), Schrock (Richard)

2006: 8 Kornberg (Roger)
2007: 4 Ertl (Gerhard)
2008: 5 Tsien (Roger) **7** Chalfie (Martin) **9** Shimomura (Osamu)
2009: 6 Steitz (Thomas), Yonath (Ada) **12** Ramakrishnan (Venkatraman)
2010: 4 Heck (Richard) **6** Suzuki (Akira) **7** Negishi (Ei-Ichi)
2011: 10 Schechtman (Dan)
2012: 7 Kobilka (Brian) **9** Lefkowitz (Robert)
2013: 6 Levitt (Michael) **7** Karplus (Martin), Warshel (Arieh)
2014: 4 Hell (Stefan) **6** Betzig (Eric) **7** Moerner (William)
2015: 6 Sancar (Aziz) **7** Lindahl (Tomas), Modrich (Paul)

economics:
1969: 6 Frisch (Ragnar) **9** Tinbergen (Jan)
1970: 9 Samuelson (Paul)
1971: 7 Kuznets (Simon)
1972: 5 Arrow (Kenneth), Hicks (John)
1973: 8 Leontief (Wassily)
1974: 5 Hayek (Friedrich von) **6** Myrdal (Gunnar)
1975: 8 Koopmans (Tjalling) **11** Kantorovich (Leonid)
1976: 8 Friedman (Milton)
1977: 5 Meade (James), Ohlin (Bertil)
1978: 5 Simon (Herbert)
1979: 5 Lewls (Arthur) **7** Schultz (Theodore)
1980: 5 Klein (Lawrence)
1981: 5 Tobin (James)
1982: 7 Stigler (George)
1983: 6 Debreu (Gerard)
1984: 5 Stone (Richard)
1985: 10 Modigliani (Franco)
1986: 8 Buchanan (James)
1987: 5 Solow (Robert)
1988: 6 Allais (Maurice)
1989: 8 Haavelmo (Trygve)
1990: 6 Miller (Merton), Sharpe (William) **9** Markowitz (Harry)
1991: 5 Coase (Ronald)
1992: 6 Becker (Gary)
1993: 5 Fogel (Robert), North (Douglass)
1994: 4 Nash (John) **6** Selten (Reinhard) **8** Harsanyi (John)
1995: 5 Lucas (Robert)
1996: 7 Vickrey (William) **8** Mirrlees (James)
1998: 3 Sen (Amartya)
1999: 7 Mundell (Robert)
2000: 7 Heckman (James) **8** McFadden (Daniel)
2001: 6 Spence (Michael) **7** Akerlof (George) **8** Stiglitz (Joseph)
2002: 5 Smith (Vernon) **8** Kahneman (Daniel)
2003: 5 Engle (Robert) **7** Granger (Clive)
2004: 7 Kydland (Finn) **8** Prescott (Edward)
2005: 6 Aumann (Robert) **9** Schelling (Thomas)
2006: 6 Phelps (Edmund)
2007: 6 Maskin (Eric) **7** Hurwicz (Leonid), Myerson (Roger)
2008: 7 Krugman (Paul)
2009: 6 Ostrom (Elinor) **10** Williamson (Oliver)
2010: 7 Diamond (Peter) **9** Mortensen (Dale) **10** Pissarides (Christopher)
2011: 4 Sims (Christopher) **7** Sargent (Thomas)
2012: 4 Roth (Alvin) **7** Shapley (Lloyd)
2013: 4 Fama (Eugene) **6** Hansen (Lars Peter) **7** Shiller (Robert)
2014: 6 Tirole (Jean)
2015: 6 Deaton (Angus)

literature:
1901: 9 Prudhomme (Sully)
1902: 7 Mommsen (Theodor)
1903: 8 Bjornson (Bjornstjerne)
1904: 7 Mistral (Frédéric) **9** Echegaray (José)
1905: 11 Sienkiewicz (Henryk)
1906: 8 Carducci (Giosue)
1907: 7 Kipling (Rudyard)
1908: 6 Eucken (Rudolf)
1909: 8 Lagerlof (Selma)
1910: 5 Heyse (Paul)
1911: 11 Maeterlinck (Maurice)
1912: 9 Hauptmann (Gerhart)
1913: 6 Tagore (Rabindranath)
1915: 7 Rolland (Romain)
1916: 10 Heidenstam (Verner von)
1917: 9 Gjellerup (Karl) **11** Pontoppidan (Henrik)
1919: 9 Spitteler (Carl)
1920: 6 Hamsun (Knut)
1921: 6 France (Anatole)
1922: 9 Benavente (Jacinto)
1923: 5 Yeats (William Butler)
1924: 7 Reymont (Wladyslaw)
1925: 4 Shaw (George Bernard)
1926: 7 Deledda (Grazia)
1927: 7 Bergson (Henri)
1928: 6 Undset (Sigrid)
1929: 4 Mann (Thomas)
1930: 5 Lewis (Sinclair)
1931: 9 Karlfeldt (Erik Axel)
1932: 10 Galsworthy (John)
1933: 5 Bunin (Ivan)
1934: 10 Pirandello (Luigi)
1936: 6 O'Neill (Eugene)
1937: 12 Martin du Gard (Roger)
1938: 4 Buck (Pearl)
1939: 9 Sillanpää (Frans Eemil)
1944: 6 Jensen (Johannes)
1945: 7 Mistral (Gabriela)
1946: 5 Hesse (Hermann)
1947: 4 Gide (André)

1948: 5 Eliot (Thomas Stearns)
1949: 8 Faulkner (William)
1950: 7 Russell (Bertrand)
1951: 10 Lagerkvist (Pär)
1952: 7 Mauriac (François)
1953: 9 Churchill (Winston)
1954: 9 Hemingway (Ernest)
1955: 7 Laxness (Halldór)
1956: 7 Jiménez (Juan Ramón)
1957: 5 Camus (Albert)
1958: 9 Pasternak (Boris)
1959: 9 Quasimodo (Salvatore)
1960: 5 Perse (Saint-John)
1961: 6 Andric (Ivo)
1962: 9 Steinbeck (John)
1963: 7 Seferis (George)
1964: 6 Sartre (Jean-Paul)
1965: 9 Sholokhov (Mikhail)
1966: 5 Agnon (Shmuel Yosef), Sachs (Nelly)
1967: 8 Asturias (Miguel Angel)
1968: 8 Kawabata (Yasunari)
1969: 7 Beckett (Samuel)
1970: 12 Solzhenitsyn (Alexander)
1971: 6 Neruda (Pablo)
1972: 4 Böll (Heinrich)
1973: 5 White (Patrick)
1974: 7 Johnson (Eyvind) **9** Martinson (Edmund)
1975: 7 Montale (Eugenio)
1976: 6 Bellow (Saul)
1977: 10 Aleixandre (Vicente)
1978: 6 Singer (Isaac Bashevis)
1979: 6 Elytis (Odysseus)
1980: 6 Milosz (Czeslaw)
1981: 7 Canetti (Elias)
1982: 13 García Márquez (Gabriel)
1983: 7 Golding (William)
1984: 7 Seifert (Jaroslav)
1985: 5 Simon (Claude)
1986: 7 Soyinka (Wole)
1987: 7 Brodsky (Joseph)
1988: 7 Mahfouz (Naguib)
1989: 4 Cela (Camilo José)
1990: 3 Paz (Octavio)
1991: 8 Gordimer (Nadine)
1992: 7 Walcott (Derek)
1993: 8 Morrison (Toni)
1994: 2 Oe (Kenzaburo)
1995: 6 Heaney (Seamus)
1996: 10 Szymborska (Wislawa)
1997: 2 Fo (Dario)
1998: 8 Saramago (José)
1999: 5 Grass (Günter)
2000: 3 Gao (Xingjian)
2001: 7 Naipaul (V. S.)
2002: 7 Kertész (Imre)
2003: 7 Coetzee (J. M.)
2004: 7 Jelinek (Elfriede)
2005: 6 Pinter (Harold)
2006: 5 Pamuk (Orhan)
2007: 7 Lessing (Doris)
2008: 8 Le Clézio (J.-M. Gustave)
2009: 6 Müller (Herta)
2010: 11 Vargas Llosa (Mario)
2011: 11 Tranströmer (Tomas)
2012: 5 Mo Yan
2013: 5 Munro (Alice)
2014: 7 Modiano (Patrick)
2015: 10 Alexievich (Svetlana)

peace:
1901: 5 Passy (Frédéric) **6** Dunant (Jean-Henri)
1902: 5 Gobat (Charles Albert) **8** Ducommun (Elie)
1903: 6 Cremer (William)
1905: 7 Suttner (Bertha von)
1906: 9 Roosevelt (Theodore)
1907: 6 Moneta (Ernesto) **7** Renault (Louis)
1908: 5 Bajer (Fredrik) **9** Arnoldson (Klas Pontus)
1909: 9 Beernaert (Auguste) **13** d'Estournelles (Paul)
1911: 5 Asser (Tobias), Fried (Alfred)
1912: 4 Root (Elihu)
1913: 10 La Fontaine (Henri)
1919: 6 Wilson (Woodrow)
1920: 9 Bourgeois (Léon)
1921: 5 Lange (Christian Louis) **8** Branting (Karl Hjalmar)
1922: 6 Nansen (Fridtjof)
1925: 5 Dawes (Charles) **11** Chamberlain (Austen)
1926: 6 Briand (Aristide) **10** Stresemann (Gustav)
1927: 6 Quidde (Ludwig) **7** Buisson (Ferdinand)
1929: 7 Kellogg (Frank)
1930: 9 Soderblom (Nathan)
1931: 6 Addams (Jane), Butler (Nicholas Murray)
1933: 6 Angell (Norman)
1934: 9 Henderson (Arthur)
1935: 9 Ossietzky (Carl von)
1936: 13 Saavedra Lamas (Carlos de)
1937: 5 Cecil (Robert)
1945: 4 Hull (Cordell)
1946: 4 Mott (John) **5** Balch (Emily Greene)
1949: 3 Orr (John Boyd)
1950: 6 Bunche (Ralph)
1951: 7 Jouhaux (Léon)
1952: 10 Schweitzer (Albert)
1953: 8 Marshall (George)
1957: 7 Pearson (Lester)
1958: 4 Pire (Dominique Georges)
1959: 9 Noel-Baker (Philip)
1960: 7 Luthuli (Albert John)

1961: **12** Hammarskjöld (Dag)
1962: **7** Pauling (Linus)
1964: **4** King (Martin Luther)
1965: **6** UNICEF
1968: **6** Cassin (René)
1969: **3** ILO
1970: **7** Borlaug (Norman)
1971: **6** Brandt (Willy)
1973: **8** Le Duc Tho **9** Kissinger (Henry)
1974: **4** Sato (Eisaku) **8** MacBride (Sean)
1975: **8** Sakharov (Andrey)
1976: **8** Corrigan (Mairead), Williams (Betty)
1978: **5** Begin (Menachem), Sadat (Anwar el-)
1979: **12** Mother Teresa
1980: **8** Esquivel (Adolfo Pérez)
1982: **6** Myrdal (Alva) **12** García Robles (Alfonso)
1983: **6** Walesa (Lech)
1984: **4** Tutu (Desmond)
1986: **6** Wiesel (Elie)
1987: **12** Arias Sánchez (Oscar)
1989: **9** Dalai Lama
1990: **9** Gorbachev (Mikhail)
1991: **13** Aung San Suu Kyi
1992: **6** Menchú (Rigoberta)
1993: **7** de Klerk (F. W.), Mandela (Nelson)
1994: **5** Peres (Shimon), Rabin (Yitzhak) **6** Arafat (Yasir)
1995: **7** Rotblat (Joseph)
1996: **10** Ramos-Horta (José) **11** Ximenes Belo (Carlos Felipe)
1997: **8** Williams (Jody)
1998: **4** Hume (John) **7** Trimble (David)
2000: **3** Kim (Dae-jung)
2001: **5** Annan (Kofi)
2002: **6** Carter (Jimmy)
2003: **5** Ebadi (Shirin)
2004: **7** Maathai (Wangari)
2005: **9** ElBaradei (Mohamed)
2006: **5** Yunus (Muhammad)
2007: **4** Gore (Al)
2008: **9** Ahtisaari (Martti)
2009: **5** Obama (Barack)
2010: **3** Liu (Xiaobo)
2011: **6** Gbowee (Leymah), Karman (Tawakkul) **7** Sirleaf (Ellen Johnson)
2012: **13** European Union
2013: **4** OPCW
2014: **6** Malala (Yousafzai)

physics:
1901: **8** Roentgen (Wilhelm)
1902: **6** Zeeman (Pieter) **7** Lorentz (Hendrik Antoon)
1903: **5** Curie (Marie, Pierre) **9** Becquerel (Antoine-Henri)
1904: **6** Strutt (John) **8** Rayleigh (Lord)
1905: **6** Lenard (Philipp von)
1906: **7** Thomson (Joseph)
1907: **9** Michelson (Albert)
1908: **8** Lippmann (Gabriel)
1909: **5** Braun (Karl) **7** Marconi (Guglielmo)
1910: **11** van der Waals (Johannes)
1911: **4** Wien (Wilhelm)
1912: **5** Dalen (Nils)
1914: **4** Laue (Max von)
1915: **5** Bragg (William)
1917: **6** Barkla (Charles)
1918: **6** Planck (Max)
1919: **5** Stark (Johannes)
1920: **9** Guillaume (Charles)
1921: **8** Einstein (Albert)
1922: **4** Bohr (Niels)
1923: **8** Millikan (Robert)
1924: **8** Siegbahn (Karl)
1925: **5** Hertz (Gustav) **6** Franck (James)
1926: **6** Perrin (Jean-Baptiste)
1927: **6** Wilson (Charles) **7** Compton (Arthur)
1928: **10** Richardson (Owen)
1929: **7** Broglie (Louis-Victor de)
1930: **5** Raman (Chandrasekhara)
1932: **10** Heisenberg (Werner)
1933: **5** Dirac (Paul) **11** Schrödinger (Erwin)
1935: **8** Chadwick (James)
1936: **4** Hess (Victor) **8** Anderson (Carl)
1937: **7** Thomson (George) **8** Davisson (Clinton)
1938: **5** Fermi (Enrico)
1939: **8** Lawrence (Ernest)
1943: **5** Stern (Otto)
1944: **4** Rabi (Isidor Isaac)
1945: **5** Pauli (Wolfgang)
1946: **8** Bridgman (Percy)
1947: **8** Appleton (Edward)
1948: **8** Blackett (Patrick)
1949: **6** Yukawa (Hideki)
1950: **6** Powell (Cecil)
1951: **6** Walton (Ernest) **9** Cockcroft (John)
1952: **5** Bloch (Felix) **7** Purcell (Edward)
1953: **7** Zernike (Frits)
1954: **4** Born (Max) **5** Bothe (Walther)
1955: **4** Lamb (Willis) **5** Kusch (Polykarp)
1956: **7** Bardeen (John) **8** Brattain (Walter), Shockley (William)
1957: **3** Lee (Tsung Dao) **4** Yang (Chen Ning)
1958: **4** Tamm (Igor) **5** Frank (Ilya) **9** Cherenkov (Pavel)
1959: **5** Segrè (Emilio) **11** Chamberlain (Owen)
1960: **6** Glaser (Donald)
1961: **9** Mossbauer (Rudolf) **10** Hofstadter (Robert)
1962: **6** Landau (Lev)
1963: **5** Mayer (Maria) **6** Jensen (J. Hans), Wigner (Eugene)
1964: **5** Basov (Nikolay) **6** Townes (Charles) **9** Prochorov (Alexander)

1965: 7 Feynman (Richard) **8** Tomonaga (Shinichiro) **9** Schwinger (Julian)
1966: 7 Kastler (Alfred)
1967: 5 Bethe (Hans)
1968: 7 Alvarez (Luis)
1969: 8 Gell-Mann (Murray)
1970: 4 Néel (Louis) **6** Alfven (Hannes)
1971: 5 Gabor (Dennis)
1972: 6 Cooper (Leon) **7** Bardeen (John) **10** Schrieffer (John)
1973: 5 Esaki (Leo) **7** Giaever (Ivar) **9** Josephson (Brian)
1974: 4 Ryle (Martin) **6** Hewish (Antony)
1975: 4 Bohr (Aage) **9** Mottelson (Ben), Rainwater (L. James)
1976: 4 Ting (Samuel) **7** Richter (Burton)
1977: 4 Mott (Nevill) **8** Anderson (Philip), Van Vleck (John)
1978: 6 Wilson (Robert) **7** Kapitsa (Pyotr), Penzias (Arno)
1979: 5 Salam (Abdus) **7** Glashow (Sheldon) **8** Weinberg (Steven)
1980: 5 Fitch (Val) **6** Cronin (James)
1981: 8 Schawlow (Arthur), Siegbahn (Kai) **11** Bloembergen (Nicholaas)
1982: 6 Wilson (Kenneth)
1983: 6 Fowler (William) **13** Chandrasekhar (Subrahmanyan)
1984: 6 Rubbia (Carlo) **11** van der Meere (Simon)
1985: 8 Klitzing (Klaus von)
1986: 5 Ruska (Ernst) **6** Binnig (Gerd), Rohrer (Heinrich)
1987: 6 Müller (K. Alex) **7** Bednorz (J. Georg)
1988: 8 Lederman (Leon), Schwartz (Melvin) **11** Steinberger (Jack)
1989: 4 Paul (Wolfgang) **6** Ramsey (Norman) **7** Dehmelt (Hans)
1990: 6 Taylor (Richard) **7** Kendall (Henry) **8** Friedman (Jerome)
1991: 8 De Gennes (Pierre-Gilles)
1992: 7 Charpak (Georges)
1993: 5 Hulse (Russell) **6** Taylor (Joseph)
1994: 5 Shull (Clifford) **10** Brockhouse (Bertram)
1995: 4 Perl (Martin) **6** Reines (Frederick)
1996: 3 Lee (David) **8** Osheroff (Douglas) **10** Richardson (Robert)
1997: 3 Chu (Steven) **8** Phillips (William) **14** Cohen-Tannoudji (Claude)
1998: 4 Tsui (Daniel) **7** Störmer (Horst) **8** Laughlin (Robert)
1999: 6 ’t Hooft (Gerardus) **7** Veltman (Martinus)
2000: 5 Kilby (Jack) **7** Alferev (Zhores), Kroemer (Herbert)
2001: 6 Wieman (Carl) **7** Cornell (Eric) **8** Ketterle (Wolfgang)
2002: 5 Davis (Raymond) **7** Koshiba (Masatoshi) **8** Giacconi (Riccardo)
2003: 7 Leggett (Anthony) **8** Ginzburg (Vitaly) **9** Abrikosov (Alexei)
2004: 5 Gross (David) **7** Wilczek (Frank) **8** Politzer (David)
2005: 4 Hall (John) **6** Hänsch (Theodor) **7** Glauber (Roy)
2006: 5 Smoot (George) **6** Mather (John)
2007: 4 Fert (Albert) **8** Grünberg (Peter)
2008: 5 Nambu (Yoichiro) **7** Maskawa (Toshihide) **9** Kobayashi (Makoto)
2009: 3 Kao (Charles K.) **5** Boyle (Willard), Smith (George)
2010: 4 Geim (Andre) **9** Novoselov (Konstantin)
2011: 5 Riess (Adam) **7** Schmidt (Brian) **10** Perlmutter (Saul)
2012: 7 Haroche (Serge) **8** Wineland (David)
2013: 5 Higgs (Peter) **7** Englert (François)
2014: 5 Amano (Hiroshi) **7** Akasaki (Isamu) **8** Nakamura (Shuji)
2015: 6 Kajita (Takaaki) **8** McDonald (Arthur)

physiology or medicine:
1901: 7 Behring (Emil von)
1902: 4 Ross (Ronald)
1903: 6 Finsen (Niels Ryberg)
1904: 6 Pavlov (Ivan)
1905: 4 Koch (Robert)
1906: 5 Golgi (Camillo) **11** Ramón y Cajal (Santiago)
1907: 7 Laveran (Alphonse)
1908: 7 Ehrlich (Paul) **11** Metchnikoff (Elie)
1909: 6 Kocher (Emil)
1910: 6 Kossel (Albrecht)
1911: 10 Gullstrand (Allvar)
1912: 6 Carrel (Alexis)
1913: 6 Richet (Charles)
1914: 6 Barany (Robert)
1919: 6 Bordet (Jules)
1920: 5 Krogh (August)
1922: 4 Hill (Archibald) **8** Meyerhof (Otto)
1923: 7 Banting (Frederick), Macleod (John)
1924: 9 Einthoven (Willem)
1926: 7 Fibiger (Johannes)
1927: 13 Wagner-Jauregg (Julius)
1928: 7 Nicolle (Charles)
1929: 7 Eijkman (Christiaan), Hopkins (Frederick)
1930: 11 Landsteiner (Karl)
1931: 7 Warburg (Otto)
1932: 6 Adrian (Edgar) **11** Sherrington (Charles)
1933: 6 Morgan (Thomas)
1934: 5 Minot (George) **6** Murphy (William) **7** Whipple (George)
1935: 7 Spemann (Hans)
1936: 4 Dale (Henry) **5** Loewi (Otto)
1937: 12 Szent-Györgyi (Albert)

1938: **7** Heymans (Corneille)
1939: **6** Domagk (Gerhard)
1943: **3** Dam (Henrik) **5** Doisy (Edward)
1944: **6** Gasser (Herbert) **8** Erlanger (Joseph)
1945: **5** Chain (Ernst) **6** Florey (Howard) **7** Fleming (Alexander)
1946: **6** Muller (Hermann)
1947: **4** Cori (Carl, Gerty) **7** Houssay (Bernardo)
1948: **7** Mueller (Paul)
1949: **4** Hess (Walter) **5** Moniz (Antonio)
1950: **5** Hench (Philip) **7** Kendall (Edward) **10** Reichstein (Tadeus)
1951: **7** Theiler (Max)
1952: **7** Waksman (Selman)
1953: **5** Krebs (Hans) **7** Lipmann (Fritz)
1954: **6** Enders (John), Weller (Thomas) **7** Robbins (Frederick)
1955: **8** Theorell (Hugo)
1956: **8** Cournand (André), Richards (Dickinson) **9** Forssmann (Werner)
1957: **5** Bovet (Daniel)
1958: **5** Tatum (Edward) **6** Beadle (George) **9** Lederberg (Joshua)
1959: **5** Ochoa (Severo) **8** Kornberg (Arthur)
1960: **6** Burnet (Macfarlane) **7** Medawar (Peter)
1961: **6** Bekesy (Georg von)
1962: **5** Crick (Francis) **6** Watson (James) **7** Wilkins (Maurice)
1963: **6** Eccles (John), Huxley (Andrew) **7** Hodgkin (Alan)
1964: **5** Bloch (Konrad), Lynen (Feodor)
1965: **5** Jacob (Francois), Lwoff (André), Monod (Jacques)
1966: **4** Rous (Francis) **7** Huggins (Charles)
1967: **4** Wald (George) **6** Granit (Ragnar) **8** Hartline (H. Keffer)
1968: **6** Holley (Robert) **7** Khorana (H. Gobind) **9** Nirenberg (Marshall)
1969: **5** Luria (Salvador) **7** Hershey (Alfred) **8** Delbruck (Max)
1970: **4** Katz (Bernard) **5** Euler (Ulf von) **7** Axelrod (Julius)
1971: **10** Sutherland (Earl)
1972: **6** Porter (Rodney) **7** Edelman (Gerald)
1973: **6** Frisch (Karl von), Lorenz (Konrad) **9** Tinbergen (Nikolaas)
1974: **4** Duve (Christian) **6** Claude (Albert), Palade (George)
1975: **5** Temin (Howard) **8** Dulbecco (Renato) **9** Baltimore (David)
1976: **8** Blumberg (Baruch), Gajdusek (D. Carleton)
1977: **5** Yalow (Rosalyn) **7** Schally (Andrew) **9** Guillemin (Roger)
1978: **5** Arber (Werner), Smith (Hamilton) **7** Nathans (Daniel)
1979: **7** Cormack (Allan) **10** Hounsfield (Godfrey)
1980: **5** Snell (George) **7** Dausset (Jean) **10** Benacerraf (Baruj)
1981: **5** Hubel (David) **6** Sperry (Roger), Wiesel (Torsten)
1982: **4** Vane (John) **9** Bergstrom (Sune) **10** Samuelsson (Bengt)
1983: **10** McClintock (Barbara)
1984: **5** Jerne (Niels) **7** Koehler (Georges) **8** Milstein (Cesar)
1985: **5** Brown (Michael) **9** Goldstein (Joseph)
1986: **5** Cohen (Stanley) **14** Levi-Montalcini (Rita)
1987: **8** Tonegawa (Susumu)
1988: **5** Black (James), Elion (Gertrude) **9** Hitchings (George)
1989: **6** Bishop (J. Michael), Varmus (Harold)
1990: **6** Murray (Joseph), Thomas (E. Donnall)
1991: **5** Neher (Erwin) **7** Sakmann (Bert)
1992: **5** Krebs (Edwin) **7** Fischer (Edmond)
1993: **5** Sharp (Phillip) **7** Roberts (Richard)
1994: **6** Gilman (Alfred) **7** Rodbell (Martin)
1995: **5** Lewis (Edward) **9** Wieschaus (Eric) **15** Nüsslein-Volhard (Christiane)
1996: **7** Doherty (Peter) **11** Zinkernagel (Rolf)
1997: **8** Prusiner (Stanley)
1998: **5** Murad (Ferid) **7** Ignarro (Louis) **9** Furchgott (Robert)
1999: **6** Blobel (Günter)
2000: **6** Kandel (Eric) **8** Carlsson (Arvid) **9** Greengard (Paul)
2001: **4** Hunt (Tim) **5** Nurse (Paul) **8** Hartwell (Leland)
2002: **7** Brenner (Sydney), Horvitz (Robert), Sulston (John)
2003: **9** Lauterbur (Paul), Mansfield (Peter)
2004: **4** Axel (Richard), Buck (Linda)
2005: **6** Warren (J. Robin) **8** Marshall (Barry)
2006: **4** Fire (Andrew) **5** Mello (Craig)
2007: **5** Evans (Martin) **8** Capecchi (Mario), Smithies (Oliver)
2008: **9** zur Hausen (Harald) **10** Montagnier (Luc) **13** Barré-Sinoussi (Françoise)
2009: **7** Greider (Carol), Szostak (Jack) **9** Blackburn (Elizabeth)
2010: **7** Edwards (Robert)
2011: **7** Beutler (Bruce) **8** Hoffmann (Jules), Steinman (Ralph)
2012: **6** Gurdon (John) **8** Yamanaka (Shinya)
2013: **6** Südhof (Thomas) **7** Rothman (James) **8** Schekman (Randy)
2014: **5** Moser (Edvard, May-Britt) **6** O'Keefe (John)
2015: **5** Omura (Satoshi) **8** Campbell (William), Tu Youyou, Youyou Tu

Nobel's invention
8 dynamite

nobility
6 virtue **7** dignity, peerage, royalty **8** eminence, noblesse **9** loftiness **10** exaltation, excellence, worthiness **11** aristocracy, superiority, uprightness

noble
4 lord, peer **5** grand, lofty, moral **6** august, lordly, titled, worthy **7** courtly, eminent, exalted, notable, stately, sublime, upright **8** baronial, elevated, generous, gracious, highborn, highbred, imposing, magnific, majestic, princely, sterling, virtuous, wellborn **9** dignified, estimable, excellent, grandiose, honorable, righteous **10** high-minded, impressive, principled **11** illustrious, magnanimous, magnificent, outstanding, right-minded **12** aristocratic

nobleman
4 duke, earl, lord, peer **5** baron, count **6** aristo, milord, prince **7** baronet, marquis **8** marquess, viscount **9** patrician **10** aristocrat
French: **5** comte **7** vicomte
German: **4** Graf **6** Herzog **8** margrave **9** landgrave
Indian: **6** sardar, sirdar **8** maharaja **9** maharajah
Islamic: **4** amir, emir **5** ameer
Italian: **8** marchese
Japanese (former): **6** daimyo
Scandinavian: **4** jarl
Spanish: **7** hidalgo

noblewoman
4 lady **7** duchess, peeress **8** baroness, countess, princess **11** marchioness, viscountess
French: **7** baronne **8** marquise
Italian: **8** marchesa

nobody
4 zero **6** cipher **7** nothing, nullity, upstart **9** nonentity **11** lightweight, small potato

nocturnal
7 nightly **9** nighttime

nocuous
3 bad **6** nocent **7** harmful, hurtful **8** damaging **9** injurious **11** deleterious, destructive, detrimental, mischievous

nod
3 bob, err **4** doze, okay **5** agree, droop, slump **6** assent, invite, signal **7** approve **8** approval **10** acceptance

nodding
6 casual, slight **7** passing **8** drooping **9** pendulous **11** superficial

noddle
3 nob, nut **4** bean, head, pate, poll **6** noggin

noddy
3 oaf **4** boob, clod, dodo, dolt, dope, fool, goof, mutt, simp, yo-yo **5** chump, dummy, dunce, moron, ninny, stupe **6** dimwit, donkey, dum-dum **7** airhead, dullard, pinhead, schnook **8** bonehead, clodpoll, dumbbell, dumbhead, imbecile, lunkhead, meathead, numskull **9** birdbrain, blockhead, ignoramus, lamebrain, numbskull, simpleton, thickhead **10** dunderhead, hammerhead, nincompoop **11** chowderhead, chucklehead, knucklehead

node
4 bump, burl, knob, knot, lump, mass **5** bulge, point **6** growth, vertex **8** swelling **11** enlargement, predicament **12** entanglement, protuberance

Noel
4 Xmas, yule **5** carol **9** Christmas

no-frills
5 plain, stark **6** simple **7** austere, spartan **9** unadorned

nog
3 ale **4** beer, brew, malt, suds **5** lager, stout

noggin
3 cup, mug, nip, nob, nut **4** bean, gill, head, pate, poll **6** noddle, noodle

no-good
3 bum, dud **4** base, vile, worm **5** loser **6** scurvy, wretch **7** dirtbag, inutile, lowlife, rounder, wastrel **8** deadbeat, fainéant, shameful, unworthy, wretched **9** no-account, valueless, worthless **10** ne'er-do-well, profligate, scapegrace **11** ignominious **12** contemptible, disreputable **13** reprehensible

noise
3 din **4** blab, talk **5** babel, rumor, sound **6** clamor, gossip, hubbub, racket, ruckus, rumpus, tattle, uproar **7** ruction, sonance, stridor **8** resonant **11** pandemonium

noiseless
4 hush, mute **5** muted, quiet, still, whist **6** hushed, silent, stilly

noisemaker
4 horn **6** rattle **7** clapper, whistle

noisome
4 foul, rank, vile **5** fetid, funky, fusty, musty, nasty **6** filthy, horrid, putrid, rancid, smelly **7** harmful, noxious, squalid **8** stinking **9** obnoxious, offensive, repulsive, revolting, sickening **10** disgusting, malodorous, nauseating

noisy
4 loud **5** aroar, rowdy **7** blatant, booming, clamant, rackety, raucous, squeaky **8** clattery, strident **9** clamorous, deafening, turbulent **10** boisterous, chattering, clangorous, tumultuous, uproarious, vociferous **11** conspicuous **12** earsplitting, obstreperous

no longer fresh
5 stale

nomad
4 bedu, hobo **5** gipsy, gypsy, rover **6** beduin, Berber, Tuareg **7** bedouin, drifter, migrant, rambler, Touareg **8** vagabond, wanderer, wayfarer **9** itinerant

nomadic
5 gipsy, gypsy **6** roving **7** roaming, vagrant **8** drifting, vagabond **9** itinerant, migratory, wandering, wayfaring **11** peripatetic **13** perambulatory

nom de plume
5 alias **7** pen name **9** pseudonym

nomen
4 name **7** moniker **11** appellation, designation

nomenclature
4 list, name **7** catalog **8** glossary, taxonomy **11** appellation, designation, phraseology, terminology **12** codification

nominal
3 low **5** given, named, rated, small **6** formal, puppet **7** alleged, minimal, seeming, titular **8** apparent, so-called, trifling **9** pretended, professed **10** ostensible **11** approximate, inexpensive **12** satisfactory **13** insignificant

nominate
3 tap **4** call, name **5** offer, put up **7** appoint, propose, suggest **9** designate, recommend

nominee
6 choice **8** aspirant **9** candidate, contender **10** contestant

nonage
5 youth **7** infancy **8** minority **9** childhood **10** immaturity, juvenility

nonchalant
4 cool, easy **5** blasé **6** casual, mellow, serene **7** offhand **8** carefree, careless, cheerful, laidback **9** easygoing **10** effortless, insouciant, untroubled **11** unconcerned, unflappable, unperturbed **12** lighthearted **13** lackadaisical

nonclerical
3 lay **4** laic

noncommittal
7 neutral **8** reserved **9** impassive **10** disengaged

nonconformist
4 anti **5** loner, rebel **7** beatnik, heretic, oddball, offbeat, radical **8** bohemian, maverick **9** dissenter, dissident, eccentric, heretical, heterodox, protester, sectarian **10** schismatic, separatist, unorthodox **11** misbeliever, schismatist

nonconformity
6 heresy, schism **7** dissent **9** misbelief, recusancy **10** dissidence, heterodoxy, opposition **11** unorthodoxy **13** individualism

nonentity
4 zero **5** aught, zilch **6** cipher, nobody **7** nothing, nullity, whiffet **8** unperson **10** figurehead, mouthpiece

nonesuch
5 ideal **7** eidolon, epitome, paragon, pattern **8** exemplar, paradigm, standard **9** archetype, beau ideal, matchless, nonpareil, unequaled, unrivaled **10** apotheosis

nonetheless
3 yet **5** still **6** anyway, though, withal **7** howbeit, however **8** although, after all **10** regardless **11** still and all

nonexistence
4 nada, void **7** nullity, vacuity **11** nothingness

nonflammable
9 fireproof **10** unburnable **13** incombustible

nonflowering plant
4 fern, moss **5** cycad **6** coleus, ginkgo, lichen **7** conifer **9** horsetail, liverwort

non-Hawaiian
5 haole

non-Jewish
3 goy **6** goyish **7** gentile

non-Muslim
6 giaour

no-no
5 taboo

no-nonsense
5 grave, sober **6** solemn **7** earnest, serious **8** resolute **9** pragmatic, realistic **10** hardheaded, sobersided **11** plainspoken **12** businesslike **13** unsentimental

nonpareil
5 ideal **6** tip-top **7** eidolon, epitome, paragon **8** exemplar, paradigm, top-notch, top-shelf **9** archetype, beau ideal, first-rate, matchless, unequaled, unrivaled **10** apotheosis, first-class **11** superlative

nonpartisan
7 neutral **8** unbiased **9** equitable, impartial, objective, uncolored **10** evenhanded, nonaligned **11** independent **12** unprejudiced

nonplus
4 faze **5** abash, stump **6** baffle, bemuse, boggle, fuddle, muddle, puzzle, rattle, stymie **7** buffalo, confuse, dilemma, flummox, fluster, mystify, perplex, stagger **8** bewilder, confound, distract, overcome, paralyze, quandary **9** discomfit, dumbfound, frustrate **10** disconcert

nonresistant
6 docile, pliant **7** passive, pliable **8** resigned, yielding **9** compliant, complying, malleable, tractable **10** conforming, submissive **11** acquiescent, complaisant, conformable **13** accommodating

nonsense
3 rot **4** blah, bosh, bull, bunk, crap, gook, guff, jazz, punk, tosh **5** bilge, crock, drool, folly, fudge, Greek, hokum, hooey, trash, tripe **6** babble, blague, bunkum, drivel, hot air, humbug, jabber, piffle **7** baloney, blather, eyewash, flubdub, foolery, fooling, hogwash, inanity, rubbish, trifles, twaddle **8** buncombe, claptrap, falderal, folderol, flimflam, malarkey, pishposh, slipslop, tommyrot, trumpery **9** gibberish, moonshine, poppycock **10** applesauce, balderdash, double-talk, flapdoodle, tomfoolery **11** jabberwocky **12** blatherskite, fiddle-faddle, fiddlesticks **13** horsefeathers
British: 10 codswallop

nonsensical
5 crazy, daffy, flaky, goofy, inane, kooky, loony, nutty, silly, wacky **6** absurd, screwy **7** foolish, idiotic, risible **9** illogical, laughable, ludicrous, senseless **10** irrational **12** preposterous, unreasonable

nonstop
7 express **8** unbroken **9** ceaseless, continual, incessant, perpetual **10** continuous

nonviolent
6 irenic **7** pacific **8** pacifist **9** peaceable **10** pacifistic

noodle
3 oaf **4** bean, boob, clod, dodo, dope, goof, head, mutt, poll, simp, yo-yo **5** chump, dummy, dunce, idiot, moron, ninny, noddy, stupe **6** dimwit, donkey, dum-dum, nitwit, noggin **7** airhead, dullard, pinhead, schnook **8** bonehead, clodpoll, dumbbell, dumbhead, imbecile, lunkhead, meathead, numskull **9** birdbrain, blockhead, ignoramus, lamebrain, numbskull, simpleton **10** dunderhead, hammerhead, nincompoop **11** chowderhead, chucklehead, knucklehead
dish: 5 pasta **7** lasagna, lasagne **8** linguine, linguini **10** fettuccine, fettuccini **11** pappardelle

nook
3 bay **4** cove **5** hutch, niche **6** alcove, cavity, corner, cranny, recess **9** cubbyhole **11** compartment

noose
3 tie **4** bait, bind, hang, loop, lure, trap **5** lasso, reata, riata, snare **6** entrap, lariat, secure

norm
3 par **4** mean, rule, type **5** gauge, maxim, model **6** median **7** average, measure, pattern **8** paradigm, standard **9** benchmark, criterion **10** touchstone

Norma
aria: 9 Casta diva
composer: 7 Bellini (Vincenzo)
librettist: 6 Romani (Felice)

Norma ____
3 Rae

normal
4 sane **5** usual **6** common **7** average, general, natural, regular, typical **8** ordinary, orthodox, standard **9** customary, prevalent **11** commonplace, traditional **12** conventional **13** perpendicular

Normandy event of 1944
4 D-day

Normandy's capital
5 Rouen

Norman of TV
4 Lear

Norns
5 fates, Skuld, Urdur **9** Verthandi

Norris novel
3 Pit (The) **4** Blix **7** Octopus (The) **8** McTeague

Norse
abode of the dead: 8 Niflheim
alphabet: 5 Runic
archer: 4 Egil
bard: 5 scald, skald
chieftain: 4 jarl, Rolf **5** Rollo
demon: 4 Mara, Surt **5** Surtr
dragon: 6 Fafnir **8** Nithhogg
epic: 4 Edda
explorer: 4 Eric, Erik, Leif **8** Ericsson (Leif), Eriksson (Leif)
first man: 3 Ask **4** Askr
first woman: 5 Embla
giant: 4 Egil, Wade, Wate, Ymer, Ymir **5** Aegir, Egill, Hymir, Jotun, Mimir **6** Fafnir, Jotunn
giantess: 4 Egia, Norn, Nott
god: 3 Asa, Ass **4** Surt, Vali, Vili **5** Aesir (plural), Surtr, Vanir (plural) **6** Hoenir, Vithar **7** Vitharr
- **blind: 4** Hoth **5** Hoder, Hodur, Hothr
- **chief: 4** Oden, Odin **5** Othin, Wodan, Woden, Wotan
- **guardian: 7** Heimdal **8** Heimdall **9** Heimdallr
- **messenger: 6** Hermod **7** Hermodr
- **of beauty: 5** Baldr **6** Balder, Baldur
- **of evil: 4** Loke, Loki
- **of fertility: 4** Frey **5** Freyr
- **of fire: 4** Loke, Loki
- **of justice: 7** Forsete, Forseti
- **of light: 3** Dag
- **of peace: 5** Baldr **6** Balder, Baldur
- **of poetry: 5** Brage, Bragi
- **of the hunt: 3** Ull **4** Ullr
- **of the seas: 5** Njord **6** Njoerd, Njorth **4** Hler **5** Aegir, Gymir
- **of the sky: 4** Odin **5** Othin, Wodan, Woden, Wotan
- **of thunder: 4** Thor **5** Donar
- **of war: 3** Tiu, Tiw, Tyr, Zio, Ziu
- **wolf: 6** Fenrir

goddess: 3 dis **4** Saga **5** disir (plural) **7** Asynjur

of fate: **3** Urd **4** Norn, Urth, Wyrd **5** Skuld **9** Verthandi
of healing: **3** Eir
of love: **5** Freya
of marriage: **5** Frigg **6** Frigga
of night: **4** Natt, Nott
of storms: **3** Ran
of the earth: **4** Erda **5** Joerd, Jorth
of the moon: **5** Nanna
of the sea: **3** Ran
of the sky: **5** Frigg **6** Frigga
of the underworld: **3** Hel **4** Hela
of youth: **4** Idun **5** Ithun **6** Ithunn
gods' abode: **6** Asgard
hall of heroes: **8** Valhalla
king: **4** Atli, Olaf
nobleman: **4** jarl
patron saint: **4** Olaf
poem: **4** rune
poet: **5** scald, skald
rainbow bridge: **7** Bifrost
sea serpent: **4** Wade, Wate **6** kraken **7** Midgard
smith: **6** Völund
tale: **4** saga
toast: **5** skoal
watchdog: **4** Garm **5** Garmr
world's destruction: **8** Ragnarok
world tree: **8** Ygdrasil **10** Yggdrasill

north
combining form: **4** arct **5** arcto

North African
country: **5** Egypt, Libya **7** Algeria, Morocco, Tunisia
fruit: **3** fig **4** date
garment: **4** haik **7** burnous **8** burnoose
grass: **4** alfa **7** esparto
jackal: **4** dieb
language: **6** Arabic, Berber
Muslim sect: **6** Sanusi **7** Senussi
people: **4** bedu **6** beduin, Berber, Hamite **7** bedouin
seaport: **4** Oran, Sfax **5** Tunis **6** Annaba **7** Algiers, Tangier **10** Casablanca

North America
country: **6** Belize, Canada, Mexico, Panama **8** Honduras **9** Costa Rica, Guatemala, Nicaragua **10** El Salvador **12** United States

North Carolina
capital: **7** Raleigh
city: **6** Durham **9** Asheville, Charlotte **10** Greensboro **12** Winston-Salem
college, university: **4** Duke, Elon **10** Chapel Hill, Wake Forest
mountain, range: **8** Mitchell **9** Blue Ridge **10** Great Smoky
nickname: **7** Tar Heel (State)
state bird: **8** cardinal
state flower: **7** dogwood
state tree: **4** pine

North Dakota
capital: **8** Bismarck
city: **5** Fargo, Minot **10** Grand Forks
nickname: **5** Sioux (State) **11** Flickertail (State)
river: **3** Red **8** Missouri
state bird: **10** meadowlark
state flower: **11** prairie rose
state tree: **3** elm (American)

North Korea
see **Korea, North**

northern
4 pike **6** boreal **11** hyperborean

Northern Ireland
6 Ulster
capital: **7** Belfast
city: **5** Derry, Newry **6** Armagh **7** Lisburn
conflict: **8** Troubles (The)
county: **4** Down **6** Antrim, Armagh, Tyrone **9** Fermanagh **11** Londonderry
lake: **10** Lough Neagh
language: **3** BSL, ISL **5** Irish **11** Ulster Scots
monetary unit: **5** pound
mountains: **6** Mourne **7** Sperrin
prison, former: **4** Maze
province: **6** Ulster
university: **6** Queens

Northern Mariana Islands
commonwealth of: **12** United States
discoverer: **8** Magellan (Ferdinand)
island: **4** Rota **6** Saipan, Tinian

North Pole toymaker
3 elf

North Star State
9 Minnesota

Northwest Territories
capital: **11** Yellowknife
gulf: **8** Amundsen
island: **5** Banks **8** Victoria
lake: **9** Great Bear **10** Great Slave
river: **9** Mackenzie
sea: **8** Beaufort

north wind
see at **wind**

Norway
Arctic region: **7** Lapland
cape: **7** Nordkyn
capital: **4** Oslo
city: **5** Hamar **6** Bergen **9** Stavanger, Trondheim
inlet: **9** Skagerrak
island: **5** Senja **6** Sørøya **8** Magerøya, Steinsøy **10** Nord-Kvaløy, Ringvassøy
island group: **7** Lofoten **10** Vesterålen
king: **4** Eric, Olaf, Olav **5** Oscar **6** Haakon, Harald, Magnus **7** Charles **9** Christian, Frederick **11** Christopher

lake: **5** Mjøsa
monetary unit: **5** krone
mountain range: **6** Kjølen **11** Jotunheimen
neighbor: **6** Russia, Sweden **7** Finland
part of: **11** Scandinavia
patron saint: **4** Olaf, Olav
port: **5** Vardø **6** Tromsø **8** Kirkenes **10** Hammerfest
river: **4** Tana **5** Glåma, Lågen **9** Dramselva
sea: **5** North

Norwegian
goblin: **5** nisse
language: **5** Norse **6** Bokmal **7** Bokmaal, Nynorsk, Riksmal **8** Landsmal, Riksmaal **9** Landsmaal
playwright: **5** Ibsen (Henrik)
saint: **4** Olaf, Olav

nose
3 pry **4** beak, bent, bump, head, poke **5** aroma, flair, knack, scent, smell, sniff, snift, snoop, snoot, snout, snuff **6** muzzle, nuzzle, schnoz, talent **7** aptness, bouquet, faculty, schnozz, smeller, sneezer **8** smell out **9** olfaction, proboscis, schnozzle
combining form: **4** naso, rhin **5** rhino
French: **3** nez
kind: **3** pug **5** Roman **8** aquiline
lengthener: **3** lie
opening: **5** nares (plural), naris **7** nostril

nosebleed
9 epistaxis

nosedive
4 drop, fall **6** header, plunge **7** plummet

nosegay
4 posy **6** flower **7** bouquet, corsage **11** boutonniere

nosh
4 bite **5** graze, munch, snack **6** nibble

nostalgic tune
5 oldie

Nostradamus
4 seer **7** prophet
birthplace: **6** St. Rémy

Nostromo author
6 Conrad (Joseph)

nostrum
4 cure **6** elixir, remedy **7** cure-all, panacea **8** antidote, medicine **10** catholicon, corrective **11** restorative

nosy
6 prying, snoopy **7** curious, peeping **8** snooping **9** intrusive **11** inquisitive, inquisitory
person: **5** prier, snoop, yenta **8** busybody

not
4 nary

notable
3 VIP **4** lion, star **5** celeb, chief, famed, mogul, nabob, power **6** big boy, biggie, big gun, bigwig, famous, fat cat, honcho, leader, prince, worthy **7** big name, big shot, eminent, magnate, pooh-bah **8** big chief, big-timer, big wheel, eminence, luminary, renowned, somebody, striking **9** big cheese, celebrity, character, chieftain, dignitary, distingué, personage, prominent, superstar **10** celebrated, celebrious, noteworthy, remarkable **11** conspicuous, heavyweight, illustrious, muckety-muck, personality **13** distinguished, high-muck-a-muck

notarize
7 certify, endorse **8** validate **12** authenticate

not at all
5 nohow, noway **6** noways, nowise

notch
3 cut, gap, jag **4** gash, kerf, mark, nick, nock, pass, rung, slit, step **5** cleft, grade, score, stage **6** degree, groove, indent, rabbet, record **7** achieve, scratch **8** incision, undercut **11** indentation

notched
5 erose

note
3 jot **4** bond, chit, heed, mark, memo, show, sign, tone **5** catch, sound, token **6** letter, notice, record, regard **7** comment, discern, jotting, missive, observe, promise, set down **8** eminence, indicate, perceive, reminder **9** attention, knowledge **10** cognizance, memorandum, reputation **11** distinction, distinguish, observation
musical: **3** sol

notebook
3 log **5** diary **7** journal

noted
5 famed **6** famous **7** eminent, leading, popular **8** esteemed, renowned, striking **9** acclaimed, prominent, well-known **10** celebrated, recognized, remarkable **11** illustrious **13** distinguished

noteworthy
7 salient **8** singular, striking **9** arresting, bodacious, memorable, prominent, red-letter **10** impressive, meaningful, remarkable **11** conspicuous, exceptional, high-profile, major-league, outstanding, significant **12** considerable **13** extraordinary

not guilty, e.g.
4 plea

not hidden
5 overt

nothing
3 nil, nix, zip **4** nada, zero **5** aught, nihil, zilch

6 cipher, naught, nobody, nought, trifle 7 nullity, whiffet 8 goose egg, whipster 9 no-account, nonentity
French: 4 rien
German: 6 nichts
Latin: 5 nihil
Spanish: 4 nada

nothingness
4 nada, void 5 death 6 vacuum 7 nullity, vacuity 9 emptiness 12 nonexistence

notice
3 eye, see 4 espy, heed, mark, memo 5 catch, sight 6 descry, regard, review 7 discern, observe, respect 8 handbill, perceive 9 attention, directive, recognize 10 cognizance, evaluation 11 declaration, information, observation 12 announcement, proclamation

noticeable
6 marked, patent, signal 7 evident, obvious, pointed, salient 8 apparent, manifest, striking 9 arresting, prominent 10 noteworthy, observable, remarkable 11 appreciable, conspicuous, eye-catching, outstanding, perceptible, significant 12 unmistakable

notify
3 cue 4 tell, warn 5 alert, brief 6 advise, clue in, fill in, inform 7 apprise 8 acquaint 9 enlighten

notion
4 clue, hint, idea, whim 5 fancy 6 belief, maggot, theory, vagary 7 caprice, conceit, concept, inkling, thought 8 crotchet 10 conception, impression, intimation, perception 11 inclination

notional
5 ideal 6 unreal 7 fancied, fictive 8 fanciful, illusory, imagined 9 imaginary, visionary, whimsical 10 capricious, conceptual 11 speculative, theoretical 12 hypothetical

notoriety
4 fame 6 infamy, renown 7 obloquy 9 disrepute 10 opprobrium, prominence 11 recognition

notorious
5 noted 6 famous 8 ill-famed, infamous 9 prominent, well-known 10 outrageous, scandalous 12 disreputable

not quite a lieut.
3 ens.

not quite closed
4 ajar

Notre Dame's Parseghian
3 Ara

Notus
6 Auster
brother: 5 Eurus 6 Boreas 8 Zephyrus
father: 6 Aeolus 8 Astraeus
mother: 3 Eos

not working
4 idle 5 kaput 6 broken, busted, unused 11 inoperative

noun
4 name 7 nominal 11 substantive
inflectional form: 4 case
verbal: 6 gerund

nourish
4 feed, rear 5 nurse, raise 6 foster 7 bring up, build up, nurture, promote, support 8 maintain 9 cultivate, encourage 10 provide for, strengthen

nourishment
3 pap 4 diet, eats, feed, food, grub 6 viands 7 aliment, pabulum, vittles 8 victuals 9 nutriment, provender 10 sustenance

____ nous
5 entre

nouveau riche
7 climber, parvenu, upstart 9 arriviste

Nova Scotia
6 Acadia
capital: 7 Halifax
city: 9 Dartmouth
island: 10 Cape Breton
lake: 7 Bras D'Or
provincial flower: 9 mayflower

novel
3 new, odd 4 book 5 fresh 6 unique 7 fiction, offbeat, unusual 8 atypical, original, peculiar, singular, uncommon 9 different, narrative 10 avant-garde, innovative, newfangled

novelist
see **author**

novelist Ferber
4 Edna

novelist Jean
4 Auel

novelist Kingsley
4 Amis

novelist Leon
4 Uris

novelist McEwan
3 Ian

novelist Rand
3 Ayn

Novello, ____
4 Ivor

novelty
5 curio 6 bauble, gewgaw, oddity, trifle 7 bibelot, gimmick, newness, trinket, whatnot 8 gimcrack, souvenir 9 bagatelle, curiosity, objet d'art 10 innovation, knickknack

novice
3 cub 4 colt, punk, tyro 5 plebe 6 newbie,

rookie **7** amateur, learner, recruit, student, trainee **8** aspirant, beginner, freshman, neophyte, newcomer, prentice **9** fledgling, greenhorn, novitiate, postulant **10** apprentice, tenderfoot **11** probationer

Novum Organum author
5 Bacon (Francis)

now
3 PDQ **4** ASAP, soon, stat **5** today **6** at once, pronto **7** anymore, present **8** directly, first off, promptly **9** forthwith, instanter, instantly, presently, right away, sometimes **11** immediately, straightway **12** straightaway

now and then
7 at times, betimes **9** sometimes **12** infrequently, occasionally, periodically, sporadically

no way
4 as if

Nox
brother: **6** Erebus
daughter: **3** Day **4** Eris **5** Light
father: **5** Chaos
husband: **6** Erebus
son: **6** Charon, Hypnos **8** Thanatos

noxious
4 foul **5** fetid, toxic **6** deadly, putrid **7** baneful, harmful, noisome **8** stinking **9** dangerous, pestilent, poisonous, unhealthy **10** corrupting, pernicious **11** deleterious, destructive, detrimental, pestiferous **12** disagreeable, pestilential

nozzle
4 nose, vent **5** spout **7** channel

nth
4 last **6** utmost **7** extreme, highest, maximal, maximum, supreme **8** greatest, ultimate

nuance
4 hint **5** shade, tinge, touch, trace **6** nicety **7** shading, soupçon **8** overtone, subtlety **9** gradation, suspicion **10** refinement, suggestion **11** distinction

nub
4 bump, core, crux, gist, knob, knot, lump, meat, node, pith **5** bulge, point, short **6** kernel, upshot **8** swelling **9** substance **10** projection **12** protuberance

Nubian
5 Mahas **6** Birked, Kenuzi, Midobi **7** Dongola **8** Cushitic **9** Chari-Nile

nubile
4 ripe **10** attractive **12** marriageable

nuchal
4 nape

nuclear agency
3 AEC, NRC

nuclear particle
4 pion **5** meson **6** proton **7** neutron

nucleus
3 bud **4** core, germ, head, kern, ring, seed **5** focus, spark **6** embryo
material: **8** karyotin

nude
3 raw **4** bald, bare **5** naked, stark **6** barren, peeled, unclad **8** disrobed, starkers, stripped **9** au naturel, buck naked, unattired, unclothed, uncovered, undressed **10** stark naked

nudge
3 dig, jab, jog **4** bump, near, poke, prod, push **5** elbow, shove **8** approach

nudnik
4 bore, drip, pest, pill, twit **8** nuisance

nugatory
4 idle, vain **5** empty, inane, vapid **6** futile, hollow, otiose **7** invalid, vacuous **8** trifling **9** fruitless, worthless **11** inoperative, meaningless

nugget
4 hunk, lump, plum **5** chunk **6** tidbit

nuisance
4 pain, pest, pill **6** bother, nudnik **7** nudnick **8** headache, irritant, pesterer, vexation **11** botheration

nuke
3 zap **4** bomb **5** crush, smash **6** attack **7** destroy **8** demolish **9** eradicate, microwave **10** annihilate **11** exterminate

null
4 void, zero **5** annul, empty **6** futile **7** invalid, useless **8** nugatory **9** worthless **10** invalidate, obliterate, unavailing **11** ineffective, ineffectual, inoperative

nullify
3 zap **4** undo, veto, void **5** abate, annul, limit, quash, scrub, trash **6** cancel, efface, negate, offset, repeal, revoke, squash **7** abolish, rescind, scratch, take out, wipe out **8** abrogate **10** annihilate, compensate, counteract, invalidate, neutralize **11** countervail

nullity
4 nada, zero **5** zilch **6** cipher, nobody **7** nothing, vacuity, whiffet **9** annulment, nonentity **11** nothingness **12** nonexistence

numb
5 chill, dazed **6** deaden, freeze **7** callous **8** deadened **9** insensate, paralyzed, stupefied, unfeeling **10** insensible, insentient **11** desensitize **12** anesthetized, desensitized

number
5 add up, count, digit, run to, sum to, tally, total **6** amount, cipher, figure **7** chiffer, include, integer, numeral, ordinal, several **8** cardinal, paginate **9** aggregate, enumerate
added to another: **6** augend
cruncher: **3** CPA

great: **4** army, host **5** horde **6** googol, legion **9** multitude **10** googolplex
irrational: **4** surd
resulting from division: **8** quotient
resulting from multiplication: **7** product
resulting from subtraction: **10** difference
science: **11** mathematics

number one
3 top **4** best, main **5** chief, first, major **6** finest, Grade A, tip-top, top dog **7** capital, highest, leading, primary, stellar **8** dominant, five-star, foremost, superior **9** excellent, first-rate, front-rank, numero uno, principal, top-drawer **10** blue-ribbon, first-class, preeminent **11** first-string, outstanding, predominant

numbness
5 shock **6** stupor **10** anesthesia **11** anaesthesia **12** stupefaction
combining form: **4** narc **5** narco

numeral
5 digit **6** cipher, figure, number **7** integer **11** whole number

numerate
4 list **5** count, tally **6** number **7** compute, itemize, tick off **8** tabulate **9** calculate

numerous
4 many **6** legion **7** profuse, umpteen **8** abundant, populous **9** plentiful **10** voluminous **13** multitudinous

Numitor
brother: **7** Amulius
daughter: **9** Rea Silvia **10** Rhea Silvia
grandson: **5** Remus **7** Romulus

numskull
3 oaf **4** boob, clod, dodo, dolt, dope, goof, mutt, simp **5** chump, dummy, dunce, idiot, moron, ninny, noddy, stupe **6** dimwit, donkey, dumdum, nitwit **7** airhead, dullard, pinhead, schnook **8** bonehead, clodpate, clodpoll, dumbbell, dumbhead, imbecile, lunkhead, meathead **9** birdbrain, blockhead, ignoramus, lamebrain, simpleton, thickhead **10** dunderhead, hammerhead, nincompoop **11** chowderhead, chucklehead, knucklehead

nun
4 buoy **6** sister
headcloth: **6** wimple

Nunavut
capital: **7** Iqaluit
island: **5** Devon **6** Baffin **9** Ellesmere **11** Southampton
mountain: **7** Barbeau (Peak)
peninsula: **7** Boothia **8** Melville
provincial flower: **11** Arctic poppy

nunnery
7 convent **8** cloister **10** sisterhood
head: **8** superior

nuptial
6 bridal, wedded **7** marital, married, spousal, wedding **8** conjugal, espousal, hymeneal, marriage **9** connubial **11** matrimonial

nurse
3 LPN, LVN **4** feed, nana, rear, suck **5** nanny, serve **6** attend, foster, pamper, suckle **7** care for, cherish, nourish, nurture **9** cultivate **10** minister to
children's: **5** nanny
English: **11** Nightingale (Florence)
Indian: **4** ayah
Chinese: **4** amah

Nurse Jackie portrayer
4 Edie (Falco)

nursemaid
4 nana **5** nanny **6** minder, sitter **9** governess **10** babysitter
Indian: **4** ayah
Chinese: **4** amah

nursery
6 crèche **7** brooder **8** hothouse **9** fosterage **10** greenhouse **12** conservatory

nurture
4 care, feed, rear, tend **5** nurse, raise, train **6** cradle, foster, parent, suckle **7** bring up, care for, develop, educate, nourish, rearing **8** breeding, instruct, training, tutelage **9** cultivate **10** upbringing

nut
3 bug **4** cola, kola, kook, loon, pili **5** acorn, betel, crank, fiend, freak, hazel, loony, pecan, piñon **6** almond, cashew, cuckoo, madman, maniac, walnut, zealot **7** buckeye, fanatic, filbert, hickory, lunatic **8** crackpot **9** bedlamite, ding-a-ling, macadamia, pistachio, screwball **10** enthusiast, Tom o' Bedlam
of a violin bow: **4** frog, heel

Nut
consort: **3** Geb, Keb
daughter: **4** Isis **8** Nephthys
son: **6** Osiris

nuthouse
6 asylum, bedlam **8** loony bin **9** funny farm **10** booby hatch **11** institution **12** insane asylum

nutmeg
4 mace

Nutmeg State
11 Connecticut

nutria
5 coypu

nutriment
4 diet, fare, food, grub, keep **6** viands **7** aliment, pabulum **8** victuals **9** provender **10** provisions, sustenance **11** comestibles, nourishment, subsistence

nutrition
4 diet **7** vittles **8** victuals **10** sustenance **11** nourishment

nutritious
9 healthful, wholesome **10** alimentary, nourishing

nuts
3 mad **4** daft, gaga, keen, loco, wild, zany **5** batty, crazy, dotty, kooky, loony, rabid, wacky **6** absurd, cuckoo, insane, screwy **7** bonkers, cracked, excited, foolish, idiotic **8** animated, demented, deranged **9** exuberant, fanatical, screwball **10** passionate, unbalanced **12** enthusiastic
on forest floor: **4** mast

nutty
see **nuts**

nuzzle
3 rub **4** root, snug **5** nudge **6** burrow, cuddle, nestle **7** snuggle

Nycteus
brother: **5** Lycus
daughter: **7** Antiope

Nykvist of cinematography
4 Sven

nymph
5 larva, sylph **6** Aegina, Egeria, maiden, sprite, Syrinx
changed into a bear: **8** Callisto
changed into a laurel: **6** Daphne
changed into a rock: **4** Echo
mountain: **5** oread **6** Oenone
sea: **6** Nereid **7** Calypso, mermaid, Oceanid
tree: **5** dryad
water: **3** nix **5** naiad, nixie **6** kelpie, undine
wood: **5** dryad

NYSE debut
3 IPO

Nyx
see **Nox**

O

oaf
3 ape, dub, lug **4** boob, boor, bull, clod, dodo, dolt, goof, goon, hulk, lout, lump, slob **5** booby, chump, clown, dummy, dunce, klutz **6** dumdum, galoot, lubber, lummox **7** fathead, palooka **8** bonehead, lunkhead, meathead **9** blockhead, blunderer, lamebrain, simpleton

oafish
5 dense **6** clumsy, klutzy, rustic **7** boorish, doltish, loutish **8** bumbling, bungling, churlish, clownish, lubberly

oak
African: **7** turtosa
fruit: **5** acorn
genus: **7** Quercus
kind: **3** bur, pin **4** cork, holm, ilex **5** roble **6** cerris, encina **7** durmast, moss-cup, valonia **9** blackjack
Mexican: **8** chaparro
young: **8** flittern

oar
3 row **4** pole, pull **5** rower, scull **6** paddle **7** paddler
part: **4** loom, palm **5** blade, shaft **6** button, collar
pin: **5** thole

oarsman
3 bow **5** rower **6** stroke **7** sculler
captain: **3** cox **8** coxswain

oasis
3 spa **4** wadi **5** haven **6** refuge, relief **12** watering hole
ancient: **4** Merv
Egypt: **4** Siwa **5** Gafsa **6** Dakhla **7** Farafra **8** Ammonium
Libya: **5** Mizda, Sebha **6** Sabhah **7** Gadames **8** Ghudamis
Niger: **5** Bilma
Saudi Arabia: **5** Hofuf, Taima **7** Al-Hufuf

oast
4 kiln, oven

oat
5 grain, grass **6** cereal
genus: **5** Avena
Scottish: **3** ait

oater
7 western **10** horse opera

oath
3 vow **4** cuss **5** curse, swear **6** pledge **7** promise **8** cussword **9** expletive, profanity, swearword
mild: **4** dang, darn, drat, egad, heck **6** jiminy, zounds

oatmeal
5 gruel **6** burgoo **8** porridge
Scottish: **8** drammock

obdurate
3 set **4** firm, hard **5** harsh, rigid, stony **6** dogged, mulish **7** adamant, callous **8** stubborn **9** heartless, immovable, unbending, unfeeling **10** hard-boiled, inflexible, unshakable, unyielding **11** coldhearted, hardhearted, insensitive **12** intransigent, stonyhearted

obeah
5 charm, magic
relative: **5** vodun **6** vodoun, voodoo **8** Santeria **9** Candomblé

Obed
father: **4** Boaz **6** Ephlal **8** Shemaiah
mother: **4** Ruth
son: **5** Jesse **7** Azariah

obedient
5 loyal **6** docile **7** devoted, duteous, dutiful, willing **8** amenable, biddable, obliging, yielding **9** compliant, tractable **10** law-abiding, manageable, respectful, submissive **11** acquiescent, cooperative, deferential, subservient

obeisance
3 bow **5** honor **6** curtsy, esteem, fealty, homage, kowtow, salaam **7** gesture, loyalty, respect **9** deference, reverence **10** allegiance, submission

obelisk
6 dagger, pillar, symbol **8** monolith

Oberon
9 fairy king
messenger: **4** Puck
wife: **7** Titania

obese
3 fat **5** bulky, gross, heavy, husky, tubby **6** fleshy, portly, rotund **7** adipose, outsize, porcine **8** heavyset, roly-poly **9** corpulent **10** overweight

obesity
7 fatness **9** adiposity **10** corpulence, embonpoint

obey
3 bow **4** heed, mind **5** agree, defer, serve, yield **6** accede, accept, assent, comply, follow, submit **7** abide by, conform, fulfill **9** acquiesce

obfuscate
4 blur **5** befog, cloud, muddy **6** darken **7** becloud, conceal, confuse, cover up, obscure **9** adumbrate

obi, e.g.
4 sash

obiter dictum
4 note **6** remark **7** comment, opinion **10** commentary, incidental **11** observation

obituary
9 necrology **11** death notice

Obi-Wan portrayer
4 Alec (Guinness)

object
3 aim, end **4** goal, item, kick, view, wish **5** demur, focus, point, thing **6** design, entity, except, intent, matter, motive, oppose, resist, target **7** article, dissent, protest, purpose **8** complain, disagree, material **9** criticize, intention, something **10** disapprove

objection
5 demur **7** protest, quibble, scruple **8** argument, demurral, demurrer, question **9** challenge, complaint, exception **10** difficulty, opposition **11** disapproval **12** disagreement, remonstrance

objectionable
5 unfit **8** unwanted **9** invidious, obnoxious, offensive, unwelcome **10** unpleasant **11** displeasing, distasteful, undesirable **12** disagreeable

objective
3 aim, end **4** fair, goal, just, lens, mark **6** actual, design, intent, target **7** mission, purpose **8** ambition, function, sensible, unbiased **9** equitable, impartial, intention **10** impersonal **11** substantial **12** unprejudiced **13** dispassionate

Objectivist Rand
3 Ayn

objet d'art
5 curio, virtu (plural) **7** bibelot, novelty **8** kickshaw **10** knickknack

objurgate
5 chide, decry, scold **6** rebuke **7** censure, reprove, upbraid **8** admonish, reproach **9** castigate, reprimand

oblate
7 lay monk **9** flattened, religious

oblation
4 gift **6** corban **8** holy gift, offering **9** sacrifice

obligate
4 bind **7** require **8** encumber, restrict **9** constrain

obligated
5 bound, owing **6** liable **8** beholden, indebted **11** accountable, responsible

obligation
3 IOU, vow **4** bond, call, debt, dues, duty, need, oath, onus **5** cause **6** burden, charge, pledge **7** promise **8** business, contract **9** committal, liability, necessity, restraint **10** commitment, compulsion, constraint **11** requirement **12** indebtedness

obligatory
7 binding **8** required **9** essential, mandatory, necessary, requisite **10** compulsory, imperative **11** unavoidable

oblige
3 aid **4** bind, help, make **5** avail, favor, force **6** assist, coerce, compel, please, profit **7** benefit, command, gratify, require **9** constrain **10** contribute **11** accommodate, necessitate

obliged
4 made **5** bound **6** forced **8** beholden, grateful, indebted, thankful **11** constrained **12** appreciative

obliging
4 kind **5** civil **7** amiable, helpful, willing **8** amenable, friendly, pleasant **9** compliant **11** complaisant, considerate, cooperative, good-humored, good-natured **12** good-tempered

oblique
4 awry **5** atilt, raked **6** sloped, tilted **7** devious, leaning, obscure, slanted, sloping, tilting **8** diagonal, inclined, indirect **9** inclining **10** roundabout

obliterate
4 raze, x out **5** erase **6** cancel, delete, efface, remove, rub out **7** blot out, destroy, expunge, wipe out **8** black out, cross out, demolish, dissolve, vaporize **9** extirpate, liquidate, pulverize **10** annihilate, extinguish

oblivion
5 lethe, limbo **7** amnesia, nirvana, nowhere **9** emptiness **11** nothingness **13** forgetfulness
producer: **6** opiate **8** nepenthe

oblivious
4 lost **5** blind **7** unaware **8** absorbed, heedless, ignorant **9** unknowing, unmindful, unwitting **10** unfamiliar, uninformed **11** incognizant, unconscious

oblong
4 oval **5** ovate **7** ellipse **8** elongate **9** elongated, rectangle **11** rectangular

obloquy
4 slam, slur **5** abuse, odium, shame **6** infamy, rebuke **7** calumny, censure **8** disgrace, dishonor, ignominy **9** aspersion, contumely, discredit, disrepute, invective, stricture **10** defamation, opprobrium, scurrility **12** billingsgate, condemnation, vituperation

obnoxious
9 invidious, offensive, vexatious **11** rebarbative

oboe
4 reed **7** hautboy **8** hautbois, woodwind **10** double reed
early: **5** shawm
relative: **7** bassoon **10** cor anglais **11** English horn

O'Brian character
6 Aubrey (Jack) **7** Maturin (Stephen)

obscene
4 foul, lewd, racy, rank, vile **5** bawdy, crude, dirty, gross, lurid, taboo **6** coarse, filthy, ribald, risqué, smutty, vulgar **7** immoral, noisome, profane, raunchy **8** indecent, scabrous **9** abhorrent, appalling, offensive, repellent, repugnant, repulsive, salacious **10** disgusting, lascivious, scurrilous **11** foulmouthed, unprintable **12** pornographic, scatological

obscure
3 dim **4** blur, hide, mask, veil **5** bedim, blind, cloak, cloud, cover, dusky, faint, minor, murky, shade, shady, vague **6** cloudy, darken, hidden, opaque, remote, screen, secret, shadow, shroud, veiled **7** clouded, conceal, cryptic, eclipse, removed, shadowy, unclear, unknown, unnoted **8** disguise, nameless, overcast, puzzling, secluded, shrouded **9** ambiguous, enigmatic, tenebrous, uncertain, undefined **10** camouflage, ill-defined, indefinite, indistinct, mysterious, overshadow **11** out-of-the-way, unimportant **12** inaccessible

obscurity
3 fog **4** dark, haze, mist, murk **5** gloom **6** enigma, miasma, puzzle **7** dimness, mystery, shadows **8** darkness **9** ambiguity

obsequies
4 rite **5** rites **6** burial **7** funeral **10** burial rite

obsequious
4 oily **6** abject, smarmy **7** fawning, fulsome, servile, slavish **8** obedient, obeisant, toadying, unctuous **9** parasitic **10** flattering, submissive **11** deferential, subservient, sycophantic

observance
4 rite, rule **6** custom, notice, regard, ritual **7** liturgy, service **8** ceremony, practice **9** adherence, attention, formality **10** ceremonial

observant
4 keen **5** alert, awake, aware, sharp **7** heedful, mindful **8** watchful **9** advertent, attentive **10** perceptive

observation
4 note **6** notice, record, remark **7** comment, finding, opinion **8** judgment, notation **9** attention, inference **10** commentary **12** obiter dictum

observatory
5 tower **7** lookout, outlook **8** overlook
famous: **4** Lick **6** Lowell, Wilson, Yerkes **7** Arecibo, Palomar
instrument: **9** telescope

observe
3 eye, see **4** espy, keep, look, mark, mind, note, obey, twig, view **5** honor, opine, sight, state, study, watch **6** behold, comply, follow, look at, notice, remark **7** abide by, comment, conform, discern, glimpse, respect **8** perceive **9** celebrate, solemnize **10** comply with **11** commemorate

obsess
5 beset, haunt, hound, rivet **6** absorb, plague **7** consume, possess, torment **9** captivate, preoccupy

obsessed
6 dogged, driven, hipped, hooked **7** gripped, haunted, plagued **8** overcome, troubled **9** dominated, possessed, tormented **11** preoccupied **12** prepossessed

obsession
5 craze, crush, mania **6** fetish, hang-up **8** fixation, idée fixe **11** infatuation **13** preoccupation

obsessive
5 rabid **8** frenetic, maniacal, neurotic **9** fanatical, possessed **10** passionate **11** preoccupied

obsolete
3 old **5** dated, passé, stale **6** old hat **7** disused, outworn, worn-out **8** outdated, outmoded, timeworn **9** out-of-date **10** antiquated, superseded **12** old-fashioned

obstacle
3 bar **4** bump, clog, snag **5** block, catch, check, crimp, hitch **6** hurdle **7** barrier **8** handicap **9** hindrance, impedance, roadblock **10** difficulty, impediment **11** encumbrance, vicissitude **12** interference

obstinate
4 firm **5** balky, fixed **6** dogged, mulish, ornery **7** staunch, willful **8** perverse, resolute, stubborn **9** pigheaded, resistant, unbudging, immovable **10** hardheaded, headstrong, inflexible, persistent, refractory, unyielding **11** intractable, stiff-necked, wrongheaded **12** intransigent, pertinacious, recalcitrant

obstreperous
4 loud, rude **5** noisy, rowdy **6** unruly **7** blatant, raucous **8** strident **9** clamorous, insistent **10** boisterous, disorderly, vociferant, vociferous **11** disobedient, loudmouthed

obstruct
3 bar, dam **4** clog, hide, plug, stop **5** block, check, choke, close **6** cut off, hamper, hinder, impede, stymie, thwart **7** congest, inhibit, occlude, prevent, shut off, shut out, trammel **9** interfere

obstruction
3 bar **4** snag **5** block, hitch **6** hamper, hurdle **7** barrier **8** blockage, obstacle, stoppage **9** hindrance, impedance, roadblock **10** impediment

obtain
3 buy, get, win **4** earn, gain, have, reap **5** annex, reach **6** come by, pick up, secure **7** achieve, acquire, chalk up, procure **8** purchase

obtrude
5 cut in **6** butt in, horn in, impose, meddle **7** presume, push out **8** chisel in, infringe **9** interfere, thrust out

obtrusive
4 nosy **5** nosey, pushy **6** prying **7** forward **8** meddling **9** bumptious, officious **10** meddlesome, protruding **11** impertinent, interfering

obtuse
4 dull, dumb, slow **5** blunt, dense, thick **6** stupid **7** rounded, unclear **11** insensitive

obverse
4 face, side **5** B side, front **8** flip side, opposite **9** other side **10** complement **11** counterpart

obviate
4 ward **5** avert, deter, block **7** forfend, prevent, rule out **8** preclude, stave off **9** forestall, interfere, interpose, intervene **10** anticipate

obvious
5 clear, overt, plain **6** patent, simple **7** blatant, evident, glaring **8** apparent, clear-cut, distinct, manifest, palpable **10** undeniable **11** conspicuous, self-evident, transparent, unambiguous, unequivocal

oca
5 tuber **6** sorrel

O'Casey, Seán
9 dramatist **10** playwright
plays: 17 Juno and the Paycock, Plough and the Stars (The)

occasion
4 call, need **5** basis, break, cause, event **6** chance, ground, reason **7** episode, instant, opening **8** ceremony, incident, instance **9** condition, happening, necessity **10** bring about, foundation, occurrence **11** celebration, opportunity **12** circumstance **13** justification

occasional
3 few, odd **4** rare **6** casual, fitful, random, scarce, seldom **7** special, unusual **8** specific, sporadic, uncommon **9** irregular **10** incidental, infrequent

occasionally
7 at times **11** now and again **12** every so often, once in a while

Occidental
7 Western **8** European **9** Westerner

occlude
4 clog, fill, hide, plug, stop **5** block, choke, close, cover **6** screen, stop up **7** close up, conceal, congest **8** block off, obstruct

occult
5 eerie, magic **6** arcane, mystic, orphic, secret **8** abstruse, esoteric, hermetic, mystical **9** recondite, unearthly **10** cabalistic, mysterious **12** supernatural

occupant
5 liver **6** inmate, tenant **7** denizen, dweller, resider **8** habitant, resident **10** inhabitant

occupation
3 job, use **4** line, work **5** trade **6** career, métier, office **7** calling **8** activity, business, position, vocation **9** residence **10** employment, habitation, possession, settlement

occupy
3 use **4** busy, fill, hold **5** seize, tie up **6** absorb, employ, engage, live in, take up, tenant **7** control, engross, immerse, inhabit **8** populate, reside in, take over

occur
3 hap **4** pass **5** arise, ensue, pop up **6** appear, befall, betide, chance, dawn on, happen, result, strike **7** come off, develop **9** take place, transpire

occurrence
3 hap **4** pass **5** event, state **7** episode **8** exigency, incident, juncture, occasion **9** adventure, condition, emergency, happening, situation

ocean
3 sea **4** blue, deep, main **5** brine, drink **6** Arctic, Indian **7** Pacific **8** Atlantic **9** Antarctic
movement: **3** ebb **4** tide, wave

Oceania
country: **4** Fiji **5** Belau, Nauru, Palau, Samoa, Tonga **6** Tuvalu **7** Vanuatu **8** Kiribati **9** Australia **10** New Zealand
territory: **7** Tokelau **12** New Caledonia **13** American Samoa
ethnic group: **6** Fijian, Papuan, Samoan **10** Melanesian, Polynesian **11** Micronesian
language: **5** Maori **6** Fijian, Papuan, Pidgin, Samoan **10** Melanesian

oceanic
4 huge, vast **5** great **6** marine **7** immense, pelagic **8** enormous, maritime **9** saltwater, thalassic

Ocean State
11 Rhode Island

Oceanus
daughter: **5** Doris **7** Oceanid **8** Eurynome
father: **6** Uranus
mother: **4** Gaea
sister: **6** Tethys
son: **6** Peneus **7** Alpheus
wife: **6** Tethys

ocellus
3 eye **7** eyespot

ocelot
3 cat **7** wildcat

O'Connor novel
9 Wise Blood

octave
5 eight, scale **6** eighth, stanza **8** interval

Octavia
brother: **8** Augustus
grandson: **8** Caligula
husband: **4** Nero **6** Antony

October birthstone
4 opal

octopus
7 mollusc, mollusk **9** devilfish **10** cephalopod
arm: **8** tentacle
genus: **7** Polypus
kin: **5** squid **10** cuttlefish

ocular
4 seen **5** optic **6** visual **7** eyelike, optical, visible **8** eyepiece, viewable **9** perceived

Odalisque painter
6 Ingres (Jean-Auguste-Dominique) **7** Matisse (Henri)

odd
4 lone, rare **5** extra, fluky, queer, rummy, weird **6** casual, chance, single, uneven **7** curious, erratic, strange, unusual **8** peculiar, singular **9** eccentric, unmatched **13** idiosyncratic

oddball
4 kook **5** kooky, weird **6** weirdo **7** bizarre, curious, offbeat, strange, unusual **8** original, peculiar **9** character, eccentric **10** outlandish **13** idiosyncratic

Odd Couple, The
author: **5** Simon (Neil)
character: **5** Felix, Oscar
star: **6** Carney (Art), Lemmon (Jack) **7** Klugman (Jack), Matthau (Walter), Randall (Tony)

oddity
5 freak, quirk **6** weirdo **7** anomaly **9** curiosity, deviation, eccentric, weirdness **10** aberration **11** abnormality, peculiarity, strangeness **12** eccentricity, idiosyncrasy, irregularity

odds
4 edge **5** favor, ratio **7** benefit, chances **8** handicap, variance **9** advantage **10** likelihood, partiality **11** probability

odds and ends
4 bits, olio **6** jumble, medley, motley, scraps **7** mélange, mixture **8** remnants, sundries **9** etceteras, leftovers, potpourri **10** assortment, hodgepodge, hotchpotch, miscellany

ode
4 hymn, poem **5** lyric, paean, psalm, verse
part: **5** epode **7** strophe **11** antistrophe

Odets play
9 Golden Boy **11** Country Girl (The) **12** Awake and Sing **15** Waiting for Lefty

odeum
4 hall **7** theater, theatre **10** auditorium **11** concert hall

Odin
brother: **4** Vili
daughter-in-law: **5** Nanna
father: **3** Bor
hall: **8** Valhalla
horse: **8** Sleipnir
maiden: **8** Valkyrie
mansion: **9** Gladsheim
mother: **6** Bestla
race: **5** Aesir
raven: **5** Hugin, Munin

ring: 8 Draupnir
son: 3 Tyr 4 Thor, Vali 5 Bragi 6 Balder, Baldur
spear: 7 Gungnir
sword: 4 Gram
wife: 4 Fria, Rind 5 Frigg 6 Frigga
wolf: 4 Geri 5 Freki

odious
4 foul, vile 6 horrid 7 hateful, heinous, noxious 8 horrible 9 abhorrent, execrable, invidious, loathsome, malicious, repellent, repugnant 10 abominable, despicable, detestable, disgusting

odium
4 hate, onus 5 shame 6 hatred, infamy, stigma 7 censure, obloquy 8 contempt, disgrace, dishonor, ignominy, loathing 9 disrepute 10 abhorrence, opprobrium 11 detestation 12 condemnation

odor
4 funk, reek 5 aroma, fetor, scent, smell, stink, whiff 6 stench 7 bouquet, perfume 9 fragrance, redolence

odorous
4 gamy 5 fetid, heady, sweet 6 foetid, smelly, strong 7 pungent, scented 8 aromatic, fragrant, perfumed, redolent, unsavory 9 offensive

Odysseus
7 Ulysses
dog: 5 Argos
enchantress: 5 Circe
father: 7 Laertes
friend: 6 Mentor
harasser: 8 Poseidon
herb: 4 moly
kingdom: 6 Ithaca, Ithaka
mother: 8 Anticlea
rescuer: 3 Ino 8 Nausicaa
son: 9 Telegonus 10 Telemachus
swineherd: 7 Eumaeus
voyage: 7 odyssey
wife: 8 Penelope

odyssey
4 trek 5 quest 6 voyage 7 journey 9 wandering 13 peregrination

Odyssey
author: 5 Homer
partner: 5 Iliad

Oedipus
brother-in-law: 5 Creon
daughter: 6 Ismene 8 Antigone
father: 5 Laius
kingdom: 6 Thebes
mother: 7 Jocasta
son: 8 Eteocles 9 Polynices 10 Polyneices
victim: 5 Laius
wife: 7 Jocasta

Oenone
husband: 5 Paris
rival: 5 Helen

oeuvre
4 work 6 corpus, output 8 lifework

of
German: 3 aus, von
Italian: 5 degli, della, delle

off
3 hit 4 away, awry, kill, slay 5 aside, snuff, whack 6 depart, murder, remote, rub out, slight 7 seaward, spoiled 8 dispatch 9 eccentric, incorrect

offal
4 guts, junk 5 gurry, trash, waste 6 debris, litter, refuse, spilth 7 carrion, garbage, innards, rubbish, viscera 8 entrails 9 sweepings 10 intestines

offbeat
3 odd 5 fresh, outré, weird 6 way out 7 bizarre, oddball, strange, unusual 8 bohemian, peculiar, singular, uncommon 9 eccentric, whimsical 10 outlandish, unorthodox 11 distinctive 13 idiosyncratic

off-color
3 ill, low 4 blue, racy 5 bawdy, salty, shady 6 ailing, peaked, poorly, risqué, sickly, unwell 7 dubious, naughty 8 improper, indecent 10 indisposed, suggestive

offend
3 dis, sin, vex 4 gall, hurt, miff, pain 5 anger, annoy, pique, repel, shock, upset 6 appall, breach, insult, nettle 7 affront, disturb, provoke, violate 8 aggrieve, distress, irritate 9 displease 10 antagonize, transgress

offender
5 felon 6 sinner 7 culprit 8 criminal, violator 9 wrongdoer 10 lawbreaker, malefactor 12 transgressor

offense
3 sin 4 huff, hurt, miff, tort, vice 5 crime, fault, pique, wrong 6 attack, breach, felony, injury, insult 7 affront, assault, dudgeon, misdeed, outrage, umbrage 9 indignity, onslaught, violation 10 aggression, infraction 11 misdemeanor

offensive
3 bad 4 foul, rank, vile 5 drive, onset 6 attack, odious 7 assault, fulsome, noisome, obscene, painful 8 nauseous, unsavory 9 loathsome, obnoxious, onslaught, repellent, repugnant, repulsive, sickening 10 aggression, aggressive, disgusting, nauseating, unpleasant 12 disagreeable, unappetizing 13 objectionable

offer
3 bid, try 4 seek, show 5 assay, essay, pitch,

put up **6** afford, extend, submit, tender **7** advance, attempt, display, exhibit, hold out, present, propose, provide, suggest **8** endeavor, proposal, threaten **9** sacrifice **10** submission **11** proposition

offering
3 IPO **4** alms, gift **5** grant **6** course, corban **7** charity, present **8** donation, oblation **9** sacrifice **11** benefaction, beneficence **12** contribution

offhand
5 ad-lib **6** blithe, breezy, casual **8** informal **9** extempore, impromptu, unstudied **10** improvised, nonchalant, unprepared **11** extemporary, spontaneous, unrehearsed

office
3 job **4** duty **5** berth, suite **6** agency, billet, bureau **7** station **8** business, cube farm, function, province **9** situation, workplace **10** department
communication: **4** memo
head: **4** boss **7** manager
holder: **9** incumbent **11** functionary
machine: **3** fax **6** copier **7** printer **10** calculator, fax machine **11** photocopier
seeker: **9** candidate **10** politician
without work: **8** sinecure
worker: **5** clerk **6** typist **9** file clerk, secretary **10** bookkeeper

officer
3 cop **4** exec **6** noncom, police **7** John Law, manager **8** brass hat, official **9** executive **10** magistrate
abbreviation: **3** Adm., Col., Ens., Gen., Maj. **4** Capt., Cmdr. **5** Comdr., Lieut.
army: **5** looey, looie, major **7** captain, colonel, general **10** lieutenant
British: **9** brigadier
court: **7** bailiff
king's: **11** chamberlain
law-enforcement: **3** cop **6** copper, deputy, police **7** marshal, sheriff **9** constable, patrolman, policeman
naval: **4** mate **6** ensign **7** admiral, captain **9** commander, commodore **10** lieutenant
noncommissioned: **5** sarge **8** corporal, sergeant
petty: **4** bos'n **5** bosun **6** yeoman **9** boatswain
prison: **5** guard **6** warden

official
4 exec **7** cleared, manager **8** approved, bona fide, endorsed **9** authentic, canonical, cathedral, certified, executive **10** accredited, authorized, ex cathedra, magistrate, sanctioned **13** administrator, authoritative
city or town: **5** mayor **8** alderman **9** councilor, selectman **10** councillor
diplomatic: **5** envoy **6** consul **7** attaché **10** ambassador
governmental: **6** syndic
parish: **6** beadle
sports: **3** ref, ump **6** umpire **7** referee **8** linesman
university: **4** dean **6** bursar **7** provost **9** registrar **10** chancellor

officiate
5 chair, serve **6** direct, umpire **7** conduct, oversee, preside, referee **9** supervise **11** superintend

officious
4 busy, nosy **5** bossy, nosey, pushy **7** forward **8** meddling **9** assertive, intrusive, obtrusive **10** meddlesome **13** self-important

offing
6 future **7** by-and-by **9** aftertime, hereafter **10** near future

off-key
3 odd **7** jarring **9** anomalous, dissonant **10** discordant **12** inharmonious

off-putting
7 irksome, jarring **8** daunting **9** dismaying, offensive, repellent **10** forbidding, irritating **11** distasteful, rebarbative **12** disagreeable, discouraging **13** disconcerting, disheartening, objectionable

off-road transport
3 ATV

offscouring
5 leper, trash **6** pariah, refuse, reject **7** outcast **8** castaway, derelict **11** untouchable

offset
6 square **7** balance, redress **8** equalize **10** balance out, compensate, neutralize **11** counterpose, countervail **12** counterpoise

offshoot
4 twig **5** scion **6** branch **7** product, spin-off **9** affiliate, by-product, outgrowth **10** derivative, descendant

offspring
3 cub, kid **4** kids, seed **5** brood, child, hatch, issue, scion, spawn, swarm, young **7** produce, product, progeny **8** children **9** posterity **10** descendant **11** progeniture

off-the-wall
4 zany **5** kooky, weird **6** far-out, way-out **7** bizarre, oddball **8** freakish **9** eccentric **10** outlandish

off-white
4 bone **5** cream, ivory **6** oyster, vellum **9** parchment

Of Human Bondage author
7 Maugham (W. Somerset)

O'Flaherty of literature
4 Liam

Of Mice and Men
author: **9** Steinbeck (John)
character: **6** George (Milton), Lennie (Small)

often
9 generally **10** frequently, habitually, repeatedly **11** recurrently

ogee
3 ess **4** arch **5** curve **7** molding

Ogier the ___
4 Dane

ogive
3 rib **4** arch **5** graph

ogle
3 eye **4** gape, gaze, leer, look **5** stare **6** goggle **7** stare at **10** rubberneck

ogre
3 orc **5** bogey, giant, Shrek **6** Grinch **7** bugbear, monster **8** bogeyman **9** boogeyman
Algonquian: **7** wendigo, windigo

ogress
5 harpy, scold, shrew, vixen **6** amazon, virago **8** fishwife **9** termagant, Xanthippe

O'Hara mansion
4 Tara

O'Hara novel
7 Pal Joey **16** Butterfield Eight

Ohio
capital: **8** Columbus
city: **5** Akron, Xenia **6** Canton, Dayton, Toledo **9** Cleveland **10** Cincinnati
college, university: **5** Miami **6** Kenyon **7** Antioch, Denison, Oberlin **9** Kent State **12** Bowling Green
nickname: **7** Buckeye (State)
river: **4** Ohio **6** Maumee **8** Sandusky
state bird: **8** cardinal
state flower: **16** scarlet carnation
state tree: **7** buckeye

Oholibamah
father: **4** Anah
husband: **4** Esau

oil
3 fat, gas **4** balm, fuel, lube, oleo **5** crude, oleum, slick **6** anoint, grease, pomade **7** blarney, incense, lanolin **8** flattery, soft soap **9** adulation, lubricant, lubricate, petroleum
cartel: **4** OPEC
combining form: **3** ole **4** olei, oleo
company: **3** Sun **4** Arco, Esso, Gulf, Hess, Hunt **5** ADNOC, Amoco, Citgo, Exxon, Getty, Mobil, Pemex, Shell, Sohio, Union, Yukos **6** Aramco, Conoco, Lukoil, Sunoco, Texaco, Valero **7** Ashland, Chevron, Gazprom, Rosneft **8** Marathon, Pennzoil, Phillips, Sinclair **9** Petrobras **10** ExxonMobil, Occidental, PetroChina
consecrated: **6** chrism
fragrant: **5** attar **6** neroli
fuel: **3** gas **6** butane, petrol **7** benzene, propane **8** gasoline, kerosene
relating to: **5** oleic
ship: **6** tanker
source: **4** rape **5** olive, shale **6** canola **7** linseed **8** flaxseed, rapeseed **9** sunflower
well: **6** gusher

oilbird
8 guacharo

oily
5 fatty, slick, soapy, suave **6** greasy, smarmy, smooth **7** fulsome **8** slippery, unctuous **10** lubricious, obsequious, oleaginous

ointment
4 balm, nard **5** cream, salve **6** lotion **7** unction, unguent **8** calamine, liniment **9** emollient, spikenard **11** embrocation

OJ trial judge
3 Ito (Lance)

OK, okay
3 aye, yea, yes **4** fine, good, safe, well, yeah **5** agree, allow, favor, licit **6** agreed, assent, decent, permit **7** approve, certify, endorse, support **8** accredit, adequate, all right, approval, blessing, high sign, passable, sanction, thumbs-up **9** authorize, hunky-dory **10** acceptable, permission **11** endorsement, permissible **12** satisfactory

O.K. Corral fighter
4 Earp (Morgan, Virgil, Wyatt) **8** Holliday (Doc)

Okinawa capital
4 Naha

Oklahoma
capital: **12** Oklahoma City
city: **3** Ada **4** Enid **5** Tulsa **6** Norman
college, university: **11** Oral Roberts
mountain: **9** Black Mesa
nickname: **6** Sooner (State)
river: **3** Red **8** Arkansas, Canadian
state bird: **10** flycatcher
state flower: **9** mistletoe
state tree: **6** redbud

okra
4 soup **5** gumbo **6** mallow

Oktoberfest vessel
5 stein

old
4 aged, gray, late, past **5** anile, dated, hoary, passé, stale **6** bygone, démodé, former, mature, senior, whilom **7** ancient, antique, archaic, elderly, lasting, onetime, overage, quondam, veteran **8** enduring, lifelong, Noachian, outmoded, timeworn **9** erstwhile, geriatric, long-lived, perennial, perpetual, venerable **10** antiquated, inveterate **13** superannuated
Scottish: **4** auld

old age
3 eld **6** dotage **8** caducity **10** senescence **11** decrepitude, elderliness, senectitude

Old Bailey
5 court
Old Colony State
13 Massachusetts
Old Curiosity Shop
author: 7 Dickens (Charles)
character: 4 Nell **10** Little Nell
Old Dominion State
8 Virginia
olden days
4 yore
Old Faithful
6 geyser
old-fashioned
4 aged **5** dated, dowdy, fusty, moldy, passé, retro, stale, tired **6** bygone, démodé, quaint, stodgy **7** ancient, antique, archaic, outworn, vintage **8** obsolete, outdated, outmoded **9** out-of-date **10** antiquated
old French coin
3 ecu, sou
old hand
3 pro, vet **6** expert, master **7** veteran **9** authority **10** past master, specialist
old hat
5 dated, passé, stale, tired, trite **6** démodé **7** antique, clichéd, vintage **8** outmoded, time-worn, well-worn **9** hackneyed, out-of-date **10** antiquated
Old Ironsides
12 Constitution (U.S.S.)
poet: 6 Holmes (Oliver Wendell)
Old Line State
8 Maryland
old maid
6 fusser **7** fusspot **8** spinster **10** fussbudget
Old Nick
3 devil, Satan **7** Lucifer **9** Beelzebub
Old North State
13 North Carolina
old-photo tint
5 sepia
Old Rough and Ready
6 Taylor (Zachary)
Olds' car
3 Reo
old-time
5 dated, retro **6** bygone **7** antique, vintage **10** antiquated **12** long-standing
old-timer
3 vet **4** fogy **5** elder, fogey **6** codger, senior **7** ancient, antique, veteran
Old World
6 Europe
oleaginous
see **oily**
oleaster
5 shrub **12** Russian olive
olecranon
9 funny bone
oleo
9 margarine
oleoresin
10 turpentine
oleum
3 oil
olfaction
5 sense, smell **8** smelling
olid
4 foul, rank **5** fetid **6** putrid, rancid, rotten, stinky **7** noisome, odorous, reeking, stenchy **8** stinking **9** offensive **10** malodorous
Olin of film
4 Lena
olio
3 mix **4** hash, stew **5** gumbo, umble **6** jumble, medley **7** farrago, grab bag, mélange, mixture **8** mishmash, mixed bag **9** potpourri **10** assortment, collection, hodgepodge, hotchpotch, macédoine, miscellany, salmagundi **11** gallimaufry
Olive of cartoons
3 Oyl
Oliver Twist
author: 7 Dickens (Charles)
character: 5 Fagin, Nancy, Sikes (Bill) **6** Bumble (Mr.) **12** Artful Dodger
Ollie's partner
4 Fran, Stan **5** Kukla
Olympian
3 god **5** deity, lofty, noble **6** lordly **7** athlete, exalted, godlike **8** majestic
Olympics site
1972: 6 Munich **7** Sapporo
1976: 8 Montreal **9** Innsbruck
1980: 6 Moscow **10** Lake Placid
1984: 10 Los Angeles **8** Sarajevo
1988: 5 Seoul **7** Calgary
1992: 9 Barcelona **11** Albertville
1994: 11 Lillehammer
1996: 7 Atlanta
1998: 6 Nagano
2000: 6 Sydney
2002: 12 Salt Lake City
2004: 6 Athens
2006: 5 Turin **6** Torino
2008: 7 Beijing
2010: 9 Vancouver
2012: 6 London
2014: 5 Sochi

2016: **3** Rio **6** Brazil **12** Rio de Janeiro
2018: **5** Korea **11** Pyeongchang
2020: **5** Japan, Tokyo

Oman
capital: **6** Masqat, Muscat
language: **6** Arabic **7** Baluchi
monetary unit: **4** rial
mountain range: **7** Al-Hajar
neighbor: **5** Yemen **11** Saudi Arabia
peninsula: **7** Arabian
sea: **7** Arabian

Omar
4 poet **7** Khayyám
country: **6** Persia
father: **7** Eliphaz
poem: **8** Rubaiyat

omega
3 end **6** ending, finale, letter
kin: **3** zed, zee

omelet ingredient
3 egg **4** eggs

omen
4 sign **5** augur, token **6** augury, boding **7** auspice, portent, presage, warning **8** bodement, prophecy **9** foretoken **10** foreboding, prediction, prognostic

ominous
4 dark, dire, grim **6** dismal **7** baleful, direful, doomful, fateful, looming **8** alarming, lowering, menacing, sinister **9** ill-boding, prophetic **10** forbidding, foreboding, portentous **11** frightening, threatening **12** inauspicious, unpropitious

omission
3 cut, gap **4** lack, skip, slip **5** blank, break, chasm, error, lapse **6** hiatus, lacuna **7** elision, failure **8** eclipsis, ellipsis, overlook **9** exclusion
mark: **5** caret **8** ellipsis **10** apostrophe

omit
4 drop, fail, skip **5** elide **6** except, forget, ignore, slight **7** exclude, neglect **8** leave out, overlook, pass over

omnibus
3 ana **4** posy **5** album **7** garland **8** analects, treasury **9** anthology **10** compendium, miscellany **11** florilegium

omnipotent
6 divine **7** godlike, supreme **8** almighty **9** unlimited **11** all-powerful

omnipresent
7 allover, endless **8** infinite, unending **9** boundless, limitless, universal **10** ubiquitous

omniscient
4 wise **7** learned **9** know-it-all **10** all-knowing

omnium-gatherum
see **olio**

Omphale
domain: **5** Lydia
slave: **8** Heracles, Hercules

omphalos
3 hub **5** focus, navel **9** umbilicus **10** focal point **11** belly button

on
4 atop, over **5** above, along, going **7** working **9** operating **11** functioning

onager
3 ass **5** kiang **8** catapult

on-and-off
6 fickle, fitful **7** erratic **8** sporadic **12** intermittent

Onan's father
5 Judah

Onassis, to his friends
3 Ari

once
4 erst, ever, late, past **5** at all **6** before, bygone, former, whilom **7** already, earlier, long ago, onetime, quondam **8** formerly, sometime

once-over
4 look **5** check **6** gander, glance, survey **10** inspection **11** examination

one
4 lone, only, sole, unit **5** monad **6** single, unique **7** numeral **8** separate, singular, solitary **9** undivided **10** individual, particular
combining form: **4** mono
French: **3** une
German: **3** ein **4** eine
prefix: **3** uni
Scottish: **3** ane, yin
Spanish: **3** una, uno

one and a half
combining form: **6** sesqui

on edge
5 antsy, jumpy, tense **6** uneasy **7** jittery, nervous, uptight

one-eyed giant
7 Cyclops **10** Polyphemus

one-handed god
3 Tiu, Tyr

one-horse town
4 burg **5** thorp **6** hamlet, Podunk **7** village **11** whistle-stop

one hundred
6 centum
years: **7** century

O'Neill, Eugene
daughter: **4** Oona
heroine: **4** Anna, Nina
play: **3** Ile **4** Gold **8** Hairy Ape (The) **12** Ah Wilderness, Anna Christie, Emperor Jones, Iceman Cometh (The) **13** Great God Brown (The),

Marco Millions **16** Strange Interlude **18** Desire Under the Elms **22** Mourning Becomes Electra **24** Long Day's Journey into Night

oneiric
6 dreamy **8** anagogic **9** dreamlike

one-name singer
4 Beck, Enya, Moby, Pink, Sade, Seal **5** Adele, Björk, Jewel **6** Eminem, Fergie, Prince **7** Beyoncé, Madonna, Shakira

oneness
3 all **5** union, unity, whole **7** harmony **8** entirety, identity, sameness, totality **9** integrity, unanimity **10** singleness, uniformity **11** singularity, unification **13** individuality

onerous
4 hard **5** heavy, tough **6** taxing, trying **7** arduous, exigent, wearing, weighty **8** exacting, grievous, imposing, pressing, toilsome **9** demanding, difficult, laborious **10** burdensome, cumbersome, oppressive **11** troublesome

one-sided
6 biased, uneven **7** colored, partial, unequal **8** inclined, partisan, weighted **10** prejudiced, unbalanced, unilateral

one-third of a WW2 film
4 Tora

onetime
3 old **4** once, past **6** bygone, former, whilom **7** quondam **8** previous **9** erstwhile

one-up
5 outdo **6** exceed **7** surpass

ongoing
7 current, growing **8** evolving **9** advancing, in process **10** continuing, continuous, developing, in progress, unfinished **11** progressing

on hand
4 here **5** ready **6** nearby **7** pending, present **9** available

onion
4 bulb **7** shallot
bulb: **3** set
genus: **6** Allium
kin: **4** leek **6** garlic
kind: **7** Bermuda, Danvers, Spanish
roll: **5** bialy
young: **8** scallion

online
5 wired **9** connected
address: **3** URL
browser: **5** Opera **6** Chrome, Safari **7** Firefox, Mozilla **8** Explorer
business: **5** e-tail
communication: **4** text **5** e-mail, tweet **7** texting
disclaimer: **4** IMHO
guffaw: **3** LOL
location: **4** site **7** Web site
publication: **5** e-zine
system: **3** Web **8** Internet

onlooker
6 viewer **7** watcher, witness **8** beholder, kibitzer, observer **9** bystander, kibbitzer, spectator **10** eyewitness **12** rubbernecker

only
3 but, few, one, yet **4** just, lone, mere, save, sole, solo **5** alone **6** and yet, at most, except, merely, simply, single, solely, unique **7** however, utterly **8** entirely, singular, solitary **11** exclusively

onomasticon
7 lexicon **8** wordbook

onomatopoeic
5 mimic **6** echoic **7** mimetic **9** emulative, imitative **10** simulative

onset
4 dawn, rush **5** birth, get-go, start **6** attack, coming, origin **7** arrival, assault, dawning, offense, opening **8** invasion **9** beginning, inception, offensive **10** aggression **12** commencement

onslaught
5 blitz **6** attack, charge, deluge **7** assault, barrage, offense, torrent **8** invasion **9** offensive **10** aggression

on-target
3 apt, fit **5** exact, right **7** correct, perfect, precise **8** accurate **11** appropriate

Ontario
bay: **8** Georgian
capital: **7** Toronto
city: **4** York **6** London, Ottawa **7** Markham, Windsor **8** Hamilton **9** Etobicoke, Kitchener, North York **10** Thunder Bay **11** Mississauga, Scarborough **13** Sault Ste. Marie
lake: **4** Erie **5** Huron **7** Nipigon, Ontario **8** Superior
provincial flower: **13** white trillium
river: **5** Moose **6** Albany, Severn, Winisk

on the go
4 busy **6** active

on the house
4 free **6** comped, gratis **13** complimentary

on the nose
5 bingo **6** dead-on, spot-on **7** exactly **8** accurate **9** precisely **10** accurately

on the ocean
4 a-sea

on the other hand
3 but **7** however **11** nonetheless **12** nevertheless

on the rocks
4 iced **7** with ice, wrecked

on the whole
6 mainly, mostly **7** usually **8** all in all **9** generally, in general, typically **10** altogether, by and large

onus
3 tax **4** duty, load, task **5** blame, brand, fault, guilt, odium, stain **6** burden, charge, stigma, weight **8** black eye **9** liability **10** obligation, oppression

onward
5 ahead, along, forth **7** forward **9** advancing

onyx
5 agate **10** chalcedony

oodles
4 a lot, gobs, lots, tons, wads **5** heaps, loads, piles, rafts, reams, scads **6** plenty

oolong
3 tea

oomph
3 pep, vim, zip **4** brio, dash, élan, push, zest, zing **5** drive, punch, verve, vigor **6** esprit, pizazz, spirit **7** pizzazz **8** strength, vitality **9** sex appeal

ooze
3 goo, mud **4** emit, goop, leak, seep, weep **5** bleed, exude, issue, marsh, slime, sweat **7** secrete, seepage **8** transude

opacity
9 murkiness, obscurity **10** obtuseness

opal
3 gem **5** jewel, stone **6** silica **7** girasol, hyalite **8** gemstone

opaque
3 dim **4** dull, hazy **5** dense, filmy, murky, vague **6** cloudy **7** clouded, obscure, unclear **8** abstruse

OPEC nation
3 UAE **4** Iran, Iraq **5** Libya, Qatar **6** Kuwait **7** Algeria, Nigeria **9** Indonesia, Venezuela **11** Saudi Arabia

open
4 ajar, bare, free, wide **5** frank, lance, overt, unzip **6** broach, candid, expand, expose, public, reveal, spread, unfold, unlock, unseal, unveil **7** convene, outdoor, uncover, unlatch **8** disclose, outdoors, unlocked, unsealed **9** available, uncovered, undecided **10** unfastened **11** susceptible, unconcealed, undisguised **12** unrestricted

open-air
7 outdoor, outside **8** alfresco, outdoors **9** out-of-door **10** out-of-doors

open-and-shut
4 easy **5** clear, plain **6** patent, simple **7** evident, obvious

openhanded
6 giving, lavish **7** liberal **8** generous **9** bounteous, bountiful, unselfish, unsparing **10** beneficent, bighearted, charitable, munificent **11** magnanimous

openhearted
4 kind, warm **5** frank, plain **6** candid, honest **8** generous **10** responsive **11** sympathetic

opening
3 gap **4** dawn, door, gate, hole, pass, pore, slit, slot, vent **5** break, chasm, chink, cleft, crack, debut, intro, mouth, onset, start, stoma **6** breach, chance, lacuna, outlet, outset **7** crevice, dawning, fissure, orifice, pinhole **8** aperture, overture **9** beginning **10** dedication **11** opportunity
ship's: **5** hatch **8** hatchway, porthole
stake in poker: **4** ante

open-minded
7 liberal **8** tolerant, unbiased **9** receptive **12** freethinking, unprejudiced

openmouthed
4 agog, awed, rapt **5** agape **6** amazed, gaping **7** stunned **9** astounded, surprised **10** astonished, speechless

open sesame
3 key **5** charm **6** ticket **8** passport, password

open up
4 fire, talk **5** shoot **6** reveal **7** cut into, divulge **8** disclose **9** make plain, spread out **11** communicate

opera
comic: **5** buffa **6** bouffe
cry: **5** brava, bravo
glasses: **9** lorgnette
house: **3** Met **7** La Scala **12** Covent Garden, Metropolitan
kind: **4** soap **5** comic, grand, horse, space
part: **3** act **4** aria **5** scena
solo: **4** aria
star: **4** diva **10** prima donna
text: **8** libretto
(see also individual titles and composers)

opera (famous)
4 Aida **5** Faust, Manon, Norma, Tosca **6** Carmen, Otello, Salome **7** Elektra, Fidelio, Macbeth, Nabucco, Walküre (Die), Wozzeck **8** Don Carlo, Falstaff, Idomeneo, La Bohème, Turandot **9** Don Carlos, Lohengrin, Rheingold (Das), Rigoletto, Siegfried **10** I Pagliacci, La Gioconda, La Traviata, Magic Flute (The), Prince Igor, Tannhäuser **11** Don Giovanni, William Tell **12** Così Fan Tutte, Manon Lescaut, Pearl Fishers (The) **14** Flying Dutchman (The) **15** Barber of Seville (The), Götterdämmerung, Madama Butterfly **16** Marriage of Figaro (The), Tristan und Isolde

opera composer Giuseppe
5 Verdi

opera star Pinza
4 Ezio

operant
8 behavior **9** effective **10** measurable, observable, productive **12** conditioning

operate
3 act, run, use **4** work **5** drive, exert, steer **6** behave, direct, effect, handle, manage **7** carry on, conduct, control, perform, produce **8** function, maneuver **9** influence **10** manipulate

operation
3 use **4** step **6** action **7** concern, mission, process, surgery **8** activity, business, exercise, exertion, function, maneuver **9** procedure **10** employment, engagement, enterprise **11** performance, transaction

operative
3 key **5** agent, alive **6** active, moving, usable **7** dynamic, in force, running, working **8** relevant **9** effective **10** functional **11** efficacious, secret agent

operator
4 user **5** agent, fixer, pilot **6** doctor, driver **7** schemer, surgeon **9** conductor

operculum
3 lid **4** flap **8** covering

operetta composer
5 Friml (Rudolf), Lehár (Franz), Suppé (Franz von) **6** Straus (Oscar) **7** Herbert (Victor), Romberg (Sigmund), Strauss (Johann) **8** Sullivan (Arthur) **9** Offenbach (Jacques)

operose
4 dull **6** boring, tiring **7** tedious **8** tiresome, toilsome, weariful **9** difficult, laborious, wearisome

Ophelia
beloved: **6** Hamlet
brother: **7** Laertes
father: **8** Polonius

ophidian
5 snake **9** snakelike

opiate
4 dope, drug **7** anodyne **8** hypnotic, narcotic, nepenthe, sedative **9** analgesic, soporific **10** anesthetic, painkiller **11** somniferous **12** somnifacient, tranquilizer
type: **7** codeine **8** morphine

opine
4 aver, deem, hold, view **5** claim, judge, state, think **6** advise, assert **7** believe, express, suppose **8** point out **9** recommend

opinion
4 idea, view **5** tenet **6** belief, notion, theory **7** feeling, thought **8** attitude, estimate, judgment, reaction **9** sentiment **10** assumption, conclusion, conjecture, conviction, estimation, hypothesis, persuasion **11** speculation, supposition
express an: **4** vote **5** judge **9** criticize
page: **4** op-ed

opium
4 dope, drug **8** narcotic
derivative: **6** heroin **7** codeine **8** laudanum, morphine **9** paregoric
source: **5** poppy

opossum
9 marsupial
kin: **8** kangaroo

opponent
3 con, foe **4** anti **5** enemy, rival **6** muscle **7** nemesis **9** adversary, assailant, combatant **10** antagonist, challenger, competitor **12** counteragent

opportune
3 apt, fit **6** timely **8** suitable **9** favorable, well-timed **10** auspicious, convenient, felicitous, propitious **11** appropriate

opportunity
4 turn **5** break, space, spell **6** chance **7** opening **8** juncture, occasion, prospect **12** circumstance

oppose
4 buck, defy, deny, duel **5** cross, fight, repel **6** attack, combat, debate, differ, object, refute, resist **7** assault, contest, counter, dispute, prevent, protest **8** confront, contrast, disagree, obstruct **9** withstand **10** contradict, contravene, controvert, disapprove

opposed (to)
3 con **4** agin, anti **6** contra **7** adverse, against **11** adversarial **12** antagonistic, antipathetic

opposite
4 foil **5** polar **6** contra, facing **7** antonym, counter, inverse, obverse, opposed, reverse **8** antipode, antipole, contrary, contrast, converse **9** antipodal, diametric **10** antipodean, antithesis **11** contrasting, counterpole **12** antithetical, counterpoint **13** contradictory
prefix: **3** dis **5** retro **6** contra **7** counter

opposition
3 con, foe **5** enemy **7** rivalry **8** conflict, defiance **9** adversary, animosity, hostility **10** antagonism, antithesis, resistance **11** contrariety, disapproval

oppress
5 abuse, crush, wrong **6** burden, injure, sadden, subdue **7** afflict, torment, torture, trouble **8** aggrieve, distress, overload **9** persecute, subjugate, weigh down

oppressive
5 harsh, heavy **6** brutal, dismal, gloomy, severe, somber, sombre, taxing **7** exigent, onerous, weighty **8** crushing, exacting, grievous, stifling **9** demanding **10** burdensome, depressing, tyrannical **11** dispiriting, overbearing, suffocating **12** discouraging, overwhelming
force: **4** onus, yoke **6** burden, weight

oppressor
5 bully 6 despot, tyrant 8 autocrat, dictator 9 strongman

opprobrious
4 evil, vile 6 odious, vulgar 7 abusive, hateful 8 infamous 9 notorious, truculent 10 despicable, scurrilous 11 disgraceful, ignominious 12 contemptible, contumelious, vituperative

opprobrium
5 abuse, blame, odium, scorn, shame 6 infamy 7 obloquy 8 contempt, disgrace, dishonor, ignominy, reproach 9 contumely, discredit, disesteem, disrepute 10 scurrility 12 vituperation

oppugn
5 argue, fight 6 battle, combat 7 contend, contest, dispute 8 question

Ops
4 Rhea
consort: 6 Cronus, Saturn
daughter: 5 Ceres 7 Demeter

opt
3 tap 4 pick 5 elect, favor 6 choose, decide, prefer, select

optical
6 ocular, visual 8 visional
debris: 7 floater
instrument: 4 lens 5 scope 7 transit 9 magnifier, periscope, telescope 10 microscope

optimal
4 best 5 ideal 6 choice, finest 7 perfect, supreme 8 choicest

optimist
4 bull 5 hoper 7 dreamer 8 idealist, Micawber 9 Pollyanna 10 positivist

optimistic
4 rosy 5 happy, merry, sunny 6 bright, hoping, upbeat 7 assured, buoyant, hopeful, roseate 8 cheerful, positive, sanguine, trusting 9 confident, promising 11 rose-colored 12 Pollyannaish

option
4 pick 5 claim, extra, grant, right 6 choice 7 license 8 contract, election 9 accessory, privilege, selection 10 preference 11 alternative, prerogative

optional
4 free 5 extra 8 elective 9 voluntary 11 alternative 13 discretionary
item: 5 add-on, extra

opulence
4 luxe 6 bounty, luxury, plenty, riches, wealth 7 fortune 9 abundance, affluence, plenitude, profusion 10 luxuriance 12 extravagance

opulent
4 lush, rich 5 plush, showy, swank 6 deluxe, lavish 7 moneyed, profuse, wealthy 8 affluent, palatial 9 luxuriant, luxurious, plentiful, sumptuous 11 extravagant 12 ostentatious

opuntia
6 cactus

opus
4 work 5 piece 6 oeuvre 7 product 8 creation 11 composition

or
4 else, gold 6 golden, yellow 9 otherwise

oracle
4 sage, seer 5 augur, sibyl 6 augury, medium, priest, Pythia, vision 7 prophet 8 haruspex, prophecy 9 priestess 10 apocalypse, revelation, soothsayer
site: 6 Claros, Delphi, Didyma, Dodona 7 Olympia 9 Epidaurus

oracular
5 vatic 6 mantic, orphic 7 cryptic, Delphic, fatidic, obscure 8 Delphian, dogmatic 9 ambiguous, arbitrary, prophetic, sibylline, vaticinal

oral
4 exam 5 vocal 6 spoken, verbal, voiced 8 narrated, viva voce 9 unwritten 11 examination

oral-health org.
3 ADA

orange
6 citrus
brownish: 6 Titian
deep: 11 bittersweet
drink: 3 ade
gem: 7 jacinth
genus: 6 Citrus
kin: 4 lime 5 lemon 7 kumquat, satsuma 8 mandarin 9 tangerine 10 grapefruit
kind: 4 sour 5 blood, chino, navel, Osage, sweet 7 Seville 8 bergamot, mandarin, Valencia
oil: 6 neroli
seed: 3 pip
skin: 4 rind

___ orange
5 Osage

orange of the South
5 Osage

orange-yellow
5 ocher, ochre

orangutan
3 ape 6 pongid 7 primate 10 anthropoid
relative: 5 chimp 6 bonobo, gibbon 7 gorilla, siamang 10 chimpanzee

Oranjestad island
5 Arutba

orate
4 rant 5 mouth, speak, spiel 6 preach 7 address, declaim, lecture 8 bloviate, harangue, perorate 9 discourse, sermonize, speechify 11 pontificate

oration
6 homily, sermon, speech 7 address, lecture 9 discourse
funeral: 6 eulogy

orator
7 speaker
American: 4 Clay (Henry) 5 Bryan (William Jennings), Henry (Patrick) 7 Calhoun (John C.), Douglas (Stephen), Webster (Daniel)
British: 5 Burke (Edmund) 8 Disraeli (Benjamin) 9 Churchill (Winston), Gladstone (William)
French: 8 Mirabeau (Comte de)
Greek: 5 Corax 8 Pericles 11 Demosthenes
Roman: 4 Cato 6 Cicero

oratory
6 chapel, speech 7 bombast 8 rhetoric 9 discourse, elocution, eloquence 10 expression 11 exhortation, speechcraft

orb
3 eye 4 ball 5 globe, round 6 circle, sphere

orbit
4 path 5 ambit, range, reach, scope, sweep, track 6 extent, radius 7 ellipse
farthest point: 4 apse 5 apsis 6 apogee 8 aphelion
nearest point: 4 apse 5 apsis 7 perigee 10 perihelion

orchard
5 trees 10 plantation

orchestra
4 band 7 gamelan 8 ensemble, symphony 12 philharmonic
instrument: 4 harp, oboe, tuba 5 celli (plural), cello, flute, viola 6 chimes, violin 7 bassoon, cymbals, piccolo, timpani, trumpet 8 bass drum, clarinet, triangle, trombone 9 castanets, snare drum, xylophone 10 double bass, French horn, kettledrum, tambourine 11 English horn, violoncello 12 glockenspiel
leader: 9 conductor
section: 5 brass 6 string 7 brasses, strings 8 woodwind 9 woodwinds 10 percussion

orchestral reed
4 oboe 7 bassoon 8 clarinet 11 English horn

orchestrate
5 blend, score, unify 6 manage 7 arrange, compose 8 organize 9 harmonize, integrate 10 coordinate

orchid
genus: 4 Disa
kind: 7 calypso, pogonia 8 cattleya, oncidium 9 cymbidium 11 cypripedium
petal: 3 lip 8 labellum
product: 5 salep
tuber: 5 salep

ordain
4 will 5 enact, order 6 decree, direct, impose, invest 7 appoint, command, conduct, destine, dictate, install, lay down 9 establish, prescribe, pronounce 10 predestine

ordeal
4 test 5 agony, cross, trial 7 calvary, torment, trouble 8 crucible 9 suffering 10 affliction, difficulty, visitation 11 tribulation

order
4 book, fiat, rank 5 array, caste, class, genre, range 6 decree, demand, diktat, lineup, method, scheme, series, system 7 command, harmony, mandate, marshal, pattern, reserve 8 classify, neatness, position, shipment, tidiness 9 directive, hierarchy, procedure, structure 10 injunction, regularity 11 progression
lack of: 5 chaos 6 ataxia 7 anarchy, clutter 9 confusion 11 pandemonium
of business: 6 agenda, docket
of preference: 8 priority

orderly
4 aide, calm, neat, tidy, trim 6 batman 7 correct, precise, regular, soldier, uniform 8 methodic, peaceful 9 attendant, organized, peaceable, regulated, shipshape 10 methodical, systematic 11 uncluttered, well-behaved 12 businesslike

ordinance
3 law 4 code, rule 5 edict 6 decree 7 precept, statute 9 direction, prescript 10 regulation

ordinary
4 so-so 5 banal, cheap, judge, plain, trite, usual 6 common, normal 7 average, humdrum, mundane, natural, popular, prelate, prosaic, regular, routine, typical 8 everyday, familiar, inferior, mediocre, workaday 9 clergyman, customary, quotidian 10 uneventful, unoriginal 11 commonplace

ordnance
4 arms, guns 6 cannon 7 weapons 8 armament, supplies, weaponry 9 artillery, munitions 10 ammunition

ore
4 gold, rock 5 metal 6 copper, silver 7 mineral 8 platinum
analysis: 5 assay
deposit: 4 lode, vein
excavation: 5 stope
iron: 5 ocher, ochre 8 goethite, hematite, limonite
lead: 6 galena
process: 8 leaching, smelting
refuse: 4 slag 5 dross, matte 6 scoria
smelted: 7 regulus

oread
5 nymph

Oregon
capital: **5** Salem
city: **4** Bend **6** Eugene **7** Coos Bay, Medford **8** Portland
college, university: **4** Reed
lake: **6** Crater
mountain, range: **4** Hood **7** Cascade
nickname: **6** Beaver (State)
river: **5** Snake **8** Columbia
state bird: **10** meadowlark
state flower: **11** Oregon grape
state tree: **10** Douglas fir

Orestes
father: **9** Agamemnon
friend: **7** Pylades
mother: **12** Clytemnestra
sister: **7** Electra **9** Iphigenia
victim: **9** Aegisthus **12** Clytemnestra
wife: **8** Hermione

org.
4 assn.

organ
5 agent, means **6** agency, medium, review **7** channel, journal, vehicle **8** magazine, ministry **9** newspaper **10** instrument, periodical
ancient: **9** hydraulus
barrel: **10** hurdy-gurdy
bodily: **3** ear, eye **4** lung, nose, skin **5** gland, heart, liver **6** kidney, larynx, spleen, tongue, tonsil, viscus **9** intestine
displacement: **8** prolapse
mouth: **9** harmonica
part: **4** pipe, reed, stop **5** pedal, valve **6** blower **7** console, tremolo **8** keyboard **9** wind chest
reed: **8** melodeon **9** harmonium
steam: **8** calliope
stop: **4** oboe, sext **5** gamba, quint, viola **6** dulcet **7** bassoon, celesta, melodia, subbass, tertian **8** carillon, diapason, dulciana, gemshorn
tactile: **6** feeler **8** tentacle

organ cactus
7 saguaro

organic
5 basic **6** innate **7** natural, primary **8** inherent, integral **9** essential **10** structural **11** fundamental
compound: **4** enol

organism
5 being, plant **6** animal
disease-producing: **4** germ **5** virus **8** pathogen **9** bacterium
single-celled: **5** monad **6** amoeba **9** protozoan

organist
American: **3** Fox (Virgil) **5** Biggs (E. Power) **6** Newman (Anthony)
Dutch: **9** Sweelinck (Jan)
English: **6** Wesley (Samuel) **7** Gibbons (Christopher, Edward, Ellis, Orlando)
French: **5** Alain (Marie-Claire), Widor (Charles) **6** Franck (César) **8** Messiaen (Olivier) **10** Schweitzer (Albert)
German: **4** Bach (Johann Sebastian) **6** Handel (George Frideric), Walcha (Helmut) **7** Richter (Anton, Ernst, Ferdinand, Johann, Karl)
Swiss: **4** Rogg (Lionel)

organization
4 body, club, unit **5** group, guild, setup **6** agency, system **7** pattern **9** framework, structure **11** arrangement, association, corporation, institution **13** establishment

organize
4 form **5** array, group, order, rally, set up, start **6** create, line up **7** arrange **8** classify, unionize **9** construct, establish, institute, integrate **10** constitute, coordinate **11** put together

orgulous
5 proud

orgy
4 rite **5** binge, revel, spree **7** blowout, carouse, debauch, rampage, revelry, splurge **8** carousal **9** bacchanal **10** indulgence, saturnalia **11** bacchanalia

oriel
3 bay **6** window

orient
3 set **4** face **5** adapt, align, pearl, sheen **6** adjust, direct, inform, locate, luster **7** arrange **8** acquaint, lustrous **9** sparkling **11** accommodate, familiarize

Orient
4 Asia, East **7** Far East

Oriental
3 rug **5** Asian **6** carpet **7** Eastern **10** Far Eastern

orientation
7 bearing **8** location, position **9** alignment, direction **10** adjustment **11** arrangement

orifice
see **opening**

oriflamme
4 flag **5** ideal **6** banner, pennon, symbol **7** pendant, pennant **8** standard, streamer

origami
12 paper folding
bird: **5** crane

origin
4 root, seed, well **5** birth, blood, start **6** source **7** descent, genesis, lineage **8** ancestry, fountain, pedigree **9** beginning, inception, maternity, parentage, paternity **10** derivation, extraction, provenance, wellspring

original
3 new **5** first, model, novel, prime **6** master, native, unique **7** initial, pattern, pioneer, primary **8** creative, earliest **9** archetype, ingenious, innovator, inventive, precursor, primitive, prototype **10** archetypal, forerunner, innovative, primordial

originally
5 first **7** at first **8** formerly **9** initially, primarily

originate
4 coin, flow, hail, make, rise, stem **5** arise, begin, found, hatch, issue, set up, start **6** create, derive, invent, launch, spring **7** emanate, proceed, produce, think up **8** commence, generate, initiate, innovate **9** institute, introduce

originator
5 maker **6** author **7** creator, founder, planner **8** inventor, producer **9** initiator, innovator **10** institutor, introducer

oriole
4 bird **8** troupial
European: **6** loriot
genus: **7** Icterus
golden: **6** loriot
kind: **6** golden **7** orchard **8** Bullock's **9** Baltimore

Orion
6 hunter **13** constellation
beloved: **3** Eos
belt: **7** Ellwand
father: **7** Hyrieus **8** Poseidon
slayer: **5** Diana **7** Artemis
star: **5** Rigel **9** Bellatrix **10** Betelgeuse

orison
6 prayer **8** entreaty, petition **12** supplication

Orithyia
lover: **6** Boreas
son: **5** Zetes **6** Calais

Orlando author
5 Woolf (Virginia)

Orlando Furioso author
7 Ariosto (Ludovico)

Orléans heroine
9 Joan of Arc

orlop
4 deck

ormolu
5 brass **6** bronze

ornament
3 gem **4** bead, deck, trim **5** adorn, jewel **6** bedeck, finial, tassel **7** dress up, garnish, jewelry, pendant, whatnot **8** beautify, decorate, filigree **9** embellish, embroider, lavaliere
Christmas tree: **4** bulb **5** angel **6** tinsel
lip: **6** labret
shoulder: **7** epaulet

ornamental case
4 etui

ornamental vase
3 urn

ornate
4 lush, rich **5** fancy, gaudy, showy **6** florid, frilly, gilded, glitzy, rococo **7** baroque, flowery, opulent **8** overdone **9** elaborate, luxuriant, sumptuous **10** flamboyant

ornery
5 balky, cross, testy **6** crabby, cranky, crusty, grumpy **7** bearish, froward, grouchy **8** contrary, perverse, stubborn, vinegary **9** crotchety, difficult, irascible, irritable **10** inflexible, vinegarish **12** cantankerous

ornithic
5 avian **8** birdlike

ornithologist
American: **4** Bond (James) **7** Audubon (John James), Bartram (William) **8** Peterson (Roger Tory)
English: **5** Gould (John)
Scottish: **6** Wilson (Alexander)

orotund
4 full, loud **5** round **7** flowery, fustian, pompous, ringing **8** resonant, sonorous **9** bombastic, high-flown, overblown **10** euphuistic, oratorical, resounding, rhetorical, stentorian **11** declamatory **12** magniloquent **13** grandiloquent

Orpah
husband: **7** Chilion
sister-in-law: **4** Ruth

orphan
4 waif **5** Annie, gamin, stray **6** bereft, gamine, urchin **7** cast-off, ignored **8** forsaken, homeless **9** abandoned, foundling, neglected **10** motherless, parentless

Orpheus
composer: **5** Gluck (Christoph Willibald)
father: **6** Apollo **7** Oeagrus
home: **6** Thrace
instrument: **4** lyre
mother: **8** Calliope
wife: **8** Euridice

orphic
6 arcane, mystic, occult **7** cryptic, Delphic, obscure **8** abstruse, Delphian, esoteric, hermetic, mystical, oracular, profound **9** enigmatic, recondite

ort
3 bit **4** bite **5** crumb, piece, scrap **6** morsel **7** remnant **8** leftover

orthodox
6 proper **8** accepted, approved, official, received, standard **9** canonical, customary **10** conformist, recognized, sanctioned

11 **established**, traditional **12** acknowledged, conservative, conventional **13** authoritative

orthography
7 writing **8** spelling

ortolan
7 bunting

Orwell novel
10 Animal Farm **18** Nineteen Eighty-four

oryx
7 gemsbok **8** antelope

os
3 ora (plural) **4** bone, ossa (plural) **5** mouth **7** orifice

Osborne play
6 Luther **11** Entertainer (The) **15** Look Back in Anger

Oscar de la ___
5 Renta

oscillate
3 wag **4** sway, vary **5** swing, waver **6** change, seesaw **7** vibrate **9** alternate, fluctuate

oscillation
4 sway **5** swing **9** variation, vibration **10** undulation **11** fluctuation, periodicity

osculate
3 lip **4** buss, kiss, peck **5** smack **6** smooch

osculation
4 buss, kiss, peck **6** smooch **7** lip-lock

osier
3 rod **6** willow **7** dogwood

Osiris
brother: **3** Set **4** Seth
father: **3** Geb, Keb, Seb
mother: **3** Nut
scribe: **5** Thoth
sister: **4** Isis
slayer: **3** Set **4** Seth
son: **5** Horus **6** Anubis
wife: **4** Isis

osmosis
4 flow **8** transfer **9** diffusion **10** absorption **12** assimilation **13** incorporation

osprey
4 hawk **8** fish hawk

OSS successor
3 CIA

osseous
4 bony **8** bonelike

ossicle
4 bone **5** incus **6** stapes **7** malleus

ossify
3 set **6** harden **7** stiffen **8** solidify **9** fossilize

osso ___
4 buco

ossuary
4 tomb **5** vault **8** boneyard, cemetery **9** sepulcher, sepulchre

ostensible
6 stated **7** alleged, seeming **8** apparent, asserted, illusive, illusory, so-called, supposed **9** pretended, professed, purported, semblable **11** superficial

ostentation
4 pomp, show **5** flash, swank **7** display **9** pomposity, showiness, vainglory **10** flashiness, pretension **11** flamboyance

ostentatious
4 loud **5** gaudy, showy, swank **6** flashy, garish, swanky **7** pompous, splashy **8** overdone, peacocky **10** flamboyant, peacockish **11** pretentious **12** vainglorious

ostiole
4 pore **7** orifice **8** aperture

ostracism
5 exile **7** removal **9** exclusion **10** banishment, relegation **11** deportation

ostracize
3 bar, cut **4** shun, snub **5** exile **6** banish, deport **7** exclude, keep out, shut out **8** throw out **9** blackball **10** expatriate **12** cold-shoulder

ostrich
6 ratite
relative: **3** emu **4** rhea

Ostrogoth king
9 Theodoric

Oswego tea
7 bee balm

otalgia
7 earache

Otello composer
5 Verdi (Giuseppe) **7** Rossini (Gioacchino)

O tempora! O ___!
5 mores

Othello
4 moor
author: **11** Shakespeare (William)
lieutenant: **6** Cassio
maid: **6** Emilia
victim, wife: **9** Desdemona
villain: **4** Iago

other, in Madrid
4 otra, otro

others
4 rest **9** remainder
and: **4** et al **6** et alia, et alii **7** et aliae

other than
3 but **4** save **6** except **7** besides **9** apart from, aside from, except for, excepting, excluding

otherwise
3 not **4** else **5** if not **6** or else **7** changed **9** different **11** differently **12** anything else **13** alternatively

otic
5 aural **8** auditory **9** auricular

otiose
4 idle, vain **5** empty **6** futile, hollow **7** surplus, useless **8** nugatory **9** fruitless, pointless, worthless **11** ineffective, purposeless, superfluous **12** functionless **13** supernumerary

Ottawa chief
7 Pontiac

ottoman
4 seat **5** couch **6** fabric **9** footstool

Ottoman
4 Turk **7** Osmanli, Turkish
council: **5** divan
governor: **3** bey
official: **3** aga, dey **4** agha **5** pasha **6** bashaw, vizier
ruler: **3** bey **5** Osman, Selim **8** Suleiman, Süleyman

Otus
5 giant
brother: **9** Ephialtes
father: **6** Aloeus **8** Poseidon
mother: **9** Iphimedia
slayer: **6** Apollo

ouch
5 bezel, jewel **6** brooch, buckle **7** setting **8** ornament **11** exclamation

ounce
3 bit, cat **4** dram **5** pinch, scrap, shred **6** amount, splash, weight **7** measure, modicum, smidgen **8** fraction, particle **11** snow leopard

our
French: **5** notre
Italian: **6** nostra
Spanish: **7** nuestro

Our Town author
6 Wilder (Thornton)

oust
4 fire, sack **5** eject, evict, expel **6** banish, deport, remove, topple, unseat **7** boot out, cast out, deprive, dismiss, kick out **8** displace, drive out, force out, relegate, supplant, take away, throw out **10** dispossess

ouster
7 removal **8** ejection, eviction **9** discharge, dismissal, expulsion **10** banishment

out
4 away, exit **5** forth, loose **6** absent, excuse
of control: **4** amok, wild **5** amuck **7** chaotic
of gas: **5** tired **7** drained **9** exhausted
of line: **4** awry, rude **5** askew, fresh
of place: **13** inappropriate
of sorts: **5** cross **7** grouchy, peevish **9** irritable
of the ordinary: **3** odd **7** bizarre, strange, unusual

outage
4 loss **5** break **7** failure **8** blackout **12** interruption

out-and-out
5 gross, sheer, total, utter **7** perfect **8** absolute, complete, positive **9** downright **10** consummate **11** unmitigated, unqualified **13** thoroughgoing

outback
4 bush **6** sticks **7** boonies **9** boondocks **10** hinterland, wilderness
call: **5** cooee
canine: **5** dingo

outboard
4 boat **5** motor **6** engine

outbreak
4 rash, rise, rush **5** burst, flare, spike, surge **6** attack, blowup, plague, revolt **7** flare-up **8** epidemic, eruption, increase, uprising **9** rebellion **12** insurrection

outbuilding
4 barn, shed

outburst
3 fit **4** gush, gust **5** flare, sally, scene, spasm, storm, surge **6** frenzy, tirade **7** flare-up, tantrum, torrent **8** eruption, paroxysm, upheaval **9** explosion

outcast
4 hobo **5** exile, leper, tramp **6** pariah **7** Ishmael, vagrant **8** castaway, derelict, vagabond **9** reprobate **10** expatriate, Ishmaelite **11** offscouring, untouchable

outclass
3 top **4** best **5** excel **6** exceed **7** surpass

outcome
3 end **5** event, fruit, issue **6** effect, result, sequel, upshot **9** aftermath **10** conclusion **11** aftereffect, consequence, development

outcrop
4 rock **5** ledge **6** appear **7** project **8** protrude **10** projection, protrusion **12** protuberance

outcry
3 hue **4** yell **5** noise, shout **6** clamor, tumult, uproar **7** auction, ferment, protest **8** upheaval **9** commotion, objection **11** exclamation

outdated
3 old **5** passé **6** bygone, démodé, old hat **7** antique, archaic, vintage **10** antiquated, oldfangled **12** old-fashioned

outdistance
3 top **4** beat, best, pass **5** excel, trump **6** better, exceed **7** eclipse, surpass

outdo
3 top **4** beat, best, pass **5** excel, trump **6** better, defeat, exceed **7** eclipse, surpass, triumph **8** overcome **9** transcend

outdoor
7 open-air **8** alfresco

outer
6 remote **7** surface **8** exoteric, exterior, external **9** extrinsic **10** extraneous **11** superficial
combining form: 3 exo

outermost
4 last **5** final **6** far-off **7** distant, extreme **8** farthest, furthest, remotest

outfit
3 kit, rig, set **4** band, firm, gear, suit, team, togs, unit **5** corps, dress, equip, getup, group, squad, troop **6** clothe, supply, tackle, troupe **7** appoint, company, concern, costume, furnish **8** accouter, accoutre, business, clothing, ensemble, matériel, tackling **9** equipment, provision **10** enterprise **12** organization **13** accouterments, accoutrements, establishment

outflank
5 evade **6** bypass **9** get around **10** circumvent

outflow
6 efflux **8** drainage, effluent **9** effluence

out-front
4 open **5** frank **6** candid, honest **10** forthright

outgoing
4 open **7** affable **8** friendly, sociable **9** departing, expansive **10** gregarious, responsive **11** extroverted

outgrowth
6 effect, result **7** product, spin-off **8** offshoot **9** by-product, offspring **10** derivative **11** aftereffect, consequence

outhouse
5 jakes, privy **7** latrine

outing
4 spin, trip **5** drive, jaunt, sally **6** junket, picnic **9** excursion **10** appearance, disclosure

outlandish
3 odd **4** wild **5** alien, outré, ultra, weird **6** exotic **7** bizarre, curious, extreme, foreign, offbeat, strange, uncouth, unusual **8** peculiar, singular **9** eccentric, fantastic, tasteless **10** ridiculous, unorthodox **11** extravagant

outlast
6 endure **7** survive, weather **9** withstand

outlaw
3 ban, con **4** wild **5** crook **6** bandit, banned, enjoin, forbid **7** exclude, illegal **8** criminal, disallow, fugitive, prohibit, renegade, restrict **9** desperado, interdict, proscribe **10** illegalize, rebellious

outlay
3 pay, tab **4** cost, give **5** spend **6** amount, expend **7** expense, payment **8** disburse **11** expenditure **12** disbursement

outlet
4 exit, hole, mart, shop, vent **5** issue, store **6** avenue, egress, escape, market, socket **7** channel, opening, passage, release **8** aperture **10** discounter, receptacle

outlet item abbrev.
3 irr.

outline
4 edge, form, limn, plan **5** brief, draft, shape, trace **6** bounds, border, précis, schema, sketch **7** contour, profile, summary **8** abstract, boundary, skeleton, syllabus, synopsis **9** delineate, summarize **10** figuration, silhouette **11** skeletonize

outlive
7 survive, weather

outlook
4 side, view **5** angle, scope, sight, slant, vista **6** aspect, future **7** promise **8** attitude, forecast, position, prospect **9** direction, viewpoint **10** standpoint **11** expectation, observatory, perspective, point of view

outlying
3 far **6** far-off, remote **7** distant, faraway, removed **8** far-flung

outmoded
4 dead **5** dated, passé, tired **6** old hat **7** antique, archaic **8** obsolete **9** moth-eaten, unstylish **10** oldfangled **11** obsolescent **12** old-fashioned

Out of Africa author
4 Isak (Dinesen)

out of control
4 amok **7** berserk

out-of-date
3 old **4** past **5** passé, stale **6** démodé, old hat, square **7** antique, archaic, old-time, vintage **8** obsolete **9** unstylish **10** antiquated, oldfangled **12** old-fashioned

out of it
4 lost **5** dazed, spacy **6** addled, spacey **7** muddled **8** confused, demented **10** bewildered

out-of-the-way
4 rare **6** remote **7** distant, obscure, removed, unusual **8** secluded, uncommon

out of work
4 idle **7** jobless **10** unemployed

outpost
4 base **6** branch, colony **7** station **8** foothold **10** detachment, settlement

outpouring
4 flow, gush, rush **5** burst, flood, spate, spurt **6** deluge, stream **7** torrent **8** effusion

output
4 crop, gain, take **5** power, yield **6** amount, profit **7** harvest, produce, product **10** production **11** achievement, information

outrage
4 fury, rape **5** abuse, shock, wrong **6** injury, insult, offend **7** affront, incense, violate **8** aggrieve, atrocity, ill-treat, mischief, violence **9** brutality, infuriate **10** resentment, scandalize

outrageous
5 awful, gross **6** horrid, insane, odious, unholy, wicked **7** beastly, ghastly, heinous, ignoble, obscene **8** dreadful, flagrant, horrible, indecent, shocking, terrible **9** atrocious, egregious, excessive, fantastic **10** abominable, inordinate, scandalous **11** intolerable

outré
3 odd **5** ultra **6** far-out **7** bizarre, extreme, offbeat, strange **8** peculiar **9** eccentric **10** off-the-wall

outrigger
4 boat, beam, prau, proa, spar

outright
4 pure **5** total, utter, whole **6** entire **7** perfect **8** absolute, complete, entirely, positive **9** on the spot **10** completely, consummate **11** unequivocal, unmitigated, unqualified **13** thoroughgoing

outrun
3 top **4** beat, pass **6** exceed **7** surpass

outset
4 dawn **5** birth, get-go, start **7** opening **9** beginning, inception **12** commencement

outshine
3 top **4** beat, best **5** excel **6** better, exceed **7** eclipse, surpass

outside
5 alien **7** foreign, open-air **8** alfresco, exterior, external
combining form: **3** ect, exo **5** extra

outsider
5 alien **7** inconnu **8** newcomer, stranger **9** foreigner

outsmart
see **outwit**

outspoken
4 free, open **5** blunt, frank, plain, vocal **6** candid, direct, honest **7** up front **8** explicit **10** forthright, point-blank, unreserved **11** unequivocal

outstanding
3 due **4** A-one, star **5** boffo, noted, owing, socko **6** signal, superb, tip-top, unpaid **7** capital, eminent, notable, overdue, salient, stellar **8** dominant, striking, superior, top-notch **9** arresting, excellent, first-rate, prominent, unsettled **10** noticeable, preeminent, remarkable, unresolved **11** conspicuous, distinctive, exceptional, magnificent, superlative, uncollected **13** extraordinary

outstrip
3 top **4** beat, best, pass **5** excel **6** better, exceed **7** surpass **8** distance, go beyond, overtake **9** transcend **11** leave behind

outward
5 overt **7** evident, visible **8** apparent, exterior, external **10** noticeable, ostensible **11** superficial

outweigh
6 exceed **8** overbear **10** overshadow **11** overbalance **12** preponderate

outworn
see **outmoded**

ouzel
6 dipper, thrush **9** blackbird

oval
5 track **6** oblong **7** ellipse **8** elliptic **9** egg-shaped, racetrack **10** elliptical **11** ellipsoidal

ovation
5 kudos **6** homage, praise **7** acclaim, tribute **8** applause, approval, cheering, clapping, plaudits **11** acclamation

oven
4 kiln, oast **5** range, stove

over
4 anew, atop, done, past, upon **5** above, again, aloft, ended **6** across, beyond **8** done with, finished, once more
French: **3** sur
German: **4** über
prefix: **3** epi, sur **5** extra, hyper, super, supra
Spanish: **5** sobre

overabundance
4 glut **6** excess **7** surfeit, surplus **8** plethora **10** surplusage **11** superfluity

overact
3 ham, mug **4** rant **5** emote **10** exaggerate

overage
6 excess **7** surplus

overall
5 smock, total **6** global, mainly, mostly **7** chiefly, general, largely **8** as a whole, sweeping **9** generally, inclusive, in general, primarily **10** far and wide **11** principally **13** comprehensive, predominantly

overalls
5 pants **8** trousers

over and above
4 also **6** as well, beyond **7** besides **8** as well as **10** in addition

over and over
3 oft **5** often **8** ofttimes **10** frequently, oftentimes, repeatedly **11** continually, recurrently

overbearing
5 bossy **6** lordly **7** haughty, pompous **8** absolute, arrogant, despotic, dominant, imperial, insolent, scornful, superior **9** imperious, tyrannous **10** autocratic, disdainful, dominating, high-handed, oppressive, peremptory, tyrannical **11** dictatorial, domineering, magisterial **12** supercilious **13** high-and-mighty

overblown
6 turgid **7** flowery, hyped up, orotund, pompous **8** inflated **9** bombastic, excessive, high-flown **10** euphuistic, oratorical, rhetorical **11** declamatory, exaggerated, pretentious **12** magniloquent **13** grandiloquent

overcast
3 sew **4** dull, gray, hazy **5** cloud, cover **6** cloudy, darken, shadow **7** becloud, blanket, clouded, obscure **8** covering, lowering **9** adumbrate

overcharge
3 pad **4** bilk, clip, rook, skin, soak **5** cheat, gouge, stick **6** fleece **7** inflate

overcoat
5 paint **6** capote, raglan, ulster **7** surtout **9** balmacaan, outerwear **12** chesterfield

overcome
4 beat, best, lick **5** drown, throw **6** defeat, hurdle, master **7** conquer, prevail, triumph **8** surmount **9** prostrate

overconfident
4 rash **5** brash, cocky, pushy **8** arrogant, cocksure, reckless **9** hubristic, presuming **12** presumptuous

overdo
7 exhaust, fatigue, wear out **9** embellish **10** exaggerate

overdo it
5 emote **7** ham it up

overdue
4 late **5** owing, tardy **6** behind, unpaid **7** belated, delayed, payable **8** dilatory **9** unsettled **10** behindhand, delinquent, unpunctual **11** outstanding

overemphasize
7 magnify **8** heighten **9** dramatize, embellish **10** exaggerate

overfill
4 sate **5** gorge, stuff

overflow
4 pour, teem **5** cover, drown, flood, slosh, spate, spill, swamp **6** deluge, engulf, excess, outlet **7** surfeit, surplus, torrent **8** flooding, inundate, spillage, submerge **10** inundation, surplusage **11** superfluity

overgrown
4 lush **5** dense, thick **6** brushy **7** hulking **8** ungainly **9** excessive, ponderous **10** junglelike

overhang
3 jut **4** eave, loom **5** bulge **6** beetle, extend, impend **7** project **8** protrude, stick out, threaten **10** projection

overhaul
3 fix **4** mend, redo **5** patch, renew **6** doctor, remake, repair, retool, revamp, revise **7** rebuild, restore **8** renovate, retrofit **11** recondition, reconstruct

overhead
4 atop **5** above, aloft, smash **7** ceiling, expense **8** expenses
trains: **3** els

overheated
5 fiery **7** fervent **8** inflated **9** perfervid **11** impassioned

overindulgence
6 excess **7** surfeit **8** gluttony **11** dissipation **12** immoderation, intemperance

overjoyed
6 elated **7** gleeful **8** blissful, ecstatic, euphoric, exultant, jubilant, thrilled **9** rapturous **11** transported

overkill
4 glut **6** excess **7** surfeit, surplus, too much **8** plethora **10** obliterate, redundancy, surplusage **11** superfluity

overlap
7 shingle **9** imbricate

overlay
3 cap **4** coat **5** cover, glaze **6** finish, veneer **7** blanket, coating, lacquer, varnish **8** covering **11** superimpose **12** transparency

overload
4 glut **5** stuff **6** burden, excess, pile on, strain **7** surfeit

overlook
4 fail, miss, omit, skip **5** check, let go **6** excuse, forget, ignore, pass by, slight, slip up, survey, wink at **7** blink at, condone, forgive, inspect, let pass, neglect **8** discount, dominate, surmount **9** disregard, supervise **11** superintend

overlord
4 czar, tsar, tzar **5** chief, mogul, ruler **6** tycoon **7** magnate **8** suzerain **9** potentate, sovereign

overly
3 too **6** too-too, unduly **11** exceedingly, excessively **12** immoderately, inordinately

overpass
5 cross **6** bridge **8** crossing, traverse **9** traversal **11** interchange

overplay
4 hype **6** expand **7** enlarge, inflate, magnify,

point up, stretch **8** maximize **9** dramatize **10** exaggerate **11** hyperbolize

overpower
4 rout **5** crush, swamp, whelm **6** defeat, master, subdue **7** conquer **8** vanquish **9** prostrate, subjugate **11** steamroller

overreach
3 con **4** beat, bilk **5** cheat, outdo **6** defeat, outfox, outwit **7** defraud **8** flimflam, outsmart **10** exaggerate **11** outmaneuver

override
4 veto **5** annul **6** cancel **7** nullify **10** counteract, neutralize

overriding
3 key **4** main **5** chief, major, prime, vital **7** central, crucial, pivotal, primary, supreme **8** cardinal, dominant, foremost **9** paramount, principal

overrule
4 undo, veto **5** upset **6** negate, revoke **7** reverse **8** set aside **11** countermand

overrun
4 beat, raid, teem, whip **5** swamp, swarm **6** defeat, excess, infest, invade, occupy, ravage, spread, thrash **7** clobber, conquer

overseas
6 abroad **11** transmarine, ultramarine **12** transoceanic, transpacific **13** transatlantic

oversee
3 run **4** boss, tend **5** watch **6** direct, manage, survey **7** command, examine, inspect **9** supervise **11** superintend

overseer
4 boss, exec, head **5** chief **7** foreman, manager **8** director **9** executive **10** supervisor **13** administrator

overshadow
4 veil **5** cloud, dwarf, shade **6** darken, exceed **7** becloud, eclipse, obscure, surpass **8** dominate, outshine, outweigh **9** adumbrate

overshoe
4 boot **6** arctic, galosh, patten, rubber

oversight
4 care, slip **5** aegis, check, error, lapse **6** charge, slip-up **7** control, failure, mistake, neglect **8** omission **10** intendance, management **11** supervision

overspread
3 cap **5** beset, cover, flood, swarm **6** infest, invade **7** blanket, obscure, pervade **8** permeate

overstate
3 pad **7** amplify, enlarge, magnify **9** embellish, embroider **10** exaggerate

overstep
6 exceed, offend **7** surpass, violate **8** infringe, trespass **10** transgress

overstock
4 glut **5** extra **6** excess **7** surplus **9** remainder **10** surplusage

overstress
7 magnify **8** maximize **10** exaggerate

overt
4 open **5** clear **6** patent **7** evident, obvious, outward, visible **8** apparent, manifest **10** observable

overtake
4 pass **5** catch **6** pass by **7** outpace, surpass **8** come upon, outstrip **11** outdistance

Over the Rainbow
composer: **5** Arlen (Harold)
lyricist: **7** Harburg (E. Y.)
movie: **10** Wizard of Oz (The)
singer: **7** Garland (Judy)

over there
3 yon **6** yonder

over-the-top
5 outré **7** extreme **8** reckless **9** egregious, excessive **10** exorbitant, flamboyant, outrageous **11** extravagant

overthrow
4 fell, oust, rout **5** evert, purge, upset **6** defeat, depose, remove, topple, unseat, usurp **7** conquer **8** dethrone, downfall **9** bring down

overtone
4 hint **5** sense **8** coloring, harmonic **9** inference **10** suggestion **11** association, connotation, implication **12** undercurrent

overture
3 bid **5** proem **7** advance, preface, prelude, present **8** approach, foreword, preamble, prologue, proposal **9** prelusion **10** initiative **11** proposition **12** introduction, presentation

overturn
3 tip **4** flip, void **5** upend, upset **6** topple, tumble **7** capsize, nullify, reverse **8** set aside **10** invalidate

overused
5 banal, musty, stale, tired, trite **7** clichéd, worn-out **9** hackneyed **10** threadbare

overview
6 aperçu, précis, survey **7** epitome, summary **10** conspectus

overweening
5 brash, pushy **6** lordly, uppish, uppity **7** forward **8** arrogant **9** conceited, presuming **10** immoderate **11** exaggerated **12** presumptuous

overweight
3 fat **5** beefy, burly, dumpy, gross, heavy, husky, obese, plump, pudgy, stout **6** chubby, chunky, flabby, fleshy, portly, rotund **7** outsize **8** heavyset, thickset **9** corpulent

overwhelm
3 mob **4** beat, bury, rout, ruin, sink, whip **5** crush, drown, flood, swamp, upset, wreck **6** boggle, defeat, deluge, engulf, thrash **7** conquer, destroy, oppress, shatter, shellac, smother **8** inundate, submerge **9** devastate, prostrate **10** demoralize **11** steamroller, subordinate

overwhelmed
6 aghast **7** shocked, stunned, touched **8** defeated, helpless **10** distressed **13** thunderstruck

overwhelming
4 huge **5** great **7** extreme **8** numerous **10** staggering

overwrought
5 hyper, upset **7** anxious, frantic, wound up **8** agitated, frenetic, stressed, troubled **9** disturbed, emotional **10** distracted, freaked out, high-strung, hysterical **11** discomposed

Ovid work
5 Fasti **6** Amores **7** Tristia **8** Heroides **13** Metamorphoses

ovine
5 sheep **9** sheeplike

ovoid
9 egg-shaped

ovule
3 egg
fertilized: **4** seed

ovum
3 egg **6** gamete **7** egg cell **11** macrogamete

owing
3 due **6** in debt, mature, unpaid **7** overdue, payable **9** unsettled **11** outstanding

owing to
4 over **7** through **9** because of **10** by reason of **11** on account of

owl
cry: **4** hoot
genus: **4** Bubo, Otus
kind: **3** elf **4** barn, gray, lulu **5** eagle, gnome, madge, pygmy, snowy **6** barred, horned **7** saw-whet, screech **9** long-eared **10** short-eared **11** great horned

Owl and the Pussycat author
4 Lear (Edward)

own
4 avow, have, hold **5** admit, allow, enjoy, grant, let on **6** accept, fess up, retain **7** concede, confess, possess **8** disclose **9** recognize **11** acknowledge

owner
6 holder **8** landlady, landlord **9** possessor, purchaser **10** proprietor

ownership
4 hand **5** title **8** dominion, property **10** possession **11** proprietary
perpetual: **8** mortmain

ox
3 yak **4** anoa, gaur, musk, zebu **5** bison, steer **6** bovine **7** banteng, buffalo
Asian: **4** zebu
attachment: **4** yoke
extinct: **4** urus **7** aurochs
family: **7** Bovidae
relating to: **6** bovine
wild: **4** anoa, gaur **7** banteng

oxeye
5 daisy **6** flower

oxford
4 shoe **5** cloth, sheep **6** cotton, fabric

oxide
calcium: **4** lime **9** quicklime
ferric: **4** rust
sodium: **4** soda

oxidize
4 rust

oxygen
3 air, gas **5** ozone **7** element
discoverer: **9** Lavoisier (Antoine)
form: **5** ozone
liquid: **3** lox

oyster
7 bivalve, mollusc, mollusk
bed: **4** park **6** claire, cultch
eggs: **5** spawn
genus: **6** Ostrea
lining: **5** nacre
Long Island: **9** bluepoint
product: **5** pearl
shell: **4** test **5** shuck
young: **4** spat

oyster plant
7 salsify

Oz
9 Australia, Down Under
creator: **4** Baum (L. Frank)
inhabitant: **8** Munchkin
princess: **4** Ozma
visitor: **7** Dorothy

Ozark State
8 Missouri

Ozem
brother: **5** David
father: **5** Jesse **9** Jerahmeel

Ozymandias author
7 Shelley (Percy Bysshe)

P

pabulum
3 pap **4** food **7** aliment **8** nutrient **9** blandness, nutriment **10** insipidity, sustenance **11** nourishment

paca
4 cavy

pace
3 set **4** beat, clip, gait, lead, rate, step, time, trot, walk **5** speed, tempo, tread **6** gallop, motion, stride, timing **7** example, fluency, measure, proceed, routine, step off **8** ambulate, movement, regulate

pachyderm
8 elephant

pacific
4 calm, mild **6** gentle, irenic, placid, serene **8** dovelike, peaceful, soothing, tranquil **9** peaceable, temperate **12** conciliatory

Pacific
island: 3 Yap **4** Wake **6** Easter, Jarvis, Saipan, Tahiti, Tarawa **7** Iwo Jima, Tokelau **8** Pitcairn, St. Helena **11** Guadalcanal
nation: 4 Fiji **5** Belau, Japan, Nauru, Palau, Tonga **6** Tuvalu **7** Vanuatu **8** Kiribati

Pacific salmon
4 coho **5** cohoe

Pacificator, Great
4 Clay (Henry)

Pacific Ocean discoverer
6 Balboa (Vasco Núñez de)

pacifist
4 dove **6** irenic **8** appeaser, peaceful, peacenik **9** peaceable **10** nonviolent **11** peacemonger

pacify
4 calm, cool, ease, lull **5** allay, quell, quiet, still **6** disarm, settle, soften, soothe, subdue, temper **7** appease, assuage, mollify, placate **9** subjugate **10** conciliate, propitiate

pack
3 jam, kit, lot, lug, ram, set, wad **4** band, bear, cram, deck, fill, gang, heap, load, lump, mass, pile, stow, tamp, tote, unit **5** bunch, carry, cover, crowd, ferry, group, store, stuff, troop **6** bundle, charge, clique, convey, gather **8** assemble, compress, knapsack **9** transport **10** collection

package
3 box **4** bale, deal, unit, wrap **5** array, combo, whole **6** bundle, parcel **7** enclose, present, wrapper **8** shipment **9** container **10** collection

pack animal
3 ass **4** mule **5** burro, camel, horse, llama **6** donkey **7** jackass **13** beast of burden

packed
4 full **5** awash, dense, flush **6** filled, jammed **7** brimful, crowded, stuffed **8** brimming **9** chock-full **10** compressed

packet
3 wad **4** boat, mass, pile **5** group **6** bundle, parcel **7** cluster

pact
4 bond, deal **6** accord, treaty **7** bargain, concord **8** alliance, contract, covenant **9** agreement

pad
3 bed, mat, wad **4** foot, mute **5** fudge, guard, paper, stuff **6** buffer, muffle, tablet **7** augment, bolster, cushion, stretch **8** dressing **9** embellish, overstate **10** exaggerate, overcharge

paddle
3 oar, row **4** beat, stir **5** spank **6** propel, thrash

paddock
5 field **7** pasture **9** enclosure

paddy wagon
10 Black Maria

padre
3 Fra **6** father, priest **8** chaplain, minister **9** clergyman, confessor

paean
3 ode **4** hymn, song **6** anthem, eulogy, praise **7** tribute **8** accolade, encomium **9** panegyric

pagan
7 heathen **8** hedonist, sybarite **9** libertine **10** voluptuary
figurine: 4 idol

page
4 beep, book, call, leaf **5** folio, sheet **6** summon **7** bellhop, equerry
left-hand: 5 verso
right-hand: 5 recto
size: 5 folio **6** octavo

pageant
4 sham, show **7** charade, display, tableau **9** spectacle **10** exhibition
wear: 4 sash **5** tiara

pageantry
4 pomp, show **7** display, panoply **8** splendor **9** spectacle **11** flamboyance, ostentation **12** magnificence

paginate
7 foliate

Pagliacci, I
character: 5 Canio, Nedda, Tonio 6 Silvio
composer: 11 Leoncavallo (Ruggero)

pagoda
6 temple

Pago Pago's land
5 Samoa

pail
3 hod 6 bucket, piggin, vessel 7 scuttle

pain
3 irk 4 ache, care, hurt, pang 5 agony, cramp, grief, sting, throe 6 stitch, twinge 7 afflict, anguish, travail 8 aggrieve, distress 9 suffering 10 affliction, discomfort
back: 7 lumbago
muscular: 7 myalgia

painful
3 raw 4 hard, sore 5 acute, sharp 6 aching, trying 7 arduous, irksome 8 annoying, piercing, stinging 9 agonizing, difficult, laborious, torturous, upsetting, vexatious 10 afflictive, tormenting

painkiller, pain reliever
4 drug 5 Advil, Aleve 6 Anacin, Motrin, opiate 7 anodyne, aspirin, codeine, Tylenol 8 Excedrin, morphine, naproxen, narcotic 9 analgesic, ibuprofen 10 anesthetic 11 anaesthetic

painstaking
5 exact 7 careful, heedful 8 diligent, exacting, thorough 9 assiduous, diligence, laborious 10 meticulous, scrupulous 11 punctilious

paint
4 coat, daub, limn, swab, tint 5 adorn, brush, color, cover, horse, pinto, rouge, stain 6 depict, makeup 7 coating, pigment, portray, touch up 8 cosmetic 9 delineate, represent

painter
6 artist
American: 4 Cole (Thomas), Haas (Richard), Katz (Alex), West (Benjamin), Wood (Grant) 5 Abbey (Edwin Austin), Davis (Stuart), Gorky (Arshile), Grosz (George), Henri (Robert), Hicks (Edward), Homer (Winslow), Johns (Jasper), Kline (Franz), Kroll (Leon), Marin (John), Marsh (Reginald), Moses (Grandma), Peale (Anna, Charles Willson, James, Raphaelle, Rembrandt, Sarah, Titian), Ryder (Albert Pinkham), Shahn (Ben), Sloan (Eric, John), Weber (Max), Wyeth (Andrew, Jamie, Newell Convers) 6 Albers (Josef), Benton (Thomas Hart), Catlin (George), Church (Frederick Edwin), Coburn (Alvin Langdon), Copley (John Singleton), Durand (Asher), Eakins (Thomas), Hassam (Childe), Hopper (Edward), Inness (George), Leutze (Emanuel), Martin (Agnes, Homer), Newman (Barnett), Rivers (Larry), Rothko (Mark), Stella (Frank), Stuart (Gilbert), Tanguy (Yves), Thorpe (Thomas), Warhol (Andy) 7 Allston (Washington), Bearden (Romare), Bellows (George), Bingham (George Caleb), Cassatt (Mary), Duchamp (Marcel), Harnett (William), Hartley (Marsden), Kinkade (Thomas), La Farge (John), O'Keeffe (Georgia), Parrish (Maxfield), Pollock (Jackson), Sargent (John Singer), Sheeler (Charles), Tiffany (Louis Comfort) 8 Basquiat (Jean-Michel), Rockwell (Norman), Trumbull (John), Whistler (James McNeill) 9 Bierstadt (Albert), de Kooning (Willem), Feininger (Lyonel), Reinhardt (Ad), Remington (Frederic), Twachtman (John Henry), Vanderlyn (John) 10 Motherwell (Robert) 12 Lichtenstein (Roy), Rauschenberg (Robert)
Austrian: 5 Klimt (Gustav) 9 Kokoschka (Oskar)
Belgian: 5 Ensor (James) 6 Campin (Robert) 8 Magritte (René)
Canadian: 4 Kane (Paul) 6 Harris (Lawren), Watson (Homer) 7 Jackson (Alexander Young), Thomson (Tom) 9 MacDonald (James Edward Hervey)
Chinese: 4 Wu Li 6 Ma Yüan 7 Wang Wei 8 Yen Li-pen
Dutch: 3 Dou (Gerrit) 4 Hals (Frans), Lely (Peter), Maas (Nicolas) 5 Bosch (Hieronymus), Hooch (Pieter de), Steen (Jan) 6 Potter (Paul) 7 de Hooch (Pieter), de Witte (Emanuel), Hobbema (Meindert), van Gogh (Vincent), Vermeer (Jan) 8 Mondrian (Piet), Ruisdael (Jacob van, Salomon), Ruysdael (Salomon), Terborch (Gerard) 9 de Kooning (Willem), Rembrandt (van Rijn), Wouwerman (Philips)
English: 4 Hunt (William Holman), John (Augustus), Lear (Edward) 5 Bacon (Francis), Blake (William), Brown (Ford Madox), Lewis (Wyndham), Watts (George Frederick) 6 Fuseli (Henry), Romney (George), Stubbs (George), Turner (Joseph Mallord William), Wilson (Richard), Wright (Joseph) 7 Hockney (David), Hogarth (William), Kneller (Godfrey), Millais (John), van Dyke (Anthony) 8 Landseer (Edwin), Lawrence (Thomas), Reynolds (Joshua), Rossetti (Dante Gabriel) 9 Constable (John), Nicholson (Ben, William) 10 Alma-Tadema (Lawrence), Burne-Jones (Edward) 12 Gainsborough (Thomas)
Finnish: 9 Järnefelt (Edvard)
Flemish: 4 Eyck (Hubert van, Jan van), Goes (Hugo van der) 6 Rubens (Peter Paul), Weyden (Rogier van der) 7 Memling (Hams), Teniers (David), Van Dyck (Anthony), van Eyck (Hubert, Jan) 8 Breughel, Brueghel (Abraham, Ambrose, Jan, Pieter)
French: 3 Arp (Hans, Jean) 4 Doré (Gustave), Dufy (Raoul), Erté, Gros (Antoine-Jean) 5 Corot

(Camille), David (Jacques-Louis), Degas (Edgar), Léger (Fernand), Manet (Edouard), Monet (Claude), Redon (Odilon), Vouet (Simon) **6** Braque (Georges), Breton (André), Claude (of Lorrain), Clouet (François, Jean), Gérôme (Jean-Léon), Greuze (Jean-Baptiste), Ingres (Jean-Auguste-Dominique), Le Brun (Charles), Le Nain (Antoine, Louis, Mathieu), Millet (Jean-François), Renoir (Pierre-Auguste), Seurat (Georges), Sisley (Alfred), Tanguy (Yves), Vernet (Carle, Horace, Joseph) **7** Balthus, Bonheur (Rosa), Bonnard (Pierre), Boucher (François), Cézanne (Paul), Chagall (Marc), Chardin (Jean-Baptiste), Courbet (Gustave), Daumier (Honoré), Duchamp (Gaston, Marcel), Gauguin (Paul), Matisse (Henri), Morisot (Berthe), Poussin (Nicolas), Rouault (Georges), Utrillo (Maurice), Watteau (Antoine) **8** Dubuffet (Jean), Magritte (René), Pissarro (Camille), Rousseau (Henri, Théodore), Vlaminck (Maurice de), Vuillard (Edouard) **9** Delacroix (Eugène), Fragonard (Jean-Honoré), Géricault (Théodore), Laurencin (Marie) **10** Bouguereau (William), Meissonier (Jean-Louis) **11** Caillebotte (Gustave) **13** Claude Lorrain
German: **3** Arp (Jean) **4** Marc (Franz) **5** Dürer (Albrecht), Ernst (Max), Grosz (George), Nolde (Emil) **6** Albers (Josef) **7** Cranach (Lucas), Holbein (Hans), Lochner (Stefan), Richter (Gerhard), Schwind (Moritz von), Zoffany (Johann) **8** Kirchner (Ernst), Kollwitz (Käthe) **9** Grünewald (Matthias), Kandinsky (Wassily) **10** Schongauer (Martin), Wohlgemuth (Michael)
Greek: **6** Zeuxis **7** Apelles **10** Polygnotus
Irish: **5** Yeats (Jack, John Butler)
Italian: **4** Reni (Guido), Rosa (Salvator), Tura (Cosme) **5** Campi (Antonio, Bernardino, Giulio, Vincenzo), Lippi (Fra Filippo, Filippino, Lorenzo), Piero (della Francesca, di Cosimo), Sarto (Andrea del) **6** Andrea (del Sarto), Cosimo (Agnolo di, Piero di), Giotto, Romano (Giulio), Sodoma (Il), Titian, Vasari (Giorgio) **7** Bellini (Gentile, Giovanni, Jacopo), Chirico (Giorgio De), Cimabue, da Vinci (Leonardo), Fiesole (Giovanni da), Martini (Simone), Orcagna, Peruzzi (Baldassare), Raphael, Tiepolo (Giovanni), Uccello (Paolo), Zuccari (Taddeo) **8** del Sarto (Andrea), Fabriano (Gentile da), Giordano (Luca), Leonardo (da Vinci), Mantegna (Andrea), Masaccio, Montagna (Bartolommeo), Perugino, Pontorno (Jacopo da), Severini (Gino), Veronese (Paolo), Vivarini (Alvise, Antonio, Bartolomeo) **9** Carpaccio (Vittore), Correggio, Francesca (Piero della) **10** Botticelli (Sandro), Caravaggio, Modigliani (Amedeo), Signorelli (Luca), Tintoretto, Verrocchio (Andrea del) **11** Ghirlandaio (Domenico) **12** Michelangelo (Buonarotti), Parmigianino
Japanese: **5** Korin **6** Sesshu
Lithuanian: **7** Soutine (Chaim)
Mexican: **6** Orozco (José Clemente), Rivera (Diego), Tamayo (Rufino) **9** Siqueiros (David Alfaro)
Norwegian: **5** Munch (Edvard)
Russian: **7** Chagall (Marc), Roerich (Nikolay) **9** Kandinsky (Wassily)
Scottish: **6** Ramsay (Allan) **7** Nasmyth (Alexander), Raeburn (Henry)
Spanish: **4** Dalí (Salvador), Goya (Francisco), Gris (Juan), Miró (Joan), Sert (José Maria) **6** Ribera (José), Rincón (Antonio del), Tapiés (Antonio) **7** El Greco, Herrera (Francisco de), Murillo (Bartolomé Esteban), Picasso (Pablo), Zuloaga (Ignacio) **8** Zurbarán (Francisco de) **9** Velázquez (Diego)
Swedish: **4** Zorn (Anders) **6** Roslin (Alexander)
Swiss: **4** Klee (Paul), Witz (Konrad) **6** Fuseli (Henry)

painter Joan
4 Miró

painter of ballerinas
5 Degas (Edgar)

painter Salvador
4 Dalí

painter's stand
5 easel

painting
3 oil **7** acrylic, picture **10** watercolor
circular: **5** tondo
one-color: **8** monotint **10** monochrome
plaster: **5** secco **6** fresco
style: **4** Dada **5** fauve **6** cubism, cubist, Gothic, pop art, rococo **7** baroque, Bauhaus, dadaism, fauvism, fauvist, realism, realist **8** Barbizon, futurism, futurist, romantic **9** Byzantine, geometric, mannerism, mannerist **10** classicism, classicist, surrealism, surrealist **11** romanticism **13** expressionism, expressionist, impressionism, impressionist
technique: **3** oil **6** fresco, pastel **7** gouache, polymer, tempera **9** encaustic **10** watercolor
three-panel: **8** triptych
tool: **5** brush, easel, knife, paint **6** canvas **7** palette
two-panel: **7** diptych
wall: **5** mural

pair
3 duo, two **4** dyad, item, join, mate, span, team, twin, yoke **5** brace, match, twins, unite **6** couple **7** doublet, twosome **8** geminate

Pakistan
capital: **9** Islamabad
city: **6** Lahore, Multan **7** Karachi **9** Hyderabad **10** Faisalabad, Rawalpindi
language: **4** Urdu
leader: **6** Bhutto (Benazir) **9** Musharraf (Pervez)

monetary unit: **5** rupee
mountain, range: **8** Himalaya **9** Himalayan, Himalayas **11** Nanga Parbat
neighbor: **4** Iran **5** China, India **11** Afghanistan
sea: **7** Arabian

pal
3 bro, bud **4** chum, mate, pard **5** amigo, buddy, crony **6** comate, friend **7** comrade, partner **9** companion

palace
5 court, manor, manse **6** castle **7** alcazar, château, mansion **8** seraglio

paladin
6 leader **8** advocate, champion, defender, official

Palamedes
brother: **6** Sforza **8** Achilles
father: **8** Nauplius
slayer: **7** Corinda, Ulysses **8** Odysseus

palatable
5 sapid, tasty **6** savory **8** pleasing, savorous, tasteful **9** agreeable, appealing, delicious, toothsome **10** acceptable, appetizing **12** satisfactory

palate
5 taste **6** liking, relish

palatial
4 rich **5** grand, large, noble, plush, regal **6** deluxe, ornate **7** opulent, stately **8** imposing, majestic, splendid **9** grandiose, luxuriant, luxurious, sumptuous **10** impressive **11** magnificent

Palau
capital: **5** Koror
former name: **5** Pelew
island: **5** Koror **6** Angaur **7** Eli Malk **10** Babelthuap, Urukthapel
language: **7** Palauan

palaver
3 gas, yak **4** blab, cant, chat, guff, talk **6** babble, cajole, hot air, jargon, parley, powwow, speech **7** chatter, prattle **8** colloquy, converse, dialogue **10** conference, discussion, rap session **12** conversation

pale
3 dim, wan **4** area, ashy, dull, fade, sick, weak **5** ashen, faded, faint, fence, field, light, livid, pasty, stake, waxen **6** anemic, blanch, chalky, doughy, feeble, pallid, picket, sallow, sickly, whiten **7** ghastly, insipid **8** blanched **9** bloodless, colorless, enclosure

palindrome
3 aha, bib, dad, dud, DVD, eke, ere, eve, ewe, eye, gag, gig, huh, mem, mom, mum, nun, pap, PCP, pep, pip, pop, pup, sis, SOS, tat, TNT, tot, tut, wow **4** deed, kook, ma'am, noon, peep, poop, toot **5** alula, civic, imami, kayak, Kazak, level, madam, minim, put-up, radar, refer, rotor, stats, Tebet, tenet, we few **6** pull-up, terret **7** deified, race car, reviver, top spot **9** Malayalam, never even **11** borrow or rob, drawn inward, Kinnikinnik, Madam I'm Adam

palindromic pop group
4 ABBA

palinode
10 retraction **11** recantation

pall
4 bore, cloy, damp, jade, sate, tire **5** cloak, cloth, cloud, drape, ennui, gloom, weary **6** coffin, damper, mantle, shadow **7** dwindle, satiate, surfeit **8** covering

palladium
9 safeguard

Pallas
6 Athena
brother: **6** Aegeus
father: **7** Pandion
slayer: **7** Theseus
wife: **4** Styx
(see also **Athena**)

palliate
4 ease **5** salve **6** soften, soothe, temper **7** assuage, cover up, lighten, relieve **8** mitigate, moderate **9** alleviate **10** ameliorate

pallid
3 wan **4** ashy, dull, pale, weak **5** ashen, pasty, waxen **6** anemic, doughy, sickly **8** blanched, lifeless **9** bloodless, colorless

pallor
8 lividity, paleness **9** pastiness, whiteness **10** etiolation

pally
4 cozy **5** close, matey **6** chummy **8** familiar, friendly

palm
5 prize, steal, swipe **6** trophy **7** conceal, triumph, victory
beverage: **4** nipa
fiber: **4** bass, bast, coir **8** piassava
fruit: **4** acai, date **7** coconut **11** coquilla nut
kind: **3** fan, wax **4** atap, coco, date, doom, hemp, nipa, sago **5** areca, betel, ivory, royal, sabal **6** miriti, raffia, rattan **7** cabbage, feather, palmyra **8** carnauba, palmetto, piassava **12** Washingtonia
leaf: **4** olla **5** frond
starch: **4** sago
vine: **6** rattan

palmer
7 pilgrim

Palmetto State
13 South Carolina

palmistry
6 augury **8** prophecy **10** divination **11** soothsaying

palm off
5 foist **7** deceive, pretend **8** disguise

palmy
6 golden **7** booming, halcyon, opulent **8** affluent, thriving **10** prospering, prosperous **11** flourishing

Palmyra's queen
7 Zenobia

palooka
3 oaf **4** boob, dolt, goon, lout, lump **5** boxer, klutz **6** baboon, galoot, lummox **7** bruiser

palpable
5 clear, plain **6** patent **7** evident, obvious, tactile **8** apparent, concrete, distinct, manifest, tangible **10** noticeable **11** discernible, perceptible

palpate
4 feel **5** touch **6** finger **7** examine

palpitate
4 beat **5** pulse, throb **6** quiver **7** flutter, pulsate **12** pitter-patter

palsy-walsy
4 cozy **5** close, thick, tight **6** chummy **10** buddy-buddy

palter
3 fib, lie **5** evade **6** dicker, haggle **7** bargain, chaffer, falsify **10** equivocate **11** prevaricate

paltry
4 mean, puny **5** cheap, petty, tatty **6** meager, measly, narrow, shabby, shoddy **7** pitiful, trivial **8** beggarly, inferior, picayune, piddling, trifling **9** worthless **10** picayunish **11** unimportant **13** insignificant

paludal place
3 fen **5** marsh

Pamela author
10 Richardson (Samuel)

pampa
5 plain **7** prairie **9** grassland
cowboy: **6** gaucho
lariat: **4** bola

pamper
3 pet **4** baby **5** humor, spoil **6** caress, cocker, coddle, cosset, cuddle, dandle, fondle **7** cater to, cherish, gratify, indulge **9** spoon-feed **11** mollycoddle

pamphlet
5 flier, flyer, tract **6** folder **7** leaflet **8** brochure, circular **9** throwaway **10** broadsheet

pan
3 pot, rap, wok **4** slam, wash **5** basin, knock, roast, trash **6** attack, vessel **7** censure, condemn, skillet **8** ridicule **9** betel leaf, criticism, criticize

Pan
5 Inuus **6** Faunus
father: **6** Hermes
invention: **6** syrinx
lower part: **4** goat
mother: **8** Penelope
pipe: **6** syrinx
seat of worship: **7** Arcadia
son: **7** Silenus

panacea
4 cure **6** elixir, remedy **7** cure-all, nostrum **10** catholicon

Panacea's father
9 Asclepius **11** Aesculapius

panache
4 brio, dash, élan, tuft, zest **5** ardor, crest, flair, style, verve, vigor **6** esprit, polish, spirit **8** aigrette, flourish, vivacity **11** flamboyance

panama
3 hat

Panama
discoverer: **6** Balboa (Vasco Núñez de) **8** Columbus (Christopher)
gulf: **7** San Blas **8** Mosquito
language: **7** Spanish
leader: **7** Noriega (Manuel)
monetary unit: **6** balboa
neighbor: **8** Colombia **9** Costa Rica
peninsula: **6** Azuero
sea: **9** Caribbean
volcano: **8** Chiriquí

pancake
8 flapjack, slapjack
chain: **4** IHOP
French: **5** crepe
Jewish: **5** latke **6** blintz **7** blintze
Russian: **4** blin **5** blini

Pandarus
6 archer **8** procuror
father: **6** Lycaon
slayer: **8** Diomedes

pandect
4 code, laws **8** treatise **10** compendium **11** compilation

pandemic
4 rife **7** rampant **9** contagion, extensive **10** contagious, widespread

pandemonium
3 din **5** babel, chaos, furor **6** bedlam, clamor, furore, hubbub, tumult, uproar **7** anarchy, discord, inferno, misrule, turmoil **8** disorder **9** confusion **10** hullabaloo

pander
4 pimp **5** cater **9** exploiter, go-between

Pandora
creator: **10** Hephaestus
husband: **10** Epimetheus

panegyric
6 eulogy, praise 7 tribute 8 citation, encomium 9 laudation 10 compliment 12 commendation

panegyrical
8 praising 9 laudative, laudatory 10 eulogistic 11 encomiastic 12 commendatory 13 complimentary

panel
4 jury 5 board, frame 6 hurdle 7 console, section 9 dashboard

panfry
5 sauté

pang
4 ache, pain, stab 5 agony, prick, spasm, throe 6 stitch, twinge 7 anguish, torment 8 distress

Pangloss's pupil
7 Candide

panhandle
3 beg, bum, tap 5 cadge, hit up, mooch, touch 6 hustle 7 solicit

panhandler
6 beggar

panic
4 fear, riot, rush 5 alarm, scare 6 frenzy, fright, terror 7 anxiety, terrify 8 hysteria, stampede

pannier
4 hoop, pack 6 basket, hamper 9 overskirt

panoply
4 pomp, show 5 armor, array 6 attire 7 display, fanfare 9 trappings

panorama
4 view 5 range, reach, scene, scope, sweep, vista 7 display, expanse, picture, purview

panoramic
8 sweeping, synoptic 12 all-inclusive, unobstructed 13 comprehensive

pan out
4 work 5 click, prove, score 7 come off, succeed

pant
4 blow, gasp, gulp, huff, puff 5 chuff, heave 6 wheeze

Pantagruel
5 giant
companion: 7 Panurge
father: 9 Gargantua
mother: 7 Badebec

pantaloon
7 buffoon, trouser

Pantaloon's daughter
9 Columbine

pantheon
4 gods 5 Aesir 6 temple 9 hierarchy 10 hall of fame

panther
4 pard, puma 6 cougar, jaguar 7 leopard 9 catamount 12 mountain lion

pantomime
5 drama, mimic 6 act out, ballet 7 charade 12 harlequinade
clown: 7 Pierrot

pantry
6 closet, larder 7 buttery 9 storeroom

pants
5 jeans 6 slacks 7 drawers, garment 8 breeches, britches, knickers, trousers
part: 3 hem 4 cuff

Panurge's companion
10 Pantagruel

Paolo's lover
9 Francesca

pap
4 food, mash, mush 7 aliment, pabulum 8 soft food 9 blandness

papal
8 pontific 9 apostolic 10 pontifical
court: 5 Curia
crown: 5 tiara
decree: 8 decretal
envoy: 6 legate, nuncio
letter: 4 bull 10 encyclical
vestment: 5 fanon, orale

paper
5 essay, sheet, theme 6 letter, report 7 article 8 document 9 monograph, newsprint 10 memorandum 11 composition, publication 12 dissertation
measure: 4 ream 5 quire
roll: 6 scroll
scrap: 4 chad
size: 3 cap 5 atlas, crown, folio, legal, royal, sexto, sixmo 6 octavo, quarto 7 emperor 8 elephant, foolscap, imperial
stiff: 7 bristol 9 cardboard 12 bristol board
strong: 5 kraft 6 manila
thin: 6 tissue 9 onionskin
transparent: 8 glassine
writing: 3 rag 6 vellum 9 parchment

paper folding
7 origami

paperwork
7 red tape

papillon
7 spaniel 9 butterfly

Papua New Guinea
archipelago: 8 Bismarck
capital: 11 Port Moresby
city: 3 Lae
island: 12 Bougainville
language: 4 Motu 8 Tok Pisin
monetary unit: 4 kina
neighbor: 9 Indonesia, Irian Jaya

par
4 mean, norm **5** equal, score, usual **6** median, normal **7** average, typical **8** equality, standard

parable
4 myth, tale **5** fable, moral, story **7** example **8** allegory

parachute
7 bailout, skydive
part: **5** riser **6** canopy **7** harness, ripcord

Paraclete
9 Holy Ghost **10** Holy Spirit

parade
4 brag, pomp **5** array, boast, flash, march, shine, strut **6** expose, flaunt, review **7** display, exhibit, fanfare, marshal, panoply, show off **8** brandish, ceremony, proclaim **9** advertise, cavalcade, pageantry, promenade **10** masquerade, procession

paradigm
5 ideal, model **6** mirror **7** example, pattern **8** exemplar, standard **9** archetype, beau ideal, framework, prototype

paradise
4 Eden, Zion **5** bliss **6** Avalon, heaven, utopia **7** arcadia, elysium, nirvana **8** empyrean **9** Shangri-la **10** wonderland **12** promised land

Paradise Lost author
6 Milton (John)

paragon
3 gem **4** tops **5** champ, cream, ideal, jewel, match, model, peach, saint **7** epitome **8** champion, class act, exemplar, last word, nonesuch **9** archetype, beau ideal, nonpareil **10** apotheosis

Paraguay
capital: **8** Asunción
lake: **4** Ypoá
language: **7** Guarani, Spanish
monetary unit: **7** guarani
neighbor: **6** Brazil **7** Bolivia **9** Argentina
river: **9** Pilcomayo

parallel
4 akin, copy, even, like **5** agree, align, alike, equal, liken, match **6** double, equate, line up **7** aligned, compare, similar **8** analogue **9** alongside, analogous, consonant, corollary, correlate, duplicate **10** comparable, comparison, equivalent, similarity **11** coextensive, counterpart, duplication **13** corresponding

parallelogram
5 rhomb **6** oblong, square **7** rhombus **8** rhomboid **9** rectangle **13** quadrilateral

paralysis
5 palsy **7** inertia **9** impotence

paralyze
3 awe **4** daze, numb, stun **6** benumb, deaden **7** cripple, disable, petrify, stupefy **8** shut down **10** immobilize **12** incapacitate

paramount
5 chief, major, ruler **6** master **7** capital, leading, primary, regnant, supreme **8** cardinal, crowning, dominant, foremost, headmost, superior **9** principal, sovereign, uppermost **10** commanding, preeminent **11** predominant

paramour
5 lover, Romeo **7** Don Juan, gallant **8** Casanova, lothario, mistress **9** courtesan, inamorata, inamorato

paranormal ability
3 ESP

parapet
4 wall **7** bastion, bulwark, rampart **10** battlement, breastwork
part: **6** merlon **12** crenellation

paraphernalia
4 gear **5** items **6** outfit, tackle **7** effects **8** property **9** equipment, trappings **10** belongings **11** accessories, furnishings **13** accouterments, accoutrements, appurtenances

paraphrase
6 reword **7** restate, version **9** interpret, rendering, translate **11** restatement, translation

parasite
5 leech, toady **6** sponge, sucker **7** sponger **8** barnacle, deadbeat, hanger-on **9** sycophant **10** freeloader **11** bloodsucker

parasitic
8 sponging, toadying **9** leechlike **11** freeloading, sycophantic **12** bloodsucking
flatworm: **5** fluke **9** trematode

parasol
8 umbrella

____ paratus
6 semper

Parcae
5 Fates, Norns **6** Moirai
name: **4** Nona **5** Morta **6** Decuma

parcel
3 box, cut, lot **4** deal, dole, land, mete, pack, plot, wrap **5** allot, array, batch, bunch, share, tract **6** bundle, divide, packet, ration **7** package, portion, prorate, section, segment **8** allocate, disburse, division **9** apportion, partition **10** distribute

parch
3 dry **4** burn, sear **5** dry up, roast, toast **6** dry out, scorch **7** shrivel **9** dehydrate, desiccate

parched
3 dry **4** arid, sere **5** dusty **7** bone-dry, thirsty, wizened **8** scorched, withered **9** shriveled, waterless **10** dehydrated

parchment
4 skin 5 paper 6 vellum 7 diploma

pardon
4 free 5 remit, spare 6 excuse, let off 7 absolve, amnesty, condone, forgive, release 8 reprieve, tolerate 9 acquittal, exculpate, indemnity, remission 10 absolution, indulgence 11 exculpation, exoneration, forgiveness

pardonable
6 venial 9 allowable, excusable 11 permissible

pare
3 cut 4 clip, crop, peel, slim, trim 5 lower, prune, shave 6 reduce, remove 7 curtail, cut back, cut down, trim off, whittle 8 diminish

parent
4 make, rear 5 beget, cause, hatch, raise, spawn 6 author, create, father, mother, origin 7 bring up, care for, produce 8 begetter, generate 9 originate, procreate 10 progenitor

parenthetically
7 by the by 8 by the bye, by the way 9 in passing 12 incidentally

parentless
6 orphan 8 orphaned

par excellence
3 top 5 prime 6 superb 7 premier, supreme 8 foremost, peerless, superior 9 matchless, number one, unmatched 10 first-class, preeminent 11 outstanding

pariah
5 leper 7 Ishmael, outcast 8 castaway 10 Ishmaelite 11 offscouring, untouchable
Japanese: 3 eta

Paris
airport: 4 Orly
ancient name: 7 Lutetia
avenue: 13 Champs-Elysées
basilica: 10 Sacré Coeur
cathedral: 9 Notre Dame
city hall: 12 Hôtel de Ville
college: 8 Sorbonne
garden: 9 Tuileries 10 Luxembourg
island: 11 Île de la Cité
museum: 5 Cluny 6 Louvre
palace: 6 Louvre 7 Bourbon
patron saint: 9 Geneviève
racecourse: 7 Auteuil
river: 5 Seine
section: 8 Left Bank 9 Right Bank 10 Montmartre, Rive Gauche 12 Latin Quarter
stock exchange: 6 Bourse
subway: 5 Métro
tower: 6 Eiffel

Paris
beloved: 5 Helen
betrothed: 6 Juliet
father: 5 Priam
home: 4 Troy
mother: 6 Hecuba
slayer: 11 Philoctetes
wife: 6 Oenone

parish
6 county 8 district 9 community 12 congregation, neighborhood

Parisian chanteuse
4 Piaf (Edith)

Parisina
author: 5 Byron (Lord)
husband: 3 Azo
lover: 4 Hugo
slayer: 3 Azo

parity
8 equality, sameness, symmetry 10 similarity, similitude 11 equivalence, equivalency

park
4 stop 5 green, plaza 7 deposit, funfair, reserve 8 carnival, preserve 9 esplanade 11 reservation

parka
6 anorak, jacket 8 pullover 9 outerwear

park designer
4 Vaux (Calvert) 6 Paxton (Joseph) 7 Alphand (Jean), Le Nôtre (André), Olmsted (Frederick Law)

Parkinson's drug
5 L-dopa

parlance
4 cant, talk 5 argot, idiom, lingo, style, usage 6 jargon, patois, phrase, speech 7 wording 8 language, locution, phrasing 11 phraseology

parlay
3 bet 5 bid up, boost, stake, wager 6 expand, extend 7 build up, enhance, enlarge, exploit 8 increase, leverage

parley
4 talk 5 speak 6 confab, confer, huddle, powwow 7 discuss, meeting 8 colloquy, converse, dialogue 9 discourse, negotiate 10 conference, discussion 11 confabulate 12 conversation 13 confabulation

parliament
see **legislature**

parliamentary
negative: 3 nay
positive: 3 yea

parlor
5 salon 11 drawing room

parlous
5 dicey, hairy, risky 6 chancy, touchy, tricky, unsafe 8 critical, ticklish 9 dangerous, hazardous 10 precarious

Parnassian
4 poet **6** poetic

parochial
5 local **6** narrow **7** insular **9** sectarian, small-town **10** provincial

parody
3 rib **4** mock **5** mimic, spoof **6** satire **7** imitate, lampoon, mockery, takeoff **8** ridicule, travesty **9** burlesque, imitation **10** caricature

parole
4 free **6** let out, pledge **7** promise, release **9** discharge, probation, watchword

paronomasia
3 pun **11** play on words

paroxysm
3 fit **4** bout **5** spasm, throe **6** attack, frenzy **7** flare-up, seizure **8** eruption, outbreak, outburst **9** explosion **10** conniption, convulsion

parrot
3 ape **4** aper, copy, echo **5** mimic **6** repeat **7** chatter, copycat, imitate
kind: **3** ara, kea **4** jako, kaka, lory **5** macaw **6** budgie, kakapo **8** cockatoo, lorikeet, lovebird, parakeet **9** cockatiel **10** budgerigar

parrot fever
11 psittacosis

parry
4 duck, fend **5** avert, avoid, block, dodge, elude, evade, repel **7** counter, deflect, fend off, prevent, respond, ward off **8** sidestep, stave off **9** turn aside

parse
4 scan **7** analyze, dissect, examine, resolve **8** construe **9** anatomize, explicate, interpret

Parseghian of Notre Dame
3 Ara

Parsi
11 Zoroastrian

Parsifal
composer: **6** Wagner (Richard)
magician: **8** Klingsor
quest: **5** Grail
son: **9** Lohengrin
temptress: **6** Kundry

parsimonious
4 mean **5** cheap, close, tight **6** frugal, stingy **7** chintzy, miserly, sparing, thrifty **9** penurious **10** restrained **11** closefisted, tightfisted **12** cheese-paring **13** penny-pinching

parsley
4 herb **7** garnish
family: **6** carrot
piece: **5** sprig

parson
6 cleric, pastor, rector **8** clerical, minister, preacher, reverend **9** clergyman

parsonage
5 manse **7** rectory

part
3 bit, cut **4** chip, role, unit **5** chunk, piece, quota, scrap, sever, share, slice **6** detail, divide, member, moiety, ration, sector **7** element, measure, portion, quantum, quarter, section, segment **8** division, fraction, fragment, function **9** component

partake of
3 eat **5** savor, share **6** accept, sample **7** acquire, consume, receive **9** enter into **11** participate

Parthenon
sculptor: **7** Phidias **8** Pheidias
sculpture: **6** frieze
site: **9** Acropolis

partial
6 biased, unfair, warped **7** colored, half-way **8** inclined, one-sided **9** jaundiced **10** fractional, incomplete, prejudiced **11** fragmentary, predisposed

partiality
4 bent, bias **5** favor, taste **6** liking **7** leaning **8** affinity, fondness, tendency **10** favoritism, preference **11** inclination **12** one-sidedness, predilection

participant
5 party **6** fellow, member, player, sharer **7** partner, sharing **11** contributor, shareholder

participate
4 join, play **5** share **6** engage, join in **7** partake **8** take part

particle
3 ace, bit, dab, dot, jot, ort, tad **4** atom, doit, dram, drop, hint, hoot, iota, mite, mote, spot, whit **5** atomy, crumb, fleck, grain, minim, ounce, scrap, shred, speck, trace **6** morsel, tittle **7** granule, modicum, smidgen, smidgin, soupçon **8** fragment, smidgeon **9** scintilla
atomic: **3** ion **5** anion **6** baryon, cation
elementary: **3** psi, tau **4** kaon, muon, pion **5** boson, meson **6** baryon, hadron, lambda, lepton, photon, proton **7** fermion, hyperon, neutron, nucleon, upsilon **8** electron, mesotron, neutrino, positron
hypothetical: **5** gluon, quark **6** parton **8** graviton
virus: **6** virion
with negative charge: **8** electron
with positive charge: **6** proton **8** positron

particular
4 item **5** exact, fussy, picky **6** detail, minute, unique **7** careful, element, feature, finicky, precise, special, unusual **8** accurate, detailed, distinct, especial, exacting, itemized, separate, specific **10** fastidious, individual, meticulous,

pernickety, scrupulous **11** distinctive, exceptional, persnickety, punctillous

particularize
4 list **6** detail **7** catalog, itemize, specify **8** spell out **9** enumerate, inventory **13** individualize

parting
4 last **5** adieu, break, congé, final **6** good-by **7** good-bye **8** division, farewell **10** divergence, separation **11** leave-taking, valedictory

partisan
6 backer, biased, warped **7** devotee, die-hard, fanatic, patriot, sectary **8** adherent, advocate, disciple, follower, guerilla, one-sided, stalwart, upholder **9** factional, guerrilla, irregular, satellite, sectarian, supporter

partition
4 wall **6** divide, screen **7** divider, section, wall off **8** disunion, division, fence off, separate **10** separation

partner
4 ally, chum, mate **5** buddy, crony **6** cohort, fellow **7** comrade **8** confrere, helpmeet, sidekick **9** assistant, associate, colleague, companion **10** accomplice **11** confederate

partnership
4 axis, firm **5** union **7** cahoots, sharing **8** alliance, marriage, relation **11** affiliation, association **12** consociation, togetherness

part of a.m.
4 ante

parturient
6 gravid, parous **8** enceinte, pregnant **9** expecting

parturition
5 birth **8** delivery **10** childbirth **12** childbearing

party
4 ball, band, bash, bevy, bloc, crew, fete, gala, luau, orgy, rave, side **5** actor, corps, covey, feast, group, revel, troop **6** fiesta, frolic, kegger, mortal, person, social, soiree, troupe **7** blowout, carouse, faction, roister, shindig **8** carousal, litigant, wingding **9** bacchanal, gathering, make merry, raise hell **10** detachment, individual, saturnalia **11** bacchanalia, celebration

parvenu
7 upstart **9** arriviste **12** nouveau riche

Pascal essay
6 Pensée

pasha
3 dey

Pasiphaë
daughter: **7** Ariadne, Phaedra
husband: **5** Minos
son: **8** Minotaur

pass
3 bye, die, end, gap **4** fare, hand **5** cease, enact, get by, lapse, notch, occur, relay, spend, while **6** crisis, depart, elapse, exceed, expire, hand on, happen, permit, push on, slight, slip by, strait **7** come off, develop, journey, proceed, succumb **8** bequeath, fork over, hand down, juncture, outshine, outstrip, transmit **9** while away
Afghanistan: **5** Murgh
Afghanistan-Pakistan: **6** Khyber
Alaska: **5** White
Alps: **5** Cenis, Loibl **7** Brenner, Ljubelj, Simplon **9** St. Bernard
California: **5** Cajon
China-India: **9** Karakoram
Colorado: **3** Ute
mountain: **3** col, gap **4** ghat **5** notch
Pakistan: **5** Kilik
Russian: **12** Caspian Gates
Tennessee: **10** Cumberland

passable
4 okay, open, so-so **6** decent **8** adequate, all right **9** tolerable, unblocked **10** accessible, good enough **12** satisfactory

passably
6 enough **8** all right, somewhat **10** moderately

passage
3 way **4** exit, fare, hall, iter, path, text **5** route, shaft, shift **6** access, arcade, avenue, course, egress, seaway, strait, travel, tunnel, voyage **7** channel, excerpt, hallway, journey, transit **8** corridor, transfer, traverse **9** enactment, quotation **10** transition **12** transference, transmission
air: **7** windway
arched: **6** arcade
Atlantic-Pacific: **9** Northwest
closing: **4** coda
narrow: **3** gut
roofed: **6** arcade **9** breezeway

Passage to India author
7 Forster (E. M.)

pass away
3 die, end **6** demise, depart, elapse, expire, perish **7** decease, succumb

pass by
4 miss, omit **6** forget, ignore **7** neglect **8** overlook **9** disregard

passé
4 dead **5** dated, stale **6** démodé, old hat **7** demoded, disused, extinct, outworn **8** obsolete, outdated, outmoded **9** out-of-date **10** antiquated, oldfangled, superseded **12** old-fashioned

passel
3 lot **4** heap, pack **5** bunch **6** bundle **9** multitude

passenger
4 fare

passing
5 brief, death, quick **6** demise, highly **7** cursory, decease **8** fleeting **9** ephemeral, fugacious, extremely, momentary, transient **10** evanescent, short-lived, transitory **11** exceedingly, superficial

pass into law
5 enact

passion
4 fire, heat, itch, love, lust, zeal **5** agony, amour, ardor, craze, crush, drive **6** desire, fervor, hunger **7** avidity, craving, ecstasy, emotion, rapture **8** appetite, devotion, yearning **9** eagerness, suffering, transport **10** enthusiasm, excitement **11** amorousness, infatuation

passionate
3 hot **5** afire, angry, fiery **6** ardent, fervid, heated **7** amorous, aroused, blazing, burning, excited, fervent, furious, intense **8** incensed, vehement **9** impetuous, steamed up **10** hot-blooded **12** enthusiastic

passive
4 idle **5** inert, stoic **6** docile, latent **8** enduring, immobile, inactive, listless, resigned, yielding **9** apathetic, compliant, lethargic, quiescent **10** motionless, nonviolent, phlegmatic, submissive **11** acquiescent, complaisant, indifferent, unresistant

pass out
3 die **5** faint, swoon **7** divvy up **8** disburse, keel over **10** distribute

pass over
4 miss, omit, skip **6** forget, ignore **7** dismiss, neglect **8** discount, leave out **9** disregard

Passover
5 Pasch **6** Pesach
bread: **5** matzo **6** matzoh
meal: **5** seder

passport endorsement
4 visa

pass up
4 skip **5** forgo **6** refuse, reject **7** decline

past
3 ago, old **4** gone, late, once, yore **5** above, after, agone, olden, prior **6** beyond, bygone, former, whilom **7** onetime, quondam **8** anterior, foretime, lang syne, previous, sometime **9** antiquity, erstwhile, foregoing, precedent, preceding, yesterday **10** antecedent, yesteryear

pasta
5 dough
kind: **4** orzo, ziti **5** penne, ruote **6** rotini **7** fusilli, gemelli, gnocchi, lasagna, lasagne, mafalda, noodles, ravioli **8** farfalle, linguine, linguini, macaroni, rigatoni **9** canneloni, capellini, cavatappi, fettucine, fettucini, manicotti, radiatore, spaghetti, tubettini **10** cannelloni, conchiglie, fettuccine, fettuccini, tortellini, vermicelli **11** cappelletti, orecchiette, pappardelle
flour: **5** durum **8** semolina
sauce: **5** pesto **8** marinara
texture: **7** al dente

paste
3 fix, hit **4** beat, clay, drub, food, glue, sock **5** affix, dough, pound, stick, stuff **6** adhere, attach, cement, defeat, fasten, thrash, wallop **7** trounce **8** adhesive, material
soybean: **4** miso

Pasternak character
4 Lara **7** Zhivago (Dr.)

pastiche
4 olio **6** jumble, medley **7** farrago, mélange, mixture **8** mishmash **9** potpourri **10** assortment, hodgepodge, hotchpotch, miscellany, salmagundi **11** gallimaufry

pastime
4 game **5** hobby, sport **9** amusement, diversion **10** recreation

past master
3 ace, pro, wiz **4** whiz **5** adept, maven **6** expert, wizard **8** virtuoso **9** authority

pastor
5 padre **6** cleric, parson **8** minister, preacher, reverend, sky pilot **9** clergyman

pastoral
4 idyl **5** idyll, rural **6** rustic **7** bucolic, crosier, idyllic **8** agrarian, clerical, innocent, peaceful **10** campestral

pastor's assistant
6 curate

pastry
3 bun, pie **4** baba, cake, flan, tart **5** torte **6** cornet, Danish, éclair, gâteau, muffin **7** baklava, beignet, bouchée, cupcake, dariole, gâteaux (plural), palmier, savarin, strudel, tartlet **8** napoleon, papillon, piroshki, pirozhki, turnover **9** barquette, cream puff, madeleine, petit four, vol-au-vent **10** cheesecake **11** profiterole **12** millefeuille
kind: **4** filo, puff **5** flaky **6** phyllo
shell: **5** crust **7** timbale **8** meringue

pasture
3 lea, ley **4** feed, land **5** field, grass, graze **6** browse, meadow **9** grassland
sound: **3** moo

pasty
3 wan **4** pale **6** doughy, pallid, sickly **7** meat pie **8** turnover

pat
3 apt, dab, set **4** firm **5** fixed, slice, stiff, trite **6** dead-on **7** apropos, fitting **8** apposite, standard, suitable **9** contrived, pertinent, rehearsed

patch
3 bit, fix **4** area, fill, mend, plot **5** cover, piece, scrap, spell **6** doctor, emblem, fill up, repair, shield **7** connect, plaster

patchwork
4 olio **5** quilt **6** jumble **7** mixture **8** covering, mishmash, mixed bag **10** assortment, hodgepodge, hotchpotch, miscellany, salmagundi

patchy
6 fitful, random, spotty, uneven **7** erratic **8** sporadic **9** haphazard, hit-or-miss, irregular **12** intermittent

pate
4 bean, dome, head, poll **5** brain, crown **6** noddle, noggin, noodle

patella
7 kneecap, kneepan

patent
4 open **5** clear, plain, right **7** evident, license, obvious, visible **8** apparent, distinct, manifest **9** exclusive, privilege, protected **11** proprietary

paternal
8 fatherly
relative: **6** agnate

paternity
7 lineage **8** ancestry **10** fatherhood, provenance **11** progenitors

Pater Noster
9 Our Father **11** Lord's Prayer

path
3 way **4** lane, line, road, tack, walk **5** byway, orbit, route, track, trail **6** avenue, bridle, course, vector **7** passage, walkway **9** direction **10** trajectory

pathetic
3 sad **4** poor **5** sorry **6** absurd, moving, paltry **7** piteous, pitiful, risible, useless **8** inferior, pitiable, poignant, touching **9** affecting, laughable, miserable **10** lamentable, ridiculous

Pathfinder, The
author: **6** Cooper (James Fenimore)
hero: **6** Bumppo (Natty)

pathogen
4 germ **5** E. coli, virus **9** bacterium

pathological
7 deviant **8** aberrant, abnormal, diseased, maniacal, schizoid **9** psychotic

pathos
4 pity **7** emotion **8** sympathy **9** poignance, poignancy

pathway
4 line, walk **5** route, track, trail **6** course **7** channel, conduit, network, passage

patience
4 cool **8** calmness, stoicism **9** composure, endurance **10** equanimity, sufferance **11** forbearance, resignation, self-control

Patience
composer: **8** Sullivan (Arthur)
librettist: **7** Gilbert (W. S.)

patient
4 case, meek **8** enduring **9** easygoing **10** persistent **11** susceptible **13** long-suffering
man: **3** Job

patina
4 aura, coat, film **6** finish, polish **7** coating **8** covering **10** appearance, coloration

patio
5 atria (plural), court **6** atrium **7** terrace **9** courtyard

patisserie
6 bakery

patois
4 cant **5** argot, lingo, slang **6** jargon **7** dialect **10** colloquial, vernacular

patriarch
4 sire **6** father, nestor **7** creator, founder **9** architect, graybeard
biblical: **5** David, Isaac, Jacob **7** Abraham

patrician
5 noble **6** aristo **9** blue blood, gentleman **10** aristocrat, upper-class

patriciate
5 elite **6** gentry **9** blue blood, gentility **10** upper crust **11** aristocracy

patrimony
6 estate, legacy **8** heritage **9** endowment **10** birthright **11** inheritance

patriot
5 jingo **8** jingoist, loyalist **9** flag-waver **10** chauvinist **11** nationalist

patriotism
8 jingoism **10** chauvinism **11** nationalism

Patroclus
friend: **8** Achilles
slayer: **6** Hector

patrol
5 guard, round, scout, troop, watch **7** protect **8** sentinel **9** keep watch

patrolman
3 cop **5** guard **6** copper, police **7** officer

patrol wagon
see **paddy wagon**

patron
5 angel **6** backer, client **7** sponsor **8** customer, guardian **9** protector, supporter **10** benefactor

patronage
4 egis, help **5** aegis, trade **6** custom **7** backing, subsidy, support, traffic **8** activity, advocacy,

auspices, business, cronyism **9** clientage, clientele, influence **11** benefaction, sponsorship **12** guardianship

patronize
3 aid, use **4** back **5** deign, favor **6** assist, shop at **7** protect, support **8** frequent **10** condescend

patron saint
of beggars, cripples: **5** Giles
of children: **8** Nicholas
of England: **6** George
of fishermen: **5** Peter
of France: **5** Denis
of Ireland: **7** Patrick
of lawyers: **4** Ives
of musicians: **7** Cecilia
of Norway: **4** Olaf
of physicians: **4** Luke
of sailors: **4** Elmo **8** Nicholas
of Scotland: **6** Andrew
of shoemakers: **7** Crispin
of Spain: **5** James **8** Santiago
of travelers: **11** Christopher
of Wales: **5** David
of winegrowers: **7** Vincent
of workers: **6** Joseph

patsy
3 sap **4** dupe, fool, mark **5** chump **6** pigeon, sucker, victim **7** fall guy **8** easy mark, pushover

patter
4 cant **5** argot, lingo, slang, spiel **6** babble, jargon, patois **7** chatter, prattle

pattern
4 copy, form, plan **5** guide, ideal, model, motif, order, plaid, shape **6** argyle, design, figure, floral, method, system **7** diagram, paisley **8** exemplar, grouping, paradigm, standard, template **9** archetype, prototype **10** stereotype **11** arrangement **12** distribution **13** configuration

paucity
4 lack, want **6** dearth **7** poverty **8** scarcity, shortage **9** scantness, smallness **10** deficiency, meagerness, meagreness

Paul the Apostle
birthplace: **6** Tarsus
companion: **5** Silas, Titus **7** Artemas, Timothy **8** Barnabas
original name: **4** Saul
place of conversion: **8** Damascus
prosecutor: **9** Tertullus
teacher: **8** Gamaliel
tribe: **8** Benjamin

paunch
3 gut, pot **5** belly, tummy **7** abdomen, stomach **8** potbelly **9** bay window, beer belly **11** breadbasket, corporation

paunchy
3 fat **5** beefy, plump, tubby **6** chunky, portly, rotund **8** thickset **10** overweight, potbellied

pauper
6 beggar **7** have-not **8** bankrupt, indigent **9** mendicant

pauperism
4 need, ruin, want **6** penury **7** beggary, poverty **9** indigence, neediness, privation **11** destitution

pause
3 gap **4** halt, hush, lull, rest, stop, wait **5** break, comma, delay, lapse, letup **6** hiatus, linger, recess **7** caesura, respite, take ten, time out **8** breather, hesitate, inaction, interval, surcease, take five **9** cessation, interlude **10** hesitation, suspension **12** intermission, interruption

Pavarotti, e.g.
5 tenor

pave
3 lay, tar **5** cover **7** asphalt, surface **8** blacktop, concrete

pavement
6 tarmac **7** asphalt, macadam, surface **8** concrete, sidewalk

pavilion
4 tent **5** kiosk **6** canopy, gazebo **9** belvedere **11** summerhouse

paving stone
4 sett

paw
4 feel, foot, grab, hand, mitt **5** grope, touch **6** fondle, handle, molest, scrape

pawn
4 hock, tool **6** pledge, puppet, stooge, victim **7** deposit, hostage, warrant **8** guaranty, security **10** chess piece

pax
5 peace **6** tablet

Pax ____
3 Dei **6** Romana **10** Britannica

pay
3 fee **4** ante, wage **5** remit, serve, spend **6** answer, ante up, defray, expend, kick in, lay out, pony up, profit, render, salary, settle, tender, reward **7** benefit, bring in, cough up, forfeit, fork out, satisfy, stipend **8** disburse, earnings, shell out **9** discharge, emolument, indemnify, reimburse **10** compensate, recompense, remunerate **12** compensation, remuneration

payable
3 due **4** owed **5** owing **6** mature, unpaid **7** overdue **9** unsettled **10** obligatory **11** outstanding, uncollected

paycheck
5 wages **6** salary

pay dirt
4 lode

payload
4 haul **5** cargo, goods **6** burden, lading, weight **7** freight, tonnage **8** shipment

payment
3 fee **4** dues **5** award, money **6** amends, outlay, return, reward **7** penance **8** defrayal, requital **11** restitution **12** compensation, remuneration, satisfaction
pledge: 3 IOU

payoff
3 fix **5** bribe, graft **6** climax, profit, result, reward, upshot **7** outcome **8** clincher, decisive **10** conclusion, conclusive, denouement **11** retribution

payola
5 bribe

pay to play
4 ante

PBS science show
4 Nova

PC
alternative: 3 Mac **4** iMac, iPad
connection: 3 LAN
display type, formerly: 3 CRT
insert: 5 CD-ROM
key: 3 Alt, Esc, Tab **4** Ctrl **5** Enter, Shift

PDQ
4 ASAP, stat **6** at once, pronto **8** directly, right now, right off **9** forthwith, instanter, instantly, right away **11** immediately

peace
3 pax **4** calm, ease, pact **5** amity, order, quiet **6** accord, repose **7** concord, harmony, silence **8** serenity **11** tranquility **12** tranquillity

peaceable
6 dovish, irenic **7** amiable, pacific **8** amicable, friendly, pacifist, tranquil **10** nonviolent **11** complaisant **12** conciliatory

peaceful
4 calm **5** still, quiet **6** irenic, placid, serene **7** equable, halcyon, pacific **8** composed, tranquil **9** unruffled **10** harmonious, nonviolent, untroubled

peacemaker
7 arbiter **8** mediator, pacifier, placater **10** arbitrator, negotiator **11** conciliator, pacificator

peace officer
3 cop **6** police **9** policeman **11** policewoman

peach
3 ace, pip, rat **4** blab, lulu, tree **5** fruit, honey **6** betray, inform, reveal, snitch, squeal **7** Elberta **8** knockout **9** freestone, humdinger, nectarine **10** clingstone **11** crackerjack
family: 4 rose

Peach State
7 Georgia

peachy
4 fine, good, neat, nice **5** dandy, neato, nifty, super, swell **8** pleasant, pleasing **9** excellent, hunky-dory, marvelous, wonderful

peacockish
5 showy, swank **6** chichi, flashy, swanky **7** splashy **8** show-offy **10** flamboyant **11** pretentious **12** ostentatious

peak
3 top **4** acme, apex, roof **5** crest, crown **6** summit, vertex, zenith **8** pinnacle
Arizona: 9 Humphreys
Bighorn Mtns.: 5 Cloud
Black Hills: 6 Harney
California: 6 Lassen **9** Telescope
Cascade Range: 6 Lassen
Colorado: 5 Grays, Longs, Pikes **6** Blanca **7** La Plata **11** Uncompahgre
Idaho: 5 Borah
Kyrgyzstan: 5 Lenin **6** Pobeda
Montana: 7 Granite **8** Electric
Nevada: 7 Wheeler **8** Boundary **10** Charleston
New Mexico: 7 Truchas, Wheeler **12** Sierra Blanca
South Dakota: 6 Harney
Sri Lanka: 5 Adam's **8** Samanala
Tajikistan: 5 Lenin **9** Communism
Utah: 5 Kings
White Mtns.: 8 Boundary
Wyoming: 5 Cloud **6** Franks **7** Gannett
(see also **mountain**)

peaked
3 ill, wan **4** ashy, pale, sick **5** acute, ashen, drawn, sharp **6** ailing, pallid, sickly **7** pointed **9** emaciated

peal
4 bell, bong, ring, toll **5** chime, knell, sound **7** ring out, ringing **8** ding-dong

peanut
4 mani **6** goober, legume, peewee, shrimp **9** pip-squeak

Peanuts
character: 4 Lucy (van Pelt) **5** Linus, Patty (Peppermint), Rerun, Sally (Brown), Spike **6** Frieda, Marcie, Pig-Pen, Snoopy **8** Franklin **9** Schroeder, Woodstock **12** Charlie Brown
creator: 6 Schulz (Charles M.)
expression: 4 rats
forerunner: 8 Li'l Folks

pear
4 Bosc, pome **5** Anjou, Hardy **6** Comice, Garber, Seckel **7** Kieffer, LeConte **8** Bartlett
cider: 5 perry

pearl
3 gem **4** dear **5** jewel **7** paragon **8** treasure
Pearl Buck heroine
4 O-Lan
Pearl Mosque site
4 Agra
pearly
8 lustrous, nacreous, precious **10** iridescent, opalescent
pear-shaped
8 pyriform
peasant
4 carl, kern, peon, serf **5** churl **6** rustic **7** bumpkin, hayseed, villein
Arab: **6** fellah
Indian: **4** ryot
Latin-American: **9** campesino
Philippine: **3** tao
Russian: **5** mujik **6** moujik, muzhik
peccary
8 javelina
genus: **7** Tayassu
peck
3 lot, nag **4** buss, carp, fuss, heap, kiss, load, mess, pile, poke **6** carp at, nibble, pick at, pick up, pierce, strike **8** quantity
pecking order
6 ladder **7** pyramid **9** food chain, hierarchy
peculate
5 steal **8** embezzle **9** defalcate **11** appropriate
peculiar
3 odd **4** rare **5** queer, weird **6** unique **7** bizarre, curious, oddball, offbeat, special, strange, unusual **8** abnormal, singular, specific, uncommon **9** eccentric **10** individual, particular **11** distinctive
peculiarity
3 tic **4** mark **5** quirk, trait **6** oddity **7** feature, quality **9** attribute, mannerism **12** eccentricity, idiosyncrasy
pecuniary
6 fiscal **8** economic, monetary **9** financial
pedagogue
5 tutor **6** pedant **7** teacher **8** educator **12** schoolmaster
pedagogy
8 teaching **9** education
pedal
5 lever **7** bicycle, treadle
digit: **3** toe
pedant
7 teacher **9** formalist, nitpicker **10** schoolmarm **12** precisionist
pedantic
3 dry **4** arid, dull **6** stodgy **7** bookish, donnish, erudite, learned, tedious **8** academic, didactic, priggish **9** ponderous **10** pedestrian, scholastic
peddle
4 hawk, push, sell, vend **5** pitch **6** monger **8** huckster
peddler
6 coster, dealer, hawker, monger, vendor **8** huckster, merchant, promoter **9** tradesman **12** costermonger
pedestal
4 base, foot **5** stand **7** footing, support **10** foundation **12** underpinning
part: **4** dado **6** plinth **7** subbase
pedestrian
4 blah, dull **5** banal **6** dreary, stodgy, walker **7** humdrum, mundane, prosaic **8** everyday, ordinary **11** commonplace **13** unimaginative
crossing: **5** zebra **10** footbridge
pedigree
6 origin, purity **7** descent, history, lineage **8** ancestry, purebred **9** bloodline, genealogy **10** background, extraction, family tree
peduncle
4 stem **5** stalk **7** pedicel
peek
3 spy **4** look **6** glance **7** glimpse
peel
4 bark, pare, rind, skin, zest **5** flake, scale, strip **7** take off **8** flake off **9** break away, exfoliate
peeled
4 bare, open **5** naked **7** denuded, exposed **8** stripped
peep
3 see, spy **4** look **5** chirp, tweet, watch **6** glance, squeak **7** glimpse, twitter **9** sandpiper
Peeping Tom
5 snoop **6** voyeur **7** prowler, snooper
peep show
5 raree
peer
3 pry **4** gaze, lord **5** equal, glare, noble, stare **6** goggle, squint **9** associate
British: **4** duke, earl **5** baron **7** marquis **8** marquess, viscount
Peer Gynt
author: **5** Ibsen (Henrik)
beloved: **7** Solveig
character: **6** Anitra
composer: **5** Grieg (Edvard)
mother: **3** Ase **4** Aase
peerless
4 best **6** unique **7** perfect, supreme **8** superior **9** matchless, nonpareil, paramount, unequaled, unmatched, unrivaled **12** incomparable, unparalleled

peeve
3 bug, irk, vex **4** miff, rile **5** anger, annoy, pique **6** bother, nettle, put out **7** disturb, provoke **8** irritate, nuisance, vexation **9** aggravate, annoyance, grievance **10** exasperate **11** aggravation

peevish
4 sour **5** cross, pouty, testy **6** crabby, cranky, grumpy, ornery, tetchy **7** fretful, grouchy, pettish, prickly, whining **8** petulant **9** fractious, irascible, irritable, obstinate, querulous **11** ill-tempered

peewee
4 runt, tike, tyke **5** dwarf, pigmy, pygmy, small **6** midget, shaver, shrimp, squirt **9** miniature **10** diminutive, flycatcher **11** lilliputian

peg
3 fix, pin, tee **4** mark, plug, step **5** dowel, prong, stake, throw **6** attach, fasten, marker **7** pin down, pretext, support **8** identify

Pegasus
5 horse, steed
rider: **11** Bellerophon

pejorative
7 adverse **8** critical, debasing **9** slighting **10** belittling, derogatory, detractive **11** denigrating, deprecatory, disparaging, opprobrious, unfavorable **12** depreciatory

pelagic
6 marine **7** oceanic **8** maritime

Peleus
brother: **7** Telamon
father: **6** Aeacus
half brother: **6** Phocus
son: **8** Achilles
victim: **8** Eurytion
wife: **6** Thetis

pelf
4 loot, swag **5** booty, lucre, money, moola **6** boodle, moolah, riches, spoils **7** plunder

Pelias
country: **6** Iolcus
father: **8** Poseidon
half brother: **5** Aeson
son: **7** Acastus

Pelican State
9 Louisiana

Pelléas
beloved: **9** Mélisande
brother, slayer: **6** Golaud

Pelles
daughter: **6** Elaine
grandson: **7** Galahad

pellet
3 wad **4** ball, shot **6** sphere **10** projectile

Pellinore
slayer: **6** Gawain
son: **5** Torre **6** Dornar **7** Lamerok **8** Percival **9** Agglovale

pell-mell
5 chaos, snarl **6** muddle, rashly **7** chaotic, clutter, hastily **8** confused, headlong, reckless **9** hurriedly **10** carelessly, heedlessly **11** hurry-scurry **13** helter-skelter

pellucid
5 clear, sheer **6** limpid **7** crystal, obvious **8** clear-cut, luminous **10** see-through **11** crystalline, transparent

Pelops
father: **8** Tantalus
son: **6** Atreus **8** Pittheus, Thyestes
wife: **10** Hippodamia

pelota
4 ball **7** jai alai
basket: **5** cesta

pelt
3 fur, run **4** beat, blow, dash, drub, hide, hurl, rush, skin, whop **5** hurry, pound, scoot, speed, strip, throw, whack **6** assail, batter, pepper, pummel, strike **7** bombard

pelvic
5 iliac
bone: **4** ilia (plural) **5** ilium

pen
3 sty **4** cage, coop, jail, swan **5** pound, quill, write **6** cooler, corral, indite, prison, shut in, stylus, writer **7** close in, confine, enclose, fence in **9** ballpoint, enclosure

penal
8 punitive **12** correctional, disciplinary

penalize
4 dock, fine **5** mulct **6** punish **7** deprive **8** handicap **10** discipline **12** disadvantage

penalty
4 fine, loss **5** mulct **7** damages, forfeit **8** hardship **10** amercement, forfeiture, punishment **12** disadvantage

penance
4 rite **7** penalty **8** hardship **9** atonement **10** punishment

penchant
4 bent **5** taste **6** liking **7** leaning **8** affinity, fondness, tendency **9** inclining **10** partiality, proclivity, propensity **11** inclination **12** predilection

pendent
7 hanging **9** suspended, undecided, unsettled **11** overhanging

pending
6 during **8** awaiting, imminent **9** undecided, unsettled **12** undetermined

___ Pendragon
5 Uther

pendulous
7 hanging **8** dangling, drooping

Penelope
father: **7** Icarius
father-in-law: **7** Laertes
husband: **7** Ulysses **8** Odysseus
mother: **8** Periboea
son: **10** Telemachus
suitor: **7** Agelaus

penetrable
6 porous **8** pervious **9** permeable

penetrate
3 jab **4** bore, go in, stab **5** break, enter **6** affect, pierce **7** pervade **8** encroach, permeate, puncture, saturate **9** percolate

penetrating
4 keen **5** acute, sharp **6** astute, shrewd **8** incisive, piercing **9** trenchant **10** discerning, insightful, perceptive **12** sharp-sighted

Peneus
daughter: **6** Daphne
father: **7** Oceanus
mother: **6** Tethys

penguin type
6 Adélie **7** emperor

___ Penh
5 Phnom

peninsula
4 neck **10** chersonese
Alaska: **5** Kenai **6** Seward
Australia: **6** Tasman
Barents Sea: **5** Kanin
British colony: **9** Gibraltar
Canada: **5** Bruce, Gaspé **6** Ungava **8** Labrador
Chile: **5** Swett
China: **8** Shandong
Costa Rica: **3** Osa
Croatia: **6** Istria
Denmark: **7** Jutland
eastern United States: **8** Delmarva
Estonia: **5** Sorve
Florida: **8** Pinellas **9** Canaveral
France: **5** Giens
Greece: **4** Acte **10** Chalcidice **11** Peloponnese **12** Peloponnesus
Guam: **5** Orote
Hong Kong: **7** Kowloon
Honshu: **3** Izu **5** Miura
Massachusetts: **7** Cape Ann, Cape Cod
Mexico: **4** Baja **7** Yucatan **14** Baja California
Michigan: **8** Keweenaw
Middle East: **5** Sinai
New Guinea: **4** Huon
New Jersey: **9** Sandy Hook
New Zealand: **5** Banks, Mahia
Nunavut: **7** Boothia **8** Melville
Ontario: **5** Bruce
Persian Gulf: **9** Ras Tanura
Quebec: **5** Gaspé
Russia: **4** Kola **5** Taman, Yamal **6** Kolski, Taimyr **9** Kamchatka
Scotland: **7** Kintyre
South Australia: **4** Eyre **5** Yorke
Southeast Asia: **5** Malay **9** Indochina
southeastern Europe: **6** Balkan
southwestern Asia: **6** Arabia **7** Arabian
southwestern Europe: **7** Iberian
Texas: **9** Matagorda
Tierra del Fuego: **5** Mitre
Turkey: **8** Anatolia **9** Asia Minor
Ukraine: **5** Kerch **6** Crimea **7** Crimean
Wales: **5** Gower, Lleyn
Washington: **7** Olympic
Wisconsin: **4** Door

Peninsular State
7 Florida

penitence
3 rue **4** ruth **6** regret, sorrow **7** anguish, remorse **8** distress, humbling **10** contrition, repentance **11** compunction, self-reproof **12** self-reproach

penitent
5 sorry **6** rueful **8** contrite **9** regretful, repentant **10** apologetic, remorseful

penitentiary
see **prison**

penman
5 clerk **6** author, scribe, writer **7** copyist **9** scrivener **12** calligrapher

penmanship
4 hand **5** style **6** script **7** writing **11** calligraphy, chirography, handwriting

pen name
5 alias **6** anonym **9** pseudonym **10** nom de plume
Addison, Joseph: **4** Clio
Arouet, François-Marie: **8** Voltaire
Beyle, Marie-Henri: **8** Stendhal
Blair, Eric: **12** George Orwell
Blixen, Karen: **4** Isak (Dinesen)
Brontë, Anne: **9** Acton Bell
Brontë, Charlotte: **10** Currer Bell
Brontë, Emily: **9** Ellis Bell
Clemens, Samuel: **9** Mark Twain
Dickens, Charles: **3** Boz
Dodgson, Charles Lutwidge: **12** Lewis Carroll
Dupin, Amandine-Aurore: **10** George Sand
Evans, Mary Ann: **11** George Eliot
Faust, Frederick: **8** Max Brand
Franklin, Benjamin: **11** Poor Richard
Gardner, Erle Stanley: **6** A. A. Fair

Geisel, Theodor: **7** Dr. Seuss
Glidden, Frederick: **9** Luke Short
Goff, Helen: **7** Travers (P. L.)
Handler (Daniel): **7** Snicket (Lemony)
Hunter, Evan: **6** McBain (Ed)
Konigsberg, Allen: **5** Allen (Woody)
Korzeniowski, Józef: **6** Conrad (Joseph)
Krentz, Jayne Ann: **5** Quick (Amanda)
Lamb, Charles: **4** Elia
Lederer, Eppie: **10** Ann Landers
Martin, Judith: **11** Miss Manners
Munro, Hector Hugh: **4** Saki
Phillips, Pauline: **8** Dear Abby (Van Buren)
Poquelin, Jean-Baptiste: **7** Molière
Porter, William Sidney: **6** O. Henry
Ramé, Maria Louise: **5** Ouida
Remi, Georges: **5** Hergé
Roberts (Nora): **4** Robb (J. D.)
Rosenbaum, Alisa: **3** Ayn (Rand)
Thibault, J.-A.-F.: **13** Anatole France
Viaud, L.-M.-J.: **10** Pierre Loti
Wofford, Chloe Anthony: **12** Toni Morrison

pennant
4 flag, jack **5** color **6** banner, ensign **8** standard, streamer **9** banderole **12** championship

penniless
4 poor **5** broke, needy **8** bankrupt, indigent **9** destitute, insolvent **11** impecunious

Penn of film
4 Sean

pennon
4 flag, jack, wing **5** color **6** banner, ensign **8** bannerol, gonfalon, streamer **9** banderole, oriflamme

Pennsylvania
capital: **10** Harrisburg
city: **4** Erie **7** Reading **8** Scranton **9** Allentown **10** Pittsburgh **12** Philadelphia
college, university: **6** Drexel, Lehigh, Temple **7** LaSalle **8** Bryn Mawr, Bucknell **9** Dickinson, Haverford, Lafayette, Villanova **10** Swarthmore
mountain range: **6** Pocono
nickname: **8** Keystone (State)
river: **9** Allegheny **10** Schuylkill **11** Monongahela, Susquehanna
state bird: **12** ruffed grouse
state flower: **14** mountain laurel
state tree: **7** hemlock

Pennsylvania sect
5 Amish

penny-pincher
5 miser **7** niggard, scrooge **8** tightwad **9** skinflint **10** cheapskate

penny-pinching
4 mean **6** frugal, stingy, thrift **7** miserly, thrifty **9** frugality, niggardly, parsimony, penurious **11** tightfisted **12** cheeseparing, parsimonious

penny-wise
5 canny, tight **6** frugal, stingy **7** prudent, sparing, thrifty **9** provident **10** economical **12** parsimonious

pen or needle
5 styli (plural) **6** stylus

pen point
3 neb, nib

pension
3 inn **5** hotel, lodge **6** hostel, reward **7** annuity, auberge, payment, stipend **8** gratuity **9** allowance **12** room and board, roominghouse **13** boardinghouse

pensioner
7 retiree

pensive
3 sad **6** dreamy, musing **7** wistful **10** meditative, melancholy, reflective, ruminative, thoughtful **11** preoccupied **13** contemplative

Pentateuch
5 Torah
books: **6** Exodus **7** Genesis, Numbers **9** Leviticus **11** Deuteronomy

Penthesilea
queen of: **7** Amazons
slayer: **8** Achilles

Pentheus
grandfather: **6** Cadmus
king of: **6** Thebes
mother: **5** Agave

penumbra
4 veil **5** cover, shade **6** fringe, screen, shadow, shroud **7** curtain

penurious
4 mean, poor **5** needy, tight **6** frugal, stingy **7** miserly **8** indigent, stinting **9** destitute, niggardly **11** impecunious, tightfisted **12** impoverished, parsimonious **13** penny-pinching

penury
4 need, want **7** beggary, poverty **9** indigence, privation, pauperism **11** destitution

peon
4 serf **5** prole, slave **6** drudge, toiler, worker **7** laborer, peasant **11** galley slave
Anglo-Saxon: **4** esne

peonage
4 yoke **6** thrall **7** bondage, helotry, serfdom, slavery **9** servitude, thralldom, villenage **11** enslavement

people
3 kin **4** folk **5** folks, plebs **6** public **7** society **8** populace **9** commoners, community, plebeians **10** commonalty **11** inhabitants, rank and file
combining form: **5** ethno

pep
3 vim, zip **4** brio, dash **5** gusto, moxie, punch, verve, vigor **6** energy, spirit **7** sparkle **8** vitality, vivacity **10** get-up-and-go, liveliness **11** high spirits

pepo
5 gourd, melon **6** squash **7** pumpkin **8** cucumber

pepper
4 kava, pelt **5** chili **6** season, shower **7** cayenne, paprika, pimento, tabasco **8** capsicum, cascabel, chipotle, habanero, jalapeño, pimiento, sprinkle **9** condiment, seasoning **12** Scotch bonnet

peppery
3 hot **5** fiery, sharp, spicy, testy, zesty **6** biting, lively, snappy, touchy **7** piquant, pungent **8** choleric, poignant, seasoned, stinging **9** irascible, irritable

peppy
4 spry **5** alert, perky **6** active, bright, lively **7** vibrant **8** animated, spirited, vigorous **9** energetic, sprightly, vivacious

Pequod
cabin boy: **3** Pip
captain: **4** Ahab
harpooner: **6** Daggoo **8** Queequeg, Tashtego
mate: **8** Starbuck
seaman: **7** Ishmael

per
3 via **4** a pop, each, with **6** apiece **7** by way of, for each, through **9** by means of **12** individually

perambulate
4 walk **6** ramble, stroll **8** traverse **9** promenade

per capita
4 each **6** apiece, by each **7** equally, for each

perceive
3 see **4** espy, feel, know, mark, note **5** grasp, seize, sense **6** detect, notice, remark **7** discern, observe, realize **8** identify **9** apprehend, recognize **10** comprehend, understand

percentage
3 cut **4** part **5** piece, share, slice **6** profit **7** portion **9** advantage **10** commission, proportion **11** probability

perceptible
5 clear **6** marked **7** visible **8** apparent, definite, distinct, palpable, sensible, tangible **10** detectable, noticeable, observable **11** appreciable, discernible **12** recognizable

perception
3 ken **4** idea **5** grasp, image **6** acumen, notion **7** concept, feeling, insight, thought **9** awareness, cognition **10** impression **11** discernment, observation

perceptive
4 keen, sage, wise **5** acute, alert, aware, sharp **7** knowing **9** intuitive, observant, sagacious, sensitive **10** discerning, insightful, responsive **13** understanding

perch
3 bar, peg, set **4** fish, land, rest, seat **5** light, roost, sit on **6** alight, settle **7** set down, sit atop, sit down

perchance
5 maybe **6** mayhap **7** perhaps **8** possibly **11** conceivably

percipience
6 acumen **8** keenness **9** cognition, intuition **10** astuteness **11** discernment **12** appreciation, perspicacity

percolate
4 drip, ooze, seep **5** exude, leach **6** charge, filter, simmer, spread **7** pervade, trickle **9** penetrate

percussion
3 jar **4** bump, jolt **5** clash, crash, shock **6** impact **9** collision **10** concussion
instrument: (see at **musical instrument**)

Perdita
father: **7** Leontes
mother: **8** Hermione

perdition
4 hell **5** hades **7** inferno **9** damnation **10** underworld **11** netherworld

Père Goriot author
6 Balzac (Honoré de)

peregrination
4 trek, trip, walk **7** journey, travels **9** traversal **10** expedition

peremptory
5 bossy, final **7** haughty **8** absolute, arrogant, decisive, dogmatic, imperial **9** imperious, masterful **10** autocratic, commanding, disdainful, high-handed, imperative **11** dictatorial, domineering, magisterial, overbearing

perennial
7 durable **8** constant, enduring, lifelong **9** continual, long-lived, permanent, perpetual, recurrent, unceasing **10** continuing, persistent, persisting, unchanging **11** long-lasting

Perez
brother: **5** Zerah
father: **5** Judah
mother: **5** Tamar

perfect
4 full, pure **5** exact, ideal, model, right, sound, total, utter **6** entire, expert, intact, polish, proper, refine, spot-on **7** correct, improve, precise, utopian **8** absolute, accurate, finished, flawless,

peerless, spotless, unbroken, unflawed **9** excellent, faultless, matchless, stainless, unalloyed, undiluted **10** consummate, impeccable

perfection
4 acme **5** ideal **6** purity, virtue **7** paragon **9** integrity, wholeness **10** excellence, excellency

perfectly
4 to a T **5** fully, quite **6** wholly **7** to a turn, utterly **8** entirely **10** altogether, completely, thoroughly

perfidious
5 false **8** disloyal **9** deceitful, dishonest, faithless **10** treasonous, traitorous, unfaithful **11** treacherous

perfidy
6 deceit **7** falsity, sellout, treason **8** betrayal **9** falseness, treachery **10** disloyalty, infidelity

perforate
3 pit **5** prick, punch **6** pierce **8** puncture

perform
3 act **4** play, work **5** enact **6** behave, comply, effect, render **7** achieve, execute, fulfill, operate, playact, present, satisfy **8** bring off, carry out, complete, function **9** discharge, entertain, implement **10** accomplish

performance
3 act **4** deed, feat, show **6** acting, action **7** conduct, display **8** behavior, exercise **9** discharge, execution, operation **10** exhibition **11** achievement, fulfillment **12** presentation

performer
4 doer, mime **5** actor, mimic **6** mummer, player **7** actress, artiste, trouper **8** thespian **9** playactor

perfume
4 balm, otto **5** aroma, attar, cense, scent, smell, spice **6** sachet **7** bouquet, incense, odorize **9** aromatize, fragrance, redolence
brand: **4** Tabu
source: **4** musk, otto **5** attar, ester, myrrh, orris **8** bergamot
type: **7** cologne **9** patchouli
with a thurible: **5** cense

perfumer
4 Dior (Christian), Nose (The) **5** Estée (Lauder) **6** Chanel (Coco), Lanvin, Lauder (Estée) **8** Guerlain (Aimé, Jacques), Guichard (Aurelien, Jean)

perfunctory
7 cursory, routine **8** careless **9** automatic **10** impersonal, mechanical **11** superficial

pergola
5 arbor, bower **7** trellis

perhaps
5 maybe **8** feasibly, possibly **9** perchance **11** conceivably

periapt
see **amulet**

Pericles
father: **10** Xanthippus
mistress: **7** Aspasia
mother: **8** Agariste

peril
4 risk **6** danger, hazard, menace **8** exposure, jeopardy **9** liability **12** endangerment

perilous
5 hairy, risky **6** chancy, unsafe **7** unsound **9** dangerous, desperate, hazardous, uncertain **11** treacherous

___ Perilous
5 Siege

perimeter
4 edge **5** limit, verge **6** border, bounds, margin **8** boundary

period
3 age, end, era **4** span, stop, term, time **5** cycle, phase, point, spell, stage **6** extent **8** division, duration, interval, sentence

periodic
6 cyclic, fitful **7** regular **8** cyclical, repeated, sporadic **9** recurrent, recurring **10** occasional **11** fluctuating **12** intermittent

periodical
3 mag **5** organ **6** cyclic, review **7** journal **8** cyclical, magazine **9** alternate, newspaper, recurrent, recurring **10** isochronal **11** isochronous, publication **12** intermittent

peripatetic
6 moving, roving **7** nomadic, walking **8** ambulant, vagabond **9** itinerant, traveling, wayfaring **10** ambulatory, pedestrian, travelling

peripheral
6 remote **7** lateral, surface **8** far-flung, marginal, outlying **9** auxiliary, secondary **10** borderline, tangential **11** out-of-the-way

perish
3 die, end **4** pass **5** cease **6** demise, expire, vanish **7** decease, decline, go under, succumb **8** pass away

perjure
3 lie **6** delude **7** deceive, distort, falsify, mislead **8** forswear **9** misinform **10** equivocate **11** prevaricate

perk
4 gain, mend, plus **5** bonus, cheer, extra **7** benefit, freshen, improve, refresh, smarten **8** brighten

perky
5 alert, cocky, happy **6** bouncy, bubbly, cheery, chirpy, frisky, jaunty, lively, upbeat **7** buoyant, chipper **8** animated, cheerful, spirited, sportive **9** energetic, sparkling, sprightly, vivacious **12** effervescent, high-spirited

Perlman of TV
4 Rhea

permanent
5 fixed 6 stable 7 abiding, durable, lasting 8 constant, enduring 9 continual, perennial 10 changeless, invariable, unchanging 11 established, everlasting

permeable
6 porous, spongy 8 pervious 9 absorbent, diffusive 10 penetrable

permeate
5 imbue 6 drench, infuse, spread 7 diffuse, pervade, suffuse 8 saturate 9 penetrate, percolate 10 impregnate, infiltrate 11 pass through

permissible
4 okay 5 legal 7 allowed 8 approved 9 allowable, tolerable, tolerated 10 acceptable, authorized, sanctioned

permission
5 leave 6 assent, permit 7 consent, license 8 approval, sanction 9 agreement, allowance 11 approbation 12 acquiescence 13 authorization

permissive
3 lax 4 open 7 lenient, liberal 8 tolerant 9 easygoing, forgiving, indulgent 10 forbearing 11 acquiescent, complaisant

permit
3 let 4 okay, pass 5 agree, allow, grant 6 accede, enable, say yes, suffer 7 consent, license, warrant 8 sanction, tolerate 9 allowance, authorize, give leave 10 permission 13 authorization

permutation
6 change 7 variety, version 9 variation 10 alteration, innovation 11 arrangement, vicissitude 12 modification

pernicious
4 evil 5 fatal, toxic 6 deadly, lethal, malign, wicked 7 baleful, baneful, harmful, hurtful, killing, malefic, noxious 8 damaging, sinister, virulent 9 injurious, malignant, offensive, poisonous 10 maleficent 11 deleterious, destructive, detrimental

Pernod flavor
5 anise 8 licorice

Perón of Argentina
3 Eva 4 Juan 5 Evita

perorate
5 speak 7 declaim, lecture 8 bloviate, harangue, proclaim 9 hold forth, speechify

perpend
5 study, weigh 6 ponder 7 examine, reflect 8 consider, think out 9 reflect on, think over 10 excogitate, think about 11 contemplate

perpendicular
5 plumb, sheer, steep 7 upright 8 straight, vertical 11 precipitate, precipitous

perpetrate
6 commit, effect 7 inflict, execute, perform 8 carry out 10 bring about

perpetual
7 endless, eternal, undying 8 constant, unending 9 ceaseless, continual, incessant, perennial, recurrent, unceasing 10 continuous 11 everlasting, unremitting

perpetuate
7 sustain 8 conserve, continue, eternize, maintain, preserve 9 keep alive 10 eternalize 11 immortalize

perplex
5 befog, mix up, stump 6 baffle, bemuse, muddle, puzzle 7 buffalo, confuse, mystify, nonplus, perturb 8 befuddle, bewilder, confound, distract, entangle 9 dumbfound 10 discompose

perplexed
5 at sea 7 at a loss, mixed up, puzzled 8 confused

Perry Mason
author: 4 Erle (Stanley Gardner)
character: 5 Della (Street)
TV star: 4 Burr (Raymond), Hale (Barbara)

Perry of popular song
4 Como

perquisite
3 tip 4 gain 5 right 6 profit 7 benefit, payment 8 gratuity 9 privilege

per se
6 as such, solely 8 in itself 11 essentially 13 intrinsically

persecute
4 bait, ride 5 annoy, harry, hound, worry, wrong 6 badger, harass, hector, injure, molest, pester, pick on, plague, punish, pursue 7 afflict, oppress, torment, torture 8 aggrieve

Persephone
4 Kore 10 Proserpina
father: 4 Zeus 7 Jupiter
husband: 5 Hades, Pluto
mother: 5 Ceres 7 Demeter

Perseus
father: 4 Zeus 7 Jupiter
grandfather: 8 Acrisius
mother: 5 Danaë
victim: 6 Medusa 8 Acrisius
wife: 9 Andromeda

perseverance
8 tenacity 9 diligence, endurance 10 dedication 11 persistence

persevere
see **persist**

Persia
4 Iran

Persian
ancient: 4 Mede
fairy: 4 peri
governor: 6 satrap
language: 5 Farsi, Parsi
mystic: 4 sufi
New Year's: 6 Nowruz
poet: 4 Omar **5** Hafez, Hafiz **7** Firdusi **8** Ferdowsi, Firdausi, Firdawsi, Firdousi **11** Omar Khayyám
prophet: 9 Zoroaster
robe: 6 caftan
sacred books: 6 Avesta
sun-god: 7 Mithras
title: 4 shah
writing: 9 cuneiform

Persian Gulf country
3 UAE **4** Iran, Iraq **5** Qatar **6** Kuwait **7** Bahrain

persiflage
6 banter, joking **7** jesting, kidding, ribbing **8** badinage, raillery, repartee

persist
4 go on, last **5** abide **6** endure, hang on, keep on, linger **7** carry on, prevail **8** continue **9** persevere

persistence
8 duration **9** endurance **10** continuity **11** continuance **12** continuation

persistent
6 dogged **7** lasting **8** enduring, obdurate, stubborn **9** continual, steadfast, tenacious **10** continuing, determined, relentless, unshakable **11** persevering, unremitting

persnickety
5 fussy, picky **6** choosy **7** finicky **8** exacting **10** fastidious, particular

person
3 guy **4** self, soul **5** being, human **6** entity, mensch, mortal **8** creature, specimen **10** individual
unique: 4 oner

personable
4 nice **6** genial **7** affable, amiable **8** charming, friendly, pleasant, pleasing **9** appealing, congenial

personage
3 VIP **5** human, mogul **6** bigwig, figure, honcho **7** big shot, magnate, notable **8** creature, luminary, somebody **9** celebrity, character, dignitary **10** individual

personal
3 own **5** privy **7** private, special **8** peculiar **10** individual, particular

personal effects
5 stuff **10** belongings **11** possessions

personality
3 ego, VIP **4** self **6** makeup, nature, temper **7** notable **8** identity, selfhood **9** celebrity, character **11** disposition, temperament

personify
6 embody, typify **8** stand for **9** actualize, epitomize, exemplify, incarnate, represent, symbolize **11** emblematize

perspective
3 POV **4** view **5** angle, scene, slant, vista **7** outlook **8** position, prospect **9** viewpoint **10** standpoint **11** point of view

perspicacious
4 keen **5** acute, savvy, sharp **6** astute, clever, shrewd **9** observant, sagacious **10** discerning, insightful, perceptive **11** penetrating

perspicacity
6 acumen **7** insight **8** keenness **10** astuteness, shrewdness **11** discernment, penetration, percipience

perspicuous
5 clear, lucid, plain **6** lucent, simple **7** crystal, precise **8** clear-cut, pellucid **11** unambiguous

perspiration
5 sweat

perspire
see **sweat**

persuadable
4 open **7** willing **9** receptive **11** suggestible, susceptible

persuade
3 win **4** coax, lead, sell, sway, urge **5** argue **6** entice, induce, prompt **7** convert, impress, win over **8** convince **9** influence, prevail on **11** bring around

persuasion
4 view **6** belief, school **7** faction, opinion **9** prejudice **10** conviction **11** affiliation

Persuasion author
6 Austen (Jane)

persuasive
6 cogent **7** telling, winning **8** credible **10** compelling, convincing **11** influential

pert
4 bold, chic, flip, trim **5** alert, cocky, fresh, lippy, sassy, saucy, smart **6** brazen, bright, cheeky, jaunty, lively **7** forward **8** animated, flippant, spirited **9** audacious, sprightly, vivacious

pertain
5 apply, refer **6** affect, bear on, belong, regard, relate **7** concern **8** bear upon **9** touch upon

pertinacious
4 firm **5** fixed **6** dogged, mulish **7** willful **8** resolute, stubborn **9** obstinate, tenacious **10** inflexible, persistent, unshakable, unyielding

pertinent
3 apt, fit **5** ad rem **7** apropos, fitting, germane **8** apposite, material, relevant **10** applicable **11** appropriate

perturb
5 upset, worry **6** bother **7** agitate, disturb, fluster, trouble **8** disorder, disquiet, unsettle **10** discompose, disconcert

perturbed
5 upset **6** uneasy **7** anxious, uptight **8** troubled

Peru
ancient civilization: **4** Inca
capital: **4** Lima
city: **5** Cusco, Cuzco **6** Callao **8** Arequipa, Trujillo
conqueror: **7** Pizarro (Francisco)
ethnic group: **7** Quechua
lake: **8** Titicaca
language: **6** Aymara **7** Quechua, Spanish
leader: **8** Fujimori (Alberto)
monetary unit: **3** sol
mountain, range: **5** Andes **9** Huascarán
neighbor: **5** Chile **6** Brazil **7** Bolivia, Ecuador **8** Colombia
river: **6** Amazon **7** Marañón
volcano: **5** Misti **7** El Misti **8** Yucamani

Peruvian Indian
4 Inca

Peruvian singer
3 Yma (Sumac)

peruse
4 read, scan **5** study **6** survey **7** examine **8** consider, look over, pore over

Peruvian singer
5 Sumac (Yma)

pervade
5 imbue **6** spread **7** diffuse **8** permeate, saturate **9** penetrate, percolate, transfuse **10** impregnate

perverse
5 balky **6** cranky, mulish, ornery **7** deviant, froward, peevish, wayward, willful **8** contrary, depraved, stubborn **9** obstinate **10** headstrong, refractory **11** stiff-necked, wrongheaded **12** cross-grained, unreasonable

pervert
4 skew, warp **5** twist **6** garble, misuse **7** corrupt, debauch, deprave, distort, falsify, vitiate

pervious
4 open **6** porous **9** permeable **10** accessible, penetrable

pesky
6 vexing **7** irksome **8** annoying **9** vexatious **10** bothersome **11** troublesome

pessimist
5 cynic **9** Cassandra, defeatist, doomsayer, worrywart **11** misanthrope

pessimistic
6 gloomy, morose **7** cynical **10** despairing **11** distrustful

pest
4 bane **5** trial, worry **6** bother, nudnik, plague, vermin **7** nudnick, trouble, varmint **8** irritant, nuisance, vexation **9** annoyance, tormentor

pester
3 bug, irk, nag **4** ride **5** annoy, harry, tease, worry **6** badger, bother, harass, hassle, plague **7** bedevil, disturb, torment **8** irritate

pestiferous
7 baneful, noxious **8** annoying, infected **9** infective, pestilent **10** pernicious **11** troublesome

pestilence
5 curse **6** plague **7** scourge

pestilential
5 fatal **6** deadly, lethal, vexing **7** baneful, deathly, noxious, ruinous **8** annoying **10** pernicious

pestle
4 mano **6** muller
vessel: **6** mortar

pet
3 cat, dog, hug **4** dear, kiss, love, neck, pout, snit, sulk **5** loved, spoon **6** caress, cosset, dandle, fondle, pamper, stroke **7** beloved, cherish, darling, indulge **8** favorite, treasure **9** cherished

petcock
3 tap **5** valve **6** faucet, spigot

Peter Fonda role
4 Ulee

Peter Grimes composer
7 Britten (Benjamin)

peter out
4 fade, wane **5** abate, cease **6** lessen, recede, run dry **7** dwindle **8** decrease, diminish, taper off **9** drain away

Peter Pan
author: **6** Barrie (James)
character: **5** Wendy **7** Michael **9** Tiger Lily **10** Tinker Bell
dog: **4** Nana
family: **7** Darling
pirate: **4** Hook, Smee

Peter the Apostle
brother: **6** Andrew
father: **5** Jonah
original name: **5** Simon
Peter the Great
father: **6** Alexis
mother: **8** Nataliya
wife: **7** Eudoxia **9** Catherine
petite
5 small **6** little **8** smallish **10** diminutive
petition
3 ask, sue **4** plea **5** plead **6** appeal **7** beseech, entreat, implore, request, solicit **8** entreaty **10** supplicate **11** application **12** supplication
Petrarch's beloved
5 Laura
petri dish substance
4 agar
petrify
4 daze, numb, stun **5** chill, scare **6** benumb, deaden, harden **7** startle **8** confound, frighten, paralyze
Petruchio's wife
9 Katharina, Katharine
pettifogger
7 shyster **8** quibbler **9** nitpicker
petty
4 mean **5** minor, small **6** measly, narrow, paltry **7** trivial **8** niggling, picayune, piddling, trifling **9** frivolous **10** irrelevant, negligible **11** small-minded, unimportant **13** insignificant
petty officer
6 noncom
petulant
5 huffy, moody, sulky, testy, whiny **6** touchy **7** grouchy, peevish **8** snappish **9** irascible, irritable, querulous **10** ill-humored
pew
3 row **4** seat **5** bench
peyote
6 cactus, mescal
drug: **9** mescaline
Peyton's brother
3 Eli
Phaedra
author: **6** Racine
father: **5** Minos
husband: **7** Theseus
mother: **8** Pasiphaë
sister: **7** Ariadne
stepson: **10** Hippolytus
Phaëthon's father
6 Helios **7** Phoebus
phalanx
4 army, host, mass **5** horde **6** myriad, throng
phantasm
5 dream, ghost **6** vision **7** fantasy, fiction, figment, specter, spectre **8** daydream, delusion, illusion **10** apparition **13** hallucination
phantom
5 dummy, ghost, shade, spook **6** goblin, shadow, spirit, vision **7** bugbear, chimera, eidolon, specter, spectre **8** illusory, spectral **9** imaginary **10** apparition, fictitious **12** will-o'-the-wisp
Phantom Tollbooth hero
4 Milo
pharaoh
3 Tut **4** Seti **5** Menes, ruler **6** Ahmose, Ramses, tyrant **8** Akhnaten, Ikhnaton, Thutmose **9** Akhenaten, Amenhotep **11** Tutankhamen, Tutankhaten
pharisee
9 hypocrite
pharmaceuticals founder Lilly
3 Eli
pharmacist
8 druggist **10** apothecary
British: **7** chemist
pharos
6 beacon **10** lighthouse
Pharsalus, battle of
vanquished: **6** Pompey
victor: **6** Caesar (Julius)
phase
4 part, side, view **5** point, stage, state **6** adjust, aspect **7** conduct **8** carry out, position **9** condition, situation, viewpoint **10** appearance
PhD exam
5 orals
Phèdre author
6 Racine (Jean)
phenomenal
6 actual **7** unusual **8** material, physical, sensible, singular, tangible, uncommon **9** corporeal, fantastic, objective **10** astounding, remarkable **11** astonishing, exceptional, outstanding, perceivable, perceptible, substantial **13** extraordinary
phenomenon
4 fact **5** event **6** marvel, object, rarity, wonder **7** miracle, reality **9** actuality, sensation **11** singularity
Phi ___ Kappa
4 Beta
philander
8 womanize
philanderer
4 rake, roué **5** satyr **6** masher **7** Don Juan, seducer **8** Casanova, lothario **9** womanizer **10** lady-killer

philanthropic
6 giving, humane **8** generous **10** altruistic, benevolent, bighearted, charitable **11** magnanimous **12** eleemosynary, humanitarian
philanthropist
5 donor
American: 4 Yale (Eli, Elihu) **5** Gates (Bill) **6** Cooper (Peter), Girard (Stephen), Mellon (Andrew) **7** Buffett (Warren), Cornell (Ezra), Eastman (George), Packard (David), Whitney (Gertrude Vanderbilt) **8** Carnegie (Andrew), Stanford (Leland) **9** Rosenwald (Julius) **10** Vanderbilt (Cornelius) **11** Rockefeller (J. D.)
English: 11 Wilberforce (William)
Swedish: 5 Nobel (Alfred)
Philemon's wife
6 Baucis
philharmonic
8 symphony **9** orchestra, symphonic
Philip of Macedonia
father: 7 Amyntas
son: 9 Alexander
philippic
4 rant **6** tirade **8** diatribe, harangue, jeremiad **12** condemnation
Philippics author
6 Cicero
Philippines
capital: 6 Manila
city: 4 Cebu **5** Davao **10** Quezon City
discoverer: 8 Magellan (Ferdinand)
guerrilla: 3 Huk **10** Hukbalahap
island: 4 Cebu **5** Leyte, Luzon, Panay, Samar **6** Negros **7** Masbate, Mindoro, Palawan **8** Mindanao
language: 7 Ilocano, Tagalog **8** Filipino, Pilipino
leader: 6 Aquino (Corazon), Marcos (Ferdinand)
liberator: 9 MacArthur (Douglas)
patriot: 5 Rizal (José)
monetary unit: 4 peso
people: 3 Ati **4** Moro
sea: 4 Sulu **5** Samar **7** Celebes, Sibuyan, Visayan **8** Mindanao **10** Philippine, South China
volcano: 4 Taal **5** Mayon
Philippi victor
6 Antony (Marc, Mark) **8** Octavian
Philip the Tetrarch
father: 5 Herod
mother: 9 Cleopatra
philistine
4 boob **7** Babbitt **9** bourgeois, vulgarian **10** capitalist **11** materialist
Philistine
champion: 7 Goliath
city: 4 Gath, Gaza **5** Ekron **6** Ashdod **8** Ashkelon
foe: 5 David **6** Samson
god: 5 Dagon
Philoctetes
father: 5 Poeas
victim: 5 Paris
Phil of folk music
4 Ochs
Philomela
11 nightingale
father: 7 Pandion
ravisher: 6 Tereus
sister: 6 Procne
philosopher
American: 5 Adler (Mortimer), Dewey (John), James (William), Quine (Willard), Rorty (Richard), Royce (Josiah) **6** Langer (Susanne), Peirce (C. S.) **7** Marcuse (Herbert), Mumford (Lewis), Strauss (Leo) **9** Santayana (George)
Arab: 8 Averroës, Avicenna
Austrian: 6 Popper (Karl) **12** Wittgenstein (Ludwig)
Chinese: 5 Laoxi, Laozi **6** Lao-tsu, Lao-tze, Lao-tzu **7** Dai Zhen, Mencius, Tai Chen **9** Confucius
Danish: 11 Kierkegaard (Soren)
Dutch: 7 Erasmus (Desiderius), Spinoza (Baruch de)
English: 4 Ayer (A. J.), Joad (C. E. M.), Mill (John Stuart), More (Henry, Thomas), Watt (James) **5** Bacon (Francis), Burke (Edmund), Locke (John), Moore (G. E.), Occam (William of), Paine (Thomas) **6** Berlin (Isaiah), Hobbes (Thomas), Huxley (Thomas), Ockham (William), Popper (Karl) **7** Bentham (Jeremy), Russell (Bertrand), Spencer (Herbert), Whewell (William) **9** Whitehead (Alfred North) **12** Wittgenstein (Ludwig)
Finnish: 11 Westermarck (Edward)
French: 4 Weil (Simone) **5** Comte (Auguste), Sorel (Georges), Taine (Hippolyte) **6** Pascal (Blaise), Sartre (Jean-Paul), Valéry (Paul) **7** Abelard (Peter), Bergson (Henri), Derrida (Jacques), Diderot (Denis), Fourier (Charles) **8** Foucault (Michel), Maritain (Jacques), Rousseau (Jean-Jacques), Voltaire **9** Descartes (René), Montaigne (Michel de) **10** Saint-Simon (Comte de) **11** Montesquieu (Baron de) **12** Merleau-Ponty (Maurice)
German: 4 Kant (Immanuel), Marx (Karl) **5** Frege (Gottlob), Hegel (Georg Wilhelm Friedrich), Wolff (Christian von) **6** Carnap (Rudolf), Fichte (Immanuel, Johann), Herder (Johann von) **7** Husserl (Edmund), Jaspers (Karl), Leibniz (Gottfried) **8** Spengler (Oswald) **9** Heidegger (Martin), Nietzsche (Friedrich), Schelling (Friedrich von) **12** Schopenhauer (Arthur) **14** Albertus Magnus

Greek: **4** Zeno **5** Plato, Timon **6** Thales **7** Gorgias, Proclus **8** Diogenes, Epicurus, Longinus, Socrates **9** Aristotle, Epictetus **10** Anaxagoras, Democritus, Empedocles, Heraclitus, Parmenides, Protagoras, Pythagoras, Xenocrates, Xenophanes **11** Anaximander **12** Theophrastus
Irish: **8** Berkeley (George)
Italian: **5** Croce (Benedetto) **6** Ficino (Marsilio) **11** Machiavelli (Niccolo)
Jewish: **5** Buber (Martin), Philo **10** Maimonides (Moses) **12** Philo Judaeus
Roman: **6** Seneca (Lucias Annaeus) **8** Boethius (Anicius), Plotinus **9** Lucretius
Scottish: **4** Hume (David), Mill (James), Reid (Thomas) **7** Stewart (Dugald)
Spanish: **6** Suárez (Francisco) **7** Unamuno (Miguel de) **13** Ortega y Gasset (José)
Swedish: **10** Swedenborg (Emanuel)

philosopher's stone
3 key **6** elixir

philosophical
4 calm **7** stoical **8** composed, rational, resigned **9** unruffled **10** thoughtful

philosophy
6 system, theory, values **7** beliefs, inquiry **8** attitude, calmness **10** discipline
component: **5** logic **6** ethics **10** aesthetics **11** metaphysics **12** epistemology

philter
4 drug **5** charm, tonic **6** potion **9** stimulant **10** love potion **11** aphrodisiac, restorative

Phineas
beloved: **9** Andromeda
tormentors: **7** Harpies
wife: **9** Cleopatra

phlegm
5 humor, mucus **6** apathy **8** calmness, coolness, dullness, serenity **9** composure, sangfroid **10** equanimity **11** impassivity, nonchalance **12** indifference

phlegmatic
4 calm, cool, dull **5** aloof, stoic **6** serene, stolid **8** detached **9** apathetic, impassive, lethargic **11** indifferent, unconcerned

Phnom ___
4 Penh

phobia
see **fear**

Phobos
4 moon **9** satellite
brother: **6** Deimos
father: **4** Ares, Mars

Phocus
father: **6** Aeacus **8** Ornytion
half brother: **6** Peleus **7** Telamon
mother: **8** Psamathe
slayer: **6** Peleus **7** Telamon
wife: **7** Antiope

Phoebe
5 Diana **7** Artemis
daughter: **4** Leto
father: **9** Leucippus
mother: **4** Gaea

Phoebus
see **Apollo**

Phoenician
city: **4** Acre, Tyre **5** Sidon
colony: **8** Carthage
god: **4** Baal **6** Eshmun
goddess: **6** Baltis **7** Astarte

Phoenix
pupil: **8** Achilles
sister: **6** Europa
team: **4** Suns **7** Coyotes **9** Cardinals **12** Diamondbacks

phonograph needle
5 styli (plural) **6** stylus

phony
4 fake, sham **5** bogus, cheat, faker, false, fraud **6** ersatz, humbug, pseudo **8** impostor, specious, spurious **9** charlatan, dishonest, pretender **10** ficticious, suspicious **11** counterfeit **12** hypocritical

photograph
3 pic **4** film, snap **5** shoot **6** glossy, selfie **7** picture, tintype **8** snapshot
three-dimensional: **8** hologram
tint: **5** sepia

photographer
8 photoist **9** cameraman **10** shutterbug
famous: **3** Ray (Man) **4** Capa (Cornell, Robert), Haas (Ernst), Hine (Lewis), Penn (Irving), Riis (Jacob) **5** Adams (Ansel), Arbus (Diane), Atget (Eugène), Brady (Mathew), Evans (Frederick, Walker), Frank (Robert), Horst (Horst Peter), Karsh (Yousuf), Lange (Dorothea), Model (Lisette), Nadar, Parks (Gordon), Ritts (Herb), Smith (W. Eugene), Weber (Bruce), White (Clarence, Minor) **6** Abbott (Berenice), Avedon (Richard), Beaton (Cecil), Brandt (Bill), Coburn (Alvin), Curtis (Edward S.), Newton (Helmut), Porter (Eliot), Rowell (Galen), Siegel (Eliot), Strand (Paul), Talbot (William Henry Fox), Weegee, Wegman (William), Weston (Brett, Edward) **7** Brassaï, Cameron (Julia Margaret), Emerson (Peter), Halsman (Philippe), Jackson (William Henry), Kertész (André), Salomon (Erich), Siskind (Aaron), Thomson (John), Watkins (Carleton) **8** Callahan (Harry), Cosindas (Marie), Daguerre (L.-J.-M.), Kasebier (Gertrude), Scavullo (Francesco), Steichen (Edward) **9** Feininger (Andreas), Leibovitz (Annie),

Meyrowitz (Joel), Muybridge (Eadweard), O'Sullivan (Timothy), Rothstein (Arthur), Stieglitz (Alfred), Winogrand (Garry) **10** Cunningham (Imogen), Moholy-Nagy (Laszlo) **11** Bourke-White (Margaret), Eisenstaedt (Alfred) **12** Mapplethorpe (Robert)

photographic
5 exact, vivid **7** graphic **8** accurate, detailed **9** pictorial **11** picturesque
solution: **4** hypo **5** fixer, toner **7** reducer **9** developer

phrase
5 couch, frame, idiom **6** slogan **7** diction, express, styling, wording **8** locution, verbiage **9** catchword, formulate, verbalism, watchword **10** expression

Phrygian
god: **4** Atys **5** Attis
goddess: **6** Cybele
king: **5** Midas **7** Gordius

phthisis
11 consumption **12** tuberculosis

phylactery
5 charm **6** amulet **7** periapt **8** talisman

physic
4 cure, heal **5** purge **6** remedy **8** medicine **9** cathartic, purgative **10** medication

physical
4 real **5** lusty, rough **6** actual, bodily, carnal, sexual **7** fleshly, natural, somatic **8** concrete, corporal, material, sensible, tangible **9** corporeal, objective **10** phenomenal **11** perceivable, perceptible, substantial

physician
3 doc **5** medic **6** doctor, medico **7** surgeon **8** sawbones
American: **4** Koop (C. Everett), Rush (Benjamin), Salk (Jonas) **5** Minot (George), Spock (Benjamin), Still (Andrew) **6** Jarvik (Robert), Murphy (John), Weller (Thomas) **7** Huggins (Charles), Robbins (Frederick), Theiler (Max) **8** Richards (Dickinson) **9** Sternberg (George Miller)
Arab: **8** Avicenna
Canadian: **5** Osler (William)
English: **4** Ross (Ronald) **6** Harvey (William), Jenner (Edward, William), Willis (Thomas) **8** Sydenham (Thomas)
French: **5** Widal (Fernand) **7** Laveran (Charles) **10** Schweitzer (Albert)
German: **7** Sylvius (Franciscus)
Greek: **5** Galen **11** Hippocrates
Italian: **7** Galvani (Luigi)
organization: **3** AMA
South African: **7** Barnard (Christiaan)
Swiss: **10** Paracelsus
(see also **Nobel Prize winner** *physiology or medicine;* **surgeon**)

physicist
American: **4** Rabi (I. I.), Ting (Samuel) **5** Fermi (Enrico), Gibbs (J. Willard), Kusch (Polykarp), Mayer (Maria-Goeppert), Pauli (Wolfgang), Pupin (Michael), Segré (Emilio), Smyth (Henry DeWolf), Stern (Otto) **6** Teller (Edward), Townes (Charles), Wigner (Eugene) **7** Alvarez (Luis), Feynman (Richard), Goddard (Robert), Purcell (Edward) **8** Einstein (Albert), Gell-Mann (Murray), McMillan (Edwin), Millikan (Clark, Robert), Mulliken (Robert), Shockley (William), Van Allen (James) **9** Michelson (Albert), Schwinger (Julian) **11** Oppenheimer (J. Robert)
Austrian: **4** Mach (Ernst) **7** Doppler (Christian) **11** Schrödinger (Erwin)
British: **4** Snow (C. P.) **5** Dirac (B. A. M.), Jeans (James), Joule (James) **6** Dalton (John), Kelvin (Baron), Newton (Isaac), Powell (Cecil), Stokes (George) **7** Faraday (Michael), Hodgkin (Dorothy), Thomson (George, Joseph, William), Tyndall (John) **8** Rayleigh (Lord), Robinson (Robert), Thompson (Benjamin, Silvanus) **9** Wollaston (William) **10** Richardson (Owen), Rutherford (Ernest), Wheatstone (Charles)
Chinese: **4** Yang (Chen-Ning)
Danish: **4** Bohr (Aage, Niels)
Dutch: **6** Zeeman (Pieter) **7** Huygens (Christian), Lorentz (Hendrik), Zernike (Frits) **11** Van der Waals (Johannes)
French: **4** Néel (Louis) **5** Arago (François) **6** Ampère (André-Marie), Perrin (Jean-Baptiste) **7** Coulomb (Charles-Augustin de), Kastler (Alfred), Réaumur (René-Antoine de) **8** Lippmann (Gabriel)
German: **3** Ohm (Georg) **4** Laue (Max von), Wien (Wilhelm) **5** Hertz (Gustav, Heinrich), Stark (Johannes), Weber (Wilhelm) **6** Jensen (Hans), Lenard (Philipp), Nernst (Walther), Planck (Max) **7** Meitner (Lise) **8** Roentgen (Wilhelm) **9** Helmholtz (Hermann von), Kirchhoff (Gustav), Mossbauer (Rudolf) **10** Fahrenheit (Daniel)
Indian: **5** Raman (Chandrasekhara)
Irish: **6** Walton (Ernest)
Italian: **5** Rossi (Bruno), Volta (Alessandro) **7** Galileo (Galilei), Galvani (Luigi) **10** Torricelli (Evangelista)
Japanese: **6** Yukawa (Hideki) **8** Tomonaga (Shinichiro)
Mexican: **8** Vallarta (Manuel)
Russian: **4** Tamm (Igor) **6** Landau (Lev)
Scottish: **4** Tait (Peter) **6** Wilson (Charles) **7** Maxwell (James Clerk)
Swedish: **8** Angstrom (Anders), Siegbahn (Kai, Karl)
Swiss: **6** Zwicky (Fritz) **7** Piccard (Auguste)
(see also **Nobel Prize winner** *physics*)

physicist Niels
4 Bohr

physiognomy
3 mug **4** face **5** front **6** aspect, visage **7** profile **8** features **9** character **10** lineaments **11** countenance, temperament

physiologist
English: **8** Starling (Ernest)
German: **5** Weber (Ernst), Wundt (Wilhelm) **7** Schwann (Theodor) **9** Helmholtz (Hermann von)
Italian: **11** Spallanzani (Lazzaro)
(see also **Nobel Prize winner**)

physique
3 bod **4** body, form **5** build, shape **6** figure, makeup **7** anatomy **9** structure **12** constitution

pianist
American: **4** Nero (Peter), Tesh (John), Wild (Earl) **5** Janis (Byron), Tatum (Art), Watts (André) **6** Duchin (Peter), Serkin (Peter, Rudolf) **7** Cliburn (Van), Istomin (Eugene), Ohlsson (Garrick), Perahia (Murray), Winston (George) **8** Graffman (Gary), Horowitz (Vladimir) **9** Fleischer (Leon) **10** Rubinstein (Arthur)
Argentinian: **8** Argerich (Martha) **9** Barenboim (Daniel)
Austrian: **6** Czerny (Karl) **7** Brendel (Alfred) **8** Schnabel (Artur)
Bulgarian: **11** Weissenberg (Alexis)
Canadian: **5** Gould (Glenn)
Chilean: **5** Arrau (Claudio)
Cuban: **5** Bolet (Jorge)
English: **4** Hess (Myra) **5** Ogdon (John) **6** Curzon (Clifford)
French: **6** Cortot (Alfred) **7** Cziffra (Gyorgy) **9** Casadesus (Robert), Entremont (Philippe)
German: **6** Kempff (Wilhelm) **8** Schumann (Clara) **9** Gieseking (Walter)
Hungarian: **5** Liszt (Franz)
Italian: **6** Busoni (Ferruccio) **7** Pollini (Maurizio)
Japanese: **6** Uchida (Mitsuko)
Polish: **7** Hofmann (Josef) **10** Paderewski (Ignacy), Rubinstein (Arthur)
Romanian: **4** Lupu (Radu) **7** Lipatti (Dinu)
Russian: **6** Berman (Lazar), Gilels (Emil), Kissin (Evgeny) **7** Richter (Sviatoslav) **8** Horowitz (Vladimir) **9** Ashkenazy (Vladimir) **10** Rubinstein (Anton)
Spanish: **6** Iturbi (José) **8** Granados (Enrique) **10** de Larrocha (Alicia)
Swiss: **4** Anda (Geza)
(see also **jazz musician**)

piano
5 grand **6** softly, spinet **7** quietly, upright **9** baby grand
builder: **5** Knabe (William), Stein (Johann), Zumpe (Johann) **7** Baldwin (Dwight) **8** Steinway (Henry) **9** Bechstein (Friedrich) **10** Chickering (Jonas), Silbermann (Johann)
inventor: **10** Cristofori (Bartolomeo)
keys: **7** ivories
pedal: **6** damper **9** sostenuto
study: **5** étude

piazza
5 patio, plaza, porch **6** square **7** balcony, gallery, portico, terrace, veranda **9** courtyard

picaro
5 rogue, rover, thief **6** pirate **7** brigand, corsair **8** bohemian, sea rover **9** buccaneer **10** freebooter

picayune
5 petty **6** measly, paltry, trifle **7** trivial **8** piddling **11** small-minded **13** insignificant

pick
3 rob, tap **4** best, carp, cull, open, pull, take, tool **5** elect, pluck, probe, prize **6** choice, choose, chosen, option, pierce, pilfer, remove, select, unlock **7** harvest, provoke **8** selected **9** exclusive, single out

picket
4 pale, post **5** fence, guard, stake, watch **6** sentry, tether **7** enclose, lookout, protest **8** palisade, sentinel, watchman **11** demonstrate

pickle
3 fix, jam **4** dill, spot **5** brine, treat **6** plight, scrape **7** dilemma, gherkin, trouble **8** marinate, preserve **10** difficulty **11** predicament

pick on
5 bully, harry, taunt, tease **6** hector, pester **9** criticize, single out

pick out
4 espy, name, spot **6** choose, descry, detect, select, take in **7** discern **8** identify, perceive **9** apprehend, ascertain, recognize **11** distinguish

pickpocket
3 dip **5** thief **6** dipper **8** cutpurse

pick up
3 buy, get **4** cull, gain, earn, land, lift, tidy **5** catch, glean, hoist, learn, raise, run in **6** arrest, detain, gather, notice, obtain, pull in, resume, revive **7** acquire, clean up, collect, restart **8** perceive **9** apprehend **10** appreciate, understand

pickup
3 ute **5** truck **9** detention **10** hitchhiker **11** improvement **12** acceleration

picky
5 fussy **6** choosy **7** finicky **10** fastidious, particular, pernickety **11** persnickety

picnic
4 snap **5** cinch **6** breeze, outing **7** cookout **8** cakewalk **11** piece of cake
pest: **3** ant

Picnic author
4 Inge (William)

picture
4 limn, show **5** image, photo, pinup **7** drawing, tableau **8** describe, painting, portrait **9** depiction, portrayal **10** simulacrum **11** delineation, description **13** spitting image
stand: **5** easel

picturesque
5 vivid **6** quaint, scenic **8** artistic, charming

piddling
4 puny **5** petty **6** meager, meagre, measly, paltry **7** trivial **8** picayune, trifling **11** Mickey Mouse, unimportant **13** insignificant

pie
4 flan, tart **5** pasty **6** pastry **7** cobbler, dessert **8** turnover

piebald
5 mixed **6** motley **7** mottled **10** multicolor, variegated

piece
4 part **5** patch, slice **6** member, parcel **7** firearm, portion, section, segment **8** division, fraction, fragment **9** allotment **10** allocation

pièce de résistance
8 main dish **9** showpiece **11** centerpiece, chef d'oeuvre, masterpiece

piecemeal
5 apart **6** slowly **7** gradual **8** bit by bit **9** by degrees, gradually **11** fragmentary

piece of cake
4 snap **5** cinch **6** breeze, picnic, shoo-in **8** duck soup, kid stuff, pushover

pied
6 motley **7** blotchy, brindle, dappled, mottled **8** brindled, speckled **9** multihued **10** variegated **11** varicolored **12** parti-colored

pier
4 anta, dock, quay, slip **5** berth, jetty, levee, wharf **6** column, pillar **8** pilaster
architectural: **4** anta

pierce
3 cut **4** gore, stab **5** probe, spear **6** impale, incise, skewer **8** puncture **9** penetrate, perforate **10** run through

piercing
4 high, keen **5** acute, sharp **6** piping, shrill **8** shooting, stabbing, strident **9** knifelike **12** earsplitting
tool: **3** awl

piety
6 fealty **7** loyalty **8** devotion, fidelity, sanctity **9** reverence **10** allegiance, dedication, devoutness **12** faithfulness

piffle
4 bosh, bunk **5** bilge, hokum, hooey **6** bunkum, drivel **7** baloney, eyewash, hogwash, rubbish, twaddle **8** malarkey, nonsense, tommyrot **9** poppycock **10** balderdash, codswallop

pig
3 hog **4** Babe, slob **5** Porky, shoat, swine **6** farrow, piglet, porker **7** casting, glutton
breed: **5** Duroc **8** Tamworth **9** Berkshire, Hampshire, Yorkshire
female: **3** sow **4** gilt
feral: **9** razorback
home: **3** sty
litter: **6** farrow
male: **4** boar **6** barrow
meat: **3** ham **4** pork **5** bacon **7** sausage **8** chitlins **12** chitterlings
sound: **3** wee
wild: **4** boar **7** peccary, warthog **8** babirusa

pigeon
3 Nun, sap **4** dupe, fool, gull, mark **5** chump, decoy, patsy **6** culver, stooge, sucker **7** fall guy, stoolie **8** rock dove
genus: **7** Columba
house: **4** cote, loft
kind: **4** barb, rock **5** homer **6** homing, pouter, roller **7** carrier, crowned, fantail, tumbler
relative: **4** dove
young: **5** squab

pigeon hawk
6 merlin

pigeonhole
4 slot, sort **5** class, cubby, grade, group, niche **6** recess, shelve **7** catalog **8** category, classify, grouping **10** categorize **11** compartment

piggish
6 greedy **7** selfish, swinish **10** gluttonous

pigheaded
5 rigid **6** dogged, mulish **7** willful **8** contrary, perverse, stubborn **9** obstinate **10** inflexible, unyielding

piglet
5 shoat

pigment
3 dye **4** tint **5** color, paint, stain **8** colorant, dyestuff, tincture
black: **9** lampblack
blue: **4** cyan **5** azure, smalt **6** indigo **7** cyanine **8** cerulean **9** verdigris **11** ultramarine
brown: **5** sepia
umber: **6** bister, sienna
combining form: **5** chrom **6** chromo
dark: **7** melanin
green: **7** celadon **8** viridian **10** biliverdin
orange: **7** realgar **8** carotene
red: **4** lake **5** eosin
skin: **7** melanin
toxic: **8** gossypol
yellow: **5** ocher, ochre **6** flavin, lutein **7** flavine, xanthin

pigpen
3 sty **4** dump, mess **5** hovel

pigskin
6 saddle **8** football

pike
4 dive, Esox, fish **5** spear **7** highway **8** pickerel

piker
5 miser **7** scrooge **8** tightwad **9** skinflint **10** cheapskate **12** penny-pincher

pilaster
4 pier **6** column, pillar

pilchard
7 herring, sardine

pile
3 fur, lot, nap **4** coat, fill, heap, hill, load, mass, much, pack, peck, pyre, rick **5** amass, crowd, drive, mound, stack **6** bundle, column, jumble **7** collect, fortune, reactor **8** quantity **9** great deal **10** assemblage, collection **11** aggregation **12** accumulation

pileup
4 mass **5** crash, smash **8** accident **9** collision **12** accumulation

pilfer
3 rob **4** lift, take **5** filch, pinch, steal, swipe **6** finger, pocket, snitch, thieve **7** purloin **11** appropriate

pilgarlic
4 butt **8** baldhead **13** laughingstock

Pilgrim
5 Alden (John) **6** Carver (John) **7** Puritan, Winslow (Edward) **8** Bradford (William), Brewster (William), Standish (Myles)
interpreter: **7** Squanto
ship: **9** Mayflower

pilgrim
5 hadji, hajji **6** palmer **8** traveler, wanderer, wayfarer

pilgrimage
4 hadj, hajj, trip **7** journey
destination: **5** Mecca **6** Assisi, Delphi, Dodona, Fátima, Medina **7** Lourdes **8** Bodh Gaya **10** Canterbury, Kusinagara

Pilgrim's Progress
8 allegory
author: **6** Bunyan (John)
hero: **9** Christian

pill
4 ball, bore, pain, pest **5** bolus **6** pellet **7** capsule, lozenge **8** medicine, nuisance **9** annoyance

pillage
4 lift, loot, sack **5** booty, prize, reave, reive, spoil, steal **6** maraud, ravage, thieve **7** despoil, plunder, purloin **8** spoliate **9** depredate, desecrate

pillar
4 pier, post, prop **5** pylon, shaft, stela, stele **6** column, stelae (plural) **7** obelisk, support, upright **8** backbone, mainstay, pedestal, pilaster

pillory
6 stocks

pillow
3 pad **4** rest **7** bolster, cushion, support
down: **5** eider

pillowcase
4 sham

pilot
3 ace **4** lead, show, tool **5** drive, flier, flyer, guide, steer **6** airman, direct, leader **7** aviator, conduct, guiding, tracing **8** aviatrix, helmsman, shepherd
announcement: **3** ETA
seat: **7** cockpit

pimple, pimples
3 dot, zit **4** acne, boil, spot, stud, zits **6** papule **7** blemish, blister, pustule, speckle **8** sprinkle, swelling **9** blackhead, whitehead

pin
3 leg, peg **4** clip, hold, join **5** affix, blame, rivet, stake **6** attach, broach, brooch, cotter, emblem, fasten, secure, trifle **8** fastener, hold down, ornament, restrain

pinafore
5 apron, dress, frock

pinch
3 bit, nab, nip **4** dash, lift, pain, take **5** filch, press, prune, run in, skimp, steal, swipe, taper, theft, tweak **6** arrest, crisis, narrow, pilfer, snatch, stress **7** confine, deficit, larceny, squeeze, straits **8** compress, exigency, hardship, juncture, pressure, stealing, straiten **9** apprehend, constrict, emergency, privation, tight spot **10** substitute

pinchbeck
4 fake, sham **5** alloy, bogus, false, phony **6** pseudo **8** spurious **9** brummagem **11** counterfeit

pinch hitter
3 sub **6** backup, fill-in, relief **7** stand-in **9** alternate, surrogate **10** substitute **11** alternative, replacement

pinchpenny
4 mean **5** cheap, close, mingy, tight **6** stingy **7** chintzy, costive, miserly, scrimpy **9** niggardly, penurious **11** closefisted, tightfisted **12** parsimonious

Pindar
5 odist
home: **6** Thebes
poem: **3** ode

pine
4 ache, long, mope, sigh, tree, wish, wood **5** brood, crave, dream, yearn **6** desire, grieve,

hanker, hunger, lament, thirst **7** conifer **8** languish **9** evergreen
textile screw: 3 ara **4** hala **7** lauhala
type: 5 pitch **8** loblolly **9** lodgepole

Pine Tree State
5 Maine

pinhead
4 dolt, dope, fool **5** dunce **6** dimwit, doofus, nitwit **7** dullard **8** dumbbell **9** birdbrain

pinion
3 cog **4** bind, gear, wing **5** quill, tie up, truss **6** fetter, tether **7** disable, feather, shackle **8** cogwheel, restrain **9** hamstring

pink
3 cut **4** best, peak, rose, stab **5** blush, coral, melon **6** flower, height, pierce **7** excited, paragon **9** perforate

pinna
3 ear, fin **4** wing **7** feather, leaflet

pinnacle
3 top, tor **4** acme, apex, peak **5** crest, crown, serac, spire **6** apogee, climax, height, summit, zenith **7** steeple **8** capsheaf, meridian **11** culmination

pinniped
4 seal **6** walrus

Pinocchio author
7 Collodi (Carlo) **9** Lorenzini (Carlo)

pinochle
card: 3 ace, ten **4** jack, king, nine **5** queen
term: 4 meld **5** widow **7** auction
two-handed: 7 goulash

pinot ___
4 noir **5** blanc

pinpoint
3 aim, fix **4** spot, tiny **5** exact, place **6** locate **7** precise **8** identify, stand out **9** determine, highlight, recognize **11** distinguish

Pinter play
8 Betrayal **9** Caretaker (The) **10** Homecoming (The)

pinto
4 pied, pony **5** horse, paint **7** mottled, piebald **8** skewbald

pint-size
3 wee **5** dwarf, small **6** midget, pocket **9** miniature **10** diminutive

Pinza of South Pacific
4 Ezio

pioneer
5 first, prime **6** maiden **7** explore, founder, initial, primary, settler **8** colonist, earliest, explorer, original **9** innovator **10** avant-garde, pathfinder **11** trailblazer **12** frontiersman
famous: 5 Boone (Daniel), Bowie (Jim), Clark (William), Lewis (Meriwether) **6** Carson (Kit), Colter (John) **7** Bridger (Jim), Chapman (John), Frémont (John C.), Whitman (Marcus) **8** Crockett (Davy)

pious
4 holy **5** godly **6** devout, worthy **7** devoted, dutiful **8** reverent, virtuous **9** hypocrite, pietistic, prayerful, religious **10** devotional **12** hypocritical

pip
3 dot **4** blip, peep, seed, spot **5** speck **9** break open

pipe
3 keg, tun **4** butt, cask, duct, flue, hose, tube **5** briar **6** barrel, convey, funnel, siphon **7** channel, conduct, conduit **8** aqueduct, hogshead **10** meerschaum
ceremonial: 7 calumet
part: 4 bowl, stem

pipe down
4 hush **5** dry up, quiet **6** shut up **7** be quiet

pipe dream
4 wish **7** chimera, fantasy **8** illusion

pipeline
5 works **6** system **7** channel, conduit, process **8** activity, supplier **10** connection

___ piper of Hamelin
4 pied

pip-squeak
4 runt **5** twerp **6** peewee, shaver, shrimp, squirt **7** tadpole **8** half-pint, small fry

piquancy
4 zest **5** gusto **6** relish

piquant
4 racy, tart **5** sharp, spicy, tangy, zesty **6** biting, lively, savory, snappy **7** peppery, pungent **8** poignant, spirited **9** flavorful, sparkling **10** appetizing **11** provocative, stimulating

pique
3 irk, pet, vex **4** huff, miff, move, snit **5** anger, annoy, peeve, pride, rouse **6** arouse, excite, nettle, offend, put out **7** dudgeon, offense, provoke, quicken **8** irritate, motivate, vexation **9** aggravate, annoyance, challenge, stimulate **10** exasperate, irritation, resentment

piracy
5 theft **7** lifting, looting, pillage, plunder, robbery **8** stealing, thievery **10** plagiarism

piranha
6 caribe

pirate
5 rover **6** looter, picaro, raider, robber, sea dog **7** brigand, corsair, sea wolf **8** marauder, picaroon, pillager, sea rover **9** buccaneer, plunderer, privateer, sea robber **10** freebooter

address: **5** matey
drink: **3** rum **4** grog
English: **4** Read (Mary) **5** Bonny (Anne), Drake (Francis), Teach (Edward) **6** Morgan (Henry) **7** Dampier (William) **10** Blackbeard
fictional: **4** Hook, Smee **6** Silver (Long John) **7** Sparrow (Jack) **8** Barbossa
flag: **10** Jolly Roger
French: **7** Laffite (Jean), Lafitte (Jean)
Scottish: **4** Kidd (William)
Welsh: **9** Black Bart

Pirates of Penzance, The
composer: **8** Sullivan (Arthur)
librettist: **7** Gilbert (W. S.)

pirogue
5 canoe **6** dugout

pirouette
4 spin, turn **5** twirl, wheel, whirl

piscator
6 angler **9** fisherman

pismire
3 ant

pistol
3 gat, rod **4** Colt **5** Glock, Luger **6** Magnum, Mauser, roscoe **7** bulldog, handgun **8** revolver, small arm **9** derringer, pepperbox
case: **7** holster

pit
3 vie **4** dent, hell, hole, scar **5** abyss, arena, hades, match, shaft, stone **6** cavity, hollow **7** counter, play off **8** pockmark
baking: **3** imu
dance: **4** mosh

Pit and the Pendulum author
3 Poe (Edgar Allan)

pitch
3 dip, set **4** buck, dive, drop, fall, hurl, line, play, plug, tilt, tone, toss **5** erect, fling, heave, lurch, put up, resin, slant, sling, slope, spiel, throw **6** encamp, go down, plunge **7** discard, incline, present, promote, sidearm **8** distance **9** advertise, declivity **13** advertisement
uneven: **3** rub

pitch-dark
3 jet **4** ebon, inky **5** black, ebony, jetty

pitcher
3 jug **4** ewer, olla, olpe, toby **5** cruse **6** beaker, flagon **7** creamer
area: **5** mound
handle: **3** ear **4** ansa
(see also **baseballer**)

pitcher Hershiser
4 Orel

pitcher's stat
3 ERA

pitchfork part
4 tine

pitch in
3 aid **4** help **5** begin, set to, start **6** fall to **8** commence, get going, start off **9** subscribe, volunteer **10** contribute

piteous
3 sad **4** poor **8** pathetic **9** affecting **10** lamentable **11** distressing

pitfall
4 risk, snag, trap **5** catch, peril, snare **6** danger, hazard **9** booby trap **10** difficulty **12** entanglement

pith
3 nub **4** core, gist, kill, meat, pulp **5** focus, heart **6** center, import, kernel **7** essence, nucleus **9** substance **10** importance **12** significance

pith helmet
4 topi **5** topee

pithy
5 brief, crisp, meaty, short, terse **6** cogent **7** compact, concise, pointed **8** succinct **12** epigrammatic **13** short and sweet

pitiable
4 poor **5** cheap, sorry **8** shameful **10** deplorable, lamentable **12** contemptible

pitiful
3 sad **4** mean, poor **5** cheap, sorry **6** meager, meagre, paltry, shabby **7** forlorn **8** beggarly, pathetic, wretched **9** miserable **10** despicable, inadequate **12** contemptible

pitiless
4 cold, hard **5** cruel, harsh, stony **6** brutal **8** inhumane, uncaring **9** barbarous, unfeeling **10** unmerciful **11** coldhearted, hardhearted

pittance
4 wage **5** scrap, trace **6** trifle **7** modicum, peanuts **9** allowance

pity
3 rue **4** ache, ruth **5** mercy **6** regret, sorrow **7** empathy, feel for, sadness **8** distress, sympathy **10** compassion, condolence, sympathize **11** commiserate

pivot
3 pin **4** slew, slue, turn **5** hinge, shaft, swing, wheel **6** center, swivel

pivotal
3 key **5** axial, chief, vital **7** central, crucial **8** critical, decisive **9** essential, important

pixie
3 elf, fay, imp **5** antic, fairy, scamp **6** elvish, impish, rascal, sprite **7** brownie, coltish, playful, puckish **8** prankish **11** mischievous

pixilated
3 fey **7** bemused, erratic, flighty, muddled, touched **9** eccentric, whimsical **10** capricious

Pizarro, Francisco
brother: 7 Gonzalo
city founded: 4 Lima
conquest: 4 Peru
victims: 5 Incas 9 Atahualpa 10 Atahuallpa

pizzazz
3 pep, vim, zip **4** bang, brio, dash, élan, snap, zest, zing **5** éclat, flair, flash, gusto, moxie, oomph, punch, spice, style, verve **6** dazzle, energy, hoopla, sizzle, spirit **7** glamour, panache **8** vitality **10** excitement

placard
4 bill, post **6** notice, plaque, poster **7** affiche **8** handbill

placate
4 calm, ease **6** pacify, soothe **7** appease, assuage, comfort, mollify, satisfy, sweeten, win over **10** conciliate, propitiate

place
3 lay, put, set **4** area, lieu, loci (plural), post, rank, site, spot, zone **5** locus, point, stead, tract **6** region, status **7** situate, station **8** district, identify, locality, location, pinpoint, position, standing **9** establish, recognize
combining form: **3** top **4** loco, topo, topy

placid
4 calm, easy, mild **5** quiet, still **6** gentle, serene **7** halcyon **8** composed, peaceful, tranquil, waveless, windless **9** unruffled **10** complacent, untroubled **11** undisturbed

plagiarize
4 copy, crib **5** steal **6** pirate **11** appropriate

plague
3 vex **4** bane, evil, pest **5** annoy, beset, curse, harry, hound, smite, trial, worry **6** blight, bother, infest, harass, hassle, hector, pester **7** afflict, bedevil, disease, disturb, scourge, torment, trouble **8** calamity, distress, epidemic, invasion, irritant, irritate, nuisance, outbreak, pandemic **9** annoyance, beleaguer **10** affliction, black death, pestilence **11** infestation

plaid
6 tartan

plain
3 lea **4** bald, bare, open, pure, veld **5** blunt, clear, field, frank, llano, pampa, usual, veldt **6** candid, common, homely, modest, pampas, patent, severe, simple, steppe, tundra **7** expanse, evident, obvious, prairie, savanna, spartan **8** apparent, distinct, everyday, homespun, manifest, ordinary, savannah **9** outspoken, unadorned **10** forthright, unaffected **11** undecorated, unvarnished

plainclothesman
3 tec **4** dick **6** shamus, sleuth **7** gumshoe **8** hawkshaw **9** detective **12** investigator

plainness
6 candor, purity **7** clarity, honesty **8** lucidity **10** simplicity

Plain People
5 Amish **10** Hutterites, Mennonites

plains home
4 tipi **5** tepee **6** teepee

Plains Indian
3 Oto, Ute **4** Otoe **5** Kiowa, Osage **6** Mandan, Pawnee **8** Cheyenne, Comanche

plainsong
5 chant **12** cantus firmus

plainspoken
4 open **5** frank **6** candid, direct, honest **8** straight, truthful **10** forthright **11** undisguised, unvarnished

plaintive
3 sad **4** glum **6** woeful **7** doleful, piteous, pitiful **8** dolorous, downcast, mournful **9** sorrowful **10** dispirited, lamentable, lugubrious, melancholy

plait
4 fold **5** braid, pleat, weave **7** pigtail **10** intertwine, interweave

plan
3 aim, map, way **4** cast, goal, idea, mean, plot **5** chart, frame **6** design, devise, intend, intent, lay out, map out, method, scheme, set out **7** arrange, diagram, drawing, outline, pattern, program, project, propose, purpose, work out **8** contrive, engineer, organize, strategy, think out **9** blueprint, formulate, intention, procedure **11** arrangement, formulation

plane
3 fly **4** even, flat, tool, tree **5** flush, level **6** joiner, smooth
(see also **airplane**)

planet
4 Mars **5** Earth, Venus **6** Saturn, Uranus **7** Jupiter, Mercury, Neptune
dwarf: **4** Eris **5** Ceres, Pluto
path: **5** orbit
satellite: **4** moon
shadow: **5** umbra
small: **8** asteroid

planetary
4 vast **6** global **7** erratic, immense **8** colossal, enormous **9** universal, wandering, worldwide **11** terrestrial

Planets composer
5 Holst (Gustav)

plangent
7 orotund, ringing, vibrant **8** resonant, sonorous

9 consonant, plaintive 10 expressive, resounding 11 reverberant

plank

4 item, wood 5 board, floor 6 lumber, timber 7 article, support

plant

3 fix, pot, set, sow 4 bury, grow, hide, mill, park, root, seed, tomb 5 cache, cover, imbed, inter, place, plunk, put in, stash, works 6 entomb, inhume, occult, screen 7 conceal, factory, install, lay away, put away, secrete 8 colonize, populate 9 cultivate

angiosperm: 5 dicot 7 monocot

aquatic: 4 reed 5 lotus, sedge 7 awlwort, cattail, fanwort, papyrus 8 duckweed, eelgrass, hornwort, pondweed 9 water lily 10 watercress 11 bladderwort 12 pickerelweed

aromatic: 4 nard 6 lovage 9 spikenard

Australian: 6 mallee 7 banksia 8 blackboy 10 eucalyptus

body: 4 stem 7 thallus

bulbous: 4 Ixia, lily 5 camas, onion, tulip 7 jonquil 8 hyacinth 9 narcissus

carnivorous: 6 sundew 10 butterwort 12 pitcher plant, Venus flytrap

cell layer: 7 phellem

climbing: 3 ivy 4 vine 5 betel, liana, vetch 6 bryony, derris, smilax 7 creeper, jasmine 8 bignonia, fumitory, moonseed, scammony, wisteria 12 morning glory

coloring agent: 8 carotene 11 chlorophyll, xanthophyll

combining form: 4 phyt 5 phyto

cone-bearing: 3 fir, yew 4 pine 5 cedar, cycad 6 ginkgo, spruce 7 conifer, cypress, redwood 10 arborvitae, gymnosperm

desert: 4 aloe 5 agave 6 cactus, cholla 8 mesquite, ocotillo 9 paloverde 11 brittlebush

disease: 3 rot 4 gall, mold, rust, scab, smut, wilt 5 edema, ergot 6 blight, mildew, mosaic 7 blister 8 clubroot 9 black spot 10 black heart

extinct: 8 calamite

flowerless: 4 alga, fern, kelp, moss 5 algae (plural), fungi (plural) 6 fungus, lichen 7 seaweed 8 clubmoss 9 bryophyte, equisetum, horsetail, liverwort

fluid: 3 gum, sap 4 milk 5 latex, resin

gland: 7 nectary

hallucinogenic: 4 hemp 5 poppy 6 mescal 8 cannabis 9 marijuana

hard-to-grow: 5 miffy

largest: 7 sequoia

life: 5 flora

marine: 4 kelp, nori 5 dulse, fucus 6 wakame 7 seaweed 8 gulfweed 10 sea lettuce

marsh: 4 reed 5 carex, sedge 7 bogbean, bulrush, calamus, cattail 8 red maple, sphagnum 10 rose mallow 11 loosestrife

medicinal: 4 aloe, sage 5 poppy, senna, tansy 6 catnip, fennel, garlic, hyssop, ipecac, nettle 7 aconite, boneset, burdock, camphor, comfrey, ginseng, hemlock, henbane, juniper, lobelia, mullein, mustard, parsley 8 camomile, capsicum, cinchona, feverfew, licorice, pilewort, plantain, wormwood 9 asafetida, chamomile, dandelion, echinacea, fenugreek, monkshood 10 asafoetida, goldenseal, peppermint

microscopic: 4 mold 6 diatom 7 euglena 8 bacteria (plural) 9 bacterium

oldest: 11 bristlecone

onion-like: 4 leek 5 chive 7 shallot 8 scallion

opening: 5 stoma 7 stomata (plural)

parasitic: 6 dodder, fungus 7 pinesap 8 gerardia 9 broomrape, mistletoe, rafflesia, witchweed 10 beechdrops

part: 3 bud, nut, sap 4 bark, bulb, cell, cone, corm, leaf, pome, root, seed, stem, wood 5 bract, drupe, fruit, grain, spore, stalk, stool, thorn, tuber, xylem 6 catkin, flower, nectar, phloem, raceme, spadix 7 rhizome 8 lenticel 9 cellulose, cotyledon 11 chlorophyll, chloroplast 13 inflorescence

pepper: 3 ava 4 kava

pest: 5 aphid, scale 6 chafer, thrips, weevil 7 cutworm 8 fruit fly, wireworm 9 gypsy moth 10 cankerworm, leafhopper, phylloxera 11 codling moth

poisonous: 4 poke, upas 5 sumac 6 castor, croton, datura 7 amanita, cassava, cowbane, henbane, lobelia, tobacco 8 foxglove, larkspur, locoweed, mayapple, oleander, pokeweed 9 baneberry, monkshood 10 belladonna, jimsonweed, manchineel, nightshade

saprophytic: 5 fungi (plural) 6 fungus 7 pinesap 9 pinedrops, snow plant 10 beechdrops, Indian pipe

succulent: 4 aloe 5 agave 6 cactus 10 bitterroot

swelling: 5 edema

thorny: 4 rose 5 briar 6 cactus, nettle, teasel 7 caltrop, thistle 9 cocklebur

tissue: 5 xylem 6 phloem 7 cambium, medulla 8 meristem

young: 5 scion, shoot 6 sprout 7 cutting 8 seedling

plantain

5 fruit 6 banana

plantation

5 manor 6 colony, estate, quinta 7 acreage, demesne 8 hacienda 10 encampment, habitation, settlement

of fiction: 4 Tara

plant louse

5 aphid

plaque

4 film 5 badge, patch 6 brooch, lesion, tablet

7 tribute **8** bacteria, memorial **13** commemoration

plaster
3 dab **4** coat **5** affix, cover, gesso **6** stucco **7** coating, conceal, overlay **8** dressing
of paris: **5** gesso **6** gypsum

plastered
3 lit **4** high **5** drunk, lit up, oiled **6** bashed, blotto, bombed, juiced, potted, soaked, soused, stewed, stoned, tanked, wasted, zonked **7** crocked, drunken, pickled, pie-eyed, sloshed, smashed, sottish **10** inebriated, liquored up **11** intoxicated

plastic
4 soft **5** vinyl **6** pliant, supple **7** ductile, pliable **8** creative, flexible, moldable, workable **9** adaptable, formative, malleable, synthetic **10** artificial, credit card, sculptural

plat
3 lot, map **4** plan **5** chart, tract **6** parcel **7** quadrat

plate
4 base, coat, disc, dish, disk, gild, tile **5** layer, paten, scute, slice **6** enamel, fascia, lamina, plaque **7** anodize, charger, lamella, overlay

plateau
4 mesa **5** table **6** upland **9** altiplano, tableland
arid: **4** puna
barren: **5** field **6** paramo
dry: **5** karoo **6** karroo

platform
3 map **4** bank, base, bema, bima, dais, deck, plan **5** bimah, forum, ledge, riser, shelf, stage, stump **6** design, pallet, perron, podium, pulpit, rostra (plural), scheme **7** almemar, balcony, pattern, rostrum **8** hustings, scaffold **9** banquette, manifesto **11** declaration
temporary: **7** staging **8** scaffold
wooden: **9** boardwalk

Plath, Sylvia
novel: **7** Bell Jar (The)
poem: **5** Ariel, Daddy

platitude
6 cliché, truism **7** bromide **8** banality, prosaism **10** shibboleth

Plato
father: **7** Ariston
literary form: **6** dialog **8** dialogue
original name: **10** Aristocles
school: **7** Academy
work: **3** Ion **4** Meno **5** Crito, Lysis **6** Laches, Phaedo **7** Apology, Gorgias **8** Phaedrus, Republic (The) **9** Charmides, Symposium

platter
5 plate **6** record **8** trencher

platypus
8 duckbill

plaudits
5 kudos **6** cheers, praise **7** acclaim, ovation **8** applause, approval, encomium **9** accolades **11** acclamation

plausible
8 credible, specious **10** believable, convincing, creditable, persuasive, reasonable

play
3 act, fun **4** game, jest, joke, romp **5** drama, feint, serve, sport, treat, trick, wager **6** cavort, comedy, fiddle, frolic, gambit, gambol, leeway, margin **7** delight, disport, perform **8** latitude, pleasure **9** amusement, diversion, enjoyment, stratagem **10** manipulate, recreation
an instrument: **3** bow **4** beat, blow, pick **5** pluck, sound, strum **6** strike **7** squeeze
kind: **5** farce **6** comedy **7** musical, tragedy **8** one-acter **9** melodrama, pantomime
part: **3** act **4** Act I **5** Act II **6** Act III **5** scene **8** epilogue, prologue
passionate: **9** melodrama
site: **8** stage set

Play-____
3 Doh

playact
5 put on **7** perform, posture, pretend **9** personate **11** impersonate, make believe

playboy
4 rake, roué **7** Don Juan, swinger **8** hedonist, lothario **9** bon vivant, libertine

play down
8 minimize **9** deprecate, soft-pedal, underrate **11** de-emphasize

player
5 actor **6** mummer **7** actress, athlete, trouper **8** musician, thespian **9** contender, performer **10** competitor, contestant **11** participant
reserve: **11** benchwarmer

player piano
7 Pianola **10** Disklavier **11** nickelodeon

play for time
5 stall

playful
5 antic, jolly, ludic, merry, pixie **6** elvish, frisky, impish, jocund, joking, jovial, lively **7** coltish, jocular, puckish, waggish **8** humorous, sportive **9** kittenish, sprightly **10** frolicsome
swimmer: **5** otter

play off
3 pit, vie **5** match **6** oppose **7** counter **8** contrast

plaything
3 toy

play up
6 stress 7 feature 9 dramatize, emphasize, highlight, overstate, underline 10 accentuate, exaggerate, underscore

playwright
9 dramatist 10 dramaturge
(see also **dramatist**)

playwright David
5 Mamet

playwright Edward
5 Albee

playwright George Bernard
4 Shaw

playwright O'Casey
4 Seán

playwright William
4 Inge

plaza
6 circus, common, square, zocalo 9 carrefour

plea
4 suit 5 alibi 6 appeal, excuse, orison, prayer 7 apology, defense, pretext, request 8 entreaty, overture, petition 12 supplication
defendant's: 4 nolo 6 guilty 8 innocent 9 not guilty

plead
3 beg 4 pray 5 argue 6 allege, answer, appeal 7 beseech, entreat, implore 8 advocate, maintain 9 importune 10 supplicate

pleasant
4 fair, fine, good, nice 5 clear, sunny, sweet 6 cheery, genial, pretty 7 affable, amiable, clarion, likable, welcome 8 amicable, charming, cheerful, engaging, gracious, grateful, likeable, pleasing, sunshine, sunshiny 9 agreeable, appealing, cloudless, congenial, convivial, enjoyable, favorable, unclouded 10 delightful, gratifying

pleasantry
3 fun 4 jest, joke 6 banter, levity 8 badinage, repartee 9 wittiness 10 jocularity

please
4 like, suit, wish 5 agree, amuse, enjoy, serve 6 choose 7 content, delight, gladden, gratify, indulge, satisfy
French: 12 s'il vous plait
German: 5 bitte
Spanish: 8 por favor

pleasing
4 good, nice 6 pretty 7 welcome 8 suitable 9 agreeable, congenial, favorable, palatable 10 attractive, delightful, gratifying

pleasure
3 fun, joy 4 will 5 bliss, fancy 6 desire, liking, relish 7 delight, gladden, gratify 8 felicity, gladness, hedonism 9 amusement, diversion, enjoyment, happiness, merriment

pleat
4 fold 5 crimp 6 crease

plebe
5 frosh 8 freshman

plebeian
3 low 4 base 5 crude, lowly 6 coarse, common, humble, menial 8 commoner, everyday, ordinary 10 lower-class

plebiscite
4 vote

plectrum
4 pick

pledge
3 vow 4 bail, bind, bond, gage, hock, oath, pawn, seal, sign, word 5 drink, swear, toast, token 6 parole, plight, surety 7 chattel, earnest, promise, warrant 8 bailment, contract, covenant, guaranty, security, warranty 9 agreement, assurance, certainty, guarantee, undertake 11 hypothecate

pledget
3 pad 8 compress

Pleiades
4 Maia 6 Merope 7 Alcyone, Celaeno, Electra, Sterope, Taygeta 8 Asterope
brightest star: 7 Alcyone

plenary
4 full 5 whole 6 entire 7 general 8 absolute, complete 9 inclusive 11 unqualified 12 unrestricted

plenitude
4 glut 6 excess 7 satiety, surfeit 8 fullness 9 abundance, profusion, repletion 11 copiousness, sufficiency, superfluity 12 completeness

plenteous
7 fertile 8 abundant, fruitful, prolific 9 abounding 10 productive

plentiful
4 full, rich, rife 5 ample, flush 7 copious, profuse 8 abundant, affluent, generous 9 abounding, bounteous, unstinted 10 sufficient

plenty
3 lot 4 enow, heap, lots, pack, peck, pile 6 stacks, wealth 8 adequacy, fullness, mountain 9 abundance, affluence, great deal 10 cornucopia

pleonasm
8 verbiage 9 prolixity, tautology, verbosity, wordiness 10 redundancy 11 periphrasis, superfluity

plethora
4 glut 5 flood 6 excess 7 overrun, surfeit, surplus 8 fullness, overflow 9 abundance, profusion, repletion 11 superfluity

plexus
4 rete **7** network

pliable
6 supple **7** plastic **9** adaptable **10** adjustable **11** complaisant, manipulable

pliant
5 lithe **6** limber, supple **7** ductile, plastic, springy **8** flexible, moldable, workable, yielding **9** adaptable, malleable, tractable **10** manageable

plica
4 fold **6** crease, groove

plight
3 fix, jam, vow **4** hole, spot, word **5** swear **6** engage, pickle, pledge, scrape **7** betroth, dilemma, promise **8** quandary **9** betrothal **10** difficulty, engagement **11** predicament

plod
4 slog, toil **5** grind, slave, tramp, tread, tromp **6** drudge, lumber, trudge **8** plug away

plot
3 map **4** area, land, mark, note, plan, ruse **5** cabal, chart, story, tract **6** design, devise, invent, lay out, locate, parcel, scheme **7** collude, compact, connive, diagram, outline **8** conspire, contrive, intrigue, scenario **9** collusion, conniving, machinate **10** complicity, connivance, conspiracy **11** machination

plotters' group
5 cabal **9** camarilla

plover
5 pewit, stilt **6** peewit **7** lapwing **8** dotterel, killdeer
relative: **9** sandpiper, turnstone

plow
3 dig **4** till, turn **5** break **6** furrow, harrow, trench **8** turn over **9** cultivate
part: **4** beam, frog **5** share **7** coulter **8** landside **9** moldboard

ploy
4 ruse, scam, wile **5** feint, trick **6** device, frolic, gambit, tactic **7** gimmick **8** artifice, escapade, maneuver **9** stratagem **11** contrivance

pluck
3 rob, tug **4** grit, guts, pick, pull, yank **5** cheek, grasp, heart, moxie, nerve, spunk **6** daring, fleece, mettle, remove, snatch, spirit, tweeze **7** bravery, courage, pull out

plucky
4 bold, game **5** brave **6** feisty, spunky **7** doughty **8** fearless, spirited, unafraid **9** dauntless

plug
3 tap **4** bung, clog, core, cork, fill, hype, pack, push, stop, tout **5** block, blurb, boost, choke, close, cry up, shoot, spile **6** device, remedy **7** congest, fitting, hydrant, promote, stopper **8** obstruct **9** advertise, publicity, publicize **10** connection

plug-ugly
4 goon, thug **5** bully, rowdy, tough **7** goombah, hoodlum, ruffian **8** enforcer **9** roughneck

plum
5 prize **6** purple, reward **7** guerdon, premium **8** dividend
dried: **5** prune
kind: **4** sloe **6** damson **7** bullace **9** greengage
spiny: **4** sloe **10** blackthorn

plumage
8 feathers
early: **4** down

plumb
5 delve, probe, sound **6** fathom, weight **7** examine, explore, install, measure **8** vertical **10** vertically **13** perpendicular

plume
4 tail **5** array, preen, pride, prize **6** column **7** feather **8** aigrette

plummet
4 dive, drop, fall **5** crash **6** plunge, tumble **8** collapse, nose-dive **11** precipitate

plump
3 fat **4** drop, fall, full **5** ample, buxom, favor, pudgy, round, stout, tubby **6** chubby, portly, rotund, zaftig **7** rounded, support **8** roly-poly **9** pneumatic **10** Rubenesque

plumply
7 frankly, plainly **8** candidly **12** forthrightly

plunder
3 rob **4** loot, sack, swag, take **5** booty, prize, reave, seize, spoil, steal, strip **6** boodle, rapine, spoils **7** despoil, pillage, ransack, relieve, stick up **9** pillaging

plunge
3 bet, ram, run **4** dive, drop, fall, jump, rush, sink, stab, swim **5** drive, lunge, pitch, stick **6** charge, gamble, hasten, hurtle, thrust, topple, tumble **7** descend, immerse, plummet **8** nose-dive, submerge **9** penetrate

plus
3 and **4** also, more, perk **5** added, asset, bonus, boost, extra **6** excess **7** benefit **8** addition, increase, positive

plush
4 full, rich **6** deluxe, fabric, lavish, velvet **7** opulent **8** luscious, palatial **9** expensive, luxuriant, luxurious, sumptuous

Pluto
3 Dis **5** Hades
brother: **4** Zeus **7** Jupiter, Neptune **8** Poseidon
father: **6** Cronus, Saturn
mother: **3** Ops **4** Rhea
wife: **10** Persephone, Proserpina

plutocrat
5 mogul **6** fat cat, tycoon **7** magnate **9** financier, moneybags **10** capitalist

plutonian
8 infernal **10** underworld

Plutus
father: **6** Iasion
god of: **6** riches, wealth
mother: **5** Ceres **7** Demeter

ply
3 use **4** bias, sail **5** apply, exert, layer, wield **6** employ, handle, strand, supply, travel, voyage **7** furnish, perform **8** maneuver, practice **11** inclination

pneuma
4 soul **5** anima **6** psyche, spirit

pneumatic
4 airy **5** ample, buxom, plump **6** aerial, zaftig **9** spiritual **10** curvaceous **11** atmospheric

poach
4 cook **5** steal **6** coddle, simmer **7** intrude **8** encroach, trespass **9** interlope **11** appropriate

Pocahontas
father: **8** Powhatan
husband: **5** Rolfe (John)

pock
3 pit **4** hole, spot **7** pustule

pocket
3 bag **4** lift, sack **5** filch, pinch, pouch, purse, steal, swipe **6** cavity, pilfer **7** capsule, dead end, impasse **8** cul-de-sac **9** condensed **10** blind alley
billiards: **4** pool

pocketbook
3 bag **4** poke **5** purse **6** clutch, income, wallet **7** handbag **8** billfold **9** clutch bag

pocket bread
4 pita **5** pitta

pocket money
6 change **9** petty cash **11** small change

pocket-size
4 tiny **5** small **9** miniature **10** diminutive

pocket-watch chain
3 fob

pod
3 bag, gam, sac **4** boll, case, hull, husk, skin **5** shell, shuck **6** cocoon **7** capsule, silique **8** seedcase
plant: **3** pea **4** bean, okra **5** chili, gumbo **6** cassia, cowpea, legume, lentil, peanut, pepper **8** capsicum, mesquite, milkweed **9** lespedeza

pod-bearing tree
5 carob **6** locust **7** catalpa

podiatry
9 chiropody

podium
4 dais **6** pulpit **7** leotern, rostrum **8** platform

___ podrida
4 olla

Poe, Edgar Allan
detective: **5** Dupin (C. Auguste)
poem: **5** Bells (The), Raven (The) **6** Lenore **7** Israfel, To Helen, Ulalume **8** Eldorado, For Annie **10** Annabel Lee
tale: **6** Ligeia, Shadow **7** Gold-Bug (The), Morella, Silence **8** Black Cat (The) **13** Tell-tale Heart (The) **15** Purloined Letter (The) **17** Cask of Amontillado (The), Pit and the Pendulum (The) **19** Masque of the Red Death (The) **21** Fall of the House of Usher (The)

poem
3 ode **4** epic, epos, idyl, rime, rune, song **5** ditty, elegy, epode, idyll, lyric, rhyme, verse **6** ballad, epopee, jingle, rondel, sonnet **7** eclogue, rondeau **8** limerick, madrigal
closing: **5** envoi, envoy
division: **4** foot, line **5** canto, epode, stich, verse **6** stanza **7** couplet, refrain **8** epilogue, prologue
Japanese: **5** haiku, tanka
of eight lines: **6** octave **7** triolet
of four lines: **8** quatrain
of fourteen lines: **6** sonnet
of six lines: **6** sestet
of three lines: **7** triplet
pastoral: **4** idyl **5** idyll **7** eclogue, georgic
short: **5** ditty **7** epigram
to a Grecian urn: **3** ode

poet
4 bard, muse, scop **5** skald **6** lyrist **7** elegist **8** idyllist, lyricist, minstrel **9** balladist, sonneteer, versifier **10** Parnassian
American: **3** Poe (Edgar Allan) **4** Dove (Rita), Hass (Robert), Nash (Ogden), Read (Thomas), Rich (Adrienne), Ryan (Kay), Tabb (John Banister), Tate (Allen) **5** Auden (Wystan Hugh), Benét (Stephen Vincent), Crane (Hart), Field (Eugene), Frost (Robert), Guest (Edgar), Moore (Marianne), Plath (Sylvia), Pound (Ezra), Riley (James Whitcomb), Wylie (Elinor) **6** Barlow (Joel), Bishop (Elizabeth), Brooks (Gwendolyn), Bryant (William Cullen), Ciardi (John), Dickey (James), Dunbar (Paul Laurence), Hughes (Langston), Kilmer (Joyce), Lanier (Sidney), Lowell (Amy, James Russell, Robert), McKuen (Rod), Millay (Edna St. Vincent), Pinsky (Robert), Ransom (John Crowe), Seeger (Alan), Strand (Mark), Taylor (Edward), Warren (Robert Penn), Wilbur (Richard) **7** Angelou (Maya), Ashbery (John), Collins (Billy), Emerson (Ralph Waldo), Freneau (Philip), Jeffers (Robinson), Lindsay (Vachel), Merrill (James), Nemerov (Howard), Roethke (Theodore), Shapiro (Karl), Stevens (Wallace),

Whitman (Walt) **8** Berryman (John), Cummings (E. E.), Ginsberg (Allen), MacLeish (Archibald), Robinson (Edwin Arlington), Sandburg (Carl), Teasdale (Sara), Wheatley (Phillis), Whittier (John Greenleaf), Williams (C. K., William Carlos) **9** Dickinson (Emily), Santayana (George) **10** Bradstreet (Anne), Longfellow (Henry Wadsworth)
Anglo-Saxon: 7 Caedmon, Cynwulf **8** Cynewulf, Kynewulf
Arab: 5 Jarir **6** Hariri **8** al-Hariri
Australian: 8 Paterson (Andrew Barton)
Belgian: 11 Maeterlinck (Maurice)
Canadian: 5 Pratt (Edwin John) **6** Carson (Anne), Hébert (Anne) **7** Roberts (Charles G. D.), Service (Robert) **8** Drummond (William Henry) **9** Fréchette (Louis-Honoré)
Chilean: 6 Neruda (Pablo) **7** Mistral (Gabriela)
Chinese: 4 Du Fu, Li Bo, Li Po, Tu Fu **5** Li Bai **7** Wang Wei
Danish: 4 Rode (Helge) **5** Ewald (Johannes)
English: 3 Gay (John) **4** Gray (Thomas), Owen (Wilfred), Pope (Alexander), Rowe (Nicholas), Tate (Nahum), Wyat (Thomas) **5** Blake (William), Byron (Lord), Carew (Thomas), Clare (John), Donne (John), Eliot (Thomas Stearns), Gower (John), Hardy (Thomas), Keats (John), Noyes (Alfred), Wilde (Oscar), Wyatt (Thomas) **6** Arnold (Matthew), Austin (Alfred), Belloc (Hilaire), Brooke (Rupert), Butler (Samuel), Clough (Arthur Hugh), Cowper (William), Dryden (John), Graves (Robert), Larkin (Philip), Milton (John), Savage (Richard), Sidney (Philip), Surrey (Earl of), Symons (Arthur), Waller (Edmund), Watson (William), Wotton (Henry) **7** Bridges (Robert), Campion (Thomas), Chaucer (Geoffrey), Gilbert (W. S.), Herbert (George), Herrick (Robert), Hopkins (Gerard Manley), Housman (A. E.), Kipling (Rudyard), Layamon, Marvell (Andrew), Patmore (Coventry), Shelley (Percy Bysshe), Skelton (John), Southey (Robert), Spender (Stephen), Spenser (Edmund) **8** Betjeman (John), Browning (Elizabeth Barrett, Robert), de la Mare (Walter), Langland (William), Lovelace (Richard), Meredith (George), Rossetti (Christina, Dante Gabriel), Tennyson (Alfred Lord), Thompson (Francis) **9** Coleridge (Samuel Taylor), Masefield (John), Swinburne (Algernon Charles) **10** Chatterton (Thomas), FitzGerald (Edward), Wordsworth (William) **11** Shakespeare (William)
Finnish: 8 Runeberg (Johan Ludvig)
French: 5 Marot (Clément) **6** Musset (Alfred de), Valéry (Paul), Villon (François) **7** Bourget (Paul), Chénier (André de, Marie-Joseph), Gautier (Théophile), Rimbaud (Arthur), Ronsard (Pierre de) **8** Malherbe (François de), Mallarmé (Stéphane), Verlaine (Paul) **9** Lamartine (Alphonse de) **10** Baudelaire (Charles) **11** Apollinaire (Guillaume)
German: 5 Heine (Heinrich), Rilke (Rainer Maria), Sachs (Hans), Storm (Theodor) **6** Brecht (Bertolt), Goethe (Johann Wolfgang von), Uhland (Ludwig) **7** Walther (von der Vogelweide), Wolfram (von Eschenbach) **8** Schiller (Friedrich von) **9** Klopstock (Friedrich Gottlieb) **10** Tannhäuser
Greek: 5 Arion, Homer **6** Elytis (Odysseus), Erinna, Hesiod, Pindar, Ritsos (Yannis), Sappho **7** Agathon, Alcaeus, Orpheus, Seferis (George), Thespis **8** Anacreon **9** Simonides **10** Apollonius, Theocritus
Hindu: 5 Naidu (Sarojini) **6** Tagore (Rabindranath) **8** Kalidasa, Tulsidas
Hungarian: 6 Petofi (Sandor), Zrinyi (Miklos)
Irish: 5 Moore (Thomas), Wolfe (Charles), Yeats (William Butler) **6** Heaney (Seamus) **7** Dunsany (Lord), Muldoon (Paul) **8** Drummond (William Henry), MacNeice (Louis)
Italian: 4 Rosa (Salvator), Vida (Marco) **5** Dante (Alighieri), Tasso (Torquato) **7** Ariosto (Ludovico), Manzoni (Alessandro), Montale (Eugenio) **8** Carducci (Giosuè), Leopardi (Giacomo), Petrarch **9** Boccaccio (Giovanni), D'Annunzio (Gabriele), Marinetti (Filippo Tommaso), Quasimodo (Salvatore), Ungaretti (Giuseppe)
Japanese: 5 Basho **6** Matsuo
medieval: 8 minstrel, trouvère **10** troubadour
Mexican: 3 Paz (Octavio)
Nicaraguan: 5 Darío (Rubén)
nonsense: 4 Lear (Edward) **7** Dr. Seuss
Norwegian: 8 Bjornson (Bjornstjerne), Welhaven (Johan) **9** Wergeland (Henrik)
Persian: 4 Omar (Khayyám), Rumi, Sadi **5** Attar, Hafez, Hafiz **11** Omar Khayyám
Roman: 4 Ovid **6** Horace, Vergil, Virgil **7** Juvenal, Martial, Statius **8** Catullus, Tibullus **9** Lucretius
Russian: 4 Blok (Aleksandr) **7** Brodsky (Joseph), Pushkin (Aleksandr), Yesenin (Sergey) **9** Akhmatova (Anna), Pasternak (Boris), Tsvetaeva (Marina) **10** Mandelstam (Osip), Mayakovsky (Vladimir) **11** Yevtushenko (Yevgeny)
Saint Lucian: 7 Walcott (Derek)
Scottish: 4 Hogg (James), Muir (Edwin) **5** Burns (Robert), Scott (Alexander, Walter) **6** Dunbar (William), Ramsay (Allan) **7** Thomson (James) **10** MacDiarmid (Hugh)
Spanish: 5 Lorca (Federico García) **7** Jiménez (Juan Ramón) **8** Figueroa (Francisco) **10** Aleixandre (Vicente) **11** García Lorca (Federico)
Swedish: 5 Sachs (Nelly) **9** Karlfeldt (Erik Axel)
Swiss: 5 Amiel (Henri Frédéric) **9** Spitteler (Carl)
Welsh: 6 Thomas (Dylan) **7** Aneurin, Watkins (Vernon)

poetic
5 lyric **6** dreamy **8** romantic **9** aesthetic, beautiful

foot: **4** iamb **6** dactyl **7** anapest, spondee, trochee **8** tribrach
meter: **6** iambic **7** pyrrhic **8** dactylic, spondaic, trochaic **9** anapestic **10** tribrachic
Muse: **5** Erato **6** Thalia **7** Euterpe **8** Calliope
rhythm: **7** prosody **8** scansion
word: **3** ere, e'er, thy **4** dost, doth, hast, hath, kine, ne'er, thee, thou, wert, wilt **5** thine **8** forsooth **9** beauteous

poet laureate
British: **3** Pye (Henry) **4** Rowe (Nicholas), Tate (Nahum) **5** Duffy (Carol Ann) **6** Austin (Alfred), Cibber (Colley), Dryden (John), Hughes (Ted), Jonson (Ben), Motion (Andrew) **7** Bridges (Robert), Southey (Robert) **8** Betjeman (John), Davenant (William), Day-Lewis (Cecil), Shadwell (Thomas), Tennyson (Alfred) **9** Masefield (John), Whitehead (William) **10** Wordsworth (William)
American: **4** Dove (Rita), Hall (Donald), Hass (Robert), Ryan (Kay) **5** Glück (Louise), Kumin (Maxine), Simic (Charles) **6** Kooser (Ted), Kunitz (Stanley), Levine (Philip), Merwin (W. S.), Pinsky (Robert), Strand (Mark), Warren (Robert Penn), Wilbur (Richard), Wright (Charles) **7** Brodsky (Joseph), Collins (Billy), Nemerov (Howard), Van Duyn (Mona) **9** Trethewey (Natasha)

poetry
5 verse

poetry term
4 iamb, mora, scan **5** arsis, canto, envoi, ictus, ionic, paeon, rhyme, stave, stich **6** dactyl, septet, sestet, stanza, thesis **7** anapest, cadence, elision, euphony, quintet, refrain, spondee, strophe, trochee **8** chiasmus, choriamb, cinquain, end rhyme, eye rhyme, quatrain, rhopalic **9** decameter, dithyramb, hexameter, near rhyme, octameter, terza rima **10** enjambment, fourteener, heptameter, ottava rima, rhyme royal **11** Alexandrine, antistrophe, heroic verse, rhyme scheme, shaped verse

poet's black
4 ebon

poet's contraction
3 e'en, e'er, o'er **4** ne'er

poet's preposition
3 ere

Pogo creator
5 Kelly (Walt)

poi source
4 taro

poignancy
6 pathos **7** emotion, sadness **9** sentiment

poignant
3 sad **4** keen **5** acute, sharp **6** biting, moving **7** painful, piquant, pointed, pungent **8** incisive, piercing, stirring, touching **9** affecting

point
3 aim, dot, end, jag, nib, tip **4** apex, crux, item, mark, show, site, spot, step, tine, turn, unit **5** motif, place, stage, theme, topic, trace, verge **6** detail, direct, intent, moment, motive, object, period, reason **7** decimal, essence, instant, meaning, purpose, subject **8** headland, juncture, locality, location, particle, position **9** direction **10** promontory **12** significance

pointed
5 acute, sharp **6** barbed, marked, signal **7** salient **8** incisive, striking **9** arresting, pertinent, prominent **11** conspicuous, penetrating
arch: **4** ogee

pointer
3 dog, tip **4** clue, hint **5** arrow, guide **6** gundog **9** indicator **10** suggestion

pointillist
6 Seurat (Georges), Signac (Paul) **8** Pissarro (Camille)

pointless
4 idle, vain **5** inane, silly **6** futile **7** useless **8** bootless **9** fruitless, senseless, worthless **10** immaterial, irrelevant, unavailing, unfruitful **11** meaningless **12** unprofitable

point of view
5 angle, slant **7** outlook **8** position, prospect **11** perspective

poise
4 ease, hang, tact **5** brace, grace, hover, skill **6** aplomb, steady **7** address, balance, bearing, dignity, support, suspend **8** carriage, elegance, serenity **9** assurance, composure, diplomacy, sangfroid **10** confidence, equanimity **11** delicatesse, equilibrium, savoir faire, tactfulness

poised
4 calm **6** at ease, serene, steady **7** assured, equable **8** composed, tranquil **9** collected, confident **13** self-possessed

poison
4 bane, upas **5** toxin, venom **6** toxoid **7** arsenic, botulin, cyanide, envenom **8** toxicant **9** botulinum, contagion **10** strychnine **13** contamination
arrow: **4** inée, upas **6** curare **7** ouabain
combining form: **3** tox **4** toxi, toxo **6** toxico

poisoning
food: **8** botulism
lead: **8** plumbism

poisonous
5 toxic **7** baneful, miasmal, nocuous, noxious **8** mephitic, venomous, virulent **9** pestilent **10** pernicious

poke
3 dig, hit, jab, jut, lag, pry **4** cuff, nose, prod, push, sock, stab, stir, urge **5** bulge, dally, delay, elbow, nudge, punch, snoop, tarry **6** dawdle,

meddle, pierce, putter, thrust **7** intrude, project, rummage **8** stick out **9** interfere, interject, interpose

poker
bet total: **3** pot
bullet: **3** ace
form: **4** stud
hand: **4** pair **5** flush **8** straight **9** full house **10** royal flush **13** straight flush
ploy: **5** bluff
stake: **4** ante
term: **3** see **4** call, draw, open **5** raise
token: **4** chip

poker-faced
5 blank, staid **7** deadpan, neutral **9** impassive **11** inscrutable, noncommital **12** inexpressive

pokey
3 can, jug, pen **4** brig, coop, jail, stir **5** clink **6** cooler, prison **7** slammer **9** calaboose

poky
4 slow **5** dingy, seedy **6** dreary, shabby **7** cramped, laggard, run-down **8** dilatory, plodding, sluggish

Poland
capital: **6** Warsaw
city: **4** Lódz **6** Gdansk, Kraków, Poznan **7** Wroclaw **8** Katowice, Szczecin
leader: **6** Walesa (Lech)
monetary unit: **5** zloty
mountain range: **10** Carpathian
national hero: **10** Kosciuszko (Thaddeus)
neighbor: **6** Russia **7** Belarus, Germany, Ukraine **8** Slovakia **9** Lithuania **13** Czech Republic
river: **4** Oder **7** Vistula
sea: **6** Baltic

Pola of film
5 Negri

polar
6 arctic **7** pivotal **8** opposite **9** diametric
hazard: **4** berg, floe **7** iceberg

pole
3 rod **4** punt, spar **5** anode, shaft, staff, stick, stilt **7** cathode
Indian: **5** totem
Scottish: **5** caber

polecat
5 fitch, skunk **6** ferret **7** fitchet

polemic
6 attack, debate, screed, tirade **7** defense **8** diatribe, harangue, jeremiad **9** assertion, philippic **11** controversy **12** denunciation

polemical
11 contentious, opinionated **12** disputatious **13** argumentative, controversial

Pole or Czech, e.g.
4 Slav

polestar
3 hub **5** focus, guide **10** focal point

police
3 law, man **4** fuzz, heat **6** govern, patrol **7** control, monitor **8** regulate
officer: **3** cop **4** bull, flic, fuzz, heat **5** bobby, garda **6** copper, lawman, peeler **7** John Law, sheriff, trooper **8** bluecoat, Dogberry, flatfoot, gendarme **9** constable, patrolman **11** carabiniere, carabinieri (plural)
vehicle: **7** cruiser **8** panda car, prowl car, squad car
weapon: **5** Taser

policy
4 plan **6** course, method, number **7** lottery, program **8** contract, practice **9** procedure **10** management

polio vaccine developer
4 Salk (Jonas) **5** Sabin (Albert)

polish
3 rub, wax **4** buff **5** glaze, glint, gloss, sheen, shine **6** luster, refine, smooth, soften **7** burnish, culture, enhance, improve, perfect, touch up **8** brighten **10** refinement

Polish
dumpling: **6** pirogi **7** pierogi
leader: **6** Walesa (Lech)
patriot: **9** Kosciusko (Thaddeus)
pope: **8** John Paul
sausage: **8** kielbasa, kielbasy
soldier: **7** Pulaski (Casimir)

polish off
5 eat up **6** devour **7** consume, put away **8** dispatch **9** dispose of

polite
5 civil **7** courtly, genteel, refined **8** cultured, mannerly, polished, well-bred **9** attentive, courteous **10** thoughtful **11** considerate

politeness
7 manners **8** civility, courtesy **10** refinement

politic
4 wise **5** suave **6** adroit, shrewd, smooth **7** prudent, tactful **8** tactical **9** advisable, expedient, judicious, sagacious **10** diplomatic

political
group: **4** bloc
meeting: **6** caucus
party: **3** GOP **4** Whig **10** Democratic, Republican
system: **7** fascism **9** communism, democracy, socialism

poll
4 cast, clip, crop, head, nape, pate **5** count, shear, tally, votes **6** noggin, record, sample,

survey **7** canvass, pollard **8** question **9** interview **10** canvassing
type: **4** exit **5** straw

pollack
4 fish **6** saithe **8** bluefish
family: **3** cod

pollard
3 top **4** crop, tree **7** cut back

pollen-producing organ
6 stamen

pollex
5 thumb

___ polloi
3 hoi

pollster
5 Roper (Elmo), Zogby (John) **6** Gallup (George), Harris (Lou)

pollute
4 foul, soil **5** dirty, spoil, stain, sully, taint **6** befoul, damage, debase, defile **7** corrupt, profane **10** adulterate **11** contaminate

pollution
4 smog **5** abuse **8** impurity **10** defilement

Pollux
10 Polydeuces
brother: **6** Castor
father: **4** Zeus
mother: **4** Leda
sister: **5** Helen **12** Clytemnestra

Pollyanna
8 optimist
author: **6** Porter (Eleanor)

Pollyannaish
6 blithe, cheery, upbeat **8** cheerful, positive **10** optimistic **11** rose-colored

pollywog
7 tadpole

Polonius
daughter: **7** Ophelia
hiding place: **5** arras
slayer: **6** Hamlet
son: **7** Laertes

poltergeist
5 ghost **6** spirit

poltroon
6 coward, craven, yellow **7** chicken, dastard, gutless **8** cowardly **9** dastardly **11** lily-livered

Polydorus
father: **5** Priam **6** Cadmus
mother: **6** Hecuba **8** Harmonia
slayer: **8** Achilles **10** Polymestor **11** Polymnestor

polygon
eight-sided: **7** octagon
five-sided: **8** pentagon
four-sided: **8** tetragon
nine-sided: **7** nonagon
seven-sided: **8** heptagon
six-sided: **7** hexagon
ten-sided: **7** decagon
three-sided: **8** triangle
twelve-sided: **9** dodecagon

Polyhymnia
4 Muse
invention: **4** lyre

polymer
5 amber, nylon **6** rubber, Teflon **7** shellac **8** Bakelite, silicone

Polynesian
5 Maori **6** Samoan, Tongan **8** Hawaiian, Tahitian **9** Marquesan
deity: **4** atua
figurine: **4** tiki
food: **3** poi

Polynices
brother: **8** Eteocles
father: **7** Oedipus
mother: **7** Jocasta
wife: **5** Argia **6** Argeia

polyp
5 tumor, zooid **6** growth **7** hydroid
freshwater: **5** hydra

Polyphemus
7 Cyclops
beloved: **7** Galatea
father: **8** Poseidon
victim: **4** Acis

pome
4 pear **5** apple, fruit

pommel
4 knob **6** handle

pomp
4 show **5** array **6** parade, ritual **7** display, fanfare, panoply **8** ceremony, grandeur, splendor **9** pageantry, vainglory **11** ostentation

pompano
4 fish **8** carangid **10** butterfish

Pompeii's volcano
8 Vesuvius

pompous
4 vain **5** proud, showy **6** lordly, ornate, stuffy **7** stuck-up **8** arrogant, boastful, inflated **9** bombastic, conceited, important, overblown **10** egocentric, flamboyant, pontifical **11** magisterial, pretentious **12** ostentatious, vainglorious

pond
4 mere, pool, tarn **5** stank **6** lagoon
growth: **4** scum **5** algae

ponder
4 mull, muse **5** study, think, weigh **6** reason **7** examine, perpend, reflect **8** appraise, cogitate, consider, evaluate, meditate, mull over, ruminate **9** reflect on, speculate **10** deliberate, think about **11** contemplate

ponderous
4 dull **5** heavy **6** clumsy, dreary, stodgy, wooden **7** labored, massive, weighty **8** cumbrous, lifeless, plodding, unwieldy **9** lumbering **10** burdensome, cumbersome, oppressive

poniard
6 dagger

Ponte Vecchio
city: **8** Florence
river: **4** Arno

Pontiac
5 chief
muscle car: **3** GTO
tribe: **6** Ottawa

pontiff
4 pope

pontifical
7 pompous **8** dogmatic **9** episcopal **11** magisterial

pontificate
5 orate **6** preach **7** declaim **8** bloviate **9** sermonize, speechify

pony
4 crib, trot **5** horse **6** bronco, cayuse **7** mustang
breed: **6** Exmoor **8** Shetland

pony up
3 pay **6** lay out, pay out **7** dish out, dole out, fork out **8** hand over, shell out, turn over **10** compensate, remunerate

pooch
3 dog, pup **4** tyke **5** hound, puppy **6** bowwow, canine

Pooh
creator: **5** Milne (A. A.)
friend: **5** Kanga **6** Eeyore, Piglet, Tigger
illustrator: **7** Shepard (Ernest)

pooh-bah
3 VIP **4** czar, king, star, tsar, tzar **5** baron, heavy, mogul **6** big gun, bigwig, honcho, kahuna, prince, worthy **7** big name, big shot, kingpin, magnate, notable **8** big wheel, eminence, luminary **9** big cheese, personage, superstar **11** heavyweight

pooh-pooh
5 scorn **6** deride **7** disdain, dismiss, sneer at **8** minimize, play down

pool
3 pot **4** mere, pond, tarn **5** chain, group, kitty, merge, trust **6** cartel, lagoon, laguna, puddle **7** combine, jackpot **9** syndicate
player: **7** Mosconi (Willie) **13** Minnesota Fats
stick: **3** cue
type: **4** gene
(see also **billiards**)

poop
4 dirt, info, tire **7** fatigue

poor
4 base, mean **5** broke, needy, scant, skimp, spare **6** humble, meager, meagre, paltry, scanty, skimpy, sparse **8** bankrupt, beggarly, indigent, strapped **9** destitute, insolvent, penniless, penurious **10** down-and-out, pauperized, stone-broke **11** impecunious, necessitous

poorly
3 ill, low **4** sick **5** badly **6** ailing, sickly, unwell **10** indisposed **11** imperfectly

pop
3 dad, dot, gun, hit, try **4** cola, dada, dart, ding, shot, slap, slog, sock, soda **5** catch, crack, daddy, drink, fling, shoot, whack, whirl **6** attack, bug out, effort, father, strike **7** assault, attempt, explode **8** backfire
brand: **3** Tab **4** Barq, Coke, Nehi **5** Barq's, Fanta, Moxie, Pepsi **6** Fresca, Sprite, Squirt **8** Dr. Pepper

pop artist
3 Max (Peter) **5** Blake (Peter), Johns (Jasper) **6** Warhol (Andy) **7** Hockney (David), Indiana (Robert) **9** Oldenburg (Claes), Wesselman (Tom) **10** Rosenquist (James) **12** Lichtenstein (Roy)
(see also **pop singer**)

pope
3 Leo **4** John, Mark, Paul, Pius **5** Caius, Conon, Donus, Felix, Gaius, Lando, Linus, Peter, Soter, Urban **6** Adrian, Agatho, Fabian, Julius, Lucius, Martin, Sixtus, Victor **7** Anterus, Clement, Damasus, Francis, Gregory, Hadrian, Hyginus, Marinus, Paschal, Pontian, Romanus, Sergius, Stephen, Zosimus **8** Agapetus, Anicetus, Benedict, Boniface, Calixtus, Eugenius, Eusebius, Formosis, Gelasius, Hilarius, Honorius, Innocent, John Paul, Liberius, Nicholas, Pelagius, Siricius, Theodore, Vigilius, Vitalian **9** Adeodatus, Alexander, Anacletus, Callistus, Celestine, Cornelius, Densdedit, Dionysius, Eutychian, Evaristus, Hormisdas, Marcellus, Miltiades, Severinus, Silverius, Silvester, Sisinnius, Sylvester, Symmachus, Valentine, Zacharias **10** Anastasius, Melchiades, Sabinianus, Simplicius, Zephyrinus **11** Christopher, Constantine, Eleutherius, Eutychianus, Marcellinus, Telesphorus
crown: **5** tiara

Pope poem
7 Dunciad (The) **10** Essay on Man (An) **13** Rape of the Lock (The)

Popeye
accessory: **4** pipe
baby: **7** Swee'Pea **8** Sweet Pea
creator: **5** Segar (E. C.)
energizer: **7** spinach
friend: **5** Wimpy **8** Olive Oyl
occupation: **6** sailor
rival: **5** Bluto

pop in
4 call **5** visit **6** drop by, look up, stop by **8** come over

popinjay
3 fop **4** toff **5** dandy, swell **7** peacock **8** macaroni

poplar
5 abele, alamo, aspen **6** balsam **9** tulip tree **10** cottonwood **12** balm of Gilead

Poppaea's husband
4 Nero

poppycock
3 rot **4** bosh, bunk, guff **5** bilge, hokum, hooey, tripe **6** bunkum **7** baloney, hogwash, rubbish **8** claptrap, malarkey, nonsense, tommyrot **10** balderdash

pop singer
3 Lee (Brenda), Ray (Johnnie), Vee (Bobby) **4** Anka (Paul), Cher, Cole (Nat "King"), Como (Perry), Dion (Celine), Enya, Gore (Lesley), Joel (Billy), Keys (Alicia), Page (Patti), Ross (Diana) **5** Abdul (Paula), Adele (Atkins), Aiken (Clay), Arden (Toni), Boone (Pat), Carey (Mariah), Cline (Patsy), Darin (Bobby), Lopez (Trini), Minaj (Nicki), Perry (Katy), Simon (Carly, Paul), Swift (Taylor), Valli (Frankie) **6** Avalon (Frankie), Bieber (Justin), Brewer (Teresa), Crosby (Bing), Fisher (Eddie), Martin (Dean, Tony), Mathis (Johnny), Midler (Bette), Murray (Billy), Pitney (Gene), Spears (Britney), Summer (Donna), Vallee (Rudy), Vinton (Bobby) **7** Bennett (Tony), Beyoncé (Knowles), Buffett (Jimmy), Diamond (Neil), Estefan (Gloria), Francis (Connie), Houston (Whitney), Jackson (Michael), Loggins (Kenny), Madonna (Ciccone), Rihanna (Fenty), Rodgers (Jimmie), Shakira (Mebarak), Simpson (Jessica), Sinatra (Frank), Warwick (Dionne) **8** Aguilera (Christina), Lady Gaga, Williams (Andy) **9** Streisand (Barbra)

pop star
4 idol

populace
5 plebs **6** masses, people, public **9** citizenry, commonage, commoners, plebeians **10** commonalty **11** commonality, rank and file, third estate

popular
5 cheap, noted **6** common, famous **7** admired, current, favored, general, leading **8** accepted, approved, favorite, ordinary **9** preferred, prevalent, prominent, well-known, well-liked **10** democratic, prevailing, widespread **11** inexpensive

populate
6 occupy, people, settle **7** inhabit

populous
6 packed **7** crowded, teeming **8** numerous **9** congested **13** multitudinous

porcelain
5 china
Chinese: **9** Lowestoft
English: **3** Bow **5** Derby, Spode **6** Minton **7** Aynsley, Belleek, Bristol, Chelsea **8** Caughley, Wedgwood
French: **6** Sèvres **7** Limoges
German: **7** Dresden, Meissen
ingredient: **6** kaolin
Italian: **6** Doccia
Japanese: **5** Imari

porch
4 deck, stoa **5** lanai, stoop **6** piazza **7** gallery, veranda **8** verandah

porcupine
8 hedgehog

pore
5 stoma **6** outlet **7** opening, orifice, reflect **8** meditate **10** interstice

pore over
4 read, scan **5** study **6** peruse **10** scrutinize

porgy
3 tai **4** fish, scup **6** sparid **8** menhaden

Porgy and Bess
composer: **8** Gershwin (George)
librettist: **7** Heyward (DuBose) **8** Gershwin (Ira)

Po River city
5 Milan, Padua, Turin **6** Milano, Padova, Torino, Verona **7** Brescia

pork
3 ham, pig **5** bacon, swine **8** sowbelly
cut: **3** ham **4** chop, jowl, loin, side **7** fatback **8** forefoot, hind foot, spare rib **9** picnic ham **10** Boston butt

pork-barreling
9 patronage

porker
3 hog, pig **5** swine (plural)
small: **5** shoat **6** piglet

pornographic
7 obscene

porous
5 leaky **6** spongy **8** pervious **9** permeable **10** penetrable

porpoise
5 whale **7** dolphin

porridge
4 mush 5 gruel, kasha 6 burgoo, cereal, congee, pablum, sowens 7 oatmeal, pabulum 8 flummery, loblolly 9 stirabout

port
4 hole, jack, left, wine 5 cover, haven 6 harbor, refuge 7 bearing, opening, retreat, shelter 8 larboard, left side 9 anchorage, harborage, roadstead, sanctuary 11 comportment
opposite: 9 starboard
(see also **seaport**)

portable
5 handy 6 mobile, wieldy

portal
4 door, gate 5 entry 7 doorway, gateway 8 approach, entrance, entryway

portcullis
4 gate 5 orgue 7 grating, lattice

portend
4 bode 5 augur 6 signal 7 betoken, predict, presage, promise, signify 8 forebode, forecast, foretell, indicate, prophesy 9 adumbrate, foretoken 10 foreshadow, vaticinate

portent
4 omen, sign 6 augury, boding 7 presage, prodigy 9 foretoken, sensation 10 foreboding, indication 11 premonition

portentous
5 grave 6 solemn 7 ominous, pompous, serious, weighty 8 inflated 9 marvelous, momentous, ponderous 10 prodigious

porter
5 hamal, stout 6 bearer, redcap, skycap 7 bellboy, bellhop, carrier 9 transport 10 doorkeeper

Porter novel
11 Ship of Fools

Porthos friend
5 Athos 6 Aramis 9 D'Artagnan

Portia
6 lawyer
husband: 6 Brutus 8 Bassanio
maid: 7 Nerissa

portico
4 stoa 9 colonnade

portion
3 cut, lot 4 bite, mete, part 5 dower, moira, piece, quota, share, slice 6 moiety, parcel 7 measure, quantum, segment 8 division
largest: 10 lion's share
unused: 8 leftover

portly
3 fat 5 bulky, heavy, large, obese, stout 6 fleshy 7 rotound, stately, weighty 8 imposing 9 corpulent 10 overweight

portmanteau
7 holdall 8 carryall, suitcase

portrait
4 bust 5 image 6 figure, statue 7 picture 8 painting 9 depiction

portray
4 draw, limn, play 5 enact, paint 6 depict, render 7 picture 8 describe 9 delineate, interpret, represent

portrayal
5 image 7 account, picture 8 likeness, painting 9 depiction 11 delineation, description, performance 12 illustration

Portugal
capital: 6 Lisbon
city: 5 Porto 6 Oporto 7 Amadora
former colony: 3 Goa 5 Macao 6 Angola, Brazil
former name: 9 Lusitania
island group: 6 Azores 7 Madeira
leader: 4 Luís 7 Salazar (Antonio de)
monetary unit: 4 euro
monetary unit, former: 6 escudo
neighbor: 5 Spain
peninsula: 6 Iberia 7 Iberian
river: 5 Tagus

pose
3 act, air, ask, set, sit 4 airs, fake, role, sham 5 feign, front, offer, place, stand, state, strut 6 affect, assume, pass as, stance 7 pass for, pass off, present, pretend, show off, suggest 8 attitude, pretense, set forth 9 mannerism 10 pretension 11 affectation

Poseidon
7 Neptune
brother: 4 Zeus 5 Hades, Pluto 7 Jupiter
consort: 4 Tyro 6 Medusa 7 Demeter
father: 6 Cronus
mother: 4 Rhea
offspring: 7 Pegasus
son: 5 Orion 6 Neleus, Pelias, Triton 7 Antaeus 10 Polyphemus
victim: 7 Laocoön
weapon: 7 trident
wife: 10 Amphitrite

poser
6 puzzle, riddle 7 problem 9 conundrum 11 brainteaser

poseur
4 fake 5 bluff, decoy, fraud, phony, pseud, quack 6 phoney 7 bluffer 8 deceiver, imposter 9 charlatan, hypocrite, pretender 10 mountebank 11 masquerader 12 impersonator

posh
4 chic, rich, tony 5 fancy, grand, smart, swank

7 elegant, stylish 9 exclusive, expensive, luxurious 11 fashionable, highfalutin, pretentious

posit
3 fix 5 offer 6 affirm, assert, assume 7 premise, present, presume, propose, suggest 9 postulate

position
3 job 4 rank, site, spot 5 locus, place, point, situs, stand, state 6 belief, locate, stance 7 emplace, footing, stature 8 attitude, capacity, location, prestige, situate, standing 10 standpoint
without work: 8 sinecure

positive
4 firm, real, sure 6 actual, useful 7 assured, certain, decided, factual, genuine, reality 8 absolute, complete, definite, forceful, outright 9 confident, doubtless, effective, favorable 10 beneficial, inarguable, optimistic, undeniable 11 categorical, irrefutable, unequivocal, unqualified 12 indisputable, unmistakable 13 incontestable
electrode: 5 anion

possess
3 own 4 have, hold, keep 5 carry 6 retain 7 acquire, control

possessed
3 mad 6 crazed, hooked 8 frenzied 9 bewitched

possession
7 control 8 property 9 occupancy, ownership 10 occupation

possessive
7 jealous 8 watchful 10 protective 11 proprietary

possibility
4 odds 6 chance 8 instance 9 potential 10 likelihood 11 contingency, feasibility

possible
6 doable, likely, viable 7 earthly 8 feasible 9 expedient, potential 10 imaginable, realizable 11 practicable

possibly
5 maybe 7 perhaps 8 by chance 9 perchance 11 conceivably

post
3 set 4 bitt, camp, mail, pole, ride, send, spot, stem, task 5 affix, after, hurry, newel, place, put up, score, stage, stake 6 advise, column, fill in, inform, notify, office, pillar 7 apprise, express, placard, publish, station 8 announce, denounce, position 9 advertise 10 assignment

post-crucifixion scene
5 pietà

poster
4 bill, sign 6 notice 7 affiche, placard 9 broadside, signboard 12 announcement 13 advertisement

posterior
4 back, butt, hind, rear, rump, seat, tail 5 after, fanny, later 6 behind, caudal, dorsal, heinie, hinder 7 ensuing, rear end, tail end 8 backside, buttocks, derriere, hindmost, rearward 9 following 10 subsequent

posterity
6 future 7 progeny 8 children 9 offspring 11 descendants

postgame summary
5 recap

posthaste
4 fast 6 at once, pronto 7 fleetly, quickly, rapidly, swiftly 8 promptly, speedily 11 immediately

Postimpressionist painter
6 Seurat (Georges) 7 Cezanne (Paul), Gauguin (Paul), Van Gogh (Vincent) 8 Pissarro (Camille), Rousseau (Henri)

postmortem
7 autopsy 8 necropsy

postpone
5 defer, delay, table 6 hold up, put off, shelve 7 hold off, lay over, suspend 8 hold over, prorogue

postulate
5 axiom, claim 6 assert, assume, demand, thesis 7 premise, suppose 10 assumption, hypothesis, presuppose 11 hypothesize, presumption, supposition

posture
4 mode, pose 5 state 6 affect, assume, manner, stance, status 7 bearing, outlook 8 attitude, carriage, position 9 condition, situation 12 attitudinize

posy
5 bloom 6 flower 7 blossom, bouquet, corsage, nosegay 9 sentiment

pot
3 bet, pan, wad 4 ante, hemp, olla, weed 5 grass, kitty, stake, wager 6 boodle, bundle, pipkin 7 marmite 8 cannabis 9 marijuana

potable
5 clean, drink, fresh 6 liquid, liquor 8 beverage 9 drinkable

Potala Palace home
5 Lhasa, Tibet

potassium ore
7 sylvite

potato
3 yam 4 spud 5 tater
bud: 3 eye

pot-au-____
3 feu 5 creme

potbelly
3 gut **5** stove **6** paunch **9** bay window, spare tire **11** corporation

Potemkin mutiny site
6 Odessa

potency
3 pep **5** force, might, power, vigor **6** energy, muscle **8** strength **9** influence, puissance **10** capability **13** effectiveness

potent
4 rich **6** mighty, robust, strong, virile **7** dynamic **8** forceful, forcible, powerful **9** effective **10** persuasive **11** influential

potential
6 latent, likely **7** ability, promise **8** capacity, possible **9** plausible, promising **10** imaginable **11** conceivable, possibility

pother
3 ado **4** flap, fret, fuss, stir, to-do **5** furor, whirl, worry **6** bustle, flurry, furore, hassle, hubbub, tumult, uproar **7** fluster, turmoil **9** agitation, annoyance, commotion, confusion

potion
6 liquid **7** mixture, philter, philtre **8** medicine **10** concoction

Potiphar's slave
6 Joseph

Potiphera
daughter: **7** Asenath
son-in-law: **6** Joseph

Potok, Chaim
character: **3** Lev (Asher)
novel: **6** Chosen (The) **16** My Name Is Asher Lev

potpourri
4 olio **5** blend **6** medley, sachet **7** grab bag, mélange, variety **8** mishmash, pastiche **10** assortment, collection, hodgepodge, hotchpotch, miscellany, salmagundi **11** gallimaufry

potshot
3 cut, dig **4** barb, gibe, jibe **5** crack, shoot, swipe **6** attack, insult **9** criticism

potter
see **putter**

Potter character
5 Mopsy, Mr. Tod **6** Flopsy, Jemima (Puddle-duck) **10** Cotton-tail, Hunca Munca **11** Peter Rabbit **12** Jeremy Fisher

potter's field
8 cemetery, God's acre **9** graveyard

pottery
4 raku **5** delft, Imari **7** redware **8** ceramics, clayware, slipware **10** lusterware, terra-cotta, yellowware **11** earthenware

pouch
3 bag, sac **4** sack **5** bulge, bursa, burse **6** pocket **7** saccule **8** sacculus

pouf
5 quilt **7** ottoman **9** comforter

poultry
4 fowl
type: **4** duck, swan **5** goose, quail **6** grouse, pigeon, turkey **7** chicken, ostrich, peacock **8** pheasant **9** partridge

pounce
5 seize, swoop, talon **6** attack, powder **7** assault, stencil

pound
4 bang, bash, beat, slam, slug, sock **5** drive, money, smite, stamp, throb, thump, tramp **6** batter, buffet, hammer, pummel, strike, thrash, wallop **7** belabor, impress, pulsate **9** enclosure

Pound of poetry
4 Ezra
work: **6** Cantos (The)

poupée
4 doll

pour
4 flow, gush, rain, rill, rush, teem **5** flood, issue, skink, spate, surge, swarm **6** decant, deluge, drench, sluice, spring, stream **7** cascade, torrent **8** inundate, overflow

pourboire
3 tip **7** cumshaw **8** gratuity **9** baksheesh

pout
3 pet **4** fish, moue, sulk **5** grump **8** protrude **10** expression, protrusion

poverty
4 need, want **6** dearth, penury **7** beggary, paucity **8** hardship, poorness, scarcity, shortage **9** indigence, neediness, pauperism, privation **10** mendicancy, scarceness **11** destitution **13** pennilessness

POW camp
6 stalag

powder
4 bray, dust, talc **5** crush **6** talcum **8** sprinkle **9** comminute, pulverize, triturate **10** besprinkle

power
3 vis **4** sway **5** force, might, sinew, steam, vigor, vires (plural) **6** energy, muscle **7** command, ability, control, potency, voltage **8** dominion, dynamism, imperium, strength **9** authority, influence, privilege, puissance, strong arm **10** ascendancy, domination **11** prerogative, sovereignty, superiority **12** jurisdiction, potentiality
combining form: **5** dynam **6** dynamo
source: **4** fuel
unit: **4** watt

powerful
5 great 6 mighty, potent, strong 7 dynamic 8 dominant, puissant, vigorous 9 energetic, strenuous 10 convincing, impressive, invincible, persuasive

powerless
4 weak 5 inert 6 feeble, unable 7 passive 8 impotent 9 incapable 11 incompetent, ineffective

powwow
4 chat, talk 6 confab, confer, huddle, parley 7 discuss, meeting 8 ceremony 9 gathering 10 discussion 11 confabulate, get-together

practicable
5 utile 6 doable, likely, usable, useful 8 feasible, possible 9 operative 10 functional

practical
5 handy, utile 6 active, useful, versed, viable 7 applied, skilled, trained, virtual 8 sensible 9 pragmatic, realistic 10 functional 11 down-to-earth, experienced 12 businesslike

practically
5 about 6 all but, almost, near to, nearly 7 close to 8 in effect 9 in essence, just about

practice
3 ply, use, way 4 form, mode, wont 5 drill, habit, usage 6 custom, manner, method, repeat, system, tryout, warm up 7 perform, process, workout 8 drilling, engage in, exercise, habitude, rehearse 9 procedure, rehearsal 10 convention
boxing: 4 spar
piece: 5 étude

PR agent
5 flack

pragmatic
7 factual, logical 8 rational 9 practical, realistic 11 down-to-earth

prairie
4 veld 5 pampa, plain, veldt 6 pampas 7 plateau 9 grassland

prairie chicken
6 grouse

prairie wolf
6 coyote

praise
4 hail, hymn, laud, puff 5 bravo, cry up, exalt, extol, honor, kudos 6 belaud, kudize 7 acclaim, adulate, applaud, commend, flatter, glorify, hosanna, magnify, ovation, plaudit, puffery 8 accolade, applause, approval, citation, encomium, eulogize, flattery 9 celebrate, laudation, panegyric, recommend 10 aggrandize, compliment, panegyrize 11 acclamation 12 commendation
poem: 3 ode 5 paean

praiseworthy
8 laudable 9 admirable, deserving, estimable 11 commendable, meritorious

prance
4 step 5 mince, strut 6 sashay, spring 8 cakewalk

prank
3 gag 4 deck, dido, lark, whim 5 adorn, antic, caper, fancy, spiff, sport, trick 6 doll up, frolic, gambol, levity, shavie, vagary, whimsy 7 caprice, deck out, doll out, dress up, garnish, rollick, spiff up 8 beautify, decorate, escapade, ornament, spruce up 9 embellish, frivolity, horseplay, smarten up 10 shenanigan, tomfoolery 11 monkeyshine

prankster
3 wag 5 cutup, joker

prate
3 gab, jaw, yak 4 blab, chat, go on 5 run on 6 babble, gabble, jabber 7 blabber, blather, chatter 9 yakety-yak

prater
5 yenta 6 gossip, magpie 10 chatterbox 12 blabbermouth

pratfall
6 mishap, tumble 7 blunder, stumble 11 humiliation

prattle
3 gab 4 blab 5 prate 6 babble, gabble, jabber, natter 7 blabber, chatter

prawn
6 shrimp 11 langoustine
French: 8 crevette

praxis
5 habit 6 action, custom, manner 7 conduct 8 exercise, habitude, practice

Praxiteles statue
5 Satyr 6 Hermes 9 Aphrodite

pray
3 ask, beg 5 plead 6 appeal 7 beseech, entreat, implore, request 8 petition 10 supplicate

prayer
4 plea, suit 6 appeal, litany, orison 7 angelus, begging, worship 8 blessing, devotion, entreaty, petition, pleading, rogation 9 adoration 11 application, imploration, imprecation 12 supplication
beads: 6 rosary
ending: 4 amen
for the dead: 7 requiem
Jewish: 7 kaddish, kiddush
period: 6 novena 7 triduum
shawl: 7 tallith

prayer book
6 missal, siddur 8 breviary

prayerful
4 holy 5 godly, pious 6 devout 7 earnest, sincere

preach
4 urge **6** exhort **7** address, deliver, lecture **8** admonish, advocate, moralize **9** sermonize **10** evangelize

preacher
5 padre **6** cleric, divine, parson, pastor **8** chaplain, clerical, minister, reverend **9** churchman, clergyman **10** evangelist, sermonizer **12** ecclesiastic

preaching friar
9 Dominican

preachy
4 smug **7** donnish **8** didactic, pedantic, sermonic, unctuous **9** homiletic, hortative, pedagogic, pietistic **10** moralizing **11** exhortative, sermonizing **13** sanctimonious, self-righteous

preamble
5 intro, proem **8** exordium, foreword, overture, prologue **12** introduction

precarious
4 iffy **5** dicey, risky, shaky **6** chancy, touchy, tricky, unsafe **7** dubious **8** delicate, doubtful, insecure, ticklish, unstable **9** dangerous, hazardous, sensitive, uncertain **10** unreliable

precaution
4 care **8** prudence **9** foresight, insurance, provision, safeguard **11** forethought

precede
4 lead, rank **5** usher **6** forego, herald **7** forerun, outrank, surpass **8** announce, antedate, go before **9** introduce

precedence
5 order **8** priority **9** seniority **10** right-of-way

precedent
4 past, rule **5** model, prior **6** former **7** earlier, example **8** anterior **9** foregoing **10** convention

preceding
4 past **5** prior **6** before, former **7** ahead of, prior to **8** anterior, hitherto **9** erstwhile **10** heretofore **11** in advance of
prefix: **4** ante

precept
3 law **4** rule **5** axiom, edict, order, tenet **6** behest, decree **7** bidding, command **8** doctrine **9** principle **10** injunction, regulation **11** fundamental

preceptive
8 didactic

preceptor
4 head **5** tutor **7** teacher **9** principal **10** headmaster

precinct
4 area **6** domain, region, sector, sphere **7** quarter, section **8** district, division, township **9** bailiwick, enclosure

precious
3 pet **4** cute, dear, nice, rare, rich, very **5** fussy, great, loved, showy **6** adored, choice, costly, la-di-da, prized **7** beloved, darling **8** affected, esteemed, favorite, valuable **9** cherished, exquisite, extremely, priceless **10** invaluable

precipice
5 brink, cliff **8** overhang

precipitancy
4 rush **5** haste, hurry **9** hastiness **10** abruptness, suddenness **11** hurriedness

precipitate
4 fall, hurl **5** hasty, sheer, steep, throw **6** abrupt, madcap, sudden, upshot **7** bring on, deposit, grounds, hurried, outcome, product **8** condense, headlong, sediment, separate **9** breakneck, impatient **10** unexpected, unforeseen **11** consequence

precipitation
4 hail, rain, snow **5** sleet **7** deposit **8** sediment

precipitous
4 rash **5** hasty, sheer, steep **6** abrupt, sudden **7** hurried, rushing **8** headlong, heedless, plunging **9** breakneck **13** perpendicular

précis
6 digest, survey **7** summary **8** abstract, overview, syllabus **10** abridgment, compendium **11** abridgement **12** condensation

precise
4 nice **5** exact, fixed, right **6** narrow, strict **7** correct, limited **8** accurate, clear-cut, definite, rigorous, specific **9** clocklike, stringent **10** particular

precisely
4 just **5** right **6** to a T **7** exactly **8** on the dot, strictly

precision
4 care **5** rigor **6** nicety **8** accuracy **9** exactness **10** exactitude, refinement **11** correctness

preclude
5 avert, deter **7** forfend, obviate, prevent, rule out **8** prohibit, stave off **9** forestall

precocious
5 smart **6** brainy, bright, mature **7** forward **8** advanced

precondition
4 must, need **7** proviso **9** essential, necessity, provision, requisite **10** sine qua non **11** requirement, stipulation

precursor
6 herald **8** ancestor, forebear **9** harbinger, indicator, prototype **10** antecedent, forerunner

predator
6 hunter, preyer, raptor **7** stalker **8** devourer **9** destroyer **10** bird of prey

predatory
6 greedy **8** ravening, ravenous **9** pillaging, rapacious **10** plundering **12** exploitative

predecessor
8 ancestor, forebear **9** precursor, prototype **10** antecedent, forerunner

predicament
3 fix, jam **4** bind, hole, spot **5** pinch, state **6** corner, muddle, pickle, plight, puzzle, scrape, strait **7** dilemma, impasse, trouble **8** hardship, nuisance, quagmire **9** condition, situation **10** difficulty

predicate
4 aver, avow, base, rest **5** found, imply **6** affirm, assert, avouch **7** declare, profess **9** establish

predict
5 augur, guess, infer **6** expect **7** forbode, foresee, portend, surmise **8** announce, conclude, forebode, forecast, foretell, indicate, prophesy, soothsay **10** conjecture, vaticinate **13** prognosticate

prediction
6 augury **8** forecast, prophecy **9** prognosis **10** expectancy **11** expectation

predilection
4 bent, bias **5** fancy, taste **6** liking **7** leaning **8** fondness, penchant, tendency **9** inclining **10** partiality, proclivity, propensity **11** inclination

predispose
4 bend, bias, tend, sway **5** prime **6** affect **7** incline **9** influence

predisposed
5 prone, ready **6** biased **7** partial, willing **8** inclined **11** susceptible

predisposition
4 bent, bias **7** leaning **8** penchant, tendency **9** inclining **10** partiality, proclivity, propensity **11** inclination

predominant
3 top **4** main **5** chief, major **6** master, ruling **7** capital, general, leading, primary, supreme **8** reigning, superior **9** number one, paramount, principal, sovereign **10** prevailing **11** outstanding

predominate
4 rule **5** reign **6** govern, master **7** command, control, prevail **8** outweigh

preeminence
6 renown **7** primacy **8** dominion, prestige **9** supremacy **10** ascendancy, domination, excellence, importance **11** distinction, superiority

preeminent
3 top **4** main **5** chief, first **7** capital, stellar, supreme **8** dominant, foremost, peerless, towering, ultimate **9** matchless, number-one, paramount, principal, unrivaled **10** surpassing, unrivalled **11** outstanding, unmatchable **12** incomparable, transcendent
prefix: 4 arch

preempt
4 bump, take **5** annex, seize, usurp **6** assume **7** acquire, replace **8** arrogate **9** forestall **10** confiscate, substitute **11** appropriate, expropriate

preen
5 gloat, groom, pride, primp, prink, swell **6** smooth

preface
4 lead, open **5** begin, intro, proem, usher **6** herald **8** exordium, foreword, overture, preamble, prologue **9** introduce **11** preliminary **12** introduction

prefatory
7 opening **8** proemial **12** introductory

prefect
7 head boy, monitor **8** head girl **10** magistrate

prefer
5 elect, favor **6** choose, opt for, select **7** advance, elevate, promote, upgrade

preferable
5 finer **6** better **8** superior, worthier

preference
4 pick **5** taste **6** choice, option **8** druthers, election, priority **9** advantage, elevation, promotion, selection, upgrading **10** favoritism, partiality

prefigure
4 hint **7** foresee **8** indicate **9** adumbrate **10** foreshadow

pregnancy
9 gestation, gravidity

pregnant
4 full, rich **5** heavy **6** gravid, parous **7** teeming, weighty **8** eloquent, enceinte, profound **9** expectant, expecting, gestating, inventive, momentous, with child **10** expressive, meaningful, parturient **11** significant

prehensile
8 grasping

prejudice
3 mar **4** bias, harm, hurt, sway **5** color, favor **6** damage, injure, injury, racism, sexism **7** bigotry, leaning **8** aversion **9** antipathy, hostility, influence **10** partiality **11** intolerance **12** one-sidedness

prejudicial
6 biased **7** bigoted **8** damaging **9** injurious **11** deleterious, detrimental

prelate
5 abbot **6** bishop **7** primate **8** cardinal, diocesan **9** patriarch **10** archbishop **12** ecclesiastic

preliminary
4 heat **5** basic, match, trial **7** initial, opening **8** proemial **9** beginning **10** qualifying **11** fundamental **12** introductory

prelude
5 intro, proem **7** opening **8** exordium, foreword, overture, prologue **12** introduction, prolegomenon

premature
5 early **8** untimely **10** beforehand

pre-meal prayer
5 grace

premeditated
5 set up **7** planned, studied, willful **8** designed, intended **9** conscious **10** calculated, considered, deliberate, thought-out **11** intentional

premier
4 head, main **5** chief, first **7** leading, primary **8** earliest, foremost, original **9** principal **13** prime minister

premiere
5 debut **7** opening **8** earliest, original **9** beginning **10** first night

Preminger of the movies
4 Otto

premise
4 base **5** posit **6** assume, thesis **8** building, property, set forth **9** postulate **10** assumption **11** postulation, proposition, supposition

premium
4 agio **5** bonus, extra, prize **6** reward **8** dividend, superior **9** excellent **10** recompense **11** exceptional

premonition
4 omen **9** misgiving, suspicion **10** foreboding **11** forewarning **12** apprehension, presentiment

prenatal
5 fetal

preoccupied
4 deep, lost, rapt **6** absent, intent **7** engaged, faraway, worried **8** absorbed, immersed **9** concerned, engrossed, wrapped up **10** abstracted, distracted **11** inattentive **12** absentminded

prep
5 basic, coach, drill, equip, groom, prime, ready, train, trial **6** warm-up **8** get ready **11** preliminary **12** introductory

preparation
4 base, plan **5** study **7** fitness, measure **8** compound, medicine, training **9** alertness, foresight, readiness **10** background, concoction

preparatory
5 basic **11** preliminary, rudimentary **12** introductory

prepare
3 fit, fix, set **4** gird **5** draft, groom, prime, ready, train **6** draw up, make up, outfit **7** arrange, fortify, furnish **9** formulate
for a bout: 4 spar
to shoot: 3 aim

prepared
3 set **4** up on **5** fixed, ready **6** primed **7** treated **9** processed

preponderance
4 bulk **8** dominion, majority, main part **9** ascendant, dominance, supremacy **10** ascendancy, domination **11** superiority

preponderant
7 supreme **8** dominant, superior **9** paramount **10** prevailing

preponderate
4 rule **5** reign **6** exceed **7** command, dictate, outrank, prevail **8** dominate, outweigh

preposition
3 for, off **4** down, from, into, like, near, onto, over, past, upon, with **5** about, above, after, along, among, below, since, under, until **6** across, around, before, behind, beside, during, except, inside, toward, within **7** against, beneath, between, outside, through, without

prepossess
4 bias, sway **5** favor **6** absorb, engage, occupy **7** engross, immerse, involve **9** influence

prepossessing
7 likable **9** appealing **10** attractive

preposterous
4 wild **5** crazy, wacky **6** absurd, insane **7** asinine, foolish, idiotic **9** fantastic, laughable, senseless **10** irrational, ridiculous **11** harebrained **12** unreasonable

prerequisite
4 must, need **5** vital **8** required **9** condition, essential, mandatory, necessary, necessity **10** imperative, sine qua non **11** requirement **13** indispensable

prerogative
5 power, right **8** appanage, immunity **9** authority, exemption, privilege **10** birthright, perquisite

presage
4 bode, omen, warn **5** augur, sense **6** augury, boding, herald, intuit **7** portend, portent, predict, promise, warning **8** announce, forebode, forecast, foretell, forewarn, indicate, prophesy, soothsay **9** foretoken, harbinger, intuition, misgiving **10** foreboding, foreshadow, prediction, prognostic, vaticinate

presbyter
5 elder **6** priest

prescience
9 foresight **12** anticipation, clairvoyance **13** foreknowledge

prescribe
3 fix, set **4** rule **5** guide, order **6** assign, choose, decide, decree, define, direct, impose, ordain, select **7** dictate, lay down, pick out, require, specify **9** designate, determine, stipulate

prescribed amount
4 dose

prescript
3 law **4** rule **5** edict, order **6** decree **10** regulation

prescription
3 med **4** drug, rule **5** claim, right, title **6** custom, remedy **8** medicine **9** direction **10** medication

presence
3 air **4** look, mien **5** poise **6** aspect, spirit **7** address, bearing **8** carriage, demeanor **9** composure

present
3 act, aim, now **4** boon, gift, give, here, pose, show **5** award, bring, favor, offer, point, stage, tense, today **6** at hand, bestow, confer, convey, direct, donate, extend, in view, modern, render, submit, tender **7** hand out, largess, perform, proffer **8** existing, nominate **9** introduce **12** contemporary

presentable
3 fit **6** decent, proper **8** becoming **9** befitting **10** acceptable **11** appropriate **12** satisfactory

present-day
6 living, recent **7** current, ongoing, popular, topical **8** contempo, existent, existing, pressing, up-to-date **9** prevalent, surviving **10** prevailing **12** contemporary

presently
3 now **4** anon, soon **5** today **6** in time, one day **7** by and by **9** forthwith, these days **10** before long

preservation
4 care **6** saving, shield **7** defense, keeping **8** pickling **10** husbanding, protection **11** conservancy, maintenance, safekeeping

preserve
3 can, jam **4** salt, save **5** jelly, put up **6** embalm, ensile, keep up, pickle **7** protect, shelter, sustain **8** keep safe, maintain **9** confiture

preside
3 run **4** head, lead **5** chair **6** direct, handle, manage **7** conduct, control, operate, oversee **8** moderate **9** officiate

president, U. S.
3 Abe, DDE, FDR, HST, Ike, JFK, LBJ, RMN **4** Bush (George, George W.), Ford (Gerald R.), Polk (James K.), Taft (William H.) **5** Adams (John, John Quincy), Grant (Ulysses S.), Hayes (Rutherford B.), Nixon (Richard M.), Obama (Barack), Tyler (John) **6** Arthur (Chester A.), Carter (Jimmy), Hoover (Herbert), Monroe (James), Pierce (Franklin), Reagan (Ronald), Taylor (Zachary), Truman (Harry S.), Wilson (Woodrow) **7** Clinton (Bill), Harding (Warren), Jackson (Andrew), Johnson (Andrew, Lyndon), Kennedy (John F.), Lincoln (Abraham), Madison (James) **8** Buchanan (James), Coolidge (Calvin), Fillmore (Millard), Garfield (James), Harrison (Benjamin, William Henry), McKinley (William), Van Buren (Martin) **9** Cleveland (Grover), Jefferson (Thomas), Roosevelt (Franklin D., Theodore) **10** Eisenhower (Dwight D.), Washington (George)
on a fiver: **3** Abe (Lincoln) **7** Lincoln (Abe, Abraham)
on a penny: **3** Abe (Lincoln) **7** Lincoln (Abe, Abraham)
on a sawbuck: **8** Hamilton (Alexander)

presidential nominee
4 Dole (Robert J.), Gore (Albert) **5** Dewey (Thomas), Kerry (John) **6** McCain (John) **7** Dukakis (Michael), Mondale (Walter) **8** Humphrey (Hubert), McGovern (George) **9** Goldwater (Barry), Stevenson (Adlai)

presidio
4 fort **7** bastion, citadel **8** fastness, fortress, garrison **10** stronghold **13** fortification

Presley, Elvis
4 King (The) **6** Pelvis (The)
daughter: **9** Lisa Marie
manager: **6** Parker (Col. Tom)
middle name: **4** Aron **5** Aaron
property: **9** Graceland
wife: **9** Priscilla

press
3 hug, jam, ram **4** cram, iron, mass, pack, pile, push, rush, urge **5** clasp, crowd, crush, drive, force, horde, hurry, media, shove **6** demand, hustle, insist, jostle, propel, squash, stress, throng, thrust **7** beseech, entreat, imprint, printer, squeeze **9** constrain, influence, multitude

press agent
5 flack

pressing
5 acute, vital **6** urgent **7** crucial, earnest, exigent, serious **8** critical **9** immediate, important, insistent **10** compelling, imperative

pressure
4 push, rush **5** drive, impel **6** burden, coerce, strain, stress **7** tension **10** constraint
combining form: 5 piezo
instrument: 9 barometer
unit: 3 bar, psi **6** pascal **7** kilobar

prestige
4 fame, rank, sway **5** power **6** cachet, credit, esteem, regard, renown, repute, status, weight **7** dignity, stature **8** eminence, position, standing **9** authority, influence **10** importance, prominence **11** consequence, distinction

prestigious
5 famed, great **6** famous **7** eminent, honored, notable **8** esteemed, renowned **9** prominent, respected **10** celebrated **11** influential **13** distinguished

presto
4 fast **7** hastily, quickly, rapidly **8** suddenly **9** posthaste **11** immediately

presumably
6 likely, surely **8** probably **9** doubtless

presume
4 dare **5** guess, imply, infer, think, trust **6** expect, gather, impose, reason **7** believe, intrude, suppose, surmise, venture **8** infringe **9** postulate **10** conjecture

presumption
4 gall **5** brass, cheek, nerve **6** belief, daring, ground, reason, thesis **7** conceit **8** audacity, chutzpah, evidence, rudeness **9** arrogance, brashness, inference, postulate **10** confidence, effrontery

presumptuous
4 bold, smug **5** brash, fresh, pushy **6** cheeky, uppity **7** forward **8** arrogant **9** audacious, confident **11** overweening, self-assured

presuppose
5 posit **6** assume, expect **7** imagine, require, surmise **9** postulate

pretend
3 act **4** fake, pose, sham **5** bluff, claim, false, feign, guess, put on **6** affect, assume, delude, invent **7** deceive, imitate, mislead, playact, profess, purport, suppose, surmise **8** simulate **9** imaginary **11** counterfeit, make-believe

pretender
4 fake, sham **5** actor, faker, fraud, phony **6** humbug **8** claimant, impostor **9** hypocrite

pretense
3 act, air **4** face, fake, mask, pose, sham **5** claim, cloak, cover, front, guise **6** deceit, facade, humbug **7** charade, fiction **8** disguise **9** deception, false show, imposture **10** masquerade, simulation **11** affectation, make-believe, ostentation

pretension
5 claim, right **6** vanity **8** ambition **10** allegation, aspiration **11** affectation

pretentious
4 arty **5** artsy, lofty, put-on, showy **6** chichi, la-de-da, la-di-da, pseudo, too-too **7** pompous, stilted **8** affected, inflated, lah-de-dah, lah-di-dah, puffed up, snobbish, specious **9** bombastic, conceited, grandiose, lah-dee-dah, overblown **10** euphuistic, hoity-toity, rhetorical **11** highfalutin **12** high-sounding, magniloquent, vainglorious

preternatural
7 psychic, unusual **8** abnormal, atypical **9** anomalous, unearthly, untypical **10** mysterious **12** inexplicable, supernatural **13** extraordinary

pretext
4 mask, ploy **5** alibi, cloak, cover, front, guise **6** device, excuse **7** apology **10** subterfuge

pretty
4 cute, fair **5** bonny, quite **6** comely, fairly, lovely, rather, sort of **7** cunning **8** graceful, pleasant, pleasing, somewhat **9** appealing, beautiful **10** attractive, more or less **11** good-looking **12** considerable

Pretty Woman star
4 Gere (Richard)

prevail
3 win **4** beat, rule **5** reign **6** master **7** conquer, impress, persist, triumph **8** convince, dominate, domineer, overcome, override, persuade **9** influence

prevalent
4 rife **6** ruling **7** favored, popular, regnant **8** accepted, dominant, superior **9** ascendant, customary, paramount, sovereign **10** accustomed, widespread

prevaricate
3 fib, lie **5** avoid, evade **6** palter **7** confuse, deceive, distort, falsify, quibble **10** equivocate **12** misrepresent

prevarication
3 fib, lie **4** tale **5** lying, story **6** canard, deceit **7** falsity **9** deception, falsehood

prevent
3 bar, dam **4** balk, foil, ward **5** avert, avoid, block, check, debar, deter, estop **6** arrest, baffle, forbid, hinder, impede, thwart **7** forfend, head off, inhibit, obviate **8** obstruct, preclude, prohibit, stave off **9** forestall, frustrate, interdict **10** anticipate

Previn of music
5 André

previous
4 fore, past **5** early, prior **6** before, former **7** earlier, onetime **8** anterior **9** erstwhile, foregoing, in advance **10** antecedent, beforehand

previously
4 once 5 afore, ahead 6 before 7 already, earlier 8 formerly 9 erstwhile 10 heretofore

prewar
10 antebellum

prey
4 feed, game, mark 5 chase 6 quarry, target, victim 8 casualty, distress

Priam
daughter: 4 Ilia 6 Creusa 8 Polyxena 9 Cassandra
father: 8 Laomedon
grandfather: 4 Ilus
kingdom: 4 Troy 5 Ilium
slayer: 7 Pyrrhus 11 Neoptolemus
son: 5 Paris 6 Hector, Lycaon 7 Helenus, Troilus 9 Deiphobus, Polydorus
wife: 6 Arisbe, Hecuba

Priapus
father: 7 Bacchus 8 Dionysus
mother: 5 Venus 9 Aphrodite

price
3 fee, fix, tab 4 cost, fare, rate, toll 6 amount, assess, charge, figure, outlay, reward, tariff 7 expense, payment 8 appraise

priceless
4 rare, rich 5 droll, funny, witty 6 absurd, costly, prized, valued 7 amusing 8 precious, valuable 9 cherished, treasured 10 invaluable

pricey
4 dear 5 steep 6 costly 9 expensive

prick
3 jab 4 goad, mark, prod, spur, urge 5 egg on, point, sting, thorn 6 affect, excite, exhort, pierce, prompt 7 pinhole 8 puncture 9 perforate

prickly
5 burry, sharp, spiny 6 briary, thorny, tetchy, tingly, touchy, trying 7 brambly, waspish 8 annoying, nettling, snappish, stinging 9 difficult, fractious, irritable, vexatious 10 bothersome, irritating, nettlesome 11 troublesome

pride
3 ego, top 4 best, brag, pack, pick 5 boast, cream, elite, exult, group, preen, prime, prize, vaunt 6 choice, egoism, hubris, vanity 7 conceit, delight, elation, dignity, disdain, egotism 8 smugness, treasure 9 arrogance, cockiness, vainglory 10 self-esteem, self-regard 11 self-respect 12 congratulate

Pride and Prejudice author
6 Austen (Jane)

prideful
6 elated 7 haughty 8 exultant 10 disdainful

prier
5 snoop 7 meddler 8 busybody, quidnunc 9 buttinsky

priest
5 padre 6 cleric, divine, father, rector 8 chaplain 9 clergyman, presbyter
ancient Roman: 6 flamen 8 pontifex
Biblical: 3 Eli
Buddhist: 4 lama
Celtic: 5 druid
Ethiopian: 3 ras
French: 4 abbé, curé
Muslim: 4 imam
prop: 4 bell, book 6 candle
tribal: 6 shaman

priestly
8 clerical, hieratic 10 sacerdotal
vestment: 3 alb 4 cope

prig
5 prude, thief 6 pedant 8 bluenose 9 Mrs. Grundy 10 goody-goody

priggish
5 fussy 6 stuffy 7 genteel, pompous, prudish 8 affected, pedantic 11 puritanical, straitlaced

prim
4 neat, nice, snug, tidy, trig 5 stiff 6 formal, prissy, proper, strict, stuffy, wooden 7 correct, genteel, orderly, precise, prudish 8 decorous, priggish 11 straitlaced

prima donna
4 diva, snob, star 7 artiste 9 chanteuse 10 narcissist 11 leading lady

prima facie
4 true 5 valid 8 apparent 11 self-evident

primal
5 basic 6 age-old 7 ancient, premier 8 cardinal, original 9 atavistic, paramount, primitive 10 preeminent 11 prehistoric

primary
4 main 5 basal, basic, chief, first 6 direct 7 initial, pioneer, radical 8 cardinal, earliest, original 9 elemental, essential, firsthand, immediate, number-one, paramount, principal 10 aboriginal, underlying 11 fundamental, rudimentary 12 foundational, introductory
combining form: 4 prot 5 proto
prefix: 4 arch 5 archi

primate
3 ape, man 5 human, lemur, loris 6 aye-aye, bishop, bonobo, monkey 7 gorilla 10 anthropoid, archbishop, chimpanzee, human being 11 Homo sapiens
nocturnal: 5 loris 7 tarsier
small: 6 galago

prime
3 top 4 best, dawn, fill, load, morn, peak, pick, rate 5 coach, cream, elite, first, paint, sunup, tonic, youth 6 choice, excite, height, spring, symbol 7 capital, highest, initial, morning, prepare, provoke, quicken 8 earliest, motivate, original,

superior **9** excellent, first-rate, principal, stimulate **10** first-class

prime minister
7 premier

primer
4 book **5** guide **6** manual, reader **8** hornbook

primeval
7 ancient **8** earliest, original **10** aboriginal

primitive
3 raw **4** rude **5** basic, crude, early **6** savage **7** archaic, Spartan **8** barbaric, original, primeval **9** atavistic, barbarian, barbarous, elemental, essential, unevolved **10** elementary, primordial, underlying **11** fundamental, preliterate, uncivilized, undeveloped **12** uncultivated
combining form: 5 palae, paleo **6** archae, archeo, palaeo **7** archaeo
prefix: 4 arch **5** arche, archi

primogenitor
4 sire **8** ancestor, forebear **9** precursor **10** forefather

primordial
5 basic, early, first **7** ancient **8** earliest, original

primp
4 fuss **5** adorn, dress, fix up, preen **7** dress up

prince
Anglo-Saxon: 8 atheling
Arab: 4 amir, emir **5** ameer
Austrian: 8 archduke
Ethiopian: 3 ras
Indian: 4 raja, rana **5** rajah
of demons: 9 Beelzebub
of Monaco: 6 Albert **7** Rainier
of opera: 4 Igor
of the church: 8 cardinal
of Wales: 7 Charles

Prince and the Pauper author
5 Twain (Mark) **7** Clemens (Samuel)

Prince Edward Island
capital: 13 Charlottetown
provincial flower: 12 lady's slipper

Prince Igor composer
7 Borodin (Aleksandr)

princely
5 grand, noble, royal **8** generous, imposing, majestic **9** dignified **11** magnificent

princess
7 infanta
fictional: 3 Ida, Mia **4** Aura, Leia, Miyu, Ozma, Xena **5** Ariel, Belle, Fiona, She-Ra, Storm, Vespa, Zelda **6** Anelle, Aurora, Kadiya **7** Camilla, Jasmine **8** Angelica, Starfire **9** Belphoebe, Blackfire, Britomart, Buttercup, Gwenevere, Snow White **10** Bradamante, Cinderella, Pocahontas **11** Casamassima
mythical: 3 Ino **5** Medea
of Monaco: 5 Grace

Prince Valiant
artist: 6 Foster (Hal)
son: 3 Arn
wife: 5 Aleta

principal
4 arch, dean, head, main, star **5** chief, first, major, prime **6** assets **7** capital, central, leading, premier, primary, stellar **8** cardinal, champion, dominant, foremost **9** paramount **10** headmaster, preeminent **11** outstanding, predominant
combining form: 4 prot **5** proto
prefix: 4 arch **5** archi

principium
3 law **5** axiom, basis **7** element, theorem **10** foundation **11** fundamental

principle
3 law **4** code, form, rule **5** axiom, basis, canon, ethic, tenet **6** ground, origin, source **7** conduct, faculty, precept **8** doctrine, polestar, rudiment **10** assumption, convention, foundation **11** fundamental

principled
5 moral, noble **6** honest **7** ethical, upright **8** virtuous **9** righteous **10** moralistic

print
4 type **5** issue, litho, stamp, write **7** engrave, impress, publish, typeset **10** impression
style: 4 bold **5** roman **6** italic **7** cursive **8** boldface

printemps follower
3 été

printer
English: 6 Caxton (William)
German: 9 Gutenberg (Johann, Johannes)
Italian: 6 Bodoni (Giambattista) **8** Manutius (Aldus)
need: 5 toner

printing
7 edition, reissue **10** impression
measure: 4 pica **5** agate
plate: 10 stereotype
process: 4 roto **7** gravure **11** lithography
tool: 6 brayer

priority
4 lead **5** order **8** ordering **9** supremacy **10** importance, precedence, preference

prior to (poetic)
3 ere

prison
3 can, jug, pen **4** brig, coop, jail, keep **5** clink, pokey **6** cooler, lockup **7** dungeon, slammer **8** bastille, big house, hoosegow, stockade **9** calaboose **11** reformatory **12** penitentiary
British: 4 gaol
California: 8 Alcatraz **10** San Quentin
knife: 4 shiv

Nazi: **6** stalag
New York: **6** Attica **8** Sing Sing **12** Rikers Island
Northern Ireland: **4** Maze
resident: **6** inmate **7** convict **8** jailbird
Russian: **5** gulag

prisoner
7 captive, convict, hostage **8** criminal, detainee, jailbird

prissy
5 picky **7** finicky, precise, prudish **8** exacting **10** fastidious, particular **11** straitlaced

pristine
4 pure **5** clean, fresh **8** earliest, original **9** unspoiled **10** immaculate

privacy
6 secret **7** retreat, secrecy **9** seclusion **11** concealment

private
5 inner **6** secret **7** soldier **8** eyes-only, hush-hush, intimate, one-on-one, personal **9** concealed **10** closed-door, restricted, unofficial **11** independent, sequestered **12** confidential

privateer
4 ship **6** pirate **7** gunship **9** mercenary

private eye
3 spy, tec **4** tail **6** sleuth, shamus **7** gumshoe **8** sherlock **9** detective **12** investigator

private jet brand
4 Lear

privately
7 sub rosa **8** covertly, in camera, in secret, secretly

privation
4 lack, loss, need, want **6** dearth, penury **7** absence, poverty **8** distress **9** indigence, neediness, suffering

privilege
4 boon **5** favor, grant, right **7** license **8** appanage **9** allowance, exemption **10** birthright, concession, perquisite **11** entitlement, opportunity, prerogative
pope-granted: **6** indult

privy
3 can, lav, loo **4** head, john **5** jakes **6** secret, toilet **7** latrine **8** bathroom, informed, lavatory, outhouse, personal **9** concealed, withdrawn **11** water closet

privy to
4 in on

prize
3 pry, top **4** best, loot, pick, plum, rate, swag **5** award, booty, cream, elite, force, lever, purse, spoil, value **6** choice, esteem, reward, spoils, trophy **7** capture, cherish, jackpot, plunder, premium **8** treasure **10** appreciate **11** outstanding

prizefighting
6 boxing **8** pugilism

pro
3 for **6** expert, master **8** skillful **9** authority, in favor of **11** affirmative
opposite: **3** con **4** anti

pro ___
4 bono, rata

probable
6 likely **7** seeming **8** apparent, credible, expected, feasible, rational, reliable **10** reasonable

probe
4 poke, quiz, test **5** delve, query, sonde, study **6** search **7** dig into, examine, explore, feel out, inquest, inquire, inquiry **8** check out, look into, research, sound out **9** delve into, penetrate **11** exploration, investigate, reconnoiter **13** investigation

probity
5 honor **6** virtue **7** honesty **8** fairness, goodness **9** integrity, rectitude **11** uprightness

problem
4 mess, snag **5** hitch, issue, poser **6** enigma, hassle, puzzle, riddle **7** dilemma, example, mystery, puzzler, trouble **8** hardship, headache, question **10** difficulty

problematic
4 iffy, moot, open **7** dubious **8** arguable, doubtful **9** debatable, uncertain, unsettled **10** precarious **12** questionable

proboscis
4 beak, nose **5** snoot, snout, trunk

procedure
4 plan, step **6** course, custom, method, policy, system **7** formula, measure, routine **8** protocol **9** operation **11** instruction

proceed
4 flow, move, rise, stem, wend **5** arise, get on, issue, segue **6** emerge, push on, spring, travel **7** advance, carry on, emanate, journey **8** continue **9** originate

proceedings
8 goings-on
recorded: **4** acta **6** annals **7** minutes

proceeds
4 gain, take **5** yield **6** profit, result, return **8** earnings

process
3 way **4** mode, wise **5** modus, treat **6** handle, manner, method, refine, system **7** fashion, prepare, recycle, routine **8** workings **9** evolution, operation, outgrowth, procedure, technique **11** development
nerve cell: **4** axon

procession
5 march, order, paseo, train **6** parade, series,

string **7** caravan, cortege **8** sequence **9** cavalcade, march-past, motorcade **11** consecution

proclaim
5 extol **6** assert, insist **7** declare, exhibit, glorify, publish **8** announce, evidence, manifest **9** advertise, broadcast, make known **10** annunciate, bruit about

proclivity
4 bent **5** taste **6** liking **7** leaning **8** affinity, fondness, penchant, tendency **9** proneness **11** inclination **12** predilection

Procne
father: **7** Pandion
husband: **6** Tereus
sister: **9** Philomela
son: **4** Itys

procrastinate
5 dally, delay, stall **6** dawdle, diddle **9** hem and haw, temporize

procreate
5 beget, breed **7** produce **8** conceive, generate, multiply **9** reproduce

Procris' husband
8 Cephalus

Procrustean ___
3 bed

proctor
7 monitor, oversee **9** supervise **10** supervisor

procure
3 buy, get **4** gain **6** obtain, pick up **7** achieve, acquire **8** purchase **10** bring about

prod
3 dig, jab, jog **4** goad, poke, push, spur, stir, urge **5** egg on, elbow, nudge, point, prick, rouse **6** excite, exhort, incite, thrust **8** motivate **9** stimulate **10** incitement

prodigal
4 lush **6** lavish **7** opulent, profuse, riotous, spender, wastrel **8** reckless, wasteful **9** exuberant, luxuriant **10** profligate, squanderer **11** extravagant, spendthrift

prodigious
4 huge, vast **6** mighty, unreal **7** amazing, immense, mammoth, massive, strange, unusual **8** colossal, enormous, gigantic **9** fantastic, marvelous, wonderful **10** astounding, impressive, monumental, phenomenal, remarkable, staggering, stupendous, surprising **11** astonishing **13** extraordinary

produce
4 bear, form, grow, make, show, sire **5** beget, breed, build, cause, erect, frame, hatch, mount, put on, raise, spawn, stage, yield **6** create, effect, father, output, parent, secure, work up **7** deliver, fashion, turn out **8** engender, generate, multiply **9** construct, fabricate, originate, procreate, propagate **10** bring about **11** manufacture, put together

product
5 fruit, issue, yield **6** effect, legacy, output, result, upshot **7** harvest, outcome, turnout **8** artifact, creation, multiple, offshoot **9** handiwork, outgrowth **11** consequence, manufacture
combining form: **3** gen

production
5 fruit, yield **6** output **7** staging, turnout **8** artifact, assembly, creation **9** execution, handiwork, rendering **11** achievement, manufacture, realization

productive
4 rich **6** fecund, useful **7** fertile **8** abundant, fruitful, prolific **9** rewarding **10** beneficial

proem
5 intro **7** preface, prelude **8** exordium, foreword, overture, prologue **11** preliminary **12** introduction

profane
3 lay **4** damn, foul **5** abuse, dirty, pagan **6** coarse, debase, defile, filthy, impure, unholy, vulgar **7** impious, obscene, secular **8** indecent, temporal, unsacred **9** desecrate **10** irreverent, unhallowed **11** blasphemous, irreligious **12** sacrilegious, unsanctified

profanity
4 oath **5** abuse, curse **7** cursing, cussing **8** swearing **9** blasphemy, sacrilege **10** execration **11** imprecation, irreverence

profess
4 aver, avow **5** claim, teach **6** affirm, allege, assert, avouch **7** declare, pretend, protest, purport **8** maintain, practice

profession
3 art, job, vow **5** craft, trade **6** avowal, career, métier **7** calling **8** business, vocation **9** assertion, specialty, statement, testimony **10** handicraft, occupation, walk of life **11** affirmation

professional
4 paid **6** expert, master **7** learned, skilled **9** authority **10** proficient, specialist **11** experienced **12** businesslike

professional org.
4 assn.

professor
3 don **6** expert **7** teacher **8** academic, educator

proffer
4 give, pose **6** extend, submit, tender **7** hold out, present, suggest **10** invitation, suggestion

proficiency
5 savvy, skill **7** ability, advance, mastery, prowess **8** facility, progress **9** adeptness, dexterity, expertise, knowledge **10** competence

proficient
4 able **5** adept **6** expert **7** capable, skilled **8** advanced, masterly, skillful **9** authority, competent, effective, masterful, qualified **11** crackerjack, experienced **12** accomplished

profile
3 bio **5** chart **6** sketch, survey **7** contour, diagram, outline **8** exposure, portrait, side view **9** biography **10** silhouette **11** description

profit
3 net **4** gain, take **5** lucre, serve, yield **6** excess, income, payoff, return **7** benefit, receipt **8** earnings, proceeds **10** percentage **12** compensation
sudden: 7 killing

profitable
6 paying, useful **7** gainful **8** fruitful **9** lucrative, rewarding **10** beneficial, well-paying, worthwhile **11** moneymaking **12** advantageous, remunerative

profligate
4 wild **6** waster **7** immoral, spender, wastrel **8** prodigal, reckless, wasteful **9** abandoned, dissolute, indulgent, reprobate **10** dissipated, immoderate, licentious, squanderer **11** extravagant, promiscuous, spendthrift **13** self-indulgent

profound
4 deep, wise **5** heavy, total, utter **7** abysmal, intense **8** absolute, abstruse, complete, esoteric, thorough **9** intensive **10** deep-seated, insightful

profundity
5 depth **6** wisdom **7** insight **8** deepness **12** abstruseness

profuse
4 lush **6** lavish **7** copious, fulsome, liberal, opulent **8** abundant, generous, prodigal **9** abounding, bounteous, bountiful, excessive, exuberant, luxuriant, plentiful **10** munificent **11** extravagant

profusion
4 glut, riot **5** flood, spate, surge **6** bounty, deluge, excess, wealth **7** nimiety, satiety, surfeit, surplus, torrent **8** overflow, overload, plethora **9** abundance, plenitude **10** lavishness, luxuriance, oversupply, plentitude, redundancy **11** copiousness, prodigality, sufficiency, superfluity **12** extravagance **13** overabundance

progenitor
4 sire **6** author, father, mother **8** ancestor, forebear **9** initiator, precursor **10** antecessor, forefather, forerunner, originator **11** predecessor

progeny
4 line **5** issue **6** litter, result, scions **7** outcome, product **8** children **9** offspring, posterity **11** descendants

prognosis
8 estimate, forecast, prophecy **9** prevision **10** estimation, prediction **11** expectation **12** anticipation

prognostic
4 omen, sign **6** augury **7** portent, presage **10** foreboding, indication

prognosticate
6 divine **7** foresee, predict, presage **8** forecast, foretell, prophesy

program
4 bill, book, plan, show **5** plans, slate **6** agenda, course, docket, lineup, policy **7** listing **8** calendar, playbill, schedule, syllabus **9** broadcast, procedure, timetable **10** bill of fare, curriculum

programming language
3 SQL **4** DASL, JADE, Java, LISP, Perl, Thue **5** Algol, BASIC, COBOL, CORAL **6** Euclid, Groovy, Inform, Pascal, Prolog, Python, Scheme, Simula **7** FORTRAN, Haskell, Miranda **10** JavaScript, PostScript **11** Visual Basic

progress
4 fare, gain, grow **5** get on, march **6** course, growth **7** advance, headway, passage, proceed **8** anabasis, get along, momentum **9** evolution, flowering, unfolding **11** advancement, development, improvement
planned: 7 telesis

progressing
5 afoot **7** en route **8** under way

progression
4 path **5** chain **6** course, growth, series **7** advance **8** sequence **9** evolution, unfolding **10** trajectory **11** development

progressive
6 modern **7** growing, liberal, radical **8** advanced, tolerant **9** advancing **10** developing, increasing

prohibit
3 ban, bar **4** stop **5** block, debar, embar, estop **6** enjoin, forbid, outlaw **7** prevent **8** preclude **9** interdict

prohibited
4 tabu **5** taboo **6** banned, barred **7** illegal, illicit **8** verboten **9** forbidden

prohibition
3 ban, bar **5** taboo **7** embargo **8** estoppel, sanction **9** interdict **10** constraint, forbidding, injunction **12** disallowance, interdiction, proscription

prohibitive
5 steep **6** costly **7** sky-high **9** excessive **10** exorbitant, forbidding **11** restrictive

project
3 jut **4** cast, feat, plan **5** bulge **6** affair, design, devise, extend, intend, scheme, vision **7** arrange, concern, emprise, exploit, feature, imagine, propose, purpose, venture **8** business, conceive, envisage, envision, game plan, overhang, protrude, stand out, stick out, strategy **9** blueprint, visualize **10** enterprise **11** proposition, undertaking

projecting window
5 oriel

projection
3 jut 4 bump, knob, snag, view 5 bulge 7 display 8 estimate, forecast, overhang, scheming, swelling 9 extension 10 jutting out, perception 11 expectation
vaulted: 4 apse

prolapse
3 sag

proletariat
6 masses 7 workers 8 laborers 9 commoners, hoi polloi 12 working class

proliferate
5 surge 7 burgeon, inflate 8 multiply, mushroom 10 accumulate

prolific
4 rich 6 fecund, gifted, lavish 7 fertile 8 abundant, creative, fruitful 9 abounding, bountiful, inventive 10 generating, generative 11 reproducing 12 reproductive

prolix
4 long 5 windy, wordy 7 diffuse, lengthy, tedious, verbose 8 drawn out, rambling, tiresome 9 redundant, wearisome 10 long-winded

prologue
7 opening, preface, prelude 8 exordium, foreword, overture, preamble 9 beginning 12 introduction

prolong
6 extend 7 drag out, draw out, spin out, stretch 8 continue, elongate, lengthen

prolonged
7 lasting, lengthy 8 drawn-out 9 lingering 10 continuing, persistent, persisting

prom
4 ball, fete, gala 5 dance 6 formal

promenade
4 deck, walk 6 parade, stroll 9 boardwalk

Prometheus
brother: 5 Atlas 9 Menoetius 10 Epimetheus
creation: 3 man 7 mankind
father: 7 Iapetus
gift: 4 fire
mother: 7 Clymene
muralist: 6 Orozco
rescuer: 8 Heracles, Hercules
tormentor: 5 eagle

prominence
4 crag, fame, rise, spur 5 bulge 6 height, renown, status 8 eminence, headland, prestige, salience, standing 9 celebrity, elevation 10 importance, projection 11 distinction

prominent
5 famed, great, noted 6 famous, marked, signal 7 eminent, jutting, leading, notable, popular, salient 8 renowned, striking 9 arresting, notorious, well-known 10 celebrated, noticeable, pronounced, remarkable 11 conspicuous, eye-catching, illustrious, outstanding 13 distinguished
person: 3 VIP 4 BMOC, lion 5 mogul, nabob 6 bigwig, honcho 7 big shot, grandee 8 luminary, mandarin, somebody 9 dignitary 13 high-muck-a-muck

promiscuous
5 mixed 6 casual, random, varied 7 immoral 8 careless 9 haphazard, hit-or-miss, irregular 10 licentious 11 unselective 12 unrestrained

promise
3 vow 4 bode, bond, oath, word 5 agree, augur, swear, vouch 6 assure, engage, ensure, expect, insure, parole, pledge, plight 7 betroth, compact, consent, declare, outlook, portend, presage, suggest 8 contract, covenant, indicate 9 assurance, betrothal, potential, undertake 11 declaration, expectation

promised land
4 Zion 6 Canaan, heaven 8 paradise 11 kingdom come

promising
6 likely 7 hopeful 9 favorable 10 auspicious 11 encouraging

promissory note
3 IOU

promontory
4 beak, bill, cape, head, ness 5 bulge, point 8 foreland, headland

promote
3 aid 4 help, hype, plug, puff, push, sell, tout 5 boost, favor, raise 6 foster, launch, prefer 7 advance, build up, elevate, endorse, forward, further, nurture, present, support 8 advocate, champion 9 advertise, encourage, publicize, recommend

promotion
6 step up, teaser 7 advance, buildup, puffery 9 elevation, publicity, upgrading 10 preference, preferment 11 advancement, advertising, improvement 13 advertisement

prompt
3 apt, cue, jog 4 fast, goad, help, hint, move, spur, urge 5 alert, quick, rapid, ready 6 assist, incite, induce, on time, remind, speedy, stir up, timely 7 suggest 8 convince, persuade, punctual, reminder 10 responsive

promulgate
5 issue 6 decree 7 declare, publish 8 announce, proclaim 9 advertise, broadcast 10 annunciate 11 disseminate

prone
3 apt 4 flat, open 5 given, level 6 liable, likely, supine 7 subject, tending, willing 8 disposed, facedown, inclined 9 lying down, reclining, prostrate, recumbent 10 horizontal 11 predisposed, susceptible

prong
4 barb, fang, fork, spur, stab, tine 5 point, thorn 6 pierce

pronghorn
8 antelope

___ pro nobis
3 ora

pronoun
archaic: 3 thy 4 thou 5 thine
demonstrative: 4 that, this 5 these, those
indefinite: 3 all, any, few, one 4 both, each, none, some 5 no one, other 6 anyone, either, nobody 7 another, anybody, neither, nothing, someone 8 anything, somebody 9 everybody, something 10 everything
personal: 3 her, him, she, you 4 them, they
possessive: 3 her, his, its, our 4 hers, mine, ours, your 5 their, yours 6 theirs
reflexive: 6 itself, myself 7 herself, himself, oneself, ourself 8 yourself 9 ourselves 10 themselves, yourselves
relative: 3 who 4 that, what, whom 5 which, whose, whoso 6 whomso 7 whoever 8 whatever, whomever 9 whichever, whosoever 10 whatsoever, whomsoever 11 whichsoever

pronounce
3 say 5 judge, sound, speak, state, utter 6 affirm, assert, decree, recite 7 declare 9 enunciate 10 articulate

pronounced
5 clear 6 marked, strong 7 assured, decided, evident, obvious 8 clear-cut, definite, distinct 12 unmistakable

pronouncement
5 edict 6 decree 9 manifesto, statement 11 declaration, publication 12 notification

pronto
3 now, PDQ 4 ASAP, fast, stat 6 at once 7 quickly 8 directly 9 forthwith, instanter, instantly, posthaste, right away 11 immediately

pronunciation
distinctive: 4 burr, lilt 5 drawl, twang 6 accent, brogue
study: 8 orthoepy 9 phonetics

proof
4 test 5 facts, goods, repro 6 galley 8 argument, evidence 9 testament, testimony 10 impression 11 attestation 12 confirmation

proofreaders' mark
4 dele, stet 5 caret

prop
4 stay 5 brace, shore 6 buoy up, hold up 7 bolster, shore up, support, sustain 8 buttress 10 strengthen 12 underpinning

propaganda
4 hype 8 agitprop, lobbying

propagandize
4 tout 5 boost, extol 7 advance, promote, trumpet 9 brainwash, catechize, inculcate 10 promulgate 11 proselytize 12 indoctrinate

propagate
5 beget, breed, raise, strew 6 extend, spread 7 diffuse, publish, radiate 8 disperse, generate, increase, multiply, transmit 9 circulate, cultivate, publicize, reproduce 10 distribute 11 disseminate

propel
4 goad, move, push, spur, urge 5 drive, egg on, power, shoot, shove 6 exhort, launch, thrust 7 actuate 8 activate

propellant
3 gas 4 fuel, spur 7 impetus, impulse 8 catalyst, stimulus 9 explosive, incentive, stimulant 10 motivation

propensity
7 leaning 8 penchant 10 preference 11 inclination

proper
3 apt, due, fit 4 good, just, meet, nice, prim, true 5 exact, right 6 au fait, decent, prissy, seemly, useful 7 correct, desired, fitting, genteel 8 becoming, decorous, priggish, rightful, rigorous, suitable 9 befitting 10 felicitous 11 appropriate, comme il faut, distinctive
combining form: 4 orth 5 ortho

property
4 land, mark 5 acres, trait, worth 6 assets, estate, realty, riches, virtue, wealth 7 acreage, chattel, effects, feature, fortune, quality 8 chattels, dominion, hallmark, holdings, premises 9 attribute, ownership, resources, substance 10 belongings, possession, real estate
claim: 4 lien
conveyor: 7 alienor
recipient: 7 alienee
seller: 7 Realtor
transfer: 8 alienate

prophecy
6 vision 8 forecast 10 divination, prediction 11 foretelling

prophesy
5 augur 6 divine, preach 7 foresee, portend, predict, presage 8 forecast, foretell, instruct, soothsay 9 adumbrate, prefigure 10 vaticinate 13 prognosticate

prophet
4 seer **5** augur, sibyl **6** auspex, oracle **7** diviner, seeress **8** foreseer, haruspex **9** predictor **10** forecaster, foreteller, prophesier, soothsayer **11** Nostradamus **13** fortune-teller
Arthurian: 6 Merlin
biblical: 4 Amos, Joel, Osee **5** Hosea, Jonah, Micah, Nahum **6** Daniel, Elijah, Haggai, Isaiah **7** Ezekiel, Malachi, Obadiah **8** Habakkuk, Jeremiah **9** Zechariah, Zephaniah

Prophet author
6 Gibran (Khalil)

prophetess
5 sibyl **6** Pythia **7** Deborah **9** Cassandra

prophetic
5 vatic **6** orphic **7** Delphic **8** Delphian, oracular **9** presaging, prescient, sibylline, vaticinal **10** predictive, revelatory **11** apocalyptic, foretelling
sign: 4 omen

propinquity
7 kinship **8** nearness **9** closeness, proximity **10** contiguity

propitiate
5 adapt, atone **6** adjust, pacify, soothe **7** appease, assuage, gratify, mollify, placate, satisfy **9** intercede, reconcile **10** conciliate

propitious
4 good, rosy **5** lucky **6** benign, bright **7** benefic, helpful **8** favoring **9** favorable, fortunate, opportune, promising **10** auspicious, beneficent, beneficial, benevolent **12** advantageous

proponent
6 backer **8** advocate, champion, defender **9** expounder, supporter **10** enthusiast

proportion
4 rate, size **5** allot, ratio, quota, share **6** adjust, divide **7** balance, conform, harmony **8** symmetry **9** dimension **10** percentage **12** relationship

proportional
5 scale **7** in scale, pro rata **8** relative **9** equalized **10** contingent, equivalent, reciprocal **11** correlative, symmetrical **12** commensurate **13** commensurable, corresponding

proposal
3 bid **4** idea, plan **6** motion, scheme **7** outline, proffer, project **8** scenario **10** invitation, suggestion **11** proposition
final: 9 ultimatum

propose
3 aim, ask, put **4** name, plan, pose **5** offer **6** design, intend, submit, tender **7** advance, move for, present, request, solicit, suggest **8** nominate, put forth, set forth, theorize **9** recommend **10** put forward

proposition
4 plan **5** offer **6** scheme, thesis **7** premise, suggest, theorem **8** proposal **10** invitation, suggestion

propound
3 put **4** pose **5** offer **7** present, suggest **8** put forth

proprietor
5 owner **8** landlord **9** possessor

propriety
7 aptness, decency, decorum, manners **8** behavior, civility, good form **9** etiquette, rightness **10** seemliness **11** correctness, fittingness, suitability **12** decorousness

propulsion
4 fuel, push **5** drive, force, power **6** energy, thrust

prorate
5 allot, divvy, quota, share, split **6** assess, divide, parcel, ration **7** divvy up, portion **9** apportion, partition **10** distribute

prorogue
3 end **4** rise, stay **5** defer, delay **6** hold up, put off, recess, shelve **7** adjourn, hold off, suspend **8** dissolve, hold over, postpone **9** terminate

prosaic
4 dull, flat **5** banal, prose, prosy, trite, vapid **6** boring, common **7** factual, literal, mundane, tedious **8** everyday, lifeless, ordinary, workaday **9** colorless **10** lackluster, uneventful **11** commonplace **13** unimaginative

proscenium
5 frame, stage **9** forestage **10** foreground

proscribe
3 ban **4** damn **6** enjoin, forbid, outlaw **7** condemn **8** prohibit, sentence **9** interdict

proscription
3 ban **4** tabu **5** taboo **8** sanction **11** prohibition **12** condemnation, interdiction

prosecute
3 sue **4** wage **5** press **6** charge, indict, pursue **7** carry on, perform **8** continue **9** bring suit, persevere

proselyte
7 convert, recruit **8** neophyte

proselytize
5 draft **6** enlist, enroll, sign up **7** convert, recruit, win over **8** convince **9** brainwash, catechize **11** prevail upon **12** indoctrinate

___ prosequi
5 nolle

prospect
4 mine, view **5** scene, vista **6** chance, survey, vision **7** dig into, explore, lookout, outlook

8 customer, exposure 9 candidate 10 expectancy 11 expectation, possibility 12 anticipation

prospective
6 coming, future, likely 7 awaited, ensuing, nearing, pending, planned, would-be 8 destined, eventual, expected, hoped-for, intended, proposed, soon-to-be 9 impending, looked-for, potential, scheduled 10 consequent, succeeding 11 anticipated, approaching, predestined, forthcoming

prospectus
4 list, plan 6 design, layout, précis 7 epitome, outline, program, summary 8 bulletin, synopsis 9 catalogue, timetable 10 projection 11 description 12 announcement

prosper
5 score, yield 6 arrive, do well, thrive 7 make out, produce, succeed, turn out 8 flourish, grow rich

prosperity
4 ease, weal 6 riches, wealth 7 success 8 thriving 9 abundance, advantage, affluence, well-being

Prospero
daughter: 7 Miranda
servant: 5 Ariel
slave: 7 Caliban

prosperous
4 rich, well 5 happy, lucky 6 robust, strong 7 booming, halcyon, opulent, wealthy, well-off 8 affluent, thriving, well-to-do 9 desirable, favorable, fortunate, promising, well-fixed 10 auspicious, successful, well-heeled 11 comfortable, flourishing

prostitute
4 bawd, doxy, drab, moll 5 abuse, B-girl, madam, quean, whore 6 callet, debase, floozy, harlot, hooker, misuse, wanton 7 chippie, cocotte, corrupt, cyprian, floozie, hustler, Paphian 8 call girl, meretrix, strumpet 9 courtesan, party girl 11 fille de joie, nightwalker 12 camp follower, street-walker
reformed: 8 magdalen 9 magdalene

prostitution
8 harlotry, whoredom 13 streetwalking
house of: 4 crib, stew 6 bagnio 7 brothel, lupanar 8 bordello, cathouse 10 bawdy house 13 sporting house

prostrate
4 fell, flat 5 abase, level, prone 6 humble, lay low, submit, supine 7 exhaust, wear out 8 helpless, overcome 9 decumbent, exhausted, overpower, overwhelm, powerless, recumbent 10 procumbent, submissive

protagonist
4 hero, lead, star 5 actor 6 leader 7 heroine, sponsor 8 advocate, champion 9 principal

protean
6 mobile, varied 7 diverse, mutable 8 variable 9 adaptable, versatile 10 changeable

protect
4 save 5 cover, guard 6 defend, screen, secure, shield 7 shelter 8 preserve, restrict 9 safeguard

protected, at sea
4 alee

protection
4 care 5 aegis, armor, bribe, graft, guard 6 safety, shield 7 bulwark, defense, shelter, support 8 armament, coverage, immunity, security 9 extortion, insurance, safeguard 11 supervision

protector
5 armor, guard 6 patron, regent, shield 8 guardian 9 caretaker

protégé
4 ward 5 pupil 7 student, trainee 8 disciple

protein
4 zein 5 actin, opsin 6 avidin, enzyme, fibrin, globin, myosin 7 albumin, elastin, fibroin, histone, keratin, legumin, sericin 8 creatine, globulin, glutelin, prolamin, protamin, proteose, vitellin
complex: 6 mucoid
derivative: 7 peptide, peptone
poisonous: 5 abrin, ricin

pro tem
6 acting 7 interim 9 ad interim, temporary

protest
4 aver, avow, beef 5 sit-in 6 affirm, assert, avouch, except, object, oppose, picket, resist 7 declare, dissent, profess 8 maintain 9 challenge, complaint, objection 10 disapprove 11 demonstrate, disapproval 13 demonstration

Protestant
5 Amish 6 Mormon, Quaker, Shaker 7 Baptist, Lollard, Pilgrim, Puritan 8 Anglican, Lutheran, Moravian 9 Adventist, Mennonite, Methodist, Unitarian 11 Pentecostal 12 Episcopalian, Presbyterian
Bohemian: 7 Hussite
French: 8 Huguenot

protocol
4 code, form, rule 6 custom, ritual 7 compact, conduct, decorum, manners 8 courtesy 9 concordat, etiquette, politesse, propriety 11 conventions, formalities

prototype
4 norm 5 model, pilot 6 design 7 example, pattern 8 original, paradigm, standard

prototypical
5 ideal, model 7 classic 9 classical, exemplary 10 archetypal

protozoan
4 cell 5 ameba 6 amoeba 7 ciliate, stentor 10 flagellate, paramecium

protract
6 drag on, extend 7 drag out, draw out, prolong, stretch 8 continue

protrude
3 jut 4 poke, pout 5 bulge 6 jut out 7 project 8 overhang, stand out, stick out

protrusion
3 jut, nub 4 bump, node 5 bulge 8 swelling 10 projection 11 protuberance

protuberance
see **protrusion**

protuberant
5 bulgy 7 bulging 9 prominent 11 conspicuous

proud
4 vain 5 huffy, lofty, noble 6 lordly, stuffy, superb 7 haughty, pleased, pompous, stuck-up, stately 8 arrogant, exultant, glorious, scornful, snobbish, spirited, splendid, superior, vigorous 9 conceited, delighted, imperious 10 disdainful, high-handed 11 magnificent, pretentious, resplendent 12 ostentatious, supercilious

Proulx novel
9 Postcards 12 Shipping News (The)

Proust character
5 Swann (Charles) 6 Marcel, Odette (de Crécy, Swann) 7 Charlus (Baron de) 8 Gilberte (Swann) 9 Albertine (Simonet)

prove
3 try 4 show, test 5 argue, check 6 attest, pan out, verify 7 bear out, certify, confirm, examine, explain, turn out 8 document, indicate, validate 9 determine, establish 11 corroborate, demonstrate 12 substantiate

provenance
4 root, well 6 origin, source 7 history 9 inception 10 derivation

provender
4 feed, food 8 victuals 10 provisions

proverb
3 saw 5 adage, axiom, maxim 6 byword, saying 7 epigram 8 aphorism

provide
4 give, hand 5 endow, endue, equip, serve, state 6 afford, outfit, render, supply 7 deliver, furnish, prepare, specify, support 8 dispense, hand over, maintain 9 stipulate

provided
5 given 6 if only 8 equipped, supplied

providence
4 care 6 thrift 7 caution, economy 8 prudence 9 foresight, frugality 11 forethought, thriftiness

provident
5 canny, chary 6 frugal, saving 7 careful, prudent, sparing, thrifty 8 prepared 10 economical, unwasteful 11 foresighted

providential
5 happy, lucky 9 benignant, fortunate 10 auspicious, fortuitous

province
4 area, duty, role, work 5 field, shire 6 canton, county, domain, office, region, sphere 7 demesne, pursuit, terrain 8 district, dominion, function 9 bailiwick, champaign, territory 10 department 12 jurisdiction

provincial
5 local, rural 6 narrow, rustic, simple 7 country, insular, limited 8 pastoral 9 parochial, sectarian, small-town 11 countrified

proving ground
10 laboratory, White Sands

provision
5 stock, store 6 supply 9 condition 11 preparation, requirement, reservation, stipulation

provisional
5 stamp 6 acting, pro tem 9 temporary 10 contingent 11 conditional

provisions
4 feed, food, grub 5 stock 6 viands 7 aliment, edibles, nurture, vittles 8 supplies, victuals 9 provender 10 sustenance 11 comestibles
dealer: 8 chandler

proviso
6 clause 7 article 9 condition 11 stipulation

provocation
5 cause, wrong 7 offense 8 stimulus, vexation 9 annoyance, incentive 10 incitement 11 instigation

provocative
4 edgy 5 heady 8 alluring, annoying, arousing, exciting 9 offensive 10 intriguing 11 challenging, stimulating

provoke
3 bug, irk, vex 4 abet, rile, stir, wake 5 anger, annoy, cause, evoke, pique, rouse, upset, waken 6 arouse, awaken, bother, excite, foment, harass, incite, induce, kindle, nettle, stir up, whip up 7 incense, inflame, inspire, outrage, quicken 8 generate, irritate, motivate, occasion 9 challenge, galvanize, instigate, stimulate

provost
4 head 6 keeper 7 marshal 8 director 10 magistrate 13 administrator

prow
3 bow **4** stem **5** front **10** projection

prowess
5 skill, valor **7** bravery, command, courage, heroism, mastery **9** expertise, gallantry **10** excellence

prowl
4 hunt, roam **5** skulk, slink, sneak, steal **6** search, wander

proximate
4 near, next **5** close **6** nearby **8** adjacent, imminent **9** following, immediate, preceding **10** near-at-hand **11** forthcoming

proximity
8 nearness, vicinity **9** adjacency, closeness, immediacy **10** contiguity **11** propinquity

proxy
5 agent **6** deputy **7** stand-in **8** attorney **9** surrogate **10** substitute

pro ___
3 tem **4** bono, rata **5** forma, tanto **7** tempore

prude
4 prig **5** priss **7** old maid, Puritan **8** bluenose **9** Mrs. Grundy

prudence
4 care **5** skill **6** acumen, reason, thrift, wisdom **7** caution, economy **8** sagacity **9** foresight, frugality **10** astuteness, discretion, expediency, precaution, providence, shrewdness **11** calculation, forethought, thriftiness

prudent
4 sage, sane, wary, wise **5** canny, chary **6** frugal **7** careful, politic **8** cautious, discreet, sensible **9** expedient, judicious **11** circumspect

Prudential rival
5 Aetna

prudish
4 prim **5** stern **6** narrow, prissy, proper, severe, strict, stuffy **7** austere, genteel **8** affected, decorous, priggish **11** puritanical, straitlaced

prune
3 cut, lop **4** clip, crop, pare, plum, thin, trim **5** shear **6** cut off, reduce, remove **7** cut away, cut back, shorten **8** pare down, truncate

prurience
4 lust **6** desire, libido **7** lechery, passion **8** cupidity **9** carnality, eroticism **11** lustfulness **13** concupiscence

prurient
4 lewd **5** bawdy **6** erotic **7** goatish, lustful, satyric, sensual **9** lickerish **10** lascivious, libidinous, passionate **12** concupiscent

pruritic
5 itchy

Prussian
aristocrat: **6** Junker **12** Hohenzollern
prime minister: **8** Bismarck (Otto von)
ruler: **7** Wilhelm **9** Frederick (the Great)

pry
4 nose, open, poke **5** jimmy, lever, snoop **6** meddle **7** inquire **9** interfere

prying
4 nosy **6** snoopy **7** curious **8** meddling, snooping **9** intrusive, obtrusive, officious **10** meddlesome **11** impertinent, inquisitive

psalm
3 ode **4** hymn, poem, song **5** paean
book: **7** psalter
selection: **6** Hallel
word: **5** selah

psalmist
4 poet **5** Asaph, David **6** cantor

pseudo
4 fake, mock, sham **5** bogus, false, phony **7** pretend **8** spurious **9** imitation **10** artificial **11** counterfeit

pseudonym
5 alias **7** pen name **9** false name, stage name **10** nom de plume **11** nom de guerre
(see also **pen name**)

pseudonym of Lamb
4 Elia

psyche
4 mind, soul **5** anima **6** animus, pneuma, spirit
part: **3** ego **8** superego

psychedelic drug
3 LSD **4** acid **9** mescaline **10** psilocybin

Psyche's beloved
4 Eros **5** Cupid

psychiatrist
6 shrink **8** alienist **11** neurologist
American: **3** May (Rollo) **5** Reich (Wilhelm) **6** Kramer (Peter), Rogers (Carl) **7** Erikson (Erik) **8** Sullivan (Harry Stack) **9** Menninger (Karl)
Austrian: **5** Adler (Alfred), Freud (Anna, Sigmund), Klein (Melanie), Reich (Wilhelm)
British: **5** Ellis (Havelock), Klein (Melanie), Laing (R. D.)
French: **5** Lacan (Jacques)
German: **5** Fromm (Erich) **6** Horney (Karen)
Swiss: **4** Jung (Carl Gustav) **9** Rorschach (Hermann)

psychic
4 seer **6** medium, mental, occult **8** cerebral **9** mentalist, prophetic, spiritual **10** mind reader, telepathic **11** clairvoyant, telekinetic **12** intellectual, supersensory
American: **5** Cayce (Edgar), Dixon (Jeane) **10** Montgomery (Ruth)
power: **3** ESP

psycho
3 nut **5** crazy, sicko, wacko **6** madman, maniac, mental, schizo, weirdo **7** berserk, haywire, lunatic, nutcase **8** crackpot, demented, deranged, head case **9** fruitcake, screwball, sociopath

psychoanalyst
4 Jung (Carl Gustav), Rank (Otto) **5** Adler (Alfred), Freud (Sigmund), Fromm (Erich), Klein (Melanie), Kohut (Heinz), Lacan (Jacques) **6** Horney (Karen) **7** Erikson (Erik) **8** Ferenczi (Sandor)

psychologist
6 shrink **9** therapist
American: **5** James (William) **6** Terman (Lewis), Maslow (Abraham), Watson (John), Yerkes (Robert) **7** Skinner (B. F.) **9** Thorndike (Edward L.)
English: **4** Ward (James) **8** Spearman (Charles), Tichener (Edward)
German: **5** Wundt (Wilhelm) **6** Müller (Georg), Stumpf (Carl) **10** Wertheimer (Max)

psychotic
3 mad **5** crazy **6** insane **8** demented, deranged, schizoid **13** schizophrenic

ptarmigan
6 grouse

ptomaine
6 poison

pub
3 bar, inn **4** dive **5** joint **6** tavern **7** barroom, gin mill, taproom **8** grogshop **9** roadhouse **11** rathskeller

pub crawler
3 sot **4** lush **5** drunk, souse **6** barfly, boozer **7** tosspot **8** drunkard **10** boozehound

pub drink
3 ale **4** beer **5** stout **8** Guinness

puberty
11 adolescence

public
4 open **5** civic, civil, state **6** common, mutual, people, shared, social **7** general, popular, society **8** communal, national, populace **9** community, municipal, universal **10** accessible, government

publican
7 barkeep **8** landlord, licensee, taverner **9** bartender, collector, innkeeper **12** tax collector

publication
4 book **7** article, journal **8** magazine, pamphlet **9** broadside, newspaper **10** periodical
list: **12** bibliography
ID: **4** ISBN

public house
3 bar, inn **6** hostel, saloon, tavern **7** auberge, hospice **8** hostelry

publicity
3 ink **4** hype, plug **5** blurb, press, promo **6** hoopla, notice **7** billing, fanfare, write-up **8** ballyhoo **9** attention, promotion **11** advertising **12** announcement **13** advertisement

publicize
3 air **4** bill, hype, plug, puff, push, tout **5** boost **7** promote, trumpet **8** announce **9** advertise, broadcast **10** press-agent, promulgate

publish
3 air **5** issue, print **6** get out, inform, put out, report **7** release **8** announce, bring out, proclaim **9** advertise, broadcast, make known **10** distribute, promulgate **11** disseminate

Puccini opera
5 Tosca **7** Le Villi **8** La Bohème, Turandot **12** Manon Lescaut **15** Madame Butterfly

puck
3 elf, imp **4** disk **5** fairy **6** spirit, sprite **9** hobgoblin, prankster

pucker
4 fold **5** purse **6** cockle, crease **7** wrinkle **8** compress, contract **9** constrict

puckish
5 antic, elfin, larky, pixie **6** elvish, impish **7** playful **8** prankish **9** whimsical **11** mischievous

Puck's master
6 Oberon

pudding
4 duff **6** burgoo **7** custard, tapioca
baked: **5** kugel **10** brown Betty
starch: **4** sago

pudgy
3 fat **5** plump, round, stout, tubby **6** chubby, chunky, flabby, rotund **8** plumpish, roly-poly

pueblo
4 town **7** village **8** dwelling
ceremonial room: **4** kiva

Pueblo tribe
3 Zia **4** Hopi, Taos, Zuni **5** Acoma, Jemez, Keres, Tigua **6** Laguna **7** Cochiti

Puente of Latin jazz
4 Tito

puerile
5 inane, silly **6** jejune **7** foolish **8** childish, immature, juvenile

Puerto Rico
capital: **7** San Juan
city: **5** Ponce **7** Bayamon **8** Mayagüez
discoverer: **8** Columbus (Christopher)
language: **7** Spanish
location: **10** West Indies

puff
3 pad **4** blow, brag, crow, drag, emit, huff, pant, plug, pouf, push, tout, waft **5** blurb, boast, boost,

elate, expel, quilt, swell, vaunt, whiff **6** exhale, pastry, praise **7** flatter, inflate **8** swelling **9** advertise, comforter, publicize **10** exaggerate

puffer
8 blowfish **9** globefish, swellfish

puffery
4 buzz, hype, plug **7** fanfare **8** ballyhoo **9** promotion, publicity **11** advertising **12** exaggeration, press-agentry

puffin
4 bird **7** seabird **9** sea parrot **10** shearwater
cousin: 3 auk

puffy
7 swollen **8** inflated **9** edematous

pug
3 bun, dog **4** nose **5** boxer, track **9** footprint

Puget Sound port
6 Tacoma **7** Seattle

pugilism
6 boxing **13** prizefighting
org.: 3 WBA

pugilist
5 boxer **7** fighter **12** prizefighter

pugnacious
7 defiant, scrappy **8** brawling, fighting, militant **9** bellicose, combative, truculent **10** aggressive, rebellious **11** belligerent, contentious, quarrelsome **13** argumentative

pugnacity
9 hostility **10** aggression, truculence, truculency **12** belligerence **13** combativeness

puisne
6 junior **8** inferior

puissance
5 force, might, power **6** energy **7** potency **8** strength

puissant
6 mighty, potent, strong **8** forceful, powerful

pukka
4 real, tops **7** genuine **8** bona fide **9** authentic **10** first-class

pule
3 cry **4** mewl **5** whine **7** whimper

Pulitzer Prize fiction winner
1918: 5 Poole (Ernest)
1919: 10 Tarkington (Booth)
1921: 7 Wharton (Edith)
1922: 10 Tarkington (Booth)
1923: 6 Cather (Willa)
1924: 6 Wilson (Margaret)
1925: 6 Ferber (Edna)
1926: 5 Lewis (Sinclair)
1927: 9 Bromfield (Louis)
1928: 6 Wilder (Thornton)
1929: 8 Peterkin (Julia)
1930: 7 La Farge (Oliver)
1931: 6 Barnes (Margaret)
1932: 4 Buck (Pearl)
1933: 9 Stribling (T. S.)
1934: 6 Miller (Caroline)
1935: 7 Johnson (Josephine)
1936: 5 Davis (Harold)
1937: 8 Mitchell (Margaret)
1938: 8 Marquand (John)
1939: 8 Rawlings (Marjorie Kinnan)
1940: 9 Steinbeck (John)
1942: 7 Glasgow (Ellen)
1943: 8 Sinclair (Upton)
1944: 6 Flavin (Martin)
1945: 6 Hersey (John)
1947: 6 Warren (Robert Penn)
1948: 8 Michener (James)
1949: 7 Cozzens (James Gould)
1950: 7 Guthrie (A. B.)
1951: 7 Richter (Conrad)
1952: 4 Wouk (Herman)
1953: 9 Hemingway (Ernest)
1955: 8 Faulkner (William)
1956: 6 Kantor (MacKinlay)
1958: 4 Agee (James)
1959: 6 Taylor (Robert Lewis)
1960: 5 Drury (Allen)
1961: 3 Lee (Harper)
1962: 7 O'Connor (Edwin)
1963: 8 Faulkner (William)
1965: 4 Grau (Shirley Ann)
1966: 6 Porter (Katherine Anne)
1967: 7 Malamud (Bernard)
1968: 6 Styron (William)
1969: 7 Momaday (N. Scott)
1970: 8 Stafford (Jean)
1972: 7 Stegner (Wallace)
1973: 5 Welty (Eudora)
1975: 6 Shaara (Michael)
1976: 6 Bellow (Saul)
1978: 9 McPherson (James Alan)
1979: 7 Cheever (John)
1980: 6 Mailer (Norman)
1981: 5 Toole (John Kennedy)
1982: 6 Updike (John)
1983: 6 Walker (Alice)
1984: 7 Kennedy (William)
1985: 5 Lurie (Alison)
1986: 8 McMurtry (Larry)
1987: 6 Taylor (Peter)
1988: 8 Morrison (Toni)
1989: 5 Tyler (Anne)
1990: 8 Hijuelos (Oscar)
1991: 6 Updike (John)
1992: 6 Smiley (Jane)
1993: 6 Butler (Robert Olen)
1994: 6 Proulx (E. Annie)

1995: **7** Shields (Carol)
1996: **4** Ford (Richard)
1997: **10** Millhauser (Steven)
1998: **4** Roth (Philip)
1999: **10** Cunningham (Michael)
2000: **6** Lahiri (Jhumpa)
2001: **6** Chabon (Michael)
2002: **5** Russo (Richard)
2003: **9** Eugenides (Jeffrey)
2004: **5** Jones (Edward P.)
2005: **8** Robinson (Marilynne)
2006: **6** Brooks (Geraldine)
2007: **8** McCarthy (Cormac)
2008: **4** Diaz (Junot)
2009: **6** Strout (Elizabeth)
2010: **7** Harding (Paul)
2011: **4** Egan (Jennifer)
2013: **7** Johnson (Adam)
2014: **5** Tartt (Donna)
2015: **5** Doerr (Anthony)

pull
3 oar, row, tow, tug **4** drag, draw, haul, jerk, lure, root, yank **5** clout, draft, drive, force, pluck, put on, wrest **6** appeal, assume, entice **7** attract, draw out, extract, stretch **9** advantage, influence **10** attraction

pull back
6 rein in **7** retreat **8** withdraw

pull down
4 draw, earn, raze, ruin **5** lower, wreck **6** reduce **7** depress, destroy **8** demolish, overcome **9** dismantle

pullet
3 hen **5** chick, frier, fryer **7** chicken

pulley
5 wheel **6** sheave
watch's: **5** fusee

pull in
3 nab **4** stop **5** check, pinch **6** arrest, arrive, collar, detain, pick up **7** inhibit **8** hold back, restrain **9** apprehend

pulling
6 towage **7** draught, haulage **8** traction
cable: **7** towline

Pullman
3 car **7** sleeper **8** suitcase **11** railroad car

pull off
6 attain, manage **7** achieve, succeed **8** carry out **10** accomplish

pull out
4 exit, quit **5** leave **6** depart **7** abandon, retreat, take off **8** shove off, withdraw

pull through
5 rally **7** get over, recover, ride out, survive, weather **9** get better

pullulate
4 teem **5** breed, crawl, swarm **6** abound, sprout **7** produce **9** germinate

pull up
4 halt, stop **5** check **6** rebuke **8** draw even **9** reprimand

pulp
4 mash, pith **5** crush **6** bruise, squash **7** tabloid **8** soft part

pulpit
4 ambo, dais **6** podium **7** lectern, rostrum **8** ministry, platform

pulpy
4 soft **5** cheap, juicy, lurid, mushy **6** spongy **11** sensational

pulsate
4 beat, pump **5** pound, throb **7** vibrate **9** oscillate, palpitate

pulse
4 beat **5** throb **6** rhythm

pulverize
4 beat, ruin **5** crush, grind, smash, wreck **6** crunch, powder **7** atomize, destroy **8** demolish **9** micronize **10** annihilate

puma
3 cat **6** cougar **7** panther **12** mountain lion

pummel
3 hit **4** beat, drub **5** pound, punch **6** batter, beat up, buffet, hammer, thrash, wallop **7** belabor

pump
4 draw, shoe, quiz **5** exert, grill, heart, raise **6** device, elicit **7** operate **8** energize, question

pumpernickel
3 rye **5** bread

pumpkin
4 pepo **6** orange, squash **12** jack-o'-lantern
family: **5** gourd

pump up
4 fill **6** excite, expand **7** enthuse, inflate **8** energize, increase, motivate **9** stimulate

pun
4 joke **11** paronomasia, play on words **13** double meaning

punch
3 box, cut, die, dig, hit, jab, jog, pep **4** bang, blow, cuff, poke, prod, push, snap, sock **5** clout, drive, notch, smack, vigor **6** buffet, emboss, energy, impact, pummel, strike, thrust **8** uppercut, vitality **9** emphasize, perforate

punch bowl
8 monteith

punch-drunk
5 dazed, dizzy, woozy **6** addled, groggy **8** unsteady **9** befuddled, slaphappy **10** staggering **11** disoriented

puncheon
3 log 4 cask, slab, tool 6 timber

puncher
5 boxer 6 cowboy

Punch's wife
4 Judy

punchy
5 dazed, dizzy, vivid 6 addled, lively 7 dynamic, vibrant 8 forceful, spirited, vigorous 9 befuddled, energetic, slaphappy 11 light-headed

punctilious
5 exact, fussy 7 careful, precise 9 attentive, observant 10 meticulous, particular, scrupulous 11 painstaking

punctual
5 ready 6 on time, prompt, timely

punctuate
4 mark 5 point 6 accent, divide, stress 8 separate 9 emphasize, interrupt 10 accentuate

punctuation mark
4 dash 5 brace, colon, comma, slant, slash 6 hyphen, parens, period 7 bracket, solidus, virgule 8 diagonal, ellipsis 9 backslash, guillemet, semicolon 10 apostrophe 11 parenthesis

puncture
3 jab 4 bore, flat, hole, stab 5 burst, drill, prick, punch 6 blow up, debunk, pierce, riddle 7 deflate, explode 8 disprove 9 discredit, perforate 11 perforation

pundit
4 guru, sage 5 maven, swami 6 critic, expert 7 teacher, wise man 9 authority, columnist 11 talking head

pungency
4 bite 5 sting 8 piquancy 9 intensity, sharpness

pungent
5 acerb, acrid, acute, harsh, sharp, spicy, tangy, zesty 6 barbed, biting 7 caustic, cutting, intense, mordant, painful, peppery, piquant, pointed 8 exciting, incisive, poignant, stinging 9 trenchant 10 irritating 11 provocative, stimulating

punish
4 fine, hurt 5 mulct, spank 6 amerce, avenge 7 chasten, correct, put down, reprove, revenge, scourge, torture 8 chastise, penalize 9 castigate, criticize 10 discipline

punishment
3 rod 4 fine 5 lumps, mulct 7 penalty, reproof 10 amercement, chastening, correction, discipline 11 castigation, comeuppance, just deserts 12 chastisement
instrument: 7 scourge

punitive
5 penal 11 castigating, vindicative 12 correctional, disciplinary

punk
4 hood, thug 5 cholo, rowdy, tough 6 novice, rookie, tinder 7 hoodlum, ruffian, toughie 8 beginner, gangster, inferior 9 roughneck 10 delinquent
rock group: 7 Ramones 10 Sex Pistols

punkah
3 fan

punt
4 boat, boot, kick, play 6 gamble, propel

Punta del ___
4 Este

puny
4 weak 5 dinky, petty, small 6 feeble, little, measly, paltry, slight 7 trivial 8 inferior, niggling, picayune, piddling, trifling

pupa
9 chrysalid, chrysalis

pupil
5 cadet, tutee 7 learner, scholar, student 8 disciple 9 schoolboy 10 apprentice, schoolgirl
French: 5 élève

puppet
4 doll, dupe, pawn, tool 6 figure, stooge 10 figurehead, marionette

puppy
3 dog 5 whelp

Puppy Love singer
4 Anka (Paul)

Purcell opera
13 Dido and Aeneas

purchase
3 buy 4 hold 6 obtain, pay for 7 acquire, procure 9 advantage 11 acquisition

pure
5 clean, fresh, plain, sheer, total, utter 6 chaste, decent 7 a priori, genuine, perfect, unmixed 8 absolute, abstract, innocent, spotless, virtuous 9 authentic, continent, exemplary, inviolate, stainless, unalloyed, undiluted, untainted 10 immaculate 11 theoretical, unblemished, unmitigated, unqualified 13 unadulterated

purebred
8 pedigree 9 full-blood, pedigreed 10 registered 11 full-blooded

puree
4 soup 5 paste

purely
4 just 5 quite 6 merely, simply, wholly 7 exactly, totally, utterly 8 entirely 10 altogether, completely 11 exclusively

purfle
4 trim 6 border 8 decorate, ornament

purgation
9 catharsis, cleansing 10 lustration

purgative
5 jalap **7** lustral **9** cathartic

purge
3 rid **4** oust **5** clear, expel **6** purify, remove **7** cleanse, wipe out **8** get rid of, lustrate **9** eliminate, liquidate

purification
8 ablution **9** catharsis, cleansing, expiation, purgation **10** absolution, lustration **11** expurgation **12** regeneration
sacrament: **7** baptism

purify
5 clean, purge **6** filter, refine **7** clarify, cleanse

Purim
11 Feast of Lots
month: **4** Adar
queen: **6** Esther

puritan
4 prig **5** prude **8** bluenose **9** Mrs. Grundy

puritanical
4 prim **5** rigid **6** severe, strict **7** ascetic, austere, prudish **8** priggish **9** bluenosed **11** straitlaced

purity
8 chastity **9** innocence

purl
4 eddy, edge, knit **5** swirl, whirl **6** border, murmur, stitch **9** embroider

purlieu
5 haunt **7** hangout

purlieus
6 bounds, limits **7** suburbs **8** boundary, confines, environs **9** outskirts, precincts **12** neighborhood

purloin
3 nip **4** lift, nick, take **5** boost, filch, pinch, steal, swipe **6** pilfer, remove, rip off, snitch **11** appropriate

purloiner
5 crook, thief **8** larcener **9** larcenist

purple
4 plum, robe **5** cloth, grape, lilac, mauve, regal **6** florid, maroon, orchid, ornate, turgid, violet **7** flowery, pigment, pompous **8** imperial, lavender **9** bombastic, high-flown, overblown **10** rhetorical

purple flower
5 lilac

Purple Heart
5 award, medal **10** decoration

purple hue
5 lilac

purport
4 gist, mean **5** claim, drift, sense, tenor **6** allege, intend, thrust **7** meaning, message, profess, purpose **8** maintain **9** substance **11** connotation, implication **12** significance, significancy

purported
7 alleged, reputed, seeming **8** apparent, so-called, supposed **9** professed **10** ostensible

purpose
3 aim, end, use **4** goal, plan, role **5** point **6** action, design, intent, object **7** meaning, mission, resolve, subject **8** ambition, function, proposal **9** direction, intention, objective **10** aspiration, resolution **13** determination

purposeful
5 telic **6** driven, intent **7** earnest, planned, studied, willful **8** resolute **9** conscious, dedicated **10** calculated, considered, deliberate, determined **11** intentional **12** premeditated

purposeless
6 random **9** desultory, haphazard, hit-or-miss, irregular, unplanned

purposely
9 expressly **10** explicitly **12** deliberately **13** intentionally

purr
3 hum **6** murmur

purse
3 bag, sum **4** knit **5** money, pouch, prize **6** pucker, wallet **7** handbag **8** reticule **9** clutch bag **10** pocketbook, prize money
Scottish: **7** sporran

pursue
3 woo **4** hunt, seek **5** chase, haunt, hound, stalk, track, trail **6** badger, follow **7** afflict, go after, proceed **8** continue, engage in **9** persecute, persevere

pursuit
3 job **4** hunt, work **5** chase, quest, trade **6** search **8** activity, business, vocation **9** avocation, following **10** employment, occupation, profession

purvey
6 obtain, peddle, supply **7** furnish, provide **9** provision

purview
3 ken **5** ambit, limit, orbit, range, reach, scope, sweep **6** extent **8** boundary

push
3 pep **4** goad, plug, prod, sell, spur, urge **5** boost, drive, elbow, exert, force, impel, press, punch, shove, vigor **6** attack, effort, energy, expand, peddle, propel, throng, thrust **7** advance, assault, impetus, promote **8** ambition, pressure, vitality **9** incentive, influence, offensive **10** enterprise, get-up-and-go, initiative

Pushkin, Alexander
novel: **12** Eugene Onegin
play: **10** Stone Guest (The) **12** Boris Godunov
story: **13** Queen of Spades (The)

push off
4 exit **5** leave, start **6** depart, set out

push on
6 travel **7** advance, journey, proceed **8** continue, progress

pushover
4 snap **5** chump, cinch, softy **6** breeze, picnic, stooge, sucker **9** soft touch

pushy
4 bold **5** brash, nervy **7** forward **8** forceful **9** assertive, obnoxious **10** aggressive **12** presumptuous

pusillanimous
5 timid **6** coward, craven **7** chicken, gutless **8** cowardly, poltroon, timorous **9** spineless **11** lily-livered

puss
3 cat, mug **4** face **6** kisser, kitten

pussycat
5 sissy, softy **6** softie **8** pushover, weakling **9** soft touch **10** namby-pamby **13** bleeding heart

pussyfoot
5 creep, dodge, evade, glide, skulk, slink, sneak, steal **6** tiptoe **10** equivocate

pustule
4 boil **6** pimple **7** abscess, blister **8** furuncle **9** carbuncle

put
3 lay, set **4** park **5** place **8** position

putative
7 assumed, reputed **8** accepted, believed, presumed, supposed **11** conjectural **12** hypothetical

put away
3 eat **4** stow **5** eat up, swill **6** commit, devour, lock up **7** confine, consume **9** polish off **11** incarcerate

put by
4 save **5** lay in, store **7** lay away **8** lay aside, salt away

put cargo on
4 lade

put down
5 abase, crush, quash, quell **6** demean, demote, depose, squash, subdue **7** squelch **8** belittle, suppress **9** criticize, disparage, downgrade, humiliate

put forth
5 exert, issue **6** assert **7** present, propose

put off
5 defer, delay **7** suspend **8** hold over, postpone

put on
3 act, don, kid **4** fake **5** apply, bluff, feign, mount, stage **6** affect, assume **7** mislead, perform, pretend, produce

put-on
3 act **4** fake, sham, show **5** faked, phony, spoof **6** parody **7** assumed, feigned **8** affected, disguise **9** pretended **10** artificial, false front

put on board
4 stow

put out
3 vex **4** gall **5** annoy, douse, evict, issue, upset **6** bother, quench **7** disturb, produce, publish, trouble **8** irritate **9** aggravate, displease, embarrass **10** disconcert, exasperate, extinguish **13** inconvenience

putrefy
3 rot **5** decay, spoil, taint **6** molder **7** corrupt **9** break down, decompose

putrid
4 foul **5** fetid **6** rancid, rotten **7** corrupt, decayed, noisome, spoiled

putsch
4 coup **6** revolt **8** takeover, uprising **9** coup d'état, overthrow, rebellion **10** usurpation

putter
4 club, idle **6** fiddle, golfer, tinker **8** golf club

putting area
5 green

putto
5 cupid **6** cherub **8** amoretto

put together
4 form, join, make **5** build, unite **7** combine, connect, fashion, produce **8** assemble **9** construct, fabricate

putty
3 mud **4** clay **6** cement

put up
4 bunk **5** board, build, erect, house, lodge, raise **6** billet, harbor **7** quarter **8** domicile **9** construct

put up with
4 bear, hack **5** abide, stand **6** endure, suffer **7** swallow **8** tolerate

Puzo novel
6 Omerta **7** Last Don (The) **8** Fools Die, Sicilian (The) **9** Godfather (The)

puzzle
3 why **4** foil, koan **5** poser, rebus **6** baffle, enigma, fuddle, muddle, riddle **7** anagram, confuse, mystery, mystify, nonplus, paradox, perplex, problem, tangram **8** acrostic, befuddle, bewilder, confound **9** conundrum, crossword, dumbfound, frustrate **10** disconcert **11** brainteaser
number: 6 Sudoku

puzzle out
5 solve **6** answer, decode **7** clarify, clear up, explain, unravel **8** decipher, unriddle

puzzling
6 knotty **7** cryptic **8** baffling **9** confusing, difficult, enigmatic **10** mystifying, perplexing **11** bewildering, paradoxical **12** inexplicable

Pygmalion
beloved: **7** Galatea
character: **5** Eliza (Doolittle) **7** Higgins (Henry)
father: **5** Belus
musical: **10** My Fair Lady
playwright: **4** Shaw (George Bernard)
sister: **4** Dido
victim: **8** Sichaeus

pygmy
4 tiny **5** dwarf **6** bantam, little, midget **8** dwarfish **10** diminutive, homunculus **11** lilliputian

Pylades
companion: **7** Orestes
father: **9** Strophius
wife: **7** Electra

Pyle of journalism
5 Ernie

pylon
4 post **5** tower **6** marker **7** gateway

Pym's creator
3 Poe (Edgar Allan)

Pynchon novel
13 Mason and Dixon **15** Gravity's Rainbow

pyramid builder
5 Khufu **6** Cheops

Pyramus' beloved
6 Thisbe

pyre
4 heap, pile

pyretic
3 hot **7** burning, febrile, fevered **8** feverish

pyromaniac
5 torch **8** arsonist **10** incendiary

pyrosis
9 heartburn

pyrotechnics
7 display **9** fireworks, spectacle

Pyrrha's husband
9 Deucalion

Pyrrhonist
7 doubter, skeptic **10** unbeliever

Pyrrhus
kingdom: **6** Epirus
victory: **7** Asculum

Pythias' friend
5 Damon

python
3 boa **5** snake
slayer: **6** Apollo

pyx
3 box **4** case **6** vessel **9** container **10** receptacle

Q

Qatar
capital: **4** Bida, Doha
gulf: **7** Persian
language: **6** Arabic
leader: **4** amir, emir **5** ameer, emeer
monetary unit: **4** rial **5** riyal
neighbor: **11** Saudi Arabia
peninsula: **7** Arabian

QED word
4 erat, quod **13** demonstrandum

q.t., on the
7 sub rosa **8** covertly, secretly **13** under the table

quack
3 cry **4** honk, sham **6** con man, humbug **7** shammer **9** charlatan **10** mountebank

quackery
4 hoax, scam **5** fraud, hokum **6** deceit **8** flimflam, pretense **9** deception, duplicity, imposture **11** dissembling

quad
see **quadrangle**

quadrangle
4 yard **5** close, court, patio **6** square **7** polygon **9** courtyard, curtilage, enclosure

quadrant
3 arc **6** fourth **9** one-fourth

quadratic
4 boxy **6** square **7** boxlike **10** foursquare

quadriga
7 chariot

quadrille
5 dance, ombre **8** card game **11** square dance

quadrivium subject
5 music **8** geometry **9** astronomy **10** arithmetic

quaestor
6 bursar **8** official **9** paymaster, treasurer

quaff
3 sip **4** swig, toss **5** drink, sup up **6** guzzle, imbibe, sup off **7** carouse, swallow

quagga
3 ass

quaggy
4 soft **5** boggy, mushy, pulpy **6** flabby, marshy, spongy **7** flaccid, squashy, squishy **8** squooshy, yielding

quagmire
3 bog, fen, fix, jam **4** mire **5** marsh, pinch, swamp **6** morass, pickle, plight, scrape, slough **7** dilemma **8** quandary **9** imbroglio, marshland, swampland

quahog
4 clam **7** mollusc, mollusk **9** shellfish **11** cherrystone

quail
5 cower, wince **6** blanch, blench, cringe, flinch, recoil, shrink **7** shudder, squinch, tremble **8** bobwhite
flock of: **4** bevy

quaint
3 odd **5** funny, queer, retro **7** antique, archaic, curious, oddball, strange, unusual **8** peculiar, singular **9** different, eccentric, whimsical **10** antiquated, unfamiliar **12** old-fashioned

quake
5 shake, waver **6** dither, quaver, quiver, shiver, tremor **7** shudder, temblor, tremble, twitter, vibrate **8** trembler

Quaker
6 Friend
city: **12** Philadelphia
colonizer: **4** Penn (William)
color: **4** gray
founder: **3** Fox (George)
poet: **6** Barton (Bernard) **8** Whittier (John Greenleaf)
pronoun: **3** thy **4** thee, thou **5** thine
State: **12** Pennsylvania

qualification
6 caveat **7** ability, fitness, proviso **8** adequacy, aptitude, capacity, standard **9** condition, criterion **10** capability, competence **11** requirement, restriction, stipulation

qualified
3 fit **4** able **6** au fait, proper, proved, proven, tested **7** capable, limited, partial, skilled, trained **8** eligible **9** competent **10** restricted **11** conditional

qualify
3 fit **5** limit **6** lessen, modify, reduce, soften, temper **7** certify, entitle, license, mollify, prepare **8** describe, mitigate

quality
4 rank **5** grade, merit, prime, savor, state, trait, value, worth **6** factor, flower, status, virtue **7** caliber, element, feature, stature **8** position, property, standing **9** attribute, character, gentility, parameter **10** excellence, patriciate

qualm
4 fear **5** demur, doubt **6** nausea, unease **7** illness, scruple **8** mistrust **9** faintness, misgiving, objection **10** conscience, foreboding, reluctance, uneasiness **11** compunction, nervousness, uncertainty

quandary
3 fix, jam **4** bind, hole, spot **5** pinch **6** pickle, plight, scrape **7** dilemma **8** quagmire **10** difficulty **11** predicament

quantity
4 body, bulk, dose, scad **5** total **6** amount, degree, volume **9** abundance, aggregate, magnitude
fixed: **8** constant
small: **3** bit, dab **4** dash **5** shred, trace **6** nugget, smidge **7** modicum, smidgen, smidgin **8** smidgeon

quantum
5 quota, share, total **6** amount, budget, ration **7** measure, portion **9** aggregate, allotment, allowance, increment
of gravity: **8** graviton
of radiant energy: **6** photon
of vibrational energy: **6** phonon
theory originator: **6** Planck (Max)

quarantine
6 detain **7** confine, isolate **8** restrain **9** isolation, restraint **10** detainment **11** confinement

quarrel
3 row **4** beef, bolt, dust, fray, fuss, miff, spar, spat, tiff **5** argue, arrow, brawl, broil, clash, fight, melee, run-in, scrap, set-to **6** affray, battle, bicker, differ, dustup, fracas, ruckus, squall, strife **7** brabble, discord, dispute, dissent, fall out, rhubarb, ruction, scuffle, wrangle **8** argument, catfight, conflict, disagree, skirmish, squabble **9** altercate, bickering, brannigan, lock horns, imbroglio, scrimmage **10** contention, difference, dissension, falling-out **11** altercation, embroilment

quarrelsome
7 adverse, scrappy **8** brawling, choleric **9** bellicose, combative, irascible, irritable, rancorous, truculent **10** pugnacious **11** bad-tempered, belligerent, contentious **12** cantankerous, disputatious **13** argumentative

quarry
3 dig, pit **4** game, mine, pane, prey **5** chase, delve **6** source, victim **8** excavate **10** excavation

quarter
4 area, bunk, part **5** board, house, lodge, mercy, put up **6** barrio, billet, canton, fourth, ghetto, harbor, sector **7** barrack, section, shelter **8** clemency, district, division, locality, precinct, quadrant
circle: **8** quadrant
note: **8** crotchet
pint: **4** gill
ship's: **6** fo'c'sle **10** forecastle

quarterback
4 boss, head, lead **6** direct, leader, player **7** athlete, oversee **8** director, overseer **9** supervise **10** footballer, supervisor

quarterback Manning
3 Eli **6** Peyton

quartet
4 four **5** group **6** tetrad **8** ensemble, foursome **10** quadruplet, quaternion

quart, metric
5 liter, litre

quartz
4 onyx, sard **5** agate **6** jasper **7** citrine, mineral **8** amethyst, sardonyx **9** cairngorm, carnelian **10** chalcedony

quash
3 axe, nix **4** undo, veto, void **5** annul, crush, quell **6** defeat, negate, quench, stifle, subdue **7** abolish, nullify, put down, repress, smother, squelch **8** abrogate, dissolve, suppress **10** extinguish, invalidate

quasi
6 almost **7** nominal, seeming, virtual **8** apparent

Quasimodo
9 hunchback
creator: **4** Hugo (Victor)
occupation: **10** bell ringer
residence: **5** Paris **9** Notre Dame

quaver
4 note **5** quake, shake, trill, waver **6** dither, shiver, tremor **7** shudder, tremble, twitter **10** eighth note

quay
4 dock, pier, slip **5** berth, jetty, levee, wharf **6** marina **7** moorage

queasy
6 qualmy, uneasy **7** dubious **8** doubtful, hesitant, nauseous, qualmish, troubled **9** hazardous, nauseated, squeamish

Quebec province
capital: **6** Quebec
city: **5** Laval **8** Montreal **9** Longueuil
island: **9** Anticosti
mountain: **9** Tremblant **10** D'Iberville
peninsula: **5** Gaspé
provincial flower: **10** fleur-de-lys **11** madonna lily
river: **10** St. Lawrence

Queeg's ship
5 Caine

queen
Austria-Hungary: **12** Maria Theresa
Belgian: **6** Astrid
Danish: **8** Margaret, Margrete
Egyptian: **9** Cleopatra **10** Hatshepsut
English: **4** Anne, Mary **8** Victoria **9** Elizabeth
French and English: **7** Eleanor
Hindu: **4** rani **5** ranee
Netherlands: **7** Beatrix, Juliana **10** Wilhelmina
of Carthage: **4** Dido
of heaven: **4** Mary, moon **7** Astarte
of Isles: **6** Albion
of Ithaca: **8** Penelope
of Navarre: **8** Margaret
of Scots: **4** Mary
of Sheba: **6** Balkis
of the Adriatic: **6** Venice
of the Antilles: **4** Cuba
of the East: **7** Zenobia
of the fairies: **3** Mab **7** Titania
of the gods: **4** Hera, Juno, Sati
of the Nile: **9** Cleopatra
of the North: **9** Edinburgh
of the underworld: **3** Hel **4** Hela **10** Persephone, Proserpina
Spanish: **7** Isabela **8** Isabella
Spartan: **4** Leda
Swedish: **9** Christina

Queen Anne's lace
6 carrot **10** wild carrot

Queen of Spades
author: **7** Pushkin (Alexander)
composer: **11** Tchaikovsky (Peter Ilyich)

Queensland
capital: **8** Brisbane
explorer: **4** Cook (Captain James)

Queens stadium
4 Ashe
former: **4** Shea

queer
3 odd **5** bogus, weird **7** bizarre, curious, dubious, oddball, strange, touched, unusual **8** peculiar, singular **9** eccentric **10** outlandish, suspicious **11** counterfeit

quell
4 calm, stop **5** allay, check, crush, quash, quiet **6** pacify, quench, squash, subdue **7** conquer, put down, squelch **8** overcome, suppress, vanquish **9** overwhelm, subjugate **10** extinguish

Quemoy's neighbor
4 Amoy **5** Matsu

quench
4 sate **5** allay, douse, quash, quell, slake **6** lessen, put out, reduce **7** appease, assuage,

gratify, lighten, put down, relieve, satiate, satisfy **8** mitigate, suppress **9** alleviate, eliminate **10** extinguish

quenelle
8 dumpling, meatball **9** forcemeat

quern
4 mill

querulous
5 whiny **7** fretful, peevish, pettish, whining **8** petulant **11** complaining

query
3 ask **4** quiz **5** doubt, grill **7** inquire, inquiry **8** question **9** catechize **11** interrogate

quest
4 hunt **5** probe **6** pursue, search **7** delving, inquire, inquiry, mission, pursuit **9** pursuance **13** investigation
object: 5 grail

question
3 ask, pry **4** poll, pump, quiz **5** doubt, grill, issue, probe, query **6** chance, matter **7** debrief, dispute, examine, inquire, inquiry, problem, suspect **8** distrust, mistrust **9** catechize, challenge, objection **10** difficulty, puzzle over **11** interrogate, possibility **13** interrogation, interrogatory
to Brutus: 4 et tu

questionable
4 iffy, moot **5** shady, vague **6** unsure **7** dubious, obscure, suspect **8** arguable, doubtful, unproven **9** debatable, equivocal, uncertain **10** disputable, fly-by-night, improbable, unreliable **11** problematic

questioning
5 probe, query **6** show-me **7** delving, dubious, inquiry, probing **8** doubtful, grilling **9** inquiring, quizzical, skeptical, uncertain **11** incredulous, inquisitive, unbelieving **12** disbelieving **13** interrogation

quetzal
4 bird, coin **6** trogon

queue
3 row **4** file, line, rank, wait **5** braid, tress **6** column **8** sequence

quibble
4 carp **5** argue, cavil **6** argufy, bicker, niggle, object **7** dispute, evasion, nitpick, wrangle **8** squabble **9** criticism, criticize, objection **10** split hairs

quick
4 core, deft, fast, keen, pith, root **5** acute, adept, agile, brisk, fleet, hasty, rapid, sharp, smart, swift **6** abrupt, bright, clever, nimble, prompt, speedy, sudden **7** hurried **9** breakneck, impetuous
combining form: 5 tachy

quick bread
6 muffin **7** biscuit

quicken
4 goad, grow, move, spur, stir, wake **5** hurry, liven, pique, rouse, speed **6** arouse, awaken, excite, hasten, induce, kindle, revive, step up, vivify **7** actuate, animate, enliven, shake up, speed up **8** activate, energize, motivate, vitalize **9** galvanize, stimulate **10** accelerate, invigorate

quickly
5 apace **6** at once, pronto **9** forthwith, posthaste **12** straightaway

quickness
5 haste, speed **8** alacrity, celerity, dispatch, legerity, rapidity, velocity **9** fleetness, rapidness, swiftness

quicksand
3 bog **4** mire **6** morass

quicksilver
7 mercury **9** mercurial **10** inconstant

quick-tempered
5 cross, fiery, ratty, testy **6** cranky, touchy **7** peppery **8** choleric, petulant **9** irascible, irritable, splenetic

quick-witted
3 apt **4** keen **5** acute, agile, alert, canny, ready, sharp, smart **6** astute, brainy, bright, clever **9** brilliant **10** perceptive **11** intelligent

quid
3 cut, wad **4** chaw, chew, coin **5** money, pound **9** sovereign

quid ___ ___
6 pro quo

quiddity
3 nub **4** gist, meat, pith **6** trifle **7** essence, quibble **8** crotchet **12** eccentricity, quintessence

quidnunc
see **rumormonger**

quiescent
4 calm **5** quiet, still **6** benign, hushed, latent, placid, serene, stilly **7** abeyant, dormant, halcyon, lurking **8** inactive, tranquil **10** untroubled

quiet
4 calm, hush, idle, lull, mute, stop **5** abate, allay, inert, muted, shush, still, whist **6** asleep, becalm, gentle, hushed, lessen, placid, serene, settle, silent, soothe, subdue **7** compose, halcyon, pacific, passive, restful, silence, subdued **8** decrease, inactive, peaceful, reserved, secluded, taciturn, tranquil **9** noiseless, soundless, stillness, unruffled **11** tranquility, tranquilize, unobtrusive

quietus
3 end **5** death, sleep **6** damper, demise, finish **7** decease, passing, silence **8** curtains **10** inactivity, settlement **11** termination

quill
3 pen **5** float, shaft, spine, spool **6** bobbin **7** feather, spindle
pen point: 3 neb, nib

quilt
4 pouf, puff **5** duvet **8** coverlet **9** comforter, eiderdown **11** counterpane
design: 8 trapunto

quince
3 bel

quintessence
4 gist, meat, pith, soul **5** ideal, model, stuff **6** marrow **7** epitome **8** exemplar, last word, quiddity, ultimate **9** substance

quintessential
5 ideal, model **7** classic, typical **8** ultimate **9** classical, exemplary **10** archetypal, consummate, prototypal **12** prototypical

quintillionth combining form
4 atto

quintuple
8 fivefold

quip
3 dig, gag, kid **4** gibe, gird, jape, jeer, jest, jibe, joke **5** crack, fleer, sally, scoff, sneer, tease **6** banter, oddity, retort, zinger **7** quibble **9** wisecrack, witticism

quipster
3 wag, wit **4** card **5** clown, comic, droll, joker **6** jester **8** comedian, funnyman, humorist, jokester **11** wisecracker

quirk
3 tic **4** bend, kink, quip, whim **5** crook, curve, twist **6** foible, groove, oddity, vagary **7** caprice **8** accident, crotchet **9** mannerism **11** peculiarity **12** idiosyncrasy

quirky
3 odd **7** erratic, offbeat **8** peculiar **9** eccentric, irregular, whimsical **10** capricious **13** idiosyncratic

quirt
4 lash, whip

quisling
5 Judas, rebel **7** traitor **8** apostate, betrayer, defector, turncoat **10** copperhead **12** collaborator

quit
3 end, pay **4** cave, drop, free, halt, stop **5** cease, chuck, leave **6** cave in, depart, desert, desist, give up, resign, retire, settle **7** abandon, drop out, forsake, release, relieve, satisfy **8** knock off, leave off, released, renounce, withdraw **9** discharge, liquidate, surrender, terminate **10** relinquish **11** discontinue

quite
3 all **4** just, very, well **5** fully, in all **6** in toto, purely, rather, wholly **7** exactly, totally, utterly **8** entirely **9** perfectly **10** absolutely, altogether, completely, positively, thoroughly **12** considerably

quittance
6 amends **7** redress **8** reprisal, requital **9** atonement, discharge, repayment **10** recompense, reparation **11** restitution **12** compensation

quitter
4 funk **6** coward, craven **7** chicken, dastard **9** defeatist

quiver
4 beat, case **5** pulse, quake, shake, throb, waver **6** arrows, dither, jitter, quaver, shiver, tremor **7** pulsate, shudder, tremble, twitter, vibrate **9** palpitate, vibration

qui vive
5 alert **7** lookout

Quixote
see **Don Quixote**

quixotic
7 foolish **8** fanciful, illusory, romantic **9** fantastic, imaginary, visionary **10** capricious, idealistic **11** impractical

quiz
3 ask **4** exam, test **5** grill, query **7** examine, inquire **8** question **9** catechize **11** interrogate **12** cross-examine

quizzical
3 odd **5** queer **6** quaint, show-me **7** curious, dubious, mocking, probing, puzzled, teasing **8** doubtful, doubting, sardonic **9** inquiring, skeptical **11** incredulous, inquisitive, questioning, unbelieving

quod ___ demonstrandum
4 erat

quodlibet
5 issue, point **6** debate, medley **7** mélange **8** fantasia, question **11** disputation

quoin
5 angle, block, wedge **6** corner **8** keystone, voussoir

quoit
4 hoop, ring **6** circle

quoits peg
3 hob

quondam
4 late, once, past **6** bygone, former, whilom **7** defunct, onetime **8** sometime **9** erstwhile **10** occasional

quorum
6 minyan **8** majority

quota
3 cut, lot **4** bite, meed, part **5** share, slice, whack **6** amount, parcel, ration **7** measure, portion, quantum **9** allotment, allowance **10** allocation, percentage, proportion

quotation
3 bid **5** offer, price **7** excerpt, extract, passage **8** citation

quotation mark, French
9 guillemet

quote
3 bid **4** cite, list **5** blurb, offer, price, refer **6** adduce, borrow, repeat **7** excerpt, extract, passage **8** citation

quotidian
5 daily, plain, usual **6** common **7** average, diurnal, prosaic, regular, routine, vanilla **8** day-to-day, everyday, ordinary, workaday **9** circadian **11** commonplace **12** unremarkable

quotient
5 ratio, share **7** caliber, portion **9** allotment, magnitude **10** percentage, proportion

R

Ra
son: **6** Khonsu
wife: **3** Mut

Raamah
father: **4** Cush
son: **5** Dedan, Sheba

Rabbi Ben Ezra author
8 Browning (Robert)

rabbit
4 cony **5** bunny, coney
female: **3** doe
fictional: **5** Fiver, Hazel, Mopsy, Peter **6** Flopsy, Harvey **7** Thumper **8** Crusader, Ricochet **9** Bugs Bunny **10** Cotton-tail **11** Easter Bunny
food: **5** salad **6** carrot **7** lettuce
fur: **4** cony **5** coney
male: **4** buck
neutered: **5** lapin
relative: **4** hare, pika
tail: **4** scut

rabble
3 mob **4** mass, rout **5** crush, horde **6** masses **8** canaille, populace, riffraff, unwashed **9** hoi polloi **10** lower class **11** proletariat, rank and file

rabble-rouser
7 inciter **8** agitator, fomenter **9** demagogue **10** incendiary **12** troublemaker

Rabelais character
7 Panurge **9** Gargantua **10** Pantagruel

rabid
3 mad **4** wild **5** crazy **6** crazed, insane **7** extreme, fanatic, frantic, furious, radical, zealous **8** demented, deranged, frenetic, frenzied, obsessed **9** delirious, extremist **10** corybantic **11** hydrophobic

rabies
11 hydrophobia

raccoon
8 ringtail
dog: **6** tanuki
relative: **5** civet, coati, panda **8** civet cat, kinkajou **10** cacomistle, coatimundi

race
3 rev **4** bolt, dart, dash, gill, lash, meet, rush, tear, type **5** brook, chase, creek, fling, hurry, match, rally, relay, shoot, speed, spurt **6** charge, course, gallop, runnel, scurry, sprint, stream **7** channel, contest, rivalry, rivulet, scamper **8** marathon **9** grand prix **11** competition, watercourse
zigzag: **6** slalom

race car
4 Elva, Lola, Ralt **5** Lotus, March, Swift **6** Abarth, Cooper, Merlyn, Royale, Turner **7** Avenger, Brabham, Chevron, Crosslé, Ferrari, Mallock, McLaren, Reynard, TransAm, Triumph **8** Corvette **9** Van Diemen **12** Austin Healey

racecourse
4 oval, turf **5** track **8** speedway
American: **7** Belmont, Hialeah **8** Saratoga **9** Keeneland
English: **5** Ascot

racehorse
5 Alsab, Kelso **6** Forego **7** Assault, Barbaro, Man O' War **8** Affirmed, Citation **9** Riva Ridge, War Emblem **10** Seabiscuit, War Admiral **11** Forward Pass, Seattle Slew, Secretariat, Smarty Jones **12** Native Dancer

Rachel
father: **5** Laban
husband: **5** Jacob
servant: **6** Bilhah
sister: **4** Leah
son: **6** Joseph **8** Benjamin

rachis
4 back 5 chine, spine 8 backbone 12 spinal column

rachitic
5 shaky 6 wobbly 7 rackety, rickety, tenuous 9 tremulous 10 ramshackle, rattletrap

___ Rachmaninoff
6 Sergei, Sergey

racing enthusiast
8 railbird

racism
7 bigotry, jim crow 9 apartheid, prejudice 11 segregation

racist
4 nazi 5 bigot 7 bigoted 10 intolerant, prejudiced 11 supremacist

rack
3 bed 4 buck, bunk, pace, pain, sack, scud 5 frame, wring 6 harass, harrow, martyr, strain, wrench 7 afflict, agonize, antlers, crucify, ratchet, sawbuck, stretch, torment, torture 8 sawhorse 10 excruciate

racket
3 con, din 4 game, scam 5 babel, fraud, hoo-ha, noise 6 clamor, hoo-hah, hubbub, rattle, scheme, tumult, uproar 7 clangor, pursuit, swindle 8 ballyhoo, brouhaha, clangour, foofaraw 10 hullabaloo 11 pandemonium

racketeer
7 goombah, mafioso, mobster 8 extorter, gangster 9 godfather, goodfella
law: 4 RICO (Act)

rack up
3 win 4 gain 5 reach, score 6 attain 7 achieve, realize 10 accomplish

raconteur
11 storyteller

racy
4 blue, gamy 5 bawdy, broad, juicy, salty, spicy, vampy, zesty 6 purple, risqué, smutty, snappy, vulgar 7 piquant, pungent 8 indecent, off-color, vigorous 10 suggestive

Radames' beloved
4 Aida

radar image
3 pip 4 blip, spot 5 trace

Raddai
brother: 5 David
father: 5 Jesse

raddled
5 at sea, dazed 7 mixed-up 8 confused

radiance
3 ray 4 aura, glow 5 glory, shine 6 luster 7 aureola, aureole 8 splendor 10 brightness, brilliance

radiant
4 glad 5 aglow, beamy, shiny 6 bright, lucent 7 beaming, fulgent, glowing, lambent 8 luminous, lustrous 9 brilliant, effulgent 10 effulgence 12 incandescent

radiate
4 beam, emit, glow 5 gleam, shine, strew 6 spread 7 diverge 8 illumine 10 illuminate

radiation unit
3 rad, rem, rep 7 langley, sievert 8 roentgen

radiator
6 cooler, heater 9 convector 11 transmitter 13 heat exchanger

radical
4 acyl, root 5 basal, basic, rebel, ultra 7 extreme, fanatic, primary 8 agitator, cardinal, militant, ultraist 9 anarchist, essential, extremist 10 subversive 11 fundamental 12 foundational, iconoclastic 13 revolutionary
mathematical: 4 surd

radicle
4 root 5 radix 9 hypocotyl

radio
4 AM-FM 8 wireless
frequency range: 8 waveband
shortwave: 3 ham 7 amateur

radioactive
3 hot 7 nuclear

radium
discoverer: 5 Curie (Marie, Pierre)

radius
5 ambit, orbit, range, reach, sweep 6 extent 7 compass, purview

radix
4 base, root 6 source

raffish
5 cocky 6 coarse, jaunty, sporty, vulgar 9 dissolute 12 devil-may-care

raffle
7 drawing, lottery

raft
3 lot, ton 4 heap, mess, pile, scad, slew 5 balsa, float 6 bundle
Maori: 4 moki

rafter
4 balk, beam, viga

rag
3 jaw, kid, rib 4 bait, jive, josh, rail, razz, rock 5 baste, cloth, scold, tease 6 berate, harass, hector, needle, pester 7 tabloid, torment 9 newspaper

ragamuffin
3 bum 4 hobo, waif 5 gamin, tramp 6 beggar, gamine, orphan, urchin 7 wastrel 8 vagabond 9 scarecrow 11 guttersnipe

rage
3 cry, fad, ire, mad, wax **4** chic, fume, fury, mode, rant **5** anger, craze, fancy, furor, go ape, mania, storm, style, vogue, wrath **6** blow up, frenzy, furore, lose it, seethe **7** fashion, madness, passion **8** boil over, hysteria **10** dernier cri

ragged
4 rent, torn **5** seedy **6** frayed, jagged, shabby, uneven **7** unkempt, worn-out **8** frazzled, straggly, tattered **10** threadbare

raging
4 wild **6** stormy **7** furious, intense, violent **8** blustery **9** ferocious, turbulent **10** blustering **11** tempestuous

ragout
4 olio, stew **5** salmi **6** burgoo, jumble, medley **7** farrago, goulash, mélange, mixture **8** mishmash **9** potpourri **10** hodgepodge, hotchpotch, salmagundi **11** gallimaufry

rags
4 duds, garb **5** dress **6** attire, shreds **7** apparel, clothes, raiment, threads **8** clothing

ragtag
see **rabble**

ragwort
7 senecio **9** cineraria, groundsel **10** butterweed

raid
4 bust, loot, sack **5** foray, harry **6** attack, forage, harass, inroad, invade, maraud, ravage, sortie **7** assault, despoil, overrun, plunder **8** invasion, spoliate **9** incursion

raider
6 pirate **10** freebooter

rail
3 bar, jaw **4** coot, sora **5** crake, fence, scold, track **6** berate, revile **7** barrier, clapper, inveigh, upbraid **8** banister, marsh hen, water hen
extinct: **4** moho

railing
8 banister **10** balustrade
part: **8** baluster

raillery
5 scorn **6** banter **7** mockery, teasing **8** badinage, derision, ridicule, taunting **10** lampoonery, persiflage

railroad
branch: **6** siding
car: **5** coach, diner, stock **6** hopper **7** caboose, gondola, Pullman
engine: **10** locomotive
locomotive: **9** iron horse
station: **5** depot
underground: **4** tube **5** metro **6** subway
worker: **6** porter **7** fireman **8** brakeman, engineer **9** conductor **11** gandy dancer

raiment
4 duds, garb, gear, togs **5** array, dress **6** attire **7** apparel, clothes, threads, vesture **8** clothing, garments, glad rags, vestiary **9** caparison, vestments **10** attirement **11** habiliments

rain
4 spit **6** deluge, mizzle, shower **7** drizzle **8** downpour, sprinkle **10** cloudburst **13** precipitation

rainbow
3 arc **4** irid, iris **5** array, gamut **7** fantasy **8** illusion, spectrum **9** pipe dream
bridge: **7** Bifrost
chaser: **9** visionary
combining form: **4** irid **5** irido
goddess: **4** Iris
shape: **3** arc

rainbow fish
5 guppy, trout **6** wrasse

raincoat
3 mac **4** mack **6** poncho, trench **7** oilskin, slicker **10** mackintosh

rain leader
9 downspout

rain tree
9 monkeypod

raise
4 ante, grow, hike, jack, jump, lift, pump, rear **5** boost, breed, erect, exalt, hoist, put up **6** foment, incite, jack up, leaven, muster, uplift **7** augment, bring up, collect, elevate, enhance, inflate, produce **8** heighten, increase **9** construct, cultivate, increment, propagate

raisin
5 grape **7** currant, sultana **10** dried grape

Raisin in the Sun author
9 Hansberry (Lorraine)

raison d' ___
4 état, être

raja
4 king **5** chief, ruler **6** prince **9** dignitary
wife: **4** rani **5** ranee

rake
3 rip **4** comb, roué, scan **5** angle, blood, pitch, rifle, scamp, scour, slope **6** forage, glance, lecher, rascal, scrape, search, strafe **7** incline, playboy, ransack, rummage, scratch **8** enfilade, lothario **9** debauchee, libertine **10** profligate

rakehell
4 fast, wild **5** blood, rogue, scamp **6** rascal, sporty **7** playboy, raffish **8** lothario, rascally **9** debauchee, dissolute, lecherous, libertine **10** licentious, profligate

rake-off
3 cut **4** bite, take **5** chunk, share **7** portion **9** baksheesh, lagniappe **10** commission, percentage

rake's look
4 leer, ogle

Rake's Progress, The
artist: 7 Hogarth (William)
composer: 10 Stravinsky (Igor)

rakish
see **rakehell**

rally
4 race, stir, wake **5** harry, renew, rouse, waken **6** arouse, awaken, bestir, kindle, muster, perk up, pick up, repair, volley **7** convene, enliven, marshal, rebound, recover **8** assemble, clambake, comeback, mobilize, recovery **9** challenge, recollect **10** invigorate, reorganize

rallying cry
5 motto **6** byword, slogan **9** watchword **10** shibboleth **11** catchphrase

ram
4 butt **5** Aries, crash, crowd, drive, pound, sheep, stuff **6** batter, plunge, strike, thrust **7** warship
mate: 3 ewe

Ramadan ending
3 Eid

Rama's wife
4 Sita

ramble
3 gad **4** roam, rove **5** drift, range, run on, stray, troll **6** stroll, wander **7** blather, digress, diverge, maunder, meander, saunter, traipse **8** divagate **9** gallivant

rambler
4 rose **5** gypsy, hiker, nomad, rover **6** roamer, walker **7** drifter, vagrant **8** stroller, vagabond, wanderer **9** itinerant **10** ranch house

rambunctious
5 rowdy **6** unruly **7** raucous, willful **10** boisterous, headstrong **12** recalcitrant, ungovernable

ramification
5 shoot **6** branch, offset **8** offshoot **9** outgrowth, offspring **11** consequence

ramify
6 branch, divide, extend **7** radiate **9** branch out, propagate **11** proliferate

Ramona author
7 Jackson (Helen Hunt)

ramose
8 branched

ramp
5 apron **7** incline

rampage
4 rage, riot, tear **5** binge, fling, spree, storm

rampageous
4 wild **6** unruly **7** riotous

rampant
4 rank, rife, wild **7** rearing, regnant **8** epidemic **9** prevalent, unbridled **10** widespread **12** uncontrolled, unrestrained

rampart
4 wall **5** ridge **7** bulwark, parapet **9** barricade **10** breastwork

ramshackle
6 flimsy **7** rickety, run-down **8** decrepit **10** tumbledown **11** dilapidated

ram's mate
3 ewe

ranch
5 finca **6** quinta, spread **8** estancia, hacienda
worker: 6 cowboy, gaucho **7** cowgirl, cowhand, cowpoke **10** cowpuncher

rancher
6 cowboy **7** breeder **9** cattleman

rancid
4 high, rank, sour **5** fetid **6** putrid, skunky, smelly **7** noisome, spoiled **8** stinking **9** offensive **10** malodorous

rancor
4 gall **6** animus, enmity, hatred **7** ill will **9** animosity, antipathy, hostility **10** antagonism, bitterness

rancorous
6 bitter **7** hateful, hostile **8** spiteful, venomous **9** malicious, malignant, vitriolic **10** malevolent **11** acrimonious **12** antagonistic

Rand, Ayn
novel: 6 Anthem **12** Fountainhead (The) **13** Atlas Shrugged

random
6 casual **7** aimless **8** slapdash **9** arbitrary, desultory, haphazard, hit-or-miss, unplanned **10** accidental, contingent, hit-and-miss, incidental **11** purposeless

randy
4 lewd **5** bawdy, lusty **7** lustful, satyric **9** lecherous, libertine, lickerish, salacious **10** lascivious, libidinous, licentious

range
3 row, run **4** area, band, roam, rove, shot, site, sort, span, vary **5** align, ambit, carry, drift, field, gamut, orbit, order, reach, realm, ridge, scale, scope, space, stove, stray, sweep, width **6** assort, domain, extent, length, limits, ramble, sierra, sphere, spread, wander **7** compass, earshot, expanse, eyeshot, habitat, meander, purview, stretch **8** confines, distance, latitude, locality, panorama, province, stovetop, traverse, vicinity **9** amplitude, extension, gallivant, magnitude, territory **12** distribution

range finder
9 telemeter

ranger
3 spy **5** scout **6** lawman, patrol, warden **8** overseer **9** caretaker, protector

rangy
4 lean **5** lanky **6** gangly **7** spindly **8** gangling

rani's mate
4 raja **5** rajah

rank
3 row **4** file, foul, lush, rate, seed, sort, tier **5** class, fetid, funky, grade, gross, humid, order, place, queue **6** assort, cachet, coarse, filthy, lavish, putrid, rancid, rating, smelly, status **7** arrange, dignity, echelon, footing, noisome, profuse, rampant, reeking, station, stature **8** classify, evaluate, flagrant, outright, position, standing, stinking **9** downright, egregious, loathsome, luxuriant, overgrown, repulsive **10** malodorous

rank and file
5 plebs **6** people, plebes **8** populace **9** commonage, commoners, plebeians **10** commonalty **11** enlisted men

rankle
3 irk, vex **4** rile **5** annoy **6** bother, fester, nettle, seethe **8** embitter, irritate **9** aggravate **10** exasperate

ransack
3 rob **4** comb, grub, loot, rake **5** rifle, scour **6** forage, ravage **7** despoil, plunder, rummage

Ran's husband
5 Aegir

ransom
3 buy **4** free **6** redeem, regain, rescue **7** deliver, recover **8** liberate

rant
3 jaw, rag **4** huff, rage, rail, rate, rave **5** mouth, scold, spout **6** screed, tirade **7** bluster, bombast, declaim, fustian **8** bloviate, harangue, perorate **10** vituperate **11** rodomontade

ranula
4 cyst

rap
3 hit, tap **4** blow, chat, swat, talk, wipe **5** blame, chide, knock, swipe **6** charge, hip-hop, patter, rebuke **7** censure, condemn **8** causerie, denounce, sentence **9** criticize, criticism, reprehend, reprimand **10** discussion **12** conversation
in Spanish: **9** reggaeton

rapacious
6 greedy **8** covetous, grasping, ravening, ravenous **9** predatory, voracious **10** gluttonous

rapacity
5 greed **7** avarice, avidity **8** cupidity, voracity **10** greediness

rape
4 ruin **5** colza, force, spoil **6** canola, defile, ravage, ravish **7** assault, debauch, despoil, outrage, plunder, violate **9** violation **10** ravishment, spoliation

Rape of the Lock, The
author: **4** Pope (Alexander)
heroine: **7** Belinda

Raphael
birthplace: **6** Urbino
subject: **7** Madonna
teacher: **8** Perugino

rapid
4 fast **5** brisk, chute, fleet, hasty, quick, swift **6** speedy **7** hurried **9** breakneck

rapidity
5 haste, hurry, speed **8** celerity, velocity

rapids
5 chute **8** cataract **10** white water

rapier
4 épée **5** blade, sword

rapine
4 loot, pelf, swag **5** booty, prize, spoil **6** boodle, spoils **7** pillage, plunder **10** spoliation

Rappaccini's Daughter
8 Beatrice
author: **9** Hawthorne (Nathaniel)

rapper
3 DMX, Eve, GZA, Jin **4** Dash (Damon), Ice T, Jay-Z **5** Cee-Lo, Combs (Sean "Diddy"), Diddy (Combs), Drake, Dr. Dre, Kanye (West), Minaj (Nicki), Rakim **6** Eminem, Heavy D, Ja Rule, KRS-ONE, Lil' Kim, Mac Dre, Mos Def, Run DMC, Twista **7** Birdman, Caushun, Ice Cube, LL Cool J, OutKast, Pitbull **8** Lil Wayne, Ludacris, Melle Mel, Paul Wall **9** Fifth Cent, Kanye West, Method Man, Snoop Dogg **10** Kool Moe Dee, Lupe Fiasco, Spoonie Gee, Tupac Shakur, Vanilla Ice **11** Busta Rhymes, Public Enemy

rapport
5 unity **6** accord **7** concord, harmony **8** affinity **9** communion

rapscallion
see **rascal**

rap session
6 confab, parley **7** palaver **8** colloquy **10** discussion

rap-sheet entry
3 aka **5** alias

rapt
6 intent **7** all ears, engaged **8** absorbed, immersed **9** engrossed **10** enthralled **11** carried away, preoccupied

raptor
3 owl **4** hawk **5** eagle **6** condor, falcon, merlin,

osprey **7** kestrel, vulture **9** gyrfalcon **10** bird of prey **11** deinonychus
claw: 5 talon

rapture
5 swoon **6** heaven **7** delight, ecstasy, nirvana **9** transport **10** exaltation **13** seventh heaven

rara ___
4 avis

rare
3 few, red **4** pink, thin **6** choice, dainty, exotic, scarce, seldom, select **7** elegant, unusual **8** delicate, singular, sporadic, superior, uncommon, unwonted **9** exquisite, recherché, underdone **10** infrequent, occasional **11** exceptional **13** extraordinary

rarefied
4 fine, thin **7** tenuous **8** esoteric **10** attenuated

rarefy
4 thin **6** refine **9** attenuate

rarely
6 little, seldom **9** extremely, unusually **12** infrequently

raring
4 avid, keen **5** eager **6** gung-ho **12** enthusiastic

rarity
5 curio **6** oddity **7** curiosa **8** scarcity **9** curiosity **10** aberration **11** collectible

rascal
3 imp **4** rake **5** devil, knave, rogue, scamp **6** varlet **7** lowlife, villain, wastrel **8** scalawag **9** miscreant, reprobate, scallywag, scoundrel, skeezicks **10** blackguard, scapegrace **11** rapscallion
Irish: 8 spalpeen

rash
5 hasty, heady **6** abrupt, brazen, daring, madcap, plague, sudden, unwary, unwise **7** foolish **8** careless, epidemic, eruption, headlong, heedless, outbreak, reckless **9** audacious, daredevil, foolhardy, hotheaded, impetuous, imprudent, impulsive **10** ill-advised, incautious, indiscreet, unthinking **11** injudicious, precipitate, temerarious, thoughtless

rasp
4 file, fret **5** annoy, chafe, grate **6** abrade, scrape **7** scratch **8** irritate

raspberry
7 catcall **8** blackcap **10** Bronx cheer

raspy
3 dry **5** harsh, rough **6** hoarse **7** grating, jarring, raucous **8** scrabbly, scratchy

rat
4 blab, fink, heel, scab, sing **5** louse **6** defect, desert, inform, rodent, snitch, squeak, squeal, tattle **7** stoolie **8** apostate, defector, informer, recreant, renegade, squealer, turncoat **9** bandicoot, repudiate, turnabout **11** stool pigeon **12** tergiversate
female: 3 doe

ratchet
4 pawl **6** detent

rate
3 fee, set, tab **4** cost, earn, rank **5** assay, class, grade, merit, price, scale, set at, value **6** amount, assess, charge, degree, esteem, regard, survey, tariff **7** apprize, deserve, valuate **8** appraise, classify, consider, estimate, evaluate, price tag **9** valuation **10** proportion

rather
4 a bit **5** quite **6** fairly, in lieu, kind of, pretty, sort of **7** instead **8** somewhat **10** more or less, preferably **11** alternately **13** alternatively

rathskeller
3 bar, inn, pub **4** dive **6** saloon, tavern **7** barroom, taproom **8** alehouse, basement

ratify
4 seal **5** enact **7** approve, certify, confirm, endorse, license **8** accredit, sanction, validate

rating
4 mark, rank **5** class, grade **6** number **8** estimate, standing

ratio
5 scale **7** percent **8** fraction, quotient **10** percentage, proportion

rational
4 sane

ratiocination
8 judgment, sequitur **9** inference, reasoning **10** conclusion

ration
4 dole, food, meal, mete **5** allot, divvy, quota, share **6** divide, parcel **7** measure, mete out, prorate **8** allocate **9** allotment, allowance **10** provisions **13** apportionment

rational
4 calm, cool, sane **5** lucid, sober, sound **6** stable **7** logical, prudent **8** sensible, thinking **9** judicious **10** consequent, reasonable **11** circumspect, intelligent, level-headed **12** intellectual

rationale
5 basis, logic **6** reason **7** grounds **9** reasoning **11** explanation **13** justification

rationalize
7 explain, justify **10** account for **11** externalize

ratite
3 emu, moa **4** kiwi, rhea **7** ostrich

rattail
3 cod **9** grenadier

rattan
4 cane, palm **6** switch **7** malacca

Rattigan play
10 Winslow Boy (The) **14** Separate Tables **15** Browning Version (The)

rattle
3 gab, jaw, yak **4** chat, faze, rale **5** abash, addle, clack, noise, rouse, run on, upset **6** babble, gabble, jangle, racket **7** chatter, clatter, confuse, disturb, flummox, perplex, unnerve **8** bewilder, confound, distract **9** discomfit, embarrass **10** disconcert, noisemaker

rattlebrained
5 ditzy, dizzy, giddy, silly **6** addled **7** flighty **9** frivolous

rattling
4 very **5** brisk, quick **6** damned, lively, mighty **8** whacking, whopping **9** energetic, extremely

ratty
4 mean **5** dowdy, dumpy, seedy, tacky **6** cheesy, scurvy, shabby **7** unkempt **8** slovenly **9** irritable

raucous
4 loud **5** harsh, noisy, rough, rowdy **6** hoarse, unruly **7** grating, jarring, squawky **8** rowdyish, strident **9** termagant, turbulent **10** boisterous, disorderly, stridulent, stridulous, tumultuous **11** cacophonous **12** rambunctious

raunchy
4 foul **5** dirty, nasty **6** coarse, filthy, smutty, vulgar **7** obscene **8** indecent **9** salacious

ravage
4 loot, raze, ruin, sack **5** foray, harry, spoil, strip, waste, wreck **6** invade **7** despoil, overrun, pillage, plunder, ransack, scourge **8** spoliate **9** depredate, desecrate, devastate

rave
4 gush, rant **5** storm **6** babble, effuse, jabber **7** enthuse **10** rhapsodize

ravel
3 run **4** fray **5** snarl **6** muddle, tangle **7** perplex, untwine **8** entangle **9** extricate **10** complicate **11** disentangle

ravelings
4 lint **7** threads

Ravel work
6 Bolero **7** La Valse **14** Daphnis et Chloé **17** Rapsodie espagnole

raven
3 jet **4** ebon, inky, prey **5** black, ebony, jetty, sable **7** despoil, plunder **9** pitch-dark **10** pitch-black
relative: **3** jay **4** crow **6** magpie **7** blue jay

Raven, The
author: **3** Poe (Edgar Allan)
lost love: **6** Lenore
refrain: **9** Nevermore

ravenous
6 greedy, hungry **7** starved **8** edacious, famished, starving **9** rapacious, voracious **10** gluttonous

ravine
3 cut, gap **4** gulf, pass, wadi **5** abyss, chasm, cleft, clove, flume, gorge, gulch, gully, notch **6** arroyo, canyon, clough, coulee, defile, gutter, nullah **7** crevice, fissure **8** barranca, crevasse
Mt. Washington's: **9** Tuckerman

raving
3 mad **5** manic, rabid, upset **6** crazed **7** frantic, lunatic, unglued **8** demented, deranged, frenetic, frenzied, maniacal, obsessed, unhinged, worked up **10** distraught, flipped out, hysterical, irrational

ravish
4 rape **5** force, spoil **6** defile **7** assault, despoil, outrage, pillage, plunder, violate **8** deflower, entrance **9** enrapture, transport

raw
4 cold, rude **5** bleak, chill, crass, crude, fresh, green, rough, young **6** callow, coarse, impure, unripe **7** uncouth **8** immature, uncooked, unformed **9** au naturel, inelegant, irritated, unbridled, unrefined **10** unfinished, unpolished **13** inexperienced

rawboned
4 bony, lank, lean **5** gaunt, gawky, lanky, spare **6** skinny **7** angular, scraggy, scrawny

raw material
3 ore

ray
4 beam **5** gleam, manta, shaft, skate, trace **6** radius, streak, stream **7** radiate, sawfish, sunbeam, torpedo **8** moonbeam **9** devilfish, thornback **10** guitarfish

raze
4 ruin **5** level **7** destroy **8** demolish, pull down, tear down

razor
6 shaver
brand: **4** Atra
sharpener: **5** strop

razz
3 rag, rib **4** bait, josh, mock, twit **5** scout, taunt **6** badger, banter, deride, heckle, hector **8** ridicule
(see also **raspberry**)

razzle-dazzle
5 gaudy **6** flashy, garish, glitzy, snazzy **10** flamboyant

re
4 as to **5** about, as for **7** apropos **9** apropos of, as regards, regarding **10** as respects, concerning, relating to, respecting **12** with regard to

reach
4 beat, gain, pass, span, tack **5** carry, get at, get to, grasp, level, range, scope **6** arrive, attain, extend, extent, rack up, thrust **7** achieve, contact, horizon, project, stretch **9** encompass

___ reaction
4 dark **5** alarm, chain, light **7** nuclear **8** chemical

reactivate
5 renew **6** revive **8** rekindle, revivify **9** resurrect **10** revitalize **11** resuscitate

read
4 scan, skim **6** peruse **8** pore over
inability to: **8** dyslexia

readable
7 legible

reader
6 lector, primer **7** proofer, scanner **8** bookworm **9** anthology

readily
4 well **6** easily, freely **7** lightly **9** willingly **12** effortlessly

readiness
4 ease **5** skill **6** DEFCON **8** alacrity, dispatch, facility **11** inclination, promptitude

reading
6 lesson **7** lection, version, vulgate **9** rendition **10** recitation

ready
3 set **4** prep, ripe, yare **5** alert, equip **6** active, gear up, make up, primed, prompt **7** prepare **8** inclined, prepared **9** available

real
4 true, very **5** pukka, sound, valid **6** actual, honest **7** genuine, sincere **8** bona fide, concrete, existent, tangible **9** authentic, undoubted, veridical **10** sure-enough, undeniable **11** substantive

real estate
abbreviation: **3** ARM, apt, flr, gar, gdn, kit, lux, mbr, MLS, TLC, vic **4** bsmt, bdrm, frpl, FSBO, furn, HVAC, PITI, util, wbfp **5** RESPA
unit: **4** acre

realism
6 verism **7** verismo **10** naturalism, pragmatism **11** objectivism, objectivity

realistic
4 sane **5** sober, sound **7** genuine, natural **8** lifelike, rational, sensible **9** practical, pragmatic **10** bottom-line, hard-boiled, hardheaded, reasonable, unromantic **11** down-to-earth **12** matter-of-fact

reality
4 fact, true **5** being, sooth, truth **9** actuality, existence, substance **13** flesh and blood

realize
4 earn, gain, reap **5** grasp, reach, score **6** attain, rack up **7** achieve, feature, imagine **8** conceive, envisage, envision **9** actualize **10** accomplish, comprehend

really
4 very **5** truly **6** indeed, verily **7** awfully, clearly **8** actually, honestly **9** assuredly, certainly, decidedly, genuinely **10** definitely, positively **11** exceedingly, indubitably, undoubtedly

realm
5 orbit, range, scope, sweep **6** domain, empire, estate, extent, radius, sphere **7** compass, demesne, kingdom, purview **8** dominion

ream
4 bore, load, scad **5** widen **7** enlarge **11** countersink

reanimation
7 rebirth, revival **10** renascence, resurgence **11** reawakening, renaissance **12** risorgimento

reap
3 cut **4** earn, gain **5** glean, shear **6** garner, gather, obtain, sickle, thresh **7** harvest

rear
3 aft **4** back, hind, ramp **5** breed, put up, raise, set up, stern **6** behind, fledge, foster **7** bring up, caboose, nurture **8** hindmost **9** posterior
of a boat: **5** stern

rear end
3 bum, bun, can **4** butt, duff, moon, rump, seat, tail, tush **5** booty, fanny, stern **6** behind, bottom, heinie **7** caboose, keister **8** backside, buttocks, derriere **9** posterior

rearmost
3 end **4** last **5** final **8** terminal, ultimate

rearrange
see **readjust**

rearward
3 aft **4** back **5** abaft **6** behind **8** backward **9** posterior **10** retrograde

Rea Silvia
father: **7** Numitor
son: **5** Remus **7** Romulus

reason
3 why, wit **4** mind, nous **5** basis, cause, infer, proof, sense, think **6** excuse, ground, motive, sanity, senses **7** account **8** argument, cogitate, conceive, persuade **9** intellect, rationale, soundness, speculate, wherefore **10** deliberate **11** explanation **12** intelligence **13** justification, ratiocination, understanding

reasonable
4 fair, just, sane **5** cheap, level, sober, sound **6** modest **7** logical, low-cost, tenable **8** credible,

feasible, moderate, rational, sensible **9** equitable, plausible **10** acceptable, affordable, restrained **11** inexpensive, intelligent

reasoning
4 case **5** logic **7** thought **8** argument **9** deduction

reata
5 lasso **6** lariat

reawaken
5 renew **6** revive **7** refresh **8** revivify **9** reanimate **10** regenerate **12** reinvigorate

rebate
6 lessen, refund, return **8** decrease, diminish, give back **9** deduction, reduction

Rebecca
beloved: 7 Ivanhoe
director: 9 Hitchcock (Alfred)

Rebekah
brother: 5 Laban
father: 7 Bethuel
husband: 5 Isaac
nurse: 7 Deborah
son: 4 Esau **5** Jacob

rebel
6 anarch, mutiny, resist, revolt **7** disobey **8** frondeur, mutineer **9** insurgent **10** malcontent

rebellion
6 émeute, mutiny, revolt, rising **8** defiance, intifada, sedition, uprising **10** insurgence, insurgency, resistance, revolution **12** insurrection

rebellious
6 unruly **8** mutinous **9** insurgent **10** refractory **11** disobedient **12** contumacious, unmanageable **13** insubordinate

rebirth
7 revival **9** awakening **10** renascence, resurgence **11** reanimation, reawakening, renaissance **12** resurrection, risorgimento

rebound
5 rally **6** bounce, reecho, recoil, repeat **7** recover **8** comeback, recovery, ricochet, snap back **10** convalesce

rebozo
5 scarf, shawl

rebuff
4 shun, slap, snub **5** repel **6** reject **7** fend off, repulse, ward off **8** turn away

rebuild
6 repair, revamp **8** overhaul, renovate, retrofit **11** reconstruct **12** rehabilitate

rebuke
3 rap **5** chide, scold, scorn **6** berate, earful, rebuff **7** bawl out, lecture, reproof, reprove **8** admonish, call down, reproach, scolding **9** reprimand, talking-to **10** tongue-lash **11** comeuppance, objurgation **12** admonishment, dressing-down **13** tongue-lashing

rebut
5 repel **6** refute, reject **7** confute, fend off, repulse, ward off **8** confound, disprove **10** controvert, disconfirm

rebuttal
5 reply **6** answer, retort **7** defense, riposte **8** argument, comeback, response **9** rejoinder **10** refutation **11** repudiation

recalcitrant
6 unruly **7** froward, willful **8** contrary, perverse, stubborn, untoward **9** fractious, obstinate, resistant **10** headstrong **11** intractable **12** ungovernable, unmanageable

recall
4 stir **5** evoke, renew, rouse, waken **6** arouse, awaken, cancel, memory, remind, repeal, revive, revoke **7** bethink, rescind, restore, retract, reverse **8** callback, remember, take back, withdraw **9** anamnesis, recollect, reinstate, reminisce **11** bring to mind, countermand

recant
5 unsay **6** abjure, revoke **7** retract **8** forswear, renounce, take back, withdraw **9** backtrack, repudiate

recap
5 sum up **6** précis, résumé, review **7** reprise, retread, summary **8** overview **9** summarize

recapitulate
5 sum up **6** resume, review **9** summarize

recapitulation
5 sum-up **6** précis, résumé, review **7** epitome, reprise, summary **9** summing-up

recede
3 ebb **4** back **5** abate, taper **6** lessen, reduce, retire **7** dwindle, regress, retract, retreat **8** decrease, diminish, fall back, withdraw **10** retrogress

receipts
4 gate, take **5** sales **6** income **7** revenue, takings **8** earnings, proceeds

receive
4 host **5** admit, catch, greet **6** accept, endure, suffer, take in **7** acquire, sustain, welcome **10** experience

received
5 plain, sound **6** common **7** popular **8** accepted, familiar, ordinary, orthodox **12** acknowledged, conventional

receiver
4 dish **5** donee, fence, pager **6** aerial **7** antenna, catcher, scanner **9** recipient, treasurer

recent
3 new **4** late **5** fresh, novel **6** latest, modern **8** neoteric

receptacle
6 hamper, holder, hopper, trough, vessel **9** container **10** repository

receptive
4 open **7** passive **8** amenable **9** sensitive **10** accessible, hospitable, open-minded, responsive **11** persuadable, persuasible, suggestible, susceptible

recess
4 cove, nook **5** break, cleft, niche **6** alcove, grotto, hiatus **7** adjourn, suspend **8** prorogue **9** prorogate **11** indentation
church: 4 apse

Recessional author
7 Kipling (Rudyard)

recessive
3 shy **8** retiring **9** reclusive, withdrawn **10** unsociable

recherché
4 rare **5** novel **6** choice, dainty, exotic, select **7** elegant, unusual **8** affected, delicate, superior, uncommon **9** exquisite **11** pretentious

recipe
7 formula **9** procedure **12** prescription
amt.: 3 tsp **4** tbsp

recipient
5 donee **7** grantee **8** receiver **11** beneficiary

reciprocal
5 match **6** double, mutual **8** requited **9** bilateral, duplicate **10** coordinate **11** interactive
prefix: 5 inter

reciprocate
5 repay **6** retort, return **7** requite **8** exchange **9** retaliate **10** compensate, recompense **11** interchange

recital
5 story **6** soiree **7** concert, reading **9** discourse, narration **10** recounting **11** performance

recite
4 tell **5** chant, count, state **6** detail, number, relate, repeat, report, set out **7** declaim, narrate, recount, reel off **8** describe, rehearse

reckless
4 rash, wild **5** brash, hasty **6** daring, madcap **8** carefree, heedless **9** audacious, daredevil, foolhardy, hotheaded **10** ill-advised, incautious **11** harebrained, temerarious **12** devil-may-care **13** irresponsible

reckon
3 sum **5** count, gauge, guess, judge, opine, tally, total **6** cipher, figure, regard **7** account, compute, suppose, surmise **8** consider, estimate **9** calculate, enumerate

reckoning
3 tab **4** bill **5** tally, score **7** account, invoice **9** statement **10** arithmetic, estimation **11** calculation

reclaim
4 save, tame **6** redeem, reform, rescue **7** deliver, recover, restore **9** restitute **11** recondition, reconstruct

recline
3 lie **4** rest, tilt **5** couch, slant, slope **6** lounge, repose **7** lie down **10** stretch out

reclining
4 flat **5** prone **6** supine **9** decumbent, prostrate, recumbent

recluse
5 loner **6** hermit, shut-in **7** eremite, stylite **8** cenobite, solitary **9** anchorite
female: 7 ancress **9** anchoress

reclusive
7 asocial **8** eremitic, hermetic, reserved, solitary **9** withdrawn **10** antisocial, eremitical, unsociable

recognition
6 credit, esteem, notice **9** attention, awareness, gratitude **10** cognizance, perception **11** realization **12** appreciation

recognize
4 note, spot **5** admit **6** notice **7** observe, realize **8** accredit, diagnose, identify **9** apprehend **10** appreciate **11** acknowledge

recoil
4 balk, kick **5** cower, dodge, quail, start, wince **6** blench, cringe, flinch, shrink **7** rebound, retract, squinch **8** reaction

recollect
5 evoke **6** recall **7** bethink **8** remember **9** reminisce

recollection
6 memory, recall **9** anamnesis, flashback **11** remembrance **12** reminiscence

recommence
5 renew **6** pick up, reopen, resume, take up **7** restart **8** continue **9** start over

recommend
4 tout **6** advise, praise, prefer **7** acclaim, commend, counsel, endorse, entrust, propose, suggest **8** advocate

recommendation
4 plug **5** pitch **6** advice **7** counsel **11** endorsement, testimonial

recompense
3 pay **4** wage **5** repay **6** amends, reward **7** guerdon, premium, redress, requite **8** gratuity, requital **9** indemnify, indemnity, quittance, reimburse **10** remunerate **11** reciprocate **12** remuneration

reconcile
4 suit, tune 5 adapt 6 accept, accord, adjust, attune, make up, resign, settle, square, submit 7 conform, get over, resolve 9 harmonize, integrate 10 conciliate, coordinate

recondite
4 deep 6 arcane, hidden, mystic, occult, orphic, secret 7 cryptic, erudite, learned, obscure 8 abstruse, academic, esoteric, hermetic, profound 9 concealed, enigmatic, scholarly

recondition
3 fix 4 mend 6 doctor, repair, revamp 7 restore 8 make over, overhaul, retrofit 9 restitute 10 rejuvenate 12 rehabilitate

reconnoiter
5 scout 6 survey

reconsider
6 review, revise 7 rethink 8 reassess 9 reexamine 10 reevaluate 13 think better of

reconstruct
6 do over, recast, re-form, remake, revamp 7 rebuild, reclaim, remodel, restore 8 make over, overhaul, renovate 9 refashion, restitute 10 reassemble, reorganize

record
4 disc, disk, tape 5 album 6 annals, enroll 7 archive, journal, platter 8 archives, document, register 9 chronicle 10 transcript
of a meeting: 7 minutes
of proceedings: 4 acta
ship's: 3 log 7 logbook

recorder
4 TiVo 5 flute 9 registrar
flight: 8 black box

record player
4 hi-fi 5 phono 6 stereo 8 Victrola 9 turntable 10 gramophone, phonograph

recount
4 tell 5 state 6 recite, relate, report, retail 7 narrate 8 describe, rehearse 9 enumerate

recoup
6 regain 7 get back, reclaim, recover 8 retrieve 9 repossess

recourse
6 backup, refuge, resort 7 standby, stopgap, support 9 expedient, makeshift

recover
4 heal, mend 5 evict, rally, renew 6 recoup, redeem, regain, revive 7 get back, get over, improve, rebound, reclaim, recycle, restore 8 retrieve, snap back 9 come round, reacquire, recapture, re-collect, repossess, restitute 10 bounce back, convalesce, recuperate

recreant
3 rat 5 false 6 coward, craven 7 chicken, dastard, unloyal 8 apostate, cowardly, defector, deserter, disloyal, poltroon, renegade, turncoat 9 dastardly, faithless, turnabout 10 perfidious, traitorous, unfaithful 13 pusillanimous

recreation
4 play 5 hobby, sport 7 leisure, pastime 9 avocation, diversion 10 relaxation 13 entertainment

recreational vehicle
3 ATV

recruit
4 boot, hire 6 engage, enlist, enroll, muster, novice, rookie 7 draftee 8 enlistee, freshman, headhunt, neophyte, newcomer 9 conscript, fledgling 10 apprentice, tenderfoot

rectifier
4 tube 5 diode 8 detector, ignitron

rectify
3 fix 4 mend 5 amend, emend 6 adjust, remedy, repair 7 correct

rectitude
6 virtue 7 honesty, probity 8 morality 9 rightness 11 uprightness 13 righteousness

recto
5 right
opposite: 4 left 5 verso

rector
6 parson, pastor, priest 9 clergyman 10 headmaster

rectory
5 manse 8 benefice 9 parsonage

recumbent
4 flat 5 prone 6 supine 7 leaning, resting 8 reposing 9 lying down, prostrate, reclining

recuperate
4 heal, mend 5 rally 6 regain, revive 7 rebound, recover 8 snap back 10 convalesce

recur
5 cycle, haunt 6 repeat, resort, return 7 iterate, revolve

recurring
7 chronic 8 periodic 10 continuous, isochronal, periodical, persistent 11 isochronous 12 intermittent

red
4 puce, ruby 5 coral, gules, rouge, ruddy 6 cerise, claret, florid, maroon 7 carmine, crimson, flushed, glowing, magenta, oxblood, scarlet, vermeil 8 burgundy, sanguine 9 vermilion
combining form: 4 rhod 5 rhodo

Red
6 Bolshy, commie 7 Bolshie, comrade 9 Bolshevik, Communist

redact
4 edit 6 censor, revise

Red and the Black author
8 Stendhal
red ape
9 orangutan
red arsenic
7 realgar
red-backed sandpiper
6 dunlin
Red Badge of Courage, The
author: 5 Crane (Stephen)
hero: 7 Fleming (Henry)
red-bellied snipe
9 dowitcher
redbird
7 tanager **8** cardinal
red blood cell
11 erythrocyte
red-blooded
5 juicy, lusty, manly **6** hearty, robust, virile **8** vigorous **9** energetic
redbreast
4 knot **5** robin **7** sunfish
red-breasted snipe
9 dowitcher
Redburn author
8 Melville (Herman)
red carp
8 goldfish
red cobalt
9 erythrite
red copper ore
7 cuprite
Red Cross
founder: 6 Barton (Clara), Dunant (Henri)
Knight: 6 George
redden
5 blush, color, flush, rouge **6** mantle, ruddle
Redding of soul
4 Otis
reddish brown
4 roan **5** henna
gem: 4 sard
red dog
5 blitz
redecorate
4 redo **5** fix up **9** refurbish
redeem
4 free, save **5** atone, renew **6** offset, pay off, ransom, reform, rescue **7** expiate, reclaim, recover, restore **9** exonerate
redeemer
6 savior **7** messiah, saviour
redemption
6 ransom **7** release **9** atonement, expiation, salvation **11** deliverance
red-eye
5 hooch **6** flight, rotgut **7** whiskey **8** home brew, rock bass **9** moonshine
red-faced
5 ruddy **6** florid, shamed **7** abashed, flushed, glowing **8** blushing, rubicund, sanguine, sheepish **9** mortified **11** embarrassed
red felt hat
3 fez
redfish
4 bass, drum **5** perch **6** salmon **10** ocean perch **11** channel bass
red hickory
6 pignut
red-hot
5 fiery **6** ardent, fervid **7** blazing, boiling, burning, fervent, flaming, glowing **8** brand-new, scalding, sizzling **9** scorching **10** blistering, passionate, sweltering
red Indian paint
9 bloodroot **11** sanguinaria
red ink
7 arrears, deficit **8** shortage
red inkberry
8 pokeweed
red ironbark
8 eucalypt **10** eucalyptus
red iron ore
5 ocher, ochre **8** hematite
red lauan
8 mahogany
red-legged crow
6 chough
red-legged sandpiper
9 turnstone
red-letter
7 notable **8** historic **9** important, memorable **10** noteworthy, observable, remarkable **11** significant
red-light district
5 stews **10** tenderloin
red mite
7 chigger
redneck
4 clod, hick, rube **5** Bubba, yahoo, yokel **6** rustic **7** bumpkin, hayseed **9** hillbilly **10** clodhopper, good old boy, good ole boy
redo
6 repeat, revamp **7** remodel, restyle **8** make over, overhaul, refinish, renovate **9** refurbish
red ocher
8 hematite
redolence
4 balm, odor **5** aroma, attar, scent, spice **7** bouquet, incense, perfume **9** fragrance

redolent
5 balmy, spicy, sweet **7** odorous, scented **8** aromatic, fragrant, perfumed **9** ambrosial, evocative

redouble
4 dupe **7** dualize, enhance, magnify **8** heighten **9** duplicate, intensify, reinforce **10** strengthen

redoubt
4 fort **7** bastion, citadel **8** fastness, fortress **10** stronghold

redoubtable
5 famed, great **6** famous, mighty **7** awesome, eminent **8** imposing, puissant, renowned **9** prominent **10** celebrated, formidable, impressive **11** illustrious **12** intimidating, overwhelming

redound
6 accrue, recoil **7** conduce, reflect

red pigment
4 lake **5** eosin, ocher, ochre **6** ruddle

Red Planet
4 Mars

redpoll
5 finch **6** linnet

redraft
6 revamp, revise, rework **7** restyle, rewrite **8** make over, overhaul, rescript, revision, work over **9** recension

redress
4 heal **6** amends, avenge, negate, offset, relief, remedy **7** correct **8** reprisal, requital **9** cancel out, indemnity, quittance, vindicate **10** compensate, counteract, neutralize, recompense, reparation **11** restitution, retribution **12** compensation

red roe
5 coral **6** caviar

redroot
7 alkanet, pigweed **9** bloodroot **12** New Jersey tea

red sable
8 kolinsky

red silver ore
9 proustite

red squirrel
9 chickaree

reduce
3 axe, cut **4** cull, diet, melt, pare **5** abate, lower, shade, shave, slash, smelt **6** humble, lessen, recede **7** abridge, curtail, cut back, cut down, dwindle, liquefy, squeeze **8** boil down, compress, contract, decrease, diminish, discount, mark down, minimize, taper off **10** depreciate, slenderize

reductio ad ____
8 absurdum

reduction
6 digest, précis, rebate **7** cutback, cutdown, epitome, summary **8** abstract, discount, markdown, synopsis **9** abatement **10** shortening **11** curtailment **12** condensation

redundancy
6 excess **7** nimiety, surfeit **8** pleonasm **9** abundance, profusion, prolixity, tautology **10** repetition **11** periphrasis, reiteration, superfluity **13** supernumerary

redundant
5 extra, spare, windy, wordy **6** de trop, prolix **7** surplus, verbose **9** excessive, iterative **11** duplicative, reiterative, repetitious, superfluous, tautologous

redux
7 revived **8** restored

redwing
6 thrush **9** blackbird

redwood
7 amboyna, sequoia **8** mahogany

Ree
7 Arikara

reed
4 di mo, pipe, tule **5** arrow, grass **7** bulrush (see also **reed instrument**)

reed instrument
3 sax **4** dizi, oboe **5** shawm **6** curtal **7** bagpipe, bassoon, dulcian **8** bagpipes, clarinet, crumhorn, melodeon **9** accordion, harmonica, krummhorn, saxophone **10** concertina **11** English horn

reedy
4 thin **6** skinny, stalky, twiggy **7** spindly

reef
3 bar, cay, key **4** lode, vein **5** atoll, ledge **6** reduce, skerry **7** sandbar

reek
4 funk **5** fetor, smell, stink **6** stench **9** effluvium

reeking
4 rank **5** fetid, funky, fusty **6** putrid, rancid, smelly, stinky **7** noisome, stenchy **10** malodorous

reel
4 spin, sway, turn **5** lurch, spool, weave, whirl **6** bobbin, careen, teeter, totter, waggle, wobble **7** stagger, stumble

reestablish
5 renew **6** revive **7** restore **9** reinstate **11** reintroduce

reevaluate
6 review **7** rethink, reweigh **8** reassess **9** reexamine **10** reconsider

reeve
4 ruff **6** thread **9** sandpiper **10** magistrate

Reeves of The Matrix
5 Keanu
reexamine
see **reevaluate**
refashion
5 alter **6** change, modify, recast, remake, revamp **7** remodel **8** make over, overhaul
refection
4 feed, meal **6** repast **11** nourishment, refreshment
refectory
7 commons **10** dining hall
refer
6 advert, allude, assign, relate, submit **7** ascribe **9** attribute
referee
3 ump **5** judge **6** umpire **7** adjudge, arbiter, mediate **8** mediator **9** arbitrate, officiate **10** adjudicate, arbitrator
reference
6 credit, source **7** meaning, mention **8** allusion, citation, innuendo, relation, resource **11** testimonial
guide: 5 index **12** bibliography
work: 3 OED **5** atlas, bible, guide **6** manual **7** almanac **8** handbook **9** directory, guidebook, thesaurus **10** dictionary **11** enchiridion **12** encyclopedia
referendum
4 poll, vote **10** plebiscite
refine
5 prune, smelt **6** polish, purify, smooth **7** elevate, improve, perfect, process **8** civilize **9** cultivate
refined
4 pure **6** subtle, urbane **7** elegant, genteel, raffiné **8** cultured, elevated, ladylike, raffinée, well-bred **9** civilized **10** cultivated, fastidious
refinement
5 couth, grace, taste **6** finish, polish **7** culture, finesse, suavity **8** breeding, civility, courtesy, elegance, subtlety, urbanity **9** politesse **10** politeness **11** cultivation **12** civilization, distillation, purification **13** clarification
reflect
4 echo, pore, show **5** weigh **6** bounce, mirror, ponder, reason **7** redound **8** chew over, cogitate, consider, ruminate **9** cerebrate **10** deliberate, retrospect **11** contemplate
reflection
4 slur **5** image **6** musing **7** replica, thought **8** reproach **9** aspersion **10** cogitation, meditation, rumination, simulacrum **11** cerebration **12** deliberation, reproduction **13** contemplation
reflective
7 pensive **9** reflexive **10** cogitative, indicative, meditative, ruminative, thoughtful **12** deliberative **13** contemplative
reflux
3 ebb **4** GERD **8** backflow
reform
5 amend, emend **6** redeem, revise **7** correct, improve, reclaim, shape up **8** make over **10** houseclean, regenerate
Reformation leader
4 Knox (John) **6** Calvin (John), Luther (Martin) **7** Zwingli (Huldrych)
reformatory
3 pen **6** prison **7** borstal **12** penitentiary
refractory
6 mulish, unruly **7** froward, restive **8** contrary, perverse, stubborn **9** obstinate **10** bullheaded, headstrong, rebellious **11** intractable, stiff-necked **12** unmanageable
refrain
4 fa-la, keep, la-la, stop **5** eieio, tra-la **6** burden, chorus, fa-la-la, shrink **7** abstain, forbear, tra-la-la **8** hold back
refresh
5 renew **6** revive **7** animate, enliven, quicken, restore **8** irrigate, recreate, renovate **9** replenish, stimulate **10** rejuvenate
refresher
5 drink, tonic **6** bracer **8** reminder **9** stimulant **11** restorative
refreshing
5 brisk, tonic **7** bracing **8** reviving **9** analeptic, animating **10** delightful, energizing **11** restorative, stimulating **12** invigorating, rejuvenating
refrigerant
3 ice **5** freon **7** coolant, cryogen **12** fluorocarbon
refrigerate
4 cool **5** chill
refrigerator
6 cooler, icebox, walk-in **9** condenser **10** Frigidaire
ref's decision
3 out, TKO **4** safe
refuge
3 den **4** lair, port **5** cover, haven **6** asylum, covert, harbor **7** hideout, retreat, shelter **8** hideaway, recourse **9** expedient, harborage, sanctuary, safe house
refugee
5 exile **6** émigré **7** evacuee **8** emigrant, fugitive **10** boat person, expatriate
refulgent
6 bright **7** glowing, radiant **8** luminous **9** brilliant
refund
5 repay **6** rebate **8** give back **9** reimburse, repayment, restitute **11** restitution
refurbish
4 redo **5** fix up, renew **6** revamp **7** restore

8 make over, overhaul, renovate, retrofit 10 redecorate, rejuvenate 11 recondition

refusal
4 veto 6 denial 7 regrets 8 negative, negation 9 disavowal 10 abnegation, thumbs-down 11 declination, repudiation

refuse
3 jib, nix 4 chum, deny, junk, marc, scum 5 dreck, dross, offal, spurn, swill, trash, waste 6 debris, litter, pomace, reject, scraps, spilth 7 decline, garbage, residue, rubbish 8 disallow, leavings, remnants, turn down, withhold 9 reprobate, repudiate, sweepings

refutation
8 disproof, elenchus, rebuttal

refute
4 deny 5 rebut 7 confute 8 confound, disprove 10 controvert, disconfirm

regain
6 recoup 7 get back, recover 8 reoccupy, retrieve 9 recapture, repossess
possession: 7 replevy 8 replevin

regal
5 grand 6 august, kingly, purple 7 queenly, stately 8 glorious, imperial, kinglike, majestic, princely 9 monarchal, sovereign 10 monarchial 11 monarchical
symbol: 3 orb 5 crown 6 throne 7 scepter, sceptre

regale
4 feed 5 amuse, feast 6 divert 9 entertain

regalia
5 array 6 finery 8 insignia 9 caparison, full dress, trappings 10 decoration 11 habiliments

Regan
father: 4 Lear
husband: 8 Cornwall
sister: 7 Goneril 8 Cordelia

regard
4 deem, heed, mark, note, rate, view 5 assay, favor, honor, judge, value 6 admire, assess, esteem, homage, liking, look at, notice, reckon, repute 7 account, concern, respect 8 approval, consider, devotion, estimate, fondness 9 attention 10 admiration, cognizance, estimation, observance, solicitude 11 approbation, contemplate, observation 12 appreciation, satisfaction

regarding
4 as to, in re 5 about, anent, as for 7 apropos 8 touching 9 apropos of 10 as respects, concerning, relative to, respecting 11 in respect to 13 with respect to

regatta
4 race
site: 6 Henley 10 Argenteuil

regenerate
5 renew 6 reform, revive 7 rebirth, restore 8 recreate 9 reproduce

regent
5 ruler 6 warden 8 governor 9 protector

reggae relative
3 dub, ska 10 rocksteady

regicide's victim
4 king 7 monarch

regime
4 rule, term 5 reign 6 empire, tenure 7 dynasty 10 government, leadership

regimen
4 diet, plan, rule 6 course

region
4 area, belt, part, zone 5 field, tract 6 domain, locale, sector, sphere 7 demesne, terrain 8 locality, province, vicinity 9 bailiwick, territory

regional
5 areal, local 9 localized, sectional 10 provincial 11 territorial

register
4 file, list, note, roll, till 5 enter, range, tally 6 annals, docket, enroll, ledger, record, roster 7 catalog, check in 9 catalogue

regnant
4 rife 6 ruling 7 current, popular 8 dominant, reigning 9 paramount, prevalent, sovereign 10 prevailing, widespread

regress
6 revert 9 backslide 10 retrograde

regret
3 rue, woe 4 care 6 bemoan, excuse, lament, repent, sorrow 7 anguish, apology, deplore, remorse 9 heartache, penitence 10 contrition, heartbreak 11 compunction

regretful
5 sorry 6 rueful 8 contrite, mournful, penitent 9 repentant, sorrowful 10 apologetic, remorseful 11 penitential

regrettable
3 sad 6 too bad, woeful 8 grievous 10 lamentable 11 distressing, unfortunate 13 heartbreaking

regular
3 due, set 4 even 5 fixed, usual 6 common, normal, steady 7 average, equable, general, natural, orderly, typical, uniform 8 constant, everyday, methodic, ordinary, standard 9 clocklike, customary, prevalent 10 methodical, systematic

regulate
5 order, scale 6 adjust, direct, govern, police, square, temper 7 arrange, control 8 organize 9 methodize, systemize 11 systematize

regulation
3 law 4 rule 5 canon, edict 6 decree 7 precept, statute 9 ordinance, prescript 11 restriction

regulator
8 governor

rehabilitate
4 cure, heal **7** reclaim, recover, restore **8** renovate **9** reeducate, restitute **11** recondition

rehash
5 reuse **6** repeat, review, rework **7** restate, version **8** chew over, talk over **9** rendering, rendition, rewording **11** restatement **12** recapitulate

rehearsal
5 trial **6** dry run, tryout **7** recital **8** dummy run, practice **10** run-through, simulation **11** reiteration **12** woodshedding

rehearse
5 drill, train **6** repeat, warm up **7** run over **8** exercise, practice **10** run through

Rehoboam
father: **7** Solomon
kingdom: **5** Judah **6** Israel
mother: **6** Naamah

reign
4 rule, sway **6** govern, regime **7** prevail **8** dominate, dominion **11** predominate, sovereignty

reimburse
3 pay **5** repay **6** recoup, refund **7** pay back, requite **9** indemnify **10** compensate, remunerate

rein (in)
4 curb, stem **5** check **6** bridle **7** control **8** hold back, restrain

reinforce
4 prop **5** brace **7** augment, bolster, enlarge, fortify, sustain **8** buttress, redouble **10** strengthen

reinstate
6 recall **7** restore **11** reestablish

reintroduce
6 recall, revive **7** restore **11** reestablish

reinvestment
4 DRIP **8** plowback

reiterate
5 renew, resay **6** repeat, resume, retell **7** reprise

reject
3 nix **4** deny, jilt, junk, shed **5** debar, scorn, scrap, spurn **6** abjure, pass up, rebuff, refuse **7** cashier, castoff, decline, discard, dismiss, exclude, outcast, repulse, shut out **8** jettison, throw out, turn away, turn down **9** eliminate, repudiate, shoot down, throw away

rejoice
5 cheer, exult, glory **7** delight, gladden **8** jubilate

rejoinder
5 reply **6** answer, retort **8** comeback, rebuttal, repartee, response

rejuvenate
5 green, renew **7** refresh **8** renovate **9** modernize **10** revitalize

rekindle
5 renew **6** revive **7** restart **8** reawaken, reignite, revivify **10** reactivate, revitalize

relate
4 link, tell **5** apply, refer **6** assign, recite, report **7** narrate, pertain, recount **8** describe, disclose **9** appertain, chronicle

related
4 akin, told **5** alike, enate **6** agnate, allied **7** cognate, connate, germane, kindred **9** analogous, pertinent **10** associated, connatural, homologous **11** consanguine

relation
3 kin **6** agnate **7** kinship, kinsman **8** affinity **9** kinswoman, reference

relationship
3 tie **4** bond, link **5** ratio, tie-in, union **6** affair **7** analogy **8** affinity, alliance **11** affiliation, association **13** consanguinity

relative
3 mom, pop, sib, sis, son **4** aunt, mama, papa **5** blood, madre, mamma, momma, niece, pappy, pater, poppa, uncle **6** agnate, cousin, father, mother, nephew, parent, sister **7** apropos, brother, cognate, germane, kinsman, sibling **8** ancestor, daughter, grandson, relation, relevant **9** ascendant, dependent, kinswoman, pertinent **10** applicable, collateral, descendant, grandchild **11** comparative, conditional, grandfather, grandmother, grandparent **13** granddaughter

relatives
3 kin **4** kith **5** folks **7** kindred, kinfolk **8** kinfolks

relax
4 bask, ease, laze, loaf, loll, rest **5** chill, let go, loose, remit **6** loosen, lounge, modify, unbend, unkink, unwind **7** slacken **8** chill out, kick back, loosen up, unbuckle, wind down **9** untighten **10** decompress

relaxation
3 fun **4** ease, rest **5** hobby **6** repose **7** leisure, pastime **9** amusement, diversion, enjoyment

relaxed
5 chill, loose, slack **6** at ease, casual, dégagé, mellow **8** informal **9** easygoing **11** low-pressure

release
4 emit, free, vent **5** issue, let go, loose, untie, yield **6** acquit, let out, loosen, pardon, ransom, remise, unbind, uncage **7** give off, give out, manumit, set free, unchain, unleash **8** liberate, unfetter **9** acquittal, discharge, exculpate, exonerate, surrender **10** emancipate **11** manumission **12** emancipation
conditional: **6** parole

relegate
5 exile, expel **6** assign, banish, charge, commit, demote, resign **7** commend, confide, consign, entrust **8** hand over, transfer, turn over

relent
3 ebb **4** cave, ease, wane **5** abate, let up, yield **6** give in, submit **7** die away, die down, ease off, slacken, subside **8** moderate **9** acquiesce **10** capitulate

relentless
5 cruel, rigid **6** dogged **7** adamant, nonstop **8** obdurate, rigorous, unabated **9** incessant, stringent **10** implacable, inexorable, inflexible, unyielding

relevant
3 apt, fit **5** ad rem **6** cogent **7** apropos, germane **8** apposite **9** pertinent **10** admissible, applicable **11** applicative, appropriate

reliable
4 safe, sure **5** solid, sound, tried, valid **6** proven, secure, trusty **7** bedrock, certain **8** verified **9** foolproof, validated **10** dependable **11** trustworthy **12** tried-and-true

reliance
4 hope **5** faith, stock, trust **10** dependence

relic
5 token **7** antique, memento, remnant, vestige **8** artefact, artifact, fragment, keepsake, memorial, reminder, souvenir

relict
5 widow **8** survivor

relief
3 aid **4** ease, fret, help **6** assist, raised, remedy, succor **7** comfort, redress, respite, support, welfare **8** breather, fretwork, repoussé **9** abatement, diversion **10** assistance, mitigation **11** alleviation, deliverance
pitcher: **6** closer **7** fireman, stopper

relieve
3 rid **4** ease, help, vent **5** allay, relax, spell **6** assist, exempt, lessen, loosen, reduce, remedy, soften, solace, soothe, succor **7** absolve, assuage, deprive, lighten, mollify **8** diminish, dispense, mitigate, moderate, palliate, unburden **9** alleviate

religion
4 cult, sect **5** Baha'i, cause, creed, dogma, faith, Islam **6** belief, church, Shinto **7** Jainism, Judaism, Sikhism **8** Buddhism, devotion, doctrine, Hinduism **9** Mormonism, Quakerism, Shintoism **12** Christianity

religious
3 nun **4** holy, monk **5** friar, godly, pious **6** devout, priest, sacral, sacred, votary **7** staunch, upright **8** cenobite, faithful, monastic, priestly, reverent **9** pietistic, prayerful, spiritual, steadfast **10** scriptural, scrupulous, worshipful
ceremony: **4** rite
offshoot: **4** cult, sect

relinquish
4 cede, quit, shed **5** forgo, leave, waive, yield **6** desert, give up, resign **7** abandon, discard, lay down, release **8** abdicate, hand over, renounce **9** quitclaim, sacrifice, surrender

relish
4 like, tang, zest **5** eat up, enjoy, fancy, flair, gusto, savor, taste **6** flavor, liking, palate **7** chutney, delight **8** chowchow, fondness, penchant, pleasure, sapidity **9** appetizer, condiment, enjoyment **10** appreciate, piccalilli **11** delectation, hors d'oeuvre

reluctant
3 shy **4** wary **5** chary, loath **6** afraid, averse **8** grudging, hesitant **9** unwilling **11** disinclined
prophet: **5** Jonah

rely
3 bet **4** bank **5** count **6** depend, gamble, reckon

rely on
5 trust **6** expect, look to **10** anticipate

remain
4 bide, last, stay, wait **5** abide, stand, tarry **6** endure, linger, loiter **7** persist, survive **8** continue **10** hang around **11** stick around

remainder
4 rest **5** dregs, trace **6** excess **7** balance, residue, remnant, surplus, vestige **8** leavings, leftover, residual, residuum

remains
4 body **5** ashes, bones, ruins **6** corpse, debris, relics **7** balance, cadaver, carcass, flotsam **8** leavings, remnants **9** reliquiae

remand
8 send back

remark
3 mot **4** gibe, note **5** aside, crack **6** bon mot **7** comment, mention **9** utterance, wisecrack, witticism **10** annotation **11** observation **12** obiter dictum

remarkable
4 rare **6** signal, unique **7** salient, strange, unusual **8** singular, striking, uncommon **9** arresting, bodacious, momentous, prominent **10** impressive, noteworthy, noticeable **11** conspicuous, exceptional, outstanding, significant **13** extraordinary

remarkably
4 unco

remedial
8 curative, salutary, sanative **9** medicinal **10** corrective **11** restorative, therapeutic **12** recuperative

remedy
3 fix 4 cure, drug, heal 5 salve 6 elixir, relief, repair 7 correct, cure-all, nostrum, panacea, rectify, redress, relieve 8 antidote, medicine, specific 9 alleviate, treatment 10 corrective, medicament, medication

remember
5 educe, evoke 6 recall, record, relive, retain, reward 7 bethink 9 flash back, recollect, reminisce 10 bear in mind 11 commemorate, memorialize

remembrance
5 relic, token 6 déjà vu, memory, recall, trophy 7 memento 8 keepsake, memorial, reminder, souvenir 9 anamnesis, flashback 12 recollection

remind
6 advise, prompt 7 bethink 8 admonish

reminder
3 cue 4 hint, memo 5 relic, token 6 prompt, trophy 7 memento 8 keepsake, memorial, monument, souvenir 9 refresher 10 admonition, memorandum

reminisce
see **remember**

reminiscence
6 memory, recall 9 anamnesis, flashback 11 remembrance 12 recollection

remise
4 cede, deed 5 alien, grant 6 assign, convey 8 make over, transfer 9 quitclaim

remiss
3 lax 4 lazy 5 slack 8 careless, derelict, heedless, indolent, slothful 9 negligent 10 delinquent, neglectful, slatternly 11 inattentive

remit
4 send, ship, stay 5 abate, defer, delay, relax 6 desist, hold up, pardon, put off, shelve 7 condone, consign, forgive, forward, hold off 8 dispatch, moderate, postpone

remnant
3 end 4 heel, husk, part, rest, rump 5 relic, trace, wrack 6 fag end, relict 7 balance, oddment, residue 8 leavings, leftover, residuum 9 remainder

remodel
4 redo 6 recast, revamp 8 make over, overhaul, redesign 9 refashion 11 reconstruct

remonstrance
5 demur 7 protest 8 demurral, demurrer, scolding 9 challenge, objection

remonstrate
5 argue, demur, plead, scold 6 combat, object, oppose, reason 7 protest 9 challenge

remora
4 clog, drag 6 sucker 9 hindrance 10 impediment 11 encumbrance, shark sucker

remorse
3 rue 4 ruth 5 guilt, smart 6 regret, sorrow 9 penitence 10 contrition, repentance 11 compunction

remorseful
see **regretful**

remote
3 far, off 4 slim 5 aloof 6 far-off, slight 7 distant, faraway, obscure, outside, slender 8 detached, far-flung, frontier, isolated, off-lying, outlying, secluded 9 backwoods, withdrawn 10 negligible 11 godforsaken, out-of-the-way
combining form: 3 tel 4 tele

remotest
6 utmost 7 extreme, outmost 8 farthest, furthest 9 outermost, uttermost 11 farthermost, furthermost

remove
4 dele, doff, skim 5 purge 6 delete, unseat 7 extract, take off, take out 8 dislodge, evacuate, take away, withdraw 9 clear away, eliminate
from office: 4 oust 6 depose, topple, unseat
hair: 8 depilate
surgically: 6 resect

removed
5 aloof, apart 6 far-off, remote 7 distant, faraway, obscure 8 detached, far-flung, isolated, outlying, separate 10 distracted 11 unconnected

remunerate
3 pay 5 repay 7 requite 9 indemnify, reimburse 10 compensate, recompense

remunerative
6 paying 7 gainful, payable 9 lucrative 10 productive, profitable 11 moneymaking

Remus
brother: 7 Romulus
father: 4 Mars
mother: 9 Rea Silvia 10 Rhea Silvia
slayer: 7 Romulus

renaissance
see **rebirth**

renal
7 nephric 9 nephritic

rend
3 rip 4 rive, tear 5 split 6 cleave, divide

render
3 pay 4 cede, limn 5 yield 6 depict, give up, impart, return, submit 7 deliver, execute, pay back, portray, present, proffer, provide, restore 8 carry out, describe, hand over, turn over 9 delineate, interpret, represent, translate, transpose 10 administer, relinquish

rendering
4 copy 7 version 9 depiction 10 paraphrase 11 description, performance, restatement, translation 12 reproduction

rendezvous
4 date **5** haunt, tryst **6** gather, muster **7** collect, hangout, meeting **8** assemble **10** congregate, engagement **11** appointment, assignation, get-together

rendition
7 reading, version **10** adaptation **11** performance, translation

renegade
3 rat **5** rebel **6** outlaw **7** heretic **8** apostate, defector, deserter, maverick, recreant, turncoat **9** turnabout **10** schismatic

renege
4 deny **5** welch, welsh **6** cry off, recall, recant, revoke **7** back off, back out, retract **8** renounce, withdraw **9** backpedal

Rene of film
5 Russo

renew
6 redeem, reform, revamp, revive **7** freshen, refresh, remodel **8** make over, overhaul, recharge, recreate, rekindle, renovate, revivify **9** refurbish, resurrect **10** reactivate, recommence, regenerate, rejuvenate, revitalize

rennet
8 abomasum

renounce
4 cede, deny, quit **5** demit **6** abjure, defect, desert, give up, recant, renege, resign **7** abandon, decline, forsake, put away, retract **8** abdicate, abnegate, disclaim, forswear, swear off **9** repudiate, sacrifice **10** apostatize

renovate
4 redo **5** renew **6** remake, repair, revamp, revive **7** furbish, refresh, restore **8** overhaul, revivify **9** modernize, refurbish, resurrect **10** rejuvenate, revitalize **12** rehabilitate

renown
4 fame **5** éclat, glory, kudos **6** repute **7** acclaim **8** eminence, prestige **9** celebrity, notoriety **10** prominence, reputation **11** distinction

renowned
5 famed, great, noted **6** fabled, famous **7** eminent, notable **9** acclaimed, legendary, notorious, prominent, well-known **10** celebrated **11** illustrious, outstanding

rent
3 let, rip **4** hire, rift, tear, torn **5** lease, split **6** breach, sublet **7** charter, fissure, rupture **8** fracture

rental
4 hire **7** tenancy

rental-car option
4 Avis **5** Hertz

renter
6 lessee, tenant **11** leaseholder

renunciation
6 denial **7** refusal **8** apostasy, eschewal **9** disavowal, sacrifice, surrender **10** abdication, abnegation, disclaimer, self-denial **11** abandonment, forswearing

reorder
5 shift **7** permute **9** rearrange, reshuffle

reorganization
7 shake-up **8** turnover

repair
3 fix **4** mend **5** patch **6** cobble, doctor **7** service **8** overhaul **9** condition **11** recondition

reparations
6 amends **7** redress **9** indemnity, quittance **10** recompense, settlement **11** restitution **12** satisfaction

repartee
3 mot **4** quip **6** banter, bon mot, retort **7** riposte **8** backchat, badinage, comeback **9** cross talk, rejoinder **10** persiflage

repast
3 eat **4** feed, meal **5** feast **9** refection

repay
6 offset, return, reward **7** requite **9** indemnify, reimburse **10** compensate, recompense, remunerate **11** get even with

repeal
4 lift, null, void **5** annul **6** recall, revoke **7** abandon, abolish, nullify, rescind, reverse **8** abrogate, renounce

repeat
4 copy, echo **5** recap, recur, rerun, resay **6** go over, parrot, reecho, recite, rehash, relate, retell **7** imitate, iterate, reprise, restate **9** duplicate, reiterate, replicate **11** reduplicate **12** recapitulate

repeated sound
4 echo

repeater
6 six-gun **7** firearm **10** recidivist

repeating
7 iterant **9** perennial, recurrent **11** reiterative, repetitious

repel
5 rebut **6** rebuff, reject, revolt, sicken **7** disgust, fend off, hold off, repulse, ward off **8** nauseate, stave off

repellent
4 DEET, foul, vile **5** nasty **7** noisome **8** aversive **9** abhorrent, loathsome, obnoxious, offensive, repulsive, revolting **10** forbidding, disgusting, off-putting **11** rebarbative

repent
3 rue **6** regret

repentance
3 rue **4** ruth **6** sorrow **7** remorse **10** contrition **11** compunction

repentant
see **regretful**

repetition
4 copy, echo **5** rerun **7** recital, reprise **9** iteration **11** duplication

repetitive learning method
4 rote

rephrase
6 recast, reword **7** restate

repine
4 beef, fuss, kick, long, moan, wail **5** gripe, yearn **6** grouse, hanker, murmur **7** grumble **8** complain

replace
7 put back, restore **8** exchange, supplant **9** supersede **10** substitute

replacement
3 sub **6** fill-in, loaner, makeup **7** stand-in **9** alternate, surrogate, temporary **10** substitute **11** locum tenens, pinch hitter

replenish
4 fill **5** renew, stock **6** refill **7** refresh, restock, restore

replete
4 full, rife **5** awash **6** packed **7** brimful, crammed, stuffed **8** brimming **9** chock-full **11** overflowing

replica
4 copy, dupe, fake **5** clone, ditto **6** carbon **9** duplicate, facsimile, imitation **10** carbon copy, simulacrum **12** reproduction

replicate
4 copy **5** clone **6** repeat **9** reproduce

reply
4 echo, RSVP **5** react **6** answer, rejoin, retort **7** respond **8** comeback, repartee, response **9** rejoinder

report
4 bang, boom, news, shot, tell **5** crack, relay, rumor, study **6** record, relate, return, review, show up **7** account, article, check in, hearsay, narrate, recount, rundown **8** advisory, bulletin, describe, dispatch **9** broadcast, chronicle, narrative, statement **11** compte rendu

reporter
7 newsman **8** pressman **9** newshound, newswoman **10** journalist
inexperienced: **3** cub

repose
3 lie **4** calm, rest **5** sleep **7** lie down, recline **8** quietude **10** inactivity, quiescence, relaxation **11** restfulness

repository
3 ark **5** depot, store **7** archive, arsenal **8** magazine, treasury **10** storehouse

repossess
see **regain**

reprehend
3 rap **4** rate **5** blame, chide, fault, knock, scold **6** berate, rebuke **7** censure, upbraid **8** admonish **9** criticize

reprehensible
4 base, evil **6** guilty, sinful, unholy, wicked **8** blamable, criminal, culpable **10** censurable **11** blameworthy, disgraceful

represent
6 denote, depict, embody, recall, relate, render, sketch, typify **7** display, exhibit, imitate, make out, narrate, picture, portray, signify **8** describe, stand for **9** delineate, epitomize, exemplify, personify, symbolize **10** constitute, illustrate **11** emblematize

representation
5 draft, image **6** effigy, symbol **7** picture **8** likeness **9** portrayal

representative
5 agent, envoy, model, proxy **6** deputy, sample **7** example, typical **8** delegate, emissary, sampling, specimen **9** exemplary, spokesman **10** ambassador, legislator, prototypal, substitute **11** congressman **12** illustrative, prototypical **13** congresswoman

repress
4 curb **5** sit on **6** bridle, muffle, stifle, subdue **7** smother, squelch **8** keep down, restrain, suppress

repression
4 curb **7** amnesia, control **8** stifling **9** clampdown, crackdown, restraint **10** constraint

reprieve
4 stay **5** grace **7** respite, suspend

reprimand
3 rap **4** rate, ream, task **5** chide, scold **6** rebuke **7** bawl out, censure, chew out, lecture, reproof, reprove **8** admonish, call down, reproach, scolding **9** talking-to **10** admonition **12** admonishment, dressing-down **13** tongue-lashing

reprisal
7 redress, revenge **8** revanche **9** tit for tat, vengeance **11** counterblow, retaliation, retribution

reprise
5 recap **6** repeat **9** reiterate **10** recurrence, repetition

reproach
3 rap **4** rail **5** blame, chide, scold **6** berate, rebuke **7** bawl out, censure, chew out, remorse, upbraid **8** admonish, call down **10** admonition **12** admonishment

reprobate
4 roué **5** scamp **6** sinner **7** lowlife, villain **8** scalawag **9** miscreant, scoundrel **10** blackguard, degenerate

reproduce
4 copy, sire **5** beget, breed **7** imitate **8** multiply **9** duplicate, procreate, propagate, replicate **10** regenerate **11** reduplicate

reproduction
see **replica**

reproductive cell
3 egg, ova (plural) **4** ovum **5** sperm, spore **6** gamete **12** spermatozoid, spermatozoon

reproof
3 rap **6** rebuke **7** censure, lecture **8** scolding **9** criticism, reprimand **10** admonition **11** castigation **12** admonishment, reprehension **13** remonstration

reprove
5 chide, scold **6** rebuke **7** censure, chasten **8** admonish, call down, lambaste, reproach **9** criticize, dress down, reprimand

Rep.'s counterpart
3 Sen.

reptile
4 croc **5** gator, skink, snake **6** caiman, cayman, gavial, iguana, lizard, turtle **7** tuatara **8** tortoise **9** alligator, crocodile, sphenodon
combining form: **6** herpet **7** herpeto
extinct: **8** dinosaur

republic
5 state **6** nation **9** democracy

Republican Party
3 GOP
symbol: **8** elephant

Republic author
5 Plato

repudiate
4 deny **5** spurn **6** abjure, disown, recant, refuse, reject **7** decline, disavow, dismiss **8** disclaim, renounce **9** disaffirm **10** apostatize

repugnance
5 odium **7** disgust **8** aversion, loathing **9** repulsion, revulsion **10** abhorrence, odiousness **11** abomination, detestation

repugnant
4 foul, icky, ugly, vile **5** nasty, yucky **6** creepy, skanky **7** noisome **8** aversive **9** abhorrent, loathsome, obnoxious, offensive, repulsive, revolting **10** disgusting

repulse
5 rebut, repel, spurn **6** rebuff, reject, revolt, sicken **7** disgust, fend off, hold off, ward off **8** nauseate, stave off

repulsion
see **repugnance**

repulsive
see **repugnant**

reputable
7 eminent, upright **8** esteemed **9** estimable, honorable **10** creditable, legitimate, recognized, sanctioned **11** respectable, trustworthy **13** well-thought-of

reputation
4 fame **5** éclat, honor **6** esteem, renown **8** position, prestige, standing **9** celebrity

reputed
7 alleged **8** supposed **9** estimable, purported **10** creditable, ostensible **12** hypothetical

request
3 ask, sue **4** pray, seek, wish **5** plead, press **6** appeal, ask for, behest, demand, invite **7** entreat, solicit **8** entreaty, petition **10** invitation

Requiem for a Nun author
8 Faulkner (William)

require
3 ask **4** lack, need **5** claim, crave **6** demand **7** call for, dictate, mandate, solicit **8** insist on **11** necessitate

required
3 due **5** vital **7** crucial **8** entailed **9** essential, mandatory, necessary, requisite **10** compulsory, obligatory **11** fundamental

requirement
4 must, need **5** claim **6** charge, demand **9** condition, essential, necessity, requisite **10** imperative, sine qua non **11** stipulation

requisite
3 due **4** must **5** vital **7** crucial, needful **8** cardinal **9** condition, essential, necessity **10** imperative, sine qua non **12** precondition **13** indispensable

requisition
5 claim **6** demand **7** solicit **11** application

requite
3 pay **5** repay **6** return **7** satisfy **9** indemnify, reimburse **10** compensate, recompense, remunerate **11** reciprocate

reredos
6 screen **9** partition

rescind
4 lift **5** annul **6** cancel, recall, repeal, revoke **7** retract, reverse **8** abrogate, roll back, take back

rescue
4 free, save **6** ransom, redeem **7** bailout, deliver, reclaim, recover, release, salvage **8** liberate **9** extricate **11** deliverance

rescuer
6 savior **7** saviour

research
5 probe, study **7** inquiry **8** look into **9** delve into **10** experiment **11** examination, investigate **13** investigation

resect
6 cut out, excise **8** amputate **9** extirpate

resemblance
7 analogy **8** likeness **9** alikeness **10** comparison, similarity, similitude **11** parallelism

resemble
5 favor **6** recall **7** smack of **8** look like, simulate **9** take after

resembling
3 à la **4** like **5** quasi **6** akin to

resent
8 begrudge

resentful
4 sore **6** bitter, piqued, sullen **7** envious

resentment
5 pique **6** animus, grudge, rancor **7** dudgeon, offense, umbrage **11** indignation

reservation
5 doubt **7** booking, enclave, proviso **8** homeland, preserve **9** condition, misgiving, sanctuary **10** limitation

reserve
4 fund, keep **5** hoard, put by, stash, stock, store, tract **6** retain, supply **7** nest egg, savings, standby **8** contract, fallback, hold back, postpone, set aside, squirrel, withhold **9** inventory, restraint, reticence, stockpile **10** discretion, diffidence **13** qualification

reserved
3 mim **4** cool **5** aloof, stiff **6** demure, formal, remote **7** distant **8** reticent, retiring, taciturn **9** diffident, secretive, withdrawn **11** tight-lipped **12** closemouthed **13** self-contained

reservoir
5 hoard, stock, store **6** supply **7** nest egg **9** inventory, stockpile

reside
3 lie **4** hive, live, stay **5** dwell, exist **6** inhere **7** consist

residence
4 home, stay **5** abode, house **7** address **8** domicile, dwelling **9** occupancy **10** habitation

resident
6 inmate, lodger, native, tenant **7** citizen, denizen, dweller **8** inherent, occupant **10** inhabitant **11** householder

residential area
6 barrio **9** community **12** neighborhood

residual
8 leftover

residue
3 ash **4** heel, lees, marc, rest, silt, slag **5** ashes, dregs, grout **6** debris, excess, scraps **7** balance, grounds, remains, remnant, surplus **8** leavings, remnants, residuum **9** leftovers, remainder, scourings

resign
4 cede, quit **5** demit, yield **6** give up, retire, submit **7** abandon **8** abdicate, hand over, relegate, renounce, step down **9** surrender **10** relinquish

resignation
8 meekness **9** demission, surrender **10** abdication, compliance, submission **12** acquiescence, renunciation

resigned
9 compliant **10** submissive **11** acquiescent, complaisant

resile
6 recede, recoil, spring **7** rebound, retract, retreat **8** draw back, snap back

resilient
6 bouncy, supple, whippy **7** buoyant, elastic, springy **8** flexible, stretchy **9** adaptable

resin
4 balm **5** copal, damar, roset **6** dammar **7** acrylic, copaiba, polymer, shellac
aromatic: **6** balsam, mastic **8** sandarac
fragrant: **5** elemi **6** storax, styrax **7** ladanum **8** labdanum
gum: **5** myrrh **7** benzoin
medicinal: **6** guaiac **8** guaiacum
of an insect: **3** lac
synthetic: **5** alkyd **8** phenolic
used by bees: **8** propolis

resist
4 buck, defy, kick **5** rebel **6** baffle, combat, oppose, revolt **7** contest, counter, gainsay **8** traverse **10** contradict, contravene

resistance
7 dissent **8** defiance, variance **10** dissension, dissidence, opposition **11** contrariety, obstruction

resistance unit
3 ohm

resistor
8 rheostat, varistor **10** thermistor

resolute
4 bold, fast, firm **6** intent, steady **7** dead set, decided, staunch **8** constant, decisive, faithful, stubborn **9** obstinate, steadfast, tenacious, undaunted **10** determined, persistent **12** pertinacious, single-minded

resolution
5 pluck, spunk **6** mettle **7** courage, outcome **8** decision, firmness, tenacity **10** conclusion **12** perseverance **13** determination, steadfastness

resolve
5 clear, crack **6** decide, settle **7** clear up, iron out, unravel, work out **8** boldness, conclude, decipher, firmness **9** breakdown, determine, intention, reconcile **10** unscramble **13** determination, steadfastness

resonant
4 deep, full, rich **6** silver **7** booming, echoing, orotund, vibrant **8** powerful, sonorous **11** reverberant

resonate
4 echo, peal, ring **7** resound, vibrate **11** reverberate

resort
3 spa **4** lido **5** haven, lodge **6** harbor, refuge **7** retreat, riviera, stopgap **8** recourse **9** expedient, makeshift **10** substitute
lake: **5** Tahoe
last: **8** pis aller

resound
4 boom, echo, peal, ring **11** reverberate

resounding
7 booming, echoing, orotund **8** emphatic, sonorous **10** clangorous, resonating, thunderous

resource
3 aid **5** asset, means **6** supply **7** standby

resourceful
5 adept **6** adroit, artful, clever, shrewd **7** capable, cunning **8** creative, skillful **9** ingenious, inventive **10** innovative **11** imaginative **12** enterprising

resources
5 funds, means, money, purse **6** assets, riches, wealth **7** capital, fortune, reserve **8** bankroll, finances, property, reserves **11** wherewithal

respect
5 favor, honor, props **6** admire, devoir, esteem, homage, regard, revere **8** venerate **9** deference **10** admiration, estimation, veneration

respectable
5 ample **6** decent, proper, worthy **8** adequate **9** admirable, estimable, honorable **10** sufficient **11** presentable **12** satisfactory **13** well-thought-of

respectful
5 civil **6** polite **8** obeisant, reverent **9** courteous **11** deferential, reverential

respecting
3 per **4** as to, in re **5** about **7** apropos **9** as regards, regarding **10** as concerns, concerning, relating to **11** considering

respire
7 breathe

respite
4 lull, rest **5** break, delay, pause, spell, truce **6** hiatus, recess, relief **8** breather, reprieve, surcease **12** intermission

resplendent
5 regal **7** glowing, shining **8** glorious, gorgeous **9** brilliant, refulgent **11** magnificent

respond
5 react, reply **6** answer, rejoin, retort **8** come back

response
5 reply **6** answer, retort, return **7** riposte **8** antiphon, comeback, reaction **9** rejoinder
involuntary: **6** reflex **7** tropism

responsibility
4 buck, duty, onus **5** blame, brief, fault **6** burden, charge, devoir **10** obligation **11** reliability

responsible
6 liable **8** amenable, reliable **10** answerable, chargeable, dependable **11** accountable, trustworthy

responsive
4 open, yare **5** alert, awake **8** sentient **9** sensitive **11** susceptible, sympathetic

rest
3 nap **4** calm, ease, laze, loaf, loll, lull **5** let up, pause, peace, quiet, relax, spell **6** catnap, depend, excess, lounge, repose **7** balance, leisure, lie down, recline, remains, remnant, surplus **8** breather, leavings **9** interlude, remainder

restate
4 echo **9** translate **10** paraphrase **12** recapitulate

restatement
10 paraphrase **11** translation

restaurant
4 café **5** diner **6** eatery **7** automat, beanery **9** brasserie, cafeteria **10** coffee shop **11** coffeehouse, greasy spoon
acronym: **4** IHOP
listing: **4** menu
price: **8** à la carte, prix fixe **10** table d'hôte
worker: **4** chef, cook **6** busboy, server, waiter **7** maître d', waitron **8** waitress **10** dishwasher, headwaiter, waitperson **12** maître d'hôtel

restaurateur Toots
4 Shor

restful
4 calm **5** quiet **6** placid **8** peaceful, tranquil

resting on
4 atop

restitute
6 refund, return **7** reclaim, recover, restore **8** give back **11** recondition, reconstruct **12** rehabilitate

restitution
6 amends, refund, return **7** redress **8** reprisal **9** indemnity, quittance **10** recompense, reparation **11** restoration **12** remuneration, satisfaction

restive
4 edgy **5** balky, nervy, tense **6** ornery, uneasy **7** fidgety, froward, wayward **8** contrary, skittish

restiveness
7 anxiety **8** disquiet **9** balkiness **10** inquietude **11** contrariety, disquietude, waywardness

restless
5 antsy, itchy, jumpy **6** fitful, uneasy **7** anxious, fidgety, fretful, jittery, nervous, unquiet **8** agitated, troubled **9** disturbed, perturbed, unsettled **12** discontented, dissatisfied

restorative
4 balm **5** tonic **7** healing **8** curative, remedial, sanative

restore
4 cure, heal, mend, stet **5** amend, remit, renew, right **6** recall, recoup, reform, remedy, render, repair, return, revive **7** get back, improve, reclaim, recover, rectify, refresh, replace **8** give back, recreate, renovate, revivify **9** refurbish, reinstate, replenish, restitute **10** regenerate, rejuvenate **11** recondition, reestablish **12** rehabilitate

restrain
3 gag **4** bate, curb, rein **5** check, leash **6** arrest, bridle, hamper, hinder, hold in, impede, muzzle **7** collect, control, harness, inhibit, repress **8** hold back, hold down, moderate, suppress

restrained
4 cool **6** low-key **5** canny, quiet **6** modest **7** subdued **8** discreet, reserved, reticent, retiring, tasteful **9** inhibited, temperate **10** controlled, reasonable

restraint
5 stint **6** bridle, tether **7** durance, embargo, reserve **8** estoppel, pullback **9** hindrance **10** deterrence, inhibition, limitation, moderation **11** confinement, forbearance **12** straitjacket

restrict
4 bind, curb **5** hem in, limit **6** hamper, hobble, impede, narrow, shrink **7** confine, curtail, delimit, inhibit, trammel **8** hold back **12** circumscribe
a will: **6** entail

restriction
4 curb **5** check, limit, stint **7** control **9** restraint **10** constraint, limitation, regulation **13** qualification

restroom
3 can, lav, loo **4** head, john **5** jakes, privy **6** toilet **7** latrine **8** lavatory

restyle
4 redo **6** revamp, revise, rework **8** make over

result
3 end **4** stem **5** ensue, issue **6** effect, emerge, finish, follow, payoff, sequel, upshot **7** outcome, product **8** sequence, solution **9** aftermath, come about, eventuate **10** conclusion, denouement **11** aftereffect, consequence, eventuality
incidental: **7** spinoff **9** byproduct

resume
4 go on **5** renew **6** pick up, reopen **7** carry on, proceed, restart **8** continue **10** recommence

résumé
4 vita **5** sum-up, vitae (plural) **6** précis **7** summary **9** summation, summing-up

resurgence
5 rally **7** rebirth, revival **8** comeback, recovery **10** renascence **11** renaissance **12** risorgimento

resurrect
5 raise, renew **6** come to, revive **8** retrieve, revivify **10** reactivate

resurrection
7 rebirth, revival **10** renascence **11** renaissance **12** risorgimento

resuscitate
see **resurrect**

retail
4 sell, tell, vend **6** market **7** narrate **11** merchandise

retailer
6 dealer, seller, trader, vendor **8** merchant **9** tradesman **10** shopkeeper **11** storekeeper **12** merchandiser

retain
4 hire, hold, keep **7** reserve **8** hold over, preserve, remember, withhold

retainer
3 fee **6** lackey, menial, minion, yeoman **7** deposit, servant **8** employee, follower **9** bite plate, dependent, pensioner

retaliate
7 get back, get even **10** strike back

retaliation
see **reprisal**

retaliatory
8 punitive, vengeful **10** vindictive

retard
4 clog, mire, slow **5** delay, stunt **6** detain, fetter, hamper, hang up, hinder, impede, slow up **7** set back, slacken **8** decrease, hold back, restrain **10** decelerate

retarded
3 dim **4** dull, dumb, slow **6** opaque, simple, stupid **8** backward **9** dim-witted **10** half-witted, slow-witted **11** exceptional

retch
3 gag **4** barf, hurl, puke, spew **5** heave, vomit **6** spit up **7** bring up, throw up, upchuck **8** disgorge

retention
6 memory **7** storage

reticent
see **reserved**

reticulate
4 vein **5** veiny **6** meshed, netted **7** netlike **10** crisscross

retinue
4 band, tail **5** suite, train **6** livery **7** company, cortege **9** entourage, following

retire
4 exit, quit **5** yield **6** bow out, depart, recede, resign, turn in **7** pension **8** step down, withdraw **9** discharge, strike out, terminate **10** relinquish

retired for the night
4 abed

retiree
6 senior **7** emerita **8** emeritus **9** pensioner **10** golden-ager **13** senior citizen

retirement allowance
3 SEP **7** pension

retiring
3 mim, shy **5** mousy, timid **6** demure, modest **7** bashful **8** reserved **9** diffident, withdrawn **11** unassertive

retool
7 reequip **8** retrofit **10** reengineer

retort
5 reply, sally **6** answer, rejoin **7** counter, respond, riposte **8** comeback, repartee, response **9** rejoinder, wisecrack

retouch
5 alter, emend, renew **6** repair **7** correct, enhance, improve, restore

retract
4 deny **5** unsay **6** abjure, recall, recant, recede, renege, resile, revoke **7** disavow, rescind, retreat, swallow **8** forswear, renounce, take back, withdraw

retreat
3 den, ebb **4** quit **5** cover, haven **6** ashram, asylum, bow out, covert, decamp, refuge, vacate **7** abandon, back off, back out, pull out, shelter **8** back down, draw back, evacuate, fall back, hideaway, withdraw **9** backtrack, climb down, sanctuary **10** give ground, withdrawal

retrench
3 cut **4** pare **5** slash **6** excise, lessen, reduce **7** abridge, curtail **9** economize

retribution
7 revenge **8** avenging, reprisal, requital, revanche **9** vengeance **10** punishment, recompense **11** counterblow, retaliation
goddess of: **3** Ate **4** Fury **7** Nemesis

retrieve
5 fetch **6** recall, recoup, redeem, rescue **7** get back, recover, restore, salvage **9** resurrect

retro
5 campy **7** antique, revival, vintage **9** nostalgic **12** old-fashioned

retrograde
4 back **7** inverse, reverse **8** backward, inverted, rearward

retrogress
see **revert**

retrospect
9 hindsight **12** recollection **13** reexamination

retrospective
6 review **8** backward **10** exhibition, reflective, ruminative

return
5 recur, repay, yield **6** answer, rebate, regain, rejoin, render, retort, revert **7** bring in, get back, rebound, recover, reprise, requite, respond, reverse, riposte **8** comeback, dividend, earnings, give back, reappear, response **9** rejoinder, repayment, reversion **10** recompense, recurrence **11** reciprocate, restitution

Return of the Native
author: **5** Hardy (Thomas)
character: **4** Clym (Yeobright) **8** Eustacia (Vye)

Reuben
brother: **6** Joseph
father: **5** Jacob
mother: **4** Leah

Réunion
capital: **7** St.-Denis
city: **6** St.-Paul **7** St.-Louis **8** St.-Pierre
department of: **6** France
ethnic group: **6** Creole
former name: **7** Bourbon **9** Bonaparte
island group: **9** Mascarene

reunion attendee
4 alum, grad **6** alumna, alumni (plural) **7** alumnae (plural), alumnus **8** graduate

revamp
4 redo **5** renew **6** remake, repair, revise, rework **7** remodel, restyle, rewrite **8** make over, overhaul, redesign, renovate **9** refurbish **11** recondition

reveal
4 bare, blab, jamb, leak, show **5** admit, let on, spill **6** betray, evince, expose, impart, unmask, unveil **7** confess, declare, display, divulge,

exhibit, publish, uncover **8** announce, decipher, disclose, discover, give away **9** broadcast, made known **11** acknowledge **12** bring to light

revel
4 bask, orgy, riot **5** binge, feast, party, spree **6** boogie, frolic, gaiety, hoopla, wallow **7** carouse, delight, indulge, jollity, roister, rollick, wassail, whoopla **8** carnival, carousal, festival **9** bacchanal, celebrate, festivity, luxuriate, merriment, whoop-de-do **11** bacchanalia, celebration, merrymaking

revelation
6 kicker **8** epiphany, giveaway, prophecy, surprise **9** discovery, punch line **10** apocalypse, disclosure **13** manifestation

reveler
7 orgiast **8** bacchant, carouser **9** bacchante, wassailer **10** merrymaker

revelry
4 orgy, riot **6** gaiety **7** carouse, jollity, wassail, whoopee, whoopla **8** carousal, partying **9** festivity, high jinks, merriment, whoop-de-do **10** whoop-de-doo **11** merrymaking

revenant
5 ghost, haunt, shade, spook **6** shadow, spirit, undead, wraith, zombie **7** phantom, specter, spectre **8** phantasm, prodigal, visitant **10** apparition

revenge
5 right **6** defend **7** get back, get even, redress, requite **8** reprisal, requital, revanche **9** retaliate, vindicate **11** retaliation, retribution

revenue
4 rent **5** gains, issue, yield **6** income, profit, return **7** comings **8** earnings, interest, proceeds, receipts, taxation

reverberant
6 hollow **7** booming, echoing **8** resonant **10** resounding

reverberate
4 echo, gong, ring **6** reecho **7** resound

reverberation
4 echo

revere
4 laud **5** adore, exalt, extol, honor, value **6** admire, esteem, hallow, regard **7** cherish, magnify, respect, worship **8** treasure, venerate

revered
6 sacred **8** esteemed **9** estimable, venerable

reverence
3 awe **5** dread, honor, piety **6** esteem, fealty, homage **7** loyalty, respect, worship **8** devotion **9** deference, obeisance **10** veneration
gesture of: 3 bow **6** kowtow **8** kneeling **12** genuflection

reverend
4 abbé, holy **5** clerk, vicar **6** clergy, cleric, deacon, divine, parson, rector **8** chaplain, clerical, minister, preacher **9** churchman, clergyman **11** clergywoman **12** ecclesiastic

reverent
5 godly, pious **6** devout **7** dutiful **9** prayerful **10** God-fearing, respectful, worshipful

reverie
4 muse **5** dream **6** trance, vision **7** fantasy **8** daydream **10** absorption, brown study, meditation **11** abstraction **13** woolgathering

reversal
4 turn **5** U-turn **6** double, switch **7** setback, undoing **8** backfire, flip-flop **9** about-face, inversion, turnabout, volte-face **10** switcheroo **12** solarization **13** change of heart

reverse
4 undo **6** change, contra, invert, repeal, revoke **7** counter, rescind **8** antipode, backward, contrary, exchange, opposite, overrule, overturn **9** about-face, backwards, diametric, overthrow, transpose, turnabout, volte-face **10** antithesis

reversion
5 lapse **6** return **7** atavism, escheat **9** about-face, throwback, turnabout, volte-face **10** succession

revert
4 turn **6** return **7** decline, devolve, escheat, inverse **8** turn back **9** backslide **10** degenerate, retrograde, retrogress

revetment
4 berm **6** bunker, riprap **9** barricade, earthwork **10** embankment

review
3 vet **4** scan **5** audit, recap, study **6** assess, go over, report, revise, survey **7** analyze, journal **8** analysis, critique, revision, scrutiny, talk over **9** criticism, reexamine, refresher **10** evaluation, inspection, periodical, reconsider, reevaluate **11** examination **13** reexamination, retrospective

revile
4 rail, rate **5** abuse, scold **6** attack, berate, defame, malign, vilify **7** asperse, bawl out, chew out, upbraid **8** belittle, disgrace, execrate **9** blaspheme **10** tongue-lash, vituperate

revise
4 edit **5** alter, amend, emend, proof, renew **6** change, polish, reform, retool, revamp **7** correct, improve, restore, rewrite **8** overhaul, redesign, work over **9** red-pencil **10** blue-pencil

revision
6 change, revamp, update **7** redraft **8** facelift, overhaul, updating **10** alteration, correction, emendation **11** overhauling **12** modification

revitalize
see **revive**

revival
7 rebirth, renewal **8** comeback **10** renascence, resurgence **11** reanimation, renaissance, restoration **12** regeneration, rejuvenation, resurrection, risorgimento **13** recrudescence, resuscitation

revive
5 rally, renew, rouse **6** arouse, awaken, come to **7** bring to, enliven, quicken, refresh, restore **8** reawaken, rekindle, renovate **9** reanimate, resurrect **10** reactivate, recuperate, regenerate, rejuvenate **11** bring around, reintroduce, resuscitate **12** reinvigorate

revoke
4 lift, void **5** annul, erase **6** abjure, cancel, recall, recant, renege, repeal **7** abolish, nullify, rescind, retract, reverse **8** abrogate, call back **10** invalidate **11** countermand

revolt
4 riot **5** rebel, repel, shock **6** mutiny, resist, sicken **7** disgust, repulse **8** nauseate, outbreak, uprising **9** jacquerie, rebellion **10** insurgence, insurgency **12** insurrection

revolter
5 rebel **6** anarch **8** frondeur, mutineer **9** anarchist, insurgent **10** malcontent

revolting
4 foul, ugly, vile **5** nasty **6** horrid **7** hideous, noisome, obscene **9** atrocious, loathsome, repellent, repugnant, repulsive **10** disgusting, nauseating

revolution
4 gyre, reel, riot, roll, spin, turn **5** cycle, orbit, twirl, wheel, whirl **6** mutiny **7** circuit **8** gyration, rotation, uprising **9** pirouette, rebellion **10** barrel roll, changeover, somersault **12** insurrection

revolutionary
5 rebel, ultra **7** extreme, radical **8** mutineer, rotating, ultraist **9** extremist, insurgent
American: **4** Emma (Goldman), Hale (Nathan), Reed (John) **5** Adams (Samuel), Allen (Ethan), Henry (Patrick), Shays (Daniel) **6** Revere (Paul)
English: **5** Paine (Thomas)
French: **5** Marat (Jean-Paul) **6** Danton (Georges) **8** Mirabeau (Comte de) **9** Saint-Just (Louis) **11** Robespierre (Maximilien)
Irish: **4** Tone (Wolfe) **6** Pearse (Padraig, Patrick) **7** Collins (Michael), Parnell (Charles Stewart) **8** Casement (Roger), de Valera (Eamon), Griffith (Arthur), O'Connell (Daniel)
Mexican: **5** Villa (Pancho) **6** Zapata (Emiliano) **7** Hidalgo (Padre Miguel)
Russian: **5** Kirov (Sergey), Lenin (Vladimir Ilyich) **7** Trotsky (Leon) **8** Kerensky (Aleksandr) **9** Kropotkin (Pyotr)

revolutionize
9 transform **11** transfigure

revolve
4 spin, turn **5** twirl, wheel, whirl **6** circle, gyrate, rotate

revolver
3 gat, gun, rod **4** Colt **5** Glock, Luger, Ruger **6** heater, Magnum, pistol, six-gun **7** firearm, handgun, shooter, sidearm **10** six-shooter

revue
4 show **9** burlesque **10** production, vaudeville **13** entertainment

revulsion
4 hate **6** hatred, horror **7** disgust **8** aversion, loathing **10** abhorrence, repugnance **11** abomination, detestation

reward
5 bonus, booty, medal, price, prize **6** bounty, carrot, payoff, trophy **7** guerdon, jackpot, premium **8** dividend **10** compensate, honorarium, recompense, remunerate **12** compensation, remuneration

rewarding
7 gainful **8** edifying, fruitful, valuable **9** lucrative **10** beneficial, fulfilling, gratifying, profitable, satisfying, worthwhile **12** advantageous, remunerative

Rex Stout's Wolfe
4 Nero

Reynard
3 fox

rhadamanthine
3 due **4** just **6** strict **7** condign, fitting, merited **8** deserved, rigorous, rightful, suitable **9** requisite, stringent

Rhadamanthus
5 judge
brother: **5** Minos
father: **4** Zeus **7** Jupiter
mother: **6** Europa

rhapsodic
5 lyric **7** fulsome, gushing **8** ecstatic, effusive

rhapsodize
4 gush, rave **5** drool **6** effuse **7** enthuse **9** wax poetic

Rhea
3 Ops
daughter: **4** Hera, Juno **5** Ceres, Vesta **6** Hestia **7** Demeter
father: **6** Uranus
husband: **6** Cronus, Saturn
mother: **4** Gaea
son: **4** Zeus **5** Hades, Pluto **7** Jupiter, Neptune **8** Poseidon

Rheingold, Das
character: **4** Loge, Loki **5** Freya, Wotan **6** Fafner, Fafnir, Fasolt **8** Alberich
composer: **6** Wagner (Richard)

rheostat
8 resistor

rhesus
6 monkey **7** macaque

rhetoric
4 rant **6** speech **7** bombast, fustian, oratory **8** rhapsody **9** elocution, eloquence, verbosity **11** rodomontade, speechcraft
term: **6** aporia, simile **7** litotes **8** metaphor **10** apostrophe, digression **12** alliteration, onomatopoeia

rhetorical
5 gassy, tumid, windy **6** florid, ornate, purple, turgid **7** aureate, flowery, orotund, pompous, stilted **8** eloquent, forensic, inflated, overdone, sonorous **9** bombastic, grandiose, high-flown, overblown, tumescent **10** euphuistic, flamboyant **11** declamatory, highfalutin, overwrought, pretentious **12** high-sounding, magniloquent **13** grandiloquent

rhetorician
6 orator, writer **7** speaker
Roman: **10** Quintilian

Rhine River
city: **4** Bonn, Köln **5** Basel, Mainz **7** Coblenz, Cologne, Koblenz **8** Duisburg, Mannheim **9** Rotterdam, Wiesbaden **10** Düsseldorf
nymph: **7** Lorelei
tributary: **3** Aar, Ill, Lek **4** Aare, Lahn, Main, Ruhr, Waal

rhizome
4 root **5** tuber

Rhode Island
bay: **12** Narragansett
capital: **10** Providence
city: **7** Newport, Warwick **9** Pawtucket
college, university: **4** RISD **5** Brown
island: **5** Block
nickname: **5** Ocean (State) **11** Little Rhody
river: **8** Pawtuxet
state bird: **14** Rhode Island red
state flower: **6** violet
state tree: **8** red maple

Rhodesia
8 Zimbabwe

rhombus
7 diamond, lozenge **13** parallelogram

rhonchus
5 snore

Rhône River
city: **4** Lyon **5** Arles, Lyons **6** Geneva **7** Avignon
lake: **6** Geneva
mountain range: **4** Jura
tributary: **5** Isère **5** Loire, Saône

rhubarb
3 row **4** flap **5** run-in **6** ruckus, tangle **7** dispute, quarrel, wrangle **8** argument, pieplant **11** altercation, controversy

rhyme
4 poem, song **5** agree, ditty, verse **6** accord, jingle, poetry **7** conform **8** dovetail **9** harmonize **10** coordinate, correspond
scheme: **4** ABAB

rhymer
4 bard, poet **5** odist **7** metrist **8** lyricist **9** poetaster, rhymester, sonneteer, versifier

rhythm
4 beat, flow, lilt, time **5** meter, pulse, swing **6** accent, groove **7** cadence, measure, pattern **8** sequence

rhythmic
7 pulsing, regular **8** measured, metrical

rialto
6 market **7** West End **8** Broadway **11** marketplace

riant
3 gay **5** jolly, merry **6** blithe, jocund, jovial **7** buoyant, gleeful **8** cheerful, mirthful **10** blithesome

riata
4 rope **5** lasso **6** lariat

rib
3 fun, kid, rag **4** band, bone, dike, fool, jape, jest, joke, josh, purl, razz, stay, wale **5** chaff, costa, ridge, tease **6** banter, costae (plural), lierne, needle

ribald
3 raw **4** blue, racy, rude, sexy **5** bawdy, crude, dirty, salty, spicy **6** coarse, earthy, filthy, purple, risqué, smutty, vulgar **7** naughty, obscene, profane, raunchy **8** indecent, off-color **9** offensive, reprobate, salacious **10** suggestive

ribbon
3 bow **4** band, tape **5** braid, shred, strip **6** cordon, fillet, stripe, tatter **7** bandeau

rice
7 arborio, basmati
dish: **5** pilaf **6** congee **7** risotto **9** jambalaya
drink: **5** mirin **6** arrack
field: **5** paddy
husk: **5** lemma
wine: **4** sake, saki

ricelike pasta
4 orzo

rich
4 lush, oily, posh **5** ample, fatty, flush, grand, heavy, plush, swank, vivid **6** costly, creamy, deluxe, gilded, lavish, loaded, monied, ornate,

potent, rococo **7** baroque, copious, elegant, fertile, filling, moneyed, opulent, orotund, profuse, wealthy, well-off **8** abundant, affluent, fruitful, palatial, well-to-do **9** abounding, bountiful, elaborate, luxuriant, luxurious, plentiful, sumptuous, well-fixed **10** productive, prosperous, wellheeled **11** extravagant
cake: **5** torte
person: **5** Midas, mogul, nabob **6** fat cat **7** Croesus, magnate **9** moneybags, plutocrat
soil: **4** loam

Richard of film
4 Gere

Richardson work
6 Pamela **8** Clarissa

Richelieu's successor
7 Mazarin

riches
4 gold, luxe, pelf **5** booty, lucre **6** bounty, mammon, wealth **7** fortune **8** opulence, treasure
demon of: **6** Mammon

rick
4 cock, heap, pile **5** shock, stack

rickety
4 weak **5** shaky **6** flimsy, wobbly **7** unsound **8** decrepit, insecure, rachitic, unstable, unsteady **10** ramshackle, rattletrap

Rick's old flame
4 Ilsa

ricochet
4 ping **5** carom **6** bounce, glance **7** rebound

rid
6 divest **7** relieve **8** unburden **11** disencumber

riddle
5 rebus **6** enigma, puzzle **7** mystery, perplex, problem **9** conundrum, perforate **10** closed book, puzzlement **11** brainteaser

ride
4 spin, tour, trip **5** drive, jaunt, mount, tease **6** travel **7** journey **8** carousel **9** excursion

ride out
6 endure **7** outlast, survive, weather **9** withstand

rider
6 clause, cowboy, jockey **7** addenda (plural), codicil **8** addendum, addition, appendix, horseman, reinsman **9** amendment **10** equestrian, horsewoman, supplement

ridge
3 rib **4** bank, berm, brow, keel, reef, ruck, seam **5** arête, arris, chine, crest, esker, knurl, plica, spine **6** crease, divide, furrow, rimple, saddle, summit **7** annulet, breaker, crinkle, hogback, wrinkle **8** shoulder **9** razorback **11** corrugation
gravelly: **5** esker
on the skin: **4** wale, weal, welt
sharp: **7** hogback

ridicule
3 pan, rib **4** gibe, haze, jape, jeer, mock, razz, ride, twit **5** chaff, flout, mimic, roast, scoff, scorn, scout, sneer, squib, taunt **6** deride, satire **7** lampoon, mockery, pillory, sarcasm **8** derision, raillery, satirize, travesty **9** burlesque **10** caricature
god of: **5** Momus
object of: **4** butt **13** laughingstock

ridiculous
5 comic, daffy, dotty, goofy, inane, silly, wacky **6** absurd, insane **7** bizarre, comical, foolish, risible **8** derisory, farcical **9** cockamamy, derisible, fantastic, laughable, ludicrous, senseless **10** cockamamie, outrageous **11** for the birds, harebrained **12** preposterous, unbelievable

riding
academy: **6** manège
costume: **5** habit
pants: **8** jodhpurs
whip: **3** bat **4** crop **5** quirt

Rienzi composer
6 Wagner (Richard)

rife
4 full **5** flush **7** replete, teeming **8** abundant, swarming **9** abounding, plentiful, prevalent **10** widespread **11** overflowing

riff
4 flip, leaf, scan, skim **5** theme, thumb **6** browse **8** ostinato

riffle
4 flip, leaf, fret, scan, skim, wave **5** shoal, thumb **6** browse, sluice **7** shallow, shuffle **10** interstice

riffraff
3 mob **6** masses, proles, rabble **8** canaille, unwashed **9** hoi polloi, multitude **11** proletariat

rifle
3 arm, gun **4** loot, sack **6** burgle, groove, weapon **7** carbine, despoil, firearm, pillage, plunder, ransack, rummage **9** chassepot
accessory: **6** ramrod
attachment: **5** scope **8** silencer
kind: **6** Garand, Mauser **7** Enfield **8** Browning **9** Remington **10** Winchester **11** Springfield

rift
3 gap **5** break, chasm, chink, cleft, crack, fault, split **6** breach, cleave, divide, hiatus, schism **7** fissure, opening, rupture **8** crevasse, division, fracture, interval **9** fault line **10** separation **12** estrangement

rig
3 arm, fit, fix **4** fake, gear, semi **5** dress, equip, getup, trick **6** adjust, clothe, doctor, outfit, tackle **7** apparel, arrange, costume, derrick, furnish, turn out **8** accouter, accoutre, clothing, equipage, platform **9** apparatus, construct, equipment **10** manipulate

rigging
3 net **4** duds, gear, togs **5** dress, lines, ropes **6** attire, chains, tackle, things **7** apparel, clothes, raiment **8** clothing **9** apparatus, equipment

right
3 apt, due, fit **4** fair, just, sane, true, well **5** amply, claim, droit, sound, title **6** decent, dexter, direct, equity, lawful, proper, square, strict **7** condign, correct, fitting, freedom, genuine, liberty, license, merited, rectify, redress **8** accurate, bona fide, orthodox, smack-dab, suitable **9** authentic, befitting, equitable, privilege, veritable **10** perquisite **11** appropriate, correctness, prerogative
combining form: **4** orth, rect **5** dextr, ortho, recti **6** dextro
feudal: **4** soke
legal: **5** droit **8** usufruct
royal: **7** regalia (plural)
turn: **3** gee

right away
3 now **6** at once, pronto **8** directly, promptly **9** forthwith, instanter, instantly **11** immediately, straight off, straightway **12** then and there

righteous
4 good, holy, just, pure **5** godly, moral, noble, pious **6** devout, worthy **7** ethical, genuine, sinless, upright **8** innocent, virtuous **9** blameless, guiltless **10** inculpable, principled

righteousness
5 honor **6** equity, virtue **7** honesty, justice, probity **8** holiness, morality **9** integrity, rectitude

rightful
3 apt, due, fit **4** fair, just, true **5** legal **6** honest, lawful, proper **7** condign, fitting **8** deserved, suitable **9** befitting, equitable, impartial **10** applicable, legitimate **11** appropriate

right-handed
6 dexter **7** dextral **9** clockwise

right-hand page
5 recto

rightist
4 tory **11** reactionary **12** conservative

right-minded
5 moral, noble **6** decent, honest **7** ethical **8** virtuous **10** upstanding

right on
4 amen **6** word up

Rights of Man author
5 Paine (Thomas)

rigid
3 set **4** firm, hard, taut **5** fixed, stiff, tense **6** severe, strict **7** austere, precise, hard-set **8** cast-iron, ironclad, obdurate, rigorous **9** draconian, immovable, inelastic, rockbound, stringent, unbending **10** adamantine, brassbound, inflexible, relentless, unyielding **11** unbudgeable **13** rhadamanthine

rigidity
6 turgor **7** buckram **8** hardness **9** stiffness
muscular: **8** myotonia

rigmarole
6 drivel, ramble **7** blather, red tape **8** nonsense **9** gibberish, procedure **10** balderdash, mumbo jumbo **12** gobbledygook

Rigoletto
composer: **5** Verdi (Giuseppe)
daughter: **5** Gilda
setting: **6** Mantua

rigor
7 cruelty **8** asperity, hardness, hardship, severity **9** austerity, exactness, harshness, roughness, sharpness, sternness **10** affliction, difficulty, exactitude, strictness **11** tribulation **13** inflexibility

rigorous
4 hard **5** exact, harsh, rigid, rough, stern, stiff **6** bitter, brutal, proper, rugged, severe, strict **7** ascetic, drastic, onerous, precise **8** accurate, exacting **9** draconian, ironbound, stringent **10** burdensome, inflexible, ironhanded, oppressive **11** punctilious **13** rhadamanthine

rile
3 bug, rub, vex **4** roil **5** anger, annoy, grate, muddy, peeve, pique, upset **6** muddle, nettle, put out, rankle **7** agitate, disturb, fluster, inflame, perturb, provoke **8** disorder, disquiet, irritate **9** aggravate **10** discompose, exasperate

rill
3 run **4** burn, purl **5** bourn, brook, creek **6** runnel, stream, valley **7** freshet, rivulet **8** brooklet **9** streamlet **11** watercourse

rim
3 hem, lip **4** bank, boss, brim, edge, ring **5** bezel, bezil, bound, brink, skirt, verge **6** border, flange, fringe, margin, shield **7** annulus, horizon, outline **8** boundary, surround **9** perimeter, periphery
of a basket: **4** hoop
of a cask: **5** chime
of an insect's wing: **6** termen
of a spoked wheel: **5** felly **6** felloe

Rimbaud work
12 Season in Hell (A) **13** Illuminations (Les)

rime
3 ice **4** hoar **5** crust, frost **7** coating, encrust **9** hoarfrost, Jack Frost **12** incrustation

Rinaldo
beloved: **8** Angelica
cousin: **7** Orlando
father: **5** Aymon
horse: **6** Bayard
mother: **3** Aya
sister: **10** Bradamante
uncle: **11** Charlemagne

rind
4 bark, husk, peel, skin **5** crust **9** crackling

ring
3 eye, hem, rim **4** band, bloc, bong, echo, gird, gyre, hoop, loop, peal, toll **5** arena, bezel, cabal, chime, clang, cycle, group, knell, knoll, phone, round, sound **6** circle, clique, collar, girdle, staple **7** annulus, clangor, combine, compass, resound, vibrate **8** bracelet, cincture, encircle, surround **9** coalition, encompass **11** combination, reverberate
around sun or moon: **6** corona
curtain: **3** eye
for a compass: **6** gimbal
harness: **3** dee **6** button, terret
heraldic: **7** annulet
in a hinge: **7** gudgeon
of chain: **4** link
of color: **8** stocking
official: **3** ref **7** referee
of leaves or flowers: **6** wreath **7** garland
of light: **4** halo **5** glory **6** corona, nimbus **7** aureole **8** halation
of rope or metal: **4** hank **6** becket **7** garland, grommet, thimble
of two hoops: **6** gimmal
relating to: **7** annular
used as a valve or diaphragm: **5** wafer
wedding: **4** band

Ring and the Book author
8 Browning (Robert)

ringed
8 annulate, bordered **9** encircled **10** surrounded

ringer
4 fake, spit **5** clone, image **6** double **7** clapper, picture **8** impostor, portrait **10** simulacrum **13** spitting image

ringing
7 orotund, vibrant **8** decisive, emphatic, plangent, resonant, sonorous **10** clangorous, resounding **11** reverberant, unequivocal

ringleader
4 boss **5** chief **6** honcho, top dog **7** kingpin **9** godfather, top banana **10** head honcho, instigator, mastermind

ringlet
4 curl, lock **5** crimp, tress **7** circlet, earlock, tendril **8** spit curl

Ring of the Nibelung composer
6 Wagner (Richard)

ring-shaped island
5 atoll

ringworm
5 tinea

rinse
4 dunk, lave, wash **5** bathe, douse, swill **6** shower, sluice **7** cleanse
the mouth: **6** gargle

Rio de la ____
5 Plata

riot
5 brawl, broil, melee, revel, spree **6** bedlam, émeute, jumble, revolt, tumult, uproar **7** carouse, debauch, rampage, revelry, roister, wassail **8** carousal, disorder, uprising **9** commotion **10** debauchery, donnybrook, revolution **11** disturbance

riotous
4 lush, wild **6** stormy, unruly, wanton **7** bacchic, profuse, untamed **8** abundant **9** abounding, clamorous, exuberant, luxuriant, plentiful, turbulent, unchecked **10** boisterous **11** saturnalian, tempestuous **12** unrestrained

rip
4 gash, hole, rend, rent, rive, spit, tear **5** shred, slash, split **6** attack, cleave **7** current, sputter **8** lacerate, undertow **9** criticize, disparage **12** undercurrent
into: **5** go for **6** assail, attack **8** lambaste
off: **3** con, rob **4** copy **5** cheat, steal, theft **7** defraud, imitate, swindle **9** imitation

ripe
4 aged, full, late **5** adult, grown, ready, ruddy, plump **6** mature, mellow, smelly, timely **7** grown-up **8** prepared, suitable **9** developed, full-blown, full-grown, offensive, opportune **10** seasonable **11** appropriate, full-fledged

ripen
3 age **4** cure, grow **6** better, grow up, mature, mellow, season **7** develop, enhance, improve, perfect **8** heighten, maturate

rip off
3 con, rob **4** copy **5** cheat, steal **7** defraud, imitate, swindle

rip-off
4 copy, scam **5** fraud, theft **7** swindle **8** stealing **9** deception, imitation **12** exploitation

riposte
5 parry, reply **6** retort, return, thrust **8** back talk, comeback, repartee **13** counterattack

ripping
4 fine **5** grand, nifty, super, swell **6** divine, peachy **7** capital **8** glorious, splendid, terrific **9** admirable, delicious, excellent, fantastic, marvelous, wonderful **10** delightful, delectable, remarkable **11** scrumptious, sensational

ripple
3 lap **4** curl, fret, riff, wave **6** cockle, dimple, lipper, popple, ruffle, spread, wimple **7** crinkle, wavelet, wrinkle **8** undulate

rip-roaring
5 noisy **6** lively **8** exciting **9** hilarious **10** boisterous, rollicking, uproarious

ripsnorter
3 ace, pip **4** lulu **5** dandy, doozy **6** doozie,

hummer **8** jim-dandy, knockout **9** humdinger **11** crackerjack

riptide
7 current **8** undertow **12** undercurrent

Rip Van Winkle
author: **6** Irving (Washington)
dog: **4** Wolf

rise
3 wax **4** grow, hill, lift, rear, soar **5** awake, get up, issue, mount, stand, surge, swell **6** ascend, ascent, awaken, emerge, expand, growth, origin, spring, uprear **7** advance, augment, develop, emanate, enhance, enlarge, hilltop, stand up, succeed, surface, upsurge **8** eminence, heighten, increase **9** ascension, beginning, increment, intensify, originate, terminate
above: **8** surmount
again: **7** resurge **9** resurrect
against: **5** rebel **6** mutiny, revolt
and fall: **4** tide **5** heave **6** welter
and shine: **5** get up
gradually: **4** loom

Rise of Silas Lapham author
7 Howells (William Dean)

riser
4 dais, step **8** platform

risible
4 rich **5** comic, droll, funny, jokey **6** absurd **7** comical **8** farcical **9** laughable, ludicrous **10** ridiculous

risk
4 ante, dare, defy **5** peril, stake, throw, wager **6** chance, danger, gamble, hazard, menace, stakes **7** imperil, jeopard, venture **8** endanger, exposure, jeopardy **9** adventure, encounter, liability **10** jeopardize

risky
4 bold **5** dicey, hairy **6** chancy, daring, touchy, tricky **7** parlous, unsound **8** delicate, perilous, ticklish **9** dangerous, hazardous, unhealthy **10** jeopardous, precarious **11** adventurous, speculative, treacherous

risqué
4 blue, lewd, racy, sexy **5** broad, crude, dirty, salty, spicy, vampy **6** coarse, daring, earthy, purple, ribald, vulgar **7** naughty, obscene, raunchy **8** indecent, off-color, scabrous **9** salacious **10** indecorous, indelicate, suggestive

rite
6 office **7** liturgy, mystery, service **8** ceremony **9** formality, ordinance, sacrament, solemnity **10** ceremonial, initiation, observance **11** celebration, sacramental
funeral: **6** exequy **7** obsequy **8** exequies **9** obsequies
Jewish: **4** bris
of initiation or purification: **7** baptism
of knighthood: **8** accolade
(see also **sacrament**)

ritual
see **rite**

ritzy
4 posh **5** fancy, swank **6** chichi, classy, modish, snazzy, swanky **7** elegant, high-hat, stylish **9** au courant, exclusive, expensive, luxurious **11** fashionable **12** ostentatious

rival
3 tie, try, vie **4** even, peer, side **5** equal, match **6** strive **7** attempt, compete, contend, contest, emulate **8** approach, opponent **9** adversary, competing, contender, measure up **10** antagonist, competitor, contending, contestant **11** comparative, competition

rivalry
6 strife **7** contest, warfare **8** conflict, jealousy, tug-of-war **9** emulation **10** contention, opposition **11** competition

rive
3 rip **4** rend, tear **5** break, burst, crack, sever, smash, split **6** cleave, divide, shiver, sunder **7** fissure, shatter **8** fracture, fragment, lacerate, separate, splinter

river
Afghanistan: **5** Kabul
Africa: **4** Bomu, Juba, Nile, Uele **5** Chari, Congo, Shari, Tsavo, Zaire **6** Atbara, Mbomou, Songwe, Ubangi **7** Aruwimi, Limpopo, Zambesi, Zambezi **9** Astaboras, Crocodile
Alabama: **5** Coosa **6** Mobile **7** Conecuh, Perdido **9** Tombigbee **10** Tallapoosa
Alaska: **5** Kobuk **6** Copper, Noatak, Tanana **7** Koyukuk, Susitna **9** Kuskokwim
Albania: **4** Drin **5** Drini
Argentina: **5** Negro **6** Paraná **7** Matanza
arm: **6** branch **9** tributary
Asia: **3** Ili **4** Amur, Lena, Oxus **5** Indus **6** Jayhun, Sutlej **7** Oedanes **8** Amu Darya **9** Dyardanes **11** Brahmaputra
Australia: **4** Daly **5** Roper, Yarra **6** Barwon, Culgoa, Dawson, DeGrey, Murray **7** Darling, Fitzroy, Lachlan **8** Victoria **10** Yarra Yarra
Austria: **4** Enns
bank: **5** levee
Belgium: **4** Leie, Yser **5** Meuse, Rupel, Senne, Weser **6** Dender, Dindar, Ourthe **8** Visurgis
Bolivia: **4** Beni **5** Abuná **6** Mamoré
Borneo: **5** Kajan
bottom: **3** bed
Brazil: **3** Ica **4** Pará, Paru **5** Negro, Xingu **6** Paraná **7** Madeira, Tapajos, Tapajoz
British Columbia: **6** Skeena **10** Bella Coola

Burma: **4** Pegu **7** Irawadi **8** Chindwin **9** Irrawaddy
California: **3** Eel, Pit **4** Kern, Yuba **6** Merced **7** Feather, Salinas, Trinity **8** Tuolumne
Cambodia: **8** Tonle Sap
Canada: **3** Bow **4** Back **5** Moose, Peace, Slave **6** Beaver, Fraser, Nelson **8** Gatineau, Saguenay **9** Athabasca, Great Fish, Mackenzie, Richelieu **11** Assiniboine
Carolinas: **7** Catawba
central United States: **3** Fox **5** Grand **6** Neosho, Platte, Wabash **8** Keya Paha, Missouri, Niobrara **9** Tennessee, Verdigris **10** Republican, Saint Croix **11** Mississippi
channel: **6** alveus
Chile: **3** Loa **5** Itata, Maule **6** Bío-Bío **8** Valdivia
China: **3** Bei, Han, Hun, Nen, Wei **4** Amur, Dong **5** Baihe, Chang, Huang, Tarim **6** Yellow **7** Kashgar, Yangtze
China-North Korea: **4** Yalu
Colombia: **4** Meta, Tomo **6** Atrato **9** Magdalena
Colorado: **5** Yampa **8** Gunnison
Connecticut: **6** Thames **7** Niantic, Shepaug **9** Naugatuck **10** Farmington, Housatonic, Quinnipiac **11** Willimantic
Crimea: **4** Alma
crossing: **4** ford
current: **4** eddy **6** rapids
Czech Republic: **4** Iser **6** Jizera, Moldau, Vltava
dam: **4** weir
Denmark: **4** Stor
dried bed: **4** wadi
East Asia: **4** Yalu **5** Amnok **7** Oryokko
Ecuador: **4** Napo **10** Esmeraldas
England: **3** Dee, Esk, Exe, Nen, Ure **4** Aire, Avon, Eden, Nene, Ouse, Tees, Tyne, Wear, Yare **5** Swale, Trent **6** Mersey, Ribble, Thames
Ethiopia: **3** Omo **4** Baro, Dawa
Europe: **4** Eger, Elbe, Labe, Oder, Ohre, Saar **5** Albis, Meuse, Saale **6** Danube, Ticino
Florida: **6** Indian **9** Kissimmee **10** Saint Johns **12** Apalachicola
Foster's: **6** Swanee
France: **3** Ain, Lot, Lys, Var **4** Aire, Aude, Aure, Cher, Eure, Gers, Loir, Oise, Orne, Saar, Tarn, Yser **5** Adour, Aisne, Drôme, Indre, Isère, Loire, Marne, Meuse, Rhône, Saare, Sâone, Seine, Somme, Yonne **6** Allier, Ariège, Scarpe, Vienne **7** Durance, Garonne, La Riège, Moselle **8** Charente, Dordogne
Georgia: **6** Etowah, Oconee **8** Altamaha, Ocmulgee **13** Chattahoochee
Germany: **3** Ems, Rur **4** Eder, Eger, Elbe, Isar, Main, Rems, Ruhr, Saar **5** Hunte, Lippe, Mosel, Rhine, Spree, Werra, Weser **6** Neckar
Germany-Poland: **4** Oder
Ghana: **5** Volta
god: **7** Alpheus, Inachus **8** Achelous
Greece: **3** Iri **4** Arta **5** Lerna, Lerne **7** Alpheus, Eurotas **8** Achelous **9** Arakhthos
Honduras: **4** Ulúa **5** Aguán **6** Patuca
Iberian: **5** Douro, Duero
Idaho: **5** Lemhi
Illinois: **8** Mackinaw
India: **4** Sind **5** Sindh, Tapti **6** Chenab, Ganges, Jhelum, Kaveri, Kistna **7** Cauvery, Krishna **8** Acesines, Godavari
inlet: **5** bayou **6** slough
Iran: **3** Kor **4** Mand, Mund **5** Karun **8** Safid Rud, Sefid Rud
Ireland: **3** Lee **4** Deel, Erne, Suir **5** Boyne, Clare, Foyle **6** Barrow, Liffey **7** Shannon
Italy: **4** Adda, Arno, Liri, Nera **5** Adige, Arnus, Etsch, Liris, Oglio, Padus, Piave, Tiber **6** Ollius, Rapido, Tevere, Trebia **7** Athesis, Rubicon, Secchia, Tiberis, Trebbia **8** Rubicone, Volturno
Kansas: **6** Pawnee
Kazakhstan-Russia: **4** Emba, Ural **5** Tobol **6** Irtysh
Kenya: **4** Athi, Tana
Kubla Khan's: **4** Alph
land: **4** holm **5** flats **7** bottoms
Latvia: **5** Gauja
Latvia-Lithuania: **7** Lielupe
Lebanon: **6** Litani
Little Rock's: **8** Arkansas
living on the bank of: **8** riparian
longest: **4** Nile
Louisiana: **11** Atchafalaya
Maine: **8** Kennebec **9** Aroostook, Penobscot
Malaysia: **9** Trengganu
Maryland: **8** Monocacy, Patapsco, Patuxent **9** Nanticoke
Massachusetts: **7** Charles, Taunton **9** Merrimack, Westfield **10** Housatonic
Mexico: **6** Pánuco, Sonora **7** Tabasco **8** Grijalva
Michigan: **4** Cass **5** Huron **7** Saginaw **8** Manistee, Muskegon **9** Cheboygan, Kalamazoo **10** Michigamme, Shiawassee
Mississippi: **5** Pearl, Yazoo **10** Pascagoula
Moldova-Ukraine: **8** Dniester
Missouri: **5** Osage
mouth: **5** delta
Myanmar: **4** Pegu **7** Irawadi **8** Chindwin **9** Irrawaddy
Nebraska: **4** Loup **6** Nemaha, Platte **7** Elkhorn
Netherlands: **4** Maas, Waal **5** Issel, Yssel **6** Amstel, IJssel **7** Vahalis
New England: **4** Saco **6** Nashua **9** Merrimack **10** Blackstone **11** Connecticut **12** Androscoggin
New Jersey: **6** Rahway **7** Passaic, Raritan **8** Tuckahoe
New York: **5** Tioga **6** Hudson, Mohawk, Oneida, Oswego, Seneca **7** Chemung, Niagara **8** Chenango

New Zealand: 7 Waikato
Nicaragua: 4 Coco 7 Segovia
Nigeria: 5 Benin
North Carolina: 3 Haw, Tar 5 Neuse 6 Chowan 8 Alamance
northeast United States: 4 Ohio 6 Hoosic 7 Genesee, Hocking 8 Delaware, Mahoning 9 Allegheny 11 Monongahela, Susquehanna
Northern Ireland: 4 Bann 6 Mourne
North Korea: 4 Yalu 5 Daido 7 Taedong
northwest United States: 5 Snake 7 Klamath 8 Columbia 11 Pend Oreille
Norway: 4 Otra, Tana, Teno
nymph: 5 naiad
of fire: 10 Phlegethon
of forgetfulness: 5 Lethe
of ice: 7 glacier
of woe: 7 Acheron
Ohio: 5 Miami 8 Cuyahoga, Sandusky 9 Muskingum 10 Tuscarawas
Oklahoma: 8 Cimarron
Oregon: 5 Rogue 6 Owyhee 7 Malheur 8 McKenzie 9 Clackamas, Deschutes 10 Willamette
Nevada: 7 Truckee
Pakistan: 4 Ravi
Panama: 5 Tuira 7 Chagres
Papua New Guinea: 3 Fly 5 Sepik
Paraguay: 3 Apa 9 Pilcomayo
Paris: 5 Seine
Pennsylvania: 6 Lehigh 10 Schuylkill
Peru: 5 Rímac, Santa 7 Marañón 8 Apurímac, Huallaga, Urubamba
Philippines: 4 Abra, Agno 5 Pasig 7 Cagayan 8 Cotabato, Mindanao, Pampanga
Poland: 3 San 7 Vistula
Portugal: 4 Sado 7 Mondego
relating to: 7 fluvial
Rhode Island: 7 Seekonk 8 Sakonnet 10 Providence
Romania: 5 Arges
Rome: 5 Tiber
Russia: 3 Don, Oka, Ufa, Usa 4 Kama, Kara, Lena, Msta, Neva, Sura, Svir 5 Onega, Terek, Volga 6 Anadyr, Angara, Belaya, Kolima, Kolyma, Ussuri, Vyatka 7 Dnieper, Pechora, Yenisey 8 Barguzin, Kostroma, Voronezh, Vychegda
Russia-Ukraine: 6 Donets
sacred: 6 Ganges
Scotland: 3 Dee, Don, Esk, Tay 4 Doon, Nith, Spey, Tyne 5 Afton, Annan, Clyde, Forth, Tweed 6 Teviot 7 Deveron 8 Findhorn
Shanghai's: 7 Huangpu, Hwang Pu
Sicily: 5 Salso 6 Simeto
siren: 7 Lorelei
Slovakia: 3 Vag, Vah 4 Gran, Hron, Waag 5 Garam, Nitra 6 Neutra, Nyitra
South Africa: 4 Vaal 6 Orange
South America: 3 Apa 6 Amazon 8 Amazonas, Orellana 9 Pilcomayo
South Carolina: 6 Saluda, Santee 7 Wateree 8 Congaree
South Dakota: 3 Bad
Southeast Asia: 6 Dza-chu, Mekong 7 Salween 8 Lan-ts'ang
southeast United States: 6 Pee Dee 7 Noxubee, Washita 8 Escambia, Ouachita, Suwannee 10 Okanoxubee
southern United States: 6 Sabine
South Korea: 3 Kum
southwest United States: 3 Red 4 Gila, Zuni 5 Pecos 8 Canadian, Colorado
Spain: 4 Ebro 5 Tagus 6 Aragon 12 Guadalquivir
Sweden: 4 Göta 5 Kalix
Switzerland: 3 Aar 4 Aare 5 Reuss 7 Obringa
Syria: 6 Khabur 7 Orontes
Tasmania: 4 Huon
Tbilisi's: 4 Kura
Texas: 5 Llano 6 Brazos, Nueces 7 San Saba, Trinity 9 Guadalupe
Texas-Mexico: 8 Rio Bravo 9 Rio Grande
tidal: 7 estuary
Tokyo's: 6 Sumida
Turkey: 4 Aras 5 Araks 6 Seihun, Seyhan
Ukraine: 3 Bug 4 Alma, Styr 8 Dniester
underworld: 4 Styx 5 Lethe 7 Acheron, Cocytus 10 Phlegethon
Uruguay: 5 Negro
Utah: 5 Provo, Uinta, Weber 6 Jordan, Sevier
valley: 6 strath
Venezuela: 5 Apure, Caura 6 Caroní 7 Orinoco
Vermont: 3 Mad 5 Onion, White 8 Winooski
Virginia: 3 Dan 5 James 7 Rapidan 9 Nansemond 10 Appomattox, Shenandoah 12 Chickahominy, Rappahannock
wailing: 7 Cocytus
Wales: 4 Dyfi 5 Clwyd, Dovey, Teifi
Washington: 6 Skagit, Yakima 9 Klickitat, Snohomish, Wenatchee
West Africa: 5 Niger 6 Gambia 7 Senegal
western United States: 7 Laramie 8 Columbia, Flathead 11 Yellowstone
West Virginia: 7 Kanawha
Wisconsin: 8 Kickapoo 9 Menominee
Wyoming: 8 Shoshone 10 Gros Ventre 11 Medicine Bow

Rivera's wife
5 Kahlo (Frida)

river duck
4 teal 6 wigeon 7 dabbler, mallard, widgeon 8 shoveler 9 greenwing

river horse
5 hippo 12 hippopotamus

riverine
8 riparian

river island
3 ait 4 eyot

river nymph
3 nix 5 naiad, nixie 6 undine

rivet
3 fix, pin 4 bolt, brad, stud 5 affix 6 absorb, attach, clinch, fasten 7 engross 8 fastener

Riviera city
4 Nice 6 Cannes, Monaco 7 Antibes, San Remo 8 St. Tropez 10 Monte Carlo

rivulet
3 run 4 beck, burn, gill, race, rill 5 bourn, brook, creek 6 runlet, runnel, stream 9 streamlet

Rizpah
father: 4 Aiah
lover: 4 Saul
son: 6 Armoni 12 Mephibosheth

roach
3 hog 6 shiner 7 sunfish

road
3 way 4 fare, lane, line, path 5 drive, going, route, track 6 artery, avenue, career, causey, course, street 7 highway, journey, passage 8 causeway, chaussée, crossway, highroad, pavement, speedway, turnpike 9 boulevard 12 thoroughfare
along a cliff: 8 corniche
around a city: 6 bypass 7 beltway
bend: 7 hairpin
division: 4 lane
edge: 4 berm 8 shoulder
French: 6 chemin
Irish: 6 boreen
machine: 5 paver 6 grader 9 bulldozer
Roman: 3 via 4 iter
shoulder: 4 berm
side: 6 branch 8 shunpike
Spanish: 6 camino
surface: 3 tar 6 gravel 7 asphalt, macadam 8 pavement

roadblock
7 barrier 8 blockade 9 barricade 11 obstruction

road book
3 map 5 atlas 9 gazetteer, itinerary

roadhouse
3 bar, inn 4 dive 5 hotel, lodge 6 tavern 9 nightclub

roadrunner
6 cuckoo 13 chaparral cock

road rut
6 kettle 7 pothole 9 chuckhole

roadside hotel
3 inn

roam
3 bat, bum, gad, run 4 rove, walk 5 drift, prowl, range, stray 6 ramble, stroll, travel, wander 7 meander, traipse 8 straggle, vagabond 9 gallivant

roamer
3 bum 5 gipsy, gypsy, nomad, rover 6 ranger, walker 7 drifter, prowler, rambler, vagrant 8 marauder, stroller, traveler, vagabond, wanderer 11 nightwalker

roar
3 din 4 bawl, bell, boom, bray, howl, yell 5 shout 6 bellow, clamor, guffaw, outcry 7 bluster 10 vociferate
bullring: 3 olé

roast
4 bake, mock, rack, sear 5 broil, grill, joint, parch 6 scathe, scorch 7 banquet, blister, mockery, swelter 8 barbecue, ridicule 9 criticize

rob
3 cop, mug 4 lift, loot, nick, raid, roll, sack 5 boost, filch, heist, pinch, pluck, reave, steal 6 burgle, fleece, hijack, hold up, pilfer, rip off, snitch, thieve 7 defraud, deprive, despoil, pillage, plunder, purloin, ransack, stick up, swindle 8 knock off 9 knock over 10 burglarize

robber
4 yegg 5 crook, thief 6 bandit, looter, mugger, pirate, reiver 7 brigand, burglar, footpad, rustler 8 hijacker, swindler 9 holdup man 10 cat burglar, highwayman, sandbagger, stickup man 12 housebreaker
grave: 5 ghoul

robbery
5 heist, theft 6 holdup, piracy 7 larceny, mugging, stickup 8 banditry

robe
3 aba 4 cape, gown, wrap 5 cloak, frock, habit 6 caftan, mantle 7 dashiki, garment, manteau 8 covering, dalmatic, vestment
baptismal: 7 chrisom
bishop's: 3 alb 7 chimere
of Roman emperors: 6 purple
Turkish: 6 dolman

Robin Goodfellow
4 Puck 6 sprite

Robinson Crusoe
author: 5 Defoe (Daniel)
character: 6 Friday

robot
5 droid, golem 7 android 8 automata (plural) 9 automaton

Rob Roy author
5 Scott (Walter)

robust
4 hale, rude 5 hardy, husky, lusty, rough, sound, stout 6 hearty, potent, rugged, sinewy, strong, sturdy 7 healthy 8 athletic, muscular, vigorous 9 energetic, strapping 10 boisterous, red-blooded, full-bodied, prosperous

robustious
4 rude **5** lusty, rough, rowdy, wooly **6** rugged **7** boorish, ill-bred, loutish **8** churlish, clownish **9** unrefined **10** boisterous, unpolished

rock
4 crag, reel, roll, sway, toss **5** geode, pitch, quake, shake, stone, swing **6** totter **7** boulder, breccia **8** astonish, convulse, undulate **9** oscillate
basaltic: **5** wacke
cavity: **3** vug
combining form: **4** lite, lith, lyte, petr **5** clast, petri, petro
debris: **5** scree, talus
decomposed: **6** gossan
fissile: **5** shale
formation: **4** sill **5** butte, nappe **6** pluton **7** rimrock, terrane **8** isocline, syncline
fragment: **8** xenolith
igneous: **4** lava, sial, sima **5** magma **6** basalt, gabbro, pumice **7** diabase, diorite, granite **8** eruptive, felstone, obsidian, porphyry, traprock **10** travertine
layer: **10** mantlerock
mass: **5** scree **9** batholith
metamorphic: **5** slate **6** gneiss, marble, schist **9** quartzite, soapstone
molten: **4** lava
sedimentary: **4** clay, coal **5** chalk, chert, coral, flint, shale **8** mudstone **9** limestone, sandstone, siltstone **10** travertine
volcanic: **4** tuff **6** basalt

rock band
3 REM, Who (The) **4** Cure (The) **5** Byrds (The), Clash (The), Cream, Doors (The), Kinks (The), Queen, ZZ Top **6** Eagles (The), Pixies (The), Police (The) **7** Animals (The), Beatles (The), Bee Gees (The), Blondie, Bon Jovi, Chicago, Genesis, Nirvana, Ramones (The), Rascals (The), Santana **8** Coldplay, Drifters (The), Green Day, Megadeth, Pearl Jam, Platters (The), Supremes (The), Van Halen **9** Aerosmith, Alice Cooper, Beach Boys (The), Metallica, Pink Floyd, Radiohead, Steely Dan, Yardbirds (The) **10** Deep Purple, Duran Duran, Guns N' Roses, Jethro Tull, Linkin Park, Moody Blues, Mötley Crüe, Sex Pistols (The), Spice Girls **11** Dire Straits, Four Seasons (The), King Crimson, Led Zeppelin, White Stripes (The) **12** Black Sabbath, Fleetwood Mac, Grateful Dead (The), Talking Heads (The) **13** Nine Inch Nails, Rolling Stones (The)

rock-band need
3 amp

rock bass
7 sunfish

rock-bottom
4 root **6** lowest **8** cheapest **9** lowermost **11** fundamental

rocket
3 fly, zip **4** soar, whiz, zoom **5** mount **6** ascend, bullet **7** missile, shoot up **8** firework, starship **10** projectile
European: **6** Ariane
landing: **7** reentry **10** splashdown
launcher: **7** bazooka
launching: **7** liftoff **8** blastoff
scientist: **5** Braun (Wernher von) **7** Goddard (Robert)
section: **5** stage

rockfish
4 cony, hind **5** coney **7** grouper, jewfish, sea bass **8** bocaccio **10** scorpaenid **11** striped bass

Rockies resort
4 Vail **5** Aspen **8** Snowmass **9** Telluride

___ Rockne
5 Knute

rock rabbit
4 cony, pika **5** coney, hyrax **6** dassie

rock-ribbed
5 rigid **8** dogmatic, obdurate **9** unbending **10** inflexible, unyielding

rocks
3 ice

rock star
3 J. Lo, Pop (Iggy) **4** Beck (Hansen), Bono, Cher, Crow (Sheryl), Dion (Celine), Flea, Gaga (Lady), Joel (Billy), John (Elton), King (Carole), Love (Courtney), Moon (Keith), Rose (Axl), Roth (David Lee) **5** Abdul (Paula), Adams (Ryan), Berry (Chuck), Bowie (David), Haley (Bill), Harry (Debbie), Holly (Buddy), Lewis (Jerry Lee), Lopez (Jennifer), Paige (Jimmy), Petty (Tom), Plant (Robert), Seger (Bob), Smith (Patti), Starr (Ringo), Sting, Tyler (Stephen), White (Jack), Wyman (Bill), Young (Neil) **6** Burdon (Eric), Cobain (Kurt), Cooper (Alice), Domino (Fats), Eminem, Garcia (Jerry), Jagger (Mick), Joplin (Janis), Lennon (John), Manson (Marilyn), Prince, Spears (Britney), Vaughn (Stevie Ray), Vedder (Eddie) **7** Bon Jovi (Jon), Clapton (Eric), Cochran (Eddie), Collins (Phil), Daltrey (Roger), Diddley (Bo), Fogerty (John), Hendrix (Jimi), Iggy Pop, Lavigne (Avril), Madonna, Mercury (Freddie), Michael (George), Perkins (Carl), Presley (Elvis), Shannon (Del), Stefani (Gwen), Stewart (Rod), Vincent (Gene), Winwood (Steve) **8** Costello (Elvis), Harrison (George), Morrison (Jim, Van), Osbourne (Ozzy), Richards (Keith), Van Halen (Eddie) **9** Boy George, McCartney (Paul), Townshend (Pete) **10** Mellencamp (John) **11** Springsteen (Bruce) **13** Little Richard

rockweed
5 algae, fucus **7** seaweed **12** bladder wrack

Rocky costar
5 Talia (Shire)
rocky hill
3 tor 5 kopje
rocky prominence
4 crag
rococo
4 busy 5 showy 6 florid, frilly, ornate 7 baroque, elegant, opulent 9 elaborate, intricate 10 decorative, flamboyant 11 overwrought
rod
3 bar, gat 4 cane, pole, wand 5 baton, dowel, rebar, spoke, staff, stave, stick 6 pistol 7 scepter 8 revolver 10 correction, discipline, punishment 11 castigation 12 chastisement
attachment: 4 reel
bundle of: 6 fasces
rodent
3 rat 4 cavy, cony, mole, paca, pika, vole 5 cavie, coney, coypu, mouse, shrew 6 agouti, beaver, gerbil, gopher, jerboa, marmot, murine, nutria, rabbit 7 hamster, lemming, leveret, muskrat 8 capybara, chipmunk, dormouse, squirrel, tuco tuco, viscacha, vizcacha, water rat 9 guinea pig, porcupine 10 chinchilla, field mouse, prairie dog 11 kangaroo rat, meadow mouse, pocket mouse 12 pocket gopher
aquatic: 5 coypu 6 beaver, nutria 7 muskrat 8 musquash
burrowing: 4 mole, paca 6 gerbil, gopher 7 hamster 8 viscacha, vizcacha
family: 5 murid 6 murine 7 sciurid
genus: 3 Mus 5 Lepus
tropical: 6 agouti
rodeo
7 contest, roundup 9 enclosure 10 exhibition 11 competition
animal: 5 horse, steer 10 Brahma bull
event: 10 calf roping 11 bulldogging 12 bronco riding
performer: 5 clown 6 cowboy
____ Rodin
7 Auguste
rodomontade
4 blow, brag, rant 5 boast, swash, vaunt 7 bluster, swagger 9 gasconade 11 braggadocio
Rodomonte
beloved: 8 Doralice
slayer: 8 Ruggiero
Rodrigo Díaz de Bivar
5 El Cid
rod-shaped
7 virgate 8 bacillar 9 bacillary
roe
4 deer, eggs 6 beluga, caviar, osetra 7 sevruga
source: 4 shad 6 beluga, salmon 8 sturgeon
Roentgen's discovery
4 X-ray
Roethke work
6 Waking (The) 8 Far Field (The)
rogation
6 litany, prayer 8 entreaty, petition 10 beseeching 12 supplication
Rogen of comedy
4 Seth
____ Rogers
3 Roy 4 Carl, Fred, Will 6 Ginger, Robert
cowgirl mate: 4 Dale (Evans)
rogue
5 cheat, gypsy, knave, scamp 6 picaro, rascal 7 lowlife, sharper, villain 8 picaroon, scalawag, swindler 9 defrauder, miscreant, reprobate, scoundrel, skeezicks, trickster 10 blackguard, mountebank 11 rapscallion
relating to: 10 picaresque
roguery
5 fraud 7 devilry, knavery, waggery 8 deviltry, mischief, trickery 9 devilment, diablerie 11 waggishness 12 sportiveness
roguish
3 sly 4 arch 6 impish, wicked 7 knavish 8 devilish, espiègle, scampish 10 picaresque 11 mischievous
roil
3 mud, vex 4 foul, rile, romp 5 annoy, dirty, grate, muddy, peeve, upset 6 befoul, muddle, nettle, stir up 7 agitate, disturb 8 disorder, irritate 9 aggravate 10 exasperate
roily
5 muddy, riley 6 turbid 9 turbulent
roister
4 riot 5 revel 6 frolic 7 carouse, reveler, wassail 9 wassailer
Roland
7 Orlando
battle site: 9 Roncevaux 12 Roncesvalles
beloved: 4 Aude
betrayer: 4 Gano 7 Ganelon
friend: 6 Oliver 7 Olivier
horn: 7 Olivant
sword: 8 Durandal, Durendal
uncle: 11 Charlemagne
role
3 bit 4 duty, lead, part, pose 5 cameo, cloak, guise, niche 6 aspect, office 7 quality 8 capacity, function, position 9 character 13 impersonation
roll
3 bun, rob 4 bolt, coil, flow, furl, gyre, list, pour, rock, toss, turn, wind, wrap 5 heave, pitch, surge 6 bundle, roster, rotate, stream, swathe, wallow,

wrap up **7** biscuit, brioche, envelop, revolve, swaddle, trundle **8** involute, register, schedule, turn over
ring-shaped: **5** bagel

roll about
6 wallow, welter

roll back
5 lower **6** reduce, repeal **7** curtail, rescind

roll-call response
3 aye, nay, yea **4** here

roller
3 rod **4** bowl, drum, wave **6** canary, caster, platen **7** breaker, carrier, tumbler **8** cylinder

Roller Derby round
3 jam

rollick
4 lark, play, romp **5** caper, frisk, party, revel, sport **6** cavort, frolic, gambol **7** disport, skylark **8** escapade **9** merriment

rollicking
4 wild **5** antic, merry **6** frisky, lively **8** sportive **10** boisterous, frolicsome **12** high-spirited

rolling stock
4 cars **7** coaches, engines **8** cabooses, Pullmans, sleepers, trailers **11** locomotives

rolling stone
4 hobo **5** gipsy, gypsy, nomad, rover, tramp **6** roamer **7** drifter, rambler, vagrant **8** vagabond, wanderer

Rolling Stones
4 Wood (Ron) **5** Jones (Brian), Watts (Charlie), Wyman (Bill) **6** Jagger (Mick), Taylor (Dick, Mick) **7** Stewart (Ian) **8** Richards (Keith)

roly-poly
see **rotund**

Rom
5 Gipsy, Gypsy

Roman
5 Latin **7** Italian
amphitheater: **9** Colosseum
assembly: **5** forum **6** senate **7** comitia
building: **5** Forum **6** Circus **8** basilica, Pantheon
clan: **4** gens
comedy writer: **7** Plautus (Titus), Terence
conspirator: **6** Brutus (Marcus Junius) **7** Cassius (Gaius) **8** Catiline
date: **4** Ides **7** calends, kalends
Doric: **6** Tuscan
emperor: **4** Nero, Otho **5** Galba (Servius Sulpicius), Nerva (Marcus Cocceius), Titus, Verus (Lucius Aurelius) **6** Julian, Trajan **7** Hadrian, Maximus (Magnus Clemens, Marcus Clodius, Petronius), Severus (Lucius Septimius) **8** Augustus, Caligula, Claudius, Commodus (Lucius Aelius), Domitian, Tiberius, Valerian **9** Caracalla, Vespasian **10** Diocletian, Theodosius **11** Constantine, Valentinian
entrance hall: **5** atria (plural) **6** atrium
epic: **6** Aeneid
epigrammatist: **7** Martial
family: **7** Gracchi
Fates: **4** Nona **5** Morta **6** Decuma, Parcae
festival: **10** Saturnalia
founder: **5** Remus **7** Romulus
fountain: **5** Trevi **6** Triton
garment: **4** toga **5** tunic
general: **5** Sulla (Lucius Cornelius), Titus **6** Antony (Marc), Marius (Gaius), Scipio (Publius Cornelius) **8** Agricola (Gnaeus Julius)
god: **3** Lar **4** deus
blind: **6** Plutus
chief: **4** Jove **7** Jupiter
messenger: **7** Mercury
of agriculture: **6** Saturn
of animals: **6** Faunus
of death: **4** Mors
of dreams: **8** Morpheus
of fire: **6** Vulcan
of gates and doors: **5** Janus
of healing: **9** Asclepius **11** Aesculapius
of heaven: **6** Uranus
of households: **3** Lar **5** Lares **7** Penates
of love: **4** Amor **5** Cupid
of medicine: **9** Asclepius **11** Aesculapius
of mirth: **5** Comus
of regeneration: **7** Priapus
of sleep: **6** Somnus
of the sea: **6** Pontus **7** Neptune, Proteus
of the sun: **3** Sol **6** Apollo
of the underworld: **3** Dis **5** Orcus, Pluto **8** Dispater
of the wind: **5** Eurus, Notus **6** Aeolus, Aquilo, Auster, Boreas **8** Favonius, Zephyrus
of war: **4** Mars **8** Quirinus
of wealth: **6** Plutus
of wine: **7** Bacchus
of woods: **6** Faunus
two-faced: **5** Janus
goddess: **3** dea
of abundance: **3** Ops
of agriculture: **5** Ceres
of beauty: **5** Venus
of dawn: **6** Aurora
of death: **5** Morta
of flowers: **5** Flora
of handicrafts: **7** Minerva
of harvests: **3** Ops
of health: **7** Minerva
of hope: **4** Spes
of hunting: **5** Diana
of justice: **7** Astraea
of love: **5** Venus

of marriage: 4 Juno
of night: 3 Nox
of peace: 3 Pax
of springs: 7 Juturna
of strife: 9 Discordia
of the earth: 5 Terra 6 Tellus
of the hearth: 5 Vesta
of the moon: 4 Luna
of the sea: 10 Amphitrite
of the underworld: 10 Proserpina
of victory: 6 Vacuna
of war: 7 Bellona
of wisdom: 7 Minerva
of womanhood: 4 Juno
greeting: 3 ave
hero: 6 Caesar (Julius) 11 Cincinnatus (Lucius Quinctius)
hill: 7 Caelian, Viminal 8 Aventine, Palatine, Quirinal 9 Esquiline 10 Capitoline
historian: 4 Livy 5 Nepos 7 Sallust, Tacitus 9 Suetonius
king: 7 Romulus, Servius, Tullius 12 Ancus Martius 13 Numa Pompilius
marketplace: 5 agora
military formation: 3 ala 6 alares (plural) 7 phalanx
miltary unit: 6 cohort, legion 7 maniple
officer: 9 centurion
official: 5 augur, edile 6 aedile, censor, consul, lictor 7 praetor, prefect, tribune 8 quaestor 9 proconsul
people: 5 Laeti, plebs 6 populi (plural) 7 populus, Sabines 9 plebeians
philosopher: 4 Cato 6 Seneca 8 Apuleius 9 Epictetus, Lucretius
physician: 9 Asclepius 11 Aesculapius
poet: 4 Ovid
port: 5 Ostia
procurator: 6 Pilate (Pontius)
province: 4 Asia 5 Lycia, Syria 6 Achaea, Africa, Arabia, Cyprus, Raetia 7 Baetica, Belgica, Galatia, Numidia, Sicilia, Thracia 8 Aegyptus, Dalmatia 9 Aquitania, Britannia, Lusitania 10 Cappadocia, Mauretania
racecourse: 6 circus
road: 3 via 4 iter
senator's robe: 4 toga
slave: 9 Spartacus
statesman: 4 Cato 5 Pliny 6 Caesar, Cicero, Pompey, Seneca 7 Agrippa 8 Augustus, Gracchus, Maecenas 9 Flaminius
symbol of authority: 6 fasces
theater: 4 odea (plural) 5 odeum

roman à ____
4 clef

romance
3 woo 4 gest, love 5 amour, court, fling, geste, novel 6 affair 7 fantasy, fiction 8 stardust 10 love affair 12 bodice ripper

romance, e.g.
5 genre

Romance language
6 French 7 Catalan, Italian, Spanish 8 Romanian, Rumanian 9 Sardinian 10 Portuguese

romance writer
4 Holt (Victoria), Robb (J. D.) 5 Brown (Sandra), Chase (Loretta), Clark (Mary Higgins), Heyer (Georgette), Steel (Danielle) 6 Dailey (Janet), Graham (Heather), Howard (Linda), Krantz (Judith), Krentz (Jayne Ann), Putney (Mary Jo), Stuart (Anne) 7 Baldwin (Faith), Collins (Jackie), Cookson (Catherine), Coulter (Catherine), Estrada (Rita Clay), Garwood (Julie), Hatcher (Robin Lee), Maxwell (Anne), Osborne (Maggie), Roberts (Nora), Spencer (LaVyrle), Stewart (Mary), Whitney (Phyllis) 8 Bradford (Barbara Taylor), Cartland (Barbara), Deveraux (Jude), Gabaldon (Diana), McNaught (Judith), Phillips (Susan Elizabeth) 9 Alsobrook (Rosalyn), Evanovich (Janet), Woodiwiss (Kathleen)

Romania
capital: 9 Bucharest
city: 4 Iasi 6 Brasov, Galati 7 Craiova 9 Constanta, Timisoara
monetary unit: 3 leu 4 bani
mountain range: 10 Carpathian
neighbor: 6 Serbia 7 Hungary, Moldova, Ukraine 8 Bulgaria
part of: 7 Balkans
peninsula: 6 Balkan
river: 5 Siret, Tisza 6 Danube
sea: 5 Black

romantic
5 gauzy, ideal, idyll, mushy 6 ardent, dreamy, exotic, gothic, poetic, unreal 7 amorous, maudlin, mawkish 8 fanciful, quixotic 9 fantastic, imaginary, visionary 10 idealistic, lovey-dovey 11 sentimental

Romany
5 Gipsy, Gypsy

Rombauer of cookery
4 Irma

Romeo
5 lover, swain 7 amorist, Don Juan, gallant 8 Casanova, lothario, paramour
beloved: 6 Juliet
enemy: 6 Tybalt
father: 8 Montague
friend: 8 Mercutio
home: 6 Verona

Rome's former port
5 Ostia

Rome's river
5 Tiber

Rommel, Erwin
9 Desert Fox

romp
4 lark, play 5 caper, frisk, sport 6 cavort, frolic, gambol, hoyden 7 rollick, runaway, skylark 8 escapade

Romulus
brother: 5 Remus
father: 4 Mars
mother: 9 Rea Silvia 10 Rhea Silvia
successor: 4 Numa
victim: 5 Remus

rondure
3 arc, orb 4 arch, ball, ring 5 curve, globe, round 6 circle, sphere 9 curvature

Ron Howard role
4 Opie

rood
5 cross 8 crucifix

roof
3 hip, top 4 apex, peak 5 cover, crest, crown 6 summit 7 ceiling 8 covering, housetop
material: 3 tar, tin 4 tile 5 slate, straw, terne 6 copper, thatch 7 pantile, shingle
of a cavern: 4 dome
of the mouth: 6 palate
part: 3 hip 4 eave 5 eaves 6 soffit 8 overhang 9 ridgepole
structure: 9 penthouse
type: 5 gable 6 hipped 7 gambrel, lamella, mansard 9 butterfly
vaulted: 4 dome

roofer
5 tiler

rook
4 bilk, colt, crow, scam, tyro 5 cheat, mulct, raven, stick 6 castle, fleece, novice 7 amateur, defraud, recruit, swindle, trainee 8 beginner, flimflam, freshman, neophyte, newcomer 10 apprentice, tenderfoot

rookery
5 roost 6 colony

rookie
4 colt, tyro 5 plebe 6 novice 7 amateur, recruit, trainee 8 beginner, freshman, neophyte, newcomer 10 apprentice, tenderfoot

room
3 den 4 cell, hall, play, rein 5 divan, house, lodge, put up, salon, scope, space 6 alcove, billet, leeway, margin, reside, studio 7 chamber, cubicle, expanse, gallery, lodging 9 clearance
ancient Roman: 5 atria (plural) 6 atrium
attic: 6 garret
eating: 4 nook 6 alcove 7 commons, kitchen 8 mess hall 9 refectory
food storage: 6 larder, pantry
for paintings: 7 gallery
harem: 3 oda
monastery: 4 cell 9 refectory 11 calefactory
prison: 4 cell
ship: 5 cabin 6 galley
round: 7 rotunda
Spanish: 4 sala
sun: 7 solaria (plural) 8 solarium

roomer
5 guest 6 lodger, renter, tenant 7 boarder

roomy
4 wide 5 ample, broad, large 8 spacious 9 capacious 10 commodious

Roosevelt, Franklin D.
birthplace: 8 Hyde Park
dog: 4 Fala
message: 12 fireside chat
mother: 4 Sara
predecessor: 6 Hoover (Herbert)
program: 7 New Deal
successor: 6 Truman (Harry)
vacation home: 10 Campobello
wife: 7 Eleanor

roost
3 sit 4 land, nest, rest 5 perch 6 alight, settle 7 rookery 8 dovecote

rooster
4 cock 5 capon 8 cockerel, gamecock 10 cockalorum 11 chanticleer

root
3 dig, fix 4 base, bulb, core, grub, pith, stem, well 5 basis, cheer, embed, grout, lodge, plant, radix, tuber 6 bottom, etymon, ground, marrow, origin, settle, source 7 applaud, bedrock, essence, footing, radical 8 radicate 9 beginning, establish, inception 10 foundation
aromatic: 7 ginseng
edible: 3 oca, yam 4 beet, taro, yuca 5 salep, yucca 6 carrot, daikon, ginger, jicama, manioc, potato, radish, turnip 7 burdock, cassava, chicory, parsnip, salsify 8 celeriac, kohlrabi, rutabaga, tuckahoe 11 horseradish
fragrant: 5 orris 7 vetiver
main: 7 taproot
medicinal: 5 jalap 7 ginseng
relating to: 7 radical
starch: 4 arum 7 tapioca
word: 6 etymon

rootlet
7 radicle, rhizoid

root out
4 grub 9 eradicate, extirpate 10 deracinate

Roots
author: **5** Haley (Alex)
character: **3** Lea (George, Tom) **4** Toby **5** Haley (Alex, Simon Alexander) **6** Bertha, Waller (Bell, John, Kizzy, Dr. William) **7** Cynthia, Matilda **8** Kintango **9** Missy Anne **10** Kunta Kinte

rootstock
4 taro **7** rhizome

rope
3 guy, tie **4** bind, cord, line, stay **5** belay, bight, brace, cable, chord, lasso, reata, riata, sheet **6** binder, fasten, halter, hawser, lariat, marlin, shroud, strand, string, tether **7** halyard, lashing, marline, painter, towline **8** buntline, lifeline
fiber: **4** coir, hemp, jute **5** abaca, sisal **6** Manila **8** henequen
loop: **7** cringle
mooring: **6** hawser
ship's: **4** vang **5** sheet **6** marlin, parral, parrel, shroud **7** lanyard, marline, ratline **9** mainsheet

ropedancer
11 funambulist

rope off
6 cordon

ropes
10 ins and outs, procedures, techniques

ropy
4 wiry **6** sinewy **7** stringy, viscous **8** muscular

roque
7 croquet

rorqual
5 whale **7** finback **8** fin whale **11** baleen whale

Rosalind's beloved
7 Orlando

rosary
5 beads **7** chaplet **8** beadroll, devotion **11** prayer beads

rose
3 gul **4** glow, pink **5** blush, color, flush, rouge **6** mantle, pinken, redden **7** crimson **10** erysipelas
Chinese: **8** Cherokee
cotton: **7** cudweed
essence: **4** otto **5** attar
feature: **5** thorn
kind: **4** moss **5** Peace, Vogue **6** Circus, damask **7** Fashion, Granada, Iceberg, New Dawn, Pascali, Tiffany **8** Rubaiyat **9** Floradora, Montezuma, polyantha, Tropicana **10** Floribunda **11** grandiflora, Mount Shasta **12** Crimson Glory
oil: **4** otto **5** attar
Persian: **3** gul

roseate
see **rosy**

rose-colored
see **rosy**

Rosenkavalier composer
7 Strauss (Richard)

rose of ___
6 Sharon

Rose Tattoo author
8 Williams (Tennessee)

rosette
7 cockade **8** ornament

Rosinante's master
7 Quixote (Don)

Rosmersholm author
5 Ibsen (Henrik)

___ Rossetti
5 Dante (Gabriel) **9** Christina
work: **8** Sing-Song **11** Annus Domini, House of Life (The), Seek and Find, Sister Helen **12** Beata Beatrix, Goblin Market

Rossini opera
6 Otello **8** Tancredi **11** Cenerentola (La), William Tell **14** Siege of Corinth (The) **15** Barber of Seville (The)

Rostand hero
6 Cyrano (de Bergerac)

roster
4 list, roll, rota **5** slate **6** muster, scroll **8** register, roll call, schedule **9** honor roll **10** muster roll **11** waiting list

Rostropovich's instrument
5 cello **11** violoncello

rostrum
4 dais **5** bimah **6** pulpit **7** lectern, tribune **8** platform

rosy
3 red **4** pink **5** sunny **6** bright, upbeat **7** beamish **8** cheerful, sanguine **10** optimistic

rot
4 bosh, bull, mold **5** decay, go bad, hooey, spoil, taint, trash **6** fester, molder **7** corrupt, crapola, crumble, eyewash, garbage, hogwash, putrefy, rubbish **8** gangrene, nonsense **9** break down, decompose, poppycock **10** balderdash, degenerate **11** deteriorate, putrescence **12** disintegrate, putrefaction **13** decomposition

rotary
6 circle **8** gyratory, spinning, whirling **10** roundabout **11** vertiginous **13** traffic circle

rotate
4 gyre, roll, spin, turn **5** pivot, twirl, wheel, whirl **6** gyrate, swivel **7** revolve, trundle **9** alternate, pirouette
a log: **4** birl

rotation
4 gyre, loop, turn **5** cycle, orbit, pivot, round, wheel, whirl **7** circuit, turning **8** gyration **10** revolution, succession

rote
5 crowd, grind **6** custom, groove, memory **7** routine **8** practice **9** automatic, treadmill **10** mechanical, repetition **12** memorization

Roth novel
11 Call It Sleep **15** Goodbye Columbus **16** American Pastoral **17** Portnoy's Complaint

rotten
4 foul **5** fetid, lousy **6** crummy, putrid **7** corrupt, decayed, spoiled, tainted **9** nefarious, offensive, putrified **10** decomposed, degenerate, putrescent

rotter
3 cad, cur **4** heel, lout **5** creep, louse **7** bounder **9** scoundrel **10** blackguard

rotund
3 fat **5** obese, plump, podgy, pudgy, round, stout, thick, tubby **6** chubby, chunky, portly, stocky **7** rounded **8** heavyset, roly-poly, thickset **9** corpulent **10** potbellied

roué
4 lech, rake, wolf **6** lecher **7** amorist, Don Juan, gallant, seducer, swinger **8** Casanova, lothario, sybarite **9** bon vivant, debauchee, libertine, womanizer **10** profligate, sensualist, voluptuary **11** philanderer

rouge
3 red **4** glow, pink, rose **5** blush, color, flush **6** mantle, pinken, redden **7** crimson

rough
3 raw **4** rude, wild **5** brute, bumpy, crass, crude, hairy, harsh, raspy, rowdy, yahoo **6** choppy, coarse, craggy, crusty, hoarse, jagged, rugged, stormy, uneven **7** cragged, grating, jarring, rasping, raucous, ruffian, scraggy, uncivil, uncouth **8** bullyboy, churlish, impolite, scabrous, unformed **9** difficult, imperfect, strenuous, turbulent, unrefined **10** boisterous, tumultuous, unfinished, unpolished **11** approximate, tempestuous

rough-and-ready
5 crude **6** make-do **7** stopgap **8** slapdash **9** expedient, impromptu, makeshift **10** improvised **11** provisional **13** quick-and-dirty

rough-hewn
4 rude **5** crude, plain **10** unfinished, unpolished **12** uncultivated

roughly
4 or so **5** about, circa **9** virtually **10** more or less **13** approximately

roughneck
see **ruffian**

rough out
5 block, chalk, draft **6** sketch **7** outline **9** adumbrate **11** skeletonize

rough up
4 beat, maul **6** batter, pummel **8** maltreat **9** brutalize, manhandle **10** slap around

roulette
bet: **4** noir, trio **5** rouge, split **7** sixline **10** straight up
term: **5** passe, tiers **6** impair, manque, mucker **7** orphans **8** croupier **9** house edge

round
4 gyre, tour, turn **5** bowed, cycle, globe, wheel **6** circle, curved, rotund **7** annular, circuit **8** circular, globular, roly-poly, rotation, sequence **9** orbicular, spherical **10** conglobate

roundabout
6 circle, detour, rotary **7** circuit, compass, curving, devious, oblique, winding **8** circular, indirect **10** circuitous, meandering **13** traffic circle

rounded
5 bowed, plump **6** arched, convex, curved, rotund, zaftig **7** concave **9** developed **10** curvaceous, Rubenesque **13** well-developed

rounder
4 rake, roué, waif **6** no-good, waster **7** wastrel **8** prodigal, vagabond **9** libertine **10** ne'er-do-well, profligate

roundly
4 well **5** fully, quite **6** widely, wholly **7** bluntly, sharply, smartly, utterly **8** candidly, entirely **9** brusquely **10** altogether, completely, rigorously, scathingly, thoroughly, vigorously

round off
3 cap, top **5** crown **6** climax, finish **8** conclude **9** culminate

round-robin
6 appeal, letter, series **7** protest **8** petition, sequence **9** statement **10** tournament

round trip
4 tour **7** circuit **9** excursion

round up
4 herd **5** drive, group **6** gather **7** cluster, collect **8** assemble

rouse
3 jog **4** call, goad, rock, stir, wake, whet **5** alarm, awake, pique, rally, roust, waken **6** awaken, bestir, excite, foment, incite, kindle, muster, rattle, recall, revive, vivify, work up **7** agitate, animate, commove, disturb, enliven, provoke, quicken **8** motivate **9** aggravate, challenge, galvanize, instigate, stimulate

rousing
5 brisk, peppy **6** lively **8** animated, exciting, spirited, stirring **9** inspiring **11** stimulating **12** exhilarating, intoxicating

Rousseau work
5 Émile

roustabout
4 hand **6** worker **7** laborer, workman **8** deckhand **10** workingman **12** longshoreman, troublemaker

rout
6 defeat **7** debacle, licking **8** drubbing, whipping

route
3 way **4** path, road, send, ship **5** guide, pilot, steer, track, trail **6** avenue, bypass, course, detour, direct, divert, escort, flyway, seaway, skyway **7** channel, circuit, conduct, consign, forward, highway, journey, passage, portage, sea-lane **8** corridor, dispatch, transmit, traverse **9** direction, itinerary

routine
3 act, bit, rut **4** dull, pace, rote **5** chore, drill, grind, habit, ho-hum, plain, round, trial, usual **6** course, groove, improv, shtick, wonted **7** chronic, formula, program, regimen, regular, utility **8** accepted, everyday, habitual, ordinary, standard, workaday **9** customary, monologue, procedure, quotidian, treadmill **10** accustomed, donkeywork, mechanical **11** commonplace, cut-and-dried, perfunctory **12** housekeeping, unremarkable

rove
3 gad **4** roam **5** drift, range, stray **6** ramble, wander **7** meander, traipse **8** straggle, vagabond **9** gallivant

rover
5 gipsy, gypsy, nomad, stray **6** picaro, pirate, roamer, viking **7** corsair, drifter, floater, rambler, vagrant **8** gadabout, picaroon, runabout, traveler, vagabond, wanderer **9** buccaneer, meanderer **10** freebooter **12** rolling stone

roving
6 errant, mobile **7** movable, nomadic, vagrant **8** straying, vagabond **9** itinerant, migratory, wayfaring **11** peripatetic

row
3 oar, way **4** bank, crew, file, fray, fuss, line, muss, rank, spat, tier, tiff **5** align, brawl, broil, chain, fight, melee, order, queue, range, run-in, scrap, scull, strip, swath **6** bicker, clamor, column, dustup, fracas, kickup, paddle, propel, ruckus, series, string, stroke **7** brabble, dispute, quarrel, rhubarb, wrangle **8** argument, diagonal, sequence, squabble **9** commotion **10** falling-out, single file, succession **11** altercation, disturbance, progression

rowdy
4 punk, rude **5** bully, crude, rough, yahoo **6** unruly **7** hoodlum, rackety, raffish, raucous, ruffian **8** bullyboy, hooligan **9** roughneck **10** boisterous, disorderly, robustious **11** rumbustious **12** rambunctious

Rowena
father: 7 Hengist
guardian: 6 Cedric
husband: 7 Ivanhoe **9** Vortigern

rowing need
3 oar

Rowling character
3 Ron (Weasley) **5** Harry (Potter), Snape (Severus) **6** Malfoy (Draco), Sirius (Black) **8** Hermione (Granger) **9** Voldemort (Lord) **10** Dumbledore (Albus)

Roxana
husband: 9 Alexander
rival: 7 Statira

Roxy Music star
3 Eno (Brian)

royal
5 grand, noble, regal **6** kingly, lordly **7** stately **8** glorious, imperial, imposing, majestic, princely, splendid **9** grandiose, monarchal, sovereign **10** monarchial **11** magnificent, monarchical

rub
4 buff **5** chafe, grate, shine **6** abrade, polish, smooth, stroke **7** burnish, massage **10** difficulty

Rubaiyat author
4 Omar (Khayyám)

rubber
4 buna **5** crepe **6** caucho, eraser **10** caoutchouc
basis: 5 latex
hard: 7 ebonite
synthetic: 8 neoprene
tree: 3 Ule **4** Para

Rubber City
5 Akron

rubberneck
3 eye **4** gape, gawk, gaze **5** crane, snoop, stare **6** goggle **8** sightsee

rubber-stamp
4 okay **7** approve, certify, endorse **9** authorize

rubbish
3 rot **4** bosh, crap, crud, junk, muck, slop, tosh **5** bilge, dreck, hooey, offal, trash, truck, waste **6** debris, litter, refuse, raffle, rubble, spilth **7** crapola, garbage, hogwash **8** nonsense, riff-raff, tommyrot **9** poppycock, sweepings **11** foolishness

rubbishy
5 cheap, tatty **6** paltry, shoddy, sleazy, trashy **9** worthless

rubble
5 ruins, scree **6** debris, litter **8** detritus, wreckage

rube
4 boor, hick, naïf **5** churl, cluck, swain, yahoo, yokel **6** rustic **7** bumpkin, hayseed, redneck **9** greenhorn, hillbilly **10** clodhopper **12** appleknocker, backwoodsman

rubicund
3 red **5** flush, ruddy **6** florid **7** glowing, reddish **8** sanguine **11** full-blooded, incarnadine

Rubik of Cube fame
4 Ernö

rub out
3 ice, off, zap 4 do in, kill, slay 5 erase, smoke, waste, whack 6 finish, murder 7 bump off, destroy, put away 8 dispatch, knock off 9 liquidate, terminate 10 extinguish, obliterate 11 assassinate

rubric
4 name, rule 5 canon, class, gloss, style, title 6 custom 7 concept, heading 8 category, headline 9 tradition 11 appellation, designation 13 interpolation

Ruby of film
3 Dee

ruck
3 mob 4 fold, heap, mass, pile 5 crimp, crowd, group, purse, ridge 6 cockle, crease, furrow, gather, jumble, pucker, rumple 7 crinkle, crumple, scrunch, wrinkle 10 generality 11 corrugation

rucksack
4 pack 6 kit bag 7 musette 8 backpack

ruckus
3 ado, din, row 4 fuss, to-do 5 brawl, furor, hooha, melee, scrap 6 fracas, furore, hassle, hoohah, pother, rumpus, shindy, uproar 7 dispute, quarrel, rhubarb, shindig, wrangle 8 foofaraw, squabble 9 commotion, kerfuffle 10 falling-out 11 altercation, controversy, disturbance

ruddle
see **redden**

ruddy
3 red 4 ripe, rosy 5 flush 6 blowsy, florid 7 flushed, glowing 8 rubicund, sanguine 11 full-blooded, incarnadine

rude
3 raw 4 curt 5 crass, gross, gruff, harsh, rough, rowdy, surly 6 abrupt, callow, clumsy, coarse, crusty, robust, rugged, rustic, sturdy, unhewn, vulgar 7 boorish, brusque, ill-bred, loutish, lowbred, uncivil, uncouth 8 arrogant, churlish, clownish, impolite, tactless 9 barbarian, barbarous, elemental, inelegant, primitive, rough-hewn, unrefined 10 ungracious, unmannered, unmannerly, unpolished 11 ill-mannered, impertinent, uncivilized 12 discourteous, presumptuous, uncultivated 13 disrespectful

rudimentary
5 basal, basic 6 simple 7 initial, primary 8 simplest 9 beginning, elemental, vestigial 10 elementary 11 fundamental, undeveloped 12 introductory

rudiments
4 ABCs 6 basics 10 essentials 12 fundamentals

rue
3 woe 4 pity, ruth 5 dolor, grief, mourn, prick 6 grieve, lament, regret, repent, sorrow 7 anguish, deplore, remorse 8 sympathy 9 heartache, penitence 10 affliction, compassion, contrition, heartbreak, repentance 11 compunction

rueful
5 sorry 6 woeful 8 contrite, penitent 9 regretful, sorrowful 10 remorseful

ruff
5 frill, perch, trump 6 collar, fringe 9 sandpiper 11 pumpkinseed
female: 5 reeve

ruffian
4 goon, hood, punk, thug 5 beast, brute, bully, rowdy, tough, yahoo 6 Apache, hector 7 gorilla, hoodlum 8 bullyboy, hooligan 9 muscleman, roughneck, swaggerer

ruffle
3 bug, irk, rub, vex 4 fret, gall, wear 5 annoy, brawl, chafe, frill, graze, jabot, pleat, ruche 6 abrade, bother, nettle, peplum, ripple 7 agitate, bristle, disturb, flounce, provoke, trouble, wrinkle 8 drumbeat, furbelow, irritate, skirmish 9 commotion

rug
3 mat, wig 6 carpet, runner, toupee 7 laprobe
kind: 3 rag, rya 6 hooked 7 braided, dhurrie, drugget, flokati, Persian 8 Aubusson, bearskin, Oriental 10 Savonnerie
type: 4 area

rugby
formation: 5 scrum 9 scrummage
goal: 7 dropped, penalty
period: 4 half
player: 6 center, hooker, winger 8 standoff 9 scrum half
scoring: 3 try 4 goal 10 conversion
team: 7 fifteen
term: 4 heel 5 match 7 convert, dribble, hand off, knock on 9 fair catch
time-out: 8 stoppage
version: 5 union 6 league

rugged
5 burly, hardy, harsh, heavy, husky, rough, tough 6 brawny, coarse, craggy, jagged, robust, severe, stable, stormy, strong, sturdy, uneven 7 arduous, austere, scraggy 8 leathery, muscular, rigorous, scabrous, stalwart, vigorous 9 difficult, inclement, strenuous, unrefined, weathered 10 formidable, unpolished 11 tempestuous
ridge: 5 arête
rock: 4 crag

Ruggiero
guardian: 7 Atlante
sister: 7 Marfisa
slayer: 11 Tisaphernes
wife: 10 Bradamante

rug rat
3 tot 4 tyke 6 moppet 7 toddler

Ruhr city
5 Essen 8 Dortmund

ruin
4 bane, bust, dash, do in, doom, fall, loss, rape, raze, sack, undo 5 decay, havoc, smash, spoil, trash, use up, waste, wrack, wreck 6 beggar, finish, pauper, perish, ravage 7 corrupt, deplete, despoil, destroy, exhaust, failure, nemesis, pillage, shatter, undoing, wipe out 8 bankrupt, collapse, decimate, demolish, downfall, spoliate 9 depredate, devastate, disrepair, overthrow, pauperize, shipwreck 10 desolation, impoverish 11 destruction, devastation, dissolution 12 degeneration 13 deterioration

ruination
4 bane, loss, rack 5 havoc 7 undoing 8 calamity, disaster, downfall 10 decimation 11 destruction, devastation

ruinous
5 fatal 7 baneful 10 calamitous, disastrous, pernicious 11 cataclysmic, destructive 12 catastrophic

rule
3 law, Raj 4 lead, sway 5 axiom, bylaw, canon, edict, habit, judge, maxim, moral, order, reign 6 assize, custom, decree, deduce, dictum, direct, govern, regime, truism 7 brocard, command, control, precept, prevail, regency, regimen, resolve, statute 8 decretum, doctrine, dominate, domineer, dominion 9 authority, determine, etiquette, ordinance, principle, procedure 10 regulation
absolute: 7 autarky 8 autarchy
by a god: 8 theonomy

Rule Britannia composer
4 Arne (Thomas)

rule out
3 bar 5 block, debar 6 forbid, refuse, reject 7 dismiss, exclude, forfend, head off, obviate, prevent 8 preclude, prohibit, stave off 9 eliminate

ruler
4 king, lord 5 queen 6 archon, dynast, ferule, gerent, prince, regent, satrap, sultan 7 emperor, monarch, viceroy 8 governor, hierarch, oligarch, pentarch, princess, theocrat 9 dominator, imperator, matriarch, patriarch, potentate, sovereign 12 straightedge
absolute: 6 despot, tyrant 8 autocrat, dictator, overlord
Arab: 4 amir, emir 5 ameer, sheik 6 sharif, sheikh, sultan
Asian: 4 khan
Byzantine Empire: 6 exarch
Egyptian: 7 pharaoh
family: 7 dynasty
Iranian: 4 shah
one of four: 8 tetrarch
one of seven: 8 heptarch
one of three: 7 triarch 8 triumvir
Persian: 6 satrap
Russian: 4 czar, tsar, tzar
Turkish: 3 bey, dey 6 sultan

ruling
3 law 4 call 5 chief, edict, order, ukase 6 decree 7 current, finding, popular, regnant, verdict 8 decision, judgment 9 directive, judgement, prevalent, statement 10 prevailing, widespread 11 predominant 12 adjudication

Rumania
see **Romania**

rumble
4 buzz, roar, roll 5 brawl, drone, fight, growl, rumor 6 murmur, report 7 hearsay, quarrel, resound, thunder 8 feedback 9 complaint 11 altercation, disturbance, reverberate, scuttlebutt

rum cake
4 baba

rum drink
4 grog 6 mojito 8 daiquiri 10 piña colada

ruminant
3 Bos, cow, yak 4 deer, goat, tahr 5 bison, camel, llama, okapi, serow, sheep, takin 6 alpaca, cattle, musk ox, vicuña 7 buffalo, chamois, chewing, giraffe, guanaco 8 antelope 9 pronghorn
stomach: 5 omasa (plural), rumen 6 omasum 8 abomasum 9 reticulum

ruminate
4 chew, mull, muse 5 champ, chomp, weigh 6 ponder 7 reflect 8 cogitate, consider, meditate 9 masticate 10 deliberate 11 contemplate

ruminative
7 pensive 8 thinking 9 pondering 10 cogitative, meditative, reflective, thoughtful 11 speculative 13 contemplative, introspective

rummage
4 comb, fish, grub, hash, hunt, poke, rake, rout, seek 5 delve, scour 6 ferret, forage, jumble, litter, search 7 clutter, ransack 8 mishmash 9 potpourri 10 hodgepodge, hotchpotch, miscellany

rummy
3 gin, odd, sot 4 lush, soak, wino 5 drunk, souse, toper 6 boozer 7 bizarre, canasta, curious, guzzler, strange, swiller, tippler, tosspot 8 drunkard, peculiar 9 eccentric, inebriate 10 boozehound

rumor
4 blab, buzz, talk 5 bruit, noise, story 6 canard, gossip, murmur, mutter, report, rumble, tattle 7 hearsay, tidings, whisper 9 grapevine 11 scuttlebutt, susurration
personified: 4 Fama

rumormonger
5 yenta **6** gossip **8** gossiper, informer, quidnunc, telltale **9** whisperer **10** talebearer, tattletale

rump
3 can **4** beam, butt, duff, hind, rear, tush **5** fanny **6** behind, bottom, breech, heinie **7** keester, keister, rear end **8** backside, buttocks, derriere, haunches **9** posterior

rumple
4 fold, muss, ruck **5** crimp, screw, touse **6** pucker, tousle **7** crimple, crinkle, scrunch, wrinkle **8** dishevel, disorder

rumpus
see **ruckus**

run
3 fly, hie, jog **4** bolt, dart, dash, flee, flow, race, rush, scud, tear **5** chase, haste, hurry, scoot, skirr, speed **6** career, gallop, hasten, manage, scurry, sprint, streak, stream **7** scamper, scuttle, smuggle **9** skedaddle

run across
4 meet **8** bump into, discover **9** encounter, stumble on

runagate
4 hobo **5** gipsy, gypsy, nomad, tramp **6** outlaw **7** drifter, floater, lamster, vagrant, wastrel **8** bohemian, fugitive, rapparee, vagabond, wanderer **11** guttersnipe

run along
5 leave, scram **6** beat it, begone, cut out, depart **7** buzz off, get lost, skiddoo, take off, vamoose **8** shove off **9** skedaddle **10** make tracks

run ___
4 amok **5** amuck

runaround
4 duck, slip **5** dodge **7** elusion, evasion

run away
4 bolt, flee, skip **5** elope, leave, scram, skirr, split, steal **6** depart, desert, escape **7** abscond, make off **8** clear out, light out, stampede, turn tail **9** skedaddle **10** make tracks

runaway
4 romp, wild **5** loose **6** outlaw **7** escapee, lamster **8** deserter, fugitive **10** delinquent **12** uncontrolled

run down
3 hit, ram, tag **5** catch, knock, trace **6** pursue **7** decline **8** belittle, derogate, diminish **9** apprehend, disparage **10** depreciate **11** catch up with

run-down
5 dingy, seedy, tacky, tired **6** beat-up, bushed, shabby **7** rickety, ruinous, worn-out **8** decrepit, tattered, untended **9** burned-out, exhausted, neglected **10** bedraggled, down-at-heel, ramshackle, uncared-for **11** dilapidated

rundown
4 dope, poop **5** recap, scoop **6** report, review, skinny, update **7** outline, summary **8** briefing, synopsis

runes
4 ogam **5** ogham **7** futhark

rung
3 bar **4** step **5** grade, notch, round, spoke, staff, stage, stair, tread **6** degree, rundle **10** crosspiece

run-in
3 row **4** tiff **5** brush, fight, set-to **6** hassle, scrape, tangle **7** dispute, quarrel, rhubarb, wrangle **8** skirmish, squabble **9** encounter **10** falling-out **11** altercation

run into
3 hit, ram **4** meet **9** encounter, stumble on **11** collide with

runner
3 rug **5** gofer, miler, racer **6** carpet, stolon **7** carrier, courier, tendril **8** smuggler, sprinter **9** go-between, messenger **10** marathoner **11** ballcarrier
(see also **track star**)

running
6 active, fluent **7** cursive, dynamic, flowing, working **9** operative **10** continuous **11** functioning

run off to wed
5 elope

run-of-the-mill
4 dull, so-so **5** usual **6** common, normal **7** average, humdrum, regular, typical **8** everyday, familiar, mediocre, middling, moderate, ordinary **9** prevalent **10** monotonous **11** commonplace, indifferent **12** intermediate **13** unexceptional

run on
3 gab, yak **4** blab **5** clack **6** babble, cackle, gabble, jabber, ramble, rattle **7** chatter, prattle **8** continue

run out of
5 use up **6** finish **7** exhaust

run over
5 spill **6** exceed, repeat **7** examine **8** overfill, overflow, rehearse

runt
5 dwarf, pygmy **6** midget, peanut, peewee, shrimp, squirt **7** manikin **8** mannikin, Tom Thumb **10** homunculus **11** hop-o'-my-thumb, lilliputian

run through
3 jab **4** blow, gore, read, scan, stab **5** spend, use up, waste **6** expend, finish, impale, pierce **7** consume, examine, exhaust **8** rehearse, squander, transfix

runty
3 wee **4** puny **6** peewee **7** stunted **8** dwarfish **10** diminutive, undersized

run up
5 build, erect, mount **6** expand **7** augment, enlarge **8** increase, multiply **9** construct **10** accumulate

runway
4 duct, path **5** strip, track, trail **6** sluice, tarmac **7** channel, conduit **8** airstrip, platform

rupture
4 rend, rent, rift, rive **5** break, burst, cleft, sever, split **6** breach, cleave, hernia, schism, sunder **7** blowout, break up, disrupt, divorce, fissure, parting, split-up **8** division, fracture, separate **9** partition **10** separation **11** dissolution **12** estrangement

R.U.R.
author: **5** Capek (Karel)
character: **5** robot

rural
6 rustic **7** bucolic, country, idyllic **8** agrarian, arcadian, down-home, pastoral **10** campestral **11** countrified

ruse
3 con, jig **4** hoax, ploy, wile **5** dodge, feint, fraud, stall, trick **6** deceit, gambit **7** gimmick, swindle **8** artifice, maneuver, trickery **9** deception, stratagem **10** subterfuge **13** double-dealing

rush
3 fly, rip, run **4** boil, bolt, dart, dash, flit, flow, hurl, lash, race, roar, scud, tear, tide, whiz **5** blitz, break, carry, chase, court, daily, flash, haste, hurry, lunge, onset, sally, scoot, sedge, shoot, spate, speed, storm, surge **6** attack, barrel, beat it, bustle, career, charge, course, hasten, hurtle, hustle, irrupt, plunge, streak, stream, thrill, whoosh **7** assault, cattail, current, rampage, torrent **8** stampede **9** whirlwind, wire grass **13** precipitation

Rushdie novel
5 Shame **13** Satanic Verses (The) **17** Midnight's Children

rushing
5 hasty **6** abrupt, sudden **7** hurried **8** headlong **9** impetuous **11** precipitate, precipitous

rusk
7 biscuit **8** biscotto

Russia
capital: **6** Moscow
city: **3** Ufa **4** Omsk, Orel, Perm' **5** Kazan', Kursk **6** Grozny, Samara **7** Groznyy, Izhevsk, Ivanovo **8** Murmansk **9** Leningrad, Volgograd **10** Stalingrad **11** Chelyabinsk, Novosibirsk, Vladivostok **12** St. Petersburg **13** Yekaterinburg
czar: **4** Ivan **5** Basil, Boris (Godunov), Peter (the Great) **6** Alexis, Dmitry, Feodor, Vasily **7** Dimitri, Godunov (Boris), Michael (Romanov), Romanov (Michael) **8** Nicholas, Romanoff, Theodore **9** Alexander
empress: **4** Anna (Ivanovna) **9** Catherine (the Great), Elizabeth (Petrovna)
ethnic group: **7** Cossack
island: **8** Sakhalin
island group: **5** Kuril **6** Kurile
lake: **5** Il'men', Onega **6** Baikal, Ladoga
leader: **5** Lenin (Vladimir), Putin (Vladimir) **6** Stalin (Joseph) **7** Trotsky (Leon), Yeltsin (Boris) **8** Brezhnev (Leonid) **9** Gorbachev (Mikhail) **10** Khrushchev (Nikita)
legislature: **4** Duma
monetary unit: **5** kopek, ruble **6** kopeck
mountain, range: **4** Ural **5** Altai, Altay, Sayan, Urals **6** Elbrus, Kolyma, Koryak **8** Caucasus, Stanovoy
neighbor: **5** China **6** Latvia, Norway **7** Belarus, Estonia, Finland, Georgia, Ukraine **8** Mongolia **9** Kazakstan **10** Azerbaijan, Kazakhstan, North Korea
peninsula: **4** Kola **5** Gydan, Kanin, Yamal **6** Taymyr **7** Chukchi **9** Kamchatka
region: **7** Siberia **9** Circassia **11** Golden Horde
revolution: **9** Bolshevik
river: **3** Don **4** Amur, Lena, Neva, Ural **5** Desna, Dvina, Vitim, Volga **6** Belaya, Kolyma, Vilyui, Vilyuy **7** Pechora, Yenisey **9** Indigirka
sea: **4** Azov, Kara **5** Black, White **6** Laptev **7** Barents, Caspian, Chukchi, Okhotsk
secret police: **3** KGB, MVD **4** NKVD
strait: **6** Bering

Russian
aristocrat: **5** boyar
caviar: **6** beluga
comrade: **8** tovarich, tovarish
country house: **5** dacha
crepe: **4** blin **5** blini (plural)
dog: **6** borzoi **7** Samoyed
drink: **5** kvass, vodka
family: **7** Romanov **9** Stroganov
farmer: **5** kulak
forest: **5** taiga
grandmother: **8** babushka
instrument: **9** balalaika
monk: **8** Rasputin
no: **4** nyet
pancakes: **5** blini
peasant: **5** kulak, mujik **6** moujik, muzhik
republic: **6** oblast
ruler: **4** czar, tsar, tzar
saint: **15** Alexander Nevsky
satellite: **3** Mir
urn: **7** samovar
vehicle: **6** troika
villa: **5** dacha

Russo of film
4 Rene

rustic
4 hick, rube, rude 5 churl, clown, plain, rough, rural, swain, yokel 6 farmer 7 bucolic, bumpkin, country, granger, hayseed, peasant, plowboy, plowman, redneck, uncouth 8 agrarian, pastoral 9 chawbacon, hillbilly 10 campestral, clodhopper, countryman, husbandman 11 countrified 12 apple-knocker, backwoodsman

rustle
5 haste, hurry, speed, steal, swish 6 forage, swoosh 7 crackle, crinkle 8 susurrus

rustler
5 thief 6 duffer, robber 7 forager 8 marauder

Rustum's son
6 Sohrab

rusty
4 slow 6 bygone, creaky 7 outworn 8 outdated, outmoded 10 antiquated, discolored 12 old-fashioned

rut
5 gouge, grind, track 6 furrow, groove 7 channel, routine 9 treadmill

rutabaga
5 swede 6 turnip

ruth
3 rue, woe 4 pity 5 grief, mercy 6 regret, sorrow 7 anguish, remorse, sadness 8 distress, sympathy 9 attrition, penitence 10 compassion, contrition, repentance 11 compunction 13 commiseration

Ruth
husband: 4 Boaz 6 Mahlon
mother-in-law: 5 Naomi
son: 4 Obed

ruthful
6 woeful 7 doleful 8 dolorous, wretched 9 miserable, sorrowful

ruthless
4 hard 5 cruel, harsh 6 brutal, savage 7 inhuman 8 pitiless 9 barbarous, cutthroat, dog-eat-dog, ferocious, heartless, merciless, unsparing 10 implacable, ironfisted 11 cold-blooded

ruttish
4 lewd 5 lusty, randy 6 wanton 7 goatish, lustful, satyric 9 lecherous, lickerish, salacious 10 lascivious, libidinous 12 concupiscent

Rwanda
capital: 6 Kigali
ethnic group: 4 Hutu 5 Tutsi
language: 6 French, Rwanda
monetary unit: 5 franc
neighbor: 5 Congo 6 Uganda 7 Burundi 8 Tanzania

Rx amount
4 dose

S

Saarinen of architecture
4 Eero 5 Eliel

sabbatical
4 rest 5 leave 7 time off 8 vacation

saber
5 sword 7 cutlass 8 scimitar

sable
3 fur 4 dark, inky 5 black, ebony, raven 6 gloomy, somber, sombre, weasel 8 mourning

sabot
4 clog, shoe 10 wooden shoe

sabotage
5 wreck 7 cripple, disable, subvert, torpedo 9 undermine, vandalize 10 subversion

sac
4 asci, caul, cyst 5 bursa, pouch 7 vesicle

saccharine
5 mushy, sweet 6 sugary, syrupy 7 candied, cloying, honeyed, maudlin, mawkish, sugared 9 oversweet, schmaltzy 11 sentimental

sacerdotal
8 hieratic, pastoral, priestly 10 priestlike

sachem
4 boss 5 chief 6 leader

sachet
9 potpourri

sack
3 axe, bag, bed, can 4 bunk, drop, fire, loot, raid 5 expel, pouch, strip, waste 6 pocket, ravage, tackle 7 boot out, cashier, despoil, dismiss, kick out, pillage, plunder 8 desolate, spoliate 9 depredate, desecrate, devastate, white wine

sackbut
8 trombone
sacked out
4 abed
sacque
6 jacket
sacrament
4 rite **6** ritual **7** baptism, penance **8** ceremony, marriage **9** Communion, Eucharist, matrimony
sacrarium
6 chapel, shrine **7** oratory, piscina **8** sacristy **9** sanctuary
sacred
4 holy **5** godly **6** divine **7** blessed, saintly **8** hallowed, numinous **9** spiritual **10** inviolable, sacrosanct, sanctified **11** consecrated
bird of Egypt: **4** ibis
bull of Egypt: **4** Apis
choral composition: **5** motet
combining form: **4** hagi, hier, sacr **5** hagio, hiero, sacro
monkey: **6** baboon, rhesus **7** hanuman
place: **7** sanctum
song: **4** hymn
weed: **7** vervain
sacrifice
4 bunt, cede, lamb, lose, loss **5** forgo **6** devote, donate, eschew, give up, martyr, victim **7** forfeit, offer up **8** hecatomb, immolate, oblation, offering
sacrilege
6 heresy **7** impiety, offense **9** blasphemy
sacrilegious
7 impious, profane, ungodly **10** irreverent **11** blasphemous
sacristan
6 sexton
sacristy
6 vestry
sacrosanct
9 inviolate **10** inviolable
sad
3 low **4** blue, down, glum **5** sorry **6** dismal, dreary, gloomy, morose, triste, woeful **7** doleful, joyless, piteous, pitiful, unhappy **8** dejected, desolate, dolorous, downbeat, downcast, grieving, mournful, pathetic, pitiable **9** depressed, sorrowful, woebegone **10** depressing, lamentable, melancholy **11** melancholic **12** heavyhearted
sadden
7 depress, oppress, trouble **8** aggrieve, dispirit **9** weigh down **10** discourage
saddle
3 tax **4** lade, load **6** burden, charge, hamper, impede **7** aparejo
adjunct: **7** stirrup
part: **6** cantle, pommel
strap: **5** cinch, girth **6** latigo **7** harness
sadness
3 woe **4** funk **5** blues, dolor, dumps, gloom, grief, mopes **6** misery, sorrow **7** dismals, megrims **8** doldrums, glumness, mourning **9** dejection, dysphoria, heartache **10** depression, desolation, melancholy **11** despondency, melancholia
safari
4 hunt, trek, trip **7** caravan, journey **10** expedition
safe
4 snug **6** secure, unhurt **7** guarded **8** defended, shielded, unharmed **9** protected, sheltered, strongbox, unscathed **10** inviolable **11** impregnable **12** invulnerable, unassailable
safecracker
4 yegg **8** picklock **9** cracksman
safeguard
4 ward **6** convoy, defend, escort, shield, surety **7** bulwark, defense, protect **8** preserve **10** precaution, protection
safety
6 asylum, refuge **7** defense, shelter **8** immunity, security **9** sanctuary **10** protection
sag
3 dip **4** bend, drop, flag, flap, flop, hang, sink, slip, wilt **5** droop, slide, slump **6** dangle, hollow, slouch **7** decline, drop off, falloff, sinkage, sinking **8** downturn, settling, sinkhole **9** downswing
saga
4 Edda, epic, myth **6** legend **9** chronicle, narrative **12** Heimskringla
sagacious
4 wise **5** acute **7** knowing, prudent, sapient **8** critical **9** far-seeing, judicious **10** discerning, insightful, perceptive **11** intelligent
sagacity
6 acuity, acumen, wisdom **7** insight **8** judgment, prudence, sapience **10** perception, shrewdness **11** discernment, penetration, percipience, perspicuity
sagamore
5 chief **6** sachem
Sagan work
6 Cosmos **16** Bonjour Tristesse
sage
4 Bias, guru, mint, wise **5** Solon, Vyasa **6** Buddha (Gautama), Chilon, expert, Gandhi (Mohandas), Lao Tzu, master, Narada, Nestor, nestor, pundit, savant, Thales **7** gnostic, learned, prudent, sapient, scholar, Solomon, Valmiki, wise man **8** polymath, sensible **9** Confucius, judicious **10** discerning, insightful, perceptive
Hindu: **6** pandit, pundit **7** mahatma

Sage
of Chelsea: **7** Carlyle (Thomas)
of Concord: **7** Emerson (Ralph Waldo)
of Emporia: **5** White (William Allen)
of Ferney: **8** Voltaire
of Monticello: **9** Jefferson (Thomas)
of Pylos: **6** Nestor

Sagebrush State
6 Nevada

Sagittarius
6 archer **7** centaur **13** constellation

sago
4 palm **6** starch

saguaro
6 cactus

Saharan
4 arid

Saharan nation
4 Chad, Mali **5** Libya, Niger, Sudan

Sahara neighbor
5 Sahel

Sahel neighbor
6 Sahara

sail
3 fly, jib **4** dart, flit, scud, skim, wing **5** fleet, float, genoa, shoot, skirr, sweep **6** cruise, mizzen **7** spencer **9** spinnaker
into the wind: **4** luff
support: **4** mast, spar **5** sprit **7** yardarm

sailing
4 a-sea

sailing term
3 aft, bow, lee, yaw **4** alee, beam, boom, port, tack, trim **5** abaft, abeam, aloft, belay, brale, stern **6** astern, adrift, batten, fouled, pay out **7** cast off, heading, rigging, sea room **8** downhaul, overhaul, sounding, underway **9** starboard **10** Cunningham, lubber line

sailing vessel
4 bark, brig, junk, moth, yawl **5** ketch, sloop, xebec, yacht **6** barque, bugeye, caïque, cutter, galley **7** caravel, clipper, frigate, galleon, pinnace, piragua, shallop **8** corvette, schooner, skipjack, trimaran **9** catamaran **10** barkentine, brigantine, windjammer **11** barquentine

sailor
3 gob, tar **4** jack, mate, salt, swab **6** hearty, sea dog, seaman **7** jack-tar, mariner, matelot, old salt, swabbie **8** flatfoot, seafarer, shipmate, water dog **9** shellback, tarpaulin, yachtsman **10** bluejacket
assent: **3** aye **6** aye-aye
British: **5** limey
cartoon: **6** Popeye
drink: **3** rum **4** grog
East Indian: **6** lascar **7** lashkar
fictional: **6** Sinbad
patron saint: **4** Elmo
song: **6** chanty, shanty **7** chantey **9** barcarole

saint
7 paragon
biography: **11** hagiography
list: **9** hagiology
Muslim: **3** pir
(see also **patron saint**)

Saint, The
7 Templar (Simon)
creator: **9** Charteris (Leslie)

Saint Anthony's cross
3 tau

Saint Elmo's Fire
9 corposant

Saint Helena
capital: **9** Jamestown
island: **9** Ascension

Saint Joan author
4 Shaw (George Bernard)

Saint John's bread
5 carob

Saint Kitts and Nevis
capital: **10** Basseterre
island group: **7** Leeward

Saint Louis
Arch architect: **4** Eero (Saarinen)
attraction: **11** Gateway Arch
baseballers: **5** Cards **9** Cardinals

Saint Lucia
capital: **8** Castries
island group: **8** Windward

saintly
4 holy, pure **5** godly, pious **6** devout **7** angelic, blessed **8** beatific, seraphic, virtuous **9** righteous
aura: **4** halo

Saint Paul's architect
4 Wren (Christopher)

Saint Peter's Basilica
architect: **7** Bernini (Gian Lorenzo) **12** Michelangelo (Buonarotti)
sculpture: **5** Pietà

Saint Teresa birthplace
5 Ávila

Saint Vincent and the Grenadines
capital: **9** Kingstown
island group: **8** Windward
volcano: **9** Soufrière

Saint Vitus' dance
6 chorea

sake
8 rice wine

Saki
5 Munro (H. H.)

salaam
3 bow 6 kowtow 9 obeisance

salacious
4 blue, lewd, racy 5 bawdy 6 erotic, ribald, risqué, smutty 7 lustful, satyric 8 indecent, off-color, prurient 9 lecherous, libertine 10 lascivious, libidinous, licentious

salad
item: 3 egg, udo 4 bean, cuke, herb 5 cress, olive, onion, pasta 6 carrot, celery, cheese, endive, pepper, potato, radish, tomato 7 anchovy, arugula, cabbage, crouton, lettuce, mesclun, niçoise, parsley, spinach 8 chickpea, cucumber, escarole, garbanzo, mushroom, scallion 9 radicchio 10 watercress
dressing: 5 ranch 6 French 7 Italian, Russian 10 blue cheese, buttermilk, gorgonzola 11 vinaigrette
type: 4 Cobb 5 chef's 6 Caesar 7 Waldorf

salamander
3 eft, olm 4 newt 7 urodele 8 mud puppy, water dog 10 hellbender
Mexican: 7 axolotl

salary
3 pay 4 take, wage 6 income 7 stipend 8 earnings 9 emolument 10 recompense

sale
6 bazaar, demand 7 auction 8 closeout, disposal, transfer 9 clearance 11 transaction
tag abbrev.: 3 irr.
tag words: 4 as is

salesperson
3 rep

salient
6 marked, signal 7 obvious 8 striking 9 arresting, important, obtrusive, pertinent, prominent 10 impressive, noticeable, projecting, pronounced, remarkable 11 conspicuous, outstanding, significant

saline
5 briny, salty 8 brackish

Salinger, J. D.
character: 4 Esmé 6 Holden (Caulfield)
novel: 14 Franny and Zooey 15 Catcher in the Rye

saliva
4 spit 6 slaver, sputum 7 spittle

salivate
5 drool 6 drivel, slaver 7 slobber

Salk of medicine
5 Jonas
creation: 7 vaccine
target: 5 polio

sallow
3 wan 4 pale, waxy 5 pasty 6 pallid, sickly, willow 7 bilious 9 jaundiced

sally
3 gag 4 gust, jape, jest, joke, quip 5 blast, burst, crack, jaunt 6 depart, junket, outing, set out, sortie, zinger 7 barrage, flare-up 8 drollery, eruption, outbreak, outburst, paroxysm 9 discharge, excursion, wisecrack, witticism

Sally Field's Norma
3 Rae

salmagundi
see **hodgepodge**

salmon
4 chum, coho, kelt 5 cohoe, smolt 6 grilse, Sebago 7 chinook, sockeye 9 brandling
cured: 4 nova 7 gravlax 8 gravlaks
male: 6 kipper
smoked: 3 lox
young: 4 parr

Salome
author: 5 Wilde (Oscar)
composer: 7 Strauss (Richard)
father: 5 Herod
mother: 8 Herodias
victim: 4 John (the Baptist)

salon
4 hall, shop 5 suite 6 parlor 7 gallery 9 apartment, reception 10 exhibition
request: 3 dye 4 perm

Salon, e.g.
5 e-zine

saloon
3 bar, pub 6 tavern 7 barroom, cantina, gin mill, taproom 9 beer joint 12 watering hole

salt
3 gob, tar 4 jack, keep, NaCl, swab 5 brine, limey 6 halite, sailor, saline, sea dog, seaman 7 jack-tar, mariner 8 seafarer

salt away
4 bank, save 5 hoard, lay by, lay up, put by, stash, store 7 deposit 8 lay aside, squirrel

saltpeter
5 niter, nitre

___ salts
5 Epsom

salty
4 blue, racy 5 briny, crude, spicy, tangy 6 earthy, purple, risqué, saline 7 caustic, mordant, pungent 8 brackish, off-color, scathing

salubrious
5 tonic 7 bracing, healthy 8 hygienic 9 healthful, wholesome 10 beneficial 11 restorative

Salus
see **Hygeia**

salutary
5 tonic **6** benign **7** bracing, healing **8** curative, remedial, sanative **9** analeptic, healthful, vulnerary, wholesome **10** beneficial **11** restorative, therapeutic

salutation
4 hail **5** hello, howdy **7** welcome **8** greeting
Arabic: **6** salaam
Hawaiian: **5** aloha
Italian: **4** ciao
Latin: **3** ave
Spanish: **4** hola

salute
4 hail **5** greet, honor **6** praise **7** address, commend **8** greeting

Salvador of surrealism
4 Dalí

salvage
4 save **6** ransom, recoup, redeem, regain, rescue **7** reclaim, recover **8** retrieve

salvation
6 saving **10** redemption **11** deliverance

Salvation Army founder
5 Booth (General William)

salve
4 balm, nard **5** cream, quiet **6** cerate, chrism, lotion, remedy **7** assuage, unction, unguent **8** ointment **9** emollient

salver
4 tray

salvo
4 hail **5** burst, spray, storm **6** attack, shower, volley **7** barrage, proviso **9** broadside, cannonade, discharge, fusillade **11** bombardment

Samaritan
6 helper **10** benefactor

same
4 idem, like, very **5** equal, exact **7** coequal, similar **8** constant **9** duplicate, identical **10** consistent, equivalent
combining form: **3** hom **4** homo

Samoa
capital: **4** Apia
island: **5** Upolu **6** Savai'i
monetary unit: **4** tala

samovar
3 urn

samp
6 cereal, hominy

sampan
4 boat **5** skiff

sample
3 try **4** case, test **5** piece, taste **7** dip into, element, example, excerpt, portion **8** fragment, instance, specimen

Samson
betrayer: **7** Delilah
deathplace: **4** Gaza

Samson Agonistes author
6 Milton (John)

samurai code
7 Bushido

San Antonio
team: **5** Spurs
landmark: **5** Alamo

sanatorium
3 spa **8** hospital, rest home

sanctify
5 bless **6** hallow, ordain, purify **8** dedicate **10** consecrate

sanctimonious
5 pious **7** canting, preachy **8** unctuous **9** pharisaic **11** pharisaical **12** hypocritical, Pecksniffian **13** self-righteous

sanction
4 fiat, okay **5** allow, bless, leave **6** assent, decree, permit, ratify **7** approve, backing, boycott, certify, consent, embargo, endorse, license, penalty, support **8** accredit, approval **9** allowance, authorize **10** permission

sanctity
8 holiness **9** godliness **11** saintliness **13** inviolability

sanctuary
5 haven **6** asylum, covert, harbor, refuge, shrine, temple **7** shelter

sanctum
6 shrine **7** retreat, shelter

sand
3 tan **4** buff, ecru, fawn, grit **5** beach, beige, camel, grind, khaki, scour, shore **6** gravel, polish, smooth **7** burnish **8** granules

sandal
4 clog, zori **5** sabot, thong **6** patten **8** flip-flop, huarache **10** espadrille

sandbag
4 stun **6** ambush, waylay

sandbar
4 reef, spit **5** shoal **7** tombolo, towhead

Sandburg, Carl
biographical subject: **7** Lincoln (Abraham)
work: **9** People Yes (The) **13** Smoke and Steel **16** Rootabaga Stories

Sand County Almanac author
7 Leopold (Aldo)

sand island
3 cay, key

Sandler of comedy
4 Adam

sandpiper
4 knot, ruff **5** reeve **6** dunlin **9** shorebird

sandstone deposit
6 flysch

sandwich
3 BLT, sub **4** club, gyro, hero, roti **5** butty, Cuban, po'boy **6** Denver, hoagie, Reuben **7** grinder, Western **9** submarine **10** muffuletta
cookie: **4** Oreo
shop: **4** deli

sandy
4 fair **5** blond **6** blonde, grainy, gritty

sane
3 fit **5** lucid, sober, sound **6** normal **7** logical, prudent, sapient **8** all there, balanced, rational, sensible **9** judicious **10** reasonable **11** levelheaded **12** compos mentis

San Francisco
hill: **3** Nob **7** Russian
tower: **4** Coit
train system: **4** BART

sangfroid
5 poise **6** aplomb, phlegm **8** serenity **9** composure **10** equanimity

sanguinary
4 gory **6** bloody **9** homicidal, murdering, murderous **12** bloodstained, bloodthirsty

sanguine
4 gory **5** flush, ruddy **6** bloody, florid, upbeat **7** assured, buoyant, flushed, hopeful **8** bloodred, cheerful, rubicund **9** confident **10** optimistic **11** self-assured **12** blood-stained, bloodthirsty, Pollyannaish

sanitary
5 clean **7** sterile **8** hygienic **9** healthful **10** antiseptic, salubrious

sanitize
5 clean, purge **6** bleach, censor, purify **7** cleanse, launder **8** black out **9** disinfect, expurgate, sterilize **10** bowdlerize

sanity
6 health, reason **7** balance **8** lucidity, prudence **9** normality, soundness, stability

San Marino
capital: **9** San Marino
monetary unit: **4** euro
monetary unit, former: **4** lira
neighbor: **5** Italy

sans
7 lacking, missing, wanting, without

sans ___ (font type)
5 serif

Sanskrit
dialect: **4** Pali
epic: **8** Ramayana
Scripture: **4** Veda **6** Purana
teaching: **5** sutra

Santa helper
3 elf

Santa ___ winds
3 Ana

São Tomé and Príncipe
language: **10** Portuguese
location: **12** Gulf of Guinea
monetary unit: **5** dobra

sap
4 dolt, dupe, fool, gull, mark **5** chump, drain, ninny **6** pigeon, sucker, weaken **7** cripple, deplete, disable, exhaust, fall guy, tomfool **8** enervate, enfeeble **9** schlemiel, undermine
pine: **5** resin, rosin

sapid
5 tasty **6** savory **9** delicious, flavorful, palatable, toothsome **10** appetizing **11** scrumptious

sapience
see **sagacity**

sapient
see **sagacious**

Sapphira's husband
7 Ananias

Sappho
island: **6** Lesbos
student: **6** Erinna

sappy
5 ditzy, flaky, mushy, silly, soupy **6** drippy, slushy, sticky, syrupy **7** cloying, maudlin, mawkish **8** bathetic **11** sentimental

Saracen hero
9 Rodomonte

Sarah
husband: **7** Abraham
maid: **5** Hagar
son: **5** Isaac

sarcasm
4 gibe **5** irony, scorn, snark **6** satire **7** mockery **8** acerbity, mordancy, ridicule, sneering **10** causticity

sarcastic
4 acid, tart **5** acerb, sharp **6** biting, ironic **7** acerbic, caustic, cutting, cynical, jeering, mocking, mordant **8** sardonic, scathing, scornful, stinging

sarcophagus
4 tomb **6** coffin

sardine
4 sild **7** anchovy, herring **8** pilchard

Sardinia
capital: **8** Cagliari
neighbor: **7** Corsica

sardonic
3 wry **6** ironic **7** caustic, cynical, jeering, mocking **8** derisive, scornful, sneering **9** corrosive, sarcastic

sarong
5 skirt **7** garment

Sarpedon
brother: **5** Minos **12** Rhadamanthus
father: **4** Zeus **7** Jupiter
mother: **6** Europa **8** Laodamia

Sartor ___
8 Resartus

Sartre work
6 Nausea, No Exit **8** Huis Clos

sash
3 obi **4** belt **6** girdle **8** ceinture, cincture **9** waistband **10** cummerbund

sashay
5 mince, strut **6** prance **7** flounce, saunter, swagger

Saskatchewan
capital: **6** Regina
city: **8** Moose Jaw **9** Saskatoon **12** Prince Albert
mountain range: **12** Cypress Hills
provincial flower: **7** red lily **11** prairie lily
river: **9** Churchill **11** Assiniboine

Sask. neighbor
3 Alb. **4** Alta.

sass
3 lip **4** guff **5** brass, cheek, mouth, sauce **8** back talk **9** impudence, insolence

sassy
4 bold, flip, pert **5** fresh, lippy, nervy, smart **6** brazen, cheeky **7** forward **8** flippant, impudent, insolent, malapert **9** audacious **11** smart-alecky

Satan
5 demon, devil, fiend **6** diablo **7** Lucifer, Old Nick, serpent, villain **9** archfiend, Beelzebub **10** Old Scratch

satanic
4 evil **6** wicked **7** demonic, hellish **8** demoniac, devilish, diabolic, fiendish, infernal

satanism
9 diabolism

satchel
3 bag **4** case, tote **5** pouch **6** valise **7** handbag **9** briefcase

sate
4 cloy, fill, glut, jade, pall **5** gorge, stuff **6** stodge **7** appease, overeat, placate, surfeit **8** overfill **9** overstuff

sated
4 full **6** filled, gorged **7** glutted, overfed, replete, stuffed **8** appeased **9** surfeited

satellite
4 moon **5** toady **6** cohort, minion **8** adherent, disciple, follower, henchman, partisan **9** attendant, supporter, sycophant, tributary
of Jupiter: **6** Europa **8** Callisto, Ganymede
of Mars: **6** Deimos, Phobos
of Neptune: **6** Nereid, Triton
of Saturn: **4** Rhea **5** Dione, Janus, Mimas, Titan **6** Phoebe, Tethys **7** Iapetus **8** Hyperion
of Uranus: **5** Ariel **6** Oberon **7** Miranda, Titania, Umbriel
Russian: **3** Mir **7** Sputnik

satiate
see **sate**

Satie of music
4 Erik

satire
5 irony, spoof, squib **6** parody **7** lampoon, mockery, takeoff **8** raillery, ridicule, spoofery, travesty **9** burlesque **10** caricature, lampoonery, pasquinade

satiric
6 ironic **7** mocking **8** farcical, ironical
TV show: **3** SNL

satirist
American: **4** Sahl (Mort) **5** Bruce (Lenny), Twain (Mark) **6** Bierce (Ambrose)
English: **4** Pope (Alexander) **5** Swift (Jonathan), Waugh (Evelyn) **7** Marston (John)
French: **7** Molière **8** Rabelais (François), Voltaire
Greek: **8** Menippus **12** Aristophanes
Italian: **7** Aretino (Pietro)
Roman: **6** Horace **7** Juvenal, Martial, Persius **8** Apuleius **9** Petronius

satirize
4 mock **5** spoof **6** parody, send up **7** lampoon **8** ridicule **10** caricature

satisfaction
6 amends **7** redress **8** pleasure, serenity **9** atonement **10** reparation **11** contentment, fulfillment, restitution, vindication **12** propitiation

satisfactory
4 fair, good, okay **5** sound **6** decent **7** alright **8** adequate, all right, passable **9** agreeable, competent, tolerable **10** acceptable, sufficient

satisfy
4 sate, suit **5** pay up **6** answer, assure, dispel, pacify, please, settle, square **7** appease, content, fulfill, gladden, gratify, indulge, placate, satiate, suffice, win over **8** convince, persuade **9** conform to, discharge, indemnify

satori
12 illumination **13** enlightenment

satrap
5 ruler **6** cohort **7** viceroy **8** governor, henchman, sidekick

saturate
3 sop, wet **4** fill, soak **5** bathe, douse, imbue, souse, steep **6** charge, drench, infuse **7** pervade, suffuse **8** permeate, waterlog **9** transfuse

Saturday Night Live
cast member: **3** Fey (Tina) **4** Rock (Chris), Wiig (Kristen) **5** Chase (Chevy), Myers (Mike), Short (Martin) **6** Carvey (Dana), Curtin (Jane), Fallon (Jimmy), Farley (Chris), Meyers (Seth), Morgan (Tracy), Murphy (Eddie), Murray (Bill), Newman (Laraine), Radner (Gilda), Rocket (Charles) **7** Aykroyd (Dan), Belushi (John), Crystal (Billy), Ferrell (Will), Franken (Al), Hartman (Phil), Poehler (Amy), Rudolph (Maya), Sandler (Adam), Shearer (Harry)
creator: **8** Michaels (Lorne)

Saturn
moon: **4** Rhea **5** Dione, Janus, Mimas, Titan **6** Phoebe, Tethys **7** Iapetus **8** Hyperion **9** Enceladus
wife: **3** Ops
(see also **Cronus**)

saturnalia
4 orgy **5** party, revel **9** bacchanal **11** bacchanalia, dissipation

saturnine
4 dour, glum, grim **5** sulky, surly **6** gloomy, moping, morose, somber, sombre, sullen **8** funereal, sardonic

satyr
4 faun, lech, rake, wolf **5** letch **6** lecher **8** Casanova, lothario

satyric
4 lewd **5** randy **6** wanton **7** goatish, lustful **8** prurient **9** lecherous, libertine, lickerish, salacious **10** lascivious, libidinous, licentious, lubricious **11** promiscuous **12** concupiscent

sauce
3 dip, lip **4** guff, sass **6** relish **7** topping **8** back talk **9** condiment, impudence
kind: **3** soy **4** hard, mayo, mole, roux **5** aioli, chili, curry, gravy, melba, pesto, ponzu, salsa **6** catsup, Mornay, panada, tamari, tartar **7** chutney, ketchup, marengo, Newburg, piquant, soubise, tartare, velouté **8** béchamel, duxelles, marinade, marinara, matelote, noisette, normande **9** béarnaise, demiglace, lyonnaise, rémoulade **10** bordelaise, Provençale **11** hollandaise, vinaigrette

saucy
see **sassy**

Saudi Arabia
capital: **6** Riyadh
city: **5** Jedda, Jidda, Mecca **6** Jeddah, Jiddah, Medina
desert: **7** Arabian **10** Rub Al-Khali **12** Empty Quarter
gulf: **7** Persian
leader: **4** Fahd **6** Salman **8** Abdullah
monetary unit: **4** rial **5** riyal
neighbor: **3** UAE **4** Iraq, Oman **5** Qatar, Yemen **6** Jordan
peninsula: **7** Arabian
sea: **3** Red

Saul
concubine: **6** Rizpah
cousin: **5** Abner
daughter: **5** Merab **6** Michal
father: **4** Kish
general: **5** Abner
son: **8** Jonathan
successor: **5** David
uncle: **3** Ner
wife: **7** Ahinoam

saunter
4 mope, roam, rove **5** amble, drift, mosey **6** loiter, ramble, sashay, stroll, wander **7** meander, traipse

sausage
5 wurst **6** banger, kishke, salami, Vienna, wiener **7** baloney, bologna, boloney, chorizo, saveloy **8** cervelat, kielbasa, kielbasy **9** andouille, bratwurst, frankfurt, pepperoni, Thuringer **10** knackwurst, knockwurst, liverwurst, mortadella **11** frankfurter

sauté
3 fry **4** sear **5** brown, grill **6** sizzle **7** frizzle

savage
4 grim, wild **5** brute, cruel, feral **6** bloody, brutal, fierce, Gothic, rugged **7** bestial, brutish, inhuman, untamed, vicious, wolfish **8** barbaric, inhumane, primeval, ravenous, unbroken **9** barbarian, barbarous, ferocious, heartless, murderous, primitive, rapacious, truculent, voracious **11** uncivilized **12** bloodthirsty, uncultivated, unsocialized

savagery
7 cruelty **8** atrocity **9** barbarity, brutality, depravity **10** bestiality, inhumanity **11** abomination, monstrosity, viciousness

savanna
4 veld **5** plain, veldt **9** grassland

savant
4 sage **7** scholar, thinker, wise man

save
3 bar **4** bank, keep, stet, stow **5** amass, cache, guard, hoard, lay by, lay in, lay up, put by, set by, skimp, spare, store **6** defend, gather, keep up, manage, ransom, redeem, rescue, scrimp, shield **7** collect, deliver, deposit, husband, lay away, protect, reclaim, reserve, salvage, store up **8** conserve, lay aside, liberate, maintain, preserve, salt away, set aside, squirrel **9** economize, excluding, safeguard, stash away, stockpile

savings option
3 IRA **7** Roth IRA

savior
7 messiah, paladin, rescuer **8** defender, redeemer **9** deliverer, liberator, preserver, protector, salvation **11** white knight

savoir faire
4 tact **5** grace, poise **6** aplomb **7** address, dignity, finesse **8** urbanity **10** confidence, refinement

savor
4 odor, tang **5** enjoy, scent, smack, smell, spice, taste, tinge **6** flavor, relish, season **8** sapidity

savory
5 sapid, spicy, tangy, tasty **7** piquant **9** flavorful, palatable, toothsome **10** appetizing
jelly: 5 aspic

savvy
4 deft **5** adept, craft, handy, knack, skill **6** clever, talent **7** ability, know-how, skilled **8** deftness **9** adeptness, expertise, handiness, ingenuity **10** capability, cleverness, competence, horse sense

saw
3 cut, hew, rip **5** adage, axiom, maxim **6** byword, cliché, cutter, saying **7** precept, proverb **8** aphorism, apothegm
type: 3 bow, jig, pit, rip **4** band, buck, buzz, fret, hack, whip **5** chain, crown, saber **6** coping, scroll **7** compass, keyhole **8** circular, crosscut

sawbones
3 doc **6** doctor **7** surgeon **9** physician

sawbuck
6 tenner **7** ten-spot, trestle **8** Hamilton

saw-toothed
7 serrate, serried **8** serrated **11** denticulate

Saxon
assembly: 4 moot **5** gemot **6** gemote
nobleman: 8 atheling
serf: 4 esne **6** thrall
warrior: 5 thane

saxophone, e.g.
4 reed

saxophonist
4 Getz (Stan), Kirk (Rahsaan Roland) **5** Ayler (Albert) **6** Bechet (Sidney), Dolphy (Eric), Gordon (Dexter), Kenny G, Parker (Charlie) **7** Coleman (Ornette), Hawkins (Coleman), Rollins (Sonny), Shorter (Wayne), Webster (Ben) **8** Adderley (Cannonball), Coltrane (John) **9** Henderson (Joe)

say
4 talk, tell **5** mouth, speak, state, utter, voice **6** affirm, assert, assume, recite, remark **7** comment, declare, express **8** announce, proclaim **9** enunciate, pronounce **10** articulate

Sayers character
6 Wimsey (Lord Peter)

saying
3 mot, saw **5** adage, axiom, maxim, motto **6** byword, dictum, truism **7** precept, proverb **8** aphorism, apothegm

scab
5 crust **6** eschar **8** blackleg **13** strikebreaker

scabbard
6 sheath

scabrous
4 lewd **5** bawdy, harsh, rough, salty, scaly **6** crusty, grubby, ribald, scurfy, sordid, uneven **7** bristly, scraggy, squalid **8** indecent, prurient **9** salacious

scads
4 gobs, lots, tons, wads **5** heaps, loads, piles, rafts, reams **6** oodles, plenty **8** slathers

scaffold
5 stage, truss **7** staging **8** platform **9** framework

Scala, La
city: 5 Milan **6** Milano
production: 5 opera

scalawag
see **scamp**

scald
4 boil, burn **6** scorch

scale
4 peel, rate, skin **5** climb, flake, gamut, gauge, mount, ratio, scute, strip **6** ascend, degree, extent, ladder, lamina, scutum, squama **7** measure, ranking **8** escalade, flake off **9** exfoliate, hierarchy **10** desquamate, proportion **11** decorticate
auxiliary: 7 vernier
earthquake: 7 Richter
syllable: 3 sol
mineral: 4 Mohs'
temperature: 6 Kelvin **7** Celsius, Réaumur **10** centigrade, Fahrenheit
wind: 8 Beaufort

scallion
4 leek **5** onion **7** shallot **10** green onion

scalp
4 flay, skin **5** cheat **6** resell, trophy

scam
3 con, gyp **4** bilk, dupe, fool, hoax **5** bunco, bunko, cheat, fraud, phish, stick, trick **6** delude, diddle, hustle, racket, take in **7** beguile, deceive, defraud, swindle **8** flimflam, hoodwink, phishing **9** shell game, swindle **11** double-cross, Ponzi scheme

scamp
3 imp **4** brat, rake, tyke **5** devil, joker, knave, rogue **6** rascal, urchin **7** hellion **8** scalawag,

slyboots **9** prankster, scoundrel, skeezicks **10** scaramouch **11** rapscallion, scaramouche

scamper
3 run **4** dash, skip **5** scoot **6** scurry **7** scuttle

scan
3 eye, MRI **4** skim, view **5** audit, check **6** browse, review, survey **7** examine, eyeball, inspect **8** glance at **10** scrutinize

scandal
5 rumor **6** gossip, infamy **7** calumny, obloquy, offense, slander **8** disgrace, dishonor **9** aspersion **10** backbiting, defamation

scandalize
5 libel, shock, smear **6** defame, malign **7** asperse, slander **9** denigrate **10** calumniate

scandalmonger
6 gossip **8** busybody, gossiper, quidnunc, telltale **9** backbiter, muckraker **10** talebearer

scandalous
7 heinous **8** infamous, libelous, shameful, shocking **9** notorious, offensive **10** defamatory, outrageous, scurrilous **11** disgraceful

Scandinavian
country: 6 Norway, Sweden **7** Denmark, Finland, Iceland
furniture chain: 4 IKEA
rug: 3 rya
(see also **Norse**)

scant
4 mere **5** skimp, spare, stint **6** meager, meagre, paltry, scarce, scrimp, skimpy, slight, sparse **7** scrimpy, wanting **8** exiguous **10** inadequate

scantiness
4 lack **6** dearth **7** deficit, paucity **8** scarcity, shortage, sparsity **10** deficiency, inadequacy

scapegoat
6 victim **7** fall guy **9** sacrifice **11** whipping boy

scapegrace
5 knave, rogue, scamp **6** bad egg, rascal, sinner **7** ruffian, varmint, villain **8** hooligan, recreant, scalawag **9** miscreant, reprobate, scoundrel **10** blackguard, black sheep, delinquent **11** rapscallion

Scapin
5 rogue, valet **6** rascal
author: 7 Molière
employer: 7 Léandre

scar
3 mar **4** flaw **5** score **6** deface, defect, keloid **7** blemish, scratch **8** cicatrix, pockmark **9** cicatrize, disfigure
on a seed: 5 hilum

scarab
6 beetle

scaramouch
see **scamp**

scarce
3 few **4** rare **5** scant **6** barely, hardly, scanty, sparse **7** limited, wanting **8** sporadic, uncommon **10** inadequate, infrequent, occasional

scarcity
see **scantiness**

scare
5 alarm, panic, spook **6** fright **7** horrify, shake up, startle, terrify **8** frighten **9** terrorize

scaredy-cat
4 wimp, wuss **5** sissy **6** coward **7** chicken, dastard **8** alarmist, poltroon **11** milquetoast, yellowbelly

scare up
4 find, snag **5** rally **6** corral, gather, locate, obtain, secure **7** procure, unearth **8** smoke out **9** ferret out, track down

scarf
3 boa **4** gulp, wolf **5** ascot, do-rag, fichu, plaid, shawl, stole **6** cravat, devour, gobble, inhale, runner **8** babushka, liripipe, mantilla, puggaree **10** lambrequin
Mexican: 6 rebozo

Scarlet Letter, The
author: 9 Hawthorne (Nathaniel)
character: 5 Pearl **6** Hester (Prynne) **10** Dimmesdale (Arthur) **13** Chillingworth (Roger)

Scarlet Pimpernel author
5 Orczy (Baroness Emmuska)

Scarlett's home
4 Tara

scary
6 creepy, spooky **8** chilling **9** frightful

scat
3 git **4** shoo **5** scram **6** beat it, bug off, skidoo **7** buzz off, get lost, vamoose

scathe
4 burn, flay, flog, harm, lash, sear **5** roast, slash **6** assail, berate, scorch, thrash **7** blister, scarify, scourge, upbraid **8** lambaste **9** castigate, excoriate

scathing
6 biting, brutal **7** caustic, mordant **8** stinging **9** trenchant

scatter
3 sow, ted **4** cast, part, shed **5** strew **6** dispel, divide, spread **7** bestrew, break up, diffuse, disband, diverge **8** disperse, sprinkle **9** broadcast, dissipate **10** distribute **11** disseminate

scatterbrained
5 ditzy, dizzy, giddy, silly **7** flighty, foolish **8** heedless **9** frivolous

scattering
8 diaspora **10** dispersion

scavenger
5 hyena **6** jackal **7** freegan, vulture

scenario
4 plot **6** script **7** outline **8** libretto, synopsis **10** screenplay

scene
3 set **4** site, spot, view **5** arena, field, place, sight, vista **6** locale, milieu, sphere **7** episode, outlook, setting, tableau **8** backdrop, locality, location, stage set **9** landscape **10** background

scenery
3 set **5** decor **7** setting **8** stage set **11** furnishings

scent
4 musk, nose, odor **5** aroma, smell, snuff, whiff **7** bouquet, essence, incense, odorize, perfume **9** aromatize, fragrance, redolence

scepter
4 mace **5** baton, staff

schedule
4 list, roll **5** chart, slate **6** agenda, docket, record, roster **7** catalog, program, reserve **8** calendar, register, roll call **9** catalogue, timetable

scheme
4 plan, plot, ploy, ruse **5** bunco, bunko, cabal, order **6** design, device **7** collude, connive, diagram, project **8** conspire, contrive, game plan, intrigue, proposal, strategy **9** blueprint, expedient, machinate **10** conspiracy, strategize **11** arrangement, contrivance, machination
type: **5** Ponzi **7** pyramid

Schiaparelli of fashion
4 Elsa

schism
4 rent, rift **5** break, chasm, cleft, split **6** breach, divide, heresy **7** discord, dissent, fissure, rupture **8** cleavage, division, fracture **10** disharmony, dissidence, divergence, falling-out, heterodoxy, separation

schlemiel
4 fool **5** chump, klutz **7** bungler

schlep
3 lug, tow **4** drag, haul, hump, plod, pull, slog, tote **5** carry, truck **6** trudge **7** shamble, shuffle

schlock
4 junk **5** cheap, dreck, gaudy, junky, tacky, tatty **6** cheesy, kitsch, shoddy, sleazy, tawdry, trashy **8** inferior, low-grade

schmaltzy
5 mushy, soppy **6** drippy **7** maudlin, mawkish **11** sentimental, tear-jerking

schmo
4 dolt, dope, dork, fool, goof, jerk, mutt, simp, twit, yo-yo **5** brute, chump, idiot, moron, ninny, noddy, scamp **6** dimwit, donkey, dumdum, nitwit, noodle, nudnik, rascal **7** dullard, halfwit, jackass, schmuck, schnook **8** bonehead, clodpoll, imbecile, lunkhead, meathead, numskull **9** birdbrain, blockhead, ignoramus, lamebrain, numbskull, thickhead

schmooze
3 gab, yak **4** chat **6** chat up, hobnob, mingle **8** converse **9** socialize

schnoz
4 beak, nose **5** snoot, snout **6** honker

scholar
4 sage, wonk **5** pupil **6** pedant, savant **7** bookman, egghead, student, wise man **8** bookworm, polymath **12** intellectual
Hindu: **6** pandit, pundit
Muslim: **5** ulama, ulema

scholarly
7 bookish, erudite, learned **8** academic, educated, studious **10** scholastic **12** intellectual

scholarship
5 award, grant **7** stipend **8** learning **9** education, erudition

scholastic
7 bookish, erudite, learned **8** academic, lettered, literary, pedantic **9** scholarly
life: **8** academia

school
3 gam, pod **5** shoal **7** academy, college **9** alma mater, institute **10** university
assignment: **5** essay
dance: **4** prom
English: **4** Eton **6** Harrow
French: **5** école, lycée
grounds: **6** campus
Jewish: **5** heder **7** yeshiva
judo: **4** dojo
organization: **3** PTA, PTO
religious: **8** seminary
term: **7** quarter **8** semester **9** trimester
type: **4** coed

schoolbook
4 text **6** primer, reader **7** speller

School for Scandal author
8 Sheridan (Richard Brinsley)

schooner
4 ship **5** stoup **6** goblet, seidel **7** tumbler **8** sailboat

Schubert forte
4 lied, song **6** lieder

science
of agriculture: **8** agronomy
of animals: **7** zoology
of criminal punishment: **8** penology

of environment: **7** ecology
of fermentation: **8** zymology
of health: **7** hygiene **9** hygienics
of heredity: **8** genetics
of human behavior: **10** psychology
of measuring time: **8** horology **11** chronometry
of motion: **8** kinetics
of mountains: **7** orology
of plants: **6** botany
of projectiles: **10** ballistics
of the earth: **7** geology

science guy of TV
3 Nye (Bill)

science show on PBS
4 Nova

scientific classification
8 taxonomy

sci-fi
author: **3** Lem (Stanislaw) **4** Card (Orson Scott), Dick (Philip K.), Pohl (Frederik) **5** Adams (Douglas), Disch (Thomas M.), Lewis (C. S.), Niven (Larry), Verne (Jules), Wells (H. G.) **6** Aldiss (Brian), Asimov (Isaac), Bester (Alfred), Bishop (Michael), Butler (Octavia), Clarke (Arthur C.), Delany (Samuel), Farmer (Philip José), Gibson (William), Le Guin (Ursula), Leiber (Fritz), L'Engle (Madeleine), Miller (Walter), Norton (Andre) **7** Ballard (J. G.), Clement (Hal), Ellison (Harlan), Herbert (Frank), Hubbard (L. Ron), Van Vogt (A. E.), Zelazny (Roger) **8** Anderson (Poul), Bradbury (Ray), Heinlein (Robert A.), Sterling (Bruce), Sturgeon (Theodore), Vonnegut (Kurt) **9** Gernsback (Hugo), Kornbluth (C. M.) **10** Silverberg (Robert)
genre: **9** cyberpunk, steampunk

sci-fi, e.g.
5 genre

scimitar
5 saber, sabre, sword **7** cutlass

scintilla
3 bit, jot **4** atom, iota, whit **5** grain, spark, speck, trace **7** smidgen **8** particle

scintillate
5 flash, gleam, glint, spark **7** glimmer, glisten, glitter, shimmer, sparkle, twinkle **9** coruscate

scion
4 heir **5** child, graft, issue **7** progeny **8** offshoot **9** inheritor, offspring, successor **10** descendant

scoff at
4 mock, twit **5** fleer, scorn **6** deride **7** contemn, disdain **8** belittle, pooh-pooh, ridicule

scold
3 rag **4** lash, rail **5** baste, blame, chide, grill, harpy, shrew, vixen **6** berate, grouch, grouse, harass, murmur, mutter, rebuke, revile, virago **7** bawl out, blister, censure, chasten, chew out, lecture, reprove, tell off, upbraid **8** admonish, execrate, fishwife, lambaste, reproach, Xantippe **9** criticize, dress down, excoriate, objurgate, reprehend, reprimand, termagant, Xanthippe **10** tongue-lash, vituperate

scoop
3 dig, dip **4** bail, beat, lift **5** gouge, ladle, spade **6** dig out, pick up, shovel **8** excavate **9** exclusive

scoot
3 fly, run, zip **4** dash, flee, race, rush, skip **5** hurry, scram, skirr, slide **6** hustle, scurry, sprint **7** scamper **9** skedaddle

scooter
5 moped

scope
3 ken **4** area, room **5** ambit, gamut, orbit, range, reach, sweep **6** extent, leeway, margin, radius **7** breadth, compass, purview **8** capacity, fullness, latitude **9** amplitude, extension

Scopes trial lawyer
5 Bryan (William Jennings) **6** Darrow (Clarence)

scorch
4 bake, burn, char, flay, sear **5** broil, roast, singe **6** scathe **7** blacken, blister, scarify, scourge, swelter **8** lambaste **9** castigate, excoriate

score
3 cut, tab, win **4** bill, gain, goal, line, mark, nick, slit **5** cleft, count, notch, reach, tally, total **6** attain, furrow, groove, grudge, rack up, record, twenty **7** account, achieve, invoice, scratch, succeed

scorn
4 gibe, jeer, mock **5** abhor, flout, scoff, spurn, taunt **6** deride **7** contemn, despise, despite, disdain, jeering, mockery **8** contempt, derision, ridicule, scoffing, taunting **9** contumely

Scorpius star
7 Antares

Scot
4 Celt, Gael

Scotch cocktail
6 Rob Roy **9** Rusty Nail

scoter
7 sea coot, sea duck

Scotland
capital: **9** Edinburgh
church: **11** the Auld Kirk
city: **6** Dundee **7** Glasgow **8** Aberdeen **9** Inverness **11** Dunfermline
emblem: **7** thistle
firth: **5** Clyde, Forth, Moray **6** Solway
former capital: **5** Perth
island, island group: **4** Iona, Jura, Mull, Skye, Uist **5** Arran, Islay **7** Orkneys **9** Shetlands **8** Hebrides
loch: **4** Ness **5** Leven **6** Lomond

mountain, range: **8** Ben Nevis **9** Grampians
patron saint: **6** Andrew
river: **3** Dee, Esk, Tay **5** Clyde

Scott, Sir Walter
novel: **6** Rob Roy **7** Ivanhoe **8** Waverley **10** Kenilworth **14** Quentin Durward
poem: **7** Marmion **13** Lady of the Lake (The)

___ Scott case
4 Dred

Scottish
4 Erse **6** Gaelic
cap: **3** tam **9** glengarry **11** tam-o'-shanter
child: **4** baba **5** bairn
coin: **6** bawbee
dance: **4** reel **5** fling **10** strathspey
Gaelic: **4** Erse
guide: **6** gillie
Highlander: **4** Gael
hero: **5** Bruce (Robert) **7** Wallace (William)
hillside: **4** brae
landowner: **5** laird
language: **4** Erse **6** Gaelic
lord: **5** thane
no: **3** nae
outlaw: **6** Rob Roy
plaid: **6** tartan
pudding: **6** haggis
skirt: **4** kilt
spirit: **6** kelpie **7** banshee
sword: **8** claymore
terrier: **4** Skye
trousers: **5** trews

scoundrel
3 cad, cur **4** heel **5** knave, rogue, scamp **6** bad guy, rascal **7** lowlife, villain **9** miscreant, reprobate **10** blackguard

scour
4 comb, rake **5** erode, purge, range, scrub **6** forage, search **7** corrode, eat away, ransack, rummage **8** wear away

scourge
4 bane, flay, flog, hide, lash, whip, whop **5** curse, flail, slash **6** plague, ravage, scathe, stripe, thrash **7** afflict, blister, despoil, pillage, scarify **8** chastise, lambaste **9** castigate, desecrate, devastate, excoriate **10** affliction, flagellate, pestilence

Scourge of God
6 Attila

scout
3 spy **6** ranger, survey **7** explore, lookout **8** searcher, watchman **11** reconnoiter

scouting group
3 BSA, GSA

scow
3 hoy **5** barge **6** garvey **7** lighter

scowl
5 frown, glare, lower **6** glower

scrabble
5 grope **6** scrawl **7** clamber **8** flounder

scrag
4 neck

scraggly
6 ragged, shaggy, uneven **7** unkempt

scraggy
4 bony, lank, lean **5** gaunt, harsh, lanky, rocky, rough **6** jagged, rugged, skinny, uneven **7** angular, spindly, unlevel **8** gangling, rawboned, scabrous

scram
3 git **4** scat, shoo **5** scoot, split **6** beat it, get out **7** buzz off, get lost, skiddoo, take off, vamoose **8** clear out **9** skedaddle

scramble
4 hash **6** jumble, muddle, scurry, tumble **7** clamber, clutter, rummage, scuttle, shuffle **8** mishmash, straggle

scrambled
7 chaotic, jumbled, mixed-up **8** confused **9** corrupted **10** disordered, disorderly

scrap
3 bit, jot, ort, row **4** chip, dump, fray, iota, junk, spat, tiff, whit **5** abort, brawl, chuck, crumb, fight, melee, piece, set-to, shred, speck **6** bicker, fracas, reject, sliver, tittle **7** brabble, cutting, discard, fall out, quarrel, scuffle, smidgen, wrangle **8** fragment, jettison, leftover, particle, squabble, throw out **9** throw away

scrape
3 fix, jam, rub **4** bark, mess, rasp **5** chafe, fight, grate, graze, pinch, scour, scuff, shave, skimp, spare, stint **6** abrade, pickle, plight, scrimp **7** dilemma, scratch **8** abrasion, struggle **11** predicament

scrappy
6 feisty **8** brawling **9** combative, truculent **10** pugnacious **11** belligerent, contentious, quarrelsome

scratch
3 mar **4** claw, rake, rasp **5** grate, money, score, scrup **6** scotch, scrape, scrawl **7** call off **8** scrabble, scribble

scratchy
5 rough **6** gritty **7** itching, prickly, rasping **8** abrasive

scrawl
6 doodle **7** scratch **8** scrabble, scribble

scrawny
4 bony, lank, lean **5** gaunt, lanky, weedy **6** skinny **7** scraggy **8** rawboned

scream
3 cry 4 yell, yowl 6 screak, shriek, shrill, squeal 7 screech

screech
6 shriek, shrill, squeal

screed
4 rant 5 level, spiel 6 letter, tirade 8 diatribe, harangue, jeremiad 9 discourse, philippic

screen
4 cull, hide, sift, veil 5 blind, sieve 6 facade, filter, movies, shroud, winnow 7 conceal, obscure, pick out 9 partition 10 camouflage
Japanese: 5 shoji

screw
9 propeller

screwball
3 nut, wag 4 kook, loco, zany 5 clown, crazy, cutup, flake, flaky, freak, gonzo, joker, kooky, loony, loopy, nutty, silly, wacko, wacky 6 madcap, weirdo 7 buffoon, dingbat, farceur 8 crackpot, jokester 9 ding-a-ling, eccentric, fruitcake

Screwtape Letters author
5 Lewis (C. S.)

screwy
3 mad 4 daft, nuts 5 batty, crazy, goofy, loony, nutty, wacky 6 absurd, insane 7 bizarre, cracked, lunatic 9 eccentric

scribble
5 write 6 scrawl 7 scratch

scribe
5 clerk, write 6 author, penman, writer 7 copyist 9 scrivener, secretary 10 amanuensis

scrimmage
4 fray 5 brawl, broil, clash, fight, melee, scrap, scrum, set-to 6 battle, fracas, ruckus, rumpus 7 scuffle 8 skirmish 10 donnybrook, free-for-all

scrimp
4 save 5 stint 6 save up 8 conserve 9 economize

script
4 hand, text 8 longhand, scenario 10 penmanship, screenplay 11 calligraphy, chirography, handwriting

scrivener
5 clerk 6 notary, scribe 7 copyist 10 amanuensis

scrooge
5 miser 7 niggard 8 tightwad 9 skinflint 10 cheapskate 12 moneygrubber

scrounge
3 beg, bum 4 grub 5 cadge, mooch, pinch, swipe 6 forage, hustle, pilfer, sponge 7 finagle, solicit, wheedle 8 freeload 9 panhandle

scroungy
5 dirty, seedy 6 grubby, grungy, scurvy, scuzzy, shabby, sleazy, sordid 7 squalid, unkempt 8 slovenly 10 slatternly

scrub
3 rub 4 buff, drop, wash 5 abort, brush, scour 6 cancel, mallee, maquis, polish 7 abandon, call off, cleanse, scratch 9 chaparral, eliminate

scrubby
4 drab, mean 5 dingy, dowdy, runty 6 paltry, ragged, shabby, shoddy 7 rundown, runtish, stunted 8 inferior 9 neglected 10 bedraggled, broken-down

scruff
4 nape, neck

scruffy
5 mangy, seedy, tacky 6 frowsy, frowzy, shabby, shaggy 7 run-down, scrubby, unkempt 8 slovenly, tattered 10 down-at-heel, threadbare

Scruggs of bluegrass
4 Earl

scrumptious
5 tasty, yummy 8 heavenly, luscious 9 ambrosial, delicious, succulent, toothsome 10 delectable 13 mouthwatering

scruple
3 bit, jot 4 balk, iota 5 demur, doubt, grain, qualm, scrap, shred, worry 7 concern, modicum 8 particle, question 9 hesitancy 11 compunction

scrupulous
5 exact, fussy 6 honest, minute, strict 7 careful, heedful, upright 8 critical, punctual, rigorous 9 honorable 10 fair-minded, fastidious, meticulous, principled, upstanding 11 painstaking, punctilious 13 conscientious

scrutinize
4 comb, scan 5 audit, probe, study 6 peruse 7 analyze, canvass, dig into, dissect, examine, eyeball, inspect 8 look over, pore over 9 check over 11 contemplate, investigate

scrutiny
4 scan 5 audit 6 review, survey 7 perusal 8 analysis 10 inspection 11 examination 12 surveillance

scuba diver
7 frogman 8 aquanaut

scud
3 fly 4 gust, race, rain, rush, sail, skim 5 brume, froth, scoot, speed, spray, spume 6 clouds, scurry, shower

scuff
6 scrape 7 scratch, shamble, shuffle

scuffle
3 row 4 fray 5 brawl, broil, fight, scrap, set-to 6 affray, fracas, hubbub, tussle 7 bobbery, grapple, shamble, shuffle, wrestle 10 roughhouse

scull
3 oar, row **4** boat **5** shell **6** propel

sculling need
3 oar

sculpt
3 hew **5** carve, shape **6** chisel

sculptor
American: **3** Lin (Maya) **4** Gabo (Naum), Judd (Donald), Taft (Lorado) **5** Andre (Carl), Koons (Jeff), Pratt (Bela), Segal (George), Serra (Richard), Smith (David), Story (William) **6** Aitkin (Robert), Calder (Alexander), Fraser (James Earle), French (Daniel Chester), Powers (Hiram), Zorach (William) **7** Borglum (Gutzon), Cornell (Joseph), Noguchi (Isamu) **8** Lachaise (Gaston), Lipchitz (Jacques), Nadelman (Elie), Nevelson (Louise) **9** Bourgeois (Louise), Mestrovic (Ivan), Oldenburg (Claes), Remington (Frederic) **12** Saint-Gaudens (Augustus)
Czech: **6** Stursa (Jan)
Danish: **11** Thorvaldsen (Bertel), Thorwaldsen (Bertel)
Dutch: **6** Sluter (Claus)
English: **5** Moore (Henry), Watts (George) **7** Epstein (Jacob), Flaxman (John) **8** Hepworth (Barbara)
French: **3** Arp (Hans, Jean) **4** Bloc (André) **5** Rodin (Auguste) **6** Dubois (Paul), Houdon (Jean-Antoine) **7** Maillol (Aristide), Pevsner (Antoine) **9** Bartholdi (Frédéric-Auguste), Roubillac (Louis-François)
German: **5** Hesse (Eva)
Greek: **5** Myron **7** Phidias **8** Pheidias **10** Polyclitus, Praxiteles **11** Polycleitus
Italian: **5** Leoni (Leone), Salvi (Niccolò, Nicola) **6** Canova (Antonio), Pisano (Andrea, Nino), Robbia (Andrea, Giovanni, Girolamo, Luca della) **7** Bernini (Gian Lorenzo), Cellini (Benvenuto), da Vinci (Leonardo), Orcagna, Quercia (Jacopo della) **8** Ghiberti (Lorenzo), Leonardo (da Vinci), Vittoria (Alessandro) **9** Donatello, Sansovino (Jacopo) **10** Giocometti (Alberto), Verrocchio (Andrea del) **12** Michelangelo (Buonarroti)
Rhodian: **9** Polydorus
Romanian: **8** Brancusi (Constantin)
Russian: **7** Zadkine (Ossip)
Swedish: **6** Milles (Carl) **9** Oldenburg (Claes)
Swiss: **10** Giacometti (Alberto)

sculptor of The Kiss
5 Rodin (Auguste)

scum
5 algae, dregs, dross **6** refuse, vermin **8** riffraff

scummy
3 low **4** base, vile **5** dirty, mucky, slimy **6** grubby, odious, sleazy, sordid **7** squalid **10** despicable **12** contemptible

scurrilous
4 foul **5** dirty, gross, nasty **6** coarse, filthy, vulgar **7** abusive, obscene, profane **8** indecent **9** insulting, offensive **10** outrageous **11** opprobrious **12** contumelious, vituperative

scurry
3 run **4** dart, dash **5** scoot, shoot **6** bustle **7** scamper, scuffle, scuttle

scurvy
see **scummy**

scut
4 tail

scuttle
3 run **4** hole, pail, sink **5** abort, scrap **6** basket, scurry **7** opening

scuttlebutt
4 buzz, talk **5** rumor **6** gossip, report **7** chatter, hearsay **9** grapevine

Scylla
4 rock
counterpart: **9** Charybdis
father: **5** Nisus
lover: **5** Minos

scythe handle
5 snath **6** snathe

sea
4 blue, deep, main **5** brine, drink, ocean
Antarctica: **4** Ross **5** Davis **7** Weddell **8** Amundsen
Arctic: **4** Kara **7** Chukchi **8** Beaufort, Karskoye **9** Chuckchee, Norwegian **11** Chukotskoye **12** East Siberian
Asia-Europe: **5** Black
Asia Minor: **7** Icarian
Atlantic: **5** North **7** Weddell **9** Caribbean
Australia-Indonesia: **7** Arafura
Balkan Peninsula-Italy: **8** Adriatic
Bay of Bengal: **7** Andaman
China-Korea: **5** Huang, Hwang **6** Yellow
combining form: **3** mer **4** mari **5** pelag **6** pelago **7** thalass **8** thalasso
Corsica-Italy: **10** Tyrrhenian
Denmark-Norway: **9** Skagerrak
Denmark-Sweden: **8** Kattegat
England-Ireland: **5** Irish
Fiji: **4** Koro
France-Italy: **8** Ligurian
Greece: **5** Crete
Greece-Italy: **6** Ionian
Greece-Turkey: **6** Aegean **8** Thracian
Honshu: **6** Sagami
Indian Ocean: **5** Timor **7** Arabian
Indonesia: **4** Bali **6** Flores
inland: **3** Red **4** Aral **7** Caspian
Japan: **3** Suo **6** Inland
Kazakhstan: **4** Aral

Malay Archipelago: **5** Banda
Mexico: **6** Cortés
Netherlands: **6** Wadden
North Atlantic: **8** Sargasso
Northern Europe: **6** Baltic, Ostsee **8** Suevicum
North Pacific: **6** Bering
off Scotland: **8** Hebrides
off Sweden: **5** Aland
Pacific: **4** Java **5** China, Coral **6** Maluku **7** Celebes, Eastern, Molucca, Solomon **9** East China **10** South China
Philippine: **4** Sulu
Russia: **5** White **7** Okhotsk
Russia-Ukraine: **4** Azov
South Pacific: **4** Ross **6** Tasman **8** Amundsen
Turkey: **7** Marmara **9** Propontis
Uzbekistan: **4** Aral
West Pacific: **5** Ceram, Japan **8** Bismarck **10** Philippine

sea anemone
5 polyp

seabird
see **bird** *aquatic*

seacoast
5 beach, shore **6** strand **7** shingle **8** littoral **9** shoreline

sea cucumber
7 trepang **11** holothurian

sea dog
see **sailor**

sea duck
5 eider, scaup **6** scoter **9** merganser

sea eagle
3 ern **4** erne **6** osprey **8** fish hawk

seafarer
3 gob, tar **4** jack, salt, swab **5** limey **6** sailor **7** jack-tar, mariner

seafood dish
4 crab **5** clams, squid **6** bisque, paella, scampi, shrimp **7** ceviche, chowder, lobster, mussels, oysters, seviche **8** calamari, scallops

seagoing
8 maritime, nautical

sea in France
3 mer

sea in Spain
3 mar

seal
5 sigil, stamp **6** cachet, signet **7** sticker
female: **3** cow
herd: **3** pod **5** patch
joint: **6** gasket
young: **3** pup

sealant
4 lute **5** caulk, grout **6** luting, mastic **8** caulking

sea lily
7 crinoid

seam
4 bond **5** joint, union **8** coupling, juncture **10** connection

seaman
see **sailor**

sea monster
3 Orc **6** kraken **9** leviathan

seamount
5 guyot

seamy
5 dirty, rough, seedy **6** sordid **7** squalid **12** disreputable

séance
7 meeting, session, sitting
holder: **6** medium

seaport
Alaska: **6** Juneau **9** Anchorage
Albania: **5** Vlorë **6** Durres, Valona
Algeria: **4** Bône, Oran **6** Annaba
Angola: **6** Lobito, Luanda **7** Cabinda **8** Benguela
Argentina: **11** Buenos Aires, Mar del Plata
Australia: **4** Eden **5** Bowen, Perth **6** Darwin, Hobart, Sydney **8** Brisbane **9** Melbourne **10** Wollongong
Azores: **5** Horta
Balearic: **5** Ibiza
Belgium: **6** Ostend **7** Antwerp
Benin: **7** Cotonou **9** Porto-Novo
Black Sea: **5** Varna **6** Burgas, Odessa **9** Constanta
Brazil: **3** Rio **4** Pará **5** Bahia, Belém, Natal **6** Recife, Santos **7** Vitoria **8** Salvador **9** Fortaleza **10** Pernambuco **11** Pôrto Alegre, São Salvador **12** Rio de Janeiro
Bulgaria: **5** Varna **6** Burgas
Cameroon: **6** Douala
Canaries: **8** Arrecife **9** Las Palmas
Chile: **5** Arica **8** Coquimbo **10** Valparaíso
China: **4** Amoy **6** Dalian, Fuzhou, Lüshun, Xiamen **7** Foochow, Hsia-men, Qingdao, Tianjin **8** Shanghai, Shenzhen, Tientsin, Tsingtao **9** Guangzhou, Zhenjiang **10** Chen-chiang, Port Arthur
Colombia: **6** Lorica **9** Cartagena **12** Barranquilla
Corsica: **5** Calvi **7** Ajaccio
Costa Rica: **5** Limón **10** Puntarenas
Crimean: **5** Kerch, Yalta **10** Sebastopol, Sevastopol
Croatia: **5** Rieka, Split **6** Rijeka **9** Dubrovnik
Cuba: **6** Havana **8** La Habana, Matanzas, Santiago
Cyprus: **9** Famagusta

Denmark: **5** Arhus **6** Aarhus, Alborg **7** Aalborg **8** Elsinore **10** Copenhagen
Ecuador: **9** Guayaquil
Egypt: **4** Said **10** Alexandria
England: **4** Hull **5** Dover **9** Liverpool **10** Portsmouth **11** Southampton
Equatorial Guinea: **4** Bata
Eritrea: **4** Aseb
Estonia: **5** Pärnu **7** Tallinn
Finland: **3** Abo **4** Kemi, Oulu, Pori, Vasa **5** Hango, Kotka, Rauma, Turku, Vaasa **6** Vyborg
Florida: **5** Miami, Tampa **9** Pensacola **12** Apalachicola, Jacksonville
France: **4** Nice **5** Brest, Havre **6** Calais, Cannes, Toulon **7** Dunkirk, Le Havre **8** Bordeaux, Boulogne **9** Cherbourg, Dunkerque, Marseille **10** Marseilles
French Polynesia: **7** Papeete
Georgia: **8** Savannah **9** Brunswick
Georgia, Republic of: **4** Pot'i
Germany: **4** Kiel **5** Emden **6** Bremen, Lübeck, Wismar **7** Hamburg, Rostock **8** Cuxhaven **11** Bremerhaven
Ghana: **4** Tema **5** Accra
Greece: **5** Pylos, Syros, Volos **7** Piraeus
Guatemala: **7** San José **10** Livingston
Haiti: **5** Cayes **10** Cap Haitien
Honduras: **7** La Ceiba **8** Trujillo
India: **3** Goa **4** Puri **5** Marud **6** Bombay, Madras, Mumbai, Old Goa **7** Calicut, Chennai **8** Calcutta **9** Jagannath **10** Trivandrum
Iran: **4** Jask **7** Bushehr
Iraq: **5** Basra
Ireland: **4** Cork **5** Sligo **6** Dingle, Dublin, Galway, Tralee **8** Drogheda, Limerick **9** Waterford **10** Balbriggan
Israel: **4** Acre, Akko, Elat, Yafo **5** Accho, Eilat, Haifa, Jaffa, Joppa **6** Ashdod **8** Ashqelon
Italy: **4** Bari **5** Anzio, Gaeta, Genoa **6** Genova, Naples, Napoli, Pesaro, Rimini, Venice **7** Leghorn, Livorno, Marsala, Messina, Rapallo, Salerno, Taranto, Trieste, Venezia **8** Brindisi, Siracusa, Sorrento, Syracuse
Ivory Coast: **5** Tabou **7** Abidjan
Jamaica: **8** Kingston **10** Montego Bay
Japan: **4** Kobe, Oita **5** Kochi, Osaka, Rumoi, Ujina, Uraga **6** Sasebo **7** Fukuoka **8** Nagasaki, Yokohama **9** Hiroshima
Java: **5** Tegal, Tuban **7** Cilacap, Jakarta **8** Semarang, Surabaya
Jordan: **5** Aqaba, Elath **6** Aelana
Latvia: **4** Riga
Lebanon: **4** Tyre **5** Saida, Sidon **6** Beirut **7** Tripoli
Libya: **6** Tobruk **7** Tripoli **8** Benghazi
Lithuania: **5** Memel **8** Klaipeda
Madagascar: **8** Tamatave
Maine: **7** Belfast **8** Portland
Malaysia: **4** Miri, Weld **5** Pekan **6** Melaka, Pinang **7** Malacca **10** George Town
Massachusetts: **6** Boston **9** Fall River **10** New Bedford
Mauritius: **9** Port Louis
Mediterranean: **4** Gaza, Oran **5** Genoa, Haifa, Jaffa **6** Beirut, Naples, Venice **7** Algiers, Bizerte, Catania, Palermo, Piraeus, Tripoli **8** Benghazi, Port Said **9** Barcelona, Marseille **10** Alexandria, Marseilles
Mexico: **7** Tampico **8** Acapulco, Mazatlán, Veracruz
Minorca: **5** Mahón
Moluccas: **5** Ambon
Montenegro: **5** Kotor
Morocco: **4** Safi, Salé **5** Ceuta **6** Agadir **7** Tangier, Tétouan **10** Casablanca
Mozambique: **5** Beira, Pemba **6** Amelia, Maputo, Xai Xai **11** Porto Amelia
New Hampshire: **10** Portsmouth
New Zealand: **8** Auckland **10** Wellington
Nicaragua: **5** Brito
Nigeria: **5** Lagos **8** Harcourt
Niger mouth: **5** Bonny
North Korea: **4** Yuki **5** Nampo, Unggi **6** Wonsan
Norway: **4** Bodo, Moss **5** Vadso **6** Bergen, Tromso **9** Stavanger, Trondheim **11** Fredrikstad
Oman: **6** Masqat, Muscat **7** Salalah
Pakistan: **5** Pasni **6** Gwadar **7** Karachi
Papua New Guinea: **3** Lea
Peru: **3** Ilo **4** Eten **5** Paita, Pisco **6** Callao
Philippines: **4** Cebu **5** Davao, Laoag **6** Aparri, Cavite, Iloilo, Manila **7** Legaspi **8** Tacloban **9** Zamboanga
Poland: **6** Danzig, Gdansk, Gdynia **7** Stettin **8** Szczecin
Portugal: **4** Faro **5** Porto **6** Oporto **7** Funchal, Setúbal
Puerto Rico: **5** Ponce **7** Arecibo, San Juan **8** Mayagüez
Russia: **6** Vyborg **8** Murmansk **11** Kaliningrad, Vladivostok
Ryukyu: **4** Naha, Nawa
Sakhalin Island: **8** Korsakov
Saudi Arabia: **5** Jedda, Jidda, Yanbu, Yenbo **6** Jeddah, Jiddah, Jubail
Scotland: **3** Ayr **5** Leith, Leven **6** Dundee **7** Glasgow **8** Aberdeen
Sicily: **7** Catania, Marsala, Messina, Palermo **8** Syracuse
Slovenia: **5** Kopar, Koper, Piran
Somalia: **7** Berbera **9** Mogadishu
South Africa: **5** Natal **6** Durban **8** Cape Town
South Carolina: **8** Savannah **10** Charleston
South Korea: **5** Masan, Mokpo, Pusan **6** Inchon **7** Incheon, Masampo

Spain: **4** Vigo **5** Cádiz, Gijón **6** Abdera, Málaga **8** Alicante **9** Algeciras, Barcelona, Cartagena, Las Palmas
Sri Lanka: **7** Colombo **10** Batticaloa
Sumatra: **5** Medan **6** Padang **9** Banda Aceh
Sweden: **4** Umea **5** Gavle, Lulea, Malmö, Pitea, Ystad **8** Göteborg **9** Stockholm **10** Gothenburg **11** Helsingborg
Tanzania: **5** Lindi, Tanga **8** Zanzibar **11** Dar es Salaam
Thailand: **4** Trat **8** Bang Phra
Tunisia: **4** Sfax **5** Gabès **6** Sousse **7** Bizerta, Bizerte
Turkey: **4** Rize **5** Izmir, Sinop **6** Samsun, Smyrna **7** Antalya **8** Istanbul
Ukraine: **5** Kerch, Yalta **6** Odessa **7** Kherson
Vanuatu: **4** Vila **8** Port-Vila
Vietnam: **3** Hue **6** Da Nang **7** Tourane **8** Haiphong, Nha Trang
Virginia: **7** Norfolk **10** Portsmouth
Yemen: **4** Aden **5** Mocha

seaport capital
4 Aden, Apia, Dili, Lomé, Suva **5** Accra, Adana, Dakar, Lagos **6** Banjul, Belize, Bissau, Dublin, Havana, Kuwait, Lisbon, Maputo, Masqat, Muscat, Roseau **7** Algiers, Batavia, Colombo, Jakarta, Moresby, San Juan **8** Castries, Djakarta, Freetown, Hamilton, Helsinki, Honolulu, Kingston, Monrovia, Valletta **9** Mogadishu, Nuku'alofa, Porto-Novo, Reykjavík, Singapore **10** Bridgetown, Daressalem, Libreville, Mogadiscio, Paramaribo **11** Dar es Salaam, Port of Spain **12** Port-au-Prince

sear
3 dry **5** brand, parch, singe **6** burn up, scorch, sizzle **7** shrivel **9** cauterize, dehydrate, desiccate

search
4 beat, comb, grub, hunt, scan, seek **5** chase, check, delve, frisk, grope, quest, rifle, scour **6** ferret, forage, google **7** fossick, hunting, manhunt, pursuit, ransack, rummage, run down **8** finecomb, scavenge, scout out **9** cast about, ferret out **10** scrutinize

searing
3 hot **5** harsh **6** severe **7** blazing, burning, intense **8** scathing **9** agonizing, scorching **10** blistering **12** excruciating

sea robber
5 rover **6** pirate **7** corsair **8** picaroon **9** buccaneer **10** freebooter

seasickness
6 nausea **8** mal de mer

season
4 fall, term, time, yule **5** spice **6** autumn, flavor, harden, pepper, period, school, spring, summer, winter **7** prepare, toughen **8** marinade, marinate **9** acclimate **10** case-harden, discipline **11** acclimatize

seasonable
3 apt **6** timely **7** welcome **9** favorable, opportune, pertinent, well-timed **10** auspicious, convenient, propitious **11** appropriate

seasonal song
5 carol

seasoned
6 inured, mature, tested, versed **7** adapted, matured, veteran **8** flavored, hardened **9** flavorful, practiced **10** acclimated, habituated **11** experienced **12** acclimatized, accomplished

seasoning
3 bay **4** dill, herb, mace, sage, salt **5** anise, basil, chili, clove, cumin, spice, thyme **6** cloves, fennel, garlic, ginger, hyssop, nutmeg, pepper, savory **7** cayenne, chervil, mustard, oregano, paprika, parsley, potherb, saffron **8** allspice, cardamom, cinnamon, rosemary, tarragon, turmeric **9** condiment, coriander

seat
4 base, beam, duff, rear, rest, rump **5** basis, chair, usher **6** behind, bottom, center, settee, tuffet **8** backside, buttocks, derriere **9** fundament, posterior **10** foundation
church: **3** pew
on a camel or elephant: **6** howdah
upholstered: **9** banquette

sea urchin
7 echinus **8** echinoid

seaweed
4 alga, kelp, limu, nori, tang, ulva **5** dulse, fucus, kombu **6** fucoid, wakame **8** sargasso **9** carrageen, Irish moss
product: **4** agar

Sea Wolf, The
author: **6** London (Jack)
captain: **6** Larsen (Wolf)
ship: **5** Ghost

Sebastian
brother: **6** Alonso
sister: **5** Viola

secco
3 dry **8** painting, staccato

secede
4 quit **5** leave **8** separate, withdraw

seclude
4 hide **6** closet, immure, retire, screen **7** confine, enclose, isolate, shut off **8** cloister, separate, withdraw **9** sequester

secluded
6 hidden, remote **7** private, recluse, shut off **8** hermetic, isolated, screened, solitary

9 concealed, reclusive, withdrawn **10** cloistered, tucked away **11** out-of-the-way, quarantined, sequestered
valley: **4** dell, glen

seclusion
6 purdah **7** privacy **8** solitude **9** isolation **10** separation, withdrawal

second
4 wink **5** flash, jiffy, place, trice **6** moment **7** endorse, instant, support **9** twinkling

secondary
3 sub **6** lesser **7** derived **8** borrowed, inferior **9** resultant, tributary **10** collateral, derivative, subsequent **11** subordinate, subservient

secondary school of England
4 Eton **6** Harrow

second-class
6 common **8** inferior, low-grade, mediocre

second-generation Japanese-American
5 nisei

secondhand
4 used, worn **7** derived **8** borrowed **10** derivative

second-rate
4 okay, so-so **8** adequate, mediocre, middling, passable **12** run-of-the-mill

second sight
3 ESP **10** sixth sense **12** clairvoyance

second-string
3 sub **6** backup **9** alternate **10** substitute

secrecy
7 silence, stealth **10** covertness, subterfuge **11** concealment, furtiveness

secret
6 arcane, closet, covert, hidden, occult **7** cryptic, furtive, obscure, sub-rosa **8** abstruse, backdoor, discreet, hermetic, hush-hush, stealthy **9** concealed, recondite **10** classified, restricted, undercover **11** clandestine, out-of-the-way, underhanded **12** confidential, hugger-mugger **13** surreptitious, under-the-table
combining form: **5** crypt, krypt **6** crypto, krypto

secret agent
3 spy **8** emissary

secretary
4 aide, desk **5** clerk **6** scribe **9** assistant **10** amanuensis, escritoire
king's: **10** chancellor

Secretary-General
3 Ban (Ki-moon), Lie (Trygve) **5** Annan (Kofi), Thant (U) **8** Waldheim (Kurt) **12** Boutros-Ghali (Boutros), Hammarskjöld (Dag)

secrete
4 bury, emit, hide **5** cache, exude, plant, stash **6** screen **7** conceal, deposit, emanate

secretion
3 pus **5** mucus

secretive
7 furtive **8** reticent, taciturn **10** backstairs, buttoned-up **11** tight-lipped **12** close-mouthed **13** unforthcoming

secretly
7 sub rosa **9** furtively **10** stealthily

secret police
East Germany: **5** Stasi
Iran: **5** SAVAK
Nazi: **7** Gestapo
Soviet Union: **3** KGB, MGB, MVD **4** NKVD, OGPU **5** Cheka

secret society
3 KKK **4** tong **5** cabal, Mafia, Triad **6** Mau Mau, Yakuza **7** camorra **9** camarilla, Carbonari **10** Cosa Nostra, Freemasons, Ku Klux Klan

sect
4 cult **5** creed, party **7** faction **8** division, religion **12** denomination

sectarian
5 local **8** splinter **9** dissident, heretical, heterodox, parochial **10** provincial, schismatic, unorthodox **13** nonconformist

sectary
5 rebel **7** heretic **8** adherent, disciple, follower, partisan **9** dissenter, dissident **10** schismatic, separatist **13** nonconformist

section
3 cut **4** area, belt, part, unit, zone **5** chunk, piece, slice, tract **6** member, moiety, parcel, region, sector, sphere **7** portion, quarter, segment **8** district, division, locality, precinct **11** subdivision

sector
4 area, zone **7** quarter **8** district, precinct **11** subdivision

secular
3 lay **4** laic **7** earthly, profane, worldly **8** temporal, unsacred **11** nonclerical, terrestrial **12** nonreligious

secure
3 fix, tie **4** bind, fast, firm, gain, land, lock, moor, nail, safe, seal **5** catch, cinch, clamp, cover, fixed, guard, solid, sound, tried **6** anchor, cement, clinch, defend, effect, ensure, fasten, insure, obtain, shield, stable **7** acquire, assured, capture, procure, protect, tie down **8** reliable, sanguine **9** confident, safeguard **10** batten down, bring about **11** established, impregnable

security
4 bail, bond, pawn **5** guard, T-note, token **6** pledge, safety, shield **7** defense, earnest, warrant **8** guaranty, immunity, warranty **9** assurance, guarantee, safeguard, soundness, stability **10** collateral, protection, steadiness

sedate
4 calm **5** grave, sober, staid **6** placid, proper, seemly, serene, steady **7** earnest, serious **8** composed, decorous, tranquil **9** dignified, unruffled **10** sobersided **13** dispassionate, imperturbable

sedative
4 balm **6** downer, Valium **7** calmant, Librium, Miltown, Seconal **8** barbital, hyoscine, Nembutal **9** calmative, soporific **10** depressant **11** barbiturate **12** sleeping pill, tranquilizer **13** tranquillizer

sedentary
4 lazy **6** seated **7** alluvia, settled, sitting **8** inactive **10** stationary

sediment
4 lees, silt **5** dregs, dross **7** bottoms, deposit, grounds, heeltap, residue **8** residuum **9** settlings **11** precipitate
layer: **5** varve

sedition
4 coup **6** mutiny, putsch, revolt, strike **7** protest, treason **8** intrigue, uprising **9** coup d'état, rebellion **10** revolution **12** insurrection

seditious
8 disloyal, factious, mutinous **9** dissident, insurgent **10** rebellious, traitorous **11** treacherous

seduce
4 bait, coax, lure **5** decoy, snare, tempt **6** allure, betray, delude, entice, entrap, lead on, ravish **7** beguile, corrupt, debauch, deceive **8** entrance, inveigle

seducer
4 rake, roué, vamp **7** Don Juan, playboy **8** Casanova, lothario **9** libertine, womanizer **11** philanderer

seduction
4 lure **8** conquest **9** siren song **10** allurement, attraction, ravishment, temptation

seductive
5 siren **8** alluring, magnetic, tempting **9** beguiling **10** attractive, bewitching, enchanting **11** captivating

seductress
4 vamp **5** siren **7** Lorelei **9** temptress **11** femme fatale

sedulous
8 diligent, tireless **9** assiduous, laborious **10** persistent **11** industrious, persevering, unremitting

see
4 espy, gaze, look, mark, peer, scan, view **5** sight, watch **6** behold, descry, divine, notice, take in **7** discern, glimpse, make out, observe, realize **8** envisage, envision, perceive **9** apprehend, ascertain, recognize, visualize

seed
3 pip, sow **4** core, germ **5** brood, grain, issue, ovule, plant, spark, spawn, spore **6** embryo, kernel, notion **7** nucleus, progeny **8** children **9** offspring **11** descendants
aromatic: **5** anise **6** fennel **8** cardamom
coating: **5** testa **6** testae (plural)
covering: **3** bur **4** aril
of a bean: **7** haricot
of a vine: **6** peanut
poisonous: **10** castor bean
poppy: **3** maw
scar: **5** hilum
small: **3** pip
vessel: **3** pod **5** fruit, pyxis **7** silicle, silique
vetch: **4** tare

seedcase
3 pod **4** aril

seedy
5 dingy, faded, mangy, ratty, tired **6** droopy, frowsy, frowzy, shabby, used up, wilted **7** rundown, scruffy, squalid, unkempt, wilting **8** decaying, decrepit, slovenly, tattered **9** neglected, overgrown **10** bedraggled, down-at-heel, threadbare **12** disreputable

see eye to eye
5 agree

seek
3 try **4** fish, hunt, root **5** assay, delve, quest, sniff **6** pursue, strive **7** attempt, inquire, look for, request **8** endeavor, smell out **9** search for, search out, undertake

seem
4 look **5** imply **6** appear, behave **8** resemble

seemly
3 fit **6** decent, proper, suited **7** apropos, correct, fitting **8** becoming, decorous, suitable **9** befitting, congenial, congruous **10** compatible, conforming **11** appropriate, comme il faut

seep
4 drip, leak, ooze, weep **5** bleed, exude, leech, sweat **6** filter, strain **7** diffuse, dribble, trickle **8** transude **9** percolate

seer
5 augur, sibyl **6** oracle **7** diviner, prophet **8** foreseer, haruspex **9** predictor **10** forecaster, foreteller, soothsayer **11** clairvoyant, Nostradamus, vaticinator **13** fortune-teller

seesaw
3 yaw **4** rock, veer **5** lurch, pitch, swing **6** teeter **7** bascule **8** flip-flop **9** alternate, fluctuate, oscillate **11** teeterboard **12** teeter-totter

seethe
3 sop **4** boil, burn, foam, fret, fume, rage, soak, stew **5** churn, erupt, froth, souse, steam, steep **6** bubble, drench, simmer, sizzle **7** bristle, ferment, parboil, smolder **8** saturate, smoulder, waterlog

see-through
5 clear **6** limpid **8** pellucid **11** translucent, transparent
see ya
4 ciao, ta-ta **5** later **6** bye-bye, so long **7** toodles **8** toodle-oo
segment
3 bit, cut, lap, leg **4** clip, part **5** phase, piece **6** divide, member, moiety **7** portion, section **8** division, fragment, separate **10** categorize
___ segno
3 dal
sego, e.g.
4 lily
segregate
6 enisle **7** isolate **8** separate **9** sequester
segregation
9 apartheid, isolation **10** jim crowism, separatism **13** ghettoization
segue
7 proceed **8** continue **10** transition **11** progression
seidel
5 stoup **8** schooner
relative: 5 stein
seine
3 net **5** trawl
Seine tributary
4 Oise, Orne **5** Marne, Yonne
seismologist
7 Richter (Charles)
seize
3 bag, nab **4** glom, grab, take **5** annex, catch, clasp, grasp, usurp, wrest **6** abduct, arrest, clinch, clutch, kidnap, occupy, secure, snatch **7** capture, grapple, impound **8** arrogate, carry off **9** apprehend, sequester **10** commandeer, confiscate **11** appropriate, expropriate
seize the day
9 carpe diem
seizure
3 fit **4** turn **5** spasm, spell, throe **6** access, attack, taking **7** capture **8** paroxysm, takeover **9** breakdown **10** annexation, convulsion, usurpation **12** confiscation
Selassie follower
5 Rasta **11** Rastafarian
seldom
6 hardly, rarely **8** scarcely **10** hardly ever **12** infrequently, occasionally, sporadically
select
3 opt, tap **4** best, cull, fine, pick, rare **5** A-list, cream, elite, prime **6** choice, choose, chosen, culled, opt for, picked **7** favored, pick out **8** screened, superior **9** exclusive, exquisite, preferred, recherché, single out
selection
6 choice **7** culling, excerpt, picking **8** choosing **10** assortment, preference
selective
5 fussy, picky **6** choosy **7** choosey, finicky **10** discerning, particular, scrupulous **11** persnickety
Selena portrayer
3 J.Lo
Selene
4 Luna **6** Hecate **7** Artemis
beloved: 8 Endymion
brother: 6 Helios
father: 8 Hyperion
mother: 4 Thea
sister: 3 Eos
self
3 ego
combining form: 3 aut **4** auto
self-absorbed
4 smug **8** egoistic **9** conceited, egotistic **10** complacent, egocentric **11** egotistical, introverted **12** narcissistic **13** inner-directed
self-acting
9 automatic
self-assertive
4 bold **5** brash, pushy **6** cheeky **7** forward **8** cocksure, militant **9** audacious, obtrusive, officious **10** aggressive **11** impertinent, overweening **12** presumptuous
self-assurance
5 poise **6** aplomb **8** coolness **9** composure, sangfroid **10** confidence, equanimity
self-assured
4 smug **6** poised **8** sanguine **9** confident
self-centered
8 egoistic **9** conceited, egotistic **10** egocentric **11** egotistical **12** narcissistic
self-composed
4 calm **6** poised, serene **7** assured **8** tranquil **9** collected, confident, possessed **10** controlled
self-confidence
5 poise **6** aplomb **9** assurance
self-confident
5 cocky **6** jaunty, poised **7** assured **8** sanguine
self-conscious
4 prim **5** stiff **6** formal, uneasy **7** awkward, stilted, studied **8** affected, mannered **9** contrived, ill at ease **10** artificial
self-contained
6 closed, formal **7** built-in **8** composed, enclosed, reserved, reticent **9** exclusive **10** restrained **11** independent
self-control
7 balance, dignity, reserve **9** restraint, stability,

willpower **10** abstinence, constraint, discipline, temperance **11** forbearance

self-defense art
4 judo **5** kendo **6** aikido, karate, kung fu **7** jujitsu, jujutsu **8** jiujitsu **9** tae kwon do

self-destruction
7 seppuku, suicide **8** felo-de-se, hara-kiri, hari-kari

self-discipline
4 will **8** stoicism **9** willpower **10** abstinence

self-educated
12 autodidactic

self-effacing
3 shy **5** timid **6** modest **7** bashful **8** retiring, sheepish **9** diffident, unassured **11** unassertive

self-esteem
5 pride **6** vanity **7** dignity, egotism **10** narcissism **11** amour propre

self-evident
5 clear, plain **6** patent **7** obvious **8** manifest, palpable **10** prima facie, undeniable **12** demonstrable, unmistakable
truth: 5 axiom

self-explanatory
5 clear, plain **7** evident, obvious **8** manifest **11** perspicuous, transparent

self-governing
7 popular **9** sovereign **10** autonomous, democratic

self-importance
3 ego **5** pride **6** egoism, hubris **7** conceit, egotism **9** arrogance, pomposity, vainglory

self-important
4 smug, vain **6** lordly **7** bloated, haughty, pompous **8** arrogant **9** conceited, egotistic **10** pontifical **11** magisterial, pretentious

self-indulgent
9 libertine, sybaritic **10** hedonistic

self-interest
6 egoism

selfish
6 stingy **8** egoistic **9** egotistic **10** egocentric, ungenerous **11** egomaniacal **12** self-centered **13** self-indulgent

selfishness
6 egoism **10** narcissism

selfless
8 generous **10** altruistic, benevolent, charitable

self-love
6 egoism, vanity **7** conceit, egotism **9** vainglory **10** narcissism **11** amour propre

self-possessed
4 calm **6** poised, serene **7** equable **8** composed, sanguine **9** collected, unruffled **11** unflappable **13** imperturbable

self-proclaimed
8 so-called **9** soi-disant **10** self-styled

Self-Reliance author
7 Emerson (Ralph Waldo)

self-respect
5 pride **7** dignity **11** amour propre

self-restraint
8 chastity, sobriety **9** willpower **10** abnegation, abstention, abstinence, continence, discipline **11** forbearance

self-righteous
5 pious **7** canting, preachy **8** unctuous **9** pharisaic **10** complacent, goody-goody **11** pharisaical **12** hypocritical, pecksniffian **13** sanctimonious

self-sacrificing
8 generous, selfless **9** unselfish **10** altruistic

self-satisfied
4 smug, vain **5** proud **8** priggish **10** complacent

self-seeking
6 greedy **8** egoistic **9** egotistic **10** egocentric **11** egotistical

self-serving
see **self-seeking**

self-starter
7 hustler **8** go-getter

self-styled
7 nominal, would-be **8** so-called **9** soi-disant

self-taught
12 autodidactic

sell
4 hawk, vend **5** trade **6** barter, deal in, hustle, market, peddle, retail, unload **7** auction **8** exchange

seller
6 broker, dealer, hawker, trader, vender, vendor **7** peddler **8** huckster, merchant, retailer, salesman

sell out
4 dump, move **6** betray, turn in, unload **7** deceive **8** inform on **11** double-cross

selvage, selvedge
3 hem **4** edge **6** border

semblance
3 air **4** face, mask, pose, show, veil **5** front, guise, image **6** aspect, facade, simile, veneer **7** analogy, modicum **8** affinity, disguise, likeness, pretense **10** apparition, appearance, false front, masquerade, similarity, similitude, simulacrum **11** countenance

Semele
father: 6 Cadmus
mother: 8 Harmonia
sister: 3 Ino **5** Agave **7** Autonoë
son: 7 Bacchus **8** Dionysus

semi
3 rig **4** demi, half, hemi **5** truck **6** big rig, partly

semicircular church section
4 apse

seminar
5 forum **8** colloquy **10** colloquium, conference, roundtable

Seminole chief
7 Osceola

Semiramis
husband: **5** Ninus
kingdom: **7** Babylon

Semite
3 Jew **4** Arab **6** Hebrew **7** Moabite **8** Akkadian, Assyrian **9** Canaanite **10** Babylonian, Phoenician

Senapo
daughter: **8** Clorinda
kingdom: **8** Ethiopia

senate
7 chamber, council **8** assembly **11** legislature
vote: **3** aye, nay, yea

senator
5 solon **8** lawmaker **10** legislator

send
4 mail, post, ship **5** relay, remit, route **6** export, launch **7** address, advance, airmail, consign, forward, traject **8** dispatch, transmit
back: **6** remand

Sendak book
17 In the Night Kitchen **21** Where the Wild Things Are

send in
5 remit **6** submit

send-up
5 roast, spoof **6** parody, satire **7** lampoon, take-off **9** burlesque **10** caricature, pasquinade

Senegal
capital: **5** Dakar
enclave: **6** Gambia
ethnic group: **5** Serer, Wolof **6** Fulani **7** Malinke
language: **5** Serer **6** French
monetary unit: **5** franc
neighbor: **4** Mali **6** Guinea **10** Mauritania **12** Guinea-Bissau
river: **6** Gambia

senescence
6 old age **8** caducity **11** senectitude

senility
6 dotage **8** dementia

senior
5 doyen, elder, older, prior **7** ancient, doyenne, oldster **8** higher-up, old-timer, superior **10** golden-ager

Sennacherib
domain: **7** Assyria
father: **6** Sargon
kingdom: **7** Assyria
slayer, son: **8** Sharezer **11** Adrammelech

sensation
4 bomb **5** éclat **6** marvel, tingle, wonder **7** feeling, miracle, prodigy, stunner **9** bombshell **10** impression, perception

sensational
3 hot **5** boffo, juicy, lurid **7** tabloid **8** dramatic, exciting, fabulous, glorious, slambang, smashing, stunning **9** hunky-dory, marvelous, thrilling **10** astounding, impressive, incredible, remarkable, scandalous **11** astonishing, extravagant, outstanding, spectacular **12** electrifying

sense
4 feel **5** sight, smell, taste, touch **6** divine, intuit, pick up, reason **7** discern, feeling, hearing, meaning, message, realize **8** consider, judgment, perceive, prudence **9** awareness, intuition **10** anticipate, cognizance, discretion, perception
sixth: **3** ESP

Sense and Sensibility author
6 Austen (Jane)

senseless
4 cold, numb **5** silly **6** absurd, simple, stupid **7** fatuous, foolish, idiotic, moronic, trivial **10** irrational

senselessness
5 folly **7** inanity **8** insanity **9** absurdity, stupidity **12** illogicality

sense of self
3 ego

sense organ
3 ear, eye **4** nose, skin **6** tongue **8** receptor

sensibility
5 taste **7** emotion, feeling, insight **8** judgment, keenness **9** affection, awareness, sensation **11** discernment, penetration **12** appreciation

sensible
4 sage, sane, wise **5** solid, sound **6** astute, shrewd **7** logical, prudent, sapient **8** rational **9** judicious, objective, sagacious **10** reasonable

sensitive
4 keen, sore **5** aware, prone **6** liable, tender, touchy, tricky **7** feeling, nervous **8** delicate, sensible, sentient, ticklish **9** emotional **10** high-strung, perceptive, precarious, responsive **11** susceptible **13** understanding

sensitive plant
6 mimosa
family: **3** pea

sensual
4 lush **6** animal, carnal, earthy **7** fleshly,

mundane, worldly **8** temporal **9** epicurean, luxurious, sybaritic **10** hedonistic, voluptuous

sensuality
4 lust **6** desire, luxury **7** lechery, license **8** hedonism, lewdness, pleasure **9** carnality, depravity, eroticism, prurience **10** debauchery, degeneracy, immorality, indulgence, profligacy, sybaritism **11** dissipation

sensuous
4 lush **6** carnal **7** fleshly **8** luscious **9** epicurean, luxurious, sybaritic **10** hedonistic, voluptuous

sentence
3 rap **4** damn, doom **5** judge **6** dictum, ordain, punish **7** adjudge, condemn, convict, verdict **8** decision, denounce, judgment, penalize **10** punishment

sententious
5 crisp, pithy, terse **7** concise, piquant, pointed **8** eloquent, succinct **10** aphoristic, expressive, moralistic, moralizing

sentient
5 alert, aware, savvy **7** knowing **8** sensible **9** attentive, cognizant, conscious, receptive, sensitive **10** conversant, discerning, perceptive, percipient, responsive **12** appreciative

sentiment
4 view **6** belief **7** emotion, feeling, leaning, opinion, posture **9** affection, sensation **10** conception, conviction, persuasion, propensity **11** disposition, inclination, sensibility

sentimental
5 corny, gooey, gushy, mushy, sappy, soupy, sweet **6** dreamy, drippy, slushy, sticky, sugary, syrupy, tender **7** cloying, gushing, insipid, maudlin, mawkish **8** bathetic, effusive, romantic **9** misty-eyed, nostalgic, schmaltzy **10** idealistic, lovey-dovey, moonstruck, saccharine, soft-boiled

sentimentality
4 mush **8** schmaltz

sentinel
see **sentry**

sentry
5 guard, watch **6** picket **7** lookout **8** sentinel, watchman

separate
4 comb, sort **5** apart, sever, split **6** cut off, detach, divide, single, unique **7** asunder, diverse, divided, divorce, isolate, several, split up, unravel, various **8** detached, discrete, disjoint, distinct, insulate, isolated, solitary, splinter, uncouple **9** different, divergent, extricate, segregate **11** distinctive, distinguish, independent, unconnected **12** disconnected, discriminate **13** differentiate

separation
3 gap **4** rift **5** break, split **6** schism **7** breakup, divorce, parting, rupture, split-up **8** disunion, disunity, division **9** apartheid, dichotomy, partition **11** disjunction, dissolution, segregation **12** dissociation, estrangement **13** disconnection, sequestration

separatism
9 apartheid **11** segregation

separatist
10 schismatic **12** secessionist

sepia
3 ink **5** brown, umber **6** sienna

sepulchral
4 grim **5** bleak, grave **6** dismal, gloomy, solemn, somber **7** doleful **8** funereal, mortuary, tomblike **9** tenebrous

sepulchre
4 tomb **5** grave, vault **9** mausoleum

sequel
3 end **5** close **6** effect, ending, finish, result, upshot **7** closing, outcome **8** epilogue **9** aftermath **10** succession **11** aftereffect, consequence, development, eventuality, progression, termination **12** continuation

sequence
3 row, run, set **4** flow **5** chain, cycle, order, train **6** course, series, string **8** disposal, ordering **9** placement **10** procession, succession **11** arrangement, disposition, progression **12** distribution

sequential
6 serial **9** succedent **10** continuous, succeeding, successive **11** consecutive **12** successional **13** chronological

sequester
4 hide, take **5** annex, seize **6** attach, cut off, enisle **7** impound, isolate, preempt, seclude, secrete **8** accroach, arrogate, cloister, close off, insulate, separate, set apart, withdraw **9** segregate **10** commandeer, confiscate, dispossess **11** appropriate, expropriate

sequoia
7 big tree, redwood **12** coast redwood

seraglio
5 harem
room: **3** oda
resident: **8** odalisc, odalisk **9** odalisque

serape
5 shawl

seraph
5 angel **8** guardian **9** messenger

seraphic
4 pure **7** angelic, sublime **8** beatific, cherubic, ethereal

Serbia
capital: **8** Belgrade
city: **3** Bar, Niš **7** Novi Sad, Pancevo **10** Kragujevac
former leader: **9** Milošević (Slobodan)
monetary unit: **4** euro **5** dinar
neighbor: **6** Bosnia, Kosovo **7** Albania, Croatia, Hungary, Romania **8** Bulgaria **9** Macedonia **10** Montenegro
part of: **7** Balkans
peninsula: **6** Balkan
province: **9** Vojvodina
province, former: **6** Kosovo
river: **4** Sava **6** Danube
sea: **8** Adriatic

Serb or Croat
4 Slav

sere
3 dry **4** arid **5** dried **7** parched, thirsty **8** withered **9** shriveled, unwatered

serenade
7 lullaby **8** shivaree **9** charivari

serendipity
4 luck **6** chance **7** fortune **8** dumb luck, good luck

serene
4 calm **5** quiet, still **6** limpid, placid, poised, sedate **7** halcyon **8** composed, tranquil **9** unruffled **10** untroubled

serenity
4 calm **5** peace **8** calmness, quietude **9** composure, placidity, stillness **10** equanimity **11** contentment, tranquility **12** peacefulness, tranquillity

serf
4 esne, peon **5** churl, helot, slave **6** thrall **7** bondman, villein
freeborn: **7** colonus

sergeant
3 NCO **6** noncom

serial
4 soap **10** sequential, successive **11** consecutive, installment

series
3 row, run, set **4** list, tier **5** chain, range, scale, train **6** catena, column, novena, parade, sequel, string **8** sequence **9** cavalcade, gradation **10** procession, succession **11** progression **12** continuation

serious
4 grim, hard **5** grave, heavy, major, sober, staid, stern, tough **6** intent, sedate, severe, solemn, somber, sombre, steady **7** austere, earnest, intense, pensive, sincere, unfunny, weighty **8** funereal, menacing, resolute, sobering **9** difficult, humorless, important, laborious, strenuous, unamusing **10** determined, formidable, meditative, no-nonsense, poker-faced, purposeful, reflective, sobersided, thoughtful, unhumorous **11** significant, threatening **12** businesslike **13** contemplative

sermon
6 homily, speech, tirade **7** address, lecture, oration **8** harangue **9** preaching **10** preachment **11** exhortation

sermonize
5 orate **6** dilate, exhort, preach **7** dissert, lecture **8** moralize **9** discourse, expatiate, preachify **10** dissertate, evangelize **11** pontificate

serpent
5 fiend, Satan, snake
fabled: **8** basilisk
mythical: **10** cockatrice
sound: **4** hiss

serpentine
4 rock, wily **5** snaky **6** snakey **7** cunning, devious, mineral, sinuous, winding **8** flexuous, tempting, tortuous **9** snakelike **10** circuitous, convoluted, meandering

serrated
7 notched, toothed **8** saw-edged, sawtooth **10** saw-toothed **11** denticulate

servant
4 maid, peon **5** slave, valet **6** butler, flunky, helper, lackey, menial **7** famulus, footman **8** domestic, handmaid, hireling, houseboy **9** attendant **11** chamberlain, chambermaid
India: **4** syce
kitchen: **8** scullion
Wodehouse: **6** Jeeves

serve
3 act, fit, use **4** help, make, play, suit, work **5** avail, nurse, spend, treat **6** foster, handle, wait on **7** advance, benefit, care for, present, promote, provide, satisfy, suffice, work for **8** deal with, function **9** encourage, officiate **10** minister to

service
3 use **4** duty, help, rite **5** favor **6** employ, repair, ritual **7** account, benefit, fitness, liturgy **8** ceremony, courtesy, disposal, maintain **10** active duty, assistance, ceremonial, observance, usefulness **11** maintenance **12** dispensation

serviceable
5 handy, utile **6** decent, usable, useful **7** durable, helpful **8** adequate, suitable **9** efficient, practical **10** acceptable, beneficial, convenient, dependable, functional **11** utilitarian **12** satisfactory

servile
6 abject, craven, humble, menial **7** fawning,

slavish **8** obedient, obeisant **9** groveling **10** obsequious, submissive **11** subservient

servility
7 bondage, helotry, peonage, serfdom, slavery **9** thralldom **11** enslavement

serving
6 dollop **7** helping, portion

servitude
5 labor **6** corvée, thrall **7** bondage, helotry, peonage, serfdom, slavery **9** captivity, indenture, thralldom, villenage **10** subjection **11** enslavement **12** enthrallment

sesame
3 til **4** teel
grass: **4** gama
seed paste: **6** tahini

Sesame Street
human character: **3** Bob, Tom **4** Alan, Gabi, Luis **5** David, Linda, Maria, Miles, Susan **6** Gordon, Savion **8** Mr. Hooper (Harold)
Muppet: **3** Zoe **4** Abby, Bert, Biff, Elmo **5** Count (The), Ernie, Oscar, Sully, Telly **6** Fluffy, Grover, Kermit, Rosita, Slimey, Snuffy **7** Barkley, Big Bird **9** Guy Smiley, Miss Piggy **13** Cookie Monster, Count von Count
puppeteer: **6** Henson (Jim)

sessile
5 fixed **6** rooted **7** settled **8** attached **11** established

session
6 assize, séance **7** hearing, meeting, sitting

set
3 aim, dry, fix, gel, lay, lot, put **4** firm, jell **5** array, batch, bunch, fixed, group, place, put on, ready, rigid, scene **6** belong, harden, impose, placed, rooted, secure, stated **7** arrange, certain, cluster, congeal, decided, deposit, dictate, jellify, lay down, located, prepare, scenery, situate, specify, station **8** prepared, resolute, resolved, situated, solidify, specific **9** confirmed, designate, establish, prescribe, specified, stipulate, tenacious **10** assortment, determined, gelatinize, inflexible, positioned, prescribed, stipulated **11** established, mise-en-scène
a gem: **6** collet
right: **7** redress

set aside
4 void **5** annul **7** discard, dismiss, reserve **8** overrule

set back
4 mire **5** delay **6** detain, hang up, hinder, retard, slow up

setback
4 snag **5** check, hitch **6** defeat, glitch, holdup, rebuff **7** reverse **8** obstacle, reversal **9** hindrance **10** impediment, regression

set down
4 land **5** light, perch, roost **6** alight, record **9** establish, touch down

set fire to
4 burn **5** light, spark **6** ignite, kindle **7** emblaze, inflame **8** enkindle, touch off

set forth
4 cite **5** state **6** adduce, affirm, allege, avouch, depart, embark, launch, submit **7** advance, declare, express, present, proffer, propose, take off **8** proclaim, spell out **9** introduce **10** account for

set free
5 loose **6** redeem, rescue, unbind **7** deliver, manumit, unchain, unloose **8** liberate, unloosen **9** unshackle **10** emancipate

Seth
brother: **4** Abel, Cain
father: **4** Adam
mother: **3** Eve
son: **4** Enos

set out
5 start **6** embark, intend **7** take off **9** undertake

Set
brother: **6** Osiris
mother: **3** Nut
opponent: **5** Horus
victim: **6** Osiris

Seton of literature
4 Anya

settee
4 seat, sofa **5** bench, divan **6** lounge

setting
5 scene **6** milieu **7** context, scenery **8** ambience **10** background **11** mise-en-scène
for a stone: **4** ouch

settle
3 fix, lay, pay, put **4** calm, sink **5** allay, judge, light, pay up, perch, place, quiet, roost, still **6** alight, clinch, decide, soothe, square, verify, wind up **7** arrange, clarify, compose, confirm, dispose, install, mediate, resolve, satisfy, work out **8** colonize, conclude, ensconce, nail down **9** determine, discharge, establish, negotiate, reconcile, touch down

settlement
4 deal, mise **6** colony, hamlet **7** outpost, quietus, village **8** decision **9** agreement, reckoning **10** conclusion, encampment, habitation, resolution **11** arrangement **13** determination
Israeli: **6** moshav

settler
7 pioneer **8** colonist, squatter **9** colonizer

set-to
3 row **4** fray, spat **5** brawl, broil, brush, fight, run-in, scrap **6** affray, blowup, fracas, tussle **7** dispute, quarrel, rhubarb, scuffle **8** argument, skirmish **9** encounter **10** falling-out **11** altercation

set up
4 open **5** erect, found, raise, start **6** create, launch **7** arrange, install **8** assemble, generate, initiate, organize **9** construct, establish, institute, originate

setup
4 plan, trap **5** array, trick **6** layout, scheme, shoo-in **7** pattern, project, setting **8** assembly, carriage, position, slam dunk **9** alignment, apparatus, structure, sure thing **11** arrangement, preparation **12** constitution

Seuss, Dr.
6 Geisel (Theodor)
character: **6** Grinch, Horton, Sam-I-Am, Yertle
work: **11** Cat in the Hat (The) **15** Green Eggs and Ham, Horton Hears a Who, Yertle the Turtle

seven
combining form: **4** hept, sept **5** hepta, septi
group of: **6** heptad **8** hebdomad

sevens
6 fan-tan

seventeen-syllable verse
5 haiku

seventeenth century
8 seicento

sever
3 cut, lop **4** part, rend **5** slice, split **6** cleave, cut off, detach, divide, lop off, sunder **7** break up, divorce **8** amputate, disjoint, separate

several
4 a few, many, some **6** divers, plural, sundry, varied **7** certain, diverse, various **8** assorted, discrete, distinct, manifold, numerous, separate, specific **9** different **10** respective

severe
4 dour, grim, hard **5** acute, grave, harsh, heavy, rigid, sober, stern, tough **6** bitter, brutal, rugged, strict **7** arduous, ascetic, austere, extreme, intense, onerous, serious, weighty **8** exacting, pitiless, rigorous **9** demanding, difficult, laborious, strenuous, stringent, unbending **10** forbidding, implacable, inflexible, iron-willed, oppressive, unyielding **11** disciplined, heavy-handed

severity
5 rigor **7** gravity, urgency **8** exigency, grimness, obduracy, rigidity **9** austerity, harshness, intensity, plainness, privation, restraint, spareness, starkness, sternness **10** strictness, stringency **11** seriousness

sew
4 darn, mend, seam **5** baste **6** needle, stitch, suture

Seward's Folly
6 Alaska

sewer
4 duct **5** ditch, drain **6** tailor **7** cesspit, conduit **8** cesspool, stitcher

sewing
aid: **7** thimble
case: **4** etui
kit: **9** housewife

sewing-machine inventor
5 Elias (Howe)

sew up
3 ice **4** darn, mend, seal **5** patch **6** clinch, decide, ensure, secure, settle, stitch, tailor **7** confirm **8** complete, conclude, finalize, nail down **9** determine

sexless
6 neuter **7** epicene **8** neutered

sex manual
9 Kama-sutra

sexton
6 deacon **9** custodian, sacristan

sexual
4 blue, lewd, racy **6** carnal, erotic, ribald, risqué, smutty **7** obscene **8** venereal **9** salacious **12** pornographic

sexual desire
4 eros, lust **6** libido

sexy
4 blue, racy **5** bawdy, spicy **6** erotic, purple, ribald, risqué, steamy, sultry **7** naughty **8** alluring, off-color, sensuous **9** appealing, salacious, seductive **10** attractive, suggestive

Seychelles
capital: **8** Victoria
island: **4** Mahé **7** La Digue, Praslin
language: **6** Creole, French
monetary unit: **5** rupee

Sganarelle
brother: **6** Ariste
daughter: **7** Lucinde
ward: **7** Leonore **8** Isabelle
wife: **7** Martine

sgt. or cpl.
3 NCO

shabby
5 dingy, dowdy, faded, mangy, ratty, seedy, sorry, tacky, tatty, tired **6** frayed, scurvy, shoddy, sleazy, sordid **7** outworn, rickety, run-down, scrubby, scruffy, squalid, worn-out **8** beggarly, decaying, decrepit, dog-eared, tattered **9** miserable, moth-eaten, neglected, worm-eaten **10** bedraggled,

down-at-heel, ramshackle, threadbare **11** dilapidated **12** deteriorated, disreputable **13** deteriorating, unrespectable

shack
3 cot, hut **4** camp, shed **5** cabin, hovel, lodge **6** shanty **7** cottage

shackle
4 gyve **5** bilbo, chain, leash, strap **6** fetter, hobble, hog-tie, impede, pinion, secure **7** enchain, leg-iron, manacle, trammel **8** handcuff **9** entrammel

shad
7 clupeid, herring

shade
3 bit, hue, tad **4** cast, tint, tone, veil **5** ghost, tinge, trace, umbra **6** awning, darken, nuance, screen **7** dimness, eclipse, phantom, shelter, specter, spectre, umbrage **8** darkness, penumbra, phantasm, tincture **9** gradation, intensity, obscurity **10** apparition **11** distinction
tree: **3** ash, elm, oak **5** maple **6** linden

shadow
3 dim, dog, tag **4** haze, hint, tail **5** cloud, shade, tinge, touch, trace, trail, umbra **6** screen, spirit, wraith **7** eidolon, obscure, phantom, specter, umbrage, vestige **8** overcast, penumbra, phantasm, revenant, tincture **9** inumbrate, overcloud, suspicion **10** apparition, intimation, suggestion **11** adumbration

shadowy
3 dim **4** dark **5** dusky, faint, murky, vague **6** gloomy, shaded **7** ghostly, obscure **9** tenebrous **10** indistinct

shady
4 dark **5** bosky, dusky, fishy **6** purple, shabby, shoddy **7** clouded, dubious, suspect **8** doubtful, screened **9** equivocal, sheltered, uncertain **10** suggestive, suspicious, umbrageous, unreliable **12** disreputable

Shaffer play
5 Equus **7** Amadeus

shaft
3 jab, ray, rod **4** axle, barb, beam, dart, pole, stem **5** arrow, lance, shoot, spear, stalk, thill **6** thrust **7** chimney, spindle **8** short end

shag
3 nap, rug **4** pile **5** chase, fetch **7** thicket, tobacco **9** cormorant

shaggy
5 bushy **7** unkempt **8** uncombed

shake
3 jar, jog, rid **4** deal, jerk, jolt, lose, rock, roil, sway **5** avoid, churn, daunt, elude, jiffy, quake, shock, waver, worry **6** escape, frappe, jiggle, joggle, quaver, quiver, shimmy, shiver, tremor, waggle **7** agitate, shingle, shudder, temblor, tremble, unnerve, vibrate **8** brandish, convulse, unsettle **9** palpitate **10** earthquake

shake down
5 frisk, gouge, screw, wrest, wring **6** coerce, extort, fleece, search **7** squeeze **9** blackmail

shakedown
3 bed **4** test **5** dance, trial **6** pallet, search, tryout **7** pursuit, testing **8** exaction **9** blackmail, extortion **10** inspection

Shaker leader
3 Lee (Ann) **9** Mother Ann

Shakespearean actor
4 Kean (Edmund) **5** Booth (Edwin), Dench (Judi), Evans (Maurice), Terry (Ellen) **6** Irving (Henry), Jacobi (Derek) **7** Branagh (Kenneth), Burbage (Richard), Garrick (David), Gielgud (John), Olivier (Laurence), Siddons (Sarah) **8** Ashcroft (Peggy), Macready (William), McKellen (Ian), Redgrave (Michael), Scofield (Paul) **9** Barrymore (Ethel, John, Lionel, Maurice) **10** Richardson (Ralph)

Shakespeare, William
4 bard
character: **3** Hal **4** Doll (Tearsheet), Hero, Iago, Kent, Lear, Puck **5** Ariel, Edgar, Feste, Harry, Percy (Henry), Poins (Ned), Regan, Romeo, Timon, Titus (Andronicus), Viola **6** Antony, Banquo, Bottom, Brutus, Caesar, Cassio, Duncan, Edmund, Emilia, Fabian, Hamlet, Hecate, Hermia, Jaques, Juliet, Oberon, Olivia, Orsino, Pistol, Portia **7** Antonio, Caliban, Cassius, Claudio, Fleance, Goneril, Horatio, Hotspur, Jessica, Laertes, Lavinia, Macbeth, Macduff, Malcolm, Miranda, Ophelia, Orlando, Othello, Perdita, Shylock, Sir Toby (Belch), Theseus, Titania, Troilus **8** Bassanio, Beatrice, Benedick, Claudius, Cordelia, Cressida, Dogberry, Falstaff (Sir John), Gertrude, Hermione, Lysander, Malvolio, Mercutio, Mortimer, Pericles, Polonius, Prospero, Rosalind **9** Cleopatra, Cymbeline, Demetrius, Desdemona, Hippolyta, Katherine, Petruchio, Sir Andrew (Aguecheek), Vincentio **10** Fortinbras, Holofernes **11** Bolingbroke, John of Gaunt, Lady Macbeth, Lady Macduff, Peter Quince **13** Queen Gertrude, Queen Margaret
contemporary: **6** Jonson (Ben) **7** Marlowe (Christopher)
forest: **5** Arden
mother: **9** Mary Arden
play: **6** Hamlet, Henry V **7** Henry IV, Henry VI, Macbeth, Othello, Tempest (The) **8** King John, King Lear, Pericles **9** Cymbeline, Henry VIII, Richard II **10** Coriolanus, Richard III **11** As You Like It, Winter's Tale (The) **12** Julius Caesar, Twelfth Night **13** Timon of Athens **14** Comedy of Errors (The), Romeo and Juliet **16** Love's

Labour's Lost, Merchant of Venice (The), Taming of the Shrew (The) **17** Measure for Measure **18** Antony and Cleopatra **19** Much Ado About Nothing **20** All's Well That Ends Well, Midsummer Night's Dream (A)
theater: **5** Globe
wife: **12** Anne Hathaway

Shakespearean
king: **4** Lear
lover: **5** Romeo **6** Juliet
sprite: **4** Puck **5** Ariel
villain: **4** Iago

Shakespeare's river
4 Avon

shaky
4 weak **6** infirm, unsure, wobbly **7** aquiver, dubious, jittery, quaking, rackety, rickety, suspect, trembly, unsound **8** doubtful, insecure, rachitic, unstable, unsteady, wavering **9** quivering, tottering, trembling, tremulous, uncertain, unsettled **10** indecisive, precarious, rattletrap, unreliable **11** problematic, vacillating

shale
4 rock **5** slate

shallot
4 herb **5** onion **10** green onion

shallow
4 idle, vain **5** petty, shoal **7** cursory, sketchy, trivial **8** trifling **9** depthless, frivolous **11** perfunctory, superficial
opposite: **4** deep **8** profound

shallows
6 lagoon, shoals

Shallum
father: **5** Shaul, Zadok **6** Jabesh, Josiah, Sismai, Tikvah **8** Colhozeh, Naphtali **9** Hallohesh
mother: **6** Bilhah
nephew: **8** Jeremiah
slayer: **7** Menahem
son: **6** Mibsam **7** Hilkiah **8** Maaseiah
victim: **9** Zechariah

shalom
5 peace

sham
3 act, ape **4** fake, hoax, mock **5** bluff, bogus, bunco, cheat, dummy, false, farce, feign, fraud, phony, pseud, put on, spoof **6** deceit, ersatz, facade, fakery, forged, invent, pseudo **7** assumed, feigned, forgery, imitate, mislead, mockery, pretend **8** affected, flimflam, simulate, spurious, travesty **9** brummagem, burlesque, deception, hypocrisy, imitation, imposture, pinchbeck, simulated **10** artificial, caricature, false front, fictitious, fraudulent, sanctimony, substitute **11** counterfeit, make-believe **12** pecksniffery
combining form: **5** pseud **6** pseudo

shaman
6 healer, priest, wizard **7** diviner **8** conjurer, conjuror, magician, sorcerer **9** enchanter, priestess **10** high priest, soothsayer **11** faith healer, necromancer, thaumaturge, witch doctor

Shamash
6 sun-god
father: **3** Sin
sister: **6** Ishtar
wife: **3** Aya

shamble
see **shuffle**

shambles
4 mess **5** chaos **6** jumble, muddle **8** disarray, disorder, wreckage **9** confusion

shame
4 pity **5** abash, guilt, odium **6** infamy, stigma **7** chagrin, mortify, obloquy, remorse, scandal **8** disgrace, dishonor, ignominy **9** disrepute, embarrass, humiliate, ill repute **10** opprobrium **11** humiliation **12** self-reproach **13** embarrassment, mortification

shamefaced
7 abashed **8** blushing, sheepish **9** mortified **10** humiliated **11** crestfallen, embarrassed

shameless
6 arrant, brazen, wanton **7** blatant, immoral **8** depraved, flagrant, immodest, impudent **9** abandoned, bald-faced, barefaced, dissolute, unabashed **10** outrageous, profligate, unblushing **11** brazen-faced, disgraceful **12** presumptuous

Shammah
brother: **5** David
father: **4** Agee **5** Jesse, Reuel
grandfather: **4** Esau **7** Ishmael
son: **7** Jonadab **8** Jonathan

Shammua
father: **5** David, Galal **6** Bilgah, Zaccur
mother: **9** Bathsheba
son: **4** Abda

shamrock land
4 Eire, Erin **7** Ireland

shamus
3 cop, tec **4** dick, tail **6** copper, shadow, sleuth **7** gumshoe **8** flatfoot, sherlock **9** constable, detective, operative, policeman **10** private eye **12** investigator **13** police officer

shanghai
6 abduct, hijack, kidnap

Shangri-la
5 Tibet **6** utopia **7** arcadia **8** paradise **9** Cockaigne, fairyland **10** wonderland

shank
3 leg **4** shin, stem **5** stalk, tibia

Shankar, Ravi
instrument: 5 sitar
music: 4 raga

shanty
3 cot, hut 4 camp, shed 5 cabin, hovel, lodge, shack 7 cottage

shape
3 fit 4 case, cast, form, mold, plan, trim 5 forge, frame, state, whack 6 aspect, devise, fettle, figure, kilter, repair, sculpt, tailor, work up 7 contour, fitness, outline, pattern, profile 8 assemble 9 condition, construct, fabricate, semblance 10 appearance, silhouette 12 conformation 13 configuration
combining form: 5 morph 6 morpho
dark: 6 shadow 10 silhouette

shapeable
6 pliant, supple 7 ductile, plastic, pliable 8 flexible 9 tractable

shapeless
8 inchoate, unformed 9 amorphous

shapely
4 trim 5 buxom 9 Junoesque 10 curvaceous, statuesque, well-turned 11 clean-limbed

shar-___
3 pei

shard
4 chip 5 chunk, scale, scrap, shell 6 sliver 7 elytron 8 carapace, fragment

share
3 cut, lot 4 part, pool 5 chunk, claim, quota, slice, stake 6 divide, parcel, ration 7 dole out, give out, helping, partake, portion, prorate, quantum 8 dispense, fraction, interest, quotient 9 allotment, allowance, apportion 10 experience, percentage, proportion 11 participate

shared
5 joint 6 common, mutual, public 8 communal, conjoint, conjunct 9 concerted 10 collective 11 cooperative

Sharezer
father, victim: 11 Sennacherib

Sharif of film
4 Omar

shark
5 cheat 8 swindler
kind: 4 gata, mako, sand, tope 5 nurse, tiger 7 basking, dogfish, leopard 8 mackerel, maneater, thresher 9 porbeagle 10 great white, hammerhead
skin: 8 shagreen

Sharon of Israel
5 Ariel

sharp
3 sly 4 acid, keen, tony, trig 5 acerb, acrid, acute, alert, canny, crisp, honed, quick, slick, smart, swank 6 astute, biting, brainy, bright, clever, jagged, nimble, peaked, shrewd, shrill, snappy, snazzy 7 caustic, dashing, intense, pointed, prickly, stylish, whetted 8 clean-cut, clear-cut, incisive 9 brilliant, ingenious, knifelike, vitriolic 10 astringent, perceptive 11 intelligent, penetrating, quick-witted, resourceful

sharpen
4 edge, file, hone, whet 5 grind, strop

sharper
5 cheat 6 con man 7 diddler 8 chiseler, swindler 9 defrauder, fraudster, trickster 10 mountebank 12 double-dealer

sharp-eyed
4 keen 5 alert 8 vigilant, watchful 9 attentive, observant 10 discerning, perceptive

sharpie
see **sharper**

sharpness
4 edge 6 acuity, acumen 9 precision

sharp ridge
5 arête

sharpshooter
6 sniper 7 deadeye 8 marksman

sharp-sighted
8 hawk-eyed, lynx-eyed 9 eagle-eyed

sharp-tongued
4 tart 5 acerb 6 barbed, biting 7 acerbic, caustic, mordant 8 sardonic

sharp-witted
4 keen 5 acute, canny, quick, smart 6 astute, clever, shrewd 11 intelligent

shatter
4 dash 5 break, burst, crush, smash 6 shiver 8 demolish, fragment, splinter 9 pulverize 10 annihilate 11 fragmentize 12 disintegrate

shatterable
7 brittle, fragile 9 breakable, frangible

shave
3 cut 4 clip, crop, pare, peel, skim, trim 5 lower, plane, prune, shear, skive 6 barber, cut off, deduct, reduce, scrape, sliver 7 cut back, whittle 8 mark down

shaver
3 boy, kid, lad, tad 4 tike, tyke 5 child, razor 6 barber, laddie, squirt 9 stripling, youngster

shawl
4 wrap 5 fichu, manta 6 afghan, chador, serape 7 tallith 8 mantilla

shawm's descendant
4 oboe

Shawnee chief
8 Tecumseh, Tecumtha 9 Cornstalk

Shaw play
6 Geneva **7** Candida **9** Pygmalion, Saint Joan **11** Misalliance **12** Major Barbara **13** Arms and the Man

shay
6 chaise **8** carriage

she
French: **4** elle
Italian: **3** lei
Spanish: **4** ella

shear
3 cut, mow **4** clip, crop, pare, snip, trim **5** prune, shave, skive **6** barber

Shearer of early film
5 Norma

shears
8 scissors

shearwater
4 bird **6** petrel **7** skimmer

sheath
4 case, skin **5** cover **7** holster **8** scabbard

sheathe
4 case, clad, face, side, skin, wrap **5** cover, panel **6** encase, jacket

Sheba
father: **6** Bichri
queen: **6** Balkis

shebang
4 mess **6** affair **7** schmear **8** business, caboodle **9** ball of wax, enchilada

shed
3 hut **4** cast, doff, drop, emit, lose, molt **5** exude, hovel, hutch, scrap, shack, stall **6** divest, lean-to, reject, slough **7** cast off, diffuse, discard, radiate, take off **8** jettison, throw out **9** throw away

sheen
5 glaze, gleam, glint, gloss, shine **6** finish, luster, lustre, polish **7** burnish, glitter, shimmer **8** radiance **9** shininess **10** brightness

sheeny
see **shiny**

sheep
5 ovine
breed: **5** Tunis **6** Dorper, Dorset, Exmoor, Merino, Navajo, No-Tail, Oxford, Panama, Romney **7** Cheviot, Colbred, Karakul, Lincoln, Ryeland, Suffolk **8** Columbia, Cotswold, Polwarth **9** Hampshire, Leicester, Montadale, Southdown **10** Corriedale, Debouillet **11** Rambouillet
coat: **4** wool **6** fleece
disease: **3** gid, orf
female: **3** ewe
genus: **4** Ovis
male: **3** ram **6** wether
meat: **6** mutton
relating to: **5** ovine
Scottish: **9** blackface
shelter: **4** cote, fold
sound: **5** bleat
tender: **8** shepherd
wild: **3** sha **5** urial **6** aoudad, argali, bharal, oorial **7** bighorn, mouflon
young: **4** lamb

sheepish
4 meek **5** timid **7** abashed, ashamed, bashful **8** timorous **9** diffident **10** shamefaced **11** embarrassed

sheepskin
4 roan **6** mouton **7** diploma **9** parchment
prepare: **3** taw

sheer
4 pure, skew, thin, turn, veer **5** filmy, gauzy, steep, utter **6** abrupt, arrant, flimsy, simple, swerve **7** chiffon, deflect, deviate, perfect, unmixed **8** absolute, complete, gossamer, outright **9** out-and-out, unalloyed, undiluted **10** diaphanous, see-through **11** precipitate, precipitous, transparent, unmitigated
fabric: **4** lawn, pina **5** tulle, voile **7** batiste

sheet
3 ply **4** film, leaf, page, sail, slab **5** cover, linen, paper **6** lamina, veneer **8** membrane **9** newspaper

sheet ___
3 ice **4** film **5** glass, metal, music **6** anchor

shelf
3 hob **4** bank, edge, reef, sill **5** ledge, shoal **6** mantel **7** counter **8** sandbank
Antarctic: **4** Ross

shell
3 pod **4** boat, bomb, case, hull, husk, rake, skin **5** blitz, conch, shuck **6** pepper **7** bombard, capsule, grenade, mollusc, mollusk **8** carapace **9** cannonade, cartridge
defective: **3** dud
explosive: **4** bomb
layer: **5** nacre
ornamental: **6** cowrie
study: **10** conchology

shellac
4 beat, drub, flay, lick, rout, trim, whap, whip, whop, whup **5** resin, smear, whomp **6** defeat, thrash **7** clobber, smother, trounce, varnish **8** lambaste, vanquish

Shelley, Percy Bysshe
friend: **5** Byron (Lord), Keats (John)
poem: **5** Cloud (The) **7** Adonais, Alastor **8** Queen Mab **10** Ozymandias, To a Skylark **16** Ode to the West Wind
wife: **4** Mary

shellfish
4 clam, crab **5** conch, cowry, prawn, snail, whelk **6** cockle, limpet, mussel, oyster, quahog, triton **7** abalone, crawdad, geoduck, lobster, mollusc, mollusk, scallop **8** barnacle, crayfish, escargot **10** crustacean, periwinkle

shell out
3 pay **4** give **5** spend **8** fork over, hand over

shell-shaped
6 spiral **9** cochleate

shelter
3 den, hut, lee **4** cote, fold, hide, port, roof, shed, tent **5** bower, cloak, cover, haven, house, shack **6** asylum, burrow, covert, defend, harbor, refuge, shield, spital **7** defense, foxhole, hideout, hospice, housing, lodging, pillbox, protect, retreat **8** hideaway, hidy-hole, security **9** dwellings, hermitage, hidey-hole, sanctuary
for aircraft: **6** hangar
for cows: **4** barn, byre

sheltered
4 alee

shelve
4 dish, drop, stay, tilt **5** defer, delay, slope, stock, waive **6** freeze, give up, hold up, put off **7** hold off, suspend **8** hold over, mothball, postpone, prorogue, set aside

Shem
brother: **3** Ham **7** Japheth
father: **4** Noah

Shema's father
4 Joel **6** Hebron

Shemida's father
6 Gilead

shenanigan
4 dido, lark **5** antic, caper, prank, stunt, trick **6** frolic **8** escapade, mischief **10** tomfoolery **11** monkeyshine

Sheol
see **hades**

shepherd
4 lead, show, tend **5** guide, pilot, route, steer, watch **6** direct, escort, leader **7** conduct **8** guardian
dog: **6** collie **12** border collie
stick: **5** crook, staff

Sheridan, Richard Brinsley
character: **8** Bob Acres, Malaprop (Mrs.) **10** Lady Teazle **13** Lady Sneerwell, Lydia Languish
play: **6** Critic (The), Rivals (The) **7** Pizarro **16** School for Scandal (The)

sheriff
5 reeve **6** lawman **7** marshal, officer
aide: **6** deputy

sherlock
4 dick, tail **5** snoop **6** shadow, shamus, sleuth **7** gumshoe **8** hawkshaw **9** detective **10** private eye **12** investigator

Sherlock Holmes
address: **11** Baker Street
creator: **5** Doyle (Arthur Conan)
sidekick: **6** Watson (Dr.)

sherry
4 fino, wine **7** oloroso **10** manzanilla **11** amontillado

shibboleth
3 saw, tag **5** axiom, maxim **6** byword, cliché, phrase, saying, slogan, truism **7** bromide **8** banality, chestnut, password, prosaism **9** catchword, platitude, watchword **11** catchphrase, commonplace

shield
4 egis, fend, roof, ward **5** aegis, armor, cover, guard, haven, house, pavis **6** buffer, defend, harbor, screen, secure **7** buckler, bulwark, defense, protect, shelter **8** defilade, insulate **9** safeguard **10** escutcheon
band: **4** fess
bullfighter's: **9** burladero
light: **5** targe
part: **4** boss, umbo **7** bordure
Roman: **7** testudo

shield-like
7 peltate

shift
3 yaw **4** bend, bout, move, stir, tack, time, tour, turn, vary, veer **5** alter, budge, get by, spell, stint, trick **6** change, make do, manage, remove, resort, swerve **7** chemise, deviate, replace, shuffle, stopgap **8** get along, relocate, resource, transfer **9** deviation, expedient, fluctuate **10** alteration, changeover, conversion, transition **11** fluctuation

shiftless
4 idle, lazy **5** inept **8** feckless, indolent, slothful **11** inefficient

shifty
3 sly **4** foxy, wily **5** cagey, lying, shady, slick **6** crafty, sneaky, tricky **7** cunning, devious, elusive, evasive, furtive **8** guileful, slippery, sneaking **9** conniving, deceitful, deceptive, dishonest, insidious, underhand **10** inconstant, untruthful **11** duplicitous, underhanded **12** equivocating

shill
5 blind, decoy, pitch **6** capper **8** promoter **10** accomplice, sales pitch

shillelagh
3 bat **4** club, cosh, mace **5** baton, billy, stick **6** cudgel **8** bludgeon **9** bastinado, billy club, blackjack, truncheon **10** nightstick

shilling
3 bob

shilly-shally
5 fudge, hedge, stall, waver 6 dawdle, dither, waffle 7 whiffle 8 hesitate 9 temporize, vacillate 11 prevaricate 12 tergiversate

Shimea
brother: 5 David
father: 5 David, Jesse
son: 7 Jonadab 8 Jonathan

shimmer
5 flash, gleam, glint, sheen 6 luster, lustre 7 glimmer, glisten, glitter, spangle, sparkle, twinkle 9 coruscate 11 coruscation, scintillate 13 scintillation

shimmy
5 dance, shake 6 quiver, shiver, tremor 7 chemise, shudder, tremble, vibrate 9 vibration

shin
3 run 4 dash 5 scoot, tibia 6 scurry, sprint 7 scamper

shinbone
5 tibia

shindig
4 ball, bash, fête, gala 5 binge, dance, party, revel 6 affair, frolic 7 blowout 8 wingding

shine
3 ray, rub 4 beam, buff, burn, glow 5 blaze, excel, flare, flash, glare, glaze, gleam, glint, gloss, sheen 6 luster, lustre, polish 7 burnish, glimmer, glisten, glitter, radiate, shimmer, sparkle, twinkle 9 luminesce 10 incandesce

shiner
4 fish 8 black eye, cyprinid

shingle
5 beach, coast, shore 7 haircut, overlap, overlay 8 detritus 9 signboard

Shinto gateway
5 torii

shiny
6 agleam, bright, glossy 7 fulgent, radiant 8 dazzling, gleaming, lustrous, polished 9 burnished, effulgent 10 glistening

ship
4 boat, send 5 craft, remit, route 6 export 7 consign, forward, freight 8 dispatch, transfer, transmit
ancient: 6 bireme, galley 7 galleon, trireme
attendant: 7 steward
beam: 7 keelson
berth: 4 dock, slip
boat: 6 dinghy 7 lighter
body: 4 hull
cabin: 9 stateroom
commercial: 5 liner, oiler 6 argosy, tanker, trader 9 freighter
crew member: 4 hand, mate 6 sailor
deck: 4 boat, main, poop 5 orlop 6 bridge 10 forecastle
fishing: 6 lugger 7 trawler
fleet: 6 armada
floor: 4 deck
front: 3 bow 4 prow, stem 8 cutwater
hoister: 4 boom 5 davit 7 capstan
Jason's: 4 Argo
kitchen: 6 galley
left side: 4 port 8 larboard
military: 6 cutter, PT boat 7 carrier, cruiser 9 destroyer, submarine
officer: 4 mate 5 bosun 6 purser 7 captain, steward 9 boatswain
of 1492: 4 Niña 5 Pinta 10 Santa Maria
part: 3 bow 4 beam, deck, helm, hold, hull, keel, mast, skeg, stem 5 bilge, hatch, stern 6 bridge, rudder 7 scupper 8 foredeck
partition: 7 bulwark 8 bulkhead
personnel: 4 crew
platform: 9 crow's nest, gangboard, gangplank
poetic: 4 bark
post: 4 bitt, mast 7 bollard
prison: 4 brig
projection: 7 sponson
rear: 5 stern
record: 3 log
right side: 9 starboard
room: 4 brig 5 cabin 6 galley
rope: 4 line 5 sheet 7 halyard
sailing: 3 hoy 4 brig, dhow, prau, proa, yawl 5 ketch, sloop, xebec, yacht 6 lugger 7 caravel, galleon 8 schooner
steerer: 4 helm 6 tiller
storage area: 4 hold
to the rear of: 3 aft 5 abaft 6 astern
valve: 7 seacock
window: 4 port 8 porthole

shipment
5 cargo 6 lading 7 freight, payload 8 delivery 11 consignment

Ship of Fools author
6 Porter (Katherine Anne)

Shipping News author
6 Proulx (Annie)

ships, group of
4 navy 5 fleet, flota 6 armada 8 flotilla

shipshape
4 neat, snug, tidy, trig, trim 7 orderly 11 spic-and-span, uncluttered 12 spick-and-span

shipworm
6 teredo

shire
5 horse 6 county 8 district 10 draft horse

Shire of Rocky
5 Talia

shirk
4 duck, lurk, shun 5 avoid, creep, dodge, elude, evade, skulk, slink, sneak, steal 8 sidestep

shirker
see **slacker**

shirt
3 tee 4 polo, sark 5 dress, kurta, sport 6 blouse, jersey 9 guayabera

shirty
3 mad 5 angry, cross, irate 6 heated, ireful 7 annoyed 8 choleric, incensed, offended 9 indignant, irritated

shiv
5 blade, knife, shank 6 dagger 8 stiletto

Shiva
consort: 3 Uma 4 Devi, Kali 5 Durga, Gauri 6 Ambika, Chandi 7 Parvati 9 Haimavati
son: 6 Ganesa, Ganesh, Skanda 7 Ganesha 10 Karttikeya

shiver
5 burst, quake, shake, smash 6 quaver, quiver, tremor 7 shatter, shudder, tremble, twitter 8 fragment, splinter, splitter

shlep
see **schlep**

shoal
3 bar 4 bank, hook, reef, spit 6 school 7 barrier, sandbar, shallow, tombolo 8 sandbank, sand reef

shoat
3 hog, pig 4 gilt 5 swine 6 piglet, porker

Shobab
father: 5 Caleb, David
mother: 6 Azubah 9 Bathsheba

shock
3 jar 4 blow, bump, daze, jolt, pile, rick, stun 5 amaze, clash, crash, mound, quake, shake, sheaf 6 appall, dismay, impact, insult, offend, trauma, tremor 7 astound, disgust, horrify, outrage, stagger, startle, stupefy, temblor 8 astonish, surprise 9 collision, electrify 10 concussion, earthquake, percussion, scandalize, traumatize 11 flabbergast 12 stupefaction

shock absorber
6 spring 7 dashpot, snubber

shocker
4 blow 7 stunner 8 surprise, thriller 9 bombshell, eye-opener, sensation 11 showstopper

shocking
5 awful, lurid 6 horrid 7 glaring, heinous 8 dreadful, horrible, horrific, shameful, terrible 9 appalling, atrocious, frightful, monstrous, revolting, traumatic 10 outrageous, scandalous 11 disgraceful, distressing, unspeakable

shoddy
4 base, mean, poor 5 cheap, dingy, gaudy, junky, seedy, tacky, tatty 6 cheesy, common, flimsy, paltry, shabby, sleazy, tawdry, trashy 7 run-down, scruffy 8 inferior, rubbishy, shameful 9 makeshift 10 broken-down, down-at-heel, jerry-built, jury-rigged 11 dilapidated, disgraceful, ignominious, pretentious 12 dishonorable, disreputable 13 discreditable

shoe
3 pac 4 boot, clog, geta, mule, pump 5 sabot, wedge 6 brogan, brogue, buskin, gaiter, galosh, gillie, kiltie, loafer, oxford, patten, sandal, slip-on, wedgie 7 chopine, ghillie, slipper, sneaker, wingtip 8 balmoral, Mary Jane, moccasin, platform, plimsoll 9 slingback 10 clodhopper, espadrille
armored: 8 solleret
athlete's: 7 sneaker
form: 4 last, tree
kind: 8 elevator, open-toed 10 high-heeled
part: 3 tip, toe 4 arch, heel, lace, lift, sole, vamp 5 cleat, shank, upper 6 box toe, collar, foxing, insole, lining, throat, tongue 7 counter, outsole 8 backstay
protective: 6 galosh, rubber
shiner: 6 polish 9 bootblack
wooden: 5 sabot 7 chopine

shoelace tip
5 aglet

shoeless
6 unshod 8 barefoot 9 discalced

shoemaker
7 cobbler
patron saint: 7 Crispin
Scottish: 6 souter
tool: 3 awl

Shogun author
7 Clavell (James)

Sholem Aleichem character
5 Golde, Tevye, Yente

shoo
3 git 4 scat 5 drive, leave, scare, scram, split 6 beat it, begone, bug off, skidoo 7 buzz off, get lost, skiddoo, vamoose 8 clear out 9 skedaddle, take a hike 10 hit the road

shoo-in
6 winner 7 sure bet 8 slam dunk 9 sure thing

shoot
3 bud, fly, gun, ray 4 beam, bolt, dart, dash, fire, lash, race, rush, sail, scud, skim, spew, tear 5 blast, chase, fling, photo, plink, shaft, skirr, snipe, spurt 6 branch 7 project 9 discharge 10 photograph

shoot down
3 pan, rap 4 bash, kill, slam 5 blast, decry, knock, scorn, trash 6 assail, deride, dump

on, reject, squash **7** deflate, squelch, torpedo **8** bad-mouth, belittle, derogate, discount, disprove, puncture, ridicule **9** discredit

shooting
4 keen **5** acute, sharp **7** gunplay **8** piercing, stabbing

shooting star
6 meteor **8** fireball

shoot up
4 soar **6** inject, rocket **7** burgeon **8** mushroom **9** skyrocket

shop
4 hunt **5** store **6** browse, market, outlet, search **8** boutique, emporium, showroom

shoplift
3 bag, cop **4** lift, palm **5** boost, filch, pinch, steal, swipe **6** pilfer, rip off, snitch

shop owner
8 merchant, retailer **9** tradesman **10** proprietor

shopworn
5 banal, faded, stale, tired, trite **6** cliché, soiled **7** clichéd **8** overused **9** hackneyed **10** threadbare

shore
4 bank, prop, stay **5** beach, brace, brink, coast **6** bear up, strand, uphold **7** bolster, shingle, support, sustain **8** buttress, littoral, seacoast **9** coastland, coastline, riverbank, riverside, waterside **10** embankment, waterfront

shorebird
see at **bird**

short
3 shy **4** curt **5** blunt, brief, crisp, scant, skimp, spare, squat, stint, terse **6** abrupt, meager, meagre, scanty, scarce, skimpy, stubby **7** brusque, compact, concise, lacking, laconic, stunted, wanting **8** abridged, succinct **9** deficient **10** inadequate **11** abbreviated **12** insufficient
jacket: **4** Eton
poem: **5** haiku

shortage
4 lack **5** pinch **6** dearth, ullage **7** deficit, paucity **8** scarcity **10** deficiency, inadequacy, scantiness

shortcoming
3 bug, sin **4** flaw, lack **5** fault, lapse **6** defect **7** demerit, failing **8** weakness **9** weak point **10** deficiency **12** imperfection

shortcut
5 macro **6** bypass, cutoff

shorten
3 bob, cut **4** clip, dock **5** elide, slash **6** lessen, reduce, shrink **7** abridge, curtail, cut back, cut down, excerpt **8** boil down, compress, condense, contract, decrease, diminish, minimize, truncate **10** abbreviate

shorthand
11 stenography
method: **5** Gregg **6** Pitman

shorthanded
7 wanting **11** undermanned **12** understaffed

short-lived
5 brief **7** passing **8** fleeting **9** ephemeral, fugacious, momentary, temporary **10** evanescent, transitory

shortly
4 anon, soon **6** pronto **7** briefly, by and by, in brief, quickly, tersely **8** directly **9** concisely, presently **10** succinctly **11** laconically

shortness
7 brevity **9** concision

shortsighted
6 myopic **8** heedless, reckless **10** astigmatic

short-spoken
4 curt **5** bluff, blunt, brief, gruff, terse **6** abrupt, crusty, snippy **7** brusque **8** snippety

short-tempered
5 testy **6** touchy **7** prickly **8** snappish **9** irascible, irritable

Shoshone chief
8 Washakie **9** Pocatello

shot
3 nip, pop, try **4** dose, dram, drop, jolt, stab **5** blast, break, carom, crack, fling, guess, ounce, photo, range, reach, snort, swipe, whack, whirl **6** chance, effort, ruined, stroke **7** attempt, snifter, worn-out **8** marksman, occasion **9** discharge **11** opportunity

shoulder
4 bear, berm, edge, push, side **5** elbow, press, shove **6** assume, hustle, jostle, take on **8** bulldoze
bone: **7** scapula **8** clavicle
covering: **6** tippet **8** scapular
muscle: **7** deltoid
relating to: **7** humeral **8** scapular

shoulder blade
7 scapula

shout
3 cry **4** bark, bawl, bray, call, roar, yell **5** blare, whoop **6** bellow, clamor, holler, scream **7** exclaim **10** vociferate

shove
3 dig, jab, jam **4** cram, prod, push **5** crowd, drive, elbow, press **6** jostle, propel, thrust **8** bulldoze, shoulder

shovel
3 dig **4** grub **5** delve, scoop, spade **6** dig out, dredge, trowel **8** excavate

shoveler
4 duck **9** broadbill

shove off
3 git **4** blow, exit **5** leave, scoot, scram, split **6** beat it, cut out, decamp, depart, move on **7** move out, pull out, vamoose **8** clear out, run along

show
4 fair, film, lead, pomp, sham **5** array, flick, front, guide, mount, movie, offer, prove, revue, sport, stage **6** appear, arrive, direct, effect, evince, expose, flaunt, lay out, parade, reveal, set out, submit, unveil **7** conduct, display, divulge, exhibit, explain, fanfare, panoply, picture, present, produce, project, trot out **8** brandish, disclose, evidence, illusion, indicate, instruct, manifest, proclaim **9** determine, establish, pageantry, represent, semblance, spectacle **10** appearance, exhibition, exposition, illustrate, production **11** demonstrate, materialize, performance

Show Boat
author: **4** Edna (Ferber)
composer: **4** Kern (Jerome)
lyricist: **11** Hammerstein (Oscar)

showcase
6 flaunt, parade **7** cabinet, exhibit, feature, vitrine

shower
4 hail, rain, wash **5** bathe, burst, party, salvo, spray, storm **6** deluge, lavish, volley **7** barrage, cascade, shatter, spatter **8** cataract, downpour, fountain, rainfall **9** broadside, cannonade, fusillade **10** cloudburst

showman
8 producer, promoter **10** impresario
famous: **4** Cody (William F.) **6** Barnum (Phineas T.)

Show Me State
8 Missouri

show off
4 brag **5** boast, flash, model, strut, vaunt **6** expose, flaunt, hotdog, parade **7** display, exhibit, swagger, trot out **8** brandish **10** grandstand

show-off
3 ham **6** hotdog **7** boaster, hotshot, peacock **8** blowhard, braggart **9** swaggerer **13** exhibitionist

showpiece
3 gem **5** jewel, prize **10** magnum opus, masterwork **11** chef d'oeuvre, masterpiece

showroom sample
4 demo

show up
4 come **6** appear, arrive, debunk, expose, reveal, unmask **8** discover **9** discredit, embarrass **10** invalidate **11** materialize

showy
4 loud **5** gaudy, jazzy **6** flashy, garish, ornate, tawdry **7** opulent, splashy **8** overdone, striking **9** luxurious, sumptuous **10** flamboyant **11** overwrought, pretentious, sensational **12** meretricious, orchidaceous, ostentatious

shred
3 bit, dag, jot, rag **4** chip, iota, whit **5** crumb, grain, grate, ounce, scrap, shave, speck, trace **6** sliver, tatter **7** modicum, smidgen, snippet **8** demolish, fragment, particle **9** scintilla

Shrek, e.g.
4 ogre

shrew
3 erd, nag **4** mole **5** harpy, scold, vixen, witch **6** dragon, gorgon, ogress, rodent, virago **7** hellcat **8** battle-ax, fishwife, harridan, she-devil, spitfire, Xantippe **9** battle-axe, termagant, Xanthippe

shrewd
3 sly **4** cagy, foxy, keen, wily, wise **5** acute, cagey, canny, savvy, sharp, slick, smart **6** artful, astute, clever, crafty, smooth **7** cunning, knowing, prudent **8** sensible **9** ingenious, judicious, sagacious **10** discerning

shrewish
5 cross, testy **6** cranky, snappy **7** nagging, peevish, peppery **8** choleric, petulant **9** crotchety, fractious, irascible, splenetic **10** ill-natured **11** contentious, intractable, quarrelsome

shriek
3 cry **4** yell, yelp **6** screak, scream, shrill, squawk, squeal **7** screech

shrill
4 keen **5** acute, sharp **6** piping **8** piercing, strident **9** deafening **12** earsplitting

shrimp
4 runt **5** prawn **6** peanut, peewee, scampi, shorty **9** pipsqueak **10** crustacean

shrine
5 altar **6** oracle, temple **7** sanctum **9** reliquary, sacrarium, sanctuary
Buddhist: **4** tope **5** stupa **7** chorten

Shriner's hat
3 fez

shrink
3 shy **4** wane **5** cower, quail, slink, start, wince **6** blench, boggle, cringe, flinch, huddle, recede, recoil, wither **7** analyst, dwindle, refrain **8** compress, condense, contract, draw back, withdraw **9** constrict, shrivel up, therapist, waste away **12** psychiatrist, psychologist

shrinking
3 shy **5** mousy, timid **7** bashful **8** retiring, skittish **9** withdrawn
Asian sea: **4** Aral

shrive
5 purge **6** pardon, purify **7** absolve, confess, expiate **8** lustrate

shrivel
4 wilt **5** dry up, parch, wizen **6** shrink, wither **7** dwindle, wrinkle **9** dehydrate, desiccate

Shropshire Lad author
7 Housman (A. E.)

shroud
4 hide, rope, veil, wrap **5** cloak, cover, shade **6** enfold, enwrap, screen **7** conceal, enclose, envelop, obscure **8** cerement, obstruct **9** cerecloth **12** winding-sheet

shroud city
5 Turin **6** Torino

shrouded
5 privy **6** covert, hidden, secret **7** obscure

shrub
4 bush **5** elder, erica, hazel **6** muskit, privet **7** arboret, dyeweed, guayule **8** barberry, bluewood, boxthorn, inkberry, ironweed, rosebush **9** bearberry **10** bladdernut
Asian: **4** bago **6** kerria **8** caragana, japonica
desert: **4** jhow **7** ephedra **8** tamarisk
dwarf: **6** bonsai
East Indian: **3** aal **4** sunn
European: **4** cade **8** woodbine
evergreen: **3** box, kat, yew **4** ilex, khat, titi **5** furze, heath, holly, pyxie, savin, taxus **6** kalmia, laurel, myrtle, nandin, protea, sabine, savine **7** boxwood, heather, jasmine, juniper, rosebay **8** lambkill, oleander, rosemary, tamarisk
flowering: **5** lilac, ribes, tiara, wahoo **6** azalea, daphne, laurel, myrtle, spirea **7** chamise, chamiso, mahonia, maybush, rhodora, spiraea, weigela **8** magnolia, mezereon, nineback, oleander, oleaster, shadblow, shadbush, snowball, snowbush, tornillo, viburnum, wisteria
genus: **3** Iva **4** Ilex, Inga, Itea, Rhus, Rosa, Ulex **7** Solanum **8** Euonymus
hardwood: **4** pelu **6** cornel, kowhai
Mexican: **8** ocotillo
New Zealand: **4** tutu
ornamental: **6** privet **7** syringa **9** bluebeard
pasture: **8** cowberry
prickly: **4** Ulex **5** briar, chico, furze, gorse **7** bramble **8** hawthorn, mesquite **9** buckthorn
thicket: **6** maquis **7** macchia **9** chaparral
tropical: **4** kava, Sida **5** henna **7** lantana **8** buddleia **10** frangipani
West Indian: **4** anil **7** acerola

shrug off
8 belittle, downplay, minimize

shtick
3 act, bag, bit **5** spiel **6** number **7** routine **9** specialty **11** performance

Shuah
father: **7** Abraham
mother: **7** Keturah

shuck
3 pod **4** case, cast, hull, husk, junk, peel, shed, skin **5** ditch, scrap, shell, strip **6** reject, remove, slough **7** discard, peel off, take off **8** jettison **11** decorticate

shudder
5 quake, shake **6** quaver, quiver, shimmy, shiver, tremor **7** frisson, tremble, twitter, vibrate

shuffle
3 mix **4** hash **5** dodge, evade, hedge, scuff, shift **6** jumble, mess up, muddle, weasel **7** clutter, reorder, rummage, shamble **8** disarray, disorder, intermix, mishmash **9** rearrange **10** disarrange, equivocate

shun
3 cut **4** duck, snub **5** avoid, dodge, elude, evade, scorn **6** escape, eschew, refuse, reject **7** decline, disdain

shunt
4 turn **5** avert, shift **6** change, divert, switch **7** deflect, shuttle **8** transfer **9** sidetrack

shush
4 hush **5** quiet, still **6** muffle, muzzle, shut up, stifle **7** repress, silence, squelch **8** suppress

shut
3 bar **4** lock, seal, slam **5** close **6** fasten **9** close down **10** batten down

shut-eye
3 nap **4** doze **5** sleep **6** snooze **7** slumber

Shute novel
10 On the Beach

shut in
3 hem, mew, pen **4** cage, coop, wall **5** fence **6** coop up, immure **7** confine, enclose **8** imprison

shut-in
7 invalid **8** confined **9** withdrawn **12** convalescent

shut out
3 bar **6** screen **7** exclude **9** ostracize

shutter
5 blind **6** screen

shuttle
5 ferry, shunt **6** bobbin **7** commute, spindle **9** alternate

shuttlecock
4 bird **5** bandy

shut up
3 gag, mew, pen **4** cage, hush, jail, mute **5** burke, choke, quiet, shush, still **6** muzzle, stifle **7** confine, enclose, impound, silence, squelch

8 choke off, imprison, pipe down, suppress 9 quiet down 11 incarcerate

shy
3 coy 4 balk, duck, meek, shun, wary 5 avoid, chary, elude, evade, mousy, quail, scant, short, timid 6 averse, blench, demure, modest, recoil, scanty, scarce, shrink 7 bashful, lacking, wanting 8 hesitant, reserved, reticent, retiring, timorous 9 diffident, withdrawn 11 introverted, unassertive

Shylock
6 usurer 9 loan shark
customer: 7 Antonio
daughter: 7 Jessica

shyster
11 pettifogger

Siam
see **Thailand**

Siamese twin
3 Eng 5 Chang

sib
3 bro, kin, sis 4 akin 6 sister 7 brother, kindred, kinsman, related 8 relation, relative 9 relatives

Sibelius composition
9 Finlandia 11 Valse Triste

Siberian
dog: 5 husky 7 Samoyed
native: 5 Tatar, Yakut 6 Tartar, Tungus 7 Chukchi 9 Mongolian
plain: 6 steppe
tent: 4 yurt

sibilate
4 buzz, fizz, hiss, whiz 6 fizzle, sizzle 7 whisper

sibling
3 bro, sis 6 sister 7 brother

sibyl
4 seer 6 oracle 7 diviner, prophet 10 prophetess, soothsayer

sic
3 set 4 thus 5 chase 6 attack

Sicily
capital: 7 Palermo
city: 4 Enna 7 Catania, Messina 8 Siracusa, Syracuse, Taormina
secret organization: 5 Mafia 10 Cosa Nostra
volcano: 4 Etna 5 Aetna

sick
3 ill 5 fed up, tired, weary 6 ailing, laid up, morbid, peaked, rotten, unwell, wobbly 7 fevered, invalid 8 confined, diseased 9 bedridden, defective, unhealthy 10 indisposed 11 debilitated

sicken
5 upset 7 afflict, disgust, fall ill 8 nauseate

sickle
5 blade, mower 6 scythe 8 crescent

sickle-shaped
7 falcate

sickly
3 ill, low, wan 4 puny, weak 5 frail 6 ailing, anemic, feeble, infirm, morbid, peaked, poorly, unwell 8 delicate, diseased 9 unhealthy 10 indisposed 11 unhealthful, unwholesome

sickness
3 bug 6 malady 7 ailment, disease, illness 8 syndrome 9 complaint, infirmity 10 affliction

sick-out
7 blue flu

sic transit gloria ___
5 mundi

side
4 clad, team 5 angle, facet, flank 6 aspect 9 direction 10 standpoint
combining form: 5 later 6 lateri, latero
exposed: 8 windward
of a coin: 7 obverse, reverse
sheltered: 3 lee

sideboard
5 table 6 buffet 8 credence, credenza
for wine: 8 cellaret 10 cellarette

sideburns
11 dundrearies, muttonchops

sidekick
3 pal 4 chun 5 buddy, crony 7 partner 9 assistant, companion 10 accomplice

sideline
5 eject, hobby 6 injure 7 disable, pastime, take out 9 avocation, diversion 10 recreation 11 distraction

sidereal
6 astral, starry 7 stellar

side road
5 byway 8 bystreet, shunpike

sideshow
9 diversion 11 distraction

sidestep
4 duck 5 avoid, burke, dodge, evade, hedge, skirt 6 bypass, swerve, weasel 10 circumvent, equivocate 12 tergiversate

sideswipe
5 brush, carom, graze, shave 6 glance, scrape

sidetrack
5 shunt 6 divert, switch 7 deflect

sidewhiskers
see **sideburns**

side with
4 back 5 favor 6 second, uphold 7 endorse, support 8 backstop

sidle
4 edge, inch, slip

siege
4 bout **5** spell **6** attack **7** assault, seizure **8** blockade **9** onslaught

Siegfried
composer: **6** Wagner (Richard)
lover: **8** Brunhild **10** Brünnhilde
mother: **9** Sieglinde
slayer: **5** Hagen
sword: **7** Balmung, Nothung
vulnerable spot: **4** back **8** shoulder
wife: **9** Kriemhild

Sienkiewicz novel
8 Quo Vadis

sierra
3 saw **4** fish **5** range **8** mackerel **13** mountain range

Sierra ___
4 Club **5** Ancha, Leone, Madre **6** Blanca, Nevada

Sierra Leone
capital: **8** Freetown
ethnic group: **5** Mende, Temne
language: **4** Krio **7** English
monetary unit: **5** leone
neighbor: **6** Guinea **7** Liberia

Sierra Nevada lake
5 Tahoe

siesta
3 nap **4** doze **5** sleep **6** catnap, snooze **10** forty winks

sieve
4 sift **6** filter, screen, sifter, winnow **8** colander, filtrate, strainer

Sif's husband
4 Thor

sift
3 pan **4** comb, cull, sort **5** glean, sieve **6** filter, screen, strain, winnow **8** filtrate, separate

sigh
3 sob **4** gasp, long, moan, pine **5** groan, sough, whine, yearn **6** exhale, grieve, hanker, murmur **7** breathe, respire, suspire

sighed word
4 alas

sight
3 aim, eye, spy **4** espy, view **5** scene, vista **6** notice, vision **7** make out, outlook
relating to: **5** optic **6** ocular, visual **7** optical

sightseer
7 tourist **10** rubberneck **12** rubbernecker

sign
3 cue, ink **4** clue, flag, hint, mark, omen **5** index, proof, token, trace **6** motion, signal, symbol **7** endorse, gesture, indicia, initial, symptom, vestige, warning **8** evidence, exponent, reminder **9** autograph, indicator **10** expression, indication, suggestion
box office: **3** SRO
gas: **4** neon
magic: **4** rune
directional: **5** arrow
of the zodiac: (see **zodiac sign**)

signal
3 cue, nod **4** flag **5** alarm, alert **6** beckon, wigwag **7** gesture **8** high sign **9** indicator, semaphore
distress: **3** SOS **6** Mayday

signature
4 name **9** autograph **11** John Hancock
flourish: **6** paraph

signet
4 ring, seal **5** stamp **6** device **8** hallmark, intaglio

significance
4 pith **5** merit, point, sense **6** credit, import, moment, weight **7** gravity, meaning **9** authority, magnitude **10** importance

significant
5 major, valid **7** notable, telling, weighty **9** important, momentous **10** compelling, convincing, meaningful, noteworthy **11** substantial **12** considerable **13** consequential

signification
4 gist **5** point, sense **6** import **7** essence, meaning, message, purport **9** substance

signify
4 mean, show **5** count, imply, spell, weigh **6** convey, denote, intend, matter **7** add up to, bespeak, connote, express, purport, suggest **8** indicate

sign on
4 book, hire, join **5** draft **6** engage, enlist, enroll, induct, join up, retain, secure **7** recruit **9** conscript
again: **4** reup

sign over
4 cede, deed **5** alien, grant **6** assign, convey, remise **7** consign **8** alienate, transfer

sign up
4 join **5** enrol, enter **6** enlist, enroll, muster

Sigourney Weaver movie
5 Alien **6** Aliens

Sigurd
horse: **5** Grani
slayer: **5** Hogni
victim: **6** Fafner, Fafnir
wife: **6** Gudrun

Sigyn's husband
4 Loki

Sikhism
deity: **4** Akal
founder: **5** Nanak **9** Guru Nanak
leader: **5** Arjan **9** Guru Arjan **11** Gobind Singh
scripture: **9** Adi Granth
shrine: **12** Golden Temple

silage
6 fodder

silence
3 gag **4** calm, hush, lull, mute **5** quash, quell, quiet, shush, still **6** dampen, deaden, muffle, muzzle, shut up, squash, stifle **7** secrecy, squelch **8** choke off, muteness, quietude, suppress **9** quietness, stillness

silent
3 mum **4** dumb, mute **5** muted, quiet, still, tacit, whist **6** hushed, stilly **8** reticent, taciturn, unspoken, wordless **9** noiseless, soundless, voiceless **10** speechless **11** tight-lipped
actor: **4** mime

Silent Night writer
4 Mohr (Joseph) **6** Gruber (Franz)

silents star
Negri: **4** Pola
Nita: **5** Naldi
Theda: **4** Bara

silent yes
3 nod

silhouette
6 shadow **7** contour, outline, profile **9** lineament, lineation **10** figuration **11** delineation

Silicon Valley city
7 San Jose **8** Palo Alto

silk
5 fiber **7** foulard **8** sarcenet, sarsenet
fabric: **4** gros **5** caffa, ninon, Pekin, satin, surah, tulle **6** mantua, pongee, samite, sendal, tussah **7** taffeta
factory: **8** filature
French: **4** soie
hat: **6** topper
maker: **4** worm
raw: **6** greige
source: **6** cocoon
waste: **4** noil **5** floss
wild: **6** tussah

sill
5 bench, ledge, shelf **9** threshold

silliness
5 folly **6** idiocy **7** inanity **9** absurdity, stupidity

silly
4 daft **5** balmy, crazy, daffy, dippy, dizzy, funny, giddy, inane, loony, sappy, wacky **6** absurd, simple **7** asinine, fatuous, flighty, foolish, idiotic, vacuous, witless **9** brainless, frivolous, ludicrous, nitwitted, senseless **10** ridiculous **11** empty-headed, harebrained, light-headed

silt
4 marl **5** dregs **7** deposit, residue **8** alluvium, sediment

silver
4 coin **5** money, shiny **6** argent, dulcet **7** bullion, element **8** flatware, lustrous, sterling **9** argentine, tableware
relating to: **9** argentine
salmon: **4** coho **5** cohoe
Spanish: **5** plata

silver-and-red fish
4 opah

silverfish
6 insect, tarpon

silversmith
6 Revere (Paul) **11** metalworker

Silverstein of children's books
4 Shel

silver-tongued
4 glib **6** fluent **7** voluble **8** eloquent

silvery
6 argent **7** shining **9** argentine, brilliant **10** shimmering

Silvia's beloved
9 Valentine

___ Simbel
3 Abu

Simenon character
7 Maigret (Inspector)

Simeon
father: **5** Jacob
mother: **4** Leah
son: **4** Ohad **6** Nemuel

simian
3 ape **5** chimp, lemur, loris **6** baboon, bonobo, galago, monkey **7** apelike, gorilla, primate, tarsier **9** orangutan **10** anthropoid, chimpanzee, monkeylike

similar
4 akin, like **5** alike **6** agnate **7** uniform **8** parallel, suchlike **9** analogous, consonant **10** comparable, reciprocal **11** correlative **13** complementary, corresponding

similarity
6 parity **7** analogy, harmony, kinship **8** affinity, likeness, parallel, sameness **9** alikeness, closeness, congruity, semblance **10** conformity, congruence **11** coincidence, correlation, homogeneity, parallelism, resemblance

similarly
8 likewise

simile
7 analogy **8** affinity, likeness, metaphor **9** alikeness, semblance **10** comparison **11** correlation, resemblance
word: **4** like

similitude
4 copy **5** image **6** double **7** analogy, kinship, replica **8** affinity, likeness, metaphor, relation, sameness **9** alikeness, congruity, semblance **10** comparison, similarity **11** correlation, counterpart, equivalence, resemblance

simmer
4 boil, fret, fume, stew, stir **5** churn **6** bubble, seethe **7** ferment, smolder

simmer down
5 relax

Simon
brother: **5** Jesus **6** Andrew
father: **5** Jonah
new name: **5** Peter
son: **5** Judas, Rufus **9** Alexander

Simon ___
5 Magus **6** Legree **8** of Cyrene **9** the Zealot

Simone of song
4 Nina

Simon play
9 Odd Couple (The) **10** Plaza Suite **11** Biloxi Blues **12** Sunshine Boys (The) **13** Lost in Yonkers **16** Come Blow Your Horn **17** Barefoot in the Park **20** Brighton Beach Memoirs **21** Last of the Red Hot Lovers

simple
4 easy, mere, pure **5** basic, lucid, naive, plain, sheer **6** modest **7** artless, natural, unmixed **8** absolute, trusting **9** childlike, credulous, ingenuous, unadorned **10** effortless, elementary, unaffected
combining form: **4** hapl **5** haplo

simpleminded
4 dull, slow **5** naive **6** stupid **7** foolish, idiotic, moronic **8** gullible, retarded **9** dim-witted, imbecilic **10** half-witted, slow-witted

simpleton
4 dolt, dope, fool **5** dummy, dunce, idiot, moron **6** cretin, dimwit, nitwit **7** dullard, half-wit, pinhead **8** bonehead, dumbbell, imbecile, lunkhead **9** blockhead, ignoramus, lamebrain **10** nincompoop

simplify
4 ease **7** clarify, clear up **8** boil down **10** facilitate, streamline, unscramble **11** disentangle **13** straighten out

simply
4 just, only **6** merely

Simpson judge
3 Ito (Lance)

Simpsons, The
character: **3** Abe, Apu, Moe **4** Bart, Lisa, Otto **5** Homer, Marge, Patty, Selma, Snake **6** Barney, Krusty, Maggie, Martin, Willie **7** Bouvier, Mr. Burns, Skinner (Principal Seymour) **8** Chalmers (Supt.), Milhouse, Smithers **9** Dr. Hibbert, Joe Quimby (Mayor) **12** Mrs. Krabappel
creator: **8** Groening (Matt)
expression: **3** d'oh **12** don't have a cow
Lisa's instrument: **3** sax **9** saxophone
setting: **11** Springfield

simulacrum
4 copy **5** clone, ditto, guise, image, trace **6** double, ersatz, mirror, ringer **7** picture, replica **8** likeness, portrait **9** facsimile, imitation, semblance **10** appearance **12** reproduction **13** impersonation, spitting image

simulate
3 ape **4** fake, sham **5** feign, mimic **6** embody, mirror, parody, parrot **7** imitate **8** resemble **9** incarnate **11** counterfeit

simulated
4 fake, mock, sham **5** bogus, dummy, false, phony **6** ersatz **8** spurious **9** imitation, insincere, pretended **10** artificial, fictitious, substitute **11** counterfeit

simultaneous
6 coeval **10** coexistent, coexisting, coincident, coinciding, concurrent, synchronic **11** synchronous **12** contemporary

simultaneously
6 at once **7** jointly **8** together **9** meanwhile

sin
3 err **4** debt, evil, no-no, tort, vice **5** crime, fault, guilt, lapse, misdo, stray, wrong **6** offend **7** demerit, misdeed, offense **8** hamartia, iniquity, trespass **10** deficiency, peccadillo, transgress, wickedness, wrongdoing **11** shortcoming
deadly: **4** envy, lust **5** anger, greed, pride, sloth **8** gluttony **12** covetousness

Sin
7 moon-god
daughter: **6** Ishtar
son: **7** Shamash
wife: **6** Ningal

since
3 ago **5** after **6** behind **7** because, whereas **8** as long as **9** following **10** inasmuch as **11** considering
Scottish: **4** syne

sincere
5 frank **6** candid, devout, honest **7** artless, earnest, genuine, serious **8** bona fide, truthful

9 authentic, heartfelt, ingenuous, unfeigned 10 aboveboard, forthright 12 wholehearted

sincerity
6 candor 7 honesty 8 goodwill, openness 9 frankness, good faith

sin city
5 Sodom 8 Gomorrah

Sinclair novel
6 Jungle (The)

sine qua non
4 must 9 condition, essential, necessity, requisite 11 requirement 12 precondition, prerequisite

sinew
6 tendon

sinewy
4 lean, ropy, wiry 5 tough 6 brawny 7 fibrous, stringy 8 muscular

sinful
4 base, evil, vile 6 guilty, unholy, wicked 7 immoral, peccant, vicious 8 blamable, culpable, damnable, depraved, shameful 9 reprobate 10 iniquitous

sing
3 rat 4 fink, hymn 5 carol, chant, chirp, croon, troll, yodel 6 inform, intone, snitch, squeal, warble 7 confess, descant, lullaby 8 serenade, vocalize 10 cantillate

singe
4 burn, char, sear 6 scorch

singer
4 alto, bass 5 mezzo, tenor 6 canary 7 crooner, soloist, soprano 8 baritone, choirboy, songbird, songster, vocalist 9 balladeer, chorister, contralto 10 troubadour 12 mezzo-soprano
cabaret: 11 chansonnier
female: 9 chanteuse
opera: 4 diva 10 cantatrice, prima donna
religious: 6 cantor
(see also **alto, baritone, bass, folksinger, mezzo-soprano, pop singer, rock star, soprano**)

singer Amos
4 Tori

singer DiFranco
3 Ani

singer Horne
4 Lena

singer Paul
4 Anka

singer-songwriter Phil
4 Ochs

singing
exercise: 7 solfège
group: 5 choir 6 chorus 7 chorale 8 glee club

singing brothers
4 Ames

singing voice
4 alto, bass 5 mezzo, tenor 7 soprano 8 baritone 9 contralto

single
3 hit, odd, one 4 free, lone, only, sole 5 unwed 6 maiden, unique 7 base hit, unitary 8 distinct, isolated, separate, solitary, specific 9 exclusive, unmarried 10 individual, particular, unattached
combining form: 3 mon 4 hapl, mono 5 haplo
prefix: 3 uni

single-minded
5 rigid 6 dogged, driven, intent 7 adamant, devoted, diehard 8 hell-bent, obdurate, resolute, resolved, stubborn 9 dedicated, steadfast, unbending 10 brassbound, determined, inexorable, inflexible, purposeful, relentless, unyielding

single out
4 cull, mark, pick 5 elect, favor 6 choose, opt for, select 9 designate 11 distinguish

singsong
4 cant

singular
3 odd 4 lone, only, rare, sole, solo 5 weird 6 unique 7 bizarre, oddball, strange, unusual 8 peculiar, solitary, uncommon 9 exclusive 10 individual, outlandish, particular, unexampled 11 exceptional

singularity
5 quirk, unity 6 oddity 7 anomaly, oneness 8 identity 9 exception 11 peculiarity, personality 12 idiosyncrasy 13 individuality, particularity

sinister
4 dark, dire, evil, left 6 creepy, malign 7 baleful, fateful, malefic, ominous 8 lowering, menacing 9 ill-omened, malicious 10 foreboding, maleficent, portentous 11 threatening

sink
3 dip, pit, sag 4 bore, bury, dive, drop, fall, sump, wane 5 basin, drill, droop, lower, sewer, slope, slump, stoop, swamp 6 hollow, invest, plunge, settle, thrust, worsen 7 capsize, cesspit, decline, depress, descend, founder, go under, immerse, let down, scuttle, subside, torpedo 8 cesspool, hellhole, submerge, submerse 9 concavity, disappear 10 depression

sinker
3 bob 5 plumb 6 weight 8 doughnut, fastball, plumb bob

sinkhole
3 dip, sag 4 bowl 5 basin 6 hollow 8 cesspool 9 concavity 10 depression

sinless
4 pure **6** chaste **8** innocent **9** righteous **10** impeccable

sinner
5 rogue, scamp **6** bad egg, outlaw, rascal, wretch **7** lowlife, villain **8** criminal, evildoer, offender **9** libertine, miscreant, reprobate, scoundrel, wrongdoer **10** black sheep, delinquent, profligate, malefactor **11** rapscallion

Sinn ___
4 Fein

sinuous
4 wavy **5** lithe, snaky **7** winding **8** flexuous, tortuous **10** convoluted, meandering, serpentine **11** anfractuous, snake-shaped

sinus
6 cavity, hollow, recess

Sioux
6 Dakota
chief: 8 Red Cloud **10** Crazy Horse **11** Sitting Bull
language: 6 Dakota, Lakota
people: 3 Ofo **4** Crow **6** Biloxi, Tutelo **7** Catawba, Hidatsa **9** Winnebago

sip
5 drink, savor, taste **6** imbibe

siphon
3 tap **4** draw, pipe, pump **5** draft, drain **6** convoy, divert, funnel **7** channel, conduct, draw off **8** transmit

sir
4 lord **5** title **6** knight, mister **9** gentleman

sire
4 lord **5** beget, breed, hatch, spawn **6** father, parent **7** founder **8** engender **9** patriarch, procreate, propagate, reproduce **10** forefather

siren
4 vamp **5** alarm **7** Lorelei **9** temptress **10** seductress **11** femme fatale
film: 4 Bara (Theda)

Siren
5 Ligea **8** Leucosia **10** Parthenope
German: 7 Lorelei

sirenian
6 dugong, sea cow **7** manatee

siren song
4 lure **5** decoy, snare **6** come-on **10** allurement, enticement, temptation

Sirius
7 Dog Star

sis
3 sib
counterpart: 3 bro

sisal source
5 agave

sister
3 nun **7** sibling
French: 5 soeur
Latin: 5 soror
Spanish: 7 hermana

Sister Carrie author
7 Dreiser (Theodore)

sisterly
7 sororal

Sisyphus
brother: 7 Athamas **9** Salmoneus
father: 6 Aeolus
mother: 7 Enarete
son: 7 Glaucus

sit
4 pose **5** perch, roost

Sita
abductor: 6 Ravana
husband, rescuer: 4 Rama

sitarist
7 Shankar (Ravi)
music: 4 raga

sitcom
3 ALF **4** MASH, Mr. Ed **5** Ellen, Maude **6** Cheers **7** Frasier, Friends, Newhart **8** Get Smart, Love Boat (The), Mister Ed, Munsters (The), Roseanne, Seinfeld **9** Bewitched, Cosby Show (The), Full House, Happy Days, I Love Lucy, Odd Couple (The) **10** Brady Bunch (The), Green Acres, Jeffersons (The), Night Court **11** Golden Girls (The), Murphy Brown, My Three Sons, Wonder Years (The) **12** Addams Family (The), Barney Miller, Fawlty Towers, Hogan's Heroes, Honeymooners (The), King of Queens (The), Modern Family, Mork and Mindy, Will and Grace **13** Big Bang Theory (The), One Day at a Time, Our Miss Brooks, Sanford and Son, Three's Company **14** All in the Family, Two and a Half Men **15** Diff'rent Strokes, Father Knows Best, Gilligan's Island, Home Improvement, I Dream of Jeannie, Leave It to Beaver, Ozzie and Harriet **17** Are You Being Served, Laverne and Shirley, My Favorite Martian, Petticoat Junction **18** Beverly Hillbillies (The), Parks and Recreation **19** Married with Children **20** Keeping Up Appearances **21** Everybody Loves Raymond

site
3 dig **4** home, spot **5** haunt, locus, place, point, scene, venue **6** locale **7** station **8** locality, location, position

sit-in
7 protest

sitting
6 séance **7** session
prolonged: 8 sederunt

Sitting Bull's tribe
5 Sioux **6** Dakota

sitting duck
4 butt, mark **6** target

situate
3 put, set **5** place **6** locate, orient **7** install **8** position

situation
3 job **4** post, rank **5** point, state **6** plight, status **7** footing, setting, station **8** location, position, standing **9** condition

sit-up muscles
3 abs

situs
5 place, venue **6** locale

Siva
see **Shiva**

six
combining form: **3** hex, sex **4** hexa, sexi **5** sexti
group of: **6** sestet, sextet **9** sextuplet
relating to: **6** senary
Spanish: **4** seis

sixfold
8 sextuple

six-pack muscles
3 abs

sixteenth of an ounce
3 tsp. **4** dram

sixth sense
3 ESP **5** hunch **7** insight **9** intuition, telepathy **12** clairvoyance

sizable
3 big **5** ample, hefty, large, major, roomy **8** spacious **9** capacious, extensive **10** commodious, large-scale **11** substantial

size
3 lge, med **4** area, bulk, mass **5** range, scope, width **6** extent, height, length, spread, volume **7** bigness, breadth, caliber, expanse, measure, stature **9** amplitude, dimension, extension, greatness, largeness, magnitude **10** dimensions, proportion **11** measurement, proportions

size up
3 peg **4** rate, read **5** assay, gauge, judge, value **6** assess, review, survey **7** adjudge, dope out **8** appraise, estimate, evaluate **9** figure out

sizzle
3 fry **4** buzz, fizz, hiss, whiz **5** grill **6** hoopla, seethe **7** pizzazz **8** sibilate **10** excitement

sizzling
3 hot **6** red-hot, torrid **7** burning **8** scalding, white-hot **9** scorching

skald
4 bard, poet

Skanda
6 war-god
brother: **6** Ganesa, Ganesh **7** Ganesha
father: **4** Siva **5** Shiva

skate
3 nag, ray **4** skid, skim **5** glide, skirr, slide **8** glissade
blade: **6** runner
kind: **6** figure, hockey, in-line **11** Rollerblade

skateboard maneuver
3 air **4** bail, hang **5** carve, grind, ollie, pivot **8** kickflip

skater
see **ice skater**

skater Midori
3 Ito

skating
area: **10** kiss and cry
game: **8** ringette **9** broomball, ice hockey **12** in-line hockey, roller hockey
site: **3** ice **4** rink
term: **3** COP **4** axel, lobe, lutz, quad **5** T-stop **6** Mohawk, rocker, spiral **7** bracket, choctaw, gliding, salchow, sit spin, swizzle, toe loop, twizzle **8** heel stop, star lift, striding, stroking, toe picks **9** camel spin, crossover, free dance, free skate, waltz jump, Zayak Rule **11** death spiral, falling leaf, hydrant lift
type: **3** ice **5** trail **6** in-line, roller

skedaddle
3 run **4** bolt, flee, skip **5** scoot, scram, split **6** beat it, begone, bug off, cut out, decamp, get out **7** make off, run away, scamper, take off, vamoose **8** clear out **10** make tracks

skein
4 coil, hank **5** flock, snarl, twist **6** tangle **12** entanglement

skeletal
4 bony **5** gaunt **6** wasted **7** angular, scraggy, starved **8** rawboned **9** emaciated **10** cadaverous

skeleton
5 bones, draft, frame **6** sketch **7** diagram, outline **9** bare bones, framework
marine: **5** coral, shell

skeptic
5 cynic **7** doubter, scoffer **8** agnostic **10** Pyrrhonist, questioner, unbeliever

skeptical
4 wary **5** leery **6** show-me **7** cynical, dubious **8** doubtful, doubting **9** quizzical **10** dissenting, suspicious **11** mistrustful, questioning, unbelieving
remark: **4** I bet **6** show me

skepticism
5 doubt **7** dubiety **8** distrust, mistrust, wariness **9** dubiosity, misgiving, suspicion

skerry
4 isle, reef **6** island

sketch
4 draw, plot **5** draft, rough, trace **6** depict, design, doodle, lay out, map out, précis **7** develop, diagram, outline, portray **8** block out, chalk out, rough out **9** blueprint, delineate

sketchy
4 iffy **5** crude, rough, vague **6** skimpy, slight **7** cursory, shallow **8** skeletal **10** incomplete **11** preliminary, superficial **12** questionable

skew
4 bias, veer **5** angle, fudge, slant, slide **6** swerve **7** distort

skewed
4 awry **5** atilt **6** aslant **7** listing **8** cockeyed, lopsided

skewer
3 rod **4** spit **5** lance, spear, spike **6** impale, pierce **8** puncture, ridicule, transfix **9** brochette, criticize

ski
5 glide, slide
lift: **4** J-bar, T-bar **5** chair **7** gondola
trail: **5** piste

____-ski
5 après

skid
5 glide, skate, slide **6** pallet, runner **7** spinout **8** sideslip

skiddoo
4 scat **5** leave, scram, split **6** beat it, begone, bug off, decamp, depart, vacate **7** buzz off, take off, vamoose **8** clear out, shove off **9** take a hike **10** hit the road, make tracks

skid row
6 bowery

skier
American: **3** Moe (Tommy) **4** Kidd (Billy), Vonn (Lindsey) **5** Mahre (Phil, Steve) **6** Ligety (Ted), Miller (Bode), Street (Picabo) **7** Johnson (Bill), Mancuso (Julia)
Austrian: **5** Maier (Hermann) **6** Proell (Annemarie), Sailer (Toni)
French: **5** Killy (Jean-Claude)
Italian: **5** Tomba (Alberto)
Swedish: **8** Stenmark (Ingemar)

skiff
4 boat **7** rowboat

skiing
area: **3** run **5** slope
cross-country: **7** touring
event: **6** slalom, super G **8** downhill **11** giant slalom
horse-drawn: **9** skijoring
kind: **6** Alpine, Nordic
position: **7** vorlage
technique: **6** schuss, wedeln **8** snowplow, telemark, traverse
turn: **7** christy **8** christie

skill
3 art **5** craft, knack **7** ability, address, command, cunning, finesse, know-how, mastery, prowess, sleight **8** deftness, facility **9** dexterity, expertise, ingenuity, readiness, technique **10** adroitness, competence **11** proficiency

skilled
3 apt **4** able **5** adept **6** expert **7** capable, trained **8** masterly, talented **9** competent, masterful, practiced **10** proficient **12** accomplished

skillet
3 pan **6** spider **9** frying pan

skillful
4 able, deft **5** adept, crack, handy **6** adroit, clever, daedal, expert **7** skilled **8** masterly **9** competent, dexterous, masterful, practiced, workmanly **10** proficient **11** crackerjack, workmanlike

skim
4 sail, scan, scud, skip **5** brush, carom, glide, graze, skirr **6** browse **8** embezzle, ricochet

skimp
4 save **5** pinch, scant, spare, stint **6** meager, scanty, scrape, sparse **7** slender **8** begrudge, conserve, withhold **9** economize

skimpy
5 scant, spare **6** meager, meagre, paltry, scanty, scarce, sparse **7** limited, wanting **8** exiguous **10** inadequate

skim through
4 scan **6** browse

skin
3 fur, pod **4** clad, clip, flay, husk, hide, pare, peel, pelt, rind **5** cover, scale, shell, stiff, strip **6** fleece, sheath, slough **7** condemn, sheathe **8** denounce **9** epidermis, sheathing **10** integument, overcharge **11** decorticate
animal: **4** coat, hide, pelt **6** hackle, peltry
art: **3** tat **6** tattoo
beaver: **4** plew
combining form: **3** cut **4** cuti, derm **5** derma, dermo, dermy **6** dermat, dermia, dermis **7** cutaneo, dermata (plural), dermato, epiderm **8** epidermo
depression: **6** dimple
disease: **4** acne **5** hives, mange **6** eczema, herpes, tetter **8** ringworm **10** dermatitis
dry: **5** scurf
fold: **5** plica

layer: **5** derma **6** corium, dermis **7** cuticle **9** epidermis
opening: **4** pore
protuberance: **3** tag, wen **4** mole, wart **6** pimple
rabbit: **5** coney
relating to: **6** dermal **9** cuticular, epidermal
spot: **7** freckle

skin care
brand: **4** Avon
ingredient: **4** aloe

skin-deep
7 shallow, trivial **11** superficial

skinflint
5 miser **7** niggard, scrooge **8** tightwad **10** cheapskate, pinchpenny

skin game
3 con **4** scam **5** bunco, bunko, cheat, fraud, sting, trick **6** hustle, racket **7** swindle **8** flimflam

skink
4 adda **6** lizard

skinny
4 bony, dope, info, lank, lean, thin **5** gaunt, lanky, scoop, spare, weedy **6** twiggy **7** angular, lowdown, scraggy, scrawny **8** rawboned, skeletal **9** emaciated
fish: **3** eel

Skin of Our Teeth author
6 Wilder (Thornton)

skip
3 dap, hop, run **4** flee, jump, leap, omit, trip **5** bound, caper, carom, frisk, leave, scoot, skirr **6** cavort, gambol, ignore, pass up, spring **7** abscond, misfire, scamper, skitter **8** leave out, overlook, pass over, ricochet **9** skedaddle

skipjack
4 boat, fish, tuna **6** bonito **8** bluefish, ladyfish, sailboat

skipper
5 pilot **6** leader **7** captain **9** butterfly, commander

ski resort
Austrian: **9** Kitzbühel
Canadian: **5** Banff **8** Big White, Sun Peaks, Whistler **9** Tremblant (Mont) **10** Lake Louise
French: **8** Chamonix
Italian: **7** Cortina
Swiss: **5** Davos **6** Gstaad **7** Verbier, Zermatt **8** St. Moritz **9** Engelberg, Sugarloaf
U. S.: **4** Alta, Taos, Vail **5** Aspen, Stowe **6** Big Sky **8** Snowbird, Snowmass **9** Camelback, Lake Tahoe, Snowbasin, Sun Valley, Telluride **10** Killington **11** Jackson Hole, Squaw Valley **12** Breckenridge

skirmish
3 row **4** fray, spar **5** broil, brush, clash, melee, run-in, scrap, set-to **6** affray, battle, dustup, fracas, tussle **7** assault, dispute **8** conflict, struggle **9** encounter, scrimmage

skirr
3 run **4** bolt, flee, sail, scud, skim, skip **5** float, scoot, shoot **7** make off, scamper **9** skedaddle

skirt
3 hem, rim **4** brim, duck, edge **5** avoid, bound, brink, burke, dodge, elude, evade, hedge, verge **6** border, bypass, define, detour, escape, fringe, ignore, margin **8** sidestep, surround **9** perimeter, periphery **10** circumvent
ballet: **4** tutu
feature: **3** hem **4** slit
length: **4** maxi, midi, mini
Polynesian: **5** pareo, pareu
Scottish: **4** kilt
style: **5** A-line **6** sheath **9** crinoline
support: **11** farthingale

skit
6 shtick, sketch **9** burlesque
show: **5** revue

skitter
3 hop **4** flit, skip, trip **6** scurry, spring **7** scamper

skittery
see **skittish**

skittish
3 coy, shy **4** edgy, wary **5** chary, dizzy, jumpy, leery **6** fickle **7** bashful, fidgety, flighty, nervous, rabbity, restive **8** unstable, volatile **9** excitable, frivolous, impulsive, mercurial, whimsical **10** capricious, unreliable

skive
4 pare **5** carve, shave, slice

skivvies
9 underwear

skoal
5 toast **6** health

skua
4 bird **6** jaeger **7** seabird

skulduggery
5 fraud **8** foul play, trickery **9** chicanery, duplicity **10** hanky-panky

skulk
4 lurk, slip **5** creep, prowl, shirk, slink, sneak, steal

skull
4 head, mind **5** brain **6** crania (plural) **7** cranium **8** brainpan **9** braincase
back of: **7** occiput
bone: **5** vomer **6** zygoma **7** ethmoid, frontal **8** parietal, sphenoid, temporal
jawless: **9** calvarium
joint: **6** suture
part: **3** jaw **5** inion

skullcap
6 beanie, pileus **7** calotte **8** yarmulke **9** calvarium, zucchetto

skunk
4 beat, drub, lick, scum, whip, whup **6** thrash, wallop **7** clobber, polecat, shellac, stinker, trounce **8** civet cat, lambaste **9** overwhelm, slaughter
genus: 8 Mephitis

sky
5 azure **6** heaven, welkin **7** heavens **8** empyrean **9** firmament

sky-blue
5 azure **8** cerulean

skylarking
5 revel **7** revelry, whoopee **9** high jinks, horseplay, rowdiness, whoop-de-do **10** roughhouse **12** roughhousing

skylight
6 window

skyline
7 horizon, outline

sky pilot
5 padre **6** cleric, parson, pastor **8** chaplain, minister, preacher **9** churchman, clergyman

skyrocket
4 rise, soar **7** shoot up **8** catapult

sky sighting
3 UFO

slab
5 block, chunk, slice, strip **8** pavement

slack
3 lax **4** lazy, slow, soft **5** inert, loose, relax **6** remiss **7** ease off, laggard, passive, relaxed **8** careless, derelict, dilatory, inactive, indolent, slothful, sluggish, stagnant **9** leisurely, lethargic, negligent **10** neglectful

slacken
3 ebb, lax **4** ease, slow, wane **5** abate, let up, loose, relax **6** detain, ease up, lessen, loosen, relent, retard, slow up **7** die down, dwindle, ease off, subside **8** diminish, moderate, slow down **9** untighten **10** decelerate

slacker
3 bum **4** slug **5** idler, sloth **6** loafer **7** goof-off, shirker, wastrel **8** deadbeat, layabout, slugabed, sluggard **9** goldbrick, lazybones **10** delinquent **11** couch potato

slack-jawed
5 agape **6** gaping

slag
4 lava **5** dross **6** cinder, debris, scoria

slake
5 allay **6** deaden, quench **7** crumble, hydrate, relieve, satisfy **9** alleviate

slam
3 bat, hit, jab, pan, rap **4** bang, bash, beat, belt, blow, boom, dash, drub, flay, slug, slur, swat, wham **5** blast, crack, crash, fling, knock, pound, slash, smack, smash, swipe, whack **6** batter, cudgel, hammer, scathe, strike, thwack, wallop **7** clobber, potshot **8** lambaste **9** castigate

slam-dance
4 mosh

slam dunk
5 cinch, setup **6** shoo-in **7** safe bet **9** certainty, sure thing

slammer
3 can, jug, pen **4** brig, coop, jail, stir **5** clink, pokey **6** cooler, lockup, prison **9** calaboose **12** penitentiary

slander
4 slur, tale **5** libel, slime, smear, sully **6** defame, malign, smirch, vilify **7** asperse, calumny, scandal, tarnish, traduce **8** besmirch **9** denigrate **10** backbiting, calumniate, defamation, detraction, scandalize **11** mud-slinging **12** backstabbing

slang
4 cant, jive **5** argot, lingo **6** jargon, patois, patter **7** dialect **10** vernacular

slant
3 tip **4** bank, bias, cant, heel, lean, list, skew, tilt, veer, warp **5** angle, aside, bevel, grade, slope, splay **7** distort, incline, leaning, outlook **8** gradient **9** prejudice, viewpoint **10** standpoint **11** inclination **12** predilection
combining form: 4 clin **5** clino

slap
3 hit, pop **4** bash, blow, cuff, shot, slam, swat **5** clout, smack, spank, whack **6** buffet, insult, rebuff, strike **7** affront, putdown **8** brickbat, lambaste, penalize **9** castigate

slapdash
5 hasty, messy **6** random, sloppy **7** cursory **8** careless, slipshod **9** half-baked, haphazard, hit-or-miss, makeshift

slap down
5 quell **6** kibosh **7** squelch **8** prohibit, suppress

slaphappy
5 dazed, dizzy, woozy **6** punchy **10** punch-drunk

slash
3 cut **4** clip, gash, hack, pare, slit **5** lower, shave, slice **6** reduce, scathe, scorch **7** abridge, blister, curtail, cut back, cut down, scarify, scourge, shorten **8** lacerate, lambaste, mark down **9** castigate, excoriate **10** abbreviate

slat
4 lath **5** board, stave, strip **6** louver, louvre **7** airfoil

slate
4 gray, list, rock, tile **6** lineup, record, tablet, ticket **7** shingle **8** schedule **9** designate

Slate, e.g.
5 e-zine

slather
5 smear **6** spread **8** squander

slattern
4 bawd, moll, slut, tart **5** hussy, tramp, wench **6** floozy, harlot **7** chippie, jezebel, trollop **8** strumpet **10** prostitute **11** painted lady **12** scarlet woman, streetwalker

slaughter
4 kill, slay **6** murder **7** butcher, carnage, killing, wipe out **8** butchery, decimate, demolish, hecatomb, massacre **9** bloodbath, bloodshed, liquidate **10** annihilate, butchering **11** destruction, exterminate, liquidation **12** annihilation

slaughterhouse
8 abattoir, shambles

Slaughter of baseball
4 Enos

Slav
4 Pole, Serb, Sorb, Wend **5** Croat, Czech **6** Bulgar, Slovak **7** Russian, Serbian, Slovene **8** Bohemian, Croatian, Moravian **9** Bulgarian, Ruthenian, Ukrainian

slave
4 grub, help, peon, plod, serf, slog, toil **5** grind, helot, swink **6** drudge, menial, thrall, toiler, vassal **7** bondman, chattel, servant
feudal: **4** serf
harem: **9** odalisque
liberated: **8** freedman
Muslim: **6** Mamluk **8** Mameluke
Spartan: **5** helot

slave driver
6 tyrant **7** foreman **8** martinet, overseer **10** taskmaster **11** Simon Legree

slaver
4 spit **5** drool, froth **6** drivel, saliva **7** dribble, slobber, spittle **8** salivate

slavery
6 thrall **7** bondage, helotry, peonage, serfdom **9** indenture, servitude, thralldom **11** subjugation

Slavic apostle
5 Cyril **9** Methodius

slavish
6 abject, menial **7** servile **8** obeisant, wretched **9** groveling, imitative, laborious **10** obsequious, unoriginal **11** subservient

slay
4 do in, kill **6** murder **7** bump off, butcher, execute, put away **8** dispatch, knock off **9** liquidate, slaughter **11** assassinate

slayer
7 butcher **11** executioner

sleazy
3 low **5** cheap, dingy, seedy, tacky, tatty **6** cheesy, flimsy, shabby, shoddy, trashy **7** run-down, squalid **8** gimcrack **10** down-at-heel **11** dilapidated **12** disreputable

sled
4 luge, pung **6** sleigh **7** coaster, travois **8** toboggan
Russian: **6** troika

sled dog
5 husky **8** malamute

sledge
4 maul **6** hammer, sleigh
Eskimo: **7** komatik
Lapp: **5** pulka

sleek
4 oily **6** glassy, glossy, smooth **7** elegant, stylish **8** lustrous, polished **10** glistening

sleep
3 nap **4** doss, doze, rest **5** sopor **6** catnap, repose, siesta, snooze **7** shut-eye, slumber **11** slumberland
bringer: **7** sandman
combining form: **4** hypn, narc **5** hypno, narco, somni
disorder: **5** apnea
god: **6** Hypnos, Somnus
noise: **5** snore

sleeper
3 tie **4** beam, mole **7** Pullman **8** long shot **11** double agent, stringpiece

sleeping
4 abed **7** dormant **8** comatose
disease: **10** narcolepsy

sleepless
7 wakeful **8** vigilant **9** insomniac

sleeplessness
8 insomnia

sleepwalker
12 somnambulist

sleepy
4 dozy **6** drowsy **7** nodding **9** somnolent **10** slumberous

sleigh
4 pung **6** sledge

sleight
4 ploy, ruse, wile **5** skill, trick **7** gimmick, prowess **8** artifice, deftness, maneuver **9** dexterity, stratagem **10** adroitness

sleight of hand
11 legerdemain

slender
4 lean, slim, thin, trim **5** lithe, reedy, spare **6** skinny, slight, svelte, twiggy **7** spindly, willowy

sleuth
3 tec **4** dick, Drew (Nancy), G-man **5** Brown (Encyclopedia, Father), Hardy (Frank, Joe), Kojak (Theo), Lupin (Arsène), McGee (Travis), Morse, Queen (Ellery), Saint (The), snoop, Spade (Sam), Tracy (Dick), Vance (Philo), Wolfe (Nero) **6** Alleyn (Roderick), Archer (Lew), Belden (Trixie), Hammer (Mike), Holmes (Sherlock), Marple (Miss), Poirot (Hercule), shamus, Wimsey (Peter) **7** Cadfael (Brother), Columbo, Fansler (Kate), gumshoe, Maigret, Marlowe (Philip), Rawlins (Easy), Templar (Simon "The Saint") **8** Drummond (Bulldog), hawkshaw, Millhone (Kinsey), Rockford (Jim), sherlock **9** Dalgliesh (Adam), detective, inspector, operative, Scarpetta (Kay), Wallander (Kurt) **10** private eye, Warshawski (V. I.) **12** investigator

slew
3 lot, mob, ton **4** army, heap, host, load, mess, pile, raft, skid, turn, veer **5** batch, bunch, crowd, flock, pivot, twist **6** myriad, passel, swerve, throng **9** abundance, multitude

slice
3 cut **4** gash, slit **5** allot, carve, divvy, quota, sever, share, slash, split, wedge **6** cleave, divide, incise, sample **7** dissect, portion, segment **8** allocate **9** allotment, allowance

slick
4 film, glib, oily, slip, wily **5** sharp, sleek, soapy **6** crafty, glossy, greasy, shrewd, smarmy, smooth, tricky **7** cunning **8** slippery, slithery, unctuous **10** lubricious, oleaginous

slicker
4 dude **5** dandy, shark **6** con man **7** cheater, diddler, grifter, oilskin, sharper **8** raincoat, swindler **9** trickster **11** flimflammer

slide
3 dip, sag **4** flow, ramp, skid, slip **5** chute, coast, chute, drift, glide, skate, slump, spill **6** scooch, stream **7** decline, slither **8** downturn **9** downswing, downtrend **12** transparency

slide over
5 elide

slight
3 dis **4** omit, skip, slim, snub, thin **5** frail, reedy, scant, scorn, small **6** flimsy, ignore, meager, meagre, modest, offend, paltry, remote, skinny **7** contemn, neglect, outside, put-down, slender, tenuous, trivial **8** brush-off, delicate, discount, overlook, smallish, trifling **9** disregard, pint-sized **10** disrespect, negligible

slightly
4 a bit, a tad **6** a touch **7** a little

slightly open
4 ajar

slim
4 thin **5** lithe, reedy, small, spare **6** meager, meagre, minute, narrow, paltry, remote, skinny, slight, svelte, twiggy **7** lissome, outside, slender, tenuous **9** lithesome **10** negligible

slim down
4 diet, fast **6** reduce **10** slenderize

slime
3 goo, mud **4** glop, gook, guck, gunk, muck, ooze, scum **5** filth **6** sleaze, sludge **7** slander

slimming option
4 lipo

slimy
4 oozy **6** mucous **7** viscous

sling
3 lob **4** cast, fire, hang, hurl, sock, toss **5** chuck, heave, march, pitch, throw **6** dangle, launch **7** suspend **8** catapult

slink
4 lurk **5** creep, prowl, skulk, slide, sneak, steal **7** gumshoe

slinky
4 sexy **5** lithe, sleek **6** svelte **7** furtive, lissome, sinuous, slender, willowy **8** graceful, sensuous, stealthy

slip
3 sag **4** dock, drop, fall, flow, flub, goof, lurk, shed, sink, skid **5** berth, boner, creep, error, fluff, gaffe, glide, lapse, slide, slink, slump, sneak, steal **6** escape **7** blooper, blunder, decline, drop off, fall off, faux pas, mistake, slither **8** downturn, throw off **9** downswing, downtrend

slipper
4 mule, shoe **5** scuff **6** bootee, bootie, sandal **8** flip-flop, pantofle

slippery
3 icy **4** eely, oily **5** slick **6** greasy, shifty, smooth **7** devious, evasive **8** illusive, slithery **10** lubricious

slipshod
6 blowsy, blowzy, flimsy, frowsy, frowzy, shabby, shoddy, sloppy, untidy **7** rumpled, scrubby, scruffy, unkempt **8** careless, ill-kempt, slapdash, slovenly, tattered **9** haphazard, makeshift, negligent **10** bedraggled, disheveled, down-at-heel

slipup
4 goof **5** boner, error, fluff, lapse **6** bungle, glitch, miscue, mishap **7** blooper, blunder, faux pas, misstep, mistake, setback, stumble **8** accident **9** mischance, oversight **10** misfortune **11** misjudgment

slip up
3 err **4** goof **7** blunder, stumble

slit
3 cut, gap **4** gash, rent **5** chink, crack, slash, slice **6** cranny, incise **7** crevice, fissure, opening

slither
4 slip **5** creep, glide, sidle, slide, slink, snake, sneak, steal **7** wriggle **8** undulate

slithery
see **slippery**

sliver
5 scrap, shard, shave, shred, slice **6** paring **7** shaving, snippet **8** splinter

slob
3 oaf **4** boor, clod, goon, lout **6** galoot, sloven

slobber
4 gush **5** drool, froth **6** drivel, effuse, slaver **7** dribble, enthuse **8** salivate

sloe
4 plum **10** blackthorn

slog
4 grub, moil, plod, plug, toil **5** chore, grind, labor, shlep, slave, sweat **6** drudge, schlep, trudge **7** schlepp

slogan
5 maxim, motto **6** byword **9** battle cry, catchword, watchword **10** shibboleth **11** catchphrase

sloop
4 boat **5** yacht **8** sailboat

slop
3 mud, pap **4** gush, muck **5** douse, dreck, dregs, offal, slosh, slush, spill, swill **6** guzzle, pablum, refuse, splash, sludge **7** garbage, pabulum, rubbish **8** splatter

slope
3 tip **4** bend, brae, cant, heel, lean, list, rise, skew, swag, sway, tilt **5** grade, pitch, scarp, slant **6** ascent, escarp, glacis **7** descent, incline, leaning, recline **8** gradient **9** acclivity, declivity, obliquity **11** inclination
combining form: **5** cline **6** clinal

sloppy
5 dowdy, gushy, messy **6** blowsy, blowzy, frowsy, frowzy, sloven, slushy, untidy **7** gushing, unkempt **8** careless, effusive, ill-kempt, slapdash, slipshod, slovenly **10** bedraggled, disheveled **11** dishevelled

slosh
4 gush, slop, wash **5** churn, swash **6** gurgle, splash **8** flounder, splatter

slot
4 vent **5** niche, notch **6** groove, keyway **7** keyhole, opening, passage **8** aperture **10** pigeonhole

sloth
4 laze **5** idler **6** acedia, apathy, idling, lazing, loafer, slouch, torpor **7** goof-off, languor, loafing, slacker **8** idleness, laziness, lethargy **9** heaviness, indolence, lassitude, lazybones, torpidity **11** couch potato **12** listlessness, sluggishness **13** shiftlessness
two-toed: **4** unau

slothful
4 idle, lazy **8** fainéant, indolent **9** shiftless

slouch
3 bum, oaf, sag **4** laze, loaf, loll, lout, mope, slug **5** droop, idler, sloth, slump, stoop **6** loafer, loiter, lounge **7** saunter, shamble, shuffle **8** fainéant, slugabed, sluggard **9** do-nothing, lazybones

slough
3 bog, fen **4** cast, mire, molt, quag, shed, sump **5** inlet, marsh, scrap, swamp **6** morass, reject **7** discard **8** jettison, quagmire, throw out **9** backwater, marshland, swampland, throw away

Slovakia
capital: **10** Bratislava
city: **6** Kosice
monetary unit: **6** koruna
mountain range: **10** Carpathian
neighbor: **6** Poland **7** Austria, Hungary, Ukraine **13** Czech Republic
river: **3** Váh **4** Hron **6** Danube, Morava

Slovenia
capital: **9** Ljubljana
city: **7** Maribor
monetary unit: **4** euro
monetary unit, former: **5** tolar
neighbor: **5** Italy **7** Austria, Croatia, Hungary
part of: **7** Balkans
peninsula: **6** Balkan

slovenly
5 dingy, messy, mussy, seedy, slack **6** frowsy, frowzy, grubby, grungy, scuzzy, shabby, skanky, sleazy, sloppy, untidy **7** squalid, unkempt **8** careless, slapdash, slipshod **10** bedraggled, slatternly

slow
4 late, poky **5** brake, check, largo, lento, pokey, tardy **6** adagio, hinder, impede, leaden, retard, torpid **7** halting, lagging, slacken **8** dilatory, dragging, plodding, sluggish, stagnant **9** leisurely, snaillike, unhurried **10** decelerate, snail-paced, straggling

slowpoke
5 sloth, snail **6** lagger **7** dawdler, laggard **8** lingerer, loiterer, tortoise **9** straggler

sludge
3 mud **4** crud, gook, guck, gunk, mire, muck, ooze, slop **5** slime **6** sewage **8** sediment

slug
3 bum, hit, nip, tot **4** bash, belt, dram, drop, jolt, shot, slam, sock, swat **5** blast, clout, idler, larva, pound, punch, smack, smash, snail, snort,

thump **6** buffet, bullet, loafer, slouch, thwack, wallop **7** clobber, goof-off, slacker **8** fainéant, toothful **9** do-nothing, lazybones **11** couch potato
genus: **5** Limax

slugfest
4 bout **5** brawl, set-to **6** rumble **8** dogfight **10** donnybrook, prizefight

sluggard
3 bum **5** idler **6** loafer, slouch **7** dawdler, goof-off, laggard, shirker, slacker **8** deadbeat, fainéant, slowpoke **9** do-nothing, goldbrick, lazybones

slugger
5 boxer **6** batter, hitter **7** palooka

slugger's stat
3 RBI

sluggish
4 lazy, logy, slow **5** inert, slack **6** draggy, leaden, stupid, torpid **7** lumpish **8** dragging, indolent, listless, slothful **9** apathetic, lethargic

sluice
4 duct, flow, gush, pour, race, wash **5** flush, surge **6** trough **7** channel **8** spillway **9** floodgate

slum
6 ghetto **7** skid row

slumber
3 nap **4** doze **5** sleep **6** catnap, drowse, snooze, stupor, torpor **8** dormancy, hebetude, lethargy **9** lassitude, torpidity

slumberous
see **sleepy**

slumgullion
4 stew **6** burgoo, ragout **7** goulash

slump
3 dip, sag **4** drop, fall, flag, funk, loll, sink, slip **5** droop, hunch, slide **6** slouch, trough **7** decline, drop off, falloff **8** collapse, downturn **9** downslide, downswing, downtrend, recession **10** depression, stagnation

slur
4 blot, blur, lisp, onus, slam, spot **5** brand, knock, libel, odium, smear, stain **6** befoul, defame, insult, malign, stigma, vilify **7** blacken, calumny, obloquy, obscure, slander, spatter, traduce **8** black eye, brickbat, innuendo, tear down **9** aspersion, bespatter, denigrate, discredit, disparage **10** accusation, calumniate

slurp
3 lap **4** gulp, suck **5** lap up, swill **6** guzzle

slush
3 mud **4** mire, muck, slop **6** drivel **8** schmaltz

sly
4 arch, foxy, wily **5** cagey, saucy, shady, slick **6** artful, clever, crafty, shifty, shrewd, smooth, sneaky, subtle, tricky **7** cunning, devious, furtive, roguish, vulpine **8** guileful, scheming, slippery, stealthy **9** designing, insidious, underhand **11** mischievous, underhanded

slyboots
see **scamp**

slyness
4 wile **5** guile **7** cunning **8** caginess, foxiness, wiliness **9** canniness **10** craftiness

smack
3 bat, bop, box **4** bang, bash, belt, biff, blow, buss, chop, clip, cuff, dash, hint, kiss, peck, reek, slam, slap, sock, tang, whop **5** clout, crack, plumb, punch, right, savor, smell, spang, spank, stink, taste, tinge, trace, whack **6** buffet, heroin, relish, smooch, square, strike, thwack **7** clobber, soupçon

smack-dab
4 bang, just **5** plumb, right, spang **6** square **7** exactly **8** squarely **9** perfectly, precisely

small
3 wee **4** mean, mini, puny, tiny **5** bitty, dinky, dwarf, micro, minor, petty, runty, short, teeny **6** bantam, little, meager, meagre, minute, monkey, narrow, paltry, petite, slight, teensy **7** cramped, stunted, trivial **8** picayune, piddling, pint-size, trifling **9** miniature, minuscule, pint-sized **10** diminutive, negligible, undersized **11** ineffectual, unimportant
combining form: **4** micr, mini **5** micro
island: **3** ait, cay, key

small fry
4 kids, tots **8** children **10** youngsters

small-minded
4 mean **5** petty **6** narrow **7** bigoted **9** hidebound, illiberal, parochial **10** brassbound, intolerant, provincial

smallpox
7 variola

small talk
4 chat **6** banter **7** chatter, palaver, prattle **8** badinage, chitchat, raillery, repartee **10** persiflage

small-time
5 minor, petty **6** paltry, two-bit **7** trivial **8** picayune, piddling, trifling **10** bush-league, negligible, shoestring **11** minor-league, unimportant **13** insignificant

smalt
4 blue

smarmy
4 glib, oily **5** slick **6** sleazy **7** buttery, fawning, fulsome **8** unctuous **10** obsequious, oleaginous **12** ingratiating

smart
3 apt **4** ache, chic, keen **5** acute, alert, canny,

fresh, natty, nobby, quick, sassy, saucy, savvy, sharp, slick, sting, swank, throb **6** brainy, bright, cheeky, clever, dapper, shrewd, spiffy, spruce, suffer **7** dashing, stylish **8** impudent **11** fashionable, intelligent, quick-witted, ready-witted, sharp-witted

smart aleck
7 show-off, wise guy **8** wiseacre **9** know-it-all **11** wisecracker, wisenheimer

smart-alecky
4 wise **5** fresh, sassy, saucy **6** cheeky **8** impudent, insolent **9** bold-faced **11** impertinent

smart set
5 elect, elite **6** bon ton, gentry **7** in crowd, quality, society, who's who **9** beau monde, haut monde **10** blue bloods, upper crust **11** aristocracy, Four Hundred, high society

smarty-pants
7 wise guy **9** know-it-all, swellhead **11** wisenheimer

smash
3 hit, jar **4** bang, bash, belt, blow, boom, clap, jolt, raze, ruin, slam, slug, sock, wham, whop **5** blast, boffo, burst, clash, crack, crash, crush, shock, whack, wreck **6** batter, impact, pileup, shiver, wallop **7** clobber, crack-up, debacle, destroy, shatter, success **8** collapse, decimate, demolish, knockout, overhand, splinter **9** breakdown, collision, pulverize, sensation, succès fou **10** annihilate **12** disintegrate

smashup
5 crash, wreck **6** fiasco, pileup **7** crack-up, debacle **8** accident, collapse, disaster **9** breakdown, collision

smattering
3 few **7** handful **10** sprinkling

smear
3 dab, tar **4** beat, coat, daub, drub, lick, slur, soil, whip **5** cover, libel, stain, sully, taint **6** befoul, defame, defile, malign, smirch, smudge, spread, thrash, vilify **7** asperse, blacken, calumny, plaster, shellac, slander, tarnish, traduce **8** besmirch **9** bespatter, denigrate **10** calumniate

smell
4 funk, nose, odor, reek **5** aroma, scent, sense, smack, sniff, snuff, stink, trace, whiff **6** detect, stench **7** bouquet, perfume **9** fragrance, redolence
rotten egg: 6 sulfur

smell, sense of
9 olfaction

smelly
4 rank **5** fetid, funky, reeky **6** foetid, putrid, rancid, stinky **7** noisome, reeking, stenchy **8** mephitic, stinking **10** malodorous

smelt
4 flux, fuse, slag **6** reduce, refine, tomcod **8** sparling **9** sand lance, whitebait

smidgen
3 bit, dab, jot **4** atom, iota, mite **5** crumb, speck, touch **6** morsel

smile
4 beam, grin **5** smirk **6** simper

smirch
see **smudge**

smirk
4 grin, leer **5** fleer, sneer **6** simper **7** grimace

smite
3 hit **4** belt, kill, sock **5** clout, whack **6** assail, attack, strike **7** afflict, assault, clobber, torment

smithereens
4 bits **6** pieces **9** fragments, particles

smitten
4 gaga **5** taken **6** hooked **8** besotted, enamored **9** enamoured, enchanted, entranced **10** captivated, enraptured, infatuated **11** intoxicated

smock
5 apron, dress, frock **8** pinafore

smoke
4 cure, fume **5** fumes, vapor **8** fastball, fumigate **9** cigarette

smoky
4 fumy, gray, hazy **5** murky, sooty **6** turbid **7** reeking **10** caliginous, smoldering

smolder
4 fume, glow, stew **5** churn **6** bubble, seethe, simmer **7** ferment **9** fulminate

smooch
4 buss, kiss, neck, peck **5** smack **8** osculate

smooth
4 easy, even, flat, oily **5** fluid, flush, level, plane, sleek, slick, suave **6** facile, fluent, glassy, glossy, polish, urbane **7** cursive, flatten, flowing, running **8** glabrous, hairless, soothing, unbroken **10** effortless, unwrinkled

smooth-spoken
4 glib **6** fluent **8** eloquent **10** articulate **13** silver-tongued

smooth transition
5 segue

smorgasbord
4 hash, olio **6** buffet, jumble, medley **7** farrago, grab bag, mélange **8** mishmash, mixed bag, pastiche **9** potpourri **10** hodgepodge, hotchpotch, miscellany, salmagundi **11** gallimaufry

smother
5 choke, douse, quell **6** hush up, muffle, quench, stifle **7** blanket, repress, squelch **8** inundate, restrain, suppress **9** overwhelm, suffocate **10** asphyxiate

smudge
3 dab **4** blot, blur, daub, foul, soil **5** dirty, smear, stain, sully, taint **6** bedaub, blotch, defile, smirch **7** begrime, besmear, blacken, blemish, splotch, tarnish **8** besmirch

smug
4 vain **9** conceited **10** complacent **13** self-satisfied

smuggle
3 run **7** bootleg

smut
4 porn **5** filth **9** obscenity **11** pornography

smutty
4 blue, foul, lewd, racy **5** bawdy, dirty, nasty, sooty **6** coarse, filthy, risqué, vulgar **7** obscene, raunchy **8** indecent, off-color, prurient **9** salacious **12** pornographic, scatological

Smyrna
5 Izmir

snack
3 tea **4** bite, nosh, tapa **6** morsel, nibble **11** refreshment

snaffle
3 bit, cop **4** lift **5** filch, pinch, swipe **6** pilfer, pocket **7** purloin

snafu
5 botch, error, mix-up, snarl **6** bungle, foul up, mess up, muddle **7** chaotic, screwup **9** confusion

snag
3 nab **4** curb, grab, hook, nail, tear **5** catch, hitch **6** glitch, holdup, hurdle, obtain, secure **7** capture **8** drawback, obstacle **9** apprehend **10** impediment **11** obstruction

snail
5 whelk **6** limpet **7** mollusc, mollusk **8** escargot, ramshorn, slowpoke **9** gastropod **10** periwinkle

snake
3 boa **4** fink **5** crawl, creep, racer, slide **6** python, writhe **7** hognose, meander, serpent, slither **8** anaconda, ophidian, undulate
combining form: **4** ophi **5** ophio
genus: **4** Eryx
poisonous: **3** asp **5** adder, cobra, coral, krait, mamba, viper **6** elapid, taipan **7** rattler **8** pit viper **10** bushmaster, copperhead, fer-de-lance **11** cottonmouth **13** water moccasin

snakebird
6 darter **7** anhinga

snake-eater
8 mongoose **13** secretary bird

snakelike
7 sinuous **8** ophidian **10** serpentine
shape: **3** ess

snakeroot
7 bugbane **10** wild ginger **11** blazing star

snakeweed
7 bistort **13** poison hemlock

snaky
7 sinuous, winding **8** flexuous, tortuous **10** convoluted, meandering, serpentine **11** anfractuous
fish: **3** eel

snap
3 pic **4** bang, bark **5** break, cinch, crack, photo **6** breeze, lose it, picnic **7** crackle **8** duck soup, kid stuff, pushover **10** child's play

snap back
6 revive **7** rebound, recover **10** convalesce, recuperate

snappish
4 edgy, tart **5** huffy, testy **6** tetchy, touchy **7** waspish **8** petulant **9** irritable

snappy
4 chic, fast **5** brisk, hasty, natty, quick, rapid, sharp, smart, swank, swift **6** dapper, lively, modish, prompt, speedy, trendy **7** dashing, stylish **8** animated, vigorous **9** breakneck, vivacious

snapshot
4 view **5** image, photo **6** précis, sketch, visual **7** picture **8** overview, synopsis **10** shadow copy

snare
3 bag, get, net **4** bait, hook, lure, trap **5** catch, decoy, noose, tempt **6** come-on, enmesh, entice, entrap, seduce, tangle **7** capture, catch up, chicane, embroil, ensnare, ensnarl, involve, mantrap, pitfail, trammel **8** entangle, inveigle **9** chicanery, deception **10** enticement, temptation

snarl
3 jam, web **4** bark, gnar, knot, maze, mesh **5** chaos, growl, ravel, skein **6** jungle, morass, muddle, tangle **7** perplex **8** disarray, disorder, entangle, gridlock, mishmash **9** confusion, labyrinth **10** complexity, complicate **12** complication, entanglement

snatch
3 bit, nab **4** grab, jerk, take, yank **5** catch, pluck, seize, swipe **6** abduct, clutch, kidnap, wrench **8** fragment

snazzy
4 chic **5** fancy, gaudy, jazzy, nobby, ritzy, sassy, sharp, smart, showy, swank **6** chichi, classy, flashy, garish, glitzy, jaunty, spiffy, swanky **7** elegant

sneak
3 cur, pad **4** lurk, slip, worm **5** crawl, creep, glide, mooch, prowl, shirk, skulk, skunk, slide, slink, steal **6** covert, secret, tiptoe, weasel **7** furtive, gumshoe, slither, smuggle **8** hush-hush,

slyboots, stealthy **9** pussyfoot, scoundrel **10** undercover **11** clandestine

sneaky
4 foxy **6** shifty, tricky **7** devious, furtive **8** guileful, indirect, slippery, stealthy **9** underhand **11** duplicitous, underhanded

sneer
4 gibe, jeer **5** fleer, scoff, smirk **7** grimace, snigger

sneeze
5 achew, achoo **6** ahchoo
cause: **5** snuff **6** dander, pollen **7** allergy **8** dust mite
French: **7** atchoum
German: **7** hatschi
Spanish: **6** atchís

snicker
5 laugh **6** giggle, titter **7** chortle, chuckle

snide
4 mean **5** nasty **8** spiteful **9** malicious **11** insinuating

sniff
4 jeer, nose **5** scent, scoff, smell, snoop **6** inhale

sniffy
4 smug **5** aloof, lofty **6** lordly, snooty, uppity **7** haughty, pompous, stuck-up **8** scornful, superior **10** disdainful, hoity-toity **12** contemptuous, supercilious

snifter
3 nip, sip, tot **4** dram, drop, jolt, shot, slug **5** glass, snort **6** finger, goblet

snip
3 bit, cut **4** clip, crop, trim **5** notch, scrap **8** fragment

snipe
4 carp **9** sandpiper

sniper
6 gunman, killer **7** shooter **8** marksman, rifleman **12** sharpshooter

snippety
see **snippy**

snippy
4 curt, tart **5** bluff, blunt, brief, gruff, short, terse **6** abrupt, crusty **7** brusque **8** snappish

snit
3 fit **4** flap, fume, huff, stew **5** panic, pique, sweat, tizzy **6** dither, frenzy, lather, pother, swivet **10** conniption

snitch
3 cop, nip, rat **4** beak, blab, fink, hook, lift, palm, sing, tell **5** filch, peach, pinch, spill, steal, swipe **6** inform, pilfer, pocket, squeal, tattle **7** purloin, rat fink, stoolie, tattler, tipster **8** betrayer, informer, squealer **11** stool pigeon

snivel
3 sob **4** weep **5** cower, whine **6** cringe, whinge **7** blubber, snuffle, whimper

snob
5 snoot **6** poseur **7** elitist, parvenu

snobbish
6 la-de-da, la-di-da, snooty, uppity **7** elitist, haughty, high-hat, stuck-up **8** lah-de-dah, lah-di-dah **9** lah-dee-dah **10** hoity-toity **11** patronizing, pretentious **12** supercilious **13** condescending

snook
5 cobia **6** robalo **12** sergeant fish

snooker
3 con **4** dupe, fool, hoax, pool **5** trick **6** delude **7** beguile, deceive, defraud **8** flimflam, hoodwink **9** bamboozle **11** hornswoggle

snoop
3 pry, spy **4** nose, peek, peep, peer, poke **5** prier, pryer **6** ferret, meddle, sleuth **7** gumshoe, intrude, meddler **8** busybody, quidnunc **9** detective, inspector, interfere **10** rubberneck

snooper
3 spy **9** detective, inspector **12** investigator

snoopy
4 nosy **6** prying **7** curious **8** meddling **9** intrusive **10** meddlesome **11** inquisitive

snoot
see **snout**

snooty
see **snobbish**

snooze
3 kip, nap **4** doze **5** sleep **6** catnap, drowse, nod off, siesta **7** drop off, slumber **10** forty winks

snore
8 rhonchus

snorkelers' site
4 reef

snort
3 nip, tot **4** dram, drop, jolt, shot, slug **5** scoff, snarl **6** exhale, inhale **7** snifter

snout
3 neb **4** beak, nose **6** muzzle, schnoz **7** schnozz **9** proboscis

snow
glacial: **4** firn, névé
melted: **5** slush
pellet: **7** graupel
ridge: **8** sastruga

snow apple
8 mushroom

snowball
5 mount, run up **6** expand **7** augment, burgeon, explode, inflate **8** increase, multiply, mushroom, viburnum **10** accumulate **11** proliferate

snowbird
5 finch, junco **6** thrush **7** bunting **9** fieldfare, ivory gull

Snow-Bound author
8 Whittier (John Greenleaf)

snow finch
9 brambling

snow grouse
9 ptarmigan

snow leopard
5 ounce

Snow Leopard author
11 Matthiessen (Peter)

snowstorm
8 blizzard

snub
3 cut **4** shun **5** blunt, scorn, spite, spurn **6** rebuff, rebuke, slight, stubby **7** put down **9** ostracize, repudiate **12** cold-shoulder

snuff
3 ice, off **4** kill, nose **5** pinch, scent, smell **6** murder, rappee **7** execute **10** extinguish **11** exterminate

snug
4 cozy, neat, taut, tidy, trim **5** comfy, cushy, tight **6** burrow, cuddle, nestle, nuzzle, secure **7** orderly **9** sheltered, shipshape **11** comfortable

snuggle
5 spoon **6** burrow, cuddle, curl up, huddle, nestle, nuzzle

so
3 sae **4** ergo, then, thus, true **5** hence **6** indeed **9** similarly, therefore **11** accordingly **12** consequently

soak
3 ret, sop, sot, wet **4** bilk, clip, lush, skin, swig, wino **5** douse, drink, gouge, imbue, souse, steep **6** boozer, drench, fleece, infuse, rip off, seethe **7** drinker, guzzler, immerse **8** drunkard, permeate, saturate, submerge **9** alcoholic, penetrate **10** boozehound, impregnate, overcharge
flax: **3** ret

soaked
5 soggy **6** sodden **7** sopping **8** drenched, dripping **9** saturated

soap
4 suds **6** stroke **7** flatter, wheedle **8** blandish, butter up, inveigle **9** sweet-talk
hard: **7** castile
ingredient: **3** lye, oil **5** scent **9** fragrance

soapbox
4 dais **6** podium **7** rostrum **8** hustings, platform, scaffold

soap bubbles
4 foam, suds

soap plant
5 amole

soapstone
4 talc **8** steatite

soapwort
7 cowherd **11** bouncing bet

soar
3 fly **4** lift, rise **5** arise, climb, glide, hover, mount, shoot **6** ascend, rocket **7** shoot up **8** increase **9** skyrocket

sob
3 cry **4** bawl, blub, wail, weep **7** blubber, whimper

sober
4 calm, cool **5** grave, staid **6** low-key, proper, sedate, solemn **7** austere, earnest, serious, subdued **8** composed, low-keyed, moderate, rational, reserved **9** abstinent, collected, practical, pragmatic, realistic, temperate **10** abstaining, abstemious, controlled, hardheaded, no-nonsense, reasonable, restrained **11** disciplined, down-to-earth **12** matter-of-fact **13** imperturbable, self-possessed

sobriety
7 gravity **10** abstinence, continence, sedateness, temperance **11** seriousness

sobriquet
3 tag **5** alias **6** byname **7** epithet, moniker **8** cognomen, nickname **10** hypocorism

so-called
6 formal **7** alleged, nominal, titular **8** supposed **9** pretended, professed, purported **10** ostensible, self-styled

soccer
cup: **5** World
official: **7** referee **8** linesman
player: **6** booter, goalie, kicker, winger **7** forward, link man, striker, sweeper **8** defender, fullback, halfback **10** goalkeeper
star: **4** Hamm (Mia), Pelé **5** Akers (Michelle), Henry (Thierry), Klose (Miroslav), Messi (Lionel) **6** Zidane (Zinedine) **7** Beckham (David), Ronaldo (Cristiano) **8** Chastain (Brandi), Maradona (Diego) **10** Ronaldinho **11** Beckenbauer (Franz)
term: **3** net **4** boot, chip, kick, trap **6** corner, header, tackle, volley **7** dribble, kickoff, throw-in **8** back-heel, free kick, goal kick, goal line **9** touchline **10** center spot, corner flag, corner kick **11** dropped ball, halfway line, penalty kick, penalty spot

sociable
5 close **6** genial **7** affable, amiable, cordial **8** familiar, gracious **9** clubbable, congenial, convivial **10** gregarious, hospitable **11** good-natured

social
5 civic, civil **8** communal **9** clubbable, convivial **10** collective, gregarious, hospitable **11** extroverted **13** companionable
class: 5 caste
position: 6 status

Social Contract author
8 Rousseau (Jean-Jacques)

socialist
American: 4 Debs (Eugene) **6** Ripley (George), Thomas (Norman)
British: 4 Owen (Robert, Robert Dale), Webb (Beatrice, Sidney) **6** Morris (William)
French: 7 Fourier (Charles), Viviani (René) **10** Saint-Simon (Henri de)
German: 4 Marx (Karl) **6** Engels (Friedrich) **9** Luxemburg (Rosa) **10** Liebknecht (Wilhelm)

socialize
3 mix **5** party, visit **6** hobnob, mingle **7** consort **9** associate **10** fraternize

social media
message: 4 post **5** tweet
site: 4 Digg **6** Flickr, Reddit, Tumblr **7** MySpace, Twitter **8** Facebook, LinkedIn **9** Instagram, Pinterest
term: 4 blog, feed, vlog, wiki **5** tweet **7** hashtag, podcast, webcast, webinar **8** flash mob, platform

social worker
4 Riis (Jacob), Wald (Lillian D.) **6** Addams (Jane) **7** Alinsky (Saul), Lathrop (Julia C.)

society
4 club **5** elite, guild **6** gentry, league, people, public **7** company, quality, who's who **8** populace, sodality **9** beau monde, community, haut monde **10** fellowship, fraternity, upper class, upper crust **11** aristocracy, association, brotherhood **13** companionship
branch: 7 chapter

sociologist
American: 4 Bell (Daniel), Park (Robert), Ward (Lester Frank) **5** Balch (Emily Green), Small (Albion), Whyte (William H.) **6** Du Bois (W. E. B.), Glazer (Nathan), Sumner (William Graham), Veblen (Thorstein) **7** Johnson (Charles Spurgeon), Riesman (David)
English: 7 Spencer (Herbert)
French: 5 Comte (Auguste) **8** Durkheim (Emile)
German: 5 Weber (Max) **6** Simmel (Georg)
Italian: 6 Pareto (Vilfredo)
Swedish: 6 Myrdal (Alva, Gunnar)

sock
3 bop, box, hit **4** bash, belt, blow, chop, cuff, ding, slap, slog **5** clout, punch, smack, smash, whack **6** argyle, buffet, strike, thwack, wallop **7** clobber **8** stocking

sock away
4 bank, save, stow **5** cache, hoard, lay by, put by, stash **8** lay aside

socket
6 outlet

socks
4 hose **7** hosiery

Socrates
birthplace: 6 Athens
poison: 7 hemlock
pupil: 5 Plato
wife: 8 Xantippe **9** Xanthippe

Socratic
8 maieutic

sod
4 land, peat, turf **5** earth, grass **6** ground

soda
3 pop **4** cola **5** tonic **7** seltzer
brand: 3 Tab **4** Barq, Coke, Nehi **5** Barq's, Fanta, Moxie, Pepsi **6** Fresca, Sprite, Squirt **8** Dr. Pepper

sodality
4 club **5** guild, lodge, order, union **6** league **7** society **9** community **10** fellowship, fraternity **11** association, brotherhood

sodden
3 wet **5** soggy, soppy **6** soaked, soused **7** soaking, sopping **8** drenched, dripping **9** saturated **11** waterlogged, wringing-wet

Sodom and ——
8 Gomorrah
visitor: 3 Lot

sofa
5 couch, divan **7** ottoman **9** banquette, davenport

so far
3 yet **5** as yet, still **6** to date **7** till now **8** hitherto, until now **10** heretofore

Sofia native
6 Bulgar **9** Bulgarian

soft
4 cozy, easy, mild, snug **5** balmy, comfy, cushy, downy, faint, mushy, silky **6** doughy, flabby, gentle, low-key, pliant, satiny, silken, simple, smooth, spongy, tender **7** cottony, lenient, pillowy, pliable, squashy, squishy, subdued, velvety **8** cushiony, workable, yielding **9** malleable **11** comfortable
cheese: 4 Brie
hail: 7 graupel
leather shoes: 4 mocs
palate: 5 velum

softcover
9 paperback

soften
4 ease, tame 5 abate, allay, relax 6 dampen, lessen, mellow, soothe, subdue, temper, weaken 7 assuage, lighten, mollify 8 diminish, mitigate, moderate, palliate, tone down 9 alleviate

softhearted
4 kind, warm 6 humane, kindly, tender 7 lenient 10 responsive 11 sympathetic 13 compassionate

soft-pedal
4 mute 6 dampen, hush up, muffle, subdue 8 minimize, play down, suppress, tone down 9 underplay 11 de-emphasize

soft-soap
3 con 4 coax 6 cajole, soothe, wangle 7 blarney, flatter, wheedle 8 blandish, butter up, inveigle 9 sweet-talk

software medium
5 CD-ROM 6 download, floppy 10 flash drive, floppy disk, thumb drive

software test phase
4 beta

soggy
3 wet 6 doughy, soaked, sodden 7 soaking, sopping 8 drenched, dripping 9 saturated 10 bedraggled 11 waterlogged

Sohrab and Rustum author
6 Arnold (Matthew)

soi-disant
7 alleged 8 putative, so-called, supposed 9 pretended, professed, purported 10 ostensible, self-styled

soil
3 mud, tar 4 daub, dirt, foul, land, loam, mess, muck, murk 5 dirty, earth, grime, muddy, smear, stain, sully, taint 6 defile, ground, smirch, smudge 7 begrime, blacken, country, pollute, tarnish 8 besmirch, discolor, homeland 10 fatherland, motherland, terra firma 11 contaminate
aggregate: 3 ped
clay: 5 gault
combining form: 3 geo 4 agro
dark: 9 chernozem
deposit: 5 loess 7 eluvium
infertile: 6 podzol
layer: 4 gley, sola (plural) 5 solum
rich: 6 hotbed
tropical: 7 latosol

soiled
5 dirty, muddy 6 filthy, grubby, grungy 7 stained, sullied, unclean

soiree
4 fete, gala 5 party 6 affair, social 7 evening, shindig 8 function 9 festivity, reception 11 celebration 13 entertainment

___ soit qui mal y pense
4 Honi

sojourn
4 bide, stay, stop 5 abide, lodge, tarry, visit 6 linger 7 layover 8 stopover

Sol
3 sun 7 daystar, phoebus
horse: 4 Eous 5 Ethon 9 Erythreos
(see also **Helios**)

solace
5 allay, amuse, cheer 6 buck up 7 comfort, console, hearten 8 inspirit 10 condolence

solar disk
4 Aten, Aton

solarium
7 sunroom

solar-system model
6 orrery

solder
4 fuse, weld 5 braze

soldier
5 grunt, sepoy 7 dogface, draftee, fighter, pikeman, private, recruit, trooper, veteran, warrior 8 bluecoat, doughboy, fusilier, rifleman 9 free lance, guerrilla, man-at-arms, mercenary 10 carabineer, carabinier, serviceman 11 condottiere, infantryman
ancient Greece: 7 hoplite
British: 5 Tommy 7 redcoat
cavalry: 6 hussar 8 chasseur
Confederate: 3 reb
French: 5 poilu 6 Zouave
German: 5 jerry
irregular: 8 guerilla 9 guerrilla
Prussian: 5 uhlan
Turkish: 9 janissary

sole
3 one 4 lone, only 5 alone 6 bottom, single, unique 8 flatfish, singular 9 exclusive

solecism
4 goof, slip 5 boner, error, gaffe, lapse 6 misuse 7 blooper, blunder, faux pas, mistake 11 impropriety

solemn
5 grand, grave, sober, staid, stern 6 august, formal, ritual, sedate, somber, sombre 7 earnest, plenary, serious, stately, weighty 8 funereal, imposing, majestic 9 dignified 10 ceremonial, impressive, no-nonsense, sobersided 11 ceremonious, magnificent
promise: 4 oath

solemnize
4 keep 5 bless, honor 6 hallow 7 dignify, observe 8 venerate 9 celebrate, ritualize 10 consecrate 11 commemorate

solicit
3 ask, beg **4** lure, tout, urge **5** apply **6** demand, drum up, entice **7** beseech, bespeak, canvass, entreat, implore, request **8** petition **9** importune **11** proposition, requisition

solicitor
6 jurist, lawyer, suitor **7** pleader **8** advocate, attorney **9** counselor

solicitous
4 avid, keen **6** ardent, tender **7** anxious, careful, devoted, fearful, worried **8** rigorous **9** assiduous, attentive, concerned **10** fastidious, meticulous, scrupulous **11** considerate, punctilious, sympathetic **12** apprehensive **13** conscientious

solicitude
4 care, heed **5** qualm, worry **7** concern, scruple **9** attention, vigilance **11** compunction **12** watchfulness **13** consideration

solid
4 firm, hard **5** dense, sound, valid **6** cogent, secure, stable, sturdy, united **7** compact **8** reliable, unbroken **9** unanimous, undivided **10** convincing

solidarity
5 union, unity **6** cement, esprit **7** concord, oneness **8** cohesion **9** integrity **13** esprit de corps

solidify
3 dry, fix, gel, set **4** cake, jell **6** freeze, harden, secure **7** compact, congeal **8** compress, contract, indurate

solitary
4 lone, lorn, only, solo **5** alone **6** hermit, lonely, single, unique **7** recluse **8** deserted, desolate, eremitic, forsaken, isolated, lonesome, separate, singular **9** reclusive, withdrawn **10** antisocial, particular, unsociable **11** standoffish **12** misanthropic **13** unaccompanied

solitude
7 privacy **8** loneness **9** aloneness, isolation, seclusion **10** detachment, loneliness, quarantine, retirement, withdrawal **11** confinement **12** separateness

solo
4 aria, lone **5** alone **6** single **7** unaided **8** solitary **13** independently, unaccompanied
operatic: **4** aria

Solo in space
3 Han

Solomon
father: **5** David
kingdom: **6** Israel
mother: **9** Bathsheba
son, successor: **8** Rehoboam
victim: **4** Joab **8** Adonijah

Solomon Islands
capital: **7** Honiara
ethnic group: **10** Melanesian
island: **8** Choiseul **11** Guadalcanal, Santa Isabel

solon
8 lawgiver **10** legislator

so long
4 by-by, ciao, ta-ta **5** adieu, adios **6** bye-bye, good-by **7** cheerio, good-bye, toodles **8** farewell, Godspeed, toodle-oo

solution
6 answer, result
salt: **6** saline

solve
3 fix **5** break, crack **6** decode, reveal, settle **7** clear up, dope out, unravel, work out **8** construe, decipher, unriddle, untangle **9** figure out, interpret, puzzle out **11** disentangle

Solzhenitsyn
archipelago: **5** gulag
character: **4** Ivan (Denisovich)

Somalia
capital: **9** Mogadishu
gulf: **4** Aden
language: **6** Arabic, Somali
location: **12** Horn of Africa
monetary unit: **8** shilling
neighbor: **5** Kenya **8** Djibouti, Ethiopia

somatic
6 bodily, carnal **7** fleshly **8** corporal, parietal, physical **9** corporeal

somber
3 dim **4** dark, drab, dull, grim **5** bleak, dusky, grave, heavy, murky, staid **6** dismal, dreary, gloomy, sedate, solemn **7** doleful, joyless, obscure, serious, weighty **8** funereal, mournful **9** tenebrous **10** caliginous, depressing, depressive, lugubrious, melancholy, sepulchral, sobersided, tenebrific

somersault
4 flip

somewhat
4 a bit, a tad **5** quite **6** fairly, kind of, rather, sort of **7** a little **8** slightly **9** partially, tolerably **10** moderately

sommelier's offering
4 wine

___ Sommer
4 Elke

somniferous
see **sleepy**

somnolent
see **sleepy**

Somnus
brother: **4** Mors
god of: **5** sleep
mother: **3** Nox

son
French: **4** fils
Italian: **6** figlio
Spanish: **4** hijo

song
3 air, lay **4** glee, tune **5** carol, chant, ditty, lyric **6** ballad, melody, number **7** chanson **8** madrigal
biblical: **8** canticle
boat: **9** barcarole **10** barcarolle
French: **7** chanson
German: **4** lied **6** lieder (plural)
lamentation: **5** dirge **8** threnode, threnody
medieval: **8** sirvente **9** sirventes
morning: **6** aubade
of joy or praise: **5** paean
operatic: **4** aria **6** arioso **7** arietta **8** cavatina **9** cabaletta
Portuguese: **4** fado
sacred: **4** hymn **5** psalm
sailor's: **6** chanty, shanty **7** chantey
short: **8** canzonet
wedding: **8** hymeneal

song and dance
5 pitch, spiel

songbird
see at **bird**

Song of Myself author
7 Whitman (Walt)

Song of Solomon
9 Canticles

songwriter
8 composer, lyricist
famous: **3** Ebb (Fred) **4** Anka (Paul), Bock (Jerry), Cahn (Sammy), Duke (Vernon), Hart (Lorenz), Joel (Billy), Kern (Jerome), King (Carole), Nyro (Laura), Webb (Jimmy), Wolf (Hugo) **5** Arlen (Harold), Berry (Chuck), Byrne (David), Cohan (George M.), Cohen (Leonard), Cooke (Sam), David (Hal), Dietz (Howard), Dylan (Bob), Evans (Ray), Green (Adolph), Holly (Buddy), Leigh (Carolyn), Loewe (Frederick), Simon (Carly, Paul), Styne (Jule), Waits (Tom), Weill (Kurt) **6** Berlin (Irving), Comden (Betty), Coward (Noel), Denver (John), Dozier (Lamont), Fields (Dorothy), Foster (Stephen), Goffin (Gerry), Herman (Jerry), Kander (John), Leiber (Jerry), Lennon (John), Lerner (Alan Jay), Lovett (Lyle), Mandel (Johnny), McHugh (Jimmy), Mercer (Johnny), Nelson (Willie), Newman (Randy), Parton (Dolly), Porter (Cole), Sedaka (Neil), Seeger (Pete), Taupin (Bernie), Taylor (James), Travis (Merle), Warren (Harry), Wonder (Stevie) **7** Bergman (Alan, Marilyn), Coleman (Cy), Diamond (Neil), Guthrie (Woody), Harburg (E. Y.), Harnick (Sheldon), Holland (Brian, Eddie), Loesser (Frank), Mancini (Henry), Manilow (Barry), Novello (Ivor), Orbison (Roy), Rodgers (Richard), Romberg (Sigmund), Spector (Phil), Stoller (Mike), Youmans (Vincent) **8** Costello (Elvis), Gershwin (George, Ira), Hamlisch (Marvin), Mayfield (Curtis), Mitchell (Joni), Morrison (Van), Robinson (Smokey), Schubert (Franz), Schwartz (Arthur), Sondheim (Stephen) **9** Bacharach (Burt), Donaldson (Walter), McCartney (Paul), Strayhorn (Billy), Von Tilzer (Albert, Harry), Van Heusen (Jimmy) **10** Carmichael (Hoagy) **11** Hammerstein (Oscar), Springsteen (Bruce)

songwriters' org.
3 BMI **5** ASCAP

Sonja ___
5 Henie

Sonnambula composer
7 Bellini (Vincenzo)

sonnet
developer: **8** Petrarch
part: **5** octet **6** octave, sestet

sonorous
7 ringing, vibrant **8** resonant **10** oratorical, resounding, rhetorical **11** declamatory **12** magniloquent **13** grandiloquent

Sons and Lovers hero
5 Morel (Paul)

Sontag novel
9 In America **12** Volcano Lover (The)

soon
4 anon **6** any day, pronto **7** betimes, by and by, shortly **8** directly, promptly **9** forthwith, presently, right away **10** before long

Sooner State
8 Oklahoma

soothe
4 balm, calm, ease, hush, lull **5** allay, quiet, salve, still **6** becalm, pacify, settle, solace, subdue **7** appease, assuage, comfort, compose, console, massage, mollify, placate, relieve **8** calm down, reassure **9** alleviate **10** conciliate, propitiate **11** tranquilize

soothsay
5 augur **8** prophesy **9** adumbrate **10** vaticinate **13** prognosticate

soothsayer
4 seer **5** sibyl **6** oracle **7** diviner, prophet **8** foreseer **9** predictor **10** forecaster, foreteller
ancient Roman: **5** augur **6** auspex **8** haruspex
blind: **8** Tiresias
(see also **prophet**)

sop
3 wet 4 gift, soak 5 bribe, douse, goody, souse, steep 6 deluge, drench, reward, seethe 7 douceur 8 gratuity, saturate, waterlog 9 incentive, lagniappe, sweetener 10 concession, enticement

sophism
see **sophistry**

sophistic
5 false, phony 7 invalid, seeming, unsound 8 delusive, illusory, spurious 9 beguiling, casuistic, deceptive, plausible 10 fallacious, fraudulent, misleading, ostensible

sophisticated
4 chic 5 blasé, jaded, suave 6 smooth, svelte, urbane 7 complex, knowing, refined, worldly 8 cultured, involved, schooled, seasoned 9 Byzantine, elaborate, intricate, practiced 10 world-weary 11 experienced, worldly-wise 12 cosmopolitan

sophistry
9 casuistry 12 equivocation 13 dissimulation, prevarication

Sophocles play
4 Ajax 7 Electra 8 Antigone 10 Oedipus Rex

Sophonisba
brother: 8 Hannibal
father: 9 Hasdrubal
husband: 6 Syphax

soporific
4 dozy 6 drowsy, opiate, sleepy 7 anodyne, calming 8 hypnotic, narcotic, sedative 9 calmative, somnolent 10 anesthetic, slumberous 11 anaesthetic, somniferous 12 somnifacient 13 tranquilizing

soprano
American: 4 Pons (Lily) 5 Costa (Mary), Gluck (Alma), Moffo (Anna), Moore (Grace), Price (Leontyne), Sills (Beverly) 6 Arroyo (Martina), Battle (Kathleen), Callas (Maria), Curtin (Phyllis), Donath (Helen), Farrar (Geraldine), Garden (Mary), Munsel (Patrice), Norman (Jessye), Peters (Roberta), Piazza (Marguerite), Resnik (Regina), Upshaw (Dawn) 7 Farrell (Eileen), Fleming (Renée), Kirsten (Dorothy), Stevens (Risë), Traubel (Helen) 8 Ponselle (Rosa)
Australian: 5 Melba (Nellie) 10 Sutherland (Joan)
Austrian: 4 Popp (Lucia) 7 Rysanek (Leonie) 8 Sembrich (Marcella)
Canadian: 7 Stratas (Teresa)
French: 7 Crespin (Régine)
German: 6 Leider (Frida) 7 Lehmann (Lilli, Lotte) 11 Schwarzkopf (Elisabeth)
Italian: 5 Freni (Mirella), Grisi (Giuditta, Giulia), Patti (Adelina) 6 Scotto (Renata) 7 Bartoli (Cecilia), Tebaldi (Renata) 10 Tetrazzini (Luisa) 11 Ricciarelli (Katia)
Korean: 6 Sumi Jo
Mexican: 8 Cruz-Romo (Gilda)
New Zealand: 8 Te Kanawa (Kiri)
Norwegian: 8 Flagstad (Kirsten)
Romanian: 8 Cotrubas (Ileana)
Russian: 8 Netrebko (Anna)
Spanish: 7 Caballé (Montserrat) 8 Berganza (Teresa) 12 de los Angeles (Victoria)
Swedish: 4 Lind (Jenny) 7 Nilsson (Birgit)
(see also **mezzo-soprano**)

Sopranos wife
4 Edie (Falco)

sorcerer
4 mage 5 magus 6 Flamel (Nicolas), Merlin, wizard 7 warlock 8 conjurer, conjuror, magician 9 enchanter 11 necromancer, thaumaturge

sorceress
3 hag, hex 5 Circe, Medea, witch

sorcery
5 magic 8 diablery, wizardry 9 conjuring 10 necromancy, witchcraft 11 bewitchment, enchantment, thaumaturgy
West Indian: 5 obeah

sordid
3 low 4 base, foul, mean, vile 5 dirty, nasty, seamy, shady, venal 6 blowsy, blowzy, filthy, frowsy, frowzy, grubby, scurvy, shabby, sleazy 7 ignoble, low-down, squalid, unclean 8 degraded, shameful, wretched 9 loathsome, mercenary 10 despicable, scandalous, slatternly 11 disgraceful 12 contemptible, disreputable 13 reprehensible

sore
3 raw 4 achy, boil 5 angry, irked, ulcer, upset, vexed 6 aching, bitter, canker, peeved, tender 7 abscess, chancre, hurting, painful 8 inflamed, smarting 9 chilblain, irritated, rancorous, resentful, sensitive

sorehead
4 crab 5 grump 6 griper, grouch 7 grouser 8 grumbler, sourpuss 10 bellyacher, complainer, crosspatch, malcontent

sorrel
3 oca 4 dock 8 chestnut, sourwood

sorrow
3 rue, sob, woe 4 moan, ruth 5 dolor, grief, mourn 6 grieve, lament, misery, regret 7 anguish, remorse, sadness 8 distress, grieving, mourning 9 dejection, heartache, suffering 10 affliction, heartbreak, melancholy 11 lamentation, unhappiness 12 mournfulness

sorrowful
3 sad 6 rueful, triste, woeful 7 doleful, forlorn, piteous, ruthful, unhappy 8 dolorous, downcast,

grieving, mournful, tristful, wretched **9** afflicted, miserable, plaintive, woebegone **10** lamentable, lugubrious, melancholy **11** heartbroken **12** disconsolate

sorry
3 bad, sad **4** mean, poor **5** cheap **6** cheesy, paltry, scummy, scurvy, shabby, shoddy **7** scruffy, unhappy **8** beggarly, contrite, mournful, penitent, pitiable, saddened, trifling, wretched **9** miserable, regretful, repentant **10** apologetic, inadequate, melancholy, remorseful **11** penitential **12** heavyhearted

sort
3 ilk, lot, set **4** comb, cull, kind, pick, sift, type **5** class, order **6** choose, screen, select, stripe, winnow **7** arrange, catalog, species, variety **8** classify, separate **9** catalogue, character **10** categorize, pigeonhole

sortie
4 dash, raid **5** foray, sally **7** assault, mission **9** excursion **10** expedition

sortilege
6 augury **7** sorcery **8** divining, witchery **10** divination, necromancy, witchcraft **11** thaumaturgy

Sorvino of film
4 Mira

so-so
4 fair, okay **6** decent, enough, fairly, medium, rather **7** average, fairish **8** adequate, mediocre, middling, moderate, passable, passably **9** tolerably **10** moderately **11** indifferent **12** run-of-the-mill

sot
4 alky, lush, wino **5** alkie, drunk, souse, toper **6** bibber, boozer, rummy **7** drinker, guzzler, tippler, tosspot **8** drunkard **9** alcoholic, inebriate **10** boozehound

Sotheby's signal
3 bid

sotto voce
3 low **5** aside **6** softly **7** faintly, mutedly, quietly **9** privately

souchong, e.g.
3 tea

sough
4 sigh **7** suspire, whisper

soul
4 pith **5** anima, being, heart **6** animus, breast, marrow, pneuma, psyche, spirit **7** essence **9** élan vital, substance **12** quintessence
combining form: **5** psych **6** psycho

soulful
6 moving, tender **7** emotive, fervent **8** poignant, stirring, touching **9** affecting, emotional **11** impassioned, sentimental

soul singer
4 Etta (James), Gaye (Marvin) **5** Bland (Bobby), Brown (James), Cooke (Sam), Flack (Roberta), Green (Al), Hayes (Isaac) **6** Butler (Jerry), Knight (Gladys), Sledge (Percy), Wonder (Stevie) **7** Charles (Ray), Pickett (Wilson), Redding (Otis) **8** Franklin (Aretha), Mayfield (Curtis)

sound
3 fit **4** firm, hale, kyle, safe, sane **5** audio, noise, plumb, probe, right, sober, solid, valid **6** cogent, fathom, intact, secure, stable, sturdy, unhurt **7** correct, earshot, healthy, logical, prudent **8** rational, reliable, sensible, unharmed **9** judicious, resonance, undamaged, vibration **10** convincing, reasonable **11** well-founded **12** satisfactory, well-grounded
combining form: **3** son **4** phon, soni, sono **5** audio, audit, phone, phono, phony **6** audito, phonia
gentle: **6** rustle
high-pitched: **4** ping, ting
pleasant: **7** euphony
quality: **6** timbre
rebound: **4** echo
repeating: **7** rat-a-tat **8** rataplan **10** rat-a-tat-tat
science: **6** sonics **7** phonics **9** acoustics

Sound
Alaska: **5** Cross
Antarctica: **7** McMurdo
Australia: **4** King **5** Broad
Bahamas: **5** Exuma
Canada: **4** Howe **6** Nansen
Connecticut-New York: **10** Long Island
English Channel: **8** Plymouth
Georgia: **8** Altamaha
Greenland: **5** Smith
Gulf of Mexico: **8** Suwannee **11** Mississippi
Massachusetts: **8** Vineyard **9** Nantucket
New England: **11** Block Island
North Carolina: **4** Core **5** Bogue **7** Pamlico, Roanoke **9** Albemarle, Currituck
Northwest Territories: **4** Peel **8** Melville **9** Lancaster **12** Prince Albert
Norwegian Sea: **8** Scoresby
Ontario: **4** Owen
Scotland: **3** Hoy **4** Jura, Mull **5** Inner
Spitsbergen: **4** Bell
Washington: **5** Puget

Sound and the Fury, The
author: **8** Faulkner (William)
character: **5** Benjy (Compson), Caddy (Compson), Jason (Compson) **6** Dilsey **7** Quentin (Compson)

soundness
6 health, sanity **7** balance **8** prudence, security, solidity, strength **9** integrity, stability **11** reliability

sound off
7 speak up 8 speak out

soup
beet: 6 borsch 7 borscht
bowl: 6 tureen
clear: 5 broth 8 bouillon, consommé, julienne
cold: 8 gazpacho 11 vichyssoise
curry: 12 mulligatawny
okra: 5 gumbo
seafood: 7 chowder
soy: 4 miso
thick: 5 gumbo, puree 6 bisque, burgoo, potage
vegetable: 10 minestrone
Vietnamese: 3 pho

soupçon
see **particle**

soupy
5 foggy, gooey, gushy, murky, mushy 6 drippy, slushy, smoggy 7 cloying, maudlin, mawkish 8 cornball 9 schmaltzy 10 saccharine 11 sentimental, tear-jerking

sour
4 acid, tart 5 acerb, acrid, tangy, testy 6 acidic, bitter, crabby, cranky, curdle, grumpy, morose, rancid, rotten, sullen, turned 7 acerbic, grouchy, peevish, prickly, spoiled, unhappy 8 vinegary 9 acidulous, fermented 12 disagreeable

source
4 font, root, well 5 basis, cause, fount, model, onset, start 6 mother, origin, spring 7 dawning, genesis 8 begetter, fountain, wellhead 9 beginning, inception, informant, precursor, prototype, reference, rootstock 10 antecedent, authorship, birthplace, derivation, originator, progenitor, provenance, wellspring 11 origination, provenience 12 fountainhead

sourness
7 acidity 8 acerbity, asperity

sourpuss
4 crab 5 crank, grump 6 griper, grouch 7 grouser, killjoy 8 grumbler, sorehead 10 bellyacher, complainer, crosspatch, curmudgeon 11 misanthrope

souse
3 dip, sop, sot 4 lush, soak, wino 5 binge, drown, steep 6 boozer, drench, pickle, plunge, seethe 7 immerse 8 drunkard, inundate, marinate, preserve, saturate, submerge, submerse 9 alcoholic, immersion, inebriate 10 boozehound, intoxicate 11 dipsomaniac

soused
3 lit 4 high 5 drunk, lit up, oiled 6 bashed, blotto, bombed, juiced, potted, soaked, soused, stewed, stoned, tanked, wasted, zonked 7 crocked, drunken, pickled, pie-eyed, sloshed, smashed, sottish 8 polluted 9 plastered 10 inebriated, liquored up 11 intoxicated

south
combining form: 5 austr 6 austro
French: 3 sud
Spanish: 3 sur

South Africa
capital: 8 Cape Town, Pretoria 12 Bloemfontein
city: 6 Durban 12 Johannesburg
desert: 8 Kalahari
enclave: 7 Lesotho
grassland: 4 veld 5 veldt
language: 5 Bantu 7 English 9 Afrikaans
monetary unit: 4 rand
mountain range: 11 Drakensberg
native: 3 San 4 Khoi, Zulu 5 Pondo, Sotho, Swazi, Venda, Xhosa 6 Tswana 7 Bushmen, Khoisan 9 Hottentot
neighbor: 7 Namibia 8 Botswana 9 Swaziland 10 Mozambique, Zimbabwe
plateau: 5 Karoo 6 Karroo
province: 7 Gauteng 8 Northern 9 Free State 10 Mpumalanga
river: 6 Molopo, Orange
settlers: 5 Boers

South America
country: 4 Peru 5 Chile 6 Brazil, Guyana 7 Bolivia, Ecuador, Uruguay 8 Colombia, Paraguay, Suriname 9 Argentina, Venezuela
ethnic group: 6 Aymara, Creole, Indian 7 mestizo, mulatto, Quechua, Spanish 10 Amerindian, Portuguese
language: 6 Aymara 7 Guaraní, Quechua, Spanish 10 Portuguese

South American
monkey: 4 titi
plain: 5 llano, pampa 6 pampas

South Asian
4 desi

South Carolina
capital: 8 Columbia
city: 10 Charleston, Greenville
college, university: 7 Citadel, Clemson
fort: 6 Sumter
island, island group: 3 Sea 6 Edisto, Parris 10 Hilton Head
nickname: 8 Palmetto (State)
river: 6 Edisto, Pee Dee, Santee 7 Tugaloo 8 Savannah
state bird: 12 Carolina wren
state flower: 13 yellow jasmine
state tree: 8 palmetto

South Dakota
capital: 6 Pierre
city: 9 Rapid City 10 Sioux Falls
mountain: 6 Harney (Peak) 8 Rushmore 10 Black Hills
nickname: 6 Coyote (State) 10 Mt. Rushmore (State)

park: **8** Badlands, Wind Cave
river: **8** Missouri **11** Belle Forche
state bird: **18** ring-necked pheasant
state flower: **12** pasqueflower
state tree: **6** spruce

Southeast Asian
4 Thai
capital: **5** Hanoi **6** Yangon **7** Bangkok, Rangoon **9** Phnom Penh, Vientiane
country: **4** Laos **5** Burma **7** Myanmar, Vietnam **8** Cambodia, Thailand

southerly
7 austral

South Korea
see **Korea, South**

South of France
4 Midi

South Pacific
country: **4** Fiji **5** Belau, Nauru, Palau, Samoa, Tonga **6** Tuvalu **7** Vanuatu **8** Kiribati
island: **4** Maui, Oahu **6** Saipan, Tahiti, Tarawa **8** Pitcairn

southpaw
5 lefty

South-West Africa
7 Namibia

Southwestern brick
5 adobe

Southwestern tribe
4 Hopi, Pima, Zuni **6** Apache, Navaho, Navajo

south wind
see at **wind**

souvenir
5 relic, token **6** trophy **7** memento **8** keepsake, memorial, reminder **11** remembrance

sovereign
4 coin, czar, free, king, tsar, tzar **5** queen, regal, royal, ruler **6** kingly, ruling **7** emperor, empress, highest, monarch, regnant, supreme **8** absolute, autarkic, autocrat, dominant, imperial, kinglike, majestic **9** ascendant, autarchic, monarchal, number one, paramount, potentate **10** autonomous, monarchial **11** independent, monarchical

soviet
7 council **9** committee

Soviet labor camp
5 gulag

Soviet Union
4 CCCP, USSR

sow
4 seed, toss **5** drill, fling, plant, strew **7** bestrew, scatter **9** broadcast **11** disseminate
young: **4** gilt

sown
4 semé

soybean
paste: **4** miso
soup: **4** miso

spa
5 baths, hydro, wells **6** hot tub, resort, spring, waters **7** springs **13** watering place
Czech: **6** Bilina **8** Karlsbad
English: **4** Bath **6** Buxton **9** Harrogate
French: **3** Dax **5** Evian
German: **3** Ems **5** Baden **6** Bad Ems **9** Kissingen
treatment: **4** peel

space
3 gap **4** area, room **5** blank, ether, plena (plural), scope **6** cavity, extent, plenum, spread, volume **7** breadth, expanse, stretch **8** capacity, distance, interval, universe **9** amplitude, expansion

space chimp
4 Enos

spaced-out
4 high **5** doped **6** stoned, zonked **7** drugged **8** hopped-up, turned on

space station
3 Mir **6** Salyut, Skylab

spacious
3 big **4** vast, wide **5** ample, large, roomy **7** immense **8** enormous, extended **9** boundless, capacious, cavernous, expansive, extensive **10** commodious, voluminous

spade
3 loy **5** scoop **6** shovel

Spade, Sam
4 dick **6** shamus, sleuth **7** gumshoe **9** detective **10** private eye
creator: **7** Hammett (Dashiell)
novel: **13** Maltese Falcon (The)

Spain
ancient name: **8** Hispania
capital: **6** Madrid
city: **6** Málaga **7** Seville **8** Pamplona, Valencia, Zaragoza **9** Barcelona, Saragossa
island: **7** Majorca, Minorca **8** Mallorca
island group: **6** Canary **8** Balearic
king: **10** Juan Carlos
leader: **6** Franco (Francisco)
monetary unit: **4** euro
monetary unit, former: **4** real **6** peseta **7** pistole
mountain: **8** Mulhacén **11** Pico de Aneto
mountain range: **8** Pyrenees
neighbor: **6** France **8** Portugal
peninsula: **7** Iberian
region: **6** Aragon, Murcia **7** Galicia **8** Valencia **9** Andalusia, Catalonia
river: **4** Ebro **12** Guadalquivir
sea: **13** Mediterranean
strait: **9** Gibraltar

___ Spake Zarathustra
4 Thus

spall
4 chip 5 flake 7 shaving 8 fragment 9 exfoliate

span
4 arch, term, time 5 cross, reach 6 extent, length, period, spread 7 compass, measure, stretch 8 duration, interval, lifetime, straddle, traverse

spangle
4 trim 5 flash, gleam 6 sequin 7 glitter, shimmer, sparkle, twinkle 9 coruscate 11 scintillate

Spaniard
9 Castilian

Spanish
accent mark: 5 tilde
aunt: 3 tia
bay: 5 bahia
bed: 4 cama 5 lecho
bird: 6 pájaro
boss: 7 cacique
bread: 3 pan
bridge: 6 puente
bull: 4 toro 6 el toro
chaperone: 6 duenna
cheer: 3 olé
church: 7 iglesia
combining form: 7 hispano
crossword puzzle: 10 crucigrama
custard: 4 flan
dance: 4 jota 5 baile, salsa 6 bailar 8 fandango, flamenco 9 zapateado
devil: 6 diablo
dictator: 8 caudillo
door: 6 puerta
dress: 7 vestido
folksong: 6 tonada
fortress: 7 alcazar
game: 5 juego
garrison: 8 presidio
gift: 6 regalo
gold: 3 oro
good-bye: 5 adiós
hello: 4 hola
hors d'oeuvre: 4 tapa
house: 4 casa
husband: 6 esposo, marido
ice cream: 6 helado
inn: 6 posada
January: 5 enero
journey: 5 viaje
library: 10 biblioteca
light: 3 luz
mayor: 7 alcalde
milk: 5 leche
Miss: 4 Srta.
money: 5 plata 6 dinero
movie: 8 pelicula
movies: 4 cine
Mrs.: 3 Sra.
number: 3 dos, uno 4 diez, doce, ocho, once, seis, tres 5 cinco, nueve, siete 6 cuatro
national hero: 3 Cid (El) 5 El Cid
nobleman: 7 grandee
operetta: 8 zarzuela
painter: 4 Dalí (Salvador), Miró (Joan) 9 Velázquez (Diego)
penal settlement: 8 presidio
plain: 4 vega 5 llano, pampa
plantation: 8 hacienda
please: 8 por favor
princess: 7 infanta
ranch: 5 finca 8 estancia
river: 3 rio
room: 4 sala 6 cuarto
saint: 7 Dominic 8 Ignatius
sale: 5 venta
scarf: 7 pañuelo 8 mantilla
school: 7 colegio, escuela
sea: 3 mar
shawl: 6 rebozo, serape
shirt: 6 camisa
shoe: 6 zapato 7 calzado
singer: 8 cantante
six: 4 seis
skirt: 5 falda
snack: 4 tapa
soccer: 6 fútbol
street: 5 calle
thank you: 7 gracias
this: 4 ésta, éste
title: 3 don, Sra. 4 doña, Srta. 5 señor 6 señora 8 señorita
tree: 5 árbol
trousers: 10 pantalones
uncle: 3 tío
water: 4 agua
wife: 6 esposa
wine: 4 sack 6 sherry
year: 3 año
you: 5 usted

Spanish fly
9 cantharis

spank
4 cane, flog, lash, slap 5 smack 6 larrup, paddle, punish, thrash 7 scourge 8 chastise

spar
3 box, vie 4 pole 5 joust, sprit, stall 7 dispute, wrangle 8 longeron
ship's: 4 boom, gaff, mast, yard 7 yardarm 8 bowsprit

spare
4 lank, lean, pity, save, slim 5 avoid, extra, gaunt, lanky 6 backup, excess, excuse, exempt, let off, meager, meagre, pardon, scanty, scrape, scrimp, skimpy, skinny, slight, unused 7 absolve,

relieve, reserve, scrawny, scrimpy, surplus **8** leftover **10** additional **11** superfluous

sparing
4 bare, wary **5** canny, chary, tight **6** frugal, meager, meagre, saving, stingy **7** prudent, thrifty **9** provident **10** economical, restrained, unwasteful **11** tightfisted **12** parsimonious

spark
3 woo **5** court, ember, glint **6** foment, incite, kindle, set off **7** provoke, trigger **8** activate, touch off **9** instigate, scintilla

sparkle
3 pep **4** élan, zing **5** flash, gleam, glint, glitz, verve **7** glimmer, glisten, glitter, shimmer, twinkle **8** vivacity **9** animation, coruscate **10** effervesce, liveliness **11** coruscation, scintillate **13** scintillation

sparkling
6 bubbly, lively **8** animated, bubbling **9** brilliant **12** effervescent

sparkling wine of Italy
4 Asti

Spark novel
11 Memento Mori **21** Prime of Miss Jean Brodie (The)

sparse
4 rare, thin **5** scant **6** meager, meagre, scanty, scarce, skimpy **7** limited, scrimpy **8** exiguous, sporadic, uncommon **9** dispersed, scattered **10** inadequate, infrequent, occasional

Sparta
10 Lacedaemon
country: **7** Laconia
general: **8** Lysander
king: **8** Leonidas, Menelaos
opponent: **5** Argos **6** Athens
queen: **4** Leda
serf: **5** helot

Spartacus
author: **4** Fast (Howard)
slayer: **7** Crassus

spasm
3 fit, tic **4** pang **5** burst, crick, throe **6** twitch **8** paroxysm **10** convulsion
muscular: **6** clonus

spasmodic
5 jerky **6** fitful, spotty **7** erratic **8** sporadic **9** desultory **10** convulsive **12** intermittent

spat
3 row **4** flap, miff, tiff **5** fight, scene, scrap **6** bicker, gaiter, hassle, oyster **7** brabble, dispute, quarrel, rhubarb, wrangle **8** argument, outburst, squabble **10** falling-out **11** altercation

spate
4 flow, flux, gush, pour, rain, rush, tide **5** flood, spurt, surge **6** deluge, series, shower, stream **7** current, freshet, torrent **8** cataract, outburst, overflow **10** inundation, outpouring

spatter
4 slop, spit **5** douse, fleck, plash, slosh, spray, spurt, swash **6** befoul, splash, splosh **7** handful, speckle, splurge, stipple **8** sprinkle

spawn
4 eggs, sire **5** beget, breed, brood, hatch, issue **6** create, father, parent **7** produce, product, progeny, provoke **8** engender, generate **9** offspring, originate, procreate, propagate, reproduce

speak
3 gab, jaw, say, yak **4** blab, chat, chin, talk **5** blurt, drawl, mouth, orate, spiel, spout, utter, voice **6** assert, convey, intone, mumble, murmur, mutter, parley **7** address, declaim, declare, lecture, phonate, whisper **8** converse, dilate on, perorate, vocalize **9** discourse, enunciate, expatiate, hold forth, verbalize
combining form: **4** phon
confusedly: **7** stammer, stutter **8** splutter
for: **7** testify

speaker
5 voice **6** orator **9** spokesman **10** mouthpiece **12** spokesperson

spear
3 gig **4** pike, spit **5** gouge, lance, spike **6** impale, pierce, skewer **7** assagai, assegai, harpoon, leister, trident **8** puncture, transfix **9** penetrate

spearhead
4 lead **5** front **6** direct

spear-thrower
6 atlatl **7** woomera

special
4 rare **6** unique **7** express, notable, unusual **8** peculiar, uncommon **10** designated, individual, noteworthy, particular **11** distinctive, exceptional, outstanding

special-effects technology
3 CGI

species
4 kind, sort, type **5** breed, class

specific
3 set **5** exact **6** strict, unique **7** express, limited, precise **8** clean-cut, clear-cut, definite, distinct, especial, explicit **10** individual, particular **11** categorical

specify
3 fix, set **4** cite, list, name **6** detail **7** itemize, mention, pin down, tick off **8** instance, spell out **9** determine, enumerate, establish, inventory, stipulate **13** particularize

specimen
4 case, sort, type **6** sample **7** example, neotype **8** exemplar, holotype, instance, sampling

specious
5 empty, false **6** hollow **8** spurious **9** casuistic, plausible, sophistic **10** misleading, ostensible **11** sophistical

speciousness
7 sophism **9** casuistry, sophistry

speck
3 bit, dot, jot **4** atom, iota, mite, mote, spot, tick, whit **5** crumb, fleck, grain, point, shred, trace **6** smidge **7** freckle, smidgen **8** molecule, particle, pinpoint, smidgeon
in the ocean: **3** cay, key **5** islet

speckle
3 dot **4** spot **5** flake, fleck **6** dapple, pepper **7** stipple

spectacle
4 pomp, show **5** drama, sight **6** parade **7** display, pageant, panoply, tableau **10** exhibition, exposition **12** extravaganza

spectacular
5 stagy **7** amazing, pageant **8** dazzling, dramatic, striking, wondrous **9** marvelous, thrilling, wonderful **10** astounding, eye-popping, histrionic, miraculous, phenomenal, prodigious, staggering, stupefying, stupendous **11** astonishing, sensational **12** extravaganza

spectator
5 gazer **6** viewer **7** watcher, witness **8** beholder, observer, onlooker **9** bystander **10** eyewitness

Spectator author
6 Steele (Richard) **7** Addison (Joseph)

specter
5 ghost, shade **6** shadow, wraith **7** eidolon, phantom **8** phantasm, revenant, visitant **10** apparition

spectral
6 spooky **7** ghastly, ghostly, phantom **9** ghostlike, unearthly **10** shadowlike **11** disembodied, phantomlike

spectrum
5 ambit, gamut, range, scale, sweep **7** compass **8** diapason **9** continuum
producer: **5** prism

speculate
4 muse **5** study, think, weigh **6** ponder, reason, review **7** reflect **8** cogitate, consider, meditate, ruminate, theorize **9** cerebrate **10** conjecture, deliberate **11** contemplate

speculation
5 guess, hunch **6** gamble, review, theory **7** surmise **9** brainwork **10** conjecture

speculative
5 risky **7** curious, pensive **8** academic **11** conjectural, theoretical **12** hypothetical

speech
4 talk **5** idiom, spiel, voice **6** debate, homily, parley, sermon, tirade, tongue **7** address, dialect, diction, lecture, monolog, oration, palaver **8** dialogue, diatribe, harangue, language, parlance, rhetoric **9** discourse, monologue, utterance **10** allocution, expression, vernacular **11** declamation **12** articulation, disquisition, vocalization
defect: **4** lisp **7** stutter

speechcraft
7 oratory **8** rhetoric **9** elocution

speechify
5 orate **6** preach **7** declaim **8** perorate

speechless
3 mum **4** dumb, mute **6** silent **7** aphonic **10** dumbstruck, tongue-tied

speed
3 fly, hie, run, zip **4** clip, gait, pace, race, rush, tear, whiz **5** chase, haste, hurry, tempo **6** barrel, burn up, career, hasten, hustle, whoosh **7** quicken **8** alacrity, celerity, dispatch, expedite, highball, legerity, momentum, rapidity, velocity **9** fleetness, quickness, swiftness **10** accelerate, cannonball, promptness

speed skater
see **ice skater**

___ Speedwagon
3 REO

speedway
5 track **8** turnpike **9** racetrack **10** racecourse

speedy
4 fast **5** brisk, fleet, hasty, quick, rapid, swift **6** nimble, prompt **8** headlong **9** breakneck **11** expeditious

spell
3 hex **4** bout, jinx, mojo, rune, time, tour, turn **5** charm, hitch, shift, stint, throe, while **6** attack, period, streak, voodoo **7** relieve, stretch **11** conjuration, incantation

spellbind
3 hex **4** grip, vamp **5** charm **7** bewitch, catch up, enchant **8** enthrall, entrance **9** enrapture, fascinate, hypnotize, mesmerize

spelling
11 orthography
bad: **10** cacography

Spelling of TV
4 Tori

spell out
7 clarify, explain, expound **8** construe, set forth **9** elucidate, explicate

spelunker
5 caver

spend
3 pay 4 blow, drop, pass 5 use up, waste 6 lavish, lay out, outlay 7 consume, exhaust, fork out, hand out, splurge 8 disburse, shell out, squander 9 dissipate, go through, throw away, while away 10 run through

spender
7 wastrel 8 prodigal 10 high roller, profligate, squanderer 11 scattergood

spendthrift
see **spender**

Spenser poem
11 Faerie Queen (The)

spent
4 shot 5 all in 6 effete, gassed, pooped, used-up, wasted 7 drained, worn-out 8 burnt out, consumed, depleted, washed-up 9 exhausted, washed-out

spew
4 gush, ooze 5 belch, egest, eject, eruct, erupt, expel, exude, flood, heave, shoot, spray, vomit 6 irrupt, spit up, squirt 7 throw up, upchuck 8 disgorge

sphagnum
4 moss

sphere
3 orb 4 area, ball, star, turf, zone 5 arena, field, globe, range, realm, round, scope 6 circle, domain, planet 7 demesne, rondure, terrain 8 dominion, province 9 bailiwick, territory 12 jurisdiction

spherical
5 orbed, round 6 global 7 globose 8 globular 9 orbicular
hairdo: 3 'fro 4 Afro

Sphinx
builder: 6 Khafre
father: 6 Typhon
mother: 7 Echidna
query: 6 riddle
site: 4 Giza 6 Thebes

spice
3 pep, zip 4 kick, mace, tang, zest 5 anise, clove, cumin, poppy, savor, smack 6 cloves, fennel, ginger, masala, nutmeg, pepper, relish, sesame 7 caraway, pimento 8 cardamom, cinnamon, piquancy 9 seasoning

Spice Islands
8 Moluccas

spick-and-span
4 mint, neat, snug, tidy, trig 5 clean 6 spruce 8 spotless 9 shipshape 10 immaculate

spicy
3 hot 4 racy 5 bawdy, fiery, salty, tangy, zesty 6 purple, ribald, risqué, savory, snappy, wicked 7 gingery, peppery, piquant, pungent, zestful 8 off-color, redolent, seasoned 9 flavorful, salacious 10 scandalous, suggestive 11 titillating
sauce: 5 salsa

spider
6 Aranea, frypan 7 skillet 8 arachnid 9 frying pan 10 black widow

spiel
4 jive, line 5 pitch 6 patter 12 song and dance

Spielberg film
4 Hook, Jaws 6 Always, Munich 7 Amistad 8 Terminal (The), War Horse 9 Lost World (The) 11 Color Purple (The) 12 Jurassic Park, Twilight Zone (The) 14 Empire of the Sun, Minority Report, Schindler's List, War of the Worlds 15 Catch Me if You Can 16 Sugarland Express (The) 17 Saving Private Ryan 19 Raiders of the Lost Ark

spieler
4 tout 6 barker, hawker, talker 8 huckster

spigot
3 tap 4 cock, gate 5 valve 6 faucet 7 hydrant, petcock, shutoff 8 stopcock

spike
3 pin 4 brob, heel, lace, nail 5 lance, piton, spear 6 antler, impale, needle, skewer 7 spindle 8 increase, mackerel, puncture, transfix

spile
4 bung 5 spout

spill
4 blab, drip, drop, fall, flow, slop, tell 5 spray 6 betray, inform, reveal, splash, squeal, tattle 7 divulge, dribble, run over, spatter 8 disclose, overflow

Spillane detective
10 Mike Hammer

spilth
5 dregs, dross, swill, trash, waste 6 debris, refuse, scraps 7 garbage, rubbish 8 leavings

spin
4 birl, gyre, reel, ride, swim, turn 5 dizzy, swirl, twirl, wheel, whirl 6 gyrate, rotate 7 revolve 8 rotation 9 pirouette, whirligig 10 revolution
a log: 4 birl
out: 6 extend 7 prolong, stretch 8 elongate, lengthen, protract

spinal column
5 chine 6 rachis
curvature: 8 lordosis
part: 8 vertebra
(see also **spine**)

spindle
3 pin, rod **5** newel, shaft, spike **6** impale, rachis

spindly
5 frail, lanky, rangy, shaky, weedy **6** flimsy, gangly, skinny, twiggy **7** fragile, rickety, tottery **8** gangling, skeletal **9** emaciated **10** jerry-built

spindrift
4 foam **5** spray

spine
4 back **6** rachis **7** spicule **8** backbone **9** vertebrae

spineless
5 timid **8** cowardly, timorous **9** weak-kneed **10** weak-willed **12** invertebrate

spinning
6 awhirl

spin-off
8 offshoot **9** by-product, outgrowth **10** derivative, descendant

Spinoza of philosophy
6 Baruch

spinster
7 old maid **10** maiden lady

spiny
6 barbed, thorny **7** prickly **8** echinate **10** nettlesome

spiral
4 coil, curl, wind **5** helix, twine, twist **6** volute **7** helical, helices (plural) **8** gyroidal, volution **9** cochleate, corkscrew
combining form: **3** gyr **4** gyro **5** helic **6** helico

spiral-horned antelope
5 eland

spire
4 coil **5** twist, whorl **7** steeple **8** pinnacle

spirit
3 pep, vim, zip **4** brio, dash, élan, gimp, grit, guts, life, mood, snap, soul, zeal, zest, zing **5** anima, ardor, drive, force, ghost, heart, moxie, oomph, pluck, shade, spunk, tenor, verve, vigor **6** animus, daemon, daimon, energy, esprit, fervor, ginger, mettle, morale, pneuma, psyche, starch, temper, wraith **7** courage, passion, phantom, specter, spectre **8** phantasm, revenant, vitality **9** animation, élan vital, substance **10** apparition, enthusiasm, get-up-and-go, liveliness
away: **6** abduct, kidnap, snatch
bottled: **5** genie
evil: **3** ker **4** aitu **5** afrit, demon **6** afreet **7** erlking, shaitan
female: **5** nymph **7** banshee
Hopi: **7** kachina
of a place: **10** genius loci
Persian: **4** peri

spirited
4 bold, game, keen **5** eager, fiery, peppy **6** ardent, gritty, lively, plucky, spunky **7** chipper, fervent, gingery, peppery, valiant, zealous **8** animated, cheerful, intrepid, resolute **9** audacious, dauntless, energetic, sprightly, vivacious **10** courageous, mettlesome **12** enthusiastic

spirits
5 booze, drink **6** liquor, tipple **9** aqua vitae, firewater
low: **5** blues, dumps, ennui **8** doldrums **10** blue devils, depression, melancholy

spiritual
6 sacred **7** saintly **8** churchly, mystical, numinous, platonic **9** religious **10** high-minded, immaterial **11** disembodied, incorporeal **12** metaphysical, supernatural, transcendent
guide: **4** guru

spiritualist
6 medium, mystic, shaman **7** psychic

spit
6 saliva, skewer, slaver, sputum **7** spatter, sputter **8** splutter **9** brochette **10** rotisserie **11** expectorate

spite
5 venom **6** grudge, malice, rancor, spleen **7** ill will, revenge **9** pettiness, vengeance **11** malevolence

spiteful
4 mean **5** catty, nasty, snide **6** malign, wicked **7** vicious, waspish **8** venomous **9** malicious, malignant, rancorous **10** malevolent, vindictive

spitfire
4 fury **5** harpy, shrew, vixen **6** dragon, virago **7** hellcat, tigress **8** fishwife, harridan **9** termagant

spitting image
4 twin **5** clone **6** double, ringer **9** duplicate **10** carbon copy, dead ringer, simulacrum

spittoon
8 cuspidor

splash
3 sop, wet **4** slop, soak **5** douse, slosh, spray, swash **6** drench **7** spatter **8** sprinkle

splashy
5 gaudy, jazzy, showy **6** flashy, garish, glitzy, tawdry **7** blatant **8** colorful, dazzling, striking **10** flamboyant **11** sensational **12** meretricious, ostentatious

splatter
4 slop **5** douse, plash, slosh, spray, swash **6** splash **8** sprinkle

splay
4 cant, tilt **5** angle, bevel, gawky, slant, slope

6 clumsy, extend, spread 7 awkward, incline 8 ungainly 9 expansion 11 inclination

spleen
see **spite**

splendid
4 fine 5 grand, showy 6 superb 7 elegant, shining 8 glorious, gorgeous 9 brilliant, excellent, marvelous, wonderful 10 first-class, impressive 11 illustrious, magnificent, outstanding 12 transcendent

splendor
4 pomp 5 glory 6 dazzle 7 majesty, panoply 8 grandeur, richness 9 pageantry, spectacle 10 brilliance, brilliancy 12 magnificence

Splendor in the Grass author
4 Inge (William)

splenetic
5 cross, surly 6 fuming 8 incensed, spiteful 9 malicious 10 ill-natured, malevolent 11 ill-tempered

splice
3 tie 4 join, mate, mesh 5 braid, graft, plait

splint
5 brace, strip 7 support 10 immobilize

splinter
4 rive 5 burst, smash 6 shiver, sliver 7 faction, shatter 8 fragment 12 disintegrate

split
3 rip 4 part, rend, rent, rift, rima, rime, rive, tear 5 break, carve, chasm, chink, cleft, crack, sever, slice 6 breach, cleave, cloven, divide, schism, sunder 7 break up, disjoin, dissect, diverge, divorce, divvy up, fission, fissure, rupture 8 cleavage, dissever, fracture, separate 11 dichotomize
combining form: 5 schiz 6 schizo 7 schisto

splotch
4 blob, blot 5 fleck, stain 6 smudge

splurge
4 orgy 5 binge, fling, spree 7 blowout, rampage 10 indulgence 12 extravagance

splutter
4 spit 6 babble, jabber 7 stammer

spoil
3 mar, rob, rot 4 baby, harm, prey, ruin, sack 5 decay, humor, taint, waste, wreck 6 coddle, cosset, curdle, damage, defile, impair, molder, pamper, ravish 7 blemish, cater to, destroy, indulge, pillage, putrefy, tarnish, vitiate 8 demolish 9 decompose 11 mollycoddle

spoiled
4 rank, sour 6 putrid, rancid, rotten, ruined 7 coddled, decayed, gone bad 8 impaired, indulged, pampered 9 indulgent
kid: 4 brat

spoils
4 haul, loot, swag 5 booty 7 pillage, plunder

spoilsport
7 killjoy

spoken
4 oral, said, told 6 verbal, voiced 7 uttered 8 phonetic, viva voce 9 delivered, unwritten 11 articulated

sponge
4 grub 5 cadge, leech, luffa, mooch 6 absorb, loofah 7 moocher 8 freeload, parasite, scrounge 10 freeloader
material: 8 mesoglea
opening: 6 oscula (plural) 7 osculum, ostiole

sponger
5 leech 7 moocher 8 parasite 10 freeloader

spongy
4 soft 5 mushy, pulpy 6 porous, quaggy 7 squashy, squishy 9 absorbent

sponsor
4 back, fund 5 angel, stake 6 backer, patron, surety 7 endorse, finance 8 advocate, bankroll, champion, Maecenas, mainstay, promoter, vouch for 9 grubstake, guarantee, guarantor, patronize, subsidize, supporter 10 benefactor, underwrite 11 underwriter

sponsorship
4 egis 5 aegis 7 backing, support 8 advocacy, auspices 9 patronage

spontaneous
5 ad-lib 7 natural, offhand 8 ad-libbed, unforced 9 automatic, extempore, impromptu, impulsive, unstudied 10 improvised, off-the-cuff, unprompted 11 instinctive, unmeditated

spontoon
4 pike 5 lance, spear

spoof
4 sham 5 farce, put-on 6 parody, satire, send-up 7 lampoon, takeoff 8 travesty

spook
3 spy 5 agent, alarm, ghost, haunt, scare 7 specter, spectre, startle, terrify 8 frighten. phantasm

spooky
5 eerie, weird 6 creepy 7 ghostly, ominous, uncanny 8 eldritch 9 unearthly

spool
4 reel, wind 6 bobbin

spoon
3 pet, woo 4 neck 5 court, ladle, scoop 6 cuddle

spoon-bending Geller
3 Uri

spoonbill
4 ibis 8 shoveler 9 ruddy duck 10 paddlefish

Spoon River poet
7 Masters (Edgar Lee)

spoony
5 mushy, silly 6 slushy, syrupy 7 fatuous, foolish, mawkish, smitten, witless 9 schmaltzy 10 saccharine 11 sentimental

spoor
5 scent, trace, track, tract, trail 7 vestige 9 droppings, footprint

sporadic
4 rare 6 fitful, random, scarce, sparse, spotty 7 erratic 8 episodic, isolated, uncommon 9 desultory, irregular, scattered, spasmodic 10 infrequent, occasional

spore
producer: 4 fern
sac: 4 asci (plural) 5 ascus

sport
3 fun 4 game, jest, joke, mock, play 6 frolic, racing, trifle 7 mockery, show off 9 diversion, high jinks, horseplay 10 recreation
horseback: 4 polo
indoor: 6 boxing, hockey, squash 7 bowling 8 handball 9 wrestling 10 acrobatics, basketball, gymnastics 11 racquetball, table tennis
Olympic: 4 judo 6 boxing, diving, hockey, rowing 7 archery, cycling, fencing, shot put 8 canoeing, football, high jump, long jump, marathon, shooting, swimming, yachting 9 decathlon, pole vault, water polo, wrestling 10 basketball, gymnastics, pentathlon, triple jump, volleyball 11 discus throw, hammer throw 12 javelin throw, steeplechase 13 weightlifting
water: 6 diving, rowing 7 sailing, surfing 8 canoeing, swimming, yachting
winter: 4 luge 6 hockey, skiing 7 curling, lugeing, skating 8 biathlon, sledding 10 ski jumping 11 bobsledding, tobogganing

sporting house
6 bagnio 7 brothel 8 bordello

sportive
5 antic 6 frisky, impish 7 playful, roguish, waggish 10 frolicsome 11 mischievous

sportiveness
7 devilry, roguery, waggery 8 deviltry, mischief 9 devilment, rascality

sports car
4 Alfa (Romeo)

sportscaster Hershiser
4 Orel

sports locale
3 gym 5 arena 7 stadium 9 gymnasium

sports source on TV
4 ESPN

sporty
4 fast 5 peppy 6 breezy, casual, jaunty, lively 7 dashing, relaxed 8 debonair, informal

spot
3 fix, jam, nip, pip, see 4 espy, post, site 5 fleck, hit on, locus, place, point, speck 6 blotch, detect, pickle, plight, scrape 7 dilemma, glimpse, smidgen, spatter, speckle 8 diagnose, flyspeck, identify, location, pinpoint, position 9 recognize 11 predicament

spotless
4 pure 5 clean 6 chaste 8 hygienic, sanitary, unsoiled 9 undefiled, unstained, unsullied 10 immaculate 11 unblemished

spotlight
5 focus 6 notice 7 feature 9 attention, public eye, publicity

spotted
3 saw 4 seen 6 calico, motley 7 flecked 7 brindle, dappled, flecked, piebald 8 brindled, speckled, stippled

spouse
4 mate, wife 5 bride, groom, hubby 7 consort, husband

spout
3 jet 4 gush 5 chute, eject, spray 6 nozzle, squirt

sprain
4 pull, tear, turn 5 twist 6 wrench 7 stretch

sprawl
4 flop, loll 5 drape, slump 6 extend, lounge, slouch, spread 7 stretch 11 spread-eagle

spray
3 fog 4 hose, mist 6 shower, spritz 7 aerosol, atomize, diffuse, spatter 8 atomizer, droplets, fumigate, nebulize 9 spindrift
banned: 4 Alar

spread
3 jam, lay, set, sow, ted 4 deal, oleo, open, pâté, push, span 5 apply, feast, jelly, space, splay, strew, sweep 6 butter, expand, extend, fan out, pass on, retail 7 banquet, breadth, diffuse, expanse, overrun, pervade, radiate, scatter, slather, stretch, suffuse 8 bedcover, coverlet, dispense, disperse, mushroom, permeate 9 amplitude, broadcast, circulate, diffusion, dissipate, expansion, extension, profusion, propagate 10 dispersion, distribute 11 counterpane, disseminate 12 transmission 13 proliferation
for bread: 4 oleo

spree
3 jag 4 bash, bust, lark, orgy, riot, tear, toot 5 binge, drunk, fling, revel 6 bender, frolic 7 blowout, carouse, rampage, splurge 8 carousal, wingding 11 bacchanalia

sprig
4 brad, heir, twig **5** scion, shoot **7** pintail **9** ruddy duck

sprightly
4 keen, spry, yare **5** agile, alert, antic, brisk, peppy, perky, zippy **6** active, breezy, chirpy, frisky, jaunty, lively, nimble **7** animate, chipper, coltish, playful **8** animated, cheerful, spirited, sportive **9** energetic, vivacious **10** frolicsome, rollicking

spring
3 hop **4** coil, flow, free, jump, leap, lope, rise, root, skip, stem, trip, well **5** arise, begin, bound, cause, fount, issue, start **6** appear, bounce, emerge, hurdle, pounce, source, uncoil, vernal **7** come out, emanate, proceed, rebound **8** commence, fountain, stimulus, wellhead **9** originate **10** incitement, resilience **12** fountainhead
back: **6** resile
flower: **5** lilac, pansy, tulip **6** crocus, scilla **8** daffodil, hyacinth, snowdrop
formal: **4** prom
mineral: **3** spa

springe
4 trap **5** noose, snare **7** pitfall **9** booby trap

springlike
6 vernal

springy
6 supple **7** elastic **8** flexible, stretchy **9** recoiling, resilient

sprinkle
3 dot **4** rain, spot **5** shake, speck, spray, strew **6** pepper, powder, sparge, spritz **7** asperse, drizzle, freckle, scatter, speckle, stipple

sprint
3 run **4** dart, dash, race, shin, tear **5** scoot **6** gallop, hurtle, scurry **7** scamper

sprite
3 elf, fay, nix **4** puck **5** Ariel, dryad, fairy, naiad, nixie, nymph, oread, pixie, sylph **6** kelpie **7** brownie **9** hamadryad, hobgoblin

spritz
3 jet **5** spray, spurt **6** shower, squirt

sprout
3 bud **4** grow **5** scion, shoot **6** ratoon, sucker **7** burgeon **8** offshoot **9** germinate

spruce
4 trim **5** natty, sassy, spiff **6** dapper, spiffy

spry
4 yare **5** agile, brisk, sound, zesty, zippy **6** active, lively, nimble, robust **7** healthy **8** animated, spirited, vigorous **9** energetic, vivacious

spud
5 tater **6** potato

____ Spumante
4 Asti

spume
4 fizz, foam, head, scum, suds **5** froth, spray, yeast **6** lather

spunk
4 grit, guts **5** moxie, nerve, pluck **6** mettle, spirit, tinder **7** cojones, courage **8** backbone, gumption **9** fortitude, toughness **10** resolution

spunky
4 bold **5** brave, fiery **6** daring **7** doughty, gingery, peppery **8** fearless, spirited **9** dauntless **10** courageous, mettlesome

spur
4 goad, prod, stir, urge **5** egg on, goose, impel, prick, rally, rouse, spine **6** arouse, branch, exhort, motive, prompt, propel **7** impetus, impulse **8** buttress, catalyst, excitant, stimulus **9** actuation, incentive, instigate, stimulant, stimulate **10** incitement, inducement, motivation, projection
part: **5** rowel

spurious
4 fake, mock, sham **5** bogus, dummy, false, phony, put-on **6** ersatz, pseudo **7** assumed, feigned, pretend **8** affected **9** brummagem, imitation, pinchbeck, pretended, simulated **10** apocryphal, artificial, substitute **11** counterfeit, make-believe **12** illegitimate
combining form: **5** pseud **6** pseudo

spurn
4 snub **5** flout, repel, scoff, scorn, scout, sneer **6** rebuff, refuse, reject **7** contemn, decline, despise, disdain, dismiss, repulse **8** turn down **9** disregard, reprobate, repudiate **10** disapprove **12** cold-shoulder

spurt
3 jet **4** gush, jump **5** burst, expel, spout, surge **6** shower, spritz, squirt **7** upsurge **8** eruption, increase **9** discharge

sputter
4 fizz, fume, rage, rant, rave, spew, spit **6** gibber, jabber **7** bluster, stammer

spy
5 agent, scout, snoop, spook **6** beagle, sleuth **7** gumshoe **8** informer, saboteur **9** detective **12** investigator **13** undercover man
name: **4** Ames (Aldrich), Bond (James), Boyd (Belle) **5** André (John), Bauer (Jack), Blunt (Anthony), Fuchs (Klaus) **6** Bourne (Matthew), Philby (Kim), Smiley (George) **7** Burgess (Guy), Hanssen (Robert), Maclean (Donald), Pollard (Jonathan) **8** Mata Hari
org.: **3** CIA, OSS **6** Mossad

spyglass
9 telescope

spying
9 espionage

Spyri's heroine
5 Heidi

squab
5 couch **6** pigeon **7** cushion

squabble
3 row **4** miff, spat, tiff **5** argue **6** bicker, dustup **7** brabble, dispute, quarrel, wrangle

squad
4 crew, side, team, unit **5** cadre **6** detail, lineup, patrol

squalid
4 base, foul, mean, vile **5** dingy, dirty, nasty, seedy **6** filthy, frowsy, frowzy, grubby, scurvy, shabby, shoddy, sleazy, slummy, sordid **7** ignoble, low-down, run-down, scrubby, unclean, unkempt **8** slovenly, wretched **10** despicable, disheveled **11** dilapidated **12** disreputable

squall
3 caw, row, yap, yip **4** bark, bawl, beef, feud, fuss, gust, howl, roar, tiff, wail, yawp, yell, yelp, yowl **5** brawl, fight, hoo-ha, shout **6** bellow, clamor, flurry, fracas, hubbub, ruckus, rumpus, scream, shriek, squeal, yammer **7** dispute, flare-up, quarrel, rhubarb, screech **8** brouhaha, squabble **9** bickering, caterwaul, commotion **10** falling-out, hullabaloo **11** altercation

squalor
5 filth **6** misery **7** neglect, poverty **8** baseness, iniquity **9** depravity, dirtiness **10** sordidness **11** degradation

squander
4 blow **5** spend, waste **7** consume, exhaust, fritter, scatter **9** dissipate, throw away **10** trifle away **11** fritter away

squanderer
see **spender**

square
3 fit, fix **4** bang, boxy, even, fair, jibe, tied **5** agree, align, equal, match, pay up, plaza, spang, tally **6** accord, adjust, settle **7** balance, conform, satisfy, settled **8** dovetail, orthodox, quadrate, smack-dab, unbiased **9** equitable, objective, quadratic, reconcile, rectangle
opposite: **3** hep, hip

squash
3 jam **4** cram, mash, pepo, pulp **5** crush, gourd, press, quell **7** flatten, put down, squeeze, squelch **8** suppress
variety: **5** acorn **6** cushaw, Sibley, turban **7** Hubbard, scallop **8** pattypan, zucchini **9** butternut, crookneck **10** Marblehead

squat
3 low **5** dumpy, hunch, stoop, stout, thick **6** chunky, crouch, hunker, stocky, stubby **8** heavyset, thickset **10** hunker down

squawfish
4 chub **8** cyprinid **10** pikeminnow

squawk
3 caw, yap, yip **4** beef, crab, fuss, yawp **5** bleat, gripe **6** yammer **7** protest **8** complain **9** bellyache, complaint

squeak
3 rat **4** blab, fink, pipe **5** cheep, creak **6** inform, snitch, tattle **10** tattletale

squeal
3 rat, yip **4** blab, howl, sing, yell, yelp, yowl **5** bleat, creak, grate, gripe, peach **6** inform, screak, scream, shriek, shrill, snitch, tattle **7** protest, screech **8** complain **10** tattletale

squealer
3 rat **4** fink **6** canary, snitch, weasel **7** ratfink, stoolie, tattler, tipster **8** betrayer, informer **10** talebearer, tattletale **11** stool pigeon

squeamish
5 fussy, upset **6** queasy **7** finical, finicky **8** nauseous **9** nauseated **10** fastidious, pernickety **11** persnickety

squeeze
3 hug, jam **4** bind, cram, grip, milk, pack, push **5** clasp, crowd, crush, exact, gouge, juice, pinch, press, screw, wring **6** clutch, coerce, compel, crunch, eke out, enfold, extort, jostle, squash, squish **7** dilemma, embrace, extract **8** compress, contract, pressure, quandary **9** shake down

squeezing snake
3 boa

squelch
5 quell, shush, sit on **6** muffle, muzzle, squash, squish, stifle, subdue **7** repress, silence, smother **8** strangle, suppress **10** extinguish

squib
6 filler **7** lampoon **8** shoot off **9** detonator **11** firecracker

squid
7 mollusc, mollusk **8** calamari, calamary **10** cephalopod
kin: **7** octopus **10** cuttlefish

squiggle
4 worm **6** doodle, scrawl, squirm, writhe **7** scratch **8** curlicue, scrabble, scribble

squinch
5 quail, start, wince **6** blench, crouch, recoil, shrink

squint
4 peek, peep, peer **10** hagioscope, strabismus

squire
6 attend, escort, lawyer **7** consort, gallant **8** cavalier, chaperon **9** accompany, landowner

squirm
4 worm **6** fidget, wiggle, writhe **7** wriggle

squirrel
4 stow **5** cache, hoard, stash **7** secrete
red: **9** chickaree

squirt
3 jet, kid, pup, tot **4** brat, tyke **5** sprat, spray, spurt, twerp **6** shaver, shrimp, splurt, spritz **7** spatter

squish
3 jam **4** cram, mash, mush, pack, push **5** crush, press, quash, smash **7** flatten, scrunch, squeeze, squelch, trample

squishy
4 soft **6** flabby, quaggy, slushy, spongy

Sri Lanka
aborigine: 5 Vedda
bay: 6 Bengal
capital: 7 Colombo
city: 5 Kandy **8** Moratuwa
ethnic group: 9 Sinhalese
former name: 6 Ceylon
language: 5 Tamil **9** Sinhalese
monetary unit: 5 rupee
shoals: 11 Adam's Bridge
strait: 4 Palk

SRO
7 sellout

SS chief
7 Himmler (Heinrich)

S-shaped
7 sigmoid
arch, molding: 4 ogee

stab
3 dig, pop, try **4** pang, poke, shot **5** crack, drive, fling, guess, prick, spear, stick, whack, whirl **6** effort, pierce, thrust, twinge **7** attempt **8** puncture **9** penetrate

Stabat ___
5 Mater

stabile
6 steady **9** sculpture **10** stationary

stabilize
3 fix, set **4** prop **5** brace **6** cement, firm up, fixate, prop up, secure, settle, steady **7** balance, ballast, support, sustain **8** solidify **9** reinforce

stable
3 set **4** barn, fast, firm, mews, safe **5** fixed, solid, sound **6** secure, steady, sturdy **7** abiding, durable, lasting, staunch **8** balanced, constant, enduring **9** immutable, permanent, steadfast, unvarying **10** perdurable, stationary, unchanging, unshakable

stack
4 cock, heap, hill, load, mass, pile, pipe, rick **5** mound, sheaf **7** chimney, pyramid

stack up
3 add **5** equal, total **6** equate, gather **7** compare, measure

stadium
4 bowl, dome, rink, ring **5** arena **6** garden **8** coliseum **10** hippodrome **12** amphitheater
level: 4 tier
Queens: 4 Ashe, Shea

staff
3 rod **4** cane, club, mace, prop, rung, team, wand **5** baton, billy, crook, stick **6** cudgel **7** faculty, support **9** personnel
bishop's: 7 crosier, crozier
medical: 8 caduceus
of office: 4 mace

staffer
4 aide

stag
4 male, solo **5** alone
mate: 3 doe

stage
3 lap, leg, lot **4** dais, play, rung, show, step **5** grade, level, mount, notch, phase, put on **6** degree, period, status **7** execute, perform, present, produce **8** platform
direction: 4 exit **5** enter **6** exeunt
front: 5 apron
part: 4 role
scenery: 3 set **8** backdrop
show: 4 play **5** drama, revue **7** musical **9** burlesque **10** vaudeville
signal: 3 cue
whisper: 5 aside

stage set
5 decor, scene **7** scenery **8** backdrop **11** mise-en-scène

stagger
4 daze, reel, stun, sway **5** amaze, lurch, pitch, stump, waver, weave **6** boggle, careen, dither, falter, teeter, topple, totter, wobble, zigzag **7** astound, nonplus, perplex, shatter, stumble, stupefy **8** astonish, bowl over **9** dumbfound, overwhelm **11** flabbergast

stagnant
5 inert, musty, stale **6** static **8** immobile, unmoving **10** motionless, stationary

stagnate
4 idle **5** stall **6** fester **8** languish, stultify, vegetate

stagy
10 artificial, histrionic, theatrical **11** pretentious **12** melodramatic

staid
5 grave, sober **6** formal, sedate, solemn, somber, sombre, stuffy **7** earnest, starchy **8** composed, priggish **9** dignified

stain
3 dye, tar **4** blot, daub, onus, slur, soil, spot **5** brand, color, odium, shame, smear, sully, taint, tinge **6** blotch, defile, embrue, imbrue, smirch,

smudge, stigma **7** blemish, pigment, tarnish **8** besmirch, colorant, discolor, dishonor, dyestuff, tincture

staircase
handrail: **8** banister **9** bannister
outdoor: **6** perron
post: **5** newel **8** baluster

stake
3 bet, lay, pot, set **4** ante, back, game, pale, play, post, risk **5** claim, put on, share, wager **6** gamble, paling, picket, pledge, tether **7** finance **8** bankroll, interest **10** investment

stalag
7 POW camp **10** prison camp

stale
5 banal, dusty, faded, fusty, moldy, musty, passé, tired, trite **7** clichéd, tedious, worn-out **8** overused, shopworn, timeworn **9** hackneyed **11** stereotyped

stalemate
3 tie **4** draw **7** impasse **8** deadlock, gridlock, standoff

stalk
4 hunt, prey, reed **5** chase, track **6** ambush, follow, pursue, stride **8** flush out
flower: **8** peduncle
leaf: **7** petiole
short: **5** stipe

stall
3 bay, pew **4** halt **5** booth, brake, delay, hedge, kiosk, stand **6** arrest, put off **7** conk out, counter, hold off **8** obstruct **9** stonewall **10** filibuster **11** compartment, prevaricate

stalwart
4 bold **5** brave, gutsy, hardy, husky, stout, tough **6** brawny, robust, sinewy, strong, sturdy **7** doughty, valiant **8** fearless, intrepid, unafraid, valorous, vigorous **9** dauntless, tenacious, undaunted **10** courageous

stamen part
6 anther **8** filament

stamina
4 legs **8** tenacity **9** endurance, fortitude, tolerance **11** persistence **12** staying power

stammer
6 gibber, jabber **7** sputter, stutter **8** hesitate, splutter

stamp
3 lot **4** etch, mark, mint, mold, seal **5** clomp, clump, pound, print, tromp **6** hammer, stripe **7** impress, imprint, trample **8** hallmark, inscribe **10** impression

stampede
4 bolt, dash, rout, rush, tear **5** crush, panic, rodeo **6** charge

stamps
7 postage

stance
4 pose **7** bearing, posture **8** attitude, carriage, position **10** deportment

stanch
4 stem, stop **5** check **6** arrest, stop up **8** hold back

stanchion
4 post, prop **5** brace **7** support

stand
4 bear, rack **5** abide, arise, booth, brook, kiosk, stall, treat **6** endure, handle, suffer **7** stomach, swallow, weather **8** attitude, platform, position, tolerate
artist's: **5** easel
three-legged: **6** tripod, trivet
ornamental: **7** étagère

standard
3 law, par **4** mean, norm, rule **5** color, gauge, ideal, model, stock, usual **6** common, ensign, median, normal **7** average, classic, example, general, measure, pattern, regular, typical, uniform **8** accepted, everyday, exemplar, familiar, ordinary, orthodox, paradigm **9** archetype, benchmark, criterion, customary, principle, yardstick **10** recognized, regulation, touchstone **11** established

standardize
6 adjust **7** conform **8** regulate **9** reconcile

stand for
4 bear, mean **5** allow **6** denote, permit **7** signify **8** indicate, tolerate **9** put up with, represent, symbolize

stand-in
3 sub **5** proxy **6** backup, second **9** alternate, surrogate **10** substitute, understudy **11** pinch hitter, replacement **12** impersonator

standing
4 rank, term **5** erect **6** cachet, credit, repute, status **7** dignity, footing, station, stature, upright **8** capacity, eminence, position, prestige **9** character, permanent, situation **10** estimation, reputation

standoff
see **stalemate**

standoffish
5 aloof **6** chilly **7** distant, haughty **8** detached, reserved **9** reclusive, withdrawn **10** unsociable

stand out
3 jut **4** bulk, loom **5** bulge **7** project **8** protrude

standpatter
4 fogy, tory **5** fogey **7** diehard **8** mossback **11** bitter-ender **12** conservative

standpoint
4 side **5** angle, slant **7** outlook **9** direction **11** perspective

standstill
4 halt, stop **5** check, pause **7** impasse **8** deadlock, dead stop **9** cessation, stalemate

Stanford site
8 Palo Alto

Stanley Kowalski's wife
6 Stella

Stanleys' car
7 steamer

Stan's partner
5 Ollie

stanza
7 strophe
combining form: **5** stich
final: **5** envoi
of eight lines: **6** octave
of four lines: **6** ballad **8** quatrain
of six lines: **6** sestet
of three lines: **6** tercet **7** triplet
Persian: **8** rubaiyat

star
4 icon, idol, lead **5** actor, chief, major **6** étoile **7** capital **8** asterisk, luminary **9** celebrity, headliner, principal **10** preeminent **11** outstanding
bright: **4** Vega **5** Algol, Deneb, Rigel, Spica **6** Altair, Castor, Pollux, Sirius **7** Antares, Canopus, Capella, Polaris, Procyon, Regulus **8** Arcturus **9** Aldebaran **10** Betelgeuse **12** Beta Centauri **13** Alpha Centauri
combining form: **4** astr **5** aster, astro **6** astero, sidero
envelope: **6** corona
exploding: **4** nova
five-pointed: **8** pentacle, stellate **9** pentagram
North: **7** Polaris
six-pointed: **8** hexagram

starch
4 sago **7** stiffen
combining form: **4** amyl **5** amylo

starchy
4 prim **5** aloof, stiff **6** doughy, formal, wooden **7** stilted
root: **4** taro

star-crossed
6 doomed **7** hapless, unlucky **8** ill-fated, luckless **11** unfortunate

Stardust composer
10 Carmichael (Hoagy)

stare
3 eye **4** gape, gawk, gawp, gaze, ogle, peer **6** goggle **10** rubberneck

stark
3 raw **4** pure **5** bleak, blunt, clear, harsh, rigid, sheer, utter **6** barren, strict, vacant **8** absolute, complete, desolate **9** au naturel, out-and-out

starry
6 astral **7** stellar **8** sidereal

starry-eyed
6 dreamy, unreal **7** utopian **8** ecstatic **9** rapturous, visionary **11** impractical, unrealistic

Star-Spangled Banner
contraction: **3** o'er
writer: **3** Key (Francis Scott)

start
4 bolt, dawn, draw **5** arise, begin, crank, found, get-go, issue, onset, quail, react, set up, wince **6** blench, create, embark, flinch, launch, outset, recoil, shrink, spring, take up **7** actuate, genesis, infancy, kickoff, opening, trigger **8** activate, commence, embark on, initiate, organize, reaction **9** beginning, establish, institute, originate **10** inaugurate **12** commencement

startle
4 jolt, jump **5** alarm, scare, shock, spook **8** astonish, frighten, surprise

Star Trek
captain: **4** Kirk (James T.) **5** Sisko (Benjamin) **6** Archer (Jonathan), Picard (Jean-Luc) **7** Janeway (Kathryn)
character: **3** Dax (Jadzia), Kim (Harry), Nog, Odo, Rom, Yar (Natasha) **4** Data, Kurn, Lore, Sulu, Troi (Deanna, Lwaxana), Worf **5** Adami (Kai Winn), Dukat, Duras (Lursa, B'Etor), McCoy ("Bones"), Nerys (Kira), Paris (Tom), Quark, Riker (Will), Sarek, Scott, Spock, Tuvok, Uhura **6** Bashir (Julian), Chekov, Doctor (The), Guinan, Gowron, O'Brien (Keiko, Miles), Torres (B'Elanna), Weyoun **7** Crusher (Dr. Beverly, Wesley), La Forge (Geordi) **8** Chakotay **9** Borg Queen
creator: **11** Roddenberry (Gene)
fan: **7** Trekker, Trekkie
race: **4** Borg, Gorn, Voth **5** Breen, Human, Trill, Vorta **6** Lurian, Pakled, Terran, Vulcan **7** Bajoran, Ferengi, Iconian, Klingon, Romulan, Tribble **8** Andorian, Betazoid, El-Aurian, Jem'Hadar **9** Nausicaan, Tellarite **10** Cardassian, Changeling
actor: **5** Nimoy (Leonard), Takei (George) **6** Kelley (DeForest) **7** Mulgrew (Kate), Shatner (William), Stewart (Patrick) **8** Fletcher (Louise), Goldberg (Whoopi)
starship: **10** Enterprise

starved
6 hungry **8** famished, ravenous, underfed

Star Wars
3 SDI

actor: **3** Lee (Christopher) **4** Ford (Harrison) **5** Jones (James Earl) **6** Fisher (Carrie), Hamill (Mark), Neeson (Liam) **7** Jackson (Samuel L.), Portman (Natalie) **8** Guinness (Alec), McGregor (Ewan), Williams (Billy Dee) **9** McDiarmid (Ian)
character: **4** Fett (Boba, Jango), Jinn (Qui-Gon), Leia (Princess), Maul (Darth), Solo (Han), Yoda (Master) **5** Binks (Jar Jar), Dooku (Count), Vader (Darth) **8** Grievous (General) **9** Chewbacca, Palpatine (Senator, Chancellor, Emperor), Skywalker (Anakin, Luke) **10** Calrissian (Lando) **12** Jabba the Hutt
composer: **8** Williams (John)
creator: **5** Lucas (George)
film: **7** New Hope (A) **13** Phantom Menace (The) **15** Return of the Jedi **16** Revenge of the Sith **17** Attack of the Clones, Empire Strikes Back (The)
group: **4** Jedi, Sith **5** Ewoks **6** Clones, Droids **8** Wookiees **13** Rebel Alliance
planet: **4** Hoth **5** Naboo **7** Dagobah **8** Alderaan, Tatooine **9** Coruscant
threat: **9** Death Star

stash
4 bury, hide, pile, stow **5** cache, hoard, plant, store **7** conceal, lay away, nest egg, secrete **8** lay aside, sock away, squirrel **9** stockpile

stasis
7 balance, inertia **9** equipoise **10** immobility, stagnation **11** equilibrium

stat
3 now, PDQ **4** ASAP **6** at once, pronto

state
3 air, put, say **4** aver, avow, mode, rank, tell, vent **5** utter **6** affirm, assert, recite, relate, report **7** declare, dignity, explain, expound, express, posture, recount **8** attitude, capacity, describe, position, set forth, standing **9** condition, enunciate, situation
French: **4** état

state
easternmost: **5** Maine
largest: **6** Alaska
smallest: **11** Rhode Island
southernmost: **6** Hawaii

stately
5 grand, lofty, noble, regal, royal **6** august, formal, kingly, lordly, solemn **7** courtly, elegant, gallant, haughty **8** gracious, imperial, imposing, majestic, palatial, princely **9** dignified **10** ceremonial, impressive, monumental **11** ceremonious, magnificent
house: **5** manor, manse **7** mansion

statement
3 tab **4** bill **5** score **6** avowal, charge, dictum, remark, report **7** account, comment, invoice, recital **8** averment **9** affidavit, assertion, manifesto, narrative, reckoning, testimony, utterance **10** deposition, expression **11** description
introductory: **7** preface **8** foreword, prologue
of belief: **5** credo

stateroom
5 cabin

statesman
8 diplomat **10** politician
American: **3** Hay (John Milton) **4** Clay (Henry), Hull (Cordell), Otis (James), Root (Elihu) **5** Adams (Samuel), Henry (Patrick), Lodge (Henry Cabot), Vance (Cyrus) **6** Bunche (Ralph), Bunker (Ellsworth), Dulles (John Foster), Kennan (George F.), Morris (Gouverneur), Powell (Colin), Sumner (Charles) **7** Acheson (Dean), Hancock (John), Kellogg (Frank B.), Lansing (Robert), Sherman (John, Roger), Stimson (Henry L.), Webster (Daniel) **8** Franklin (Benjamin), Hamilton (Alexander), Harriman (Averell), Pinckney (Charles, Thomas), Randolph (Edmund Jennings, John, Payton), Rutledge (John), Trumbull (Jonathan, Joseph) **9** Kissinger (Henry), Stevenson (Adlai) **10** Stettinius (Edward Reilly)
Australian: **9** Wentworth (William Charles)
Austrian: **6** Renner (Karl) **7** Kaunitz (Wenzel von) **8** Dollfuss (Engelbert) **10** Metternich (Klemens von) **13** Schwarzenberg (Felix zu)
Canadian: **4** King (W. L. Mackenzie) **7** Laurier (Wilfrid) **8** Thompson (John Sparrow) **9** Macdonald (John Alexander, John Sandfield), Mackenzie (Alexander, William Lyon)
Chinese: **3** Yen (Hsishan) **4** Deng (Xiaoping), Kung (Hsiang-hsi), Teng (Hsiao-p'ing), Wang (Anshih, Chingwei), Yuan (Shih-kai) **9** Sun Yat-Sen
Dutch: **6** de Witt (Johan de) **7** Grotius (Hugo), Stikker (Dirk)
East German: **8** Ulbricht (Walter)
English: **3** Fox (Charles, Henry) **4** Eden (Anthony, George, William), More (Thomas), Peel (Arthur, Robert, William), Pitt (William), Vane (Henry) **5** Cecil (Robert, William), North (Francis, Frederick, Roger) **6** Morley (John), Sidney (Algernon, Henry, Philip, Robert), Temple (Henry, William), Wolsey (Thomas) **7** Halifax (Earl of), Reading (Marquis of), Russell (John, William), Stanley (Edward George, Edward Henry), Stewart (Robert), Warwick (Earl of) **8** Cromwell (Oliver, Thomas), Disraeli (Benjamin), Robinson (George Frederick Samuel), Villiers (George) **9** Cavendish (Spencer, William), Churchill (Randolph, Winston), Gladstone (William), Salisbury (Earl, Marquis of), Strafford (Earl of), Wellesley (Arthur, Richard Colley) **10** Palmerston (Lord), Rockingham (Marquis of), Sunderland (Earl of), Walsingham (Francis), Wellington (Duke of)

11 Chamberlain (Austen, Joseph, Neville), Shaftesbury (Earl of) **12** Chesterfield (Earl of)
Finnish: **9** Stahlberg (Kaarlo Juho)
French: **5** Sully (Duc de) **6** Guizot (François-Pierre-Guillaume), Thiers (Louis-Adolphe), Turgot (Anne-Robert-Jacques) **7** Herriot (Edouard), Mazarin (Jules), Schuman (Robert), Viviani (René) **8** Hanotaux (Gabriel) **9** Lafayette (Marquis de), Millerand (Alexandre), Richelieu (Duc de) **10** Clemenceau (Georges) **11** Tocqueville (Alexis de)
German: **5** Wirth (Joseph) **10** Stresemann (Gustav)
German-Danish: **9** Struensee (Johann Friedrich)
Greek: **6** Zaimis (Alexandros) **8** Pericles **9** Aristides **11** Cleisthenes, Demosthenes **12** Themistocles
Israeli: **4** Eban (Abba) **5** Begin (Menachem), Dayan (Moshe), Peres (Shimon), Rabin (Yitzhak) **7** Sharett (Moshe) **9** Ben-Gurion (David)
Italian: **6** Cavour (Conte di), Crispi (Francesco) **7** Orlando (Vittorio Emanuele) **11** Machiavelli (Niccolo)
Japanese: **3** Ito (Hirobumi) **5** genro, Kanoe **6** Kanoye
Norwegian: **6** Nansen (Fridtjof)
Polish: **7** Zaleski (August) **9** Pilsudski (Jozef) **10** Paderewski (Ignacy)
Prussian: **5** Stein (Karl)
Roman: **4** Cato (Marcus Porcius) **6** Cicero (Marcus Tullius), Pompey, Seneca (Lucius Annaeus) **7** Agrippa (Marcus Vipsanius) **8** Gracchus (Gaius, Tiberius), Maecenas (Gaius) **9** Symmachus (Quintus Aurelius)
Russian: **5** Witte (Sergey) **7** Molotov (Vyacheslav) **8** Potemkin (Grigory) **9** Vyshinsky (Andrey)
Scottish: **4** Knox (John)
South American: **7** Bolívar (Simón) **9** San Martín (José de)
Swiss: **4** Ador (Gustave) **5** Welti (Emil)

static
5 fixed, inert, still **6** stable, steady **7** stabile, stalled, stopped **8** constant, immobile, inactive, stagnant, unmoving **9** immovable, unvarying **10** changeless, unchanging

station
4 base, post, rank, site, spot **5** depot, locus, place, point **6** assign **7** footing **8** capacity, standing **9** character **10** white noise

stationary
5 fixed **6** static **8** immobile, stagnant, unmoving **9** immovable **10** motionless, stock-still

stats, e.g.
4 data

statue
base: **6** plinth **8** pedestal
gigantic: **8** Colossus
Greek: **5** atlas **7** telamon **8** caryatid
religious: **5** Pietà
small: **8** figurine

stature
see **status**

status
4 rank **5** merit, place, worth **6** cachet, rating, renown **7** caliber, dignity, footing, posture, quality **8** capacity, eminence, position, prestige, standing **9** character, condition, situation **10** prominence

statute
3 act, law **4** bill **5** canon, edict **9** enactment, ordinance

staunch
4 firm, true **5** liege, loyal, solid, sound **6** trusty **8** constant, faithful, reliable, resolute, stalwart **9** steadfast **10** dependable **11** trustworthy

stave off
4 foil **5** avert, block, deter, parry, rebut, repel **6** rebuff, thwart **7** forfend, obviate, prevent, repulse **8** preclude **9** forestall

____ Stavro Blofeld
5 Ernst

stay
3 guy, lag **4** bide, halt, prop, rest, stop, wait **5** abide, brace, check, defer, delay, dwell, lodge, tarry, visit **6** linger, put off, remain **7** sojourn, support, suspend **8** hold over, postpone, stop over **9** interrupt **10** suspension **11** stick around

stead
4 lieu **5** place **9** advantage

steadfast
4 firm, sure, true **5** fixed, liege, loyal **7** abiding, adamant, patient, staunch **8** constant, enduring, faithful, immobile, reliable, resolute, stubborn **9** immovable, unbending, unmovable **10** dependable, unwavering, unyielding **11** unfaltering, unflinching **12** single-minded, wholehearted

steady
3 set **4** beau, even, fast, firm, sure **5** fixed, liege, loyal, sober **6** stable, static **7** abiding, ballast, certain, durable, equable, nonstop, regular, stabile, staunch, uniform **8** constant, enduring, faithful, habitual, reliable, resolute, unbroken, unshaken **9** ceaseless, incessant, stabilize, unvarying **10** changeless, consistent, continuous, dependable, persistent, sweetheart, unchanging, unswerving, unwavering **11** unfaltering

steak
4 club, cube, loin **5** chuck, flank, round, T-bone **6** rib eye **7** brisket, sirloin **9** Delmonico, hamburger, Salisbury **10** tenderloin **11** filet mignon, London broil, porterhouse **13** chateaubriand
order: **4** rare

steal
3 bag, cop, nab, nip, rob **4** glom, grab, hook, kite, lift, loot, lurk, slip, take **5** boost, creep, filch, glide, heist, pinch, poach, prowl, seize, shirk, sidle, skulk, slide, slink, sneak, swipe **6** burgle, fleece, hijack, pilfer, pocket, snatch, snitch, thieve, tiptoe **7** bargain, pillage, plunder, purloin **8** embezzle, shanghai, shoplift **9** pussyfoot **10** burglarize, plagiarize **11** appropriate
a vehicle: **6** hijack **8** highjack

stealing
5 theft **6** piracy **7** larceny, robbery **8** burglary

stealthy
3 sly **4** wily **6** covert, crafty, feline, shifty, silent, slinky, sneaky **7** catlike, cunning, furtive, subrosa **8** hush-hush, skulking, slinking, sneaking **10** undercover **11** clandestine **13** surreptitious

steam
3 gas, pep, zip **4** foam, fume, mist, rage **5** anger, force, might, power, vapor **6** energy, seethe

steam bath
5 sauna

steamboat structure
5 texas

steamer
4 boat, clam, ship

steam organ
8 calliope

steamy
3 hot **5** humid, muggy **6** erotic, sticky, sultry, torrid **8** stifling

steed
5 horse, mount **7** charger, courser

steel
4 gird **5** brace, nerve, rally **6** buck up, harden **7** fortify, hearten, stiffen **8** embolden, inspirit **9** reinforce
joist: **4** I bar

steep
3 sop **4** high, soak **5** bathe, dizzy, imbue, sheer **6** abrupt, drench, infuse **7** arduous, extreme, immerse, suffuse **8** elevated, marinate, saturate **10** exorbitant, immoderate, impregnate, inordinate **11** precipitate, precipitous
rock: **4** crag

steeple
5 spire, tower **6** flèche

steer
4 helm, lead **5** guide, pilot, point, route **6** direct, escort, tip-off **7** channel, conduct, skipper **8** shepherd
a ship: **4** conn, helm, luff

steer clear of
4 duck **5** avert, avoid, dodge, elude, evade **6** bypass

steersman
3 cox **7** captain **8** coxswain

stein
3 mug **5** stoup **6** flagon, goblet **7** tankard

Steinbeck novel
5 Pearl (The) **10** Cannery Row, East of Eden **12** Of Mice and Men, Tortilla Flat **13** Grapes of Wrath (The)

Stein's companion
6 Toklas (Alice B.)

Steinway product
5 piano

stellar
6 astral, starry **7** leading, shining **8** sidereal, standout, starlike **10** preeminent **11** outstanding, predominant, superlative

stem
4 flow, head, rise, stop **5** abate, arise, check, issue **6** arrest, derive, spring, stanch **7** control, develop, emanate, proceed **8** peduncle **9** originate
plant: **4** axis **5** haulm
underground: **5** tuber **7** rhizome

stench
4 funk, reek **5** fetor, smell, stink **7** malodor

stentorian
4 loud **7** blaring, booming, orotund, roaring **8** sonorous **9** deafening **10** thundering

step
4 hoof, pace, rung, walk **5** grade, level, notch, stage, stair, stile, track, tread **6** degree **7** measure, traipse **8** footfall **9** gradation
dance: **3** pas

step-by-step
7 gradual **9** piecemeal

Stephen of film
3 Rea

steppe
5 plain **6** tundra

Steppenwolf author
5 Hesse (Hermann)

stereo forerunner
4 mono

stereotype
4 mold **5** plate **7** pattern **10** categorize, pigeonhole **11** standardize

stereotypical
4 hack **5** banal, stale, trite **7** clichéd **8** shopworn, timeworn **9** hackneyed **11** commonplace

sterile
4 arid, bare, vain **6** barren, fallow **7** aseptic, worn-out **8** desolate, hygienic, impotent, lifeless, sanitary **9** fruitless, infertile **10** antiseptic, unfruitful **11** disinfected **12** unproductive

sterilize
3 fix 4 geld, spay 5 alter 6 neuter, purify 7 cleanse 9 disinfect 10 emasculate

sterilized
7 aseptic

sterling
4 pure, true 5 noble 6 worthy 8 virtuous 9 estimable, exemplary, honorable

stern
4 grim 5 harsh, rigid, sober, stony 6 gloomy, severe, strict 7 ascetic, austere 8 obdurate 10 forbidding, implacable, inexorable, inflexible

Sterne novel
14 Tristram Shandy

sternutation
8 sneezing

sternward
3 aft 5 abaft

Sterope
father: 5 Atlas
mother: 7 Pleione
sisters: 8 Pleiades

stevedores' union
3 ILA

Stevenson, Robert Louis
character: 3 Jim (Hawkins) 4 Hyde (Mr.) 5 David (Balfour) 6 Jekyll (Dr.), Silver (Long John)
novel: 9 Kidnapped 14 Treasure Island

Stevenson of Illinois
5 Adlai

stew
4 boil, brew, flap, fret, fume, fuss, hash, olio, olla, snit 5 daube, gumbo, salmi, sweat, tizzy, worry 6 burgoo, dither, jumble, lather, medley, menudo, pother, ragout, seethe, simmer, swivet, tumult 7 brothel, goulash, mélange, mixture, parboil, swelter, turmoil 8 bordello, mishmash, mulligan, pot-au-feu 9 Brunswick, cassoulet, commotion, confusion, fricassee, pasticcio, potpourri 10 hodgepodge, hotchpotch, miscellany, turbulence 11 gallimaufry, olla podrida, ratatouille, slumgullion 13 bouillabaisse
vegetable: 4 okra

steward
6 manage 7 manager 8 overseer 10 supervisor

stewed
3 lit 4 high 5 drunk, lit up, oiled 6 bashed, blotto, bombed, cooked, juiced, potted, soaked, soused, stewed, stoned, tanked, wasted, zonked 7 crocked, drunken, pickled, pie-eyed, sloshed, smashed, sottish 8 simmered 9 plastered 10 inebriated, liquored up 11 intoxicated

stewpot
4 olla

stick
3 put, rod 4 glue, pole, stab 5 affix, baton, cling 6 adhere, attach, cleave, cohere, fasten 7 scruple

stick around
4 bide, stay, wait 5 abide, dally, tarry 6 linger, remain

sticker
3 pin 4 barb, seal, shiv, spur 5 decal, point, prong, shank, spike, spine, stamp 6 dagger 8 stiletto

stick-in-the-mud
4 fogy 5 fogey 6 fossil 8 mossback 10 fuddy-duddy

stick out
3 jut 5 bulge 6 beetle 7 project 8 overhang, protrude

stick up
3 mug, rob 6 waylay 7 project 8 protrude

sticky
5 gluey, gooey, gummy, humid, muggy, tacky 6 clammy, knotty, slushy, sultry, thorny, viscid 7 awkward, viscous 8 adhesive, clinging, romantic 9 difficult 11 problematic
stuff: 3 goo 4 gunk

stiff
3 lit, set 4 body, firm, hard, lush 5 cheat, drunk, harsh, oiled, rigid, stark, steep, stick, tense, tight, tipsy 6 buzzed, corpse, frozen, jelled, juiced, person, plowed, potent, potted, severe, soused, stewed, wooden 7 cadaver, carcass, sloshed, starchy, stilted 8 reserved, stubborn 9 cardboard, inelastic, petrified, plastered, unbending 10 inflexible, mechanical, unyielding 11 intoxicated

stiffen
5 tense 6 harden 7 thicken 8 rigidify, solidify 9 stabilize 10 immobilize

stifle
3 gag 4 hush, mute 5 burke, choke, deter 6 dampen, deaden, hush up, muffle, muzzle 7 repress, silence, smother, squelch 8 stultify, suppress 9 suffocate 10 discourage

stigma
4 blot, onus, spot 5 brand, odium, shame, stain, taint 6 smudge, smutch 8 black eye, disgrace, dishonor, petechia, tainting

stigmatize
5 brand, label, stamp

still
3 but, yet 4 calm, even, hush, lull 5 allay, inert, quiet, shush, whist 6 even so, hushed, placid, serene, settle, silent, static, though, withal 7 alembic, halcyon, silence 8 peaceful, stagnant, tranquil 9 noiseless, soundless 10 motionless,

stationary **11** furthermore, nonetheless **12** nevertheless

stilt
4 bird, pile, pole **8** longlegs **9** shorebird

stilted
4 prim **5** stiff **6** formal, wooden **7** pompous, starchy **8** affected **9** cardboard

stilt-like bird
6 avocet

Stimpy's pal
3 Ren

stimulant
4 goad, spur **5** tonic **7** impetus, impulse **8** caffeine, catalyst, excitant **9** analeptic, energizer, incentive **10** incitement, motivation

stimulate
4 fire, goad, move, prod, spur, urge, whet **5** impel, pique, rouse, set up, spark **6** arouse, excite, fire up, foment, incite, prompt, vivify, work up **7** agitate, enliven, inspire, provoke, quicken, trigger **8** activate, energize, motivate, vitalize **9** galvanize

stimulus
4 goad, kick, push, spur **5** boost, cause **6** charge, motive **7** impetus, impulse **8** catalyst **9** incentive **10** incitement, inducement, motivation **11** instigation, provocation **13** encouragement

sting
3 con **4** scam, trap **5** cheat, prick, smart, snare **6** hustle, tingle **7** con game **8** skin game

stinging
8 aculeate

stingy
4 mean **5** close, tight **6** frugal, paltry, skimpy **7** chintzy, costive, miserly, niggard, scrimpy, sparing, thrifty **8** grudging **9** niggardly, penny-wise, penurious **10** ironfisted, pinchpenny, ungenerous **11** tightfisted **12** cheeseparing, parsimonious **13** penny-pinching

stink
3 ado **4** flap, funk, fuss, reek, to-do **5** smell **6** stench **7** malodor

stinker
3 dog, dud **4** bomb, bust, flop **5** lemon, loser, skunk **6** petrel, turkey **7** washout

stinking
see **smelly**

stinky
see **smelly**

stint
3 job **4** bout, task, time, tour, turn **5** chore, cramp, pinch, scant, share, shift, skimp, spare, spell **6** amount, scrape, scrimp **8** restrict **9** allotment **10** assignment

stipend
3 fee, pay **4** hire, wage **5** award **6** salary **7** payment **9** allowance, emolument

stipple
3 dot **5** fleck, speck **6** pepper **7** freckle, speckle **8** sprinkle

stipulate
5 state **6** detail **7** specify **8** contract, spell out

stipulation
5 limit, terms **7** proviso, strings **9** condition, provision **11** requirement

stir
3 ado, din, mix **4** fuss, rout, to-do, wake, whet **5** blend, budge, churn, impel, rally, rouse, roust, spark, waken **6** arouse, bustle, excite, flurry, foment, hubbub, incite, kindle, pother, seethe, simmer, tumult, whip up **7** agitate, disturb, ferment, inspire, provoke, quicken **8** activity **9** agitation, commotion, galvanize, stimulate **11** disturbance

stirrup
6 stapes **8** footrest

stir up
4 roil **6** arouse, incite **7** provoke

stithy
5 anvil

stoat
6 ermine, weasel

stock
4 butt, fund, hope, race **5** brace, carry, faith, goods, hoard, store, talon, trunk, trust **6** family, supply **7** furnish, lineage **8** pedigree, reliance **9** inventory, selection **10** confidence, dependence **11** merchandise

stockade
4 jail **5** fence **6** paling, prison **8** palisade **9** enclosure, guardroom

stock exchange
4 AMEX, FTSE, NYSE **6** bourse, NASDAQ

stockings
4 hose **5** socks **7** hosiery
shade: 4 ecru **5** beige, taupe

stock-market debut
3 IPO

stockpile
4 bank, heap, mass **5** amass, cache, hoard, lay up, store **6** garner, supply **7** backlog, collect, nest egg, reserve, store up **9** inventory, reservoir **10** accumulate, repository

stocky
3 fat **5** beefy, burly, dumpy, husky, plump, pudgy, squat, stout, thick **6** chunky, stubby, stumpy **8** heavyset, thickset **9** corpulent

stodge
4 fill, sate **5** gorge, stuff **7** overeat, surfeit

stodgy
5 fusty **6** stuffy **9** hidebound, out-of-date **12** old-fashioned

stogie
4 shoe **5** cigar **6** brogan

stoic
4 Zeno **6** stolid **7** Spartan **9** apathetic, impassive **10** phlegmatic

stoicism
9 stolidity **11** impassivity
founder: **4** Zeno

stoke
3 fan **4** feed, fuel, poke, stir, tend **6** supply

Stoker novel
7 Dracula

stole
4 took **5** fichu, manta, scarf, shawl **6** tippet **7** tallith

stolid
3 dry **4** dull, flat **5** stoic **6** wooden **8** rocklike **9** apathetic, impassive, unruffled **10** phlegmatic **11** unemotional

stomach
3 gut, maw **4** bear, craw **5** abide, belly, brook, stand, taste, tummy **6** digest, endure, paunch, venter **7** abdomen, swallow **8** appetite, tolerate
combining form: **5** gastr **6** gastro, ventri, ventro
enzyme: **6** pepsin, rennin
muscle: **7** pylorus
ruminant: **6** omasum **8** abomasum **9** reticulum
Scottish: **4** kyte

stomachache
5 colic, gripe **12** collywobbles

stomp
5 clump, pound, tramp **7** trample

stone
3 gem **4** rock **5** lapis **6** pebble **7** boulder
base: **6** plinth
block of: **8** monolith
carving: **7** epitaph
chip: **5** spall
combining form: **4** lite, lith, lyte
cosmic: **6** meteor **9** chondrite, meteorite
facing: **6** ashlar
for grinding grains: **6** metate
fruit: **5** drupe
marker: **5** cairn
memorial: **5** cairn, stela, stele **7** obelisk
monument: **6** dolmen **8** megalith
of a fruit: **3** pit
paving: **3** set **4** sett
pillar: **5** stela, stele

___ Stone
7 Blarney, Rosetta

stonecrop
5 sedum

stoned
3 lit **4** high **5** boozy, doped, drunk, fried, oiled, tight, tipsy **6** buzzed, canned, juiced, loaded, plowed, potted, soused, tanked, wasted, zonked **7** crocked, drugged, muddled, pickled, pie-eyed, sloshed, smashed **8** hopped-up, turned on, wiped out **9** pixilated, plastered, spaced-out, strung out **10** inebriated, tripped out **11** intoxicated

stonewall
5 delay, stall **6** hamper, hinder, impede, stymie **8** obstruct

stood up
4 rose **5** arose

stooge
3 sap **4** dupe, foil, gull, mark, pawn, tool **5** chump, dummy, patsy, proxy **6** puppet, sucker, victim **7** fall guy **8** sidekick **11** stool pigeon, straight man

Stooge of TV
3 Moe (Howard) **5** Curly (Howard), Larry (Fine)

stool pigeon
3 rat **4** fink, nark **5** decoy **6** canary, snitch **7** ratfink, tipster **8** informer

stoop
3 dip **4** bend, duck, sink **5** deign, hunch, porch, slump **6** resort, slouch **7** descend **8** stairway **10** condescend

stop
3 bar, can, dam, end **4** clog, fill, halt, plug, quit, stay, stem, whoa **5** block, brake, cease, check, close, deter, stall, tarry **6** arrest, desist, ending, kibosh, stanch **7** disrupt, occlude, prevent, sojourn, suspend **8** knock off, obstruct **9** interrupt, terminate **11** discontinue
up: **4** cork, plug **7** occlude

stopgap
5 shift **6** resort **8** recourse, resource **9** expedient, makeshift **10** expediency, substitute

stopover
4 stay **5** visit **7** sojourn

stoppage
4 halt **6** cutoff, strike **7** walkout **8** shutdown **10** standstill **11** obstruction

Stoppard play
7 Jumpers **9** Real Thing (The) **10** Travesties **13** Coast of Utopia (The)

stopper
4 bung, cork, fill, plug **5** close

storage building
4 shed, silo

store
3 bin **4** fund, mart, pack, shop, stow, tank **5** amass, cache, depot, hoard, lay up, stash

6 ensile, garner, market, outlet, shoppe, supply 7 arsenal, backlog, deposit, reserve 8 boutique, cumulate, emporium, mothball, showroom, squirrel 9 abundance, inventory, reservoir, stockpile, warehouse 10 accumulate, depository, five-and-ten, repository 11 five-and-dime
display: 6 endcap 8 showcase

storehouse
5 depot 7 arsenal, granary 8 magazine 9 stockpile 10 depository, repository

storekeeper
8 merchant, retailer 9 tradesman

storeroom
6 larder, pantry 7 buttery

storm
3 row 4 fury, gale, hail, rage, rant, rave, roar, rush, to-do 5 beset, blast, blitz, burst, furor, onset, salvo 6 assail, attack, charge, clamor, fall on, flurry, furore, hubbub, outcry, pother, racket, shower, squall, tumult 7 assault, bluster, cyclone, monsoon, ruction, tempest, thunder, tornado, turmoil, twister, typhoon 8 blizzard, downpour, fall upon, outbreak, outburst, paroxysm, upheaval 9 broadside, commotion, hurricane, nor'easter, onslaught 10 cloudburst 11 northeaster, northwester

storm trooper
10 brownshirt

stormy
4 foul 5 rainy, rough 6 raging 7 furious 8 blustery 9 turbulent 10 tumultuous 11 tempestuous, threatening

Stormy Weather
composer: 5 Arlen (Harold)
singer: 4 Lena (Horne)

story
3 fib, lie 4 epic, saga, tale, yarn 5 conte, fable 6 canard, legend, report 7 account, fiction, märchen, parable, version 8 allegory, anecdote, folktale, megillah, tall tale 9 chronicle, fairy tale, narration, narrative

storyteller
4 liar 6 fibber 8 fabulist, narrator 9 raconteur

stoup
4 font 5 basin, stein 6 flagon, goblet 7 chalice, tankard

stout
3 ale, fat 4 brew 5 beefy, bulky, burly, heavy, husky, obese, plump, thick 6 fleshy, porter, portly, strong, sturdy 9 corpulent 10 overweight

Stout detective
5 Wolfe (Nero)

stouthearted
4 bold, game 5 brave, gutsy 7 doughty, valiant 8 fearless, intrepid, resolute, stalwart, stubborn, unafraid 9 audacious, dauntless, undaunted 10 courageous

stove
4 kiln, oven 5 range 8 Franklin, potbelly

stow
3 bin 4 lade, load, pack 5 stash, store 7 arrange, deposit

stower
9 stevedore

Stowe work
4 Dred

strabismus
6 squint

straddle
4 span 6 sprawl 8 bestride 11 spread-eagle

strafe
4 rake 6 attack 8 enfilade 10 machine-gun

straggle
3 lag 4 poke, roam, rove 5 drift, range, stray 6 dawdle, loiter, ramble, wander 7 maunder, meander 8 trail off 9 string out

straight
4 even, fair, neat, pure, true 5 erect, plain, plumb, right 6 at once, candid, direct, honest, linear, square 7 unmixed, upright 8 orthodox 9 bourgeois, forthwith, undiluted 10 aboveboard, button-down, forthright
combining form: 4 orth, rect 5 ortho, recti

straightaway
3 now 4 ASAP 6 at once, pronto 7 stretch 8 directly, first off, promptly 9 forthwith, instanter 11 immediately

straighten
4 even, tidy 5 align 6 neaten, unbend, uncurl 7 rectify

straightforward
5 frank, lucid 6 candid, direct, honest 7 genuine, precise, sincere 8 clear-cut 9 outspoken 10 forthright 11 undeviating

strain
3 air, tax, try 4 hint, kind, pull, sort, toil, tune, vein 5 exert, stock, sweat, tinge, touch, trace, twist 6 filter, melody, screen, streak, stress, strive, wrench 7 overtax, tension, trouble 8 exertion, overwork, pressure 9 overexert

strait
4 bind, kyle, pass 5 pinch 6 crisis, plight 7 channel, dilemma, narrows, squeeze 8 exigency, hardship, juncture 9 crossroad, emergency 10 difficulty 11 contingency
Adriatic Sea-Ionian Sea: 7 Otranto
Alaska: 3 Icy
Alaska-Russia: 6 Bering
Albania-Greece: 5 Corfu
Asia-Europe: 11 Dardanelles

Atlantic-Baffin Island: **5** Davis
Atlantic-Mediterranean: **9** Gibraltar
Atlantic-Nantucket Sound: **8** Muskeget
Atlantic-North Sea: **7** English
Atlantic-Pacific: **5** Drake **8** Magellan
Atlantic-Saint Lawrence: **5** Cabot
Baffin Island-Quebec: **6** Hudson
Bering Sea-Sea of Okhotsk: **5** Kuril **6** Kurile
Bismarck Sea-Solomon Sea: **6** Vitiaz
Canada: **3** Rae **5** Dease
East China Sea: **5** Korea **8** Tsushima
East China-South China: **6** Taiwan **7** Formosa
England-France: **5** Dover
Flores Sea-Indian Ocean: **4** Sape
Flores Sea-Savu Sea: **4** Alor
Indian Ocean-Java Sea: **5** Sunda
India-Sri Lanka: **4** Palk
Indonesia: **4** Alas, Alor, Bali **5** Tioro **6** Lombok **7** Dampier **8** Macassar, Makassar, Surabaya
Inner Hebrides: **5** Tiree
Iran-Oman: **6** Hormuz
Italy: **7** Messina
Japan: **4** Yura **5** Bungo, Kitan **7** Hayasui
Japan-Sakhalin Island: **4** Soya
Lake Huron: **10** Mississagi
Lake Huron-Lake Michigan: **8** Mackinac
Malay Archipelago: **5** Wetar
Malaysia-Singapore: **6** Johore
Malay-Sumatra: **7** Malacca
New Jersey-Staten Island: **7** van Kull
New South Wales-Tasmania: **4** Bass
New Zealand: **4** Cook
Northwest Territories: **6** Barrow **8** Franklin, Victoria **13** Prince of Wales
Nova Scotia: **5** Canso
Pacific-San Francisco Bay: **10** Golden Gate
Pacific-South China Sea: **5** Luzon
Philippines: **5** Bohol, Tanon **6** Iloilo **7** Basilan
Russia: **4** Kara
Suvu Sea-Timor Sea: **4** Roti
Sea of Azov-Black Sea: **5** Kerch **7** Enikale
Sea of Japan: **5** Tatar
Solomon Islands: **12** Bougainville
South China Sea: **7** Mindoro **9** Singapore
Turkey: **8** Bosporus **9** Bosphorus, Karadeniz
Vancouver-Washington: **10** Juan de Fuca
Wales: **5** Menai
Washington Sound: **4** Haro

straitened
7 lacking, pinched, wanting **8** deprived, strapped **9** deficient, destitute **10** distressed, inadequate **12** impoverished

straitlaced
4 prim **5** staid, stiff **6** formal, narrow, prissy, strict, stuffy **7** genteel, prudish, starchy, stilted **8** priggish **9** hidebound, Victorian **11** puritanical

strand
4 bank **5** beach, coast, fiber, leave, shore, wreck **6** desert, enisle, maroon, thread **7** abandon, shingle **8** cast away, filament, littoral, seacoast, seashore **9** shipwreck **10** run aground, waterfront

strange
3 odd **5** alien, crazy, eerie, fishy, funny, kinky, kooky, nutty, outré, queer, weird **6** exotic, far-out, freaky **7** bizarre, curious, oddball, offbeat, uncanny, unknown, unusual **8** aberrant, abnormal, atypical, peculiar, singular **9** eccentric, fantastic, grotesque **10** mysterious, off-the-wall, outlandish, unfamiliar

Strange Interlude author
6 O'Neill (Eugene)

stranger
5 alien, guest **7** visitor **8** newcomer, outsider, wanderer **9** auslander, foreigner, immigrant, transient

strangle
5 burke, choke, scrag, shush **6** muffle, quelch, stifle **7** garotte, garrote **8** suppress, throttle **10** asphyxiate

strap
4 band, beat, belt, bind, rein **5** leash **6** attach, latigo, punish, secure, suffer **7** binding, leather **8** distress **9** constrict

strapping
5 beefy, burly, hardy, husky **6** brawny, robust, rugged, sturdy **8** muscular, vigorous **10** able-bodied

stratagem
4 play, plot, ploy, ruse, wile **5** feint, trick **6** device, gambit, scheme, tactic **8** artifice, intrigue, maneuver **10** conspiracy, subterfuge **11** machination

strategy
4 plan **6** design, method, scheme **7** project, tactics **8** game plan **9** blueprint

Stratford's river
4 Avon

stratum
3 bed **4** rank **5** class, grade, layer, level

Strauss, Richard
opera: **6** Salome **7** Elektra **13** Rosenkavalier (Der) **15** Ariadne auf Naxos **16** Frau ohne Schatten (Die)
tone poem: **7** Don Juan **10** Don Quixote **11** Heldenleben (Ein) **20** Thus Spake Zarathustra **23** Death and Transfiguration

Strauss of jeans fame
4 Levi

straw
3 hay **5** blond **6** flaxen, golden, thatch
braided: **6** sennit
mat: **6** tatami
plaited: **7** leghorn

straw man
4 dupe, foil, sham

stray
3 err, gad **4** lost, roam, rove, waif **5** drift, range **6** depart, errant, ramble, random, wander **7** deviate, digress, diverge, erratic, meander, runaway, traipse, vagrant **8** divagate, homeless, sporadic **9** gallivant

streak
4 hint, vein **5** fleck, tinge, trace **6** dapple, marble, mottle, strain, stripe **7** striate **8** tincture

streaked
5 upset **7** brindle, marbled, striped **8** brindled, grizzled

stream
4 beck, burn, flow, flux, gill, gush, pour, race, rill, rush, sike **5** bourn, brook, creek, spate **6** bourne, branch, rindle, runlet, runnel, sluice **7** current, freshet, rivulet, torrent

streambed
4 wadi, wash **5** gully **6** arroyo

streamer
4 flag, jack **6** banner, burgee, ensign, pennon **7** pennant **8** banderol, bannerol, standard **9** banderole

streamline
7 contour **8** organize, simplify **9** modernize

street
3 way **4** drag, road, wynd **5** alley, drive **6** artery, avenue **7** roadway **9** boulevard **12** thoroughfare
border: **4** curb **7** curbing
French: **3** rue
material: **6** cobble **7** asphalt, macadam **11** cobblestone

streetcar
4 tram **7** trolley

Streetcar Named Desire, A
author: **8** Williams (Tennessee)
character: **6** Stella (Kowalski) **7** Blanche (DuBois), Stanley (Kowalski)

street performer
4 mime **6** busker

Street Scene author
4 Rice (Elmer)

strength
5 brawn, force, forte, might, power, sinew, vigor **6** energy, muscle **7** potency **8** security **9** fortitude, intensity, soundness, stability, toughness

strengthen
4 gird **5** brace, steel **6** anneal, beef up, harden, prop up **7** bolster, enhance, fortify, support, toughen **8** buttress, embolden, energize **9** intensify, reinforce, undergird

strenuous
4 hard **5** tough **6** taxing, uphill **7** arduous, operose **9** demanding, difficult, effortful, Herculean, laborious **12** backbreaking

Strephon
8 shepherd
beloved: **5** Chloe **6** Urania

stress
6 accent, burden, import, play up, strain, weight **7** anxiety, feature, tension, urgency **8** emphasis, pressure **9** emphasize, italicize, underline **10** accentuate, underscore
in poetry: **5** ictus

stretch
5 crane, range, reach, scope, space, spell, sweep, tract **6** extend, extent, length, limber, region, spread **7** breadth, draw out, expanse, magnify, prolong, purview, spin out, tighten **8** distance, elongate, lengthen, protract **9** embellish, embroider, expansion **10** exaggerate
on a frame: **6** tenter
out: **6** sprawl **7** lie down, recline

stretchable
7 ductile, elastic, tensile

stretched
4 taut

stretcher
4 yarn **6** gurney, litter **8** tall tale

strew
3 sow **4** dust **5** cover **6** pepper, spread **7** scatter **8** disperse, sprinkle **9** broadcast, circulate, propagate **10** distribute **11** disseminate

strewn
4 semé

stricken
3 hit, ill **4** hurt, sick **6** bereft **7** injured, wounded **9** afflicted **11** overwhelmed

strict
4 firm **5** exact, harsh, rigid, stern, tough **6** narrow, severe **7** precise **8** exacting, faithful, rigorous **9** draconian, stringent, unsparing **10** inflexible, ironhanded, meticulous, scrupulous **11** hard-and-fast, punctilious

stricture
5 cramp, stint **7** censure, reproof **8** reproach **9** aspersion, criticism, reprimand **10** constraint, limitation

stride
4 gait, pace, step **5** march, stalk **7** advance **8** straddle

strident
4 loud **5** harsh **6** shrill **7** grating, jarring, rasping, raucous, squawky **8** piercing **9** clamorous, insistent, obtrusive **10** boisterous, discordant, stentorian, vociferous **12** obstreperous

strife
4 fray **5** broil, fight **6** battle, combat **7** discord,

dispute, dissent, quarrel, rivalry, warfare, wrangle **8** argument, conflict, disunity, friction, struggle, tug-of-war **10** contention, dissension, dissidence

strike
3 hit, pop, rap **4** bash, beat, poke, slam, slap, slug, sock, swat, whap, whop **5** clout, knock, punch, smack, smite, swipe, thump, whack **6** assail, attack, cudgel, delete, hammer, pummel, thrash **7** assault, impress, inflict, wildcat **8** stoppage

strike out
4 dele **5** elide **6** delete, efface **7** expunge

striking
5 showy, vivid **6** cogent, marked, signal **7** salient, telling **9** arresting, prominent **10** compelling, noticeable, remarkable **11** conspicuous, outstanding

Strindberg play
9 Miss Julie **11** Ghost Sonata (The) **12** Dance of Death (The)

string
3 row **4** cord, file, line, rank, tier **5** chain, chord, order, queue, train, twine **6** sequel, series **7** echelon **8** sequence **10** succession
together: **4** bead
up: **4** hang **5** noose, scrag **6** gibbet

stringed instrument
4 harp, viol **5** banjo, celli (plural), cello, gamba, viola **6** fiddle, guitar, violin **8** mandolin **9** mandoline **10** bass fiddle, double bass, pedal steel

stringent
see **strict**

string tie
4 bolo

stringy
4 lean, ropy, wiry **6** sinewy **7** fibrous

strip
4 band, bare, doff, flay, husk, peel, sack, skin **5** scale **6** billet, denude, divest, expose, fillet, ravage, ribbon **7** bandeau, deprive, disrobe, pillage, uncover, undress **8** unclothe
leather: **5** thong
of wood: **4** lath, slat
skin, blubber: **5** scarf **6** flense

stripe
3 ilk **4** band, kind, lash, sort, type **5** order **6** strake, streak **7** banding, chevron, lineate, striate, variety

striped African mammal
5 okapi, zebra

striped gemstone
4 onyx **5** agate

stripling
3 boy, lad **5** youth **9** youngster **10** adolescent

stripper
6 peeler, teaser **9** ecdysiast

stripteaser
see **stripper**

strive
3 try, vie **4** seek **5** labor **6** strain **7** attempt, contend **8** endeavor, struggle **9** undertake

stroke
3 fit, hit, pet, rub **4** blow, hone, whet **5** swing **6** attack, caress, fondle, soothe **7** flatter **8** apoplexy, ischemia **9** heartbeat

stroll
4 rove, turn, walk **5** amble, drift, mosey, paseo **6** cruise, linger, ramble, wander **7** saunter, traipse **9** promenade

stroller
4 pram **6** go-cart **8** carriage **12** baby carriage, perambulator

strong
4 fast, firm **5** burly, hardy, lusty, solid, stout, tough **6** brawny, hearty, heroic, mighty, potent, robust, rugged, sinewy, stable, sturdy **7** durable, intense, staunch **8** forceful, muscular, powerful, stalwart, vigorous **9** resilient, strapping **10** able-bodied, spirituous

strong-arm
5 bully **6** bounce, coerce, hector, lean on **7** assault, dragoon **8** browbeat, bulldoze, bullyrag **9** terrorize **10** intimidate

strongbox
4 arca, safe, till **5** chest **6** coffer **9** reliquary **13** treasure chest

stronghold
4 fort **7** bastion, bulwark, citadel, redoubt **8** fastness, fortress

strongman
4 Amin (Idi), Tito **5** Assad (Hafez), Perón (Juan), Putin (Vladimir) **6** Castro (Fidel), Chávez (Hugo), despot, Marcos (Ferdinand), Mobutu (Sese Seko), Samson, tyrant **7** Batista (Fulgencio), Hussein (Saddam), Noriega (Manuel), Suharto **8** caudillo, Pinochet (Augusto) **9** Milošević (Slobodan), Mussolini (Benito)

strong point
5 asset, forte **6** métier

strong suit
see **strong point**

strophe
5 verse **6** stanza

struck
3 hit **5** smote

structure
4 form **5** frame **6** format, makeup, system **7** anatomy, complex, edifice, network **8** building, erection, skeleton **9** framework **10** morphology **11** arrangement

struggle
3 try, vie **4** agon **5** trial **6** battle, effort, hassle, strain, strife, strive, tussle **7** attempt, compete, contend, contest, grapple, scuffle **8** endeavor, exertion, flounder, skirmish, striving

strumpet
4 bawd, jade, slut, tart **5** hussy, tramp, trull, wench **6** floozy, harlot, hooker, wanton **7** jezebel, trollop **8** slattern

strut
6 flaunt, parade, prance, sashay **7** flounce, peacock, show off, swagger

stub
3 end **4** butt, tail **5** stump **6** put out, strike **7** remnant **10** extinguish

stubborn
5 balky, rigid **6** cussed, dogged, mulish, ornery **7** adamant, lasting, willful **8** obdurate, perverse **9** obstinate, pigheaded, steadfast, unbending **10** bullheaded, determined, headstrong, inexorable, inflexible, persistent, rebellious, refractory, relentless, unyielding **11** intractable **12** contumacious, pertinacious, single-minded

stubby
5 dumpy, short, squat, stout **6** stocky, stumpy **8** heavyset, thickset

stuck
5 clung, glued **6** jammed, wedged **7** adhered, blocked, saddled, stabbed, stumped **8** attached, held fast

stuck-up
4 vain **6** sniffy, snippy, snooty **7** haughty **8** snobbish **9** conceited **12** narcissistic, supercilious

stud
3 guy **4** dude, hunk, male, nail, post **5** cleat, he-man, himbo, macho **6** button, pillar **7** earring, speckle, upright **8** sprinkle, stallion
site: **4** lobe

student
4 tiro, tyro **5** pupil, tutee **6** novice **7** protégé, scholar **8** disciple, neophyte **10** apprentice
assignment: **5** essay
college: **9** undergrad **13** undergraduate
female: **4** coed
first-year: **5** frosh **8** freshman
fourth-year: **6** senior
French: **5** élève **8** étudiant
military: **5** cadet, middy **10** midshipman
second-year: **4** soph **9** sophomore
third-year: **6** junior
wandering: **7** goliard

studio
4 shop **7** atelier **8** workroom, workshop
sign: **5** on air
stand: **5** easel

studious
7 bookish, learned **9** scholarly

Studs Lonigan creator
7 Farrell (James T.)

study
3 con, den, vet **4** case, cram, muse **5** étude **6** ponder, survey **7** analyze, examine, inspect, reverie **10** excogitate, scrutinize

stuff
3 jam, ram **4** cram, fill, glut, junk, pack, sate, tamp **5** crowd, gorge, shove **6** matter, things **7** essence, jam-pack, squeeze, surfeit **8** material, overfill **9** substance **11** possessions

stuffy
4 dull, prim **5** close, fuggy, heavy, humid, stale **6** narrow, stodgy **7** airless, bloated, genteel, pompous, prudish, stilted **8** priggish, stagnant, stifling **9** hidebound, Victorian **11** puritanical, suffocating **13** self-righteous

stultify
4 dull **6** deaden, impair, stifle, weaken **7** inhibit, nullify, repress, smother, trammel **8** restrain, stagnate, suppress **9** suffocate **10** discourage, invalidate

stumble
3 err **4** goof, reel, slip, trip **5** error, fluff, gaffe, lapse, lurch **6** falter, mess up, muddle, slipup, totter **7** blunder, faux pas, mistake, stagger, stammer **8** flounder

stump
3 end **4** beat, butt, dare, defy, plod, stub **6** baffle, outwit, stymie, trudge **7** buffalo, flummox, mystify, nonplus, perplex **8** bewilder, campaign, confound, hustings, politick **9** barnstorm, challenge **11** electioneer

stun
4 daze **5** amaze, floor, shock **6** dazzle **7** astound, nonplus, stagger, stupefy **8** astonish, bewilder, bowl over, knock out, paralyze **9** dumbfound **11** flabbergast

stun gun
5 Taser

stunning
6 superb **7** amazing, awesome **8** gorgeous, striking **9** excellent, wonderful **10** astounding, impressive, remarkable, staggering, surprising **11** astonishing

stunt
4 curb, feat **5** antic, caper, check, dwarf, prank, trick **6** hinder, impair, retard **8** escapade, hold back, suppress

stuntman Knievel
4 Evel

stupefy
4 daze, dull, faze, stun **5** addle, amaze **6** muddle,

rattle **7** astound, nonplus, petrify, stagger **8** astonish, bewilder, paralyze **9** disorient, dumbfound **11** flabbergast

stupendous
4 huge **7** amazing, awesome, massive, titanic **8** colossal, enormous, gigantic, stunning, towering, wondrous **9** fantastic, humongous, marvelous, monstrous, wonderful **10** astounding, miraculous, monumental, phenomenal, prodigious, staggering, tremendous **11** astonishing, spectacular

stupid
3 dim **4** dull, dumb, slow **5** dense, dopey, inane, silly, thick **6** oafish, obtuse, simple, torpid **7** asinine, brutish, doltish, fatuous, foolish, idiotic, moronic, witless **8** backward, ignorant, mindless, retarded **9** brainless, fatheaded, imbecilic, laughable, ludicrous, pinheaded, senseless, vexatious **10** half-witted, slow-witted

stupor
6 torpor, trance **7** languor **8** dullness, hebetude, lethargy, narcosis **9** lassitude **10** anesthesia, somnolence
combining form: **4** narc **5** narco

sturdy
5 hardy, solid, sound, stout, tough **6** robust, rugged, secure, strong **7** durable, healthy, staunch **8** stalwart, vigorous **9** strapping

sturgeon
6 beluga
eggs: **3** roe **6** caviar

Sturm und Drang
6 unrest **7** ferment, turmoil **9** agitation **10** turbulence

St. Vitus' ___
5 dance

sty
3 pen **4** coop, cyst **6** pigpen **7** piggery

stygian
4 dark **6** gloomy **7** hellish, sunless **8** infernal, plutonic **9** Cimmerian, plutonian

style
3 fad, way **4** chic, élan, mode, rage, vein **5** craze, decor, flair, trend, vogue **6** manner **7** fashion, panache **11** savoir-faire
hair: **4** coif **8** coiffure

stylish
3 mod **4** chic, posh, tony, trig **5** doggy, natty, ritzy, sassy, sharp, showy, sleek, slick, smart, swank, swell **6** chichi, dapper, dressy, modern, modish, snappy, snazzy, spiffy, trendy, with-it **7** à la mode, dashing, doggish **8** spiffing, up-to-date **10** newfangled **11** fashionable

stymie
4 stop **5** block **6** hamper, hinder, impede, thwart **7** flummox, prevent **8** confound, obstruct **9** frustrate, hamstring

Stymphalides' slayer
8 Heracles, Hercules

styptic
4 alum

Styron novel
13 Sophie's Choice

Styx
counterpart: **5** Lethe **7** Acheron, Cocytus **10** Phlegethon
ferryman: **6** Charon
location: **5** Hades

suave
4 oily **5** slick **6** smarmy, smooth, urbane **7** cordial, courtly, gallant, politic, refined, worldly **8** debonair, gracious, polished, unctuous, well-bred **10** cultivated, diplomatic **13** sophisticated

sub
4 hero **5** below, po'boy, proxy, U-boat, under **6** backup, fill-in, hoagie **7** grinder, stand-by, stand-in, torpedo **8** pinch-hit **9** alternate, secondary, surrogate **10** understudy **11** locum tenens, pinch hitter, replacement

subaltern
8 inferior **9** secondary, underling

subatomic particle
3 ion

subdue
4 curb, tame **5** crush, quash, quell **6** defeat, master, quench **7** conquer, control, enslave, put down, repress, squelch **8** beat down, overcome, suppress, tone down, vanquish **9** overpower, overthrow

subdued
4 soft, tame **5** muted, quiet, sober **6** low-key, mellow, subtle **7** neutral, serious **8** low-keyed, softened, tasteful, tempered **9** moderated, toned down **10** controlled, restrained, submissive

subjacent
3 low **5** lower, under **6** lesser, nether **8** inferior

subject
3 apt **4** core **5** liege, motif, point, prone, theme, topic **6** expose, liable, likely, matter, motive, vassal **7** citizen, exposed, lay open, problem **8** argument, inferior, material, question **9** dependent, leitmotif, secondary, sensitive, tributary **11** susceptible

subjective
6 biased **10** prejudiced

subjugate
see **subdue**

sublime
4 holy **5** ideal, lofty, noble, proud **6** august, divine, sacred **7** blessed, exalted **8** elevated, glorious, heavenly, majestic, splendid **9** celestial, spiritual **11** magnificent, resplendent **12** transcendent

submachine gun
3 Uzi **4** Sten
submarine
4 hero **5** po'boy, U-boat **6** hoagie **7** grinder, torpedo **8** undersea
detector: 5 sonar
submerge
3 dip **4** duck, dunk, sink **5** drown, flood, swamp **6** deluge, engulf, plunge **7** founder, go under, immerse **8** inundate, overflow
submerged
4 sunk **6** sunken
submissive
4 meek, tame **6** abject, docile, pliant **7** servile, slavish **8** amenable, obedient, obeisant, yielding **9** compliant, tractable **10** obsequious **11** acquiescent, deferential
submit
3 bow **4** cave, fold, obey **5** defer, yield **6** accede, comply, give in, hand in, relent, send in, tender **7** concede, deliver, go under, present, proffer, provide, subject, succumb, suggest **9** acquiesce, surrender **10** capitulate
subordinate
5 minor, scrub, under **6** junior **7** adjunct, subject **8** inferior **9** accessory, ancillary, auxiliary, dependent, secondary, tributary, underling **10** collateral
sub rosa
6 covert, secret **7** furtive, private **8** covertly, in camera, secretly, stealthy **9** by stealth, furtively, privately, secretive, underhand **10** stealthily **11** clandestine, underhanded **13** surreptitious
subsequent
4 next **5** after, later **6** serial **7** ensuing **9** following, resultant, resulting **10** sequential, succeeding, successive **11** consecutive
prefix: 4 post
subsequently
4 next, then **5** after, later, since **9** afterward **10** afterwards, thereafter
subservient
6 abject, docile **7** fawning, servile, slavish **8** adjuvant, obeisant **9** accessory, ancillary, auxiliary, compliant, truckling **10** collateral, obsequious **11** acquiescent, deferential, sycophantic
subside
3 ebb **4** bate, ease, lull, lyse, sink, wane **5** abate, let up, taper **6** ease up, recede, settle **7** decline, descend, die away, die down, dwindle, ease off, slacken **8** decrease, diminish
subsidiary
5 minor **6** backup, branch **7** subject **8** adjuvant **9** accessory, ancillary, auxiliary, secondary, tributary
subsidize
4 back, fund **5** endow, stake **7** finance, promote, sponsor, support **8** bankroll **10** underwrite
subsidy
4 gift **5** grant **6** reward
subsistence
4 keep, salt **5** bread, means **6** income, living **7** support **9** resources **10** livelihood, sustenance
substance
3 nub **4** bulk, core, crux, gist, mass, meat, pith, soul **5** being, drift, focus, heart, point, sense, stuff, tenor **6** amount, burden, entity, import, kernel, marrow, matter, nubbin, object, thrust, upshot, wealth **7** essence, meaning, nucleus **8** material, property, sum total **9** resources **12** quintessence
substantial
5 ample, hefty, meaty, solid **6** sturdy **7** massive, sizable, weighty **8** abundant, concrete, material, physical, sensible, tangible **9** corporeal, important **10** meaningful, phenomenal **11** significant **12** considerable
substantiate
5 prove **6** embody, evince, verify **7** bear out, confirm, justify **8** evidence, manifest, validate **9** establish, objectify, vindicate **11** corroborate, demonstrate **12** authenticate
substitute
4 mock, sham, swap, temp **5** dummy, locum, proxy, trade **6** acting, backup, deputy, double, ersatz, fill-in, refuge, resort, second, switch **7** replace, reserve, standby, stand-in, stopgap **8** exchange, recourse, resource, spurious **9** alternate, expedient, imitation, makeshift, simulated, surrogate **10** artificial, expediency, understudy **11** alternative, locum tenens, pinch hitter, replacement, succedaneum
substratum
4 base **5** basis **6** bottom, ground **7** bedrock, footing **10** foundation, groundwork **12** underpinning
substructure
4 base, seat **5** basis **6** bottom **7** footing **10** foundation, groundwork **12** underpinning
subsume
6 embody, take in **7** contain, embrace, include, involve **8** comprise **9** encompass
subterfuge
4 ploy, ruse, scam, sham **5** cheat, feint, fraud **6** deceit, dupery **7** chicane **8** trickery **9** chicanery, deception
subterranean
11 underground
subtle
4 fine **5** faint **6** artful, astute **7** refined **8** delicate, finespun, skillful **9** insidious
subtract
6 deduct, remove **7** take off **8** discount, knock off, take away, withdraw, withhold

subtraction
6 rebate **8** discount **9** abatement, deduction **10** diminution, withdrawal
term: **7** minuend **9** remainder **10** subtrahend

suburbs
7 fringes **8** environs, purlieus **9** outskirts

subversion
8 sabotage

subvert
7 vitiate **8** sabotage **9** undermine

subway
British: **4** tube **11** underground
French: **5** métro
New York: **3** BMT, IND, IRT
relatives: **3** els
San Francisco: **4** BART

succeed
3 win **4** boom **5** click, ensue, go far, score **6** arrive, follow, go over, make it, pan out, thrive, win out **7** catch on, come off, make out, prevail, prosper, replace, triumph **8** displace, flourish, get ahead, make good, supplant **9** supervene

succes ____
3 fou **7** d'estime

success
3 hit **4** coup, fame **5** smash, éclat **6** wealth **7** arrival, fortune, killing, triumph, victory **8** fruition **10** attainment, prosperity **11** achievement, fulfillment

successful
5 boffo, smash, socko **7** booming **8** fruitful, thriving **9** effective, lucrative **10** prosperous, triumphant, victorious **11** flourishing

succession
3 row **5** chain, cycle, march, order, suite, train **6** course, sequel, series, string **8** sequence **11** progression

successive
4 next **7** ensuing **9** following **10** subsequent

successor
4 heir **8** claimant, follower **9** inheritor **11** beneficiary

succinct
5 blunt, brief, pithy, short, terse **7** brusque, compact, concise, laconic, summary

succor
3 aid **4** help, lift **6** assist, relief **7** comfort, relieve, support

succotash bean
4 lima

succulent
5 juicy **8** luscious
plant: **4** aloe, hoya **5** agave, ficus, yucca **6** cactus, cereus, hoodia, viscum **7** begonia

succumb
3 bow, die **4** cave, fold, wilt **5** defer, yield **6** accede, buckle, cave in, expire, give in, perish, relent, resign, submit **7** give out, go under, knuckle **8** collapse **9** break down, surrender **10** capitulate

sucker
3 con, gyp, sap **4** bilk, dupe, fool, gull, mark, rook **5** cheat, chump, patsy, shoot **6** diddle, pigeon **7** defraud, fall guy, swindle **8** hoodwink, pushover **9** bamboozle

suckle
5 nurse **7** nourish, nurture **10** breast-feed

suction preceder
4 lipo

Sudan
capital: **8** Khartoum
desert: **6** Libyan
language: **6** Arabic
monetary unit: **5** dinar
neighbor: **4** Chad **5** Congo, Egypt, Kenya, Libya **6** Uganda **7** Eritrea **8** Ethiopia
river: **4** Nile
sea: **3** Red

sudden
4 rash **5** hasty, swift **6** abrupt, prompt **7** hurried **8** headlong **9** impetuous, impromptu, impulsive **10** unexpected, unforeseen **11** precipitant, precipitate, precipitous

suddenly
5 aback **7** hastily, unaware **8** abruptly, promptly, unawares **9** all at once **10** by surprise

suds
4 beer, fizz, foam, head, soap **5** froth, spume **6** lather **7** brewski

sue
8 litigate

suer
8 litigant

suet
3 fat **4** lard **6** tallow

Suez Canal
builder: **7** Lesseps (Ferdinand de)
city: **8** Ismailia, Port Said

suffer
3 ail **4** ache, bear, lump **5** abide, admit, allow, brook **6** accept, endure, permit, submit **7** agonize, anguish, stomach, sustain, swallow, undergo **8** tolerate **10** experience

sufferer
6 victim

suffering
5 agony, dolor **6** misery, ordeal **7** anguish, passion, torment, torture **8** distress **10** affliction, misfortune

suffice
5 avail, serve

sufficient
3 due **5** ample **6** decent, enough, plenty **8** adequate, all right **9** tolerable **10** acceptable **12** commensurate, satisfactory
poetic: 4 enow

suffocate
5 burke, choke **6** stifle **7** smother **8** snuff out, strangle **10** asphyxiate

suffrage
4 vote **5** voice **6** ballot **9** franchise

suffragist
4 Catt (Carrie Chapman), Howe (Julia Ward), Mott (Lucretia), Paul (Alice) **5** Stone (Lucy) **7** Anthony (Susan B.), Bloomer (Amelia), Stanton (Elizabeth Cady) **8** Woodhull (Victoria Claflin) **9** Pankhurst (Emmeline)

suffuse
4 fill **5** bathe, flush, imbue, steep **7** pervade **8** permeate, saturate

sugar
6 aldose, fucose, ribose, xylose **7** glucose, lactose, maltose, mannose, pentose, sorbose, sucrose, sweeten **8** fructose, furanose, levulose **10** saccharose
burnt: 7 caramel
combining form: 4 gluc, glyc, sucr **5** gluco, glyco, sucro **7** sacchar **8** sacchari, saccharo
from palm sap: 7 jaggery
Mexican: 7 panocha, penuche
source: 4 beet, cane, corn **5** maple
substitute: 6 stevia **7** steevia **8** sorbitol **9** aspartame

sugarcane refuse
7 bagasse

sugarcoat
5 candy, glaze **6** veneer **7** sweeten, varnish **8** palliate **9** extenuate, gloss over, gloze over, whitewash

sugary
6 syrupy **7** cloying, honeyed, mawkish **10** saccharine **11** sentimental

suggest
4 hint **5** evoke, imply **6** submit **7** connote, propose, signify **8** indicate, intimate **9** adumbrate, insinuate

suggestion
3 cue **4** clue, hint **5** shade, smack, tinge, trace **6** advice **7** inkling **8** allusion, innuendo, overtone, reminder **9** suspicion **10** indication, intimation **11** implication, insinuation

suggestive
4 racy **5** salty, spicy **6** ribald, risqué **8** off-color **9** evocative

suicidal pilot
8 kamikaze

suicide
8 felo-de-se **10** self-murder **13** self-slaughter
Japanese: 7 seppuku **8** hara-kiri, hari-kari

suit
3 fit **4** case, jibe, plea **5** adapt, agree, befit, cause, check, serve, tally **6** accord, action, adjust, appeal, become, go with, please, prayer, square, tailor **7** conform, enhance, flatter, lawsuit, request, satisfy **8** entreaty, petition **9** agree with, reconcile
card: 5 clubs **6** hearts, spades **8** diamonds
type: 4 zoot **6** monkey, vested **9** paternity **10** pin-striped **11** class-action

suitable
3 apt, due, fit **4** just, meet **5** right **6** proper, seemly, useful **7** condign, fitting **8** apposite, becoming, deserved, eligible **9** pertinent, qualified, requisite **10** acceptable **11** appropriate

suitcase
3 bag **4** grip **6** valise **7** carry-on, holdall **8** carryall

suite
3 lot, row, set **4** flat **5** array, rooms, train **6** sequel, series, string **7** lodging **8** chambers, sequence **9** apartment, following

suitor
4 beau **5** lover, spark, swain, wooer **7** admirer, gallant, sparker **8** cavalier, paramour **9** boyfriend **10** petitioner

sulfur
9 brimstone

sulk
4 mope, pout **5** brood, gloom

sulky
4 cart, dour, glum **5** moody **6** gloomy, morose, sullen

sullen
4 dour, glum, mean, sour **5** moody, pouty, surly **6** crabby, dismal, gloomy, grumpy, morose, somber, sombre **7** crabbed, pouting **8** lowering, scowling **9** glowering, saturnine **10** ill-humored **11** pessimistic

Sullivan's partner
7 Gilbert (William Schwenk)

sully
3 tar **4** soil **5** dirty, shame, smear, stain, taint **6** defame, defile, malign, vilify **7** asperse, blacken, pollute, slander, tarnish, traduce **8** besmirch, disgrace, dishonor **9** denigrate

Sultan of Swat
8 Babe Ruth

sultry
3 hot **4** sexy **5** close, humid, muggy **6** steamy,

sticky, stuffy, torrid **7** airless **8** stifling **9** seductive **10** sweltering, voluptuous

sum
3 add, all, tot **4** mass, tote **5** gross, total, whole **6** amount, digest, entity, figure, resumé **7** epitome **8** entirety, integral, nutshell, totality **9** aggregate

Sumac of Peru
3 Yma

Sumatra
country: **9** Indonesia
highest peak: **7** Kerinci **8** Kerintji
largest city: **5** Medan
shrew: **4** tana

Sumerian
city: **4** Kish, Umma **5** Erech **6** Lagash, Nippur
dragon: **3** Kur
god: **3** Abu, Kur, Utu **4** Enki **5** Enlil, Lahar, Nanna, Nintu **6** Dumuzi, Nergal, Ninazu **7** Enkimdu
goddess: **6** Ningal, Ninlil

summarize
5 recap **6** digest **7** abridge, outline **8** boil down, condense **9** epitomize, synopsize **11** encapsulate **12** recapitulate

summary
5 recap **6** aperçu, digest, précis, résumé, review, wrap-up **7** compend, epitome, outline, roundup, rundown **8** abstract, overview, scenario, synopsis **9** inventory **10** abridgment, compendium, conspectus **11** abridgement **12** condensation

summer
cooler: **3** ade
French: **3** été
Spanish: **6** verano

summerhouse
6 alcove, gazebo, pagoda **9** belvedere

summery
7 estival

summit
3 top **4** acme, apex, peak, roof **5** crest, crown **6** apogee, climax, height, vertex, zenith **8** capstone, meridian, pinnacle **11** culmination

summon
3 bid **4** call, cite **5** evoke, order **6** beckon, call in, invite, muster **7** arraign, command, conjure, convene, convoke, ring for, send for **8** assemble, subpoena

sump
4 sink **8** cesspool

sumptuous
4 lush, rich **5** grand **6** costly, deluxe, lavish, superb **7** opulent **8** gorgeous, luscious, palatial, splendid **9** grandiose, luxurious **11** extravagant, resplendent

sum up
5 recap

sun
3 orb, Sol **4** bask, star **7** daystar, phoebus **8** daylight, luminary, radiance **9** radiation
combining form: **4** heli **5** helio
disk: **4** Aten
god: **3** Lug, Sol, Tem, Utu **4** Amen, Atmu, Atum, Inti, Lleu, Llew, Lugh, Utug **5** Horus, Sunna, Surya **6** Apollo, Babbar, Helios, Marduk **7** Khepera, Ninurta, Phoebus, Shamash **8** Hyperion, Merodach

Sun Also Rises, The
author: **9** Hemingway (Ernest)
character: **6** Ashley (Brett), Barnes (Jake)

sunder
3 cut **4** rend, rive **5** break, sever, slice, split **6** cleave, divide **8** dissever, disunite, separate

sundial part
6 gnomon

sundown
4 dusk **7** evening **8** eventide, gloaming, twilight

sun-dried brick
5 adobe

sundries
7 notions **8** oddments **9** etceteras **11** odds and ends

sundry
4 many, some **6** varied **7** diverse, several, various **8** assorted, manifold **9** different, disparate **12** multifarious **13** miscellaneous

sunfish
4 opah **7** pompano **8** bluegill **11** pumpkinseed

Sunflower State
6 Kansas

Sun King
8 Louis XIV

sunny
4 fair, fine, warm **5** clear, happy **6** blithe, bright, cheery, chirpy, golden **7** beaming, clarion, radiant **8** cheerful, pleasant **9** brilliant, cloudless, unclouded **10** optimistic

sunrise
4 dawn, morn **6** aurora **7** dawning, morning **8** cockcrow, daybreak, daylight
goddess: **3** Eos **6** Aurora

sunroom
8 solarium

sunscreen ingredient
4 PABA

sunset
3 eve **4** dusk **7** evening **8** gloaming, twilight

Sunset State
6 Oregon

Sunshine State
7 Florida
sunup
see **sunrise**
sup
3 eat 4 dine 5 feast
super
4 very 5 great 8 powerful, splendid, terrific 9 excellent, extremely, fantastic, first-rate, wonderful 11 outstanding
superannuated
4 aged 5 hoary, passé 6 bygone 7 ancient, archaic, elderly, outworn 8 obsolete, outdated, outmoded 9 out-of-date 10 antiquated 11 obsolescent 12 old-fashioned
superb
4 A-one, rich 5 grand, noble, prime, primo 7 elegant, exalted, optimal, optimum, opulent, sublime, supreme 8 glorious, gorgeous, imposing, majestic, peerless, splendid, standout 9 excellent, marvelous, matchless, wonderful 11 magnificent, outstanding, resplendent, sensational, splendorous
supercilious
5 lofty 6 lordly, sniffy, snippy 7 haughty, stuck-up 8 cavalier, scornful, snobbish, superior 10 disdainful 11 patronizing 13 condescending, high-and-mighty
superficial
5 hasty 6 breezy, casual, slight 7 cursory, shallow, sketchy, surface, trivial 8 external, skin-deep 9 depthless, frivolous 11 perfunctory
superfluity
4 glut 5 frill 6 excess 7 nimiety, overrun, surfeit, surplus 8 overflow, overkill, overload, overmuch, overplus, plethora 10 oversupply, redundancy, surplusage 11 prodigality 13 overabundance
superfluous
5 extra, spare 6 de trop, excess, otiose 7 surplus 8 needless 9 excessive, redundant 10 gratuitous 11 uncalled-for, unnecessary
superintend
4 boss 6 direct, manage 7 control, oversee 10 administer
superintendence
4 care 6 charge 7 conduct, running 8 handling 9 authority, direction, oversight 10 management
superior
4 rare 5 above, lofty, major, prime, proud, upper 6 better, choice, higher, lordly, select, sniffy, snippy, snooty 7 capital, greater, haughty, premium, stuck-up 8 arrogant, brass hat, cavalier, dominant, higher-up, insolent 9 excellent, first-rate, marvelous 10 disdainful, first-class, preeminent, preferable, remarkable 11 exceptional, overbearing, patronizing, predominant
superiority
9 advantage, dominance, seniority, supremacy, upper hand 10 ascendancy
superjacent
4 over 6 higher 7 greater 9 overlying
superlative
3 ace 4 A-one, best 8 peerless, standout 9 matchless 10 consummate 11 magnificent, outstanding
Superman
9 Clark Kent
actor: 4 Alyn (Kirk), Cain (Dean) 5 Reeve (Christopher), Routh (Brandon) 6 Reeves (George) 7 Collyer (Bud)
bane: 10 kryptonite
birthplace: 7 Krypton
creator: 7 Shuster (Joe)
employer: 11 Daily Planet (The)
father: 5 Jor-El
foe: 3 Zod (General) 6 Luthor (Lex) 7 Bizarro 8 Brainiac, Darkseid, Doomsday, Mxyzptlk (Mr.)
friend: 5 Olsen (Jimmy)
girlfriend: 8 Lois Lane
mother: 4 Lara
original name: 5 Kal-El
supermarket section
4 deli
supernatural
5 magic 6 divine, mystic 7 magical, psychic, uncanny 8 heavenly 9 celestial, unearthly 10 miraculous, paranormal, phenomenal 12 metaphysical, transcendent 13 extraordinary
supernatural being
3 elf, fay, god, hob, imp, nix 4 jinn, ogre, peri, puck 5 afrit, angel, bogle, deity, demon, fairy, gnome, jinni, lamia, naiad, nixie, nymph, pixie, satyr, sylph, Titan, troll 6 afreet, goblin, kelpie, seraph, spirit, sprite 7 banshee, brownie, bugbear, goddess, incubus, silenus, vampire, wendigo, windigo 8 bogeyman, demiurge, succubus 9 boogeyman, hobgoblin 10 leprechaun
supernatural force
4 mana
supernumerary
5 extra, spare 6 de trop, excess, walk-on 7 reserve, surplus 8 leftover 9 redundant
supersede
5 usurp 7 replace, succeed 8 displace, supplant
supervene
5 ensue, occur 6 befall, follow, result 7 succeed 9 eventuate, transpire
supervise
3 run 4 boss 5 steer 6 direct, govern, manage 7 conduct, monitor, oversee, proctor, referee 8 chaperon, overlook

supervision
7 control, running **8** auspices, handling **9** oversight **10** intendance, management

supervisor
7 foreman, manager **8** director, overseer **13** administrator

supine
5 inert, prone, slack **7** passive **8** inactive, indolent **9** prostrate, recumbent **10** horizontal **12** outstretched

supper club
6 nitery **7** cabaret **9** night spot

supplant
4 oust **5** usurp **6** cut out, unseat **7** replace, succeed **8** crowd out, displace, force out **9** overthrow, supersede

supple
5 agile, lithe, withy **6** limber, nimble, pliant, whippy **7** ductile, elastic, lissome, plastic, pliable, springy, willowy **8** flexible, graceful, moldable **9** malleable, resilient

supplement
3 add, pad **4** coda **5** rider **6** append, beef up, enrich, extend, sequel **7** adjunct, augment, codicil, enhance, fill out, fortify **8** addendum, addition, appendix, buttress, increase **9** accessory, reinforce **10** postscript

suppliant
5 asker **6** beggar, suitor **9** solicitor **10** petitioner

supplicant
see **suppliant**

supplicate
3 ask, beg, sue **4** pray **5** crave, plead **6** appeal, invoke **7** beseech, entreat, implore, solicit **8** petition **9** importune

supplication
4 plea, suit **6** appeal, orison, prayer **8** entreaty, petition **11** application

supplies
6 stores **8** matériel **9** equipment, materials **10** provisions

supply
5 cache, equip, hoard, stock, store **6** outfit, purvey **7** deliver, fulfill, furnish, provide, reserve, surplus **8** dispense, hand over, transfer, turn over **9** inventory, provision, reservoir, stockpile **10** contribute

support
3 aid **4** back, base, bear, hand, help, lift, prop, root, side, stay **5** abide, adopt, boost, brace, bread, brook, carry, favor, shore, strut, truss **6** anchor, assist, bear up, buoy up, column, crutch, defend, endure, girder, pillar, prop up, second, suffer, uphold, verify **7** alimony, applaud, approve, backing, bolster, comfort, confirm, embrace, endorse, espouse, fortify, fulcrum, nourish, nurture, pull for, shore up, stiffen, sustain, trestle **8** abutment, advocate, backstop, buttress, mainstay, maintain, sanction, side with, tide over, underpin **9** encourage, reinforce, underprop **10** assistance, foundation, livelihood, provide for, strengthen, sustenance **11** corroborate, maintenance, subsistence **12** underpinning

support beam
4 I bar

supporter
3 fan **4** ally **6** patron **7** booster, sectary **8** adherent, advocate, champion, disciple, exponent, follower, henchman, partisan **9** proponent

suppose
4 deem **5** allow, guess, infer, opine, posit, think **6** assume, expect, gather, reckon **7** believe, imagine, presume, pretend, surmise, suspect **8** consider **9** postulate, speculate **10** conjecture **11** hypothesize

supposed
7 alleged, seeming **8** apparent, putative, so-called **10** ostensible

supposition
5 guess, hunch, posit **6** notion, theory, thesis **7** premise, surmise **9** postulate **10** assumption, conjecture, hypothesis **11** postulation, presumption, speculation

suppress
4 curb, stop **5** burke, check, choke, crush, drown, quash, quell, shush, spike, stunt **6** censor, cut off, hush up, muffle, muzzle, quench, retard, squash, stifle, subdue **7** abolish, conceal, prevent, put down, smother, squelch **8** prohibit, restrain, snuff out, withhold **9** overthrow

suppurate
6 fester

supra
5 above

supremacy
7 control, mastery **8** dominion **9** authority, dominance **10** ascendancy, domination, prepotency **11** preeminence, sovereignty **12** predominance

supreme
4 best **5** chief, final, prime **6** superb, utmost **7** highest, leading, maximum, perfect **8** absolute, cardinal, crowning, foremost, greatest, peerless, towering, ultimate **9** matchless, paramount, principal, sovereign, unequaled, unmatched, unrivaled **10** preeminent, surpassing **11** culminating, predominant, superlative, unmatchable, unsurpassed **12** incomparable, transcendent, unparalleled

Supreme Being
3 God **5** Allah **7** creator, Jehovah **8** Almighty
belief in: 5 deism

Supreme Court justice
3 Jay (John) **4** Taft (William Howard) **5** Alito (Samuel), Black (Hugo), Chase (Salmon P.), Kagan (Elena), Stone (Harlan Fiske), Story (Joseph), Taney (Roger B.) **6** Breyer (Stephen G.), Burger (Warren), Holmes (Oliver Wendell), Hughes (Charles Evans), Scalia (Antonin), Souter (David), Thomas (Clarence), Vinson (Fred), Warren (Earl) **7** Brennan (William), Cardozo (Benjamin), Douglas (William O.), O'Connor (Sandra Day), Roberts (John G.), Stevens (John Paul), Kennedy (Anthony M.) **8** Blackmun (Harry), Brandeis (Louis), Ginsburg (Ruth Bader), Marshall (John, Thurgood) **9** Rehnquist (William), Sotomayor (Sonia) **11** Frankfurter (Felix)

surcease
3 end **4** halt, rest, stay, stop **6** desist **7** respite **8** postpone, stoppage **9** cessation, remission **10** suspension

sure
5 fixed **6** indeed, secure, stable, steady **7** certain, staunch **8** absolute, definite, enduring, positive, reliable, unerring **9** confident, convinced, steadfast **10** dependable, inevitable, infallible, undeniable, unshakable, unwavering **11** indubitable, unequivocal

surefire
7 assured, certain **8** reliable **10** dependable, guaranteed

sure thing
4 cert, lock **5** cinch **6** shoo-in, winner **8** slam dunk **9** certainty

surety
4 bail, bond **5** angel **6** backer, patron, pledge **7** sponsor **8** guaranty, security, warranty **9** certainty, certitude, guarantee, guarantor **10** confidence, conviction

surf
4 scan, skim **6** browse **9** bodyboard, kneeboard

surface
6 crop up, emerge, facade **8** exterior **11** superficial

surfing term
4 deck, tube **5** leash **6** A-frame, barrel, drop in, hollow, turtle **7** bail out, carving, cutback, grommet, hang ten, snaking, wipeout **8** backdoor, blown out **9** goofy foot **10** impact zone **12** kneeboarding

surface
3 top **4** face, pave, rise, skin **5** cover **6** appear, come up, emerge, facade, facing, finish, patina, show up, veneer **7** outside **8** covering, exterior **11** superficial

surfeit
4 cloy, fill, glut, jade, pall, sate **5** gorge, stuff **6** excess **7** replete, satiate, surplus **8** overfill, overflow, overkill, overmuch, overplus, plethora **10** surplusage **11** overindulge, superfluity **13** overabundance

surfer wannabe
5 hodad **7** hodaddy

surge
4 flow, gush, pour, rise, roll, rush, soar, tide, wave **5** flood, swell **6** billow, deluge, sluice, stream **7** torrent

surgeon
8 sawbones
American: **4** Mayo (Charles, William), Reed (Walter) **7** Cushing (Harvey), DeBakey (Michael)
English: **6** Lister (Joseph)
French: **4** Paré (Ambroise) **5** Broca (Paul)
South African: **7** Barnard (Christiaan)

surgery
9 operation
instrument: **5** clamp, curet, laser **6** gorget, lancet, splint, stylet, trocar **7** forceps, scalpel

surgical removal
8 ablation
combining form: **6** ectomy

Suriname
capital: **10** Paramaribo
former name: **11** Dutch Guiana
monetary unit: **7** guilder
mountain range: **10** Tumac-Humac
neighbor: **6** Guyana **12** French Guiana
river: **6** Maroni **10** Courantyne

surly
4 dour, glum **5** cross, gruff, sulky **6** crusty, grumpy, morose, sullen **7** bearish, crabbed, grouchy **8** churlish, menacing, snappish **9** irritable, saturnine **10** ungracious

surmise
see **suppose**

surmount
5 clear, climb, crest, crown, excel, outdo, vault **6** hurdle, master **7** conquer, surpass **8** outstrip, overcome, vanquish **9** negotiate, transcend

surpass
3 cap, top **4** beat, best **5** excel, outdo, trump **6** better, exceed, outrun **7** eclipse, outpace **8** go beyond, outclass, outshine, outstrip, outweigh, overstep, overtake **9** transcend **10** overshadow

surplice
5 cotta, ephod **8** vestment

surplus
5 extra, spare **6** excess **7** overage, overrun, reserve, surfeit **8** leftover, overflow, overkill, overmuch, plethora **9** overstock, remainder **10** oversupply

surprise
4 faze, stun **5** amaze, floor **6** ambush, dismay, rattle, waylay, wonder **7** astound, capture, nonplus, stagger, startle, stupefy **8** astonish, bewilder, bowl over **9** amazement, dumbfound, overpower, take aback **11** flabbergast **12** astonishment, stupefaction

surreal
5 weird **7** bizarre **9** dreamlike, fantastic **10** outlandish

surrealist
3 Arp (Jean), Ray (Man) **4** Dalí (Salvador), Miró, Népo **5** Ernst (Max) **6** Breton (André), Tanguy (Yves) **8** Magritte (René) **9** de Chirico (Giorgio)

surrender
4 cave, cede, fold **5** waive, yield **6** cave in, give in, give up, resign, submit **7** abandon, concede, succumb **8** cry uncle, hand over **10** abdication, capitulate, relinquish, submission **12** capitulation
sign: **7** hands up **9** white flag

surreptitious
see **stealthy**

surrogate
3 sub **5** proxy **6** acting, deputy, fill-in **7** stand-in, stopgap **9** makeshift **10** substitute **11** locum tenens, pinch hitter, replacement

surround
3 hem, rim **4** edge, gird, girt, loop, ring **5** beset, bound, hem in, limit, verge **6** border, circle, engird, fringe, girdle, margin **7** besiege, confine, enclose, envelop **8** encircle **9** encompass **12** circumscribe

surrounded by
4 amid **6** amidst **7** amongst

surrounding
5 about **7** ambient **12** circumjacent
glow: **4** aura, halo
prefix: **4** peri **6** circum

surroundings
6 milieu **7** ambient **8** ambience **11** environment

surveillance
5 vigil **7** lookout **8** scrutiny, stakeout **9** vigilance **11** supervision

survey
3 con, vet **4** case, poll, scan, view **5** assay, audit **6** assess, précis, review, size up **7** canvass, examine, inspect, pandect, perusal, preview **8** analysis, appraise, estimate, evaluate, look over, overlook, overview, scrutiny, syllabus **9** check over **10** scrutinize **11** reconnoiter

surveyor's map
4 plat

survive
4 last **6** endure **7** carry on, hold out, outlast, outlive, outwear, persist, recover, ride out, weather **8** live down **9** withstand **11** come through, live through, pull through

Surya
6 sun-god
son: **4** Manu, Yama **5** Karna **6** Asvins
temple site: **7** Konarak

susceptible
5 naive, prone **6** liable **7** exposed, pliable **8** disposed, inclined, sensible **9** malleable, receptive, sensitive **10** responsive, vulnerable

sushi
condiment: **6** wasabi
fish: **4** tuna **5** unagi
sauce: **5** shoyu
type: **7** sashimi
wrapping: **4** nori

sushi-bar drink
4 sake, saki

suspect
5 doubt, fishy, guess **6** assume, unsure **7** believe, dubious, imagine, suppose, surmise **8** distrust, doubtful, mistrust **9** uncertain **10** disbelieve

suspect's out
5 alibi

suspend
3 bar **4** bate, halt, hang, stay **5** debar, defer, delay, hover **6** dangle, depend, hold up, put off, shelve **7** adjourn, hold off **8** intermit, postpone, prorogue **11** discontinue

suspended
4 hung **6** frozen **7** hanging, pendant, pendent, stopped **8** dangling, swinging **9** pendulous

suspenders
6 braces **8** galluses

suspense
7 anxiety, mystery, tension **10** expectancy **11** expectation, uncertainty

suspension
5 delay, letup, pause **6** cutoff, freeze **7** latency, respite, time-out **8** abeyance, dormancy, stoppage **9** remission **10** moratorium, quiescence **11** cold storage **12** intermission, interruption, postponement

suspicion
5 doubt, dread, guess, hunch, qualm, shade, tinge, trace, whiff **7** concern, dubiety, surmise **8** distrust, mistrust, wariness **9** chariness, misgiving **10** foreboding, intimation, skepticism **11** premonition, supposition, uncertainty

suspicious
4 wary **5** chary, fishy, leery **7** dubious, jealous, suspect **8** doubtful, watchful **9** doubtable, skeptical **11** distrustful, mistrustful, problematic **12** apprehensive, questionable

suspire
4 sigh 5 sough

sustain
4 bear, feed, prop 5 brace, carry, incur, stand 6 bear up, buoy up, foster, hold up, keep up, succor, uphold 7 bolster, confirm, nourish, nurture, prolong, relieve, shore up, support, undergo 8 buttress, preserve

sustenance
3 pap 4 food, keep, meat 5 bread, means 6 living, viands 7 aliment, alimony, pabulum, support 8 victuals 9 nutriment, provender 10 livelihood, provisions 11 nourishment, subsistence, wherewithal

susurration
4 purr 6 mumble, murmur, mutter, rustle 7 whisper 9 undertone

suture
3 sew 4 seam 6 stitch

suzerain
5 ruler 8 overlord 9 sovereign

svelte
4 slim 5 lithe, sleek, suave 6 smooth, urbane 7 elegant, slender 8 graceful

swab
3 mop 4 Q-Tip 5 clean 6 sponge

swaddle
4 roll, wrap 5 drape 6 enfold, swathe, wrap up 7 blanket 8 enshroud, enswathe

swag
3 sag, yaw 4 loot, sway, tilt 5 booty, droop, lurch, money, prize 6 boodle, spoils 7 festoon, garland, pillage, plunder 10 contraband

swagger
5 strut, swank, swash, swell 6 sashay 7 bluster, bravado, peacock, saunter 9 arrogance, cockiness, gasconade 11 braggadocio, swashbuckle

swagman
4 hobo 5 rover, tramp 7 drifter, vagrant 8 vagabond, wanderer

swain
4 beau 5 lover, spark, wooer 6 rustic, suitor 7 admirer 8 shepherd 9 boyfriend

swallow
3 buy, eat, sip 4 bear, belt, bolt, down, gulp, swig, take, toss, wolf 5 abide, brook, drink, quaff, slurp, stand, swill 6 absorb, accept, digest, endure, guzzle, imbibe, ingest, inhale 7 believe, consume, fall for, repress, retract, stomach 8 chugalug, take back, tolerate

swamp
3 bog, fen 4 holm, mire, moss, muck, quag 5 drown, flood, glade, marsh, whelm 6 deluge, engulf, morass, muskeg, slough 7 bottoms 8 inundate, overcome, overflow, quagmire, submerge 9 everglade, marshland, overwhelm
Everglades: 10 Big Cypress
Georgia: 10 Okefenokee
North Carolina-Virginia: 6 Dismal
plant: 5 sedge
snapper: 4 croc 5 gator

swamped
5 awash 7 brimful, flooded, overrun 8 engulfed 9 inundated, submerged 11 overflowing, overwhelmed

Swamp Fox
6 Marion (Francis)

swan
female: 3 pen
genus: 4 Olor 6 Cygnus
male: 3 cob 4 cobb
young: 6 cygnet

swank
4 posh, tony, trig 5 boast, fancy, ritzy, sharp, showy, smart, swell, swish 6 chichi, classy, dapper, deluxe, lavish, plushy, snappy, trendy 7 elegant, peacock, show off, splashy, stylish, swagger 8 peacocky 9 glamorous, luxurious 10 flamboyant, peacockish

Swan Lake
character: 5 Odile 6 Odette 9 Siegfried (Prince) 11 Von Rothbart
composer: 11 Tchaikovsky (Pyotr Ilyich)
skirt: 4 tutu

swan lover
4 Leda

swap
5 trade, truck 6 barter, change, switch 7 bargain, traffic 8 exchange 10 substitute

swarm
3 jam, mob 4 army, bevy, herd, host, mass, pack, push, shin, teem 5 crawl, crowd, crush, drove, flock, group, horde, mount, press 6 abound, gather, myriad, throng 7 climb up, cluster, overrun 9 multitude, pullulate 10 congregate

swarthy
4 dark 5 dusky, sooty 6 brunet 8 bistered

swash
4 dash, gush, slop 5 boast, churn, douse, froth, plash 6 bubble, burble, gurgle, seethe, splash 7 bluster, channel, saunter, spatter, splurge, swagger

swat
3 bat, box, hit 4 bash, belt, blow, cuff, lick, slap, slog, slug, sock 5 blast, clout, homer, knock, smack, smash, smite, swipe, whack 6 buffet, larrup, strike, wallop 7 clobber

swath
4 belt, path 5 strip, sweep 6 stroke

swathe
see **swaddle**

sway
4 bend, bias, rock, rule **5** lurch, range, reach, scope, sweep, swing, waver, weave **6** affect, careen, direct, govern, totter, wobble **7** command, control, dispose, impress, incline, mastery, stagger, win over **8** dominate, dominion, overrule, persuade, undulate **9** authority, dominance, fluctuate, influence, oscillate, vacillate

Swaziland
capital: 7 Lobamba, Mbabane
language: 5 Swazi
monetary unit: 9 lilangeni
neighbor: 10 Mozambique **11** South Africa
river: 5 Usutu **6** Komati **8** Umbeluzi

swear
3 vow **4** avow, bind, cuss, damn, oath, rail, rant **5** abuse, curse, vouch **6** adjure, affirm, assert, attest, depone, depose, pledge, plight **7** declare, promise, testify, warrant **8** covenant, maintain **9** blaspheme, imprecate **10** asseverate

swearword
4 cuss, oath **5** curse **9** expletive, obscenity

sweat
4 emit, glow, moil, ooze, seep, toil, weep **5** exude, grind, labor **6** strain, swivet **7** excrete **8** perspire, transude **12** perspiration

sweater
8 cardigan, pullover, slipover **10** turtleneck

sweater girl Turner
4 Lana

sweaty
6 clammy, sticky **7** glowing **10** perspiring

Sweden
Arctic region: 7 Lapland
capital: 9 Stockholm
city: 5 Malmö **8** Göteborg
gulf: 7 Bothnia **8** Kattegat
island: 5 Öland **7** Gotland
lake: 6 Vänern **7** Mälaren, Vättern **9** Hjälmaren
monetary unit: 5 krona **6** kronur (plural)
mountain range: 5 Kölen
neighbor: 6 Norway **7** Finland
part of: 11 Scandinavia
river: 3 Dal
sea: 6 Baltic

Swedish
cinematographer Nykvist: 4 Sven
Nightingale: 4 Lind (Jenny)
pop group: 4 ABBA

Sweeney of Anything Goes
4 Reno

sweep
3 arc, fly, mop, win **4** flit, sail, scud, skim, wing **5** ambit, broom, brush, clean, clear, curve, drive, gamut, orbit, range, reach, scope, surge, whisk **6** extent, radius, search **7** compass, purview

sweeping
4 epic **5** broad **6** all-out **7** blanket, general, overall, radical **8** thorough, whole-hog **9** extensive, inclusive, out-and-out, universal, wholesale **11** far-reaching

sweepings
4 dust **5** trash, waste **6** debris, litter, refuse **7** garbage, residue, rubbish **8** detritus

sweet
5 candy, honey **6** bonbon, dulcet, lovely, sugary, syrupy **7** angelic, cloying, dessert, melodic, scented, sugared, winning, winsome **8** aromatic, fragrant, heavenly, luscious, perfumed **9** ambrosial, delicious **10** delectable, saccharine
combining form: 4 glyc **5** glyco

Sweet ___
7 Adeline, Charity **8** Caroline **12** Georgia Brown

sweeten
5 candy, honey, sugar **6** soften **7** appease, assuage, enhance, mollify, placate **9** sugarcoat, sugar over **10** conciliate, propitiate

sweetheart
3 gra **4** dear, love **5** flame, honey **7** beloved, darling, tootsie **10** heartthrob, honeybunch

Sweetheart of ___ Chi
5 Sigma

sweetmeat
5 candy **6** comfit **8** delicacy, preserve **10** confection

sweet potato
3 yam **7** boniato, ocarina

sweetsop
4 anon, ates **10** sugar apple

sweet-talk
4 coax **5** charm **6** banter, cajole, wangle **7** blarney, flatter, wheedle **8** blandish, butter up, inveigle, soft-soap

swell
3 fop **4** fine, grow, keen, neat, pout, puff **5** bloat, bulge, dandy, neato, nifty, pouch, super, surge, swank **6** abound, billow, blow up, dilate, expand, groovy, peachy **7** amplify, augment, balloon, distend, enlarge, inflate, peacock, swagger, upsurge **8** increase, jim-dandy, terrific **9** crescendo, marvelous, wonderful
British: 3 nob **4** toff

swelled head
3 ego **5** pride **6** egoism, vanity **7** conceit,

egotism **8** smugness **9** arrogance, vainglory **10** narcissism **11** amour propre, self-conceit

swelling
3 sty **4** boil, bubo, bump, corn, gall, node **5** bulge, edema, tumid, tumor **6** bunion, growth, nodule **7** gibbous **8** tubercle **9** carbuncle, chilblain, expansion, tumescent **10** tumescence **11** excrescence **12** inflammation, protuberance

sweltering
3 hot **5** fiery **6** baking, sultry, torrid **7** burning **8** broiling, roasting, sizzling **9** scorching

swerve
3 yaw **4** skew, turn, veer **5** sheer, shift, stray, waver **6** depart, wander **7** deflect, deviate

swift
4 fast **5** fleet, hasty, quick, rapid, ready **6** prompt, snappy, speedy, sudden **8** full-tilt, headlong **9** breakneck

___ Swift
3 Tom **8** Jonathan
character: 8 Gulliver

swiftness
4 gait, pace **5** haste, hurry, speed **6** hustle **8** celerity, dispatch, legerity, rapidity, velocity

swig
4 belt, chug, down, drag, gulp, pull, slug **5** booze, draft, drain, drink, quaff, swill **6** guzzle, imbibe, tipple **7** swallow, swizzle

swill
4 bolt, gulp, slop, swig, tope, wolf **5** booze, draft, drink, gorge, scarf, scoff, slops **6** debris, gobble, guzzle, inhale, spilth, tank up, tipple **7** consume, garbage, hogwash, rubbish, swizzle

swim
3 dip **4** reel, spin, turn **5** bathe, crawl, float, swoon, whirl **9** dizziness, dog-paddle

swimmingly
6 easily **8** smoothly **10** splendidly

swimming unit
3 lap

swimming stroke
5 crawl **7** dolphin, trudgen **9** butterfly, dog paddle

swindle
3 con, gyp **4** bilk, clip, dupe, fake, hoax, rook, scam, sell, sham, skin, soak **5** bunco, bunko, cheat, cozen, fraud, gouge, grift, phony, rogue, shaft, skunk, sting **6** chouse, diddle, fleece, humbug, hustle, take in **7** con game, defraud **8** flimflam, hoodwink **9** bamboozle, imposture, victimize **11** hornswoggle

swindler
5 cheat, crook, ganef, gonif, shark **6** con man, goniff **7** grifter, sharper, shyster **8** deceiver **9** charlatan, defrauder **10** mountebank

swine
see **hog**

swing
4 jive, lilt, slew, slue, sway, veer **5** flail, lurch, pivot, twirl, waver, weave, whirl, wield **6** dangle, divert, rhythm, rotate, seesaw, stroke, swerve, switch **7** revolve, suspend **8** brandish **9** alternate, fluctuate, oscillate, vacillate

swinish
5 feral **6** coarse **7** beastly, bestial, porcine

swipe
3 cop, hit, nab, rap **4** blow, clip, conk, grab, hook, lick, lift, nick, sock, swat, wipe **5** clout, filch, heist, knock, pinch, smack, steal **6** pilfer, snatch, snitch, strike, wallop

swirl
4 eddy, purl, roil **5** curve, twist, whirl, whorl **6** swoosh, vortex **9** whirlpool **11** convolution

swish
4 buzz, chic, fizz, hiss, posh, tony, whiz **5** ritzy, smart, swank, whisk **6** classy, dressy, sizzle, trendy, whoosh **7** elegant, stylish **8** sibilate

Swiss Family Robinson author
4 Wyss (Johann David)

Swiss mathematician
5 Euler (Leonhard)

Swiss painter
4 Klee (Paul)

switch
3 rod, wag **4** beat, flay, flog, lash, swap, veer, wand, whip **5** shift, shunt, trade, whisk **6** change, strike, toggle, waggle **7** scourge **8** exchange, flip-flop, reversal **9** about-face, sidetrack **10** substitute **12** substitution

Switzerland
canton: 3 Uri, Zug **4** Jura, Vaud **5** Berne **6** Geneva, Ticino, Valais
capital: 4 Bern **5** Berne
city: 5 Basel **6** Geneva, Zürich **8** Lausanne
lake: 6 Geneva, Wallen **7** Lucerne **9** Constance, Neuchâtel, Thunersee, Zürichsee
language: 6 French, German **7** Italian
monetary unit: 5 franc
mountain, range: 3 Alp **4** Alps, Jura **9** Monte Rosa
neighbor: 5 Italy **6** France **7** Austria, Germany **13** Liechtenstein
resort: 5 Davos, Vevey **7** Zermatt **8** Montreux, St. Moritz **10** Interlaken
river: 3 Aar **4** Aare **5** Rhine, Rhône
state: 6 canton

swivel
4 spin, turn **5** pivot, swing, twirl, whirl **6** rotate **7** revolve **9** pirouette

swivet
see **snit**

swizzle
3 mix **4** stir **5** swill **6** guzzle, tipple

swollen
5 puffy, tumid **6** turgid **7** bloated, bulbous, bulging **8** enlarged, inflated, varicose **9** distended, tumescent

swoon
4 coma, daze, fade **5** droop, faint **6** torpor **7** pass out, rapture, syncope **8** black out

swoosh
4 eddy, gush, purl, rush **5** swirl, whirl, whorl

sword
4 épée, foil **5** saber, sabre **6** barong, bilboa, rapier, Toledo **7** cutlass **8** claymore, falchion, scimitar, yataghan
part: 4 haft, hilt **6** pommel **10** cross guard

sword-shaped
6 ensate **8** ensiform

sworn
6 avowed **7** devoted **8** affirmed **9** committed, confirmed

sybarite
7 epicure **8** hedonist **9** libertine **10** sensualist, voluptuary

sybaritic
6 carnal **7** sensual **8** sensuous **9** epicurean, libertine, luxurious **10** hedonistic, voluptuous

sycophancy
7 fawning **8** flattery, toadying **9** truckling **11** bootlicking

sycophant
5 leech, toady **6** flunky, lackey, minion, yes-man **8** groveler, hanger-on, parasite, truckler **9** easy rider, flatterer, toadeater **10** bootlicker, self-seeker **11** lickspittle

sycophantic
7 fawning, servile, slavish **8** toadying, unctuous **9** groveling, kowtowing, parasitic, truckling **10** obsequious **11** bootlicking

Sycorax's son
7 Caliban

syllable
deletion: 7 apocope
last: 6 ultima
lengthening of: 7 ectasis
musical: 3 sol
next to last: 6 penult
shortening: 7 elision, systole
stressed: 5 arsis

syllabus
6 aperçu, digest, précis, sketch, survey **7** epitome, outline, pandect, summary **8** abstract, headnote, synopsis

sylph
5 fairy, nymph **6** sprite

sylvan
5 bosky, woody **6** rustic, wooded
deity: 3 Pan **4** faun **5** dryad, satyr **6** Faunus **7** Silenus **8** Arethusa

symbol
4 icon, logo, mark, sign **5** badge, glyph, motif, stamp, token **6** design, device, emblem, mascot
chemical: see individual element
musical: 4 clef, flat, hold, note, rest, turn **5** shake, sharp **7** fermata, mordent, natural
of power: 3 orb **7** scepter, sceptre

symbolic
5 token **10** emblematic **11** allegorical

symbolist poet
7 Rimbaud (Arthur) **8** Mallarmé (Stéphane), Verlaine (Paul) **10** Baudelaire (Charles)

symbolize
4 mean **6** embody, mirror, typify **7** signify **8** stand for **9** epitomize, exemplify, personify, represent

symmetrical
5 equal **7** regular **8** balanced

symmetry
5 order **6** parity **7** balance, harmony **8** equality, evenness **9** agreement, congruity **10** conformity, proportion, regularity

sympathetic
4 kind, warm **6** benign, caring, humane, kindly, tender **8** amenable, friendly **9** agreeable, approving, benignant, receptive **10** compatible, consistent, responsive **11** considerate, kind-hearted, softhearted, warmhearted

sympathize
4 pity **7** condole **11** commiserate

sympathy
4 pity, ruth **5** heart **6** accord, solace, warmth **7** comfort, harmony, rapport **8** affinity, kindness **10** benignancy, compassion, condolence, kindliness, tenderness **11** consolation

symphonic
10 orchestral

Symphonie Espagnole composer
4 Lalo (Édouard)

symphony
9 orchestra **12** philharmonic
movement: 5 rondo **6** minuet

symposium
5 forum **7** meeting, seminar **9** gathering **10** conference, discussion

symptom
4 mark, sign **5** index, token **8** evidence **10** indication

symptoms
7 indicia **8** syndrome

synagogue
4 shul **6** temple
platform: 4 bema, bima **5** bimah **7** almemar
quorum: 6 minyan
singer: 6 cantor

sync
4 jibe **5** agree, match **7** harmony **8** coincide **9** harmonize **10** concurrent **12** simultaneous

synchronize
5 agree **6** concur **8** coincide

synchronous
6 coeval **7** in phase **10** coetaneous, coexistent, coexisting, coincident, concurrent **11** concomitant **12** contemporary, simultaneous **13** geostationary

syncope
4 coma **5** faint, swoon **8** blackout

syndicate
3 mob **4** pool **5** chain, group, mafia, trust, union **6** cartel, league **7** combine **11** association, partnership **12** conglomerate, organization

syndrome
3 ill **6** malady **7** ailment, disease **8** disorder, sickness **9** complaint, condition, infirmity

synergic
5 joint **6** shared **8** coacting, coactive, conjoint **9** collusive, concerted **11** cooperating, cooperative, coordinated

synod
4 body, diet **7** council, meeting **8** assembly, conclave, congress **10** conference, convention **11** convocation

synonym expert
5 Roget (Peter Mark)

synopsis
5 brief, recap **6** aperçu, digest, précis, review **7** capsule, epitome, outline, rundown, summary **8** abstract, breviary, syllabus **10** abridgment, compendium, conspectus

synopsize
5 recap, sum up **6** digest **7** outline, summate **8** abstract, boil down, compress, condense **9** epitomize, inventory, summarize

synthesis
5 blend, union **6** fusion, merger **7** amalgam **8** blending, compound **9** composite

synthesize
4 fuse, meld **5** blend, merge, unify **7** combine **8** compound **9** harmonize, integrate **10** amalgamate

synthetic
6 ersatz **7** man-made, plastic **9** imitation, unnatural **10** artificial, fabricated **11** counterfeit
fiber: 3 PBI, PLA **5** Modal, Mylar, Nomex, nylon, Orlon, saran, Zylon **6** Kevlar, olefin, sulfar, Twaron, vinyon **7** acetate, acrylic, lyocell, spandex, vectran, vinalon **9** polyester **10** modacrylic

Syria
capital: 8 Damascus
city: 4 Homs **6** Aleppo
language: 6 Arabic, French
monetary unit: 5 pound
neighbor: 4 Iraq **6** Israel, Jordan, Turkey **7** Lebanon

syringe
4 hypo **6** needle **10** hypodermic

Syrinx
5 nymph
pursuer: 3 Pan

syrinx
7 panpipe **8** panpipes

syrup
6 orgeat **9** grenadine

syrupy
5 gooey, mushy, sappy, sweet **6** drippy, dulcet, slushy, sticky, sugary **7** cloying, maudlin, mawkish **9** schmaltzy **10** saccharine **11** sentimental

system
3 way **4** mode, plan **5** modus, order, setup **6** entity, manner, method, scheme **7** complex, network, pattern, process, regimen, routine **8** strategy **9** procedure, structure, technique

systematic
7 logical, ordered, orderly, regular **8** arranged **9** organized **10** analytical, methodical

systematize
5 array, order **6** codify **7** arrange, catalog, dispose, marshal **8** classify, organize, regiment **9** catalogue, methodize

system of weights
4 troy **11** avoirdupois **12** apothecaries

T

tab
4 bill, cost, list, loop, rate **5** check **6** charge, record **7** account, invoice **8** price tag

tabard
4 cape, coat **5** tunic **10** coat of arms

tabby
3 cat **6** feline, cement **8** brindled

tabernacle
4 tent **5** hovel **6** church, temple

tabes
7 atrophy, wasting

Tabitha's Greek name
6 Dorcas

table
4 fare, list **5** bench, board, chart, defer, stand **6** buffet, put off, record, shelve, teapoy **7** counter **8** mahogany, postpone **9** sideboard
constellation: **5** Mensa
ornament: **7** epergne
writing: **4** desk **9** secretary **10** escritoire

table d' ___
4 hôte

tableland
4 mesa **5** butte **6** upland **7** plateau
(see also **plateau**)

table scrap
3 ort

tablet
3 pad **4** disk, pill, slab **5** slate **6** pellet, plaque, troche **7** lozenge, notepad **8** steno pad
from Apple: **4** iPad

tableware
4 cups **5** bowls, china, forks **6** dishes, knives, plates, silver, spoons **7** glasses, saucers **8** settings, utensils **9** stainless

tabloid
3 rag **5** lurid, pulpy **9** newspaper **11** sensational **12** scandal sheet

taboo
3 ban **4** no-no **6** banned, enjoin, forbid, outlaw **7** inhibit **9** forbidden, ineffable, interdict, off-limits, restraint
Muslim: **5** haram

tabor
4 drum

tabulation
4 list **5** chart, tally **6** record **7** account

tabula ___
4 rasa

tacit
6 silent, unsaid **7** assumed, implied **8** implicit, inferred, unspoken **9** intimated, suggested **10** subtextual, undeclared, underlying, understood **11** unexpressed

taciturn
4 dumb **6** silent **7** laconic **8** reserved, reticent

Tacitus work
7 Annales **9** Historiae

tack
3 pin, yaw **4** brad, gear, nail, turn **5** baste, shift **6** attach, course, stitch, swerve, zigzag **7** push-pin, tangent **8** put about **9** come about, deviation **10** digression, sea biscuit

tackle
3 rig **4** gear, sack **6** outfit, take on, take up **7** halyard, lineman, rigging **8** set about **9** apparatus, equipment, undertake **10** footballer, line-backer

tack on
3 add **5** affix **6** append, attach **7** subjoin

tacky
5 cheap, gaudy **6** kitsch, sticky, tawdry, vulgar **9** inelegant, tasteless, unstylish

tact
5 poise **7** address, finesse, suavity **8** civility, courtesy, delicacy, urbanity **9** diplomacy, politesse **10** politeness, smoothness **11** savoir faire, sensitivity

tactful
5 suave **6** adroit, urbane **7** politic **8** delicate, discreet, polished **9** courteous, sensitive **10** diplomatic, perceptive **11** considerate

tactic
4 plan, play, ploy, ruse **5** dodge, feint **6** gambit, method **7** sleight **8** approach, artifice, maneuver, strategy **9** procedure, stratagem

tactical
7 politic, prudent **9** advisable, expedient, strategic

tactics
4 plan **6** method, scheme **8** maneuver, playbook, strategy **9** stratagem

tactile
8 palpable, tangible **9** touchable

tactless
4 rude **5** blunt, inept **6** clumsy, gauche **7** awkward **8** impolite **9** impolitic, maladroit **10** indiscreet **11** insensitive

tad
3 bit, boy, lad, son **4** drop, lick, mite, snap, spot, whit **5** child, crumb, shade, sonny, speck **6** laddie, nipper, shaver **7** smidgen

tadpole
8 polliwog, pollywog

tag
3 bit, dog, end **4** cost, logo, mark, name, tail **5** brand, label, price, trail **6** append, charge, select, slogan, tassel, tatter, ticket **7** license **8** graffito, identify, insignia

tagline
5 motto **6** byword, slogan

Tahiti
city: **7** Papeete
painter: **7** Gauguin (Paul)
war god: **3** Oro

tai ——
3 chi

tail
3 dog, end, tag **4** butt, rear **5** hound, stalk **6** follow, pursue, shadow **7** hind end, rear end **8** backside, buttocks **9** posterior
bone: **6** coccyx
relating to: **6** caudal
short: **4** scut

tailed
7 oaudate

tailor
3 fit, hem, sew **4** suit **5** adapt, alter, style **7** fashion **8** clothier, seamster **11** haberdasher

tailor-made
6 fitted, suited **7** bespoke, fitting **8** suitable **10** well-suited

taint
3 rot **4** blot, blur, foul, smut, soil, spot, vice **5** brand, cloud, decay, dirty, fault, smear, spoil, stain, sully **6** befoul, defile, smudge, smutch **7** blacken, blemish, corrupt, pollute, putrefy, tarnish **8** besmirch, discolor **9** discredit **10** adulterate, stigmatize **11** contaminate

taipan
5 snake **8** merchant **11** businessman

Taiwan
7 Formosa
capital: **6** Taipei
channel: **5** Bashi
leader: **6** Chiang (Kai-shek)
monetary unit: **4** yuan
mountain: **6** Yü Shan

Taiwanese computer brand
4 Acer

Tajikistan
capital: **8** Dushanbe
monetary unit: **5** diram **6** somoni
monetary unit, former: **5** ruble, tanga
mountain, range: **6** Pamirs **9** Trans Alai
river: **8** Amu Dar'ya, Syr Dar'ya

Taj Mahal
9 mausoleum
builder: **9** Shah Jahan
site: **4** Agra

take
3 cop, get, nab **4** glom, grab **5** annex, catch, seize, steal, swipe **6** endure, gather, ingest, obtain, secure **7** capture, receive **8** proceeds, receipts
account of: **6** notice
advantage of: **5** abuse **7** exploit
after: **6** follow **8** resemble
apart: **7** analyze, dissect **9** dismantle
care: **6** beware
care of: **3** fix **4** tend **5** nurse **6** attend
exception: **6** object
five: **4** rest **5** break, relax
from: **7** deprive, detract **8** subtract
it easy: **5** relax
on the: **7** corrupt, crooked
part: **4** join **5** share **11** participate
place: **5** occur **6** happen
to task: **5** scold **7** reprove
turns: **9** alternate
unawares: **8** surprise

take a load off
3 sit

take away
4 grab **5** wrest **6** arrest, commit, deduct, detach, detain, remove, revoke **7** deprive, detract **8** diminish, discount, minimize, subtract, withdraw

take back
5 unsay **6** abjure, recall, recant, return, revoke **7** replace, restore, retract, swallow **8** forswear, withdraw **9** repossess

take down
4 note **5** lower **6** humble, record, reduce **7** deflate **8** dismount **9** dismantle

take in
3 con **4** dupe, earn, fool, furl **5** admit, bluff, board, house, trick **6** absorb, accept, arrest, attend, betray, delude, embody, incept, ingest **7** beguile, deceive, embrace, include, mislead, observe, receive, shelter, snooker, subsume **8** flimflam, hoodwink, perceive **9** apprehend, bamboozle, encompass, four-flush **10** assimilate, comprehend **11** double-cross

take off
4 doff, exit, quit, soar 5 leave, scram 6 begone, deduct, depart, remove, set out 7 pull out, skiddoo, vamoose 8 clear out, discount, hightail, light out, subtract, withdraw 9 skedaddle

takeoff
5 spoof 6 launch, parody, satire, send-up 7 lampoon 8 travesty 9 burlesque 10 caricature
area: 3 pad 6 runway

take on
4 face, hire 5 adopt, annex, fight 6 accept, append, assume, attack, battle, employ, engage, strike, tackle 7 contest, embrace, espouse, venture

take out
4 date, dele, kill, omit 5 loose, whack 6 deduct, excise, remove 7 unleash 8 discount, knock off, separate, subtract, withdraw, withhold 9 eliminate

take over
5 seize, spell, usurp 6 assume 7 capture, relieve

take up
3 use 4 fill, open 5 adopt, begin, enter, raise, renew, set to, start 6 absorb, accept, assume, gather, occupy, resume, shrink, tackle 7 embrace, espouse, kick off, restart, shorten, tighten 8 commence, continue, initiate

talc
6 powder 8 steatite 9 soapstone

tale
3 fib, lie 4 epic, gest, myth, saga, yarn 5 fable, geste, rumor, story 6 canard, legend 7 fiction 8 anecdote 9 narration, narrative

talebearer
5 yenta 6 canary, gossip, snitch 7 rat fink, tattler 8 busybody, gossiper, informer, quidnunc, squealer 9 informant 10 newsmonger 11 rumormonger, stool pigeon 12 blabbermouth 13 scandalmonger

talent
4 bent, gift 5 dowry, flair, forte, knack, skill 6 genius 7 ability, aptness, faculty 8 aptitude

talented
4 able 6 clever, expert, gifted 8 skillful

Tale of Two Cities, A
author: 7 Dickens (Charles)
character: 5 Lucie (Manette) 6 Carton (Sidney), Darnay (Charles) 7 Defarge (Madame), Manette (Alexander)

talisman
4 juju, luck 5 charm 6 amulet, fetish, grigri, mascot, scarab 7 periapt 8 gris-gris 10 phylactery

talk
3 gab, rap, yak 4 blab, buzz, chat, chin, yarn 5 prate, rumor, run on, speak, utter, voice 6 babble, gabble, gossip, natter, parley, patter, report, speech 7 address, chatter, declaim, hearsay, lecture, prattle 8 colloquy, converse, dialogue, harangue 9 discourse, utterance 10 discussion 12 conversation
about: 7 discuss
back: 4 sass
empty: 3 gas 6 hot air 7 bombast
foolish: 4 bunk 6 babble 7 chatter, palaver
indistinctly: 6 mumble, mutter
over: 7 discuss
shop: 5 argot
slowly: 5 drawl
small: 6 banter 8 chitchat 10 persiflage
wildly: 4 rant, rave

talkative
4 glib 5 gabby, vocal, windy 6 chatty, fluent, prolix 7 gossipy, verbose, voluble 9 garrulous 10 loquacious

talking horse
4 Mr. Ed

talk over
6 debate 7 discuss, hash out 9 thrash out 10 deliberate

talk-show host Jack
4 Paar

tall
4 high 5 lofty, rangy 8 towering 10 statuesque

tallow
3 fat 4 lard, suet 6 grease

tally
4 jibe, list 5 agree, count, match, score, total 6 accord, census, number, reckon, square 7 account, balance, catalog, compute, conform, itemize 8 check off, register, tabulate 9 agreement, catalogue, enumerate, harmonize, inventory, reckoning

talon
4 claw, hand 5 stock 6 finger

talus
5 ankle, scree, slope 9 anklebone 10 astragalus

tam
3 cap

Tamar
brother: 7 Absalom
father: 5 David 7 Absalom
seducer: 5 Amnon
son: 5 Perez, Zerah

tamarisk
9 salt cedar

tame
4 meek, mild 5 break 6 bridle, docile, gentle, subdue 7 harness, subdued 8 domestic, obedient 9 tractable 10 housebreak, submissive 11 domesticate, housebroken 12 domesticated

Taming of the Shrew, The
character: 6 Bianca 8 Baptista 9 Katharina, Petruchio
locale: 5 Padua

Tammany boss
5 Tweed (William)

Tammuz's lover
6 Ishtar

tam-o'-shanter
3 cap

tamp
3 ram 4 pack 5 pound, press, stuff

Tampa Bay footballers
4 Bucs 10 Buccaneers

tampion
4 plug 5 cover

tan
3 sun, taw 4 beat, ecru, flog, whip 5 beige, brown, taupe, tawny, toast 6 bronze, darken, thrash 7 biscuit

tanager
7 redbird

Tancred, Tancredi
beloved: 8 Clorinda
composer: 7 Rossini (Gioacchino)
father: 3 Odo
mother: 4 Emma
victim: 8 Clorinda

tandem
4 pair 7 bicycle, concert 8 carriage

tang
3 nip 4 bite, fang, odor, ring, zest 5 aroma, clang, prong, sapor, savor, shank, smack, taste, trace 6 flavor, relish 8 piquancy, pungency, sapidity 9 spiciness

tangible
4 real 7 tactile 8 concrete, palpable, physical 9 corporeal, touchable 10 detectable, observable 11 appreciable, discernible, perceptible, substantial

tangle
3 mat, web 4 foul, knot, maze, mesh, shag 5 ravel, skein, snare, snarl 6 entrap, hamper, jumble, jungle, morass, muddle, pileup 7 dispute, embroil, ensnare, ensnarl, involve, thicket 8 obstruct 9 implicate

tangy
7 piquant, pungent, zestful 9 flavorful

tank
3 vat 5 basin 7 cistern 8 aquarium 9 reservoir
American: 6 Abrams 7 Bradley, Sherman
German: 6 panzer
part: 6 turret

tankard
3 mug 5 stein, stoup 6 flagon, goblet 7 chalice 9 blackjack

tanked
3 lit 4 high, lost 5 drunk, lit up, oiled 6 bashed, blotto, bombed, failed, gave up, juiced, potted, soaked, soused, stewed, stoned, tanked, wasted, zonked 7 crocked, drunken, fizzled, flopped, pickled, pie-eyed, sloshed, smashed, sottish 8 cratered, squiffed 9 flamed out, plastered 10 inebriated, liquored up 11 intoxicated

tanker
4 ship 5 oiler

Tannhäuser
character: 5 Venus 9 Elisabeth
composer: 6 Wagner (Richard)
locale: 8 Wartburg 9 Venusberg

tantalize
3 rag 4 bait, lure 5 tease, tempt 6 entice, needle 7 torment 9 frustrate

Tantalus
daughter: 5 Niobe
father: 4 Zeus
son: 6 Pelops

tantara
5 blare 7 fanfare

tantivy
3 run 6 gallop

tantrum
3 fit 4 rage 6 blowup 8 outburst, paroxysm 9 hysterics 10 conniption

Tanzania
capital: 6 Dodoma 11 Dar es Salaam
former name: 10 Tanganyika
island: 8 Zanzibar
lake: 8 Victoria 10 Tanganyika
language: 7 Swahili
monetary unit: 8 shilling
mountain: 11 Kilimanjaro
plain: 9 Serengeti

Taoism founder
5 Laozi 6 Lao-tzu

tap
3 pat 4 cock, draw, flap, plug, tick 5 chuck, draft, drain, nudge, touch, valve 6 faucet, select, siphon, spigot 7 draw off, hydrant, percuss, petcock 8 drumbeat, half sole, nominate, stopcock

tape
4 band, belt, bind 5 strip 6 fillet, ribbon 7 bandage
kind: 5 inkle 6 ferret 7 masking 8 adhesive
machine: 4 deck 8 recorder

taper
4 wane, wick 5 abate, spire 6 candle, lessen, narrow 7 dwindle, glimmer 8 decrease, diminish

tapering
5 conic, spiry **6** spired, terete **7** conical **8** ensiform, fusiform, napiform, subulate **9** acuminate **10** lanceolate

tapestry
5 arras, kilim **6** dossal **7** curtain, Gobelin, hanging
pattern: 7 cartoon

tapioca
4 yuca **5** yucca **6** manioc **7** cassava, farinha, pudding

tapir
4 anta

taproom
3 bar, pub **4** café **6** bodega, saloon, tavern **7** cantina **8** dramshop **9** roadhouse

tapster
6 barman **7** barkeep, barmaid, skinker **9** barkeeper, bartender **10** mixologist

tar
3 gob **4** jack, salt, soil, swab **5** pitch, smear, stain, sully, taint **6** defile, hearty, sailor, seaman **7** asphalt, besmear, mariner, shipman **8** besmirch, creosote, deckhand, flatfoot

taradiddle
3 fib, lie **5** hooey, story, trash **6** bunkum, canard **7** baloney, falsity **8** claptrap, nonsense **9** falsehood **10** balderdash

tarboosh
3 fez, hat

tardy
4 dull, late, lazy, slow **7** belated, delayed, laggard, overdue **8** dilatory, sluggish **10** behindhand, delinquent, unpunctual

tare
4 seed, weed **5** vetch, weigh **6** darnel, weight **13** counterweight

target
3 aim **4** butt, goal, mark, prey **5** aim at **6** object, quarry, victim **9** objective **11** sitting duck
center: 8 bull's-eye
shooter's: 10 clay pigeon

tariff
3 tax **4** duty, levy **6** charge, impost **10** assessment

tarn
4 lake, pool

tarnish
3 dim, mar **4** dull, foul, harm, hurt, soil **5** dirty, muddy, smear, spoil, stain, sully, taint **6** damage, darken, defile, injure, smirch, smudge, smutch **7** begrime, besmear, blemish, vitiate **8** besmirch, discolor

taro
3 yam **4** eddo **5** aroid **6** yautia **7** cocoyam, dasheen, malanga
product: 3 poi
root: 4 eddo

tarpaulin
3 gob **4** jack, salt, swab **5** cover, sheet **6** hearty, sailor, seaman **7** mariner, shipman **9** shellback

tar pit
6 La Brea

tarpon
8 ladyfish **10** silverfish

tarry
3 lag **4** bide, drag, stay, wait **5** abide, dally, delay, visit **6** dawdle, linger, loiter, pitchy, remain **7** sojourn

tarsus
5 ankle

Tarsus native
4 Saul

tart
3 pie **4** acid, bawd, moll, slut, sour **5** acerb, quean, sharp, tramp, trull, whore **6** biting, harlot, pastry **7** acerbic, cutting, piquant, pungent, tootsie **8** chess pie, strumpet **10** prostitute

tartar
5 argol **6** plaque **8** calculus

Tartar
see **Tatar**

Tarzan
chimpanzee: 7 Cheetah
creator: 9 Burroughs (Edgar Rice)
mate: 4 Jane
son: 4 Jack **5** Korak

task
3 job **4** duty, lade, load, post, slog, toil, work **5** chare, chore, labor, stint **6** assign, burden, charge, detail, devoir **7** mission, project **8** business, function **9** challenge **10** assignment, commission **11** undertaking
list: 4 to-do

Tasmanian
4 wolf **5** devil
capital: 6 Hobart
pine: 4 Huon

tassel
3 tag **4** tuft **6** fringe **7** pendant, tzitzit **8** ornament

tasseled hat
3 fez **11** mortarboard

taste
3 eat, sip, try **4** tang, zest **5** sapor, savor, smack **6** flavor, liking, palate, relish **8** appetite, elegance, fondness, sapidity, soft spot, weakness

10 partiality, preference, refinement 11 inclination
kind: 4 salt, sour 5 sweet, umami 6 bitter
organ: 3 bud

tasteful
4 fine 7 elegant, genteel, refined, stylish 8 artistic, becoming 9 aesthetic

tasteless
4 dull, flat 5 bland, crass, gaudy, showy, stale, tacky, vapid 6 vulgar 7 insipid 8 off-color, unsavory 9 inelegant, savorless, unrefined

tasty
5 sapid, yummy 6 dainty, delish, savory 8 luscious 9 delicious, flavorful, palatable, succulent, toothsome 10 appetizing, delectable, flavorsome 11 scrumptious

ta-ta
4 by-by, ciao 6 bye-bye 7 cheerio, toodles 8 toodle-oo

Tatar
6 Mongol, Turkic 7 Turkish 9 Mongolian
leader: 4 Vatu

tater
4 spud 6 murphy

tat-tat preceder
4 rat-a

tattered
4 torn 5 dingy, seedy 6 frayed, ragged, ripped, shabby 7 raggedy, run-down, worn-out 10 bedraggled, threadbare

tattle
3 rat, wag, yak 4 blab, buzz, dish, tell 5 clack, prate, rumor 6 gossip, inform, report, snitch, squeal 7 chatter, hearsay, prattle 8 chitchat 9 grapevine 11 scuttlebutt

tattletale
see **talebearer**

tatty
5 cheap, dingy, dowdy, dumpy, seedy, tacky 6 beat-up, cheesy, paltry, scuzzy, shabby, shoddy, sleazy, trashy 7 run-down, scrubby 8 rubbishy 10 threadbare 11 dilapidated

taunt
3 jab 4 gibe, jeer, mock, quip, razz, twit 5 scout, tease 6 deride, insult 7 affront, provoke 8 ridicule 9 challenge

taurine
6 bovine 8 bull-like

Taurus
4 bull
star: 9 Aldebaran

taut
4 firm, snug, trim 5 rigid, tense, tight

tautology
8 iterance, pleonasm 9 iteration 10 redundancy, repetition

tavern
3 bar, inn, pub 4 café, dive 6 bistro, bodega, saloon 7 barroom, cantina, gin mill, taproom 8 alehouse, pothouse, wineshop 9 roadhouse 11 public house, rathskeller 12 watering hole

taverner
7 barkeep 8 boniface, publican 9 barkeeper, bartender, innkeeper 12 saloonkeeper

taw
3 tan 6 marble 7 partner

tawdry
5 cheap, gaudy, tacky 6 brazen, flashy, garish, glitzy, tinsel 7 chintzy, ignoble, kitschy 9 brummagem, dime-store, tasteless 12 meretricious

tawny
3 tan 4 buff 5 beige, brown, sandy 6 copper, tanned

tax
4 cess, duty, lade, levy, load, onus, scot, toll 5 drain, tithe 6 assess, burden, cumber, impost, saddle, strain, tariff, weight 7 tribute 8 encumber 9 overexert 10 imposition
agency: 3 IRS
expert: 3 CPA
feudal: 7 scutage, tallage
kind: 4 geld 5 sales, tithe 6 excise, income 8 property 9 ad valorem, surcharge

taxi
3 cab, car 4 hack 5 cyclo

taxi driver
5 cabby 6 cabbie, hackie 7 hackman

taxing
5 tough 6 trying 7 exigent, onerous, wearing 8 exacting, grueling 9 demanding, difficult 10 burdensome, oppressive

tazza
3 cup 4 vase

Tchaikovsky, Pyotr Ilyich
ballet: 8 Swan Lake 10 Nutcracker (The) 14 Sleeping Beauty
opera: 12 Eugene Onegin 13 Queen of Spades (The)

tchotchke
5 curio 6 gewgaw 7 bibelot 8 gimcrack, kickshaw 9 objet d'art 10 knickknack

tea
5 party 6 repast 8 beverage 9 reception
black: 5 bohea, pekoe 8 souchong
box: 5 caddy
bread: 5 scone
brand: 6 Lipton, Salada 8 Twinings

cake: 6 cookie
genus: 4 Thea
herbal: 6 ptisan, tisane
kind: 4 chai, herb, Java, maté 5 Assam, black, bohea, green, hyson, pekoe 6 Ceylon, congou, herbal, oolong, tisane 7 cambric, rooibos 8 Earl Grey, souchong 9 chamomile, sassafras 10 Darjeeling

teach
5 coach, edify, guide, train, tutor 6 impart, school 7 educate, instill, profess 8 instruct 9 enlighten, inculcate

teacher
4 guru, prof 5 coach, guide, tutor 6 docent, master, mentor, pedant 7 maestro, trainer 8 educator 9 pedagogue, preceptor, professor 10 instructor 12 schoolmaster
Hindu: 5 swami
Jewish: 5 rabbi, rebbe
Muslim: 6 mullah
organization: 3 NEA
religious: 9 catechist 10 mystagogue

team
4 band, club, crew, gang, join, pair, side, yoke 5 group, squad, troop, wagon 6 stable, troupe 8 carriage
baseball: 4 nine
basketball: 4 five 7 quintet
football: 6 eleven
kind: 6 jayvee 7 varsity

teamster
6 driver 7 trucker

Téa of TV and film
5 Leoni

tear
3 cry, cut, fly, rip, run 4 bolt, claw, dash, drop, flaw, gash, hole, lash, pull, race, rend, rift, rive, rush, slit, snag, weep 5 chase, hurry, shoot, shred, slash, speed, split, spree 6 career, charge, course, sunder, tatter, wrench 7 droplet, fissure, rupture 8 lacerate 10 laceration

tear down
4 raze, ruin 5 smash, wreck 7 destroy, shatter 8 demolish 9 take apart 10 annihilate

tearful
5 misty, moist, weepy 6 crying, watery 7 bawling, sobbing, weeping 8 pathetic 9 lamenting, sniveling 10 blubbering, lachrymose

tear-jerking
5 mushy 6 drippy, sticky 7 maudlin, mawkish 8 touching 9 schmaltzy 11 sentimental

teary-eyed
4 dewy 5 blear, moist

tease
3 kid, rag, rib, rip 4 bait, coax, comb, gibe, jive, josh, ride, twit 5 chaff, chivy, shred, taunt, worry 6 cajole, harass, needle, pester, pick on 7 torment 8 ridicule 9 tantalize

teaser
4 lure 5 promo 7 preview

teched
3 mad 4 daft 5 batty, crazy 6 insane 7 cracked, lunatic 8 demented

technicality
6 detail 8 loophole

technique
5 modus, style 6 method, system 8 approach 9 procedure 13 modus operandi

ted
5 strew 6 spread 7 scatter

tedious
4 dull 5 ho-hum 6 boring, dreary 7 operose 8 drudging, tiresome 9 dryasdust, wearisome 10 monotonous

tedium
5 ennui 7 boredom 8 doldrums, dullness, monotony

teem
4 flow, pour 5 crawl, swarm 6 abound, bustle 9 pullulate

teeming
4 lush, rife 6 aswarm 7 replete 8 abundant, swarming, thronged 9 abounding 11 overflowing

teen
5 youth 10 adolescent
woe: 4 acne

tee off
4 open 5 begin, drive, enter, start 8 commence, initiate

teeter
4 rock, sway 5 waver 6 falter, seesaw, wobble 9 vacillate

telamon
5 atlas
counterpart: 8 caryatid

Telamon
brother: 6 Peleus
father: 6 Aeacus
half-brother: 6 Phocus
son: 4 Ajax 6 Teucer

Telegonus
father: 7 Ulysses 8 Odysseus
mother: 5 Circe

telegraph
4 wire 5 cable
code: 5 Morse
inventor: 5 Morse (Samuel F. B.)

Telemachus
father: 7 Ulysses 8 Odysseus
mother: 8 Penelope

telephone
4 buzz, call, cell, dial, ring **6** mobile, ring up **8** cordless, landline
inventor: **4** Bell (Alexander Graham)

telescope
5 glass **6** finder **7** compact **8** compress, condense, contract, spyglass **9** reflector, refractor
part: **4** lens

television
4 tube **5** video **8** boob tube, idiot box
antenna: **10** rabbit ears
award: **4** Emmy
British: **5** telly
children's: **6** kidvid
frequency: **3** UHF, VHF
network: **3** ABC, BBC, CBS, Fox, HBO, NBC, NET, PBS, QVC, TNT **4** ESPN, INHD
pioneer: **5** Baird (John Logie) **8** De Forest (Lee), Goldmark (Peter Carl), Zworykin (Vladimir) **10** Farnsworth (Philo T.)
program: **4** news **5** pilot, rerun **6** series, sitcom **7** western **8** game show, talk show **9** broadcast, docudrama, soap opera **11** infomercial
tube: **9** kinescope

tell
3 rat, say **4** blab, clue **5** count, mound, order, spill, state, utter **6** advise, betray, fill in, inform, notify, relate, report, retail, reveal, tattle **7** confess, declare, divulge, narrate, recount **8** disclose, give away

teller
5 clerk **6** banker **7** cashier, counter **8** informer, narrator

telling
5 solid, sound, valid **6** cogent **7** weighty **8** powerful **9** effective **10** convincing

tell off
4 flay, rate, ream **5** chide, scold **6** berate, rebuke **7** bawl out, chew out, reprove, upbraid **8** admonish, call down **9** dress down, excoriate, reprimand **10** take to task, tongue-lash, vituperate

tell on
6 inform, snitch, tattle

telltale
3 cue **4** clue, fink, lead, sign **5** proof **6** canary, gossip, signal, snitch, tip-off **7** rat fink, tattler **8** evidence, gossiper, informer, quidnunc, signpost, squealer **12** blabbermouth, gossipmonger **13** scandalmonger

Tell-Tale Heart author
3 Poe (Edgar Allan)

telluric
6 earthy **7** earthly, mundane, terrene, worldly **9** sublunary **11** terrestrial

temblor
5 quake, shake, shock **6** tremor **8** upheaval **10** aftershock, earthquake

temerarious
4 rash **6** daring **8** heedless, reckless **9** audacious, daredevil, foolhardy **11** adventurous, venturesome

temerity
4 gall **5** cheek, nerve **6** daring **8** audacity, chutzpah, rashness **9** brashness, hardihood, hardiness **10** effrontery **12** recklessness

temper
4 heat, mean, mood, tone **5** admix, alloy, anger, grain **6** anneal, attune, dander, dilute, govern, hackle, medium, season, soften, strain **7** mollify, passion, toughen **8** hardness, moderate, modulate, restrain **9** character, composure, condition

temperament
4 mood **5** humor, nature **11** disposition, personality

temperamental
5 moody **7** erratic **8** contrary, ticklish, unstable, variable, volatile **9** mercurial **10** capricious, changeable, high-strung, inconstant **13** unpredictable

temperance
8 sobriety **9** austerity, restraint **10** abstinence, continence, moderation, self-denial **11** self-control
advocate: **6** Nation (Carry)

temperate
4 calm, even, mild **5** sober **6** modest, steady **7** clement **8** discreet, moderate **9** abstinent **10** abstemious, restrained **11** abstentious

temperature
4 heat **5** fever **6** degree, warmth **7** hotness **8** coldness

tempered
7 diluted, treated **8** adjusted, hardened, softened **9** mitigated, moderated, qualified

tempest
3 din **4** blow, gale, rage, wind **5** furor, hurly, storm **6** hubbub, squall, tumult, uproar **8** brouhaha, foofaraw **9** commotion, hurricane **10** hullabaloo, hurly-burly

Tempest character
5 Ariel **6** Alonso **7** Caliban, Miranda **8** Prospero **9** Ferdinand

tempestuous
5 roily **6** raging, stormy **7** furious, moiling, violent **8** blustery **9** turbulent

temple
4 fane **6** church **9** synagogue **10** tabernacle
ancient: **8** pantheon
Aztec: **8** teocalli

Buddhist: **3** wat
Eastern: **6** pagoda
Greek: **9** Parthenon
sanctuary: **4** naos **5** cella, Nemea **6** adytum **10** penetralia

tempo
4 pace, rate, time **5** speed, lento **6** adagio, presto, rhythm, vivace **7** allegro, andante

temporal
3 lay **4** laic **5** civil **6** carnal **7** earthly, mundane, profane, secular, worldly **13** chronological, synchronistic

temporary
5 ad hoc **6** acting **7** interim **8** fleeting **9** ad interim, makeshift, transient **10** short-lived, substitute, transitory **11** provisional

temporize
5 delay, stall, yield **6** palter **7** draw out **8** gain time **10** equivocate **11** prevaricate

tempt
4 bait, lure, risk, sway **5** court **6** allure, entice, entrap, lead on, seduce **7** provoke **8** inveigle **9** tantalize

temptation
4 bait, lure, trap **5** decoy, siren, snare **6** allure, come-on **9** seduction **10** attraction, enticement

tempting
8 alluring **9** appealing, delicious, seductive **10** attractive, come-hither

temptress
4 vamp **5** siren **7** Delilah, Lorelei **8** Mata Hari **10** seductress **11** femme fatale

ten
cents: **4** dime
combining form: **3** dec, dek **4** deca, deka **5** decem
dollars: **7** sawbuck
mills: **4** cent
thousand: **6** myriad
years: **6** decade

tenacious
4 firm **5** fixed **6** dogged, sturdy **8** adhesive, clinging, resolute, stalwart, stubborn **9** obstinate, steadfast **10** persistent

tenacity
4 grit **5** moxie, pluck **6** mettle **8** firmness **10** resolution **11** persistence

tenant
6 holder, lessee, lodger, renter **7** boarder, dweller **8** occupant
feudal: **6** vassal

Ten Commandments
9 Decalogue
director: **7** DeMille (Cecil B.)

tend
4 lean **5** guard, labor, nurse, serve, watch **6** foster **7** babysit, care for, incline, nurture, oversee **8** minister **9** cultivate, look after, watch over

tendency
4 bent, bias **5** drift, tenor, trend **7** current, leaning **8** penchant **10** partiality, proclivity, propensity **11** disposition, inclination **12** predilection

tendentious
6 biased **7** colored, partial **8** one-sided, partisan **10** prejudiced

tender
3 bid **4** fond, mild, soft, sore, warm **5** green, money, mushy, offer **6** gentle, humane, loving, submit, touchy **7** fragile, lenient, painful, proffer, propose **8** delicate, proposal **9** sensitive, succulent **11** considerate, warmhearted **12** affectionate

tenderfoot
4 colt, punk, tiro, tyro **6** novice, rookie **7** amateur **8** beginner, freshman, neophyte, newcomer **9** cheechako, fledgling, greenhorn, novitiate **10** apprentice

tenderhearted
6 kindly **11** sympathetic **13** compassionate

tendon
4 band, cord **5** nerve, sinew **6** leader **9** hamstring

tendril
4 curl, vine **6** cirrus, spiral **7** ringlet

tenebrous
3 dim **4** dark, dusk, hazy **5** dusky, foggy, muddy, murky, vague **6** cloudy, gloomy **7** cryptic, obscure, shadowy, unclear **9** ambiguous **10** caliginous

tenement
4 flat **6** rental, walk-up, warren **7** lodging, rookery **9** apartment

tenet
3 ism **5** canon, creed, dogma **6** belief **8** doctrine **9** principle

tenfold
7 decuple

Tennessee
capital: **9** Nashville
city: **7** Memphis **9** Knoxville **11** Chattanooga
college, university: **10** Vanderbilt
mountain, range: **7** Lookout **10** Great Smoky **13** Clingmans Dome
nickname: **9** Volunteer (State)
public works: **3** TVA **9** Norris Dam
river: **9** Tennessee **11** Mississippi
state bird: **11** mockingbird
state flower: **4** iris
state tree: **11** tulip poplar

tennis
award: **8** Davis Cup
item: **3** net **6** racket **7** racquet
put-away: **3** ace
score: **4** ad-in, love **5** add-in, ad-out, deuce **6** add-out
serve: **3** ace
shoe: **7** sneaker
stroke: **3** cut, lob **4** chop, drop **5** serve, slice **6** volley **8** backhand, forehand
term: **3** let, set **5** court, fault **7** service **9** advantage, backcourt

tennis champ
4 Ashe (Arthur), Borg (Bjorn), Graf (Steffi), King (Billie Jean), Noah (Yannick), Wade (Virginia) **5** Budge (Don), Court (Margaret Smith), Evert (Chris), Henin (Justine), Laver (Rod), Lendl (Ivan), Nadal (Rafael), Perry (Fred), Seles (Monica), Wills (Helen) **6** Agassi (André), Becker (Boris), Edberg (Stefan), Gibson (Althea), Hingis (Martina), Kramer (Jack), Murray (Andy), Muster (Thomas), Stolle (Fred), Tilden (Bill) **7** Connors (Jimmy), Emerson (Roy), Federer (Roger), Lacoste (René), McEnroe (John), Nastase (Ilie), Roddick (Andy), Sampras (Pete) **8** Connolly (Maureen), Djokovic (Novak), González (Pancho), Newcombe (John), Rosewall (Ken), Wilander (Mats), Williams (Serena, Venus) **11** Navratilova (Martina)

Tennyson, Alfred
hero: **5** Enoch (Arden)
poem: **4** Maud **7** Ulysses **10** Enoch Arden, In Memoriam **12** Locksley Hall

tenor
4 mood, tone **5** drift, voice **6** singer **7** meaning, purport
American: **5** Lanza (Mario) **6** Peerce (Jan), Tucker (Richard)
Canadian: **7** Vickers (Jon)
Danish: **8** Melchior (Lauritz)
English: **5** Pears (Peter)
German: **10** Wunderlich (Fritz)
Irish: **9** McCormack (John)
Italian: **6** Alagna (Roberto), Caruso (Enrico) **7** Bocelli (Andrea), Corelli (Franco) **8** Bergonzi (Carlo) **9** del Monaco (Mario), di Stefano (Giuseppe), Pavarotti (Luciano)
Spanish: **7** Domingo (Plácido) **8** Carreras (José)
Swedish: **5** Gedda (Nicolai) **8** Björling (Jussi) **9** Bjoerling (Jussi)

tenpins
7 bowling

tense
4 edgy, taut **5** hyper, nervy, tight, wired **6** on edge, uneasy **7** anxious, jittery, nervous, restive, uptight **8** strained, stressed **10** high-strung
grammatical: **4** past **6** future **7** perfect, present **8** preterit **9** preterite **10** pluperfect **11** progressive

tension
6 nerves, strain, stress, unease **7** anxiety **8** edginess, pressure, tautness **9** agitation, stiffness **10** discomfort, uneasiness

tent
4 camp **6** canopy, encamp, laager **7** bivouac, shelter
kind: **3** ger, pup **4** yurt **5** Baker, tepee **6** teepee **7** marquee **8** pavilion, umbrella
maker: **4** Omar
material: **6** canvas
part: **3** fly, guy, peg **4** pole **5** stake

tentacle
3 arm **6** barbel, feeler

tenth
5 tithe
combining form: **4** deci

tenuous
5 reedy, shaky **6** feeble, flimsy, slight, stalky **7** fragile, sketchy **10** precarious

tenure
4 term **5** lease **6** estate **10** incumbency
feudal: **7** burgage

tepid
4 mild, warm **7** warmish **8** lukewarm **9** apathetic **11** halfhearted, indifferent

tequila
relative: **6** mescal, mezcal
source: **5** agave

tergiversate
3 haw, hem **5** dodge, evade, hedge **6** defect, desert, waffle, weasel **7** abandon, shuffle **8** renounce, sidestep **9** pussyfoot, repudiate **10** apostatize, equivocate

term
3 end **4** name, span, tour, word **5** label, spell, stint, title **6** detail, period, tenure **7** quarter, session **8** duration, semester **9** designate **10** conclusion, expression, particular

termagant
5 harpy, scold, shrew, vixen **6** ogress, virago **8** fishwife, harridan **9** Xanthippe

terminal
3 end, lag **4** last **5** anode, depot, fatal, final **6** finial, latest, latter, lethal **7** cathode, closing, extreme, station **8** eventual, hindmost, junction, ultimate **9** extremity **10** concluding
negative: **7** cathode
positive: **5** anode

terminate
3 end **4** drop, fire, halt, kill, quit, sack, stop **5** abort, cease, close, leave **6** cut off, finish, wind

up **7** abolish, dead-end, dismiss **8** complete, conclude, dissolve **9** determine, discharge **10** extinguish **11** discontinue

terminology
4 cant **5** argot, idiom, lingo **6** jargon, patois **7** lexicon **10** vernacular, vocabulary **12** nomenclature

termite
5 alate **8** white ant

ternary
5 third **6** triple **9** threefold

Terpsichore
see **Muse**

terrace
4 bank, mesa **5** bench, porch, shelf **7** balcony, sundeck, veranda **8** platform, verandah **9** promenade

terra-cotta
4 clay **7** pottery

terra firma
4 dirt, land, soil **5** earth **6** ground

terrain
4 area, land, turf **6** domain, milieu, sphere **8** province **9** bailiwick, territory **10** topography **11** environment

terrapin
6 turtle

terrestrial
6 earthy **7** earthly, mundane, worldly **8** telluric **9** earthlike, planetary, sublunary **10** earthbound

terrible
4 dire **5** awful, dread **6** grisly, horrid **7** dreaded, fearful, ghastly, heinous, hideous, macabre, violent **8** dreadful, gruesome, horrible, horrific, shocking **9** abhorrent, appalling, atrocious, frightful, harrowing, monstrous **10** disastrous, formidable, horrendous, horrifying

terrible czar
4 Ivan

terrier
breed: 3 fox **4** blue, bull, Skye **5** cairn, Irish, Welsh **6** Boston **8** Airedale, Lakeland **9** Yorkshire
movie: 4 Asta **6** Skippy
White House: 4 Fala

terrific
5 boffo, socko, super, swell **6** superb **7** amazing, awesome **8** dynamite, glorious **9** fantastic, marvelous, wonderful **10** formidable, incredible **11** magnificent, sensational **13** extraordinary

terrify
5 alarm, scare **7** startle **8** affright, frighten

terrifying
4 grim **5** scary **6** grisly, horrid **7** ghastly, hideous, macabre **8** alarming, dreadful, fearsome, gruesome, horrible, horrific **9** frightful **10** formidable, horrifying

territory
4 area, belt, land, turf, zone **5** route, tract **6** domain, region, sphere **7** country, demesne, terrain **8** district, dominion, province **9** bailiwick **12** jurisdiction

terror
5 alarm, dread, panic **6** fright, horror **9** nightmare

terrorize
3 cow **5** alarm, bully, scare **6** coerce, fright, menace **7** scarify **8** browbeat, bulldoze, frighten, threaten **9** strong-arm

terry
4 loop **5** cloth **6** fabric

terse
4 curt **5** brief, crisp, pithy **7** brusque, compact, concise, laconic, summary **8** polished, succinct **11** compendious, sententious, telegraphic

tertiary
5 third

terza ___
4 rima

tessera
3 die **4** tile **6** tablet, ticket

test
3 try **4** exam, quiz **5** assay, check, essay, final, taste, touch, trial, try on **6** sample, tryout, verify **7** confirm, examine, midterm **8** evaluate, gut check, sounding, trial run **9** benchmark **10** evaluation, experiment, touchstone **11** examination
type: 5 essay

testa
6 cupule **7** coating **8** envelope, seed coat, tegument **10** integument

testament
4 will **5** credo, creed **7** tribute, witness **8** evidence **9** scripture **11** attestation **12** confirmation

tester
4 coin **6** canopy, prover **7** analyst, assayer **8** examiner **12** investigator

testifier
7 witness **8** deponent

testify
5 swear **6** affirm, attest, depone, depose **7** certify, witness

testimonial
5 proof **6** salute **7** tribute, witness **9** affidavit, character, reference **11** attestation

testimony
6 avowal **7** witness **8** evidence **9** affidavit **10** deposition **11** affirmation, attestation, declaration

testy
6 cranky, ornery, touchy **7** fretful, grouchy, peevish **8** choleric **9** crotchety, irascible, irritable **10** ill-humored, out of sorts **12** cantankerous

tetanus
7 lockjaw, trismus

tête-à-tête
4 chat, talk **5** à deux **7** vis-à-vis **8** causerie **10** face-to-face **12** conversation

tether
3 tie **4** bind, rope **5** cable, chain, stake **6** fasten, fetter, lariat, picket **8** restrain **9** restraint

tetrad
4 four **7** quartet **8** foursome **10** quaternion

Teutonic
6 German **8** Germanic
language: 5 Dutch **6** Danish, German, Gothic **7** English, Flemish, Frisian, Swedish **9** Afrikaans, Norwegian

Texas
capital: 6 Austin
city: 4 Waco **6** Dallas, El Paso **7** Houston **8** Amarillo **9** Fort Worth **10** San Antonio
college, university: 3 SMU **4** Rice **6** Baylor **9** Texas Tech
island: 5 Padre
mountain: 9 Guadalupe (Peak)
nickname: 8 Lone Star (State)
park: 7 Big Bend
river: 5 Pecos **6** Brazos **9** Rio Grande
state bird: 11 mockingbird
state flower: 10 bluebonnet
state tree: 5 pecan

text
6 script

textbook
6 primer

texter's disclaimer
3 IMO **4** IMHO

texter's guffaw
3 LOL

textile
5 cloth **6** fabric
dealer: 6 draper, mercer
machine: 8 calender
pattern: 7 paisley **11** houndstooth
shop: 7 mercery
starch: 4 sago
treat: 9 mercerize

texture
3 web **4** feel, hand, wale, woof **5** weave **6** fabric

Thackeray novel
9 Pendennis **10** Vanity Fair **11** Barry Lyndon, Henry Esmond

Thailand
capital: 7 Bangkok
former name: 4 Siam
monetary unit: 4 baht
sea: 7 Andaman

Thaïs
7 hetaera, hetaira **9** courtesan
author: 6 France (Anatole)
composer: 8 Massenet (Jules)
husband: 7 Ptolemy
lover: 9 Alexander (the Great)

thalassic
6 marine **7** oceanic **8** maritime

Thalia
see **Graces; Muse**

Thanatos
5 death
brother: 6 Hypnos
mother: 3 Nyx

thankful
4 glad **8** grateful **12** appreciative

thanks
9 gratitude **12** appreciation

Thanksgiving
5 feast **7** holiday
first celebrant: 6 Indian **7** Pilgrim
food: 6 turkey

thatch
3 mop **4** hair, nipa, roof **5** cover

that is (Latin)
5 id est

That's ___ (Dean Martin hit)
5 Amore

thaumaturgic
5 magic **6** Magian, mystic, witchy **7** magical **8** wizardly **10** miraculous **11** necromantic

thaumaturgy
5 magic **7** sorcery **8** cabbalah, kabbalah, witchery, wizardry **10** necromancy

thaw
4 melt **5** deice, relax **6** unbend **7** defrost, liquefy **8** dissolve, unfreeze **10** condescend, deliquesce

the
French: 3 les, une
German: 3 das, der, die, ein **4** eine
Italian: 3 una, uno
Spanish: 3 las, los, una, uno

theater
4 nabe **5** drama, stage **6** boards **9** playhouse **10** footlights
award: 4 Obie, Tony
district: 6 rialto
drop: 5 scrim
entrance: 5 foyer, lobby
Greek: 4 odea (plural) **5** odeum

movie: **6** cinema **8** cineplex, megaplex **9** multiplex
name: **4** Roxy **5** Bijou **6** Rialto
outdoor: **7** drive-in
part: **3** box, pit **4** loge, tier **5** apron, stage, wings **6** stalls **7** balcony, parquet **8** parterre **9** greenroom, mezzanine, orchestra **10** proscenium

theatrical
5 stagy **6** staged **8** dramatic, thespian **10** artificial, flamboyant, histrionic **11** dramaturgic **12** melodramatic
agent: **6** Morris (William)
device: **4** prop
group: **6** troupe

Theban Eagle
6 Pindar

Thebes
founder: **6** Cadmus
king: **5** Laius **7** Oedipus
queen: **5** Niobe **7** Jocasta

Theda of silent film
4 Bara

theft
5 heist, pinch **6** holdup, piracy **7** break-in, larceny, robbery **8** burglary, stealing **9** pilferage
combining form: **5** klept **6** klepto

theme
4 stem, text, tune **5** essay, lemma, motif, point, topic, topos **6** burden, matter, melody, mythos, thesis **7** article, conceit, message, subject **8** argument

Themis
father: **6** Uranus
goddess of: **3** law **7** justice
husband: **4** Zeus **7** Jupiter
mother: **4** Gaea

then
4 also, anon, ergo, next, thus, when **5** again, hence, later **7** besides, further **8** moreover **9** therefore, thereupon

thence
4 away **7** thereof **9** from there, therefrom

Theogony poet
6 Hesiod

theologian
American: **6** Merton (Thomas) **7** Edwards (Jonathan), Niebuhr (Reinhold), Tillich (Paul)
Dutch: **6** Jansen (Cornelis)
English: **4** Bede (Venerable) **5** Pusey (Edward) **6** Alcuin, Wesley (John) **7** Langton (Stephen) **8** Wycliffe (John)
French: **6** Calvin (John) **7** Abelard (Peter) **8** Maritain (Jacques), Teilhard (de Chardin, Pierre)
German: **7** Eckhart (Meister) **8** Albertus (Magnus) **9** Niemöller (Martin) **10** Bonhoeffer (Dietrich)
Italian: **7** Aquinas (Thomas)
Scottish: **10** Duns Scotus (John)
Swiss: **4** Küng (Hans) **5** Barth (Karl) **6** Calvin (John), Cauvin (Jean)

___ Theologica
5 Summa

theorbo
4 lute

theorem
5 axiom **9** principle **11** fundamental, proposition

theoretical
5 ideal **8** abstract, academic, notional, unproved **11** conjectural, speculative **12** hypothetical

theorize
9 formulate, postulate, speculate **10** conjecture **11** hypothesize

theory
7 perhaps, premise, surmise **8** supposal **10** conjecture, hypothesis
astronomical: **7** big bang
suffix: **3** ism

therapeutic
5 tonic **7** healing, helpful **8** curative, remedial, salutary, sanative **9** healthful, medicinal, vulnerary **10** beneficial, corrective **11** restorative

therefore
4 ergo, thus **5** hence **6** hereat, thence

thereupon
4 ergo, then, thus **6** at once, at that, thence **8** directly **9** right away, therefore, wherefore **11** accordingly, straightway

thermal unit
3 Btu **6** degree **7** calorie

thermometer
5 gauge
kind: **4** oral **7** Celsius, Réaumur **10** centigrade, Fahrenheit

thermos
5 dewar **10** Dewar flask

Thersites' slayer
8 Achilles

thesaurus editor
5 Roget (Peter Mark)

Theseus
beloved: **7** Ariadne
son: **10** Hippolytus
victim: **8** Minotaur **10** Procrustes
wife: **7** Phaedra

thesis
5 essay, point, theme **6** belief **7** premise **8** downbeat, position, tractate, treatise

9 discourse, monograph, postulate, synthesis 11 proposition, supposition 12 dissertation

thespian
5 actor 6 mummer, player 7 actress, trouper 8 dramatic 9 performer

Thespis' forte
5 drama 7 tragedy

Thessalian hero
5 Jason 8 Achilles

Thetis
6 Nereid
father: 6 Nereus
husband: 6 Peleus
mother: 5 Doris
son: 8 Achilles

theurgist
5 witch 7 warlock 8 magician, sorcerer 12 wonder-worker

thew
4 beef 5 brawn, might, power, sinew, vigor 6 muscle

thick
3 fat 4 wide 5 broad, bulky, burly, dense, dumpy, husky, squat, stout 6 chunky, packed, stocky 7 compact, crammed, crowded, viscous 8 familiar, heavyset

thicken
3 set 4 blur, clot, jell 6 curdle 7 broaden, compact, congeal 8 condense 9 coagulate 10 inspissate 11 concentrate

thickening agent
4 agar

thicket
4 bosk, bush, shaw 5 clump, copse, grove, hedge 6 bosket, covert, mallee, tangle 7 boscage, bosquet, coppice, spinney 8 hedgerow, quickset 9 brushwood, canebrake, chaparral

thickness
3 ply 4 bulk, loft 5 depth, gauge, layer, sheet 7 density 9 viscosity

thickset
5 bulky, burly, heavy, husky, plump, pudgy, stout, tubby 6 chubby, chunky, portly, stocky, sturdy 7 compact 9 corpulent

thief
4 yegg 5 ganef, gonif 6 bandit, goniff, looter, pirate, robber 7 burglar, filcher, stealer 8 hijacker, larcener, pilferer 9 larcenist, purloiner 10 cat burglar, highwayman, pickpocket, shoplifter 12 housebreaker

thieve
3 rob 4 hook, lift 5 boost, filch, pinch, pluck, steal, swipe 6 pilfer, rip off, snitch 7 purloin 8 knock off 9 knock over

thievery
see **theft**

thievish
7 corrupt, crooked 9 larcenous 13 light-fingered

thigh
3 ham 5 flank 6 gammon
bone: 5 femur
relating to: 6 crural 7 femoral

thimble
3 cup 5 cover

thin
4 fine, lank, lean, slim 5 gaunt, lanky, reedy, scant, sharp, sheer, spare 6 dilute, flimsy, meager, meagre, rarefy, scanty, skimpy, skinny, slight, sparse, stalky, twiggy, watery 7 diluted, scraggy, scrawny, slender, spindly, squinny, subtile, tenuous 8 rarefied, skeletal 9 attenuate, emaciated, extenuate 10 attenuated

thing
4 item, unit 5 being, event 6 entity, matter, object 7 article, concern, element 10 occurrence, phenomenon
in law: 3 res

thingamajig
5 gismo, gizmo 6 dingus, doodad, gadget, hickey, jigger, widget 7 whatsit 9 doohickey

things
4 gear 5 goods, stock, stuff 7 baggage, clothes, effects, luggage 8 chattels, clothing, matériel, movables, property, supplies 10 belongings, provisions 11 impedimenta, merchandise

think
4 mull, muse 5 brood, study 6 ideate, ponder, reason 7 believe, imagine, reflect, suppose, surmise 8 cogitate, consider, meditate, ruminate 9 cerebrate, speculate 10 conjecture, deliberate, excogitate 11 contemplate
alike: 5 agree

Thinker sculptor
5 Rodin (Auguste)

think tank since 1948
4 Rand

Thin Man, The
actor: 3 Loy (Myrna) 6 Powell (William), Skippy 9 O'Sullivan (Maureen)
author: 7 Hammett (Dashiell)
character: 4 Nick (Charles), Nora (Charles)
dog: 4 Asta

third
4 show 8 tertiary
combining form: 3 tri
power: 4 cube

third degree
7 torture 8 grilling 11 inquisition, questioning 13 interrogation

third estate
5 plebs **6** people, plebes **8** populace **9** commonage, commoners, plebeians **10** commonalty **11** rank and file

Third Man author
6 Greene (Graham)

thirst
3 yen **4** itch, long, lust, pine **5** crave, yearn **6** desire, hanker, hunger **7** craving, dryness, longing **8** appetite

thirsty
3 dry **4** arid, avid **5** eager **6** ardent **7** anxious, bone-dry, parched **8** droughty **9** absorbent

this, in Mexico
4 esta, este, esto

this and that
8 oddments, sundries **9** etceteras **11** miscellanea, odds and ends

Thisbe's lover
7 Pyramus

thistle
4 weed **7** caltrop
Russian: **10** tumbleweed

thistlebird
9 goldfinch

thither
3 yon **5** there **6** yonder

thole
3 peg, pin **6** endure

Thomas à ____
6 Becket, Kempis

Thomas ____ Edison
4 Alva

thong
4 band, lace, lash, rein, zori **5** lasso, strap, strip, whang **6** sandal **7** latchet **8** flip-flop

Thor
5 Donar
father: **4** Odin **5** Wotan
god of: **7** thunder
hammer: **8** Mjollnir

thorax
5 chest, trunk **6** pereon

Thoreau, Henry David
friend: **7** Emerson (Ralph Waldo)
pond: **6** Walden
town: **7** Concord
work: **6** Walden

thorn
4 barb **5** briar, spike, spine **7** prickle, spinule

thorny
5 sharp, spiny **6** briary, touchy, tricky **7** awkward, prickly, spinous **8** ticklish **9** difficult, vexatious

thorough
6 minute **7** careful, in-depth **8** complete, detailed, diligent, whole-hog **9** downright **10** blow-by-blow, exhaustive, meticulous **11** painstaking

thoroughbred
5 racer **8** pedigree **9** pedigreed, pureblood **10** bloodstock **11** full-blooded

thoroughfare
6 artery, avenue, street **7** highway, parkway **8** corridor **9** boulevard

thoroughgoing
5 utter **6** all-out **7** extreme **8** absolute, complete, outright, whole-hog **9** out-and-out **10** consummate, exhaustive **11** straight-out

though
3 yet **5** still, while **6** albeit **7** however, whereas **8** after all **11** nonetheless **12** nevertheless

thought
4 idea **6** notion, reason **7** concept, opinion **8** ideation **9** brainwork **10** cogitation, conception, meditation, reflection, rumination

thoughtful
6 polite **7** gallant, heedful, mindful, pensive, serious **8** gracious, studious, thinking **9** attentive, courteous **10** cogitative, meditative, reflective, ruminative, solicitous **11** considerate **12** deliberative, intellectual **13** contemplative

thoughtless
4 rash, rude **5** brash, hasty **6** madcap **7** selfish **8** impolite, uncaring **9** insensate **10** incautious, ungracious **12** discourteous **13** inconsiderate

thousand
combining form: **4** kilo
cubed: **7** billion
dollars: **5** grand
squared: **7** million
years: **10** millennium

thousandth
10 millesimal
combining form: **5** milli

thrall
4 peon, serf, yoke **5** helot, slave **7** bondage, bondman, helotry, peonage, serfdom, slavery, villein **9** servitude, villenage **10** absorption

thrash
3 tan **4** beat, belt, drub, flog, hide, lash, lick, maul, pelt, trim, whip **5** baste, flail, pound, smear, swing, thump, whale, whang **6** batter, buffet, larrup, pummel, stripe, wallop **7** scourge, shellac **8** flounder, lambaste, work over **10** flagellate

thrash out
4 moot **5** argue **6** debate **7** discuss, dispute

thread
4 line, vein, yard **5** fiber, trail, weave **6** strand, stream, string **8** filament

ball of: 4 clew
dental: 5 floss
holder: 6 bobbin
kind: 4 silk, yarn 5 floss, lisle 6 cotton 8 surgical
loose: 8 raveling 9 ravelling
surgical: 6 catgut, suture

threadbare
4 hack, worn 5 dingy, faded, seedy, stale, tacky, tatty, tired, trite 6 beat-up, cheesy, cliché, frayed, ragged, shabby, shoddy 7 clichéd, run-down, tedious, worn-out 8 shopworn, slipshod, tattered, timeworn, well-worn 9 hackneyed 10 down-at-heel 11 dilapidated, down-at-heels

threadlike
6 filate 11 filamentous

threads
4 duds 7 clothes 8 clothing, garments

threat
6 danger, duress, menace, or else 7 warning 8 big stick, coercion

threaten
3 cow 4 loom, warn 5 augur, lower 6 coerce, menace 7 caution, portend, presage 8 endanger, forebode, forewarn, overhang 10 intimidate

three
5 crowd
combining form: 3 ter, tri
in games: 4 trey

threefold
5 trine 6 thrice, treble, trinal, triple 7 triplex

Three Musketeers
5 Athos 6 Aramis 7 Porthos
author: 5 Dumas (Alexandre)
friend: 9 D'Artagnan

Threepenny Opera, The
author: 6 Brecht (Bertolt)
composer: 5 Weill (Kurt)

threescore
5 sixty

Three Sisters, The
4 Olga 5 Irina, Masha
author: 7 Chekhov (Anton)

threesome
4 trio 5 triad, trine 6 triple, triune, troika 7 trinity 8 triangle 11 triumvirate

three-wheeler
5 trike 7 pedicab 8 tricycle 10 velocipede

threnody
5 dirge, elegy 6 lament

thresh
5 flail 6 winnow

threshold
3 eve 4 cusp, door, edge, gate, sill 5 brink, limen, verge 6 outset 8 boundary

thrift
6 saving 7 economy, sea pink 8 prudence 9 frugality, parsimony

thrifty
5 canny 6 frugal 7 sparing 9 provident 10 economical 12 cheeseparing, parsimonious

thrill
3 wow 4 bang, boot, kick, rush 5 throb 6 charge, excite, shiver, tingle 7 frisson, tremble, vibrate 9 electrify 10 excitement 11 titillation

thriller
6 gothic 7 mystery, shocker 8 whodunit 9 dime novel

thrive
4 boom, grow 7 advance, burgeon, develop, prosper, succeed 8 flourish, get ahead

throat
3 maw 4 tube 5 gorge 6 groove, gullet 7 channel, weasand
infection: 5 strep 12 epiglottitis
inflammation: 5 croup 6 angina, quinsy 10 laryngitis 11 pharyngitis
relating to: 8 guttural
warmer: 5 scarf

throat-clearing sound
4 ahem

throaty
5 gruff, husky, thick 6 hoarse 8 gravelly, guttural

throb
4 ache, beat, drum 5 pound, pulse 6 thrill 7 pulsate, vibrate 9 palpitate

throe
3 fit 4 pain, pang 5 agony, spasm 6 attack 7 seizure 10 convulsion 11 contraction

thrombus
4 clot 8 blockage, coagulum

throne
5 chair, crown, power, reign 8 cathedra, dominion 11 sovereignty

throng
3 jam, mob 4 host, pack, rout 5 bunch, crowd, crush, drove, flock, group, horde, press, scrum, shoal, swarm 9 multitude

throttle
3 gun 5 choke 6 throat 7 garrote, trachea 8 strangle, suppress 11 accelerator, strangulate

through
3 per, via 4 done, past 5 ended 6 direct 7 done for 8 complete, finished, washed-up 9 completed, concluded 10 terminated, throughout
prefix: 3 dia, per

throughout
3 mid 4 amid 5 midst 6 during 7 all over, overall 10 everywhere, far and near, far and wide, high and low

throve
9 burgeoned, prospered 10 flourished

throw
3 lob, peg, put 4 cast, fire, hurl, toss 5 chuck, fling, heave, pitch, sling 6 afghan, launch, propel 7 buck off, project

throw away
4 blow, cast, dump, junk, shed 5 chuck, ditch, scrap, waste 6 unload 7 deep-six, discard, fritter 8 jettison, squander

throwback
7 atavism 9 reversion 11 anachronism

throw in
3 add

throw in the towel
4 quit 6 give up, resign

throw out
4 emit, junk, shed 5 chuck, eject, evict, scrap 6 reject 7 discard 8 jettison

throw up
4 barf, cast, hurl, lose, puke, quit, spew, toss 5 heave, retch, vomit 7 upchuck 8 disgorge 11 regurgitate

thrush
4 omao 5 mavis, ouzel, robin, veery 6 mistle 8 bluebird, throstle 9 blackbird, fieldfare, mistle-toe 11 nightingale

thrust
3 dig, jab, ram 4 barb, butt, cram, poke, prod, push, stab, tilt 5 barge, crowd, cut in, drive, force, lunge, press, punch, sense, shove, spear, stick 6 pierce, plunge, propel 7 assault, obtrude, project 8 pressure

thud
3 jar 4 bump, jolt, plop 5 clunk, throb, thump 6 impact

thug
3 mug 4 goon, hood 5 bravo, bully, rowdy 6 Apache, Capone, gunman, hit man 7 hoodlum, mobster, ruffian 8 enforcer, gangster, hooligan, plug-ugly 9 cutthroat, roughneck

thumb
4 leaf, turn 5 digit, hitch, ovolo 6 pollex, riffle 8 pollices (plural) 9 hitchhike

thumbs-up
3 AOK, nod 4 okay 7 go-ahead 10 green light

thumb through
4 scan 6 browse, riffle 7 dip into

thump
3 bop, hit 4 bash, beat, belt, blow, drub, jolt, pelt, whip, whup 5 knock, paste, pound, punch, shock, smack, sound, whack 6 batter, buffet, defeat, impact, pummel, strike, thrash, thwack, wallop 7 clobber, shellac, trounce

thunder
4 bang, boom, clap, peal, roar 6 rumble 7 re-sound 8 rumbling 9 fulminate
god: 4 Thor
lizard: 11 apatosaurus 12 brontosaurus

thunderbolt
9 lightning

thunderstruck
5 agape 6 aghast, amazed 7 shocked, stunned 8 appalled, dismayed 9 astounded, staggered 10 astonished 11 dumbfounded

Thurber character
5 Mitty (Walter)

thurible
6 censer

Thurman of Pulp Fiction
3 Uma

thus
3 sic 4 ergo, then 5 hence 9 therefore
French: 5 ainsi

thwack
3 bop 4 belt, biff, blow, pelt, sock, whop 5 crack, pound, smack, thump, whack 6 wallop 7 clobber

thwart
4 balk, beat, dash, foil 5 bench, block, deter 6 baffle, hamper, hinder, oppose, scotch, sty-mie 7 flummox, prevent 8 confound, obstruct 9 checkmate, frustrate 10 circumvent, contravene

tiara
5 crown 6 diadem 8 headband

Tibetan
animal: 3 yak 5 takin
capital: 5 Lhasa
coin: 5 tanga
dog: 9 Lhasa apso
monk: 4 lama
monster: 4 yeti
people: 6 Bhotia, Sherpa

tibia
8 shinbone

tic
5 quirk, spasm 6 twitch 9 twitching

tick
5 check 8 arachnid, parasite 9 checkmark 11 bloodsucker

ticked off
4 sore 5 irate, riled 7 annoyed 8 provoked 9 indignant, irritated

ticker
4 bomb 5 clock, heart, watch

ticket
3 key, tag 4 comp, pass, vote 5 slate 6 ballot 7 receipt, summons 8 passport, password
seller: 7 scalper

tickle
5 amuse, goose, tease, touch **6** arouse, excite, tingle **7** delight, gratify, provoke **9** stimulate, titillate

tickled
5 happy **6** amused **7** pleased **9** delighted

ticklish
5 dicey **6** tender, thorny, touchy, tricky **8** delicate, unstable **9** sensitive **10** precarious

ticklish Muppet
4 Elmo

tick off
3 ire, irk **5** anger **6** rankle **7** incense, provoke **9** aggravate

tidal flood
4 bore **5** eagre

tidbit
3 ort **4** bite **5** goody, treat **6** dainty, morsel, nugget

tide
4 bore, flow, flux, rush **5** drift, flood, spate, surge **6** stream **7** current, holiday
type: **3** ebb **4** neap **5** flood **6** spring

tidings
4 news, word **6** advice **7** message **11** information

tidy
4 neat, snug, trim **5** kempt **6** pick up **7** clean up, orderly, precise **9** shipshape **11** respectable, spic-and-span, uncluttered, well-groomed **12** spick-and-span

tie
3 rod **4** band, bind, bolo, bond, cord, gird, join, knit, knot, lash, link, moor, rope, yoke **5** equal, leash, match, truss **6** attach, clip-on, cravat, fasten, fetter, hamper, oxford, ribbon, secure **7** connect, harness, shackle **8** dead heat, deadlock, fastener, ligament, ligature, shoelace, standoff, vinculum **9** stalemate **10** four-in-hand
alternative: **5** ascot

tied
4 even **5** bound **6** joined, united **8** attached, fastened **9** connected

tier
3 row **4** bank, deck, file, line, rank **5** class, grade, story **6** league **7** echelon **8** category

tie-up
3 jam **4** snag **5** crimp, delay, hitch, snarl **6** glitch **7** problem **8** gridlock, slowdown, stoppage **10** traffic jam

tiff
3 row **4** fuss, spat **5** run-in, scrap **6** bicker, dustup **7** brabble, dispute, quarrel, wrangle **8** argument, squabble **10** falling-out **11** altercation

tiffany
5 gauze **11** cheesecloth

tiger
3 cat **6** feline **9** carnivore
young: **3** cub

tight
4 fast, firm, snug, taut, trim **5** cheap, close, fixed **6** firmly, secure, stingy **7** compact, crowded, miserly **8** intimate **9** tenacious **11** closefisted **12** cheeseparing, parsimonious

tighten
5 choke, close, cramp, pinch, screw **6** clench, narrow, secure, shrink **8** compress, restrict **9** clamp down, constrict

tight-lipped
6 silent **8** reserved, reticent, taciturn **12** close-mouthed

tightwad
5 miser, piker **7** niggard, scrooge **9** skinflint **10** cheapskate **12** penny-pincher

tile
5 plate, slate **6** domino **7** tessera **8** linoleum

till
3 hoe, sow **4** disk, plow, tend, turn, up to, work **6** before, harrow **7** cashbox, prior to **9** cultivate **12** cash register

tillable
6 arable

tillage
4 farm, land **7** culture **11** cultivation

tiller
4 helm **5** stalk **6** farmer, sprout **7** planter, steerer **9** sodbuster **10** cultivator

tilt
3 tip **4** bank, bent, bias, cant, cock, heel, lean, list, toss **5** grade, joust, level, lurch, pitch, slant, slope, speed **6** attack, charge, thrust **7** dispute, incline, leaning, recline **8** gradient

timber
3 log **4** balk, beam, stud, tree, wood **5** board, joist, plank, trees, woods **6** forest, girder, lumber, rafter **8** woodland
uncut: **8** stumpage
wolf: **4** lobo

timbre
4 tone **6** temper **7** quality **9** resonance, tone color

timbrel
4 drum **10** tambourine

Timbuktu's country
4 Mali

time
3 age, era **4** bout, date, hour, pace, span, term **5** clock, epoch, shift, space, spell, stint, tempo,

while **6** moment, period, season **7** instant, stretch **8** duration, occasion **11** opportunity
abbreviation: 3 CDT, CST, EDT, EST, MDT, MST, PDT, PST
combining form: 5 chron **6** chrono
gone by: 3 ago **4** past **9** yesterday **10** yesteryear **12** auld lang syne
long: 3 age, eon, era **4** aeon
of day: 4 dawn, dusk, noon **5** night **6** sunset **7** evening, morning, sunrise **8** daybreak, twilight **9** afternoon
olden: 4 yore **10** yesteryear
period: 3 age, day, eon, era **4** aeon, hour, week, year **5** epoch, month **6** decade, minute, moment, second **7** century, instant **9** fortnight **10** millennium
present: 3 now **5** nonce
relating to: 8 temporal
short: 5 jiffy **6** moment, second **7** instant
to come: 6 future **8** tomorrow
waste: 4 loaf **5** dally **6** loiter

time and again
3 oft **5** often **8** commonly, ofttimes **10** constantly, frequently, oftentimes, repeatedly **11** continually, over and over

Time founder
4 Luce (Henry R.) **6** Hadden (Briton)

timeless
7 ageless, eternal, unaging **8** unageing **9** atemporal, perpetual **11** everlasting

timely
6 prompt **8** punctual, suitable **9** opportune **10** seasonable

Time Machine, The
author: 5 Wells (H. G.)
race: 4 Eloi

time-out
4 rest **5** break, pause **6** hiatus, recess **7** respite **8** breather **9** interlude **12** interruption

timepiece
5 clock, watch **7** sundial **8** horologe **9** clepsydra, metronome, stopwatch **10** water clock **11** chronograph, chronometer

timetable
6 agenda, docket **7** program **8** calendar, schedule

timeworn
3 old **4** aged, hack **5** hoary, stale, trite **6** age-old **7** ancient **8** dog-eared, Noachian **9** hackneyed **10** threadbare

time zone
7 Central, Eastern, Pacific **8** Mountain

timid
3 shy **4** wary **5** chary, mousy **6** afraid **7** bashful, chicken, fearful **8** cowardly, retiring **9** diffident, trepidant **12** apprehensive, fainthearted

timidity
4 fear **7** modesty, shyness **8** meekness **9** hesitancy, reticence **10** diffidence

Timon's servant
7 Flavius

timorous
4 wary **5** timid **6** afraid, trepid **7** fearful **8** retiring **9** shrinking, tremulous **12** apprehensive

Timothy's associate
4 Paul **5** Titus

tin
mining region: 8 stannary
relating to: 7 stannic **8** stannous
sheet: 6 latten

tincture
3 dye **4** cast, hint, tint **5** color, shade, smack, stain, tinge, touch, trace **6** iodine, streak **8** colorant, dyestuff, laudanum **9** paregoric

tinder
4 punk **5** spunk **8** kindling

tine
5 point, prong, spike **6** branch

tinge
3 dye, hue **4** cast, hint, tint, tone **5** color, imbue, shade, stain, tinct, touch **8** tincture **10** intimation

tingle
5 sting **6** thrill **7** prickle **9** sensation

tinker
3 fix **4** mend, muck **5** gypsy **6** adjust, diddle, fiddle, mender, potter, putter, repair **7** bungler, twiddle

tinkle
4 ring, ting **5** chink, clink, plink **6** jingle

Tin Man's need
3 oil

tinny
4 thin **5** cheap, harsh **8** metallic

Tin Pan Alley org.
3 BMI **5** ASCAP

tinsel
5 gaudy **6** flashy, garish, tawdry **7** chintzy, glaring, trinket **8** ornament, specious **9** clinquant

tint
3 dye, hue **4** cast, tone, wash **5** color, shade, tinge, touch **8** tincture

tiny
3 wee **4** itsy **5** bitsy, bitty, elfin, micro, pygmy, weeny **6** minute, peewee, pocket, weensy **8** pint-size **9** itsy-bitsy, itty-bitty, miniature, minuscule **10** diminutive, pocket-size **11** lilliputian, microscopic **12** teensy-weensy **13** infinitesimal
amount: 3 bit, jot, tad **4** drop, iota, mite, whit **5** speck, trace **6** smidge **7** scintilla, smidgen **8** smidgeon

tip
3 cap, cue **4** apex, cant, clue, cusp, doff, hint, lean, list, peak, perk, tilt **5** point, slant, slope, steer, upset **6** advice, topple **7** cumshaw, incline **8** gratuity, overturn, turn over **9** baksheesh, lagniappe, pourboire

tip off
4 warn **5** alert

tip-off
4 clue, hint, sign **5** alert **6** advice **7** pointer, red flag, warning **8** giveaway, jump ball

Tippecanoe and ___ too
5 Tyler

tippet
4 cape **5** scarf **8** liripipe

tipple
3 bib, sip **4** swig, tope **5** booze, drink **6** guzzle, imbibe **7** swizzle

tippler
3 sot **4** lush, soak **5** drunk **6** bibber, boozer **7** tosspot **8** drunkard **9** inebriate

tipstaff
7 bailiff

tipster
4 fink, tout **6** canary, snitch **7** adviser, rat fink, stoolie, tattler **8** informer, squealer **11** stool pigeon

tipsy
3 lit **4** high **5** askew, drunk, lit up, oiled, tight **7** drunken, fuddled, sloshed **8** unsteady **10** inebriated **11** intoxicated

tiptoe
5 creep, skulk, slink, sneak, steal **9** pussyfoot

tirade
4 rant **6** screed **8** diatribe, harangue, jeremiad **9** philippic

tire
3 sap **4** bore, fail, flag, jade, pall, poop, wear **5** drain, droop, ennui, weary, wheel **6** tucker, weaken **7** exhaust, fatigue, wear out **8** enervate, wear down
airless: **4** flat **7** blowout
kind: **4** bias, snow **6** radial **7** retread **9** whitewall
pressure measure: **3** psi

tired
4 beat, limp, worn **5** spent, weary **6** bushed, done in **7** drained, run-down, worn out **8** fatigued, flagging **9** enervated, exhausted

tiredness
7 fatigue **9** lassitude **10** enervation, exhaustion **11** prostration

Tiresias
4 seer **10** soothsayer

tiresome
4 dull **6** boring **7** operose, tedious

Tirol
capital: **9** Innsbruck
country: **7** Austria
mountains: **4** Alps

tissue
3 web **4** film, mesh **5** fiber, gauze, paper **6** fabric
anatomical: **4** tela **5** fiber **6** diploe **8** ganglion **10** epithelium
connective: **4** tela **6** stroma, tendon **9** cartilage
layer: **6** dermis **7** stratum
plant: **4** bast, wood **5** xylem **6** phloem

titan
5 giant **8** colossus

Titan
father: **6** Uranus
female: **4** Rhea **6** Tethys, Themis
male: **6** Cronus **7** Iapetus, Oceanus
mother: **4** Gaea

Titania's husband
6 Oberon

titanic
4 huge, vast **5** great **6** mighty **7** immense, mammoth, massive **8** colossal, enormous, gigantic **9** cyclopean, Herculean, monstrous **10** gargantuan, tremendous

Titanic
star: **3** Leo (DiCaprio) **7** Winslet (Kate) **8** DiCaprio (Leonardo)
director: **7** Cameron (James)
line: **9** White Star
rescuing vessel: **9** Carpathia
sister ship: **7** Olympic **9** Britannic

tithe
3 tax **4** levy **5** tenth **12** contribution

titillate
6 arouse, excite, stir up, thrill, tickle **9** stimulate

title
3 dub, due **4** call, deed, dibs, name, term **5** claim, merit, nomen **7** baptize, caption, heading **8** cognomen **9** designate **10** denominate **11** appellation, appellative, designation **12** championship, compellation, denomination
academic: **4** dean, Prof. **7** provost **9** president, professor
Dutch: **7** mynheer
ecclesiastic: **3** Rev. **5** abbot **6** bishop **8** cardinal, reverend **10** archbishop
Etruscan: **3** lar
feminine: **3** Mrs. **4** dame, lady, ma'am, miss **5** madam **6** abbess, madame, milady, missus **8** mistress

French: **6** madame **8** monsieur **12** mademoiselle
German: **4** Frau, Herr **8** Fräulein
Hindu: **4** babu, raja, rani **5** baboo, rajah, ranee
holder: **5** noble **8** champion
Indian: **3** sri **5** sahib
Islamic: **4** amir, emir, imam **5** ameer, hadji, hajji **6** sayyid **9** ayatollah
Italian: **5** donna **6** signor **7** signora **9** signorina
masculine: **6** mister
monk's: **3** fra **7** brother
of nobility: **3** sir **4** duke, earl, king, lady, lord, sire **5** baron, count, queen **6** prince **7** baronet, duchess, marquis **8** Archduke, baroness, countess, marchesa, marchese, marquise, princess, viscount **11** marchioness, viscountess
Oriental: **4** khan
Persian: **5** mirza
Portuguese: **3** dom **4** dona **6** senhor **7** senhora **9** senhorita
Spanish: **3** don **4** doña
Turkish: **3** aga, bey

titmouse
4 bird **6** tomtit **7** bushtit **9** chickadee

Tito
4 Broz (Josip)

titter
6 giggle **7** chortle, chuckle, snicker, snigger

tittle
3 bit, jot **4** atom, iota, mite **5** minim, speck **6** smidge **7** smidgen, smidgin **8** particle **9** diacritic

titular
6 titled **7** nominal **8** so-called

Tityus
father: **4** Zeus
slayer: **6** Apollo

Tiu
see **Tyr**

tizzy
4 flap, fume, snit, stew **6** dither, swivet

T-man
5 agent **8** revenuer

to (Scottish)
3 tae

toad
4 agua, hyla **6** anuran, peeper **9** amphibian **10** batrachian
genus: **4** Bufo, Hyla

toady
4 fawn **5** cower, leech **6** cringe, flunky, grovel, kowtow, lackey, sponge **7** truckle **8** bootlick, parasite, truckler **9** brownnose, sycophant **10** bootlicker **11** apple-polish, lickspittle

toast
5 bread, drink, salud, singe, skoal **6** cheers, health, l'chaim, pledge, prosit, salute **7** wassail **8** mazel tov **9** celebrate
kind: **4** rusk **5** melba **8** zwieback

toastmaster
5 emcee

tobacco
4 leaf, weed
cask: **8** hogshead
chewing: **4** chaw, quid
ingredient: **8** nicotine
juice: **6** ambeer
kiln: **4** oast
kind: **4** shag **5** flake, snuff **6** burley **7** caporal, latakia, perique **9** broadleaf, mundungus
pipe: **4** heel **6** dottle
residue: **3** tar
rolled: **5** cigar **9** cigarette
Turkish: **7** latakia

to be
Latin: **4** esse

to be sure
6 indeed **7** granted **9** certainly

toby
3 jug, mug **7** pitcher

tocsin
3 SOS **5** alarm, alert **6** signal

toddler
3 tot **4** tike, tyke **6** rug rat

to-do
4 flap, fuss, rout **5** hoo-ha **6** bother, bustle, clamor, furore, hoo-hah, hubbub, pother, ruckus, rumpus, tumult, uproar **7** turmoil **8** foofaraw **9** agitation, commotion **10** hurly-burly

toe
5 digit
big: **6** hallux
combining form: **6** dactyl

toehold
7 footing

toff
3 fop **4** beau **5** blade, dandy, swell **7** coxcomb, peacock **8** macaroni, popinjay **9** exquisite

tofu bean
3 soy **4** soya

toga
4 gown, robe, wrap

together
5 as one **6** at once, joined, united **7** jointly **8** mutually **10** conjointly **12** coincidently, collectively, concurrently

toggle
3 pin **6** fasten, switch **9** alternate **10** crosspiece

Togo
capital: **4** Lomé
language: **3** Ewe
monetary unit: **5** franc

togs
3 rig **4** duds, suit **5** dress **6** attire, outfit **7** apparel, clothes, raiment, rigging, threads **8** clothing, ensemble, garments

toil
3 fag, net, tug **4** grub, plod, plug, slog, trap, work **5** grind, labor, slave, snare, sweat **6** drudge **7** slavery, travail **8** drudgery

toiler
4 peon **5** slave **6** drudge, slavey **9** workhorse

toilet
3 lav, loo **4** head, john **5** bidet, jakes, potty, privy **6** johnny **7** latrine **8** bathroom, lavatory, restroom **11** water closet

toilsome
6 uphill **7** arduous, labored **9** difficult, effortful, laborious, strenuous

token
4 buck, chip, gift, sign **5** badge, favor, plume, prize, relic, scrip **6** copper, emblem, pledge, symbol, ticket, trophy **7** earnest, gesture, memento, symptom, warrant **8** evidence, keepsake, memorial, reminder, security, souvenir **9** indicator **11** perfunctory, remembrance

To Kill a Mockingbird
author: **3** Lee (Harper)
character: **3** Boo (Radley), Jem (Finch), Tom (Robinson) **4** Dill (Harris) **5** Scout (Finch) **7** Atticus (Finch)
town: **7** Maycomb

Tokyo
formerly: **3** Edo
island: **6** Honshu

Toledo's lake
4 Erie

tolerable
4 fair, okay **6** common, decent **7** livable **8** adequate, all right, bearable, passable **9** endurable **10** acceptable, sufferable **11** respectable **12** satisfactory

tolerably
4 so-so **5** quite **6** fairly, pretty, rather **8** passably **9** averagely **10** moderately

tolerance
6 leeway **8** patience **9** allowance **10** indulgence, sufferance **11** forbearance

tolerant
7 lenient, liberal **8** placable **9** easygoing, eurytopic, forgiving, indulgent, tractable **10** open-minded, permissive **11** broad-minded, sympathetic

tolerate
4 bear, bide, hack **5** abide, allow, brook, stand **6** accept, endure, pardon, permit, suffer **7** condone, stomach, swallow **8** bear with, live with **9** put up with **11** countenance

Tolkien creature
3 Ent, Orc **4** Warg **5** Ainur, Huorn, Troll **6** Balrog, Hobbit, Nazgul, Shelob

toll
3 fee, tax **4** bell, bong, cost, levy, peal, ring **5** chime, knell, price, sound **6** charge, summon, tariff **7** expense **8** casualty **10** assessment

tollbooth
11 customhouse

Tolstoy, Leo
novel: **11** War and Peace **12** Anna Karenina

tomato
9 love apple
kind: **4** roma

tomb
5 crypt, grave **6** burial **9** mausoleum, sepulcher, sepulchre, sepulture
ancient Egyptian: **7** mastaba
empty: **8** cenotaph
Neolithic: **4** cist

tomboy
6 gamine, hoyden

Tomb Raider heroine
4 Lara

tombstone
4 slab **8** memorial, monument **11** grave marker
inscription: **3** RIP **8** hic jacet

Tombstone lawman
4 Earp (Wyatt)

tome
4 book **6** volume

tomfool
3 ass **4** dolt, fool, jerk **5** crazy, idiot, loony, ninny, silly, wacky **6** absurd, donkey, stupid **7** doltish, foolish, jackass **8** clodpoll, dummkopf, imbecile **9** blockhead, fantastic, thickhead **10** dunderhead, nincompoop

tomfoolery
4 dido, lark **5** antic, caper, prank, shine, trick **6** frolic **8** escapade, fandango **9** high jinks **10** shenanigan **11** monkeyshine

tommyrot
4 bosh, bull, bunk **5** bilge, hooey, trash **7** baloney, eyewash, hogwash, rubbish **8** claptrap, nonsense **9** poppycock **10** balderdash **13** horsefeathers

Tom o'Bedlam
3 nut **4** loon **5** loony **6** madman, maniac **7** lunatic

tomorrow
6 future, mañana

Tom Sawyer
author: 5 Twain (Mark) **7** Clemens (Samuel)
character: 5 Becky (Thatcher) **8** Huck Finn, Injun Joe **9** Aunt Polly **10** Muff Potter

Tom Thumb
4 runt **5** dwarf, pygmy **6** midget, peewee **7** manikin **8** half-pint, mannikin **10** homunculus **11** lilliputian

ton
3 lot **4** heap, load, pile, raft, scad, slew **5** bunch **6** bundle

tone
3 hue **4** cast, mode, mood, note, tint, vein **5** color, pitch, shade, sound, style, tinge **6** accent, manner, spirit, strain, temper, timbre **7** fashion **10** inflection

toned
3 cut, fit **4** buff, firm, trim **6** buffed **7** defined **8** muscular

toned down
5 muted, quiet, sober **6** low-key, mellow **7** subdued **8** laid-back, low-keyed, softened **10** restrained **11** understated

Tonga
capital: 9 Nuku'alofa
explorer: 4 Cook (Capt. James) **6** Tasman (Abel)
monetary unit: 6 pa'anga

tongue
4 lick, pole, tang **6** glossa, lingua, speech **7** clapper, dialect, languet **8** language **10** vernacular
combining form: 4 glot **5** gloss, lingu **6** glossa, glosso, lingua, lingui, linguo **7** glossia

tongue-lash
4 lash, rail **5** chide, scold **6** berate, rebuke, revile **7** bawl out, chew out, tell off, reprove, upbraid **8** admonish, call down, reproach **9** castigate, reprimand **10** vituperate

tongue-lashing
6 rebuke, tirade **7** censure, reproof **8** scolding **9** reprimand, talking-to **11** castigation **12** dressing-down

tongue-tied
3 mum, shy **4** mute **6** silent **7** bashful **9** diffident **10** speechless **12** inarticulate

tonic
3 pop **4** cola, soda **5** brisk **7** bracing, soda pop **8** curative, salutary **10** refreshing **11** restorative, stimulating **12** exhilarating, invigorating
extract: 4 cola **9** berberine

Tonight Show host
4 Leno (Jay), Paar (Jack) **5** Allen (Steve) **6** Fallon (Jimmy), O'Brien (Conan)

tons
4 gobs, lots **5** heaps, loads, piles, reams, scads **6** oodles

tony
4 chic, posh **5** smart, swank, swish **6** classy, modish, uptown **7** à la mode, elegant, stylish **9** exclusive **11** fashionable

too
4 also, ever, over, very **5** along **6** as well, overly, unduly, withal **7** awfully, besides, further, greatly **8** likewise, moreover, overmuch **9** extremely, immensely **10** in addition, remarkably, strikingly **11** exceedingly, excessively, furthermore

toodle-oo
4 by-by, ciao, ta-ta **6** bye-bye, so long **7** cheerio

tool
4 pawn **5** means **6** puppet, rimmer, stooge **7** cat's-paw, hayfork, machine, rounder, utensil **8** picklock **9** appliance, implement, mechanism **10** instrument
axlike: 3 adz **4** adze
boring: 5 auger, drill
carving: 6 veiner
cleaving: 4 froe
cobbler's: 3 awl
cooper's: 3 adz **4** adze
cutting: 3 adz, axe, saw **4** adze **5** edger, knife **6** shears **8** billhook
digging: 4 pick **5** spade **6** shovel **7** mattock
engraving: 5 burin
farm: 6 seeder
filing: 4 rasp **7** riffler
garden: 3 hoe **4** rake **5** spade **6** trowel, weeder
grasping: 6 pincer **7** tweezer **8** tweezers
mining: 3 gad **6** trepan
piercing: 3 awl
prehistoric: 6 eolith
pruning: 6 shears **9** secateurs
rubbing: 9 burnisher
scooping: 6 router
toothed: 3 saw **7** rippler
twisting: 6 wrench **7** spanner
woodworking: 3 adz, saw **4** adze **5** bevel, plane **6** chisel, hammer

toon frame
3 cel

toot
3 bat, jag **4** bout, bust, honk, tear **5** binge, blast, drunk, snort, sound, souse, spree **6** bender **7** carouse

tooth
5 molar **7** incisor **8** bicuspid, premolar
combining form: 4 dent **5** denti, dento
cuspid: 6 canine **8** dogtooth, eyetooth
cutting: 10 carnassial
decay: 6 caries
doctor: 7 dentist

gear: **3** cog
horse: **4** tush
material: **4** pulp **6** dentin, enamel **8** cementum
pointed: **4** fang **6** canine, cuspid
small: **8** denticle

toothless
7 useless **8** edentate **10** edentulous **11** ineffective, ineffectual

toothpaste endorser
3 ADA

toothsome
5 sapid, tasty **6** delish, savory **8** luscious, pleasant, pleasing, tasteful **9** agreeable, delicious, palatable, succulent **10** appetizing, attractive **11** scrumptious

too-too
6 la-di-da **7** extreme **8** affected, overdone, overmuch, precious **9** excessive **10** hoity-toity, inordinate **11** exaggerated, overrefined, pretentious

Toots ____
4 Shor

tootsie
3 pet **4** dear **5** honey, sugar **7** beloved, darling, sweetie **10** sweetheart, sweetie pie

top
3 cap **4** acme, apex, best, cusp, head, peak, roof **5** cream, crest, crown, elite, point, prime **6** apical, choice, climax, height, summit, utmost, vertex **7** capital, dreidel, highest, maximal, maximum, surface **8** five-star, loftiest, pinnacle, superior **9** first-rate, uppermost **10** first-class **11** culmination

tope
3 nip **4** soak **5** booze, drink, shark, stupa **6** guzzle, imbibe, tipple **7** swizzle **8** liquor up

toper
3 sot **4** lush, soak, wino **5** drunk, rummy, souse **6** bibber, boozer **7** tippler, tosspot **8** drunkard **9** inebriate **10** boozehound

Tophet
4 hell **5** hades, Sheol **6** blazes **7** Gehenna, inferno **9** perdition **10** underworld

topic
5 issue, motif, point, score, theme **6** burden, matter, motive, thread **7** content, subject

topical
5 local **7** current, nominal **8** regional **9** temporary **11** superficial

topmost
7 highest, leading, supreme **8** crowning, ultimate **9** paramount, principal **10** consummate, preeminent

top-notch
4 A-one **5** elite, prime, primo **6** choice, grade A **7** capital **8** five-star, superior **9** excellent, first-rate **10** first-class **11** first-string

top off
3 cap **5** crown **6** climax, finish, refill **8** complete, conclude, resupply **9** culminate

topple
3 tip **4** drop, fall **5** crash, lurch, pitch, slump, upset **6** defeat, falter, plunge, totter **8** collapse, keel over, overturn **9** overthrow

tops
4 A-one, best **5** primo **6** at most **7** highest, supreme **8** peerless, superior **9** at the most, first-rate, matchless, nonpareil **11** outstanding

topsy-turvy
7 chaotic, jumbled, mixed-up **8** cockeyed, confused, inverted **10** disjointed, disordered, upside down

toque
3 cap, hat

tor
4 crag, hill, peak **5** butte, cliff, mound, talus

Torah
10 Pentateuch

torch
4 fire **5** flame, light **6** ignite **7** firebug **8** arsonist, flambeau, guidance **10** flashlight

toreador
6 torero **7** matador **11** bullfighter

torero
see **toreador**

torment
3 rag, vex **4** bait, bane, hell, pain, pang, rack **5** abuse, agony, curse, grill, harry, tease, wring **6** harass, harrow, heckle, misery, molest, needle, plague **7** afflict, agonize, anguish, bedevil, crucify, distort, hagride, torture, travail **8** distress **9** persecute, tantalize **10** affliction, excruciate

Tormé of song
3 Mel

torn
4 rent **5** split **6** ragged, ripped, unsure **7** mangled **8** tattered, wrenched **9** lacerated, uncertain, undecided

tornado
6 funnel **7** cyclone, twister **9** windstorm, whirlwind

toro
4 bull

torpedo
3 gun, ray **4** thug **5** blast, bravo, smash, wreck **6** gunman, gunsel, hit man, killer, weapon **7** destroy, nullify, scuttle **8** assassin **10** hatchet man, projectile, triggerman

torpid
4 dull, lazy, numb **5** dopey, inert **6** sodden, stupid **7** dormant **8** comatose, inactive, sluggish **9** apathetic, lethargic

torpor
4 coma, daze **5** swoon **6** apathy, stupor **7** inertia, languor **8** dopiness, dullness, hebetude, lethargy **9** lassitude, passivity, stolidity **10** stagnation **12** listlessness

torque
5 twist

torrent
4 rush **5** flood, spate **6** deluge, stream **7** cascade, Niagara **8** cataract, flooding **9** cataclysm **10** inundation, outpouring

torrid
3 hot **5** fiery **6** ardent, fervid, heated, red-hot, sultry **7** boiling, burning, flaming, parched **8** broiling, white-hot **9** scorching **10** hot-blooded, passionate, sweltering

tort
5 crime, wrong **7** offense **10** wrongdoing

tortilla dish
4 taco **6** flauta **7** burrito, chalupa, tostada **9** enchilada **10** quesadilla **11** chimichanga

tortoise
6 turtle **8** terrapin **9** chelonian
beak: **3** neb
shell: **8** carapace

tortuous
5 snaky **6** tricky **7** crooked, devious, sinuous, winding **8** flexuous, involute, involved **9** meandrous **10** circuitous, convoluted, meandering, serpentine **11** anfractuous, vermiculate **12** labyrinthine

torture
4 rack, warp **5** agony, wring **6** harrow, martyr **7** afflict, agonize, anguish, crucify **9** martyrdom **10** excruciate **11** third degree

tortured
4 bent **6** racked, warped **7** twisted **8** deformed **9** distorted

tory
5 right **7** old-line **8** loyalist, old guard, orthodox, rightist, royalist **12** conservative

Tosca
character: **5** Mario (Cavaradossi) **7** Scarpia (Baron)
composer: **7** Puccini (Giacomo)

tosh
3 rot **4** bosh, bunk **5** bilge, hooey **6** bunkum, drivel, humbug **7** baloney, eyewash, hogwash, twaddle **8** malarkey, nonsense, tommyrot, trumpery

toss
4 cast, flap, flip, hurl, rock **5** bandy, chuck, drink, fling, heave, match, pitch, quaff, sling, surge, throw, vomit **6** imbibe, tumble, welter, writhe **7** discard **9** throw away

tosspot
see **tippler**

tot
3 add, kid, nip, sum **4** dram, shot, slug, tike, tyke **5** child, snort **6** figure, infant, nipper, shaver, squirt **7** snifter, toddler

total
3 add, all, sum **4** full **5** add up, equal, gross, in all, run to, smash, sum to, utter, whole, wreck, yield **6** all-out, amount, entire, figure, number **7** crack up, destroy, overall, perfect, quantum **8** absolute, complete, demolish, entirety, outright, quantity **9** aggregate, full-blown, full-scale, inclusive, unlimited

totalitarian
8 absolute, despotic **10** autocratic **11** dictatorial **13** authoritarian

totality
3 all, sum **4** lump **5** whole **7** oneness **8** entirety **9** aggregate, wholeness **12** completeness

totalize
3 add, sum **5** sum up **6** figure **7** summate

tote
3 lug **4** cart, haul, load, pack **5** carry, ferry, shlep, sum up **6** burden, convey, figure, schlep, shlepp **7** schlepp, summate **9** transport **10** pari-mutuel

totem
6 emblem, symbol

totter
4 reel, sway **5** lurch, shake, waver **6** falter, toddle, topple, wobble **7** stagger

touch
3 dab, tad **4** abut, feel, meet, move, stir **5** brush, graze **6** adjoin, border, caress, finger, stroke **7** contact, palpate, smidgen **9** palpation, tactility

touchable
7 tactile **8** palpable, tangible

touch down
4 land **5** light, perch, roost **6** alight, settle

touched
3 odd, off **5** batty, crazy, moved **7** stirred **8** affected **9** emotional
down: **4** alit

touching
4 as to, in re **5** anent, as for **6** moving, tender **7** apropos, emotive, piteous, pitiful, tangent **8** abutting, adjacent, pitiable, poignant **9** adjoining, affecting, apropos of, as regards, bordering, immediate, impinging, regarding **10** back-to-back, concerning, contiguous, respecting, tangential **11** coterminous

touch off
5 erupt, spark, start **6** ignite, incite, kindle

7 explode, inflame, provoke, trigger **8** initiate **9** instigate **11** precipitate

touchstone
4 test **5** check, gauge, proof, trial **7** measure **8** standard **9** barometer, benchmark, criterion, yardstick

touch up
3 fix **5** patch **6** rework **7** improve, perfect

touchy
5 dicey, huffy, risky, testy **6** tender, tricky **7** peppery **8** delicate, ticklish **9** explosive, hazardous, irascible, irritable, sensitive **10** precarious **11** inflammable, quarrelsome, thin-skinned **13** oversensitive, temperamental

tough
3 mug **4** goon, hard, hood, lout, punk, thug **5** bully, hardy, harsh **6** rugged, severe **7** arduous, hoodlum, onerous, ruffian **8** bullyboy, hooligan, obdurate **9** arbitrary, demanding, difficult, effortful, hard-nosed, hidebound, laborious, resistant, strenuous **10** hard-bitten, hard-boiled, hardheaded, refractory

toughen
5 inure **6** anneal, harden, temper **9** acclimate, habituate **10** strengthen

toughie
4 goon, hood, lout, punk, thug **5** poser, rowdy **7** hoodlum, ruffian, stumper **8** bullyboy, hooligan, plug-ugly **9** roughneck

toupee
3 rug, wig **6** peruke, wiglet **7** periwig **8** postiche **9** hairpiece

tour
4 bout, trip, turn **5** jaunt, round, shift, spell, stint **6** junket, period, travel, troupe **7** circuit, journey **8** progress **9** barnstorm, excursion **10** expedition, rubberneck

tour de force
4 deed, feat **7** classic, display, exploit **10** magnum opus, masterwork **11** achievement, chef d'oeuvre, masterpiece

Tour de France winner
4 Riis (Bjarne) **5** Roche (Stephen) **6** Fignon (Laurent), Landis (Floyd), LeMond (Greg), Merckx (Eddy), Sastre (Carlos) **7** Delgado (Pedro), Hinault (Bernard), Pantani (Marco), Pereiro (Oscar), Ullrich (Jan) **8** Anquetil (Jacques), Contador (Alberto), Induráin (Miguel) **9** Armstrong (Lance)

tour guide
8 cicerone

tourist
7 tripper, visitor **8** traveler **9** sightseer, traveller **10** day-tripper, rubberneck, vacationer **12** excursionist, globe-trotter

tournament
4 meet, tilt **5** pro-am **6** jousts **7** contest **8** carousel **10** round-robin **11** competition **12** championship

tourney
4 meet **5** event, games, match **7** contest **8** concours **11** competition

tousle
4 mess, muss **6** rumple **8** dishevel, disorder

tout
3 spy, tip **4** brag, hype, laud, plug **5** watch **6** blow up, peddle, praise, talk up **7** acclaim, crack up, promote, solicit **8** ballyhoo, persuade, proclaim **9** publicize

tovarich
7 comrade

tow
3 lug, tug **4** drag, draw, haul, pull, rope, yarn **5** chain, trail **6** hawser
truck: **7** wrecker

towel word
3 his **4** hers

tower
4 loom **5** spire **6** turret **8** overlook
biblical: **4** Edar **5** Babel
mosque: **7** minaret

towering
4 high, tall **5** lofty **6** aerial **7** soaring **8** imposing, majestic **10** monumental **11** skyscraping **12** altitudinous

towhee
5 finch **7** chewink

to wit
3 viz **6** namely, that is **8** scilicet **9** c'est-à-dire, videlicet

town
4 burg **6** hamlet, podunk **7** borough, village
medieval: **5** bourg

town and ___
4 gown **7** country

townsman
7 burgher, citizen

town square
5 plaza
Italian: **6** piazza

toxic
6 poison **7** harmful, noxious **8** venomous, virulent **9** poisonous **10** infectious

toxin
5 venom **6** poison

toy
3 top **4** fool, play, yo-yo **5** antic, curio, dally, flirt, knack, mouse, tease **6** bauble, caress, coquet, diddle, fiddle, gewgaw, puzzle, rattle, Slinky, trifle

7 bibelot, Frisbee, foot bag, novelty, pastime, trinket, whatnot **8** gimcrack **9** plaything, pogo stick **10** diminutive, knickknack, Silly Putty, sock monkey, Spirograph, View-Master **11** jumping jack **12** kaleidoscope
block: 4 Lego

Toyota-GM line
3 Geo

trace
3 jot, ray, run, tug **4** blip, echo, hint, iota, mark, path, scan, wisp **5** relic, shade, spoor, tinge, trail, tread **6** derive, detect, nuance, shadow, strain, streak **7** outline, remnant, run down, soupçon, vestige **8** discover, tincture, traverse **9** delineate, footprint, remainder, scintilla, suspicion **10** intimation, suggestion

trachea
6 larynx, throat, vessel **7** weasand **8** throttle, windpipe

track
3 way **4** drag, oval, path, rail, road, sign, slot, step, tail **5** chase, cover, print, spoor, trace, trail, tread **6** artery, follow, pursue, shadow, travel **7** footway, imprint, monitor, pathway, vestige **8** footpath, footstep **9** footprint **10** racecourse
circuit: 3 lap
cycle: 9 velodrome
deer: 4 slot

track-and-field event
4 dash **5** relay **6** discus **7** javelin, hurdles, shot put **8** footrace, high jump, long jump **9** broad jump, decathlon, pole vault **10** heptathlon, triple jump **11** discus throw **12** steeplechase

track star
3 Coe (Sebastian) **4** Bolt (Usain) **5** Flo-Jo, Jones (Marion), Lewis (Carl), Moses (Edwin), Nurmi (Paavo), Ovett (Steve), Owens (Jesse), Viren (Lasse) **6** Beamon (Bob), Jenner (Bruce), Oerter (Al), Thorpe (Jim) **7** Fosbury (Dick), Johnson (Michael, Rafer), Mathias (Bob), Rudolph (Wilma), Shorter (Frank), Zátopek (Emil) **8** Thompson (Daley), Zaharias (Babe Didrikson) **9** Bannister (Roger), Didrikson (Babe)

tract
3 lot **4** area, belt, land, plat, plot, zone **6** parcel **7** leaflet, portion, terrain **8** pamphlet, preserve **9** territory

tractable
4 tame **6** docile, gentle, pliant **7** ductile, plastic, pliable **8** amenable, biddable, flexible, obedient, workable **9** adaptable, malleable **10** manageable

tractate
5 summa **6** memoir, thesis **7** pandect **8** hornbook, monument, treatise **9** discourse, monograph **10** commentary

traction
4 drag, pull **5** force **7** drawing, tension **8** friction

tractor maker
4 Case **5** Deere (John) **6** Kubota **7** Farmall

trade
4 deal, sell, swap **5** craft, truck **6** barter, change, custom, market, métier, peddle, switch **7** bargain, calling, pursuit, traffic **8** business, commerce, exchange, industry, vocation **10** employment, occupation, profession, substitute **11** merchandise, transaction
illicit: 11 black market

trademark
3 tag **4** logo **5** brand, label, stamp **6** patent, symbol **8** colophon, logotype **9** brand name

trader
4 ship **6** broker, dealer, vendor **8** merchant

trade route
7 sea-lane

trade show
4 expo **10** exhibition, exposition

tradition
4 lore **6** belief, custom, legacy, legend **7** folkway **8** folklore, heritage, practice **10** convention

traditional
5 usual **7** classic, old-line **8** habitual, orthodox **9** classical, customary, old-school, unwritten **11** established **12** conservative, conventional

traditionalist
4 tory **6** purist **7** old-line **8** orthodox, standpat **12** conservative

traduce
4 slur **5** libel, smear, wrong **6** betray, breach, defame, malign, vilify **7** asperse, slander, violate **8** disgrace, tear down **9** denigrate **10** calumniate

Trafalgar commander
6 Nelson (Horatio)

traffic
4 deal **5** cargo, fence, trade, truck **6** barter, custom **7** bootleg, freight **8** commerce, dealings, exchange **9** patronage, transport **11** black-market
circle: 6 rotary **10** roundabout
cone: 5 pylon
jam: 5 tie-up **6** holdup **8** blockage, gridlock **10** bottleneck

trafficker
6 dealer, trader

tragedy
3 woe **8** calamity, disaster **9** cataclysm **10** misfortune **11** catastrophe

trail
3 dog, lag, tag **4** drag, flag, path, plod, poke **5** chase, dally, delay, tarry, trace, track **6** dawdle,

follow, linger, pursue, shadow **7** draggle, gumshoe, pathway, traipse **8** footpath, footwalk **10** bridle path
Florida: **7** Tamiami
Georgia-Maine: **11** Appalachian
mix: **4** gorp

trailer
5 truck **6** teaser **7** preview **9** motor home, transport **10** mobile home

trailer truck
3 rig **4** semi **6** big rig

train
5 coach, drill, teach, track **6** column, convoy, course, school, sequel, series, thread **7** caravan, cortege, educate, prepare, retinue **8** exercise, instruct, sequence **9** entourage, following, habituate **10** succession **11** progression
fast: **5** Acela

trainee
4 tiro, tyro **5** cadet **6** novice **7** learner **8** beginner, neophyte **10** apprentice

training
7 tuition **8** tutelage **9** education **11** instruction
horse: **6** manège

traipse
3 gad **4** hoof, pace, roam, rove, step, walk **5** amble, range, trail, tramp, tread **6** ramble, stroll, wander **7** maunder, meander **8** ambulate **9** gallivant

trait
4 mark **5** quirk, touch, trace **6** oddity, stroke **7** feature, quality **8** hallmark, specific **9** attribute

traitor
3 rat **5** Judas **8** apostate, betrayer, defector, deserter, quisling, renegade, turncoat **9** turnabout

traitorous
5 Punic **8** apostate, disloyal, mutinous, recreant, renegade **9** faithless **10** perfidious, rebellious, unfaithful

trajectory
3 arc **4** path **5** curve **11** progression

tram
7 trolley **9** streetcar

trammel
3 tie **4** bind, curb **5** check, gauge, leash **6** fetter, hamper, hobble **7** compass, confine, ensnare, manacle, pothook, shackle **8** entangle, handcuff **9** restraint

tramontane
8 outsider **9** foreigner, outlander **11** transalpine

tramp
3 bum **4** hike, hobo, jade, plod, slog **5** bimbo, caird, clump, gipsy, gypsy, march, stamp, stomp, tread **6** ramble, stroll, travel, trudge, wander **7** chippie, drifter, floater, saunter, traipse, vagrant **8** clochard, derelict, footslog, stroller, vagabond, wanderer

trample
4 mash **5** crush, pound, stamp, stomp, tread, tromp

trance
4 daze, muse **5** swoon **7** ecstasy, rapture, reverie **8** hypnosis **9** catalepsy, enrapture **10** absorption, brown study

tranquil
4 calm **5** quiet, still **6** dreamy, placid, poised, serene **7** restful **8** composed, peaceful **10** untroubled

tranquilize
4 calm, hush, lull **5** quiet, relax, still **6** becalm, pacify, sedate, settle, soothe, subdue **7** compose, mollify

tranquilizer
6 downer **8** diazepam, pacifier, sedative **10** depressant **11** barbiturate

tranquillity
4 calm **5** peace, quiet **8** calmness, serenity **9** composure, placidity

transaction
4 deal **5** trade **7** bargain, dealing **8** contract, covenant **9** agreement

transcend
3 top **4** beat, best **5** excel, outdo **6** better, exceed **7** surpass **8** outshine, outstrip, overcome, surmount

transcendent
5 ideal **7** perfect, sublime, supreme **8** abstract, immanent **10** consummate, surpassing

Transcendentalist
6 Alcott (Bronson), Fuller (Margaret) **7** Emerson (Ralph Waldo), Thoreau (Henry David)

transcribe
4 copy **5** write **6** record **9** write down

transfer
4 cede, deed, hand, pass, ship **5** carry, grant, shift **6** assign, convey, remove, supply **7** consign, convert, deliver, devolve, dispose **8** alienate, hand over, make over, relocate, turn over **9** carry over **10** assignment, conveyance **11** disposition

transfix
3 pin **4** spit **5** lance, rivet, spear, spike, stick **6** impale, skewer **7** spindle **8** entrance **9** fascinate, hypnotize, mesmerize

transform
5 alter, morph **6** change, mutate **7** commute, convert **12** metamorphose

transformation
8 reaction **10** changeover, conversion **13** metamorphosis

transfuse
5 endue, imbue 7 pervade, suffuse, traject 8 permeate, saturate 9 penetrate, percolate 10 impregnate

transgress
3 err, sin 6 breach, exceed, offend 7 violate 8 infringe, overpass, overstep, trespass

transgression
3 sin 5 crime, error, lapse, wrong 6 breach 7 misdeed, offense 9 violation 12 infringement

transient
4 hobo 5 brief, tramp 7 drifter, migrant, passing 8 fleeting, flitting, fugitive, volatile 9 ephemeral, fugacious, momentary, temporary 10 evanescent, fly-by-night, short-lived

transit
7 passage 8 traverse
loss allowance: 4 tret

transition
4 cusp, leap 5 morph, segue, shift 6 change 7 passage 10 conversion

transitory
see **transient**

translate
6 render 7 convert 10 paraphrase

translation
10 conversion

transmarine
7 oversea 8 overseas

transmission
7 gearbox 8 handover 9 broadcast, infection

transmit
3 air 4 beam, hand, pass, pipe, send 6 convey, hand on, impart, pass on, render, signal 7 channel, conduct, consign, diffuse, forward, traject 8 bequeath, dispatch, hand down 9 broadcast

transmogrify
see **transform**

transmute
see **transform**

transoceanic message
4 wire 5 cable 9 cablegram

transparent
5 clear, filmy, gauzy, sheer 6 limpid 8 clear-cut, gossamer, pellucid 10 diaphanous, see-through

transpire
4 leak 5 exude, occur, sweat 6 chance, emerge, happen 7 develop 9 come about, take place 11 come to light

transplant
6 ecesis 8 relocate, resettle

transport
3 bus, fly, lag, lug, zap, zip 4 haul, hump, lift, pack, pass, send, ship, taxi, tote 5 carry, ferry, motor, truck 6 convey, ravish, remove, thrill 7 delight, ecstasy, freight, rapture, sealift, trundle, vehicle 8 carriage, displace, railroad, rhapsody 9 carry away, troopship 10 conveyance, helicopter

transportation
6 moving 7 freight, hauling, vehicle 8 carriage, carrying 10 conveyance

transpose
6 invert 7 convert, permute, reorder 9 rearrange 11 interchange

transude
4 ooze, reek, seep, weep 5 bleed, sweat 7 diffuse, give off 8 permeate

transverse
5 cross 6 across, lintel, thwart 8 crossbar, crossing 9 crossbeam, crosswise 10 crosspiece

trap
3 bag, gin, net 4 bait, snag 5 catch, decoy, set up, snare 6 ambush, enmesh, tangle 7 ensnare, pitfall 8 birdlime, deadfall, entangle, quagmire

trappings
4 gear 6 finery 8 equipage 9 caparison, equipment 11 habiliments 13 accouterments, accoutrements, paraphernalia

Trappist
4 monk
writer: 6 Merton (Thomas)

trash
3 rag, rot 4 bosh, bunk, junk, ruin, scum, slop 5 bilge, blast, dreck, dregs, hokum, offal, spoil, tripe, waste, wreck 6 bunkum, debris, litter, refuse, rubble 7 clutter, destroy, garbage, hogwash, put down, rubbish 8 claptrap, malarkey, nonsense, tommyrot 9 disparage, poppycock, throw away, vandalize 10 balderdash 11 guttersnipe
barge: 4 scow

trash can
7 dustbin

trashy
5 cheap, tatty 6 cruddy, shoddy, sleazy 8 rubbishy

trattoria course
5 pasta

trauma
4 blow, pain 5 shock, wound 6 crisis, injury, stress

travail
4 grub, moil, task, toil, work 5 grind, labor, pains 6 drudge, effort 7 slavery, torment 8 drudgery, struggle

travel
4 fare, pass, roam, tour, trek, trip, wend 5 jaunt, range, tramp 6 junket, push on, voyage 7 explore, journey, passage, proceed, traffic, transit 8 movement, traverse 9 gallivant 10 hit the road

traveler
5 gipsy, gypsy, nomad, rover 7 drifter, drummer, tourist, trekker, voyager 8 explorer, runabout, runagate, salesman, vagabond, wayfarer 9 itinerant, sightseer, transient 10 journeyman 11 peripatetic

traveler's need
4 visa 8 passport

traveling library
10 bookmobile

traverse
4 ride, span, walk 5 cover, cross, march, trace, track 6 course, travel, voyage 7 examine, transit 8 crossing, navigate, pass over

travesty
3 ape 4 mock, sham 5 farce, mimic, spoof 6 parody 7 imitate, lampoon, mimicry, mockery, take off 8 ridicule 9 burlesque 10 caricature, distortion
satanic: 9 Black Mass

Traviata, La
character: 7 Alfredo (Germont), Germont (Giorgio) 8 Violetta (Valéry)
composer: 5 Verdi (Giuseppe)

trawl
3 net 4 fish 7 setline

tray
6 salver, server 7 platter 8 teaboard
revolving: 9 lazy Susan

treacherous
5 false, Punic, risky 6 chancy, tricky 8 disloyal, perilous, recreant 9 deceptive, faithless, hazardous, insidious 10 perfidious, traitorous, unfaithful, unreliable

treachery
7 perfidy, treason 8 bad faith, betrayal 9 duplicity 10 disloyalty, infidelity 11 double-cross 13 double-dealing

treacle
4 mush 5 slush, syrup 6 bathos 8 molasses, schmaltz

tread
4 hoof, pace, plod, step, walk 5 march, stamp, stomp, trace, track, tramp, tromp, troop 6 stride 7 footing, traipse, trample 8 footstep

treadle
5 lever, pedal

treadmill
3 rut 4 rote 5 chore, grind 6 groove 7 routine 8 drudgery, turnspit

treason
7 perfidy 8 betrayal, sedition 9 treachery 10 disloyalty, misprision 11 lèse-majesté

treasure
4 haul, loot, save, swag 5 adore, booty, cache, hoard, pearl, prize, trove, value 6 esteem, revere, riches, wealth 7 apprize, cherish, idolize, worship 8 conserve, preserve, venerate 9 reverence 10 appreciate

Treasure Island
author: 9 Stevenson (Robert Louis)
character: 7 Ben Gunn 8 Long John (Silver)
narrator: 10 Jim Hawkins

treasurer
6 bursar, purser 7 curator 8 receiver 11 chamberlain

Treasure State
7 Montana

treasure trove
7 bonanza, pay dirt 8 El Dorado, Golconda, gold mine

treasury
4 fisc, mine 5 cache, chest, hoard 6 argosy, coffer, museum 7 bonanza, gallery 8 El Dorado, Golconda, gold mine, war chest 9 exchequer 10 depositary, depository, repository

treat
5 goody, nurse 6 bonbon, dainty, doctor, goodie, handle, manage, morsel, tidbit 7 care for 8 deal with, delicacy, medicate 10 minister to
animals: 3 vet
leather: 3 tan, taw 7 tanning

treatise
6 thesis 8 tractate 9 discourse, monograph 12 disquisition, dissertation

treatment
4 care 7 therapy

treaty
4 pact 6 accord 7 charter, compact, concord 8 alliance, contract, covenant 9 agreement, concordat 10 convention

treble
4 high 6 shrill, triple 7 descant, soprano 9 threefold 11 high-pitched

tree
3 apa, ash, box, dao, dar, elm, eng, fir, koa, kou, lin, oak, sal, ule, yew 4 ague, atle, copa, dhak, kaki, lime, linn, mora, mugo, neem, pine, poon, sorb, tawa, teak, teil, titi, tung, upas, wych, yate 5 aalii, abele, alamo, alder, athel, beech, birch, carob, cedar, ebony, holly, larch, lemon, maire, maple, mugho, osier, pipal, roble, rowan, sauch, saugh, sumac, taxus, yulan 6 arbute, banyan, cherry, cornel, deodar, ginkgo, kamala, linden, loquat, lychee, mallee, medlar, mimosa, myrtle, orange, poplar, redbud, sapota, spruce, tan oak, tupelo 7 arariba, arbutus, camphor, catalpa, conifer, cypress, deodara, dogwood, hemlock, inkwood, juniper, kumquat, lentisk, madrona, madrone, murmast, redwood, sequoia, seringa, wallaba, zelkova 8 basswood, bergamot, black gum, bluejack, cinchona, corkwood, laburnum, loblolly, longleaf, magnolia, mahogany, sourwood,

sweetgum, sycamine, sycamore, tamarisk **9** balsam fir, sassafras **10** candlewood, chinaberry, chinquapin **11** bald cypress **12** rhododendron
African: **4** akee, cola, shea **5** limba, sassy **6** baobab **7** avodire, bubinga **8** sasswood **9** berberine
Australian: **4** toon, yate **5** wilga **7** blue gum **8** lacewood, quandong **9** casuarina **10** eucalyptus **11** bottlebrush
branch: **5** bough
combining form: **3** dry **4** dryo **5** arbor, dendr **6** arbori, dendra (plural), dendro
genus: **4** Acer, Cola, Maba, Olea, Para **5** Abies **11** Callistemon
miniature: **6** bonsai
palm: **4** coco, nipa **5** ratan **6** pinang, raffia, rattan **7** coquito **8** carnauba
tropical: **3** ake, ama **4** akee, copa, dita, ohia, palm, pili, sago, teak, upas, yaya **5** areca, assai, balsa, cacao, ceiba, cycad, lehua, mamey **6** acajou, balata, baobab, bataan, citrus **7** genipap, logwood, majagua, palmyra, quassia, soursop **8** allspice, barbasco, mahogany, mangrove, milkwood, palmetto, rosewood, soapbark, sweetsop, tamarind **9** candlenut, jacaranda, sapodilla **10** breadfruit, calamondin, manchineel **11** candleberry, coconut palm
trunk: **4** bole
young: **7** sapling

tree creature
3 ent **5** dryad

tree house
4 aery, nest **5** aerie, eyrie

tree juice
3 sap

tree trunk
4 bole

trefoil
4 leaf **6** clover **8** ornament
part: **3** arc

trek
4 hike **6** trudge **7** journey **9** migration **10** expedition

trellis
5 arbor **6** screen **7** lattice, pergola **8** espalier **11** latticework

tremble
5 quake, shake **6** dither, quaver, quiver, shiver **7** shudder, twitter, vibrate

tremblor
see **temblor**

tremendous
4 huge, vast **6** mighty **7** awesome, immense, massive, titanic **8** colossal, enormous, fearsome, gigantic, terrific, towering **9** fantastic, monstrous **10** formidable, gargantuan, incredible, monumental, prodigious, stupendous **13** extraordinary

tremolo
7 vibrato

tremor
5 quake, shake, shock **6** quaver, quiver, shiver **7** shudder, temblor **10** earthquake
muscular: **8** dystaxia

tremulous
5 shaky **7** aquiver, quaking, shivery **9** quivering, shivering

trench
4 sink **5** ditch, fosse, gully, verge **6** border, furrow, trough
Caribbean: **6** Cayman
Pacific: **7** Mariana

trenchant
4 acid, keen **5** acerb, crisp, sharp **6** biting **7** acerbic, caustic, cutting, mordant, probing, satiric **8** incisive, sardonic, scathing **9** sarcastic

trencher
4 tray **7** platter

trencherman
5 eater **7** glutton **8** gourmand

trend
3 fad **4** mode **5** curve, drift, shift, style, swing, vogue **6** course **7** current, fashion, incline **8** movement, tendency **9** direction

trendy
3 hep, hip, hot **4** chic, cool, tony **5** faddy **6** groovy, modish, with-it **7** à la mode, faddish, stylish **8** downtown, nouvelle, up-to-date **11** fashionable, ultramodern

trepang
10 bêche-de-mer **11** sea cucumber

trepidation
4 fear **5** alarm, dread **6** dismay, unease **7** anxiety **12** apprehension

trespass
3 err, sin **4** debt **5** lapse, poach **6** breach, invade, offend **7** impinge, intrude **8** encroach, entrench, infringe **9** interlope **10** transgress

tress
4 curl, lock **5** braid, plait

trestle
4 buck **5** frame **6** bridge **7** sawbuck, support **8** sawhorse **9** framework

trey
5 three

triad
4 trio **5** chord **6** triple, troika **7** harmony, trinity **9** threesome **11** triumvirate

trial
3 woe **4** test **5** cross, rigor, worry **6** dry run, hassle, misery, ordeal, tryput **7** anguish, attempt,

contest, trouble **8** crucible, distress, gauntlet, hardship, struggle, vexation **9** adversity, rehearsal, suffering **10** affliction, coup d'essai, difficulty, experiment, misfortune, proceeding, temptation **11** preliminary, tribulation

trial balloon
6 feeler, tryout

trial run
4 test **5** essay **7** break-in **10** experiment

triangle type
5 acute, delta, right **6** obtuse **7** scalene **9** isosceles **11** equilateral

triangular sail
3 jib

tribal unit
6 moiety **7** phratry

tribe
4 clan, folk, race **5** house, phyle, stock **6** family **7** kindred, lineage
(see also **Indian, American**)

tribulation
3 woe **5** cross, trial **6** burden, ordeal **9** adversity **10** affliction

tribunal
3 bar **4** dais, rota **5** bench, court **10** consistory

tributary
5 bayou, creek **6** branch, feeder, stream **8** influent **9** backwater, confluent, dependent, satellite

tribute
5 paean, toast **6** eulogy, homage **8** citation, encomium **9** panegyric **10** salutation **11** recognition, testimonial

trice
4 lash, wink **5** blink, flash, jiffy, shake **6** moment, second, secure **7** instant **9** twinkling **11** split second

trick
4 bilk, dido, dupe, fool, gull, hoax, hose, lark, ploy, ruse, scam, sham, wile **5** antic, caper, dodge, feint, fraud, prank, stunt **6** gambit, outwit, scheme **7** chicane, finagle, gimmick, sleight, wrinkle **8** artifice, escapade, flimflam, hoodwink **9** bamboozle, deception, stratagem, victimize **10** shenanigan, tomfoolery **11** hornswoggle, monkeyshine

trickery
4 scam, wile **5** cheat, fraud **6** deceit **7** chicane **9** chicanery, deception **10** subterfuge **11** double cross **13** double-dealing, jiggery-pokery

trickle
4 drip, seep **5** creep, trill **7** dribble

trickster
5 cheat, shark **6** con man **7** cheater, diddler, grifter, sharper **8** deceiver, swindler **9** defrauder **11** flimflammer **12** double-dealer

tricksy
5 rough **6** trying **7** arduous **8** prankish

tricky
3 sly **4** foxy, wily **5** dodgy **6** catchy, clever, crafty, shifty, sticky, thorny, touchy **7** cunning, knavish **8** delusive, guileful, slippery, ticklish, tortuous, unstable **9** deceptive, dishonest, ingenious, intricate **10** misleading, nettlesome, precarious, unreliable **11** treacherous

trident
5 spear
part: **4** tine

tried and true
5 loyal **6** proven, secure, steady, tested, trusty **8** faithful, reliable, stalwart **9** steadfast **10** dependable **11** trustworthy

trifle
3 fig, pin, toy **4** doit, fool, play **5** curio, dally, flirt, sport, waste **6** bauble, coquet, diddle, doodle, fiddle, fidget, footle, frivol, gewgaw, niggle **7** bibelot, conceit, fribble, fritter, novelty, trinket, twiddle, whatnot **8** folderol, gimcrack, kickshaw, nonsense, squander **9** bagatelle, cream puff, dalliance **10** knickknack **11** small change

trifling
4 mere, tiny **5** minor, petty **6** measly, paltry, piddly, slight **7** trivial **8** niggling, nugatory, picayune, piddling, piffling **9** frivolous, worthless **10** negligible **11** Mickey Mouse, unimportant

trifolium
6 clover **8** shamrock

trig
4 chic, neat, prim, snug, tidy **5** sharp, smart, swank, trick **6** classy, modish, snappy **7** chipper, dashing, orderly, precise, stylish **9** shipshape

trigger
5 cause, spark, start **6** ignite, kindle, set off **7** actuate, release **8** activate, initiate, touch off

triggerman
3 gun **5** bravo **6** gunsel, killer, sniper **7** torpedo **8** assassin **9** cutthroat, pistolero

trigonometric function
see at **function**

trill
4 burr, roll **5** chirr, shake, twirl **6** quaver, warble **7** dribble, twitter, vibrato

trillion combining form
4 tera, treg **5** trega

trillionth combining form
4 pico

trim
4 buff, clip, crop, deck, neat, pare, snug, tidy, trig **5** adorn, order, prune, shape, shave, shear, skive, toned **6** barber, dapper, fettle, kilter, repair, spruce **7** chipper, dress up, garnish,

orderly, shapely **8** clean-cut, decorate, manicure **9** shipshape **11** spic-and-span, streamlined, well-groomed **12** spick-and-span
a tree: **5** prune **7** pollard

Trinidad and Tobago
capital: **11** Port of Spain
sea: **9** Caribbean

trinity
see **triad**

trinket
3 toy **5** bijou, curio, jewel **6** bauble, doodad, gewgaw, trifle **7** bibelot, novelty, whatnot **8** gimcrack, kickshaw **9** bagatelle, plaything, tchotchke **10** knickknack

trinkets
10 bijouterie

trio of goddesses
5 Fates **6** Furies, Graces

trip
3 hop **4** fall, ride, skip, step, tour, trek **5** caper, dance **6** junket, outing, sashay, travel, voyage **7** journey, misstep, stumble **9** excursion **10** expedition
type: **3** ego

tripe
4 guts **5** bilge, trash **6** menudo, waffle, viscus **7** innards, viscera (plural) **8** entrails, stuffing **9** internals

triple
4 trio **5** triad, trine **6** triune, troika **7** triform, trilogy, trinity **8** trifecta **9** threefold, threesome **11** three-bagger, triumvirate

Triple Crown
race: **5** Derby (Kentucky) **7** Belmont (Stakes) **9** Preakness (Stakes)
site: **7** Pimlico **9** Baltimore **10** Louisville **11** Belmont Park
winner:
1919: **9** Sir Barton
1930: **10** Gallant Fox
1935: **5** Omaha
1937: **10** War Admiral
1941: **9** Whirlaway
1943: **10** Count Fleet
1946: **7** Assault
1948: **8** Citation
1973: **11** Secretariat
1977: **11** Seattle Slew
1978: **8** Affirmed

tripped out
4 high **5** doped **6** stoned, zonked **7** drugged **8** hopped-up, turned on

Tristan's beloved
6 Iseult, Isolde

Tristan und Isolde composer
6 Wagner (Richard)

triste
3 sad **7** doleful, pensive, wistful **8** mournful **9** depressed, sorrowful **10** melancholy **11** melancholic

Tristram Shandy author
6 Sterne (Laurence)

trite
4 dull, flat, hack **5** banal, corny, musty, slick, stale, stock, vapid **6** cliché, jejune, old-hat **7** prosaic, worn-out **8** bathetic, bromidic, flyblown, ordinary, shopworn, timeworn, well-worn **9** hackneyed **10** threadbare **11** commonplace, stereotyped

triton
5 conch

Triton
6 merman
attribute: **5** conch
father: **7** Neptune **8** Poseidon
mother: **10** Amphitrite

triturate
4 bray **5** crush, grind **6** powder **9** comminute, pulverize

triumph
3 joy, win **4** crow, palm **5** exult, glory, vaunt **6** master **7** conquer, prevail, succeed, success, victory **8** conquest, overcome, surmount **10** exultation, jubilation

triumphant
8 exultant, exulting, jubilant **10** conquering, victorious

triumvirate
see **triad**

Triumvirate member
6 Antony (Marc, Mark), Caesar (Julius), Pompey **7** Anthony (Mark), Crassus (Marcus Licinius), Lepidus (Marcus Aemilius) **8** Octavius (Gaius)

trivet
4 rack **5** stand **6** tripod

trivia
8 factoids, minutiae **9** small beer **11** small change

trivial
5 dinky, minor, petty **6** casual, measly, paltry, piddly, slight **8** nugatory, picayune, piddling, piffling, trifling **10** negligible **11** Mickey Mouse, unimportant **13** insignificant

troche
6 tablet **7** lozenge **8** pastille **9** cough drop

troglodyte
6 hermit **7** caveman, recluse **11** cave dweller

Troilus
beloved: **8** Cressida, Criseyde
father: **5** Priam
mother: **6** Hecuba
slayer: **8** Achilles

Trojan
king: **5** Priam
priest: **7** Laocoön
princess: **4** Ilia **9** Cassandra
queen: **6** Hecuba
soothsayer: **9** Cassandra
warrior: **5** Paris **6** Aeneas, Hector **7** Troilus **8** Sarpedon

troll
4 fish, lure, sing, spin **5** angle, dwarf, prowl **6** goblin, search

trolley
3 car **4** cart, tram **8** carriage **9** streetcar

Trollope novel
11 Phineas Finn **12** Way We Live Now (The) **15** Eustace Diamonds (The) **16** Barchester Towers

trombone
7 sackbut

tromp
4 beat, drub, hike, pelt, slog, walk, whup **5** pound, stamp, stomp, stump **6** batter, buffet, pummel, thrash, trudge, wallop **7** belabor, clobber

troop
4 army, band, crew, host **5** corps, crowd, flock **6** legion, outfit **7** brigade, company, soldier **8** assembly **9** associate, battalion, gathering, multitude

trooper
3 cop **5** horse **7** soldier **9** policeman **10** cavalryman

trope
6 cliché, simile **8** metaphor, metonymy **10** synecdoche

trophy
3 cup **5** award, prize, relic, scalp, token **6** spoils **7** memento **8** hardware, keepsake, memorial, reminder, souvenir **9** loving cup

tropical
3 hot **4** lush, warm **5** humid **6** jungly, steamy, sultry, torrid **10** equatorial
root: **4** taro **6** manioc **7** cassava, tapioca
vine: **5** liana

tropical storm
see **typhoon**

Tropic of Cancer author
6 Miller (Henry)

trot
3 jog **4** gait, lope, pony, rack **5** amble, hurry **7** setline **11** translation

troth
6 commit, engage, pledge **7** loyalty **8** affiance, contract, espousal, fidelity **10** engagement **12** faithfulness

trot out
4 show **6** expose, parade **7** display, disport, exhibit, show off

Trotsky, Leon
associate: **5** Lenin (Vladimir)
rival: **6** Stalin (Joseph)

troubadour
4 bard, poet **6** singer **8** jongleur, minstrel, musician **9** balladist **10** folksinger

trouble
3 ado, ail, ill, irk, vex, woe **4** bind, care **5** annoy, beset, grief, harry, pains, trial, upset, worry **6** bother, effort, hassle, harass, kiaugh, misery, pester, plague, ruffle, strain, stress, unrest **7** afflict, agitate, ailment, bedevil, concern, disturb, oppress, perturb, torment **8** aggrieve, disquiet, distress, hardship, hot water, irritate, vexation **9** suffering **10** difficulty, disconcert

troubled
6 uneasy **7** anxious, worried **9** concerned, disturbed **10** distressed

troublemaker
7 hellion **8** agitator **9** firebrand **10** instigator **11** provocateur **12** rabble-rouser

troublesome
5 pesky **6** thorny, tricky, trying, vexing **7** onerous **8** annoying **9** difficult, upsetting, vexatious **10** bothersome, burdensome, disturbing **11** disquieting, importunate, pestiferous

trough
3 hod **4** bowl, tank **5** basin, drain **6** vessel **7** channel **10** depression

trounce
4 beat, drub, lick, rout, whip, whup **5** crush, whomp **6** defeat, larrup, punish, thrash, thresh, wallop **7** clobber, shellac

troupe
4 band **5** corps, party **6** outfit **7** company

trouper
4 mime **5** actor, mimic **6** mummer, player **7** actress, artiste **8** thespian **9** performer **11** entertainer

trousers
5 pants **6** slacks **7** drawers **8** breeches, britches
skirtlike: **7** culotte
tartan: **5** trews

trout
kind: **4** char **5** brook **7** rainbow **8** speckled **9** steelhead

Trovatore, Il
character: **7** Azucena, Leonora, Manrico **11** Count di Luna
composer: **5** Verdi (Giuseppe)

trove
4 find, haul **5** cache, hoard, store **8** treasure **10** collection

Troy
5 Ilium
epic of: 5 Iliad
excavator: 10 Schliemann (Heinrich)
founder: 4 Ilus
modern site: 9 Hissarlik 11 Dardanelles
(see also **Trojan**)

truant
4 idle 5 shirk 7 shirker, slacker 8 shirking 10 delinquent

truce
4 lull 5 letup, pause, peace 6 accord 7 respite 9 armistice, cease-fire

truck
3 rig, ute, van 4 semi 5 lorry 6 big rig, pickup
military: 6 camion

Truckee River city
4 Reno

truckle
4 fawn 5 cower, defer, toady 6 cringe, grovel, kowtow 8 bootlick

truckler
5 leech, toady 6 lackey, sponge 7 spaniel 8 parasite 9 sycophant 10 bootlicker 11 lickspittle

truculent
4 grim 5 cruel, harsh 6 brutal, deadly, fierce, savage, severe 7 abusive, warlike 9 barbarous, bellicose, combative, ferocious 10 pernicious, pugnacious 11 belligerent, destructive, quarrelsome

trudge
4 plod, slog, trek 5 march, tramp 8 footslog

true
4 real, very 5 valid 6 actual, trusty 7 factual, genuine, staunch 8 accurate, bona fide, rightful 9 authentic, undoubted, veracious, veritable 10 legitimate, undeniable 11 indubitable 12 indisputable

true-blue
5 loyal 6 proven, steady, trusty 7 genuine 8 bona fide, constant, faithful, reliable, stalwart 9 steadfast 10 unswerving

truism
3 saw 5 adage, axiom, gnome, maxim, moral 6 cliché, dictum, saying, verity 8 aphorism, apothegm 9 platitude 10 shibboleth 11 commonplace

truly
6 easily, indeed, really, surely, verily 7 de facto 8 actually 9 doubtless, genuinely, sincerely, veritably 10 absolutely, definitely, positively, truthfully, undeniably

Truman, Harry S
birthplace: 5 Lamar 8 Missouri
predecessor: 3 FDR
successor: 3 DDE
wife: 4 Bess

trump
3 cap, top 4 beat, best, pass, ruff 5 excel, outdo 6 better 7 manille, surpass 8 clincher, outstrip, override, spadille
up: 6 invent 7 concoct 9 fabricate

trumpery
4 bosh, junk, muck, slop, tosh 5 bilge, dreck, hokum, trash 6 bunkum, humbug, piffle 7 baloney, twaddle 8 claptrap, flimflam, malarkey, nonsense, tommyrot 10 double-talk

trumpet
4 horn, tout 6 herald 7 clarion 8 ballyhoo
call: 4 Taps 6 sennet 7 clarion
ram's horn: 6 shofar

trumpeter
4 Byrd (Donald), Hirt (Al) 5 André (Maurice), Baker (Chet), Botti (Chris), Brown (Clifford), Davis (Miles), James (Harry), Terry (Clark) 6 Alpert (Herb), Balsom (Alison), Bolden (Buddy), Faddis (John), Farmer (Art), Morgan (Lee), Oliver (King), Voisin (Roger) 7 Hubbard (Freddie), Navarro (Fats), Satchmo, Schwarz (Gerard) 8 Eldridge (Roy), Ferguson (Maynard), Marsalis (Wynton), Masekela (Hugh), Sandoval (Arturo) 9 Armstrong (Louis), Blanchard (Terence), Gillespie (Dizzy)

Trump's ex
5 Ivana, Marla (Maples)

truncate
3 lop, top 4 crop, trim 5 prune, shear 6 cut off 7 abridge, shorten 10 abbreviate

truncheon
3 bat 4 club 5 baton, billy 6 cudgel, warder 8 bludgeon 9 billy club, shillalah 10 nightstick, shillelagh

trundle
3 bed, tub 4 cart, haul, roll, spin 5 churn, wheel 6 rotate 7 revolve

trunk
4 body, bole, case, stem 5 chest, torso 7 channel, circuit, luggage
elephant: 9 proboscis
tree: 4 bole 5 stump

truss
4 band, bind 5 brace 7 bandage, bracket, support 9 framework, supporter

trust
4 hope, pool, rely 5 faith, stock 6 assume, bank on, belief, cartel, charge, commit, credit, rely on 7 build on, combine, confide, consign, count on, custody, keeping, presume 8 credence, depend on, reckon on, reliance 9 assurance, certainty, certitude, syndicate 10 confidence, dependence

trustee
8 guardian 9 custodian, protector 10 supervisor

trusting
8 gullible 9 credulous
trustworthy
5 tried, valid 6 honest, proven, secure 8 accurate, credible, faithful, reliable, stalwart, true-blue 9 authentic, realistic, steadfast, veracious 10 dependable 11 responsible 12 tried and true
trusty
5 tried 6 proven, secure, stable, steady 7 certain, convict 8 faithful, reliable 9 steadfast, truepenny 10 dependable 11 responsible 12 tried and true
truth
5 sooth 6 candor, gospel, verity 7 lowdown, reality, veritas 8 veracity
truth drug
4 sera (plural) 5 serum
truthful
5 frank 6 candid, honest 7 factual, sincere 8 accurate 9 realistic, veracious, veridical
truthfulness
6 candor, verity 7 honesty 8 veracity
try
3 aim 4 seek, shot, stab, test 5 assay, essay, judge, offer, prove, study, whirl 6 aspire, sample, strive 7 adjudge, attempt 8 endeavor, struggle 9 undertake 10 adjudicate
trying
6 taxing, thorny, tricky, vexing 7 arduous, onerous 8 annoying, exacting, grueling 9 demanding, difficult, strenuous, vexatious 10 irritating
try out
4 test 5 check, prove 6 verify 8 audition
tryst
4 date 7 meeting 10 rendezvous 11 assignation
tsar
see **czar**
T-shaped cross
3 tau
tsunami
9 tidal wave
tub
3 vat 4 boat 9 container
hot: 3 spa 7 Jacuzzi
tuba
7 helicon 9 bombardon, euphonium 10 sousaphone
tubby
3 fat 5 plump, podgy, porky, pudgy 6 chubby, chunky, rotund 8 roly-poly
tube
4 duct, flue, hose, pipe 5 buret 6 siphon, subway, tunnel 7 burette, cuvette, pipette, syringe 8 cylinder, pipeline 10 television
anatomical: 3 vas 4 duct, vasa (plural) 7 salpinx 9 salpinges (plural)
tuber
3 oca, set, yam 4 bulb, corm, eddo, root, stem, taro, yamp, yuca 5 salep, yucca 6 jicama, manioc, mashua, potato, yautia 7 cassava, cocoyam, rhizome 9 arrowroot
tuberculosis
8 phthisis, scrofula 11 consumption
tubular pasta
4 ziti 5 penne
tucker out
4 do in, poop, tire 5 drain, weary 7 exhaust
tuft
5 clump, mound 7 cluster
of feathers: 7 panache
ornamental: 6 pom-pom
vascular: 6 glomus
tufted
7 crested
tug
3 tow 4 drag, draw, haul, moil, pull, toil 5 labor 6 strain, strive
tug-of-war
5 match 6 strife 7 contest, grapple, rivalry 8 conflict, struggle 11 competition
tuition
3 fee 6 charge 8 teaching, training, tutelage 9 education, schooling 11 instruction
collector: 6 bursar
tumble
4 drop, fall, trip 5 upset 6 plunge, topple 8 collapse, keel over
tumbledown
8 decrepit 10 ramshackle 11 dilapidated
tumbler
5 glass 6 roller 7 acrobat, gymnast 11 cartwheeler
tumbrel
4 cart 5 wagon 7 tipcart
tumescent
6 turgid 7 aureate, bloated, bulging, flowery, swollen 8 inflated, swelling 9 bombastic, dropsical, overblown 10 euphuistic, rhetorical
tummy
3 gut 5 belly 6 paunch 7 abdomen, stomach 8 potbelly 9 bay window 11 breadbasket
tumult
3 din 4 flap, riot, to-do 5 babel, broil, hoo-ha, hurly 6 clamor, dither, hoo-hah, hubbub, lather, pother, racket, uproar 7 ferment, tempest, turmoil 8 disorder, foofaraw, paroxysm, upheaval 9 agitation, commotion, confusion, kerfuffle 10 convulsion, hullabaloo, hurly-burly, turbulence
tumultuous
5 rowdy 6 stormy, unruly 7 raucous, riotous 9 clamorous, turbulent 10 boisterous, disorderly 11 rumbustious, tempestuous 12 rambunctious

tumulus
5 grave, knoll, mound 6 barrow 7 hillock

tun
3 keg, vat 4 butt, cask, pipe 6 barrel 8 hogshead, puncheon

tuna
3 ahi 4 pear 6 bigeye, bonito 7 bluefin 8 albacore, skipjack 9 scombroid, yellowfin

tune
3 air 4 dial, lilt, song 5 theme, tweak 6 accord, adjust, amount, attune, extent, jingle, melody, strain, temper 7 descant 8 modulate, regulate

tuneful
5 sweet 6 dulcet 7 melodic 9 melodious

tungsten
7 wolfram 9 scheelite 10 wolframite

tunic
4 jama 5 jupon 6 kirtle, tabard 7 hauberk
Greek: 6 chiton

tunicate
4 salp 8 ascidian, chordate 9 sea squirt

Tunisia
capital: 5 Tunis
language: 6 Arabic
monetary unit: 5 dinar
neighbor: 5 Libya 7 Algeria
ruins: 8 Carthage

tunnel
4 tube 6 burrow 7 conduit 8 crawlway
Alps: 7 Simplon
France: 4 Rove
Hudson river: 7 Holland, Lincoln
Nevada: 5 Sutro
railroad: 6 Hoosac 7 Cascade

Turandot
character: 3 Liu 5 Calaf
author: 5 Gozzi (Carlo)
composer: 6 Busoni (Ferruccio) 7 Puccini (Giacomo)

turban
7 bandana, pugaree 8 bandanna 9 headdress

turbid
5 dense, mucky, muddy, murky, riley, roily, smoky 6 cloudy, opaque, roiled 7 clouded, obscure

turbot
8 flatfish

turbulence
3 din 4 flap, stew 5 babel, fight, hoo-ha 6 dither, fracas, lather, pother, tumult, uproar 8 foofaraw 9 agitation, commotion

turbulent
5 bumpy, roily, rough, rowdy 6 raging, stormy, unruly 7 furious, moiling, raucous, riotous, roaring 8 agitated, blustery, swirling 9 clamorous 10 boisterous, tumultuous

tureen
3 pot 4 bowl 5 crock 9 casserole

turf
3 sod 4 area, nabe, peat 5 grass, sward, track 6 domain, region 7 terrain 9 racetrack, territory

Turgenev of literature
4 Ivan

turgid
see **tumescent**

Turkey
capital: 6 Ankara
city: 8 Istanbul
lake: 3 Van
leader: 7 Atatürk (Kemal)
monetary unit: 4 lira, lire (plural)
mountain, range: 6 Ararat, Taurus
peninsula: 6 Balkan 9 Asia Minor
river: 6 Tigris 8 Menderes 9 Euphrates
sea: 6 Aegean 7 Marmara 13 Mediterranean

turkey
buzzard: 7 vulture
disease: 9 blackhead
head growth: 5 snood 7 dewbill
male: 3 tom 7 gobbler
throat pouch: 6 wattle
young: 5 poult

Turkish
cavalryman: 5 spahi
empire: 7 Osmanli, Ottoman
governor: 4 vali
hat: 3 fez
inn: 4 kahn 6 imaret
soldier: 5 nizam 9 janissary
sword: 8 yataghan
title: 3 aga, bey 4 agha 5 pasha 6 vizier 7 effendi

Turkmenistan
capital: 8 Ashgabat 9 Ashkhabad
desert: 7 Kara-Kum
monetary unit: 5 manat, tenne
river: 6 Murgab 7 Murghab 8 Amu Dar'ya
sea: 7 Caspian

Turks and Caicos Islands
capital: 9 Grand Turk
passage: 8 Mouchoir
territory of: 7 Britain

turmeric
3 dye 4 herb 5 spice 6 ginger

turmoil
4 riot, stew, to-do 5 chaos 6 clamor, dither, hubbub, lather, pother, strife, tumult, unrest, uproar, welter 7 ferment 8 disorder, upheaval 9 agitation, commotion, confusion 10 disruption, hurly-burly, turbulence 11 pandemonium 13 Sturm und Drang

turn
3 yaw, zag, zig **4** bend, bias, bout, cast, gyre, reel, slue, spin, tack, tour, veer, whip, wind **5** angle, curve, go bad, pivot, refer, shunt, spell, stint, swirl, train, twirl, whirl **6** detour, divert, gyrate, revert, rotate, switch, swivel **7** circuit, deflect, deviate, digress, diverge, reverse, revolve **8** gyration, rotation **9** about-face, deviation, pirouette, volte-face

turnabout
7 reverse **8** apostate, defector, recreant, reversal **9** about-face, reversion, volte-face **11** retaliation **12** merry-go-round

turn aside
4 veer, sway, veer **5** repel, shunt, stave **6** divert, swerve **7** deflect, deviate, digress, diverge, fend off, reflect, ward off **9** sidetrack

turncoat
3 rat **5** Judas **7** traitor **8** apostate, betrayer, defector, deserter, quisling, recreant, renegade

turn down
4 deny, jilt, veto **5** spurn **6** rebuff, refuse, reject **7** decline, dismiss **9** repudiate

turned on
4 high **5** doped **6** stoned, zonked **7** aroused, drugged, excited **8** hopped-up, tripping **9** activated, spaced-out, zonked-out

Turner of Hollywood
4 Lana

Turner of song
4 Tina

turn in
5 crash, rat on **6** betray, inform, rat out, retire, submit **7** deliver, produce, sack out **8** hand over **9** hit the hay **10** hit the sack, relinquish

turning point
4 cusp **5** pivot **6** climax, crisis **8** landmark **11** climacteric

turn inside out
5 evert

turnip
5 swede **8** rutabaga
Scottish: **4** neep

turnkey
6 jailer

turn left
3 haw

Turn of the Screw, The
author: **5** James (Henry)
character: **5** Flora, Miles **10** Peter Quint
composer: **7** Britten (Benjamin)

turn on
5 start **6** excite, ignite **7** start up **8** activate, motivate **9** stimulate

turn over
4 cede, plow, roll **5** upend, upset **6** assign, commit, give up, rotate **7** capsize, consign, deliver, entrust, furnish, provide, revolve **8** delegate, transfer **9** overthrow, surrender **10** relinquish

turnpike
7 highway
fee: **4** toll

turn right
3 gee

turn sharply
4 veer **6** swerve

turn up
4 find **6** appear, arrive, reveal **7** uncover, unearth **8** discover **11** materialize

turpentine
7 galipot, solvent, thinner
ingredient: **6** pinene
tree: **4** pine **9** terebinth

turret
5 tower **6** cupola, louver, louvre **7** mirador **8** bartizan **9** belvedere

turtle
8 terrapin, tortoise **9** chelonian
edible part: **7** calipee **8** calipash
genus: **4** Emys
sea: **6** ridley **8** hawkbill
shell: **8** carapace
shell part: **8** plastron

Tuscany
city: **4** Pisa **8** Florence
formerly: **7** Etruria
river: **4** Arno
tower: **4** Pisa

tusk
4 fang **5** ivory, tooth

tusker
6 dugong, walrus **7** mammoth, muntjac, narwhal, warthog **8** elephant, musk deer

tussle
4 spar **5** scrap, scrum **6** hassle, scrape **7** scuffle, wrangle, wrestle **8** skirmish, struggle **9** scrimmage

tussock
4 tuft **5** clump, mound

tutelage
see **tuition**

tutor
3 don **5** coach, teach **6** docent, mentor **7** teacher **9** pedagogue, preceptor **10** instructor

Tut's tomb discoverer
6 Carter (Howard)

tutti
3 all **8** everyone **9** everybody

tutu material
5 tulle

Tuvalu
capital: 8 Funafuti
former name: 6 Ellice (Islands)

TVA dam
5 Ocoee

TV Tarzan
3 Ely (Ron)

TV watchdog
3 FCC

twaddle
3 jaw, yak 4 bosh, bull, bunk, guff, muck, tosh 5 clack, drool, hooey, prate, run on 6 babble, bunkum, burble, drivel, gabble, hot air, humbug, jabber, tattle 7 baloney, blabber, blarney, blather, chatter, hogwash, prattle, rubbish 8 claptrap, malarkey, nonsense, tommyrot, trumpery 9 poppycock 10 applesauce, balderdash

Twain, Mark
birth name: 7 Clemens (Samuel L.)
character: 3 Jim 5 Becky (Thatcher) 8 Huck Finn, Injun Joe 9 Aunt Polly, Joe Harper, Tom Sawyer
portrayer: 3 Hal (Holbrook)

tweak
4 jerk, zing 5 pinch, pluck 6 adjust, modify, twitch 8 fine-tune

tweet
4 call, note 5 cheep, chirp 7 chirrup, twitter

Twelfth Night character
5 Viola 6 Olivia, Orsino (Duke) 7 Antonio, Cesario 8 Malvolio 9 Sebastian, Toby Belch

twelve
5 dozen
combining form: 5 dodec 6 dodeca

twenty
5 score
combining form: 4 icos 5 icosa, icosi

twerp
4 brat, drip, fool, jerk, nerd, twit 5 dweeb 6 squirt

twibil
3 axe

twice
3 bis 7 twofold
combining form: 3 bis
prefix: 3 dis

twice a day
3 b.i.d. 8 bis in die

twice a year
8 biannual 10 semiannual

twig
5 shoot, sprig, withe

twiggy
4 slim, thin 5 reedy 6 skinny, stalky 9 sticklike

twilight
3 e'en, eve 4 dusk 5 gloam, gloom 6 sunset 7 decline 8 evenfall, eventide, gloaming 9 nightfall 10 crepuscule

Twilight of the Gods
8 Ragnarok
composer: 6 Wagner (Richard)

twill
5 chino, cloth, serge, toile, tweed, weave 6 fabric 7 cheviot 8 dungaree 9 bombazine, gabardine 11 herringbone

twin
4 dual, like, mate 5 clone, match 6 bifold, binary, double, paired 7 matched, similar, twofold 8 matching 9 duplicate, identical
of Chang: 3 Eng
of Jacob: 4 Esau

Twin City
6 St. Paul 11 Minneapolis

twine
4 coil, cord, curl, wind, wrap 5 twist, weave 6 spiral, string 7 embrace, meander, wreathe 8 entangle 9 interlace 10 interweave

twinge
4 ache, pain, pang, stab 5 pluck, shoot 6 stitch

twinkle
4 flit, wink 5 flash, flirt, gleam, glint, light, shake, shine, trice 7 flicker, flutter, glimmer, glisten, glitter, shimmer, sparkle 9 coruscate, nictitate 11 coruscation, scintillate

twin stars
6 Castor, Pollux

twirl
4 coil, gyre, spin 5 pitch, trill 6 gyrate 7 revolve 9 pirouette

twist
4 coil, curl, skew, turn, warp, wind 5 belie, gnarl, pivot, snake, twine, twirl, wring 6 garble, spiral, sprain, squirm, torque, wrench, writhe 7 contort, distort, entwine, falsify, pervert, wriggle

twisted
3 wry 4 awry, sick 5 askew, kinky, slued 6 swirly, warped 9 perverted

twister
6 funnel 7 tornado 9 dust devil, whirlwind 10 waterspout

twit
4 dolt, fool, gibe, jeer, jive, josh, mock, quiz, razz 5 chide, rally, scout, taunt, tease, twerp 6 deride 8 bonehead, numskull, ridicule 9 blockhead, numbskull

twitch
3 tic **4** jerk, pang, pull, yank **5** pluck, spasm, throe, tweak **6** quiver **10** quack grass

twitter
4 peep **5** cheep, chirp, quake, tweet **6** giggle, quiver, shiver, titter, tremor, warble **7** chirrup

Twitter term
5 tweep, tweet **7** hashtag

two
3 duo **4** duet, dyad, pair **5** twain **6** couple
combining form: **3** bis, duo, dyo
divide into: **4** fork **6** bisect **9** bifurcate
prefix: **3** twi

two-faced
9 deceitful, dishonest, insincere **11** duplicitous **12** hypocritical
god: **5** Janus

twofold
4 dual, twin **5** binal, duple **6** binary, double, duplex, dyadic, paired **9** dualistic

two-footed
7 bipedal

Two Gentlemen of Verona
author: **11** Shakespeare (William)
character: **5** Julia **6** Silvia, Thurio **7** Proteus **9** Valentine

two-sided
9 bilateral

twosome
3 duo **4** dyad, item, pair **5** brace **6** couple **7** doublet

two-time
4 dupe **6** betray, delude, humbug, take in **7** beguile, cheat on, deceive, mislead **9** bamboozle **11** double-cross

two-toed sloth
4 unau

two-wheeler
4 bike **5** cycle **7** bicycle, scooter **10** motorcycle

Tybalt
cousin: **6** Juliet
family: **7** Capulet
slayer: **5** Romeo
victim: **8** Mercutio

tycoon
5 mogul, nabob **7** magnate

tyke
3 dog, kid **5** child, hound, puppy **6** canine, moppet, nipper, shaver

Tylenol alternative
5 Advil, Aleve **6** Anacin, Motrin **7** aspirin

tympanum
7 eardrum **9** middle ear

Tyndareus
kingdom: **6** Sparta
wife: **4** Leda

type
3 cut, ilk, key, lot, way **4** cast, form, kind, mold, sort **5** breed, class, genre, order, print, serif, stamp **6** kidney, nature, stripe **7** feather, species, variety **8** category, keyboard
bar: **4** slug
font: **5** Arial, Goudy **6** Bodoni **7** Courier **8** Garamond, Palatino **9** Helvetica **10** Times Roman
measure: **4** pica **5** point
set: **7** compose
setter: **10** compositor
size: **4** pica **5** agate, elite, pearl
stroke: **5** serif
style: **4** bold **5** roman, serif **6** Gothic, italic **7** Fraktur **8** boldface **9** lightface, sans serif
tray: **6** galley

Typee
author: **8** Melville (Herman)
character: **4** Toby
sequel: **4** Omoo

typewriter
part: **3** key **6** platen, spacer
type size: **4** pica **5** elite

typhoon
7 cyclone **9** hurricane **13** tropical storm

typical
5 ideal, model, usual **6** common, normal **7** classic, general, regular

typify
6 embody, mirror **9** epitomize, represent, symbolize **10** illustrate **11** emblematize **12** characterize

typo
5 error **7** erratum **8** misprint **11** corrigendum

typographer
7 printer **10** compositor

tyrannical
8 absolute, despotic **9** arbitrary **10** absolutist, autocratic, oppressive **11** dictatorial

tyrannize
7 oppress **8** dominate, domineer, overbear

tyrannous
5 harsh **6** brutal, severe **8** absolute, despotic **9** arbitrary, fascistic **10** autocratic **11** dictatorial

tyranny
7 fascism **9** autocracy, despotism, monocracy **10** absolutism, domination, oppression **12** dictatorship

tyrant
4 czar, duce, tsar, tzar **5** ruler **6** despot, führer **7** fuehrer, pharaoh, usurper **8** autocrat, dictator **9** oppressor, strongman **10** absolutist

Tyrian ___
6 purple

tyro
4 naïf, punk 6 novice, rookie 7 amateur, dabbler, student 8 beginner, freshman, neophyte, newcomer 9 novitiate 10 apprentice, dilettante, tenderfoot 11 abecedarian

Tyrol
see **Tirol**

tzar
see **czar**

tzigane
3 Rom 5 gypsy 6 Romany

U

UAE ruler
4 amir, emir 5 ameer, emeer

übermensch
8 superman

ubiquitous
7 allover 9 pervasive, universal 10 everywhere, widespread 11 omnipresent

U-boat
3 sub 9 submarine

Uganda
capital: 7 Kampala
falls: 5 Ripon
lake: 8 Victoria
leader: 4 Amin (Idi) 5 Obote (Milton)
monetary unit: 8 shilling
mountain range: 9 Ruwenzori
river: 4 Nile

ugly
4 vile 7 hideous 8 deformed 9 loathsome, misshapen, offensive, repugnant, repulsive, unsightly

Ugly Duckling author
8 Andersen (Hans Christian)

ukase
4 fiat 5 edict, order 6 decree, dictum, ruling 7 command, dictate, mandate 9 directive 10 injunction

Ukraine
capital: 4 Kiev
city: 4 Lviv, Lvov 5 Yalta 6 Odessa 7 Kharkiv 9 Chernobyl
ethnic group: 7 Cossack
monetary unit: 6 hryvny
mountain range: 10 Carpathian
peninsula: 5 Kerch 6 Crimea 7 Crimean
river: 5 Tisza 6 Donets 7 Dnieper 8 Dniester
sea: 4 Azov 5 Black

ulcer
4 sore 6 fester 7 corrupt
kind: 6 peptic 8 duodenal
mouth: 10 canker sore

Ulster hero
6 Fergus 7 Deirdre 9 Conchobar, Cuchulain, Cuchullin 10 Cú Chulainn

ulterior
5 privy 6 covert, future, hidden, latent 7 further, obscure 9 ambiguous, concealed 11 undisclosed

ultimate
3 end, nth 4 last 5 basic, final, utter 6 utmost 7 closing, extreme, maximum, primary, supreme, topmost 8 absolute, deciding, decisive, eventual, farthest, furthest, greatest, original, terminal 9 elemental, paramount 10 concluding, conclusive, consummate, preeminent 11 categorical, fundamental, furthermost

ultra
5 rabid 7 extreme, fanatic, radical 9 excessive, extremist, fanatical

ultraconservative
11 reactionary

ultraist
5 rabid 6 zealot 7 extreme, fanatic, radical 9 extremist

ultramarine
7 oversea, sea-blue 8 overseas 11 lapis lazuli

Ulysses
author: 5 Joyce (James)
character: 5 Bloom (Leopold), Molly (Bloom) 6 Blazes (Boylan) 7 Dedalus (Stephen)
last word: 3 yes
(see also **Odysseus**)

umber
5 brown, sepia, shade 6 darken, shadow

Umberto of literature
3 Eco

umbilicus
3 hub 4 core 5 heart, hilum, navel 6 center

umbra
5 shade 6 shadow

umbrage
4 huff 5 anger, pique 7 chagrin, dudgeon, offense 9 annoyance, suspicion 10 irritation, resentment 11 displeasure, indignation

umbrageous
5 shady 6 shaded, touchy 7 shadowy 8 shadowed 9 defensive, sensitive

umbrella
5 cover, guard, shade 6 brolly, pileus, screen 7 parasol, protect, shelter 8 sunshade 10 protection 11 bumbershoot

ump equivalent
3 ref

umph
see **oomph**

umpire
3 ref 5 judge 6 decide, settle 7 arbiter, referee 9 arbitrate 10 arbitrator
call: 3 out 4 balk, ball, safe 6 strike

unabashed
5 blunt, brash, frank, overt 6 arrant, brassy, brazen, candid 7 blatant, forward 8 outright 9 audacious, barefaced, shameless

unable
5 inept 8 helpless, impotent 9 incapable, maladroit, powerless 11 incompetent

unabridged
5 whole 6 entire, intact 8 complete 10 full-length

unacceptable
11 intolerable 12 inadmissible 13 exceptionable, inappropriate, insupportable, objectionable

unaccompanied
4 lone, sole, solo, stag 5 alone, apart 6 single 8 detached, solitary 9 a cappella

unaccountable
5 eerie, weird 6 arcane, mystic 7 strange 8 baffling, puzzling 9 enigmatic 10 mysterious, mystifying 12 impenetrable, inexplicable

unaccustomed
3 new 5 alien, novel 7 strange 8 singular

unadorned
4 bald, bare 5 plain, spare, stark 6 rustic, severe, simple 7 austere, natural, spartan

unadulterated
4 neat, pure 5 sheer, utter 7 genuine 8 absolute, straight

unaffected
5 naive 6 candid, simple 7 artless, callous, genuine, natural, sincere 9 guileless, impassive, ingenuous 10 impervious

unagi
3 eel

unalloyed
4 pure 5 sheer, total 7 genuine 8 absolute, straight 9 authentic, out-and-out

unalterable
5 fixed 7 binding, certain, decided 8 constant, required 9 immutable, mandatory, necessary 10 compulsory, invariable 13 predetermined

unambiguous
5 clear, lucid, plain 6 patent 7 evident, express, obvious, precise 8 apparent, clean-cut, clear-cut, decisive, definite, distinct, explicit, manifest, specific, univocal 10 definitive, forthright 11 categorical, translucent, transparent

unanimous
5 as one 6 united 8 univocal 9 unopposed 10 collective 11 uncontested

unanimously
5 as one 6 wholly 7 en masse 10 altogether

unanticipated
10 surprising 12 out of the blue

unappeasable
4 grim 7 adamant 8 obdurate, resolute 9 insatiate 10 implacable, insatiable, relentless

unappetizing
4 icky 5 gross, yucky 7 insipid 9 repugnant

unapproachable
5 aloof 6 remote, offish 7 distant 8 reserved 11 standoffish 12 inaccessible

unasked
7 willing 9 voluntary 10 gratuitous 11 spontaneous, voluntarily

unassailable
6 secure 8 airtight 10 invincible, inviolable 11 impregnable, irrefutable 12 indisputable, invulnerable 13 incontestable

unassertive
3 shy 4 meek 5 mousy, timid 6 modest, mousey 7 bashful 8 backward, reticent, retiring, sheepish, timorous 9 diffident, shrinking 10 submissive 12 self-effacing

unassuming
3 shy 6 humble, modest, simple 8 ordinary, retiring 9 diffident 12 self-effacing

unattached
4 free 5 loose 6 single 8 separate 12 disconnected, freestanding

unattainable
7 elusive 10 impossible 12 inaccessible

unattractive
4 drab, dull, ugly 5 dowdy, plain 6 homely 8 frumpish

unavailable
4 busy 6 absent, tied up 7 missing 8 occupied

unavailing
4 idle, vain 5 empty 6 barren, futile 7 useless 8 abortive, bootless 9 fruitless, pointless 11 ineffective, ineffectual

unavoidable
5 fated 8 destined 9 impending, necessary 10 compulsory, inevitable, obligatory 11 ineluctable, inescapable

unavoidably
8 perforce 10 helplessly, inevitably, willy-nilly 11 inescapably, necessarily, whether or no

unaware, unawares
5 aback 8 abruptly, clueless, heedless, ignorant, nescient, off guard, suddenly 9 oblivious, unknowing 10 by surprise

unbalance
11 destabilize

unbalanced
3 mad 4 daft 5 batty, nutty 6 crazed, insane, wobbly 8 demented, deranged, lopsided 9 psychotic 10 disordered, moonstruck

unbearable
11 intolerable 12 excruciating, insufferable

unbecoming
8 improper 9 inelegant, tasteless 10 indecorous, indelicate, malapropos 11 disgraceful 13 inappropriate

unbelievable
7 amazing, awesome 9 fantastic 10 astounding, improbable, incredible, phenomenal, staggering, stupendous 11 astonishing, implausible 13 extraordinary, inconceivable

unbeliever
5 pagan 6 giaour 7 atheist, doubter, gentile, heathen, heretic, infidel, scoffer, skeptic 8 agnostic 10 Pyrrhonist 11 freethinker

unbelieving
5 leery 6 show-me 8 agnostic, apostate, doubting 9 quizzical, skeptical 10 dissenting, suspicious 11 incredulous, mistrustful, questioning

unbending
5 rigid, stern, stiff 6 severe 8 hard-line, obdurate, resolute 9 inelastic 10 brassbound, inexorable, inflexible

unbiased
4 fair, just 5 equal 7 neutral 8 detached, tolerant 9 equitable, impartial, objective 10 even-handed, open-minded 11 broad-minded 13 disinterested, dispassionate

unbidden
7 willing 9 impromptu, voluntary 10 gratuitous 11 spontaneous

unbind
4 free 5 loose 6 detach, loosen 7 manumit, release 8 dissolve, liberate 9 discharge, disengage 10 emancipate

unblemished
4 pure 7 perfect 8 flawless, spotless, virtuous 9 exemplary, faultless, stainless 10 immaculate

unbosom
4 bare, open, tell 6 betray, expose, reveal 7 divulge, express 8 disclose

unbound
4 free 5 freed, loose 6 loosed

unbounded
4 open 7 endless 8 infinite 9 excessive, limitless 10 immoderate, indefinite, inordinate 11 extravagant, measureless 12 immeasurable, incalculable

unbreakable
7 durable, lasting 11 everlasting

unbridled
4 free 5 loose 6 madcap 8 reckless 9 dissolute 10 immoderate, licentious 11 spontaneous

unbroken
5 solid, sound, whole 6 entire, intact, single 8 complete, constant, enduring 9 ceaseless, steadfast 10 continuous

unburden
3 rid 4 dump, ease, lose 5 shake 6 reveal 7 cast off, confess, confide, off-load, relieve 8 shake off, throw off 9 discharge 10 relinquish 11 disencumber

uncalled-for
8 baseless, needless 10 gratuitous, groundless

uncanny
5 eerie, weird 6 creepy, spooky 7 ghostly, strange 10 mysterious, mystifying, superhuman 11 supernormal, supranormal 12 supernatural

uncared-for
5 dingy 6 beat-up, shabby 7 run-down, worn-out 8 decrepit, derelict, deserted, desolate, forsaken, tattered 9 neglected 10 broken-down, down-at-heel, ramshackle, tumble-down 11 dilapidated

uncaring
4 cold 7 callous 9 heartless, negligent, oblivious 11 coldhearted, hard-hearted, indifferent, insensitive, thoughtless 13 inconsiderate

unceasing
7 abiding, endless, eternal, nonstop 8 constant, enduring 9 continual, perennial, perpetual 10 continuous 11 amaranthine, everlasting 12 imperishable, interminable

unceremonious
4 curt, rude 5 bluff, blunt, frank, hasty, sharp, short, terse 6 abrupt, breezy, casual, sudden 7 brusque, hurried, offhand 8 familiar, informal 11 precipitate, precipitous

uncertain
4 hazy, iffy, moot 5 vague 6 chancy, fitful, unsure, wobbly 7 dubious, erratic, halting 8 arguable, doubtful, insecure, slippery, variable 9 ambiguous, debatable 10 ambivalent, disputable, inconstant, indefinite, precarious

11 problematic, speculative **12** questionable **13** indeterminate, problematical

uncertainty
5 doubt **6** anomie **7** dubiety **8** distrust, mistrust **9** ambiguity, suspicion **10** indecision, perplexity, puzzlement, skepticism **11** ambivalence

unchain
4 free **5** loose **6** loosen **7** manumit, release **8** liberate **9** discharge **10** emancipate **11** disenthrall

unchangeable
3 set **4** firm **5** fixed **7** settled **8** constant **9** immutable, permanent **10** continuing, inflexible, invariable **11** established, inalterable

unchanging
5 fixed **6** stable, static, steady **7** abiding, equable, eternal, settled, stabile, uniform **8** constant, enduring **9** immutable, steadfast **10** consistent, continuing, invariable

unchaste
4 lewd **5** bawdy, loose **6** impure, vulgar, wanton **7** immoral, lustful, obscene, scarlet **8** depraved, prurient **9** debauched, dissolute, lecherous, salacious **10** adulterous, lascivious, libidinous, licentious, profligate **11** promiscuous

unchecked
5 loose **7** rampant **9** spreading **10** widespread

uncivil
4 rude **5** crass, crude **6** coarse, savage, vulgar **7** boorish, ill-bred **8** barbaric, impolite **9** barbarous **10** indecorous **11** ill-mannered **12** discourteous **13** disrespectful

uncivilized
4 rude, wild **6** brutal, coarse, Gothic, savage **7** boorish, Hunnish, ill-bred, loutish, lowbred **8** barbaric, churlish **9** barbarian, barbarous, primitive **10** mannerless

uncle
3 eme
cry: **6** give up **9** surrender
mate: **4** aunt
Scottish: **3** eme
Spanish: **3** tío
U.S. symbol: **3** Sam

unclean
4 foul **5** dingy, dirty, grimy **6** filthy, grubby, grungy, impure, soiled, sordid **7** corrupt, defiled, immoral, obscene, squalid, stained, sullied, tainted **8** befouled, indecent, polluted **9** tarnished **10** besmirched, desecrated **12** contaminated

unclear
3 dim **4** hazy **5** murky, vague **6** bleary, blurry, cloudy, opaque **7** clouded, cryptic, dubious, obscure, shadowy **8** doubtful, nebulous, overcast, puzzling **9** ambiguous, enigmatic, tenebrous **10** ill-defined, indistinct, indefinite, inexplicit

Uncle Remus creator
6 Harris (Joel Chandler)

Uncle Tom's Cabin
author: **5** Stowe (Harriet Beecher)
character: **5** Eliza, Topsy **6** Legree (Simon) **9** Little Eva

unclothe
5 strip **6** denude, divest, expose **7** display, disrobe

unclothed
4 bare, nude **5** naked **6** peeled **7** denuded, exposed **8** in the raw, stripped **9** au naturel, buck-naked **10** stark naked

unclouded
4 fair **5** clear, lucid, sunny **6** bright **7** halcyon **8** rainless, sunshiny

uncluttered
4 neat, tidy, trig, trim **7** orderly **9** organized, shipshape **11** spic-and-span, well-ordered **12** spick-and-span

uncombed
5 messy, mussy **6** matted, mussed **7** ruffled, snarled, tangled, tousled **10** disheveled

uncommon
3 odd **4** rare **5** novel **6** choice, scarce, unique **7** special **8** esoteric, singular, sporadic **10** infrequent, noteworthy, remarkable **11** distinctive, exceptional **13** extraordinary

uncommunicative
3 mum **4** dumb **5** aloof **6** offish, silent **7** distant, guarded **8** reserved, reticent, taciturn **9** reclusive, secretive, withdrawn **10** antisocial, poker-faced, speechless, tongue-tied **11** inscrutable, standoffish, tight-lipped **12** closemouthed, tight-mouthed

uncomplicated
4 easy **5** basic, clear, plain **6** simple **8** clear-cut **10** effortless, elementary, manageable

uncomplimentary
7 adverse **8** critical **9** degrading **10** belittling, derogatory, pejorative **11** deprecatory, disparaging **12** depreciative, depreciatory

uncompromising
4 firm **5** rigid **8** hard-line, obdurate, resolute, stubborn **9** hard-nosed, immovable, insistent **10** brassbound, determined, inexorable, inflexible **12** intransigent, single-minded

unconcealed
4 bald, bare, open **5** frank, naked, overt, plain **6** candid **7** blatant, evident, exposed, express, obvious, visible **8** apparent, explicit, manifest, palpable **10** forthright **11** openhearted, transparent

unconcern
6 apathy **7** neglect **9** aloofness, disregard **10** alienation, detachment, dispassion **11** disinterest, inattention, insouciance, nonchalance **12** carelessness, heedlessness, indifference **13** preoccupation

unconcerned
4 cool **6** remote **8** careless, detached, heedless **9** alienated, apathetic, oblivious **10** insouciant, neglectful **11** inattentive, indifferent **13** disinterested, dispassionate

unconditional
5 sheer, total, utter **8** absolute, definite, explicit, outright **9** downright, out-and-out

unconfined
4 free, vast **5** loose **7** at large **9** at liberty, boundless, limitless

uncongenial
6 at odds **8** unfitted **9** repellent, repugnant **10** discordant **11** conflicting, displeasing **12** antipathetic, disagreeable, incompatible

unconnected
5 alone, apart **8** discrete, detached, disjoint, disjunct, distinct, separate **11** independent **13** discontinuous, noncontinuous

unconquerable
10 invincible, inviolable **11** bulletproof, impregnable, indomitable, insuperable **12** invulnerable

unconscionable
5 undue **6** unfair, unholy, unjust, wanton, wicked **7** immoral **8** barbaric, criminal **9** barbarous **10** exorbitant, inordinate, outrageous **11** inexcusable

unconscious
3 out **6** asleep, chance **7** out cold, stunned **8** comatose **9** insensate, passed out **10** blacked out, insensible, knocked out **11** inadvertent, instinctual, involuntary

unconsciousness
4 coma **5** faint **6** stupor, torpor, trance **7** syncope **13** obliviousness

unconsidered
4 rash **5** brash, hasty **6** casual **7** offhand **8** careless, reckless, slapdash **9** desultory, haphazard, hit-or-miss, hotheaded, impetuous **10** ill-advised, incautious **11** thoughtless

unconstrained
4 free, open **6** blithe, dégagé, wanton **7** buoyant, gushing, relaxed **8** animated, carefree, effusive, informal, outgoing **9** easygoing, expansive, liberated **10** expressive, nonchalant

uncontrollable
4 wild **6** unruly **7** wayward, willful **9** fractious **10** headstrong, refractory, self-willed **11** intractable **12** overwhelming, recalcitrant **13** irrepressible

uncontrolled
4 free, wild **5** loose **6** wanton **9** automatic, excessive **10** autonomous, immoderate, licentious **11** independent, instinctual, involuntary **12** disorganized **13** self-governing

unconventional
3 odd **4** beat, boho **5** kinky, kooky, outré **6** casual, far-out, freaky, quirky, unique, way-out, weirdo **7** bizarre, deviant, oddball, offbeat, wayward **8** aberrant, abnormal, atypical, bohemian, freakish, original, peculiar **9** anomalous, eccentric, irregular **10** avant-garde

unconvinced
5 leery **7** dubious **8** doubtful **9** skeptical **10** suspicious

unconvincing
4 lame **6** feeble, flimsy, forced **7** dubious, suspect **8** doubtful, strained **10** farfetched, improbable, incredible **11** implausible

uncooked
3 raw

uncool one
4 dink, dork, geek, nerd, wonk **6** weenie

uncouple
4 part **6** detach, divide **7** disjoin, divorce **8** separate **9** disengage **10** disconnect, dissociate **12** disaffiliate

uncouth
3 raw **4** rude **5** crass, crude, gross, rough **6** clumsy, coarse, vulgar **7** awkward, bizarre, boorish, ill-bred, loutish **8** impolite **9** eccentric, graceless, inelegant **10** outlandish **11** ill-mannered **12** discourteous
person: **3** oaf **4** boor, dolt, lout **5** clown **7** bumpkin **9** barbarian

uncover
4 bare **5** strip **6** betray, detect, divest, expose, remove, reveal **7** display, divulge **8** disclose

uncritical
5 naive **9** credulous **11** perfunctory

unction
3 oil **4** balm **5** cream, salve **6** balsam, cerate, chrism **7** suavity **8** liniment, ointment **9** emollient **11** embrocation

unctuous
4 oily **5** fatty, slick, soapy, suave **6** greasy, smarmy **7** cloying, fawning, fulsome **8** slippery **9** wheedling **10** flattering, oleaginous, saccharine **11** sycophantic

uncultivated
4 wild **5** crass, crude **6** coarse, desert, fallow, savage, vulgar **7** boorish, lowbrow **8** barbaric **9** barbarian, barbarous, inelegant

uncultured
3 raw **4** rude **5** crass, crude, gross **6** coarse, vulgar **7** artless, boorish, ill-bred, loutish,

lowbred, lowbrow, natural **8** barbaric, churlish, cloddish **9** barbarian, barbarous, benighted, inelegant

uncut
5 whole **6** entire, intact **8** complete **10** full-length

undamaged
5 sound, whole **6** intact

undaunted
4 bold **5** brave **6** daring, heroic **7** doughty, Spartan, valiant **8** fearless, intrepid, resolute, valorous **9** audacious **10** courageous **11** lionhearted **12** stouthearted

____ und Drang
5 Sturm

undeceive
8 disabuse **11** disillusion

undecided
4 iffy, moot, open, torn **7** dubious, pending **8** doubtful, wavering **9** equivocal, tentative **10** ambivalent, indefinite

undeclared
5 tacit **6** unsaid **7** assumed, implied **8** accepted, implicit, inferred, presumed **10** understood

undecorated
4 bare **5** plain, stark **6** homely, severe, simple **8** no-frills

undefiled
4 pure **6** chaste, intact, vestal, virgin **8** innocent, spotless, virginal, virtuous **9** stainless **10** immaculate

undefined
3 dim **4** hazy **5** faint, vague **6** bleary **7** obscure, shadowy, unclear **8** inchoate, nebulous **9** amorphous, shapeless **10** indistinct

undemonstrative
4 calm, cold, cool **5** aloof, chill **7** distant, laconic **8** reserved, retiring **9** contained, inhibited, shrinking, withdrawn **10** restrained **11** emotionless, passionless, standoffish **12** matter-of-fact **13** self-contained

undeniable
6 patent **7** certain, evident, genuine, obvious **8** manifest **9** veridical **10** inarguable **11** indubitable, irrefutable **12** indisputable **13** incontestable

undependable
6 fickle, tricky **7** erratic **10** capricious, fly-by-night, inconstant **12** inconsistent, questionable **13** irresponsible

under
3 low, sub **4** down, less **5** below, lower, short **6** lesser **7** beneath, covered, subject **8** downward, inferior **9** dependent, receiving, secondary, subjacent **11** subordinate
prefix: 3 hyp, sub **4** hypo

undercarriage
5 frame **9** framework **11** landing gear

undercover
6 covert, hidden, secret **7** furtive, stealth, sub-rosa **8** hush-hush, stealthy **11** clandestine **12** confidential **13** surreptitious
person: 3 spy **4** mole **5** agent, spook **6** sleuth **9** detective, operative **10** counterspy **11** double agent, secret agent **12** counteragent

undercroft
5 crypt, vault **7** chamber **8** catacomb

undercut
7 subvert **8** sabotage

underdeveloped
4 poor **7** dwarfed, stunted **8** backward, immature **9** unevolved **10** third-world

underdog
5 loser **6** victim **7** also-ran, fall guy, wannabe **9** dark horse

underdone
3 raw, red **4** rare

underestimate
6 slight **7** dismiss **8** belittle, discount, disprize, minimize **9** deprecate, disparage, sell short **10** depreciate

undergarment
3 bra **4** BVDs, slip **5** teddy **6** bikini, bodice, briefs, corset, girdle, shorts, undies **7** chemise, drawers, panties, stammel, step-ins **8** lingerie, pretties, Skivvies, woollies **9** brassiere, jockstrap, long johns, petticoat, underwear **10** foundation

undergo
4 bear, face **5** abide, brave, brook **6** endure, suffer **7** sustain, weather **8** submit to, tolerate **9** withstand **10** experience

undergraduate
4 coed, soph **5** frosh **6** junior, senior **8** freshman **9** collegian, sophomore

underground
4 tube **5** metro, train **6** buried, hidden, nether, secret, subway **7** illegal, off-beat, railway **8** hypogeal, hypogean **11** alternative, clandestine **12** subterranean **13** surreptitious

underhanded
3 sly **4** wily **5** shady **6** covert, crafty, secret, shifty, sneaky, tricky **7** cunning, devious, elusive, evasive, furtive, sub-rosa **8** guileful, sneaking, stealthy **9** deceitful, deceptive **10** circuitous **11** clandestine, duplicitous **13** surreptitious

underlie
4 bear **6** prop up **7** subtend, support **8** buttress

underline
4 mark **6** play up, stress **9** emphasize, italicize **10** accentuate

underling
4 aide, peon, serf **5** gofer, scrub, slave **6** flunky, gopher, lackey, menial, minion **7** fall guy **8** inferior **9** assistant, attendant, subaltern **11** subordinate

underlying
4 root **5** basal, basic **7** primary **8** implicit **9** elemental, essential **11** fundamental

undermine
3 sap **4** foil **5** blunt, erode **6** impair, thwart, weaken **7** cripple, disable, subvert **8** sabotage **9** attenuate, frustrate **10** debilitate, demoralize

undermost
6 bottom, lowest **10** rock-bottom

underneath
4 sole **5** below, lower **6** bottom **7** covered

underpin
4 back, base, prop, root **5** brace **6** uphold **7** bolster, justify, shore up, support **8** buttress, validate **10** strengthen **11** corroborate

underpinning
4 base, prop, root, stay **5** basis, brace **7** bedrock, footing, seating, support **8** buttress **10** foundation, groundwork **12** substructure

underprivileged
4 poor **5** needy **8** deprived **11** handicapped, unfortunate **13** disadvantaged

underrate
7 devalue **8** discount, mark down, minimize, write off **9** devaluate, write down **10** depreciate

underscore
6 accent, play up, stress **9** emphasize, italicize **10** accentuate

underside
4 sole **6** bottom **7** reverse

undersized
3 toy **4** baby, mini, puny **5** dinky, dwarf, pygmy, runty, short, small **6** bantam, little, pocket, slight **7** scrubby, stunted **9** miniature **10** diminutive **11** Lilliputian

understand
3 con, dig, ken, see **4** grok, know **5** grasp, infer, savvy, sense **6** accept, assume, deduce, fathom, figure, follow, gather, reason, reckon, take in, take it **7** believe, discern, imagine, presume, realize, suppose, surmise, suspect, suss out **8** conclude, consider, perceive **9** apprehend **10** appreciate, comprehend, conjecture

understandable
5 clear, lucid, plain **8** clear-cut, coherent, knowable **9** excusable, graspable, plausible **10** articulate, believable, defensible, fathomable, reasonable **11** justifiable, perceivable, unambiguous **12** intelligible **13** apprehensible

understanding
3 ken, wit **4** deal, pact **5** grasp, sense **6** accord, humane, kindly **7** compact, empathy, entente, insight, mastery **8** sympathy **9** agreement, awareness, knowledge, tolerance **10** acceptance, impression, perception **11** considerate, discernment, explanation, sympathetic **12** apprehension, relationship **13** comprehension

understatement
7 litotes

understood
3 got **5** tacit **7** assumed, implied **8** accepted, implicit, inferred, unspoken

understudy
6 double, backup, fill-in **7** standby, stand-in **9** surrogate **10** substitute **11** replacement

undertake
3 try **4** dare **5** assay, begin, essay, start **6** accept, assume, pledge, strive, tackle **7** attempt, certify, execute, perform, promise, warrant **8** commence, contract, covenant, endeavor, set about, set forth, shoulder **9** guarantee

undertaker
8 embalmer **9** mortician

undertaking
3 job **4** task **6** affair, charge, effort **7** calling, emprise, exploit, mission, project, pursuit, venture **8** endeavor **9** adventure, guarantee, operation **10** enterprise

under-the-table
6 covert, hidden, secret, sneaky **7** furtive, on the q.t., sub-rosa **8** hush-hush, stealthy **9** concealed **11** clandestine **13** surreptitious

under the weather
3 ill **4** sick **6** ailing, unwell

undertone
3 hue, hum **4** buzz, cast, hint, tint **5** drone, shade **6** mumble, murmur, mutter, rumble **7** inkling **10** suggestion **11** association, connotation, implication

undertow
4 eddy **7** current, riptide, sea puss

undervalue
see **underrate**

underwater
9 submarine **10** subaquatic, subaqueous
breathing apparatus: 5 scuba
captain: 4 Nemo
chamber: 7 caisson
device: 8 paravane
missile: 7 torpedo
sound detector: 5 sonar

underwear
see **undergarment**

underwood
5 brush, copse, hedge, scrub 7 boscage, coppice, thicket 9 shrubbery

underworld
4 hell 5 hades, Sheol 6 Erebus, Tophet 7 Gehenna, inferno 8 gangland 9 antipodes 11 Pandemonium
boatman: 6 Charon
deity: 3 Dis 4 Bran 5 Pluto 6 Osiris
goddess: 6 Hecate 10 Persephone
organization: 4 tong 5 Mafia, Triad 6 Yakuza 10 Cosa Nostra
relating to: 8 chthonic
watchdog: 8 Cerberus

underwrite
4 back, fund, sign 5 endow, stake 6 assure, insure, pay for, secure 7 agree to, endorse, finance, sponsor, support 8 bankroll 9 grubstake, guarantee 11 subscribe to

undesirable
8 annoying 9 offensive 10 ill-favored 11 displeasing, inadvisable, troublesome 12 disagreeable 13 inappropriate, objectionable

undetermined
5 vague 7 dubious, obscure, pending, unclear 8 doubtful 9 ambiguous, equivocal 10 ill-defined, indefinite, indistinct 12 inconclusive

undeveloped
5 crude, green, rough 6 latent 8 backward, immature, inchoate 9 embryonic, incipient, primitive

undiluted
4 neat, pure 5 sheer, utter 7 genuine 8 absolute, straight 9 authentic

undiplomatic
4 rash, rude 5 brash 8 impudent, tactless 9 audacious, impolitic, impulsive, maladroit 10 ill-advised, indiscreet 11 impertinent, injudicious, insensitive, thoughtless 12 presumptuous

undisciplined
4 wild 6 wanton 7 froward, restive, wayward, willful 8 contrary 9 fractious 10 disorderly, rebellious, refractory 11 intractable 12 contumacious, noncompliant, obstreperous, recalcitrant

undisclosed
6 hidden, sealed, secret 8 ulterior, withheld 9 anonymous 11 clandestine 12 confidential

undisguised
4 bald, open, pure 5 frank, naked, overt, sheer, stark 6 candid, patent 7 obvious 8 apparent, explicit, manifest, palpable 9 barefaced 11 open-hearted

undistinguished
5 stock 6 common 7 humdrum, obscure, routine 8 everyday, inferior, low-grade, mediocre, middling, ordinary, workaday 10 second-rate 11 commonplace, nondescript, second-class 12 run-of-the-mill

undivided
3 one 4 full 5 fixed, total, whole 6 entire, intact, united 8 complete 9 unanimous 10 continuous 11 indivisible 12 concentrated

undo
4 free, open, stet, veto 5 annul, loose 6 cancel, defeat, loosen, negate, repeal, stymie 7 nullify, release, reverse, vitiate 8 abrogate, disallow, overturn 9 disengage 10 contravene, invalidate 11 disentangle, outmaneuver

undoing
4 bane, doom, ruin, slip 5 shame 7 misstep 8 downfall, reversal 9 destroyer, overthrow, ruination 10 misfortune 11 destruction, humiliation

undoubted
4 real, sure, true 7 certain, genuine 8 definite, positive 9 authentic

undoubtedly
5 truly 6 indeed, really, surely 7 clearly 8 of course 9 assuredly, certainly 10 definitely, positively, presumably 11 indubitably

undress
see **unclothe**

undressed
4 nude, rude 5 naked 7 exposed 8 in the raw, stripped 9 au naturel

undue
5 inapt 7 extreme 8 ill-timed, improper, needless 9 excessive 10 immoderate, indecorous, inordinate 11 extravagant 13 inappropriate

undulant fever
11 brucellosis

undulate
4 roll, swag, sway, wave 5 heave, snake, swell, swing 6 billow, ripple 7 slither 9 fluctuate, oscillate

unduly
3 too 6 overly 9 extremely, immensely 11 excessively 12 immoderately, inordinately

undying
7 abiding, ageless, endless, eternal 8 enduring, immortal 9 continual, deathless, perennial, perpetual 10 continuing 11 amaranthine, everlasting 12 imperishable

unearth
4 find 5 dig up 6 exhume, expose, reveal 7 exhibit, find out, root out 8 come upon, disclose, discover, dredge up, excavate 9 ascertain, determine 10 come across

unearthly
5 eerie, weird 6 spooky 7 ghostly 8 abnormal, ethereal, heavenly, numinous, spectral 9 appalling, fantastic 10 miraculous, mysterious,

outlandish, superhuman, suprahuman **12** preposterous, supermundane, supernatural **13** preternatural

unease
4 care, fear **5** agita, angst, worry **6** strain, stress **7** anxiety, concern, tension **8** disquiet, distress **9** abashment, confusion, misgiving **10** discomfort, discontent, solicitude **11** disquietude, fretfulness, nervousness, uncertainty, uptightness

uneasy
4 edgy **5** tense **7** anxious, awkward, fearful, fidgety, fretful, nervous, restive, worried **8** agitated, doubtful, insecure, restless **9** ambiguous, disturbed, perturbed **10** disquieted **12** apprehensive

uneducated
5 crude, rough **8** ignorant **9** benighted **10** illiterate

unembellished
4 bald, bare **5** blunt, plain, spare, stark **6** severe **7** austere

unemotional
4 cold, cool **5** stoic, stony **6** frigid, sedate, serene, stolid **7** deadpan, equable, glacial, stoical **8** composed, obdurate, reserved, reticent **9** apathetic, impassive **10** hard-boiled, phlegmatic **11** insensitive, passionless **12** intellectual, thick-skinned **13** dispassionate

unemployed
4 idle **5** fired **6** otiose **7** jobless, laid off, loafing **8** inactive, leisured, workless

unending
7 eternal **8** constant, immortal, infinite, timeless **9** boundless, ceaseless, continual, incessant, limitless, perennial, perpetual **10** continuous **11** amaranthine, everlasting **12** interminable

unenlightened
5 naive **8** backward, ignorant, nescient **9** benighted

unenthusiastic
4 cool **5** tepid **8** grudging, listless, lukewarm **9** apathetic **10** lackluster, lacklustre, spiritless **11** halfhearted, indifferent, perfunctory

unequal
3 odd **7** diverse **8** inferior, lopsided, one-sided **9** different, disparate, divergent, irregular **10** asymmetric, dissimilar, mismatched

unequaled
6 unique **7** supreme **8** foremost, nonesuch, peerless **9** matchless, paramount **10** preeminent, surpassing **12** incomparable, transcendent

unequivocal
5 clear **6** direct, patent **7** certain, evident **8** absolute, apparent, definite, distinct, explicit, manifest, palpable **11** categorical, indubitable **12** indisputable

unerring
5 exact **6** dead-on **7** certain, correct, perfect, precise **8** accurate, reliable **9** faultless, unfailing **10** dependable, infallible

unessential
8 marginal, needless, unneeded **9** redundant **10** expendable, gratuitous, irrelevant, peripheral **11** dispensable, superfluous

unethical
5 venal, wrong **7** corrupt, crooked, immoral **9** dishonest, reprobate **12** disreputable

uneven
3 odd **4** wavy **5** bumpy, erose, harsh, jaggy, rough **6** craggy, jagged, patchy, ragged, random, rugged, spotty **7** scraggy, varying **8** lopsided, scabrous, scraggly, variable **9** haphazard, hit-or-miss, irregular **10** asymmetric, imbalanced

unevenness
4 bump, wave **7** anomaly **8** imparity **9** disparity, imbalance, roughness, variation **10** inequality **12** irregularity, lopsidedness **13** disproportion

uneventful
5 usual **6** placid **7** humdrum, prosaic, routine **8** ordinary **11** commonplace

unexampled
4 lone, only, sole, solo **5** alone **6** unique **8** singular, solitary **10** consummate, inimitable, sui generis **12** incomparable

unexcited
4 calm **5** blasé, stoic **6** placid, sedate, serene **7** relaxed, stoical **8** composed, tranquil **9** apathetic **10** nonchalant **11** indifferent **13** dispassionate

unexciting
4 arid, dull, tame **5** banal, bland, ho-hum **6** boring, stodgy **7** humdrum, insipid, prosaic, tedious **8** lifeless, tiresome **10** monotonous **11** commonplace

unexpected
10 surprising
defeat: **5** upset

unexpectedly
5 aback, short **6** sudden **8** abruptly, suddenly **9** forthwith **12** accidentally **13** inadvertently

unexpended
5 saved **7** reserve, surplus **8** left over, reserved **9** remaining

unexpired
5 valid **9** operative

unexpressed
5 tacit **6** silent **7** assumed, implied **8** implicit, presumed, wordless

unfailing
4 fast, sure **7** certain, devoted **8** constant, faithful, reliable, resolute, surefire **9** steadfast **10** consistent, dependable, infallible, invariable,

persistent **11** everlasting, persevering **12** tried-and-true **13** inexhaustible

unfair
4 foul **5** wrong **6** biased, shabby **8** wrongful **9** arbitrary, dishonest **10** prejudiced

unfaithful
5 false **6** untrue **8** cheating, disloyal, recreant, turncoat **9** faithless, two-timing **10** adulterous, inaccurate, perfidious, traitorous **11** treacherous

unfaltering
3 set **4** firm **6** steady **7** abiding **8** constant, enduring, resolute, tireless **9** steadfast **10** continuous **11** persevering **12** never-failing, wholehearted

unfamiliar
3 new, odd **5** alien, novel, weird **6** exotic **7** foreign, strange **8** abnormal, peculiar **11** incognizant, out-of-the-way

unfashionable
5 dated, dowdy, passé, stale **6** bygone, démodé, old-hat, shabby **7** outworn **8** outdated, outmoded **9** out-of-date **10** antiquated, oldfangled

unfasten
4 free, open **5** loose **6** detach, loosen **7** release **9** disengage

unfathomable
7 abysmal, obscure **8** profound **9** boundless, enigmatic **10** bottomless, fathomless **11** inscrutable **12** immeasurable, impenetrable

unfavorable
3 bad, ill **4** poor **6** averse **7** adverse, hostile, opposed **8** contrary, damaging, inimical, negative **9** disliking, troubling **11** detrimental, displeasing **12** antagonistic, disapproving, inauspicious
prefix: 3 dys

unfavorably
4 awry **5** amiss, badly **6** astray, poorly **7** wrongly **10** negatively

unfeasible
8 quixotic **9** visionary **10** chimerical, impossible **11** impractical, speculative, theoretical **13** impracticable

unfeeling
4 cold, hard, numb **5** cruel, harsh, stern, stony **6** brutal, leaden, marble, numbed, severe, stolid **7** callous **8** benumbed, deadened, hardened, obdurate, pitiless, ruthless **9** apathetic, heartless, indurated, insensate, senseless **10** hard-boiled, insensible, insentient **11** cold-blooded, coldhearted, hardhearted, insensitive **12** anesthetized

unfeigned
4 real, true **6** actual, hearty, honest **7** artless, earnest, genuine, natural, sincere **8** innocent **9** guileless, heartfelt, ingenuous **12** wholehearted

unfinished
3 raw **5** crude, rough **7** sketchy **9** imperfect, roughhewn **10** incomplete

unfit
4 weak **5** inapt, inept **6** faulty **7** deprive, disable, useless **8** disabled, improper **9** ill-suited, incapable, maladroit **10** disqualify, ill-adapted, inadequate, ineligible **11** ill-equipped, incompetent **12** disqualified, incompatible **13** inappropriate, incapacitated

unfitting
5 inapt **8** improper **9** imprudent **10** ill-advised, inapposite, malapropos **11** inadvisable **13** inappropriate

unfix
4 part **5** loose, sever **6** cut off, detach, loosen, sunder **9** disengage **10** disconnect, dissociate

unflagging
6 steady **7** staunch **8** constant, tireless **11** persevering **13** indefatigable, inexhaustible

unflappable
4 calm, cool **5** stoic **6** poised, serene **7** assured, equable **8** composed, laid-back **9** collected **10** deliberate, nonchalant **11** self-assured **13** imperturbable, self-possessed

unfledged
5 green, young **6** callow, jejune **7** puerile **8** immature, juvenile **13** inexperienced

unflinching
4 firm, grim **6** dogged **7** doughty, staunch, valiant **8** fearless, intrepid, resolute **9** dauntless, steadfast **10** courageous, relentless **12** stouthearted

unfold
4 open **6** deduce, evolve, expand, expose, extend, flower, mature, reveal **7** blossom, burgeon, clear up, develop, display, dope out, exhibit, explain, resolve **8** decipher, disclose, evidence, manifest **9** elaborate, explicate, figure out, puzzle out, transpire **10** effloresce, outstretch **11** come to light

unforced
4 easy **7** natural, willing, witting **8** elective, optional **9** available, easygoing, voluntary **10** deliberate, volitional **11** intentional **13** discretionary, noncompulsory

unforeseen
6 chance **8** surprise **10** accidental, surprising

unforgivable
10 censurable, inexpiable, outrageous **11** blameworthy, inexcusable, intolerable **12** indefensible **13** insupportable, reprehensible

unformed
4 rude **5** crude, rough, vague **6** callow **8** immature, inchoate, nebulous **9** amorphous, roughhewn, shapeless **10** indefinite

unfortunate
3 bad, sad **4** dire, poor **6** woeful **7** adverse, awkward, hapless **8** grievous, ill-fated, luckless, wretched **9** ill-chosen, miserable **10** afflictive, calamitous, deplorable, disastrous, ill-starred, lamentable **11** distressing, regrettable, star-crossed **12** disagreeable, inauspicious, infelicitous

unfounded
4 idle, vain **5** false **8** baseless, spurious **9** deceptive, dishonest **10** fabricated, fallacious, gratuitous, groundless, mendacious, misleading

unfriendly
3 icy **4** cold, cool **5** alien, aloof, chill, gruff, surly **6** chilly, frosty, remote **7** distant, grouchy, hostile, opposed **8** inimical **10** antisocial, inimicable **11** ill-disposed **12** antagonistic, disagreeable, inhospitable, misanthropic

unfruitful
4 idle **6** barren, desert, effete, fallow, futile, wasted **7** sterile, useless **8** abortive, bootless, depleted, impotent **9** infertile, pointless **10** unavailing **11** ineffective, ineffectual

unfurl
4 open **6** expose, reveal, spread **7** develop, display, exhibit **8** disclose **9** elaborate, spread out

unfurnished
4 bare **5** empty **6** vacant

unfussy
5 loose **6** breezy, casual, common, dégagé, folksy, mellow **7** cursory, relaxed **8** familiar, informal, laid-back **9** easygoing **11** low-pressure, pococurante

ungainly
5 gawky, lanky, splay **6** clumsy, klutzy, oafish **7** awkward, boorish, hulking, loutish, lumpish **8** bungling, clownish, lubberly **9** lumbering, maladroit **10** blundering

ungarnished
5 plain **6** modest, simple

ungenerous
4 mean **5** petty, tight **6** paltry, shabby, skimpy, stingy **7** chintzy, miserly **8** grudging, picayune **9** illiberal, niggardly, penurious **10** pinchpenny **11** closefisted, tightfisted **12** parsimonious **13** penny-pinching

ungodly
see **unholy**

ungovernable
4 wild **6** unruly **7** froward, lawless, willful **8** mutinous **9** fractious, turbulent **10** disorderly, headstrong, rebellious, refractory, tumultuous **11** intractable **12** recalcitrant **13** irrepressible

ungraceful
5 crude, gawky, inept, stiff **6** clumsy, gauche, klutzy, oafish, wooden **7** artless, awkward, halting, labored, stilted **8** bumbling, bungling **9** all thumbs, inelegant, lumbering, maladroit **10** blundering

ungracious
4 rude **5** gruff **6** crusty **7** brusque **8** churlish, impolite **9** offensive **11** disobliging, ill-mannered, impertinent, thoughtless **12** disagreeable, discourteous **13** disrespectful, inconsiderate

unguarded
5 frank, hasty **6** candid, direct **7** offhand **8** careless, heedless, reckless **9** impolitic, imprudent, impulsive **10** incautious, indiscreet **11** defenseless, thoughtless

unguent
4 balm **5** cream, salve **6** balsam, cerate, chrism, lotion **8** ointment **9** emollient, lubricant **11** embrocation

ungulate
3 hog, pig **4** deer **5** horse, tapir **6** hoofed **8** elephant **10** rhinoceros

unhallowed
4 evil **6** impure, wicked **7** immoral, impious, profane **8** infernal **9** nefarious **10** desecrated, iniquitous, irreverent

unhampered
4 free, open **5** frank, loose **6** direct

unhand
5 let go **7** release

unhandy
5 bulky, inept **6** clumsy, gauche, klutzy **7** awkward, halting, hulking **8** bumbling, bungling, cumbrous **9** all thumbs, ham-handed, maladroit, ponderous **10** cumbersome **12** inconvenient

unhappiness
3 woe **5** blues, dolor, dumps, gloom, grief **6** misery, sorrow **7** anxiety, sadness **8** distress **9** dejection **10** depression, desolation, discontent, heartbreak, melancholy **11** despondency, dolefulness **12** mournfulness, wretchedness

unhappy
3 sad **4** down, glum **5** sorry **6** dismal, dreary, gloomy **7** joyless **8** dejected, downcast, mournful, saddened, troubled, wretched **9** cheerless, depressed, sorrowful, woebegone **10** despondent, dispirited, melancholy **11** melancholic **12** disconsolate, heavyhearted

unharmed
4 safe **5** sound **6** intact, secure, unhurt

unhealthy
3 ill **4** sick **6** ailing, infirm, sickly, unwell **7** baneful, noisome, noxious **8** diseased **9** injurious **11** deleterious **12** insalubrious

unheard-of
3 new **6** unique **7** obscure **8** nameless **10** phenomenal **13** extraordinary

unhinge
5 addle, craze 6 madden, ruffle 7 derange

unhinged
3 mad 4 daft, loco, nuts 5 balmy, crazy, loony, wacky 6 insane 7 lunatic 8 demented, deranged 9 disturbed

unholy
4 base, evil, vile 6 impure, sinful, wicked 7 heinous, immoral, impious, profane 8 dreadful, fiendish, god-awful, shocking 9 atheistic, barbarous 10 iniquitous, irreverent, outrageous, scandalous 11 irreligious 12 sacrilegious 13 reprehensible

unhurried
4 easy, slow 6 casual 7 laggard, relaxed 8 dilatory, laid-back 9 easygoing, leisurely 10 deliberate 11 low-pressure

unhurt
4 safe 5 sound, whole 6 entire, intact 7 perfect

unification
5 union 6 fusion, hookup, merger 7 amalgam, joining, linkage, melding, merging 8 alliance, coupling 9 coalition 10 connection, federation 11 affiliation, coalescence, combination 12 amalgamation 13 confederation, consolidation

uniform
4 even, like, suit 5 alike, equal, level 6 attire, outfit, stable, steady 7 ordered, orderly, regular, similar, stabile 8 constant, unvaried 9 consonant, unvarying 10 comparable, consistent, invariable, unchanging 11 homogeneous
combining form: 3 iso
type: 3 BDU 5 blues, habit, khaki 6 livery, whites

uniformity
6 parity 7 oneness 8 equality, evenness, identity, monotony, sameness 9 agreement, congruity, constancy 11 consistency 13 invariability

uniformly
6 always, evenly 7 equally 8 smoothly 10 comparably 11 analogously, identically 12 equivalently

unify
3 tie 4 bind, bond, fuse, knit, link, mesh 5 blend, merge, unite 6 cement 7 combine, conjoin 8 coalesce, compound, federate 9 integrate 10 amalgamate, centralize, synthesize 11 consolidate

unimaginable
10 incredible 12 mind-boggling 13 extraordinary, inconceivable, indescribable

unimaginative
4 dull, flat 5 banal, bland, trite, vapid 6 common 7 literal, prosaic, routine, vanilla 8 bromidic 10 derivative, pedestrian 11 commonplace

unimpaired
4 safe 5 sound 6 intact 7 perfect

unimpeachable
5 valid 7 correct 8 flawless, reliable, virtuous 9 blameless, exemplary, faultless 10 conclusive, impeccable 13 authoritative

unimportant
4 mere 5 minor, petty 6 casual, minute, paltry 7 trivial 8 piddling 9 small-beer, worthless 10 expendable, immaterial, irrelevant, negligible 11 dispensable, meaningless, superfluous 13 insignificant

uninformed
8 ignorant, nescient 9 oblivious 11 incognizant, superficial

uninhabited
5 empty, waste 6 barren, vacant 7 vacated 8 deserted, desolate, forsaken 9 abandoned, evacuated

uninhibited
3 lax 4 free 5 loose 9 expansive, fancy-free, liberated 10 boisterous

uninjured
4 safe 5 sound, whole 6 intact

uninspired
4 blah, drab, dull 5 banal, stock, trite, vapid 6 boring 7 humdrum, insipid, sterile 8 bromidic, lifeless, ordinary 9 colorless 10 lackluster, lacklustre, pedestrian 11 commonplace

unintelligent
4 dumb 5 dense 6 obtuse, stupid 7 asinine, brutish, doltish, fatuous, foolish, moronic, vacuous, witless 8 mindless 9 brainless, ludicrous 10 half-witted, ill-advised, irrational, ridiculous, weak-minded 11 harebrained, lamebrained

unintentional
6 chance, random 9 haphazard 10 accidental, fortuitous, incidental 11 inadvertent 12 adventitious, coincidental

uninterested
5 aloof, blasé, bored, jaded 9 apathetic, incurious 11 indifferent

uninteresting
3 dry 4 arid, blah, drab, dull, flat 5 banal, dusty, ho-hum, stale 6 boring, jejune 7 humdrum, insipid, prosaic, tedious 8 bromidic, plodding, tiresome 9 colorless, dryasdust, wearisome 10 monotonous, pedestrian

uninterrupted
6 direct 7 endless, nonstop 8 constant 9 ceaseless, continual, incessant, perpetual, sustained 10 continuous

union
4 bloc, bond, club 5 alloy, artel, group, guild, joint 6 fusion, league, merger 7 amalgam,

joining, melding, merging, society **8** alliance, congress, coupling, junction, juncture, marriage, sodality **9** coalition **10** connection, federation, fellowship **11** association, brotherhood, coalescence, combination, confederacy, cooperative, unification **13** confederation, consolidation
branch: **5** local
labor: **3** AFL, CIO, ILA, UAW, UFW, UMW **4** ILWU **5** ILGWU

Union's foe
3 CSA

unique
3 odd **4** lone, only, sole, solo **5** novel **6** single **7** special **8** peculiar, peerless, singular, solitary, uncommon, unwonted **9** anomalous, exclusive, matchless, unequaled, unmatched, unrivaled **10** inimitable, particular, sui generis, unequalled, unexampled, unrivalled **11** distinctive, exceptional **12** incomparable, unparalleled, unrepeatable

uniqueness
8 identity **10** singleness **11** singularity **13** individuality

___-Unis
5 Etats

unit
3 arm, one **4** area, item, part, wing **5** digit, group, monad, piece, whole **6** entity **7** element, measure **8** molecule **9** component **10** individual **11** constituent
administrative: **6** agency, bureau, sector **8** district
boy scout: **5** troop
educational: **6** course
military: (see at **military**)
of acceleration: **3** gal
of action: **7** episode
of advertising space: **4** line **6** column
of an element: **4** atom **8** molecule
of angular measure: **6** radian
of area: **3** are **4** acre **6** morgen **7** hectare **9** square rod **10** square mile, square yard
of astronomical distance: **6** parsec **9** light-year
of brightness: **7** lambert
of capacitance: **5** farad
of capacity: **3** cup, tun **4** cord, dram, gill, peck, pint **5** liter, litre, minim, ounce, quart **6** barrel, bushel, firkin, gallon
of computer information: **3** bit, gig, meg **4** byte **8** gigabyte, megabyte
of conductance: **3** mho **7** siemens
of distance: **4** mile **6** league, parsec **7** furlong **9** kilometer
of electricity: **3** amp **4** volt, watt **6** ampere **7** coulomb
of energy: **3** erg **5** joule **7** quantum **8** watt-hour
of explosive force: **7** megaton
of fineness: **5** carat, karat
of force: **4** dyne **6** newton **7** poundal
of frequency: **5** hertz **7** fresnel
of grain: **5** sheaf
of heat: **3** Btu **5** therm **6** kelvin **7** calorie
of illumination: **3** lux **5** lumen
of impedance: **3** ohm
of inductance: **5** henry
of length: **3** mil, rod **4** foot, hand, inch, rood, yard **5** chain, fermi, meter **6** fathom, micron **8** angstrom
historic: **5** cubit
of loudness: **4** sone **7** decibel
of lumber: **9** board foot
of magnetic flux: **5** gamma, gauss, tesla, weber **7** maxwell
of magnetic intensity: **7** oersted
of magnetomotive force: **7** gilbert
of pressure: **3** bar, psi **4** torr **6** pascal **10** atmosphere
of radiation: **3** rad **8** roentgen
of radioactivity: **5** curie
of resistance: **3** ohm
of solar radiation: **7** langley
of sound absorption: **5** sabin
of speech: **4** word **6** toneme **7** phoneme **8** morpheme, syllable
of speed: **3** CPS, MPH, RPM **4** knot
of temperature: **6** degree, kelvin
of time: **3** age, day, eon **4** beat, bell, hour, week, year **5** month **6** minute, season, second **8** svedberg
of viscosity: **5** poise
of volume: **5** stere **9** cubic foot, cubic yard **10** cubic meter
of weight: **3** cwt, ton **4** dram, gram, rotl, tael **5** carat, grain, ounce, pound, tonne **6** drachm **7** gigaton, kiloton, quintal, scruple **8** kilogram, millieme **9** metric ton, microgram, milligram
historic: **3** tod **5** gerah, libra
Indian: **4** tola
Russian: **4** pood
of work: **3** erg **5** ergon, joule
social: **4** clan **5** tribe **6** family **7** chapter

unitary
5 whole **9** undivided **11** indivisible

unite
3 mix, tie, wed **4** ally, band, bind, bond, fuse, join, knit, link, meld, pool, weld **5** blend, graft, marry, merge, unify **6** cement, couple, gather, league, mingle, splice **7** combine, conjoin, connect **8** assemble, coadjute, coalesce, compound, federate **9** affiliate, aggregate, commingle **10** amalgamate, federalize **11** confederate, incorporate

united
3 one, wed **5** joint **6** allied, linked, merged, wedded **7** made one **8** agreeing, combined, in accord **10** harmonious

United Arab Emirates
capital: **8** Abu Dhabi
city: **5** Dubai **6** Dubayy
emirate: **5** Dubai **6** Dubayy **8** Abu Dhabi
former name: **13** Trucial States
monetary unit: **6** dirham
peninsula: **7** Arabian
strait: **6** Hormuz

United Kingdom
capital: **6** London
city: **3** Ely **4** Bath **5** Derby, Dover, Leeds **6** Exeter, Oxford **7** Bristol, Cardiff, Glasgow, Paisley **8** Bradford, Brighton, Coventry, Plymouth **9** Cambridge, Edinburgh, Leicester, Liverpool, Newcastle, Sheffield **10** Birmingham, Manchester, Nottingham
component: **5** Wales **7** England **8** Scotland **12** Great Britain
conqueror: **6** Caesar (Julius) **7** William (the Conqueror)
county: **4** Kent **5** Devon, Essex **6** Dorset, Surrey, Sussex **7** Norfolk, Suffolk **8** Cornwall, Somerset **9** Berkshire, Wiltshire, Yorkshire
island: **3** Man **4** Jura, Skye **5** Islay, Lewis, Wight **6** Jersey **8** Anguilla, Guernsey
island group: **6** Orkney **7** Channel **8** Hebrides, Shetland
language: **5** Welsh **6** Gaelic
monarch: **4** Anne, Mary **5** Henry, James **6** Alfred (the Great), Edward, George **7** Charles, Richard, William **8** Victoria **9** Elizabeth
monetary unit: **5** pence, penny, pound
monetary unit, former: **3** bob **5** crown, groat **6** florin, guinea **7** ha'penny **8** farthing, shilling, sixpence **9** halfpenny **10** threepence
mountain, range: **7** Scafell (Peak), Snowdon **8** Ben Nevis, Cumbrian, Grampian **12** Cheviot Hills
peninsula: **7** Kintyre
prehistoric site: **7** Avebury **9** Skara Brae **10** Stonehenge
river: **3** Dee, Exe, Wye **4** Aire, Avon, Ouse, Tyne **5** Clyde **6** Mersey, Severn, Thames

United Nations secretary-general
3 Ban (Ki-moon), Lie (Trygve) **5** Annan (Kofi), Thant (U) **8** Waldheim (Kurt) **12** Boutros-Ghali (Boutros), Hammarskjöld (Dag)

United States
desert: **6** Mojave **7** Sonoran **8** Colorado
highest point: **6** Denali (Mt.) **8** McKinley (Mt.)
island group: **6** Hawaii **8** Aleutian, Pribilof, Thousand
lowest point: **11** Death Valley
mountain range: **5** Ozark, Rocky **7** Cascade, Olympic **8** Catskill **9** Blue Ridge **10** Adirondack, Great Smoky **11** Appalachian **12** Sierra Nevada
possession: **10** Puerto Rico
state: **4** Iowa, Ohio, Utah **5** Idaho, Maine, Texas **6** Alaska, Hawaii, Kansas, Nevada, Oregon **7** Alabama, Arizona, Florida, Georgia, Indiana, Montana, New York, Vermont, Wyoming **8** Arkansas, Colorado, Delaware, Illinois, Kentucky, Maryland, Michigan, Missouri, Nebraska, Oklahoma, Virginia **9** Louisiana, Minnesota, New Jersey, New Mexico, Tennessee, Wisconsin **10** California, Washington **11** Connecticut, Mississippi, North Dakota, Rhode Island, South Dakota **12** New Hampshire, Pennsylvania, West Virginia **13** Massachusetts, North Carolina, South Carolina
territory: **4** Guam **13** American Samoa, Virgin Islands

unity
5 union **6** accord **7** concord, harmony, oneness **8** identity, soleness **9** agreement, consensus **10** continuity, singleness, solidarity

universal
3 all **5** broad, total, whole **6** common, cosmic, entire, global **7** general, generic **8** catholic **9** extensive, planetary, unlimited, worldwide **10** ecumenical, ubiquitous **11** omnipresent **12** all-embracing, all-inclusive, cosmopolitan **13** comprehensive
combining form: **4** omni

universe
3 all **5** whole, world **6** cosmos, system **8** creation **9** macrocosm

unjust
5 wrong **6** biased, shabby **7** partial **8** one-sided, improper, wrongful **9** inequable **10** prejudiced **11** inequitable

unjustifiable
7 invalid **8** baseless **10** groundless **11** inexcusable **12** indefensible

unkempt
5 messy **6** frowsy, frowzy, ragtag, shaggy, sloppy **7** ruffled, rumpled, scruffy, tousled **8** scraggly, slipshod, slovenly **10** bedraggled, disarrayed, disheveled, disordered **11** disarranged

unkind
4 mean, vile **5** cruel, harsh, rough, stern **6** severe **7** callous **9** inclement, malicious **11** insensitive, thoughtless

unknowable
6 arcane, hidden, mystic, occult, secret **7** cryptic **8** mystical, numinous **9** enigmatic, recondite **10** mysterious **11** inscrutable **12** impenetrable

unknowing
8 heedless, ignorant **9** oblivious **10** insensible **11** incognizant

unknown
6 hidden, nobody, secret **7** obscure, strange **8** nameless **9** anonymous, incognito
author: **4** Anon.

unlawful
6 banned **7** bootleg, corrupt, illegal, illicit **8** criminal, outlawed, verboten **9** forbidden, felonious **10** contraband, flagitious, indictable, prohibited, proscribed **11** black-market **12** illegitimate

unlearned
5 naive **8** ignorant, nescient **10** illiterate **11** instinctive

unleash
4 free, vent **5** let go, loose, untie, visit, wreak **7** inflict, release **8** carry out, liberate **10** bring about

unless
3 but **4** save **6** except, saving **7** barring, but that, without **9** excepting, excluding

unlettered
see **uneducated**

unlikable
9 obnoxious, offensive, repellent **11** displeasing, distasteful **12** disagreeable

unlike
5 mixed **6** varied **7** diverse, unequal, various **8** assorted **9** different, disparate, divergent **10** dissimilar **11** contrasting, distinctive, diversified **13** heterogeneous

unlikely
5 faint, unfit **6** remote, slight **7** distant, dubious **8** doubtful **10** farfetched, improbable **11** implausible **12** questionable

unlimited
4 full, vast **5** total **7** endless, immense **8** absolute, infinite, wide-open **9** boundless **12** immeasurable, interminable **13** comprehensive

unlit
4 dark, inky **6** gloomy **7** shadowy **9** lightless, tenebrous

unload
4 drop, dump, junk **5** chuck, ditch, empty **6** debark, remove **7** confess, confide, deep-six, deliver, discard, divulge, lighten, relieve **8** disclose, disgorge, jettison **9** disburden, discharge, disembark, eighty-six, stevedore **11** disencumber

unloose
4 free, undo **5** let go, relax **6** detach **7** break up, manumit, release, set free, slacken **8** liberate **9** disengage, extricate **10** disconnect

unlucky
6 jinxed **7** hapless, ominous **8** ill-fated **9** ill-boding **10** ill-starred **11** detrimental, inopportune, regrettable, star-crossed **12** inauspicious

unmanageable
4 wild **5** balky, bulky **7** awkward **8** contrary, cumbrous, perverse, stubborn **9** fractious **10** cumbersome, disorderly, headstrong, rebellious, refractory **11** intractable **12** obstreperous, recalcitrant

unmannered
4 rude **5** crude, rough **6** coarse, gauche **7** boorish, ill-bred, loutish **8** impolite **10** indecorous **12** discourteous **13** disrespectful

unmarred
5 sound, whole **6** intact **7** perfect **8** pristine

unmask
6 debunk, detect, expose, reveal, show up **7** deflate **8** disclose, discover, disprove **9** demystify

unmatched
3 odd **4** only **5** alone **6** unique **8** peerless, singular **10** inimitable **11** exceptional **12** incomparable

unmerciful
5 cruel, harsh **6** brutal **7** callous, extreme **8** inhumane, pitiless, ruthless, vengeful **9** heartless **10** relentless

unmindful
8 careless, heedless **9** forgetful, negligent, oblivious **10** abstracted, distracted, neglectful **11** inattentive

unmistakable
5 clear, frank, plain **6** patent **7** certain, decided, evident, express, obvious **8** apparent, definite, distinct, explicit, manifest, palpable

unmitigated
4 pure, rank **5** gross, sheer, utter **6** arrant **7** perfect **8** absolute, clearcut, complete, outright **9** downright, out-and-out **10** consummate **11** straight-out **13** thoroughgoing

unmixed
4 mere, neat, pure **5** plain, sheer, utter **6** simple **7** perfect, sincere **8** absolute, straight

unmoved
4 calm, cool, firm **5** aloof, stony **6** in situ, stolid **7** adamant, callous, stoical **8** obdurate **9** impassive **10** insensible

unnamed
5 incog **6** secret **7** obscure **9** anonymous, incognito

unnatural
8 aberrant, abnormal **9** anomalous, contrived, irregular, synthetic **10** artificial, fabricated, factitious

unnecessary
6 excess **7** surplus **8** needless, optional, prodigal **9** avoidable, redundant **10** expendable, extraneous, gratuitous **11** dispensable, inessential, superfluous **12** nonessential

unnerve
5 daunt, upset, worry **6** dismay, rattle **7** agitate, disturb, fluster, perturb, trouble **8** distress **10** disconcert, discourage, dishearten, intimidate

unobstructed
4 open **5** clear **8** passable

unobtrusive
5 quiet **6** modest **7** subdued **8** reserved, retiring, tasteful **10** restrained **13** inconspicuous

unoccupied
4 free, idle **5** empty **6** vacant **7** jobless, vacated **8** deserted **9** abandoned, available **10** employable

unofficial
7 pirated, private, wildcat **8** informal **9** irregular

unorganized
7 aimless, chaotic, muddled **8** confused, inchoate, nebulous, rambling **9** amorphous, arbitrary, haphazard, shapeless **10** disjointed, disordered, incoherent, incohesive **11** spontaneous

unoriginal
5 banal, stock **6** copied, old-hat **7** clichéd, humdrum, prosaic, sterile **8** borrowed, ordinary **9** hackneyed, imitative **10** derivative **11** commonplace, plagiarized **12** conventional

unornamented
4 bare **5** plain, spare, stark **6** chaste, modest, severe, simple **7** austere

unorthodox
3 odd **5** kinky, novel, weird **6** far-out **7** offbeat, strange **8** abnormal, maverick **9** different, dissident, eccentric, heretical, irregular, sectarian **10** schismatic **13** nonconformist

unorthodoxy
6 heresy, schism **7** dissent **8** variance **9** ingenuity, recusancy **10** contention, dissidence, innovation **13** nonconformism, nonconformity

unpaid
3 due **5** owing **6** mature **7** donated, overdue, payable, pro-bono **8** freewill, honorary, wageless **9** voluntary, volunteer **10** delinquent, gratuitous, receivable **11** contributed, outstanding

unpalatable
10 flavorless **11** distasteful

unparalleled
6 unique **8** peerless, singular **9** matchless **10** inimitable **11** exceptional **12** incomparable

unplanned
5 fluky **6** chance, random **7** aimless **9** desultory, haphazard, hit-or-miss **10** accidental **11** inadvertent **12** adventitious, coincidental

unpolished
4 rude **5** crude, gruff, rough **6** crusty, vulgar **7** brusque **8** homespun **9** inelegant, roughhewn **10** amateurish **11** ill-mannered

unpredictable
4 iffy **5** dicey, fluky **6** chancy, fickle, random, touchy **7** erratic, mutable **8** unstable, variable, volatile **9** arbitrary, mercurial, whimsical **10** capricious, changeable

unprejudiced
4 fair, just **5** equal **8** balanced **9** equitable, impartial, objective **10** even-handed, fair-minded, open-minded **11** nonpartisan **13** disinterested, dispassionate

unpressed
7 rumpled, wrinkly **8** crinkled, puckered, wrinkled

unpretentious
5 frank, plain **6** candid, honest, modest, simple **7** genuine **8** ordinary **10** forthright **11** plain-spoken

unprincipled
5 venal **7** corrupt, crooked, immoral **9** deceitful, dishonest, dissolute, mercenary, reprobate **10** inconstant, iniquitous, profligate

unproductive
4 vain **6** barren, futile **7** sterile, useless **8** bootless, depleted, feckless, impotent **9** fruitless, infertile **11** ineffectual **12** hardscrabble

unprofitable
4 idle, vain **6** barren, futile **7** useless **8** bootless **9** fruitless **11** ineffective

unprotected
7 exposed **8** helpless, insecure **10** endangered, vulnerable **11** defenseless, susceptible

unproved
10 postulated **11** conjectural, preliminary, provisional, speculative, theoretical **12** experimental, hypothetical

unpunctual
4 late **5** tardy **6** remiss **7** belated, delayed, overdue **10** behindhand, delinquent

unqualified
4 firm, rank **5** sheer, total, utter **7** express **8** absolute, explicit **9** incapable, out-and-out, steadfast **10** ineligible **11** ill-equipped, incompetent **12** wholehearted

unquenchable
7 exigent **9** demanding, insatiate, insistent **10** insatiable **12** effervescent **13** irrepressible

unquestionable
4 real, sure, true **7** certain, genuine **8** absolute, bona fide **9** authentic **10** sure-enough **11** established, indubitable, self-evident, well-founded **12** indisputable, well-grounded **13** authoritative, incontestable

unquestioning
8 gullible, trusting **9** accepting, believing, credulous

unravel
4 fray **5** break, solve **6** answer, decode **7** clear up, dope out, explain, resolve **8** decipher, dissolve **9** elucidate, figure out, interpret, puzzle out **11** disentangle

unreadable
7 deadpan **9** illegible **10** poker-faced **11** inscrutable **12** hieroglyphic **13** cacographical

unreal
4 fake **5** bogus, false **6** fabled **7** fictive **8** chimeric, fanciful, illusory, mythical **9** fantastic, fictional, imaginary, imitation **10** artificial, chimerical, fictitious, improbable, incredible **11** nonexistent
combining form: 5 pseud **6** pseudo

unrealistic
7 blue-sky, idyllic, utopian **8** fanciful, quixotic, romantic **9** distorted, idealized, overblown **10** farfetched, ivory-tower, overstated, starry-eyed **11** exaggerated, extravagant, impractical, sensational

unreasonable
6 absurd **7** invalid **9** arbitrary, excessive, illogical, senseless **10** exorbitant, fallacious, headstrong, immoderate, inordinate, irrational, peremptory, ridiculous **11** extravagant, incongruous **12** preposterous

unrefined
3 raw **4** rude **5** crass, crude, rough, tacky **6** coarse, earthy, impure, vulgar **7** natural **9** graceless, inelegant, maladroit, roughhewn **11** ill-mannered

unreflective
6 casual **7** offhand **8** careless, feckless, heedless, mindless **9** imprudent, impulsive, oblivious **10** indiscreet, nonchalant **11** inadvertent, perfunctory, thoughtless **13** ill-considered

unrehearsed
5 ad-lib **7** offhand **8** ad-libbed, informal **9** extempore, impromptu **10** improvised, off-the-cuff **11** extemporary, spontaneous **12** extemporized

unrelated
8 discrete, separate **9** disparate **10** dissimilar, extraneous, irrelevant **11** independent

unrelenting
3 set **4** grim **7** adamant, endless **8** constant, resolute, ruthless, tireless **9** ceaseless, continual, hard-nosed, incessant, tenacious **10** continuous, determined, implacable, inexorable, inflexible, persistent

unreliable
6 fickle, shifty, tricky **7** dubious **8** fallible, slippery, two-faced **9** deceitful, deceptive, faithless, trustless **10** capricious, fly-by-night, inaccurate, inconstant, perfidious **11** vacillating **12** false-hearted, questionable **13** irresponsible

unremarkable
4 so-so **5** plain, usual **6** common, decent, normal **7** average, mundane, prosaic, routine **8** adequate, everyday, familiar, habitual, mediocre, ordinary, workaday **9** customary, quotidian **11** commonplace, nondescript **12** run-of-the-mill

unremitting
7 abiding, chronic, endless, lasting, nonstop, ongoing **8** constant, enduring **9** ceaseless, continual, incessant, perennial, perpetual, sustained **10** continuous, persistent, persisting, relentless **12** interminable

unrepresentative
7 deviant, unusual **8** aberrant, abnormal, atypical **9** anomalous, divergent, eccentric, irregular **11** exceptional, heteroclite **13** nonconforming

unreserved
4 open **5** frank, plain **6** candid **8** effusive, explicit, outgoing, outright **9** expansive, talkative **10** definitive **11** forthcoming, openhearted

unresolved
4 moot **7** pending **8** hesitant, wavering **9** faltering, tentative **10** ambivalent, hesitating, indecisive, irresolute **11** vacillating

unrespectable
5 shady **6** shabby, shoddy **8** shameful, unworthy **10** inglorious **11** disgraceful, ignominious **12** dishonorable, disreputable **13** discreditable

unresponsive
4 cold **5** aloof, stoic **6** frigid, remote, stolid **7** distant, passive **8** detached, reserved **9** inhibited, withdrawn **10** forbidding, insentient **11** insensitive, passionless **13** insusceptible

unrest
6 strife, tumult **7** anarchy, anxiety, ferment, tension, turmoil **8** disorder, disquiet, distress, edginess, upheaval **9** agitation, commotion, confusion **10** inquietude, turbulence **11** disquietude, disturbance, instability **12** perturbation **13** Sturm und Drang

unrestrained
6 wanton **7** rampant **9** audacious, excessive **10** immoderate, inordinate **11** extravagant, intemperate, spontaneous **13** demonstrative, irrepressible, overindulgent

unrestricted
4 free, full, open **9** boundless, extensive **10** accessible **11** far-reaching, wide-ranging

unripe
3 raw **5** green, young **6** callow, jejune **8** emergent, immature, juvenile, youthful **13** inexperienced

unrivaled
4 sole **6** unique **7** leading, stellar, supreme **8** champion, foremost, greatest, peerless **9** matchless, paramount, principal **10** inimitable, preeminent **11** outstanding, predominant **12** incomparable

unroll
6 expose, extend, reveal **7** exhibit, open out **8** disclose **9** spread out

unromantic
5 sober **8** sensible **9** practical, pragmatic, realistic **10** hard-boiled, hardheaded **11** down-to-earth, level-headed, utilitarian **12** businesslike, matter-of-fact

unruffled
4 calm, cool **5** stoic **6** poised, placid, serene, smooth **7** equable **8** composed, tranquil **9** collected **10** nonchalant **13** imperturbable, self-possessed

unruly
4 wild **5** rowdy **7** froward, raucous, wayward, willful **8** contrary, perverse **9** fractious, obstinate, turbulent **10** boisterous, disorderly, headstrong, ill-behaved, rebellious, refractory, tumultuous **11** disobedient, intractable **12** contumacious, incorrigible, obstreperous, rambunctious, recalcitrant

unsafe
5 risky, shaky **6** chancy **7** erratic, harmful, parlous, rickety, tottery **8** insecure, perilous, slippery **9** dangerous, hazardous **10** precarious, ramshackle, vulnerable **11** threatening, treacherous

unsaid
5 known, tacit **6** silent **7** assumed, implied **8** accepted, implicit, indirect, inferred, presumed, wordless **9** customary **10** insinuated **11** traditional

unsatisfactory
3 bum **4** lame **8** mediocre **9** defective, deficient **10** inadequate **11** displeasing, substandard **13** disappointing

unsavory
4 rank **5** gross, shady **7** insipid **9** repugnant, repulsive, sickening, tasteless **11** distasteful, ill-flavored **12** disagreeable

unsay
4 lift, void **6** abjure, cancel, disown, recall, recant, revoke **7** nullify, rescind, retract, reverse, suspend **8** abnegate, abrogate, disclaim, forswear, renounce, take back, withdraw **11** countermand

unscathed
4 safe **5** sound, whole **6** intact

unschooled
5 naive **7** artless, natural, vacuous **8** ignorant **9** ingenuous **10** illiterate **11** empty-headed

unscramble
5 solve **6** decode **7** clarify, clear up, resolve, restore, sort out **8** decipher **9** extricate, figure out **11** disentangle

unscrupulous
5 shady, venal **7** corrupt, crooked, knavish **8** scheming, wrongful **9** deceitful, dishonest, mercenary, shameless, underhand **11** underhanded **12** exploitative

unseasoned
3 raw **4** flat **5** bland, fresh, green, young **6** callow **8** immature **9** credulous, tasteless **10** flavorless **13** inexperienced

unseat
3 axe, can **4** boot, buck, fire, oust, sack **5** eject, pitch, purge, throw **6** depose, recall, remove **7** buck off, dismiss **8** dethrone, dislodge, displace **9** ostracize

unseemly
8 improper **9** inelegant **10** indecorous, indelicate, malapropos **13** inappropriate

unseen
6 hidden **9** concealed, invisible **10** overlooked

unselfish
8 generous **10** altruistic, munificent, open-handed

unsentimental
see **unromantic**

unserviceable
7 useless **10** inoperable **11** impractical **13** impracticable, nonfunctional

unsettle
3 jar, vex **4** faze **5** spook, upset **6** bother, flurry, jumble, rattle, ruffle **7** agitate, disturb, fluster, perturb, trouble **8** bewilder, confound, disarray, disorder, disquiet **9** discomfit **10** discompose, disconcert

unsettled
4 open **5** fluid, owing, shaky **6** mobile, queasy, shaken **7** anxious, dubious, mutable, overdue, payable, pending, restive **8** agitated, bothered, doubtful, frontier, restless, troubled, variable **9** disturbed **10** changeable **11** outstanding, problematic

unsex
3 fix **4** geld, spay **5** alter **6** change, neuter **8** castrate **9** sterilize **10** emasculate

unshackle
4 free **5** loose **6** loosen **7** manumit, release **8** liberate **10** emancipate

unshakable
4 firm, sure **5** fixed **6** stable, steady **7** abiding, adamant, settled, staunch **8** resolute **9** steadfast, tenacious **10** determined, persistent

unshaped
5 vague **7** nascent **8** formless, inchoate **9** amorphous, embryonic **10** incoherent **11** preliminary

unshared
4 sole **6** single, unique **7** private **8** singular **9** exclusive **10** individual **11** distinctive

unshod
8 barefoot, shoeless **9** discalced **10** barefooted

unsightly
4 ugly **5** gross **6** grisly **7** hideous **9** repulsive **10** ill-favored

unskilled laborer
4 peon **6** coolie

unskillful
5 inept **6** clumsy, gauche **7** awkward **8** bumbling, bungling, inexpert **9** ham-handed, incapable, maladroit, stumbling

unsnarl
see **untangle**

unsociable
3 shy **4** cool **5** aloof, timid **6** offish, remote, shut-in **7** distant **8** reserved, secluded, solitary **9** diffident, reclusive, withdrawn **11** introverted, standoffish **12** inaccessible

unsoiled
5 clean **8** spotless **10** immaculate

unsophisticated
5 corny, green, naive **6** callow, folksy, rustic, simple **7** artless, natural, sincere, uncouth **8** gullible, innocent **9** childlike, ingenuous

unsorted
5 mixed **6** divers, motley, sundry, varied **7** diverse, jumbled, mingled **9** disparate, scrambled **10** variegated **11** diversified **12** multifarious **13** heterogeneous, miscellaneous

unsought
7 willing **9** voluntary **10** gratuitous **11** spontaneous

unsound
3 mad **4** weak **5** frail, shaky, wrong **6** faulty, flawed, flimsy, infirm, insane, sickly **7** damaged, fragile, invalid **8** decrepit, specious **9** defective, erroneous, imperfect, incorrect **13** insubstantial

unsparing
5 ample, harsh, stern, tough **6** lavish, severe, strict **7** copious, liberal, onerous, profuse **8** abundant, exacting, generous, prolific, rigorous, ruthless **9** bounteous, bountiful, demanding, plenteous **10** freehanded, munificent, openhanded **11** magnanimous

unspeakable
4 dire, evil **5** awful **6** grisly **7** beastly, ghastly, hateful, heinous, hideous **8** dreadful, ghoulish, gruesome, horrific, shocking **9** appalling, atrocious, execrable, frightful, loathsome, monstrous, obnoxious, repugnant, repulsive, revolting **10** abominable, detestable, disgusting, horrendous, outrageous, scandalous **13** inexpressible

unspoiled
5 ideal **6** intact, virgin **7** halcyon, idyllic, perfect **8** arcadian, pastoral, pristine, virginal **9** idealized

unspoken
4 mute **5** tacit **6** hinted, silent **7** assumed, implied **8** implicit, inferred, presumed, wordless **9** intimated, suggested

unstable
5 fluid, rocky, shaky **6** fickle, shifty, tricky, wobbly **7** astatic, dubious, rickety, suspect **8** insecure, slippery, variable, volatile, wavering **9** ambiguous, changeful, fluctuant, irregular, mercurial, teetering **10** capricious, inconstant, precarious **11** vacillating **13** temperamental

unstated
5 tacit **6** latent **7** assumed, implied **8** implicit **10** understood

unsteady
5 rocky, shaky, tippy **6** uneven, wobbly **7** erratic, mutable, rickety, varying **8** shifting, variable **9** changeful, irregular, tottering **10** changeable, inconstant
British: 5 wonky

unstinting
4 generous **10** munificent, openhanded

unstudied
5 naive **6** casual **7** artless, natural, offhand **8** careless, informal **9** extempore, guileless, impromptu, ingenuous, makeshift **10** improvised, nonchalant **11** extemporary, spontaneous **13** improvisatory

unstylish
4 drab, dull **5** dated, dowdy, fusty, passé, ratty, tacky **6** démodé, frumpy, old-hat, shabby, stodgy **7** vintage **8** outdated, outmoded **9** inelegant, moth-eaten, out-of-date **10** antiquated, oldfangled **12** old-fashioned

unsubstantial
4 thin **5** frail, shaky **6** feeble, flimsy, infirm **7** fragile, shadowy, tenuous **8** ethereal, illusory **9** dreamlike, imaginary **10** immaterial, impalpable, intangible **11** implausible, incorporeal, nonmaterial, nonphysical

unsuitable
5 inapt 7 awkward, jarring 8 ill-timed, improper 9 ill-suited 10 ill-adapted, inadequate, inapposite, malapropos, mismatched 11 inadvisable, inopportune 12 incompatible, infelicitous 13 inappropriate

unsullied
4 pure 5 clean 6 chaste 8 flawless, spotless 9 blameless, exemplary, guiltless, stainless, taintless 10 immaculate

unsure
5 dicey, shaky 6 wobbly 7 dubious 8 doubtful, insecure, wavering 9 fluctuant, skeptical 10 ambivalent, indecisive, irresolute 11 vacillating 12 questionable

unsurpassable
7 supreme 8 ultimate 9 matchless 10 consummate, preeminent 12 transcendent

unsusceptible
6 immune, inured 8 hardened 9 impassive, resistant 10 impervious 11 insensitive 12 invulnerable

unsuspecting
5 naive 8 gullible, trustful, trusting 9 confiding, credulous, imprudent 10 incautious

unswerving
see **unfaltering**

unsympathetic
4 cold, cool 5 chill, stony 6 averse 7 callous 8 detached 9 apathetic 10 hard-boiled 11 coldhearted, hardhearted, indifferent, insensitive 12 stonyhearted 13 disinterested

untactful
4 flip, rash, rude 5 brash 6 brazen 8 flippant, insolent 9 audacious, impolitic, imprudent, maladroit 10 indiscreet 11 impertinent, thoughtless 12 presumptuous

untamed
4 wild 5 brute, feral 6 carnal, fierce, savage 7 bestial, brutish 8 barbaric 9 primitive

untangle
5 solve 7 clear up, explain, resolve 9 elucidate, extricate, interpret 10 disembroil, disentwine, straighten 11 disencumber 12 disembarrass

untaught
5 naive 7 natural 8 ignorant, nescient 9 intuitive 11 empty-headed, instinctual, spontaneous

untempered
6 wanton 7 extreme 9 excessive 10 gratuitous, immoderate, inordinate 11 extravagant

untenable
5 wrong 6 faulty, flimsy 10 inadequate 12 indefensible

untended
5 seedy 7 rickety, run-down 8 decrepit, derelict, deserted, forsaken, tattered 9 neglected 10 ramshackle, tumbledown 11 dilapidated

Unter den ___
6 Linden

unthinkable
10 impossible, incredible, outlandish 12 preposterous 13 extraordinary, inconceivable

unthinking
8 careless, feckless, habitual, heedless, knee-jerk 9 automatic, reflexive 10 distracted 11 inattentive, inadvertent, instinctive, instinctual, involuntary, perfunctory, spontaneous, thoughtless

unthrifty
6 lavish, wanton 8 prodigal, wasteful 9 imprudent 10 profligate 11 extravagant, improvident

untidy
5 messy 6 sloppy 7 chaotic, jumbled 8 confused, littered, slapdash, slipshod, slovenly 9 cluttered 10 disheveled, disordered, disorderly, topsy-turvy 11 disarranged, dishevelled 12 disorganized

untie
5 let go 6 loosen 7 release, resolve, set free 9 extricate 11 disencumber, disentangle 12 disembarrass

until
4 up to 6 before 7 prior to 11 in advance of

untimely
5 early 9 premature 10 malapropos 11 ill-seasoned, inopportune

untiring
7 devoted, patient 8 diligent, enduring 9 assiduous, ceaseless, dedicated, energetic 10 determined, persistent 11 persevering 13 indefatigable, inexhaustible

untold
4 huge, vast 7 immense 8 enormous, gigantic 9 countless 10 prodigious 11 innumerable 12 incalculable

untouchable
5 dalit, leper 6 pariah 7 harijan, outcast 8 outcaste

Untouchables leader
4 Ness (Eliot)

untouched
4 pure 5 sound, whole 6 intact, virgin 8 flawless, pristine, virginal

untoward
7 adverse, awkward, froward 8 ill-fated, improper, indecent, luckless 9 vexatious 10 ill-starred, indecorous, indelicate 11 intractable 12 inconvenient, recalcitrant

untrained
see **unskilled**

untried
3 raw **5** fresh, green **6** callow, rookie **10** innovative, pioneering **13** inexperienced

untroubled
4 calm **5** still **6** blithe, placid, serene **7** halcyon **8** carefree, composed, peaceful, tranquil **9** easygoing **10** insouciant, nonchalant **12** lighthearted

untrue
4 fake **5** false, wrong **8** disloyal, specious **9** erroneous, faithless, incorrect **10** fictitious, inaccurate
combining form: 5 pseud **6** pseudo

untrustworthy
5 shady **6** shifty **7** devious, dubious **8** disloyal, slippery, two-faced **9** deceptive, negligent, two-timing **10** fly-by-night **11** duplicitous **12** questionable **13** double-dealing, irresponsible

untruth
3 fib, lie **4** sham **5** error **6** canard, deceit **7** blarney, fallacy, falsity, fiction, hogwash **9** deception, duplicity, falsehood, falseness, hypocrisy, mendacity **11** fabrication, insincerity **12** misstatement

untruthful
4 sham **5** bogus, false, lying, phony **7** knavish **8** specious **9** deceitful, dishonest, erroneous, incorrect **10** fictitious, inaccurate, mendacious

untutored
see **unschooled**

unusable
7 outworn, useless **8** obsolete **9** worthless **10** inoperable **11** impractical **12** inapplicable **13** nonfunctional

unused
3 new **4** idle **5** fresh **6** excess **7** dormant, surplus **8** leftover, residual

unusual
3 odd **4** rare **5** outré **6** quaint, unique **7** bizarre, curious, special, strange **8** aberrant, abnormal, atypical, peculiar, singular **9** anomalous, different, eccentric, irregular **11** exceptional **13** extraordinary

unusually
4 very **5** extra **6** highly, rarely, seldom **8** markedly **9** curiously, extremely, strangely **10** abnormally, especially, peculiarly, remarkably, strikingly **11** exceedingly **12** infrequently, particularly

unutterable
5 taboo **7** awesome **9** ineffable **13** indescribable, inexpressible

unvaried
4 like, same **5** alike **7** uniform **9** identical **10** consistent

unvarnished
see **undisguised**

unvarying
see **unchanging**

unveil
see **uncover**

unversed
3 raw **5** green **6** callow **8** inexpert **13** inexperienced

unwarranted
8 baseless **9** misguided **10** gratuitous, groundless, immoderate **11** extravagant, inexcusable, injudicious **13** insupportable

unwary
5 brash, hasty **8** careless, gullible, heedless, reckless **9** credulous, impetuous, imprudent **10** ill-advised, incautious, indiscreet **11** thoughtless

unwavering
see **unfaltering**

unwed
6 single

unwell
3 ill **4** sick **5** frail, shaky **6** ailing, feeble, infirm, offish, peaked, queasy, sickly, wobbly **8** diseased, stricken **9** afflicted, enfeebled **10** indisposed **11** debilitated

unwholesome
4 foul **5** toxic **6** sickly **7** adverse, corrupt, harmful, immoral, noisome, noxious **8** diseased **9** injurious, loathsome, offensive **10** pernicious, subversive **11** deleterious, detrimental **12** insalubrious

unwieldy
5 bulky **7** awkward, massive **8** cumbrous **9** ponderous **10** burdensome, cumbersome

unwilling
5 loath **6** averse **8** grudging, hesitant **9** obstinate, reluctant **10** indisposed **11** disinclined

unwind
4 rest **5** let go, relax **6** loosen **7** ease off, slacken, unravel **8** calm down, kick back, loosen up

unwise
4 rash **5** silly **6** stupid **7** asinine, fatuous, foolish, idiotic, witless **8** reckless **9** brainless, foolhardy, ill-judged, imbecilic, impolitic, imprudent, ludicrous, misguided, senseless **10** ill-advised, indiscreet, ridiculous **11** impractical, injudicious, thoughtless

unwitting
6 chance **8** ignorant, innocent **9** haphazard, oblivious **11** inadvertent

unwonted
4 rare **6** signal, unique **7** notable **8** singular **10** remarkable **11** exceptional **13** extraordinary

unworkable
7 useless **8** quixotic **9** half-baked **10** impossible, infeasible, inoperable **11** impractical **12** inapplicable **13** impracticable, nonfunctional

unworldly
5 naive **6** astral, dreamy, simple **7** artless, natural **8** ethereal, innocent, trusting **9** celestial, ingenuous, spiritual, visionary **11** impractical **13** inexperienced

unworthy
6 no-good **7** ignoble **8** shameful **9** no-account, worthless **11** disgraceful, inexcusable

unwrap
see **uncover**

unwritten
4 oral **5** blank, tacit **6** latent, spoken, verbal **7** assumed **8** accepted, implicit **10** understood **11** traditional, word-of-mouth **12** conventional

unyielding
4 firm, grim, hard, iron **5** fixed, rigid, stern, stiff, stony, tough **6** dogged, mulish **7** adamant **8** hard-core, obdurate, stubborn **9** hard-nosed, immovable, insistent, obstinate, pigheaded, steadfast **10** determined, headstrong, implacable, inexorable, inflexible, persistent, relentless **11** intractable **12** pertinacious, single-minded

up-and-coming
7 go-ahead, hot-shot **8** aspiring **9** promising **11** presumptive, prospective **12** enterprising

upbeat
4 rosy **5** arsis **6** cheery **7** buoyant, hopeful **8** cheerful, positive, sanguine **9** confident, expectant, promising **10** heartening, optimistic **12** Pollyannaish

upbraid
3 rap **4** lash, rate **5** chide, scold **6** berate, rail at, rebuke, revile, scorch **7** bawl out, censure, chasten, chew out, reprove, scourge, tell off **8** admonish, chastise, reproach **9** castigate, criticize, dress down, reprimand **10** tongue-lash, vituperate

upbringing
7 nurture, rearing **8** training **9** schooling

upchuck
4 barf, hurl, puke, spew, toss **5** heave, retch, vomit **6** spit up **7** bring up, throw up **8** disgorge **11** regurgitate

upcoming
7 looming, nearing, pending **8** expected, foreseen, imminent **9** advancing, impending, onrushing **11** anticipated, approaching, forthcoming, prospective

up-country
4 bush **6** inland, sticks, upland **7** outback **8** backland, frontier, interior, outlying, woodland **9** backwater, backwoods, boondocks **10** hinterland, timberland

update
5 amend, brief, renew **6** inform, revamp, revise, revive **7** apprise, enhance, improve, refresh, restore, rundown, upgrade **8** renovate **9** modernize, refurbish **10** rejuvenate

Updike, John
character: 6 Rabbit (Angstrom)
novel: 7 Couples **9** Rabbit Run **11** Rabbit Redux **12** Rabbit at Rest, Rabbit Is Rich **17** Witches of Eastwick (The)

upend
4 beat, best, drub, flip, lick, skin, trim, whip **5** cream, crush, upset **6** invert, subdue, thrash, topple, unseat, wallop **7** capsize, clobber, conquer, overrun, shellac, trounce **8** dethrone, lambaste, overcome, overturn, vanquish **9** overpower, overwhelm, subjugate

upgrade
4 hike, rise **5** boost, raise **6** prefer **7** advance, elevate, enhance, improve, promote **8** increase **9** promotion **10** betterment **11** advancement, improvement **12** breakthrough

upheaval
6 clamor, outcry, tumult, upturn **7** ferment, turmoil **8** churning, disaster, disorder **9** cataclysm, commotion **10** alteration, convulsion, disruption **11** catastrophe

uphill
4 hard **6** rising, rugged, taxing **7** arduous, labored, operose, tedious **8** climbing, grueling, toilsome **9** ascending, difficult, effortful, gruelling, laborious, punishing, strenuous, wearisome

uphold
3 aid **4** back, help, lift, prop **5** brace, carry, hoist, raise **6** assist, back up, bear up, buoy up, defend, second **7** bolster, elevate, justify, shore up, support, sustain **8** advocate, backstop, buttress, champion, maintain, side with **9** vindicate

upkeep
4 cost **7** expense **8** overhead **11** expenditure, maintenance

upland
4 mesa **5** table **7** plateau

uplift
4 buoy **5** cheer, edify, elate, hoist, raise **6** take up **7** animate, elevate, enliven, gladden, hearten **8** brighten, embolden, inspirit **9** encourage **10** exhilarate, strengthen

upon
4 atop
prefix: 3 epi

upper class
4 rank **5** elite **6** gentry **7** peerage, quality, society, who's who **8** affluent, nobility, noblesse, well-to-do **9** blue blood, gentility, haut monde

10 patricians, patriciate 11 aristocracy 13 carriage trade, Establishment

upper hand
4 edge, sway 5 leg up 7 control, mastery 8 leverage 9 advantage, dominance 10 ascendancy 11 superiority 12 predominance

uppermost
3 top 6 apical 7 highest 8 loftiest

uppity
4 smug 5 aloof, brash 6 lordly, sniffy, snippy, snooty, snotty 7 forward, haughty, pompous 8 arrogant, cavalier 9 conceited, egotistic, imperious, know-it-all, presuming 10 disdainful, high-handed 11 overweening, pretentious 12 contemptuous, presumptuous, supercilious 13 self-asserting, self-assertive, self-important

upright
4 fair, good, just, pure, true 5 erect, moral, noble, on end, piano 6 honest, raised 7 correct, ethical 8 elevated, goalpost, standing, vertical, virtuous 9 equitable, exemplary, honorable, impartial 10 principled, scrupulous 13 conscientious, perpendicular

uprightness
5 honor 6 repute, virtue 7 honesty, probity 8 morality, nobility 9 character, integrity, rectitude 13 righteousness

uprising
4 riot 6 mutiny, revolt 8 upheaval 9 rebellion 10 insurgence, revolution 12 insurrection

uproar
3 din, row 4 coil, fuss, to-do, riot 5 babel, brawl, broil, chaos, furor, hoo-ha, melee, whirl 6 bedlam, clamor, fracas, furore, hassle, hoo-hah, hubbub, mayhem, pother, racket, ruckus, rumpus, shindy, tumult 7 shindig, turmoil 8 brouhaha, disorder, foofaraw 9 commotion, confusion 10 hullabaloo, hurly-burly, turbulence 11 pandemonium

uproarious
5 noisy, rowdy 7 comical, rackety, raucous, riotous 8 brawling, clattery, mirthful, strident 9 clamorous, hilarious 10 clangorous, hysterical, resounding, rollicking, tumultuous 12 obstreperous 13 sidesplitting

uproot
4 grub, move, weed 8 displace, overturn, supplant 9 eradicate, extirpate, overthrow, supersede 10 annihilate, transplant 11 exterminate

upset
3 ail, ill, irk, vex 4 rile, roil 5 annoy, evert, worry 6 bother, defeat, dismay, invert, jumble, muddle, topple, tumble 7 afflict, agitate, capsize, disrupt, disturb, fluster, invalid, jittery, jumbled, muddled, perturb, rattled, reverse, shook up, tip over, toppled, trouble, unnerve, worried 8 agitated, bewilder, bothered, confound, confused, disarray, dismayed, disorder, distress, overturn, troubled, turn over, unnerved 9 afflicted, confusion, disturbed, flustered, knock over, overthrow, perturbed 10 bewildered, confounded, disconcert, disordered, distracted, distressed, indisposed, invalidate, overthrown, overturned, tipped over 11 overwrought 12 apprehensive, disconcerted

upshot
5 issue 6 burden, climax, effect, ending, finish, result 7 outcome, purport 9 substance 10 conclusion, denouement 11 consequence, culmination, termination 12 significance

upside-down
7 chaotic, haywire, jumbled 8 backward, confused, inverted, pell-mell, reversed 10 disordered, overturned, topsy-turvy 13 helter-skelter

upstanding
see **upright**

upstart
5 comer 7 parvenu 8 outsider 9 arriviste, pretender 12 nouveau riche 13 social climber

upsurge
4 gain, jump, rise, rush, tide, wave 5 boost, flood, spurt, swell 6 deluge, growth 7 advance 8 increase

uptight
4 edgy 5 riled, tense 6 uneasy 7 anxious, nervous, restive, worried 8 stressed 10 high-strung

up to
4 till 5 until 6 before 11 in advance of

up-to-date
6 modern, modish, timely, trendy, with-it 7 abreast, à la mode, current, stylish 8 advanced, brand-new, contempo 9 au courant, plugged-in 10 avant-garde 11 cutting-edge, fashionable 12 contemporary 13 state-of-the-art

upturn
4 jump, rise 6 growth 8 increase 11 improvement

Uranus
6 planet
moon: 5 Ariel 6 Oberon 7 Titania
mother, wife: 4 Gaea
offspring: 6 Titans 8 Cyclopes
overthrower, son: 6 Cronus

urban
9 municipal 12 metropolitan

urbane
5 suave 6 poised, smooth 7 elegant, genteel, politic, refined 8 cultured, debonair, gracious, polished 9 civilized, distingué 10 cultivated, diplomatic 12 cosmopolitan 13 sophisticated

urbanize
6 citify

urchin
3 imp **4** brat **5** child, gamin, scamp **10** ragamuffin

urge
3 egg, sic, yen **4** coax, goad, itch, lust, prod, push, spur, wish **5** drive, egg on, goose, impel, press, prick, set on, tar on **6** adjure, cajole, compel, demand, desire, exhort, incite, induce, needle, prompt, propel **7** beseech, conjure, craving, entreat, implore, impulse, inspire, longing, passion, promote, propose, provoke, solicit, wheedle **8** advocate, appetite, blandish, pressure, yearning **9** encourage, instigate, stimulate **12** high-pressure

urgency
5 haste **6** duress, stress **8** exigence, exigency, pressure **9** necessity **10** compulsion, insistence

urgent
5 vital **6** crying **7** burning, clamant, crucial, driving, exigent, instant, present **8** critical, pressing **9** clamorous, demanding, immediate, impelling, insistent, momentous **10** compelling, imperative **11** importunate

Uris novel
6 Exodus

urn
4 vase **6** vessel **7** ossuary, samovar
Greek: **7** amphora

Ursa Major
9 Great Bear **11** Great Dipper

Ursa Minor
10 Little Bear **12** Little Dipper
star: **7** Polaris **8** polestar **9** North Star

Uruguay
capital: **10** Montevideo
monetary unit: **4** peso
river: **7** La Plata **8** Río Negro

usable
6 liquid **7** running, working **9** adaptable, available, operative **10** accessible, applicable, employable, expendable, functional, marketable, negotiable **11** exploitable, functioning, operational, serviceable

usage
3 way **4** form, mode, wont **5** habit, sense **6** action, amount, custom, manner, method, praxis **7** process **8** habitude, practice **9** formality, procedure **10** convention

use
3 ply **4** wont, work **5** apply, avail, habit, serve, treat, value, wield, worth **6** custom, demand, employ, handle, liking, manage, manner **7** benefit, exploit, operate, purpose, service, utility, utilize **8** deal with, exercise, exertion, function, impose on, occasion, practice, regulate **9** advantage, habituate, objective, relevance **10** employment, manipulate **11** application

used
8 pre-owned, shopworn **10** secondhand

used up
5 all in, spent **6** bleary, effete, sapped, wasted **7** drained, emptied, far-gone, worn-out **8** consumed, depleted **9** exhausted, washed-out

useful
3 fit **4** meet **5** handy, utile **7** helpful **8** fruitful, suitable, valuable **9** favorable, practical **10** beneficial, convenient, functional, productive, profitable, propitious, worthwhile **11** appropriate, practicable, serviceable, utilitarian **12** advantageous

usefulness
5 value, worth **7** fitness, service, utility **8** function **9** advantage, relevance, substance **10** expedience, expediency **12** practicality **13** applicability

useless
4 idle, vain **5** inept **6** futile **7** inutile **8** bootless, hopeless, unusable **9** fruitless, pointless, worthless **10** unavailing, unworkable **11** impractical, ineffective, ineffectual, inoperative **12** unproductive, unprofitable **13** impracticable, nonfunctional

user
5 buyer **6** addict **8** consumer, customer, utilizer

use up
5 drain, spend **6** devour, expend **7** consume, deplete, exhaust **8** draw down **10** run through

usher
4 lead, seat **5** guide **6** escort **7** conduct, precede **9** conductor **10** doorkeeper

usher in
5 begin, greet, start **6** launch **7** kick off, trumpet, welcome **8** announce, commence, initiate, proclaim **9** institute, introduce, originate **10** inaugurate

usual
5 stock **6** common, normal, wonted **7** average, regular, routine, typical **8** accepted, everyday, expected, familiar, habitual, ordinary, standard, workaday **9** customary, prevalent, quotidian **10** accustomed, prevailing **11** commonplace, established **12** conventional, unremarkable

usually
6 mainly, mostly **7** as a rule **8** commonly, normally **9** generally, routinely **10** habitually, ordinarily **11** customarily

usurer
7 Shylock 9 loan shark 11 moneylender

usurp
4 take 5 seize, wrest 6 assume 7 preempt 8 arrogate, displace, supplant 10 commandeer 11 appropriate

Utah
capital: 12 Salt Lake City
city: 4 Orem 5 Ogden, Provo
college, university: 12 Brigham Young
lake: 6 Powell 9 Great Salt
motto: 8 Industry
mountain: 5 Kings (Peak)
nickname: 7 Beehive (State)
park: 4 Zion 5 Bryce 6 Arches 11 Canyonlands
river: 6 Sevier
ski resort: 4 Alta
state bird: 14 California gull
state flower: 4 sego (lily)
state tree: 10 blue spruce

utensil
3 pan, pot 4 fork, tool 5 knife, spoon 6 device, vessel 8 saucepan, teaspoon 9 implement 10 instrument

uterus
4 womb

Uther Pendragon
son: 6 Arthur
wife: 6 Ygerne 7 Igraine

utile
5 handy 6 useful 7 working 9 available, operative, practical 10 accessible, convenient, dependable, functional 11 practicable, serviceable

utilitarian
6 useful 9 practical, pragmatic 10 functional
philosopher: 4 Mill (John Stuart) 7 Bentham (Jeremy)

utility
3 use 7 benefit, fitness, service 8 function 9 advantage, relevance 10 efficiency, usefulness 12 practicality 13 applicability

utilize
3 use 5 apply, spend 6 bestow, deploy, employ, handle, occupy 7 exploit 8 exercise 11 appropriate

utmost
3 nth, top 4 acme, apex, best, peak 6 height, zenith 7 extreme, highest, maximal, maximum, supreme 8 farthest, furthest, greatest, pinnacle, remotest, ultimate 9 damnedest, extremity

utopia
4 Eden, Zion 5 bliss 6 heaven 7 Elysium 8 paradise 9 Cockaigne, dreamland, Shangri-la 10 dreamworld 12 promised land 13 Elysian fields

Utopia author
4 More (Thomas)

utopian
5 ideal, lofty 6 edenic 7 dreamer 8 arcadian, fanciful, idealist, quixotic 9 grandiose, ideologue, visionary 10 chimerical, idealistic, impossible, millennial, unfeasible 11 impractical 12 otherworldly 13 castle-builder, impracticable

utter
3 say 4 damn, dang, darn, rank, talk, tell 5 sheer, speak, stark, state, total, voice 6 arrant, dashed, deuced, reveal 7 blasted, blessed, declare, deliver, divulge, express, flat-out 8 absolute, bring out, complete, crashing, disclose, infernal, outright, positive, throw out 9 downright, out-and-out, pronounce, verbalize 10 articulate, confounded, consummate 11 come out with, straight-out, unmitigated, unqualified 13 thoroughgoing

utterance
4 rant, vent, word 5 voice 6 speech 7 oration 8 delivery, speaking 9 assertion, discourse, statement 10 expression, revelation 11 declaration 12 announcement, articulation 13 pronouncement, verbalization

utterly
4 just 5 plumb, quite 6 in toto 7 totally 8 entirely 9 perfectly 10 absolutely, altogether, completely, thoroughly

uttermost
4 last 5 final 7 extreme, outmost 8 farthest, furthest, remotest

Utu
see **Shamash**

UV blocker
4 PABA

Uzbekistan
capital: 8 Tashkent
city: 7 Bokhara, Bukhara 9 Samarkand, Samarqand
desert: 8 Kyzyl Kum
enclave: 10 Karakalpak
monetary unit: 3 som 5 tiyin
river: 8 Amu Dar'ya, Syr Dar'ya
sea: 4 Aral

V

vacancy
4 void **6** vacuum **7** opening **9** emptiness

vacant
4 bare, free, idle, open, void **5** blank, clear, empty, inane, stark **6** unused **7** deadpan **8** deserted, unfilled **9** abandoned **10** tenantless, unoccupied **11** empty-headed

vacate
4 quit, void **5** annul, clear, empty, leave **6** bow out, give up, repeal, revoke **7** abandon, rescind, retract, reverse **8** abrogate, check out, dissolve, evacuate **9** discharge **10** relinquish

vacation
4 rest, trip **5** break, leave **6** recess **7** holiday, leisure, respite, time off **8** furlough, interval **10** sabbatical **12** intermission

vacationer
7 tourist, tripper **9** weekender **10** rubberneck **12** holidaymaker

vaccination
4 shot **7** booster **9** injection **11** inoculation

vaccine
4 shot **5** serum **9** antiserum **11** preparation
inventor: **4** Salk (Jonas), Zhou (Jian) **5** Cohen (Joe), Sabin (Albert) **6** Frazer (Ian), Jenner (Edward), Talwar (Gursaran) **8** Hilleman (Maurice)
target: **5** polio **8** smallpox

vacillate
4 sway, yo-yo **5** waver **6** dither, falter, seesaw, teeter, waffle, waggle **7** swither, whiffle **8** hesitate **9** alternate, fluctuate **10** equivocate **12** shilly-shally

vacillating
4 weak **6** fickle, unsure, wobbly **8** hesitant, shifting, unstable, unsteady **9** fluctuant, tentative, uncertain, undecided, unsettled **10** changeable, inconstant, indecisive, irresolute **12** shilly-shally

vacillation
5 doubt **8** to-and-fro, wavering **9** hesitancy **10** fickleness, indecision **12** irresolution, shilly-shally

vacuity
4 hole, void **6** cavity, hollow, vacuum **7** inanity **9** black hole, blankness, ditsiness, ditziness, emptiness, stupidity **10** hollowness **11** nothingness

vacuous
4 idle, void **5** blank, empty, inane, silly **6** stupid, vacant **7** foolish, shallow **11** birdbrained, empty-headed, superficial

vacuum
4 void **5** space **7** suction **9** emptiness **11** nothingness
bottle: **5** dewar **7** thermos

vacuum tube
5 diode **6** triode **7** tetrode
casing: **4** bulb

vade mecum
5 guide **6** manual **8** Baedeker, handbook **9** guidebook **11** enchiridion

____ Vadis
3 Quo

vagabond
3 bum **4** hobo **5** gipsy, gypsy, idler, nomad, rogue, rover, tramp **6** picaro, roamer **7** drifter, floater, migrant, nomadic, vagrant, wastrel **8** bohemian, clochard, picaroon, runabout, runagate, traveler, wanderer **9** itinerant, transient, wandering **11** peripatetic

vagarious
6 fickle **7** erratic, flighty, mutable, wayward **8** unstable, volatile **9** impulsive, mercurial, whimsical **10** capricious, inconstant **13** unpredictable

vagary
3 bee **4** whim **5** crank, fancy, freak, humor, quirk **6** megrim, whimsy **7** caprice, fantasy **8** crotchet

vagrancy
6 roving **7** roaming **8** drifting, nomadism, rambling **9** wandering **10** itinerancy

vagrant
see **vagabond**

vague
3 dim **4** hazy **5** blear, faint, foggy, fuzzy, gauzy, misty, muddy, woozy **6** bleary, blurry, cloudy, dreamy, slight, vacant **7** inexact, obscure, shadowy, unclear **8** confused, nebulous, vaporous **9** ambiguous, dreamlike, enigmatic, imprecise, uncertain **10** diaphanous, ill-defined, indefinite, indistinct **13** indeterminate, unsubstantial

vain
4 idle **5** empty, proud **6** futile, hollow, otiose **7** foppish, haughty, stuck-up, trivial, useless **8** abortive, arrogant, boastful, bootless, nugatory **9** conceited, fruitless, valueless, worthless **10** egocentric, profitless, sophomoric, unavailing **11** egotistical, ineffective, ineffectual **12** narcissistic, unproductive, unprofitable, unsuccessful **13** self-important

vainglorious
8 arrogant, boastful, bragging, puffed-up, vaunting **9** conceited, egotistic **10** swaggering **11** egotistical **12** supercilious

vainglory
4 pomp **5** pride **6** egoism, vanity **7** conceit, egotism **9** arrogance **10** pretension **11** haughtiness **12** boastfulness

valance
5 drape **6** pelmet **7** curtain, drapery **10** lambrequin

vale
4 dale, dell, glen **5** combe **6** dingle, hollow, valley

valediction
5 adieu **7** good-bye **8** farewell **11** leave-taking
Latin: **3** ave

valedictory
see **valediction**

valentine
4 card, dear, love **7** beloved, darling, tribute **10** sweetheart

valet
7 servant **9** attendant **10** manservant

Valhalla chief
4 Odin **5** Wotan

valiant
4 bold **5** brave **6** heroic, plucky **7** doughty, gallant, valiant **8** fearless, intrepid **9** dauntless **10** chivalrous, courageous **11** lionhearted **12** greathearted, stouthearted

valid
4 just, true **5** legal, solid, sound **6** cogent, lawful, potent, proven **7** binding, in force, logical, telling **8** attested, bona fide, credible, forceful **9** effective, effectual, operative **10** acceptable, compelling, convincing, legitimate, persuasive **11** justifiable, trustworthy **12** well-grounded

validate
4 okay **5** prove **6** affirm, ratify, verify **7** approve, bear out, certify, confirm, endorse, justify, probate **8** legalize, sanction **10** legitimate, legitimize **11** corroborate, rubber-stamp **12** authenticate, substantiate

validity
5 force, proof **7** cogency, potency **8** efficacy **9** soundness **10** lawfulness **13** effectiveness

valise
3 bag **4** grip **6** kit bag, suiter **7** handbag, Pullman **8** gripsack, suitcase **9** gladstone, two-suiter **10** weekend bag **11** portmanteau **12** overnight bag, traveling bag **13** traveling case

Valjean's pursuer
6 Javert

Valkyrie
6 maiden **8** Brynhild
mother: **4** Erda

valley
4 dale, dell, dene, glen, vale, wadi **5** basin, combe, gulch, gully, swale **6** canyon, dingle, hollow, ravine **10** depression
Africa-Asia: **4** Rift **9** Great Rift
Alps: **11** Grindelwald
ancient Greece: **5** Nemea
Asia: **7** Fergana
California: **3** Noe **4** Napa **5** Death, Squaw **7** Central **8** Imperial, Yosemite **10** San Joaquin **11** San Fernando
Dead Sea area: **6** Arabah
Dominican Republic: **5** Cibao
Egypt: **6** Kharga
England: **5** Doone
Germany: **4** Ruhr
Greece: **5** Tembi, Tempe
India: **4** Kulu **7** Kashmir (Vale of)
Ireland: **5** Avoca, Ovoca
Israel: **4** Elah
Lebanon: **4** Biqa **5** Bekaa
moon: **4** rill **5** rille
New York: **12** Sleepy Hollow
Pennsylvania: **7** Nittany
Scotland: **7** Glen Roy
Switzerland: **5** Hasli **8** Engadine **11** Grindelwald
Virginia: **10** Shenandoah
Washington: **11** Grand Coulee

Valmiki's epic
8 Ramayana

valor
4 guts **6** mettle, spirit, virtue **7** bravery, courage, heroism, prowess, stomach **8** chivalry, valiance, valiancy **9** fortitude, gallantry **10** resolution

valorous
see **valiant**

valse
5 waltz

valuable
4 dear **5** utile **6** costly, prized, useful, worthy **8** precious **9** expensive, important, rewarding, treasured **10** satisfying, worthwhile

valuate
4 rate **5** assay, price **6** assess, survey **7** adjudge **8** appraise, estimate

valuation
4 cost, rate **5** price, worth **6** rating **7** opinion **8** estimate, judgment **9** appraisal **10** assessment, estimation **12** appreciation

value
4 cost, rate **5** assay, gauge, judge, price, prize,

scale, worth **6** assess, assign, charge, esteem, figure, reckon, regard, return, survey **7** account, apprize, care for, cherish, compute, quality, respect, utility **8** appraise, estimate, evaluate, quantity, treasure **9** appraisal, principle **10** appreciate, assessment, equivalent, importance **11** market price **12** denomination

valve
3 tap **4** cock, flap, gate **6** device, faucet, poppet, spigot **7** hydrant, petcock, shutoff **8** stopcock **9** regulator
cardiac: **6** mitral **8** bicuspid

vamoose
3 git **4** scat, shoo **5** leave, scram, split **6** beat it, begone, cut out, decamp, depart, get out **7** run away, skiddoo, take off **8** clear out **9** skedaddle

vamp
3 fix **4** fake, lure, mend, wile **5** ad-lib, flirt, intro, patch, siren, tempt **6** cook up, entice, groove, lead-in, make up, repair, seduce **7** beguile, charmer, rebuild **8** inveigle **9** fabricate, formulate, improvise, refurbish, temptress **10** gold digger, seductress **11** enchantress, extemporize, femme fatale
famous: **4** Bara (Theda) **5** Negri (Pola) **6** Golden (Eve), Harlow (Jean), Lamarr (Hedy), Salome **7** Delilah, Jezebel **8** Dietrich (Marlene), Mata Hari **9** Cleopatra

vampire
3 bat **5** lamia **6** Lestat, undead **7** Dracula **9** Nosferatu **11** bloodsucker
novelist: **4** Rice (Anne) **5** Meyer (Stephenie) **6** Stoker (Bram)

van
3 car **4** head, lead, wing **5** front, truck, wagon **7** minibus **9** forefront **11** cutting edge, leading edge

vandal
3 Hun **5** yahoo **6** looter **8** pillager **9** despoiler, destroyer, plunderer, spoliator

vandalize
5 smash, trash, wreck **6** damage, deface, ravage, tear up **7** destroy **8** demolish, sabotage

Vandal king
8 Gaiseric, Genseric

Vandyke
5 beard **6** border, collar, edging, goatee

vane
3 web **7** feather, wind tee **8** vexillum **10** bellwether **11** weathercock

Van Gogh, Vincent
brother: **4** Theo
friend: **7** Gauguin (Paul)
residence: **5** Arles
subject: **10** sunflowers

vanguard
4 lead **5** front **9** forefront **11** cutting edge, leading edge

vanilla
4 tame **5** beige, cream, plain **7** extract **8** ordinary **9** innocuous **10** white-bread **12** conventional **13** garden-variety

vanish
3 die, fly **4** fade, flee, melt **5** clear **8** dissolve, evanesce **9** disappear, dissipate, evaporate **13** dematerialize

vanishing Asian sea
4 Aral

vanity
3 ego **5** pride **6** egoism **7** conceit, egotism **8** self-love, smugness **9** vainglory **10** narcissism, pretension **13** dressing table

Vanity Fair author
9 Thackeray (William Makepeace)

vanquish
4 beat, best, drub, lick, rout **5** cream, crush, quell **6** defeat, humble, subdue, thrash **7** clobber, conquer, destroy, smother, trounce **8** surmount **9** overpower, overthrow, subjugate **10** annihilate

vantage
4 edge, odds **8** handicap **9** head start, upper hand
point: **3** POV **5** perch **7** lookout, outlook **8** position **10** watchtower

Vanuatu
capital: **8** Port-Vila
ethnic group: **10** Melanesian
explorer: **4** Cook (Capt. James)
former name: **11** New Hebrides
island: **3** Epi **5** Efate, Maéwo, Tanna **6** Ambrim **8** Aneityum, Malekula **9** Erromango, Pentecost **13** Espíritu Santo
language: **6** French
monetary unit: **4** vatu

vapid
4 dull, flat, weak **5** banal, bland, ditsy, ditzy, inane, silly **6** jejune **7** fatuous, insipid, sapless, vacuous **9** brainless, colorless, innocuous **10** namby-pamby, wishy-washy **13** uninteresting

vapor
3 fog, gas **4** brag, haze, mist, smog **5** brume, cloud, smoke, steam **6** breath, miasma, nimbus **7** bluster **8** phantasm
condensed: **3** dew
frozen: **4** hoar, rime **5** frost **9** hoarfrost

vaporize
5 steam **6** ablate **8** disperse, dissolve, evanesce **9** dissipate, evaporate

vaporous
4 airy, fumy, hazy **5** foggy, misty, vague, wispy **6** cloudy, unreal **7** gaseous **8** ethereal, illusory, volatile **10** evanescent **13** unsubstantial

vaquero
5 waddy **6** cowboy, gaucho, herder, waddie **7** cowpoke **8** buckaroo, herdsman, wrangler **10** cowpuncher
lasso: **5** reata, riata

varia
6 medley **7** mélange, mixture, omnibus **8** treasury **9** anthology **10** compendium, miscellany **11** compilation

variable
5 fluid **6** fickle, fitful, mobile, symbol **7** mutable, protean **8** unstable, unsteady, volatile **9** irregular, mercurial, uncertain, unsettled, versatile **10** capricious, changeable, inconstant **13** temperamental

variance
3 war **4** odds **6** change, strife **7** discord, dispute, dissent **8** conflict, disunity, division **9** variation **10** contention, difference, dissension, dissidence **11** fluctuation **12** disagreement

variation
4 riff **5** shade, shift **6** change, nuance **7** partita **8** mutation **9** disparity **10** alteration, difference, divergence **11** fluctuation, declination, discrepancy, oscillation **12** modification **13** dissimilarity

varicolored
see **variegated**

varicose
7 bulging, dilated, swollen

varied
5 mixed **6** motley, sundry **7** diverse, various **8** assorted **9** different, disparate, divergent **10** dissimilar **12** multifarious **13** heterogeneous, kaleidoscopic, miscellaneous

variegated
4 pied **5** mixed, pinto **6** calico, motley **7** checked, dappled, diverse, mottled, piebald, spotted **8** skewbald, stippled, streaked **9** checkered, multihued **10** multicolor, parti-color, polychrome **12** multicolored, parti-colored **13** kaleidoscopic, polychromatic

variety
3 ilk **4** kind, mode, sort, type **5** array, breed **6** flavor, medley, nature, stripe **8** mixed bag **9** diversity, variation **10** assortment, collection, miscellany, subspecies **12** multiformity, multiplicity

variety show
5 revue

various
4 some **5** mixed **6** divers, sundry, unlike **7** diverse, several, unalike **8** assorted, separate **9** different, disparate, divergent, unsimilar **10** dissimilar **12** multifarious **13** heterogeneous, miscellaneous

varlet
3 cur **4** page **5** knave, rogue, skunk **6** menial, rascal, wretch **8** coistrel **9** attendant, miscreant, scoundrel **10** blackguard

varmint
4 pest **5** knave, rogue, scamp, skunk, sneak **6** rascal **7** critter **9** scoundrel

varnish
4 coat **5** adorn, cover, glaze, gloss, japan **6** veneer **7** coating, conceal, cover up, lacquer, shellac **8** covering **9** embellish, gloss over, sugarcoat, whitewash
component: **3** lac **5** elemi, resin

varsity squad
5 A team

vary
5 alter, range **6** change, depart, differ, modify, mutate **7** deviate, digress, diverge **8** modulate **9** diversify

vase
3 urn **5** tazza **6** crater, krater, vessel **7** amphora

vase-shaped jug
4 ewer

Vashni's father
6 Samuel

Vashti's husband
6 Xerxes **9** Ahasuerus

vassal
4 leud, serf **5** helot, liege, slave **6** tenant **7** bondman, homager, peasant, servant, subject **8** bondsman, liege man **9** dependent, underling **11** subordinate **12** feudal tenant
high-ranking: **7** vavasor **8** vavasour

vast
4 huge, mega **5** giant, great, jumbo **6** cosmic, untold **7** immense, mammoth, oceanic, titanic **8** colossal, enormous, gigantic, spacious, whopping **9** boundless, expansive, humongous **10** gargantuan, tremendous, widespread **12** astronomical

vastness
5 sweep **8** enormity, hugeness **9** immensity, magnitude **13** expansiveness

vat
3 tub, tun **4** beck, butt, cask, kier, tank **5** keeve, kieve **6** barrel, liquor, vessel **7** cistern **8** cauldron
cheese: **7** chessel

vatic
6 mantic **7** fatidic **8** oracular **9** fatidical, prophetic, sibylline **10** predictive **11** apocalyptic

Vatican City
10 papal state
army: 11 Swiss Guards
chapel: 7 Sistine
church: 11 Saint Peter's
court: 4 Rota
ruler: 4 Pope
site: 4 Rome

Vaticano's home
4 Roma

vaticinal
see **vatic**

vaticinate
5 augur 6 divine 7 portend, predict, presage 8 forebode, forecast, foretell, prophesy, soothsay 9 adumbrate 13 prognosticate

vaudeville
5 revue 9 burlesque, music hall 11 variety show 12 song and dance

vaudevillian
11 entertainer

vault
3 pit, sky 4 arch, cave, dome, jump, leap, room, safe, tomb 5 bound, crypt 6 cavern, cellar, cupola, hurdle, spring, welkin 7 archway, dungeon 8 catacomb, overleap 9 firmament 10 undercroft

vaulting
4 arch, dome 7 emulous 8 aspiring 9 ambitious 12 enthusiastic 13 opportunistic

vaunt
4 blow, brag, crow, puff, rant 5 boast, strut 6 flaunt, parade 7 bluster, display, exhibit, show off 8 brandish 9 gasconade 11 rodomontade

VCR's successor
4 TiVo

veal
4 calf
cutlet: 9 schnitzel
roasted: 10 fricandeau
shank: 8 osso buco

vector
5 agent 7 carrier 9 direction 10 pollinator

Vedic religion
country: 5 India
god: 4 Agni, deva, Soma 5 Indra 6 Varuna
language: 8 Sanskrit
priest: 7 Brahman
treatise: 9 Upanishad
writing: 7 Rig Veda, Samhita

veer
3 yaw 4 cast, chop, slew, sway, turn 5 fetch, sheer, shift, trend 6 depart, swerve 7 deflect, deviate, digress, diverge

Vegas game
4 keno 5 bingo, craps, poker 8 baccarat, roulette 9 blackjack

vegetable
3 pea, soy, udo, yam 4 bean, beet, corn, kale, leek, okra, soya, spud, taro, wort 5 chard, chive, cress, green, onion, plant 6 carrot, celery, cowpea, endive, garlic, legume, lentil, peanut, pepper, potato, radish, sorrel, squash, tomato, turnip 7 cabbage, chayote, dullard, edamame, lettuce, mustard, parsley, parsnip, pumpkin, rhubarb, salsify, shallot, soybean, spinach 8 broccoli, collards, cucumber, eggplant, kohlrabi, lima bean, rutabaga, scallion, snap bean 9 artichoke, asparagus, muskmelon 10 watermelon 11 cauliflower, horseradish, sweet potato
bog: 6 muskeg
covering: 4 peel, rind, skin
dish: 5 salad
mold: 5 humus
seller: 6 grocer 7 grocery 12 costermonger
sponge: 5 luffa 6 loofah
spread: 4 oleo 9 margarine

vegetarian
9 herbivore 11 herbivorous

vegetate
4 idle, laze, loaf, loll 5 chill, slack 6 loiter, lounge 7 goof off, hang out 8 chill out, languish, lollygag, slack off, stagnate 9 goldbrick, hibernate

vegetation
5 flora 6 growth, plants 7 verdure 8 greenery 9 plant life
floating: 4 sudd 8 pleuston

veg out
4 hang, idle, laze, loaf, loll 5 chill, relax 8 kick back

vehement
3 hot 4 wild 5 fiery, rabid 6 ardent, bitter, fervid, fierce, heated 7 excited, fervent, vicious, violent, zealous 8 forceful, powerful 9 perfervid 10 passionate 11 impassioned 12 antagonistic

vehicle
3 ATV, bus, cab, car, SUV, van 4 auto, bike, taxi, tool 5 agent, buggy, means, organ, plane, sedan, train, truck, wagon 6 agency, binder, medium, pickup, vector 7 bicycle, carrier, channel, machine, solvent, travois 8 airplane, ministry 9 ambulance, implement, motor home, transport 10 automobile, conveyance, instrument, motorcycle
baby's: 4 pram 8 carriage, stroller 9 baby buggy
child's: 5 trike 7 scooter 8 tricycle
farm: 4 wain 7 tractor
horse-drawn: 4 cart, dray 5 buggy, lorry, sulky, wagon 6 hansom, landau, troika 7 calèche, phaeton 8 carriage 9 buckboard
military: 4 jeep, tank 6 Humvee
one-wheeled: 8 unicycle
passenger: 3 bus, cab, car 4 auto, taxi 7 ricksha 8 cable car, rickshaw

public: **3** bus **4** tram **5** train **6** subway **7** omnibus, trolley
Roman: **7** chariot
winter: **4** sled **6** sleigh **8** snowplow **10** snowmobile

veil
4 caul, hide, mask, wrap **5** cloak, cloth, cloud, cover, velum **6** chador, mantle, screen, shield, shroud **7** conceal, cover up, curtain, obscure, secrete, yashmak **8** covering, disguise, enshroud **10** camouflage, false front
chalice: **3** aer
Muslim: **7** yashmak
netting: **6** maline **7** malines

vein
3 bed, way **4** line, lode, mind, mode, mood, seam, tone, tube **5** style, tenor **6** manner, nature, spirit, strain, streak, vessel **7** channel, fashion, pattern, quality, stratum **8** aptitude **11** blood vessel
combining form: **3** ven **4** veni, veno
deposit: **3** ore
fluid: **5** blood
heart: **8** vena cava
leaf: **3** rib
leg: **7** saphena **9** saphenous
neck: **7** jugular
small: **6** venule
varicose: **5** varix

velar
8 guttural
nasal consonant: **3** eng **4** agma

veld
7 prairie **9** grassland

velleity
4 bent, wish **5** fancy **6** desire, liking **7** leaning **10** propensity **11** inclination

velocipede
4 bike **5** cycle, trike **6** tandem **7** bicycle, pedicab **8** tricycle

velocity
4 pace **5** haste, speed, tempo **7** headway **8** celerity, rapidity **9** quickness, swiftness **12** acceleration

velum
4 caul, veil **8** membrane **10** soft palate

velvet
4 gain, mild, rich, soft **5** cloth, panne **6** fabric, profit, smooth **8** winnings **10** antler skin

velvety
4 mild, soft **5** mossy, plush **6** smooth

venal
4 paid **6** sordid **7** corrupt **8** bribable **9** mercenary, unethical **11** corruptible, purchasable **12** unprincipled, unscrupulous

vend
4 hawk, sell, toot **6** market, monger, peddle, retail **8** huckster **9** advertise, broadcast

vendee
5 buyer **6** client **8** customer **9** purchaser

vendetta
4 feud **7** rivalry **9** blood feud

vendible
7 salable **8** sellable **10** marketable **12** merchantable

vendor
6 dealer, duffer, hawker, seller **7** packman, peddler **8** huckster, merchant, retailer, salesman

vendue
4 sale **7** auction **10** public sale

veneer
3 ply **4** burl, coat, face, mask, show, veil **5** cover, front, gloss, layer, plate **6** facade, facing **7** conceal, overlay **8** disguise

venomous snake
3 asp **5** adder, cobra, krait, mamba, viper **6** elapid, taipan **7** rattler **10** colubrid, copperhead **11** cottonmouth

venerable
3 old **4** aged **5** hoary **6** sacred **7** ancient, antique, elderly, honored, revered, stately **8** esteemed **9** admirable, dignified, estimable, honorable, respected

venerate
5 adore, honor, prize **6** admire, esteem, hallow, revere **7** cherish, idolize, respect, worship **8** treasure **9** reverence

veneration
3 awe **5** honor **6** esteem, homage **7** respect, worship **9** adoration, reverence **10** admiration **11** hero worship

venery
3 sex **4** game, prey **5** chase **7** hunting

venesection
10 phlebotomy

Venetian
boat: **7** gondola
boatman: **9** gondolier
product: **5** glass **9** glassware
ruler: **4** doge
school: **6** Titian **7** Bellini, Tiepolo **8** Veronese **9** Giorgione **10** Tintoretto
street: **5** canal
suburb: **6** Murano

Venezuela
capital: **7** Caracas
city: **8** Valencia **9** Maracaibo **12** Barquisimeto
island: **9** Margarita
lake: **8** Valencia **9** Maracaibo
language: **7** Spanish

monetary unit: 7 bolívar
mountain, range: 5 Andes 6 Parima (Serra, Sierra) 7 Bolívar (Pico) 9 Pacaraima 11 Pico Bolívar, Serra Parima 12 Sierra Parima
neighbor: 6 Brazil, Guyana 8 Colombia
peninsula: 9 Paraguaná
river: 7 Orinoco
sea: 9 Caribbean
waterfall: 10 Angel Falls

Venezuelan
herdsman: 7 llanero
liberator: 7 Bolívar (Simón)
people: 5 Carib 6 Timote

vengeance
6 payoff 7 payback, redress, revenge 8 reprisal, revanche 9 repayment 10 punishment 11 retaliation, retribution

vengeful
8 punitive 10 vindictive 11 retaliatory

venial
5 minor 7 trivial 8 harmless, trifling 9 allowable, excusable, tolerable 10 condonable, forgivable, pardonable, remissible, remittable 13 insignificant

Venice of the East
7 Bangkok, Udaipur

Venice of the North
6 Bruges, Brugge 9 Amsterdam, Stockholm 12 St. Petersburg

Veni, Creator ___
8 Spiritus

venison
4 deer

veni, vidi, ___
4 vici

venom
4 bane, hate 5 spite 6 malice, poison, rancor 7 ill will, vitriol 8 embitter 9 contagion, malignity, virulence 11 malevolence

venomous
5 toxic 6 deadly, malign, poison 7 baneful, malefic, noxious 8 spiteful, viperish, viperous, virulent 9 malicious, malignant, poisonous 10 malevolent, pernicious 12 vituperative

vent
3 air 4 emit, flue, hole, pipe, pour, slit 5 burst, expel, issue, loose, utter, voice 6 broach, nozzle, outlet 7 chimney, exhaust, express, give off, opening, orifice, release, take out, unleash, volcano 8 breather, fumarole, spiracle 9 discharge 11 black smoker

venter
3 gut 5 belly 6 paunch 7 abdomen, stomach

ventilate
3 air 5 state, utter 6 aerate, expose 7 discuss, express 9 advertise, broadcast, circulate, verbalize 11 investigate

ventral area
7 abdomen, stomach

ventricle
6 cavity 7 chamber

ventriloquist
9 performer 11 entertainer
companion: 5 dummy
famous: 6 Bergen (Edgar)

venture
3 bet, try 4 dare, face, feat, gest, risk 5 brave, peril, stake, wager 6 chance, expose, gamble, hazard 7 attempt, daresay, emprise, exploit 8 endanger, jeopardy, long shot, make bold 9 challenge, crapshoot, speculate 10 enterprise 11 speculation, undertaking

venturesome
4 bold, rash 5 brave 6 daring 8 reckless 9 audacious, daredevil, foolhardy 11 adventurous, temerarious

venue
4 site 5 arena, forum, place, scene 6 locale, outlet 7 setting 8 locality

Venus
6 planet, Vesper 7 daystar, Lucifer 8 Hesperus
husband: 6 Vulcan
son: 4 Amor 5 Cupid 6 Aeneas
(see also **Aphrodite**)

Venus de ___
4 Milo

___ vera
4 aloe

veracious
4 just, true 5 exact, frank, right, valid 6 candid, honest 7 correct, factual, sincere 8 accurate, truthful

veracity
4 fact 5 truth 6 candor 7 honesty 8 accuracy, trueness 9 actuality, exactness 11 correctness 12 truthfulness

veranda
5 lanai, porch, stoop 6 piazza 7 gallery, portico

verb
auxiliary: 3 are, can, did, had, has, may, was 4 have, must, were, will, word 5 could, might, shall, would 6 should
form: 6 active, gerund 7 passive 10 infinitive, participle
kind: 10 transitive 12 intransitive
Latin: 3 amo
linking: 6 copula
mood: 8 optative 10 imperative, indicative 11 subjunctive
tense: 4 past 6 aorist, future 7 perfect, present 9 predicate 10 pluperfect

verbal
4 oral **5** wordy **6** gerund, spoken **7** literal **9** unwritten **10** infinitive, participle, rhetorical **11** word-for-word

verbalism
4 term **6** phrase **7** wording **8** phrasing **9** prolixity, windiness, wordiness **11** phraseology

verbalization
4 talk **6** speech **8** speaking **9** discourse, utterance **12** articulation, vocalization

verbalize
3 air, say **4** talk **5** speak, state, utter, voice, write **6** broach **7** express **8** bloviate, vocalize **9** ventilate

verbatim
5 exact **6** direct **7** exactly, literal, precise **8** directly **9** literally, literatim, precisely **10** accurately **11** word-for-word

verbiage
4 talk **6** phrase **7** diction, wording **8** parlance, phrasing, pleonasm **9** wordiness **10** redundancy **11** phraseology

verbose
5 gassy, windy, wordy **6** prolix **7** diffuse **9** garrulous, redundant, talkative **10** loquacious, pleonastic **11** tautologous

verbosity
9 prolixity, windiness, wordiness **10** redundancy

verboten
5 taboo **6** banned **7** illegal **8** outlawed **9** forbidden **10** prohibited

verdant
4 lush **5** green, leafy, naive **6** grassy, unripe

verdict
6 assize, ruling **7** finding, opinion **8** decision, judgment **9** judgement

Verdi opera
4 Aida **6** Ernani, Oberto, Otello **7** Nabucco **8** Don Carlo, Falstaff, Lombardi (I), Traviata (La) **9** Don Carlos, Rigoletto, Trovatore (Il) **15** Simon Boccanegra

Verdon's husband
5 Fosse (Bob)

verdure
7 foliage **8** greenery **9** greenness **10** vegetation

verge
3 hem, lip, rim **4** abut, cusp, edge, sink **5** bound, brink, skirt, staff, touch **6** adjoin, border, fringe, margin **7** selvage **8** approach, shoulder **9** threshold **10** borderline

veridical
see **veracious**

verifiable
4 true **6** proven **7** certain **8** provable **9** undoubted

verification
5 proof **10** validation **11** attestation **12** confirmation **13** corroboration

verify
4 aver, test **5** check, prove, vouch **6** attest, settle **7** bear out, confirm **8** document, validate **9** establish, fact-check **11** corroborate, demonstrate **12** authenticate, substantiate

verily
5 truly **6** indeed **7** in truth **9** assuredly, certainly **11** confidently, undoubtedly

veritable
4 real, true **6** actual **7** factual, genuine **8** bona fide **9** authentic, undoubted **10** sure-enough **11** indubitable

verity
5 truth **6** gospel, truism **7** honesty, reality **9** actuality **12** truthfulness

vermiform
8 wormlike

vermilion
3 red

vermin
4 lice, mice, pest, rats, scum **5** fleas, pests, trash **7** bedbugs, varmint

Vermont
capital: **10** Montpelier
city: **5** Barre, Stowe **7** Rutland **10** Burlington
college, university: **7** Norwich **8** Marlboro **10** Bennington, Middlebury
mountain, range: **5** Green **9** Mansfield
nickname: **13** Green Mountain (State)
river: **11** Connecticut
state bird: **12** hermit thrush
state flower: **9** red clover
state tree: **10** sugar maple

vernacular
4 cant **5** argot, idiom, lingo, slang **6** common, jargon, patois, patter, speech, tongue, vulgar **7** dialect, vulgate **8** language **9** dialectal **10** colloquial **12** mother tongue

vernal
5 fresh, green **6** spring **8** youthful **10** springlike

Verne, Jules
character: **4** Fogg (Phileas), Nemo (Captain) **12** Passepartout
submarine: **8** Nautilus
work: **16** Mysterious Island (The) **21** From the Earth to the Moon **26** Around the World in Eighty Days **28** Journey to the Center of the Earth

versant
see **conversant**

versatile
5 handy **6** adroit, facile **7** protean **8** variable **9** all-around, competent, many-sided **10** changeable **11** well-rounded **12** ambidextrous

verse
3 lay, ode 4 epic, poem, rune 5 lyric, poesy, rhyme 6 ballad, jingle, poetry, sonnet, stanza 7 passage 8 acquaint 11 composition, familiarize
amateurish: 8 doggerel
analysis: 8 scansion
four-line: 8 quatrain
free: 5 blank 8 unrhymed
humorous: 8 limerick
six-line: 6 sestet
three-line: 6 tercet
two-line: 7 couplet
writer: 4 poet

versed
5 adept 6 au fait 7 abreast, skilled, veteran 8 familiar, informed, seasoned 9 au courant, competent, practiced 10 acquainted 11 experienced 13 knowledgeable

versifier
4 bard, poet 6 rhymer 9 poetaster, rhymester, sonneteer

version
4 copy 5 draft, model 6 flavor, remake 7 account, edition, reading, variant 8 revision 9 iteration, narrative, redaction, rendition, rewording 10 adaptation, paraphrase 11 arrangement, description, incarnation, restatement, translation

verso opposite
5 recto

versus
4 anti 6 contra 7 against, vis-à-vis 11 over against

vertebra
7 centrum, segment
kind: 6 dorsal, lumbar, sacral 8 cervical, thoracic 9 coccygeal

vertebrae
4 back 5 spine 6 coccyx, rachis, sacrum 8 backbone, tailbone 12 spinal column

vertebrate
6 animal
characteristic: 5 spine 7 cranium 12 spinal column
kind: 4 bird, fish, frog 6 mammal 7 reptile 9 amphibian

vertex
3 cap, top 4 acme, apex, peak 5 crest, crown 6 apogee, summit, tip-top, zenith

vertical
5 erect, plumb, sheer, steep 7 upright 8 straight 10 lengthwise, straight-up 13 perpendicular

vertiginous
5 dizzy, giddy, woozy 6 fickle, rotary 11 light-headed

vertigo
6 megrim 9 dizziness, giddiness

verve
3 pep, vim, zip 4 brio, dash, élan, fire, life, zest, zing 5 flair, gusto, moxie, oomph, style, vigor 6 bounce, energy, esprit, spirit, spring 7 panache 8 vitality, vivacity 10 enthusiasm, liveliness 13 sprightliness

very
3 too 4 bare, mere, most, much, pure, real, same, true 5 exact, ideal, model, plain, quite, sheer, super, truly, utter 6 actual, ever so, highly, hugely, mighty, really, simple 7 awfully, genuine, greatly, notably, perfect, precise, special 8 absolute, actually, bona fide, selfsame, terribly 9 authentic, decidedly, extremely, genuinely, identical, undoubted 10 absolutely, particular 11 exceedingly
French: 4 très
German: 4 sehr
Italian: 5 assai, molto
Scottish: 3 gey
Spanish: 3 muy

vesicle
3 sac 4 cell, cyst 5 bulla 6 cavity 7 blister, vacuole

Vespasian's son
5 Titus

vespertilion
7 bat-like

vespers
8 evensong

____ Vespucci
7 Amerigo

vessel
3 ama, can, cup, jar, pan, pot, tub, urn 4 boat, bowl, cask, drum, duct, ewer, olla, pail, ship, tank, tube, vase, vein 5 canal, churn, craft, cruse 6 artery, barrel, bottle, bucket, censer, firkin, flagon, kettle, krater, pottle 7 cresset, pitcher 8 crucible 9 container 10 receptacle, watercraft
Arab: 4 dhow
combining form: 3 vas 4 angi, vaso 5 angio
drinking: 3 cup, mug 4 toby 5 flask, glass, gourd, stein, stoup 6 goblet, seidel 7 tankard, tumbler
Indian: 4 lota 5 lotah
Scottish: 6 quaich, quaigh

vest
6 weskit 9 waistcoat

Vesta
see **Hestia**

vestal
4 pure 6 chaste, virgin 8 celibate, virginal, virtuous

vestibule
5 entry, foyer, lobby 6 cavity 7 hallway, narthex, passage 8 anteroom, entrance, entryway 10 antechapel 11 antechamber

vestige
4 echo **5** dregs (plural), relic, scrap, stump, trace, track **6** shadow **7** memento, remains, remnant **8** leftover **9** remainder **10** hide or hair **11** hide nor hair

vestment
3 alb **4** cope, garb, gown, robe **5** amice, cotta, dress, fanon, habit, orale, stole, tunic **6** attire, rochet **7** apparel, cassock, garment, maniple, pallium, tunicle **8** chasuble, cincture, clothing, covering, dalmatic, parament, surplice
ancient Hebrew: 5 ephod **11** breastplate

vestry
6 closet **8** sacristy **9** sacrarium

vesture
4 robe **6** clothe **7** apparel, garment **8** clothing **10** habiliment

Vesuvius
7 volcano

vet
5 check **6** go over, review **7** analyze, examine, inspect **8** appraise, check out, evaluate, look over **10** old soldier

vetch
3 ers **4** herb, tare **6** legume
type: 4 milk (vetch) **5** crown (vetch), hairy (vetch)

veteran
4 ex-GI **5** adept **6** expert, master **7** old hand, skilled **8** old-timer, warhorse **9** practiced, shellback **10** past master **11** experienced

veto
3 axe, nix **4** kill, void **5** quash **6** defeat, forbid, refuse, reject **7** decline, nullify **8** abrogate, disallow, negative, prohibit **9** blackball **10** disapprove **11** prohibition **12** interdiction

vex
3 bug, irk **4** fret, gall, itch, rile, roil **5** annoy, chafe, gripe, harry, rowel, tease, worry **6** badger, baffle, bother, harass, harrow, nettle, pester, plague, puzzle, rankle, ruffle **7** chagrin, torment, trouble **8** bullyrag, distress, irritate

vexation
4 fret, sore **5** chafe, trial **6** bother **7** problem, torment **8** distress, headache **9** annoyance, troubling **10** affliction, harassment, irritation **11** aggravation, bedevilment, provocation

vexatious
5 pesky **7** prickly **8** annoying, tiresome **9** troublous **10** bothersome, irritating **11** distressing, troublesome **12** exasperating

vexed
6 sticky, touchy **7** debated, weighty **8** ticklish **9** difficult, discussed, troubling

vexing
5 tough **7** irksome **8** annoying **9** difficult, harassing, upsetting **10** bothersome, irritating **11** distressing, troublesome

via
3 per **4** over, with **5** along **7** by way of, through **9** by means of

viable
6 doable **7** capable **8** feasible, possible, workable **11** practicable, sustainable

vial
6 ampule **7** ampoule

viands
4 eats, fare, feed, food, grub **7** aliment, edibles, vittles **8** victuals **9** provender **10** provisions **11** comestibles

vibe
3 chi **4** aura **6** energy **9** emanation

vibrant
5 alive, vital, vivid **6** bright, lively, punchy **7** ringing **8** resonant **9** consonant, pulsating **10** resounding **11** oscillating **12** effervescent

vibrate
3 jar **4** ring **5** quake, shake, swing, throb, waver **6** quiver, shimmy, thrill, tremor **7** flutter, pulsate **8** undulate **9** fluctuate, oscillate, vacillate

vibration
4 aura **5** quake, shake, trill **6** motion, quaver, quiver, shimmy, spirit, tremor **7** flutter, shaking **8** fremitus, wavering **9** emanation, trembling **11** fluctuation, oscillation, vacillation

vicar
6 pastor, priest **8** minister, reverend **9** clergyman

Vicar of Wakefield, The
author: 9 Goldsmith (Oliver)
character: 8 Primrose

vice
3 sin **4** evil, flaw **5** crime, fault **6** defect **7** devilry, failing, frailty, offense, scandal **8** iniquity **9** deformity, depravity, indecency **10** corruption, debauchery, immorality, perversion, wickedness **11** shortcoming

vice president
4 veep **6** deputy **7** officer **9** executive
American: 4 Burr (Aaron), Bush (George), Ford (Gerald), Gore (Albert), King (William) **5** Adams (John), Agnew (Spiro), Biden (Joseph), Dawes (Charles), Gerry (Elbridge), Nixon (Richard), Tyler (John) **6** Arthur (Chester), Cheney (Dick), Colfax (Schuyler), Curtis (Charles), Dallas (George), Garner (John Nance), Hamlin (Hannibal), Hobart (Garret), Morton (Levi), Quayle (Dan), Truman (Harry), Wilson (Woodrow)

7 **Barkley** (Alben), Calhoun (John Caldwell), Clinton (George), Johnson (Andrew, Lyndon Baines, Richard Mentor), Mondale (Walter), Sherman (James Schoolcraft), Wallace (Henry), Wheeler (William) **8** Coolidge (Calvin), Fillmore (Millard), Humphrey (Hubert Horatio), Marshall (Thomas), Tompkins (Daniel), Van Buren (Martin) **9** Fairbanks (Charles), Hendricks (Thomas), Jefferson (Thomas), Roosevelt (Theodore), Stevenson (Adlai) **11** Rockefeller (Nelson) **12** Breckinridge (John)

viceroy
5 nabob **6** exarch, satrap **7** khedive **8** alderman, governor **9** butterfly **11** stadtholder

vice versa
10 conversely **12** contrariwise

vicinity
4 area, nabe **5** range **6** extent, locale, region, shadow **7** suburbs **8** ballpark, district, environs, locality, nearness, precinct **9** closeness, magnitude, proximity **12** neighborhood

vicious
4 evil, mean, vile **5** cruel **6** fierce, malign, savage, sinful, wicked **7** brutish, corrupt, hateful, immoral, noxious, violent **8** depraved, horrible, perverse, spiteful **9** barbarous, ferocious, malicious, malignant, monstrous, nefarious, reprobate **10** degenerate, flagitious, iniquitous, malevolent, villainous, vindictive

vicissitude
5 rigor, trial **6** chance, change **7** weather **8** hardship, mutation, reversal **9** adversity, mischance **10** affliction, difficulty, misfortune, mutability **11** fluctuation, permutation, progression, tribulation

victim
4 butt, dupe, gull, mark, prey **5** chump, patsy **6** pigeon, martyr, quarry, sucker **7** fall guy **8** casualty, fatality, offering, underdog **9** sacrifice

victimize
4 dupe, fool, gull, hoax **5** cheat, cozen, trick **6** prey on **7** deceive, swindle **8** flimflam, hoodwink **9** bamboozle, sacrifice **11** hornswoggle

victor
5 champ **6** top dog, winner **7** subduer **8** champion **9** conqueror **10** vanquisher

Victorian
4 prim **6** prissy, stuffy **7** prudish **8** priggish **11** puritanical, straitlaced **12** old-fashioned

Victoria, Queen
family: **7** Hanover
father: **6** Edward
husband: **6** Albert
prime minister: **8** Disraeli (Benjamin) **9** Gladstone (William), Melbourne (Lord)
son: **6** Edward

victory
3 win **4** rout **5** sweep **6** defeat **7** mastery, success, triumph **8** conquest, walkaway, walkover **10** overcoming **11** superiority
costly: **7** Pyrrhic
easy: **4** romp **7** runaway **8** cakewalk, walkaway
monument: **4** arch **13** Arc de Triomphe
reward: **6** spoils
sign: **3** vee
symbol: **4** flag **6** laurel, wreath

Victory author
6 Conrad (Joseph)

victuals
4 chow, eats, feed, food, grub, prog **6** viands **7** edibles, vittles **9** provender **10** provisions **11** comestibles

____ Vidal
4 Gore

videlicet
3 viz **5** to wit **6** namely, that is **8** scilicet **11** that is to say

video game
4 Doom, Myst **6** Pac-Man, Tetris **7** SimCity **9** Minecraft **10** Call of Duty, Donkey Kong **12** Mortal Kombat
maker: **3** THQ **4** Sega **5** Atari, Namco, Raven, Shaba, Z-Axis **6** Capcom, Konami **7** Ubisoft, Vivendi **8** Luxoflux, Nintendo, Treyarch, Williams **9** Neversoft **10** Activision, Square Enix

vie
3 pit **5** match **6** oppose, strive **7** compete, contend, contest, counter **8** struggle

Viennese
city hall: **7** Rathaus
family: **8** Habsburg, Hapsburg
palace: **7** Hofburg
park: **6** Prater
river: **6** Danube

Vietnam
capital: **5** Hanoi
city: **3** Hue **6** Da Nang, Saigon **8** Haiphong **13** Ho Chi Minh City
delta: **6** Mekong
gulf: **6** Tonkin **8** Thailand
monetary unit: **3** hao **4** dong
mountain: **8** Fan-si-pan
neighbor: **4** Laos **5** China **8** Cambodia **9** Kampuchea
river: **3** Red **6** Mekong
sea: **10** South China

Vietnamese
New Year: **3** Tet
soup: **3** pho

view
3 eye, see **4** espy, look, plan, scan **5** scene, sight, vista, watch **6** behold, belief, look at,

notice, notion, regard, review, survey **7** close-up, examine, inspect, lookout, observe, opinion, outlook, picture, scenery, vantage **8** judgment, panorama, perceive, prospect, scrutiny, snapshot **10** conviction, inspection, scrutinize **11** contemplate, examination

viewer
7 witness **8** looker-on, onlooker **9** bystander, spectator **10** eyewitness

viewing instrument
5 glass, scope **6** binocs **7** glasses **9** telescope **10** binoculars, microscope **12** field glasses
combining form: **5** scope

viewpoint
3 eye **5** angle, slant, stand **6** stance **7** outlook **8** attitude, position **9** direction **11** perspective

vigil
4 wake **5** watch **7** lookout, prayers **9** devotions **10** deathwatch **11** wakefulness **12** surveillance, watch and ward

vigilance
5 watch **9** alertness **12** surveillance, watchfulness

vigilant
4 keen, wary **5** alert, awake, aware, chary, sharp **7** careful, jealous, on guard **8** cautious, open-eyed, watchful **9** attentive, sharp-eyed, wide-awake

vignette
5 scene **6** sketch **7** glimpse, picture **8** ornament

vigor
3 pep, vim, zip **4** brio, push, snap, tuck **5** ardor, drive, force, gusto, moxie, oomph **6** energy, mettle, muscle, spirit, starch **7** potency **8** dynamism, strength, tonicity, virility, vitality **9** hardihood, lustiness, puissance **10** get-up-and-go, robustness, sturdiness

vigorous
4 hale, spry **5** brisk, hardy, lusty, stout, tough, vital **6** active, hearty, lively, potent, robust, strong, sturdy, virile **7** dashing, driving, dynamic, healthy **8** athletic, forceful, muscular, powerful, spirited, youthful **9** energetic, strenuous **10** mettlesome, red-blooded

Viking
see **Norse**

vile
4 base, evil, foul, mean, ugly **5** gross, nasty, slimy **6** filthy, horrid, sordid, vulgar, wicked **7** low-down, noisome, obscene, squalid **8** depraved, wretched **9** abhorrent, loathsome, obnoxious, offensive, perverted, repugnant, repulsive, revolting **10** despicable, disgusting **12** contemptible

vilify
5 abuse, libel, smear **6** assail, attack, berate, defame, malign **7** asperse, run down, slander, spatter, traduce **8** denounce, tear down **9** denigrate, disparage **10** calumniate

villa
5 dacha, manor **6** estate, quinta **7** château, mansion **9** residence

village
4 burg, town **5** bourg, thorp **6** hamlet **7** townlet
African: **4** dorp **5** kraal
Indian: **6** pueblo
Japanese: **4** mura
Jewish: **6** shtetl
Malay: **7** kampong
Russian: **3** mir

Village Blacksmith author
10 Longfellow (Henry Wadsworth)

villain
4 boor, heel, ogre **5** demon, devil, heavy, knave, rogue **6** baddie, bad guy, rascal, sinner **7** lowlife **8** antihero, criminal, evildoer, offender, scalawag **9** character, miscreant, reprobate, scoundrel **10** blackguard, malefactor
classic: **4** Iago **5** Judas (Iscariot) **6** Brutus (Marcus Junius) **8** Quisling (Vidkun)

villainous
4 evil **6** rotten, wicked **7** corrupt, debased, heinous, vicious **8** depraved, wretched **9** atrocious, felonious, miscreant, nefarious **10** detestable, diabolical, flagitious, iniquitous, perfidious, traitorous **11** treacherous

villainy
4 vice **5** crime **8** evilness **9** depravity, treachery, turpitude **10** corruption, wickedness

villein
7 peasant **8** villager

villenage
4 yoke **6** tenure, thrall **7** bondage, serfdom **9** servitude, thralldom

vim
3 zip **4** brio, dash, élan, gimp, zing **5** gusto, oomph, verve, vigor **6** bounce, energy, esprit, spirit **7** vinegar **9** animation **10** enthusiasm, razzmatazz

____ vincit omnia
4 Amor

vinculum
3 tie **4** bond, knot, link, yoke **5** nexus **8** ligament, ligature

vindicable
7 tenable **9** excusable **10** condonable, defendable, defensible, pardonable **11** justifiable, warrantable

vindicate
4 free **5** clear, guard, prove, right **6** acquit, avenge, defend, excuse, refute, shield, uphold, verify **7** absolve, bear out, confirm, deliver, justify, redress, revenge, support, warrant **8** maintain **9** exculpate, exonerate, safeguard **11** corroborate **12** substantiate

vindictive
5 catty, nasty **6** malign **7** hateful, hurtful, vicious **8** punitive, spiteful, vengeful, venomous **9** malicious, malignant, poisonous

vine
3 aka, hop, ivy, iyo, pea **5** grape, kudzu, liana, liane, maile, plant **6** maypop **7** chayote, climber, creeper **8** catbrier, clematis **11** bittersweet
Asian: **6** pikake
East Indian: **4** soma

vinegar
3 pep, vim **6** liquid **8** ill humor, sourness **9** condiment **12** preservative
relating to: **10** acetic acid
steep in: **6** pickle

vinegarish
4 sour **6** bitter, cranky, ornery **7** bearish, waspish **8** snappish **9** crotchety, irascible **12** cantankerous, cross-grained, disagreeable

Vinegar Joe
8 Stilwell (Joseph)

vineyard
French: **3** cru **7** château, domaine

Vinland discoverer
4 Leif (Ericsson, Eriksson) **12** Leif Ericsson, Leif Eriksson

vintage
3 age, old **4** crop, wine **5** retro, yield **7** antique, classic, harvest **8** outdated **9** classical **10** antiquated **12** old-fashioned
auto: **3** REO

vintner
city: **4** Asti
prefix: **4** oeno
region: **4** Napa **6** Sonoma

Viola
brother: **9** Sebastian
husband: **6** Orsino
play: **12** Twelfth Night

viola da ____
5 gamba

violate
4 rape **5** break, wrong **6** breach, defile, offend, ravish **7** disturb, outrage, profane, traduce **8** fracture, infringe, trespass **9** desecrate, disregard **10** contravene, transgress

violation
4 foul, rape **5** break, crime, wrong **6** breach, injury **7** offense, outrage, perjury, scandal **8** trespass **9** blasphemy, injustice, sacrilege **10** illegality, infraction, ravishment **11** desecration, disturbance, misdemeanor, profanation **12** encroachment, infringement, interruption **13** contravention, transgression

violence
4 fury, riot **5** clash **6** frenzy, mayhem **7** assault, outrage, rampage **8** foul play, savagery **9** onslaught **10** distortion, roughhouse

violent
5 cruel, harsh, rabid **6** fierce, raging, savage, stormy **7** berserk, furious, intense, vicious **8** slam-bang, vehement **9** explosive, ferocious **10** hellacious **11** acrimonious, destructive

violet
5 mauve **6** purple **8** amethyst, lavender **10** heliotrope

violin
6 fiddle **10** instrument
kind: **5** Amati, Strad **8** Guarneri **10** Guarnerius, Stradivari **12** Stradivarius
part: **3** bow, nut, peg **4** neck **6** bridge, scroll, string **8** chin rest **9** tailpiece **10** soundboard **11** fingerboard
precursor: **5** rebec **6** rebeck
relative: **5** celli (plural), cello, viola

violinist
American: **4** Hahn (Hilary) **5** Elman (Mischa), Fodor (Eugene), Ricci (Ruggiero), Stern (Isaac) **6** Midori, Powell (Maud) **7** Heifetz (Jascha), Menuhin (Yehudi) **8** Kreisler (Fritz), Milstein (Nathan) **9** Zimbalist (Efrem)
Belgian: **5** Ysayë (Eugene) **8** Grumiaux (Arthur)
Czech: **3** Suk (Josef)
Dutch: **4** Rieu (André)
English: **7** Kennedy (Nigel), Menuhin (Yehudi)
French: **9** Grappelli (Stéphane) **12** Francescatti (Zino)
German: **6** Mutter (Anne-Sophie)
Hungarian: **4** Auer (Leopold) **7** Joachim (Joseph), Szigeti (Joseph)
Israeli: **5** Mintz (Shlomo) **6** Shaham (Gil) **7** Perlman (Itzhak) **8** Zukerman (Pinchas)
Italian: **6** Viotti (Giovanne Battista) **7** Corelli (Arcangelo), Vivaldi (Antonio) **8** Paganini (Niccolo) **9** Geminiani (Francesco)
Japanese: **6** Midori (Goto)
Korean: **5** Chang (Sarah)
Latvian: **6** Kremer (Gidon)
Romanian: **6** Enescu (George)
Russian: **8** Oistrakh (David, Igor)

violin maker
4 Salò (Gasparo da) **5** Amati (Andrea, Antonio, Girolamo, Nicolo) **7** Maggini (Giovanni Paolo), Stainer (Jacob) **8** Guarneri (Andrea, del Gesù, Giuseppe, Pietro) **10** Guarnerius (Andrea, Giuseppe, Pietro), Stradivari (Antonio, Francesco, Omobono) **12** Stradivarius (Antonio, Francesco, Omobono)

VIP
3 CEO **4** BMOC, lion **5** celeb, mogul, nabob **6** big gun, biggie, bigwig, fat cat, honcho **7** big shot, notable, someone **8** big wheel, luminary, mandarin, somebody **9** big cheese, celebrity, dignitary **10** panjandrum **13** high-muck-a-muck

viper
3 asp **5** adder, snake **7** serpent **10** bushmaster, copperhead, fer-de-lance **11** rattlesnake **13** water moccasin

virago
3 hag **5** harpy, scold, shrew, vixen **6** amazon, dragon, gorgon, ogress **8** battle-ax, fishwife, harridan, Xantippe **9** battle-axe, termagant, Xanthippe

Virgil
4 poet **5** guide **6** orator **8** cicerone
epic: **6** Aeneid
hero: **6** Aeneas
poems: **8** Eclogues, Georgics

virgin
3 new **4** pure **5** first, fresh, unwed **6** chaste, intact, maiden, modest, unused, vestal **7** initial **8** celibate, innocent, primeval, pristine, spotless **9** abstinent, undefiled, unmarried, unspoiled, unsullied, untouched **10** immaculate

virginal
4 pure **5** fresh **6** chaste, intact, maiden, spinet **8** pristine, virtuous **9** undefiled, unspoiled, unsullied, untouched

Virgin Goddess
5 Diana **6** Hestia **7** Artemis

Virginia
capital: **8** Richmond
city: **7** Norfolk, Roanoke **10** Alexandria **11** Newport News **13** Virginia Beach
college, university: **3** VMI **7** Hampton **10** Sweet Briar **11** George Mason, Old Dominion **12** James Madison **13** Randolph-Macon **14** William and Mary
historical site: **10** Monticello **11** Mount Vernon **12** Williamsburg
mountain, range: **6** Rogers **9** Blue Ridge
nickname: **11** Old Dominion
river: **5** James **7** Potomac **10** Shenandoah
state bird: **8** cardinal
state flower: **7** dogwood (American)
state tree: **7** dogwood (American)

Virginian, The
author: **6** Wister (Owen)
character: **7** Trampas

Virgin Island
5 Peter **6** Norman, St. John **7** Anegada, St. Croix, Tortola **8** St. Thomas

Virgin Islands (U.S.)
capital: **15** Charlotte Amalie
island: **6** St. John **7** St. Croix **8** St. Thomas
location: **10** West Indies
territory of: **12** United States

Virgin Islands, British
capital: **8** Road Town
island: **5** Peter **6** Norman **7** Anegada, Tortola **11** Jost Van Dyke, Virgin Gorda
location: **10** West Indies

virginity
6 purity **8** celibacy, chastity **10** chasteness, maidenhead, maidenhood

Virgin Queen
9 Elizabeth

Virgo star
5 Spica

virgule
5 comma, slant, slash **6** solidi (plural) **7** solidus **8** diagonal

viridity
5 green **7** naïveté **9** freshness, greenness, innocence

virile
4 male **5** macho, manly **6** manful, potent, robust **7** manlike **8** forceful, vigorous **9** energetic, masculine

virtual
5 moral, quasi, tacit **7** de facto **8** implicit **9** essential, practical **10** electronic **11** fundamental

virtuality
4 core, pith, soul **5** being, juice, stuff **6** effect, marrow, nature **7** essence, makings **8** quiddity **9** substance **10** capability **12** essentiality, quintessence, potentiality

virtually
4 nigh **6** all but, almost, fairly, nearly, next to **7** morally **8** as good as, in effect, well-nigh **9** basically, in essence, literally **10** implicitly **11** effectively, essentially, practically **13** approximately, fundamentally, substantially

virtue
5 merit, power, right, trait, valor, value, vigor, worth **7** courage, feature, potency, probity, quality **8** chastity, goodness, morality, strength **9** attribute, character, puissance, rectitude, rightness **10** excellence, excellency, perfection **11** uprightness
cardinal: **4** hope, love **5** faith **7** charity, justice **8** prudence **9** fortitude **10** temperance

virtuosic
5 showy **6** expert, flashy **7** hotshot, skilled **9** brilliant, masterful **10** consummate, prodigious **12** razzle-dazzle

virtuoso
3 ace **4** whiz **6** expert, master, savant, wizard, wonder **7** artiste, hotshot, maestro, prodigy **10** past master, wunderkind

virtuous
4 good, pure **5** moral, noble, pious, right **6** chaste, decent, modest, proper **7** ethical, saintly, sinless **8** innocent, spotless **9** blameless, faultless, guiltless, righteous, unsullied, untainted **10** inculpable, moralistic **11** respectable, right-minded, untarnished

virulent
5 harsh, toxic **6** biting, bitter, malign, poison **7** cutting, hateful, hostile, noxious **8** scathing, spiteful, venomous **9** malicious, malignant, pestilent, poisonous, rancorous, vitriolic **10** pathogenic

virus
3 bug **8** pathogen **9** contagion, infection

vis
5 force, might, power

visage
3 mug, pan **4** cast, face, look, mien, phiz, puss **6** aspect, kisser **8** features **9** semblance **10** expression **11** countenance

vis-à-vis
4 date **6** escort, facing, toward, versus **7** against **8** fronting, opposite, together **9** tête-à-tête **10** compared to, face-to-face **11** counterpart

visceral
3 gut **4** deep **5** inner **8** internal, intimate **9** intuitive **10** intestinal **11** instinctive, instinctual

viscid
see **viscous**

viscount
4 lord, peer **8** nobleman

viscous
4 limy, ropy **5** gluey, gooey, gummy, limey, slimy, thick **9** glutinous, semifluid **10** gelatinous **12** mucilaginous

vise
5 clamp, screw **7** squeeze

Vishnu
4 Hari
avatar: **4** Rama **5** Kurma **6** Buddha, Matsya, Vamena, Varaha **7** Krishna **9** Narasinha
consort: **3** Sri **4** Shri **7** Lakshmi
home: **4** Meru

visible
6 patent **7** obvious **8** apparent, viewable **9** available, well-known **10** detectable, observable **11** conspicuous, discernible, macroscopic, perceivable, perceptible **12** recognizable

Visigoth
conquest: **4** Rome
king: **6** Alaric

vision
3 eye **5** dream, fancy, image, sense, sight **6** beauty, seeing **7** concept, fantasy, feature, picture, specter **8** daydream, eyesight, phantasm, presence, prophecy **9** foresight, nightmare **10** apparition, perception, phenomenon, revelation **13** manifestation
combining form: **4** opia, opto **5** opsis
deceptive: **6** mirage
relating to: **5** optic **6** visual **7** optical

visionary
4 seer **5** ideal, lofty, noble **6** unreal **7** blue-sky, dreamer, utopian **8** fanciful, idealist, illusory, quixotic, romantic **9** ambitious, ideologue, imaginary **10** abstracted, daydreamer, idealistic, starry-eyed **11** impractical

visionless
5 blind

visit
3 gam, see **4** call, chat, stay, talk, tour **5** haunt, pop in, run in **6** call on, come by, drop by, drop in, look in, look up, stay at, stop by, stop in **7** force on, sojourn **8** come over, converse, stay with, stopover **10** social call

visitation
3 woe **4** wake **5** cross, trial **6** misery, ordeal, plague **8** calamity **9** martyrdom **10** affliction **11** tribulation

visitor
5 alien, guest **6** caller, drop-in **7** company, invitee **8** stranger, visitant **9** transient **10** houseguest

visor
4 bill, mask **6** domino **8** eyeshade, disguise, face mask, sunshade

Vissi d'____
4 arte

vista
4 view **5** scene, sight **7** lookout, outlook **8** panorama, prospect **9** landscape **11** perspective

visual
5 optic **6** ocular **7** graphic, optical, seeable **8** viewable **9** pictorial **11** discernible, perceivable, perceptible

visualize
3 see **4** view **5** fancy, image **6** call up **7** feature, imagine, picture **8** conceive, envisage, envision **9** conjure up

vital
4 dire **5** alive **6** lively, living, mortal, urgent

7 animate, crucial, pivotal **8** animated, cardinal, critical, decisive, integral, pressing, required, vigorous **9** essential, important, necessary, requisite **10** imperative, red-blooded **11** fundamental, life-or-death **12** invigorating **13** indispensable
energy: 3 chi

vitality
see **vigor**

vitalize
5 liven **6** arouse, excite, infuse, perk up, spirit, vivify **7** animate, enliven, quicken **8** energize **9** encourage, galvanize, stimulate **10** invigorate

vitals
see **viscera**

vitamin
6 biotin, niacin **7** choline, folacin, retinal, retinol **8** thiamine **9** carnitine, cobalamin, folic acid **10** calciferol, pyridoxine, riboflavin, tocopherol **12** ascorbic acid

Vita Nuova author
5 Dante (Alighieri)

vitelline
5 yolky **6** yellow

vitiate
3 mar **4** harm, soil, undo **5** annul, spoil, sully, taint **6** damage, debase, defile, impair, negate **7** blemish, corrupt, debauch, deprave, nullify, pervert, tarnish **8** abrogate **9** undermine **10** bastardize, demoralize, invalidate

vitreous
6 glassy

vitriol
4 acid, bile **5** spite, venom **6** malice, rancor **7** sulfate **8** acrimony **9** virulence **12** sulfuric acid

vitriolic
4 acid **5** acrid **7** acerbic, caustic, cutting, mordant **8** scathing, stinging, virulent **9** rancorous, truculent

vituperate
3 rag **4** lash, rail, rant, rate **5** abuse, baste, curse, scold, score **6** berate, malign, revile, scorch **7** asperse, bawl out, chew out, condemn, cuss out, upbraid **8** lambaste **9** castigate **10** tongue-lash

vituperation
5 abuse **6** rebuke **7** censure, obloquy, reproof **8** scolding **9** contumely, invective **10** scurrility **11** fulmination, mudslinging **12** billingsgate **13** tongue-lashing

vituperative
7 abusive, railing, scurril **8** scathing, scolding, scurrile, venomous, viperish **9** invective **10** censorious, scurrilous **11** opprobrious **12** contumelious

vivace
5 brisk **6** lively **8** animated, spirited

vivacious
3 gay **4** airy, pert **5** perky, spicy, sunny, zesty **6** bouncy, breezy, bubbly, jaunty, lively, sparky **7** buoyant, chipper **8** animated, pixieish, spirited **9** ebullient, sprightly **12** effervescent, high-spirited

vivacity
see **verve**

Vivaldi epithet
9 Red Priest (the)

___ vivant
3 bon

vivarium
9 terrarium

viva voce
4 oral **6** orally, spoken **11** word-of-mouth

viverrid
5 civet, fossa, genet **7** linsang

vivid
5 alive, sharp **6** bright, garish, lively, punchy, visual **7** graphic, intense, vibrant **8** animated, colorful, eloquent, lifelike **9** chromatic, pictorial **10** expressive **11** picturesque

vivify
5 liven, renew **6** excite, infuse, kindle, revive **7** animate, enliven, quicken, refresh, restore **9** stimulate

vixen
3 fox, nag **5** harpy, scold, shrew **6** ogress, virago **8** fishwife, harridan, Xantippe **9** termagant, Xanthippe

viz
5 to wit **6** namely, that is **8** scilicet **9** videlicet **12** in other words

vizard
4 face, mask **5** guise, visor **6** domino **8** disguise

vocabulary
4 cant **5** argot, lingo, slang, words **6** jargon, patois **7** lexicon **8** glossary **9** word-hoard **10** vernacular **11** terminology

vocal
4 oral **5** blunt, frank **6** phonic, spoken, voiced **7** uttered **8** eloquent **9** outspoken **10** articulate, expressive, free-spoken

vocalic
5 vowel

vocalist
4 diva **6** belter, canary, singer **7** crooner, warbler, yodeler **8** minstrel, songbird **9** balladeer, chanteuse, chorister **10** cantatrice, prima donna

vocalization
4 song **5** voice **6** speech **7** diction **8** speaking

9 utterance 11 enunciation 12 articulation 13 pronunciation

vocalize
3 air, hem 4 sing, talk 5 chant, croon, speak, state, utter, voice 6 warble 7 express 9 enunciate, pronounce

vocal organ
6 larynx 8 voice box
bird: 6 syrinx

vocation
3 art, job 4 call, work 5 craft, trade 6 career, métier 7 calling, mission, pursuit 8 business, lifework 10 employment, handicraft, occupation, profession

vociferate
3 bay, cry 4 bark, bray, call, roar, yawp, yell 5 shout 6 bellow, clamor, holler 7 thunder

vociferous
4 loud 5 noisy 6 shrill 7 blatant, clamant, raucous 8 strident 9 clamorous 11 openmouthed 12 obstreperous

vodka
brand: 5 Stoli 7 Absolut 8 Smirnoff 11 Stolichnaya
source: 3 rye 4 corn 5 wheat 6 barley, potato

vogue
3 cry, fad, ton 4 chic, mode, pose, rage 5 craze, favor, furor, style, trend 6 furore 7 fashion 10 dernier cri, popularity 11 stylishness

voice
3 put, say 4 part, talk, tell, vent 5 say-so, sound, speak, state, utter 6 assert, choice, medium, singer, speech 7 declare, express, opinion, present 8 vocalize 9 condition, enunciate, formulate, pronounce, statement, utterance, verbalize 10 articulate, expression, instrument
female: 4 alto 5 mezzo 7 soprano 9 contralto
high: 5 tenor 7 soprano 8 falsetto
in grammar: 6 active 7 passive
Latin: 3 vox
male: 4 bass 5 tenor 8 baritone
quality: 5 pitch 6 timbre
quiet: 7 whisper
relating to: 5 vocal 8 phonetic
without: 4 dumb, mute

voice box
6 larynx

voiced
4 oral 5 vocal 6 sonant, spoken 7 uttered 8 phonated 9 expressed

voiceless
3 mum 4 dumb, mute, surd 6 silent 8 breathed 12 inarticulate

void
3 gap, nix 4 emit, hole, idle, lack, null, undo 5 abyss, annul, blank, clear, empty, inane, quash 6 bereft, cancel, cavity, hollow, negate, remove, vacant, vacate, vacuum 7 absence, give off, negated, nullify, rescind, reverse, vacuity, vacuous 8 abrogate, deserted, evacuate 9 black hole, discharge, eliminate, emptiness 10 extinguish 11 nothingness

voilà
4 ta-da 5 ta-dah, there

volant
4 fast, spry, yare 5 agile, fleet, quick, zippy 6 flying, lively, nimble 9 dexterous, sprightly

volar
6 palmar

volatile
5 flaky 6 fickle, flakey, flying, lively 7 erratic, essence, flighty 8 fleeting, fugitive, skittery, skittish, unstable, variable, volcanic 9 ephemeral, explosive, fugacious, mercurial, momentary, transient 10 capricious, changeable, evanescent, inconstant, short-lived, transitory 11 impermanent 13 temperamental

volatility
10 fickleness 11 flightiness, inconstancy, instability 13 changeability

volcanic
7 violent 8 volatile 9 explosive
crater: 4 maar
explosion: 8 eruption
glass: 8 obsidian
matter: 3 ash 4 lava, tufa, tuff 5 magma 6 scoria
mound: 4 cone
passage: 6 throat 7 conduit
rock: 6 basalt
vent: 8 fumarole 9 solfatara

volcano
4 hill, vent 8 mountain
Alaska: 6 Katmai (Mount) 8 Wrangell (Mount) 9 Aniakchak (Crater)
Andes: 5 Omate 12 Huaina Putina
Antarctica: 6 Erebus (Mount)
Azores: 4 Alto (Pico)
California: 6 Lassen (Peak)
Canaries: 5 Teide (Pico de), Teyde (Pico de) 8 Tenerife (Pico de)
Colombia: 5 Huila (Nevado del), Pasto 6 Purace 7 Galeras
Costa Rica: 4 Poás 5 Barba, Irazú
Ecuador: 6 Sangay 8 Antisana, Cotopaxi
extinct: 4 Popa (Mount) 5 Iriga, Kenya (Mount) 8 Mauna Kea 9 Haleakala (Crater)
Guatemala: 4 Agua 5 Fuego 7 Atitlán
Hawaii: 7 Kilauea 8 Mauna Kea, Mauna Loa
Honshu: 4 Nasu 5 Asama, Azuma 6 Bandai 8 Nasudake 9 Asamayama

Iceland: **5** Askja, Hecla, Hekla
Indonesia: **3** Awu (Gunung) **5** Agung (Gunung) **7** Tambora (Gunung)
island: **5** Thera, Thira **8** Krakatau, Krakatoa, Santorin **9** Santorini
Italy: **4** Etna **5** Aetna **8** Vesuvius **9** Stromboli
Iwo Jima: **9** Suribachi (Mount)
Japan: **3** Aso **5** Unzen **6** Asosan
Java: **4** Gede (Gunung) **5** Bromo, Gedeh (Gunung), Kelud (Gunung), Salak (Gunung)
Madeira: **5** Ruivo (Pico)
Martinique: **5** Pelée (Mount)
Mexico: **6** Colima **7** Orizaba **9** Paricutín **12** Popocatepetl
mud: **5** salse
New Zealand: **7** Ruapehu (Mount) **9** Ngauruhoe, Tongariro
Peru: **5** Misti (El)
Philippines: **3** Apo (Mount) **4** Taal **5** Mayon (Mount) **8** Pinatubo (Mount)
Sicily: **4** Etna **5** Aetna
Solomons: **5** Balbi
South America: **5** Lanín, Maipo, Maipu
Sumatra: **5** Dempo (Gunung) **7** Kerinci **8** Kerintji
type: **6** shield **10** cinder cone
Washington: **11** Saint Helens (Mount)
West Indies: **9** Soufrière

volcano goddess
4 Pele

___ volente
3 Deo

volition
4 will **6** choice, desire, intent, option **8** decision, election **9** selection **10** preference

volley
4 hail, shot **5** burst, round, salvo, storm **6** return, shower **7** barrage **8** drumfire **9** broadside, cannonade, discharge, fusillade

volplane
5 glide

Volpone
3 Fox (The)
author: **6** Jonson (Ben)
servant: **5** Mosca

Volsung
grandson: **6** Sigurd **9** Siegfried
great-grandfather: **4** Odin
son: **7** Sigmund

voltage
5 power **6** energy **9** intensity

Voltaire
drama: **5** Zaïre **6** Alzire, Brutus, Mèrope, Oedipe **7** Mahomet **8** Tancrède
novel: **5** Zadig **7** Candide
real name: **6** Arouet (François Marie)

volte-face
5 U-turn **8** flip-flop, reversal, turnover **9** about-face, inversion, turnabout **10** switcheroo **13** change of heart

voluble
4 glib **5** gabby, talky, windy **6** chatty, fluent, mouthy, prolix **7** verbose **8** effusive, vocative **9** garrulous, talkative **10** long-winded, loquacious

volume
4 body, book, bulk, mass, size, tome **5** album, flood, folio, space **6** amount, scroll **7** content **8** capacity, loudness, quantity **9** aggregate **12** displacement

voluminous
4 full **5** bulky **6** legion, prolix **7** copious **8** numerous, prolific **9** capacious **10** convoluted **13** multitudinous

Volumnia's son
10 Coriolanus

voluntary
4 free **7** willful, willing, witting **8** elective, free-will, optional **10** autonomous, deliberate, volitional **11** independent, intentional, spontaneous **13** discretionary

volunteer
5 offer **6** enlist, join up, sign up **7** present, propose, suggest
hospital: **12** candy striper

Volunteer State
9 Tennessee

voluptuous
4 sexy **5** ample, buxom **6** wanton **7** languid, sensual **8** luscious, sensuous **9** bodacious, luxurious **10** curvaceous

volute
5 helix, shell **6** scroll, spiral **7** mollusc, mollusk **8** curlicue

vomit
3 gag **4** barf, cast, gush, hurl, lose, puke, spew, toss **5** expel, retch **6** spit up **7** bring up, throw up, upchuck **8** disgorge **11** regurgitate

vomiting
6 emesis

von Bismarck of Prussia
4 Otto

Vonnegut work
9 Galapagos, Timequake **10** Cat's Cradle, Hocus Pocus **11** Player Piano **13** Sirens of Titan (The) **18** Slaughterhouse Five **20** Breakfast of Champions **22** Happy Birthday Wanda June

voodoo
3 hex **4** jinx, juju, mojo **5** charm, magic, spell, vodun **6** amulet, whammy **7** bewitch, enchant, sorcery **8** ensorcel, wizardry **9** ensorcell

10 hocus-pocus, mumbo jumbo, necromancy, witchcraft 11 abracadabra, implausible, unrealistic
relative: 5 obeah 8 santeria 9 Candomblé
spirit: 3 loa

voracious
4 avid 5 eager 6 ardent, greedy, hungry 7 piggish, starved 8 edacious, famished, ravenous, starving 9 rapacious 10 gluttonous, insatiable, omnivorous, quenchless

vortex
4 eddy, gyre 5 swirl 7 tornado 9 hurricane, maelstrom, whirlpool, whirlwind 11 tourbillion

votary
3 bug, fan, nut 4 buff 5 lover 6 addict, zealot 7 admirer, apostle, devotee, groupie, habitué 8 adherent, advocate, believer, disciple, follower 9 worshiper 10 aficionado, enthusiast, worshipper

vote
3 opt 4 poll 5 elect, judge, offer 6 ballot, choice, choose, decide, ratify, select, ticket 7 adjudge, declare, endorse, express, opinion, propose, suggest, verdict 8 election, suffrage 9 franchise 10 expression
affirmative: 3 aye, nod, yea, yes 6 placet
kind: 5 proxy, straw, voice 6 secret 7 write-in 8 absentee 10 plebiscite, referendum
negative: 2 no 3 nay
right to: 8 suffrage 9 franchise

voting group
4 bloc

votive
8 grateful 10 devotional

vouch
5 prove 6 affirm, assert, assure, attest, uphold, verify 7 certify, confirm, support, witness 8 accredit 9 guarantee 11 corroborate 12 substantiate

voucher
3 IOU 4 chit 5 proof 6 coupon, surety 7 receipt 9 affidavit, indenture 10 credential 11 certificate 13 authorization

vouchsafe
4 give 5 award, favor, grant 6 accord, bestow, confer, oblige 7 concede, furnish

vow
3 I do 4 aver, oath, word 5 swear, troth 6 assert, attest, pledge, plight 7 confirm, declare, promise, warrant 8 covenant 9 assertion, guarantee 10 obligation 11 declaration

vowel
6 letter, symbol 11 speech sound
kind: 4 high, long 5 glide, schwa, short 9 diphthong 11 monophthong
omission: 7 aphesis 11 contraction
variation: 6 ablaut, umlaut

voyage
4 sail, trek, trip 5 jaunt 6 cruise, junket, outing, travel 7 journey, odyssey, set sail 8 traverse 9 excursion 10 expedition, pilgrimage

voyeur
6 peeper 10 peeping Tom

Vronski's lover
12 Anna Karenina

Vulcan
see **Hephaestus**

vulgar
3 low, raw 4 base, lewd, loud, rude, vile 5 crass, crude, gaudy, gross, rough, showy, tacky 6 coarse, earthy, flashy, garish, ribald, sordid, tawdry 7 chintzy, kitschy, lowbred, lowbrow, obscene, profane, uncouth 8 churlish, improper, indecent, off-color, unseemly 9 barbarous, graceless, low-minded, offensive, tasteless, unrefined 10 indecorous, indelicate, scurrilous, unpolished, vernacular 11 pretentious

vulgate
10 vernacular

Vulgate translator
6 Jerome

vulnerability
8 exposure, soft spot, weakness 10 underbelly 12 Achilles' heel

vulnerable
4 open, weak 6 liable 7 exposed 10 assailable 11 susceptible

vulnerary
4 balm 5 salve, tonic 7 healing, unguent 8 curative, ointment, remedial, salutary, sanative 9 medicinal, wholesome 10 salubrious 11 restorative, therapeutic 12 healthgiving

vulpine
3 sly 4 foxy, wily 5 slick 6 artful, astute, crafty, shrewd, tricky 7 cunning, foxlike 8 guileful

vulture
4 bird 6 condor 11 lammergeier, lammergeyer
food: 7 carrion
relative: 4 hawk 5 eagle 6 falcon 7 buzzard

vulturine
8 ravenous 9 predatory, rapacious, raptorial 10 predaceous, predacious, scavenging

W

wacko
3 mad, nut **4** kook, loon, nuts **5** crazy, loony, nutty, raver **6** cuckoo, madman, maniac, psycho **7** bonkers, dingbat, haywire, lunatic, nutcase **8** crackpot, deranged **9** fruitcake, screwball

wacky
3 fey, mad **4** daft, nuts **5** batty, daffy, crazy, flaky, kooky, loony, loopy, silly **6** absurd, fruity, insane, screwy **7** bonkers, cracked, foolish, idiotic, lunatic, offbeat **8** crackers, demented **9** eccentric **10** irrational **11** harebrained **12** preposterous

wad
3 gob, jam **4** chaw, cram, lump, mint, pile, plug, quid, roll, swab **5** chunk, stuff **6** boodle, bundle, packet, pellet **7** fortune **8** bankroll

waddle
6 toddle

waddy
4 club, cosh **6** cowboy, cudgel **7** rustler **8** bludgeon

wade
4 ford, plod **5** labor **6** drudge, plodge, trudge
into: **5** set to **6** attack, plunge, tackle **9** undertake

Wade opponent
3 Roe

wadi
3 bed **4** wash **5** gully **6** arroyo, coulee, course, ravine **9** streambed **10** depression **11** watercourse

wading bird
4 ibis, rail, sora **5** crane, crake, egret, heron, snipe, stilt, stork **6** avocet, godwit **8** flamingo **9** spoonbill

wafer
4 chip, disk, host **5** matzo, obley, slice **6** matzoh **7** cracker

waffle
4 yo-yo **5** tripe, waver **6** dither, drivel, seesaw **7** blather **8** flip-flop **9** fluctuate, vacillate **10** equivocate

waft
4 flag, gust, puff, waif, wave **5** carry, drift, float, hover **7** pennant

wag
3 bob, nod, wit **4** card, lash, wave **5** clown, cutup, joker, shake, swing, whisk **6** kidder, switch, twitch, waddle **8** brandish, comedian, funnyman, jokester

wage
3 fee, pay **6** income, reward, salary **7** carry on, payment, stipend **8** earnings, pittance, receipts **9** emolument **10** recompense **12** compensation, remuneration

wager
3 bet, lay, pot **4** ante, game, risk **5** stake **6** chance, gamble, hazard **7** venture

waggery
3 gag **4** jest, joke **5** prank, sport **7** devilry, kidding, roguery **8** deviltry, drollery, mischief **10** impishness, pleasantry **11** roguishness **12** sportiveness **13** practical joke

waggish
4 arch, pert **5** antic, comic, droll, saucy, witty **6** impish, jocose **7** comical, jocular, playful, puckish, roguish **8** humorous, prankish, sportive **9** facetious **10** frolicsome **11** mischievous

waggle
3 bob **4** reel, sway

Wagner, Richard
birthplace: **7** Leipzig
father-in-law: **5** Liszt (Franz)
festival site: **8** Bayreuth
hero: **9** Siegfried
opera: **4** Ring **6** Rienzi **7** Walküre (Die) **8** Parsifal **9** Lohengrin, Rheingold (Das), Siegfried **10** Die Walküre, Tannhäuser **12** Das Rheingold **13** Meistersinger (Die) **14** Flying Dutchman (The) **15** Götterdämmerung **16** Tristan und Isolde **17** Ring of the Nibelung (The)
patron: **6** Ludwig
recurring theme: **9** leitmotif, leitmotiv
wife: **5** Minna **6** Cosima

wagon
3 van **4** cart, dray, tram, trek, wain **7** caravan, coaster, hayrack **9** Conestoga

wahoo
3 ono **8** mackerel **9** winged elm **11** burning bush

waif
5 gamin, stray **6** gamine, orphan, urchin **8** wanderer **9** foundling **10** ragamuffin **11** guttersnipe

wail
3 bay, cry **4** bawl, blub, fuss, howl, keen, weep, yowl **5** mourn, whine **6** bemoan, lament, plaint, repine **7** blubber, ululate **8** complain **9** complaint **11** lamentation

wain
5 wagon **9** Big Dipper
wainscot
4 dado
waistband
3 obi **4** belt, sash **6** girdle **8** ceinture, cincture **10** cummerbund
waistcoat
4 vest **5** gilet **6** jerkin, weskit
wait
4 bide, idle, lurk, stay **5** abide, dally, delay, serve, tarry, watch **6** expect, hold on, linger, remain **8** hang fire, mark time, sit tight **10** anticipate **11** stick around
waiter
4 tray **6** carhop, garçon, salver, server **7** servant **9** attendant
Waiting for ——
5 Godot, Lefty
wait on
4 tend **5** serve **6** attend, tend to **7** care for, cater to **9** look after
waitperson
6 server
waive
4 cede, stay **5** allow, defer, delay, forgo, table, yield **6** give up, hold up, put off, shelve **7** abandon, concede, dismiss, hold off, suspend **8** hand over, hold over, postpone **9** surrender **10** relinquish
wake
4 path, stir, wash **5** alert, arise, get up, rally, rouse, track, vigil, watch **6** arouse, bestir, excite, kindle, stir up **7** roll out **8** activate, backwash **9** aftermath, stimulate
wakeful
5 alert **8** restless, vigilant **9** insomniac, sleepless
waken
see **wake**
Walden author
7 Thoreau (Henry David)
wale
3 rib **4** bend, welt **5** brace, ridge **6** strake
Wales
capital: **7** Cardiff
city: **6** Bangor **7** Newport, Swansea **8** St. David's
island: **8** Anglesey
mountain: **7** Snowdon
patron saint: **5** David
river: **3** Dee
strait: **5** Menai
symbol: **4** leek **6** dragon **8** daffodil
(see also **Cymric**)
Walesa of Poland
4 Lech
walk
3 pad **4** gait, hike, hoof, pace, path, plod, roam, slog, step, trip **5** alley, amble, clump, mince, paseo, stave, strut, stump, trail, tramp, tread, troop **6** hoof it, prance, ramble, sashay, stride, stroll, toddle, trudge, waddle, wander **7** saunter, shamble, shuffle, stumble, swagger, traipse **8** ambulate, traverse **9** promenade **11** base on balls, perambulate, peregrinate
walkaway
4 romp, rout
walking shorts
8 Bermudas
walking stick
4 cane **5** staff **6** crutch, insect **7** phasmid, whangee
Walkman successor
4 iPod
walk out
5 leave **6** strike
walk out on
5 leave **6** desert **7** abandon, forsake
Walküre composer
6 Wagner (Richard)
walkway
4 path **7** alameda, passage **9** esplanade, promenade
wall
3 bar, hem **4** side, stop **5** block, close, fence, hedge **6** immure **7** barrier, close in, enclose **8** blockade, surround **9** barricade, enclosure, roadblock, structure
bearing: **7** support
hanging: **8** tapestry
painting: **5** mural **6** fresco
protective: **7** parapet, rampart
top of: **6** coping
wallaby
8 kangaroo
Wallach of film
3 Eli
wallet
5 funds **6** folder **8** billfold **9** accessory, resources **10** pocketbook
Wallis and Futuna Islands
capital: **7** Matautu
island: **4** Uvéa
territory of: **6** France
wallop
3 bop, hit, tan **4** bang, bash, beat, belt, blow, boil, bust, clip, drub, kayo, lick, pelt, slam, slug, sock, whip, whop, whup **5** baste, paste, pound, punch, smack, whack **6** buffet, pummel, thrash, thwack **7** shellac, trounce **8** lambaste

walloping
4 huge **5** giant **7** immense, mammoth, monster **8** colossal, enormous, gigantic, smashing **10** gargantuan, impressive, incredible, prodigious
wallow
4 bask, roll **5** enjoy, revel **6** billow, welter **7** delight, indulge **9** luxuriate
Wall Street debut
3 IPO
___ Walpole
4 Hugh **6** Horace
___ Walton
3 Sam **5** Izaak
waltz
5 dance, valse
Waltz King
7 Strauss (Johann)
Wampanoag chief
9 Massasoit, Metacomet **10** King Philip
wampum
4 peag **5** beads, money **6** shells
wan
3 dim **4** ashy, gray, pale, waxy, weak, worn **5** ashen, faint, livid, lurid, pasty, waxen **6** anemic, doughy, feeble, infirm, pallid, peaked, sallow, sickly **7** ghastly, languid **8** blanched **9** bloodless, colorless, washed-out **10** cadaverous, white-faced
wand
3 rod **4** pole, tube **5** baton, staff
wander
3 bat, bum, gad **4** mill, roam, rove, swan **5** amble, dally, drift, float, gypsy, mooch, prowl, range, stray, tramp **6** ramble, stroll **7** deviate, digress, diverge, maunder, meander, saunter, traipse **8** divagate, straggle, vagabond **9** expatiate, gallivant **10** kick around
wanderer
4 waif **5** gypsy, nomad, rover, stray **7** pilgrim, vagrant **8** runabout, vagabond
wandering
7 erratic, migrant, nomadic, vagrant **8** vagabond **9** itinerant, migratory, walkabout, wayfaring **10** roundabout **11** peripatetic
wane
3 dim, ebb **4** fail, fall **5** abate, let up **6** lessen, recede, reduce, relent, shrink, weaken **7** decline, dwindle, slacken, subside **8** decrease, diminish, moderate, slack off, taper off
wangle
6 scheme **7** finagle, wheedle **8** inveigle, scrounge **10** manipulate
wannabe
5 clone **7** also-ran, copycat, hopeful, wishful **8** apparent, aspiring, desiring, desirous **9** ambitious, look-alike, potential
want
4 lack, like, need, void, wish **5** covet, crave, fault **6** dearth, desire, penury **7** absence, poverty, require **8** exigency **9** indigence, necessity, neediness, privation **10** deficiency, desiderate, inadequacy, scantiness **11** destitution, requirement **13** insufficiency
wanted-poster abbr.
3 aka
wanting
4 away, less, sans **5** minus, scant, short **6** absent, scanty, scarce **7** lacking, missing, without **9** deficient **10** inadequate, incomplete **12** insufficient
wanton
4 doxy, jade, lewd, minx, rank, slut **5** bawdy, cruel, hussy, loose, tramp, trull, wench **6** coquet, floozy, harlot, lavish, trifle, unruly **7** baggage, cyprian, immoral, jezebel, lustful, obscene, Paphian, sensual, trollop, wayward **8** inhumane, pitiless, ruthless, slattern, spiteful, sportive, strumpet **9** dissolute, luxuriant, malicious, merciless **10** gratuitous, lascivious, malevolent, outrageous, prostitute **11** extravagant, mischievous, uncalled-for
wapiti
3 elk **4** stag **7** red deer
war
4 feud, odds **5** fight **6** battle, combat, strife **7** contest **8** conflict, struggle, variance **9** hostility **10** antagonism **11** competition
German: **5** Krieg **10** blitzkrieg
god: **3** Tiu, Tyr **4** Ares, Mars, Odin **5** Woden, Wotan
goddess: **4** Enyo **5** Anath **6** Inanna, Ishtar **7** Bellona
Latin: **6** bellum
Muslim: **5** jehad, jihad
relating to: **7** martial
War and Peace
author: **7** Tolstoy (Leo)
character: **6** Andrey (Prince), Pierre (Bezukhov) **7** Natasha (Rostova)
composer: **9** Prokofiev (Sergey)
warble
4 sing **5** carol, chirp, trill, tweet **6** gadfly, maggot, quaver **7** descant, melisma, twitter
warbler
4 bird **6** singer **7** kinglet **8** songster **9** blackpoll **11** gnatcatcher
European: **10** chiffchaff
___ Warbucks
5 Daddy
war casualties group
3 DAV
war cry
5 motto **6** slogan
Greek: **5** alala
Japanese: **6** banzai

ward
4 care 5 aegis, stave 6 barrio, charge 7 custody, defense, keeping 8 district, division, precinct, security 9 bishopric 10 protection 11 safekeeping 12 guardianship

warden
6 jailer, keeper, regent 7 provost 8 governor, guardian, official 9 castellan, constable, custodian, protector 10 commandant, supervisor

ward off
5 avert, parry, rebut, repel 6 divert 7 deflect 8 turn away 9 forestall

Ward of TV
4 Sela

wardrobe
5 trunk 6 closet 7 apparel, armoire, clothes 8 clothing 9 garderobe 12 clothespress
assistant: 7 dresser

warehouse
4 stow 5 depot, lodge, stock, store 7 confine, deposit, shelter, storage, stowage 8 building 9 stockroom, storeroom 10 depository, repository 11 accommodate
oriental: 6 godown

wares
4 line 5 goods, stock 9 vendibles 11 commodities, marketables, merchandise

warfare
6 battle, combat, strife 8 conflict, struggle 10 operations 11 hostilities
type: 4 germ 6 trench 10 biological

warhorse
4 hack 5 steed 7 charger, courser, veteran 8 chestnut, standard

warlike
7 hawkish, martial 8 militant, military 9 bellicose, combative, truculent 10 aggressive, pugnacious 11 belligerent

warlock
3 wiz 4 mage 5 magus 6 wizard 8 conjurer, conjuror, magician, satanist, sorcerer 9 diabolist, enchanter 11 necromancer

warm
4 bask, heat, kind 5 angry, fresh 6 ardent, genial, heated, heat up, loving, reheat, secure, tender 7 affable, cordial, excited, fervent, sincere 8 friendly, gracious, spirited 9 heartfelt 10 passionate, responsive 11 kindhearted, sympathetic 12 affectionate, enthusiastic, wholehearted 13 compassionate
air: 7 thermal

warmed-over
5 banal, stale, tired, trite 6 old-hat 7 clichéd 8 shopworn, timeworn 9 hackneyed

warmhearted
4 kind 6 benign, kindly, loving, tender 7 cordial 8 generous 9 benignant, unselfish 10 benevolent 11 magnanimous, sympathetic 12 affectionate 13 compassionate

warmth
4 glow, heat 7 comfort 8 fondness 9 affection 10 cordiality

warmup
4 prep 5 run-up 6 lead-in, opener 7 kickoff, preface, prelude, preview 8 overture, preamble, prologue 9 countdown, rehearsal 10 run-through 11 preliminary 12 introduction

warn
3 tip 4 clew, clue 5 alert 6 advise, inform, notify, tip off 7 apprise, caution, counsel 8 admonish

warning
3 tip 4 hint, omen 5 alarm, alert 6 alarum, caveat, notice, signal, tip-off 7 caution, counsel, summons 8 monition, monitory 10 admonition, cautionary 12 admonishment
legal: 6 caveat

War of the Worlds author
5 Wells (H. G.)

warp
4 base, bend, cast, kink, rope, wind 5 color, curve, twist 6 buckle, debase, deform, wrench 7 confuse, contort, corrupt, deflect, distort, pervert, torture, vitiate 10 bastardize 12 misrepresent

warrant
4 pawn, writ 5 proof, prove, token 6 affirm, assert, assure, attest, avouch, ensure, ground, insure, pledge, secure 7 certify, contend, declare, justify, precept 8 guaranty, maintain, mittimus, sanction, security 9 assurance, authority, authorize, guarantee 10 foundation 11 certificate 12 confirmation 13 justification

warranty
4 bail, bond 6 surety 8 covenant, security 9 guarantee

warren
4 maze 7 network, rabbits 8 tenement

Warren novel
14 All the King's Men

warrior
4 hero 7 battler, fighter, soldier 8 champion 9 combatant 10 serviceman
female: 6 Amazon
Japanese: 5 ronin 7 samurai
princess: 4 Xena 7 Lawless (Lucy)

Warsaw
castle: 5 Zamek
river: 7 Vistula

wart
4 flaw 6 defect, growth 7 blemish, verruca 11 excrescence

warty amphibian
4 toad

wary
5 alert, cagey, canny, chary, leery **7** careful, dubious, guarded, mindful **8** cautious, skittish, vigilant, watchful **10** suspicious **11** circumspect, distrustful

wash
3 lap, pan, tub **4** hose, lave, suds, wadi **5** bathe, clean, creek, douse, drift, float, flush, gully, marsh, scrub, slosh, swill **6** drench, shower, sluice, splash **7** cleanse, coating, launder, laundry, shampoo, suffuse **8** backwash

washbasin
6 lavabo

Wash. bigwig
3 Sen.

washboard muscles
3 abs

washed-out
4 beat **5** all in, faded, spent, tired, weary **6** bushed, effete, sapped, used-up, wasted **7** drained **8** depleted **9** exhausted

washed-up
4 beat, done **5** kaput, spent **6** done in **7** also-ran, defunct, done for, through **8** finished

washing
4 bath **6** lavage **7** laundry **8** ablution, lavation
ceremonial: **6** lavabo

Washington
capital: **7** Olympia
city: **6** Tacoma **7** Seattle, Spokane **9** Vancouver **10** Walla Walla
college, university: **7** Gonzaga, Whitman **9** Evergreen
dam: **11** Grand Coulee
mountain, range: **7** Cascade, Olympic, Rainier **8** St. Helens
nickname: **9** Evergreen (State)
river: **6** Yakima **8** Columbia
state bird: **9** goldfinch
state flower: **12** rhododendron
state tree: **7** hemlock

Washington, D.C., designer
7 L'Enfant (Pierre-Charles)

Washington, George
home: **11** Mount Vernon
portraitist: **6** Stuart (Gilbert)
wife: **6** Martha

Washington Redskins nickname
4 Hogs

Washington Square author
5 James (Henry)

wasp
5 mason **6** digger, hornet, vespid **8** braconid **9** ichneumon, mud dauber **12** yellow jacket

waspish
5 testy **6** snappy, snarky, snippy, touchy **7** peevish, vespine **8** petulant, snappish, vinegary **9** crotchety, fractious, irritable, querulous **10** vinegarish **12** cantankerous, cross-grained

wassail
5 binge, carol, drink, revel, spree, toast **6** bender **7** carouse, revelry, roister **8** carousal, drinking

Wasserstein play
15 Heidi Chronicles (The) **17** Sisters Rosenzweig (The)

waste
4 arid, fail, kill, loss, ruin, sack, wild **5** empty, offal, scrap, trash **6** barren, damage, debris, desert, devour, litter, ravage, refuse, sewage, shrink, weaken **7** badland, consume, despoil, destroy, fritter, garbage, pillage, plunder, rubbish **8** decrease, desolate, emaciate, enfeeble, misspend, prodigal, spoilage, squander, wear away, wildland **9** devastate, dissipate, excrement, sweepings, throw away **10** desolation, wilderness **11** prodigality **12** extravagance, extravagancy
maker: **5** haste
time: **5** dally **6** dawdle, footle, piddle, trifle

waste allowance
4 tret

waste away
4 fade, fail **6** molder, shrink **7** atrophy, decline, dwindle, shrivel **10** degenerate

wasted
3 lit **4** high **5** drunk, gaunt **6** peaked, sickly, stoned **7** elapsed, ravaged **8** skeletal **9** emaciated **10** cadaverous, skeletonic **11** intoxicated

wasteful
6 lavish **8** prodigal **9** throwaway **10** profligate, thriftless, uneconomic **11** extravagant, improvident, inefficient, spendthrift

wastefulness
6 excess **10** lavishness **11** prodigality **12** extravagance, immoderation

wasteland
4 wild **5** heath **6** barren **10** desolation, wilderness

Waste Land author
3 T.S.E. **5** Eliot (T. S.)

wastrel
3 rip **4** rake, roué **7** rounder, spender **8** prodigal **9** fritterer, libertine **10** dissipater, high roller, ne'er-do-well, profligate, squanderer **11** scattergood, spendthrift

watch
3 eye, see, spy **4** bide, look, mind, tend, tout, wait, wake, ward **5** guard, shift, vigil **6** attend, follow, look at, notice, sentry **7** care for, lookout,

monitor, observe, surveil **8** bulletin, eagle eye, scrutiny, sentinel, watchman **9** attention, timepiece, vigilance **10** duty period, observance **11** chronometer, observation **12** surveillance
chain: **3** fob
maker: **5** Timex **6** Piaget **10** horologist

watchdog
5 guard **6** keeper **8** Cerberus, guardian **9** custodian, protector

watcher
6 viewer **7** guarder, lookout **8** beholder, follower, guardian, observer, onlooker **9** spectator

watchful
4 wary **5** alert, chary **7** on guard, wakeful **8** cautious, vigilant **9** attentive, observant, sleepless, wide-awake **10** unsleeping
Scottish: **5** tenty **6** tentie

watchman
5 guard, scout **6** patrol, picket, sentry, warder **7** lookout **8** sentinel

watch out
4 fore **6** beware **8** take care

watchtower
6 turret **7** lookout **8** barbican, bartizan **10** lighthouse

watchword
3 cry **5** motto **6** mantra, parole, signal, slogan **8** password **9** principle **10** shibboleth **11** catchphrase, countersign

water
4 hose, soak, thin, tide **5** drink, fluid, spray **6** dilute, liquid, supply **7** moisten **8** irrigate, moisture, snowmelt, sprinkle **10** excellence **13** amniotic fluid
body: **3** bay, sea **4** gulf, lake, pool **5** ocean **6** lagoon, strait **9** reservoir
combining form: **4** aqui, aquo, hydr **5** hydro
French: **3** eau
goddess: **4** Nina **7** Anahita, Anaitis
Latin: **4** aqua
Spanish: **4** agua

water buffalo
4 arna **5** bovid **7** carabao
female: **5** arnee

water clock
9 clepsydra

water closet
3 can, lav, loo **4** head, john **5** jakes, privy **6** toilet **7** latrine **8** bathroom, lavatory

water color
4 aqua

watercourse
4 dike, duct **5** bayou, canal, ditch **6** arroyo **7** channel, conduit **8** aqueduct, headrace, tailrace **9** streambed

water cow
6 dugong **7** manatee

watered-down
5 washy **6** dilute **7** anodyne, diluted

waterfall
4 linn **5** chute, sault, shoot **7** cascade **8** cataract
Brazil: **6** Iguaçú (Falls), Iguazú (Falls)
California: **8** Yosemite (Falls)
Canada: **5** Grand (Falls) **8** Takkakaw **9** Churchill (Falls)
Canada-U.S.: **7** Niagara (Falls)
Congo: **6** Boyoma (Falls) **7** Stanley (Falls)
former Nile: **4** Owen (Falls) **5** Ripon (Falls)
Kentucky: **10** Cumberland (Falls)
New Zealand: **10** Sutherland (Falls)
Niagara: **8** American, Canadian **9** Horseshoe
Norway: **6** Rjukan (Falls)
Oregon: **9** Multnomah (Falls)
South Africa: **6** Tugela (Falls)
Snake River: **4** Twin (Falls) **8** Shoshone (Falls)
Venezuela: **5** Angel (Falls)
Washington: **10** Snoqualmie (Falls)
world's highest: **5** Angel (Falls)
Wyoming: **11** Yellowstone (Falls)
Zambezi River: **8** Victoria (Falls)

water finder
6 dowser **11** divining rod

waterfront
8 seacoast **9** lakeshore, riverside

Watergate judge
6 Sirica (John)

water hole
5 oasis

watering hole
3 bar, pub **4** café **5** oasis **6** lounge, nitery, resort, saloon, tavern **7** barroom, cabaret, gin mill, taproom **9** nightclub, nightspot, roadhouse **10** supper club **11** rathskeller

waterless
3 dry **4** arid, sere **7** bone-dry, parched **8** droughty **9** anhydrous **10** dehydrated

waterlog
8 saturate

waterloo
4 ruin **6** defeat **7** failure **8** disaster, downfall

Waterloo group
4 ABBA

water nymph
3 nix **4** lily **5** naiad, nixie **6** mayfly, Nereid, undine **7** Oceanid **9** dragonfly

water oscillation
6 seiche

water pipe
4 bong **5** spout **6** hookah **8** narghile, nargileh **12** hubble-bubble

water plant
7 aquatic, seaweed **8** duckweed, wild rice **9** arrowhead, tape grass **10** hydrophyte, manna grass **11** bladderwort

water rat
6 nutria

watershed
6 crisis, divide **12** turning point

water spirit
3 nix **5** nixie, nymph **6** sprite, undine

water tank
7 cistern

water-to-wine site
4 Cana

waterway
5 canal, river **7** channel

waterwheel
5 noria

watery
4 pale, thin, weak **5** banal, bland, vapid, washy **6** dilute, serous **7** diluted, insipid
swelling: **5** edema

wattle
4 gill, grid, jowl **5** frame **6** dewlap **8** caruncle **9** framework, interlace **10** interweave

wattle and ___
4 daub

wave
3 wag **4** flag, flap **5** heave, ridge, surge, sweep, swell **6** comber, influx, marcel, motion, period, ripple, signal, waggle **7** breaker, dismiss, flutter, gesture, upsurge **8** activity, brandish, flourish, undulate **9** disregard
large: **7** tsunami

waver
4 reel, sway **5** swing, weave **6** dither, falter, quaver, quiver, teeter, totter, wobble **7** flicker, stagger, whiffle **8** hesitate, undulate **9** fluctuate, oscillate, vacillate **12** shilly-shally

wavering
4 weak **5** shake, shaky **6** unsure, wobbly **7** halting **8** doubtful, insecure, to-and-fro, unstable **9** equivocal, faltering, fluctuant, hesitancy, undecided, vibration, whiffling **10** hesitating, hesitation, indecision, irresolute **11** fluctuating, vacillating, vacillation **12** irresolution, shilly-shally

Waverley novels
6 Rob Roy **7** Ivanhoe **10** Kenilworth **14** Quentin Durward
author: **5** Scott (Walter)

wavy
4 ondé, undé **7** rolling **8** rippling, swelling **9** fluctuant **10** undulating **11** fluctuating

wavy pattern
5 moiré **8** squiggle **10** undulation **11** crenulation

wax
4 cere, come, grow, rise **5** boost, build, mount **6** become, expand, record **7** augment, enlarge **8** heighten, increase, multiply, paraffin, simonize **9** secretion, substance
Chinese: **4** pela

wax-covered cheese
4 Edam **5** Gouda

wax eloquent
5 orate **8** perorate **9** hold forth, sermonize

waxen
3 wan **4** ashy, pale **5** ashen, livid **6** pallid, smooth **7** pliable **8** blanched, moldable **9** colorless

way
3 ilk **4** door, kind, mode, much, path, road, sort, type, very **5** entry, habit, means, order, route, state, style, usage **6** access, artery, action, avenue, course, custom, degree, manner, method, street **7** ability, fashion, feature, ingress, opening, outcome, respect **8** distance, entrance, practice **9** boulevard, condition, direction, procedure, technique **11** opportunity, possibility **12** thoroughfare

wayfarer
4 hobo **5** gipsy, gypsy, hiker, nomad, rover, tramp **7** rambler **8** traveler, vagabond **9** itinerant, journeyer, traveller

wayfaring
6 roving **7** nomadic, vagrant **8** vagabond **9** itinerant, traveling, wandering **10** travelling **11** peripatetic **13** perambulatory

waylay
4 jump **5** brace **6** ambush, attack **8** surprise **9** bushwhack, still-hunt

Wayne's World
actor: **5** Myers (Mike) **6** Carvey (Dana)
character: **5** Garth, Wayne

Way of All Flesh author
6 Butler (Samuel)

way off
4 afar

Way of the World author
8 Congreve (William)

wayward
5 balky **6** fickle, unruly **7** froward, restive, vagrant, willful **8** contrary, perverse, untoward **9** whimsical **10** capricious, headstrong **11** intractable, wrongheaded **12** ungovernable **13** unpredictable

we
French: **4** nous
German: **3** wir
Italian: **3** noi
Spanish: **8** nosotros

weak
3 dim, wan **4** lame, puny, soft, thin **5** faint, frail, shaky, timid **6** dilute, feeble, flimsy, infirm, sickly,

unsure, watery, wobbly **7** brittle, diluted, fragile, rickety, spindly, tenuous, unsound **8** decrepit, delicate, helpless, impotent, inferior, insecure, timorous, unstable, wavering **9** deficient, enfeebled, inaudible, powerless, spineless, uncertain **10** improbable, inadequate, unreliable, unstressed **11** debilitated, implausible, ineffective, ineffectual, vacillating, watered-down **12** unconvincing, undependable **13** insubstantial, unsubstantial

weaken
3 lag, sap **4** fail, flag, thin, wane **5** abate **6** damage, dilute, impair, lessen, reduce, soften **7** corrode, decline, disable, dwindle, subvert, unbrace **8** enervate, enfeeble, moderate **9** attenuate, grind down, honeycomb, undermine **10** debilitate, demoralize, invalidate

weak-kneed
5 timid **6** wobbly **7** gutless **8** cowardly, wavering **9** faltering, uncertain, whiffling **10** irresolute **11** lily-livered, vacillating **12** fainthearted, shilly-shally **13** pusillanimous

weakling
4 wimp, wuss **5** mouse, sissy **7** doormat, milksop, sad sack **8** pushover **9** cream puff, jellyfish **10** namby-pamby **11** milquetoast, mollycoddle **12** invertebrate

weakness
4 flaw, hole, vice **5** crack, fault, taste **6** defect, desire, liking, relish **7** failing, frailty **8** appetite, debility, fondness, soft spot **9** infirmity **10** feebleness **11** decrepitude, shortcoming **12** Achilles' heel

weal
4 welt **5** ridge **7** welfare **9** well-being

weald
5 woods **6** forest **8** woodland **10** timberland, wilderness

wealth
5 goods, worth **6** assets, estate, mammon, plenty, riches **7** capital, fortune **8** holdings, opulence, property **9** abundance, affluence, profusion, resources **11** possessions

Wealth of Nations author
5 Smith (Adam)

wealthy
4 rich **5** flush **6** loaded **7** moneyed, opulent, well-off **8** affluent, well-to-do **9** well-fixed **10** prosperous, well-heeled **12** silk-stocking

wean
4 free, part **5** alien **6** detach **8** accustom, estrange, separate

weapon
3 bow, gun **4** bill, bolo, bomb, club, dart, dirk, mace, nuke, pike, shiv **5** A-bomb, arrow, H-bomb, knife, lance, prick, rifle, saber, sabre, sling, spear, steel, sword **6** cudgel, dagger, Magnum, musket, pistol, poleax, rapier, rocket **7** bazooka, broadax, car bomb, carbine, firearm, gisarme, halberd, handgun, javelin, machete, missile, shotgun, sidearm, stun gun, torpedo, war club **8** battle-ax, bludgeon, broadaxe, catapult, crossbow, death ray, nerve gas, nunchaku, partisan, partizan, petronel, revolver, spontoon, tomahawk **9** battle-axe, blackjack, boomerang, derringer, slingshot **10** atomic bomb, machine gun, projectile **11** blunderbuss, depth charge, nuclear bomb **12** quarterstaff **13** brass knuckles

weapons
4 arms **7** arsenal, battery **8** ordnance **9** armaments, artillery, munitions **13** armamentarium

wear
3 rub **4** fray, tire **5** chafe, dress, erode, grind, sport **6** abrade, attire, endure, have on, impair **7** corrode, exhibit, fatigue, fashion **8** abrasion, clothing
and tear: **12** depreciation
thin: **4** fray **5** chafe **6** tatter **7** hackney

wear down
5 drain, erode, grind **6** abrade, weaken **7** corrode, degrade, exhaust, fatigue

weariness
5 ennui **7** boredom, fatigue, languor **8** lethargy **9** lassitude **10** enervation, exhaustion **12** taedium vitae

wearing
6 taxing, tiring, trying **9** difficult, fatiguing

wearisome
see **tiresome**

wear out
3 fag **4** bust, do in, fray, jade, poop, tire **5** drain **6** efface, tucker **7** consume, deplete, exhaust, frazzle **8** overstay

weary
4 beat, jade, limp, tire, worn **5** drain, jaded, spent, tired **6** bushed, done in, pooped, tucker, wasted **7** drained, fatigue, worn-out **8** dog-tired, fatigued, tiresome **9** apathetic, overtaxed

weasand
6 gullet, throat **7** trachea **8** windpipe **9** esophagus

weasel
4 mink **5** dodge, evade, hedge, sable, slink, sneak, stoat **6** ermine, escape, ferret, mammal, marten **7** sneaker **8** sidestep **9** pussyfoot **10** equivocate
Scottish: **8** whittret

weather
4 rain **5** storm **6** bear up, endure, expose **7** climate, ride out, undergo **9** withstand
forecaster: **4** NOAA
forecasting: **11** meteorology

weathercock
4 vane

weathered
8 hardened, seasoned, tempered

weave
4 cane, lawn, leno, spin, sway 5 braid, cloth, lurch, twine, waver 6 careen, fabric, pleach, raddle, wobble, zigzag 7 pattern, stagger, textile, texture 8 contrive 9 interlace 10 crisscross, intertwine

weaver
4 loom 7 Arachne, webster

web
3 net 4 mesh, vane 5 snare, snarl 6 enmesh, fabric, tangle 7 ensnare, netting, network 8 entangle 10 enmeshment 12 entanglement

Weber opera
6 Oberon 9 Euryanthe 10 Freischütz (Der)

Web message
4 post 5 e-mail, tweet

Web publication
5 e-zine

Web-site test phase
4 beta

___ Webster
4 Noah 6 Daniel

Web vending
5 e-tail 9 e-commerce

wed
4 join, link, mate, yoke 5 hitch, marry, merge, unite 6 splice 7 combine, conjoin, connect, espouse 10 tie the knot
on the run: 5 elope

wedded
7 marital, nuptial 8 conjugal, hymeneal 9 connubial 11 matrimonial

wedding
5 union 6 bridal 7 spousal 8 espousal, marriage, nuptials
words: 3 I do

wedding anniversary
fifteenth: 7 crystal
fifth: 6 wooden
fiftieth: 6 golden
first: 5 paper
seventy-fifth: 7 diamond
tenth: 3 tin
twentieth: 5 china
twenty-fifth: 6 silver

wedding-cake layer
4 tier

wedding-notice word
3 née

wedge
4 shim 5 chock, stuff 8 golf club, golf shot, keystone 10 force apart

wedge-shaped
7 cuneate 8 cottered, sphenoid 9 cuneiform
mark: 5 caret

wedlock
4 knot, yoke 8 espousal, marriage 9 matrimony 11 conjugality 12 connubiality

wee
4 tiny 5 bitsy, bitty, early, small, teeny 6 little, minute, teensy 9 itty-bitty, miniature 10 diminutive, teeny-weeny 11 Lilliputian, little bitty 12 teensy-weensy
drink: 4 dram

weed
4 dock 5 chess, clear, plant, tansy 6 cockle, darnel, dodder, nettle, remove 7 burdock, burseed, ragweed, ruderal 8 amaranth, charlock, purslane 9 buckthorn, chickweed, cocklebur, dandelion, knotgrass, marijuana, poison ivy, poison oak, stickseed 10 cheatgrass, lady's thumb, sow thistle
biblical: 4 tare
European: 6 spurry 7 spurrey
killer: 8 paraquat 9 herbicide
Western: 4 loco

weedy
4 lean, thin 5 lanky 6 skinny 7 scrawny, stringy, willowy 8 untended 9 overgrown

week
6 period 8 hebdomad
two weeks: 9 fortnight

week-ending phrase
4 TGIF

weep
3 cry, sob 4 drip, moan, ooze, tear, wail 5 bleed, exude, sweat 6 lament 7 blubber, dribble, trickle 8 transude

weeper
5 Niobe

weepy
5 misty, moist, teary 7 tearful 10 lachrymose

weevil
7 billbug 8 curculio

weft
3 web 4 pick, woof, yarn 6 fabric, thread

weigh
3 way 4 heft, rate, tare 5 count, judge, scale, study 6 burden, ponder 7 balance, measure, oppress, perpend 8 appraise, bear down, consider, evaluate, militate 11 contemplate

weigh down
4 load 5 press 6 burden, sadden 7 depress, oppress 8 encumber 10 discourage, overburden

weight
3 tax 4 heft, lade, load, mass, onus, task 5 class, force, power 6 amount, assign, burden,

charge, credit, import, moment, saddle **7** oppress, potency, quality **8** encumber, poundage, pressure, prestige, quantity **9** authority, influence, magnitude **10** corpulence, importance **11** consequence **12** significance
allowance: **4** tare
ancient: **4** mina
apothecary: **4** dram **5** grain, pound **7** scruple
Asian: **4** tael **5** catty
deduction: **4** tare
gem: **5** carat
measure of: **3** fun, kin, kip, oke, tan, tod, ton, vis, yin **4** dram, gram, mina, rotl, tael **5** grain, libra, ounce, picul, pound **7** long ton, scruple **8** kilogram, short ton **9** metric ton
system: **3** net **4** troy **6** metric **10** apothecary **11** avoirdupois

weightiness
4 pith **6** import, moment **7** dignity, gravity **9** heaviness, magnitude, solemnity **10** importance **11** consequence, massiveness **12** significance **13** momentousness

weight lifting term
4 curl, pull, push **5** clean, press, shrug, squat **6** snatch **8** deadlift **12** clean and jerk

weightlifter
4 Kono (Tommy), Tang (Gonghong) **5** Dimas (Pyrros), Mutlu (Halil) **6** Weller (Ronny) **7** Krastev (Antonio) **8** Alexeyev (Vasily), Pechalov (Nikolay) **9** Chemerkin (Andrei), Reza Zadeh (Hossein), Taranenko (Leonid) **10** Schemansky (Norbert)

weighty
3 fat **5** grave, gross, heavy, hefty, obese, sober, staid **6** fleshy, portly, sedate, severe, solemn, somber **7** massive, serious, telling **8** cumbrous, grievous, powerful **9** corpulent, effective, important, momentous, ponderous **10** burdensome, convincing, cumbersome **11** significant, substantial **12** considerable **13** consequential
book: **4** tome

weir
3 dam **5** stank

weird
3 odd **5** eerie, queer **6** creepy, freaky, spooky **7** bizarre, curious, oddball, strange, uncanny **8** freakish, peculiar, singular, sinister **9** eccentric, fantastic, unearthly **10** mysterious **11** inscrutable **12** supernatural **13** preternatural

weirdo
4 geek, kook, loon **5** freak **7** nutcase, oddball **8** crackpot **9** eccentric, screwball

welcome
4 hail **5** cheer, greet, hello, howdy **6** accept, invite, salute **7** embrace, invited, receive **8** greeting, pleasant, pleasing **9** agreeable, favorable, reception **10** gratifying, hospitable **11** hospitality, pleasurable

weld
4 bond, fuse, join **5** braze, joint, merge, unite **6** solder

welfare
3 aid **4** dole, help, weal **5** pogey **6** health, relief, succor **7** benefit, fortune, success, support **8** interest **9** advantage, happiness, well-being **10** assistance, commonweal, prosperity

welkin
3 sky **5** ether, vault **6** heaven **7** heavens **8** empyrean **9** firmament

well
3 far, fit, pit **4** easy, emit, hale, hole, pool, rise, sane **5** amply, clear, cured, fully, quite, shaft, sound, truly **6** easily, freely, healed, indeed, justly, kindly, likely, nicely, origin, rather, really, source, spring, wholly **7** clearly, healthy, perhaps, readily, rightly **8** entirely, expertly, pleasing, possibly, probably, properly, sensibly, smoothly, suitably **9** advisable, correctly, desirable, elegantly, favorably, fittingly, fortunate, perfectly, wholesome

well-being
4 weal **6** health **7** welfare **8** thriving **9** happiness **10** prosperity

well-bred
6 urbane **7** genteel, refined **8** cultured, highborn, polished **9** civilized, patrician **10** cultivated **11** blue-blooded, gentlemanly

well-built
4 buff **5** hunky, solid **8** muscular **9** strapping

well-developed
5 curvy **7** fulsome, rounded, shapely **8** advanced **9** Junoesque **10** curvaceous

well-disposed
7 amiable **8** friendly **9** favorable, receptive **11** sympathetic **13** understanding

Welles movie
5 Trial (The) **7** Macbeth, Othello **8** Jane Eyre, Stranger (The), Third Man (The) **11** Citizen Kane, Touch of Evil **15** Journey into Fear **16** Chimes at Midnight, Lady from Shanghai (The) **20** Magnificent Ambersons (The)

well-favored
4 fair **5** bonny **6** comely, lovely, pretty **7** winsome **8** gorgeous, handsome **9** beauteous, beautiful **10** attractive **11** good-looking

well-fixed
see **well-to-do**

well-founded
5 sound, valid **6** cogent **8** rational **9** justified **10** convincing

well-groomed
4 neat, snug, tidy, trig, trim **5** natty, smart **6** dapper, snappy, spiffy, spruce, sprucy **7** orderly **8** clean-cut **9** shipshape

well-heeled
see **well-to-do**

Wellington
4 duke **7** general **8** Iron Duke
horse: 10 Copenhagen
original name: 9 Wellesley (Arthur)
victory: 7 Vitoria **8** Talavera, Waterloo **9** Salamanca

well-known
5 famed, noted **6** famous **7** big-name, eminent, popular **8** renowned **9** notorious, prominent **10** celebrated **11** illustrious

well-liked
7 beloved, favored, popular **8** favorite **9** cherished, preferred

well-mannered
5 civil, suave **6** poised, polite, proper, urbane **7** genteel, tactful **9** courteous **10** diplomatic

wellness
6 health

well-nigh
6 all but, almost, fairly, nearly, next to **8** as good as **9** just about, virtually **11** essentially, practically

well-off
see **well-to-do**

well-paying
7 gainful **9** lucrative, rewarding **10** profitable, worthwhile **11** moneymaking **12** advantageous, remunerative

well-read
7 bookish, erudite, learned **8** lettered **9** scholarly

Wells novel
11 Time Machine (The) **12** Invisible Man (The) **14** War of the Worlds (The)

wellspring
4 font, root **5** fount **6** origin, source **7** genesis **8** fountain **10** provenance **11** provenience **12** fountainhead

well-thought-of
6 valued, worthy **7** admired, reputed **9** estimable, reputable **10** creditable **11** respectable

well-timed
6 timely **7** apropos, fitting, timeous **9** favorable, opportune **10** auspicious, felicitous, fortuitous, propitious, seasonable

well-to-do
4 rich **5** flush **6** loaded, monied **7** moneyed, upscale, wealthy **8** affluent **10** prosperous **11** comfortable

well-turned
4 trim **5** plump **7** rounded, shapely **10** curvaceous, felicitous, Rubenesque, statuesque **11** clean-limbed

well-worn
5 banal, musty, stale, stock, tired, trite **6** frayed, old-hat, shabby **7** clichéd **8** bromidic, cobwebby, dog-eared, overused **9** hackneyed **10** threadbare **11** commonplace, stereotyped

Welsh
see **Cymric**

welsh
5 dodge **6** renege, resile **7** back out, default

welt
4 blow, edge, seam, wale, weal **5** ridge, wheal, whelk **6** insert

welter
4 coil, moil, toss **5** chaos, churn, steep, surge **6** flurry, hassle, hubbub, jumble, lather, ruckus, seethe, thrash, wallow, writhe **7** ferment, turmoil **8** disorder **9** confusion

____ Welty
6 Eudora

wen
4 bleb, cyst **5** blain **6** growth **7** vesicle **11** excrescence

wench
3 gal **4** girl, jade, lass, maid, minx, miss, puss, slut, tart **5** hussy, nymph, tramp, trull, whore, woman **6** damsel, gamine, harlot, hoyden, lassie, maiden, wanton **7** jezebel, servant, trollop **8** slattern, strumpet

wend
3 hie **4** fare, pass **6** direct, push on, repair, travel **7** journey, proceed

werewolf
9 loup-garou **11** lycanthrope

Werther's beloved
5 Lotte **9** Charlotte

Wesleyan
9 Methodist

West
8 Occident

West African capital
4 Lomé **5** Abuja, Dakar **6** Bissau, Niamey **7** Conakry, Cotonou, Malabo

western
5 oater **9** Hesperian **10** horse opera, occidental
hemisphere: 8 Americas, New World

Western alliance
4 NATO

Western neckwear
4 bolo

Western novelist
4 Grey (Zane), Ross (Dana Fuller) **5** Brand (Max), Faust (Frederick), Short (Luke) **6** Judson (E. Z. C.), Kelton (Elmer), L'Amour (Louis), Patten (Lewis), Wister (Owen) **7** Guthrie (A. B.), Leonard (Elmore) **8** Buntline (Ned), McCarthy (Cormac), McMurtry (Larry)

West Indies
country: **4** Cuba **5** Haiti **7** Bahamas, Grenada, Jamaica **8** Barbados, Dominica **10** Guadeloupe, Martinique, Puerto Rico, Saint Lucia **17** Dominican Republic
island group: **6** Virgin (Islands) **7** Bahamas, Leeward (Islands) **8** Antilles (Greater, Lesser), Windward (Islands)

West of Hollywood
3 Mae

West Point
father of: **6** Thayer (Sylvanus)
freshman: **5** plebe
student: **5** cadet

West Side Story
composer: **9** Bernstein (Leonard)
heroine: **5** Maria
lyricist: **8** Sondheim (Stephen)

West Virginia
capital: **10** Charleston
city: **8** Wheeling **10** Huntington
mountain: **10** Spruce Knob
nickname: **8** Mountain (State)
river: **4** Ohio
state bird: **8** cardinal
state flower: **12** rhododendron
state tree: **10** sugar maple

west wind
see at **wind**

wet
3 sop **4** damp, dank, rain, soak, wash, weak **5** douse, drown, drunk, humid, moist, rainy, soggy, soppy, souse, water **6** dampen, drench, soaked, sodden, soused, sweaty, watery **7** moisten, raining, soaking, sopping **8** drenched, dripping, humidify, irrigate, moisture, saturate, slippery **9** saturated, spineless
combining form: **4** hygr **5** hygro

wet blanket
6 grinch **7** killjoy **8** sourpuss **9** pessimist **10** spoilsport **11** party pooper

wether
4 goat **5** sheep

wetland
3 bog, fen **4** mire, quag **5** marsh, swamp **6** morass, muskeg, slough

whack
3 bat, hit, pop, try **4** bash, belt, biff, blow, chop, cuff, kill, pelt, shot, sock, stab, wham, whap, whop **5** crack, punch, smack, smash, smite **6** attack, defeat, murder, strike, wallop **7** bump off **8** knock off, lambaste
up: **4** part **5** divvy, split **6** divide **7** portion **9** apportion

whacked, biblically
5 smote

whale
3 hit **4** beat, cete, flog, hide, lash, whip **5** giant, Shamu **6** defeat, strike, stripe, thrash **7** mammoth **8** cetacean, behemoth, Moby Dick **9** leviathan **10** flagellate
arctic: **7** bowhead
group: **3** gam, pod
killer: **4** orca
kind: **3** sei **4** blue **5** right, sperm **6** baleen, beluga, killer **7** narwhal, rorqual **8** cachalot
toothed: **5** pilot (whale) **9** blackfish
white: **4** huso
young: **4** calf

whalebone
9 scrimshaw

wham
3 hit, pow **4** bang, beat, blow, boom, clap, slam **5** blast, burst, crack, crash, smash, whack **6** impact, propel, strike **7** explode

whammy
3 hex, zap **4** jinx, juju **5** curse, spell **6** hoodoo, voodoo **7** evil eye

wharf
4 dock, pier, quay **5** jetty, levee

Wharton of literature
5 Edith
novel: **10** Ethan Frome **12** House of Mirth (The) **14** Age of Innocence (The) **18** Custom of the Country (The)

whatever
5 at all **9** in any case

whatnot
7 étagère

whatsit
5 gizmo **6** dingus, doodad, gadget, gewgaw, hickey, jigger, widget **9** doohickey

wheal
4 lump, welt **5** ridge, whelk

wheat
4 crop **5** emmer, flour, grain, grass, spelt **6** cereal **7** einkorn
beard: **3** awn
beat: **6** thresh
bundle: **5** sheaf
chaff: **4** bran
crushed: **6** bulgur
disease: **4** rust, smut
type: **4** club **5** durum

wheedle
3 con **4** coax **5** cozen **6** cajole, entice, seduce **7** blarney, flatter **8** blandish, inveigle, scrounge, soft-soap **9** sweet-talk

wheel
3 VIP **4** auto, gyre, move, reel, spin, turn **5** cycle, drive, motor, pilot, pivot, round, whirl **6** bigwig, circle, gyrate, league, rotate, totter, travel **7** big shot, circuit, revolve **8** rotation **9** about-face, volte-face
part: **3** hub, rim **4** tire **5** felly, spoke
shaft: **4** axle
spoke: **6** radius
toothed: **3** cog **4** gear

wheeze
3 saw, yuk **4** gasp, hiss, joke, puff, rasp **5** adage, cough **6** saying **7** proverb, whistle **8** chestnut, rhonchus

whelk
4 wale, weal, welt **5** wheal

whelm
4 bury, sink **5** cover, drown, flood, swamp **6** deluge, engulf **8** bear down, inundate, overbear, overcome, submerge **9** devastate

whelp
3 cub, kid, pup **4** bear **5** child, puppy **9** youngster

whereas
5 since, while **6** seeing, though **7** howbeit **8** although **11** considering

wherefore
3 why **4** thus **5** proof **6** ground, reason, whence **8** argument **11** explanation

Where the Sidewalk Ends author
4 Shel (Silverstein)

wherewithal
5 funds, means, money **9** resources

wherry
4 boat **5** barge, scull **7** lighter, rowboat

whet
4 edge, goad, hone **5** drink, rally, rouse, waken **6** arouse, awaken, excite, kindle **7** sharpen, starter **8** aperitif **9** appetizer, challenge, stimulate **10** incitement **11** hors d'oeuvre

whiff
3 fan **4** blow, gust, hint, puff, waft **5** expel, smoke, tinge, trace **6** breath, exhale, inhale **7** soupçon, whisper **9** strikeout **10** indication, inhalation

whiffet
6 nobody, squirt **9** nonentity

whiffle
4 blow, gust, puff **5** waver **6** dither, falter **9** fluctuate, vacillate **12** shilly-shally

while
4 pass, time, when **5** spell **6** albeit, moment, though **7** howbeit, stretch, whereas **8** although, as long as, so long as
prefix: **4** erst

whilom
4 past **6** bygone, former **7** onetime, quondam **8** formerly, previous, sometime **9** erstwhile

whim
3 bee **4** idea, kink **5** dream, fancy, freak, humor **6** maggot, megrim, notion, vagary **7** caprice, capstan, conceit, thought **8** crotchet

whimper
3 cry **4** fret, mewl, pule, wail **5** bleat, whine **6** snivel

whimsical
4 iffy, zany **5** ditsy, ditzy, droll, fancy, flaky **6** chancy, fickle, fitful, flakes, quirky, random **7** erratic, flighty, mutable, puckish, wayward **8** fanciful, freakish, volatile **9** eccentric, impulsive, mercurial, pixilated, screwball, uncertain, vagarious **10** capricious, pixillated **13** unpredictable

whimsy
3 bee **4** play **5** dream, fancy, freak, humor **6** levity, maggot, megrim, notion, vagary **7** caprice, conceit, fantasy **9** capriccio, frivolity

whim-wham
4 dido **5** curio, fancy, frill **6** bauble, gewgaw, ruffle, trifle **7** bibelot, flounce, trinket, whatnot **8** furbelow, gimcrack, kickshaw **9** objet d'art **10** knickknack

whine
3 cry **4** cant, fret, fuss, kick, moan, pule, wail **5** bleat, gripe **6** grouse, repine, snivel, whinge, yammer **7** grumble, snuffle, whimper **8** complain **9** bellyache

whinny
5 neigh **6** nicker **7** whicker

whiny
5 fussy **7** fretful, grouchy, peevish **8** petulant **9** irritable, querulous

whip
3 cut, hem, set, tan **4** beat, cane, crop, dash, flog, hide, jerk, lash, lick, pull, rout, wind, wrap **5** abuse, mop up, quirt, spank, sting, whale, whisk **6** defeat, lather, snatch, strike, stroke, subdue, switch, thrash, urge on **7** agitate, dessert, provoke, rawhide, shellac, trounce, utensil **8** coachman, lambaste, overcome, vanquish **9** instigate, overwhelm **10** flagellate **13** cat-o'-nine-tails
braided: **10** blacksnake

whippersnapper
see **whiffet**

whipping boy
4 goat 5 patsy 7 fall guy 9 scapegoat

whippy
6 supple 7 elastic, springy 8 flexible 9 resilient

whir
3 fly, hum 4 burr, buzz, whiz 5 chirr, churr, drone, whizz 7 revolve, vibrate 9 bombinate

whirl
3 ado, gig, pop, try 4 eddy, flit, fuss, gyre, moil, reel, shot, spin, stab, stir, swim, turn, veer 5 hurry, pivot, swirl, whack, wheel 6 bustle, circle, gyrate, hassle, hubbub, pother, rotate 7 circuit, dervish, turmoil 8 ballyhoo, gyration, rotation 9 commotion, pirouette 10 revolution

whirligig
4 gyre, spin 6 beetle, gyrate 8 carousel 9 pirouette 12 merry-go-round

whirlpool
3 ado 4 eddy, fuss 6 bustle, flurry, furore, tumult, vortex 7 turmoil 8 vortices (plural) 9 commotion, maelstrom
bath: 6 hot tub 7 Jacuzzi

Whirlpool rival
5 Amana

whirlwind
4 rush, stir, to-do 5 hasty, spout, swift 6 bustle 7 cyclone, tornado, twister, typhoon 8 headlong 9 commotion, dust devil, dust storm, hurricane 10 waterspout 11 tourbillion

whish
4 fizz, hiss 6 fizzle 8 sibilate

whisk
3 mix, nip, wag, zip 4 beat, flit, whip 5 broom, brush, fluff, hurry, speed 6 switch

whisker
4 hair 7 bristle 8 filament, vibrissa 9 outrigger 11 hairbreadth

whiskered
5 hairy 6 pilose 7 bearded, bristly, hirsute 8 stubbled, unshaven

whiskers
5 beard 6 goatee 7 stubble, weepers 8 bristles 9 burnsides, peach fuzz, sideburns 11 dundrearies, muttonchops

whiskey
3 rye 6 liquor, Scotch 7 alcohol, bourbon
with beer chaser: 11 boilermaker

whisper
4 buzz, hint, hiss, whiz 5 rumor, shade, tinge, touch, trace, whiff 6 breath, gossip, murmur, mutter 8 sibilate, susurrus 9 suspicion, undertone 11 susurration

whist
4 game, hush 5 quiet, still 6 silent 9 noiseless, soundless

whistle
4 pipe, toot 5 flute, whiff 6 signal, tootle, wheeze

whistle-stop
5 stump 8 campaign, politick 9 barnstorm 11 electioneer

whit
3 bit, fig, jot, rap 4 atom, damn, hoot, iota, mite 5 crumb, scrap, shred, speck, whoop 7 dribble, modicum, smidgen 8 molecule, particle

white
4 pure 5 cream, ivory, livid, milky, snowy 6 albino, blanch, bleach, pallid 7 silvery 9 colorless
combining form: 4 leuc, leuk 5 leuco, leuko
egg's: 5 glair 6 glaire 7 albumen
heron: 5 egret

White novel
12 Stuart Little 13 Charlotte's Web

white cliffs of ___
5 Dover

White Fang author
6 London (Jack)

whitefish on the menu
3 cod 5 scrod 7 haddock, halibut

Whitehorse's territory
5 Yukon

White House
daughter: 5 Jenna, Malia, Sasha 7 Barbara, Chelsea
designer: 5 Hoban (James)
dog: 4 Fala
first occupant: 5 Adams (Abigail, John)

white lightning
5 hooch 7 bootleg, whiskey 9 moonshine 10 bathtub gin 11 mountain dew

whiten
4 fade, pale 5 frost 6 blanch, bleach, blench 8 etiolate 10 decolorize

white plague
8 phthisis 11 consumption 12 tuberculosis

whitewash
6 parget 7 cover up 9 gloss over, gloze over, sugarcoat

whither
5 where 7 whereto 9 whereunto

whiting
3 cod 4 hake 10 silver hake

Whitman work
13 Leaves of Grass

Whitney of cotton-gin fame
3 Eli

Whitsunday
9 Pentecost

Whittier poem
9 Snow-Bound 10 Maud Muller 11 Barefoot Boy 16 Barbara Frietchie

whittle
3 hew 4 chip, form, fret, pare, trim 5 carve, shape, shave, skive 6 reduce, sculpt 8 diminish

whiz
3 ace, fly, hum, zip 4 buzz, flit, hiss, zoom 5 hurry, speed, swish, whirl 6 expert, fizzle, genius, phenom, rotate, whoosh 8 virtuoso 10 wunderkind

whoa
3 hey 4 slow, stop 6 hold up

whodunit hint
4 clue

whole
3 all, fit, sum 4 full, hale, sane 5 sound, total, uncut, unity 6 entire, entity, healed, intact, system, unhurt 7 corrupt, healthy, perfect, plenary, unitary 8 complete, entirely, entirety, flawless, restored, totality, unbroken, unmarred
combining form: 3 hol, pan 4 holo

wholehearted
6 ardent 7 devoted, earnest, fervent, sincere 8 bona fide 9 committed, heartfelt, steadfast, unfeigned 10 passionate, unwavering 11 impassioned 12 enthusiastic 13 unquestioning

whole-hog
6 all-out, gung-ho 8 complete, thorough 9 full-scale 11 straight-out 13 thoroughgoing

wholeness
7 oneness 8 entirety, totality 9 integrity, soundness 10 intactness, perfection

whole note
9 semibreve

whole number
5 digit 6 cipher 7 integer, numeral

wholesome
3 fit 4 good, hale, safe, sane, well 5 right, sound 6 benign 7 healthy 8 hygienic, salutary 9 favorable, healthful 10 beneficial, salubrious

wholly
3 all 4 only 6 in toto, singly, solely, purely 7 totally 8 entirely 10 altogether, completely 11 exclusively

whomp
3 hit 4 beat, drub, slap, whip, whup 5 crash, thump 6 crunch, strike, thrash, wallop 7 clobber, shellac, trounce 8 lambaste

whomp up
4 stir 5 rouse, spark 6 arouse, excite, foment

whoopee
3 fun 5 revel, yahoo 6 gaiety, hoopla, hooray, yippee 7 jollity, revelry, wassail, whoopla 8 hilarity 9 festivity, high jinks, merriment 10 hurly-burly 11 merrymaking

whoopla
see **hoopla**

whop
3 bat, bop 4 bash, beat, biff, blow, drub, lick, sock 5 baste, pound, smack, thump, whack 6 batter, buffet, defeat, hammer, pummel, strike, thrash, thwack, wallop 7 trounce 8 lambaste

whopper
3 lie 4 lulu 5 beaut, doozy, whale 6 doozie 8 knockout, tall tale 9 humdinger

whopping
4 huge, vast 6 mighty 7 amazing, immense, massive 8 colossal, enormous, gigantic, whacking 9 bodacious, humongous, monstrous 10 gargantuan, incredible, prodigious 13 extraordinary

whorl
4 coil, eddy, turn 5 swirl 6 spiral

Who's Afraid of Virginia Woolf playwright
5 Albee (Edward)

why
5 cause 6 enigma, motive, puzzle, reason, riddle 7 mystery, problem, what for 9 conundrum, rationale, therefore, wherefore 10 puzzlement 11 explanation

wicked
4 evil, mean, very, vile 5 awful, black, wrong 6 fierce, malign, sinful, unholy 7 corrupt, hateful, heinous, immoral, naughty, ungodly, vicious 8 depraved, devilish, fiendish, sinister 9 atrocious, barbarous, dangerous, extremely, hazardous, injurious, malicious, malignant, nefarious 10 iniquitous, malevolent, outrageous 11 treacherous

wickedness
3 sin 4 evil, vice 7 devilry 8 enormity, iniquity, satanism 9 depravity 10 corruption, immorality 12 devilishness, fiendishness

wicker
4 twig 5 osier, withe 6 branch, rattan

wicket
4 arch, door, gate, hoop 6 window
sticky: 3 fix, jam 4 knot 7 toughie 9 conundrum, tight spot

wide
4 vast 5 broad, fully 8 extended, spacious, straying, sweeping 9 deviating, expansive, extensive, inclusive 10 completely 13 comprehensive
shoe size: 3 EEE

widen
4 ream 6 dilate, expand, extend, open up, spread 7 broaden, distend, enlarge

widespread
4 rife, vast 6 common 7 current, general, popular, rampant, regnant 8 far-flung 9 extensive, pervasive, prevalent 10 far-ranging, ubiquitous

widget
5 gismo, gizmo **6** device, dingus, doodad, gadget, hickey, jigger **7** gimmick, whatsit **9** doohickey, thingummy **11** contraption, thingamabob, thingamajig, thingumajig

width
4 gape, kerf, span **5** depth, range **6** spread **7** breadth **9** extension

wield
3 use **5** exert **6** handle **7** control **8** brandish, exercise **10** manipulate
the gavel: **7** preside

wiener
3 dog **5** frank **6** hot dog **7** sausage **11** frankfurter **13** Vienna sausage

Wiesel of literature
4 Elie

wife
3 Mrs. **4** mate **5** bride, woman **6** female, matron, missis, missus, spouse **7** consort, partner **8** helpmate, helpmeet
Latin: **4** uxor
of a rajah: **4** rani **5** ranee
of Geraint: **4** Enid
of Nick: **4** Nora
of Prince Valiant: **5** Aleta

wifely
7 uxorial

wig
3 jaw, rap, rug **4** flip, rail, rate **5** chide, freak, scold **6** berate, peruke, rebuke, revile, toupee **7** bawl out, chew out, reproof, upbraid **8** postiche, reproach **9** hairpiece, reprimand **10** tongue-lash

wiggle
4 jerk **5** shake, twist **6** fidget, squirm, writhe
Scottish: **5** hotch

wight
3 man **5** human **6** animal, mortal, person **7** critter **8** creature **10** human being, individual

Wight, e.g.
4 isle

wigwam relative
5 tepee

wild
3 mad **4** fast **5** crazy, feral **6** barren, raging, savage, stormy, unruly **7** erratic, frantic, furious, natural, untamed, vicious **8** barbaric, blustery, desolate, frenetic, frenzied, reckless **9** barbarian, barbarous, delirious, fantastic, turbulent, wasteland **10** incautious, outlandish **11** extravagant, intractable, sensational, tempestuous, uncivilized, uninhabited **12** preposterous, uncontrolled, uncultivated, ungovernable, unmanageable **13** irresponsible, undisciplined

wild ass
5 klang **6** onager

wildcat
4 eyra, lynx **6** ocelot, strike **10** jaguarundi

wild dog of Australia
5 dingo

Wild Duck author
5 Ibsen (Henrik)

wildebeest
3 gnu

wilderness
4 bush **5** heath, waste **6** barren, desert **9** backlands, wasteland **10** hinterland **11** backcountry

Wilder play
7 Our Town **10** Matchmaker (The) **14** Skin of Our Teeth (The)

wild-eyed
6 raving **7** blue-sky, radical **9** visionary

wild goat
4 ibex

wild ox
4 anoa

wile
4 ploy, ruse, vamp **5** charm, feint, guile, trick **6** allure, deceit, entice, gambit **7** attract, beguile, bewitch, chicane, cunning, enchant, gimmick **8** artifice, inveigle, maneuver, trickery **9** captivate, chicanery, fascinate, magnetize, stratagem **10** subterfuge

wiliness
5 guile **7** cunning

will
4 like, wish **5** cause, elect, leave, order **6** choice, choose, decree, desire, direct, intend, intent, liking, option, ordain, please **7** bequest, consent, control, passion, purpose **8** appetite, bequeath, pleasure, volition **9** intention, testament **10** discipline **11** disposition, inclination, self-control **13** determination, self-restraint
addition: **7** codicil
maker: **8** testator **9** testatrix
without: **9** intestate

willful
5 heady **6** dogged, mulish, ornery, unruly **7** froward, wayward **8** perverse, stubborn **9** obstinate, pigheaded, voluntary **10** deliberate, hardheaded, headstrong, purposeful, self-willed **11** intentional, intractable, wrongheaded **12** contumacious, pertinacious, ungovernable

Williams play
10 Camino Real, Rose Tattoo (The) **14** Glass Menagerie (The), Summer and Smoke **16** Cat on a Hot Tin Roof, Night of the Iguana (The), Sweet Bird of Youth **18** Suddenly Last Summer **20** Streetcar Named Desire (A)

William Tell
canton: **3** Uri
composer: **7** Rossini (Gioacchino)

willies
6 creeps, shakes **7** jimjams, jitters, shivers **9** whim-whams **10** goose bumps **13** heebie-jeebies

willing
3 apt **4** fain, game, glad, open **5** prone, ready **6** minded **7** forward, witting **8** amenable, disposed, inclined, obliging, unforced **9** agreeable, compliant, favorable, receptive, voluntary **10** deliberate, volitional **11** intentional, predisposed

williwaw
4 gust, wind **5** blast **8** outburst, paroxysm **9** commotion

will-o'-the-wisp
7 fantasy, figment, phantom **8** daydream, delusion **11** ignis fatuus

willow
5 osier, salix **6** sallow **10** cricket bat
flower cluster: **6** catkin
kind: **5** crack, pussy, white **6** basket **7** weeping
Virginia: **4** Itea

willowy
4 slim, tall **5** lithe **6** pliant, supple, svelte **7** lissome, pliable, slender **8** graceful

Wilson play
6 Fences **11** Piano Lesson (The) **12** Talley's Folly **13** Hot l Baltimore (The) **20** Ma Rainey's Black Bottom

wilt
3 sag **4** swag **5** droop, dry up, wizen **6** wither **7** shrivel **8** languish

wily
3 sly **4** cagy, foxy **5** cagey, canny, slick **6** artful, astute, clever, crafty, shrewd, tricky **7** cunning, devious, vulpine **8** guileful, scheming **10** serpentine

wimble
4 bore **5** auger, borer, brace, drill **6** gimlet

Wimbledon's game
6 tennis

wimp
4 nerd, wuss **5** sissy **6** weenie **7** doormat, nebbish **9** jellyfish **11** milquetoast

wimple
4 bend, veil, wrap **5** cover, curve **6** ripple
wearer: **3** nun

wimp out
6 beg off, cave in, give in **8** back down

wimpy
4 lame, puny, weak **5** dinky, inept, timid **6** craven, feeble **7** gutless **8** cowardly, feckless, impotent, pathetic **9** spineless **10** namby-pamby, wishy-washy **11** ineffective, ineffectual

win
3 get **4** beat, earn, gain, kayo **5** reach, score **6** attain, defeat, obtain, secure **7** achieve, acquire, conquer, procure, produce, realize, succeed, success, triumph, victory **8** conquest, persuade **9** influence **10** accomplish
over: **6** disarm, induce **8** convince, persuade, talk into **9** prevail on

wince
5 cower, quail, start **6** blanch, blench, cringe, flinch, recoil, shrink **7** squinch

wind
3 air, dry, fan, gas **4** bend, blow, clue, coil, curl, gale, gird, gust, haul, hint, reel, rest, talk, turn, warp, wrap **5** cover, crank, curve, force, hoist, raise, sound, spool, twine, twist **6** breath, breeze, circle, enlace, girdle, notion, zephyr **7** enclose, entwine, envelop, inkling, involve, monsoon, nothing, tighten **8** easterly, encircle, entangle, surround, tendency, westerly **9** direction, idle words, influence, insinuate **10** indication, intimation, suggestion
Adriatic: **4** bora
cold: **4** bora **7** mistral, pampero **8** williwaw
combining form: **4** anem **5** anemo, venti, vento
desert: **6** simoom
gentle: **6** breeze, zephyr
god: **6** Boreas (north) **8** Favonius, Zephyrus (west)
hot: **6** simoom **7** sirocco **8** scirocco
instrument: **4** vane **10** anemometer **11** weather vane
into: **8** aweather
measure of speed: **4** knot
Mediterranean: **4** bora **7** sirocco **8** levanter, libeccio, scirocco
scale: **8** Beaufort
stormy: **4** gale **7** cyclone, tornado, twister **9** hurricane **11** northeaster
warm: **4** föhn **5** foehn **7** chinook

windbag
6 gabber **7** blabber **8** bigmouth, blowhard, braggart

windfall
4 boon, gain **5** break **7** jackpot **8** fortuity

winding
4 curl, kink **5** snaky **6** spiral **7** coiling, curving, devious, sinuous **8** flexuous, indirect, tortuous, twisting **9** meandrous **10** circuitous, convoluted, meandering, roundabout, serpentine **11** anfractuous **12** labyrinthine

wind instrument
3 sax **4** horn, oboe, pipe, tuba **5** flute, shawm **6** cornet **7** bagpipe, bassoon, panpipe, piccolo, sackbut, trumpet **8** bagpipes, clarinet, crumhorn, recorder, trombone **9** krummhorn, saxophone **10** cor anglais, flugelhorn, French horn, sousaphone **11** English horn

windmill
4 spin **5** wheel **7** machine
fighter: **10** Don Quixote
blade: **4** vane

window
3 eye **4** pane **7** opening **8** aperture, casement, jalousie
cover: **5** blind **7** curtain, shutter
French: **7** fenêtre
over a door: **7** transom **8** fanlight
part: **4** pane, sash, sill **5** frame
projecting: **3** bay **5** oriel
roof's: **6** dormer **7** lucarne **8** skylight
round: **5** oxeye
Scottish: **7** winnock
ship's: **4** port **8** porthole

windpipe
7 trachea
combining form: **6** trache **7** tracheo

windrow
4 bank, heap, hill, mass, pile **5** mound, ridge, stack

wind up
3 end **4** halt **5** close **6** finish, settle **8** complete, conclude **9** terminate

windup
3 end **5** close **6** ending, finale, finish **9** backswing **10** completion, conclusion **11** termination

windward opposite
4 alee

windy
4 airy **5** blowy, gassy, gusty, inane, tumid, wordy **6** breezy, prolix, stormy, turgid **7** diffuse, orotund, pompous, verbose **8** blustery, inflated **9** bombastic, overblown **11** tempestuous **13** grandiloquent, unsubstantial

wine
4 vino **5** drink, juice **8** beverage
aromatized: **8** vermouth **9** hippocras
beverage: **5** negus, punch **6** bishop, cooler **7** sangria **8** sangaree, spritzer **9** hippocras
bottle: **6** fiasco, magnum **8** decanter, jeroboam **10** methuselah
cabinet: **8** cellaret
cask: **3** tun, vat **4** butt, pipe
cellar: **6** bodega
cheap: **5** plonk
combining form: **3** eno, oen **4** oeno
discoverer: **4** Noah
distillate: **6** brandy, cognac
dry: **3** sec **4** brut
flavor: **4** mull
fortified: **4** port **5** Tokay **6** Malaga, Muscat, sherry **7** Madeira, marsala, oloroso **8** muscatel
fragrance: **4** nose **7** bouquet
Greek: **7** retsina
lover: **9** oenophile **11** oenophilist
maker: **7** vintner **8** vigneron **10** winegrower **13** viticulturist
merchant: **7** vintner
pink: **4** rosé **5** blush
red: **4** port **5** Gamay, Macon, Medoc, Rioja **6** Barolo, Beaune, claret, merlot, Shiraz **7** Chianti **8** Bordeaux, Burgundy, cabernet, Sancerre **9** Lambrusco, Pinot Noir, St. Emilion, zinfandel **10** Beaujolais, Sangiovese **11** Petite Sirah **12** Valpolicella
region: **3** Ahr **4** Asti, Cuzo, Jura, Nahe, Napa, Saar, Toro **5** Baden, Douro, Jerez, Loire, Mosel, Pfalz, Rhône, Ruwer **6** Alsace, Sonoma, Veneto **7** Mendoza, Tuscany **8** Bordeaux, Burgundy, Rheingau **9** Champagne **10** Napa Valley **11** Finger Lakes, Rheinhessen
relating to: **6** vinous
residue: **4** marc
rice: **4** sake
richness: **4** body
rosé: **5** blush
sediment: **4** lees **5** dregs
shop: **6** bistro, bodega, tavern
sparkling: **4** Asti **7** Vouvray **8** cold duck, sparkler, Spumante **9** champagne, Lambrusco
specialist: **9** enologist **10** oenologist
spiced: **5** negus **6** mulled (wine) **9** hippocras
steward: **9** sommelier
study of: **7** enology **8** oenology
sweet: **4** port **5** Tokay **6** canary, Malaga, muscat **7** Catawba, Madeira, malmsey, marsala, oloroso, Vouvray **8** Malvasia, muscatel, sauterne **9** Sauternes **11** scuppernong
sweeten: **4** mull
vessel: **7** chalice
white: **4** hock **5** Rhine, Soave **7** Catawba, Chablis, Moselle, Orvieto, Vouvray **8** Bordeaux, muscadet, Riesling, Semillon, vermouth **9** champagne, Hermitage, Meursault, pinot gris **10** chardonnay, Montrachet **11** Chenin Blanc, pinot grigio, scuppernong **13** liebfraumilch **14** sauvignon blanc
year: **7** vintage

wing
3 ala, arm, ell, fly **4** sail, unit, vane **5** annex, flank, fleet, pinna, wound **6** flight **7** airfoil, faction, flanker, section **9** appendage, expansion, extension, improvise
combining form: **3** ali **4** pter **5** ptero
relating to: **4** alar **5** alary

wingding
4 bash, fete, gala **5** binge, party **7** blowout, shindig **9** festivity

winged
5 alate, fleet, rapid, swift **7** soaring **8** elevated
deity: **4** Amor, Eros, Nike **5** Cupid **6** Hermes **7** Mercury
horse: **7** Pegasus
monster: **5** harpy

wingless
8 apterous

winglike
4 alae (plural), alar **5** alary
part: 3 ala **4** alae (plural)

wink
3 bat, nap **5** flash, jiffy, shake, trice **6** moment, second, signal **7** connive, flicker, instant, twinkle **9** nictitate, twinkling **11** split second

winner
3 ace **4** lulu **5** beaut, doozy **6** doozie, top dog, victor **7** success **8** champion **9** conqueror, humdinger **11** titleholder

Winnie-the-Pooh
author: 5 Milne (A. A.)
character: 3 Roo **5** Kanga **6** Eeyore, Piglet, Tigger

winning
8 charming, engaging, pleasing **9** agreeable **10** delightful, successful, triumphant, victorious **11** captivating **13** prepossessing

winnow
3 fan **4** blow, cull, pare, sift, sort **6** delete, filter, narrow, reduce, remove, screen, select **8** separate

winsome
4 cute **5** sweet **6** dulcet, lovely **8** charming, cheerful, engaging, pleasing **9** easygoing **12** lighthearted

winter
6 season **9** hibernate
French: 5 hiver
Spanish: 8 invierno
transport: 4 sled

Winter's Tale, A
author: 11 Shakespeare (William)
character: 7 Camillo, Leontes, Paulina, Perdita **8** Florizel, Hermione **9** Antigonus, Autolycus, Polixenes

wintry
3 icy **4** cold **5** bleak, hoary, nippy, snowy **6** frigid, frosty **8** chilling, freezing, hibernal **12** bone-chilling
covering: 4 hoar, rime **5** frost

wipe
3 dry, rub **4** swab **5** towel, whisk **6** napkin, smudge, sponge **8** squeegee

wipe clean
5 erase

wipe out
4 rout **5** crash, erase, smear, sweep **6** efface **7** blot out, destroy, expunge **8** decimate **9** eradicate, extirpate **10** annihilate, obliterate

wipeout
4 fall, rout **5** crash **8** drubbing **11** destruction **12** annihilation

wire
3 rod **4** cord, line, send **5** cable, metal **6** thread **7** message **8** meshwork, telegram **9** cablegram, telegraph **10** finish line
measure: 3 mil **5** gauge
nail: 4 brad

wiry
4 lean, ropy **6** sinewy, supple **7** fibrous, stringy

Wisconsin
capital: 7 Madison
city: 6 Racine **7** Kenosha **8** Green Bay **9** Milwaukee
college, university: 5 Ripon **6** Beloit **9** Marquette
lake: 7 Mendota
motto: 7 Forward
nickname: 6 Badger (State)
peninsula: 4 Door
river: 7 St. Croix **9** Menominee, Wisconsin **11** Mississippi
state bird: 5 robin
state flower: 6 violet
state tree: 10 sugar maple

wisdom
5 sense **7** insight, science **8** judgment, learning, sagacity, sageness, sapience **9** good sense, knowledge **10** horse sense **11** common sense, information

wise
4 sage **5** brash, cagey, canny, cocky, fresh, nervy, sassy **6** astute, cheeky, crafty, fill in, inform, notify, shrewd, sophic **7** gnostic, knowing, politic, prudent, sapient **8** discreet, flippant, impudent, insolent, sensible, tactical **9** advisable, expedient, judicious, sagacious, scholarly **10** discerning, insightful, perceptive, thoughtful **11** foresighted, impertinent, intelligent, smart-alecky **13** contemplative, knowledgeable, perspicacious
old man: 6 Nestor
person: 4 guru, sage **5** magus **6** savant **7** scholar
saying: 5 adage, maxim **6** truism **7** epigram, precept, proverb **8** apothegm

wiseacre
see **wise guy**

wisecrack
3 dig, gag **4** barb, gibe, jape, jest, joke, quip **5** sally **6** zinger **9** witticism

wise guy
6 smarty **7** mobster **8** gangster, smart-ass **9** know-it-all, swellhead **10** smart aleck **11** smarty-pants, wisenheimer

Wise Men
see **Magi**

wish
3 bid **4** care, goal, like, long, lust, want **5** covet, crave, fancy, foist, order, yearn **6** desire, impose **7** request **10** desiderate

wishbone
7 furcula

wishful
5 eager **7** anxious, hopeful, longing **8** desirous

wishy-washy
4 lame, weak **5** banal, bland, vapid, wimpy **6** jejune, watery **7** insipid, languid **10** namby-pamby **11** ineffective, ineffectual **13** characterless

wisp
3 bit **5** shred, strip, trace **6** sliver, snatch, streak **7** smidgen, snippet **8** fragment **9** scintilla

wispy
4 slim **5** frail **6** flimsy, slight **7** slender, tenuous **8** fleeting, nebulous **10** evanescent

Wister novel
9 Virginian (The)

wistful
3 sad **6** dreamy, triste **7** longing, pensive **8** yearning **9** nostalgic **10** melancholy

wit
3 wag **5** brain, comic, droll, humor, irony, joker **6** banter, esprit, jester, reason, satire, wisdom **7** farceur, punster **8** banterer, comedian, funnyman, judgment, humorist, jokester, quipster, repartee **9** alertness, ingenuity, intellect **10** cleverness, persiflage

witch
3 hag, hex **5** crone, dowse, spell **6** voodoo, Wiccan **7** charmer **8** magician, sorcerer **9** sorceress **11** enchantress
companion: **3** cat
group: **5** coven
male: **6** wizard **7** warlock
meeting: **6** sabbat **7** sabbath
town: **5** Endor
vehicle: **5** broom

witchcraft
5 magic, wicca **6** hoodoo, voodoo **7** devilry, hexerei, sorcery **8** wizardry **9** diablerie, sortilege, voodooism **10** black magic, hocus-pocus, mumbo jumbo, necromancy **11** abracadabra, thaumaturgy

witch hazel
5 shrub **6** lotion

witchy
6 Wiccan **7** magical **8** wizardly **9** sorcerous **11** necromantic **12** thaumaturgic

with
3 for, per, pro, via **4** over, upon **5** about **6** having **7** against, by way of, through **8** as well as **9** by means of, in favor of **10** by virtue of
French: **4** avec
German: **3** mit
Italian, Spanish: **3** con
Latin: **3** cum

withal
3 too, yet **4** also **5** still **6** as well, though **7** besides, howbeit, however **8** after all, moreover **11** furthermore, nonetheless **12** additionally, nevertheless

withdraw
4 exit, quit **5** demit, leave, unsay **6** depart, bow out, call in, cash in, desert, detach, recall, recant, recede, recoil, retire, secede, shrink **7** back out, drop out, pull out, retract, retreat, scratch, take off, take out **8** back down, evacuate, fall back, pull away, push back, separate, take back, turn away **9** disengage, stand down **10** disconnect, give ground

withdrawal
4 exit **6** exodus **7** exiting, pullout, removal, retreat **9** departure **10** alienation, detachment, retirement, retraction, revocation

withdrawn
4 cool **5** aloof **6** casual, remote **7** distant, removed **8** detached, isolated, reserved, retiring, solitary **9** incurious, unaffable, uncurious **10** unsociable **11** indifferent, introverted, standoffish, unconcerned, unexpansive **12** uninterested, unresponsive

wither
3 age, dry **4** fade, sear, wilt **5** dry up, parch, quail, wizen **6** scorch **7** mummify, shrivel

withered
4 sere **7** sapless **8** shrunken, wrinkled **9** shriveled

withhold
4 deny **5** check **6** deduct, detain, refuse, retain **7** abstain, deprive, forbear, inhibit, refrain, reserve **8** restrain, subtract **9** constrain

within
4 into **5** among **6** inside **7** indoors, inwards **8** enclosed, interior, inwardly **10** inner place
prefix: **3** ent **4** endo, ento **5** infra, intra, intro

with-it
6 modern, modish, trendy **7** à la mode, current, faddish, stylish **8** up-to-date **9** au courant **11** fashionable **12** contemporary

without
4 less, open, past, sans **5** minus **6** absent **7** lacking, open air, outside, wanting **8** outdoors **10** externally, out-of-doors
Latin: **4** sine

with respect to
4 as to, in re **5** as for **7** apropos **8** touching **9** as regards, regarding **10** concerning

withstand
4 bear, buck, defy **5** fight, repel **6** endure, oppose, resist, suffer **7** hold off, survive, sustain **8** tolerate, traverse

withy
4 twig **5** osier **6** branch, willow **8** flexible **9** resilient

witless
3 mad **4** daft, nuts **5** crazy, daffy, dotty, nutty, silly **6** insane, simple, stupid **7** asinine, cracked, foolish, idiotic **8** demented, deranged, mindless **9** bedlamite, brainless, senseless **10** weak-minded, unbalanced

witlessness
5 folly **6** idiocy, lunacy **7** inanity **8** insanity **9** absurdity, stupidity

witness
3 see **4** note, sign, view **5** proof, vouch **6** attest, depone, depose, notice, viewer **7** bear out, confirm, betoken, certify, testify, watcher **8** attester, beholder, deponent, evidence, looker-on, observer, onlooker **9** bystander, spectator, testament, testifier, testimony **11** affirmation, attestation, corroborate, testimonial **12** confirmation

witticism
3 dig, gag, mot **4** gibe, jape, jest, jibe, joke, quip **5** crack, sally **6** bon mot **8** one-liner, repartee **9** throwaway, wisecrack

witting
5 aware **7** knowing, willful **8** sensible, sentient **9** cognizant, conscious, voluntary **10** deliberate **11** intentional

witty
5 funny **6** clever, jocose **7** amusing, jocular **8** humorous **9** facetious **13** scintillating

wiz
3 ace **5** adept, fiend **6** artist, expert, phenom **7** artiste **8** virtuoso

wizard
3 ace **4** mage **5** adept, druid, fiend, magus **6** expert, phenom **7** warlock **8** conjurer, magician, sorcerer, virtuoso **9** enchanter **10** past master **11** necromancer, thaumaturge **13** thaumaturgist

wizardly
5 magic **6** mystic, witchy **7** magical **9** sorcerous **10** mysterious **11** necromantic **12** thaumaturgic

Wizard of Menlo Park
6 Edison (Thomas Alva)

Wizard of Oz
actor: 4 Lahr (Bert)
author: 4 Baum (L. Frank)
character: 6 Tin Man **7** Dorothy **9** Scarecrow **11** Tin Woodsman **12** Cowardly Lion
dog: 4 Toto
composer: 5 Arlen (Harold)

wizardry
5 magic **6** voodoo **7** sorcery **8** witchery **9** diablerie, sortilege **10** black magic, necromancy, witchcraft **11** bewitchment, conjuration, enchantment

wizen
3 dry **4** sere, wilt **5** dry up **6** shrink, wither **7** dried-up, shrivel, wrinkle

wizened
4 aged, sere **5** dried **6** shrunk **7** pinched **8** shrunken, withered, wrinkled

wobble
4 reel, rock, sway **5** quake, shake, waver, weave **6** dither, falter, quaver, shimmy, teeter, totter **7** stagger, stumble, tremble **8** nutation **9** vacillate

wobbly
4 weak **5** rocky, shaky **6** unsure **7** rackety, rickety **8** insecure, rachitic, unstable, unsteady, wavering **9** faltering, teetering, tottering **10** nutational **11** vacillating

Wodehouse, P. G.
castle: 9 Blandings
character: 6 Bertie (Wooster), Gussie (Fink-Nottle), Jeeves, Psmith **7** Wooster (Bertie) **8** Emsworth (Lord), Mulliner (Mr.) **10** Threepwood (Clarence, Freddie) **12** Lord Emsworth
club: 6 Drones

Woden
see **Odin**

woe
3 rue **4** bale, bane, care **5** grief **6** misery, regret, sorrow **7** anguish, sadness, trouble **8** calamity **9** heartache **10** affliction, heartbreak **11** lamentation, unhappiness **12** wretchedness

woebegone
3 low, sad **4** blue, down, worn **6** shabby **7** doleful, forlorn, ruthful **8** dejected, dolorous, downcast, wretched **9** depressed, miserable, sorrowful **10** despondent, melancholy **11** crestfallen, downhearted, low-spirited

woeful
3 sad **5** heavy, sorry **6** dismal, rueful, tragic, triste **7** ruthful **8** dejected, dolorous, downcast, grievous, mournful, stricken, tortured, wretched **9** afflicted, aggrieved, depressed, heartsick, miserable, plaintive, sorrowful **10** deplorable, lamentable, lugubrious, melancholy **11** distressing, downhearted, low-spirited **12** disconsolate

woe is me
4 alas

wolf
4 bolt, lobo, rake, roué **5** canid **6** canine, coyote, devour, gobble, masher **7** Don Juan, poverty **8** Casanova, lothario **10** starvation

genus: 5 Canis
group: 4 pack
young: 5 whelp

Wolfe novel
17 Look Homeward Angel, Of Time and the River 18 You Can't Go Home Again 20 Bonfire of the Vanities (The)

Wolfe of detective fiction
4 Nero

wolfish
4 wild 5 cruel, feral 6 fierce, lupine, savage 7 bestial, brutish, vicious 9 ferocious

Wolf Man portrayer
3 Lon (Cheney)

wolframite
3 cal

wolfsbane
7 aconite

wolverine
European: 7 glutton
genus: 4 Gulo

Wolverine State
8 Michigan

woman
4 dame, lady 5 madam 6 female, matron 8 mistress 10 girlfriend
attractive: 5 belle, vixen 6 beauty, eyeful, looker 7 stunner 8 knockout
combining form: 4 gyny 5 gynec 6 gynaec, gyneco, gynous 7 gynaeco
courageous: 7 heroine
dignified: 6 matron 7 dowager 10 grande dame
dowdy: 5 frump
English: 6 milady
first, biblical: 3 Eve
first, mythological: 7 Pandora
French: 5 femme
German: 4 Frau 8 Fräulein
Hawaiian: 6 wahine
Indian: 5 squaw
Italian: 5 donna 7 signora
old: 3 hag 4 dame 5 crone 6 beldam, carlin, gammer, granny
Polynesian: 6 wahine
pregnant: 7 gravida
resembling: 8 gynecoid
royal: 5 queen 8 princess
sailor: 4 Wave
servant: 4 maid
soldier: 3 Wac
Spanish: 4 doña 5 mujer 6 señora
strong: 6 amazon, virago
surfer: 6 wahine
unmarried: 4 miss 6 maiden 8 spinster
young: 4 girl, lass 6 lassie, maiden 7 ingenue

womanize
4 wolf 9 gallivant, philander 10 fool around, mess around

womanizer
4 rake, roué, stud, wolf 5 satyr 6 lecher, masher, tomcat 7 Don Juan, gallant, playboy 8 Casanova, lothario 9 ladies' man, mack daddy 10 lady-killer 11 philanderer

womb
6 uterus
combining form: 6 hyster 7 hystero

women
hatred of: 8 misogyny
organization of: 3 DAR, NOW 8 sorority
seclusion of: 6 purdah

wonder
3 awe 4 muse 5 doubt 6 marvel 7 dubiety, miracle, portent, prodigy 8 mistrust, question 9 amazement, speculate, suspicion 10 admiration, skepticism 12 astonishment

wonderful
4 keen 5 grand, great, nifty, super, swell 6 divine, groovy, peachy, spiffy 7 amazing, strange, too much, topping 8 dynamite, fabulous, glorious, spiffing, terrific 9 admirable, excellent, marvelous, wunderbar 10 astounding, delightful, miraculous, out-of-sight, stupendous 11 astonishing, outstanding

wondrous
6 mystic 7 amazing, awesome, strange 9 marvelous 10 astounding, formidable, miraculous, portentous, prodigious, remarkable, stupendous, surprising 11 astonishing, spectacular 13 extraordinary

wonk
4 dork, geek, nerd, swot 5 dweeb, grind

wonky
4 awry 5 geeky, nerdy, shaky 7 bookish 8 unsteady

wont
3 apt 4 used 5 habit, usage 6 custom, manner 8 accustom, habitude, inclined, practice 10 accustomed, consuetude

wonted
5 usual 7 routine 8 habitual, ordinary 9 customary 10 accustomed

woo
3 sue 5 court 6 pursue 7 address, entreat

wood
5 weald 6 forest, lumber, timber 8 golf club
combining form: 3 xyl 4 lign, xylo 5 ligni, ligno
decayed: 4 punk
eater: 7 termite
for burning: 5 fagot 6 tinder 8 kindling
fragrant: 5 cedar

golf: **6** driver
hard: **3** ash, elm, oak **4** ebon, rata, teak **5** aalii, alder, aspen, beech, birch, ebony, maple **6** cherry, poplar, walnut **7** hickory **8** chestnut, hornbeam, ironwood, mahogany, sycamore
imperfection: **4** knot **5** gnarl
light: **5** balsa **8** corkwood
made of: **5** treen
measure: **4** cord **5** stere
pattern in: **5** grain **6** figure
product: **3** tar **5** paper **10** turpentine
soft: **3** fir, yew **4** pine **5** cedar, larch **6** spruce **7** cypress, hemlock, redwood

wood alcohol
6 methyl **8** carbinol, methanol

Woodard of film
5 Alfre

woodchuck
6 marmot **9** groundhog

wood coal
7 lignite

wooded
5 bosky, treed **6** sylvan **8** forested, timbered

wooden
5 rigid, stiff **6** clumsy **7** awkward, stilted **8** ligneous **10** inflexible

wooden shoe
4 clog **5** sabot

wooden strip
4 lath, slat

woodland
5 copse, taiga, weald **6** forest, pinery **7** coppice
deity: **3** Pan **4** faun **5** satyr **6** Faunus **7** silenus

wood nymph
5 dryad

woodpecker
4 bird **7** flicker, wryneck **9** sapsucker
genus: **5** Picus
kind: **5** downy, green, hairy **8** imperial, pileated **9** redheaded **11** ivory-billed

woodsman
6 logger **8** forester **10** bushranger

wood sorrel
3 oca **6** oxalis **8** shamrock **9** carambola

woodsy
6 rustic, sylvan

woodwind
3 sax **4** oboe, reed **5** flute, shawm **7** bassoon, piccolo **8** clarinet **9** saxophone **10** cor anglais, instrument **11** English horn **13** contrabassoon

woodworker
9 carpenter **12** cabinetmaker

woody
8 ligneous **12** station wagon

Woody's son
4 Arlo (Guthrie)

wooer
4 beau **5** lover, spark, swain **6** suitor **7** admirer, gallant, sparker

woof
4 bark, crow, weft, yarn **5** boast, weave **6** fabric, thread **7** texture

wool
3 fur **4** coat, hair **6** fabric, fleece
comb: **4** card
cut: **5** shear
fabric: **4** felt **5** baize, crepe, loden, serge, tweed **6** covert, duffel, duffle, kersey, mohair, poplin, shoddy, velour **7** flannel, worsted **8** cashmere, chenille **9** gabardine **10** broadcloth
fat: **7** lanolin
kind: **4** hogg **6** angora, hogget, virgin
low-quality: **5** mungo **6** shoddy
musk-ox: **6** qiviut
process: **7** carding
short fiber: **4** noil
source: **4** goat, lamb **5** camel, llama, sheep **6** alpaca

Woolf, Virginia
home: **10** Bloomsbury
husband: **7** Leonard
novel: **5** Waves (The), Years (The) **7** Orlando **11** Mrs. Dalloway **13** Room of One's Own (A) **15** To the Lighthouse

woolly
5 fuzzy, hairy, nappy **6** fleecy, shaggy **7** hirsute

woozy
4 hazy, sick, weak **5** dazed, dizzy, faint, fuzzy, muzzy, vague **6** addled, blurry, groggy, punchy **8** confused **9** slaphappy **11** light-headed

word
3 vow **4** oath, term **5** logos **6** pledge **7** promise **8** locution **9** utterance **10** expression
connective: **11** conjunction
group: **6** clause, phrase **8** sentence
last: **4** Amen
misused: **8** malaprop **11** malapropism
naming: **4** noun
new: **7** coinage **9** neologism
of action: **4** verb
of honor: **4** oath **7** promise
origin: **9** etymology
part: **8** syllable
root: **6** etymon
scrambled: **7** anagram
shortened: **11** contraction **12** abbreviation
square: **10** palindrome
ultimatum: **4** else
with opposite meaning: **7** antonym
with same meaning: **7** synonym

with same pronunciation: **7** homonym **9** homophone
with same spelling: **7** homonym **9** homograph

wordbook
5 vocab **7** lexicon **8** glossary **9** thesaurus **10** dictionary, vocabulary

word-for-word
7 literal **8** ad verbum, verbally, verbatim

wordiness
8 verbiage **9** logorrhea, prolixity, verbosity **10** bloviation

word-of-mouth
4 oral **6** spoken, verbal **8** viva voce **9** unwritten

Wordsworth, William
friend: **9** Coleridge (Samuel T.)
poem: **7** Prelude (The)
sister: **7** Dorothy

wordy
5 windy **6** prolix, verbal **7** diffuse, verbose **9** dictional, garrulous, iterative, redundant, vocabular **10** long-winded, logorrheic, loquacious, rhetorical

work
3 act, fix, job, run, use **4** duty, line, opus, task, tend, till, toil **5** chore, craft, drive, forge, grind, guide, labor, shape, solve, sweat, trade **6** effect, effort, métier, result, strain, strive **7** arrange, calling, control, fashion, operate, perform, product, provoke, pursuit, resolve, travail **8** activity, business, contrive, drudgery, exertion, function, vocation **10** assignment, employment, occupation, profession
unit: **3** erg **5** joule

workaday
5 plain, usual **7** mundane, prosaic, routine **8** ordinary **9** quotidian **11** commonplace

worker
4 doer, hand, peon, serf **5** prole **6** coolie, toiler, wallah **7** artisan, laborer **8** employee, mechanic, operator **9** operative **11** proletarian
fellow: **7** comrade, partner **9** colleague
group: **4** crew, gang **5** artel, shift, staff, union
hard: **5** slave **6** beaver, drudge
insect: **3** ant, bee **4** wasp **7** termite
itinerant: **6** boomer **7** migrant
unskilled: **4** peon **7** jackleg, laborer

workers' rights group
3 ILO **4** NLRB

working
4 busy, live **6** active, useful, viable **7** dynamic, engaged, running **8** employed, occupied **9** operative **11** functioning
not: **5** kaput **6** broken

work out
3 fix **5** solve, train **6** devise, settle **7** arrange, develop, resolve **8** exercise

workout
4 test **5** drill **8** exercise, practice **10** daily dozen
goal: **3** bod

work over
4 beat, redo **5** scrag, study **6** beat up, mess up, redraw, rehash, revamp, revise **7** examine, redraft, restyle, rewrite, rough up **9** manhandle

workplace safety agency
4 OSHA

workroom
3 lab **4** shop **6** studio **7** atelier **10** laboratory

Works and Days author
6 Hesiod

world
5 class, earth, globe, realm **6** career, cosmos, nature, planet, public, sphere, system **7** kingdom, society **8** creation, division, everyone, renowned, universe **9** human race, macrocosm, microcosm **13** distinguished
combining form: **4** cosm **5** cosmo

worldly
5 blasé **6** carnal, earthy, urbane **7** earthly, fleshly, mundane, profane, secular, sensual, terrene **8** material, telluric, temporal **9** sublunary **11** terrestrial **12** cosmopolitan **13** sophisticated

worldly-wise
12 cosmopolitan **13** sophisticated

World Series winner
1990: **4** Reds
1991: **5** Twins
1992, 1993: **8** Blue Jays
1995: **6** Braves
1996, 1998, 1999, 2000: **7** Yankees
1997: **7** Marlins
2001: **12** Diamondbacks
2002: **6** Angels
2003: **7** Marlins
2004: **6** Red Sox
2005: **8** White Sox
2006: **9** Cardinals
2007: **6** Red Sox
2008: **8** Phillies
2009: **7** Yankees
2010: **6** Giants
2011: **9** Cardinals
2012: **6** Giants
2013: **6** Red Sox
2014: **6** Giants
2015: **6** Royals

World War I
battle: **5** Aisne, Marne, Somme, Ypres **6** Isonzo, Verdun **7** Jutland **9** Caporetto **10** Tannenberg **11** Dardanelles
battle line: **9** Siegfried
general: **4** Foch (Ferdinand), Haig (Douglas) **6** Joffre (Joseph), Pétain (Philippe) **7** Allenby

(Edmund) **8** Pershing (John) **10** Hindenburg (Paul von), Ludendorff (Erich)
hero: **4** York (Alvin) **8** Red Baron (The) **10** Richthofen (Manfred von) **12** Rickenbacker (Eddie)
treaty: **10** Versailles

World War II
admiral: **6** Dönitz (Karl), Halsey (William "Bull"), Nimitz (Chester), Nimitz (Chester) **8** Yamamoto (Isoroku)
alliance: **4** Axis **6** Allies
battle: **4** St.-Lô **5** Anzio, Bulge **6** Bataan, Midway, Tarawa, Warsaw **7** Britain, Iwo Jima, Okinawa, Saint-Lô **8** Coral Sea, Normandy **9** El Alamein, Leyte Gulf **10** Stalingrad **11** Guadalcanal
general: **4** Jodl (Alfred), Tojo (Hideki) **5** Clark (Mark) **6** Arnold (Hap), Keitel (Wilhelm), Patton (George), Rommel (Erwin), Zhukov (Georgy) **7** Bradley (Omar) **8** Marshall (George) **9** MacArthur (Douglas), Rundstedt (Gerd von) **10** Eisenhower (Dwight), Kesselring (Albert), Montgomery (Bernard)
hero: **6** Murphy (Audie)
journalist: **4** Pyle (Ernie)
milestone: **4** D-day
weapon: **5** A-bomb **6** rocket **8** buzz bomb

world-weary
5 blasé, jaded **7** cynical **9** apathetic, exhausted

worldwide
6 cosmic, global **8** catholic **9** planetary, universal **10** ecumenical **12** cosmopolitan

worm
3 cad, cur **4** grub, lout **5** borer, creep, fluke, leech, louse, screw, treat **6** edge in, maggot, no-good, squirm, thread, wiggle, wretch, writhe **7** extract, triclad, wriggle **8** helminth, nematode, squiggle **9** planarium, trematode
African: **3** Loa
marine: **6** nereid **7** annelid, tubifex
parasitic: **5** fluke, leech **7** ascarid, ascaris, cestode, filaria **8** helminth, trichina **9** strongyle

worn
3 old, wan **4** aged, beat **5** drawn, jaded, tatty, tired, weary **6** eroded, frayed, ragged, shabby **7** haggard **8** fatigued **9** woebegone **10** threadbare

worn-out
4 beat, shot **5** all in, spent, tired, weary **6** bleary, bushed, ragged, used-up **7** drained, run-down **8** decrepit, depleted, fatigued, overused **9** exhausted, worm-eaten **10** broken-down, threadbare, tumbledown **11** debilitated, dilapidated

worried
6 afraid, on edge **7** anxious, nervous **8** bothered, distrait, troubled **9** concerned, tormented **10** distracted, distraught, distressed

worry
3 nag, try, vex **4** care, fret, fuss, gnaw, goad, pain, stew, test **5** angst, annoy, beset, shake, tease, trial, upset **6** assail, attack, bother, harass, needle, pester, plague, pull at, unease **7** afflict, anguish, anxiety, concern, disturb, oppress, torment, trouble **8** aggrieve, distress, irritate **9** agitation, annoyance, misgiving

worrywart
7 fusspot **9** Cassandra, doomsayer, pessimist **10** fussbudget

worse
8 inferior

worsen
4 sink **7** decline **10** degenerate **11** deteriorate

worship
4 love **5** adore, honor **6** admire, dote on, homage, revere **7** idolize, lionize, liturgy, respect **8** devotion, idolatry, venerate **9** adoration, affection, reverence **10** admiration, veneration
object of: **3** god **4** icon, idol **5** deity **7** goddess
place of: **5** altar **6** church, mosque, shrine, temple **9** cathedral, synagogue **10** tabernacle

worshipper
3 fan **6** votary **7** admirer, devotee **8** adherent, believer, disciple **10** enthusiast

worsted
4 yarn **5** stuff **6** caddis, fabric **7** cheviot, etamine, flannel, lasting **8** shalloon **9** bombazine, sharkskin **10** broadcloth

worth
4 rate **5** merit, price, value **6** regard, riches, wealth **7** caliber, calibre, fortune, quality, stature **9** resources, substance, valuation **10** excellence

worthless
4 vain **6** futile, no-good, otiose **7** inutile **8** nugatory **9** no-account

worthwhile
6 paying **7** gainful **9** estimable, honorable, lucrative **10** profitable, well-paying

worthy
4 good **5** noble **8** laudable, standout **9** admirable, deserving, desirable, estimable, honorable **10** acceptable, creditable **11** commendable, meritorious

Wotan
see **Odin**

Wouk novel
10 Winds of War (The) **11** Caine Mutiny (The)

would-be
7 hopeful, wishful **8** apparent, aspiring, desiring, desirous **9** ambitious, potential

wound
3 cut **4** blow, harm, hurt, pain, rift **6** damage, injure, injury, insult, lesion, trauma **8** lacerate **10** laceration
sign: 4 scab, scar **5** blood **7** blister

wow
3 hit **4** boff, gosh, grab **5** amaze, boffo, golly, smash **6** dazzle **7** astound, impress, success **8** bedazzle

Wozzeck composer
4 Berg (Alban)

wrack
4 kelp, raze, ruin **5** smash, total **7** destroy, flotsam, remnant, seaweed **8** decimate, demolish, shambles, wreckage **11** destruction

wraith
5 ghost, shade, spook **6** double, shadow, spirit **7** phantom, specter, spectre **8** phantasm **10** apparition

wrangle
3 row **4** spar, spat, tiff **5** argue, brawl, fight, scrap **6** bicker, fracas, haggle, hassle **7** brabble, dispute, fall out, finagle, quarrel, quibble **8** squabble **11** altercation

wrangler
6 cowboy **8** buckaroo **9** ranch hand

Wrangler rival
3 Lee **4** Levi

wrap
3 fur **4** bind, cape, cere, coat, roll **5** cloak, drape, pareu, shawl, stole **6** bundle, clothe, enfold, invest, mantle, muffle, parcel, shroud, swathe **7** bandage, blanket, conceal, dress up, embrace, enclose, engross, envelop, involve, package, swaddle **8** bundle up, enshroud, lavalava

wrapped up
4 deep **6** intent **7** engaged **8** absorbed, consumed, immersed **9** engrossed **11** preoccupied

wrapper
5 cover **6** jacket **10** dust jacket **12** dressing gown

wrap up
6 muffle **8** close out, complete, conclude **9** summarize

wrap-up
4 coda **5** close **6** capper, closer, finale, report **7** closing **8** epilogue **9** summation **10** denouement

wrath
3 ire **4** fury, rage **5** anger **6** choler **8** ferocity **9** vengeance **10** punishment **11** retribution

wrathful
3 mad **5** angry, irate **6** heated, raging **7** enraged, furious **8** choleric, incensed, inflamed **10** infuriated

wreak
5 cause, exact, visit **6** effect, impose **7** inflict

wreath
3 bay, lei **5** crown **6** anadem, laurel **7** chaplet, circlet, coronal, coronet, garland, laurels

wreathe
4 coil, curl, wind **5** twine, twist **6** spiral **7** entwine **9** corkscrew **10** interweave

wreck
4 do in, heap, hulk, raze, ruin **5** beach, crack, crash, cream, smash, total, trash **6** beater, damage, jalopy, junker, pileup, ravage, strand **7** clunker, crack-up, destroy, scuttle, smashup, torpedo **8** decimate, demolish **9** vandalize

wreckage
5 wrack **6** debris **7** flotsam **8** detritus, shambles **11** destruction

wrecker
8 salvager, tow truck

wrench
4 jerk, pull, rack, tool, turn, warp, yank **5** force, twist, wrest, wring **6** change, injure, injury, snatch, socket, sprain, strain **7** disable, distort, pervert, spanner, squeeze **8** distress, twisting
kind: 5 Allen **6** monkey **7** ratchet **8** Stillson

wrest
4 rend, rive **5** exact, twist, wring **6** elicit, extort, snatch, wrench **7** extract, squeeze

wrestle
6 combat, strain, strive, tussle **7** contend, grapple, scuffle **8** struggle

wrestling
champion: 4 Ladd (Ernie), Race (Harley) **5** Gagne (Verne), Hogan (Hulk), Studd (Big John) **7** Ventura (Jesse) **8** Kowalski (Killer) **9** Slaughter (Sgt.) **13** André the Giant
hold: 4 lock **6** nelson **8** headlock, scissors
kind: 4 sumo
pad: 3 mat
term: 3 pin **4** fall **5** throw **8** takedown

wretch
3 cur, dog **4** scum, toad, worm **5** devil, knave, louse, rogue, skunk, snake **6** rascal, rotter **7** caitiff, hangdog, lowlife, outcast, rat fink, stinker, villain **8** scalawag, stinkard **9** scoundrel **10** blackguard, sleazeball **11** rapscallion

wretched
3 low, sad **4** base, foul, mean, vile **6** abject, dismal, horrid, scurvy, sordid, woeful **7** abysmal, doleful, forlorn, ignoble, ruthful, servile, squalid, unhappy **8** dejected, dolorous, hopeless, inferior **9** afflicted, execrable, miserable, sorrowful **10** despairing, despicable, deplorable

wretchedness
3 woe **6** misery **7** anguish **8** distress

wriggle
4 worm **5** slink **6** squirm, writhe

Wright, Richard
character: **6** Bigger (Thomas)
novel: **8** Black Boy **9** Native Son

wring
3 wry **5** choke, exact, screw, twist, wrest **6** extort, squirm, wrench, writhe **7** afflict, draw out, extract, squeeze, torment
the neck: **5** scrag

wringing-wet
5 soppy **6** soaked, sodden, soused **7** soaking, sopping **8** drenched, dripping **9** saturated

wrinkle
4 fold, ruck, ruga, seam **5** crimp, crisp, plica, ridge, wizen **6** cockle, crease, furrow, pucker, rumple **7** crumple, scrunch, shrivel **9** corrugate, crow's-foot, worry line **11** corrugation

wrinkled
5 lined **6** rugose, rumply **7** creased **8** puckered, rugulose
fruit: **4** Ugli

wrist
5 joint **6** carpus
bone: **6** carpal, hamate **8** pisiform

writ
5 brief, order **6** assize, capias, decree, elegit, extent **7** mandate, process, summons, warrant **8** detainer, document, mandamus, mittimus, praecipe, replevin, subpoena **9** execution **10** attachment, certiorari, court order, injunction **11** fieri facias, scire facias, supersedeas **12** habeas corpus, venire facias

write
3 ink, jot, pen **4** note **5** chalk, draft, print, score, spell **6** answer, author, byline, draw up, indite, ordain, pencil, record, scrawl, scribe **7** compose, dissert, engross, fire off, put down, scratch, set down **8** inscribe, scribble, spell out **9** autograph, transpose **10** correspond

write down
4 note **6** record, reduce **10** transcribe

write off
6 cancel **7** dismiss, expense **8** amortize, discount **9** eliminate **10** depreciate

write-off
4 debt, loss **7** expense **8** donation **9** allowance, deduction, reduction

writer
4 poet **6** author, penman, scribe **8** composer, novelist **9** scribbler, wordsmith
bad: **4** hack
(see also **author**)

writer James
4 Agee

writer Leon
4 Uris

write-up
5 blurb, story **7** account, article

writhe
4 curl, worm **5** twist **6** squirm, suffer, wallow, welter, wiggle, wrench **7** agonize, contort, distort, wriggle **8** convolve, squiggle

writing
4 book, hand, note **5** essay, paper, print, prose, style, words **6** letter, notice, record, script **8** document, longhand **10** literature, penmanship **11** calligraphy, composition, inscription
character: **6** letter **9** cuneiform **10** hieroglyph
combining form: **4** gram **6** grapho, graphy
for the blind: **7** braille
instrument: **3** pen **5** chalk, quill **6** pencil, stylus
sacred: **5** Bible, Koran, Quran **6** Talmud, Tantra **9** scripture
surface: **5** board, paper, slate **6** scroll **9** parchment

wrong
3 bad, ill, off, sin **4** awry, evil, harm, hurt, tort **5** abuse, amiss, badly, crime, false, inapt, unfit **6** afield, astray, injure, injury, malign, offend, sinful, unfair, unjust, untrue **7** defraud, immoral, oppress, outrage, violate **8** aggrieve, ill-treat, improper, inequity, iniquity, mistaken, opposite **9** erroneous, grievance, incorrect, injustice, misguided, unethical, violation

wrongdoer
5 felon **6** sinner **8** criminal, offender **9** miscreant, reprobate **10** accomplice, delinquent, malefactor **12** transgressor

wrongdoing
3 sin **4** evil **5** crime **7** misdeed, offense **8** iniquity **10** misconduct **11** malefaction, malfeasance, misbehavior

wrongful
6 unjust, unfair **7** illegal, illicit, lawless **8** criminal, improper, unlawful **12** illegitimate
act: **4** tort

wrongheaded
6 mulish **7** froward **8** contrary, perverse **9** obstinate

wrought
4 made **6** formed, shaped, worked **7** created **8** finished, hammered **9** decorated, fashioned
up: **7** excited, stirred

wry
4 bent **5** askew, twist, wrest **6** ironic, wrench **7** crooked, twisted **8** humorous, sardonic

wryneck
10 woodpecker **11** torticollis

wurst
7 sausage

Wuthering Heights
author: 6 Brontë (Emily)
character: 5 Cathy 9 Catherine 10 Heathcliff
family: 6 Linton 8 Earnshaw

Wyatt of Western fame
4 Earp

Wycliffite
7 Lollard

Wyoming
capital: 8 Cheyenne
city: 6 Casper 7 Laramie
mountain, range: 5 Rocky 7 Gannett (Peak) 9 Wind River 10 Grand Teton
nickname: 8 Equality (State)
river: 5 Green, Snake 6 Powder 7 Bighorn
state bird: 10 meadowlark
state flower: 16 Indian paintbrush
state tree: 10 cottonwood

X

x
3 chi, ten 4 kiss 5 annul, cross, erase, error, times, wrong 6 cancel, delete, efface 7 mistake, unknown 8 abscissa 9 signature

Xanthippe
3 nag 5 scold, shrew 6 nagger, virago 8 battle-ax, harridan 9 termagant
husband: 8 Socrates

Xenophon work
8 Anabasis 9 Cyropedia, Hellenica

xerophyte
6 cactus

Xerxes
crossing site: 10 Hellespont
defeat: 7 Plataea, Salamis
father: 6 Darius
kingdom: 6 Persia
mother: 6 Atossa
victory: 11 Thermopylae

Xmas
4 Noel, yule 8 Nativity, yuletide

X-ray
discoverer: 8 Roentgen (Wilhelm)
science: 9 radiology

xylophone relative
7 marimba 10 vibraphone

Y

yacht
4 race, sail 6 cruise 7 cruiser 8 sailboat 12 cabin cruiser

Yaga of Russian lore
4 Baba

yahoo
3 hun, yay 4 boor, clod, dolt, hood, lout, punk, thug 5 brute, chuff, churl, clown, rough, rowdy, tough 6 hoorah, hooray, hurrah, savage, terror, vandal, yippie 7 buffoon, bumpkin, hoodlum, ruffian, toughie 8 bullyboy, hooligan 9 roughneck 10 clodhopper

Yahweh
3 God 6 Adonai, Elohim 7 Jehovah

yak
3 gab, jaw 4 blab, chat 5 clack, prate 6 babble, gabble, jabber, natter, yammer 7 blabber, blather, chatter, palaver, prattle 11 confabulate

Yale
founder: 3 Eli 5 Elihu
student: 3 Eli

Yalta participant
6 Stalin (Joseph) 9 Churchill (Winston), Roosevelt (Franklin Delano)

yam
4 taro 7 boniato 11 sweet potato

yammer
3 cry, gab 4 bawl, crab, fuss, moan, wail, yawp,

yell **5** bleat, gripe, whine **6** babble, bellow, clamor, gabble, grouch, grouse, jabber, natter, snivel, squawk **7** blather, prattle, whimper **8** complain **9** bellyache, caterwaul

yank
3 tug **4** grab, jerk, pull, tear **5** hoick **6** snatch, wrench **7** extract

Yankees star
4 A-Rod

yank's counterpart
3 reb

yap
3 gab **4** bark, hick **5** mouth, prate **6** babble, bowwow, gabble, jabber, natter, rustic, yammer **7** blather, bumpkin, chatter, hayseed, prattle **9** hillbilly **10** clodhopper

yard
3 pen **4** herd, quad, spar, unit **5** court, garth, glass **6** length **7** grounds, measure **9** curtilage, enclosure **10** playground, quadrangle
five and one-half: **3** rod
part of: **4** foot
two hundred and twenty: **7** furlong

yardstick
4 norm, test **5** basis, gauge, model **7** measure, pattern **8** paradigm, standard **9** barometer, benchmark, criterion, guideline **10** touchstone

yare
4 deft, spry **5** agile, brisk, handy, lithe, quick, ready, zippy **6** lively, nimble, volant **7** lissome **9** sprightly

yarn
4 tale, talk **5** fiber, story **6** caddis, cotton, crewel, strand, thread **7** account, caddice **8** anecdote, tall tale **9** adventure, narration, narrative
ball of: **4** clew
coil: **5** skein **6** skeane
cotton: **10** candlewick
for fastening a sail: **6** roband
metallic: **6** tinsel
woolen: **6** crewel **7** worsted **8** shetland

yaw
4 rock, swag, veer **5** lurch **6** swerve **7** deviate **9** alternate, deviation **10** deflection

yawn
3 gap **4** bore, gape **5** ennui **6** cavity, tedium **7** boredom, bromide **10** dullsville

yawning
4 deep **5** agape **6** gaping **7** abyssal **9** cavernous

yawp
3 bay, cry, nag **4** bark, bawl, beef, crab, fuss, gape, wail **5** bleat, gripe **6** clamor, outcry, squall, squawk, yammer **8** complain **9** bellyache

yaws
9 frambesia

yclept
5 named **6** called

yea
3 aye, too **4** also, amen, even, more, okay **5** truly **6** agreed, assent, as well, indeed, really, verily **7** besides, granted **8** likewise, moreover, positive **9** certainly **10** definitely **11** affirmation, affirmative **12** additionally

yeah, right
4 as if

yeanling
3 kid **4** lamb

year
4 time **5** cycle **6** period
academic division: **4** term **7** quarter, session **8** semester **9** trimester
French: **5** année
kind: **4** leap **5** solar **6** fiscal **8** academic, calendar, sidereal
Latin: **5** annus
Scottish: **7** towmond
Spanish: **3** año

yearbook
5 annal **6** annual **7** almanac

yearling
4 colt, foal **5** filly

Yearling, The
author: **8** Rawlings (Marjorie Kinnan)
character: **4** Jody
fawn: **4** Flag

yearly
6 annual **8** annually

yearn
4 ache, burn, itch, long, lust, pant, pine, sigh, wish **5** dream, spoil **6** hanker, hunger, thirst

yearning
3 yen **4** itch, urge, wish **5** ardor, drive, eager **6** desire, hunger, thirst **7** craving, passion, wistful **8** appetite **10** aspiration

years
3 age, era
five: **7** lustrum **12** quinquennial, quinquennium
four: **11** quadrennial, quadrennium
one hundred: **7** century **9** centenary **10** centennial
one thousand: **10** millennium
ten: **6** decade **9** decennial, decennium
three: **9** triennial, triennium
two: **8** biennial, biennium

yeast
4 barm, foam, suds **5** froth, spume **6** lather, leaven **7** ferment

yeasty
5 dizzy, giddy, light **6** frothy **7** flighty **8** immature, restless, seething **9** exuberant, frivolous, unsettled **11** light-headed

Yeats, William Butler
beloved: **9** Maud Gonne
birthplace: **6** Dublin
play: **7** Deirdre **9** Herne's Egg (The) **16** Countess Cathleen (The)
poetry: **5** Tower (The) **12** Second Coming (The) **16** Wild Swans at Coole (The) **18** Sailing to Byzantium
theater: **5** Abbey

yegg
5 thief **6** robber **7** burglar **8** picklock **11** safecracker

yell
3 cry **4** bawl, call, howl, roar, wail **5** cheer, hallo, hollo, shout, whoop **6** bellow, clamor, holler, outcry, scream, shriek, squall **10** vociferate

yellow
3 age **4** buff, mean, weak, yolk **5** amber, blond, color, lemon, straw, tawny, topaz **6** canary, coward, craven, flaxen, golden, sallow **7** citrine, gutless, ignoble, jasmine, mustard, saffron **8** cowardly, discolor **9** dastardly, jaundiced, spunkless **11** sensational **12** dishonorable **13** pusillanimous
brownish: **3** dun **5** amber, ocher
dye: **7** annatto
greenish: **5** olive **6** acacia **10** chartreuse

yellowhammer
5 finch **7** bunting, flicker

yellow-orange
5 ocher, ochre

yelp
3 cry, yap **4** bark **6** outcry, squeal

Yemen
capital: **4** Sana **5** Sanaa
city: **4** Aden **5** Ta'izz
desert: **10** Rub' al-Khali
gulf: **4** Aden
island: **7** Socotra
island group: **7** Kamaran
language: **6** Arabic
monetary unit: **4** rial
neighbor: **4** Oman **11** Saudi Arabia
peninsula: **7** Arabian
sea: **3** Red **7** Arabian

yen
4 ache, itch, long, lust, pine, sigh, urge **5** taste, yearn **6** desire, hanker, hunger, thirst **7** craving, longing, passion **8** appetite, yearning **9** hankering

yeoman
5 clerk **6** farmer **7** freeman **8** retainer **9** attendant, beefeater, landowner **10** freeholder **11** homesteader

yeomanly
5 loyal **6** sturdy **8** faithful

Yerby novel
13 Foxes of Harrow (The)

yes
3 aye, yea, yeh, yep, yup **4** okay, yeah **5** agree **6** agreed, assent, gladly **7** consent, exactly **8** all right **9** assuredly, certainly, willingly **11** affirmation, affirmative, undoubtedly
French: **3** oui

yeshiva
6 school **8** seminary

yes-man
5 toady **6** flunky, lap dog, minion, stooge **7** flunkey, spaniel **8** groveler, truckler **9** flatterer, sycophant **10** bootlicker **13** apple-polisher

yesterday
4 past, yore **8** recently **10** recent time
French: **4** hier
Spanish: **4** ayer

yesteryear
4 past, yore **7** history **8** foretime, lang syne **12** auld lang syne

yet
3 but, too **4** also, even, more, only, save **5** so far, still **6** as well, though, withal **7** besides, earlier, finally, howbeit, however, someday, thus far **8** after all, hitherto, moreover, sometime **10** eventually, ultimately **11** furthermore, nonetheless, still and all **12** additionally, nevertheless

Yevtushenko poem
7 Babi Yar, Baby Yar

Ygerne
see **Igraine**

Yiddish
bit: **5** shtik **6** shtick **7** schtick
bargain: **7** metziah
bore: **6** nudnik **7** nudnick
burst: **5** plotz
busybody: **5** yenta
cash: **6** mezuma
celebration: **6** simcha
comment: **6** kibitz **7** kibbitz
converse: **7** shmooze **8** schmooze
craziness: **8** meshugas, mishegas
crazy: **7** meshuga **8** meshugge
crazy person: **11** meshuggener
dirt: **7** schmutz
drag: **5** shlep **6** schlep, shlepp **7** schlepp
expert: **5** maven, mavin **6** mayvin
fool: **10** shmendrick
garbage: **5** dreck
gentile: **3** goy **5** goyim (plural)
go away: **7** gay avek
good deed: **7** mitzvah
gossip: **5** yenta
go to sleep: **10** gay shlafen
grandpa: **5** zayde
gripe: **6** kvetch

jerk: 5 schmo 6 schmoe, shmuck 7 schmuck
knickknack: 9 tchotchke
long story: 8 megillah
loser: 5 shlub 6 schlub 7 nebbish 8 shlemiel 9 schlemiel, schlemihl
man of integrity: 6 mensch
matchmaker: 8 shadchen
meddler: 5 yenta
money: 4 gelt
munch: 4 nosh
nerve, gall: 7 chutzpa 8 chutzpah
nothing: 6 bubkes, bupkes, bupkus
pleasure, pride: 6 noches
plump: 6 zaftig, zoftig
rejoice: 5 kvell
routine: 6 shtick 7 schtick
subhuman: 5 golem
thief: 5 ganef, gonif 6 goniff
unlucky person: 9 shlemazel

yield
3 bow, net, pay 4 bear, bend, cave, cede, crop, earn, fold 5 defer, grant, waive 6 accede, bounty, buckle, comply, impart, output, profit, relent, render, resign, return, reward, submit, supply, tender 7 abandon, bring in, concede, consent, deliver, furnish, harvest, produce, product, proffer, provide, revenue, succumb 8 abdicate, collapse, generate, hand over 9 acquiesce, surrender 10 bring forth, capitulate, production, relinquish

yielding
4 soft 6 docile, pliant, supple 7 bearing, passive, pliable 8 flexible 9 adaptable, malleable, tractable 10 manageable, productive, submissive 11 acquiescent, unresistant

yikes
3 gee, wow 4 gosh, uh-oh

yin and ___
4 yang

yip
3 cry 4 bark, yelp

yippee
3 yay 6 hoorah, hooray, hurrah, hurray 10 hallelujah

yoga posture
5 asana

yoga pad
3 mat

yoke
3 bar, tie, wed 4 bond, join, link, pair, span, team 5 clamp, frame, hitch, marry, unite 6 attach, couple, inspan 7 bondage, connect, control, harness, peonage, serfdom, slavery 8 marriage 9 servitude 10 crosspiece, oppression
combining form: 3 zyg 4 zygo
part: 5 oxbow

yoked pair
4 oxen

yokel
3 oaf, yap 4 boor, clod, hick, rube 5 churl, swain 6 rustic 7 bucolic, bumpkin, hayseed 9 chawbacon, hillbilly 10 clodhopper, countryman

Yoko from Tokyo
3 Ono

yolk
4 food 6 yellow

yon
see **yonder**

yonder
5 there 7 farther, further, thither 8 outlying

yore
3 old 7 history 8 foretime, lang syne 9 antiquity, yesterday 10 yesteryear

Yorkshire river
4 Ouse

you
3 one 4 thee, thou
French: 4 vous
German: 3 Sie
Spanish: 5 usted 7 ustedes

young
3 fry, new 4 baby, tyro 5 brood, fresh, green 6 babies, callow, infant, junior, litter, tender, unripe 7 untried 8 childish, immature, juvenile, unformed, youthful 9 unfledged 10 unfinished, unseasoned 11 unpracticed 13 inexperienced
animal: 3 cub, fry, kid, kit, pup 4 calf, colt, fawn, foal, joey 5 puppy 6 kitten, heifer, piglet
bird: 5 chick 7 gosling
bring forth: 3 ean 4 yean
hare: 7 leveret
sheep, goat: 4 lamb 8 yeanling

younger
6 junior

Young Frankenstein's assistant
4 Igor

young hog
5 shoat 6 piglet

Young partner
5 Ernst

young salmon
4 parr

youngster
3 boy, cub, kid, lad, tad, tot 4 girl, lass, tike, tyke 5 chick, child 6 moppet, shaver, squirt 8 juvenile 9 fledgling

your
3 thy

youth
3 lad **5** prime **6** period, spring **8** juvenile, preadult, teenager **9** stripling **10** adolescent, springtide, springtime **12** inexperience
ancient Greek: **6** ephebe **7** ephebus
goddess of: **4** Hebe
mythological: **6** Adonis, Apollo, Icarus **8** Ganymede
time of: **9** salad days

youthful
5 fresh, green, young **6** boyish, callow, maiden, unripe **7** puerile **8** immature, juvenile, virginal **9** beardless, unfledged

yowl
3 bay, cry **4** bawl, howl, wail **6** scream, squall, squeal **7** ululate **9** caterwaul

Yo-Yo's instrument
5 cello

yucca
5 agave **7** cassava **9** bear grass
relative: **4** aloe

yuck
3 ugh

Yugoslavia region
6 Bosnia, Kosovo, Serbia **7** Croatia

Yugoslav leader
4 Tito (Josip Broz)

Yukon
bay: **9** Mackenzie
capital: **10** Whitehorse
city: **6** Dawson
mountain: **5** Logan
river: **5** Yukon **8** Klondike

yule
4 Noel, Xmas **8** Nativity **9** Christmas **13** Christmastide
song: **4** noel **5** carol

Z

Zambia
capital: **6** Lusaka
city: **5** Kitwe, Ndola **11** Livingstone
lake: **5** Mweru **9** Bangweulu **10** Tanganyika
monetary unit: **6** kwacha
mountain range: **8** Muchinga
neighbor: **5** Congo **6** Angola, Malawi **7** Namibia **8** Tanzania, Zimbabwe **10** Mozambique
river: **5** Kafue **7** Luangwa, Zambezi
waterfall: **13** Victoria Falls

zany
3 nut, wag **4** card, fool, kook **5** antic, campy, clown, comic, crazy, cutup, dotty, goofy, idiot, joker, kooky, loony, nutty, wacky **6** jester, madcap **7** buffoon, farceur, half-wit **8** clowning, clownish, comedian, funnyman, jokester **9** harlequin, prankster, screwball, simpleton, trickster **11** merry-andrew

zap
3 hit **4** blow, kill, lase, nuke **5** blast, snuff **6** attack **7** destroy, wipe out **8** dissolve **9** eliminate, irradiate, liquidate **10** annihilate

Zátopek of running fame
4 Emil

Zauberflöte composer
6 Mozart (Wolfgang Amadeus)

zeal
4 brio, fire, zest **5** ardor, drive, mania **6** desire, energy, esprit, fervor, spirit **7** avidity, passion, urgency **8** devotion, dynamism, keenness **9** eagerness, intensity, vehemence **10** enthusiasm, fanaticism, fierceness

zealot
3 bug, fan, nut **4** buff **5** fiend, freak **6** maniac, votary **7** devotee, fanatic, sectary **8** partisan **10** aficionado, enthusiast **12** true believer

zealous
4 avid, keen **5** afire, eager, fiery, fired, nutty, rabid **6** ardent, fervid, gung-ho **7** devoted, fanatic, fervent **8** frenetic, obsessed, wild-eyed **9** dedicated, fanatical, possessed **10** passionate **11** impassioned **12** enthusiastic

zebra
6 equine **7** referee **9** crosswalk
extinct: **6** quagga
type: **6** Grevy's **8** mountain **9** Burchell's

zebra-striped mammal
5 okapi

zebu
4 oxen
Zebulun
9 lost tribe
brother: 4 Levi 5 Judah 6 Simeon
father: 5 Jacob
mother: 4 Leah
zecchino
6 sequin
Zechariah
7 prophet
Zedekiah
9 Mattaniah
father: 6 Josiah
zen
divine law: 6 dharma
enlightenment: 6 satori
paradox: 4 koan
school: 4 dojo
teacher: 6 sensei
zenana
5 harem, serai 8 seraglio
zenith
3 top 4 acme, apex, peak 6 apogee, height, summit, vertex 8 capstone, pinnacle 11 culmination 12 highest point
opposite: 5 nadir
Zenobia
husband: 9 Odenathus
kingdom: 7 Palmyra
Zeno
follower: 5 Stoic
home: 4 Elea
Zephaniah
7 prophet 9 Sophonias
zephyr
6 breeze 8 west wind
Zephyrus
father: 8 Astraeus
mother: 3 Eos 6 Aurora
zeppelin
5 blimp 7 airship 9 dirigible
zero
3 aim, nil, nix, zip 4 love, nada, none, null, void 5 aught, nadir, zilch 6 cipher, naught, nobody 7 nothing, nullity 8 goose egg 9 nonentity
zest
4 élan, peel, tang, zeal 5 gusto, spice, taste 6 flavor, relish 7 delight, passion, sparkle 8 appetite, piquancy, pleasure 9 eagerness, enjoyment 10 enthusiasm
zesty
4 racy, tart 5 brisk, sharp, spicy, tangy 6 biting, lively, savory, snappy 7 peppery, piquant, pungent 8 exciting, poignant, seasoned, spirited 9 flavorful
Zetes
brother: 6 Calais
father: 6 Boreas
mother: 8 Orithyia
slayer: 8 Heracles, Hercules
Zethus
brother: 7 Amphion
father: 4 Zeus 7 Jupiter
mother: 7 Antiope
Zeus
7 Jupiter
birthplace: 5 Mt. Ida
breastplate: 4 egis 5 aegis
brother: 5 Hades 8 Poseidon
daughter: 3 Ate 4 Hebe 5 Helen 6 Athena 7 Artemis 9 Aphrodite 10 Persephone, Proserpina
father: 6 Cronus
home: 7 Olympus (Mt.)
lover: 4 Leda, Leto, Maia 5 Danaë, Dione, Metis 6 Aegina, Europa, Latona, Semele, Themis 7 Alcmene, Antiope, Demeter 8 Callisto, Eurynome
mother: 4 Rhea
nurse: 9 Almathaea
oracle: 6 Dodona
shield: 5 aegis
sister: 4 Hera, Juno
son: 4 Ares 5 Arcas, Argus, Minos 6 Aeacus, Apollo, Hermes, Zethus 7 Amphion, Perseus 8 Dionysus, Heracles, Hercules, Sarpedon, Tantalus
tree: 3 oak
wife: 4 Hera, Juno
weapon: 11 thunderbolt
Zhivago's love
4 Lara
zigzag
4 tack, turn 5 angle, crank, weave 6 jagged, ricrac 7 chevron 8 flexuous, indirect, rickrack, serrated
course: 6 slalom
zilch
3 nil, zip 4 nada, zero 5 aught, squat 6 cipher, diddly, naught, nobody 7 nothing, nullity 8 goose egg 9 nonentity 11 diddly-squat
Zimbabwe
capital: 6 Harare
city: 5 Gweru 6 Kwekwe, Mutare 8 Bulawayo, Maxvingo 11 Chitungwiza
dictator: 6 Mugabe (Robert)
ethnic group: 5 Shona 7 Ndebele
former name: 8 Rhodesia
lake: 6 Kariba
language: 5 Bantu
neighbor: 6 Zambia 8 Botswana 10 Mozambique 11 South Africa
river: 4 Sabi 7 Limpopo, Zambezi
waterfall: 13 Victoria Falls

zinc
7 element
ingot: **7** spelter
ore: **6** blende **10** sphalerite

zing
3 pan, pep, rap, vim, zap, zip **4** brio, dash, élan, slam, snap, zeal **5** ardor, flair, oomph, verve, vigor **6** energy, esprit, fervor, spirit **7** panache, passion, sparkle **8** dynamism, vitality **9** animation, eagerness **10** ebullience, enthusiasm

zinger
3 dig **4** barb, gibe, jibe, slam **6** retort **7** riposte

Zion
5 bliss **6** heaven, Israel **7** Elysium **8** eternity, paradise **12** New Jerusalem, promised land

Zionist
American: **5** Szold (Henrietta)
English: **7** Sokolow (Nahum) **8** Zangwill (Israel)
German: **6** Nordau (Max Simon)
Hungarian: **5** Herzl (Theodor)
Israeli: **5** Buber (Martin) **8** Weizmann (Chaim)

zip
3 fly, nil, nix, pep, run, vim **4** brio, dash, hiss, rush, nada, snap, tear, whiz, zero, zest, zing, zoom **5** drive, gusto, hurry, oomph, speed, squat, whisk, zilch **6** bustle, energy, hasten, hustle **7** nothing **8** vitality **10** excitement, liveliness **11** diddly-squat

zippy
4 keen, spry, yare **5** agile, alert, brisk, peppy, quick, ready **6** lively, nimble, snappy, speedy **7** dynamic **8** spirited **9** sprightly

zircon
6 jargon **7** jargoon, mineral
variety: **7** jacinth **8** hyacinth

zit
6 pimple

zither
10 instrument
Chinese: **3** kin **4** ch'in
Japanese: **4** koto
relative: **8** autoharp, dulcimer

ziti relative
5 penne

zodiac sign
3 Leo (Lion) **5** Aries (Ram), Libra (Balance, Scales), Virgo (Virgin) **6** Cancer (Crab), Gemini (Twins), Pisces (Fishes), Taurus (Bull) **7** Scorpio (Scorpion) **8** Aquarius (Water Bearer) **9** Capricorn (Goat) **11** Sagittarius (Archer)

Zola of literature
5 Émile
work: **4** Nana **7** J'accuse **8** Drunkard (The), Germinal **9** La Débâcle **10** L'Assommoir **13** Thérèse Raquin

zombie
5 robot **8** cocktail **9** automaton

zone
4 area, band, belt **5** layer, tract **6** region, sector **7** portion, quarter, section, segment, stretch **8** district, division, encircle, surround **9** partition, territory

zonked
4 high **5** dazed, doped, drunk, tight **6** ripped, stoned **7** drugged, drunken, smashed **8** hopped-up, tripping, turned on, wiped out **9** spaced-out, strung out, stupefied **10** inebriated, tripped out **11** intoxicated

zoologist
American: **5** Clark (Eugenie), Hyatt (Alpheus) **6** Carson (Rachel), Fossey (Dian), Osborn (Henry Fairfield), Yerkes (Robert) **7** Agassiz (Alexander), Ditmars (Raymond), Merriam (Clinton) **8** Hornaday (William)
Austrian: **6** Frisch (Karl von)
British: **6** Darwin (Charles), Huxley (Julian, Thomas) **7** Goodall (Jane), Medawar (Peter) **9** Lankester (Edwin)
Dutch: **10** Swammerdam (Jan)
French: **6** Buffon (G.-L. Leclerc), Cuvier (Georges)
German: **7** Haeckel (Ernst)
Norwegian: **6** Nansen (Fridtjof)
South African: **5** Broom (Robert)
Swedish: **8** Linnaeus (Carolus)

zoom
3 hum, zip **4** buzz, dash, whiz, zero **5** focus, speed, whizz **6** streak **7** shoot up **9** skyrocket

zoophyte
5 coral **6** sponge **8** bryozoan **9** gorgonian **10** sea anemone

Zoroastrian
demon: **4** deva
god: **10** Ahura Mazda
sacred writings: **6** Avesta

zounds
3 gad **4** egad **8** gadzooks **11** odd's bodkins

Zubin on the podium
5 Mehta

zucchetto
7 calotte **8** skullcap

zwieback
5 toast **7** biscuit

zygomatic bone
5 malar **9** cheekbone

zygote
4 cell **6** oocyst